Official 2009 National Football League Record & Fact Book

National Football League
280 Park Avenue, New York, N.Y. 10017 (212) 450-2000. NFL Internet Address: http://www.NFL.com

Printed in the United States of America.

A National Football League Book.

Compiled by the NFL Communications Department and Seymour Siwoff, Elias Sports Bureau.
Statistics by Elias Sports Bureau.

Edited by Jon Zimmer, NFL Communications Department, and Matt Marini. Layout by William Tham. Cover design by NFL Creative.
Produced by NFL Communications Department.

Cover photograph of Santonio Holmes of the Super Bowl XLIII champion Pittsburgh Steelers by Timothy A. Clary, AFP/GETTY IMAGES.

Time Inc. Home Entertainment
1271 Avenue of the Americas, New York, N.Y. 10020
Manufactured in the United States of America.
First printing, July 2009.
10 9 8 7 6 5 4 3 2 1

TABLE OF CONTENTS

Additional sections available online at www.NFLmedia.com.

2009 SCHEDULE AND NOTE CALENDAR

All times local. Dates and times subject to change.
Nationally televised games indicated by network in parentheses.

	Sunday, August 9	Hall of Fame Game at Canton, Ohio Buffalo _____ at Tennessee _____	(NBC) 8:00
PRESEASON/WEEK 1	**Thursday, August 13**	New England _____ at Philadelphia _____	7:00
		Washington _____ at Baltimore _____	7:30
		Arizona _____ at Pittsburgh _____	(ESPN) 8:00
		Dallas _____ at Oakland _____	7:00
	Friday, August 14	St. Louis _____ at N.Y. Jets _____	7:00
		Minnesota _____ at Indianapolis _____	7:30
		Cincinnati _____ at New Orleans _____	7:00
		Denver _____ at San Francisco _____	7:00
	Saturday, August 15	Atlanta _____ at Detroit _____	4:00
		Chicago _____ at Buffalo _____	7:00
		Cleveland _____ at Green Bay _____	7:00
		Tampa Bay _____ at Tennessee _____	7:00
		Houston _____ at Kansas City _____	7:00
		Seattle _____ at San Diego _____	7:00
	Monday, August 17	Jacksonville _____ at Miami _____	7:30
		Carolina _____ at N.Y. Giants _____	(ESPN) 8:15
PRESEASON/WEEK 2	**Thursday, August 20**	Cincinnati _____ at New England _____	7:30
		Philadelphia _____ at Indianapolis _____	(FOX) 8:00
	Friday, August 21	Tennessee _____ at Dallas _____	(FOX) 7:00
		Atlanta _____ at St. Louis _____	7:00
		Kansas City _____ at Minnesota _____	7:00
	Saturday, August 22	Detroit _____ at Cleveland _____	7:30
		Carolina _____ at Miami _____	7:30
		Pittsburgh _____ at Washington _____	7:30
		Tampa Bay _____ at Jacksonville _____	7:30
		New Orleans _____ at Houston _____	7:00
		Buffalo _____ at Green Bay _____	7:00
		N.Y. Giants _____ at Chicago _____	7:00
		Oakland _____ at San Francisco _____	5:15
		San Diego _____ at Arizona _____	7:00
		Denver _____ at Seattle _____	7:30
	Monday, August 24	N.Y. Jets _____ at Baltimore _____	(ESPN) 8:00
PRESEASON/WEEK 3	**Thursday, August 27**	Jacksonville _____ at Philadelphia _____	7:00
		St. Louis _____ at Cincinnati _____	7:35
		Miami _____ at Tampa Bay _____	(FOX) 8:00
	Friday, August 28	New England _____ at Washington _____	(CBS) 8:00
		Green Bay _____ at Arizona _____	7:00
	Saturday, August 29	Indianapolis _____ at Detroit _____	1:00
		New Orleans _____ at Oakland _____	1:00
		Buffalo _____ at Pittsburgh _____	7:30
		Tennessee _____ at Cleveland _____	7:30
		San Francisco _____ at Dallas _____	7:00
		San Diego _____ at Atlanta _____	(CBS) 8:00
		Baltimore _____ at Carolina _____	8:00
		N.Y. Jets _____ at N.Y. Giants _____	8:00
		Seattle _____ at Kansas City _____	7:00
	Sunday, August 30	Chicago _____ at Denver _____	(NBC) 6:00
	Monday, August 31	Minnesota _____ at Houston _____	(ESPN) 7:00

PRESEASON/WEEK 4	**Thursday, September 3**	Detroit _____ at Buffalo _____	6:30
		Philadelphia _____ at N.Y. Jets _____	7:00
		Washington _____ at Jacksonville _____	7:30
		Indianapolis _____ at Cincinnati _____	7:30
		N.Y. Giants _____ at New England _____	7:30
		Baltimore _____ at Atlanta _____	7:30
		Miami _____ at New Orleans _____	7:00
		Green Bay _____ at Tennessee _____	7:00
		Kansas City _____ at St. Louis _____	7:00
		Cleveland _____ at Chicago _____	7:00
		Pittsburgh _____ at Carolina _____	8:00
		Arizona _____ at Denver _____	7:00
		Oakland _____ at Seattle _____	7:00
	Friday, September 4	Houston _____ at Tampa Bay _____	7:00
		Dallas _____ at Minnesota _____	6:00
		San Francisco _____ at San Diego _____	7:00

NFL KICKOFF 2009	**Thursday, September 10**	Tennessee _____ at Pittsburgh _____	(NBC) 8:30
	Sunday, September 13	Miami _____ at Atlanta _____	1:00
	FOX-TV National Weekend	Kansas City _____ at Baltimore _____	1:00
		Philadelphia _____ at Carolina _____	1:00
KICKOFF WEEKEND		Denver _____ at Cincinnati _____	1:00
		Minnesota _____ at Cleveland _____	1:00
		N.Y. Jets _____ at Houston _____	12:00
		Jacksonville _____ at Indianapolis _____	1:00
		Detroit _____ at New Orleans _____	12:00
		Dallas _____ at Tampa Bay _____	1:00
		San Francisco _____ at Arizona _____	1:15
		Washington _____ at N.Y. Giants _____	4:15
		St. Louis _____ at Seattle _____	1:15
		Chicago _____ at Green Bay _____	(NBC) 7:20
	Monday, September 14	Buffalo _____ at New England _____	(ESPN) 7:00
		San Diego _____ at Oakland _____	(ESPN) 7:15

SECOND WEEK	**Sunday, September 20**	Carolina _____ at Atlanta _____	1:00
	CBS-TV National Weekend	Minnesota _____ at Detroit _____	1:00
		Cincinnati _____ at Green Bay _____	12:00
		Arizona _____ at Jacksonville _____	1:00
		Oakland _____ at Kansas City _____	12:00
		New England _____ at N.Y. Jets _____	1:00
		New Orleans _____ at Philadelphia _____	1:00
		Houston _____ at Tennessee _____	12:00
		St. Louis _____ at Washington _____	1:00
		Tampa Bay _____ at Buffalo _____	4:05
		Seattle _____ at San Francisco _____	1:05
		Pittsburgh _____ at Chicago _____	3:15
		Cleveland _____ at Denver _____	2:15
		Baltimore _____ at San Diego _____	1:15
		N.Y. Giants _____ at Dallas _____	(NBC) 7:20
	Monday, September 21	Indianapolis _____ at Miami _____	(ESPN) 8:30

THIRD WEEK	**Sunday, September 27**	Cleveland _____ at Baltimore _____	1:00
	CBS-TV National Weekend	Washington _____ at Detroit _____	1:00
		Jacksonville _____ at Houston _____	12:00
		San Francisco _____ at Minnesota _____	12:00
		Atlanta _____ at New England _____	1:00
		Tennessee _____ at N.Y. Jets _____	1:00
		Kansas City _____ at Philadelphia _____	1:00
		Green Bay _____ at St. Louis _____	12:00
		N.Y. Giants _____ at Tampa Bay _____	1:00
		New Orleans _____ at Buffalo _____	4:05
		Chicago _____ at Seattle _____	1:05
		Pittsburgh _____ at Cincinnati _____	4:15
		Denver _____ at Oakland _____	1:15
		Miami _____ at San Diego _____	1:15
		Indianapolis _____ at Arizona _____	(NBC) 5:20
	Monday, September 28	Carolina _____ at Dallas _____	(ESPN) 7:30

FOURTH WEEK
Open Date: Arizona, Atlanta, Carolina, Philadelphia

Sunday, October 4	Detroit _____ at Chicago _____	12:00
FOX-TV National Weekend	Cincinnati _____ at Cleveland _____	1:00
	Oakland _____ at Houston _____	12:00
	Seattle _____ at Indianapolis _____	1:00
	Tennessee _____ at Jacksonville _____	1:00
	N.Y. Giants _____ at Kansas City _____	12:00
	Baltimore _____ at New England _____	1:00
	Tampa Bay _____ at Washington _____	1:00
	Buffalo _____ at Miami _____	4:05
	N.Y. Jets _____ at New Orleans _____	3:05
	Dallas _____ at Denver _____	2:15
	St. Louis _____ at San Francisco _____	1:15
	San Diego _____ at Pittsburgh _____	(NBC) 8:20
Monday, October 5	Green Bay _____ at Minnesota _____	(ESPN) 7:30

FIFTH WEEK
Open Date: Chicago, Green Bay, New Orleans, San Diego

Sunday, October 11	Cincinnati _____ at Baltimore _____	1:00
CBS-TV National Weekend	Cleveland _____ at Buffalo _____	1:00
	Washington _____ at Carolina _____	1:00
	Pittsburgh _____ at Detroit _____	1:00
	Dallas _____ at Kansas City _____	12:00
	Oakland _____ at N.Y. Giants _____	1:00
	Tampa Bay _____ at Philadelphia _____	1:00
	Minnesota _____ at St. Louis _____	12:00
	Atlanta _____ at San Francisco _____	1:05
	Houston _____ at Arizona _____	1:15
	New England _____ at Denver _____	2:15
	Jacksonville _____ at Seattle _____	1:15
	Indianapolis _____ at Tennessee _____	(NBC) 7:20
Monday, October 12	N.Y. Jets _____ at Miami _____	(ESPN) 8:30

SIXTH WEEK
Open Date: Dallas, Indianapolis, Miami, San Francisco

Sunday, October 18	Houston _____ at Cincinnati _____	1:00
CBS-TV National Weekend	Detroit _____ at Green Bay _____	12:00
	St. Louis _____ at Jacksonville _____	1:00
	Baltimore _____ at Minnesota _____	12:00
	N.Y. Giants _____ at New Orleans _____	12:00
	Cleveland _____ at Pittsburgh _____	1:00
	Carolina _____ at Tampa Bay _____	1:00
	Kansas City _____ at Washington _____	1:00
	Philadelphia _____ at Oakland _____	1:05
	Arizona _____ at Seattle _____	1:05
	Tennessee _____ at New England _____	4:15
	Buffalo _____ at N.Y. Jets _____	4:15
	Chicago _____ at Atlanta _____	(NBC) 8:20
Monday, October 19	Denver _____ at San Diego _____	(ESPN) 5:30

SEVENTH WEEK
Open Date: Baltimore, Denver, Detroit, Jacksonville, Seattle, Tennessee

NFL INTERNATIONAL SERIES 2009

Sunday, October 25	Chicago _____ at Cincinnati _____	1:00
FOX-TV National Weekend	Green Bay _____ at Cleveland _____	1:00
	San Francisco _____ at Houston _____	12:00
	San Diego _____ at Kansas City _____	12:00
	Minnesota _____ at Pittsburgh _____	1:00
	Indianapolis _____ at St. Louis _____	12:00
	New England _____ at Tampa Bay _____ (London)	5:00
	Buffalo _____ at Carolina _____	4:05
	N.Y. Jets _____ at Oakland _____	1:05
	Atlanta _____ at Dallas _____	3:15
	New Orleans _____ at Miami _____	4:15
	Arizona _____ at N.Y. Giants _____	(NBC) 8:20
Monday, October 26	Philadelphia _____ at Washington _____	(ESPN) 8:30

EIGHTH WEEK **Open Date: Cincinnati, Kansas City, New England, Pittsburgh, Tampa Bay, Washington**	**Sunday, November 1** **FOX-TV National Weekend**	Denver _____ at Baltimore _____	1:00
		Houston _____ at Buffalo _____	1:00
		Cleveland _____ at Chicago _____	12:00
		Seattle _____ at Dallas _____	12:00
		St. Louis _____ at Detroit _____	1:00
		Minnesota _____ at Green Bay _____	12:00
		San Francisco _____ at Indianapolis _____	1:00
		Miami _____ at N.Y. Jets _____	1:00
		Oakland _____ at San Diego _____	1:05
		Jacksonville _____ at Tennessee _____	3:05
		Carolina _____ at Arizona _____	2:15
		N.Y. Giants _____ at Philadelphia _____	4:15
	Monday, November 2	Atlanta _____ at New Orleans _____	(ESPN) 7:30

NINTH WEEK **Open Date: Buffalo, Cleveland, Minnesota, N.Y. Jets, Oakland, St. Louis**	**Sunday, November 8** **CBS-TV National Weekend**	Washington _____ at Atlanta _____	1:00
		Arizona _____ at Chicago _____	12:00
		Baltimore _____ at Cincinnati _____	1:00
		Houston _____ at Indianapolis _____	1:00
		Kansas City _____ at Jacksonville _____	1:00
		Miami _____ at New England _____	1:00
		Green Bay _____ at Tampa Bay _____	1:00
		Carolina _____ at New Orleans _____	3:05
		Detroit _____ at Seattle _____	1:05
		San Diego _____ at N.Y. Giants _____	4:15
		Tennessee _____ at San Francisco _____	1:15
		Dallas _____ at Philadelphia _____	(NBC) 8:20
	Monday, November 9	Pittsburgh _____ at Denver _____	(ESPN) 6:30

TENTH WEEK **Open Date: Houston, N.Y. Giants**	**Thursday, November 12**	Chicago _____ at San Francisco _____	(NFLN) 5:20
	Sunday, November 15 **FOX-TV National Weekend**	Atlanta _____ at Carolina _____	1:00
		Tampa Bay _____ at Miami _____	1:00
		Detroit _____ at Minnesota _____	12:00
		Jacksonville _____ at N.Y. Jets _____	1:00
		Cincinnati _____ at Pittsburgh _____	1:00
		New Orleans _____ at St. Louis _____	12:00
		Buffalo _____ at Tennessee _____	12:00
		Denver _____ at Washington _____	1:00
		Kansas City _____ at Oakland _____	1:05
		Seattle _____ at Arizona _____	2:15
		Dallas _____ at Green Bay _____	3:15
		Philadelphia _____ at San Diego _____	1:15
		New England _____ at Indianapolis _____	(NBC) 8:20
	Monday, November 16	Baltimore _____ at Cleveland _____	(ESPN) 8:30

ELEVENTH WEEK	**Thursday, November 19**	Miami _____ at Carolina _____	(NFLN) 8:20
	Sunday, November 22 **CBS-TV National Weekend**	Indianapolis _____ at Baltimore _____	1:00
		Washington _____ at Dallas _____	12:00
		Cleveland _____ at Detroit _____	1:00
		San Francisco _____ at Green Bay _____	12:00
		Buffalo _____ at Jacksonville _____	1:00
		Pittsburgh _____ at Kansas City _____	12:00
		Seattle _____ at Minnesota _____	12:00
		Atlanta _____ at N.Y. Giants _____	1:00
		New Orleans _____ at Tampa Bay _____	1:00
		Arizona _____ at St. Louis _____	3:05
		San Diego _____ at Denver _____	2:15
		N.Y. Jets _____ at New England _____	4:15
		Cincinnati _____ at Oakland _____	1:15
		Philadelphia _____ at Chicago _____	(NBC) *7:20
	Monday, November 23	Tennessee _____ at Houston _____	(ESPN) 7:30

**Sunday Night Games In Weeks 11-16 Subject to Change*

2009 SCHEDULE AND NOTE CALENDAR

TWELFTH WEEK

THANKSGIVING 2009

	Game	Time
Thursday, November 26	Green Bay _____ at Detroit _____	(FOX) 12:30
	Oakland _____ at Dallas _____	(CBS) 3:15
	N.Y. Giants _____ at Denver _____	(NFLN) 6:20
Sunday, November 29	Tampa Bay _____ at Atlanta _____	1:00
FOX-TV National Weekend	Miami _____ at Buffalo _____	1:00
	Cleveland _____ at Cincinnati _____	1:00
	Indianapolis _____ at Houston _____	12:00
	Chicago _____ at Minnesota _____	12:00
	Carolina _____ at N.Y. Jets _____	1:00
	Washington _____ at Philadelphia _____	1:00
	Seattle _____ at St. Louis _____	12:00
	Arizona _____ at Tennessee _____	12:00
	Kansas City _____ at San Diego _____	1:05
	Jacksonville _____ at San Francisco _____	1:05
	Pittsburgh _____ at Baltimore _____	(NBC) *8:20
Monday, November 30	New England _____ at New Orleans _____	(ESPN) 7:30

**Sunday Night Games In Weeks 11-16 Subject to Change*

THIRTEENTH WEEK

	Game	Time
Thursday, December 3	N.Y. Jets _____ at Buffalo _____ (Toronto)	(NFLN) 8:20
Sunday, December 6	Philadelphia _____ at Atlanta _____	1:00
FOX-TV National Weekend	Tampa Bay _____ at Carolina _____	1:00
	St. Louis _____ at Chicago _____	12:00
	Detroit _____ at Cincinnati _____	1:00
	Tennessee _____ at Indianapolis _____	1:00
	Houston _____ at Jacksonville _____	1:00
	Denver _____ at Kansas City _____	12:00
	Oakland _____ at Pittsburgh _____	1:00
	New Orleans _____ at Washington _____	1:00
	San Diego _____ at Cleveland _____	4:05
	Minnesota _____ at Arizona _____	2:15
	Dallas _____ at N.Y. Giants _____	4:15
	San Francisco _____ at Seattle _____	1:15
	New England _____ at Miami _____	(NBC) *8:20
Monday, December 7	Baltimore _____ at Green Bay _____	(ESPN) 7:30

**Sunday Night Games In Weeks 11-16 Subject to Change*

FOURTEENTH WEEK

	Game	Time
Thursday, December 10	Pittsburgh _____ at Cleveland _____	(NFLN) 8:20
Sunday, December 13	New Orleans _____ at Atlanta _____	1:00
CBS-TV National Weekend	Detroit _____ at Baltimore _____	1:00
	Green Bay _____ at Chicago _____	12:00
	Seattle _____ at Houston _____	12:00
	Denver _____ at Indianapolis _____	1:00
	Miami _____ at Jacksonville _____	1:00
	Buffalo _____ at Kansas City _____	12:00
	Cincinnati _____ at Minnesota _____	12:00
	Carolina _____ at New England _____	1:00
	N.Y. Jets _____ at Tampa Bay _____	1:00
	St. Louis _____ at Tennessee _____	12:00
	Washington _____ at Oakland _____	1:05
	San Diego _____ at Dallas _____	3:15
	Philadelphia _____ at N.Y. Giants _____	(NBC) *8:20
Monday, December 14	Arizona _____ at San Francisco _____	(ESPN) 5:30

**Sunday Night Games In Weeks 11-16 Subject to Change*

FIFTEENTH WEEK	**Thursday, December 17**	Indianapolis _____ at Jacksonville _____	(NFLN) 8:20
	Saturday, December 19	Dallas _____ at New Orleans _____	(NFLN) 7:20
	Sunday, December 20	Chicago _____ at Baltimore _____	1:00
	FOX-TV National Weekend	New England _____ at Buffalo _____	1:00
		Arizona _____ at Detroit _____	1:00
		Cleveland _____ at Kansas City _____	12:00
		Atlanta _____ at N.Y. Jets _____	1:00
		San Francisco _____ at Philadelphia _____	1:00
		Green Bay _____ at Pittsburgh _____	1:00
		Houston _____ at St. Louis _____	12:00
		Miami _____ at Tennessee _____	12:00
		Oakland _____ at Denver _____	2:05
		Cincinnati _____ at San Diego _____	1:05
		Tampa Bay _____ at Seattle _____	1:15
		Minnesota _____ at Carolina _____	(NBC) *8:20
	Monday, December 21	N.Y. Giants _____ at Washington _____	(ESPN) 8:30

**Sunday Night Games In Weeks 11-16 Subject to Change*

SIXTEENTH WEEK	**Friday, December 25**	San Diego _____ at Tennessee _____	(NFLN) 6:30
	Sunday, December 27	Buffalo _____ at Atlanta _____	1:00
	CBS-TV National Weekend	Kansas City _____ at Cincinnati _____	1:00
		Oakland _____ at Cleveland _____	1:00
		Seattle _____ at Green Bay _____	12:00
		Houston _____ at Miami _____	1:00
		Jacksonville _____ at New England _____	1:00
		Tampa Bay _____ at New Orleans _____	12:00
		Carolina _____ at N.Y. Giants _____	1:00
		Denver _____ at Philadelphia _____	1:00
		Baltimore _____ at Pittsburgh _____	1:00
		St. Louis _____ at Arizona _____	2:05
		Detroit _____ at San Francisco _____	1:05
		N.Y. Jets _____ at Indianapolis _____	4:15
		Dallas _____ at Washington _____	(NBC) *8:20
	Monday, December 28	Minnesota _____ at Chicago _____	(ESPN) 7:30

**Sunday Night Games In Weeks 11-16 Subject to Change*

SEVENTEENTH WEEK*	**Sunday, January 3**	Indianapolis _____ at Buffalo _____	1:00
	CBS-TV and FOX-TV National Weekend	New Orleans _____ at Carolina _____	1:00
		Jacksonville _____ at Cleveland _____	1:00
		Philadelphia _____ at Dallas _____	12:00
		Chicago _____ at Detroit _____	1:00
		New England _____ at Houston _____	12:00
		Pittsburgh _____ at Miami _____	1:00
		N.Y. Giants _____ at Minnesota _____	12:00
		Cincinnati _____ at N.Y. Jets _____	1:00
		San Francisco _____ at St. Louis _____	12:00
		Atlanta _____ at Tampa Bay _____	1:00
		Green Bay _____ at Arizona _____	2:15
		Kansas City _____ at Denver _____	2:15
		Baltimore _____ at Oakland _____	1:15
		Washington _____ at San Diego _____	1:15
		Tennessee _____ at Seattle _____	1:15

**Sunday Night Game In Week 17 TBD*

Wild Card Playoff Games
Site Priorities
Two Wild Card teams (division non-champions with best two records) from each conference and the division champions with the third and fourth-best record in each conference will enter the first round of the playoffs. The division champion with the third-best record will play host to the Wild Card team with the second-best record. The division champion with the fourth-best record will play host to the Wild Card team with the best record. There are no restrictions on intra-division games.

Saturday, January 9, 2010 American Football Conference

__________ at __________ (NBC)

National Football Conference

__________ at __________ (NBC)

Sunday, January 10, 2010 American Football Conference

__________ at __________ (CBS)

National Football Conference

__________ at __________ (FOX)

Divisional Playoff Games
Site Priorities
In each conference, the two division champions with the highest won-lost-tied percentage during the regular season will play host to the Wild Card winners. The division champion with the best record in each conference is assured of playing the lowest seeded Wild Card survivor. There are no restrictions on intra-division games.

Saturday, January 16, 2010 American Football Conference

__________ at __________ (CBS)

National Football Conference

__________ at __________ (FOX)

Sunday, January 17, 2010 American Football Conference

__________ at __________ (CBS)

National Football Conference

__________ at __________ (FOX)

Championship Games
Site Priorities for Championship Games
The home teams will be the surviving playoff winners with the highest seeds. A Wild Card team cannot play host unless two Wild Card teams are in the game, in which case the Wild Card team that was seeded highest in the first round of the playoffs will be the home team.

Sunday, January 24, 2010 American Football Conference

__________ at __________ (CBS)

National Football Conference

__________ at __________ (FOX)

AFC-NFC Pro Bowl

Sunday, January 31, 2010 AFC-NFC Pro Bowl at Dolphin Stadium, South Florida

AFC__________ vs. NFC __________ (ESPN)

Super Bowl XLIV

Sunday, February 7, 2010 Super Bowl XLIV at Dolphin Stadium, South Florida

__________ vs. __________ (CBS)

2009 NATIONALLY TELEVISED PRIME-TIME GAMES

All times ET.

Thursday, Sept. 10	Tennessee at Pittsburgh (NBC)	8:30
Sunday, Sept. 13	Chicago at Green Bay (NBC)	8:20
Monday, Sept. 14	Buffalo at New England (ESPN)	7:00
	San Diego at Oakland (ESPN)	10:15
Sunday, Sept. 20	N.Y. Giants at Dallas (NBC)	8:20
Monday, Sept. 21	Indianapolis at Miami (ESPN)	8:30
Sunday, Sept. 27	Indianapolis at Arizona (NBC)	8:20
Monday, Sept. 28	Carolina at Dallas (ESPN)	8:30
Sunday, Oct. 4	San Diego at Pittsburgh (NBC)	8:20
Monday, Oct. 5	Green Bay at Minnesota (ESPN)	8:30
Sunday, Oct. 11	Indianapolis at Tennessee (NBC)	8:20
Monday, Oct. 12	N.Y. Jets at Miami (ESPN)	8:30
Sunday, Oct. 18	Chicago at Atlanta (NBC)	8:20
Monday, Oct. 19	Denver at San Diego (ESPN)	8:30
Sunday, Oct. 25	Arizona at N.Y. Giants (NBC)	8:20
Monday, Oct. 26	Philadelphia at Washington (ESPN)	8:30
Monday, Nov. 2	Atlanta at New Orleans (ESPN)	8:30
Sunday, Nov. 8	Dallas at Philadelphia (NBC)	8:20
Monday, Nov. 9	Pittsburgh at Denver (ESPN)	8:30
Thursday, Nov. 12	Denver at Cleveland (NFL Network)	8:20
Sunday, Nov. 15	New England at Indianapolis (NBC)	8:20
Monday, Nov. 16	Baltimore at Cleveland (ESPN)	8:30
Thursday, Nov. 19	Miami at Carolina (NFL Network)	8:20
Sunday, Nov. 22	Philadelphia at Chicago (NBC)*	8:20
Monday, Nov. 23	Tennessee at Houston (ESPN)	8:30
Thursday, Nov. 26	Green Bay at Detroit (CBS)	12:30
	Oakland at Dallas (FOX)	4:15
	N.Y. Giants at Denver (NFL Network)	8:20
Sunday, Nov. 29	Pittsburgh at Baltimore (NBC)*	8:20
Monday, Nov. 30	New England at New Orleans (ESPN)	8:30
Thursday, Dec. 3	N.Y. Jets at Buffalo (CBS)	12:30
Sunday, Dec. 6	New England at Miami (NBC)*	8:20
Monday, Dec. 7	Baltimore at Green Bay (ESPN)	8:30
Thursday, Dec. 10	Pittsburgh at Cleveland (NFL Network)	8:20
Sunday, Dec. 13	Philadelphia at N.Y. Giants (NBC)*	8:20
Monday, Dec. 14	Arizona at San Francisco (ESPN)	8:30
Thursday, Dec. 17	Indianapolis at Jacksonville (NFL Network)	8:20
Saturday, Dec. 19	Dallas at New Orleans (NFL Network)	8:20
Sunday, Dec. 20	Minnesota at Carolina (NBC)*	8:20
Monday, Dec. 21	N.Y. Giants at Washington (ESPN)	8:30
Friday, Dec. 25	San Diego at Tennessee (NFL Network)	7:30
Sunday, Dec. 27	Dallas at Washington (NBC)*	8:20
Monday, Dec. 28	Minnesota at Chicago (ESPN)	8:30
Sunday, Jan. 3	To be determined (NBC)*	8:20

POSTSEASON GAMES

Saturday, January 9	AFC and NFC Wild Card Playoffs (NBC)
Sunday, January 10	AFC and NFC Wild Card Playoffs (CBS and FOX)
Saturday, January 16	AFC and NFC Divisional Playoffs (CBS and FOX)
Sunday, January 17	AFC and NFC Divisional Playoffs (CBS and FOX)
Sunday, January 24	AFC and NFC Championship Games (CBS and FOX)
Sunday, January 31	AFC-NFC Pro Bowl in South Florida (ESPN)
Sunday, February 7	Super Bowl XLIV in South Florida (CBS)

**The NFL again will utilize "flexible scheduling" in 2009.*

Flexible scheduling moves will be announced at least 12 days before games in Weeks 11-16. In Week 17, the flexible scheduling move will be announced at least six days before the game. Flexible scheduling will ensure quality matchups on Sunday night in those weeks and give "surprise" teams a chance to play their way on to primetime.

IMPORTANT DATES

2009

July 6 — Claiming period of 24 hours begins in waiver system.

Mid-July — Preseason training camps open. Clubs not permitted to open official preseason camp earlier than July 5. Veteran players cannot be required to report earlier than 15 days prior to club's first preseason game.

July 15 — Deadline at 4 P.M., New York time, for any club that designated a Franchise Player to sign such player to a multi-year contract or extension. After this date, the player may sign only a one-year ctonract with the designating club for the 2009 season, and such contract cannot be extended until after the Club's last regular season game.

July 22 — Signing period ends at 4 P.M., New York time, for Transition Players with outstanding tenders. After this date and through 4 P.M., New York time, on the Tuesday after the 10th regular season weekend, Old Club has exclusive negotiating rights to these players.

July 22# — Signing period ends at 4 P.M., New York time, for Unrestricted Free Agents to whom a June 1 tender was made by Old Club. After this date and through 4 P.M., New York time, on the Tuesday after the 10th regular season weekend, Old Club has exclusive negotiating rights to these players.
#or the first scheduled day of the first NFL training camp, whichever is later.

August 7 — Deadline for players under contract to report to earn a season of free-agency credit.

August 7-9 — Hall of Fame Weekend.

August 9 — Pro Football Hall of Fame Game, Canton, Ohio:
Buffalo vs. Tennessee

August 13-17 — First Preseason Weekend.

August 14 — If a Drafted Rookie has not signed with his club by this date, he may not be traded to any other club in 2009.

August 15-19 — Deadline for club to provide written notice to certain unsigned players and the NFLPA of its intent to place them on the Exempt List if they fail to report no later than one day prior to the club's second preseason game. Any player who fails to report prior to the deadline will be ineligible to play or receive compensation for at least three games (preseason or regular season) from the time that he reports.

September 1 — Roster cut-down to maximum of 75 players on Active List by 4 P.M., New York time.

September 2 — All tryouts on this date and for the remainder of the season must be reported to the League office.

September 5 — Roster cut-down to maximum of 53 players on Active/Inactive List by 4 P.M., New York time. Clubs may dress minimum of 42 and maximum of 45 players and Third Quarterback for each regular-season and postseason game.

September 5 — Simultaneously with the cut-down to 53, clubs that have players in the categories of Active/Physically Unable to Perform or Active/Non-Football Injury or Illness must take one of the following options: place player on Reserve/Physically Unable to Perform or Reserve/Non-Football Injury or Illness, whichever is applicable; ask waivers; terminate; trade; or continue to count him on Active List.

September 6 — After 12 noon, New York time, clubs may establish a Practice Squad of eight players by signing free agents who do not have an accrued season of free-agency credit or who were on the 45-player Active List for less than nine regular-season games during their only Accrued Season(s). A player cannot participate on the Practice Squad for more than three seasons.

September 9 — All clubs are required to file a personnel (injury) report with their conference information manager by 4:00 p.m., New York time. Reports are to be filed every Wednesday, Thursday and Friday before a regular-season game by 4:00 p.m., New York time (or as soon as possible after the completion of practice). An update must also be reported if there is any change in a player's condition after Friday.

September 9 — Beginning at 4 P.M., New York time, Team Salary includes all players receiving compensation under their 2009 contracts. Top 51 rule is no longer in effect.

September 10-14 — Regular Season opens.

September 10-14 — Beginning on these dates vested veterans terminated from the Active List or Inactive List (and from Reserve/Injured if the player is placed on Reserve/Injured after the beginning of the regular season) are entitled to receive, after the end of the regular-season schedule, Termination Pay pursuant to the terms of the CBA.

September 29 — Priority on multiple waiver claims is now based on the current season's standing.

October 20 — Beginning the day after the conclusion of the sixth regular-season weekend and continuing through the day after the conclusion of the ninth regular-season weekend, clubs are permitted to begin practicing players on Reserve/Physically Unable to Perform and Reserve/Non-Football Injury or Illness for a period not to exceed 21 days. Players may be activated during the 21-day practice period or until 4 P.M., New York time, on the day after the conclusion of the 21-day period.

October 20 — All trading ends at 4 P.M., New York time.

October 21 — Players with at least four previous pension-credited seasons are subject to the waiver system for the remainder of the regular season and postseason.

November 17 — Signing period ends at 4 P.M., New York time, for Franchise Players who are eligible to receive Offer Sheets.

November 17 — Deadline for clubs to sign by 4 P.M., New York time, their unsigned Franchise and Transition Players, including Franchise Players who were eligible to receive Offer Sheets until this date. If still unsigned after this date, such players are prohibited from playing in NFL in 2009.

November 17 — Deadline for clubs to sign by 4 P.M., New York time, their Unrestricted Free Agents to whom June 1 tender was made. If still unsigned after this date, such players are prohibited from playing in NFL in 2009.

November 17 — Deadline for clubs to sign by 4 P.M., New York time, their Restricted Free Agents to whom June 1 tender was made. If such players remain unsigned, they are prohibited from playing in NFL in 2009.

November 17 — Deadline for clubs to sign Drafted players by 4 P.M., New York time. If such players remain unsigned, they are prohibited from playing in NFL in 2009.

December 4 — Deadline for reinstatement of players in Reserve List categories of Retired, Did Not Report, and Exclusive Rights, and of players who were placed on Reserve/Left Squad in a previous season.

2010

January 1 — Deadline for waiver requests in 2009, except for "special waiver requests," which have a 10-day claiming period, with termination or assignment delayed until after the Super Bowl.

January 4 — Clubs may begin signing free-agent players for the 2010 season.

January 9-10 — Wild Card Playoff Games.

January 16-17 — Divisional Playoff Games.

January 24 — AFC and NFC Championship Games.

January 31 — AFC-NFC Pro Bowl, Dolphin Stadium, South Florida.

February 7 — Super Bowl XLIV, Dolphin Stadium, South Florida.

2011

February 6 — Super Bowl XLV, Cowboys Stadium, North Texas.

2012

February 5 — Super Bowl XLVI, Lucas Oil Stadium, Indianapolis, Indiana.

2013

February 3* — Super Bowl XLVII, Louisiana Superdome, New Orleans, Louisiana.

**Tentative date.*

NFL ON THE INTERNET

The NFL is online to provide fans and media quick and easy access to all the latest professional football information.

NFL.COM—(http://NFL.com)
NFL.com, the league's year-round home page on the Internet, enters its 13th season in cyberspace. The site provides NFL information during the regular season, postseason, and offseason, including:

NEWS/STATS: Up-to-the-minute news from around the league, plus game previews, injury reports, and player and team stats.

GAMEDAY COVERAGE: Live game coverage with play-by-play, scores, and statistics, including graphical drive charts and comprehensive scoreboard that reloads automatically with the latest information.

VIDEO HIGHLIGHTS: The site showcases NFL Films video highlights of the previous week's games as well as upcoming matchups. Video also supports feature stories and team highlight clips from every game last season. In addition, exclusive NFL Network programming is featured.

TEAM AREAS: Customized areas for all 32 clubs, featuring updated rosters, depth charts, and all the latest news from the teams.

SUPERBOWL.COM—(http://SuperBowl.com)
Look for SuperBowl.com in late December for complete coverage of the playoffs and Super Bowl XLIV. The multimedia site follows all postseason action and features audio and video clips of past Super Bowls.

During the week leading up to Super Bowl XLIV, the site will go "live" from South Florida, providing coverage of events, press conferences, and chats with Super Bowl players and coaches. On Super Bowl Sunday, SuperBowl.com will showcase a live Internet cybercast, complete with online commentators calling the action. The site also features digital photos from the game, live public address audio and press box announcements, and live audio from foreign broadcasts.

NFLATINO.COM POWERED BY UNIVISION.COM—(http://NFLatino.com)
The official U.S. Spanish-language site of the NFL provides in depth information on teams and players, and is the only destination online for NFL video highlights in Spanish. In addition, the site includes Hispanic player diaries, live radio broadcasts, up-to-date stats, fantasy football, and Tu Pasión, the NFL's interactive community for Hispanic fans.

NFLYOUTHFOOTBALL.COM—(http://nflyouthfootball.com)
NFLyouthfootball.com is the NFL's website focused on league-sponsored youth football programs and initiatives, which supports the NFL Play 60 campaign by encouraging kids to be active for at least 60 minutes a day. Boys and girls ages 5-17 nationwide have the opportunity to display their skills in competitive environments with one of the NFL's Youth Football programs. Coaches, parents, and youth organizations can learn how to host their own local NFL Punt, Pass, and Kick event and can learn how to get children involved with an NFL FLAG league in their local community. Our website is also a resource for coaches and parents to help them promote a positive experience for youth participants.

NFLRUSH.COM—(http://www.NFLRUSH.com)
NFLRUSH.com is the official kids' website of the National Football League. The site offers an NFL experience solely for kids, with unique customizable content, games, contests, fun daily features on NFL players and information on the NFL's Youth Football programs. NFLRUSH.com also features fun and interactive fitness information as part of the NFL PLAY 60 campaign, which encourages kids to be active for 60 minutes a day. The NFLRUSH ZONE, a role playing game on NFLRUSH.com, was launched in December 2007. The NFLRUSH ZONE is an immersive virtual world where kids are able to create avatars, join their favorite team, play games, chat, watch cartoons and compete with friends in safe and fun environment. NFLRUSH.com, which is targeted to kids 6-15, provides an environment where kids can share their interest in their NFL and delivers the NFL experience they want to have – as fans, athletes and gamers.

USAFOOTBALL.COM—(http://usafootball.com)
USA Football is an independent, non-profit organization which is leading the growth and development of youth, high school and international amateur football. USA Football helps youth and amateur football organizations keep the sport fun, safe, and accessible by offering resources focused on coaching education, league enhancement, officiating development and health and safety awareness. The organization also serves as the designated United States representatives to the International Federation of American Football. Based near Washington, D.C., USA Football was endowed by the NFL and NFLPA in 2002.

JOINTHETEAM.COM—(http://JoinTheTeam.com)
JoinTheTeam.com is the official website dedicated to the off-the-field community work of the NFL and the member clubs. The site provides news and information regarding how the NFL gives back and serves as a useful tool for individuals who are looking for a way to make a difference in their communities. The site also serves as the online home for NFL Charities, and provides opportunities to learn about and apply for funding. JoinTheTeam.com highlights the ways the league, our teams and our fans come together to make a difference through community involvement.

PROFOOTBALLHOF.COM—(http://profootballhof.com)
Profootballhof.com is the official site of the Pro Football Hall of Fame in Canton, Ohio. In addition to a complete visitor's guide to the Hall, the site features bios, stories and Q & A's with Hall of Fame inductees, a detailed archive of football history, and information on appearances by members of the Hall.

OFFICIAL NFL TEAM SITES
In addition to a dedicated area on NFL.com, all 32 teams have their own Websites, which have separate URLs, and are linked from NFL.com.

Arizona Cardinals (www.azcardinals.com)
Atlanta Falcons (www.atlantafalcons.com)
Baltimore Ravens (www.baltimoreravens.com)
Buffalo Bills (www.buffalobills.com)
Carolina Panthers (www.panthers.com)
Chicago Bears (www.chicagobears.com)
Cincinnati Bengals (www.bengals.com)
Cleveland Browns (www.clevelandbrowns.com)
Dallas Cowboys (www.dallascowboys.com)
Denver Broncos (www.denverbroncos.com)
Detroit Lions (www.detroitlions.com)
Green Bay Packers (www.packers.com)
Houston Texans (www.houstontexans.com)
Indianapolis Colts (www.colts.com)
Jacksonville Jaguars (www.jaguars.com)
Kansas City Chiefs (www.kcchiefs.com)
Miami Dolphins (www.miamidolphins.com)
Minnesota Vikings (www.vikings.com)
New England Patriots (www.patriots.com)
New Orleans Saints (www.neworleanssaints.com)
New York Giants (www.giants.com)
New York Jets (www.newyorkjets.com)
Oakland Raiders (www.raiders.com)
Philadelphia Eagles (www.philadelphiaeagles.com)
Pittsburgh Steelers (www.steelers.com)
St. Louis Rams (www.stlouisrams.com)
San Diego Chargers (www.chargers.com)
San Francisco 49ers (www.sf49ers.com)
Seattle Seahawks (www.seahawks.com)
Tampa Bay Buccaneers (www.buccaneers.com)
Tennessee Titans (www.titansonline.com)
Washington Redskins (www.redskins.com)

NFL Network provides fans with a network to call their own. Seven days a week, 24 hours a day, 365 days a year, fans turn to NFL Network to receive information and insight straight from the field, team headquarters, league offices and everywhere the NFL is making news.

NFL Network gives fans unprecedented year-round access to all NFL events, including the Super Bowl, Playoffs, regular season, preseason, Pro Bowl, Pro Football Hall of Fame induction weekend, NFL Draft, Scouting Combine, Senior Bowl, Insight Bowl, Texas Bowl, league meetings, minicamps and training camps.

In addition, NFL Network is the only place on television for fans to view NFL games outside their initial live airings. From original broadcast versions of past Super Bowls, in-week replays of current games, original network telecasts of classic NFL regular season and postseason games, to live telecasts of college bowl games, preseason games, and regular season *Thursday Night Football* games—NFL Network is truly the year-round destination for football fans. NFL Network is available on cable, telcos and satellite television through your local service provider. If your provider doesn't currently offer NFL Network, please call (866) NFL-NETWORK or log on to IWantNFLNetwork.com for more information.

KEY PROGRAMMING

EXCLUSIVE LIVE PRIMETIME GAMES
NFL Network's eight-game, regular-season Thursday Night primetime schedule kicks off in high definition on November 12. Each game, at 8:00 PM ET, will be preceded by a two-hour pregame show and followed by a live post-game show.

NFL TOTAL ACCESS
NFL Network's signature show is the football show of record. *NFL Total Access* is uniquely structured to see the game through the participants' eyes, airing at 7:00 PM ET Monday through Saturday.

Covering all 32 teams, *NFL Total Access* features interviews with players, coaches and other key league personnel. Using cameras at every facility, *NFL Total Access* has the ability to go live to any NFL team headquarters at any time.

NFL GAMEDAY MORNING
The information packed *NFL GameDay Morning* is the first NFL pregame show on the air Sundays at 9:00 AM ET during the regular season and playoffs, providing fans with the earliest news and notes as well as live reports from around the league. Expert analysts Warren Sapp, Marshall Faulk and Emmy-nominated Steve Mariucci join host Spero Dedes each week.

NFL GAMEDAY RED ZONE
NFL Network provides the best place on television to get up-to-the-minute scores, statistics and news each game day during the season. Airing at 1:00 PM ET on Sundays, *NFL GameDay Red Zone* features continuously scrolling real-time game statistics with audio from Sirius NFL Radio's *Around the League* program.

NFL GAMEDAY SCOREBOARD
After Sunday's early games conclude, *NFL GameDay Scoreboard* takes viewers around the league for post-game press conferences and game highlights. *NFL GameDay Scoreboard* airs at 4:00 PM ET on Sundays and continues through the Sunday afternoon games.

NFL GAMEDAY FINAL
After each Sunday's final game, the 90-minute *NFL GameDay Final* delivers comprehensive coverage of the day's action. Host Rich Eisen is joined by Steve Mariucci and Deion Sanders. *NFL GameDay Final* kicks off at 11:30 PM ET and features highlights, post-game press conferences, on-field interviews, analysis and more in wrapping up each NFL Sunday.

NFL REPLAY
NFL games will be re-aired with the original television announcers and cameras. This offering features the most exciting games each week in a 90-minute format (eliminating halftime and other non-critical elements) at 8:00 PM ET and 9:30 PM ET each Tuesday and Wednesday. Enhancements to each broadcast include additional camera angles, sideline sound and post-game interviews.

In addition, each Monday at 6:00 PM ET, *NFL Replay Real-Time* gives fans a unique minute-by-minute look at what happened in the previous afternoon's games as they unfolded in real time.

PLAYBOOK
NFL Network uses the "all 22" game film watched each week by coaches and players to present football's ultimate chalkboard show. Twice each week – at 8:00 PM ET Thursday and Friday – *Playbook* offers 60-minute strategy sessions with Brian Baldinger, Sterling Sharpe and Solomon Wilcots, who analyze each week's key matchups and discuss technique and game planning with coaches and players.

AMERICA'S GAME
The Sports Emmy-winning original series continues its profiles of Super Bowl champions with the 2008 Pittsburgh Steelers.

NFL's TOP 10
Putting a fresh twist on the countdown genre, *NFL's Top 10* is a fast-paced series airing Saturdays at 9:00 PM ET. *NFL's Top 10* provides an irreverent look at some of the most intriguing subjects in the NFL, creating and debating a top ten list for each category. Each 60-minute episode counts down from No. 10 to the top ranking in each category.

LIVE WIRE
The sounds of the game that only NFL Films can capture – with exclusive on-field and sideline microphone access – will be featured on *Live Wire* each Wednesday at 6:00 PM ET.

NFL CLASSIC GAMES
The only place on television to catch the complete network broadcasts of classic NFL regular season and playoff games is on NFL Network every Friday at 9:00 PM ET. Each *NFL Classic Games* telecast features the original network announcers and graphics.

PRESEASON GAMES
NFL Network is the only place on television where fans can view the majority of NFL preseason games. This summer, NFL Network televises 54 preseason games—every game that does not appear on the four NFL broadcast partners (CBS, FOX, NBC, and ESPN).

SCHEDULING FORMULA

The NFL expanded to 32 teams in 2002 with the addition of the Houston Texans. In addition, the NFL realigned for the first time since 1970—into eight divisions of four teams each—and the scheduling formula that was introduced guarantees for the first time that all teams play each other on a regular, rotating basis. Although the number of teams has increased to 32, the number of playoff teams remains the same at 12.

Under the NFL scheduling formula, every team within a division plays 16 games as follows:

- Home and away against its three division opponents (6 games).
- The four teams from another division within its conference on a rotating three-year cycle (4 games).
- The four teams from a division in the other conference on a rotating four-year cycle (4 games).
- Two intraconference games based on the prior year's standings (2 games). These games will match a first-place team against the first-place teams in the two same-conference divisions the team is not scheduled to play that season. The second-place, third-place, and fourth-place teams in a conference will be matched in the same way each year.

The schedule format takes each team through a cycle of games—home and away—against every other team in the league. From 2002-2009, every team will play every other team at least twice—once home and once away. After the 2008 season, a decision was made to continue with the same rotation in 2010.

In determining how to begin the divisional rotation in 2002, the displacement of teams from their old divisions in the new alignment was taken into account. Preference was given to scheduling games with former division rivals and other regional opponents for clubs realigned from otherwise intact divisions.

FUTURE SCHEDULING ROTATION

		2009	2010
AFC	Intraconference	AFCS	AFCN
EAST	Interconference	NFCS	NFCN
AFC	Intraconference	AFCW	AFCE
NORTH	Interconference	NFCN	NFCS
AFC	Intraconference	AFCE	AFCW
SOUTH	Interconference	NFCW	NFCE
AFC	Intraconference	AFCN	AFCS
WEST	Interconference	NFCE	NFCW
NFC	Intraconference	NFCS	NFCN
EAST	Interconference	AFCW	AFCS
NFC	Intraconference	NFCW	NFCE
NORTH	Interconference	AFCN	AFCE
NFC	Intraconference	NFCE	NFCW
SOUTH	Interconference	AFCE	AFCN
NFC	Intraconference	NFCN	NFCS
WEST	Interconference	AFCS	AFCW

AFC EAST NON-DIVISIONAL OPPONENTS 2009-2010

BUFFALO BILLS

	2009 Home	2009 Away	2010 Home	2010 Away
Intraconference by Division	HOU	JAX	CLE	BALT
	IND	TENN	PITT	CIN
Interconference by Division	NO	ATL	CHI	GB
	TB	CAR	DET	MINN
Intraconference by Position	AFCN	AFCW	AFCS	AFCW

MIAMI DOLPHINS

	2009 Home	2009 Away	2010 Home	2010 Away
Intraconference by Division	HOU	JAX	CLE	BALT
	IND	TENN	PITT	CIN
Interconference by Division	NO	ATL	CHI	GB
	TB	CAR	DET	MINN
Intraconference by Position	AFCN	AFCW	AFCS	AFCW

NEW ENGLAND PATRIOTS

	2009 Home	2009 Away	2010 Home	2010 Away
Intraconference by Division	JAX	HOU	BALT	CLE
	TENN	IND	CIN	PITT
Interconference by Division	ATL	NO	GB	CHI
	CAR	TB	MINN	DET
Intraconference by Position	AFCN	AFCW	AFCS	AFCW

NEW YORK JETS

	2009 Home	2009 Away	2010 Home	2010 Away
Intraconference by Division	JAX	HOU	BALT	CLE
	TENN	IND	CIN	PITT
Interconference by Division	ATL	NO	GB	CHI
	CAR	TB	MINN	DET
Intraconference by Position	AFCN	AFCW	AFCS	AFCW

AFC NORTH NON-DIVISIONAL OPPONENTS 2009-2010

BALTIMORE RAVENS

	2009 Home	2009 Away	2010 Home	2010 Away
Intraconference by Division	DEN	OAK	BUFF	NE
	KC	SD	MIA	NYJ
Interconference by Division	CHI	GB	NO	ATL
	DET	MINN	TB	CAR
Intraconference by Position	AFCS	AFCE	AFCW	AFCS

CINCINNATI BENGALS

	2009 Home	2009 Away	2010 Home	2010 Away
Intraconference by Division	DEN	OAK	BUFF	NE
	KC	SD	MIA	NYJ
Interconference by Division	CHI	GB	NO	ATL
	DET	MINN	TB	CAR
Intraconference by Position	AFCS	AFCE	AFCW	AFCS

CLEVELAND BROWNS

	2009 Home	2009 Away	2010 Home	2010 Away
Intraconference by Division	OAK	DEN	NE	BUFF
	SD	KC	NYJ	MIA
Interconference by Division	GB	CHI	ATL	NO
	MINN	DET	CAR	TB
Intraconference by Position	AFCS	AFCE	AFCW	AFCS

PITTSBURGH STEELERS

	2009 Home	2009 Away	2010 Home	2010 Away
Intraconference by Division	OAK	DEN	NE	BUFF
	SD	KC	NYJ	MIA
Interconference by Division	GB	CHI	ATL	NO
	MINN	DET	CAR	TB
Intraconference by Position	AFCS	AFCE	AFCW	AFCS

SCHEDULING FORMULA

AFC SOUTH NON-DIVISIONAL OPPONENTS 2009-2010

HOUSTON TEXANS	2009 Home	2009 Away	2010 Home	2010 Away
Intraconference by Division	NE	BUFF	KC	DEN
	NYJ	MIA	SD	OAK
Interconference by Division	SF	ARIZ	DALL	PHIL
	SEA	STL	NYG	WASH
Intraconference by Position	AFCW	AFCN	AFCN	AFCE

INDIANAPOLIS COLTS	2009 Home	2009 Away	2010 Home	2010 Away
Intraconference by Division	NE	BUFF	KC	DEN
	NYJ	MIA	SD	OAK
Interconference by Division	SF	ARIZ	DALL	PHIL
	SEA	STL	NYG	WASH
Intraconference by Position	AFCW	AFCN	AFCN	AFCE

JACKSONVILLE JAGUARS	2009 Home	2009 Away	2010 Home	2010 Away
Intraconference by Division	BUFF	NE	DEN	KC
	MIA	NYJ	OAK	SD
Interconference by Division	ARIZ	SF	PHIL	DALL
	STL	SEA	WASH	NYG
Intraconference by Position	AFCW	AFCN	AFCN	AFCE

TENNESSEE TITANS	2009 Home	2009 Away	2010 Home	2010 Away
Intraconference by Division	BUFF	NE	DEN	KC
	MIA	NYJ	OAK	SD
Interconference by Division	ARIZ	SF	PHIL	DALL
	STL	SEA	WASH	NYG
Intraconference by Position	AFCW	AFCN	AFCN	AFCE

AFC WEST NON-DIVISIONAL OPPONENTS 2009-2010

DENVER BRONCOS	2009 Home	2009 Away	2010 Home	2010 Away
Intraconference by Division	CLE	BALT	HOU	JAX
	PITT	CIN	IND	TENN
Interconference by Division	DALL	PHIL	STL	ARIZ
	NYG	WASH	SEA	SF
Intraconference by Position	AFCE	AFCS	AFCE	AFCN

KANSAS CITY CHIEFS	2009 Home	2009 Away	2010 Home	2010 Away
Intraconference by Division	CLE	BALT	JAX	HOU
	PITT	CIN	TENN	IND
Interconference by Division	DALL	PHIL	ARIZ	STL
	NYG	WASH	SF	SEA
Intraconference by Position	AFCE	AFCS	AFCE	AFCN

OAKLAND RAIDERS	2009 Home	2009 Away	2010 Home	2010 Away
Intraconference by Division	BALT	CLE	HOU	JAX
	CIN	PITT	IND	TENN
Interconference by Division	PHIL	DALL	STL	ARIZ
	WASH	NYG	SEA	SF
Intraconference by Position	AFCE	AFCS	AFCE	AFCN

SAN DIEGO CHARGERS	2009 Home	2009 Away	2010 Home	2010 Away
Intraconference by Division	BALT	CLE	JAX	HOU
	CIN	PITT	TENN	IND
Interconference by Division	PHIL	DALL	ARIZ	STL
	WASH	NYG	SF	SEA
Intraconference by Position	AFCE	AFCS	AFCE	AFCN

NFC EAST NON-DIVISIONAL OPPONENTS 2009-2010

DALLAS COWBOYS

	2009 Home	2009 Away	2010 Home	2010 Away
Intraconference by Division	ATL	NO	CHI	GB
	CAR	TB	DET	MINN
Interconference by Division	OAK	DEN	JAX	HOU
	SD	KC	TENN	IND
Intraconference by Position	NFCW	NFCN	NFCS	NFCW

NEW YORK GIANTS

	2009 Home	2009 Away	2010 Home	2010 Away
Intraconference by Division	ATL	NO	CHI	GB
	CAR	TB	DET	MINN
Interconference by Division	OAK	DEN	JAX	HOU
	SD	KC	TENN	IND
Intraconference by Position	NFCW	NFCN	NFCS	NFCW

PHILADELPHIA EAGLES

	2009 Home	2009 Away	2010 Home	2010 Away
Intraconference by Division	NO	ATL	GB	CHI
	TB	CAR	MINN	DET
Interconference by Division	DEN	OAK	HOU	JAX
	KC	SD	IND	TENN
Intraconference by Position	NFCW	NFCN	NFCS	NFCW

WASHINGTON REDSKINS

	2009 Home	2009 Away	2010 Home	2010 Away
Intraconference by Division	NO	ATL	GB	CHI
	TB	CAR	MINN	DET
Interconference by Division	DEN	OAK	HOU	JAX
	KC	SD	IND	TENN
Intraconference by Position	NFCW	NFCN	NFCS	NFCW

NFC NORTH NON-DIVISIONAL OPPONENTS 2009-2010

CHICAGO BEARS

	2009 Home	2009 Away	2010 Home	2010 Away
Intraconference by Division	ARIZ	SF	PHIL	DALL
	STL	SEA	WASH	NYG
Interconference by Division	CLE	BALT	NE	BUFF
	PITT	CIN	NYJ	MIA
Intraconference by Position	NFCE	NFCS	NFCW	NFCS

DETROIT LIONS

	2009 Home	2009 Away	2010 Home	2010 Away
Intraconference by Division	ARIZ	SF	PHIL	DALL
	STL	SEA	WASH	NYG
Interconference by Division	CLE	BALT	NE	BUFF
	PITT	CIN	NYJ	MIA
Intraconference by Position	NFCE	NFCS	NFCW	NFCS

GREEN BAY PACKERS

	2009 Home	2009 Away	2010 Home	2010 Away
Intraconference by Division	SF	ARIZ	DALL	PHIL
	SEA	STL	NYG	WASH
Interconference by Division	BALT	CLE	BUFF	NE
	CIN	PITT	MIA	NYJ
Intraconference by Position	NFCE	NFCS	NFCW	NFCS

MINNESOTA VIKINGS

	2009 Home	2009 Away	2010 Home	2010 Away
Intraconference by Division	SF	ARIZ	DALL	PHIL
	SEA	STL	NYG	WASH
Interconference by Division	BALT	CLE	BUFF	NE
	CIN	PITT	MIA	NYJ
Intraconference by Position	NFCE	NFCS	NFCW	NFCS

NFC SOUTH NON-DIVISIONAL OPPONENTS 2009-2010

ATLANTA FALCONS

	2009 Home	2009 Away	2010 Home	2010 Away
Intraconference by Division	PHIL	DALL	ARIZ	STL
	WASH	NYG	SF	SEA
Interconference by Division	BUFF	NE	BALT	CLE
	MIA	NYJ	CIN	PITT
Intraconference by Position	NFCN	NFCW	NFCN	NFCE

CAROLINA PANTHERS

	2009 Home	2009 Away	2010 Home	2010 Away
Intraconference by Division	PHIL	DALL	ARIZ	STL
	WASH	NYG	SF	SEA
Interconference by Division	BUFF	NE	BALT	CLE
	MIA	NYJ	CIN	PITT
Intraconference by Position	NFCN	NFCW	NFCN	NFCE

NEW ORLEANS SAINTS

	2009 Home	2009 Away	2010 Home	2010 Away
Intraconference by Division	DALL	PHIL	STL	ARIZ
	NYG	WASH	SEA	SF
Interconference by Division	NE	BUFF	CLE	BALT
	NYJ	MIA	PITT	CIN
Intraconference by Position	NFCN	NFCW	NFCN	NFCE

TAMPA BAY BUCCANEERS

	2009 Home	2009 Away	2010 Home	2010 Away
Intraconference by Division	DALL	PHIL	STL	ARIZ
	NYG	WASH	SEA	SF
Interconference by Division	NE	BUFF	CLE	BALT
	NYJ	MIA	PITT	CIN
Intraconference by Position	NFCN	NFCW	NFCN	NFCE

NFC WEST NON-DIVISIONAL OPPONENTS 2009-2010

ARIZONA CARDINALS

	2009 Home	2009 Away	2010 Home	2010 Away
Intraconference by Division	GB	CHI	NO	ATL
	MINN	DET	TB	CAR
Interconference by Division	HOU	JAX	DEN	KC
	IND	TENN	OAK	SD
Intraconference by Position	NFCS	NFCE	NFCE	NFCN

ST. LOUIS RAMS

	2009 Home	2009 Away	2010 Home	2010 Away
Intraconference by Division	GB	CHI	ATL	NO
	MINN	DET	CAR	TB
Interconference by Division	HOU	JAX	KC	DEN
	IND	TENN	SD	OAK
Intraconference by Position	NFCS	NFCE	NFCE	NFCN

SAN FRANCISCO 49ERS

	2009 Home	2009 Away	2010 Home	2010 Away
Intraconference by Division	CHI	GB	NO	ATL
	DET	MINN	TB	CAR
Interconference by Division	JAX	HOU	DEN	KC
	TENN	IND	OAK	SD
Intraconference by Position	NFCS	NFCE	NFCE	NFCN

SEATTLE SEAHAWKS

	2009 Home	2009 Away	2010 Home	2010 Away
Intraconference by Division	CHI	GB	ATL	NO
	DET	MINN	CAR	TB
Interconference by Division	JAX	HOU	KC	DEN
	TENN	IND	SD	OAK
Intraconference by Position	NFCS	NFCE	NFCE	NFCN

TOP ACTIVE PASSERS

1,000 or more attempts

		Yrs.	Att.	Comp.	Pct. Comp.	Yards	TD	Pct. TD	Had Int.	Pct. Int.	Ratings Pts.
1.	Peyton Manning, Ind.	11	5,960	3,839	64.4	45,628	333	5.6	165	2.8	94.7
2.	Tony Romo, Dal.	5	1,307	831	63.6	10,562	81	6.2	46	3.5	94.7
3.	Kurt Warner, Ari.	11	3,557	2,327	65.4	28,591	182	5.1	114	3.2	93.8
4.	Philip Rivers, S.D.	5	1,428	890	62.3	10,697	78	5.5	36	2.5	92.9
5.	Tom Brady, N.E.	9	3,653	2,301	63.0	26,446	197	5.4	86	2.4	92.9
6.	Chad Pennington, Mia.	9	2,395	1,580	66.0	17,391	101	4.2	62	2.6	90.6
7.	Ben Roethlisberger, Pit.	5	1,905	1,189	62.4	14,974	101	5.3	69	3.6	89.4
8.	Drew Brees, N.O.	8	3,650	2,334	63.9	26,258	168	4.6	99	2.7	89.4
9.	Daunte Culpepper, Det.	10	3,042	1,927	63.3	23,208	146	4.8	100	3.3	89.0
10.	Carson Palmer, Cin.	5	2,165	1,380	63.7	15,630	107	4.9	67	3.1	88.9
11.	Jeff Garcia, Oak.	10	3,676	2,264	61.6	25,537	161	4.4	83	2.3	87.5
12.	Jay Cutler, Chi.	3	1,220	762	62.5	9,024	54	4.4	37	3.0	87.1
13.	Trent Green, *	11	3,740	2,266	60.6	28,475	162	4.3	114	3.0	86.0
14.	Donovan McNabb, Phi.	10	4,303	2,534	58.9	29,320	194	4.5	90	2.1	85.9
15.	Marc Bulger, St.L.	7	2,924	1,829	62.6	21,345	117	4.0	87	3.0	85.6
16.	David Garrard, Jac.	7	1,399	856	61.2	9,672	51	3.6	29	2.1	85.4
17.	Jake Delhomme, Car.	8	2,434	1,452	59.7	17,877	115	4.7	76	3.1	85.1
18.	Matt Hasselbeck, Sea.	10	3,347	2,013	60.1	23,549	147	4.4	94	2.8	84.5
19.	Mark Brunell, N.O.	15	4,594	2,738	59.6	31,826	182	4.0	106	2.3	84.2
20.	Brian Griese, T.B.	11	2,796	1,752	62.7	19,440	119	4.3	99	3.5	82.7
21.	Brad Johnson, *	15	4,326	2,668	61.7	29,054	166	3.8	122	2.8	82.5
22.	Jason Campbell, Was.	3	1,130	675	59.7	7,242	35	3.1	23	2.0	80.4
23.	Byron Leftwich, T.B.	6	1,438	842	58.6	9,624	54	3.8	38	2.6	80.3
24.	Charlie Batch, Pit.	11	1,459	818	56.1	10,033	57	3.9	44	3.0	77.9
25.	Jon Kitna, Dal.	12	4,114	2,462	59.8	27,293	152	3.7	151	3.7	76.6

TOP ACTIVE SCORERS

(number in parentheses represents 2-point conversions scored)

		Yrs.	TD	FG	PAT	TP
1.	John Carney, *	21	0	460	575	1,955
2.	Matt Stover, *	18	0	462	558	1,944
3.	Jason Elam, Atl.	16	0	424	643	1,915
4.	Jason Hanson, Det.	17	0	406	529	1,747
5.	John Kasay, Car.	18	0	386	476	1,634
6.	Adam Vinatieri, Ind.	13	0	331	497(1)	1,492
7.	Ryan Longwell, Min.	12	0	296	482	1,370
8.	Olindo Mare, Sea.	12	0	279	377	1,214
9.	David Akers, Phi.	11	0	230	353	1,043
10.	Kris Brown, Hou.	10	0	231	304	997
11.	Joe Nedney, S.F.	13	0	228	295	979
12.	Sebastian Janikowski, Oak.	9	0	203	296	905
13.	Phil Dawson, Cle.	10	1	212	255	897
	Rian Lindell, Buf.	9	0	205	282	897
15.	Jay Feely, NYJ	8	0	201	288	891
16.	Terrell Owens, Buf.	13	141	0	0(3)	852
17.	LaDainian Tomlinson, S.D.	8	141	0	0	846
18.	Randy Moss, N.E.	11	136	0	0(3)	822
19.	Neil Rackers, Ari.	9	0	189	253	820
20.	Marvin Harrison, *	13	128	0	0(5)	778
21.	Shayne Graham, Cin.	8	0	173	248	767
22.	Jeff Reed, Pit.	7	0	162	247	733
23.	Martin Gramatica, *	9	0	155	228	693
24.	Josh Brown, St.L.	6	0	147	242	683
25.	Nate Kaeding, S.D.	5	0	118	253	607

**Free agent; subject to developments.*

TOP ACTIVE SCORERS (TOUCHDOWNS)

		Yrs.	Rush	Rec.	Ret.	Tot.
1.	Terrell Owens, Buf.	13	2	139	0	141
	LaDainian Tomlinson, S.D.	8	126	15	0	141
3.	Randy Moss, N.E.	11	0	135	1	136
4.	Marvin Harrison, *	13	0	128	0	128
5.	Isaac Bruce, S.F.	15	0	91	0	91
	Edgerrin James, *	10	80	11	0	91
7.	Joey Galloway, N.E.	14	1	77	5	83
8.	Tony Gonzalez, Atl.	12	0	76	0	76
	Clinton Portis, Was.	7	72	4	0	76
10.	Torry Holt, Jac.	10	0	74	0	74
11.	Ahman Green, *	11	59	14	0	73
	Hines Ward, Pit.	11	1	72	0	73
13.	Fred Taylor, N.E.	11	62	8	0	70
14.	Brian Westbrook, Phi.	7	36	28	2	66
15.	Warrick Dunn, *	12	49	15	0	64
16.	Jamal Lewis, Cle.	8	58	4	0	62
17.	Larry Johnson, K.C.	6	55	6	0	61
	Muhsin Muhammad, Car.	13	0	61	0	61
19.	Amani Toomer, *	13	1	54	3	58
20.	Ricky Williams, Mia.	8	51	5	0	56
21.	Plaxico Burress, *	9	0	55	0	55
	Derrick Mason, Bal.	12	0	52	3	55
	Deuce McAllister, *	8	49	5	1	55
24.	Chad Ochocinco, Cin.	8	0	53	0	53
	Reggie Wayne, Ind.	8	0	53	0	53

NFL ACTIVE STATISTICAL LEADERS

TOP ACTIVE RUSHERS

		Yrs.	Att.	Yards	TD
1.	Edgerrin James, *	10	2,982	12,121	80
2.	LaDainian Tomlinson, S.D.	8	2,657	11,760	126
3.	Fred Taylor, N.E.	11	2,428	11,271	62
4.	Warrick Dunn, *	12	2,669	10,967	49
5.	Jamal Lewis, Cle.	8	2,399	10,107	58
6.	Clinton Portis, Was.	7	2,052	9,202	72
7.	Ahman Green, *	11	2,015	9,045	59
8.	Thomas Jones, NYJ	9	1,949	7,815	48
9.	Ricky Williams, Mia.	8	1,923	7,771	51
10.	Deuce McAllister, *	8	1,429	6,096	49
11.	Rudi Johnson, *	8	1,517	5,979	49
12.	Brian Westbrook, Phi.	7	1,247	5,721	36
13.	Larry Johnson, K.C.	6	1,243	5,638	55
14.	Michael Pittman, *	11	1,392	5,627	25
15.	Steven Jackson, St.L.	5	1,224	5,291	37
16.	Willis McGahee, Bal.	5	1,332	5,243	38
17.	Willie Parker, Pit.	5	1,155	4,989	24
18.	Frank Gore, S.F.	4	939	4,441	22
19.	Julius Jones, Sea.	5	1,043	4,182	20
20.	Chester Taylor, Min.	7	934	4,058	21
21.	LaMont Jordan, Den.	8	872	3,648	28
22.	Michael Bennett, S.D.	8	817	3,627	13
23.	Reuben Droughns, *	8	929	3,602	19
24.	DeShaun Foster, *	6	927	3,570	11
25.	Ronnie Brown, Mia.	4	781	3,433	23

TOP ACTIVE SCRIMMAGE YARDS LEADERS

		Yrs.	Rush	Rec	Total	TD
1.	LaDainian Tomlinson, S.D.	8	11,760	3,801	15,561	141
2.	Edgerrin James, *	10	12,121	3,345	15,466	91
3.	Warrick Dunn, *	12	10,967	4,339	15,306	64
4.	Isaac Bruce, S.F.	15	147	14,944	15,091	91
5.	Marvin Harrison, *	13	28	14,580	14,608	128
6.	Terrell Owens, Buf.	13	197	14,122	14,319	141
7.	Fred Taylor, N.E.	11	11,271	2,361	13,632	70
8.	Randy Moss, N.E.	11	159	13,201	13,360	135
9.	Torry Holt, Jac.	10	57	12,660	12,717	74
10.	Ahman Green, *	11	9,045	2,865	11,910	73
11.	Jamal Lewis, Cle.	8	10,107	1,791	11,898	62
12.	Joey Galloway, N.E.	14	496	10,710	11,206	78
13.	Clinton Portis, Was.	7	9,202	1,906	11,108	76
14.	Tony Gonzalez, Atl.	12	14	10,940	10,954	76
15.	Muhsin Muhammad, Car.	13	64	10,857	10,921	61
16.	Hines Ward, Pit.	11	430	9,780	10,210	73
17.	Derrick Mason, Bal.	12	1	10,061	10,062	52
18.	Ricky Williams, Mia.	8	7,771	2,118	9,889	56
19.	Thomas Jones, NYJ	9	7,815	1,800	9,615	51
20.	Amani Toomer, *	13	110	9,497	9,607	55
21.	Brian Westbrook, Phi.	7	5,721	3,609	9,330	64
22.	Michael Pittman, *	11	5,627	3,512	9,139	33
23.	Chad Ochocinco, Cin.	8	143	8,905	9,048	53
24.	Laveranues Coles, Cin.	9	221	8,095	8,316	44
25.	Donald Driver, G.B.	10	204	7,989	8,193	44

TOP ACTIVE PASS RECEIVERS

		Yrs.	No.	Yards	TD
1.	Marvin Harrison, *	13	1,102	14,580	128
2.	Isaac Bruce, S.F.	15	1,003	14,944	91
3.	Terrell Owens, Buf.	13	951	14,122	139
4.	Tony Gonzalez, Atl.	12	916	10,940	76
5.	Torry Holt, Jac.	10	869	12,660	74
6.	Randy Moss, N.E.	11	843	13,201	135
7.	Muhsin Muhammad, Car.	13	807	10,857	61
8.	Hines Ward, Pit.	11	800	9,780	72
9.	Derrick Mason, Bal.	12	790	10,061	52
10.	Joey Galloway, N.E.	14	682	10,710	77
11.	Amani Toomer, *	13	668	9,497	54
12.	Bobby Engram, K.C.	13	645	7,690	35
13.	Laveranues Coles, Cin.	9	631	8,095	44
14.	Chad Ochocinco, Cin.	8	612	8,905	53
15.	Donald Driver, G.B.	10	577	7,989	43
16.	Reggie Wayne, Ind.	8	576	8,129	53
17.	Ike Hilliard, *	12	546	6,397	35
18.	Marty Booker, *	10	523	6,522	36
19.	Warrick Dunn, *	12	510	4,339	15
	LaDainian Tomlinson, S.D.	8	510	3,801	15
21.	Steve Smith, Car.	8	509	7,348	43
22.	T.J. Houshmandzadeh, Sea.	8	507	5,782	37
23.	Plaxico Burress, *	9	505	7,845	55
24.	Anquan Boldin, Ari.	6	502	6,496	40
25.	Darrell Jackson, *	9	499	7,132	51

TOP ACTIVE INTERCEPTORS

		Yrs.	No.	Yards	TD
1.	Darren Sharper, N.O.	12	54	1,036	8
2.	Ty Law, *	14	52	791	7
3.	Champ Bailey, Den.	10	43	428	4
	Ed Reed, Bal.	7	43	1,144	5
5.	Sammy Knight, *	12	42	664	4
6.	Aaron Glenn, *	15	41	560	6
7.	Dre' Bly, S.F.	10	40	586	5
8.	Sam Madison, *	12	38	595	2
9.	Ronde Barber, T.B.	12	37	653	7
	Patrick Surtain, *	11	37	430	2
11.	Charles Woodson, G.B.	11	36	606	6
12.	Walt Harris, S.F.	13	35	332	4
13.	Brian Dawkins, Den.	13	34	515	2
	Rodney Harrison, *	15	34	361	2
	Deltha O'Neal, *	9	34	452	3
16.	Shawn Springs, N.E.	12	32	421	2
17.	Samari Rolle, Bal.	11	31	425	1
18.	Nate Clements, S.F.	8	29	428	5
	Anthony Henry, Det.	8	29	507	3
20.	Donnie Edwards, *	13	28	347	4
	Ray Lewis, Bal.	13	28	464	2
22.	Mike McKenzie, *	10	27	425	4
23.	Chris McAlister, *	10	26	486	5
	Asante Samuel, Phi.	6	26	377	4
25.	Derrick Brooks, *	14	25	530	6
	Rashean Mathis, Jac.	6	25	441	3
	Lawyer Milloy, *	13	25	205	1

TOP ACTIVE PUNT RETURNERS

40 or more punt returns

	Yrs.	No.	Yards	Avg.	TD
1. Roscoe Parrish, Buf.	4	94	1,312	14.0	3
2. Santana Moss, Was.	8	101	1,216	12.0	3
3. Devin Hester, Chi.	3	121	1,449	12.0	7
4. Will Blackmon, G.B.	3	44	504	11.5	3
5. Jacoby Jones, Hou.	2	62	672	10.8	2
6. Josh Cribbs, Cle.	4	65	689	10.6	1
7. Johnnie Lee Higgins, Oak.	2	64	673	10.5	3
8. Dante Hall, *	9	216	2,261	10.5	6
9. Bobby Engram, K.C.	13	102	1,059	10.4	2
10. Dennis Northcutt, Jac.	9	233	2,403	10.3	3
11. Hank Poteat, Cle.	8	77	788	10.2	1
12. Allen Rossum, S.F.	11	295	2,972	10.1	3
13. Nate Burleson, Sea.	6	126	1,269	10.1	3
14. Nate Clements, S.F.	8	78	778	10.0	2
15. James Thrash, Was.	12	42	418	10.0	0
16. Deltha O'Neal, *	9	138	1,370	9.9	2
17. Mewelde Moore, Pit.	5	80	789	9.9	2
18. Reggie Bush, N.O.	3	51	498	9.8	4
19. Wes Welker, N.E.	5	176	1,718	9.8	0
20. Amani Toomer, *	13	109	1,060	9.7	3
21. Adam Jones, *	3	84	807	9.6	4
22. Kevin Faulk, N.E.	10	94	901	9.6	0
23. Joey Galloway, N.E.	14	141	1,349	9.6	5
24. Leon Washington, NYJ	3	62	583	9.4	0
25. Mark Jones, Ten.	5	156	1,460	9.4	0

TOP ACTIVE KICKOFF RETURNERS

40 or more kickoff returns

	Yrs.	No.	Yards	Avg.	TD
1. Danieal Manning, Chi.	3	40	1,151	28.8	1
2. Leodis McKelvin, Buf.	1	52	1,468	28.2	1
3. Ellis Hobbs, Phi.	4	105	2,913	27.7	3
4. Justin Miller, Oak.	4	141	3,745	26.6	5
5. Josh Cribbs, Cle.	4	209	5,507	26.3	5
6. Terrence McGee, Buf.	6	206	5,420	26.3	5
7. Maurice Jones-Drew, Jac.	3	75	1,952	26.0	2
8. Josh Wilson, Sea.	2	83	2,138	25.8	1
9. Adam Jones, *	3	70	1,803	25.8	0
10. Leon Washington, NYJ	3	101	2,601	25.8	4
11. Darren Sproles, S.D.	4	153	3,912	25.6	2
12. Jerious Norwood, Atl.	3	116	2,948	25.4	0
13. Quintin Demps, Phi.	1	52	1,314	25.3	1
14. Michael Turner, Atl.	5	44	1,111	25.3	0
15. Derek Stanley, St.L.	2	45	1,129	25.1	0
16. Pierre Thomas, N.O.	2	67	1,658	24.7	0
17. Chris Carr, Bal.	4	236	5,825	24.7	0
18. Koren Robinson, *	8	84	2,070	24.6	1
19. Rock Cartwright, Was.	7	183	4,464	24.4	1
20. Glenn Holt, Min.	3	122	2,961	24.3	1
21. Miles Austin, Dal.	3	82	1,989	24.3	0
22. Deuce McAllister, *	8	45	1,091	24.2	0
23. Mark Jones, Ten.	5	58	1,405	24.2	0
24. Reuben Droughns, *	8	72	1,743	24.2	0
25. Steve Smith, Car.	8	98	2,371	24.2	2

TOP ACTIVE PUNTERS

50 or more punts

	Yrs.	No.	Avg.	LG
1. Shane Lechler, Oak.	9	682	46.8	73
2. Donnie Jones, St.L.	5	359	45.2	80
3. Mat McBriar, Dal.	5	299	45.0	75
4. Jon Ryan, Sea.	3	222	44.9	72
5. Chris Kluwe, Min.	4	318	44.5	70
6. Andy Lee, S.F.	5	455	44.4	82
7. Mike Scifres, S.D.	6	341	44.1	71
8. Sam Koch, Bal.	3	248	43.8	74
9. Dustin Colquitt, K.C.	4	301	43.7	81
10. Brandon Fields, Mia.	2	151	43.5	71
11. Ben Graham, Ari.	4	249	43.5	69
12. Steven Weatherford, Jac.	3	199	43.5	61
13. Hunter Smith, Was.	10	577	43.4	69
14. Brian Moorman, Buf.	8	610	43.2	84
15. Mitch Berger, Pit.	14	796	43.0	75
16. Chris Hanson, N.E.	9	521	42.8	74
17. Craig Hentrich, Ten.	15	1,141	42.8	78
18. Josh Bidwell, T.B.	9	727	42.8	68
19. Sav Rocca, Phi.	2	150	42.7	65
20. Dave Zastudil, Cle.	7	532	42.6	67
21. Jason Baker, Car.	8	561	42.5	70
22. Matt Turk, Hou.	13	970	42.4	77
23. Adam Podlesh, Jac.	2	100	42.4	76
24. Daniel Sepulveda, Pit.	2	68	42.4	59
25. Michael Koenen, Atl.	4	305	42.3	67

TOP ACTIVE QUARTERBACK SACKERS

	Yrs.	No.
1. Jason Taylor, Mia.	12	120.5
2. Kevin Carter, *	14	104.5
3. Willie McGinest, *	15	86.0
4. John Abraham, Atl.	9	84.0
5. La'Roi Glover, *	13	83.5
Trevor Pryce, Bal.	12	83.5
7. Joey Porter, Mia.	10	83.0
8. Leonard Little, St.L.	11	81.0
9. Patrick Kerney, Sea.	10	77.5
10. Greg Ellis, Dal.	11	77.0
11. Jevon Kearse, Ten.	10	73.0
12. Dwight Freeney, Ind.	7	70.5
Julius Peppers, Car.	7	70.5
14. Aaron Schobel, Buf.	8	68.0
15. Shaun Ellis, NYJ	9	61.5
16. Darren Howard, Phi.	9	60.5
Adewale Ogunleye, Chi.	8	60.5
18. Bertrand Berry, Ari.	11	59.0
Phillip Daniels, Was.	13	59.0
20. Jared Allen, Min.	5	57.5
21. Junior Seau, N.E.	19	56.5
22. Vonnie Holliday, *	11	55.0
Mike Vrabel, K.C.	12	55.0
24. Robert Mathis, Ind.	6	53.5
DeMarcus Ware, Dal.	4	53.5

COACHES RECORDS

ACTIVE COACHES' CAREER RECORDS (Order Based on Career Victories)
Start of 2009 Season

			Regular Season				Postseason			Career			
Coach	**Team(s)**	**Yrs.**	**Won**	**Lost**	**Tied**	**Pct.**	**Won**	**Lost**	**Pct.**	**Won**	**Lost**	**Tied**	**Pct.**
Bill Belichick	Cleveland Browns, New England Patriots	14	138	86	0	.616	15	4	.789	153	90	0	.630
Jeff Fisher	Houston-Tennessee Oilers, Tennessee Titans	14	128	102	0	.557	5	6	.455	133	108	0	.552
Tom Coughlin	Jacksonville Jaguars, New York Giants	13	115	93	0	.553	8	7	.533	123	100	0	.552
Andy Reid	Philadelphia Eagles	10	97	62	1	.609	10	7	.588	107	69	1	.607
Norv Turner	Washington Redskins, Oakland Raiders, San Diego Chargers	11	77	95	1	.448	4	3	.571	81	98	1	.453
Wade Phillips	New Orleans Saints, Denver Broncos, Buffalo Bills, Atlanta Falcons, Dallas Cowboys	9	70	49	0	.588	0	4	.000	70	53	0	.569
John Fox	Carolina Panthers	7	63	49	0	.563	5	3	.625	68	52	0	.567
Dick Jauron	Chicago Bears, Detroit Lions, Buffalo Bills	9	57	76	0	.429	0	1	.000	57	77	0	.425
Jack Del Rio	Jacksonville Jaguars	6	50	46	0	.521	1	2	.333	51	48	0	.515
Lovie Smith	Chicago Bears	5	45	35	0	.563	2	2	.500	47	37	0	.560
Marvin Lewis	Cincinnati Bengals	6	46	49	1	.484	0	1	.000	46	50	1	.479
Mike McCarthy	Green Bay Packers	3	27	21	0	.563	1	1	.500	28	22	0	.560
Jim Mora	Atlanta Falcons, Seattle Seahawks	3	26	22	0	.542	1	1	.500	27	23	0	.540
Sean Payton	New Orleans Saints	3	25	23	0	.521	1	1	.500	26	24	0	.520
Mike Tomlin	Pittsburgh Steelers	2	22	10	0	.688	3	1	.750	25	11	0	.694
Brad Childress	Minnesota Vikings	3	24	24	0	.500	0	1	.000	24	25	0	.490
Eric Mangini	New York Jets, Cleveland Browns	3	23	25	0	.479	0	1	.000	23	26	0	.469
Gary Kubiak	Houston Texans	3	22	26	0	.458	0	0	—	22	26	0	.458
Ken Whisenhunt	Arizona Cardinals	2	17	15	0	.531	3	1	.750	20	16	0	.556
John Harbaugh	Baltimore Ravens	1	11	5	0	.688	2	1	.667	13	6	0	.684
Mike Smith	Atlanta Falcons	1	11	5	0	.688	0	1	.000	11	6	0	.647
Tony Sparano	Miami Dolphins	1	11	5	0	.688	0	1	.000	11	6	0	.647
Jim Zorn	Washington Redskins	1	8	8	0	.500	0	0	—	8	8	0	.500
Mike Singletary	San Francisco 49ers	1	5	4	0	.556	0	0	—	5	4	0	.556
Tom Cable	Oakland Raiders	1	4	8	0	.333	0	0	—	4	8	0	.333
Jim Caldwell	Indianapolis Colts	0	0	0	0	—	0	0	—	0	0	0	—
Todd Haley	Kansas City Chiefs	0	0	0	0	—	0	0	—	0	0	0	—
Josh McDaniels	Denver Broncos	0	0	0	0	—	0	0	—	0	0	0	—
Raheem Morris	Tampa Bay Buccaneers	0	0	0	0	—	0	0	—	0	0	0	—
Rex Ryan	New York Jets	0	0	0	0	—	0	0	—	0	0	0	—
Jim Schwartz	Detroit Lions	0	0	0	0	—	0	0	—	0	0	0	—
Steve Spagnuolo	St. Louis Rams	0	0	0	0	—	0	0	—	0	0	0	—

COACHES WITH 100 CAREER VICTORIES (Order Based on Career Victories)
Start of 2009 Season

Coach	Team(s)	Yrs.	Regular Season Won	Lost	Tied	Pct.	Postseason Won	Lost	Pct.	Career Won	Lost	Tied	Pct.
Don Shula	Baltimore Colts, Miami Dolphins	33	328	156	6	.677	19	17	.528	347	173	6	.666
George Halas	Chicago Bears	40	318	148	31	.682	6	3	.667	324	151	31	.682
Tom Landry	Dallas Cowboys	29	250	162	6	.607	20	16	.556	270	178	6	.603
Earl (Curly) Lambeau	Green Bay Packers, Chicago Cardinals, Washington Redskins	33	226	132	22	.631	3	2	.600	229	134	22	.631
Chuck Noll	Pittsburgh Steelers	23	193	148	1	.566	16	8	.667	209	156	1	.572
Marty Schottenheimer	Cleveland Browns, Kansas City Chiefs, Washington Redskins, San Diego Chargers	21	200	126	1	.613	5	13	.278	205	139	1	.596
Dan Reeves	Denver Broncos, New York Giants, Atlanta Falcons	23	190	165	2	.535	11	9	.550	201	174	2	.536
Chuck Knox	Los Angeles Rams, Buffalo Bills, Seattle Seahawks	22	186	147	1	.558	7	11	.389	193	158	1	.550
Bill Parcells	New York Giants, New England Patriots, New York Jets, Dallas Cowboys	19	172	130	1	.569	11	8	.579	183	138	1	.570
Mike Holmgren	Green Bay Packers, Seattle Seahawks	17	161	111	0	.592	13	11	.542	174	122	0	.588
Joe Gibbs	Washington Redskins	16	154	94	0	.621	17	7	.708	171	101	0	.629
Paul Brown	Cleveland Browns, Cincinnati Bengals	21	166	100	6	.624	4	8	.333	170	108	6	.612
Bud Grant	Minnesota Vikings	18	158	96	5	.621	10	12	.455	168	108	5	.608
Bill Cowher	Pittsburgh Steelers	15	149	90	1	.623	12	9	.571	161	99	1	.619
Mike Shanahan	Los Angeles Raiders, Denver Broncos	16	146	98	0	.598	8	5	.615	154	103	0	.599
Marv Levy	Kansas City Chiefs, Buffalo Bills	17	143	112	0	.561	11	8	.579	154	120	0	.562
Bill Belichick	Cleveland Browns, New England Patriots	14	138	86	0	.616	15	4	.789	153	90	0	.630
Steve Owen	New York Giants	23	151	100	17	.602	2	8	.200	153	108	17	.586
Tony Dungy	Tampa Bay Buccaneers, Indianapolis Colts	13	139	69	0	.668	9	10	.474	148	79	0	.652
Hank Stram	Kansas City Chiefs, New Orleans Saints	17	131	97	10	.574	5	3	.625	136	100	10	.576
Weeb Ewbank	Baltimore Colts, New York Jets	20	130	129	7	.502	4	1	.800	134	130	7	.508
Jeff Fisher	Houston-Tennessee Oilers, Tennessee Titans	14	128	102	0	.557	5	6	.455	133	108	0	.552
Mike Ditka	Chicago Bears, New Orleans Saints	14	121	95	0	.560	6	6	.500	127	101	0	.557
Dick Vermeil	Philadelphia Eagles, St. Louis Rams, Kansas City Chiefs	15	120	109	0	.524	6	5	.545	126	114	0	.525
Jim Mora	New Orleans Saints, Indianapolis Colts	15	125	106	0	.541	0	6	.000	125	112	0	.527
George Seifert	San Francisco 49ers, Carolina Panthers	11	114	62	0	.648	10	5	.667	124	67	0	.649
Tom Coughlin	Jacksonville Jaguars, New York Giants	13	115	93	0	.553	8	7	.533	123	100	0	.552
Sid Gillman	Los Angeles Rams, Los Angeles-San Diego Chargers, Houston Oilers	18	122	99	7	.552	1	5	.167	123	104	7	.542
George Allen	Los Angeles Rams, Washington Redskins	12	116	47	5	.712	2	7	.222	118	54	5	.686
Dennis Green	Minnesota Vikings, Arizona Cardinals	13	113	94	0	.546	4	8	.333	117	102	0	.534
Don Coryell	St. Louis Cardinals, San Diego Chargers	14	111	83	1	.572	3	6	.333	114	89	1	.561
John Madden	Oakland Raiders	10	103	32	7	.759	9	7	.563	112	39	7	.739
Andy Reid	Philadelphia Eagles	10	97	62	1	.609	10	7	.588	107	69	1	.607
Ray (Buddy) Parker	Chicago Cardinals, Detroit Lions, Pittsburgh Steelers	15	104	75	9	.581	3	1	.750	107	76	9	.585
Vince Lombardi	Green Bay Packers, Washington Redskins	10	96	34	6	.739	9	1	.900	105	35	6	.750
Tom Flores	Oakland-Los Angeles Raiders, Seattle Seahawks	12	97	87	0	.527	8	3	.727	105	90	0	.538
Bill Walsh	San Francisco 49ers	10	92	59	1	.609	10	4	.714	102	63	1	.617
Jon Gruden	Oakland Raiders, Tampa Bay Buccaneers	11	95	81	0	.540	5	4	.556	100	85	0	.541

Active coaches in bold.
From 1920-71, tie games were not included in winning percentage.

WHAT TO LOOK FOR IN 2009

The **Green Bay Packers** need seven regular-season victories to become the second NFL team with 650 regular-season victories (Chicago, 686). Green Bay's all-time regular-season record is 643-513-36.

The **Detroit Lions** need five victories to reach 500 total victories. Detroit's all-time record is 495-579-32.

The **Indianapolis Colts** need six victories to reach 450 total victories. Indianapolis' all-time record is 444-406-7.

Indianapolis needs 12 regular-season wins to become the first team in NFL history with seven consecutive 12-win seasons. Indianapolis is the only team to accomplish the feat in six consecutive seasons.

The **New England Patriots** need two victories to reach 400 total victories. New England's all-time record is 398-367-9.

The **Minnesota Vikings** need five regular-season victories to reach 400 regular-season victories. Minnesota's all-time regular-season record is 395-322-9.

Minnesota can become the second team in history to lead the league in fewest rushing yards allowed for four consecutive seasons. Dallas (1966-69) is the only team to have accomplished the feat.

The **Buffalo Bills** need two regular-season victories to reach 350 regular-season victories. Buffalo's all-time regular-season record is 348-384-8.

The **Denver Broncos** need to score in their first 14 games to surpass Cleveland (274 games, 1950-1971) for the second-longest scoring streak in NFL history. The Broncos' current streak began on November 30, 1992 and stands at 261 games.

Bill Belichick, New England, needs nine victories to pass Marv Levy (154), Mike Shanahan (154) and Bill Cowher (161) for 14th place all-time in career victories. In 14 seasons, Belichick has 153 career victories.

Andy Reid, Philadelphia, needs three regular-season victories to reach 100 regular-season victories. In 10 seasons, Reid has 97 regular-season victories.

Peyton Manning, Indianapolis, needs 4,000 passing yards to become the first quarterback in NFL history with 10 4,000-yard seasons. Manning is the only quarterback to accomplish the feat in nine seasons.

Manning needs 25 touchdown passes to become the first player in NFL history to throw 25 touchdown passes in 12 consecutive seasons. Manning is the only player to have 11 consecutive seasons with 25 touchdown passes.

Manning has passed for 3,000 yards in each of the past 11 seasons and owns the second-longest streak of consecutive 3,000-yard seasons (Brett Favre, 17). Manning is the only player in NFL history to start a career with 11 consecutive 3,000-yard seasons.

Manning has led the league in touchdown passes three times in his career and can tie Brett Favre, Johnny Unitas, Len Dawson and Steve Young (4) for the most seasons leading the league in touchdown passes.

Manning has passed for 400 yards in a game seven times in his career. Manning needs one 400-yard passing game to surpass Joe Montana and Warren Moon (7) for the second-most games with 400 passing yards in NFL history (Dan Marino, 13).

Manning needs 10 touchdown passes to surpass Fran Tarkenton (342) to move into third place all-time. In 11 seasons, Manning has thrown 333 touchdown passes.

Manning needs 285 completions to surpass Drew Bledsoe (3,839), Warren Moon (3,988) and John Elway (4,123) to move into third place all-time. In 11 seasons, Manning has completed 3,839 passes.

Manning needs 3,698 passing yards to surpass Vinny Testaverde (46,233), Fran Tarkenton (47,003) and Warren Moon (49,325) to move into fourth place all-time. In 11 seasons, Manning has passed for 45,628 yards.

Kerry Collins, Tennessee, needs 2,607 passing yards to become the 12th quarterback in NFL history with 40,000 career passing yards. In 14 seasons, Collins has 37,393 passing yards.

LaDainian Tomlinson, San Diego, needs 10 rushing touchdowns to extend his NFL-record streak of consecutive 10-touchdown seasons to begin a career to nine.

Tomlinson needs five touchdowns to surpass Terrell Owens (141) and Marcus Allen (145) to move into third place all-time (see Owens note). In eight seasons, Tomlinson has scored 141 touchdowns.

Tomlinson has gained 2,000 scrimmage yards three times in his eight-year career. With one more 2,000-scrimmage yard season, Tomlinson will tie Eric Dickerson, Marshall Faulk and Walter Payton (4) for the most all-time (see James note).

Tomlinson has gained 2,000 combined yards three times in his career. Tomlinson needs one more season with 2,000 combined yards to tie Tiki Barber, Eric Dickerson, Marshall Faulk, Dante Hall, Brian Mitchell and Walter Payton (4) for the most all-time (see Hall and James notes).

Tomlinson has four 200-yard rushing games in his career. Tomlinson needs two to surpass Tiki Barber (5) and tie O.J. Simpson (6) for the most all-time.

Tomlinson needs 1,000 rushing yards to become the fourth player in NFL history with nine consecutive 1,000-yard rushing seasons. Only Emmitt Smith (11), Barry Sanders and Curtis Martin (10) have accomplished the feat.

Tomlinson needs 439 scrimmage yards to become the 10th player in NFL history with 16,000 scrimmage yards (see Bruce, Dunn and James notes). In eight seasons, Tomlinson has 15,561 scrimmage yards.

Edgerrin James has gained 2,000 scrimmage yards three times in his 10-year career. With one more 2,000-scrimmage yard season, James will tie Eric Dickerson, Marshall Faulk and Walter Payton (4) for the most all-time (see Tomlinson note).

James has gained 2,000 combined yards three times in his career. James needs one more season with 2,000 combined yards to tie Tiki Barber, Eric Dickerson, Marshall Faulk, Dante Hall, Brian Mitchell and Walter Payton (4) for the most all-time (see Hall and Tomlinson notes).

James needs 1,139 rushing yards to surpass Marcus Allen (12,243), Marshall Faulk (12,279), Jim Brown (12,312), Tony Dorsett (12,739) and Eric Dickerson (13,259) to move into sixth place all-time. In 10 seasons, James has 12,121 rushing yards.

James needs 554 scrimmage yards to become the 10th player in NFL history with 16,000 scrimmage yards (see Bruce, Dunn and Tomlinson notes). In 10 seasons, James has 15,446 scrimmage yards.

Warrick Dunn needs 694 scrimmage yards to become the 10th player in NFL history with 16,000 scrimmage yards (see Bruce, James and Tomlinson notes). In 12 seasons, Dunn has 15,306 scrimmage yards.

Marvin Harrison needs 100 receptions to pass Jerry Rice (4) to become the first player in NFL history with five 100-catch seasons. In 13 seasons, Harrison has four seasons with 100 receptions.

Harrison needs 365 receiving yards to surpass Tim Brown (14,934) and Isaac Bruce (14,944) to move into second place all-time (see Bruce and Owens notes). In 13 seasons, Harrison has 14,580 receiving yards.

Harrison needs eight receiving touchdowns to surpass Cris Carter (130) and Randy Moss (135) for fourth place all-time (see Moss note). In 13 seasons, Harrison has 128 touchdown receptions.

Harrison needs to catch a pass in each of his first 10 games to join Jerry Rice (274 games) as the only other player in NFL history to register a catch in 200 consecutive games (see Owens note). Harrison has caught a pass in 190 consecutive games.

Isaac Bruce, San Francisco, needs 56 receiving yards to join Jerry Rice (22,895) as the only other player in NFL history with 15,000 receiving yards (see Harrison and Owens notes). In 15 seasons, Bruce has 14,944 receiving yards.

Bruce needs 909 scrimmage yards to become the 10th player in NFL history with 16,000 scrimmage yards (see Dunn, James and Tomlinson notes). In 15 seasons, Bruce has 15,091 scrimmage yards.

Terrell Owens, Buffalo, needs 11 receiving touchdowns to become the second player in NFL history with 150 receiving TDs. Owens can join Jerry Rice (197) as the only other player in NFL history with 150 receiving touchdowns (see Moss note). In 13 seasons, Owens has 139 receiving touchdowns.

Owens needs five touchdowns to surpass LaDainian Tomlinson (141) and Marcus Allen (145) to move into third place all-time (see Tomlinson note). In 13 seasons, Owens has scored 141 touchdowns.

Owens has recorded 1,000 receiving yards in a season nine times in his 13-year NFL career. Owens can join Jerry Rice (14) as the only players in NFL history with 10 seasons with 1,000 receiving yards (see Moss note).

Owens needs 823 yards to surpass Marvin Harrison (14,580), Tim Brown (14,934) and Isaac Bruce (14,944) to move into second place all-time (see Bruce and Harrison notes). In 13 seasons, Owens has 14,122 receiving yards.

Owens needs 49 receptions to become the sixth player in NFL history with 1,000 receptions. In 13 seasons, Owens has 951 receptions.

Owens needs to catch a pass in each of his first eight games to surpass Art Monk (183) and Marvin Harrison (190) for the second-longest streak in NFL history (see Harrison note). Owens has caught a pass in 183 consecutive games.

Randy Moss, New England, needs 15 receiving touchdowns to become the second player in NFL history with 150 receiving TDs. Moss can join Jerry Rice (197) as the only other player in NFL history with 150 receiving touchdowns (see Owens note). In 11 seasons, Moss has 135 touchdown receptions.

Moss has recorded 1,000 receiving yards in a season nine times in his 11-year NFL career. Moss can join Jerry Rice (14) as the only players in NFL history with 10 seasons with 1,000 receiving yards (see Owens note).

Moss needs 799 receiving yards to become the seventh player in NFL history with 14,000 receiving yards. In 11 seasons, Moss has 13,201 receiving yards.

Wes Welker, New England, has caught at least 100 passes in each of the past two seasons. Welker can join Herman Moore (3) and Marvin Harrison (4) as the only players to catch 100 passes in three consecutive seasons (see Marshall note).

Brandon Marshall, Denver, has caught at least 100 passes in each of the past two seasons. Marshall can join Herman Moore (3) and Marvin Harrison (4) as the only players to catch 100 passes in three consecutive seasons (see Welker note).

Dante Hall has six kickoff-return touchdowns in his nine-year career, tied for the most all-time. Hall needs one kickoff-return touchdown to pass Mel Gray, Ollie Matson, Gale Sayers and Travis Williams (6) for sole possession of first place in NFL history.

Hall has 12 combined kick-return touchdowns (six kickoff, six punt) in his nine-year career, tied for the second-most all-time. Hall needs two combined kick-return touchdowns to pass Brian Mitchell (13) for first place in NFL history (see Hester note).

Hall has gained 2,000 combined yards four times in his nine-year career, tied for the most in NFL history. Hall needs one more season with 2,000 combined yards to pass Tiki Barber, Eric Dickerson, Marshall Faulk, Brian Mitchell and Walter Payton (4) for the most all-time.

Devin Hester, Chicago, has 11 combined kick-return touchdowns (seven punt, four kickoff) in his three-year career, the fourth-most all-time. Hester needs three combined kick-return touchdowns to pass Dante Hall, Eric Metcalf (12) and Brian Mitchell (13) for first place in NFL history (see Hall note).

Tony Gonzalez, Atlanta, needs 84 receptions to become the first tight end in NFL history with 1,000 receptions. In 12 seasons, Gonzalez has 916 receptions – the most ever by a tight end.

Gonzalez needs 50 receptions to become the first tight end in NFL history with 12 consecutive 50-reception seasons. Gonzalez is the only tight end in NFL history with 11 consecutive 50-reception seasons.

Ray Lewis, Baltimore, can become the first player in NFL history with 35 sacks and 30 interceptions in a career. In 13 seasons, Lewis has 33.5 sacks and 28 interceptions.

Jason Taylor, Miami, needs 12.5 sacks to pass Clyde Simmons (121.5), Simeon Rice (122.0), Derrick Thomas (126.5), Rickey Jackson (128.0), Leslie O'Neal and Lawrence Taylor (132.5) to move into eighth place all-time. In 12 seasons, Taylor has 120.5 sacks.

Darren Sharper, New Orleans, needs five interceptions to pass Eric Allen, Willie Brown, Darrell Green (54), Aeneas Williams (55), Lem Barney, Pat Fischer (56), Mel Blount, Bobby Boyd, Eugene Robinson, Johnny Robinson, Everson Walls (57) and Emmitt Thomas (58) to move into ninth place all-time. In 12 seasons, Sharper has 54 interceptions.

Jason Elam, Atlanta, has scored 100 points in each of his first 16 seasons and needs 100 points to extend his NFL record streak for consecutive 100-point seasons to 17. Elam is the only player in NFL history to score 100 points in 16 seasons.

Elam needs 85 points to become the fourth player with 2,000 career points (see Carney and Stover notes). In 16 seasons, Elam has 1,915 points.

Matt Stover has successfully kicked 389 consecutive points after touchdowns, the longest streak in NFL history. Stover needs to convert 11 in a row to become the 1st player in NFL history to make 400 consecutive PATs.

Stover needs 56 points to become the fourth player with 2,000 career points (see Carney and Elam notes). In 19 seasons, Stover has 1,944 points.

Adam Vinatieri, Indianapolis, has scored 100 points in each of his first 13 seasons and needs 100 points to become the second player (Jason Elam, 16) in NFL history with 100 points in each of his first 14 seasons.

John Carney needs 45 points to become the fourth player with 2,000 career points (see Elam and Stover notes). In 20 seasons, Carney has 1,955 points.

DRAFT LIST FOR 2009

74th Annual NFL Draft, April 25-26, 2009
+Denotes Compensatory Selection
#Denotes Underclassman Selection

ARIZONA CARDINALS
1.# Beanie Wells—31, RB, Ohio State
2. Cody Brown—63, LB, Connecticut
3. Rashad Johnson—95, DB, Alabama
4. Gregory Toler—131, DB, St. Paul's, Va.
5. Herman Johnson—167, G, Louisiana State
6. Will Davis—204, LB, Illinois
7. LaRod Stephens-Howling—240, RB, Pittsburgh
+ Trevor Canfield—254, G, Cincinnati

ATLANTA FALCONS
1. Peria Jerry—24, DT, Mississippi
2. William Moore—55, DB, Missouri
3. Christopher Owens—90, DB, San Jose State
4. Lawrence Sidbury—125, DE, Richmond
5. William Middleton—138, DB, Furman, from St. Louis
Garrett Reynolds—156, T, North Carolina, from Dallas
6. Spencer Adkins—176, LB, Miami
7. Vance Walker—210, DT, Georgia Tech,
from Detroit through Dallas

BALTIMORE RAVENS
1. Michael Oher—23, T, Mississippi, from New England
2.# Paul Kruger—57, DE, Utah
3. Lardarius Webb—88, DB, Nicholls State
5. Jason Phillips—137, LB, Texas Christian
from Detroit through Seattle, Philadelphia,
and New England
Davon Drew—149, TE, East Carolina
6. Cedric Perrman—185, RB, Virginia

BUFFALO BILLS
1.# Aaron Maybin—11, DE, Penn State
Eric Wood—28, C, Louisville,
from Carolina through Philadelphia
2.# Jairus Byrd—42, DB, Oregon
Andy Levitre—51, G, Oregon State, from Dallas
4. Shawn Nelson—121, TE, Southern Mississippi,
from Philadelphia
5. Nic Harris—147, LB, Oklahoma
6. Cary Harris—183, DB, Southern California
7. Ellis Lankster—220, DB, West Virginia

CAROLINA PANTHERS
2.# Everette Brown—43, DE, Florida State, from San Francisco
Sherrod Martin—59, DB, Troy
3. Corvey Irvin—93, DT, Georgia
4.# Mike Goodson—111, RB, Texas A&M, from San Francisco
Tony Fiammetta—128, RB, Syracuse
5. Duke Robinson—163, G, Oklahoma
7.# Captain Munnerlyn—216, DB, South Carolina, from Oakland

CHICAGO BEARS
3. Jarron Gilbert—68, DT, San Jose State, from Seattle
+ Juaquin Iglesias—99, WR, Oklahoma
4. Henry Melton—105, DE, Texas, From Seattle
D.J. Moore—119, DB, Vanderbilt
5. Johnny Knox—140, WR, Abilene Christian,
from Seattle through Denver
Marcus Freeman—154, LB, Ohio State
6. Al Afalava—190, DB, Oregon State
7.+ Lance Louis—246, TE, San Diego State
+ Derek Kinder—251, WR, Pittsburgh

CINCINNATI BENGALS
1.# Andre Smith—6, T, Alabama
2. Rey Maualuga—38, LB, Southern California
3. Michael Johnson—70, DE, Georgia Tech
+ Chase Coffman—98, TE, Missouri
4. Jonathan Luigs—106, C, Arkansas
5. Kevin Huber—142, P, Cincinnati
6. Morgan Trent—179, DB, Michigan
+ Bernard Scott—209, RB, Abilene Christian
7. Fui Vakapuna—215, RB, Brigham Young
+ Clinton McDonald—249, DT, Memphis
+ Freddie Brown—252, WR, Utah

CLEVELAND BROWNS
1. Alex Mack—21, C, California, from Philadelphia
2. Brian Robiskie—36, WR, Ohio State
Mohamed Massaquoi—50, WR, Georgia, from Tampa Bay
David Veikune—52, DE, Hawaii
4. Kaluka Maiava—104, LB, Southern California
6. Don Carey—177, DB, Norfolk State
Coye Francies—191, DB, San Jose State, from Tampa Bay
James Davis—195, RB, Clemson
from Minnesota through Philadelphia

DALLAS COWBOYS
3. Jason Williams—69, LB, Western Illinois, from Cleveland
Robert Brewster—75, T, Ball State, from Buffalo
4. Stephen McGee—101, QB, Texas A&M, from Detroit
Victor Butler—110, LB, Oregon State
Brandon Williams—120, LB, Texas Tech, from Tampa Bay
5. DeAngelo Smith—143, DB, Cincinnati,
from Oakland through Atlanta
Michael Hamlin—166, DB, Clemson, from Tennessee
+ David Buehler—172, K, Southern California
6. Stephen Hodge—197, LB, Texas Christian, from Miami
+ John Phillips—208, TE, Virginia
7. Mike Mickens—227, DB, Cincinnati
Manuel Johnson—229, WR, Oklahoma,
from Chicago through Tampa Bay

DENVER BRONCOS
1.# Knowshon Moreno—12, RB, Georgia
Robert Ayers—18, DE, Tennessee, from Chicago
2. Alphonso Smith—37, DB, Wake Forest, from Seattle
Darcel McBath—48, DB, Texas Tech
Richard Quinn—64, TE, North Carolina, from Pittsburgh
4. David Bruton—114, DB, Notre Dame
Seth Olsen—132, G, Iowa, from Pittsburgh
5. Kenny McKinley—141, WR, South Carolina,
from Cleveland through Philadelphia,
New England, and Baltimore
6. Tom Brandstater—174, QB, Fresno State, from Detroit
7. Blake Schlueter—225, C, Texas Christian

DETROIT LIONS
1.#Matthew Stafford—1, QB, Georgia
Brandon Pettigrew—20, TE, Oklahoma State, from Dallas
2. Louis Delmas—33, DB, Western Michigan
3. DeAndre Levy—76, LB, Wisconsin, from New Orleans through New York Jets
Derrick Williams—82, WR, Penn State, from Dallas
4. Sammie Lee Hill—115, DT, Stillman, from Washington through New York Jets
6. Aaron Brown—192, RB, Texas Christian, from Dallas
7. Lydon Murtha—228, T, Nebraska, from N.Y. Jets
Zack Follett—235, LB, California, from Atlanta through Denver
+ Dan Gronkowski—255, TE, Maryland

GREEN BAY PACKERS
1. B.J. Raji—9, DT, Boston College
Clay Matthews—26, LB, Southern California, from Baltimore through New England
4. T.J. Lang—109, G, Eastern Michigan
5. Quinn Johnson—145, RB, Louisiana State
Jamon Meredith—162, T, South Carolina, from Baltimore through New England
6. Jarius Wynn—182, DE, Georgia
Brandon Underwood—187, DB, Cincinnati, from New Orleans
7. Brad Jones—218, LB, Colorado

HOUSTON TEXANS
1. Brian Cushing—15, LB, Southern California
2. Connor Barwin—46, DE, Cincinnati
3. Antoine Caldwell—77, C, Alabama
4. Glover Quin—112, DB, New Mexico
Anthony Hill—122, TE, North Carolina State, from Minnesota
5.#James Casey—152, TE, Rice
6. Brice McCain—188, DB, Utah
7. Troy Nolan—223, DB, Arizona State

INDIANAPOLIS COLTS
1.#Donald Brown—27, RB, Connecticut
2. Fili Moala—56, DT, Southern California, from Miami
3.#Jerraud Powers—92, DB, Auburn
4.#Austin Collie—127, WR, Brigham Young
+ Terrance Taylor—136, DT, Michigan
6. Curtis Painter—201, QB, Purdue
7. Pat McAfee—222, P, West Virginia, from New Orleans through Philadelphia
Jaimie Thomas—236, G, Maryland

JACKSONVILLE JAGUARS
1. Eugene Monroe—8, T, Virginia
2.#Eben Britton—39, T, Arizona
3. Terrance Knighton—72, DT, Temple
Derek Cox—73, DB, William & Mary, from Green Bay through New England
4. Mike Thomas—107, WR, Arizona
5. Jarett Dillard—144, WR, Rice
6. Zach Miller—180, TE, Nebraska-Omaha
7.+Rashad Jennings—250, RB, Liberty
+ Tiquan Underwood—253, WR, Rutgers

KANSAS CITY CHIEFS
1. Tyson Jackson—3, DE, Louisiana State
3. Alex Magee—67, DE, Purdue
4.#Donald Washington—102, DB, Ohio State
5. Colin Brown—139, T, Missouri
6. Quinten Lawrence—175, WR, McNeese State
7. Javarris Williams—212, RB, Tennessee State
Jake O'Connell—237, TE, Miami (Ohio), from Carolina through Miami
+ Ryan Succop—256, K, South Carolina

MIAMI DOLPHINS
1.#Vonate Davis—25, DB, Illinois
2. Pat White—44, QB, West Virginia, from Washington
Sean Smith—61, DB, Utah, from Indianapolis
3. Patrick Turner—87, WR, Southern California
4.#Brian Hartline—108, WR, Ohio State, from Oakland
5. John Nalbone—161, TE, Monmouth
Chris Clemons—165, DB, Clemson, from Indianapolis
6. Andrew Gardner—181, T, Georgia Tech, from Oakland
7. J.D. Folsom—214, LB, Weber State

MINNESOTA VIKINGS
1.#Percy Harvin—22, WR, Florida
2. Phil Loadholt—54, T, Oklahoma
3.#Asher Allen—86, DB, Georgia
5. Jasper Brinkley—150, LB, South Carolina, from Washington
7. Jamarca Sanford—231, DB, Mississippi

NEW ENGLAND PATRIOTS
2. Patrick Chung—34, DB, Oregon, from Kansas City
Ron Brace—40, DT, Boston College, from Oakland
Darius Butler—41, DB, Connecticut, from Green Bay
Sebastian Vollmer—58, T, Houston
3. Brandon Tate—83, WR, North Carolina, from N.Y. Jets through Green Bay
+ Tyrone McKenzie—97, LB, South Florida
4. Rich Ohrnberger—123, G, Penn State, from Baltimore
5.+George Bussey—170, T, Louisville
6. Jake Ingram—198, LS, Hawaii, from Baltimore
+ Myron Pryor—207, DT, Kentucky
7. Julian Edelman—232, WR, Kent State, from Miami through Jacksonville
Darryl Richard—234, DT, Georgia Tech

NEW ORLEANS SAINTS
1. Malcolm Jenkins—14, DB, Ohio State
4. Chip Vaughn—116, DB, Wake Forest
Stanley Arnoux—118, LB, Wake Forest, from N.Y. Jets
5. Thomas Morstead—164, P, Southern Methodist, from N.Y. Giants through Philadelphia

NEW YORK GIANTS
1.#Hakeem Nicks—29, WR, North Carolina
2. Clint Sintim—45, LB, Virginia, from New Orleans
Will Beatty—60, T, Connecticut
3. Ramses Barden—85, WR, Cal Poly, from Philadelphia
+ Travis Beckum—100, TE, Wisconsin
4. Andre Brown—129, RB, North Carolina State
5. Rhett Bomar—151, QB, Sam Houston State, from New Orleans
6. DeAndre Wright—200, DB, New Mexico
7. Stoney Woodson—238, DB, South Carolina

DRAFT LIST FOR 2009

NEW YORK JETS
1.#Mark Sanchez—5, QB, Southern California, from Cleveland
3.#Shonn Greene—65, RB, Iowa, from Detroit
6. Matt Slauson—193, G, Nebraska

OAKLAND RAIDERS
1.#Darrius Heyward-Bey—7, WR, Maryland
2. Michael Mitchell—47, DB, Ohio,
from San Diego through New England
3. Matt Shaughnessy—71, DE, Wisconsin
4. Louis Murphy—124, WR, Florida, from New England
Slade Norris—126, LB, Oregon State, from Miami
6. Stryker Sulak—199, DE, Missouri, from New England
Brandon Myers—202, TE, Iowa, from Carolina

PHILADELPHIA EAGLES
1.#Jeremy Maclin—19, WR, Missouri,
from Tampa Bay through Cleveland
2.#LeSean McCoy—53, RB, Pittsburgh
5. Cornelius Ingram—153, TE, Florida, from N.Y. Jets
Victor Harris—157, DB, Virginia Tech
Fenuki Tupou—159, T, Oregon, from New England
6. Brandon Gibson—194, WR, Washington State
7. Paul Fanaika—213, G, Arizona State, from Seattle
Moise Fokou—230, LB, Maryland

PITTSBURGH STEELERS
1. Evander Hood—32, DE, Missouri
3. Kraig Urbik—79, G, Wisconsin, from Denver
Mike Wallace—84, WR, Mississippi,
from Chicago through Denver
Keenan Lewis—96, DB, Oregon State
5. Joe Burnett—168, DB, Central Florida
+ Frank Summer—169, RB, Nevada-Las Vegas
6. Ra'Shon Harris—205, DE, Oregon
7. A.Q. Shipley—226, C, Penn State, from Tampa Bay
David Johnson—241, TE, Arkansas State

ST. LOUIS RAMS
1. Jason Smith—2, T, Baylor
2. James Laurinaitis—35, LB, Ohio State
3. Bradley Fletcher—66, DB, Iowa
4. Dorell Scott—103, DT, Clemson
5. Brooks Foster—160, WR, North Carolina, from Atlanta
6. Keith Null—196, QB, West Texas A&M, from Atlanta
7. Chris Ogbonnaya—211, RB, Texas

SAN DIEGO CHARGERS
1. Larry English—16, LB, Northern Illinois
3. Louis Vasquez—78, G, Texas Tech
4.#Vaughn Martin—113, DT, Western Ontario
+ Tyronne Green—133, C, Auburn
+ Gartrell Johnson—134, RB, Colorado State
5. Brandon Hughes—148, DB, Oregon State
6. Kevin Ellison—189, DB, Southern California
7. Demetrius Byrd—224, WR, Louisiana State

SAN FRANCISCO 49ERS
1.#Michael Crabtree—10, WR, Texas Tech
3.#Glen Coffee—74, RB, Alabama
5. Scott McKillop—146, LB, Pittsburgh
#+Nate Davis—171, QB, Ball State
6. Bear Pascoe—184, TE, Fresno State
7. Curtis Taylor—219, DB, Louisiana State
#+Ricky Jean Francois—244, DE, Louisiana State

SEATTLE SEAHAWKS
1. Aaron Curry—4, LB, Wake Forest
2. Max Unger—49, C, Oregon, from Chicago
3. Deon Butler—91, WR, Penn State,
from N.Y. Giants through Philadelphia
6. Mike Teel—178, QB, Rutgers
7.+Courtney Greene—245, DB, Rutgers
+ Nick Reed—247, DE, Oregon
#+Cameron Morrah—248, TE, California

TAMPA BAY BUCCANEERS
1.#Josh Freeman—17, QB, Kansas State,
from N.Y. Jets through Cleveland
3. Roy Miller—81, DT, Texas
4. Kyle Moore—117, DE, Southern California, from Dallas
5. Xavier Fulton—155, T, Illinois
7. E.J. Biggers—217, DB, Western Michigan,
from Jacksonville
Sammie Stroughter—233, WR, Oregon State,
from Baltimore

TENNESSEE TITANS
1.#Kenny Britt—30, WR, Rutgers
2.#Sen'Derrick Marks—62, DT, Auburn
3.#Jared Cook—89, TE, South Carolina, from New England
Ryan Mouton—94, DB, Hawaii
4.#Gerald McRath—130, LB, Southern Mississippi
+ Troy Kropog—135, T, Tulane
5.+Javon Ringer—173, RB, Michigan State
6. Jason McCourty—203, DB, Rutgers
+ Dominique Edison—206, WR, Stephen F. Austin
7. Ryan Durand—239, G, Syracuse
+ Nick Schommer—242, DB, North Dakota State

WASHINGTON REDSKINS
1. Brian Orakpo—13, DE, Texas
3. Kevin Barnes—80, DB, Maryland
5. Cody Glenn—158, LB, Nebraska, from Minnesota
6. Robert Henson—186, LB, Texas Christian
7. Eddie Williams—221, RB, Idaho,
reacquired through Minnesota
+ Marko Mitchell—243, WR, Nevada

NUMBER OF PLAYERS DRAFTED—2009

BY POSITION:

Position	Number
Defensive Backs	55
Wide Receivers	34
Linebackers	31
Running Backs	23
Defensive Ends	20
Tight Ends	20
Tackles	18
Defensive Tackles	17
Guards	13
Quarterbacks	11
Centers	8
Punters	3
Kickers	2
Long Snapper	1

BY COLLEGE:

Southern California	11
Ohio State	7
Oregon State	7
South Carolina	7
Cincinnati	6
Georgia	6
Louisiana State	6
Missouri	6
Oregon	6
Maryland	5
North Carolina	5
Oklahoma	5
Penn State	5
Rutgers	5
Texas Christian	5
Alabama	4
Clemson	4
Connecticut	4
Georgia Tech	4
Iowa	4
Mississippi	4
Pittsburgh	4
Texas	4
Texas Tech	4
Utah	4
Virginia	4
Wake Forest	4
Wisconsin	4
Auburn	3
California	3
Florida	3
Hawaii	3
Illinois	3
Nebraska	3
San Jose State	3
West Virginia	3
Abilene Christian	2
Arizona	2
Arizona State	2
Ball State	2
Boston College	2
Brigham Young	2
Fresno State	2
Louisville	2
Michigan	2
New Mexico	2
North Carolina State	2
Purdue	2
Rice	2
Southern Mississippi	2
Syracuse	2
Texas A&M	2
Western Michigan	2
Arkansas	1
Arkansas State	1
Baylor	1
Cal Poly	1
Central Florida	1
Colorado	1
Colorado State	1
East Carolina	1
Eastern Michigan	1
Florida State	1
Furman	1
Houston	1
Idaho	1
Kansas State	1
Kent State	1
Kentucky	1
Liberty	1
McNeese State	1
Memphis	1
Miami	1
Miami (Ohio)	1
Michigan State	1
Monmouth	1
Nebraska-Omaha	1
Nevada	1
Nevada-Las Vegas	1
Nicholls State	1
Norfolk State	1
North Dakota State	1
Northern Illinois	1
Notre Dame	1
Ohio	1
Oklahoma State	1
Richmond	1
St. Paul's (Va.)	1
Sam Houston State	1
San Diego State	1
South Florida	1
Southern Methodist	1
Stephen F. Austin	1
Stillman	1
Temple	1
Tennessee	1
Tennessee State	1
Troy	1
Tulane	1
Vanderbilt	1
Virginia Tech	1
Washington State	1
Weber State	1
West Texas A&M	1
Western Ontario	1
Western Illinois	1
William & Mary	1

BY CONFERENCE:

Southeastern	37
Atlantic Coast	33
Pacific 10	32
Big 12	28
Big Ten	28
Big East	27
Mountain West	16
Conference USA	10
Mid-American	10
Western Athletic	10
Southland	4
Lone Star	3
Colonial Athletic	2
Sun Belt	2
Big Sky	1
Big South	1
Central Intercollegiate Athletic	1
Gateway Football	1
Great West Football	1
Independent	1
Mid-America Intercollegiate Athletic	1
Mid-Eastern Athletic	1
Missouri Valley Football	1
Northeast	1
Ohio Valley	1
Ontario Universities Athletic	1
Southern	1
Southern Intercollegiate Athletic	1

UNDERCLASSMEN IN THE DRAFT

Year	Entered	Drafted	In Top 10
1989	25	12	3
1990	38	18	5
1991	33	22	2
1992	48	25	5
1993	46	24	5
1994	43	27	6
1995	42	22	2
1996	46	21	4
1997	44	27	7
1998	41	20	3
1999	42	27	5
2000	31	20	4
2001	54	31	5
2002	43	26	5
2003	54	32	5
2004	44	35	5
2005	57	38	4
2006	62	34	6
2007	40	29	4
2008	53	39	4
2009	46	41	5

WAIVERS
The waiver system is a procedure by which player contracts or NFL rights to players are made available by a club to other clubs in the League. During the procedure, the 31 other clubs either file claims to obtain the players or waive the opportunity to do so—thus the term "waiver." Claiming clubs are assigned players on a priority based on the inverse of won-and-lost standing. The claiming period is 24 hours from the first business day after the Super Bowl through the last business day prior to June 1. From June 1 through the last business day prior to July 4, the claiming period is three days. From the first business day after July 4 through the conclusion of the regular season, the claiming period is 24 hours. If a player passes through waivers unclaimed, he becomes a free agent. All waivers are no recall and no withdrawal. Under the Collective Bargaining Agreement, from the beginning of the waiver system each year through the trading deadline (October 20, 2009), any veteran who has acquired four years of pension credit is not subject to the waiver system if the club desires to release him. After the trading deadline, such players are subject to the waiver system.

ACTIVE/INACTIVE LIST
The Active/Inactive List is the principal status for players participating for a club. It consists of all players under contract who are eligible for preseason, regular-season, and postseason games. Teams are permitted to open training camp with no more than 80 players under contract and thereafter must meet two mandatory roster reductions prior to the season opener. Teams will be permitted an Active List of 45 players and an Inactive List of eight players for each regular-season and postseason game. Provided that a club has two quarterbacks on its 45-player Active List, a third quarterback from its Inactive List is permitted to dress for the game, but if he enters the game during the first three quarters, the other two quarterbacks are thereafter prohibited from playing. Teams also are permitted to establish Practice Squads of up to eight players who are eligible to participate in practice, but these players remain free agents and are eligible to sign with any other team in the league.

September 1................Roster reduction to 75 players
September 5................Roster reduction to 53 players
September 6................Teams establish a Practice Squad of up to eight players

In addition to the squad limits described above, the overall roster limit of 80 players remains in effect throughout the regular season and postseason. The overall limit is applicable to players on a team's Active, Inactive, and certain Exempt Lists, players on the Practice Squad, and players on the Reserve List as Injured, Physically Unable to Perform, Non-Football Illness/Injury, and Suspended by Club.

RESERVE LIST
The Reserve List is a status for players who, for reasons of injury, retirement, military service, or other circumstances, are not immediately available for participation with a club. Players on Reserve/Injured are not eligible to practice or return to the Active/Inactive List in the same season that they are placed on Reserve. Players in the category of Reserve/Retired, Reserve/Did Not Report, Reserve/Exclusive Rights, and players who were placed in the category of Reserve/Left Squad in a previous season may not be reinstated during the period from 30 days before the end of the regular season through the postseason.

TRADES
Unrestricted trading between the AFC and NFC is allowed in 2009 through October 20, after which trading will end until 2010.

ANNUAL ACTIVE PLAYER LIMITS
NFL

Year(s)	Limit
1991-2009	45**
1985-90	45
1983-84	49
1982	45†-49
1978-81	45
1975-77	43
1974	47
1964-73	40
1963	37
1961-62	36
1960	38
1959	36
1957-58	35
1951-56	33
1949-50	32
1948	35
1947	35*-34
1945-46	33
1943-44	28
1940-42	33
1938-39	30
1936-37	25
1935	24
1930-34	20
1926-29	18
1925	16

** 45 plus a third quarterback
† 45 for first two games
* 35 for first three games

AFL

Year(s)	Limit
1966-69	40
1965	38
1964	34
1962-63	33
1960-61	35

NFL FREE AGENCY MOVEMENT
The following chart details veteran free agents who signed with new teams:

	Unrestricted	Restricted	Transition	Franchise	TOTALS
1993	108	8	4	1	121
1994	121	7	4	0	132
1995	171	6	2	0	179
1996	100	4	2	0	106
1997	86	2	2	0	90
1998	112	4	1	2	119
1999	115	2	1	0	118
2000	107	4	0	0	111
2001	93	4	0	0	97
2002	130	1	0	0	131
2003	111	5	1	0	117
2004	124	1	1	0	126
2005	104	3	0	0	107
2006	149	4	1	0	154
2007	126	4	0	0	130
2008	132	3	0	0	135

The following procedures will be used to break standings ties for postseason playoffs and to determine regular-season schedules.
Note: Tie games count as one-half win and one-half loss for both clubs.

TO BREAK A TIE WITHIN A DIVISION
If, at the end of the regular season, two or more clubs in the same division finish with the best won-lost-tied percentage, the following steps will be taken until a champion is determined:
TWO CLUBS
1. Head-to-head (best won-lost-tied percentage in games between the clubs.)
2. Best won-lost-tied percentage in games played within the division.
3. Best won-lost-tied percentage in common games.
4. Best won-lost-tied percentage in games played within the conference.
5. Strength of victory.
6. Strength of schedule.
7. Best combined ranking among conference teams in points scored and points allowed.
8. Best combined ranking among all teams in points scored and points allowed.
9. Best net points in common games.
10. Best net points in all games.
11. Best net touchdowns in all games
12. Coin toss.

THREE OR MORE CLUBS
(Note: If two clubs remain tied after a third club is eliminated during any step, tie-breaker reverts to Step 1 of the two-club format.)
1. Head-to-head (best won-lost-tied percentage in games among the clubs.)
2. Best won-lost-tied percentage in games played within the division.
3. Best won-lost-tied percentage in common games.
4. Best won-lost-tied percentage in games played within the conference.
5. Strength of victory.
6. Strength of schedule.
7. Best combined ranking among conference teams in points scored and points allowed.
8. Best combined ranking among all teams in points scored and points allowed.
9. Best net points in common games.
10. Best net points in all games.
11. Best net touchdowns in all games.
12. Coin toss.

TO BREAK A TIE FOR THE WILD-CARD TEAM
If it is necessary to break ties to determine the two Wild Card clubs from each conference, the following steps will be taken:
A. If all the tied clubs are from the same division, apply division tie-breaker.
B. If the tied clubs are from different divisions, apply the following steps:

TWO CLUBS
1. Head-to-head, if applicable.
2. Best won-lost-tied percentage in the games played within the conference.
3. Best won-lost-tied percentage in common games, minimum of four.
4. Strength of victory.
5. Strength of schedule.
6. Best combined ranking among conference teams in points scored and points allowed.
7. Best combined ranking among all teams in points scored and points allowed.
8. Best net points in conference games.
9. Best net points in all games.
10. Best net touchdowns in all games.
11. Coin toss.

THREE OR MORE CLUBS
1. Apply division tie-breaker to eliminate all but highest ranked club in each division prior to proceeding to Step 2. The original seeding within a division upon application of the division tie-breaker remains the same for all subsequent applications of the procedure that are necessary to identify the Wild Card participants.
2. Head-to-head sweep (apply only if one club has defeated each of the others or one club has lost to each of the others).
3. Best won-lost-tied percentage in games played within the conference.
4. Best won-lost-tied percentage in common games, minimum of four.
5. Strength of victory.
6. Strength of schedule.
7. Best combined ranking among conference teams in points scored and points allowed.
8. Best combined ranking among all teams in points scored and points allowed.
9. Best net points in conference games.
10. Best net points in all games.
11. Best net touchdowns in all games.
12. Coin toss.

When the first Wild Card team has been identified, the procedure is repeated to name the second Wild Card (i.e., eliminate all but the highest ranked club in each division prior to proceeding to Step 2.) In situations where three teams from the same division are involved in the procedure, the original seeding of the teams remains the same for subsequent applications of the tie-breaker if the top-ranked team in that division qualifies for a Wild Card berth.

OTHER TIE-BREAKING PROCEDURES
1. Only one club advances to the playoffs in any tie-breaking step. Remaining tied clubs revert to the first step of the applicable division or Wild Card tie-breakers. As an example, if two clubs remain tied in any tie-breaker step after all other clubs have been eliminated, the procedure reverts to Step 1 of the two-club format to determine the winner. When one club wins the tie-breaker, all other clubs revert to Step 1 of the applicable two-club or three-club format.
2. In comparing records against common opponents among tied teams, the best won-lost-tied percentage is the deciding factor since teams may have played an unequal number of games.
3. To determine home-field priority among division-titlists, apply Wild Card tie-breakers.
4. To determine home-field priority for Wild Card qualifiers, apply division tie-breakers (if teams are from the same division) or Wild Card tie-breakers (if teams are from different divisions).
5. To determine the best combined ranking among conference teams in points scored and points allowed, add a team's position in the two categories, and the lowest score wins. For example, if Team A is first in points scored and second in points allowed, its combined ranking is "3." If Team B is third in points scored and first in points allowed, its combined ranking is "4." Team A then wins the tiebreaker. If two teams are tied for a position, both teams are awarded the ranking as if they held it solely. For example, if Team A and Team B are tied for first in points scored, each team is assigned a ranking of "1" in that category, and if Team C is third, its ranking will still be "3."

TIE-BREAKING PROCEDURE FOR SELECTION MEETING
1. Clubs not participating in the playoffs shall select in the first through 20th positions in reverse standings order.
2. The Super Bowl winner is last and Super Bowl loser is next-to-last.
3. The losers of the Conference Championship games shall select 29th and 30th based on won-lost-tied percentage.
4. The losers of the Divisional playoff games shall select 25th through 28th based on won-lost-tied percentage.
5. The losers of the Wild Card games shall select 21st through 24th based on won-lost-tied percentage.

If ties exist in any grouping except (2) above, such ties shall be broken by strength-of-schedule. If any ties cannot be broken by strength-of-schedule, the divisional or conference tie-breakers, if applicable, shall be applied. Any ties that still exist shall be broken by a coin flip.

INSTANT REPLAY

The NFL utilizes a system of Referee Replay Review to aid officiating.

Prior to the two-minute warning of each half, a Coaches' Challenge System will be in effect. After the two-minute warning, and throughout any overtime period, a Referee Review will be initiated by a Replay Assistant from a Replay Booth.

The following procedures will be used:

Reviews by Referee: All Replay Reviews will be conducted by the Referee on a field-level monitor after consultation with the other covering official(s), prior to review. A decision will be reversed only when the Referee has *indisputable visual evidence* available to him that warrants the change.

Coaches' Challenge: In each game, a team will be permitted two challenges that will initiate Referee Replay reviews. Each challenge will require the use of a team time out. If a challenge is upheld, the time out will be restored to the challenging team. If both challenges are upheld, a third challenge will be awarded to the challenging team. No challenges will be recognized from a team that has exhausted its time outs.

Replay Assistant's Request for Review: After the two-minute warning of each half, and throughout any overtime period, any review will be initiated by a Replay Assistant. There is no limit to the number of reviews that may be initiated by the Replay Assistant. His ability to initiate a review will be unrelated to the number of time outs that either team has remaining, and no time out will be charged for any review initiated by the Replay Assistant.

Time Limit: Each review will be a maximum of 60 seconds in length, timed from when the Referee begins his review of the replay at the field-level monitor.

Reviewable Plays: The Replay System will cover the following play situations only:

A) Plays Governed by Sideline, Goal Line, End Zone, End Line, and Goal Posts:

1. Scoring plays, including a runner breaking the plane of the goal line.
2. Pass complete/incomplete/intercepted at sideline, goal line, end zone, and end line.
3. Runner/receiver in or out of bounds.
4. Recovery of loose ball in or out of bounds.

B) Passing Plays:

1. Pass ruled complete/incomplete/intercepted in the field of play.
2. Touching of a forward pass by an ineligible receiver.
3. Touching of a forward pass by a defensive player.
4. Quarterback (Passer) forward pass or fumble.
5. Illegal forward pass beyond line of scrimmage.
6. Illegal forward pass after change of possession.
7. Forward or backward pass thrown from behind line of scrimmage.

C) Other Reviewable Plays:

1. Runner ruled not down by defensive contact.
2. Runner ruled down by defensive contact and there is a recovery by defense.
3. Forward progress with respect to first down.
4. Touching of a kick.
5. Number of players on the field.
6. Recovery of loose ball in the field of play, including those ruled to have hit sideline.
7. A field goal or try attempt when it is lower than the top of the uprights.
8. Illegal forward handoff.

INSTANT REPLAY HISTORY

From 1986-1991, a limited system of Instant Replay was used on a year-by-year basis. Replay also was experimented with during the 1996 and 1998 preseasons. For the 1999 season, the NFL introduced a system of Referee Replay Review to aid officiating. That system was extended on a one-year basis for the 2000 season and then approved for the next three years through 2003. The system was extended on a five-year basis in March 2004 and was later installed permanently in March 2007.

Following are the results of the different systems:

REGULAR SEASON, 1986-1991

Year	Games	Plays Closely Reviewed	Reversals
1986	224	374	38
1987	210	490	57
1988	224	537	53
1989	224	492	65
1990	224	504	73
1991	224	570	90
TOTAL	1,330	2,967	376

PRESEASON, 1996, 1998

Year	Games	Challenges	Reversals
1996	10	13	3
1998	10	10	3
TOTAL	20	23	6

REGULAR SEASON, 1999-2008

Year	Games	Total Replay Reviews	Challenges	Reversals
1999	248	195	133	57
2000	248	247	179	84
2001	248	258	191	89
2002	256	294	208	94
2003	256	255	184	66
2004	256	283	233	88
2005	256	295	223	92
2006	256	311	237	107
2007	256	327	250	122
2008	256	315	229	117
TOTAL	2,536	2,780	2,067	916

The AFC

American Football Conference
North Division
Team Colors: Black, Purple, and Metallic Gold
1 Winning Drive
Owings Mills, Maryland 21117
Telephone: (410) 701-4000

2009 SCHEDULE

PRESEASON

Aug. 13 **Washington** 7:30
Aug. 24 **N.Y. Jets** 8:00
Aug. 29 at Carolina.......................... 8:00
Sep. 3 at Atlanta............................ 7:30

REGULAR SEASON

Sep. 13 **Kansas City** 1:00
Sep. 20 at San Diego 1:15
Sep. 27 **Cleveland** 1:00
Oct. 4 at New England 1:00
Oct. 11 **Cincinnati** 1:00
Oct. 18 at Minnesota 12:00
Oct. 25 BYE
Nov. 1 **Denver** 1:00
Nov. 8 at Cincinnati 1:00
Nov. 16 at Cleveland (Mon.) 8:30
Nov. 22 **Indianapolis** 1:00
Nov. 29 **Pittsburgh** *...................... 8:20
Dec. 7 at Green Bay (Mon.) 7:30
Dec. 13 **Detroit** 1:00
Dec. 20 **Chicago** 1:00
Dec. 27 at Pittsburgh 1:00
Jan. 3 at Oakland 1:15

** Sunday night games in Weeks 11-17 subject to change*

Stadium: M&T Bank Stadium (opened in 1998)
• **Capacity:** 71,008
1101 Russell Street
Baltimore, Maryland 21230
Playing Surface: Sportexe Momentum
Training Camp: McDaniel College
2 College Hill
Westminster, MD 21157

M&T BANK STADIUM

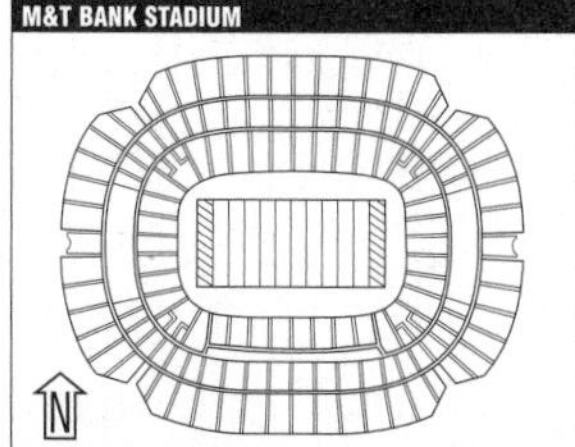

CLUB OFFICIALS

Owner: Steve Bisciotti
President: Dick Cass
Executive Vice President/General Manager: Ozzie Newsome
Senior Vice President/Public and Community Relations: Kevin Byrne
Vice President of Football Administration: Pat Moriarty
Vice President of Medical Services/ Head Certified Athletic Trainer: Bill Tessendorf
Vice President, Corporate Sales: Mark Burdett
Vice President and Chief Financial Officer: Jeff Goering
Vice President, Regional Partnerships and Sales: Ed Burchell
Vice President, Marketing: Gabrielle Dow
Vice President, Operations: Bob Eller
Vice President, Information Technology: Bill Jankowski
Vice President, Ticket Sales and Operations: Baker Koppelman
Vice President, National Partnerships and Sales: Kevin Rochlitz
Vice President, Broadcasting: Larry Rosen
Vice President, Stadium Operations: Roy Sommerhof
Director of Player Personnel: Eric DeCosta
Director of College Scouting: Joe Hortiz
Director of Pro Personnel: Vincent Newsome
Director of Player Development: O.J. Brigance
Director of Media Relations: Chad Steele
Assistant Director of Player Development: Harry Swayne
Scouts: Chad Alexander, Joe Douglas, Jack Glowik, Milt Hendrickson, Jeremiah Washburn, Andrew Weidl, Lonnie Young
Equipment Manager: Ed Carroll
Director of Football Video Operations: Jon Dubé
Assistant Director of Football Video Operations: Mark Bienvenu
Senior Director, Fields & Grounds/Head Groundskeeper: Don Follett
Director of Premium Services/Suites: Theresa Abato
Director, New Media: Michelle Andres
Controller: Jim Coller
Director, Broadcasting Administration: Don DiRaddo
Director, Information Technology: Nick Fusee
Director, Human Resources: Elizabeth Jackson
Director of Community Relations: Melanie LeGrande
Director, Security: Darren Sanders

COACHING HISTORY
(114-104-1)

Records include postseason games

1996-98 Ted Marchibroda 16-31-1
1999-2007 Brian Billick................ 85-67-0
2008 John Harbaugh 13-6-0

PAID ATTENDANCE

Home 557,792 Away 537,424
Total 1,095,216
Single-game home record, 71,382 (12/03/07)
Single-season home record, 557,792 (2008)

2009 DRAFT CHOICES

Round	Name	Pos.	College
1	Michael Oher	T	Mississippi
2	Paul Kruger	DE	Utah
3	Lardarius Webb	DB	Nicholls State
5	Jason Phillips	LB	Texas Christian
	Davon Drew	TE	East Carolina
6	Cedric Peerman	RB	Virginia

BALTIMORE RAVENS

2008 TEAM RECORD

PRESEASON (2-2)

Date	Result	Opponent
8/7	L 10-24	New Orleans
8/16	W 27-17	at Kansas City
8/23	W 24-0	at Oakland
8/29	L 14-28	Denver

REGULAR SEASON (11-5)

Date	Result	Opponent
9/7	W 17-10	Cincinnati
9/21	W 28-10	Cleveland
9/29	L 20-23	at Pittsburgh (OT)
10/5	L 10-13	Tennessee
10/12	L 3-31	at Indianapolis
10/19	W 27-13	at Miami
10/26	W 29-10	Oakland
11/2	W 37-27	at Cleveland
11/9	W 41-13	at Houston
11/16	L 10-30	at New York Giants
11/23	W 36-7	Philadelphia
11/30	W 34-3	at Cincinnati
12/7	W 24-10	Washington
12/14	L 9-13	Pittsburgh
12/20	W 33-24	at Dallas
12/28	W 27-7	Jacksonville

(OT) Overtime

POSTSEASON (2-1)

Date	Result	Opponent
1/4	W 27-9	at Miami
1/10	W 13-10	at Tennessee
1/18	L 14-23	at Pittsburgh

SCORE BY PERIODS

	1	2	3	4	OT	Total
Ravens	58	115	97	115	0	— 385
Opponents	57	58	66	60	3	— 244

2008 TEAM STATISTICS

	Ravens	Opp.
Total First Downs	300	228
Rushing	132	58
Passing	147	152
Penalty	21	18
3rd Down: Made/Att	95/232	71/212
3rd Down Pct.	40.9	33.5
4th Down: Made/Att	7/11	3/16
4th Down Pct.	63.6	18.8
Possession Avg.	33:10	26:50
Total Net Yards	5184	4177
Avg. Per Game	324.0	261.1
Total Plays	1058	928
Avg. Per Play	4.9	4.5
Net Yards Rushing	2376	1302
Avg. Per Game	148.5	81.4
Total Rushes	592	366
Net Yards Passing	2808	2875
Avg. Per Game	175.5	179.7
Sacked/Yards Lost	33/277	34/257
Gross Yards	3085	3132
Att./Completions	433/261	528/276
Completion Pct.	60.3	52.3
Had Intercepted	12	26
Punts/Average	84/45.0	92/42.8
Net Punting Avg.	84/39.9	92/37.0
Penalties/Yards	103/785	114/792
Fumbles/Ball Lost	28/9	21/8
Touchdowns	42	26
Rushing	20	4
Passing	16	17
Returns	6	5

2008 INDIVIDUAL STATISTICS

PASSING	Att.	Comp.	Yds.	Pct.	TD	Int.	Tkld.	Rate
Flacco	428	257	2971	60.0	14	12	32/276	80.3
T. Smith	4	3	82	75.0	1	0	1/1	156.3
Clayton	1	1	32	100.0	1	0	0/0	158.3
Ravens	433	261	3085	60.3	16	12	33/277	82.8
Opponents	528	276	3132	52.3	17	26	34/257	60.6

SCORING	TD R	TD P	TD Rt	PAT	FG	Saf	PTS
Stover	0	0	0	41/41	27/33	0	122
L. McClain	10	1	0	0/0	0/0	0	66
McGahee	7	0	0	0/0	0/0	0	42
D. Mason	0	5	0	0/0	0/0	0	32
Clayton	1	3	0	0/0	0/0	0	24
Heap	0	3	0	0/0	0/0	0	18
Reed	0	0	3	0/0	0/0	0	18
Flacco	2	0	0	0/0	0/0	0	12
Suggs	0	0	2	0/0	0/0	0	12
Wilcox	0	2	0	0/0	0/0	0	12
Figurs	0	1	0	0/0	0/0	0	6
Leonhard	0	0	1	0/0	0/0	0	6
D. Williams	0	1	0	0/0	0/0	0	6
J. McClain	0	0	0	0/0	0/0	2	4
Hauschka	0	0	0	0/0	1/2	0	3
Ravens	20	16	6	41/41	28/35	3	385
Opponents	4	17	5	25/25	21/22	0	244

2-Pt. Conversions: D. Mason.
Ravens 1-1, Opponents 0-1.

RUSHING	No.	Yds	Avg	LG	TD
L. McClain	232	902	3.9	82t	10
McGahee	170	671	3.9	77t	7
Rice	107	454	4.2	60	0
Flacco	52	180	3.5	38t	2
Clayton	6	81	13.5	42t	1
Parmele	2	27	13.5	31	0
Neal	12	25	2.1	5	0
T. Smith	9	24	2.7	8	0
Koch	1	9	9.0	9	0
D. Mason	1	3	3.0	3	0
Ravens	592	2376	4.0	82t	20
Opponents	366	1302	3.6	77	4

RECEIVING	No.	Yds	Avg	LG	TD
D. Mason	80	1037	13.0	54	5
Clayton	41	695	17.0	70t	3
Heap	35	403	11.5	30	3
Rice	33	273	8.3	40	0
McGahee	24	173	7.2	35	0
L. McClain	19	123	6.5	25	1
D. Williams	13	180	13.8	70t	1
Neal	7	35	5.0	13	0
Wilcox	5	19	3.8	8	2
Figurs	1	43	43.0	43t	1
Flacco	1	43	43.0	43	0
T. Smith	1	36	36.0	36	0
Jones	1	25	25.0	25	0
Ravens	261	3085	11.8	70t	16
Opponents	276	3132	11.3	67t	17

INTERCEPTIONS	No.	Yds	Avg	LG	TD
Reed	9	264	29.3	107t	2
Lewis	3	43	14.3	29	0
McAlister	3	28	9.3	16	0
Rolle	3	5	1.7	3	0
Suggs	2	86	43.0	44t	2
Ngata	2	8	4.0	7	0
Leonhard	1	35	35.0	35t	1
Washington	1	12	12.0	12	0
Walker	1	0	0.0	0	0
Bannan	1	-4	-4.0	-4	0
Ravens	26	477	18.3	107t	5
Opponents	12	104	8.7	50t	1

PUNTING	No.	Yds.	Avg.	In 20	LG
Koch	84	3777	45	34	74
Ravens	84	3777	45	34	74
Opponents	92	3938	42.8	21	59

PUNT RETURNS	Ret	FC	Yds	Avg	LG	TD
Figurs	23	11	138	6.0	35	0
Leonhard	20	9	232	11.6	46	0
Reed	1	0	8	8.0	8	0
Ravens	44	20	378	8.6	46	0
Opponents	38	12	245	6.4	33	0

KICKOFF RETURNS	No.	Yds	Avg	LG	TD
Figurs	29	608	21.0	39	0
Leonhard	8	163	20.4	30	0
Rice	7	161	23.0	30	0
Zbikowski	2	48	24.0	26	0
J. Johnson	1	13	13.0	13	0
Clayton	1	12	12.0	12	0
Neal	1	2	2.0	2	0
Jones	1	0	0.0	0	0
Ravens	50	1007	20.1	39	0
Opponents	76	1720	22.6	100t	2

FIELD GOALS	1-19	20-29	30-39	40-49	50+
Stover	0/0	11/11	11/12	5/9	0/1
Hauschka	0/0	0/0	0/0	0/0	1/2
Ravens	0/0	11/11	11/12	5/9	1/3
Opponents	2/2	7/7	6/6	5/6	1/1

SACKS	No.
Suggs	8.0
J. Johnson	5.0
Pryce	4.5
Lewis	3.5
Ivy	2.5
J. McClain	2.5
Scott	1.5
Ayanbadejo	1.0
Bannan	1.0
Leonhard	1.0
Ngata	1.0
Reed	1.0
(group)	1.0
Jones	0.5
Ravens	34.0
Opponents	33.0

RECORD HOLDERS

INDIVIDUAL RECORDS—CAREER

Category	Name	Performance
Rushing (Yds.)	Jamal Lewis, 2000-06	7,801
Passing (Yds.)	Kyle Boller, 2003-08	7,846
Passing (TDs)	Vinny Testaverde, 1996-97	51
Receiving (No.)	Todd Heap, 2001-08	374
Receiving (Yds.)	Todd Heap, 2001-08	4,300
Interceptions	Ed Reed, 2002-08	43
Punting (Avg.)	Sam Koch, 2006-08	43.8
Punt Return (Avg.)	Jermaine Lewis, 1996-2001	11.8
Kickoff Return (Avg.)	Corey Harris, 1998-2001	24.0
Field Goals	Matt Stover, 1996-2008	354
Touchdowns (Tot.)	Jamal Lewis, 2000-06	47
Points	Matt Stover, 1996-2008	1,464
*Sacks	Peter Boulware, 1997-2005	70.0

INDIVIDUAL RECORDS—SINGLE SEASON

Category	Name	Performance
Rushing (Yds.)	Jamal Lewis, 2003	2,066
Passing (Yds.)	Vinny Testaverde, 1996	4,177
Passing (TDs)	Vinny Testaverde, 1996	33
Receiving (No.)	Derrick Mason, 2007	103
Receiving (Yds.)	Michael Jackson, 1996	1,201
Interceptions	Ed Reed, 2004, 2008	9
Punting (Avg.)	Sam Koch, 2008	45.0
Punt Return (Avg.)	Jermaine Lewis, 2000	16.1
Kickoff Return (Avg.)	Corey Harris, 1998	27.6
Field Goals	Matt Stover, 2000	35
Touchdowns (Tot.)	Michael Jackson, 1996	14
	Jamal Lewis, 2003	14
Points	Matt Stover, 2000	135
*Sacks	Peter Boulware, 2001	15.0

INDIVIDUAL RECORDS—SINGLE GAME

Category	Name	Performance
Rushing (Yds.)	Jamal Lewis, 9-14-03	295
Passing (Yds.)	Vinny Testaverde, 10-27-96	429
Passing (TDs)	Tony Banks, 9-10-00	5
Receiving (No.)	Priest Holmes, 10-11-98	13
Receiving (Yds.)	Qadry Ismail, 12-12-99	268
Interceptions	Many times	2
	Last time by Ed Reed, 12-28-08	
Field Goals	Matt Stover, 9-21-97, 12-26-99, 10-28-00, 10-14-07	5
Touchdowns (Tot.)	Marcus Robinson, 11-23-03	4
Points	Marcus Robinson, 11-23-03	24
*Sacks	Michael McCrary, 11-8-98	4.0
	Peter Boulware, 1-7-02	4.0

**Sacks became an official statistic in 1982.*

BALTIMORE RAVENS

2009 VETERAN ROSTER

No.	Name	Pos.	Ht.	Wt.	Birthdate	NFL Exp.	College	Hometown	How Acq.	'08 Games/ Starts
79	Anderson, Willie	T	6-5	340	7/11/75	14	Auburn	Mobile, Ala	FA-'08	14/11
51	Ayanbadejo, Brendon	LB	6-1	228	9/6/76	7	UCLA	Santa Cruz, Calif.	UFA(Chi)-'08	16/0
94	Bannan, Justin	DT	6-3	310	4/18/79	8	Colorado	Orangevale, Calif.	UFA(Buff)-'06	16/15
50	Barnes, Antwan	LB	6-1	240	10/19/84	3	Florida International	Miami, Fla.	D4a-'07	13/0
9	Beck, John	QB	6-2	215	8/21/81	3	Brigham Young	Mesa, Ariz.	FA-'09	0*
77	Birk, Matt	C	6-4	309	7/23/76	12	Harvard	St. Paul, Minn.	UFA(Minn)-'09	16/16*
54	Burgess, Prescott	LB	6-3	240	3/6/84	3	Michigan	Warren, Ohio	D6-'07	0*
30	Carr, Chris	CB	5-10	180	4/30/83	5	Boise State	Reno, Nev.	UFA(Tenn)-'09	16/2*
65	Chester, Chris	G/C	6-3	305	1/12/83	4	Oklahoma	Tustin, Calif.	D2-'06	16/13
89	Clayton, Mark	WR	5-10	195	7/2/82	5	Oklahoma	Arlington, Texas	D1-'05	16/13
64	Cousins, Oniel	T	6-4	310	6/29/84	2	Texas-El Paso	Fullerton, Calif.	D3c-'08	6/0
96	Divens, Lamar	DT	6-3	333	11/12/85	2	Tennessee State	Fayetteville, Tenn.	FA-'08	3/0
93	Edwards, Dwan	DT	6-3	315	5/16/81	6	Oregon State	Columbus, Mont.	D2-'04	0*
16	Figurs, Yamon	WR/RS	5-11	175	1/10/82	3	Kansas State	Fort Pierce, Fla.	D3a-'07	12/0
5	Flacco, Joe	QB	6-6	230	1/16/85	2	Delaware	Audubon, N.J.	D1-'08	16/16
24	Foxworth, Domonique	CB	5-11	180	3/27/83	5	Maryland	Randallstown, Md.	UFA(Atl)-'09	14/10*
71	Gaither, Jared	T	6-9	350	3/18/86	3	Maryland	White Plains, Md.	SD5-'07	16/15
56	Gooden, Tavares	LB	6-1	235	10/7/84	2	Miami	Fort Lauderdale, Fla.	D3a-'08	4/0
97	Gregg, Kelly	DT	6-0	310	11/1/76	10	Oklahoma	Edmond, Okla.	FA-'00	0*
66	Grubbs, Ben	G	6-3	315	3/10/84	3	Auburn	Eclectic, Ala.	D1-'07	16/16
62	Hale, David	G/T	6-6	315	3/3/83	2	Weber State	Plain City, Utah	D4b-'08	6/0
14	Harper, Justin	WR	6-3	215	2/24/85	2	Virginia Tech	Catawba, N.C.	D7a-'08	0*
6	Hauschka, Steve	K	6-4	210	6/29/85	2	North Carolina St.	Needham, Mass.	FA-'08	8/0
86	Heap, Todd	TE	6-5	252	3/16/80	9	Arizona State	Mesa, Ariz.	D1-'01	16/16
95	Johnson, Jarret	DE	6-3	270	8/14/81	7	Alabama	Cedar Key, Fla.	D4a-'03	16/16
84	Jones, Edgar	LB/TE	6-3	263	12/1/84	3	Southeast Missouri	Rayville, La.	FA-'07	7/0
70	Katula, Matt	LS	6-6	272	8/22/82	5	Wisconsin	Brookfield, Wisc.	FA-'05	16/0
4	Koch, Sam	P	6-1	230	8/13/82	4	Nebraska	Seward, Neb.	D6a-'06	16/0
26	Landry, Dawan	S	6-0	220	12/30/82	4	Georgia Tech	Ama, La.	D5a-'06	2/2
52	Lewis, Ray	LB	6-1	250	5/15/75	14	Miami	Lakeland, Fla.	D1b-'96	16/16
29	Martin, Derrick	CB	5-10	202	5/16/85	4	Wyoming	Denver, Colo.	D6b-'06	4/0
85	Mason, Derrick	WR	5-10	192	1/17/74	13	Michigan State	Detroit, Mich.	FA-'05	16/16
72	Mattison, Bryan	OL	6-3	272	5/15/84	2	Iowa	Mishawaka, Ind.	FA-'08	0*
17	Maxwell, Marcus	WR	6-3	210	7/3/83	4	Oregon	Hercules, Calif.	FA-'08	0*
53	McClain, Jameel	LB	6-1	250	7/25/85	2	Syracuse	Philadelphia, Pa.	FA-'08	16/0
33	McClain, Le'Ron	FB	6-0	260	12/27/84	3	Alabama	Northport, Ala.	D4b-'07	16/16
23	McGahee, Willis	RB	6-0	232	10/21/81	7	Miami	Miami, Fla.	T(Buff)-'07	13/8
91	McKinney, Brandon	DT	6-2	324	8/24/83	4	Michigan State	Dayton, Ohio	FA-'08	11/0
43	Nakamura, Haruki	S	5-10	205	4/18/86	2	Cincinnati	Cleveland, Ohio	D6-'08	16/0
92	Ngata, Haloti	NT	6-4	340	1/21/84	4	Oregon	Salt Lake City, Utah	D1-'06	16/16
25	Oglesby, Evan	CB	5-11	188	12/18/81	4	North Alabama	Toccoa, Ga.	FA-'08	9/0
34	Parmele, Jalen	RB	5-11	220	12/30/85	2	Toledo	Midland, Mich.	FA-'08	1/0
90	Pryce, Trevor	DT	6-5	286	8/3/75	13	Clemson	Winter Park, Fla.	FA-'06	16/16
20	Reed, Ed	S	5-11	200	9/11/78	8	Miami	St. Rose, La.	D1-'02	16/16
76	Reitz, Joe	T	6-7	270	8/24/85	2	Western Michigan	Fishers, Ind.	FA-'08	0*
27	Rice, Ray	RB	5-8	205	1/22/87	2	Rutgers	New Rochelle, N.Y.	D2-'08	13/4
22	Rolle, Samari	CB	6-0	175	8/10/76	12	Florida State	Miami, Fla.	FA-'05	10/10
82	Smith, L.J.	TE	6-3	258	5/13/80	7	Rutgers	Highland Park, N.J.	UFA(Phil)-'09	13/12*
81	Smith, Marcus	WR	6-1	215	1/11/85	2	New Mexico	San Diego, Calif.	D4a-'08	5/0
10	Smith, Troy	QB	6-0	225	7/20/84	3	Ohio State	Cleveland, Ohio	D5-'07	6/0
63	Stallings, Tre	T	6-3	315	1/8/83	2	Mississippi	Magnolia, Miss.	FA-'08	0*
55	Suggs, Terrell	LB	6-3	260	10/11/82	7	Arizona State	Chandler, Ariz.	D1a-'03	16/16
88	Sypniewski, Quinn	TE	6-6	270	4/14/82	4	Colorado	Johnston, Iowa	D5b-'06	0*
98	Talavou, Kelly	NT	6-2	340	10/4/84	2	Utah	Fountain Valley, Calif.	FA-'08	0*
78	Terry, Adam	T	6-8	330	9/1/82	5	Syracuse	Queensbury, N.Y.	D2b-'05	12/7
41	Walker, Frank	CB	5-11	196	8/6/81	7	Tuskegee	Tuskegee, Ala.	UFA(GB)-'08	15/5
31	Washington, Fabian	CB	5-11	185	6/9/83	5	Nebraska	Bradenton, Fla.	T(Oak)-'08	12/12
87	Williams, Demetrius	WR	6-2	197	3/28/83	4	Oregon	Concord, Calif.	D4a-'06	7/0
73	Yanda, Marshal	G/T	6-3	310	9/15/84	3	Iowa	Anamosa, Iowa	D3b-'07	5/5
28	Zbikowski, Tom	S	5-11	215	5/22/85	2	Notre Dame	Arlington Heights, Ill.	D3b-'08	16/0

* Beck inactive for 16 games with Miami; Birk played 16 games for Minnesota in '08; Burgess missed '08 season because of injury; Carr played 16 games for Tennessee; Edwards missed '08 season because of injury; Foxworth played 14 games for Atlanta; Gregg inactive for 4 games and missed rest of season because of injury; Harper missed '08 season because of injury; Maxwell inactive for 6 games; Reitz missed '08 season because of injury; Smith played 13 games for Philadelphia; Stallings last active with Kansas City in '07; Sypniewski missed '08 season because of injury: Talavou missed '08 season because of injury.

Players lost through free agency (6): QB Kyle Boller (StL; 0 games in '08), C Jason Brown (StL; 16), WR Terrance Copper (KC; 7), CB Corey Ivy (Cle; 16), S Jim Leonhard (NYJ; 16), LB Bart Scott (NYJ; 16).

Also played with Ravens in '08—DE Marques Douglas (16 games), LB Nick Greisen (14), T Mike Kracalik (1), CB Chris McAlister (6), LB Robert McCune (1), FB Lorenzo Neal (16), Anwar Phillips (1), T Chad Slaughter (6), K Matt Stover (16); TE Daniel Wilcox (13).

2009 FIRST-YEAR ROSTER

Name	Pos.	Ht.	Wt.	Birthdate	College	Hometown	How Acq.
Cook, Jason	FB	6-0	235	1/28/86	Mississippi	Suwanee, Ga.	FA
Drew, Davon	TE	6-4	260	12/9/85	East Carolina	New Bern, N.C.	D5b
Ellerbe, Dannell	LB	6-1	228	11/29/85	Georgia	Hamlet, N.C.	FA
Gano, Graham	K	6-1	192	4/9/87	Florida State	Pensacola, Fla.	FA
Gerard, Kevin "K.J."	CB	6-1	187	4/22/86	Northern Arizona	Fountain Valley, Calif.	FA
Johnson, Brian (1)	G	6-4	307	3/24/84	Louisiana State	Godby, Fla.	FA-'08
Johnson, Will	DL	6-5	285	11/10/85	Michigan	Oakland, Mich.	FA
Jones, David	CB	5-10	185	10/29/85	Kentucky	Red Jacket, W. Va.	FA
Kruger, Paul	LB/DE	6-4	265	31458	Utah	Orem, Utah	D2
Lawrence, Matt (1)	RB	6-1	204	5/5/85	Massachusetts	Bloomfield, Conn.	FA-'08
Oher, Michael	T	6-4	309	5/28/86	Mississippi	Memphis, Tenn.	D1
Peerman, Cedric	RB	5-9	220	10/10/86	Virginia	Gladys, Va.	D6
Phillips, Anwar (1)	CB	6-0	187	10/25/82	Penn State	Germantown, Md.	FA-'08
Phillips, Jason	LB	6-1	240	2/14/86	Texas Christian	Waller, Texas	D5a
Riley, Eron	WR	6-3	200	8/5/87	Duke	Savannah, Ga.	FA
Ryan, Greg	C	6-4	295	9/22/85	Western Kentucky	Murray, Ky.	FA
Smolko, Isaac (1)	TE	6-5	260	2/28/83	Penn State	Youngstown, Ohio	FA-'08
VanDeSteeg, William	LB/DE	6-4	256	9/22/85	Minnesota	Silver Lake, Minn.	FA
Vasquez, Luis	LB/DE	6-3	260	4/23/86	Arizona State	Gales Ferry, Conn.	FA
Webb, Lardarius	DB	5-10	180	10/12/85	Nicholls State	Opelika, Ala.	D3
Wheelwright, Ernie (1)	WR	6-5	220	7/10/84	Minnesota	Columbus, Ohio	FA-'08
Williams, Edward (1)	WR	6-4	215	11/24/82	Lane	Montgomery, Ala.	FA-'08
Williams, Isaiah	WR	6-3	200	1/30/87	Maryland	Montclair, N.J.	FA
Willy, Drew	QB	6-4	214	11/13/86	Buffalo	Randolph, N.J.	FA

The term NFL Rookie is defined as a player who is in his first season of professional football and has not been on the roster of another professional football team for any regular-season or postseason games. A Rookie is designated by an "R" on NFL rosters. Players who have been active in another professional football league or players who have NFL experience, including either preseason training camp or being on an Active List or Inactive List, or on Reserve/Injured or Reserve/Physically Unable to Perform for fewer than six regular-season games, are termed NFL First-Year Players. An NFL First-Year Player is designated by a "1" on NFL rosters. Thereafter, a player is credited with an additional year of experience for each season in which he accumulates six games on the Active List or Inactive List, or on Reserve/Injured or Reserve/Physically Unable to Perform.

Log on to www.baltimoreravens.com for an up-to-date roster.

BALTIMORE RAVENS

COACHING STAFF

Head Coach,

John Harbaugh

Pro Career: John Harbaugh became the third head coach in Baltimore Ravens history on January 19, 2008. In his first season in Baltimore, Harbaugh led the Ravens to an 11-5 record and a berth in the AFC Championship game. Baltimore set an NFL record for most wins by a team with both a rookie head coach and a rookie quarterback (Joe Flacco). Harbaugh spent the previous 10 seasons (1998-2007) with the Philadelphia Eagles. He was the team's secondary coach in 2007, after 9 seasons as its special teams coordinator. Under his leadership, Harbaugh's special teams units were consistently ranked among the NFL's best. From 2000-04, Philadelphia was the only team to rank in the top 10 in the comprehensive annual special teams report created by *The Dallas Morning News*' Rick Gosselin. (Gosselin's report is recognized by NFL teams as the special teams measuring stick.) In 2001 and 2003, the Eagles were ranked first by Gosselin, who compiles his report based on 22 kicking-game categories. Following the 2001 season, Harbaugh was voted the NFL's Special Teams Coach of the Year by his coaching peers. He was also named *The Dallas Morning News* Special Teams Coach of the Year that season. Career record: 13-6.

Background: Harbaugh played defensive back at Miami (Ohio) from 1980-83, while earning his degree in political science. He coached on the collegiate level at Western Michigan (1984-86), Pittsburgh (1987), Morehead State (1988), Cincinnati (1989-1996), and Indiana (1997).

Personal: Born in Perrysburg, Ohio on September 23, 1962, Harbaugh and his wife, Ingrid, have a daughter, Alison. He is the son of longtime college coach Jack Harbaugh, and his brother, Jim, the current Stanford head coach, played quarterback in the NFL for 14 years, including a season in Baltimore (1998). John's brother-in-law, Tom Crean, Indiana University's head basketball coach, is married to his sister, Joani.

ASSISTANT COACHES

Roy Anderson, defensive assistant; born October 5, 1979, Tallahassee, Fla. Quarterback Howard 1997-2001. No pro playing experience. Pro coach: Joined Ravens in 2009.

Clarence Brooks, defensive line; born May 20, 1951, New York, N.Y. Guard Massachusetts 1970-73. No pro playing experience. College coach: Massachusetts 1976-1980, Syracuse 1981-89, Arizona 1990-92. Pro coach: Chicago Bears 1993-98, Cleveland Browns 1999, Miami Dolphins 2000-04, joined Ravens in 2005.

Cam Cameron, offensive coordinator; born February 6, 1961, Chapel Hill, N.C. Quarterback Indiana 1980-83. No pro playing experience. College coach: Michigan 1984-1993, Indiana 1997-2001 (head coach). Pro coach: Washington Redskins 1994-96, San Diego Chargers 2002-06, Miami Dolphins 2007 (head coach), joined Ravens in 2008.

Mark Carrier, defensive backs; born April 28, 1968, Lake Charles, La. Cornerback Southern California 1987-89. Pro cornerback Chicago Bears, 1990-96, Detroit Lions 1997-99, Washington Redskins 2000. College coach: Arizona State 2004-05. Pro coach: Joined Ravens in 2006.

John Dunn, asst. strength and conditioning; born July 22, 1965, Great Barrington, Mass. Guard Penn State 1974-77. No pro playing experience. College coach: Penn State 1978. Pro coach: Washington Redskins 1984-86, Los Angeles Raiders 1987-89, San Diego Chargers 1990-96, New York Giants 1997-2003, Washington Redskins 2004-05, joined Ravens in 2008.

Vic Fangio, linebackers; born August 22, 1958, Dunmore, Pa. Attended East Stroudsburg State. No pro playing experience. College coach: North Carolina 1983. Pro coach: Philadelphia/Baltimore Stars (USFL) 1984-85, New Orleans Saints 1986-1994, Carolina Panthers 1995-98, Indianapolis Colts 1999-2001, Houston Texans 2002-2005, joined Ravens in 2006.

Wade Harman, tight ends; born October 1, 1963, Corydon, Iowa. Linebacker Drake 1985, Utah State 1986. No pro playing experience. College coach: Utah State 1987-1991, Pacific 1992-95, Morningside 1996. Pro coach: Minnesota Vikings 1997-98, joined Ravens in 1999.

Jim Hostler, wide receivers; born November 11, 1966, Pittsburgh. Defensive back Indiana (Pa.) 1986-89. College coach: Indiana (Pa.) 1990-92, 1994-99, Juniata (Pa.) 1993. Pro coach: Kansas City Chiefs 2000, New Orleans Saints 2001-02, New York Jets 2003-04, San Francisco 49ers 2005-07, joined Ravens in 2008.

Hue Jackson, quarterbacks; born October 22, 1965, Los Angeles. Quarterback Pacific 1985-86. No pro playing experience. College coach: Pacific 1987-89, Cal State-Fullerton 1990, Arizona State 1992-95, California 1996, Southern California 1997-2000. Pro coach: London Monarchs (WFL) 1991, Washington Redskins 2001-03, Cincinnati Bengals 2004-06, Atlanta Falcons 2007, joined Ravens in 2008.

Marwan Maalouf, asst. special teams; born November 26, 1976, Beirut, Lebanon. Guard Baldwin-Wallace 1997-99. No pro playing experience. College coach: Baldwin-Wallace 2000, Fordham 2001, Rutgers 2002-03. Pro coach: Cleveland Browns 2004-06, joined Ravens in 2008.

John Matsko, offensive line; born February 2, 1951, Cleveland. Fullback Kent State 1970-73. No pro playing experience. College coach: Kent State 1973, Miami (Ohio) 1974-75, 1977, North Carolina 1978-1984, Navy 1985, Arizona 1986, Southern California 1987-1991. Pro coach: Phoenix Cardinals 1992-93, New Orleans Saints 1994-96, N.Y. Giants 1997-98, St. Louis Rams 1999-2005, Kansas City Chiefs 2006-07, joined Ravens in 2008.

Greg Mattison, defensive coordinator; born November 15, 1949, Madison, Wisc. Guard Wisconsin-LaCrosse 1967-1970. No pro playing experience. College coach: Illinois 1976, Cornell 1977, Northwestern 1978-1980, Western Michigan 1981-86, Navy 1987-88, Texas A&M 1989-1991, Michigan 1992-96, Notre Dame 1997-2004, Florida 2005-07. Pro coach: Joined Ravens in 2008.

Andy Moeller, asst. offensive line; June 15, 1964, Grand Rapids, Mich. Linebacker Michigan 1983-86. No pro playing experience. College coach: Indiana 1987, Army 1988-1993, Missouri 1994-99, Michigan 2000-07. Pro coach: Joined Ravens in 2008.

Wilbert Montgomery, running backs; born September 16, 1954, Greenville, Miss. Running back Abilene Christian 1973-76. Pro running back Philadelphia Eagles 1977-1984, Detroit Lions 1985. Pro Coach: St. Louis Rams 1997-2005, Detroit Lions 2006-07, joined Ravens in 2008.

Chuck Pagano, secondary; born October 2, 1960, Boulder, Colo. Safety Wyoming 1980-83. No pro playing experience. College coach: Southern California 1984-85, Miami 1986, Boise State 1987-88, East Carolina 1989, Nevada-Las Vegas 1990-91, East Carolina 1992-94, Miami 1995-2000, North Carolina 2007. Pro coach: Cleveland Browns 2001-04, Oakland Raiders 2005-06, joined Ravens in 2008.

Bob Rogucki, strength and conditioning; born September 27, 1953, Clarksburg, W.Va. No college or pro playing experience. College coach: Penn State 1981, Weber State 1982, Army 1983-89. Pro coach: Arizona Cardinals 1990-2003, Jacksonville Jaguars 2004, Philadelphia Eagles 2006-07, joined Ravens in 2008.

Jerry Rosburg, special teams coordinator/asst. head coach; born November 24, 1955, Fairmont, Minn. Linebacker North Dakota State 1974-77. No pro playing experience. College coach: Northern Michigan 1981-86, Western Michigan 1987-1991, Cincinnati 1992-95, Minnesota 1996, Boston College 1997-98, Notre Dame 1999-2000. Pro coach: Cleveland Browns 2001-06, Atlanta Falcons 2007, joined Ravens in 2008.

Craig Ver Steeg, offensive assistant; born September 11, 1960, Inglewood, Calif. No college or pro playing experience. College coach: Southern California 1984-85, Utah 1986-89, Cincinnati 1990-93, Harvard 1994-95, Illinois 1998-2000, Utah 2001-02, Rutgers 2003-07. Pro coach: Chicago Bears 1996-97, joined Ravens in 2008.

Matt Weiss, coaching assistant; born March 1, 1983, New Haven, Conn. Punter Vanderbilt 2001-02. No pro playing experience. College coach: Stanford 2008. Pro coach: Joined Ravens in 2009.

American Football Conference
East Division
Team Colors: Dark Navy, Red, Royal, and Nickel
One Bills Drive
Orchard Park, New York 14127-2296
Telephone: (716) 648-1800

2009 SCHEDULE
PRESEASON

Aug. 9	vs. Tennessee at Canton, OH	8:00
Aug. 15	**Chicago**	7:00
Aug. 22	at Green Bay	7:00
Aug. 29	at Pittsburgh	7:30
Sep. 3	**Detroit**	6:30

REGULAR SEASON

Sep. 14	at New England (Mon.)	7:00
Sep. 20	**Tampa Bay**	4:05
Sep. 27	**New Orleans**	4:05
Oct. 4	at Miami	4:05
Oct. 11	**Cleveland**	1:00
Oct. 18	at N.Y. Jets	4:15
Oct. 25	at Carolina	4:05
Nov. 1	**Houston**	1:00
Nov. 8	BYE	
Nov. 15	at Tennessee	12:00
Nov. 22	at Jacksonville	1:00
Nov. 29	**Miami**	1:00
Dec. 3	**N.Y. Jets** (Thu. – Toronto)	8:20
Dec. 13	at Kansas City	12:00
Dec. 20	**New England**	1:00
Dec. 27	at Atlanta	1:00
Jan. 3	**Indianapolis**	1:00

Stadium: Ralph Wilson Stadium (opened in 1973) • **Capacity:** 73,967 One Bills Drive Orchard Park, New York 14127-2296
Playing Surface: AstroPlay
Training Camp: St. John Fisher College Rochester, N.Y. 14618

RALPH WILSON STADIUM

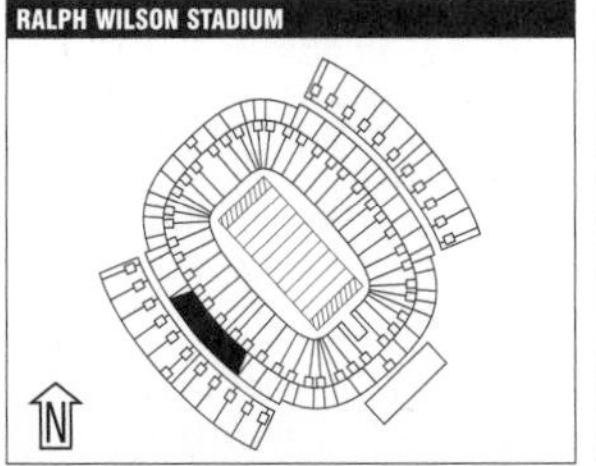

CLUB OFFICIALS
Owner and President: Ralph C. Wilson, Jr.
Chief Operating Officer/General Manager: Russ Brandon
Treasurer: Jeffrey C. Littmann
Senior Vice President of Marketing and Broadcasting: Marc Honan
Senior Vice President of Football Administration: Jim Overdorf
Senior Vice President of Business Development: Bruce Popko
Senior Vice President of Business Operations and Ticketing: Dave Wheat
Vice President of Communications: Scott Berchtold
Vice President of Stadium Operations: Joe Frandina
Vice President of Community Relations: Gretchen Geitter
Vice President of Pro Personnel: John Guy
Vice President of College Scouting: Tom Modrak
Vice President of Government Relations/External Affairs: Bill Munson
Vice President of Strategic Planning: Mary Owen
Consultant: Christy Wilson Hofmann
Executive Director of Information Technology: Dan Evans
Director of Security: Chris Clark
Director of Stadium Operations: Perry Dix
Director of Merchandise: Tim Kehoe
Director of Player Programs: Paul Lancaster
Controller: Frank Wojnicki
Strength and Conditioning Assistant: Dan Liburd
Equipment Manager: Dave Hojnowski
Assistant Equipment Managers: Randy Ribbeck, Jeff Mazurek
Head Athletic Trainer: Bud Carpenter
Athletic Trainers: Chris Fischetti, Shone Gipson, Greg McMillen
Video Director: Henry Kunttu
Assistant Video Director: Greg Estes
Video Assistant: Wes Burnard
Scouts: Rashaan Curry, Brian Fisher, Brad Forsyth, Matt Hand (BLESTO), Shawn Heilen, Doug Majeski, Buddy Nix, Tom Roth, (emeritus) David G. Smith, (emeritus) David W. Smith

COACHING HISTORY
(362-399-8)
Records include postseason games

1960-61	Buster Ramsey	11-16-1
1962-65	Lou Saban	38-18-3
1966-68	Joe Collier*	13-17-1
1968	Harvey Johnson	1-10-1
1969-1970	John Rauch	7-20-1
1971	Harvey Johnson	1-13-0
1972-76	Lou Saban**	32-29-1
1976-77	Jim Ringo	3-20-0
1978-1982	Chuck Knox	38-38-0
1983-85	Kay Stephenson***	10-26-0
1985-86	Hank Bullough****	4-17-0
1986-1997	Marv Levy	123-78-0
1998-2000	Wade Phillips	29-21-0
2001-03	Gregg Williams	17-31-0
2004-05	Mike Mularkey	14-18-0
2006-08	Dick Jauron	21-27-0

*Released after two games in 1968
**Resigned after five games in 1976
***Released after four games in 1985
****Released after nine games in 1986

PAID ATTENDANCE
Home 541,882 Away 532,420
Total 1,074,302
Single-game home record, 80,368 (10/4/92)
Single-season home record, 635,889 (1991)

2009 DRAFT CHOICES

Round	Name	Pos.	College
1	Aaron Maybin	DE	Penn State
	Eric Wood	OL	Louisville
2	Jairus Byrd	DB	Oregon
	Andy Levitre	OL	Oregon State
4	Shawn Nelson	TE	Southern Mississippi
5	Nic Harris	LB	Oklahoma
6	Cary Harris	DB	Southern California
7	Ellis Lankster	DB	West Virginia

BUFFALO BILLS

2008 TEAM RECORD

PRESEASON (2-2)

Date	Result	Opponent
8/9	L 14-17	at Washington
8/14	W 24-21	Pittsburgh
8/24	W 20-7	at Indianapolis
8/28	L 6-14	Detroit

REGULAR SEASON (7-9)

Date	Result	Opponent
9/7	W 34-10	Seattle
9/14	W 20-16	at Jacksonville
9/21	W 24-23	Oakland
9/28	W 31-14	at St. Louis
10/5	L 17-41	at Arizona
10/19	W 23-14	San Diego
10/26	L 16-25	at Miami
11/2	L 17-26	New York Jets
11/9	L 10-20	at New England
11/17	L 27-29	Cleveland
11/23	W 54-31	at Kansas City
11/30	L 3-10	San Francisco
12/7	L 3-16	Miami
12/14	L 27-31	at New York Jets
12/21	W 30-23	at Denver
12/28	L 0-13	New England

SCORE BY PERIODS

Bills	46	113	73	104	0 —	336
Opponents	108	76	81	77	0 —	342

2008 TEAM STATISTICS

	Bills	Opp.
Total First Downs	287	293
Rushing	107	113
Passing	167	167
Penalty	13	13
3rd Down: Made/Att	81/203	73/202
3rd Down Pct.	39.9	36.1
4th Down: Made/Att	7/16	8/16
4th Down Pct.	43.8	50.0
Possession Avg.	30:04	29:57
Total Net Yards	4882	5217
Avg. Per Game	305.1	326.1
Total Plays	956	971
Avg. Per Play	5.1	5.4
Net Yards Rushing	1842	1946
Avg. Per Game	115.1	121.6
Total Rushes	439	455
Net Yards Passing	3040	3271
Avg. Per Game	190.0	204.4
Sacked/Yards Lost	38/262	24/170
Gross Yards	3302	3441
Att./Completions	479/309	492/301
Completion Pct.	64.5	61.2
Had Intercepted	15	10
Punts/Average	58/44.1	64/45.6
Net Punting Avg.	58/39.1	64/36.8
Penalties/Yards	71/538	72/540
Fumbles/Ball Lost	33/15	21/12
Touchdowns	35	34
Rushing	16	18
Passing	14	14
Returns	5	2

2008 INDIVIDUAL STATISTICS

PASSING	Att.	Comp.	Yds.	Pct.	TD	Int.	Tkld.	Rate
Edwards	374	245	2699	65.5	11	10	23/143	85.4
Losman	104	63	584	60.6	2	5	15/119	62.3
Moorman	1	1	19	100.0	1	0	0/0	158.3
Bills	479	309	3302	64.5	14	15	38/262	81.3
Opponents	492	301	3441	61.2	14	10	24/170	83.2

SCORING	TD R	TD P	TD Rt	PAT	FG	Saf	PTS
Lindell	0	0	0	34/34	30/38	0	124
Lynch	8	1	0	0/0	0/0	0	54
Evans	0	3	0	0/0	0/0	0	20
Edwards	3	0	0	0/0	0/0	0	18
Jackson	3	0	0	0/0	0/0	0	18
Greer	0	0	2	0/0	0/0	0	12
Hardy	0	2	0	0/0	0/0	0	12
St. Johnson	0	2	0	0/0	0/0	0	12
Losman	2	0	0	0/0	0/0	0	12
McKelvin	0	0	2	0/0	0/0	0	12
Parrish	0	1	1	0/0	0/0	0	12
Denney	0	1	0	0/0	0/0	0	6
Fine	0	1	0	0/0	0/0	0	6
Reed	0	1	0	0/0	0/0	0	6
Royal	0	1	0	0/0	0/0	0	6
Schouman	0	1	0	0/0	0/0	0	6
Bills	16	14	5	34/34	30/38	0	336
Opponents	18	14	2	34/34	34/41	1	342

2-Pt. Conversions: Evans.
Bills 1-1, Opponents 0-0.

RUSHING	No.	Yds	Avg	LG	TD
Lynch	250	1036	4.1	50	8
Jackson	130	571	4.4	32	3
Edwards	36	117	3.3	15t	3
Losman	12	70	5.8	17	2
Evans	1	22	22.0	22	0
Parrish	2	9	4.5	9	0
Ellison	1	6	6.0	6	0
St. Johnson	1	6	6.0	6	0
Omon	6	5	0.8	2	0
Bills	439	1842	4.2	50	16
Opponents	455	1946	4.3	72t	18

RECEIVING	No.	Yds	Avg	LG	TD
Evans	63	1017	16.1	87t	3
Reed	56	597	10.7	24	1
Lynch	47	300	6.4	42	1
Jackson	37	317	8.6	65	0
Royal	33	351	10.6	30t	1
Parrish	24	232	9.7	22	1
Schouman	15	153	10.2	21	1
Steve Johnson	10	102	10.2	21	2
Fine	10	94	9.4	20	1
Hardy	9	87	9.7	17	2
Barnes	2	34	17.0	25	0
McIntyre	2	-1	-.5	0	0
Denney	1	19	19.0	19t	1
Bills	309	3302	10.7	87t	14
Opponents	301	3441	11.4	84t	14

INTERCEPTIONS	No.	Yds	Avg	LG	TD
McGee	3	36	12.0	36	0
Greer	2	75	37.5	42t	2
McKelvin	2	64	32.0	64t	1
Mitchell	2	33	16.5	32	0
Posluszny	1	9	9.0	9	0
Bills	10	217	21.7	64t	3
Opponents	15	169	11.3	92t	1

PUNTING	No.	Yds.	Avg.	In 20	LG
Moorman	58	2557	44.1	23	63
Bills	58	2557	44.1	23	63
Opponents	64	2920	45.6	22	65

PUNT RETURNS	Ret	FC	Yds	Avg	LG	TD
Parrish	21	10	322	15.3	63t	1
Jackson	7	0	116	16.6	35	0
McKelvin	2	0	26	13.0	14	0
Bills	30	10	464	15.5	63t	1
Opponents	18	12	187	10.4	21	0

KICKOFF RETURNS	No.	Yds	Avg	LG	TD
McKelvin	52	1468	28.2	98t	1
Jackson	12	181	15.1	30	0
Sp. Johnson	3	40	13.3	19	0
McGee	3	62	20.7	27	0
Parrish	2	40	20.0	25	0
McIntyre	1	18	18.0	18	0
Wilson	1	7	7.0	7	0
St. Johnson	1	0	0.0	0	0
Bills	75	1816	24.2	98t	1
Opponents	63	1247	19.8	69	0

FIELD GOALS	1-19	20-29	30-39	40-49	50+
Lindell	1/1	7/8	11/11	10/15	1/3
Bills	1/1	7/8	11/11	10/15	1/3
Opponents	0/0	8/9	14/15	8/11	4/6

SACKS	No.
Denney	4.0
Mitchell	4.0
Stroud	2.5
Sp. Johnson	2.0
Kelsay	2.0
Williams	2.0
Wilson	1.5
Bryan	1.0
Schobel	1.0
B. Scott	1.0
Whitner	1.0
Youboty	1.0
(group)	1.0
Bills	24.0
Opponents	38.0

RECORD HOLDERS

INDIVIDUAL RECORDS—CAREER

Category	Name	Performance
Rushing (Yds.)	Thurman Thomas, 1988-1999	11,938
Passing (Yds.)	Jim Kelly, 1986-1996	35,467
Passing (TDs)	Jim Kelly, 1986-1996	237
Receiving (No.)	Andre Reed, 1985-1999	941
Receiving (Yds.)	Andre Reed, 1985-1999	13,095
Interceptions	George (Butch) Byrd, 1964-1970	40
Punting (Avg.)	Brian Moorman, 2001-08	43.2
Punt Return (Avg.)	Roscoe Parrish, 2005-08	**14.0
Kickoff Return (Avg.)	O.J. Simpson, 1969-1977	30.0
Field Goals	Steve Christie, 1992-2000	234
Touchdowns (Tot.)	Andre Reed, 1985-1999	87
	Thurman Thomas, 1988-1999	87
Points	Steve Christie, 1992-2000	1,011
*Sacks	Bruce Smith, 1985-1999	**171.0

INDIVIDUAL RECORDS—SINGLE SEASON

Category	Name	Performance
Rushing (Yds.)	O.J. Simpson, 1973	2,003
Passing (Yds.)	Drew Bledsoe, 2002	4,359
Passing (TDs)	Jim Kelly, 1991	33
Receiving (No.)	Eric Moulds, 2002	100
Receiving (Yds.)	Eric Moulds, 1998	1,368
Interceptions	Billy Atkins, 1961	10
	Tom Janik, 1967	10
Punting (Avg.)	Brian Moorman, 2005	45.7
Punt Return (Avg.)	Roscoe Parrish, 2007	16.3
Kickoff Return (Avg.)	Terrence McGee, 2005	30.24
Field Goals	Steve Christie, 1998	33
Touchdowns (Tot.)	O.J. Simpson, 1975	23
Points	Steve Christie, 1998	140
*Sacks	Bruce Smith, 1990	19.0

INDIVIDUAL RECORDS—SINGLE GAME

Category	Name	Performance
Rushing (Yds.)	O.J. Simpson, 11-25-76	273
Passing (Yds.)	Drew Bledsoe, 9-15-02	463
Passing (TDs)	Jim Kelly, 9-8-91	6
Receiving (No.)	Andre Reed, 11-20-94	15
Receiving (Yds.)	Lee Evans, 11-19-06	265
Interceptions	Many times	3
	Last time by Nate Clements, 10-20-02	
Field Goals	Steve Christie, 10-20-96	6
Touchdowns (Tot.)	Cookie Gilchrist, 12-8-63	5
Points	Cookie Gilchrist, 12-8-63	30
*Sacks	Cornelius Bennett, 12-27-87	4.0
	Bruce Smith, 12-9-90, 9-18-94	4.0

**Sacks became an official statistic in 1982.*
***NFL Record*

BUFFALO BILLS

2009 VETERAN ROSTER

No.	Name	Pos.	Ht.	Wt.	Birthdate	NFL Exp.	College	Hometown	How Acq.	'08 Games/ Starts
16	Baker, Matt	QB	6-2	217	5/11/83	2	North Carolina	East Lansing, Mich.	FA-'08	0*
77	Bell, Demetrius	T	6-5	307	5/3/84	2	Northwestern State	Summerfield, La.	D7a-'08	0*
50	Bowen, Alvin	LB	6-1	222	12/24/83	2	Iowa State	East Orange, N.J.	D5-'08	0*
96	Bryan, Copeland	DE	6-4	253	7/14/83	2	Arizona	San Jose, Calif.	FA-'07	15/0
53	Buggs, Marcus	LB	5-10	223	9/21/85	2	Vanderbilt	Madison, Tenn.	UFA-'08	4/0
60	Butler, Brad	OL	6-7	315	9/18/83	4	Virginia	Lynchburg, Va.	D5b-'06	13/13
73	Chambers, Kirk	OL	6-7	315	3/19/79	5	Stanford	Provo, Utah	FA-'07	16/4
27	Corner, Reggie	CB	5-9	175	11/17/83	2	Akron	Canton, Ohio	D4a-'08	12/2
57	Corto, Jon	LB	6-0	208	9/3/84	2	Sacred Heart	Orchard Park, N.Y.	FA-'08	16/0
54	Costanzo, Blake	LB	6-2	235	4/14/184	3	Lafayette	Franklin Lakes, N.J.	FA-'07	16/0
92	Denney, Ryan	DE	6-7	264	6/15/77	8	Brigham Young	Thornton, Colo.	D2b-'02	16/11
52	DiGiorgio, John	LB	6-2	229	6/29/82	4	Saginaw Valley State	Shelby Twp., Mich.	FA-'06	6/0
5	Edwards, Trent	QB	6-4	231	10/30/83	3	Stanford	Los Gatos, Calif.	D3-'07	14/14
93	Ellis, Chris	DE	6-4	261	2/11/85	2	Virginia Tech	Hampton, Va.	D3-'08	7/0
56	Ellison, Keith	LB	6-0	229	2/6/84	4	Oregon State	Redondo Beach, Calif.	D6-'06	16/14
83	Evans, Lee	WR	5-10	197	3/11/81	6	Wisconsin	Bedford, Ohio	D1a-'04	16/16
86	Fine, Derek	TE	6-3	247	8/24/83	2	Kansas	Sallisaw, Okla.	D4b-'08	10/5
14	Fitzpatrick, Ryan	QB	6-2	225	11/24/82	4	Harvard	Gilbert, Ariz.	UFA(Cin)-'09	13/12*
21	Florence, Drayton	CB	6-0	195	12/19/80	7	Tuskegee	Waycross, Ga.	FA-'09	15/8*
35	Fox, Dustin	DB	5-11	200	10/8/82	4	Ohio State	Canton, Ohio	FA-'07	5/0
10	Hamdan, Gibran	QB	6-4	220	2/8/81	3	Indiana	San Diego, Calif.	FA-'07	0*
63	Hangartner, Geoff	C	6'5	301	4/22/82	5	Texas A&M	New Braunfels, Texas	UFA(Car)-'09	16/8*
84	Hardy, James	WR	6-5	220	12/24/85	2	Indiana	Fort Wayne, Ind.	D2-'08	14/4
22	Jackson, Fred	RB	6-1	215	2/20/81	3	Coe College	Fort Worth, Texas	FA-'06	16/3
17	Jenkins, Justin	WR	6-0	207	12/10/80	3	Mississippi State	Pearl, Miss.	FA-'07	13/0
91	Johnson, Spencer	DT	6-3	286	12/12/81	6	Auburn	Waynesboro, Miss.	UFA(Minn)-'08	16/0
13	Johnson, Steve	WR	6-2	202	7/22/86	2	Kentucky	San Francisco, Calif.	D7b-'08	10/1
90	Kelsay, Chris	DE	6-4	261	10/31/79	7	Nebraska	Auburn, Neb.	D2-'03	16/16
9	Lindell, Rian	K	6-3	233	1/20/77	10	Washington State	Vancouver, Wash.	FA-'03	16/0
23	Lynch, Marshawn	RB	5-11	215	4/22/86	3	California	Oakland, Calif.	D1-'07	15/15
97	McCargo, John	DT	6-2	307	8/19/83	4	North Carolina State	Drakes Branch, Va.	D1b-'06	7/0
24	McGee, Terrence	CB	5-9	198	10/14/80	7	Northwestern State	Athens, Texas	D4a-'03	14/13
38	McIntyre, Corey	FB	6-0	258	1/25/79	5	West Virginia	Indiantown, Fla.	FA-'08	11/2
28	McKelvin, Leodis	CB	5-10	184	9/1/85	2	Troy	Waycross, Ga.	D1-'08	16/6
66	McKinney, Seth	OL	6-3	310	6/12/79	8	Texas A&M	Buffalo, Texas	UFA(Cle)-'09	16/3*
59	Mitchell, Kawika	LB	6-1	253	10/10/79	7	South Florida	Winter Springs, Fla.	UFA(NYG)-'08	16/15
8	Moorman, Brian	P	6-0	172	2/5/76	9	Pittsburg State	Sedgwick, Kan.	FA-'01	16/0
72	Neill, Ryan	DL	6-3	253	12/12/82	3	Rutgers	Wayne Hills, N.J.	FA-'06	16/0
44	Omon, Xavier	RB	5-11	227	2/15/85	2	NW Missouri	Beatrice, Neb.	D6-'08	2/0
81	Owens, Terrell	WR	6-3	224	12/7/73	14	Tennessee-Chattanooga	Alexander City, Ala.	FA-'09	16/16*
11	Parrish, Roscoe	WR	5-9	171	7/16/82	5	Miami	Miami, Fla.	D2-'05	13/1
51	Posluszny, Paul	LB	6-1	238	10/10/84	3	Penn State	Aliquippa, Pa.	D2-'07	16/16
82	Reed, Josh	WR	5-10	210	5/1/80	8	Louisiana State	Rayne, La.	D2a-'02	13/13
33	Rhodes, Dominic	RB	5-9	203	1/17/79	9	Midwestern State	Waco, Texas	UFA(Ind)-'09	15/4*
94	Schobel, Aaron	DE	6-4	243	9/1/77	9	Texas Christian	Columbus, Texas	D2a-'01	5/5
80	Schouman, Derek	TE	6-2	223	3/11/85	3	Boise State	Eagle, Idaho	D7a-'07	16/12
43	Scott, Bryan	S	6-1	219	4/13/81	7	Penn State	Doylestown, Pa.	FA-'07	16/7
79	Scott, Jonathan	T	6-6	318	1/10/83	3	Texas	Dallas, Texas	FA-'08	0*
30	Simpson, Ko	S	6-1	202	11/9/83	3	South Carolina	Rock Hill, S.C.	D4-'06	16/11
99	Stroud, Marcus	DT	6-6	310	6/25/78	9	Georgia	Thomasville, Ga.	T(Jax)-'08	16/16
59	Thomas, Pat	LB	6-1	237	1/26/83	5	North Carolina State	Vallejo, Calif.	UFA(KC)-'09	12/9
68	Walker, Langston	OL	6-8	366	9/3/79	8	California	Oakland, Calif.	FA-'07	16/16
29	Wendling, John	S	6-1	222	6/4/83	3	Wyoming	Cody, Wyo.	D6-'07	16/0
20	Whitner, Donte	S	5-10	208	7/24/85	4	Ohio State	Cleveland, Ohio	D1a-'06	13/13
95	Williams, Kyle	DT	6-1	306	6/10/83	4	Louisiana State	Ruston, La.	D5a-'06	16/16
37	Wilson, George	S	6-0	212	3/14/81	4	Arkansas	Paducah, Kent.	FA-'04	16/3
26	Youboty, Ashton	CB	5-11	189	7/7/84	4	Ohio State	Klein, Texas	D3-'06	5/2

* Baker missed '08 season because of injury; Bell inactive for 16 games; Bowen missed '08 season because of injury; Fitzpatrick played 13 games with Cincinnati in '08; Florence played 15 games with Jacksonville; Hamdan inactive for 12 games; Hangartner played 16 games with Carolina; McKinney played 16 games with Cleveland; Owens played 16 games with Dallas; Rhodes played 15 games with Indianapolis; Scott inactive for 2 games; Thomas played 12 games with Kansas City.

Traded—T Jason Peters (13 games in '08) to Philadelphia.

Players lost through free agency (3): LB Angelo Crowell (TB; 0 games in '08), CB Jabari Greer (NO; 10), C Duke Preston (GB; 15).

Also played with Bills in '08—FB Darian Barnes (3 games), G Derrick Dockery (16), C Melvin Fowler (15), LB Teddy Lehman (4), QB JP Losman (5), DE Corey Mace (3), LT Jason Peters (13), TE Robert Royal (15), OL Jason Whittle (9).

2009 FIRST-YEAR ROSTER

Name	Pos.	Ht.	Wt.	Birthdate	College	Hometown	How Acq.
Bell, Joel	OL	6-6	315	7/29/85	Furman	Spartanburg, S.C.	FA
Byrd, Jairus	DB	5-10	200	10/7/86	Oregon	Clayton, Mo.	D2a
Denman, Chris (1)	OL	6-7	315	10/7/83	Fresno State	Tehachapi, Calif.	FA-'08
Faletoese, John	DL	6-2	286	7/5/86	UC Davis	Carmichael, Calif.	FA
Hall, Bruce (1)	RB	5-11	210	3/18/85	Mississippi	Milton, Fla.	FA-'08
Harris, Cary	DB	5-11	187	3/22/87	Southern California	Pacoima, Calif.	D6
Harris, Nic	LB	6-2	232	10/6/86	Oklahoma	Alexandria, La.	D5
Hawthorne, CJ (1)	WR	5-11	168	12/15/83	Hawaii	Biloxi, Miss.	FA-'07
Hennessey, Nick	OL	6'5	291	7/2/86	Colgate	Danvers, Mass.	FA
Huggins, Felton (1)	WR	6-2	186	2/15/83	Southeastern Louisiana	Zachary, La.	FA-'07
Jefferson, Mike (1)	WR	6-1	206	12/28/82	Montana State	El Paso, Texas	FA-'08
Jenkins, Ventrell	DL	6'1	286	11/16/84	Kentucky	Columbia, S.C.	FA
Lankster, Ellis	DB	5-9	190	6/3/87	West Virginia	Whistler, Ala.	D7
Levitre, Andy	OL	6-2	305	5/15/86	Oregon State	Ben Lomand, Calif.	D2b
Lindquist, David	DL	6'2	292	12/16/85	Illinois	Highland Park, Ill.	FA
Maybin, Aaron	DE	6-4	250	4/6/88	Penn State	Ellicott City, Md.	D1a
McCall, Travis	TE	6'2	276	4/6/85	Alabama	Prattville, Ala.	FA
McGhee, Jermaine (1)	DE	6-2	257	12/31/83	Prairie View A&M	Oakland, Calif.	FA
Nelson, Shawn	TE	6-5	240	10/5/85	Southern Mississippi	Gonzales, La.	D4
Palmer, Ashlee	LB	6-1	236	4/7/86	Mississippi	Compton, Calif.	FA
Philip, Marvin (1)	C	6-1	307	2/3/82	California	Redwood City, Calif.	FA
Rodd, Brandon (1)	OL	6-4	305	11/1/85	Arizona State	Honolulu, Hawaii	FA-'08
Sam, PK (1)	WR	6-3	217	2/26/83	Florida State	Denver, Colo.	FA
Sanborn, Garrison	LS	6-0	240	7/31/85	Florida State	Tampa, Fla.	FA
Sargeant, Lydell	DB	6-1	187	1/31/87	Penn State	Lompoc, Calif.	FA
Smith, Marcus (1)	DE	6-4	295	2/7/84	Arizona	San Diego, Calif.	FA
Stupar, Jonathan (1)	TE	6-3	254	7/24/84	Virginia	State College, Pa.	FA-'08
Urrego, Dan	K	5-11	190	11/1/85	Portland State	Fort Lauderdale, Fla.	FA
Ward, Kyle (1)	DB	6-1	198	12/15/84	Louisiana-Lafayette	Dallas, Texas	FA
Washington, Gerald	DL	6-5	262	4/23/82	Southern California	Vallejo, Calif.	FA
Wood, Eric	OL	6-3	310	3/18/86	Louisville	Cincinnati, Ohio	D1b

The term NFL Rookie is defined as a player who is in his first season of professional football and has not been on the roster of another professional football team for any regular-season or postseason games. A Rookie is designated by an "R" on NFL rosters. Players who have been active in another professional football league or players who have NFL experience, including either preseason training camp or being on an Active List or Inactive List, or on Reserve/Injured or Reserve/Physically Unable to Perform for fewer than six regular-season games, are termed NFL First-Year Players. An NFL First-Year Player is designated by a "1" on NFL rosters. Thereafter, a player is credited with an additional year of experience for each season in which he accumulates six games on the Active List or Inactive List, or on Reserve/Injured or Reserve/Physically Unable to Perform.

Log on to www.buffalobills.com for an up-to-date roster.

BUFFALO BILLS

COACHING STAFF

Head Coach,
Dick Jauron

Pro Career: Now in his fourth season, Jauron was named Buffalo's fourteenth head coach on January 23, 2006. He enters 2009 with a 21-27 record over his first three seasons. Jauron is in his third stint as an NFL head coach after serving as the head coach of the Chicago Bears (1999-2003) and as interim head coach of the Detroit Lions for the final five games of 2005. The highlight of his Bears' tenure career came in 2001 when Chicago finished 13-3 and claimed its first division championship since 1990. Under Jauron's leadership, the 2001 Bears were 8-0 in games decided by seven points or less, and engineered five second half, come-from-behind victories. The Bears defense ranked first in the NFL in points allowed and second in rushing yards allowed. For his efforts, Jauron was selected as the *Associated Press* NFL Coach of the Year. He was just the third coach in team history to win 13 games in a season. The 2001 season marked the greatest single-season turnaround in team history improving from 5-11 in 2000 to 13-3. In his five seasons in Chicago, Jauron posted a 35-46 record. He became the first Bears coach to defeat the Green Bay Packers in Lambeau Field on his first two trips. He began his coaching career with the Buffalo Bills (1985, defensive backs), Green Bay Packers (1986-1994, defensive backs), and Jacksonville Jaguars (1995-98, defensive coordinator). As Jacksonville's inaugural defensive coordinator, the Jaguars made three playoff berths. He served as the Lions' defensive coordinator from 2004-05. Career record: 57-77.

Background: A three-sport (football, basketball, and baseball) standout at Swampscott (Mass.) High School. Named one of the top 10 prep athletes of the 20th Century in the state of Massachusetts by the *Boston Globe*. Played running back at Yale (1970-72) where, for 27 years, he held the school's career rushing mark with 2,947 yards. Drafted by the Detroit Lions in the fourth round of the 1973 draft. Played defensive back for Detroit (1973-77) and was named to the Pro Bowl following the 1974 season after leading the NFC in punt return average (16.8). He finished his career with the Cincinnati Bengals (1978-1980).

Personal: Born October 7, 1950, Peoria, Ill. Dick and his wife Gail have two daughters—Kacy and Amy.

ASSISTANT COACHES

John Allaire, strength and conditioning; born December 3, 1970, Woonsocket, R.I. Attended Springfield College. No college or pro playing experience. College coach: Boston College 1992, Clemson 1993-95, Tulsa 1996-2001. Pro coach: Joined Bills in 2002.

Bobby April, asst. head coach/special teams; born April 15, 1963, New Orleans. Linebacker/defensive end Nicholls State 1972-75. No pro playing experience. College coach: Southern Mississippi 1978, Tulane 1979, Arizona 1980-86, Southern California 1987-1990. Pro coach: Atlanta Falcons 1991-93, Pittsburgh Steelers 1994-95, New Orleans Saints 1996-99, St. Louis Rams 2001-02, joined Bills in 2004.

Ray Brown, asst. offensive line; born December 12, 1962, Marion, Ark. Offensive lineman Arkansas State 1982-85. Pro offensive lineman St. Louis/Phoenix Cardinals 1986-88, Washington Redskins 1989-1995, 2004-05, San Francisco 49ers 1996-2001, Detroit Lions 2002-03. Pro coach: Washington Redskins 2006, joined Bills in 2008.

George Catavolos, defensive backs; born May 8, 1945, Chicago. Defensive back Purdue 1964-67. No pro playing experience. College coach: Purdue 1967-68, 1971-76, Middle Tennessee State 1969, Louisville 1970, Kentucky 1977-1981, Tennessee 1982-83. Pro coach: Indianapolis Colts 1984-1994, 1998-2001, Carolina Panthers 1995-97, Washington Redskins 2002-03, Detroit Lions 2004-05, joined Bills in 2006.

Charlie Coiner, tight ends; born April 24, 1960, Waynesboro, Va. Attended Catawba College, Appalachian State. No college or pro playing experience. College coach: Appalachian State 1983-86, Minnesota 1987, Louisville 1995-97, Tennessee-Chattanooga 1998, Louisiana State 1999, Texas Southern 2000. Pro coach: Chicago Bears 2001-05, joined Bills in 2006.

DeMontie Cross, asst. linebackers/special teams; born February 26, 1974, St. Louis, Mo. Free safety Missouri 1994-96. No pro playing experience. College coach: Missouri 1998-99, Sam Houston State 2000, Iowa State 2001-05. Pro coach: Joined Bills in 2006.

Perry Fewell, defensive coordinator; born September 7, 1962, Gastonia, N.C. Defensive back Lenoir-Rhyne 1981-84. No pro playing experience. College coach: North Carolina 1985-86, Army 1987, 1992-94, Kent State 1988-1991, Vanderbilt 1995-97. Pro coach: Jacksonville Jaguars 1998-2002, St. Louis Rams 2003-04, Chicago Bears 2005, joined Bills in 2006.

Nathaniel Hackett, offensive quality control; born December 19, 1979, Fullerton, Calif. Linebacker/long snapper U.C. Davis 1999-2002. No pro playing experience. College coach: U.C. Davis 2003, Stanford 2003-05. Pro coach: Tampa Bay Buccaneers 2006-07, joined Bills in 2008.

Sean Hayes, asst. strength and conditioning; born October 25, 1975, Peabody, Mass. No college or pro playing experience. College coach: Springfield College 1997-98, Tulsa 1999-2000, Harvard 2001-03, Clemson 2004-05. Pro coach: Joined Bills in 2006.

Sean Kugler, offensive line; born August 9, 1966, Lockport, N.Y. Offensive line Texas-El Paso 1985-89. No pro playing experience. College coach: Texas-El Paso 1993-2000, Boise State 2006. Pro coach: Detroit Lions 2001-05, joined Bills in 2007.

Chuck Lester, asst. to the head coach/special projects; born May 18, 1955, Chicago. Linebacker Oklahoma 1974. No pro playing experience. College coach: Iowa State 1980-81, Oklahoma 1982-84. Pro coach: Kansas City Chiefs 1984-86 (scout), joined Bills in 1987.

Bob Sanders, defensive line; born December 5, 1953, Jacksonville, N.C. Linebacker Davidson College 1973-75. No pro playing experience. College coach: Georgia Tech 1978, East Carolina 1980-82, Richmond 1983-84, Duke 1985-89, Florida 1990-2000. Pro coach: Miami Dolphins 2001-04, Green Bay Packers 2005-08, joined Bills in 2009.

Turk Schonert, offensive coordinator; born January 15, 1957, Torrance, Calif. Quarterback Stanford 1975-79. Pro quarterback Cincinnati Bengals 1980-85, 1987-89, Atlanta Falcons 1986. Pro coach: Tampa Bay Buccaneers 1992-95, Buffalo Bills 1998-2000, Carolina Panthers 2001, New York Giants 2003, New Orleans Saints 2005, rejoined Bills in 2006.

Matt Sheldon, linebackers; born February 26, 1969, Berwyn, Ill. Cornerback Minnesota 1987-1991. No pro playing experience. College coach: Wisconsin 1997-99. Pro coach: St. Louis Rams 2001-05, joined Bills in 2006.

Eric Studesville, running game coordinator/running backs; born May 29, 1967, Madison, Wis. Defensive back Wisconsin-Whitewater 1985-88. No pro playing experience. College coach: Wingate 1994, Kent State 1995-96. Pro coach: Chicago Bears 1997-2000, New York Giants 2001-03, joined Bills in 2004.

Tyke Tolbert, wide receivers; born September 15, 1967, Conroe, Texas. Wide receiver Louisiana State 1988-1990. No pro playing experience. College coach: Louisiana-Monroe 1994-97, Auburn 1998, Louisiana-Lafayette 1999-2001, Florida 2002. Pro coach: Arizona Cardinals 2003, joined Bills in 2004.

Alex Van Pelt, quarterbacks; born May 1, 1970, Pittsburgh. Quarterback Pittsburgh 1990-94. Pro quarterback Buffalo Bills 1995-2003. College coach: Buffalo 2005. Pro coach: Frankfurt Galaxy (NFLE) 2005, joined Bills in 2006.

Adrian White, defensive quality control; born April 6, 1964, Orange Park, Fla. Defensive back Southern Illinois 1983, Florida 1985-86. Pro defensive back: New York Giants 1987-1991, Green Bay Packers 1992, New England Patriots 1993. No college coaching experience. Pro coach: Rhein Fire (NFLE) 2001-07, joined Bills in 2008.

American Football Conference
North Division
Team Colors: Black, Orange, and White
One Paul Brown Stadium
Cincinnati, Ohio 45202-3492
Telephone: (513) 621-3550
Ticket Office (513) 621-TDTD (8383)

2009 SCHEDULE

PRESEASON

Aug. 14	at New Orleans	7:00
Aug. 20	at New England	7:30
Aug. 27	**St. Louis**	7:35
Sep. 3	**Indianapolis**	7:30

REGULAR SEASON

Sep. 13	**Denver**	1:00
Sep. 20	at Green Bay	12:00
Sep. 27	**Pittsburgh**	4:15
Oct. 4	at Cleveland	1:00
Oct. 11	at Baltimore	1:00
Oct. 18	**Houston**	1:00
Oct. 25	**Chicago**	1:00
Nov. 1	BYE	
Nov. 8	**Baltimore**	1:00
Nov. 15	at Pittsburgh	1:00
Nov. 22	at Oakland	1:15
Nov. 29	**Cleveland**	1:00
Dec. 6	**Detroit**	1:00
Dec. 13	at Minnesota	12:00
Dec. 20	at San Diego	1:05
Dec. 27	**Kansas City**	1:00
Jan. 3	at N.Y. Jets	1:00

Stadium: Paul Brown Stadium (opened in 2000) • **Capacity:** 65,515
One Paul Brown Stadium
Cincinnati, Ohio 45202-3492
Playing Surface: Synthetic
Training Camp: Georgetown College
Georgetown, KY 40324

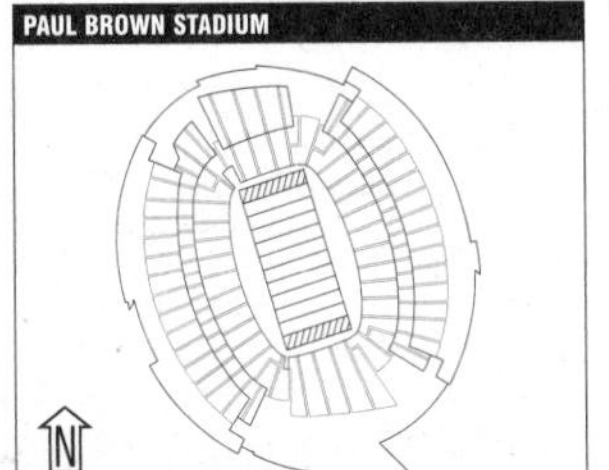

CLUB OFFICIALS

President: Mike Brown
Senior Vice President: Pete Brown
Executive Vice President: Katie Blackburn
Vice President: Paul Brown
Vice President: John Sawyer
Vice President: Troy Blackburn
Business Manager: Bill Connelly
Chief Financial Officer: Bill Scanlon
Director of Development—Paul Brown Stadium: Bob Bedinghaus
Managing Director of Paul Brown Stadium: Eric Brown
Directors of Technology: Michael Kayes, Jo Ann Ralstin
Bengals.com Editor: Geoff Hobson
Director of Security: Rusty Guy
Director of Sales and Public Affairs: Jeff Berding
Director of Corporate Sales and Marketing: Vince Cicero
Ticket Manager: Tim Kelly
Director of Player Relations: Eric Ball
Director of Football Operations: Jim Lippincott
Director of Player Personnel: Duke Tobin
Public Relations Director: Jack Brennan
Athletic Trainer: Paul Sparling
Equipment Manager: Jeff Brickner
Video Director: Travis Brammer

COACHING HISTORY

(277-362-2)

Records include postseason games

1968-1975	Paul Brown	55-59-1
1976-78	Bill Johnson*	18-15-0
1978-79	Homer Rice	8-19-0
1980-83	Forrest Gregg	34-27-0
1984-1991	Sam Wyche	64-68-0
1992-96	Dave Shula**	19-52-0
1996-2000	Bruce Coslet***	21-39-0
2000-02	Dick LeBeau	12-33-0
2003-08	Marvin Lewis	46-50-1

* Resigned after five games in 1978
** Released after seven games in 1996
*** Resigned after three games in 2000

PAID ATTENDANCE

Home 504,506 Away 552,788
Total 1,057,294
Single-game home record, 66,188 (10/28/07)
Single-season home record, 516,154 (2006)

2009 DRAFT CHOICES

Round	Name	Pos.	College
1	Andre Smith	T	Alabama
2	Rey Maualuga	LB	Southern California
3	Michael Johnson	DE	Georgia Tech
	Chase Coffman	TE	Missouri
4	Jonathan Luigs	C	Arkansas
5	Kevin Huber	P	Cincinnati
6	Morgan Trent	CB	Michigan
	Bernard Scott	RB	Abilene Christian
7	Fui Vakapuna	FB	Brigham Young
	Clinton McDonald	DT	Memphis
	Freddie Brown	WR	Utah

CINCINNATI BENGALS

2008 TEAM RECORD

PRESEASON (2-2)

Date	Result	Opponent
8/11	W 20-17	at Green Bay
8/17	L 10-27	Detroit
8/23	L 0-13	New Orleans
8/28	W 27-7	at Indianapolis

REGULAR SEASON (4-11-1)

Date	Result	Opponent
9/7	L 10-17	at Baltimore
9/14	L 7-24	Tennessee
9/21	L 23-26	at New York Giants (OT)
9/28	L 12-20	Cleveland
10/5	L 22-31	at Dallas
10/12	L 14-26	at New York Jets
10/19	L 10-38	Pittsburgh
10/26	L 6-35	at Houston
11/2	W 21-19	Jacksonville
11/16	T 13-13	Philadelphia (OT)
11/20	L 10-27	at Pittsburgh
11/30	L 3-34	Baltimore
12/7	L 3-35	at Indianapolis
12/14	W 20-13	Washington
12/21	W 14-0	at Cleveland
12/28	W 16-6	Kansas City

(OT) Overtime

SCORE BY PERIODS

Bengals	51	92	20	41	0 —	204
Opponents	54	94	82	131	3 —	364

2008 TEAM STATISTICS

	Bengals	Opp.
Total First Downs	245	296
Rushing	80	106
Passing	145	169
Penalty	20	21
3rd Down: Made/Att	82/236	93/218
3rd Down Pct.	34.7	42.7
4th Down: Made/Att	7/14	5/11
4th Down Pct.	50.0	45.5
Possession Avg.	28:40	31:20
Total Net Yards	3926	5208
Avg. Per Game	245.4	325.5
Total Plays	984	1013
Avg. Per Play	4.0	5.1
Net Yards Rushing	1520	1921
Avg. Per Game	95.0	120.1
Total Rushes	420	490
Net Yards Passing	2406	3287
Avg. Per Game	150.4	205.4
Sacked/Yards Lost	51/271	17/122
Gross Yards	2677	3409
Att./Completions	513/303	506/315
Completion Pct.	59.1	62.3
Had Intercepted	15	12
Punts/Average	101/39.1	79/43.6
Net Punting Avg.	101/34.1	79/37.6
Penalties/Yards	75/591	102/772
Fumbles/Ball Lost	27/11	20/12
Touchdowns	20	43
Rushing	6	15
Passing	11	23
Returns	3	5

2008 INDIVIDUAL STATISTICS

PASSING	Att.	Comp.	Yds.	Pct.	TD	Int.	Tkld.	Rate
Fitzpatrick	372	221	1905	59.4	8	9	38/193	70.0
C. Palmer	129	75	731	58.1	3	4	11/67	69.0
J. Palmer	12	7	41	58.3	0	2	2/11	25.3
Bengals	513	303	2677	59.1	11	15	51/271	68.0
Opponents	506	315	3409	62.3	23	12	17/122	87.3

SCORING	TD R	TD P	TD Rt	PAT	FG	Saf	PTS
Graham	0	0	0	15/15	21/24	0	78
Houshmandzadeh	0	4	0	0/0	0/0	0	24
Ochocinco	0	4	0	0/0	0/0	0	24
Benson	2	0	0	0/0	0/0	0	12
Fitzpatrick	2	0	0	0/0	0/0	0	12
Henry	0	2	0	0/0	0/0	0	12
Perry	2	0	0	0/0	0/0	0	12
Hall	0	0	1	0/0	0/0	0	6
Holt	0	1	0	0/0	0/0	0	6
Joseph	0	0	1	0/0	0/0	0	6
Ndukwe	0	0	1	0/0	0/0	0	6
Rayner	0	0	0	3/3	1/1	0	6
Bengals	6	11	3	18/18	22/25	0	204
Opponents	15	23	5	40/40	22/23	0	364

2-Pt. Conversions: None.
Bengals 0-2, Opponents 0-3.

RUSHING	No.	Yds	Avg	LG	TD
Benson	214	747	3.5	46	2
Fitzpatrick	60	304	5.1	22	2
Perry	104	269	2.6	25t	2
Watson	13	55	4.2	7	0
Caldwell	5	53	10.6	26	0
C. Palmer	6	38	6.3	15	0
Ja. Johnson	9	29	3.2	12	0
Houshmandzadeh	1	9	9.0	9	0
Dorsey	5	8	1.6	7	0
Chatman	2	4	2.0	2	0
J. Palmer	1	4	4.0	4	0
Bengals	420	1520	3.6	46	6
Opponents	490	1921	3.9	51	15

RECEIVING	No.	Yds	Avg	LG	TD
Houshmandzadeh	92	904	9.8	46	4
Ochocinco	53	540	10.2	26	4
Kelly	31	207	6.7	31	0
Chatman	21	194	9.2	25	0
Benson	20	185	9.3	79	0
Perry	20	71	3.6	12	0
Henry	19	220	11.6	22	2
Utecht	16	123	7.7	14	0
Caldwell	11	78	7.1	15	0
Ja. Johnson	6	47	7.8	16	0
Holt	3	26	8.7	10t	1
Watson	3	4	1.3	3	0
Dorsey	2	49	24.5	36	0
Coats	2	19	9.5	11	0
Lawrie	2	11	5.5	7	0
Simpson	1	2	2.0	2	0
Fitzpatrick	1	-3	-3.0	-3	0
Bengals	303	2677	8.8	79	11
Opponents	315	3409	10.8	70t	23

INTERCEPTIONS	No.	Yds	Avg	LG	TD
Hall	3	87	29.0	50t	1
B. Johnson	2	35	17.5	35	0
Rivers	1	39	39.0	39	0
Crocker	1	22	22.0	22	0
Joseph	1	22	22.0	22	0
Dh. Jones	1	13	13.0	13	0
Ndukwe	1	12	12.0	12	0
Lynch	1	6	6.0	6	0
White	1	0	0.0	0	0
Bengals	12	236	19.7	50t	1
Opponents	15	279	18.6	85t	2

PUNTING	No.	Yds.	Avg.	In 20	LG
Larson	100	3945	39.5	28	57
Bengals	101	3945	39.1	28	57
Opponents	79	3443	43.6	22	70

PUNT RETURNS	Ret	FC	Yds	Avg	LG	TD
Chatman	21	5	158	7.5	34	0
Houshmandzadeh	8	2	79	9.9	15	0
Hall	3	0	16	5.3	12	0
Bengals	32	7	253	7.9	34	0
Opponents	48	22	436	9.1	73t	1

KICKOFF RETURNS	No.	Yds	Avg	LG	TD
Holt	46	1110	24.1	60	0
Caldwell	13	338	26.0	43	0
Watson	4	63	15.8	24	0
Coats	1	18	18.0	18	0
Ja. Johnson	1	13	13.0	13	0
Simpson	1	8	8.0	8	0
Hall	1	1	1.0	1	0
Bengals	67	1551	23.1	60	0
Opponents	47	1059	22.5	87	0

FIELD GOALS	1-19	20-29	30-39	40-49	50+
Graham	1/1	5/5	6/7	9/11	0/0
Rayner	0/0	1/1	0/0	0/0	0/0
Bengals	1/1	6/6	6/7	9/11	0/0
Opponents	0/0	12/12	6/6	3/4	1/1

SACKS	No.
Ndukwe	3.0
Odom	3.0
Thornton	3.0
Geathers	2.5
Crocker	1.5
B. Johnson	1.5
Rucker	1.0
Sims	1.0
Peko	0.5
Bengals	17.0
Opponents	51.0

RECORD HOLDERS

INDIVIDUAL RECORDS—CAREER

Category	Name	Performance
Rushing (Yds.)	Corey Dillon, 1997-2003	8,061
Passing (Yds.)	Ken Anderson, 1971-1986	32,838
Passing (TDs)	Ken Anderson, 1971-1986	197
Receiving (No.)	Chad Ochocinco, 2001-08	612
Receiving (Yds.)	Chad Ochocinco, 2001-08	8,905
Interceptions	Ken Riley, 1969-1983	65
Punting (Avg.)	Dave Lewis, 1970-73	43.8
Punt Return (Avg.)	Mike Martin, 1983-89	9.9
Kickoff Return (Avg.)	Lemar Parrish, 1970-77	24.7
Field Goals	Jim Breech, 1980-1992	225
Touchdowns (Tot.)	Pete Johnson, 1977-1983	70
Points	Jim Breech, 1980-1992	1,151
*Sacks	Eddie Edwards, 1977-1988	47.5

INDIVIDUAL RECORDS—SINGLE SEASON

Category	Name	Performance
Rushing (Yds.)	Rudi Johnson, 2005	1,458
Passing (Yds.)	Carson Palmer, 2007	4,131
Passing (TDs)	Carson Palmer, 2005	32
Receiving (No.)	T.J. Houshmandzadeh, 2007	112
Receiving (Yds.)	Chad Ochocinco, 2007	1,440
Interceptions	Deltha O'Neal, 2005	10
Punting (Avg.)	Dave Lewis, 1970	46.2
Punt Return (Avg.)	Lemar Parrish, 1974	18.8
Kickoff Return (Avg.)	Tremain Mack, 1999	27.1
Field Goals	Shayne Graham, 2007	31
Touchdowns (Tot.)	Carl Pickens, 1995	17
Points	Shayne Graham, 2005	131
*Sacks	Eddie Edwards, 1983	13.0

INDIVIDUAL RECORDS—SINGLE GAME

Category	Name	Performance
Rushing (Yds.)	Corey Dillon, 10-22-00	278
Passing (Yds.)	Boomer Esiason, 10-7-90	490
Passing (TDs)	Carson Palmer, 9-16-07	6
Receiving (No.)	Carl Pickens, 10-11-98	13
Receiving (Yds.)	Chad Ochocinco, 11-12-06	260
Interceptions	Many times	3
	Last time by Leon Hall, 12-21-08	
Field Goals	Shayne Graham, 11-11-07	7
Touchdowns (Tot.)	Larry Kinnebrew, 10-28-84	4
	Corey Dillon, 12-4-97	4
Points	Larry Kinnebrew, 10-28-84	24
	Corey Dillon, 12-4-97	24
*Sacks	Alfred Williams, 10-16-94	4.0

**Sacks became an official statistic in 1982.*

CINCINNATI BENGALS

2009 VETERAN ROSTER

No.	Name	Pos.	Ht.	Wt.	Birthdate	NFL Exp.	College	Hometown	How Acq.	'08 Games/ Starts
32	Benson, Cedric	HB	5-11	220	12/28/82	5	Texas	Midland, Texas	FA-'08	12/10
56	Blackstock, Darryl	LB/DE	6-3	255	5/30/83	5	Virginia	Newport News, Va.	FA-'08	12/4
87	Caldwell, Andre	WR	6-0	204	4/15/85	2	Florida	Tampa, Fla.	D3b-'08	7/4
21	Castille, Simeon	CB	6-0	195	10/12/85	2	Alabama	Birmingham, Ala.	FA-'08	8/0
83	Chatman, Antonio	WR	5-8	185	2/12/79	7	Cincinnati	Los Angeles, Calif.	FA-'06	10/1
86	Coats, Daniel	TE	6-3	264	4/16/84	3	Brigham Young	Layton, Utah	FA-'07	16/4
11	Coles, Laveranues	WR	5-11	193	12/29/77	10	Florida State	Jacksonville, Fla.	UFA(NYJ)-'09	16/16*
73	Collins, Anthony	T	6-5	317	11/2/85	2	Kansas	Beaumont, Texas	D4-'08	9/6
64	Cook, Kyle	C	6-3	306	7/25/83	2	Michigan State	Macomb, Mich.	FA-'07	5/0
42	Crocker, Chris	S	5-11	200	3/9/80	7	Marshall	Chesapeake, Va.	FA-'08	8/6
60	Crummey, Andrew	C	6-5	301	10/22/84	2	Maryland	Van Wert, Ohio	PS(Wash)-'08	6/0
27	Dorsey, DeDe	HB	5-11	203	8/1/84	4	Lindenwood	Broken Arrow, Okla.	FA-'07	4/0
68	Fanene, Jonathan	DE	6-4	295	3/19/82	5	Utah	Pago Pago, American Samoa	D7-'05	16/4
25	#Fletcher, Jamar	CB	5-10	185	8/28/79	9	Wisconsin	St. Louis, Mo.	FA-'08	11/2
91	Geathers, Robert	DE	6-3	272	8/11/83	6	Georgia	Georgetown, S.C.	D4b-'04	11/11
17	Graham, Shayne	K	6-0	205	12/9/77	9	Virginia Tech	Dublin, Va.	W(Car)-'03	14/0
29	Hall, Leon	CB	5-11	199	12/9/84	3	Michigan	Vista, Calif.	D1-'07	16/16
34	Hebert, Kyries	S	6-3	220	10/9/80	2	Louisiana-Lafayette	Lafayette, La.	FA-'08	16/2
15	Henry, Chris	WR	6-4	200	5/17/83	5	West Virginia	Belle Chasse, La.	FA-'08	12/1
52	Hodge, Abdul	LB	6-0	236	9/9/82	4	Iowa	Lauderdale Lakes, Fla.	FA-'08	6/0
53	Jeanty, Rashad	LB	6-2	245	4/17/83	4	Central Florida	Miami, Fla.	FA-'06	16/15
59	Johnson, Brandon	LB	6-5	245	4/5/83	4	Louisville	Birmingham, Ala.	FA-'08	16/9
35	Johnson, Jeremi	FB	5-11	270	9/4/80	7	Western Kentucky	Louisville, Ky.	FA-'09	0*
99	Johnson, Tank	DT	6-3	305	12/7/81	6	Washington	Tempe, Ariz.	UFA(Dall)-'09	16/1*
20	Jones, David	CB	6-0	196	9/19/85	3	Wingate	Greenville, S.C.	W(NO)-'07	14/7
57	Jones, Dhani	LB	6-1	240	2/22/78	10	Michigan	Potomac, Md.	FA-'07	16/16
22	Joseph, Johnathan	CB	5-11	193	4/16/84	4	South Carolina	Rock Hill, S.C.	D1-'06	8/7
82	Kelly, Reggie	TE	6-4	256	2/22/77	11	Mississippi State	Aberdeen, Miss.	UFA(Atl)-'03	16/15
75	Kooistra, Scott	G/T	6-6	335	10/14/80	7	North Carolina State	Cary, N.C.	D7a-'03	10/0
40	Leonard, Brian	HB	6-1	229	2/3/84	3	Rutgers	Gouverneur, N.Y.	T(StL)-'09	2/0*
62	Livings, Nate	G	6-5	335	3/16/82	2	Louisiana State	Lake Charles, La.	FA-'06	6/6
47	Lynch, Corey	S	6-0	206	5/7/85	2	Appalachian State	Cape Coral, Fla.	D6a-'08	7/0
66	Mathis, Evan	G	6-5	310	11/1/81	5	Alabama	Homewood, Ala.	FA-'08	1/0
51	Maxwell, Jim	LB	6-4	240	8/8/81	5	Gardner-Webb	Johnsonville, S.C.	FA-'08	2/0
41	Ndukwe, Chinedum	S	6-2	220	3/4/85	3	Notre Dame	Powell, Ohio	D7b-'07	11/11
85	Ochocinco, Chad	WR	6-1	192	1/9/78	9	Oregon State	Miami, Fla.	D2-'01	13/10
98	Odom, Antwan	DE	6-5	260	9/24/81	6	Alabama	Bayou La Batre, Ala.	UFA(Tenn)-'08	12/8
4	O'Sullivan, J.T.	QB	6-2	227	8/25/79	7	California, Davis	Burbank, Calif.	UFA(SF)-'09	9/8*
9	Palmer, Carson	QB	6-5	230	12/27/79	7	Southern California	Mission Viejo, Calif.	D1-'03	4/4
5	Palmer, Jordan	QB	6-5	232	5/30/84	2	Texas-El Paso	Mission Viejo, Calif.	FA-'08	3/0
94	Peko, Domata	DT	6-3	325	11/27/84	4	Michigan State	Pago Pago (American Samoa)	D4-'06	16/16
24	Pope, Geoffrey	CB	6-0	186	6/21/84	2	Howard	Detroit, Mich.	FA-'08	8/0
55	Rivers, Keith	LB	6-2	241	5/5/86	2	Southern California	Lake Mary, Fla.	D1-'08	7/7
74	Roland, Dennis	T	6-9	325	3/10/83	2	Georgia	Bolivar, Mo.	FA-'08	2/1
92	Rucker, Frostee	DE	6-3	280	9/14/83	4	Southern California	Tustin, Calif.	D3-'06	11/4
38	Runnels, J.D.	FB	5-11	242	10/26/81	3	Oklahoma	Midwest City, Okla.	FA-'08	0*
48	St. Louis, Brad	LS/TE	6-3	243	8/19/76	10	Southwest Missouri State	Belton, Mo.	D7-'00	16/0
65	Santucci, Dan	C	6-4	304	9/6/83	3	Notre Dame	Harwood Heights, Ill.	PS(Ind)-'07	0*
88	Sherry, Matt	TE	6-4	250	12/11/84	2	Villanova	Rumford, R.I.	D6b-'08	0*
97	Shirley, Jason	DT	6-5	338	9/30/85	2	Fresno State	Fontana, Calif.	D5-'08	3/0
89	Simpson, Jerome	WR	6-2	195	2/4/86	2	Coastal Carolina	Reidsville, N.C.	D2-'08	6/1
90	Sims, Pat	DT	6-2	320	11/29/85	2	Auburn	Ft. Lauderdale, Fla.	D3a-'08	11/6
97	#Thornton, John	DT	6-3	297	10/2/76	11	West Virginia	Philadelphia, Pa.	UFA(Tenn)-'03	15/11
81	Utecht, Ben	TE	6-6	250	6/30/81	5	Minnesota	Hastings, Minn.	RFA(Ind)-'08	10/6
33	Watson, Kenny	HB	6-0	220	3/13/78	8	Penn State	Harrisburg, Pa.	FA-'03	10/0
26	White, Marvin	S	6-1	199	12/5/83	3	Texas Christian	Port Barre, La.	D4-'07	12/10
77	Whitworth, Andrew	G	6-7	330	12/12/81	4	Louisiana State	West Monroe, La.	D2-'06	10/10
63	Williams, Bobbie	G/C	6-4	345	9/25/76	10	Arkansas	Jefferson, Texas	UFA(Phil)-'04	16/16
31	Williams, Roy	S	6-0	221	8/14/80	8	Oklahoma	Union City, Calif.	FA-'09	3/2*

* Coles played 16 games for N.Y. Jets in '08; Je. Johnson missed '08 season because of injury; T. Johnson played 16 games with Dallas; Leonard played 2 games with St. Louis; O'Sullivan played 9 games for San Francisco; Runnels was last active with Chicago in '06; Santucci missed '08 season because of injury; Sherry missed '08 season because of injury; R. Williams played 3 games with Dallas.

\# Unrestricted free agent; subject to developments.

t- Bengals traded for Leonard (StL).

Traded—DT Orien Harris (14 games in '08) to St. Louis.

Players lost through free agency (4): T Stacy Andrews (Phil; 15 games in '08), QB Ryan Fitzpatrick (Buff; 13), C Eric Ghiaciuc (KC; 16), WR T.J. Houshmandzadeh (Sea; 15).

Also played with Bengals in '08—S John Busing (8 games), S Mike Doss (3), DE Chris Harrington (3), DE Eric Henderson (2), LB Victor Hobson (2), WR Glenn Holt (15), S Dexter Jackson (3), S Herana-Daze Jones (3), T Levi Jones (10), P Kyle Larson (16), TE Nate Lawrie (8), DE Josh Mallard (2), FB Reagan Maui'a (2), LB Corey Mays (1), HB Chris Perry (13), K Dave Rayner (2).

2009 FIRST-YEAR ROSTER

Name	Pos.	Ht.	Wt.	Birthdate	College	Hometown	How Acq.
Brown, Freddie	WR	6-4	213	6/24/86	Utah	La Verne, Calif.	D7c
Bujnoch, Digger (1)	C/G	6-5	285	6/19/85	Cincinnati	Cincinnati, Ohio	FA-'08
Coffman, Chase	TE	6-6	244	11/10/86	Missouri	Peculiar, Mo.	D3b
Cosby, Quan	WR	5-9	196	12/23/82	Texas	Mart, Texas	FA
Dow, Colin	G	6-5	310	2/25/86	Montana	Billings, Mont.	FA
Farris, Billy	QB	6-3	234	3/2/85	Colorado State	Baton Rouge, La.	FA
Harrington, Chris (1)	DE	6-5	265	1/19/85	Texas A&M	Houston, Texas	PS(Ariz)-'08
Hill, Darius	TE	6-7	247	8/26/85	Ball State	Blue Springs, Mo.	FA
Huber, Kevin	P	6-1	220	7/16/85	Cincinnati	Cincinnati, Ohio	D5
Johnson, James (1)	HB	5-11	202	9/6/84	Kansas State	Port Arthur, Texas	FA-'08
Johnson, Michael	DE	6-7	266	2/7/87	Georgia Tech	Selma, Ala.	D3a
Lucky, Marlon	HB	5-11	216	2/28/86	Nebraska	North Hollywood, Calif.	FA
Luigs, Jonathan	C	6-4	301	8/11/86	Arkansas	Little Rock, Ark.	D4
Maualuga, Rey	LB	6-2	249	1/20/87	Southern California	Eureka, Calif.	D2
McDonald, Clinton	DT	6-2	283	1/6/87	Memphis	Jacksonville, Ark.	D7b
Murray, Rico	CB	5-11	191	8/21/87	Kent State	Cincinnati, Ohio	FA
Nelson, Tom	S	5-11	200	12/4/86	Illinois State	Arlington Heights, Ill.	FA
Orton, Greg	WR	6-3	207	12/17/86	Purdue	Dayton, Ohio	FA
Phillips, Pernell	DT	6-0	311	4/5/85	Central State	Cincinnati, Ohio	FA
Pressley, Chris	FB	5-11	257	8/8/86	Wisconsin	Woodbury, N.J.	FA
Purify, Maurice (1)	WR	6-3	224	1/17/86	Nebraska	Eureka, Calif.	FA-'08
Richmond, David	WR	6-2	197	4/1/87	San Jose State	Anaheim, Calif.	FA
Scott, Bernard	HB	5-10	200	2/10/84	Abilene Christian	Vernon, Texas	D6b
Skuta, Dan	LB	6-2	251	4/21/86	Grand Valley State	Flint, Mich.	FA
Smith, Andre	T	6-4	332	1/25/87	Alabama	Birmingham, Ala.	D1
Smith, James	LS	6-2	244	10/31/85	Florida	Gainesville, Fla.	FA
Trent, Morgan	CB	6-1	193	12/14/85	Michigan	San Diego, Calif.	D6a
Urrutia, Mario (1)	WR	6-5	232	1/18/86	Louisville	Louisville, Ky.	D7b-'08
Vakapuna, Fui	FB	5-11	244	3/9/84	Brigham Young	Glendale, Utah	D7a

The term NFL Rookie is defined as a player who is in his first season of professional football and has not been on the roster of another professional football team for any regular-season or postseason games. A Rookie is designated by an "R" on NFL rosters. Players who have been active in another professional football league or players who have NFL experience, including either preseason training camp or being on an Active List or Inactive List, or on Reserve/Injured or Reserve/Physically Unable to Perform for fewer than six regular-season games, are termed NFL First-Year Players. An NFL First-Year Player is designated by a "1" on NFL rosters. Thereafter, a player is credited with an additional year of experience for each season in which he accumulates six games on the Active List or Inactive List, or on Reserve/Injured or Reserve/Physically Unable to Perform.

Log on to www.bengals.com for an up-to-date roster.

CINCINNATI BENGALS

COACHING STAFF

Head Coach,
Marvin Lewis

Pro Career: After establishing himself as a record-setting NFL defensive coordinator, Lewis was named the ninth head coach in Bengals history on January 14, 2003. Now in his seventh season, Lewis is one year from tying Paul Brown and Sam Wyche for the franchise's longest tenure (eight seasons). Lewis ranks third as well in Bengals head coaching victories, and his log includes an AFC North Division championship in 2005. With a record of 46-50-1 (including 0-1 in postseason), Lewis needs nine victories to tie Paul Brown (55-59-1) and is 18 wins behind Wyche (64-68). Lewis starts 2009 ranked tied for fifth in the NFL for current consecutive seasons as a head coach, and he ranks tied for ninth among active coaches for most total seasons as an NFL head coach. Prior to joining the Bengals, Lewis was Washington Redskins defensive coordinator (2002), serving as assistant head coach in addition to his coordinator's role. He spent six seasons (1996-2001) as defensive coordinator with the Baltimore Ravens, a tenure that included a Super Bowl victory in the 2000 season. In 2000, Lewis' defense set the NFL record for fewest points allowed in a 16-game campaign (165), and the unit has been widely considered as one of the best NFL defenses of all time. Baltimore's 970 rushing yards allowed in 2000 was the fewest in NFL history for a 16-game season. The Ravens' four shutouts were the most in the NFL since 1976. Prior to joining Baltimore, Lewis spent four seasons (1992-95) with the Pittsburgh Steelers as linebackers coach, guiding the careers of Pro Bowl selections Chad Brown, Kevin Greene, Levon Kirkland and Gregg Lloyd. Career record: 46-50-1.

Background: Earned All-Big Sky Conference honors as a linebacker at Idaho State (1978-1980), and saw action at quarterback and free safety. Received his bachelor's degree in physical education from Idaho State in 1981, and earned his Master's degree in athletic administration in 1982. Inducted into Idaho State's Hall of Fame in 2001. Began his coaching career at Idaho State (1981-84). The team finished 12-1 during his first season and won the NCAA Division I-AA championship. Was also the linebackers coach at Long Beach State (1985-86), New Mexico (1987-89), and Pittsburgh (1990-91).

Personal: Born September 23, 1958, McDonald, Pa. Lewis and his wife, Peggy, have two children—Whitney and Marcus.

ASSISTANT COACHES

Paul Alexander, asst. head coach/offensive line; born February 12, 1960, Rochester, N.Y. Tackle Cortland State 1979-1981. No pro playing experience. College coach: Penn State 1982-84, Michigan 1985-86, Central Michigan 1987-1991. Pro coach: New York Jets 1992-93, joined Bengals in 1994.

Jim Anderson, running backs; born March 27, 1948, Harrisburg, Pa. Linebacker/defensive end California Western 1967-69. No pro playing experience. College coach: California Western 1970-71, Scottsdale (Ariz.) C.C. 1973, Nevada-Las Vegas 1974-75, Southern Methodist 1976-1980, Stanford 1981-83. Pro coach: Joined Bengals in 1984.

Bob Bratkowski, offensive coordinator; born December 2, 1955, San Angelo, Texas. Wide receiver Washington State 1975-77. No pro playing experience. College coach: Missouri 1978-1980, Weber State 1981-85, Wyoming 1986, Washington State 1987-88, Miami 1989-1991. Pro coach: Seattle Seahawks 1992-98, Pittsburgh Steelers 1999-2000, joined Bengals in 2001.

Louie Cioffi, asst. defensive backs; born September 21, 1973, Greenlawn, N.Y. Attended SUNY-Stony Brook. No college or pro playing experience. College coach: C.W. Post 1995-96. Pro coach: New York Jets 1993-94, joined Bengals in 1997.

Kevin Coyle, defensive backs; born January 14, 1956, Staten Island, N.Y. Defensive back Massachusetts 1975-77. No pro playing experience. College coach: Cincinnati 1978-79, Arkansas 1980, U.S. Merchant Marine Academy 1981, Holy Cross 1982-1990, Syracuse 1991-93, Maryland 1994-96, Fresno State 1997-2000. Pro coach: Joined Bengals in 2001.

Jeff FitzGerald, linebackers; born April 18, 1960, Burbank, Calif. Linebacker Oregon State 1980. No pro playing experience. College coach: Cincinnati 1985, Alabama 1986-89, San Diego State 1994-97. Pro coach: Tampa Bay Buccaneers 1990-93, Washington Redskins 1998-99, Arizona Cardinals 2000-03, Baltimore Ravens 2004-07, joined Bengals in 2008.

Paul Guenther, staff assistant; born Nov. 22, 1971, Richboro, Pa. Linebacker Ursinus College 1990-93. No pro playing experience. College coach: Western Maryland 1994-95, Ursinus College 1996, 1997-2001 (head coach 1997-2001), Jacksonville 1997. Pro coach: Washington Redskins 2002-03, joined Bengals in 2005.

Jay Hayes, defensive line; born March 3, 1960, South Fayette, Pa. Defensive end Idaho 1978-1981. Pro defensive end/linebacker Michigan Panthers (USFL) 1984, Memphis Showboats (USFL) 1985. College coach: Notre Dame 1988-1991, California 1992-94, Wisconsin 1995-98. Pro coach: Pittsburgh Steelers 1999-2001, Minnesota Vikings 2002, joined Bengals in 2003.

Jonathan Hayes, tight ends; born Aug. 11, 1962, South Fayette, Pa. Linebacker/tight end Iowa 1981-84. Pro tight end Kansas City Chiefs 1985-1993, Pittsburgh Steelers 1994-96. College coach: Oklahoma 1999-2002. Pro coach: Joined Bengals in 2003.

Chip Morton, strength and conditioning; born November 27, 1962, Hamden, Conn. Attended North Carolina. No college or pro playing experience. College coach: Ohio State 1985-86, Penn State 1987-1991. Pro coach: San Diego Chargers 1992-94, Carolina Panthers 1995-98, Baltimore Ravens 1999-2001, Washington Redskins 2002, joined Bengals in 2003.

Ray Oliver, asst. strength and conditioning; born June 6, 1961, Cincinnati. Defensive back Ohio State 1980-81. College coach: Pittsburgh 1985-88, Kentucky 1989-1991, South Carolina 1993-95, Memphis 2001-03. Pro coach: Tampa Bay Buccaneers 1992, New Jersey Nets (NBA) 1996-97, joined Bengals in 2004.

Mike Sheppard, wide receivers; born October 29, 1951, Tulsa, Okla. Wide receiver Cal Lutheran 1969-1972. No pro playing experience. College coach: Cal Lutheran 1974-76, Brigham Young 1977-78, U.S. International 1979, Idaho State 1980-81, Long Beach State 1982, 1984-86, Kansas 1983, New Mexico 1987-1991, California 1992. Pro coach: Cleveland Browns 1993-95, Baltimore Ravens 1996, San Diego Chargers 1997-98, Seattle Seahawks 1999-2000, Buffalo Bills 2001, New Orleans Saints 2002-05, joined Bengals in 2007.

Darrin Simmons, special teams; born April 9, 1973, Elkhart, Kan. Punter Kansas 1993-95. No pro playing experience. College coach: Kansas 1996, Minnesota 1997. Pro coach: Baltimore Ravens 1998, Carolina Panthers 1999-2002, joined Bengals in 2003.

Bob Surace, offensive assistant; born April 25, 1968, Harrisburg, Pa. Center Princeton 1987-89. No pro playing experience. College coach: Springfield College 1990-91, Maine Maritime Academy 1992-93, Rensselaer Polytechnic Institute 1995, Western Connecticut State 1996-2001 (head coach 2000-01). Pro coach: Shreveport Pirates (CFL) 1994, joined Bengals in 2002.

Ken Zampese, quarterbacks; born July 19, 1967, Santa Maria, Calif. Wide receiver San Diego 1985-88. No pro playing experience. College coach: San Diego 1989, Southern California 1990-91, Northern Arizona 1992-95, Miami (Ohio) 1996-97. Pro coach: Philadelphia Eagles 1998, Green Bay Packers 1999, St. Louis Rams 2000-02, joined Bengals in 2003.

Mike Zimmer, defensive coordinator; born June 5, 1956, Peoria, Ill. Quarterback/linebacker Illinois State 1974-76. No pro playing experience. College coach: Missouri 1979-1980, Weber State 1981-88, Washington State 1989-1993. Pro coach: Dallas Cowboys 1994-2006, Atlanta Falcons 2007, joined Bengals in 2008.

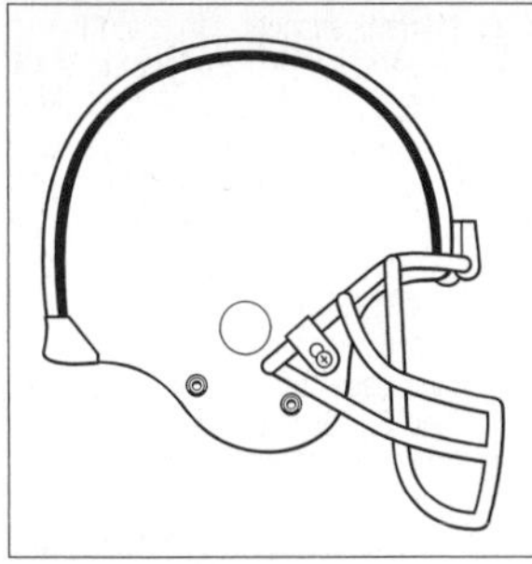

American Football Conference
North Division
Team Colors: Brown, Orange, and White
76 Lou Groza Blvd.
Berea, Ohio 44017
Telephone: (440) 891-5000

2009 SCHEDULE

PRESEASON

Aug. 15	at Green Bay	7:00
Aug. 22	**Detroit**	7:30
Aug. 29	**Tennessee**	7:30
Sep. 3	at Chicago	7:00

REGULAR SEASON

Sep. 13	**Minnesota**	1:00
Sep. 20	at Denver	2:15
Sep. 27	at Baltimore	1:00
Oct. 4	**Cincinnati**	1:00
Oct. 11	at Buffalo	1:00
Oct. 18	at Pittsburgh	1:00
Oct. 25	**Green Bay**	1:00
Nov. 1	at Chicago	12:00
Nov. 8	BYE	
Nov. 16	**Baltimore** (Mon.)	8:30
Nov. 22	at Detroit	1:00
Nov. 29	at Cincinnati	1:00
Dec. 6	**San Diego**	4:05
Dec. 10	**Pittsburgh** (Thu.)	8:20
Dec. 20	at Kansas City	12:00
Dec. 27	**Oakland**	1:00
Jan. 3	**Jacksonville**	1:00

Stadium: Cleveland Browns Stadium (opened in 1999) • **Capacity:** 73,300
100 Alfred Lerner Way
Cleveland, Ohio 44114
Playing Surface: Grass
Headquarters/Training Camp:
76 Lou Groza Boulevard
Berea, Ohio 44017

CLEVELAND BROWNS STADIUM

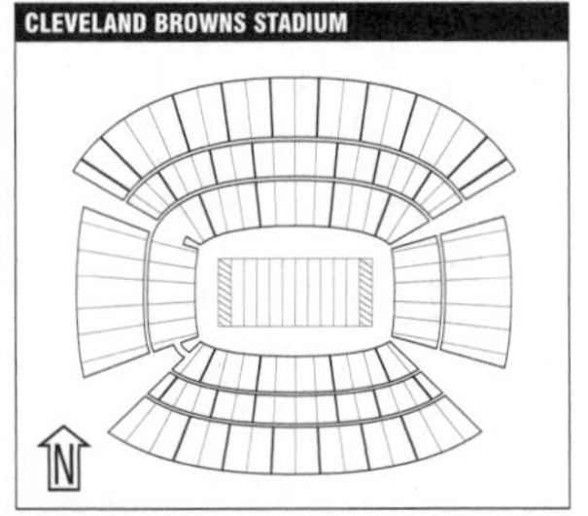

CLUB OFFICIALS

Owner: Randy Lerner
President: Mike Keenan
Head Coach: Eric Mangini
General Manager: George Kokinis
Senior Vice President: Lew Merletti
Vice President, Football Administration: Dawn Aponte
Vice President, Communications: Bill Bonsiewicz
Executive Advisor: Jim Brown
Vice President, Finance & Administration: David A. Jenkins
Vice President, Security: Carl Meyer
Vice President, Sales & Marketing: Brett Reynolds
Director, Stadium Operations: Todd Argust
Director, New Media: Reagan Berube
Director, Player Development: Jerry Butler
Director, Information Technology: Brandon Covert
Director, Public Relations: Neal Gulkis
Director, Community Relations: Renee Harvey
Director, Corporate Sales & Client Services: Scott Klein
Director, Alumni Relations: Dino Lucarelli
Director, Football Administration: Trip McCracken
Director, Scoreboard: Kathy McLain
Director, Marketing Services: George Muller
Director, Human Resources: Mike Nikolaus
Director, Team Operations: Erin O'Brien
Director, Suite Operations: Joe Ricciuti
Controller: Laura Rice
Director, Finance: Gregory Rush
Director, Pro Personnel: Steve Sabo
Director, Direct Marketing and Customer Service: John Schulze
Head Athletic Trainer: Marty Lauzon
Equipment Manager: Brad Melland
Head Groundskeeper: Chris Powell

COACHING HISTORY
(439-392-10)
Records include postseason games

1950-1962	Paul Brown	115-49-5
1963-1970	Blanton Collier	79-38-2
1971-74	Nick Skorich	30-26-2
1975-77	Forrest Gregg*	18-23-0
1977	Dick Modzelewski	0-1-0
1978-1984	Sam Rutigliano**	47-52-0
1984-88	Marty Schottenheimer	46-31-0
1989-1990	Bud Carson***	12-14-1
1990	Jim Shofner	1-6-0
1991-95	Bill Belichick	37-45-0
1999-2000	Chris Palmer	5-27-0
2001-04	Butch Davis****	24-36-0
2004	Terry Robiskie	1-4-0
2005-08	Romeo Crennel	24-40-0

*Resigned after 13 games in 1977
**Released after eight games in 1984
***Released after nine games in 1990
****Resigned after 11 games in 2004

PAID ATTENDANCE

Home 568,477 Away 551,592
Total 1,120,069
Single-game home record, 85,073 (9/21/70)
Single-season home record, 620,496 (1980)

2009 DRAFT CHOICES

Round	Name	Pos.	College
1	Alex Mack	C	California
2	Brian Robiskie	WR	Ohio State
	Mohamed Massaquoi	WR	Georgia
	David Veikune	DE	Hawaii
4	Kaluka Maiava	LB	Southern California
6	Don Carey	DB	Norfolk State
	Coye Francies	DB	San Jose State
	James Davis	RB	Clemson

CLEVELAND BROWNS

2008 TEAM RECORD

PRESEASON (0-4)

Date	Result		Opponent
8/7	L	20-24	New York Jets
8/18	L	34-37	at New York Giants
8/23	L	6-26	at Detroit
8/28	L	10-16	Chicago

REGULAR SEASON (4-12)

Date	Result		Opponent
9/7	L	10-28	Dallas
9/14	L	6-10	Pittsburgh
9/21	L	10-28	at Baltimore
9/28	W	20-12	at Cincinnati
10/13	W	35-14	New York Giants
10/19	L	11-14	at Washington
10/26	W	23-17	at Jacksonville
11/2	L	27-37	Baltimore
11/6	L	30-34	Denver
11/17	W	29-27	at Buffalo
11/23	L	6-16	Houston
11/30	L	6-10	Indianapolis
12/7	L	9-28	at Tennessee
12/15	L	10-30	at Philadelphia
12/21	L	0-14	Cincinnati
12/28	L	0-31	at Pittsburgh

SCORE BY PERIODS

Browns	45	76	29	82	0 —	232
Opponents	51	119	74	106	0 —	350

2008 TEAM STATISTICS

	Browns	Opp.
Total First Downs	233	315
Rushing	84	125
Passing	127	176
Penalty	22	14
3rd Down: Made/Att	72/212	95/207
3rd Down Pct.	34.0	45.9
4th Down: Made/Att	6/14	11/17
4th Down Pct.	42.9	64.7
Possession Avg.	27:33	32:27
Total Net Yards	3985	5704
Avg. Per Game	249.1	356.5
Total Plays	921	1004
Avg. Per Play	4.3	5.7
Net Yards Rushing	1605	2431
Avg. Per Game	100.3	151.9
Total Rushes	409	541
Net Yards Passing	2380	3273
Avg. Per Game	148.8	204.6
Sacked/Yards Lost	24/157	17/90
Gross Yards	2537	3363
Att./Completions	488/238	446/286
Completion Pct.	48.8	64.1
Had Intercepted	20	23
Punts/Average	76/45.3	59/40.7
Net Punting Avg.	76/39.3	59/34.1
Penalties/Yards	100/669	95/770
Fumbles/Ball Lost	17/6	19/8
Touchdowns	20	42
Rushing	6	16
Passing	11	19
Returns	3	7

2008 INDIVIDUAL STATISTICS

PASSING	Att.	Comp.	Yds.	Pct.	TD	Int.	Tkld.	Rate
Anderson	283	142	1615	50.2	9	8	14/87	66.5
Dorsey	91	43	370	47.3	0	7	5/43	26.4
Quinn	89	45	518	50.6	2	2	1/9	66.6
Gradkowski	21	7	26	33.3	0	3	4/18	2.8
Cribbs	4	1	8	25.0	0	0	0/0	39.6
Browns	488	238	2537	48.8	11	20	24/157	54.8
Opponents	446	286	3363	64.1	19	23	17/90	79.7

SCORING	TD R	TD P	TD Rt	PAT	FG	Saf	PTS
Dawson	0	0	0	18/18	30/36	0	108
Lewis	4	0	0	0/0	0/0	0	24
Edwards	0	3	0	0/0	0/0	0	22
Cribbs	1	1	1	0/0	0/0	0	18
Winslow	0	3	0	0/0	0/0	0	18
Harrison	1	1	0	0/0	0/0	0	12
Dinkins	0	1	0	0/0	0/0	0	6
McDonald	0	0	1	0/0	0/0	0	6
Stallworth	0	1	0	0/0	0/0	0	6
E. Wright	0	0	1	0/0	0/0	0	6
J. Wright	0	1	0	0/0	0/0	0	6
Browns	6	11	3	18/18	30/36	0	232
Opponents	16	19	7	41/41	19/28	0	350

2-Pt. Conversions: Edwards 2.
Browns 2-2, Opponents 0-1

RUSHING	No.	Yds	Avg	LG	TD
Lewis	279	1002	3.6	29	4
Harrison	34	246	7.2	72t	1
Cribbs	29	167	5.8	27	1
J. Wright	23	85	3.7	11	0
Anderson	25	55	2.2	15	0
Vickers	10	31	3.1	10	0
Quinn	5	21	4.2	12	0
Gradkowski	1	2	2.0	2	0
Dorsey	2	0	0.0	0	0
Stallworth	1	-4	-4.0	-4	0
Browns	409	1605	3.9	72t	6
Opponents	541	2431	4.5	60	16

RECEIVING	No.	Yds	Avg	LG	TD
Edwards	55	873	15.9	70	3
Winslow	43	428	10.0	30	3
Heiden	23	249	10.8	51	0
Lewis	23	178	7.7	18	0
J. Wright	22	156	7.1	17	1
Steptoe	19	182	9.6	53	0
Stallworth	17	170	10.0	19	1
Harrison	12	116	9.7	23	1
Vickers	10	78	7.8	21	0
Dinkins	5	41	8.2	22t	1
Ali	4	13	3.3	12	0
Cribbs	2	18	9.0	17	1
Rucker	2	17	8.5	9	0
Sanders	1	18	18.0	18	0
Browns	238	2537	10.7	70	11
Opponents	286	3363	11.8	93t	19

INTERCEPTIONS	No.	Yds	Avg	LG	TD
McDonald	5	146	29.2	98	1
Jones	4	27	6.8	20	0
E. Wright	3	131	43.7	94t	1
Pool	3	45	15.0	24	0
Jackson	3	29	9.7	16	0
Adams	2	18	9.0	18	0
Cousin	1	4	4.0	4	0
Davis	1	4	4.0	4	0
Wimbley	1	2	2.0	2	0
Browns	23	406	17.7	98	2
Opponents	20	381	19.1	50t	5

PUNTING	No.	Yds.	Avg.	In 20	LG
Zastudil	75	3410	45.5	23	65
Dawson	1	33	33	1	33
Browns	76	3443	45.3	24	65
Opponents	59	2403	40.7	18	59

PUNT RETURNS	Ret	FC	Yds	Avg	LG	TD
Cribbs	28	7	228	8.1	32	0
Steptoe	2	0	23	11.5	14	0
Browns	30	7	251	8.4	32	0
Opponents	32	7	235	7.3	44	0

KICKOFF RETURNS	No.	Yds	Avg	LG	TD
Cribbs	44	1110	25.2	92t	1
Lawson	3	72	24.0	43	0
Steptoe	3	61	20.3	23	0
Dinkins	3	37	12.3	14	0
J. Wright	1	15	15.0	15	0
Ali	1	10	10.0	10	0
Cieslak	1	7	7.0	7	0
McKinney	1	0	0.0	0	0
Sowells	1	0	0.0	0	0
Browns	58	1312	22.6	92t	1
Opponents	53	1228	23.2	98t	1

FIELD GOALS	1-19	20-29	30-39	40-49	50+
Dawson	0/0	10/10	12/14	5/6	3/6
Browns	0/0	10/10	12/14	5/6	3/6
Opponents	0/0	4/4	10/13	4/9	1/2

SACKS	No.
Rogers	4.5
Wimbley	4.0
Hall	3.0
Jackson	2.0
McGinest	1.0
Pool	1.0
Sorensen	0.5
S. Thomas	0.5
C. Williams	0.5
Browns	17.0
Opponents	24.0

RECORD HOLDERS

INDIVIDUAL RECORDS—CAREER

Category	Name	Performance
Rushing (Yds.)	Jim Brown, 1957-1965	12,312
Passing (Yds.)	Brian Sipe, 1974-1983	23,713
Passing (TDs)	Brian Sipe, 1974-1983	154
Receiving (No.)	Ozzie Newsome, 1978-1990	662
Receiving (Yds.)	Ozzie Newsome, 1978-1990	7,980
Interceptions	Thom Darden, 1972-74, 1976-1981	45
Punting (Avg.)	Dave Zastudil, 2006-08	44.0
Punt Return (Avg.)	Greg Pruitt, 1973-1981	11.8
Kickoff Return (Avg.)	Joshua Cribbs, 2005-08	26.3
Field Goals	Lou Groza, 1950-59, 1961-67	234
Touchdowns (Tot.)	Jim Brown, 1957-1965	126
Points	Lou Groza, 1950-59, 1961-67	1,349
*Sacks	Clay Matthews, 1978-1993	62.0

INDIVIDUAL RECORDS—SINGLE SEASON

Category	Name	Performance
Rushing (Yds.)	Jim Brown, 1963	1,863
Passing (Yds.)	Brian Sipe, 1980	4,132
Passing (TDs)	Brian Sipe, 1980	30
Receiving (No.)	Ozzie Newsome, 1983	89
	Ozzie Newsome, 1984	89
	Kellen Winslow, 2006	89
Receiving (Yds.)	Braylon Edwards, 2007	1,289
Interceptions	Thom Darden, 1978	10
	Anthony Henry, 2001	10
Punting (Avg.)	Gary Collins, 1965	46.7
Punt Return (Avg.)	Leroy Kelly, 1965	15.6
Kickoff Return (Avg.)	Billy Lefear, 1975	31.7
Field Goals	Phil Dawson, 2008	30
Touchdowns (Tot.)	Jim Brown, 1965	21
Points	Jim Brown, 1965	126
*Sacks	Reggie Camp, 1984	14.0

INDIVIDUAL RECORDS—SINGLE GAME

Category	Name	Performance
Rushing (Yds.)	Jim Brown, 11-24-57	237
	Jim Brown, 11-19-61	237
Passing (Yds.)	Brian Sipe, 10-25-81	444
Passing (TDs)	Frank Ryan, 12-12-64	5
	Bill Nelsen, 11-2-69	5
	Brian Sipe, 10-7-79	5
	Kelly Holcomb, 11-28-04	5
	Derek Anderson, 9-16-07	5
Receiving (No.)	Ozzie Newsome, 10-14-84	14
Receiving (Yds.)	Ozzie Newsome, 10-14-84	191
Interceptions	Many times	3
	Last time by Anthony Henry, 11-18-01	
Field Goals	Phil Dawson, 11-5-06	6
Touchdowns (Tot.)	Dub Jones, 11-25-51	**6
Points	Dub Jones, 11-25-51	30
*Sacks	Andra Davis, 11-9-03	4.0

**Sacks became an official statistic in 1982.*
***NFL Record*

CLEVELAND BROWNS

2009 VETERAN ROSTER

No.	Name	Pos.	Ht.	Wt.	Birthdate	NFL Exp.	College	Hometown	How Acq.	'08 Games/ Starts
42	Abdullah, Hamza	S	6-2	216	8/20/83	5	Washington State	Pomona, Calif.	FA-'08	0*
20	Adams, Mike	DB	5-11	195	3/24/81	6	Delaware	Paterson, N.J.	UFA(SF)-'07	14/5
41	Ali, Charles	FB	6-2	255	8/23/84	3	Arkansas-Pine Bluff	St. Louis, Mo.	FA-'07	15/4
3	Anderson, Derek	QB	6-6	230	6/15/83	5	Oregon State	Portland, Ore.	W(Bal)-'05	10/9
50	Barton, Eric	LB	6-2	245	9/29/77	11	Maryland	Alexandria, Va.	UFA(NYJ)-'09	16/16*
58	Bell, Beau	LB	6-1	250	5/26/86	2	Nevada-Las Vegas	Tustin, Calif.	D4a-'08	4/0
96	Bowens, David	LB	6-3	265	7/3/77	10	Western Illinois	Detroit, Mich.	FA-'09	16/5*
90	t- Coleman, Kenyon	DE	6-5	295	4/10/79	8	UCLA	Alta Loma, Calif.	T(NYJ)-'09	16/15*
16	Cribbs, Joshua	WR	6-1	215	6/9/83	5	Kent State	Washington, D.C.	FA-'05	15/2
4	Dawson, Phil	K	5-11	200	1/23/75	11	Texas	Dallas, Texas	FA-'99	16/0
17	Edwards, Braylon	WR	6-3	215	2/21/83	5	Michigan	Detroit, Mich.	D1-'05	16/16
26	t- Elam, Abram	DB	6-0	207	10/15/81	4	Kent State	Riviera Beach, Fla.	T(NYJ)-'09	16/9*
83	Ellis, Devale	WR	5-10	174	4/2/84	3	Hofstra	Brooklyn, N.Y.	FA-'09	0*
66	Fraley, Hank	OL	6-2	310	9/21/77	10	Robert Morris	Gaithersburg, Md.	T(Phil)-'06	16/16
	# Friedman, Lennie	OL	6-3	290	8/13/76	10	Duke	Milford, N.J.	T(Chi)-'06	0*
62	Fry, Dustin	OL	6-3	326	10/3/83	2	Clemson	Summerville, S.C.	FA-'08	0*
	Furrey, Mike	WR	6-0	195	5/12/77	7	Northern Iowa	Grove City, Ohio	FA-'09	9/2*
	# Griffin, Kris	LB	6-3	245	5/27/82	4	Indiana (Pa.)	Beaver, Pa.	W(KC)-'07	10/0
70	Hadnot, Rex	OL	6-2	320	1/28/82	6	Houston	Lufkin, Texas	UFA(Mia)-'08	15/15
51	Hall, Alex	LB	6-5	250	8/17/85	2	St. Augustine	Glenarden, Md.	D7-'08	16/2
35	Harrison, Jerome	RB	5-9	205	2/26/83	4	Washington State	Kalamazoo, Mich.	D5a-'06	15/0
82	Heiden, Steve	TE	6-5	270	9/21/76	11	South Dakota St.	Rushford, Minn.	T(SD)-'02	14/11
33	Herron, Noah	RB	5-11	218	4/3/82	4	Northwestern	Mattawan, Mich.	FA-'09	0*
	# Holly, Daven	DB	5-10	185	8/8/82	4	Cincinnati	Clairton, Pa.	FA-'06	0*
29	Ivy, Corey	DB	5-9	190	3/21/77	9	Oklahoma	Moore, Okla.	UFA(Balt)-'09	16/1*
52	Jackson, D'Qwell	LB	6-0	240	9/26/83	4	Maryland	Largo, Fla.	D2-'06	16/16
30	Lawson, Gerard	DB	5-10	195	1/12/85	2	Oregon State	Las Vegas, Nev.	FA-'08	15/0
93	Leonard, Louis	DL	6-4	325	7/16/84	3	Fresno State	Los Angeles, Calif.	W(StL)-'07	16/4
31	Lewis, Jamal	RB	5-11	245	8/26/79	10	Tennessee	Atlanta, Ga.	UFA(Balt)-'07	16/16
85	Madsen, John	TE	6-5	240	5/9/83	4	Utah	West Valley City, Utah	FA-'08	3/0*
22	McDonald, Brandon	DB	5-10	185	8/26/85	3	Memphis	Collins, Miss.	D5-'07	16/15
	# McGinest, Willie	LB	6-5	270	12/11/71	15	Southern California	Long Beach, Calif.	UFA(NE)-'06	14/14
69	Mosley, C.J.	DL	6-3	305	8/6/83	5	Missouri	Fort Leonard Wood, Mo.	UFA(NYJ)-'09	16/1*
	# Orr, Shantee	LB	6-1	245	5/28/81	5	Michigan	Detroit, Mich.	UFA(Jax)-'08	15/1
81	Patten, David	WR	5-10	190	8/19/74	13	Western Carolina	Hopkins, S.C.	FA-'09	5/3*
64	Pontbriand, Ryan	LS	6-2	255	10/1/79	7	Rice	Houston, Texas	D5a-'03	16/0
21	Pool, Brodney	DB	6-2	205	5/24/84	5	Oklahoma	Houston, Texas	D2-'05	15/15
23	Poteat, Hank	DB	5-10	195	8/31/77	8	Pittsburgh	Harrisburg, Pa.	UFA(NYJ)-'09	13/1*
10	Quinn, Brady	QB	6-3	235	10/27/84	3	Notre Dame	Dublin, Ohio	D1b-'07	3/3
92	Rogers, Shaun	DL	6-4	350	3/12/79	9	Texas	LaPorte, Texas	T(Det)-'08	16/16
84	Royal, Robert	TE	6-4	257	5/15/78	8	Louisiana State	New Orleans, La.	FA-'09	15/7*
71	Rubin, Ahtyba	DL	6-2	330	7/25/86	2	Iowa State	Fort Belvoir, Virg.	D6a-'08	12/0
86	Rucker, Martin	TE	6-4	260	5/4/85	2	Missouri	St. Joseph, Mo.	D4b-'08	5/1
43	Ruud, Bo	LB	6-3	255	9/2/84	2	Nebraska	Lincoln, Neb.	W(NE)-'09	0*
98	Smith, Robaire	DL	6-4	310	11/15/77	10	Michigan State	Flint, Mich.	UFA(Tenn)-'07	2/2
91	Smith, Shaun	DL	6-2	325	8/19/81	6	South Carolina	Brooklyn, N.Y.	RFA(Cin)-'07	11/9
27	Sorensen, Nick	DB	6-3	210	7/31/78	9	Virginia Tech	Winter Haven, Fla.	FA-'07	16/0
61	Sowells, Isaac	OL	6-3	320	5/4/82	4	Indiana	Louisville, Ky.	D4b-'06	16/0
78	St. Clair, John	OL	6-5	315	7/15/77	10	Virginia	Roanoke, Va.	UFA(Chi)-'09	16/16*
18	Stallworth, Donte'	WR	6-0	200	11/10/80	8	Tennessee	Sacramento, Calif.	UFA(NE)-'08	11/7
65	Steinbach, Eric	OL	6-6	295	4/4/80	7	Iowa	Lockport, Ill.	UFA(Cin)-'07	14/14
12	Steptoe, Syndric	WR	5-9	200	12/6/84	2	Arizona	Bryan, Texas	D7b-'07	16/5
73	Thomas, Joe	OL	6-6	305	12/4/84	3	Wisconsin	Brookfield, Wisc.	D1a-'07	16/16
97	Thomas, Santonio	DL	6-4	305	7/2/81	3	Miami	Belle Glade, Fla.	FA-'08	11/1
72	Tucker, Ryan	OL	6-6	315	6/12/75	13	Texas Christian	Midland, Texas	UFA(StL)-'02	1/1
47	Vickers, Lawrence	FB	6-0	250	5/8/83	4	Colorado	Houston, Texas	D6a-'06	12/8
87	Walker, Aaron	TE	6-6	270	3/14/80	5	Florida	Titusville, Fla.	FA-'09	0*
99	Williams, Corey	DL	6-4	320	8/17/80	6	Arkansas State	Camden, Ark.	T(GB)-'08	16/16
94	Williams, Leon	LB	6-2	250	7/30/83	4	Miami	Brooklyn, N.Y.	D4a-'06	14/0
95	Wimbley, Kamerion	LB	6-3	255	10/13/83	4	Florida State	Wichita, Kan.	D1-'06	16/16
77	Womack, Floyd	OL	6-4	328	11/15/78	9	Mississippi State	Cleveland, Miss.	UFA(Sea)-'09	15/14*
24	Wright, Eric	DB	5-10	190	7/24/85	3	Nevada-Las Vegas	San Francisco, Calif.	D2-'07	16/16
15	Zastudil, Dave	P	6-3	220	10/26/78	8	Ohio University	Bay Village, Ohio	UFA(Balt)-'06	16/0

* Abdullah inactive for 12 games; Barton played 16 games with New York Jets in '08; Bowens played 16 games with New York Jets; Coleman played 16 games with New York Jets; Elam played 16 games with New York Jets; Ellis last active with Detroit in '06; Friedman missed '08 season because of injury; Fry last active with St. Louis in '07; Furrey played 9 games with Detroit; Herron last active with Green Bay in '06; Holly missed '08 season because of injury; Ivy played 16 games with Baltimore; Madsen played 3 games with Oakland; Mosley played 16 games with New York Jets; Patten played 5 games with New Orleans; Poteat played 13 games with New York Jets; Royal played 15 games with Buffalo; Ruud missed '08 season because of injury with New England; St. Clair played 16 games with Chicago; Walker last active with St. Louis in '07; Womack played 15 games with Seattle.

Unrestricted free agent; subject to developments.

t- Browns traded for Coleman (NYJ), Elam (NYJ), and Ratliff (NYJ).

Traded—TE Kellen Winslow (10 games in '08) to Tampa Bay.

Players lost through free agency (7): LB Andra Davis (Den; 16 games in '08), DB Travis Daniels (KC; 7), TE Darnell Dinkins (NO; 14), DB Sean Jones (Phil; 12), OL Seth McKinney (Buff; 16), RB Jason Wright (Ariz; 15), OL Scott Young (Den; 1).

Also played with Browns in '08—Titus Brown (4 games), TE Brad Cieslak (1), DB Terry Cousin (16), QB Ken Dorsey (4), QB Bruce Gradkowski (2), WR Steve Sanders (5), OL Kevin Shaffer (15).

2009 FIRST-YEAR ROSTER

Name	Pos.	Ht.	Wt.	Birthdate	College	Hometown	How Acq.
Bartel, Richard (1)	QB	6-3	233	2/3/83	Tarleton State	Grapevine, Texas	FA-'08
Benard, Marcus	LB	6-2	256	7/26/85	Jackson State	Ypsilanti, Mich.	FA
Braxton, Branndon	OL	6-6	312	12/9/85	Oklahoma	Youngstown, Ohio	FA
Brown, Titus (1)	LB	6-3	245	3/27/86	Mississippi State	Tuscaloosa, Ala.	FA-'08
Carey, Don	DB	5-11	192	2/14/87	Norfolk State	Norfolk, Va.	D6a
Davis, James	RB	5-11	218	1/1/86	Clemson	Atlanta, Ga.	D6c
Davis, Marlon	OL	6-2	309	11/2/86	Alabama	Columbus, Ga.	FA
Foster, Jonathan	LB	6-4	246	7/31/87	Central State	Ann Arbor, Mich.	FA
Francies, Coye	DB	6-0	185	11/15/86	San Jose State	Sacramento, Calif.	D6b
Holloway, David (1)	LB	6-2	234	12/4/83	Maryland	Stephentown, N.Y.	FA-'08
Hoppel, Adam	DL	6-1	307	5/20/85	Cincinnati	Lisbon, Ohio	FA
Hubbard, Paul	WR	6-2	225	6/12/85	Wisconsin	Colorado Springs, Colo.	D6b-'08
Hunt, Phillip	LB	6-0	244	1/9/86	Houston	Fort Worth, Texas	FA
Leggett, Lance (1)	WR	6-3	200	2/11/85	Miami	Bartow, Fla.	FA-'08
Lockett, Bret	DB	6-1	211	10/7/86	UCLA	Diamond Bar, Calif.	FA
Mack, Alex	C	6-4	311	11/19/85	California	Santa Barbara, Calif.	D1
Maiava, Kaluka	LB	6-0	229	3/22/87	Southern California	Wailuku, Hawaii	D4
Massaquoi, Mohamed	WR	6-2	207	11/24/86	Georgia	Charlotte, N.C.	D2b
Ness, Nate	DB	6-0	193	9/3/86	Arizona	Gardena, Calif.	FA
Norwood, Jordan	WR	5-11	179	9/28/86	Penn State	State College, Pa.	FA
Purcell, Melila (1)	DL	6-5	295	2/5/84	Hawaii	Pago Pago, American Samoa	FA-'08
Quarterman, Kurt (1)	OL	6-5	348	10/5/85	Louisville	Albany, Ga.	FA-'08
Ratliff, Brett (1)	QB	6-4	224	8/8/85	Utah	Chico, Calif.	T(NYJ)
Robiskie, Brian	WR	6-3	209	12/3/87	Ohio State	Cleveland, Ohio	D2a
Thomas, Marcus (1)	RB	6-0	215	5/28/84	Texas-El Paso	Phoenix, Ariz.	FA
Veikune, David	LB	6-2	257	12/12/85	Hawaii	Wahiawa, Hawaii	D2c
Venson, Jason	DB	5-9	211	10/13/85	Central Florida	Marietta, Ga.	FA
Williams, Bryan	DB	5-11	197	9/17/87	Akron	Akron, Ohio	FA

The term NFL Rookie is defined as a player who is in his first season of professional football and has not been on the roster of another professional football team for any regular-season or postseason games. A Rookie is designated by an "R" on NFL rosters. Players who have been active in another professional football league or players who have NFL experience, including either preseason training camp or being on an Active List or Inactive List, or on Reserve/Injured or Reserve/Physically Unable to Perform for fewer than six regular-season games, are termed NFL First-Year Players. An NFL First-Year Player is designated by a "1" on NFL rosters. Thereafter, a player is credited with an additional year of experience for each season in which he accumulates six games on the Active List or Inactive List, or on Reserve/Injured or Reserve/Physically Unable to Perform.

Log on to www.clevelandbrowns.com for an up-to-date roster.

COACHING STAFF

Head Coach,
Eric Mangini

Pro Career: Eric Mangini was named the twelfth full-time head coach in Browns history on January 8, 2009. This is Mangini's fourth season as an NFL head coach, having led the Jets to a three-year record of 23-25. The Jets put together winning marks in two of Mangini's three seasons at the helm, including a record of 10-6 in 2006, when the Jets earned the 12th postseason berth in franchise history. Overall, Mangini is entering his 15th season in the NFL. Prior to joining the Jets, he spent six seasons (2000-05) on the staff of the New England Patriots, the first five as defensive backs coach and the final one as defensive coordinator. During Mangini's tenure there, the Patriots captured three Super Bowl titles. Mangini's first NFL coaching position came as an assistant on the Browns' staff in 1995. He moved with the team to Baltimore in 1996, serving as a quality control/offensive assistant for the Ravens that year. He joined Bill Parcells' staff with the Jets in 1997, serving as a defensive assistant/quality control coach for three seasons. While completing his Wesleyan degree in Melbourne, Australia, Mangini served as the head coach and defensive coordinator for the Kewe Colts, a semi-professional football team, and led them to back-to-back titles. Career record: 23-26.

Background: Mangini set a school record with 36.5 sacks as a nose tackle in college for Wesleyan (Conn.) from 1989-1990, 1992-93. He was voted a first-team all-star by NESCAC and ECAC New England Division III.

Personal: Born January 19, 1971, Hartford, Conn. Mangini and his wife, Julie, have three sons, Jake, Luke and Zack.

ASSISTANT COACHES

Gary Brown, running backs; born July 1, 1969, Williamsport, Pa. Running back Penn State 1987-1990. Pro running back Houston Oilers 1991-95, San Diego Chargers 1995, New York Giants 1998-99. College coach: Lycoming 2003-04, Susquehanna 2006-07, Rutgers 2008. Pro coach: New York Giants 2005, joined Browns in 2009.

Bryan Cox, defensive line; born February 17, 1968, East St. Louis, Mo. Linebacker Western Illinois 1987-1990. Pro linebacker Miami Dolphins 1991-95, Chicago Bears 1996-97, New York Jets 1998-2000, New England Patriots 2001, New Orleans Saints 2002. Pro coach: New York Jets 2006-08, joined Browns in 2009.

Brian Daboll, offensive coordinator; born April 14, 1975, Welland, Ontario, Canada. Safety Rochester 1995-97. No pro playing experience. College coach: William & Mary 1997, Michigan State 1998-99. Pro coach: New England Patriots 2000-06, New York Jets 2007-08, joined Browns in 2009.

Alan DeGennaro, asst. strength and conditioning coach; born January 21, 1977, Altoona, Pa. Attended Pittsburgh. No college or pro playing experience. Pro coach: Joined Browns in 2007.

Andy Dickerson, defensive quality control; born January 29, 1982, Wilmington, Del. Offensive lineman Tufts 1999-2002. No pro playing experience. College coach: Tufts 2003. Pro coach: New York Jets 2006-08, joined Browns in 2009.

Matt Eberflus, linebackers; born May 17, 1970, Toledo, Ohio. Linebacker Toledo 1988-1991. No pro playing experience. College coach: Toledo 1992-2000, Missouri 2001-08. Pro coach: Joined Browns in 2009.

Steve Hagen, tight ends; born September 15, 1961, Forest City, Iowa. Wide receiver Cal Lutheran 1979-1982. No pro playing experience. College coach: Illinois 1983, Kansas 1984-85, Northern Arizona 1986-88, Notre Dame 1989-1990, Kent State 1991, Nevada 1992-93, Nevada-Las Vegas 1994-95, Wartburg 1996, San Jose State 1997-98, California 1999-2000, Fresno State 2006, North Carolina 2007-08. Pro coach: Cleveland Browns 2001-04, re-joined Browns in 2009.

Jerome Henderson, defensive backs; born August 8, 1969, Portsmouth, Va. Defensive back Clemson 1987-1990. Pro cornerback New England Patriots 1991-93, 1996, Buffalo Bills 1993-94, Philadelphia Eagles 1995, New York Jets 1997-98. Pro coach: New York Jets 2006-08, joined Browns in 2009.

Rick Lyle, asst. strength and conditioning; born February 26, 1971, Monroe, La. Defensive lineman Missouri 1989-1993. Pro defensive lineman Cleveland Browns 1994-95, Baltimore Ravens 1996, New York Jets 1997-2001, New England Patriots 2002-03. Pro coach: New York Jets 2006-08, joined Browns in 2009.

George McDonald, wide receivers; born May 10, 1976, Buena Park, Calif. Wide receiver Illinois 1995-98. No pro playing experience. College coach: Ball State 2000, Northern Illinois 2001-03, Stanford 2004, Western Michigan 2005-06, Minnesota 2007-08. Pro coach: Joined Browns in 2009.

Tom Myslinski, strength and conditioning; born December 7, 1968, Rome, N.Y. Guard Tennessee 1989-1992. Pro guard Chicago Bears 1993-94, Pittsburgh Steelers 1996-97, 2000, Indianapolis Colts 1998. College coach: North Florida 1996, Pittsburgh 1998-2001, 2007, Robert Morris 2005-06. Pro coach: Cleveland Browns 2001-04, re-joined Browns in 2007.

Rob Ryan, defensive coordinator; born December 13, 1962, Ardmore, Okla. Linebacker Oklahoma State 1984, Southwestern Oklahoma State 1985-86. No pro playing experience. College coach: Western Kentucky 1987, Ohio State 1988, Tennessee State 1989-1993, Hutchinson (Kan.) C.C. 1996, Oklahoma State 1997-99. Pro coach: Arizona Cardinals 1994-95, New England Patriots 2000-03, Oakland Raiders 2004-08, joined Browns in 2009.

Brad Seely, asst. head coach/special teams coordinator; born September 6, 1956, Vinton, Iowa. Tackle/guard South Dakota State 1974-77. No pro playing experience. College coach: Colorado State 1979-1980, Southern Methodist 1981, North Carolina State 1982, Pacific 1983, Oklahoma State 1984-88. Pro coach: Indianapolis Colts 1989-1993, New York Jets 1994, Carolina Panthers 1995-98, New England Patriots 1999-2008, joined Browns in 2009.

Carl Smith, quarterbacks; born April 26, 1948, Wasco, Calif. Quarterback Bakersfield 1966-67, defensive back Cal Poly-San Luis Obispo 1969-1970. No pro playing experience. College coach: Cal Poly-San Luis Obispo 1971, Colorado 1972-73, Southwestern Louisiana 1974-78, Lamar 1979-1981, North Carolina State 1982, Southern California 2004. Pro coach: Philadelphia/Baltimore Stars 1983-85, New Orleans Saints 1986-1996, New England Patriots 1997-99, Cleveland Browns 2001-03, Jacksonville Jaguars 2005-06, re-joined Browns in 2009.

George Warhop, offensive line; born September 19, 1961, Riverside, Calif. Guard/center Mt. San Jacinto (Calif.) J.C. 1979-1980, Cincinnati 1981-82. No pro playing experience. College coach: Cincinnati 1983, Kansas 1984-86, Vanderbilt 1987-89, New Mexico 1990, Southern Methodist 1993, Boston College 1994-95. Pro coach: London Monarchs (World League) 1991-92, St. Louis Rams 1996-97, Arizona Cardinals 1998-2002, Dallas Cowboys 2003-04, San Francisco 49ers 2005-08, joined Browns in 2009.

American Football Conference
West Division
Team Colors: Orange,
Broncos Navy Blue, and White
13655 Broncos Parkway
Englewood, Colorado 80112
Telephone: (303) 649-9000

2009 SCHEDULE

PRESEASON

Aug. 14	at San Francisco	7:00
Aug. 22	at Seattle	7:30
Aug. 30	**Chicago**	6:00
Sep. 3	**Arizona**	7:00

REGULAR SEASON

Sep. 13	at Cincinnati	1:00
Sep. 20	**Cleveland**	2:15
Sep. 27	at Oakland	1:15
Oct. 4	**Dallas**	2:15
Oct. 11	**New England**	2:15
Oct. 19	at San Diego (Mon.)	5:30
Oct. 25	BYE	
Nov. 1	at Baltimore	1:00
Nov. 9	**Pittsburgh** (Mon.)	6:30
Nov. 15	at Washington	1:00
Nov. 22	**San Diego**	2:15
Nov. 26	**N.Y. Giants** (Thu.)	6:20
Dec. 6	at Kansas City	12:00
Dec. 13	at Indianapolis	1:00
Dec. 20	**Oakland**	2:05
Dec. 27	at Philadelphia	1:00
Jan. 3	**Kansas City**	2:15

Stadium: INVESCO Field at Mile High (opened in 2001) •**Capacity:** 76,125
1701 Bryant Street
Denver, Colorado 80204
Playing Surface: DD Grassmaster
Training Camp: 13655 Broncos Parkway
Englewood, Colorado 80112

INVESCO FIELD AT MILE HIGH

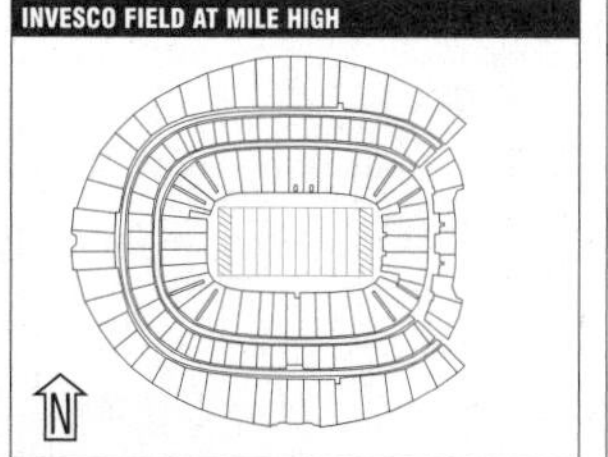

CLUB OFFICIALS

President-Chief Executive Officer: Pat Bowlen
Head Coach: Josh McDaniels
Chief Operating Officer: Joe Ellis

FOOTBALL STAFF

General Manager: Brian Xanders
Director of Football Administration: Mike Bluem
Head Athletic Trainer: Steve Antonopulos
Director of Football Technology: Kent Erickson

BUSINESS STAFF

General Counsel/Senior Vice President of Administration: Rich Slivka
Vice President of Public Relations: Jim Saccomano
Vice President of Marketing: Greg Carney
Vice President of Finance: Jim Barlow
Vice President of Community Development: Cindy Kellogg

STADIUM MANAGEMENT COMPANY

Vice President of Stadium Operations: Mac Freeman

COACHING HISTORY (403-359-10)

Records include postseason games

1960-61	Frank Filchock	7-20-1
1962-64	Jack Faulkner*	9-22-1
1964-66	Mac Speedie**	6-19-1
1966	Ray Malavasi	4-8-0
1967-1971	Lou Saban***	20-42-3
1971	Jerry Smith	2-3-0
1972-76	John Ralston	34-33-3
1977-1980	Robert (Red) Miller	42-25-0
1981-1992	Dan Reeves	117-79-1
1993-94	Wade Phillips	16-17-0
1995-2008	Mike Shanahan	146-91-0

*Released after four games in 1964
**Resigned after two games in 1966
***Resigned after nine games in 1971

PAID ATTENDANCE

Home 590,661 Away 556,306
Total 1,146,967
Single-game home record, 76,645 (10/29/07)
Single-season home record, 597,984 (2007)

2009 DRAFT CHOICES

Round	Name	Pos.	College
1	Knowshon Moreno	RB	Georgia
	Robert Ayers	DE	Tennessee
2	Alphonso Smith	DB	Wake Forest
	Darcel McBath	DB	Texas Tech
	Richard Quinn	TE	North Carolina
4	David Bruton	DB	Notre Dame
	Seth Olsen	G	Iowa
5	Kenny McKinley	WR	South Carolina
6	Tom Brandstater	QB	Fresno State
7	Blake Schlueter	C	Texas Christian

DENVER BRONCOS

2008 TEAM RECORD

PRESEASON (2-2)

Date	Result	Opponent
8/9	L 16-19	at Houston
8/16	W 23-13	Dallas
8/22	L 24-27	Green Bay
8/29	W 28-14	at Arizona

REGULAR SEASON (8-8)

Date	Result	Opponent
9/8	W 41-14	at Oakland
9/14	W 39-38	San Diego
9/21	W 34-32	New Orleans
9/28	L 19-33	at Kansas City
10/5	W 16-13	Tampa Bay
10/12	L 17-24	Jacksonville
10/20	L 7-41	at New England
11/2	L 17-26	Miami
11/6	W 34-30	at Cleveland
11/16	W 24-20	at Atlanta
11/23	L 10-31	Oakland
11/30	W 34-17	at New York Jets
12/7	W 24-17	Kansas City
12/14	L 10-30	at Carolina
12/21	L 23-30	Buffalo
12/28	L 21-52	at San Diego

SCORE BY PERIODS

Broncos	106	86	70	108	0 —	370
Opponents	84	145	88	131	0 —	448

2008 TEAM STATISTICS

	Broncos	Opp.
Total First Downs	354	327
Rushing	103	122
Passing	223	186
Penalty	28	19
3rd Down: Made/Att	95/200	89/202
3rd Down Pct.	47.5	44.1
4th Down: Made/Att	4/10	10/18
4th Down Pct.	40.0	55.6
Possession Avg.	28:44	31:16
Total Net Yards	6333	5993
Avg. Per Game	395.8	374.6
Total Plays	1019	990
Avg. Per Play	6.2	6.1
Net Yards Rushing	1862	2337
Avg. Per Game	116.4	146.1
Total Rushes	387	469
Net Yards Passing	4471	3656
Avg. Per Game	279.4	228.5
Sacked/Yards Lost	12/74	26/141
Gross Yards	4545	3797
Att./Completions	620/386	495/333
Completion Pct.	62.3	67.3
Had Intercepted	18	6
Punts/Average	46/46.7	52/46.4
Net Punting Avg.	46/37.8	52/39.6
Penalties/Yards	77/739	83/738
Fumbles/Ball Lost	18/12	15/7
Touchdowns	42	50
Rushing	15	26
Passing	25	20
Returns	2	4

2008 INDIVIDUAL STATISTICS

PASSING	Att.	Comp.	Yds.	Pct.	TD	Int.	Tkld.	Rate
Cutler	616	384	4526	62.3	25	18	11/69	86.0
Ramsey	3	2	19	66.7	0	0	1/5	84.0
Royal	1	0	0	0.0	0	0	0/0	39.6
Broncos	620	386	4545	62.3	25	18	12/74	85.9
Opponents	495	333	3797	67.3	20	6	26/141	98.5

SCORING	TD R	TD P	TD Rt	PAT	FG	Saf	PTS
Prater	0	0	0	39/40	25/34	0	114
Hillis	5	1	0	0/0	0/0	0	36
Marshall	0	6	0	0/0	0/0	0	36
Royal	0	5	0	0/0	0/0	0	32
Graham	0	4	0	0/0	0/0	0	24
Pittman	4	0	0	0/0	0/0	0	24
Scheffler	0	3	0	0/0	0/0	0	18
Stokley	0	3	0	0/0	0/0	0	18
Cutler	2	0	0	0/0	0/0	0	14
T. Bell	2	0	0	0/0	0/0	0	12
Fox	0	0	1	0/0	0/0	0	6
D. Jackson	0	1	0	0/0	0/0	0	6
N. Jackson	0	1	0	0/0	0/0	0	6
Pope	0	1	0	0/0	0/0	0	6
Torain	1	0	0	0/0	0/0	0	6
Webster	0	0	1	0/0	0/0	0	6
Young	1	0	0	0/0	0/0	0	6
Broncos	15	25	2	39/40	25/34	0	370
Opponents	26	20	4	48/48	32/35	1	448

2-Pt. Conversions: Cutler, Royal.
Broncos 2-2, Opponents 1-2.

RUSHING	No.	Yds	Avg	LG	TD
Hillis	68	343	5.0	19	5
Pittman	76	320	4.2	20	4
Young	61	303	5.0	49	1
T. Bell	44	249	5.7	37t	2
Cutler	57	200	3.5	18	2
Hall	35	144	4.1	16	0
Pope	17	130	7.6	24	0
Royal	11	109	9.9	71	0
Torain	15	69	4.6	19	1
Scheffler	1	-1	-1.0	-1	0
Marshall	2	-4	-2.0	7	0
Broncos	387	1862	4.8	71	15
Opponents	469	2337	5.0	65	26

RECEIVING	No.	Yds	Avg	LG	TD
Marshall	104	1265	12.2	47	6
Royal	91	980	10.8	93t	5
Stokley	49	528	10.8	36t	3
Scheffler	40	645	16.1	72	3
Graham	32	389	12.2	28t	4
Hillis	14	179	12.8	47	1
D. Jackson	12	190	15.8	48t	1
N. Jackson	11	84	7.6	19	1
Pittman	10	112	11.2	40	0
T. Bell	10	57	5.7	12	0
Martinez	3	32	10.7	12	0
Hall	3	25	8.3	11	0
Pope	3	24	8.0	16	1
Young	3	16	5.3	8	0
C. Jackson	1	19	19.0	19	0
Broncos	386	4545	11.8	93t	25
Opponents	333	3797	11.4	74	20

INTERCEPTIONS	No.	Yds	Avg	LG	TD
Bly	2	5	2.5	5	0
Barrett	1	34	34.0	34	0
Paymah	1	13	13.0	13	0
Thomas	1	11	11.0	11	0
C. Bailey	1	0	0.0	0	0
Broncos	6	63	10.5	34	0
Opponents	18	153	8.5	32t	2

PUNTING	No.	Yds.	Avg.	In 20	LG
Kern	46	2150	46.7	13	64
Broncos	46	2150	46.7	13	64
Opponents	52	2413	46.4	22	71

PUNT RETURNS	Ret	FC	Yds	Avg	LG	TD
Royal	14	10	140	10.0	36	0
Martinez	5	0	56	11.2	27	0
Haggan	1	0	0	0.0	0	0
Broncos	20	10	196	9.8	36	0
Opponents	28	6	330	11.8	89t	1

KICKOFF RETURNS	No.	Yds	Avg	LG	TD
Royal	23	600	26.1	95	0
Hall	21	469	22.3	28	0
C. Jackson	8	162	20.3	24	0
Young	8	176	22.0	31	0
Hillis	4	65	16.3	25	0
Russell	2	44	22.0	25	0
Mustard	1	17	17.0	17	0
Engelberger	1	9	9.0	9	0
T. Bell	1	8	8.0	8	0
Martinez	1	0	0.0	0	0
Putzier	1	0	0.0	0	0
Broncos	71	1550	21.8	95	0
Opponents	63	1554	24.7	103t	1

FIELD GOALS	1-19	20-29	30-39	40-49	50+
Prater	0/0	7/8	8/9	5/11	5/6
Broncos	0/0	7/8	8/9	5/11	5/6
Opponents	0/0	10/10	10/10	11/13	1/2

SACKS	No.
Dumervil	5.0
Ekuban	5.0
Peterson	3.0
Moss	2.5
D. Williams	2.5
Webster	2.0
Robertson	1.5
C. Bailey	1.0
Engelberger	1.0
Haggan	1.0
(group)	1.0
Winborn	0.5
Broncos	26.0
Opponents	12.0

RECORD HOLDERS

INDIVIDUAL RECORDS—CAREER

Category	Name	Performance
Rushing (Yds.)	Terrell Davis, 1995-2002	7,607
Passing (Yds.)	John Elway, 1983-1998	51,475
Passing (TDs)	John Elway, 1983-1998	300
Receiving (No.)	Rod Smith, 1995-2007	849
Receiving (Yds.)	Rod Smith, 1995-2007	11,389
Interceptions	Steve Foley, 1976-1986	44
Punting (Avg.)	Jim Fraser, 1962-64	45.2
Punt Return (Avg.)	Darrien Gordon, 1997-98	12.5
Kickoff Return (Avg.)	Abner Haynes, 1965-66	26.3
Field Goals	Jason Elam, 1993-2007	395
Touchdowns (Tot.)	Rod Smith, 1995-2007	71
Points	Jason Elam, 1993-2007	1,786
*Sacks	Simon Fletcher, 1985-1995	97.5

INDIVIDUAL RECORDS—SINGLE SEASON

Category	Name	Performance
Rushing (Yds.)	Terrell Davis, 1998	2,008
Passing (Yds.)	Jay Cutler, 2008	4,526
Passing (TDs)	John Elway, 1997	27
	Jake Plummer, 2004	27
Receiving (No.)	Rod Smith, 2001	113
Receiving (Yds.)	Rod Smith, 2000	1,602
Interceptions	Goose Gonsoulin, 1960	11
Punting (Avg.)	Tom Rouen, 1998	46.9
Punt Return (Avg.)	Floyd Little, 1967	16.9
Kickoff Return (Avg.)	Bill Thompson, 1969	28.5
Field Goals	Jason Elam, 1995, 2001	31
Touchdowns (Tot.)	Terrell Davis, 1998	23
Points	Terrell Davis, 1998	138
*Sacks	Simon Fletcher, 1992	16.0

INDIVIDUAL RECORDS—SINGLE GAME

Category	Name	Performance
Rushing (Yds.)	Mike Anderson, 12-3-00	251
Passing (Yds.)	Jake Plummer, 10-31-04	499
Passing (TDs)	Frank Tripucka, 10-28-62	5
	John Elway, 11-18-84	5
	Gus Frerotte, 11-19-00	5
Receiving (No.)	Brandon Marshall, 9-14-08	18
Receiving (Yds.)	Shannon Sharpe, 10-20-02	214
Interceptions	Goose Gonsoulin, 9-18-60	**4
	Willie Brown, 11-15-64	**4
	Deltha O'Neal, 10-7-01	**4
Field Goals	Gene Mingo, 10-6-63	5
	Rich Karlis, 11-20-83	5
	Jason Elam, 9-3-95, 10-13-02	5
Touchdowns (Tot.)	Clinton Portis, 12-7-03	5
Points	Clinton Portis, 12-7-03	30
*Sacks	Karl Mecklenburg, 9-15-85, 12-1-85	4.0
	Simon Fletcher, 11-4-90	4.0

**Sacks became an official statistic in 1982.*
***NFL Record*

DENVER BRONCOS

2009 VETERAN ROSTER

No.	Name	Pos.	Ht.	Wt.	Birthdate	NFL Exp.	College	Hometown	How Acq.	'08 Games/ Starts
31	Arrington, J.J.	RB	5-9	212	1/23/83	5	California	Rocky Mount, N.C.	UFA(Ariz)-'09	11/3*
99	Askew, Matthias	DT	6-5	302	7/1/82	3	Michigan State	Fort Lauderdale, Fla.	FA-'08	0*
97	Bailey, Boss	LB	6-3	232	10/14/79	7	Georgia	Folkston, Ga.	UFA(Det)-'08	6/6
24	Bailey, Champ	CB	6-0	192	6/22/78	11	Georgia	Folkston, Ga.	T(Wash)-'04	9/9
36	Barrett, Josh	S	6-3	225	11/22/84	2	Arizona State	Reno, Nev.	D7-'08	6/3
25	Bell, Josh	CB	5-11	177	1/8/85	2	Baylor	Dallas, Texas	FA-'08	9/5
28	Buckhalter, Correll	RB	6-0	217	10/6/78	9	Nebraska	Collins, Miss.	UFA(Phil)-'09	14/2*
78	Clady, Ryan	T	6-6	325	9/6/86	2	Boise State	Rialto, Calif.	D1-'08	16/16
93	Clemons, Nic	DT	6-6	300	2/3/80	3	Georgia	Griffin, Ga.	FA-'08	16/16
96	Crowder, Tim	DE	6-4	275	6/30/85	3	Texas	Tyler, Texas	D2-'07	6/0
54	Davis, Andra	LB	6-1	250	12/23/78	8	Florida	Live Oak, Fla.	UFA(Cle)-'09	16/16*
20	Dawkins, Brian	S	6-0	210	10/13/73	14	Clemson	Jacksonville, Fla.	UFA(Phil)-'09	16/16*
92	Dumervil, Elvis	DE	5-11	260	1/19/84	4	Louisville	Miami, Fla.	D4b-'06	16/15
91	Fields, Ronald	DT	6-2	315	9/13/81	5	Mississippi State	Bogalusa, La.	UFA(SF)-'09	16/0*
39	Fox, Vernon	S	5-10	203	10/9/79	8	Fresno State	Las Vegas, Nev.	FA-'08	10/3
10	Gaffney, Jabar	WR	6-1	200	12/1/80	8	Florida	Jacksonville, Fla.	UFA(NE)-'09	16/7*
21	Goodman, Andre	CB	5-10	190	8/11/78	8	South Carolina	Greenville, S.C.	UFA(Mia)-'09	16/16*
77	Gorin, Brandon	T	6-6	308	7/17/78	9	Purdue	Muncie, Ind.	UFA(StL)-'09	0*
89	Graham, Daniel	TE	6-3	257	11/16/78	8	Colorado	Denver, Colo.	UFA(NE)-'07	16/16
52	Green, Louis	LB	6-3	237	9/23/79	6	Alcorn State	Fayette, Miss.	FA-'03	12/0
58	Greisen, Nick	LB	6-1	250	8/10/79	8	Wisconsin	Sturgeon Bay, Wisc.	FA-'09	14/1*
57	Haggan, Mario	LB	6-3	252	3/3/80	7	Mississippi State	Clarksdale, Miss.	FA-'08	8/0
50	Hamilton, Ben	G/C	6-4	290	8/18/77	9	Minnesota	Minneapolis, Minn.	D4a-'01	16/16
74	Harris, Ryan	T	6-5	300	3/11/85	3	Notre Dame	St. Paul, Minn.	D3-'07	16/16
23	Hill, Renaldo	S	5-11	205	11/12/78	9	Michigan State	Detroit, Mich.	UFA(Mia)-'09	16/15*
22	Hillis, Peyton	FB	6-2	250	1/21/86	2	Arkansas	Conway, Ark.	D7b-'08	12/6
16	Jackson, Chad	WR	6-1	215	3/6/85	4	Florida	Hoover, Ala.	FA-'08	4/0
29	Jones, Herana-Daze	S	5-11	205	4/15/82	4	Indiana	Louisville, Ky.	FA-'08	5/0*
32	Jordan, LaMont	RB	5-10	230	11/11/78	9	Maryland	Forestville, Md.	UFA(NE)-'09	8/8*
1	Kern, Brett	P	6-3	205	2/17/86	2	Toledo	Grand Island, N.Y.	FA-'08	16/0
73	Kuper, Chris	G	6-4	302	12/19/82	4	North Dakota	Anchorage, Alaska	D5-'06	16/16
46	Larsen, Spencer	FB/LB	6-2	240	3/4/84	2	Arizona	Gilbert, Ariz.	D6-'08	14/3
67	Lichtensteiger, Kory	C	6-3	295	3/22/85	2	Bowling Green St.	Van Wert, Ohio	D4a-'08	16/0
15	Marshall, Brandon	WR	6-4	230	3/23/84	4	Central Florida	Winter Park, Fla.	D4a-'06	15/15
98	McBean, Ryan	DE	6-5	290	4/23/84	2	Oklahoma State	Euless, Texas	FA-'08	0*
60	McChesney, Matt	G	6-4	307	11/6/81	3	Colorado	Niwot, Colo.	FA-'09	1/0*
94	Moss, Jarvis	DE	6-6	265	8/3/84	3	Florida	Denton, Texas	D1-'07	12/0
72	Murray, Pat	G	6-3	310	10/31/84	2	Truman State	Pocahontas, Iowa	PS(Sea)-'08	0*
71	Oldenburg, Clint	T	6-5	300	9/9/83	2	Colorado State	Campbell County, Wyo.	FA-'08	0*
8	t- Orton, Kyle	QB	6-4	216	11/14/82	5	Purdue	Runnels, Iowa	T(Chi)-'09	15/15
69	Parker, J'Vonne	DT	6-4	325	6/7/82	5	Rutgers	Newark, N.J.	FA-'09	1/0*
66	Paxton, Lonie	LS	6-2	260	3/13/78	10	Sacramento State	Corona, Calif.	UFA(NE)-'09	16/0*
90	Peterson, Kenny	DT	6-3	300	11/21/78	7	Ohio State	Canton, Ohio	FA-'06	16/1
76	Polumbus, Tyler	T	6-8	310	4/10/85	2	Colorado	Greenwood Village, Colo.	FA-'08	15/0
75	Powell, Carlton	DT	6-2	300	8/14/85	2	Virginia Tech	Chesapeake, Va.	D5b-'08	0*
5	Prater, Matt	K	5-10	188	8/10/84	3	Central Florida	Estero, Fla.	PS(Mia)-'07	16/0
87	Putzier, Jeb	TE	6-4	251	1/20/79	8	Boise State	Eagle, Idaho	FA-'08	8/1*
95	Reid, Darrell	DL/LB	6-2	288	6/20/82	5	Minnesota	Freehold, N.J.	UFA(Ind)-'09	16/0*
19	Royal, Eddie	WR	5-10	182	5/21/86	2	Virginia Tech	Chantilly, Va.	D2-'08	15/15
88	Scheffler, Tony	TE	6-5	250	2/15/83	4	Western Michigan	Chelsea, Mich.	D2-'06	13/7
2	Simms, Chris	QB	6-4	220	8/29/80	7	Texas	Franklin Lakes, N.J.	UFA(Tenn)-'09	1/0*
14	Stokley, Brandon	WR	5-11	192	6/23/76	11	Southwestern Louisiana	Lafayette, La.	FA-'07	15/2
79	Thomas, Marcus	DT	6-3	305	9/23/85	3	Florida	Jacksonville, Fla.	D4-'07	16/16
42	Torain, Ryan	RB	6-1	225	8/10/86	2	Arizona State	Shawnee Mission, Kan.	D5a-'08	2/1
43	Walker, Darius	RB	5-11	205	10/21/85	2	Notre Dame	Buford, Ga.	FA-'09	0*
62	Wiegmann, Casey	C	6-2	285	7/20/73	14	Iowa	Parkersburg, Iowa	UFA(KC)-'08	16/16
55	Williams, D.J.	LB	6-1	242	7/20/82	6	Miami	Concord, Calif.	D1-'04	11/11
26	Williams, Jack	CB	5-9	185	3/27/85	2	Kent State	Norfolk, Va.	D4b-'08	14/0
17	Willis, Matt	WR	5-11	190	4/13/84	2	UCLA	Anaheim, Calif.	FA-'08	0*
59	Woodyard, Wesley	LB	6-1	230	7/21/86	2	Kentucky	LaGrange, Ga.	FA-'08	16/6

* Arrington played 11 games with Arizona in '08; Askew last active with Cincinnati in '05; Buckhalter played 14 games with Philadelphia; Davis played 16 games with Cleveland; Dawkins played 16 games with Philadelphia; Fields played 16 games with San Francisco; Gaffney played 16 games with New England; Goodman played 16 games with Miami; Gorin missed '08 season with St. Louis because of injury; Greisen played 14 games with Baltimore; Hill played 16 games with Miami; Jones played 3 games with Cincinnati and 2 with Denver; Jordan played 8 games with New England; McBean last active with Pittsburgh in '07; McChesney played 1 game with Miami; Oldenburg last active with N.Y. Jets in '07; Orton played 15 games with Chicago; Parker played 1 game with Carolina; Paxton played 16 games with New England; Powell missed '08 season because of injury; Putzier played 6 games with Seattle; Reid played 16 games with Indianapolis; Simms played 1 game with Tennessee; Walker inactive for 5 games with Houston; Willis last active with Baltimore in '07.

t- Broncos traded for Orton (Chi).

Players lost through free agency (2)—CB Karl Paymah (Minn; 16 games in '08), QB Patrick Ramsey (Tenn; 1).

Traded—QB Jay Cutler (16 games in '08) to Chicago.

Also played with Broncos in '08—S Hamza Abdullah (1 game), RB Tatum Bell (7), CB Dre' Bly (16), RB Cory Boyd (1), DE Ebenezer Ekuban (15), DE John Engelberger (15), RB Andre Hall (8), WR Darrell Jackson (12), TE Nate Jackson (10), LB Niko Koutouvides (14), TE/LS Mike Leach (16), S Calvin Lowry (11), S Marquand Manuel (16), WR Glenn Martinez (2), S Marlon McCree (8), TE Chad Mustard (8), RB Michael Pittman (8), RB P.J. Pope (5), DT Dewayne Robertson (15), S Roderick Rogers (3), WR Clifford Russell (2), DT Josh Shaw (5), LB Nate Webster (13), LB Jamie Winborn (16), RB Selvin Young (8).

2009 FIRST-YEAR ROSTER

Name	Pos.	Ht.	Wt.	Birthdate	College	Hometown	How Acq.
Ayers, Robert	DE	6-3	272	9/6/85	Tennessee	Bennettsville, S.C.	D1b
Baker, Chris	NT	6-2	326	10/8/87	Hampton	Windsor, Conn.	FA
Brandstater, Tom	QB	6-5	222	10/21/84	Fresno State	Turlock, Calif.	D6
Branson, Marquez	TE	6-3	248	2/14/87	Central Arkansas	Starkville, Miss.	FA
Bruton, David	S	6-2	219	7/23/87	Notre Dame	Miamisburg, Ohio	D4a
Bryant, Stanley	T	6-5	282	5/7/85	East Carolina	Goldsboro, N.C.	FA
Carter, Tony	CB	5-9	177	5/24/86	Florida State	Jacksonville, Fla.	FA
Colquitt, Britton	P	6-3	205	3/20/85	Tennessee	Knoxville, Tenn.	FA
Davis, Rulon	DE	6-5	281	6/16/83	California	Covina, Calif.	FA
Erickson, Mitch (1)	G	6-6	290	5/14/85	South Dakota State	Hutchinson, Minn.	FA-'08
Gordon, Marcus	T	6-5	298	6/20/84	Kentucky State	Memphis, Tenn.	FA
Grimes, David	WR	5-10	177	12/31/86	Notre Dame	Detroit, Mich.	FA
Johnson, D.J.	CB	6-2	200	11/7/85	Jackson State	LaMarque, Texas	FA
Kelley, Braxton	LB	6-0	230	10/24/86	Kentucky	LaGrange, Ga.	FA
McBath, Darcel	S	6-0	198	10/28/85	Texas Tech	Gainesville, Texas	D2b
McKinley, Kenny	WR	6-0	189	1/31/87	South Carolina	Austell, Ga.	D5
Moore, Kestahn	WR	5-10	207	4/13/87	Florida	Arlington, Texas	FA
Moreno, Knowshon	RB	5-11	205	7/16/87	Georgia	Middletown, N.J.	D1a
Moulton, Rashod (1)	CB	5-11	184	11/6/79	Fort Valley State	St. Petersburg, Fla.	FA-'08
Olsen, Seth	G	6-4	306	12/17/85	Iowa	Omaha, Neb.	D4b
Pedescleaux, Everette	DE	6-6	305	1/19/85	Northern Iowa	Plymouth, Minn.	FA
Quinn, Richard	TE	6-4	260	9/6/86	North Carolina	Maple Heights, Ohio	D2c
Robinson, Lee	LB	6-3	245	4/23/87	Alcorn State	Liberty, Miss.	FA
Schlueter, Blake	C	6-3	284	4/22/86	Texas Christian	Ganado, Texas	D7
Schweiger, Jeffrey	LB	6-5	276	1/1/86	San Jose State	San Jose, Calif.	FA
Shelton, Travis	WR	5-11	185	4/23/85	Temple	Plantation, Fla.	FA
Smith, Alphonso	CB	5-9	193	10/20/85	Wake Forest	Pahokee, Fla.	D2a
Swift, Nate	WR	6-2	195	8/24/85	Nebraska	Hutchinson, Minn.	FA
Taylor, Lucas	WR	6-0	185	9/28/86	Tennessee	Lafayette, La.	FA

The term NFL Rookie is defined as a player who is in his first season of professional football and has not been on the roster of another professional football team for any regular-season or postseason games. A Rookie is designated by an "R" on NFL rosters. Players who have been active in another professional football league or players who have NFL experience, including either preseason training camp or being on an Active List or Inactive List, or on Reserve/Injured or Reserve/Physically Unable to Perform for fewer than six regular-season games, are termed NFL First-Year Players. An NFL First-Year Player is designated by a "1" on NFL rosters. Thereafter, a player is credited with an additional year of experience for each season in which he accumulates six games on the Active List or Inactive List, or on Reserve/Injured or Reserve/Physically Unable to Perform.

Log on to www.denverbroncos.com for an up-to-date roster.

DENVER BRONCOS

COACHING STAFF

Head Coach, Josh McDaniels

Pro Career: Became the twelfth head coach in Broncos history on January 12, 2009. McDaniels joins the Broncos after spending the previous eight seasons (2001-08) with the New England Patriots, including the last three years (2006-08) as the club's offensive coordinator/quarterbacks coach. McDaniels helped the Patriots win three Super Bowls, four AFC championships and six division titles while posting the NFL's best overall record (111-34) during his eight years in New England. The Patriots had seven 10-win seasons with McDaniels on staff, including the 2007 campaign when New England became the first team in NFL history to post a 16-0 regular-season record. McDaniels joined the Patriots in 2001 as a personnel/coaching assistant. In 2003 he acquired additional responsibility working with the defensive backs. In 2004 he acted as the club's quarterbacks coach and on January 20, 2006 the Patriots promoted McDaniels to offensive coordinator/quarterbacks coach. McDaniels is the fifth-youngest coach in NFL history (32 years, 8 months) at the time of his hire. He is the youngest active coach in the league and the youngest in the history of the Denver Broncos. Career record: 0-0.

Background: McDaniels was a quarterback and kicker at Canton McKinley High School (Canton, Ohio). Was a quarterback/wide receiver at John Carroll from 1995-98. No pro playing experience. He was a college coach at Michigan State in 1999.

Personal: Born in Barberton, Ohio on April 22, 1976. He and his wife, Laura, have one son Jack Thomas, and one daughter, Maddie.

ASSISTANT COACHES

Clancy Barone, tight ends; born July 26, 1963, San Andreas, Calif. Offensive lineman Cal State-Sacramento 1981-82, Nevada 1985-86. No pro playing experience. College coach: American River (Calif.) J.C. 1987-89, Cal State-Sacramento 1990-92, Texas A&M 1993, Eastern Illinois 1994-96, Wyoming 1997-99, Houston 2000-02, Texas State 2003. Pro coach: Atlanta Falcons 2004-06, San Diego Chargers 2007-08, joined Broncos in 2009.

Keith Burns, coaching assistant/special teams; born May 16, 1972, Greeleyville, S.C. Linebacker Oklahoma State 1991-94. Pro linebacker Denver Broncos 1994-98, 2000-03, 2005-06, Chicago Bears 1999, Tampa Bay Buccaneers 2004. Pro coach: Joined Broncos in 2007.

Rick Dennison, offensive line; born June 22, 1958, Kalispell, Mont. Tight end Colorado State 1976-79. Pro linebacker Denver Broncos 1982-1990. Pro coach: Joined Broncos in 1995.

Ed Donatell, secondary; born February 4, 1957, Akron, Ohio. Defensive back Glenville (W. Va.) State 1975-78. College coach: Kent State 1979-1980, Washington 1981-82, 2008, Pacific 1983-85, Idaho 1986-88, Cal State-Fullerton 1989. Pro coach: New York Jets 1990-94, Denver Broncos 1995-99, Green Bay Packers 2000-03, Atlanta Falcons 2004-06, re-joined Broncos in 2009.

Adam Gase, wide receivers; born March 29, 1978, Ypsilanti, Mich. Attended Michigan State. No college or pro playing experience. College coach: Louisiana State 2000-02. Pro coach: Detroit Lions 2003-07, San Francisco 49ers 2008, joined Broncos in 2009.

Don Martindale, linebackers, born May 19, 1963, Dayton, Ohio. Linebacker Defiance College 1984-86. No pro playing experience. College coach: Defiance 1987, Notre Dame 1994-95, Cincinnati 1996-98, Western Illinois 1999, Western Kentucky 2000-02. Pro coach: Oakland Raiders 2004-08, joined Broncos in 2009.

Mike McCoy, offensive coordinator/quarterbacks; born April 1, 1972, San Francisco. Quarterback Long Beach State 1990-91, Utah 1992-94. Pro quarterback Amsterdam Admirals (NFLE) 1997, Calgary Stampeders (CFL) 1999. Pro coach: Carolina Panthers 1999-2008, joined Broncos in 2009.

Ben McDaniels, coaching assistant, born June 6, 1980, Barberton, Ohio. Quarterback Kent State 1999-2002. No pro playing experience. College coach: Minnesota 2004-05. Pro coach: Joined Broncos in 2009.

Mike Nolan, defensive coordinator; born March 7, 1965, Haverhill, Mass. Safety Oregon 1978-1980. No pro playing experience. College Coach: Oregon 1981, Stanford 1982-83, Rice 1984-85, Louisiana State 1986. Pro coach: Denver Broncos 1987-1992, New York Giants 1993-96, Washington Redskins 1997-99, New York Jets 2000, Baltimore Ravens 2001-04, San Francisco 2005-08 (head coach), re-joined Broncos in 2009.

Wayne Nunnely, defensive line, born March 29, 1952, Los Angeles. Fullback Nevada-Las Vegas 1972-75. No pro playing experience. College coach: Nevada-Las Vegas 1976, 1982-89 (head coach 1986-89), Cal Poly-Pomona 1977-78, Cal State-Fullerton 1979, Pacific 1980-81, Southern California 1991-92, UCLA 1993-94. Pro coach: New Orleans Saints 1995-96, San Diego Chargers 1997-2008, joined Broncos in 2009.

Roman Phifer, asst. coach/linebackers, born March 5, 1968, Charlotte, N.C. Linebacker UCLA 1987-1990. Linebacker Los Angeles/St. Louis Rams 1991-98, New York Jets 1999-2000, New England Patriots 2001-04, New York Giants 2005. Pro coach: Joined Broncos in 2009.

Mike Priefer, special teams; born August 21, 1966, Cleveland. Attended U.S. Naval Academy. No college or pro playing experience. College coach: Navy 1994-96, Youngstown State 1997-98, Virginia Military Institute 1999, Northern Illinois 2000-01. Pro coach: Jacksonville Jaguars 2002, New York Giants 2003-05, Kansas City Chiefs 2007-08, joined Broncos in 2009.

Jay Rodgers, coaching assistant, born August 29, 1976, St. Paul, Minn. Quarterback Indiana 1996-98, Missouri State 1999. No pro playing experience. College coach: Missouri State 2004, Stephen F. Austin 2005-06, Iowa State 2007-08. Pro coach: Joined Broncos in 2009.

Greg Saporta, asst. strength and conditioning; born February 2, 1957, New York, N.Y. Wide receiver Buffalo State 1977-79. No pro playing experience. College coach: Florida 1981-88, 1993-94, North Carolina 1989-1992. Pro coach: Joined Broncos in 1995.

Mark Thewes, asst. to the head coach; born September 13, 1976, Canton, Ohio. Attended Miami (Ohio). No college or pro playing experience. Pro coach: Joined Broncos in 2009.

Bobby Turner, running backs; born May 6, 1949, East Chicago, Ind. Defensive back Indiana State 1968-1971. No pro playing experience. College coach: Indiana State 1975-1982, Fresno State 1983-88, Ohio State 1989-1990, Purdue 1991-94. Pro coach: Joined Broncos in 1995.

Rich Tuten, strength and conditioning; born December 30, 1953, Columbia, S.C. Nose guard Clemson 1976-78. No pro playing experience. College coach: Florida 1979-1988, 1993-94, North Carolina 1989-1992. Pro coach: Joined Broncos in 1995.

American Football Conference
South Division
Team Colors: Deep Steel Blue, Battle Red, and Liberty White
Two Reliant Park
Houston, Texas 77054
Telephone: (832) 667-2000

2009 SCHEDULE

PRESEASON

Aug. 15	at Kansas City	7:00
Aug. 22	**New Orleans**	7:00
Aug. 31	**Minnesota**	7:00
Sep. 4	at Tampa Bay	6:00

REGULAR SEASON

Sep. 13	**N.Y. Jets**	12:00
Sep. 20	at Tennessee	12:00
Sep. 27	**Jacksonville**	12:00
Oct. 4	**Oakland**	12:00
Oct. 11	at Arizona	1:15
Oct. 18	at Cincinnati	1:00
Oct. 25	**San Francisco**	12:00
Nov. 1	at Buffalo	1:00
Nov. 8	at Indianapolis	1:00
Nov. 15	BYE	
Nov. 23	**Tennessee** (Mon.)	7:30
Nov. 29	**Indianapolis**	12:00
Dec. 6	at Jacksonville	1:00
Dec. 13	**Seattle**	12:00
Dec. 20	at St. Louis	12:00
Dec. 27	at Miami	1:00
Jan. 3	**New England**	12:00

Stadium: Reliant Stadium (opened in 2002) • **Capacity:** 71,054 Houston, Texas 77054
Playing Surface: Grass
Training Camp: Methodist Training Center

RELIANT STADIUM

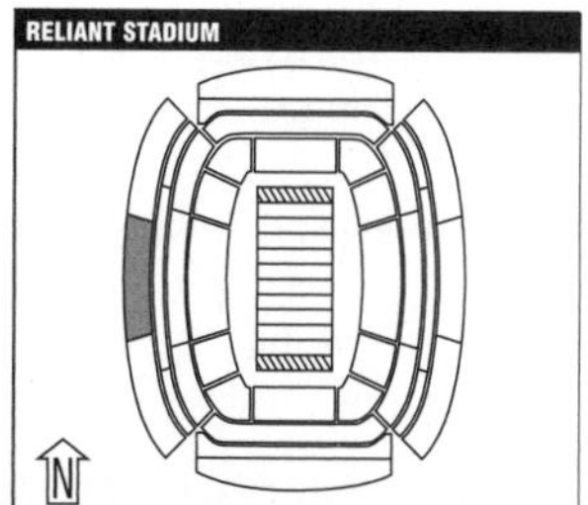

CLUB OFFICIALS

Chairman and CEO: Robert C. McNair
Vice Chairman: Philip J. Burguiéres
Vice Chairman: D. Cal McNair
General Manager: Rick Smith
President: Jamey Rootes
Senior Vice President, Treasurer and CFO: Scott Schwinger
Senior Vice President, General Counsel and CAO: Suzie Thomas
Vice President and Controller: Marilan Logan
Vice President of Security: Ryan Reichert
Vice President, Ticketing and Event Management: John Schriever
Vice President, Sales and Marketing: John Vidalin
Vice President, Finance: Greg Watson
Vice President, Communications: Tony Wyllie
Director of Football Administration: Chris Olsen
Director of Football Operations: Lloyd Richards
Director of Player Development: Sean Washington
Director of College Scouting: Dale Strahm
Director of Pro Personnel: Brian Gardner
Associate Director of Pro Scouting: Bobby Grier
Pro Scouts: Brandon Hunt, Kevin Murphy
Coordinator of College Scouting: Mike Maccagnan
National College Scout: Ed Lambert
College Scouts: Bob Beers, Larry Bryan, Jon Carr, Mike Martin, Bob Merritt
Head Athletic Trainer: Geoff Kaplan
Coordinator of Rehabilitation: Roland Ramirez
Assistant Athletic Trainer: Jon Ishop
Director of Equipment Services: Jay Brunetti
Equipment Services Assistant: Mike Parson
Equipment Services Assistant: Christian Snell
Director of Video Operations: Joe Malota
Assistant Director of Video Operations: Bob Ford
Video Operations Assistant: Robert Wells
Director of Public Relations: Kevin Cooper
Director of Corporate Development: Greg Grissom
Risk Manager: Jan Kelly
Corporate Counsel: Greg Kondritz
Director of Human Resources: Glenda Morrison
Director of Event Services: Diane Crossey
Director of Advertising and Branding: Melissa Rentz
Director of Media Products: Nick Schenck
Director of Information Technology: Jeff Schmitz
Assistant Treasurer: Jon Southern
Director of Premium Seating: Brian Varnadoe

COACHING HISTORY
(40-72-0)

2002-05	Dom Capers	18-46-0
2006-08	Gary Kubiak	22-26-0

PAID ATTENDANCE

Home 548,894 Away 498,805
Total 1,047,699
Single-game home record, 70,758 (12/21/03)
Single-season home record, 555,421 (2004)

2009 DRAFT CHOICES

Round	Name	Pos.	College
1	Brian Cushing	LB	Southern California
2	Connor Barwin	DE	Cincinnati
3	Antoine Caldwell	C	Alabama
4	Glover Quin	DB	New Mexico
	Anthony Hill	TE	North Carolina St.
5	James Casey	TE	Rice
6	Brice McCain	DB	Utah
7	Troy Nolan	S	Arizona State

HOUSTON TEXANS

2008 TEAM RECORD

PRESEASON (2-2)

Date	Result	Opponent
8/9	W 19-16	Denver
8/16	W 31-27	at New Orleans
8/22	L 22-23	at Dallas
8/28	L 6-16	Tampa Bay

REGULAR SEASON (8-8)

Date	Result	Opponent
9/7	L 17-38	at Pittsburgh
9/21	L 12-31	at Tennessee
9/28	L 27-30	at Jacksonville (OT)
10/5	L 27-31	Indianapolis
10/12	W 29-28	Miami
10/19	W 28-21	Detroit
10/26	W 35-6	Cincinnati
11/2	L 21-28	at Minnesota
11/9	L 13-41	Baltimore
11/16	L 27-33	at Indianapolis
11/23	W 16-6	at Cleveland
12/1	W 30-17	Jacksonville
12/7	W 24-21	at Green Bay
12/14	W 13-12	Tennessee
12/21	L 16-27	at Oakland
12/28	W 31-24	Chicago

(OT) Overtime

SCORE BY PERIODS

Texans	77	109	78	102	0 —	366
Opponents	84	85	86	136	3 —	394

2008 TEAM STATISTICS

	Texans	Opp.
Total First Downs	340	300
Rushing	106	114
Passing	210	167
Penalty	24	19
3rd Down: Made/Att	83/197	74/188
3rd Down Pct.	42.1	39.4
4th Down: Made/Att	14/23	10/13
4th Down Pct.	60.9	76.9
Possession Avg.	31:57	28:03
Total Net Yards	6113	5385
Avg. Per Game	382.1	336.6
Total Plays	1019	935
Avg. Per Play	6.0	5.8
Net Yards Rushing	1846	1962
Avg. Per Game	115.4	122.6
Total Rushes	432	439
Net Yards Passing	4267	3423
Avg. Per Game	266.7	213.9
Sacked/Yards Lost	32/207	25/175
Gross Yards	4474	3598
Att./Completions	555/367	471/294
Completion Pct.	66.1	62.4
Had Intercepted	20	12
Punts/Average	53/42.3	67/44.4
Net Punting Avg.	53/35.2	67/37.2
Penalties/Yards	80/664	81/659
Fumbles/Ball Lost	28/12	19/10
Touchdowns	40	45
Rushing	16	18
Passing	21	24
Returns	3	3

2008 INDIVIDUAL STATISTICS

PASSING	Att.	Comp.	Yds.	Pct.	TD	Int.	Tkld.	Rate
Schaub	380	251	3043	66.1	15	10	23/149	92.7
Rosenfels	174	116	1431	66.7	6	10	9/58	79.5
Turk	1	0	0	0.0	0	0	0/0	39.6
Texans	555	367	4474	66.1	21	20	32/207	88.4
Opponents	471	294	3598	62.4	24	12	25/175	92.3

SCORING	TD R	TD P	TD Rt	PAT	FG	Saf	PTS
K. Brown	0	0	0	37/37	29/33	0	124
Slaton	9	1	0	0/0	0/0	0	60
A. Johnson	0	8	0	0/0	0/0	0	50
Walter	0	8	0	0/0	0/0	0	48
Green	3	0	0	0/0	0/0	0	18
Anderson	0	2	0	0/0	0/0	0	12
Daniels	0	2	0	0/0	0/0	0	12
Jones	0	0	2	0/0	0/0	0	12
Schaub	2	0	0	0/0	0/0	0	12
Leach	1	0	0	0/0	0/0	0	6
Moats	1	0	0	0/0	0/0	0	6
Reeves	0	0	1	0/0	0/0	0	6
Texans	16	21	3	37/37	29/33	0	366
Opponents	18	24	3	43/43	25/29	1	394

2-Pt. Conversions: A. Johnson.
Texans 1-3, Opponents 2-2.

RUSHING	No.	Yds	Avg	LG	TD
Slaton	268	1282	4.8	71t	9
Green	74	294	4.0	14	3
Moats	26	94	3.6	12	1
Schaub	31	68	2.2	10	2
Rosenfels	11	37	3.4	15	0
Taylor	14	37	2.6	17	0
Walter	3	23	7.7	13	0
Turk	1	18	18.0	18	0
Leach	1	1	1.0	1t	1
Sapp	2	-3	-1.5	0	0
Jones	1	-5	-5.0	-5	0
Texans	432	1846	4.3	71t	16
Opponents	439	1962	4.5	41t	18

RECEIVING	No.	Yds	Avg	LG	TD
A. Johnson	115	1575	13.7	65	8
Daniels	70	862	12.3	35	2
Walter	60	899	15.0	61	8
Slaton	50	377	7.5	46	1
Anderson	19	241	12.7	65	2
An. Davis	13	213	16.4	49	0
Leach	12	103	8.6	22	0
Dreessen	11	77	7.0	13	0
Green	11	32	2.9	8	0
Jones	3	81	27.0	45	0
Moats	3	14	4.7	5	0
Texans	367	4474	12.2	65	21
Opponents	294	3598	12.2	96t	24

INTERCEPTIONS	No.	Yds	Avg	LG	TD
Reeves	4	108	27.0	44t	1
Wilson	2	36	18.0	19	0
Bennett	2	26	13.0	23	0
Du. Robinson	2	0	0.0	0	0
Weaver	1	8	8.0	8	0
Diles	1	0	0.0	0	0
Texans	12	178	14.8	44t	1
Opponents	20	221	11.1	99t	1

PUNTING	No.	Yds.	Avg.	In 20	LG
Turk	53	2240	42.3	17	59
Texans	53	2240	42.3	17	59
Opponents	67	2978	44.4	25	74

PUNT RETURNS	Ret	FC	Yds	Avg	LG	TD
Jones	32	17	386	12.1	73t	2
Texans	32	17	386	12.1	73t	2
Opponents	21	14	235	11.2	80t	1

KICKOFF RETURNS	No.	Yds	Avg	LG	TD
An. Davis	43	993	23.1	50	0
Jones	13	280	21.5	30	0
Moats	9	212	23.6	32	0
Leach	3	34	11.3	15	0
Taylor	1	17	17.0	17	0
Sapp	1	7	7.0	7	0
White	1	7	7.0	7	0
Walter	1	0	0.0	0	0
Texans	72	1550	21.5	50	0
Opponents	73	1630	22.3	49	0

FIELD GOALS	1-19	20-29	30-39	40-49	50+
K. Brown	0/0	9/10	10/10	8/10	2/3
Texans	0/0	9/10	10/10	8/10	2/3
Opponents	0/0	3/3	11/12	7/9	4/5

SACKS	No.
M. Williams	12.0
Bulman	4.0
Cochran	2.0
Barber	1.0
Bentley	1.0
Diles	1.0
T. Johnson	1.0
Okoye	1.0
Ryans	1.0
Thompson	1.0
Texans	25.0
Opponents	32.0

RECORD HOLDERS

INDIVIDUAL RECORDS—CAREER

Category	Name	Performance
Rushing (Yds.)	Domanick Williams, 2003-06	3,195
Passing (Yds.)	David Carr, 2002-06	13,391
Passing (TDs)	David Carr, 2002-06	59
Receiving (No.)	Andre Johnson, 2003-08	486
Receiving (Yds.)	Andre Johnson, 2003-08	6,379
Interceptions	Dunta Robinson, 2004-08	13
Punting (Avg.)	Chad Stanley, 2002-06	41.0
Punt Return (Avg.)	Jacoby Jones, 2007-08	10.8
Kickoff Return (Avg.)	André Davis, 2007-08	26.1
Field Goals	Kris Brown, 2002-08	151
Touchdowns (Tot.)	Andre Johnson, 2003-08	33
Points	Kris Brown, 2002-08	661
*Sacks	Mario Williams, 2006-08	30.5

INDIVIDUAL RECORDS—SINGLE SEASON

Category	Name	Performance
Rushing (Yds.)	Steve Slaton, 2008	1,282
Passing (Yds.)	David Carr, 2004	3,531
Passing (TDs)	David Carr, 2004	16
Receiving (No.)	Andre Johnson, 2008	115
Receiving (Yds.)	Andre Johnson, 2008	1,575
Interceptions	Marcus Coleman, 2003	7
Punting (Avg.)	Matt Turk, 2008	42.3
Punt Return (Avg.)	Jacoby Jones, 2008	12.1
Kickoff Return (Avg.)	André Davis, 2007	30.3
Field Goals	Kris Brown, 2008	29
Touchdowns (Tot.)	Domanick Williams, 2004	14
Points	Kris Brown, 2008	124
*Sacks	Mario Williams, 2007	14.0

INDIVIDUAL RECORDS—SINGLE GAME

Category	Name	Performance
Rushing (Yds.)	Domanick Williams, 12-26-04	158
Passing (Yds.)	Matt Schaub, 12-7-08	414
Passing (TDs)	Sage Rosenfels, 10-21-07	4
Receiving (No.)	Andre Johnson, 10-10-04, 11-27-05	12
	Kevin Walter, 10-14-07	12
Receiving (Yds.)	Andre Johnson, 12-14-08	207
Interceptions	Aaron Glenn, 12-8-02	2
	Marcus Coleman, 9-7-03	2
	Kenny Wright, 9-28-03	2
	Dunta Robinson, 10-3-04	2
Field Goals	Kris Brown, 9-7-03, 12-4-05, 10-7-07	5
Touchdowns (Tot.)	Many times	2
	Last time by Andre Johnson, 12-28-08	
Points	Kris Brown, 10-7-07	16
*Sacks	Mario Williams, 12-13-07	3.5

**Sacks became an official statistic in 1982.*

HOUSTON TEXANS

2009 VETERAN ROSTER

No.	Name	Pos.	Ht.	Wt.	Birthdate	NFL Exp.	College	Hometown	How Acq.	'08 Games/ Starts
52	Adibi, Xavier	LB	6-2	232	10/18/84	2	Virginia Tech	Hampton, Va.	D4-'08	7/5
89	Anderson, David	WR	5-10	196	7/28/83	4	Colorado State	Thousand Oaks, Calif.	D7-'06	16/1
34	Barber, Dominique	S	6-0	212	8/2/86	2	Minnesota	Wayzata, Minn.	D6-'08	12/0
32	Bennett, Fred	CB	6-1	201	12/31/83	3	South Carolina	Manning, S.C.	D4-'07	16/6
57	Bentley, Kevin	LB	6-0	240	12/29/79	8	Northwestern	North Hills, Calif.	UFA(Sea)-'08	16/7
65	Brisiel, Mike	G	6-5	295	3/14/83	2	Colorado State	Fayetteville, Ark.	FA-'06	16/16
22	Brown, Chris	RB	6-3	235	4/17/81	7	Colorado	Naperville, Ill.	UFA(Tenn)-'08	0*
76	Brown, Duane	T	6-4	329	8/30/85	2	Virginia Tech	Richmond, Va.	D1-'08	16/16
3	Brown, Kris	K	5-11	206	12/23/76	11	Nebraska	Southlake, Texas	RFA(Pitt)-'02	16/0
87	#Bruener, Mark	TE	6-4	253	9/16/72	15	Washington	Olympia, Wash.	UFA(Pitt)-'04	2/0
93	Bulman, Tim	DE	6-4	275	10/31/82	3	Boston College	Dorchester, Mass.	FA-'06	14/0
78	Butler, Rashad	T	6-4	309	2/10/83	4	Miami	West Palm Beach, Fla.	W(Car)-07	0*
96	#Cochran, Earl	DE	6-5	282	4/19/81	4	Alabama State	Bessemer, Ala.	FA-'06	8/1
95	Cody, Shaun	DT	6-4	310	1/22/83	5	Southern California	Hacienda Heights, Calif.	UFA(Det)-'09	16/5*
53	Coley, Kevis	LB	6-1	241	6/23/82	2	Southern Mississippi	Palatka, Fla.	FA-'07	3/0
81	Daniels, Owen	TE	6-3	246	11/9/82	4	Wisconsin	Naperville, Ill.	D4-'06	16/16
11	Davis, André	WR	6-1	196	6/12/79	8	Virginia Tech	Niskayuna, N.Y.	UFA(Buff)-'07	12/0
58	Davis, Buster	LB	5-9	239	10/20/83	2	Florida State	Daytona Beach, Fla.	FA-'09	6/3*
54	Diles, Zac	LB	6-2	246	6/11/85	3	Kansas State	Tulare, Calif.	D7-'07	8/8
85	Dreessen, Joel	TE	6-4	244	7/26/82	4	Colorado State	Fort Morgan, Colo.	FA-'07	16/3
25	Ferguson, Nick	SS	5-11	201	11/27/74	10	Georgia Tech	Miami, Fla.	UFA(Den)-'08	14/9
46	Grigsby, Boomer	FB	5-11	249	11/15/81	5	Illinois State	Canton, Ill.	FA-'09	1/0*
31	Harrison, Brandon	FS	6-2	227	4/29/84	3	Stanford	Baton Rouge, La.	D5a-'07	16/6
62	#Jackson, Scott	T	6-4	294	1/19/79	5	Brigham Young	Rancho Palos Verdes, Calif.	FA-'06	0*
80	Johnson, Andre	WR	6-3	223	7/11/81	7	Miami	Miami, Fla.	D1-'03	16/16
99	Johnson, Travis	DT	6-3	311	4/26/82	5	Florida State	Sherman Oaks, Calif.	D1-'05	16/15
12	Jones, Jacoby	WR	6-2	200	7/11/84	3	Lane College	New Orleans, La.	D3-'07	16/0
50	June, Cato	LB	6-0	227	11/18/79	7	Michigan	Riverside, Calif.	FA-'09	16/14*
44	Leach, Vonta	FB	6-0	253	11/6/81	6	East Carolina	Rowland, N.C.	FA-'06	16/12
17	Martinez, Glenn	WR	6-1	190	11/30/81	4	Saginaw Valley	Tampa, Fla.	FA-'09	2/0*
75	McClover, Stanley	DE	6-2	263	12/16/84	4	Auburn	Ft. Lauderdale, Fla.	W(Car)-'08	1/0
21	Moats, Ryan	RB	5-8	210	12/17/82	5	Louisiana Tech	Dallas, Texas	FA-'08	9/0
28	Molden, Antwaun	CB	6-1	196	1/23/85	2	Eastern Kentucky	Cleveland, Ohio	D3a-'08	14/0
55	Myers, Chris	C	6-4	287	9/15/81	5	Miami	Miami, Fla.	T(Den)-'08	16/16
72	Nading, Jesse	DE	6-5	259	7/3/85	2	Colorado State	Highlands Ranch, Colo.	FA-'08	6/0
97	Okam, Frank	DT	6-5	337	10/16/85	2	Texas	Dallas, Texas	D5-'08	5/0
91	Okoye, Amobi	DT	6-2	306	6/10/87	3	Louisville	Huntsville, Ala.	D1-'07	14/12
7	Orlovsky, Dan	QB	6-5	230	8/18/83	5	Connecticut	Shelton, Conn.	UFA(Det)-'09	10/7*
48	#Pittman, Bryan	LS	6-3	265	1/20/77	7	Washington	Auburn, Wash.	FA-'03	12/0
42	Pittman, David	CB	5-11	185	10/14/83	4	Northwestern St. (La.)	Gramercy, La.	FA-'08	0*
69	Pitts, Chester	G	6-4	308	6/26/79	8	San Diego State	Inglewood, Calif.	D2-'02	16/16
35	Reeves, Jacques	CB	5-11	194	10/8/82	6	Purdue	Lancaster, Texas	UFA(Dall)-'08	16/16
66	Robinson, DelJuan	DT	6-3	303	7/1/84	2	Mississippi State	Hernando, Miss.	FA-'07	16/3
23	Robinson, Dunta	CB	5-10	182	4/11/82	6	South Carolina	Athens, Ga.	D1a-'04	11/6
59	Ryans, DeMeco	LB	6-1	245	7/28/84	4	Alabama	Bessemer, Ala.	D2-'06	16/16
37	#Sapp, Cecil	FB	5-11	229	12/23/78	7	Colorado State	Miami, Fla.	FA-'08	12/0
8	Schaub, Matt	QB	6-5	234	6/25/81	6	Virginia	West Chester, Pa.	T(Atl)-'07	11/11
20	Slaton, Steve	RB	5-9	203	1/4/86	2	West Virginia	Levittown, Pa.	D3b-'08	16/15
94	Smith, Antonio	DE	6-4	285	10/21/81	6	Oklahoma State	Oklahoma City, Okla.	UFA(Ariz)-'09	16/10*
68	Stevenson, Dan	G	6-5	300	10/4/82	2	Notre Dame	Barrington, Ill.	FA-'07	0*
64	Studdard, Kasey	G	6-3	299	7/1/84	3	Texas	Lone Tree, Colo.	D6-'07	2/0
51	Thompson, Chaun	LB	6-2	246	5/22/80	7	West Texas A&M	Mount Pleasant, Texas	UFA(Cle)-'08	15/0
1	Turk, Matt	P	6-5	245	6/16/68	14	Wisconsin-Whitewater	Greenfield, Wisc.	FA-'07	16/0
83	Walter, Kevin	WR	6-3	215	8/4/81	7	Eastern Michigan	Vernon Hills, Ill.	RFA(Cin)-'06	16/16
63	White, Chris	C	6-2	292	2/28/83	5	Southern Mississippi	Winona, Miss.	FA-'06	8/0
41	#Williams, Jimmy	CB	5-11	193	3/10/79	8	Vanderbilt	Baton Rouge, La.	FA-'08	0*
90	Williams, Mario	DE	6-6	283	1/31/85	4	North Carolina State	Richlands, N.C.	D1-'06	16/16
26	Wilson, Eugene	S	5-10	195	8/17/80	7	Illinois	Merrillville, Ind.	FA-'08	12/10
73	Winston, Eric	T	6-5	309	11/17/83	4	Miami	Midland, Texas	D3b-'06	16/16
92	#Zgonina, Jeff	DT	6-2	281	5/24/70	17	Purdue	Chicago, Ill.	UFA(Mia)-'07	16/2

* C. Brown missed '08 season because of injury; Butler was inactive for 16 games; Cody played 16 games with Detroit in '08; B. Davis played 6 games with Indianapolis; Grigsby played 1 game with Miami; Jackson missed '08 season because of injury; June played 16 games with Tampa Bay; Martinez played 2 games with Denver; Orlovsky played 10 games with Detroit; D. Pittman was inactive for 4 games with New Orleans and 2 games with Houston; Smith played 16 games with Arizona; Stevenson missed '08 season because of injury; J. Williams missed '08 season because of injury.

\# Unrestricted free agent; subject to developments.

Players lost through free agency (2): S C.C. Brown (NYG; 3 games in '08); CB DeMarcus Faggins (Tenn; 16).

Traded—QB Sage Rosenfels (6 games in '08) to Minnesota.

Also played with Texans in '08—S Will Demps (9 games), RB Ahman Green (8), LB Morlon Greenwood (15), DE N.D. Kalu (2), T Ephraim Salaam (13), RB Chris Taylor (3), DE Anthony Weaver (16).

2009 FIRST-YEAR ROSTER

Name	Pos.	Ht.	Wt.	Birthdate	College	Hometown	How Acq.
Barwin, Connor	DE	6-4	256	10/15/86	Cincinnati	Detroit, Mich.	D2
Bell, Aubrey	WR	6-3	216	12/9/86	Mississippi State	Prichard, Ala.	FA
Brantly, Justin	P	6-3	241	3/28/86	Texas A&M	Sealy, Texas	FA
Brink, Alex (1)	QB	6-2	212	6/2/85	Washington State	Eugene, Ore.	D7-'08
Caldwell, Antoine	C	6-3	307	4/19/86	Alabama	Montgomery, Ala.	D3
Casey, James	TE	6-3	243	9/22/84	Rice	Azle, Texas	D5
Cushing, Brian	LB	6-3	243	1/24/87	Southern California	Oradell, N.J.	D1
Davis, A.J. (1)	CB	5-10	192	5/29/83	North Carolina State	Durham, N.C.	FA
Dedrick, Doug	T	6-5	285	12/20/86	Iowa State	Tempe, Ariz.	FA
Foster, Arian	RB	6-1	215	8/24/86	Tennessee	San Diego, Calif.	FA
Harris, Clark (1)	TE	6-5	256	7/10/84	Rutgers	Manahawkin, N.J.	FA-'08
Helms, Brett	C	6-2	270	4/16/86	Louisiana State	Stuttgart, Ark.	FA
Hill, Anthony	TE	6-6	265	1/2/85	North Carolina State	Houston, Texas	D4b
Jamison, Tim	DE	6-3	263	2/26/86	Michigan	Riverdale, Ill.	FA
Jenkins, Darnell (1)	WR	5-10	188	12/31/82	Miami	Miami, Fla.	FA-'08
Johnson, Jeremiah	RB	5-9	210	2/15/87	Oregon	Los Angeles, Calif.	FA
Jones, Mike	WR	6-4	210	9/9/86	Arizona State	Sugar Land, Texas	FA
Leonard, Josh	DT	6-3	305	7/22/87	Hawaii	Elverta, Calif.	FA
McCain, Brice	CB	5-9	182	12/10/86	Utah	Terrell, Texas	D6
Nolan, Troy	S	6-2	207	9/7/86	Arizona State	Woodland Hills, Calif.	D7
Quin, Glover	CB	6-0	200	1/15/86	New Mexico	Summitt, Miss.	D4a
Richardson, Matterral (1)	CB	6-0	195	6/30/85	Arkansas	Marlin, Texas	FA-'08
Simmons, Mark (1)	WR	5-10	187	1/16/84	Kansas	DeSoto, Texas	FA-'08
Stenavich, Adam (1)	T	6-4	308	3/11/83	Michigan	Marshfield, Wisc.	FA-'08
Verdell, Toddrick	LB	6-3	225	11/21/85	Florida State	Hartwell, Ga.	FA
Visser, Jake	DT	6-2	275	2/20/86	Ferris State	Coopersville, Mich.	FA
Walker, Brandon	G	6-3	284	12/26/85	Oklahoma	Detroit, Mich.	FA
Washburn, Cliff (1)	T	6-5	293	1/25/80	The Citadel	Harriet, N.C.	FA
Watkins, Jason	T	6-6	302	6/10/85	Florida	Lakeland, Fla.	FA

The term NFL Rookie is defined as a player who is in his first season of professional football and has not been on the roster of another professional football team for any regular-season or postseason games. A Rookie is designated by an "R" on NFL rosters. Players who have been active in another professional football league or players who have NFL experience, including either preseason training camp or being on an Active List or Inactive List, or on Reserve/Injured or Reserve/Physically Unable to Perform for fewer than six regular-season games, are termed NFL First-Year Players. An NFL First-Year Player is designated by a "1" on NFL rosters. Thereafter, a player is credited with an additional year of experience for each season in which he accumulates six games on the Active List or Inactive List, or on Reserve/Injured or Reserve/Physically Unable to Perform.

Log on to www.houstontexans.com for an up-to-date roster.

HOUSTON TEXANS

COACHING STAFF

Head Coach,
Gary Kubiak

Pro Career: Gary Kubiak was introduced as the second head coach in Houston Texans history on January 26, 2006. Kubiak returned to Houston after spending 20 of the previous 23 years in the Denver area. Kubiak's record as Texans head coach is 22-26, making him the franchise's winningest head coach. In his first year as a head coach, Kubiak guided the Texans to a 6-10 record, tripling the team's win total of the year before. In 2007, the Texans broke even for the first time, finishing at 8-8. Houston went 7-3 outside of the AFC West and set a franchise record with a 6-2 mark at home. It was the first time the Texans posted a winning mark at Reliant Stadium. In 2008, the Texans overcame an 0-4 start that was due in part to the damage inflicted by Hurricane Ike and finished 8-8. Houston's 8-4 record over the last 12 games was the third-best in the league, and the team became just the ninth squad in NFL history to finish .500 or better after an 0-4 start. Kubiak spent the previous 11 years (1995-2005) as Denver's offensive coordinator, helping guide the Broncos to back-to-back World Championships in Super Bowls XXXII and XXXIII and three AFC West Division titles. Kubiak began his coaching career as the running backs coach at Texas A&M (1992-93). Kubiak started his NFL coaching career with the San Francisco 49ers as the quarterbacks coach, winning Super Bowl XXIX in his only season (1994). Kubiak is a veteran of six Super Bowls—three as a player and three as a coach. Career record: 22-26.

Background: Kubiak starred at quarterback for Texas A&M from 1979-1982, earning all-Southwest Conference honors as a senior. He played for the Broncos from 1983-1991 as John Elway's backup. Kubiak played in 119 career games, tossed 14 touchdowns, and was a part of three teams that reached the Super Bowl.

Personal: Born August 15, 1961 in Houston. He and his wife, Rhonda, have three sons—Klint, Klay, and Klein.

ASSISTANT COACHES

John Benton, offensive line; born December 13, 1963, Los Angeles. Offensive lineman Colorado State 1986-1990. No pro playing experience. College coach: California University (Pa.) 1990-94, Colorado State 1996-2003. Pro coach: St. Louis Rams 2004-05, joined Texans in 2006.

Frank Bush, defensive coordinator; born January 10, 1963, Athens, Ga. Linebacker North Carolina State 1981-84. Pro linebacker Houston Oilers 1985-86. Pro coach: Houston Oilers 1987-1991 (scout), 1992-94, Denver Broncos 1995-2003, Arizona Cardinals 2004-06, joined Texans in 2007.

Perry Carter, defensive assistant; born August 15, 1971, McComb, Miss. Defensive back Southern Mississippi 1989-1993. Pro defensive back Arizona Cardinals 1994, Kansas City Chiefs 1995, Oakland Raiders 1996-98, Edmonton Eskimos (CFL) 2000-01, Montreal Alouettes (CFL) 2002, British Columbia Lions (CFL) 2003-04. College coach: Texas A&M-Commerce 2004. Pro coach: Hamburg Sea Devils (NFLEL) 2006, joined Texans in 2006.

Alex Gibbs, asst. head coach/offense; born February 22, 1941, Morganton, N.C. Running back/defensive back Davidson College 1959-1963. No pro playing experience. College coach: Duke 1969-1970, Kentucky 1971-72, West Virginia 1973-74, Ohio State 1975-78, Auburn 1979-1981, Georgia 1982-83. Pro coach: Denver Broncos 1984-87, Oakland Raiders 1988-89, San Diego Chargers 1990-91, Indianapolis Colts 1992, Kansas City Chiefs 1993-94, Denver Broncos 1995-2003, Atlanta Falcons 2004-06, joined Texans in 2008.

David Gibbs, defensive backs; born January 10, 1968, Mount Airy, N.C. Defensive back Colorado 1987-1990. No pro playing experience. College coach: Oklahoma 1991-92, Colorado 1993-94, Kansas 1995-96, Minnesota 1997-2000, Auburn 2005. Pro coach: Denver Broncos 2001-04, Kansas City Chiefs 2006-08, joined Texans in 2009.

Chick Harris, running backs; born September 21, 1945, Durham, N.C. Running back Northern Arizona 1966-69. No pro playing experience. College coach: Colorado State 1970-71, Long Beach State 1972-73, Washington 1975-1980. Pro coach: Detroit Wheels (WFL) 1974, Buffalo Bills 1981-82, Seattle Seahawks 1983-1991, Los Angeles Rams 1992-94, Carolina Panthers 1995-2001, joined Texans in 2002.

Johnny Holland, linebackers; born March 11, 1965, Belleville, Texas. Linebacker Texas A&M 1983-86. Pro linebacker Green Bay Packers 1987-1993. Pro coach: Green Bay Packers 1995-99, Seattle Seahawks 2000-02, Detroit Lions 2003-05, joined Texans in 2006.

Larry Kirksey, wide receivers; born January 6, 1951, Harlan, Ky. Wide receiver Eastern Kentucky 1970-73. No pro playing experience. College coach: Miami (Ohio) 1974-76, Kentucky 1977-1981, Kansas 1982, Kentucky State 1983 (head coach), Florida 1984-88, Pittsburgh 1989, Alabama 1990-93, Texas A&M 2000, Middle Tennessee State 2006. Pro coach: San Francisco 49ers 1994-99, Detroit Lions 2001-02, Jacksonville Jaguars 2003, Denver Broncos 2004, joined Texans in 2007.

Bill Kollar, asst. head coach/defensive line; born November 27, 1952, Warren, Ohio. Defensive end Montana State 1971-73. Pro defensive end Cincinnati Bengals 1974-76, Tampa Bay Buccaneers 1977-1981. College coach: Illinois 1985-87, Purdue 1988-89. Pro coach: Tampa Bay Buccaneers 1984, Atlanta Falcons 1990-2000, St. Louis Rams 2001-05, Buffalo Bills 2006-08, joined Texans in 2009.

Matt LaFleur, offensive assistant; born November 3, 1979, Mt. Pleasant, Mich. QB/WR Western Michigan 1998-99, Saginaw Valley State 2000-02. Pro QB Omaha Beef (NIFL) 2002, Billings Outlaws (NIFL) 2002. College coach: Saginaw Valley State 2003, Central Michigan 2004-05, Northern Michigan 2006, Ashland 2007. Pro coach: Joined Texans in 2006.

Joe Marciano, special teams coordinator; born February 10, 1954, Dunmore, Pa. Quarterback Temple 1972-75. No pro playing experience. College coach: East Stroudsburg State 1977, Rhode Island 1978-79, Villanova 1980, Penn State 1981, Temple 1982. Pro coach: Philadelphia/Baltimore Stars (USFL) 1983-85, New Orleans Saints 1986-1995, Tampa Bay Buccaneers 1996-2001, joined Texans in 2002.

Bruce Matthews, offensive assistant; born August 8, 1961, Raleigh, N.C. Offensive lineman Southern California, 1979-1982. Pro offensive lineman Houston Oilers/Tennessee Titans 1983-2001. Inducted into Pro Football Hall of Fame in 2007. Pro coach: Joined Texans in 2009

Brian Pariani, tight ends; born July 2, 1965, San Francisco. No college or pro playing experience. College coach: UCLA 1989, Syracuse 2005. Pro coach: San Francisco 49ers 1991-94, Denver Broncos 1994-2004, joined Texans in 2006.

Frank Pollack, asst. offensive line; born November 5, 1967, Camp Springs, Md. Offensive lineman Northern Arizona 1985-89. Pro offensive lineman San Francisco 49ers 1990-97. College coach: Northern Arizona 2005-06. Pro coach: Joined Texans in 2007.

Ray Rhodes, senior defensive assistant; born October 20, 1950, Mexia, Texas. Running back Texas Christian 1969-1970, wide receiver/defensive back/kick returner Tulsa 1972-73. Pro wide receiver/defensive back New York Giants 1974-79, San Francisco 49ers 1980. Pro coach: San Francisco 49ers 1981-1991, 1994, Green Bay Packers 1992-93, 1999 (head coach 1999), Philadelphia Eagles 1995-98 (head coach), Washington Redskins 2000, Denver Broncos 2001-02, Seattle Seahawks 2003-07, joined Texans in 2008.

Robert Saleh, asst. linebackers; born January 31, 1979, Dearborn, Mich. Tight end Northern Michigan 1997-2000. No pro playing experience. College coach: Michigan State 2002-03, Central Michigan 2004. Pro coach: Joined Texans in 2005.

Kyle Shanahan, offensive coordinator/quarterbacks; born December 14, 1979, Minneapolis. Wide receiver Duke 1998-99, Texas 2000-02. No pro playing experience. College coach: UCLA 2003. Pro coach: Tampa Bay Buccaneers 2004-05, joined Texans in 2006.

American Football Conference
South Division
Team Colors: Royal Blue and White
P.O. Box 535000
Indianapolis, Indiana 46253
Telephone: (317) 297-2658

2009 SCHEDULE

PRESEASON

Aug. 14	**Minnesota**	7:30
Aug. 20	**Philadelphia**	8:00
Aug. 29	at Detroit	1:00
Sep. 3	at Cincinnati	7:30

REGULAR SEASON

Sep. 13	**Jacksonville**	1:00
Sep. 21	at Miami (Mon.)	8:30
Sep. 27	at Arizona	5:20
Oct. 4	**Seattle**	1:00
Oct. 11	at Tennessee	7:20
Oct. 18	BYE	
Oct. 25	at St. Louis	12:00
Nov. 1	**San Francisco**	1:00
Nov. 8	**Houston**	1:00
Nov. 15	**New England**	8:20
Nov. 22	at Baltimore	1:00
Nov. 29	at Houston	12:00
Dec. 6	**Tennessee**	1:00
Dec. 13	**Denver**	1:00
Dec. 17	at Jacksonville (Thu.)	8:20
Dec. 27	**N.Y. Jets**	4:15
Jan. 3	at Buffalo	1:00

Stadium: Lucas Oil Stadium (opened in 2008) • **Capacity:** 63,000
500 South Capitol Avenue
Indianapolis, Indiana 46225
Playing Surface: FieldTurf
Training Camp: Rose-Hulman Institute
5500 Wabash Avenue
Terre Haute, IN 47803

LUCAS OIL STADIUM

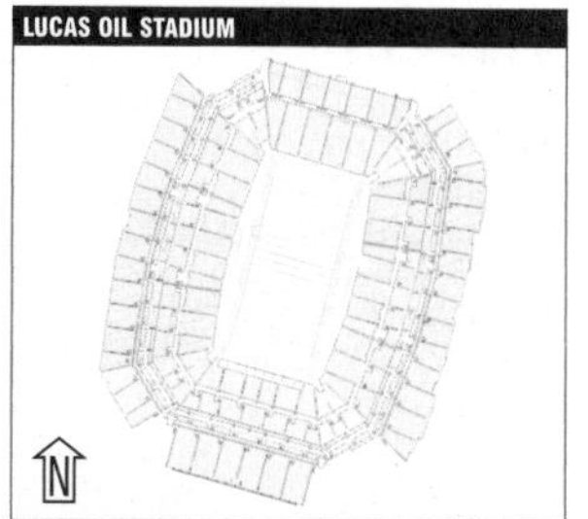

CLUB OFFICIALS

Owner and CEO: James Irsay
President: Bill Polian
Head Coach: Jim Caldwell
Vice President: Casey Irsay
Vice President: Carlie Irsay
Senior Executive Vice President: Pete Ward
Senior Vice President of Sales and Marketing: Tom Zupancic
Vice President of Football Operations: Chris Polian
Vice President-Finance: Kurt Humphrey
Vice President-Ticket Operations/Guest Services: Larry Hall
Vice President-Public Relations: Craig Kelley
Vice President of Sponsorship Sales: Jay Souers
Vice President of Premium Seating and Ticket Sales: Greg Hylton
Director of Football Administration: Steve Champlin
Director of Player Personnel: Tom Telesco
Director of Pro Player Personnel: Clyde Powers
Equipment Manager: Jon Scott
Video Director: Marty Heckscher
Head Athletic Trainer: Dave Hammer
Assistant Director of Public Relations: Vernon Cheek
Manager of Publicity: Justin Dickens
Assistant Equipment Managers: Mike Mays, Sean Sullivan, Brian Seabrooks
Assistant Trainers: Dave Walston, Bryant Baugh
Assistant Video Director: John Starliper

COACHING HISTORY

Baltimore 1953-1983
(444-406-7)
Records include postseason games

1953	Keith Molesworth	3-9-0
1954-1962	Weeb Ewbank	61-52-1
1963-69	Don Shula	73-26-4
1970-72	Don McCafferty*	26-11-1
1972	John Sandusky	4-5-0
1973-74	Howard Schnellenberger**	4-13-0
1974	Joe Thomas	2-9-0
1975-79	Ted Marchibroda	41-36-0
1980-81	Mike McCormack	9-23-0
1982-84	Frank Kush***	11-28-1
1984	Hal Hunter	0-1-0
1985-86	Rod Dowhower****	5-24-0
1986-1991	Ron Meyer#	36-36-0
1991	Rick Venturi	1-10-0
1992-95	Ted Marchibroda	32-35-0
1996-97	Lindy Infante	12-21-0
1998-2001	Jim Mora	32-34-0
2002-08	Tony Dungy	92-33-0

*Released after five games in 1972
**Released after three games in 1974
***Resigned after 15 games in 1984
****Released after 13 games in 1986
#Released after five games in 1991

PAID ATTENDANCE

Home 515,627 Away 533,204
Total 1,048,831
Single-game home record, 66,822 (9/7/08)
Single-season home record, 515,627 (2008)

2009 DRAFT CHOICES

Round	Name	Pos.	College
1	Donald Brown	RB	Connecticut
2	Fili Moala	DT	Southern California
3	Jerraud Powers	DB	Auburn
4	Austin Collie	WR	Brigham Young
	Terrance Taylor	DT	Michigan
6	Curtis Painter	QB	Purdue
7	Pat McAfee	P	West Virginia
	Jaimie Thomas	G	Maryland

INDIANAPOLIS COLTS

2008 TEAM RECORD

PRESEASON (1-4)

Date	Result	Opponent
8/3	L 16-30	at Washington
8/9	L 20-23	at Carolina (OT)
8/16	W 16-9	at Atlanta
8/24	L 7-20	Buffalo
8/28	L 7-27	Cincinnati

REGULAR SEASON (12-4)

Date	Result	Opponent
9/7	L 13-29	Chicago
9/14	W 18-15	at Minnesota
9/21	L 21-23	Jacksonville
10/5	W 31-27	at Houston
10/12	W 31-3	Baltimore
10/19	L 14-34	at Green Bay
10/27	L 21-31	at Tennessee
11/2	W 18-15	New England
11/9	W 24-20	at Pittsburgh
11/16	W 33-27	Houston
11/23	W 23-20	at San Diego
11/30	W 10-6	at Cleveland
12/7	W 35-3	Cincinnati
12/14	W 31-21	Detroit
12/18	W 31-24	at Jacksonville
12/28	W 23-0	Tennessee

POSTSEASON (0-1)

1/3 L 17-23 at San Diego (OT)

(OT) Overtime

SCORE BY PERIODS

Colts	98	71	81	127	0 —	377
Opponents	45	111	67	75	0 —	298

2008 TEAM STATISTICS

	Colts	Opp.
Total First Downs	321	305
Rushing	80	119
Passing	220	165
Penalty	21	21
3rd Down: Made/Att	101/201	100/211
3rd Down Pct.	50.2	47.4
4th Down: Made/Att	11/16	3/7
4th Down Pct.	68.8	42.9
Possession Avg.	28:39	31:21
Total Net Yards	5368	4975
Avg. Per Game	335.5	310.9
Total Plays	969	983
Avg. Per Play	5.5	5.1
Net Yards Rushing	1274	1966
Avg. Per Game	79.6	122.9
Total Rushes	370	472
Net Yards Passing	4094	3009
Avg. Per Game	255.9	188.1
Sacked/Yards Lost	14/86	30/200
Gross Yards	4180	3209
Att./Completions	585/393	481/329
Completion Pct.	67.2	68.4
Had Intercepted	12	15
Punts/Average	53/44.2	53/44.9
Net Punting Avg.	53/38.8	53/39.0
Penalties/Yards	86/619	68/543
Fumbles/Ball Lost	13/5	24/11
Touchdowns	45	28
Rushing	13	18
Passing	27	6
Returns	5	4

2008 INDIVIDUAL STATISTICS

PASSING	Att.	Comp.	Yds.	Pct.	TD	Int.	Tkld.	Rate
Manning	555	371	4002	66.8	27	12	14/86	95.0
Sorgi	30	22	178	73.3	0	0	0/0	87.9
Colts	585	393	4180	67.2	27	12	14/86	94.7
Opponents	481	329	3209	68.4	6	15	30/200	78.0

SCORING	TD R	TD P	TD Rt	PAT	FG	Saf	PTS
Vinatieri	0	0	0	43/43	20/25	0	103
Rhodes	6	3	0	0/0	0/0	0	56
Addai	5	2	0	0/0	0/0	0	42
Wayne	0	6	0	0/0	0/0	0	38
Clark	0	6	0	0/0	0/0	0	36
Harrison	0	5	0	0/0	0/0	0	30
Gonzalez	0	4	0	0/0	0/0	0	24
Brackett	0	0	1	0/0	0/0	0	6
Hayden	0	0	1	0/0	0/0	0	6
Manning	1	0	0	0/0	0/0	0	6
Mathis	0	0	1	0/0	0/0	0	6
Ratliff	0	0	1	0/0	0/0	0	6
Richard	0	0	1	0/0	0/0	0	6
Santi	0	1	0	0/0	0/0	0	6
Simpson	1	0	0	0/0	0/0	0	6
Colts	13	27	5	43/43	20/25	0	377
Opponents	18	6	4	25/25	33/38	1	298

2-Pt. Conversions: Rhodes, Wayne.
Colts 2-2, Opponents 2-3

RUSHING	No.	Yds	Avg	LG	TD
Addai	155	544	3.5	23	5
Rhodes	152	538	3.5	38	6
Ball	13	83	6.4	23	0
Simpson	15	45	3.0	10	1
Davenport	8	26	3.3	8	0
Manning	20	21	1.1	12	1
Hart	2	9	4.5	7	0
Sorgi	5	8	1.6	12	0
Colts	370	1274	3.4	38	13
Opponents	472	1966	4.2	71t	18

RECEIVING	No.	Yds	Avg	LG	TD
Wayne	82	1145	14.0	65t	6
Clark	77	848	11.0	33	6
Harrison	60	636	10.6	67t	5
Gonzalez	57	664	11.6	58	4
Rhodes	45	302	6.7	29	3
Addai	25	206	8.2	55t	2
Robinson	19	166	8.7	23	0
Santi	10	64	6.4	13	1
Davenport	4	54	13.5	33	0
Garcon	4	23	5.8	12	0
Simpson	3	30	10.0	15	0
Tamme	3	12	4.0	6	0
Hart	1	18	18.0	18	0
Hall	1	9	9.0	9	0
Ball	1	5	5.0	5	0
Ch. Johnson	1	-2	-2.0	-2	0
Colts	393	4180	10.6	75	27
Opponents	329	3209	9.8	61	6

INTERCEPTIONS	No.	Yds	Avg	LG	TD
Bullitt	4	7	1.8	3	0
Hayden	3	135	45.0	85t	1
Ratliff	2	37	18.5	35t	1
Jennings	2	9	4.5	6	0
Bethea	2	0	0.0	0	0
Hughes	1	16	16.0	16	0
Sanders	1	0	0.0	0	0
Colts	15	204	13.6	85t	2
Opponents	12	294	24.5	99t	3

PUNTING	No.	Yds.	Avg.	In 20	LG
H. Smith	53	2343	44.2	23	64
Colts	53	2343	44.2	23	64
Opponents	53	2381	44.9	17	75

PUNT RETURNS	Ret	FC	Yds	Avg	LG	TD
Ratliff	16	12	89	5.6	19	0
Forsett	4	1	36	9.0	25	0
Garcon	1	0	5	5.0	5	0
Harrison	1	0	2	2.0	2	0
Colts	22	13	132	6.0	25	0
Opponents	27	11	249	9.2	39	0

KICKOFF RETURNS	No.	Yds	Avg	LG	TD
Garcon	22	475	21.6	39	0
Simpson	15	344	22.9	46	0
Forsett	11	248	22.5	28	0
Davenport	5	107	21.4	26	0
Roby	5	101	20.2	25	0
Reid	1	12	12.0	12	0
K. Dawson	1	11	11.0	11	0
Tamme	1	11	11.0	11	0
Harrison	1	3	3.0	3	0
Wheeler	1	0	0.0	0	0
Colts	63	1312	20.8	46	0
Opponents	70	1700	24.3	50	0

FIELD GOALS	1-19	20-29	30-39	40-49	50+
Vinatieri	0/0	3/3	11/13	4/7	2/2
Colts	0/0	3/3	11/13	4/7	2/2
Opponents	1/1	11/11	9/11	9/12	3/3

SACKS	No.
Mathis	11.5
Freeney	10.5
Brock	3.5
Reid	2.0
Howard	1.5
Cu. Johnson	1.0
Colts	30.0
Opponents	14.0

RECORD HOLDERS

INDIVIDUAL RECORDS—CAREER

Category	Name	Performance
Rushing (Yds.)	Edgerrin James, 1999-2005	9,226
Passing (Yds.)	Peyton Manning, 1998-2008	45,628
Passing (TDs)	Peyton Manning, 1998-2008	333
Receiving (No.)	Marvin Harrison, 1996-2008	1,102
Receiving (Yds.)	Marvin Harrison, 1996-2008	14,580
Interceptions	Bob Boyd, 1960-68	57
Punting (Avg.)	Chris Gardocki, 1995-98	44.8
Punt Return (Avg.)	Ron Gardin, 1970-71	13.5
Kickoff Return (Avg.)	Jim Duncan, 1969-1971	32.6
Field Goals	Mike Vanderjagt, 1998-2005	217
Touchdowns (Tot.)	Marvin Harrison, 1996-2008	128
Points	Mike Vanderjagt, 1998-2005	995
*Sacks	Dwight Freeney, 2002-08	70.5

INDIVIDUAL RECORDS—SINGLE SEASON

Category	Name	Performance
Rushing (Yds.)	Edgerrin James, 2000	1,709
Passing (Yds.)	Peyton Manning, 2004	4,557
Passing (TDs)	Peyton Manning, 2004	49
Receiving (No.)	Marvin Harrison, 2002	**143
Receiving (Yds.)	Marvin Harrison, 2002	1,722
Interceptions	Tom Keane, 1953	11
Punting (Avg.)	Rohn Stark, 1985	45.9
Punt Return (Avg.)	T.J. Rushing, 2007	13.1
Kickoff Return (Avg.)	Jim Duncan, 1970	35.4
Field Goals	Mike Vanderjagt, 2003	37
Touchdowns (Tot.)	Lenny Moore, 1964	20
Points	Mike Vanderjagt, 2003	157
*Sacks	Dwight Freeney, 2004	16.0

INDIVIDUAL RECORDS—SINGLE GAME

Category	Name	Performance
Rushing (Yds.)	Edgerrin James, 10-15-00	219
Passing (Yds.)	Peyton Manning, 10-31-04	472
Passing (TDs)	Peyton Manning, 9-28-03, 11-25-04	6
Receiving (No.)	Marvin Harrison, 12-26-99, 11-17-02	14
Receiving (Yds.)	Raymond Berry, 11-10-57	224
Interceptions	Many times Last time by Mike Prior, 12-20-92	3
Field Goals	Many times Last time by Mike Vanderjagt, 12-7-03	5
Touchdowns (Tot.)	Many times Last time by Joseph Addai, 11-26-06	4
Points	Many times Last time by Joseph Addai, 11-26-06	24
*Sacks	Johnie Cooks, 11-25-84	4.5

**Sacks became an official statistic in 1982.*
***NFL Record*

INDIANAPOLIS COLTS

2009 VETERAN ROSTER

No.	Name	Pos.	Ht.	Wt.	Birthdate	NFL Exp.	College	Hometown	How Acq.	'08 Games/ Starts
29	Addai, Joseph	RB	5-11	214	5/3/83	4	Louisiana State	Houston, Texas	D1-'06	12/12
41	Bethea, Antoine	DB	5-11	203	7/7/84	4	Howard	Newport News, Va.	D6b-'06	16/16
58	Brackett, Gary	LB	5-11	235	5/23/80	7	Rutgers	Glassboro, N.J.	FA-'03	12/12
79	Brock, Raheem	DE	6-4	274	6/10/78	8	Temple	Philadelphia, Pa.	FA-'02	16/15
33	Bullitt, Melvin	DB	6-1	201	11/13/84	3	Texas A&M	Bryan, Texas	FA-'07	15/9
44	Clark, Dallas	TE	6-3	252	6/12/79	7	Iowa	Livermore, Iowa	D1-'03	15/15
25	Coe, Michael	DB	6-0	190	12/17/83	3	Alabama State	Memphis, Tenn.	D5b-'07	0*
42	Condren, Brannon	DB	6-1	205	8/19/83	3	Troy	Ft. Walton Beach, Fla.	FA-'09	4/0*
96	Dawson, Keyunta	DT	6-3	254	9/13/85	3	Texas Tech	Shreveport, La.	D7-'07	14/14
71	Diem, Ryan	T	6-6	320	7/ 1/79	9	Northern Illinois	Carol Stream, Ill.	D4-'01	16/16
76	Federkeil, Dan	T	6-6	290	11/9/83	4	Calgary	Medicine Hat, Alberta, Canada	FA-'06	12/3
68	Foster, Eric	DT	6-2	265	4/5/85	2	Rutgers	Homestead, Fla.	FA-'08	13/11
93	Freeney, Dwight	DE	6-1	268	2/19/80	8	Syracuse	Hartford, Conn.	D1-'02	15/14
85	Garcon, Pierre	WR	6-0	210	8/8/86	2	Mount Union	West Palm Beach, Fla.	D6d-'08	14/0
43	Giordano, Matt	DB	5-11	200	10/16/82	5	California	Fresno, Ca.	D4b-'05	16/1
11	Gonzalez, Anthony	WR	6-0	193	9/18/84	3	Ohio State	Cleveland, Ohio	D1-'07	16/2
37	Graham, Nick	DB	5-10	191	1/19/84	3	Tulsa	Oklahoma City, Okla.	FA-'08	4/0
56	Hagler, Tyjuan	LB	6-0	236	12/3/81	4	Cincinnati	Kankakee, Ill.	D5c-'05	9/3
81	Hall, Roy	WR	6-3	240	12/8/83	3	Ohio State	Lyndhurst, Ohio	D5a-'07	4/0
32	Hart, Mike	RB	5-9	206	4/9/86	2	Michigan	Syracuse, N.Y.	D6c-'08	5/0
26	Hayden, Kelvin	DB	6-0	195	7/23/83	5	Illinois	Chicago, Ill.	D2-'05	10/10
72	Hilliard, Corey	T	6-6	305	4/26/85	3	Oklahoma State	New Orleans, La.	FA-'09	2/0
92	Howard, Marcus	DE	6-0	237	10/12/85	2	Georgia	Huger, S.C.	D5-'08	9/0
20	Hughes, Dante	DB	5-10	190	9/21/85	3	California	Los Angeles, Ca.	D3a-'07	14/0
28	Jackson, Marlin	DB	6-0	196	6/30/83	5	Michigan	Sharon, Pa.	D1-'05	7/7
23	Jennings, Tim	DB	5-8	185	12/24/83	4	Georgia	Orangeburg, S.C.	D2-'06	16/12
99	Johnson, Antonio	DT	6-3	310	12/8/84	3	Mississippi State	Leland, Miss.	FA-'08	8/4
74	Johnson, Charlie	T	6-4	305	5/2/84	4	Oklahoma State	Sherman, Texas	D6a-'06	16/16
94	Johnson, Curtis	DE	6-3	237	2/16/85	2	Clark Atlanta	Lauderhill, Fla.	FA-'08	7/0
66	Johnson, Ed	DT	6-2	296	12/18/83	2	Penn State	Detroit, Mich.	FA-'09	1/1
53	Justice, Steve	C	6-3	293	5/26/84	2	Wake Forest	Lancaster, Pa.	D6b-'08	8/1
54	Keiaho, Freddy	LB	5-11	226	12/18/82	4	San Diego State	Ventura, Calif.	D3-'06	14/14
65	Lilja, Ryan	G	6-2	290	10/15/81	6	Kansas State	Shawnee, Kan.	W(KC)-04	0*
18	Manning, Peyton	QB	6-5	230	3/24/76	12	Tennessee	New Orleans, La.	D1-98	16/16
98	Mathis, Robert	DE	6-2	245	2/26/81	7	Alabama A&M	Atlanta, Ga.	D5a-'03	15/2
90	Muir, Daniel	DT	6-2	312	9/12/83	3	Kent State	Riverdale, Md.	W(GB)-'08	6/0
78	Pollak, Mike	G	6-3	301	2/16/85	2	Arizona State	Scottsdale, Ariz.	D2-'08	13/13
61	Richard, Jamey	G	6-5	295	10/9/84	2	Buffalo	Weston, Conn.	D7-'08	15/7
47	Robinson, Gijon	TE	6-1	255	10/12/84	2	Missouri West. State	Waynesville, Mo.	FA-'08	15/14
34	Rushing, T.J.	DB	5-9	186	6/8/83	4	Stanford	Pauls Valley, Okla.	D7-'06	0*
21	Sanders, Bob	DB	5-8	206	2/24/81	6	Iowa	Erie, Pa.	D2b-'04	6/6
86	Santi, Tom	TE	6-3	250	11/22/85	2	Virginia	Nashville, Tenn.	D6a-'08	6/2
63	Saturday, Jeff	C	6-2	295	6/8/75	11	North Carolina	Tucker, Ga.	FA-99	12/12
51	Senn, Jordan	LB	5-11	224	6/11/84	2	Portland State	Beaverton, Ore.	FA-'08	15/0
55	Session, Clint	LB	6-0	235	9/22/84	3	Pittsburgh	Pompano Beach, Fla.	D4c-'07	16/15
52	Seward, Adam	LB	6-3	250	6/15/82	5	Nevada-Las Vegas	Las Vegas, Nev.	UFA(Car)-'09	9/0*
40	Silva, Jamie	DB	5-11	204	12/14/84	2	Boston College	East Providence, R.I.	FA-'08	11/0
35	Simpson, Chad	RB	5-9	216	8/22/85	2	Morgan State	Miami, Fla.	FA-'08	11/0
48	Snow, Justin	TE	6-3	240	12/21/76	10	Baylor	Abilene, Texas	FA-'00	16/0
12	Sorgi, Jim	QB	6-5	196	12/ 3/80	6	Wisconsin	Fraser, Mich.	D6b-'04	1/0
84	Tamme, Jacob	TE	6-3	236	3/15/85	2	Kentucky	Danville, Ky.	D4-'08	12/0
91	#Thomas, Josh	DE	6-5	271	6/26/81	6	Syracuse	Orchard Park, N.Y.	FA-'04	16/3
75	Toudouze, Michael	T	6-6	303	4/27/83	3	Texas Christian	San Antonio, Texas	D5-'06	0*
67	Ugoh, Tony	T	6-5	301	11/17/83	3	Arkansas	Houston, Texas	D2a-'07	15/12
4	Vinatieri, Adam	K	6-0	202	12/28/72	14	South Dakota State	Rapid City, S.D.	UFA(NE)-'06	16/0
87	Wayne, Reggie	WR	6-0	198	11/17/78	9	Miami	New Orleans, La.	D1b-'01	16/16
50	Wheeler, Philip	LB	6-2	240	12/12/84	2	Georgia Tech	Columbus, Ga.	D3-'08	16/0

Coe missed '08 season because of injury; Condren played 4 games with Miami in '08; Lilja missed '08 season because of injury; Rushing missed '08 because of injury; Seward played 9 games with Carolina; Toudouze spent '08 season on practice squad.

\# Unrestricted free agent; subject to developments.

Players lost through free agency (3): DE Darrell Reid (Den; 16 games in '08); DB Keiwan Ratliff (Pitt; 13); RB Dominic Rhodes (Buff; 15).

Also played with Colts in '08—RB Lance Ball (1 game), RB Najeh Davenport (2), LB Buster Davis (6), RB Clifton Dawson (2), RB Justin Forsett (3), WR Marvin Harrison (15), DT LaJuan Ramsey (4), WR Courtney Roby (1), P Hunter Smith (16).

2009 FIRST-YEAR ROSTER

Name	Pos.	Ht.	Wt.	Birthdate	College	Hometown	How Acq.
Anderson, Brandon	DB	5-10	179	12/10/85	Akron	Dublin, Va.	FA
Ball, Lance (1)	RB	5-9	220	6/19/85	Maryland	Teaneck, N.J.	FA-'08
Barnes, Brandon (1)	T	6-2	315	2/28/85	Grand Valley State	Detroit, Mich.	FA
Brown, Donald	RB	5-10	210	4/11/87	Connecticut	Atlantic Highlands, N.J.	D1
Cloherty, Colin	TE	6-2	245	9/16/87	Brown	Bethesda, Md.	FA
Collie, Austin	WR	6-0	200	11/11/85	Brigham Young	El Dorado Hills, Calif.	D4a
Crane, Chris	QB	6-4	236	4/18/86	Boston College	Mechanicsburg, Penn.	FA
DeVan, Kyle (1)	OL	6-2	306	2/10/85	Oregon State	Vacaville, Calif.	FA
Foster, Brandon (1)	DB	5-8	185	12/25/84	Texas	Arlington, Texas	FA
Giguere, Sam (1)	WR	5-11	215	7/11/85	Sherbrooke	Sherbrooke, Quebec, Canada	FA
Grady, Adrian	DT	6-1	290	11/21/85	Louisville	Nicholls, Ga.	FA
Harrison, Brandon	DB	5-9	197	11/6/86	Michigan	Dayton, Ohio	FA
Humber, Ramon	LB	5-11	232	8/10/87	North Dakota State	Brooklyn Park, Minn.	FA
Key, Travis (1)	DB	5-9	190	12/31/85	Michigan State	Harvey, Ill.	FA
Kuntz, Pat	DT	6-2	276	4/15/86	Notre Dame	Indianapolis, Ind.	FA
Lacey, Jacob	DB	5-10	177	5/28/87	Oklahoma State	Garland, Texas	FA
Lewis, Cornelius	G	6-3	324	8/1/86	Tennessee State	Jacksonville, Fla.	FA
Masthay, Tim	P/K	6-1	198	3/16/87	Kentucky	Murray, Ky.	FA
Matthews, John	WR	6-0	197	4/19/86	San Diego	Aurora, Colo.	FA
McAfee, Pat	P	6-1	220	5/2/86	West Virginia	Plum, Pa.	D7a
McDermott, Brett	WR	6-0	201	9/21/87	Holy Cross	Mansfield, Mass.	FA
Moala, Fili	DT	6-4	303	6/23/85	Southern California	Buena Park, Calif.	D2a
Okwo, Michael (1)	LB	6-0	225	11/24/85	Stanford	Manchester, England	FA
Painter, Curtis	QB	6-4	230	6/24/85	Purdue	Vincennes, Ind.	D6
Pestock, Tom	G	6-6	317	9/13/84	Northwest Missouri State	Lenexa, Kan.	FA
Petrowski, Jamie (1)	TE	6-4	262	7/12/82	Indiana State	Terre Haute, Ind.	FA
Powers, Jerraud	DB	5-10	192	7/19/87	Auburn	Decatur, Ala.	D3
Sales, Tyrell	LB	6-2	230	1/1/86	Penn State	Butler, Pa.	FA
Smith, Taj (1)	WR	6-0	192	9/30/83	Syracuse	Newark, N.J.	FA
Tauiliili, Michael	LB	5-11	235	10/29/86	Duke	Houston, Texas	FA
Taylor, Terrance	DT	6-0	319	5/14/86	Michigan	Muskegon, Mich.	D4b
Thomas, Jaime	G	6-4	330	8/24/86	Maryland	Harrisburg, Pa.	D7b

The term NFL Rookie is defined as a player who is in his first season of professional football and has not been on the roster of another professional football team for any regular-season or postseason games. A Rookie is designated by an "R" on NFL rosters. Players who have been active in another professional football league or players who have NFL experience, including either preseason training camp or being on an Active List or Inactive List, or on Reserve/Injured or Reserve/Physically Unable to Perform for fewer than six regular-season games, are termed NFL First-Year Players. An NFL First-Year Player is designated by a "1" on NFL rosters. Thereafter, a player is credited with an additional year of experience for each season in which he accumulates six games on the Active List or Inactive List, or on Reserve/Injured or Reserve/Physically Unable to Perform.

Log on to www.colts.com for an up-to-date roster.

COACHING STAFF

Head Coach, Jim Caldwell

Pro Career: Jim Caldwell was named head coach of the club on January 13, 2009 and enters his first season as head coach of the Colts. Caldwell has served with Indianapolis for the past seven years. He was elevated to associate head coach with the club on January 21, 2008. Caldwell spent his first three seasons as quarterbacks coach before earning the expanded title of assistant head coach prior to the 2005 season. Caldwell's leadership has helped the Colts annually have one of the NFL's most prolific offenses. The Colts have ranked in the top four in NFL scoring offense in eight of the past 10 years, while the Colts have ranked in the top three in AFC passing offense, and top six in the NFL, for 11 consecutive seasons, including six times as the conference leader. The offensive performance has helped the franchise earn historic accomplishments. Indianapolis (2003-08) extended its NFL mark to six consecutive seasons with at least 12 victories. The club also led the NFL with a seventh consecutive playoff appearance, a span that includes Caldwell's tenure in Indianapolis. The Colts extended their streak of double-digit victory seasons to seven, tying the second-longest streak in NFL history. Indianapolis produced a nine-game winning streak over the last half of the 2008 season, making the franchise the only one in NFL history to win seven or more consecutive regular-season games in five consecutive seasons. Indianapolis' recent success includes a 32-10 record in AFC South play, and Indianapolis is the only NFL team to post double-digit victory totals and playoff appearances each season since the 2002 NFL Realignment. Caldwell joined Indianapolis from Tampa Bay, where he served as quarterbacks coach during the 2001 season. Caldwell has more than 20 years of collegiate coaching experience. Caldwell spent 1993-2000 as head coach at Wake Forest and served as an assistant coach at Southern Illinois (1978-1980), Northwestern (1981), Colorado (1982-84), Louisville (1985) and Penn State (1986-1992). Career record: 0-0.

Background: Caldwell was a four-year starter (1973-76) as a defensive back at Iowa and worked as a graduate assistant for the Hawkeyes in 1977. He holds a bachelor's degree from Iowa.

Personal: Born January 16, 1955 in Beloit, Wis. Jim and his wife, Cheryl, have four children: Jimmy, Jermaine, Jared, and Natalie.

ASSISTANT COACHES

Clyde Christensen, asst. head coach/wide receivers; born January 28, 1956, Covina, Calif. Quarterback Fresno City College 1975, North Carolina 1976-78. No pro playing experience. College coach: Mississippi 1979, East Tennessee State 1980-82, Temple 1983-85, East Carolina 1986-88, Holy Cross 1989-1990, South Carolina 1991, Maryland 1992-93, Clemson 1994-95. Pro coach: Tampa Bay Buccaneers 1996-2001, joined Colts in 2002.

Larry Coyer, defensive coordinator; born April 19, 1943, Huntington, W.Va. Quarterback Marshall 1961-64. No pro playing experience. College coach: Marshall 1965-67, Bowling Green 1968-1973, Iowa 1974-77, Oklahoma State 1978, Iowa State 1979-1982, 1995-96, UCLA 1987-89, Houston 1990, Ohio State 1991-92, East Carolina 1993, Pittsburgh 1997-99. Pro coach: Michigan Panthers (USFL) 1983-84, Memphis Showboats (USFL) 1985, New York Jets 1994, Denver Broncos 2000-06, Tampa Bay Buccaneers 2007-08, joined Colts in 2009.

Richard Howell, asst. strength and conditioning; born February 19, 1972, Bladenboro, N.C. Quarterback Davidson 1990-93. No pro playing experience. College coach: Davidson 1994-98, North Carolina 1998-99. Pro coach: Barcelona Dragons (NFLE) 1999, joined Colts in 2000.

Gene Huey, running backs; born July 20, 1947, Uniontown, Pa. Defensive back-wide receiver Wyoming 1965-68. Pro running back San Diego Chargers 1969. College coach: Wyoming 1970-73, New Mexico 1974-76, Nebraska 1977-1986, Arizona State 1987, Ohio State 1988-1991. Pro coach: Joined Colts in 1992.

Pete Metzelaars, offensive quality control/asst. offensive line; born May 24, 1960, Three Rivers, Mich. Tight end Wabash College 1978-1981. Pro tight end Seattle Seahawks 1982-84, Buffalo Bills 1985-1994, Carolina Panthers 1995, Detroit Lions 1996-97. College coach: Wingate 2003. Pro coach: Barcelona Dragons (NFLE) 2003, joined Colts in 2004.

Tom Moore, offensive coordinator; born November 7, 1938, Owatonna, Minn. Quarterback Iowa 1957-1960. No pro playing experience. College coach: Iowa 1961-62, Dayton 1965-68, Wake Forest 1969, Georgia Tech 1970-71, Minnesota 1972-73, 1975-76. Pro coach: New York Stars (WFL) 1974, Pittsburgh Steelers 1977-1989, Minnesota Vikings 1990-93, Detroit Lions 1994-96, New Orleans Saints 1997, joined Colts in 1998.

Howard Mudd, offensive line; born February 10, 1942, Midland, Mich. Guard Hillsdale (Mich.) College 1960-63. Pro offensive lineman San Francisco 49ers 1964-69, Chicago Bears 1969-1971. College coach: California 1972-73. Pro coach: San Diego Chargers 1974-76, San Francisco 49ers 1977, Seattle Seahawks 1978-1982, 1993-97, Cleveland Browns 1983-88, Kansas City Chiefs 1989-1992, joined Colts in 1998.

Mike Murphy, linebackers; born September 25, 1944, New York, N.Y. Guard/linebacker Huron (S.D.) 1963-66. No pro playing experience. College coach: Vermont 1970-73, Idaho State 1974-76, Western Illinois 1977-78. Pro coach: Saskatchewan Roughriders (CFL) 1979-1983, Chicago Blitz (USFL) 1984, Detroit Lions 1985-89, Arizona Cardinals 1990-93, Seattle Seahawks 1995-97, joined Colts in 1998.

Rod Perry, special assistant to the defense; born September 11, 1953, Fresno, Calif. Defensive back Colorado 1972-74. Pro cornerback Los Angeles Rams 1975-1982, Cleveland Browns 1983-84. College coach: Columbia 1985, Fresno City College 1986, Fresno State 1987-88. Pro coach: Seattle Seahawks 1989-1991, Los Angeles Rams 1992-94, Houston Oilers 1995-96, San Diego Chargers 1997-2001, Carolina Panthers 2002-06, joined Colts in 2007.

Frank Reich, quarterbacks; born December 4, 1961, Freeport, N.Y. Quarterback Maryland 1981-84. Pro quarterback Buffalo Bills 1985-1994, Carolina Panthers 1995, New York Jets 1996, Detroit Lions 1997-98. Pro coach: Joined Colts in 2008.

Ray Rychleski, special teams; born September 27, 1957, Old Forge, Pa. Attended Millersville (Pa.) State College. No college or pro playing experience. College coach: Temple 1981-88, Northeastern 1989-1990, Penn State 1991, East Stroudsburg 1992, Wake Forest 1993-2000, Maryland 2001-07, South Carolina 2008. Pro coach: Joined Colts in 2009.

Bill Teerlinck, defensive assistant; born July 23, 1978, Champaign, Ill. Defensive end Chadron State 2000-02. No pro playing experience. College coach: Indiana 2003-04, Illinois State 2005-06. Pro coach: Joined Colts in 2007.

John Teerlinck, defensive line; born April 9, 1951, Rochester, N.Y. Defensive lineman Western Illinois 1970-73. Pro defensive tackle San Diego Chargers 1974-77. College coach: Iowa Lakes J.C. 1977, Eastern Illinois 1978-79, Illinois 1980-82. Pro coach: Chicago Blitz (USFL) 1983-84, Arizona Wranglers/Outlaws (USFL) 1985-86, Cleveland Browns 1989-1990, Los Angeles Rams 1991, Minnesota Vikings 1992-94, Detroit Lions 1995-96, Denver Broncos 1997-2001, joined Colts in 2002.

Ricky Thomas, tight ends; born March 29, 1965, London, England. Safety Alabama 1983-86. No pro playing experience. College coach: Kentucky 1996, Gardner-Webb 1997. Pro coach: Tampa Bay Buccaneers 1997-2001, joined Colts in 2002.

Jon Torine, strength and conditioning; born November 16, 1973, Livingston, N.J. Linebacker Springfield (Mass.) College 1991. No pro playing experience. Pro coach: Buffalo Bills 1995-97, joined Colts in 1998.

Alan Williams, defensive backs; born November 4, 1969, Norfolk, Va. Running back William & Mary 1988-1991. No pro playing experience. College coach: William & Mary 1996-2000. Pro coach: Tampa Bay Buccaneers 2001, joined Colts in 2002.

American Football Conference
South Division
Team Colors: Teal, Black, and Gold
Jacksonville Municipal Stadium
One Stadium Place
Jacksonville, Florida 32202
Telephone: (904) 633-6000

2009 SCHEDULE

PRESEASON

Aug. 17	at Miami	7:30
Aug. 22	**Tampa Bay**	7:30
Aug. 27	at Philadelphia	7:00
Sep. 3	**Washington**	7:30

REGULAR SEASON

Sep. 13	at Indianapolis	1:00
Sep. 20	**Arizona**	1:00
Sep. 27	at Houston	12:00
Oct. 4	**Tennessee**	1:00
Oct. 11	at Seattle	1:15
Oct. 18	**St. Louis**	1:00
Oct. 25	BYE	
Nov. 1	at Tennessee	3:05
Nov. 8	**Kansas City**	1:00
Nov. 15	at N.Y. Jets	1:00
Nov. 22	**Buffalo**	1:00
Nov. 29	at San Francisco	1:05
Dec. 6	**Houston**	1:00
Dec. 13	**Miami**	1:00
Dec. 17	**Indianapolis** (Thu.)	8:20
Dec. 27	at New England	1:00
Jan. 3	at Cleveland	1:00

Stadium: Jacksonville Municipal Stadium (opened in 1995)
•**Capacity:** 67,164
One Stadium Place
Jacksonville, Florida 32202
Playing Surface: Grass
Training Camp: Jacksonville Municipal Stadium
One Stadium Place
Jacksonville, Florida 32202

JACKSONVILLE MUNICIPAL STADIUM

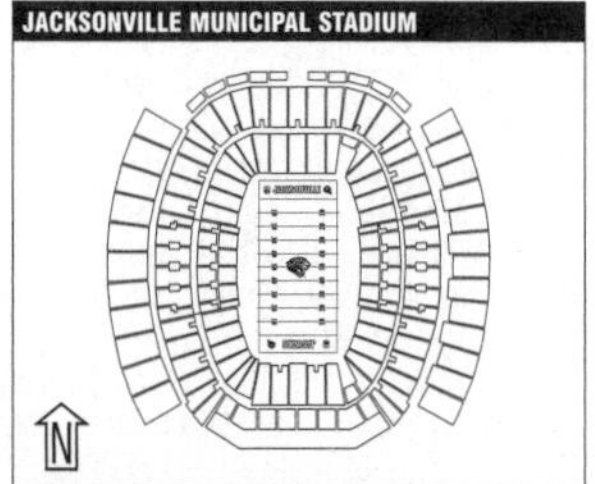

CLUB OFFICIALS

Chairman and Chief Executive Officer: Wayne Weaver
Senior Vice President/Football Operations: Paul Vance
Senior Vice President/Chief Financial Officer: Bill Prescott
Senior Vice President/Business Development: Tim Connolly
Vice President/Communications and Media: Dan Edwards

General Manager/Senior Vice President, Player Personnel: Gene Smith
Director, Player Personnel: Terry McDonough
Assistant Director, College Personnel: Tim Mingey
Assistant Director, Pro Personnel: Louis Clark
National Scout: Andy Dengler
Regional Scouts: Chris Driggers, Marty Miller and Chris Prescott
BLESTO Scout: Jason DesJarlais
Scouting Assistant, Player Personnel: Jake Peetz

Executive Director of Corporate Sponsorship: Macky Weaver
Executive Director of Football Operations: Skip Richardson
Executive Director of Information Technology: Bruce Swindell
Director of Ticket Operations: Tim Bishko
Associate General Counsel: Sashi Brown
Director of Football Administration: Tim Walsh
Head Athletic Trainer: Michael Ryan
Video Director: Mike Perkins
Equipment Manager: Drew Hampton
Manager, Communications: Ryan Robinson
Executive Assistant to VP, Communications and Media: Alisa Abbott

Chair & Chief Executive Officer, Jaguars Foundation: Delores Barr Weaver
Executive Director: Peter Racine

COACHING HISTORY

(123-112-0)

Records include postseason games

1995-2002	Tom Coughlin	72-64-0
2003-08	Jack Del Rio	51-48-0

PAID ATTENDANCE

Home 483,446 Away 517,805
Total 1,001,251
Single-game home record, 74,143 (12/28/98)
Single-season home record, 561,472 (1998)

2009 DRAFT CHOICES

Round	Name	Pos.	College
1	Eugene Monroe	T	Virginia
2	Eben Britton	T	Arizona
3	Terrance Knighton	DT	Temple
	Derek Cox	DB	William & Mary
4	Mike Thomas	WR	Arizona
5	Jarett Dillard	WR	Rice
6	Zach Miller	TE	Nebraska-Omaha
7	Rashad Jennings	RB	Liberty
	Tiquan Underwood	WR	Rutgers

JACKSONVILLE JAGUARS

2008 TEAM RECORD

PRESEASON (3-1)

Date	Result	Opponent
8/9	W 20-17	Atlanta
8/16	L 14-19	Miami
8/23	W 23-17	at Tampa Bay
8/28	W 24-3	at Washington

REGULAR SEASON (5-11)

Date	Result	Opponent
9/7	L 10-17	at Tennessee
9/14	L 16-20	Buffalo
9/21	W 23-21	at Indianapolis
9/28	W 30-27	Houston (OT)
10/5	L 21-26	Pittsburgh
10/12	W 24-17	at Denver
10/26	L 17-23	Cleveland
11/2	L 19-21	at Cincinnati
11/9	W 38-14	at Detroit
11/16	L 14-24	Tennessee
11/23	L 12-30	Minnesota
12/1	L 17-30	at Houston
12/7	L 10-23	at Chicago
12/14	W 20-16	Green Bay
12/18	L 24-31	Indianapolis
12/28	L 7-27	at Baltimore

(OT) Overtime

SCORE BY PERIODS

Jaguars	58	88	62	91	3	— 302
Opponents	101	102	50	114	0	— 367

2008 TEAM STATISTICS

	Jaguars	Opp.
Total First Downs	312	289
Rushing	107	98
Passing	183	166
Penalty	22	25
3rd Down: Made/Att	87/213	82/200
3rd Down Pct.	40.8	41.0
4th Down: Made/Att	14/24	5/11
4th Down Pct.	58.3	45.5
Possession Avg.	31:22	28:38
Total Net Yards	5106	5295
Avg. Per Game	319.1	330.9
Total Plays	1005	922
Avg. Per Play	5.1	5.7
Net Yards Rushing	1774	1709
Avg. Per Game	110.9	106.8
Total Rushes	426	428
Net Yards Passing	3332	3586
Avg. Per Game	208.3	224.1
Sacked/Yards Lost	42/288	29/191
Gross Yards	3620	3777
Att./Completions	537/335	465/297
Completion Pct.	62.4	63.9
Had Intercepted	13	13
Punts/Average	67/43.3	67/42.9
Net Punting Avg.	67/36.9	67/36.7
Penalties/Yards	104/813	80/691
Fumbles/Ball Lost	23/11	15/4
Touchdowns	35	41
Rushing	17	14
Passing	15	25
Returns	3	2

2008 INDIVIDUAL STATISTICS

PASSING	Att.	Comp.	Yds.	Pct.	TD	Int.	Tkld.	Rate
Garrard	535	335	3620	62.6	15	13	42/288	81.7
Lemon	2	0	0	0.0	0	0	0/0	39.6
Jaguars	537	335	3620	62.4	15	13	42/288	81.4
Opponents	465	297	3777	63.9	25	13	29/191	95.4

SCORING	TD R	TD P	TD Rt	PAT	FG	Saf	PTS
Scobee	0	0	0	33/33	19/25	0	90
Jones-Drew	12	2	0	0/0	0/0	0	84
Owens	2	0	1	0/0	0/0	0	18
R. Williams	0	3	0	0/0	0/0	0	18
Garrard	2	0	0	0/0	0/0	0	12
M. Jones	0	2	0	0/0	0/0	0	12
M. Lewis	0	2	0	0/0	0/0	0	12
Mathis	0	0	2	0/0	0/0	0	12
Northcutt	0	2	0	0/0	0/0	0	12
G. Jones	0	1	0	0/0	0/0	0	6
Pearman	0	1	0	0/0	0/0	0	6
Porter	0	1	0	0/0	0/0	0	6
Taylor	1	0	0	0/0	0/0	0	6
Williamson	0	1	0	0/0	0/0	0	6
Jaguars	17	15	3	33/33	19/25	1	302
Opponents	14	25	2	40/40	27/30	0	367

2-Pt. Conversions: Jaguars 0-2, Opponents 0-1

RUSHING	No.	Yds	Avg	LG	TD
Jones-Drew	197	824	4.2	46t	12
Taylor	143	556	3.9	34	1
Garrard	73	322	4.4	24	2
Owens	2	43	21.5	41t	2
G. Jones	2	13	6.5	13	0
Northcutt	1	9	9.0	9	0
Washington	4	9	2.3	6	0
Williamson	1	1	1.0	1	0
R. Williams	1	0	0.0	0	0
Lemon	2	-3	-1.5	-1	0
Jaguars	426	1774	4.2	46t	17
Opponents	428	1709	4.0	40t	14

RECEIVING	No.	Yds	Avg	LG	TD
M. Jones	65	761	11.7	35	2
Jones-Drew	62	565	9.1	26	2
Northcutt	44	545	12.4	41	2
M. Lewis	41	489	11.9	30t	2
R. Williams	37	364	9.8	32	3
Walker	16	217	13.6	32	0
Taylor	16	98	6.1	17	0
G. Jones	13	116	8.9	22	1
Porter	11	181	16.5	33	1
Estandia	10	113	11.3	23	0
Angulo	8	63	7.9	17	0
Williamson	5	30	6.0	10t	1
Wrighster	2	35	17.5	27	0
Owens	2	17	8.5	10	0
Pearman	1	23	23.0	23t	1
Washington	1	9	9.0	9	0
Garrard	1	-6	-6.0	-6	0
Jaguars	335	3620	10.8	41	15
Opponents	297	3777	12.7	56t	25

INTERCEPTIONS	No.	Yds	Avg	LG	TD
Mathis	4	151	37.8	72t	2
Sensabaugh	4	38	9.5	23	0
B. Williams	2	31	15.5	27	0
Nelson	2	0	0.0	0	0
Harvey	1	0	0.0	0	0
Jaguars	13	220	16.9	72t	2
Opponents	13	181	13.9	42	1

PUNTING	No.	Yds.	Avg.	In 20	LG
Weatherford	21	915	43.6	2	57
Podlesh	46	1989	43.2	12	60
Jaguars	67	2904	43.3	14	60
Opponents	67	2877	42.9	25	61

PUNT RETURNS	Ret	FC	Yds	Avg	LG	TD
Witherspoon	17	9	192	11.3	38	0
Jones-Drew	7	1	69	9.9	15	0
Northcutt	5	7	14	2.8	9	0
Jaguars	29	17	275	9.5	38	0
Opponents	31	19	269	8.7	28	0

KICKOFF RETURNS	No.	Yds	Avg	LG	TD
Witherspoon	52	1250	24.0	51	0
Jones-Drew	13	281	21.6	33	0
Williamson	4	84	21.0	26	0
Owens	2	30	15.0	20	0
G. Jones	2	19	9.5	10	0
Reyes	1	14	14.0	14	0
Jaguars	74	1678	22.7	51	0
Opponents	51	1015	19.9	52	0

FIELD GOALS	1-19	20-29	30-39	40-49	50+
Scobee	0/0	7/7	3/6	5/7	4/5
Jaguars	0/0	7/7	3/6	5/7	4/5
Opponents	0/0	9/9	10/12	6/7	2/2

SACKS	No.
Hayward	4.5
Harvey	3.5
Spicer	3.5
Groves	2.5
D. Smith	2.5
Henderson	2.0
Ingram	2.0
Landri	2.0
Meier	2.0
Kennedy	1.0
Mathis	1.0
Mincey	1.0
Peterson	1.0
McDaniel	0.5
Jaguars	29.0
Opponents	42.0

RECORD HOLDERS

INDIVIDUAL RECORDS—CAREER

Category	Name	Performance
Rushing (Yds.)	Fred Taylor, 1998-2008	11,271
Passing (Yds.)	Mark Brunell, 1995-2003	25,698
Passing (TDs)	Mark Brunell, 1995-2003	144
Receiving (No.)	Jimmy Smith, 1995-2005	862
Receiving (Yds.)	Jimmy Smith, 1995-2005	12,287
Interceptions	Rashean Mathis, 2003-08	25
Punting (Avg.)	Bryan Barker, 1995-2000	43.5
Punt Return (Avg.)	Bobby Shaw, 2002	12.4
Kickoff Return (Avg.)	Maurice Jones-Drew, 2006-08	26.0
Field Goals	Mike Hollis, 1995-2001	175
Touchdowns (Tot.)	Fred Taylor, 1998-2008	70
Points	Mike Hollis, 1995-2001	764
*Sacks	Tony Brackens, 1996-2003	55.0

INDIVIDUAL RECORDS—SINGLE SEASON

Category	Name	Performance
Rushing (Yds.)	Fred Taylor, 2003	1,572
Passing (Yds.)	Mark Brunell, 1996	4,367
Passing (TDs)	Mark Brunell, 1998	20
Receiving (No.)	Jimmy Smith, 1999	116
Receiving (Yds.)	Jimmy Smith, 1999	1,636
Interceptions	Rashean Mathis, 2006	8
Punting (Avg.)	Bryan Barker, 1998	45.0
Punt Return (Avg.)	Reggie Barlow, 1998	12.9
Kickoff Return (Avg.)	Maurice Jones-Drew, 2006	27.7
Field Goals	Mike Hollis, 1997, 1999	31
Touchdowns (Tot.)	Fred Taylor, 1998	17
Points	Mike Hollis, 1997	134
*Sacks	Tony Brackens, 1999	12.0

INDIVIDUAL RECORDS—SINGLE GAME

Category	Name	Performance
Rushing (Yds.)	Fred Taylor, 11-19-00	234
Passing (Yds.)	Mark Brunell, 9-22-96	432
Passing (TDs)	Mark Brunell, 11-29-98	4
	Quinn Gray, 12-30-07	4
Receiving (No.)	Keenan McCardell, 10-20-96	16
Receiving (Yds.)	Jimmy Smith, 9-10-00	291
Interceptions	Many times	2
	Last time by Rashean Mathis, 11-5-06	
Field Goals	Mike Hollis, 12-1-96, 11-30-97, 9-10-00	5
	Josh Scobee, 11-25-07	5
Touchdowns (Tot.)	James Stewart, 10-12-97	5
Points	James Stewart, 10-12-97	30
*Sacks	Kelvin Pritchett, 10-5-97	3.0
	John Henderson, 10-6-02	3.0
	Paul Spicer, 9-25-05	3.0

**Sacks became an official statistic in 1982.*

JACKSONVILLE JAGUARS

2009 VETERAN ROSTER

No.	Name	Pos.	Ht.	Wt.	Birthdate	NFL Exp.	College	Hometown	How Acq.	'08 Games/ Starts
85	Angulo, Richard	TE	6-8	266	11/30/80	6	Western New Mexico	Albuquerque, N.M.	FA-'07	15/7
78	Black, Jordan	T	6-5	310	1/28/80	6	Notre Dame	Garland, Texas	FA-'08	0*
4	Bouman, Todd	QB	6-2	226	8/1/72	11	St. Cloud State	Ruthton, Minn.	FA-'09	0*
37	Considine, Sean	S	6-0	212	12/17/82	5	Iowa	Byron, Ill.	UFA(Phil)-'09	16/0
56	Durant, Justin	LB	6-1	232	9/20/85	3	Hampton	Florence, S.C.	D2-'07	14/12
99	Ellison, Atiyyah	DT	6-3	318	9/29/81	3	Missouri	St. Louis, Mo.	PS(SF)-'08	0*
83	Estandia, Greg	TE	6-8	265	11/18/82	3	Nevada-Las Vegas	Moorpark, Calif.	FA-'06	16/2
9	Garrard, David	QB	6-1	245	2/14/78	8	East Carolina	Durham, N.C.	D4-'02	16/16
54	Groves, Quentin	DE	6-3	259	7/5/84	2	Auburn	Greenville, Miss.	D2-'08	16/0
91	Harvey, Derrick	DE	6-5	271	11/9/86	2	Florida	Greenbelt, Md.	D1-'08	16/9
97	Hayward, Reggie	DE	6-5	275	3/14/79	9	Iowa State	Dolton, Ill.	UFA(Den)-'05	16/13
98	Henderson, John	DT	6-7	335	1/9/79	8	Tennessee	Nashville, Tenn.	D1-'02	14/14
81	Holt, Torry	WR	6-0	190	6/5/76	11	North Carolina State	Gibsonville, N.C.	FA-'09	16/14*
51	Ingram, Clint	LB	6-2	238	3/21/83	4	Oklahoma	Hallsville, Texas	D3-'06	16/12
59	Iwuh, Brian	LB	6-0	235	3/8/84	4	Colorado	Houston, Texas	FA-'06	15/0
22	James, William	CB	6-0	200	6/15/79	9	Western Illinois	Brownsville, Pa.	FA-'08	8/1
33	Jones, Greg	FB/RB	6-1	254	5/9/81	6	Florida State	Beaufort, S.C.	D2b-'04	12/7
32	Jones-Drew, Maurice	RB/KR	5-7	208	3/23/85	4	UCLA	Antioch, Calif.	D2-'06	16/3
66	Landri, Derek	DT	6-2	282	9/21/83	3	Notre Dame	Huntington Beach, Calif.	D5c-'07	15/0
17	Lemon, Cleo	QB	6-2	215	8/16/79	6	Arkansas State	Greenwood, Miss.	UFA(Mia)-'08	1/0
95	Lewis, Jonathan	DT	6-0	304	7/12/84	3	Virginia Tech	Richmond, Va.	FA-'08	0*
89	Lewis, Marcedes	TE	6-6	275	5/19/84	4	UCLA	Lakewood, Calif.	D1-'06	16/15
30	Lowry, Calvin	DB	5-11	200	2/13/83	4	Penn State	Fayetteville, N.C.	FA-'08	11/3
67	Manuwai, Vince	G	6-2	329	7/12/80	7	Hawaii	Honolulu, Hawaii	D3-'03	1/1
27	Mathis, Rashean	CB	6-1	190	8/27/80	7	Bethune-Cookman	Jacksonville, Fla.	D2-'03	12/12
63	Meester, Brad	C	6-3	295	3/23/77	10	Northern Iowa	Parkersburg, Iowa	D2-'00	10/10
92	Meier, Rob	DT/DE	6-5	308	8/29/77	10	Washington State	W. Vancouver, B.C., Canada	D7b-'00	15/15
61	Miller, Drew	C/G	6-5	303	7/6/85	2	Florida	Sarasota, Fla.	FA-'08	0*
94	Mincey, Jeremy	DL	6-3	272	12/14/83	3	Florida	Statesboro, Ga.	FA-'06	3/0
25	Nelson, Reggie	S	5-11	202	9/21/83	3	Florida	Melbourne, Fla.	D1-'07	13/13
42	Nkang, Chad	DB	5-11	215	7/1/85	3	Elon	Hyattsville, Mary.	D7b-'07	7/0
62	Norman, Dennis	OL	6-5	322	1/26/80	9	Princeton	Marlton, N.J.	FA-'04	16/14
86	Northcutt, Dennis	WR/KR	5-11	172	12/22/77	10	Arizona	Los Angeles, Calif.	UFA(Cle)-'07	14/2
77	Nwaneri, Uche	G/C	6-3	330	3/20/84	3	Purdue	Garland, Texas	D5a-'07	16/15
24	Owens, Montell	FB	5-10	225	5/4/84	4	Maine	Wilmington, Del.	FA-'06	16/0
79	Pashos, Tony	T	6-6	325	8/3/80	7	Illinois	Lock Port, Ill.	UFA(Balt)-'07	16/16
39	Pearman, Alvin	RB	5-10	204	9/10/82	4	Virginia	Princeton, N.J.	FA-'08	1/0
3	Podlesh, Adam	P	5-11	198	8/11/83	3	Maryland	Pittsford, N.Y.	D4a-'07	11/0
10	Scobee, Josh	K	6-1	192	6/23/82	6	Louisiana Tech	Longview, Texas	D5a-'04	16/0
57	Shaw, Tim	LB	6-1	236	3/27/84	2	Penn State	Livonia, Mich.	FA-'08	3/0
52	Smith, Daryl	LB	6-2	245	3/14/82	6	Georgia Tech	Albany, Ga.	D2a-'04	14/14
31	Starks, Scott	CB	5-9	176	6/27/83	5	Wisconsin	St. Louis, Mo.	D3-'05	1/0
72	Thomas, Tra	T	6-7	317	11/20/74	12	Florida State	DeLand, Fla.	UFA(Phil)-'09	16/16
11	Walker, Mike	WR	6-2	208	11/21/84	3	Central Florida	Orlando, Fla.	D3-'07	9/1
34	Washington, Chauncey	RB	5-11	224	4/29/86	2	Southern California	Torrance, Calif.	D7-'08	6/0
6	Weatherford, Steve	P	6-3	215	12/17/82	4	Illinois	Terre Haute, Ind.	FA-'08	14/0
29	Williams, Brian	DB	5-11	202	7/2/79	8	North Carolina State	High Point, N.C.	UFA(Minn)-'06	16/16
74	Williams, Maurice	G/T	6-5	302	1/26/79	9	Michigan	Detroit, Mich.	D2-'01	1/1
53	Williams, Thomas	LB	6-1	225	12/25/84	2	Southern California	Vacaville, Calif.	D5a-'08	6/0
84	Williamson, Troy	WR	6-1	203	4/30/83	5	South Carolina	Jackson, S.C.	T(Minn)-'08	8/2
38	Witherspoon, Brian	CB	5-10	175	6/5/85	2	Stillman	Butler, Ala.	FA-'08	14/0
93	Wyche, James	DE	6-5	275	4/19/82	4	Syracuse	Roosevelt, N.Y.	D7a-'06	0*
88	Zelenka, Joe	LS	6-3	256	3/9/76	11	Wake Forest	Cleveland, Ohio	FA-'01	16/0

* Black inactive for 1 game; Bouman inactive for 10 games with Baltimore in '08; Considine played 16 games with Philadelphia in '08; Ellison inactive for 3 games; Holt played 16 games with St. Louis; J. Lewis missed '08 season because of injury; Lowry played 11 games with Denver; Miller inactive for 8 games; Thomas played 16 games with Philadelphia; Weatherford played 7 games with New Orleans, 2 with Kansas City, 5 with Jacksonville; Wyche missed '08 season because of injury.

Players lost through free agency (4): T Khalif Barnes (Oak; 16 games in '08), LB Mike Peterson (Atl; 15), S Pierson Prioleau (NO; 16), S Gerald Sensabaugh (Dall; 16).

Also played with Jaguars in '08—G Milford Brown (6 games), CB Drayton Florence (15), WR Matt Jones (12), DT Jimmy Kennedy (6), DB Omare Lowe (5), DT Tony McDanniel (10), WR Jerry Porter (10), G Tutan Reyes (15), DE Paul Spicer (16), RB Fred Taylor (13), WR Reggie Williams (16), TE George Wrighster (5).

2009 FIRST-YEAR ROSTER

Name	Pos.	Ht.	Wt.	Birthdate	College	Hometown	How Acq.
Abdallah, Nader	DT	6-4	289	10/25/85	Ohio State	Metairie, La.	FA
Allen, Russell	LB	6-3	230	5/5/86	San Diego State	Oceanside, Calif.	FA
Bell, Kyle	FB	6-1	233	6/16/85	Colorado State	Keenesburg, Colo.	FA
Bolen, Brock	FB	6-0	233	3/24/85	Louisville	Germantown, Ohio	FA
Britton, Eben	T	6-6	310	10/14/87	Arizona	Brooklyn, N.Y.	D2
Brown, Weldon	CB	5-10	185	5/12/87	Louisiana Tech	Bossier City,La.	FA
Bruce, Mkristo (1)	DE	6-6	260	10/16/84	Washington State	Renton, Wash.	FA-'08
Cox, Derek	CB	6-1	188	9/22/86	William & Mary	Greenville, N.C.	D3b
Cox, Kennard (1)	DB	6-0	200	8/17/85	Pittsburgh	Miami, Fla.	PS(GB)-'08
Davis, Charles (1)	TE	6-6	260	3/13/83	Purdue	Fraser, Michigan	FA-'07
Desormeaux, Michael	S	6-0	204	9/29/85	Louisiana-Lafayette	New Iberia, La.	FA
Dillard, Jarett	WR	5-10	187	12/21/85	Rice	San Antonio, Texas	D5
Dupree, Maurice	WR	5-10	168	3/7/85	Jacksonville State	Centre, Ala.	FA
English, Jason	WR	5-10	188	2/17/86	Tuskegee	Mobile, Ala.	FA
Forrester, Mesphin	DB	6-2	201	3/10/86	Washington	Los Angeles, Calif.	FA
Hughes, Nate (1)	WR	6-2	190	1/18/85	Alcorn State	Starkville, Miss.	FA-'08
Hypolite,George	DT	6-1	299	8/1/87	Colorado	Los Angeles, Calif.	FA
Ittersagen, Pete	CB	5-10	191	9/28/85	Wheaton	Wheaton, Ill.	FA
Jennings, Rashad	RB	6-1	231	3/26/85	Liberty	Forest, Va.	D7a
Knighton, Terrance	DT	6-3	317	7/4/86	Temple	Windsor, Conn.	D3a
Lorenzen, Tyler	TE	6-5	226	12/24/85	Connecticut	Fremont, Iowa	FA
McLendon, Mike	RB	5-9	196	4/16/85	North Alabama	Quitman, Miss.	FA
Miller, Zach	TE	6-4	240	10/4/84	Nebraska-Omaha	Wahoo, Neb.	D6
Monroe, Eugene	T	6-5	309	4/18/87	Virginia	Plainfield, N.J.	D1
Myles, Lamar (1)	LB	5-11	230	1/7/86	Louisville	Winterhaven, Fla.	FA-'08
Navarre, Jeremy	DE	6-3	283	3/16/87	Maryland	Joppatowne, Md.	FA
Newton, Cecil	C	6-2	300	3/20/86	Tennessee State	Atlanta, Ga.	FA
Patterson, Kevin	S	5-10	185	4/9/86	Wake Forest	Kingsland, Ga.	FA
Peterson,Todd	WR	6-4	215	10/26/85	Nebraska	Grand Island, Neb.	FA
Smith, Paul (1)	QB	6-1	208	7/2/84	Tulsa	Owasso, Okla.	FA-'08
Stephenson, Cameron (1)	G	6-3	314	6/18/83	Rutgers	Inglewood, Calif.	ps(NO)-'08
Thomas, Mike	WR	5-8	193	6/4/87	Arizona	DeSota, Texas	D4
Underwood, Tiquan	WR	6-1	178	2/17/87	Rutgers	Lawrenceville, N.J.	D7b
Williams, Johnny	LB	6-2	236	2/20/86	Kentucky	Jacksonville, Fla.	FA
Williams, Julius	DE	6-2	260	7/19/86	Connecticut	Decatur, Ga.	FA
Woods, D'Juan (1)	WR	6-1	210	6/11/84	Oklahoma State	Oklahoma City, Okla.	FA-'07

The term NFL Rookie is defined as a player who is in his first season of professional football and has not been on the roster of another professional football team for any regular-season or postseason games. A Rookie is designated by an "R" on NFL rosters. Players who have been active in another professional football league or players who have NFL experience, including either preseason training camp or being on an Active List or Inactive List, or on Reserve/Injured or Reserve/Physically Unable to Perform for fewer than six regular-season games, are termed NFL First-Year Players. An NFL First-Year Player is designated by a "1" on NFL rosters. Thereafter, a player is credited with an additional year of experience for each season in which he accumulates six games on the Active List or Inactive List, or on Reserve/Injured or Reserve/Physically Unable to Perform.

Log on to www.jaguars.com for an up-to-date roster.

JACKSONVILLE JAGUARS

COACHING STAFF

Head Coach,
Jack Del Rio

Pro Career: Jack Del Rio was named head coach of the Jaguars on January 17, 2003, becoming the second head coach in franchise history. He earned his 50th career win in 2008 and is one of nine active coaches to win 50 games. In 2007, the Jaguars posted an 11-5 record and won the franchise's first playoff game since 1999. In 2006, the Jaguars finished second in the NFL in total defense and third in rushing offense but fell just shy of the playoffs with an 8-8 record. Jacksonville finished with a 12-4 record in 2005 and Del Rio guided the franchise to its first postseason appearance since 1999. In 2004, the Jaguars registered a 9-7 record for the franchise's first winning season since 1999. In 2003, six of the Jaguars' eleven losses were by seven points or less. Del Rio was the defensive coordinator for the Carolina Panthers in 2002, and the team's defense ranked second in the league after finishing thirty-first in 2001. From 1999-2001, he was the linebackers coach for the Baltimore Ravens, helping the team win Super Bowl XXXV. Del Rio previously coached in New Orleans (1997-98). He previously spent 11 years as an NFL linebacker. In 1985, he was a third-round choice of the New Orleans Saints and was named to the NFL's All-Rookie team. Del Rio also played for the Kansas City Chiefs (1987-88), Dallas Cowboys (1989-1991), and Minnesota Vikings (1992-95). He played in the Pro Bowl following the 1994 season. Career record: 51-48.

Background: Four-year starter at linebacker from 1981-84 at Southern California, where he earned consensus All-America honors as a senior and was runner-up for the Lombardi Award. He was co-MVP of the 1985 Rose Bowl. Drafted by baseball's Toronto Blue Jays in 1981, Del Rio batted .340 while playing catcher on USC's baseball team. He has a political science degree from Kansas.

Personal: Born April 4, 1963 in Castro Valley, Calif. Jack and his wife, Linda, live in Jacksonville, and have three daughters, Lauren, Hope, and Aubrey, and a son, Luke.

ASSISTANT COACHES

Johnny Cox, quality control/ offense; born February 5, 1972, Denver. Wide receiver Fort Lewis College 1990-93. No pro playing experience. College coach: Fort Lewis College 1994, North Dakota State 1996, Texas 1997-98, Fort Lewis College 1999, North Dakota State 2000-02, Holy Cross 2007. Pro coach: Tampa Bay Buccaneers 2008, joined Jaguars in 2009.

Mark Duffner, linebackers; born July 19, 1953, Annandale, Va. Defensive lineman William & Mary 1972-74. No pro playing experience. College coach: Ohio State 1975-76, Cincinnati 1977-1980, Holy Cross 1981-1991 (head coach 1986-1991), Maryland 1992-1996 (head coach). Pro coach: Cincinnati Bengals 1997-2002, Green Bay Packers 2003-2005, joined Jaguars in 2006.

Jason George, asst. strength and conditioning; born October 3, 1968, Winnipeg, Manitoba, Canada. Safety Manitoba 1991-1992. No pro playing experience. College coach: Kansas 1997-98, Fordham 1998-2008. Pro coach: Joined Jaguars in 2009.

Andy Heck, offensive line; born January 1, 1967, Fargo, N.D. Tackle Notre Dame 1985-88. Pro tackle Seattle 1989-1993, Chicago 1994-98, Washington 1999-2000. College coach: Virginia 2001-03. Pro coach: Joined Jaguars in 2003.

Nate Kaczor, asst. special teams; born April 8, 1967, Scott City, Kan. Center Utah State 1986-89. No pro playing experience. College coach: Utah State 1991-99, Nebraska-Kerney 2000-03, Idaho 2004-05, Louisiana-Monroe 2006-07. Pro coach: Joined Jaguars in 2008.

Thom Kaumeyer, asst. defensive backs; born March 17, 1967, LaJolla, Calif. Safety Palomar (JC) College 1985-86, Oregon 1987-88. Pro safety Seattle Seahawks 1989-1990, New York Giants 1991-92. College coach: Palomar College 1991-94, 1998-2000 (head coach 1994), Onward Kashiyama Ltd. (head coach, Tokyo, Japan) 1995-96, San Diego State 2002-06, Tulane 2007, Kentucky 2008. Pro coach: Atlanta Falcons 2001-02, joined Jaguars in 2008.

Dirk Koetter, offensive coordinator; born February 5, 1959, Pocatello, Idaho. Quarterback Idaho State 1978-1981. No pro playing experience. College coach: San Francisco State 1985, Texas El-Paso 1986-88, Missouri 1989-1993, Boston College 1994-95, Oregon 1996-97, Boise State 1998-2000 (head coach), Arizona State 2001-06 (head coach). Pro coach: Joined Jaguars in 2007.

Ted Monachino, defensive line; born October 15, 1966, Council Bluffs, Iowa. Defensive lineman Missouri 1988-1990. No pro playing experience. College coach: Texas Christian 1998, Southwest Missouri State 1999, Boise State 2000, Arizona State 2001-2005. Pro coach: Joined Jaguars in 2006.

Todd Monken, wide receivers; born February 2, 1966, Wheaton, Ill. Quarterback Knox College 1987-1989. No pro playing experience. College coach: Grand Valley State 1989-1990, Notre Dame 1991-92, Eastern Michigan 1993-99, Louisiana Tech 2000-01, Oklahoma State 2002-04, Louisiana State 2005-06. Pro coach: Joined Jaguars in 2007.

Kennedy Pola, running backs; born November 22, 1963, Pago, Pago, American Samoa. Fullback Southern California 1982-85. No pro playing experience. College coach: UCLA 1992-93, San Diego State 1994-96, Colorado 1997-98, San Diego State 1999, Southern California 2000-2003. Pro coach: Cleveland Browns 2004, joined Jaguars in 2005.

Russ Purnell, special teams coordinator; born June 12, 1948, Chicago. Center Orange Coast (Calif.) J.C. 1966-67, Whittier College 1968-69. No pro playing experience. College coach: Whittier College 1970-71, Southern California 1982-85. Pro coach: Seattle Seahawks 1986-1994, Houston Oilers/Tennessee Titans 1995-98, Baltimore Ravens 1999-2001, Indianapolis Colts 2002-2008, joined Jaguars in 2009.

Luke Richesson, strength and conditioning; born April 29, 1974, Kansas City, Missouri. Defensive back Kansas 1992-96. No pro playing experience. College coach: Wyoming 1998, Arizona State 1999-2000. Pro coach: Joined Jaguars in 2009.

Mike Shula, quarterbacks; born June 3, 1965, Baltimore. Quarterback Alabama 1984-86. No pro playing experience. College coach: Alabama 2003-06 (head coach). Pro coach: Miami Dolphins 1991-92, Chicago Bears 1993-95, Tampa Bay Buccaneers 1996-99, Miami Dolphins 2000-02, joined Jaguars in 2007.

Mike Tice, asst. head coach/offense; born February 2, 1959, Bayshore, N.Y. Quarterback Maryland 1977-1980. Pro tight end Seattle Seahawks 1981-1988, 1990-91, Washington Redskins 1989, Minnesota Vikings 1992-1993, 1995. Pro coach: Minnesota Vikings 1996-2005 (head coach 2001-2005), joined Jaguars in 2006.

Mel Tucker, defensive coordinator; born January 4, 1972, Cleveland. Defensive back Wisconsin 1992-95. No pro playing experience. College coach: Michigan State 1997-98, Miami (Ohio) 1999, Louisiana State 2000, Ohio State 2001-04. Pro coach: Cleveland Browns 2005-08, joined Jaguars in 2009.

Cory Undlin, defensive assistant; born June 29, 1971, St. Cloud, Minn. Defensive back California Lutheran 1990-94. No pro playing experience. College coach: California Lutheran 1998-2001, Fresno State 2002-03. Pro coach: New England Patriots 2004, Cleveland Browns 2005-08, joined Jaguars in 2009.

American Football Conference
West Division
Team Colors: Red, Gold, and White
One Arrowhead Drive
Kansas City, Missouri 64129
Telephone: (816) 920-9300

2009 SCHEDULE
PRESEASON

Aug. 15	**Houston**	7:00
Aug. 21	at Minnesota	7:00
Aug. 29	**Seattle**	7:00
Sep. 3	at St. Louis	7:00

REGULAR SEASON

Sep. 13	at Baltimore	1:00
Sep. 20	**Oakland**	12:00
Sep. 27	at Philadelphia	1:00
Oct. 4	**N.Y. Giants**	12:00
Oct. 11	**Dallas**	12:00
Oct. 18	at Washington	1:00
Oct. 25	**San Diego**	12:00
Nov. 1	BYE	
Nov. 8	at Jacksonville	1:00
Nov. 15	at Oakland	1:05
Nov. 22	**Pittsburgh**	12:00
Nov. 29	at San Diego	1:05
Dec. 6	**Denver**	12:00
Dec. 13	**Buffalo**	12:00
Dec. 20	**Cleveland**	12:00
Dec. 27	at Cincinnati	1:00
Jan. 3	at Denver	2:15

Stadium: Arrowhead Stadium (opened in 1972) •**Capacity:** 79,451
One Arrowhead Drive
Kansas City, Missouri 64129
Playing Surface: Grass
Training Camp: University of Wisconsin-River Falls
River Falls, WI 54022

ARROWHEAD STADIUM

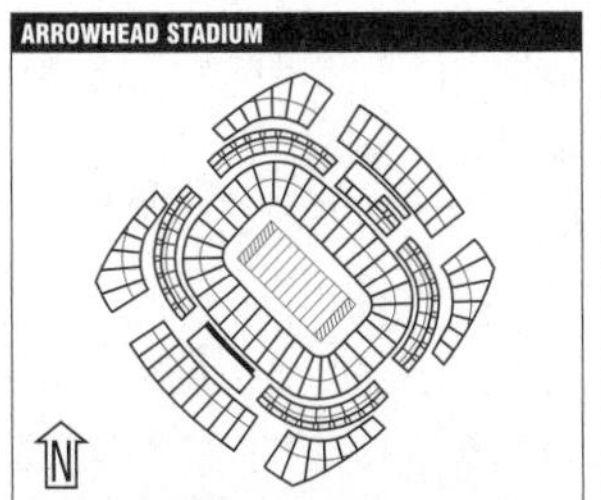

CLUB OFFICIALS
Chairman of the Board: Clark Hunt
President: Denny Thum
General Manager: Scott Pioli
Senior Vice President of Administration: Bill Newman
Secretary: Jim Seigfreid
Director of Finance/Treasurer: Dale Young
Vice President of Sales and Marketing: Tammy Fruits
Director of College Scouting: Phil Emery
Director of Public Relations: Bob Moore
Associate Director of Public Relations: Pete Moris
Director of Stadium Operations: Steve Schneider
Director of Logistics: Ken Blume
Director of Special Events: Gary Spani
Executive Director of Player Development: Lamonte Winston
Director of Community Relations: Brenda Sniezek
Director of Ticket Operations: Doug Hopkins
Director of Salary Cap/General Counsel: Woodie Dixon
Director of Sales and Marketing: David Steffano
Equipment Manager: Mike Davidson
Asst. Equipment Managers: Allen Wright, Chris Shropshire, Kyle Crumbaugh
Head Athletic Trainer: David Price
Assistant Athletic Trainers: David Glover, Jimmy Ntelekos, Owen Stanley
Director of Video Operations: Pat Brazil
Assistant Director Video Operations: Ken Radino
Video Assistant: Josh Shmidt

COACHING HISTORY
Dallas Texans 1960-62
(389-360-12)
Records include postseason games

1960-1974	Hank Stram	129-79-10
1975-77	Paul Wiggin*	11-24-0
1977	Tom Bettis	1-6-0
1978-1982	Marv Levy	31-42-0
1983-86	John Mackovic	30-35-0
1987-88	Frank Gansz	8-22-1
1989-1998	Marty Schottenheimer	104-65-1
1999-2000	Gunther Cunningham	16-16-0
2001-05	Dick Vermeil	44-37-0
2006-08	Herm Edwards	15-34-0

*Released after seven games in 1977

PAID ATTENDANCE
Home 533,609 Away 542,761
Total 1,076,370
Single-game home record, *82,893 (10/2/00)
Single-season home record, 629,569 (1999)
*Arrowhead Stadium attendance: 78,502
Kauffman Stadium attendance: 4,391

2009 DRAFT CHOICES

Round	Name	Pos.	College
1	Tyson Jackson	DE	Louisiana State
3	Alex Magee	DT	Purdue
4	Donald Washington	DB	Ohio State
5	Colin Brown	T	Missouri
6	Quinten Lawrence	WR	McNeese State
7	Javarris Williams	RB	Tennessee State
	Jake O'Connell	TE	Miami (Ohio)
	Ryan Succop	K	South Carolina

KANSAS CITY CHIEFS

2008 TEAM RECORD

PRESEASON (2-2)

Date	Result	Opponent
8/7	W 24-20	at Chicago
8/16	L 17-27	Arizona
8/23	L 0-24	at Miami
8/28	W 21-17	St. Louis

REGULAR SEASON (2-14)

Date	Result	Opponent
9/7	L 10-17	at New England
9/14	L 8-23	Oakland
9/21	L 14-38	at Atlanta
9/28	W 33-19	Denver
10/5	L 0-34	at Carolina
10/19	L 10-34	Tennessee
10/26	L 24-28	at New York Jets
11/2	L 27-30	Tampa Bay (OT)
11/9	L 19-20	at San Diego
11/16	L 20-30	New Orleans
11/23	L 31-54	Buffalo
11/30	W 20-13	at Oakland
12/7	L 17-24	at Denver
12/14	L 21-22	San Diego
12/21	L 31-38	Miami
12/28	L 6-16	at Cincinnati

(OT) Overtime

SCORE BY PERIODS

Chiefs	68	102	33	88	0	— 291
Opponents	77	141	106	113	3	— 440

2008 TEAM STATISTICS

	Chiefs	Opp.
Total First Downs	273	344
Rushing	94	133
Passing	161	195
Penalty	18	16
3rd Down: Made/Att	82/214	100/211
3rd Down Pct.	38.3	47.4
4th Down: Made/Att	7/18	6/14
4th Down Pct.	38.9	42.9
Possession Avg.	27:56	32:04
Total Net Yards	4939	6291
Avg. Per Game	308.7	393.2
Total Plays	957	1041
Avg. Per Play	5.2	6.0
Net Yards Rushing	1810	2543
Avg. Per Game	113.1	158.9
Total Rushes	379	509
Net Yards Passing	3129	3748
Avg. Per Game	195.6	234.3
Sacked/Yards Lost	37/229	10/62
Gross Yards	3358	3810
Att./Completions	541/310	522/348
Completion Pct.	57.3	66.7
Had Intercepted	16	13
Punts/Average	82/44.2	50/43.9
Net Punting Avg.	82/37.5	50/37.3
Penalties/Yards	78/645	81/588
Fumbles/Ball Lost	20/8	30/16
Touchdowns	35	49
Rushing	9	25
Passing	23	21
Returns	3	3

2008 INDIVIDUAL STATISTICS

PASSING	Att.	Comp.	Yds.	Pct.	TD	Int.	Tkld.	Rate
Thigpen	420	230	2608	54.8	18	12	26/162	76.0
Huard	81	50	477	61.7	2	4	9/56	65.7
Croyle	29	20	151	69.0	0	0	1/10	81.3
Gray	8	7	76	87.5	1	0	0/0	145.8
Bradley	1	1	37	100.0	1	0	0/0	158.3
Hagans	1	1	5	100.0	0	0	1/1	87.5
L. Johnson	1	1	4	100.0	1	0	0/0	122.9
Chiefs	541	310	3358	57.3	23	16	37/229	77.5
Opponents	522	348	3810	66.7	21	13	10/62	91.1

SCORING	TD R	TD P	TD Rt	PAT	FG	Saf	PTS
Gonzalez	0	10	0	0/0	0/0	0	60
Barth	0	0	0	24/24	10/12	0	54
Bowe	0	7	0	0/0	0/0	0	42
L. Johnson	5	0	0	0/0	0/0	0	30
Novak	0	0	0	7/7	6/10	0	25
Thigpen	3	1	0	0/0	0/0	0	24
Bradley	0	3	0	0/0	0/0	0	18
Leggett	0	0	2	0/0	0/0	0	12
Charles	0	1	0	0/0	0/0	0	6
Darling	0	1	0	0/0	0/0	0	6
Flowers	0	0	1	0/0	0/0	0	6
K. Smith	1	0	0	0/0	0/0	0	6
Cox	0	0	0	0/0	0/0	0	2
Chiefs	9	23	3	31/31	16/22	0	291
Opponents	25	21	3	45/45	33/36	0	440

2-Pt. Conversions: Cox.
Chiefs 1-4, Opponents 1-4.

RUSHING	No.	Yds	Avg	LG	TD
L. Johnson	193	874	4.5	65	5
Thigpen	62	386	6.2	32	3
Charles	67	357	5.3	30	0
K. Smith	35	100	2.9	19	1
Savage	15	53	3.5	11	0
Gray	1	27	27.0	27	0
Huard	4	13	3.3	15	0
Hagans	1	2	2.0	2	0
Cox	1	-2	-2.0	-2	0
Chiefs	379	1810	4.8	65	9
Opponents	509	2543	5.0	80t	25

RECEIVING	No.	Yds	Avg	LG	TD
Gonzalez	96	1058	11.0	35	10
Bowe	86	1022	11.9	36	7
Bradley	30	380	12.7	56	3
Charles	27	272	10.1	75	1
Darling	17	247	14.5	68	1
L. Johnson	12	74	6.2	20	0
K. Smith	10	52	5.2	8	0
Cox	8	19	2.4	5	0
Franklin	7	83	11.9	42	0
Cottam	7	63	9.0	19	0
Webb	5	46	9.2	15	0
Savage	2	0	0.0	2	0
Thigpen	1	37	37.0	37t	1
Hagans	1	7	7.0	7	0
Battle	1	-2	-2.0	-2	0
Chiefs	310	3358	10.8	75	23
Opponents	348	3810	10.9	70t	21

INTERCEPTIONS	No.	Yds	Avg	LG	TD
Page	4	2	0.5	2	0
Flowers	2	118	59.0	91t	1
Carr	2	67	33.5	35	0
Surtain	1	50	50.0	50	0
Leggett	1	27	27.0	27t	1
D. Johnson	1	7	7.0	7	0
McGraw	1	4	4.0	4	0
Pollard	1	0	0.0	0	0
Chiefs	13	275	21.2	91t	2
Opponents	16	323	20.2	64t	2

PUNTING	No.	Yds.	Avg.	In 20	LG
Colquitt	70	3110	44.4	27	73
Weatherford	12	512	42.7	1	58
Chiefs	82	3622	44.2	28	73
Opponents	50	2196	43.9	19	70

PUNT RETURNS	Ret	FC	Yds	Avg	LG	TD
Robinson	11	0	94	8.5	32	0
Savage	8	2	17	2.1	11	0
Sams	7	3	58	8.3	16	0
Chiefs	26	5	169	6.5	32	0
Opponents	33	16	307	9.3	37	0

KICKOFF RETURNS	No.	Yds	Avg	LG	TD
Savage	26	633	24.3	59	0
Robinson	19	420	22.1	36	0
Charles	15	321	21.4	40	0
Sams	9	180	20.0	36	0
Leggett	5	103	20.6	30	0
Cox	3	11	3.7	8	0
Franklin	1	16	16.0	16	0
McGraw	1	18	18.0	18	0
Taylor	1	14	14.0	14	0
Chiefs	80	1716	21.5	59	0
Opponents	62	1465	23.6	97t	1

FIELD GOALS	1-19	20-29	30-39	40-49	50+
Barth	0/0	6/6	3/4	1/1	0/1
Novak	0/0	3/3	1/3	2/3	0/1
Chiefs	0/0	9/9	4/7	3/4	0/2
Opponents	0/0	8/9	15/16	6/7	4/4

SACKS	No.
Hali	3.0
Babin	2.0
D. Johnson	1.5
Boone	1.0
Dorsey	1.0
R. Edwards	1.0
Thomas	0.5
Chiefs	10.0
Opponents	37.0

RECORD HOLDERS

INDIVIDUAL RECORDS—CAREER

Category	Name	Performance
Rushing (Yds.)	Priest Holmes, 2001-07	6,070
Passing (Yds.)	Len Dawson, 1962-1975	28,507
Passing (TDs)	Len Dawson, 1962-1975	237
Receiving (No.)	Tony Gonzalez, 1997-2008	916
Receiving (Yds.)	Tony Gonzalez, 1997-2008	10,940
Interceptions	Emmitt Thomas, 1966-1978	58
Punting (Avg.)	Dustin Colquitt, 2005-08	43.7
Punt Return (Avg.)	Noland Smith, 1967-69	11.1
Kickoff Return (Avg.)	Noland Smith, 1967-69	26.8
Field Goals	Nick Lowery, 1980-1993	329
Touchdowns (Tot.)	Priest Holmes, 2001-07	83
Points	Nick Lowery, 1980-1993	1,466
*Sacks	Derrick Thomas, 1989-1999	126.5

INDIVIDUAL RECORDS—SINGLE SEASON

Category	Name	Performance
Rushing (Yds.)	Larry Johnson, 2006	1,789
Passing (Yds.)	Trent Green, 2004	4,591
Passing (TDs)	Len Dawson, 1964	30
Receiving (No.)	Tony Gonzalez, 2004	102
Receiving (Yds.)	Derrick Alexander, 2000	1,391
Interceptions	Emmitt Thomas, 1974	12
Punting (Avg.)	Dustin Colquitt, 2007	45.5
Punt Return (Avg.)	Dante Hall, 2003	16.3
Kickoff Return (Avg.)	Dave Grayson, 1962	29.7
Field Goals	Nick Lowery, 1990	34
Touchdowns (Tot.)	Priest Holmes, 2003	27
Points	Priest Holmes, 2003	162
*Sacks	Derrick Thomas, 1990	20.0

INDIVIDUAL RECORDS—SINGLE GAME

Category	Name	Performance
Rushing (Yds.)	Larry Johnson, 11-20-05	211
Passing (Yds.)	Elvis Grbac, 11-5-00	504
Passing (TDs)	Len Dawson, 11-1-64	6
Receiving (No.)	Tony Gonzalez, 1-2-05	14
Receiving (Yds.)	Stephone Paige, 12-22-85	309
Interceptions	Bobby Ply, 12-16-62	**4
	Bobby Hunt, 10-4-64	**4
	Deron Cherry, 9-29-85	**4
Field Goals	Many times	5
	Last time by Nick Lowery, 9-20-93	
Touchdowns (Tot.)	Abner Haynes, 11-26-61	5
Points	Abner Haynes, 11-26-61	30
*Sacks	Derrick Thomas, 11-11-90	**7.0

**Sacks became an official statistic in 1982.*
***NFL Record*

KANSAS CITY CHIEFS

2009 VETERAN ROSTER

No.	Name	Pos.	Ht.	Wt.	Birthdate	NFL Exp.	College	Hometown	How Acq.	'08 Games/ Starts
76	Albert, Branden	T	6-5	316	11/4/84	2	Virginia	Glen Burnie, Md.	D1b-'08	15/15
5	Barth, Connor	K	5-11	193	4/11/86	2	North Carolina	Wilmington, N.C.	FA-'08	10/0
26	Battle, Jackie	RB	6-2	238	10/1/83	2	Houston	Humble, Texas	FA-'08	9/0
52	Beisel, Monty	LB	6-3	244	8/20/78	9	Kansas State	Douglass, Kan.	UFA(Ariz)-'09	16/0*
70	Boone, Alfonso	DE	6-3	305	1/11/76	9	Mt. San Antonio (Calif.) J.C.	Saginaw, Mich.	UFA(Chi)-'07	15/4
82	Bowe, Dwayne	WR	6-2	221	9/21/84	3	Louisiana State	Miami, Fla.	D1-'07	16/16
83	Bradley, Mark	WR	6-1	201	1/29/82	5	Oklahoma	Pine Bluff, Ark.	FA-'08	12/8*
39	Carr, Brandon	CB	6-0	207	5/19/86	2	Grand Valley State	Flint, Mich.	D5-'08	16/16
7	t- Cassel, Matt	QB	6-4	230	5/17/82	5	Southern California	Chatsworth, Calif.	T(NE)-'09	16/15*
25	Charles, Jamaal	RB	5-11	199	12/27/86	2	Texas	Port Arthur, Texas	D3a-'08	16/2
30	Colclough, Ricardo	CB	5-11	194	9/26/83	6	Tusculum	Sumter, S.C.	FA-'08	6/1
2	Colquitt, Dustin	P	6-3	210	5/6/82	5	Tennessee	Knoxville, Tenn.	D3-'05	14/0
10	Copper, Terrance	WR	6-0	207	3/12/82	6	East Carolina	Washington, N.C.	UFA(Balt)-'09	7/0*
87	Cottam, Brad	TE	6-7	269	11/28/84	2	Tennessee	Germantown, Tenn.	D3b-'08	16/7
42	Cox, Mike	FB	6-0	252	7/11/85	2	Georgia Tech	Woodbury, N.J.	FA-'08	16/5
12	Croyle, Brodie	QB	6-2	206	2/6/83	4	Alabama	Rainbow City, Ala.	D3-'06	2/2
85	Curtis, Tony	TE	6-5	251	2/11/83	4	Portland State	Seaside, Calif.	FA-'09	16/6*
57	Dacus, Weston	LB	6-1	232	9/19/85	2	Arkansas	Searcy, Ark.	FA-'08	8/0
23	Daniels, Travis	CB	6-1	195	9/8/82	5	Louisiana State	Hollywood, Fla.	UFA(Cle)-'09	7/1*
81	Darling, Devard	WR	6-1	213	4/16/82	6	Washington State	Nassau, Bahamas	UFA(Balt)-'08	16/9
60	De La Puente, Brian	G	6-2	308	5/13/85	2	California	San Clemente, Calif.	W(SF)-'08	0*
72	Dorsey, Glenn	DT	6-1	297	8/1/85	2	Louisiana State	Gonzales, La.	D1a-'08	16/16
95	Edwards, Ron	DT	6-3	315	7/12/79	9	Texas A&M	Houston, Texas	UFA(Buff)-'06	16/0
84	Engram, Bobby	WR	5-10	192	1/7/73	14	Penn State	Camden, S.C.	UFA(Sea)-'09	13/11*
24	Flowers, Brandon	CB	5-9	187	2/18/86	2	Virginia Tech	Delray Beach, Fla.	D2-'08	14/13
48	Gafford, Thomas	LS	6-2	235	1/29/83	2	Houston	Webster, Texas	FA-'08	9/0
73	Ghiaciuc, Eric	C	6-4	303	5/28/81	5	Central Michigan	Oxford, Mich.	UFA(Cin)-'09	16/16*
92	Gilberry, Wallace	DE	6-2	268	12/5/84	2	Alabama	Bay Minette, Ala.	FA-'08	5/0
79	Goff, Mike	G	6-5	311	1/6/76	12	Iowa	Peru, Ill.	UFA(SD)-'09	16/16*
91	Hali, Tamba	DE	6-3	275	11/3/83	4	Penn State	Ghanga, Liberia	D1-'06	15/15
99	Jackson, T.J.	DT	6-0	304	12/12/83	3	Auburn	Opelika, Ala.	FA-'08	4/0
56	Johnson, Derrick	LB	6-3	242	11/22/82	5	Texas	Waco, Texas	D1-'05	14/14
27	Johnson, Larry	RB	6-1	230	11/19/79	7	Penn State	State College, Pa.	D1-'03	12/12
97	Johnston, Brian	DE	6-4	269	5/2/86	2	Gardner-Webb	San Diego, Calif.	D7a-'08	9/0
17	Jones, C.J.	WR	5-11	195	9/20/80	2	Iowa	Santaluces, Fla.	FA-'09	0*
31	Leggett, Maurice	CB	5-11	188	10/2/86	2	Valdosta State	McKeesport, Pa.	FA-'08	12/3
15	Martin, Ingle	QB	6-2	220	8/15/82	3	Furman	Nashville, Tenn.	FA-'08	0*
51	Mays, Corey	LB	6-1	245	11/27/83	4	Notre Dame	Chicago, Ill.	FA-'09	12/0*
90	McBride, Turk	DE	6-2	278	5/30/85	3	Tennessee	Camden, N.J.	D2-'07	9/9
47	McGraw, Jon	S	6-3	208	4/2/79	8	Kansas State	Louisville, Ky.	UFA(Det)-'07	16/0
77	McIntosh, Damion	T	6-4	320	3/25/77	10	Kansas State	Kingston, Jamaica	UFA(Mia)-'07	16/16
38	Morgan, DaJuan	S	6-0	203	10/21/85	2	North Carolina State	Riviera Beach, Fla.	D3c-'08	15/0
64	Niswanger, Rudy	C	6-5	301	11/9/82	4	Louisiana State	Monroe, La.	FA-'06	15/15
44	Page, Jarrad	S	6-0	225	10/19/84	4	UCLA	Oakland, Calif.	D7-'06	16/16
49	Pollard, Bernard	S	6-1	224	12/23/84	4	Purdue	Ft. Wayne, Ind.	D2-'06	16/16
67	Richardson, Barry	T	6-6	319	5/15/86	2	Clemson	Mount Pleasant, S.C.	D6a-'08	6/0
89	Ryan, Sean	TE	6-5	260	3/27/80	6	Boston College	Buffalo, N.Y.	UFA(SF)-'09	8/1*
29	Savage, Dantrell	RB	5-8	182	2/15/85	2	Oklahoma State	Columbus, Ga.	CFA-'08	8/0
21	Smith, Kolby	RB	5-11	219	12/15/84	3	Louisville	Tallahassee, Fla.	D5a-'07	7/3
74	Smith, Wade	G	6-4	296	4/26/81	7	Memphis	Dallas, Texas	UFA(NYJ)-'08	15/7
96	Studebaker, Andy	DE	6-3	248	9/16/85	2	Wheaton	Congerville, Ill.	FA-'08	6/0
75	Taylor, Herb	T	6-3	295	9/22/84	3	Texas Christian	Houston, Texas	D6-'07	16/1
4	Thigpen, Tyler	QB	6-1	224	4/14/84	3	Coastal Carolina	Winnsboro, S.C.	W(Minn)-'07	14/11
55	Thomas, Zach	LB	5-11	242	9/1/73	14	Texas Tech	Pampa, Texas	UFA(Dall)-'09	16/14*
93	Tyler, Tank	DT	6-2	306	2/14/85	3	North Carolina State	Fayetteville, N.C.	D3-'07	16/16
50	t- Vrabel, Mike	LB	6-4	261	8/14/75	13	Ohio State	Stowe, Ohio	T(NE)-'09	16/14*
54	Waters, Brian	G	6-3	320	2/18/77	10	North Texas	Waxahachie, Texas	FA-'00	16/16
80	Webb, Jeff	WR	6-2	211	1/31/82	4	San Diego State	Pontiac, Mich.	D6b-'06	5/1
53	Williams, Demorrio	LB	6-1	232	7/6/80	6	Nebraska	Carthage, Texas	UFA(Atl)-'08	16/9

* Beisel played 16 games with Arizona in '08; Bradley played 2 games with Chicago and 10 games with Kansas City; Cassel played 16 games with New England; Copper played 5 games with New Orleans and 2 games with Baltimore; Curtis played 16 games with Dallas; Daniels played 7 games with Cleveland; De La Puente inactive for 7 games; Engram played 13 games with Seattle; Ghiaciuc played 16 games with Cincinnati; Goff played 16 games with San Diego; Jones inactive for 1 game with New England; Martin inactive for 6 games, Mays played 12 games with Cincinnati; Ryan played 1 game with Miami, 1 game with New Orleans and 6 games with San Francisco; Thomas played 16 games with Dallas; Vrabel played 16 games with New England.

t- Chiefs traded for Cassel and Vrabel (NE).

Traded—TE Tony Gonzalez (16 games in '08) to Atlanta.

Players lost through free agency (1): LB Pat Thomas (Buff; 12 games in '08).

Also played with Chiefs in '08—DE Jason Babin (7 games), LB Rocky Boiman (11), CB Tyron Brackenridge (1), DT Antwon Burton (1), S Oliver Celestin (8), LS Jean-Philippe Darche (7), LB Donnie Edwards (7), TE John Paul Foschi (7), WR Will Franklin (13), LB Curtis Gatewood (6), QB Quinn Gray (1), WR Marques Hagans (2), QB Damon Huard (5), G Adrian Jones (11), DT Derek Lokey (1), CB David Macklin (4), K Nick Novak (6), CB Dimitri Patterson (7), WR Kevin Robinson (8), KR B.J. Sams (3), CB Patrick Surtain (8), LB Erik Walden (9), G Tavares Washington (2), P Steve Weatherford (2).

2009 FIRST-YEAR ROSTER

Name	Pos.	Ht.	Wt.	Birthdate	College	Hometown	How Acq.
Bates, Jackie	CB	5-10	180	10/12/86	Hampton	Concord, Calif.	FA
Belcher, Jovan	LB	6-2	228	7/24/87	Maine	West Babylon, N.Y.	FA
Brown, Colin	T	6-7	335	8/29/85	Missouri	Braymer, Mo.	D5
Collins, Jed (1)	TE/FB	6-1	249	3/3/86	Washington State	Mission Viejo, Calif.	FA
Crabtree, Tom	TE	6-5	244	11/4/85	Miami (Ohio)	Carroll, Ohio	FA
Fryar, Londen	CB	5-11	192	5/19/86	Western Michigan	Jobstown, N.J.	FA
Gales, Dion	DE	6-5	259	8/17/85	Troy State	New Orleans, La.	FA
Goldberg, Cameron	T	6-6	265	11/17/85	Duke	Owings Mills, Md.	FA
Greenwood, Robert	DE	6-5	278	3/2/87	Alabama	Prattville, Ala.	FA
Harris, Darryl	G	6-4	300	1/14/85	Mississippi	Clarksdale, Miss.	FA
Harrison, Edwin (1)	G	6-3	314	11/18/84	Colorado	Houston, Texas	FA-'08
Jackson, Tyson	DE	6-4	296	6/6/86	Louisiana State	Edgard, La.	D1
Johnson, Taurus	WR	6-1	205	4/13/86	South Florida	Cape Coral, Fla.	FA
Lawrence, Quinten	WR	6-0	184	9/21/84	McNeese State	Carencro, La.	D6
Lokey, Derek (1)	DT	6-1	287	11/25/85	Texas	Denton, Texas	FA-'08
Magee, Alex	DT	6-3	298	4/28/87	Purdue	Oswego, Ill.	D3
O'Connell, Jake	TE	6-3	250	11/6/85	Miami (Ohio)	Naples, Fla.	D7b
Price, Ricky	S	6-1	195	9/16/87	Oklahoma State	Houston, Texas	FA
Purdum, Tanner	LS	6-3	270	8/15/84	Baker	Hewitt, Texas	FA
Robertson, Darrell (1)	LB	6-4	246	4/15/86	Georgia Tech	Jonesboro, Ga.	FA
Smith, Corey	LB	6-1	225	1/17/87	Cincinnati	Salem, N.J.	FA
Succop, Ryan	K	6-2	218	9/19/86	South Carolina	Hickory, N.C.	D7c
Walters, Pierre	LB	6-5	269	3/25/86	Eastern Illinois	Westchester, Ill.	FA
Washington, Donald	CB	6-1	197	7/28/86	Ohio State	Indianapolis, Ind.	D4
Washington, Tavares (1)	G	6-4	315	4/20/83	Florida	Rolling Fork, Miss.	FA-'08
Williams, Javarris	RB	5-10	223	4/8/86	Tennessee State	Richmond, Texas	D7a
Wright, Rodney (1)	WR	5-9	181	11/28/79	Fresno State	Bakersfield, Calif.	FA

The term NFL Rookie is defined as a player who is in his first season of professional football and has not been on the roster of another professional football team for any regular-season or postseason games. A Rookie is designated by an "R" on NFL rosters. Players who have been active in another professional football league or players who have NFL experience, including either preseason training camp or being on an Active List or Inactive List, or on Reserve/Injured or Reserve/Physically Unable to Perform for fewer than six regular-season games, are termed NFL First-Year Players. An NFL First-Year Player is designated by a "1" on NFL rosters. Thereafter, a player is credited with an additional year of experience for each season in which he accumulates six games on the Active List or Inactive List, or on Reserve/Injured or Reserve/Physically Unable to Perform.

Log on to www.kcchiefs.com for an up-to-date roster.

COACHING STAFF

Head Coach,
Todd Haley

Pro Career: Todd Haley was named head coach of the Kansas City Chiefs by Chairman of the Board Clark Hunt on February 6, 2009. At age 42, he is the second-youngest head coach in franchise history. Haley joined the Chiefs after a two-year stint as the offensive coordinator of the Arizona Cardinals (2007-08). He is entering his 15th season in the NFL and his 13th campaign in a coaching capacity in 2009. Haley has been on the coaching staff of four different franchises that have reached the playoffs—Arizona, Dallas, Chicago and the N.Y. Jets—serving under head coach Bill Parcells in both Dallas and with the N.Y. Jets. In 2008, Haley helped the Cardinals claim their first division crown since 1975 as Arizona earned a berth in Super Bowl XLIII. The Cardinals offense tied for third in the league in scoring, registering a franchise-record 427 points. Arizona also ranked second in the league in passing offense, and fourth in total offense. Under Haley in 2007, the Cardinals were fifth in the league in passing and set a single-season franchise record with 32 touchdown passes. He served three seasons as passing game coordinator/wide receivers coach for Dallas (2004-06). In 2006, the Cowboys offense was second in third-down efficiency and fourth in both scoring and passing. Haley joined Dallas after a three-year tour of duty as wide receivers coach for Chicago (2001-03). In 2001, the Bears went 13-3 and won the NFC Central. He served as the N.Y. Jets wide receivers coach (1999-2000) after serving as an offensive assistant/quality control coach (1997-98). Haley began his NFL career with the Jets as an assistant in the scouting department (1995). Career record: 0-0.

Background: Haley was a member of the collegiate golf squads at Florida and Miami. He later earned a degree in Communications from North Florida in 1991. He is the son of longtime NFL personnel man Dick Haley, who was one of the architects of the great Steelers teams of the 1970s.

Personal: Born on February 28, 1967 in Atlanta, Georgia. He and his wife, Chrissy, have four daughters: Taylor, Peyton, Kady, and Ella and one son, Richard Todd, Jr.

ASSISTANT COACHES

Bob Bicknell, tight ends; born November 13, 1969, Holliston, Mass. Tight end Boston College 1988-1991. No pro playing experience. College coach: Boston 1993-97, Temple 2006. Pro coach: Frankfurt Galaxy (NFLEL) 1998-99, Berlin Thunder (NFLEL) 2000-03, Cologne Centurions (NFLEL) 2004-05, joined Chiefs in 2007.

Ronnie Bradford, defensive assistant; born October 1, 1970, Minot, N.D. Defensive back Colorado 1989-1992. Pro defensive back Denver Broncos 1993-95, Arizona Cardinals 1996, Atlanta Falcons 1997-2001, Minnesota Vikings 2002. Pro coach: Denver Broncos 2003-08, joined Chiefs in 2009.

Maurice Carthon, asst. head coach; born April 24, 1961, Chicago. Running back Arkansas State 1979-1982. Pro running back New Jersey Generals (USFL) 1983-85, New York Giants 1985-1991, Indianapolis Colts 1992. Pro coach: New England Patriots 1994-96, New York Jets 1997-2000, Detroit Lions 2001-02, Dallas Cowboys 2003-04, Cleveland Browns 2005-06, Arizona Cardinals 2007-08, joined Chiefs in 2009.

Joel Collier, TBA; born December 25, 1963, Buffalo. Linebacker Northern Colorado 1984-87. No pro playing experience. College coach: Syracuse 1988-89. Pro coach: Tampa Bay Buccaneers 1990, New England Patriots 1991-93, 2005-07, Miami Dolphins 1994-2004, joined Chiefs in 2009.

Joe D'Alessandris, asst. offensive line, born April 29, 1954, Aliquippa, Pa. Guard Western Carolina 1972-76. No pro playing experience. College coach: Western Carolina 1977-78, Livingston 1979-1983, Memphis 1984-85, UT-Chattanooga 1986-89, Samford 1993, Texas A&M 1994, Pittsburgh 1996, Duke 1997-2001, Georgia Tech 2002-07. Pro coach: Ottawa Rough Riders (CFL) 1990, Birmingham Fire (WLAF) 1991-92, Memphis 1995, joined Chiefs in 2008.

Chan Gailey, offensive coordinator; born January 5, 1952, Gainesville, Ga. Quarterback Florida 1971-73. No pro playing experience. College coach: Florida 1974-75, Troy State 1976-78, 1983-84 (head coach 1983-84), Air Force 1979-1982, Samford 1993 (head coach), Georgia Tech 2002-07 (head coach). Pro coach: Denver Broncos 1985-1990, Birmingham Fire (WLAF) 1991-92 (head coach), Pittsburgh Steelers 1994-97, Dallas Cowboys 1998-99 (head coach), Miami Dolphins 2000-01, joined Chiefs in 2008.

Gary Gibbs, linebackers; born August 13, 1952, Beaumont, Texas. Linebacker Oklahoma 1972-74. No pro playing experience. College coach: Oklahoma 1975-1994 (head coach 1989-1994), Georgia 2000, Louisiana State 2001. Pro coach: Dallas Cowboys 2002-04, New Orleans Saints 2006-08, joined Chiefs in 2009.

Steve Hoffman, special teams; born September 8, 1958, Camden, N.J. Quarterback/running back/wide receiver Dickinson College 1977-1980. Pro punter Washington Federals (USFL) 1983. College coach: Miami 1985-87. Pro coach: Dallas Cowboys 1989-2004, Atlanta Falcons 2006, Miami Dolphins 2007-08, joined Chiefs in 2009.

Tim Krumrie, defensive line; born May 20, 1960, Menomonie, Wis. Defensive tackle Wisconsin 1979-1982, Pro defensive tackle Cincinnati Bengals 1983-1994. Pro coach: Cincinnati Bengals 1995-2002, Buffalo Bills 2003-05, joined Chiefs in 2006.

Bill Muir, offensive line; born October 26, 1942, Pittsburgh. Tackle Susquehanna 1962-64. No pro playing experience. College coach: Susquehanna 1965, Delaware Valley 1966-67, Rhode Island 1970-71, Idaho State 1972-73, Southern Methodist 1976-77. Pro coach: Orlando (Continental Football League) 1968-69, Houston/Shreveport Steamer (WFL) 1974-75, New England Patriots 1982-84, Detroit Lions 1985-88, Indianapolis Colts 1989-1991, Philadelphia Eagles 1992-94, New York Jets 1995-2001, Tampa Bay Buccaneers 2002-08, joined Chiefs in 2009.

Clancy Pendergast, defensive coordinator; born November 29, 1967, Phoenix. Attended Arizona. No college or playing experience. College coach: Mississippi State 1991, Southern California 1992, Oklahoma 1993-94. Pro coach: Houston Oilers 1995, Dallas Cowboys 1996-2002, Cleveland Browns 2003, Arizona Cardinals 2004-08, joined Chiefs in 2009.

Pat Perles, defensive quality control; born October 2, 1963, Detroit. Defensive tackle Michigan State 1982-85. No pro playing experience. College coach: Toledo 1989-1991, Michigan State 2000-02, North Dakota State 2003-08. Pro coach: L.A. Rams 1992-93, Saskatchewan Roughriders (CFL) 1994-96, Winnipeg Blue Bombers (CFL) 1997, Hamilton Tigercats (CFL) 1998-99, joined Chiefs in 2009.

Brent Salazar, asst. strength and conditioning; born May 22, 1980, Denver. Attended New Mexico. No college or pro playing experience. College coach: New Mexico 2002-03, Nevada-Las Vegas 2004, Pacific 2006. Pro coach: Joined Chiefs in 2007.

Nick Sirianni, offensive quality control; born June 15, 1981, Jamestown, N.Y. Wide receiver Mount Union 2000-03. No pro playing experience. College coach: Mount Union 2004-05, Indiana (Pa.) 2006-08. Pro coach: Joined Chiefs in 2009.

Cedric Smith, strength and conditioning; born May 27, 1968, Enterprise, Alabama. Fullback Florida 1986-89. Pro fullback Minnesota Vikings 1990, New Orleans Saints 1991, Washington Redskins 1994-95, Arizona Cardinals 1996-98. Pro coach: Denver Broncos 2001-06, joined Chiefs in 2007.

Dedric Ward, wide receivers; born September 29, 1974, Cedar Rapids, Iowa. Wide receiver Northern Iowa 1993-96. Pro wide receiver New York Jets 1997-2000, Miami Dolphins 2001-02, Baltimore Ravens 2003, New England Patriots 2003, Dallas Cowboys 2004. College coach: Missouri State 2006. Pro coach: Arizona Cardinals 2007-08, joined Chiefs in 2009.

American Football Conference
East Division
Team Colors: Aqua, Coral, Blue, and White
7500 S.W. 30th Street
Davie, Florida 33314
Telephone: (954) 452-7000

2009 SCHEDULE

PRESEASON

Aug. 17	**Jacksonville**	7:30
Aug. 22	**Carolina**	7:30
Aug. 27	at Tampa Bay	8:00
Sep. 3	at New Orleans	7:00

REGULAR SEASON

Sep. 13	at Atlanta	1:00
Sep. 21	**Indianapolis** (Mon.)	8:30
Sep. 27	at San Diego	1:15
Oct. 4	**Buffalo**	4:05
Oct. 12	**N.Y. Jets** (Mon.)	8:30
Oct. 18	BYE	
Oct. 25	**New Orleans**	4:15
Nov. 1	at N.Y. Jets	1:00
Nov. 8	at New England	1:00
Nov. 15	**Tampa Bay**	1:00
Nov. 19	at Carolina (Thu.)	8:20
Nov. 29	at Buffalo	1:00
Dec. 6	**New England** *	8:20
Dec. 13	at Jacksonville	1:00
Dec. 20	at Tennessee	12:00
Dec. 27	**Houston**	1:00
Jan. 3	**Pittsburgh**	1:00

** Sunday night games in Weeks 11-17 subject to change*

Stadium: Land Shark Stadium
(opened in 1987)
• **Capacity:** 75,192
2269 Dan Marino Blvd.
Miami Gardens, Florida 33056
Playing Surface: Grass (PAT)
Training Camp: Nova Southeastern Univ.
7500 S.W. 30th Street
Davie, Florida 33314

LAND SHARK STADIUM

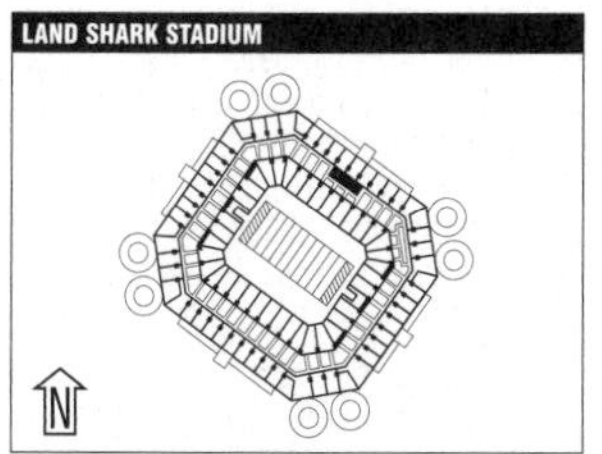

CLUB OFFICIALS

Owner/Chairman of the Board: Stephen M. Ross
Chief Executive Officer, Miami Dolphins: Michael Dee
President & Chief Operating Officer: Bryan Wiedmeier
Executive Vice President-Football Operations: Bill Parcells
General Manager: Jeff Ireland
Head Coach: Tony Sparano
Senior Vice President-Finance & Administration: Jill R. Strafaci
Senior Vice President-Operations: Bill Galante
Senior Vice President-Media Relations: Harvey Greene
Vice President-Information Technology: Tery Howard
General Counsel/Football Administration: Matt Thomas
Assistant Director of Player Personnel: Brian Gaine
Director of College Scouting: Chris Grier
Director of Player Development: John Gamble
Senior Director of Internet & Publications: Scott Stone
Alumni, Youth & Special Projects: Nat Moore
Director of Youth Programs: Twan Russell
Director of Communications: Fitz Ollison
Director of Media Relations: Jason Jenkins
Director of Event Entertainment: Dorie Grogan
Director of Programming & Production: Jeff Griffith
Director of Cheerleaders: Emily Newton
Director of Records & Archives: Kristin Hingston
Director of Community Relations: Ilona Wolpin
Head Athletic Trainer: Kevin O'Neill
Equipment Manager: Joe Cimino
Video Director: Bob Hack
Team Security Investigator: Stuart Weinstein

COACHING HISTORY (400-292-4)

Records include postseason games

1966-69	George Wilson	15-39-2
1970-1995	Don Shula	274-147-2
1996-99	Jimmy Johnson	38-31-0
2000-04	Dave Wannstedt*	43-33-0
2004	Jim Bates	3-4-0
2005-06	Nick Saban	15-17-0
2007	Cam Cameron	1-15-0
2008	Tony Sparano	11-6-0

*Resigned after nine games in 2004

PAID ATTENDANCE

Home 523,919 Away 524,384
Total 1,048,303
Single-game home record, 75,283 (10/27/96)
Single-season home record, 592,161 (1999)

2009 DRAFT CHOICES

Round	Name	Pos.	College
1	Vontae Davis	DB	Illinois
2	Pat White	QB	West Virginia
	Sean Smith	DB	Utah
3	Patrick Turner	WR	Southern California
4	Brian Hartline	WR	Ohio State
5	John Nalbone	TE	Monmouth
	Chris Clemons	DB	Clemson
6	Andrew Gardner	T	Georgia Tech
7	J.D. Folsom	LB	Weber State

MIAMI DOLPHINS

2008 TEAM RECORD

PRESEASON (3-1)

Date	Result	Opponent
8/9	L 6-17	Tampa Bay
8/16	W 19-14	at Jacksonville
8/23	W 24-0	Kansas City
8/28	W 14-10	at New Orleans

REGULAR SEASON (11-5)

Date	Result	Opponent
9/7	L 14-20	New York Jets
9/14	L 10-31	at Arizona
9/21	W 38-13	at New England
10/5	W 17-10	San Diego
10/12	L 28-29	at Houston
10/19	L 13-27	Baltimore
10/26	W 25-16	Buffalo
11/2	W 26-17	at Denver
11/9	W 21-19	Seattle
11/16	W 17-15	Oakland
11/23	L 28-48	New England
11/30	W 16-12	at St. Louis
12/7	W 16-3	at Buffalo
12/14	W 14-9	San Francisco
12/21	W 38-31	at Kansas City
12/28	W 24-17	at New York Jets

POSTSEASON (0-1)

Date	Result	Opponent
1/4	L 9-27	Baltimore

SCORE BY PERIODS

Dolphins	85	113	65	82	0	— 345
Opponents	62	102	91	62	0	— 317

2008 TEAM STATISTICS

	Dolphins	Opp.
Total First Downs	308	296
Rushing	111	96
Passing	184	173
Penalty	13	27
3rd Down: Made/Att	71/192	79/209
3rd Down Pct.	37.0	37.8
4th Down: Made/Att	10/15	11/19
4th Down Pct.	66.7	57.9
Possession Avg.	31:03	28:57
Total Net Yards	5529	5264
Avg. Per Game	345.6	329.0
Total Plays	965	979
Avg. Per Play	5.7	5.4
Net Yards Rushing	1897	1620
Avg. Per Game	118.6	101.3
Total Rushes	448	388
Net Yards Passing	3632	3644
Avg. Per Game	227.0	227.8
Sacked/Yards Lost	26/129	40/218
Gross Yards	3761	3862
Att./Completions	491/330	551/320
Completion Pct.	67.2	58.1
Had Intercepted	7	18
Punts/Average	74/43.9	61/46.7
Net Punting Avg.	74/35.5	61/39.7
Penalties/Yards	81/669	86/615
Fumbles/Ball Lost	18/6	27/12
Touchdowns	40	33
Rushing	18	11
Passing	20	18
Returns	2	4

2008 INDIVIDUAL STATISTICS

PASSING	Att.	Comp.	Yds.	Pct.	TD	Int.	Tkld.	Rate
Pennington	476	321	3653	67.4	19	7	24/121	97.4
Henne	12	7	67	58.3	0	0	0/0	74.0
R. Brown	3	2	41	66.7	1	0	1/8	149.3
Williams	0	0	0	—	0	0	1/0	—
Dolphins	491	330	3761	67.2	20	7	26/129	97.6
Opponents	551	320	3862	58.1	18	18	40/218	77.0

SCORING	TD R	TD P	TD Rt	PAT	FG	Saf	PTS
Carpenter	0	0	0	40/40	21/25	0	103
R. Brown	10	0	0	0/0	0/0	0	60
Fasano	0	7	0	0/0	0/0	0	42
Williams	4	1	0	0/0	0/0	0	30
Ginn	2	2	0	0/0	0/0	0	24
Cobbs	1	2	0	0/0	0/0	0	18
Martin	0	3	0	0/0	0/0	0	18
Camarillo	0	2	0	0/0	0/0	0	12
W. Allen	0	0	1	0/0	0/0	0	6
Bess	0	1	0	0/0	0/0	0	6
Cramer	0	1	0	0/0	0/0	0	6
Haynos	0	1	0	0/0	0/0	0	6
Merling	0	0	1	0/0	0/0	0	6
Pennington	1	0	0	0/0	0/0	0	6
Anderson	0	0	0	0/0	0/0	1	2
Dolphins	18	20	2	40/40	21/25	1	345
Opponents	11	18	4	28/28	29/32	1	317

2-Pt. Conversions: None.
Dolphins 0-0, Opponents 1-5.

RUSHING	No.	Yds	Avg	LG	TD
R. Brown	214	916	4.3	62t	10
Williams	160	659	4.1	51t	4
Cobbs	12	88	7.3	44	1
Polite	23	85	3.7	14	0
Ginn	5	73	14.6	40t	2
Pennington	30	62	2.1	16	1
Bess	1	13	13.0	13	0
Camarillo	2	1	0.5	6	0
Fields	1	0	0.0	0	0
Dolphins	448	1897	4.2	62t	18
Opponents	388	1620	4.2	33	11

RECEIVING	No.	Yds	Avg	LG	TD
Ginn	56	790	14.1	64	2
Camarillo	55	613	11.1	33	2
Bess	54	554	10.3	37	1
Fasano	34	454	13.4	24	7
R. Brown	33	254	7.7	39	0
Martin	31	450	14.5	61t	3
Williams	29	219	7.6	47	1
Cobbs	19	275	14.5	80t	2
Polite	6	24	4.0	9	0
Hagan	3	51	17.0	20	0
London	3	30	10.0	14	0
Wilford	3	25	8.3	15	0
Haynos	2	22	11.0	19t	1
Cramer	2	3	1.5	2t	1
Satele	0	-3	—	-3	0
Dolphins	330	3761	11.4	80t	20
Opponents	320	3862	12.1	79t	18

INTERCEPTIONS	No.	Yds	Avg	LG	TD
Goodman	5	53	10.6	55	0
W. Allen	3	62	20.7	32t	1
Hill	3	34	11.3	17	0
Ayodele	2	29	14.5	17	0
Merling	1	25	25.0	25t	1
Starks	1	8	8.0	8	0
J. Allen	1	2	2.0	2	0
Culver	1	1	1.0	1	0
Jones	1	0	0.0	0	0
Dolphins	18	214	11.9	55	2
Opponents	7	130	18.6	44t	2

PUNTING	No.	Yds.	Avg.	In 20	LG
Fields	74	3249	43.9	24	71
Dolphins	74	3249	43.9	24	71
Opponents	61	2848	46.7	23	67

PUNT RETURNS	Ret	FC	Yds	Avg	LG	TD
Bess	21	10	231	11.0	27	0
Ginn	7	1	54	7.7	15	0
Dolphins	28	11	285	10.2	27	0
Opponents	37	15	485	13.1	93t	2

KICKOFF RETURNS	No.	Yds	Avg	LG	TD
Ginn	32	657	20.5	41	0
Bess	14	311	22.2	32	0
Cobbs	8	189	23.6	60	0
London	2	28	14.0	17	0
Ndukwe	1	14	14.0	14	0
Ryan	1	14	14.0	14	0
Fasano	1	0	0.0	0	0
Jones	1	0	0.0	0	0
Dolphins	60	1213	20.2	60	0
Opponents	68	1655	24.3	95	0

FIELD GOALS	1-19	20-29	30-39	40-49	50+
Carpenter	0/0	4/4	7/7	9/13	1/1
Dolphins	0/0	4/4	7/7	9/13	1/1
Opponents	1/1	9/9	10/11	7/9	2/2

SACKS	No.
Porter	17.5
Roth	5.0
Holliday	3.5
Jones	3.0
Starks	3.0
Anderson	2.5
Langford	2.0
W. Allen	1.0
Bell	1.0
Merling	1.0
Torbor	0.5
Dolphins	40.0
Opponents	26.0

RECORD HOLDERS

INDIVIDUAL RECORDS—CAREER

Category	Name	Performance
Rushing (Yds.)	Larry Csonka, 1968-1974, 1979	6,737
Passing (Yds.)	Dan Marino, 1983-1999	61,361
Passing (TDs)	Dan Marino, 1983-1999	420
Receiving (No.)	Mark Clayton, 1983-1992	550
Receiving (Yds.)	Mark Duper, 1982-1992	8,869
Interceptions	Jake Scott, 1970-75	35
Punting (Avg.)	John Kidd, 1994-97	44.2
Punt Return (Avg.)	Jeff Ogden, 2000-01	13.7
Kickoff Return (Avg.)	Mercury Morris, 1969-1975	26.5
Field Goals	Olindo Mare, 1997-2006	245
Touchdowns (Tot.)	Mark Clayton, 1983-1992	82
Points	Olindo Mare, 1997-2006	1,048
*Sacks	Jason Taylor, 1997-2007	117.0

INDIVIDUAL RECORDS—SINGLE SEASON

Category	Name	Performance
Rushing (Yds.)	Ricky Williams, 2002	1,853
Passing (Yds.)	Dan Marino, 1984	**5,084
Passing (TDs)	Dan Marino, 1984	48
Receiving (No.)	O.J. McDuffie, 1998	90
Receiving (Yds.)	Mark Clayton, 1984	1,389
Interceptions	Dick Westmoreland, 1967	10
Punting (Avg.)	John Kidd, 1996	46.3
Punt Return (Avg.)	Jeff Ogden, 2000	17.0
Kickoff Return (Avg.)	Duriel Harris, 1976	32.9
Field Goals	Olindo Mare, 1999	39
Touchdowns (Tot.)	Mark Clayton, 1984	18
Points	Olindo Mare, 1999	144
*Sacks	Jason Taylor, 2002	18.5

INDIVIDUAL RECORDS—SINGLE GAME

Category	Name	Performance
Rushing (Yds.)	Ricky Williams, 12-1-02	228
Passing (Yds.)	Dan Marino, 10-23-88	521
Passing (TDs)	Bob Griese, 11-24-77	6
	Dan Marino, 9-21-86	6
Receiving (No.)	Chris Chambers, 12-4-05	15
Receiving (Yds.)	Chris Chambers, 12-4-05	238
Interceptions	Dick Anderson, 12-3-73	**4
Field Goals	Olindo Mare, 10-17-99	6
Touchdowns (Tot.)	Paul Warfield, 12-15-73	4
	Mark Ingram, 11-27-94	4
	Ronnie Brown, 9-21-08	4
Points	Paul Warfield, 12-15-73	24
	Mark Ingram, 11-27-94	24
	Ronnie Brown, 9-21-08	24
*Sacks	Doug Betters, 9-4-83	4.0
	E.J. Junior, 10-6-91	4.0
	Joey Porter, 9-21-08	4.0

**Sacks became an official statistic in 1982.*
***NFL Record*

MIAMI DOLPHINS

2009 VETERAN ROSTER

No.	Name	Pos.	Ht.	Wt.	Birthdate	NFL Exp.	College	Hometown	How Acq.	'08 Games/ Starts
57	Alleman, Andy	C/G	6-4	310	11/20/83	3	Akron	Massillon, Ohio	W(NO)-'08	15/4
32	Allen, Jason	CB	6-1	200	7/5/83	4	Tennessee	Muscle Shoals, Ala.	D1-'06	15/2
25	Allen, Will	CB	5-10	195	8/5/78	9	Syracuse	Syracuse, N.Y.	UFA(NYG)-'06	16/16
56	Anderson, Charlie	LB	6-4	250	12/8/81	6	Mississippi	Jackson, Miss.	UFA(Hou)-'08	16/1
51	Ayodele, Akin	LB	6-2	245	9/17/79	8	Purdue	Irving, Texas	T(Dall)-'08	16/13
37	Bell, Yeremiah	S	6-0	205	3/3/78	6	Eastern Kentucky	Winchester, Ky.	D6c-'03	16/16
67	Berger, Joe	G	6-5	315	5/25/82	5	Michigan Tech	Newaygo, Mich.	UFA(Dall)-'09	3/0*
15	Bess, Davone	WR	5-10	190	9/13/85	2	Hawaii	Oakland, Calif.	FA-'08	16/6
23	Brown, Ronnie	RB	6-0	230	12/12/81	5	Auburn	Cartersville, Ga.	D1-'05	16/13
47	Bryan, Courtney	S	6-0	210	10/2/84	3	New Mexico State	San Jose, Calif.	FA-'07	7/0
83	Camarillo, Greg	WR	6-1	190	4/18/82	4	Stanford	Menlo Park, Calif.	W(SD)-'07	11/11
72	Carey, Vernon	T	6-5	350	7/31/81	6	Miami	Miami, Fla.	D1-'04	16/16
5	Carpenter, Dan	K	6-2	220	11/25/85	2	Montana	Helena, Mont.	FA-'08	16/0
38	Cobbs, Patrick	RB	5-8	205	1/31/83	4	North Texas	Tecumseh, Okla.	FA-'06	16/2
62	Cohen, Joe	DT	6-2	315	6/6/84	2	Florida	Melbourne, Fla.	FA-'09	0*
52	Crowder, Channing	LB	6-2	250	12/2/83	5	Florida	Atlanta, Ga.	D3-'05	15/14
29	Culver, Tyrone	S	6-1	210	7/6/83	4	Fresno State	Palmdale, Calif.	FA-'08	15/0
92	Denney, John	LS	6-5	255	12/13/78	5	Brigham Young	Thornton, Colo.	FA-'05	16/0
71	Dotson, Lionel	DE	6-4	290	2/11/85	2	Arizona	Houston, Texas	D7-'08	2/0
80	Fasano, Anthony	TE	6-4	255	4/20/84	4	Notre Dame	Verona, N.J.	T(Dall)-'08	16/16
95	Ferguson, Jason	DT	6-3	305	11/28/74	13	Georgia	Tupelo, Miss.	T(Dall)-'08	16/13
2	Fields, Brandon	P	6-5	235	5/21/84	3	Michigan State	Toledo, Ohio	D7b-'07	16/0
76	Frye, Brandon	T	6-4	305	1/23/83	3	Virginia Tech	Myrtle Beach, S.C.	FA-'08	7/0
75	Garner, Nate	T	6-7	320	1/18/85	2	Arkansas	Roland, Ark.	W(NYJ)-'08	0*
19	Ginn, Ted Jr.	WR	5-11	180	4/12/85	3	Ohio State	Cleveland, Ohio	D1-'07	16/14
21	Green, Eric	CB	5-11	196	3/16/82	5	Virginia Tech	Clewiston, Fla.	UFA(Ariz) -'09	13/9*
64	Grove, Jake	C	6-4	300	1/22/80	6	Virginia Tech	Forest, Va.	UFA(Oak)-'09	12/12*
81	Haynos, Joey	TE	6-8	270	8/28/84	2	Maryland	Rockville, Md.	FA-'08	7/0
7	Henne, Chad	QB	6-3	230	7/2/85	2	Michigan	Wyomissing, Pa.	D2b-'08	3/0
33	Jones, Nathan	CB	5-10	185	6/15/82	6	Rutgers	Scotch Plains, N.J.	UFA(Dall)-'08	16/1
43	Kilmer, Ethan	S	6-0	205	1/31/83	3	Penn State	Wyalusing, Pa.	FA-'09	0*
70	Langford, Kendall	DE	6-6	290	1/27/86	2	Hampton	Petersburg, Va.	D3-'08	16/13
17	London, Brandon	WR	6-4	210	10/16/84	2	Massachusetts	Charlottesville, Va.	W(NYG)-'08	14/1
77	Long, Jake	T	6-7	310	5/9/85	2	Michigan	Lapeer, Mich.	D1-'08	16/16
88	Martin, David	TE	6-4	265	3/13/79	9	Tennessee	Norfolk, Va.	UFA-'07	16/7
78	t-McDaniel, Tony	DT	6-7	310	1/20/85	4	Tennessee	Columbia, SC	T(Jax) -'09	10/3*
97	Merling, Phillip	DE	6-4	290	4/19/85	2	Clemson	St. Matthews, S.C.	D2a-'08	16/2
74	Moses, Quentin	LB	6-5	260	11/18/83	3	Georgia	Athens, Ga.	FA-'07	12/1
61	Murphy, Shawn	G	6-4	315	12/17/82	2	Utah State	Alpine, Utah	D4-'08	0*
68	Ndukwe, Ikechuku	G/C	6-4	325	7/17/82	3	Northwestern	Dublin, Ohio	FA-'07	16/15
10	Pennington, Chad	QB	6-3	225	6/26/76	10	Marshall	Knoxville, Tenn.	FA-'08	16/16
36	Polite, Lousaka	FB	6-0	245	9/14/81	5	Pittsburgh	Pittsburgh, Pa.	FA-'08	11/5
55	Porter, Joey	LB	6-3	255	3/22/77	11	Colorado State	Bakersfield, Calif.	FA-'07	16/16
98	Roth, Matt	LB	6-4	275	10/14/82	5	Iowa	Villa Park, Ill.	D2-'05	16/14
65	Smiley, Justin	G	6-3	310	11/11/81	6	Alabama	Ellabell, Ga.	UFA(SF)-'08	12/12
96	Soliai, Paul	DT	6-4	355	12/30/83	3	Utah	Pago Pago, American Samoa	D4-'07	14/0
94	Starks, Randy	DE	6-3	305	12/14/83	6	Maryland	Waldorf, Md.	UFA(Tenn)-'08	16/3
99	Taylor, Jason	LB	6-5	244	9/1/74	12	Akron	Pittsburgh, Pa.	FA-'09	13/8*
66	Thomas, Donald	G	6-4	310	9/25/85	2	Connecticut	New Haven, Conn.	D6b-'08	1/1
22	Thomas, Joey	CB	6-1	195	8/29/80	4	Montana State	Burien, Wash.	FA-'08	6/0
53	Torbor, Reggie	LB	6-2	245	1/25/81	6	Auburn	Baton Rouge, La.	UFA(NYG)-'08	16/1
50	Walden, Erik	LB	6-2	245	8/21/85	2	Middle Tennessee	Dublin, Ga.	W(KC)-'08	15/0
18	Wilford, Ernest	WR	6-4	225	1/14/79	6	Virginia Tech	Richmond, Va.	UFA(Jax)-'08	7/0
34	Williams, Ricky	RB	5-10	230	5/21/77	9	Texas	San Diego, Calif.	T(NO)-'02	16/3
28	Wilson, Gibril	S	6-0	210	11/12/81	6	Tennessee	San Jose, Calif.	FA-'09	16/15*
90	Wright, Rodrique	DE	6-5	310	7/31/84	3	Texas	Houston, Texas	D7b-'06	0

* Berger played 3 games with Dallas in '08; Cohen missed '07 season because of injury with San Francisco; Garner inactive for 16 games; Green played 13 games with Arizona; Grove played 12 games with Oakland; Kilmer last active with Cincinnati in '06; McDaniel played 10 games with Jacksonville; Murphy inactive for 16 games; Taylor played 13 games with Washington; Wilson played 16 games with Oakland.

t- Dolphins traded for McDaniel (Jax).

Traded—C Samson Satele (16 games in '08) to Oakland.

Players lost through free agency (4): CB Andre' Goodman (Den; 16 games in '08), S Renaldo Hill (Den; 16), C Al Johnson (NE; 4), G Seth McKinney (Buff; 0).

Also played with Dolphins in '08—CB Brannon Condren (4 games), RB Casey Cramer (9), S Chris Crocker (6), FB Boomer Grigsby (1), WR Derek Hagan (4), DE/DT Vonnie Holliday (16), LB William Kershaw (1), CB Michael Lehan (5), G Evan Mathis (7), G Matt McChesney (1), DE Rob Ninkovich (1),TE Sean Ryan (1), LB Derek Smith (1).

2009 FIRST-YEAR ROSTER

Name	Pos.	Ht.	Wt.	Birthdate	College	Hometown	How Acq.
Armstrong, Anthony (1)	WR	5-11	175	3/29/83	West Texas A&M	Carrollton, Texas	FA
Babers, Scorpio (1)	CB	5-11	185	11/6/83	Sam Houston State	Italy, Texas	FA
Baker, Ryan	DE	6-5	295	11/25/84	Purdue	Indianapolis, Ind.	FA
Billingsley, Will (1)	CB	5-10	195	4/23/84	North Carolina A&T	Ft. Wayne, Ind.	FA
Bond, Jy (1)	P	6-2	212	4/22/79	No College	Melbourne, Australia	FA
Bronson, Jared	TE	6-4	255	12/24/84	Central Washington	Kent, Wash.	FA
Brown, Chris (1)	FB	6-0	240	6/23/86	Tennessee	Destrehan, La.	FA
Clemons, Chris	S	6-1	210	9/15/85	Clemson	Arcadia, Fla.	D5b
Davis, Vontae	CB	5-11	203	5/27/88	Illinois	Washington, D.C.	D1
Ellis, Louis	NT	6-2	320	10/7/85	Shaw	Jackson, Miss.	FA
Folsom, J.D.	LB	6-3	230	8/19/84	Weber State	Salmon, Idaho	D7a
Gardner, Andrew	T	6-6	305	4/4/86	Georgia Tech	Tyrone, Ga.	D6
George, Tearrius (1)	LB	6-4	260	12/3/82	Kansas State	Fayetteville, N.C.	W(NO)
Hartline, Brian	WR	6-2	186	11/22/86	Ohio State	North Canton, Ohio	D4
Hilliard, Lex (1)	RB	5-11	230	7/30/84	Montana	Kalispell, Mont.	D6c-'08
Kershaw, William (1)	LB	6-3	240	12/15/83	Maryland	Raeford, N.C.	FA-'08
Kimble, Anthony	RB	6-0	215	4/9/86	Stanford	Baton Rouge, La.	FA
Lewis, Mark	G	6-3	305	7/17/85	Oregon	Pasadena, Calif.	FA
Lowber, Todd (1)	WR	6-3	205	1/26/82	Ramapo	Camden, N.J.	FA
Marion, Brennan	WR	5-11	190	8/25/87	Tulsa	Greensburg, Pa.	FA
Martin, Orion	LB	6-2	260	9/2/85	Virginia Tech	Martinsville, Va.	FA
Nalbone, John	TE	6-4	255	5/14/86	Monmouth	Lawrenceville, N.J.	D5a
Quinn, J.D.	G	6-4	300	2/23/86	Montana	Garland, Texas	FA
Rogers, SirVincent	T	6-4	310	5/9/86	Houston	Jasper, Texas	FA
Smith, Sean	CB	6-3	214	7/14/87	Utah	Pasadena, Calif.	D2b
Turner, Patrick	WR	6-5	220	5/19/87	Southern California	West Madison, Tenn.	D3
Wake, Cameron (1)	LB	6-3	240	1/30/82	Penn State	Hyattsville, Md.	FA
White, Pat	QB	6-0	190	2/25/86	West Virginia	Daphne, Ala	D2a
Williams, Chris	WR	5-8	175	9/16/87	New Mexico State	Rio Rancho, N.M.	FA

The term NFL Rookie is defined as a player who is in his first season of professional football and has not been on the roster of another professional football team for any regular-season or postseason games. A Rookie is designated by an "R" on NFL rosters. Players who have been active in another professional football league or players who have NFL experience, including either preseason training camp or being on an Active List or Inactive List, or on Reserve/Injured or Reserve/Physically Unable to Perform for fewer than six regular-season games, are termed NFL First-Year Players. An NFL First-Year Player is designated by a "1" on NFL rosters. Thereafter, a player is credited with an additional year of experience for each season in which he accumulates six games on the Active List or Inactive List, or on Reserve/Injured or Reserve/Physically Unable to Perform.

Log on to www.miamidolphins.com for an up-to-date roster.

MIAMI DOLPHINS

COACHING STAFF

Head Coach,

Tony Sparano

Pro Career: Became the eighth head coach in Dolphins history on January 16, 2008. In his first season led the Dolphins to the greatest turnaround in NFL history as Miami posted an 11-5 regular season record while capturing the teams first AFC East Division title since 2000. Sparano had spent the previous five seasons(2003-07) on the staff of the Dallas Cowboys, during which time the team made three playoff appearances. He tutored the Cowboys' offensive line the last three years while also holding the title of assistant head coach the past two seasons. He coached the team's tight ends his first two seasons in Dallas. Prior to joining the Cowboys, Sparano had NFL stops in Cleveland (1999-2000), Washington (2001) and Jacksonville (2002). Career record: 11-6.

Background: Sparano was a four-year letterman as a center at the University of New Haven, where he earned his degree in criminal law. He began his coaching career at his alma mater in 1984 before moving on to Boston University as offensive coordinator in 1989. He returned to New Haven as the school's head coach in 1994, and manned that spot for the next five years.

Personal: Born October 7, 1961 in West Haven, Conn. He and his wife, Jeanette, have two sons, Tony and Andrew, and one daughter, Ryan Leigh.

ASSISTANT COACHES

John Bonamego, special teams coordinator; born August 14, 1963, Waynesboro, Pa. Wide receiver/quarterback Central Michigan 1985-86. No pro playing experience. College coach: Maine 1988-91, Lehigh 1992, Army 1993-98. Pro coach: Jacksonville Jaguars 1999-2002, Green Bay Packers 2003-05, New Orleans Saints 2006-07, joined Dolphins in 2008.

Todd Bowles, asst. head coach/secondary; born November 18, 1963, Elizabeth, N.J. Defensive back Temple 1982-85. Pro defensive back Washington Redskins 1986-1990, 1992-93, San Francisco 49ers 1991. College coach: Morehouse College 1997, Grambling State 1998-99. Pro coach: New York Jets 2000, Cleveland Browns 2001-04, Dallas Cowboys 2005-07, joined Dolphins in 2008.

Steve Bush, offensive quality control; born December 21, 1959, Denville, N.J. Defensive back Southern Connecticut State 1978-1981. No pro playing experience. College coach: Southern Connecticut State 1982-83, Springfield College 1984-85, New Haven 1986-87, Boston University 1988-89, Syracuse 2000-04. Pro coach: Joined Dolphins in 2008.

David Corrao, defensive quality control; born June 11, 1974. Running back University of San Diego 1992. No pro playing experience. College coach: Syracuse 2000-03, Northeastern 2004, Mississippi 2005-07. Pro coach: Joined Dolphins in 2008.

Dave DeGuglielmo, offensive line; born July 15, 1968, Cambridge, Mass. Attended Boston University. No college or pro playing experience. College coach: Boston College 1991-92, Boston University 1993-96, Connecticut 1997-98, South Carolina 1999-2003. Pro coach: New York Giants 2004–08, joined Dolphins in 2009.

George DeLeone, tight ends; born May 9, 1948, New Haven, Conn. Offensive lineman Connecticut 1966-67. No pro playing experience. College coach: Southern Connecticut State 1970-79, Rutgers 1980-83, Holy Cross 1984, Syracuse 1985-1996, 1998-2004, Mississippi 2005, Temple 2006-07. Pro coach: San Diego Chargers 1997, joined Dolphins in 2008.

Karl Dorrell, wide receivers; born December 18, 1968, Alameda, Calif. Wide receiver UCLA 1982-86. No pro playing experience. College coach: UCLA 1988, 2003-07 (head coach 2003-07), Central Florida 1989, Northern Arizona 1990-91, Colorado 1992-93, 1995-98, Arizona State 1994, Washington 1999. Pro coach: Denver Broncos 2000-02, joined Dolphins in 2008.

George Edwards, inside linebackers; born January 16, 1967, Siler City, N.C. Linebacker Duke 1985-89. No pro playing experience. College coach: Florida 1990-91, Appalachian State 1992-95, Duke 1996, Georgia 1997. Pro coach: Dallas Cowboys 1998-2001, Washington Redskins 2002-03, Cleveland Browns 2004, joined Dolphins in 2005.

Dan Henning, offensive coordinator; born June 21, 1942, Bronx, N.Y. Quarterback William & Mary 1962-64. Pro quarterback San Diego Chargers 1964, 1966-67. College coach: Florida State 1968-1970, 1974, Virginia Tech 1971, 1973, Boston College 1994-96 (head coach). Pro coach: Houston Oilers 1972, New York Jets 1976-78, 1998-2000, Miami Dolphins 1979-1980, Washington Redskins 1981-82, 1987-88, Atlanta Falcons 1983-86 (head coach), San Diego Chargers 1989-1991 (head coach), Detroit Lions 1992-93, Buffalo Bills 1997, Carolina Panthers 2002-06, re-joined Dolphins in 2008.

David Lee, quarterbacks; born July 2, 1953, Cape Girardeau, Mo. Quarterback Vanderbilt 1971-74. No pro playing experience. College coach: Tennessee-Martin 1975-76, Vanderbilt 1977, Mississippi 1978-1982, New Mexico 1983, Arkansas 1984-88, 2001-02, 2007, Texas-El Paso 1989-1993 (head coach), Rice 1994-2000. Pro coach: Dallas Cowboys 2003-06, joined Dolphins in 2008.

Evan Marcus, head strength and conditioning; born January 2, 1968, Cranford, N.J. Tackle Ithaca College 1986-1990. No pro playing experience. College coach: Arizona State 1991-92, Rutgers 1993, Maryland 1994, Texas 1995-97, Louisville 1998-99, Virginia 2003-06. Pro coach: New Orleans Saints 2000-02, Atlanta Falcons 2007, joined Dolphins in 2008.

Paul Pasqualoni, defensive coordinator; born August 16, 1949, New Haven, Conn. Linebacker Penn State 1968-1971. No pro playing experience. College coach: Southern Connecticut State 1976-81, Western Connecticut 1982-86 (head coach), Syracuse 1987-2004 (head coach 1991-2004). Pro coach: Dallas Cowboys 2005-07, joined Dolphins in 2008.

Dave Puloka, asst. strength and conditioning; born January 12, 1979, Arlington, Mass. Linebacker Holy Cross 1997-2000. No pro playing experience College coach: Stevens Institute of Technology 2005, Virginia 2006. Pro coach: Atlanta Falcons 2007, joined Dolphins in 2008.

Jim Reid, outside linebackers; born December 1, 1950. Defensive back Maine 1970-72. No pro playing experience. College coach: Massachusetts 1973-1991, Richmond 1992-93, 1995-2003 (head coach 1995-2003), Boston College 1994, Syracuse 2004, Bucknell 2005, VMI 2006-07 (head coach). Pro coach: Joined Dolphins in 2008.

Darren Rizzi, asst. special teams; born July 21, 1970, Hillsdale, N.J. Tight end Rhode Island 1988-1991. College coach: Rhode Island 1992, Colgate 1993, New Haven 1993-97, Northeastern 1998, New Haven 1999-2001 (head coach), Rutgers 2002-07, Rhode Island 2008 (head coach). Pro coach: Joined Dolphins in 2009.

Kacy Rodgers, defensive line; born June 24, 1969, Humboldt, Tennessee. Linebacker/defensive end Tennessee 1988-1991. Pro linebacker Shreveport Pirates (CFL) 1994. College coach: Tennessee-Martin 1994-97, Louisiana-Monroe 1998, Middle Tennessee State 1999-2001, Arkansas 2002. Pro coach: Dallas Cowboys 2003-07, joined Dolphins in 2008.

James Saxon, running backs; born March 23, 1966, Beaufort, S.C. Running back American River (Calif.) J.C. 1984-85, San Jose State 1986-87. Pro running back Kansas City Chiefs 1988-1991, Miami Dolphins 1992-94, Philadelphia Eagles 1995. College coach: Rutgers 1997-98, Menlo College 1999. Pro coach: Buffalo Bills 2000, Kansas City Chiefs 2001-07, joined Dolphins in 2008.

American Football Conference
East Division
Team Colors: Blue, Red, Silver, and White
Gillette Stadium
One Patriot Place
Foxborough, Massachusetts 02035
Telephone: (508) 543-8200

2009 SCHEDULE

PRESEASON

Aug. 13	at Philadelphia	7:00
Aug. 20	**Cincinnati**	7:30
Aug. 28	at Washington	8:00
Sep. 3	**N.Y. Giants**	7:30

REGULAR SEASON

Sep. 14	**Buffalo** (Mon.)	7:00
Sep. 20	at N.Y. Jets	1:00
Sep. 27	**Atlanta**	1:00
Oct. 4	**Baltimore**	1:00
Oct. 11	at Denver	2:15
Oct. 18	**Tennessee**	4:15
Oct. 25	at Tampa Bay (London)	5:00
Nov. 1	BYE	
Nov. 8	**Miami**	1:00
Nov. 15	at Indianapolis	8:20
Nov. 22	**N.Y. Jets**	4:15
Nov. 30	at New Orleans (Mon.)	7:30
Dec. 6	at Miami *	8:20
Dec. 13	**Carolina**	1:00
Dec. 20	at Buffalo	1:00
Dec. 27	**Jacksonville**	1:00
Jan. 3	at Houston	12:00

** Sunday night games in Weeks 11-17 subject to change*

Stadium: Gillette Stadium
(opened in 2002)
• **Capacity:** 68,756
One Patriot Place
Foxborough, Massachusetts 02035
Playing Surface: FieldTurf
Training Camp: Gillette Stadium
Foxborough, MA 02035

GILLETTE STADIUM

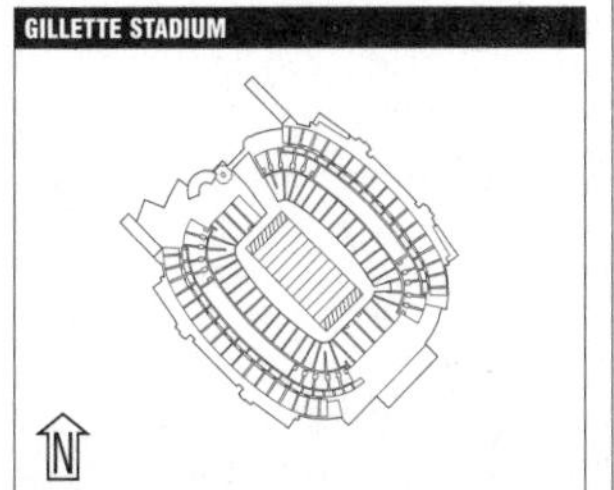

CLUB OFFICIALS

Chairman & CEO: Robert K. Kraft
President: Jonathan A. Kraft
Chief Administrative Officer: Jim Hausmann
Director of Strategic Initiatives and Retail Operations: Brian Bilello
Vice President of Human Resources: Robin Boudreau
Chief Operating Officer of TeamOps Security: Mark Briggs
Equipment Manager: Don Brocher
Director of Player Personnel: Nick Caserio
Vice President of Information Technology: Pat Curley
Video Director: Jimmy Dee
Vice President of Marketing Operations: Jennifer Ferron
Director of New Business Development & Operational Initiatives: Jessica Gelman
Senior Advisor: Robyn Glaser
Director of Ticket Operations: Maryruth Hughey
Vice President of Media Relations: Stacey James
General Counsel: Richard Karelitz
Publisher / Editor-in-Chief and Director of Interactive Media: Fred Kirsch
Vice President of Sales: Murray Kohl
President of New England Patriots Charitable Foundation: Josh Kraft
Director of Research: Richard Miller
Vice President of Stadium Business Development and External Affairs: Dan Murphy
Director of Football / Head Coach Administration: Berj Najarian
Vice President of Stadium Operations: Jim Nolan
Vice President of Marketing Integration and Events: David Pearlstein
Senior Football Advisor: Floyd Reese
Executive Producer of Broadcast Production: Matt Smith
Director of Cheerleaders: Tracy Sormanti
Executive Director of Community Affairs: Andre Tippett
Head Athletic Trainer: Jim Whalen
Vice President of Finance: Jim Wilson

COACHING HISTORY

Boston 1960-1970
(398-367-9)
Records include postseason games

1960-61	Lou Saban*	7-12-0
1961-68	Mike Holovak	53-47-9
1969-1970	Clive Rush**	5-16-0
1970-72	John Mazur***	9-21-0
1972	Phil Bengtson	1-4-0
1973-78	Chuck Fairbanks****	46-41-0
1978	Hank Bullough-Ron Erhardt#	0-1-0
1979-1981	Ron Erhardt	21-27-0
1982-84	Ron Meyer##	18-16-0
1984-89	Raymond Berry	51-41-0
1990	Rod Rust	1-15-0
1991-92	Dick MacPherson	8-24-0
1993-96	Bill Parcells	34-34-0
1997-99	Pete Carroll	28-23-0
2000-08	Bill Belichick	116-45-0

*Released after five games in 1961
**Released after seven games in 1970
***Resigned after nine games in 1972
****Suspended for final regular-season game in 1978
#Co-coaches
##Released after eight games in 1984

PAID ATTENDANCE

Home 565,706 Away 539,121
Total 1,104,827
Single-game home record, 71,768 (11/30/08)
Single-season home record, 579,182 (2007)

2009 DRAFT CHOICES

Round	Name	Pos.	College
2	Patrick Chung	DB	Oregon
	Ron Brace	DT	Boston College
	Darius Butler	DB	Connecticut
	Sebastian Vollmer	T	Houston
3	Brandon Tate	WR	North Carolina
	Tyrone McKenzie	LB	South Florida
4	Rich Ohrnberger	G	Penn State
5	George Bussey	T	Louisville
6	Jake Ingram	LS	Hawaii
	Myron Pryor	DT	Kentucky
7	Julian Edelman	WR	Kent State
	Darryl Richard	DT	Georgia Tech

NEW ENGLAND PATRIOTS

2008 TEAM RECORD

PRESEASON (0-4)

Date	Result		Opponent
8/7	L	15-16	Baltimore
8/17	L	10-27	at Tampa Bay
8/22	L	17-27	Philadelphia
8/28	L	14-19	at New York Giants

REGULAR SEASON (11-5)

Date	Result		Opponent
9/7	W	17-10	Kansas City
9/14	W	19-10	at New York Jets
9/21	L	13-38	Miami
10/5	W	30-21	at San Francisco
10/12	L	10-30	at San Diego
10/20	W	41-7	Denver
10/26	W	23-16	St. Louis
11/2	L	15-18	at Indianapolis
11/9	W	20-10	Buffalo
11/13	L	31-34	New York Jets (OT)
11/23	W	48-28	at Miami
11/30	L	10-33	Pittsburgh
12/7	W	24-21	at Seattle
12/14	W	49-26	at Oakland
12/21	W	47-7	Arizona
12/28	W	13-0	at Buffalo

(OT) Overtime

SCORE BY PERIODS

Patriots	84	123	106	97	0 —	410
Opponents	75	79	61	91	3 —	309

2008 TEAM STATISTICS

	Patriots	Opp.
Total First Downs	356	268
Rushing	145	78
Passing	186	176
Penalty	25	14
3rd Down: Made/Att	96/222	91/205
3rd Down Pct.	43.2	44.4
4th Down: Made/Att	17/22	2/10
4th Down Pct.	77.3	20.0
Possession Avg.	32:09	27:51
Total Net Yards	5847	4944
Avg. Per Game	365.4	309.0
Total Plays	1095	920
Avg. Per Play	5.3	5.4
Net Yards Rushing	2278	1722
Avg. Per Game	142.4	107.6
Total Rushes	513	415
Net Yards Passing	3569	3222
Avg. Per Game	223.1	201.4
Sacked/Yards Lost	48/221	31/239
Gross Yards	3790	3461
Att./Completions	534/339	474/288
Completion Pct.	63.5	60.8
Had Intercepted	11	14
Punts/Average	50/44.0	75/43.0
Net Punting Avg.	50/36.8	75/36.2
Penalties/Yards	57/501	81/636
Fumbles/Ball Lost	17/10	17/8
Touchdowns	43	37
Rushing	21	8
Passing	21	27
Returns	1	2

2008 INDIVIDUAL STATISTICS

PASSING	Att.	Comp.	Yds.	Pct.	TD	Int.	Tkld.	Rate
Cassel	516	327	3693	63.4	21	11	47/219	89.4
Brady	11	7	76	63.6	0	0	0/0	83.9
O'Connell	6	4	23	66.7	0	0	1/2	73.6
Faulk	1	1	-2	100.0	0	0	0/0	79.2
Patriots	534	339	3790	63.5	21	11	48/221	89.1
Opponents	474	288	3461	60.8	27	14	31/239	89.8

SCORING	TD R	TD P	TD Rt	PAT	FG	Saf	PTS
Gostkowski	0	0	0	40/40	36/40	0	148
Moss	0	11	0	0/0	0/0	0	66
Morris	7	0	0	0/0	0/0	0	42
Faulk	3	3	0	0/0	0/0	0	36
Green-Ellis	5	0	0	0/0	0/0	0	30
Jordan	4	0	0	0/0	0/0	0	24
Welker	0	3	0	0/0	0/0	0	20
Gaffney	0	2	0	0/0	0/0	0	14
Cassel	2	0	0	0/0	0/0	0	12
Watson	0	2	0	0/0	0/0	0	12
Hobbs	0	0	1	0/0	0/0	0	6
Patriots	21	21	1	40/40	36/40	0	410
Opponents	8	27	2	34/35	17/21	0	309

2-Pt. Conversions: Gaffney, Welker.
Patriots 2-3, Opponents 1-2.

RUSHING	No.	Yds	Avg	LG	TD
Morris	156	727	4.7	35	7
Faulk	83	507	6.1	41	3
Jordan	80	363	4.5	49t	4
Green-Ellis	74	275	3.7	15	5
Cassel	73	270	3.7	19	2
Maroney	28	93	3.3	17	0
Welker	3	26	8.7	19	0
Evans	11	23	2.1	4	0
Moss	2	0	0.0	2	0
O'Connell	3	-6	-2.0	-2	0
Patriots	513	2278	4.4	49t	21
Opponents	415	1722	4.1	62t	8

RECEIVING	No.	Yds	Avg	LG	TD
Welker	111	1165	10.5	64	3
Moss	69	1008	14.6	76t	11
Faulk	58	486	8.4	22	3
Gaffney	38	468	12.3	37	2
Watson	22	209	9.5	29	2
Morris	17	161	9.5	42	0
D. Thomas	9	93	10.3	18	0
Aiken	8	101	12.6	43	0
Evans	3	59	19.7	28	0
Green-Ellis	3	37	12.3	20	0
Washington	1	3	3.0	3	0
Patriots	339	3790	11.2	76t	21
Opponents	288	3461	12.0	78t	27

INTERCEPTIONS	No.	Yds	Avg	LG	TD
Meriweather	4	25	6.3	19	0
O'Neal	3	49	16.3	47	0
Hobbs	3	0	0.0	4	0
Wilhite	1	16	16.0	16	0
J. Sanders	1	9	9.0	9	0
Vrabel	1	5	5.0	5	0
Harrison	1	0	0.0	0	0
Patriots	14	104	7.4	47	0
Opponents	11	186	16.9	89	0

PUNTING	No.	Yds.	Avg.	In 20	LG
Hanson	49	2143	43.7	19	70
Cassel	1	57	57	1	57
Patriots	50	2200	44	20	70
Opponents	75	3228	43	20	82

PUNT RETURNS	Ret	FC	Yds	Avg	LG	TD
Welker	24	6	237	9.9	44	0
Faulk	10	9	132	13.2	24	0
O'Neal	2	1	2	1.0	2	0
Patriots	36	16	371	10.3	44	0
Opponents	11	13	158	14.4	30	0

KICKOFF RETURNS	No.	Yds	Avg	LG	TD
Hobbs	45	1281	28.5	95t	1
Slater	11	155	14.1	31	0
Morris	2	37	18.5	24	0
Faulk	2	36	18.0	25	0
Neal	1	27	27.0	27	0
Welker	1	26	26.0	26	0
Patriots	62	1562	25.2	95t	1
Opponents	75	1672	22.3	92t	2

FIELD GOALS	1-19	20-29	30-39	40-49	50+
Gostkowski	0/0	10/12	16/16	9/11	1/1
Patriots	0/0	10/12	16/16	9/11	1/1
Opponents	0/0	10/10	3/4	3/6	1/1

SACKS	No.
Seymour	8.0
A. Thomas	5.0
Vrabel	4.0
Wright	2.5
Green	2.0
Meriweather	2.0
Warren	2.0
Wilfork	2.0
Hobbs	1.5
Woods	1.0
(group)	1.0
Patriots	31.0
Opponents	48.0

RECORD HOLDERS

INDIVIDUAL RECORDS—CAREER

Category	Name	Performance
Rushing (Yds.)	Sam Cunningham, 1973-79, 1981-82	5,453
Passing (Yds.)	Drew Bledsoe, 1993-2001	29,657
Passing (TDs)	Tom Brady, 2000-08	197
Receiving (No.)	Troy Brown, 1993-2007	557
Receiving (Yds.)	Stanley Morgan, 1977-1989	10,352
Interceptions	Raymond Clayborn, 1977-1989	36
	Ty Law, 1995-2004	36
Punting (Avg.)	Tom Tupa, 1996-98	44.7
Punt Return (Avg.)	Mack Herron, 1973-75	12.0
Kickoff Return (Avg.)	Laurence Maroney, 2006-08	28.0
Field Goals	Adam Vinatieri, 1996-2005	263
Touchdowns (Tot.)	Stanley Morgan, 1977-1989	68
Points	Adam Vinatieri, 1996-2005	1,158
*Sacks	Andre Tippett, 1982-1993	100.0

INDIVIDUAL RECORDS—SINGLE SEASON

Category	Name	Performance
Rushing (Yds.)	Corey Dillon, 2004	1,635
Passing (Yds.)	Tom Brady, 2007	4,806
Passing (TDs)	Tom Brady, 2007	*50
Receiving (No.)	Wes Welker, 2007	112
Receiving (Yds.)	Randy Moss, 2007	1,493
Interceptions	Ron Hall, 1964	11
Punting (Avg.)	Tom Tupa, 1997	45.8
Punt Return (Avg.)	Mack Herron, 1974	14.8
Kickoff Return (Avg.)	Raymond Clayborn, 1977	31.0
Field Goals	Stephen Gostkowski, 2008	36
Touchdowns (Tot.)	Randy Moss, 2007	23
Points	Gino Cappelletti, 1964	155
*Sacks	Andre Tippett, 1984	18.5

INDIVIDUAL RECORDS—SINGLE GAME

Category	Name	Performance
Rushing (Yds.)	Tony Collins, 9-18-83	212
Passing (Yds.)	Drew Bledsoe, 11-13-94	426
Passing (TDs)	Tom Brady, 10-21-07	6
Receiving (No.)	Troy Brown, 9-22-02	16
Receiving (Yds.)	Terry Glenn, 10-3-99	214
Interceptions	Many times	3
	Last time by Asante Samuel, 11-26-06	
Field Goals	Gino Cappelletti, 10-4-64	6
Touchdowns (Tot.)	Randy Moss, 11-18-07	4
Points	Gino Cappelletti, 12-18-65	24
*Sacks	Andre Tippett, 10-26-86	3.5
	Chris Slade, 11-20-94	3.5

**Sacks became an official statistic in 1982.*
***NFL Record*

NEW ENGLAND PATRIOTS

2009 VETERAN ROSTER

No.	Name	Pos.	Ht.	Wt.	Birthdate	NFL Exp.	College	Hometown	How Acq.	'08 Games/ Starts
88	Aiken, Sam	WR	6-2	215	12/14/80	7	North Carolina	Kenansville, N.C.	UFA(Buff)-'08	14/2
52	Alexander, Eric	LB	6-2	240	2/8/82	5	Louisiana State	Port Arthur, Texas	FA-'04	1/0
87	Baker, Chris	TE	6-3	258	11/18/79	8	Michigan State	St. Albans, N.Y.	FA-'09	16/13*
95	Banta-Cain, Tully	LB	6-2	250	8/28/80	7	California	Sunnyvale, Calif.	FA-'09	12/0*
23	Bodden, Leigh	CB	6-1	193	9/24/81	7	Duquesne	Hyattsville, Md.	FA-'09	16/15*
12	Brady, Tom	QB	6-4	225	8/3/77	10	Michigan	San Mateo, Calif.	D6b-'00	1/1
65	Britt, Wesley	T	6-8	320	11/21/81	4	Alabama	Cullman, Ala.	FA-'05	2/0
54	Bruschi, Tedy	LB	6-1	247	6/9/73	14	Arizona	Roseville, Calif.	D3-'96	13/12
50	Ciurciu, Vinny	LB	6-0	240	5/2/80	7	Boston College	Paramus, N.J.	FA-'09	14/1*
	#Colvin, Rosevelt	LB	6-3	250	9/5/77	11	Purdue	Indianapolis, Ind.	FA-'08	4/3
63	Connolly, Dan	G/C	6-4	313	9/2/82	4	Southeast Missouri State	St. Louis, Mo.	FA-'08	1/0
98	Crable, Shawn	LB	6-5	243	12/26/84	2	Michigan	Massillon, Ohio	D3a-'08	0*
85	DeVree, Tyson	TE	6-6	245	11/12/84	2	Colorado	Hudsonville, Mich.	FA-'08	2/0
66	Duckett, Damane	T	6-6	329	1/21/81	5	East Carolina	Lexington, N.C.	UFA(SF)-'09	0*
33	Faulk, Kevin	RB	5-8	202	6/5/76	11	Louisiana State	Carencro, La.	D2-'99	15/3
13	Galloway, Joey	WR	5-11	197	11/20/71	15	Ohio State	Bellaire, Ohio	FA-'09	9/4*
3	Gostkowski, Stephen	K	6-1	210	1/28/84	4	Memphis	Madison, Miss.	D4b-'06	16/0
97	Green, Jarvis	DL	6-3	285	1/12/79	8	Louisiana State	Donaldsonville, La.	D4b-'02	14/3
42	Green-Ellis, BenJarvus	RB	5-11	215	7/2/85	2	Mississippi	New Orleans, La.	FA-'08	9/3
7	Gutierrez, Matt	QB	6-4	230	6/9/84	3	Idaho State	Concord, Calif.	FA-'07	0*
59	Guyton, Gary	LB	6-3	242	11/14/85	2	Georgia Tech	Hinesville, Ga.	FA-'08	14/2
6	Hanson, Chris	P	6-2	202	10/25/76	11	Marshall	Sharpsburg, Ga.	FA-'07	16/0
	#Harrison, Rodney	S	6-1	220	12/15/72	16	Western Illinois	Chicago, Ill.	FA-'03	6/6
71	Hochstein, Russ	G/C	6-4	305	10/7/77	9	Nebraska	Hartington, Neb.	FA-'02	15/2
45	Hodel, Nathan	LS	6-2	238	11/12/77	8	Illinois	Fairview Heights, Ill.	FA-'09	16/0*
60	Johnson, Al	C/G	6-5	305	1/27/79	7	Wisconsin	Brussels, Wisc.	UFA(Mia)-'09	4/0*
77	Kaczur, Nick	T	6-4	315	7/28/79	5	Toledo	Brantford, Ontario, Canada	D3b-'05	14/14
67	Koppen, Dan	C	6-2	296	9/12/79	7	Boston College	Whitehall, Pa.	D5-'03	16/16
64	LeVoir, Mark	T	6-7	306	7/29/82	3	Notre Dame	Eden Prairie, Minn.	W(StL)-'08	15/2
17	t-Lewis, Greg	WR	6-0	180	2/12/80	7	Illinois	Matteson, Ill	T(Phil)-'09	16/0*
72	Light, Matt	T	6-4	305	6/23/78	9	Purdue	Greenville, Ohio	D2-'01	16/16
70	Mankins, Logan	G	6-4	310	3/10/82	5	Fresno State	Catheys Valley, Calif.	D1-'05	16/16
39	Maroney, Laurence	RB	5-11	220	2/5/85	4	Minnesota	St. Louis, Mo.	D1-'06	3/3
51	Mayo, Jerod	LB	6-1	242	2/23/86	2	Tennessee	Hampton, Va.	D1-'08	16/16
43	McGowan, Brandon	S	5-11	207	9/26/83	5	Maine	Jersey City, N.J.	UFA(Chi)-'09	2/1*
31	Meriweather, Brandon	S	5-11	200	1/14/84	3	Miami	Apopka, Fla.	D1-'07	16/11
34	Morris, Sammy	RB	6-0	220	3/23/77	10	Texas Tech	San Antonio, Texas	UFA(Mia)-'07	13/7
81	Moss, Randy	WR	6-4	210	2/13/77	12	Marshall	Rand, W. Va.	T(Oak)-'07	16/16
61	Neal, Stephen	G	6-4	305	10/9/76	8	Cal State-Bakersfield	San Diego, Calif.	FA-'01	11/9
68	O'Callaghan, Ryan	T	6-7	330	7/19/83	4	California	Redding, Calif.	D5-'06	0*
5	O'Connell, Kevin	QB	6-5	225	5/25/85	2	San Diego State	Carlsbad, Calif.	D3b-'08	2/0
	#O'Neal, Deltha	CB	5-11	194	1/30/77	10	California	Milpitas, Calif.	FA-'08	16/10
49	Redd, Vince	LB	6-6	260	9/1/85	2	Liberty	Elizabethton, Tenn.	FA-'08	5/0
35	Richardson, Mike	CB	5-11	190	2/18/84	3	Notre Dame	Warner Robins, Ga.	D6b-'07	10/0
91	Ruud, Bo	LB	6-3	235	9/2/84	2	Nebraska	Lincoln, Neb.	D6-'08	0*
36	Sanders, James	S	5-10	210	11/11/83	5	Fresno State	Porterville, Calif.	D4-'05	14/14
	#Sanders, Lewis	CB	6-1	210	6/22/78	10	Maryland	Staten Island, N.Y.	FA-'08	10/4
	#Seau, Junior	LB	6-3	250	1/19/69	20	Southern California	Oceanside, Calif.	FA-'06	4/2
93	Seymour, Richard	DL	6-6	310	10/6/79	9	Georgia	Gadsden, S.C.	D1-'01	15/15
18	Slater, Matthew	WR	6-0	198	9/9/85	2	UCLA	Anaheim, Calif.	D5-'08	14/0
80	t-Smith, Alex	TE	6-4	258	5/22/82	5	Stanford	Denver, Colo.	T(TB)-'09	14/12*
92	Smith, Kenny	DL	6-4	303	9/8/77	7	Alabama	Meridian, Miss.	FA-'08	0*
90	Smith, Le Kevin	DL	6-3	308	7/21/82	4	Nebraska	Macon, Ga.	D6c-'06	15/0
28	Spann, Antwain	S	6-0	195	2/22/83	4	Louisiana-Lafayette	Oceanside, Calif.	FA-'06	10/0
29	Springs, Shawn	CB	6-0	204	3/11/75	13	Ohio State	Silver Spring, Md.	FA-'09	9/7*
	#Stokes, Barry	OL	6-4	310	12/20/73	12	Eastern Michigan	Flint, Mich.	FA-'08	0*
21	Taylor, Fred	RB	6-1	228	1/27/76	12	Florida	Pahokee, Fla.	FA-'09	13/13*
96	Thomas, Adalius	LB	6-2	270	8/18/77	10	Southern Mississippi	Equality, Ala.	UFA(Balt)-'07	9/9
86	Thomas, David	TE	6-3	248	7/5/83	4	Texas	Wolfforth, Texas	D3-'06	15/10
41	Ventrone, Ray	S	5-10	200	10/21/82	4	Villanova	Pittsburgh, Pa.	FA-'07	15/0
94	Warren, Ty	DL	6-5	300	2/6/81	7	Texas A&M	Bryan, Texas	D1-'03	13/13
84	Watson, Benjamin	TE	6-3	255	12/18/80	6	Georgia	Rock Hill, S.C.	D1b-'04	14/0
	#Webster, Jason	CB	5-9	187	9/8/77	10	Texas A&M	Houston, Texas	UFA(Buff)-'08	3/0
83	Welker, Wes	WR	5-9	185	5/1/81	6	Texas Tech	Oklahoma City, Okla.	T(Mia)-'07	16/14
22	Wheatley, Terrence	CB	5-9	183	5/5/85	2	Colorado	Plano, Texas	D2-'08	6/1
75	Wilfork, Vince	NT	6-2	325	11/4/81	6	Miami	Boynton Beach, Fla.	D1a-'04	16/16

No.	Name	Pos.	Ht.	Wt.	Birthdate	NFL Exp.	College	Hometown	How Acq.	'08 Games/ Starts
24	Wilhite, Jonathan	CB	5-11	185	2/23/84	2	Auburn	Monroe, La.	D4-'08	16/4
76	Williams, Steve	DL	6-2	306	9/21/81	2	Northwest Missouri St.	Bolingbrook, Ill.	FA-'09	0*
26	Williams, Tank	S	6-2	223	6/30/80	8	Stanford	Bay St. Louis, Miss.	UFA(Minn)-'08	0*
58	Woods, Pierre	LB	6-5	250	1/6/82	4	Michigan	Cleveland, Ohio	FA-'06	12/3
99	Wright, Mike	DL	6-4	295	3/1/82	5	Cincinnati	Cincinnati, Ohio	FA-'05	16/2
74	Yates, Billy	G	6-2	305	4/15/80	6	Texas A&M	Fort Worth, Texas	FA-'04	7/7

* Baker played 16 games with N.Y. Jets in '08; Banta-Cain played 12 games with San Francisco; Bodden played 16 games with Detroit; Ciurciu played 14 games with Minnesota; Crable inactive for 8 games and missed rest of season because of injury; Duckett last active with San Francisco in '06; Galloway played 9 games with Tampa Bay; Gutierrez inactive for 14 games; Hodel played 16 games with Arizona; Johnson played 4 games with Miami; Lewis played 16 games with Philadelphia; McGowan played 2 games with Chicago; O'Callaghan missed '08 season because of injury; Ruud missed '08 season because of injury; A. Smith played 14 games with Tampa Bay; K. Smith missed '08 season because of injury; Springs played 9 games with Washington; Stokes missed '08 season because of injury; Taylor played 13 games with Jacksonville; S. Williams last active with Kansas City in '06; T. Williams missed '08 season because of injury.

\# Unrestricted free agent; subject to developments.

t- Patriots traded for Lewis (Phil) and A. Smith (TB).

Traded—QB Matt Cassel (16 games in '08) to Kansas City, CB Ellis Hobbs (16) to Philadelphia, LB Mike Vrabel (16) to Kansas City.

Players lost through free agency (5): FB Heath Evans (NO; 16 games in '08); WR Jabar Gaffney (Den; 16), LB Larry Izzo (NYJ; 16), RB LaMont Jordan (Den; 8), LS Lonie Paxton (Den; 16).

Also played with Patriots in '08—TE Stephen Spach (2 games), WR Kelley Washington (10).

2009 FIRST-YEAR ROSTER

Name	Pos.	Ht.	Wt.	Birthdate	College	Hometown	How Acq.
Adams, Titus (1)	DL	6-4	305	1/28/83	Nebraska	Omaha, Neb.	FA-'08
Appleby, Antonio	LB	6-3	245	1/25/87	Virginia	Virginia Beach, Va.	FA
Barnes, Tyree	WR	6-0	196	4/15/86	Navy	Hampton, Va.	FA
Brace, Ron	DL	6-3	330	12/18/86	Boston College	Worcester, Mass.	D2b
Bussey, George	OL	6-2	306	10/24/84	Louisville	Louisville, Ky.	D5
Butler, Darius	DB	5-10	183	3/18/86	Connecticut	Ft. Lauderdale, Fla.	D2c
Chung, Patrick	S	5-11	212	4/19/87	Oregon	Rancho Cucamonga, Calif.	D2a
Craig, Angelo (1)	LB	6-5	242	9/5/85	Cincinnati	Cleveland, Ohio	FA-'08
Cuff, Omar (1)	RB	5-9	195	9/24/84	Delaware	Springdale, Md.	FA
Edelman, Julian	WR	6-0	198	5/22/86	Kent State	Redwood City, Calif.	D7a
Hoyer, Brian	QB	6-2	215	10/13/85	Michigan State	North Olmstead, Ohio	FA
Ingram, Jake	LS	6-3	232	10/23/85	Hawaii	Mililani, Hawaii	D6a
Kettani, Eric	RB	5-11	235	3/26/87	Navy	Kirtland, Ohio	FA
Listorti, Brad (1)	TE	6-4	255	10/11/84	Massachusetts	West Haven, Conn.	FA
Love, Jamar	DB	6-0	191	11/8/86	Arkansas	North Little Rock, Ark.	FA
McClinton, Marcus	DB	6-0	210	12/6/85	Kentucky	Ft. Campbell, Ky.	FA
McKenzie, Tyrone	LB	6-2	243	12/11/85	South Florida	Riverview, Fla.	D3b
Nunn, Terrence	WR	6-0	190	7/25/86	Nebraska	Houston, Texas	FA
Ohrnberger, Rich	OL	6-2	291	2/13/86	Penn State	East Meadow, N.Y.	D4
Ortiz, Robert (1)	WR	6-1	188	5/30/83	San Diego State	San Diego, Calif.	FA
Perez, Aaron	P	6-2	231	8/28/86	UCLA	Covina, Calif.	FA
Porter, Jermail	OL	6-5	310	5/24/86	Kent State	Akron, Ohio	FA
Pryor, Myron	DL	6-1	310	6/13/86	Kentucky	Louisville, Ky.	D6b
Richard, Darryl	DL	6-4	290	6/17/86	Georgia Tech	Destrehan, La.	D7b
Tate, Brandon	WR	6-1	210	10/5/87	North Carolina	Burlington, N.C.	D3a
Vollmer, Sebastian	OL	6-8	315	7/10/84	Houston	Kaarst, Germany	D2d
Wendell, Ryan (1)	G	6-2	275	3/4/86	Fresno State	Diamond Bar, Calif.	FA-'08
White, Shun	WR	5-8	195	12/9/85	Navy	Memphis, Tenn.	FA

The term NFL Rookie is defined as a player who is in his first season of professional football and has not been on the roster of another professional football team for any regular-season or postseason games. A Rookie is designated by an "R" on NFL rosters. Players who have been active in another professional football league or players who have NFL experience, including either preseason training camp or being on an Active List or Inactive List, or on Reserve/Injured or Reserve/Physically Unable to Perform for fewer than six regular-season games, are termed NFL First-Year Players. An NFL First-Year Player is designated by a "1" on NFL rosters. Thereafter, a player is credited with an additional year of experience for each season in which he accumulates six games on the Active List or Inactive List, or on Reserve/Injured or Reserve/Physically Unable to Perform.

Log on to www.patriots.com for an up-to-date roster.

NEW ENGLAND PATRIOTS

COACHING STAFF

Head Coach,
Bill Belichick

Pro Career: Bill Belichick is in his 35th season as an NFL coach and is the only head coach in NFL history to win three Super Bowl titles in a four-year span. In his first nine seasons as Patriots head coach, he has won 116 games—more than any other head coach in NFL history through his first nine years with a team. Belichick's Patriots teams own the all-time NFL records for consecutive total victories (21 from 2003-04), consecutive regular-season victories (21 from 2006-08) and consecutive playoff victories (10 from 2001-05). Over a 100-game span from 2003-08, he directed the Patriots to an 82-18 record—the best record for any 100-game span in NFL history. Hired by Chairman and CEO Robert Kraft on January 27, 2000, Belichick is in his 10th season as New England's head coach in 2009. Through nine seasons, Belichick has delivered three Super Bowl championships, four conference titles, six division crowns and 14 playoff victories, while posting an overall record of 116-45. Belichick directed the Patriots to victories in Super Bowls XXXVI (2001), XXXVIII (2003) and XXXIX (2004), and in 2007 he became the first NFL head coach to guide his team to a 16-0 regular season. Only one coach (Pittsburgh's Chuck Noll, 4) has won more Super Bowls than Belichick, and his three Super Bowl titles tie Washington's Joe Gibbs and San Francisco's Bill Walsh for second place on the NFL's all-time list. Belichick owns the second-best postseason record in NFL history (15-4) and is the winningest NFL head coach since 2001 (111-34). Coach Belichick's overall career winning percentage of .630 (153-90-0) ranks fourth among the 17 NFL coaches with 150 or more wins, trailing only George Halas (324-151-31, .682), Don Shula (347-173-6, .677) and Curly Lambeau (226-132-22, .631). Belichick's recent accomplishments are the latest triumphs in a career during which he has helped produce five Super Bowl titles, seven conference championships and 13 division titles since entering the NFL in 1975. He won his first two Super Bowls as the defensive coordinator for the New York Giants in 1986 and 1990 before claiming three Super Bowl championships with the Patriots. George Seifert is the only other man to have won multiple Super Bowls both as a head coach and as an assistant coach. Belichick launched his career in 1975 as a special assistant with the Baltimore Colts, then became an assistant special teams coach with Detroit (1976-77) and Denver (1978). In 1979, he joined the New York Giants to begin a 12-season stint in which he contributed to two Super Bowl championships as New York's defensive coordinator. Belichick was named head coach of the Cleveland Browns in 1991, becoming the youngest head coach in the NFL at age 38. By 1994, Belichick brought the Browns back to the playoffs, finishing 11-5 and advancing to the second round of the playoffs, while allowing a league-low 204 total points. In 1996, Belichick joined New England and was a key contributor to the team's rebound from a 6-10 season in 1995 to an 11-5 season and the team's first division title in 10 years en route to the Patriots' appearance in Super Bowl XXXI. Belichick then spent three seasons with the New York Jets from 1997 to 1999, helping New York improve from a 1-15 season in 1996 to an appearance in the AFC Championship Game in 1998. Career record: 153-90.

Background: Belichick was a center/tight end at Wesleyan 1971-74.

Personal: Born April 16, 1952, Nashville.

ASSISTANT COACHES

Josh Boyer, defensive backs; born January 21, 1977, Heath, Ohio. Wide receiver/defensive back Muskingum College 1996-99. No pro playing experience. College coach: King's College (Pa.) 2000, Dayton 2001, Kent State 2002-03, Bryant University 2004, South Dakota School of Mines and Technology 2005. Pro coach: Joined Patriots in 2006.

Ivan Fears, running backs; born November 15, 1954, Portsmouth, Va. Running back William & Mary 1973-75. No pro playing experience. College coach: William & Mary 1977-79, Syracuse 1980-1990. Pro coach: New England Patriots 1991-92, Chicago Bears 1993-98, re-joined Patriots in 1999.

Pepper Johnson, defensive line; born July 29, 1964, Detroit. Linebacker Ohio State 1982-85. Pro linebacker New York Giants 1986-1992, Cleveland Browns 1993-95, Detroit Lions 1996, New York Jets 1997-98. Pro coach: Joined Patriots in 2001.

Harold Nash, asst. strength and conditioning; born May 5, 1970, New Orleans. Defensive back Louisiana-Lafayette 1988-1993. Pro defensive back Shreveport Pirates (CFL) 1994-95, Montreal Alouettes (CFL) 1996-99, Winnipeg Blue Bombers (CFL) 1999-2003, Edmonton Eskimos (CFL) 2004. Pro coach: Joined Patriots in 2005.

Bill O'Brien, quarterbacks; born October 23, 1969, Andover, Mass. Linebacker/defensive end Brown 1990-92. No pro playing experience. College coach: Brown 1993-94, Georgia Tech 1995-2002, Maryland 2003-04, Duke 2005-06. Pro Coach: Joined Patriots in 2007.

Scott O'Brien, special teams; born June 25, 1957, Superior, Wisc. Linebacker Wisconsin-Superior 1975-78. No pro playing experience. College coach: Wisconsin-Superior 1980-82, Nevada-Las Vegas 1983-85, Rice 1986, Pittsburgh 1987-1990. Pro coach: Cleveland Browns 1991-95, Baltimore Ravens 1996-98, Carolina Panthers 1999-2004, Miami Dolphins 2005-06, Denver Broncos 2007-08, joined Patriots in 2009.

Chad O'Shea, receivers; born December 18, 1972, Houston. Quarterback Marshall 1991-93, Houston 1994-95. No pro playing experience. College coach: Houston 1996-99, Southern Mississippi 2000-02. Pro coach: Kansas City Chiefs 2003-05, Minnesota Vikings 2006-08, joined Patriots in 2009.

Matt Patricia, linebackers; born Sept. 13, 1974. Center-guard Rensselaer 1992-96. No pro playing experience. College coach: Rensselaer 1996, Amherst 1999-2000, Syracuse 2001-03. Pro coach: Joined Patriots in 2004.

Dean Pees, defensive coordinator; born September 4, 1949, Dunkirk, Ohio. Attended Bowling Green. No college or pro playing experience. College coach: Findlay 1979-1982, Miami (Ohio) 1983-86, Navy 1987-89, Toledo 1990-93, Notre Dame 1994, Michigan State 1995-97, Kent State 1998-2003. Pro coach: Joined Patriots in 2004.

Dante Scarnecchia, asst. head coach/offensive line; born February 15, 1948, Los Angeles. Center/guard California Western 1968-1970. No pro playing experience. College coach: California Western 1970-72, Iowa State 1973-74, Southern Methodist 1975-76, Pacific 1977-78, Northern Arizona 1979, Southern Methodist 1980-81. Pro coach: New England Patriots 1982-88, Indianapolis Colts 1989-1990, re-joined Patriots in 1991.

Shane Waldron, tight ends; born August 17, 1979, Portland, Ore. Tight end Tufts University 1999-2001. No pro playing experience. College coach: Notre Dame 2005-07. Pro coach: Joined Patriots in 2008.

Mike Woicik, strength and conditioning; born September 26, 1956, Baltimore. Attended Boston College. No college or pro playing experience. College coach: Springfield College 1978-1980, Syracuse 1980-89. Pro coach: Dallas Cowboys 1990-96, New Orleans Saints 1997-99, joined Patriots in 2000.

American Football Conference
East Division
Team Colors: Green and White
1 Jets Drive
Florham Park, New Jersey 07932
Telephone (973) 549-4800

2009 SCHEDULE

PRESEASON

Aug. 14	**St. Louis**	7:00
Aug. 24	at Baltimore	8:00
Aug. 29	at N.Y. Giants	8:00
Sep. 3	**Philadelphia**	7:00

REGULAR SEASON

Sep. 13	at Houston	12:00
Sep. 20	**New England**	1:00
Sep. 27	**Tennessee**	1:00
Oct. 4	at New Orleans	3:05
Oct. 12	at Miami (Mon.)	8:30
Oct. 18	**Buffalo**	4:15
Oct. 25	at Oakland	1:05
Nov. 1	**Miami**	1:00
Nov. 8	BYE	
Nov. 15	**Jacksonville**	1:00
Nov. 22	at New England	4:15
Nov. 29	**Carolina**	1:00
Dec. 3	at Buffalo (Thu. – Toronto)	8:20
Dec. 13	at Tampa Bay	1:00
Dec. 20	**Atlanta**	1:00
Dec. 27	at Indianapolis	4:15
Jan. 3	**Cincinnati**	1:00

Stadium: Meadowlands
(opened in 1976)
• **Capacity:** 80,062
East Rutherford, New Jersey
07073
Playing Surface: FieldTurf
Training Camp: SUNY Cortland
Cortland, New York 13045

MEADOWLANDS

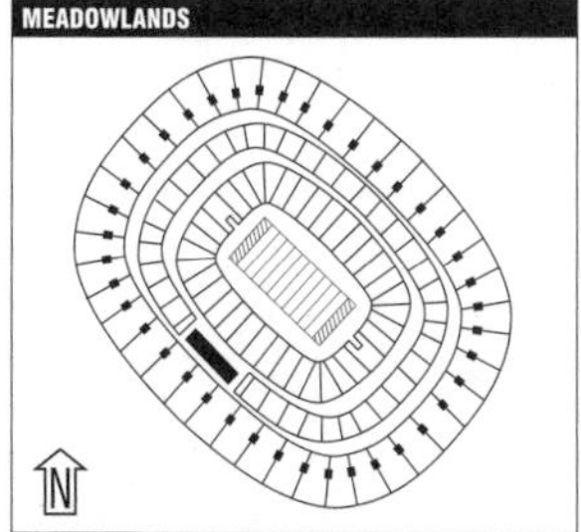

CLUB OFFICIALS

Chairman and CEO:
Robert Wood Johnson IV
Executive V.P., Business Operations:
Matt Higgins
Executive V.P., Finance & Stadium
Development: Thad Sheely
Executive V.P., General Manager:
Mike Tannenbaum
Assistant General Manager: Scott Cohen
Associate General Counsel/ Director,
Legal Affairs: Hymie Elhai
V.P., College Scouting: Joey Clinkscales
V.P., Finance/ Chief Financial Officer:
Mike Gerstle
V.P., Broadcasting & Production:
Bob Parente
V.P., Corporate Sales: Marc Riccio
V.P., Consumer Sales & Service:
Robert Sullivan
V.P., Security: Steve Yarnell
Senior Personnel Executive:
Terry Bradway
Assistant Director, Player Personnel:
JoJo Wooden
Director, Pro Personnel:
Brendan Phophett
Pro Scout: Brock Sunderland
Assistant, Pro Personnel: Cole Hufnagel
Assistant Director, College Scouting:
Michael Davis
National Scout: Jim Cochran
Personnel Scouts: Jeff Bauer,
Matt Bazirgan, Joe Bommarito,
Jesse Kaye, Jay Mandolesi,
Gary Smith
Assistant, Player Personnel:
Kathryn Smith
Director, Football Administration:
Ari Nissim
Manager, Football Administration:
Jacqueline Davidson
Senior Director, Sales: Bob Brennfleck
Senior Director, Multimedia & Production:
Rich Gentile
Senior Director, Operations: Clay Hampton
Senior Director, Ticket Operations:
Jeff Hecker
Senior Director, Athletic Training:
John Mellody
Assistant Athletic Trainers: Josh Koch,
Dave Zuffelato
Senior Director, Corporate Partnerships:
Jennifer Linn
Senior Director, IT: Tom Murphy
Senior Director, Merchandising:
Chris Pierce
Senior Director, Media Relations:
Bruce Speight
Senior Director, Marketing:
Victoria Vitarelli
Director, Equipment: Gus Granneman
Manager, Equipment: Vito Contento
Coordinator, Equipment: Cortez Robinson
Director, Community Relations:
Jesse Linder
Director, Events & Game Operations:
Brian Mulligan
Director, Player Development: David Szott
Director, Video: Tim Tubito

COACHING HISTORY

New York Titans 1960-62
(339-412-8)
Records include postseason games

1960-61	Sammy Baugh	14-14-0
1962	Clyde (Bulldog) Turner	5-9-0
1963-1973	Weeb Ewbank	73-78-6
1974-75	Charley Winner*	9-14-0
1975	Ken Shipp	1-4-0
1976	Lou Holtz**	3-10-0
1976	Mike Holovak	0-1-0
1977-1982	Walt Michaels	41-49-1
1983-89	Joe Walton	54-59-1
1990-93	Bruce Coslet	26-39-0
1994	Pete Carroll	6-10-0
1995-96	Rich Kotite	4-28-0
1997-99	Bill Parcells	30-20-0
2000	Al Groh	9-7-0
2001-05	Herman Edwards	41-44-0
2006-08	Eric Mangini	23-26-0

*Released after nine games in 1975
**Resigned after 13 games in 1976

PAID ATTENDANCE

Home 613,627 Away 534,214
Total 1,147,841
Single-game home record,
79,572 (11/19/06)
Single-season home record,
628,773 (2002)

2009 DRAFT CHOICES

Round	Name	Pos.	College
1	Mark Sanchez	QB	Southern California
3	Shonn Greene	RB	Iowa
6	Matt Slauson	G	Nebraska

NEW YORK JETS

2008 TEAM RECORD

PRESEASON (3-1)

Date	Result	Opponent
8/7	W 24-20	at Cleveland
8/16	L 10-13	Washington
8/23	W 10-7	New York Giants
8/28	W 27-20	at Philadelphia

REGULAR SEASON (9-7)

Date	Result	Opponent
9/7	W 20-14	at Miami
9/14	L 10-19	New England
9/22	L 29-48	at San Diego
9/28	W 56-35	Arizona
10/12	W 26-14	Cincinnati
10/19	L 13-16	at Oakland (OT)
10/26	W 28-24	Kansas City
11/2	W 26-17	at Buffalo
11/9	W 47-3	St. Louis
11/13	W 34-31	at New England (OT)
11/23	W 34-13	at Tennessee
11/30	L 17-34	Denver
12/7	L 14-24	at San Francisco
12/14	W 31-27	Buffalo
12/21	L 3-13	at Seattle
12/28	L 17-24	Miami

(OT) Overtime

SCORE BY PERIODS

NY Jets	102	137	55	108	3 —	405
Opponents	60	117	75	101	3 —	356

2008 TEAM STATISTICS

	Jets	Opp.
Total First Downs	308	315
Rushing	94	86
Passing	186	209
Penalty	28	20
3rd Down: Made/Att	81/197	81/210
3rd Down Pct.	41.1	38.6
4th Down: Made/Att	9/16	13/18
4th Down Pct.	56.3	72.2
Possession Avg.	30:28	29:32
Total Net Yards	5307	5270
Avg. Per Game	331.7	329.4
Total Plays	981	1020
Avg. Per Play	5.4	5.2
Net Yards Rushing	2004	1518
Avg. Per Game	125.3	94.9
Total Rushes	422	407
Net Yards Passing	3303	3752
Avg. Per Game	206.4	234.5
Sacked/Yards Lost	30/213	41/253
Gross Yards	3516	4005
Att./Completions	529/347	572/368
Completion Pct.	65.6	64.3
Had Intercepted	23	14
Punts/Average	59/42.2	69/43.4
Net Punting Avg.	59/35.6	69/36.4
Penalties/Yards	77/569	93/663
Fumbles/Ball Lost	22/8	37/16
Touchdowns	48	40
Rushing	20	10
Passing	22	23
Returns	6	7

2008 INDIVIDUAL STATISTICS

PASSING	Att.	Comp.	Yds.	Pct.	TD	Int.	Tkld.	Rate
Favre	522	343	3472	65.7	22	22	30/213	81.0
Clemens	5	3	26	60.0	0	1	0/0	34.2
B. Smith	2	1	18	50.0	0	0	0/0	81.3
NY Jets	529	347	3516	65.6	22	23	30/213	80.2
Opponents	572	368	4005	64.3	23	14	41/253	88.1

SCORING	TD R	TD P	TD Rt	PAT	FG	Saf	PTS
Feely	0	0	0	39/39	24/28	0	111
Jones	13	2	0	0/0	0/0	0	90
Washington	6	2	1	0/0	0/0	0	56
Coles	0	7	0	0/0	0/0	0	42
Cotchery	0	5	0	0/0	0/0	0	32
Keller	0	3	0	0/0	0/0	0	18
Stuckey	0	3	0	0/0	0/0	0	18
Barrett	0	0	1	0/0	0/0	0	6
Elam	0	0	1	0/0	0/0	0	6
Ellis	0	0	1	0/0	0/0	0	6
Favre	1	0	0	0/0	0/0	0	6
Pace	0	0	1	0/0	0/0	0	6
Revis	0	0	1	0/0	0/0	0	6
Nugent	0	0	0	2/2	0/1	0	2
NY Jets	20	22	6	41/41	24/29	0	405
Opponents	10	23	7	37/37	25/28	0	356

2-Pt. Conversions: Cotchery, Washington. Jets 2-7, Opponents 2-3.

RUSHING	No.	Yds	Avg	LG	TD
Jones	290	1312	4.5	59t	13
Washington	76	448	5.9	61t	6
B. Smith	12	113	9.4	36	0
Richardson	10	65	6.5	16	0
Favre	21	43	2.0	27	1
Coles	2	9	4.5	6	0
Chatman	5	8	1.6	5	0
Cotchery	2	8	4.0	8	0
Stuckey	1	1	1.0	1	0
Clemens	3	-3	-1.0	-1	0
NY Jets	422	2004	4.7	61t	20
Opponents	407	1518	3.7	35	10

RECEIVING	No.	Yds	Avg	LG	TD
Cotchery	71	858	12.1	56t	5
Coles	70	850	12.1	54	7
Keller	48	535	11.1	54	3
Washington	47	355	7.6	40	2
Jones	36	207	5.8	19	2
Stuckey	32	359	11.2	31	3
Baker	21	194	9.2	29	0
B. Smith	12	64	5.3	18	0
Franks	6	47	7.8	25	0
Chatman	2	5	2.5	3	0
Clowney	1	26	26.0	26	0
Richardson	1	4	4.0	4	0
Carroll	0	11	—	11	0
Favre	0	2	—	2	0
Revis	0	-1	—	-1	0
NY Jets	347	3516	10.1	56t	22
Opponents	368	4005	10.9	60	23

PUNTING	No.	Yds.	Avg.	In 20	LG
Hodges	44	1884	42.8	14	61
Graham	14	606	43.3	2	56
NY Jets	59	2490	42.2	16	61
Opponents	69	2992	43.4	23	65

INTERCEPTIONS	No.	Yds	Avg	LG	TD
Revis	5	38	7.6	32t	1
Rhodes	2	50	25.0	50	0
Poteat	2	47	23.5	41	0
Elam	1	92	92.0	92t	1
Barrett	1	25	25.0	25t	1
Bowens	1	24	24.0	24	0
E. Smith	1	6	6.0	6	0
Lowery	1	0	0.0	0	0
NY Jets	14	282	20.1	92t	3
Opponents	23	351	15.3	91t	4

PUNT RETURNS	Ret	FC	Yds	Avg	LG	TD
Washington	29	9	303	10.4	37	0
NY Jets	29	9	303	10.4	37	0
Opponents	29	13	288	9.9	56	0

KICKOFF RETURNS	No.	Yds	Avg	LG	TD
Washington	48	1231	25.6	94	1
B. Smith	4	39	9.8	26	0
Bowens	4	37	9.3	14	0
Cotchery	1	54	54.0	54	0
Miller	1	22	22.0	22	0
Keller	1	9	9.0	9	0
Turner	1	9	9.0	9	0
Franks	1	6	6.0	6	0
NY Jets	61	1407	23.1	94	1
Opponents	73	1568	21.5	44	0

FIELD GOALS	1-19	20-29	30-39	40-49	50+
Feely	0/0	9/9	9/12	4/5	2/2
Nugent	0/0	0/0	0/1	0/0	0/0
NY Jets	0/0	9/9	9/13	4/5	2/2
Opponents	0/0	5/5	11/12	7/9	2/2

SACKS	No.
Ellis	8.0
Pace	7.0
Thomas	5.5
Bowens	4.0
Jenkins	3.5
Elam	2.0
Barton	1.5
Mosley	1.5
D. Coleman	1.0
Harris	1.0
Poteat	1.0
Revis	1.0
Rhodes	1.0
(group)	1.0
Barrett	0.5
K. Coleman	0.5
Devito	0.5
Pouha	0.5
Jets	41.0
Opponents	30.0

RECORD HOLDERS

INDIVIDUAL RECORDS—CAREER

Category	Name	Performance
Rushing (Yds.)	Curtis Martin, 1998-2005	10,302
Passing (Yds.)	Joe Namath, 1965-1976	27,057
Passing (TDs)	Joe Namath, 1965-1976	170
Receiving (No.)	Don Maynard, 1960-1972	627
Receiving (Yds.)	Don Maynard, 1960-1972	11,732
Interceptions	Bill Baird, 1963-69	34
Punting (Avg.)	Ben Graham, 2005-08	43.6
Punt Return (Avg.)	Dick Christy, 1961-63	16.2
Kickoff Return (Avg.)	Justin Miller, 2005-07	27.1
Field Goals	Pat Leahy, 1974-1991	304
Touchdowns (Tot.)	Don Maynard, 1960-1972	88
Points	Pat Leahy, 1974-1991	1,470
*Sacks	Mark Gastineau, 1979-1988	74.0

INDIVIDUAL RECORDS—SINGLE SEASON

Category	Name	Performance
Rushing (Yds.)	Curtis Martin, 2004	1,697
Passing (Yds.)	Joe Namath, 1967	4,007
Passing (TDs)	Vinny Testaverde, 1998	29
Receiving (No.)	Al Toon, 1988	93
Receiving (Yds.)	Don Maynard, 1967	1,434
Interceptions	Dainard Paulson, 1964	12
Punting (Avg.)	Curley Johnson, 1965	45.3
Punt Return (Avg.)	Dick Christy, 1961	21.3
Kickoff Return (Avg.)	Bobby Humphery, 1984	30.7
Field Goals	Jim Turner, 1968	34
Touchdowns (Tot.)	Thomas Jones, 2008	15
Points	Jim Turner, 1968	145
*Sacks	Mark Gastineau, 1984	22.0

INDIVIDUAL RECORDS—SINGLE GAME

Category	Name	Performance
Rushing (Yds.)	Curtis Martin, 12-3-00	203
Passing (Yds.)	Joe Namath, 9-24-72	496
Passing (TDs)	Joe Namath, 9-24-72	6
	Brett Favre, 9-28-08	6
Receiving (No.)	Clark Gaines, 9-21-80	17
Receiving (Yds.)	Don Maynard, 11-17-68	228
Interceptions	Many times	3
	Last time by Ty Law, 1-1-06	
Field Goals	Jim Turner, 11-3-68	6
	Bobby Howfield, 12-3-72	6
Touchdowns (Tot.)	Wesley Walker, 9-21-86	4
Points	Wesley Walker, 9-21-86	24
*Sacks	Mark Gastineau, 11-6-83, 9-2-84	4.0
	John Abraham, 11-4-01	4.0

**Sacks became an official statistic in 1982.*

NEW YORK JETS

2009 VETERAN ROSTER

No.	Name	Pos.	Ht.	Wt.	Birthdate	NFL Exp.	College	Hometown	How Acq.	'08 Games/ Starts
10	Ainge, Erik	QB	6-5	221	6/12/86	2	Tennessee	Hillsboro, Ore.	D5-'08	0*
36	#Barrett, David	CB	5-10	185	12/22/77	10	Maryland	Alexandria, Va.	UFA(Ariz)-'04	11/1
32	Brackenridge, Tyron	CB	5-11	189	6/30/84	2	Washington State	Ontario, Calif.	FA-'09	1/0*
84	Brown, Kareem	TE	6-4	295	1/30/84	3	Miami	Miami, Fla.	W(NE)-'07	0*
31	Carroll, Ahmad	DB	5-10	190	8/4/83	5	Arkansas	Atlanta, Ga.	UFA-'09	16/0
22	#Chatman, Jesse	RB	5-8	225	9/22/79	7	Eastern Washington	Seattle, Wash.	UFA(Mia)-'08	3/0
11	Clemens, Kellen	QB	5-2	223	6/7/83	4	Oregon	Burns, Ore.	D2-'06	2/0
87	Clowney, David	WR	6-0	188	7/7/85	2	Virginia Tech	Delray Beach, Fla.	FA-'07	2/0
30	Coleman, Drew	CB	5-9	175	4/22/83	4	Texas Christian	Henderson, Texas	D6-'06	9/0
89	Cotchery, Jerricho	WR	6-0	207	6/16/82	6	North Carolina State	Birmingham, Ala.	D4a-'04	16/16
85	Dearth, James	TE/LS	6-4	270	1/22/76	9	Tarleton State	Scurry, Texas	FA-01	16/0
70	DeVito, Mike	DE	6-3	298	6/10/84	3	Maine	Wellfleet, Mass.	FA-'07	16/0
93	Douglas, Marques	DE	6-2	292	5/5/77	8	Howard	Greensboro, N.C.	FA-'09	16/0*
92	Ellis, Shaun	DE	6-5	285	10/15/81	10	Tennessee	Anderson, S.C.	D1a-'00	16/16
66	Faneca, Alan	G	6-5	307	6/24/77	12	Louisiana State	New Orleans, La.	UFA(Pitt)-'08	16/16
3	Feely, Jay	K	5-10	205	5/23/76	9	Michigan	Tampa, Fla.	FA-'08	15/0
60	Ferguson, D'Brickashaw	T	6-6	312	12/10/83	4	Virginia	Freeport, N.Y.	D1a-'08	15/0
88	Franks, Bubba	TE	6-6	265	1/6/78	10	Miami	Riverside, Calif.	FA-'09	13/0
50	Gholston, Vernon	LB	6-3	264	3/28/85	2	Ohio State	Detroit, Mich.	D2-'07	11/11
95	Green, Howard	DT	6-2	320	1/12/79	6	Louisiana State	Donaldsonville, La.	UFA(Sea)-'09	13/0*
52	Harris, David	LB	6-2	243	1/21/84	3	Michigan	Grand Rapids, Mich.	FA-'07	10/10
58	Harris, Nate	T	6-0	230	3/8/83	2	Louisville	Miami, Fla.	FA-'09	0*
78	Hunter, Wayne	T	6-5	303	7/2/81	6	Hawaii	Honolulu, Hawaii	FA-'07	14/0
44	Ihedigbo, James	DB	6-1	202	12/3/83	3	Massachusetts	Amherst, Mass.	FA-'08	8/0
53	Izzo, Larry	LB	5-10	228	9/26/74	14	Rice	Fort Belvoir, Va.	UFA(NE)-'09	16/0*
77	Jenkins, Kris	DT	6-4	349	8/3/79	9	Maryland	Ypsilanti, Mich.	T(Car)-'08	16/16
20	Jones, Thomas	RB	5-10	215	8/19/78	10	Virginia	Big Stone Gap, Va.	T(Chi)-'07	16/14
81	Keller, Dustin	TE	6-2	248	9/25/84	2	Purdue	Lafayette, Ind.	D1b-'08	16/4
22	#Law, Ty	CB	5-8	200	2/10/74	15	Michigan	Aliquippa, Pa.	FA-'08	7/6
36	Leonhard, Jim	S	5-11	186	10/27/82	5	Wisconsin	Ladysmith, Wisc.	UFA(Balt)-'09	16/13*
21	Lowery, Dwight	CB	5-8	201	1/23/86	2	San Jose State	Santa Cruz, Calif.	D4-'08	16/10
74	Mangold, Nick	C	6-4	300	1/13/84	4	Ohio State	Centerville, Ohio	D1b-'06	16/16
65	Moore, Brandon	G	6-3	295	6/3/80	7	Illinois	Gary, Ind.	FA-'03	16/16
94	Murrell, Marques	LB	6-2	250	3/20/85	3	Appalachian State	Fayetteville, N.C.	FA-'07	12/0
97	Pace, Calvin	LB	6-4	270	10/28/80	7	Wake Forest	Douglasville, Ga.	UFA(Ariz)-'08	16/16
91	Pouha, Sione	DT	6-3	325	2/3/79	5	Utah	Salt Lake City, Utah	D3-'05	16/0
32	#Reed, J.R.	S	5-11	202	2/11/82	6	South Florida	Tampa, Fla.	FA-'08	5/0*
24	Revis, Darrelle	DB/PR	5-11	204	7/14/85	3	Pittsburgh	Aliquippa, Pa.	D1-'07	16/16
25	Rhodes, Kerry	S	6-3	220	8/2/82	5	Louisville	Bessemer, Ala.	D4-'05	16/16
49	Richardson, Tony	FB	6-1	238	12/17/71	15	Auburn	Daleville, Ala.	UFA(Minn)-'08	16/7
57	Scott, Bart	LB	6-2	240	8/18/80	8	Southern Illinois	Detroit, Mich.	UFA(Balt)-'09	16/16*
26	t- Sheppard, Lito	CB	5-10	194	4/8/81	8	Florida	Jacksonville, Fla.	T(Phil)-'09	16/3*
16	Smith, Brad	WR	6-2	210	12/12/83	4	Missouri	Youngstown, Ohio	D4a-'06	15/1
33	Smith, Eric	S	6-1	209	3/17/83	4	Michigan State	Groveport, Ohio	D3b-'06	15/1
27	Strickland, Donald	CB	5-10	185	11/24/80	7	Colorado	Redwood City, Calif.	UFA(SF)-'09	14/3*
83	Stuckey, Chansi	WR	6-0	196	10/4/83	3	Clemson	Warner Robins, Ga.	D7-'07	15/2
99	Thomas, Bryan	LB	6-4	266	6/7/79	8	Alabama-Birmingham	Birmingham, Ala.	D1-'02	16/15
96	Trusnik, Jason	LB	6-4	250	6/6/84	3	Ohio Northern	Macedonia, Ohio	FA-'07	7/0
75	Turner, Robert	OL	6-4	308	8/20/84	2	New Mexico	Austin, Texas	FA-'07	10/0
29	Washington, Leon	RB/KR	5-8	202	8/29/82	4	Florida State	Jacksonville, Fla.	D4b-'06	16/1
22	Woodhead, Danny	RB	5-9	200	12/3/83	2	Chadron State	North Platte, Neb.	FA-'08	0*
67	Woody, Damien	OL	6-3	335	11/3/77	11	Boston College	Beaverdam, Va.	UFA(Det)-'08	16/16
15	Wright, Wallace	WR	6-1	191	2/1/84	3	North Carolina	Fayetteville, N.C.	FA-'06	16/0

* Ainge inactive for 7 games; Brackenridge played 1 game with Kansas City; Brown inactive for 7 games; Douglas played 16 games with Baltimore in '08; Green played 13 games with Seattle; N. Harris last active with Kansas City in '07; Izzo played 16 games with New England; CB Leonhard played 16 games with Baltimore; Reed played 5 games with Philadelphia; Scott played 16 games with Baltimore; Sheppard played 16 games with Philadelphia; Strickland played 14 games with San Francisco in '08; Woodhead missed '08 season because of injury.

Retired—Brett Favre, 18-year quarterback, 16 games.

t- Jets traded for Lito Sheppard (Phil).

Traded—DE Kenyon Coleman (16 games in '08) to Cleveland; S Abram Elam (16) to Cleveland; QB Brett Ratliff (0) to Cleveland.

Players lost through free agency (6): LB Eric Barton (Cle; 16 games in '08), WR Laveranues Coles (Cin; 16), DT C.J. Mosley (Cle; 16), K Mike Nugent (TB; 1), CB Hank Poteat (Cle; 13), LB Cody Spencer (Det; 14).

Also played with Jets in '08—TE Chris Baker (16 games), LB David Bowens (16), P Ben Graham (4), P Reggie Hodges (12), CB Ty Law (7), CB Justin Miller (1).

2009 FIRST-YEAR ROSTER

Name	Pos.	Ht.	Wt.	Birthdate	College	Hometown	How Acq.
Bullock, J'Nathan	TE	6-5	240	6/25/87	Cleveland State	Flint, Mich.	FA
Caulcrick, Jehuu (1)	RB	6-0	254	8/6/83	Michigan State	Findley Lake, N.Y.	FA-'08
Cole, Marquice (1)	CB	5-10	190	11/13/83	Northwestern	Hazel Crest, Ill.	FA
Conley, T.J.	P	6-3	220	8/29/85	Idaho	Walla Walla, Wash.	FA
Cook, Emanuel	S	5-10	214	1/20/88	South Carolina	Riviera Beach, Fla.	FA
Cummings, Kenwin (1)	LB	6-3	270	7/23/86	Wingate	Maxton, N.C.	FA-'08
Daniels, Stanley (1)	OL	6-4	320	11/30/84	Washington	San Diego, Calif.	FA-'08
Davie, Andrew	TE/LS	6-6	275	1/5/83	Arkansas	Little Rock, Ark.	FA
Davis, Britt	WR	6-3	205	4/23/86	Northern Illinois	Broadview, Ill.	FA
Fitzhugh, Keith	S	5-11	205	11/11/86	Mississippi State	Lovejoy, Ga.	FA
Greene, Shonn	RB	5-11	227	8/21/85	Iowa	Sicklerville, N.J.	D3
Harris, Anthony (1)	LS/DT	6-3	287	12/24/81	Western New Mexico	Rollins Fork, Miss.	FA
Henry, Marcus (1)	WR	6-4	207	2/21/86	Kansas	Lawton, Okla.	D6-'08
Kracalik, Michael (1)	T	6-8	337	9/8/82	San Diego State	San Diego, Calif.	FA
Kroul, Matt	DL	6-3	281	2/25/86	Iowa	Mount Vernon, Iowa	FA
Link, Kyle	T	6-6	300	6/19/86	McNeese State	Lake Charles, La.	FA
McKee, Ryan	T	6-6	291	11/4/86	Southern Mississippi	Spanish Fort, Ala.	FA
Myers, Rob	TE	6-4	240	4/9/86	Utah State	Houston, Texas	FA
Parenton, Michael	C	6-2	287	11/2/85	Tulane	Thibodaux, La.	FA
Pitoitua, Ropati (1)	DE	6-8	290	4/6/85	Washington State	Spanaway, Wash.	FA-'08
Pizzotti, Chris	QB	6-5	225	6/29/86	Harvard	Reading, Mass.	FA
Potter, Zach	DE	6-7	280	5/4/86	Nebraska	Omaha, Neb.	FA
Raymond, Paul (1)	WR	5-10	185	5/5/86	Brown	Miami, Fla.	FA
Renkart, Brandon (1)	DB/PR	5-11	204	12/29/84	Pittsburgh	Aliquippa, Pa.	FA-'08
Sanchez, Mark	QB	6-2	227	11/11/86	Southern California	Mission Viejo, Calif.	D1
Schaefering, Brian (1)	DL	6-5	295	8/20/83	Lindenwood	St. Louis, Mo.	FA-'08
Simmons, Jack	TE	6-4	246	2/21/86	Minnesota	Libertyville, Ill.	FA
Slauson, Matt	G	6-5	316	2/18/86	Nebraska	Colorado Springs, Colo.	D6
Southerland, Brannan	FB	6-0	244	11/12/85	Georgia	Dacula, Ga.	FA
Steinkuhler, Ty	DL	6-3	280	9/11/85	Nebraska	Lincoln, Neb.	FA
Thompson, Tavita	T	6-5	309	12/26/85	Oregon State	Honolulu, Hawaii	FA
Westerman, Jamaal	DE	6-3	265	2/21/85	Rutgers	Brampton, Ontario, Canada	FA
Whittaker, Huey (1)	WR	6-2	220	6/19/81	South Florida	Springstead, Fla.	FA
Wilbur, Eric (1)	P	6-2	200	12/12/84	Florida	Orlando, Fla.	FA

The term NFL Rookie is defined as a player who is in his first season of professional football and has not been on the roster of another professional football team for any regular-season or postseason games. A Rookie is designated by an "R" on NFL rosters. Players who have been active in another professional football league or players who have NFL experience, including either preseason training camp or being on an Active List or Inactive List, or on Reserve/Injured or Reserve/Physically Unable to Perform for fewer than six regular-season games, are termed NFL First-Year Players. An NFL First-Year Player is designated by a "1" on NFL rosters. Thereafter, a player is credited with an additional year of experience for each season in which he accumulates six games on the Active List or Inactive List, or on Reserve/Injured or Reserve/Physically Unable to Perform.

Log on to www.newyorkjets.com for an up-to-date roster.

NEW YORK JETS

COACHING STAFF

Head Coach,
Rex Ryan

Pro Career: Named the 15th full-time head coach of the New York Jets on January 19, 2009. Spent the past 10 seasons with the Baltimore Ravens, including 2008 as the assistant head coach/defensive coordinator. Since becoming defensive coordinator in 2005, the Ravens never finished lower than sixth in total defense. From 1999-2008, the Ravens ranked first in the NFL for fewest points allowed, fewest rushing yards allowed, most takeaways, most interceptions and most interceptions returned for touchdowns. Ravens allowed fewest points in NFL history for 16-game season (165) in 2000 en route to winning Super Bowl XXXV. Began NFL career with Arizona under his father, Buddy Ryan, as coach for defensive line (1994) and linebackers (1995). Career record: 0-0.

Background: Coached at Eastern Kentucky (1987-88), New Mexico Highlands (1989), Morehead State (1990-93), Cincinnati (1996-97) and Oklahoma (1998). Played defensive end at Southwestern Oklahoma State with his twin brother, Rob, who is currently the Cleveland defensive coordinator. Earned his Bachelor's and Master's Degree in Physical Education at Eastern Kentucky.

Personal: Born December 13, 1963, Ardmore, Okla. Ryan and his wife Michelle have two sons, Payton and Seth.

ASSISTANT COACHES

Sal Alosi, head strength and conditioning; born May 11, 1977, Massapequa, N.Y. Linebacker Hofstra 1996-2000. No pro playing experience. College coach: Hofstra 2001. Pro coach: New York Jets 2002-05, Atlanta Falcons 2006, re-joined Jets in 2007.

Mike Bloomgren, offensive assistant; born January 25, 1977, Tallahassee, Fla. Culver-Stockton tight end 1996. No pro playing experience. College coach: Florida State 1997-98 Alabama 1999-2001, Catawba College 2002-04, Delta State 2005-06. Pro coach: Joined Jets in 2007.

Bill Callahan, asst. head coach/offense; born July, 31 1956, Chicago. Quarterback Benedictine 1975-77. No pro playing experience. College coach: Illinois 1980-86, Northern Arizona 1987-88, Southern Illinois 1989, Wisconsin 1990-94, Nebraska 2004-2007 (head coach). Pro coach: Philadelphia Eagles 1995-97, Oakland Raiders 1998-2003 (head coach 2002-03), joined Jets in 2008.

Matt Cavanaugh, quarterbacks; born October 27, 1956, Youngstown, Ohio. Quarterback Pittsburgh 1974-77. Pro quarterback New England Patriots 1978-1982, San Francisco 49ers 1983-85, Philadelphia Eagles 1986-89, New York Giants 1990-91. College coach: Pittsburgh 1991-93, 2005-08. Pro coach: Arizona Cardinals 1994-95, San Francisco 49ers 1996, Chicago Bears 1997-98, Baltimore Ravens 1999-2004, joined Jets in 2009.

Ryan Cidzik, asst. strength and conditioning; born January 20, 1979, Rome, N.Y. Fullback Susquehanna 1997-2001. College coach: Louisiana Tech 2003-05, Northwestern State 2006-07. Pro coach: Cleveland Browns 2008, joined Jets in 2009.

John DeFilippo, asst. quarterbacks; born April 12, 1978, Youngstown, Ohio. Quarterback James Madison 1996-99. No pro playing experience. College coach: Fordham 2000, Notre Dame 2001-02, Columbia 2003-04. Pro coach: New York Giants 2005-06, Oakland Raiders 2007-08, joined Jets in 2009.

Mike Devlin, tight ends/asst. offensive line; born November 16, 1969, Blacksburg, Va. Offensive line Iowa 1989-1992. Pro offensive lineman Buffalo Bills 1993-95, Arizona Cardinals 1996-99. College coach: Toledo 2004-05. Pro coach: Arizona Cardinals 2000-03, joined Jets in 2006.

Henry Ellard, wide receivers; born July 21, 1961, Fresno, Calif. Wide receiver Fresno State 1979-1982. Pro wide receiver/punt returner Los Angeles Rams 1983-1993, Washington Redskins 1994-98, New England Patriots 1998. College coach: Fresno State 2000. Pro coach: St. Louis Rams 2001-08, joined Jets in 2009.

Ben Kotwica, asst. special teams; born December 8, 1974, Tinley Park, Ill. Linebacker Army 1995-97. No pro playing experience. Pro coach: Joined Jets in 2007.

Kerry Locklin, defensive line; born September 9, 1959, Las Cruces, N.M. Tight end New Mexico State 1978-1981. Pro tight end Los Angeles Rams 1982-83, Arizona (USFL) 1984-85, Denver Broncos 1987. College coach: Western New Mexico 1988, Utah 1989, Morehead State 1990-94, Eastern Michigan 1995-99, Fresno State 2000-08. Pro coach: Shreveport (CFL) 1995, joined Jets in 2009.

Anthony Lynn, running backs; born December 21, 1968, McKinney, Texas. Running back Texas Tech 1987-1990. Pro running back Denver Broncos 1993, 1997-99, San Francisco 49ers 1995-96. Pro coach: Denver Broncos 2000-02, Jacksonville Jaguars 2003-04, Dallas Cowboys 2005-06, Cleveland Browns 2007, joined Jets in 2009.

Kevin O'Dea, special teams; born June 9, 1960, Williamsport, Pa. Wide receiver/defensive back Lock Haven 1984-85. No pro playing experience. College coach: Lock Haven 1986, Cornell 1987, Virginia 1988-1990, Penn State 1991-93. Pro coach: San Diego Chargers 1994-95, Tampa Bay Buccaneers 1996-2001, Detroit Lions 2002-03, Arizona Cardinals 2004-05, Chicago Bears 2006-07, joined Jets in 2008.

Jim O'Neil, quality control/defense; born Oct. 26, 1978, Philadelphia. Defensive end Towson University 1997-2000. No pro playing experience. College coach: SUNY-Albany 2001, Pennsylvania 2002, Northwestern 2003-04, Towson University 2005, Eastern Michigan 2006-08. Pro coach: Joined Jets in 2009.

Mike Pettine, defensive coordinator; born September 25, 1966, Doyelstown, Pa. Safety Virginia 1984-87. No pro playing experience. College coach: Pittsburgh 1993-94. Pro coach: Baltimore Ravens 2003-08, joined Jets in 2009.

Doug Plank, asst. defensive backs; born March 4, 1953, Greensburg, Pa. Safety Ohio State 1972-74. Pro safety Chicago Bears 1975-1982, Chicago Blitz (AFL) 1983, Arizona Rattlers (AFL) 2002-04, Georgia Force (AFL) 2005-08, Atlanta Falcons 2008, joined Jets in 2009.

Brian Schottenheimer, offensive coordinator; born October 16, 1973, Denver. Quarterback Kansas 1992, Florida 1993-96. No pro playing experience. College coach: Syracuse 1999, Southern California 2000. Pro coach: St. Louis Rams 1997, Kansas City Chiefs 1998, Washington Redskins 2001, San Diego Chargers 2002-05, joined Jets in 2006.

Brian Smith, quality control/defense; born July 15, 1979, Wilmington, Del. Defensive back Massachusetts 1997-2000. No pro playing experience. College coach: Massachusetts 2004-06. Pro coach: Joined Jets in 2007.

Bob Sutton, defensive assistant/linebackers; born January 28, 1951, Ypsilanti, Mich. Attended Eastern Michigan. No college or pro playing experience. College coach: Michigan 1972-73, Syracuse 1974, Western Michigan 1975-76, 1980-81, Illinois 1977-79, North Carolina State 1982, Army 1983-1999 (head coach 1991-99). Pro coach: Joined Jets in 2000.

Kyle Thorne, asst. strength and conditioning; born August 4, 1980, Tucson, Ariz. Linebacker Hofstra 2000-01. Pro linebacker/wide receiver Hawaiian Islanders (AF2) 2004. Pro coach: Billings Outlaws (IFL) 2005, Everton Football Club (EPL) 2007-09, joined Jets in 2009.

Dennis Thurman, defensive backs; born April 13, 1956, Los Angeles, Calif. Defensive back Southern California 1974-77. Pro defensive back Dallas Cowboys 1978-1985, St. Louis Cardinals 1986. College coach: Southern California 1993-2000. Pro coach: Ohio Glory (WLAF) 1992, Baltimore Ravens 2002-08, joined Jets in 2009.

Jeff Weeks, defensive assistant; born May 30, 1962, Denver. Wide receiver Southwest Oklahoma State 1982-84, Northwest Oklahoma State 1985. College coach: Western Kentucky 1987-88, Morehead State 1990-91, Phoenix CC 1996, Oklahoma 1999, Fort Scott (Kan.) C.C. 2001-04, Southeast Oklahoma State 2005, Texas A&M- Kingsville 2006. Pro coach: Oakland Raiders 2008, joined Jets in 2009.

Mike Westhoff, special teams coordinator; born January 10, 1948, Pittsburgh. Linebacker Wyoming 1965, center/linebacker Wichita State 1967-69. College coach: Indiana 1974-75, Dayton 1976, Indiana State 1977, Northwestern 1978-1980, Texas Christian 1981. Pro coach: Baltimore Colts 1982-83, Indianapolis Colts 1984, Arizona Outlaws (USFL) 1985, Miami Dolphins 1986-2000, joined Jets in 2001.

American Football Conference
West Division
Team Colors: Silver and Black
1220 Harbor Bay Parkway
Alameda, California 94502
Telephone: (510) 864-5000

2009 SCHEDULE
PRESEASON

Aug. 13	**Dallas**	7:00
Aug. 22	at San Francisco	5:15
Aug. 29	**New Orleans**	1:00
Sep. 3	at Seattle	7:00

REGULAR SEASON

Sep. 14	**San Diego** (Mon.)	7:15
Sep. 20	at Kansas City	12:00
Sep. 27	**Denver**	1:15
Oct. 4	at Houston	12:00
Oct. 11	at N.Y. Giants	1:00
Oct. 18	**Philadelphia**	1:05
Oct. 25	**N.Y. Jets**	1:05
Nov. 1	at San Diego	1:05
Nov. 8	BYE	
Nov. 15	**Kansas City**	1:05
Nov. 22	**Cincinnati**	1:15
Nov. 26	at Dallas (Thu.)	3:15
Dec. 6	at Pittsburgh	1:00
Dec. 13	**Washington**	1:05
Dec. 20	at Denver	2:05
Dec. 27	at Cleveland	1:00
Jan. 3	**Baltimore**	1:15

Stadium: Oakland Coliseum
(opened in 1966)
• **Capacity:** 63,132
7000 Coliseum Way
Oakland, CA 94621-1917
Playing Surface: Grass
Training Camp: Napa Valley Marriott
Napa, California 94558

OAKLAND COLISEUM

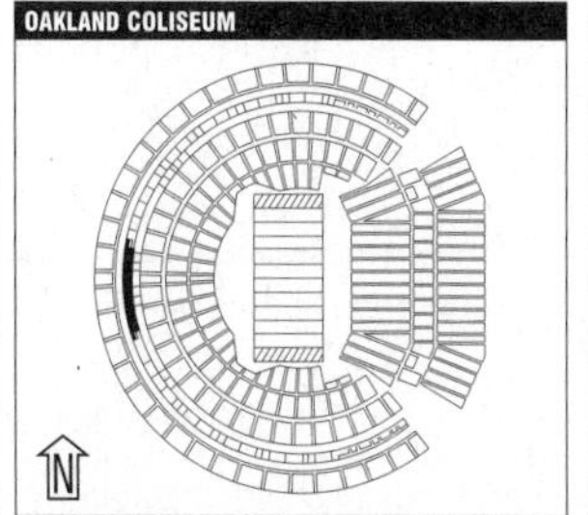

CLUB OFFICIALS
Owner: Al Davis
Chief Executive: Amy Trask
Legal: Jeff Birren, Dan Ventrelle
Finance: Marc Badain, Tom Blanda, Ed Villanueva, Derek Person
Special Projects: Jim Otto
Senior Administrator: Morris Bradshaw
Senior Executive: John Herrera
Public Relations: Mike Taylor, Will Kiss
Tickets, Suites & Premium Seats: Jarrod Dillon, Mark Shearer
Multi-Cultural Initiatives: Patty Herrera, Elena Valenzuela
Internet: Jerry Knaak
Marketing: Robert Kinnard
Community Relations: Scott Fink
Youth Initiatives: Rosie Bone
Raiderettes: Karen Kovac
Trainers: H. Rod Martin, Scott Touchet
Equipment: Bob Romanski, Richard Romanski, Danny Molina
Video Operations: Dave Nash, Jim Otten, John Otten
Broadcasting: Vittorio DeBartolo, Brad Phinney
Computer Operations: Matt Pasco

COACHING HISTORY
Oakland 1960-1981
Los Angeles 1982-1994
(430-342-11)
Records include postseason games

1960-61	Eddie Erdelatz*	6-10-0
1961-62	Marty Feldman**	2-15-0
1962	Red Conkright	1-8-0
1963-65	Al Davis	23-16-3
1966-68	John Rauch	35-10-1
1969-1978	John Madden	112-39-7
1979-1987	Tom Flores	91-56-0
1988-89	Mike Shanahan***	8-12-0
1989-1994	Art Shell	56-41-0
1995-96	Mike White	15-17-0
1997	Joe Bugel	4-12-0
1998-2001	Jon Gruden	40-28-0
2002-03	Bill Callahan	17-18-0
2004-05	Norv Turner	9-23-0
2006	Art Shell	2-14-0
2007-08	Lane Kiffin****	5-15-0
2008	Tom Cable	4-8-0

* Released after two games in 1961
** Released after five games in 1962
*** Released after four games in 1989
**** Released after four games in 2008

PAID ATTENDANCE
Home 449,373 Away 549,759
Total 999,132
Single-game home record, 62,660 (11/3/02)
Single-season home record, 471,151 (2002)

2009 DRAFT CHOICES

Round	Name	Pos.	College
1	Darrius Heyward-Bey	WR	Maryland
2	Michael Mitchell	DB	Ohio
3	Matt Shaughnessy	DE	Wisconsin
4	Louis Murphy	WR	Florida
	Slade Norris	LB	Oregon State
6	Stryker Sulak	DE	Missouri
	Brandon Myers	TE	Iowa

OAKLAND RAIDERS

2008 TEAM RECORD

PRESEASON (1-3)

Date	Result	Opponent
8/8	W 18-6	San Francisco
8/15	L 16-17	at Tennessee
8/23	L 0-24	Arizona
8/29	L 16-23	at Seattle

REGULAR SEASON (5-11)

Date	Result	Opponent
9/8	L 14-41	Denver
9/14	W 23-8	at Kansas City
9/21	L 23-24	at Buffalo
9/28	L 18-28	San Diego
10/12	L 3-34	at New Orleans
10/19	W 16-13	New York Jets (OT)
10/26	L 10-29	at Baltimore
11/2	L 0-24	Atlanta
11/9	L 6-17	Carolina
11/16	L 15-17	at Miami
11/23	W 31-10	at Denver
11/30	L 13-20	Kansas City
12/4	L 7-34	at San Diego
12/14	L 26-49	New England
12/21	W 27-16	Houston
12/28	W 31-24	at Tampa Bay

(OT) Overtime

SCORE BY PERIODS

Raiders	46	54	73	87	3	— 263
Opponents	81	115	58	134	0	— 388

2008 TEAM STATISTICS

	Raiders	Opp.
Total First Downs	225	325
Rushing	87	129
Passing	123	166
Penalty	15	30
3rd Down: Made/Att	61/214	103/232
3rd Down Pct.	28.5	44.4
4th Down: Made/Att	9/21	9/13
4th Down Pct.	42.9	69.2
Possession Avg.	28:09	31:51
Total Net Yards	4356	5775
Avg. Per Game	272.3	360.9
Total Plays	919	1045
Avg. Per Play	4.7	5.5
Net Yards Rushing	1987	2555
Avg. Per Game	124.2	159.7
Total Rushes	459	542
Net Yards Passing	2369	3220
Avg. Per Game	148.1	201.3
Sacked/Yards Lost	39/270	32/188
Gross Yards	2639	3408
Att./Completions	421/222	471/266
Completion Pct.	52.7	56.5
Had Intercepted	11	16
Punts/Average	90/48.8	74/43.2
Net Punting Avg.	90/41.2	74/34.2
Penalties/Yards	109/823	74/633
Fumbles/Ball Lost	28/12	21/8
Touchdowns	27	45
Rushing	9	23
Passing	13	20
Returns	5	2

2008 INDIVIDUAL STATISTICS

PASSING	Att.	Comp.	Yds.	Pct.	TD	Int.	Tkld.	Rate
Russell	368	198	2423	53.8	13	8	31/210	77.1
Walter	49	22	204	44.9	0	3	5/39	31.3
Bush	2	1	8	50.0	0	0	0/0	60.4
Tuiasosopo	2	1	4	50.0	0	0	2/16	56.3
McFadden	0	0	0	—	0	0	1/5	—
Raiders	421	222	2639	52.7	13	11	39/270	71.6
Opponents	471	266	3408	56.5	20	16	32/188	79.3

SCORING	TD R	TD P	TD Rt	PAT	FG	Saf	PTS
Janikowski	0	0	0	25/26	24/30	0	97
Higgins	0	4	3	0/0	0/0	0	42
McFadden	4	0	0	0/0	0/0	0	24
Bush	3	0	0	0/0	0/0	0	18
Curry	0	2	0	0/0	0/0	0	12
Lelie	0	2	0	0/0	0/0	0	12
J. Miller	0	0	2	0/0	0/0	0	12
Schilens	0	2	0	0/0	0/0	0	12
Fargas	1	0	0	0/0	0/0	0	6
Griffith	0	1	0	0/0	0/0	0	6
Z. Miller	0	1	0	0/0	0/0	0	6
Russell	1	0	0	0/0	0/0	0	6
Walker	0	1	0	0/0	0/0	0	6
Richardson	0	0	0	0/0	0/0	1	2
G. Wilson	0	0	0	0/0	0/0	1	2
Raiders	9	13	5	25/26	24/30	2	263
Opponents	23	20	2	43/43	23/31	1	388

2-Pt. Conversions: None.
Raiders 0-1, Opponents 2-2.

RUSHING	No.	Yds	Avg	LG	TD
Fargas	218	853	3.9	42	1
McFadden	113	499	4.4	50	4
Bush	95	421	4.4	67t	3
Russell	17	127	7.5	24	1
Higgins	3	34	11.3	18	0
Alston	1	22	22.0	22	0
Walter	5	19	3.8	13	0
Tuiasosopo	2	11	5.5	11	0
Griffith	2	2	1.0	2	0
Curry	1	1	1.0	1	0
Lechler	1	0	0.0	0	0
Schilens	1	-2	-2.0	-2	0
Raiders	459	1987	4.3	67t	9
Opponents	542	2555	4.7	69t	23

RECEIVING	No.	Yds	Avg	LG	TD
Z. Miller	56	778	13.9	63t	1
McFadden	29	285	9.8	27	0
Higgins	22	366	16.6	84t	4
Curry	19	181	9.5	16	2
Bush	19	162	8.5	25	0
Schilens	15	226	15.1	60	2
Walker	15	196	13.1	29	1
Lelie	11	197	17.9	51	2
Stewart	11	81	7.4	17	0
Fargas	10	52	5.2	12	0
Griffith	9	85	9.4	24	1
Lawton	6	30	5.0	12	0
Raiders	222	2639	11.9	84t	13
Opponents	266	3408	12.8	72	20

INTERCEPTIONS	No.	Yds	Avg	LG	TD
Johnson	3	68	22.7	44	0
De. Hall	3	31	10.3	21	0
Baker	3	8	2.7	8	0
G. Wilson	2	5	2.5	5	0
Branch	1	36	36.0	36	0
Asomugha	1	0	0.0	0	0
Morrison	1	0	0.0	0	0
Williams	1	0	0.0	0	0
Howard	1	-3	-3.0	-3	0
Raiders	16	145	9.1	44	0
Opponents	11	163	14.8	84	0

PUNTING	No.	Yds.	Avg.	In 20	LG
Lechler	90	4391	48.8	33	70
Raiders	90	4391	48.8	33	70
Opponents	74	3199	43.2	23	73

PUNT RETURNS	Ret	FC	Yds	Avg	LG	TD
Higgins	44	12	570	13.0	93t	3
Raiders	44	12	570	13.0	93t	3
Opponents	43	11	425	9.9	55	0

KICKOFF RETURNS	No.	Yds	Avg	LG	TD
Higgins	36	842	23.4	69	0
J. Miller	32	794	24.8	92t	2
Branch	6	89	14.8	20	0
Lawton	2	29	14.5	15	0
Bush	1	14	14.0	14	0
Gunheim	1	9	9.0	9	0
Raiders	78	1777	22.8	92t	2
Opponents	44	1074	24.4	95t	1

FIELD GOALS	1-19	20-29	30-39	40-49	50+
Janikowski	0/0	11/11	8/8	2/4	3/7
Raiders	0/0	11/11	8/8	2/4	3/7
Opponents	0/0	6/6	8/9	7/12	2/4

SACKS	No.
Edwards	5.0
Scott	5.0
Kelly	4.5
Warren	4.0
Burgess	3.5
Richardson	3.0
Sands	2.0
G. Wilson	1.5
Gunheim	1.0
Howard	1.0
Morrison	1.0
De. Hall	0.5
Raiders	32.0
Opponents	39.0

RECORD HOLDERS

INDIVIDUAL RECORDS—CAREER

Category	Name	Performance
Rushing (Yds.)	Marcus Allen, 1982-1992	8,545
Passing (Yds.)	Ken Stabler, 1970-79	19,078
Passing (TDs)	Ken Stabler, 1970-79	150
Receiving (No.)	Tim Brown, 1988-2003	1,070
Receiving (Yds.)	Tim Brown, 1988-2003	14,734
Interceptions	Willie Brown, 1967-1978	39
	Lester Hayes, 1977-1986	39
Punting (Avg.)	Shane Lechler, 2000-08	**46.8
Punt Return (Avg.)	Claude Gibson, 1963-65	12.6
Kickoff Return (Avg.)	Jack Larscheid, 1960-61	28.4
Field Goals	Chris Bahr, 1980-88	162
Touchdowns (Tot.)	Tim Brown, 1988-2003	104
Points	George Blanda, 1967-1975	863
*Sacks	Greg Townsend, 1983-1993, 1997	107.5

INDIVIDUAL RECORDS—SINGLE SEASON

Category	Name	Performance
Rushing (Yds.)	Marcus Allen, 1985	1,759
Passing (Yds.)	Rich Gannon, 2002	4,689
Passing (TDs)	Daryle Lamonica, 1969	34
Receiving (No.)	Tim Brown 1997	104
Receiving (Yds.)	Tim Brown, 1997	1,408
Interceptions	Lester Hayes, 1980	13
Punting (Avg.)	Shane Lechler, 2007	49.1
Punt Return (Avg.)	Claude Gibson, 1964	14.4
Kickoff Return (Avg.)	Harold Hart, 1975	30.5
Field Goals	Jeff Jaeger, 1993	35
Touchdowns (Tot.)	Marcus Allen, 1984	18
Points	Jeff Jaeger, 1993	132
*Sacks	Derrick Burgess, 2005	16.0

INDIVIDUAL RECORDS—SINGLE GAME

Category	Name	Performance
Rushing (Yds.)	Napoleon Kaufman, 10-19-97	227
Passing (Yds.)	Cotton Davidson, 10-25-64	427
Passing (TDs)	Tom Flores, 12-22-63	6
	Daryle Lamonica, 10-19-69	6
Receiving (No.)	Tim Brown, 12-21-97	14
Receiving (Yds.)	Art Powell, 12-22-63	247
Interceptions	Many times	3
	Last time by Rod Woodson, 9-29-02	
Field Goals	Jeff Jaeger, 12-11-94	5
	Sebastian Janikowski, 10-29-00, 10-5-03, 11-18-07	5
Touchdowns (Tot.)	Art Powell, 12-22-63	4
	Marcus Allen, 9-24-84	4
	Harvey Williams, 11-16-97	4
Points	Art Powell, 12-22-63	24
	Marcus Allen, 9-24-84	24
	Harvey Williams, 11-16-97	24
*Sacks	Howie Long, 10-2-83	5.0

**Sacks became an official statistic in 1982.*
***NFL Record*

OAKLAND RAIDERS

2009 VETERAN ROSTER

No.	Name	Pos.	Ht.	Wt.	Birthdate	NFL Exp.	College	Hometown	How Acq.	'08 Games/ Starts
55	Alston, Jon	LB	6-0	225	6/4/83	4	Stanford	Shreveport, La.	FA-'07	14/4
21	Asomugha, Nnamdi	CB	6-2	210	7/6/81	7	California	Los Angeles, Calif.	D1-'03	15/15
70	Barnes, Khalif	T	6-5	325	4/21/82	5	Washington	Spring Valley, Calif.	UFA(Jax)-'09	16/16*
73	Boschetti, Ryan	DT	6-4	310	10/7/81	6	UCLA	Belmont, Calif.	UFA(Wash)-'09	0*
35	Bowie, John	CB	5-11	190	5/11/84	3	Cincinnati	Columbus, Ohio	D4-'07	0*
33	Branch, Tyvon	DB	6-0	205	12/11/86	2	Connecticut	Cicero, N.Y.	D4-'08	8/0
39	Brown, Darrick	DB	6-4	200	2/18/84	2	McNeese State	Tangipahoa, La.	FA-'08	0*
57	Brown, Ricky	LB	6-2	235	12/27/83	4	Boston College	Cincinnati, Ohio	FA-'06	7/6
56	Burgess, Derrick	DE	6-2	260	8/12/78	9	Mississippi	Greenbelt, Md.	UFA(Phil)-'05	10/10
29	Bush, Michael	RB	6-1	245	6/16/84	2	Louisville	Louisville, Ky.	D4-'07	14/0
66	Carlisle, Cooper	G	6-5	295	8/11/77	10	Florida	McComb, Miss.	UFA(Den)-'07	15/15
18	#Carter, Drew	WR	6-4	205	9/5/81	6	Ohio State	Solon, Ohio	UFA(Car)-'08	0*
59	Condo, Jon	LS/LB	6-3	250	8/26/81	3	Maryland	Philipsburg, Pa.	FA-'06	16/0
50	Ekejiuba, Isaiah	LB	6-4	240	10/5/81	5	Virginia	Somerset, N.J.	FA-'05	16/0
31	Eugene, Hiram	S	6-2	200	11/24/80	4	Louisiana Tech	Jeanerette, La.	FA-'06	16/10
25	Fargas, Justin	RB	6-1	220	1/25/80	7	Southern California	Sherman Oaks, Calif.	D3-'03	14/14
76	Gallery, Robert	G	6-7	325	7/26/80	6	Iowa	Masonville, Iowa	D1-'04	16/16
7	Garcia, Jeff	QB	6-1	205	2/24/70	11	San Jose State	Gilroy, Calif.	UFA(TB)-'09	12/11*
5	Gradkowski, Bruce	QB	6-1	220	1/27/83	4	Toledo	Pittsburgh, Pa.	FA-09	2/1*
74	Green, Cornell	T	6-6	315	8/25/76	11	Central Florida	St. Petersburg, Fla.	UFA(TB)-'07	16/16
97	Gunheim, Greyson	DE	6-5	265	4/4/86	2	Washington	Sebastopol, Calif.	FA-'08	3/0
75	Henderson, Mario	T	6-7	300	10/29/84	3	Florida State	Lehigh Acres, Fla.	D3-'07	11/4
15	Higgins, Johnnie Lee	WR	5-11	185	9/8/83	3	Texas-El Paso	Sweeny, Texas	D3-'07	16/3
10	Holland, Jonathan	WR	6-1	195	2/18/85	3	Louisiana Tech	Archibald, La.	D7-'07	3/0
27	Horton, Jason	CB	6-0	190	2/16/80	3	North Carolina A&T	Ahoskie, N.C.	FA-'09	0*
53	Howard, Thomas	LB	6-3	240	7/14/83	4	Texas-El Paso	Lubbock, Texas	D2-'06	16/16
24	Huff, Michael	S	6-1	205	3/6/83	4	Texas	Irving, Texas	D1-'06	16/7
11	Janikowski, Sebastian	K	6-2	250	3/2/78	10	Florida State	Daytona Beach, Fla.	D1-'00	16/0
37	Johnson, Chris	CB	6-1	200	9/25/79	7	Louisville	Longview, Texas	UFA(KC)-'07	15/7
78	Johnson, Marcus	G	6-6	320	12/1/81	5	Mississippi	Greenville, Miss.	UFA(Minn)-'09	7/0*
94	Joseph, William	DT	6-5	310	9/3/79	7	Miami	Miami, Fla.	FA-'08	8/0
93	Kelly, Tommy	DT	6-6	300	12/27/80	6	Mississippi State	Jackson, Miss.	FA-'04	16/16
44	Lawton, Luke	RB	6-0	240	8/26/80	4	McNeese State	New Iberia, La.	FA-'08	16/8
9	Lechler, Shane	P	6-2	225	8/7/76	10	Texas A&M	Sealy, Texas	D5-'00	16/0
87	#Lelie, Ashley	WR	6-3	195	6/16/80	8	Hawaii	Honolulu, Hawai'i	FA-'08	13/6
69	Marten, James	T	6-8	310	4/18/84	3	Boston College	Indianapolis, Ind.	W(Dall)-'08	2/0
20	McFadden, Darren	RB	6-2	210	8/27/87	2	Arkansas	North Little Rock, Ark.	D1-'08	13/5
79	McQuistan, Paul	G	6-6	315	4/30/83	4	Weber State	Lebanon, Ore.	D3-'06	1/0
22	Miller, Justin	CB	5-10	195	2/14/84	5	Clemson	Owensboro, Ky.	W(NYJ)-'08	8/0
80	Miller, Zach	TE	6-5	255	12/11/85	3	Arizona State	Phoenix, Ariz.	D2-'07	16/15
51	Morris, Chris	C	6-4	305	2/2/83	4	Michigan State	Temperance, Mich.	D7-'06	16/1
52	Morrison, Kirk	LB	6-2	240	2/19/82	5	San Diego State	Oakland, Calif.	D3-'05	16/16
41	Neal, Lorenzo	FB	5-11	255	12/27/70	17	Fresno State	Lemoore, Calif.	UFA(Balt)-'09	16/5*
46	O'Neal, Oren	RB	5-11	245	9/8/83	3	Arkansas State	Stuttgart, Ark.	D6-'07	0*
85	Parker, Samie	WR	5-11	195	3/25/81	6	Oregon	Long Beach, Calif.	FA-'09	0*
72	Pears, Erik	T	6-8	305	6/25/82	4	Colorado State	Denver, Colo.	FA-'09	0*
40	Rankin, Louis	RB	6-1	205	5/4/85	2	Washington	Stockton, Calif.	FA-'08	0*
45	Reece, Marcel	RB	6-2	240	6/23/85	2	Washington	Hesperia, Calif.	FA-'08	0*
98	Richardson, Jay	DE	6-6	280	1/27/84	3	Ohio State	Washington, D.C	D5-'07	16/11
26	Routt, Stanford	CB	6-1	195	7/26/83	5	Houston	Austin, Texas	D2-'05	15/4
23	Russell, Gary	RB	5-11	215	9/6/86	3	Minnesota	Columbus, Ohio	FA-'09	12/0*
2	Russell, JaMarcus	QB	6-6	260	8/9/85	3	Louisiana State	Mobile, Ala.	D1-'07	15/15
90	Sands, Terdell	DT	6-7	335	10/31/79	7	Tenn.-Chattanooga	Chattanooga, Tenn.	W(KC)-'03	16/0
64	t-Satele, Sampson	C	6-3	300	11/29/84	3	Hawaii	Kailua, Hawai'i	T(Mia)-'09	16/16*
81	Schilens, Chaz	WR	6-4	225	11/7/85	2	San Diego State	Mesa, Ariz.	D7-'08	16/6
91	Scott, Trevor	DE	6-5	255	8/30/84	2	Buffalo	Potsdam, N.Y.	D6-'08	16/0
14	Shields, Arman	WR	6-1	195	7/10/85	2	Richmond	Washington, D.C.	D4-'08	0*
86	Stewart, Tony	TE	6-5	260	8/9/79	9	Penn State	Allentown, Pa.	UFA(Cin)-'07	16/4
82	Strong, Darrell	TE	6-5	265	5/21/86	2	Pittsburgh	Plantation, Fla.	FA-'08	0*
8	#Tuiasosopo, Marques	QB	6-1	220	3/22/79	9	Washington	Woodinville, Wash.	UFA(NYJ)-08	2/0
71	Wade, John	C	6-5	300	1/25/75	12	Marshall	Harrisonburg, Va.	UFA(TB)-'08	5/4
84	Walker, Javon	WR	6-3	215	10/14/78	8	Florida State	Lafayette, La.	FA-'08	8/7
16	Walter, Andrew	QB	6-6	230	5/11/82	5	Arizona State	Grand Junction, Colo.	D3-'05	2/1
61	Warren, Gerard	DT	6-4	325	7/25/78	9	Florida	Lake City, Fla.	T(Den)-'07	16/16
19	Watkins, Todd	WR	6-3	195	6/22/83	2	Brigham Young	La Mesa, Calif.	FA-'08	8/0
54	Williams, Sam	LB	6-7	260	7/28/80	7	Fresno State	Clayton, Calif.	D3-'03	16/1
63	Wilson, Mark	T	6-6	320	11/11/80	4	California	McArthur, Calif.	FA-'06	0*

* Barnes played 16 games with Jacksonville in '08; Boschetti played 3 games with Washington; Bowie missed '08 season because of injury: D. Brown inactive for 4 games; Carter missed '08 season because of injury; Garcia played 12 games with Tampa Bay; Gradkowski played 2 games with Cleveland; Horton last active with Green Bay in '05; M. Johnson played 7 games with Minnesota; Neal played 16 games with Baltimore; O'Neal missed '08 season because of injury; Parker last active with Kansas City in '07; Pears inactive for 7 games with Denver; Rankin inactive for 3 games; Reece inactive for 1 game; G. Russell played 12 games with Pittsburgh; Satele played 16 games with Miami; Shields missed '08 season because of injury; Wilson missed '08 season because of injury.

t- Raiders traded for Satele (Mia).

\# Unrestricted free agent; subject to developments.

Players lost through free agency (2): S Rashad Baker (Phil; 10 games in '08), C Jake Grove (Mia; 12).

Also played with Raiders in '08—LB Marquis Cooper (8 games), FB Jason Davis (1), DE Kalimba Edwards (14), FB Justin Griffith (7), CB DeAngelo Hall (8), T Kwame Harris (14), TE John Madsen (4), LB Robert Thomas (2), CB Michael Waddell (1), TE Fred Wakefield (7), T Seth Wand (1), S Gibril Wilson (16).

2009 FIRST-YEAR ROSTER

Name	Pos.	Ht.	Wt.	Birthdate	College	Hometown	How Acq.
Bayes, Shawn	WR	5-10	180	7/8/87	San Jose State	Memphis, Tenn.	FA
Boyd, Jerome	DB	6-2	225	5/26/86	Oregon	Los Angeles, Calif.	FA
Bryant, Desmond	DL	6-5	290	12/15/85	Harvard	Elizabethtown, N.C.	FA
Compas, Jonathan	OL	6-3	300	1/9/86	UC Davis	Carlsbad, Calif.	FA
Gray, Derrick (1)	DL	6-4	265	11/11/85	Texas Southern	Silver Spring, Md.	FA-'08
Heyward-Bey, Darrius	WR	6-2	210	2/26/87	Maryland	Silver Spring, Md.	D1
Joseph, Frantz	LB	6-3	235	6/12/86	Florida Atlantic	Ft. Lauderdale, Fla.	FA
Miller, Nick	WR	5-9	180	3/29/87	Southern Utah	Mesa, Ariz.	FA
Mitchell, Mike	S	6-1	220	6/10/87	Ohio	Florence, Ky.	D2
Murphy, Louis	WR	6-2	200	5/11/87	Florida	St. Petersburg, Fla.	D4
Myers, Brandon	TE	6-4	250	9/4/85	Iowa	Iowa City, Iowa	D6
Nixon, David	LB	6-3	225	3/16/85	Brigham Young	College Station, Texas	FA
Norris, Slade	LB	6-3	245	10/25/85	Oregon State	Portland, Ore.	D4
O'Neill, Chris	TE	6-3	250	2/21/86	Boise State	Orinda, Calif.	FA
Schmidt, Ricky (1)	P	6-3	210	8/17/85	Shephard	Virginia Beach, Va.	FA-'08
Shaughnessy, Matt	DE	6-5	270	9/23/86	Wisconsin	Norwich, Conn.	D3
Southwick, Danny (1)	QB	6-1	210	9/28/81	Occidental	Provo, Utah	FA
Sulak, Stryker	DE	6-5	250	6/17/86	Missouri	Round Rock, Texas	D6

The term NFL Rookie is defined as a player who is in his first season of professional football and has not been on the roster of another professional football team for any regular-season or postseason games. A Rookie is designated by an "R" on NFL rosters. Players who have been active in another professional football league or players who have NFL experience, including either preseason training camp or being on an Active List or Inactive List, or on Reserve/Injured or Reserve/Physically Unable to Perform for fewer than six regular-season games, are termed NFL First-Year Players. An NFL First-Year Player is designated by a "1" on NFL rosters. Thereafter, a player is credited with an additional year of experience for each season in which he accumulates six games on the Active List or Inactive List, or on Reserve/Injured or Reserve/Physically Unable to Perform.

Log on to www.raiders.com for an up-to-date roster.

OAKLAND RAIDERS

COACHING STAFF
Head Coach,
Tom Cable

Pro Career: In 2008, named the seventeenth head coach in Raiders history. Cable, who has 21 years of coaching experience, including four as a head coach at the college level, joined the team as the Raiders offensive line coach in 2007. He spent the 2006 season as offensive line coach for Atlanta. In 1987, Cable spent one season with the Indianapolis Colts as an offensive lineman. Career record: 4-8.

Background: Offensive lineman Idaho 1982-86. College coach: Idaho 1987-88, San Diego State 1989, Cal State-Fullerton 1990, Nevada-Las Vegas 1991, California 1992-97, Colorado 1998-99, Idaho 2000-03 (head coach 2001-03), UCLA 2004-05.

Personal: Born November 26, 1964, in Merced, Calif.

ASSISTANT COACHES

Dwaine Board, defensive line; born November 29, 1956, Rocky Mount, Va. Defensive lineman North Carolina A&T 1974-77. Pro defensive lineman San Francisco 49ers 1979-1987, New Orleans Saints 1988. Pro coach: San Francisco 49ers 1990-2002, Seattle Seahawks 2003-08, joined Raiders in 2009.

Willie Brown, squad development, defensive backs; born December 2, 1940, Yazoo City, Miss. Defensive back Grambling State 1959-1962. Pro defensive back Denver Broncos 1963-66, Oakland Raiders 1967-1978. Inducted into Pro Football Hall of Fame in 1984. College coach: Long Beach State 1990-91 (head coach 1991). Pro coach: Oakland/Los Angeles Raiders 1979-1988, re-joined Raiders in 1995.

John Fassel, special teams coordinator; born January 10, 1974, Anaheim, Calif. Wide receiver/quarterback Pacific 1994-95, Weber State 1996-98. No pro playing experience. College coach: Bucknell 1999, 2001, Idaho State 2000, New Mexico Highlands 2002-03. Pro coach: Amsterdam Admirals (NFLE) 2000, Baltimore Ravens 2005-07; joined Raiders in 2008.

Paul Hackett, quarterbacks; born July 5, 1947, Burlington, Vt. Quarterback Cal-Davis 1965-68. No pro playing experience. College coach: Cal-Davis 1969-1971, California 1972-75, Southern California 1976-1980, 1998-2000 (head coach 1998-2000), Pittsburgh 1989-1992 (head coach 1990-92). Pro coach: Cleveland Browns 1981-82, San Francisco 49ers 1983-85, Dallas Cowboys 1986-88, Kansas City Chiefs 1993-97, New York Jets 2001-04, Tampa Bay Buccaneers 2005-07, joined Raiders in 2008.

Mike Haluchak, linebackers; born Nov. 28, 1949, Concord, Calif. Linebacker Southern California 1967-1970. No pro playing experience. College coach: Southern California 1976-77, Cal State-Fullerton 1978, Pacific 1979-1980, California 1981, North Carolina State 1982. Pro coach: Oakland Invaders (USFL) 1983-85, San Diego Chargers 1986-1991, Cincinnati Bengals 1992-93, Washington Redskins 1994-96, New York Giants 1997-99, St. Louis Rams 2000-02, Jacksonville Jaguars 2003-04, Cleveland Browns 2005-08, joined Raiders in 2009.

Randy Hanson, defensive assistant; born January 17, 1968, Burlington, Wash. Quarterback Delta (Calif.) J.C. 1987, Walla Walla (Wash.) 1988-89, Pacific University (Ore.) 1990-91. No pro playing experience. College coach: Eastern Washington 1993-95, 1998-99, Washington 1996-97, Portland State 2000-02. Pro coach: Minnesota Vikings 2003-05, St. Louis Rams 2006, joined Raiders in 2007.

Adam Henry, tight ends; born April 27, 1972, Beaumont, Texas. Wide receiver McNeese State 1992-93. Pro receiver New Orleans Saints 1995. College coach: McNeese State 1996-2006. Pro coach: Joined Raiders in 2007.

Sanjay Lal, wide receivers; born July 23, 1969, London, England. Wide receiver UCLA 1989, Washington 1990-92. Pro wide receiver St. Louis Rams 1998, Scottish Claymores (World League) 1999. College coach: Los Medanos (Calif.) College 2003, Saint Mary's College 2004, California 2005-06, joined Raiders in 2007.

Bert Leone, quality control, defense; born Jan. 20, 1983, Garfield Heights, Ohio. Attended Ohio State. No college or pro playing experience. Pro coach: Cleveland Browns 2005-08, joined Raiders in 2009.

John Marshall, defensive coordinator; born October 2, 1945, Arroyo Grande, Calif. Linebacker Washington State 1964. No pro playing experience. College coach: Oregon 1970-76, Southern California 1977-79. Pro coach: Green Bay Packers 1980-82, Indianapolis Colts 1986-88, San Francisco 49ers 1989-1998, Carolina Panthers 1999-2001, Detroit Lions 2002, Seattle Seahawks 2003-08, joined Raiders in 2009.

Jim Michalczik, offensive line; born June 7, 1966, Port Angeles, Wash. Offensive lineman Washington State 1995-1998. Pro offensive lineman Arizona Cardinals 1989. College coach: Miami 1990-91, Montana State 1992-98, Oregon State 1999-2001, California 2002-08, Washington 2009. Pro coach: Joined Raiders in 2009.

Chris Morgan, asst. offensive line; born September 24 1976, Killeen, Texas. Offensive lineman Colorado 1996-99. No pro playing experience. College coach: Idaho 2003. Pro coach: Joined Raiders in 2009.

Aaron Pelch, asst. special teams; born September 9, 1977, Sandy, Utah. Wide receiver Weber State. No pro playing experience. College coach: New Mexico Highlands 2002-04, Millsaps College 2006-08. Pro coach: Joined Raiders in 2009.

Brad Roll, strength & conditioning; July 4, 1958, Houston. Center Blinn (Tex.) J.C. 1976-77, Stephen F. Austin 1978-79. No pro playing experience. College coach: Stephen F. Austin 1980, Southwestern Louisiana 1981-86, Kansas 1987-88, Miami 1989-1992. Pro coach: Tampa Bay Buccaneers 1993-95, Miami Dolphins 1996-2003, Buffalo Bills 2004-05, St. Louis Rams 2006-07, joined Raiders in 2008.

Rich Scangarello, quality control, offense; born April 15, 1972. Roseville, Calif. Attended Sacramento State. No college or pro playing experience. College coach: U.C. Davis 1998-99; 2004-08, Idaho 2000, 2002-03, Carleton College 2001. Pro coach: Joined Raiders in 2009.

Kelly Skipper, tight ends; born July 25, 1967, Brawley, Calif. Running back Fresno State 1985-88. No pro playing experience. College coach: Fresno State 1989-1997, UCLA 1998-2002, Washington State 2003-06. Pro coach: Joined Raiders in 2007.

Ted Tollner, passing game coordinator; born May 29, 1940, San Francisco, Calif. Quarterback Cal Poly-San Luis Obispo 1959-61. No pro playing experience. College coach: College of San Mateo 1971-72 (head coach), San Diego State 1973-1980, 1994-2001 (head coach 1994-2001), Brigham Young 1981, Southern California 1982-86 (head coach 1983-86). Pro coach: Buffalo Bills 1987-88, San Diego Chargers 1989-1991, San Francisco 2002-04, Detroit Lions 2005, San Francisco 49ers 2007-08, joined Raiders in 2009.

Lionel Washington, defensive backs; born October 21, 1960, New Orleans. Defensive back Tulane 1979-1982. Pro defensive back St. Louis Cardinals 1983-86, Los Angeles/Oakland Raiders 1987-1994, 1997, Denver Broncos 1995-96. Pro coach: Green Bay Packers 1999-2008, joined Raiders in 2009.

American Football Conference
North Division
Team Colors: Black and Gold
3400 South Water Street
Pittsburgh, Pennsylvania 15203
Telephone: (412) 432-7800

2009 SCHEDULE

PRESEASON

Aug. 13	**Arizona**	8:00
Aug. 22	at Washington	7:30
Aug. 29	**Buffalo**	7:30
Sep. 3	at Carolina	8:00

REGULAR SEASON

Sep. 10	**Tennessee** (Thu.)	8:30
Sep. 20	at Chicago	3:15
Sep. 27	at Cincinnati	4:15
Oct. 4	**San Diego**	8:20
Oct. 11	at Detroit	1:00
Oct. 18	**Cleveland**	1:00
Oct. 25	**Minnesota**	1:00
Nov. 1	BYE	
Nov. 9	at Denver (Mon.)	6:30
Nov. 15	**Cincinnati**	1:00
Nov. 22	at Kansas City	12:00
Nov. 29	at Baltimore *	8:20
Dec. 6	**Oakland**	1:00
Dec. 10	at Cleveland (Thu.)	8:20
Dec. 20	**Green Bay**	1:00
Dec. 27	**Baltimore**	1:00
Jan. 3	at Miami	1:00

** Sunday night games in Weeks 11-17 subject to change*

Stadium: Heinz Field (opened in 2001)
•**Capacity:** 65,050
100 Art Rooney Avenue
Pittsburgh, Pennsylvania 15212
Playing Surface: DD GrassMaster
Training Camp: St. Vincent College
Latrobe, PA 15650

HEINZ FIELD

CLUB OFFICIALS

Chairman: Daniel M. Rooney
President: Arthur J. Rooney II
Vice President: John R. McGinley
Vice President: Arthur J. Rooney Jr.
Administration Advisor: Charles H. Noll
Director of Business: Mark Hart
Business Operations: Omar Khan
Director of Football Operations: Kevin Colbert
College Scouting Coordinator: Ron Hughes
Pro Scouting Coordinator: Doug Whaley
Head Athletic Trainer: John Norwig
Director of Marketing: Tony Quatrini
Communications Coordinator: Dave Lockett
Public Relations/Media Manager: Burt Lauten
Director of Stadium Management: Jim Sacco
Video Coordinator: Bob McCartney
Human Relations/Office Coordinator: Geraldine Glenn
Ticket Manager: Ben Lentz

COACHING HISTORY

Pittsburgh Pirates 1933-39
(556-521-21)
Records include postseason games

1933	Forrest (Jap) Douds	3-6-2
1934	Luby DiMelio	2-10-0
1935-36	Joe Bach	10-14-0
1937-39	Johnny (Blood) McNally*	6-19-0
1939-1940	Walt Kiesling	3-13-3
1941	Bert Bell**	0-2-0
	Aldo (Buff) Donelli***	0-5-0
1941-44	Walt Kiesling****	13-20-2
1945	Jim Leonard	2-8-0
1946-47	Jock Sutherland	13-10-1
1948-1951	Johnny Michelosen	20-26-2
1952-53	Joe Bach	11-13-0
1954-56	Walt Kiesling	14-22-0
1957-1964	Raymond (Buddy) Parker	51-47-6
1965	Mike Nixon	2-12-0
1966-68	Bill Austin	11-28-3
1969-1991	Chuck Noll	209-156-1
1992-2006	Bill Cowher	161-99-1
2007-08	Mike Tomlin	25-11-0

*Released after three games in 1939
**Resigned after two games in 1941
***Released after five games in 1941
****Co-coach with Earle (Greasy) Neale in Philadelphia-Pittsburgh merger in 1943 and with Phil Handler in Chicago Cardinals-Pittsburgh merger in 1944

PAID ATTENDANCE

Home 517,235 Away 564,334
Total 1,081,569
Single-game home record, 64,810 (10/26/08)
Single-season home record, 517,235 (2008)

2009 DRAFT CHOICES

Round	Name	Pos.	College
1	Evander Hood	DE	Missouri
3	Kraig Urbik	G	Wisconsin
	Mike Wallace	WR	Mississippi
	Keenan Lewis	DB	Oregon State
5	Joe Burnett	DB	Central Florida
	Frank Summers	RB	Nevada-Las Vegas
6	Ra'Shon Harris	DE	Oregon
7	A.Q. Shipley	C	Penn State
	David Johnson	TE	Arkansas State

PITTSBURGH STEELERS

2008 TEAM RECORD

PRESEASON (3-1)

Date	Result	Opponent
8/8	W 16-10	Philadelphia
8/14	L 21-24	at Buffalo
8/23	W 12-10	at Minnesota
8/28	W 19-16	Carolina

REGULAR SEASON (12-4)

Date	Result	Opponent
9/7	W 38-17	Houston
9/14	W 10-6	at Cleveland
9/21	L 6-15	at Philadelphia
9/29	W 23-20	Baltimore (OT)
10/5	W 26-21	at Jacksonville
10/19	W 38-10	at Cincinnati
10/26	L 14-21	New York Giants
11/3	W 23-6	at Washington
11/9	L 20-24	Indianapolis
11/16	W 11-10	San Diego
11/20	W 27-10	Cincinnati
11/30	W 33-10	at New England
12/7	W 20-13	Dallas
12/14	W 13-9	at Baltimore
12/21	L 14-31	at Tennessee
12/28	W 31-0	Cleveland

(OT) Overtime

POSTSEASON (3-0)

Date	Result	Opponent
1/11	W 35-24	San Diego
1/18	W 23-14	Baltimore
2/1	W 27-23	vs. Arizona, at Tampa, Florida

SCORE BY PERIODS

Steelers	47	106	87	104	3	— 347
Opponents	54	65	29	75	0	— 223

2008 TEAM STATISTICS

	Steelers	Opp.
Total First Downs	290	240
Rushing	93	73
Passing	179	149
Penalty	18	18
3rd Down: Made/Att	92/224	71/226
3rd Down Pct.	41.1	31.4
4th Down: Made/Att	3/12	10/21
4th Down Pct.	25.0	47.6
Possession Avg.	31:29	28:31
Total Net Yards	4991	3795
Avg. Per Game	311.9	237.2
Total Plays	1015	974
Avg. Per Play	4.9	3.9
Net Yards Rushing	1690	1284
Avg. Per Game	105.6	80.3
Total Rushes	460	390
Net Yards Passing	3301	2511
Avg. Per Game	206.3	156.9
Sacked/Yards Lost	49/306	51/350
Gross Yards	3607	2861
Att./Completions	506/303	533/301
Completion Pct.	59.9	56.5
Had Intercepted	15	20
Punts/Average	78/39.8	91/42.5
Net Punting Avg.	78/35.6	91/38.5
Penalties/Yards	95/812	91/801
Fumbles/Ball Lost	28/10	22/9
Touchdowns	38	21
Rushing	16	7
Passing	19	12
Returns	3	2

2008 INDIVIDUAL STATISTICS

PASSING	Att.	Comp.	Yds.	Pct.	TD	Int.	Tkld.	Rate
Roethlisberger	469	281	3301	59.9	17	15	46/284	80.1
Leftwich	36	21	303	58.3	2	0	3/22	104.3
Dixon	1	1	3	100.0	0	0	0/0	79.2
Steelers	506	303	3607	59.9	19	15	49/306	81.9
Opponents	533	301	2861	56.5	12	20	51/350	63.4

SCORING	TD R	TD P	TD Rt	PAT	FG	Saf	PTS
Reed	0	0	0	36/37	27/31	0	117
Ward	0	7	0	0/0	0/0	0	42
Moore	5	1	0	0/0	0/0	0	36
Holmes	0	5	0	0/0	0/0	0	30
Parker	5	0	0	0/0	0/0	0	30
Miller	0	3	0	0/0	0/0	0	18
Russell	3	0	0	0/0	0/0	0	18
Washington	0	3	0	0/0	0/0	0	18
Roethlisberger	2	0	0	0/0	0/0	0	12
Carter	0	0	1	0/0	0/0	0	6
Leftwich	1	0	0	0/0	0/0	0	6
Townsend	0	0	1	0/0	0/0	0	6
Woodley	0	0	1	0/0	0/0	0	6
J. Harrison	0	0	0	0/0	0/0	1	2
Steelers	16	19	3	36/37	27/31	1	347
Opponents	7	12	2	21/21	24/27	2	223

2-Pt. Conversions: None.
Steelers 0-1, Opponents 0-0

RUSHING	No.	Yds	Avg	LG	TD
Parker	210	791	3.8	34t	5
Moore	140	588	4.2	32t	5
Roethlisberger	34	101	3.0	17	2
Russell	28	77	2.8	15	3
Mendenhall	19	58	3.1	12	0
C. Davis	12	35	2.9	11	0
Washington	5	18	3.6	8	0
Holmes	2	9	4.5	10	0
Leftwich	4	7	1.8	8t	1
Davenport	2	5	2.5	3	0
Ward	1	4	4.0	4	0
Berger	1	0	0.0	0	0
Dixon	2	-3	-1.5	-1	0
Steelers	460	1690	3.7	34t	16
Opponents	390	1284	3.3	41	7

RECEIVING	No.	Yds	Avg	LG	TD
Ward	81	1043	12.9	49	7
Holmes	55	821	14.9	48	5
Miller	48	514	10.7	22	3
Washington	40	631	15.8	65t	3
Moore	40	320	8.0	25	1
Spaeth	17	136	8.0	13	0
Sweed	6	64	10.7	17	0
C. Davis	5	27	5.4	14	0
McHugh	3	24	8.0	15	0
Parker	3	13	4.3	5	0
Mendenhall	2	17	8.5	11	0
Baker	1	6	6.0	6	0
Russell	1	-2	-2.0	-2	0
Roethlisberger	1	-7	-7.0	-7	0
Steelers	303	3607	11.9	65t	19
Opponents	301	2861	9.5	65t	12

INTERCEPTIONS	No.	Yds	Avg	LG	TD
Polamalu	7	59	8.4	23	0
Carter	3	64	21.3	32t	1
Townsend	2	27	13.5	25t	1
McFadden	2	0	0.0	0	0
Timmons	1	89	89.0	89	0
J. Harrison	1	33	33.0	33	0
Gay	1	12	12.0	12	0
Woodley	1	6	6.0	6	0
Clark	1	0	0.0	0	0
Taylor	1	0	0.0	0	0
Steelers	20	290	14.5	89	2
Opponents	15	234	15.6	83t	2

PUNTING	No.	Yds.	Avg.	In 20	LG
Berger	66	2728	41.3	19	61
Ernster	12	379	31.6	4	43
Steelers	78	3107	39.8	23	61
Opponents	91	3868	42.5	28	64

PUNT RETURNS	Ret	FC	Yds	Avg	LG	TD
Holmes	34	7	226	6.6	35	0
Moore	6	12	21	3.5	12	0
Sweed	1	0	0	0.0	0	0
Steelers	41	19	247	6.0	35	0
Opponents	40	17	247	6.2	46	0

KICKOFF RETURNS	No.	Yds	Avg	LG	TD
Russell	16	371	23.2	43	0
Davenport	10	217	21.7	27	0
Moore	10	185	18.5	24	0
Mendenhall	6	115	19.2	27	0
C. Davis	6	106	17.7	24	0
Carter	1	16	16.0	16	0
Spaeth	1	3	3.0	3	0
Steelers	50	1013	20.3	43	0
Opponents	71	1357	19.1	40	0

FIELD GOALS	1-19	20-29	30-39	40-49	50+
Reed	1/1	9/9	8/9	8/10	1/2
Steelers	1/1	9/9	8/9	8/10	1/2
Opponents	0/0	11/12	9/9	4/5	0/1

SACKS	No.
J. Harrison	16.0
Woodley	11.5
Aa. Smith	5.5
Timmons	5.0
Farrior	3.5
Kirschke	2.0
Eason	1.5
Foote	1.5
Frazier	1.0
Hampton	1.0
Keisel	1.0
McFadden	1.0
Hoke	0.5
Steelers	51.0
Opponents	49.0

RECORD HOLDERS

INDIVIDUAL RECORDS—CAREER

Category	Name	Performance
Rushing (Yds.)	Franco Harris, 1972-1983	11,950
Passing (Yds.)	Terry Bradshaw, 1970-1983	27,989
Passing (TDs)	Terry Bradshaw, 1970-1983	212
Receiving (No.)	Hines Ward, 1998-2008	800
Receiving (Yds.)	Hines Ward, 1998-2008	9,780
Interceptions	Mel Blount, 1970-1983	57
Punting (Avg.)	Bobby Joe Green, 1960-61	45.7
Punt Return (Avg.)	Bobby Gage, 1949-1950	14.9
Kickoff Return (Avg.)	Lynn Chandnois, 1950-56	29.6
Field Goals	Gary Anderson, 1982-1994	309
Touchdowns (Tot.)	Franco Harris, 1972-1983	100
Points	Gary Anderson, 1982-1994	1,343
*Sacks	Jason Gildon, 1994-2003	77.0

INDIVIDUAL RECORDS—SINGLE SEASON

Category	Name	Performance
Rushing (Yds.)	Barry Foster, 1992	1,690
Passing (Yds.)	Terry Bradshaw, 1979	3,724
Passing (TDs)	Ben Roethlisberger, 2007	32
Receiving (No.)	Hines Ward, 2002	112
Receiving (Yds.)	Yancey Thigpen, 1997	1,398
Interceptions	Mel Blount, 1975	11
Punting (Avg.)	Bobby Joe Green, 1961	47.0
Punt Return (Avg.)	Bobby Gage, 1949	16.0
Kickoff Return (Avg.)	Lynn Chandnois, 1952	35.2
Field Goals	Norm Johnson, 1995	34
Touchdowns (Tot.)	Willie Parker, 2006	16
Points	Norm Johnson, 1995	141
*Sacks	James Harrison, 2008	16.0

INDIVIDUAL RECORDS—SINGLE GAME

Category	Name	Performance
Rushing (Yds.)	Willie Parker, 12-7-06	223
Passing (Yds.)	Tommy Maddox, 11-10-02	473
Passing (TDs)	Terry Bradshaw, 11-15-81	5
	Mark Malone, 9-8-85	5
	Ben Roethlisberger, 11-5-07	5
Receiving (No.)	Courtney Hawkins, 11-1-98	14
Receiving (Yds.)	Plaxico Burress, 11-10-02	253
Interceptions	Jack Butler, 12-13-53	**4
Field Goals	Gary Anderson, 10-23-88	6
	Jeff Reed, 12-1-02	6
Touchdowns (Tot.)	Ray Mathews, 10-17-54	4
	Roy Jefferson, 11-3-68	4
Points	Ray Mathews, 10-17-54	24
	Roy Jefferson, 11-3-68	24
*Sacks	Chad Brown, 10-13-96	4.5

**Sacks became an official statistic in 1982.*
***NFL Record*

PITTSBURGH STEELERS

2009 VETERAN ROSTER

No.	Name	Pos.	Ht.	Wt.	Birthdate	NFL Exp.	College	Hometown	How Acq.	'08 Games/ Starts
55	Bailey, Patrick	LB	6-4	235	7/27/85	2	Duke	Elmendorf, Texas	FA-'08	12/0
81	Baker, Dallas	WR	6-3	206	11/10/82	2	Florida	New Smyrna Beach, Fla.	D7-'07	8/0
16	Batch, Charlie	QB	6-2	216	12/5/74	12	Eastern Michigan	Homestead, Pa.	FA-'02	0*
17	#Berger, Mitch	P	6-4	228	6/24/72	14	Colorado	Kamloops, Canada	FA-'08	13/0
31	Bryant, Fernando	CB	5-10	175	3/26/77	11	Alabama	Murfreesboro, Tenn.	FA-'08	2/0
69	Capizzi, Jason	T	6-9	330	6/19/83	3	Indiana (Pa.)	Gibsonia, Pa.	FA-'08	0*
23	Carter, Tyrone	S	5-9	195	3/31/76	10	Minnesota	Pompano Beach, Fla.	FA-'04	16/2
25	Clark, Ryan	S	5-11	205	10/12/79	8	Louisiana State	Merraro, La.	UFA(Wash)-'06	14/14
74	Colon, Willie	T	6-3	315	4/9/83	4	Hofstra	Bronx, N.Y.	D4a-'06	16/16
53	Davis, Bruce	LB	6-3	252	9/2/85	2	UCLA	Houston, Texas	D3-'08	5/0
38	Davis, Carey	FB	5-10	225	3/27/81	4	Illinois	St. Louis, Mo.	FA-'06	14/4
2	Dixon, Dennis	QB	6-3	195	1/11/85	2	Oregon	San Leandro, Calif.	D5-'08	1/0
93	Eason, Nick	DE	6-3	305	5/29/80	7	Clemson	Lyons, Ga.	FA-'07	15/0
79	Essex, Trai	T	6-4	324	12/5/82	5	Northwestern	Fort Wayne, Ind.	D3-'05	9/0
51	Farrior, James	LB	6-2	243	1/6/75	13	Virginia	Ettrick, Va.	UFA(NYJ)-'02	16/16
57	Fox, Keyaron	LB	6-3	235	1/24/82	6	Georgia Tech	Atlanta, Ga.	FA-'08	13/0
54	Frazier, Andre	LB	6-5	245	6/29/82	5	Cincinnati	Cincinnati, Ohio	FA-'07	15/0
22	Gay, William	CB	5-10	190	1/1/85	3	Louisville	Tallahassee, Fla.	D5b-'07	16/4
98	Hampton, Casey	NT	6-1	325	9/3/77	9	Texas	Galveston, Texas	D1-'01	13/13
97	Harrison, Arnold	LB	6-3	241	9/20/82	4	Georgia	Augusta, Ga.	FA-'05	0*
92	Harrison, James	LB	6-0	242	5/4/78	6	Kent State	Akron, Ohio	FA-'04	15/15
62	Hartwig, Justin	C	6-4	312	11/21/78	8	Kansas	Mankato, Minn.	UFA(Car)-'08	16/16
66	Hills, Tony	T	6-5	304	11/4/84	2	Texas	Houston, Texas	D4-'08	0*
76	Hoke, Chris	NT	6-2	305	4/6/76	9	Brigham Young	Long Beach, Calif.	FA-'01	16/3
10	Holmes, Santonio	WR	5-11	192	3/3/84	4	Ohio State	Belle Glade, Fla.	D1-'06	15/15
6	Johnson, Dirk	P	6-0	210	6/1/75	8	Northern Colorado	Hoxie, Kan.	FA-'09	12/0*
99	Keisel, Brett	DE	6-5	285	9/19/78	8	Brigham Young	Greybull, Wyo.	D7b-'02	10/10
68	Kemoeatu, Chris	G	6-3	344	1/4/83	5	Utah	Kahuka, Hawaii	D6-'05	16/16
90	Kirschke, Travis	DE	6-3	298	9/6/74	13	UCLA	Highland Ranch, Colo.	UFA(SF)-'04	16/6
30	Lewis, Roy	CB	5-10	190	5/19/85	2	Washington	Los Angeles, Calif.	FA-'08	1/0
37	Madison, Anthony	CB	5-9	180	10/8/81	4	Alabama	Thomasville, Ala.	FA-'07	16/0
87	McDonald, Shaun	WR	5-10	183	6/30/81	7	Arizona State	Phoenix, Ariz.	FA-'09	12/7*
49	McHugh, Sean	TE	6-5	265	5/27/82	6	Penn State	University Heights, Ohio	FA-'08	15/3
34	Mendenhall, Rashard	RB	5-10	225	6/19/87	2	Illinois	Skokie, Ill.	D1-'08	4/1
83	Miller, Heath	TE	6-5	256	10/22/82	5	Virginia	Swords Creek, Va.	D1-'05	14/14
21	Moore, Mewelde	RB	5-11	209	7/24/82	6	Tulane	Hammond, La.	UFA(Min)-'08	16/4
39	Parker, Willie	RB	5-10	209	11/11/80	6	North Carolina	Clinton, N.C.	FA-'04	11/11
77	Parquet, Jeremy	OL	6-6	321	4/11/82	5	Southern Mississippi	Norco, La.	FA-'07	4/0
71	Paxson, Scott	DT	6-4	292	2/3/83	2	Penn State	Philadelphia, Pa.	FA-'06	1/0
43	Polamalu, Troy	S	5-10	207	4/19/81	7	Southern California	Tenmile, Ore.	D1-'03	16/16
35	Powdrell, Ryan	FB	5-11	254	12/20/83	2	Southern California	Albuquerque, N.M.	FA-'09	0*
27	Ratliff, Keiwan	CB	5-11	188	4/19/81	6	Florida	Youngstown, Ohio	UFA(Ind)-'09	13/4*
3	Reed, Jeff	K	5-11	225	4/9/79	8	North Carolina	Charlotte, N.C.	FA-'02	16/0
7	Roethlisberger, Ben	QB	6-5	241	3/2/82	6	Miami (Ohio)	Findlay, Ohio	D1-'04	16/16
96	#Roye, Orpheus	DE	6-4	330	1/21/73	13	Florida State	Miami, Fla.	FA-'08	6/0
9	Sepulveda, Daniel	P	6-3	230	1/12/84	3	Baylor	Austin, Texas	D4a-'07	0*
91	Smith, Aaron	DE	6-5	298	4/19/76	11	Northern Colorado	Colorado Springs, Colo.	D4-'99	16/16
89	Spaeth, Matt	TE	6-7	270	11/24/84	3	Minnesota	St. Michael, Minn.	D3-'07	16/13
72	Stapleton, Darnell	G/C	6-3	305	9/21/85	3	Rutgers	Union, N.J.	FA-'07	16/12
78	Starks, Max	T	6-8	345	1/10/82	6	Florida	Orlando, Fla.	D3-'04	16/11
14	Sweed, Limas	WR	6-4	220	12/25/84	2	Texas	Brenham, Texas	D2-'08	11/0
24	Taylor, Ike	CB	6-2	195	5/5/80	7	Louisiana-Lafayette	Gretna, La.	D4-'03	16/16
94	Timmons, Lawrence	LB	6-1	234	3/14/86	3	Florida State	Florence, S.C.	D1-'07	16/2
26	Townsend, Deshea	CB	5-10	190	9/8/75	12	Alabama	Batesville, Miss.	D4a-'98	12/4
86	Ward, Hines	WR	6-0	205	3/8/76	12	Georgia	Forest Park, Ga.	D3b-'98	16/14
60	Warren, Greg	LS	6-3	252	10/18/81	5	North Carolina	Goldsboro, N.C.	FA-'05	7/0
82	Williams, Brandon	WR	5-11	170	2/24/84	4	Wisconsin	St. Louis, Mo.	FA-'09	0*
56	Woodley, LaMarr	LB	6-2	265	11/3/84	3	Michigan	Saginaw, Mich.	D2-'07	15/15
95	Woods, Donovan	LB	6-2	230	7/27/85	2	Oklahoma State	Oklahoma City, Okla.	FA-'08	5/0

* Batch missed '08 season because of injury; Capizzi inactive for 1 game; A. Harrison missed '08 season because of injury; Hills inactive 16 games; Johnson played 12 games with Arizona in '08; McDonald played 12 games with Detroit; Powdrell spent 2 weeks on Tampa Bay practice squad; Ratliff played 13 games with Indianapolis; Sepulveda missed '08 season because of injury; Williams last active with St. Louis in '07.

Players lost through free agency (5): QB Byron Leftwich (TB; 5 games in '08), CB Bryant McFadden (Ariz; 10), S Anthony Smith (GB; 14), T Marvel Smith (SF; 5), WR Nate Washington (Tenn; 16).

Also played with Steelers in '08—RB Najeh Davenport (4 games), P Paul Ernster (3), LB Larry Foote (16), RB Gary Russell (12), P Jared Retkofsky (9), G Kendall Simmons (4).

2009 FIRST-YEAR ROSTER

Name	Pos.	Ht.	Wt.	Birthdate	College	Hometown	How Acq.
Black, Steven	WR	6-3	213	12/11/86	Memphis	Birmingham, Ala.	FA
Bradley, Jeff	DT	6-2	275	7/3/85	Western Carolina	Lewisville, N.C.	FA
Burnett, Joe	CB	5-9	192	11/28/86	Central Florida	Eustis, Fla.	D5a
Czech, Piotr	K	6-5	210	8/17/86	Wagner College	Olesnica, Poland	FA
Estermyer, Mark	LS	6-2	245	10/17/85	Pittsburgh	Chippewa, Pa.	FA
Foster, Jayson (1)	WR	5-7	175	7/22/85	Georgia Southern	Canton, Ga.	FA
Foster, Ramon	T	6-6	325	1/7/86	Tennessee	Henning, Tenn.	FA
Goodman, Cedric	WR	6-2	190	3/17/86	Georgia	Newnan, Ga.	FA
Grisham, Tyler	WR	5-11	180	6/11/87	Clemson	Birmingham, Ala.	FA
Harris, Ra'Shon	DE	6-4	298	8/26/86	Oregon	Pensacola, Fla.	D6
Hood, Ziggy	DE	6-3	300	2/16/87	Missouri	Amarillo, Texas	D1
Johnson, David	TE	6-2	260	8/26/87	Arkansas State	Pine Bluff, Ark.	D7b
Korte, Tom	LB	6-0	239	7/26/86	Hillsdale (Mich.)	Grand Rapids, Mich.	FA
Legursky, Doug (1)	G	6-1	323	6/9/86	Marshall	Frankfurt, Germany	FA-'08
Lewis, Keenan	CB	6-0	208	5/17/86	Oregon State	New Orleans, La.	D3b
Logan, Stefan (1)	RB	5-7	185	6/2/81	South Dakota	Miami, Fla.	FA
McCabe, Kevin	QB	6-2	220	11/12/84	California (Pa.)	Gibsonia, Pa.	FA
McLendon, Steve	DT	6-4	280	1/3/86	Troy	Ozark, Ala.	FA
Mundy, Ryan (1)	S	6-1	215	2/11/85	West Virginia	Pittsburgh, Pa.	D6b-'08
Nance, Martin (1)	WR	6-3	212	5/26/83	Miami (Ohio)	Maryland Heights, Mo.	FA-'08
Redman, Isaac	RB	6-0	230	11/10/84	Bowie State	Paulsboro, N.J.	FA
Reffett, Jordan (1)	DE	6-4	292	9/9/84	Washington	Moses Lake, Wash.	FA
Reilly, Mike	QB	6-3	212	1/1/85	Central Washington	Kalispell, Mont.	FA
Richardson, Derrick	S	5-11	190	4/3/86	New Mexico State	Denver, Colo.	FA
Schantz, Andrew	LB	6-1	235	8/23/86	Portland State	Santa Clarita, Calif.	FA
Sherrod, Dezmond (1)	TE	6-2	250	5/11/85	Mississippi State	Newport, R.I.	FA-'08
Shipley, A.Q.	C	6-0	298	5/22/86	Penn State	Coraopolis, Pa.	D7a
Summers, Frank	RB	5-10	230	9/6/85	Nevada-Las Vegas	Oakland, Calif.	D5b
Urbik, Kraig	G	6-5	323	9/23/85	Wisconsin	Hudson, Wisc.	D3a
Vincent, Justin (1)	RB	5-10	219	1/25/83	Louisiana State	Lake Charles, La.	FA-'07
Wallace, Mike	WR	6-0	199	8/1/86	Mississippi	New Orleans, La.	D3c

The term NFL Rookie is defined as a player who is in his first season of professional football and has not been on the roster of another professional football team for any regular-season or postseason games. A Rookie is designated by an "R" on NFL rosters. Players who have been active in another professional football league or players who have NFL experience, including either preseason training camp or being on an Active List or Inactive List, or on Reserve/Injured or Reserve/Physically Unable to Perform for fewer than six regular-season games, are termed NFL First-Year Players. An NFL First-Year Player is designated by a "1" on NFL rosters. Thereafter, a player is credited with an additional year of experience for each season in which he accumulates six games on the Active List or Inactive List, or on Reserve/Injured or Reserve/Physically Unable to Perform.

Log on to www.steelers.com for an up-to-date roster.

PITTSBURGH STEELERS

COACHING STAFF

Head Coach,
Mike Tomlin

Pro Career: Named the sixteenth head coach in Steelers history when he replaced Bill Cowher on January 22, 2007. Became the youngest coach (36 years, 323 days) in NFL history to win a Super Bowl when the Steelers defeated the Arizona Cardinals, 27-23, in Super Bowl XLIII on February 1, 2009. The only coach in Steelers' history to win division titles each of his first two seasons, Tomlin directed the Steelers to a 12-4 record in 2008, winning his second-consecutive AFC North title. In his first season, Tomlin guided the Steelers to a 10-6 record and their first AFC North title since 2004. Tomlin was the Minnesota Vikings defensive coordinator in 2006 after spending the previous five seasons (2001-05) as defensive backs coach for the Tampa Bay Buccaneers. Tomlin coached one of the top defensive backfields in the NFL for the Buccaneers, culminating with its performance in Super Bowl XXXVII. The secondary recorded four interceptions, returning two for touchdowns to help Tampa Bay capture the franchise's first Super Bowl title. Tomlin served two seasons as the defensive backs coach at the University of Cincinnati (1999-2000) before going to Tampa Bay. Prior to joining the Cincinnati staff, Tomlin had a short stint on the coaching staff at Tennessee-Martin and then spent two seasons at Arkansas State. He spent the 1996 season as a graduate assistant at Memphis. Tomlin began his coaching career in 1995 as wide receivers coach at Virginia Military Institute. Career record: 25-11.

Background: Was a three-year starter at wide receiver at William & Mary (1990-94) and finished his career with 101 receptions for 2,046 yards and a school-record 20 touchdown receptions. A first-team All-Yankee Conference selection in 1994, he established a school record with a 20.2 yards per catch average. Tomlin was a teammate of current Viking Pro Bowl safety Darren Sharper at William and Mary. Graduated in 1994 with a degree in sociology.

Personal: Born in Hampton, Va., on March 15, 1972. He and his wife, Kiya, have two sons, Dino and Mason, and a daughter Harlyn Quinn.

ASSISTANT COACHES

Ken Anderson, quarterbacks; born February 15, 1949, Batavia, Ill. Quarterback Augustana (Ill.) 1967-1970. Pro quarterback Cincinnati Bengals 1971-1986. Pro coach: Cincinnati Bengals 1992-2002, Jacksonville Jaguars 2003-2006, joined Steelers in 2007.

Bruce Arians, offensive coordinator; born October 3, 1952, Paterson, N.J. Quarterback Virginia Tech 1970-74. No pro playing experience. College coach: Virginia Tech 1975-77, Mississippi State 1978-1980, Alabama 1981-82, Temple 1983-88 (head coach), Mississippi State 1993-95, Alabama 1997. Pro coach: Kansas City Chiefs 1989-1992, New Orleans Saints 1996, Indianapolis Colts 1998-2000, Cleveland Browns 2001-03, joined Steelers in 2004.

Keith Butler, linebackers; born May 16, 1956, Anniston, Ala. Linebacker Memphis 1974-77. Pro linebacker Seattle Seahawks 1978-1987. College coach: Memphis 1990-97, Arkansas State 1998. Pro coach: Cleveland Browns 1999-2002, joined Steelers in 2003.

James Daniel, tight ends; born January 17, 1953, Wetumpka, Ala. Guard Alabama State 1970-73. No pro playing experience. College coach: Auburn 1981-1992. Pro coach: New York Giants 1993-96, Atlanta Falcons 1997-2003, joined Steelers in 2004.

Randy Fichtner, wide receivers; born November 7, 1963, Cleveland. Defensive back Purdue 1982-85. No pro playing experience. College coach: Michigan 1986-87, Southern California 1988, Nevada-Las Vegas 1989, Memphis 1990-93, Purdue 1994-96, Arkansas State 1997-2000, Memphis 2001-06. Pro coach: Joined Steelers in 2007.

Ray Horton, defensive backs; born April 12, 1960, Tacoma, Wash. Defensive back Washington 1979-1982. Pro defensive back Cincinnati Bengals 1983-88, Dallas Cowboys 1989-1992. Pro coach: Washington Redskins 1994-96, Cincinnati Bengals 1997-2001, Detroit Lions 2002-03, joined Steelers in 2004.

Amos Jones, asst. special teams; born December 31, 1959, Tallahassee, Fla.. Safety/running back Alabama 1978-1980. No pro playing experience. College coach: Alabama 1981-82, Temple 1983-88, Alabama 1990-91, Pittsburgh 1992, Tulane 1995-96, Cincinnati 1999-2002, James Madison 2003, Mississippi State 2004-06. Pro coach: British Columbia (CFL) 1997, joined Steelers in 2007.

Dick LeBeau, defensive coordinator; born September 9, 1937, London, Ohio. Defensive back Ohio State 1955-58. Pro cornerback Detroit Lions 1959-1972. Pro coach: Philadelphia Eagles 1973-75, Green Bay Packers 1976-79, Cincinnati Bengals 1980-1991, 1997-2002 (head coach 2000-02), Pittsburgh Steelers 1992-96, Buffalo Bills 2003, re-joined Steelers in 2004.

Bob Ligashesky, special teams; born June 2, 1962, Pittsburgh. Linebacker Indiana (Pa.) 1983-84. No pro playing experience. College coach: Wake Forest 1985, Arizona State 1986-89, Kent State 1990, Bowling Green 1991-99, Pittsburgh 2000-03. Pro coach: Jacksonville Jaguars 2004, St. Louis Rams 2005-06, joined Steelers in 2007.

John Mitchell, defensive line; born October 14, 1951, Mobile, Ala. Defensive end Eastern Arizona J.C. 1969-1970, Alabama 1971-72. No pro playing experience. College coach: Alabama 1973-76, Arkansas 1977-1982, Temple 1986, Louisiana State 1987-1990. Pro coach: Birmingham Stallions (USFL) 1983-85, Cleveland Browns 1991-93, joined Steelers in 1994.

Kirby Wilson, running backs; born August 24, 1961, Los Angeles. Running back/wide receiver Pasadena (Calif.) C.C. 1979-1980, Illinois 1981-82. Pro cornerback Winnipeg Blue Bombers (CFL) 1983, Toronto Argonauts (CFL) 1984. College coach: Pasadena (Calif.) C.C. 1989-1990, Southern Illinois 1991-92, Wyoming 1993-94, Iowa State 1995-96, Southern California 2001. Pro coach: New England Patriots 1997-99, Washington Redskins 2000, Tampa Bay Buccaneers 2002-03, Arizona Cardinals 2004-06, joined Steelers in 2007.

Larry Zierlein, offensive line; born July 12, 1945, Norton, Kan. Linebacker/tight end Pratt (Kan.) J.C. 1967-68, linebacker Fort Hays State (Kan.) 1969-1970. No pro playing experience. College coach: Fort Hays State (Kan.) 1970-71, Houston 1978-1986, Tulane 1988-1990, 1995-96, Louisiana State 1993-94, Cincinnati 1997-2000. Pro coach: Washington (AFL) 1987, New York/New Jersey Knights (WLAF) 1991-92, Cleveland Browns 2001-04, Buffalo Bills 2006, joined Steelers in 2007.

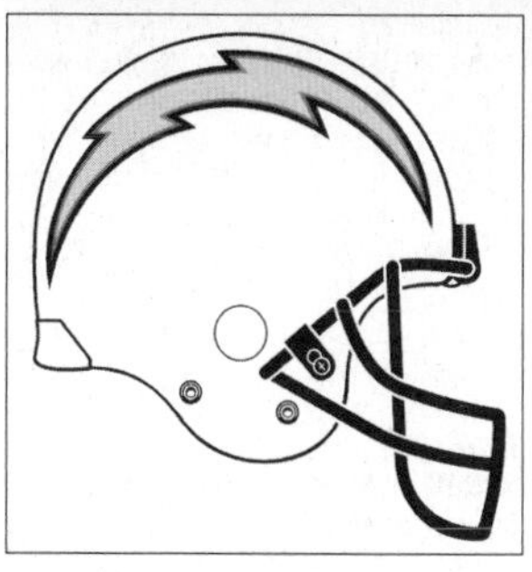

American Football Conference
West Division
Team Colors: Navy Blue, Powder Blue, White, and Gold
P.O. Box 609609
San Diego, California 92160-9609
Telephone: (858) 874-4500

2009 SCHEDULE
PRESEASON

Aug. 15	**Seattle**	7:00
Aug. 22	at Arizona	7:00
Aug. 29	at Atlanta	8:00
Sep. 4	**San Francisco**	7:00

REGULAR SEASON

Sep. 14	at Oakland (Mon.)	7:15
Sep. 20	**Baltimore**	1:15
Sep. 27	**Miami**	1:15
Oct. 4	at Pittsburgh	8:20
Oct. 11	BYE	
Oct. 19	**Denver** (Mon.)	5:30
Oct. 25	at Kansas City	12:00
Nov. 1	**Oakland**	1:05
Nov. 8	at N.Y. Giants	4:15
Nov. 15	**Philadelphia**	1:15
Nov. 22	at Denver	2:15
Nov. 29	**Kansas City**	1:05
Dec. 6	at Cleveland	4:05
Dec. 13	at Dallas	3:15
Dec. 20	**Cincinnati**	1:05
Dec. 25	at Tennessee (Fri.)	6:30
Jan. 3	**Washington**	1:15

Stadium: Qualcomm Stadium (opened in 1967)
• **Capacity:** 70,000 (app.)
9449 Friars Road
San Diego, California 92108
Playing Surface: Grass
Training Camp: Chargers Park
4020 Murphy Canyon Rd.
San Diego, CA 92123

QUALCOMM STADIUM

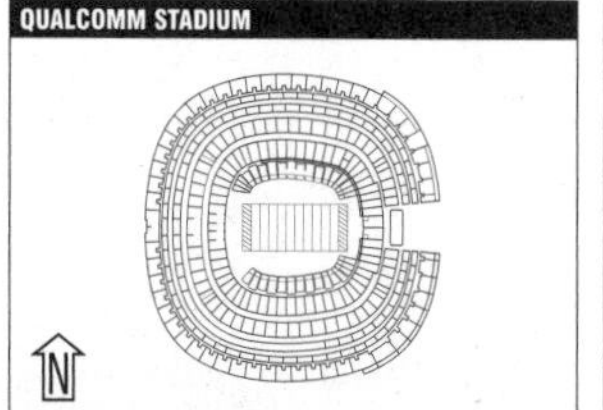

CLUB OFFICIALS
Owner: Alex G. Spanos
President/CEO: Dean A. Spanos
Executive Vice President: Michael A. Spanos
Executive Vice President-Executive Officer: A.G. Spanos
Executive Vice President-General Manager: A.J. Smith
Executive Vice President-Chief Operating Officer: Jim Steeg
Executive Vice President: Jeremiah T. Murphy
Executive Vice President of Football Operations-Assistant General Manager: Ed McGuire
Executive Vice President-Chief Financial Officer: Jeanne M. Bonk
Vice President-Chief Marketing Officer: Ken Derrett
Director of Player Personnel: Jimmy Raye
Director of College Scouting: John Spanos
Director of Pro Scouting: Dennis Abraham
Senior Executive: Randy Mueller
Head Athletic Trainer: James Collins
Director of Video Operations: Brian Duddy
Equipment Manager: Bob Wick
Director of Player Development: Arthur Hightower
Senior Director of Marketing Partnerships: Dennis O'Leary
Senior Director of Ticket Sales and Service: Todd Poulsen
Director of Business Operations: John Hinek
Director of Public Relations: Bill Johnston
Director of Public Affairs & Corporate/Community Relations: Kimberley Layton
Director of Security: Dick Lewis
Director of Stadium/Game Operations & Events: Sean O'Connor
Controller: Marsha Wells
Director of Ticket Operations: Michael L. Dougherty

COACHING HISTORY
Los Angeles 1960
(372-382-11)
Records include postseason games

1960-69	Sid Gillman*	83-51-6
1969-1970	Charlie Waller	9-7-3
1971	Sid Gillman**	4-6-0
1971-73	Harland Svare***	7-17-2
1973	Ron Waller	1-5-0
1974-78	Tommy Prothro****	21-39-0
1978-1986	Don Coryell#	72-60-0
1986-88	Al Saunders	17-22-0
1989-1991	Dan Henning	16-32-0
1992-96	Bobby Ross	50-36-0
1997-98	Kevin Gilbride	6-16-0
1998	June Jones	3-7-0
1999-2001	Mike Riley	14-34-0
2002-06	Marty Schottenheimer	47-35-0
2007-08	Norv Turner	22-15-0

*Retired after nine games in 1969
**Resigned after 10 games in 1971
***Resigned after eight games in 1973
****Resigned after four games in 1978
#Resigned after eight games in 1986
##Released after six games in 1998

PAID ATTENDANCE
Home 545,043 Away 541,751
Total 1,086,794
Single-game home record, 69,288 (11/7/99)
Single-season home record, 547,937 (2005)

2009 DRAFT CHOICES

Round	Name	Pos.	College
1	Larry English	LB	Northern Illinois
3	Louis Vasquez	G	Texas Tech
4	Vaughn Martin	DT	Western Ontario
	Tyronne Green	C	Auburn
	Gartrell Johnson	RB	Colorado State
5	Brandon Hughes	DB	Oregon State
6	Kevin Ellison	DB	Southern California
7	Demetrius Byrd	WR	Louisiana State

SAN DIEGO CHARGERS

2008 TEAM RECORD

PRESEASON (3-1)

Date	Result	Opponent
8/9	W 31-17	Dallas
8/16	L 6-7	at St. Louis
8/25	W 18-17	Seattle
8/29	W 20-17	at San Francisco

REGULAR SEASON (8-8)

Date	Result	Opponent
9/7	L 24-26	Carolina
9/14	L 38-39	at Denver
9/22	W 48-29	New York Jets
9/28	W 28-18	at Oakland
10/5	L 10-17	at Miami
10/12	W 30-10	New England
10/19	L 14-23	at Buffalo
10/26	L 32-37	at New Orleans
11/9	W 20-19	Kansas City
11/16	L 10-11	at Pittsburgh
11/23	L 20-23	Indianapolis
11/30	L 16-22	Atlanta
12/4	W 34-7	Oakland
12/14	W 22-21	at Kansas City
12/21	W 41-24	at Tampa Bay
12/28	W 52-21	Denver

POSTSEASON (1-1)

Date	Result	Opponent
1/3	W 23-17	Indianapolis (OT)
1/11	L 24-35	at Pittsburgh

(OT) Overtime

SCORE BY PERIODS

Chargers	77	126	84	152	0	— 439
Opponents	64	141	59	83	0	— 347

2008 TEAM STATISTICS

	Chargers	Opp.
Total First Downs	301	339
Rushing	92	98
Passing	191	213
Penalty	18	28
3rd Down: Made/Att	89/194	84/207
3rd Down Pct.	45.9	40.6
4th Down: Made/Att	8/11	13/24
4th Down Pct.	72.7	54.2
Possession Avg.	28:53	31:07
Total Net Yards	5584	5599
Avg. Per Game	349.0	349.9
Total Plays	924	1041
Avg. Per Play	6.0	5.4
Net Yards Rushing	1726	1641
Avg. Per Game	107.9	102.6
Total Rushes	421	408
Net Yards Passing	3858	3958
Avg. Per Game	241.1	247.4
Sacked/Yards Lost	25/151	28/132
Gross Yards	4009	4090
Att./Completions	478/312	605/411
Completion Pct.	65.3	67.9
Had Intercepted	11	15
Punts/Average	51/45.7	60/43.9
Net Punting Avg.	51/40.9	60/38.7
Penalties/Yards	95/748	78/708
Fumbles/Ball Lost	18/9	18/9
Touchdowns	51	39
Rushing	13	11
Passing	34	25
Returns	4	3

2008 INDIVIDUAL STATISTICS

PASSING	Att.	Comp.	Yds.	Pct.	TD	Int.	Tkld.	Rate
Rivers	478	312	4009	65.3	34	11	25/151	105.5
Chargers	478	312	4009	65.3	34	11	25/151	105.5
Opponents	605	411	4090	67.9	25	15	28/132	90.3

SCORING	TD R	TD P	TD Rt	PAT	FG	Saf	PTS
Kaeding	0	0	0	46/46	27/32	0	127
Tomlinson	11	1	0	0/0	0/0	0	72
Gates	0	8	0	0/0	0/0	0	48
Sproles	1	5	1	0/0	0/0	0	44
Jackson	0	7	0	0/0	0/0	0	42
Chambers	0	5	0	0/0	0/0	0	30
Floyd	0	4	0	0/0	0/0	0	24
Hester	1	1	0	0/0	0/0	0	12
Manumaleuna	0	2	0	0/0	0/0	0	12
Cason	0	0	1	0/0	0/0	0	6
Cromartie	0	0	1	0/0	0/0	0	6
Tolbert	0	1	0	0/0	0/0	0	6
Weddle	0	0	1	0/0	0/0	0	6
Naanee	0	0	0	0/0	0/0	0	2
Chargers	13	34	4	46/46	27/32	1	439
Opponents	11	25	3	31/33	24/31	3	347

2-Pt. Conversions: Naanee, Sproles.
Chargers 2-5, Opponents 2-6

RUSHING	No.	Yds	Avg	LG	TD
Tomlinson	292	1110	3.8	45	11
Sproles	61	330	5.4	37	1
Hester	19	95	5.0	28	1
Rivers	31	84	2.7	11	0
Jackson	4	69	17.3	31	0
Tolbert	13	37	2.8	11	0
Chambers	1	1	1.0	1	0
Chargers	421	1726	4.1	45	13
Opponents	408	1641	4.0	49	11

RECEIVING	No.	Yds	Avg	LG	TD
Gates	60	704	11.7	34	8
Jackson	59	1098	18.6	60	7
Tomlinson	52	426	8.2	32	1
Chambers	33	462	14.0	48t	5
Sproles	29	342	11.8	66t	5
Floyd	27	465	17.2	49t	4
Manumaleuna	15	127	8.5	17	2
Tolbert	13	171	13.2	67	1
Hester	12	91	7.6	16	1
Naanee	8	64	8.0	18	0
Davis	4	59	14.8	20	0
Chargers	312	4009	12.8	67	34
Opponents	411	4090	10.0	71t	25

INTERCEPTIONS	No.	Yds	Avg	LG	TD
Cooper	4	11	2.8	10	0
Cason	2	69	34.5	59t	1
Cromartie	2	66	33.0	52t	1
Jammer	2	2	1.0	2	0
Wilhelm	1	8	8.0	8	0
Castillo	1	4	4.0	4	0
Dobbins	1	4	4.0	4	0
Weddle	1	3	3.0	3	0
Oliver	1	0	0.0	0	0
Chargers	15	167	11.1	59t	2
Opponents	11	189	17.2	50	1

PUNTING	No.	Yds.	Avg.	In 20	LG
Scifres	51	2332	45.7	19	67
Chargers	51	2332	45.7	19	67
Opponents	60	2633	43.9	25	70

PUNT RETURNS	Ret	FC	Yds	Avg	LG	TD
Sproles	22	12	249	11.3	43	0
Davis	2	0	15	7.5	10	0
Cromartie	1	0	4	4.0	4	0
Weddle	1	1	1	1.0	1	0
Chargers	26	13	269	10.3	43	0
Opponents	23	12	146	6.3	32	0

KICKOFF RETURNS	No.	Yds	Avg	LG	TD
Sproles	53	1376	26.0	103t	1
Hester	3	42	14.0	20	0
Cromartie	3	37	12.3	26	0
Manumaleuna	2	14	7.0	9	0
Gordon	1	18	18.0	18	0
Naanee	0	-2	—	-2	0
Chargers	62	1485	24.0	103t	1
Opponents	86	1943	22.6	94	1

FIELD GOALS	1-19	20-29	30-39	40-49	50+
Kaeding	0/0	13/13	10/10	3/8	1/1
Chargers	0/0	13/13	10/10	3/8	1/1
Opponents	0/0	6/6	8/9	8/10	2/6

SACKS	No.
Phillips	7.5
Tucker	5.5
Harris	2.5
Cesaire	2.0
Olshansky	2.0
Bingham	1.5
Castillo	1.5
Cooper	1.5
Williams	1.5
Weddle	1.0
(group)	1.0
Applewhite	0.5
Chargers	28.0
Opponents	25.0

RECORD HOLDERS

INDIVIDUAL RECORDS—CAREER

Category	Name	Performance
Rushing (Yds.)	LaDainian Tomlinson, 2001-08	11,760
Passing (Yds.)	Dan Fouts, 1973-1987	43,040
Passing (TDs)	Dan Fouts, 1973-1987	254
Receiving (No.)	Charlie Joiner, 1976-1986	586
Receiving (Yds.)	Lance Alworth, 1962-1970	9,585
Interceptions	Gill Byrd, 1983-1992	42
Punting (Avg.)	Mike Scifres, 2003-08	44.1
Punt Return (Avg.)	Darrien Gordon, 1993-96	13.6
Kickoff Return (Avg.)	Darren Sproles, 2005-08	25.6
Field Goals	John Carney, 1990-2000	261
Touchdowns (Tot.)	LaDainian Tomlinson, 2001-08	141
Points	John Carney, 1990-2000	1,076
*Sacks	Leslie O'Neal, 1986-1995	105.5

INDIVIDUAL RECORDS—SINGLE SEASON

Category	Name	Performance
Rushing (Yds.)	LaDainian Tomlinson, 2006	1,815
Passing (Yds.)	Dan Fouts, 1981	4,802
Passing (TDs)	Philip Rivers, 2008	34
Receiving (No.)	LaDainian Tomlinson, 2003	100
Receiving (Yds.)	Lance Alworth, 1965	1,602
Interceptions	Antonio Cromartie, 2007	10
Punting (Avg.)	Darren Bennett, 2000	46.2
Punt Return (Avg.)	Leslie (Speedy) Duncan, 1965	15.5
Kickoff Return (Avg.)	Keith Lincoln, 1962	28.4
Field Goals	John Carney, 1994	34
Touchdowns (Tot.)	LaDainian Tomlinson, 2006	**31
Points	LaDainian Tomlinson, 2006	**186
*Sacks	Leslie O'Neal, 1992	17.0
	Shawne Merriman, 2006	17.0

INDIVIDUAL RECORDS—SINGLE GAME

Category	Name	Performance
Rushing (Yds.)	LaDainian Tomlinson, 12-28-03	243
Passing (Yds.)	Dan Fouts, 10-19-80, 12-11-82	444
Passing (TDs)	Dan Fouts, 11-22-81	6
Receiving (No.)	Kellen Winslow, 10-7-84	15
Receiving (Yds.)	Wes Chandler, 12-20-82	260
Interceptions	Many times	3
	Last time by Antonio Cromartie, 11-11-07	
Field Goals	John Carney, 9-5-93, 9-18-93	6
	Greg Davis, 10-5-97	6
Touchdowns (Tot.)	Kellen Winslow, 11-22-81	5
Points	Kellen Winslow, 11-22-81	30
*Sacks	Leslie O'Neal, 11-16-86	5.0

**Sacks became an official statistic in 1982.*
***NFL Record*

SAN DIEGO CHARGERS

2009 VETERAN ROSTER

No.	Name	Pos.	Ht.	Wt.	Birthdate	NFL Exp.	College	Hometown	How Acq.	'08 Games/ Starts
90	Applewhite, Antwan	LB	6-3	246	12/31/85	2	San Diego State	Los Angeles, Calif.	FA-'07	14/0
29	Bennett, Michael	RB	5-9	207	8/13/78	9	Wisconsin	Milwaukee, Wisc.	W(TB)-'08	5/0*
97	Bingham, Ryon	DE/DT	6-3	303	6/6/81	5	Nebraska	Sandy, Utah	D7A-'04	16/0
50	Binn, David	LS	6-3	228	2/6/72	16	California	San Mateo, Calif.	FA-'94	16/0
99	Burnett, Kevin	LB	6-3	240	12/24/82	5	Tennessee	Compton, Calif.	UFA(Dall)-'09	16/2*
20	Cason, Antoine	CB	6-0	190	7/9/86	2	Arizona	Long Beach, Calif.	D1-'08	16/3
93	Castillo, Luis	DE	6-3	290	8/4/83	5	Northwestern	Garfield, N.J.	D1B-'05	15/15
74	Cesaire, Jacques	DE	6-2	295	8/30/80	7	So. Connecticut State	Gardner, Mass.	FA-'03	16/2
89	Chambers, Chris	WR	5-11	210	8/12/78	9	Wisconsin	Bedford, Ohio	T(Mia)-'07	14/9
75	Clark, Corey	T	6-5	325	6/21/84	2	Texas A&M	Spring Branch, Texas	D7-'08	0*
66	Clary, Jeromey	T	6-6	320	11/5/83	3	Kansas State	Mansfield, Texas	D6A-'06	16/16
54	Cooper, Stephen	LB	6-1	235	6/19/79	7	Maine	Wareham, Mass.	FA-'03	12/12
31	Cromartie, Antonio	CB	6-2	203	4/15/84	4	Florida State	Tallahassee, Fla.	D1-'06	16/15
84	Davis, Buster	WR	6-1	210	10/2/85	3	Louisiana State	New Orleans, La.	D1-'07	4/0
68	Dielman, Kris	G	6-4	320	2/3/81	7	Indiana	Troy, Ohio	FA-'03	15/15
51	Dobbins, Tim	LB	6-1	246	12/10/82	4	Iowa State	Nashville, Tenn.	D5-'06	16/8
80	Floyd, Malcom	WR	6-5	225	9/8/81	4	Wyoming	Sacramento, Calif.	FA-'04	13/2
67	Forney, Kynan	G	6-3	302	9/8/78	9	Hawaii	Nacogdoches, Texas	FA-'08	0*
85	Gates, Antonio	TE	6-4	260	6/18/80	7	Kent State	Detroit, Mich.	FA-'03	16/16
24	Gordon, Cletis	CB	6-1	205	4/23/83	4	Jackson State	Amite City, La.	FA-'06	14/1
28	Gregory, Steve	CB/S	5-11	195	1/8/83	4	Syracuse	Staten Island, N.Y.	FA-'06	15/3
96	Grennan, Keith	DE	6-4	298	5/20/84	2	Eastern Washington	Edmonds, Wash.	FA-'07	1/0
61	Hardwick, Nick	C	6-4	295	9/2/81	6	Purdue	Indianapolis, Ind.	D3B-'04	13/13
42	Hart, Clinton	S	6-0	208	7/20/77	7	Central Florida CC	Bushnell, Fla.	W(Phil)-'04	14/14
22	Hester, Jacob	FB	5-11	225	5/8/85	2	Louisiana State	Shreveport, La.	D3-'08	16/3
83	Jackson, Vincent	WR	6-5	230	1/14/83	5	Northern Colorado	Colorado Springs, Colo.	D2-'05	16/16
23	Jammer, Quentin	CB	6-0	204	6/19/79	8	Texas	Angleton, Texas	D1-'02	16/16
10	Kaeding, Nate	K	6-0	187	3/26/82	6	Iowa	Coralville, Iowa	D3A-'04	16/0
86	Manumaleuna, Brandon	TE	6-2	295	1/4/80	9	Arizona	Torrance, Calif.	T(StL)-'06	16/11
73	McNeill, Marcus	T	6-7	336	11/16/83	4	Auburn	Ellenwood, Ga.	D2-'06	14/14
56	Merriman, Shawne	LB	6-4	265	5/25/84	5	Maryland	Upper Marlboro, Md.	D1A-'05	1/1
63	Mruczkowski, Scott	C	6-5	325	4/5/82	5	Bowling Green	Garfield Heights, Ohio	D7-'05	16/1
11	Naanee, Legedu	WR	6-2	220	9/16/83	3	Boise State	Portland, Ore.	D5-'07	16/0
27	Oliver, Paul	CB	5-10	210	3/30/84	3	Georgia	Kennesaw, Ga.	D4(Supp)-'07	12/0
81	Osgood, Kassim	WR	6-5	220	5/20/80	7	San Diego State	Salinas, Calif.	FA-'03	16/0
95	Phillips, Shaun	LB	6-3	262	5/13/81	6	Purdue	Willingboro, N.J.	D4-'04	16/16
17	Rivers, Philip	QB	6-5	228	12/8/81	6	North Carolina State	Athens, Ala.	T(NYG)-'04	16/16
5	Scifres, Mike	P	6-2	221	10/8/80	7	Western Illinois	Destrehan, La.	D5-'03	16/0
98	Scott, Ian	DT	6-3	315	11/8/81	7	Florida	Gainesville, Fla.	FA-'08	4/0
70	Shelton, L.J.	T	6-6	345	3/21/76	11	Eastern Michigan	Rochester, Mich.	FA-'08	16/12
59	Siler, Brandon	LB	6-2	239	12/5/85	3	Florida	Orlando, Fla.	D7-'07	15/0
43	Sproles, Darren	RB/KR	5-6	185	6/20/83	5	Kansas State	Olathe, Kan.	D4-'05	16/0
35	Tolbert, Mike	FB	5-9	243	11/23/85	2	Coastal Carolina	Douglasville, Ga.	FA-'08	13/7
21	Tomlinson, LaDainian	RB	5-10	221	6/23/79	9	Texas Christian	Waco, Texas	D1-'01	16/16
94	Tucker, Jyles	LB	6-3	258	9/18/83	3	Wake Forest	Dover, N.J.	FA-'07	13/12
7	Volek, Billy	QB	6-2	214	4/28/76	10	Fresno State	Fresno, Calif.	T(Tenn)-'06	0*
32	Weddle, Eric	S	5-11	200	1/4/85	3	Utah	Alta Loma, Calif.	D2-'07	16/16
6	Whitehurst, Charlie	QB	6-4	220	8/6/82	4	Clemson	Alpharetta, Ga.	D3-'06	0*
57	Wilhelm, Matt	LB	6-4	245	2/2/81	7	Ohio State	Lorain, Ohio	D4-'03	16/7
76	Williams, Jamal	DT	6-3	348	4/28/76	12	Oklahoma State	Washington, D.C.	D2(Supp)-'98	16/15
88	Wilson, Kris	TE	6-2	245	8/22/81	6	Pittsburgh	Lancaster, Pa.	FA-'08	3/0

* Bennett played in 5 games with Tampa Bay in '08; Burnett played 16 games with Dallas; Clark inactive for 13 games; Forney inactive for 13 games; Volek did not play in 16 games; Whitehurst inactive for 16 games.

Players lost through free agency (3): G Mike Goff (KC; 16 games in '08), LB Marquis Harris (SF; 15), DE Igor Olshansky (Dall; 16).

Also played with Chargers in '08—S Tra Battle (1 game), C Jeremy Newberry (16), LB Derek Smith (5), LB Anthony Waters (7).

2009 FIRST-YEAR ROSTER

Name	Pos.	Ht.	Wt.	Birthdate	College	Hometown	How Acq.
Allen, Sam	G	6-4	290	5/11/86	Grand Valley State	Lansing, Mich.	FA
Bakhtiari, Eric (1)	LB	6-3	255	12/2/84	San Diego	Burlingame, Calif.	FA
Banks, Gary (1)	WR	6-0	193	11/4/81	Troy	Melvin, Ala.	FA-'08
Beckwith, Darry	LB	6-0	234	5/15/87	Louisiana State	Baton Rouge, La.	FA
Brinkley, Curtis	RB	5-9	208	9/20/85	Syracuse	Philadelphia, Pa.	FA
Brown, Ramarcus	CB	5-11	179	10/10/84	Georgia	East Point, Ga.	FA
Byrd, Demetrius	WR	6-0	200	6/30/86	Louisiana State	Miami, Fla.	D7
Carr, Greg	WR	6-5	217	10/8/85	Florida State	Reddick, Fla.	FA
Childs, Jeremy	WR	6-0	196	6/29/87	Boise State	Los Alamitos, Calif.	FA
Coleman, Andre (1)	DE	6-3	287	7/26/84	Albany	Buffalo, N.Y.	FA-'07
Dombrowski, Brandyn (1)	T	6-5	323	4/3/85	San Diego State	Henderson, Nev.	FA-'08
Ellison, Kevin	S	6-1	221	1/8/87	Southern California	Inglewood, Calif.	D6
English, Larry	LB	6-2	255	1/22/86	Northern Illinois	Aurora, Ill.	D1
Felder, Anthony	LB	6-2	235	3/16/87	California	Seattle, Wash.	FA
Gay, Dan	T	6-4	303	8/29/86	Baylor	Lafayette, La.	FA
Green, Tyronne	G	6-2	308	4/6/86	Auburn	Pensacola, Fla.	D4b
Holt, James	LB	6-2	223	11/24/86	Kansas	Altus, Okla.	FA
Hughes, Brandon	CB	5-11	181	5/23/86	Oregon State	Bloomington, Ill.	D5
Jackson, Rashaad	DT	6-2	298	1/25/85	Clemson	Union, S.C.	FA
Johnson, Gartrell	RB	5-11	218	6/21/86	Colorado State	Miami Springs, Fla.	D4c
Latsko, Billy (1)	FB	5-10	233	2/16/84	Florida	Gainesville, Fla.	FA-'08
Martin, Charly	WR	6-1	212	3/20/84	West Texas A&M	Farmington, N.M.	FA
Martin, Vaughn	DE	6-4	327	4/18/86	Western Ontario	London, Ontario	D4a
McDonald, Ryan	C	6-4	293	8/21/85	Illinois	Holland, Mich.	FA
Muth, Ben	G	6-6	304	7/17/85	Stanford	Phoenix, Ariz.	FA
Nwagbuo, Ogemdi (1)	DT	6-4	303	12/24/85	Michigan State	Spring Valley, Calif.	FA-'08
Osaisai, Wopamo	CB	5-10	201	9/13/86	Stanford	Pinole, Calif.	FA
Rentmeester, Bill	FB	6-0	247	4/25/86	Wisconsin	Beaver Dam, Wis.	FA
Smith, Rodgeriqus	WR	6-0	200	9/8/85	Auburn	Snellville, Ga.	FA
Sperry, Kory	TE	6-5	244	4/10/85	Colorado State	Vineland, Colo.	FA
Spillman, C.J.	S	6-0	196	5/6/86	Marshall	Louisville, Ky.	FA
Vasquez, Louis	G	6-5	325	4/11/87	Texas Tech	Corsicana, Texas	D3

The term NFL Rookie is defined as a player who is in his first season of professional football and has not been on the roster of another professional football team for any regular-season or postseason games. A Rookie is designated by an "R" on NFL rosters. Players who have been active in another professional football league or players who have NFL experience, including either preseason training camp or being on an Active List or Inactive List, or on Reserve/Injured or Reserve/Physically Unable to Perform for fewer than six regular-season games, are termed NFL First-Year Players. An NFL First-Year Player is designated by a "1" on NFL rosters. Thereafter, a player is credited with an additional year of experience for each season in which he accumulates six games on the Active List or Inactive List, or on Reserve/Injured or Reserve/Physically Unable to Perform.

Log on to www.chargers.com for an up-to-date roster.

SAN DIEGO CHARGERS

COACHING STAFF

Head Coach,
Norv Turner

Pro Career: A veteran coach of 24 NFL seasons, Turner became the 14th head coach in team history on February 19, 2007. In his first two seasons, Turner has led the Chargers to consecutive AFC West titles. In the postseason, he led the Chargers to the 2007 AFC Championship Game and the 2008 Divisional Playoffs. A two-time Super Bowl champion as an offensive coordinator with the Dallas Cowboys, Turner was the offensive coordinator for the San Francisco 49ers in 2006. A Bay Area native from Martinez, California, this is Turner's second stint with the Chargers. He spent the 2001 season as the Bolts' offensive coordinator. Turner's previous 24 years of coaching experience include 11 as a head coach—seven for the Washington Redskins (1994-2000), two with the Oakland Raiders (2004-05), and two with the Chargers (2007-08). In 1999, he led the Redskins to a division title. He spent 13 seasons as an NFL assistant coach, including seven as an offensive coordinator with the Cowboys (1991-93), Chargers (2001), Dolphins (2002-03), and 49ers (2006). Turner began his NFL coaching career as an assistant with the Rams in 1985. He coached wide receivers from 1985-86 before adding the responsibility of the team's tight ends from 1987-1990. Turner made his coaching mark during his three seasons in Dallas as the Cowboys won back-to-back Super Bowls (XXVII and XXVIII) following the 1992 and 1993 seasons. Career record: 81-98-1.

Background: Turner played quarterback at Oregon, spending two seasons behind former Charger and NFL Hall of Fame quarterback Dan Fouts. Turner coached at Oregon (1975) and Southern California (1976-1984). During his nine-year tenure at USC, the Trojans played in four Rose Bowls, winning all four. One of those was a win over Michigan after the 1978 season that capped a 12-1 season and gave USC the National Championship.

Personal: Born in LeJeune, N.C., May 17, 1952. Turner and his wife, Nancy, have three children—Scott, Stephanie, and Drew.

ASSISTANT COACHES

Rob Chudzinski, tight ends/asst. head coach; born May 12, 1968, Toledo, Ohio. Tight end Miami 1986-90. No pro playing experience. College coach: Miami 1994-2003. Pro coach: Cleveland Browns 2004, 2007-08, San Diego Chargers 2005-06, rejoined Chargers in 2009.

Steve Crosby, special teams; born July 3, 1950, Great Bend, Kan. Running back Fort Hayes State 1970-73. Pro running back New York Giants 1974-76. College coach: Vanderbilt 1998-2001. Pro coach: Miami Dolphins 1979-1982, Atlanta Falcons 1983-84, 1986-89, Cleveland Browns 1985, 1991-95, New England Patriots 1990, joined Chargers in 2002.

Cris Dishman, asst. secondary; born August 13, 1965, Louisville, Kentucky. Cornerback Purdue 1984-87. Pro cornerback Houston Oilers 1988-1996, Washington Redskins 1997-98, Kansas City Chiefs 1999, Minnesota Vikings 2000. College coach: Menlo College 2006-08. Pro coach: Joined Chargers in 2009.

Hal Hunter, offensive line; born July 8, 1959, Canonsburg, Pa. Linebacker Northwestern 1978. College coach: William & Mary 1982, Pittsburgh 1983-84, Columbia 1985, Indiana (Pa.) 1986, Akron 1987-1990, Vanderbilt 1991-94, Louisiana State 1995-99, Indiana 2000-01, North Carolina 2002-05. Pro coach: Joined Chargers in 2006.

Jeff Hurd, strength and conditioning; born April 24, 1958, Pomona, Calif. No college or pro playing experience. College coach: Fort Hays State 1984, Delta State 1985-86, Clemson 1986-87, Western Michigan 1987-1992, Tulsa 1994. Pro coach: Jacksonville Jaguars 1995-97, Kansas City Chiefs 1998-2006, joined Chargers in 2007.

Don Johnson, defensive line; born November 3, 1954, Newark, N.J. Linebacker Jersey City State 1973-76. College coach: Jersey City State 1984-85. Riverside (Calif.) C.C. 1987-1990, Cal State-Fullerton 1991-92, Nevada 1995-98, UCLA 1999-2004. Pro coach: Chicago Bears 2005-06, Oakland Raiders 2007-08, joined Chargers in 2009.

Charlie Joiner, receivers; born October 14, 1947, Many, La. Wide receiver Grambling State 1965-68. Pro defensive back/wide receiver Houston Oilers 1969-1972, Cincinnati Bengals 1972-75, San Diego Chargers 1976-1986. Inducted into Pro Football Hall of Fame 1996. Pro coach: San Diego Chargers 1987-1991, Buffalo Bills 1992-2000, Kansas City Chiefs 2001-07, re-joined Chargers in 2008.

John Pagano, outside linebackers; born March 30, 1967, Boulder, Colo. Linebacker Mesa State College 1985-88. No pro playing experience. College coach: Mesa State College 1989, Nevada-Las Vegas 1990-91, Louisiana Tech 1994, Mississippi 1995. Pro coach: New Orleans Saints 1996-97, Indianapolis Colts 1998-2001, joined Chargers in 2002.

John Ramsdell, quarterbacks; born August 16, 1954, Lafayette, Ind. Running back Springfield (Mass.) College 1972-75. No pro playing experience. College coach: San Francisco State 1976-77, Long Beach State 1978, Pacific 1979-1982, Oregon 1983-1994. Pro coach: St. Louis Rams 1995-2005, joined Chargers in 2006.

Ron Rivera, defensive coordinator; born January 7, 1962, Fort Ord, Calif. Linebacker California 1980-83. Pro linebacker Chicago Bears 1984-1992. Pro coach: Chicago Bears 1997-98, 2004-06, Philadelphia Eagles 1999-2003, joined Chargers in 2007.

Clarence Shelmon, offensive coordinator; born September 17, 1952, Bossier City, La. Running back Houston 1971-75. No pro playing experience. College coach: Army 1978-1980, Indiana 1981-83, Arizona 1984-86, Southern California 1987-1990. Pro coach: Los Angeles Rams 1991, Seattle Seahawks 1992-97, Dallas Cowboys 1998-2001, joined Chargers in 2002.

Vernon Stephens, asst. strength and conditioning; born November 30, 1974, Jacksonville. No college or pro playing experience. College coach: North Florida 1999-2002, Colorado 2003-06. Pro coach: Jacksonville Jaguars 2002-03, joined Chargers in 2007.

Mike Sullivan, offensive line; born December 22, 1967, Chicago. Offensive lineman Miami 1986-90. Pro offensive lineman Dallas Cowboys 1991, Tampa Bay Buccaneers 1992-95. College coach: Miami 2000, Western Michigan 2005-06. Pro coach: Cleveland Browns 2001-04, 2007-08, joined Chargers in 2009.

Steven Wilks, secondary; born August 8, 1969, Charlotte. Defensive back Appalachian State 1987-1991. Pro defensive back/wide receiver Charlotte Rage (AFL) 1993. College coach: Johnson C. Smith 1995-96, Savannah State 1997-99, Illinois State 2000, Appalachian State 2001, East Tennessee State 2002, Bowling Green State 2003, Notre Dame 2004, Washington 2005. Pro coach: Chicago Bears 2006-08, joined Chargers in 2009.

Greg Williams, asst. linebackers; born March 12, 1976, Chicago. Wide receiver/defensive back North Carolina 1994-97. Pro defensive back Amsterdam Admirals (NFL Europe) 1999-2000, San Francisco Demons (XFL) 2001, Indiana Firebirds (AFL) 2001-03, Chicago Rush (AFL) 2004. College coach: Arizona State 2003, College of DuPage 2004-05, Arkansas Tech 2006-07, Pittsburgh 2008. Pro coach: Joined Chargers in 2009.

Ollie Wilson, running backs; born March 3, 1951, Worcester, Mass. Wide receiver Springfield 1971-73. No pro playing experience. College coach: Springfield 1975, Northeastern 1976-1982, California 1983-1990. Pro coach: Atlanta Falcons 1991-96, 2002-07, San Diego Chargers 1997-2001, re-joined Chargers in 2008.

American Football Conference
South Division
Team Colors: Navy, Titans Blue, Red, Silver
460 Great Circle Road
Nashville, Tennessee 37228
Telephone: (615) 565-4000

2009 SCHEDULE
PRESEASON

Aug. 9	vs. Buffalo at Canton, OH	8:00
Aug. 15	**Tampa Bay**	7:00
Aug. 21	at Dallas	7:00
Aug. 29	at Cleveland	7:30
Sep. 3	**Green Bay**	7:00

REGULAR SEASON

Sep. 10	at Pittsburgh (Thu.)	8:30
Sep. 20	**Houston**	12:00
Sep. 27	at N.Y. Jets	1:00
Oct. 4	at Jacksonville	1:00
Oct. 11	**Indianapolis**	7:20
Oct. 18	at New England	4:15
Oct. 25	BYE	
Nov. 1	**Jacksonville**	3:05
Nov. 8	at San Francisco	1:15
Nov. 15	**Buffalo**	12:00
Nov. 23	at Houston (Mon.)	7:30
Nov. 29	**Arizona**	12:00
Dec. 6	at Indianapolis	1:00
Dec. 13	**St. Louis**	12:00
Dec. 20	**Miami**	12:00
Dec. 25	**San Diego** (Fri.)	6:30
Jan. 3	at Seattle	1:15

Stadium: LP Field
(opened in 1999)
• **Capacity:** 69,143
One Titans Way
Nashville, Tennessee 37213
Playing Surface: Natural Grass
Training Camp: Baptist Sports Park
460 Great Circle Road
Nashville, TN 37228

LP FIELD

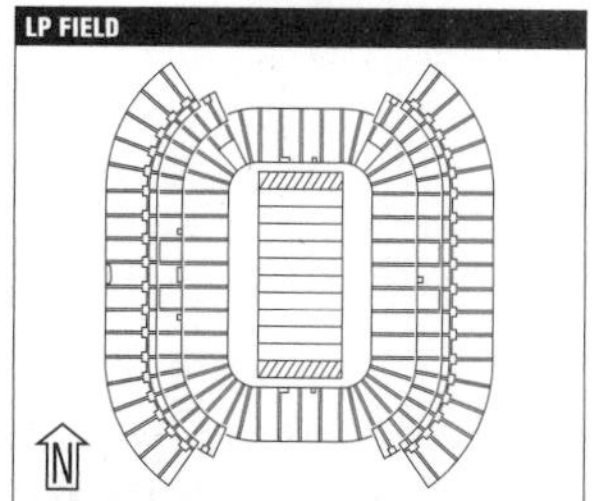

CLUB OFFICIALS
Owner/Chairman of the Board/CEO/ President: K.S. (Bud) Adams, Jr.
Senior Executive V.P./General Counsel: Steve Underwood
Executive V.P./Head Coach: Jeff Fisher
Executive V.P./General Manager: Mike Reinfeldt
Executive V.P. of Administration/Facilities: Don MacLachlan
Vice President/Asst. General Counsel: Elza Bullock
Vice President/Community Affairs: Bob Hyde
Vice President/CFO: Jenneen Kaufman
Senior Director of Football Administration: Vincent Marino
National Supervisor of College Scouting: C.O. Brocato
Eastern Director of College Scouting: Mike Ackerley
Senior Director of Sales and Operations: Stuart Spears
Operations Manager: Brent Akers
Director of Broadcasting: Mike Keith
Vice President/Marketing: Ralph Ockenfels
Director of Information Systems: Russ Hudson
Director of Internet Operations/Publications: Gary Glenn
Director of Media Relations: Robbie Bohren
Asst. Director of Media Relations: Dwight Spradlin
Director of Security: Steve Berk
Senior Director of Ticketing: Marty Collins
Director of Pro Personnel: Lake Dawson
Director of Player Development: Tina Tuggle
Director of Cheerleading: Stacie Kinder
Director of Suite and Club Services: Bill Wainwright
Marketing Manager: Brad McClanahan
Head Athletic Trainer: Brad Brown
Assistant Athletic Trainers: Don Moseley
Equipment Manager: Paul Noska
Video Director: Anthony Pastrana
General Manager of LP Field: Walter Overton
Manager of Community Relations: Tresa Halbrooks
Club Member Manager: Anthony Hall
Head Groundskeeper: Terry Porch

COACHING HISTORY
Houston 1960-1996
(377-390-6)
Records include postseason games

1960-61	Lou Rymkus*	12-7-1
1961	Wally Lemm	10-0-0
1962-63	Frank (Pop) Ivy	17-12-0
1964	Sammy Baugh	4-10-0
1965	Hugh Taylor	4-10-0
1966-1970	Wally Lemm	28-40-4
1971	Ed Hughes	4-9-1
1972-73	Bill Peterson**	1-18-0
1973-74	Sid Gillman	8-15-0
1975-1980	O.A. (Bum) Phillips	59-38-0
1981-83	Ed Biles***	8-23-0
1983	Chuck Studley	2-8-0
1984-85	Hugh Campbell****	8-22-0
1985-89	Jerry Glanville	35-35-0
1990-94	Jack Pardee#	44-35-0
1994-2008	Jeff Fisher	133-108-0

* Released after five games in 1961
** Released after five games in 1973
*** Resigned after six games in 1983
**** Released after 14 games in 1985
\# Released after 10 games in 1994

PAID ATTENDANCE
Home 537,315 Away 512,412
Total 1,049,727
Single-game home record, 69,149, many times (last: 12/18/05)
Single-season home record, 553,192 (2005)

2009 DRAFT CHOICES

Round	Name	Pos.	College
1	Kenny Britt	WR	Rutgers
2	Sen'Derrick Marks	DT	Auburn
3	Jared Cook	TE	South Carolina
	Ryan Mouton	DB	Hawaii
4	Gerald McRath	LB	Southern Mississippi
	Troy Kropog	T	Tulane
5	Javon Ringer	RB	Michigan State
6	Jason McCourty	DB	Rutgers
	Dominique Edison	WR	Stephen F. Austin
7	Ryan Durand	G	Syracuse
	Nick Schommer	DB	North Dakota St.

TENNESSEE TITANS

2008 TEAM RECORD

PRESEASON (3-1)

Date	Result	Opponent
8/9	W 34-13	St. Louis
8/15	W 17-16	Oakland
8/22	L 3-17	at Atlanta
8/28	W 23-21	at Green Bay

REGULAR SEASON (13-3)

Date	Result	Opponent
9/7	W 17-10	Jacksonville
9/14	W 24-7	at Cincinnati
9/21	W 31-12	Houston
9/28	W 30-17	Minnesota
10/5	W 13-10	at Baltimore
10/19	W 34-10	at Kansas City
10/27	W 31-21	Indianapolis
11/2	W 19-16	Green Bay (OT)
11/9	W 21-14	at Chicago
11/16	W 24-14	at Jacksonville
11/23	L 13-34	New York Jets
11/27	W 47-10	at Detroit
12/7	W 28-9	Cleveland
12/14	L 12-13	at Houston
12/21	W 31-14	Pittsburgh
12/28	L 0-23	at Indianapolis

(OT) Overtime

POSTSEASON (0-1)

Date	Result	Opponent
1/10	L 10-13	Baltimore

SCORE BY PERIODS

Titans	63	119	67	123	3	—	375
Opponents	49	87	34	64	0	—	234

2008 TEAM STATISTICS

	Titans	Opp.
Total First Downs	268	276
Rushing	108	81
Passing	143	166
Penalty	17	29
3rd Down: Made/Att	78/216	79/226
3rd Down Pct.	36.1	35.0
4th Down: Made/Att	5/11	8/18
4th Down Pct.	45.5	44.4
Possession Avg.	29:09	30:51
Total Net Yards	5018	4698
Avg. Per Game	313.6	293.6
Total Plays	973	1022
Avg. Per Play	5.2	4.6
Net Yards Rushing	2199	1502
Avg. Per Game	137.4	93.9
Total Rushes	508	403
Net Yards Passing	2819	3196
Avg. Per Game	176.2	199.8
Sacked/Yards Lost	12/83	44/262
Gross Yards	2902	3458
Att./Completions	453/265	575/342
Completion Pct.	58.5	59.5
Had Intercepted	9	20
Punts/Average	87/42.8	87/42.3
Net Punting Avg.	87/36.5	87/36.2
Penalties/Yards	108/855	93/750
Fumbles/Ball Lost	18/8	28/11
Touchdowns	41	25
Rushing	24	12
Passing	13	12
Returns	4	1

2008 INDIVIDUAL STATISTICS

PASSING	Att.	Comp.	Yds.	Pct.	TD	Int.	Tkld.	Rate
Collins	415	242	2676	58.3	12	7	8/60	80.2
Young	36	22	219	61.1	1	2	3/13	64.5
Simms	2	1	7	50.0	0	0	1/10	58.3
Titans	453	265	2902	58.5	13	9	12/83	78.8
Opponents	575	342	3458	59.5	12	20	44/262	69.2

SCORING	TD R	TD P	TD Rt	PAT	FG	Saf	PTS
Bironas	0	0	0	40/40	29/33	0	127
White	15	0	0	0/0	0/0	0	90
C. Johnson	9	1	0	0/0	0/0	0	60
Gage	0	6	0	0/0	0/0	0	36
Hall	0	2	0	0/0	0/0	0	14
Scaife	0	2	0	0/0	0/0	0	12
Ball	0	0	1	0/0	0/0	0	6
Bulluck	0	0	1	0/0	0/0	0	6
Crumpler	0	1	0	0/0	0/0	0	6
Finnegan	0	0	1	0/0	0/0	0	6
Griffin	0	0	1	0/0	0/0	0	6
B. Jones	0	1	0	0/0	0/0	0	6
Titans	24	13	4	40/40	29/33	0	375
Opponents	12	12	1	24/24	20/30	0	234

2-Pt. Conversions: Hall.
Titans 1-1, Opponents 0-1.

RUSHING	No.	Yds	Avg	LG	TD
C. Johnson	251	1228	4.9	66t	9
White	200	773	3.9	80t	15
Ganther	9	61	6.8	22	0
Collins	25	49	2.0	17	0
B. Jones	2	35	17.5	28	0
Young	8	27	3.4	8	0
Hall	8	21	2.6	6	0
McCareins	2	8	4.0	4	0
Henry	1	3	3.0	3	0
Hentrich	2	-6	-3.0	0	0
Titans	508	2199	4.3	80t	24
Opponents	403	1502	3.7	61t	12

RECEIVING	No.	Yds	Avg	LG	TD
Scaife	58	561	9.7	44	2
C. Johnson	43	260	6.0	25	1
B. Jones	41	449	11.0	40	1
Gage	34	651	19.1	56t	6
McCareins	30	412	13.7	37	0
Crumpler	24	257	10.7	28	1
Hall	13	138	10.6	54	2
Hawkins	7	68	9.7	19	0
Ganther	6	43	7.2	15	0
White	5	16	3.2	7	0
C. Davis	2	31	15.5	21	0
Stevens	1	9	9.0	9	0
P. Williams	1	7	7.0	7	0
Titans	265	2902	11.0	56t	13
Opponents	342	3458	10.1	65	12

INTERCEPTIONS	No.	Yds	Avg	LG	TD
Griffin	7	172	24.6	83t	1
Finnegan	5	100	20.0	99t	1
Hope	4	53	13.3	39	0
Harper	2	11	5.5	11	0
Ball	1	15	15.0	15t	1
Carr	1	0	0.0	0	0
Titans	20	351	17.6	99t	3
Opponents	9	88	9.8	33	0

PUNTING	No.	Yds.	Avg.	In 20	LG
Hentrich	87	3725	42.8	27	75
Titans	87	3725	42.8	27	75
Opponents	87	3676	42.3	28	66

PUNT RETURNS	Ret	FC	Yds	Avg	LG	TD
Carr	32	20	323	10.1	44	0
C. Davis	2	1	6	3.0	9	0
Titans	34	21	329	9.7	44	0
Opponents	32	20	290	9.1	34	0

KICKOFF RETURNS	No.	Yds	Avg	LG	TD
Carr	35	984	28.1	52	0
Hawkins	7	130	18.6	23	0
C. Davis	4	119	29.8	33	0
Griffin	2	32	16.0	28	0
Hall	2	21	10.5	13	0
C. Johnson	1	17	17.0	17	0
Stevens	1	16	16.0	16	0
Titans	52	1319	25.4	52	0
Opponents	61	1524	25.0	59	0

FIELD GOALS	1-19	20-29	30-39	40-49	50+
Bironas	0/0	6/6	7/7	15/19	1/1
Titans	0/0	6/6	7/7	15/19	1/1
Opponents	0/0	9/10	6/10	4/8	1/2

SACKS	No.
Haynesworth	8.5
Ford	7.0
J. Jones	5.0
Ball	4.5
Vanden Bosch	4.5
Brown	4.0
Kearse	3.5
Vickerson	1.5
Finnegan	1.0
Griffin	1.0
Hayes	1.0
Hope	1.0
Tulloch	1.0
Bulluck	0.5
Titans	44.0
Opponents	12.0

RECORD HOLDERS

INDIVIDUAL RECORDS—CAREER

Category	Name	Performance
Rushing (Yds.)	Eddie George, 1996-2003	10,009
Passing (Yds.)	Warren Moon, 1984-1993	33,685
Passing (TDs)	Warren Moon, 1984-1993	196
Receiving (No.)	Ernest Givins, 1986-1994	542
Receiving (Yds.)	Ernest Givins, 1986-1994	7,935
Interceptions	Jim Norton, 1960-68	45
Punting (Avg.)	Greg Montgomery, 1988-1993	43.6
Punt Return (Avg.)	Billy Johnson, 1974-1980	13.2
Kickoff Return (Avg.)	Bobby Jancik, 1962-67	26.5
Field Goals	Al Del Greco, 1991-2000	246
Touchdowns (Tot.)	Eddie George, 1996-2003	74
Points	Al Del Greco, 1991-2000	1,060
*Sacks	Ray Childress, 1985-1995	75.5

INDIVIDUAL RECORDS—SINGLE SEASON

Category	Name	Performance
Rushing (Yds.)	Earl Campbell, 1980	1,934
Passing (Yds.)	Warren Moon, 1991	4,690
Passing (TDs)	George Blanda, 1961	36
Receiving (No.)	Charley Hennigan, 1964	101
Receiving (Yds.)	Charley Hennigan, 1961	1,746
Interceptions	Fred Glick, 1963	12
	Mike Reinfeldt, 1979	12
Punting (Avg.)	Craig Hentrich, 1998	47.2
Punt Return (Avg.)	Billy Johnson, 1977	15.4
Kickoff Return (Avg.)	Ken Hall, 1960	31.3
Field Goals	Al Del Greco, 1998	36
Touchdowns (Tot.)	Earl Campbell, 1979	19
Points	Al Del Greco, 1998	136
*Sacks	William Fuller, 1991	15.0

INDIVIDUAL RECORDS—SINGLE GAME

Category	Name	Performance
Rushing (Yds.)	Billy Cannon, 12-10-61	216
	Eddie George, 8-31-97	216
Passing (Yds.)	Warren Moon, 12-16-90	527
Passing (TDs)	George Blanda, 11-19-61	**7
Receiving (No.)	Charley Hennigan, 10-13-61	13
	Haywood Jeffires, 10-13-91	13
	Drew Bennett, 12-19-04	13
Receiving (Yds.)	Charley Hennigan, 10-13-61	272
Interceptions	Many times	3
	Last time by Keith Bulluck, 9-24-07	
Field Goals	Rob Bironas, 10-21-07	**8
Touchdowns (Tot.)	Billy Cannon, 12-10-61	5
Points	Billy Cannon, 12-10-61	30
*Sacks	William Fuller, 11-28-93	4.0

**Sacks became an official statistic in 1982.*
***NFL Record*

TENNESSEE TITANS

2009 VETERAN ROSTER

No.	Name	Pos.	Ht.	Wt.	Birthdate	NFL Exp.	College	Hometown	How Acq.	'08 Games/ Starts
56	Allred, Colin	LB	6-1	238	4/15/83	2	Baylor	Dallas, Texas	FA-'07	12/0
54	Amano, Eugene	G/C	6-3	310	3/1/82	6	Southeast Missouri State	San Diego, Calif.	D7-'04	16/16
58	Amato, Ken	LB/LS	6-2	245	5/18/77	7	Montana State	Miami, Fla.	FA-'03	16/0
98	Ball, Dave	DE	6-5	277	1/4/81	5	UCLA	Fairfield, Calif.	FA-'08	15/3
92	Birdine, Larry	DE	6-4	265	10/6/83	2	Oklahoma	Altus, Okla.	FA-'09	0*
2	Bironas, Rob	K	6-0	215	1/29/78	5	Georgia Southern	Louisville, Ky.	FA-'05	16/0
97	Brown, Tony	DT	6-3	290	9/29/80	5	Memphis	Chattanooga, Tenn.	FA-'06	15/15
53	Bulluck, Keith	LB	6-3	235	4/4/77	10	Syracuse	New City, N.Y.	D1-'00	16/16
5	Collins, Kerry	QB	6-5	245	12/30/72	15	Penn State	Lebanon, Pa.	UFA(Oak)-'06	16/15
48	Cramer, Casey	FB	6-2	250	1/5/82	5	Dartmouth	Middleton, Wis.	FA-'08	9/2*
83	Crumpler, Alge	TE	6-2	262	12/23/77	9	North Carolina	Wilmington, N.C.	FA-'08	15/15
67	Datish, Doug	C/G	6-4	305	8/1/83	2	Ohio State	Warren, Ohio	FA-'08	0*
17	Davis, Chris	WR	5-10	181	1/23/84	3	Florida State	St. Petersburg, Fla.	D4b-'07	5/0
38	Faggins, DeMarcus	CB	5-10	178	6/13/79	8	Kansas State	Irving, Texas	UFA(Hou)-'09	16/5*
31	Finnegan, Cortland	CB	5-10	188	2/2/84	4	Samford	Milton, Fla.	D7a-'06	16/16
78	Ford, Jacob	DE	6-4	256	7/20/83	3	Central Arkansas	Memphis, Tenn.	D6b-'07	14/3
52	Fowler, Ryan	LB	6-3	250	5/20/82	6	Duke	Redington Shores, Fla.	RFA(Dall)-'07	16/4
22	Fuller, Vincent	S	6-1	190	8/3/82	5	Virginia Tech	Baltimore, Md.	D4a-'05	16/1
12	Gage, Justin	WR	6-4	212	1/24/81	7	Missouri	Jefferson City, Mo.	UFA(Chi)-'07	12/11
35	Ganther, Quinton	RB	5-9	214	7/15/84	2	Utah	Richmond, Calif.	D7c-'06	13/0
33	Griffin, Michael	S	6-0	202	1/4/85	3	Texas	Austin, Texas	D1-'07	16/16
45	Hall, Ahmard	FB	5-11	242	11/13/79	4	Texas	Angleton, Texas	FA-'06	16/11
20	Harper, Nick	CB	5-10	182	9/10/74	9	Fort Valley State	Baldwin, Ga.	UFA(Ind)-'07	13/12
64	Harris, Leroy	G/C	6-3	302	6/6/84	3	North Carolina State	Raleigh, N.C.	D4a-'07	16/1
26	Harris, Tuff	DB	6-0	198	1/23/83	3	Montana	Colstrip, Mont.	FA-'08	6/0
87	Hawkins, Lavelle	WR	5-11	190	7/12/86	2	California	Stockton, Calif.	D4b-'08	13/1
75	Haye, Jovan	DT	6-2	285	6/21/82	5	Vanderbilt	Sunrise, Fla.	UFA(TB)-'09	15/14*
95	Hayes, William	DE	6-3	272	5/2/85	2	Winston-Salem State	High Point, N.C.	D4a-'08	8/0
42	Henry, Chris	RB	5-11	230	6/6/85	3	Arizona	Oakland, Calif.	D2-'07	1/0
15	Hentrich, Craig	P/K	6-3	213	5/18/71	16	Notre Dame	Alton, Ill.	UFA(GB)-'98	16/0
21	#Hill, Reynaldo	CB	5-11	185	8/28/82	5	Florida	Ft. Lauderdale, Fla.	D7-'05	5/0
24	Hope, Chris	S	6-0	208	9/29/80	8	Florida State	Rock Hill, S.C.	UFA(Pitt)-'06	16/16
28	Johnson, Chris	RB	5-11	200	9/23/85	2	East Carolina	Orlando, Fla.	D1-'08	15/14
91	Jones, Jason	DT	6-5	275	5/23/86	2	Eastern Michigan	Detroit, Mich.	D2-'08	13/3
84	Jones, Mark	WR	5-9	185	11/3/80	6	Tennessee	Wallingford, Pa.	UFA(Car)-'09	16/0*
90	Kearse, Jevon	DE	6-4	265	9/3/76	11	Florida	Ft. Myers, Fla.	FA-'08	16/16
59	Keglar, Stanford	LB	6-2	240	7/4/85	2	Purdue	Indianapolis, Ind.	D4c-'08	13/0
36	Little, Rafael	RB	5-9	195	9/23/86	2	Kentucky	Anderson, S.C.	FA-'08	0*
68	Mawae, Kevin	C	6-4	289	1/23/71	16	Louisiana State	Leesville, La.	UFA(NYJ)-'06	15/15
19	#McCareins, Justin	WR	6-2	215	12/1/78	9	Northern Illinois	Naperville, Ill.	FA-'08	14/10
37	Morton, Christian	CB	6-0	190	4/28/81	4	Illinois	St. Louis, Mo.	FA-'09	0*
23	Nickey, Donnie	S	6-3	210	4/25/80	7	Ohio State	Plain City, Ohio	D5-'03	16/0
66	Otto, Mike	T	6-5	308	7/24/83	2	Purdue	Kokomo, Ind.	D7-'07	1/0
38	#Poole, Tyrone	CB	5-8	190	2/3/72	12	Fort Valley State	LaGrange, Ga.	FA-'08	2/0
99	Ramsey, LaJuan	DT	6-3	300	3/19/84	3	Southern California	Compton, Calif.	FA-'09	4/0*
7	Ramsey, Patrick	QB	6-2	225	2/14/79	8	Tulane	Ruston, La.	UFA(Den)-'09	1/0*
71	Roos, Michael	T	6-7	315	10/5/82	5	Eastern Washington	Vancouver, Wash.	D2-'05	16/16
80	Scaife, Bo	TE	6-3	249	1/6/81	5	Texas	Denver, Colo.	D6-'05	16/7
73	Scott, Jake	G	6-5	295	4/16/81	6	Idaho	Lewiston, Idaho	UFA(Ind)-'08	16/16
57	Stamer, Josh	LB	6-2	242	10/11/77	7	South Dakota	Sutherland, Iowa	UFA(Buff)-'08	16/1
88	Stevens, Craig	TE	6-3	255	9/1/84	2	California	San Pedro, Calif.	D3-'08	16/2
76	Stewart, David	T	6-7	318	8/28/82	5	Mississippi State	Moulton, Ala.	D4b-'05	16/16
50	Thornton, David	LB	6-2	225	11/1/78	8	North Carolina	Goldsboro, N.C.	UFA(Ind)-'06	15/15
14	Thorpe, Craphonso	WR	6-0	187	6/27/83	2	Florida State	Tallahassee, Fla.	FA-'09	0*
55	Tulloch, Stephen	LB	5-11	235	1/1/85	4	North Carolina State	Miami, Fla.	D4b-'06	16/12
93	Vanden Bosch, Kyle	DE	6-4	278	11/17/78	9	Nebraska	Larchwood, Iowa	UFA(Ariz)-'05	10/10
96	Vickerson, Kevin	DT	6-5	305	1/8/83	4	Michigan State	Detroit, Mich.	FA-'07	7/0
85	Washington, Nate	WR	6-1	185	8/28/83	5	Tiffin	Toledo, Ohio	UFA(Pitt)-'09	16/1*
25	White, LenDale	RB	6-1	235	12/20/84	4	Southern California	Park Hill, Colo.	D2-'06	16/2
11	Williams, Paul	WR	6-1	205	12/2/83	3	Fresno State	Avenal, Calif.	D3-'07	5/0
79b	Winkler, Ulrich	DE	6-5	265	1/4/84	2	None	Munich, Germany	FA-'07	0*
10	Young, Vince	QB	6-5	233	5/18/83	4	Texas	Houston, Texas	D1-'06	3/1

* Birdine last active with Denver in '07; Cramer played 9 games with Miami; Datish last active with Atlanta in '07; Faggins played 16 games with Houston in '08; Haye played 15 games with Tampa Bay; M. Jones played 16 games with Carolina; Little spent entire season on reserve/non-football injury list; Morton last active with Carolina in '06; L. Ramsey played 4 games with Indianapolis; P. Ramsey played 1 game with Denver; Thorpe last active with Indianapolis in '07; Washington played 16 games with Pittsburgh; Winkler missed '08 season because of injury.

\# Unrestricted free agent; subject to developments.

Players lost through free agency (6): DB Chris Carr (Balt; 16 games in '08), DT Albert Haynesworth (Wash; 14), WR Brandon Jones (SF; 16), CB Eric King (Det; 10), T/G Daniel Loper (Det; 16), QB Chris Simms (Den; 1).

Also played with Titans in '08—DT Amon Gordon (2 games), CB Cary Williams (1).

2009 FIRST-YEAR ROSTER

Name	Pos.	Ht.	Wt.	Birthdate	College	Hometown	How Acq.
Bennett, Charles (1)	DE	6-4	245	4/4/83	Clemson	Camden, S.C.	FA-'08
Britt, Kenny	WR	6-3	218	9/19/88	Rutgers	Bayonne, N.J.	D1
Clifford, Pete (1)	T	6-7	312	4/3/84	Michigan State	Salem, N.H.	FA
Cook, Jared	TE	6-5	246	4/7/87	South Carolina	Suwanee, Ga.	D3a
Davis, Tanard (1)	CB	5-9	184	1/27/83	Miami	Miami, Fla.	FA-'08
Durand, Ryan	G	6-5	305	11/17/85	Syracuse	Leominster, Mass.	D7a
Edison, Dominique	WR	6-2	204	7/16/86	Stephen F. Austin	San Augustine, Texas	D6b
Ferguson, Rodney	RB	5-11	245	8/25/86	New Mexico	Albuquerque, N.M.	FA
Guice, Dudley	WR	6-3	209	5/28/86	Northwestern State	Fayette, Miss.	FA
Haynes, Jeremy	CB	5-10	185	3/2/86	McNeese State	Waller, Texas	FA
Jones, Derrick (1)	DT	6-4	282	11/14/84	Grand Valley State	Barstow, Calif.	FA-'08
King, Mitch	DT	6-2	280	5/5/86	Iowa	Burlington, Iowa	FA
Kropog, Troy	T/G	6-6	309	7/31/86	Tulane	Metairie, La.	D4b
Marks, Sen'Derrick	DT	6-2	306	2/23/87	Auburn	Mobile, Ala.	D2
McCourty, Jason	CB	6-0	193	8/13/87	Rutgers	Nanuet, N.Y.	D6a
McRath, Gerald	LB	6-3	231	6/16/86	Southern Mississippi	Powder Springs, Ga.	D4a
Morris, Phillip	WR	6-3	175	7/2/86	South Carolina State	Timmonsville, S.C.	FA
Mortensen, Alex	QB	6-1	222	11/24/85	Arkansas	Fairburn, Ga.	FA
Mouton, Ryan	CB	5-9	187	9/23/86	Hawaii	Katy, Texas	D3b
Mulligan, Matthew (1)	TE	6-4	265	1/18/85	Maine	Enfield, Maine	FA-'08
Murphy, Jason (1)	C	6-2	304	8/7/82	Virginia Tech	Baltimore, Md.	FA-'07
Ringer, Javon	RB	5-9	205	2/2/87	Michigan State	Dayton, Ohio	D5
Schmidt, Ryan	G	6-4	330	8/30/86	South Florida	Boca Raton, Fla.	FA
Schommer, Nick	S	6-0	201	1/3/86	North Dakota State	Prescott, Wis.	D7b
Trapasso, A.J.	P	5-11	225	2/6/86	Ohio State	Pickerington, Ohio	FA
Velasco, Fernando (1)	C/G	6-4	304	2/22/85	Georgia	Wrens, Ga.	FA-'08
Williams, Cary (1)	CB	6-1	185	12/23/84	Washburn	Hollywood, Fla.	D7-'08

The term NFL Rookie is defined as a player who is in his first season of professional football and has not been on the roster of another professional football team for any regular-season or postseason games. A Rookie is designated by an "R" on NFL rosters. Players who have been active in another professional football league or players who have NFL experience, including either preseason training camp or being on an Active List or Inactive List, or on Reserve/Injured or Reserve/Physically Unable to Perform for fewer than six regular-season games, are termed NFL First-Year Players. An NFL First-Year Player is designated by a "1" on NFL rosters. Thereafter, a player is credited with an additional year of experience for each season in which he accumulates six games on the Active List or Inactive List, or on Reserve/Injured or Reserve/Physically Unable to Perform.

Log on to www.titansonline.com for an up-to-date roster.

COACHING STAFF
Head Coach,
Jeff Fisher

Pro Career: Officially became the franchise's fifteenth head coach on January 5, 1995, after closing his first campaign with the Oilers as head coach/defensive coordinator. He replaced Jack Pardee on November 14, 1994, coaching the remaining six games as head coach. Fisher holds the franchise mark for wins with 133 over his 14-year coaching career. In 2008, Fisher, the NFL's current leader in head coaching tenure, led the Titans to their sixth playoff appearance in the past 10 years. Tennessee's 13-3 record, which included a franchise-best 10 consecutive wins to start the season, matched the best record in franchise history and led to an AFC South title. He moved into 22nd place in NFL history in career wins among head coaches, and he ranks 10th in league history in games coached with one team (240). Fisher has led the Titans to two AFC Championship Games and a berth in Super Bowl XXXIV. In 2000, Fisher became only the fifth coach in NFL history to lead his team to consecutive 13-win seasons, joining Mike Holmgren, George Seifert, Marv Levy, and Mike Ditka. Fisher originally joined the Oilers in 1994 as the defensive coordinator, after serving as defensive backs coach for the San Francisco 49ers (1992-93). Prior to heading up the 49ers secondary, Fisher served as the defensive coordinator for the Los Angeles Rams (1991). He began his coaching career with the Philadelphia Eagles in 1986, where he handled defensive backs until becoming the NFL's youngest defensive coordinator in 1988. Drafted by Chicago in seventh round in 1981, he spent five seasons as a cornerback and kick returner for the Bears (1981-85). Assisted defensive coordinator Buddy Ryan in Bears' 1985 Super Bowl championship season after being placed on injured reserve with ankle injury. Career record: 120-104.

Background: Played at Southern California (1977-1980) for John Robinson in a star-studded defensive backfield that included Ronnie Lott, Dennis Smith, and Joey Browner. Member of the USC team that won the national championship in 1978. Also served as the Trojans' backup placekicker and was a Pac-10 All-Academic selection in 1980.

Personal: Born February 25, 1958, in Culver City, Calif. Fisher has three children, sons Brandon and Trenton, and daughter Tara.

ASSISTANT COACHES

Earnest Byner, running backs; born September 15, 1962, Milledgeville, Ga. Running back East Carolina 1980-83. Pro running back Cleveland Browns 1984-88, 1994-95, Washington Redskins 1989-1993, Baltimore Ravens 1996-97. Pro coach: Washington Redskins 2004-07, joined Titans in 2008.

Chuck Cecil, defensive coordinator; born November 8, 1964, Red Bluff, Calif. Defensive back Arizona 1983-87. Pro safety Green Bay Packers 1988-1992, Phoenix Cardinals 1993, Houston Oilers 1995. Pro coach: Joined Titans in 2001.

Marty Galbraith, asst. special teams; born February 3, 1950, Joplin, Mo. Defensive back Missouri Southern 1971-73. No pro playing experience. College coach: Purdue 1977, Wake Forest 1978-1982, Louisiana State 1987-88, Wake Forest 1989-1990, Pittsburgh 1991, Georgia Tech 1992-93, Marshall 1998-99, North Carolina State 2000-02, Duke 2004. Pro coach: Tampa Bay Bandits (USFL) 1983-84, Kansas City Chiefs 1985, Arizona Outlaws (USFL) 1986, Arizona Cardinals 2003, joined Titans in 2005.

Fred Graves, wide receivers; born March 2, 1950, Los Angeles, Calif. Halfback/split end Utah 1968-1971. Pro halfback California Suns 1973 (World Football League). College coach: Northeast Missouri State 1975-76, Western Illinois 1977-78, New Mexico State 1979-1981, Utah 1982-2000. Pro coach: Buffalo Bills 2001-03, Cleveland Browns 2004, Detroit Lions 2005, joined Titans in 2007.

Tim Hauck, asst. secondary; born December 20, 1966, Butte, Mont. Defensive back Pacific 1985, Montana 1986-89. Pro safety New England Patriots 1990, Green Bay Packers 1991-94, Denver Broncos 1995-96, Seattle Seahawks 1997, Indianapolis Colts 1998, Philadelphia Eagles 1999-2002, San Francisco 49ers 2002. College coach: Montana 2004-07, UCLA 2008. Pro coach: Joined Titans in 2009.

Mike Heimerdinger, offensive coordinator; born October 13, 1952, DeKalb, Ill. Wide receiver Eastern Illinois 1970-74. No pro playing experience. College coach: Florida 1980, Air Force 1981, North Texas State 1982, Florida 1983-87, Cal State-Fullerton 1988, Rice 1989-1993, Duke 1994. Pro coach: Denver Broncos 1995-99, Tennessee Titans 2000-04, N.Y. Jets 2005, Denver Broncos 2006-07, re-joined Titans in 2008.

Craig Johnson, quarterbacks; born March 3, 1960, Rome, N.Y. Quarterback Wyoming 1978-1982. No pro playing experience. College coach: Wyoming 1983, Arkansas 1984, Army 1985, Rutgers 1986-88, Virginia Military Institute 1989-1991, Northwestern 1992-96, Maryland 1997-99. Pro coach: Joined Titans in 2000.

Dowell Loggains, offensive quality control; born October 1, 1980, Newport, Ark. Quarterback Arkansas 2000-04. No pro playing experience. Pro coach: Dallas Cowboys 2005, joined Titans in 2006.

Alan Lowry, special teams; born November 21, 1950, Miami, Okla. Defensive back/quarterback Texas 1970-72. No pro playing experience. College coach: Virginia Tech 1974, Wyoming 1975, Texas 1977-1981. Pro coach: Dallas Cowboys 1982-1990, Tampa Bay Buccaneers 1991, San Francisco 49ers 1992-95, joined Titans/Oilers in 1996.

Dave McGinnis, linebackers; born August 7, 1951, Independence, Kan. Defensive back Texas Christian 1970-72. No pro playing experience. College coach: Texas Christian 1973-74, 1982, Missouri 1975-77, Indiana State 1978, 1980-81, Kansas State 1983-85. Pro coach: Chicago Bears 1986-1995, Arizona Cardinals 1996-2003 (head coach 2000-2003), joined Titans in 2004.

Mike Munchak, offensive line; born March 5, 1960, Scranton, Pa. Guard-tackle Penn State 1979-1981. Pro guard Houston Oilers 1982-1993. Inducted into Pro Football Hall of Fame 2001. Pro coach: Joined Titans/Oilers in 1994.

Marcus Robertson, defensive backs; born October 2, 1969, Pasadena, Calif. Defensive back Iowa State 1987-1990. Pro safety Houston Oilers/Tennessee Titans 1991-2000, Seattle Seahawks 2001-02. Pro coach: Joined Titans in 2007.

Rayna Stewart, defensive quality control; born June 18, 1973, Oklahoma City, Okla. Defensive back/linebacker Northern Arizona 1992-95. Pro defensive back Houston/Tennessee Oilers 1996-97, Miami Dolphins 1998, Jacksonville Jaguars 1999-2000. College coach: Northwestern 2007-08. Pro coach: Joined Titans in 2009.

Jim Washburn, defensive line; born December 2, 1949, Shelby, N.C. Offensive lineman Gardner-Webb 1969-1973. No pro playing experience. College coach: Southern Methodist 1976, Lees McRae (N.C.) J.C. 1977-78, Livingston 1979, New Mexico 1980-82, South Carolina 1983-88, Purdue 1989, Arkansas 1994-97, Houston 1998. Pro coach: London Monarchs (WLAF) 1991, Charlotte Rage (AFL) 1993, joined Titans in 1999.

Steve Watterson, strength and rehabilitation; born November 27, 1956, Newport, R.I. Attended Rhode Island. No college or pro playing experience. Pro coach: Philadelphia Eagles 1984-85, joined Titans/Oilers in 1986.

John Zernhelt, tight ends, born January 4, 1954, Pottsville, Pa. Offensive lineman Maryland 1974-77. No pro playing experience. College coach: Ferrum 1977-1980, Marshall 1981, East Carolina 1982-86, Maryland 1987-1991, Rice 1992-93, Duke 1994-95, South Carolina 1996-98, James Madison 1999-2002, The Citadel 2003-04. Pro coach: New York Jets 2005, joined Titans in 2006.

The NFC

National Football Conference
West Division
Team Colors: Cardinal Red, Black, and White
P.O. Box 888
Phoenix, Arizona 85001-0888
Telephone: (602) 379-0101

2009 SCHEDULE

PRESEASON

Aug. 13	at Pittsburgh	8:00
Aug. 22	**San Diego**	7:00
Aug. 28	**Green Bay**	7:00
Sep. 3	at Denver	7:00

REGULAR SEASON

Sep. 13	**San Francisco**	1:15
Sep. 20	at Jacksonville	1:00
Sep. 27	**Indianapolis**	5:20
Oct. 4	BYE	
Oct. 11	**Houston**	1:15
Oct. 18	at Seattle	1:05
Oct. 25	at N.Y. Giants	8:20
Nov. 1	**Carolina**	2:15
Nov. 8	at Chicago	12:00
Nov. 15	**Seattle**	2:15
Nov. 22	at St. Louis	3:05
Nov. 29	at Tennessee	12:00
Dec. 6	**Minnesota**	2:15
Dec. 14	at San Francisco (Mon.)	5:30
Dec. 20	at Detroit	1:00
Dec. 27	**St. Louis**	2:05
Jan. 3	**Green Bay**	2:15

Stadium: University of Phoenix Stadium (opened in 2006)
• **Capacity:** 65,000
1 Cardinals Drive
Glendale, Arizona 85305
Playing Surface: Grass
Training Camp: Northern Arizona University Flagstaff, Arizona 86011

UNIVERSITY OF PHOENIX STADIUM

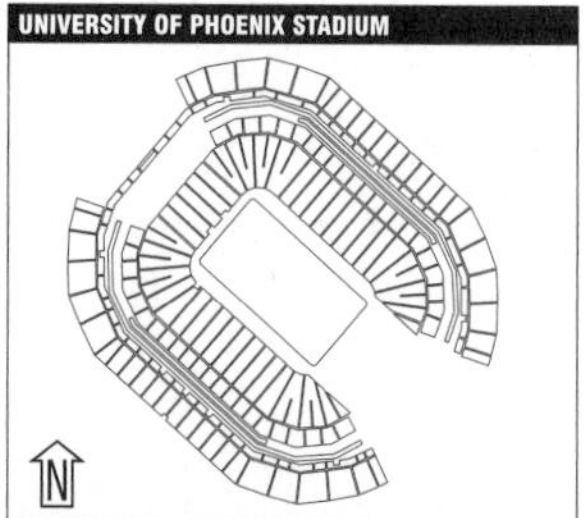

CLUB OFFICIALS

Owner: William V. Bidwill
President: Michael Bidwill
General Manager: Rod Graves
Executive Vice President/Chief Operating Officer: Ron Minegar
Chief Financial Officer: Adrian Bracy
Vice President, Media Relations: Mark Dalton
Vice President, Marketing: Lisa Manning
Vice President, Business Development: Steve Ryan
Vice President, Information Technology: Mark Feller
Vice President, Security: Rick Knight
Vice President, Stadium Operations: John Drum
Senior Director, Player Programs: Anthony Edwards
Senior Director, Community Relations: Luis Zendejas
Senior Director, Ticketing: Steve Bomar
Senior Director, Ticket Sales: Ron Campbell
Director, Player Personnel: Steve Keim
Director, Pro Personnel: T.J. McCreight
Director, Football Administration: Reggie Terry
Director, Cardinals Charities: Pat Tankersley
Director, Broadcasting/Executive Producer: Tim DeLaney
Director, Cheerleading: Heather Karberg
Website Manager: Darren Urban
Video Director: Rob Brakel
Head Athletic Trainer: Tom Reed
Assistant Athletic Trainers: Jim Shearer, Jeff Herndon, Freddie Carbajal
Equipment Manager: Mark Ahlemeier
Assistant Equipment Manager: Steve Christensen

COACHING HISTORY

Chicago 1920-1959, St. Louis 1960-1987 (478-680-39)

Records include postseason games

1920-22	John (Paddy) Driscoll	17-8-4
1923-24	Arnold Horween	13-8-1
1925-26	Norman Barry	16-8-2
1927	Guy Chamberlin	3-7-1
1928	Fred Gillies	1-5-0
1929	Dewey Scanlon	6-6-1
1930	Ernie Nevers	5-6-2
1931	LeRoy Andrews*	0-1-0
1931	Ernie Nevers	5-3-0
1932	Jack Chevigny	2-6-2
1933-34	Paul Schissler	6-15-1
1935-38	Milan Creighton	16-26-4
1939	Ernie Nevers	1-10-0
1940-42	Jimmy Conzelman	8-22-3
1943-45	Phil Handler**	1-29-0
1946-48	Jimmy Conzelman	27-10-0
1949	Phil Handler-Buddy Parker***	2-4-0
1949	Raymond (Buddy) Parker	4-1-1
1950-51	Earl (Curly) Lambeau****	7-15-0
1951	Phil Handler-Cecil Isbell#	1-1-0
1952	Joe Kuharich	4-8-0
1953-54	Joe Stydahar	3-20-1
1955-57	Ray Richards	14-21-1
1958-1961	Frank (Pop) Ivy##	15-31-2
1961	Chuck Drulis-Ray Prochaska-Ray Willsey###	2-0-0
1962-65	Wally Lemm	27-26-3
1966-1970	Charley Winner	35-30-5
1971-72	Bob Hollway	8-18-2
1973-77	Don Coryell	42-29-1
1978-79	Bud Wilkinson####	9-20-0
1979	Larry Wilson	2-1-0
1980-85	Jim Hanifan	39-50-1
1986-89	Gene Stallings@	23-34-1
1989	Hank Kuhlmann	0-5-0
1990-93	Joe Bugel	20-44-0
1994-95	Buddy Ryan	12-20-0
1996-2000	Vince Tobin@@	29-44-0
2000-03	Dave McGinnis	17-40-0
2004-06	Dennis Green	16-32-0
2007-08	Ken Whisenhunt	20-16-0

* Resigned after one game in 1931
** Co-coach with Walt Kiesling in Chicago Cardinals-Pittsburgh merger in 1944
*** Co-coaches for first six games in 1949
**** Resigned after 10 games in 1951
\# Co-coaches
\## Resigned after 12 games in 1961
\### Co-coaches
\#### Released after 13 games in 1979
@ Released after 11 games in 1989
@@ Released after seven games in 2000

PAID ATTENDANCE

Home 500,077 Away 556,885
Total 1,056,962
Single-game home record, 73,025* (9/19/93)
Single-season home record, 516,646 (2007)
*Team holds NFL attendance record of 103,467 for home game at Azteca Stadium, Mexico City, Mexico

2009 DRAFT CHOICES

Round	Name	Pos.	College
1	Beanie Wells	RB	Ohio State
2	Cody Brown	LB	Connecticut
3	Rashad Johnson	DB	Alabama
4	Gregory Toler	DB	St. Paul's (Va.)
5	Herman Johnson	G	Louisiana State
6	Will Davis	LB	Illinois
7	LaRod Stephens-Howling	RB	Pittsburgh
	Trevor Canfield	G	Cincinnati

ARIZONA CARDINALS

2008 TEAM RECORD

PRESEASON (2-2)

Date	Result	Opponent
8/7	L 10-24	New Orleans
8/16	W 27-17	at Kansas City
8/23	W 24-0	at Oakland
8/29	L 14-28	Denver

REGULAR SEASON (9-7)

Date	Result	Opponent
9/07	W 23-13	at San Francisco
9/14	W 31-10	Miami
9/21	L 17-24	at Washington
9/28	L 35-56	at New York Jets
10/5	W 41-17	Buffalo
10/12	W 30-24	Dallas (OT)
10/26	L 23-27	at Carolina
11/2	W 34-13	at St. Louis
11/10	W 29-24	San Francisco
11/16	W 26-20	at Seattle
11/23	L 29-37	New York Giants
11/27	L 20-48	at Philadelphia
12/7	W 34-10	St. Louis
12/14	L 14-35	Minnesota
12/21	L 7-47	at New England
12/28	W 34-21	Seattle

(OT) Overtime

POSTSEASON (3-1)

Date	Result	Opponent
1/3	W 30-24	Atlanta
1/10	W 33-13	at Carolina
1/18	W 32-25	Philadelphia
2/1	L 23-27	vs. Pittsburgh, at Tampa, Florida

SCORE BY PERIODS

	1	2	3	4	OT	Total
Cardinals	64	117	154	86	6	— 427
Opponents	84	150	81	111	0	— 426

2008 TEAM STATISTICS

	Cardinals	Opp.
Total First Downs	328	312
Rushing	72	117
Passing	231	172
Penalty	25	23
3rd Down: Made/Att	83/198	92/207
3rd Down Pct.	41.9	44.4
4th Down: Made/Att	8/16	13/17
4th Down Pct.	50.0	76.5
Possession Avg.	30:09	29:51
Total Net Yards	5852	5304
Avg. Per Game	365.8	331.5
Total Plays	998	993
Avg. Per Play	5.9	5.3
Net Yards Rushing	1178	1764
Avg. Per Game	73.6	110.3
Total Rushes	340	445
Net Yards Passing	4674	3540
Avg. Per Game	292.1	221.3
Sacked/Yards Lost	28/201	31/191
Gross Yards	4875	3731
Att./Completions	630/418	517/323
Completion Pct.	66.3	62.5
Had Intercepted	15	13
Punts/Average	60/41.8	61/45.5
Net Punting Avg.	60/34.1	61/40.0
Penalties/Yards	107/781	98/816
Fumbles/Ball Lost	27/15	26/17
Touchdowns	51	52
Rushing	14	13
Passing	31	36
Returns	6	3

2008 INDIVIDUAL STATISTICS

PASSING	Att.	Comp.	Yds.	Pct.	TD	Int.	Tkld.	Rate
Warner	598	401	4583	67.1	30	14	26/182	96.9
Leinart	29	15	264	51.7	1	1	2/19	80.2
Arrington	1	0	0	0.0	0	0	0/0	39.6
D. Johnson	1	1	10	100.0	0	0	0/0	108.3
Urban	1	1	18	100.0	0	0	0/0	118.8
Cardinals	630	418	4875	66.3	31	15	28/201	96.1
Opponents	517	323	3731	62.5	36	13	31/191	96.9

SCORING	TD R	TD P	TD Rt	PAT	FG	Saf	PTS
Rackers	0	0	0	44/44	25/28	0	119
Fitzgerald	0	12	0	0/0	0/0	0	72
Boldin	0	11	0	0/0	0/0	0	66
Hightower	10	0	0	0/0	0/0	0	60
Urban	0	4	0	0/0	0/0	0	24
James	3	0	0	0/0	0/0	0	20
Arrington	1	1	1	0/0	0/0	0	18
Breaston	0	3	0	0/0	0/0	0	18
Beisel	0	0	1	0/0	0/0	0	6
Dockett	0	0	1	0/0	0/0	0	6
Hood	0	0	1	0/0	0/0	0	6
Rodgers-Cromartie	0	0	1	0/0	0/0	0	6
Rolle	0	0	1	0/0	0/0	0	6
Cardinals	14	31	6	44/44	25/28	0	427
Opponents	13	36	3	49/49	21/27	0	426

2-Pt. Conversions: James.
Cardinals 1-6, Opponents 1-3.

RUSHING	No.	Yds	Avg	LG	TD
James	133	514	3.9	35	3
Hightower	143	399	2.8	30t	10
Arrington	31	187	6.0	30	1
Boldin	9	67	7.4	30	0
Breaston	2	8	4.0	4	0
Leinart	4	5	1.3	8	0
Warner	18	-2	-0.1	11	0
Cardinals	340	1178	3.5	35	14
Opponents	445	1764	4.0	41t	13

RECEIVING	No.	Yds	Avg	LG	TD
Fitzgerald	96	1431	14.9	78t	12
Boldin	89	1038	11.7	79t	11
Breaston	77	1006	13.1	58	3
Urban	34	448	13.2	56t	4
Hightower	34	237	7.0	26	0
Arrington	29	255	8.8	35	1
Doucet	14	90	6.4	12	0
James	12	85	7.1	16	0
Patrick	11	104	9.5	19	0
Pope	9	77	8.6	25	0
Castille	4	11	2.8	5	0
Tuman	3	41	13.7	18	0
T. Smith	2	24	12.0	18	0
Spach	2	15	7.5	8	0
Rolle	1	9	9.0	9	0
L. Brown	1	4	4.0	4	0
Cardinals	418	4875	11.7	79t	31
Opponents	323	3731	11.6	87t	36

INTERCEPTIONS	No.	Yds	Avg	LG	TD
Rodgers-Cromartie	4	157	39.3	99t	1
Dansby	2	47	23.5	34	0
Wilson	2	37	18.5	28	0
Rolle	1	40	40.0	40t	1
Okeafor	1	39	39.0	39	0
Green	1	1	1.0	1	0
R. Brown	1	0	0.0	0	0
Hood	1	0	0.0	0	0
Cardinals	13	321	24.7	99t	2
Opponents	15	276	18.4	58	1

PUNTING	No.	Yds.	Avg.	In 20	LG
D. Johnson	40	1670	41.8	13	59
Graham	20	839	42	7	59
Cardinals	60	2509	41.8	20	59
Opponents	61	2777	45.5	20	63

PUNT RETURNS	Ret	FC	Yds	Avg	LG	TD
Breaston	33	10	237	7.2	25	0
Cardinals	33	10	237	7.2	25	0
Opponents	29	13	381	13.1	82t	1

KICKOFF RETURNS	No.	Yds	Avg	LG	TD
Arrington	36	923	25.6	93t	1
Breaston	33	667	20.2	38	0
Morey	2	23	11.5	15	0
Campbell	2	16	8.0	16	0
Urban	2	1	0.5	1	0
Cardinals	75	1630	21.7	93t	1
Opponents	69	1724	25.0	104t	1

FIELD GOALS	1-19	20-29	30-39	40-49	50+
Rackers	0/0	9/9	9/11	6/6	1/2
Cardinals	0/0	9/9	9/11	6/6	1/2
Opponents	0/0	4/4	9/11	5/8	3/4

SACKS	No.
Berry	5.0
Okeafor	4.5
Dansby	4.0
Dockett	4.0
LaBoy	4.0
A. Smith	3.5
Wilson	2.5
Haggans	1.0
Robinson	1.0
Watson	1.0
Hayes	0.5
Cardinals	31.0
Opponents	28.0

RECORD HOLDERS

INDIVIDUAL RECORDS—CAREER

Category	Name	Performance
Rushing (Yds.)	Ottis Anderson, 1979-1986	7,999
Passing (Yds.)	Jim Hart, 1966-1983	34,639
Passing (TDs)	Jim Hart, 1966-1983	209
Receiving (No.)	Larry Centers, 1990-98	535
Receiving (Yds.)	Roy Green, 1979-1990	8,497
Interceptions	Larry Wilson, 1960-1972	52
Punting (Avg.)	Jerry Norton, 1959-1961	44.9
Punt Return (Avg.)	Charley Trippi, 1947-1955	13.7
Kickoff Return (Avg.)	Ollie Matson, 1952, 1954-58	28.5
Field Goals	Jim Bakken, 1962-1978	282
Touchdowns (Tot.)	Roy Green, 1979-1990	70
Points	Jim Bakken, 1962-1978	1,380
*Sacks	Freddie Joe Nunn, 1985-1993	66.5

INDIVIDUAL RECORDS—SINGLE SEASON

Category	Name	Performance
Rushing (Yds.)	Ottis Anderson, 1979	1,605
Passing (Yds.)	Neil Lomax, 1984	4,614
Passing (TDs)	Kurt Warner, 2008	30
Receiving (No.)	Larry Fitzgerald, 2005	103
Receiving (Yds.)	David Boston, 2001	1,598
Interceptions	Bob Nussbaumer, 1949	12
Punting (Avg.)	Jerry Norton, 1960	45.6
Punt Return (Avg.)	John (Red) Cochran, 1949	20.9
Kickoff Return (Avg.)	Ollie Matson, 1958	35.5
Field Goals	Neil Rackers, 2005	**40
Touchdowns (Tot.)	John David Crow, 1962	17
Points	Neil Rackers, 2005	140
*Sacks	Simeon Rice, 1999	16.5

INDIVIDUAL RECORDS—SINGLE GAME

Category	Name	Performance
Rushing (Yds.)	LeShon Johnson, 9-22-96	214
Passing (Yds.)	Boomer Esiason, 11-10-96 (OT)	522
Passing (TDs)	Jim Hardy, 10-2-50	6
	Charley Johnson, 9-26-65, 11-2-69	6
Receiving (No.)	Sonny Randle, 11-4-62	16
Receiving (Yds.)	Sonny Randle, 11-4-62	256
Interceptions	Bob Nussbaumer, 11-13-49	**4
	Jerry Norton, 11-20-60	**4
	Kwamie Lassiter, 12-27-98	**4
Field Goals	Jim Bakken, 9-24-67	7
Touchdowns (Tot.)	Ernie Nevers, 11-28-29	**6
Points	Ernie Nevers, 11-28-29	**40
*Sacks	Curtis Greer, 12-18-83	4.5

**Sacks became an official statistic in 1982.*
***NFL Record*

ARIZONA CARDINALS

2009 VETERAN ROSTER

No.	Name	Pos.	Ht.	Wt.	Birthdate	NFL Exp.	College	Hometown	How Acq.	'08 Games/ Starts
27	Adams, Michael	CB	5-8	181	6/17/85	3	Louisiana-Lafayette	Dallas, Texas	FA-'07	5/1
84	Becht, Anthony	TE	6-6	270	8/8/77	10	West Virginia	Drexel Hill, Pa.	FA-'09	16/11*
92	Berry, Bertrand	DE	6-3	254	8/15/75	12	Notre Dame	Houston, Texas	UFA(Den)-'04	14/4
81	Boldin, Anquan	WR	6-1	217	10/3/80	7	Florida State	Pahokee, Fla.	D2-'03	12/11
78	Branch, Alan	DT	6-5	338	12/29/84	3	Michigan	Rio Rancho, N.M.	D2-'07	4/0
15	Breaston, Steve	WR	6-0	189	8/20/83	3	Michigan	North Braddock, Pa.	D5-'07	16/10
61	Brown, Elton	G/T	6-5	338	5/22/82	5	Virginia	Hampton, Va.	D4-'05	16/0
75	Brown, Levi	T	6-5	324	3/16/84	3	Penn State	Norfolk, Va.	D1-'07	16/16
20	Brown, Ralph	CB	5-10	185	9/16/78	10	Nebraska	LaPuenta, Calif.	UFA(Cle)-'07	16/3
39	Byrd, Dominique	TE	6-3	255	2/7/84	3	Southern California	Minneapolis, Minn.	FA-'09	0*
93	Campbell, Calais	DE	6-8	290	9/1/86	2	Miami	Aurora, Colo.	D2-'08	16/0
46	Castille, Tim	FB	5-11	238	5/29/84	3	Alabama	Birmingham, Ala.	FA-'07	14/0
62	Claxton, Ben	C	6-2	301	7/30/80	3	Mississippi	Dublin, Ga.	FA-'09	0*
58	Dansby, Karlos	LB	6-4	250	11/3/81	6	Auburn	Birmingham, Ala.	D2-'04	16/16
90	Dockett, Darnell	DT	6-4	285	5/27/81	6	Florida State	Burtonsville, Md.	D3-'04	16/16
80	Doucet, Early	WR	6-0	212	10/28/85	2	Louisiana State	St. Martinville, La	D3-'08	7/0
11	Fitzgerald, Larry	WR	6-3	217	8/31/83	6	Pittsburgh	Minneapolis, Minn.	D1-'04	16/16
47	Francisco, Aaron	FS	6-2	207	7/5/83	5	Brigham Young	Laie, Hawaii	FA-'05	16/4
69	Gandy, Mike	T	6-4	316	1/3/79	9	Notre Dame	Dallas, Texas	UFA(Buff)-'07	16/16
5	Graham, Ben	P	6-5	235	11/2/73	5	Deakin (Australia)	Geelong, Australia	FA-'08	4/0
33	Green, Justin	FB	6-0	246	4/30/82	4	Montana	San Diego, Calif.	FA-'09	0*
53	Haggans, Clark	LB	6-4	243	1/10/77	10	Colorado State	Torrance, Calif.	UFA(Pitt)-'08	11/0
54	Hayes, Gerald	MLB	6-1	246	10/10/80	7	Pittsburgh	Paterson, N.J.	D3-'03	16/14
95	Highsmith, Ali	LB	6-1	230	1/20/85	2	Louisiana State	Miami, Fla.	FA-'08	6/0
34	Hightower, Tim	RB	6-0	222	5/23/86	2	Richmond	Alexandria, Va.	D5-'08	16/7
57	Hobson, Victor	LB	6-0	254	2/3/80	7	Michigan	Mt. Laurel, N.J.	FA-'08	1/0
91	Iwebema, Kenny	DE	6-4	280	2/6/85	2	Iowa	Arlington, Texas	D4-'08	13/0
72	Keith, Brandon	T	6-5	338	11/21/84	2	Northern Iowa	McAlester, Okla.	D7-'08	0*
35	Kreider, Dan	FB	5-11	250	3/11/77	10	New Hampshire	Lancaster, Pa.	FA-09	11/4*
48	Leach, Mike	LS	6-2	238	10/18/76	10	William & Mary	Jefferson Township, N.J.	FA-'09	16/0*
7	Leinart, Matt	QB	6-5	232	5/11/83	4	Southern California	Santa Ana, Calif.	D1-'06	4/0
94	Leisle, Rodney	DT	6-3	315	2/5/81	5	UCLA	Bakersfield, Calif.	FA-'09	0*
28	Lewis, Keith	S	6-1	222	10/20/81	6	Oregon	Sacramento, Calif.	FA-'09	16/0*
76	Lutui, Deuce	G	6-4	338	5/5/83	4	Southern California	Mesa, Ariz.	D2-'06	16/16
25	McFadden, Bryant	CB	6-0	190	11/21/81	5	Florida State	Florence, S.C.	UFA(Pitt)-'09	10/8*
87	Morey, Sean	WR	5-11	193	2/26/76	8	Brown	Marshfield, Mass.	UFA(Pitt)-'07	16/0
56	Okeafor, Chike	OLB	6-5	256	3/27/76	11	Purdue	Grand Rapids, Mich.	UFA(Sea)-'05	16/16
3	Palko, Tyler	QB	6-1	215	8/9/83	2	Pittsburgh	Imperial, Pa.	FA-'09	0*
89	Patrick, Ben	TE	6-3	264	8/23/84	3	Delaware	Savannah, Ga.	D7-'07	10/3
82	Pope, Leonard	TE	6-8	264	9/10/83	4	Georgia	Americus, Ga.	D3-'06	13/8
1	Rackers, Neil	K	6-1	206	8/16/76	10	Illinois	St. Louis, Mo.	FA-'03	16/0
97	Robinson, Bryan	DT	6-4	304	6/22/74	13	Fresno State	Toledo, Ohio	UFA(Cin)-'08	16/15
29	Rodgers-Cromartie, Dominique	CB	6-2	182	4/7/86	2	Tennessee State	Bradenton, Fla.	D1-'08	16/11
21	Rolle, Antrel	S	6-0	208	12/16/82	5	Miami	Homestead, Fla.	D1-'05	16/16
79	Ross, Oliver	T	6-5	315	9/27/74	12	Iowa State	Los Angeles, Calif.	FA-'09	0*
63	Sendlein, Lyle	C	6-3	305	3/16/84	3	Texas	Scottsdale, Ariz.	FA-'07	16/16
83	Spach, Stephen	TE	6-4	260	7/18/82	4	Fresno State	Clovis, Calif.	FA-'08	9/6
2	St. Pierre, Brian	QB	6-3	224	11/28/79	7	Boston College	Salem, Mass.	UFA(Pitt)-'08	0*
51	Togafau, Pago	LB	5-11	240	1/10/84	3	Idaho State	Long Beach, Calif.	FA-'08	6/0
85	Urban, Jerheme	WR	6-3	207	11/26/80	6	Trinity	Victoria, Texas	W(Dall)-'07	16/2
68	Vallejo, Elliot	T	6-7	312	5/17/84	2	UC Davis	Salinas, Calif.	FA-'07	0*
22	Ware, Matt	S	6-2	215	12/2/82	6	UCLA	Los Angeles, Calif.	W(Phil)-'06	13/1
13	Warner, Kurt	QB	6-2	214	6/22/71	12	Northern Iowa	Burlington, Iowa	UFA(NYG)-'05	16/16
98	Watson, Gabe	DT	6-4	329	9/24/83	4	Michigan	Southfield, Mich.	D4-'06	11/0
74	Wells, Reggie	G	6-4	312	11/3/80	7	Clarion (Pa.)	Library, Pa.	D6a-'03	16/16
24	Wilson, Adrian	SS	6-3	226	10/12/79	9	North Carolina State	High Point, N.C.	D3-'01	15/14
31	Wright, Jason	RB	5-10	212	7/12/82	5	Northwestern	Diamond Bar, Calif.	UFA(Cle)-'09	15/0*

* Becht played 16 games with St. Louis in '08; Byrd last active with St. Louis in '07; Claxton last on injured reserve for Atlanta in '06; Green last active with Baltimore in '07; Keith was inactive for 16 games; Kreider played 11 games with St. Louis; Leach played 16 games for Denver; Lewis played 16 games with San Francisco; Leisle last active with New Orleans in '06; McFadden played 10 games with Pittsburgh; Palko did not play in 4 games with New Orleans in '07; Ross missed '08 season because of injury with New England; St. Pierre inactive for 16 games; Vallejo did not play in 4 games; Wright played 15 games with Cleveland.

Players lost through free agency (5): RB J.J. Arrington (Den; 11 games in '08), LB Monty Beisel (KC; 16), CB Eric Green (Mia; 13), DE Antonio Smith (Hou; 16), FB Terrelle Smith (Det; 15).

Also played with Cardinals in '08—S Oliver Celestin (2 games), LS Nathan Hodel (16), CB Roderick Hood (15), RB Edgerrin James (13), P Dirk Johnson (12), DE Travis LaBoy (13), TE Jerame Tuman (3).

2009 FIRST-YEAR ROSTER

Name	Pos.	Ht.	Wt.	Birthdate	College	Hometown	How Acq.
Banks, Jason (1)	DE	6-5	296	5/8/85	Grambling State	Baton Rouge, La.	FA-'08
Brown, Cody	LB	6-3	244	11/9/86	Connecticut	Coral Springs, Fla.	D2
Brown, Justin	WR	6-2	200	3/11/87	Hampton	Dover, N.J.	FA
Bullock, Chase	LB	6-3	234	2/13/86	Maryland	Durham, N.C.	FA
Canfield, Trevor	G	6-5	307	1/10/86	Cincinnati	Cincinnati, Ohio	D7b
Davis, Tony	CB	5-10	195	9/9/86	Penn State	Warren, Ohio	FA
Davis, Will	LB	6-2	261	6/2/86	Illinois	Greenbelt, Md.	D6
Dykes, Keilen (1)	DT	6-3	305	9/6/84	West Virginia	Youngstown, Ohio	FA-'08
Dowling, Jameel	CB	6-3	205	12/29/84	Hawaii	Tacoma, Wash.	FA
Fontenot, Wilrey (1)	CB	5-10	169	10/14/84	Arizona	Dallas, Texas	FA-'08
Garvin, Michael Ray	WR	5-8	182	9/29/86	Florida State	Upper Saddle River, N.J.	FA
Johnson, Herman	G/T	6-7	382	1/29/85	Louisiana State	Denton, Texas	D5
Johnson, Rashad	S	5-11	203	1/2/86	Alabama	Sulligent, Ala.	D3
Jones, Onrea (1)	WR	6-0	202	12/22/83	Hampton	Williamsburg, Va.	FA-'08
Keyes, Dennis (1)	S	6-2	203	3/26/85	UCLA	Canoga Park, Calif.	FA-'08
Long, Lance (1)	WR	5-11	186	5/4/85	Mississippi State	Macomb, Mich.	FA-'08
Medder, Carlton (1)	G	6-5	315	12/1/84	Florida	Clermont, Fla.	FA
Morales, Shane	WR	6-1	209	12/12/86	Oregon State	Valencia, Calif.	FA
Pearce, Brandon	T	6-6	290	8/28/85	Memphis	Memphis, Tenn.	FA
Prather, Waylon (1)	P	6-3	225	2/16/85	San Jose State	Felton, Calif.	FA
Raiola, Donovan (1)	C	6-2	300	12/13/82	Wisconsin	Honolulu, Hawaii	FA
Shor, Alex (1)	TE	6-8	254	1/29/83	Syracuse	Panama City, Fla.	FA-'06
Stephens-Howling, LaRod	RB	5-7	180	4/26/87	Pittsburgh	Johnstown, Pa.	D7a
Toler, Greg	CB	6-0	191	1/2/85	Saint Paul's (Va.)	Washington, D.C.	D4
Vincent, Chris (1)	RB	6-1	218	9/3/81	Oregon	Philadelphia, Pa.	FA
Walker, Reggie	LB	6-0	238	12/15/86	Kansas State	Sacramento, Calif.	FA
Wells, Beanie	RB	6-1	228	8/7/88	Ohio State	Akron, Ohio	D1

The term NFL Rookie is defined as a player who is in his first season of professional football and has not been on the roster of another professional football team for any regular-season or postseason games. A Rookie is designated by an "R" on NFL rosters. Players who have been active in another professional football league or players who have NFL experience, including either preseason training camp or being on an Active List or Inactive List, or on Reserve/Injured or Reserve/Physically Unable to Perform for fewer than six regular-season games, are termed NFL First-Year Players. An NFL First-Year Player is designated by a "1" on NFL rosters. Thereafter, a player is credited with an additional year of experience for each season in which he accumulates six games on the Active List or Inactive List, or on Reserve/Injured or Reserve/Physically Unable to Perform.

Log on to www.azcardinals.com for an up-to-date roster.

COACHING STAFF

Head Coach, Ken Whisenhunt

Pro Career: Became an NFL head coach for the first time when hired by Arizona on January 14, 2007, bringing 10 years of experience as an NFL assistant and nine as a tight end. Arizona's 8-8 mark in his first season was the team's best record since going 9-7 in 1998. The 2008 season brought the franchise's first postseason appearance since 1998, first division crown since 1975, and first home playoff game since 1947. It ended with the team's first-ever conference title and Super Bowl appearance. Arizona's 12 total wins in 2008 were the most in team history and the Cardinals won more postseason contests in January (3) than they had in their entire history (2). In the 36 total games played in Whisenhunt's two seasons as head coach, the Cardinals have scored 20-or-more points in 29 of them (80.6%) and 30-plus points in 16 (44.4%). Whisenhunt is just the second Cardinals head coach to go .500 or better in each of his first two seasons (Arnie Horween 1923-24) and the team's 12-4 home record in that span is the best in the NFC. In 2007, Arizona set a franchise record for passing TDs in a season (32) and the team's point total of 404 was the second-highest in team history. In 2008, the Cardinals' offense was again explosive and scored a franchise record 427 total points. They added 188 more points in the postseason, the third-highest total in NFL postseason history. Prior to joining the Cardinals, Whisenhunt spent the previous six seasons as an assistant on Bill Cowher's staff with the Pittsburgh Steelers, the first three as tight ends coach and the last three as offensive coordinator. Whisenhunt took over as Pittsburgh's offensive coordinator in 2004, the same year the team drafted quarterback Ben Roethlisberger, who went on to set an NFL record with wins in his first 13 career starts en route to Offensive Rookie of the Year honors. The next season he became the youngest quarterback in NFL history to win a Super Bowl and finished third in the league in passer rating (98.6). He joined the Steelers in January of 2001 as tight ends coach. Whisenhunt previously coached at the pro level with the New York Jets (tight ends, 2000), Cleveland Browns (special teams, 1999) and Baltimore Ravens (tight ends, 1997-98). He began his coaching career in the collegiate ranks with Vanderbilt for two seasons (1995-96). Whisenhunt was selected in the 12th round of the 1985 NFL Draft by the Atlanta Falcons out of Georgia Tech. He went on to play nine NFL seasons with the Falcons (1985-88), Washington Redskins (1989-90), and New York Jets (1991-93). In 74 career games (37 starts), he caught 62 passes for 601 yards and 6 touchdowns. Career record: 20-16.

Background: After going to Georgia Tech as a walk-on, he played four seasons as a tight end/H-back. He finished his college playing career ranked second on the Yellow Jackets' receiving yardage list (1,264 yards) and fourth in career receptions (82). Whisenhunt was a consensus All-ACC and honorable mention All-America selection as a senior in 1984 when he averaged 19.1 yards-per-catch.

Personal: Born February 28, 1962 in Atlanta. Whisenhunt earned a degree in civil engineering from Georgia Tech. Ken and his wife, Alice, have two children—son, Kenneth, Jr. and daughter, Mary Ashley.

ASSISTANT COACHES

Ron Aiken, defensive line; born August 18, 1955, Moncks Corner, S.C. Guard/center North Carolina A&T 1973-76. No pro playing experience. College coach: Bethany College 1979-1981, Tarkio College 1982-84, Rensselaer Polytechnic Institute 1985, Langston 1986-89, New Mexico 1990-94, Vanderbilt 1995-96, Texas 1997, San Diego State 1998, Iowa 1999-2006. Pro coach: Joined Cardinals in 2007.

Teryl Austin, defensive backs; born March 3, 1965, Sharon, Pa. Defensive back Pittsburgh 1984-87. Pro defensive back Montreal Machine (WLAF) 1991. College coach: Penn State 1991-92, Wake Forest 1993-95, Syracuse 1996-98, Michigan 1999-2002. Pro coach: Seattle Seahawks 2003-06, joined Cardinals in 2007.

Rick Courtright, asst. defensive backs; born January 4, 1961, Miami. Linebacker Wheaton College 1980-83. No pro playing experience. College coach: Washington 1991-92, Minnesota-Morris 1993, Ohio 1994, Idaho State 1995, Idaho 1996-99, Murray State 2000, Western Illinois 2001-03. Pro coach: Joined Cardinals in 2004.

Bill Davis, defensive coordinator; born November 5, 1965, Youngstown, Ohio. Quarterback Cincinnati 1984-88. College coach: Michigan State 1990-91. Pro coach: Pittsburgh Steelers 1992-94, Carolina Panthers 1995-98, Cleveland Browns 1999, Green Bay Packers 2000, Atlanta Falcons 2001-03, New York Giants 2004, San Francisco 49ers 2005-06, joined Cardinals in 2007.

Chad Grimm, offensive quality control; born May 18, 1985, Fairfax, Va. Linebacker Virginia Tech 2003-06. No pro playing experience. Pro coach: Joined Cardinals in 2009.

Russ Grimm, asst. head coach/run game coordinator/offensive line; born May 2, 1959, Scottdale, Pa. Center Pittsburgh 1977-1980. Pro guard Washington Redskins 1981-1991. Pro coach: Washington Redskins 1992-2000, Pittsburgh Steelers 2001-06, joined Cardinals in 2007.

Freddie Kitchens, tight ends; born November 29, 1974, Gadsden, Ala. Quarterback Alabama 1994-97. No pro playing experience. College coach: Glenville State College 1999, Louisiana State 2000, North Texas 2001-03, Mississippi State 2004-05. Pro coach: Dallas Cowboys 2006, joined Cardinals in 2007.

John Lott, strength and conditioning; born May 9, 1964, Denton, Texas. Offensive lineman North Texas 1983-86. Pro offensive lineman Pittsburgh Steelers 1987. College coach: North Texas 1989-1990, Houston 1991-96. Pro coach: New York Jets 1997-2004, Cleveland Browns 2005-06, joined Cardinals in 2007.

John McNulty, wide receivers; born May 29, 1968, Scranton, Pa. Safety Penn State 1988-1990. No pro playing experience. College coach: Michigan 1991-94, Connecticut 1995-97, Rutgers 2004-08. Pro coach: Jacksonville Jaguars 1998-2002, Dallas Cowboys 2003, joined Cardinals in 2009.

Chris Miller, quarterbacks; born August 9, 1965, Pomona, Calif. Quarterback Oregon 1983-86. Pro quarterback Atlanta Falcons 1987-1993, St. Louis Rams 1994-95, Denver Broncos 1999. Pro coach: Joined Cardinals in 2009.

Mike Miller, passing game coordinator; born April 9, 1970, Plum Borough, Pa. Attended Clarion. No college or pro playing experience. College coach: Robert Morris 1997-98, 2006. Pro coach: Pittsburgh Steelers 1999-2003, Buffalo Bills 2004-05, Berlin Thunder (NFLE) 2006, joined Cardinals in 2007.

Curtis Modkins, running backs; born November 15, 1970, Marlin, Texas. Running back TCU 1989-1992. No pro playing experience. College coach: TCU 1995-97, New Mexico 1998-2001, Georgia Tech 2002-07. Pro coach: Kansas City Chiefs 2008, joined Cardinals in 2009.

Matt Raich, linebackers; born August 16, 1970, Monaca, Pa. Middle linebacker Westminster College 1989-1992. No pro playing experience. College coach: Westminster 1993-94, Robert Morris 1996-98, 2000-02, Glenville State 1999. Pro coach: Pittsburgh Steelers 2004-06, joined Cardinals in 2007.

Ryan Slowik, defensive quality control; born Dec. 27, 1980, Chicago. Safety Wisconsin-Oshkosh 2002-03. No pro playing experience. College coach: Wisconsin-Oshkosh 2004. Pro coach: Denver Broncos 2005-08, joined Cardinals in 2009.

Kevin Spencer, special teams; born November 2, 1953, Queens, N.Y. Outside linebacker Springfield College 1971. No pro playing experience. College coach: SUNY-Cortland 1975-76, Cornell 1979-1980, Ithaca 1981-86, Wesleyan 1987-1991. Pro coach: Cleveland Browns 1991-94, Oakland Raiders 1995-97, Indianapolis Colts 1998-2001, Pittsburgh Steelers 2002-06, joined Cardinals in 2007.

National Football Conference
South Division
Team Colors: Black, Red, Silver, and White
4400 Falcon Parkway
Flowery Branch, Georgia 30542
Telephone: (770) 965-3115

2009 SCHEDULE

PRESEASON

Aug. 15	at Detroit	4:00
Aug. 21	at St. Louis	7:00
Aug. 29	**San Diego**	8:00
Sep. 3	**Baltimore**	7:30

REGULAR SEASON

Sep. 13	**Miami**	1:00
Sep. 20	**Carolina**	1:00
Sep. 27	at New England	1:00
Oct. 4	BYE	
Oct. 11	at San Francisco	1:05
Oct. 18	**Chicago**	8:20
Oct. 25	at Dallas	3:15
Nov. 2	at New Orleans (Mon.)	7:30
Nov. 8	**Washington**	1:00
Nov. 15	at Carolina	1:00
Nov. 22	at N.Y. Giants	1:00
Nov. 29	**Tampa Bay**	1:00
Dec. 6	**Philadelphia**	1:00
Dec. 13	**New Orleans**	1:00
Dec. 20	at N.Y. Jets	1:00
Dec. 27	**Buffalo**	1:00
Jan. 3	at Tampa Bay	1:00

Stadium: Georgia Dome
(opened in 1992)
• **Capacity:** 71,228
One Georgia Dome Drive
Atlanta, Georgia 30313
Playing Surface: FieldTurf
Training Camp: Atlanta Falcons
4400 Falcon Parkway
Flowery Branch, GA 30542

GEORGIA DOME

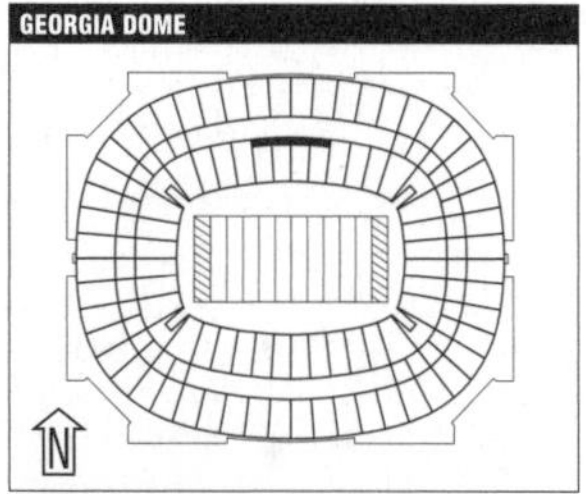

CLUB OFFICIALS

Owner & CEO: Arthur M. Blank
President: Rich McKay
General Manager: Thomas Dimitroff
Head Coach: Mike Smith
Director of Human Resources: Karen Walters
Vice President & CFO: Greg Beadles
Controller: Rob Geoffroy
Vice President of Football Communications: Reggie Roberts
Vice President of Information Technology: Danny Branch
Vice President of Marketing: Jim Smith
Vice President of Sales: Dave Cohen
Senior Director of Media Relations: Frank Kleha
Senior Director of Player Development: Kevin Winston
Director of Logistics and Facilities: Spencer Treadwell
Director of Ticket Operations: Mike Gilsenan
Director of Event Marketing: Roddy White
Director of Football Operations: Nick Polk
Director of Player Personnel: Les Snead
Director of College Scouting: David Caldwell
Director of Community Relations: Kendyl Baugh Moss
Assistant Director of Player Personnel: Lionel Vital
Eastern Regional Scout: Marvin Allen
Western Regional Scout: Mark Olson
Area Scouts: Bob Harrison, Shepley Heard, Bob Kronenberg, Taylor Morton, Robinson Payne, Bruce Plummer
Pro Scouts: Ran Carthon, DeJuan Polk
Scouting Assistant: Anthony Robinson
Head Athletic Trainer: Ron Medlin
Assistant Athletic Trainer: Andre Tucker
Rehabilitation Coordinator: Scott Kneller
Video Director: Mike Crews
Video Assistants: Phil Tieman, Daniel Wayne
Equipment Manager: Brian Boigner
Director of Sponsorship Sales: Tim Zulawski
Director of Retail: Chris DiPierri
Director of New Media: Dan Levak
Football Communications Manager: Matt Conti
Football Communications Coordinator: Brian Cearns

COACHING HISTORY
(273-392-6)

Records include postseason games

1966-68	Norb Hecker*	4-26-1
1968-1974	Norm Van Brocklin**	37-49-3
1974-76	Marion Campbell***	6-19-0
1976	Pat Peppler	3-6-0
1977-1982	Leeman Bennett	47-44-0
1983-86	Dan Henning	22-41-1
1987-89	Marion Campbell****	11-32-0
1989	Jim Hanifan	0-4-0
1990-93	Jerry Glanville	28-38-0
1994-96	June Jones	19-30-0
1997-2003	Dan Reeves#	52-61-1
2003	Wade Phillips	2-1-0
2004-06	Jim Mora	27-23-0
2007	Bobby Petrino##	3-10-0
2007	Emmitt Thomas	1-2-0
2008	Mike Smith	11-6-0

*Released after three games in 1968
**Released after eight games in 1974
***Released after five games in 1976
****Retired after 12 games in 1989
#Released after 13 games in 2003
##Resigned after 13 games in 2007

PAID ATTENDANCE

Home 500,970 Away 526,760
Total 1,027,730
Single-game home record, 71,151 (10/22/06)
Single-season home record, 553,979 (1992)

2009 DRAFT CHOICES

Round	Name	Pos.	College
1	Peria Jerry	DT	Mississippi
2	William Moore	DB	Missouri
3	Christopher Owens	DB	San Jose State
4	Lawrence Sidbury	DE	Richmond
5	William Middleton	DB	Furman
	Garrett Reynolds	T	North Carolina
6	Spencer Adkins	LB	Miami
7	Vance Walker	DT	Georgia Tech

ATLANTA FALCONS

2008 TEAM RECORD

PRESEASON (2-2)

Date	Result	Opponent
8/9	L 17-20	at Jacksonville
8/16	L 9-16	Indianapolis
8/22	W 17-3	Tennessee
8/28	W 10-9	at Baltimore

REGULAR SEASON (11-5)

Date	Result	Opponent
9/7	W 34-21	Detroit
9/14	L 9-24	at Tampa Bay
9/21	W 38-14	Kansas City
9/28	L 9-24	at Carolina
10/5	W 27-24	at Green Bay
10/12	W 22-20	Chicago
10/26	L 14-27	at Philadelphia
11/2	W 24-0	at Oakland
11/9	W 34-20	New Orleans
11/16	L 20-24	Denver
11/23	W 45-28	Carolina
11/30	W 22-16	at San Diego
12/7	L 25-29	at New Orleans
12/14	W 13-10	Tampa Bay (OT)
12/21	W 24-17	at Minnesota
12/28	W 31-27	St. Louis

(OT) Overtime

POSTSEASON (0-1)

Date	Result	Opponent
1/3	L 24-30	at Arizona

SCORE BY PERIODS

	1	2	3	4	OT		Total
Falcons	114	120	43	111	3	—	391
Opponents	52	87	60	126	0	—	325

2008 TEAM STATISTICS

	Falcons	Opp.
Total First Downs	313	309
Rushing	131	108
Passing	157	189
Penalty	25	12
3rd Down: Made/Att	95/219	79/208
3rd Down Pct.	43.4	38.0
4th Down: Made/Att	6/13	10/20
4th Down Pct.	46.2	50.0
Possession Avg.	30:49	29:11
Total Net Yards	5779	5572
Avg. Per Game	361.2	348.3
Total Plays	1011	998
Avg. Per Play	5.7	5.6
Net Yards Rushing	2443	2046
Avg. Per Game	152.7	127.9
Total Rushes	560	415
Net Yards Passing	3336	3526
Avg. Per Game	208.5	220.4
Sacked/Yards Lost	17/104	34/245
Gross Yards	3440	3771
Att./Completions	434/265	549/325
Completion Pct.	61.1	59.2
Had Intercepted	11	10
Punts/Average	65/39.5	76/45.5
Net Punting Avg.	65/37.5	76/39.2
Penalties/Yards	71/591	109/854
Fumbles/Ball Lost	18/10	18/8
Touchdowns	43	38
Rushing	23	17
Passing	16	20
Returns	4	1

2008 INDIVIDUAL STATISTICS

PASSING	Att.	Comp.	Yds.	Pct.	TD	Int.	Tkld.	Rate
Ryan	434	265	3440	61.1	16	11	17/104	87.7
Falcons	434	265	3440	61.1	16	11	17/104	87.7
Opponents	549	325	3771	59.2	20	10	34/245	84.6

SCORING	TD R	TD P	TD Rt	PAT	FG	Saf	PTS
Elam	0	0	0	42/42	29/31	0	129
Turner	17	0	0	0/0	0/0	0	102
White	0	7	0	0/0	0/0	0	42
Norwood	4	2	0	0/0	0/0	0	36
Jenkins	0	3	0	0/0	0/0	0	20
Douglas	1	1	1	0/0	0/0	0	18
Peelle	0	2	0	0/0	0/0	0	12
Blalock	0	0	1	0/0	0/0	0	6
Finneran	0	1	0	0/0	0/0	0	6
Houston	0	0	1	0/0	0/0	0	6
C. Jackson	0	0	1	0/0	0/0	0	6
Ryan	1	0	0	0/0	0/0	0	6
Falcons	23	16	4	42/42	29/31	1	391
Opponents	17	20	1	35/35	20/25	0	325

2-Pt. Conversions: Jenkins.
Falcons 1-1, Opponents 1-3.

RUSHING	No.	Yds	Avg	LG	TD
Turner	376	1699	4.5	70	17
Norwood	95	489	5.1	45t	4
Ryan	55	104	1.9	17	1
Douglas	12	69	5.8	33	1
Snelling	15	62	4.1	13	0
Mughelli	5	16	3.2	9	0
White	2	4	2.0	2	0
Falcons	560	2443	4.4	70	23
Opponents	415	2046	4.9	68t	17

RECEIVING	No.	Yds	Avg	LG	TD
White	88	1382	15.7	70t	7
Jenkins	50	777	15.5	62t	3
Norwood	36	338	9.4	67t	2
Douglas	23	320	13.9	69	1
Finneran	21	169	8.0	14	1
Peelle	15	159	10.6	18t	2
Snelling	8	89	11.1	27	0
Mughelli	8	57	7.1	18	0
Turner	6	41	6.8	18	0
Robinson	5	52	10.4	23	0
Hartsock	3	26	8.7	17	0
Rader	1	26	26.0	26	0
Weems	1	4	4.0	4	0
Falcons	265	3440	13.0	70t	16
Opponents	325	3771	11.6	56t	20

INTERCEPTIONS	No.	Yds	Avg	LG	TD
Coleman	3	48	16.0	32	0
Houston	2	10	5.0	10t	1
C. Jackson	1	95	95.0	95t	1
Milloy	1	38	38.0	38	0
Grimes	1	25	25.0	25	0
Boley	1	16	16.0	16	0
Foxworth	1	1	1.0	1	0
Falcons	10	233	23.3	95t	2
Opponents	11	74	6.7	23	0

PUNTING	No.	Yds.	Avg.	In 20	LG
Koenen	63	2566	40.7	25	60
Falcons	65	2566	39.5	25	60
Opponents	76	3458	45.5	21	64

PUNT RETURNS	Ret	FC	Yds	Avg	LG	TD
Jennings	23	6	151	6.6	37	0
Douglas	19	3	226	11.9	61t	1
Finneran	1	3	2	2.0	2	0
Falcons	43	12	379	8.8	61t	1
Opponents	20	27	49	2.5	12	0

KICKOFF RETURNS	No.	Yds	Avg	LG	TD
Norwood	51	1311	25.7	92	0
Douglas	4	46	11.5	22	0
Weems	1	19	19.0	19	0
Mughelli	1	17	17.0	17	0
Wilkerson	1	10	10.0	10	0
Finneran	1	5	5.0	5	0
Falcons	59	1408	23.9	92	0
Opponents	71	1536	21.6	88	0

FIELD GOALS	1-19	20-29	30-39	40-49	50+
Elam	0/0	11/11	7/8	10/10	1/2
Falcons	0/0	11/11	7/8	10/10	1/2
Opponents	1/1	9/9	6/7	3/5	1/3

SACKS	No.
Abraham	16.5
Davis	4.0
Babineaux	3.5
Anderson	2.0
Biermann	2.0
G. Jackson	2.0
Lofton	1.0
Moorehead	1.0
Nicholas	1.0
(Group)	1.0
Falcons	34.0
Opponents	17.0

RECORD HOLDERS

INDIVIDUAL RECORDS—CAREER

Category	Name	Performance
Rushing (Yds.)	Gerald Riggs, 1982-88	6,631
Passing (Yds.)	Steve Bartkowski, 1975-1985	23,468
Passing (TDs)	Steve Bartkowski, 1975-1985	154
Receiving (No.)	Terance Mathis, 1994-2001	573
Receiving (Yds.)	Terance Mathis, 1994-2001	7,349
Interceptions	Rolland Lawrence, 1973-1980	39
Punting (Avg.)	Rick Donnelly, 1985-89	42.6
Punt Return (Avg.)	Darrien Gordon, 2001	14.1
Kickoff Return (Avg.)	Darrick Vaughn, 2000-01	25.7
Field Goals	Morten Andersen, 1995-2000, 2006-07	184
Touchdowns (Tot.)	Terance Mathis, 1994-2001	57
Points	Morten Andersen, 1995-2000, 2006-07	806
Sacks*	Chuck Smith, 1992-99	58.5

INDIVIDUAL RECORDS—SINGLE SEASON

Category	Name	Performance
Rushing (Yds.)	Jamal Anderson, 1998	1,846
Passing (Yds.)	Jeff George, 1995	4,143
Passing (TDs)	Steve Bartkowski, 1980	31
Receiving (No.)	Terance Mathis, 1994	111
Receiving (Yds.)	Roddy White, 2008	1,382
Interceptions	Scott Case, 1988	10
Punting (Avg.)	Billy Lothridge, 1968	44.3
Punt Return (Avg.)	Darrien Gordon, 2001	14.1
Kickoff Return (Avg.)	Darrick Vaughn, 2000	27.7
Field Goals	Jay Feely, 2002	32
Touchdowns (Tot.)	Michael Turner, 2008	17
Points	Jay Feely, 2002	138
Sacks*	John Abraham, 2008	16.5

INDIVIDUAL RECORDS—SINGLE GAME

Category	Name	Performance
Rushing (Yds.)	Michael Turner, 9-7-08	220
Passing (Yds.)	Steve Bartkowski, 11-15-81	416
Passing (TDs)	Wade Wilson, 12-13-92	5
Receiving (No.)	William Andrews, 11-15-81	15
Receiving (Yds.)	Terance Mathis, 12-13-98	198
Interceptions	Many times	2
	Last time by DeAngelo Hall, 9-17-06	
Field Goals	Norm Johnson, 11-13-94	6
Touchdowns (Tot.)	T.J. Duckett, 12-12-04	4
	Michael Turner, 11-23-08	4
Points	T.J. Duckett, 12-12-04	24
	Michael Turner, 11-23-08	24
Sacks*	Chuck Smith, 10-12-97	5.0

**Sacks became an official statistic in 1982.*

ATLANTA FALCONS

2009 VETERAN ROSTER

No.	Name	Pos.	Ht.	Wt.	Birthdate	NFL Exp.	College	Hometown	How Acq.	'08 Games/ Starts
55	Abraham, John	DE	6-4	263	5/6/78	10	South Carolina	Timmonsville, S.C.	T(NYJ)-'06	16/16
98	Anderson, Jamaal	DE	6-6	282	2/6/86	3	Arkansas	Little Rock, Ark.	D1-'07	15/15
95	Babineaux, Jonathan	DT	6-2	284	10/12/81	5	Iowa	Port Arthur, Texas	D2-'05	16/16
72	Baker, Sam	T	6-5	312	5/30/85	2	Southern California	Tustin, Calif.	D1b-'08	8/5
71	Biermann, Kroy	DE	6-3	241	9/12/85	2	Montana	Hardin, Mont.	D5b-'08	16/6
63	Blalock, Justin	G	6-4	333	12/20/83	3	Texas	Dallas, Texas	D2a-'07	16/16
77	Clabo, Tyson	T	6-6	332	10/17/81	4	Wake Forest	Knoxville, Tenn.	FA-'06	16/16
26	Coleman, Erik	S	5-10	206	5/16/82	6	Washington State	Sacramento, Calif.	FA-'08	16/16
73	Dahl, Harvey	G	6-5	308	6/24/81	3	Nevada-Reno	Fallon, Nev.	FA-'07	16/16
92	Davis, Chauncey	DE	6-2	274	1/27/83	5	Florida State	Bartow, Fla.	D4-'05	16/1
28	DeCoud, Thomas	S	6-0	197	3/19/85	2	California	Vallejo, Calif.	D3c-'08	10/0
83	Douglas, Harry	WR	5-11	171	9/16/84	2	Louisville	Jonesboro, Ga.	D3b-'08	16/0
1	Elam, Jason	K	5-11	194	3/8/70	17	Hawaii	Ft. Walton Beach, Fla.	UFA(Den)-'08	16/0
86	Finneran, Brian	WR	6-5	206	1/31/76	9	Villanova	Mission Viejo, Calif.	FA-'00	16/0
79	Foster, Renardo	OL	6-7	340	7/15/84	2	Louisville	Ripley, Tenn.	FA-'07	0*
29	Fudge, Jamaal	S	5-9	194	5/17/83	4	Clemson	Jacksonville, Fla.	W(Jax)-'08	11/1
51	Gilbert, Tony	LB	6-0	248	10/16/79	6	Georgia	Macon, Ga.	FA-'08	0*
88	Gonzalez, Tony	TE	6-5	251	2/27/76	13	California	Torrance, Calif.	T(KC)-'09	16/16
20	Grimes, Brent	CB	5-10	185	7/19/83	2	Shippensburg	Philadelphia, Pa.	FA-'07	12/6
41	Harris, Antoine	S	5-10	197	4/8/82	3	Louisville	Columbus, Ohio	FA-'07	12/0
89	Hartsock, Ben	TE	6-4	264	7/5/80	6	Ohio State	Chillicothe, Ohio	FA-'08	11/11
36	Haynes, Verron	RB	5-9	222	2/17/79	7	Georgia	Atlanta, Ga.	FA-'09	0*
23	Houston, Chris	CB	5-11	175	10/18/84	3	Arkansas	Austin, Texas	D2b-'07	16/16
25	Hutchins, Von	CB	5-10	185	2/14/81	5	Mississippi	Natchez, Miss.	FA-'08	0*
30	Irons, David	CB	5-11	197	10/9/82	3	Auburn	Dacula, Ga.	D6b-'07	5/0
22	Jackson, Chevis	CB	5-11	185	12/11/85	2	Louisiana State	Mobile, Ala.	D3a-'08	16/1
99	Jefferson, Jason	DT	6-1	295	12/20/81	5	Wisconsin	Chicago, Ill.	W(Buff)-'08	13/1
12	Jenkins, Michael	WR	6-4	215	6/18/82	6	Ohio State	Tampa, Fla.	D1b-'04	16/12
93	Johnson, Thomas	DT	6-2	305	6/24/81	2	Middle Tennessee State	Memphis, Tenn.	FA-'09	7/0
9	Koenen, Michael	P	5-11	199	7/13/82	5	Western Washington	Ferndale, Wash.	FA-'05	16/0
97	Lewis, Trey	DT	6-3	323	5/23/85	2	Washburn	Topeka, Kan.	D6a-'07	0*
50	Lofton, Curtis	LB	6-0	248	6/2/86	2	Oklahoma	Kingfisher, Okla.	D2-'08	16/16
62	McClure, Todd	C	6-1	301	2/16/77	11	Louisiana State	Baton Rouge, La.	D7a-'99	16/16
43	Miles, Edmond	LB	6-0	240	7/6/84	2	Iowa	Tallahassee, Fla.	FA-'09	2/0*
34	Mughelli, Ovie	FB	6-1	245	6/10/80	7	Wake Forest	Boston, Mass.	UFA(Balt)-'07	16/13
54	Nicholas, Stephen	LB	6-3	232	5/1/83	3	South Florida	Jacksonville, Fla.	D4a-'07	16/0
32	Norwood, Jerious	RB	5-11	202	7/29/83	4	Mississippi State	Jackson, Miss.	D3-'06	16/0
76	Ojinnaka, Quinn	T	6-5	305	4/23/84	4	Syracuse	Seabrook, Md.	D5-'06	8/0
87	Peelle, Justin	TE	6-4	250	3/15/79	8	Oregon	Fresno, Calif.	FA-'08	16/11
53	Peterson, Mike	LB	6-1	238	6/17/76	11	Florida	Gainesville, Fla.	UFA(Jax)-'09	15/10*
39	Prude, Ronnie	CB	5-11	180	6/4/82	3	Louisiana State	Shreveport, La.	FA-'09	0*
85	Rader, Jason	TE	6-4	271	4/12/81	4	Marshall	St. Albans, W. Va.	FA-'08	6/1
8	Redman, Chris	QB	6-3	221	7/7/77	7	Louisville	Louisville, Ky.	FA-'07	0*
65	Romberg, Brett	C	6-2	298	10/10/79	6	Miami	Windsor, Ontario, Canada	UFA(StL)-'09	0*
2	Ryan, Matt	QB	6-4	220	5/17/85	2	Boston College	Exton, Pa.	D1a-'08	16/16
46	Schneck, Mike	LS	6-1	234	8/4/77	11	Wisconsin	Whitefish Bay, Wis.	FA-'07	16/0
3	Shockley, D.J.	QB	6-0	222	3/23/83	3	Georgia	College Park, Ga.	D7-'06	0*
44	Snelling, Jason	RB	5-11	229	12/29/83	3	Virginia	Chester, Va.	D7-'07	16/1
69	Stepanovich, Alex	C	6-4	296	9/25/81	6	Ohio State	Berea, Ohio	UFA(Cin)-'08	4/0
74	Svitek, Will	T	6-6	300	1/8/82	4	Stanford	Prague, Czech Republic	FA-'09	0*
33	Turner, Michael	RB	5-10	244	2/13/82	6	Northern Illinois	Waukegan, Ill.	UFA(SD)-'08	16/16
14	Weems, Eric	WR	5-9	191	7/4/85	2	Bethune-Cookman	Ormond Beach, Fla.	FA-'07	6/0
84	White, Roddy	WR	6-0	208	11/2/81	5	Alabama-Birmingham	James Island, S.C.	D1-'05	16/1
67	Wilkerson, Ben	C	6-4	310	11/22/82	4	Louisiana State	Port Arthur, Texas	FA-'07	13/0
52	Wire, Coy	LB	6-0	228	11/7/78	8	Stanford	Camp Hill, Pa.	FA-'08	16/4

* Foster missed '08 season because of injury; Gilbert inactive for 16 games; Haynes last active with Pittsburgh in '07; Hutchins missed '08 season because of injury; Miles played 2 games with N.Y. Giants; Peterson played 10 games with Jacksonville in '08; Prude last active with Baltimore in '07; Redman did not play in 16 games; Romberg played 14 games with St. Louis; Shockley inactive for 16 games; Svitek last active with Kansas City in '07.

Traded—WR Laurent Robinson (16 games in '08) to St. Louis.

Players lost through free agency (4): LB Michael Boley (NYG; 16 games in '08), LB Keith Brooking (Dall; 16), CB Dominique Foxworth (Balt; 14), DT Grady Jackson (Det; 15).

Also played with Falcons in '08—Eric Brock (1 game), S Lawyer Milloy (15), DT Kindal Moorehead (14).

2009 FIRST-YEAR ROSTER

Name	Pos.	Ht.	Wt.	Birthdate	College	Hometown	How Acq.
Adkins, Spencer	LB	5-11	246	5/16/87	Miami	Naples, Fla.	D6
Bergeron, Troy (1)	WR	6-4	198	12/3/83	None	New Orleans, La.	FA
Bobino, Rashad	LB	5-9	228	9/2/85	Texas	Galveston, Texas	FA
Brock, Eric (1)	S	6-0	202	4/24/85	Auburn	Alexander City, Ala.	FA-'08
Brown, Thomas (1)	RB	5-8	200	1/7/85	Georgia	Tucker, Ga.	D6-'08
Butterworth, Michael (1)	OL	6-7	298	9/11/86	Slippery Rock	Northern Cambria, Pa.	FA-'08
Christopher, Brock	LB	6-2	235	5/15/86	Missouri	Kearney, Mo.	FA
Dehaze, Robbie	K/P	6-3	193	1/3/86	Northern Arizona	Sherwood, Ore.	FA
Evans, Willie (1)	DE	6-1	267	3/5/84	Mississippi State	Waynesboro, Miss.	FA-'08
James, Robert (1)	LB	5-11	218	12/26/83	Arizona State	Glendale, Ariz.	D5a-'08
Jerry, Peria	DT	6-2	290	8/23/84	Mississippi	Batesville, Miss.	D1
Kelley, Aaron	WR	6-5	190	4/2/86	Clemson	Marietta, Ga.	FA
Lucas, Maurice	DE	6-4	260	3/26/87	Colorado	Denver, Colo.	FA
Middleton, William	CB	5-11	186	7/28/86	Furman	Atlanta, Ga.	D5a
Moore, William	S	6-0	221	5/18/85	Missouri	Hayti, Mo.	D2
Mougey, Darren	WR	6-6	230	4/7/85	San Diego State	Scottsdale, Ariz.	FA
Myles, Tywain (1)	DT	6-2	305	10/1/84	Tarleton State	Nacogdoches, Texas	FA-'08
Nicholson, Derek	LB	6-2	233	12/30/88	Florida State	Winston-Salem, N.C.	FA
Owens, Chris	CB	5-9	181	12/1/86	San Jose State	Los Angeles, Calif.	D3
Paschal, Marcus (1)	S	6-0	201	8/31/84	Iowa	Clearwater, Fla.	FA
Reynolds, Garrett	T	6-7	310	7/1/87	North Carolina	Knoxville, Tenn.	D5b
Sharpe, Glenn (1)	CB	6-0	185	2/27/84	Miami	Miami, Fla.	FA-'08
Shiver, Robert	LS	6-3	225	8/4/85	Auburn	Thomasville, Ga.	FA
Sidbury, Lawrence	DE	6-2	266	2/6/86	Richmond	Cheltenham, Md.	D4
Stanchek, Ryan	G	6-3	305	6/26/85	West Virginia	Cincinnati, Ohio	FA
Tiller, Tony (1)	CB	6-0	185	12/20/81	East Tennessee State	Stone Mountain, Ga.	FA
Valdez, Jose	G	6-6	310	12/13/86	Arkansas	St. Francis, Wisc.	FA
Walker, Vance	DT	6-2	293	4/25/87	Georgia Tech	Fort Mill, S.C.	D7
Williams, Chandler (1)	WR	5-11	178	8/9/85	Florida International	Miami, Fla.	FA-'08
Wilson, John Parker	QB	6-2	211	10/17/85	Alabama	Hoover, Ala.	FA
Zinger, Keith (1)	TE	6-4	268	10/9/84	Louisiana State	Leesville, La.	D7b-'08

The term NFL Rookie is defined as a player who is in his first season of professional football and has not been on the roster of another professional football team for any regular-season or postseason games. A Rookie is designated by an "R" on NFL rosters. Players who have been active in another professional football league or players who have NFL experience, including either preseason training camp or being on an Active List or Inactive List, or on Reserve/Injured or Reserve/Physically Unable to Perform for fewer than six regular-season games, are termed NFL First-Year Players. An NFL First-Year Player is designated by a "1" on NFL rosters. Thereafter, a player is credited with an additional year of experience for each season in which he accumulates six games on the Active List or Inactive List, or on Reserve/Injured or Reserve/Physically Unable to Perform.

Log on to www.atlantafalcons.com for an up-to-date roster.

ATLANTA FALCONS

COACHING STAFF

Head Coach,
Mike Smith

Pro Career: Mike Smith was named the 14th head coach in Atlanta Falcons franchise history on January 23, 2008. In his first season, Smith guided the Falcons to an 11-5 record as the team earned its first playoff berth since 2004. The 11 wins in 2008 marked a seven-plus win turnaround from the 2007 campaign and also equaled the best record ever for a rookie head coach in the NFL taking over a team that finished below .500 the previous season. For his efforts, Smith was named the Associated Press NFL Coach of the Year. Atlanta's rushing attack finished second in the league with a 152.7 average, while the Falcons also posted a 24.4 points per game average in 2008, which was an 8.2-point upgrade from 2007. From 2003-07, Smith served as the defensive coordinator for the Jacksonville Jaguars following a four-year stint with the Baltimore Ravens from 1999-2002, which included the team's 2000 Super Bowl season. Before joining the NFL ranks, Smith coached at San Diego State (1982-85), Morehead State (1986), and Tennessee Tech (1987-1998). Career record: 11-6.

Background: Smith played linebacker for the Winnipeg Blue Bombers of the CFL in 1982. He played at East Tennessee (1977-1981) and was named defensive MVP twice at his position. Smith led the team with 186 tackles as a senior.

Personal: A native of Daytona Beach, Florida, Smith was born on November 30, 1959 in Chicago, Illinois. He and his wife Julie have one daughter, Logan, who is seven years old.

ASSISTANT COACHES

Keith Armstrong, special teams coordinator; born December 15, 1963, Levittown, Pa. Running back Temple 1983-86. No pro playing experience. College coach: Temple 1987, Miami 1988, Akron 1989, Oklahoma State 1990-92, Notre Dame 1993. Pro coach: Atlanta Falcons 1994-96, Chicago Bears 1997-2000, Miami Dolphins 2001-2007, re-joined Falcons 2008.

Jonas Beauchemin, asst. director of athletic performance; born October 11, 1984, Burlington, Vt. Attended Keene State. No college or pro playing experience. Pro coach: Joined Falcons in 2009.

Paul Boudreau, offensive line; born December 30, 1949, Arlington, Mass. Guard Boston College 1970-73. No pro playing experience. Pro coach: New Orleans Saints 1987-1993, Detroit Lions 1994-96, New England Patriots 1997-98, Miami Dolphins 1999-2000, Carolina Panthers 2001-02, Jacksonville Jaguars 2003-05, St. Louis Rams 2006-07, joined Falcons in 2008.

Gerald Brown, running backs; born September 4, 1959, Sweetwater, Tenn. Attended Memphis State. No college or pro playing experience. College coach: Tennessee Tech 1991-2000, Indiana 2002-07. Pro coach: Joined Falcons in 2008.

Joe Danna, defensive assistant; born April 3, 1977, Midland, Mich. Wide receiver Central Michigan 1995-98. No pro playing experience. College coach: Central Michigan 1999-2000, 2002-05, Georgia 2001, Georgia Southern 2006, James Madison 2007. Pro coach: Joined Falcons in 2008.

Paul Dunn, asst. offensive line; born July 7, 1960, Philadelphia. Offensive lineman Pittsburgh 1978-1982. No pro playing experience. College coach: Pittsburgh 1983, 2005-07, Penn State 1984-85, Edinboro 1986-88, Rutgers 1989, Maine 1990-93, Cincinnati 1994-95, Vanderbilt 1996-97, Kansas State 1998-2002, Kentucky 2003-04. Pro coach: Joined Falcons in 2008.

Jeff Fish, director of athletic performance; born June 6, 1966, Ithaca, N.Y. Wide receiver Western Carolina 1985-88. No pro playing experience. College coach: Western Michigan 1989, Clemson 1991-92, Kent State 1993-94, Tulsa 1995-97, Missouri 2001-03. Pro coach: Tampa Bay Buccaneers 1997, Kansas City Chiefs 1998-2000, Oakland Raiders 2004-07, joined Falcons in 2008.

Ray Hamilton, defensive line; born January 20, 1951, Omaha, Neb. Nose tackle Oklahoma 1969-1972. Pro defensive lineman New England Patriots 1973-1981. College coach: Tennessee 1992. Pro coach: New England Patriots 1985-89, Tampa Bay Buccaneers 1991, Los Angeles Raiders 1993-94, New York Jets 1994-96, 2000, New England Patriots 1997-99, Cleveland Browns 2001-02, Jacksonville Jaguars 2003-07, joined Falcons in 2008.

Bill Hughan, asst. director of athletic performance; born February 8, 1975, Oxford, Conn. Attended Springfield College. No college or pro playing experience. College coach: Yale 1997-98, Columbia 1999-2000, Missouri 2001-03. Pro coach: Oakland Raiders 2004-07, joined Falcons in 2008.

Mike Mularkey, offensive coordinator; born November 19, 1961, Ft. Lauderdale, Fla. Tight end Florida 1979-1982. Pro tight end Minnesota Vikings 1983-88, Pittsburgh Steelers 1989-1991. College coach: Concordia 1993. Pro coach: Tampa Bay Buccaneers 1994-1995, Pittsburgh Steelers 1996-2003, Buffalo Bills 2004-05 (head coach), Miami Dolphins 2006-07, joined Falcons in 2008.

Bill Musgrave, quarterbacks; born November 11, 1967, Grand Junction, Colo. Quarterback Oregon 1987-1990. Pro quarterback San Francisco 49ers 1991-94, Denver Broncos 1995-96. College coach: Virginia 2001-02. Pro coach: Oakland Raiders 1997, Philadelphia Eagles 1998, Carolina Panthers 1999-2000, Jacksonville Jaguars 2003-04, Washington Redskins 2005, joined Falcons in 2006.

Glenn Pires, linebackers; born September 13, 1958, New Bedford, Mass. Offensive lineman Springfield College 1976-79. No pro playing experience. College coach: Dartmouth 1985-88, Syracuse 1989-1994, Michigan State 1995. Pro coach: Arizona Cardinals 1996-2000, Detroit Lions 2001-02, Miami Dolphins 2003-07, joined Falcons in 2008.

Alvin Reynolds, defensive backs; born June 24, 1959, Pineville, La. Safety Indiana State 1978-1981. No pro playing experience. College coach: Indiana State 1982-1992. Pro coach: Denver Broncos 1993-95, Baltimore Ravens 1996-98, Carolina Panthers 1999-2002, Jacksonville Jaguars 2003-07, joined Falcons in 2008.

Terry Robiskie, wide receivers; born November 12, 1954, New Orleans. Running back Louisiana State 1973-76. Pro running back Oakland Raiders 1977-79, Miami Dolphins 1980-81. Pro coach: Los Angeles Raiders 1982-1993, Washington Redskins 1994-2000 (interim head coach 2000), Cleveland Browns 2001-06 (interim head coach 2004), Miami Dolphins 2007, joined Falcons in 2008.

Chris Scelfo, tight ends; born September 30, 1963, New Iberia, La. Center Northeast Louisiana 1981-84. No pro playing experience. College coach: Northeast Louisiana 1986-87, Oklahoma 1988-89, Marshall 1990-95, Georgia 1996-98, Tulane 1998-2006. Pro coach: Joined Falcons in 2008.

Eric Sutulovich, asst. special teams; born February 28, 1974, Kansas City, Kan. Tight end Louisiana Tech 1993-95. No pro playing experience. College coach: Louisiana Tech 1997-99, Pittsburgh 2000, Kansas 2006. Pro coach: Houston Texans 2002-05, Detroit Lions 2008, joined Falcons in 2009.

Emmitt Thomas, asst. head coach/secondary; born June 3, 1943, Angleton, Texas. Quarterback/receiver Bishop (Texas) College 1963-65. Pro defensive back Kansas City Chiefs 1966-1978. College coach: Central Missouri State 1979-1980. Pro coach: St. Louis Cardinals 1981-85, Washington Redskins 1986-1994, Philadelphia Eagles 1995-1998, Green Bay Packers 1999, Minnesota Vikings 2000-01, joined Falcons in 2002 (interim head coach 2007).

Glenn Thomas, offensive assistant; born September 22, 1977, Eastland, Texas. Attended Texas Tech. No college or pro playing experience. College coach: Texas Tech 1998-2001, Midwestern State 2001-07. Pro coach: Joined Falcons in 2008.

Brian VanGorder, defensive coordinator; born April 17, 1959, Jackson, Mich. Linebacker Wayne State 1979-1980. No pro playing experience. College coach: Grand Valley State 1989-1991, Wayne State 1992-94 (head coach), Central Florida 1995-97, Central Michigan 1998-99, Western Illinois 2000, Georgia 2001-04, Georgia Southern 2006 (head coach). Pro coach: Jacksonville Jaguars 2005, joined Falcons in 2007.

National Football Conference
South Division
Team Colors: Black, Panther Blue, and Silver
800 South Mint Street
Charlotte, North Carolina 28202-1502
Telephone: (704) 358-7000

2009 SCHEDULE

PRESEASON

Aug. 17	at N.Y. Giants	8:15
Aug. 22	at Miami	7:30
Aug. 29	**Baltimore**	8:00
Sep. 3	**Pittsburgh**	8:00

REGULAR SEASON

Sep. 13	**Philadelphia**	1:00
Sep. 20	at Atlanta	1:00
Sep. 28	at Dallas (Mon.)	7:30
Oct. 4	BYE	
Oct. 11	**Washington**	1:00
Oct. 18	at Tampa Bay	1:00
Oct. 25	**Buffalo**	4:05
Nov. 1	at Arizona	2:15
Nov. 8	at New Orleans	3:05
Nov. 15	**Atlanta**	1:00
Nov. 19	**Miami** (Thu.)	8:20
Nov. 29	at N.Y. Jets	1:00
Dec. 6	**Tampa Bay**	1:00
Dec. 13	at New England	1:00
Dec. 20	**Minnesota** *	8:20
Dec. 27	at N.Y. Giants	1:00
Jan. 3	**New Orleans**	1:00

** Sunday night games in Weeks 11-17 subject to change*

Stadium: Bank of America Stadium (opened in 1996) • **Capacity:** 73,504 Charlotte, North Carolina 28202-1502
Playing Surface: Grass
Training Camp: Wofford College Spartanburg, South Carolina 29303

BANK OF AMERICA STADIUM

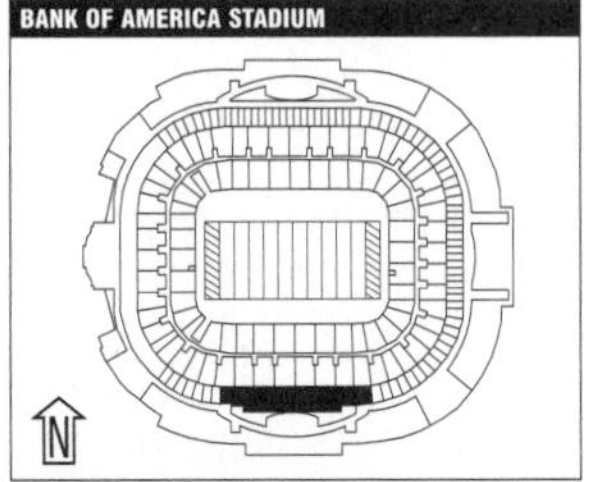

CLUB OFFICIALS

Owner/Founder: Jerry Richardson
President, Panthers Football LLC: Mark Richardson
President Panthers Stadium LLC: Jon Richardson
General Manager: Marty Hurney
General Counsel: Richard Thigpen
Chief Financial Officer: Dave Olsen
Controller: Mike Dudan
Director of Pro Scouting: Mark Koncz
Pro Scouts: Trent Kirchner
Director of College Scouting: Don Gregory
College Scouts: Brian Adams, Jeff Beathard, Ryan Cowden, Khary Darlington, Jeff Morrow, John Peterson, Pete Russell, Mike Szabo
Director of Communications: Charlie Dayton
Media Relations Manager: Steven Drummond
Public Relations Assistant: Deedee Mills
Director of Ticket Operations: Phil Youtsey
Director of Community Relations and Cheerleader/Mascot Programs: Riley Fields
Director of Sponsor Sales and Services: John Berger
Director of Broadcast Administration: Henry Thomas
Executive Producer-Television: Greg Brannon
Executive Producer-Radio: David Langton
Director of Team Administration: Rob Rogers
Director of Team Operations: Brandon Beane
Video Director: Mark Hobbs
Assistant Video Director: Jeff Mueller
Head Trainer: Ryan Vermillion
Assistant Trainers: Mark Shermansky, Reggie Scott
Equipment Manager: Jackie Miles
Assistant Equipment Manager: Don Toner
Director of Security: Gene Brown
Stadium Operations Manager: Scott Paul
Director of Entertainment and Panthervision: Kyle Ritchie
Facility Manager: Matthew Getz
Head Groundskeeper: Tom Vaughan
Director of Human Resources: Jackie Jeffries

COACHING HISTORY (115-119-0)

Records include postseason games

1995-98	Dom Capers	31-35-0
1999-2001	George Seifert	16-32-0
2002-08	John Fox	68-52-0

PAID ATTENDANCE

Home 576,144 Away 516,194
Total 1,092,338
Single-game home record, 76,136 (12/10/95)
Single-season home record, 579,192 (2006)

2009 DRAFT CHOICES

Round	Name	Pos.	College
2	Everette Brown	DE	Florida State
	Sherrod Martin	DB	Troy
3	Corvey Irvin	DT	Georgia
4	Mike Goodson	RB	Texas A&M
	Tony Fiammetta	RB	Syracuse
5	Duke Robinson	G	Oklahoma
7	Captain Munnerlyn	DB	South Carolina

CAROLINA PANTHERS

2008 TEAM RECORD

PRESEASON (2-2)

Date	Result	Opponent
8/9	W 23-20	Indianapolis (OT)
8/14	L 13-24	at Philadelphia
8/23	W 47-3	Washington
8/28	L 16-19	at Pittsburgh

REGULAR SEASON (12-4)

Date	Result	Opponent
9/7	W 26-24	at San Diego
9/14	W 20-17	Chicago
9/21	L 10-20	at Minnesota
9/28	W 24-9	Atlanta
10/5	W 34-0	Kansas City
10/12	L 3-27	at Tampa Bay
10/19	W 30-7	New Orleans
10/26	W 27-23	Arizona
11/9	W 17-6	at Oakland
11/16	W 31-22	Detroit
11/23	L 28-45	at Atlanta
11/30	W 35-31	at Green Bay
12/8	W 38-23	Tampa Bay
12/14	W 30-10	Denver
12/21	L 28-34	at New York Giants (OT)
12/28	W 33-31	at New Orleans

(OT) Overtime

POSTSEASON (0-1)

Date	Result	Opponent
1/10	L 13-33	Arizona

SCORE BY PERIODS

Panthers	60	149	99	106	0 —	414
Opponents	57	92	71	103	6 —	329

2008 TEAM STATISTICS

	Panthers	Opp.
Total First Downs	287	296
Rushing	118	100
Passing	152	178
Penalty	17	18
3rd Down: Made/Att	78/197	87/219
3rd Down Pct.	39.6	39.7
4th Down: Made/Att	3/8	9/20
4th Down Pct.	37.5	45.0
Possession Avg.	29:19	30:41
Total Net Yards	5595	5299
Avg. Per Game	349.7	331.2
Total Plays	938	1026
Avg. Per Play	6.0	5.2
Net Yards Rushing	2437	1912
Avg. Per Game	152.3	119.5
Total Rushes	504	432
Net Yards Passing	3158	3387
Avg. Per Game	197.4	211.7
Sacked/Yards Lost	20/130	37/230
Gross Yards	3288	3617
Att./Completions	414/246	557/333
Completion Pct.	59.4	59.8
Had Intercepted	12	12
Punts/Average	76/42.3	80/45.9
Net Punting Avg.	76/37.4	80/37.7
Penalties/Yards	94/637	88/736
Fumbles/Ball Lost	12/7	25/13
Touchdowns	47	37
Rushing	30	14
Passing	15	19
Returns	2	4

2008 INDIVIDUAL STATISTICS

PASSING	Att.	Comp.	Yds.	Pct.	TD	Int.	Tkld.	Rate
Delhomme	414	246	3288	59.4	15	12	20/130	84.7
Panthers	414	246	3288	59.4	15	12	20/130	84.7
Opponents	557	333	3617	59.8	19	12	37/230	81.4

SCORING	TD R	TD P	TD Rt	PAT	FG	Saf	PTS
Kasay	0	0	0	46/46	28/31	0	130
D. Williams	18	2	0	0/0	0/0	0	122
Stewart	10	0	0	0/0	0/0	0	60
St. Smith	0	6	0	0/0	0/0	0	36
Muhammad	0	5	0	0/0	0/0	0	30
Delhomme	2	0	0	0/0	0/0	0	12
Gamble	0	0	1	0/0	0/0	0	6
King	0	1	0	0/0	0/0	0	6
Rosario	0	1	0	0/0	0/0	0	6
Wesley	0	0	1	0/0	0/0	0	6
Panthers	30	15	2	46/46	28/31	0	414
Opponents	14	19	4	31/32	24/28	0	329

2-Pt. Conversions: D. Williams.
Panthers 1-1, Opponents 2-4.

RUSHING	No.	Yds	Avg	LG	TD
D. Williams	273	1515	5.5	69t	18
Stewart	184	836	4.5	41	10
St. Smith	5	40	8.0	23	0
Delhomme	20	21	1.1	12t	2
Hoover	9	18	2.0	5	0
Goings	9	10	1.1	4	0
McCown	4	-3	-0.8	0	0
Panthers	504	2437	4.8	69t	30
Opponents	432	1912	4.4	51	14

RECEIVING	No.	Yds	Avg	LG	TD
St. Smith	78	1421	18.2	65t	6
Muhammad	65	923	14.2	60	5
D. Williams	22	121	5.5	25t	2
King	21	195	9.3	31	1
Rosario	18	209	11.6	24	1
Hackett	13	181	13.9	37	0
Jarrett	10	119	11.9	25	0
Stewart	8	47	5.9	15	0
Hoover	6	39	6.5	12	0
Goings	3	1	0.3	3	0
Jones	2	32	16.0	19	0
Panthers	246	3288	13.4	65t	15
Opponents	333	3617	10.9	69	19

INTERCEPTIONS	No.	Yds	Avg	LG	TD
Beason	3	52	17.3	44	0
Gamble	3	23	7.7	19	0
Lucas	2	74	37.0	43	0
Godfrey	1	16	16.0	16	0
Harris	1	16	16.0	16	0
Marshall	1	11	11.0	11	0
Diggs	1	0	0.0	0	0
Panthers	12	192	16.0	44	0
Opponents	12	167	13.9	58	0

PUNTING	No.	Yds.	Avg.	In 20	LG
Baker	73	3217	44.1	30	63
Panthers	76	3217	42.3	30	63
Opponents	80	3671	45.9	18	63

PUNT RETURNS	Ret	FC	Yds	Avg	LG	TD
Jones	39	20	443	11.4	55	0
Salley	1	0	0	0.0	0	0
St. Smith	1	0	10	10.0	10	0
Wesley	1	0	0	0.0	0	0
Panthers	42	20	453	10.8	55	0
Opponents	41	13	276	6.7	61t	1

KICKOFF RETURNS	No.	Yds	Avg	LG	TD
Jones	40	958	24.0	59	0
Stewart	15	349	23.3	38	0
Rosario	2	26	13.0	18	0
Bridges	1	15	15.0	15	0
Hoover	1	12	12.0	12	0
King	1	12	12.0	12	0
Panthers	60	1372	22.9	59	0
Opponents	59	1292	21.9	46	0

FIELD GOALS	1-19	20-29	30-39	40-49	50+
Kasay	0/0	7/7	9/9	11/12	1/3
Panthers	0/0	7/7	9/9	11/12	1/3
Opponents	1/1	8/8	7/7	7/9	1/3

SACKS	No.
Peppers	14.5
C. Johnson	6.0
Brayton	4.5
Davis	3.5
Lewis	3.5
Marshall	2.0
Diggs	1.0
Godfrey	1.0
Taylor	1.0
Panthers	37.0
Opponents	20.0

RECORD HOLDERS

INDIVIDUAL RECORDS—CAREER

Category	Name	Performance
Rushing (Yds.)	DeShaun Foster, 2002-07	3,336
Passing (Yds.)	Jake Delhomme, 2003-08	17,243
Passing (TDs)	Jake Delhomme, 2003-08	112
Receiving (No.)	Muhsin Muhammad, 1996-2004, 2008	643
Receiving (Yds.)	Muhsin Muhammad, 1996-2004, 2008	8,674
Interceptions	Eric Davis, 1996-2000	25
Punting (Avg.)	Todd Sauerbrun, 2001-04	45.5
Punt Return (Avg.)	Winslow Oliver, 1996-98	10.7
Kickoff Return (Avg.)	Michael Bates, 1996-2000	25.7
Field Goals	John Kasay, 1995-2008	304
Touchdowns (Tot.)	Steve Smith, 2001-08	51
Points	John Kasay, 1995-2008	1,293
*Sacks	Julius Peppers, 2002-08	70.5

INDIVIDUAL RECORDS—SINGLE SEASON

Category	Name	Performance
Rushing (Yds.)	DeAngelo Williams, 2008	1,515
Passing (Yds.)	Steve Beuerlein, 1999	4,436
Passing (TDs)	Steve Beuerlein, 1999	36
Receiving (No.)	Steve Smith, 2005	103
Receiving (Yds.)	Steve Smith, 2005	1,563
Interceptions	Doug Evans, 2001	8
Punting (Avg.)	Todd Sauerbrun, 2001	47.5
Punt Return (Avg.)	Winslow Oliver, 1996	11.5
Kickoff Return (Avg.)	Michael Bates, 1996	30.2
Field Goals	John Kasay, 1996	37
Touchdowns (Tot.)	DeAngelo Williams, 2008	20
Points	John Kasay, 1996	145
*Sacks	Kevin Greene, 1998	15.0

INDIVIDUAL RECORDS—SINGLE GAME

Category	Name	Performance
Rushing (Yds.)	DeAngelo Williams, 12-8-08	186
Passing (Yds.)	Chris Weinke, 12-10-06	423
Passing (TDs)	Steve Beuerlein, 1-2-00	5
Receiving (No.)	Steve Smith, 11-20-05	14
Receiving (Yds.)	Steve Smith, 10-30-05	201
Interceptions	Deon Grant, 9-22-02	3
Field Goals	John Kasay, 12-5-04	6
Touchdowns (Tot.)	DeAngelo Williams, 11-30-08, 12-21-08	4
Points	DeAngelo Williams, 11-30-08, 12-21-08	24
*Sacks	Many times	3.0
	Julius Peppers, 11-9-08	

**Sacks became an official statistic in 1982.*

CAROLINA PANTHERS

2009 VETERAN ROSTER

No.	Name	Pos.	Ht.	Wt.	Birthdate	NFL Exp.	College	Hometown	How Acq.	'08 Games/ Starts
50	Anderson, James	LB	6-2	235	9/26/83	4	Virginia Tech	Chesapeake, Va.	D3a-'06	8/0
7	Baker, Jason	P	6-2	205	5/17/78	9	Iowa	Fort Wayne, Ind.	T(Den)-'05	16/0
82	Barnidge, Gary	TE	6-5	247	9/22/85	2	Louisville	Middleburg, Fla.	D5-'08	14/0
52	Beason, Jon	LB	6-0	237	1/14/85	3	Miami	Miramar, Fla.	D1-'07	16/16
73	Bernadeau, Mackenzy	G	6-4	308	1/3/86	2	Bentley	Waltham, Mass.	D7c-'08	0*
96	Brayton, Tyler	DE	6-6	280	11/20/79	7	Colorado	Pasco, Wash.	UFA(Oak)-'08	16/16
11	Carter, Jason	WR	6-0	205	9/15/82	3	Texas A&M	Caldwell, Texas	FA-'07	0*
57	Connor, Dan	LB	6-2	231	11/2/85	2	Penn State	Wallingford, Pa.	D3b-'08	3/0
58	Davis, Thomas	LB	6-0	240	3/22/83	5	Georgia	Shellman, Ga.	D1-'05	16/16
17	Delhomme, Jake	QB	6-2	215	1/10/75	11	Louisiana-Lafayette	Lafayette, La.	UFA(NO)-'03	16/16
53	Diggs, Na'il	LB	6-4	240	7/8/78	9	Ohio State	Los Angeles, Calif.	FA-'06	16/16
20	Gamble, Chris	CB	6-1	200	3/11/83	6	Ohio State	Sunrise, Fla.	D1-'04	16/16
63	Geisinger, Justin	G	6-2	315	5/24/82	4	Vanderbilt	Pittsburgh, Pa.	FA-'09	4/0*
30	Godfrey, Charles	S	5-11	205	11/15/85	2	Iowa	Baytown, Texas	D3a-'08	16/16
69	Gross, Jordan	T	6-4	305	7/20/80	7	Utah	Fruitland, Idaho	D1-'03	15/15
43	Harris, Chris	S	6-0	205	8/6/82	5	Louisiana-Monroe	Little Rock, Ark.	T(Chi)-'07	16/16
98	Hayden, Nick	DT	6-4	292	2/4/86	2	Wisconsin	Hartland, Wisc.	D6-'08	2/1
45	Hoover, Brad	FB	6-0	245	11/11/76	10	Western Carolina	Thomasville, N.C.	FA-'00	16/12
44	Jansen, J.J.	LS	6-2	256	1/20/86	2	Notre Dame	Phoenix, Ariz.	T(GB)-'09	0*
80	Jarrett, Dwayne	WR	6-4	219	9/11/86	3	Southern California	New Brunswick, N.J.	D2a-'07	9/1
95	Johnson, Charles	DE	6-2	275	7/10/86	3	Georgia	Hawkinsville, Ga.	D3-'07	16/0
59	Johnson, Landon	LB	6-2	232	3/13/81	6	Purdue	Lubbock, Texas	UFA(Cin)-'08	15/0
67	Kalil, Ryan	C	6-2	295	3/29/85	3	Southern California	Corona, Calif.	D2b-'07	12/12
4	Kasay, John	K	5-10	210	10/27/69	19	Georgia	Athens, Ga.	UFA(Sea)-'95	16/0
99	Kemoeatu, Maake	DT	6-5	345	1/10/79	8	Utah	Kahuku, Hawaii	UFA(Balt)-'06	14/14
47	King, Jeff	TE	6-3	260	2/19/83	4	Virginia Tech	Pulaski, Va.	D5-'06	16/15
92	Lewis, Damione	DT	6-2	301	3/1/78	9	Miami	Sulphur Springs, Texas	UFA(StL)-'06	15/15
5	Lloyd, Rhys	K	5-11	231	6/5/82	3	Minnesota	Dover, England	WV-'07	16/0
31	Marshall, Richard	CB	5-11	189	12/12/84	4	Fresno State	Los Angeles, Calif.	D2-'06	16/0
12	McCown, Josh	QB	6-4	215	7/4/79	8	Sam Houston State	Jacksonville, Texas	T(Mia)-'08	2/0
81	Moore, Kenneth	WR	5-11	195	2/19/85	2	Wake Forest	Charlotte, N.C.	FA-'08	0*
3	Moore, Matt	QB	6-3	202	8/9/84	3	Oregon State	Valencia, Calif.	WV-'07	0*
87	Muhammad, Muhsin	WR	6-2	215	5/5/73	14	Michigan State	Lansing, Mich.	FA-'08	16/15
79	Otah, Jeff	T	6-6	330	6/17/86	2	Pittsburgh	New Castle, Del.	D1b-'08	12/12
90	Peppers, Julius	DE	6-7	283	1/18/80	8	North Carolina	Bailey, N.C.	D1-'02	16/16
10	Robinson, Ryne	WR	5-9	179	11/4/84	3	Miami (Ohio)	Toledo, Ohio	D4-'07	0*
88	Rosario, Dante	TE	6-4	250	10/25/84	3	Oregon	Dayton, Ore.	D5a-'07	16/5
25	Salley, Nate	S	6-1	216	2/5/84	4	Ohio State	Ft. Lauderdale, Fla.	D4-'06	16/0
89	Smith, Steve	WR	5-9	185	5/12/79	9	Utah	Lynwood, Calif.	D3-'01	14/14
28	Stewart, Jonathan	RB	5-10	235	3/21/87	2	Oregon	Fort Lewis, Wash.	D1a-'08	16/0
66	Taylor, Hilee	DE	6-2	250	7/18/86	2	North Carolina	Laurinburg, N.C.	D7a-'08	9/0
26	Teal, Quinton	S	6-1	187	3/8/84	3	Coastal Carolina	Bennettsville, S.C.	FA-'07	13/0
68	Vincent, Keydrick	G	6-5	325	4/13/78	9	Mississippi	Lakeland, Fla.	UFA(Ariz)-'08	14/14
21	Wesley, Dante	CB	6-1	210	4/5/79	8	Arkansas Pine-Bluff	Pine Bluff, Ark.	FA-'07	16/0
70	Wharton, Travelle	G	6-4	312	5/19/81	6	South Carolina	Simpsonville, S.C.	D3-'04	14/14
34	Williams, DeAngelo	RB	5-9	217	4/25/83	4	Memphis	Wynne, Ark.	D1-'06	16/16
27	Wilson, C.J.	CB	6-1	195	4/2/85	3	Baylor	Terrell, Texas	FA-'07	4/0

* Bernadeau inactive for 11 games; Carter missed '08 season because of injury; Geisinger played 4 games with Washington in '08; Jansen missed '08 season because of injury with Green Bay; K. Moore inactive for 11 games; M. Moore inactive for 16 games; Robinson missed '08 season because of injury.

Players lost through free agency (3): G/C Geoff Hangartner (Buff; 16 games in '08), WR Mark Jones (Tenn; 16), T Frank Omiyale (Chi; 10).

Also played with Panthers in '08—LB Donte Curry (13), RB Nick Goings (16), WR D.J. Hackett (9), LB Jason Kyle (16), CB Ken Lucas (16), DT J'Vonne Parker (1), LB Adam Seward (9), DT Darwin Walker (10).

2009 FIRST-YEAR ROSTER

Name	Pos.	Ht.	Wt.	Birthdate	College	Hometown	How Acq.
Beavers, Larry	WR	5-10	167	10/7/85	Wesley	Annapolis, Md.	FA
Birmingham, Decori (1)	RB	5-10	210	11/22/82	Arkansas	Atlanta, Texas	FA-'07
Brinkley, Casper (1)	DE	6-2	259	7/12/85	South Carolina	Thomson, Ga.	FA-'08
Brock, Kevin	TE	6-5	255	4/9/86	Rutgers	Hackensack, N.J.	FA
Brown, Everette	DE	6-1	256	8/7/87	Florida State	Stantonsburg, N.C.	D2a
Brown, Patrick	T	6-5	303	12/25/86	Central Florida	St. Charles, Ill.	FA
Cadogan, Gerald	T	6-5	310	1/16/86	Penn State	Portsmouth, Ohio	FA
Cantwell, Hunter	QB	6-4	236	12/30/85	Louisville	Paducah, Ky.	FA
Chery, Jason	WR	5-10	185	5/31/85	Louisiana-Lafayette	Delray Beach, Fla.	FA
Clark, D.J.	CB	6-1	200	11/30/86	Idaho State	Oceanside, Calif.	FA
Davis, C.J.	G	6-2	308	2/2/87	Pittsburgh	Imperial, Pa.	FA
Favorite, Marlon	DT	6-1	317	6/22/86	Louisiana State	Harvey, La.	FA
Fiammetta, Tony	FB	6-0	242	8/22/86	Syracuse	Walkersville, Md.	D4a
Fields, Joe (1)	S	6-0	201	10/5/85	Syracuse	Houston, Texas	FA-'08
Goodson, Mike	RB	6-0	212	5/23/87	Texas A&M	Klein, Texas	D4b
Gray, Keith	C	6-1	294	8/28/86	Connecticut	Allen, Texas	FA
Harvey, Lonnie	DT	6-3	342	1/20/87	Morgan State	Baltimore, Md.	FA
Heygood, Anthony	LB	6-1	225	4/3/86	Purdue	Chester, Pa.	FA
Irvin, Corvey	DT	6-3	302	5/3/85	Georgia	Augusta, Ga.	D3
Ivy, Mortty	LB	6-1	239	4/26/86	West Virginia	Monroeville, Pa.	FA
Juergens, Mike	LB	6-3	230	12/30/84	Wyoming	Westminster, Colo.	FA
Kershaw, Justin	DT	6-4	271	9/18/85	Michigan State	Columbus, Ohio	FA
Lee, Jamall	RB	6-1	225	3/13/87	Bishop's	Port Coquitlan, B.C., Canada	FA
Leman, Jeremy	LB	6-2	240	3/1/85	Illinois	Champaign, Ill.	FA
MacDonald, Patrick (1)	DT	6-2	265	2/20/82	Alberta	Toronto, Ontario, Canada	FA-'08
Martin, Sherrod	CB	6-1	198	10/12/84	Troy	Griffin, Ga.	D2b
McMahan, Kevin	WR	6-2	192	3/2/83	Maine	Rochester, N.Y.	FA
Miller, Brit	LB	6-0	243	9/15/86	Illinois	Decatur, Ill.	FA
Monk, Marcus	WR	6-4	212	4/26/86	Arkansas	Lepanto, Ark.	FA
Munnerlyn, Captain	CB	5-8	186	4/10/88	South Carolina	Mobile, Ala.	D7
Oshinowo, Babatunde	DT	6-1	325	1/14/83	Stanford	Naperville, Ill.	FA
Palmer, Jonathan (1)	T	6-4	336	12/3/83	Auburn	Ellenwood, Ga.	FA-'08
Robinson, Duke	G	6-5	330	10/10/86	Oklahoma	Atlanta, Ga.	D5
Schwartz, Geoff (1)	T	6-6	331	7/11/86	Oregon	Los Angeles, Calif.	D7b-'08
Scirrotto, Anthony	S	6-0	202	10/21/86	Penn State	West Deptford, N.J.	FA
Sundberg, Nick	LS	6-0	245	7/29/87	California	Phoenix, Ariz.	FA
Williams, Garry	T	6-3	296	8/20/86	Kentucky	Louisville, Ky.	FA
Williams, Lorenzo	DT	6-0	310	10/23/84	Missouri	Midwest City, Okla.	FA

The term NFL Rookie is defined as a player who is in his first season of professional football and has not been on the roster of another professional football team for any regular-season or postseason games. A Rookie is designated by an "R" on NFL rosters. Players who have been active in another professional football league or players who have NFL experience, including either preseason training camp or being on an Active List or Inactive List, or on Reserve/Injured or Reserve/Physically Unable to Perform for fewer than six regular-season games, are termed NFL First-Year Players. An NFL First-Year Player is designated by a "1" on NFL rosters. Thereafter, a player is credited with an additional year of experience for each season in which he accumulates six games on the Active List or Inactive List, or on Reserve/Injured or Reserve/Physically Unable to Perform.

Log on to www.panthers.com for an up-to-date roster.

COACHING STAFF

Head Coach,

John Fox

Pro Career: Became third coach in Carolina Panthers history on January 25, 2002. In 2008, guided the Panthers to the third division title in franchise history. During tenure from 2002-07, 68 overall victories stand as the second-highest total in the NFC. Since arrival in 2002, the Panthers have ranked among the NFL's top 10 in total defense in four of the seven seasons. In 2005, directed team to second NFC championship appearance in three seasons. Became the fifth head coach in NFL history to record four career postseason road wins. Equaled an NFL record with four consecutive postseason road wins. In 2004, directed Carolina team that overcame a 1-7 record to end the regular season with mark of 7-9. Of the 28 NFL teams that began season with 1-7 record since 1990, Panthers became only third team to finish season with seven victories. In 2003, guided Panthers to Super Bowl XXXVIII two years after inheriting team that won one game in 2001. Joined Vince Lombardi and Bill Parcells as the only coaches in NFL history to inherit a one-win team and guide it to the playoffs in their second season. In 2002, engineered a six-game turn-around that ranks second for rookie head coaches since 1978. In 2002, the Panthers became the only team since 1970 to improve from thirty-first to second in total defense in one season. Prior to joining Carolina he served as the defensive coordinator for the N.Y. Giants (1997-2001). In 2000, Fox helped the Giants reach Super Bowl XXXV, including posting the first shutout in a conference title game since 1986. Before joining the Giants, Fox was a consultant for the Rams (1996), defensive coordinator for the Raiders (1994-95), defensive backs coach for the Chargers (1992-93) and Steelers (1989-1991), and secondary coach for the USFL's Los Angeles Express (1985). Career record: 68-52.

Background: Defensive back at San Diego State (1976-77). Coached at San Diego State (1978), U.S. International (1979) Boise State (1980), Long Beach State (1981), Utah (1982), Kansas (1983), Iowa State (1984), and Pittsburgh (1986-88). Received bachelor's degree in physical education and earned a teaching credential from San Diego State.

Personal: Born February 8, 1955, in Virginia Beach, Va. He and his wife, Robin, have four children—Mathew, Mark, Cody, and Halle.

ASSISTANT COACHES

Brian Baker, defensive line; born June 20, 1962, Baltimore. Linebacker Maryland 1981-83. College coach: Maryland 1984-85, Army 1986, Georgia Tech 1987-1995. Pro coach: San Diego Chargers 1996, Detroit Lions 1997-2000, Minnesota Vikings 2001-05, St. Louis Rams 2006-08, joined Panthers in 2009.

Geep Chryst, tight ends/quality control-offense; born June 25, 1962, Madison, Wis. Linebacker Princeton 1981-84. Pro linebacker Orlando Thunder (WFL) 1992. College coach: Wisconsin-Platteville 1987, Wisconsin 1988, Wyoming 1989-1990. Pro coach: Orlando Thunder (WL) 1991, Chicago Bears 1991-95, Arizona Cardinals 1996-98, 2001-03, San Diego Chargers 1999-2000, joined Panthers in 2006.

Danny Crossman, special teams; born January 17, 1967, El Paso, Texas. Defensive back Kansas 1985, Pittsburgh 1987-89. Pro defensive back Washington Redskins 1990, Detroit Lions 1991-92. College coach: U.S. Coast Guard Academy 1993, Western Kentucky 1994-96, Central Florida 1997-98, Georgia Tech 1999-2001, Michigan State 2002. Pro coach: Joined Panthers in 2003.

Jeff Davidson, offensive coordinator; born Oct. 3, 1967, Akron, Ohio. Offensive lineman Ohio State 1986-89. Pro offensive lineman Denver Broncos 1990-92, New Orleans Saints 1994. Pro coach: New Orleans Saints 1995-96, New England Patriots 1997-2004, Cleveland Browns 2005-06, joined Panthers in 2007.

Mike Gillhamer, secondary; born February 20, 1956, Oakland. Defensive back Carroll College 1972, Wenatchee (Wash.) J.C. 1973, Humboldt State 1974-75. No pro playing experience. College coach: College of the Sequoias 1979-1983, Weber State 1984, Utah 1985-89, San Jose State 1990-93, Nevada 1994-95, Oregon 2001-02, Louisville 2003. Pro coach: New York Giants 1997-2000, joined Panthers in 2004.

David Magazu, offensive line; born June 10, 1957, Taunton Mass. Defensive tackle Springfield College 1976-79. No pro playing experience. College coach: Ithaca 1980, Western Michigan 1981, Eastern Michigan 1982, Michigan 1983, Northern Illinois 1984, Ball State 1985-86, Navy 1987-89, Indiana State 1990-91, Colorado State 1992-94, Kentucky 1995-96, Memphis 1997-98, Boston College 1999-2002. Pro coach: Joined Panthers in 2003.

Ron Meeks, defensive coordinator; born August 27, 1954, Jacksonville. Defensive back Arkansas State 1972-76. Pro defensive back Hamilton Tiger-Cats (CFL) 1977-79, Ottawa Rough Riders (CFL) 1979, Toronto Argonauts (CFL) 1980-81. College coach: Arkansas State 1984-85, Miami 1986-87, New Mexico State 1988, Fresno State 1989-1990. Pro coach: Dallas Cowboys 1991, Cincinnati Bengals 1992-96, Atlanta Falcons 1997-99, Washington Redskins 2000, St. Louis Rams 2001, Indianapolis Colts 2002-08, joined Panthers in 2009.

Sam Mills III, quality control/defense; born May 20, 1978, Long Branch, N.J. Cornerback Montclair State 1997-98. No pro playing experience. Pro coach: Joined Panthers in 2006.

Ron Milus, secondary; born November 25, 1963, Tacoma, Wash. Cornerback Washington 1982-85. College coach: Washington 1991-98, Texas A&M 1999. Pro coach: Denver Broncos 2000-02, Arizona Cardinals 2003, New York Giants 2004-05, St. Louis Rams 2006-08, joined Panthers in 2009.

Jeff Rodgers, asst. special teams; January 12, 1978, St. Paul, Minn. Linebacker North Texas 1996-99. College coach: Arizona 2001-02, Kansas State 2008. Pro coach: San Francisco 49ers 2003-07, joined Panthers in 2009.

Rip Scherer, quarterbacks, passing game coordinator; born August 3, 1952, Quarterback: William & Mary 1970-73. College coach: Penn State 1974-75, North Carolina State 1976, Hawaii 1977-78, Virginia 1979, Georgia Tech 1980-86, Alabama 1987, Arizona 1988-1990, James Madison 1991-94 (head coach), Memphis 1995-2000 (head coach), Kansas 2001, Southern Mississippi 2003-04. Pro coach: Cleveland Browns 2005-2008, joined Panthers in 2009.

Jerry Simmons, strength and conditioning; born June 15, 1954, Elkhart, Kan. Linebacker Fort Hays State 1976-77. No pro playing experience. College coach: Fort Hays State 1978, Clemson 1980, Rice 1981-82, Southern California 1983-87. Pro coach: New England Patriots 1988-1990, Cleveland Browns/Baltimore Ravens 1991-98, joined Panthers in 1999.

Jim Skipper, asst. head coach/running backs; born January 23, 1949, Breaux Bridge, La. Defensive back Whittier College 1971-72. No pro playing experience. College coach: Cal Poly-Pomona 1974-76, San Jose State 1977-78, Pacific 1979, Oregon 1980-82. Pro coach: Philadelphia/Baltimore Stars (USFL) 1983-85, New Orleans Saints 1986-1995, Arizona Cardinals 1996, New York Giants 1997-2000, San Francisco Demons (XFL) 2001 (head coach), joined Panthers in 2002.

Richard Smith, linebackers; born October 17, 1955, Los Angeles. Offensive lineman Rio Hondo (Calif.) J.C. 1975-76, Fresno State 1977-78. College coach: Rio Hondo (Calif.) J.C. 1979-1980, Cal State-Fullerton 1981-83, California 1984-86, Arizona 1987. Pro coach: Houston Oilers 1988-1992, Denver Broncos 1993-96, San Francisco 49ers 1997-2002, Detroit Lions 2003-04, Miami Dolphins 2005, Houston Texans 2006-08, joined Panthers in 2009.

Richard Williamson, wide receivers; born April 13, 1941, Ft. Deposit, Ala. Receiver Alabama 1961-62. No pro playing experience. College coach: Alabama 1963-67, 1970-71, Arkansas 1968-69, 1972-74, Memphis State 1975-1980 (head coach). Pro coach: Kansas City Chiefs 1983-86, Tampa Bay Buccaneers 1987-1991 (interim head coach 1990, head coach 1991), Cincinnati Bengals 1992-94, joined Panthers in 1995.

National Football Conference
North Division
Team Colors: Navy Blue, Orange, and White
Halas Hall at Conway Park
1000 Football Drive
Lake Forest, Illinois 60045
Telephone: (847) 295-6600

2009 SCHEDULE

PRESEASON

Aug. 15	at Buffalo	7:00
Aug. 22	**N.Y. Giants**	7:00
Aug. 30	at Denver	6:00
Sep. 3	**Cleveland**	7:00

REGULAR SEASON

Sep. 13	at Green Bay	7:20
Sep. 20	**Pittsburgh**	3:15
Sep. 27	at Seattle	1:05
Oct. 4	**Detroit**	12:00
Oct. 11	BYE	
Oct. 18	at Atlanta	8:20
Oct. 25	at Cincinnati	1:00
Nov. 1	**Cleveland**	12:00
Nov. 8	**Arizona**	12:00
Nov. 12	at San Francisco (Thu.)	5:20
Nov. 22	**Philadelphia** *	7:20
Nov. 29	at Minnesota	12:00
Dec. 6	**St. Louis**	12:00
Dec. 13	**Green Bay**	12:00
Dec. 20	at Baltimore	1:00
Dec. 28	**Minnesota** (Mon.)	7:30
Jan. 3	at Detroit	1:00

** Sunday night games in Weeks 11-17 subject to change*

Stadium: Soldier Field (opened in 1924) •**Capacity:** 61,500
1410 S. Museum Campus Dr.
Chicago, Illinois 60605
Playing Surface: Natural Grass
Training Camp: Olivet-Nazarene Univ.
Bourbonnais, Illinois 60901

SOLDIER FIELD

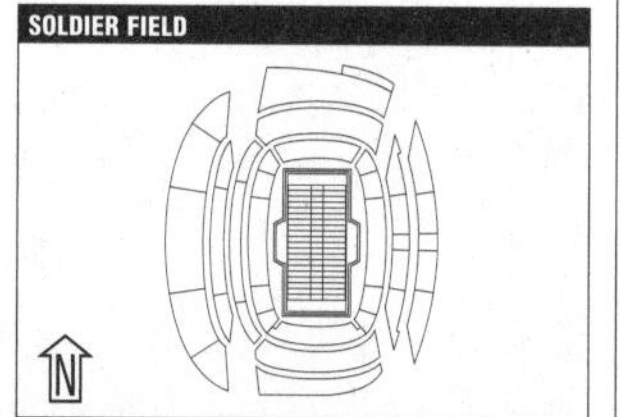

CLUB OFFICIALS

Chairman of the Board: Michael B. McCaskey
Secretary: Virginia H. McCaskey
President and CEO: Ted Phillips
General Manager: Jerry Angelo
Vice President: Tim McCaskey
Senior Director of Special Projects: Pat McCaskey
Senior Director of Ticket Operations: George McCaskey
Senior Director of Business Development & Alumni Relations: Brian McCaskey
Senior Director of Administration: John Bostrom
Senior Director of Finance & Treasurer: Karen Murphy
Senior Director of Corporate Sales & Marketing: Chris Hibbs
Senior Director of Corporate Communications: Scott Hagel
Senior Director of Pro Personnel: Bobby DePaul
Director of College Scouting: Greg Gabriel
Senior Director of Football Administration and General Counsel: Cliff Stein
Assistant Director of Pro Personnel: Kevin Turks
Director of Player Development: Isaiah Harris
Director of Community Relations: Caroline Guip
Director of Broadcasting & Scoreboard Operations: Greg Miller
Media Services Manager: Jim Christman
Media Relations Coordinator: Mike Corbo
Media Relations Assistant: Cary Dohman
Director of Video Services: Dave Hendrickson
Assistant Video Director: Dean Pope
College Video Coordinator: Dan Tuohy
Head Athletic Trainer: Tim Bream
Assistant Trainers: Chris Hanks, Jeremy Smith
Director of Rehabilitation: Bobby Slater
Head Equipment Manager: Tony Medlin
Assistant Equipment Managers: Carl Piekarski, John Perkins
Scouts: Chris Ballard, Marty Barrett, Rex Hogan, Ted Monago, Mark Sadowski, Jeff Shiver
Director of Human Resources: Ann Quint
Director of Finance: Jake Jones
Director of Security & Safety Services: Tom Dillon
Director of Stadium Operations: Bryan Pett
Director of Football Systems Technology: Brian Wright
Director of Corporate Sales: Ryan Huzjak
Director of Client Services: Rebecca Coffey
Director of Stadium Sales & Services: Adam Kellner
Director of Creative Services: John Conroy
Director of Events & Advertising: Julie White
Director of Bears Care: Marge Hamm

COACHING HISTORY

Decatur Staleys 1920, Chicago Staleys 1921 (702-515-42)

Records include postseason games

1920-29	George Halas	84-31-19
1930-32	Ralph Jones	24-10-7
1933-1942	George Halas*	88-24-4
1942-45	Hunk Anderson-Luke Johnsos**	24-12-2
1946-1955	George Halas	76-43-2
1956-57	John (Paddy) Driscoll	14-10-1
1958-1967	George Halas	76-53-6
1968-1971	Jim Dooley	20-36-0
1972-74	Abe Gibron	11-30-1
1975-77	Jack Pardee	20-23-0
1978-1981	Neill Armstrong	30-35-0
1982-1992	Mike Ditka	112-68-0
1993-98	Dave Wannstedt	41-57-0
1999-2003	Dick Jauron	35-46-0
2004-08	Lovie Smith	47-37-0

*Retired after five games to enter U.S. Navy
**Co-coaches

PAID ATTENDANCE

Home 484,501 Away 519,389
Total 1,003,890
Single-game home record, 66,900 (9/5/93)
Single-season home record, 527,769 (1999)

2009 DRAFT CHOICES

Round	Name	Pos.	College
3	Jarron Gilbert	DT	San Jose State
	Juaquin Iglesias	WR	Oklahoma
4	Henry Melton	DE	Texas
	D.J. Moore	DB	Vanderbilt
5	Johnny Knox	WR	Abilene Christian
	Marcus Freeman	LB	Ohio State
6	Al Afalava	DB	Oregon State
7	Lance Louis	TE	San Diego State
	Derek Kinder	WR	Pittsburgh

CHICAGO BEARS

2008 TEAM RECORD

PRESEASON (1-3)

Date	Result	Opponent
8/7	L 20-24	Kansas City
8/16	L 26-29	at Seattle (OT)
8/21	L 30-37	San Francisco
8/28	W 16-10	at Cleveland

REGULAR SEASON (9-7)

Date	Result	Opponent
9/7	W 29-13	at Indianapolis
9/14	L 17-20	at Carolina
9/21	L 24-27	Tampa Bay (OT)
9/28	W 24-20	Philadelphia
10/5	W 34-7	at Detroit
10/12	L 20-22	at Atlanta
10/19	W 48-41	Minnesota
11/2	W 27-23	Detroit
11/9	L 14-21	Tennessee
11/16	L 3-37	at Green Bay
11/23	W 27-3	at St. Louis
11/30	L 14-34	at Minnesota
12/7	W 23-10	Jacksonville
12/11	W 27-24	New Orleans (OT)
12/22	W 20-17	Green Bay (OT)
12/28	L 24-31	at Houston

(OT) Overtime

SCORE BY PERIODS

Bears	109	101	88	71	6 —	375
Opponents	47	128	72	100	3 —	350

2008 TEAM STATISTICS

	Bears	Opp.
Total First Downs	264	314
Rushing	98	93
Passing	153	208
Penalty	13	13
3rd Down: Made/Att	78/219	81/232
3rd Down Pct.	35.6	34.9
4th Down: Made/Att	6/14	10/21
4th Down Pct.	42.9	47.6
Possession Avg.	28:07	31:53
Total Net Yards	4734	5355
Avg. Per Game	295.9	334.7
Total Plays	991	1087
Avg. Per Play	4.8	4.9
Net Yards Rushing	1673	1496
Avg. Per Game	104.6	93.5
Total Rushes	434	437
Net Yards Passing	3061	3859
Avg. Per Game	191.3	241.2
Sacked/Yards Lost	29/168	28/217
Gross Yards	3229	4076
Att./Completions	528/304	622/383
Completion Pct.	57.6	61.6
Had Intercepted	14	22
Punts/Average	96/41.2	83/42.5
Net Punting Avg.	96/38.1	83/37.4
Penalties/Yards	78/610	100/827
Fumbles/Ball Lost	19/13	17/10
Touchdowns	42	39
Rushing	15	16
Passing	20	21
Returns	7	2

2008 INDIVIDUAL STATISTICS

PASSING	Att.	Comp.	Yds.	Pct.	TD	Int.	Tkld.	Rate
Orton	465	272	2972	58.5	18	12	27/160	79.6
Grossman	62	32	257	51.6	2	2	2/8	59.7
Maynard	1	0	0	0.0	0	0	0/0	39.6
Bears	528	304	3229	57.6	20	14	29/168	77.1
Opponents	622	383	4076	61.6	21	22	28/217	77.2

SCORING	TD R	TD P	TD Rt	PAT	FG	Saf	PTS
Gould	0	0	0	41/41	26/29	0	119
Forté	8	4	0	0/0	0/0	0	72
Olsen	0	5	0	0/0	0/0	0	30
Lloyd	0	2	1	0/0	0/0	0	20
R. Davis	0	2	1	0/0	0/0	0	18
Hester	0	3	0	0/0	0/0	0	18
McKie	2	1	0	0/0	0/0	0	18
Orton	3	0	0	0/0	0/0	0	18
Booker	0	2	0	0/0	0/0	0	12
Grossman	2	0	0	0/0	0/0	0	12
Bowman	0	0	1	0/0	0/0	0	6
Briggs	0	0	1	0/0	0/0	0	6
Clark	0	1	0	0/0	0/0	0	6
Manning	0	0	1	0/0	0/0	0	6
Tillman	0	0	1	0/0	0/0	0	6
Wolfe	0	0	1	0/0	0/0	0	6
Ogunleye	0	0	0	0/0	0/0	1	2
Bears	15	20	7	41/41	26/29	1	375
Opponents	16	21	2	38/39	26/33	0	350

2-Pt. Conversions: Lloyd.
Bears 1-1, Opponents 0-0.

RUSHING	No.	Yds	Avg	LG	TD
Forté	316	1238	3.9	50t	8
Jones	34	109	3.2	16	0
Peterson	20	100	5.0	16	0
Wolfe	15	69	4.6	38	0
Hester	6	61	10.2	20	0
Orton	24	49	2.0	12	3
McKie	11	26	2.4	6	2
R. Davis	3	14	4.7	17	0
Grossman	3	4	1.3	2	2
Booker	1	3	3.0	3	0
J. Davis	1	0	0.0	0	0
Bears	434	1673	3.9	50t	15
Opponents	437	1496	3.4	59	16

RECEIVING	No.	Yds	Avg	LG	TD
Forté	63	477	7.6	19	4
Olsen	54	574	10.6	52	5
Hester	51	665	13.0	65t	3
Clark	41	367	9.0	35	1
R. Davis	35	445	12.7	36	2
Lloyd	26	364	14.0	32	2
Booker	14	211	15.1	51t	2
McKie	11	64	5.8	12	1
Peterson	6	45	7.5	19	0
Jones	2	5	2.5	3	0
J. Davis	1	12	12.0	12	0
Bears	304	3229	10.6	65t	20
Opponents	383	4076	10.6	99t	21

INTERCEPTIONS	No.	Yds	Avg	LG	TD
Payne	4	147	36.8	50	0
Tillman	3	52	17.3	26t	1
Briggs	3	12	4.0	9	0
Urlacher	2	11	5.5	11	0
M. Brown	2	0	0.0	0	0
Steltz	1	44	44.0	44	0
Manning	1	42	42.0	42	0
Graham	1	6	6.0	6	0
Bowman	1	0	0.0	0	0
McBride	1	0	0.0	0	0
Ogunleye	1	0	0.0	0	0
Vasher	1	0	0.0	0	0
A. Brown	1	-2	-2.0	-2	0
Bears	22	312	14.2	50	1
Opponents	14	219	15.6	45t	1

PUNTING	No.	Yds.	Avg.	In 20	LG
Maynard	96	3957	41.2	40	67
Bears	96	3957	41.2	40	67
Opponents	83	3525	42.5	22	65

PUNT RETURNS	Ret	FC	Yds	Avg	LG	TD
Hester	32	14	198	6.2	25	0
Vasher	6	1	46	7.7	18	0
Bennett	1	0	17	17.0	17	0
Bears	39	15	261	6.7	25	0
Opponents	36	27	203	5.6	31	0

KICKOFF RETURNS	No.	Yds	Avg	LG	TD
Manning	36	1070	29.7	83t	1
Hester	31	679	21.9	51	0
Wolfe	5	98	19.6	33	0
McKie	2	38	19.0	20	0
K. Davis	1	13	13.0	13	0
Peterson	1	11	11.0	11	0
R. Davis	1	10	10.0	10	0
Bears	77	1919	24.9	83t	1
Opponents	68	1656	24.4	85	0

FIELD GOALS	1-19	20-29	30-39	40-49	50+
Gould	0/0	6/6	12/12	8/11	0/0
Bears	0/0	6/6	12/12	8/11	0/0
Opponents	0/0	8/8	8/10	8/12	2/3

SACKS	No.
A. Brown	6.0
Harris	5.0
Ogunleye	5.0
Idonije	3.5
Harrison	2.0
Anderson	1.0
M. Brown	1.0
Hillenmeyer	1.0
Manning	1.0
Payne	1.0
(group)	1.0
Briggs	0.5
Bears	28.0
Opponents	29.0

RECORD HOLDERS

INDIVIDUAL RECORDS—CAREER

Category	Name	Performance
Rushing (Yds.)	Walter Payton, 1975-1987	16,726
Passing (Yds.)	Sid Luckman, 1939-1950	14,686
Passing (TDs)	Sid Luckman, 1939-1950	137
Receiving (No.)	Walter Payton, 1975-1987	492
Receiving (Yds.)	Johnny Morris, 1958-1967	5,059
Interceptions	Gary Fencik, 1976-1987	38
Punting (Avg.)	George Gulyanics, 1947-1952	44.5
Punt Return (Avg.)	George McAfee, 1940-41, 1945-1950	12.8
Kickoff Return (Avg.)	Gale Sayers, 1965-1971	**30.6
Field Goals	Kevin Butler, 1985-1995	243
Touchdowns (Tot.)	Walter Payton, 1975-1987	125
Points	Kevin Butler, 1985-1995	1,116
*Sacks	Richard Dent, 1983-1993, 1995	124.5

INDIVIDUAL RECORDS—SINGLE SEASON

Category	Name	Performance
Rushing (Yds.)	Walter Payton, 1977	1,852
Passing (Yds.)	Erik Kramer, 1995	3,838
Passing (TDs)	Erik Kramer, 1995	29
Receiving (No.)	Marty Booker, 2001	100
Receiving (Yds.)	Marcus Robinson, 1999	1,400
Interceptions	Mark Carrier, 1990	10
Punting (Avg.)	Bobby Joe Green, 1963	46.5
Punt Return (Avg.)	Harry Clark, 1943	15.8
Kickoff Return (Avg.)	Gale Sayers, 1967	37.7
Field Goals	Robbie Gould, 2006	32
Touchdowns (Tot.)	Gale Sayers, 1965	22
Points	Kevin Butler, 1985	144
*Sacks	Richard Dent, 1984	17.5

INDIVIDUAL RECORDS—SINGLE GAME

Category	Name	Performance
Rushing (Yds.)	Walter Payton, 11-20-77	275
Passing (Yds.)	Johnny Lujack, 12-11-49	468
Passing (TDs)	Sid Luckman, 11-14-43	**7
Receiving (No.)	Jim Keane, 10-23-49	14
Receiving (Yds.)	Harlon Hill, 10-31-54	214
Interceptions	Many times	3
	Last time by Mark Carrier, 12-9-90	
Field Goals	Roger LeClerc, 12-3-61	5
	Mac Percival, 10-20-68	5
Touchdowns (Tot.)	Gale Sayers, 12-12-65	**6
Points	Gale Sayers, 12-12-65	36
*Sacks	Richard Dent, 11-4-84, 12-27-87	4.5

**Sacks became an official statistic in 1982.*
***NFL Record*

CHICAGO BEARS

2009 VETERAN ROSTER

No.	Name	Pos.	Ht.	Wt.	Birthdate	NFL Exp.	College	Hometown	How Acq.	'08 Games/ Starts
95	Adams, Anthony	DT	6-0	307	6/18/80	7	Penn State	Detroit, Mich.	UFA(SF)-'07	9/4
97	Anderson, Mark	DE	6-4	255	5/26/83	4	Alabama	Tulsa, Okla.	D5-'06	16/0
19	Aromashodu, Devin	WR	6-2	201	5/23/84	3	Auburn	Miami, Fla.	FA-'08	0*
99	Baldwin, Ervin	DE	6-2	260	8/25/86	2	Michigan State	Oglethorpe, Ga.	D7a-'08	0*
14	Basanez, Brett	QB	6-2	210	5/11/83	2	Northwestern	Arlington Heights, Ill.	FA-'09	0*
67	Beekman, Josh	G/C	6-2	310	6/30/83	3	Boston College	Amsterdam, N.Y.	D4-'07	16/16
80	Bennett, Earl	WR	6-0	203	3/23/87	2	Vanderbilt	Birmingham, Ala.	D3a-'08	10/0
35	Bowman, Zackary	S	6-1	193	11/18/84	2	Nebraska	Anchorage, Alaska	D5a-'08	1/0
55	Briggs, Lance	LB	6-1	240	11/12/80	7	Arizona	Sacramento, Calif.	D3-'03	16/16
15	Broussard, John	WR	6-1	176	12/18/83	2	San Jose State	Kingwood, Texas	FA-'08	0*
96	Brown, Alex	DE	6-3	260	6/4/79	8	Florida	White Springs, Fla.	D4-'02	16/16
30	#Brown, Mike	S	5-10	207	2/13/78	10	Nebraska	Scottsdale, Ariz.	D2-'00	15/15
72	Buenning, Dan	G	6-4	320	10/26/81	5	Wisconsin	Green Bay, Wis.	T(TB)-'08	10/0
36	Bullocks, Josh	S	6-1	207	2/28/83	5	Nebraska	Chattanooga, Tenn.	UFA(NO)-'09	16/6*
88	Clark, Desmond	TE	6-3	249	4/20/77	11	Wake Forest	Lakeland, Fla.	UFA(Mia)-'03	16/16
6	t-Cutler, Jay	QB	6-3	233	4/29/83	4	Vanderbilt	Santa Claus, Ind.	T(Den)-'09	16/16*
43	Davis, Jason	FB	5-10	245	11/2/83	2	Illinois	St. Louis, Mo.	FA-'08	5/3
87	Davis, Kellen	TE	6-7	262	10/11/85	2	Michigan State	Adrian, Mich.	D5b-'08	16/0
81	Davis, Rashied	WR	5-9	187	7/24/79	5	San Jose State	Granada Hills, Calif.	FA-'05	16/12
98	Dvoracek, Dusty	DT	6-3	303	3/3/83	4	Oklahoma	Lake Dallas, Texas	D3-'06	12/12
32	Earl, Glenn	S	6-1	213	6/10/81	5	Notre Dame	Naperville, Ill.	FA-'09	0*
22	Forté, Matt	RB	6-2	216	12/10/85	2	Tulane	Slidell, La.	D2-'08	16/16
	Gaines, Michael	TE	6-4	277	3/30/80	6	Central Florida	Tallahassee, Fla.	FA-'09	16/6*
63	Garza, Roberto	G/C	6-2	310	3/26/79	9	Texas A&M-Kingsville	Rio Hondo, Texas	UFA(Atl)-'05	16/16
9	Gould, Robbie	K	6-0	185	12/30/81	5	Penn State	Lock Haven, Pa.	FA-'05	16/0
21	Graham, Corey	CB	6-0	193	7/25/85	3	New Hampshire	Buffalo, N.Y.	D5b-'07	16/9
8	#Grossman, Rex	QB	6-1	217	8/23/80	7	Florida	Bloomington, Ind.	D1b-'03	4/1
24	Hamilton, Marcus	CB	5-11	188	2/17/84	2	Virginia	Fairfax, Va.	W(TB)-'08	9/0*
12	Hanie, Caleb	QB	6-2	225	9/11/85	2	Colorado State	Forney, Texas	FA-'08	0*
91	Harris, Tommie	DT	6-3	295	4/29/83	6	Oklahoma	Killeen, Texas	D1-'04	14/13
94	Harrison, Marcus	DT	6-3	310	7/10/84	2	Arkansas	Little Rock, Ark.	D3b-'08	16/0
23	Hester, Devin	WR/PR	5-11	190	11/4/82	4	Miami	Riviera Beach, Fla.	D2b-'06	15/8
92	Hillenmeyer, Hunter	LB	6-4	238	10/28/80	7	Vanderbilt	Nashville, Tenn.	FA-'03	13/6
71	Idonije, Israel	DL	6-6	297	11/17/80	6	Manitoba	Lagos, Nigeria	FA-'03	16/3
27	Jones, Kevin	RB	6-0	228	8/21/82	6	Virginia Tech	Chester, Pa.	FA-'08	11/0
57	Kreutz, Olin	C	6-2	292	6/9/77	12	Washington	Honolulu, Hawaii	D3-'98	16/16
90	LaRocque, Joey	LB	6-2	226	3/15/86	2	Oregon State	Agoura, Calif.	D7c-'08	14/0
80	#Lloyd, Brandon	WR	6-0	194	7/5/81	7	Illinois	Blue Springs, Mo.	FA-'08	11/5
65	Mannelly, Patrick	LS	6-5	265	4/18/75	12	Duke	Atlanta, Ga.	D6b-'98	16/0
38	Manning, Danieal	S	5-11	200	8/9/82	4	Abilene Christian	Corsicana, Texas	D2a-'06	14/1
4	Maynard, Brad	P	6-1	188	2/9/74	13	Ball State	Sheridan, Ind.	UFA(NYG)-'01	16/0
26	McBride, Trumaine	CB	5-9	185	9/24/85	3	Mississippi	Clarksdale, Miss.	D7a-'07	16/1
58	#McClover, Darrell	LB	6-1	226	8/25/81	6	Miami	Coconut Creek, Fla.	FA-'06	10/0
37	McKie, Jason	FB	5-11	245	5/22/80	8	Temple	Gulf Breeze, Fla.	W(Dall)-'03	11/8
69	#Miller, Fred	T	6-7	314	2/6/73	14	Baylor	Aldine, Texas	FA-'05	6/0
93	Ogunleye, Adewale	DE	6-4	260	8/9/77	9	Indiana	Staten Island, N.Y.	T(Mia)-'04	16/16
82	Olsen, Greg	TE	6-5	255	3/11/85	3	Miami	Wayne, N.J.	D1-'07	16/7
68	Omiyale, Frank	G	6-4	310	11/23/82	5	Tennessee Tech	Whites Creek, Tenn.	UFA(Car)-'09	10/1*
76	Pace, Orlando	T	6-7	325	11/4/74	13	Ohio State	Sandusky, Ohio	FA-'09	14/14*
44	Payne, Kevin	S	6-0	212	12/5/83	3	Louisiana-Monroe	Junction City, Ark.	D5a-'07	16/16
29	Peterson, Adrian	RB	5-10	212	7/1/79	8	Georgia Southern	Alachua, Fla.	D6a-'02	15/0
84	Rideau, Brandon	WR	6-3	198	10/18/82	3	Kansas	Beaumont, Texas	FA-'06	2/0
53	Roach, Nick	LB	6-1	234	6/16/85	3	Northwestern	Milwaukee, Wis.	FA-'07	14/9
78	Shaffer, Kevin	T	6-5	315	3/2/80	8	Tulsa	Lancaster, Pa.	FA-'09	15/15*
20	Steltz, Craig	S	6-1	210	5/7/86	2	Louisiana State	Metairie, La.	D4-'08	11/0
33	Tillman, Charles	CB	6-1	198	2/23/81	7	Louisiana-Lafayette	Copperas Cove, Texas	D2-'03	15/15
75	Toeaina, Matt	DT	6-2	308	10/9/84	2	Oregon	Utulei, American Samoa	FA-'07	1/0
54	Urlacher, Brian	LB	6-4	258	5/25/78	10	New Mexico	Lovington, N.M.	D1-'00	16/16
31	Vasher, Nathan	CB	5-10	187	11/17/81	6	Texas	Texarkana, Texas	D4a-'04	8/7
74	Williams, Chris	T	6-6	312	8/26/85	2	Vanderbilt	Glynn, La.	D1-'08	9/0
52	Williams, Jamar	LB	6-0	237	6/14/84	4	Arizona State	Houston, Texas	D4-'06	16/0
25	Wolfe, Garrett	RB	5-7	186	8/17/84	3	Northern Illinois	Chicago, Ill.	D3a-'07	13/0
45	#Worrell, Cameron	S	5-11	194	12/14/79	7	Fresno State	Chowchilla, Calif.	FA-'08	1/0

* Aromashodu inactive for 3 games; Baldwin inactive 7 games; Basanez last active with Carolina in '06; Broussard last active with Jacksonville in '07; Bullocks played 16 games with New Orleans in '08; Cutler played 16 games with Denver; Earl last active with Houston in '06; Gaines played 16 games with Detroit; Hamilton played 1 game with Tampa Bay; Hanie inactive 15 games; Omiyale played 10 games with Carolina; Pace played 14 games with St. Louis; Shaffer played 15 games with Cleveland.

\# Unrestricted free agent; subject to development.

t - Traded for Cutler (Den).

Traded—QB Kyle Orton (15 games in '08) to Denver.

Retired—John Tait, 10-year tackle, 16 games in '08.

Players lost through free agency (2): T John St. Clair (Cle; 16 games in '08), S Brandon McGowan (NE; 2).

Also played with Bears in '08—T Kirk Barton (1 game), WR Marty Booker (13), WR Mark Bradley (2), DT Gilbert Gardner (1), G Terrence Metcalf (6).

2009 FIRST-YEAR ROSTER

Name	Pos.	Ht.	Wt.	Birthdate	College	Hometown	How Acq.
Afalava, Al	S	5-10	213	1/20/87	Oregon State	Laie, Hawai'i	D6
Asiata, Johan	G	6-4	310	12/19/85	Nevada-Las Vegas	Kalihi, Hawai'i	FA
Balogh, Cody (1)	T	6-6	303	2/14/86	Montana	Steilacoom, Wash.	FA-'08
Burgess, Rudy (1)	CB	5-10	186	9/19/84	Arizona State	Edwards, Calif.	FA-'08
Clermond, Joe (1)	DE	6-2	250	11/13/84	Pittsburgh	Tampa, Fla.	FA-'08
Conley, Dennis	G	6-4	303	7/13/85	Hampton	Suffolk, Va.	FA
Deleston, Dahna	S	6-0	211	12/6/85	Connecticut	East Hartford, Conn.	FA
Freeman, Marcus	LB	6-0	239	1/10/86	Ohio State	Huber Heights, Ohio	D5b
Gilbert, Jarron	DT	6-5	288	9/30/86	San Jose State	Chino, Calif.	D3a
Iglesias, Juaquin	WR	6-0	210	8/22/87	Oklahoma	Killeen, Texas	D3b
Kinder, Derek	WR	6-1	210	3/25/86	Pittsburgh	Albion, N.Y.	D7b
Knox, Johnny	WR	5-11	185	11/3/86	Abilene Christian	Houston, Texas	D5a
Louis, Lance	TE	6-3	200	4/24/85	San Diego State	New Orleans, La.	D7a
Malast, Kevin	LB	6-0	225	6/6/86	Rutgers	Manchester, N.J.	FA
Melton, Henry	DE	6-3	260	10/11/86	Texas	Grapevine, Texas	D4a
Mines, Fontel (1)	TE	6-4	244	2/26/85	Virginia	Richmond, Va.	FA-'07
Moore, D.J.	CB	5-8	192	3/22/87	Vanderbilt	Spartanburg, S.C.	D4b
Peterman, Eric	WR	6-1	200	11/18/86	Northwestern	Sherman, Ill.	FA
Reed, Tyler (1)	G	6-4	303	10/6/82	Penn State	Jefferson Borough, Pa.	D6b-'06
Rivera, Mike	LB	6-3	255	1/10/86	Kansas	Shawnee Mission, Kan.	FA
Ta'ufo'ou, Will	FB	5-11	253	6/19/86	California	San Carlos, Calif.	FA
Turenne, Woodny	CB	6-1	182	1/25/87	Louisville	Ft. Lauderdale, Fla.	FA

The term NFL Rookie is defined as a player who is in his first season of professional football and has not been on the roster of another professional football team for any regular-season or postseason games. A Rookie is designated by an "R" on NFL rosters. Players who have been active in another professional football league or players who have NFL experience, including either preseason training camp or being on an Active List or Inactive List, or on Reserve/Injured or Reserve/Physically Unable to Perform for fewer than six regular-season games, are termed NFL First-Year Players. An NFL First-Year Player is designated by a "1" on NFL rosters. Thereafter, a player is credited with an additional year of experience for each season in which he accumulates six games on the Active List or Inactive List, or on Reserve/Injured or Reserve/Physically Unable to Perform.

Log on to www.chicagobears.com for an up-to-date roster.

COACHING STAFF

Head Coach,
Lovie Smith

Pro Career: Named the thirteenth head coach in Chicago Bears history on January 15, 2004. Smith enters his sixth season as the head coach of the Chicago Bears with a regular season coaching record of 45-35 (.563). Those 45 wins are third most in franchise history, trailing only Hall of Famers George Halas and Mike Ditka. Smith also has a 2-2 postseason record, including an NFC Championship and the Bears first Super Bowl appearance in 21 years (2006), to give him the third-most playoff victories in team history behind the six of Halas and Ditka. Registering a career-high 13 wins in 2006 to tie predecessor Dick Jauron for the most victories by a Bears head coach in his third season, Smith led Chicago to home-field advantage in the NFC Playoffs and the team's first NFC Championship since its Super Bowl season of 1985. A year earlier, Smith earned the 2005 AP NFL Coach of the Year Award after turning a 1-3 start to the season into 11 victories, the most by a second-year coach in club annals, and the second seed in the NFC Playoffs. Fueled by an eight-game win streak, Smith led a worst-to-first revival in the NFC North division as the Bears six-win improvement from the previous season was tied for the biggest in the NFL in 2005. In Smith's first season, Chicago posted a 5-11 record. The Bears rank second in the NFL from 2004-07 with 140 takeaways and 14 touchdowns scored via defensive return. Smith came to Chicago from St. Louis (2001-03), where he served as defensive coordinator. In 2001 he helped the Rams return to the Super Bowl after missing the playoffs the previous season. Smith previously coached the linebackers for the Tampa Bay Buccaneers (1996-2000). Career record: 47-37.

Background: Played at Tulsa (1976-79), where he was a linebacker before moving to strong safety and earning two-time All-America and three-time All-Missouri Conference defensive back honors. Began his coaching career at his hometown high school (Big Sandy, Texas) in 1980 before moving to Cascia Hall Prep in Tulsa the following year. Two years later Smith began coaching collegiately at Tulsa (1983-86), Wisconsin (1987), Arizona State (1988-1991), Kentucky (1992), Tennessee (1993-94), and Ohio State (1995).

Personal: Born May 8, 1958, Gladewater, Texas. Lovie and his wife MaryAnne have three sons—Mikal, Matthew and Miles and twin grandsons—Malachi and Noah.

ASSISTANT COACHES

Jim Arthur, strength and conditioning assistant; born July 12, 1978. Attended Springfield (Mass.) College. No college or pro playing experience. College coach: Springfield (Mass.) College 2000, Louisiana Tech 2001, Boston College 2002. Pro coach: Joined Bears in 2005.

Bob Babich, defensive coordinator; born February 20, 1961, Aliquippa, Pa. Linebacker Mesa (Colo.) C.C. 1979-1980, Tulsa 1981-82. No pro playing experience. College coach: Tulsa 1984-87, 1990, Wisconsin 1988-89, Bowling Green 1991, East Carolina 1992-93, Pittsburgh 1994-96, North Dakota State 1997-2002 (head coach). Pro coach: St. Louis Rams 2003, joined Bears in 2004.

Rob Boras, tight ends; born September 30, 1970, Glen Ellyn, Ill. Center DePauw 1988-1991. No pro playing experience. College coach: DePauw 1992-93, Texas 1994-97, Benedictine 1998 (head coach), Nevada-Las Vegas 1999-2003. Pro coach: Joined Bears in 2004.

Luke Butkus, offensive assistant/asst. offensive line; born June 26, 1979, Steger, Ill. Center Illinois 1998-2001. Pro center San Diego Chargers 2002-03. College coach: Oregon 2005-06. Pro coach: Joined Bears in 2007.

Gill Byrd, asst. defensive backs/safeties; born February 20, 1961, San Francisco. Cornerback San Jose State 1979-1982. Pro cornerback San Diego Chargers 1983-1992. Pro coach: St. Louis Rams 2003-05, joined Bears in 2006.

Darryl Drake, wide receivers; born December 11, 1956, Louisville, Ky. Wide receiver Western Kentucky 1975-78. Pro wide receiver Washington Redskins 1979, Ottawa Rough Riders (CFL) 1981, Cincinnati Bengals 1983. College coach: Western Kentucky 1983-1991, Georgia 1992-96, Baylor 1997, Texas 1998-2003. Pro coach: Joined Bears in 2004.

Pep Hamilton, quarterbacks; born September 19, 1974, Charlotte, N.C. Quarterback Howard 1993-96. No pro playing experience. College coach: Howard 1997-2002. Pro coach: New York Jets 2003-05, San Francisco 49ers 2006, joined Bears in 2007.

Harry Hiestand, offensive line; born November 19, 1958, Malvern, Pa. Offensive lineman Springfield College 1978-79, East Stroudsburg 1980. No pro playing experience. College coach: East Stroudsburg 1981-85, Pennsylvania 1986, Southern California 1987, Toledo 1988, Cincinnati 1989-1993, Missouri 1994-96, Illinois 1997-2004. Pro coach: Joined Bears in 2005.

Jon Hoke, defensive backs; born January 24, 1957, Kettering, Ohio. Defensive back Ball State 1976-79. Pro defensive back Chicago Bears 1980. College coach: Bowling Green 1983-86, San Diego State 1987-88, Kent State 1989-1993, Missouri 1994-98, Florida 1999-2001. Pro coach: Houston Texans 2002-08, joined Bears in 2009.

Rusty Jones, director of physical development; born August 14, 1953. Attended Springfield (Mass.) College. No college or pro playing experience. College coach: Springfield (Mass.) College 1979-1982. Pro coach: Buffalo Bills 1985-2004, joined Bears in 2005.

Charles London, offensive assistant/asst. wide receivers; born August 12, 1975, Dunwoody, Ga. Running back Duke 1994-96. No pro playing experience. College coach: Duke 2004-06. Pro coach: Joined Bears in 2007.

Rod Marinelli, asst. head coach/defensive line; born July 13, 1949, Rosemead, Calif. Offensive/defensive tackle Utah 1968, offensive tackle California Lutheran 1970-72. No pro playing experience. College coach: Utah State 1976, California 1983-1991, Arizona State 1992-94, Southern California 1995. Pro coach: Tampa Bay Buccaneers 1996-2005, Detroit Lions 2006-08 (head coach), joined Bears in 2009.

Tim Spencer, running backs; born December 10, 1960, Martin Ferry, Ohio. Running back Ohio State 1979-1982. Pro running back Chicago Blitz (USFL) 1983, Arizona Wranglers (USFL) 1984, Memphis Showboats (USFL) 1985, San Diego Chargers 1985-1990. College coach: Ohio State 1994-2003. Pro coach: Joined Bears in 2004.

Chris Tabor, asst. special teams; born March 4, 1971, St. Joseph, Mo. Quarterback Benedictine College 1989-1992. No pro playing experience. College coach: Hutchinson (Kan.) C.C. 1994, Central Methodist College 1995-96, Missouri 1997-2000, Culver-Stockton College 2001 (head coach), Utah State 2002-04, Western Michigan 2005-07. Pro coach: Joined Bears in 2008.

Dave Toub, special teams coordinator; born June 1, 1962, Ossining, N.Y. Offensive lineman Springfield College 1980-81, Texas-El Paso 1983-84. No pro playing experience. College coach: Texas El-Paso 1987-89, Missouri 1989-2000. Pro coach: Philadelphia Eagles 2001-03, joined Bears in 2004.

Ron Turner, offensive coordinator; born December 5, 1953, Martinez, Calif. Wide receiver Diablo Valley (Calif.) C.C. 1973-74, Pacific 1975-76. No pro playing experience. College coach: Pacific 1977, Arizona 1978-1980, Northwestern 1981-82, Pittsburgh 1983-84, Southern California 1985-87, Texas A&M 1988, Stanford 1989-1991, San Jose State 1992 (head coach), Illinois 1997-2004 (head coach). Pro coach: Chicago Bears 1993-96, re-joined Bears in 2005.

Eric Washington, defensive assistant/asst. defensive line; born October 29, 1969, Shreveport, La. Grambling State 1989-1991. No pro playing experience. College coach: Texas A&M 1997-98, Ohio 2001-03, Northwestern 2004-07. Pro coach: Joined Bears in 2008.

National Football Conference
East Division
Team Colors: Royal Blue, Metallic Silver Blue, and White
Cowboys Center
One Cowboys Parkway
Irving, Texas 75063
Telephone: (972) 556-9900

2009 SCHEDULE

PRESEASON

Aug. 13	at Oakland	7:00
Aug. 21	**Tennessee**	7:00
Aug. 29	**San Francisco**	7:00
Sep. 4	at Minnesota	7:00

REGULAR SEASON

Sep. 13	at Tampa Bay	1:00
Sep. 20	**N.Y. Giants**	7:20
Sep. 28	**Carolina** (Mon.)	7:30
Oct. 4	at Denver	2:15
Oct. 11	at Kansas City	12:00
Oct. 18	BYE	
Oct. 25	**Atlanta**	3:15
Nov. 1	**Seattle**	12:00
Nov. 8	at Philadelphia	8:20
Nov. 15	at Green Bay	3:15
Nov. 22	**Washington**	12:00
Nov. 26	**Oakland** (Thu.)	3:15
Dec. 6	at N.Y. Giants	4:15
Dec. 13	**San Diego**	3:15
Dec. 19	at New Orleans (Sat.)	7:20
Dec. 27	at Washington *	8:20
Jan. 3	**Philadelphia**	12:00

** Sunday night games in Weeks 11-17 subject to change*

Stadium: Cowboys Stadium (opens in 2009)
•**Capacity:** 80,000 (expandable to 100,000 for special events)
One Legends Way
Arlington, Texas 76011
Playing Surface: Sportfield Softtop
Training Camp: Alamodome
San Antonio, TX 78203

COWBOYS STADIUM

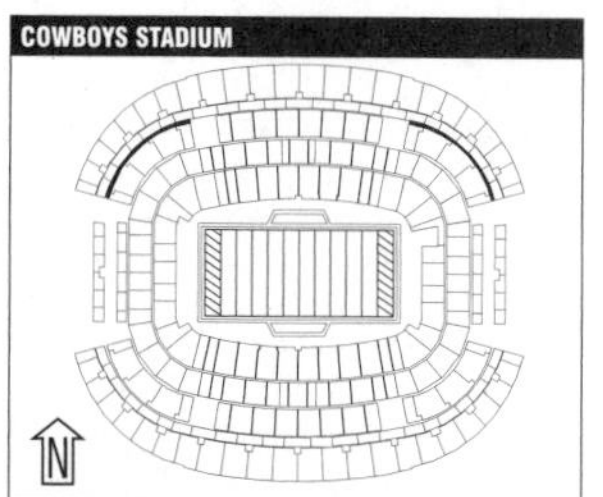

CLUB OFFICIALS

Owner/President/General Manager: Jerry Jones
Chief Operating Officer/Executive Vice President/Director of Player Personnel: Stephen Jones
Executive Vice President/VP of Brand Management/President Charity Foundation: Charlotte Anderson
Executive Vice President/Chief Sales and Marketing Officer: Jerry Jones Jr.
CFO: George Mitchell
Senior Vice President, Sales and Marketing: Greg McElroy
Senior Vice President and General Counsel: Alec Scheiner
Director of Public Relations: Rich Dalrymple
Director of Client Services and Corporate Communications: Brett Daniels
Director of Community Relations: Emily Robbins
Director of College and Pro Scouting: Tom Ciskowski
Director of Operations: Bruce Mays
Director of Player Development: Bryan Wansley
Director of Information Technology: Peter Walsh
Director of Broadcasting: Scott Purcel
Internet Director: Derek Eagleton
Director of Ticket Operations: Ann Bihari
Head Athletic Trainer: Jim Maurer
Equipment Manager: Mike McCord
Video Director: Robert Blackwell
Cheerleader Director: Kelli Finglass

COACHING HISTORY

(455-333-6)

Records include postseason games

1960-1988	Tom Landry	270-178-6
1989-1993	Jimmy Johnson	51-37-0
1994-97	Barry Switzer	45-26-0
1998-99	Chan Gailey	18-16-0
2000-02	Dave Campo	15-33-0
2003-06	Bill Parcells	34-32-0
2007-08	Wade Phillips	22-11-0

PAID ATTENDANCE

Home 506,944 Away 569,943
Total 1,076,887
Single-game home record, 65,180 (11/12/95)
Single-season home record, 518,167 (1995)

2009 DRAFT CHOICES

Round	Name	Pos.	College
3	Jason Williams	LB	Western Illinois
	Robert Brewster	T	Ball State
4	Stephen McGee	QB	Texas A&M
	Victor Butler	LB	Oregon State
	Brandon Williams	LB	Texas Tech
5	DeAngelo Smith	DB	Cincinnati
	Michael Hamlin	DB	Clemson
	David Buehler	K	Southern California
6	Stephen Hodge	LB	Texas Christian
	John Phillips	TE	Virginia
7	Mike Mickens	DB	Cincinnati
	Manuel Johnson	WR	Oklahoma

DALLAS COWBOYS

2008 TEAM RECORD

PRESEASON (2-2)

Date	Result	Opponent
8/9	L 17-31	at San Diego
8/16	L 13-23	at Denver
8/22	W 23-22	Houston
8/28	W 16-10	Minnesota

REGULAR SEASON (9-7)

Date	Result	Opponent
9/7	W 28-10	at Cleveland
9/15	W 41-37	Philadelphia
9/21	W 27-16	at Green Bay
9/28	L 24-26	Washington
10/5	W 31-22	Cincinnati
10/12	L 24-30	at Arizona (OT)
10/19	L 14-34	at St. Louis
10/26	W 13-9	Tampa Bay
11/2	L 14-35	at New York Giants
11/16	W 14-10	at Washington
11/23	W 35-22	San Francisco
11/27	W 34-9	Seattle
12/7	L 13-20	at Pittsburgh
12/14	W 20-8	New York Giants
12/20	L 24-33	Baltimore
12/28	L 6-44	at Philadelphia

(OT) Overtime

SCORE BY PERIODS

Cowboys	72	117	62	111	0 —	362
Opponents	79	109	67	104	6 —	365

2008 TEAM STATISTICS

	Cowboys	Opp.
Total First Downs	291	276
Rushing	102	85
Passing	171	163
Penalty	18	28
3rd Down: Made/Att	91/212	77/216
3rd Down Pct.	42.9	35.6
4th Down: Made/Att	7/12	8/14
4th Down Pct.	58.3	57.1
Possession Avg.	30:00	30:00
Total Net Yards	5512	4709
Avg. Per Game	344.5	294.3
Total Plays	979	969
Avg. Per Play	5.6	4.9
Net Yards Rushing	1723	1706
Avg. Per Game	107.7	106.6
Total Rushes	401	402
Net Yards Passing	3789	3003
Avg. Per Game	236.8	187.7
Sacked/Yards Lost	31/199	59/374
Gross Yards	3988	3377
Att./Completions	547/328	508/308
Completion Pct.	60.0	60.6
Had Intercepted	20	8
Punts/Average	78/43.4	74/44.3
Net Punting Avg.	78/36.4	74/39.0
Penalties/Yards	119/952	87/601
Fumbles/Ball Lost	29/13	28/14
Touchdowns	43	36
Rushing	12	11
Passing	29	19
Returns	2	6

2008 INDIVIDUAL STATISTICS

PASSING	Att.	Comp.	Yds.	Pct.	TD	Int.	Tkld.	Rate
Romo	450	276	3448	61.3	26	14	20/123	91.4
B. Johnson	78	41	427	52.6	2	5	8/54	50.5
Bollinger	17	10	71	58.8	1	1	3/22	63.6
Crayton	1	0	0	0.0	0	0	0/0	39.6
Witten	1	1	42	100.0	0	0	0/0	118.8
Cowboys	547	328	3988	60.0	29	20	31/199	84.9
Opponents	508	308	3377	60.6	19	8	59/374	86.2

SCORING	TD R	TD P	TD Rt	PAT	FG	Saf	PTS
Folk	0	0	0	42/42	20/22	0	102
Owens	0	10	0	0/0	0/0	0	60
Barber	7	2	0	0/0	0/0	0	54
Bennett	0	4	0	0/0	0/0	0	24
Crayton	0	4	0	0/0	0/0	0	24
F. Jones	3	0	1	0/0	0/0	0	24
Witten	0	4	0	0/0	0/0	0	24
Austin	0	3	0	0/0	0/0	0	18
Choice	2	0	0	0/0	0/0	0	12
Roy E. Williams	0	1	0	0/0	0/0	0	6
Anderson	0	1	0	0/0	0/0	0	6
Jenkins	0	0	1	0/0	0/0	0	6
Polk	0	0	0	0/0	0/0	1	2
Cowboys	12	29	2	42/42	20/22	1	362
Opponents	11	19	6	33/33	38/44	1	365

2-Pt. Conversions: None
Cowboys 0-1, Opponents 0-2

RUSHING	No.	Yds	Avg	LG	TD
Barber	238	885	3.7	35	7
Choice	92	472	5.1	38t	2
F. Jones	30	266	8.9	60t	3
Romo	28	41	1.5	15	0
Owens	7	33	4.7	8	0
Roy E. Williams	1	13	13.0	13	0
Crayton	1	11	11.0	11	0
Anderson	2	3	1.5	3	0
B. Johnson	2	-1	-0.5	0	0
Cowboys	401	1723	4.3	60t	12
Opponents	402	1706	4.2	82t	11

RECEIVING	No.	Yds	Avg	LG	TD
Witten	81	952	11.8	42	4
Owens	69	1052	15.2	75t	10
Barber	52	417	8.0	70t	2
Crayton	39	550	14.1	55t	4
Choice	21	185	8.8	50	0
Bennett	20	283	14.2	37	4
Roy E. Williams	19	198	10.4	38	1
Austin	13	278	21.4	63	3
Curtis	8	32	4.0	8	0
Stanback	2	24	12.0	15	0
F. Jones	2	10	5.0	7	0
Anderson	2	7	3.5	6	1
Cowboys	328	3988	12.2	75t	29
Opponents	308	3377	11.0	60	19

INTERCEPTIONS	No.	Yds	Avg	LG	TD
Newman	4	2	0.5	2	0
Jenkins	1	23	23.0	23t	1
Ellis	1	11	11.0	11	0
Hamlin	1	0	0.0	0	0
Henry	1	0	0.0	0	0
Cowboys	8	36	4.5	23t	1
Opponents	20	349	17.5	61	1

PUNTING	No.	Yds.	Avg.	In 20	LG
Paulescu	53	2213	41.8	14	70
McBriar	24	1175	49.0	5	66
Cowboys	78	3388	43.4	19	70
Opponents	74	3281	44.3	20	65

PUNT RETURNS	Ret	FC	Yds	Avg	LG	TD
A. Jones	21	0	95	4.5	18	0
Crayton	15	9	143	9.5	33	0
Battle	1	0	0	0.0	0	0
Cowboys	37	9	238	6.4	33	0
Opponents	37	17	390	10.5	35	0

KICKOFF RETURNS	No.	Yds	Avg	LG	TD
Austin	29	624	21.5	36	0
F. Jones	16	434	27.1	98t	1
Stanback	10	218	21.8	58	0
A. Jones	7	155	22.1	41	0
Scandrick	4	81	20.3	25	0
M. Thomas	4	93	23.3	27	0
Spencer	1	18	18.0	18	0
Crayton	1	11	11.0	11	0
Anderson	1	9	9.0	9	0
Curtis	1	4	4.0	4	0
Cowboys	70	1554	22.2	98t	1
Opponents	71	1510	21.3	93t	1

FIELD GOALS	1-19	20-29	30-39	40-49	50+
Folk	0/0	1/1	7/8	10/11	2/2
Cowboys	0/0	1/1	7/8	10/11	2/2
Opponents	0/0	9/9	16/16	11/14	2/5

SACKS	No.
Ware	20.0
Ellis	8.0
James	8.0
Ratliff	7.5
Canty	3.0
Burnett	2.0
Henry	2.0
Spencer	1.5
Hamlin	1.0
Hatcher	1.0
T. Johnson	1.0
Scandrick	1.0
Spears	1.0
Z. Thomas	1.0
(group)	1.0
Cowboys	59.0
Opponents	31.0

RECORD HOLDERS

INDIVIDUAL RECORDS—CAREER

Category	Name	Performance
Rushing (Yds.)	Emmitt Smith, 1990-2002	**17,162
Passing (Yds.)	Troy Aikman, 1989-2000	32,942
Passing (TDs)	Troy Aikman, 1989-2000	165
Receiving (No.)	Michael Irvin, 1988-1999	750
Receiving (Yds.)	Michael Irvin, 1988-1999	11,904
Interceptions	Mel Renfro, 1964-1977	52
Punting (Avg.)	Mat McBriar, 2004-08	45.0
Punt Return (Avg.)	Deion Sanders, 1995-99	13.3
Kickoff Return (Avg.)	Mel Renfro, 1964-1977	26.4
Field Goals	Rafael Septien, 1978-1986	162
Touchdowns (Tot.)	Emmitt Smith, 1990-2002	164
Points	Emmitt Smith, 1990-2002	986
*Sacks	Jim Jeffcoat, 1983-1994	94.5

INDIVIDUAL RECORDS—SINGLE SEASON

Category	Name	Performance
Rushing (Yds.)	Emmitt Smith, 1995	1,773
Passing (Yds.)	Tony Romo, 2007	4,211
Passing (TDs)	Tony Romo, 2007	36
Receiving (No.)	Michael Irvin, 1995	111
Receiving (Yds.)	Michael Irvin, 1995	1,603
Interceptions	Everson Walls, 1981	11
Punting (Avg.)	Mat McBriar, 2006	48.2
Punt Return (Avg.)	Bob Hayes, 1968	20.8
Kickoff Return (Avg.)	Mel Renfro, 1965	30.0
Field Goals	Richie Cunningham, 1997	34
Touchdowns (Tot.)	Emmitt Smith, 1995	25
Points	Emmitt Smith, 1995	150
*Sacks	DeMarcus Ware, 2008	20.0

INDIVIDUAL RECORDS—SINGLE GAME

Category	Name	Performance
Rushing (Yds.)	Emmitt Smith, 10-31-93	237
Passing (Yds.)	Don Meredith, 11-10-63	460
Passing (TDs)	Many times	5
	Last time by Tony Romo, 11-23-06	
Receiving (No.)	Jason Witten, 12-9-07	15
Receiving (Yds.)	Bob Hayes, 11-13-66	246
Interceptions	Many times	3
	Last time by Terance Newman, 12-14-03	
Field Goals	Chris Boniol, 11-18-96	7
	Billy Cundiff, 9-15-03	7
Touchdowns (Tot.)	Many times	4
	Last time by Terrell Owens, 11-18-07	
Points	Many times	24
	Last time by Terrell Owens, 11-18-07	
*Sacks	Jim Jeffcoat, 11-10-85	5.0

**Sacks became an official statistic in 1982.*
***NFL Record*

DALLAS COWBOYS

2009 VETERAN ROSTER

No.	Name	Pos.	Ht.	Wt.	Birthdate	NFL Exp.	College	Hometown	How Acq.	'08 Games/ Starts
76	Adams, Flozell	T	6-7	340	5/18/75	12	Michigan State	Bellwood, Ill.	D2-'98	16/16
34	Anderson, Deon	FB	5-10	245	1/27/83	3	Connecticut	Providence, R.I	D6b-'07	14/5
95	Anderson, Tim	DT	6-4	315	11/22/80	6	Ohio State	Clyde, Ohio	FA-'09	0*
19	Austin, Miles	WR	6-3	216	6/30/84	4	Monmouth	Garfield, N.J.	FA-'06	12/1
20	Ball, Alan	CB	6-1	186	3/29/85	2	Illinois	Detroit, Mich.	D7b-'07	10/1
24	Barber, Marion	RB	6-1	225	6/10/83	5	Minnesota	Wayzata, Minn.	D4a-'05	15/13
35	Battle, Tra	S	5-11	173	1/5/85	2	Georgia	Forsyth, Ga.	FA-'08	5/0
80	Bennett, Martellus	TE	6-6	265	3/10/87	2	Texas A&M	Alief, Texas	D2-'08	16/7
72	Bowen, Stephen	DE	6-5	304	3/28/84	4	Hofstra	Wheatley Heights, N.Y.	FA-'06	14/0
51	Brooking, Keith	LB	6-2	241	10/30/75	12	Georgia Tech	Senoia, Ga.	UFA(Atl)-'09	16/16*
27	Brown, Courtney	S	6-1	204	2/10/84	3	Cal Poly	Berkeley, Calif.	D7a-'07	9/1
54	Carpenter, Bobby	LB	6-2	250	8/1/83	4	Ohio State	Lancaster, Ohio	D1-'06	13/0
42	Carter, Jerome	S	5-11	219	10/25/82	5	Florida State	Lake City, Fla.	FA-'09	0*
23	Choice, Tashard	RB	5-10	208	11/20/84	2	Georgia Tech	Riverdale, Ga.	D4-'08	16/3
75	Colombo, Marc	T	6-8	315	10/8/78	8	Boston College	Bridgewater, Mass.	FA-'05	16/16
84	Crayton, Patrick	WR	6-1	203	4/7/79	6	Northwestern Okla. St.	DeSoto, Texas	D7b-'04	16/7
70	Davis, Leonard	G	6-6	353	9/5/78	9	Texas	Wortham, Texas	UFA(Ariz)-'07	16/16
98	#Ellis, Greg	LB	6-6	262	8/14/75	12	North Carolina	Wendell, N.C.	D1-'98	16/16
6	Folk, Nick	K	6-1	225	11/5/84	3	Arizona	Sherman Oaks, Calif.	D6a-'07	16/0
68	Free, Doug	T	6-6	311	1/6/84	3	Northern Illinois	Manitowoc, Wis.	D4b-'07	0*
65	Gurode, Andre	C	6-4	318	3/6/78	8	Colorado	Houston, Texas	D2a-'02	16/16
26	Hamlin, Ken	S	6-2	208	1/20/81	7	Arkansas	Memphis, Tenn.	UFA(Sea)-'07	16/16
97	Hatcher, Jason	DE	6-6	304	7/13/82	4	Grambling State	Alexandria, La.	D3-'06	16/0
37	Hawkins, Michael	CB	6-1	188	7/15/83	4	Oklahoma	Carrollton, Texas	FA-'09	0*
64	Holland, Montrae	G	6-2	322	5/21/80	7	Florida State	Ore, Texas	T(Den)-'08	7/2
17	Hurd, Sam	WR	6-2	205	4/24/85	4	Northern Illinois	San Antonio, Texas	FA-'06	3/0
56	James, Bradie	LB	6-2	245	1/17/81	7	Louisiana State	Monroe, La.	D4-'03	16/16
21	Jenkins, Mike	CB	5-10	190	3/22/85	2	South Florida	Bradenton, Fla.	D1b-'08	14/3
28	Jones, Felix	RB	6-1	212	5/8/87	2	Arkansas	Tulsa, Okla.	D1a-'08	6/0
3	t-Kitna, Jon	QB	6-2	220	9/21/72	13	Central Washington	Tacoma, Wash.	T(Det)-'09	4/4*
63	Kosier, Kyle	G	6-5	305	11/27/78	8	Arizona State	Peoria, Ariz.	UFA(Det)-'06	3/3
91	Ladouceur, Louis-Philippe	LS	6-4	256	3/13/81	5	California	Pointe-Claire, Quebec	FA-'05	16/0
1	McBriar, Mat	P	6-1	222	7/8/79	6	Hawaii	East Brighton, Australia	FA-'04	6/0
77	McQuistan, Pat	T	6-6	315	4/30/83	4	Weber State	Lebanon, Ore.	D7-'06	16/0
41	Newman, Terence	CB	5-11	190	9/4/78	7	Kansas State	Salina, Kan.	D1-'03	10/10
99	Olshansky, Igor	DE	6-6	309	5/3/82	6	Oregon	San Francisco, Calif.	UFA(SD)-'09	16/13*
71	Procter, Cory	C	6-4	308	10/18/82	5	Montana	Gig Harbor, Wash.	FA-'05	16/11
90	Ratliff, Jay	NT	6-4	302	8/29/81	5	Auburn	Valdosta. Ga.	FA-'05	16/16
50	Rogers, Justin	LB	6-4	250	8/31/83	3	Southern Methodist	Commerce, Texas	FA-'07	15/0
9	Romo, Tony	QB	6-2	224	4/21/80	7	Eastern Illinois	Burlington, Wis.	FA-'03	13/13
32	Scandrick, Orlando	CB	5-10	192	2/10/87	2	Boise State	Los Alamitos, Calif.	D5-'08	16/3
43	Sensabaugh, Gerald	S	6-1	204	6/13/83	6	North Carolina	Kingsport, Tenn.	UFA(Jax)-'09	16/13*
78	Siavii, Junior	NT	6-5	320	11/14/78	4	Oregon	Pago Pago, African Samoa	FA-'09	0*
96	Spears, Marcus	DE	6-4	315	3/8/83	5	Louisiana State	Baton Rouge, La.	D1b-'05	16/16
93	Spencer, Anthony	LB	6-3	255	1/23/84	3	Purdue	Fort Wayne, Ind.	D1-'07	12/0
86	Stanback, Isaiah	WR	6-2	208	8/16/84	3	Washington	Seattle, Wash.	D4a-'07	8/0
52	#Stewart, Matt	LB	6-3	239	8/31/79	8	Vanderbilt	Columbus, Ohio	FA-'09	0*
94	Ware, DeMarcus	LB	6-4	262	7/31/82	5	Troy	Auburn, Ala.	D1a-'05	16/16
25	Watkins, Patrick	S	6-5	215	12/18/82	4	Florida State	Tallahassee, Fla.	D5-'06	8/0
11	Williams, Roy	WR	6-3	220	12/20/81	6	Texas	Odessa, Texas	T(Det)-'08	15/11*
10	Wilson, Travis	WR	6-1	210	2/11/84	4	Oklahoma	Carrollton, Texas	FA-'08	0*
82	Witten, Jason	TE	6-5	262	5/6/82	7	Tennessee	Elizabethton, Tenn.	D3-'03	16/16

* T. Anderson last active with Atlanta in '07; Brooking played 16 games with Atlanta in '08; Carter last active with St. Louis in '07; Free inactive for 13 games; Hawkins last active with Cleveland in '06; Kitna played 4 games with Detroit; Olshansky played 16 games with San Diego; Sensabaugh played 16 games with Jacksonville; Siavii last active with Kansas City in '05; Stewart last active with Cleveland in '06; Wilson last active with Cleveland in '06; Williams played 5 games with Detroit.

t- Cowboys traded for Kitna (Det).

\# Unrestricted free agent; subject to development.

Players lost through free agency (5): G Joe Berger (Mia; 5 games in '08), LB Kevin Burnett (SD; 16), DE Chris Canty (NYG; 16), DT Tank Johnson (Cin; 16), LB Zach Thomas (KC; 16).

Also played with Cowboys in '08—QB Brooks Bollinger (2 games), RB Alonzo Coleman (1), TE Tony Curtis (16), S Keith Davis (16), CB Anthony Henry (16), QB Brad Johnson (16), CB Adam Jones (9), LB Steve Octavien (2), WR Terrell Owens (16), P Sam Paulescu (10), LB Carlos Polk (10), S Roy Williams (3).

2009 FIRST-YEAR ROSTER

Name	Pos.	Ht.	Wt.	Birthdate	College	Hometown	How Acq.
Brewster, Robert	T	6-4	325	7/30/86	Ball State	Cincinnati, Ohio	D3b
Bright, Travis	G	6-4	321	1/5/83	Brigham Young	Queen Creek, Ariz.	FA
Buehler, David	K	6-2	227	2/5/87	Southern California	Anaheim, Calif.	D5c
Butler, Victor	LB	6-2	248	7/29/87	Oregon State	Rialto, Calif.	D4b
Carpenter, Rudy	QB	6-2	217	4/15/86	Arizona State	Westlake, Calif.	FA
Coleman, Alonzo (1)	RB	5-9	210	1/27/84	Hampton	South Boston, Va.	FA-'07
Crosslin, Julius (1)	FB	5-11	245	11/2/83	Oklahoma State	Amarillo, Texas	FA-'08
Dixon, Marcus (1)	DE	6-4	285	9/16/84	Hampton	Rome, Ga.	FA-'08
Gibbons, Ryan (1)	G	6-4	318	3/13/83	Northeastern	Marshfield, Mass.	FA-'08
Hamlin, Michael	S	6-2	214	11/21/85	Clemson	Lamar, S.C.	D5b
Hannah, Rodney (1)	TE	6-6	258	8/9/84	Houston	Roseville, Calif.	FA-'07
Hawkins, Julian	WR	6-2	215	7/18/86	Boise State	Long Beach, Calif.	FA
Hodge, Stephen	LB	6-0	234	7/17/87	Texas Christian	Tatum, Texas	D6a
Hunt, Jamar	TE	6-7	253	12/4/82	Texas-El Paso	Mesa, Ariz.	FA
Isdaner, Greg	G	6-3	325	2/25/86	West Virginia	Gladwyne, Pa.	FA
Johnson, Manuel	WR	5-11	189	10/14/86	Oklahoma	Gilmer, Texas	D7b
Lattimore, Keon (1)	RB	5-11	222	7/6/84	Maryland	Owings Mills, Md.	FA
McGee, Stephen	QB	6-3	225	9/27/85	Texas A&M	Burnet, Texas	D4a
Mickens, Mike	CB	6-1	186	7/24/87	Cincinnati	Huber Heights, Ohio	D7a
Ogletree, Kevin	WR	6-0	196	8/5/87	Virginia	Queens, N.Y.	FA
Phillips, John	TE	6-5	251	6/11/87	Virginia	Warm Springs, Va.	D6b
Schwapp, Asaph	FB	5-11	251	1/26/87	Notre Dame	Hartford, Conn.	FA
Smith, DeAngelo	S	5-11	197	7/17/86	Cincinnati	Columbus, Ohio	D5a
Spanos, Matt (1)	C	6-5	310	12/31/84	Southern California	Corona, Calif.	FA-'08
Turkovich, Michael	T	6-6	316	11/27/86	Notre Dame	Bedford, Pa.	FA
Tyler, Casey (1)	DT	6-5	304	7/25/85	Portland State	Edmonds, Wash.	FA
Williams, Brandon	LB	6-3	254	6/21/88	Texas Tech	Fort Worth, Texas	D4c
Williams, Jason	LB	6-1	238	2/21/86	Western Illinois	Woodbridge, Va.	D3a

The term NFL Rookie is defined as a player who is in his first season of professional football and has not been on the roster of another professional football team for any regular-season or postseason games. A Rookie is designated by an "R" on NFL rosters. Players who have been active in another professional football league or players who have NFL experience, including either preseason training camp or being on an Active List or Inactive List, or on Reserve/Injured or Reserve/Physically Unable to Perform for fewer than six regular-season games, are termed NFL First-Year Players. An NFL First-Year Player is designated by a "1" on NFL rosters. Thereafter, a player is credited with an additional year of experience for each season in which he accumulates six games on the Active List or Inactive List, or on Reserve/Injured or Reserve/Physically Unable to Perform.

Log on to www.dallascowboys.com for an up-to-date roster.

COACHING STAFF

Head Coach, Wade Phillips

Pro Career: Was named the seventh coach in club history on February 8, 2007. He led the Cowboys to a 13-3 record in 2007 becoming the third head coach since the NFL merger to reach 13 wins in his first season with a club. In guiding the Cowboys to the playoffs, he has now reached the playoffs in the first season in each of the last seven times he has taken over as a head coach or defensive coordinator. Phillips brought 30 years of NFL coaching experience, including five as a head coach and 20 as a defensive coordinator, to the Cowboys. In his seven full seasons as a head coach, Phillips has produced a 67-45 record and guided his teams to four playoff appearances. He has had only one non-winning season as a head coach. His .588 career winning percentage in the regular season is third among active NFL head coaches with 40 or more games. Over the last 20 years as a head coach or coordinator, he has been a part of only four teams that have had non-winning records. During that time he has worked with a defense that ranked in the NFL's top 10 ten times. Phillips served as the defensive coordinator for the San Diego Chargers (2004-06) and Atlanta Falcons (2002-03), finishing the 2003 season as interim head coach for the Falcons (posting a 2-1 record). Phillips also served as interim head coach in New Orleans for four games in 1985 (1-3 record) and Atlanta for three games in 2003 (2-1). During the 1998-2000 seasons as head coach in Buffalo, the Bills compiled a record of 29-19. Phillips took the reins after a 6-10 finish in 1997 and reversed the team's fortunes by leading it to a 10-6 record and the playoffs in 1998. His 1999 team led the NFL in total defense, went 11-5 and earned another trip to the postseason. Before becoming the Bills head coach in 1998, he was the team's defensive coordinator (1995-97). Phillips had a two-year stint as Denver's head coach (1993-94), after serving as defensive coordinator the previous four seasons. He led the Broncos to a playoff berth in his first season (1993). He was the Philadelphia Eagles defensive coordinator and linebackers coach (1986-88). His first coordinator's position came with the New Orleans Saints (1981-85). He began his NFL coaching career with the Houston Oilers (1976-1980) under his father, longtime NFL coach Bum Phillips. Career record: 70-53.

Background: Played linebacker at Houston (1966-68). Served as a college coach at Houston (1969), Oklahoma State (1973-74), and Kansas (1975).

Personal: Born June 21, 1947, in Orange, Texas. He and his wife Laurie, have one son, Wesley, and one daughter, Tracy.

ASSISTANT COACHES

Dave Campo, secondary; born July 18, 1947, Groton, Conn. Defensive back Central Connecticut State 1967-1970. No pro playing experience. College coach: Central Connecticut State 1971-72, Albany 1973, Bridgeport 1974, Pittsburgh 1975, Washington State 1976, Boise State 1977-79, Oregon State 1980, Weber State 1981-82, Iowa State 1983, Syracuse 1984-86, Miami 1987-88. Pro coach: Dallas Cowboys 1989-2002 (head coach 2000-02), Cleveland Browns 2003-04, Jacksonville Jaguars 2005-07, re-joined Cowboys in 2008.

Joe DeCamillis, special teams; born June 29, 1965, Arvada, Colo. Attended Wyoming. No college or pro playing experience. Pro coach: Denver Broncos 1988-1992, New York Giants 1993-96, Atlanta Falcons 1997-2006, Jacksonville Jaguars 2007-08, joined Cowboys in 2009.

Jason Garrett, asst. head coach/offensive coordinator; born March 28, 1966, Abington, Pa. Quarterback Princeton 1987-88. Pro quarterback San Antonio Riders (World League) 1991, Ottawa RoughRiders (CFL) 1991, Dallas Cowboys 1993-99, New York Giants 2000-03, Tampa Bay Buccaneers 2004, Miami Dolphins 2004. College coach: Princeton 1990. Pro coach: Miami Dolphins 2005-06, joined Cowboys in 2007.

John Garrett, tight ends; born March 2, 1965, Danville, Pa. Wide receiver Columbia 1983-85, Princeton 1986-87. Pro wide receiver Cincinnati Bengals 1989, Buffalo Bills 1991, San Antonio Riders (World League) 1991. College coach: Virginia 2004-06. Pro coach: Cincinnati Bengals 1995-98, 2001-02, Arizona Cardinals 1999-2000, joined Cowboys in 2007.

Todd Grantham, defensive line; born September 13, 1966, Pulaski, Va. Offensive lineman Virginia Tech 1984-88. No pro playing experience. College coach: Virginia Tech 1990-95, Michigan State 1996-98. Pro coach: Indianapolis Colts 1999-2001, Houston Texans 2002-04, Cleveland Browns 2005-07, joined Cowboys in 2008.

Reggie Herring, linebackers; born July 3, 1959, Myrtle Beach, S.C. Linebacker Florida State 1978-1980. No pro playing experience. College coach: Oklahoma State 1981-85, Auburn 1986-1991, Texas Christian 1992-93, Clemson 1994-2001, North Carolina State 2004, Arkansas 2005-07 (interim head coach 2007). Pro coach: Houston Texans 2002-03, joined Cowboys in 2008.

Hudson Houck, offensive line; born January 7, 1943, Los Angeles. Center Southern California 1962-64. No pro playing experience. College coach: Southern California 1970-72, 1976-1982, Stanford 1973-75. Pro coach: Los Angeles Rams 1983-1991, Seattle Seahawks 1992, Dallas Cowboys 1993-2001, San Diego Chargers 2002-04, Miami Dolphins 2005-07, re-joined Cowboys in 2008.

Joe Juraszek, strength and conditioning; born June 8, 1958, Chicago. Linebacker/defensive end New Mexico 1976-1980. No pro playing experience. College coach: Oklahoma 1981-86, 1993-96, Texas Tech 1987-1992. Pro coach: Joined Cowboys in 1997.

Brett Maxie, secondary/safeties; born January 13, 1962, Dallas. Safety Texas Southern 1982-84. Pro safety New Orleans Saints 1985-1993, Atlanta Falcons 1994, Carolina Panthers 1995-96, San Francisco 49ers 1997. Pro coach: Carolina Panthers 1998, San Francisco 49ers 1999-2003, Miami Dolphins 2007, joined Cowboys in 2008.

Dat Nguyen, asst. linebackers/defensive quality control; born November 25, 1975, Rockport, Texas. Linebacker Texas A&M 1994-1998. Pro linebacker Dallas Cowboys 1999-2005. Pro coach: Joined Cowboys in 2007.

Skip Peete, running backs; born January 30, 1963, Mesa, Ariz. Wide receiver Arizona 1981-82, Kansas 1984-85. Pro wide receiver New York Jets 1987. College coach: Pittsburgh 1988-1992, Michigan State 1993-94, Rutgers 1995, UCLA 1996-97. Pro coach: Oakland Raiders 1998-2006, joined Cowboys in 2007.

Wes Phillips, offensive assistant/offensive quality control; born February 17, 1979, Houston. Quarterback Texas-El Paso 1997-2001. Pro quarterback San Diego Riptide (AFL2) 2002-03. College coach: Texas-El Paso 2003, West Texas A&M 2004-05, Baylor 2006. Pro coach: Joined Cowboys in 2007.

Bruce Read, special teams; born January 1, 1962, Santa Rosa, Calif. No pro playing experience. College coach: Montana 1985-1996, Oregon State 1997-98, 2004-06. Pro coach: San Diego Chargers 1999-2001, New York Giants 2002-03, joined Cowboys in 2007.

Ray Sherman, wide receivers; born November 27, 1951, Berkeley, Calif. Wide receiver/defensive back Fresno State 1971-72. No pro playing experience. College coach: San Jose State 1974, California 1975, 1981, Michigan State 1976-77, Wake Forest 1978-1980, Purdue 1982-85, Georgia 1986-87. Pro coach: Houston Oilers 1988-89, Atlanta Falcons 1990, San Francisco 49ers 1991-93, New York Jets 1994, Minnesota Vikings 1995-97, 1999, Pittsburgh Steelers 1998, Green Bay Packers 2000-04, Tennessee Titans 2005-06, joined Cowboys in 2007.

Wade Wilson, quarterbacks; born February 1, 1959, Commerce, Texas. Quarterback East Texas State 1977-1980. Pro quarterback Minnesota Vikings 1981-1991, Atlanta Falcons 1992, New Orleans Saints 1993-94, Dallas Cowboys 1995-97, Oakland Raiders 1998-99. Pro coach: Dallas Cowboys 2000-02, Chicago Bears 2004-06, re-joined Cowboys in 2007.

National Football Conference
North Division
Team Colors: Honolulu Blue and Silver
Detroit Lions Practice & Training Facility
222 Republic Drive
Allen Park, Michigan 48101
Telephone: (313) 216-4000

2009 SCHEDULE

PRESEASON

Aug. 15	**Atlanta**	4:00
Aug. 22	at Cleveland	7:30
Aug. 29	**Indianapolis**	1:00
Sep. 3	at Buffalo	6:30

REGULAR SEASON

Sep. 13	at New Orleans	12:00
Sep. 20	**Minnesota**	1:00
Sep. 27	**Washington**	1:00
Oct. 4	at Chicago	12:00
Oct. 11	**Pittsburgh**	1:00
Oct. 18	at Green Bay	12:00
Oct. 25	BYE	
Nov. 1	**St. Louis**	1:00
Nov. 8	at Seattle	1:05
Nov. 15	at Minnesota	12:00
Nov. 22	**Cleveland**	1:00
Nov. 26	**Green Bay** (Thu.)	12:30
Dec. 6	at Cincinnati	1:00
Dec. 13	at Baltimore	1:00
Dec. 20	**Arizona**	1:00
Dec. 27	at San Francisco	1:05
Jan. 3	**Chicago**	1:00

Stadium: Ford Field (opened in 2002) •**Capacity:** 64,500
2000 Brush Street
Detroit, Michigan 48226
Playing Surface: FieldTurf
Training Camp: 222 Republic Drive
Allen Park, Michigan 48101

FORD FIELD

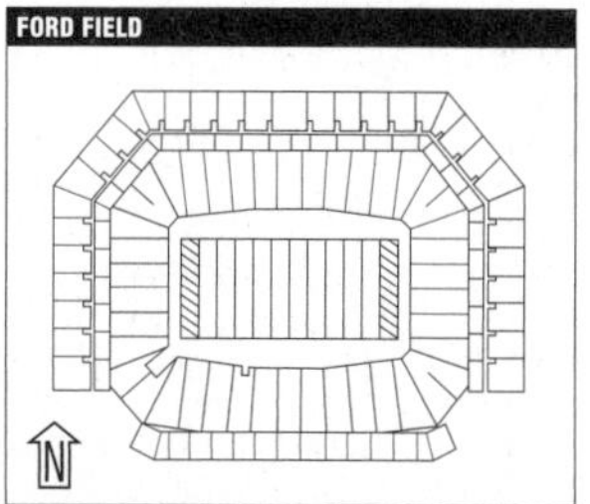

CLUB OFFICIALS

Chairman and Owner: William Clay Ford
Vice Chairman: William Clay Ford, Jr.
President: Tom Lewand
General Manager: Martin Mayhew
Senior Vice President: Bill Keenist
Senior Vice President/CFO: Tom Lesnau
Corporate Secretary: David Hempstead
Senior Personnel Executive: James Harris
Vice President of Football Operations: Cedric Saunders
Director of Pro Personnel: Sheldon White
Director of College Scouting: Scott McEwen
Scouts: Mike Butler, Dennis Gentry, Chad Henry, Rob Lohman, Silas McKinnie, Lance Newmark, Charlie Sanders, Dave Sears, Dave Uyrus
Senior Director of Community Affairs: Tim Pendell
Director of Media Relations: Matt Barnhart
Director of Broadcasting and Production: Bryan Bender
Director of Ticket Operations: Mark Graham
Coordinator of Athletic Medicine/ Athletic Trainer: Dean Kleinschmidt
Athletic Trainer: Al Bellamy
Equipment Manager: Tim O'Neill
Video Director: Robert Yanagi

COACHING HISTORY

Portsmouth Spartans 1930-33
(495-579-32)
Records include postseason games

1930	Hal (Tubby) Griffen	5-6-3
1931-36	George (Potsy) Clark	49-20-6
1937-38	Earl (Dutch) Clark	14-8-0
1939	Elmer (Gus) Henderson	6-5-0
1940	George (Potsy) Clark	5-5-1
1941-42	Bill Edwards*	4-9-1
1942	John Karcis	0-8-0
1943-47	Charles (Gus) Dorais	20-31-2
1948-1950	Alvin (Bo) McMillin	12-24-0
1951-56	Raymond (Buddy) Parker	50-24-2
1957-1964	George Wilson	55-45-6
1965-66	Harry Gilmer	10-16-2
1967-1972	Joe Schmidt	43-35-7
1973	Don McCafferty	6-7-1
1974-76	Rick Forzano**	15-17-0
1976-77	Tommy Hudspeth	11-13-0
1978-1984	Monte Clark	43-63-1
1985-88	Darryl Rogers***	18-40-0
1988-1996	Wayne Fontes	67-71-0
1997-2000	Bobby Ross****	27-32-0
2000	Gary Moeller	4-3-0
2001-02	Marty Mornhinweg	5-27-0
2003-05	Steve Mariucci#	15-28-0
2005	Dick Jauron	1-4-0
2006-08	Rod Marinelli	10-38-0

*Released after three games in 1942
**Resigned after four games in 1976
***Released after 11 games in 1988
****Resigned after nine games in 2000
#Released after 11 games in 2005

PAID ATTENDANCE

Home 415,124 Away 516,598
Total 931,722
Single-game home record, 80,444 (12/20/81)
Single-season home record, 644,904 (1980)

2009 DRAFT CHOICES

Round	Name	Pos.	College
1	Matthew Stafford	QB	Georgia
	Brandon Pettigrew	TE	Oklahoma State
2	Louis Delmas	DB	Western Michigan
3	DeAndre Levy	LB	Wisconsin
	Derrick Williams	WR	Penn State
4	Sammie Lee Hill	DT	Stillman
6	Aaron Brown	RB	Texas Christian
7	Lydon Murtha	T	Nebraska
	Zack Follett	LB	California
	Dan Gronkowski	TE	Maryland

DETROIT LIONS

2008 TEAM RECORD

PRESEASON (4-0)

Date	Result	Opponent
8/7	W 13-10	New York Giants
8/17	W 27-10	at Cincinnati
8/23	W 26-6	Cleveland
8/28	W 14-6	at Buffalo

REGULAR SEASON (0-16)

Date	Result	Opponent
9/7	L 21-34	at Atlanta
9/14	L 25-48	Green Bay
9/21	L 13-31	at San Francisco
10/5	L 7-34	Chicago
10/12	L 10-12	at Minnesota
10/19	L 21-28	at Houston
10/26	L 17-25	Washington
11/2	L 23-27	at Chicago
11/9	L 14-38	Jacksonville
11/16	L 22-31	at Carolina
11/23	L 20-38	Tampa Bay
11/27	L 10-47	Tennessee
12/7	L 16-20	Minnesota
12/14	L 21-31	at Indianapolis
12/21	L 7-42	New Orleans
12/28	L 21-31	at Green Bay

SCORE BY PERIODS

Lions	47	92	57	72	0	—	268
Opponents	126	163	109	119	0	—	517

2008 TEAM STATISTICS

	Lions	Opp.
Total First Downs	234	350
Rushing	70	147
Passing	143	188
Penalty	21	15
3rd Down: Made/Att	59/205	90/197
3rd Down Pct.	28.8	45.7
4th Down: Made/Att	10/20	6/10
4th Down Pct.	50.0	60.0
Possession Avg.	26:59	33:01
Total Net Yards	4292	6470
Avg. Per Game	268.3	404.4
Total Plays	913	1009
Avg. Per Play	4.7	6.4
Net Yards Rushing	1332	2754
Avg. Per Game	83.3	172.1
Total Rushes	352	536
Net Yards Passing	2960	3716
Avg. Per Game	185.0	232.3
Sacked/Yards Lost	52/339	30/191
Gross Yards	3299	3907
Att./Completions	509/281	443/303
Completion Pct.	55.2	68.4
Had Intercepted	19	4
Punts/Average	90/43.9	59/43.6
Net Punting Avg.	90/38.0	59/38.4
Penalties/Yards	88/729	91/753
Fumbles/Ball Lost	31/10	31/16
Touchdowns	29	63
Rushing	10	31
Passing	18	25
Returns	1	7

2008 INDIVIDUAL STATISTICS

PASSING	Att.	Comp.	Yds.	Pct.	TD	Int.	Tkld.	Rate
Orlovsky	255	143	1616	56.1	8	8	14/95	72.6
Kitna	120	68	758	56.7	5	5	15/89	72.2
Culpepper	115	60	786	52.2	4	6	14/95	63.9
Stanton	17	9	119	52.9	1	0	6/35	95.0
Henson	2	1	20	50.0	0	0	3/25	85.4
Lions	509	281	3299	55.2	18	19	52/339	71.3
Opponents	443	303	3907	68.4	25	4	30/191	110.9

SCORING	TD R	TD P	TD Rt	PAT	FG	Saf	PTS
Hanson	0	0	0	25/26	21/22	0	88
C. Johnson	0	12	0	0/0	0/0	0	74
Kev. Smith	8	0	0	0/0	0/0	0	48
R. Johnson	1	1	0	0/0	0/0	0	12
Fitzsimmons	0	1	0	0/0	0/0	0	8
Bullocks	0	0	1	0/0	0/0	0	6
Culpepper	1	0	0	0/0	0/0	0	6
Gaines	0	1	0	0/0	0/0	0	6
McDonald	0	1	0	0/0	0/0	0	6
Owens	0	1	0	0/0	0/0	0	6
Williams	0	1	0	0/0	0/0	0	6
Lions	10	18	1	25/26	21/22	1	268
Opponents	31	25	7	62/62	25/29	1	517

2-Pt. Conversions: Fitzsimmons, C. Johnson. Lions 2-3, Opponents 0-1.

RUSHING	No.	Yds	Avg	LG	TD
Kev. Smith	238	976	4.1	50	8
R. Johnson	76	237	3.1	27	1
Kitna	6	34	5.7	10	0
Orlovsky	7	29	4.1	10	0
Culpepper	12	25	2.1	9	1
Stanton	3	20	6.7	15	0
Cason	4	7	1.8	4	0
Felton	2	4	2.0	4	0
Norris	1	1	1.0	1	0
C. Johnson	3	-1	-0.3	7	0
Lions	352	1332	3.8	50	10
Opponents	536	2754	5.1	73t	31

RECEIVING	No.	Yds	Avg	LG	TD
C. Johnson	78	1331	17.1	96t	12
Kev. Smith	39	286	7.3	27	0
McDonald	35	332	9.5	26	1
Gaines	23	260	11.3	33	1
Furrey	18	181	10.1	25	0
Williams	17	232	13.6	25	1
Standeford	15	244	16.3	36	0
R. Johnson	12	88	7.3	34t	1
Fitzsimmons	12	85	7.1	16	1
Felton	9	53	5.9	12	0
Owens	8	56	7.0	19	1
Colbert	5	64	12.8	28	0
Cason	4	27	6.8	15	0
Norris	4	16	4.0	6	0
Middleton	1	23	23.0	23	0
D. Campbell	1	21	21.0	21	0
Lions	281	3299	11.7	96t	18
Opponents	303	3907	12.9	86t	25

INTERCEPTIONS	No.	Yds	Avg	LG	TD
Nece	1	18	18.0	18	0
Bodden	1	2	2.0	2	0
C. Smith	1	0	0.0	0	0
White	1	-4	-4.0	-4	0
Lions	4	16	4.0	18	0
Opponents	19	364	19.2	65t	5

PUNTING	No.	Yds.	Avg.	In 20	LG
Harris	90	3952	43.9	24	66
Lions	90	3952	43.9	24	66
Opponents	59	2573	43.6	23	60

PUNT RETURNS	Ret	FC	Yds	Avg	LG	TD
McDonald	11	8	104	9.5	27	0
Furrey	5	5	36	7.2	20	0
Cason	3	0	27	9.0	13	0
Standeford	1	0	1	1.0	1	0
Jennings	1	0	0	0.0	0	0
Lions	21	13	168	8.0	27	0
Opponents	51	22	414	8.1	80t	2

KICKOFF RETURNS	No.	Yds	Avg	LG	TD
Middleton	39	864	22.2	42	0
Cason	32	746	23.3	46	0
Thomas	4	93	23.3	27	0
Fitzsimmons	3	41	13.7	16	0
Furrey	2	30	15.0	16	0
C. Smith	2	26	13.0	17	0
Cody	1	7	7.0	7	0
Lions	83	1807	21.8	46	0
Opponents	57	1332	23.4	60	0

FIELD GOALS	1-19	20-29	30-39	40-49	50+
Hanson	0/0	3/3	4/5	6/6	8/8
Lions	0/0	3/3	4/5	6/6	8/8
Opponents	0/0	6/6	7/8	10/11	2/4

SACKS	No.
White	6.5
Avril	5.0
Redding	3.0
C. Smith	3.0
DeVries	2.0
(group)	2.0
Darby	1.5
Lenon	1.5
Nece	1.5
Alama-Francis	1.0
L. Moore	1.0
Pearson	1.0
Sims	1.0
Lions	30.0
Opponents	52.0

RECORD HOLDERS

INDIVIDUAL RECORDS—CAREER

Category	Name	Performance
Rushing (Yds.)	Barry Sanders, 1989-1998	15,269
Passing (Yds.)	Bobby Layne, 1950-58	15,710
Passing (TDs)	Bobby Layne, 1950-58	118
Receiving (No.)	Herman Moore, 1991-2001	670
Receiving (Yds.)	Herman Moore, 1991-2001	9,174
Interceptions	Dick LeBeau, 1959-1972	62
Punting (Avg.)	Yale Lary, 1952-53, 1956-1964	44.3
Punt Return (Avg.)	Jack Christiansen, 1951-58	12.8
Kickoff Return (Avg.)	Pat Studstill, 1961-67	25.7
Field Goals	Jason Hanson, 1992-2008	406
Touchdowns (Tot.)	Barry Sanders, 1989-1998	109
Points	Jason Hanson, 1992-2008	1,747
*Sacks	Robert Porcher, 1992-2003	95.5

INDIVIDUAL RECORDS—SINGLE SEASON

Category	Name	Performance
Rushing (Yds.)	Barry Sanders, 1997	2,053
Passing (Yds.)	Scott Mitchell, 1995	4,338
Passing (TDs)	Scott Mitchell, 1995	32
Receiving (No.)	Herman Moore, 1995	123
Receiving (Yds.)	Herman Moore, 1995	1,686
Interceptions	Don Doll, 1950	12
	Jack Christiansen, 1953	12
Punting (Avg.)	Yale Lary, 1963	48.9
Punt Return (Avg.)	Pat Studstill, 1962	15.8
Kickoff Return (Avg.)	Mel Gray, 1994	28.4
Field Goals	Jason Hanson, 1993	34
Touchdowns (Tot.)	Barry Sanders, 1991	17
Points	Jason Hanson, 1995	132
*Sacks	Robert Porcher, 1999	15.0

INDIVIDUAL RECORDS—SINGLE GAME

Category	Name	Performance
Rushing (Yds.)	Barry Sanders, 11-13-94	237
Passing (Yds.)	Charlie Batch, 11-18-01	436
Passing (TDs)	Gary Danielson, 12-9-78	5
Receiving (No.)	Herman Moore, 12-4-95	14
Receiving (Yds.)	Cloyce Box, 12-3-50	302
Interceptions	Don Doll, 10-23-49	**4
Field Goals	Garo Yepremian, 11-13-66	6
	Jason Hanson, 10-17-99	6
Touchdowns (Tot.)	Dutch Clark, 10-22-34	4
	Cloyce Box, 12-3-50	4
	Barry Sanders, 11-24-91	4
Points	Dutch Clark, 10-22-34	24
	Cloyce Box, 12-3-50	24
	Barry Sanders, 11-24-91	24
*Sacks	Bill Gay, 9-4-83	5.5

**Sacks became an official statistic in 1982.*
***NFL Record*

DETROIT LIONS

2009 VETERAN ROSTER

No.	Name	Pos.	Ht.	Wt.	Birthdate	NFL Exp.	College	Hometown	How Acq.	'08 Games/ Starts
97	Alama-Francis, Ikaika	DE	6-5	280	12/4/84	3	Hawaii	Oahu, Hawaii	D2b-'07	13/2
42	Alexander, Gerald	S	6-2	204	6/28/84	3	Boise State	Rancho Cucamonga, Calif.	D2c-'07	5/1
92	Avril, Cliff	DE	6-3	253	4/8/86	2	Purdue	Green Cove Springs, Fla.	D3c-'08	15/4
76	Backus, Jeff	T	6-5	305	9/21/77	9	Michigan	Norcross, Ga.	D1-'01	16/16
46	Bing, Darnell	LB	6-2	220	9/10/84	2	Southern California	Lakewood, Calif.	FA-'08	1/0
40	Bradley, Jon	FB	6-0	301	1/13/81	6	Arkansas State	Barton, Ark.	FA-'07	0*
31	Buchanon, Phillip	CB	5-11	186	9/19/80	8	Miami	Ft. Myers, Fla.	UFA(TB)-'09	16/16*
27	Bullocks, Daniel	S	6-0	212	2/28/83	4	Nebraska	Chattanooga, Tenn.	D2-'06	16/15
36	Cason, Aveion	RB	5-10	204	7/12/79	9	Illinois State	St. Petersburg, Fla.	FA-'08	6/0
77	Cherilus, Gosder	T	6-7	319	6/28/84	2	Boston College	Somerville, Mass.	D1-'08	16/13
98	Cohen, Landon	DT	6-3	296	8/3/86	2	Ohio	Spartanburg, S.C.	D7-'08	6/0
49	Conover, Sean	TE	6-5	275	7/31/84	3	Bucknell	Whitman, Mass.	UFA(NYJ)-'09	0*
74	Cook, Damion	T	6-5	330	4/16/79	9	Bethune-Cookman	Nashville, Tenn.	FA-'08	8/4
62	Coston, Junius	G	6-3	313	11/5/83	4	North Carolina A&T	Framingham, Mass.	FA-'08	0*
11	Culpepper, Daunte	QB	6-4	260	1/28/77	11	Central Florida	Ocala, Fla.	FA-'08	5/5
87	Curry, Ronald	WR	6-2	210	5/28/79	8	North Carolina	Hampton, Va.	FA-'09	13/10*
91	Darby, Chuck	DT	6-0	297	10/22/75	9	South Carolina State	North, S.C.	UFA(Sea)-'08	15/15
95	DeVries, Jared	DE	6-4	275	6/11/76	11	Iowa	Aplington, Iowa	D3 '99	10/10
57	Dizon, Jordon	LB	6-0	229	1/16/86	2	Colorado	Kauai, Hawaii	D2-'08	12/0
45	Felton, Jerome	FB	6-0	246	7/3/86	2	Furman	Madisonville, Tenn.	D5b-'08	12/6
82	FitzSimmons, Casey	TE	6-4	258	10/10/80	7	Carroll College (Mont.)	Helena, Mont.	FA-'03	14/1
96	Fluellen, Andre	DT	6-2	296	3/7/85	2	Florida State	Cartersville, Ga.	D3b-'08	8/2
72	Foster, George	T	6-5	338	6/9/80	7	Georgia	Macon, Ga.	T(Den)-'07	4/3
19	Franklin, William	WR	6-0	209	10/13/85	2	Missouri	St. Louis, Mo.	FA-'09	13/1*
65	Gandy, Dylan	C	6-3	290	3/8/82	4	Texas Tech	Harlingen, Texas	FA-'09	0*
58	Gatewood, Curtis	LB	6-2	248	5/18/85	3	Vanderbilt	Memphis, Tenn.	W(KC)-'09	6/0*
4	Hanson, Jason	K	6-0	190	6/17/70	18	Washington State	Spokane, Wash.	D2b '92	16/0
2	Harris, Nick	P	6-2	218	7/23/78	9	California	Avondale, Ariz.	W(Cin)-'03	16/0
89	Heller, Will	TE	6-6	270	2/28/81	8	Georgia Tech	Dunwoody, Ga.	UFA(Sea)-'09	12/0*
32	Henry, Anthony	CB	6-1	207	11/3/76	9	South Florida	Fort Myers, Fla.	T(Dall)-'09	16/15*
71	Hicks, Eric	DE	6-6	280	6/17/76	11	Maryland	Erie, Pa.	FA-'09	0*
35	Hicks, LaMarcus	S	6-0	189	4/15/83	3	Iowa State	Clarksdale, Miss.	FA-'08	7/0
90	Jackson, Grady	DT	6-2	345	1/21/73	12	Knoxville College	Greensboro, Ala.	UFA(Atl)-'09	15/14*
83	Jennings, Adam	WR	5-9	176	11/17/82	4	Fresno State	Granite Bay, Calif.	FA-'08	7/0*
80	Johnson, Bryant	WR	6-3	211	3/7/81	7	Penn State	Baltimore City, Md.	UFA(SF)-'09	16/12*
81	Johnson, Calvin	WR	6-5	239	9/25/85	3	Georgia Tech	Tyrone, Ga.	D1-'07	16/16
25	King, Eric	CB	5-10	185	5/10/82	5	Wake Forest	Owings Mills, Md.	UFA(Tenn)-'09	10/1*
52	Lewis, Alex	LB	6-0	230	6/11/81	6	Wisconsin	Delran, N.J.	D5-'04	11/4
70	Loper, Daniel	T	6-6	320	1/15/82	5	Texas Tech	Houston, Texas	UFA(Tenn)-'09	16/0*
28	Morris, Maurice	RB	5-11	216	12/1/79	8	Oregon	Chester, S.C.	UFA(Sea)-'09	13/6*
48	Muhlbach, Don	LS	6-4	265	8/17/81	6	Texas A&M	Lufkin, Texas	FA-'04	16/0
24	Pearson, Kalvin	S	5-10	200	10/22/78	5	Grambling State	Town Creek, Ala.	RFA(TB)-'08	16/10
66	Peterman, Stephen	G	6-4	323	1/11/82	5	Louisiana State	Gulfport, Miss.	FA-'06	14/14
59	Peterson, Julian	LB	6-3	240	7/28/78	8	Michigan State	Washington, D.C.	T(Sea)-'09	16/16*
51	Raiola, Dominic	C	6-1	295	12/30/78	9	Nebraska	Honolulu, Hawaii	D2a-'01	12/12
63	Ramirez, Manny	G	6-3	326	2/13/83	3	Texas Tech	Houston, Texas	D4b-'07	4/3
33	Roberson, Chris	CB	5-11	190	6/3/83	4	Eastern Michigan	Farmington Hills, Mich.	FA-'08	1/0
38	Robinson, Ramzee	CB	5-10	186	2/20/84	3	Alabama	Huntsville, Ala.	FA-'07	13/0
39	Schweigert, Stuart	S	6-1	210	6/21/81	6	Purdue	Saginaw, Mich.	FA-'08	6/0
50	Sims, Ernie	LB	6-0	225	12/23/84	4	Florida State	Tallahassee, Fla.	D1-'06	16/16
23	Smith, Keith	CB	5-11	191	3/20/80	6	McNeese State	Leesville, La.	D3-'04	10/0
34	Smith, Kevin	RB	6-1	217	12/17/86	2	Central Florida	Miami, Fla.	D3-'08	16/12
44	Smith, Terrelle	FB	6-0	246	3/12/78	10	Arizona State	West Covina, Calif.	UFA(Ariz)-'09	15/6*
53	Spencer, Cody	LB	6-2	245	6/1/81	6	North Texas	Port Lavaca, Texas	UFA(NYJ)-'09	14/0*
16	Standeford, John	WR	6-4	206	4/15/82	2	Purdue	Monrovia, Ind.	FA-'08	9/4
5	Stanton, Drew	QB	6-3	226	5/7/84	3	Michigan State	Farmington Hills, Mich.	D2a-'07	3/0
99	White, Dewayne	DE	6-2	273	10/19/79	7	Louisville	Marbury, Ala.	UFA(TB)-'07	12/11
30	Wynn, Dexter	CB	5-9	175	2/25/81	5	Colorado State	Sumpter, S.C.	FA-'08	2/0

* Bradley missed '08 season because of injury; Buchanon played 16 games with Tampa Bay; Conover last active with Tennessee in '07; Coston inactive 1 game; Curry played 13 games with Oakland; Franklin played 13 games with Kansas City; Gandy last active with Indianapolis in '07; Gatewood played 6 games with Kansas City; Heller played 12 games with Seattle; Henry played 16 games with Dallas; E. Hicks last active with N.Y. Jets in '07; Jackson played 15 games with Atlanta; Jennings played 7 games with Atlanta; Johnson played 16 games with San Francisco; King played 10 games with Tennessee; Loper played 16 games with Tennessee; Morris played 13 games with Seattle; Peterson played 16 games with Seattle; T. Smith played 15 games with Arizona; Spencer played 14 games with New York Jets.

Traded—QB Jon Kitna (Dall; 4 games in '08), DT Cory Redding (Sea, 13 games in '08), WR Roy Williams (Dall; 5 games in '08).

Players lost through free agency (5): DT Shaun Cody (Hou; 16), WR Shaun McDonald (Pitt; 12), FB Moran Norris (SF; 11), QB Dan Orlovsky (Hou; 10), TE John Owens (Sea; 16).

Also played with Lions in '08—Darian Barnes (2 games), CB Leigh Bodden (16), TE Dan Campbell (1), LB Anthony Cannon (9), WR Keary Colbert (4), CB Travis Fisher (15), WR Mike Furrey (9), TE Michael Gaines (16), LB Gilbert Gardner (2), QB Drew Henson (2), RB Rudi Johnson (14), CB Brian Kelly (11), LB Paris Lenon (16), C Andy McCollum (11), WR Brandon Middleton (7), DT Langston Moore (9), G Edwin Mulitalo (11), LB Ryan Nece (16), CB Chris Roberson (1), DE Corey Smith (12), S Dwight Smith (10), RB Marcus Thomas (3).

2009 FIRST-YEAR ROSTER

Name	Pos.	Ht.	Wt.	Birthdate	College	Hometown	How Acq.
Barton, Kirk (1)	T	6-6	300	11/4/84	Ohio State	Massillon, Ohio	W(Cin)
Blair, James (1)	G	6-3	338	8/10/85	Western Michigan	Detroit, Mich.	FA
Boldin, Demir	WR	5-11	205	6/20/86	Wake Forest	Pahokee, Fla.	FA
Brown, Aaron	RB	6-1	196	10/10/85	Texas Christian	Katy, Texas	D6
Delmas, Louis	S	5-11	202	4/12/87	Western Michigan	North Miami Beach, Fla.	D2
Downey, Andrew	LB	6-1	231	3/9/87	Maine	Kingston, N.Y.	FA
Ervin, Allen (1)	RB	5-10	224	3/19/85	Lambuth	Memphis, Tenn.	FA-'08
Follett, Zack	LB	6-1	236	7/30/87	California	Clovis, Calif.	D7b
Fowler, Eric (1)	WR	6-3	210	10/17/84	Grand Valley State	New Haven, Mich.	FA-'08
Gerberry, Dan	C	6-3	302	11/10/85	Ball State	Austintown, Ohio	FA
Gill, John	DT	6-3	302	10/28/86	Northwestern	Los Altos Hills, Calif.	FA
Graham, Chris (1)	LB	5-11	232	9/30/84	Michigan	Indianapolis, Ind.	FA-'08
Gronkowski, Dan	TE	6-5	255	1/21/85	Maryland	Amherst, N.Y.	D7c
Hannon, Chris (1)	WR	6-3	205	2/18/84	Tennessee	Sarasota, Fla.	FA-'08
Hardie, Rudolph (1)	DE	6-2	269	10/8/85	Howard	Hartford, Conn.	FA-'08
Hill, Sammie Lee	DT	6-4	329	11/8/86	Stillman	West Blockton, Ala.	D4
Levy, Deandre	LB	6-2	236	3/26/87	Wisconsin	Milwaukee, Wisc.	D3a
Murtha, Lydon	T	6-7	315	11/13/85	Nebraska	Hutchinson, Minn.	D7a
Nordin, Jake (1)	TE	6-3	262	7/8/84	Northern Illinois	Lake Lillian, Minn.	FA-'08
Pettigrew, Brandon	TE	6-5	263	2/23/85	Oklahoma State	Tyler, Texas	D1b
Smith, Antonio (1)	CB	5-9	192	6/12/84	Ohio State	Columbus, Ohio	FA
Stafford, Matthew	QB	6-3	237	2/7/88	Georgia	Highland Park, Texas	D1a
Waters, Swayze	K	5-11	178	5/18/87	Alabama-Birmingham	Jackson, Miss.	FA
Williams, Derrick	WR	5-11	197	7/6/86	Penn State	Greenbelt, Md.	D3b

The term NFL Rookie is defined as a player who is in his first season of professional football and has not been on the roster of another professional football team for any regular-season or postseason games. A Rookie is designated by an "R" on NFL rosters. Players who have been active in another professional football league or players who have NFL experience, including either preseason training camp or being on an Active List or Inactive List, or on Reserve/Injured or Reserve/Physically Unable to Perform for fewer than six regular-season games, are termed NFL First-Year Players. An NFL First-Year Player is designated by a "1" on NFL rosters. Thereafter, a player is credited with an additional year of experience for each season in which he accumulates six games on the Active List or Inactive List, or on Reserve/Injured or Reserve/Physically Unable to Perform.

Log on to www.detroitlions.com for an up-to-date roster.

DETROIT LIONS

COACHING STAFF
Head Coach,
Jim Schwartz

Pro Career: Named Lions' twenty-fifth head coach on January 16, 2009. Schwartz begins his tenure in Detroit following 10 seasons with the Tennessee Titans, including the past eight as defensive coordinator. As the Titans' defensive coordinator since 2001, Schwartz's defensive unit held firm in two major defensive categories that factored significantly in the team's overall success; rushing defense and third-down conversion. From 2001-08, Tennessee ranked fifth in rushing yards allowed per game (103.5) and sixth in third-down conversion percentage (36.1). Before joining the Titans in 1999, he spent three years (1996-98) as a defensive assistant/quality control coach with the Baltimore Ravens. During his tenure in Baltimore, he also coached the team's outside linebackers. After the Cleveland Browns moved to Baltimore following the 1995 season, Schwartz made the transition from player personnel to coaching. From 1993-95, he worked in the Browns' player personnel department, serving as both a college and pro scout. Career record: 0-0.

Background: Schwartz worked on the college level for four years before moving onto the NFL. He began his coaching career as a graduate assistant coach at the University of Maryland, tutoring the Terrapins' linebackers in 1989 and then served as graduate assistant at the University of Minnesota (1990). He became a position coach in the secondary at North Carolina Central (1991) before moving to Colgate (1992) as linebackers coach. Played collegiately at Georgetown University where he lettered four years at linebacker. In 1988 he earned numerous honors that include Division III CoSIDA/GTE Academic All-America, All-America and team captain.

Personal: Born June 2, 1966, in Baltimore, Md. He and his wife, Kathy, have twins Christian and Allison along with a younger daughter Maria. He earned a degree in economics at Georgetown as well as Distinguished Economics Graduate honors.

ASSISTANT COACHES

Jason Arapoff, director of physical development; born July 8, 1965, Weymouth, Mass. Defensive back Springfield College 1985-88. No college or pro playing experience. Pro coach: Washington Redskins 1992-2000, joined Lions in 2001.

Bradford Banta, asst. special teams; born December 14, 1979, Baton Rouge, La. Tight end Southern California 1990-93, Pro tight end/long snapper Indianapolis Colts 1993-99, New York Jets 2000, Detroit Lions 2001-03, Buffalo Bills 2004. College coach: Tennessee-Chattanooga 2007. Pro coach: Joined Lions in 2008.

Malcolm Blacken, strength and conditioning; born October 12, 1965, Richmond, Va. Running back Virginia Tech 1984-88. No pro playing experience. College coach: South Carolina 1990-91, George Mason 1992-94, Virginia 1995. Pro coach: Washington Redskins 1996-2000, joined Lions in 2001.

Matt Burke, linebackers; born March 25, 1976, Hudson, Mass. Safety Dartmouth 1994-97. No pro playing experience. College coach: Boston College 2000-02, Harvard 2003. Pro coach: Tennessee Titans 2006-08, joined Lions in 2009.

Don Clemons, defensive quality control; born February 15, 1954, Newark, N.J. Defensive end Muhlenberg (Pa.) 1973-76. No pro playing experience. College coach: Kutztown State 1977-78, New Mexico 1979, Arizona State 1980-84. Pro coach: Joined Lions in 1985.

Gunther Cunningham, defensive coordinator; born June 19, 1946, Munich, Germany. Linebacker/placekicker Oregon 1966-68. No pro playing experience. College coach: Oregon 1969-1971, Arkansas 1972, Stanford 1973-76, California 1977-1980. Pro coach: Hamilton Tiger-Cats (CFL) 1981, Baltimore/Indianapolis Colts 1982-84, San Diego Chargers 1985-1990, L.A. Raiders 1991-94, Kansas City Chiefs 1995-2000, 2004-08 (head coach 1999-2000), Tennessee Titans 2001-03, joined Lions in 2009.

Todd Downing, offensive quality control: born July 22, 1980, Eden Prairie, Minn. Attended Minnesota. No college or pro playing experience. Pro coach: Minnesota Vikings 2003-05, St. Louis Rams 2006-08, joined Lions in 2009.

Sam Gash, running backs; born March 7, 1969, Henderson, N.C. Fullback Penn State 1987-1991. Pro fullback New England Patriots 1992-97, Buffalo Bills 1998-99, 2003, Baltimore Ravens 2000-02. Pro coach: New York Jets 2005-06, joined Lions in 2007.

Jeff Horton, quarterbacks: born July 13, 1957, Tulsa, Okla. Attended Nevada. No college or pro playing experience. College coach: Minnesota 1984, Nevada 1985-89, 1992-93, Nevada-Las Vegas 1990-91, 1994-98 (head coach 1994-98), Wisconsin 1999-2005, Iowa State 2006. Pro coach: St. Louis Rams 2006-08, joined Lions in 2009.

Shawn Jefferson, wide receivers; born February 22, 1969, Jacksonville. Wide receiver Central Florida 1988-1990. Pro wide receiver San Diego Chargers 1991-95, New England Patriots 1996-99, Atlanta Falcons 2000-02, Detroit Lions 2003. Pro coach: Joined Lions in 2005.

Bob Karmelowicz, defensive line; born July 22, 1949, New Britain, Conn. Nose tackle Bridgeport 1968-1971. No pro playing experience. College coach: Arizona State 1975-79, Massachusetts 1980, Texas El-Paso 1981, Nevada-Las Vegas 1982, Illinois 1983-86, Washington State 1987-88, Miami 1989-1991. Pro coach: Cincinnati Bengals 1992-93, Washington Redskins 1994-96, Kansas City Chiefs 1997-2005, Houston Texans 2006, joined Lions in 2009.

Kris Kocurek, asst. defensive line; born November 15, 1978. Defensive tackle Texas Tech 1997-2000. Pro defensive tackle Seattle Seahawks 2001, Tennessee Titans 2002. College coach: Texas Tech 2003, Texas A&M-Kingsville 2004-05, Texas A&M-Commerce 2006, West Texas A&M 2007, Stephen F. Austin State 2008. Pro coach: Joined Lions in 2009.

Stan Kwan, special teams; born November 2, 1967, Phoenix. Attended South Mountain (Ariz.) C.C., San Diego State. No college or pro playing experience. Pro coach: San Diego Chargers 1991-96, Detroit Lions 1997-2000, Arizona Cardinals 2001-2003, re-joined Lions in 2004.

Tim Lappano, tight ends: born October 14, 1956, Spokane, Wash. Running back Idaho 1978-1981. No pro playing experience. College coach: Idaho 1982-85, Wyoming 1986, Washington State 1987-1991, California 1992-95, Wyoming 1996, Purdue 1997, Oregon State 2000-02, Washington 2005-08. Pro coach: Seattle Seahawks 1998, San Francisco 49ers 2003-04, joined Lions in 2009.

Scott Linehan, offensive coordinator; born September 17, 1963, Sunnyside, Wash. Quarterback Idaho 1982-86. No pro playing experience. College coach: Idaho 1989-1990, 1992-93, Nevada-Las Vegas 1991, Washington 1994-98, Louisville 1999-2001. Pro coach: Minnesota Vikings 2002-04, Miami Dolphins 2005, St Louis Rams 2006-08 (head coach), joined Lions in 2009.

Daron Roberts, asst. secondary; born November 29, 1978, Mt. Pleasant, Texas. Attended Texas. No college or pro playing experience. Pro coach: Kansas City Chiefs 2007-08, joined Lions in 2009.

Tim Walton, secondary; born March 11, 1971. Defensive back Ohio State 1990-94. No pro playing experience. College coach: Bowling Green 1995-99, Memphis 2000-01, 2008, Syracuse 2002, Louisiana State 2003, Miami 2004-07. Pro coach: Joined Lions in 2009.

George Yarno, offensive line; born August 12, 1957, Spokane, Wash. Offensive line Washington State 1975-78. Pro offensive line Tampa Bay Buccaneers 1979-1983, 1985-87, Denver Gold (USFL) 1984-85, Atlanta Falcons 1988, Houston Oilers 1989, Green Bay Packers 1990. College coach: Louisiana State 2001-02, Washington State 2003-07. Pro coach: Tampa Bay Buccaneers 2008, joined Lions in 2009.

National Football Conference
North Division
Team Colors: Dark Green, Gold, and White
Lambeau Field Atrium
1265 Lombardi Avenue
Green Bay, Wisconsin 54304
Telephone: (920) 569-7500

2009 SCHEDULE

PRESEASON

Aug. 15	**Cleveland**	7:00
Aug. 22	**Buffalo**	7:00
Aug. 28	at Arizona	7:00
Sep. 3	at Tennessee	7:00

REGULAR SEASON

Sep. 13	**Chicago**	7:20
Sep. 20	**Cincinnati**	12:00
Sep. 27	at St. Louis	12:00
Oct. 5	at Minnesota (Mon.)	7:30
Oct. 11	BYE	
Oct. 18	**Detroit**	12:00
Oct. 25	at Cleveland	1:00
Nov. 1	**Minnesota**	12:00
Nov. 8	at Tampa Bay	1:00
Nov. 15	**Dallas**	3:15
Nov. 22	**San Francisco**	12:00
Nov. 26	at Detroit (Thu.)	12:30
Dec. 7	**Baltimore** (Mon.)	7:30
Dec. 13	at Chicago	12:00
Dec. 20	at Pittsburgh	1:00
Dec. 27	**Seattle**	12:00
Jan. 3	at Arizona	2:15

Stadium: Lambeau Field (opened in 1957)
•**Capacity:** 72,928
1265 Lombardi Avenue
Green Bay, Wisconsin 54304
Playing Surface: DD GrassMaster
Training Camp: St. Norbert College
De Pere, Wisconsin 54115

LAMBEAU FIELD

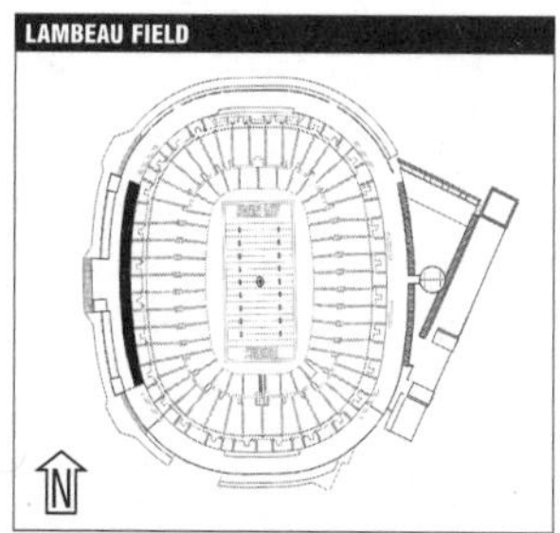

CLUB OFFICIALS

President and Chief Executive Officer: Mark Murphy
Executive Vice President/General Manager/Director of Football Operations: Ted Thompson
Vice President of Football Administration/Player Finance: Russ Ball
Senior Vice President of Marketing & Sales: Laura Sankey
Vice President of Organizational/Staff Development: Betsy Mitchell
Vice President of Administration/General Counsel: Jason Wied
Director of College Scouting: John Dorsey
Director-Football Operations: Reggie McKenzie
Director-Football Operations: John Schneider
Director of Player Development: Rob Davis
Director of Public Relations: Jeff Blumb
Assistant Directors of Public Relations: Sarah Quick, Adam Woullard
Public Relations Coordinator: Rob Crane
Manager of Corporate Communications: Aaron Popkey
Ticket Director: Mark Wagner
Director of Marketing and Corporate Sales: Craig Benzel
Director of Premium Sales and Guest Services: Jennifer Ark
Director of Retail Operations: Kate Hogan
Director of Information Technology: Wayne Wichlacz
Director of Facility Operations: Ted Eisenreich
Director of Corporate Security/Risk Management: Doug Collins
Manager of Community Outreach: Cathy Dworak
Internet Coordinator: Duke Bobber
Assistant Director of College Scouting: Shaun Herock
College Scouts: Lee Gissendaner, Brian Gutekunst, Alonzo Highsmith, Sam Seale, Jon-Eric Sullivan, Richmond Williams
Scouting Coordinator: Danny Mock
Assistant Directors of Pro Personnel: Tim Terry, Eliot Wolf
Director of Research and Development: Mike Eayrs
Strength and Conditioning Assistant: Mondray Gee
Director of Football Administration/Communications: Mark Schiefelbein
Football Administration Coordinator: Matt Klein
Video Director: Bob Eckberg
Head Athletic Trainer: Pepper Burruss
Equipment Manager: Gordon (Red) Batty

COACHING HISTORY
(668-528-36)

Records include postseason games

1921-1949	Earl (Curly) Lambeau	212-106-21
1950-53	Gene Ronzani*	14-31-1
1953	Hugh Devore-Ray (Scooter) McLean**	0-2-0
1954-57	Lisle Blackbourn	17-31-0
1958	Ray (Scooter) McLean	1-10-1
1959-1967	Vince Lombardi	98-30-4
1968-1970	Phil Bengtson	20-21-1
1971-74	Dan Devine	25-28-4
1975-1983	Bart Starr	53-77-3
1984-87	Forrest Gregg	25-37-1
1988-1991	Lindy Infante	24-40-0
1992-98	Mike Holmgren	84-42-0
1999	Ray Rhodes	8-8-0
2000-05	Mike Sherman	59-43-0
2006-08	Mike McCarthy	28-22-0

*Resigned after 10 games in 1953
**Co-coaches

PAID ATTENDANCE

Home 565,462 Away 501,589
Total 1,067,051
Single-game home record, 71,113 (9/21/08)
Single-season home record, 566,418 (2007)

2009 DRAFT CHOICES

Round	Name	Pos.	College
1	B.J. Raji	DT	Boston College
	Clay Matthews	LB	Southern California
4	T.J. Lang	G	Eastern Michigan
5	Quinn Johnson	RB	Louisiana State
	Jamon Meredith	T	South Carolina
6	Jarius Wynn	DE	Georgia
	Brandon Underwood	DB	Cincinnati
7	Brad Jones	LB	Colorado

GREEN BAY PACKERS

2008 TEAM RECORD

PRESEASON (1-3)

Date	Result	Opponent
8/11	L 17-20	Cincinnati
8/16	L 6-34	at San Francisco
8/22	W 27-24	at Denver
8/28	L 21-23	Tennessee

REGULAR SEASON (6-10)

Date	Result	Opponent
9/8	W 24-19	Minnesota
9/14	W 48-25	at Detroit
9/21	L 16-27	Dallas
9/28	L 21-30	at Tampa Bay
10/5	L 24-27	Atlanta
10/12	W 27-17	at Seattle
10/19	W 34-14	Indianapolis
11/2	L 16-19	at Tennessee (OT)
11/9	L 27-28	at Minnesota
11/16	W 37-3	Chicago
11/24	L 29-51	at New Orleans
11/30	L 31-35	Carolina
12/7	L 21-24	Houston
12/14	L 16-20	at Jacksonville
12/22	L 17-20	at Chicago (OT)
12/28	W 31-21	Detroit

(OT) Overtime

SCORE BY PERIODS

Packers	61	133	75	150	0 —	419
Opponents	65	103	71	135	6 —	380

2008 TEAM STATISTICS

	Packers	Opp.
Total First Downs	299	295
Rushing	99	121
Passing	182	141
Penalty	18	33
3rd Down: Made/Att	99/224	80/210
3rd Down Pct.	44.2	38.1
4th Down: Made/Att	8/18	17/23
4th Down Pct.	44.4	73.9
Possession Avg.	31:20	28:40
Total Net Yards	5618	5349
Avg. Per Game	351.1	334.3
Total Plays	1012	1003
Avg. Per Play	5.6	5.3
Net Yards Rushing	1805	2105
Avg. Per Game	112.8	131.6
Total Rushes	437	458
Net Yards Passing	3813	3244
Avg. Per Game	238.3	202.8
Sacked/Yards Lost	34/231	27/140
Gross Yards	4044	3384
Att./Completions	541/343	518/287
Completion Pct.	63.4	55.4
Had Intercepted	13	22
Punts/Average	65/41.4	76/44.3
Net Punting Avg.	65/35.7	76/37.4
Penalties/Yards	110/984	89/721
Fumbles/Ball Lost	25/8	20/6
Touchdowns	48	43
Rushing	11	20
Passing	28	22
Returns	9	1

2008 INDIVIDUAL STATISTICS

PASSING	Att.	Comp.	Yds.	Pct.	TD	Int.	Tkld.	Rate
Rodgers	536	341	4038	63.6	28	13	34/231	93.8
Flynn	5	2	6	40.0	0	0	0/0	47.9
Packers	541	343	4044	63.4	28	13	34/231	93.3
Opponents	518	287	3384	55.4	22	22	27/140	71.9

SCORING	TD R	TD P	TD Rt	PAT	FG	Saf	PTS
Crosby	0	0	0	46/46	27/34	0	127
Jennings	0	9	0	0/0	0/0	0	56
Driver	0	5	0	0/0	0/0	0	30
Grant	4	1	0	0/0	0/0	0	30
D. Lee	0	5	0	0/0	0/0	0	30
Rodgers	4	0	0	0/0	0/0	0	24
Collins	0	0	3	0/0	0/0	0	18
Kuhn	1	2	0	0/0	0/0	0	18
Blackmon	0	0	2	0/0	0/0	0	12
Nelson	0	2	0	0/0	0/0	0	12
Woodson	0	0	2	0/0	0/0	0	12
Martin	0	1	0	0/0	0/0	0	8
Finley	0	1	0	0/0	0/0	0	6
Hall	0	1	0	0/0	0/0	0	6
Hunter	0	0	1	0/0	0/0	0	6
Jackson	1	0	0	0/0	0/0	0	6
Jones	0	1	0	0/0	0/0	0	6
Rouse	0	0	1	0/0	0/0	0	6
Wynn	1	0	0	0/0	0/0	0	6
Packers	11	28	9	46/46	27/34	0	419
Opponents	20	22	1	39/39	25/30	3	380

2-Pt. Conversions: Jennings, Martin. Packers 2-2, Opponents 1-4.

RUSHING	No.	Yds	Avg	LG	TD
Grant	312	1203	3.9	57	4
Jackson	45	248	5.5	32	1
Rodgers	56	207	3.7	21	4
Wynn	8	110	13.8	73t	1
Lumpkin	1	19	19.0	19	0
Kuhn	8	10	1.3	3	1
Driver	2	4	2.0	6	0
Flynn	4	4	1.0	6	0
Frost	1	0	0.0	0	0
Packers	437	1805	4.1	73t	11
Opponents	458	2105	4.6	60t	20

RECEIVING	No.	Yds	Avg	LG	TD
Jennings	80	1292	16.2	63	9
Driver	74	1012	13.7	71t	5
D. Lee	39	303	7.8	26	5
Nelson	33	366	11.1	29t	2
Jackson	30	185	6.2	18	0
Jones	20	274	13.7	46	1
Grant	18	116	6.4	17t	1
Martin	15	149	9.9	17	1
Humphrey	11	162	14.7	37	0
Hall	7	38	5.4	11	1
Finley	6	74	12.3	35	1
Kuhn	4	21	5.3	13	2
Wynn	3	30	10.0	16	0
Lumpkin	3	22	7.3	12	0
Packers	343	4044	11.8	71t	28
Opponents	287	3384	11.8	70t	22

INTERCEPTIONS	No.	Yds	Avg	LG	TD
Collins	7	295	42.1	62t	3
Woodson	7	169	24.1	62t	2
Williams	5	78	15.6	39	0
Rouse	2	136	68.0	99t	1
Bigby	1	7	7.0	7	0
Packers	22	685	31.1	99t	6
Opponents	13	70	5.4	42	0

PUNTING	No.	Yds.	Avg.	In 20	LG
Frost	48	2021	42.1	8	65
Kapinos	17	667	39.2	7	55
Packers	65	2688	41.4	15	65
Opponents	76	3364	44.3	25	65

PUNT RETURNS	Ret	FC	Yds	Avg	LG	TD
Blackmon	36	11	398	11.1	76t	2
Bush	1	0	0	0.0	0	0
Packers	37	11	398	10.8	76t	2
Opponents	33	9	249	7.5	24	0

KICKOFF RETURNS	No.	Yds	Avg	LG	TD
Blackmon	55	1157	21.0	45	0
Nelson	11	208	18.9	45	0
Barbre	1	17	17.0	17	0
Hunter	1	7	7.0	7	0
Woodson	1	-2	-2.0	-2	0
Packers	69	1387	20.1	45	0
Opponents	72	1687	23.4	70	0

FIELD GOALS	1-19	20-29	30-39	40-49	50+
Crosby	1/1	8/8	10/13	5/6	3/6
Packers	1/1	8/8	10/13	5/6	3/6
Opponents	0/0	6/6	10/10	6/10	3/4

SACKS	No.
Kampman	9.5
Hawk	3.0
Woodson	3.0
Jenkins	2.5
Montgomery	2.5
Hunter	2.0
Pickett	1.5
Bishop	1.0
Chillar	1.0
Cole	0.5
Gbaja-Biamila	0.5
Packers	27.0
Opponents	34.0

RECORD HOLDERS

INDIVIDUAL RECORDS—CAREER

Category	Name	Performance
Rushing (Yds.)	Jim Taylor, 1958-1966	8,207
Passing (Yds.)	Brett Favre, 1992-2007	**61,655
Passing (TDs)	Brett Favre, 1992-2007	**442
Receiving (No.)	Sterling Sharpe, 1988-1994	595
Receiving (Yds.)	James Lofton, 1978-1986	9,656
Interceptions	Bobby Dillon, 1952-59	52
Punting (Avg.)	Craig Hentrich, 1994-97	42.8
Punt Return (Avg.)	Desmond Howard, 1996, 1999	13.8
Kickoff Return (Avg.)	Travis Williams, 1967-1970	26.7
Field Goals	Ryan Longwell, 1997-2005	226
Touchdowns (Tot.)	Don Hutson, 1935-1945	105
Points	Ryan Longwell, 1997-2005	1,054
*Sacks	Kabeer Gbaja-Biamila, 2000-08	74.5

INDIVIDUAL RECORDS—SINGLE SEASON

Category	Name	Performance
Rushing (Yds.)	Ahman Green, 2003	1,883
Passing (Yds.)	Lynn Dickey, 1983	4,458
Passing (TDs)	Brett Favre, 1996	39
Receiving (No.)	Sterling Sharpe, 1993	112
Receiving (Yds.)	Robert Brooks, 1995	1,497
Interceptions	Irv Comp, 1943	10
Punting (Avg.)	Craig Hentrich, 1997	45.0
Punt Return (Avg.)	Billy Grimes, 1950	19.1
Kickoff Return (Avg.)	Travis Williams, 1967	**41.1
Field Goals	Chester Marcol, 1972	33
	Ryan Longwell, 2000	33
Touchdowns (Tot.)	Ahman Green, 2003	20
Points	Paul Hornung, 1960	176
*Sacks	Tim Harris, 1989	19.5

INDIVIDUAL RECORDS—SINGLE GAME

Category	Name	Performance
Rushing (Yds.)	Ahman Green, 12-28-03	218
Passing (Yds.)	Lynn Dickey, 10-12-80	418
Passing (TDs)	Many times	5
	Last time by Brett Favre, 9-27-98	
Receiving (No.)	Don Hutson, 11-22-42	14
Receiving (Yds.)	Billy Howton, 10-21-56	257
Interceptions	Bobby Dillon, 11-26-53	**4
	Willie Buchanon, 9-24-78	**4
Field Goals	Chris Jacke, 11-11-90, 10-14-96	5
	Ryan Longwell, 9-24-00	5
Touchdowns (Tot.)	Paul Hornung, 12-12-65	5
Points	Paul Hornung, 10-8-61	33
*Sacks	Vonnie Holliday, 12-22-02	5.0

**Sacks became an official statistic in 1982.*
***NFL Record*

GREEN BAY PACKERS

2009 VETERAN ROSTER

No.	Name	Pos.	Ht.	Wt.	Birthdate	NFL Exp.	College	Hometown	How Acq.	'08 Games/ Starts
78	Barbre, Allen	G/T	6-4	305	6/22/84	3	Missouri Southern St.	Granby, Mo.	D4-'07	8/0
56	Barnett, Nick	LB	6-2	236	5/27/81	7	Oregon State	Fontana, Calif.	D1-'03	9/9
20	Bigby, Atari	S	5-11	213	9/19/81	4	Central Florida	Miami, Fla.	FA-'05	7/6
55	Bishop, Desmond	LB	6-2	238	7/24/84	3	California	Fairfield, Calif.	D6b-'07	15/1
27	Blackmon, Will	CB	6-0	206	10/27/84	4	Boston College	Warwick, R.I.	D4b-'06	16/1
11	Brohm, Brian	QB	6-3	223	9/23/85	2	Louisville	Louisville, Ky.	D2b-'08	0*
8	Brooks, Durant	P	6-0	204	4/15/85	2	Georgia Tech	Macon, Ga.	FA-'08	6/0*
24	Bush, Jarrett	CB/S	6-0	200	5/21/84	4	Utah State	Vacaville, Calif.	W(Car)-'06	16/0
54	Chillar, Brandon	LB	6-3	243	10/21/82	6	UCLA	Carlsbad, Calif.	FA-'08	14/7
76	Clifton, Chad	T	6-5	320	6/26/76	10	Tennessee	Martin, Tenn.	D2-'00	15/15
73	Colledge, Daryn	G/T	6-4	308	2/11/82	4	Boise State	North Pole, Alaska	D2a-'06	16/16
36	Collins, Nick	S	5-11	207	8/16/83	5	Bethune-Cookman	Cross City, Fla.	D2a-'05	16/16
2	Crosby, Mason	K	6-1	207	9/3/84	3	Colorado	Georgetown, Texas	D6c-'07	16/0
80	Driver, Donald	WR	6-0	194	2/2/75	11	Alcorn State	Houston, Texas	D7b-'99	16/16
88	Finley, Jermichael	TE	6-5	247	3/26/87	2	Texas	Diboll, Texas	D3-'08	14/1
10	Flynn, Matt	QB	6-2	222	6/20/85	2	Louisiana State	Tyler, Texas	D7a-'08	7/0
68	Giacomini, Breno	T	6-7	311	9/27/85	2	Louisville	Malden, Mass.	D5-'08	1/0
61	Goode, Brett	LS	6-1	261	11/2/84	2	Arkansas	Fort Smith, Ark.	FA-'08	16/0
25	Grant, Ryan	RB	6-1	226	12/9/82	3	Notre Dame	Ramsey, N.J.	T(NYG)-'07	16/14
35	Hall, Korey	FB	6-0	243	8/5/83	3	Boise State	Glenns Ferry, Idaho	D6a-'07	11/5
91	Harrell, Justin	DE	6-4	320	2/14/84	3	Tennessee	Martin, Tenn.	D1-'07	6/0
31	Harris, Al	CB	6-1	190	12/7/74	12	Texas A&M-Kingsville	Pompano Beach, Fla.	T(Phil)-'03	12/12
50	Hawk, A.J.	LB	6-1	248	1/6/84	4	Ohio State	Centerville, Ohio	D1-'06	16/16
84	Humphrey, Tory	TE	6-2	255	1/20/83	4	Central Michigan	Saginaw, Mich.	FA-'05	16/7
32	Jackson, Brandon	RB	5-10	220	10/2/85	3	Nebraska	Horn Lake, Miss.	D2-'07	13/0
77	Jenkins, Cullen	DE	6-2	305	1/20/81	6	Central Michigan	Belleville, Mich.	FA-'04	4/0
85	Jennings, Greg	WR	5-11	198	9/21/83	4	Western Michigan	Kalamazoo, Mich.	D2b-'06	16/15
97	Jolly, Johnny	DE	6-3	320	2/21/83	4	Texas A&M	Houston, Texas	D6a-'06	16/16
89	Jones, James	WR	6-1	218	3/31/84	3	San Jose State	San Jose, Calif.	D3a-'07	10/2
74	Kampman, Aaron	LB	6-4	265	11/30/79	8	Iowa	Parkersburg, Iowa	D5a-'02	16/16
30	Kuhn, John	FB	6-0	259	9/9/82	4	Shippensburg	York, Pa.	W(Pitt)-'07	16/3
58	Lansanah, Danny	LB	6-1	248	8/28/85	2	Connecticut	Harrisburg, Pa.	FA-'08	5/0
86	Lee, Donald	TE	6-4	248	8/31/80	7	Mississippi State	Maben, Miss.	D2c-'08	16/14
22	Lee, Pat	CB	6-0	194	2/20/84	2	Auburn	Miami, Fla.	FA-'05	5/0
28	Lumpkin, Kregg	RB	5-11	228	5/15/84	2	Georgia	Stone Mountain, Ga.	FA-'08	2/0
98	Malone, Alfred	DE	6-4	312	2/21/82	2	Troy	Frisco City, Ala.	FA-'07	4/0
82	Martin, Ruvell	WR	6-4	220	8/10/82	4	Saginaw Valley State	Muskegon, Mich.	FA-'06	13/1
75	Moll, Tony	T/G	6-5	306	8/23/83	4	Nevada	Sonoma, Calif.	D5b-'06	14/5
96	Montgomery, Michael	DE	6-5	273	8/18/83	5	Texas A&M	Center, Texas	D6a-'05	14/8
44	Moore, Evan	TE	6-6	247	1/3/85	2	Stanford	Brea, Calif.	FA-'08	0*
87	Nelson, Jordy	WR	6-3	217	5/31/85	2	Kansas State	Riley, Kan.	D2a-'08	16/2
26	Peprah, Charlie	S	5-11	203	2/24/83	4	Alabama	Plano, Texas	W(NYG)-'06	13/1
79	Pickett, Ryan	NT	6-2	330	10/8/79	9	Ohio State	Zephyrhills, Fla.	UFA(StL)-'06	16/16
51	Poppinga, Brady	LB	6-3	247	9/21/79	5	Brigham Young	Evanston, Wyo.	D4b-'05	16/12
60	Preston, Duke	C/G	6-5	315	6/12/82	5	Illinois	San Diego, Calif.	UFA(Buff)-'09	15/11*
12	Rodgers, Aaron	QB	6-2	220	12/2/83	5	California	Chico, Calif.	D1-'05	16/16
37	Rouse, Aaron	S	6-4	223	1/8/84	3	Virginia Tech	Virginia Beach, Va.	D3b-'07	14/6
71	Sitton, Josh	G	6-3	317	6/6/86	2	Central Florida	Pensacola, Fla.	D4b-'08	11/2
29	Smith, Anthony	S	6-0	200	9/20/83	4	Syracuse	Hubbard, Ohio	FA-'09	14/0*
72	Spitz, Jason	C/G	6-3	302	12/19/82	4	Louisville	Jacksonville, Fla.	D3b-'06	16/16
99	Thompson, Jeremy	LB	6-4	270	10/9/85	2	Wake Forest	Charlotte, N.C.	D4a-'08	9/3
63	Wells, Scott	C	6-2	303	1/7/81	6	Tennessee	Brentwood, Tenn.	FA-'04	13/13
38	Williams, Tramon	CB	5-11	191	3/16/83	3	Louisiana Tech	Napoleonville, La.	FA-'06	16/9
21	Woodson, Charles	CB	6-1	202	10/7/76	12	Michigan	Fremont, Ohio	UFA(Oak)-'06	16/16
42	Wynn, DeShawn	RB	5-10	238	10/9/83	3	Florida	Cincinnati, Ohio	FA-'08	5/0

* Brohm inactive 16 games; Brooks played 6 games with Washington in '08; Moore missed '08 season because of injury; Preston played 15 games with Buffalo; Smith played 14 games with Pittsburgh.

Player lost through free agency (1): DT Colin Cole (Sea; 16 games in '08).

Also played with Packers in '08—Derrick Frost (12 games), DE Kabeer Gbaja-Biamila (7), LB Jason Hunter (12), DE Kenny Pettway (8), T Mark Tauscher (13), LB Tracy White (5).

2009 FIRST-YEAR ROSTER

Name	Pos.	Ht.	Wt.	Birthdate	College	Hometown	How Acq.
Abrams, Joshua (1)	CB	5-11	196	1/18/86	Ohio	Dunwoody, Ga.	FA-'08
Allen, Jake (1)	WR	6-4	196	1/18/85	Mississippi College	Waynesboro, Miss.	FA-'08
Butler, Carson	TE	6-4	255	8/21/87	Michigan	Detroit, Mich.	FA
Dekker, Travis	TE	6-4	256	10/21/85	Air Force	Albuquerque, N.M.	FA
Dietrich-Smith, Evan	G/C	6-2	305	7/19/86	Idaho State	Salinas, Calif.	FA
Ford, Trevor	CB	6-0	188	2/19/86	Troy	Miami, Fla.	FA
Graessle, Adam	P	6-4	232	11/25/84	Pittsburgh	Dublin, Ohio	FA
Harris, JaRon	WR	6-0	193	5/6/86	South Dakota State	Sioux Falls, S.D.	FA
Hartline, Andrew	G/T	6-5	297	9/1/85	Central Michigan	Harrisburg, Pa.	FA
Havner, Spencer (1)	LB	6-3	248	2/2/83	UCLA	Grass Valley, Calif.	FA-'08
Heckendorf, Kole	WR	6-2	191	11/20/84	North Dakota State	Mosinee, Wisc.	FA
Johnson, Quinn	FB	6-1	250	9/30/86	Louisiana State	Edgard, La.	D5a
Jones, Brad	LB	6-3	232	4/1/86	Colorado	East Lansing, Mich.	D7
Kapinos, Jeremy (1)	P	6-1	230	8/23/84	Penn State	Springfield, Va.	FA-'08
Lang, T.J.	G/T	6-4	316	9/20/87	Eastern Michigan	Birmingham, Mich.	D4
Matthews, Clay	LB	6-3	245	5/14/86	Southern California	Agoura Hills, Calif.	D1b
McCaskill, Nevin (1)	G	6-4	315	12/29/83	Hampton	Tallahassee, Fla.	FA-'08
Meredith, Jamon	T	6-5	304	5/11/86	South Carolina	Simpsonville, S.C.	D5b
Muhtadi, Dean	NT/DE	6-3	296	7/17/86	Maryland	Alexandria, Va.	FA
Obiozor, Cyril	LB	6-4	267	9/26/86	Texas A&M	Pearland, Texas	FA
Porter, Joe (1)	CB	5-10	203	11/27/85	Rutgers	Franklin, N.J.	FA-'07
Raji, B.J.	NT	6-2	337	7/11/86	Boston College	Washington Township, N.J.	D1a
Randolph, Dane	T	6-5	300	9/4/86	Maryland	Columbia, Md.	FA
Sam, Lorne (1)	WR	6-3	220	12/5/84	Texas-El Paso	Buford, Ga.	FA-'08
Simmons, Jamarko	WR	6-2	231	9/23/86	Western Michigan	Flint, Mich.	FA
Soi, Brian (1)	NT	6-3	334	5/3/85	Utah State	Honolulu, Hawaii	FA
Sutton, Tyrell	RB	5-8	213	12/19/86	Northwestern	Akron, Ohio	FA
Swain, Brett (1)	WR	6-0	203	6/21/85	San Diego State	Carlsbad, Calif.	D7b-'08
Talley, Ronald	DE	6-3	282	2/21/86	Delaware	Detroit, Mich.	FA
Toribio, Anthony (1)	NT	6-1	304	3/1/85	Carson-Newman	Miami, Fla.	FA-'08
Underwood, Brandon	CB	6-1	198	6/24/86	Cincinnati	Hamilton, Ohio	D6b
Williams, Patrick	WR	6-1	204	1/13/86	Colorado	DeSoto, Texas	FA-'06
Wynn, Jarius	DE	6-3	277	8/29/86	Georgia	Lincolnton, Ga.	D6a

The term NFL Rookie is defined as a player who is in his first season of professional football and has not been on the roster of another professional football team for any regular-season or postseason games. A Rookie is designated by an "R" on NFL rosters. Players who have been active in another professional football league or players who have NFL experience, including either preseason training camp or being on an Active List or Inactive List, or on Reserve/Injured or Reserve/Physically Unable to Perform for fewer than six regular-season games, are termed NFL First-Year Players. An NFL First-Year Player is designated by a "1" on NFL rosters. Thereafter, a player is credited with an additional year of experience for each season in which he accumulates six games on the Active List or Inactive List, or on Reserve/Injured or Reserve/Physically Unable to Perform.

Log on to www.packers.com for an up-to-date roster.

GREEN BAY PACKERS

COACHING STAFF
Head Coach,
Mike McCarthy
Pro Career: Named the fourteenth head coach in team history January 12, 2006. Team has ranked in Top 10 in total yards on offense each of his three years as head coach. Named Motorola Coach of the Year, matched a franchise record with 13 wins, and won NFC North Division title in 2007. Became the first coach since Vince Lombardi to lead team to a championship game in his second season. Had returned to Green Bay after serving as the team's quarterbacks coach in 1999. Subsequently was a highly successful offensive coordinator for the New Orleans Saints (2000-04). With McCarthy calling plays, the Saints racked up 10 offensive team records and 26 individual marks. He was named NFC Assistant Coach of the Year by *USA Today* in 2000, and New Orleans led the league with 432 points and 49 touchdowns in 2002. The list of quarterbacks he has coached includes Joe Montana, Elvis Grbac, Rich Gannon, Brett Favre, Matt Hasselbeck, Aaron Brooks, Jake Delhomme, Marc Bulger, Steve Bono, and Jeff Blake—a collection that combines for 34 career Pro Bowl selections and eight Super Bowl starts. Career record: 28-22.
Background: Graduated with a degree in business administration from Baker University following a two-year playing career (1985-86). Was an all-conference tight end, helping the school to a NAIA Division II runner-up finish as a senior captain. Coached collegiately at Fort Hays State (1987-88) and Pittsburgh (1989-1992), before moving to the NFL with the Kansas City Chiefs (1993-98), Green Bay Packers (1999), New Orleans Saints (2000-04) and San Francisco 49ers (2005).
Personal: Born November 10, 1963, in Pittsburgh. Family includes daughters Alexandra and Gabrielle, wife Jessica and boys Jack and George.

ASSISTANT COACHES
Edgar Bennett, running backs; born February 15, 1969, Jacksonville. Running back Florida State 1987, 1989-1991. Pro running back Green Bay Packers 1992-96, Chicago Bears 1998-99. Pro coach: Joined Packers in 2001.
James Campen, offensive line; born June 11, 1964, Sacramento, Calif. Center Sacramento City (Calif.) J.C. 1982-83, Tulane 1984-85. Pro center New Orleans Saints 1987-88, Green Bay Packers 1989-1993. Pro coach: Joined Packers in 2004.
Dom Capers, defensive coordinator; born August 5, 1950, Cambridge, Ohio. Defensive back Mount Union 1968-1971. No pro playing experience. College coach: Kent State 1972-74, Hawaii 1975-76, San Jose State 1977, California 1978-79, Tennessee 1980-81, Ohio State 1982-83. Pro coach: Philadelphia/Baltimore Stars (USFL) 1984-85, New Orleans Saints 1986-1991, Pittsburgh Steelers 1992-94, Carolina Panthers 1995-98 (head coach), Jacksonville Jaguars 1999-2000, Houston Texans 2001-05 (head coach), Miami Dolphins 2006-07, New England Patriots 2008, joined Packers in 2009.
Tom Clements, quarterbacks; born June 18, 1953, McKees Rocks, Pa. Quarterback Notre Dame 1972-74. Pro quarterback Ottawa Rough Riders (CFL) 1975-78, Hamilton Tiger-Cats (CFL) 1979, 1981-82, Kansas City Chiefs 1980, Winnipeg Blue Bombers (CFL) 1983-87. College coach: Notre Dame 1992-95. Pro coach: New Orleans Saints 1997-99, Kansas City Chiefs 2000, Pittsburgh Steelers 2001-03, Buffalo Bills 2004-05, joined Packers in 2006.
Jerry Fontenot, asst. offensive line; born November 21, 1966, Lafayette, La. Guard Texas A&M 1985-88. Pro center Chicago Bears 1989-1996, New Orleans Saints 1997-2003, Cincinnati Bengals 2004. Pro coach: Joined Packers in 2006.
Curtis Fuller, asst. special teams; born July 5, 1978, Fort Worth, Texas. Defensive back Tyler (Texas) J.C. 1997, Texas Christian 1998-2000. Pro defensive back Seattle Seahawks 2001-02, Green Bay Packers 2003-04, Carolina Panthers 2004. Pro coach: Oakland Raiders 2007, joined Packers in 2009.
Kevin Greene, outside linebackers; born July 31, 1962, Schenectady, N.Y. Linebacker Auburn 1980-85. Pro linebacker Los Angeles Rams 1985-1992, Pittsburgh Steelers 1993-95, Carolina Panthers 1996, San Francisco 49ers 1997, Carolina Panthers 1998-99. Pro coach: Joined Packers in 2009.
Mark Lovat, asst. strength & conditioning; born Oct. 9, 1969, Pocatello, Idaho. Attended Butler. No college or pro playing experience. Pro coach: Joined Packers in 1999.
Ben McAdoo, tight ends; born July 7, 1977, Homer City, Pa. Attended Indiana University (Pa.). No college or pro playing experience. College coach: Michigan State 2001, Fairfield 2002, Pittsburgh 2003, Akron 2004, Stanford 2005. Pro coach: New Orleans Saints 2004, San Francisco 49ers 2005, joined Packers in 2006.
Scott McCurley, defensive quality control; born August 1, 1980, New Castle, Pa. Linebacker Pittsburgh 1998-2002. No pro playing experience. College coach: Pittsburgh 2003-05. Pro coach: Joined Packers in 2006.
Winston Moss, asst. head coach/ inside linebackers; born December 24, 1965, Miami. Linebacker Miami 1983-86. Pro linebacker Tampa Bay Buccaneers 1987-1990, Los Angeles Raiders 1991-94, Seattle Seahawks 1995-97. Pro coach: Seattle Seahawks 1998, New Orleans Saints 2000-05, joined Packers in 2006.
Darren Perry, secondary-safeties; born December 29, 1968, Norfolk, Va. Safety Penn State 1989-1991. Pro safety Pittsburgh Steelers 1992-98, San Diego Chargers 1999, New Orleans Saints 2000. Pro coach: Cincinnati Bengals 2002, Pittsburgh Steelers 2003-06, Oakland Raiders 2007-08, joined Packers in 2009.
Joe Philbin, offensive coordinator; born July 2, 1961, Springfield, Mass. Tight end Washington & Jefferson 1980. No pro playing experience. College coach: Tulane 1984-85, Worcester Tech 1986-87, U.S. Merchant Marine Academy 1988-89, Allegheny 1990-93, Ohio University 1994, Northeastern 1995-96, Harvard 1997-98, Iowa 1999-2002. Pro coach: Joined Packers in 2003.
Dave Redding, strength & conditioning; born June 14, 1952, Holdenville, Okla. Defensive end Nebraska 1971-75. No pro playing experience. College coach: Nebraska 1976, Washington State 1977, Missouri 1978-1981. Pro coach: Cleveland Browns 1982-88, Kansas City Chiefs 1989-1997, Washington Redskins 2001, San Diego Chargers 2002-06, joined Packers in 2009.
Jimmy Robinson, wide receivers; born January 3, 1953, Atlanta. Wide receiver Georgia Tech 1972-74. Pro wide receiver New York Giants 1976-79, San Francisco 49ers 1980, Denver Broncos 1981. College coach: Georgia Tech 1987-89. Pro coach: Memphis Showboats (USFL) 1984-85, Atlanta Falcons 1990-93, Indianapolis Colts 1994-97, New York Giants 1998-2003, New Orleans Saints 2004-05, joined Packers in 2006.
John Rushing, offensive quality control; born February 26, 1972, Merced, Calif. Defensive back Washington State 1991-94. No pro playing experience. College coach: Willamette (Ore.) 1996-97, Boise State 1998-99, Montana State 2000-02, Utah State 2003-08. Pro coach: Joined Packers in 2009.
Shawn Slocum, special teams coordinator; born February 21, 1965, Bryan, Texas. Linebacker Texas A&M 1983-84. No pro playing experience. College coach: Texas A&M 1989, 1991-97, 2000-02, Pittsburgh 1990, Southern California 1998-99, Mississippi 2005. Pro coach: Joined Packers in 2006.
Mike Trgovac, defensive line; born February 27, 1959, Youngstown, Ohio. Defensive lineman Michigan 1977-1980. No pro playing experience. College coach: Michigan 1984-85, Ball State 1986-88, Navy 1989, Colorado State 1990-91, Notre Dame 1992-94. Pro coach: Philadelphia Eagles 1995-98, Green Bay Packers 1999, Washington Redskins 2000-01, Carolina Panthers 2002-08, re-joined Packers in 2009.
Joe Whitt, Jr., secondary-cornerbacks; born July 19, 1978, Auburn, Ala. Wide receiver Auburn 1997-99. No pro playing experience. College coach: Auburn 2000-01, The Citadel 2002, Louisville 2003-06. Pro coach: Atlanta Falcons 2007, joined Packers in 2008.

National Football Conference
North Division
Team Colors: Purple, Gold, and White
9520 Viking Drive
Eden Prairie, Minnesota 55344
Telephone: (952) 828-6500

2009 SCHEDULE

PRESEASON

Aug. 14	at Indianapolis	7:00
Aug. 21	**Kansas City**	7:00
Aug. 31	at Houston	7:00
Sep. 3	**Dallas**	7:00

REGULAR SEASON

Sep. 13	at Cleveland	1:00
Sep. 20	at Detroit	1:00
Sep. 27	**San Francisco**	12:00
Oct. 5	**Green Bay** (Mon.)	7:30
Oct. 11	at St. Louis	12:00
Oct. 18	**Baltimore**	12:00
Oct. 25	at Pittsburgh	1:00
Nov. 1	at Green Bay	12:00
Nov. 8	BYE	
Nov. 15	**Detroit**	12:00
Nov. 22	**Seattle**	12:00
Nov. 29	**Chicago**	12:00
Dec. 6	at Arizona	2:15
Dec. 13	**Cincinnati**	12:00
Dec. 20	at Carolina *	8:20
Dec. 28	at Chicago (Mon.)	7:30
Jan. 3	**N.Y. Giants**	12:00

** Sunday night games in Weeks 11-17 subject to change*

Stadium: Hubert H. Humphrey Metrodome (opened in 1982)
• **Capacity:** 64,121
500 11th Avenue South
Minneapolis, Minnesota 55415

Playing Surface: FieldTurf

Training Camp: Minnesota State-Mankato
Mankato, Minnesota
56001

HUBERT H. HUMPHREY METRODOME

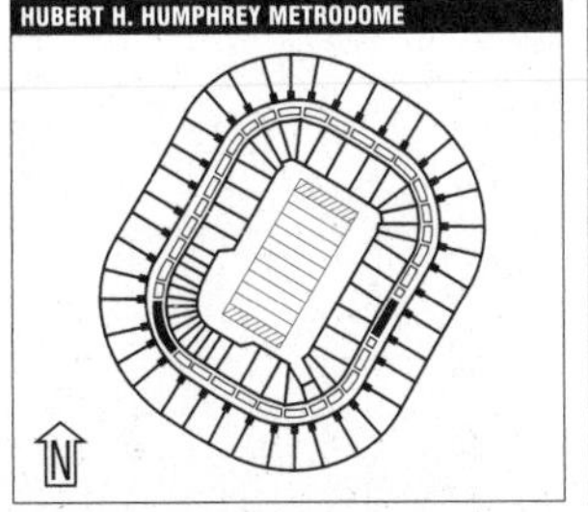

CLUB OFFICIALS

Owner/Chairman: Zygi Wilf
Owner/President: Mark Wilf
Owner/Vice Chairman: Leonard Wilf
Ownership Partners: Reggie Fowler, Alan Landis, David Mandelbaum
Vice President of Public Affairs/Stadium Development: Lester Bagley
Vice President of Football Operations: Rob Brzezinski
Vice President of Sales and Marketing: Steve LaCroix
Vice President of Finance: Steve Poppen
Vice President of Player Personnel: Rick Spielman
Vice President of Operations and Legal Counsel: Kevin Warren
Director of College Scouting: Scott Studwell
Director of Public Relations: Bob Hagan
Director of Community Relations: Brad Madson
Director of Operations/Team Travel: Luther Hippe
Director of Operations/Stadium and Logistics: Chad Lundeen
Director of Ticketing and Hospitality: Phil Huebner
Director of Video: Bob Marcus
Executive Director of Player Development/Legal: Les Pico
Director of Security: Kim Klawiter
Head Athletic Trainer: Eric Sugarman
Equipment Manager: Dennis Ryan
Director of Marketing & Business Development: Dannon Hulskotter
Director of Corporate Sales: Mike Slates
Director of Civic and Business Affairs: Kimberly Fields
Facilities Director: Nick Tigue

COACHING HISTORY
(413-347-9)

Records include postseason games

1961-66	Norm Van Brocklin	29-51-4
1967-1983	Bud Grant	161-99-5
1984	Les Steckel	3-13-0
1985	Bud Grant	7-9-0
1986-1991	Jerry Burns	55-46-0
1992-2001	Dennis Green*	101-70-0
2001-05	Mike Tice	33-34-0
2006-08	Brad Childress	24-25-0

*Resigned after 15 games in 2001

PAID ATTENDANCE

Home 492,536 Away 501,253
Total 993,789
Single-game home record, 64,482 (11/2/03)
Single-season home record, 510,741 (1998)

2009 DRAFT CHOICES

Round	Name	Pos.	College
1	Percy Harvin	WR	Florida
2	Phil Loadholt	T	Oklahoma
3	Asher Allen	DB	Georgia
5	Jasper Brinkley	LB	South Carolina
7	Jamarca Sanford	DB	Mississippi

MINNESOTA VIKINGS

2008 TEAM RECORD

PRESEASON (1-3)

Date	Result	Opponent
8/8	L 17-34	Seattle
8/16	W 23-15	at Baltimore
8/23	L 10-12	Pittsburgh
8/28	L 10-16	at Dallas

REGULAR SEASON (10-6)

Date	Result	Opponent
9/8	L 19-24	at Green Bay
9/14	L 15-18	Indianapolis
9/21	W 20-10	Carolina
9/28	L 17-30	at Tennessee
10/6	W 30-27	at New Orleans
10/12	W 12-10	Detroit
10/19	L 41-48	at Chicago
11/2	W 28-21	Houston
11/9	W 28-27	Green Bay
11/16	L 13-19	at Tampa Bay
11/23	W 30-12	at Jacksonville
11/30	W 34-14	Chicago
12/7	W 20-16	at Detroit
12/14	W 35-14	at Arizona
12/21	L 17-24	Atlanta
12/28	W 20-19	New York Giants

POSTSEASON (0-1)

Date	Result	Opponent
1/4	L 14-26	Philadelphia

SCORE BY PERIODS

Vikings	94	114	61	110	0 —	379
Opponents	78	74	115	66	0 —	333

2008 TEAM STATISTICS

	Vikings	Opp.
Total First Downs	292	255
Rushing	119	72
Passing	150	163
Penalty	23	20
3rd Down: Made/Att	86/218	68/203
3rd Down Pct.	39.4	33.5
4th Down: Made/Att	9/18	5/13
4th Down Pct.	50.0	38.5
Possession Avg.	31:19	28:41
Total Net Yards	5294	4679
Avg. Per Game	330.9	292.4
Total Plays	1014	946
Avg. Per Play	5.2	4.9
Net Yards Rushing	2338	1230
Avg. Per Game	146.1	76.9
Total Rushes	519	371
Net Yards Passing	2956	3449
Avg. Per Game	184.8	215.6
Sacked/Yards Lost	43/261	45/304
Gross Yards	3217	3753
Att./Completions	452/267	530/324
Completion Pct.	59.1	61.1
Had Intercepted	17	12
Punts/Average	74/46.9	80/43.5
Net Punting Avg.	74/35.0	80/39.1
Penalties/Yards	90/692	109/1002
Fumbles/Ball Lost	31/14	34/13
Touchdowns	41	36
Rushing	15	10
Passing	22	15
Returns	4	11

2008 INDIVIDUAL STATISTICS

Passing	Att.	Comp.	Yds.	Pct.	TD	Int.	Tkld.	Rate
Frerotte	301	178	2157	59.1	12	15	29/164	73.7
Jackson	149	88	10586	59.1	9	2	14/97	95.4
Taylor	1	1	4	100.0	1	0	0/0	122.9
Rice	1	0	0	0.0	0	0	0/0	39.6
Vikings	452	267	3217	59.1	22	17	43/261	81.5
Opponents	530	324	3753	61.1	15	12	45/304	82.5

SCORING	TD R	TD P	TD Rt	PAT	FG	Saf	PTS
Longwell	0	0	0	40/40	29/34	0	127
Peterson	10	0	0	0/0	0/0	0	60
Berrian	0	7	1	0/0	0/0	0	48
Shiancoe	0	7	0	0/0	0/0	0	42
Taylor	4	2	0	0/0	0/0	0	36
Rice	0	4	0	0/0	0/0	0	24
Wade	0	2	0	0/0	0/0	0	12
Winfield	0	0	2	0/0	0/0	0	12
Frerotte	1	0	0	0/0	0/0	0	6
Harris	0	0	1	0/0	0/0	0	6
J. Allen	0	0	0	0/0	0/0	2	4
Vikings	15	22	4	40/40	29/34	3	379
Opponents	10	15	11	35/35	26/36	1	333

2-Pt. Conversions: None
Vikings 0-1, Opponents 1-1

RUSHING	No.	Yds	Avg	LG	TD
Peterson	363	1760	4.8	67t	10
Taylor	101	399	4.0	21t	4
Jackson	26	145	5.6	29	0
Berrian	4	26	6.5	14	0
Dugan	4	7	1.8	2	0
Frerotte	19	7	0.4	5	1
Allison	1	1	1.0	1	0
Kluwe	1	-7	-7.0	-7	0
Vikings	519	2338	4.5	67t	15
Opponents	371	1230	3.3	57	10

RECEIVING	No.	Yds	Avg	LG	TD
Wade	53	645	12.2	59t	2
Berrian	48	964	20.1	99t	7
Taylor	45	399	8.9	47t	2
Shiancoe	42	596	14.2	40	7
Peterson	21	125	6.0	16	0
Tahi	16	37	2.3	7	0
Rice	15	141	9.4	23t	4
Allison	10	109	10.9	21	0
Kleinsasser	6	92	15.3	34	0
Mills	5	65	13.0	23	0
Ferguson	3	25	8.3	9	0
Dugan	2	12	6.0	9	0
Tapeh	1	7	7.0	7	0
Vikings	267	3217	12.0	99t	22
Opponents	324	3753	11.6	75	15

INTERCEPTIONS	No.	Yds	Avg	LG	TD
Leber	2	29	14.5	28	0
Sapp	2	13	6.5	14	0
Winfield	2	5	2.5	4	0
M. Williams	2	-1	-0.5	0	0
Sharper	1	12	12.0	12	0
Gordon	1	0	0.0	0	0
T. Johnson	1	0	0.0	0	0
Griffin	1	-2	-2.0	-2	0
Vikings	12	56	4.7	28	0
Opponents	17	329	19.4	59t	2

PUNTING	No.	Yds.	Avg.	In 20	LG
Kluwe	73	3473	47.6	23	62
Vikings	74	3473	46.9	23	62
Opponents	80	3481	43.5	4	29

PUNT RETURNS	Ret	FC	Yds	Avg	LG	TD
Gordon	15	11	66	4.4	20	0
Allison	9	4	58	6.4	27	0
Berrian	7	5	114	16.3	82t	1
Wade	3	3	35	11.7	20	0
Vikings	34	23	273	8.0	82t	1
Opponents	42	8	624	14.9	76t	4

KICKOFF RETURNS	No.	Yds	Avg	LG	TD
M. Hicks	29	690	23.8	38	0
Taylor	10	234	23.4	37	0
Reynaud	8	201	25.1	49	0
Allison	6	100	16.7	22	0
Kleinsasser	3	36	12.0	14	0
Gordon	2	61	30.5	42	0
Tahi	2	31	15.5	20	0
Peterson	1	16	16.0	16	0
Vikings	61	1369	22.4	49	0
Opponents	78	1830	23.5	58	0

FIELD GOALS	1-19	20-29	30-39	40-49	50+
Longwell	0/0	10/10	7/9	6/9	6/6
Vikings	0/0	10/10	7/9	6/9	6/6
Opponents	0/0	10/10	5/8	9/15	2/3

SACKS	No.
J. Allen	14.5
K. Williams	8.5
Greenway	5.5
Edwards	5.0
Robison	2.5
Wyms	2.5
Winfield	2.0
Leber	1.5
Harris	1.0
E.J. Henderson	1.0
P. Williams	1.0
Vikings	45.0
Opponents	43.0

RECORD HOLDERS

INDIVIDUAL RECORDS—CAREER

Category	Name	Performance
Rushing (Yds.)	Robert Smith, 1993-2000	6,818
Passing (Yds.)	Fran Tarkenton, 1961-66, 1972-78	33,098
Passing (TDs)	Fran Tarkenton, 1961-66, 1972-78	239
Receiving (No.)	Cris Carter, 1990-2001	1,004
Receiving (Yds.)	Cris Carter, 1990-2001	12,383
Interceptions	Paul Krause, 1968-1979	53
Punting (Avg.)	Chris Kluwe, 2005-08	44.5
Punt Return (Avg.)	Mewelde Moore, 2004-07	10.4
Kickoff Return (Avg.)	Charlie West, 1968-1973	25.5
Field Goals	Fred Cox, 1963-1977	282
Touchdowns (Tot.)	Cris Carter, 1990-2001	110
Points	Fred Cox, 1963-1977	1,365
*Sacks	John Randle, 1990-2000	114.0

INDIVIDUAL RECORDS—SINGLE SEASON

Category	Name	Performance
Rushing (Yds.)	Adrian Peterson, 2008	1,760
Passing (Yds.)	Daunte Culpepper, 2004	4,717
Passing (TDs)	Daunte Culpepper, 2004	39
Receiving (No.)	Cris Carter, 1994, 1995	122
Receiving (Yds.)	Randy Moss, 2003	1,632
Interceptions	Paul Krause, 1975	10
Punting (Avg.)	Chris Kluwe, 2008	47.6
Punt Return (Avg.)	David Palmer, 1995	13.2
Kickoff Return (Avg.)	John Gilliam, 1972	26.3
Field Goals	Gary Anderson, 1998	35
Touchdowns (Tot.)	Chuck Foreman, 1975	22
Points	Gary Anderson, 1998	164
*Sacks	Chris Doleman, 1989	21.0

INDIVIDUAL RECORDS—SINGLE GAME

Category	Name	Performance
Rushing (Yds.)	Adrian Peterson, 11-4-07	**296
Passing (Yds.)	Tommy Kramer, 11-2-86	490
Passing (TDs)	Joe Kapp, 9-28-69	**7
Receiving (No.)	Rickey Young, 12-16-79	15
Receiving (Yds.)	Sammy White, 11-7-76	210
Interceptions	Many Times	3
	Last time by Darren Sharper, 11-13-05	
Field Goals	Rich Karlis, 11-5-89	7
Touchdowns (Tot.)	Chuck Foreman, 12-20-75	4
	Ahmad Rashad, 9-2-79	4
Points	Chuck Foreman, 12-20-75	24
	Ahmad Rashad, 9-2-79	24
*Sacks	Randy Holloway, 9-16-84	5.0

**Sacks became an official statistic in 1982.*
***NFL Record*

MINNESOTA VIKINGS

2009 VETERAN ROSTER

No.	Name	Pos.	Ht.	Wt.	Birthdate	NFL Exp.	College	Hometown	How Acq.	'08 Games/ Starts
39	Abdullah, Husain	S	6-0	204	7/27/85	2	Washington State	Pomona, Calif.	FA-'08	16/0
69	Allen, Jared	DE	6-6	270	4/3/82	6	Idaho State	Los Gatos, Calif.	T(KC)-'08	16/16
84	Allison, Aundrae	WR	6-0	198	6/25/84	3	East Carolina	Kannapolis, N.C.	D5-'07	15/0
87	Berrian, Bernard	WR	6-1	185	12/27/80	6	Fresno State	Winton, Calif.	UFA(Chi)-'08	16/13
4	Booty, John David	QB	6-3	213	1/3/85	2	Southern California	Shreveport, La.	D5a-'08	0*
62	Cook, Ryan	T	6-6	328	5/8/83	4	New Mexico	Albuquerque, N.M.	D2b-'06	16/14
63	Daniels, Brian	G	6-4	303	10/31/84	2	Colorado	Denver, Colo.	FA-'07	0*
83	Dugan, Jeff	FB	6-4	258	4/8/81	6	Maryland	Pittsburgh, Pa.	D7-'04	9/2
91	Edwards, Ray	DE	6-5	268	1/1/85	4	Purdue	Cincinnati, Ohio	D4-'06	15/15
90	Evans, Fred	DT	6-4	305	11/6/83	4	Texas St.-San Marcos	Morgan Park, Ill.	FA-'07	16/2
59	Farwell, Heath	LB	6-0	235	12/31/81	5	San Diego State	Corona, Calif.	FA-'05	0*
37	Frampton, Eric	S	5-11	205	2/6/84	3	Washington State	San Jose, Calif.	W(Det)-'07	16/0
41	Gordon, Charles	CB	5-11	180	7/18/84	4	Kansas	Santa Monica, Calif.	FA-'06	9/2
52	Greenway, Chad	LB	6-2	242	1/12/83	4	Iowa	Mt. Vernon, S.D.	D1-'06	16/15
23	Griffin, Cedric	CB	6-0	203	11/11/82	4	Texas	San Antonio, Texas	D2a-'06	16/15
99	Grigsby, Otis	DE	6-3	260	11/19/80	3	Kentucky	Converse, Texas	PS(Car)-'07	8/1
98	Guion, Letroy	DT	6-4	303	6/21/87	2	Florida State	Starke, Fla.	D5b-'08	2/0
56	Henderson, E.J.	LB	6-1	245	8/3/80	7	Maryland	Aberdeen, Md.	D2-'03	4/3
50	Henderson, Erin	LB	6-3	244	7/1/86	2	Maryland	Aberdeen, Md.	FA-'08	10/0
64	Herrera, Anthony	G	6-2	315	6/14/80	6	Tennessee	Naples, Fla.	FA-'04	16/16
58	Herron, David	LB	6-1	239	6/17/84	2	Michigan State	Warren, Ohio	FA-'07	14/3
79	Hicks, Artis	G	6-4	335	11/28/78	8	Memphis	Jackson, Tenn.	T(Phil)-'06	12/6
16	Holt, Glenn	WR	6-1	193	7/31/84	4	Kentucky	Miami, Fla.	FA-'09	15/2*
76	Hutchinson, Steve	G	6-5	313	11/1/77	9	Michigan	Ft. Lauderdale, Fla.	RFA(Sea)-'06	16/16
7	Jackson, Tarvaris	QB	6-2	225	4/21/83	4	Alabama State	Montgomery, Ala.	D2c-'06	9/5
25	Johnson, Tyrell	S	6-0	207	5/19/85	2	Arkansas State	Rison, Ark.	D2-'08	16/7
73	Kennedy, Jimmy	DT	6-5	320	11/15/79	7	Penn State	Yonkers, N.Y.	FA(Jax)-'08	8/0*
40	Kleinsasser, Jim	TE	6-3	272	1/31/77	11	North Dakota	Carrington, N.D.	D2-'99	16/11
5	Kluwe, Chris	P	6-4	215	12/24/81	5	UCLA	Los Alamitos, Calif.	W(Sea)-'05	16/0
51	Leber, Ben	LB	6-3	244	12/7/78	8	Kansas State	Vermillion, S.D.	UFA(SD)-'06	16/15
46	Loeffler, Cullen	LS	6-5	241	1/27/81	6	Texas	Ingram, Texas	FA-'04	16/0
8	Longwell, Ryan	K	6-0	200	8/16/74	13	California	Bend, Ore.	UFA(GB)-'06	16/0
21	McCauley, Marcus	CB	6-1	203	9/3/83	3	Fresno State	Sacramento, Calif.	D3-'07	10/1
74	McKinnie, Bryant	T	6-8	335	9/23/79	8	Miami	Woodbury, N.J.	D1-'02	12/12
3	Mehlhaff, Taylor	K	5-10	184	8/25/85	2	Wisconsin	Aberdeen, S.D.	FA-'09	3/0*
45	Mills, Garrett	TE	6-1	235	10/12/83	4	Tulsa	Jenks, Okla.	W(NE)-'07	8/0
92	Mitchell, Jayme	DE	6-6	285	3/15/84	4	Mississippi	Jackson, Miss.	FA-'06	0*
31	Paymah, Karl	CB	6-0	195	11/29/82	4	Washington State	Culver City, Calif.	UFA(Den)-'09	16/2*
28	Peterson, Adrian	RB	6-1	217	3/21/85	3	Oklahoma	Palestine, Texas	D1-'07	16/15
60	Radovich, Drew	T	6-5	305	6/20/85	2	Southern California	Mission Viejo, Calif.	FA-'08	0*
82	Reynaud, Darius	WR	5-9	201	12/29/84	2	West Virginia	Boutte, La.	FA-'08	3/0
18	Rice, Sidney	WR	6-4	202	9/1/86	3	South Carolina	Gaffney, S.C.	D2-'07	13/3
96	Robison, Brian	DE	6-3	259	4/27/83	3	Texas	Splendora, Texas	D4-'07	15/0
85	Rogers, Roderick	WR	6-2	187	9/7/84	3	Wisconsin	Stone Mountain, Ga.	FA-'08	3/1*
2	t-Rosenfels, Sage	QB	6-4	225	3/6/78	9	Iowa State	Maquoketa, Iowa	T(Hou)-'09	6/5*
22	Sapp, Benny	CB	5-9	190	1/20/81	6	Northern Iowa	Ft. Lauderdale, Fla.	UFA(KC)-'08	14/4
81	Shiancoe, Visanthe	TE	6-4	250	6/18/80	7	Morgan State	Laurel, Md.	UFA(NYG)-'07	16/15
65	Sullivan, John	C	6-4	301	8/8/85	2	Notre Dame	Old Greenwich, Conn.	D6a-'08	16/0
38	Tahi, Naufahu	FB	6-0	254	10/30/81	4	Brigham Young	West Valley City, Utah	PS(Cin)-'06	16/5
29	Taylor, Chester	RB	5-11	213	9/22/79	8	Toledo	River Rouge, Mich.	UFA(Balt)-'06	16/1
95	Udeze, Kenechi	DE	6-3	281	3/5/83	6	Southern California	Los Angeles, Calif.	D1-'04	0*
19	Wade, Bobby	WR	5-10	186	2/25/81	7	Arizona	Phoenix, Ariz.	UFA(Tenn)-'07	16/14
93	Williams, Kevin	DT	6-5	311	8/16/80	7	Oklahoma State	Fordyce, Ark.	D1-'03	16/16
20	Williams, Madieu	S	6-1	203	10/18/81	6	Maryland	Lanham, Md.	UFA(Cin)-'08	9/9
94	Williams, Pat	DT	6-3	317	10/24/72	13	Texas A&M	Monroe, La.	UFA(Buff)-'05	14/14
26	Winfield, Antoine	CB	5-9	180	6/24/77	11	Ohio State	Akron, Ohio	UFA(Buff)-'04	16/16

* Booty inactive for 15 games; Daniels on practice squad for entire '08 season; Farwell missed '08 season because of injury; Holt played 15 games with Cincinnati in '08; Kennedy played six games with Jacksonville; Mehlhaff played 3 games with New Orleans; Mitchell missed '08 season because of injury; Paymah played 16 games with Denver; Radovich was inactive for 6 games and then missed the rest of '08 season because of injury; Rogers played 3 games with Denver; Rosenfels played 6 games with Houston; Udeze missed entire '08 season because of non-football illness.

t- Vikings traded for Rosenfels (Hou).

Players lost through free agency (3): C Matt Birk (16 games in '08), T Marcus Johnson (Oak; 7), S Darren Sharper (NO; 16).

Also played with Vikings in '08—LB Rufus Alexander (1 game), LB Vinny Ciurciu (14), WR Robert Ferguson (8), QB Gus Frerotte (11), LB Napoleon Harris (10), RB Maurice Hicks (11), LB Dontarrious Thomas (4), DT Ellis Wyms (16).

2009 FIRST-YEAR ROSTER

Name	Pos.	Ht.	Wt.	Birthdate	College	Hometown	How Acq.
Allen, Asher	CB	5-9	194	1/22/88	Georgia	Tucker, Ga.	D3
Anderson, Colt	S	5-10	194	10/25/85	Montana	Butte, Mont.	FA
Bell, Kahlil	RB	5-11	212	12/10/86	UCLA	San Anselmo, Calif.	FA
Brinkley, Jasper	LB	6-1	252	7/12/85	South Carolina	Thomson, Ga.	D5
Burnett, Martail (1)	DE	6-3	262	1/10/85	Utah	Los Angeles, Calif.	FA-'08
Clark, Chris (1)	T	6-5	315	10/1/85	Southern Mississippi	New Orleans, La.	FA-'08
Cooper, Jon	C	6-2	291	10/1/86	Oklahoma	Fort Collins, Colo.	FA-
Francois, Robert	LB	6-2	244	5/14/85	Boston College	Highlands, Texas	FA
Garcia, Juan	C	6-3	294	4/24/84	Washington	Yakima, Wash.	FA
Glennon, Sean	QB	6-4	220	9/5/85	Virginia Tech	Centreville, Va.	FA
Hall, De'von	S	6-3	212	9/8/87	Utah State	Reseda, Calif.	FA
Harvin, Percy	WR	5-11	184	5/28/88	Florida	Virginia Beach, Va.	D1
Holmes, Antoine	DT	6-2	289	3/25/86	North Carolina State	Williamsburg, Va.	FA
Johnson, Ian	RB	5-11	212	10/10/86	Boise State	San Dimas, Calif.	FA
Johnson, Jaymar (1)	WR	6-0	176	7/10/84	Jackson State	Gary, Ind.	D6b-'08
Johnson, Tremaine	DT	6-2	285	9/26/85	Louisiana State	Galena Park, Texas	FA
Kemp, Andy	G	6-5	313	3/12/87	Wisconsin	Menasha, Wisc.	FA
Lepori, Bobby	T	6-4	297	9/27/85	Fresno State	Reno, Nev.	FA
Loadholt, Phil	T	6-8	343	1/21/86	Oklahoma	Fountain, Colo.	D2
Moore, Nick	WR	6-2	186	6/25/86	Toledo	Westerville, Ohio	FA
Onatolu, Kenny (1)	LB	6-2	225	10/8/82	Nebraska-Omaha	Papillion, Neb.	FA
Perretta, Vinny	WR	5-9	186	10/14/85	Boise State	Encitas, Calif.	FA
Roberson, Derrick (1)	CB	5-10	182	3/12/85	Rutgers	Ft. Lauderdale, Fla.	FA
Sanford, Jamarca	S	5-10	200	8/27/85	Mississippi	Batesville, Miss.	D7
Urban, Nick	G	6-4	309	4/22/86	Winona Satae	Brookfield, Wisc.	FA
Walker, Marcus (1)	CB	5-11	191	5/23/86	Oklahoma	Waco, Texas	FA-'08
Walker, Nick	TE	6-4	253	11/19/85	Alabama	Brundidge, Ala.	FA
Young, Albert (1)	RB	5-10	209	2/25/85	Iowa	Moorestown, N.J.	FA-'08

The term NFL Rookie is defined as a player who is in his first season of professional football and has not been on the roster of another professional football team for any regular-season or postseason games. A Rookie is designated by an "R" on NFL rosters. Players who have been active in another professional football league or players who have NFL experience, including either preseason training camp or being on an Active List or Inactive List, or on Reserve/Injured or Reserve/Physically Unable to Perform for fewer than six regular-season games, are termed NFL First-Year Players. An NFL First-Year Player is designated by a "1" on NFL rosters. Thereafter, a player is credited with an additional year of experience for each season in which he accumulates six games on the Active List or Inactive List, or on Reserve/Injured or Reserve/Physically Unable to Perform.

Log on to www.vikings.com for an up-to-date roster.

COACHING STAFF

Head Coach,
Brad Childress

Pro Career: Named the seventh head coach in Vikings' history on January 6, 2006. This marks Childress' 32nd season coaching, including his twelfth on an NFL sideline, and his fourth with the Vikings. Childress led Minnesota to its first NFC North title with a 10-6 record, earning the Vikings its first division title and home playoff game since 2000. The Vikings have led the NFL in rush defense for three consecutive years under Childress, a league first since the 1970 AFL-NFL merger. In 2008 under Childress, Adrian Peterson became the Vikings' first-ever NFL rushing leader. The 2007 Vikings became the first team in franchise history to rank No. 1 in the NFL in rushing offense and rushing defense. Was an assistant coach with the Eagles (the last four as offensive coordinator), when the Eagles reached Super Bowl XXXIX and played in four straight NFC Championship Games. He began his NFL coaching career as the Colts' quarterbacks coach (1985). Career record: 24-25.

Background: Coached at Illinois (1978-1984), Northern Arizona (1986-89), Utah (1990), and Wisconsin (1991-98). Childress played quarterback and wide receiver at Illinois before transferring to Eastern Illinois, where he graduated with a bachelor's degree in psychology.

Personal: Born June 27, 1956 in Aurora, Ill. He and his wife Dru-Ann have four children: Cara, Kyle, Andrew, and Christopher.

ASSISTANT COACHES

Juney Barnett, asst. strength and conditioning; born January 11, 1979, Philadelphia. Defensive back Bloomsburg 1997-2000. College coach: Bloomsburg 2001, Army 2005. Pro coach: Rhein Fire (NFLE) 2004-05, joined Vikings in 2006.

Darrell Bevell, offensive coordinator; born January 6, 1970, Yuma, Ariz. Quarterback Northern Arizona 1989, Wisconsin 1992-95. No pro playing experience. College coach: Westmar 1996, Iowa State 1997, Connecticut 1998-99. Pro coach: Green Bay Packers 2000-05, joined Vikings in 2006.

Eric Bieniemy, running backs; born August 15, 1969, New Orleans. Running back Colorado 1987-1990. Pro running back San Diego Chargers 1991-94, Cincinnati Bengals 1995-98, Philadelphia Eagles 1999. College coach: Colorado 2001-02, UCLA 2003-05. Pro coach: Joined Vikings in 2006.

Karl Dunbar, defensive line; born May 18, 1967, Plaisance, La. Defensive lineman Louisiana State 1986-89. Pro defensive lineman Pittsburgh Steelers 1990, New Orleans Saints 1992-93, Arizona Cardinals 1994-95. College coach: Nicholls State 1998-99, Louisiana State 2000-01, 2005, Oklahoma State 2002-03. Pro coach: Chicago Bears 2004, joined Vikings in 2006.

Ryan Ficken, quality control-offense/wide receivers; born February 20, 1980, Aurora, Colo. Wide receiver Arizona State 1998-99. No pro playing experience. College coach: UCLA 2004-06. Pro coach: Joined Vikings in 2007.

Leslie Frazier, defensive coordinator/asst. head coach; born April 3, 1959, Columbus, Miss. Defensive back Alcorn State 1977-1980. Pro defensive back Chicago Bears 1981-86. College coach: Trinity (Ill.) College 1988-1996 (head coach), Illinois 1997-98. Pro coach Philadelphia Eagles 1999-2002, Cincinnati Bengals 2003-04, Indianapolis Colts 2005-06, joined Vikings in 2007.

Jason Glenn, special teams assistant/player development assistant; born August 20, 1979, Humble, Texas. Safety/linebacker Texas A&M 1997-2000. Pro linebacker New York Jets 2001-04, Miami Dolphins 2005, Minnesota Vikings 2006. Pro coach: Joined Vikings in 2009.

Jim Hueber, asst. offensive line; born August 14, 1948, Philadelphia. Center South Dakota 1966-67. No pro playing experience. College coach: Cincinnati 1974, Dodge City (Kan.) C.C. 1975-78, Wichita State 1979-1980, Temple 1981-82, Memphis State 1983, Minnesota 1984-1991, Wisconsin 1992-2005. Pro coach: Joined Vikings in 2006.

Jeff Imamura, quality control-defense/linebackers; born May 22, 1974, Lubbock, Texas. Attended Texas Christian. No college or pro playing experience. College coach: Texas Christian 1997-99, Northern Arizona 2000-02, Saginaw Valley State 2003. Pro coach: Joined Vikings in 2006.

Jimmie Johnson, tight ends; born October 6, 1966, Augusta, Ga. Tight end Howard 1985-88. Pro tight end Washington Redskins 1989-1991, Detroit Lions 1992-93, Kansas City Chiefs 1994, Philadelphia Eagles 1995-98. College coach: South Carolina State 2001, Shaw 2002-03, Texas Southern 2004-05. Pro coach: Joined Vikings in 2006.

Tom Kanavy, strength and conditioning; born April 8, 1970, Archibald, Pa. Attended Penn State. No college or pro playing experience. College coach: Miami 1993, Penn State 1993-95. Pro coach: Philadelphia Eagles 1995-2005, joined Vikings in 2006.

Derek Mason, asst. defensive backs; born September 29, 1969, Phoenix. Defensive back Northern Arizona 1987-1991. No pro playing experience. College coach: Mesa C.C. 1994, Weber State 1995-96, Idaho State 1997-98, Bucknell 1999-2001, Utah 2002, St. Mary's 2003, New Mexico State 2004, Ohio 2005-06. Pro coach: Joined Vikings in 2007.

Pat Morris, offensive line; born April 7, 1954, Cleveland. Offensive lineman Southern California 1972-75. College coach: Southern California 1976-77, 1983-86, Northern Arizona 1978, Minnesota 1979-1982, Michigan State 1987-1994, Stanford 1995-96. Pro coach: San Francisco 49ers 1997-2003, Detroit Lions 2004-05, joined Vikings in 2006.

Brian Murphy, special teams coordinator; born July 17, 1969, Elmwood Park, Ill. Defensive lineman Lehigh 1988-1991. No pro playing experience. College coach: Benedictine 1992, Wisconsin 1994-96, 2002-05, Baylor 1997, San Diego 1998, Lehigh 1999. Pro coach: Joined Vikings in 2006.

Fred Pagac, linebackers; born April 26, 1952, Richeyville, Pa. Tight end Ohio State 1971-73. Pro tight end Chicago Bears 1974, Tampa Bay Buccaneers 1976. College coach: Ohio State 1978-2000. Pro coach: Oakland Raiders 2001-03, Kansas City Chiefs 2004-05, joined Vikings in 2006.

Dennis Polian, asst. to head coach; born November 10, 1976, Bronx, N.Y. Attended Villanova and Boston College. No college or pro playing experience. Pro coach: Hamilton Tiger-Cats (CFL) 2008, joined Vikings in 2009.

Diron Reynolds, defensive assistant/defensive line; born February 23, 1971, Aiken, S.C. Linebacker Wake Forest 1990-93. No pro playing experience. College coach: Wake Forest 1997-2000, Indiana 2001. Pro coach: Indianapolis Colts 2002-06, Miami Dolphins 2007, joined Vikings in 2009.

Kevin Rogers, quarterbacks; born September 7, 1951, Brooklyn, N.Y. Linebacker Massanutten Academy 1969-1970, William & Mary 1971-73. College coach: Ohio State 1977-78, William & Mary 1980-82, Navy 1983-1990, Syracuse 1991-98, Notre Dame 1999-2001, Virginia Tech 2002-05. Pro coach: Joined Vikings in 2006.

Ryan Silverfield, quality control-defense; born August 4, 1980, Jacksonville, Fla. Attended Hampden-Sydney. No college or pro playing experience. College coach: Hampden-Sydney 2000-03, Jacksonville 2005, Central Florida 2006-07. Pro coach: Joined Vikings in 2008.

Kevin Stefanski, quality control-offense/quarterbacks; born May 8, 1982, Philadelphia. Safety Pennsylvania 2000-04. College coach: Pennsylvania 2005. Pro coach: Joined Vikings in 2006.

George Stewart, wide receivers; born December 29, 1958, Little Rock, Ark. Guard Arkansas 1977-1980. No pro playing experience. College coach: Minnesota 1984-85, Notre Dame 1986-88. Pro coach: Pittsburgh Steelers 1989-1991, Tampa Bay Buccaneers 1992-95, San Francisco 49ers 1996-2002, Atlanta Falcons 2003-06, joined Vikings in 2007.

Martin Streight, asst. strength and conditioning; born June 20, 1969, Trenton, N.J. Attended Indiana (Penn.). No college or pro playing experience. College coach: Penn State 1994, Princeton 1995-96. Pro coach: Philadelphia Eagles 1995-96, Arizona Cardinals 1997-2003, Scottish Claymores (NFLE) 2003, Berlin Thunder (NFLE) 2004-05, joined Vikings in 2006.

Chris White, asst. special teams; born June 29, 1967, Haverhill, Mass. Quarterback Colby College 1986-89. No pro playing experience. College coach: Syracuse 1990-92, 2000-08, Arkansas State 1992-93, Holy Cross 1993-94, UNLV 1996-98, Cal Poly-San Luis Obispo 1999. Pro coach: Joined Vikings in 2009.

Joe Woods, defensive backs; born June 25, 1970, Natrona Heights, Pa. Safety Illinois State 1988-1991. College coach: Muskingum 1992, Eastern Michigan 1993, Northwestern (La.) State 1994, Grand Valley State 1994-96, Kent State 1997, Hofstra 1998-2000, Western Michigan 2001-03. Pro coach: Tampa Bay Buccaneers 2004-05, joined Vikings in 2006.

National Football Conference
South Division
Team Colors: Old Gold, Black, and White
5800 Airline Drive
Metairie, Louisiana 70003
Telephone: (504) 733-0255

2009 SCHEDULE

PRESEASON

Aug. 14	**Cincinnati**	7:00
Aug. 22	at Houston	7:00
Aug. 29	at Oakland	1:00
Sep. 3	**Miami**	7:00

REGULAR SEASON

Sep. 13	**Detroit**	12:00
Sep. 20	at Philadelphia	1:00
Sep. 27	at Buffalo	4:05
Oct. 4	**N.Y. Jets**	3:05
Oct. 11	BYE	
Oct. 18	**N.Y. Giants**	12:00
Oct. 25	at Miami	4:15
Nov. 2	**Atlanta** (Mon.)	7:30
Nov. 8	**Carolina**	3:05
Nov. 15	at St. Louis	12:00
Nov. 22	at Tampa Bay	1:00
Nov. 30	**New England** (Mon.)	7:30
Dec. 6	at Washington	1:00
Dec. 13	at Atlanta	1:00
Dec. 19	**Dallas** (Sat.)	7:20
Dec. 27	**Tampa Bay**	12:00
Jan. 3	at Carolina	1:00

Stadium: Louisiana Superdome
(opened in 1975)
•**Capacity:** 68,000
1500 Poydras Street
New Orleans, Louisiana 70112
Playing Surface: Sportexe Momentum
Training Camp: New Orleans Saints
Metairie, Louisiana 70003

LOUISIANA SUPERDOME

CLUB OFFICIALS

Owner/President: Tom Benson
Owner/Executive Vice President: Rita Benson LeBlanc
Executive Vice President/General Manager: Mickey Loomis
Senior Vice President/Chief Financial Officer: Dennis Lauscha
Vice President of Communications: Greg Bensel
Vice President of Marketing and Business Development: Ben Hales
Vice President/General Counsel: Vicky Neumeyer
Vice President of Ticket and Suite Sales: Mike Stanfield
Director of Football Administration: Khai Harley
Director of Operations: James Nagaoka
Pro Scouting Director: Ryan Pace
Pro Scouts: Terry Fontenot, Ryan Powell
Director of College Scouting: Rick Reiprish
Assistant Director of College Scouting: Brian Adams
College Scouting Coordinator: Jason Mitchell
Area Scouts: Mike Baugh, David Hinson, Dwaune Jones, Josh Lucas, Jim Monos, Terry Wooden
Combine Scout: Ryan Hollern
Player Personnel Assistant: Joseph Laine
Equipment Manager: Dan Simmons
Assistant Equipment Manager: Glennon (Silky) Powell
Equipment Assistant: John Baumgartner
Head Athletic Trainer: Scottie B. Patton
Assistant Athletic Trainers: Duane Brooks, Kevin Mangum
Video Director: Dave Desposito
Director of Player Development: Fred McAfee
Senior Director of New Media: Doug Miller
Director of Communications: Ricky Zeller
Communications Manager: Justin Macione
Communications Assistant: Dave Lawrence
Director of Security: Geoff Santini
Director of Photography: Michael C. Hebert
Director of Community Affairs: Nick Karl
Information Technology/Network Manager: Jeff Huffman
Facilities Manager: Terry Ashburn

COACHING HISTORY
(264-381-5)

Records include postseason games

1967-70	Tom Fears*	13-34-2
1970-72	J.D. Roberts	7-25-3
1973-75	John North**	11-23-0
1975	Ernie Hefferle	1-7-0
1976-77	Hank Stram	7-21-0
1978-80	Dick Nolan***	15-29-0
1980	Dick Stanfel	1-3-0
1981-85	O.A. (Bum) Phillips****	27-42-0
1985	Wade Phillips	1-3-0
1986-96	Jim Mora#	93-78-0
1996	Rick Venturi	1-7-0
1997-99	Mike Ditka	15-33-0
2000-05	Jim Haslett	46-52-0
2006-08	Sean Payton	26-24-0

*Released after seven games in 1970
**Released after six games in 1975
***Released after 12 games in 1980
****Resigned after 12 games in 1985
#Resigned after eight games in 1996

PAID ATTENDANCE

Home 546,755 Away 535,099
Total 1,081,854
Single-game home record, 70,940 (9/2/79)
Single-season home record, 548,728 (1992)

2009 DRAFT CHOICES

Round	Name	Pos.	College
1	Malcolm Jenkins	DB	Ohio State
4	Chip Vaughn	DB	Wake Forest
	Stanley Arnoux	LB	Wake Forest
5	Thomas Morstead	P	Southern Methodist

NEW ORLEANS SAINTS

2008 TEAM RECORD

PRESEASON (2-2)

Date	Result	Opponent
8/7	W 24-10	at Arizona
8/16	L 27-31	Houston
8/23	W 13-0	at Cincinnati
8/28	L 10-14	Miami

REGULAR SEASON (8-8)

Date	Result	Opponent
9/7	W 24-20	Tampa Bay
9/14	L 24-29	at Washington
9/21	L 32-34	at Denver
9/28	W 31-17	San Francisco
10/6	L 27-30	Minnesota
10/12	W 34-3	Oakland
10/19	L 7-30	at Carolina
10/26	W 37-32	San Diego
11/9	L 20-34	at Atlanta
11/16	W 30-20	at Kansas City
11/24	W 51-29	Green Bay
11/30	L 20-23	at Tampa Bay
12/7	W 29-25	Atlanta
12/11	L 24-27	at Chicago (OT)
12/21	W 42-7	at Detroit
12/28	L 31-33	Carolina

(OT) Overtime

SCORE BY PERIODS

Saints	67	154	115	127	0	— 463
Opponents	80	141	69	100	3	— 393

2008 TEAM STATISTICS

	Saints	Opp.
Total First Downs	354	299
Rushing	103	100
Passing	232	180
Penalty	19	19
3rd Down: Made/Att	97/200	82/206
3rd Down Pct.	48.5	39.8
4th Down: Made/Att	10/18	8/14
4th Down Pct.	55.6	57.1
Possession Avg.	30:23	29:37
Total Net Yards	6571	5432
Avg. Per Game	410.7	339.5
Total Plays	1047	999
Avg. Per Play	6.3	5.4
Net Yards Rushing	1594	1885
Avg. Per Game	99.6	117.8
Total Rushes	398	445
Net Yards Passing	4977	3547
Avg. Per Game	311.1	221.7
Sacked/Yards Lost	13/92	28/161
Gross Yards	5069	3708
Att./Completions	636/413	526/299
Completion Pct.	64.9	56.8
Had Intercepted	18	15
Punts/Average	53/44.6	66/41.1
Net Punting Avg.	53/35.9	66/35.2
Penalties/Yards	86/797	84/637
Fumbles/Ball Lost	18/8	16/7
Touchdowns	57	41
Rushing	20	14
Passing	34	21
Returns	3	6

2008 INDIVIDUAL STATISTICS

PASSING	Att.	Comp.	Yds.	Pct.	TD	Int.	Tkld.	Rate
Brees	635	413	5069	65.0	34	17	13/92	96.2
Moore	1	0	0	0.0	0	1	0/0	0.0
Saints	636	413	5069	64.9	34	18	13/92	95.4
Opponents	526	299	3708	56.8	21	15	28/161	80.3

SCORING	TD R	TD P	TD Rt	PAT	FG	Saf	PTS
P. Thomas	9	3	0	0/0	0/0	0	72
Hartley	0	0	0	28/28	13/13	0	67
Moore	0	10	0	0/0	0/0	0	60
Bush	2	4	3	0/0	0/0	0	54
McAllister	5	1	0	0/0	0/0	0	36
Gramatica	0	0	0	16/16	6/10	0	34
Colston	0	5	0	0/0	0/0	0	30
Meachem	1	3	0	0/0	0/0	0	24
Henderson	0	3	0	0/0	0/0	0	18
Mehlhaff	0	0	0	9/10	3/4	0	18
Campbell	0	2	0	0/0	0/0	0	12
Karney	2	0	0	0/0	0/0	0	12
Bell	1	0	0	0/0	0/0	0	6
Miller	0	1	0	0/0	0/0	0	6
Patten	0	1	0	0/0	0/0	0	6
Stecker	0	1	0	0/0	0/0	0	6
Grant	0	0	0	0/0	0/0	1	2
Saints	20	34	3	53/54	22/27	1	463
Opponents	14	21	6	37/37	34/39	1	393

2-Pt. Conversions: None.
Saints 0-3, Opponents 3-4.

RUSHING	No.	Yds	Avg	LG	TD
P. Thomas	129	625	4.8	42t	9
McAllister	107	418	3.9	19	5
Bush	106	404	3.8	43	2
Stecker	8	43	5.4	12	0
Bell	13	42	3.2	15	1
Henderson	4	33	8.3	30	0
Meachem	1	20	20.0	20t	1
Karney	8	10	1.3	3	2
Brees	22	-1	0.0	9	0
Saints	398	1594	4.0	43	20
Opponents	445	1885	4.2	46	14

RECEIVING	No.	Yds	Avg	LG	TD
Moore	79	928	11.7	70t	10
Bush	52	440	8.5	42t	4
Shockey	50	483	9.7	26	0
Colston	47	760	16.2	70t	5
Miller	45	579	12.9	41	1
Henderson	32	793	24.8	84t	3
P. Thomas	31	284	9.2	24	3
McAllister	18	128	7.1	20	1
Meachem	12	289	24.1	74	3
Campbell	12	121	10.1	29	2
Patten	11	162	14.7	39t	1
Stecker	9	52	5.8	12	1
Karney	9	18	2.0	7	0
Sobomehin	2	8	4.0	10	0
Ryan	2	7	3.5	5	0
Bell	1	14	14.0	14	0
Ortega	1	3	3.0	3	0
Saints	413	5069	12.3	84t	34
Opponents	299	3708	12.4	67t	21

INTERCEPTIONS	No.	Yds	Avg	LG	TD
David	5	83	16.6	42	0
Fujita	2	19	9.5	17	0
Kaesviharn	2	13	6.5	13	0
U. Young	2	3	1.5	3	0
Porter	1	25	25.0	25	0
Bullocks	1	23	23.0	23	0
McKenzie	1	14	14.0	14	0
Vilma	1	8	8.0	8	0
Saints	15	188	12.5	42	0
Opponents	18	270	15.0	95t	2

PUNTING	No.	Yds.	Avg.	In 20	LG
Weatherford	26	1094	42.1	5	61
Pakulak	24	1144	47.7	3	70
Graham	3	126	42	1	44
Saints	53	2364	44.6	9	70
Opponents	66	2711	41.1	23	65

PUNT RETURNS	Ret	FC	Yds	Avg	LG	TD
Bush	20	3	270	13.5	71t	3
Moore	6	13	40	6.7	11	0
Green	0	1	0	—	—	0
Saints	26	17	310	11.9	71t	3
Opponents	34	7	363	10.7	42	0

KICKOFF RETURNS	No.	Yds	Avg	LG	TD
P. Thomas	31	793	25.6	88	0
Roby	19	472	24.8	62	0
Green	4	133	33.3	60	0
Copper	2	35	17.5	18	0
Stecker	2	10	5.0	10	0
Campbell	1	0	0.0	0	0
Meachem	1	9	9.0	9	0
Moore	1	36	36.0	36	0
Ortega	1	8	8.0	8	0
Saints	62	1496	24.1	88	0
Opponents	76	1827	24.0	83t	1

FIELD GOALS	1-19	20-29	30-39	40-49	50+
Hartley	0/0	5/5	4/4	4/4	0/0
Gramatica	0/0	0/0	3/3	2/5	1/2
Mehlhaff	0/0	1/1	1/2	1/1	0/0
Saints	0/0	6/6	8/9	7/10	1/2
Opponents	0/0	13/13	15/16	5/7	1/3

SACKS	No.
McCray	6.0
Ellis	4.0
Charleston	3.0
Grant	3.0
Smith	3.0
Clancy	2.0
Shanle	2.0
Gay	1.0
Porter	1.0
Reis	1.0
Vilma	1.0
B. Young	1.0
Saints	28.0
Opponents	13.0

RECORD HOLDERS

INDIVIDUAL RECORDS—CAREER

Category	Name	Performance
Rushing (Yds.)	Deuce McAllister, 2001-08	6,096
Passing (Yds.)	Archie Manning, 1971-1982	21,734
Passing (TDs)	Aaron Brooks, 2000-05	120
Receiving (No.)	Eric Martin, 1985-1993	532
Receiving (Yds.)	Eric Martin, 1985-1993	7,854
Interceptions	Dave Waymer, 1980-89	37
Punting (Avg.)	Mark Royals, 1997-98	45.8
Punt Return (Avg.)	Mel Gray, 1986-88	13.4
Kickoff Return (Avg.)	Walter Roberts, 1967	26.3
Field Goals	Morten Andersen, 1982-1994	302
Touchdowns (Tot.)	Deuce McAllister, 2001-08	55
Points	Morten Andersen, 1982-1994	1,318
*Sacks	Rickey Jackson, 1981-1993	115.0

INDIVIDUAL RECORDS—SINGLE SEASON

Category	Name	Performance
Rushing (Yds.)	George Rogers, 1981	1,674
Passing (Yds.)	Drew Brees, 2008	5,069
Passing (TDs)	Drew Brees, 2008	34
Receiving (No.)	Marques Colston, 2007	98
Receiving (Yds.)	Joe Horn, 2004	1,399
Interceptions	Dave Whitsell, 1967	10
Punting (Avg.)	Mark Royals, 1997	45.9
Punt Return (Avg.)	Mel Gray, 1987	14.7
Kickoff Return (Avg.)	John Gilliam, 1967	30.1
Field Goals	Morten Andersen, 1985	31
	John Carney, 2002	31
Touchdowns (Tot.)	Dalton Hilliard, 1989	18
Points	John Carney, 2002	130
*Sacks	Pat Swilling, 1991	17.0
	La'Roi Glover, 2000	17.0

INDIVIDUAL RECORDS—SINGLE GAME

Category	Name	Performance
Rushing (Yds.)	George Rogers, 9-4-83	206
Passing (Yds.)	Drew Brees, 11-19-06	510
Passing (TDs)	Billy Kilmer, 11-2-69	6
Receiving (No.)	Tony Galbreath, 9-10-78	14
Receiving (Yds.)	Wes Chandler, 9-2-79	205
Interceptions	Tommy Myers, 9-3-78	3
	Dave Waymer, 10-6-85	3
	Reggie Sutton, 10-18-87	3
	Gene Atkins, 12-22-91	3
	Sammy Knight, 9-9-01	3
Field Goals	Many times	5
	Last time by John Carney, 9-26-04	
Touchdowns (Tot.)	Joe Horn, 12-14-03	4
	Reggie Bush, 12-3-06	4
Points	Joe Horn, 12-14-03	24
	Reggie Bush, 12-3-06	24
*Sacks	Many times	4.0
	Last time by Wayne Martin, 9-21-97	

**Sacks became an official statistic in 1982.*

NEW ORLEANS SAINTS

2009 VETERAN ROSTER

No.	Name	Pos.	Ht.	Wt.	Birthdate	NFL Exp.	College	Hometown	How Acq.	'08 Games/ Starts
87	Arrington, Adrian	WR	6-3	192	9/9/86	2	Michigan	Cedar Rapids, Iowa	D7-'08	0*
92	Ayodele, Remi	DT	6-2	318	11/7/85	3	Oklahoma	Grand Prairie, Texas	FA-'08	6/0
36	Barnes, Darian	FB	6-0	255	2/29/80	8	Hampton	Toms River, N.J.	FA-'08	9/2*
21	Bell, Mike	RB	6-0	225	4/23/83	4	Arizona	Tolleson, Ariz.	FA-'08	4/0
9	Brees, Drew	QB	6-0	209	1/15/79	9	Purdue	Austin, Texas	UFA(SD)-'06	16/16
70	Brown, Jammal	T	6-6	313	3/30/81	5	Oklahoma	Lawton, Okla.	D1-'05	15/15
11	Brunell, Mark	QB	6-1	217	9/17/70	17	Washington	Santa Maria, Calif.	FA-'08	2/0
25	Bush, Reggie	RB	6-0	203	3/2/85	4	Southern California	Spring Valley, Calif.	D1-'06	10/9
74	Bushrod, Jermon	T	6-5	315	8/19/84	3	Towson	King George, Va.	D4b-'07	2/0
89	Campbell, Dan	TE	6-5	265	4/13/76	11	Texas A&M	Glen Rose, Texas	FA-'09	1/0*
97	Charleston, Jeff	DE	6-4	265	1/19/83	3	Idaho State	Oregon City, Ore.	FA-'09	10/0
71	Clancy, Kendrick	DT	6-1	305	8/17/78	10	Mississippi	Tuscaloosa, Ala.	FA-'07	14/14
72	Coleman, Rod	DT	6-2	285	8/16/76	10	East Carolina	Philadelphia, Pa.	FA-'09	0*
12	Colston, Marques	WR	6-4	225	6/5/83	4	Hofstra	Harrisburg, Pa.	D7b-'06	11/6
29	David, Jason	CB	5-8	180	6/12/82	6	Washington State	Covina, Calif.	RFA(Ind)-'07	14/6
80	Dinkins, Darnell	TE	6-4	260	1/20/77	8	Pittsburgh	Pittsburgh, Pa.	UFA(Cle)-'09	14/2*
56	Dunbar, Jo-Lonn	LB	6-0	226	3/13/85	2	Boston College	Syracuse, N.Y.	FA-'08	15/2
98	Ellis, Sedrick	DT	6-1	307	7/9/85	2	Southern California	Chino, Calif.	D1-'08	13/13
44	Evans, Heath	FB	6-0	250	12/30/78	9	Auburn	West Palm Beach, Fla.	UFA(NE)-'09	16/4*
73	Evans, Jahri	G	6-4	318	8/22/83	4	Bloomsburg	Philadelphia, Pa.	D4-'06	16/16
54	Evans, Troy	LB	6-3	238	12/3/77	8	Cincinnati	Cincinnati, Ohio	UFA(Hou)-'07	15/0
55	Fujita, Scott	LB	6-5	250	4/28/79	8	California	Oxnard, Calif.	UFA(Dall)-'06	14/13
20	Gay, Randall	CB	5-11	190	5/5/82	6	Louisiana State	Brusly, La.	UFA(NE)-'08	14/13
76	Goodwin, Jonathan	C	6-3	318	12/2/78	8	Michigan	Richland, S.C.	UFA(NYJ)-'06	13/13
94	Grant, Charles	DE	6-3	285	9/3/78	8	Georgia	Colquitt, Ga.	D1b-'02	8/8
10	Green, Skyler	WR	5-9	190	9/12/84	3	Louisiana State	Avondale, La.	FA-'08	2/0
32	Greer, Jabari	CB	5-11	180	2/11/82	6	Tennessee	Jackson, Tenn.	UFA(Buff)-'09	10/10*
41	Harper, Roman	S	6-1	200	12/11/82	4	Alabama	Prattville, Ala.	D2-'06	15/15
3	Harrington, Joey	QB	6-4	210	10/21/78	8	Oregon	Portland, Ore.	FA-'08	0*
5	Hartley, Garrett	K	5-8	196	5/16/86	2	Oklahoma	Southlake, Texas	FA-'08	8/0
19	Henderson, Devery	WR	5-11	200	3/26/82	6	Louisiana State	Opelousas, La.	D2a-'04	16/13
47	Houser, Kevin	LS	6-2	252	8/23/77	10	Ohio State	Westlake, Ohio	D7-'00	16/0
60	Leckey, Nick	C	6-3	291	3/12/82	6	Kansas State	Grapevine, Texas	UFA(StL)-'09	10/10*
93	McCray, Bobby	DE	6-6	260	8/8/81	6	Florida	Homestead, Fla.	UFA(Jax)-'08	16/8
17	Meachem, Robert	WR	6-2	210	9/28/84	3	Tennessee	Tulsa, Okla.	D1-'07	14/3
83	Miller, Billy	TE	6-3	252	4/24/77	10	Southern California	Westlake Village, Calif.	FA-'08	15/5
50	Mitchell, Marvin	LB	6-3	249	10/21/84	3	Tennessee	Norfolk, Va.	FA-'07	15/0
16	Moore, Lance	WR	5-9	190	8/31/83	4	Toledo	Westerville, Ohio	FA-'07	16/6
52	Morgan, Dan	LB	6-2	245	12/19/78	8	Miami	Coral Springs, Fla.	FA-'08	0*
67	Nesbit, Jamar	G	6-4	328	12/17/76	11	South Carolina	Summerville, S.C.	UFA(Jax)-'04	7/3
77	Nicks, Carl	G/T	6-5	343	5/14/85	2	Nebraska	Salinas, Calif.	D5b-'08	16/13
79	Ninkovich, Rob	DE	6-2	255	2/1/84	3	Purdue	New Lenox, Ill.	FA-'08	1/0*
86	Ortega, Buck	TE	6-4	250	11/22/81	2	Miami	Miami, Fla.	FA-'08	11/1
4	Pakulak, Glenn	P	6-3	220	4/9/80	2	Kentucky	Lapeer, Mich.	FA-'08	8/0
22	Porter, Tracy	CB	5-11	186	8/11/86	2	Indiana	Port Allen, La.	D2-'08	5/5
90	Pressley, DeMario	DT	6-3	301	11/3/85	2	North Carolina State	Greensboro, N.C.	D5a-'08	0*
31	Prioleau, Pierson	S	5-11	188	8/6/77	11	Virginia Tech	Alvin, S.C.	UFA(Jax)-'09	16/1*
39	Reis, Chris	S	6-1	215	9/19/83	3	Georgia Tech	Roswell, Ga.	FA-'07	15/0
15	Roby, Courtney	WR	6-0	189	1/10/83	4	Indiana	Indianapolis, Ind.	FA-'08	6/0*
95	Savage, Josh	DE	6-4	276	9/28/80	4	Utah	Midvale, Utah	FA-'07	3/0
58	Shanle, Scott	LB	6-2	245	11/23/79	7	Nebraska	St. Edward, Neb.	T(Dall)-'06	16/16
42	Sharper, Darren	S	6-2	210	11/3/75	13	William & Mary	Richmond, Va.	UFA(Minn)-'09	16/16*
88	Shockey, Jeremy	TE	6-5	251	8/18/80	8	Miami	Ada, Okla.	T(NYG)-'08	12/11
53	Simoneau, Mark	LB	6-0	245	1/16/77	10	Kansas State	Smith Center, Kan.	T(Phil)-'06	0*
91	Smith, Will	DE	6-3	282	7/4/81	6	Ohio State	Utica, N.Y.	D1-'04	16/16
33	Sobomehin, Olaniyi	FB	6-1	230	10/11/84	2	Portland State	Portland, Ore.	FA-'08	1/0
96	Spicer, Paul	DE	6-4	295	8/18/75	10	Saginaw Valley State	Indianapolis, Ind.	FA-'09	16/10*
78	Stinchcomb, Jon	T	6-5	315	8/27/79	7	Georgia	Lilburn, Ga.	D2-'03	16/16
64	Strief, Zach	T	6-7	320	9/22/83	4	Northwestern	Milford, Ohio	D7a-'06	16/1
23	Thomas, Pierre	RB	5-11	215	12/18/84	3	Illinois	Lynwood, Ill.	FA-'07	15/5
24	Torrence, Leigh	CB	5-11	179	1/4/82	4	Stanford	Atlanta, Ga.	W(Wash)-'08	16/0*
51	Vilma, Jonathan	LB	6-1	230	4/16/82	6	Miami	Coral Gables, Fla.	T(NYJ)-'08	16/16
59	Waters, Anthony	LB	6-3	238	7/25/84	3	Clemson	Lake View, S.C.	FA-'09	7/0*
28	Young, Usama	CB	6-0	200	5/8/85	3	Kent State	Largo, Md.	D3a-'07	15/2

* Arrington missed '08 season because of injury; Barnes played 3 games with Buffalo and 2 with Detroit in addition to 4 for New Orleans in '08; Campbell played 1 game with Detroit; Coleman last active with Atlanta in '07; Dinkins played 14 games with Cleveland; H. Evans played 16 games with New England; Greer played 10 games with Buffalo; Harrington inactive for 12 games; Leckey played 10 games with St. Louis; Morgan last active with Carolina in '07; Ninkovich played 1 game with Miami; Pressley missed '08 season because of injury; Prioleau played 16 games with Jacksonville; Roby played 1 game with Indianapolis in addition to 5 for New Orleans; Sharper played 16 games with Minnesota; Spicer played 16 games with Jacksonville; Torrence played 9 games with Washington in addition to 7 for New Orleans; Waters played 7 games with San Diego.

Players lost to free agency (1): S Josh Bullocks (Chi; 16 games in '08).

Also played with Saints in '08—TE Mark Campbell (9 games), WR Terrance Copper (5), CB Jason Craft (2), CB Aaron Glenn (4), P Ben Graham (1), K Martín Gramatica (5), RB Lynell Hamilton (1), S Terrence Holt (2), S Kevin Kaesviharn (11), FB Mike Karney (12), DT Antwan Lake (11), C Matt Lehr (13), RB Deuce McAllister (13), CB Mike McKenzie (7), DT Alvin McKinley (1), K Taylor Mehlhaff (3), WR David Patten (5), TE Sean Ryan (1), DT Montavious Stanley (1), RB Aaron Stecker (6), DT Hollis Thomas (8), P Steve Weatherford (7), DT Brian Young (8).

2009 FIRST-YEAR ROSTER

Name	Pos.	Ht.	Wt.	Birthdate	College	Hometown	How Acq.
Arnoux, Stanley	LB	6-0	232	9/9/86	Wake Forest	Sunrise, Fla.	D4b
Brown, Michael	T	6-5	300	4/23/86	Mississippi State	College Park, Ga.	FA
Casillas, Jonathan	LB	6-1	227	6/3/87	Wisconsin	New Brunswick, N.J.	FA
Cowan, Patrick	QB	6-4	226	3/23/86	UCLA	Pico Rivera, Calif.	FA
Donaldson, Herb	RB	5-10	226	12/13/85	Western Illinois	St. Louis, Mo.	FA
Duckworth, Tim (1)	G	6-4	318	9/14/82	Auburn	Taylorsville, Miss.	FA-'07
Flanagan, Shawn	G	6-5	302	7/10/83	Sioux Falls	Pendleton, Ore.	FA
Fletcher, Alex	C	6-2	297	9/5/85	Stanford	Old Brookville, N.Y.	FA
Gorrer, Danny	CB	6-0	185	6/1/86	Texas A&M	Port Arthur, Texas	FA
Hamilton, Lynell (1)	RB	6-0	235	8/5/85	San Diego State	Stockton, Calif.	FA-'08
Harris, Kenneth	WR	6-3	205	8/10/86	Georgia	Cherryville, N.C.	FA
Heyman, Earl	DT	6-1	289	9/15/87	Louisville	Louisville, Ky.	FA
Hill, P.J.	RB	5-10	218	1/3/87	Wisconsin	East Elmhurst, N.Y.	FA
Jenkins, Malcolm	CB	6-0	204	12/20/87	Ohio State	Piscataway, N.J.	D1
Jones, Reggie	CB	6-0	193	3/15/86	Portland State	Federal Way, Wash.	FA
Morstead, Thomas	P	6-4	225	3/7/86	Southern Methodist	Pearland, Texas	D5
Parnell, Jermey	DE	6-6	278	7/20/86	Mississippi	Gosnell, Ark.	FA
Parrish, Augustus	T	6-4	302	3/19/87	Kent State	Temple Hills, Md.	FA
Simon, Matt	WR	6-1	199	12/4/85	Northern Illinois	Farmington, Minn.	FA
Vaughn, Chip	S	6-2	221	10/26/85	Wake Forest	Fairfax, Va.	D4a

The term NFL Rookie is defined as a player who is in his first season of professional football and has not been on the roster of another professional football team for any regular-season or postseason games. A Rookie is designated by an "R" on NFL rosters. Players who have been active in another professional football league or players who have NFL experience, including either preseason training camp or being on an Active List or Inactive List, or on Reserve/Injured or Reserve/Physically Unable to Perform for fewer than six regular-season games, are termed NFL First-Year Players. An NFL First-Year Player is designated by a "1" on NFL rosters. Thereafter, a player is credited with an additional year of experience for each season in which he accumulates six games on the Active List or Inactive List, or on Reserve/Injured or Reserve/Physically Unable to Perform.

Log on to www.neworleanssaints.com for an up-to-date roster.

COACHING STAFF

Head Coach, Sean Payton

Pro Career: Named the fourteenth head coach in Saints history on Jan. 18, 2006 and in his opening season led the Saints to the NFC Championship Game for the first time in club history. A unanimous choice for NFL coach of the year honors after also guiding the team to a 10-6 record and the NFC South title following a dramatic roster overhaul. Considered one of the NFL's brightest offensive minds, the Saints have ranked among the league's most productive offenses each season since his arrival, including finishing first in the NFL in both 2008 and 2006 and ranking fourth in 2007. He arrived in New Orleans following a three-year stint with Dallas Cowboys, serving as the assistant head coach/passing game coordinator in 2005 after spending his first two seasons as assistant head coach/quarterbacks. Additional experience includes four years with the New York Giants (1999-2002), the last three seasons as offensive coordinator. Also previously worked for the Philadelphia Eagles (1997-98) as quarterbacks coach. Career record: 26-24.

Background: Earned a degree in communications at Eastern Illinois, where he departed with a school-record 10,665 passing yards, then the third-highest total in NCAA Division I-AA history. A three-time All-American, Payton had brief playing stops with Chicago of the Arena Football League, the Ottawa Rough Riders of the Canadian Football League and the Chicago Bears in 1987. Inducted into the Eastern Illinois Hall of Fame in 2000, Payton coached collegiately at San Diego State (1988-89, 1992-93), Indiana State (1990-91), and Miami (Ohio) in 1994-95.

Personal: Born Dec. 29, 1963 in San Mateo, Calif. and raised in Naperville, Ill, Payton and his wife, Beth, have a daughter, Meghan, and a son, Connor.

ASSISTANT COACHES

Dennis Allen, secondary; born Sept. 22, 1972, Atlanta. Safety Texas A&M 1992-95. No pro playing experience. College coach: Texas A&M 1996-99, Tulsa 2000-01. Pro coach: Atlanta Falcons 2002-05, joined Saints in 2006.

Adam Bailey, asst. strength and conditioning; born March 30, 1976, Tyler, Texas. Attended Louisville. No college or pro playing experience. College coach: Texas 1996-1997, Louisville 1998-1999, Auburn 2000-2001, Missouri 2002-2003. Pro coach: New Orleans VooDoo (AFL) 2004-2005, joined Saints in 2005.

Pete Carmichael Jr., offensive coordinator; born October 6, 1971, Framingham, Mass. Attended Boston College. No college or pro playing experience. College coach: New Hampshire 1994, Louisiana Tech 1995-99. Pro coach: Cleveland Browns 2000, Washington Redskins 2001, San Diego Chargers 2002-05, joined Saints in 2006.

Mike Cerullo, coaching assistant; born March 15, 1967, Boston. Running back Central Connecticut State 1986-1990. No pro playing experience. College coach: Central Connecticut State 1991-92, Curry College 2000-01, Northeastern 2001-03, Syracuse 2003-06. Pro coach: Joined Saints in 2007.

Dan Dalrymple, head strength and conditioning; born Aug. 26, 1965, Cleveland. Offensive lineman Miami (Ohio) 1983-86. No pro playing experience. College coach: Miami (Ohio) 1987-2005. Pro coach: Joined Saints in 2006.

Bret Ingalls, running backs; born Aug. 19, 1960, San Jose, Calif. Running back Wichita State 1979-1981. No pro playing experience. College coach: Idaho 1982-88, San Diego State 1989-1993, Eastern Michigan 1994, Louisville 1995-96, Northern Iowa 1997-99, Idaho 2000-03, Indiana State 2004, Miami (Ohio) 2005, Northwestern 2006-08. Pro coach: Joined Saints in 2009.

Bill Johnson, defensive line; born June 23, 1955, Monroe, La. Defensive lineman Northwestern (La.) State 1976-79. No pro playing experience. College coach: Northwestern (La.) 1980-84, McNeese State 1985-86, Miami 1987, Louisiana Tech 1988-89, Arkansas 1990-91, 2000, Texas A&M 1992-99. Pro coach: Atlanta Falcons 2001-06, Denver Broncos 2007-08, joined Saints in 2009.

Curtis Johnson, wide receivers; born November 5, 1961, New Orleans. Wide receiver Idaho 1979-1983. No pro playing experience. College coach: Idaho 1987-88, San Diego State 1989-1993, Southern Methodist 1994, California 1995, Miami 1996-2005. Pro coach: Joined Saints in 2006.

Travis Jones, asst. defensive line; born June 6, 1972, Milledgeville, Ga. Linebacker Georgia 1991-94. Pro linebacker Baltimore Stallions (CFL) 1995. College coach: Georgia: 1997, Appalachian State 1998-2000, Kansas 2001-02, Louisiana State 2003-04. Pro coach: Miami Dolphins 2005-07, joined Saints in 2008.

Aaron Kromer, offensive line/running game; born April 30, 1967, Sandusky, Ohio. Offensive tackle Miami (Ohio) 1986-89. No pro playing experience. College coach: Miami (Ohio) 1990-98, Northwestern 1999-2000. Pro coach: Oakland Raiders 2001-04, Tampa Bay Buccaneers 2005-07, joined Saints in 2008.

Joe Lombardi, quarterbacks; born June 6, 1981, Seattle. Tight end Air Force 1992-94. No pro playing experience. College coach: Dayton 1996-98, Virginia Military Institute 1999, Bucknell 2000, Mercyhurst 2002-05. Pro coach: New York/New Jersey Hitmen (XFL) 2001, Atlanta Falcons 2006, joined Saints in 2007.

Mike Mallory, asst. special teams; born Nov. 16, 1962, Bowling Green, Ohio. Linebacker Michigan 1982-85. No pro playing experience. College coach: Indiana 1986-87, Kent State 1989-1990, Eastern Illinois 1991-92, Rhode Island 1993-95, Northern Illinois 1996-99, Maryland 2000, Illinois 2001-05, Kansas 2006, Louisville 2007. Pro coach: Joined Saints in 2008.

Terry Malone, tight ends; born February 26, 1960, Buffalo. Tight end Holy Cross 1978-1982. No pro playing experience. College coach: Arizona 1983-84, Holy Cross 1985, Bowling Green 1986-1995, Boston College 1996, Michigan 1997-2005. Pro coach: Joined Saints in 2006.

Greg McMahon, special teams coordinator; born Jan. 2, 1960, Rantoul, Ill. Defensive back Eastern Illinois 1978-1981. No pro playing experience. College coach: Eastern Illinois 1982, Minnesota 1983-84, North Alabama 1985-87, Southern Illinois 1988, Valdosta State 1989, Nevada Las-Vegas 1990-91, Illinois 1992-2004, East Carolina 2005. Pro coach: Joined Saints in 2006.

Tony Oden, asst. secondary; born June 30, 1973, Cleveland. Linebacker Baldwin-Wallace College 1991-95. No pro playing experience. College coach: Millersville (Penn.) 1996, Boston College 1997, Army 1998-99, East Carolina 2000-02, Eastern Michigan 2003. Pro coach: Houston Texans 2004-05, joined Saints in 2006.

Carter Sheridan, offensive assistant/asst. player programs; born Nov. 20, 1977, New Orleans. Defensive back Florida A&M 1996-98. No pro playing experience. Pro coach: Joined Saints in 2006.

Joe Vitt, asst. head coach/linebackers, born August 23, 1954, Syracuse, N.Y. Linebacker Towson State 1974-78. No pro playing experience. Pro coach: Baltimore Colts 1979-1981, Seattle Seahawks 1982-1991, Los Angeles Rams 1992-94, Philadelphia Eagles 1995-98, Green Bay Packers 1999, Kansas City Chiefs 2000-03, St. Louis Rams 2004-05 (head coach, final 11 games of 2005), joined Saints in 2006.

Blake Williams, coaching assistant; born Dec. 30, 1984, Independence, Mo. Defensive back Princeton 2003-07. No pro playing experience. Pro coach: Washington Redskins 2006-07, Jacksonville Jaguars 2008, joined Saints in 2009.

Gregg Williams, defensive coordinator; born July 15, 1958, Excelsior Springs, Mo. Quarterback Northeastern Missouri State 1976-79. No pro playing experience. College coach: Houston 1988-89. Pro coach: Houston Oilers/Tennessee Titans 1990-2000, Buffalo Bills 2001-03 (head coach), Washington Redskins 2004-07, Jacksonville Jaguars 2008, joined Saints in 2009.

Adam Zimmer, defensive assistant/linebackers; born Jan. 13, 1984, Ogden, Utah. Defensive back Trinity University (Texas) 2002-05. No pro playing experience. Pro coach: Joined Saints in 2006.

National Football Conference
East Division
Team Colors: Blue, Red, and White
Giants Training Facility
50 Route 120
East Rutherford, New Jersey 07073
Telephone: (201) 935-8111

2009 SCHEDULE

PRESEASON

Aug. 17	**Carolina**	8:15
Aug. 22	at Chicago	7:00
Aug. 29	**N.Y. Jets**	8:00
Sep. 3	at New England	7:30

REGULAR SEASON

Sep. 13	**Washington**	4:15
Sep. 20	at Dallas	7:20
Sep. 27	at Tampa Bay	1:00
Oct. 4	at Kansas City	12:00
Oct. 11	**Oakland**	1:00
Oct. 18	at New Orleans	12:00
Oct. 25	**Arizona**	8:20
Nov. 1	at Philadelphia	4:15
Nov. 8	**San Diego**	4:15
Nov. 15	BYE	
Nov. 22	**Atlanta**	1:00
Nov. 26	at Denver (Thu.)	6:20
Dec. 6	**Dallas**	4:15
Dec. 13	**Philadelphia** *	8:20
Dec. 21	at Washington (Mon.)	8:30
Dec. 27	**Carolina**	1:00
Jan. 3	at Minnesota	12:00

** Sunday night games in Weeks 11-17 subject to change*

Stadium: Giants Stadium (opened in 1976) •**Capacity:** 80,242
East Rutherford, New Jersey 07073
Playing Surface: FieldTurf
Training Camp: University at Albany
1400 Washington Avenue
Albany, New York 12222

GIANTS STADIUM

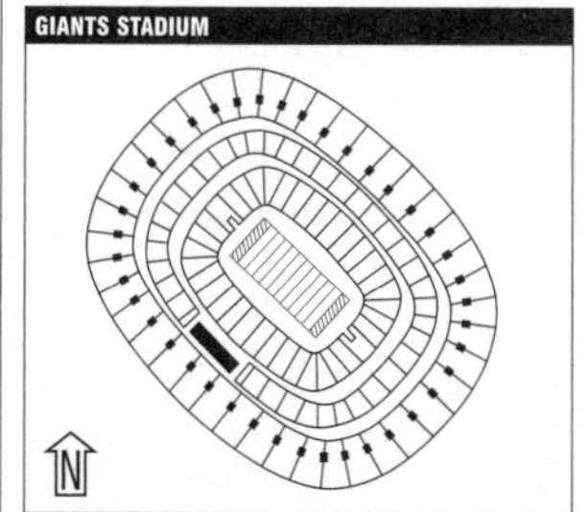

CLUB OFFICIALS

President/CEO: John K. Mara
Chairman/EVP: Steve Tisch
Treasurer: Jonathan Tisch
Senior Vice President-General Manager: Jerry Reese
Senior Vice President and Chief Marketing Officer: Michael Stevens
Vice President-Player Evaluations: Chris Mara
Vice President and Chief Financial Officer: Christine Procops
Senior Vice President-Marketing: John Maguire
Vice President-Marketing: Rusty Hawley
VP/Medical Services: Ronnie Barnes
Vice President-Communications: Pat Hanlon
Vice President, Media and Partnerships: Dan Lynch
Vice President and Executive Producer, Giants Entertainment: Don Sperling
Assistant General Manager: Kevin Abrams
Director of Pro Player Personnel: David Gettleman
Assistant Director of Pro Player Personnel: Ken Sternfeld
Director of College Scouting: Marc Ross
Director of Research and Development: Raymond J. Walsh, Jr.
Director of Player Development: Charles Way
Pro Personnel Assistants: Jeremy Breit, Matthew Shauger
Director of Promotions: Frank Mara
Ticket Manager: John Gorman
Director of Administration: Jim Phelan
Controller: Steven Hamrahi
Director of Community Relations: Allison Stangeby
Director of Creative Services: Doug Murphy
Director of Public/Media Relations: Peter John-Baptiste
Assistant Director of Communications: Avis Roper
Head Athletic Trainer: Ronnie Barnes
Assistant Athletic Trainers: Steve Kennelly, Byron Hansen, Leigh Weiss
Equipment/Locker Room Manager: Ed Wagner, Jr.
Equipment Director: Joseph Skiba
Assistant Equipment Managers: Ed Skiba, Tim Slaman
Video Director: Dave Maltese
Assistant Video Directors: Carmen Pizzano, Ed Triggs, Steve Venditti
Assistant Director of Community Relations: Ethan Medley
Directors of Information Technology: Julie Glisky, Justin Warren
Director of Marketing Services & Youth Programs: Beth Roche

COACHING HISTORY
(638-534-33)

Records include postseason games

1925	Bob Folwell	8-4-0
1926	Joe Alexander	8-4-1
1927-28	Earl Potteiger	15-8-3
1929-1930	LeRoy Andrews*	24-5-1
1930	Benny Friedman-Steve Owen	2-0-0
1931-1953	Steve Owen	153-108-17
1954-1960	Jim Lee Howell	55-29-4
1961-68	Allie Sherman	57-54-4
1969-1973	Alex Webster	29-40-1
1974-76	Bill Arnsparger**	7-28-0
1976-78	John McVay	14-23-0
1979-1982	Ray Perkins	24-35-0
1983-1990	Bill Parcells	85-52-1
1991-92	Ray Handley	14-18-0
1993-96	Dan Reeves	32-34-0
1997-2003	Jim Fassel	60-56-1
2004-08	Tom Coughlin	51-36-0

*Released after 15 games in 1930
**Released after seven games in 1976

PAID ATTENDANCE

Home 628,605 Away 540,613
Total 1,169,218
Single-game home record, 79,378 (1/8/06)
Single-season home record, 629,874 (2004)

2009 DRAFT CHOICES

Round	Name	Pos.	College
1	Hakeem Nicks	WR	North Carolina
2	Clint Sintim	LB	Virginia
	Will Beatty	T	Connecticut
3	Ramses Barden	WR	Cal Poly
	Travis Beckum	TE	Wisconsin
4	Andre Brown	RB	North Carolina St.
5	Rhett Bomar	QB	Sam Houston St.
6	DeAndre Wright	DB	New Mexico
7	Stoney Woodson	DB	South Carolina

NEW YORK GIANTS

2008 TEAM RECORD

PRESEASON (2-2)

Date	Result	Opponent
8/7	L 10-13	at Detroit
8/18	W 37-34	Cleveland
8/23	L 7-10	at New York Jets
8/28	W 19-14	New England

REGULAR SEASON (12-4)

Date	Result	Opponent
9/4	W 16-7	Washington
9/14	W 41-13	at St. Louis
9/21	W 26-23	Cincinnati (OT)
10/5	W 44-6	Seattle
10/13	L 14-35	at Cleveland
10/19	W 29-17	San Francisco
10/26	W 21-14	at Pittsburgh
11/2	W 35-14	Dallas
11/9	W 36-31	at Philadelphia
11/16	W 30-10	Baltimore
11/23	W 37-29	at Arizona
11/30	W 23-7	at Washington
12/7	L 14-20	Philadelphia
12/14	L 8-20	at Dallas
12/21	W 34-28	Carolina (OT)
12/28	L 19-20	at Minnesota

POSTSEASON (0-1)

Date	Result	Opponent
1/11	L 23-11	Philadelphia

(OT) Overtime

SCORE BY PERIODS

	1	2	3	4	OT		Total
NY Giants	91	138	76	113	9	—	427
Opponents	39	121	38	96	0	—	294

2008 TEAM STATISTICS

	Giants	Opp.
Total First Downs	338	268
Rushing	130	78
Passing	176	165
Penalty	32	25
3rd Down: Made/Att	88/204	83/204
3rd Down Pct.	43.1	40.7
4th Down: Made/Att	5/11	5/16
4th Down Pct.	45.5	31.3
Possession Avg.	32:56	27:04
Total Net Yards	5695	4672
Avg. Per Game	355.9	292.0
Total Plays	1021	931
Avg. Per Play	5.6	5.0
Net Yards Rushing	2518	1533
Avg. Per Game	157.4	95.8
Total Rushes	502	386
Net Yards Passing	3177	3139
Avg. Per Game	198.6	196.2
Sacked/Yards Lost	28/176	42/288
Gross Yards	3353	3427
Att./Completions	491/298	503/296
Completion Pct.	60.7	58.8
Had Intercepted	10	17
Punts/Average	64/44.0	76/43.4
Net Punting Avg.	64/40.2	76/36.6
Penalties/Yards	102/821	111/866
Fumbles/Ball Lost	18/3	22/5
Touchdowns	45	34
Rushing	19	14
Passing	23	17
Returns	3	3

2008 INDIVIDUAL STATISTICS

PASSING	Att.	Comp.	Yds.	Pct.	TD	Int.	Tkld.	Rate
Manning	479	289	3238	60.3	21	10	27/174	86.4
Carr	12	9	115	75.0	2	0	1/2	144.1
Giants	491	298	3353	60.7	23	10	28/176	88.2
Opponents	503	296	3427	58.8	17	17	42/288	76.7

SCORING	TD R	TD P	TD Rt	PAT	FG	Saf	PTS
Carney	0	0	0	38/38	35/38	0	143
Jacobs	15	0	0	0/0	0/0	0	90
Boss	0	6	0	0/0	0/0	0	36
Burress	0	4	0	0/0	0/0	0	24
Toomer	0	4	0	0/0	0/0	0	24
Hixon	0	2	0	0/0	0/0	0	14
Bradshaw	1	1	0	0/0	0/0	0	12
D. Johnson	0	2	0	0/0	0/0	0	12
Moss	0	2	0	0/0	0/0	0	12
Ward	2	0	0	0/0	0/0	0	12
Dockery	0	0	1	0/0	0/0	0	6
Hedgecock	0	1	0	0/0	0/0	0	6
Manning	1	0	0	0/0	0/0	0	6
Ross	0	0	1	0/0	0/0	0	6
Smith	0	1	0	0/0	0/0	0	6
Tuck	0	0	1	0/0	0/0	0	6
Tynes	0	0	0	3/3	1/1	0	6
Kiwanuka	0	0	0	0/0	0/0	1	2
Giants	19	23	3	41/41	36/39	3	427
Opponents	14	17	3	31/31	19/26	0	294

2-Pt. Conversions: Hixon.
Giants 1-3, Opponents 1-3.

RUSHING	No.	Yds	Avg	LG	TD
Jacobs	219	1089	5.0	44	15
Ward	182	1025	5.6	51	2
Bradshaw	67	355	5.3	77	1
Hixon	2	26	13.0	15	0
Ware	2	15	7.5	9	0
Carr	8	10	1.3	7	0
Manning	20	10	0.5	13	1
Hedgecock	1	0	0.0	0	0
Manningham	1	-12	-12.0	-12	0
Giants	502	2518	5.0	77	19
Opponents	386	1533	4.0	67t	14

RECEIVING	No.	Yds	Avg	LG	TD
Smith	57	574	10.1	30	1
Toomer	48	580	12.1	40t	4
Hixon	43	596	13.9	41	2
Ward	41	384	9.4	48	0
Burress	35	454	13.0	33t	4
Boss	33	384	11.6	28	6
Moss	12	153	12.8	27	2
Hedgecock	8	52	6.5	13	1
Jacobs	6	36	6.0	9	0
Bradshaw	5	42	8.4	18t	1
D. Johnson	4	46	11.5	26	2
Manningham	4	26	6.5	11	0
Matthews	2	26	13.0	13	0
Giants	298	3353	11.3	48	23
Opponents	296	3427	11.6	70	17

INTERCEPTIONS	No.	Yds	Avg	LG	TD
Webster	3	65	21.7	57	0
J. Butler	3	62	20.7	47	0
Ross	3	58	19.3	50t	1
M. Johnson	2	18	9.0	18	0
Dockery	1	44	44.0	44	0
Tuck	1	41	41.0	41t	1
Madison	1	21	21.0	21	0
Kehl	1	17	17.0	17	0
Thomas	1	13	13.0	13	0
Phillips	1	0	0.0	0	0
Giants	17	339	19.9	57	2
Opponents	10	189	18.9	94t	2

PUNTING	No.	Yds.	Avg.	In 20	LG
Feagles	64	2814	44.0	23	61
Giants	64	2814	44.0	23	61
Opponents	76	3297	43.4	23	63

PUNT RETURNS	Ret	FC	Yds	Avg	LG	TD
Hixon	24	9	242	10.1	50	0
McQuarters	13	9	86	6.6	15	0
Bradshaw	1	0	6	6.0	6	0
Webster	1	0	3	3.0	3	0
Giants	39	18	337	8.6	50	0
Opponents	24	13	140	5.8	21	0

KICKOFF RETURNS	No.	Yds	Avg	LG	TD
Bradshaw	39	867	22.2	58	0
Moss	8	162	20.3	27	0
Hixon	3	180	60.0	83	0
D. Johnson	2	2	1.0	2	0
Droughns	1	34	34.0	34	0
Ward	1	21	21.0	21	0
McQuarters	1	18	18.0	18	0
Giants	55	1284	23.3	83	0
Opponents	85	1912	22.5	55	0

FIELD GOALS	1-19	20-29	30-39	40-49	50+
Carney	0/0	15/15	14/15	5/7	1/1
Tynes	1/1	0/0	0/0	0/0	0/0
Giants	1/1	15/15	14/15	5/7	1/1
Opponents	0/0	7/7	5/8	3/4	4/7

SACKS	No.
Tuck	12.0
Kiwanuka	8.0
Robbins	5.5
Tollefson	3.5
Cofield	3.0
Alford	2.5
Wynn	2.0
Pierce	1.5
Blackburn	1.0
M. Johnson	1.0
Kehl	1.0
Webster	1.0
Giants	42.0
Opponents	28.0

RECORD HOLDERS

INDIVIDUAL RECORDS—CAREER

Category	Name	Performance
Rushing (Yds.)	Tiki Barber, 1997-2006	10,449
Passing (Yds.)	Phil Simms, 1979-1993	33,462
Passing (TDs)	Phil Simms, 1979-1993	199
Receiving (No.)	Amani Toomer, 1996-2008	668
Receiving (Yds.)	Amani Toomer, 1996-2008	9,497
Interceptions	Emlen Tunnell, 1948-1958	74
Punting (Avg.)	Don Chandler, 1956-1964	43.8
Punt Return (Avg.)	Ward Cuff, 1941-45	12.1
Kickoff Return (Avg.)	Rocky Thompson, 1971-73	27.2
Field Goals	Pete Gogolak, 1966-1974	126
Touchdowns (Tot.)	Frank Gifford, 1952-1964	78
Points	Pete Gogolak, 1966-1974	646
*Sacks	Michael Strahan, 1993-2007	141.5

INDIVIDUAL RECORDS—SINGLE SEASON

Category	Name	Performance
Rushing (Yds.)	Tiki Barber, 2005	1,860
Passing (Yds.)	Kerry Collins, 2002	4,073
Passing (TDs)	Y.A. Tittle, 1963	36
Receiving (No.)	Amani Toomer, 2002	82
Receiving (Yds.)	Amani Toomer, 2002	1,343
Interceptions	Otto Schnellbacher, 1951	11
	Jim Patton, 1958	11
Punting (Avg.)	Don Chandler, 1959	46.6
Punt Return (Avg.)	Merle Hapes, 1942	15.5
Kickoff Return (Avg.)	John Salscheider, 1949	31.6
Field Goals	Ali Haji-Sheikh, 1983	35
	Jay Feely, 2005	35
	John Carney, 2008	35
Touchdowns (Tot.)	Ali Morris, 1985	21
Points	Jay Feely, 2005	148
*Sacks	Michael Strahan, 2001	**22.5

INDIVIDUAL RECORDS—SINGLE GAME

Category	Name	Performance
Rushing (Yds.)	Tiki Barber, 12-30-06	234
Passing (Yds.)	Phil Simms, 10-13-85	513
Passing (TDs)	Y.A. Tittle, 10-28-62	**7
Receiving (No.)	Tiki Barber, 1-2-00	13
Receiving (Yds.)	Del Shofner, 10-28-62	269
Interceptions	Many times	3
	Last time by Terry Kinard, 9-20-87	
Field Goals	Joe Danelo, 10-18-81	6
Touchdowns (Tot.)	Ron Johnson, 10-2-72	4
	Earnest Gray, 9-7-80	4
	Rodney Hampton, 9-24-95	4
Points	Ron Johnson, 10-2-72	24
	Earnest Gray, 9-7-80	24
	Rodney Hampton, 9-24-95	24
*Sacks	Osi Umenyiora, 9-30-07	6.0

**Sacks became an official statistic in 1982.*
***NFL Record*

NEW YORK GIANTS

2009 VETERAN ROSTER

No.	Name	Pos.	Ht.	Wt.	Birthdate	NFL Exp.	College	Hometown	How Acq.	'08 Games/ Starts
93	Alford, Jay	DT	6-3	304	5/28/83	3	Penn State	Orange, N.J.	D3-'07	16/3
33	Barksdale, Rashad	CB	6-0	208	5/11/84	2	Albany	Hudson, N.Y.	FA-'08	0*
95	Bernard, Rocky	DT	6-3	308	4/19/79	8	Texas A&M	Baytown, Texas	UFA(Sea)-'09	15/15*
19	Biddle, Taye	WR	6-1	185	2/27/83	2	Mississippi	Decatur, Ala.	FA-'08	0*
57	Blackburn, Chase	LB	6-3	247	6/10/83	5	Akron	Marysville, Ohio	FA-'05	16/8
2	Bodiford, Shaun	WR	5-11	186	5/4/82	4	Portland State	Federal Way, Wisc.	FA-'09	0*
52	Boley, Michael	LB	6-3	223	8/24/82	5	Southern Miss	Elkmont, Ala.	UFA(Atl)-'09	16/12*
77	Boothe, Kevin	G	6-5	315	7/5/83	4	Cornell	Fort Lauderdale, Fla.	W(Oak)-'07	16/0
89	Boss, Kevin	TE	6-6	253	1/11/84	3	Western Oregon	Philomath, Ore.	D5-'07	15/15
44	Bradshaw, Ahmad	RB	5-9	198	3/19/86	3	Marshall	Bluefield, Va.	D7b-'07	15/0
41	Brown, C.C.	S	6-0	208	1/27/83	5	Louisiana-Lafayette	Greenwood, Miss.	UFA(Hou)-'09	3/3*
75	Bryant, Anthony	DT	6-3	337	11/16/81	3	Alabama	Greensboro, N.C.	FA-'09	0*
99	Canty, Chris	DL	6-7	304	11/10/82	5	Virginia	Charlotte, N.C.	UFA(Dall)-'09	16/16*
38	Cargile, Steve	S	6-2	215	6/2/82	3	Columbia	Akron, Ohio	FA-'09	0*
8	Carr, David	QB	6-3	216	7/21/79	8	Fresno State	Bakersfield, Calif.	FA-'08	3/0
55	Clark, Danny	LB	6-2	245	5/9/77	10	Illinois	Country Club Hills, Ill.	UFA-'08	16/15
73	Clark, Jeremy	DT	6-3	309	9/6/83	2	Alabama	Dephne, Ala.	FA-'08	4/0
96	Cofield, Barry	DT	6-4	306	3/19/84	4	Northwestern	Cleveland Heights, Ohio	D4a-'06	15/15
51	DeOssie, Zak	LB	6-4	249	5/24/84	3	Brown	No. Andover, Mass.	D4-'07	16/0
66	Diehl, David	T	6-5	319	9/15/80	7	Illinois	Oak Lawn, Ill.	D5-'03	16/16
35	Dockery, Kevin	CB	5-8	188	1/8/84	4	Mississippi State	Hernando, Miss.	FA-'06	13/1
78	Douzable, Leger	DL	6-4	305	5/31/86	2	Central Florida	Tampa, Fla.	FA-'08	0*
18	Feagles, Jeff	P	6-1	215	3/7/66	22	Miami	Phoenix, Ariz.	UFA(Sea)-'03	16/0
54	Goff, Jonathan	LB	6-2	236	12/12/85	2	Vanderbilt	Lynn, Mass.	D5-'08	5/0
80	Hagan, Derek	WR	6-2	215	9/21/84	4	Arizona State	Palmdale, Calif.	FA-'08	4/0*
39	Hedgecock, Madison	FB	6-3	266	8/27/81	5	North Carolina	Wallburg, N.C.	W(StL)-'07	16/10
90	Henderson, Robert	DE	6-3	278	11/9/83	2	Southern Mississippi	Ponchatoula, La.	D6b-'08	0*
87	Hixon, Domenik	WR	6-2	182	10/8/84	4	Akron	Columbus, Ohio	W(Den)-'07	16/6
27	Jacobs, Brandon	RB	6-4	264	7/6/82	5	Southern Illinois	Napoleonville, La.	D4-'05	13/13
84	Johnson, Darcy	TE	6-5	252	2/11/83	3	Central Florida	Palatka, Fla.	FA-'06	16/2
20	Johnson, Michael	S	6-2	207	5/9/84	3	Arizona	Round Rock, Texas	D7a-'07	16/16
53	Kehl, Bryan	LB	6-2	237	6/16/84	2	Brigham Young	Salt Lake City, Utah	D4-'08	16/2
97	Kiwanuka, Mathias	DE	6-5	265	3/8/83	4	Boston College	Indianapolis, Ind.	D1-'06	16/16
61	Koets, Adam	T	6-5	300	1/7/84	3	Oregon State	Santa Ana, Calif.	D6-'07	1/0
10	Manning, Eli	QB	6-4	225	1/3/81	6	Mississippi	New Orleans, La.	T(SD)-'04	16/16
82	Manningham, Mario	WR	5-11	183	5/25/86	2	Michigan	Warren, Ohio	D3-'08	7/0
88	Matthews, Michael	TE	6-4	270	10/9/83	3	Georgia Tech	Cincinnati, Ohio	FA-'07	16/5
67	McKenzie, Kareem	T	6-6	327	5/24/79	9	Penn State	Willingboro, N.J.	UFA(NYJ)-'05	16/16
86	Milner, Martrez	TE	6-4	259	8/9/84	2	Georgia	Oakwood, Ga.	FA-'08	0*
83	Moss, Sinorice	WR	5-8	185	12/28/83	4	Miami	Miami, Fla.	D2-'06	10/0
60	O'Hara, Shaun	C	6-3	303	6/23/77	10	Rutgers	Hillsborough, N.J.	UFA(Cle)-'04	16/16
74	Pennington, Terrance	OL	6-7	315	9/25/83	3	New Mexico	Los Angeles, Calif.	FA-'09	0*
21	Phillips, Kenny	S	6-2	210	11/24/86	2	Miami	Miami, Fla.	D1-'08	16/3
58	Pierce, Antonio	LB	6-1	238	10/26/78	9	Arizona	Ontario, Calif.	UFA(Wash)-'05	15/15
98	Robbins, Fred	DT	6-4	317	3/25/77	10	Wake Forest	Pensacola, Fla.	UFA(Minn)-'04	14/14
31	Ross, Aaron	CB	6-0	197	9/15/82	9	Texas	Tyler, Texas	D1-'07	15/15
69	Seubert, Rich	G	6-3	310	3/30/79	9	Western Illinois	Marshfield, Wis.	FA-'01	16/16
12	Smith, Steve	WR	5-11	195	5/6/85	3	Southern California	Woodland Hills, Calif.	D2-'07	16/4
76	Snee, Chris	G	6-3	317	1/18/82	6	Boston College	Montrose, Pa.	D2-'04	16/16
24	Thomas, Terrell	CB	6-0	199	1/8/85	2	Southern California	Alto Loma, Calif.	D2-'08	12/2
71	Tollefson, Dave	DE	6-4	255	7/10/82	3	N.W. Missouri State	Concord, Calif.	FA-'07	13/0
91	Tuck, Justin	DE	6-5	274	3/29/83	5	Notre Dame	Kellyton, Ala.	D3-'05	16/16
9	Tynes, Lawrence	K	6-1	202	6/3/78	6	Troy State	Milton, Fla.	T(KC)-'07	2/0
85	Tyree, David	WR	6-0	206	1/3/80	7	Syracuse	Montclair, N.J.	D6c-'03	0*
72	Umenyiora, Osi	DE	6-3	261	11/16/81	7	Troy State	Auburn, Ala.	D2-'03	0*
49	Vickers, Lee	TE	6-6	275	3/13/81	3	North Alabama	Athens' Ala.	FA-'09	0*
28	Ware, Danny	RB	6-0	234	2/18/85	3	Georgia	Rockmart, Ga.	FA-'07	6/0
23	Webster, Corey	CB	6-0	202	3/2/82	5	Louisiana State	Vacherie, La.	D2-'05	16/16
79	Whimper, Guy	T	6-5	302	5/21/83	4	East Carolina	Havelock, N.C.	D4b-'06	0*
59	Wilkinson, Gerris	LB	6-3	231	4/5/83	4	Georgia Tech	Oakland, Calif.	D3-'06	8/5
48	Wrighster, George	TE	6-3	265	4/1/81	7	Oregon	Memphis, TN	FA-'09	5/3*

* Barksdale last active with Kansas City in '07; Bernard played 15 games with Seattle in '08; Biddle inactive for 1 game; Bodiford last active wtih Green Bay in '07; Boley played 16 games with Atlanta; Brown played in 3 games with Houston; Bryant was inactive for 16 games; Canty played 16 games with Cowboys in '08; Cargile was inactive for all games in '08; Douzable inactive for 4 games; Hagan played 4 games with Miami; Henderson missed '08 season because of injury; Koets played 1 postseason game; Milner last active with

Atlanta in '07; Pennington last active with Atlanta in '07; Tyree missed '08 season because of injury; Umenyiora missed '08 season because of injury; Vickers last active with Baltimore in '07; Whimper missed '08 season because of injury; Wrighster played 5 games with Jacksonville.

Players lost through free agency (3): S James Butler (StL; 15 games in '08), RB Derrick Ward (TB; 15), DE Renaldo Wynn (Wash; 16).

Also played with Giants in '08—WR Plaxico Burress (10 games), S Sammy Knight (9), CB Sam Madison (6), DE Jerome McDougle (3), CB R.W. McQuarters (9), LB Edmond Miles (1), G Grey Ruegamer (16), WR Amani Toomer (16).

2009 FIRST-YEAR ROSTER

Name	Pos.	Ht.	Wt.	Birthdate	College	Hometown	How Acq.
Anderson, Vince	CB	6-2	205	12/8/84	Webber International	Lake City, Fla.	FA
Barden, Ramses	WR	6-6	227	1/1/86	Cal Poly	La Canada Flintridge, Calif.	D3
Beatty, William	T	6-6	307	3/2/85	Connecticut	York, Pa.	D2
Beckum, Travis	TE	6-3	239	1/24/87	Wisconsin	Milwaukee, Wisc.	D3
Bomar, Rhett	QB	6-2	225	7/2/85	Sam Houston State	Grand Prairie, Texas	D5
Brown, Andre	RB	6-0	224	12/15/86	North Carolina State	Greenville, N.C.	D4
Derenthal, Alex	C	6-4	298	4/20/86	Temple	Davie, Fla.	FA
Evans, Maurice	DE	6-2	264	8/14/88	Penn State	Brooklyn, N.Y.	FA
Field, Alex	DL	6-7	270	12/23/86	Virginia	Ashburn, Va.	FA
Hendricks, Dwayne	DT	6-4	300	3/17/86	Miami	Millville, N.J.	FA
Hill, Tommie	DE	6-6	245	11/28/85	Colorado State	Englewood, Colo.	FA
Ingram, Kenny	LB	6-5	239	2/27/86	Florida State	Orlando, Fla.	FA
Johnson, Bruce	CB	5-11	182	12/18/87	Miami	Live Oak, Fla.	FA
Louis, Cliff (1)	OL	6-8	315	8/24/84	Morgan State	Westhill, Conn.	FA-'08
Nicks, Hakeem	WR	6-0	212	11/14/88	North Carolina	Charlotte, N.C.	D1
Patrick, Allen (1)	RB	6-1	196	2/15/84	Oklahoma	Conway, S.C.	FA
Rashad, Sha'reff	S	6-0	198	10/6/86	Central Florida	Jacksonville, Fla.	FA
Rucker, Micah (1)	WR	6-6	221	1/4/85	Eastern Illinois	Estero, Fla.	FA-'08
Sintim, Clint	LB	6-2	256	2/21/86	Virginia	Woodbridge, Va.	D2
Smith, Kelvin	LB	6-2	240	3/20/84	Syracuse	Suffern, N.Y.	FA
Thompson, Orrin (1)	OL	6-6	320	11/11/82	Duke	Charlotte, N.C.	FA
Woodson, Andre' (1)	QB	6-4	230	4/25/84	Kentucky	Radcliff, Ky.	FA-'08
Woodson, Stoney	CB	5-10	198	10/11/85	South Carolina	Tampa, Fla.	D7
Wright, DeAndre	CB	5-10	198	4/13/86	New Mexico	Clinton, Md.	D6

The term NFL Rookie is defined as a player who is in his first season of professional football and has not been on the roster of another professional football team for any regular-season or postseason games. A Rookie is designated by an "R" on NFL rosters. Players who have been active in another professional football league or players who have NFL experience, including either preseason training camp or being on an Active List or Inactive List, or on Reserve/Injured or Reserve/Physically Unable to Perform for fewer than six regular-season games, are termed NFL First-Year Players. An NFL First-Year Player is designated by a "1" on NFL rosters. Thereafter, a player is credited with an additional year of experience for each season in which he accumulates six games on the Active List or Inactive List, or on Reserve/Injured or Reserve/Physically Unable to Perform.

Log on to www.giants.com for an up-to-date roster.

NEW YORK GIANTS

COACHING STAFF

Head Coach,
Tom Coughlin

Pro Career: Was named the sixteenth head coach in Giants history on January 6, 2004. This season marks Coughlin's sixth with the Giants and fourteenth as an NFL head coach. The Coughlin-led Giants finished the 2008 season with a 12-4 record, which won the NFC East division. Coughlin directed the Giants 17-14 win over the New England Patriots in Super Bowl XLII on February 3, 2008, the third championship in the teams history. Coached the Giants to an 11-5 record, the NFC East title and the playoffs in 2005-06, his second and third seasons with the team. Coughlin previously spent eight years (1995-2002) with the Jacksonville Jaguars. Under Coughlin, the Jaguars had the most victories of any NFL expansion team in its first seven seasons. They were also the only expansion team in NFL history to advance to the playoffs four times in their first five seasons. Coughlin's team went 9-7 in 1996 and an NFL-best 14-2 in 1999, both times reaching the AFC Championship Game. Coughlin previously coached the Philadelphia Eagles (1984-85), Green Bay Packers (1986-87), and Giants (1988-1990). He was a member of the Giants' Super Bowl XXV champion coaching staff. Career record: 123-100.

Background: Served as head coach at Boston College (1991-93), and coached at Syracuse (1969, 1974-1980), Rochester Institute of Technology 1970-73 (head coach), and Boston College (1981-83). Played wingback for Syracuse (1965-67).

Personal: Born August 31, 1946, Waterloo, N.Y. Tom and his wife Judy have two daughters, Keli and Katie; two son-in-laws named Chris; two sons, Brian and Tim; two daughters-in-law, Andrea (Tim's wife) and Susie (Brian's wife); and five grandchildren, Emma Rose, Dylan, Shea, Cooper, and Caroline.

ASSISTANT COACHES

Jack Bicknell, Jr., asst. offensive line; born Feb 7, 1963, North Plainfield, N.J. Center Boston College 1981-85. No pro playing experience. College coach: Boston College 1985-87, 2007-08, New Hampshire 1987-1996, Louisiana Tech 1997-2006 (head coach 1999-2006). Pro coach: Joined Giants in 2009.

Pat Flaherty, offensive line; born April 27, 1956, Hanover, Pa. Center East Stroudsburg 1974-77. No pro playing experience. College coach: East Stroudsburg 1980-81, Penn State 1982-83, Rutgers 1984-1991, East Carolina 1992, Wake Forest 1993-98, Iowa 1999. Pro coach: Washington Redskins 2000, Chicago Bears 2001-03, joined Giants in 2004.

Kevin Gilbride, offensive coordinator; born August 27, 1951, New Haven, Conn. Quarterback/tight end Southern Connecticut State 1971-73. No pro playing experience. College coach: Idaho State 1974-75, Tufts 1976-77, American International 1978-79. Southern Connecticut State 1980-84, East Carolina 1987-88. Pro coach: Ottawa Rough Riders (CFL) 1985-86, Houston Oilers 1989-1994, Jacksonville Jaguars 1995-96, San Diego Chargers 1997-98 (head coach), Pittsburgh Steelers 1999-2000, Buffalo Bills 2002-2003, joined Giants in 2004.

Peter Giunta, secondary/corners; born August 11, 1956, Salem, Mass. Running back/defensive back Northeastern 1974-77. No pro playing experience. College coach: Penn State 1981-83, Brown 1984-87, Lehigh 1988-1990. Pro coach: Philadelphia Eagles 1991-94, N.Y. Jets 1995-96, St. Louis Rams 1997-2000, Kansas City Chiefs 2001-2005, joined Giants in 2006.

Jim Hermann, linebackers; born December 8, 1960, Hollywood, Calif. Linebacker Michigan 1979-1982. No pro playing experience. College coach: Michigan 1983, 1986-2005. Pro coach: New York Jets 2006-2008, joined Giants in 2009.

Al Holcomb, defensive quality control; born October 22, 1970, Queens, N.Y. Attended West Virginia. No college or pro playing experience. College coach: Temple 1995-96, Colby College 1997, Bloomsburg 1998-2003, Kutztown 2004-05, Lafayette 2006-08. Pro coach: Joined Giants in 2009.

Jerald Ingram, running backs; born December 24, 1960, Dayton, Ohio. Fullback Michigan 1979-1983. College coach: Michigan 1984, Ball State 1985-1990, Boston College 1991-93. Pro coach: Jacksonville Jaguars 1994-2002, joined Giants in 2004.

Thomas McGaughey, asst. special teams coordinator; born May 8, 1973, Chicago. Safety Houston 1991-95. Pro safety Philadelphia Eagles 1996, Barcelona Dragons (NFLE) 1997. College coach Houston 1997, 2003-04. Pro coach: Scottish Claymores (NFLE) 2002, Kansas City Chiefs 2002, Denver Broncos 2005-06, joined Giants in 2007.

David Merritt Sr., secondary/safeties; born September 8, 1971, Raleigh, N.C. Linebacker North Carolina State 1989-1992. Pro linebacker Miami Dolphins 1993, Arizona Cardinals 1993-96, Rhein Fire (NFLE) 1997. College coach: Chattanooga 1997, Virginia Military Institute 1998-2000. Pro coach: New York Jets 2001-2003, joined Giants in 2004.

Chris Palmer, quarterbacks; born September 23, 1949, Brewster, N.Y. Quarterback Southern Connecticut State 1968-1971. No pro playing experience. College coach: Connecticut 1972-74, Lehigh 1975, Colgate 1976-1982, New Haven 1986-87 (head coach), Boston 1988-89 (head coach). Pro coach: Montreal Concordes (CFL) 1983, New Jersey Generals (USFL) 1984-85, Houston Oilers 1990-92, New England Patriots 1993-96, Jacksonville Jaguars 1997-98, Cleveland Browns 1999-2000 (head coach), Houston Texans 2001-05, Dallas Cowboys 2006, joined Giants in 2007.

Jerry Palmieri, strength and conditioning; born October 30, 1958, Englewood, N.J. Attended Montclair State. No college or pro playing experience. College coach: North Carolina 1982-83, Oklahoma State 1984-86, Kansas State 1987-1992, Boston College 1993-94. Pro coach: Jacksonville Jaguars 1995-2002, New Orleans Saints 2003, joined Giants in 2004.

Marcus Paul, asst. strength and conditioning; born April 1, 1966, Orlando, Fla. Safety Syracuse 1984-88. Pro safety Chicago Bears 1989-1993, Tampa Buccaneers 1993. Pro coach: New Orleans Saints 1998-99, New England Patriots 2000-04, New York Jets 2005-2006, joined Giants in 2007.

Michael Pope, tight ends; born March 15, 1942, Monroe, N.C. Quarterback Lenoir-Rhyne 1962-64. No pro playing experience. College coach: Florida State 1970-74, Texas Tech 1975-77, Mississippi 1978-1982. Pro coach: New York Giants 1983-1991, Cincinnati Bengals 1992-93, New England Patriots 1994-96, Washington Redskins 1997-99, re-joined Giants in 2000.

Tom Quinn, special teams coordinator; born January 27, 1968, Pasadena, Calif. Linebacker Arizona 1986-1990. No pro playing experience. College coach; Davidson College 1991, James Madison 1992-94, Boston 1995, Holy Cross 1996-98, San Jose State 1999-2001, Stanford 2002-05. Pro coach: Joined Giants in 2006.

Sean Ryan, offensive quality control; born May 1, 1972, Glenn Falls, N.Y. Defensive back Hamilton College 1994. No pro playing experience. College coach: Albany 1998-99, Colgate 2000, Boston College 2001-02, Columbia 2003-04, Harvard 2006. Pro coach: Joined Giants in 2007.

Bill Sheridan, defensive coordinator; born January 27, 1959, Detroit. Linebacker Grand Valley State 1979-1982. No pro playing experience. College coach: Michigan 1985-86, Maine 1987-88, Cincinnati 1989-1991, Army 1992-97, Michigan State 1998-2000, Notre Dame 2001, Michigan 2002-04. Pro coach: Joined Giants in 2005.

Mike Sullivan, wide receivers; born January 28, 1967, Santa Maria, Calif. Defensive back Army 1987-88. No pro playing experience. College coach: Mt. San Jacinto (Calif.) J.C. 1993, Humboldt State 1993-94, Army 1995-96, 1999-2000, Youngstown State 1997-98, Ohio 2001. Pro coach: Jacksonville Jaguars 2002-03, joined Giants in 2004.

Mike Waufle, defensive line; born June 27, 1954, Hornell, N.Y. U.S. Marines 1972-75. Defensive lineman Bakersfield (Calif.) J.C. 1975-76, Utah State 1977-78. No pro playing experience. College coach: Alfred 1979, Utah State 1980-84, Fresno State 1985-88, UCLA 1989, Oregon State 1990-91, California 1992-97. Pro coach: Oakland Raiders 1998-2003, joined Giants in 2004.

National Football Conference
East Division
Team Colors: Midnight Green, Silver, Black, and White
NovaCare Complex
One NovaCare Way
Philadelphia, Pennsylvania 19145
Telephone: (215) 463-2500

2009 SCHEDULE

PRESEASON

Aug. 13	**New England**	7:00
Aug. 20	at Indianapolis	8:00
Aug. 27	**Jacksonville**	7:00
Sep. 3	at N.Y. Jets	7:00

REGULAR SEASON

Sep. 13	at Carolina	1:00
Sep. 20	**New Orleans**	1:00
Sep. 27	**Kansas City**	1:00
Oct. 4	BYE	
Oct. 11	**Tampa Bay**	1:00
Oct. 18	at Oakland	1:05
Oct. 26	at Washington (Mon.)	8:30
Nov. 1	**N.Y. Giants**	4:15
Nov. 8	**Dallas**	8:20
Nov. 15	at San Diego	1:15
Nov. 22	at Chicago *	7:20
Nov. 29	**Washington**	1:00
Dec. 6	at Atlanta	1:00
Dec. 13	at N.Y. Giants *	8:20
Dec. 20	**San Francisco**	1:00
Dec. 27	**Denver**	1:00
Jan. 3	at Dallas	12:00

** Sunday night games in Weeks 11-17 subject to change*

Stadium: Lincoln Financial Field (opened in 2003) •**Capacity:** 69,144
One Lincoln Financial Field Way
Philadelphia, Pennsylvania 19148
Playing Surface: Natural Grass
Training Camp: Lehigh University
Bethlehem, PA 18015

LINCOLN FINANCIAL FIELD

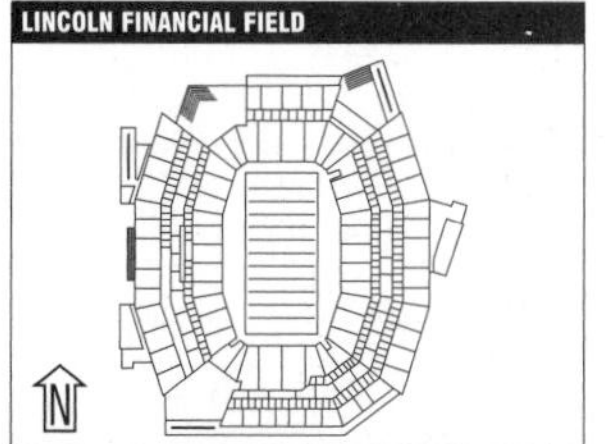

CLUB OFFICIALS

Chairman/Chief Executive Officer: Jeffrey Lurie
President: Joe Banner
Head Coach/Executive Vice President of Football Operations: Andy Reid
General Manager: Tom Heckert
Vice President of Player Personnel: Howie Roseman
Senior Vice President/Public Affairs and Government Relations: Pamela Browner Crawley
Senior Vice President of Business Operations: Mark Donovan
Senior Vice President/Chief Financial Officer: Don Smolenski
Vice President of Sales and Service: Marlyse Fant
Executive Director of Eagles Youth Partnership: Sarah Martinez-Helfman
Director of Pro Personnel: Jon Sandusky
Director of Football Media Relations: Derek Boyko
Director of Marketing: Mike Malo
Director of Human Resources: Kristie Pappal
Manager of Community Relations: Julie Hirshey
Director of Stadium Operations: Dave Duernberger
Director, Broadcasting: Rob Alberino
Director of Events: Leonard Bonacci
Director of Ticket Operations: Laini Delawter
Director of Ticket Client Relations: Leo Carlin
Director of Merchandise: Brendan McQuillen
Travel Manager: Tracey Leinen
Director of Team Security: Anthony (Butch) Buchanico
Head Athletic Trainer: Rick Burkholder
Asst. Athletic Trainers: Steve Condon, Chris Peduzzi
Video Director: Mike Dougherty
Head Equipment Manager: John Hatfield

COACHING HISTORY
(507-548-26)

Records include postseason games

1933-35	Lud Wray	9-21-1
1936-1940	Bert Bell	10-44-2
1941-1950	Earle (Greasy) Neale*	66-44-5
1951	Alvin (Bo) McMillin**	2-0-0
1951	Wayne Millner	2-8-0
1952-55	Jim Trimble	25-20-3
1956-57	Hugh Devore	7-16-1
1958-1960	Lawrence (Buck) Shaw	20-16-1
1961-63	Nick Skorich	15-24-3
1964-68	Joe Kuharich	28-41-1
1969-1971	Jerry Williams***	7-22-2
1971-72	Ed Khayat	8-15-2
1973-75	Mike McCormack	16-25-1
1976-1982	Dick Vermeil	57-51-0
1983-85	Marion Campbell****	17-29-1
1985	Fred Bruney	1-0-0
1986-1990	Buddy Ryan	43-38-1
1991-94	Rich Kotite	37-29-0
1995-98	Ray Rhodes	30-36-1
1999-2008	Andy Reid	107-69-1

*Co-coach with Walt Kiesling in Philadelphia-Pittsburgh merger in 1943
**Retired after two games in 1951
***Released after three games in 1971
****Released after 15 games in 1985

PAID ATTENDANCE

Home 541,000 Away 552,132
Total 1,093,132
Single-game home record, 72,111 (11/1/81)
Single-season home record, 557,325 (1980)

2009 DRAFT CHOICES

Round	Name	Pos.	College
1	Jeremy Maclin	WR	Missouri
2	LeSean McCoy	RB	Pittsburgh
5	Cornelius Ingram	TE	Florida
	Victor Harris	DB	Virginia Tech
	Fenuki Tupou	T	Oregon
6	Brandon Gibson	WR	Washington St.
7	Paul Fanaika	G	Arizona State
	Moise Fokou	LB	Maryland

PHILADELPHIA EAGLES

2008 TEAM RECORD

PRESEASON (2-2)

Date	Result	Opponent
8/8	L 10-16	at Pittsburgh
8/14	W 24-13	Carolina
8/22	W 27-17	at New England
8/28	L 20-27	New York Jets

REGULAR SEASON (9-6-1)

Date	Result	Opponent
9/7	W 38-3	St. Louis
9/15	L 37-41	at Dallas
9/21	W 15-6	Pittsburgh
9/28	L 20-24	at Chicago
10/5	L 17-23	Washington
10/12	W 40-26	at San Francisco
10/26	W 27-14	Atlanta
11/2	W 26-7	at Seattle
11/9	L 31-36	New York Giants
11/16	T 13-13	at Cincinnati (OT)
11/23	L 7-36	at Baltimore
11/27	W 48-20	Arizona
12/7	W 20-14	at New York Giants
12/15	W 30-10	Cleveland
12/21	L 3-10	at Washington
12/28	W 44-6	Dallas

POSTSEASON (2-1)

Date	Result	Opponent
1/4	W 26-14	at Minnesota
1/11	W 23-11	at New York Giants
1/18	L 25-32	at Arizona

(OT) Overtime

SCORE BY PERIODS

Eagles	85	150	73	108	0	— 416
Opponents	53	100	49	87	0	— 289

2008 TEAM STATISTICS

	Eagles	Opp.
Total First Downs	318	248
Rushing	94	79
Passing	204	144
Penalty	20	25
3rd Down: Made/Att	93/225	73/227
3rd Down Pct.	41.3	32.2
4th Down: Made/Att	4/9	5/14
4th Down Pct.	44.4	35.7
Possession Avg.	30:55	29:05
Total Net Yards	5608	4389
Avg. Per Game	350.5	274.3
Total Plays	1056	994
Avg. Per Play	5.3	4.4
Net Yards Rushing	1697	1476
Avg. Per Game	106.1	92.3
Total Rushes	427	421
Net Yards Passing	3911	2913
Avg. Per Game	244.4	182.1
Sacked/Yards Lost	23/149	48/312
Gross Yards	4060	3225
Att./Completions	606/362	525/284
Completion Pct.	59.7	54.1
Had Intercepted	16	15
Punts/Average	78/42.7	101/42.5
Net Punting Avg.	78/37.9	101/36.5
Penalties/Yards	74/635	80/593
Fumbles/Ball Lost	16/10	26/14
Touchdowns	45	31
Rushing	15	7
Passing	23	19
Returns	7	5

2008 INDIVIDUAL STATISTICS

PASSING	Att.	Comp.	Yds.	Pct.	TD	Int.	Tkld.	Rate
McNabb	571	345	3916	60.4	23	11	23/149	86.4
Kolb	34	17	144	50.0	0	4	0/0	21.8
D. Jackson	1	0	0	0.0	0	1	0/0	0.0
Eagles	606	362	4060	59.7	23	16	23/149	81.4
Opponents	525	284	3225	54.1	19	15	48/312	72.9

SCORING	TD R	TD P	TD Rt	PAT	FG	Saf	PTS
Akers	0	0	0	45/45	33/40	0	144
Westbrook	9	5	0	0/0	0/0	0	84
Buckhalter	2	2	0	0/0	0/0	0	24
D. Jackson	1	2	1	0/0	0/0	0	24
Baskett	0	3	0	0/0	0/0	0	18
L. Smith	0	3	0	0/0	0/0	0	18
Avant	0	2	0	0/0	0/0	0	12
Curtis	0	2	0	0/0	0/0	0	12
McNabb	2	0	0	0/0	0/0	0	12
R. Brown	0	1	0	0/0	0/0	0	6
Celek	0	1	0	0/0	0/0	0	6
Clemons	0	0	1	0/0	0/0	0	6
Demps	0	0	1	0/0	0/0	0	6
Gocong	0	0	1	0/0	0/0	0	6
Hanson	0	0	1	0/0	0/0	0	6
Herremans	0	1	0	0/0	0/0	0	6
Hunt	1	0	0	0/0	0/0	0	6
Lewis	0	1	0	0/0	0/0	0	6
Parker	0	0	1	0/0	0/0	0	6
Samuel	0	0	1	0/0	0/0	0	6
Eagles	15	23	7	45/45	33/40	1	416
Opponents	7	19	5	29/29	24/28	1	289

2-Pt. Conversions: None.
Eagles 0-0, Opponents 0-2.

RUSHING	No.	Yds	Avg	LG	TD
Westbrook	233	936	4.0	39t	9
Buckhalter	76	369	4.9	33	2
McNabb	39	147	3.8	17	2
D. Jackson	17	96	5.6	21	1
Eckel	24	79	3.3	14	0
Booker	20	53	2.7	8	0
Hunt	4	9	2.3	6	1
R. Brown	1	6	6.0	6	0
Kolb	13	2	0.2	8	0
Eagles	427	1697	4.0	39t	15
Opponents	421	1476	3.5	28	7

RECEIVING	No.	Yds	Avg	LG	TD
D. Jackson	62	912	14.7	60	2
Westbrook	54	402	7.4	47	5
L. Smith	37	298	8.1	25	3
Baskett	33	440	13.3	90t	3
Curtis	33	390	11.8	32	2
Avant	32	377	11.8	31	2
Celek	27	318	11.8	44	1
Buckhalter	26	324	12.5	59	2
Lewis	19	247	13.0	52	1
R. Brown	18	252	14.0	40	1
Hunt	6	42	7.0	18	0
Klecko	6	36	6.0	12	0
Booker	6	11	1.8	8	0
Schobel	2	10	5.0	5	0
Herremans	1	1	1.0	1t	1
Eagles	362	4060	11.2	90t	23
Opponents	284	3225	11.4	90t	19

INTERCEPTIONS	No.	Yds	Avg	LG	TD
Samuel	4	64	16.0	50t	1
Mikell	3	53	17.7	41	0
Parker	1	55	55.0	55t	1
Dawkins	1	25	25.0	25	0
S. Brown	1	23	23.0	23	0
Patterson	1	21	21.0	21	0
Bradley	1	17	17.0	17	0
Hanson	1	13	13.0	13	0
Howard	1	8	8.0	8	0
Sheppard	1	0	0.0	0	0
Eagles	15	279	18.6	55t	2
Opponents	16	434	27.1	107t	2

PUNTING	No.	Yds.	Avg.	In 20	LG
Rocca	77	3334	43.3	24	65
Eagles	78	3334	42.7	24	65
Opponents	101	4294	42.5	38	67

PUNT RETURNS	Ret	FC	Yds	Avg	LG	TD
D. Jackson	50	16	440	8.8	68t	1
Hanson	1	0	0	0.0	0	0
Lewis	1	0	6	6.0	6	0
Eagles	52	16	446	8.6	68t	1
Opponents	41	12	296	7.2	45	0

KICKOFF RETURNS	No.	Yds	Avg	LG	TD
Demps	52	1314	25.3	100t	1
Lewis	3	43	14.3	31	0
Buckhalter	1	14	14.0	14	0
Avant	1	13	13.0	13	0
D. Jackson	1	12	12.0	12	0
Klecko	1	12	12.0	12	0
Abiamiri	1	3	3.0	3	0
Eagles	60	1411	23.5	100t	1
Opponents	75	1698	22.6	98t	1

FIELD GOALS	1-19	20-29	30-39	40-49	50+
Akers	2/2	11/11	10/12	8/10	2/5
Eagles	2/2	11/11	10/12	8/10	2/5
Opponents	0/0	6/6	5/5	9/11	4/6

SACKS	No.
Howard	10.0
T. Cole	9.0
Parker	5.0
Clemons	4.0
Dawkins	3.0
Gaither	2.5
Abiamiri	2.0
Bunkley	2.0
Gocong	2.0
Klecko	2.0
Mikell	2.0
Bradley	1.0
S. Brown	1.0
Demps	1.0
Hanson	1.0
Patterson	0.5
Eagles	48.0
Opponents	23.0

RECORD HOLDERS

INDIVIDUAL RECORDS—CAREER

Category	Name	Performance
Rushing (Yds.)	Wilbert Montgomery, 1977-1984	6,538
Passing (Yds.)	Donovan McNabb, 1999-2008	26,320
Passing (TDs)	Donovan McNabb, 1999-2008	194
Receiving (No.)	Harold Carmichael, 1971-1983	589
Receiving (Yds.)	Harold Carmichael, 1971-1983	8,978
Interceptions	Bill Bradley, 1969-1976	34
	Eric Allen, 1988-1994	34
	Brian Dawkins, 1996-2008	34
Punting (Avg.)	Joe Muha, 1946-1950	42.9
Punt Return (Avg.)	Ernie Steele, 1942-48	16.8
Kickoff Return (Avg.)	Steve Van Buren, 1944-1951	26.7
Field Goals	David Akers, 1999-2008	230
Touchdowns (Tot.)	Harold Carmichael, 1971-1983	79
Points	David Akers, 1999-2008	1,041
*Sacks	Reggie White, 1985-1992	124.0

INDIVIDUAL RECORDS—SINGLE SEASON

Category	Name	Performance
Rushing (Yds.)	Wilbert Montgomery, 1979	1,512
Passing (Yds.)	Donovan McNabb, 2004	3,875
Passing (TDs)	Sonny Jurgensen, 1961	32
Receiving (No.)	Brian Westbrook, 2007	90
Receiving (Yds.)	Mike Quick, 1983	1,409
Interceptions	Bill Bradley, 1971	11
Punting (Avg.)	Joe Muha, 1948	47.2
Punt Return (Avg.)	Steve Van Buren, 1944	15.3
Kickoff Return (Avg.)	Al Nelson, 1972	29.1
Field Goals	Paul McFadden, 1984	30
	David Akers, 2002	30
Touchdowns (Tot.)	Steve Van Buren, 1945	18
Points	David Akers, 2002	133
*Sacks	Reggie White, 1987	21.0

INDIVIDUAL RECORDS—SINGLE GAME

Category	Name	Performance
Rushing (Yds.)	Steve Van Buren, 11-27-49	205
Passing (Yds.)	Donovan McNabb, 12-5-04	464
Passing (TDs)	Adrian Burk, 10-17-54	**7
Receiving (No.)	Don Looney, 12-1-40	14
	Brian Westbrook, 11-4-07	14
Receiving (Yds.)	Tommy McDonald, 12-10-60	237
Interceptions	Russ Craft, 9-24-50	**4
Field Goals	Tom Dempsey, 11-12-72	6
Touchdowns (Tot.)	Many times	4
	Last time by Brian Westbrook, 11-27-08	
Points	Bobby Walston, 10-17-54	25
*Sacks	Clyde Simmons, 9-15-91	4.5
	Hugh Douglas, 10-18-98	4.5

**Sacks became an official statistic in 1982.*
***NFL Record*

PHILADELPHIA EAGLES

2009 VETERAN ROSTER

No.	Name	Pos.	Ht.	Wt.	Birthdate	NFL Exp.	College	Hometown	How Acq.	'08 Games/ Starts
95	Abiamiri, Victor	DE	6-4	267	1/14/86	3	Notre Dame	Baltimore, Md.	D2b-'07	10/0
2	Akers, David	K	5-10	200	12/9/74	11	Louisville	Lexington, Ky.	FA-'99	16/0
73	Andrews, Shawn	G/T	6-4	335	12/25/82	6	Arkansas	Camden, Ark.	D1-'04	2/2
76	Andrews, Stacy	T/G	6-7	342	6/2/81	6	Mississippi	Camden, Ark.	UFA(Cin)-'09	15/15*
81	Avant, Jason	WR	6-0	212	4/20/83	4	Michigan	Chicago, Ill.	D4b-'06	15/6
30	Baker, Rashad	S	5-10	200	2/22/82	6	Tennessee	Camden, N.J.	UFA(Oak)-'09	10/1*
84	Baskett, Hank	WR	6-4	220	9/4/82	4	New Mexico	Clovis, N.M.	T(Minn)-'06	15/6
25	Booker, Lorenzo	RB	5-10	191	6/14/84	3	Florida State	Ventura, Calif.	T(Mia)-'08	10/1
55	Bradley, Stewart	LB	6-4	255	11/2/83	3	Nebraska	Salt Lake City, Utah	D3a-'07	16/16
86	Brown, Reggie	WR	6-1	197	1/13/81	5	Georgia	Carrollton, Ga.	D2a-'05	10/3
24	Brown, Sheldon	CB	5-10	200	3/19/79	8	South Carolina	Ft. Lawn, S.C.	D2b-'02	16/15
97	Bunkley, Brodrick	DT	6-2	306	11/23/83	4	Florida State	Tampa, Fla.	D1-'06	16/16
87	Celek, Brent	TE	6-4	255	1/25/85	3	Cincinnati	Cincinnati, Ohio	D5b-'07	16/7
91	Clemons, Chris	DE	6-2	240	10/30/81	6	Georgia	Griffin, Ga.	UFA(Oak)-'08	16/0
59	Cole, Nick	C	6-0	350	7/28/84	4	New Mexico State	Lawton, Okla.	FA-'06	16/5
58	Cole, Trent	LB/DE	6-3	270	10/5/82	5	Cincinnati	Xenia, Ohio	D5a-'05	16/16
80	Curtis, Kevin	WR	6-0	186	7/17/78	7	Utah State	South Jordan, Utah	UFA(StL)-'07	9/8
50	Daniels, Tank	LB	6-3	248	12/27/81	4	Harding	Clarendon, Ark.	W(NYG)-'08	16/0
39	Demps, Quintin	S	5-11	206	6/29/85	2	Texas-El Paso	San Antonio, Texas	D4b-'08	16/0
46	Dorenbos, Jon	LS	6-0	250	7/21/80	7	Texas-El Paso	Garden Grove, Calif.	FA-'06	16/0
65	Dunlap, King	T	6-8	310	9/9/85	2	Auburn	Brentwood, Tenn.	D7-'08	0*
32	Eckel, Kyle	FB	5-11	237	12/30/81	3	Navy	Merion, Pa.	FA-'08	5/0
14	Feeley, A.J.	QB	6-3	220	5/16/77	9	Oregon	Ontario, Ore.	FA-'06	0*
96	Gaither, Omar	LB	6-2	245	3/18/84	4	Tennessee	Charlotte, N.C.	D5b-'06	16/10
61	Gibson, Mike	G	6-3	305	11/18/85	2	California	Napa, Calif.	D6a-'08	0*
57	Gocong, Chris	LB	6-2	263	11/16/83	4	Cal Poly San Luis Obispo	Carpinteria, Calif.	D3-'06	16/12
66	Gordon, Amon	DT	6-2	305	10/31/81	4	Stanford	San Diego, Calif.	W(Tenn)-'09	2/0*
21	Hanson, Joselio	CB	5-9	185	8/13/81	5	Texas Tech	Playa Del Rey, Calif.	FA-'06	16/3
79	Herremans, Todd	G/T	6-6	321	10/13/82	5	Saginaw Valley State	Ravenna, Mich.	D4b-'05	16/15
37	t- Hobbs, Ellis	CB	5-9	195	5/16/83	5	Iowa State	DeSoto, Texas	T(NE)-'09	16/16*
90	Howard, Darren	DE	6-3	260	11/19/76	10	Kansas State	St. Petersburg, Fla.	UFA(NO)-'06	16/0
33	Ikegwuonu, Jack	CB	5-10	194	1/7/86	2	Wisconsin	Madison, Wisc.	D4c-'08	0*
10	Jackson, DeSean	WR	5-10	175	12/1/86	2	California	Long Beach, Calif.	D2b-'08	16/15
67	Jackson, Jamaal	C	6-4	330	5/8/80	6	Delaware State	Miami, Fla.	FA-'03	16/16
62	Jean-Gilles, Max	G	6-3	358	11/19/83	4	Georgia	Miami, Fla.	D4a-'06	12/10
26	Jones, Sean	S	6-1	220	3/2/82	6	Georgia	Atlanta, Ga.	UFA(Cle)-'09	12/12*
56	Jordan, Akeem	LB	6-1	230	8/17/85	3	James Madison	Harrisonburg, Va.	FA-'07	16/6
74	Justice, Winston	T	6-6	320	9/14/84	4	Southern California	Long Beach, Calif.	D2-'06	5/0
68	Klecko, Dan	DT	5-11	275	1/12/81	7	Temple	Marlboro, N.J.	FA(Ind)-'08	16/3
4	Kolb, Kevin	QB	6-3	218	8/24/84	3	Houston	Stephenville, Texas	D2a-'07	6/0
93	Laws, Trevor	DT	6-1	304	6/14/85	2	Notre Dame	Apple Valley, Minn.	D2a-'08	16/0
51	Mays, Joe	LB	5-11	246	7/6/85	2	North Dakota State	Chicago, Ill.	D6b-'08	2/0
77	McGlynn, Mike	G	6-4	311	3/8/85	2	Pittsburgh	Austintown, Ohio	D4a-'08	3/0
5	McNabb, Donovan	QB	6-2	240	11/25/76	11	Syracuse	Chicago, Ill.	D1-'99	16/16
27	Mikell, Quintin	S	5-10	206	9/16/80	7	Boise State	Eugene, Ore.	FA-'03	16/16
75	Parker, Juqua	DE	6-2	250	5/15/78	9	Oklahoma State	Houston, Texas	FA-'05	16/16
23	Patterson, Dimitri	CB	5-10	190	6/18/83	4	Tuskegee	Orlando, Fla.	FA-'09	7/0*
98	Patterson, Mike	DT	6-0	292	9/1/83	5	Southern California	Los Alamitos, Calif.	D1-'05	16/16
71	t- Peters, Jason	T	6-4	340	1/22/82	6	Arkansas	Queen City, Texas	T(Buff)-'09	13/13*
6	Rocca, Sav	P	6-5	265	11/20/73	3	None	Lakeside, Australia	FA-'07	16/0
69	Runyan, Jon	T	6-7	330	11/27/73	14	Michigan	Flint, Mich.	UFA(Tenn)-'00	16/16
22	Samuel, Asante	CB	5-10	185	1/6/81	7	Central Florida	Lauderdale Lakes, Fla.	UFA(NE)-'08	15/15
89	Schobel, Matt	TE	6-5	247	11/4/78	8	Texas Christian	Columbus, Texas	UFA(Cin)-'06	5/1
63	Smith, Bryan	DE	6-2	245	11/29/83	2	McNeese State	Newton, Texas	D3-'08	0*
43	Weaver, Leonard	FB	6-0	242	9/23/82	5	Carson-Newman	Satellite, Fla.	UFA(Sea)-'09	14/7*
36	Westbrook, Brian	RB	5-10	203	9/2/79	8	Villanova	Ft. Washington, Md.	D3-'02	14/14
54	White, Tracy	LB	6-0	238	4/14/81	7	Howard	St. Stephen, SC..	FA-'08	15/0*

* St. Andrews played 15 games with Cincinnati in '08; Baker played 10 games with Oakland; Dunlap missed '08 season because of injury; Feeley inactive for 16 games; Gibson missed '08 season because of injury; Gordon played 2 games with Tennessee; Hobbs played 16 games with New England; Ikegwuonu missed '08 season on the non-football injury list; Jones played 12 games with Cleveland; D. Patterson played 7 games with Kansas City; Peters played 13 games with Buffalo; Smith inactive for 16 games; Weaver played 14 games with Philadelphia; White played 5 games with Green Bay and 10 with Philadelphia.

t- Eagles traded for Hobbs (NE) and Peters (Buff).

Players lost through free agency (5): RB Correll Buckhalter (Den; 14 games in '08), S Sean Considine (Jax; 16), S Brian Dawkins (Den; 16), TE L.J. Smith (Balt; 13), T Tra Thomas (Jax; 16).

Also played with Eagles in '08—FB Tony Hunt (6 games), WR Greg Lewis (16), J.R. Reed (5), CB Lito Sheppard (16).

2009 FIRST-YEAR ROSTER

Name	Pos.	Ht.	Wt.	Birthdate	College	Hometown	How Acq.
Amendola, Danny (1)	WR	5-11	186	11/2/85	Texas Tech	The Woodlands, Texas	FA
Bright, Eugene	TE	6-4	254	4/18/85	Purdue	Bryn Mawr, Pa.	FA
Buckley, Eldra (1)	RB	5-9	207	6/23/85	Tennessee-Chattanooga	Charleston, Miss.	W(SD)
Fanaika, Paul	G	6-5	327	4/9/86	Arizona State	Millbrae, Calif.	D7a
Fokou, Moise	LB	6-1	233	8/28/85	Maryland	Potomac, Md.	D7b
Gaines, Josh	DE	6-1	274	9/27/85	Penn State	Fort Wayne, Ind.	FA
Gibson, Brandon	WR	6-0	210	8/13/87	Washington State	Puyallup, Wash.	D6
Harris, Macho	CB	5-11	198	2/16/86	Virginia Tech	Highland Springs, Va.	D5b
Hughes, Charleston (1)	LB	6-1	244	12/14/83	Northwood	Saginaw, Mich.	FA
Ingram, Cornelius	TE	6-4	245	6/10/85	Florida	Hawthorne, Fla.	D5a
Langford, Reshard	S	6-1	213	2/6/86	Vanderbilt	Tanner, Ala.	FA
Maclin, Jeremy	WR	6-0	198	5/11/88	Missouri	Kirkwood, Mo.	D1
Mailei, Marcus	FB	6-0	255	10/30/86	Weber State	Salt Lake City, Utah	FA
McBride, Shaheer (1)	WR	6-2	205	2/6/85	Delaware State	Chester, Pa.	FA-'08
McCoy, LeSean	RB	5-10	198	7/12/88	Pittsburgh	Harrisburg, Pa.	D2
Mendenhall, Walter	RB	6-0	225	1/22/86	Illinois State	Skokie, Ill.	FA
Parker, Byron (1)	S	5-11	193	3/7/81	Tulane	Stone Mountain, Ga.	FA
Patrick, Chris (1)	T	6-4	280	8/22/84	Nebraska	Ithaca, Mich.	FA-'08
Reynolds, Dallas	G	6-4	314	4/23/84	Brigham Young	Provo, Utah	FA
Robinson, Brandon	WR	5-10	198	8/2/85	Boston College	Minneapolis, Minn.	FA
Robinson, Courtney	CB	5-11	200	12/7/86	Massachusetts	Delray Beach, Fla.	FA
Swank, Sam	K	6-2	201	10/5/85	Wake Forest	Neptune Beach, Fla.	FA
Thigpen, Marcus	WR	5-9	193	5/15/86	Indiana	Detroit, Mich.	FA
Tupou, Fenuki	T	6-5	314	5/1/85	Oregon	Antelope, Calif.	D5c
Williams, Trae (1)	CB	5-10	195	1/30/85	South Florida	Plant City, Fla.	FA-'08

The term NFL Rookie is defined as a player who is in his first season of professional football and has not been on the roster of another professional football team for any regular-season or postseason games. A Rookie is designated by an "R" on NFL rosters. Players who have been active in another professional football league or players who have NFL experience, including either preseason training camp or being on an Active List or Inactive List, or on Reserve/Injured or Reserve/Physically Unable to Perform for fewer than six regular-season games, are termed NFL First-Year Players. An NFL First-Year Player is designated by a "1" on NFL rosters. Thereafter, a player is credited with an additional year of experience for each season in which he accumulates six games on the Active List or Inactive List, or on Reserve/Injured or Reserve/Physically Unable to Perform.

Log on to www.philadelphiaeagles.com for an up-to-date roster.

PHILADELPHIA EAGLES

COACHING STAFF

Head Coach/Executive Vice President of Football Operations, Andy Reid

Pro Career: Reid has earned NFL coach of the year honors twice, compiled the best win total (107), winning percentage (.607), and playoff victory total (10) in team history. He has captured five division titles and five trips to the NFC Championship game. Since he was hired in 1999, no other franchise has earned more divisional playoff round appearances (7) than Philadelphia. Among coaches with 100 games under their belt entering 2009, Reid's .607 overall winning percentage is 15th in NFL history and second among active coaches behind New England's Bill Belichick (.632). In his 17-year NFL coaching career, Reid's teams have made the playoffs 13 times (19-12 record). He has coached in the Super Bowl three times, the NFC Championship game eight times, and the Pro Bowl five times. Reid became the 20th head coach in franchise history on January 11, 1999, and was promoted to head coach/executive vice president of football operations in 2001. He was named NFL coach of the year in 2000 and 2002. He joined the Eagles after a seven-year stint as an assistant coach with Green Bay (1992-98) under Mike Holmgren. With Green Bay, Reid helped the Packers earn a Super Bowl XXXI victory over New England. Career record: 107-69-1

Background: Coached at Brigham Young (1982), San Francisco State (1983-85), Northern Arizona (1986), Texas-El Paso (1987-88), and Missouri (1989-1991). Reid first met Holmgren, who was a member of BYU's coaching staff, when Reid was an offensive tackle and guard on three Cougar Holiday Bowl teams. Reid graduated with a bachelor's degree in physical education. He also received a master's degree in professional leadership in physical education and athletics.

Personal: Born in Los Angeles on March 19, 1958, Reid and his wife Tammy have five children—Garrett, Britt, Crosby, Drew Ann, and Spencer.

ASSISTANT COACHES

Mike Caldwell, defensive quality control; born August 31, 1971. Linebacker Middle Tennessee State 1989-1992. Pro linebacker Cleveland Browns 1993-95, Baltimore Ravens 1996, Arizona Cardinals 1997, Philadelphia Eagles 1998-2001, Chicago Bears 2002, Carolina Panthers 2003. Pro coach: Joined Eagles in 2008.

Juan Castillo, offensive line; born October 8, 1959, Port Isabel, Texas. Linebacker Texas A&I (now Texas A&M-Kingsville) 1978-1980. Pro linebacker San Antonio Gunslingers (USFL) 1984-85. College coach: Texas A&I/Texas A&M-Kingsville 1982-85, 1990-94. Pro coach: Joined Eagles in 1995.

David Culley, wide receivers; born September 17, 1955, Sparta, Tenn. Quarterback Vanderbilt 1973-77. No pro playing experience. College coach: Austin Peay 1978, Vanderbilt 1979-1981, Middle Tennessee State 1982, Tennessee-Chattanooga 1983, Western Kentucky 1984, Southwestern Louisiana 1985-88, Texas-El Paso 1989-1990, Texas A&M 1991-93. Pro coach: Tampa Bay Buccaneers 1994-95, Pittsburgh Steelers 1996-1998, joined Eagles in 1999.

Ted Daisher, special teams coordinator; born February 2, 1955, Taylor, Mich. Wide receiver/defensive back Western Michigan 1975-77. No pro playing experience. College coach: Illinois 1980-84, Eastern Michigan 1985-88, Cincinnati 1989-1992, Army 1995-97, Indiana 1998-2000, East Carolina 2001-02. Pro coach: Philadelphia Eagles 2004-05, Oakland Raiders 2006, Cleveland Browns 2007-08, re-joined Eagles in 2009.

Jim Johnson, defensive coordinator; born May 26, 1941, Maywood, Ill. Quarterback Missouri 1959-1962. Pro tight end Buffalo Bills 1963-64. College coach: Missouri Southern 1967-68 (head coach), Drake 1969-1972, Indiana 1973-76, Notre Dame 1977-1980. Pro coach: Oklahoma Outlaws (USFL) 1984, Jacksonville Bulls (USFL) 1985, Phoenix Cardinals 1986-1993, Indianapolis Colts 1994-97, Seattle Seahawks 1998, joined Eagles in 1999.

Sean McDermott, secondary; born March 21, 1974, Omaha, Neb. Safety William & Mary 1994-97. No pro playing experience. College coach: William & Mary 1998. Pro coach: Joined Eagles in 1998.

Tom Melvin, tight ends; born October 1, 1961, Redwood City, Calif. Offensive lineman San Francisco State 1982-83. No pro playing experience. College coach: San Francisco State 1984-85, Northern Arizona 1986-87, California-Santa Barbara 1988-1990, Occidental College 1991-98. Pro coach: Joined Eagles in 1999.

Marty Mornhinweg, asst. head coach/\offensive coordinator; born March 29, 1962, Edmond, Okla. Quarterback Montana 1981-84. Pro quarterback Denver Dynamite (AFL) 1987. College coach: Montana 1985, Texas-El Paso 1986-87, Northern Arizona 1988, 1994, Southeast Missouri State 1989-1990, Missouri 1991-93. Pro coach: Green Bay Packers 1995-96, San Francisco 49ers 1997-2000, Detroit Lions 2001-02 (head coach), joined Eagles in 2003.

Jeff Nixon, special teams quality control; born October 16, 1974, Rochester, Pa. Running back West Virginia 1993-94, Penn State 1996. No pro playing experience. College coach: Penn State 1997, Princeton 1998, Shippensburg 1999-2002, Tennessee-Chattanooga 2003-05, Temple 2006. Pro coach: Joined Eagles in 2007.

Doug Pederson, offensive quality control; born January 31, 1968, Bellingham, Wash. Quarterback Louisiana-Monroe 1987-1990. Pro experience: Miami Dolphins 1993-95, Green Bay Packers 1995-98, 2001-04, Philadelphia Eagles 1999, Cleveland Browns 2000. Pro coach: Joined Eagles in 2009.

Rory Segrest, defensive line; born May 20, 1973, Waycross, Ga. Tackle Alabama 1991-93. No pro playing experience. College coach: Alabama 1994-97, Auburn 1997-98, Southeast Missouri State 1999-2001, Samford 2002-05. Pro coach: Joined Eagles in 2006.

Bill Shuey, linebackers; born October 5, 1974, Bethlehem, Pa. Attended Slippery Rock. No college or pro playing experience. Pro coach: Joined Eagles in 2003.

Otis Smith, assistant secondary; born October 22, 1965. Cornerback Missouri 1988-89. Pro cornerback Philadelphia Eagles 1991-94, New York Jets 1995, 1997-99, New England Patriots 1996, 2000-02, Detroit Lions 2003. Pro coach: Joined Eagles in 2008.

James Urban, quarterbacks; born December 1, 1973, Mechanicsburg, Pa. Wide receiver Washington and Lee 1993-96. No pro playing experience. College coach: Clarion 1997-98, Pennsylvania 1999-2004. Pro coach: Joined Eagles in 2007.

Ted Williams, running backs; born November 17, 1943, Lyons, Texas. Attended Cal Poly-Pomona. No college or pro playing experience. College coach: UCLA 1980-89, Washington State 1991-93, Arizona 1994. Pro coach: Joined Eagles in 1995.

Mike Wolf, strength and conditioning; born May 15, 1965, Allentown, Pa. Center Penn State 1983-87. No pro playing experience. College coach: Vanderbilt 1988-89, Lehigh 1990, Penn State 1991. Pro coach: Minnesota Vikings 1992-94, joined Eagles in 1995.

National Football Conference
West Division
Team Colors: New Century Gold, Millennium Blue, and White
One Rams Way
St. Louis, Missouri 63045
Telephone: (314) 982-7267

2009 SCHEDULE

PRESEASON

Aug. 14	at N.Y. Jets	7:00
Aug. 21	**Atlanta**	7:00
Aug. 27	at Cincinnati	7:35
Sep. 3	**Kansas City**	7:00

REGULAR SEASON

Sep. 13	at Seattle	1:15
Sep. 20	at Washington	1:00
Sep. 27	**Green Bay**	12:00
Oct. 4	at San Francisco	1:15
Oct. 11	**Minnesota**	12:00
Oct. 18	at Jacksonville	1:00
Oct. 25	**Indianapolis**	12:00
Nov. 1	at Detroit	1:00
Nov. 8	BYE	
Nov. 15	**New Orleans**	12:00
Nov. 22	**Arizona**	3:05
Nov. 29	**Seattle**	12:00
Dec. 6	at Chicago	12:00
Dec. 13	at Tennessee	12:00
Dec. 20	**Houston**	12:00
Dec. 27	at Arizona	2:05
Jan. 3	**San Francisco**	12:00

Stadium: Edward Jones Dome (opened in 1995) •**Capacity:** 66,000
901 N. Broadway
St. Louis, Missouri 63101
Playing Surface: FieldTurf
Training Camp: Russell Training Center
1 Rams Way
St. Louis, Missouri 63045

EDWARD JONES DOME

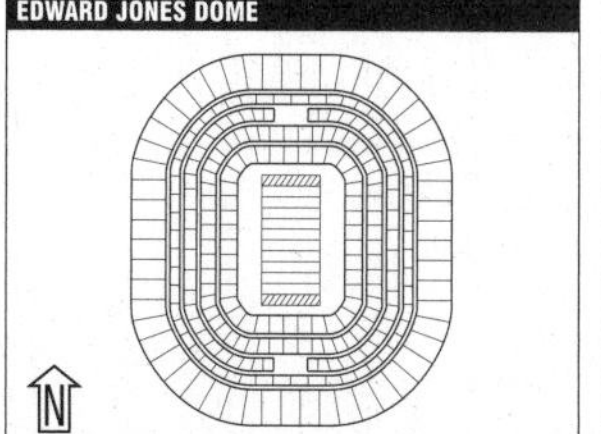

CLUB OFFICIALS

Owner/Chairman: Dale "Chip" Rosenbloom
Owner/Partner: Lucia Rodriguez
Owner/Vice Chairman: Stan Kroenke
General Manager: Billy Devaney
Executive Vice President Of Football Operations/Chief Operating Officer: Kevin Demoff
Director of Player Personnel: Lawrence McCutcheon
Treasurer: Jeff Brewer
Executive Vice President of Marketing and Sales: Bob Reif
Vice President of Finance: Michael T. Naughton
Vice President of Operations: John Oswald
Vice President of Ticketing: Mike O'Keefe
Senior Director of Communications: Ted Crews
Director of Media Relations: Artis Twyman
Director of Corporate Sales: Chad Watson
Director of Marketing: Adam Jacobs
Vice President of Corporate Communications and Civic Affairs: Molly Higgins
Director of Community Relations: Michael Yarbrough
Vice President of Player Personnel: Tony Softli
Director of Pro Personnel: Mike Williams
Head Trainer: Jim Anderson
Assistant Trainers: Dake Walden, James Lomax
Equipment Manager: Todd Hewitt
Assistant Equipment Manager: Jim Lake
Scouts: Ray Agnew, Drew Casani, Luke Driscoll, Brad Holmes, Steve Kazor, John Mancini, Joel Patten

COACHING HISTORY

Cleveland 1937-1945, Los Angeles 1946-1994 (522-492-20)

Records include postseason games

1937-38	Hugo Bezdek*	1-13-0
1938	Art Lewis	4-4-0
1939-1942	Earl (Dutch) Clark	16-26-2
1944	Aldo (Buff) Donelli	4-6-0
1945-46	Adam Walsh	16-5-1
1947	Bob Snyder	6-6-0
1948-49	Clark Shaughnessy	14-8-3
1950-52	Joe Stydahar**	19-9-0
1952-54	Hamp Pool	23-11-2
1955-59	Sid Gillman	28-32-1
1960-62	Bob Waterfield***	9-24-1
1962-65	Harland Svare	14-31-3
1966-1970	George Allen	49-19-4
1971-72	Tommy Prothro	14-12-2
1973-77	Chuck Knox	57-20-1
1978-1982	Ray Malavasi	43-36-0
1983-1991	John Robinson	79-74-0
1992-94	Chuck Knox	15-33-0
1995-96	Rich Brooks	13-19-0
1997-99	Dick Vermeil	25-26-0
2000-05	Mike Martz****	56-36-0
2005	Joe Vitt	4-7-0
2006-08	Scott Linehan#	11-25-0
2008	Jim Haslett	2-10-0

* Released after three games in 1938
** Resigned after one game in 1952
*** Resigned after eight games in 1962
**** Took medical leave after five games in 2005
# Released after four games in 2008

PAID ATTENDANCE

Home 466,242 Away 555,914
Total 1,022,156
Single-game home record, 66,273 (12/10/00)
Single-season home record, 520,926 (1999)

2009 DRAFT CHOICES

Round	Name	Pos.	College
1	Jason Smith	T	Baylor
2	James Laurinaitis	LB	Ohio State
3	Bradley Fletcher	DB	Iowa
4	Dorell Scott	DT	Clemson
5	Brooks Foster	WR	North Carolina
6	Keith Null	QB	West Texas A&M
7	Chris Ogbonnaya	RB	Texas

ST. LOUIS RAMS

2008 TEAM RECORD

PRESEASON (2-2)

Date	Result	Opponent
8/9	L 13-34	at Tennessee
8/16	W 7-6	San Diego
8/23	W 24-10	Baltimore
8/28	L 17-21	at Kansas City

REGULAR SEASON (2-14)

Date	Result	Opponent
9/7	L 3-38	at Philadelphia
9/14	L 13-41	New York Giants
9/21	L 13-37	at Seattle
9/28	L 14-31	Buffalo
10/12	W 19-17	at Washington
10/19	W 34-14	Dallas
10/26	L 16-23	at New England
11/2	L 13-34	Arizona
11/9	L 3-47	at New York Jets
11/16	L 16-35	at San Francisco
11/23	L 3-27	Chicago
11/30	L 12-16	Miami
12/7	L 10-34	at Arizona
12/14	L 20-23	Seattle
12/21	L 16-17	San Francisco
12/28	L 27-31	at Atlanta

SCORE BY PERIODS

Rams	61	82	35	54	0 —	232
Opponents	130	144	57	134	0 —	465

2008 TEAM STATISTICS

	Rams	Opp.
Total First Downs	249	320
Rushing	95	146
Passing	140	158
Penalty	14	16
3rd Down: Made/Att	69/216	74/187
3rd Down Pct.	31.9	39.6
4th Down: Made/Att	11/23	4/6
4th Down Pct.	47.8	66.7
Possession Avg.	29:32	30:28
Total Net Yards	4596	5950
Avg. Per Game	287.3	371.9
Total Plays	982	975
Avg. Per Play	4.7	6.1
Net Yards Rushing	1649	2475
Avg. Per Game	103.1	154.7
Total Rushes	417	501
Net Yards Passing	2947	3475
Avg. Per Game	184.2	217.2
Sacked/Yards Lost	45/321	30/201
Gross Yards	3268	3676
Att./Completions	520/292	444/278
Completion Pct.	56.2	62.6
Had Intercepted	19	12
Punts/Average	83/49.6	67/45.2
Net Punting Avg.	83/40.8	67/38.3
Penalties/Yards	97/718	89/654
Fumbles/Ball Lost	18/12	24/14
Touchdowns	20	53
Rushing	8	26
Passing	11	20
Returns	1	7

2008 INDIVIDUAL STATISTICS

PASSING	Att.	Comp.	Yds.	Pct.	TD	Int.	Tkld.	Rate
Bulger	440	251	2720	57.0	11	13	38/263	71.4
Green	72	38	525	52.8	0	6	6/58	41.7
Berlin	3	1	6	33.3	0	0	0/0	42.4
Looker	3	2	17	66.7	0	0	1/0	81.3
D. Hall	1	0	0	0.0	0	0	0/0	39.6
D. Jones	1	0	0	0.0	0	0	0/0	39.6
Rams	520	292	3268	56.2	11	19	45/321	66.9
Opponents	444	278	3676	62.6	20	12	30/201	92.5

SCORING	TD R	TD P	TD Rt	PAT	FG	Saf	PTS
J. Brown	0	0	0	19/19	31/36	0	112
Jackson	7	1	0	0/0	0/0	0	48
Avery	1	3	0	0/0	0/0	0	24
Holt	0	3	0	0/0	0/0	0	18
Looker	0	2	0	0/0	0/0	0	12
Atogwe	0	0	1	0/0	0/0	0	6
K. Burton	0	1	0	0/0	0/0	0	6
Stanley	0	1	0	0/0	0/0	0	6
Rams	8	11	1	19/19	31/36	0	232
Opponents	26	20	7	52/52	31/32	0	465

2-Pt. Conversions: None.
Rams 0-1, Opponents 1-1.

RUSHING	No.	Yds	Avg	LG	TD
Jackson	253	1042	4.1	56t	7
Pittman	79	296	3.7	24	0
Darby	32	140	4.4	14	0
Avery	10	69	6.9	37t	1
Bulger	14	41	2.9	16	0
Minor	13	29	2.2	13	0
D. Hall	4	9	2.3	10	0
K. Burton	3	8	2.7	5	0
Leonard	2	7	3.5	5	0
Gado	2	4	2.0	3	0
Green	3	4	1.3	3	0
Kreider	1	0	0.0	0	0
Stanley	1	0	0.0	0	0
Rams	417	1649	4.0	56t	8
Opponents	501	2475	4.9	70	26

RECEIVING	No.	Yds	Avg	LG	TD
Holt	64	796	12.4	45t	3
Avery	53	674	12.7	69t	3
Jackson	40	379	9.5	53	1
Looker	23	271	11.8	30	2
Darby	19	183	9.6	30	0
Pittman	18	132	7.3	27	0
K. Burton	13	172	13.2	30t	1
D. Hall	12	105	8.8	20	0
McMichael	11	139	12.6	31	0
Klopfenstein	11	123	11.2	29	0
Fells	7	81	11.6	26	0
Stanley	6	119	19.8	80t	1
Becht	6	39	6.5	11	0
Minor	5	35	7.0	16	0
Bulger	2	17	8.5	11	0
Bennett	1	4	4.0	4	0
Gado	1	-1	-1.0	-1	0
Rams	292	3268	11.2	80t	11
Opponents	278	3676	13.2	90t	20

INTERCEPTIONS	No.	Yds	Avg	LG	TD
Atogwe	5	91	18.2	43	0
Bartell	3	29	9.7	24	0
F. Brown	1	16	16.0	16	0
Craft	1	16	16.0	16	0
Wade	1	8	8.0	8	0
Witherspoon	1	2	2.0	2	0
Rams	12	162	13.5	43	0
Opponents	19	452	23.8	99t	4

PUNTING	No.	Yds.	Avg.	In 20	LG
D. Jones	82	4100	50	20	68
J. Brown	1	20	20	1	20
Rams	83	4120	49.6	21	68
Opponents	67	3029	45.2	22	62

PUNT RETURNS	Ret	FC	Yds	Avg	LG	TD
Stanley	11	4	101	9.2	33	0
D. Hall	9	1	93	10.3	34	0
Looker	9	5	51	5.7	14	0
Rams	29	10	245	8.4	34	0
Opponents	57	7	590	10.4	60	0

KICKOFF RETURNS	No.	Yds	Avg	LG	TD
D. Hall	37	763	20.6	41	0
Stanley	25	620	24.8	75	0
Darby	7	173	24.7	32	0
Minor	7	155	22.1	34	0
Avery	1	21	21.0	21	0
Greco	1	14	14.0	14	0
Wade	1	11	11.0	11	0
Looker	1	4	4.0	4	0
Rams	80	1761	22.0	75	0
Opponents	56	1469	26.2	92	0

FIELD GOALS	1-19	20-29	30-39	40-49	50+
J. Brown	0/0	8/8	7/7	10/13	6/8
Rams	0/0	8/8	7/7	10/13	6/8
Opponents	0/0	7/7	12/12	10/11	2/24

SACKS	No.
J. Hall	6.5
Little	6.0
Long	4.0
Craft	3.0
Tinoisamoa	3.0
Adeyanju	2.0
Bartell	1.0
F. Brown	1.0
Manning	1.0
Moore	1.0
Witherspoon	1.0
Glover	0.5
Rams	30.0
Opponents	45.0

RECORD HOLDERS

INDIVIDUAL RECORDS—CAREER

Category	Name	Performance
Rushing (Yds.)	Eric Dickerson, 1983-87	7,245
Passing (Yds.)	Jim Everett, 1986-1993	23,758
Passing (TDs)	Roman Gabriel, 1962-1972	154
Receiving (No.)	Isaac Bruce, 1994-2007	942
Receiving (Yds.)	Isaac Bruce, 1994-2007	14,109
Interceptions	Ed Meador, 1959-1970	46
Punting (Avg.)	Danny Villanueva, 1960-64	44.3
Punt Return (Avg.)	Az-Zahir Hakim, 1998-2001	11.4
Kickoff Return (Avg.)	Ron Brown, 1984-89, 1991	26.3
Field Goals	Jeff Wilkins, 1997-2007	265
Touchdowns (Tot.)	Marshall Faulk, 1999-2005	85
Points	Jeff Wilkins, 1997-2007	1,223
*Sacks	Leonard Little, 1998-2008	81.0

INDIVIDUAL RECORDS—SINGLE SEASON

Category	Name	Performance
Rushing (Yds.)	Eric Dickerson, 1984	**2,105
Passing (Yds.)	Kurt Warner, 2001	4,830
Passing (TDs)	Kurt Warner, 1999	41
Receiving (No.)	Isaac Bruce, 1995	119
Receiving (Yds.)	Isaac Bruce, 1995	1,781
Interceptions	Dick (Night Train) Lane, 1952	**14
Punting (Avg.)	Donnie Jones, 2008	50.0
Punt Return (Avg.)	Woodley Lewis, 1952	18.5
Kickoff Return (Avg.)	Verda (Vitamin T) Smith, 1950	33.7
Field Goals	Jeff Wilkins, 2003	39
Touchdowns (Tot.)	Marshall Faulk, 2000	26
Points	Jeff Wilkins, 2003	163
*Sacks	Kevin Carter, 1999	17.0

INDIVIDUAL RECORDS—SINGLE GAME

Category	Name	Performance
Rushing (Yds.)	Willie Ellison, 12-5-71	247
Passing (Yds.)	Norm Van Brocklin, 9-28-51	**554
Passing (TDs)	Many times	5
	Last time by Kurt Warner, 10-10-99	
Receiving (No.)	Tom Fears, 12-3-50	18
Receiving (Yds.)	Willie Anderson, 11-26-89	**336
Interceptions	Many times	3
	Last time by Keith Lyle, 12-15-96	
Field Goals	Bob Waterfield, 12-9-51	5
	Jeff Wilkins, 10-1-00	5
Touchdowns (Tot.)	Many times	4
	Last time by Marshall Faulk, 10-20-02	
Points	Many times	24
	Last time by Marshall Faulk, 10-20-02	
*Sacks	Gary Jeter, 9-18-88	5.0

**Sacks became an official statistic in 1982.*
***NFL Record*

ST. LOUIS RAMS

2009 VETERAN ROSTER

No.	Name	Pos.	Ht.	Wt.	Birthdate	NFL Exp.	College	Hometown	How Acq.	'08 Games/ Starts
94	Adeyanju, Victor	DE	6-4	280	2/11/83	4	Indiana	Chicago, Ill.	D4-'06	16/9
21	#Atogwe, Oshiomogho	S	5-11	210	6/23/81	5	Stanford	Windsor, Ontario, Canada	D3a-'05	16/16
17	Avery, Donnie	WR	5-11	184	6/12/84	2	Houston	Alief, Texas	D2-'08	15/12
47	Bajema, Billy	TE	6-4	256	10/31/82	5	Oklahoma State	Oklahoma City, Okla.	UFA(SF)-'09	16/11*
70	Barron, Alex	T	6-7	315	9/28/82	5	Florida State	Orangeburg, S.C.	D1-'05	16/15
24	Bartell, Ron	CB	6-1	205	2/22/82	5	Howard	Detroit, Mich.	D2-'05	16/16
41	Bassey, Eric	S	6-1	200	1/3/83	3	Oklahoma	Garland, Texas	FA-'07	10/0
63	Bell, Jacob	G	6-5	295	3/2/81	6	Miami (Ohio)	Cleveland, Ohio	UFA(Tenn)-'08	13/13
13	Berlin, Brock	QB	6-1	215	7/4/81	2	Miami	Shreveport, La.	FA-'07	1/0
12	Boller, Kyle	QB	6-3	220	6/17/81	7	California	Newhall, Calif.	UFA(Balt)-'09	0*
60	Brown, Jason	C	6-3	320	5/5/83	5	North Carolina	Henderson, N.C.	UFA(Balt)-'09	16/16*
3	Brown, Josh	K	6-0	212	4/29/79	7	Nebraska	Foyil, Okla.	UFA(Sea)-'08	16/0
10	Bulger, Marc	QB	6-3	212	4/5/77	9	West Virginia	Pittsburgh, Pa.	FA-'01	15/15
99	Burton, Antwon	DT	6-2	325	7/11/83	3	Temple	Cheektowaga, N.Y.	FA-'08	0*
14	Burton, Keenan	WR	6-0	202	10/29/84	2	Kentucky	Louisville, Ky.	D4b-'08	13/1
37	Butler, James	S	6-3	215	9/7/82	5	Georgia Tech	Bainbridge, Ga.	UFA(NYG)-'09	15/14*
36	Butler, Quincy	CB	6-1	190	11/25/81	2	Texas Christian	San Antonio, Texas	W(Dall)-'08	1/0
90	Carriker, Adam	DL	6-6	296	5/6/84	3	Nebraska	Kennewick, Wash.	D1-'07	15/9
15	Carter, Tim	WR	6-0	187	9/21/79	7	Auburn	St. Petersburg, Fla.	FA-'09	0*
57	Chamberlain, Chris	LB	6-1	230	9/30/85	2	Tulsa	Bethany, Okla.	D7a-'08	16/0
53	Culberson, Quinton	LB	6-1	236	10/21/85	3	Mississippi State	Jackson, Miss.	FA-'07	16/10
43	Dahl, Craig	S	6-1	211	6/17/85	3	North Dakota State	Madison Lake, Minn.	FA-'09	0*
34	Darby, Kenneth	RB	5-10	211	12/26/82	2	Alabama	Huntsville, Ala.	FA-'08	10/0
52	Draft, Chris	LB	5-11	232	2/26/76	11	Stanford	Placentia, Calif.	UFA(Car)-'07	12/9
46	Fells, Daniel	TE	6-4	252	9/23/83	3	California-Davis	Fullerton, Calif.	FA-'08	12/1
38	Gado, Samkon	RB	5-10	226	11/13/82	4	Liberty	Columbia, S.C.	FA-'08	1/0
71	Gibson, Gary	DT	6-3	285	5/5/82	4	Rutgers	Jamesville, N.Y.	FA-'09	11/0*
73	Goldberg, Adam	T	6-7	318	8/12/80	7	Wyoming	Edina, Minn.	T(Minn)-'06	16/6
79	Greco, John	T	6-4	315	3/24/85	2	Toledo	Youngstown, Ohio	D3-'08	9/1
96	Hall, James	DE	6-2	280	2/4/77	10	Michigan	New Orleans, La.	T(Det)-'07	16/
61	t-Harris, Orien	DT	6-3	300	6/3/83	2	Miami	Newark, Del.	T(Cin)-'09	14/1*
26	Hill, Tye	CB	5-10	185	6/3/82	4	Clemson	St. George, S.C.	D1-'06	4/4
68	Incognito, Richie	G	6-3	330	7/5/83	5	Nebraska	Glendale, Ariz.	D3b-'05	15/15
39	Jackson, Steven	RB	6-2	231	7/22/83	6	Oregon State	Las Vegas, Nev.	D1-'04	12/11
35	Johnson, Todd	S	6-1	200	12/18/78	7	Florida	Sarasota, Fla.	UFA(Chi)-'07	14/3
5	Jones, Donnie	P	6-2	222	7/5/80	6	Louisiana State	Baton Rouge, La.	RFA(Mia)-'07	16/0
44	Karney, Mike	FB	5-11	255	7/6/81	6	Arizona State	Kent, Wash.	FA-'09	12/8*
32	King, Justin	CB	5-11	188	5/11/87	2	Penn State	Pittsburgh, Pa.	D4a-'08	0*
88	Klopfenstein, Joe	TE	6-5	262	11/9/83	4	Colorado	Aurora, Colo.	D2-'06	16/10
91	Little, Leonard	DE	6-3	263	10/19/74	12	Tennessee	Asheville, N.C.	D3-'98	14/5
72	Long, Chris	DE	6-3	263	3/28/85	2	Virginia	Charlottesville, Va.	D1-'08	16/16
45	Massey, Chris	LS	6-0	245	8/21/79	8	Marshall	Chesapeake, W. Va.	D7-'02	16/0
84	McMichael, Randy	TE	6-3	255	6/28/79	8	Georgia	Fort Valley, Ga.	FA-'07	4/4
92	Moore, Eric	DE	6-4	268	2/28/81	5	Florida State	Pahokee, Fla.	FA-'06	7/0
25	Pittman, Antonio	RB	5-11	195	12/19/85	3	Ohio State	Akron, Ohio	W(NO)-'07	12/5
11	t-Robinson, Laurent	WR	6-2	194	5/20/85	3	Illinois State	Rockledge, Fla.	T(Atl)-'09	6/0*
95	Ryan, Clifton	DT	6-3	310	2/18/84	3	Michigan State	Saginaw, Mich.	D5B-'07	16/12
67	Schuening, Roy	G	6-3	315	4/8/84	2	Oregon State	Pendleton, Ore.	D5-'08	1/0
66	Setterstrom, Mark	G	6-4	314	3/3/84	4	Minnesota	Northfield, Minn.	D7b-'06	0*
19	Stanley, Derek	WR	5-11	179	8/27/85	2	Wisconsin-Whitewater	Verona, Wisc.	D7b-'07	10/0
58	Vobora, David	LB	6-1	238	4/8/86	2	Idaho	Eugene, Ore.	D7b-'08	8/1
20	Wade, Jonathan	CB	5-10	195	3/27/84	3	Tennessee	Shreveport, La.	D3-'07	16/1
51	Witherspoon, Will	LB	6-1	240	8/19/80	8	Georgia	Panama City, Fla.	UFA(Car)-'06	16/12

* Bajema played 16 games with San Francisco in '08; Boller missed '08 season because of injury with Baltimore; Ja. Brown played 16 games with Baltimore; J. Butler played 15 games with N.Y. Giants; Carter last active with Cleveland in '07; Dahl missed '08 season because of injury with N.Y. Giants; Gibson played 11 games with Carolina; Harris played 14 games with Cincinnati; Karney played 12 games with New Orleans; King missed '08 season because of injury; Robinson played 6 games with Atlanta; Setterstrom missed '08 season because of injury.

\# Unrestricted free agent; subject to developments.

t- Rams traded for Harris (Cin) and Robinson (Atl).

Traded—RB Brian Leonard (2 games in '08) to Cincinnati.

Players lost through free agency (3): T Brandon Gorin (Den; 0 games in '08), C Nick Leckey (NO; 10), C Brett Romberg (Atl; 14).

Also played with Rams in '08—TE Anthony Becht (16 games), WR Drew Bennett (1), S Corey Chavous (16), CB Jason Craft (13), NT La'Roi Glover (13), Larry Grant (2), QB Trent Green (3), WR Dante Hall (8), WR Torry Holt (16), WR Eddie Kennison (3), FB Dan Kreider (11), WR Dane Looker (13), CB Ricky Manning (5), RB Travis Minor (13), T Orlando Pace (14), DT Gary Stills (14), LB Pisa Tinoisamoa (16), C/G Cory Withrow (1).

2009 FIRST-YEAR ROSTER

Name	Pos.	Ht.	Wt.	Birthdate	College	Hometown	How Acq.
Ah You, C.J. (1)	DE	6-4	275	7/7/82	Oklahoma	Highland, Utah	FA-'07
Allen III, Roger	G	6-3	326	2/10/86	Missouri Western State	Raytown, Mo.	FA
Asiodu, K.C.	LB	6-2	225	11/24/86	Central Oklahoma	Chino Hills, Calif.	FA
Brown, Marcus	CB	6-2	200	4/2/86	McNeese State	Kentwood, La.	FA
Brown, Travis (1)	WR	6-3	202	7/26/86	New Mexico	West Covina, Calif.	FA-'08
Butler, Eric	TE	6-2	255	9/13/84	Mississippi State	Moss Point, Miss.	FA
Byers, Jarrett	WR	5-10	191	8/30/85	Northeastern State	Kansas City, Kan.	FA
Campbell, Ian	DL	6-4	263	5/15/85	Kansas State	Cimarron, Kan.	FA
Douglas, Dominic	LB	6-1	229	1/13/87	Mississippi State	Clinton, Miss.	FA
Feinga, Ray	G	6-4	337	5/8/86	Brigham Young	West Valley City, Utah	FA
Fletcher, Bradley	CB	6-0	196	6/25/86	Iowa	Youngstown, Ohio	D3
Foster, Brooks	WR	6-1	204	4/9/86	North Carolina	Boiling Springs, S.C.	D5
Gant, Horace	WR	6-3	218	4/7/85	St. Olaf	Pensacola, Fla.	FA
Grant, Larry (1)	LB	6-1	235	2/16/85	Ohio State	Sacramento, Calif.	FA-'08
Heerspink, Daren	T	6-6	315	4/2/84	Portland State	Bellingham, Wash.	FA
Johnson, Jerome	FB	6-0	258	1/19/85	Nevada	Los Angeles, Calif.	FA
Jones, Nate (1)	WR	6-2	195	12/30/85	Texas	Texarkana, Texas	FA-'08
Laurinaitis, James	LB	6-2	244	12/3/86	Ohio State	Plymouth, Minn.	D2
Lucas, Chad	WR	6-1	201	11/7/81	Alabama State	Auburn, Ala.	FA
Mattran, Tim	C	6-5	298	10/23/84	Stanford	Chanhassen, Minn.	FA
Newkirk, Mike	DL	6-3	264	8/12/86	Wisconsin	Ladysmith, Wis.	FA
Null, Keith	QB	6-4	220	9/24/85	West Texas A&M	Lampasas, Texas	D6
Ogbonnaya, Chris	RB	6-0	220	5/20/86	Texas	Houston, Texas	D7
Parks, Cordelius	CB	5-10	178	11/12/86	Northeastern	Stone Mountain, Ga.	FA
Pittman, Kirston	DL	6-3	250	1/18/85	Louisiana State	Garyville, La.	FA
Roach, David (1)	S	6-2	215	8/9/85	Texas Christian	Abilene, Texas	FA-'08
Rubin, Mark	S	6-3	223	10/24/85	Penn State	Amherst, N.Y.	FA
Sanders, Daniel	C	6-2	316	2/3/86	Colorado	Vista, Calif.	FA
Scott, Darell	DT	6-3	312	3/15/86	Clemson	Columbia, S.C.	D4
Smith, Jason	T	6-5	306	4/30/86	Baylor	Dallas, Texas	D1
Trautwein, Phillip	T	6-6	308	4/15/86	Florida	Voorhees, N.J.	FA
Williams, Willie (1)	DT	6-4	305	9/19/84	Louisville	Thomson, Ga.	FA-'08
Young, Eric	T	6-3	305	11/22/83	Tennessee	Union, S.C.	FA

The term NFL Rookie is defined as a player who is in his first season of professional football and has not been on the roster of another professional football team for any regular-season or postseason games. A Rookie is designated by an "R" on NFL rosters. Players who have been active in another professional football league or players who have NFL experience, including either preseason training camp or being on an Active List or Inactive List, or on Reserve/Injured or Reserve/Physically Unable to Perform for fewer than six regular-season games, are termed NFL First-Year Players. An NFL First-Year Player is designated by a "1" on NFL rosters. Thereafter, a player is credited with an additional year of experience for each season in which he accumulates six games on the Active List or Inactive List, or on Reserve/Injured or Reserve/Physically Unable to Perform.

Log on to www.stlouisrams.com for an up-to-date roster.

COACHING STAFF

Head Coach,

Steve Spagnuolo

Pro Career: Named the twenty-fifth head coach in franchise history on January 19, 2009. Spagnuolo was defensive coordinator of the New York Giants from 2007-08. In 2007, the Giants' defense ranked seventh in the NFL in yards allowed after ranking 25th in 2006. The Giants were in the NFL's top 10 in eight statistical categories and led the league with 53 quarterback sacks. The Giants beat the undefeated New England Patriots 17-14 in Super Bowl XLII. The Giants' defense held the Patriots to nearly 130 yards less than their season average. New England scored 14 points in the Super Bowl after averaging more than 36 points per game in the regular season. In 2008, Spagnuolo's defense improved from seventh to fifth in the NFL in total defense as the Giants won the NFC East. Spagnuolo spent eight seasons (1999-2006) with the Philadelphia Eagles, serving as defensive assistant/safeties from 1999-2000, defensive backs coach from 2001-03 and linebackers coach from 2004-06. From 1999-2005, the Eagles played in four NFC Championship games and one Super Bowl. Spagnuolo served as defensive line/special teams coach with the Barcelona Dragons of the WLAF in 1992 and was defensive coordinator/linebackers coach for NFL Europe's Frankfurt Galaxy in 1998. Spagnuolo worked as pro personnel intern with the Washington Redskins in 1983 and as a scout with the San Diego Chargers in 1993. Career record: 0-0.

Background: Wide receiver at Springfield (Mass.) College (1978-1981). Coached collegiately at Massachusetts (1982-83), Lafayette (1984-86), Connecticut (1987-1991), Maine (1993-94), Rutgers (1994-95), and Bowling Green (1996-97).

Personal: Born December 21, 1959 in Whitinsville, Mass. He is married to wife, Maria.

ASSISTANT COACHES

Charlie Baggett, wide receivers; born January 21, 1953, Fayetteville, N.C. Quarterback North Carolina 1971, Michigan State 1973-75. Pro Quarterback Hamilton Tiger-Cats (CFL) 1976. College coach: Bowling Green 1977-1980, Minnesota 1981-82, Michigan State 1983-1992, 1995-98, Washington 2007-08. Pro coach: Houston Oilers 1993-94, Green Bay Packers 1999, Minnesota Vikings 2000-04, Miami Dolphins 2005-06, joined Rams in 2009.

Sylvester Croom, running backs; born September 25, 1954, Tuscaloosa, Ala. Linebacker/tight end/center Alabama 1971-74. Pro center New Orleans Saints 1975. College coach: Alabama 1976-1986, Mississippi State 2004-08 (head coach). Pro coach: Tampa Bay Buccaneers 1987-1990, Indianapolis Colts 1991, San Diego Chargers 1992-96, Detroit Lions 1997-2000, Green Bay Packers 2001-03, joined Rams in 2009.

Richard Curl, asst. head coach/quarterbacks; born May 4, 1940, Chester, Pa. Quarterback Richmond 1958-1962. No pro playing experience. College coach: Trenton State 1973-74, Rutgers 1975-1980, 1983-89, Virginia 1981-82, Boston College 1990. Pro coach: Barcelona Dragons (NFLE) 1991-97, Frankfurt Galaxy (NFLE) 1998-2000, New York Jets 2003-05, Kansas City Chiefs 2006-08, joined Rams in 2009.

Andre Curtis, secondary/safeties; born December 8, 1976, Beaverdam, Va. Linebacker Virginia Military Institute 1996-99. No pro playing experience. College coach: Virginia Military Institute 2000-03, Georgia Southern 2004-05. Pro coach: New York Giants 2006-08, joined Rams in 2009.

Brendan Daly, defensive line; born September 10, 1975, Springfield, Ill. Tight End Drake 1993-96. No pro playing experience. College coach: Drake 1998, Villanova 1999, 2005, Maryland 2000, Oklahoma State 2001-2003, Illinois State 2004. Pro coach: Minnesota Vikings 2006-08, joined Rams in 2009.

Chuck Faucette, asst. strength; born October 7, 1963, Willingboro, N.J. Linebacker Maryland 1983-86. Pro linebacker San Diego Chargers 1987-89. College coach: Texas 1999-2001, 2007, Southern Methodist 2002-06. Pro coach: Hamilton TigerCats (CFL) 1990-92, joined Rams in 2008.

Paul Ferraro, linebackers; born April 30, 1959, Ridgewood, N.J. Safety Springfield College 1978-1981. No pro playing experience. College coach: Massachusetts 1982, Syracuse 1983, Villanova 1984-86, Dartmouth 1987, Catholic University 1988, Maine 1989, Ohio University 1990, Bowling Green 1991-98, Georgia Tech 1999-2000, Rutgers 2001-04. Pro coach: Carolina Panthers 2005, Minnesota Vikings 2006-08, joined Rams in 2009.

Ken Flajole, defensive coordinator; born October 4, 1954, Seattle. Linebacker Carroll College 1972, Wenatchee Valley Community College 1973, Pacific Lutheran 1974-75. No pro playing experience. College coach: Pacific Lutheran 1977-78, Washington 1979, Montana 1980-85, Texas-El Paso 1986-88, Missouri 1989-1993, Richmond 1994, Hawaii 1995, Nevada 1996-97. Pro coach: Green Bay Packers 1998, Seattle Seahawks 1999-2002, Carolina Panthers 2003-08, joined Rams in 2009.

Rock Gullickson, strength; born April 11, 1955, Moorhead, Minn. Guard Moorhead State 1973-76. No pro playing experience. College coach: Moorhead State 1978, Maryville State (N.D.) 1979-1980, South Dakota State 1981, Montana State 1982-89, Rutgers 1990-92, Texas 1993-97, Louisville 1998-99. Pro coach: New Orleans Saints 2000-05, Green Bay Packers 2006-08, joined Rams in 2009.

Matt House, defensive quality control; born May 17, 1978, Harrison, Mich. No pro playing experience. College coach: Michigan State 2001-02, North Carolina 2003-04, Gardner-Webb 2005, Buffalo 2006-07. Pro coach: Carolina Panthers 2008, joined Rams in 2009.

Frank Leonard, tight ends; born April 5, 1958, Wethersfield, Conn. Cornerback Central Connecticut State 1976, 1978-1980. No pro playing experience. College coach: Western Connecticut 1982-84, Central Connecticut State 1985-86, Western Connecticut 1987-89, Connecticut 1990-93, Richmond 1994-2003, Kansas State 2007-08. Pro coach: Joined Rams in 2009.

Steve Loney, offensive line; born April 26, 1952, Marshalltown, Iowa. Guard Iowa State 1971-72. No pro playing experience. College coach: Iowa State 1974, 1995-97, Missouri Western 1975-76, Morehead State 1979-1983, Citadel 1984-86, Colorado State 1989-1992, Connecticut 1994, Minnesota 1998-99, Iowa State 2000-01, Drake 2007. Pro coach: Arizona Cardinals 1993, Minnesota Vikings 2002-05, Arizona Cardinals 2006, joined Rams in 2008.

Clayton Lopez, secondary/cornerbacks; born May 26, 1970, Los Angeles. Defensive back Nevada 1991-94. No pro playing experience. College coach: Nevada 1995-98. Pro coach: Seattle Seahawks 1999-2003, Oakland Raiders 2004-05, Detroit Lions 2006-08, joined Rams in 2009.

Tom McMahon, special teams coordinator; born July 12, 1969, Helena, Mont. Corner Carroll College 1988-1992. No pro playing experience. College coach: Carroll College 1992, 1994, Utah State 1995-2005, Louisville 2006. Pro coach: Atlanta Falcons 2007-08, joined Rams in 2009.

Pat Shurmur, offensive coordinator; born April 14, 1965, Ann Arbor, Mich. Center/linebacker Michigan State 1983-87. No pro playing experience. College coach: Michigan State 1988-1997, Stanford 1998. Pro coach: Philadelphia Eagles 1999-2008, joined Rams in 2009.

Andy Sugarman, quality control/offense; born May 23, 1972, Lafayette, Calif. No college or pro playing experience. College coach: California-Berkeley 1991-97. Pro coach: San Francisco 49ers 1998-2002, Detroit Lions 2003-05, Atlanta Falcons 2007, joined Rams in 2009.

Derius Swinton, quality control special teams; born April 26, 1985, Newport News, Va. Safety Hampton 2003-06. No pro playing experience. College coach: Tennessee 2007-08. Pro coach: Joined Rams in 2009.

Art Valero, asst. offensive line; born May 12, 1958, La Mirada, Calif. Guard Boise State 1979-1980. No pro playing experience. College coach: Boise State 1981-82, Iowa State 1983, Long Beach State 1984-86, New Mexico 1987-89, Idaho 1990-94, Utah State 1995-97, Louisville 1998-2001. Pro coach: Tampa Bay Buccaneers 2002-2007, joined Rams in 2008.

National Football Conference
West Division
Team Colors: 49ers Gold, 49ers Red, and Beige
4949 Centennial Boulevard
Santa Clara, California 95054
Telephone: (408) 562-4949

2009 SCHEDULE

PRESEASON

Aug. 14	**Denver**	7:00
Aug. 22	**Oakland**	5:15
Aug. 29	at Dallas	7:00
Sep. 4	at San Diego	7:00

REGULAR SEASON

Sep. 13	at Arizona	1:15
Sep. 20	**Seattle**	1:05
Sep. 27	at Minnesota	12:00
Oct. 4	**St. Louis**	1:15
Oct. 11	**Atlanta**	1:05
Oct. 18	BYE	
Oct. 25	at Houston	12:00
Nov. 1	at Indianapolis	1:00
Nov. 8	**Tennessee**	1:15
Nov. 12	**Chicago** (Thu.)	5:20
Nov. 22	at Green Bay	12:00
Nov. 29	**Jacksonville**	1:05
Dec. 6	at Seattle	1:15
Dec. 14	**Arizona** (Mon.)	5:30
Dec. 20	at Philadelphia	1:00
Dec. 27	**Detroit**	1:05
Jan. 3	at St. Louis	12:00

Stadium: Candlestick Park (opened in 1960) •**Capacity:** 69,732 San Francisco, California 94124
Playing Surface: Natural Grass
Training Camp: Marie P. DeBartolo Sports Center 4949 Centennial Boulevard Santa Clara, CA 95054

CANDLESTICK PARK

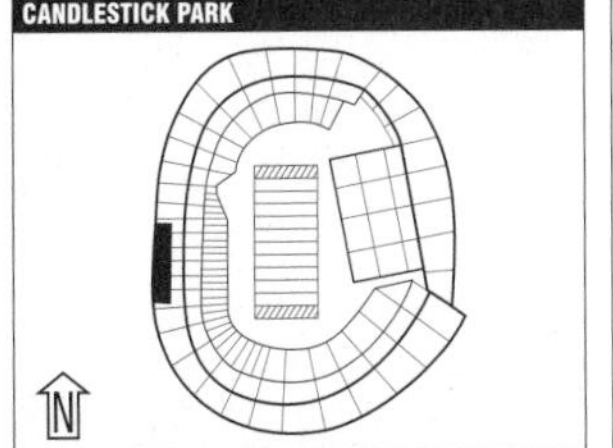

CLUB OFFICIALS

OWNERSHIP

Co-Chairman/Owner: Denise DeBartolo York
Co-Chairman/Owner: John York
Team President/Owner: Jed York
Limited Partner: Franklin Mieuli
Limited Partner: Rick and Carla Morabito

MANAGEMENT

General Manager: Scot McCloughan
Chief Operating Officer: Andy Dolich
Executive Vice President of Football Operations: Lal Heneghan
Vice President of Football Operations: Paraag Marathe
Director of Player Personnel: Trent Baalke
Director of Pro Personnel: Tom Gamble
Director of College Scouting: David McCloughan
Vice President of Football Affairs: Keena Turner
Vice President/CFO: Larry MacNeil
Vice President of Marketing: Michael P. Williams
Vice President of Stadium Operations & Security: Jim Mercurio
Vice President Communications: Lisa Lang
Senior Manager of Ticket Office: Lynn Carrozzi
Director of Security: Fred Formosa
Director of Information Technology: Alexander Ignacio
Director of Football Public Relations: Bob Lange
Director of Player Development: Guy McIntrye
Director of Business Partnerships: Patrick Streko
Director of Ticket Sales: Jamie Brandt
Senior Human Resources Director: Tina De Vora Rojas
Executive Director of 49ers Foundation: Reginald Duhe
Director of Communications: Steve Fine
Director of Video Operations: Keith Yanagi
Controller: Debye Whelchel
Head Athletic Trainer: Jeff Ferguson
Equipment Manager: Steve Urbaniak

COACHING HISTORY

(475-396-13)

Records include postseason games

1950-54	Lawrence (Buck) Shaw	33-25-2
1955	Norman (Red) Strader	4-8-0
1956-58	Frankie Albert	19-17-1
1959-1963	Howard (Red) Hickey*	27-27-1
1963-67	Jack Christiansen	26-38-3
1968-1975	Dick Nolan	56-56-5
1976	Monte Clark	8-6-0
1977	Ken Meyer	5-9-0
1978	Pete McCulley**	1-8-0
1978	Fred O'Connor	1-6-0
1979-1988	Bill Walsh	102-63-1
1989-1996	George Seifert	108-35-0
1997-2002	Steve Mariucci	60-43-0
2003-04	Dennis Erickson	9-23-0
2005-08	Mike Nolan***	18-37-0
2008	Mike Singletary	5-4-0

* Resigned after three games in 1963
** Released after nine games in 1978
*** Released after seven games in 2008

PAID ATTENDANCE

Home 497,443 Away 525,061
Total 1,022,504
Single-game home record, 69,014 (11/13/94)
Single-season home record, 544,228 (1999)

2009 DRAFT CHOICES

Round	Name	Pos.	College
1	Michael Crabtree	WR	Texas Tech
3	Glen Coffee	RB	Alabama
5	Scott McKillop	LB	Pittsburgh
	Nate Davis	QB	Ball State
6	Bear Pascoe	TE	Fresno State
7	Curtis Taylor	DB	Louisiana State
	Ricky Jean Francois	DE	Louisiana State

SAN FRANCISCO 49ERS

2008 TEAM RECORD

PRESEASON (1-3)

Date	Result	Opponent
8/8	L 6-18	at Oakland
8/16	W 34-6	Green Bay
8/21	W 37-30	at Chicago
8/29	L 17-20	San Diego

REGULAR SEASON (7-9)

Date	Result	Opponent
9/7	L 13-23	Arizona
9/14	W 33-30	at Seattle (OT)
9/21	W 31-13	Detroit
9/28	L 17-31	at New Orleans
10/5	L 21-30	New England
10/12	L 26-40	Philadelphia
10/19	L 17-29	at New York Giants
10/26	L 13-34	Seattle
11/10	L 24-29	at Arizona
11/16	W 35-16	St. Louis
11/23	L 22-35	at Dallas
11/30	W 10-3	at Buffalo
12/7	W 24-14	New York Jets
12/14	L 9-14	at Miami
12/21	W 17-16	at St. Louis
12/28	W 27-24	Washington

(OT) Overtime

SCORE BY PERIODS

49ers	90	102	53	91	3	— 339
Opponents	54	160	64	103	0	— 381

2008 TEAM STATISTICS

	49ers	Opp.
Total First Downs	287	293
Rushing	83	104
Passing	176	170
Penalty	28	19
3rd Down: Made/Att	75/198	83/219
3rd Down Pct.	37.9	37.9
4th Down: Made/Att	5/11	12/19
4th Down Pct.	45.5	63.2
Possession Avg.	29:22	30:38
Total Net Yards	4978	5216
Avg. Per Game	311.1	326.0
Total Plays	961	1027
Avg. Per Play	5.2	5.1
Net Yards Rushing	1599	1709
Avg. Per Game	99.9	106.8
Total Rushes	397	452
Net Yards Passing	3379	3507
Avg. Per Game	211.2	219.2
Sacked/Yards Lost	55/345	30/161
Gross Yards	3724	3668
Att./Completions	509/309	545/331
Completion Pct.	60.7	60.7
Had Intercepted	19	12
Punts/Average	67/47.1	72/42.4
Net Punting Avg.	67/39.0	72/35.8
Penalties/Yards	98/732	111/869
Fumbles/Ball Lost	36/16	16/6
Touchdowns	36	39
Rushing	10	14
Passing	21	22
Returns	5	3

2008 INDIVIDUAL STATISTICS

PASSING	Att.	Comp.	Yds.	Pct.	TD	Int.	Tkld.	Rate
S. Hill	288	181	2046	62.8	13	8	23/148	87.5
O'Sullivan	220	128	1678	58.2	8	11	32/197	73.6
Bruce	1	0	0	0.0	0	0	0/0	39.6
49ers	509	309	3724	60.7	21	19	55/345	81.4
Opponents	545	331	3668	60.7	22	12	30/161	85.0

SCORING	TD R	TD P	TD Rt	PAT	FG	Saf	PTS
Nedney	0	0	0	34/34	29/33	0	121
Gore	6	2	0	0/0	0/0	0	50
Bruce	0	7	0	0/0	0/0	0	42
Johnson	0	3	0	0/0	0/0	0	18
Morgan	0	3	0	0/0	0/0	0	18
Davis	0	2	0	0/0	0/0	0	12
Foster	1	1	0	0/0	0/0	0	12
J. Hill	0	2	0	0/0	0/0	0	12
S. Hill	2	0	0	0/0	0/0	0	12
Rossum	1	0	1	0/0	0/0	0	12
Clements	0	0	1	0/0	0/0	0	6
Staley	0	0	1	0/0	0/0	0	6
Strickland	0	0	1	0/0	0/0	0	6
Walker	0	1	0	0/0	0/0	0	6
Willis	0	0	1	0/0	0/0	0	6
49ers	10	21	5	34/34	29/33	0	339
Opponents	14	22	3	38/38	35/42	2	381

2-Pt. Conversions: Gore.
49ers 1-2, Opponents 0-1.

RUSHING	No.	Yds	Avg	LG	TD
Gore	240	1036	4.3	41t	6
Foster	76	234	3.1	18	1
O'Sullivan	30	145	4.8	18	0
S. Hill	24	115	4.8	24	2
Robinson	19	50	2.6	10	0
Battle	1	18	18.0	18	0
Davis	1	11	11.0	11	0
J. Hill	2	5	2.5	9	0
Rossum	1	1	1.0	1t	1
Bruce	1	-3	-3.0	-3	0
Walker	2	-13	-6.5	-3	0
49ers	397	1599	4.0	41t	10
Opponents	452	1709	3.8	50	14

RECEIVING	No.	Yds	Avg	LG	TD
Bruce	61	835	13.7	63	7
Johnson	45	546	12.1	42	3
Gore	43	373	8.7	26	2
Davis	31	358	11.5	57	2
J. Hill	30	317	10.6	33	2
Battle	24	318	13.3	36	0
Morgan	20	319	16.0	48t	3
Robinson	17	202	11.9	36	0
Foster	16	133	8.3	31	1
Walker	10	155	15.5	53	1
Zeigler	5	97	19.4	31	0
Keasey	3	25	8.3	12	0
Bajema	2	34	17.0	29	0
Ryan	1	8	8.0	8	0
Rossum	1	4	4.0	4	0
49ers	309	3724	12.1	63	21
Opponents	331	3668	11.1	81	22

INTERCEPTIONS	No.	Yds	Avg	LG	TD
Harris	3	25	8.3	24	0
Spikes	3	14	4.7	13	0
Clements	2	13	6.5	13	0
Brown	2	1	0.5	1	0
Willis	1	86	86.0	86t	1
J. Smith	1	0	0.0	0	0
49ers	12	139	11.6	86t	1
Opponents	19	358	18.8	75t	2

PUNTING	No.	Yds.	Avg.	In 20	LG
Lee	66	3155	47.8	13	82
49ers	67	3155	47.1	13	82
Opponents	72	3054	42.4	23	70

PUNT RETURNS	Ret	FC	Yds	Avg	LG	TD
Rossum	15	7	223	14.9	45	0
Battle	6	2	29	4.8	19	0
Clements	6	0	46	7.7	16	0
Zeigler	2	3	0	0.0	0	0
49ers	29	12	298	10.3	45	0
Opponents	39	11	364	9.3	30	0

KICKOFF RETURNS	No.	Yds	Avg	LG	TD
Rossum	47	1259	26.8	104t	1
Walker	13	257	19.8	35	0
Robinson	6	135	22.5	34	0
Balmer	5	47	9.4	14	0
Bajema	2	27	13.5	14	0
Ryan	1	14	14.0	14	0
Battle	1	28	28.0	28	0
Spikes	1	0	0.0	0	0
49ers	76	1767	23.3	104t	1
Opponents	65	1515	23.3	63	0

FIELD GOALS	1-19	20-29	30-39	40-49	50+
Nedney	0/0	9/9	10/10	8/11	2/3
49ers	0/0	9/9	10/10	8/11	2/3
Opponents	1/1	9/10	9/11	14/17	2/3

SACKS	No.
Haralson	8.0
J. Smith	7.0
Green	3.5
Lawson	3.0
M. Lewis	2.0
Franklin	1.0
Harris	1.0
McDonald	1.0
Sopoaga	1.0
Spikes	1.0
Willis	1.0
Banta-Cain	0.5
49ers	30.0
Opponents	55.0

RECORD HOLDERS

INDIVIDUAL RECORDS—CAREER

Category	Name	Performance
Rushing (Yds.)	Joe Perry, 1950-1960, 1963	7,344
Passing (Yds.)	Joe Montana, 1979-1992	35,124
Passing (TDs)	Joe Montana, 1979-1992	244
Receiving (No.)	Jerry Rice, 1985-2000	1,281
Receiving (Yds.)	Jerry Rice, 1985-2000	19,247
Interceptions	Ronnie Lott, 1981-1990	51
Punting (Avg.)	Tommy Davis, 1959-1969	44.7
Punt Return (Avg.)	Dana McLemore, 1982-87	10.8
Kickoff Return (Avg.)	Abe Woodson, 1958-1964	29.4
Field Goals	Ray Wersching, 1977-1987	190
Touchdowns (Tot.)	Jerry Rice, 1985-2000	187
Points	Jerry Rice, 1985-2000	1,130
*Sacks	Bryant Young, 1994-2007	89.5

INDIVIDUAL RECORDS—SINGLE SEASON

Category	Name	Performance
Rushing (Yds.)	Frank Gore, 2006	1,695
Passing (Yds.)	Jeff Garcia, 2000	4,278
Passing (TDs)	Steve Young, 1998	36
Receiving (No.)	Jerry Rice, 1995	122
Receiving (Yds.)	Jerry Rice, 1995	**1,848
Interceptions	Dave Baker, 1960	10
	Ronnie Lott, 1986	10
Punting (Avg.)	Andy Lee, 2007	47.8
Punt Return (Avg.)	Dana McLemore, 1982	22.3
Kickoff Return (Avg.)	Joe Arenas, 1953	34.4
Field Goals	Jeff Wilkins, 1996	30
Touchdowns (Tot.)	Jerry Rice, 1987	23
Points	Jerry Rice, 1987	138
*Sacks	Fred Dean, 1983	17.5

INDIVIDUAL RECORDS—SINGLE GAME

Category	Name	Performance
Rushing (Yds.)	Frank Gore, 11-19-06	212
Passing (Yds.)	Joe Montana, 10-14-90	476
Passing (TDs)	Joe Montana, 10-14-90	6
Receiving (No.)	Terrell Owens, 12-17-00	**20
Receiving (Yds.)	Jerry Rice, 12-18-95	289
Interceptions	Dave Baker, 12-4-60	**4
Field Goals	Ray Wersching, 10-16-83	6
	Jeff Wilkins, 9-29-96	6
Touchdowns (Tot.)	Jerry Rice, 10-14-90	5
Points	Jerry Rice, 10-14-90	30
*Sacks	Fred Dean, 11-13-83	6.0

**Sacks became an official statistic in 1982.*
***NFL Record*

SAN FRANCISCO 49ERS

2009 VETERAN ROSTER

No.	Name	Pos.	Ht.	Wt.	Birthdate	NFL Exp.	College	Hometown	How Acq.	'08 Games/ Starts
64	Baas, David	G	6-4	330	9/28/81	5	Michigan	Sarasota, Fla.	D2-'05	16/9
96	Balmer, Kentwan	DE	6-5	315	10/15/86	2	North Carolina	Weldon, N.C.	D1-'08	16/0
83	Battle, Arnaz	WR	6-1	208	2/22/80	7	Notre Dame	Shreveport, La.	D6-'03	9/0
77	Bender, Jacob	T	6-6	315	4/25/85	2	Nicholls State	Mayo, Md.	FA-'08	0*
55	Brooks, Ahmad	LB	6-3	259	3/14/84	4	Virginia	Fairfax, Va.	W(Cin)-'08	0*
25	Brown, Tarell	CB	5-10	193	1/6/85	3	Texas	Mesquite, Texas	D5-'07	15/1
88	Bruce, Isaac	WR	6-0	188	11/10/72	16	Memphis	Fort Lauderdale, Fla.	FA-'08	16/15
22	Clements, Nate	CB	6-0	205	12/12/79	9	Ohio State	Shaker Heights, Ohio	UFA(Buff)-'07	15/15
85	Davis, Vernon	TE	6-3	250	1/31/84	4	Maryland	Washington, D.C.	D1a-'06	16/16
93	Evans, Demetric	DE	6-4	275	9/3/79	8	Georgia	Haynesville, La.	UFA(Wash)-'09	16/11*
92	Franklin, Aubrayo	DT	6-1	317	8/27/80	7	Tennessee	Johnson City, Tenn.	UFA(Balt)-'07	16/15
38	Goldson, Dashon	S	6-2	200	9/18/84	3	Washington	Carson, Calif.	D4b-'07	9/2
21	Gore, Frank	RB	5-9	217	5/14/83	5	Miami	Coral Gables, Fla.	D3a-'05	14/13
98	Haralson, Parys	LB	6-0	255	1/24/84	4	Tennessee	Flora, Miss.	D5a-'06	161/0
54	Harris, Marques	LB	6-1	235	9/20/81	5	Southern Utah	Salt Lake City, Utah	UFA(SD)-'09	15/3*
27	Harris, Walt	CB	5-11	196	8/10/74	14	Mississippi State	LaGrange, Ga.	FA-'06	16/16
66	Heitmann, Eric	C	6-3	312	2/24/80	8	Stanford	Katy, Texas	D7a-'02	16/16
89	Hill, Jason	WR	6-0	202	2/20/85	3	Washington State	San Francisco, Calif.	D3a-'07	16/2
13	Hill, Shaun	QB	6-3	220	1/9/80	8	Maryland	Parsons, Kan.	FA-'06	9/8
14	Huard, Damon	QB	6-3	218	7/9/73	13	Washington	Yakima, Wash.	FA-'09	5/3*
23	Hudson, Marcus	CB	6-2	200	11/15/82	4	North Carolina State	Miami, Fla.	D6b-'06	9/0
86	Jennings, Brian	TE/LS	6-5	242	10/14/76	10	Arizona State	Mesa, Ariz.	D7b-'00	16/0
81	Jones, Brandon	WR	6-1	212	10/6/82	5	Oklahoma	Texarkana, Texas	UFA(Tenn)-'09	16/7*
45	Keasey, Zak	FB	6-0	235	3/19/82	3	Princeton	Lake Orion, Mich.	FA-'07	6/3
99	Lawson, Manny	LB	6-5	240	7/3/84	4	North Carolina State	Goldsboro, N.C.	D1b-'06	14/10
4	Lee, Andy	P	6-0	178	8/11/82	6	Pittsburgh	Westminster, S.C.	D6a-'04	16/0
32	Lewis, Michael	S	6-1	222	4/29/80	8	Colorado	Houston, Texas	UFA(Phil)-'07	16/16
91	McDonald, Ray	DE	6-3	290	9/2/84	3	Florida	Belle Glade, Fla.	D3b-'07	15/9
58	Moore, Jay	LB	6-4	256	8/16/83	3	Nebraska	Elkhorn, Neb.	D4a-'07	0*
84	Morgan, Josh	WR	6-0	219	6/20/85	2	Virginia Tech	Washington, D.C.	D6-'08	12/1
6	Nedney, Joe	K	6-5	234	3/22/73	14	San Jose State	San Jose, Calif.	FA-'05	16/0
44	Norris, Moran	FB	6-1	250	6/16/78	9	Kansas	Houston, Texas	UFA(Det)-'06	11/8*
62	Rachal, Chilo	T/G	6-4	315	3/15/86	2	Southern California	Compton, Calif.	D2-'08	8/6
24	Robinson, Michael	RB	6-1	223	2/6/83	4	Penn State	Richmond, Va.	D4-'06	16/1
26	Roman, Mark	S	5-11	205	3/26/77	10	Louisiana State	Lafayette, La.	FA-'06	16/16
20	Rossum, Allen	KR/PR	5-8	178	10/22/75	12	Notre Dame	Dallas, Texas	FA-'08	13/1
65	Sims, Barry	T	6-5	300	12/1/74	11	Utah	Park City, Utah	FA-'08	14/8
11	Smith, Alex	QB	6-4	217	5/7/84	5	Utah	San Diego, Calif.	D1-'05	0*
94	Smith, Justin	DE	6-4	285	9/30/79	9	Missouri	Jefferson City, Mo.	UFA(Cin)-'08	16/16
71	Smith, Marvel	T	6-5	321	8/6/78	10	Arizona State	Oakland, Calif.	UFA(Pitt)-'09	5/5*
31	Smith, Reggie	CB	6-1	200	9/3/86	2	Oklahoma	Edmond, Okla.	D3-'08	3/0
68	Snyder, Adam	T/G	6-6	325	1/30/82	5	Oregon	Fullerton, Calif.	D3b-'05	14/13
90	Sopoaga, Isaac	DE/DT	6-2	330	9/4/81	6	Hawaii	Pago Pago, American Samoa	D4a-'04	16/15
36	Spencer, Shawntae	CB	6-1	190	2/22/82	6	Pittsburgh	Rankin, Pa.	D2b-'04	2/0
51	Spikes, Takeo	LB	6-2	242	12/17/76	12	Auburn	Sandersville, Ga.	FA-'08	16/13
18	Spurlock, Micheal	WR	5-11	200	1/31/83	2	Mississippi	Indianola, Miss.	FA-'09	0*
74	Staley, Joe	T	6-5	315	8/30/84	3	Central Michigan	Rockford, Mich.	D1b-'07	16/16
61	Toledo, Joe	T	6-5	330	10/20/82	3	Washington	Omaha, Neb.	FA-'09	0*
53	Ulbrich, Jeff	LB	6-0	240	2/17/77	10	Hawaii	San Jose, Calif.	D3b-'00	16/3
46	Walker, Delanie	TE	6-0	242	8/12/84	4	Central Missouri	Pomona, Calif.	D6a-'06	15/2
59	Wallace, Cody	C	6-4	300	11/26/84	2	Texas A&M	Cuero, Texas	D4-'08	0*
41	Williams, Jimmy	CB	6-3	220	3/8/84	3	Virginia Tech	Hampton, Va.	FA-'09	0*
52	Willis, Patrick	LB	6-1	240	1/25/85	3	Mississippi	Bruceton, Tenn.	D1a-'07	16/16
69	Wragge, Tony	G	6-4	310	8/14/79	5	New Mexico State	Creighton, Neb.	FA-'05	16/10
17	Zeigler, Dominique	WR	6-3	185	10/11/84	2	Baylor	Kalamazoo, Mich.	FA-'07	8/0

* Bender inactive five games; Brooks inactive 14 games; Evans played 16 games with Washington in '08; M. Harris played 15 games with San Diego; Huard played 5 games with Kansas City; Jones played 16 games with Tennessee; Moore missed '08 season because of injury; Norris played 11 games with Detroit; A. Smith missed '08 season because of injury; M. Smith played 5 games with Pittsburgh; Spurlock last active with Tampa Bay '07; Toledo last active with Miami '07; Wallace inactive 16 games; Williams last active with Atlanta '07.

Players lost through free agency (7): TE Billy Bajema (StL; 16 games in '08), DT Damane Duckett (0; NE), DT Ronald Fields (Den; 16), WR Bryant Johnson (Det; 16), QB J.T. O'Sullivan (Cin; 9), TE Sean Ryan (KC; 6), CB Donald Strickland (NYJ; 14).

Also played with 49ers in '08—LB Tully Banta-Cain (12 games), RB DeShaun Foster (16), LB Roderick Green (13), T Jonas Jennings (2), FB David Kirtman (1), S Keith Lewis (16).

2009 FIRST-YEAR ROSTER

Name	Pos.	Ht.	Wt.	Birthdate	College	Hometown	How Acq.
Baker, Lewis (1)	S	6-2	202	10/12/84	Oklahoma	Bremerhaven, Germany	FA
Boone, Alex	T	6-7	328	5/4/87	Ohio State	Lakewood, Ohio	FA
Bradford, Mark (1)	WR	6-2	205	10/7/84	Stanford	Los Angeles, Calif.	FA
Briggs, Diyral	LB	6-4	230	10/31/85	Bowling Green	Mt. Healthy, Ohio	FA
Clayton, Thomas (1)	RB	5-11	222	4/26/84	Kansas State	Alexandria, Va.	D6-'07
Coffee, Glen	RB	6-0	209	5/1/87	Alabama	Fort Walton Beach, Fla.	D3
Collins, Dobson	WR	6-2	178	7/12/87	Gardner-Webb	Stone Mountain, Ga.	FA
Crabtree, Michael	WR	6-1	214	9/14/87	Texas Tech	Dallas, Texas	D1
Davis, Nate	QB	6-1	226	5/5/87	Ball State	Bellaire, Ohio	D5b
Egboh, Pannel	DE	6-6	276	3/23/86	Stanford	Mesquite, Texas	FA
Finley, J.J. (1)	TE	6-6	251	1/30/85	Oklahoma	Arlington, Texas	FA
Howard, Kyle	T	6-7	312	5/13/86	Wyoming	Colorado Springs, Colo.	FA
Huners, Matthew	G	6-3	290	10/15/85	South Florida	Dunedin, Fla.	FA
Jean-Francois, Ricky	DT	6-3	295	11/23/86	Louisiana State	Miami, Fla.	D7b
Lambert, Terrail	CB	5-11	195	12/1/85	Notre Dame	Los Angeles, Calif.	FA
Long, Brandon	LB	6-3	254	9/6/86	Michigan State	Canton, Ohio	FA
McKillop, Scott	LB	6-1	244	3/4/86	Pittsburgh	Export, Pa.	D5a
Mitchell, Khalif	DT	6-5	318	4/7/85	East Carolina	Virginia Beach, Va.	FA
Pascoe, Bear	TE	6-5	251	2/23/86	Fresno State	Porterville, Calif.	D6
Price, Maurice (1)	WR	6-1	200	9/11/85	Charleston Southern	Orlando, Fla.	FA
Roland, Justin (1)	LB	5-11	242	1/14/86	Kansas State	Ponca City, Okla.	FA
Sheets, Kory	RB	5-11	208	3/31/85	Purdue	Manchester, Conn.	FA
Taylor, Curtis	S	6-2	209	7/13/85	Louisiana State	Bogalusa, La.	D7a
Thomas, Carlos	CB	5-11	197	5/1/87	South Carolina	College Park, Ga.	FA
Washington, Mark (1)	LB	6-3	245	8/20/85	Texas State-San Marcos	Harbor City, Calif.	FA
Word-Daniels, Jahi	CB	6-0	194	11/19/86	Georgia Tech	Hoover, Ala.	FA

The term NFL Rookie is defined as a player who is in his first season of professional football and has not been on the roster of another professional football team for any regular-season or postseason games. A Rookie is designated by an "R" on NFL rosters. Players who have been active in another professional football league or players who have NFL experience, including either preseason training camp or being on an Active List or Inactive List, or on Reserve/Injured or Reserve/Physically Unable to Perform for fewer than six regular-season games, are termed NFL First-Year Players. An NFL First-Year Player is designated by a "1" on NFL rosters. Thereafter, a player is credited with an additional year of experience for each season in which he accumulates six games on the Active List or Inactive List, or on Reserve/Injured or Reserve/Physically Unable to Perform.

Log on to www.sf49ers.com for an up-to-date roster.

SAN FRANCISCO 49ERS

COACHING STAFF
Head Coach,
Mike Singletary

Pro Career: Named the sixteenth head coach in 49ers history on October 20, 2008, Mike Singletary enters his second season at the helm of the San Francisco 49ers. Singletary is in his seventh season as an NFL coach after a 12-year Pro Football Hall of Fame playing career with the Chicago Bears. Prior to being named head coach of the 49ers, Singletary served as the assistant head coach/defense for San Francisco from 2006 to 2008 after spending one year as the assistant head coach/linebackers in 2005 under head coach Mike Nolan. Under Singletary's direction, LB Patrick Willis was named Defensive Rookie of the Year to go along with All-Pro and Pro Bowl honors. Singletary joined the 49ers after serving as the inside linebackers coach for the Baltimore Ravens from 2003 to 2004 under head coach Brian Billick. Inducted into the Hall of Fame in 1998, Singletary played linebacker for 12 seasons as a member of the Chicago Bears (1981-1992) after being drafted in the second round of the 1981 NFL Draft out of Baylor. The former Bears captain played in a team-record 10 consecutive Pro Bowls and was also named All-Pro eight times. Career record: 5-4.

Background: Singletary earned All-America honors as both a junior and senior at Baylor, where he totaled 662 career tackles. He was the only junior selected to the All-Southwest Conference Team of the 1970s. Singletary is a graduate of Evan E. Worthing (Tex.) High School in Houston.

Personal: Born October 9, 1958, Houston. He and wife Kim have seven children.

ASSISTANT COACHES

Duane Carlisle, strength and conditioning; born Nov. 13, 1965, Haverhill, Mass. Attended Maryland. No college or pro playing experience. Pro coach: Speed development consultant for Philadelphia Eagles 2000-04, joined 49ers in 2005.

Shane Day, quality control; born September 27, 1974, Manhattan, Kan. Attended Kansas State. Wide receiver Rhodes College 1995-96. No pro playing experience. College coach: Michigan 2005-06. Pro coach: Joined 49ers in 2007.

Al Everest, special teams coordinator; born August 22, 1950, Santa Barbara, Calif. Safety Southern Methodist 1970-71. No pro playing experience. College coach: Southern Methodist 1972, North Texas 1973-74, Cameron University 1974-75. Pro coach: Arizona Cardinals 1996-99, New Orleans Saints 2000-05, joined 49ers in 2007.

Dave Fipp, asst. special teams; born August 8, 1974, Albuquerque, N.M. Safety Arizona 1994-97. No pro playing experience. College coach: Holy Cross 1998-99, Arizona 2000, Cal Poly 2001-03, Nevada 2004, San Jose State 2005-07. Pro coach: Joined 49ers in 2008.

Chris Foerster, offensive line; born October 12, 1961, Milwaukee, Wis. Center Colorado State 1979-1982. No pro playing experience. College coach: Colorado State 1983-87, Stanford 1988-1991, Minnesota 1992. Pro coach: Minnesota Vikings 1993-95, Tampa Bay Buccaneers 1996-2001, Indianapolis Colts 2002-03, Miami Dolphins 2004, Baltimore Ravens 2005-07, joined 49ers in 2008.

Al Harris, pass rush specialist; born December 31, 1956, Bangor, Me. Defensive end Arizona State 1975-78. Pro defensive end Chicago Bears 1979-1988, Philadelphia Eagles 1989-1990. Pro coach: Joined 49ers in 2009.

Pete Hoener, tight ends; born June 14, 1954, Peoria, Ill. Tight end/defensive end Bradley 1969-1970. College coach: Missouri 1975-76, Illinois State 1977, Indiana State 1978-1984, Illinois 1986-88, Purdue 1989-1990, Texas Christian 1991-97, Iowa State 1998-99, Texas A&M 2000. Pro coach: St. Louis Cardinals 1985-86, Arizona Cardinals 2003, Chicago Bears 2004, joined 49ers in 2005.

Mike Johnson, quarterbacks; born May 2, 1967, Los Angeles. Quarterback Arizona State 1985-86, Akron 1988-89. Pro quarterback Arizona Cardinals 1990, San Antonio Riders (WLAF) 1991-92, British Columbia Lions (CFL) 1992-93, Shreveport Pirates (CFL) 1994-95. College coach: Oregon State 1997-99. Pro coach: San Diego Chargers 2000-01, Atlanta Falcons 2002-05, Baltimore Ravens 2006-07, joined 49ers in 2009.

Vance Joseph, secondary assistant; born September 20, 1972, Marrero, La. Defensive back Colorado 1990-94. Pro defensive back New York Jets 1995, Indianapolis Colts 1996. College coach: Colorado 1999-2001, 2002-03, Wyoming 2002, Bowling Green State 2004. Pro coach: Joined 49ers in 2005.

Johnnie Lynn, secondary; born December 19, 1956, Los Angeles. Defensive back UCLA 1975-78. Pro defensive back New York Jets 1979-1986. College coach: Arizona 1988-1993. Pro coach: Tampa Bay Buccaneers 1994-95, San Francisco 49ers 1996, New York Giants 1997-2003, Baltimore Ravens 2004-05, joined 49ers in 2006.

Greg Manusky, defensive coordinator; born August 12, 1966, Wilkes-Barre, Pa. Linebacker Colgate 1983-87. Pro linebacker Washington Redskins 1988-1990, Minnesota Vikings 1991-93, Kansas City Chiefs 1994-99. Pro coach: Washington Redskins 2001, San Diego Chargers 2002-06, joined 49ers in 2007.

Jason Michael, offensive assistant; born October 15, 1978, Portsmouth, Ohio. Quarterback Western Kentucky 1999-2002. No pro playing experience. College coach: Tennessee 2003-04, 2008. Pro coach: Oakland Raiders 2005, New York Jets 2006-07, joined 49ers in 2009.

Tom Rathman, running backs; born October 7, 1962, Grand Island, Neb. Running back Nebraska 1983-85. Pro running back San Francisco 49ers 1986-1993, Los Angeles Raiders 1994. College coach: Menlo College (Calif.) 1996. Pro coach: San Francisco 1997-2002, Detroit Lions 2003-05, Oakland Raiders 2007-08, re-joined 49ers in 2009.

Jimmy Raye, offensive coordinator; born March 26, 1946, Fayetteville, N.C. Quarterback Michigan State 1964-68. Pro defensive back Philadelphia Eagles 1969. College coach: Michigan State 1971-75, Wyoming 1976. Pro coach: San Francisco 49ers 1977, Detroit Lions 1978-79, Atlanta Falcons 1980-82, 1987-89, Los Angeles Rams 1983-84, 1991, Tampa Bay Buccaneers 1985-86, New England Patriots 1990, Kansas City Chiefs 1992-2000, Washington Redskins 2001, New York Jets 2002-03, Oakland Raiders 2004-05, New York Jets 2006-08, re-joined 49ers in 2009.

Vantz Singletary, inside linebackers; born November 23, 1965, Houston, Texas. Linebacker Blinn College 1985-86, Kansas State 1987-88. No pro playing experience. College coach: Trinity International 1992-96, Southern 1997-98, Hawaii 1999-2005, Tennessee-Chattanooga 2006-07, Buffalo 2008. Pro coach: Joined 49ers in 2009.

Jerry Sullivan, wide receivers/senior assistant; born July 13, 1944, Miami, Fla. Quarterback Florida State 1963-64. No pro playing experience. College coach: Kansas State 1971-72, Texas Tech 1973-75, South Carolina 1976-1982, Indiana 1983, Louisiana State 1984-1990, Ohio State 1991. Pro coach: San Diego Chargers 1992-96, Detroit Lions 1997-2000, Arizona Cardinals 2001-03, Miami Dolphins 2004, joined 49ers in 2005.

Jason Tarver, outside linebackers/defensive assistant; born August 28, 1974, Stanford, Calif. Defensive back West Valley College 1994-95. No pro playing experience. College coach: West Valley College 1996-97, UCLA 1998-2000. Pro coach: Joined 49ers in 2001.

Jim Tomsula, defensive line; born April 14, 1967, Homestead, Pa. Middle Tennessee State 1985-86, Catawba College 1987-1990. No pro playing experience College coach: Charleston Southern 1997. Pro coach: England Monarchs (NFL Europe) 1998, Scottish Claymores (NFL Europe) 1999-2003, Berlin Thunder (NFL Europe) 2004-05, Rhein Fire (NFL Europa head coach) 2006, joined 49ers in 2007.

Mark Uyeyama, asst. strength and conditioning; born December 2, 1975, Vancouver, B.C. Nose Guard Butte C.C. 1994-95, Northern State 1996-97. No pro playing experience. College coach: Arizona State 2001-03, Utah State 2004-07. Pro coach: joined 49ers in 2008.

National Football Conference
West Division
Team Colors: Seahawks Blue, Seahawks Navy, Seahawks Bright Green
Virginia Mason Athletic Center
12 Seahawks Way
Renton, Washington 98056
Telephone: (425) 203-8000

2009 SCHEDULE

PRESEASON

Aug. 15	at San Diego	7:00
Aug. 22	**Denver**	7:30
Aug. 29	at Kansas City	7:00
Sep. 3	**Oakland**	7:00

REGULAR SEASON

Sep. 13	**St. Louis**	1:15
Sep. 20	at San Francisco	1:05
Sep. 27	**Chicago**	1:05
Oct. 4	at Indianapolis	1:00
Oct. 11	**Jacksonville**	1:15
Oct. 18	**Arizona**	1:05
Oct. 25	BYE	
Nov. 1	at Dallas	12:00
Nov. 8	**Detroit**	1:05
Nov. 15	at Arizona	2:15
Nov. 22	at Minnesota	12:00
Nov. 29	at St. Louis	12:00
Dec. 6	**San Francisco**	1:15
Dec. 13	at Houston	12:00
Dec. 20	**Tampa Bay**	1:15
Dec. 27	at Green Bay	12:00
Jan. 3	**Tennessee**	1:15

Stadium: Qwest Field
(opened in 2002)
• **Capacity:** 67,000
Playing Surface: FieldTurf
Training Camp: VMAC
Renton, WA 98056

QWEST FIELD

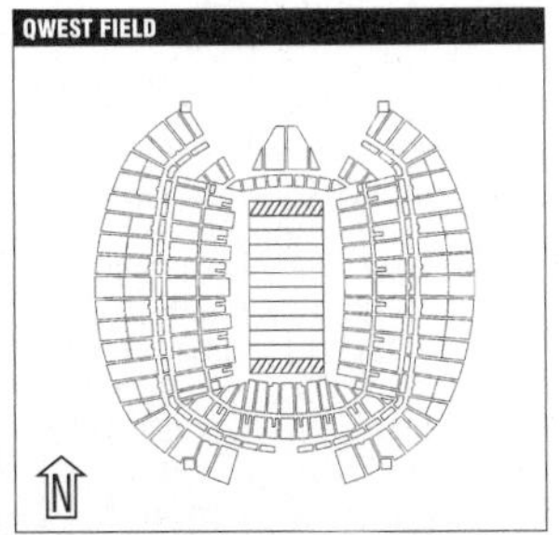

CLUB OFFICIALS

Chairman: Paul Allen
CEO: Tod Leiweke
President of Football Operations: Tim Ruskell
Head Coach: Jim Mora
Senior VP/COO: John Rizzardini
Senior VP/CFO: Martha Fuller
VP/Football Administration: John Izdik
VP/Player Personnel: Ruston Webster
VP/Community Outreach: Mike Flood
VP/Corporate Partnership/Legal Affairs: Lance Lopes
VP/Corporate Partnerships: Ron Jenkins
Director of Marketing: Bill Chapin
Director of Corp. Hospitality, Suite Sales & Service: Amy Sprangers
Director of Pro Personnel: Will Lewis
Director of Communications and Broadcasting: Dave Pearson
Director of Communications: Lane Gammel
Director of Community Outreach: Sandy Gregory
Director of Ticket Sales/Operations: Chuck Arnold
Gameday Presentation: Rick Crawford
Video Director Football: Thom Fermstad
Head Athletic Trainer: Sam Ramsden
Equipment Manager: Erik Kennedy
Team Travel: Jeremy Young

COACHING HISTORY
(257-276-0)

Records include postseason games

1976-1982	Jack Patera*	35-59-0
1982	Mike McCormack	4-3-0
1983-1991	Chuck Knox	83-67-0
1992-94	Tom Flores	14-34-0
1995-98	Dennis Erickson	31-33-0
1999-2008	Mike Holmgren	90-80-0

*Released after two games in 1982

PAID ATTENDANCE

Home 531,014 Away 515,940
Total 1,046,954
Single-game home record, 68,681 (12/16/00)
Single-season home record, 533,657 (2007)

2009 DRAFT CHOICES

Round	Name	Pos.	College
1	Aaron Curry	LB	Wake Forest
2	Max Unger	C	Oregon
3	Deon Butler	WR	Penn State
6	Mike Teel	QB	Rutgers
7	Courtney Greene	DB	Rutgers
	Nick Reed	DE	Oregon
	Cameron Morrah	TE	California

SEATTLE SEAHAWKS

2008 TEAM RECORD

PRESEASON (3-1)

Date	Result	Opponent
8/8	W 34-17	at Minnesota
8/16	W 29-26	Chicago (OT)
8/25	L 17-18	at San Diego
8/29	W 23-16	Oakland

REGULAR SEASON (4-12)

Date	Result	Opponent
9/7	L 10-34	at Buffalo
9/14	L 30-33	San Francisco (OT)
9/21	W 37-13	St. Louis
10/5	L 6-44	at New York Giants
10/12	L 17-27	Green Bay
10/19	L 10-20	at Tampa Bay
10/26	W 34-13	at San Francisco
11/2	L 7-26	Philadelphia
11/9	L 19-21	at Miami
11/16	L 20-26	Arizona
11/23	L 17-20	Washington
11/27	L 9-34	at Dallas
12/7	L 21-24	New England
12/14	W 23-20	at St. Louis
12/21	W 13-3	New York Jets
12/28	L 21-34	at Arizona

(OT) Overtime

SCORE BY PERIODS

Seahawks	74	95	38	87	0 —	294
Opponents	78	137	105	69	3	392

2008 TEAM STATISTICS

	Seahawks	Opp.
Total First Downs	265	324
Rushing	104	98
Passing	142	207
Penalty	19	19
3rd Down: Made/Att	62/198	94/222
3rd Down Pct.	31.3	42.3
4th Down: Made/Att	10/12	8/13
4th Down Pct.	83.3	61.5
Possession Avg.	26:30	33:30
Total Net Yards	4385	6048
Avg. Per Game	274.1	378.0
Total Plays	927	1058
Avg. Per Play	4.7	5.7
Net Yards Rushing	1768	1899
Avg. Per Game	110.5	118.7
Total Rushes	417	457
Net Yards Passing	2617	4149
Avg. Per Game	163.6	259.3
Sacked/Yards Lost	36/214	35/193
Gross Yards	2831	4342
Att./Completions	474/262	566/366
Completion Pct.	55.3	64.7
Had Intercepted	15	9
Punts/Average	90/44.5	68/44.3
Net Punting Avg.	90/36.9	68/38.2
Penalties/Yards	79/601	81/671
Fumbles/Ball Lost	20/12	26/11
Touchdowns	32	40
Rushing	10	13
Passing	18	25
Returns	4	2

2008 INDIVIDUAL STATISTICS

PASSING	Att.	Comp.	Yds.	Pct.	TD	Int.	Tkld.	Rate
S. Wallace	242	141	1532	58.3	11	3	14/76	87.0
Hasselbeck	209	109	1216	52.2	5	10	19/119	57.8
Frye	23	12	83	52.2	2	2	3/19	53.4
Seahawks	474	262	2831	55.3	18	15	36/214	72.5
Opponents	566	366	4342	64.7	25	9	35/193	96.0

SCORING	TD R	TD P	TD Rt	PAT	FG	Saf	PTS
Mare	0	0	0	30/30	24/27	0	102
Duckett	8	0	0	0/0	0/0	0	48
Carlson	0	5	0	0/0	0/0	0	30
Branch	0	4	0	0/0	0/0	0	24
Babineaux	0	0	2	0/0	0/0	0	12
J. Jones	2	0	0	0/0	0/0	0	12
Morris	0	2	0	0/0	0/0	0	12
K. Robinson	0	2	0	0/0	0/0	0	12
Weaver	0	2	0	0/0	0/0	0	12
Bumpus	0	1	0	0/0	0/0	0	6
Burleson	0	1	0	0/0	0/0	0	6
Colbert	0	1	0	0/0	0/0	0	6
Terrill	0	0	1	0/0	0/0	0	6
Wilson	0	0	1	0/0	0/0	0	6
Seahawks	10	18	4	30/30	24/27	0	294
Opponents	13	25	2	39/39	37/41	0	392

2-Pt. Conversions: None.
Seahawks 0-2, Opponents 1-1.

RUSHING	No.	Yds	Avg	LG	TD
J. Jones	158	698	4.4	33	2
Morris	132	574	4.3	45	0
Duckett	62	172	2.8	29	8
Weaver	30	130	4.3	15	0
S. Wallace	16	78	4.9	23	0
Hasselbeck	11	69	6.3	15	0
Frye	2	30	15.0	27	0
O. Schmitt	5	21	4.2	14	0
K. Robinson	1	-4	-4.0	-4	0
Seahawks	417	1768	4.2	45	10
Opponents	457	1899	4.2	51t	13

RECEIVING	No.	Yds	Avg	LG	TD
Carlson	55	627	11.4	33	5
Engram	47	489	10.4	37	0
K. Robinson	31	400	12.9	90t	2
Branch	30	412	13.7	63	4
Weaver	20	222	11.1	62t	2
Morris	19	136	7.2	13t	2
J. Jones	14	66	4.7	17	0
Taylor	9	98	10.9	26	0
McMullen	7	124	17.7	34	0
Colbert	7	52	7.4	11	1
O. Schmitt	6	29	4.8	7	0
Burleson	5	60	12.0	20t	1
Bumpus	5	48	9.6	19	1
Heller	4	29	7.3	14	0
Payne	3	39	13.0	22	0
Seahawks	262	2831	10.8	90t	18
Opponents	366	4342	11.9	63	25

INTERCEPTIONS	No.	Yds	Avg	LG	TD
Wilson	4	135	33.8	75t	1
Grant	2	31	15.5	31	0
Babineaux	1	35	35.0	35t	1
Tatupu	1	16	16.0	16	0
Trufant	1	0	0.0	0	0
Seahawks	9	217	24.1	75t	2
Opponents	15	261	17.4	86t	1

PUNTING	No.	Yds.	Avg.	In 20	LG
Ryan	78	3557	45.6	22	63
Plackemeier	11	450	40.9	2	56
Seahawks	90	4007	44.5	24	63
Opponents	68	3009	44.3	20	68

PUNT RETURNS	Ret	FC	Yds	Avg	LG	TD
Forsett	23	9	227	9.9	29	0
Bumpus	7	2	66	9.4	30	0
Burleson	3	3	54	18.0	21	0
Engram	1	2	6	6.0	6	0
S. Wallace	1	1	0	0.0	0	0
Seahawks	35	17	353	10.1	30	0
Opponents	44	8	444	10.1	63t	1

KICKOFF RETURNS	No.	Yds	Avg	LG	TD
Wilson	69	1753	25.4	61	0
Forsett	7	174	24.9	32	0
Duckett	1	21	21.0	21	0
Seahawks	77	1948	25.3	61	0
Opponents	47	1205	25.6	58	0

FIELD GOALS	1-19	20-29	30-39	40-49	50+
Mare	0/0	7/7	9/10	5/6	3/4
Seahawks	0/0	7/7	9/10	5/6	3/4
Opponents	0/0	15/15	8/8	11/14	3/4

SACKS	No.
Mebane	5.5
Tapp	5.5
Kerney	5.0
Peterson	5.0
R. Bernard	4.0
Atkins	2.0
Jackson	2.0
Terrill	2.0
Green	1.0
Hill	1.0
Russell	1.0
Wilson	1.0
Seahawks	35.0
Opponents	36.0

RECORD HOLDERS

INDIVIDUAL RECORDS—CAREER

Category	Name	Performance
Rushing (Yds.)	Shaun Alexander, 2000-07	9,429
Passing (Yds.)	Dave Krieg, 1980-1991	26,132
Passing (TDs)	Dave Krieg, 1980-1991	195
Receiving (No.)	Steve Largent, 1976-1989	819
Receiving (Yds.)	Steve Largent, 1976-1989	13,089
Interceptions	Dave Brown, 1976-1986	50
Punting (Avg.)	Rick Tuten, 1991-97	43.8
Punt Return (Avg.)	Charlie Rogers, 1999-2001	12.7
Kickoff Return (Avg.)	Steve Broussard, 1995-98	23.2
Field Goals	Norm Johnson, 1982-1990	159
Touchdowns (Tot.)	Shaun Alexander, 2000-07	112
Points	Norm Johnson, 1982-1990	810
*Sacks	Jacob Green, 1980-1991	97.5

INDIVIDUAL RECORDS—SINGLE SEASON

Category	Name	Performance
Rushing (Yds.)	Shaun Alexander, 2005	1,880
Passing (Yds.)	Matt Hasselbeck, 2007	3,966
Passing (TDs)	Dave Krieg, 1984	32
Receiving (No.)	Bobby Engram, 2007	94
Receiving (Yds.)	Steve Largent, 1985	1,287
Interceptions	John Harris, 1981	10
	Kenny Easley, 1984	10
Punting (Avg.)	Ryan Plackemeier, 2006	45.0
Punt Return (Avg.)	Charlie Rogers, 1999	14.5
Kickoff Return (Avg.)	Charlie Rogers, 2000	24.9
Field Goals	Todd Peterson, 1999	34
Touchdowns (Tot.)	Shaun Alexander, 2005	28
Points	Shaun Alexander, 2005	168
*Sacks	Michael Sinclair, 1998	16.5

INDIVIDUAL RECORDS—SINGLE GAME

Category	Name	Performance
Rushing (Yds.)	Shaun Alexander, 11-11-01	266
Passing (Yds.)	Matt Hasselbeck, 12-29-02	449
Passing (TDs)	Dave Krieg, 12-2-84, 9-15-85, 11-28-88	5
	Warren Moon, 10-26-97	5
	Matt Hasselbeck, 11-23-03, 9-24-06	5
Receiving (No.)	Steve Largent, 10-18-87	15
Receiving (Yds.)	Steve Largent, 10-18-87	261
Interceptions	Kenny Easley, 9-3-84	3
	Eugene Robinson, 12-6-92	3
	Darryl Williams, 9-21-97	3
	Lofa Tatupu, 12-2-07	3
	Marcus Trufant, 12-9-07	3
Field Goals	Norm Johnson, 9-20-87, 12-18-88	5
Touchdowns (Tot.)	Shaun Alexander, 9-29-02	5
Points	Shaun Alexander, 9-29-02	30
*Sacks	Many times	4.0
	Last time by Darryl Tapp, 10-21-07	

**Sacks became an official statistic in 1982.*

SEATTLE SEAHAWKS

2009 VETERAN ROSTER

No.	Name	Pos.	Ht.	Wt.	Birthdate	NFL Exp.	College	Hometown	How Acq.	'08 Games/ Starts
36	Adams, Jamar	S	6-2	212	11/29/85	2	Michigan	Charlotte, N.C.	FA-'08	1/0
91	Atkins, Baraka	DE	6-4	268	9/28/84	3	Miami	Sarasota, Fla.	D4a-'07	9/0
27	Babineaux, Jordan	S	6-0	206	8/31/82	6	Southern Arkansas	Port Arthur, Texas	FA-'04	14/1
83	Branch, Deion	WR	5-9	192	7/18/79	8	Louisville	Albany, Ga.	T(NE)-'06	8/8
72	Brown, Kevin	DT	6-2	303	7/8/85	2	UCLA	Los Angeles, Calif.	FA-'08	0*
79	Bryant, Red	DT	6-4	318	4/18/84	2	Texas A&M	Jasper, Texas	D4-'08	4/0
16	Bumpus, Michael	WR	5-11	194	12/13/85	2	Washington State	Culver City, Calif.	FA-'08	4/1
81	Burleson, Nate	WR	6-0	198	8/19/81	7	Nevada	Seattle, Wash.	RFA(Minn)-'06	1/1
89	Carlson, John	TE	6-5	251	5/12/84	2	Notre Dame	Litchfield, Minn.	D2-'08	16/9
90	Cole, Colin	DT	6-1	330	6/24/80	7	Iowa	Ft. Lauderdale, Fla.	UFA(GB)-'09	16/0*
7	Coutu, Brandon	K	5-11	188	9/29/84	2	Georgia	Lawrenceville, Ga.	D7b-'08	0*
44	Duckett, T.J.	RB	6-0	254	2/17/81	8	Michigan State	Kalamazoo, Mich.	UFA(Det)-'08	16/0
29	Floyd, Marquis	CB	6-0	190	3/17/80	2	West Georgia	Monroe, Ga.	FA-'08	0*
20	Forsett, Justin	RB	5-8	194	10/14/85	2	California	Arlington, Texas	D7a-'08	11/0
70	Goddard, Na'Shan	T	6-5	315	4/23/83	3	South Carolina	Dayton, Ohio	PS(NYG)-'08	2/0
24	Grant, Deon	S	6-2	215	3/14/79	10	Tennessee	Augusta, Ga.	UFA(Jax)-'07	16/16
	Griffith, Justin	FB	6-0	230	7/21/80	7	Mississippi State	Magee, Miss.	UFA(Oak)-'09	7/3*
14	Hass, Mike	WR	6-1	206	1/2/83	3	Oregon State	Portland, Ore.	FA-'09	0*
8	Hasselbeck, Matt	QB	6-4	225	9/25/75	11	Boston College	Westwood, Mass.	T(GB)-'01	7/7
59	Hawthorne, David	LB	6-0	240	5/14/85	2	Texas Christian	Corsicana, Texas	FA-'08	14/0
54	Herring, Will	LB	6-3	235	8/28/83	3	Auburn	Opelika, Ala.	D5-'07	11/1
56	Hill, Leroy	LB	6-1	238	9/14/82	5	Clemson	Haddock, Ga.	D3b-'05	12/12
32	Hobbs, Kevin	CB	6-0	188	4/30/83	3	Auburn	Tampa, Fla.	FA-'07	14/0
84	Houshmandzadeh, T.J.	WR	6-2	203	9/26/77	9	Oregon State	Barstow, Calif.	UFA(Cin)-'09	15/15*
95	Jackson, Lawrence	DE	6-4	271	8/30/85	2	Southern California	Inglewood, Calif.	D1-'08	16/14
21	Jennings, Kelly	CB	5-11	180	11/30/82	4	Miami	Live Oak, Fla.	D1-'06	16/6
22	Jones, Julius	RB	5-10	208	8/14/81	6	Notre Dame	Big Stone Gap, Va.	UFA(Dall)-'08	15/10
71	Jones, Walter	T	6-5	325	1/19/74	13	Florida State	Aliceville, Ala.	D1b-'97	12/12
82	Kent, Jordan	WR	6-4	219	7/24/84	3	Oregon	Eugene, Ore	D6b-'07	9/1
97	Kerney, Patrick	DE	6-5	272	12/30/76	11	Virginia	Newtown, Pa.	UFA(Atl)-'07	7/7
50	Laury, Lance	LB	6-2	237	1/17/82	4	South Carolina	Hopkins, S.C.	FA-'06	16/0
52	Lewis, D.D.	LB	6-1	241	1/8/79	8	Texas	Houston, Texas	FA-'08	14/2
75	Locklear, Sean	T	6-4	308	5/29/81	6	North Carolina State	Lumberton, N.C.	D3-'04	12/11
	Lucas, Ken	CB	6-0	205	1/23/79	9	Mississippi	Cleveland, Miss.	UFA(Car)-'09	16/16*
10	Mare, Olindo	K	5-11	190	6/6/73	14	Syracuse	Cooper City, Fla.	FA-'08	16/0
17	McMullen, Billy	WR	6-4	215	3/8/80	6	Virginia	Richmond, Va.	FA-'08	4/2
92	Mebane, Brandon	DT	6-1	314	1/15/85	3	California	Los Angeles, Calif.	D3-'07	16/16
99	Miller, Brandon	DE	6-4	259	1/21/86	2	Georgia	Colquitt, Ga.	W(Atl)-'08	1/0
46	Newton, Joe	TE	6-7	258	10/15/83	3	Oregon State	Roseburg, Ore.	FA-'07	0*
87	Obomanu, Ben	WR	6-0	206	10/30/83	4	Auburn	Selma, Ala.	D7b-'06	0*
47	Owens, John	TE	6-3	255	1/10/80	8	Notre Dame	Gulfport, Miss.	UFA(Det)-'09	16/7*
19	Payne, Logan	WR	6-2	205	1/21/85	3	Minnesota	Lutz, Fla.	FA-'07	2/2
94	t- Redding, Cory	DT	6-4	292	11/15/80	7	Texas	Houston, Texas	T(Det)-'09	13/12*
73	Robinson, William	T	6-5	297	12/20/84	2	San Diego State	Pomona, Calif.	FA-'08	0*
3	Rowe, Jeff	QB	6-5	221	3/21/84	3	Nevada	Reno, Nev.	PS(Cin)-'08	0*
25	Russell, Brian	S	6-2	210	2/5/78	8	San Diego State	West Covina, Calif.	UFA(Cle)-'07	16/16
9	Ryan, Jon	P	6-0	222	11/26/81	4	Regina	Regina, Saskatchewan, Canada	FA-'08	15/0
35	Schmitt, Owen	FB	6-2	247	2/13/85	2	West Virginia	Fairfax, Va.	D5-'08	15/1
67	Sims, Rob	G	6-3	312	12/6/83	4	Ohio State	Macedonia, Ohio	D4-'06	1/1
65	Spencer, Chris	C	6-3	312	3/28/82	5	Mississippi	Madison, Miss.	D1-'05	11/11
55	Tapp, Darryl	DE	6-1	270	9/13/84	4	Virginia Tech	Chesapeake, Va.	D2-'06	16/10
51	Tatupu, Lofa	LB	6-0	242	11/15/82	5	Southern California	Wrentham, Mass.	D2-'05	15/15
86	Taylor, Courtney	WR	6-1	205	4/7/84	3	Auburn	Carrollton, Ala.	D6a-'07	10/4
93	Terrill, Craig	DT	6-2	295	6/27/80	6	Purdue	Lebanon, Ind.	D6-'04	16/1
23	Trufant, Marcus	CB	5-11	197	12/25/80	7	Washington State	Tacoma, Wash.	D1-'03	16/16
69	Vallos, Steve	C	6-3	312	12/28/83	3	Wake Forest	Boardman, Ohio	D7-'07	16/5
68	Wahle, Mike	G	6-6	304	3/29/77	12	Navy	Lake Arrowhead, Calif.	FA-'08	10/10
39	Wallace, C.J.	S	6-0	218	4/17/85	3	Washington	Sacramento, Calif.	FA-'07	12/0
15	Wallace, Seneca	QB	5-11	205	8/6/80	7	Iowa State	Sacramento, Calif.	D4a-'03	10/8
78	Williams, Kyle	T	6-6	295	3/19/84	3	Southern California	Dallas, Texas	FA-'07	4/2
74	Willis, Ray	G	6-6	315	8/13/82	5	Florida State	Angleton, Texas	D4-'05	16/10
26	Wilson, Josh	CB	5-9	192	3/11/85	3	Maryland	Upper Marlboro, Md.	D2-'07	16/12
66	Wrotto, Mansfield	G	6-3	320	10/12/84	3	Georgia Tech	Snellville, Ga.	D4b-'07	7/4

* Brown was on Seattle's practice squad in '08; Cole played 16 games with Green Bay; Coutu was inactive for 16 games; Floyd on practice squad; Griffith played 7 games with Oakland; Hass was on Chicago's practice squad; Houshmandzadeh played 15 games with Cincinnati; Lucas played 16 games with Carolina; Newton was on Seattle's practice squad; Obomanu missed season due to injury; Owens played 16 games with Detroit; Redding played 13 games with Detroit; Robinson missed season due to injury; Rowe was inactive for 2 games.

t- Seahawks traded for Redding (Det).

Players lost through free agency (7): DT Rocky Bernard (NYG; 15 games in '08), WR Bobby Engram (KC; 13), DT Howard Green (NYJ; 13), TE Will Heller (Det; 12), RB Maurice Morris (Det; 13), FB Leonard Weaver (Phil; 14), G/T Floyd Womack (Cle; 14).

Retired—Chris Gray, 16-year guard, missed '08 season due to injury.

Also played with Seahawks in '08—DE Jason Babin (2 games), WR Keary Colbert (7), QB Charlie Frye (2), LB Julian Peterson (16), P Ryan Plackemeier (1), TE Jeb Putzier (6), LS Jeff Robinson (16), WR Koren Robinson (12).

2009 FIRST-YEAR ROSTER

Name	Pos.	Ht.	Wt.	Birthdate	College	Hometown	How Acq.
Bennett, Michael	DE	6-3	274	11/13/85	Texas A&M	Alief, Texas	FA
Butler, Deon	WR	5-10	182	1/4/86	Penn State	Woodbridge, Va.	D3
Curry, Aaron	LB	6-2	254	4/6/86	Wake Forest	Fayetteville, N.C.	D1
Fein, Tony	LB	6-2	242	7/13/82	Mississippi	Port Orchard, Wash.	FA
Greene, Courtney	S	6-0	212	11/23/86	Rutgers	New Rochelle, N.Y.	D7a
Moore, Devin	RB	5-9	191	11/6/85	Wyoming	Indianapolis, Ind.	FA
Morrah, Cameron	TE	6-3	244	3/18/87	California	Claremont, Calif.	D7c
Philistin, Dave	LB	6-1	235	9/24/86	Maryland	Manchester, N.H.	FA
Ramsey, Andre	T	6-5	322	7/24/87	Ball State	Cordele, Ga.	FA
Reed, Nick	DE	6-1	247	9/1/87	Oregon	Trabuco Canyon, Calif.	D7b
Roehl, Tyler	RB	5-10	233	1/29/86	North Dakota State	West Fargo, N.D.	FA
Senser, Ryan (1)	LS	6-3	241	7/21/84	Ohio	Westerville, Ohio	FA
Teel, Mike	QB	6-3	230	1/6/86	Rutgers	Ramsey, N.J.	D6
Tereshinski, John (1)	TE	6-3	245	2/10/85	Wake Forest	Athens, Ga.	FA
Unger, Max	C	6-5	309	4/14/86	Oregon	Kailua-Kona, Hawaii	D2

The term NFL Rookie is defined as a player who is in his first season of professional football and has not been on the roster of another professional football team for any regular-season or postseason games. A Rookie is designated by an "R" on NFL rosters. Players who have been active in another professional football league or players who have NFL experience, including either preseason training camp or being on an Active List or Inactive List, or on Reserve/Injured or Reserve/Physically Unable to Perform for fewer than six regular-season games, are termed NFL First-Year Players. An NFL First-Year Player is designated by a "1" on NFL rosters. Thereafter, a player is credited with an additional year of experience for each season in which he accumulates six games on the Active List or Inactive List, or on Reserve/Injured or Reserve/Physically Unable to Perform.

Log on to www.seahawks.com for an up-to-date roster.

COACHING STAFF

Head Coach,
Jim Mora

Pro Career: Named as Seahawks seventh head coach on February 6, 2008, to take over following the 2008 season. He has held the assistant head coach and defensive backs coaching titles since 2007. In 2007, the Seahawks' defense led the league in fewest touchdown passes allowed (15) and led the NFC (fourth in the NFL) with 20 interceptions. Before joining the Seahawks, Mora was the executive vice president/head coach of the Atlanta Falcons (2004-06). His teams recorded a 26-22 regular-season record (.542) during that time. In 2004, he was the eighth rookie head coach in NFL history to win 11 games. In that year, the Falcons won the NFC South. From 1997-2003, Mora coached for the San Francisco 49ers, first as their secondary coach (1997-98) and then as their defensive coordinator (1999-2003). In his last two seasons with the 49ers, the defense finished no worse than fourth in the NFC against the run. Prior to that, he coached the secondary for the New Orleans Saints (1992-96). During his first two years in New Orleans, the Saints boasted the top-ranked pass defense in the NFL. Mora began his NFL coaching career with the San Diego Chargers in 1985, where he was the quality control coach for the defense. From 1986-88, he was the Chargers' defensive assistant and secondary coach, and from 1989-91, he coached San Diego's defensive backs. Career record: 27-23.

Background: Mora was a walk-on linebacker at the University of Washington (1981-83), where he played on two Rose Bowl teams. He began his coaching career at Washington as the defensive assistant in 1984, helping the Huskies reach the Orange Bowl that year.

Personal: Born November 19, 1961 in Los Angeles. He and his wife, Shannon, have four children: daughter Lillia and sons Cole, Ryder, and Trey. He has two brothers, Stephen and Michael.

ASSISTANT COACHES

Chris Beake, offensive assistant/asst. special teams; born September 10, 1972, Kansas City, Mo. Quarterback Air Force 1991-92. No pro playing experience. College coach: Air Force 1993-94. Pro coach: San Francisco 49ers 1999-2003, Atlanta Falcons 2004-2007, joined Seahawks in 2008.

Casey (Gus) Bradley, defensive coordinator; born July 5, 1966, Zumbrota, Minn. Safety/punter North Dakota State 1984-88. No pro playing experience. College coach: North Dakota State 1990-91, 1996-2005, Fort Lewis College 1992-96. Pro coach: Tampa Bay Buccaneers 2006-2008, joined Seahawks in 2009.

Mike Clark, head strength and conditioning; born August 22, 1954, Wichita, Kan. Linebacker Ottawa College 1973-76. No pro playing experience. College coach: Kansas 1977-78, 1982, Wyoming 1981, Oregon 1983-87, Southern California 1988-89, Texas A&M 2000-2003. Pro coach: Joined Seahawks in 2004.

Mike DeBord, tight ends; born February 7, 1956, Muncie, Ind. No college or pro playing experience. College coach: Franklin 1982-83, Fort Hays State 1984-86, Eastern Illinois 1987-88, Ball State 1989, Colorado State 1990-91, Northwestern 1992, Michigan 1992-99, Central Michigan 2000-03 (head coach), Michigan 2004-2007. Pro coach: Joined Seahawks in 2008.

Bruce DeHaven, special teams; born September 6, 1948, Trousdale, Kan. Attended Southwestern (Kan.) College. No college or pro playing experience. College coach: Kansas 1979-1981, New Mexico State 1982. Pro coach: New Jersey Generals (USFL) 1983, Pittsburgh Maulers (USFL) 1984, Orlando Renegades (USFL) 1985, Buffalo Bills 1987-1999, San Francisco 49ers 2000-02, Dallas Cowboys 2003-2006, joined Seahawks in 2007.

Kasey Dunn, running backs; born July 22, 1969, San Diego. Wide receiver Idaho 1987-1991. Pro wide receiver Houston Oilers 1992, British Columbia Lions (CFL) 1992, Edmonton Eskimos (CFL) 1993. College coach: Idaho 1993, 1995, San Diego 1994, New Mexico 1996-97, Washington State 1998-2002, Texas Christian 2003, Arizona 2004-2006, Baylor 2007, Maryland 2008. Pro coach: Joined Seahawks in 2008.

Tom Headlee, quality control/defense; born November 6, 1976, Bothell, Wash. Attended Washington State. No college or pro playing experience. Pro coach: Joined Seahawks in 2006.

Greg Knapp, offensive coordinator; born March 5, 1963, Long Beach, Calif. Quarterback Sacramento State 1982-85. No pro playing experience. College coach: Sacramento State 1986-1994. Pro coach: San Francisco 49ers 1995-2003, Atlanta Falcons 2004-06, Oakland Raiders 2007-08, joined Seahawks in 2009.

Darren Krein, asst. strength & conditioning; born July 7, 1971, Aurora, Colo. Linebacker/defensive end Miami 1989-1993. Pro linebacker San Diego Chargers 1994, Barcelona Dragons (NFLE) 1996. Pro coach: Seattle Seahawks 1997-98, re-joined Seahawks in 2002.

Bill Lazor, quarterbacks; born June 14, 1972, Scranton, Pa. Quarterback Cornell 1991-93. No pro playing experience. College coach: Cornell 1994-2000, Buffalo 2001-02. Pro coach: Atlanta Falcons 2003, Washington Redskins 2004-2007, joined Seahawks in 2008.

Tim Lewis, secondary; born December 18, 1961, Quakertown, Pa. Defensive back Pittsburgh 1979-1982. Pro cornerback Green Bay Packers 1983-86. College coach: Texas A&M 1987-88, Southern Methodist 1989-1992, Pittsburgh 1993-94. Pro coach: Pittsburgh Steelers 1995-2003, New York Giants 2004-06, Carolina Panthers 2007-08, joined Seahawks in 2009.

Larry Marmie, asst. defensive backs; born October 17, 1942, Berea, Kent. Quarterback Eastern Kentucky 1962-65. No pro playing experience. College coach: Morehead State 1968-1971, Eastern Kentucky 1972-76, Tulsa 1977-78, North Carolina 1979-1982, Tennessee 1983-84, Arizona State 1985-1991 (head coach 1988-1991), Tennessee 1992-94, UCLA 1995. Pro coach: Arizona Cardinals 1996-2003, St. Louis Rams 2004-05, joined Seahawks in 2006.

Mike Phair, asst. defensive line; born November 8, 1969, Mesa, Ariz. Linebacker Mesa (Ariz.) C.C. 1988-89, Arizona State 1990-91. No pro playing experience. College coach: Arizona State 1999-2000, Tiffin University 2001. Pro coach: Joined Seahawks in 2008.

Robert Prince, wide receivers; born May 9, 1965, Okinawa, Japan. Wide receiver Humboldt State 1985-86. No pro playing experience. College coach: Humboldt State 1989-1990, Montana State 1991, Sacramento State,1992-93, Fort Lewis College 1994-95, Recruit Seagulls (Japan) 1996-97, Portland State 1998-2000, Boise State 2001-03. Pro coach: Atlanta Falcons, 2004-06, Jacksonville Jaguars 2007-08, joined Seahawks in 2009.

Dan Quinn, asst. head coach/defensive line; born September 11, 1970, Orange, N.J. Defensive lineman Salisbury State 1990-93. No pro playing experience. College coach: William & Mary 1994, Virginia Military Institute 1995, Hofstra 1997-2000. Pro coach: San Francisco 49ers 2001-04, Miami Dolphins 2005-06, New York Jets 2007-08, joined Seahawks in 2009.

Zerick Rollins, linebackers; born June 20, 1975, Houston. Defensive end Texas A&M 1995-97. No pro playing experience. Graduate assistant Texas A&M 1997-2000. Pro coach: Joined Seahawks in 2001.

Mike Solari, offensive line; born January 16, 1955, Daly City, Calif. Offensive lineman San Diego State 1972-75. No pro playing experience. College coach: Mira Costa (Calif.) J.C. 1978, U.S. International 1979, Boise State 1980, Cincinnati 1981-82, Kansas 1983-85, Pittsburgh 1986, Alabama 1990-91. Pro coach: Dallas Cowboys 1987-88, Phoenix Cardinals 1989, San Francisco 49ers 1992-1996, Kansas City Chiefs 1997-2007, joined Seahawks in 2008.

National Football Conference
South Division
Team Colors: Buccaneer Red, Pewter, Black, and Orange
One Buccaneer Place
Tampa, Florida 33607
Telephone: (813) 870-2700

2009 SCHEDULE

PRESEASON

Aug. 15	at Tennessee	7:00
Aug. 22	at Jacksonville	7:30
Aug. 27	**Miami**	8:00
Sep. 4	**Houston**	7:00

REGULAR SEASON

Sep. 13	**Dallas**	1:00
Sep. 20	at Buffalo	4:05
Sep. 27	**N.Y. Giants**	1:00
Oct. 4	at Washington	1:00
Oct. 11	at Philadelphia	1:00
Oct. 18	**Carolina**	1:00
Oct. 25	**New England** (London)	5:00
Nov. 1	BYE	
Nov. 8	**Green Bay**	1:00
Nov. 15	at Miami	1:00
Nov. 22	**New Orleans**	1:00
Nov. 29	at Atlanta	1:00
Dec. 6	at Carolina	1:00
Dec. 13	**N.Y. Jets**	1:00
Dec. 20	at Seattle	1:15
Dec. 27	at New Orleans	12:00
Jan. 3	**Atlanta**	1:00

Stadium: Raymond James Stadium (opened in 1998) • **Capacity:** 65,908 Tampa, Florida 33607
Playing Surface: Grass
Training Camp: One Buccaneer Place Tampa, Florida 33607

RAYMOND JAMES STADIUM

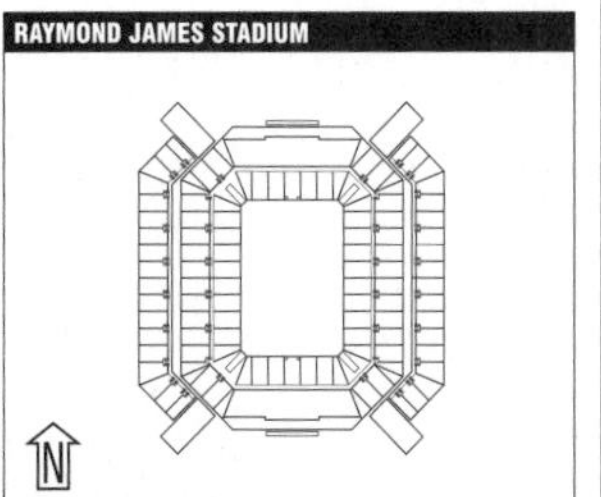

CLUB OFFICIALS

Owner/President: Malcolm Glazer
Co-Chairman: Bryan Glazer
Co-Chairman: Joel Glazer
Co-Chairman: Edward Glazer
General Manager: Mark Dominik
Vice President of Business Administration: Brian Ford
Director of College Scouting: Dennis Hickey
Coordinator of Pro Personnel: Doug Williams
Director of Player Development: Eric Vance
Director of Football Administration: Digger Daley
National College Scout: Jim Abrams
College Scouts: Reggie Cobb, Frank Dorazio, Dominic Green, Thomas Throckmorton, Seth Turner
National Combine Scout: Byron Kiefer
Pro Scout: Shelton Quarles
Senior Director of Sales and Finance: Jason Layton
General Counsel: Manny Alvare
Director of Accounting: Anne Ansley
Director of Community Relations: Miray Holmes
Director of Creative Services: Darren Morgan
Director of Marketing and Business Development: Jeff Ajluni
Director of Public Relations: Jeff Kamis
Director of Security and Facilities: Andre Trescastro
Director of Special Events and Team Operations: Killeen Mullen
Trainer: Todd Toriscelli
Director of Rehabilitation: Shannon Merrick
Equipment Manager: James Sorenson
Assistant Equipment Manager: Mike Myrick
Video Director: Dave Levy
Assistant Video Director: Chris Bryan
Broadcasting Operations Manager: Jeff Ryan
IT Manager: Ed Johnston
Public Relations Manager: Jason Wahlers
Purchasing Manager: Brian Mathiews
Ticket Operations Manager: Alex Bohne
Website Manager: Scott Smith

COACHING HISTORY
(211-319-1)

Records include postseason games

1976-1984	John McKay	45-91-1
1985-86	Leeman Bennett	4-28-0
1987-1990	Ray Perkins*	19-41-0
1990-91	Richard Williamson	4-15-0
1992-95	Sam Wyche	23-41-0
1996-2001	Tony Dungy	56-46-0
2002-08	Jon Gruden	60-57-0

*Released after 13 games in 1990

PAID ATTENDANCE

Home 505,940 Away 511,555
Total 1,017,495
Single-game home record, 73,523 (12/7/97)
Single-season home record, 545,980 (1979)

2009 DRAFT CHOICES

Round	Name	Pos.	College
1	Josh Freeman	QB	Kansas State
3	Roy Miller	DT	Texas
4	Kyle Moore	DE	Southern California
5	Xavier Fulton	T	Illinois
7	E.J. Biggers	DB	Western Michigan
	Sammie Stroughter	WR	Oregon State

TAMPA BAY BUCCANEERS

2008 TEAM RECORD

PRESEASON (3-1)

Date	Result	Opponent
8/9	W 17-6	at Miami
8/17	W 27-10	New England
8/23	L 17-23	Jacksonville
8/28	W 16-6	at Houston

REGULAR SEASON (9-7)

Date	Result	Opponent
9/7	L 20-24	at New Orleans
9/14	W 24-9	Atlanta
9/21	W 27-24	at Chicago (OT)
9/28	W 30-21	Green Bay
10/5	L 13-16	at Denver
10/12	W 27-3	Carolina
10/19	W 20-10	Seattle
10/26	L 9-13	at Dallas
11/2	W 30-27	at Kansas City (OT)
11/16	W 19-13	Minnesota
11/23	W 38-20	at Detroit
11/30	W 23-20	New Orleans
12/8	L 23-38	at Carolina
12/14	L 10-13	at Atlanta (OT)
12/21	L 24-41	San Diego
12/28	L 24-31	Oakland

(OT) Overtime

SCORE BY PERIODS

Buccaneers	61	112	86	96	6 —	361
Opponents	77	86	51	106	3 —	323

2008 TEAM STATISTICS

	Buccaneers	Opp.
Total First Downs	298	259
Rushing	100	87
Passing	184	153
Penalty	14	19
3rd Down: Made/Att	88/229	81/214
3rd Down Pct.	38.4	37.9
4th Down: Made/Att	10/18	5/13
4th Down Pct.	55.6	38.5
Possession Avg.	31:23	28:37
Total Net Yards	5456	4898
Avg. Per Game	341.0	306.1
Total Plays	1045	945
Avg. Per Play	5.2	5.2
Net Yards Rushing	1837	1901
Avg. Per Game	114.8	118.8
Total Rushes	451	441
Net Yards Passing	3619	2997
Avg. Per Game	226.2	187.3
Sacked/Yards Lost	32/169	29/190
Gross Yards	3788	3187
Att./Completions	562/355	475/276
Completion Pct.	63.2	58.1
Had Intercepted	13	22
Punts/Average	77/44.5	81/43.6
Net Punting Avg.	77/37.6	81/35.4
Penalties/Yards	95/834	88/660
Fumbles/Ball Lost	21/13	16/8
Touchdowns	38	34
Rushing	13	8
Passing	18	23
Returns	7	3

2008 INDIVIDUAL STATISTICS

PASSING	Att.	Comp.	Yds.	Pct.	TD	Int.	Tkld.	Rate
Garcia	376	244	2712	64.9	12	6	23/100	90.2
Griese	184	110	1073	59.8	5	7	9/69	69.4
Graham	1	1	3	100.0	1	0	0/0	118.8
McCown	1	0	0	0.0	0	0	0/0	39.6
Buccaneers	562	355	3788	63.2	18	13	32/169	83.8
Opponents	475	276	3187	58.1	23	22	29/190	75.3

SCORING	TD R	TD P	TD Rt	PAT	FG	Saf	PTS
M. Bryant	0	0	0	35/36	32/38	0	131
A. Bryant	0	7	0	0/0	0/0	0	42
Graham	4	0	0	0/0	0/0	0	24
Hilliard	0	4	0	0/0	0/0	0	24
Williams	4	0	0	0/0	0/0	0	24
A. Smith	0	3	0	0/0	0/0	0	20
Askew	2	0	0	0/0	0/0	0	12
Dunn	2	0	0	0/0	0/0	0	12
C. Smith	0	0	2	0/0	0/0	0	12
Stevens	0	2	0	0/0	0/0	0	12
Adams	0	0	1	0/0	0/0	0	6
Barber	0	0	1	0/0	0/0	0	6
Buchanon	0	0	1	0/0	0/0	0	6
Clayton	0	1	0	0/0	0/0	0	6
Garcia	1	0	0	0/0	0/0	0	6
Gilmore	0	1	0	0/0	0/0	0	6
Hayes	0	0	1	0/0	0/0	0	6
Phillips	0	0	1	0/0	0/0	0	6
Buccaneers	13	18	7	35/36	32/38	0	361
Opponents	8	23	3	33/33	28/30	0	323

2-Pt. Conversions: A. Smith.
Buccaneers 1-2, Opponents 1-1.

RUSHING	No.	Yds	Avg	LG	TD
Dunn	186	786	4.2	40	2
Graham	132	563	4.3	68t	4
Williams	63	233	3.7	28	4
Garcia	35	148	4.2	20	1
C. Smith	8	40	5.0	10	0
A. Bryant	2	22	11.0	13	0
McCown	3	15	5.0	12	0
Askew	7	14	2.0	3	2
Bennett	7	12	1.7	4	0
Clayton	2	5	2.5	4	0
Hilliard	1	0	0.0	0	0
Griese	5	-1	-0.2	3	0
Buccaneers	451	1837	4.1	68t	13
Opponents	441	1901	4.3	67t	8

RECEIVING	No.	Yds	Avg	LG	TD
A. Bryant	83	1248	15.0	71t	7
Hilliard	47	424	9.0	36t	4
Dunn	47	330	7.0	36	0
Clayton	38	484	12.7	58t	1
Stevens	36	397	11.0	31	2
Graham	23	174	7.6	24	0
A. Smith	21	250	11.9	34	3
Gilmore	15	147	9.8	36	1
Galloway	13	138	10.6	22	0
Askew	13	66	5.1	18	0
Williams	7	43	6.1	25	0
C. Smith	4	24	6.0	13	0
Stovall	3	25	8.3	9	0
Cook	3	24	8.0	12	0
Clark	1	12	12.0	12	0
Bennett	1	2	2.0	2	0
Buccaneers	355	3788	10.7	71t	18
Opponents	276	3187	11.5	84t	23

INTERCEPTIONS	No.	Yds	Avg	LG	TD
Barber	4	69	17.3	65t	1
Talib	4	32	8.0	19	0
Phillips	3	72	24.0	58	0
Piscitelli	2	106	53.0	84	0
Adams	2	50	25.0	45t	1
Buchanon	2	33	16.5	26t	1
Ruud	2	10	5.0	10	0
T. Jackson	1	25	25.0	25	0
June	1	1	1.0	1	0
Brooks	1	-2	-2.0	-2	0
Buccaneers	22	396	18.0	84	3
Opponents	13	233	17.9	62t	2

PUNTING	No.	Yds.	Avg.	In 20	LG
Bidwell	77	3426	44.5	27	64
Buccaneers	77	3426	44.5	27	64
Opponents	81	3528	43.6	15	70

PUNT RETURNS	Ret	FC	Yds	Avg	LG	TD
C. Smith	23	4	324	14.1	70t	1
D. Jackson	20	0	97	4.9	19	0
Hilliard	3	7	19	6.3	11	0
Talib	1	0	0	0.0	0	0
Buccaneers	47	11	440	9.4	70t	1
Opponents	39	10	392	10.1	43	0

KICKOFF RETURNS	No.	Yds	Avg	LG	TD
C. Smith	36	992	27.6	97t	1
D. Jackson	14	327	23.4	45	0
Clayton	3	69	23.0	29	0
Clark	3	54	18.0	22	0
A. Smith	2	17	8.5	17	0
Stovall	1	15	15.0	15	0
Gilmore	1	12	12.0	12	0
Buccaneers	60	1486	24.8	97t	1
Opponents	74	1542	20.8	61	0

FIELD GOALS	1-19	20-29	30-39	40-49	50+
M. Bryant	0/0	12/12	15/15	5/8	0/3
Buccaneers	0/0	12/12	15/15	5/8	0/3
Opponents	0/0	10/10	8/9	8/9	2/2

SACKS	No.
Adams	6.5
White	5.0
Wilkerson	5.0
Carter	4.0
Ruud	3.0
Barber	2.0
Sims	1.5
Hovan	1.0
T. Jackson	1.0
Buccaneers	29.0
Opponents	32.0

RECORD HOLDERS

INDIVIDUAL RECORDS—CAREER

Category	Name	Performance
Rushing (Yds.)	James Wilder, 1981-89	5,957
Passing (Yds.)	Vinny Testaverde, 1987-1992	14,820
Passing (TDs)	Vinny Testaverde, 1987-1992	77
Receiving (No.)	James Wilder, 1981-89	430
Receiving (Yds.)	Mark Carrier, 1987-1992	5,018
Interceptions	Ronde Barber, 1997-2008	37
Punting (Avg.)	Josh Bidwell, 2004-08	44.0
Punt Return (Avg.)	Clifton Smith, 2008	14.1
Kickoff Return (Avg.)	Aaron Stecker, 2000-03	23.8
Field Goals	Martín Gramatica, 1999-2004	137
Touchdowns (Tot.)	Mike Alstott, 1996-2006	71
Points	Martín Gramatica, 1999-2004	592
*Sacks	Warren Sapp, 1995-2003	77.0

INDIVIDUAL RECORDS—SINGLE SEASON

Category	Name	Performance
Rushing (Yds.)	James Wilder, 1984	1,544
Passing (Yds.)	Brad Johnson, 2003	3,811
Passing (TDs)	Brad Johnson, 2003	26
Receiving (No.)	Keyshawn Johnson, 2001	106
Receiving (Yds.)	Mark Carrier, 1989	1,422
Interceptions	Ronde Barber, 2001	10
Punting (Avg.)	Josh Bidwell, 2005	45.6
Punt Return (Avg.)	Karl Williams, 1996	21.1
Kickoff Return (Avg.)	Mark Jones, 2007	28.6
Field Goals	Martín Gramatica, 2002	32
	Matt Bryant, 2008	32
Touchdowns (Tot.)	James Wilder, 1984	13
Points	Matt Bryant, 2008	131
*Sacks	Warren Sapp, 2000	16.5

INDIVIDUAL RECORDS—SINGLE GAME

Category	Name	Performance
Rushing (Yds.)	James Wilder, 11-6-83	219
Passing (Yds.)	Doug Williams, 11-16-80	486
Passing (TDs)	Steve DeBerg, 9-13-87	5
	Brad Johnson, 11-3-02	5
Receiving (No.)	James Wilder, 9-15-85	13
	Earnest Graham, 10-21-07	13
Receiving (Yds.)	Mark Carrier, 12-6-87	212
Interceptions	Ronde Barber, 12-23-01, 12-4-05	3
Field Goals	Martín Gramatica, 12-29-02	5
Touchdowns (Tot.)	Jimmie Giles, 10-20-85	4
Points	Jimmie Giles, 10-20-85	24
*Sacks	Marcus Jones, 10-19-00	4.0
	Simeon Rice, 10-12-03	4.0

**Sacks became an official statistic in 1982.*

TAMPA BAY BUCCANEERS

2009 VETERAN ROSTER

No.	Name	Pos.	Ht.	Wt.	Birthdate	NFL Exp.	College	Hometown	How Acq.	'08 Games/ Starts
90	Adams, Gaines	DE	6-5	258	6/8/83	3	Clemson	Greenwood, S.C.	D1-'07	16/16
73	Alabi, Anthony	T	6-5	315	2/16/81	4	Texas Christian	San Antonio, Texas	FA-'09	0*
26	Allen, Will	S	6-1	200	6/17/82	6	Ohio State	Dayton, Ohio	D4-'04	16/0
35	Askew, B.J.	FB	6-3	233	8/19/80	7	Michigan	Cincinnati, Ohio	UFA(NYJ)-'07	10/4
20	Barber, Ronde	CB	5-10	184	4/7/75	13	Virginia	Roanoke, Va.	D3b-'97	16/16
9	Bidwell, Josh	P	6-3	220	3/13/76	10	Oregon	Winston, Ore.	UFA(GB)-'04	16/0
58	Black, Quincy	LB	6-2	240	2/28/84	3	New Mexico	Chicago, Ill.	D3-'07	16/0
89	Bryant, Antonio	WR	6-1	205	3/9/81	7	Pittsburgh	Miami, Fla.	FA-'08	16/15
3	Bryant, Matt	K	5-9	200	5/29/75	8	Baylor	Orange, Texas	FA-'05	16/0
17	Campbell, Kelly	WR	5-10	175	7/23/80	4	Georgia Tech	Atlanta, Ga.	FA-'09	0*
87	Clark, Brian	WR	6-2	204	12/26/83	3	North Carolina State	Tampa, Fla.	FA-'07	9/0
80	Clayton, Michael	WR	6-4	215	10/13/82	6	Louisiana State	Baton Rouge, La.	D1-'04	15/9
43	Cook, Jameel	FB	5-10	237	2/8/79	9	Illinois	Miami, Fla.	FA-'08	10/1
27	Cox, Torrie	CB	5-10	192	10/29/80	7	Pittsburgh	Miami, Fla.	D6-'03	0*
59	Crowell, Angelo	LB	6-1	246	8/16/81	7	Virginia	North Forsythe, N.C.	UFA(Buff)-'09	0*
48	Economos, Andrew	LS	6-1	250	6/24/82	4	Georgia Tech	Atlanta, Ga.	FA-'06	16/0
52	Faine, Jeff	C	6-3	291	4/6/81	7	Notre Dame	Sanford, Fla.	UFA(NO)-'08	16/16
88	Gilmore, John	TE	6-5	257	9/21/79	8	Penn State	West Lawn, Pa.	UFA(Chi)-'08	16/10
34	Graham, Earnest	RB	5-9	225	1/15/80	6	Florida	Ft. Myers, Fla.	FA-'03	10/10
8	Griese, Brian	QB	6-3	214	3/18/75	12	Michigan	Miami, Fla.	T(Chi)-'08	5/5
16	Hankton, Cortez	WR	6-0	200	1/20/81	6	Texas-Southern	New Orleans, La.	FA-'08	0*
54	Hayes, Geno	LB	6-1	226	8/10/87	2	Florida State	Greenville, Fla.	D6-'08	9/0
57	Hayward, Adam	LB	6-1	240	6/23/84	3	Portland State	Westminster, Calif.	D6-'07	16/0
95	Hovan, Chris	DT	6-2	296	5/12/78	10	Boston College	Rocky River, Ohio	FA-'05	15/15
10	Jackson, Dexter	WR	5-9	182	8/5/86	2	Appalachian State	Dunwoody, Ga.	D2-'08	7/0
36	Jackson, Tanard	S	6-0	200	7/21/85	3	Syracuse	Potomac, Md.	D4-'07	16/16
11	Johnson, Josh	QB	6-2	201	5/15/86	2	San Diego	Oakland, Calif.	D5-'08	0*
75	Joseph, Davin	G	6-3	313	11/22/83	4	Oklahoma	Hallandale, Fla.	D1-'06	12/12
53	Koutouvides, Niko	LB	6-2	238	3/25/81	6	Purdue	Plainville, Conn.	FA-'09	14/0*
77	Lee, James	T	6-4	305	8/17/85	2	South Carolina State	Belle Glade, Fla.	W(Cle)-'08	1/0
7	Leftwich, Byron	QB	6-5	250	1/14/80	7	Marshall	Washington, D.C.	UFA(Pitt)-'09	5/0*
33	Mack, Elbert	CB	5-10	175	7/14/86	2	Troy	Wichita, Kan.	FA-'08	15/0
79	Mahan, Sean	C/G	6-3	301	5/28/80	7	Notre Dame	Tulsa, Okla.	T(Pitt)-'08	15/0(t)
12	McCown, Luke	QB	6-3	212	7/12/81	6	Louisiana Tech	Jacksonville, Texas	T(Cle)-'05	2/0
50	McCoy, Matt	LB	6-0	235	10/14/82	5	San Diego State	Tustin, Calif.	UFA(NO)-'08	5/0
30	Nicholson, Donte	S	6-1	216	12/18/81	3	Oklahoma	Diamond Bar, Calif.	D5a-'05	5/0
4	Nugent, Mike	K	5-10	190	3/2/82	5	Ohio State	Centerville, Ohio	UFA(NYJ)-'09	1/0*
70	Penn, Donald	T	6-5	305	4/27/83	4	Utah State	Playa Del Rey, Calif.	FA-'06	16/16
96	Peterson, Greg	DT	6-5	286	1/21/84	3	North Carolina Central	East Duplin, N.C.	D5-'07	2/0
23	Phillips, Jermaine	S	6-2	230	3/27/79	8	Georgia	Roswell, Ga.	D5-'02	11/11
21	Piscitelli, Sabby	S	6-3	224	8/24/83	3	Oregon State	Boca Raton, Fla.	D2b-'07	15/5
84	Pociask, Jason	TE	6-2	259	2/9/83	3	Wisconsin	Plainfield, Ind.	FA-'08	0*
51	Ruud, Barrett	LB	6-2	241	5/20/83	5	Nebraska	Lincoln, Neb.	D2-'05	16/16
78	Sears, Arron	G	6-3	319	10/25/84	3	Tennessee	Russellville, Ala.	D2a-'07	15/15
98	Sims, Ryan	DT	6-4	315	5/4/80	8	North Carolina	Spartanburg, S.C.	T(KC)-'07	15/2
22	Smith, Clifton	RB	5-8	190	7/4/85	2	Fresno State	Fresno, Calif.	FA-'08	9/0
86	Stevens, Jerramy	TE	6-7	260	11/13/79	8	Washington	Olympia, Wash.	UFA(Sea)-'07	14/3
44	Storer, Byron	FB	6-1	219	5/1/84	3	California	Modesto, Calif.	FA-'07	6/3
85	Stovall, Maurice	WR	6-5	220	2/21/85	4	Notre Dame	Philadelphia, Pa.	D3-'06	5/0
25	Talib, Aqib	CB	6-1	205	2/13/86	2	Kansas	Richardson, Texas	D1-'08	15/2
65	Trueblood, Jeremy	T	6-8	320	5/10/83	4	Boston College	Indianapolis, Ind.	D2-'06	16/16
28	Ward, Derrick	RB	5-11	228	8/30/80	6	Ottawa (KS)	Moreno Valley, Calif.	UFA(NYG)-'09	16/3*
91	White, Stylez G.	DE	6-3	270	7/25/79	3	Minnesota	Newark, N.J.	FA-'07	16/0
97	Wilkerson, Jimmy	DE/DT	6-2	270	1/4/81	7	Oklahoma	Naples, Texas	UFA(KC)-'08	16/1
24	Williams, Carnell	RB	5-11	217	4/21/82	5	Auburn	Attalla, Ala.	D1-'05	6/1
56	Wilson, Rod	LB	6-2	230	11/12/81	3	South Carolina	Cross, S.C.	FA-'08	0*
82 t	Winslow, Kellen	TE	6-4	250	7/21/83	6	Miami	San Diego, Calif.	T(Cle)-'09	10/8*
76	Zuttah, Jeremy	OL	6-4	303	6/1/86	2	Rutgers	Edison, N.J.	D3-'08	12/5

* Alabi last active with Miami in '07; Campbell last active with Minnesota in '04; Cox missed '08 season because of injury; Crowell missed '08 season because of injury with Buffalo; Hankton missed '08 season because of injury; J. Johnson inactive for 16 games: Koutouvides played 14 games with Denver; Leftwich played 5 games with Pittsburgh; Nugent played 1 game with N.Y. Jets; Pociask last active with N.Y. Jets in '07; Ward played 16 games with N.Y. Giants; Winslow played 10 games with Cleveland Browns; Wilson inactive for 2 games.

t- Buccaneers traded for Winslow (Cle).

Traded—TE Alex Smith (14 games in '08) to New England.

Players lost through free agency (3): CB Phillip Buchanon (Det; 16 games in '08), QB Jeff Garcia (Oak; 12), DT Jovan Haye (Tenn; 15).

Also played with Buccaneers in '08—RB Michael Bennett (5 games), LB Derrick Brooks (16), DE Kevin Carter (16), G/T Anthony Davis (4), RB Warrick Dunn (15), WR Joey Galloway (10), CB Marcus Hamilton (1), WR Ike Hilliard (16), LB Cato June (16), TE Ben Troupe (2).

2009 FIRST-YEAR ROSTER

Name	Pos.	Ht.	Wt.	Birthdate	College	Hometown	How Acq.
Arrington, Kyle (1)	CB	5-10	196	8/12/86	Hofstra	Accokeek, Md.	FA-'08
Biggers, E.J.	CB	6-0	180	6/13/87	Western Michigan	North Miami Beach, Fla.	D7a
Bradwell, Chris (1)	DT	6-5	280	12/17/83	Troy	Johns Creek, Ga.	FA-'08
Bruggeman, Rob	C	6-4	293	3/2/86	Iowa	Cedar Rapids, Iowa	FA
Buie, Jarriett	DE	6-4	250	9/7/85	South Florida	Tampa, Fla.	FA
Byrd, C.J.	S	6-2	187	11/17/86	Georgia	North Augusta, S.C.	FA
Carter, Pat (1)	WR	6-3	215	2/6/85	Louisville	St. Petersburg, Fla.	FA
Dile, Marc	T	6-4	300	5/5/86	South Florida	Miami, Fla.	FA
Dotson, Demar	T	6-9	268	10/11/85	Southern Mississippi	Alexandria, La.	FA
Duncan, Rashaad	DT	6-2	295	12/10/86	Pittsburgh	Belle Glade, Fla.	FA
Freeman, Josh	QB	6-6	248	1/13/88	Kansas State	Kansas City, Mo.	D1
Fulton, Xavier	T	6-4	301	4/18/86	Illinois	Flossmoor, Ill.	D5
Holmes, Louis (1)	DE	6-4	275	2/24/85	Arizona	Memphis, Tenn.	FA
Huggins, Kareem (1)	RB	5-9	189	5/24/86	Hofstra	Irvington, N.J.	FA
Jackson, Amarri (1)	WR	6-5	202	5/18/85	South Florida	Sarasota, Fla.	FA
Johnson, Jamall (1)	LB	6-1	222	10/12/82	Northwestern State	Norco, La.	FA
McCollough, Evan	S	5-10	190	9/2/87	James Madison	Springdale, Md.	FA
McDuffie, Marshall	CB	6-2	207	7/31/86	Florida International	Valrico, Fla.	FA
Miller, Maurice	G	6-3	327	1/22/86	Mississippi	West Helena, Ark.	FA
Miller, Roy	DT	6-2	310	7/9/87	Texas	Killeen, Texas	D3
Moore, Dre (1)	DT	6-4	305	6/9/85	Maryland	Charlotte, N.C.	D4-'08
Moore, Kyle	DE	6-5	272	10/25/86	Southern California	Warner Robins, Ga.	D4
Purvis, Ryan	TE	6-4	260	5/8/86	Boston College	Reinholds, Pa.	FA
Stroughter, Sammie	WR	5-9	189	1/3/86	Oregon State	Sacramento, Calif.	D7b
Vaughan, Josh	RB	6-0	232	12/3/86	Richmond	Richmond, Va.	FA
Willingham, DeAngelo	CB	6-0	200	1/15/87	Tennessee	Calhoun, S.C.	FA
Wilson, Julius (1)	G	6-4	327	10/17/83	Alabama-Birmingham	Bradenton, Fla.	FA-'08

The term NFL Rookie is defined as a player who is in his first season of professional football and has not been on the roster of another professional football team for any regular-season or postseason games. A Rookie is designated by an "R" on NFL rosters. Players who have been active in another professional football league or players who have NFL experience, including either preseason training camp or being on an Active List or Inactive List, or on Reserve/Injured or Reserve/Physically Unable to Perform for fewer than six regular-season games, are termed NFL First-Year Players. An NFL First-Year Player is designated by a "1" on NFL rosters. Thereafter, a player is credited with an additional year of experience for each season in which he accumulates six games on the Active List or Inactive List, or on Reserve/Injured or Reserve/Physically Unable to Perform.

Log on to www.buccaneers.com for an up-to-date roster.

COACHING STAFF

Head Coach,
Raheem Morris

Pro Career: Morris was named the eighth head coach in Buccaneers history on January 17, 2009. Prior to being named the head coach, he worked as the Buccaneers defensive backs coach from 2007-08, as assistant defensive back coach from 2004-05, as defensive assistant in 2003 and as a defensive quality control coach in 2002. After Tampa Bay fell to 19th in the NFL in pass defense in 2006, Morris led a resurgence in his return as he guided the Buccaneers pass defense to the league's top ranking en route to the NFC South division title in 2007. In five of his seasons with Tampa Bay, the Bucs ranked in the top five in the NFL in total defense, including No. 1 rankings in 2005 and 2002, when the club captured its first world title in Super Bowl XXXVII. He spent time with the New York Jets serving a defensive minority internship in 2001. Career record: 0-0.

Background: Safety at Hofstra (1994-97), graduating with a degree in physical education. Coached collegiately at Hofstra (1998, 2000-01), Cornell (1999) and Kansas State (2006).

Personal: Born September 3, 1976 in Irvington, New Jersey.

ASSISTANT COACHES

Joe Baker, defensive backs; born June 29, 1969, Glen Ridge, N.J. Wide receiver Princeton 1987-1990. No pro playing experience. College coach: East Stroudsburg 1991, Samford 1993, Wisconsin 1999. Pro coach: Birmingham Fire (WFL) 1992, Jacksonville Jaguars 1995-98, New Orleans Saints 2000-04, Green Bay Packers 2005, St. Louis Rams 2006, Denver Broncos 2007-08, joined Buccaneers in 2009.

Joe Barry, linebackers; born July 5, 1970, Boulder, Colo. Linebacker Michigan 1989-1990, Southern California 1991-93. No pro playing experience. College coach: Southern California 1994-95, Northern Arizona 1996-98, Nevada-Las Vegas 1999. Pro coach: San Francisco 49ers 2000, Tampa Bay Buccaneers 2001-06, Detroit Lions 2007-08, re-joined Buccaneers in 2009.

Jim Bates, defensive coordinator; born May 31, 1946, Pontiac, Mich. Linebacker Tennessee 1964-67. No pro playing experience. College coach: Tennessee 1968, 1989, Southern Mississippi 1972, Villanova 1973-74, Kansas State 1975-76, West Virginia 1977, Texas Tech 1978-1983, Florida 1990. Pro coach: San Antonio Gunslingers (USFL) 1984-85, Arizona Outlaws (USFL) 1986, Detroit Drive (AFL) 1988, Cleveland Browns 1991-93, 1995, Atlanta Falcons 1994, Dallas Cowboys 1996-99, Miami Dolphins 2000-04, Green Bay Packers 2005, Denver Broncos 2007, joined Buccaneers in 2009.

Tim Berbenich, asst. wide receivers; born December 19, 1979, Huntington, N.Y. Wide receiver Hamilton College 1998-2001. No pro playing experience. Pro coach: New York Jets 2003-05, joined Buccaneers in 2006.

Richard Bisaccia, associate head coach/special teams coordinator; born June 3, 1960, Yonkers, N.Y. Defensive back Yankton College 1979-1982. Pro defensive back Philadelphia Stars (USFL) 1983. College coach: Wayne State College 1983-87, South Carolina 1988-1993, Clemson 1994-98, Mississippi 1999-2001. Pro coach: Joined Buccaneers in 2002.

Ejiro Evero, defensive quality control; born January 6, 1981, Colchester, England. Safety California-Davis 2000-2003. No pro playing experience. College coach: California-Davis 2005-2006. Pro coach: Joined Buccaneers in 2007.

Jeff Jagodzinski, offensive coordinator; born October 12, 1963, Milwaukee, Wis. Fullback Wisconsin-Whitewater 1981-84. No pro playing experience. College coach: Wisconsin-Whitewater 1985, Northern Illinois 1986, Lousiana State 1987-88, East Carolina 1989-1996, Boston College 1997-98, 2007-08 (head coach 2007-08). Pro coach: Green Bay Packers 1999-2003, 2006, Atlanta Falcons 2004-05, joined Buccaneers in 2009.

Chris Keenan, asst. strength and conditioning; born November 3, 1980, Creston, Iowa. Fullback Drake 1999-2001. No pro playing experience. College coach: Iowa State 2003, Tulane 2006-2008. Pro coach: Minnesota Vikings 2004-05, Tampa Bay Buccaneers 2006, re-joined Buccaneers in 2009.

Steve Logan, running backs; born February 3, 1953, Lawton, Okla. No college or pro playing experience. College coach: Oklahoma State 1980, Hutchinson J.C. 1981-82, Tulsa 1983-84, Colorado 1985-86, Mississippi State 1987-88, East Carolina 1989-2002, Boston College 2007-08. Pro coach: Berlin Thunder (NFL Europe) 2004-05, Rhein Fire (NFL Europe) 2006, joined Buccaneers in 2009.

Pete Mangurian, offensive line; born June 17, 1955, Los Angeles. Defensive tackle Louisiana State 1975-78. No pro playing experience. College coach: Southern Methodist 1979-1980, New Mexico State 1981, Stanford 1982-83, Louisiana State 1984-87, Cornell 1998-2000. Pro coach: Denver Broncos 1988-1992, New York Giants 1993-96, Atlanta Falcons 1997, 2001-03, New England Patriots 2005-08, joined Buccaneers in 2009.

Richard Mann, asst. head coach/wide receivers; born April 20, 1947, Aliquippa, Pa. Wide receiver Arizona State 1966-68. No pro playing experience. College coach: Arizona State 1974-79, Louisville 1980-81. Pro coach: Baltimore/Indianapolis Colts 1982-84, Cleveland Browns 1985-1993, New York Jets 1994-96, Baltimore Ravens 1997-98, Kansas City Chiefs 1999-2000, Washington Redskins 2001, joined Buccaneers in 2002.

Chris Mosley, asst. offensive line; born December 5, 1977, Jacksonville. Running back Southeast Missouri State 1997-98, Washington & Jefferson 1999-2001. No pro playing experience. College coach: Boston College 2007, Princeton 2008. Pro coach: Joined Buccaneers in 2009.

Robert Nunn, defensive line; born June 10, 1965, Apache, Okla. Linebacker Oklahoma State 1984-87. No pro playing experience. College coach: Northeastern Oklahoma 1988, Tennessee 1989-1990, Georgia Military 1991-99. Pro coach: Miami Dolphins 2000-02, 2004, Washington Redskins 2003, Green Bay Packers 2005-08, joined Buccaneers in 2009.

Greg Olson, quarterbacks; born March 1, 1963, Richland, Wash. Quarterback, Spokane Falls (Wash.) J.C. 1981-82. No pro playing experience. College coach: Washington State 1987-1989, Central Washington 1990-1993, Idaho 1994-1996, Purdue 1997-2000, 2002. Pro coach: San Francisco 49ers 2001, Chicago Bears 2003, Detroit Lions 2004-2005, St. Louis Rams 2006-2007, joined Buccaneers in 2008.

Alfredo Roberts, tight ends; born March 17, 1965, Fort Lauderdale, Fla. Tight end Miami 1983-87. Pro tight end Kansas City Chiefs 1988-1990, Dallas Cowboys 1991-93. College coach: Florida Atlantic 1999-2002. Pro coach: Jacksonville Jaguars 2003-06, Cleveland Browns 2007-08, joined Buccaneers in 2009.

Kurtis Shultz, head strength and conditioning; born March 10, 1972, Baltimore. Attended Maryland. No college or pro playing experience. College coach: Loyola (Md.) 1995-98, Maryland and Johns Hopkins 1999-2002. Pro coach: Cincinnati Bengals 2003, Minnesota Vikings 2004-05, joined Buccaneers in 2006.

Dwayne Stukes, asst. defensive backs; born January 24, 1977, Portsmith, Va. Cornerback/safety Virginia 1996-1999. Pro safety Berlin Thunder (NFL Europe) 2001-2002, Colorado Crush (AFL) 2004. Pro coach: Joined Buccaneers in 2006.

Todd Wash, defensive line; born July 19, 1968, Miles City, Mont. Linebacker North Dakota State 1988-1991. No pro playing experience. College coach: Fort Lewis College 1996-99, Nebraska-Kearney 2000-01, North Dakota State 2002-03, 2005-06, Missouri Southern State 2004. Pro coach: Joined Buccaneers in 2006.

National Football Conference
East Division
Team Colors: Burgundy and Gold
Redskins Park
21300 Redskins Park Drive
Ashburn, Virginia 20147
Telephone: (703) 726-7000

2009 SCHEDULE

PRESEASON

Aug. 13	at Baltimore	7:30
Aug. 22	**Pittsburgh**	7:30
Aug. 28	**New England**	8:00
Sep. 3	at Jacksonville	7:30

REGULAR SEASON

Sep. 13	at N.Y. Giants	4:15
Sep. 20	**St. Louis**	1:00
Sep. 27	at Detroit	1:00
Oct. 4	**Tampa Bay**	1:00
Oct. 11	at Carolina	1:00
Oct. 18	**Kansas City**	1:00
Oct. 26	**Philadelphia** (Mon.)	8:30
Nov. 1	BYE	
Nov. 8	at Atlanta	1:00
Nov. 15	**Denver**	1:00
Nov. 22	at Dallas	12:00
Nov. 29	at Philadelphia	1:00
Dec. 6	**New Orleans**	1:00
Dec. 13	at Oakland	1:05
Dec. 21	**N.Y. Giants** (Mon)	8:30
Dec. 27	**Dallas** *	8:20
Jan. 3	at San Diego	1:15

** Sunday night games in Weeks 11-17 subject to change*

Stadium: FedExField (opened in 1997)
•Capacity: 91,704
1600 FedEx Way
Landover, Maryland 20785
Playing Surface: Natural Grass
Training Camp: Redskins Park
Ashburn, Virginia 20147

FEDEXFIELD

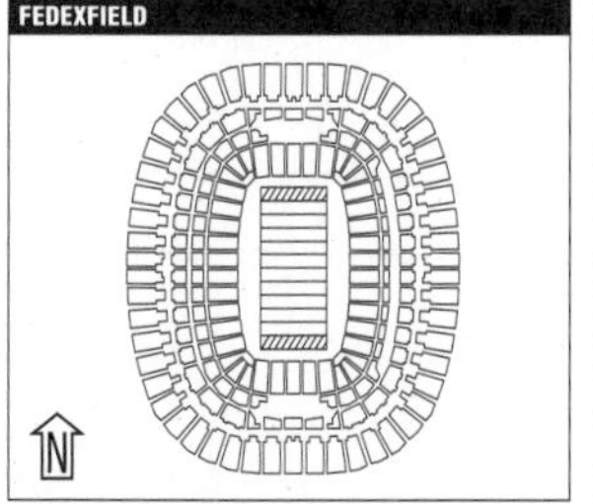

CLUB OFFICIALS

Owner: Daniel M. Snyder
Chief Operating Officer: Mitch Gershman
Chief Financial Officer: Nico Foris
Executive Vice President/Football Operations: Vinny Cerrato
General Counsel: Dave Donovan
Senior Vice President: Karl Swanson
Senior Vice President, Marketing: Janice Schmidt
Senior Vice President, Stadium Operations: Michael Dillow
Director of Player Personnel: Scott Campbell
Director of Pro Personnel: Morocco Brown
Pro Scouts: Donnie Warren, Alex Santos
College Scouts: Chip Flanagan, Tim Gribble, Shemy Schembechler, Jim Zeches
National Scouts: Russ Bolinger, Joel Patten
Vice President, Football Administration: Eric Schaffer
Director of Player Development: Bobby Crumpler
Executive Director of Communications: Zack Bolno
Leadership Council/Community Affairs: BJ Corriveau
Director of Team Administration: Derrick Crawford
Video Director: Mike Bracken
Video Department: Todd Davis, George Claiborne
Head Athletic Trainer: John Burrell
Assistant Athletic Trainers: Eric Steward, Larry Hess, Elliott Jermyn
Equipment Manager: Brad Berlin
Assistant Equipment Manager: Anders Beutel, Chris Collins

COACHING HISTORY

Boston 1932-36
(560-511-27)
Records include postseason games

1932	Lud Wray	4-4-2
1933-34	William (Lone Star) Dietz	11-11-2
1935	Eddie Casey	2-8-1
1936-1942	Ray Flaherty	56-23-3
1943	Arthur (Dutch) Bergman	7-4-1
1944-45	Dudley DeGroot	14-6-1
1946-48	Glen (Turk) Edwards	16-18-1
1949	John Whelchel*	3-3-1
1949-1951	Herman Ball**	4-16-0
1951	Dick Todd	5-4-0
1952-53	Earl (Curly) Lambeau	10-13-1
1954-58	Joe Kuharich	26-32-2
1959-1960	Mike Nixon	4-18-2
1961-65	Bill McPeak	21-46-3
1966-68	Otto Graham	17-22-3
1969	Vince Lombardi	7-5-2
1970	Bill Austin	6-8-0
1971-77	George Allen	69-35-1
1978-1980	Jack Pardee	24-24-0
1981-1992	Joe Gibbs	140-65-0
1993	Richie Petitbon	4-12-0
1994-2000	Norv Turner***	50-60-1
2000	Terry Robiskie	1-2-0
2001	Marty Schottenheimer	8-8-0
2002-03	Steve Spurrier	12-20-0
2004-07	Joe Gibbs	31-36-0
2008	Jim Zorn	8-8-0

*Released after seven games in 1949
**Released after three games in 1951
***Released after 13 games in 2000

PAID ATTENDANCE

Home 710,049 Away 525,135
Total 1,235,184
Single-game home record, 90,910 (12/30/07)
Single-season home record, * 711,471 (2007)
**NFL Record*

2009 DRAFT CHOICES

Round	Name	Pos.	College
1	Brian Orakpo	DE	Texas
3	Kevin Barnes	DB	Maryland
5	Cody Glenn	LB	Nebraska
6	Robert Henson	LB	Texas Christian
7	Eddie Williams	RB	Idaho
	Marko Mitchell	WR	Nevada

WASHINGTON REDSKINS

2008 TEAM RECORD

PRESEASON (3-2)

Date	Result	Opponent
8/3	W 30-16	vs. Indianapolis at Canton, OH
8/9	W 17-14	Buffalo
8/16	W 13-10	at New York Jets
8/23	L 3-47	at Carolina
8/28	L 3-24	Jacksonville

REGULAR SEASON (8-8)

Date	Result	Opponent
9/4	L 7-16	at New York Giants
9/14	W 29-24	New Orleans
9/21	W 24-17	Arizona
9/28	W 26-24	at Dallas
10/5	W 23-17	at Philadelphia
10/12	L 17-19	St. Louis
10/19	W 14-11	Cleveland
10/26	W 25-17	at Detroit
11/3	L 6-23	Pittsburgh
11/16	L 10-14	Dallas
11/23	W 20-17	at Seattle
11/30	L 7-23	New York Giants
12/7	L 10-24	at Baltimore
12/14	L 13-20	at Cincinnati
12/21	W 10-3	Philadelphia
12/28	L 24-27	at San Francisco

SCORE BY PERIODS

Redskins	33	92	57	83	0	— 265
Opponents	89	66	66	75	0	— 296

2008 TEAM STATISTICS

	Redskins	Opp.
Total First Downs	295	259
Rushing	109	86
Passing	165	159
Penalty	21	14
3rd Down: Made/Att	76/216	74/208
3rd Down Pct.	35.2	35.6
4th Down: Made/Att	10/16	8/12
4th Down Pct.	62.5	66.7
Possession Avg.	31:31	28:29
Total Net Yards	5120	4621
Avg. Per Game	320.0	288.8
Total Plays	1026	933
Avg. Per Play	5.0	5.0
Net Yards Rushing	2095	1526
Avg. Per Game	130.9	95.4
Total Rushes	478	398
Net Yards Passing	3025	3095
Avg. Per Game	189.1	193.4
Sacked/Yards Lost	38/266	24/141
Gross Yards	3291	3236
Att./Completions	510/318	511/290
Completion Pct.	62.4	56.8
Had Intercepted	6	13
Punts/Average	82/40.5	87/42.8
Net Punting Avg.	82/33.4	87/37.0
Penalties/Yards	83/644	80/639
Fumbles/Ball Lost	20/12	16/5
Touchdowns	27	32
Rushing	12	12
Passing	14	16
Returns	1	4

2008 INDIVIDUAL STATISTICS

PASSING	Att.	Comp.	Yds.	Pct.	TD	Int.	Tkld.	Rate
J. Campbell	506	315	3245	62.3	13	6	38/266	84.3
Randle El	4	3	46	75.0	1	0	0/0	152.1
Redskins	510	318	3291	62.4	14	6	38/266	85.2
Opponents	511	290	3236	56.8	16	13	24/141	75.6

SCORING	TD R	TD P	TD Rt	PAT	FG	Saf	PTS
Suisham	0	0	0	25/25	26/36	0	103
Portis	9	0	0	0/0	0/0	0	54
Moss	0	6	1	0/0	0/0	0	42
Randle El	0	4	0	0/0	0/0	0	24
Betts	1	0	0	0/0	0/0	0	6
J. Campbell	1	0	0	0/0	0/0	0	6
Cooley	0	1	0	0/0	0/0	0	6
Sellers	0	1	0	0/0	0/0	0	6
D. Thomas	1	0	0	0/0	0/0	0	6
Thrash	0	1	0	0/0	0/0	0	6
Yoder	0	1	0	0/0	0/0	0	6
Redskins	12	14	1	25/25	26/36	0	265
Opponents	12	16	4	30/31	24/28	0	296

2-Pt. Conversions: None.
Redskins 0-2, Opponents 1-1.

RUSHING	No.	Yds	Avg	LG	TD
Portis	342	1487	4.3	31	9
J. Campbell	47	258	5.5	23	1
Betts	61	206	3.4	14	1
D. Thomas	3	53	17.7	29t	1
Moss	1	27	27.0	27	0
S. Alexander	11	24	2.2	8	0
Sellers	6	24	4.0	10	0
Cartwright	5	14	2.8	7	0
Randle El	1	5	5.0	5	0
Davis	1	-3	-3.0	-3	0
Redskins	478	2095	4.4	31	12
Opponents	398	1526	3.8	44	12

RECEIVING	No.	Yds	Avg	LG	TD
Cooley	83	849	10.2	28	1
Moss	79	1044	13.2	67t	6
Randle El	53	593	11.2	31	4
Portis	28	218	7.8	29	0
Betts	22	200	9.1	27	0
D. Thomas	15	120	8.0	18	0
Sellers	12	98	8.2	20	1
Thrash	9	81	9.0	29	1
Yoder	8	50	6.3	14	1
Davis	3	27	9.0	15	0
Kelly	3	18	6.0	7	0
S. Alexander	1	9	9.0	9	0
Cartwright	1	-7	-7.0	-7	0
Kendall	1	-9	-9.0	-9	0
Redskins	318	3291	10.3	67t	14
Opponents	290	3236	11.2	79	16

INTERCEPTIONS	No.	Yds	Avg	LG	TD
Horton	3	13	4.3	10	0
Rogers	2	73	36.5	42	0
Landry	2	18	9.0	13	0
Hall	2	6	3.0	4	0
McIntosh	1	4	4.0	4	0
Griffin	1	0	0.0	0	0
Smoot	1	0	0.0	0	0
Springs	1	0	0.0	0	0
Redskins	13	114	8.8	42	0
Opponents	6	23	3.8	14	0

PUNTING	No.	Yds.	Avg.	In 20	LG
Plackemeier	55	2291	41.7	15	62
Brooks	26	1030	39.6	9	60
Redskins	82	3321	40.5	24	62
Opponents	87	3721	42.8	24	59

PUNT RETURNS	Ret	FC	Yds	Avg	LG	TD
Randle El	39	21	254	6.5	36	0
Moss	6	0	124	20.7	80t	1
Redskins	45	21	378	8.4	80t	1
Opponents	33	18	385	11.7	68t	2

KICKOFF RETURNS	No.	Yds	Avg	LG	TD
Cartwright	51	1307	25.6	87	0
Sellers	2	32	16.0	17	0
Moss	1	26	26.0	26	0
Thrash	1	17	17.0	17	0
Redskins	55	1382	25.1	87	0
Opponents	55	1103	20.1	55	0

FIELD GOALS	1-19	20-29	30-39	40-49	50+
Suisham	0/0	7/7	7/9	11/16	1/4
Redskins	0/0	7/7	7/9	11/16	1/4
Opponents	0/0	6/6	10/10	7/8	1/4

SACKS	No.
Carter	4.0
Evans	3.5
Taylor	3.5
L. Alexander	2.0
Golston	2.0
McIntosh	2.0
A. Montgomery	2.0
Griffin	1.0
Horton	1.0
Springs	1.0
Wilson	1.0
Fletcher	0.5
Landry	0.5
Redskins	24.0
Opponents	38.0

RECORD HOLDERS

INDIVIDUAL RECORDS—CAREER

Category	Name	Performance
Rushing (Yds.)	John Riggins, 1976-79, 1981-85	7,472
Passing (Yds.)	Joe Theismann, 1974-1985	25,206
Passing (TDs)	Sammy Baugh, 1937-1952	187
Receiving (No.)	Art Monk, 1980-1993	888
Receiving (Yds.)	Art Monk, 1980-1993	12,028
Interceptions	Darrell Green, 1983-2001	54
Punting (Avg.)	Sammy Baugh, 1937-1952	45.1
Punt Return (Avg.)	Johnny Williams, 1952-53	12.8
Kickoff Return (Avg.)	Bobby Mitchell, 1962-68	28.5
Field Goals	Mark Moseley, 1974-1986	263
Touchdowns (Tot.)	Charley Taylor, 1964-1977	90
Points	Mark Moseley, 1974-1986	1,206
*Sacks	Dexter Manley, 1981-89	91.0

INDIVIDUAL RECORDS—SINGLE SEASON

Category	Name	Performance
Rushing (Yds.)	Clinton Portis, 2005	1,516
Passing (Yds.)	Jay Schroeder, 1986	4,109
Passing (TDs)	Sonny Jurgensen, 1967	31
Receiving (No.)	Art Monk, 1984	106
Receiving (Yds.)	Santana Moss, 2005	1,483
Interceptions	Dan Sandifer, 1948	13
Punting (Avg.)	Sammy Baugh, 1940	**51.4
Punt Return (Avg.)	Johnny Williams, 1952	15.3
Kickoff Return (Avg.)	Mike Nelms, 1981	29.7
Field Goals	Mark Moseley, 1983	33
Touchdowns (Tot.)	John Riggins, 1983	24
Points	Mark Moseley, 1983	161
*Sacks	Dexter Manley, 1986	18.5

INDIVIDUAL RECORDS—SINGLE GAME

Category	Name	Performance
Rushing (Yds.)	Gerald Riggs, 9-17-89	221
Passing (Yds.)	Sammy Baugh, 10-31-43	446
Passing (TDs)	Sammy Baugh, 10-31-43, 11-23-47	6
	Mark Rypien, 11-10-91	6
Receiving (No.)	Art Monk, 12-15-85, 11-4-90	13
	Kelvin Bryant, 12-7-86	13
Receiving (Yds.)	Anthony Allen, 10-4-87	255
Interceptions	Sammy Baugh, 11-14-43	**4
	Dan Sandifer, 10-31-48	**4
Field Goals	Many times	5
	Last time by Shaun Suisham, 11-4-07	
Touchdowns (Tot.)	Dick James, 12-17-61	4
	Larry Brown, 12-16-73	4
Points	Dick James, 12-17-61	24
	Larry Brown, 12-16-73	24
*Sacks	Dexter Manley, 10-2-88	4.0
	Ken Harvey, 11-23-97	4.0
	Phillip Daniels, 12-18-05	4.0

**Sacks became an official statistic in 1982.*
***NFL Record*

WASHINGTON REDSKINS

2009 VETERAN ROSTER

No.	Name	Pos.	Ht.	Wt.	Birthdate	NFL Exp.	College	Hometown	How Acq.	'08 Games/ Starts
67	Albright, Ethan	LS	6-5	248	5/1/71	15	North Carolina	Greensboro, N.C.	UFA(Buff)-'01	16/0
79	Alexander, Lorenzo	DT	6-1	297	5/31/83	3	California	Berkeley, Calif.	FA-'07	15/0
39	Alridge, Anthony	RB	5-9	175	11/24/83	2	Houston	Denton, Texas	W(Den)-'09	0*
78	Batiste, D'Anthony	OL	6-4	314	3/29/82	2	Louisiana-Lafayette	Marksville, LA	FA-'08	0*
46	Betts, Ladell	RB	5-11	224	8/27/79	8	Iowa	Blue Springs, Mo.	D2-'02	13/0
54	Blades, H.B.	LB	5-10	242	9/30/84	3	Pittsburgh	Plantation, Fla.	D6-'07	16/5
#	Boschetti, Ryan	DT	6-4	311	10/7/81	6	UCLA	Belmont, Calif.	FA-'04	3/0
5	Brennan, Colt	QB	6-3	206	8/16/83	2	Hawaii	Irvine, Calif.	D6-'08	0*
73	Bridges, Jeremy	G	6-4	326	4/19/80	6	Southern Mississippi	Fort Wayne, Ind.	FA-'09	14/4*
90	Buzbee, Alex	DE	6-3	272	11/27/84	2	Georgetown	Chester, N.J.	FA-'07	0*
38	Cain, Jeremy	LS	6-1	240	3/24/80	3	Massachusetts	Fort Lauderdale, Fla.	FA-'08	0*
17	Campbell, Jason	QB	6-5	231	12/31/81	5	Auburn	Taylorsville, Miss.	D1-'05	16/16
#	Campbell, Khary	LB	6-2	224	4/4/79	8	Bowling Green	Toledo, Ohio	FA-'03	14/0
99	Carter, Andre	DE	6-4	253	5/12/79	9	California	San Jose, Calif.	UFA(SF)-'06	16/14
31	Cartwright, Rock	RB	5-8	213	12/3/79	8	Kansas State	Conroe, Texas	D7-'02	16/0
62	Clark, Devin	T	6-4	325	5/22/86	2	New Mexico	Mesa, Ariz.	FA-'08	2/0
15	Collins, Todd	QB	6-4	223	11/5/71	15	Michigan	Walpole, Mass.	UFA(KC)-'06	0*
47	Cooley, Chris	TE	6-3	250	7/11/82	5	Utah State	Logan, Utah	D3-'04	16/16
93	Daniels, Phillip	DE	6-6	311	3/4/73	14	Georgia	Donalson, Ga.	UFA(Chi)-'04	0*
86	Davis, Fred	TE	6-4	257	1/15/86	2	Southern California	Toledo, Ohio	D2-'08	11/2
66	Dockery, Derrick	G	6-6	326	9/7/80	7	Texas	Lakeview, Texas	FA-'09	16/16*
37	Doughty, Reed	S	6-1	205	11/4/82	4	Northern Colorado	Johnstown, Colo.	D6-'06	4/3
#	Evans, Demetric	DE	6-4	287	9/3/79	8	Georgia	Haynesville, La.	FA-'08	16/11
#	Fabini, Jason	G/T	6-7	312	8/25/74	12	Cincinnati	Fort Wayne, Ind.	FA-'08	7/2
51	Fincher, Alfred	LB	6-1	250	8/15/83	5	Connecticut	Norwood, Mass.	FA-'08	15/0
59	Fletcher, London	LB	5-10	245	5/19/75	12	John Carroll	Cleveland, Ohio	UFA(Buff)-'07	16/16
#	Geisinger, Justin	OL	6-4	317	5/24/82	3	Vanderbilt	Pittsburgh, Pa.	FA-'07	8/0
64	Golston, Kedric	DT	6-4	290	5/30/83	4	Georgia	Tyrone, Ga.	D6-'06	13/12
#	Green, Mike	S	6-0	200	12/6/76	9	Northwestern State	Rustin, La.	FA-'08	8/2
96	Griffin, Cornelius	DT	6-3	303	12/3/76	10	Alabama	Brundidge, Ala.	UFA(NYG)-'04	14/14
80	Hagans, Marques	WR	5-10	205	12/29/82	2	Virginia	Hampton, Va.	FA-'08	2/0*
23	Hall, DeAngelo	CB	5-10	195	11/19/83	6	Virginia Tech	Chesapeake, Va.	FA-'08	15/12
92	Haynesworth, Albert	DT	6-6	350	6/17/81	8	Tennessee	Hartsville, S.C.	UFA(Tenn)-'09	14/14*
74	Heyer, Stephon	T	6-6	330	1/16/84	3	Maryland	Lawrenceville, Ga.	FA-'07	9/7
48	Horton, Chris	S	6-1	211	12/29/84	2	UCLA	New Orleans. La.	D7-'08	14/10
91	Jackson, Rob	DE	6-4	269	11/3/85	2	Kansas State	West Haven, Conn.	D7-'08	3/0
76	Jansen, Jon	T	6-6	306	1/28/76	11	Michigan	Clawson, Mich.	D2-'99	14/11
12	Kelly, Malcolm	WR	6-4	227	12/30/86	2	Oklahoma	Longview, Texas	D2-'08	5/0
#	Kendall, Pete	G	6-5	286	7/9/73	14	Boston College	Weymouth, Mass.	T(NYJ)-'07	16/16
30	Landry, LaRon	S	6-0	210	10/14/84	3	Louisiana State	Ama, La.	D1-'07	16/16
24	Mason, Marcus	RB	5-9	215	6/23/84	2	Youngstown State	Potomac, Md.	W(NYJ)-'09	0*
52	McIntosh, Rocky	LB	6-2	238	11/15/82	4	Miami	Gaffney, S.C.	D2-'06	16/15
94	Montgomery, Anthony	DT	6-6	330	3/8/84	4	Minnesota	Cleveland, Ohio	D5-'06	14/6
63	Montgomery, Will	G	6-3	305	2/13/83	3	Virginia Tech	Clifton, Va.	FA-'08	0*
41	Moore, Kareem	S	5-11	218	8/13/84	2	Nicholls State	Okolona, Miss.	D6-'08	14/1
89	Moss, Santana	WR	5-10	200	6/1/79	9	Miami	Miami, Fla.	T(NYJ)-'05	16/16
26	Portis, Clinton	RB	5-11	221	9/1/81	8	Miami	Gainesville, Fla.	T(Den)-'04	16/16
61	Rabach, Casey	CB	6-4	295	9/24/77	9	Wisconsin	Sturgeon Bay, Wisc.	UFA(Balt)-'05	16/16
82	Randle El, Antwaan	WR	5-10	185	8/17/79	9	Indiana	Riverdale, Ill.	UFA(Pitt)-'06	15/13
4	Rayner, Dave	K	6-2	210	10/26/82	4	Michigan State	Oxford, Mich.	FA-'09	2/0*
75	Rinehart, Chad	G/T	6-5	310	5/4/85	2	Northern Iowa	Boone, Iowa	D3-'08	0*
22	Rogers, Carlos	CB	6-0	190	7/2/81	5	Auburn	Augusta, Ga.	D1-'05	16/14
60	Samuels, Chris	T	6-5	314	7/28/77	10	Alabama	Mobile, Ala.	D1-'00	12/12
45	Sellers, Mike	FB	6-3	280	7/21/75	10	Walla Walla (Wash.) C.C.	North Thurston, Wash.	FA-'04	16/6
3	Smith, Hunter	P	6-2	209	8/9/77	11	Notre Dame	Sherman, Texas	FA-'09	16/0*
56	Smith, Tyson	LB	6-2	250	10/9/81	2	Iowa State	West Des Moines, Iowa	FA-'08	0*
27	Smoot, Fred	CB	5-11	185	4/17/79	9	Mississippi State	Jackson, Miss.	FA-'07	16/9
6	Suisham, Shaun	K	6-0	200	12/29/81	4	Bowling Green	Wallaceburg, Ontario	FA-'06	16/0
11	Thomas, Devin	WR	6-2	215	11/15/86	2	Michigan State	Ann Arbor, Mich.	D2-'08	16/1
77	Thomas, Randy	G	6-5	308	1/19/76	11	Mississippi State	East Point, Ga.	UFA(NYJ)-'03	16/16
55	Thomas, Robert	LB	6-0	235	7/17/80	8	UCLA	El Centro, Calif.	FA-'09	2/1*
83	Thrash, James	WR	6-0	203	4/28/75	13	Missouri Southern	Wewoka, Okla.	T(Phil)-'04	16/5
20	Tryon, Justin	CB	5-9	183	5/29/84	2	Arizona State	Palmdale, Calif.	D4-08	14/0
#	Wallace, Rian	LB	6-3	243	5/24/82	3	Temple	Pottstown, Pa.	FA-'08	0*
71	Williams, Mike	T	6-7	370	1/11/80	5	Texas	Dallas, Texas	FA-'09	0*
88	Williams, Roydell	WR	6-0	187	3/14/81	4	Tulane	New Orleans, La.	FA-'09	0*
95	Wilson, Chris	DE	6-4	247	7/10/82	3	Northwood	Flint, Mich.	FA-'07	16/0

97	Wynn, Renaldo	DE	6-3	296	9/3/74	13	Notre Dame	Chicago, Ill.	UFA(NYG)-'09	16/0*
87	Yoder, Todd	TE	6-4	251	3/18/78	10	Vanderbilt	New Palestine, Ind.	FA-'06	16/2

* Alridge missed '08 season because of injury; Bridges played 14 games with N.Y. Giants in '08; Cain was last active with Tennessee in '07; Daniels missed '08 season because of injury; Dockery played 16 games with Buffalo; Hagans played 2 games with Kansas City; Haynesworth played 14 games with Tennessee; Mason inactive 6 games with N.Y. Jets in '08; W. Montgomery inactive for 3 games; Rayner played 2 games with Cincinnati; H. Smith played 16 games with Indianapolis; R. Thomas played 2 games with Oakland; Wallace last active with Pittsburgh in '06; M. Williams was last active with Buffalo in '05; R. Williams last active with Tennessee in '07; Wynn played 16 games with the N.Y. Giants.

Players lost through free agency (2): DT Ryan Boschetti (Oak; 3 games in '08), DE Demetric Evans (SF; 16).

Also played with Redskins in '08—RB Shaun Alexander (4 games), P Durant Brooks (6), S Justin Hamilton (2), DE Erasmus James (5), P Ryan Plackemeier (10), CB/S Shawn Springs (9), LB/DE Jason Taylor (13), CB Leigh Torrence (9), LB Marcus Washington (10).

2009 FIRST-YEAR ROSTER

Name	Pos.	Ht.	Wt.	Birthdate	College	Hometown	How Acq.
Agnone, Robbie	TE	6-6	260	10/2/85	Delaware	Etters, Pa.	FA
Barnes, Kevin	CB	6-1	188	9/15/86	Maryland	Glen Burnie, Md.	D3
Burley, Scott	T	6-5	335	1/2/86	Maryland	Baltimore, Md.	FA
Daniel, Chase	QB	6-0	225	10/7/86	Missouri	Southlake, Texas	FA
Dixon, Antonio	DT	6-3	322	7/17/85	Miami	Miami, Fla.	FA
Dorsey, Dominique (1)	RB	5-7	170	5/7/83	Nevada-Las Vegas	Tulare, Calif.	FA
Dutch, Doug	CB	5-11	199	2/15/86	Michigan	Bowie, Md.	FA
Eloi, Keith	WR	5-10	190	11/1/84	Nebraska-Omaha	Naples, Fla.	FA
Evans, Jonathan (1)	FB	6-1	245	10/10/81	Baylor	Duncanville, Texas	FA
Glenn, Cody	LB	6-0	240	10/6/86	Nebraska	Rusk, Texas	D5
Grant, Michael (1)	DB	5-11	182	3/20/86	Arkansas	Stone Mountain, Ga.	FA-'08
Henson, Robert	LB	6-0	242	1/27/86	Texas Christian	Longview, Texas	D6
Holmes, Lendy	S	6-1	201	10/28/85	Oklahoma	Dallas, Texas	FA
Manupuna, Vaka (1)	DT	6-0	300	6/30/82	Colorado	Honolulu, Hawaii	FA
Mitchell, Marko	WR	6-4	218	3/11/85	Nevada	York, Ala.	D7
Orakpo, Brian	LB/DE	6-4	260	7/31/86	Texas	Houston, Texas	D1
Riley, Rueben (1)	G	6-4	305	9/20/84	Michigan	Marksville, La.	FA-'08
Shelton, Trent (1)	WR	6-0	202	9/21/84	Baylor	Little Rock, Ark.	FA
Skolnitsky, J.D.	DL	6-5	255	11/6/86	James Madison	Fairfax, Va.	FA
Walker, Derek	DE	6-4	268	9/16/86	Illinois	Glendale Heights, Ill.	FA
Westbrook, Byron	CB	5-10	200	12/26/84	Salisbury	Washington, D.C.	FA-'07
Williams, Eddie	FB	6-1	249	8/22/87	Idaho	San Mateo, Calif.	D7
Williams, Edwin	C	6-3	315	12/10/86	Maryland	Washington, D.C.	FA
Williams, Jaison	WR	6-5	237	4/14/86	Oregon	Culver City, Calif.	FA
Young, Darrel	LB	5-11	245	4/8/87	Villanova	Amityville, NY	FA

The term NFL Rookie is defined as a player who is in his first season of professional football and has not been on the roster of another professional football team for any regular-season or postseason games. A Rookie is designated by an "R" on NFL rosters. Players who have been active in another professional football league or players who have NFL experience, including either preseason training camp or being on an Active List or Inactive List, or on Reserve/Injured or Reserve/Physically Unable to Perform for fewer than six regular-season games, are termed NFL First-Year Players. An NFL First-Year Player is designated by a "1" on NFL rosters. Thereafter, a player is credited with an additional year of experience for each season in which he accumulates six games on the Active List or Inactive List, or on Reserve/Injured or Reserve/Physically Unable to Perform.

Log on to www.washingtonredskins.com for an up-to-date roster.

WASHINGTON REDSKINS

COACHING STAFF

Head Coach,
Jim Zorn

Pro Career: Became the twenty-seventh coach in franchise history when he replaced Joe Gibbs on February 9, 2008. In his first season, Zorn led the Redskins to an 8-8 record. Zorn began his NFL coaching career as an offensive assistant with the Seattle Seahawks (1997), and then moved to the Detroit Lions as quarterbacks coach (1998-2000), where he was instrumental in the development of rookie quarterback Charlie Batch. Zorn returned to the Seattle Seahawks in 2001, as quarterbacks coach, where he remained until 2007 while helping to develop quarterbacks Matt Hasselbeck, Trent Dilfer, and Brock Huard. Career record: 8-8.

Background: Played quarterback at Cal Poly-Pomona. Broke into the NFL in 1976 as the first quarterback for the expansion Seahawks. Played nine years for Seattle, then one year each with the Green Bay Packers (1985), the Winnipeg Blue Bombers of the CFL (1986), and the Tampa Bay Buccaneers (1987). Coached at Boise State (1989-1991), Utah State (1992-1994), and Minnesota (1995-1996).

Personal: Born May 10, 1953 in Whittier, Calif. Jim and his wife, Joy, have four children, daughters, Rachel, Sarah, Danielle, and son, Isaac. Rachel is married to Neal Mitchell, and they have a daughter: Hollis Joy.

ASSISTANT COACHES

Harrison Bernstein, strength and conditioning; born May 14, 1978, Brooklyn, N.Y. Defensive back Johns Hopkins 1996-99. No pro playing experience. Pro coach: Joined Redskins in 2007.

Greg Blache, defensive coordinator; born March 9, 1949, New Orleans. Attended Notre Dame. No college or pro playing experience. College coach: Notre Dame 1972-75, 1981-83, Tulane 1976-1980, Southern 1986, Kansas 1987. Pro coach: Jacksonville Bulls (USFL) 1984-85, Green Bay Packers 1988-1993, Indianapolis Colts 1994-98, Chicago Bears 1999-2003, joined Redskins in 2004.

Joe Bugel, offensive line; born March 10, 1940, Pittsburgh. Guard/linebacker Western Kentucky 1960-63. No pro playing experience. College coach: Western Kentucky 1964-68, Navy 1969-1972, Iowa State 1973, Ohio State 1974. Pro coach: Detroit Lions 1975-76, Houston Oilers 1977-1980, Washington Redskins 1981-89, Phoenix Cardinals 1990-1993 (head coach), Oakland Raiders 1995-97 (head coach 1997), San Diego Chargers 1998-2001, re-joined Redskins in 2004.

Bobby Crumpler, strength and conditioning; born April 23, 1965, Newton Grove, N.C. Running back North Carolina State 1983-87. No pro playing experience. College coach: North Carolina State 1989, 1992-96, 2000-01, Kansas 2002. Pro coach: Joined Redskins in 2003.

Chip Garber, defensive quality control; May 7, 1955, Winchester, Va. Linebacker Maryland 1975-77. No pro playing experience. College coach: Southern Methodist 1980-81, Kentucky 1982-89, Mississippi State 1990, TCU 1991, Minnesota 1992-95, Virginia Military Institute 1996-98, Hofstra 1999, Army 2000-03, Hofstra 2004-05, North Texas 2006. Pro coach: Hamilton Tiger-Cats (CFL) 2008, joined Redskins in 2009.

Jerry Gray, secondary; born December 16, 1962, Lubbock, Texas. Safety Texas 1981-84. Pro defensive back Los Angeles Rams 1985-1991, Houston Oilers 1992, Tampa Bay Buccaneers 1993. College coach: Southern Methodist 1995-96. Pro coach: Tennessee Titans 1997-2000, Buffalo Bills 2001-05, joined Redskins in 2006.

John Hastings, strength and conditioning; born July 5, 1964, Newport News, Va. Attended Ohio University. No college or pro playing experience. Pro coach: San Diego Chargers 1990-2001, joined Redskins in 2002.

Stan Hixon, wide receivers; born July 24, 1957, Lakeland, Fla. Wide receiver Iowa State 1975-78. No pro playing experience. College coach: Morehead State 1980-82, Appalachian State 1983-88, South Carolina 1989-1992, Wake Forest 1993-94, Georgia Tech 1995-99, Louisiana State 2000-03. Pro coach: Joined Redskins in 2004.

Steve Jackson, safeties; born April 8, 1969, Houston. Defensive back Purdue 1987-1990. Pro defensive back Houston Oilers/Tennessee Titans 1991-99. Pro coach: Buffalo Bills 2001-03, joined Redskins in 2004.

Bill Khayat, offensive quality control; born March 26, 1973, York, Pa. Tight end Duke 1992-95. Pro tight end Kansas City Chiefs 1996, Carolina Panthers 1997, Barcelona Dragons (NFLE) 1998. College coach: Tennessee State 2000-03. Pro coach: Arizona Cardinals 2004-06, joined Redskins in 2007.

Chris Meidt, offensive assistant; born June 1, 1969, Fergus Falls, Minn. Attended Bethel College. No college or pro playing experience. College coach: Bethel University 1995-2001, St. Olaf College 2002-07. Pro coach: Joined Redskins in 2008.

Stump Mitchell, asst. head coach/running backs; born March 15, 1959, St. Mary's, Ga. Tailback The Citadel 1977-1980. Pro running back St. Louis/Phoenix Cardinals 1981-89. College coach: Morgan State 1995-98 (head coach 1996-98). Pro coach: San Antonio Rough Riders (WLAF) 1991, Seattle Seahawks 1999-2007, joined Redskins in 2008.

Kirk Olivadotti, linebackers; born January 1, 1974, Wilmington, Del. Wide receiver Purdue 1992-1996. No pro playing experience. College coach: Maine Maritime Academy 1997, Indiana State 1998-99. Pro coach: Joined Redskins in 2000.

John Palermo, defensive line; born March 27, 1952, Newburgh, N.Y. Defensive tackle Florida State 1972-73. No pro playing experience. College coach: Memphis State 1980-82, Appalachian State 1983-84, Minnesota 1984-87, Notre Dame 1988-89, Austin Peay 1990, Wisconsin 1991-2005, Miami 2006, Tennessee Tech 2007. Pro coach: Joined Redskins in 2008.

Danny Smith, special teams; born September 7, 1953, Pittsburgh. Defensive back Edinboro State 1972-75. No pro playing experience. College coach: Edinboro State 1976, Clemson 1979, William & Mary 1980-83, The Citadel 1984-86, Georgia Tech 1987-1994. Pro coach: Philadelphia Eagles 1995-98, Detroit Lions 1999-2000, Buffalo Bills 2001-03, joined Redskins in 2004.

Sherman Smith, offensive coordinator; born November 1, 1954, Youngstown, Ohio. Quarterback Miami (Ohio) 1972-75. Pro running back Seattle Seahawks 1976-1982, San Diego Chargers 1983-84. College coach: Miami (Ohio) 1990-91, Illinois 1992-94. Pro coach: Houston Oilers/Tennessee Titans 1995-2007, joined Redskins in 2008.

Scott Wachenheim, tight ends; born August 13, 1962, Woodland Hills, Calif. Offensive lineman Air Force Academy 1980-83. No pro playing experience. College coach: Arkansas 1989-1990, Colorado 1991, Utah State 1992-93, Rice 1994-2005, Liberty 2006-08. Pro coach: Joined Redskins in 2009.

2008 Season in Review

2008 TRADES

Defensive tackle **Kris Jenkins** from Carolina to N.Y. Jets for the Jets' third-round selection in 2008 (DB **Charles Godfrey**) and the Jets' fifth-round selection in 2008 (TE **Gary Barnidge**). (2/29)

Defensive tackle **Jason Ferguson** and the Cowboys' sixth-round selection in 2008 (G **Donald Thomas**) from Dallas to Miami for the Dolphins' sixth-round selection in 2008 (LB **Erik Walden**). (2/29)

Wide receiver **Troy Williamson** from Minnesota to Jacksonville for the Jaguars' sixth-round selection in 2008 (WR **Jaymar Johnson**). (2/29)

Linebacker **Jonathan Vilma** from N.Y. Jets to New Orleans for the Saints' fourth-round selection in 2008 (DB **Dwight Lowery**). (2/29)

Defensive back **Leigh Bodden** and the Browns' third-round selection in 2008 (DT **Andre Fluellen**) from Cleveland to Detroit for defensive tackle **Shaun Rogers**. (3/1)

Defensive tackle **Corey Williams** from Green Bay to Cleveland for the Browns' second-round selection in 2008 (QB **Brian Brohm**). (3/1)

Defensive tackle **Marcus Stroud** from Jacksonville to Buffalo for the Ravens' third-round selection in 2008 (#71) and the Bears' fifth-round selection in 2008 (#143). (3/1)

Quarterback **Brian Griese** from Chicago to Tampa Bay for two unannounced selections. (3/3)

Center **Chris Myers** from Denver to Houston for the Texans' sixth-round selection in 2008 (LB **Spencer Larsen**). (3/17)

Defensive back **DeAngelo Hall** from Atlanta to Oakland for the Raiders' second-round selection in 2008 (#34) and an unannounced selection. (3/21)

Defensive end **Jared Allen** and the Buccaneers' sixth-round selection in 2008 (C **John Sullivan**) from Kansas City to Minnesota for the Vikings' first-round selection in 2008 (#17), the Broncos' third-round selection in 2008 (RB **Jamaal Charles**), the Vikings' third-round selection in 2008 (DB **DaJuan Morgan**), and the Vikings' sixth-round selection in 2008 (WR **Kevin Robinson**). (4/23)

Defensive tackle **Dewayne Robertson** from N.Y. Jets to Denver for an unannounced selection. (4/26)

Linebacker **Akin Ayodele** and tight end **Anthony Fasano** from Dallas to Miami for the Dolphins' fourth-round selection in 2008 (#100). (4/26)

New Orleans' first-round selection in 2008 (LB **Jerod Mayo**) and third-round selection in 2008 (LB **Shawn Crable**) from New Orleans to New England for the 49ers' first-round selection in 2008 (DT **Sedrick Ellis**) and the Patriots' fifth-round selection in 2008 (T **Carl Nicks**). (4/26)

Baltimore's first-round selection in 2008 (DE **Derrick Harvey**) from Baltimore to Jacksonville for the Jaguars' first-round selection in 2008 (#26), the Ravens' third-round selection in 2008 (LB **Tavares Gooden**), the Jaguars' third-round selection in 2008 (#89), and the Jaguars' fourth-round selection in 2008 (#125). (4/26)

Detroit's first-round selection in 2008 (T **Branden Albert**) and the Lions' third-round selection in 2008 (TE **Brad Cottam**) from Detroit to Kansas City for the Vikings' first-round selection in 2008 (T **Gosder Cherilus**), the Chiefs' third-round selection in 2008 (#66), and the Dolphins' fifth-round selection in 2008 (WR **Kenneth Moore**). (4/26)

Houston's first-round selection in 2008 (QB **Joe Flacco**) from Houston to Baltimore for the Jaguars' first-round selection in 2008 (#26), the Jaguars' third-round selection in 2008 (RB **Steve Slaton**), and the Ravens' sixth-round selection in 2008 (DB **Dominique Barber**). (4/26)

Philadelphia's first-round selection in 2008 (T **Jeff Otah**) from Philadelphia to Carolina for the Panthers' second-round selection in 2008 (#43), the Panthers' fourth-round selection in 2008 (G **Mike McGlynn**), and the Panthers' first-round selection in 2009 (#28). (4/26)

Washington's first-round selection in 2008 (T **Sam Baker**), the Redskins' third-round selection in 2008 (WR **Harry Douglas**), and the Redskins' fifth-round selection in 2008 (DE **Kroy Biermann**) from Washington to Atlanta for the Raiders' second-round selection in 2008 (WR **Devin Thomas**), the Texans' second-round selection (TE **Fred Davis**), and the Falcons' fourth-round selection (#103). (4/26)

Seattle's first-round selection in 2008 (DB **Mike Jenkins**) from Seattle to Dallas for the Cowboys' first-round selection in 2008 (DE **Lawrence Jackson**), fifth-round selection in 2008 (RB **Owen Schmitt**), and seventh-round selection in 2008 (K **Brandon Coutu**). (4/26)

Green Bay's first-round selection in 2008 (DT **Dustin Keller**) from Green Bay to N.Y. Jets for the Jets' second-round selection in 2008 (WR **Jordy Nelson**) and the Saints' fourth-round selection in 2008 (#113). (4/26)

Baltimore's second-round selection in 2008 (TE **John Carlson**) from Baltimore to Seattle for the Seahawks' second-round selection in 2008 (RB **Ray Rice**), and third-round selection in 2008 (DB **Tom Zbikowski**). (4/26)

Running back **Lorenzo Booker** from Miami to Philadelphia for the Eagles' fourth-round selection in 2008 (#115). (4/26)

Minnesota's second-round selection in 2008 (DT **Trevor Laws**) and fourth-round selection in 2008 (DB **Quintin Demps**) from Minnesota to Philadelphia for the Panthers' second-round selection in 2008 (DB **Tyrell Johnson**) and the Eagles' fifth-round selection in 2008 (DT **Letroy Guion**). (4/26)

Tampa Bay's second-round selection in 2008 (DE **Quentin Groves**) from Tampa Bay to Jacksonville for the Jaguars' second-round selection in 2008 (WR **Dexter Jackson**), the Seahawks' fifth-round selection in 2008 (#158), and the Jaguars' seventh-round selection in 2009 (DB **E.J. Biggers**). (4/26)

Miami's third-round selection in 2008 (RB **Kevin Smith**) from Miami to Detroit for the Chiefs' third-round selection in 2008 (DE **Kendall Langford**) and the Lions' sixth-round selection in 2008 (RB **Jalen Parmele**). (4/27)

New England's third-round selection in 2008 (RB **Jacob Hester**) from New England to San Diego for the Chargers' fifth-round selection in 2008 (#160) and second-round selection in 2009 (#47). (4/27)

Dallas' third-round selection in 2008 (DE **Cliff Avril**) from Dallas to Detroit for the Lions' fourth-round selection in 2008 (#111) and fourth-round selection in 2009 (QB **Stephen McGee**). (4/27)

Defensive back **Adam Jones** from Tennessee to Dallas for the Cowboys' fourth-round selection in 2008 (WR **Lavelle Hawkins**). (4/27)

Tennessee's fourth-round selection in 2008 (DB **Justin Tryon**) and fifth-round selection in 2008 (#157) from Tennessee to Washington for the Falcons' fourth-round selection in 2008 (DE **William Hayes**). (4/27)

Oakland's fourth-round selection in 2008 (#104) and seventh-round selection in 2008 (#213) from Oakland to Dallas for the Dolphins' fourth-round selection in 2008 (DB **Tyvon Branch**). (4/27)

New York Jets' fourth-round selection in 2008 (DE **Jeremy Thompson**) from N.Y. Jets to Green Bay for the Saints' fourth-round selection in 2008 (DB **Dwight Lowery**) and the Packers' fifth-round selection in 2008 (QB **Erik Ainge**). (4/27)

Cleveland's fourth-round selection in 2008 (RB **Tashard Choice**) and fifth-round selection in 2008 (#155) from Cleveland to Dallas for the Raiders' fourth-round selection in 2008 (LB **Beau Bell**). (4/27)

Defensive back **Fabian Washington** from Oakland to Baltimore for the Jaguars' fourth-round selection in 2008 (WR **Arman Shields**). (4/27)

Chicago's fourth-round selection in 2008 (G **Shawn Murphy**) from Chicago to Miami for the Eagles' fourth-round selection in 2008 (#115), and the Dolphins' seventh-round selection in 2008 (DE **Ervin Baldwin**). (4/27)

Cleveland's third-round selection in 2009 (LB **Jason Williams**) from Cleveland to Dallas for the Lions' fourth-round selection in 2008 (TE **Martin Rucker**). (4/27)

Tampa Bay's fourth-round selection in 2008 (DB **Craig Steltz**) and the Seahawks' fifth-round selection in 2008 (TE **Kellen Davis**) from Tampa Bay to Chicago for the Eagles' fourth-round selection in 2008 (DT **Dre Moore**) and the Bears' sixth-round selection in 2008 (LB **Geno Hayes**). (4/27)

Pittsburgh's fourth-round selection in 2008 (LB **Bryan Kehl**) from Pittsburgh to N.Y. Giants for the Giants' fourth-round selection in 2008 (T **Tony Hills**) and the Packers' sixth-round selection in 2008 (#194). (4/27)

Green Bay's fourth-round selection in 2008 (WR **Keenan Burton**) from Green Bay to St. Louis for the Rams' fifth-round selection in 2008 (#137) and the Bengals' seventh-round selection in 2008 (WR **Brett Swain**). (4/27)

Minnesota's fifth-round selection in 2008 (T **Breno Giacomini**) and the Rams' seventh-round selection in 2008 (QB **Matt Flynn**) from Minnesota to Green Bay for the Rams' fifth-round selection in 2008 (QB **John David Booty**). (4/27)

Bears' fifth-round selection in 2008 (DB **Orlando Scandrick**) from Jacksonville to Dallas for the Browns' fifth-round selection in 2008 (LB **Thomas Williams**) and the Raiders' seventh-round selection in 2008 (RB **Chauncey Washington**). (4/27)

Detroit's fifth-round selection in 2008 (DT **DeMario Pressley**) from Detroit to New Orleans for the Saints' fifth-round selection in 2008 (RB **Jerome Felton**) and seventh-round selection in 2008 (DB **Caleb Campbell**). (4/27)

Tampa Bay's fifth-round selection in 2008 (WR **Matt Slater**) from Tampa Bay to New England for the Chargers' fifth-round selection in 2008 (QB **Josh Johnson**) and the Patriots' seventh-round selection in 2008 (RB **Cory Byrd**). (4/27)

St. Louis' sixth-round selection in 2008 (P **Durant Brooks**) and the Broncos' sixth-round selection in 2008 (DB **Kareem Moore**) from St. Louis to Washington for the Titans' fifth-round selection in 2008 (G **Roy Schuening**) and the Redskins' seventh-round selection in 2008 (LB **Chris Chamberlain**). (4/27)

Cleveland's fifth-round selection in 2009 from Cleveland to Philadelphia for the Browns' sixth-round selection in 2008 (WR **Paul Hubbard**). (4/27)

Green Bay's seventh-round selection in 2008 (WR **Adrian Arrington**) from Green Bay to New Orleans for the Saints' sixth-round selection in 2009 (DB **Brandon Underwood**). (4/27)

Defensive end **Erasmus James** from Minnesota to Washington for Redskins' unannounced selection. (5/27)

Running back **Luke Lawton** from Indianapolis to Philadelphia for an Eagles' unannounced selection. (6/6)

Defensive end **Jason Taylor** from Miami to Washington for Redskins' unannounced selections. (7/21)

Tight end **Jeremy Shockey** from the New York Giants to New Orleans for Saints' unannounced selections. (7/21)

Quarterback **Brett Favre** from Green Bay to the New York Jets for an unannounced selection. (8/7)

Defensive back **Travis Daniels** from Miami

to Cleveland for a Browns' unannounced selection. (8/20)

Defensive end **Marques Douglas** from Tampa Bay to Baltimore for a Ravens' unannounced selection. (8/27)

Guard **Montrae Holland** from Denver to Dallas for a Cowboys' unannounced selection. (8/28)

Quarterback **Josh McCown** from Miami to Carolina for a Panthers' unannounced selection. (8/30)

Defensive back **Domonique Foxworth** from Denver to Atlanta for a Falcons' unannounced selection. (9/2)

Center **Sean Mahan** from Pittsburgh to Tampa Bay for a Buccaneers' unannounced selection. (9/2)

Guard **Dan Buenning** from Tampa Bay to Chicago for a Bears' unannounced selection. (9/2)

Wide receiver **Keary Colbert** from Denver to Seattle for a Seahawks' unannounced selection. (9/16)

Defensive tackle **John McCargo** from Buffalo to Indianapolis for a Colts' unannounced selection. (10/14)

Wide receiver **Roy Williams** and a Detroit unannounced selection from the Lions to Dallas for Cowboys' unannounced selections. (10/14)

** Draft choice number is listed if club later traded the pick.*

2009 TRADES

Tight end **Kellen Winslow** from Cleveland to Tampa Bay for the Buccaneers' second-round selection in 2009 (WR **Mohamed Massaquoi**) and sixth-round selection in 2009 (DB **Coye Francies**). (2/27)

Quarterback **Sage Rosenfels** from Houston to Minnesota for the Vikings' fourth-round selection in 2009 (TE **Anthony Hill**). (2/27)

Defensive back **Anthony Henry** from Dallas to Detroit for quarterback **Jon Kitna**. (2/28)

Quarterback **Matt Cassel** and linebacker **Mike Vrabel** from New England to Kansas City for the Chiefs' second-round selection in 2009 (DB **Patrick Chung**). (2/28)

Defensive back **Lito Sheppard** from Philadelphia to N.Y. Jets for the Jets' fifth-round selection in 2009 (TE **Cornelius Ingram**). (2/28)

Wide receiver **Greg Lewis** and an unannounced choice from Philadelphia to New England for the Patriots' fifth-round selection in 2009 (T **Fenuki Tupou**). (3/5)

Defensive tackle **Cory Redding** and the Lions' fifth-round selection in 2009 (#137) from Detroit to Seattle for linebacker **Julian Peterson**. (3/16)

Defensive tackle **Tony McDaniel** from Jacksonville to Miami for the Dolphins' seventh-round selection in 2009 (#232). (4/9)

Center **Samson Satele** and the Dolphins' fourth-round selection in 2009 (LB **Slade Norris**) from Miami to Oakland for the Raiders' fourth-round selection in 2009 (WR **Brian Hartline**) and sixth-round selection in 2009 (T **Andrew Gardner**). (3/23)

Quarterback **Jay Cutler** and the Seahawks' fifth-round selection in 2009 (WR **Johnny Knox**) from Denver to Chicago for quarterback **Kyle Orton**, the Bears' first-round selection in 2009 (DE **Robert Ayers**), third-round selection in 2009 (#84), and an unannounced selection. (4/3)

Wide receiver **Laurent Robinson**, the Falcons' fifth-round selection in 2009 (WR **Foster Brooks**), and sixth-round selection in 2009 (QB **Keith Null**) from Atlanta to St. Louis for the Rams' fifth-round selection in 2009 (DB **William Middleton**) and sixth-round selection in 2009 (LB **Spencer Adkins**). (4/9)

Long snapper **J.J. Jansen** from Green Bay to Carolina for an unannounced selection. (4/13)

Tackle **Jason Peters** from Buffalo to Philadelphia for the Eagles' first-round selection in 2009 (C **Eric Wood**) and fourth-round selection in 2009 (TE **Shawn Nelson**). (4/20)

Tight end **Tony Gonzalez** from Kansas City to Atlanta for an unannounced selection. (4/23)

Defensive end **Kenyon Coleman**, defensive back **Abram Elam**, quarterback **Brett Ratliff**, the Jets' first-round selection in 2009 (#17) and second-round selection in 2009 (DE **David Veikune**) from N.Y. Jets to Cleveland for the Browns' first-round selection in 2009 (QB **Mark Sanchez**). (4/25)

Tampa Bay's first-round selection in 2009 (#19) and the Buccaneers' sixth-round selection in 2009 (DB **Coye Francies**) from Tampa Bay to Cleveland for the Jets' sixth-round selection in 2009 (QB **Josh Freeman**). (4/25)

Philadelphia's first-round selection in 2009 (C **Alex Mack**) and Vikings' sixth-round selection in 2009 (RB **James Davis**) from Philadelphia to Cleveland for the Buccaneers' first-round selection in 2009 (WR **Jeremy Maclin**). (4/25)

New England's first-round selection in 2009 (T **Michael Oher**) from New England to Baltimore for the Ravens' first-round selection in 2009 (#26) and fifth-round selection in 2009 (#162). (4/25)

Green Bay's second-round selection in 2009 (DB **Darius Butler**), third-round selection in 2009 (#73), and the Jets' third-round selection in 2009 (WR **Brandon Tate**) from Green Bay to New England for the Ravens' first-round selection in 2009 (LB **Clay Matthews**) and Ravens' sixth-round selection in 2009 (T **Jamon Meredith**). (4/25)

Seattle's second-round selection in 2009 (DB **Alphonso Smith**) from Seattle to Denver for the Broncos' first-round selection in 2010. (4/25)

Oakland's second-round selection in 2009 (DT **Ron Brace**) from Oakland to New England for the Chargers' second-round selection in 2009 (DB **Michael Mitchell**), the Patriots' fourth-round selection in 2009 (WR **Louis Murphy**), and the Patriots' sixth-round selection in 2009 (DE **Stryker Sulak**). (4/25)

San Francisco trades 49ers' second-round selection in 2009 (DE **Everette Brown**) and fourth-round selection in 2009 (RB **Mike Goodson**) from San Francisco to Carolina for the Panthers' first-round selection in 2010. (4/25)

Chicago trades Bears' second-round selection in 2009 (C **Max Unger**) from Chicago to Seattle for the Seahawks' third-round selection in 2009 (DT **Jarron Gilbert**) and fourth-round selection in 2009 (DE **Henry Melton**). (4/25)

Dallas trades Cowboys' second-round selection in 2009 (G **Andy Levitre**) from Dallas to Buffalo for the Bills' third-round selection in 2009 (T **Robert Brewster**) and fourth-round selection in 2009 (LB **Victor Butler**). (4/25)

Miami trades Dolphins' second-round selection in 2009 (DT **Fili Moala**) from Miami to Indianapolis for the Colts' second-round selection in 2009 (DB **Sean Smith**) and fifth-round selection in 2009 (DB **Chris Clemons**). (4/25)

Denver trades Broncos' third-round selection in 2009 (TE **Richard Quinn**) and Bears' third-round selection in 2009 (G **Seth Olsen**) from Denver to Pittsburgh for the Steelers' second-round selection in 2009 (G **Kraig Urbik**) and fourth-round selection in 2009 (WR **Mike Wallace**). (4/25)

Detroit trades Lions' third-round selection in 2009 (RB **Shonn Greene**) from Detroit to N.Y. Jets for the Saints' third-round selection in 2009 (LB **DeAndre Levy**), Redskins' fourth-round selection in 2009 (DT **Sammie Lee Hill**), and Jets' seventh-round selection in 2009 (T **Lydon Murtha**). (4/26)

New England trades Packers' third-round selection in 2009 (DB **Derek Cox**) from New England to Jacksonville for the Dolphins' seventh-round selection in 2009 (WR **Julian Edelman**) and second-round selection in 2010. (4/26)

Philadelphia trades Eagles' third-round selection in 2009 (WR **Ramses Barden**) from Philadelphia to N.Y. Giants for the Giants' third-round selection in 2009 (#91) and fifth-round selection in 2009 (#164). (4/26)

New England trades Patriots' third-round selection in 2009 (TE **Jared Cook**) from New England to Tennessee for the Titans' second-round selection in 2010. (4/26)

Philadelphia trades Giants' third-round selection in 2009 (WR **Deon Butler**) from Philadelphia to Seattle for the Lions' fifth-round selection in 2009 (#137), the Seahawks' seventh-round selection in 2009 (G **Paul Fanaika**), and the Seahawks' third-round selection in 2010. (4/26)

Dallas trades Cowboys' fourth-round selection in 2009 (DE **Kyle Moore**) from Dallas to Tampa Bay for the Buccaneers' fourth-round selection in 2009 (LB **Brandon Williams**) and Bears' seventh-round selection in 2009 (WR **Manuel Johnson**). (4/26)

Defensive back **Ellis Hobbs** from New England to Philadelphia for the Lions' fifth-round selection in 2009 (#137) and the Browns' fifth-round selection in 2009 (#141). (4/26)

New England trades Lions' fifth-round selection in 2009 (LB **Jason Phillips**) and the Browns' fifth-round selection in 2009 (#141) from New England to Baltimore for the Ravens' fourth-round selection in 2009 (G **Rich Ohrnberger**) and sixth-round selection in 2009 (LS **Jake Ingram**). (4/26)

Baltimore trades Browns' fifth-round selection in 2009 (WR **Kenny McKinley**) from Baltimore to Denver for the Broncos' fifth-round selection in 2009 (TE **Davon Drew**) and sixth-round selection in 2009 (RB **Cedric Peerman**). (4/26)

Atlanta trades Raiders' fifth-round selection in 2009 (DB **DeAngelo Smith**) from Atlanta to Dallas for the Cowboys' fifth-round selection in 2009 (T **Garrett Reynolds**) and Lions' seventh-round selection in 2009 (DT **Vance Walker**). (4/26)

Washington trades Redskins' fifth-round selection in 2009 (LB **Jasper Brinkley**) from Washington to Minnesota for the Vikings' fifth-round selection in 2009 (LB **Cody Glenn**) and Redskins' seventh-round selection in 2009 (RB **Eddie Williams**). (4/26)

Philadelphia trades Giants' fifth-round selection in 2009 (P **Thomas Morstead**) from Philadelphia to New Orleans for the Saints' seventh-round selection in 2009 (#222) and Saints' fifth-round selection in 2010. (4/26)

Detroit trades Lions' sixth-round selection in 2009 (QB **Tom Brandstater**) from Detroit to Denver for the Falcons' seventh-round selection in 2009 (LB **Zack Follett**) and Broncos' fifth-round selection in 2010. (4/26)

Carolina trades Panthers' sixth-round selection in 2009 (TE **Brandon Myers**) from Carolina to Oakland for the Raiders' seventh-round selection in 2009 (DB **Captain Munnerlyn**) and Raiders' sixth-round selection in 2010. (4/26)

Indianapolis trades Colts' sixth-round selection in 2010 from Indianapolis to Philadelphia for the Saints' seventh-round selection in 2009 (P **Pat McAfee**). (4/26)

Kansas City trades Chiefs' seventh-round selection in 2010 from Kansas City to Miami for the Panthers' seventh-round selection in 2009 (TE **Jake O'Connell**). (4/26)

Tight end **Alex Smith** from Tampa Bay to New England for an unannounced selection. (4/30)

Defensive tackle **Orien Harris** from Cincinnati to St. Louis for running back **Brian Leonard**. (5/7)

** Draft choice number is listed if club later traded the pick.*

2008 PRESEASON STANDINGS/RESULTS

PRESEASON STANDINGS

AMERICAN FOOTBALL CONFERENCE

East Division

	W	L	T	Pct.	Pts.	OP
Miami	3	1	0	.750	63	41
New York Jets	3	1	0	.750	71	60
Buffalo	2	2	0	.500	64	59
New England	0	4	0	.000	56	89

North Division

	W	L	T	Pct.	Pts.	OP
Pittsburgh	3	1	0	.750	68	60
Cincinnati	2	2	0	.500	57	64
Baltimore	1	3	0	.250	50	72
Cleveland	0	4	0	.000	70	103

South Division

	W	L	T	Pct.	Pts.	OP
Jacksonville	3	1	0	.750	81	56
Tennessee	3	1	0	.750	77	67
Houston	2	2	0	.500	78	82
Indianapolis	1	4	0	.200	66	109

West Division

	W	L	T	Pct.	Pts.	OP
San Diego	3	1	0	.750	75	58
Denver	2	2	0	.500	91	73
Kansas City	2	2	0	.500	62	88
Oakland	1	3	0	.250	50	70

AFC PRESEASON RECORDS—TEAM BY TEAM

East Division

BUFFALO (2-2)

14	at Washington	17
24	Pittsburgh	21
20	at Indianapolis	7
6	Detroit	14
64		59

MIAMI (3-1)

6	Tampa Bay	17
19	at Jacksonville	14
24	Kansas City	0
14	at New Orleans	10
63		41

NEW ENGLAND (0-4)

15	Baltimore	16
10	at Tampa Bay	27
17	Philadelphia	27
14	at New York Giants	19
56		89

N.Y. JETS (3-1)

24	at Cleveland	20
10	Washington	13
10	New York Giants	7
27	at Philadelphia	20
71		60

North Division

BALTIMORE (1-3)

16	at New England	15
15	Minnesota	23
10	at St. Louis	24
9	Atlanta	10
50		62

CINCINNATI (2-2)

20	at Green Bay	17
10	Detroit	27
0	New Orleans	13
27	at Indianapolis	7
57		64

CLEVELAND (0-4)

20	New York Jets	24
34	at New York Giants	37
6	at Detroit	26
10	Chicago	16
70		103

PITTSBURGH (3-1)

16	Philadelphia	10
21	at Buffalo	24
12	at Minnesota	10
19	Carolina	16
68		60

South Division

HOUSTON (2-2)

19	Denver	16
31	at New Orleans	27
22	at Dallas	23
6	Tampa Bay	16
78		82

INDIANAPOLIS (1-4)

16	Washington (a)	30
20	at Carolina	(OT) 23
16	at Atlanta	9
7	Buffalo	20
7	Cincinnati	27
66		109

JACKSONVILLE (3-1)

20	Atlanta	17
14	Miami	19
23	at Tampa Bay	17
24	at Washington	3
81		56

TENNESSEE (3-1)

34	St. Louis	13
17	Oakland	16
3	at Atlanta	17
23	at Green Bay	21
77		67

West Division

DENVER (2-2)

16	at Houston	19
23	Dallas	13
24	Green Bay	27
28	at Arizona	14
91		73

KANSAS CITY (2-2)

24	at Chicago	20
17	Arizona	27
0	at Miami	24
21	St. Louis	17
32		67

OAKLAND (1-3)

18	San Francisco	6
16	at Tennessee	17
0	Arizona	24
16	at Seattle	23
50		70

SAN DIEGO (3-1)

31	Dallas	17
6	at St. Louis	7
18	Seattle	17
20	at San Francisco	17
75		58

(a) Pro Football Hall of Fame Game at Canton, Ohio

NFC PRESEASON RECORDS—TEAM BY TEAM

East Division

DALLAS (2-2)

17	at San Diego	31
13	at Denver	23
23	Houston	22
16	Minnesota	10
69		86

N.Y. GIANTS (2-2)

10	at Detroit	13
37	Cleveland	34
7	at New York Jets	10
19	New England	14
70		71

PHILADELPHIA (2-2)

10	at Pittsburgh	16
24	Carolina	13
27	at New England	17
20	New York Jets	27
81		73

WASHINGTON (3-2)

30	Indianapolis (a)	16
17	Buffalo	14
13	at New York Jets	10
3	at Carolina	47
3	Jacksonville	24
66		111

North Division

CHICAGO (1-3)

20	Kansas City	24
26	at Seattle	(OT) 29
30	San Francisco	37
16	at Cleveland	10
92		100

DETROIT (4-0)

13	New York Giants	10
27	at Cincinnati	10
26	Cleveland	6
14	at Buffalo	6
80		32

GREEN BAY (1-3)

17	Cincinnati	20
6	at San Francisco	34
27	at Denver	24
21	Tennessee	23
71		101

MINNESOTA (1-3)

17	Seattle	34
23	at Baltimore	15
10	Pittsburgh	12
10	at Dallas	16
50		77

South Division

ATLANTA (2-2)

17	at Jacksonville	20
9	Indianapolis	16
17	Tennessee	3
10	at Baltimore	9
53		48

CAROLINA (2-2)

23	Indianapolis	(OT) 20
13	at Philadelphia	24
47	Washington	3
16	at Pittsburgh	19
99		66

NEW ORLEANS (2-2)

24	at Arizona	10
27	Houston	31
13	at Cincinnati	0
10	Miami	14
74		55

TAMPA BAY (3-1)

17	at Miami	6
27	New England	10
17	Jacksonville	23
16	at Houston	6
77		45

West Division

ARIZONA (2-2)

10	New Orleans	24
27	at Kansas City	17
24	at Oakland	0
14	Denver	28
75		69

ST. LOUIS (2-2)

13	at Tennessee	34
7	San Diego	6
24	Baltimore	10
17	at Kansas City	21
61		71

SAN FRANCISCO (2-2)

6	at Oakland	18
34	Green Bay	6
37	at Chicago	30
17	San Diego	20
94		74

SEATTLE (3-1)

34	at Minnesota	17
29	Chicago	(OT) 26
17	at San Diego	18
23	Oakland	16
103		77

(a) Pro Football Hall of Fame Game at Canton, Ohio

PRESEASON STANDINGS

NATIONAL FOOTBALL CONFERENCE

East Division

	W	L	T	Pct.	Pts.	OP
Washington	3	2	0	.600	66	111
Dallas	2	2	0	.500	69	86
New York Giants	2	2	0	.500	73	71
Philadelphia	2	2	0	.500	81	73

North Division

	W	L	T	Pct.	Pts.	OP
Detroit	4	0	0	1.000	80	32
Chicago	1	3	0	.250	92	100
Green Bay	1	3	0	.250	71	101
Minnesota	1	3	0.	250	60	77

South Division

	W	L	T	Pct.	Pts.	OP
Tampa Bay	3	1	0	.750	77	45
Atlanta	2	2	0	.500	53	48
Carolina	2	2	0	.500	99	66
New Orleans	2	2	0	.500	74	55

West Division

	W	L	T	Pct.	Pts.	OP
Seattle	3	1	0	.750	103	77
Arizona	2	2	0	.500	75	69
St. Louis	2	2	0	.500	61	71
San Francisco	2	2	0	.500	94	74

2008 AFC RESULTS

AMERICAN FOOTBALL CONFERENCE

BALTIMORE (11-5)		
17	Cincinnati	10
28	Cleveland	10
20	at Pittsburgh (OT)	23
10	Tennessee	13
3	at Indianapolis	31
27	at Miami	13
29	Oakland	10
37	at Cleveland	27
41	at Houston	13
10	at New York Giants	30
36	Philadelphia	7
34	at Cincinnati	3
24	Washington	10
9	Pittsburgh	13
33	at Dallas	24
27	Jacksonville	7
385		244

BUFFALO (7-9)		
34	Seattle	10
20	at Jacksonville	16
24	Oakland	23
31	at St. Louis	14
17	at Arizona	41
23	San Diego	14
16	at Miami	25
17	New York Jets	26
10	at New England	20
27	Cleveland	29
54	at Kansas City	31
3	San Francisco	10
3	Miami	16
27	at New York Jets	31
30	at Denver	23
0	New England	13
336		342

CINCINNATI (4-11-1)		
10	at Baltimore	17
7	Tennessee	24
23	at New York Giants (OT)	26
12	Cleveland	20
22	at Dallas	31
14	at New York Jets	26
10	Pittsburgh	38
6	at Houston	35
21	Jacksonville	19
13	Philadelphia (OT)	13
10	at Pittsburgh	27
3	Baltimore	34
3	at Indianapolis	35
20	Washington	13
14	at Cleveland	0
16	Kansas City	6
204		364

CLEVELAND (4-12)		
10	Dallas	28
6	Pittsburgh	10
10	at Baltimore	28
20	at Cincinnati	12
35	New York Giants	14
11	at Washington	14
23	at Jacksonville	17
27	Baltimore	37
30	Denver	34
29	at Buffalo	27
6	Houston	16
6	Indianapolis	10
9	at Tennessee	28
10	at Philadelphia	30
0	Cincinnati	14
0	at Pittsburgh	31
232		350

DENVER (8-8)		
41	at Oakland	14
39	San Diego	38
34	New Orleans	32
19	at Kansas City	33
16	Tampa Bay	13
17	Jacksonville	24
7	at New England	41
17	Miami	26
34	at Cleveland	30
24	at Atlanta	20
10	Oakland	31
34	at New York Jets	17
24	Kansas City	17
10	at Carolina	30
23	Buffalo	30
21	at San Diego	52
370		448

HOUSTON (8-8)		
17	at Pittsburgh	38
12	at Tennessee	31
27	at Jacksonville (OT)	30
27	Indianapolis	31
29	Miami	28
28	Detroit	21
35	Cincinnati	6
21	at Minnesota	28
13	Baltimore	41
27	at Indianapolis	33
16	at Cleveland	6
30	Jacksonville	17
24	at Green Bay	21
13	Tennessee	12
16	at Oakland	27
31	Chicago	24
366		394

INDIANAPOLIS (12-4)		
13	Chicago	29
18	at Minnesota	15
21	Jacksonville	23
31	at Houston	27
31	Baltimore	3
14	at Green Bay	34
21	at Tennessee	31
18	New England	15
24	at Pittsburgh	20
33	Houston	27
23	at San Diego	20
10	at Cleveland	6
35	Cincinnati	3
31	Detroit	21
31	at Jacksonville	24
23	Tennessee	0
377		298

JACKSONVILLE (5-11)		
10	at Tennessee	17
16	Buffalo	20
23	at Indianapolis	21
30	Houston (OT)	27
21	Pittsburgh	26
24	at Denver	17
17	Cleveland	23
19	at Cincinnati	21
38	at Detroit	14
14	Tennessee	24
12	Minnesota	30
17	at Houston	30
10	at Chicago	23
20	Green Bay	16
24	Indianapolis	31
7	at Baltimore	27
302		367

KANSAS CITY (2-14)		
10	at New England	17
8	Oakland	23
14	at Atlanta	38
33	Denver	19
0	at Carolina	34
10	Tennessee	34
24	at New York Jets	28
27	Tampa Bay (OT)	30
19	at San Diego	20
20	New Orleans	30
31	Buffalo	54
20	at Oakland	13
17	at Denver	24
21	San Diego	22
31	Miami	38
6	at Cincinnati	16
291		440

MIAMI (11-5)		
14	New York Jets	20
10	at Arizona	31
38	at New England	13
17	SAN DIEGO	10
28	at Houston	29
13	BALTIMORE	27
25	BUFFALO	16
26	at Denver	17
21	SEATTLE	19
17	OAKLAND	15
28	NEW ENGLAND	48
16	at St. Louis	12
16	at Buffalo	3
14	SAN FRANCISCO	9
38	at Kansas City	31
24	at New York Jets	17
345		317

NEW ENGLAND (11-5)		
17	Kansas City	10
19	at New York Jets	10
13	Miami	38
30	at San Francisco	21
10	at San Diego	30
41	Denver	7
23	St. Louis	16
15	at Indianapolis	18
20	Buffalo	10
31	New York Jets (OT)	34
48	at Miami	28
10	Pittsburgh	33
24	at Seattle	21
49	at Oakland	26
47	Arizona	7
13	at Buffalo	0
410		309

NEW YORK JETS (9-7)		
20	at Miami	14
10	New England	19
29	at San Diego	48
56	Arizona	35
26	Cincinnati	14
13	at Oakland (OT)	16
28	Kansas City	24
26	at Buffalo	17
47	St. Louis	3
34	at New England (OT)	31
34	at Tennessee	13
17	Denver	34
14	at San Francisco	24
31	Buffalo	27
3	at Seattle	13
17	Miami	24
405		356

OAKLAND (5-11)		
14	Denver	41
23	at Kansas City	8
23	at Buffalo	24
18	San Diego	28
3	at New Orleans	34
16	New York Jets (OT)	13
10	at Baltimore	29
0	Atlanta	24
6	Carolina	17
15	at Miami	17
31	at Denver	10
13	Kansas City	20
7	at San Diego	34
26	New England	49
27	Houston	16
31	at Tampa Bay	24
263		388

PITTSBURGH (12-4)		
38	Houston	17
10	at Cleveland	6
6	at Philadelphia	15
23	Baltimore (OT)	20
26	at Jacksonville	21
38	at Cincinnati	10
14	New York Giants	21
23	at Washington	6
20	Indianapolis	24
11	San Diego	10
27	Cincinnati	10
33	at New England	10
20	Dallas	13
13	at Baltimore	9
14	at Tennessee	31
31	Cleveland	0
347		223

SAN DIEGO (8-8)		
24	Carolina	26
38	at Denver	39
48	New York Jets	29
28	at Oakland	18
10	at Miami	17
30	New England	10
14	at Buffalo	23
32	at New Orleans	37
20	Kansas City	19
10	at Pittsburgh	11
20	Indianapolis	23
16	Atlanta	22
34	Oakland	7
22	at Kansas City	21
41	at Tampa Bay	24
52	Denver	21
439		347

TENNESSEE (13-3)		
17	Jacksonville	10
24	at Cincinnati	7
31	Houston	12
30	Minnesota	17
13	at Baltimore	10
34	at Kansas City	10
31	Indianapolis	21
19	Green Bay (OT)	16
21	at Chicago	14
24	at Jacksonville	14
13	New York Jets	34
47	at Detroit	10
28	Cleveland	9
12	at Houston	13
31	Pittsburgh	14
0	at Indianapolis	23
375		234

NATIONAL FOOTBALL CONFERENCE

ARIZONA (9-7)

23	at San Francisco	13
31	Miami	10
17	at Washington	24
35	at New York Jets	56
41	Buffalo	17
30	Dallas (OT)	24
23	at Carolina	27
34	at St. Louis	13
29	San Francisco	24
26	at Seattle	20
29	New York Giants	37
20	at Philadelphia	48
34	St. Louis	10
14	Minnesota	35
7	at New England	47
34	Seattle	21
427		426

ATLANTA (11-5)

34	Detroit	21
9	at Tampa Bay	24
38	Kansas City	14
9	at Carolina	24
27	at Green Bay	24
22	Chicago	20
14	at Philadelphia	27
24	at Oakland	0
34	New Orleans	20
20	Denver	24
45	Carolina	28
22	at San Diego	16
25	at New Orleans	29
13	Tampa Bay (OT)	10
24	at Minnesota	17
31	ST. LOUIS	27
391		325

CAROLINA (12-4)

26	at San Diego	24
20	Chicago	17
10	at Minnesota	20
24	Atlanta	9
34	Kansas City	0
3	at Tampa Bay	27
30	New Orleans	7
27	Arizona	23
17	at Oakland	6
31	Detroit	22
28	at Atlanta	45
35	at Green Bay	31
38	Tampa Bay	23
30	Denver	10
28	at New York Giants (OT)	34
33	at New Orleans	31
414		329

CHICAGO (9-7)

29	at Indianapolis	13
17	at Carolina	20
24	Tampa Bay (OT)	27
24	Philadelphia	20
34	at Detroit	7
20	at Atlanta	22
48	Minnesota	41
27	Detroit	23
14	Tennessee	21
3	at Green Bay	37
27	at St. Louis	3
14	at Minnesota	34
23	Jacksonville	10
27	New Orleans (OT)	24
20	Green Bay (OT)	17
24	at Houston	31
375		350

DALLAS (9-7)

28	at Cleveland	10
41	Philadelphia	37
27	at Green Bay	16
24	Washington	26
31	Cincinnati	22
24	at Arizona (OT)	30
14	at St. Louis	34
13	Tampa Bay	9
14	at New York Giants	35
14	at Washington	10
35	San Francisco	22
34	Seattle	9
13	at Pittsburgh	20
20	New York Giants	8
24	Baltimore	33
6	at Philadelphia	44
362		365

DETROIT (0-16)

21	at Atlanta	34
25	Green Bay	48
13	at San Francisco	31
7	Chicago	34
10	at Minnesota	12
21	at Houston	28
17	Washington	25
23	at Chicago	27
14	Jacksonville	38
22	at Carolina	31
20	Tampa Bay	38
10	Tennessee	47
16	Minnesota	20
21	at Indianapolis	31
7	New Orleans	42
21	at Green Bay	31
268		517

GREEN BAY (6-10)

24	Minnesota	19
48	at Detroit	25
16	Dallas	27
21	at Tampa Bay	30
24	Atlanta	27
27	at Seattle	17
34	Indianapolis	14
16	at Tennessee (OT)	19
27	at Minnesota	28
37	Chicago	3
29	at New Orleans	51
31	Carolina	35
21	Houston	24
16	at Jacksonville	20
17	at Chicago (OT)	20
31	Detroit	21
419		380

MINNESOTA (10-6)

19	at Green Bay	24
15	Indianapolis	18
20	Carolina	10
17	at Tennessee	30
30	at New Orleans	27
12	Detroit	10
41	at Chicago	48
28	Houston	21
28	Green Bay	27
13	at Tampa Bay	19
30	at Jacksonville	12
34	Chicago	14
20	at Detroit	16
35	at Arizona	14
17	Atlanta	24
20	New York Giants	19
379		333

NEW ORLEANS (8-8)

24	Tampa Bay	20
24	at Washington	29
32	at Denver	34
31	San Francisco	17
27	Minnesota	30
34	Oakland	3
7	at Carolina	30
37	San Diego	32
20	at Atlanta	34
30	at Kansas City	20
51	Green Bay	29
20	at Tampa Bay	23
29	Atlanta	25
24	at Chicago (OT)	27
42	at Detroit	7
31	Carolina	33
463		393

NEW YORK GIANTS (12-4)

16	Washington	7
41	at St. Louis	13
26	Cincinnati (OT)	23
44	Seattle	6
14	at Cleveland	35
29	San Francisco	17
21	at Pittsburgh	14
35	Dallas	14
36	at Philadelphia	31
30	Baltimore	10
37	at Arizona	29
23	at Washington	7
14	Philadelphia	20
8	at Dallas	20
34	Carolina (OT)	28
19	at Minnesota	20
427		294

PHILADELPHIA (9-6-1)

38	St. Louis	3
37	at Dallas	41
15	Pittsburgh	6
20	at Chicago	24
17	Washington	23
40	at San Francisco	26
27	Atlanta	14
26	at Seattle	7
31	New York Giants	36
13	at Cincinnati (OT)	13
7	at Baltimore	36
48	Arizona	20
20	at New York Giants	14
30	Cleveland	10
3	at Washington	10
44	Dallas	6
416		289

ST. LOUIS (2-14)

3	at Philadelphia	38
13	New York Giants	41
13	at Seattle	37
14	Buffalo	31
19	at Washington	17
34	Dallas	14
16	at New England	23
13	Arizona	34
3	at New York Jets	47
16	at San Francisco	35
3	Chicago	27
12	Miami	16
10	at Arizona	34
20	Seattle	23
16	San Francisco	17
27	at Atlanta	31
232		465

SAN FRANCISCO (7-9)

13	Arizona	23
33	at Seattle (OT)	30
31	Detroit	13
17	at New Orleans	31
21	New England	30
26	Philadelphia	40
17	at New York Giants	29
13	Seattle	34
24	at Arizona	29
35	St. Louis	16
22	at Dallas	35
10	at Buffalo	3
24	New York Jets	14
9	at Miami	14
17	at St. Louis	16
27	Washington	24
339		381

SEATTLE (4-12)

10	at Buffalo	34
30	San Francisco (OT)	33
37	St. Louis	13
6	at New York Giants	44
17	Green Bay	27
10	at Tampa Bay	20
34	at San Francisco	13
7	Philadelphia	26
19	at Miami	21
20	Arizona	26
17	Washington	20
9	at Dallas	34
21	New England	24
23	at St. Louis	20
13	New York Jets	3
21	at Arizona	34
294		392

TAMPA BAY (9-7)

20	at New Orleans	24
24	Atlanta	9
27	at Chicago (OT)	24
30	Green Bay	21
13	at Denver	16
27	Carolina	3
20	Seattle	10
9	at Dallas	13
30	at Kansas City (OT)	27
19	Minnesota	13
38	at Detroit	20
23	New Orleans	20
23	at Carolina	38
10	at Atlanta (OT)	13
24	San Diego	41
24	Oakland	31
361		323

WASHINGTON (8-8)

7	at New York Giants	16
29	New Orleans	24
24	Arizona	17
26	at Dallas	24
23	at Philadelphia	17
17	St. Louis	19
14	Cleveland	11
25	at Detroit	17
6	Pittsburgh	23
10	Dallas	14
20	at Seattle	17
7	New York Giants	23
10	at Baltimore	24
13	at Cincinnati	20
10	Philadelphia	3
24	at San Francisco	27
265		296

2008 NFL STANDINGS

FINAL STANDINGS

AMERICAN FOOTBALL CONFERENCE

East Division	**W**	**L**	**T**	**Pct.**	**Pts.**	**OP**
* Miami	11	5	0	.688	345	317
New England	11	5	0	.688	410	309
New York Jets	9	7	0	.563	405	356
Buffalo	7	9	0	.438	363	342
North Division	**W**	**L**	**T**	**Pct.**	**Pts.**	**OP**
* Pittsburgh	12	4	0	.750	347	223
# Baltimore	11	5	0	.688	385	244
Cincinnati	4	11	1	.281	204	364
Cleveland	4	12	0	.250	232	350
South Division	**W**	**L**	**T**	**Pct.**	**Pts.**	**OP**
* Tennessee	13	3	0	.813	375	234
# Indianapolis	12	4	0	.750	377	298
Houston	8	8	0	.500	366	394
Jacksonville	5	11	0	.313	302	367
West Division	**W**	**L**	**T**	**Pct.**	**Pts.**	**OP**
* San Diego	8	8	0	.500	439	347
Denver	8	8	0	.500	370	448
Oakland	5	11	0	.313	263	388
Kansas City	2	14	0	.125	291	440

NATIONAL FOOTBALL CONFERENCE

East Division	**W**	**L**	**T**	**Pct.**	**Pts.**	**OP**
* New York Giants	12	4	0	.750	427	294
# Philadelphia	9	6	1	.594	416	289
Dallas	9	7	0	.563	362	365
Washington	8	8	0	.500	265	296
North Division	**W**	**L**	**T**	**Pct.**	**Pts.**	**OP**
* Minnesota	10	6	0	.625	379	333
Chicago	9	7	0	.563	375	350
Green Bay	6	10	0	.375	419	380
Detroit	0	16	0	.000	268	517
South Division	**W**	**L**	**T**	**Pct.**	**Pts.**	**OP**
* Carolina	12	4	0	.750	414	329
# Atlanta	11	5	0	.688	391	325
Tampa Bay	9	7	0	.563	361	323
New Orleans	8	8	0	.500	463	393
West Division	**W**	**L**	**T**	**Pct.**	**Pts.**	**OP**
* Arizona	9	7	0	.563	427	426
San Francisco	7	9	0	.438	339	381
Seattle	4	12	0	.250	294	392
St. Louis	2	14	0	.125	232	465

* *Division champion*
\# *Wild Card team*

Miami finished ahead of New England based on better conference record (8-4 to Patriots' 7-5). Baltimore was second Wild Card ahead of New England based on better conference record (8-4 to Patriots' 7-5). San Diego finished ahead of Denver based on better division record (5-1 to Broncos' 3-3). N.Y. Giants finished ahead of Carolina based on head-to-head victory.

WILD-CARD PLAYOFFS
AFC
SAN DIEGO 23, Indianapolis 17
Baltimore 27, MIAMI 9
NFC
ARIZONA 30, Atlanta 24
Philadelphia 26, MINNESOTA 14

DIVISIONAL PLAYOFFS
AFC
Baltimore 13, TENNESSEE 10
PITTSBURGH 35, San Diego 24
NFC
Arizona 33, CAROLINA 13
Philadelphia 23, N.Y. GIANTS 11

CHAMPIONSHIP GAMES
AFC
PITTSBURGH 23, Baltimore 14
NFC
ARIZONA 32, Philadelphia 25

SUPER BOWL XLIII
Pittsburgh (AFC) 27, Arizona (NFC) 23
at Raymond James Stadium, Tampa, Florida

AFC-NFC PRO BOWL
NFC 30, AFC 21
at Aloha Stadium, Honolulu, Hawaii

Home teams in playoff games are indicated in CAPS.

FIRST WEEK STANDINGS

American Football Conference

East Division	W	L	T	Pct.	Pts.	OP
Buffalo	1	0	0	1.000	34	10
New England	1	0	0	1.000	17	10
New York Jets	1	0	0	1.000	20	14
Miami	0	1	0	.000	14	20
North Division	**W**	**L**	**T**	**Pct.**	**Pts.**	**OP**
Baltimore	1	0	0	1.000	17	10
Pittsburgh	1	0	0	1.000	38	17
Cincinnati	0	1	0	.000	10	17
Cleveland	0	1	0	.000	10	28
South Division	**W**	**L**	**T**	**Pct.**	**Pts.**	**OP**
Tennessee	1	0	0	1.000	17	10
Houston	0	1	0	.000	17	38
Indianapolis	0	1	0	.000	13	29
Jacksonville	0	1	0	.000	10	17
West Division	**W**	**L**	**T**	**Pct.**	**Pts.**	**OP**
Denver	1	0	0	1.000	41	14
Kansas City	0	1	0	.000	10	17
Oakland	0	1	0	.000	14	41
San Diego	0	1	0	.000	24	26

National Football Conference

East Division	W	L	T	Pct.	Pts.	OP
Dallas	1	0	0	1.000	28	10
New York Giants	1	0	0	1.000	16	7
Philadelphia	1	0	0	1.000	38	3
Washington	0	1	0	.000	7	16
North Division	**W**	**L**	**T**	**Pct.**	**Pts.**	**OP**
Chicago	1	0	0	1.000	29	13
Green Bay	1	0	0	1.000	24	19
Detroit	0	1	0	.000	21	34
Minnesota	0	1	0	.000	19	24
South Division	**W**	**L**	**T**	**Pct.**	**Pts.**	**OP**
Atlanta	1	0	0	1.000	34	21
Carolina	1	0	0	1.000	26	24
New Orleans	1	0	0	1.000	24	20
Tampa Bay	0	1	0	.000	20	24
West Division	**W**	**L**	**T**	**Pct.**	**Pts.**	**OP**
Arizona	1	0	0	.000	23	13
St. Louis	0	1	0	.000	3	38
San Francisco	0	1	0	.000	13	23
Seattle	0	1	0	.000	10	34

WEEK 1 RESULTS

Thursday, September 4

N.Y. GIANTS 16, Washington 7

Sunday, September 7

ATLANTA 34, Detroit 21
NEW ORLEANS 24, Tampa Bay 20
N.Y. Jets 20, MIAMI 14
BUFFALO 34, Seattle 10
BALTIMORE 17, Cincinnati 10
TENNESSEE 10, Jacksonville 10
PITTSBURGH 38, Houston 17
Dallas 28, CLEVELAND 10
NEW ENGLAND 17, Kansas City 10
PHILADELPHIA 38, St. Louis 3
Arizona 23, SAN FRANCISCO 13
Carolina 26, SAN DIEGO 24
Chicago 29, INDIANAPOLIS 13

Monday, September 8

GREEN BAY 24, Minnesota 19
Denver 41, OAKLAND 14

In the 2008 Week By Week section, home teams are indicated by ALL CAPS.

**For game recaps, box scores, and video highlights, please visit www.NFL.com/scores.*

SECOND WEEK STANDINGS

American Football Conference

East Division	W	L	T	Pct.	Pts.	OP
Buffalo	2	0	0	1.000	54	26
New England	2	0	0	1.000	36	20
New York Jets	1	1	0	.500	30	33
Miami	0	2	0	.000	24	51
North Division	**W**	**L**	**T**	**Pct.**	**Pts.**	**OP**
Pittsburgh	2	0	0	1.000	48	23
Baltimore	1	0	0	1.000	17	10
Cincinnati	0	2	0	.000	17	41
Cleveland	0	2	0	.000	16	38
South Division	**W**	**L**	**T**	**Pct.**	**Pts.**	**OP**
Tennessee	2	0	0	1.000	41	17
Indianapolis	1	1	0	.500	31	44
Houston	0	1	0	.000	17	38
Jacksonville	0	2	0	.000	26	37
West Division	**W**	**L**	**T**	**Pct.**	**Pts.**	**OP**
Denver	2	0	0	1.000	80	52
Oakland	1	1	0	.500	37	49
Kansas City	0	2	0	.000	18	40
San Diego	0	2	0	.000	62	65

National Football Conference

East Division	W	L	T	Pct.	Pts.	OP
Dallas	2	0	0	1.000	69	47
New York Giants	2	0	0	1.000	57	20
Philadelphia	1	1	0	.500	75	44
Washington	1	1	0	.500	36	40
North Division	**W**	**L**	**T**	**Pct.**	**Pts.**	**OP**
Green Bay	2	0	0	1.000	72	44
Chicago	1	1	0	.500	46	33
Detroit	0	2	0	.000	46	82
Minnesota	0	2	0	.000	34	42
South Division	**W**	**L**	**T**	**Pct.**	**Pts.**	**OP**
Carolina	2	0	0	1.000	46	41
Atlanta	1	1	0	.500	43	45
New Orleans	1	1	0	.500	48	49
Tampa Bay	1	1	0	.500	44	33
West Division	**W**	**L**	**T**	**Pct.**	**Pts.**	**OP**
Arizona	2	0	0	1.000	54	23
San Francisco	1	1	0	.500	46	53
St. Louis	0	2	0	.000	16	79
Seattle	0	2	0	.000	40	67

WEEK 2 RESULTS

Sunday, September 14

CAROLINA 20, Chicago 17
Tennessee 24, CINCINNATI 7
Oakland 23, KANSAS CITY 8
Buffalo 20, JACKSONVILLE 16
Green Bay 48, DETROIT 25
WASHINGTON 29, New Orleans 24
N.Y. Giants 41, ST. LOUIS 13
Indianapolis 18, MINNESOTA 15
ARIZONA 31, Miami 10
TAMPA BAY 24, Atlanta 9
San Francisco 33, SEATTLE 30 (OT)
New England 19, N.Y. JETS 10
DENVER 39, San Diego 38
Pittsburgh 10, CLEVELAND 6

Monday, September 15

DALLAS 41, Philadelphia 37

Note: Baltimore at Houston game postponed until November 9 due to Hurricane Ike.

THIRD WEEK STANDINGS

American Football Conference

East Division	W	L	T	Pct.	Pts.	OP
Buffalo	3	0	0	1.000	78	49
New England	2	1	0	.667	49	58
Miami	1	2	0	.333	62	64
New York Jets	1	2	0	.333	59	81
North Division	**W**	**L**	**T**	**Pct.**	**Pts.**	**OP**
Baltimore	2	0	0	1.000	45	20
Pittsburgh	2	1	0	.667	54	38
Cincinnati	0	3	0	.000	40	67
Cleveland	0	3	0	.000	26	66
South Division	**W**	**L**	**T**	**Pct.**	**Pts.**	**OP**
Tennessee	3	0	0	1.000	72	29
Indianapolis	1	2	0	.333	52	67
Jacksonville	1	2	0	.333	49	58
Houston	0	2	0	.000	29	69
West Division	**W**	**L**	**T**	**Pct.**	**Pts.**	**OP**
Denver	3	0	0	1.000	114	84
Oakland	1	2	0	.333	60	73
San Diego	1	2	0	.333	110	94
Kansas City	0	3	0	.000	32	78

National Football Conference

East Division	W	L	T	Pct.	Pts.	OP
Dallas	3	0	0	1.000	96	63
New York Giants	3	0	0	1.000	83	43
Philadelphia	2	1	0	.667	90	50
Washington	2	1	0	.667	60	57
North Division	**W**	**L**	**T**	**Pct.**	**Pts.**	**OP**
Green Bay	2	1	0	.667	88	71
Chicago	1	2	0	.333	70	60
Minnesota	1	2	0	.333	54	52
Detroit	0	3	0	.000	59	113
South Division	**W**	**L**	**T**	**Pct.**	**Pts.**	**OP**
Atlanta	2	1	0	.667	81	590
Carolina	2	1	0	.667	56	61
Tampa Bay	2	1	0	.667	71	57
New Orleans	1	2	0	.333	80	83
West Division	**W**	**L**	**T**	**Pct.**	**Pts.**	**OP**
Arizona	2	1	0	.667	71	47
San Francisco	2	1	0	.667	77	66
Seattle	1	2	0	.333	77	80
St. Louis	0	3	0	.000	29	116

WEEK 3 RESULTS

Sunday, September 21

Tampa Bay 27, CHICAGO 24 (OT)
BUFFALO 24, Oakland 23
ATLANTA 38, Kansas City 14
N.Y. GIANTS 26, Cincinnati 23 (OT)
Miami 38, NEW ENGLAND 13
MINNESOTA 20, Carolina 10
DENVER 34, New Orleans 32
WASHINGTON 24, Arizona 17
TENNESSEE 31, Houston 12
BALTIMORE 28, Cleveland 10
SEATTLE 37, St. Louis 13
SAN FRANCISCO 31, Detroit 13
Jacksonville 23, INDIANAPOLIS 21
PHILADELPHIA 15, Pittsburgh 6
Dallas 27, GREEN BAY 16

Monday, September 22

SAN DIEGO 48, N.Y. Jets 29

FOURTH WEEK STANDINGS

American Football Conference

East Division	W	L	T	Pct.	Pts.	OP
Buffalo	4	0	0	1.000	109	63
New England	2	1	0	.667	49	58
New York Jets	2	2	0	.500	115	116
Miami	1	2	0	.333	62	64
North Division	**W**	**L**	**T**	**Pct.**	**Pts.**	**OP**
Pittsburgh	3	1	0	.750	77	58
Baltimore	2	1	0	.667	65	43
Cleveland	1	3	0	.250	46	78
Cincinnati	0	4	0	.000	52	87
South Division	**W**	**L**	**T**	**Pct.**	**Pts.**	**OP**
Tennessee	4	0	0	1.000	102	46
Jacksonville	2	2	0	.500	79	85
Indianapolis	1	2	0	.333	52	67
Houston	0	3	0	.000	56	99
West Division	**W**	**L**	**T**	**Pct.**	**Pts.**	**OP**
Denver	3	1	0	.750	133	117
San Diego	2	2	0	.500	138	112
Kansas City	1	3	0	.250	65	97
Oakland	1	3	0	.250	78	101

National Football Conference

East Division	W	L	T	Pct.	Pts.	OP
New York Giants	3	0	0	1.000	83	43
Dallas	3	1	0	.750	120	89
Washington	3	1	0	.750	86	81
Philadelphia	2	2	0	.500	110	74
North Division	**W**	**L**	**T**	**Pct.**	**Pts.**	**OP**
Chicago	2	2	0	.500	94	80
Green Bay	2	2	0	.500	109	101
Minnesota	1	3	0	.250	71	82
Detroit	0	3	0	.000	59	113
South Division	**W**	**L**	**T**	**Pct.**	**Pts.**	**OP**
Carolina	3	1	0	.750	80	70
Tampa Bay	3	1	0	.750	101	78
Atlanta	2	2	0	.500	90	83
New Orleans	2	2	0	.500	111	100
West Division	**W**	**L**	**T**	**Pct.**	**Pts.**	**OP**
Arizona	2	2	0	.500	106	103
San Francisco	2	2	0	.500	94	97
Seattle	1	2	0	.333	77	80
St. Louis	0	4	0	.000	43	147

WEEK 4 RESULTS

Sunday, September 28

JACKSONVILLE 30, Houston 27 (OT)
Cleveland 20, CINCINNATI 12
CAROLINA 24, Atlanta 9
N.Y. JETS 56, Arizona 35
NEW ORLEANS 31, San Francisco 17
KANSAS CITY 33, Denver 19
San Diego 28, OAKLAND 18
TENNESSEE 30, Minnesota 17
TAMPA BAY 30, Green Bay 21
Buffalo 31, ST. LOUIS 14
Washington 26, DALLAS 24
CHICAGO 24, Philadelphia 20

Monday, September 29

PITTSBURGH 23, Baltimore 20 (OT)

Byes: Detroit, Indianapolis, Miami, New England, N.Y. Giants, Seattle

FIFTH WEEK STANDINGS

American Football Conference

East Division	W	L	T	Pct.	Pts.	OP
Buffalo	4	1	0	.800	126	104
New England	3	1	0	.750	79	79
Miami	2	2	0	.500	79	74
New York Jets	2	2	0	.500	115	116
North Division	**W**	**L**	**T**	**Pct.**	**Pts.**	**OP**
Pittsburgh	4	1	0	.800	103	79
Baltimore	2	2	0	.500	75	56
Cleveland	1	3	0	.250	46	78
Cincinnati	0	5	0	.000	74	118
South Division	**W**	**L**	**T**	**Pct.**	**Pts.**	**OP**
Tennessee	5	0	0	1.000	115	56
Indianapolis	2	2	0	.500	83	94
Jacksonville	2	3	0	.400	100	111
Houston	0	4	0	.000	83	130
West Division	**W**	**L**	**T**	**Pct.**	**Pts.**	**OP**
Denver	4	1	0	.800	149	130
San Diego	2	3	0	.400	148	129
Oakland	1	3	0	.250	78	101
Kansas City	1	4	0	.200	65	131

National Football Conference

East Division	W	L	T	Pct.	Pts.	OP
New York Giants	4	0	0	1.000	127	49
Dallas	4	1	0	.800	151	111
Washington	4	1	0	.800	109	98
Philadelphia	2	3	0	.400	127	97
North Division	**W**	**L**	**T**	**Pct.**	**Pts.**	**OP**
Chicago	3	2	0	.600	128	87
Green Bay	2	3	0	.400	133	128
Minnesota	2	3	0	.400	101	109
Detroit	0	4	0	.000	66	147
South Division	**W**	**L**	**T**	**Pct.**	**Pts.**	**OP**
Carolina	4	1	0	.800	114	70
Atlanta	3	2	0	.600	117	107
Tampa Bay	3	2	0	.600	114	94
New Orleans	2	3	0	.400	138	130
West Division	**W**	**L**	**T**	**Pct.**	**Pts.**	**OP**
Arizona	3	2	0	.600	147	120
San Francisco	2	3	0	.400	115	127
Seattle	1	3	0	.250	83	124
St. Louis	0	4	0	.000	43	147

WEEK 5 RESULTS

Sunday, October 5

Tennessee 13, BALTIMORE 10
Atlanta 27, GREEN BAY 24
Chicago 34, DETROIT 7
CAROLINA 34, Kansas City 0
N.Y. GIANTS 44, Seattle 6
MIAMI 17, San Diego 10
Indianapolis 31, HOUSTON 27
ARIZONA 41, Buffalo 17
DENVER 16, Tampa Bay 13
Washington 23, PHILADELPHIA 17
DALLAS 31, Cincinnati 22
New England 30, SAN FRANCISCO 21
Pittsburgh 26, JACKSONVILLE 21

Monday, October 6

Minnesota 30, NEW ORLEANS 27

Byes: Cleveland, N.Y Jets, Oakland, St. Louis

SIXTH WEEK STANDINGS

American Football Conference

East Division	W	L	T	Pct.	Pts.	OP
Buffalo	4	1	0	.800	126	104
New England	3	2	0	.600	89	109
New York Jets	3	2	0	.600	141	130
Miami	2	3	0	.400	107	103
North Division	**W**	**L**	**T**	**Pct.**	**Pts.**	**OP**
Pittsburgh	4	1	0	.800	103	79
Baltimore	2	3	0	.400	78	87
Cleveland	2	3	0	.400	81	92
Cincinnati	0	6	0	.000	88	144
South Division	**W**	**L**	**T**	**Pct.**	**Pts.**	**OP**
Tennessee	5	0	0	1.000	115	56
Indianapolis	3	2	0	.600	114	97
Jacksonville	3	3	0	.500	124	128
Houston	1	4	0	.200	112	158
West Division	**W**	**L**	**T**	**Pct.**	**Pts.**	**OP**
Denver	4	2	0	.667	166	154
San Diego	3	3	0	.500	178	139
Kansas City	1	4	0	.200	65	131
Oakland	1	4	0	.200	81	135

National Football Conference

East Division	W	L	T	Pct.	Pts.	OP
New York Giants	4	1	0	.800	141	84
Dallas	4	2	0	.667	175	141
Washington	4	2	0	.667	126	117
Philadelphia	3	3	0	.500	167	123
North Division	**W**	**L**	**T**	**Pct.**	**Pts.**	**OP**
Chicago	3	3	0	.500	148	109
Green Bay	3	3	0	.500	160	145
Minnesota	3	3	0	.500	113	119
Detroit	0	5	0	.000	76	159
South Division	**W**	**L**	**T**	**Pct.**	**Pts.**	**OP**
Atlanta	4	2	0	.667	139	127
Carolina	4	2	0	.667	117	97
Tampa Bay	4	2	0	.667	141	97
New Orleans	3	3	0	.500	172	133
West Division	**W**	**L**	**T**	**Pct.**	**Pts.**	**OP**
Arizona	4	2	0	.667	177	144
San Francisco	2	4	0	.333	141	167
St. Louis	1	4	0	.200	62	164
Seattle	1	4	0	.200	100	151

WEEK 6 RESULTS

Sunday, October 12

ATLANTA 22, Chicago 20
NEW ORLEANS 34, Oakland 3
INDIANAPOLIS 31, Baltimore 3
HOUSTON 29, Miami 28
TAMPA BAY 27, Carolina 3
St. Louis 19, WASHINGTON 17
N.Y. JETS 26, Cincinnati 14
Green Bay 27, SEATTLE 17
Jacksonville 24, DENVER 17
MINNESOTA 12, Detroit 10
Philadelphia 40, SAN FRANCISCO 26
ARIZONA 30, Dallas 24 (OT)
SAN DIEGO 30, New England 10

Monday, October 13

CLEVELAND 35, N.Y. Giants 14

Byes: Buffalo, Kansas City, Pittsburgh, Tennessee

SEVENTH WEEK STANDINGS

American Football Conference

East Division	W	L	T	Pct.	Pts.	OP
Buffalo	5	1	0	.833	149	118
New England	4	2	0	.667	130	116
New York Jets	3	3	0	.500	154	146
Miami	2	4	0	.333	120	130
North Division	**W**	**L**	**T**	**Pct.**	**Pts.**	**OP**
Pittsburgh	5	1	0	.833	141	89
Baltimore	3	3	0	.500	105	100
Cleveland	2	4	0	.333	92	106
Cincinnati	0	7	0	.000	98	182
South Division	**W**	**L**	**T**	**Pct.**	**Pts.**	**OP**
Tennessee	6	0	0	1.000	149	66
Indianapolis	3	3	0	.500	128	131
Jacksonville	3	3	0	.500	124	128
Houston	2	4	0	.333	140	179
West Division	**W**	**L**	**T**	**Pct.**	**Pts.**	**OP**
Denver	4	3	0	.571	173	195
San Diego	3	4	0	.429	192	162
Oakland	2	4	0	.333	97	148
Kansas City	1	5	0	.167	75	165

National Football Conference

East Division	W	L	T	Pct.	Pts.	OP
New York Giants	5	1	0	.833	170	101
Washington	5	2	0	.714	140	128
Dallas	4	3	0	.571	189	175
Philadelphia	3	3	0	.500	167	123
North Division	**W**	**L**	**T**	**Pct.**	**Pts.**	**OP**
Chicago	4	3	0	.571	196	150
Green Bay	4	3	0	.571	194	159
Minnesota	3	4	0	.429	154	167
Detroit	0	6	0	.000	97	187
South Division	**W**	**L**	**T**	**Pct.**	**Pts.**	**OP**
Carolina	5	2	0	.714	147	104
Tampa Bay	5	2	0	.714	161	107
Atlanta	4	2	0	.667	139	127
New Orleans	3	4	0	.429	179	163
West Division	**W**	**L**	**T**	**Pct.**	**Pts.**	**OP**
Arizona	4	2	0	.667	177	144
St. Louis	2	4	0	.333	96	178
San Francisco	2	5	0	.286	158	196
Seattle	1	5	0	.167	110	171

WEEK 7 RESULTS

Sunday, October 19

BUFFALO 23, San Diego 14
Pittsburgh 38, CINCINNATI 10
CHICAGO 48, Minnesota 41
CAROLINA 30, New Orleans 7
N.Y. GIANTS 29, San Francisco 17
Baltimore 27, MIAMI 13
Tennessee 34, KANSAS CITY 10
GREEN BAY 34, Indianapolis 14
HOUSTON 28, Detroit 21
ST. LOUIS 34, Dallas 14
OAKLAND 16, N.Y. Jets 13 (OT)
WASHINGTON 14, Cleveland 11
TAMPA BAY 20, Seattle 10

Monday, October 20

NEW ENGLAND 41, Denver 7

Byes: Arizona, Atlanta, Jacksonville, Philadelphia

EIGHTH WEEK STANDINGS

American Football Conference

East Division	W	L	T	Pct.	Pts.	OP
Buffalo	5	2	0	.714	165	143
New England	5	2	0	.714	153	132
New York Jets	4	3	0	.571	182	170
Miami	3	4	0	.429	145	146
North Division	**W**	**L**	**T**	**Pct.**	**Pts.**	**OP**
Pittsburgh	5	2	0	.714	155	110
Baltimore	4	3	0	.571	134	110
Cleveland	3	4	0	.429	115	123
Cincinnati	0	8	0	.000	104	217
South Division	**W**	**L**	**T**	**Pct.**	**Pts.**	**OP**
Tennessee	7	0	0	1.000	180	87
Houston	3	4	0	.429	175	185
Indianapolis	3	4	0	.429	149	162
Jacksonville	3	4	0	.429	141	151
West Division	**W**	**L**	**T**	**Pct.**	**Pts.**	**OP**
Denver	4	3	0	.571	173	195
San Diego	3	5	0	.375	224	199
Oakland	2	5	0	.286	107	177
Kansas City	1	6	0	.143	99	193

National Football Conference

East Division	W	L	T	Pct.	Pts.	OP
New York Giants	6	1	0	.857	191	115
Washington	6	2	0	.750	165	145
Dallas	5	3	0	.625	202	184
Philadelphia	4	3	0	.571	194	137
North Division	**W**	**L**	**T**	**Pct.**	**Pts.**	**OP**
Chicago	4	3	0	.571	196	150
Green Bay	4	3	0	.571	194	159
Minnesota	3	4	0	.429	154	167
Detroit	0	7	0	.000	114	212
South Division	**W**	**L**	**T**	**Pct.**	**Pts.**	**OP**
Carolina	6	2	0	.750	174	127
Tampa Bay	5	3	0	.625	170	120
Atlanta	4	3	0	.571	153	154
New Orleans	4	4	0	.500	216	195
West Division	**W**	**L**	**T**	**Pct.**	**Pts.**	**OP**
Arizona	4	3	0	.571	200	171
St. Louis	2	5	0	.286	112	201
Seattle	2	5	0	.286	144	184
San Francisco	2	6	0	.250	171	230

WEEK 8 RESULTS

Sunday, October 26

BALTIMORE 29, Oakland 10
Washington 25, DETROIT 17
DALLAS 13, Tampa Bay 9
CAROLINA 27, Arizona 23
NEW ORLEANS 37, San Diego 32 (London)
NEW ENGLAND 23, St. Louis 16
MIAMI 25, Buffalo 16
Cleveland 23, JACKSONVILLE 17
PHILADELPHIA 27, Atlanta 14
N.Y. JETS 28, Kansas City 24
HOUSTON 35, Cincinnati 6
N.Y. Giants 21, PITTSBURGH 14
Seattle 34, SAN FRANCISCO 13

Monday, October 27

TENNESSEE 31, Indianapolis 21

Byes: Chicago, Denver, Green Bay, Minnesota

NINTH WEEK STANDINGS

American Football Conference

East Division	W	L	T	Pct.	Pts.	OP
Buffalo	5	3	0	.625	182	169
New England	5	3	0	.625	168	150
New York Jets	5	3	0	.625	208	187
Miami	4	4	0	.500	171	163
North Division	**W**	**L**	**T**	**Pct.**	**Pts.**	**OP**
Pittsburgh	6	2	0	.750	178	116
Baltimore	5	3	0	.625	171	137
Cleveland	3	5	0	.375	142	160
Cincinnati	1	8	0	.111	125	236
South Division	**W**	**L**	**T**	**Pct.**	**Pts.**	**OP**
Tennessee	8	0	0	1.000	199	103
Indianapolis	4	4	0	.500	167	177
Houston	3	5	0	.375	196	213
Jacksonville	3	5	0	.375	160	172
West Division	**W**	**L**	**T**	**Pct.**	**Pts.**	**OP**
Denver	4	4	0	.500	190	221
San Diego	3	5	0	.375	224	199
Oakland	2	6	0	.250	107	201
Kansas City	1	7	0	.125	126	223

National Football Conference

East Division	W	L	T	Pct.	Pts.	OP
New York Giants	7	1	0	.875	226	129
Washington	6	3	0	.667	171	168
Philadelphia	5	3	0	.625	220	144
Dallas	5	4	0	.556	216	219
North Division	**W**	**L**	**T**	**Pct.**	**Pts.**	**OP**
Chicago	5	3	0	.625	223	173
Green Bay	4	4	0	.500	210	178
Minnesota	4	4	0	.500	182	188
Detroit	0	8	0	.000	137	239
South Division	**W**	**L**	**T**	**Pct.**	**Pts.**	**OP**
Carolina	6	2	0	.750	174	127
Tampa Bay	6	3	0	.667	200	147
Atlanta	5	3	0	.625	177	154
New Orleans	4	4	0	.500	216	195
West Division	**W**	**L**	**T**	**Pct.**	**Pts.**	**OP**
Arizona	5	3	0	.625	234	184
St. Louis	2	6	0	.250	125	235
San Francisco	2	6	0	.250	171	230
Seattle	2	6	0	.250	151	210

WEEK 9 RESULTS

Sunday, November 2

N.Y. Jets 26, BUFFALO 17
Baltimore 37, CLEVELAND 27
CINCINNATI 21, Jacksonville 19
CHICAGO 27, Detroit 23
Tampa Bay 30, KANSAS CITY 27 (OT)
MINNESOTA 28, Houston 21
Arizona 34, ST. LOUIS 13
N.Y. GIANTS 35, Dallas 14
Miami 26, DENVER 17
TENNESSEE 19, Green Bay 16 (OT)
Atlanta 24, OAKLAND 0
Philadelphia 26, SEATTLE 7
INDIANAPOLIS 18, New England 15

Monday, November 3

Pittsburgh 23, WASHINGTON 6

Byes: Carolina, New Orleans, San Diego, San Francisco

TENTH WEEK STANDINGS

American Football Conference

East Division	W	L	T	Pct.	Pts.	OP
New England	6	3	0	.667	188	160
New York Jets	6	3	0	.667	255	190
Buffalo	5	4	0	.556	192	189
Miami	5	4	0	.556	192	182
North Division	**W**	**L**	**T**	**Pct.**	**Pts.**	**OP**
Baltimore	6	3	0	.667	212	150
Pittsburgh	6	3	0	.667	198	140
Cleveland	3	6	0	.333	172	194
Cincinnati	1	8	0	.111	125	236
South Division	**W**	**L**	**T**	**Pct.**	**Pts.**	**OP**
Tennessee	9	0	0	1.000	220	117
Indianapolis	5	4	0	.556	191	197
Jacksonville	4	5	0	.444	198	186
Houston	3	6	0	.333	209	254
West Division	**W**	**L**	**T**	**Pct.**	**Pts.**	**OP**
Denver	5	4	0	.556	224	251
San Diego	4	5	0	.444	244	218
Oakland	2	7	0	.222	113	218
Kansas City	1	8	0	.111	145	243

National Football Conference

East Division	W	L	T	Pct.	Pts.	OP
New York Giants	8	1	0	.889	262	160
Washington	6	3	0	.667	171	168
Dallas	5	4	0	.556	216	219
Philadelphia	5	4	0	.556	251	180
North Division	**W**	**L**	**T**	**Pct.**	**Pts.**	**OP**
Chicago	5	4	0	.556	237	194
Minnesota	5	4	0	.556	210	215
Green Bay	4	5	0	.444	237	206
Detroit	0	9	0	.000	151	277
South Division	**W**	**L**	**T**	**Pct.**	**Pts.**	**OP**
Carolina	7	2	0	.778	191	133
Atlanta	6	3	0	.667	211	174
Tampa Bay	6	3	0	.667	200	147
New Orleans	4	5	0	.444	236	229
West Division	**W**	**L**	**T**	**Pct.**	**Pts.**	**OP**
Arizona	6	3	0	.667	263	208
St. Louis	2	7	0	.222	128	282
San Francisco	2	7	0	.222	195	259
Seattle	2	7	0	.222	170	231

WEEK 10 RESULTS

Thursday, November 6
Denver 34, CLEVELAND 30

Sunday, November 9
ATLANTA 34, New Orleans 20
MINNESOTA 28, Green Bay 27
MIAMI 21, Seattle 19
N.Y. JETS 47, St. Louis 3
Baltimore 41, HOUSTON 13
Tennessee 21, CHICAGO14
Carolina 17, OAKLAND 6
Jacksonville 38, DETROIT 14
NEW ENGLAND 20, Buffalo 10
Indianapolis 24, PITTSBURGH 20
SAN DIEGO 20, Kansas City 19
N.Y. Giants 36, PHILADELPHIA 31

Monday, November 10
ARIZONA 29, San Francisco 24

Byes: Cincinnati, Dallas, Tampa Bay, Washington

ELEVENTH WEEK STANDINGS

American Football Conference

East Division	W	L	T	Pct.	Pts.	OP
New York Jets	7	3	0	.700	289	221
Miami	6	4	0	.600	209	197
New England	6	4	0	.600	219	194
Buffalo	5	5	0	.500	219	218
North Division	**W**	**L**	**T**	**Pct.**	**Pts.**	**OP**
Pittsburgh	7	3	0	.700	209	150
Baltimore	6	4	0	.600	222	180
Cleveland	4	6	0	.400	201	221
Cincinnati	1	8	1	.150	138	249
South Division	**W**	**L**	**T**	**Pct.**	**Pts.**	**OP**
Tennessee	10	0	0	1.000	244	131
Indianapolis	6	4	0	.600	224	224
Jacksonville	4	6	0	.400	212	210
Houston	3	7	0	.300	236	287
West Division	**W**	**L**	**T**	**Pct.**	**Pts.**	**OP**
Denver	6	4	0	.600	248	271
San Diego	4	6	0	.400	254	229
Oakland	2	8	0	.200	128	235
Kansas City	1	9	0	.100	165	273

National Football Conference

East Division	W	L	T	Pct.	Pts.	OP
New York Giants	9	1	0	.900	292	170
Dallas	6	4	0	.600	230	229
Washington	6	4	0	.600	181	182
Philadelphia	5	4	1	.550	264	193
North Division	**W**	**L**	**T**	**Pct.**	**Pts.**	**OP**
Chicago	5	5	0	.500	240	231
Green Bay	5	5	0	.500	274	209
Minnesota	5	5	0	.500	223	234
Detroit	0	10	0	.000	173	308
South Division	**W**	**L**	**T**	**Pct.**	**Pts.**	**OP**
Carolina	8	2	0	.800	222	155
Tampa Bay	7	3	0	.700	219	160
Atlanta	6	4	0	.600	231	198
New Orleans	5	5	0	.500	266	249
West Division	**W**	**L**	**T**	**Pct.**	**Pts.**	**OP**
Arizona	7	3	0	.700	289	228
San Francisco	3	7	0	.300	230	275
St. Louis	2	8	0	.200	144	317
Seattle	2	8	0	.200	190	257

WEEK 11 RESULTS

Thursday, November 13
N.Y. Jets 34, NEW ENGLAND 31 (OT)

Sunday, November 16
CAROLINA 31, Detroit 22
Denver 24, ATLANTA 20
New Orleans 30, KANSAS CITY 20
INDIANAPOLIS 33, Houston 27
CINCINNATI 13, Philadelphia 13 (tie, OT)
N.Y. GIANTS 30, Baltimore 10
TAMPA BAY 19, Minnesota 13
MIAMI 17, Oakland 15
Arizona 26, SEATTLE 20
SAN FRANCISCO 35, St. Louis 16
GREEN BAY 37, Chicago 3
Tennessee 24, JACKSONVILLE 14
PITTSBURGH 11, San Diego 10
Dallas 14, WASHINGTON 10

Monday, November 17
Cleveland 29, BUFFALO 27

TWELFTH WEEK STANDINGS

American Football Conference

East Division	W	L	T	Pct.	Pts.	OP
New York Jets	8	3	0	.727	323	234
New England	7	4	0	.636	267	222
Buffalo	6	5	0	.545	273	249
Miami	6	5	0	.545	237	245
North Division	**W**	**L**	**T**	**Pct.**	**Pts.**	**OP**
Pittsburgh	8	3	0	.727	236	160
Baltimore	7	4	0	.636	258	187
Cleveland	4	7	0	.364	207	237
Cincinnati	1	9	1	.136	148	276
South Division	**W**	**L**	**T**	**Pct.**	**Pts.**	**OP**
Tennessee	10	1	0	.909	257	165
Indianapolis	7	4	0	.636	247	244
Houston	4	7	0	.364	252	293
Jacksonville	4	7	0	.364	224	240
West Division	**W**	**L**	**T**	**Pct.**	**Pts.**	**OP**
Denver	6	5	0	.545	258	302
San Diego	4	7	0	.364	274	252
Oakland	3	8	0	.273	159	245
Kansas City	1	10	0	.091	196	327

National Football Conference

East Division	W	L	T	Pct.	Pts.	OP
New York Giants	10	1	0	.909	329	199
Dallas	7	4	0	.636	265	251
Washington	7	4	0	.636	201	199
Philadelphia	5	5	1	.500	271	229
North Division	**W**	**L**	**T**	**Pct.**	**Pts.**	**OP**
Chicago	6	5	0	.545	267	234
Minnesota	6	5	0	.545	253	246
Green Bay	5	6	0	.455	303	260
Detroit	0	11	0	.000	193	346
South Division	**W**	**L**	**T**	**Pct.**	**Pts.**	**OP**
Carolina	8	3	0	.727	250	200
Tampa Bay	8	3	0	.727	257	180
Atlanta	7	4	0	.636	276	226
New Orleans	6	5	0	.545	317	278
West Division	**W**	**L**	**T**	**Pct.**	**Pts.**	**OP**
Arizona	7	4	0	.636	318	265
San Francisco	3	8	0	.273	252	310
St. Louis	2	9	0	.182	147	344
Seattle	2	9	0	.182	207	277

WEEK 12 RESULTS

Thursday, November 20
PITTSBURGH 27, Cincinnati 10

Sunday, November 23
BALTIMORE 36, Philadelphia 7
New England 48, MIAMI 28
N.Y. Jets 34, TENNESSEE 13
DALLAS 35, San Francisco 22
Houston 16, CLEVELAND 6
Buffalo 54, KANSAS CITY 31
Chicago 27, ST. LOUIS 3
Minnesota 30, JACKSONVILLE 12
ATLANTA 45, Carolina 28
Oakland 31, DENVER 10
Tampa Bay 38, DETROIT 20
Washington 20, SEATTLE 17
N.Y. Giants 37, ARIZONA 29
Indianapolis 23, SAN DIEGO 20

Monday, November 24
NEW ORLEANS 51, Green Bay 29

THIRTEENTH WEEK STANDINGS

American Football Conference

East Division	W	L	T	Pct.	Pts.	OP
New York Jets	8	4	0	.667	340	268
Miami	7	5	0	.583	253	257
New England	7	5	0	.583	277	255
Buffalo	6	6	0	.500	276	259
North Division	**W**	**L**	**T**	**Pct.**	**Pts.**	**OP**
Pittsburgh	9	3	0	.750	269	170
Baltimore	8	4	0	.667	292	190
Cleveland	4	8	0	.333	213	247
Cincinnati	1	10	1	.125	151	310
South Division	**W**	**L**	**T**	**Pct.**	**Pts.**	**OP**
Tennessee	11	1	0	.917	304	175
Indianapolis	8	4	0	.667	257	250
Houston	5	7	0	.417	282	310
Jacksonville	4	8	0	.333	241	270
West Division	**W**	**L**	**T**	**Pct.**	**Pts.**	**OP**
Denver	7	5	0	.583	292	319
San Diego	4	8	0	.333	290	274
Oakland	3	9	0	.250	172	265
Kansas City	2	10	0	.167	216	340

National Football Conference

East Division	W	L	T	Pct.	Pts.	OP
New York Giants	11	1	0	.917	352	206
Dallas	8	4	0	.667	299	260
Washington	7	5	0	.583	208	222
Philadelphia	6	5	1	.542	319	249
North Division	**W**	**L**	**T**	**Pct.**	**Pts.**	**OP**
Minnesota	7	5	0	.583	287	260
Chicago	6	6	0	.500	281	268
Green Bay	5	7	0	.417	334	295
Detroit	0	12	0	.000	203	393
South Division	**W**	**L**	**T**	**Pct.**	**Pts.**	**OP**
Carolina	9	3	0	.750	285	231
Tampa Bay	9	3	0	.750	280	200
Atlanta	8	4	0	.667	298	242
New Orleans	6	6	0	.500	337	301
West Division	**W**	**L**	**T**	**Pct.**	**Pts.**	**OP**
Arizona	7	5	0	.583	338	313
San Francisco	4	8	0	.333	262	313
St. Louis	2	10	0	.167	159	360
Seattle	2	10	0	.167	216	311

WEEK 13 RESULTS

Thursday, November 27
Tennessee 47, DETROIT 10
DALLAS 34, Seattle 9
PHILADELPHIA 48, Arizona 20

Sunday, November 30
Carolina 35, GREEN BAY 31
Baltimore 34, CINCINNATI 3
San Francisco 10, BUFFALO 3
Miami 16, ST. LOUIS 12
Indianapolis 10, CLEVELAND 6
TAMPA BAY 23, New Orleans 20
Denver 34, N.Y. JETS 17
Atlanta 22, SAN DIEGO 16
N.Y. Giants 23, WASHINGTON 7
Kansas City 20, OAKLAND 13
Pittsburgh 33, NEW ENGLAND 10
MINNESOTA 34, Chicago 14

Monday, December 1
HOUSTON 30, Jacksonville 17

FOURTEENTH WEEK STANDINGS

American Football Conference

East Division	W	L	T	Pct.	Pts.	OP
Miami	8	5	0	.615	269	260
New England	8	5	0	.615	301	276
New York Jets	8	5	0	.615	354	292
Buffalo	6	7	0	.462	279	275
North Division	**W**	**L**	**T**	**Pct.**	**Pts.**	**OP**
Pittsburgh	10	3	0	.769	289	183
Baltimore	9	4	0	.692	316	200
Cleveland	4	9	0	.308	222	275
Cincinnati	1	11	1	.115	154	345
South Division	**W**	**L**	**T**	**Pct.**	**Pts.**	**OP**
Tennessee*	12	1	0	.923	332	184
Indianapolis	9	4	0	.692	292	253
Houston	6	7	0	.462	306	331
Jacksonville	4	9	0	.308	251	293
West Division	**W**	**L**	**T**	**Pct.**	**Pts.**	**OP**
Denver	8	5	0	.615	316	336
San Diego	5	8	0	.385	324	281
Oakland	3	10	0	.231	179	299
Kansas City	2	11	0	.154	233	364

National Football Conference

East Division	W	L	T	Pct.	Pts.	OP
New York Giants*	11	2	0	.846	366	226
Dallas	8	5	0	.615	312	280
Philadelphia	7	5	1	.577	339	263
Washington	7	6	0	.538	218	246
North Division	**W**	**L**	**T**	**Pct.**	**Pts.**	**OP**
Minnesota	8	5	0	.615	307	276
Chicago	7	6	0	.538	304	278
Green Bay	5	8	0	.385	355	319
Detroit	0	13	0	.000	219	413
South Division	**W**	**L**	**T**	**Pct.**	**Pts.**	**OP**
Carolina	10	3	0	.769	323	254
Tampa Bay	9	4	0	.692	303	238
Atlanta	8	5	0	.615	323	271
New Orleans	7	6	0	.538	366	326
West Division	**W**	**L**	**T**	**Pct.**	**Pts.**	**OP**
Arizona*	8	5	0	.615	372	323
San Francisco	5	8	0	.385	286	327
St. Louis	2	11	0	.154	169	394
Seattle	2	11	0	.154	237	335

**Clinched division title*

WEEK 14 RESULTS

Thursday, December 4
SAN DIEGO 34, Oakland 7

Sunday, December 7
Minnesota 20, DETROIT 16
CHICAGO 23, Jacksonville 10
Philadelphia 20, N.Y. GIANTS 14
INDIANAPOLIS 35, Cincinnati 3
Houston 24, GREEN BAY 21
TENNESSEE 28, Cleveland 9
NEW ORLEANS 29, Atlanta 25
Miami 16, BUFFALO 3 (Toronto)
SAN FRANCISCO 24, N.Y. Jets 14
DENVER 24, Kansas City 17
New England 24, SEATTLE 21
ARIZONA 34, St. Louis 10
PITTSBURGH 20, Dallas 13
BALTIMORE 24, Washington 10

Monday, December 8
CAROLINA 38, Tampa Bay 23

FIFTEENTH WEEK STANDINGS

American Football Conference

East Division	W	L	T	Pct.	Pts.	OP
Miami	9	5	0	.643	283	269
New England	9	5	0	.643	350	302
New York Jets	9	5	0	.643	385	319
Buffalo	6	8	0	.429	306	306
North Division	**W**	**L**	**T**	**Pct.**	**Pts.**	**OP**
Pittsburgh*	11	3	0	.786	302	192
Baltimore	9	5	0	.643	325	213
Cleveland	4	10	0	.286	232	305
Cincinnati	2	11	1	.179	174	358
South Division	**W**	**L**	**T**	**Pct.**	**Pts.**	**OP**
Tennessee*	12	2	0	.857	344	197
Indianapolis	10	4	0	.714	323	274
Houston	7	7	0	.500	319	343
Jacksonville	5	9	0	.357	271	309
West Division	**W**	**L**	**T**	**Pct.**	**Pts.**	**OP**
Denver	8	6	0	.571	326	366
San Diego	6	8	0	.429	346	302
Oakland	3	11	0	.214	205	348
Kansas City	2	12	0	.143	254	386

National Football Conference

East Division	W	L	T	Pct.	Pts.	OP
New York Giants*	11	3	0	.786	374	246
Dallas	9	5	0	.643	332	288
Philadelphia	8	5	1	.607	369	273
Washington	7	7	0	.500	231	266
North Division	**W**	**L**	**T**	**Pct.**	**Pts.**	**OP**
Minnesota	9	5	0	.643	342	290
Chicago	8	6	0	.571	331	302
Green Bay	5	9	0	.357	371	339
Detroit	0	14	0	.000	240	444
South Division	**W**	**L**	**T**	**Pct.**	**Pts.**	**OP**
Carolina	11	3	0	.786	353	264
Atlanta	9	5	0	.643	336	281
Tampa Bay	9	5	0	.643	313	251
New Orleans	7	7	0	.500	390	353
West Division	**W**	**L**	**T**	**Pct.**	**Pts.**	**OP**
Arizona*	8	6	0	.571	386	358
San Francisco	5	9	0	.357	295	341
Seattle	3	11	0	.214	260	355
St. Louis	2	12	0	.143	189	417

**Clinched division title*

WEEK 15 RESULTS

Thursday, December 11
CHICAGO 27, New Orleans 24 (OT)

Sunday, December 14
ATLANTA 13, Tampa Bay 10 (OT)
CINCINNATI 20, Washington 13
JACKSONVILLE 20, Green Bay 16
HOUSTON 13, Tennessee 12
INDIANAPOLIS 31, Detroit 21
MIAMI 14, San Francisco 9
Seattle 23, ST. LOUIS 20
N.Y. JETS 31, Buffalo 27
Pittsburgh 13, BALTIMORE 9
Minnesota 35, ARIZONA 14
San Diego 22, KANSAS CITY 21
New England 49, OAKLAND 26
CAROLINA 30, Denver 10
DALLAS 20, N.Y. Giants 8

Monday, December 15
PHILADELPHIA 30, Cleveland 10

SIXTEENTH WEEK STANDINGS

American Football Conference

East Division	W	L	T	Pct.	Pts.	OP
Miami	10	5	0	.667	321	300
New England	10	5	0	.667	397	309
New York Jets	9	6	0	.600	388	332
Buffalo	7	8	0	.467	336	329
North Division	**W**	**L**	**T**	**Pct.**	**Pts.**	**OP**
Pittsburgh*	11	4	0	.733	316	223
Baltimore	10	5	0	.667	358	237
Cleveland	4	11	0	.267	232	319
Cincinnati	3	11	1	.233	188	358
South Division	**W**	**L**	**T**	**Pct.**	**Pts.**	**OP**
Tennessee*	13	2	0	.867	375	211
Indianapolis#	11	4	0	.733	354	298
Houston	7	8	0	.467	335	370
Jacksonville	5	10	0	.333	295	340
West Division	**W**	**L**	**T**	**Pct.**	**Pts.**	**OP**
Denver	8	7	0	.533	349	396
San Diego	7	8	0	.467	387	326
Oakland	4	11	0	.267	232	364
Kansas City	2	13	0	.133	285	424

National Football Conference

East Division	W	L	T	Pct.	Pts.	OP
New York Giants*	12	3	0	.800	408	274
Dallas	9	6	0	.600	356	321
Philadelphia	8	6	1	.567	372	283
Washington	8	7	0	.533	241	269
North Division	**W**	**L**	**T**	**Pct.**	**Pts.**	**OP**
Chicago	9	6	0	.600	351	319
Minnesota	9	6	0	.600	359	314
Green Bay	5	10	0	.333	388	359
Detroit	0	15	0	.000	247	486
South Division	**W**	**L**	**T**	**Pct.**	**Pts.**	**OP**
Carolina#	11	4	0	.733	381	298
Atlanta#	10	5	0	.667	360	298
Tampa Bay	9	6	0	.600	337	292
New Orleans	8	7	0	.533	432	360
West Division	**W**	**L**	**T**	**Pct.**	**Pts.**	**OP**
Arizona*	8	7	0	.533	393	405
San Francisco	6	9	0	.400	312	357
Seattle	4	11	0	.267	273	358
St. Louis	2	13	0	.133	205	434

**Clinched division title*
#Clinched playoff berth

WEEK 16 RESULTS

Thursday, December 18
Indianapolis 31, JACKSONVILLE 24

Saturday, December 20
Baltimore 33, DALLAS 24

Sunday, December 21
Cincinnati 14, CLEVELAND 0
San Diego 41, TAMPA BAY 24
San Francisco 17, ST. LOUIS 16
TENNESSEE 31, Pittsburgh 14
Miami 38, KANSAS CITY 31
New Orleans 42, DETROIT 7
NEW ENGLAND 47, Arizona 7
SEATTLE 13, N.Y. Jets 3
Buffalo 30, DENVER 23
OAKLAND 27, Houston 16
Atlanta 24, MINNESOTA 17
WASHINGTON 10, Philadelphia 3
N.Y. GIANTS 34, Carolina 28 (OT)

Monday, December 22
CHICAGO 20, Green Bay 17 (OT)

SEVENTEENTH WEEK STANDINGS

American Football Conference

East Division	W	L	T	Pct.	Pts.	OP
Miami*	11	5	0	.688	345	317
New England	11	5	0	.688	410	309
New York Jets	9	7	0	.563	405	356
Buffalo	7	9	0	.438	336	342
North Division	**W**	**L**	**T**	**Pct.**	**Pts.**	**OP**
Pittsburgh*	12	4	0	.750	347	223
Baltimore#	11	5	0	.688	385	244
Cincinnati	4	11	1	.281	204	364
Cleveland	4	12	0	.250	232	350
South Division	**W**	**L**	**T**	**Pct.**	**Pts.**	**OP**
Tennessee*	13	3	0	.813	375	234
Indianapolis#	12	4	0	.750	377	298
Houston	8	8	0	.500	366	394
Jacksonville	5	11	0	.313	302	367
West Division	**W**	**L**	**T**	**Pct.**	**Pts.**	**OP**
San Diego*	8	8	0	.500	439	347
Denver	8	8	0	.500	370	448
Oakland	5	11	0	.313	263	388
Kansas City	2	14	0	.125	291	440

National Football Conference

East Division	W	L	T	Pct.	Pts.	OP
New York Giants*	12	4	0	.750	427	294
Philadelphia#	9	6	1	.594	416	289
Dallas	9	7	0	.563	362	365
Washington	8	8	0	.500	265	296
North Division	**W**	**L**	**T**	**Pct.**	**Pts.**	**OP**
Minnesota*	10	6	0	.625	379	333
Chicago	9	7	0	.563	375	350
Green Bay	6	10	0	.375	419	380
Detroit	0	16	0	.000	268	517
South Division	**W**	**L**	**T**	**Pct.**	**Pts.**	**OP**
Carolina*	12	4	0	.750	414	329
Atlanta#	11	5	0	.688	391	325
Tampa Bay	9	7	0	.563	361	323
New Orleans	8	8	0	.500	463	393
West Division	**W**	**L**	**T**	**Pct.**	**Pts.**	**OP**
Arizona*	9	7	0	.563	427	426
San Francisco	7	9	0	.438	339	381
Seattle	4	12	0	.250	294	392
St. Louis	2	14	0	.125	232	465

**Clinched division title*
#Clinched playoff berth

WEEK 17 RESULTS

Sunday, December 28
ATLANTA 31, St. Louis 27
HOUSTON 31, Chicago 24
CINCINNATI 16, Kansas City 6
New England 13, BUFFALO 0
MINNESOTA 20, N.Y. Giants 19
Carolina 33, NEW ORLEANS 31
PITTSBURGH 31, Cleveland 0
GREEN BAY 31, Detroit 21
INDIANAPOLIS 23, Tennessee 0
Oakland 31, TAMPA BAY 24
BALTIMORE 27, Jacksonville 7
ARIZONA 34, Seattle 21
SAN FRANCISCO 27, Washington 24
PHILADELPHIA 44, Dallas 6
Miami 24, N.Y. JETS 17
SAN DIEGO 52, Denver 21

2008 NFL PAID ATTENDANCE BREAKDOWN

Games	Attendance	Average
NFL Preseason Total		
65	3,995,942	61,476
NFL Regular-Season Total		
256	17,055,982	66,625
NFL Postseason Total		
12	806,840	67,237
NFL All Games		
333	21,858,764	66,629

1.1-MILLION CLUB

During the 2008 season, six teams drew more than 1.1 million paid attendance home and away during the regular season. For the ninth consecutive year, the Washington Redskins led the league in regular-season paid attendance (1,235,184) and home paid attendance (710,049).

Team	Total Paid Home Attendance	Total Paid Visiting Attendance	Total Paid Attendance
Washington	710,049	525,135	1,235,184
New York Giants	628,605	540,613	1,169,218
New York Jets	613,627	534,214	1,147,841
Denver	590,661	556,306	1,146,967
Cleveland	568,477	551,592	1,120,069
New England	565,706	539,121	1,104,827

For complete year-by-year attendance records, see pages 539-540.

2008 AFC PLAYERS OF THE WEEK

	Offense		Defense		Special Teams	
Week 1	RB	Willie Parker, Pittsburgh	CB	Cortland Finnegan, Tennessee	WR/KR	Roscoe Parrish, Buffalo
Week 2	WR	Brandon Marshall, Denver	S	Troy Polamalu, Pittsburgh	LB	Keith Bulluck, Tennessee
Week 3	RB	Ronnie Brown, Miami	CB	Antonio Cromartie, San Diego	K	Josh Scobee, Jacksonville
Week 4	QB	Brett Favre, N.Y. Jets	LB	Derrick Johnson, Kansas City	K	Jeff Reed, Pittsburgh
Week 5	QB	Ben Roethlisberger, Pittsburgh	LB	Gary Brackett, Indianapolis	K	Matt Prater, Denver
Week 6	QB	Peyton Manning, Indianapolis	CB	Eric Wright, Cleveland	WR/PR	Jacoby Jones, Houston
Week 7	QB	Matt Cassel, New England	LB	Terrell Suggs, Baltimore	K	Sebastian Janikowski, Oakland
Week 8	QB	Chad Pennington, Miami	S	Chris Hope, Tennessee	WR/PR	Jacoby Jones, Houston
Week 9	QB	Joe Flacco, Baltimore	DT	Kris Jenkins, N.Y. Jets	K	Adam Vinatieri, Indianapolis
Week 10	QB	Jay Cutler, Denver	LB	Ray Lewis, Baltimore	P	Craig Hentrich, Tennessee
Week 11	QB	Peyton Manning, Indianapolis	LB	James Harrison, Pittsburgh	KR/RB	Leon Washington, N.Y. Jets
Week 12	QB	Matt Cassel, New England	S	Ed Reed, Baltimore	PR/WR	Johnnie Lee Higgins, Oakland
Week 13	RB	Steve Slaton, Houston	DE	Robert Mathis, Indianapolis	CB	Maurice Leggett, Kansas City
Week 14	QB	Matt Schaub, Houston	S	Ed Reed, Baltimore	K	Dan Carpenter, Miami
Week 15	QB	Philip Rivers, San Diego	DE	Aaron Smith, Pittsburgh	KR/CB	Ellis Hobbs, New England
Week 16	QB	Peyton Manning, Indianapolis	CB	Leon Hall, Cincinnati	P	Sam Koch, Baltimore
Week 17	QB	Chad Pennington, Miami	S	Tyrone Carter, Pittsburgh	P	Chris Hanson, New England

2008 AFC PLAYERS OF THE MONTH

	Offense		Defense		Special Teams	
September	QB	Jay Cutler, Denver	DT	Albert Haynesworth, Tennessee	RB/KR	Darren Sproles, San Diego
October	WR	Andre Johnson, Houston	LB	Joey Porter, Miami	K	Stephen Gostkowski, New England
November	RB	Thomas Jones, N.Y. Jets	DE	Dwight Freeney, Indianapolis	K	Dan Carpenter, Miami
December	QB	Philip Rivers, San Diego	S	Ed Reed, Baltimore	KR/CB	Justin Miller, Oakland

2008 NFC PLAYERS OF THE WEEK

	Offense		Defense		Special Teams	
Week 1	RB	Michael Turner, Atlanta	DE	Adewale Ogunleye, Chicago	PR/KR	Will Blackmon, Green Bay
Week 2	QB	Kurt Warner, Arizona	S	Chris Horton, Washington	KR/RB	Felix Jones, Dallas
Week 3	RB	Michael Turner, Atlanta	S	Brian Dawkins, Philadelphia	K	John Carney, N.Y. Giants
Week 4	QB	Jake Delhomme, Carolina	LB	Derrick Brooks, Tampa Bay	K	Matt Bryant, Tampa Bay
Week 5	RB	Clinton Portis, Washington	CB	Antoine Winfield, Minnesota	PR/RB	Reggie Bush, New Orleans
Week 6	QB	Drew Brees, New Orleans	S	Oshiomogho Atogwe, St. Louis	WR	Sean Morey, Arizona
Week 7	RB	Steven Jackson, St. Louis	S	Aaron Rouse, Green Bay	S	Zackary Bowman, Chicago
Week 8	QB	Drew Brees, New Orleans	DE	Mathias Kiwanuka, N.Y. Giants	WR/PR	Santana Moss, Washington
Week 9	QB	Matt Ryan, Atlanta	S	Antrel Rolle, Arizona	KR/RB	Clifton Smith, Tampa Bay
Week 10	RB	Adrian Peterson, Minnesota	DE	Julius Peppers, Carolina	LB	Chase Blackburn, N.Y. Giants
Week 11	QB	Shaun Hill, San Francisco	CB	Aaron Ross, N.Y. Giants	K	Neil Rackers, Arizona
Week 12	QB	Drew Brees, New Orleans	CB	Ronde Barber, Tampa Bay	WR/PR	Harry Douglas, Atlanta
Week 13	RB	Brian Westbrook, Philadelphia	DE	Jared Allen, Minnesota	KR/PR	Mark Jones, Carolina
Week 14	RB	DeAngelo Williams, Carolina	LB	Gerald Hayes, Arizona	RB/KR	Pierre Thomas, New Orleans
Week 15	QB	Tarvaris Jackson, Minnesota	LB	DeMarcus Ware, Dallas	KR/S	Danieal Manning, Chicago
Week 16	RB	Derrick Ward, N.Y. Giants	CB	Josh Wilson, Seattle	P	Ryan Plackemeier, Washington
Week 17	RB	Michael Turner, Atlanta	DE	Chris Clemons, Philadelphia	K	Ryan Longwell, Minnesota

2008 NFC PLAYERS OF THE MONTH

	Offense		Defense		Special Teams	
September	QB	Drew Brees, New Orleans	CB	Charles Woodson, Green Bay	P	Sav Rocca, Philadelphia
October	RB	Clinton Portis, Washington	LB	Jon Beason, Carolina	K	Josh Brown, St. Louis
November	QB	Eli Manning, N.Y. Giants	DE	Julius Peppers, Carolina	RB/KR/PR	Clifton Smith, Tampa Bay
December	RB	DeAngelo Williams, Carolina	S	Brian Dawkins, Philadelphia	K	Robbie Gould, Chicago

2008 NFL ROOKIES OF THE MONTH

	Offense (College)		Defense (College)	
September	RB	Chris Johnson, Tennessee (East Carolina)	S	Chris Horton, Washington (UCLA)
October	QB	Matt Ryan, Atlanta (Boston College)	LB	Jerod Mayo, New England (Tennessee)
November	QB	Joe Flacco, Baltimore (Delaware)	CB	Leodis McKelvin, Buffalo (Troy)
December	RB	Steve Slaton, Houston (West Virginia)	CB	Dominique Rodgers-Cromartie, Arizona (Tennessee State)

2008 PRO FOOTBALL AWARDS/ALL-PRO TEAMS

2008 PRO FOOTBALL AWARDS

ASSOCIATED PRESS

Most Valuable Player	Peyton Manning
Offensive Player of the Year	Drew Brees
Defensive Player of the Year	James Harrison
Offensive Rookie of the Year	Matt Ryan
Defensive Rookie of the Year	Jerod Mayo
Coach of the Year	Mike Smith
Comeback Player of the Year	Chad Pennington

THE SPORTING NEWS

Offensive Player of the Year	Drew Brees
Defensive Player of the Year	Albert Haynesworth
Rookie of the Year	Matt Ryan
Coach of the Year	Mike Smith

PRO FOOTBALL WEEKLY/PFWA

Executive of the Year	Bill Parcells
Most Valuable Player	Peyton Manning
Defensive Most Valuable Player	James Harrison
Offensive Rookie of the Year	Matt Ryan
Defensive Rookie of the Year	Jerod Mayo
Coach of the Year	Tony Sparano
Assistant Coach of the Year	Dick LeBeau
Golden Toe	Jason Hanson
Comeback Player of the Year	Chad Pennington
Most Improved Player of the Year	DeAngelo Williams

SPORTS ILLUSTRATED

Most Valuable Player	Peyton Manning
Offensive Rookie of the Year	Matt Ryan
Defensive Rookie of the Year	Jerod Mayo
Coach of the Year	Mike Smith

MAXWELL CLUB PLAYER OF THE YEAR

(Bert Bell Trophy)	Adrian Peterson

MAXWELL CLUB COACH OF THE YEAR

(Earle "Greasy" Neale Trophy)	Jeff Fisher

DIET PEPSI ROOKIE OF THE YEAR

Rookie of the Year	Joe Flacco

FEDEX AIR & GROUND NFL PLAYERS OF THE YEAR

FedEx Express NFL Player of the Year	Drew Brees
FedEx Ground NFL Player of the Year	Adrian Peterson

GMC SIERRA DEFENSIVE PLAYER OF THE YEAR

Defensive Player of the Year	James Harrison

MOTOROLA NFL COACH OF THE YEAR

Motorola Coach of the Year	Mike Tomlin

WALTER PAYTON/ NFL MAN OF THE YEAR

Man of the Year	Kurt Warner
Man of the Year Finalist	Matt Birk
Man of the Year Finalist	Brian Dawkins

SUPER BOWL XLIII MOST VALUABLE PLAYER

Pete Rozelle Trophy	Santonio Holmes

AFC-NFC 2009 PRO BOWL MOST VALUABLE PLAYER

Dan McGuire Award	Larry Fitzgerald

2008 ALL-PRO TEAMS

2008 PFW/PFWA ALL-PRO TEAM

Selected by *Pro Football Weekly* and the Professional Football Writers of America

Offense:

Peyton Manning, Indianapolis	Quarterback
Adrian Peterson, Minnesota	Running Back
Michael Turner, Atlanta	Running Back
Tony Gonzalez, Kansas City	Tight End
Andre Johnson, Houston	Wide Receiver
Larry Fitzgerald, Arizona	Wide Receiver
Michael Roos, Tennessee	Tackle
Jordan Gross, Carolina	Tackle
Chris Snee, New York Giants	Guard
Steve Hutchinson, Minnesota	Guard
Kevin Mawae, Tennessee	Center

Defense:

Justin Tuck, New York Giants	End
John Abraham, Atlanta	End
Albert Haynesworth, Tennessee	Tackle
Kevin Williams, Minnesota	Tackle
DeMarcus Ware, Dallas	Outside Linebacker
James Harrison, Pittsburgh	Outside Linebacker
Ray Lewis, Baltimore	Middle Linebacker
Cortland Finnegan, Tennessee	Cornerback
Nnamdi Asomugha, Oakland	Cornerback
Ed Reed, Baltimore	Safety
Troy Polamalu, Pittsburgh	Safety

Special Teams:

Stephen Gostkowski, New England	Kicker
Shane Lechler, Oakland	Punter
Danieal Manning, Chicago	Kick Returner
Johnnie Lee Higgins, Oakland	Punt Returner
Brendon Ayanbadejo, Baltimore	Special Teams Player

2008 ASSOCIATED PRESS ALL-PRO TEAM

Selected by the Associated Press

Offense:

Peyton Manning, Indianapolis	Quarterback
Adrian Peterson, Minnesota	Running Back
Michael Turner, Atlanta	Running Back
Le'Ron McClain, Baltimore	Fullback
Tony Gonzalez, Kansas City	Tight End
Andre Johnson, Houston	Wide Receiver
Larry Fitzgerald, Arizona	Wide Receiver
Jordan Gross, Carolina	Tackle
Michael Roos, Tennessee	Tackle
Steve Hutchinson, Minnesota	Guard
Chris Snee, New York Giants	Guard
Kevin Mawae, Tennessee	Center

Defense:

Justin Tuck, New York Giants	End
Jared Allen, Minnesota	End
Albert Haynesworth, Tennessee	Tackle
Kevin Williams, Minnesota	Tackle
DeMarcus Ware, Dallas	Outside Linebacker
James Harrison, Pittsburgh	Outside Linebacker
Ray Lewis, Baltimore	Inside Linebacker
Jon Beason, Carolina	Inside Linebacker
Nnamdi Asomugha, Oakland	Cornerback
Cortland Finnegan, Tennessee	Cornerback
Ed Reed, Baltimore	Safety
Troy Polamalu, Pittsburgh	Safety

Special Teams:

Stephen Gostkowski, New England	Kicker
Shane Lechler, Oakland	Punter

2008 ALL-NFL TEAM

Selected by the Associated Press, *Pro Football Weekly,* and the Professional Football Writers of America

Offense:

Peyton Manning, Indianapolis (PFW, AP)	Quarterback
Adrian Peterson, Minnesota (PFW, AP)	Running Back
Michael Turner, Atlanta (PFW, AP)	Running Back
Le'Ron McClain, Baltimore (AP)	Fullback
Tony Gonzalez, Kansas City (PFW, AP)	Tight End
Andre Johnson, Houston (PFW, AP)	Wide Receiver
Larry Fitzgerald, Arizona (PFW, AP)	Wide Receiver
Jordan Gross, Carolina (PFW, AP)	Tackle
Michael Roos, Tennessee (PFW, AP)	Tackle
Steve Hutchinson, Minnesota (PFW, AP)	Guard
Chris Snee, New York Giants (PFW, AP)	Guard
Kevin Mawae, Tennessee (PFW, AP)	Center

Defense:

Justin Tuck, New York Giants (PFW, AP)	End
John Abraham, Atlanta (PFW)	End
Jared Allen, Minnesota (AP)	End
Albert Haynesworth, Tennessee (PFW, AP)	Tackle
Kevin Williams, Minnesota (PFW, AP)	Tackle
DeMarcus Ware, Dallas (PFW, AP)	Outside Linebacker
James Harrison, Pittsburgh (PFW, AP)	Outside Linebacker
Ray Lewis, Baltimore (PFW, AP)	Inside Linebacker
Jon Beason, Carolina (AP)	Inside Linebacker
Nnamdi Asomugha, Oakland (PFW, AP)	Cornerback
Cortland Finnegan, Tennessee (PFW, AP)	Cornerback
Ed Reed, Baltimore (PFW, AP)	Safety
Troy Polamalu, Pittsburgh (PFW, AP)	Safety

Special Teams:

Stephen Gostkowski, New England (PFW, AP)	Kicker
Shane Lechler, Oakland (PFW, AP)	Punter
Danieal Manning, Chicago (PFW)	Kick Returner
Johnnie Lee Higgins, Oakland (PFW)	Punt Returner
Brendon Ayanbadejo, Baltimore (PFW)	Special Teams Player

2008 PFW/PFWA ALL-ROOKIE TEAM

Selected by *Pro Football Weekly* and the Professional Football Writers of America

Offense:

Matt Ryan, Atlanta	Quarterback
Matt Forté, Chicago	Running Back
Chris Johnson, Tennessee	Running Back
John Carlson, Seattle	Tight End
Eddie Royal, Denver	Wide Receiver
DeSean Jackson, Philadelphia	Wide Receiver
Ryan Clady, Denver	Tackle
Jake Long, Miami	Tackle
Mike Pollak, Indianapolis	Guard
Carl Nicks, New Orleans	Guard
Jamey Richard, Indianapolis	Center

Defense:

Chris Long, St. Louis	Defensive Lineman
Kendall Langford, Miami	Defensive Lineman
Sedrick Ellis, New Orleans	Defensive Lineman
Jason Jones, Tennessee	Defensive Lineman
Jerod Mayo, New England	Outside Linebacker
Curtis Lofton, Atlanta	Outside Linebacker
Xavier Adibi, Houston	Middle Linebacker
Dominique Rodgers-Cromartie, Arizona	Cornerback
Brandon Flowers, Kansas City	Cornerback
Chris Horton, Washington	Safety
Kenny Phillips, New York Giants	Safety

Special Teams:

Dan Carpenter, Miami	Kicker
Brett Kern, Denver	Punter
Clifton Smith, Tampa Bay	Punt Returner
Leodis McKelvin, Buffalo	Kickoff Returner

TEN BEST RUSHING PERFORMANCES, 2008

		Att.	Yards	TD
1.	Michael Turner Atlanta vs. Detroit, Sept. 7	22	220	2
2.	Derrick Ward N.Y. Giants vs. Carolina, Dec. 21	15	215	0
3.	Michael Turner Atlanta vs. St. Louis, Dec. 28	25	208	1
4.	Larry Johnson Kansas City vs. Denver, Sept. 28	28	198	2
5.	Adrian Peterson Minnesota vs. Green Bay, Nov. 9	30	192	1
6.	DeAngelo Williams Carolina vs. Tampa Bay, Dec. 8	19	186	2
7.	DeAngelo Williams Carolina vs. New Orleans, Dec. 28	25	178	0
8.	Michael Bush Oakland vs. Tampa Bay, Dec. 28	27	177	2
9.	Clinton Portis Washington vs. Cleveland, Oct. 19	27	175	1
10.	Cedric Benson Cincinnati vs. Cleveland, Dec. 21	38	171	0

There were 129 100-yard rushing performances in 2008.

MOST 100-YARD RUSHING PERFORMANCES, 2008

Player, Team	100-Yd. Games
Adrian Peterson, Minnesota	10
Michael Turner, Atlanta	8
DeAngelo Williams, Carolina	8
Clinton Portis, Washington	6
Thomas Jones, N.Y. Jets	5
Steve Slaton, Houston	5
Ryan Grant, Green Bay	4
Brandon Jacobs, N.Y. Giants	4
Chris Johnson, Tennessee	4
Willie Parker, Pittsburgh	4
Marion Barber III, Dallas	3
Cedric Benson, Cincinnati	3
Ronnie Brown, Miami	3
Matt Forté, Chicago	3
Frank Gore, San Francisco	3
Steven Jackson, St. Louis	3
Larry Johnson, Kansas City	3
Marshawn Lynch, Buffalo	3
Willis McGahee, Baltimore	3
Brian Westbrook, Philadelphia	3
Earnest Graham, Tampa Bay	2
Edgerrin James, Arizona	2
Julius Jones, Seattle	2
Maurice Morris, Seattle	2
Sammy Morris, New England	2
Kevin Smith, Detroit	2
Jonathan Stewart, Carolina	2
LaDainian Tomlinson, San Diego	2
Derrick Ward, N.Y. Giants	2
LenDale White, Tennessee	2
By many players	1

100-YARD RUSHING, 2008 POSTSEASON

Wild Card
Darren Sproles, San Diego — 105 yards vs. Indianapolis
Divisional
Willie Parker, Pittsburgh — 146 yards vs. San Diego
Championship
None
Super Bowl XLIII
None

TEN BEST PASSING PERFORMANCES, 2008

		Att.	Comp.	Yds.	TD
1.	Kurt Warner Arizona vs. N.Y. Jets, Sept. 28	57	40	472	2
2.	Jay Cutler Denver vs. Cleveland, Nov. 6	42	24	447	3
3.	Drew Brees New Orleans vs. Atlanta, Nov. 9	58	31	422	2
4.	Drew Brees New Orleans vs. Denver, Sept. 21	48	39	421	1
5.	Matt Cassel New England vs. Miami, Nov. 23	43	30	415	3
6.	Matt Schaub Houston vs. Green Bay, Dec. 7	42	28	414	2
7.	Brian Griese Tampa Bay vs. Chicago, Sept. 21	67	38	407	2
8.	Matt Cassel New England vs. N.Y. Jets, Nov. 13	51	30	400	3
9.	Kurt Warner Arizona vs. Seattle, Nov. 16	44	32	395	1
10.	Drew Brees New Orleans vs. Carolina, Dec. 28	49	30	386	4

There were 76 300-yard passing performances in 2008.

MOST 300-YARD PASSING PERFORMANCES, 2008

Player, Team	300-Yd. Games
Drew Brees, New Orleans	10
Jay Cutler, Denver	8
Kurt Warner, Arizona	7
Tony Romo, Dallas	6
Philip Rivers, San Diego	5
Peyton Manning, Indianapolis	4
Aaron Rodgers, Green Bay	4
Matt Schaub, Houston	4
Matt Cassel, New England	3
Jeff Garcia, Tampa Bay	3
Donovan McNabb, Philadelphia	3
Ben Roethlisberger, Pittsburgh	3
Jason Campbell, Washington	2
David Garrard, Jacksonville	2
Chad Pennington, Miami	2
Matt Ryan, Atlanta	2
Derek Anderson, Cleveland	1
Marc Bulger, St. Louis	1
Brian Griese, Tampa Bay	1
Shaun Hill, San Francisco	1
Eli Manning, N.Y. Giants	1
Kyle Orton, Chicago	1
J.T. O'Sullivan, San Francisco	1
Tyler Thigpen, Kansas City	1

300-YARD PASSING, 2008 POSTSEASON

Wild Card
Peyton Manning, Indianapolis — 310 yards vs. San Diego
Donovan McNabb, Philadelphia — 300 yards vs. Minnesota
Divisional
Philip Rivers, San Diego — 308 yards vs. Baltimore
Championship
Donovan McNabb, Philadelphia — 375 yards vs. Arizona
Super Bowl XLIII
Kurt Warner, Arizona — 377 yards vs. Pittsburgh

TEN BEST RECEIVING PERFORMANCES, 2008

	No.	Yards	TD
1. Terrell Owens Dallas vs. San Francisco, Nov. 23	7	213	1
2. Andre Johnson Houston vs. Tennessee, Dec. 14	11	207	1
3. Antonio Bryant Tampa Bay vs. Carolina, Dec. 8	9	200	2
4. Anquan Boldin Arizona vs. Seattle, Nov. 16	13	186	0
5. Andre Johnson Houston vs. Miami, Oct. 12	10	178	1
6. Ted Ginn Jr. Miami vs. Buffalo, Oct. 26	7	175	0
7. Steve Smith Carolina vs. Atlanta, Nov. 23	8	168	0
8. Greg Jennings Green Bay vs. Detroit, Sept. 14	6	167	0
9. Brandon Marshall Denver vs. San Diego, Sept. 14	18	166	1
10. Steve Smith Carolina vs. Denver, Dec. 14	9	165	1

There were 162 100-yard receiving performances in 2008.

MOST 100-YARD RECEIVING PERFORMANCES, 2008

Player, Team	100-Yd. Games
Steve Smith, Carolina	8
Larry Fitzgerald, Arizona	7
Andre Johnson, Houston	7
Roddy White, Atlanta	7
Antonio Bryant, Tampa Bay	6
Greg Jennings, Green Bay	5
Bernard Berrian, Minnesota	4
Chad Ochocinco, Cincinnati	4
Hines Ward, Pittsburgh	4
Reggie Wayne, Indianapolis	4
Wes Welker, New England	4
Anquan Boldin, Arizona	3
Steve Breaston, Arizona	3
Marques Colston, New Orleans	3
Braylon Edwards, Cleveland	3
Lee Evans, Buffalo	3
Tony Gonzalez, Kansas City	3
Vincent Jackson, San Diego	3
Brandon Marshall, Denver	3
Lance Moore, New Orleans	3
Randy Moss, New England	3
Santana Moss, Washington	3
Dwayne Bowe, Kansas City	2
Isaac Bruce, San Francisco	2
Dallas Clark, Indianapolis	2
Mark Clayton, Baltimore	2
Owen Daniels, Houston	2
Donald Driver, Green Bay	2
Justin Gage, Tennessee	2
T.J. Houshmandzadeh, Cincinnati	2
Matt Jones, Jacksonville	2
Derrick Mason, Baltimore	2
Dennis Northcutt, Jacksonville	2
Terrell Owens, Dallas	2
Eddie Royal, Denver	2
Jason Witten, Dallas	2
By many players	1

100-YARD RECEIVING, 2008 POSTSEASON

Wild Card

Reggie Wayne, Indianapolis	129 yards vs. San Diego
Larry Fitzgerald, Arizona	101 yards vs. Atlanta

Divisional

Larry Fitzgerald, Arizona	166 yards vs. Carolina
Justin Gage, Tennessee	135 yards vs. Baltimore

Championship

Larry Fitzgerald, Arizona	152 yards vs. Philadelphia
Kevin Curtis, Philadelphia	122 yards vs. Arizona

Super Bowl XLIII

Santonio Holmes, Pittsburgh	131 yards vs. Arizona
Larry Fitzgerald, Arizona	127 yards vs. Pittsburgh

TOP QUARTERBACK SACK PERFORMANCES, 2008

	No.
1. Joey Porter Miami vs. New England, Sept. 21	4.0
Kevin Williams Minnesota vs. Detroit, Oct. 12	4.0
3. Jason Jones Tennessee vs. Pittsburgh, Dec. 21	3.5
4. John Abraham Atlanta vs. Detroit, Sept. 7	3.0
John Abraham Atlanta vs. Oakland, Nov. 2	3.0
John Abraham Atlanta vs. Tampa Bay, Dec. 14	3.0
James Harrison Pittsburgh vs. Houston, Sept. 7	3.0
Robert Mathis Indianapolis vs. Baltimore, Oct. 12	3.0
Julius Pepper Carolina vs. Oakland, Nov. 9	3.0
DeMarcus Ware Dallas vs. St. Louis, Oct. 19	3.0
DeMarcus Ware Dallas vs. Seattle, Nov. 27	3.0
DeMarcus Ware Dallas vs. N.Y. Giants, Dec. 14	3.0
Mario Williams Houston vs. Jacksonville, Dec. 1	3.0

There were 13 3.0-plus sack performances in 2008.

MOST 3.0-PLUS SACK PERFORMANCES, 2008

Player, Team	3.0-Sack Games
John Abraham, Atlanta	3
DeMarcus Ware, Dallas	3
James Harrison, Pittsburgh	1
Jason Jones, Tennessee	1
Robert Mathis, Indianapolis	1
Julius Peppers, Carolina	1
Joey Porter, Miami	1
Kevin Williams, Minnesota	1
Mario Williams, Houston	1

3.0 SACK PERFORMANCES, 2008 POSTSEASON

Wild Card

None

Divisional

None

Championship

None

Super Bowl XLIII

Darnell Dockett, Arizona	3.0 vs. Pittsburgh

For week-by-week listings of top performances from 1970 to the present, please visit www.NFL.com/stats/topperformers.

AMERICAN FOOTBALL CONFERENCE OFFENSE

	Balt.	Buff.	Cin.	Cle.	Den.	Hou.	Ind.	Jax.	KC	Mia.	NE	NYJ	Oak.	Pitt.	SD	Tenn.
First Downs	300	287	245	233	354	340	321	312	273	308	356	308	225	290	301	268
Rushing	132	107	80	84	103	106	80	107	94	111	145	94	87	93	92	108
Passing	147	167	145	127	223	210	220	183	161	184	186	186	123	179	191	143
Penalty	21	13	20	22	28	24	21	22	18	13	25	28	15	18	18	17
Rushes	592	439	420	409	387	432	370	426	379	448	513	422	459	460	421	508
Net Yds. Gained	2376	1842	1520	1605	1862	1846	1274	1774	1810	1897	2278	2004	1987	1690	1726	2199
Avg. Gain	4.0	4.2	3.6	3.9	4.8	4.3	3.4	4.2	4.8	4.2	4.4	4.7	4.3	3.7	4.1	4.3
Avg. Yds. per Game	148.5	115.1	95.0	100.3	116.4	115.4	79.6	110.9	113.1	118.6	142.4	125.3	124.2	105.6	107.9	137.4
Passes Attempted	433	479	513	488	620	555	585	537	541	491	534	529	421	506	478	453
Completed	261	309	303	238	386	367	393	335	310	330	339	347	222	303	312	265
% Completed	60.3	64.5	59.1	48.8	62.3	66.1	67.2	62.4	57.3	67.2	63.5	65.6	52.7	59.9	65.3	58.5
Total Yds. Gained	3085	3302	2677	2537	4545	4474	4180	3620	3358	3761	3790	3516	2639	3607	4009	2902
Times Sacked	33	38	51	24	12	32	14	42	37	26	48	30	39	49	25	12
Yds. Lost	277	262	271	157	74	207	86	288	229	129	221	213	270	306	151	83
Net Yds. Gained	2808	3040	2406	2380	4471	4267	4094	3332	3129	3632	3569	3303	2369	3301	3858	2819
Avg. Yds. per Game	175.5	190.0	150.4	148.8	279.4	266.7	255.9	208.3	195.6	227.0	223.1	206.4	148.1	206.3	241.1	176.2
Net Yds. per Pass Play	6.03	5.88	4.27	4.65	7.07	7.27	6.83	5.75	5.41	7.03	6.13	5.91	5.15	5.95	7.67	6.06
Yds. Gained per Comp.	11.82	10.69	8.83	10.66	11.77	12.19	10.64	10.81	10.83	11.40	11.18	10.13	11.89	11.90	12.85	10.95
Combined Net Yds. Gained	5184	4882	3926	3985	6333	6113	5368	5106	4939	5529	5847	5307	4356	4991	5584	5018
% Total Yds. Rushing	45.8	37.7	38.7	40.3	29.4	30.2	23.7	34.7	36.6	34.3	39.0	37.8	45.6	33.9	30.9	43.8
% Total Yds. Passing	54.2	62.3	61.3	59.7	70.6	69.8	76.3	65.3	63.4	65.7	61.0	62.2	54.4	66.1	69.1	56.2
Avg. Yds. per Game	324.0	305.1	245.4	249.1	395.8	382.1	335.5	319.1	308.7	345.6	365.4	331.7	272.3	311.9	349.0	313.6
Ball Control Plays	1058	956	984	921	1019	1019	969	1005	957	965	1095	981	919	1015	924	973
Avg. Yds. per Play	4.9	5.1	4.0	4.3	6.2	6.0	5.5	5.1	5.2	5.7	5.3	5.4	4.7	4.9	6.0	5.2
Avg. Time of Poss.	33:10	30:04	28:40	27:33	28:44	31:57	28:39	31:22	27:56	31:03	32:09	30:28	28:09	31:29	28:53	29:09
Third Down Efficiency	40.9	39.9	34.7	34.0	47.5	42.1	50.2	40.8	38.3	37.0	43.2	41.1	28.5	41.1	45.9	36.1
Had Intercepted	12	15	15	20	18	20	12	13	16	7	11	23	11	15	11	9
Yds. Opp Returned	104	169	279	381	153	221	294	181	323	130	186	351	163	234	189	88
Ret. by Opp. for TD	1	1	2	5	2	1	3	1	2	2	0	4	0	2	1	0
Punts	84	58	101	76	46	53	53	67	82	74	50	59	90	78	51	87
Yds. Punted	3777	2557	3945	3443	2150	2240	2343	2904	3622	3249	2200	2490	4391	3107	2332	3725
Avg. Yds. per Punt	45.0	44.1	39.1	45.3	46.7	42.3	44.2	43.3	44.2	43.9	44.0	42.2	48.8	39.8	45.7	42.8
Punt Returns	44	30	32	30	20	32	22	29	26	28	36	29	44	41	26	34
Yds. Returned	378	464	253	251	196	386	132	275	169	285	371	303	570	247	269	329
Avg. Yds. per Return	8.6	15.5	7.9	8.4	9.8	12.1	6.0	9.5	6.5	10.2	10.3	10.4	13.0	6.0	10.3	9.7
Returned for TD	0	1	0	0	0	2	0	0	0	0	0	0	3	0	0	0
Kickoff Returns	50	75	67	58	71	72	63	74	80	60	62	61	78	50	62	52
Yds. Returned	1007	1816	1551	1312	1550	1550	1312	1678	1716	1213	1562	1407	1777	1013	1485	1319
Avg. Yds. per Return	20.1	24.2	23.1	22.6	21.8	21.5	20.8	22.7	21.5	20.2	25.2	23.1	22.8	20.3	24.0	25.4
Returned for TD	0	1	0	1	0	0	0	0	0	0	1	1	2	0	1	0
Fumbles	28	33	27	17	18	28	13	23	20	18	17	22	28	28	18	18
Lost	9	15	11	6	12	12	5	11	8	6	10	8	12	10	9	8
Out of Bounds	4	1	2	1	2	1	3	2	1	5	0	1	1	5	2	2
Own Rec. for TD	0	0	0	0	0	0	1	0	0	0	0	0	0	0	0	0
Opp. Rec. by	8	12	12	8	7	10	11	4	16	12	8	16	8	9	9	11
Opp. Rec. for TD	1	0	2	0	2	0	2	1	1	0	0	2	0	1	1	0
Penalties	103	71	75	100	77	80	86	104	78	81	57	77	109	95	95	108
Yds. Penalized	785	538	591	669	739	664	619	813	645	669	501	569	823	812	748	855
Total Points Scored	385	336	204	232	370	366	377	302	291	345	410	405	263	347	439	375
Total TDs	42	35	20	20	42	40	45	35	35	40	43	48	27	38	51	41
TDs Rushing	20	16	6	6	15	16	13	17	9	18	21	20	9	16	13	24
TDs Passing	16	14	11	11	25	21	27	15	23	20	21	22	13	19	34	13
TDs on Ret. and Rec.	6	5	3	3	2	3	5	3	3	2	1	6	5	3	4	4
Extra Point Kicks	41	34	18	18	39	37	43	33	31	40	40	41	25	36	46	40
Extra Point Kicks Att.	41	34	18	18	40	37	43	33	31	40	40	41	26	37	46	40
2Pt Conversions	1	1	0	2	2	1	2	0	1	0	2	2	0	0	2	1
2Pt Conversions Att.	1	1	2	2	2	3	2	2	4	0	3	7	1	1	5	1
Safeties	3	0	0	0	0	0	0	1	0	1	0	0	2	1	1	0
Field Goals Made	28	30	22	30	25	29	20	19	16	21	36	24	24	27	27	29
Field Goals Attempted	35	38	25	36	34	33	25	25	22	25	40	29	30	31	32	33
% Successful	80.0	78.9	88.0	83.3	73.5	87.9	80.0	76.0	72.7	84.0	90.0	82.8	80.0	87.1	84.4	87.9

AMERICAN FOOTBALL CONFERENCE DEFENSE

	Balt.	Buff.	Cin.	Cle.	Den.	Hou.	Ind.	Jax.	KC	Mia.	NE	NYJ	Oak.	Pitt.	SD	Tenn.
First Downs	228	293	296	315	327	300	305	289	344	296	268	315	325	240	339	276
Rushing	58	113	106	125	122	114	119	98	133	96	78	86	129	73	98	81
Passing	152	167	169	176	186	167	165	166	195	173	176	209	166	149	213	166
Penalty	18	13	21	14	19	19	21	25	16	27	14	20	30	18	28	29
Rushes	366	455	490	541	469	439	472	428	509	388	415	407	542	390	408	403
Net Yds. Gained	1302	1946	1921	2431	2337	1962	1966	1709	2543	1620	1722	1518	2555	1284	1641	1502
Avg. Gain	3.6	4.3	3.9	4.5	5.0	4.5	4.2	4.0	5.0	4.2	4.1	3.7	4.7	3.3	4.0	3.7
Avg. Yds. per Game	81.4	121.6	120.1	151.9	146.1	122.6	122.9	106.8	158.9	101.3	107.6	94.9	159.7	80.3	102.6	93.9
Passes Attempted	528	492	506	446	495	471	481	465	522	551	474	572	471	533	605	575
Completed	276	301	315	286	333	294	329	297	348	320	288	368	266	301	411	342
% Completed	52.3	61.2	62.3	64.1	67.3	62.4	68.4	63.9	66.7	58.1	60.8	64.3	56.5	56.5	67.9	59.5
Total Yds. Gained	3132	3441	3409	3363	3797	3598	3209	3777	3810	3862	3461	4005	3408	2861	4090	3458
Times Sacked	34	24	17	17	26	25	30	29	10	40	31	41	32	51	28	44
Yds. Lost	257	170	122	90	141	175	200	191	62	218	239	253	188	350	132	262
Net Yds. Gained	2875	3271	3287	3273	3656	3423	3009	3586	3748	3644	3222	3752	3220	2511	3958	3196
Avg. Yds. per Game	179.7	204.4	205.4	204.6	228.5	213.9	188.1	224.1	234.3	227.8	201.4	234.5	201.3	156.9	247.4	199.8
Net Yds. per Pass Play	5.12	6.34	6.28	7.07	7.02	6.90	5.89	7.26	7.05	6.17	6.38	6.12	6.40	4.30	6.25	5.16
Yds. Gained per Comp.	11.35	11.43	10.82	11.76	11.40	12.24	9.75	12.72	10.95	12.07	12.02	10.88	12.81	9.50	9.95	10.11
Combined Net Yds. Gained	4177	5217	5208	5704	5993	5385	4975	5295	6291	5264	4944	5270	5775	3795	5599	4698
% Total Yds. Rushing	31.2	37.3	36.9	42.6	39.0	36.4	39.5	32.3	40.4	30.8	34.8	28.8	44.2	33.8	29.3	32.0
% Total Yds. Passing	68.8	62.7	63.1	57.4	61.0	63.6	60.5	67.7	59.6	69.2	65.2	71.2	55.8	66.2	70.7	68.0
Avg. Yds. per Game	261.1	326.1	325.5	356.5	374.6	336.6	310.9	330.9	393.2	329.0	309.0	329.4	360.9	237.2	349.9	293.6
Ball Control Plays	928	971	1013	1004	990	935	983	922	1041	979	920	1020	1045	974	1041	1022
Avg. Yds. per Play	4.5	5.4	5.1	5.7	6.1	5.8	5.1	5.7	6.0	5.4	5.4	5.2	5.5	3.9	5.4	4.6
Avg. Time of Poss.	26:50	29:57	31:20	32:27	31:16	28:03	31:21	28:38	32:04	28:57	27:51	29:32	31:51	28:31	31:07	30:51
Third Down Efficiency	33.5	36.1	42.7	45.9	44.1	39.4	47.4	41.0	47.4	37.8	44.4	38.6	44.4	31.4	40.6	35.0
Intercepted By	26	10	12	23	6	12	15	13	13	18	14	14	16	20	15	20
Yds. Returned By	477	217	236	406	63	178	204	220	275	214	104	282	145	290	167	351
Returned for TD	5	3	1	2	0	1	2	2	2	2	0	3	0	2	2	3
Punts	92	64	79	59	52	67	53	67	50	61	75	69	74	91	60	87
Yds. Punted	3938	2920	3443	2403	2413	2978	2381	2877	2196	2848	3228	2992	3199	3868	2633	3676
Avg. Yds. per Punt	42.8	45.6	43.6	40.7	46.4	44.4	44.9	42.9	43.9	46.7	43.0	43.4	43.2	42.5	43.9	42.3
Punt Returns	38	18	48	32	28	21	27	31	33	37	11	29	43	40	23	32
Yds. Returned	245	187	436	235	330	235	249	269	307	485	158	288	425	247	146	290
Avg. Yds. per Return	6.4	10.4	9.1	7.3	11.8	11.2	9.2	8.7	9.3	13.1	14.4	9.9	9.9	6.2	6.3	9.1
Returned for TD	0	0	1	0	1	1	0	0	0	2	0	0	0	0	0	0
Kickoff Returns	76	63	47	53	63	73	70	51	62	68	75	73	44	71	86	61
Yds. Returned	1720	1247	1059	1228	1554	1630	1700	1015	1465	1655	1672	1568	1074	1357	1943	1524
Avg. Yds. per Return	22.6	19.8	22.5	23.2	24.7	22.3	24.3	19.9	23.6	24.3	22.3	21.5	24.4	19.1	22.6	25.0
Returned for TD	2	0	0	1	1	0	0	0	1	0	2	0	1	0	1	0
Fumbles	21	21	20	19	15	19	24	15	30	27	17	37	21	22	18	28
Lost	8	12	12	8	7	10	11	4	16	12	8	16	8	9	9	11
Out of Bounds	4	4	2	1	1	3	2	1	4	0	2	4	2	0	2	1
Own Rec. for TD	0	0	0	0	0	0	0	0	0	0	0	1	0	0	0	1
Opp. Rec. by	9	15	11	6	12	12	5	11	8	6	10	8	12	10	9	8
Opp. Rec. for TD	2	1	1	1	0	1	1	1	0	0	0	2	1	0	1	0
Penalties	114	72	102	95	83	81	68	80	81	86	81	93	74	91	78	93
Yds. Penalized	792	540	772	770	738	659	543	691	588	615	636	663	633	801	708	750
Total Points Scored	244	342	364	350	448	394	298	367	440	317	309	356	388	223	347	234
Total TDs	26	34	43	42	50	45	28	41	49	33	37	40	45	21	39	25
TDs Rushing	4	18	15	16	26	18	18	14	25	11	8	10	23	7	11	12
TDs Passing	17	14	23	19	20	24	6	25	21	18	27	23	20	12	25	12
TDs on Ret. and Rec.	5	2	5	7	4	3	4	2	3	4	2	7	2	2	3	1
Extra Point Kicks	25	34	40	41	48	43	25	40	45	28	34	37	43	21	31	24
Extra Point Kicks Att.	25	34	40	41	48	43	25	40	45	28	35	37	43	21	33	24
2Pt Conversions	0	0	0	0	1	2	2	0	1	1	1	2	2	0	2	0
2Pt Conversions Att.	1	0	3	1	2	2	3	1	4	5	2	3	2	0	6	1
Safeties	0	1	0	0	1	1	1	0	0	1	0	0	1	2	3	0
Field Goals Made	21	34	22	19	32	25	33	27	33	29	17	25	23	24	24	20
Field Goals Attempted	22	41	23	28	35	29	38	30	36	32	21	28	31	27	31	30
% Successful	95.5	82.9	95.7	67.9	91.4	86.2	86.8	90.0	91.7	90.6	81.0	89.3	74.2	88.9	77.4	66.7

2008 TEAM STATISTICS

NATIONAL FOOTBALL CONFERENCE OFFENSE

	Ariz.	Atl.	Car.	Chi.	Dall.	Det.	GB	Minn.	NO	NYG	Phil.	StL	SF	Sea.	TB	Wash.
First Downs	328	313	287	264	291	234	299	292	354	338	318	249	287	265	298	295
Rushing	72	131	118	98	102	70	99	119	103	130	94	95	83	104	100	109
Passing	231	157	152	153	171	143	182	150	232	176	204	140	176	142	184	165
Penalty	25	25	17	13	18	21	18	23	19	32	20	14	28	19	14	21
Rushes	340	560	504	434	401	352	437	519	398	502	427	417	397	417	451	478
Net Yds. Gained	1178	2443	2437	1673	1723	1332	1805	2338	1594	2518	1697	1649	1599	1768	1837	2095
Avg. Gain	3.5	4.4	4.8	3.9	4.3	3.8	4.1	4.5	4.0	5.0	4.0	4.0	4.0	4.2	4.1	4.4
Avg. Yds. per Game	73.6	152.7	152.3	104.6	107.7	83.3	112.8	146.1	99.6	157.4	106.1	103.1	99.9	110.5	114.8	130.9
Passes Attempted	630	434	414	528	547	509	541	452	636	491	606	520	509	474	562	510
Completed	418	265	246	304	328	281	343	267	413	298	362	292	309	262	355	318
% Completed	66.3	61.1	59.4	57.6	60.0	55.2	63.4	59.1	64.9	60.7	59.7	56.2	60.7	55.3	63.2	62.4
Total Yds. Gained	4875	3440	3288	3229	3988	3299	4044	3217	5069	3353	4060	3268	3724	2831	3788	3291
Times Sacked	28	17	20	29	31	52	34	43	13	28	23	45	55	36	32	38
Yds. Lost	201	104	130	168	199	339	231	261	92	176	149	321	345	214	169	266
Net Yds. Gained	4674	3336	3158	3061	3789	2960	3813	2956	4977	3177	3911	2947	3379	2617	3619	3025
Avg. Yds. per Game	292.1	208.5	197.4	191.3	236.8	185.0	238.3	184.8	311.1	198.6	244.4	184.2	211.2	163.6	226.2	189.1
Net Yds. per Pass Play	7.10	7.40	7.28	5.50	6.56	5.28	6.63	5.97	7.67	6.12	6.22	5.22	5.99	5.13	6.09	5.52
Yds. Gained per Comp.	11.66	12.98	13.37	10.62	12.16	11.74	11.79	12.05	12.27	11.25	11.22	11.19	12.05	10.81	10.67	10.35
Combined Net Yds. Gained	5852	5779	5595	4734	5512	4292	5618	5294	6571	5695	5608	4596	4978	4385	5456	5120
% Total Yds. Rushing	20.1	42.3	43.6	35.3	31.3	31.0	32.1	44.2	24.3	44.2	30.3	35.9	32.1	40.3	33.7	40.9
% Total Yds. Passing	79.9	57.7	56.4	64.7	68.7	69.0	67.9	55.8	75.7	55.8	69.7	64.1	67.9	59.7	66.3	59.1
Avg. Yds. per Game	365.8	361.2	349.7	295.9	344.5	268.3	351.1	330.9	410.7	355.9	350.5	287.3	311.1	274.1	341.0	320.0
Ball Control Plays	998	1011	938	991	979	913	1012	1014	1047	1021	1056	982	961	927	1045	1026
Avg. Yds. per Play	5.9	5.7	6.0	4.8	5.6	4.7	5.6	5.2	6.3	5.6	5.3	4.7	5.2	4.7	5.2	5.0
Avg. Time of Poss.	30:09	30:49	29:19	28:07	30:00	26:59	31:20	31:19	30:23	32:56	30:55	29:32	29:22	26:30	31:23	31:31
Third Down Efficiency	41.9	43.4	39.6	35.6	42.9	28.8	44.2	39.4	48.5	43.1	41.3	31.9	37.9	31.3	38.4	35.2
Had Intercepted	15	11	12	14	20	19	13	17	18	10	16	19	19	15	13	6
Yds. Opp Returned	276	74	167	219	349	364	70	329	270	189	434	452	358	261	233	23
Ret. by Opp. for TD	1	0	0	1	1	5	0	2	2	2	2	4	2	1	2	0
Punts	60	65	76	96	78	90	65	74	53	64	78	83	67	90	77	82
Yds. Punted	2509	2566	3217	3957	3388	3952	2688	3473	2364	2814	3334	4120	3155	4007	3426	3321
Avg. Yds. per Punt	41.8	39.5	42.3	41.2	43.4	43.9	41.4	46.9	44.6	44.0	42.7	49.6	47.1	44.5	44.5	40.5
Punt Returns	33	43	42	39	37	21	37	34	26	39	52	29	29	35	47	45
Yds. Returned	237	379	453	261	238	168	398	273	310	337	446	245	298	353	440	378
Avg. Yds. per Return	7.2	8.8	10.8	6.7	6.4	8.0	10.8	8.0	11.9	8.6	8.6	8.4	10.3	10.1	9.4	8.4
Returned for TD	0	1	0	0	0	0	2	1	3	0	1	0	0	0	1	1
Kickoff Returns	75	59	60	77	70	83	69	61	62	55	60	80	76	77	60	55
Yds. Returned	1630	1408	1372	1919	1554	1807	1387	1369	1496	1284	1411	1761	1767	1948	1486	1382
Avg. Yds. per Return	21.7	23.9	22.9	24.9	22.2	21.8	20.1	22.4	24.1	23.3	23.5	22.0	23.3	25.3	24.8	25.1
Returned for TD	1	0	0	1	1	0	0	0	0	0	1	0	1	0	1	0
Fumbles	27	18	12	19	29	31	25	31	18	18	16	18	36	20	21	20
Lost	15	10	7	13	13	10	8	14	8	3	10	12	16	12	13	12
Out of Bounds	0	2	1	2	3	4	1	5	2	2	5	1	3	4	0	2
Own Rec. for TD	0	1	0	1	0	0	0	0	0	0	0	0	1	1	0	0
Opp. Rec. by	17	8	13	10	14	16	6	13	7	5	14	14	6	11	8	5
Opp. Rec. for TD	1	0	2	2	0	1	1	2	0	0	3	1	0	1	1	0
Penalties	107	71	94	78	119	88	110	90	86	102	74	97	98	79	95	83
Yds. Penalized	781	591	637	610	952	729	984	692	797	821	635	718	732	601	834	644
Total Points Scored	427	391	414	375	362	268	419	379	463	427	416	232	339	294	361	265
Total TDs	51	43	47	42	43	29	48	41	57	45	45	20	36	32	38	27
TDs Rushing	14	23	30	15	12	10	11	15	20	19	15	8	10	10	13	12
TDs Passing	31	16	15	20	29	18	28	22	34	23	23	11	21	18	18	14
TDs on Ret. and Rec.	6	4	2	7	2	1	9	4	3	3	7	1	5	4	7	1
Extra Point Kicks	44	42	46	41	42	25	46	40	53	41	45	19	34	30	35	25
Extra Point Kicks Att.	44	42	46	41	42	26	46	40	54	41	45	19	34	30	36	25
2Pt Conversions	1	1	1	1	0	2	2	0	0	1	0	0	1	0	1	0
2Pt Conversions Att.	6	1	1	1	1	3	2	1	3	3	0	1	2	2	2	2
Safeties	0	1	0	1	1	1	0	3	1	3	1	0	0	0	0	0
Field Goals Made	25	29	28	26	20	21	27	29	22	36	33	31	29	24	32	26
Field Goals Attempted	28	31	31	29	22	22	34	34	27	39	40	36	33	27	38	36
% Successful	89.3	93.5	90.3	89.7	90.9	95.5	79.4	85.3	81.5	92.3	82.5	86.1	87.9	88.9	84.2	72.2

NATIONAL FOOTBALL CONFERENCE DEFENSE

	Ariz.	Atl.	Car.	Chi.	Dall.	Det.	GB	Minn.	NO	NYG	Phil.	StL	SF	Sea.	TB	Wash.
First Downs	312	309	296	314	276	350	295	255	299	268	248	320	293	324	259	259
Rushing	117	108	100	93	85	147	121	72	100	78	79	146	104	98	87	86
Passing	172	189	178	208	163	188	141	163	180	165	144	158	170	207	153	159
Penalty	23	12	18	13	28	15	33	20	19	25	25	16	19	19	19	14
Rushes	445	415	432	437	402	536	458	371	445	386	421	501	452	457	441	398
Net Yds. Gained	1764	2046	1912	1496	1706	2754	2105	1230	1885	1533	1476	2475	1709	1899	1901	1526
Avg. Gain	4.0	4.9	4.4	3.4	4.2	5.1	4.6	3.3	4.2	4.0	3.5	4.9	3.8	4.2	4.3	3.8
Avg. Yds. per Game	110.3	127.9	119.5	93.5	106.6	172.1	131.6	76.9	117.8	95.8	92.3	154.7	106.8	118.7	118.8	95.4
Passes Attempted	517	549	557	622	508	443	518	530	526	503	525	444	545	566	475	511
Completed	323	325	333	383	308	303	287	324	299	296	284	278	331	366	276	290
% Completed	62.5	59.2	59.8	61.6	60.6	68.4	55.4	61.1	56.8	58.8	54.1	62.6	60.7	64.7	58.1	56.8
Total Yds. Gained	3731	3771	3617	4076	3377	3907	3384	3753	3708	3427	3225	3676	3668	4342	3187	3236
Times Sacked	31	34	37	28	59	30	27	45	28	42	48	30	30	35	29	24
Yds. Lost	191	245	230	217	374	191	140	304	161	288	312	201	161	193	190	141
Net Yds. Gained	3540	3526	3387	3859	3003	3716	3244	3449	3547	3139	2913	3475	3507	4149	2997	3095
Avg. Yds. per Game	221.3	220.4	211.7	241.2	187.7	232.3	202.8	215.6	221.7	196.2	182.1	217.2	219.2	259.3	187.3	193.4
Net Yds. per Pass Play	6.46	6.05	5.70	5.94	5.30	7.86	5.95	6.00	6.40	5.76	5.08	7.33	6.10	6.90	5.95	5.79
Yds. Gained per Comp.	11.55	11.60	10.86	10.64	10.96	12.89	11.79	11.58	12.40	11.58	11.36	13.22	11.08	11.86	11.55	11.16
Combined Net Yds. Gained	5304	5572	5299	5355	4709	6470	5349	4679	5432	4672	4389	5950	5216	6048	4898	4621
% Total Yds. Rushing	33.3	36.7	36.1	27.9	36.2	42.6	39.4	26.3	34.7	32.8	33.6	41.6	32.8	31.4	38.8	33.0
% Total Yds. Passing	66.7	63.3	63.9	72.1	63.8	57.4	60.6	73.7	65.3	67.2	66.4	58.4	67.2	68.6	61.2	67.0
Avg. Yds. per Game	331.5	348.3	331.2	334.7	294.3	404.4	334.3	292.4	339.5	292.0	274.3	371.9	326.0	378.0	306.1	288.8
Ball Control Plays	993	998	1026	1087	969	1009	1003	946	999	931	994	975	1027	1058	945	933
Avg. Yds. per Play	5.3	5.6	5.2	4.9	4.9	6.4	5.3	4.9	5.4	5.0	4.4	6.1	5.1	5.7	5.2	5.0
Avg. Time of Poss.	29:51	29:11	30:41	31:53	30:00	33:01	28:40	28:41	29:37	27:04	29:05	30:28	30:38	33:30	28:37	28:29
Third Down Efficiency	44.4	38.0	39.7	34.9	35.6	45.7	38.1	33.5	39.8	40.7	32.2	39.6	37.9	42.3	37.9	35.6
Intercepted By	13	10	12	22	8	4	22	12	15	17	15	12	12	9	22	13
Yds. Returned By	321	233	192	312	36	16	685	56	188	339	279	162	139	217	396	114
Returned for TD	2	2	0	1	1	0	6	0	0	2	2	0	1	2	3	0
Punts	61	76	80	83	74	59	76	80	66	76	101	67	72	68	81	87
Yds. Punted	2777	3458	3671	3525	3281	2573	3364	3481	2711	3297	4294	3029	3054	3009	3528	3721
Avg. Yds. per Punt	45.5	45.5	45.9	42.5	44.3	43.6	44.3	43.5	41.1	43.4	42.5	45.2	42.4	44.3	43.6	42.8
Punt Returns	29	20	41	36	37	51	33	42	34	24	41	57	39	44	39	33
Yds. Returned	381	49	276	203	390	414	249	624	363	140	296	590	364	444	392	385
Avg. Yds. per Return	13.1	2.5	6.7	5.6	10.5	8.1	7.5	14.9	10.7	5.8	7.2	10.4	9.3	10.1	10.1	11.7
Returned for TD	1	0	1	0	0	2	0	4	0	0	0	0	0	1	0	2
Kickoff Returns	69	71	59	68	71	57	72	78	76	85	75	56	65	47	74	55
Yds. Returned	1724	1536	1292	1656	1510	1332	1687	1830	1827	1912	1698	1469	1515	1205	1542	1103
Avg. Yds. per Return	25.0	21.6	21.9	24.4	21.3	23.4	23.4	23.5	24.0	22.5	22.6	26.2	23.3	25.6	20.8	20.1
Returned for TD	1	0	0	0	1	0	0	0	1	0	1	0	0	0	0	0
Fumbles	26	18	25	17	28	31	20	34	16	22	26	24	16	26	16	16
Lost	17	8	13	10	14	16	6	13	7	5	14	14	6	11	8	5
Out of Bounds	1	2	0	1	3	5	5	1	1	4	2	3	1	3	1	4
Own Rec. for TD	0	0	0	0	0	0	0	2	0	0	0	0	1	0	0	0
Opp. Rec. by	15	10	7	13	13	10	8	14	8	3	10	12	16	12	13	12
Opp. Rec. for TD	0	1	1	1	3	0	1	1	2	0	0	3	0	0	1	2
Penalties	98	109	88	100	87	91	89	109	84	111	80	89	111	81	88	80
Yds. Penalized	816	854	736	827	601	753	721	1002	637	866	593	654	869	671	660	639
Total Points Scored	426	325	329	350	365	517	380	333	393	294	289	465	381	392	323	296
Total TDs	52	38	37	39	36	63	43	36	41	34	31	53	39	40	34	32
TDs Rushing	13	17	14	16	11	31	20	10	14	14	7	26	14	13	8	12
TDs Passing	36	20	19	21	19	25	22	15	21	17	19	20	22	25	23	16
TDs on Ret. and Rec.	3	1	4	2	6	7	1	11	6	3	5	7	3	2	3	4
Extra Point Kicks	49	35	31	38	33	62	39	35	37	31	29	52	38	39	33	30
Extra Point Kicks Att.	49	35	32	39	33	62	39	35	37	31	29	52	38	39	33	31
2Pt Conversions	1	1	2	0	0	0	1	1	3	1	0	1	0	1	1	1
2Pt Conversions Att.	3	3	4	0	2	1	4	1	4	3	2	1	1	1	1	1
Safeties	0	0	0	0	1	1	3	1	1	0	1	0	2	0	0	0
Field Goals Made	21	20	24	26	38	25	25	26	34	19	24	31	35	37	28	24
Field Goals Attempted	27	25	28	33	44	29	30	36	39	26	28	32	42	41	30	28
% Successful	77.8	80.0	85.7	78.8	86.4	86.2	83.3	72.2	87.2	73.1	85.7	96.9	83.3	90.2	93.3	85.7

2008 TEAM STATISTICS

AFC, NFC, AND NFL SUMMARY

	AFC Offense Total	AFC Offense Average	AFC Defense Total	AFC Defense Average	NFC Offense Total	NFC Offense Average	NFC Defense Total	NFC Defense Average	NFL Total	NFL Average
First Downs	4721	295.1	4756	297.3	4712	294.5	4677	292.3	9433	294.8
Rushing	1623	101.4	1629	101.8	1627	101.7	1621	101.3	3250	101.6
Passing	2775	173.4	2795	174.7	2758	172.4	2738	171.1	5533	172.9
Penalty	323	20.2	332	20.8	327	20.4	318	19.9	650	20.3
Rushes	7085	442.8	7122	445.1	7034	439.6	6997	437.3	14119	441.2
Net Yds. Gained	29690	1855.6	29959	1872.4	29686	1855.4	29417	1838.6	59376	1855.5
Avg. Gain	—	4.2	—	4.2	—	4.2	—	4.2	—	4.2
Avg. Yds. per Game	—	116.0	—	117.0	—	116.0	—	114.9	—	116.0
Passes Attempted	8163	510.2	8187	511.7	8363	522.7	8339	521.2	16526	516.4
Completed	5020	313.8	5075	317.2	5061	316.3	5006	312.9	10081	315.0
% Completed	—	61.5	—	62.0	—	60.5	—	60.0	—	61.0
Total Yds. Gained	56002	3500.1	56681	3542.6	58764	3672.8	58085	3630.3	114766	3586.4
Times Sacked	512	32.0	479	29.9	524	32.8	557	34.8	1036	32.4
Yds. Lost	3224	201.5	3050	190.6	3365	210.3	3539	221.2	6589	205.9
Net Yds. Gained	52778	3298.6	53631	3351.9	55399	3462.4	54546	3409.1	108177	3380.5
Avg. Yds. per Game	—	206.2	—	209.5	—	216.4	—	213.1	—	211.3
Net Yds. per Pass Play	—	6.08	—	6.19	—	6.23	—	6.13	—	6.16
Yds. Gained per Comp.	—	11.16	—	11.17	—	11.61	—	11.60	—	11.38
Combined Net Yds. Gained	82468	5154.3	83590	5224.4	85085	5317.8	83963	5247.7	167553	5236.0
% Total Yds. Rushing	—	36.0	—	35.8	—	34.9	—	35.0	—	35.4
% Total Yds. Passing	—	64.0	—	64.2	—	65.1	—	65.0	—	64.6
Avg. Yds. per Game	—	322.1	—	326.5	—	332.4	—	328.0	—	327.3
Ball Control Plays	15760	985.0	15788	986.8	15921	995.1	15893	993.3	31681	990.0
Avg. Yds. per Play	—	5.2	—	5.3	—	5.3	—	5.3	—	5.3
Third Down Efficiency	—	40.0	—	40.6	—	39.0	—	38.4	—	39.5
Interceptions	228	14.3	247	15.4	237	14.8	218	13.6	465	14.5
Yds. Returned	3446	215.4	3829	239.3	4068	254.3	3685	230.3	7514	234.8
Returned for TD	27	1.7	30	1.9	25	1.6	22	1.4	52	1.6
Punts	1109	69.3	1100	68.8	1198	74.9	1207	75.4	2307	72.1
Yds. Punted	48475	3029.7	47993	2999.6	52291	3268.2	52773	3298.3	100766	3148.9
Avg. Yds. per Punt	—	43.7	—	43.6	—	43.6	—	43.7	—	43.7
Punt Returns	503	31.4	491	30.7	588	36.8	600	37.5	1091	34.1
Yds. Returned	4878	304.9	4532	283.3	5214	325.9	5560	347.5	10092	315.4
Avg. Yds. per Return	—	9.7	—	9.2	—	8.9	—	9.3	—	9.3
Returned for TD	6	0.4	5	0.3	10	0.6	11	0.7	16	0.5
Kickoff Returns	1035	64.7	1036	64.8	1079	67.4	1078	67.4	2114	66.1
Yds. Returned	23268	1454.3	23411	1463.2	24981	1561.3	24838	1552.4	48249	1507.8
Avg. Yds. per Return	—	22.5	—	22.6	—	23.2	—	23.0	—	22.8
Returned for TD	7	0.4	9	0.6	6	0.4	4	0.3	13	0.4
Fumbles	356	22.3	354	22.1	359	22.4	361	22.6	715	22.3
Lost	152	9.5	161	10.1	176	11.0	167	10.4	328	10.3
Out of Bounds	33	2.1	33	2.1	37	2.3	37	2.3	70	2.2
Own Rec. for TD	1	0.1	2	0.1	4	0.3	3	0.2	5	0.2
Opp. Rec.	161	10.1	152	9.5	167	10.4	176	11.0	328	10.3
Opp. Rec. for TD	13	0.8	12	0.8	15	0.9	16	1.0	28	0.9
Penalties	1396	87.3	1372	85.8	1471	91.9	1495	93.4	2867	89.6
Yds. Penalized	11040	690.0	10899	681.2	11758	734.9	11899	743.7	22798	712.4
Total Points Scored	5447	340.4	5421	338.8	5832	364.5	5858	366.1	11279	352.5
Total TDs	602	37.6	598	37.4	644	40.3	648	40.5	1246	38.9
TDs Rushing	239	14.9	236	14.8	237	14.8	240	15.0	476	14.9
TDs Passing	305	19.1	306	19.1	341	21.3	340	21.3	646	20.2
TDs on Ret. and Rec.	58	3.6	56	3.5	66	4.1	68	4.3	124	3.9
Extra Point Kicks	562	35.1	559	34.9	608	38.0	611	38.2	1170	36.6
Extra Point Kicks Att.	565	35.3	562	35.1	611	38.2	614	38.4	1176	36.8
2Pt Conversions	17	1.1	14	0.9	11	0.7	14	0.9	28	0.9
2Pt Conversions Att.	37	2.3	36	2.3	31	1.9	32	2.0	68	2.1
Safeties	9	0.6	11	0.7	12	0.8	10	0.6	21	0.7
Field Goals Made	407	25.4	408	25.5	438	27.4	437	27.3	845	26.4
Field Goals Attempted	493	30.8	482	30.1	507	31.7	518	32.4	1000	31.3
% Successful	—	82.6	—	84.6	—	86.4	—	84.4	—	84.5

CLUB LEADERS

	Offense	Defense
First Downs	New England 356	Baltimore 228
Rushing	New England 145	Baltimore 58
Passing	New Orleans 232	Green Bay 141
Penalty	N.Y. Giants 32	Atlanta 12
Rushes	Baltimore 592	Baltimore 366
Net Yds. Gained	N.Y. Giants 2518	Minnesota 1230
Avg. Gain	N.Y. Giants 5.0	Pittsburgh 3.3
Passes Attempted	New Orleans 636	Detroit 443
Completed	Arizona 418	Oakland 266
% Completed	Miami 67.2	Baltimore 52.3
Total Yds. Gained	New Orleans 5069	Pittsburgh 2861
Times Sacked	Denver, Tennessee 12	Dallas 59
Yds. Lost	Denver 74	Dallas 374
Net Yds. Gained	New Orleans 4977	Pittsburgh 2511
Net Yds. per Pass Play	San Diego 7.7	Pittsburgh 4.3
Yds. Gained per Comp.	Carolina 13.4	Pittsburgh 9.5
Combined Net Yds. Gained	New Orleans 6571	Pittsburgh 3795
% Total Yds. Rushing	Baltimore 45.8	Minnesota 26.3
% Total Yds. Passing	Arizona 79.9	Oakland 55.8
Ball Control Plays	New England 1095	New England 920
Avg. Yds. per Play	New Orleans 6.3	Pittsburgh 3.9
Avg. Time of Poss.	Baltimore 33:10	—
Third Down Efficiency	Indianapolis 50.2	Pittsburgh 31.4
Interceptions	—	Baltimore 26
Yds. Returned	—	Green Bay 685
Returned for TD	—	Green Bay 6
Punts	Cincinnati 101	—
Yds. Punted	Oakland 4391	—
Avg. Yds. per Punt	St. Louis 49.6	—
Punt Returns	Philadelphia 52	New England 11
Yds. Returned	Oakland 570	Atlanta 49
Avg. Yds. per Return	Buffalo 15.5	Atlanta 2.5
Returned for TD	New Orleans, Oakland 3	—
Kickoff Returns	Detroit 83	Oakland 44
Yds. Returned	Seattle 1948	Jacksonville 1015
Avg. Yds. per Return	Tennessee 25.4	Pittsburgh 19.1
Returned for TD	Oakland 2	—
Total Points Scored	New Orleans 463	Pittsburgh 223
Total TDs	New Orleans 57	Pittsburgh 21
TDs Rushing	Carolina 30	Baltimore 4
TDs Passing	New Orleans, San Diego 34	Indianapolis 6
TDs on Ret. and Rec.	Green Bay 9	Atlanta, Green Bay, Tennessee 1
Extra Point Kicks	New Orleans 53	Pittsburgh 21
2-Point Conversions	Cleveland, Denver, Detroit, Green Bay, Indianapolis, New England, N.Y. Jets, San Diego 2	—
Safeties	Baltimore, Minnesota, N.Y. Giants 3	—
Field Goals Made	New England, N.Y. Giants 36	New England 17
Field Goals Attempted	New England, Philadelphia 40	New England 21
% Successful	Detroit 95.5	Tennessee 66.7

NFL CLUB RANKINGS BY YARDS

	Offense			Defense		
	Total	Rush	Pass	Total	Rush	Pass
Arizona	4	32	2	19	16	22
Atlanta	6	2	14	24	25	21
Baltimore	18	4	28	2	3	2
Buffalo	25	14	22	14	22	13
Carolina	10	3	19	18	20	16
Chicago	26	24	21	21	5	30
Cincinnati	32	29	30	12	21	15
Cleveland	31	26	31	26	28	14
Dallas	13	21	9	8	12	5
Denver	2	12	3	29	27	26
Detroit	30	30	24	32	32	27
Green Bay	8	17	8	20	26	12
Houston	3	13	4	22	23	17
Indianapolis	15	31	5	11	24	6
Jacksonville	20	18	15	17	13T	24
Kansas City	24	16	20	31	30	28
Miami	12	11	10	15	10	25
Minnesota	17	5	25	6	*1	18
New England	5	6	12	10	15	11
New Orleans	*1	28	*1	23	17	23
New York Giants	7	*1	18	5	9	8
New York Jets	16	9	16	16	7	29
Oakland	29	10	32	27	31	10
Philadelphia	9	22	6	3	4	3
Pittsburgh	22	23	17	*1	2	*1
St. Louis	27	25	26	28	29	19
San Diego	11	20	7	25	11	31
San Francisco	23	27	13	13	13T	20
Seattle	28	19	29	30	18	32
Tampa Bay	14	15	11	9	19	4
Tennessee	21	7	27	7	6	9
Washington	19	8	23	4	8	7

T = Tied for position * = League Leader

AFC TAKEAWAYS/GIVEAWAYS

	Takeaways			Giveaways			Net
	Int	Fum	Total	Int	Fum	Total	Diff.
Miami	18	12	30	7	6	13	+17
Tennessee	20	11	31	9	8	17	+14
Baltimore	26	8	34	12	9	21	+13
Indianapolis	15	11	26	12	5	17	+9
Cleveland	23	8	31	20	6	26	+5
Kansas City	13	16	29	16	8	24	+5
Pittsburgh	20	9	29	15	10	25	+4
San Diego	15	9	24	11	9	20	+4
New England	14	8	22	11	10	21	+1
Oakland	16	8	24	11	12	23	+1
N.Y. Jets	14	16	30	23	8	31	-1
Cincinnati	12	12	24	15	11	26	-2
Jacksonville	13	4	17	13	11	24	-7
Buffalo	10	12	22	15	15	30	-8
Houston	12	10	22	20	12	32	-10
Denver	6	7	13	18	12	30	-17
Totals	247	161	408	228	152	380	+28

NFC TAKEAWAYS/GIVEAWAYS

	Takeaways			Giveaways			Net
	Int	Fum	Total	Int	Fum	Total	Diff.
N.Y. Giants	17	5	22	10	3	13	+9
Green Bay	22	6	28	13	8	21	+7
Carolina	12	13	25	12	7	19	+6
Chicago	22	10	32	14	13	27	+5
Tampa Bay	22	8	30	13	13	26	+4
Philadelphia	15	14	29	16	10	26	+3
Arizona	13	17	30	15	15	30	0
Washington	13	5	18	6	12	18	0
Atlanta	10	8	18	11	10	21	-3
New Orleans	15	7	22	18	8	26	-4
St. Louis	12	14	26	19	12	31	-5
Minnesota	12	13	25	17	14	31	-6
Seattle	9	11	20	15	12	27	-7
Detroit	4	16	20	19	10	29	-9
Dallas	8	14	22	20	13	33	-11
San Francisco	12	6	18	19	16	35	-17
NFC Totals	218	167	385	237	176	413	-28

SCORING

POINTS

AFC: 148 Stephen Gostkowski, New England
NFC: 144 David Akers, Philadelphia

TOUCHDOWNS

NFC: 20 DeAngelo Williams, Carolina
AFC: 15 Thomas Jones, N.Y. Jets
15 LenDale White, Tennessee

EXTRA POINT KICKS

AFC: 46 Nate Kaeding, San Diego
NFC: 46 Mason Crosby, Green Bay
46 John Kasay, Carolina

TWO-POINT EXTRA POINT PLAYS

AFC: 2 Braylon Edwards, Cleveland
NFC: 1 Casey FitzSimmons, Detroit
1 Frank Gore, San Francisco
1 Domenik Hixon, N.Y. Giants
1 Edgerrin James, Arizona
1 Michael Jenkins, Atlanta
1 Greg Jennings, Green Bay
1 Calvin Johnson, Detroit
1 Brandon Lloyd, Chicago
1 Ruvell Martin, Green Bay
1 Alex Smith, Tampa Bay
1 DeAngelo Williams, Carolina

FIELD GOALS

AFC: 36 Stephen Gostkowski, New England
NFC: 35 John Carney, N.Y. Giants

FIELD GOAL ATTEMPTS

AFC: 40 Stephen Gostkowski, New England
NFC: 40 David Akers, Philadelphia

LONGEST FIELD GOAL

AFC: 57 Sebastian Janikowski, Oakland vs. N.Y. Jets, October 19 - (OT)
57 Nate Kaeding, San Diego at Tampa Bay, December 21
NFC: 56 Jason Hanson, Detroit at Carolina, November 16

MOST POINTS, GAME

AFC: 24 Ronnie Brown, Miami at New England, September 21 (4 TD)
NFC: 24 Michael Turner, Atlanta vs. Carolina, November 23 (4 TD)
24 Brian Westbrook, Philadelphia vs. Arizona, November 27 (4 TD)
24 DeAngelo Williams, Carolina at Green Bay, November 30 (4 TD)
24 DeAngelo Williams, Carolina at N.Y. Giants, December 21 (4 TD) - (OT)

TEAM LEADERS, POINTS

AFC: BALTIMORE, 122, Matt Stover; BUFFALO, 124, Rian Lindell; CINCINNATI, 78, Shayne Graham; CLEVELAND, 108, Phil Dawson; DENVER, 114, Matt Prater; HOUSTON, 124, Kris Brown; INDIANAPOLIS, 103, Adam Vinatieri; JACKSONVILLE, 90, Josh Scobee; KANSAS CITY, 60, Tony Gonzalez; MIAMI, 103, *Dan Carpenter; NEW ENGLAND, 148, Stephen Gostkowski; N.Y. JETS, 111, Jay Feely; OAKLAND, 97, Sebastian Janikowski; PITTSBURGH, 117, Jeff Reed; SAN DIEGO, 127, Nate Kaeding; TENNESSEE, 127, Rob Bironas

NFC: ARIZONA, 119, Neil Rackers; ATLANTA, 129, Jason Elam; CAROLINA, 130, John Kasay; CHICAGO, 119, Robbie Gould; DALLAS, 102, Nick Folk; DETROIT, 88, Jason Hanson; GREEN BAY, 127, Mason Crosby; MINNESOTA, 127, Ryan Longwell; NEW ORLEANS, 72, Pierre Thomas; N.Y. GIANTS, 143, John Carney; PHILADELPHIA, 144, David Akers; ST. LOUIS, 112, Josh Brown; SAN FRANCISCO, 121, Joe Nedney; SEATTLE, 102, Olindo Mare; TAMPA BAY, 131, Matt Bryant; WASHINGTON, 103, Shaun Suisham

TEAM CHAMPION

NFC: 463 New Orleans
AFC: 439 San Diego

NFL TOP TEN SCORERS—KICKERS

	XP	XPA	FG	FGA	PTS
Gostkowski, Stephen, N.E.	40	40	36	40	148
Akers, David, Phi.	45	45	33	40	144
Carney, John, NY-G	38	38	35	38	143
Bryant, Matt, T.B.	35	36	32	38	131
Kasay, John, Car.	46	46	28	31	130
Elam, Jason, Atl.	42	42	29	31	129
Bironas, Rob, Ten.	40	40	29	33	127
Crosby, Mason, G.B.	46	46	27	34	127
Kaeding, Nate, S.D.	46	46	27	32	127
Longwell, Ryan, Min.	40	40	29	34	127

NFL TOP TEN SCORERS—NONKICKERS

	TD	TDR	TDP	TDM	2-PT.	PTS
Williams, DeAngelo, Car.	20	18	2	0	1	122
Turner, Michael, Atl.	17	17	0	0	0	102
Jacobs, Brandon, NY-G	15	15	0	0	0	90
Jones, Thomas, NYJ	15	13	2	0	0	90
White, LenDale, Ten.	15	15	0	0	0	90
Jones-Drew, Maurice, Jac.	14	12	2	0	0	84
Westbrook, Brian, Phi.	14	9	5	0	0	84
Johnson, Calvin, Det.	12	0	12	0	1	74
Fitzgerald, Larry, Ariz	12	0	12	0	0	72
Forté, Matt, Chi.	12	8	4	0	0	72
Thomas, Pierre, N.O.	12	9	3	0	0	72
Tomlinson, LaDainian, S.D.	12	11	1	0	0	72

AFC—INDIVIDUAL SCORERS

KICKERS

	XP	XPA	FG	FGA	PTS
Gostkowski, Stephen, N.E.	40	40	36	40	148
Bironas, Rob, Ten.	40	40	29	33	127
Kaeding, Nate, S.D.	46	46	27	32	127
Brown, Kris, Hou.	37	37	29	33	124
Lindell, Rian, Buf.	34	34	30	38	124
Stover, Matt, Bal.	41	41	27	33	122
Reed, Jeff, Pit.	36	37	27	31	117
Prater, Matt, Den.	39	40	25	34	114
Feely, Jay, NYJ	39	39	24	28	111
Dawson, Phil, Cle.	18	18	30	36	108
* Carpenter, Dan, Mia.	40	40	21	25	103
Vinatieri, Adam, Ind.	43	43	20	25	103
Janikowski, Sebastian, Oak.	25	26	24	30	97
Scobee, Josh, Jac.	33	33	19	25	90
Graham, Shayne, Cin.	15	15	21	24	78
* Barth, Connor, K.C.	24	24	10	12	54
Novak, Nick, K.C.	7	7	6	10	25
Rayner, Dave, Cin.	3	3	1	1	6
* Hauschka, Steven, Bal.	0	0	1	2	3
Nugent, Mike, NYJ	2	2	0	1	2

NONKICKERS

	TD	TDR	TDP	TDM	2-PT.	PTS
Jones, Thomas, NYJ	15	13	2	0	0	90
White, LenDale, Ten.	15	15	0	0	0	90
Jones-Drew, Maurice, Jac.	14	12	2	0	0	84
Tomlinson, LaDainian, S.D.	12	11	1	0	0	72
McClain, Le'Ron, Bal.	11	10	1	0	0	66
Moss, Randy, N.E.	11	0	11	0	0	66
Brown, Ronnie, Mia.	10	10	0	0	0	60
Gonzalez, Tony, K.C.	10	0	10	0	0	60
* Johnson, Chris, Ten.	10	9	1	0	0	60
* Slaton, Steve, Hou.	10	9	1	0	0	60
Rhodes, Dominic, Ind.	9	6	3	0	1	56
Washington, Leon, NYJ	9	6	2	1	1	56
Lynch, Marshawn, Buf.	9	8	1	0	0	54
Johnson, Andre, Hou.	8	0	8	0	1	50
Gates, Antonio, S.D.	8	0	8	0	0	48
Walter, Kevin, Hou.	8	0	8	0	0	48
Sproles, Darren, S.D.	7	1	5	1	1	44
Addai, Joseph, Ind.	7	5	2	0	0	42
Bowe, Dwayne, K.C.	7	0	7	0	0	42
Coles, Laveranues, NYJ	7	0	7	0	0	42
Fasano, Anthony, Mia.	7	0	7	0	0	42
Higgins, Johnnie Lee, Oak.	7	0	4	3	0	42
Jackson, Vincent, S.D.	7	0	7	0	0	42
McGahee, Willis, Bal.	7	7	0	0	0	42
Morris, Sammy, N.E.	7	7	0	0	0	42
Ward, Hines, Pit.	7	0	7	0	0	42
Wayne, Reggie, Ind.	6	0	6	0	1	38
Clark, Dallas, Ind.	6	0	6	0	0	36
Faulk, Kevin, N.E.	6	3	3	0	0	36
Gage, Justin, Ten.	6	0	6	0	0	36
* Hillis, Peyton, Den.	6	5	1	0	0	36
Marshall, Brandon, Den.	6	0	6	0	0	36
Moore, Mewelde, Pit.	6	5	1	0	0	36
Cotchery, Jerricho, NYJ	5	0	5	0	1	32
Mason, Derrick, Bal.	5	0	5	0	1	32
* Royal, Eddie, Den.	5	0	5	0	1	32
Chambers, Chris, S.D.	5	0	5	0	0	30
* Green-Ellis, BenJarvus, N.E.	5	5	0	0	0	30
Harrison, Marvin, Ind.	5	0	5	0	0	30
Holmes, Santonio, Pit.	5	0	5	0	0	30
Johnson, Larry, K.C.	5	5	0	0	0	30
Parker, Willie, Pit.	5	5	0	0	0	30
Williams, Ricky, Mia.	5	4	1	0	0	30
Clayton, Mark, Bal.	4	1	3	0	0	24
Floyd, Malcom, S.D.	4	0	4	0	0	24
Ginn, Ted Jr., Mia.	4	2	2	0	0	24
Gonzalez, Anthony, Ind.	4	0	4	0	0	24
Graham, Daniel, Den.	4	0	4	0	0	24
Houshmandzadeh, T.J., Cin.	4	0	4	0	0	24
Jordan, LaMont, N.E.	4	4	0	0	0	24
Lewis, Jamal, Cle.	4	4	0	0	0	24
* McFadden, Darren, Oak.	4	4	0	0	0	24
Ochocinco, Chad, Cin.	4	0	4	0	0	24
Pittman, Michael, Den.	4	4	0	0	0	24
Thigpen, Tyler, K.C.	4	3	1	0	0	24
Edwards, Braylon, Cle.	3	0	3	0	2	22
Evans, Lee, Buf.	3	0	3	0	1	20
Welker, Wes, N.E.	3	0	3	0	1	20
Bradley, Mark, K.C.	3	0	3	0	0	18
Bush, Michael, Oak.	3	3	0	0	0	18
Cobbs, Patrick, Mia.	3	1	2	0	0	18
Cribbs, Josh, Cle.	3	1	1	1	0	18
Edwards, Trent, Buf.	3	3	0	0	0	18
Green, Ahman, Hou.	3	3	0	0	0	18
Heap, Todd, Bal.	3	0	3	0	0	18
Jackson, Fred, Buf.	3	3	0	0	0	18
* Keller, Dustin, NYJ	3	0	3	0	0	18
Martin, David, Mia.	3	0	3	0	0	18
Miller, Heath, Pit.	3	0	3	0	0	18
Owens, Montell, Jac.	3	2	0	1	0	18
Reed, Ed, Bal.	3	0	0	3	0	18
Russell, Gary, Pit.	3	3	0	0	0	18
Scheffler, Tony, Den.	3	0	3	0	0	18
Stokley, Brandon, Den.	3	0	3	0	0	18
Stuckey, Chansi, NYJ	3	0	3	0	0	18
Washington, Nate, Pit.	3	0	3	0	0	18
Williams, Reggie, Jac.	3	0	3	0	0	18
Winslow, Kellen, Cle.	3	0	3	0	0	18
Cutler, Jay, Den.	2	2	0	0	1	14
Gaffney, Jabar, N.E.	2	0	2	0	1	14
Hall, Ahmard, Ten.	2	0	2	0	1	14
Anderson, David, Hou.	2	0	2	0	0	12
Bell, Tatum, Den.	2	2	0	0	0	12
Benson, Cedric, Cin.	2	2	0	0	0	12
Camarillo, Greg, Mia.	2	0	2	0	0	12
Cassel, Matt, N.E.	2	2	0	0	0	12
Curry, Ronald, Oak.	2	0	2	0	0	12
Daniels, Owen, Hou.	2	0	2	0	0	12
Fitzpatrick, Ryan, Cin.	2	2	0	0	0	12
* Flacco, Joe, Bal.	2	2	0	0	0	12
Garrard, David, Jac.	2	2	0	0	0	12
Greer, Jabari, Buf.	2	0	0	2	0	12
* Hardy, James, Buf.	2	0	2	0	0	12
Harrison, Jerome, Cle.	2	1	1	0	0	12
Henry, Chris, Cin.	2	0	2	0	0	12
* Hester, Jacob, S.D.	2	1	1	0	0	12
* Johnson, Steve, Buf.	2	0	2	0	0	12
Jones, Jacoby, Hou.	2	0	0	2	0	12
Jones, Matt, Jac.	2	0	2	0	0	12
* Leggett, Maurice, K.C.	2	0	0	2	0	12
Lelie, Ashley, Oak.	2	0	2	0	0	12
Lewis, Marcedes, Jac.	2	0	2	0	0	12
Losman, J.P., Buf.	2	2	0	0	0	12
Manumaleuna, Brandon, S.D.	2	0	2	0	0	12
Mathis, Rashean, Jac.	2	0	0	2	0	12
* McKelvin, Leodis, Buf.	2	0	0	2	0	12
Miller, Justin, Oak.	2	0	0	2	0	12
Northcutt, Dennis, Jac.	2	0	2	0	0	12
Parrish, Roscoe, Buf.	2	0	1	1	0	12
Perry, Chris, Cin.	2	2	0	0	0	12
Roethlisberger, Ben, Pit.	2	2	0	0	0	12
Scaife, Bo, Ten.	2	0	2	0	0	12
Schaub, Matt, Hou.	2	2	0	0	0	12
* Schilens, Chaz, Oak.	2	0	2	0	0	12
Suggs, Terrell, Bal.	2	0	0	2	0	12
Watson, Benjamin, N.E.	2	0	2	0	0	12
Wilcox, Daniel, Bal.	2	0	2	0	0	12
Allen, Will, Mia.	1	0	0	1	0	6
Ball, Dave, Ten.	1	0	0	1	0	6
Barrett, David, NYJ	1	0	0	1	0	6
* Bess, Davone, Mia.	1	0	1	0	0	6
Brackett, Gary, Ind.	1	0	0	1	0	6
Bulluck, Keith, Ten.	1	0	0	1	0	6
Carter, Tyrone, Pit.	1	0	0	1	0	6
* Cason, Antoine, S.D.	1	0	0	1	0	6
* Charles, Jamaal, K.C.	1	0	1	0	0	6
Cramer, Casey, Mia.	1	0	1	0	0	6
Cromartie, Antonio, S.D.	1	0	0	1	0	6
Crumpler, Alge, Ten.	1	0	1	0	0	6
Darling, Devard, K.C.	1	0	1	0	0	6
Denney, Ryan, Buf.	1	0	1	0	0	6
Dinkins, Darnell, Cle.	1	0	1	0	0	6
Elam, Abram, NYJ	1	0	0	1	0	6
Ellis, Shaun, NYJ	1	0	0	1	0	6
Fargas, Justin, Oak.	1	1	0	0	0	6
Favre, Brett, NYJ	1	1	0	0	0	6
Figurs, Yamon, Bal.	1	0	1	0	0	6

2008 INDIVIDUAL STATISTICS—SCORING

	TD	TDR	TDP	TDM	2-PT.	PTS
* Fine, Derek, Buf.	1	0	1	0	0	6
Finnegan, Cortland, Ten.	1	0	0	1	0	6
* Flowers, Brandon, K.C.	1	0	0	1	0	6
Fox, Vernon, Den.	1	0	0	1	0	6
Griffin, Michael, Ten.	1	0	0	1	0	6
Griffith, Justin, Oak.	1	0	1	0	0	6
Hall, Leon, Cin.	1	0	0	1	0	6
Hayden, Kelvin, Ind.	1	0	0	1	0	6
* Haynos, Joey, Mia.	1	0	1	0	0	6
Hobbs, Ellis, N.E.	1	0	0	1	0	6
Holt, Glenn, Cin.	1	0	1	0	0	6
Jackson, Darrell, Den.	1	0	1	0	0	6
Jackson, Nate, Den.	1	0	1	0	0	6
Jones, Brandon, Ten.	1	0	1	0	0	6
Jones, Greg, Jac.	1	0	1	0	0	6
Joseph, Johnathan, Cin.	1	0	0	1	0	6
Leach, Vonta, Hou.	1	1	0	0	0	6
Leftwich, Byron, Pit.	1	1	0	0	0	6
Leonhard, Jim, Bal.	1	0	0	1	0	6
Manning, Peyton, Ind.	1	1	0	0	0	6
Mathis, Robert, Ind.	1	0	0	1	0	6
McDonald, Brandon, Cle.	1	0	0	1	0	6
* Merling, Phillip, Mia.	1	0	0	1	0	6
Miller, Zach, Oak.	1	0	1	0	0	6
Moats, Ryan, Hou.	1	1	0	0	0	6
Ndukwe, Chinedum, Cin.	1	0	0	1	0	6
Pace, Calvin, NYJ	1	0	0	1	0	6
Pearman, Alvin, Jac.	1	0	1	0	0	6
Pennington, Chad, Mia.	1	1	0	0	0	6
Pope, P.J., Den.	1	0	1	0	0	6
Porter, Jerry, Jac.	1	0	1	0	0	6
Ratliff, Keiwan, Ind.	1	0	0	1	0	6
Reed, Josh, Buf.	1	0	1	0	0	6
Reeves, Jacques, Hou.	1	0	0	1	0	6
Revis, Darrelle, NYJ	1	0	0	1	0	6
* Richard, Jamey, Ind.	1	0	0	1	0	6
Royal, Robert, Buf.	1	0	1	0	0	6
Russell, JaMarcus, Oak.	1	1	0	0	0	6
* Santi, Tom, Ind.	1	0	1	0	0	6
Schouman, Derek, Buf.	1	0	1	0	0	6
* Simpson, Chad, Ind.	1	1	0	0	0	6
Smith, Kolby, K.C.	1	1	0	0	0	6
Stallworth, Donte', Cle.	1	0	1	0	0	6
Taylor, Fred, Jac.	1	1	0	0	0	6
* Tolbert, Mike, S.D.	1	0	1	0	0	6
* Torain, Ryan, Den.	1	1	0	0	0	6
Townsend, Deshea, Pit.	1	0	0	1	0	6
Walker, Javon, Oak.	1	0	1	0	0	6
Webster, Nate, Den.	1	0	0	1	0	6
Weddle, Eric, S.D.	1	0	0	1	0	6
Williams, Demetrius, Bal.	1	0	1	0	0	6
Williamson, Troy, Jac.	1	0	1	0	0	6
Woodley, LaMarr, Pit.	1	0	0	1	0	6
Wright, Eric, Cle.	1	0	0	1	0	6
Wright, Jason, Cle.	1	0	1	0	0	6
Young, Selvin, Den.	1	1	0	0	0	6
* McClain, Jameel, Bal.	0	0	0	0	0	^4
Anderson, Charlie, Mia.	0	0	0	0	0	^2
* Cox, Mike, K.C.	0	0	0	0	1	2
Harrison, James, Pit.	0	0	0	0	0	^2
Naanee, Legedu, S.D.	0	0	0	0	1	2
Richardson, Jay, Oak.	0	0	0	0	0	^2
Wilson, Gibril, Oak.	0	0	0	0	0	^2

*^ Safety; *Player that was a rookie in 2008*
Team safety credited to Baltimore, Jacksonville, and San Diego

NFC—INDIVIDUAL SCORERS

KICKERS

	XP	XPA	FG	FGA	PTS
Akers, David, Phi.	45	45	33	40	144
Carney, John, NY-G	38	38	35	38	143
Bryant, Matt, T.B.	35	36	32	38	131
Kasay, John, Car.	46	46	28	31	130
Elam, Jason, Atl.	42	42	29	31	129
Crosby, Mason, G.B.	46	46	27	34	127
Longwell, Ryan, Min.	40	40	29	34	127
Nedney, Joe, S.F.	34	34	29	33	121
Gould, Robbie, Chi.	41	41	26	29	119
Rackers, Neil, Ariz	44	44	25	28	119
Brown, Josh, St.L	19	19	31	36	112
Suisham, Shaun, Was.	25	25	26	36	103
Folk, Nick, Dal.	42	42	20	22	102
Mare, Olindo, Sea.	30	30	24	27	102
Hanson, Jason, Det.	25	26	21	22	88
* Hartley, Garrett, N.O.	28	28	13	13	67
Gramatica, Martin, N.O.	16	16	6	10	34
* Mehlhaff, Taylor, N.O.	9	10	3	4	18
Tynes, Lawrence, NY-G	3	3	1	1	6

NONKICKERS

	TD	TDR	TDP	TDM	X2G	PTS
Williams, DeAngelo, Car.	20	18	2	0	1	122
Turner, Michael, Atl.	17	17	0	0	0	102
Jacobs, Brandon, NY-G	15	15	0	0	0	90
Westbrook, Brian, Phi.	14	9	5	0	0	84
Johnson, Calvin, Det.	12	0	12	0	1	74
Fitzgerald, Larry, Ariz	12	0	12	0	0	72
* Forté, Matt, Chi.	12	8	4	0	0	72
Thomas, Pierre, N.O.	12	9	3	0	0	72
Boldin, Anquan, Ariz	11	0	11	0	0	66
* Hightower, Tim, Ariz	10	10	0	0	0	60
Moore, Lance, N.O.	10	0	10	0	0	60
Owens, Terrell, Dal.	10	0	10	0	0	60
Peterson, Adrian, Min.	10	10	0	0	0	60
* Stewart, Jonathan, Car.	10	10	0	0	0	60
Jennings, Greg, G.B.	9	0	9	0	1	56
Barber, Marion, Dal.	9	7	2	0	0	54
Bush, Reggie, N.O.	9	2	4	3	0	54
Portis, Clinton, Was.	9	9	0	0	0	54
Gore, Frank, S.F.	8	6	2	0	1	50
Berrian, Bernard, Min.	8	0	7	1	0	48
Duckett, T.J., Sea.	8	8	0	0	0	48
Jackson, Steven, St.L	8	7	1	0	0	48
* Smith, Kevin, Det.	8	8	0	0	0	48
Bruce, Isaac, S.F.	7	0	7	0	0	42
Bryant, Antonio, T.B.	7	0	7	0	0	42
Moss, Santana, Was.	7	0	6	1	0	42
Shiancoe, Visanthe, Min.	7	0	7	0	0	42
White, Roddy, Atl.	7	0	7	0	0	42
Boss, Kevin, NY-G	6	0	6	0	0	36
McAllister, Deuce, N.O.	6	5	1	0	0	36
Norwood, Jerious, Atl.	6	4	2	0	0	36
Smith, Steve, Car.	6	0	6	0	0	36
Taylor, Chester, Min.	6	4	2	0	0	36
* Carlson, John, Sea.	5	0	5	0	0	30
Colston, Marques, N.O.	5	0	5	0	0	30
Driver, Donald, G.B.	5	0	5	0	0	30
Grant, Ryan, G.B.	5	4	1	0	0	30
Lee, Donald, G.B.	5	0	5	0	0	30
Muhammad, Muhsin, Car.	5	0	5	0	0	30
Olsen, Greg, Chi.	5	0	5	0	0	30
* Avery, Donnie, St.L	4	1	3	0	0	24
* Bennett, Martellus, Dal.	4	0	4	0	0	24
Branch, Deion, Sea.	4	0	4	0	0	24
Buckhalter, Correll, Phi.	4	2	2	0	0	24

	TD	TDR	TDP	TDM	2-PT.	PTS
Burress, Plaxico, NY-G	4	0	4	0	0	24
Crayton, Patrick, Dal.	4	0	4	0	0	24
Graham, Earnest, T.B.	4	4	0	0	0	24
Hilliard, Ike, T.B.	4	0	4	0	0	24
* Jackson, DeSean, Phi.	4	1	2	1	0	24
* Jones, Felix, Dal.	4	3	0	1	0	24
Meachem, Robert, N.O.	4	1	3	0	0	24
Randle El, Antwaan, Was.	4	0	4	0	0	24
Rice, Sidney, Min.	4	0	4	0	0	24
Rodgers, Aaron, G.B.	4	4	0	0	0	24
Toomer, Amani, NY-G	4	0	4	0	0	24
Urban, Jerheme, Ariz	4	0	4	0	0	24
Williams, Cadillac, T.B.	4	4	0	0	0	24
Witten, Jason, Dal.	4	0	4	0	0	24
James, Edgerrin, Ariz	3	3	0	0	1	20
Jenkins, Michael, Atl.	3	0	3	0	1	20
Lloyd, Brandon, Chi.	3	0	2	1	1	20
Smith, Alex, T.B.	3	0	3	0	1	20
Arrington, J.J., Ariz	3	1	1	1	0	18
Austin, Miles, Dal.	3	0	3	0	0	18
Baskett, Hank, Phi.	3	0	3	0	0	18
Breaston, Steve, Ariz	3	0	3	0	0	18
Collins, Nick, G.B.	3	0	0	3	0	18
Davis, Rashied, Chi.	3	0	2	1	0	18
* Douglas, Harry, Atl.	3	1	1	1	0	18
Henderson, Devery, N.O.	3	0	3	0	0	18
Hester, Devin, Chi.	3	0	3	0	0	18
Holt, Torry, St.L	3	0	3	0	0	18
Johnson, Bryant, S.F.	3	0	3	0	0	18
Kuhn, John, G.B.	3	1	2	0	0	18
McKie, Jason, Chi.	3	2	1	0	0	18
* Morgan, Josh, S.F.	3	0	3	0	0	18
Orton, Kyle, Chi.	3	3	0	0	0	18
Smith, L.J., Phi.	3	0	3	0	0	18
Hixon, Domenik, NY-G	2	0	2	0	1	14
Askew, B.J., T.B.	2	2	0	0	0	12
Avant, Jason, Phi.	2	0	2	0	0	12
Babineaux, Jordan, Sea.	2	0	0	2	0	12
Blackmon, Will, G.B.	2	0	0	2	0	12
Booker, Marty, Chi.	2	0	2	0	0	12
Bradshaw, Ahmad, NY-G	2	1	1	0	0	12
Campbell, Mark, N.O.	2	0	2	0	0	12
* Choice, Tashard, Dal.	2	2	0	0	0	12
Curtis, Kevin, Phi.	2	0	2	0	0	12
Davis, Vernon, S.F.	2	0	2	0	0	12
Delhomme, Jake, Car.	2	2	0	0	0	12
Dunn, Warrick, T.B.	2	2	0	0	0	12
Foster, DeShaun, S.F.	2	1	1	0	0	12
Grossman, Rex, Chi.	2	2	0	0	0	12
Hill, Jason, S.F.	2	0	2	0	0	12
Hill, Shaun, S.F.	2	2	0	0	0	12
Johnson, Darcy, NY-G	2	0	2	0	0	12
Johnson, Rudi, Det.	2	1	1	0	0	12
Jones, Julius, Sea.	2	2	0	0	0	12
Karney, Mike, N.O.	2	2	0	0	0	12
Looker, Dane, St.L	2	0	2	0	0	12
McNabb, Donovan, Phi.	2	2	0	0	0	12
Morris, Maurice, Sea.	2	0	2	0	0	12
Moss, Sinorice, NY-G	2	0	2	0	0	12
* Nelson, Jordy, G.B.	2	0	2	0	0	12
Peelle, Justin, Atl.	2	0	2	0	0	12
Robinson, Koren, Sea.	2	0	2	0	0	12
Rossum, Allen, S.F.	2	1	0	1	0	12
* Smith, Clifton, T.B.	2	0	0	2	0	12
Stevens, Jerramy, T.B.	2	0	2	0	0	12
Wade, Bobby, Min.	2	0	2	0	0	12
Ward, Derrick, NY-G	2	2	0	0	0	12
Weaver, Leonard, Sea.	2	0	2	0	0	12
Williams, Roy E., Det-Dal	2	0	2	0	0	12
Winfield, Antoine, Min.	2	0	0	2	0	12
Woodson, Charles, G.B.	2	0	0	2	0	12
Fitzsimmons, Casey, Det.	1	0	1	0	1	8
Martin, Ruvell, G.B.	1	0	1	0	1	8
Adams, Gaines, T.B.	1	0	0	1	0	6
Anderson, Deon, Dal.	1	0	1	0	0	6
Atogwe, Oshiomogho, St.L	1	0	0	1	0	6
Barber, Ronde, T.B.	1	0	0	1	0	6
Beisel, Monty, Ariz	1	0	0	1	0	6
Bell, Mike, N.O.	1	1	0	0	0	6
Betts, Ladell, Was.	1	1	0	0	0	6
Blalock, Justin, Atl.	1	0	0	1	0	6
* Bowman, Zack, Chi.	1	0	0	1	0	6
Briggs, Lance, Chi.	1	0	0	1	0	6
Brown, Reggie, Phi.	1	0	1	0	0	6
Buchanon, Phillip, T.B.	1	0	0	1	0	6
Bullocks, Daniel, Det.	1	0	0	1	0	6
* Bumpus, Michael, Sea.	1	0	1	0	0	6
Burleson, Nate, Sea.	1	0	1	0	0	6
* Burton, Keenan, St.L	1	0	1	0	0	6
Campbell, Jason, Was.	1	1	0	0	0	6
Celek, Brent, Phi.	1	0	1	0	0	6
Clark, Desmond, Chi.	1	0	1	0	0	6
Clayton, Michael, T.B.	1	0	1	0	0	6
Clements, Nate, S.F.	1	0	0	1	0	6
Clemons, Chris, Phi.	1	0	0	1	0	6
Colbert, Keary, Den/Sea/Det	1	0	1	0	0	6
Cooley, Chris, Was.	1	0	1	0	0	6
Culpepper, Daunte, Det.	1	1	0	0	0	6
* Demps, Quintin, Phi.	1	0	0	1	0	6
Dockery, Kevin, NY-G	1	0	0	1	0	6
Dockett, Darnell, Ariz	1	0	0	1	0	6
* Finley, Jermichael, G.B.	1	0	1	0	0	6
Finneran, Brian, Atl.	1	0	1	0	0	6
Frerotte, Gus, Min.	1	1	0	0	0	6
Gaines, Michael, Det.	1	0	1	0	0	6
Gamble, Chris, Car.	1	0	0	1	0	6
Garcia, Jeff, T.B.	1	1	0	0	0	6
Gilmore, John, T.B.	1	0	1	0	0	6
Gocong, Chris, Phi.	1	0	0	1	0	6
Hall, Korey, G.B.	1	0	1	0	0	6
Hanson, Joselio, Phi.	1	0	0	1	0	6
Harris, Napoleon, Min.	1	0	0	1	0	6
* Hayes, Geno, T.B.	1	0	0	1	0	6
Hedgecock, Madison, NY-G	1	0	1	0	0	6
Herremans, Todd, Phi.	1	0	1	0	0	6
Hood, Roderick, Ariz	1	0	0	1	0	6
Houston, Chris, Atl.	1	0	0	1	0	6
Hunt, Tony, Phi.	1	1	0	0	0	6
Hunter, Jason, G.B.	1	0	0	1	0	6
Jackson, Brandon, G.B.	1	1	0	0	0	6
* Jackson, Chevis, Atl.	1	0	0	1	0	6
* Jenkins, Mike, Dal.	1	0	0	1	0	6
Jones, James, G.B.	1	0	1	0	0	6
King, Jeff, Car.	1	0	1	0	0	6
Lewis, Greg, Phi.	1	0	1	0	0	6
Manning, Danieal, Chi.	1	0	0	1	0	6
Manning, Eli, NY-G	1	1	0	0	0	6
McDonald, Shaun, Det.	1	0	1	0	0	6
Miller, Billy, N.O.	1	0	1	0	0	6
Owens, John, Det.	1	0	1	0	0	6
Parker, Juqua, Phi.	1	0	0	1	0	6
Patten, David, N.O.	1	0	1	0	0	6
Phillips, Jermaine, T.B.	1	0	0	1	0	6
* Rodgers-Cromartie, Domin, Ariz	1	0	0	1	0	6
Rolle, Antrel, Ariz	1	0	0	1	0	6
Rosario, Dante, Car.	1	0	1	0	0	6

2008 INDIVIDUAL STATISTICS—SCORING

	TD	TDR	TDP	TDM	2-PT.	PTS
Ross, Aaron, NY-G	1	0	0	1	0	6
Rouse, Aaron, G.B.	1	0	0	1	0	6
* Ryan, Matt, Atl.	1	1	0	0	0	6
Samuel, Asante, Phi.	1	0	0	1	0	6
Sellers, Mike, Was.	1	0	1	0	0	6
Smith, Steve, NY-G	1	0	1	0	0	6
Staley, Joe, S.F.	1	0	0	1	0	6
Stanley, Derek, St.L	1	0	1	0	0	6
Stecker, Aaron, N.O.	1	0	1	0	0	6
Strickland, Donald, S.F.	1	0	0	1	0	6
Terrill, Craig, Sea.	1	0	0	1	0	6
* Thomas, Devin, Was.	1	1	0	0	0	6
Thrash, James, Was.	1	0	1	0	0	6
Tillman, Charles, Chi.	1	0	0	1	0	6
Tuck, Justin, NY-G	1	0	0	1	0	6
Walker, Delanie, S.F.	1	0	1	0	0	6
Wesley, Dante, Car.	1	0	0	1	0	6
Willis, Patrick, S.F.	1	0	0	1	0	6
Wilson, Josh, Sea.	1	0	0	1	0	6
Wolfe, Garrett, Chi.	1	0	0	1	0	6
Wynn, DeShawn, G.B.	1	1	0	0	0	6
Yoder, Todd, Was.	1	0	1	0	0	6
Allen, Jared, Min.	0	0	0	0	0	^4
Grant, Charles, N.O.	0	0	0	0	0	^2
Kiwanuka, Mathias, NY-G	0	0	0	0	0	^2
Ogunleye, Adewale, Chi.	0	0	0	0	0	^2
Polk, Carlos, Dal.	0	0	0	0	0	^2

^ Safety

Team safety credited to Atlanta, Detroit, Minnesota, New York (2), and Philadelphia

* *Player that was a rookie in 2008*

AMERICAN FOOTBALL CONFERENCE—SCORING

	TD	TDR	TDP	TDM	XKG	XKAtt	X2G	X2Att	FG	FGA	SAF	POINTS
San Diego	51	13	34	4	46	46	2	5	27	32	1	439
New England	43	21	21	1	40	40	2	3	36	40	0	410
N.Y. Jets	48	20	22	6	41	41	2	7	24	29	0	405
Baltimore	42	20	16	6	41	41	1	1	28	35	3	385
Indianapolis	45	13	27	5	43	43	2	2	20	25	0	377
Tennessee	41	24	13	4	40	40	1	1	29	33	0	375
Denver	42	15	25	2	39	40	2	2	25	34	0	370
Houston	40	16	21	3	37	37	1	3	29	33	0	366
Pittsburgh	38	16	19	3	36	37	0	1	27	31	1	347
Miami	40	18	20	2	40	40	0	0	21	25	1	345
Buffalo	35	16	14	5	34	34	1	1	30	38	0	336
Jacksonville	35	17	15	3	33	33	0	2	19	25	1	302
Kansas City	35	9	23	3	31	31	1	4	16	22	0	291
Oakland	27	9	13	5	25	26	0	1	24	30	2	263
Cleveland	20	6	11	3	18	18	2	2	30	36	0	232
Cincinnati	20	6	11	3	18	18	0	2	22	25	0	204
AFC Total	602	239	305	58	562	565	17	37	407	493	9	5447
AFC Average	37.6	14.9	19.1	3.6	35.1	35.3	1.1	2.3	25.4	30.8	0.6	340.4

NATIONAL FOOTBALL CONFERENCE—SCORING

	TD	TDR	TDP	TDM	XKG	XKAtt	X2G	X2Att	FG	FGA	SAF	POINTS
New Orleans	57	20	34	3	53	54	0	3	22	27	1	463
Arizona	51	14	31	6	44	44	1	6	25	28	0	427
N.Y. Giants	45	19	23	3	41	41	1	3	36	39	3	427
Green Bay	48	11	28	9	46	46	2	2	27	34	0	419
Philadelphia	45	15	23	7	45	45	0	0	33	40	1	416
Carolina	47	30	15	2	46	46	1	1	28	31	0	414
Atlanta	43	23	16	4	42	42	1	1	29	31	1	391
Minnesota	41	15	22	4	40	40	0	1	29	34	3	379
Chicago	42	15	20	7	41	41	1	1	26	29	1	375
Dallas	43	12	29	2	42	42	0	1	20	22	1	362
Tampa Bay	38	13	18	7	35	36	1	2	32	38	0	361
San Francisco	36	10	21	5	34	34	1	2	29	33	0	339
Seattle	32	10	18	4	30	30	0	2	24	27	0	294
Detroit	29	10	18	1	25	26	2	3	21	22	1	268
Washington	27	12	14	1	25	25	0	2	26	36	0	265
St. Louis	20	8	11	1	19	19	0	1	31	36	0	232
NFC Total	644	237	341	66	608	611	11	31	438	507	12	5832
NFC Average	40.3	14.8	21.3	4.1	38.0	38.2	0.7	1.9	27.4	31.7	0.8	364.5
NFL Total	1246	476	646	124	1170	1176	28	68	845	1000	21	11279
NFL Average	38.9	14.9	20.2	3.9	36.6	36.8	0.9	2.1	26.4	31.3	0.7	352.5

FIELD GOALS

FIELD GOAL PERCENTAGE

NFC: .955 Jason Hanson, Detroit
AFC: .900 Stephen Gostkowski, New England

FIELD GOALS

AFC: 36 Stephen Gostkowski, New England
NFC: 35 John Carney, N.Y. Giants

FIELD GOAL ATTEMPTS

AFC: 40 Stephen Gostkowski, New England
NFC: 40 David Akers, Philadelphia

FIELD GOALS, GAME

AFC: 5 Phil Dawson, Cleveland at Buffalo, November 17 (5 attempts)
NFC: 5 Ryan Longwell, Minnesota vs. Indianapolis, September 14 (6 attempts)
5 Jason Elam, Atlanta vs. Chicago, October 12 (6 attempts)

LONGEST FIELD GOAL

AFC: 57 Sebastian Janikowski, Oakland vs. N.Y. Jets, October 19 - (OT)
57 Nate Kaeding, San Diego at Tampa Bay, December 21
NFC: 56 Jason Hanson, Detroit at Carolina, November 16

AVERAGE YARDS MADE

NFC: 42.9 Jason Hanson, Detroit
AFC: 38.2 * Dan Carpenter, Miami

AMERICAN FOOTBALL CONFERENCE—FIELD GOALS

	FG	FGA	Pct	Long
New England	36	40	.900	50
Cincinnati	22	25	.880	45
Houston	29	33	.879	53
Tennessee	29	33	.879	51
Pittsburgh	27	31	.871	53
San Diego	27	32	.844	57
Miami	21	25	.840	50
Cleveland	30	36	.833	56
N.Y. Jets	24	29	.828	55
Baltimore	28	35	.800	54
Indianapolis	20	25	.800	52
Oakland	24	30	.800	57
Buffalo	30	38	.789	53
Jacksonville	19	25	.760	53
Denver	25	34	.735	56
Kansas City	16	22	.727	45
AFC Total	407	493	—	57
AFC Average	25.4	30.8	.826	—

NATIONAL FOOTBALL CONFERENCE—FIELD GOALS

	FG	FGA	Pct	Long
Detroit	21	22	.955	56
Atlanta	29	31	.935	50
N.Y. Giants	36	39	.923	51
Dallas	20	22	.909	52
Carolina	28	31	.903	50
Chicago	26	29	.897	48
Arizona	25	28	.893	54
Seattle	24	27	.889	51
San Francisco	29	33	.879	53
St. Louis	31	36	.861	54
Minnesota	29	34	.853	54
Tampa Bay	32	38	.842	49
Philadelphia	33	40	.825	51
New Orleans	22	27	.815	53
Green Bay	27	34	.794	53
Washington	26	36	.722	50
NFC Total	438	507	—	56
NFC Average	27.4	31.7	.864	—
League Total	845	1000	—	57
League Average	26.4	31.3	.845	—

2008 INDIVIDUAL STATISTICS—FIELD GOALS

AFC—INDIVIDUAL FIELD GOALS

	1-19 Yards	20-29 Yards	30-39 Yards	40-49 Yards	50 or Longer	Totals	Avg Yds Att	Avg Yds Made	Avg Yds Miss	Long
Gostkowski, Stephen, N.E.	0-0	10-12	16-16	9-11	1-1	36-40	34.8	34.4	37.5	50
	—	.833	1.000	.818	1.000	.900				
Bironas, Rob, Ten.	0-0	6-6	7-7	15-19	1-1	29-33	39.2	38.1	46.8	51
	—	1.000	1.000	.789	1.000	.879				
Brown, Kris, Hou.	0-0	9-10	10-10	8-10	2-3	29-33	35.6	34.6	43.0	53
	—	.900	1.000	.800	.667	.879				
Graham, Shayne, Cin.	1-1	5-5	6-7	9-11	0-0	21-24	34.9	33.6	44.0	45
	1.000	1.000	.857	.818	—	.875				
Reed, Jeff, Pit.	1-1	9-9	8-9	8-10	1-2	27-31	34.7	33.6	42.3	53
	1.000	1.000	.889	.800	.500	.871				
Feely, Jay, NYJ	0-0	9-9	9-12	4-5	2-2	24-28	33.0	32.4	37.0	55
	—	1.000	.750	.800	1.000	.857				
Kaeding, Nate, S.D.	0-0	13-13	10-10	3-8	1-1	27-32	34.1	32.3	44.0	57
	—	1.000	1.000	.375	1.000	.844				
* Carpenter, Dan, Mia.	0-0	4-4	7-7	9-13	1-1	21-25	39.5	38.2	46.3	50
	—	1.000	1.000	.692	1.000	.840				
Dawson, Phil, Cle.	0-0	10-10	12-14	5-6	3-6	30-36	36.4	34.6	45.8	56
	—	1.000	.857	.833	.500	.833				
Stover, Matt, Bal.	0-0	11-11	11-12	5-9	0-1	27-33	34.6	32.3	45.0	47
	—	1.000	.917	.556	.000	.818				
Janikowski, Sebastian, Oak.	0-0	11-11	8-8	2-4	3-7	24-30	37.6	33.0	56.0	57
	—	1.000	1.000	.500	.429	.800				
Vinatieri, Adam, Ind.	0-0	3-3	11-13	4-7	2-2	20-25	37.5	36.9	40.0	52
	—	1.000	.846	.571	1.000	.800				
Lindell, Rian, Buf.	1-1	7-8	11-11	10-15	1-3	30-38	37.9	36.4	43.4	53
	1.000	.875	1.000	.667	.333	.789				
Scobee, Josh, Jac.	0-0	7-7	3-6	5-7	4-5	19-25	38.7	37.6	42.2	53
	—	1.000	.500	.714	.800	.760				
Prater, Matt, Den.	0-0	7-8	8-9	5-11	5-6	25-34	38.8	36.6	44.8	56
	—	.875	.889	.455	.833	.735				
(Nonqualifiers)										
* Barth, Connor, K.C.	0-0	6-6	3-4	1-1	0-1	10-12	32.1	30.1	42.0	45
	—	1.000	.750	1.000	.000	.833				
Novak, Nick, K.C.	0-0	3-3	1-3	2-3	0-1	6-10	35.5	31.0	42.3	43
	—	1.000	.333	.667	.000	.600				
* Hauschka, Steven, Bal.	0-0	0-0	0-0	0-0	1-2	1-2	53.5	54.0	53.0	54
	—	—	—	—	.500	.500				
Nugent, Mike, NYJ	0-0	0-0	0-1	0-0	0-0	0-1	32.0	—	32.0	0
	—	—	.000	—	—	.000				
Rayner, Dave, Cin.	0-0	1-1	0-0	0-0	0-0	1-1	26.0	26.0	—	26
	—	1.000	—	—	—	1.000				
AFC Totals	3-3	131-136	141-159	104-150	28-45	407-493	36.4	34.7	44.0	57
	1.000	.963	.887	.693	.622	.826				
NFL Totals	7-7	261-266	286-321	225-302	66-104	845-1000	36.7	35.3	44.5	57
	1.000	.981	.891	.745	.635	.845				

Leader based on overall percentage, minimum 16 field goals

NFC—INDIVIDUAL FIELD GOALS

	1-19 Yards	20-29 Yards	30-39 Yards	40-49 Yards	50 or Longer	Totals	Avg Yds Att	Avg Yds Made	Avg Yds Miss	Long
Hanson, Jason, Det.	0-0	3-3	4-5	6-6	8-8	21-22	42.4	42.9	33.0	56
	—	1.000	.800	1.000	1.000	.955				
Elam, Jason, Atl.	0-0	11-11	7-8	10-10	1-2	29-31	35.2	34.8	42.0	50
	—	1.000	.875	1.000	.500	.935				
Carney, John, NY-G	0-0	15-15	14-15	5-7	1-1	35-38	33.3	32.4	43.3	51
	—	1.000	.933	.714	1.000	.921				
Folk, Nick, Dal.	0-0	1-1	7-8	10-11	2-2	20-22	40.8	40.8	41.5	52
	—	1.000	.875	.909	1.000	.909				
Kasay, John, Car.	0-0	7-7	9-9	11-12	1-3	28-31	37.5	36.4	48.3	50
	—	1.000	1.000	.917	.333	.903				
Gould, Robbie, Chi.	0-0	6-6	12-12	8-11	0-0	26-29	36.6	35.5	46.3	48
	—	1.000	1.000	.727	—	.897				
Rackers, Neil, Ariz	0-0	9-9	9-11	6-6	1-2	25-28	35.0	33.6	46.7	54
	—	1.000	.818	1.000	.500	.893				
Mare, Olindo, Sea.	0-0	7-7	9-10	5-6	3-4	24-27	37.5	36.7	44.3	51
	—	1.000	.900	.833	.750	.889				
Nedney, Joe, S.F.	0-0	9-9	10-10	8-11	2-3	29-33	37.0	35.7	46.3	53
	—	1.000	1.000	.727	.667	.879				
Brown, Josh, St.L	0-0	8-8	7-7	10-13	6-8	31-36	40.1	39.0	47.0	54
	—	1.000	1.000	.769	.750	.861				
Longwell, Ryan, Min.	0-0	10-10	7-9	6-9	6-6	29-34	38.0	37.1	43.0	54
	—	1.000	.778	.667	1.000	.853				
Bryant, Matt, T.B.	0-0	12-12	15-15	5-8	0-3	32-38	35.6	33.2	48.0	49
	—	1.000	1.000	.625	.000	.842				
Akers, David, Phi.	2-2	11-11	10-12	8-10	2-5	33-40	34.8	32.8	43.9	51
	1.000	1.000	.833	.800	.400	.825				
Crosby, Mason, G.B.	1-1	8-8	10-13	5-6	3-6	27-34	37.5	35.1	46.7	53
	1.000	1.000	.769	.833	.500	.794				
Suisham, Shaun, Was.	0-0	7-7	7-9	11-16	1-4	26-36	38.7	36.3	45.0	50
	—	1.000	.778	.688	.250	.722				
(Nonqualifiers)										
* Hartley, Garrett, N.O.	0-0	5-5	4-4	4-4	0-0	13-13	32.6	32.6	—	47
	—	1.000	1.000	1.000	—	1.000				
Gramatica, Martin, N.O.	0-0	0-0	3-3	2-5	1-2	6-10	43.1	40.8	46.5	53
	—	—	1.000	.400	.500	.600				
* Mehlhaff, Taylor, N.O.	0-0	1-1	1-2	1-1	0-0	3-4	32.8	33.3	31.0	44
	—	1.000	.500	1.000	—	.750				
Tynes, Lawrence, NY-G	1-1	0-0	0-0	0-0	0-0	1-1	19.0	19.0	—	19
	1.000	—	—	—	—	1.000				
NFC Totals	4-4	130-130	145-162	121-152	38-59	438-507	37.0	35.8	45.1	56
	1.000	1.000	.895	.796	.644	.864				
NFL Totals	7-7	261-266	286-321	225-302	66-104	845-1000	36.7	35.3	44.5	57
	1.000	.981	.891	.745	.635	.845				

Leader based on overall percentage, minimum 16 field goals
** Player that was a rookie in 2008*

RUSHING

YARDS

NFC: 1760 Adrian Peterson, Minnesota
AFC: 1312 Thomas Jones, N.Y. Jets

YARDS, GAME

NFC: 220 Michael Turner, Atlanta vs. Detroit, September 7 (22 attempts, 2 TD)
AFC: 198 Larry Johnson, Kansas City vs. Denver, September 28 (28 attempts, 2 TD)

LONGEST

AFC: 82 Le'Ron McClain, Baltimore at Dallas, December 20 - TD
NFC: 77 Ahmad Bradshaw, N.Y. Giants vs. Baltimore, November 16

ATTEMPTS

NFC: 376 Michael Turner, Atlanta
AFC: 292 LaDainian Tomlinson, San Diego

ATTEMPTS, GAME

AFC: 38 Cedric Benson, Cincinnati at Cleveland, December 21 (171 yards, 0 TD)
NFC: 33 Ryan Grant, Green Bay at Seattle, October 12 (90 yards, 0 TD)
33 Brian Westbrook, Philadelphia at N.Y. Giants, December 7 (131 yards, 1 TD)

YARDS PER ATTEMPT

NFC: 5.6 Derrick Ward, N.Y. Giants
AFC: 4.9* Chris Johnson, Tennessee

TOUCHDOWNS

NFC: 18 DeAngelo Williams, Carolina
AFC: 15 LenDale White, Tennessee

TEAM LEADERS, YARDS

AFC: BALTIMORE, 902, Le'Ron McClain; BUFFALO, 1036, Marshawn Lynch; CINCINNATI, 747, Cedric Benson; CLEVELAND, 1002, Jamal Lewis; DENVER, 343, * Peyton Hillis; HOUSTON, 1282, * Steve Slaton; INDIANAPOLIS, 544, Joseph Addai; JACKSONVILLE, 824, Maurice Jones-Drew; KANSAS CITY, 874, Larry Johnson; MIAMI, 916, Ronnie Brown; NEW ENGLAND, 727, Sammy Morris; N.Y. JETS, 1312, Thomas Jones; OAKLAND, 853, Justin Fargas; PITTSBURGH, 791, Willie Parker; SAN DIEGO, 1110, LaDainian Tomlinson; TENNESSEE, 1228, * Chris Johnson

NFC: ARIZONA, 514, Edgerrin James; ATLANTA, 1699, Michael Turner; CAROLINA, 1515, DeAngelo Williams; CHICAGO, 1238, * Matt Forté; DALLAS, 885, Marion Barber; DETROIT, 976, * Kevin Smith; GREEN BAY, 1203, Ryan Grant; MINNESOTA, 1760, Adrian Peterson; NEW ORLEANS, 625, Pierre Thomas; N.Y. GIANTS, 1089, Brandon Jacobs; PHILADELPHIA, 936, Brian Westbrook; ST. LOUIS, 1042, Steven Jackson; SAN FRANCISCO, 1036, Frank Gore; SEATTLE, 698, Julius Jones; TAMPA BAY, 786, Warrick Dunn; WASHINGTON, 1487, Clinton Portis

TEAM CHAMPION

NFC: 2518 N.Y. Giants
AFC: 2376 Baltimore

**Player that was a rookie in 2008*

NFL TOP TEN RUSHERS

	Att	Yards	Avg	Long	TD
Peterson, Adrian, Min.	363	1760	4.8	67t	10
Turner, Michael, Atl.	376	1699	4.5	70	17
Williams, DeAngelo, Car.	273	1515	5.5	69t	18
Portis, Clinton, Was.	342	1487	4.3	31	9
Jones, Thomas, NYJ	290	1312	4.5	59t	13
* Slaton, Steve, Hou.	268	1282	4.8	71t	9
* Forté, Matt, Chi.	316	1238	3.9	50t	8
* Johnson, Chris, Ten.	251	1228	4.9	66t	9
Grant, Ryan, G.B.	312	1203	3.9	57	4
Tomlinson, LaDainian, S.D.	292	1110	3.8	45	11

AFC—INDIVIDUAL RUSHERS

	Att	Yards	Avg	Long	TD
Jones, Thomas, NYJ	290	1312	4.5	59t	13
* Slaton, Steve, Hou	268	1282	4.8	71t	9
* Johnson, Chris, Ten	251	1228	4.9	66t	9
Tomlinson, LaDainian, S.D.	292	1110	3.8	45	11
Lynch, Marshawn, Buf.	250	1036	4.1	50	8
Lewis, Jamal, Cle.	279	1002	3.6	29	4
Brown, Ronnie, Mia.	214	916	4.3	62t	10
McClain, Le'Ron, Bal.	232	902	3.9	82t	10
Johnson, Larry, K.C.	193	874	4.5	65	5
Fargas, Justin, Oak.	218	853	3.9	42	1
Jones-Drew, Maurice, Jac.	197	824	4.2	46t	12
Parker, Willie, Pit.	210	791	3.8	34t	5
White, LenDale, Ten.	200	773	3.9	80t	15
Benson, Cedric, Cin.	214	747	3.5	46	2
Morris, Sammy, N.E.	156	727	4.7	35	7
McGahee, Willis, Bal.	170	671	3.9	77t	7
Williams, Ricky, Mia.	160	659	4.1	51t	4
Moore, Mewelde, Pit.	140	588	4.2	32t	5
Jackson, Fred, Buf.	130	571	4.4	32	3
Taylor, Fred, Jac.	143	556	3.9	34	1
Addai, Joseph, Ind.	155	544	3.5	23	5
Rhodes, Dominic, Ind.	152	538	3.5	38	6
Faulk, Kevin, N.E.	83	507	6.1	41	3
* McFadden, Darren, Oak.	113	499	4.4	50	4
* Rice, Ray, Bal.	107	454	4.2	60	0
Washington, Leon, NYJ	76	448	5.9	61t	6
Bush, Michael, Oak.	95	421	4.4	67t	3
Thigpen, Tyler, K.C.	62	386	6.2	32	3
Jordan, LaMont, N.E.	80	363	4.5	49t	4
* Charles, Jamaal, K.C.	67	357	5.3	30	0
* Hillis, Peyton, Den.	68	343	5.0	19	5
Sproles, Darren, S.D.	61	330	5.4	37	1
Garrard, David, Jac.	73	322	4.4	24	2
Pittman, Michael, Den.	76	320	4.2	20	4
Fitzpatrick, Ryan, Cin.	60	304	5.1	22	2
Young, Selvin, Den.	61	303	5.0	49	1
Green, Ahman, Hou.	74	294	4.0	14	3
* Green-Ellis, BenJarvus, N.E.	74	275	3.7	15	5
Cassel, Matt, N.E.	73	270	3.7	19	2
Perry, Chris, Cin.	104	269	2.6	25t	2
Bell, Tatum, Den.	44	249	5.7	37t	2
Harrison, Jerome, Cle.	34	246	7.2	72t	1
Cutler, Jay, Den.	57	200	3.5	18	2
* Flacco, Joe, Bal.	52	180	3.5	38t	2
Cribbs, Josh, Cle.	29	167	5.8	27	1
Hall, Andre, Den.	35	144	4.1	16	0
Pope, P.J., Den.	17	130	7.6	24	0
Russell, JaMarcus, Oak.	17	127	7.5	24	1
Edwards, Trent, Buf.	36	117	3.3	15t	3
Smith, Brad, NYJ	12	113	9.4	36	0
* Royal, Eddie, Den.	11	109	9.9	71	0
Roethlisberger, Ben, Pit.	34	101	3.0	17	2
Smith, Kolby, K.C.	35	100	2.9	19	1
* Hester, Jacob, S.D.	19	95	5.0	28	1
Moats, Ryan, Hou.	26	94	3.6	12	1

	Att	Yards	Avg	Long	TD
Maroney, Laurence, N.E.	28	93	3.3	17	0
Cobbs, Patrick, Mia.	12	88	7.3	44	1
Polite, Lousaka, Mia.	23	85	3.7	14	0
Wright, Jason, Cle.	23	85	3.7	11	0
Rivers, Philip, S.D.	31	84	2.7	11	0
* Ball, Lance, Ind.	13	83	6.4	23	0
Clayton, Mark, Bal.	6	81	13.5	42t	1
Russell, Gary, Pit.	28	77	2.8	15	3
Ginn, Ted Jr., Mia.	5	73	14.6	40t	2
Losman, J.P., Buf.	12	70	5.8	17	2
Jackson, Vincent, S.D.	4	69	17.3	31	0
* Torain, Ryan, Den.	15	69	4.6	19	1
Schaub, Matt, Hou.	31	68	2.2	10	2
Richardson, Tony, NYJ	10	65	6.5	16	0
Pennington, Chad, Mia.	30	62	2.1	16	1
Ganther, Quinton, Ten.	9	61	6.8	22	0
* Mendenhall, Rashard, Pit.	19	58	3.1	12	0
Anderson, Derek, Cle.	25	55	2.2	15	0
Watson, Kenny, Cin.	13	55	4.2	7	0
* Caldwell, Andre, Cin.	5	53	10.6	26	0
* Savage, Dantrell, K.C.	15	53	3.5	11	0
Collins, Kerry, Ten.	25	49	2.0	17	0
* Simpson, Chad, Ind.	15	45	3.0	10	1
Favre, Brett, NYJ	21	43	2.0	27	1
Owens, Montell, Jac.	2	43	21.5	41t	2
Palmer, Carson, Cin.	6	38	6.3	15	0
Rosenfels, Sage, Hou.	11	37	3.4	15	0
Taylor, Chris, Hou.	14	37	2.6	17	0
* Tolbert, Mike, S.D.	13	37	2.8	11	0
Davis, Carey, Pit.	12	35	2.9	11	0
Jones, Brandon, Ten.	2	35	17.5	28	0
Higgins, Johnnie Lee, Oak.	3	34	11.3	18	0
Davenport, Najeh, Pit.-Ind.	10	31	3.1	8	0
Vickers, Lawrence, Cle.	10	31	3.1	10	0
* Johnson, James, Cin.	9	29	3.2	12	0
Gray, Quinn, K.C.	1	27	27.0	27	0
* Parmele, Jalen, Bal.	2	27	13.5	31	0
Young, Vince, Ten.	8	27	3.4	8	0
Welker, Wes, N.E.	3	26	8.7	19	0
Neal, Lorenzo, Bal.	12	25	2.1	5	0
Smith, Troy, Bal.	9	24	2.7	8	0
Evans, Heath, N.E.	11	23	2.1	4	0
Walter, Kevin, Hou.	3	23	7.7	13	0
Alston, Jon, Oak.	1	22	22.0	22	0
Evans, Lee, Buf.	1	22	22.0	22	0
Hall, Ahmard, Ten.	8	21	2.6	6	0
Manning, Peyton, Ind.	20	21	1.1	12	1
Quinn, Brady, Cle.	5	21	4.2	12	0
Walter, Andrew, Oak.	5	19	3.8	13	0
Turk, Matt, Hou.	1	18	18.0	18	0
Washington, Nate, Pit.	5	18	3.6	8	0
* Bess, Davone, Mia.	1	13	13.0	13	0
Huard, Damon, K.C.	4	13	3.3	15	0
Jones, Greg, Jac.	2	13	6.5	13	0
Tuiasosopo, Marques, Oak.	2	11	5.5	11	0
Coles, Laveranues, NYJ	2	9	4.5	6	0
* Hart, Mike, Ind.	2	9	4.5	7	0
Holmes, Santonio, Pit.	2	9	4.5	10	0
Houshmandzadeh, T.J., Cin.	1	9	9.0	9	0
Koch, Sam, Bal.	1	9	9.0	9	0
Northcutt, Dennis, Jac.	1	9	9.0	9	0
Parrish, Roscoe, Buf.	2	9	4.5	9	0
* Washington, Chauncey, Jac.	4	9	2.3	6	0
Chatman, Jesse, NYJ	5	8	1.6	5	0
Cotchery, Jerricho, NYJ	2	8	4.0	8	0
Dorsey, DeDe, Cin.	5	8	1.6	7	0
McCareins, Justin, Ten.	2	8	4.0	4	0
Sorgi, Jim, Ind.	5	8	1.6	12	0
Leftwich, Byron, Pit.	4	7	1.8	8t	1
Ellison, Keith, Buf.	1	6	6.0	6	0
* Johnson, Steve, Buf.	1	6	6.0	6	0
* Omon, Xavier, Buf.	6	5	0.8	2	0
Chatman, Antonio, Cin.	2	4	2.0	2	0
Palmer, Jordan, Cin.	1	4	4.0	4	0
Ward, Hines, Pit.	1	4	4.0	4	0
Henry, Chris, Ten.	1	3	3.0	3	0
Mason, Derrick, Bal.	1	3	3.0	3	0
Gradkowski, Bruce, Cle.	1	2	2.0	2	0
Griffith, Justin, Oak.	2	2	1.0	2	0
Hagans, Marques, K.C.	1	2	2.0	2	0
Camarillo, Greg, Mia.	2	1	0.5	6	0
Chambers, Chris, S.D.	1	1	1.0	1	0
Curry, Ronald, Oak.	1	1	1.0	1	0
Leach, Vonta, Hou.	1	1	1.0	1t	1
Stuckey, Chansi, NYJ	1	1	1.0	1	0
Williamson, Troy, Jac.	1	1	1.0	1	0
Berger, Mitch, Pit.	1	0	0.0	0	0
Dorsey, Ken, Cle.	2	0	0.0	0	0
Fields, Brandon, Mia.	1	0	0.0	0	0
Lechler, Shane, Oak.	1	0	0.0	0	0
Moss, Randy, N.E.	2	0	0.0	2	0
Williams, Reggie, Jac.	1	0	0.0	0	0
Scheffler, Tony, Den.	1	-1	-1.0	-1	0
* Cox, Mike, K.C.	1	-2	-2.0	-2	0
* Schilens, Chaz, Oak.	1	-2	-2.0	-2	0
Clemens, Kellen, NYJ	3	-3	-1.0	-1	0
* Dixon, Dennis, Pit.	2	-3	-1.5	-1	0
Lemon, Cleo, Jac.	2	-3	-1.5	-1	0
Sapp, Cecil, Hou.	2	-3	-1.5	0	0
Marshall, Brandon, Den.	2	-4	-2.0	7	0
Stallworth, Donte', Cle.	1	-4	-4.0	-4	0
Jones, Jacoby, Hou.	1	-5	-5.0	-5	0
Hentrich, Craig, Ten.	2	-6	-3.0	0	0
* O'Connell, Kevin, N.E.	3	-6	-2.0	-2	0

t = Touchdown
Leader based on most yards gained
** Player that was a rookie in 2008*

NFC—INDIVIDUAL RUSHERS

	Att	Yards	Avg	Long	TD
Peterson, Adrian, Min.	363	1760	4.8	67t	10
Turner, Michael, Atl.	376	1699	4.5	70	17
Williams, DeAngelo, Car.	273	1515	5.5	69t	18
Portis, Clinton, Was.	342	1487	4.3	31	9
* Forté, Matt, Chi.	316	1238	3.9	50t	8
Grant, Ryan, G.B.	312	1203	3.9	57	4
Jacobs, Brandon, NY-G	219	1089	5.0	44	15
Jackson, Steven, St.L	253	1042	4.1	56t	7
Gore, Frank, S.F.	240	1036	4.3	41t	6
Ward, Derrick, NY-G	182	1025	5.6	51	2
* Smith, Kevin, Det.	238	976	4.1	50	8
Westbrook, Brian, Phi.	233	936	4.0	39t	9
Barber, Marion, Dal.	238	885	3.7	35	7
* Stewart, Jonathan, Car.	184	836	4.5	41	10
Dunn, Warrick, T.B.	186	786	4.2	40	2
Jones, Julius, Sea.	158	698	4.4	33	2
Thomas, Pierre, N.O.	129	625	4.8	42t	9
Morris, Maurice, Sea.	132	574	4.3	45	0
Graham, Earnest, T.B.	132	563	4.3	68t	4
James, Edgerrin, Ariz	133	514	3.9	35	3
Norwood, Jerious, Atl.	95	489	5.1	45t	4
* Choice, Tashard, Dal.	92	472	5.1	38t	2
McAllister, Deuce, N.O.	107	418	3.9	19	5
Bush, Reggie, N.O.	106	404	3.8	43	2
* Hightower, Tim, Ariz	143	399	2.8	30t	10

2008 INDIVIDUAL STATISTICS—RUSHING

	Att	Yards	Avg	Long	TD
Taylor, Chester, Min.	101	399	4.0	21t	4
Buckhalter, Correll, Phi.	76	369	4.9	33	2
Bradshaw, Ahmad, NY-G	67	355	5.3	77	1
Pittman, Antonio, St.L	79	296	3.7	24	0
* Jones, Felix, Dal.	30	266	8.9	60t	3
Campbell, Jason, Was.	47	258	5.5	23	1
Jackson, Brandon, G.B.	45	248	5.5	32	1
Johnson, Rudi, Det.	76	237	3.1	27	1
Foster, DeShaun, S.F.	76	234	3.1	18	1
Williams, Cadillac, T.B.	63	233	3.7	28	4
Rodgers, Aaron, G.B.	56	207	3.7	21	4
Betts, Ladell, Was.	61	206	3.4	14	1
Arrington, J.J., Ariz	31	187	6.0	30	1
Duckett, T.J., Sea.	62	172	2.8	29	8
Garcia, Jeff, T.B.	35	148	4.2	20	1
McNabb, Donovan, Phi.	39	147	3.8	17	2
Jackson, Tarvaris, Min.	26	145	5.6	29	0
O'Sullivan, J.T., S.F.	30	145	4.8	18	0
Darby, Kenneth, St.L	32	140	4.4	14	0
Weaver, Leonard, Sea.	30	130	4.3	15	0
Hill, Shaun, S.F.	24	115	4.8	24	2
Wynn, DeShawn, G.B.	8	110	13.8	73t	1
Jones, Kevin, Chi.	34	109	3.2	16	0
* Ryan, Matt, Atl.	55	104	1.9	17	1
Peterson, Adrian, Chi.	20	100	5.0	16	0
* Jackson, DeSean, Phi.	17	96	5.6	21	1
Eckel, Kyle, Phi.	24	79	3.3	14	0
Wallace, Seneca, Sea.	16	78	4.9	23	0
* Avery, Donnie, St.L	10	69	6.9	37t	1
* Douglas, Harry, Atl.	12	69	5.8	33	1
Hasselbeck, Matt, Sea.	11	69	6.3	15	0
Wolfe, Garrett, Chi.	15	69	4.6	38	0
Boldin, Anquan, Ariz	9	67	7.4	30	0
Snelling, Jason, Atl.	15	62	4.1	13	0
Hester, Devin, Chi.	6	61	10.2	20	0
Booker, Lorenzo, Phi.	20	53	2.7	8	0
* Thomas, Devin, Was.	3	53	17.7	29t	1
Robinson, Michael, S.F.	19	50	2.6	10	0
Orton, Kyle, Chi.	24	49	2.0	12	3
Stecker, Aaron, N.O.	8	43	5.4	12	0
Bell, Mike, N.O.	13	42	3.2	15	1
Bulger, Marc, St.L	14	41	2.9	16	0
Romo, Tony, Dal.	28	41	1.5	15	0
* Smith, Clifton, T.B.	8	40	5.0	10	0
Smith, Steve, Car.	5	40	8.0	23	0
Kitna, Jon, Det.	6	34	5.7	10	0
Henderson, Devery, N.O.	4	33	8.3	30	0
Owens, Terrell, Dal.	7	33	4.7	8	0
Frye, Charlie, Sea.	2	30	15.0	27	0
Minor, Travis, St.L	13	29	2.2	13	0
Orlovsky, Dan, Det.	7	29	4.1	10	0
Moss, Santana, Was.	1	27	27.0	27	0
Berrian, Bernard, Min.	4	26	6.5	14	0
Hixon, Domenik, NY-G	2	26	13.0	15	0
McKie, Jason, Chi.	11	26	2.4	6	2
Culpepper, Daunte, Det.	12	25	2.1	9	1
Alexander, Shaun, Was.	11	24	2.2	8	0
Sellers, Mike, Was.	6	24	4.0	10	0
Bryant, Antonio, T.B.	2	22	11.0	13	0
Delhomme, Jake, Car.	20	21	1.1	12t	2
* Schmitt, Owen, Sea.	5	21	4.2	14	0
Meachem, Robert, N.O.	1	20	20.0	20t	1
Stanton, Drew, Det.	3	20	6.7	15	0
* Lumpkin, Kregg, G.B.	1	19	19.0	19	0
Battle, Arnaz, S.F.	1	18	18.0	18	0
Hoover, Brad, Car.	9	18	2.0	5	0
Mughelli, Ovie, Atl.	5	16	3.2	9	0
McCown, Luke, T.B.	3	15	5.0	12	0
Ware, Danny, NY-G	2	15	7.5	9	0
Askew, B.J., T.B.	7	14	2.0	3	2
Cartwright, Rock, Was.	5	14	2.8	7	0
Davis, Rashied, Chi.	3	14	4.7	17	0
Williams, Roy E., Dal.	1	13	13.0	13	0
Bennett, Michael, T.B.	7	12	1.7	4	0
Crayton, Patrick, Dal.	1	11	11.0	11	0
Davis, Vernon, S.F.	1	11	11.0	11	0
Carr, David, NY-G	8	10	1.3	7	0
Goings, Nick, Car.	9	10	1.1	4	0
Karney, Mike, N.O.	8	10	1.3	3	2
Kuhn, John, G.B.	8	10	1.3	3	1
Manning, Eli, NY-G	20	10	0.5	13	1
Hall, Dante, St.L	4	9	2.3	10	0
Hunt, Tony, Phi.	4	9	2.3	6	1
Breaston, Steve, Ariz	2	8	4.0	4	0
* Burton, Keenan, St.L	3	8	2.7	5	0
Cason, Aveion, Det.	4	7	1.8	4	0
Dugan, Jeff, Min.	4	7	1.8	2	0
Frerotte, Gus, Min.	19	7	0.4	5	1
Leonard, Brian, St.L	2	7	3.5	5	0
Brown, Reggie, Phi.	1	6	6.0	6	0
Clayton, Michael, T.B.	2	5	2.5	4	0
Hill, Jason, S.F.	2	5	2.5	9	0
Leinart, Matt, Ariz	4	5	1.3	8	0
Randle El, Antwaan, Was.	1	5	5.0	5	0
Driver, Donald, G.B.	2	4	2.0	6	0
* Felton, Jerome, Det.	2	4	2.0	4	0
* Flynn, Matt, G.B.	4	4	1.0	6	0
Gado, Samkon, St.L	2	4	2.0	3	0
Green, Trent, St.L	3	4	1.3	3	0
Grossman, Rex, Chi.	3	4	1.3	2	2
White, Roddy, Atl.	2	4	2.0	2	0
Anderson, Deon, Dal.	2	3	1.5	3	0
Booker, Marty, Chi.	1	3	3.0	3	0
Kolb, Kevin, Phi.	13	2	0.2	8	0
Allison, Aundrae, Min.	1	1	1.0	1	0
Norris, Moran, Det.	1	1	1.0	1	0
Rossum, Allen, S.F.	1	1	1.0	1t	1
Davis, Jason, Chi.	1	0	0.0	0	0
Frost, Derrick, G.B.	1	0	0.0	0	0
Hedgecock, Madison, NY-G	1	0	0.0	0	0
Hilliard, Ike, T.B.	1	0	0.0	0	0
Kreider, Dan, St.L	1	0	0.0	0	0
Stanley, Derek, St.L	1	0	0.0	0	0
Brees, Drew, N.O.	22	-1	0.0	9	0
Griese, Brian, T.B.	5	-1	-0.2	3	0
Johnson, Calvin, Det.	3	-1	-0.3	7	0
Johnson, Brad, Dal.	2	-1	-0.5	0	0
Warner, Kurt, Ariz	18	-2	-0.1	11	0
Bruce, Isaac, S.F.	1	-3	-3.0	-3	0
* Davis, Fred, Was.	1	-3	-3.0	-3	0
McCown, Josh, Car.	4	-3	-0.8	0	0
Robinson, Koren, Sea.	1	-4	-4.0	-4	0
Kluwe, Chris, Min.	1	-7	-7.0	-7	0
* Manningham, Mario, NY-G	1	-12	-12.0	-12	0
Walker, Delanie, S.F.	2	-13	-6.5	-3	0

t = Touchdown
Leader based on most yards gained
** Player that was a rookie in 2008*

AMERICAN FOOTBALL CONFERENCE—RUSHING

	Att	Yards	Avg	Long	TD
Baltimore	592	2376	4.0	82t	20
New England	513	2278	4.4	49t	21
Tennessee	508	2199	4.3	80t	24
N.Y. Jets	422	2004	4.7	61t	20
Oakland	459	1987	4.3	67t	9
Miami	448	1897	4.2	62t	18
Denver	387	1862	4.8	71	15
Houston	432	1846	4.3	71t	16
Buffalo	439	1842	4.2	50	16
Kansas City	379	1810	4.8	65	9
Jacksonville	426	1774	4.2	46t	17
San Diego	421	1726	4.1	45	13
Pittsburgh	460	1690	3.7	34t	16
Cleveland	409	1605	3.9	72t	6
Cincinnati	420	1520	3.6	46	6
Indianapolis	370	1274	3.4	38	13
AFC Total	7085	29690	4.2	82t	239
AFC Average	442.8	1855.6	4.2	—	14.9

NATIONAL FOOTBALL CONFERENCE—RUSHING

	Att	Yards	Avg	Long	TD
N.Y. Giants	502	2518	5.0	77	19
Atlanta	560	2443	4.4	70	23
Carolina	504	2437	4.8	69t	30
Minnesota	519	2338	4.5	67t	15
Washington	478	2095	4.4	31	12
Tampa Bay	451	1837	4.1	68t	13
Green Bay	437	1805	4.1	73t	11
Seattle	417	1768	4.2	45	10
Dallas	401	1723	4.3	60t	12
Philadelphia	427	1697	4.0	39t	15
Chicago	434	1673	3.9	50t	15
St. Louis	417	1649	4.0	56t	8
San Francisco	397	1599	4.0	41t	10
New Orleans	398	1594	4.0	43	20
Detroit	352	1332	3.8	50	10
Arizona	340	1178	3.5	35	14
NFC Total	7034	29686	4.2	77	237
NFC Average	439.6	1855.4	4.2	—	14.8
League Total	14119	59376	—	82t	476
League Average	441.2	1855.5	4.2	—	14.9

PASSING

HIGHEST RATING
AFC: 105.5 Philip Rivers, San Diego
NFC: 96.9 Kurt Warner, Arizona

COMPLETION PERCENTAGE
AFC: 67.4 Chad Pennington, Miami
NFC: 67.1 Kurt Warner, Arizona

ATTEMPTS
NFC: 635 Drew Brees, New Orleans
AFC: 616 Jay Cutler, Denver

COMPLETIONS
NFC: 413 Drew Brees, New Orleans
AFC: 384 Jay Cutler, Denver

YARDS
NFC: 5069 Drew Brees, New Orleans
AFC: 4526 Jay Cutler, Denver

YARDS, GAME
NFC: 472 Kurt Warner, Arizona at N.Y. Jets, September 28 (40-57, 2 TD)
AFC: 447 Jay Cutler, Denver at Cleveland, November 6 (24-42, 3 TD)

LONGEST
NFC: 99 Gus Frerotte (to Bernard Berrian) Minnesota vs. Chicago, November 30 - TD
AFC: 93 Jay Cutler (to Eddie Royal*) Denver at Cleveland, November 6 - TD

YARDS PER ATTEMPT
AFC: 8.39 Philip Rivers, San Diego
NFC: 7.98 Drew Brees, New Orleans

TOUCHDOWN PASSES
AFC: 34 Philip Rivers, San Diego
NFC: 34 Drew Brees, New Orleans

TOUCHDOWN PASSES, GAME
AFC: 6 Brett Favre, N.Y. Jets vs. Arizona, September 28 (24-34, 289 yards)
NFC: 4 Drew Brees, New Orleans vs. Green Bay, November 24 (20-26, 323 yards)
4 Donovan McNabb, Philadelphia vs. Arizona, November 27 (27-39, 260 yards)
4 Tarvaris Jackson, Minnesota at Arizona, December 14 (11-17, 163 yards)
4 Drew Brees, New Orleans vs. Carolina, December 28 (30-49, 386 yards)
4 Kurt Warner, Arizona vs. Seattle, December 28 (19-30, 263 yards)

LOWEST INTERCEPTION PERCENTAGE
AFC: 1.5 Chad Pennington, Miami
NFC: 1.2 Jason Campbell, Washington

TEAM CHAMPION (MOST NET YARDS)
NFC: 4977 New Orleans
AFC: 4471 Denver

NFL TOP TEN PASSERS

	Att	Comp	Pct Comp	Yds	Avg Gain	TD	Pct TD	Long	Int	Pct Int	Sack	Yds Lost	Rating Points
Rivers, Philip, S.D.	478	312	65.3	4009	8.39	34	7.1	67	11	2.3	25	151	105.5
Pennington, Chad, Mia.	476	321	67.4	3653	7.67	19	4.0	80t	7	1.5	24	121	97.4
Warner, Kurt, Ariz	598	401	67.1	4583	7.66	30	5.0	79t	14	2.3	26	182	96.9
Brees, Drew, N.O.	635	413	65.0	5069	7.98	34	5.4	84t	17	2.7	13	92	96.2
Manning, Peyton, Ind.	555	371	66.8	4002	7.21	27	4.9	75	12	2.2	14	86	95.0
Rodgers, Aaron, G.B.	536	341	63.6	4038	7.53	28	5.2	71t	13	2.4	34	231	93.8
Schaub, Matt, Hou.	380	251	66.1	3043	8.01	15	3.9	65	10	2.6	23	149	92.7
Romo, Tony, Dal.	450	276	61.3	3448	7.66	26	5.8	75t	14	3.1	20	123	91.4
Garcia, Jeff, T.B.	376	244	64.9	2712	7.21	12	3.2	71t	6	1.6	23	100	90.2
Cassel, Matt, N.E.	516	327	63.4	3693	7.16	21	4.1	76t	11	2.1	47	219	89.4

AMERICAN FOOTBALL CONFERENCE—PASSING

	Att	Comp	Pct Comp	Gross Yards	Sacked	Yds Lost	Net Yards	Yds/ Att	Yards/ Comp	TD	Pct TD	Long	Int	Pct Int
Denver	620	386	62.3	4545	12	74	4471	7.33	11.77	25	4.03	93t	18	2.9
Houston	555	367	66.1	4474	32	207	4267	8.06	12.19	21	3.78	65	20	3.6
Indianapolis	585	393	67.2	4180	14	86	4094	7.15	10.64	27	4.62	75	12	2.1
San Diego	478	312	65.3	4009	25	151	3858	8.39	12.85	34	7.11	67	11	2.3
New England	534	339	63.5	3790	48	221	3569	7.10	11.18	21	3.93	76t	11	2.1
Miami	491	330	67.2	3761	26	129	3632	7.66	11.40	20	4.07	80t	7	1.4
Jacksonville	537	335	62.4	3620	42	288	3332	6.74	10.81	15	2.79	41	13	2.4
Pittsburgh	506	303	59.9	3607	49	306	3301	7.13	11.90	19	3.75	65t	15	3.0
N.Y. Jets	529	347	65.6	3516	30	213	3303	6.65	10.13	22	4.16	56t	23	4.3
Kansas City	541	310	57.3	3358	37	229	3129	6.21	10.83	23	4.25	75	16	3.0
Buffalo	479	309	64.5	3302	38	262	3040	6.89	10.69	14	2.92	87t	15	3.1
Baltimore	433	261	60.3	3085	33	277	2808	7.12	11.82	16	3.70	70t	12	2.8
Tennessee	453	265	58.5	2902	12	83	2819	6.41	10.95	13	2.87	56t	9	2.0
Cincinnati	513	303	59.1	2677	51	271	2406	5.22	8.83	11	2.14	79	15	2.9
Oakland	421	222	52.7	2639	39	270	2369	6.27	11.89	13	3.09	84t	11	2.6
Cleveland	488	238	48.8	2537	24	157	2380	5.20	10.66	11	2.25	70	20	4.1
AFC Total	8163	5020	—	56002	512	3224	52778	—	—	305	—	93t	228	—
AFC Average	510.2	313.8	61.5	3500.1	32.0	201.5	3298.6	6.86	11.16	19.1	3.7	—	14.3	2.8

NATIONAL FOOTBALL CONFERENCE—PASSING

	Att	Comp	Pct Comp	Gross Yards	Sacked	Yds Lost	Net Yards	Yds/ Att	Yards/ Comp	TD	Pct TD	Long	Int	Pct Int
New Orleans	636	413	64.9	5069	13	92	4977	7.97	12.27	34	5.35	84t	18	2.8
Arizona	630	418	66.3	4875	28	201	4674	7.74	11.66	31	4.92	79t	15	2.4
Philadelphia	606	362	59.7	4060	23	149	3911	6.70	11.22	23	3.80	90t	16	2.6
Green Bay	541	343	63.4	4044	34	231	3813	7.48	11.79	28	5.18	71t	13	2.4
Dallas	547	328	60.0	3988	31	199	3789	7.29	12.16	29	5.30	75t	20	3.7
Tampa Bay	562	355	63.2	3788	32	169	3619	6.74	10.67	18	3.20	71t	13	2.3
San Francisco	509	309	60.7	3724	55	345	3379	7.32	12.05	21	4.13	63	19	3.7
Atlanta	434	265	61.1	3440	17	104	3336	7.93	12.98	16	3.69	70t	11	2.5
N.Y. Giants	491	298	60.7	3353	28	176	3177	6.83	11.25	23	4.68	48	10	2.0
Detroit	509	281	55.2	3299	52	339	2960	6.48	11.74	18	3.54	96t	19	3.7
Washington	510	318	62.4	3291	38	266	3025	6.45	10.35	14	2.75	67t	6	1.2
Carolina	414	246	59.4	3288	20	130	3158	7.94	13.37	15	3.62	65t	12	2.9
St. Louis	520	292	56.2	3268	45	321	2947	6.28	11.19	11	2.12	80t	19	3.7
Chicago	528	304	57.6	3229	29	168	3061	6.12	10.62	20	3.79	65t	14	2.7
Minnesota	452	267	59.1	3217	43	261	2956	7.12	12.05	22	4.87	99t	17	3.8
Seattle	474	262	55.3	2831	36	214	2617	5.97	10.81	18	3.80	90t	15	3.2
NFC Total	8363	5061	—	58764	524	3365	55399	—	—	341	—	99t	237	—
NFC Average	522.7	316.3	60.5	3672.8	32.8	210.3	3462.4	7.03	11.61	21.3	4.1	—	14.8	2.8
League Total	16526	10081	—	114766	1036	6589	108177	—	—	646	—	99t	465	—
League Average	516.4	315.0	61.0	3586.4	32.4	205.9	3380.5	6.94	11.38	20.2	3.9	—	14.5	2.8

2008 INDIVIDUAL STATISTICS—PASSING

AFC—INDIVIDUAL PASSERS

	Att	Comp	Pct Comp	Yds	Avg Gain	TD	Pct TD	Long	Int	Pct Int	Sack	Yds Lost	Rating Points
Rivers, Philip, S.D.	478	312	65.3	4009	8.39	34	7.1	67	11	2.3	25	151	105.5
Pennington, Chad, Mia.	476	321	67.4	3653	7.67	19	4.0	80t	7	1.5	24	121	97.4
Manning, Peyton, Ind.	555	371	66.8	4002	7.21	27	4.9	75	12	2.2	14	86	95.0
Schaub, Matt, Hou.	380	251	66.1	3043	8.01	15	3.9	65	10	2.6	23	149	92.7
Cassel, Matt, N.E.	516	327	63.4	3693	7.16	21	4.1	76t	11	2.1	47	219	89.4
Cutler, Jay, Den.	616	384	62.3	4526	7.35	25	4.1	93t	18	2.9	11	69	86.0
Edwards, Trent, Buf.	374	245	65.5	2699	7.22	11	2.9	65	10	2.7	23	143	85.4
Garrard, David, Jac.	535	335	62.6	3620	6.77	15	2.8	41	13	2.4	42	288	81.7
Favre, Brett, NYJ	522	343	65.7	3472	6.65	22	4.2	56t	22	4.2	30	213	81.0
* Flacco, Joe, Bal.	428	257	60.0	2971	6.94	14	3.3	70t	12	2.8	32	276	80.3
Collins, Kerry, Ten.	415	242	58.3	2676	6.45	12	2.9	56t	7	1.7	8	60	80.2
Roethlisberger, Ben, Pit.	469	281	59.9	3301	7.04	17	3.6	65t	15	3.2	46	284	80.1
Russell, JaMarcus, Oak.	368	198	53.8	2423	6.58	13	3.5	84t	8	2.2	31	210	77.1
Thigpen, Tyler, K.C.	420	230	54.8	2608	6.21	18	4.3	75	12	2.9	26	162	76.0
Fitzpatrick, Ryan, Cin.	372	221	59.4	1905	5.12	8	2.2	79	9	2.4	38	193	70.0
Anderson, Derek, Cle.	283	142	50.2	1615	5.71	9	3.2	70	8	2.8	14	87	66.5
(Nonqualifiers)													
Leftwich, Byron, Pit.	36	21	58.3	303	8.42	2	5.6	50	0	0.0	3	22	104.3
Sorgi, Jim, Ind.	30	22	73.3	178	5.93	0	0.0	33	0	0.0	0	0	87.9
Brady, Tom, N.E.	11	7	63.6	76	6.91	0	0.0	26	0	0.0	0	0	83.9
Croyle, Brodie, K.C.	29	20	69.0	151	5.21	0	0.0	22	0	0.0	1	10	81.3
Rosenfels, Sage, Hou.	174	116	66.7	1431	8.22	6	3.4	61	10	5.7	9	58	79.5
* Henne, Chad, Mia.	12	7	58.3	67	5.58	0	0.0	19	0	0.0	0	0	74.0
Palmer, Carson, Cin.	129	75	58.1	731	5.67	3	2.3	36	4	3.1	11	67	69.0
Quinn, Brady, Cle.	89	45	50.6	518	5.82	2	2.2	42	2	2.2	1	9	66.6
Huard, Damon, K.C.	81	50	61.7	477	5.89	2	2.5	68	4	4.9	9	56	65.7
Young, Vince, Ten.	36	22	61.1	219	6.08	1	2.8	54	2	5.6	3	13	64.5
Losman, J.P., Buf.	104	63	60.6	584	5.62	2	1.9	87t	5	4.8	15	119	62.3
Walter, Andrew, Oak.	49	22	44.9	204	4.16	0	0.0	28	3	6.1	5	39	31.3
Dorsey, Ken, Cle.	91	43	47.3	370	4.07	0	0.0	28	7	7.7	5	43	26.4
Palmer, Jordan, Cin.	12	7	58.3	41	3.42	0	0.0	13	2	16.7	2	11	25.3
Gradkowski, Bruce, Cle.	21	7	33.3	26	1.24	0	0.0	12	3	14.3	4	18	2.8
(Fewer than 10 attempts)													
Bradley, Mark, K.C.	1	1	100.0	37	37.00	1	100.0	37t	0	0.0	0	0	158.3
Brown, Ronnie, Mia.	3	2	66.7	41	13.67	1	33.3	22	0	0.0	1	8	149.3
Bush, Michael, Oak.	2	1	50.0	8	4.00	0	0.0	8	0	0.0	0	0	60.4
Clayton, Mark, Bal.	1	1	100.0	32	32.00	1	100.0	32t	0	0.0	0	0	158.3
Clemens, Kellen, NYJ	5	3	60.0	26	5.20	0	0.0	11	1	20.0	0	0	34.2
Cribbs, Josh, Cle.	4	1	25.0	8	2.00	0	0.0	8	0	0.0	0	0	39.6
* Dixon, Dennis, Pit.	1	1	100.0	3	3.00	0	0.0	3	0	0.0	0	0	79.2
Faulk, Kevin, N.E.	1	1	100.0	-2	-2.00	0	0.0	-2	0	0.0	0	0	79.2
Gray, Quinn, K.C.	8	7	87.5	76	9.50	1	12.5	26	0	0.0	0	0	145.8
Hagans, Marques, K.C.	1	1	100.0	5	5.00	0	0.0	5	0	0.0	1	1	87.5
Johnson, Larry, K.C.	1	1	100.0	4	4.00	1	100.0	4t	0	0.0	0	0	122.9
Lemon, Cleo, Jac.	2	0	0.0	0	0.00	0	0.0	—	0	0.0	0	0	39.6
* McFadden, Darren, Oak.	0	0	—	0	—	0	—	—	0	—	1	5	—
Moorman, Brian, Buf.	1	1	100.0	19	19.00	1	100.0	19t	0	0.0	0	0	158.3
* O'Connell, Kevin, N.E.	6	4	66.7	23	3.83	0	0.0	12	0	0.0	1	2	73.6
Ramsey, Patrick, Den.	3	2	66.7	19	6.33	0	0.0	10	0	0.0	1	5	84.0
* Royal, Eddie, Den.	1	0	0.0	0	0.00	0	0.0	—	0	0.0	0	0	39.6
Simms, Chris, Ten.	2	1	50.0	7	3.50	0	0.0	7	0	0.0	1	10	58.3
Smith, Brad, NYJ	2	1	50.0	18	9.00	0	0.0	18	0	0.0	0	0	81.3
Smith, Troy, Bal.	4	3	75.0	82	20.50	1	25.0	43	0	0.0	1	1	156.3
Tuiasosopo, Marques, Oak.	2	1	50.0	4	2.00	0	0.0	4	0	0.0	2	16	56.3
Turk, Matt, Hou.	1	0	0.0	0	0.00	0	0.0	—	0	0.0	0	0	39.6
Williams, Ricky, Mia.	0	0	—	0	—	0	—	—	0	—	1	0	—

t = Touchdown
Leader based on rating points, minimum 224 attempts
* *Player that was a rookie in 2008*

NFC—INDIVIDUAL PASSERS

	Att	Comp	Pct Comp	Yds	Avg Gain	TD	Pct TD	Long	Int	Pct Int	Sack	Yds Lost	Rating Points
Warner, Kurt, Ariz	598	401	67.1	4583	7.66	30	5.0	79t	14	2.3	26	182	96.9
Brees, Drew, N.O.	635	413	65.0	5069	7.98	34	5.4	84t	17	2.7	13	92	96.2
Rodgers, Aaron, G.B.	536	341	63.6	4038	7.53	28	5.2	71t	13	2.4	34	231	93.8
Romo, Tony, Dal.	450	276	61.3	3448	7.66	26	5.8	75t	14	3.1	20	123	91.4
Garcia, Jeff, T.B.	376	244	64.9	2712	7.21	12	3.2	71t	6	1.6	23	100	90.2
* Ryan, Matt, Atl.	434	265	61.1	3440	7.93	16	3.7	70t	11	2.5	17	104	87.7
Hill, Shaun, S.F.	288	181	62.8	2046	7.10	13	4.5	48t	8	2.8	23	148	87.5
Wallace, Seneca, Sea.	242	141	58.3	1532	6.33	11	4.5	90t	3	1.2	14	76	87.0
Manning, Eli, NY-G	479	289	60.3	3238	6.76	21	4.4	48	10	2.1	27	174	86.4
McNabb, Donovan, Phi.	571	345	60.4	3916	6.86	23	4.0	90t	11	1.9	23	149	86.4
Delhomme, Jake, Car.	414	246	59.4	3288	7.94	15	3.6	65t	12	2.9	20	130	84.7
Campbell, Jason, Was.	506	315	62.3	3245	6.41	13	2.6	67t	6	1.2	38	266	84.3
Orton, Kyle, Chi.	465	272	58.5	2972	6.39	18	3.9	65t	12	2.6	27	160	79.6
Frerotte, Gus, Min.	301	178	59.1	2157	7.17	12	4.0	99t	15	5.0	29	164	73.7
Orlovsky, Dan, Det.	255	143	56.1	1616	6.34	8	3.1	96t	8	3.1	14	95	72.6
Bulger, Marc, St.L	440	251	57.0	2720	6.18	11	2.5	80t	13	3.0	38	263	71.4
(Nonqualifiers)													
Carr, David, NY-G	12	9	75.0	115	9.58	2	16.7	27	0	0.0	1	2	144.1
Jackson, Tarvaris, Min.	149	88	59.1	1056	7.09	9	6.0	59t	2	1.3	14	97	95.4
Stanton, Drew, Det.	17	9	52.9	119	7.00	1	5.9	41	0	0.0	6	35	95.0
Leinart, Matt, Ariz	29	15	51.7	264	9.10	1	3.4	78t	1	3.4	2	19	80.2
O'Sullivan, J.T., S.F.	220	128	58.2	1678	7.63	8	3.6	63	11	5.0	32	197	73.6
Kitna, Jon, Det.	120	68	56.7	758	6.32	5	4.2	47t	5	4.2	15	89	72.2
Griese, Brian, T.B.	184	110	59.8	1073	5.83	5	2.7	38	7	3.8	9	69	69.4
Culpepper, Daunte, Det.	115	60	52.2	786	6.83	4	3.5	70t	6	5.2	14	95	63.9
Bollinger, Brooks, Dal.	17	10	58.8	71	4.18	1	5.9	24	1	5.9	3	22	63.6
Grossman, Rex, Chi.	62	32	51.6	257	4.15	2	3.2	29	2	3.2	2	8	59.7
Hasselbeck, Matt, Sea.	209	109	52.2	1216	5.82	5	2.4	34	10	4.8	19	119	57.8
Frye, Charlie, Sea.	23	12	52.2	83	3.61	2	8.7	19	2	8.7	3	19	53.4
Johnson, Brad, Dal.	78	41	52.6	427	5.47	2	2.6	36	5	6.4	8	54	50.5
Green, Trent, St.L	72	38	52.8	525	7.29	0	0.0	53	6	8.3	6	58	41.7
Kolb, Kevin, Phi.	34	17	50.0	144	4.24	0	0.0	16	4	11.8	0	0	21.8
(Fewer than 10 attempts)													
Arrington, J.J., Ariz	1	0	0.0	0	0.00	0	0.0	—	0	0.0	0	0	39.6
Berlin, Brock, St.L	3	1	33.3	6	2.00	0	0.0	6	0	0.0	0	0	42.4
Bruce, Isaac, S.F.	1	0	0.0	0	0.00	0	0.0	—	0	0.0	0	0	39.6
Crayton, Patrick, Dal.	1	0	0.0	0	0.00	0	0.0	—	0	0.0	0	0	39.6
* Flynn, Matt, G.B.	5	2	40.0	6	1.20	0	0.0	3	0	0.0	0	0	47.9
Graham, Earnest, T.B.	1	1	100.0	3	3.00	1	100.0	3t	0	0.0	0	0	118.8
Hall, Dante, St.L	1	0	0.0	0	0.00	0	0.0	—	0	0.0	0	0	39.6
Henson, Drew, Det.	2	1	50.0	20	10.00	0	0.0	20	0	0.0	3	25	85.4
* Jackson, DeSean, Phi.	1	0	0.0	0	0.00	0	0.0	—	1	100.0	0	0	0.0
Johnson, Dirk, Ariz	1	1	100.0	10	10.00	0	0.0	10	0	0.0	0	0	108.3
Jones, Donnie, St.L	1	0	0.0	0	0.00	0	0.0	—	0	0.0	0	0	39.6
Looker, Dane, St.L	3	2	66.7	17	5.67	0	0.0	11	0	0.0	1	0	81.3
Maynard, Brad, Chi.	1	0	0.0	0	0.00	0	0.0	—	0	0.0	0	0	39.6
McCown, Luke, T.B.	1	0	0.0	0	0.00	0	0.0	—	0	0.0	0	0	39.6
Moore, Lance, N.O.	1	0	0.0	0	0.00	0	0.0	—	1	100.0	0	0	0.0
Randle El, Antwaan, Was.	4	3	75.0	46	11.50	1	25.0	18t	0	0.0	0	0	152.1
Rice, Sidney, Min.	1	0	0.0	0	0.00	0	0.0	—	0	0.0	0	0	39.6
Taylor, Chester, Min.	1	1	100.0	4	4.00	1	100.0	4t	0	0.0	0	0	122.9
Urban, Jerheme, Ariz	1	1	100.0	18	18.00	0	0.0	18	0	0.0	0	0	118.8
Witten, Jason, Dal.	1	1	100.0	42	42.00	0	0.0	42	0	0.0	0	0	118.8

t = Touchdown
Leader based on rating points, minimum 224 attempts
** Player that was a rookie in 2008*

PASS RECEIVING

RECEPTIONS
AFC: 115 Andre Johnson, Houston
NFC: 96 Larry Fitzgerald, Arizona

RECEPTIONS, GAME
AFC: 18 Brandon Marshall, Denver vs. San Diego, September 14 (166 yards, 1 TD)
NFC: 13 Anquan Boldin, Arizona at Seattle, November 16 (186 yards, 0 TD)

YARDS
AFC: 1575 Andre Johnson, Houston
NFC: 1431 Larry Fitzgerald, Arizona

YARDS, GAME
NFC: 213 Terrell Owens, Dallas vs. San Francisco, November 23 (7 receptions, 1 TD)
AFC: 207 Andre Johnson, Houston vs. Tennessee, December 14 (11 receptions, 1 TD)

LONGEST
NFC: 99 Bernard Berrian (from Gus Frerotte), Minnesota vs. Chicago, November 30 - TD
AFC: 93 * Eddie Royal (from Jay Cutler), Denver at Cleveland, November 6 - TD

YARDS PER RECEPTION
NFC: 24.8 Devery Henderson, New Orleans
AFC: 19.1 Justin Gage, Tennessee

TOUCHDOWNS
NFC: 12 Larry Fitzgerald, Arizona
Calvin Johnson, Detroit
AFC: 11 Randy Moss, New England

TEAM LEADERS, RECEPTIONS
AFC: BALTIMORE, 80, Derrick Mason; BUFFALO, 63, Lee Evans; CINCINNATI, 92, T.J. Houshmandzadeh; CLEVELAND, 55, Braylon Edwards; DENVER, 104, Brandon Marshall; HOUSTON, 115, Andre Johnson; INDIANAPOLIS, 82, Reggie Wayne; JACKSONVILLE, 65, Matt Jones; KANSAS CITY, 96, Tony Gonzalez; MIAMI, 56, Ted Ginn Jr.; NEW ENGLAND, 111, Wes Welker; N.Y. JETS, 71, Jerricho Cotchery; OAKLAND, 56, Zach Miller; PITTSBURGH, 81, Hines Ward; SAN DIEGO, 60, Antonio Gates; TENNESSEE, 58, Bo Scaife

NFC: ARIZONA, 96, Larry Fitzgerald; ATLANTA, 88, Roddy White; CAROLINA, 78, Steve Smith; CHICAGO, 63, *Matt Forté; DALLAS, 81, Jason Witten; DETROIT, 78, Calvin Johnson; GREEN BAY, 80, Greg Jennings; MINNESOTA, 53, Bobby Wade; NEW ORLEANS, 79, Lance Moore; N.Y. GIANTS, 57, Steve Smith; PHILADELPHIA, 62, *DeSean Jackson; ST. LOUIS, 64, Torry Holt; SAN FRANCISCO, 61, Isaac Bruce; SEATTLE, 55, *John Carlson; TAMPA BAY, 83, Antonio Bryant; WASHINGTON, 83, Chris Cooley

** Player that was a rookie in 2008*

NFL TOP TEN PASS RECEIVERS

	No	Yards	Avg	Long	TD
Johnson, Andre, Hou.	115	1575	13.7	65	8
Welker, Wes, N.E.	111	1165	10.5	64	3
Marshall, Brandon, Den.	104	1265	12.2	47	6
Fitzgerald, Larry, Ariz	96	1431	14.9	78t	12
Gonzalez, Tony, K.C.	96	1058	11.0	35	10
Houshmandzadeh, T.J., Cin.	92	904	9.8	46	4
* Royal, Eddie, Den.	91	980	10.8	93t	5
Boldin, Anquan, Ariz	89	1038	11.7	79t	11
White, Roddy, Atl.	88	1382	15.7	70t	7
Bowe, Dwayne, K.C.	86	1022	11.9	36	7

NFL TOP TEN RECEIVERS BY YARDS

	Yards	No	Avg	Long	TD
Johnson, Andre, Hou.	1575	115	13.7	65	8
Fitzgerald, Larry, Ariz	1431	96	14.9	78t	12
Smith, Steve, Car.	1421	78	18.2	65t	6
White, Roddy, Atl.	1382	88	15.7	70t	7
Johnson, Calvin, Det.	1331	78	17.1	96t	12
Jennings, Greg, G.B.	1292	80	16.2	63	9
Marshall, Brandon, Den.	1265	104	12.2	47	6
Bryant, Antonio, T.B.	1248	83	15.0	71t	7
Welker, Wes, N.E.	1165	111	10.5	64	3
Wayne, Reggie, Ind.	1145	82	14.0	65t	6

AFC—INDIVIDUAL RECEIVERS

	No	Yards	Avg	Long	TD
Johnson, Andre, Hou.	115	1575	13.7	65	8
Welker, Wes, N.E.	111	1165	10.5	64	3
Marshall, Brandon, Den.	104	1265	12.2	47	6
Gonzalez, Tony, K.C.	96	1058	11.0	35	10
Houshmandzadeh, T.J., Cin.	92	904	9.8	46	4
* Royal, Eddie, Den.	91	980	10.8	93t	5
Bowe, Dwayne, K.C.	86	1022	11.9	36	7
Wayne, Reggie, Ind.	82	1145	14.0	65t	6
Ward, Hines, Pit.	81	1043	12.9	49	7
Mason, Derrick, Bal.	80	1037	13.0	54	5
Clark, Dallas, Ind.	77	848	11.0	33	6
Cotchery, Jerricho, NYJ	71	858	12.1	56t	5
Daniels, Owen, Hou.	70	862	12.3	35	2
Coles, Laveranues, NYJ	70	850	12.1	54	7
Moss, Randy, N.E.	69	1008	14.6	76t	11
Jones, Matt, Jac.	65	761	11.7	35	2
Evans, Lee, Buf.	63	1017	16.1	87t	3
Jones-Drew, Maurice, Jac.	62	565	9.1	26	2
Walter, Kevin, Hou.	60	899	15.0	61	8
Gates, Antonio, S.D.	60	704	11.7	34	8
Harrison, Marvin, Ind.	60	636	10.6	67t	5
Jackson, Vincent, S.D.	59	1098	18.6	60	7
Scaife, Bo, Ten.	58	561	9.7	44	2
Faulk, Kevin, N.E.	58	486	8.4	22	3
Gonzalez, Anthony, Ind.	57	664	11.6	58	4
Ginn, Ted Jr., Mia.	56	790	14.1	64	2
Miller, Zach, Oak.	56	778	13.9	63t	1
Reed, Josh, Buf.	56	597	10.7	24	1
Edwards, Braylon, Cle.	55	873	15.9	70	3
Holmes, Santonio, Pit.	55	821	14.9	48	5
Camarillo, Greg, Mia.	55	613	11.1	33	2
* Bess, Davone, Mia.	54	554	10.3	37	1
Ochocinco, Chad, Cin.	53	540	10.2	26	4
Tomlinson, LaDainian, S.D.	52	426	8.2	32	1
* Slaton, Steve, Hou.	50	377	7.5	46	1
Stokley, Brandon, Den.	49	528	10.8	36t	3
* Keller, Dustin, NYJ	48	535	11.1	54	3
Miller, Heath, Pit.	48	514	10.7	22	3
Washington, Leon, NYJ	47	355	7.6	40	2
Lynch, Marshawn, Buf.	47	300	6.4	42	1
Rhodes, Dominic, Ind.	45	302	6.7	29	3
Northcutt, Dennis, Jac.	44	545	12.4	41	2
Winslow, Kellen, Cle.	43	428	10.0	30	3

	No	Yards	Avg	Long	TD
* Johnson, Chris, Ten.	43	260	6.0	25	1
Clayton, Mark, Bal.	41	695	17.0	70t	3
Lewis, Marcedes, Jac.	41	489	11.9	30t	2
Jones, Brandon, Ten.	41	449	11.0	40	1
Scheffler, Tony, Den.	40	645	16.1	72	3
Washington, Nate, Pit.	40	631	15.8	65t	3
Moore, Mewelde, Pit.	40	320	8.0	25	1
Gaffney, Jabar, N.E.	38	468	12.3	37	2
Williams, Reggie, Jac.	37	364	9.8	32	3
Jackson, Fred, Buf.	37	317	8.6	65	0
Jones, Thomas, NYJ	36	207	5.8	19	2
Heap, Todd, Bal.	35	403	11.5	30	3
Gage, Justin, Ten.	34	651	19.1	56t	6
Fasano, Anthony, Mia.	34	454	13.4	24	7
Chambers, Chris, S.D.	33	462	14.0	48t	5
Royal, Robert, Buf.	33	351	10.6	30t	1
* Rice, Ray, Bal.	33	273	8.3	40	0
Brown, Ronnie, Mia.	33	254	7.7	39	0
Graham, Daniel, Den.	32	389	12.2	28t	4
Stuckey, Chansi, NYJ	32	359	11.2	31	3
Martin, David, Mia.	31	450	14.5	61t	3
Kelly, Reggie, Cin.	31	207	6.7	31	0
McCareins, Justin, Ten.	30	412	13.7	37	0
Bradley, Mark, K.C.	30	380	12.7	56	3
Sproles, Darren, S.D.	29	342	11.8	66t	5
* McFadden, Darren, Oak.	29	285	9.8	27	0
Williams, Ricky, Mia.	29	219	7.6	47	1
Floyd, Malcom, S.D.	27	465	17.2	49t	4
* Charles, Jamaal, K.C.	27	272	10.1	75	1
Addai, Joseph, Ind.	25	206	8.2	55t	2
Crumpler, Alge, Ten.	24	257	10.7	28	1
Parrish, Roscoe, Buf.	24	232	9.7	22	1
McGahee, Willis, Bal.	24	173	7.2	35	0
Heiden, Steve, Cle.	23	249	10.8	51	0
Lewis, Jamal, Cle.	23	178	7.7	18	0
Higgins, Johnnie Lee, Oak.	22	366	16.6	84t	4
Watson, Benjamin, N.E.	22	209	9.5	29	2
Wright, Jason, Cle.	22	156	7.1	17	1
Baker, Chris, NYJ	21	194	9.2	29	0
Chatman, Antonio, Cin.	21	194	9.2	25	0
Benson, Cedric, Cin.	20	185	9.3	79	0
Perry, Chris, Cin.	20	71	3.6	12	0
Cobbs, Patrick, Mia.	19	275	14.5	80t	2
Anderson, David, Hou.	19	241	12.7	65	2
Henry, Chris, Cin.	19	220	11.6	22	2
Steptoe, Syndric, Cle.	19	182	9.6	53	0
Curry, Ronald, Oak.	19	181	9.5	16	2
Robinson, Gijon, Ind.	19	166	8.7	23	0
Bush, Michael, Oak.	19	162	8.5	25	0
McClain, Le'Ron, Bal.	19	123	6.5	25	1
Darling, Devard, K.C.	17	247	14.5	68	1
Stallworth, Donte', Cle.	17	170	10.0	19	1
Morris, Sammy, N.E.	17	161	9.5	42	0
Spaeth, Matt, Pit.	17	136	8.0	13	0
Walker, Mike, Jac.	16	217	13.6	32	0
Utecht, Ben, Cin.	16	123	7.7	14	0
Taylor, Fred, Jac.	16	98	6.1	17	0
* Schilens, Chaz, Oak.	15	226	15.1	60	2
Walker, Javon, Oak.	15	196	13.1	29	1
Schouman, Derek, Buf.	15	153	10.2	21	1
Manumaleuna, Brandon, S.D.	15	127	8.5	17	2
* Hillis, Peyton, Den.	14	179	12.8	47	1
Davis, Andre, Hou.	13	213	16.4	49	0
Williams, Demetrius, Bal.	13	180	13.8	70t	1
* Tolbert, Mike, S.D.	13	171	13.2	67	1
Hall, Ahmard, Ten.	13	138	10.6	54	2
Jones, Greg, Jac.	13	116	8.9	22	1
Jackson, Darrell, Den.	12	190	15.8	48t	1
Harrison, Jerome, Cle.	12	116	9.7	23	1
Leach, Vonta, Hou.	12	103	8.6	22	0
* Hester, Jacob, S.D.	12	91	7.6	16	1
Johnson, Larry, K.C.	12	74	6.2	20	0
Smith, Brad, NYJ	12	64	5.3	18	0
Lelie, Ashley, Oak.	11	197	17.9	51	2
Porter, Jerry, Jac.	11	181	16.5	33	1
Jackson, Nate, Den.	11	84	7.6	19	1
Stewart, Tony, Oak.	11	81	7.4	17	0
* Caldwell, Andre, Cin.	11	78	7.1	15	0
Dreessen, Joel, Hou.	11	77	7.0	13	0
Green, Ahman, Hou.	11	32	2.9	8	0
Estandia, Greg, Jac.	10	113	11.3	23	0
Pittman, Michael, Den.	10	112	11.2	40	0
* Johnson, Steve, Buf.	10	102	10.2	21	2
* Fine, Derek, Buf.	10	94	9.4	20	1
Vickers, Lawrence, Cle.	10	78	7.8	21	0
* Santi, Tom, Ind.	10	64	6.4	13	1
Bell, Tatum, Den.	10	57	5.7	12	0
Fargas, Justin, Oak.	10	52	5.2	12	0
Smith, Kolby, K.C.	10	52	5.2	8	0
Thomas, David, N.E.	9	93	10.3	18	0
* Hardy, James, Buf.	9	87	9.7	17	2
Griffith, Justin, Oak.	9	85	9.4	24	1
Aiken, Sam, N.E.	8	101	12.6	43	0
Naanee, Legedu, S.D.	8	64	8.0	18	0
Angulo, Richard, Jac.	8	63	7.9	17	0
* Cox, Mike, K.C.	8	19	2.4	5	0
* Franklin, Will, K.C.	7	83	11.9	42	0
* Hawkins, Lavelle, Ten.	7	68	9.7	19	0
* Cottam, Brad, K.C.	7	63	9.0	19	0
Neal, Lorenzo, Bal.	7	35	5.0	13	0
* Sweed, Limas, Pit.	6	64	10.7	17	0
Franks, Bubba, NYJ	6	47	7.8	25	0
* Johnson, James, Cin.	6	47	7.8	16	0
Ganther, Quinton, Ten.	6	43	7.2	15	0
Lawton, Luke, Oak.	6	30	5.0	12	0
Polite, Lousaka, Mia.	6	24	4.0	9	0
Webb, Jeff, K.C.	5	46	9.2	15	0
Dinkins, Darnell, Cle.	5	41	8.2	22t	1
Williamson, Troy, Jac.	5	30	6.0	10t	1
Davis, Carey, Pit.	5	27	5.4	14	0
Wilcox, Daniel, Bal.	5	19	3.8	8	2
White, LenDale, Ten.	5	16	3.2	7	0
Davis, Craig, S.D.	4	59	14.8	20	0
Davenport, Najeh, Ind.	4	54	13.5	33	0
* Garcon, Pierre, Ind.	4	23	5.8	12	0
Ali, Charles, Cle.	4	13	3.3	12	0
Jones, Jacoby, Hou.	3	81	27.0	45	0
Evans, Heath, N.E.	3	59	19.7	28	0
Hagan, Derek, Mia.	3	51	17.0	20	0
* Green-Ellis, BenJarvus, N.E.	3	37	12.3	20	0
Martinez, Glenn, Den.	3	32	10.7	12	0
London, Brandon, Mia.	3	30	10.0	14	0
* Simpson, Chad, Ind.	3	30	10.0	15	0
Holt, Glenn, Cin.	3	26	8.7	10t	1
Hall, Andre, Den.	3	25	8.3	11	0
Wilford, Ernest, Mia.	3	25	8.3	15	0
McHugh, Sean, Pit.	3	24	8.0	15	0
Pope, P.J., Den.	3	24	8.0	16	1
Young, Selvin, Den.	3	16	5.3	8	0
Moats, Ryan, Hou.	3	14	4.7	5	0
Parker, Willie, Pit.	3	13	4.3	5	0
* Tamme, Jacob, Ind.	3	12	4.0	6	0
Watson, Kenny, Cin.	3	4	1.3	3	0
Dorsey, DeDe, Cin.	2	49	24.5	36	0
Wrighster, George, Jac.	2	35	17.5	27	0
Barnes, Darian, Buf.	2	34	17.0	25	0
Davis, Chris, Ten.	2	31	15.5	21	0
* Haynos, Joey, Mia.	2	22	11.0	19t	1

2008 INDIVIDUAL STATISTICS—PASS RECEIVING

	No	Yards	Avg	Long	TD
Coats, Daniel, Cin.	2	19	9.5	11	0
Cribbs, Josh, Cle.	2	18	9.0	17	1
* Mendenhall, Rashard, Pit.	2	17	8.5	11	0
Owens, Montell, Jac.	2	17	8.5	10	0
* Rucker, Martin, Cle.	2	17	8.5	9	0
Lawrie, Nate, Cin.	2	11	5.5	7	0
Chatman, Jesse, NYJ	2	5	2.5	3	0
Cramer, Casey, Mia.	2	3	1.5	2t	1
* Savage, Dantrell, K.C.	2	0	0.0	2	0
McIntyre, Corey, Buf.	2	-1	-0.5	0	0
Figurs, Yamon, Bal.	1	43	43.0	43t	1
* Flacco, Joe, Bal.	1	43	43.0	43	0
Thigpen, Tyler, K.C.	1	37	37.0	37t	1
Smith, Troy, Bal.	1	36	36.0	36	0
Clowney, David, NYJ	1	26	26.0	26	0
Jones, Edgar, Bal.	1	25	25.0	25	0
Pearman, Alvin, Jac.	1	23	23.0	23t	1
Denney, Ryan, Buf.	1	19	19.0	19t	1
Jackson, Chad, Den.	1	19	19.0	19	0
* Hart, Mike, Ind.	1	18	18.0	18	0
Sanders, Steve, Cle.	1	18	18.0	18	0
Hall, Roy, Ind.	1	9	9.0	9	0
* Stevens, Craig, Ten.	1	9	9.0	9	0
* Washington, Chauncey, Jac.	1	9	9.0	9	0
Hagans, Marques, K.C.	1	7	7.0	7	0
Williams, Paul, Ten.	1	7	7.0	7	0
Baker, Dallas, Pit.	1	6	6.0	6	0
* Ball, Lance, Ind.	1	5	5.0	5	0
Richardson, Tony, NYJ	1	4	4.0	4	0
Washington, Kelley, N.E.	1	3	3.0	3	0
* Simpson, Jerome, Cin.	1	2	2.0	2	0
Battle, Jackie, K.C.	1	-2	-2.0	-2	0
Johnson, Charlie, Ind.	1	-2	-2.0	-2	0
Russell, Gary, Pit.	1	-2	-2.0	-2	0
Fitzpatrick, Ryan, Cin.	1	-3	-3.0	-3	0
Garrard, David, Jac.	1	-6	-6.0	-6	0
Roethlisberger, Ben, Pit.	1	-7	-7.0	-7	0
Carroll, Ahmad, NYJ	0	11	—	11	0
Favre, Brett, NYJ	0	2	—	2	0
Revis, Darrelle, NYJ	0	-1	—	-1	0
Satele, Samson, Mia.	0	-3	—	-3	0

*t = Touchdown; * Player that was a rookie in 2008*
Leader based on receptions

NFC—INDIVIDUAL RECEIVERS

	No	Yards	Avg	Long	TD
Fitzgerald, Larry, Ariz	96	1431	14.9	78t	12
Boldin, Anquan, Ariz	89	1038	11.7	79t	11
White, Roddy, Atl.	88	1382	15.7	70t	7
Bryant, Antonio, T.B.	83	1248	15.0	71t	7
Cooley, Chris, Was.	83	849	10.2	28	1
Witten, Jason, Dal.	81	952	11.8	42	4
Jennings, Greg, G.B.	80	1292	16.2	63	9
Moss, Santana, Was.	79	1044	13.2	67t	6
Moore, Lance, N.O.	79	928	11.7	70t	10
Smith, Steve, Car.	78	1421	18.2	65t	6
Johnson, Calvin, Det.	78	1331	17.1	96t	12
Breaston, Steve, Ariz	77	1006	13.1	58	3
Driver, Donald, G.B.	74	1012	13.7	71t	5
Owens, Terrell, Dal.	69	1052	15.2	75t	10
Muhammad, Muhsin, Car.	65	923	14.2	60	5
Holt, Torry, St.L	64	796	12.4	45t	3
* Forté, Matt, Chi.	63	477	7.6	19	4
* Jackson, DeSean, Phi.	62	912	14.7	60	2
Bruce, Isaac, S.F.	61	835	13.7	63	7
Smith, Steve, NY-G	57	574	10.1	30	1
* Carlson, John, Sea.	55	627	11.4	33	5
Olsen, Greg, Chi.	54	574	10.6	52	5
Westbrook, Brian, Phi.	54	402	7.4	47	5
* Avery, Donnie, St.L	53	674	12.7	69t	3
Wade, Bobby, Min.	53	645	12.2	59t	2
Randle El, Antwaan, Was.	53	593	11.2	31	4
Bush, Reggie, N.O.	52	440	8.5	42t	4
Barber, Marion, Dal.	52	417	8.0	70t	2
Hester, Devin, Chi.	51	665	13.0	65t	3
Jenkins, Michael, Atl.	50	777	15.5	62t	3
Shockey, Jeremy, N.O.	50	483	9.7	26	0
Berrian, Bernard, Min.	48	964	20.1	99t	7
Toomer, Amani, NY-G	48	580	12.1	40t	4
Colston, Marques, N.O.	47	760	16.2	70t	5
Engram, Bobby, Sea.	47	489	10.4	37	0
Hilliard, Ike, T.B.	47	424	9.0	36t	4
Dunn, Warrick, T.B.	47	330	7.0	36	0
Miller, Billy, N.O.	45	579	12.9	41	1
Johnson, Bryant, S.F.	45	546	12.1	42	3
Taylor, Chester, Min.	45	399	8.9	47t	2
Hixon, Domenik, NY-G	43	596	13.9	41	2
Gore, Frank, S.F.	43	373	8.7	26	2
Shiancoe, Visanthe, Min.	42	596	14.2	40	7
Ward, Derrick, NY-G	41	384	9.4	48	0
Clark, Desmond, Chi.	41	367	9.0	35	1
Jackson, Steven, St.L	40	379	9.5	53	1
Crayton, Patrick, Dal.	39	550	14.1	55t	4
Lee, Donald, G.B.	39	303	7.8	26	5
* Smith, Kevin, Det.	39	286	7.3	27	0
Clayton, Michael, T.B.	38	484	12.7	58t	1
Smith, L.J., Phi.	37	298	8.1	25	3
Williams, Roy E., Det-Dal	36	430	11.9	38	2
Stevens, Jerramy, T.B.	36	397	11.0	31	2
Norwood, Jerious, Atl.	36	338	9.4	67t	2
Burress, Plaxico, NY-G	35	454	13.0	33t	4
Davis, Rashied, Chi.	35	445	12.7	36	2
McDonald, Shaun, Det.	35	332	9.5	26	1
Urban, Jerheme, Ariz	34	448	13.2	56t	4
* Hightower, Tim, Ariz	34	237	7.0	26	0
Baskett, Hank, Phi.	33	440	13.3	90t	3
Curtis, Kevin, Phi.	33	390	11.8	32	2
Boss, Kevin, NY-G	33	384	11.6	28	6
* Nelson, Jordy, G.B.	33	366	11.1	29t	2
Henderson, Devery, N.O.	32	793	24.8	84t	3
Avant, Jason, Phi.	32	377	11.8	31	2
Robinson, Koren, Sea.	31	400	12.9	90t	2
Davis, Vernon, S.F.	31	358	11.5	57	2
Thomas, Pierre, N.O.	31	284	9.2	24	3
Branch, Deion, Sea.	30	412	13.7	63	4
Hill, Jason, S.F.	30	317	10.6	33	2
Jackson, Brandon, G.B.	30	185	6.2	18	0
Arrington, J.J., Ariz	29	255	8.8	35	1
Portis, Clinton, Was.	28	218	7.8	29	0
Celek, Brent, Phi.	27	318	11.8	44	1
Lloyd, Brandon, Chi.	26	364	14.0	32	2
Buckhalter, Correll, Phi.	26	324	12.5	59	2
Battle, Arnaz, S.F.	24	318	13.3	36	0
* Douglas, Harry, Atl.	23	320	13.9	69	1
Looker, Dane, St.L	23	271	11.8	30	2
Gaines, Michael, Det.	23	260	11.3	33	1
Graham, Earnest, T.B.	23	174	7.6	24	0
Betts, Ladell, Was.	22	200	9.1	27	0
Williams, DeAngelo, Car.	22	121	5.5	25t	2
Smith, Alex, T.B.	21	250	11.9	34	3
King, Jeff, Car.	21	195	9.3	31	1
* Choice, Tashard, Dal.	21	185	8.8	50	0
Finneran, Brian, Atl.	21	169	8.0	14	1
Peterson, Adrian, Min.	21	125	6.0	16	0
* Morgan, Josh, S.F.	20	319	16.0	48t	3
* Bennett, Martellus, Dal.	20	283	14.2	37	4
Jones, James, G.B.	20	274	13.7	46	1

	No	Yards	Avg	Long	TD
Weaver, Leonard, Sea.	20	222	11.1	62t	2
Lewis, Greg, Phi.	19	247	13.0	52	1
Darby, Kenneth, St.L	19	183	9.6	30	0
Morris, Maurice, Sea.	19	136	7.2	13t	2
Brown, Reggie, Phi.	18	252	14.0	40	1
Rosario, Dante, Car.	18	209	11.6	24	1
Furrey, Mike, Det.	18	181	10.1	25	0
Pittman, Antonio, St.L	18	132	7.3	27	0
McAllister, Deuce, N.O.	18	128	7.1	20	1
Grant, Ryan, G.B.	18	116	6.4	17t	1
Robinson, Michael, S.F.	17	202	11.9	36	0
Foster, DeShaun, S.F.	16	133	8.3	31	1
Tahi, Naufahu, Min.	16	37	2.3	7	0
Standeford, John, Det.	15	244	16.3	36	0
Peelle, Justin, Atl.	15	159	10.6	18t	2
Martin, Ruvell, G.B.	15	149	9.9	17	1
Gilmore, John, T.B.	15	147	9.8	36	1
Rice, Sidney, Min.	15	141	9.4	23t	4
* Thomas, Devin, Was.	15	120	8.0	18	0
Booker, Marty, Chi.	14	211	15.1	51t	2
* Doucet, Early, Ariz	14	90	6.4	12	0
Jones, Julius, Sea.	14	66	4.7	17	0
Austin, Miles, Dal.	13	278	21.4	63	3
Hackett, D.J., Car.	13	181	13.9	37	0
* Burton, Keenan, St.L	13	172	13.2	30t	1
Galloway, Joey, T.B.	13	138	10.6	22	0
Askew, B.J., T.B.	13	66	5.1	18	0
Meachem, Robert, N.O.	12	289	24.1	74	3
Moss, Sinorice, NY-G	12	153	12.8	27	2
Campbell, Mark, N.O.	12	121	10.1	29	2
Colbert, Keary, Den/Sea/Det	12	116	9.7	28	1
Hall, Dante, St.L	12	105	8.8	20	0
Sellers, Mike, Was.	12	98	8.2	20	1
Johnson, Rudi, Det.	12	88	7.3	34t	1
Fitzsimmons, Casey, Det.	12	85	7.1	16	1
James, Edgerrin, Ariz	12	85	7.1	16	0
Humphrey, Tory, G.B.	11	162	14.7	37	0
Patten, David, N.O.	11	162	14.7	39t	1
McMichael, Randy, St.L	11	139	12.6	31	0
Klopfenstein, Joe, St.L	11	123	11.2	29	0
Patrick, Ben, Ariz	11	104	9.5	19	0
McKie, Jason, Chi.	11	64	5.8	12	1
Walker, Delanie, S.F.	10	155	15.5	53	1
Jarrett, Dwayne, Car.	10	119	11.9	25	0
Allison, Aundrae, Min.	10	109	10.9	21	0
Taylor, Courtney, Sea.	9	98	10.9	26	0
Thrash, James, Was.	9	81	9.0	29	1
Pope, Leonard, Ariz	9	77	8.6	25	0
* Felton, Jerome, Det.	9	53	5.9	12	0
Stecker, Aaron, N.O.	9	52	5.8	12	1
Karney, Mike, N.O.	9	18	2.0	7	0
Snelling, Jason, Atl.	8	89	11.1	27	0
Mughelli, Ovie, Atl.	8	57	7.1	18	0
Owens, John, Det.	8	56	7.0	19	1
Hedgecock, Madison, NY-G	8	52	6.5	13	1
Yoder, Todd, Was.	8	50	6.3	14	1
* Stewart, Jonathan, Car.	8	47	5.9	15	0
Curtis, Tony, Dal.	8	32	4.0	8	0
McMullen, Billy, Sea.	7	124	17.7	34	0
Fells, Daniel, St.L	7	81	11.6	26	0
Williams, Cadillac, T.B.	7	43	6.1	25	0
Hall, Korey, G.B.	7	38	5.4	11	1
Stanley, Derek, St.L	6	119	19.8	80t	1
Kleinsasser, Jimmy, Min.	6	92	15.3	34	0
* Finley, Jermichael, G.B.	6	74	12.3	35	1
Peterson, Adrian, Chi.	6	45	7.5	19	0
Hunt, Tony, Phi.	6	42	7.0	18	0
Turner, Michael, Atl.	6	41	6.8	18	0
Becht, Anthony, St.L	6	39	6.5	11	0
Hoover, Brad, Car.	6	39	6.5	12	0
Jacobs, Brandon, NY-G	6	36	6.0	9	0
Klecko, Dan, Phi.	6	36	6.0	12	0
* Schmitt, Owen, Sea.	6	29	4.8	7	0
Booker, Lorenzo, Phi.	6	11	1.8	8	0
Zeigler, Dominique, S.F.	5	97	19.4	31	0
Mills, Garrett, Min.	5	65	13.0	23	0
Burleson, Nate, Sea.	5	60	12.0	20t	1
Robinson, Laurent, Atl.	5	52	10.4	23	0
* Bumpus, Michael, Sea.	5	48	9.6	19	1
Bradshaw, Ahmad, NY-G	5	42	8.4	18t	1
Minor, Travis, St.L	5	35	7.0	16	0
Johnson, Darcy, NY-G	4	46	11.5	26	2
Heller, Will, Sea.	4	29	7.3	14	0
Cason, Aveion, Det.	4	27	6.8	15	0
* Manningham, Mario, NY-G	4	26	6.5	11	0
* Smith, Clifton, T.B.	4	24	6.0	13	0
Kuhn, John, G.B.	4	21	5.3	13	2
Norris, Moran, Det.	4	16	4.0	6	0
Castille, Tim, Ariz	4	11	2.8	5	0
Tuman, Jerame, Ariz	3	41	13.7	18	0
Payne, Logan, Sea.	3	39	13.0	22	0
Wynn, DeShawn, G.B.	3	30	10.0	16	0
* Davis, Fred, Was.	3	27	9.0	15	0
Hartsock, Ben, Atl.	3	26	8.7	17	0
Ferguson, Robert, Min.	3	25	8.3	9	0
Keasey, Zak, S.F.	3	25	8.3	12	0
Stovall, Maurice, T.B.	3	25	8.3	9	0
Cook, Jameel, T.B.	3	24	8.0	12	0
* Lumpkin, Kregg, G.B.	3	22	7.3	12	0
* Kelly, Malcolm, Was.	3	18	6.0	7	0
Ryan, Sean, N.O.-S.F.	3	15	5.0	8	0
Goings, Nick, Car.	3	1	0.3	3	0
Bajema, Billy, S.F.	2	34	17.0	29	0
Jones, Mark, Car.	2	32	16.0	19	0
Matthews, Michael, NY-G	2	26	13.0	13	0
Smith, Terrelle, Ariz	2	24	12.0	18	0
Stanback, Isaiah, Dal.	2	24	12.0	15	0
Bulger, Marc, St.L	2	17	8.5	11	0
Spach, Stephen, Ariz	2	15	7.5	8	0
Dugan, Jeff, Min.	2	12	6.0	9	0
* Jones, Felix, Dal.	2	10	5.0	7	0
Schobel, Matt, Phi.	2	10	5.0	5	0
* Sobomehin, Olaniyi, N.O.	2	8	4.0	10	0
Anderson, Deon, Dal.	2	7	3.5	6	1
Jones, Kevin, Chi.	2	5	2.5	3	0
Rader, Jason, Atl.	1	26	26.0	26	0
Middleton, Brandon, Det.	1	23	23.0	23	0
Campbell, Dan, Det.	1	21	21.0	21	0
Bell, Mike, N.O.	1	14	14.0	14	0
Clark, Brian, T.B.	1	12	12.0	12	0
Davis, Jason, Chi.	1	12	12.0	12	0
Alexander, Shaun, Was.	1	9	9.0	9	0
Rolle, Antrel, Ariz	1	9	9.0	9	0
Tapeh, Thomas, Min.	1	7	7.0	7	0
Bennett, Drew, St.L	1	4	4.0	4	0
Brown, Levi, Ariz	1	4	4.0	4	0
Rossum, Allen, S.F.	1	4	4.0	4	0
Weems, Eric, Atl.	1	4	4.0	4	0
Ortega, Buck, N.O.	1	3	3.0	3	0
Bennett, Michael, T.B.	1	2	2.0	2	0
Herremans, Todd, Phi.	1	1	1.0	1t	1
Gado, Samkon, St.L	1	-1	-1.0	-1	0
Cartwright, Rock, Was.	1	-7	-7.0	-7	0
Kendall, Pete, Was.	1	-9	-9.0	-9	0

*t = Touchdown; * Player that was a rookie in 2008*
Leader based on receptions

2008 INDIVIDUAL STATISTICS—INTERCEPTIONS

INTERCEPTIONS

INTERCEPTIONS

AFC: 9 Ed Reed, Baltimore
NFC: 7 Nick Collins, Green Bay
7 Charles Woodson, Green Bay

INTERCEPTIONS, GAME

AFC: 3 Leon Hall, Cincinnati at Cleveland, December 21 (87 yards, 1 TD)
NFC: 2 Charles Woodson, Green Bay at Detroit, September 14 (41 yards, 1 TD)
2 * Chris Horton, Washington vs. New Orleans, September 14 (10 yards, 0 TD)
2 Michael Johnson, N.Y. Giants vs. San Francisco, Oct. 19 (18 yards, 0 TD)
2 Oshiomogho Atogwe, St. Louis vs. Dallas, October 19 (59 yards, 0 TD)
2 Corey Webster, N.Y. Giants vs. Dallas, November 2 (58 yards, 0 TD)
2 Aaron Ross, N.Y. Giants vs. Baltimore, November 16 (60 yards, 1 TD)
2 * Dominique Rodgers-Cromartie, Arizona at Seattle, Nov. 16 (6 yards, 0 TD)
2 Ronde Barber, Tampa Bay at Detroit, November 23 (67 yards, 1 TD)
2 Lance Briggs, Chicago at St. Louis, November 23 (9 yards, 0 TD)
2 Jason David, New Orleans vs. Green Bay, November 24 (42 yards, 0 TD)
2 Terence Newman, Dallas vs. N.Y. Giants, December 14 (2 yards, 0 TD)
2 Ronald Bartell, St. Louis vs. San Francisco, December 21 (5 yards, 0 TD)
2 Josh Wilson, Seattle vs. N.Y. Jets, December 21 (2 yards, 0 TD)

YARDS

NFC: 295 Nick Collins, Green Bay
AFC: 264 Ed Reed, Baltimore

LONGEST

AFC: 107 Ed Reed, Baltimore vs. Philadelphia, November 23 - TD
NFC: 99 Aaron Rouse, Green Bay vs. Indianapolis, October 19 - TD
99 * Dominique Rodgers-Cromartie, Arizona vs. St. Louis, December 7 - TD

TOUCHDOWNS

NFC: 3 Nick Collins, Green Bay
AFC: 2 Jabari Greer, Buffalo
2 Rashean Mathis, Jacksonville
2 Ed Reed, Baltimore
2 Terrell Suggs, Baltimore

TEAM LEADERS, INTERCEPTIONS

AFC: BALTIMORE, 9, Ed Reed; BUFFALO, 3, Terrence McGee; CINCINNATI, 3, Leon Hall; CLEVELAND, 5, Brandon McDonald; DENVER, 2, Dré Bly; HOUSTON, 4, Jacques Reeves; INDIANAPOLIS, 4, Melvin Bullitt; JACKSONVILLE, 4, Rashean Mathis, Gerald Sensabaugh; KANSAS CITY, 4, Jarrad Page; MIAMI, 5, Andre' Goodman; NEW ENGLAND, 4, Brandon Meriweather; N.Y. JETS, 5, Darrelle Revis; OAKLAND, 3, Rashad Baker, DeAngelo Hall; Chris Johnson; PITTSBURGH, 7, Troy Polamalu; SAN DIEGO, 4, Stephen Cooper; TENNESSEE, 7, Michael Griffin

NFC: ARIZONA, 4, *Dominique Rodgers-Cromartie; ATLANTA, 3, Erik Coleman; CAROLINA, 3, Jon Beason, Chris Gamble; CHICAGO, 4, Kevin Payne; DALLAS, 4, Terence Newman; DETROIT, 1, Leigh Bodden, Ryan Nece; Corey Smith, Dewayne White; GREEN BAY, 7, Nick Collins, Charles Woodson; MINNESOTA, 2, Ben Leber, Benny Sapp; Madieu Williams, Antoine Winfield; NEW ORLEANS, 5, Jason David; N.Y. GIANTS, 3, James Butler, Aaron Ross, Corey Webster; PHILADELPHIA, 4, Asante Samuel; ST. LOUIS, 5, Oshiomogho Atogwe; SAN FRANCISCO, 3, Walt Harris, Takeo Spikes; SEATTLE, 4, Josh Wilson; TAMPA BAY, 4, Ronde Barber, *Aqib Talib; WASHINGTON, 3, *Chris Horton

TEAM CHAMPION

AFC: 26 Baltimore
NFC: 22 Chicago
22 Green Bay
22 Tampa Bay

NFL TOP TEN INTERCEPTORS

	No	Yards	Avg	Long	TD
Reed, Ed, Bal	9	264	29.3	107t	2
Collins, Nick, G.B.	7	295	42.1	62t	3
Griffin, Michael, Ten.	7	172	24.6	83t	1
Polamalu, Troy, Pit.	7	59	8.4	23	0
Woodson, Charles, G.B.	7	169	24.1	62t	2
Atogwe, Oshiomogho, St.L	5	91	18.2	43	0
David, Jason, N.O.	5	83	16.6	42	0
Finnegan, Cortland, Ten.	5	100	20.0	99t	1
Goodman, Andre', Mia.	5	53	10.6	55	0
Hall, DeAngelo, Oak.-Was.	5	37	7.4	21	0
McDonald, Brandon, Cle.	5	146	29.2	98	1
Revis, Darrelle, NYJ	5	38	7.6	32t	1
Williams, Tramon, G.B.	5	78	15.6	39	0

AFC—INDIVIDUAL INTERCEPTORS

	No	Yards	Avg	Long	TD
Reed, Ed, Bal.	9	264	29.3	107t	2
Griffin, Michael, Ten.	7	172	24.6	83t	1
Polamalu, Troy, Pit.	7	59	8.4	23	0
McDonald, Brandon, Cle.	5	146	29.2	98	1
Finnegan, Cortland, Ten.	5	100	20.0	99t	1
Goodman, Andre', Mia.	5	53	10.6	55	0
Revis, Darrelle, NYJ	5	38	7.6	32t	1
Mathis, Rashean, Jac.	4	151	37.8	72t	2
Reeves, Jacques, Hou.	4	108	27.0	44t	1
Hope, Chris, Ten.	4	53	13.3	39	0
Sensabaugh, Gerald, Jac.	4	38	9.5	23	0
Jones, Sean, Cle.	4	27	6.8	20	0
Meriweather, Brandon, N.E.	4	25	6.3	19	0
Cooper, Stephen, S.D.	4	11	2.8	10	0
Bullitt, Melvin, Ind.	4	7	1.8	3	0
Page, Jarrad, K.C.	4	2	0.5	2	0
Hayden, Kelvin, Ind.	3	135	45.0	85t	1
Wright, Eric, Cle.	3	131	43.7	94t	1
Hall, Leon, Cin.	3	87	29.0	50t	1
Johnson, Chris, Oak.	3	68	22.7	44	0
Carter, Tyrone, Pit.	3	64	21.3	32t	1
Allen, Will, Mia.	3	62	20.7	32t	1
O'Neal, Deltha, N.E.	3	49	16.3	47	0
Pool, Brodney, Cle.	3	45	15.0	24	0
Lewis, Ray, Bal.	3	43	14.3	29	0
McGee, Terrence, Buf.	3	36	12.0	36	0
Hill, Renaldo, Mia.	3	34	11.3	17	0
Jackson, D'Qwell, Cle.	3	29	9.7	16	0
McAlister, Chris, Bal.	3	28	9.3	16	0
Baker, Rashad, Oak.	3	8	2.7	8	0
Rolle, Samari, Bal.	3	5	1.7	3	0

	No	Yards	Avg	Long	TD
Hobbs, Ellis, N.E.	3	0	0.0	4	0
* Flowers, Brandon, K.C.	2	118	59.0	91t	1
Suggs, Terrell, Bal.	2	86	43.0	44t	2
Greer, Jabari, Buf.	2	75	37.5	42t	2
* Cason, Antoine, S.D.	2	69	34.5	59t	1
* Carr, Brandon, K.C.	2	67	33.5	35	0
Cromartie, Antonio, S.D.	2	66	33.0	52t	1
* McKelvin, Leodis, Buf.	2	64	32.0	64t	1
Rhodes, Kerry, NYJ	2	50	25.0	50	0
Poteat, Hank, NYJ	2	47	23.5	41	0
Ratliff, Keiwan, Ind.	2	37	18.5	35t	1
Wilson, Eugene, Hou.	2	36	18.0	19	0
Johnson, Brandon, Cin.	2	35	17.5	35	0
Mitchell, Kawika, Buf.	2	33	16.5	32	0
Williams, Brian, Jac.	2	31	15.5	27	0
Ayodele, Akin, Mia.	2	29	14.5	17	0
Townsend, Deshea, Pit.	2	27	13.5	25t	1
Bennett, Fred, Hou.	2	26	13.0	23	0
Adams, Mike, Cle.	2	18	9.0	18	0
Harper, Nick, Ten.	2	11	5.5	11	0
Jennings, Tim, Ind.	2	9	4.5	6	0
Ngata, Haloti, Bal.	2	8	4.0	7	0
Bly, Dre', Den.	2	5	2.5	5	0
Wilson, Gibril, Oak.	2	5	2.5	5	0
Jammer, Quentin, S.D.	2	2	1.0	2	0
Bethea, Antoine, Ind.	2	0	0.0	0	0
McFadden, Bryant, Pit.	2	0	0.0	0	0
Nelson, Reggie, Jac.	2	0	0.0	0	0
Robinson, Dunta, Hou.	2	0	0.0	0	0
Elam, Abram, NYJ	1	92	92.0	92t	1
Timmons, Lawrence, Pit.	1	89	89.0	89	0
Surtain, Patrick, K.C.	1	50	50.0	50	0
* Rivers, Keith, Cin.	1	39	39.0	39	0
* Branch, Tyvon, Oak.	1	36	36.0	36	0
Leonhard, Jim, Bal.	1	35	35.0	35t	1
* Barrett, Josh, Den.	1	34	34.0	34	0
Harrison, James, Pit.	1	33	33.0	33	0
* Leggett, Maurice, K.C.	1	27	27.0	27t	1
Barrett, David, NYJ	1	25	25.0	25t	1
* Merling, Phillip, Mia.	1	25	25.0	25t	1
Bowens, David, NYJ	1	24	24.0	24	0
Crocker, Chris, Cin.	1	22	22.0	22	0
Joseph, Johnathan, Cin.	1	22	22.0	22	0
Hughes, Dante, Ind.	1	16	16.0	16	0
* Wilhite, Jonathan, N.E.	1	16	16.0	16	0
Ball, Dave, Ten.	1	15	15.0	15t	1
Jones, Dhani, Cin.	1	13	13.0	13	0
Paymah, Karl, Den.	1	13	13.0	13	0
Gay, William, Pit.	1	12	12.0	12	0
Ndukwe, Chinedum, Cin.	1	12	12.0	12	0
Washington, Fabian, Bal.	1	12	12.0	12	0
Thomas, Marcus, Den.	1	11	11.0	11	0
Posluszny, Paul, Buf.	1	9	9.0	9	0
Sanders, James, N.E.	1	9	9.0	9	0
Starks, Randy, Mia.	1	8	8.0	8	0
Weaver, Anthony, Hou.	1	8	8.0	8	0
Wilhelm, Matt, S.D.	1	8	8.0	8	0
Johnson, Derrick, K.C.	1	7	7.0	7	0
* Lynch, Corey, Cin.	1	6	6.0	6	0
Smith, Eric, NYJ	1	6	6.0	6	0
Woodley, LaMarr, Pit.	1	6	6.0	6	0
Vrabel, Mike, N.E.	1	5	5.0	5	0
Castillo, Luis, S.D.	1	4	4.0	4	0
Cousin, Terry, Cle.	1	4	4.0	4	0
Davis, Andra, Cle.	1	4	4.0	4	0
Dobbins, Tim, S.D.	1	4	4.0	4	0
McGraw, Jon, K.C.	1	4	4.0	4	0
Weddle, Eric, S.D.	1	3	3.0	3	0
Allen, Jason, Mia.	1	2	2.0	2	0
Wimbley, Kamerion, Cle.	1	2	2.0	2	0
Culver, Tyrone, Mia.	1	1	1.0	1	0
Asomugha, Nnamdi, Oak.	1	0	0.0	0	0
Bailey, Champ, Den.	1	0	0.0	0	0
Carr, Chris, Ten.	1	0	0.0	0	0
Clark, Ryan, Pit.	1	0	0.0	0	0
Diles, Zach, Hou.	1	0	0.0	0	0
Harrison, Rodney, N.E.	1	0	0.0	0	0
* Harvey, Derrick, Jac.	1	0	0.0	0	0
Jones, Nate, Mia.	1	0	0.0	0	0
* Lowery, Dwight, NYJ	1	0	0.0	0	0
Morrison, Kirk, Oak.	1	0	0.0	0	0
Oliver, Paul, S.D.	1	0	0.0	0	0
Pollard, Bernard, K.C.	1	0	0.0	0	0
Sanders, Bob, Ind.	1	0	0.0	0	0
Taylor, Ike, Pit.	1	0	0.0	0	0
Walker, Frank, Bal.	1	0	0.0	0	0
White, Marvin, Cin.	1	0	0.0	0	0
Williams, Sam, Oak.	1	0	0.0	0	0
Howard, Thomas, Oak.	1	-3	-3.0	-3	0
Bannan, Justin, Bal.	1	-4	-4.0	-4	0

*t = Touchdown; *Player that was a rookie in 2008*
Leader based on interceptions

NFC—INDIVIDUAL INTERCEPTORS

	No	Yards	Avg	Long	TD
Collins, Nick, G.B.	7	295	42.1	62t	3
Woodson, Charles, G.B.	7	169	24.1	62t	2
Atogwe, Oshiomogho, St.L	5	91	18.2	43	0
David, Jason, N.O.	5	83	16.6	42	0
Williams, Tramon, G.B.	5	78	15.6	39	0
Hall, DeAngelo, Oak.-Was.	5	37	7.4	21	0
* Rodgers-Cromartie, Domin, Ariz	4	157	39.3	99t	1
Payne, Kevin, Chi.	4	147	36.8	50	0
Wilson, Josh, Sea.	4	135	33.8	75t	1
Barber, Ronde, T.B.	4	69	17.3	65t	1
Samuel, Asante, Phi.	4	64	16.0	50t	1
* Talib, Aqib, T.B.	4	32	8.0	19	0
Newman, Terence, Dal.	4	2	0.5	2	0
Phillips, Jermaine, T.B.	3	72	24.0	58	0
Webster, Corey, NY-G	3	65	21.7	57	0
Butler, James, NY-G	3	62	20.7	47	0
Ross, Aaron, NY-G	3	58	19.3	50t	1
Mikell, Quintin, Phi.	3	53	17.7	41	0
Beason, Jon, Car.	3	52	17.3	44	0
Tillman, Charles, Chi.	3	52	17.3	26t	1
Coleman, Erik, Atl.	3	48	16.0	32	0
Bartell, Ronald, St.L	3	29	9.7	24	0
Harris, Walt, S.F.	3	25	8.3	24	0
Gamble, Chris, Car.	3	23	7.7	19	0
Spikes, Takeo, S.F.	3	14	4.7	13	0
* Horton, Chris, Was.	3	13	4.3	10	0
Briggs, Lance, Chi.	3	12	4.0	9	0
Rouse, Aaron, G.B.	2	136	68.0	99t	1
Piscitelli, Sabby, T.B.	2	106	53.0	84	0
Lucas, Ken, Car.	2	74	37.0	43	0
Rogers, Carlos, Was.	2	73	36.5	42	0
Adams, Gaines, T.B.	2	50	25.0	45t	1
Dansby, Karlos, Ariz	2	47	23.5	34	0
Wilson, Adrian, Ariz	2	37	18.5	28	0
Buchanon, Phillip, T.B.	2	33	16.5	26t	1
Grant, Deon, Sea.	2	31	15.5	31	0
Leber, Ben, Min.	2	29	14.5	28	0
Fujita, Scott, N.O.	2	19	9.5	17	0
Johnson, Michael, NY-G	2	18	9.0	18	0
Landry, LaRon, Was.	2	18	9.0	13	0
Clements, Nate, S.F.	2	13	6.5	13	0
Kaesviharn, Kevin, N.O.	2	13	6.5	13	0

2008 INDIVIDUAL STATISTICS—INTERCEPTIONS

	No	Yards	Avg	Long	TD
Sapp, Benny, Min.	2	13	6.5	14	0
Urlacher, Brian, Chi.	2	11	5.5	11	0
Houston, Chris, Atl.	2	10	5.0	10t	1
Ruud, Barrett, T.B.	2	10	5.0	10	0
Winfield, Antoine, Min.	2	5	2.5	4	0
Young, Usama, N.O.	2	3	1.5	3	0
Brown, Tarell, S.F.	2	1	0.5	1	0
Brown, Mike, Chi.	2	0	0.0	0	0
Williams, Madieu, Min.	2	-1	-0.5	0	0
* Jackson, Chevis, Atl.	1	95	95.0	95t	1
Willis, Patrick, S.F.	1	86	86.0	86t	1
Parker, Juqua, Phi.	1	55	55.0	55t	1
Dockery, Kevin, NY-G	1	44	44.0	44	0
* Steltz, Craig, Chi.	1	44	44.0	44	0
Manning, Danieal, Chi.	1	42	42.0	42	0
Tuck, Justin, NY-G	1	41	41.0	41t	1
Rolle, Antrel, Ariz	1	40	40.0	40t	1
Okeafor, Chike, Ariz	1	39	39.0	39	0
Milloy, Lawyer, Atl.	1	38	38.0	38	0
Babineaux, Jordan, Sea.	1	35	35.0	35t	1
Dawkins, Brian, Phi.	1	25	25.0	25	0
Grimes, Brent, Atl.	1	25	25.0	25	0
Jackson, Tanard, T.B.	1	25	25.0	25	0
* Porter, Tracy, N.O.	1	25	25.0	25	0
Brown, Sheldon, Phi.	1	23	23.0	23	0
Bullocks, Josh, N.O.	1	23	23.0	23	0
* Jenkins, Mike, Dal.	1	23	23.0	23t	1
Madison, Sam, NY-G	1	21	21.0	21	0
Patterson, Mike, Phi.	1	21	21.0	21	0
Nece, Ryan, Det.	1	18	18.0	18	0
Bradley, Stewart, Phi.	1	17	17.0	17	0
* Kehl, Bryan, NY-G	1	17	17.0	17	0
Boley, Michael, Atl.	1	16	16.0	16	0
Brown, Fakhir, St.L	1	16	16.0	16	0
Craft, Jason, St.L	1	16	16.0	16	0
* Godfrey, Charles, Car.	1	16	16.0	16	0
Harris, Chris, Car.	1	16	16.0	16	0
Tatupu, Lofa, Sea.	1	16	16.0	16	0
McKenzie, Mike, N.O.	1	14	14.0	14	0
Hanson, Joselio, Phi.	1	13	13.0	13	0
* Thomas, Terrell, NY-G	1	13	13.0	13	0
Sharper, Darren, Min.	1	12	12.0	12	0
Ellis, Greg, Dal.	1	11	11.0	11	0
Marshall, Richard, Car.	1	11	11.0	11	0
Howard, Darren, Phi.	1	8	8.0	8	0
Vilma, Jonathan, N.O.	1	8	8.0	8	0
Wade, Jonathan, St.L	1	8	8.0	8	0
Bigby, Atari, G.B.	1	7	7.0	7	0
Graham, Corey, Chi.	1	6	6.0	6	0
McIntosh, Rocky, Was.	1	4	4.0	4	0
Bodden, Leigh, Det.	1	2	2.0	2	0
Witherspoon, Will, St.L	1	2	2.0	2	0
Foxworth, Domonique, Atl.	1	1	1.0	1	0
Green, Eric, Ariz	1	1	1.0	1	0
June, Cato, T.B.	1	1	1.0	1	0
* Bowman, Zack, Chi.	1	0	0.0	0	0
Brown, Ralph, Ariz	1	0	0.0	0	0
Diggs, Na'il, Car.	1	0	0.0	0	0
Gordon, Charles, Min.	1	0	0.0	0	0
Griffin, Cornelius, Was.	1	0	0.0	0	0
Hamlin, Ken, Dal.	1	0	0.0	0	0
Henry, Anthony, Dal.	1	0	0.0	0	0
Hood, Roderick, Ariz	1	0	0.0	0	0
* Johnson, Tyrell, Min.	1	0	0.0	0	0
McBride, Trumaine, Chi.	1	0	0.0	0	0
Ogunleye, Adewale, Chi.	1	0	0.0	0	0
* Phillips, Kenny, NY-G	1	0	0.0	0	0
Sheppard, Lito, Phi.	1	0	0.0	0	0
Smith, Corey, Det.	1	0	0.0	0	0
Smith, Justin, S.F.	1	0	0.0	0	0
Smoot, Fred, Was.	1	0	0.0	0	0
Springs, Shawn, Was.	1	0	0.0	0	0
Trufant, Marcus, Sea.	1	0	0.0	0	0
Vasher, Nathan, Chi.	1	0	0.0	0	0
Brooks, Derrick, T.B.	1	-2	-2.0	-2	0
Brown, Alex, Chi.	1	-2	-2.0	-2	0
Griffin, Cedric, Min.	1	-2	-2.0	-2	0
White, Dewayne, Det.	1	-4	-4.0	-4	0

t = Touchdown; Leader based on interceptions
** Player that was a rookie in 2008*

AMERICAN FOOTBALL CONFERENCE—INTERCEPTIONS

	No	Yards	Avg	Long	TD
Baltimore	26	477	18.3	107t	5
Cleveland	23	406	17.7	98	2
Pittsburgh	20	290	14.5	89	2
Tennessee	20	351	17.6	99t	3
Miami	18	214	11.9	55	2
Oakland	16	145	9.1	44	0
Indianapolis	15	204	13.6	85t	2
San Diego	15	167	11.1	59t	2
New England	14	104	7.4	47	0
N.Y. Jets	14	282	20.1	92t	3
Jacksonville	13	220	16.9	72t	2
Kansas City	13	275	21.2	91t	2
Cincinnati	12	236	19.7	50t	1
Houston	12	178	14.8	44t	1
Buffalo	10	217	21.7	64t	3
Denver	6	63	10.5	34	0
AFC Total	247	3829	15.5	107t	30
AFC Average	15.4	239.3	15.5	—	1.9

NATIONAL FOOTBALL CONFERENCE—INTERCEPTIONS

	No	Yards	Avg	Long	TD
Chicago	22	312	14.2	50	1
Green Bay	22	685	31.1	99t	6
Tampa Bay	22	396	18.0	84	3
N.Y. Giants	17	339	19.9	57	2
New Orleans	15	188	12.5	42	0
Philadelphia	15	279	18.6	55t	2
Arizona	13	321	24.7	99t	2
Washington	13	114	8.8	42	0
Carolina	12	192	16.0	44	0
Minnesota	12	56	4.7	28	0
St. Louis	12	162	13.5	43	0
San Francisco	12	139	11.6	86t	1
Atlanta	10	233	23.3	95t	2
Seattle	9	217	24.1	75t	2
Dallas	8	36	4.5	23t	1
Detroit	4	16	4.0	18	0
NFC Total	218	3685	16.9	99t	22
NFC Average	13.6	230.3	16.9	—	1.4
League Total	465	7514	—	107t	52
League Average	14.5	234.8	16.2	—	1.6

KICKOFF RETURNS

YARDS PER RETURN
NFC: 29.7 Danieal Manning, Chicago
AFC: 28.5 Ellis Hobbs, New England

YARDS
NFC: 1753 Josh Wilson, Seattle
AFC: 1468 * Leodis McKelvin, Buffalo

YARDS, GAME
NFC: 247 * Felix Jones, Dallas vs. Philadelphia, September 15 (6 returns, 1 TD)
AFC: 237 Ellis Hobbs, New England vs. Miami, September 21 (6 returns, 0 TD)
237 Josh Cribbs, Cleveland vs. Baltimore, November 2 (7 returns, 1 TD)

LONGEST
NFC: 104 Allen Rossum, San Francisco at Arizona, November 10 - TD
AFC: 103 Darren Sproles, San Diego at Denver, September 14 - TD

RETURNS
NFC: 69 Josh Wilson, Seattle
AFC: 53 Darren Sproles, San Diego

RETURNS, GAME
NFC: 9 Allen Rossum, San Francisco vs. Philadelphia, October 12 (194 yards, 0 TD)
9 Steve Breaston, Arizona at New England, December 21 (141 yards, 0 TD)
AFC: 8 Darren Sproles, San Diego at New Orleans, October 26 (201 yards, 0 TD)
8 Ted Ginn Jr., Miami vs. New England, November 23 (154 yards, 0 TD)
8 Chad Jackson, Denver at San Diego, December 28 (162 yards, 0 TD)

TOUCHDOWNS
AFC: 2 Justin Miller, N.Y. Jets-Oakland
NFC: 1 J.J. Arrington, Arizona
1 * Quintin Demps, Philadelphia
1 * Felix Jones, Dallas
1 Danieal Manning, Chicago
1 Allen Rossum, San Francisco
1 * Clifton Smith, Tampa Bay

TEAM CHAMPION
AFC: 25.4 Tennessee
NFC: 25.3 Seattle

NFL TOP TEN KICKOFF RETURNERS

	No	Yards	Avg	Long	TD
Manning, Danieal, Chi.	36	1070	29.7	83t	1
Hobbs, Ellis, N.E.	45	1281	28.5	95t	1
* McKelvin, Leodis, Buf.	52	1468	28.2	98t	1
Carr, Chris, Ten.	35	984	28.1	52	0
* Smith, Clifton, T.B.	36	992	27.6	97t	1
Rossum, Allen, S.F.	47	1259	26.8	104t	1
* Royal, Eddie, Den.	23	600	26.1	95	0
Sproles, Darren, S.D.	53	1376	26.0	103t	1
Norwood, Jerious, Atl.	51	1311	25.7	92	0
Washington, Leon, NYJ	48	1231	25.6	94	1

AFC—INDIVIDUAL KICKOFF RETURNERS

	No	Yards	Avg	Long	TD
Hobbs, Ellis, N.E.	45	1281	28.5	95t	1
* McKelvin, Leodis, Buf.	52	1468	28.2	98t	1
Carr, Chris, Ten.	35	984	28.1	52	0
* Royal, Eddie, Den.	23	600	26.1	95	0
Sproles, Darren, S.D.	53	1376	26.0	103t	1
Washington, Leon, NYJ	48	1231	25.6	94	1
Cribbs, Josh, Cle.	44	1110	25.2	92t	1
Miller, Justin, NYJ-Oak.	33	816	24.7	92t	2
Savage, Dantrell, K.C.	26	633	24.3	59	0
Holt, Glenn, Cin.	46	1110	24.1	60	0
* Witherspoon, Brian, Jac.	52	1250	24.0	51	0
Higgins, Johnnie Lee, Oak.	36	842	23.4	69	0
Davis, Andre, Hou.	43	993	23.1	50	0
Hall, Andre, Den.	21	469	22.3	28	0
* Garcon, Pierre, Ind.	22	475	21.6	39	0
Figurs, Yamon, Bal.	29	608	21.0	39	0
Ginn, Ted Jr., Mia.	32	657	20.5	41	0
(Nonqualifiers)					
* Robinson, Kevin, K.C.	19	420	22.1	36	0
Russell, Gary, Pit.	16	371	23.2	43	0
* Simpson, Chad, Ind.	15	344	22.9	46	0
Davenport, Najeh, Pit.-Ind.	15	324	21.6	27	0
* Charles, Jamaal, K.C.	15	321	21.4	40	0
* Bess, Davone, Mia.	14	311	22.2	32	0
* Caldwell, Andre, Cin.	13	338	26.0	43	0
Jones-Drew, Maurice, Jac.	13	281	21.6	33	0
Jones, Jacoby, Hou.	13	280	21.5	30	0
Jackson, Fred, Buf.	12	181	15.1	30	0
* Slater, Matt, N.E.	11	155	14.1	31	0
Moore, Mewelde, Pit.	10	185	18.5	24	0
Moats, Ryan, Hou.	9	212	23.6	32	0
Sams, B.J., K.C.	9	180	20.0	36	0
Cobbs, Patrick, Mia.	8	189	23.6	60	0
Young, Selvin, Den.	8	176	22.0	31	0
Leonhard, Jim, Bal.	8	163	20.4	30	0
Jackson, Chad, Den.	8	162	20.3	24	0
* Rice, Ray, Bal.	7	161	23.0	30	0
* Hawkins, Lavelle, Ten.	7	130	18.6	23	0
* Mendenhall, Rashard, Pit.	6	115	19.2	27	0
Davis, Carey, Pit.	6	106	17.7	24	0
* Branch, Tyvon, Oak.	6	89	14.8	20	0
* Leggett, Maurice, K.C.	5	103	20.6	30	0
Davis, Chris, Ten.	4	119	29.8	33	0
Williamson, Troy, Jac.	4	84	21.0	26	0
* Hillis, Peyton, Den.	4	65	16.3	25	0
Watson, Kenny, Cin.	4	63	15.8	24	0
Smith, Brad, NYJ	4	39	9.8	26	0
Bowens, David, NYJ	4	37	9.3	14	0
* Lawson, Gerard, Cle.	3	72	24.0	43	0
McGee, Terrence, Buf.	3	62	20.7	27	0
Steptoe, Syndric, Cle.	3	61	20.3	23	0
* Hester, Jacob, S.D.	3	42	14.0	20	0
Johnson, Spencer, Buf.	3	40	13.3	19	0
Cromartie, Antonio, S.D.	3	37	12.3	26	0
Dinkins, Darnell, Cle.	3	37	12.3	14	0
Leach, Vonta, Hou.	3	34	11.3	15	0
* Cox, Mike, K.C.	3	11	3.7	8	0
* Zbikowski, Tom, Bal.	2	48	24.0	26	0
Russell, Cliff, Den.	2	44	22.0	25	0
Parrish, Roscoe, Buf.	2	40	20.0	25	0
Morris, Sammy, N.E.	2	37	18.5	24	0
Faulk, Kevin, N.E.	2	36	18.0	25	0
Griffin, Michael, Ten.	2	32	16.0	28	0
Owens, Montell, Jac.	2	30	15.0	20	0
Lawton, Luke, Oak.	2	29	14.5	15	0
London, Brandon, Mia.	2	28	14.0	17	0
Hall, Ahmard, Ten.	2	21	10.5	13	0
Jones, Greg, Jac.	2	19	9.5	10	0
Manumaleuna, Brandon, S.D.	2	14	7.0	9	0
Cotchery, Jerricho, NYJ	1	54	54.0	54	0
Neal, Stephen, N.E.	1	27	27.0	27	0

2008 INDIVIDUAL STATISTICS—KICKOFF RETURNS

	No	Yards	Avg	Long	TD
Welker, Wes, N.E.	1	26	26.0	26	0
Coats, Daniel, Cin.	1	18	18.0	18	0
Gordon, Cletis, S.D.	1	18	18.0	18	0
McGraw, Jon, K.C.	1	18	18.0	18	0
McIntyre, Corey, Buf.	1	18	18.0	18	0
* Johnson, Chris, Ten.	1	17	17.0	17	0
Mustard, Chad, Den.	1	17	17.0	17	0
Taylor, Chris, Hou.	1	17	17.0	17	0
Carter, Tyrone, Pit.	1	16	16.0	16	0
* Franklin, Will, K.C.	1	16	16.0	16	0
* Stevens, Craig, Ten.	1	16	16.0	16	0
Wright, Jason, Cle.	1	15	15.0	15	0
Bush, Michael, Oak.	1	14	14.0	14	0
Ndukwe, Ike, Mia.	1	14	14.0	14	0
Reyes, Tutan, Jac.	1	14	14.0	14	0
Taylor, Herb, K.C.	1	14	14.0	14	0
* Johnson, James, Cin.	1	13	13.0	13	0
Johnson, Jarret, Bal.	1	13	13.0	13	0
Clayton, Mark, Bal.	1	12	12.0	12	0
Reid, Darrell, Ind.	1	12	12.0	12	0
Dawson, Keyunta, Ind.	1	11	11.0	11	0
* Tamme, Jacob, Ind.	1	11	11.0	11	0
Ali, Charles, Cle.	1	10	10.0	10	0
Engelberger, John, Den.	1f	9	9.0	9	0
* Gunheim, Greyson, Oak.	1	9	9.0	9	0
* Keller, Dustin, NYJ	1	9	9.0	9	0
Turner, Robert, NYJ	1	9	9.0	9	0
Bell, Tatum, Den.	1	8	8.0	8	0
* Simpson, Jerome, Cin.	1	8	8.0	8	0
Cieslak, Brad, Cle.	1	7	7.0	7	0
Sapp, Cecil, Hou.	1	7	7.0	7	0
White, Chris, Hou.	1	7	7.0	7	0
Wilson, George, Buf.	1	7	7.0	7	0
Franks, Bubba, NYJ	1	6	6.0	6	0
Harrison, Marvin, Ind.	1	3	3.0	3	0
Spaeth, Matt, Pit.	1f	3	3.0	3	0
Neal, Lorenzo, Bal.	1	2	2.0	2	0
Hall, Leon, Cin.	1	1	1.0	1	0
Fasano, Anthony, Mia.	1	0	0.0	0	0
* Johnson, Steve, Buf.	1	0	0.0	0	0
Jones, Edgar, Bal.	1	0	0.0	0	0
Jones, Nate, Mia.	1	0	0.0	0	0
Martinez, Glenn, Den.	1	0	0.0	0	0
McKinney, Seth, Cle.	1	0	0.0	0	0
Putzier, Jeb, Den.	1	0	0.0	0	0
Sowells, Isaac, Cle.	1	0	0.0	0	0
Walter, Kevin, Hou.	1	0	0.0	0	0
* Wheeler, Philip, Ind.	1	0	0.0	0	0
Stewart, Tony, Oak.	0f	0	—	—	0
Naanee, Legedu, S.D.	0	-2	—	-2	0

t = Touchdown; f = Fair Catch
Leader based on average return, minimum 20 returns
* *Player that was a rookie in 2008*

NFC—INDIVIDUAL KICKOFF RETURNERS

	No	Yards	Avg	Long	TD
Manning, Danieal, Chi.	36	1070	29.7	83t	1
* Smith, Clifton, T.B.	36	992	27.6	97t	1
Rossum, Allen, S.F.	47	1259	26.8	104t	1
Norwood, Jerious, Atl.	51	1311	25.7	92	0
Arrington, J.J., Ariz	36	923	25.6	93t	1
Cartwright, Rock, Was.	51	1307	25.6	87	0
Thomas, Pierre, N.O.	31	793	25.6	88	0
Wilson, Josh, Sea.	69	1753	25.4	61	0
* Demps, Quintin, Phi.	52	1314	25.3	100t	1
Stanley, Derek, St.L	25	620	24.8	75	0
Jones, Mark, Car.	40	958	24.0	59	0
Roby, Courtney, Ind.-N.O.	24	573	23.9	62	0
Hicks, Maurice, Min.	29	690	23.8	38	0
Cason, Aveion, Det.	32	746	23.3	46	0
Bradshaw, Ahmad, NY-G	39	867	22.2	58	0
Middleton, Brandon, Det.	39	864	22.2	42	0
Hester, Devin, Chi.	31	679	21.9	51	0
Austin, Miles, Dal.	29	624	21.5	36	0
Blackmon, Will, G.B.	55	1157	21.0	45	0
Hall, Dante, St.L	37	763	20.6	41	0
Breaston, Steve, Ariz	33	667	20.2	38	0
(Nonqualifiers)					
* Forsett, Justin, Sea.-Ind.-Sea.	18	422	23.4	32	0
* Jones, Felix, Dal.	16	434	27.1	98t	1
* Stewart, Jonathan, Car.	15	349	23.3	38	0
* Jackson, Dexter, T.B.	14	327	23.4	45	0
Walker, Delanie, S.F.	13	257	19.8	35	0
* Nelson, Jordy, G.B.	11	208	18.9	45	0
Taylor, Chester, Min.	10	234	23.4	37	0
Stanback, Isaiah, Dal.	10	218	21.8	58	0
* Reynaud, Darius, Min.	8	201	25.1	49	0
Moss, Sinorice, NY-G	8	162	20.3	27	0
Darby, Kenneth, St.L	7	173	24.7	32	0
Jones, Adam, Dal.	7	155	22.1	41	0
Minor, Travis, St.L	7	155	22.1	34	0
Robinson, Michael, S.F.	6	135	22.5	34	0
Allison, Aundrae, Min.	6	100	16.7	22	0
Wolfe, Garrett, Chi.	5	98	19.6	33	0
* Balmer, Kentwan, S.F.	5	47	9.4	14	0
Green, Skyler, N.O.	4	133	33.3	60	0
* Thomas, Marcus, Det.	4	93	23.3	27	0
* Scandrick, Orlando, Dal.	4	81	20.3	25	0
* Douglas, Harry, Atl.	4	46	11.5	22	0
Hixon, Domenik, NY-G	3	180	60.0	83	0
Clayton, Michael, T.B.	3	69	23.0	29	0
Clark, Brian, T.B.	3	54	18.0	22	0
Lewis, Greg, Phi.	3	43	14.3	31	0
Fitzsimmons, Casey, Det.	3	41	13.7	16	0
Kleinsasser, Jimmy, Min.	3	36	12.0	14	0
Gordon, Charles, Min.	2	61	30.5	42	0
McKie, Jason, Chi.	2	38	19.0	20	0
Copper, Terrance, N.O.	2	35	17.5	18	0
Sellers, Mike, Was.	2	32	16.0	17	0
Tahi, Naufahu, Min.	2	31	15.5	20	0
Furrey, Mike, Det.	2	30	15.0	16	0
Ryan, Sean, Mia.-S.F.	2	28	14.0	14	0
Bajema, Billy, S.F.	2	27	13.5	14	0
Rosario, Dante, Car.	2	26	13.0	18	0
Smith, Corey, Det.	2	26	13.0	17	0
Morey, Sean, Ariz	2	23	11.5	15	0
Smith, Alex, T.B.	2	17	8.5	17	0
* Campbell, Calais, Ariz	2f	16	8.0	16	0
Stecker, Aaron, N.O.	2	10	5.0	10	0
Johnson, Darcy, NY-G	2	2	1.0	2	0
Urban, Jerheme, Ariz	2	1	0.5	1	0
Moore, Lance, N.O.	1	36	36.0	36	0
Droughns, Reuben, NY-G	1	34	34.0	34	0
Battle, Arnaz, S.F.	1	28	28.0	28	0
Moss, Santana, Was.	1	26	26.0	26	0
* Avery, Donnie, St.L	1	21	21.0	21	0
Duckett, T.J., Sea.	1	21	21.0	21	0
Ward, Derrick, NY-G	1	21	21.0	21	0
Weems, Eric, Atl.	1	19	19.0	19	0
McQuarters, R.W., NY-G	1	18	18.0	18	0
Spencer, Anthony, Dal.	1	18	18.0	18	0
Barbre, Allen, G.B.	1	17	17.0	17	0
Mughelli, Ovie, Atl.	1	17	17.0	17	0
Thrash, James, Was.	1	17	17.0	17	0
Peterson, Adrian, Min.	1	16	16.0	16	0
Bridges, Jeremy, Car.	1	15	15.0	15	0
Stovall, Maurice, T.B.	1	15	15.0	15	0

	No	Yards	Avg	Long	TD
Buckhalter, Correll, Phi.	1	14	14.0	14	0
* Greco, John, St.L	1	14	14.0	14	0
Avant, Jason, Phi.	1	13	13.0	13	0
* Davis, Kellen, Chi.	1	13	13.0	13	0
Gilmore, John, T.B.	1	12	12.0	12	0
Hoover, Brad, Car.	1	12	12.0	12	0
* Jackson, DeSean, Phi.	1	12	12.0	12	0
King, Jeff, Car.	1	12	12.0	12	0
Klecko, Dan, Phi.	1	12	12.0	12	0
Crayton, Patrick, Dal.	1	11	11.0	11	0
Peterson, Adrian, Chi.	1	11	11.0	11	0
Wade, Jonathan, St.L	1	11	11.0	11	0
Davis, Rashied, Chi.	1	10	10.0	10	0
Wilkerson, Ben, Atl.	1	10	10.0	10	0
Anderson, Deon, Dal.	1	9	9.0	9	0
Meachem, Robert, N.O.	1	9	9.0	9	0
Ortega, Buck, N.O.	1	8	8.0	8	0
Cody, Shaun, Det.	1	7	7.0	7	0
Hunter, Jason, G.B.	1	7	7.0	7	0
Finneran, Brian, Atl.	1	5	5.0	5	0
Curtis, Tony, Dal.	1	4	4.0	4	0
Looker, Dane, St.L	1	4	4.0	4	0
Abiamiri, Victor, Phi.	1	3	3.0	3	0
Campbell, Mark, N.O.	1	0	0.0	0	0
Spikes, Takeo, S.F.	1	0	0.0	0	0
Woodson, Charles, G.B.	1	-2	-2.0	-2	0
Boschetti, Ryan, Was.	0f	0	—	—	0
Heller, Will, Sea.	0f	0	—	—	0
Karney, Mike, N.O.	0f	0	—	—	0

t = Touchdown; f = Fair Catch
Leader based on average return, minimum 20 returns
** Player that was a rookie in 2008*

AMERICAN FOOTBALL CONFERENCE—KICKOFF RETURNS

	No	Yards	Avg	Long	TD
Tennessee	52	1319	25.4	52	0
New England	62	1562	25.2	95t	1
Buffalo	75	1816	24.2	98t	1
San Diego	62	1485	24.0	103t	1
Cincinnati	67	1551	23.1	60	0
N.Y. Jets	61	1407	23.1	94	1
Oakland	78	1777	22.8	92t	2
Jacksonville	74	1678	22.7	51	0
Cleveland	58	1312	22.6	92t	1
Denver	71	1550	21.8	95	0
Houston	72	1550	21.5	50	0
Kansas City	80	1716	21.5	59	0
Indianapolis	63	1312	20.8	46	0
Pittsburgh	50	1013	20.3	43	0
Miami	60	1213	20.2	60	0
Baltimore	50	1007	20.1	39	0
AFC Total	1035	23268	22.5	103t	7
AFC Average	64.7	1454.3	22.5	—	0.4

NATIONAL FOOTBALL CONFERENCE—KICKOFF RETURNS

	No	Yards	Avg	Long	TD
Seattle	77	1948	25.3	61	0
Washington	55	1382	25.1	87	0
Chicago	77	1919	24.9	83t	1
Tampa Bay	60	1486	24.8	97t	1
New Orleans	62	1496	24.1	88	0
Atlanta	59	1408	23.9	92	0
Philadelphia	60	1411	23.5	100t	1
N.Y. Giants	55	1284	23.3	83	0
San Francisco	76	1767	23.3	104t	1
Carolina	60	1372	22.9	59	0
Minnesota	61	1369	22.4	49	0
Dallas	70	1554	22.2	98t	1
St. Louis	80	1761	22.0	75	0
Detroit	83	1807	21.8	46	0
Arizona	75	1630	21.7	93t	1
Green Bay	69	1387	20.1	45	0
NFC Total	1079	24981	23.2	104t	6
NFC Average	67.4	1561.3	23.2	—	0.4
League Total	2114	48249	—	104t	13
League Average	66.1	1507.8	22.8	—	0.4

2008 INDIVIDUAL STATISTICS—PUNTING

PUNTING

AVERAGE YARDS PER PUNT

NFC: 50.0 Donnie Jones, St. Louis
AFC: 48.8 Shane Lechler, Oakland

NET AVERAGE YARDS PER PUNT

AFC: 41.2 Shane Lechler, Oakland
NFC: 41.1 Donnie Jones, St. Louis

LONGEST

NFC: 82 Andy Lee, San Francisco vs. New England, October 5
AFC: 75 Craig Hentrich, Tennessee vs. Indianapolis, October 27

PUNTS

AFC: 100 Kyle Larson, Cincinnati
NFC: 96 Brad Maynard, Chicago

PUNTS, GAME

AFC: 11 Shane Lechler, Oakland vs. Carolina, November 9 (556 yards)
11 Kyle Larson, Cincinnati vs. Philadelphia, November 16 (397 yards) - (OT)
11 Kyle Larson, Cincinnati vs. Baltimore, November 30 (480 yards)
NFC: 11 Ryan Plackemeier, Seattle at Buffalo, September 7 (450 yards)
11 Jon Ryan, Seattle vs. Philadelphia, November 2 (508 yards)

TEAM CHAMPION

NFC: 49.6 St. Louis
AFC: 48.8 Oakland

AMERICAN FOOTBALL CONFERENCE—PUNTING

	Total Punts	Yards	Long	Avg	TB	Blk	Opp Ret	Return Yards	In 20	Net Avg
Oakland	90	4391	70	48.8	13	0	43	425	33	41.2
Denver	46	2150	64	46.7	4	0	28	330	13	37.8
San Diego	51	2332	67	45.7	5	0	23	146	19	40.9
Cleveland	76	3443	65	45.3	11	0	32	235	24	39.3
Baltimore	84	3777	74	45.0	9	0	38	245	34	39.9
Indianapolis	53	2343	64	44.2	2	0	27	249	23	38.8
Kansas City	82	3622	73	44.2	12	0	33	307	28	37.5
Buffalo	58	2557	63	44.1	5	0	18	187	23	39.1
New England	50	2200	70	44.0	10	0	11	158	20	36.8
Miami	74	3249	71	43.9	7	0	37	485	24	35.5
Jacksonville	67	2904	60	43.3	8	0	31	269	14	36.9
Tennessee	87	3725	75	42.8	13	0	32	290	27	36.5
Houston	53	2240	59	42.3	7	0	21	235	17	35.2
N.Y. Jets	59	2490	61	42.2	5	1	29	288	16	35.6
Pittsburgh	78	3107	61	39.8	4	0	40	247	23	35.6
Cincinnati	101	3945	57	39.1	3	1	48	436	28	34.1
AFC Total	1109	48475	75	—	118	2	491	4532	366	—
AFC Average	69.3	3029.7	--	43.7	7.4	0.1	30.7	283.3	22.9	37.5

NATIONAL FOOTBALL CONFERENCE—PUNTING

	Total Punts	Yards	Long	Avg	TB	Blk	Opp Ret	Return Yards	In 20	Net Avg
St. Louis	83	4120	68	49.6	7	0	57	590	21	40.8
San Francisco	67	3155	82	47.1	9	1	39	364	13	39.0
Minnesota	74	3473	62	46.9	13	1	42	624	23	35.0
New Orleans	53	2364	70	44.6	5	0	34	363	9	35.9
Seattle	90	4007	63	44.5	12	1	44	444	24	36.9
Tampa Bay	77	3426	64	44.5	7	0	39	392	27	37.6
N.Y. Giants	64	2814	61	44.0	5	0	24	140	23	40.2
Detroit	90	3952	66	43.9	6	0	51	414	24	38.0
Dallas	78	3388	70	43.4	8	1	37	390	19	36.4
Philadelphia	78	3334	65	42.7	4	1	41	296	24	37.9
Carolina	76	3217	63	42.3	5	3	41	276	30	37.4
Arizona	60	2509	59	41.8	4	0	29	381	20	34.1
Green Bay	65	2688	65	41.4	6	0	33	249	15	35.7
Chicago	96	3957	67	41.2	5	0	36	203	40	38.1
Washington	82	3321	62	40.5	10	1	33	385	24	33.4
Atlanta	65	2566	60	39.5	4	2	20	49	25	37.5
NFC Total	1198	52291	82	—	110	11	600	5560	361	—
NFC Average	74.9	3268.2	--	43.6	6.9	0.7	37.5	347.5	22.6	37.2
NFL Total	2307	100766	82	—	228	13	1091	10092	727	—
NFL Average	72.1	3148.9	--	43.7	7.1	0.4	34.1	315.4	22.7	37.3

NFL TOP TEN PUNTERS

	No	Yards	Long	Avg	Total Punts	TB	Blk	Opp Ret	Return Yards	In 20	Net Avg
Jones, Donnie, St.L	82	4100	68	50.0	82	7	0	57	590	20	41.1
Lechler, Shane, Oak.	90	4391	70	48.8	90	13	0	43	425	33	41.2
Lee, Andy, S.F.	66	3155	82	47.8	67	9	1	39	364	13	39.0
Kluwe, Chris, Min.	73	3473	62	47.6	74	13	1	42	624	23	35.0
*Kern, Brett, Den.	46	2150	64	46.7	46	4	0	28	330	13	37.8
Scifres, Mike, S.D.	51	2332	67	45.7	51	5	0	23	146	19	40.9
Ryan, Jon, Sea.	78	3557	63	45.6	79	12	1	38	324	22	37.9
Zastudil, Dave, Cle.	75	3410	65	45.5	75	11	0	32	235	23	39.4
Koch, Sam, Bal.	84	3777	74	45.0	84	9	0	38	245	34	39.9
Bidwell, Josh, T.B.	77	3426	64	44.5	77	7	0	39	392	27	37.6

AFC—INDIVIDUAL PUNTERS

	No	Yards	Long	Avg	Total Punts	TB	Blk	Opp Ret	Return Yards	In 20	Net Avg
Lechler, Shane, Oak.	90	4391	70	48.8	90	13	0	43	425	33	41.2
* Kern, Brett, Den.	46	2150	64	46.7	46	4	0	28	330	13	37.8
Scifres, Mike, S.D.	51	2332	67	45.7	51	5	0	23	146	19	40.9
Zastudil, Dave, Cle.	75	3410	65	45.5	75	11	0	32	235	23	39.4
Koch, Sam, Bal.	84	3777	74	45.0	84	9	0	38	245	34	39.9
Colquitt, Dustin, K.C.	70	3110	73	44.4	70	8	0	28	209	27	39.2
Smith, Hunter, Ind.	53	2343	64	44.2	53	2	0	27	249	23	38.8
Moorman, Brian, Buf.	58	2557	63	44.1	58	5	0	18	187	23	39.1
Fields, Brandon, Mia.	74	3249	71	43.9	74	7	0	37	485	24	35.5
Hanson, Chris, N.E.	49	2143	70	43.7	49	10	0	11	158	19	36.4
Podlesh, Adam, Jac.	46	1989	60	43.2	46	5	0	24	206	12	36.6
Hodges, Reggie, NYJ	44	1884	61	42.8	45	5	1	20	187	14	35.5
Hentrich, Craig, Ten.	87	3725	75	42.8	87	13	0	32	290	27	36.5
Weatherford, Steven, N.O.-K.C.-Jac.	59	2521	61	42.7	59	10	0	26	307	8	34.1
Turk, Matt, Hou.	53	2240	59	42.3	53	7	0	21	235	17	35.2
Berger, Mitch, Pit.	66	2728	61	41.3	66	4	0	38	243	19	36.4
Larson, Kyle, Cin.	100	3945	57	39.5	101	3	1	48	436	28	34.1
(Nonqualifiers)											
Ernster, Paul, Pit.	12	379	43	31.6	12	0	0	2	4	4	31.3
Cassel, Matt, N.E.	1	57	57	57.0	1	0	0	0	0	1	57.0
Dawson, Phil, Cle.	1	33	33	33.0	1	0	0	0	0	1	33.0

Leader based on average, minimum 40 punts

NFC—INDIVIDUAL PUNTERS

	No	Yards	Long	Avg	Total Punts	TB	Blk	Opp Ret	Return Yards	In 20	Net Avg
Jones, Donnie, St.L	82	4100	68	50.0	82	7	0	57	590	20	41.1
Lee, Andy, S.F.	66	3155	82	47.8	67	9	1	39	364	13	39.0
Kluwe, Chris, Min.	73	3473	62	47.6	74	13	1	42	624	23	35.0
Ryan, Jon, Sea.	78	3557	63	45.6	79	12	1	38	324	22	37.9
Bidwell, Josh, T.B.	77	3426	64	44.5	77	7	0	39	392	27	37.6
Baker, Jason, Car.	73	3217	63	44.1	76	5	3	41	276	30	37.4
Feagles, Jeff, NY-G	64	2814	61	44.0	64	5	0	24	140	23	40.2
Harris, Nick, Det.	90	3952	66	43.9	90	6	0	51	414	24	38.0
Rocca, Sav, Phi.	77	3334	65	43.3	78	4	1	41	296	24	37.9
Frost, Derrick, G.B.	48	2021	65	42.1	48	5	0	24	189	8	36.1
Paulescu, Sam, Dal.	53	2213	70	41.8	53	5	0	21	246	14	35.2
Johnson, Dirk, Ariz	40	1670	59	41.8	40	4	0	19	182	13	35.2
Plackemeier, Ryan, Sea.-Was.	66	2741	62	41.5	67	10	1	27	310	17	33.3
Maynard, Brad, Chi.	96	3957	67	41.2	96	5	0	36	203	40	38.1
Koenen, Michael, Atl.	63	2566	60	40.7	65	4	2	20	49	25	37.5
(Nonqualifiers)											
Graham, Ben, NYJ-N.O.-Ariz	37	1571	59	42.5	37	0	0	21	320	10	33.8
* Brooks, Durant, Was.	26	1030	60	39.6	26	0	0	12	195	9	32.1
McBriar, Mat, Dal.	24	1175	66	49.0	25	3	1	16	144	5	38.8
Pakulak, Glenn, N.O.	24	1144	70	47.7	24	2	0	18	197	3	37.8
Kapinos, Jeremy, G.B.	17	667	55	39.2	17	1	0	9	60	7	34.5
Brown, Josh, St.L	1	20	20	20.0	1	0	0	0	0	1	20.0

Leader based on average, minimum 40 punts
** Player that was a rookie in 2008*

2008 INDIVIDUAL STATISTICS—PUNT RETURNS

PUNT RETURNS

YARDS PER RETURN

AFC:	15.3	Roscoe Parrish, Buffalo
NFC:	14.1*	Clifton Smith, Tampa Bay

YARDS

AFC:	570	Johnnie Lee Higgins, Oakland
NFC:	443	Mark Jones, Carolina

YARDS, GAME

NFC:	176	Reggie Bush, New Orleans vs. Minnesota, October 6 (5 returns, 2 TD)
AFC:	120	Roscoe Parrish, Buffalo vs. Seattle, September 7 (6 returns, 1 TD)

LONGEST

AFC:	93	Johnnie Lee Higgins, Oakland at Miami, November 16 - TD
NFC:	82	Bernard Berrian, Minnesota at Arizona, December 14 - TD

RETURNS

NFC:	50	* DeSean Jackson, Philadelphia
AFC:	44	Johnnie Lee Higgins, Oakland

RETURNS, GAME

NFC:	8	* DeSean Jackson, Philadelphia vs. St. Louis, September 7 (97 yards, 0 TD)
AFC:	7	Johnnie Lee Higgins, Oakland vs. Carolina, November 9 (17 yards, 0 TD)

FAIR CATCHES

NFC:	21	Antwaan Randle El, Washington
AFC:	20	Chris Carr, Tennessee

TOUCHDOWNS

AFC:	3	Johnnie Lee Higgins, Oakland
NFC:	3	Reggie Bush, New Orleans

TEAM CHAMPION

AFC:	15.5	Buffalo
NFC:	11.9	New Orleans

NFL TOP TEN PUNT RETURNERS

	No	FC	Yards	Avg	Long	TD
Parrish, Roscoe, Buf.	21	10	322	15.3	63t	1
* Smith, Clifton, T.B.	23	4	324	14.1	70t	1
Bush, Reggie, N.O.	20	3	270	13.5	71t	3
Higgins, Johnnie Lee, Oak.	44	12	570	13.0	93t	3
Jones, Jacoby, Hou.	32	17	386	12.1	73t	2
Leonhard, Jim, Bal.	20	9	232	11.6	46	0
Jones, Mark, Car.	39	20	443	11.4	55	0
Sproles, Darren, S.D.	22	12	249	11.3	43	0
Blackmon, Will, G.B.	36	11	398	11.1	76t	2
* Bess, Davone, Mia.	21	10	231	11.0	27	0

AFC—INDIVIDUAL PUNT RETURNERS

	No	FC	Yards	Avg	Long	TD
Parrish, Roscoe, Buf.	21	10	322	15.3	63t	1
Higgins, Johnnie Lee, Oak.	44	12	570	13.0	93t	3
Jones, Jacoby, Hou.	32	17	386	12.1	73t	2
Leonhard, Jim, Bal.	20	9	232	11.6	46	0
Sproles, Darren, S.D.	22	12	249	11.3	43	0
* Bess, Davone, Mia.	21	10	231	11.0	27	0
Washington, Leon, NYJ	29	9	303	10.4	37	0
Carr, Chris, Ten.	32	20	323	10.1	44	0
Welker, Wes, N.E.	24	6	237	9.9	44	0
Cribbs, Josh, Cle.	28	7	228	8.1	32	0
Chatman, Antonio, Cin.	21	5	158	7.5	34	0
Holmes, Santonio, Pit.	34	7	226	6.6	35	0
Figurs, Yamon, Bal.	23	11	138	6.0	35	0
(Nonqualifiers)						
* Witherspoon, Brian, Jac.	17	9	192	11.3	38	0
Ratliff, Keiwan, Ind.	16	12	89	5.6	19	0
* Royal, Eddie, Den.	14	10	140	10.0	36	0
* Robinson, Kevin, K.C.	11	0	94	8.5	32	0
Faulk, Kevin, N.E.	10	9	132	13.2	24	0
Houshmandzadeh, T.J., Cin.	8	2	79	9.9	15	0
* Savage, Dantrell, K.C.	8	2	17	2.1	11	0
Jackson, Fred, Buf.	7	0	116	16.6	35	0
Jones-Drew, Maurice, Jac.	7	1	69	9.9	15	0
Sams, B.J., K.C.	7	3	58	8.3	16	0
Ginn, Ted Jr., Mia.	7	1	54	7.7	15	0
Moore, Mewelde, Pit.	6	12	21	3.5	12	0
Martinez, Glenn, Den.	5	0	56	11.2	27	0
Northcutt, Dennis, Jac.	5	7	14	2.8	9	0
Hall, Leon, Cin.	3	0	16	5.3	12	0
* McKelvin, Leodis, Buf.	2	0	26	13.0	14	0
Steptoe, Syndric, Cle.	2	0	23	11.5	14	0
Davis, Craig, S.D.	2	0	15	7.5	10	0
Davis, Chris, Ten.	2	1	6	3.0	9	0
O'Neal, Deltha, N.E.	2	1	2	1.0	2	0
Reed, Ed, Bal.	1	0	8	8.0	8	0
* Garcon, Pierre, Ind.	1	0	5	5.0	5	0
Cromartie, Antonio, S.D.	1	0	4	4.0	4	0
Harrison, Marvin, Ind.	1	0	2	2.0	2	0
Weddle, Eric, S.D.	1	1	1	1.0	1	0
Haggan, Mario, Den.	1	0	0	0.0	0	0
* Sweed, Limas, Pit.	1	0	0	0.0	0	0

t = Touchdown
Leader based on average return, minimum 20 returns
* *Player that was a rookie in 2008*

NFC—INDIVIDUAL PUNT RETURNERS

	No	FC	Yards	Avg	Long	TD
* Smith, Clifton, T.B.	23	4	324	14.1	70t	1
Bush, Reggie, N.O.	20	3	270	13.5	71t	3
Jones, Mark, Car.	39	20	443	11.4	55	0
Blackmon, Will, G.B.	36	11	398	11.1	76t	2
Hixon, Domenik, NY-G	24	9	242	10.1	50	0
* Forsett, Justin, Sea.-Ind.-Sea.	27	10	263	9.7	29	0
* Jackson, DeSean, Phi.	50	16	440	8.8	68t	1
Breaston, Steve, Ariz	33	10	237	7.2	25	0
Randle El, Antwaan, Was.	39	21	254	6.5	36	0
Jennings, Adam, Atl.-Det.	24	6	151	6.3	37	0
Hester, Devin, Chi.	32	14	198	6.2	25	0
* Jackson, Dexter, T.B.	20	0	97	4.9	19	0
Jones, Adam, Dal.	21	0	95	4.5	18	0
(Nonqualifiers)						
* Douglas, Harry, Atl.	19	3	226	11.9	61t	1
Rossum, Allen, S.F.	15	7	223	14.9	45	0
Crayton, Patrick, Dal.	15	9	143	9.5	33	0
Gordon, Charles, Min.	15	11	66	4.4	20	0
McQuarters, R.W., NY-G	13	9	86	6.6	15	0
McDonald, Shaun, Det.	11	8	104	9.5	27	0
Stanley, Derek, St.L	11	4	101	9.2	33	0
Hall, Dante, St.L	9	1	93	10.3	34	0
Allison, Aundrae, Min.	9	4	58	6.4	27	0
Looker, Dane, St.L	9	5	51	5.7	14	0
Berrian, Bernard, Min.	7	5	114	16.3	82t	1
* Bumpus, Michael, Sea.	7	2	66	9.4	30	0
Moss, Santana, Was.	6	0	124	20.7	80t	1
Clements, Nate, S.F.	6	0	46	7.7	16	0
Vasher, Nathan, Chi.	6	1	46	7.7	18	0
Moore, Lance, N.O.	6	13	40	6.7	11	0
Battle, Arnaz, S.F.	6	2	29	4.8	19	0
Furrey, Mike, Det.	5	5	36	7.2	20	0
Burleson, Nate, Sea.	3	3	54	18.0	21	0
Wade, Bobby, Min.	3	3	35	11.7	20	0
Cason, Aveion, Det.	3	0	27	9.0	13	0
Hilliard, Ike, T.B.	3	7	19	6.3	11	0
Zeigler, Dominique, S.F.	2	3	0	0.0	0	0
* Bennett, Earl, Chi.	1	0	17	17.0	17	0
Smith, Steve, Car.	1	0	10	10.0	10	0
Bradshaw, Ahmad, NY-G	1	0	6	6.0	6	0
Engram, Bobby, Sea.	1	2	6	6.0	6	0
Lewis, Greg, Phi.	1	0	6	6.0	6	0
Webster, Corey, NY-G	1	0	3	3.0	3	0
Finneran, Brian, Atl.	1	3	2	2.0	2	0
Standeford, John, Det.	1	0	1	1.0	1	0
Battle, Tra, Dal.	1	0	0	0.0	0	0
Bush, Jarrett, G.B.	1	0	0	0.0	0	0
Hanson, Joselio, Phi.	1	0	0	0.0	0	0
Salley, Nate, Car.	1	0	0	0.0	0	0
* Talib, Aqib, T.B.	1	0	0	0.0	0	0
Wallace, Seneca, Sea.	1	1	0	0.0	0	0
Wesley, Dante, Car.	1	0	0	0.0	0	0
Green, Skyler, N.O.	0	1	0	—	—	0

t = Touchdown
Leader based on average return, minimum 20 returns
** Player that was a rookie in 2008*

AMERICAN FOOTBALL CONFERENCE—PUNT RETURNS

	No	FC	Yards	Avg	Long	TD
Buffalo	30	10	464	15.5	63t	1
Oakland	44	12	570	13.0	93t	3
Houston	32	17	386	12.1	73t	2
N.Y. Jets	29	9	303	10.4	37	0
San Diego	26	13	269	10.3	43	0
New England	36	16	371	10.3	44	0
Miami	28	11	285	10.2	27	0
Denver	20	10	196	9.8	36	0
Tennessee	34	21	329	9.7	44	0
Jacksonville	29	17	275	9.5	38	0
Baltimore	44	20	378	8.6	46	0
Cleveland	30	7	251	8.4	32	0
Cincinnati	32	7	253	7.9	34	0
Kansas City	26	5	169	6.5	32	0
Pittsburgh	41	19	247	6.0	35	0
Indianapolis	22	13	132	6.0	25	0
AFC Total	503	207	4878	9.7	93t	6
AFC Average	31.4	12.9	304.9	9.7	—	0.4

NATIONAL FOOTBALL CONFERENCE—PUNT RETURNS

	No	FC	Yards	Avg	Long	TD
New Orleans	26	17	310	11.9	71t	3
Carolina	42	20	453	10.8	55	0
Green Bay	37	11	398	10.8	76t	2
San Francisco	29	12	298	10.3	45	0
Seattle	35	17	353	10.1	30	0
Tampa Bay	47	11	440	9.4	70t	1
Atlanta	43	12	379	8.8	61t	1
N.Y. Giants	39	18	337	8.6	50	0
Philadelphia	52	16	446	8.6	68t	1
St. Louis	29	10	245	8.4	34	0
Washington	45	21	378	8.4	80t	1
Minnesota	34	23	273	8.0	82t	1
Detroit	21	13	168	8.0	27	0
Arizona	33	10	237	7.2	25	0
Chicago	39	15	261	6.7	25	0
Dallas	37	9	238	6.4	33	0
NFC Total	588	235	5214	8.9	82t	10
NFC Average	36.8	14.7	325.9	8.9	—	0.6
League Total	1091	442	10092	—	93t	16
League Average	34.1	13.8	315.4	9.3	—	0.5

2008 INDIVIDUAL STATISTICS—SACKS

SACKS

MOST SACKS

NFC:	20.0	DeMarcus Ware, Dallas
AFC:	17.5	Joey Porter, Miami

MOST SACKS, GAME

AFC:	4.0	Joey Porter, Miami at New England, September 21
NFC:	4.0	Kevin Williams, Detroit vs. Minnesota, October 12

TEAM LEADERS, SACKS

AFC: BALTIMORE, 8, Terrell Suggs; BUFFALO, 4, Ryan Denney, Kawika Mitchell; CINCINNATI, 3, Chinedum Ndukwe; Antwan Odom, John Thornton; CLEVELAND, 4.5, Shaun Rogers; DENVER, 5, Elvis Dumervil, Ebenezer Ekuban; HOUSTON, 12, Mario Williams; INDIANAPOLIS, 11.5, Robert Mathis; JACKSONVILLE, 4.5, Reggie Hayward; KANSAS CITY, 3, Tamba Hali; MIAMI, 17.5, Joey Porter; NEW ENGLAND, 8, Richard Seymour; N.Y. JETS, 8, Shaun Ellis; OAKLAND, 5, Kalimba Edwards, *Trevor Scott; PITTSBURGH, 16, James Harrison; SAN DIEGO, 7.5, Shaun Phillips; TENNESSEE, 8.5, Albert Haynesworth

NFC: ARIZONA, 5, Bertrand Berry; ATLANTA, 16.5, John Abraham; CAROLINA, 14.5, Julius Peppers; CHICAGO, 6, Alex Brown; DALLAS, 20, DeMarcus Ware; DETROIT, 6.5, Dewayne White; GREEN BAY, 9.5, Aaron Kampman; MINNESOTA, 14.5, Jared Allen; NEW ORLEANS, 6, Bobby McCray; N.Y. GIANTS, 12, Justin Tuck; PHILADELPHIA, 10, Darren Howard; ST. LOUIS, 6.5, James Hall; SAN FRANCISCO, 8, Parys Haralson; SEATTLE, 5.5, Brandon Mebane, Darryl Tapp; TAMPA BAY, 6.5, Gaines Adams; WASHINGTON, 4, Andre Carter

TEAM CHAMPION

NFC:	59	Dallas
AFC:	51	Pittsburgh

NFL TOP TEN LEADERS—SACKS

	Sacks
Ware, DeMarcus, Dal.	20.0
Porter, Joey, Mia.	17.5
Abraham, John, Atl.	16.5
Harrison, James, Pit.	16.0
Allen, Jared, Min.	14.5
Peppers, Julius, Car.	14.5
Tuck, Justin, NY-G	12.0
Williams, Mario, Hou.	12.0
Mathis, Robert, Ind.	11.5
Woodley, LaMarr, Pit.	11.5

AMERICAN FOOTBALL CONFERENCE—SACKS

	Sacks	Yards
Pittsburgh	51	350
Tennessee	44	262
N.Y. Jets	41	253
Miami	40	218
Baltimore	34	257
Oakland	32	188
New England	31	239
Indianapolis	30	200
Jacksonville	29	191
San Diego	28	132
Denver	26	141
Houston	25	175
Buffalo	24	170
Cincinnati	17	122
Cleveland	17	90
Kansas City	10	62
AFC Total	479	3050
AFC Average	29.9	190.6

NATIONAL FOOTBALL CONFERENCE—SACKS

	Sacks	Yards
Dallas	59	374
Philadelphia	48	312
Minnesota	45	304
N.Y. Giants	42	288
Carolina	37	230
Seattle	35	193
Atlanta	34	245
Arizona	31	191
Detroit	30	191
St. Louis	30	201
San Francisco	30	161
Tampa Bay	29	190
Chicago	28	217
New Orleans	28	161
Green Bay	27	140
Washington	24	141
NFC Total	557	3539
NFC Average	34.8	221.2
League Total	1036	6589
League Average	32.4	205.9

AFC—INDIVIDUAL SACKS

	Sacks
Porter, Joey, Mia.	17.5
Harrison, James, Pit.	16.0
Williams, Mario, Hou.	12.0
Mathis, Robert, Ind.	11.5
Woodley, LaMarr, Pit.	11.5
Freeney, Dwight, Ind.	10.5
Haynesworth, Albert, Ten.	8.5
Ellis, Shaun, NYJ	8.0
Seymour, Richard, N.E.	8.0
Suggs, Terrell, Bal.	8.0
Phillips, Shaun, S.D.	7.5
Ford, Jacob, Ten.	7.0
Pace, Calvin, NYJ	7.0
Smith, Aaron, Pit.	5.5
Thomas, Bryan, NYJ	5.5
Tucker, Jyles, S.D.	5.5
Dumervil, Elvis, Den.	5.0
Edwards, Kalimba, Oak.	5.0
Ekuban, Ebenezer, Den.	5.0
Johnson, Jarret, Bal.	5.0
* Jones, Jason, Ten.	5.0
Roth, Matt, Mia.	5.0
* Scott, Trevor, Oak.	5.0
Thomas, Adalius, N.E.	5.0
Timmons, Lawrence, Pit.	5.0
Ball, Dave, Ten.	4.5
Hayward, Reggie, Jac.	4.5
Kelly, Tommy, Oak.	4.5
Pryce, Trevor, Bal.	4.5
Rogers, Shaun, Cle.	4.5
Vanden Bosch, Kyle, Ten.	4.5
Bowens, David, NYJ	4.0
Brown, Tony, Ten.	4.0
Bulman, Tim, Hou.	4.0
Denney, Ryan, Buf.	4.0
Mitchell, Kawika, Buf.	4.0
Vrabel, Mike, N.E.	4.0
Warren, Gerard, Oak.	4.0
Wimbley, Kamerion, Cle.	4.0
Brock, Raheem, Ind.	3.5
Burgess, Derrick, Oak.	3.5
Farrior, James, Pit.	3.5
* Harvey, Derrick, Jac.	3.5
Holliday, Vonnie, Mia.	3.5
Jenkins, Kris, NYJ	3.5
Kearse, Jevon, Ten.	3.5
Lewis, Ray, Bal.	3.5
Spicer, Paul, Jac.	3.5
Hali, Tamba, K.C.	3.0
* Hall, Alex, Cle.	3.0
Jones, Nate, Mia.	3.0
Ndukwe, Chinedum, Cin.	3.0
Odom, Antwan, Cin.	3.0
Peterson, Kenny, Den.	3.0
Richardson, Jay, Oak.	3.0
Starks, Randy, Mia.	3.0
Thornton, John, Cin.	3.0
Anderson, Charlie, Mia.	2.5
Geathers, Robert, Cin.	2.5
* Groves, Quentin, Jac.	2.5
Harris, Marques, S.D.	2.5
Ivy, Corey, Bal.	2.5
* McClain, Jameel, Bal.	2.5
Moss, Jarvis, Den.	2.5
Smith, Daryl, Jac.	2.5
Stroud, Marcus, Buf.	2.5
Williams, D.J., Den.	2.5
Wright, Mike, N.E.	2.5

	Sacks
Babin, Jason, K.C.	2.0
Cesaire, Jacques, S.D.	2.0
Cochran, Earl, Hou.	2.0
Elam, Abram, NYJ	2.0
Green, Jarvis, N.E.	2.0
Henderson, John, Jac.	2.0
Ingram, Clint, Jac.	2.0
Jackson, D'Qwell, Cle.	2.0
Johnson, Spencer, Buf.	2.0
Kelsay, Chris, Buf.	2.0
Kirschke, Travis, Pit.	2.0
Landri, Derek, Jac.	2.0
* Langford, Kendall, Mia.	2.0
Meier, Rob, Jac.	2.0
Meriweather, Brandon, N.E.	2.0
Olshansky, Igor, S.D.	2.0
Reid, Darrell, Ind.	2.0
Sands, Terdell, Oak.	2.0
Warren, Ty, N.E.	2.0
Webster, Nate, Den.	2.0
Wilfork, Vince, N.E.	2.0
Williams, Kyle, Buf.	2.0
Barton, Eric, NYJ	1.5
Bingham, Ryon, S.D.	1.5
Castillo, Luis, S.D.	1.5
Cooper, Stephen, S.D.	1.5
Crocker, Chris, Cin.	1.5
Eason, Nick, Pit.	1.5
Foote, Larry, Pit.	1.5
Hobbs, Ellis, N.E.	1.5
* Howard, Marcus, Ind.	1.5
Johnson, Brandon, Cin.	1.5
Johnson, Derrick, K.C.	1.5
Mosley, C.J., NYJ	1.5
Robertson, Dewayne, Den.	1.5
Scott, Bart, Bal.	1.5
Vickerson, Kevin, Ten.	1.5
Williams, Jamal, S.D.	1.5
Wilson, George, Buf.	1.5
Wilson, Gibril, Oak.	1.5
Allen, Will, Mia.	1.0
Ayanbadejo, Brendon, Bal.	1.0
Bailey, Champ, Den.	1.0
Bannan, Justin, Bal.	1.0
* Barber, Dominique, Hou.	1.0
Bell, Yeremiah, Mia.	1.0
Bentley, Kevin, Hou.	1.0
Boone, Alfonso, K.C.	1.0
Bryan, Copeland, Buf.	1.0
Coleman, Drew, NYJ	1.0
Diles, Zach, Hou.	1.0
* Dorsey, Glenn, K.C.	1.0
Edwards, Ron, K.C.	1.0
Engelberger, John, Den.	1.0
Finnegan, Cortland, Ten.	1.0
Frazier, Andre, Pit.	1.0
Griffin, Michael, Ten.	1.0
* Gunheim, Greyson, Oak.	1.0
Haggan, Mario, Den.	1.0
Hampton, Casey, Pit.	1.0
Harris, David, NYJ	1.0
* Hayes, William, Ten.	1.0
Hope, Chris, Ten.	1.0
Howard, Thomas, Oak.	1.0
* Johnson, Curtis, Ind.	1.0
Johnson, Travis, Hou.	1.0
Keisel, Brett, Pit.	1.0
Kennedy, Jimmy, Jac.	1.0
Leonhard, Jim, Bal.	1.0

	Sacks
Mathis, Rashean, Jac.	1.0
McFadden, Bryant, Pit.	1.0
McGinest, Willie, Cle.	1.0
* Merling, Phillip, Mia.	1.0
Mincey, Jeremy, Jac.	1.0
Morrison, Kirk, Oak.	1.0
Ngata, Haloti, Bal.	1.0
Okoye, Amobi, Hou.	1.0
Peterson, Mike, Jac.	1.0
Pool, Brodney, Cle.	1.0
Poteat, Hank, NYJ	1.0
Reed, Ed, Bal.	1.0
Revis, Darrelle, NYJ	1.0
Rhodes, Kerry, NYJ	1.0
Rucker, Frostee, Cin.	1.0
Ryans, DeMeco, Hou.	1.0
Schobel, Aaron, Buf.	1.0
Scott, Bryan, Buf.	1.0
* Sims, Pat, Cin.	1.0
Thompson, Chaun, Hou.	1.0
Tulloch, Stephen, Ten.	1.0
Weddle, Eric, S.D.	1.0
Whitner, Donte, Buf.	1.0
Woods, Pierre, N.E.	1.0
Youboty, Ashton, Buf.	1.0
Applewhite, Antwan, S.D.	0.5
Barrett, David, NYJ	0.5
Bulluck, Keith, Ten.	0.5
Coleman, Kenyon, NYJ	0.5
Devito, Mike, NYJ	0.5
Hall, DeAngelo, Oak.	0.5
Hoke, Chris, Pit.	0.5
Jones, Edgar, Bal.	0.5
McDaniel, Tony, Jac.	0.5
Peko, Domata, Cin.	0.5
Pouha, Sione, NYJ	0.5
Sorensen, Nick, Cle.	0.5
Thomas, Pat, K.C.	0.5
Thomas, Santonio, Cle.	0.5
Torbor, Reggie, Mia.	0.5
Williams, Corey, Cle.	0.5
Winborn, Jamie, Den.	0.5

** Player that was a rookie in 2008*

NFC—INDIVIDUAL SACKS

	Sacks
Ware, DeMarcus, Dal.	20.0
Abraham, John, Atl.	16.5
Allen, Jared, Min.	14.5
Peppers, Julius, Car.	14.5
Tuck, Justin, NY-G	12.0
Howard, Darren, Phi.	10.0
Kampman, Aaron, G.B.	9.5
Cole, Trent, Phi.	9.0
Williams, Kevin, Min.	8.5
Ellis, Greg, Dal.	8.0
Haralson, Parys, S.F.	8.0
James, Bradie, Dal.	8.0
Kiwanuka, Mathias, NY-G	8.0
Ratliff, Jay, Dal.	7.5
Smith, Justin, S.F.	7.0
Adams, Gaines, T.B.	6.5
Hall, James, St.L	6.5
White, Dewayne, Det.	6.5
Brown, Alex, Chi.	6.0
Johnson, Charles, Car.	6.0
Little, Leonard, St.L	6.0
McCray, Bobby, N.O.	6.0
Greenway, Chad, Min.	5.5
Mebane, Brandon, Sea.	5.5
Robbins, Fred, NY-G	5.5
Tapp, Darryl, Sea.	5.5
* Avril, Cliff, Det.	5.0
Berry, Bertrand, Ariz	5.0
Edwards, Ray, Min.	5.0
Harris, Tommie, Chi.	5.0
Kerney, Patrick, Sea.	5.0
Ogunleye, Adewale, Chi.	5.0
Parker, Juqua, Phi.	5.0
Peterson, Julian, Sea.	5.0
White, Greg, T.B.	5.0
Wilkerson, Jimmy, T.B.	5.0
Brayton, Tyler, Car.	4.5
Okeafor, Chike, Ariz	4.5
Bernard, Rocky, Sea.	4.0
Carter, Andre, Was.	4.0
Carter, Kevin, T.B.	4.0
Clemons, Chris, Phi.	4.0
Dansby, Karlos, Ariz	4.0
Davis, Chauncey, Atl.	4.0
Dockett, Darnell, Ariz	4.0
* Ellis, Sedrick, N.O.	4.0
LaBoy, Travis, Ariz	4.0
* Long, Chris, St.L	4.0
Babineaux, Jonathan, Atl.	3.5
Davis, Thomas, Car.	3.5
Evans, Demetric, Was.	3.5
Green, Roderick, S.F.	3.5
Idonije, Israel, Chi.	3.5
Lewis, Damione, Car.	3.5
Smith, Antonio, Ariz	3.5
Taylor, Jason, Was.	3.5
Tollefson, Dave, NY-G	3.5
Canty, Chris, Dal.	3.0
Charleston, Jeff, N.O.	3.0
Cofield, Barry, NY-G	3.0
Craft, Jason, St.L	3.0
Dawkins, Brian, Phi.	3.0
Grant, Charles, N.O.	3.0
Hawk, A.J., G.B.	3.0
Lawson, Manny, S.F.	3.0
Redding, Cory, Det.	3.0
Ruud, Barrett, T.B.	3.0
Smith, Corey, Det.	3.0

2008 INDIVIDUAL STATISTICS—SACKS

	Sacks
Smith, Will, N.O.	3.0
Tinoisamoa, Pisa, St.L	3.0
Woodson, Charles, G.B.	3.0
Alford, Jay, NY-G	2.5
Gaither, Omar, Phi.	2.5
Jenkins, Cullen, G.B.	2.5
Montgomery, Mike, G.B.	2.5
Robison, Brian, Min.	2.5
Wilson, Adrian, Ariz	2.5
Wyms, Ellis, Min.	2.5
Abiamiri, Victor, Phi.	2.0
Adeyanju, Victor, St.L	2.0
Alexander, Lorenzo, Was.	2.0
Anderson, Jamaal, Atl.	2.0
Atkins, Baraka, Sea.	2.0
Barber, Ronde, T.B.	2.0
* Biermann, Kroy, Atl.	2.0
Bunkley, Brodrick, Phi.	2.0
Burnett, Kevin, Dal.	2.0
Clancy, Kendrick, N.O.	2.0
DeVries, Jared, Det.	2.0
Gocong, Chris, Phi.	2.0
Golston, Kedric, Was.	2.0
* Harrison, Marcus, Chi.	2.0
Henry, Anthony, Dal.	2.0
Hunter, Jason, G.B.	2.0
Jackson, Grady, Atl.	2.0
* Jackson, Lawrence, Sea.	2.0
Klecko, Dan, Phi.	2.0
Lewis, Michael, S.F.	2.0
Marshall, Richard, Car.	2.0
McIntosh, Rocky, Was.	2.0
Mikell, Quintin, Phi.	2.0
Montgomery, Anthony, Was.	2.0
Shanle, Scott, N.O.	2.0
Terrill, Craig, Sea.	2.0
Winfield, Antoine, Min.	2.0
Wynn, Renaldo, NY-G	2.0
Darby, Chartric, Det.	1.5
Leber, Ben, Min.	1.5
Lenon, Paris, Det.	1.5
Nece, Ryan, Det.	1.5
Pickett, Ryan, G.B.	1.5
Pierce, Antonio, NY-G	1.5
Sims, Ryan, T.B.	1.5
Spencer, Anthony, Dal.	1.5
Alama-Francis, Ikaika, Det.	1.0
Anderson, Mark, Chi.	1.0
Bartell, Ronald, St.L	1.0
Bishop, Desmond, G.B.	1.0
Blackburn, Chase, NY-G	1.0
Bradley, Stewart, Phi.	1.0
Brown, Fakhir, St.L	1.0
Brown, Mike, Chi.	1.0
Brown, Sheldon, Phi.	1.0
Chillar, Brandon, G.B.	1.0
* Demps, Quintin, Phi.	1.0
Diggs, Na'il, Car.	1.0
Franklin, Aubrayo, S.F.	1.0
Gay, Randall, N.O.	1.0
* Godfrey, Charles, Car.	1.0
Green, Howard, Sea.	1.0
Griffin, Cornelius, Was.	1.0
Haggans, Clark, Ariz	1.0
Hamlin, Ken, Dal.	1.0
Hanson, Joselio, Phi.	1.0
Harris, Napoleon, Min.	1.0
Harris, Walt, S.F.	1.0
Hatcher, Jason, Dal.	1.0
Henderson, E.J., Min.	1.0
Hill, Leroy, Sea.	1.0
Hillenmeyer, Hunter, Chi.	1.0
* Horton, Chris, Was.	1.0
Hovan, Chris, T.B.	1.0
Jackson, Tanard, T.B.	1.0
Johnson, Michael, NY-G	1.0
Johnson, Tank, Dal.	1.0
* Kehl, Bryan, NY-G	1.0
* Lofton, Curtis, Atl.	1.0
Manning, Danieal, Chi.	1.0
Manning, Ricky, St.L	1.0
McDonald, Ray, S.F.	1.0
Moore, Eric, St.L	1.0
Moore, Langston, Det.	1.0
Moorehead, Kindal, Atl.	1.0
Nicholas, Stephen, Atl.	1.0
Payne, Kevin, Chi.	1.0
Pearson, Kalvin, Det.	1.0
* Porter, Tracy, N.O.	1.0
Reis, Chris, N.O.	1.0
Robinson, Bryan, Ariz	1.0
Russell, Brian, Sea.	1.0
* Scandrick, Orlando, Dal.	1.0
Sims, Ernie, Det.	1.0
Sopoaga, Isaac, S.F.	1.0
Spears, Marcus, Dal.	1.0
Spikes, Takeo, S.F.	1.0
Springs, Shawn, Was.	1.0
* Taylor, Hilee, Car.	1.0
Thomas, Zach, Dal.	1.0
Vilma, Jonathan, N.O.	1.0
Watson, Gabe, Ariz	1.0
Webster, Corey, NY-G	1.0
Williams, Pat, Min.	1.0
Willis, Patrick, S.F.	1.0
Wilson, Chris, Was.	1.0
Wilson, Josh, Sea.	1.0
Witherspoon, Will, St.L	1.0
Young, Brian, N.O.	1.0
Banta-Cain, Tully, S.F.	0.5
Briggs, Lance, Chi.	0.5
Cole, Colin, G.B.	0.5
Fletcher, London, Was.	0.5
Gbaja-Biamila, Kabeer, G.B.	0.5
Glover, La'Roi, St.L	0.5
Hayes, Gerald, Ariz	0.5
Landry, LaRon, Was.	0.5
Patterson, Mike, Phi.	0.5

** Player that was a rookie in 2008*

2009 PLAYER RANKINGS AND PROJECTIONS

The *NFL.com 2009 Fantasy Football Preview*, available at newsstands now, contains 160 pages of fantasy football facts, tips, and projections for the upcoming season. The following eight pages display the projections for the running backs, wide receivers, quarterbacks, tight ends, and kickers for the 2009 season, as devised by the magazine's experts. Page 296 provides the statistical average for each team's defense over the past three seasons, allowing you a comprehensive look at which team defense can consistently help lead your fantasy team to the title. Pick up a copy of the *NFL.com 2009 Fantasy Football Preview* today.

RUNNING BACKS	Rushing Yards	Rushing Touchdowns	Receiving	Receiving Yards	Receiving Touchdowns	Total Touchdowns
1. Adrian Peterson, Minnesota	1670	16	23	175	0	16
2. Matt Forté, Chicago	1265	9	67	540	4	13
3. Michael Turner, Atlanta	1525	15	8	55	0	8
4. Maurice Jones-Drew, Jacksonville	1120	13	59	540	1	14
5. DeAngelo Williams, Carolina	1345	12	21	180	2	14
6. Chris Johnson, Tennessee	1290	8	51	325	2	10
7. Steven Jackson, St. Louis	1205	8	51	465	1	9
8. Brian Westbrook, Philadelphia	995	7	56	540	3	10
9. Frank Gore, San Francisco	1255	7	41	355	2	9
10. Marion Barber, Dallas	995	10	43	360	2	12
11. Steve Slaton, Houston	1210	7	41	305	1	8
12. Clinton Portis, Washington	1200	8	23	195	1	9
13. LaDainian Tomlinson, San Diego	1025	8	43	355	1	9
14. Brandon Jacobs, N.Y. Giants	1070	12	14	105	0	12
15. Ronnie Brown, Miami	1065	8	38	295	1	9
16. Kevin Smith, Detroit	1070	7	44	295	1	8
17. Pierre Thomas, New Orleans	940	8	38	325	1	9
18. Joseph Addai, Indianapolis	1005	7	33	280	1	7
19. Knowshon Moreno, Denver	1025	6	35	320	1	7
20. Derrick Ward, Tampa Bay	1100	6	41	300	0	6
21. Thomas Jones, N.Y. Jets	1065	7	27	195	0	7
22. Marshawn Lynch, Buffalo	1010	6	39	265	1	7
23. Larry Johnson, Kansas City	1095	8	17	125	0	8
24. Ryan Grant, Green Bay	1180	6	21	105	0	6
25. Darren McFadden, Oakland	875	6	38	325	0	6
26. Reggie Bush, New Orleans	520	3	79	615	4	7
27. Willie Parker, Pittsburgh	1090	6	12	75	0	6
28. LenDale White, Tennessee	810	10	9	45	0	10
29. Cedric Benson, Cincinnati	925	5	23	190	0	5
30. Beanie Wells, Arizona	940	7	6	35	0	7
31. Jonathan Stewart, Carolina	880	8	13	75	0	8
32. Sammy Morris, New England	870	6	19	155	0	6
33. Le'Ron McClain, Baltimore	835	8	17	0	0	8
34. Jamal Lewis, Cleveland	880	5	16	110	0	2
35. Willis McGahee, Baltimore	815	6	20	135	0	6
36. Julius Jones, Seattle	925	4	21	125	0	4
37. Donald Brown, Indianapolis	675	5	33	250	0	5
38. Leon Washington, N.Y. Jets	500	4	42	340	2	6
39. Tim Hightower, Arizona	585	6	38	280	0	6
40. Earnest Graham, Tampa Bay	545	3	25	200	0	3
41. Felix Jones, Dallas	660	4	18	145	0	4
42. Darren Sproles, San Diego	365	2	31	330	4	6
43. Fred Jackson, Buffalo	585	0	29	285	1	1
44. Jerious Norwood, Atlanta	455	3	31	325	1	4
45. Chester Taylor, Minnesota	365	5	41	335	1	6
46. Ahmad Bradshaw, N.Y. Giants	710	3	11	110	0	3
47. LeSean McCoy, Philadelphia	560	3	17	165	1	4
48. Rashard Mendenhall, Pittsburgh	580	4	8	65	0	4
49. Fred Taylor, New England	615	3	11	105	0	3
50. Ricky Williams, Miami	545	3	25	170	0	3
51. Correll Buckhalter, Denver	325	4	3	35	0	4
52. Michael Bush, Oakland	295	2	8	75	0	2
53. Ray Rice, Baltimore	435	1	41	345	1	2
54. Shonn Greene, N.Y. Jets	235	3	5	65	0	3
55. Kevin Faulk, New England	290	1	46	375	2	3
56. Justin Fargas, Oakland	565	2	7	60	0	2
57. Jamaal Charles, Kansas City	395	1	33	260	1	2
58. LaMont Jordan, Denver	475	3	8	75	0	3

	Rushing Yards	Rushing Touchdowns	Receiving	Receiving Yards	Receiving Touchdowns	Total Touchdowns
59. Laurence Maroney, New England	445	3	9	125	0	3
60. Ladell Betts, Washington	395	2	23	215	0	2
61. Tashard Choice, Dallas	395	2	18	190	0	2
62. Dominic Rhodes, Buffalo	360	3	16	185	0	3
63. Maurice Morris, Detroit	425	2	21	185	0	2
64. Mewelde Moore, Pittsburgh	325	2	34	285	0	2
65. T.J. Duckett, Seattle	325	6	5	25	0	6
66. Edgerrin James, Free Agent	485	3	14	60	0	3
67. Jerome Harrison, Cleveland	250	1	20	250	1	2
68. Antonio Pitman, St. Louis	285	2	9	65	0	2
69. Brandon Jackson, Green Bay	265	1	5	40	0	1
70. Glen Coffee, San Francisco	225	2	13	120	0	2
71. Greg Jones, Jacksonville	320	3	9	85	0	3
72. Kolby Smith, Kansas City	255	2	14	90	0	2
73. Kevin Jones, Chicago	175	4	5	45	0	4
74. J.J. Arrington, Denver	255	2	10	80	0	2
75. Lorenzo Booker, Philadelphia	225	1	10	85	1	2
76. Chris Brown, Houston	75	0	25	275	1	1
77. Michael Bennett, San Diego	125	1	20	205	0	1
78. Peyton Hillis, Denver	126	1	10	125	1	2
79. Jacob Hester, San Diego	125	1	15	175	0	1
80. Mike Bell, New Orleans	120	0	10	180	1	1
81. Patrick Cobbs, Miami	100	0	20	185	1	1
82. Andre Brown, N.Y. Giants	75	1	15	125	0	1
83. DeShawn Wynn, Green Bay	140	1	5	45	0	1
84. Leonard Weaver, Philadelphia	75	0	15	175	0	0
85. Kenneth Darby, St. Louis	75	1	10	110	0	1
86. Jason Wright, Arizona	125	1	5	45	0	1
87. Chauncey Washington, Jacksonville	125	1	5	45	0	1
88. Michael Robinson, San Francisco	145	1	1	10	0	1
89. Carnell Williams, Tampa Bay	125	1	5	30	0	1
90. Mike Hart, Indianapolis	15	1	15	145	0	1
91. BenJarvus Green-Ellis, New England	125	0	8	80	0	0
92. DeDe Dorsey, Cincinnati	75	1	8	65	0	1
93. Ryan Moats, Houston	125	1	5	27	0	1
94. Aaron Stecker, New Orleans	125	1	0	0	0	1
95. Adrian Peterson, Chicago	100	0	5	35	0	0
96. Heath Evans, New Orleans	55	1	0	0	0	1
97. Brian Leonard, Cincinnati	45	0	3	20	0	0
98. Garrett Wolfe, Chicago	50	0	3	19	0	0
99. Montrell Owens, Jacksonville	25	1	3	25	0	1
100. Darius Walker, Houston	40	0	2	18	0	0

For more in-depth analysis, pick up a copy of the NFL.com 2009 Fantasy Football Preview, *available at newsstands today.*

WIDE RECEIVERS	Receiving	Yards	Touchdowns
1. Larry Fitzgerald, Arizona	94	1405	13
2. Andre Johnson, Houston	107	1490	10
3. Calvin Johnson, Detroit	85	1395	11
4. Randy Moss, New England	91	1255	13
5. Anquan Boldin, Arizona	83	1295	10
6. Steve Smith, Carolina	83	1380	8
7. Reggie Wayne, Indianapolis	98	1335	8
8. Greg Jennings, Green Bay	77	1260	8
9. Roddy White, Atlanta	85	1245	8
10. Dwayne Bowe, Kansas City	92	1235	8
11. Wes Welker, New England	107	1215	7
12. Roy Williams, Dallas	73	1155	8
13. Marques Colston, New Orleans	82	1130	8
14. Brandon Marshall, Denver	82	1185	6
15. Terrell Owens, Buffalo	71	1070	8
16. T.J. Houshmandzadeh, Seattle	78	1045	7
17. Chad Ochocinco, Cincinnati	75	1040	7
18. Antonio Bryant, Tampa Bay	75	1105	6
19. Vincent Jackson, San Diego	64	1060	6
20. DeSean Jackson, Philadelphia	73	1035	6
21. Eddie Royal, Denver	82	995	6
22. Braylon Edwards, Cleveland	68	1035	7
23. Bernard Berrian, Minnesota	55	985	7
24. Santonio Holmes, Pittsburgh	64	975	7
25. Anthony Gonzalez, Indianapolis	76	1055	6
26. Hines Ward, Pittsburgh	72	1005	6
27. Lee Evans, Buffalo	67	955	6
28. Santana Moss, Washington	68	1010	5
29. Lance Moore, New Orleans	65	900	7
30. Derrick Mason, Baltimore	76	1020	5
31. Donald Driver, Green Bay	71	1020	5
32. Jerricho Cotchery, N.Y. Jets	75	980	5
33. Laveranues Coles, Cincinnati	74	955	5
34. Devin Hester, Chicago	69	890	5
35. Steve Breaston, Arizona	68	965	4
36. Donald Avery, St. Louis	65	880	4
37. Torry Holt, Jacksonville	65	885	5
38. Michael Crabtree, San Francisco	62	860	5
39. Domenik Hixon, N.Y. Giants	64	860	5
40. Kevin Curtis, Philadelphia	54	820	5
41. Kevin Walter, Houston	62	815	6
42. Deion Branch, Seattle	62	805	5
43. Ted Ginn Jr., Miami	61	855	4
44. Muhsin Muhammad, Carolina	58	825	3
45. Chris Chambers, San Diego	51	745	4
46. Patrick Crayton, Dallas	52	640	6
47. Justin Gage, Tennessee	52	700	5
48. Percy Harvin, Minnesota	31	460	3
49. Michael Jenkins, Atlanta	51	665	5
50. Nate Burleson, Seattle	57	685	4
51. Steve Smith, N.Y. Giants	65	765	3
52. Darrius Heyward-Bey, Oakland	41	615	3
53. Mark Bradley, Kansas City	55	695	4
54. Nate Washington, Tennessee	52	705	3
55. Mark Clayton, Baltimore	54	680	3
56. Devery Henderson, New Orleans	36	715	3
57. Bryant Johnson, Detroit	50	715	3
58. Isaac Bruce, San Francisco	48	630	4
59. Davone Bess, Miami	62	695	3
60. Miles Austin, Dallas	46	640	4
61. Sidney Rice, Minnesota	45	580	5
62. Jeremy Maclin, Philadelphia	42	520	4
63. Chris Henry, Cincinnati	43	615	4
64. Antwaan Randle El, Washington	55	645	3
65. Earl Bennett, Chicago	48	635	3
66. Greg Camarillo, Miami	61	695	2
67. Bobby Engram, Kansas City	56	650	3
68. Johnnie Lee Higgins, Oakland	41	540	3
69. Hakeem Nicks, N.Y. Giants	41	550	3

WIDE RECEIVERS	Receiving	Yards	Touchdowns
70. Joey Galloway, New England	41	495	4
71. Jabar Gaffney, Denver	46	545	3
72. Brandon Jones, San Francisco	51	585	2
73. Bobby Wade, Minnesota	48	575	2
74. Mike Walker, Jacksonville	39	495	3
75. Dennis Northcutt, Jacksonville	40	500	3
76. Josh Morgan, San Francisco	35	530	2
77. Laurent Robinson, St. Louis	45	555	2
78. Jerheme Urban, Arizona	45	555	2
79. Ronald Curry, Detroit	47	495	2
80. Jason Avant, Philadelphia	40	480	2
81. Harry Douglas, Atlanta	37	435	2
82. Josh Reed, Buffalo	47	520	1
83. Michael Clayton, Tampa Bay	42	490	1
84. Malcom Floyd, San Diego	37	445	2
85. Rashied Davis, Chicago	30	425	2
86. Will Franklin, Kansas City	32	420	2
87. James Jones, Green Bay	35	425	2
88. Brian Robiskie, Cleveland	35	425	2
89. Kenny Britt, Tennessee	25	365	3
90. Mario Manningham, N.Y. Giants	35	425	2
91. Devin Thomas, Washington	35	385	1
92. Chansi Stuckey, N.Y. Jets	45	410	2
93. David Clowney, N.Y. Jets	32	420	1
94. Roscoe Parrish, Buffalo	22	285	1
95. Josh Cribbs, Cleveland	15	240	1
96. Brandon Stokley, Denver	32	405	1
97. Jordy Nelson, Green Bay	35	380	1
98. Hank Baskett, Philadelphia	30	375	1
99. Robert Meachem, New Orleans	25	310	2
100. David Patten, Cleveland	30	375	1

For more in-depth analysis, pick up a copy of the NFL.com 2009 Fantasy Football Preview, *available at newsstands today.*

QUARTERBACKS

	Player	Passing Yards	Passing Touchdowns	Rushing Yards	Rushing Touchdowns
1.	Drew Brees, New Orleans	4575	32	30	1
2.	Tom Brady, New England	4355	30	70	1
3.	Peyton Manning, Indianapolis	4100	29	55	2
4.	Philip Rivers, San Diego	3975	30	70	1
5.	Aaron Rodgers, Green Bay	3900	27	195	3
6.	Kurt Warner, Arizona	4425	29	10	0
7.	Tony Romo, Dallas	4025	25	95	2
8.	Matt Ryan, Atlanta	3950	25	90	0
9.	Jay Cutler, Chicago	3925	23	195	1
10.	Donovan McNabb, Philadelphia	3825	21	165	2
11.	Carson Palmer, Cincinnati	3950	23	35	0
12.	Matt Cassel, Kansas City	3725	19	175	1
13.	Matt Schaub, Houston	3875	21	55	1
14.	Ben Roethlisberger, Pittsburgh	3250	19	165	2
15.	Matt Hasselbeck, Seattle	3475	19	95	0
16.	Kyle Orton, Denver	3370	20	40	1
17.	Trent Edwards, Buffalo	3375	18	130	1
18.	Joe Flacco, Baltimore	3150	17	195	2
19.	Chad Pennington, Miami	3475	17	65	0
20.	Eli Manning, N.Y. Giants	3350	20	25	0
21.	David Garrard, Jacksonville	3325	14	215	2
22.	Shaun Hill, San Francisco	3225	17	155	1
23.	Jason Campbell, Washington	3125	14	205	1
24.	JaMarcus Russell, Oakland	2775	15	115	1
25.	Brady Quinn, Cleveland	3000	14	125	0
26.	Jake Delhomme, Carolina	3075	16	25	0
27.	Marc Bulger, St. Louis	3050	15	35	0
28.	Sage Rosenfels, Minnesota	3000	14	55	1
29.	Daunte Culpepper, Detroit	2750	15	70	1
30.	Kerry Collins, Tennessee	2525	14	45	0
31.	Kellen Clemens, N.Y. Jets	2375	13	55	1
32.	Luke McCown, Tampa Bay	2325	13	95	0
33.	Mark Sanchez, N.Y. Jets	1975	11	155	1
34.	Byron Leftwich, Tampa Bay	1950	7	25	0
35.	Derek Anderson, Cleveland	1775	9	45	0
36.	Tarvaris Jackson, Minnesota	1125	4	45	0
37.	Matthew Stafford, Detroit	1155	4	10	0
38.	Matt Leinart, Arizona	950	3	20	0
39.	Vince Young, Tennessee	850	4	85	0
40.	Tyler Thigpen, Kansas City	1000	3	85	1
41.	Jon Kitna, Dallas	925	4	35	0
42.	Jeff Garcia, Oakland	765	3	90	0
43.	Kyle Boller, St. Louis	750	4	25	0
44.	Chris Simms, Denver	635	6	5	0
45.	Dan Orlovsky, Houston	725	4	25	0
46.	Josh Freeman, Tampa Bay	725	3	10	0
47.	J.P. Losman, Free Agent	750	2	15	0
48.	Alex Smith, San Francisco	680	2	25	0
49.	J.T. O'Sullivan, Cincinnati	375	2	55	0
50.	Matt Flynn, Green Bay	345	2	20	0
51.	Charlie Batch, Pittsburgh	350	2	5	0
52.	Troy Smith, Baltimore	240	1	30	0
53.	David Carr, N.Y. Giants	175	2	15	0
54.	Seneca Wallace, Seattle	230	1	15	0
55.	Brian Griese, Tampa Bay	175	2	10	0
56.	Ryan Fitzpatrick, Buffalo	145	1	35	0
57.	Jim Sorgi, Indianapolis	155	1	2	0
58.	Kevin O'Connell, New England	135	1	10	0
59.	Todd Collins, Washington	125	1	-3	0
60.	Kevin Kolb, Philadelphia	125	1	0	0

FANTASY SECTION

TIGHT ENDS	Receiving	Yards	Touchdowns
1. Jason Witten, Dallas	90	1045	7
2. Antonio Gates, San Diego	74	940	8
3. Tony Gonzalez, Atlanta	84	975	6
4. Dallas Clark, Indianapolis	71	805	7
5. Chris Cooley, Washington	76	810	6
6. Greg Olsen, Chicago	68	730	7
7. Kellen Winslow, Tampa Bay	73	845	5
8. Owen Daniels, Houston	67	820	4
9. Josh Carlson, Seattle	64	690	6
10. Zach Miller, Oakland	64	800	4
11. Dustin Keller, N.Y. Jets	61	630	4
12. Kevin Boss, N.Y. Giants	47	505	5
13. Heath Miller, Pittsburgh	55	560	4
14. Anthony Fasano, Miami	42	460	5
15. Vernon Davis, San Francisco	54	545	4
16. Visanthe Shiancoe, Minnesota	39	535	4
17. Tony Scheffler, Denver	45	570	3
18. Jeremy Shockey, New Orleans	61	560	3
19. Brent Celek, Philadelphia	43	485	3
20. Brandon Pettigrew, Detroit	46	505	3
21. Bo Scaife, Tennessee	52	540	2
22. Todd Heap, Baltimore	41	450	4
23. Donald Lee, Green Bay	43	335	5
24. Marcedes Lewis, Jacksonville	47	510	2
25. Randy McMichael, St. Louis	50	515	2
26. Billy Miller, New Orleans	40	505	2
27. Desmond Clark, Chicago	44	475	2
28. Daniel Graham, Denver	30	425	2
29. Benjamin Watson, New England	35	365	2
30. Martellus Bennett, Dallas	35	390	1

For more in-depth analysis, pick up a copy of the NFL.com 2009 Fantasy Football Preview, *available at newsstands today.*

KICKERS	PTS	XP/XPA	FG/FGA
1. Rob Bironas, Tennessee	145	37/37	36/40
2. Stephen Gostkowski, New England	141	51/51	30/34
3. Mason Crosby, Green Bay	138	42/42	32/38
4. Jason Elam, Atlanta	131	47/47	28/32
5. David Akers, Philadelphia	129	48/48	27/34
6. Garrett Hartley, New Orleans	127	52/52	25/28
7. Ryan Longwell, Minnesota	125	44/44	27/32
8. Nick Folk, Dallas	124	46/46	26/30
9. John Kasay, Carolina	121	43/43	26/30
10. Matt Bryant, Tampa Bay	120	33/33	29/36
11. Nate Kaeding, San Diego	120	42/42	26/30
12. Neil Rackers, Arizona	119	41/41	26/33
13. Josh Brown, St. Louis	118	25/25	31/36
14. Kris Brown, Houston	118	40/40	26/31
15. Shayne Graham, Cincinnati	118	37/37	27/31
16. Robbie Gould, Chicago	118	37/37	27/31
17. Adam Vinatieri, Indianapolis	117	45/45	24/28
18. Rian Lindell, Buffalo	115	40/40	25/30
19. Matt Prater, Denver	112	37/37	25/32
20. Jeff Reed, Pittsburgh	112	37/37	25/30
21. Lawrence Tynes, N.Y. Giants	111	34/34	25/31
22. Joe Nedney, San Francisco	110	29/29	27/33
23. Phil Dawson, Cleveland	110	26/26	28/33
24. Dan Carpenter, Miami	107	38/38	23/27
25. Shaun Suisham, Washington	105	24/24	27/33
26. Jason Hanson, Detroit	104	32/32	24/27
27. Josh Scobee, Jacksonville	99	36/36	21/25
28. Sebastian Janikowski, Oakland	102	33/33	23/28
29. Jay Feely, N.Y. Jets	96	30/30	22/26
30. Olindo Mare, Seattle	99	36/36	21/26

DEFENSE/ SPECIAL TEAMS*	Yards Per Game	Points Per Game	Takeaways	Sacks	Touchdowns DEF & RET
1. Steelers	268.0	16.8	29	42	3
2. Giants	313.1	21.0	26	42	4
3. Vikings	310.2	20.2	30	38	7
4. Jets	331.0	21.0	33	35	5
5. Titans	318.3	19.4	27	37	5
6. Ravens	275.6	17.3	31	42	5
7. Eagles	304.6	19.1	28	42	5
8. Cowboys	308.2	21.7	28	46	4
9. Patriots	297.2	17.1	26	41	3
10. Dolphins	320.1	21.6	30	39	3
11. Bears	327.8	19.9	32	36	8
12. Cardinals	337.0	25.3	31	35	6
13. Packers	322.8	21.6	28	36	7
14. Redskins	316.5	20.5	21	25	2
15. Colts	307.6	19.2	29	28	3
16. Bills	339.5	21.0	27	30	5
17. Buccaneers	304.6	19.7	27	29	4
18. Panthers	317.4	20.5	29	34	2
19. Chargers	323.9	19.5	28	44	5
20. Falcons	345.5	22.2	23	32	2
21. 49ers	338.8	24.1	21	22	3
22. Jaguars	309.4	19.7	22	34	3
23. Seahawks	343.4	21.3	25	40	4
24. Raiders	329.1	23.3	26	31	4
25. Browns	353.6	22.7	30	24	3
26. Bengals	343.1	22.5	30	25	3
27. Texans	339.4	23.8	26	28	4
28. Saints	331.6	23.0	25	33	4
29. Chiefs	347.2	22.7	28	26	2
30. Rams	349.4	26.8	30	32	2
31. Lions	375.9	28.3	25	32	2
32. Broncos	345.7	24.2	19	31	2

**Defense/Special Team statistics reflect an average of the past three seasons (2006-08); clubs are ranked in projected order.*

For more in-depth analysis, pick up a copy of the NFL.com 2009 Fantasy Football Preview, *available at newsstands today.*

Inside the Numbers

GREATEST COMEBACKS IN NFL HISTORY
(Most Points Overcome To Win Game)

REGULAR SEASON GAMES

FROM 28 POINTS BEHIND TO WIN:
December 7, 1980, at San Francisco

New Orleans	14	21	0	0	0	—	35
San Francisco	0	7	14	14	3	—	38

NO — Harris 33 pass from Manning (Ricardo kick)
NO — Childs 21 pass from Manning (Ricardo kick)
NO — Holmes 1 run (Ricardo kick)
SF — Solomon 57 punt return (Wersching kick)
NO — Holmes 1 run (Ricardo kick)
NO — Harris 41 pass from Manning (Ricardo kick)
SF — Montana 1 run (Wersching kick)
SF — Clark 71 pass from Montana (Wersching kick)
SF — Solomon 14 pass from Montana (Wersching kick)
SF — Elliott 7 run (Wersching kick)
SF — FG Wersching 36

FROM 26 POINTS BEHIND TO WIN:
September 21, 1997, at Buffalo

Indianapolis	14	12	0	9	—	35
Buffalo	0	10	6	21	—	37

Ind — Bailey 10 pass from Harbaugh (Blanchard kick)
Ind — Faulk 10 run (Blanchard kick)
Ind — FG Blanchard 39
Ind — FG Blanchard 36
Ind — FG Blanchard 49
Ind — FG Blanchard 22
Buff — Johnson 16 pass from Collins (Christie kick)
Buff — FG Christie 27
Buff — A. Smith 15 run (2-pt attempt failed)
Ind — FG Blanchard 25
Buff — Early 4 pass from Collins (Christie kick)
Buff — A. Smith 1 run (Christie kick)
Buff — A. Smith 54 run (Christie kick)
Ind — Harrison 2 pass from Justin (2-pt attempt failed)

FROM 25 POINTS BEHIND TO WIN:
November 8, 1987, at St. Louis

Tampa Bay	7	7	14	0	—	28
St. Louis	0	3	0	28	—	31

TB — Carrier 5 pass from DeBerg (Igwebuike kick)
TB — Carter 3 pass from DeBerg (Igwebuike kick)
StL — FG Gallery 31
TB — Smith 34 pass from DeBerg (Igwebuike kick)
TB — Smith 3 run (Igwebuike kick)
StL — Awalt 4 pass from Lomax (Gallery kick)
StL — Noga 23 fumble recovery (Gallery kick)
StL — J. Smith 11 pass from Lomax (Gallery kick)
StL — J. Smith 17 pass from Lomax (Gallery kick)

FROM 24 POINTS BEHIND TO WIN:
October 27, 1946, at Washington

Philadelphia	0	0	14	14	—	28
Washington	10	14	0	0	—	24

Wash — Rosato 2 run (Poillon kick)
Wash — FG Poillon 28
Wash — Rosato 4 run (Poillon kick)
Wash — Lapka recovered fumble in end zone (Poillon kick)
Phil — Steele 1 run (Lio kick)
Phil — Pritchard 45 pass from Thompson (Lio kick)
Phil — Steinke 7 pass from Thompson (Lio kick)
Phil — Ferrante 30 pass from Thompson (Lio kick)

FROM 24 POINTS BEHIND TO WIN:
October 20, 1957, at Detroit

Baltimore	7	14	6	0	—	27
Detroit	0	3	7	21	—	31

Balt — Mutscheller 15 pass from Unitas (Rechichar kick)
Det — FG Martin 47
Balt — Moore 72 pass from Unitas (Rechichar kick)
Balt — Mutscheller 52 pass from Unitas (Rechichar kick)
Balt — Moore 4 pass from Unitas (kick failed)
Det — Junker 14 pass from Rote (Layne kick)
Det — Cassady 26 pass from Layne (Layne kick)
Det — Johnson 1 run (Layne kick)
Det — Cassady 29 pass from Layne (Layne kick)

FROM 24 POINTS BEHIND TO WIN:
October 25, 1959, at Minneapolis

Philadelphia	0	0	21	7	—	28
Chicago Cardinals	7	10	7	0	—	24

Cardinals — Crow 10 pass from Roach (Conrad kick)
Cardinals — J. Hill 77 blocked field goal return (Conrad kick)
Cardinals — FG Conrad 15
Cardinals — Lane 37 interception return (Conrad kick)
Phil — Barnes 1 run (Walston kick)
Phil — McDonald 29 pass from Van Brocklin (Walston kick)
Phil — Barnes 2 run (Walston kick)
Phil — McDonald 22 pass from Van Brocklin (Walston kick)

FROM 24 POINTS BEHIND TO WIN:
October 23, 1960, at Denver

Boston	10	7	7	0	—	24
Denver	0	0	14	17	—	31

Bos — FG Cappelletti 12
Bos — Colclough 10 pass from Songin (Cappelletti kick)
Bos — Wells 6 pass from Songin (Cappelletti kick)
Bos — Miller 47 pass from Songin (Cappelletti kick)
Den — Carmichael 21 pass from Tripucka (Mingo kick)
Den — Jessup 19 pass from Tripucka (Mingo kick)
Den — Carmichael 35 lateral from Taylor, pass from Tripucka (Mingo kick)
Den — Taylor 8 pass from Tripucka (Mingo kick)
Den — FG Mingo 9

FROM 24 POINTS BEHIND TO WIN:
December 15, 1974, at Miami

New England	21	3	0	3	—	27
Miami	0	17	7	10	—	34

NE — Hannah recovered fumble in end zone (J. Smith kick)
NE — Sanders 23 interception return (J. Smith kick)
NE — Herron 4 pass from Plunkett (J. Smith kick)
NE — FG J. Smith 46
Mia — Nottingham 1 run (Yepremian kick)
Mia — Baker 37 pass from Morrall (Yepremian kick)
Mia — FG Yepremian 28
Mia — Baker 46 pass from Morrall (Yepremian kick)
NE — FG J. Smith 34
Mia — Nottingham 2 run (Yepremian kick)
Mia — FG Yepremian 40

FROM 24 POINTS BEHIND TO WIN:
December 4, 1977, at Minnesota

San Francisco	0	10	14	3	—	27
Minnesota	0	0	7	21	—	28

SF — Delvin Williams 2 run (Wersching kick)
SF — FG Wersching 31
SF — Dave Williams 80 kickoff return (Wersching kick)
SF — Delvin Williams 5 run (Wersching kick)
Minn — McClanahan 15 pass from Lee (Cox kick)
Minn — Rashad 8 pass from Kramer (Cox kick)
Minn — Tucker 9 pass from Kramer (Cox kick)
SF — FG Wersching 31
Minn — S. White 69 pass from Kramer (Cox kick)

FROM 24 POINTS BEHIND TO WIN:
September 23, 1979, at Denver

Seattle	10	10	14	0	—	34
Denver	0	10	21	6	—	37

Sea — FG Herrera 28
Sea — Doornink 5 run (Herrera kick)
Den — FG Turner 27
Sea — Doornink 5 run (Herrera kick)
Den — Armstrong 2 run (Turner kick)
Sea — FG Herrera 22
Sea — McCullum 13 pass from Zorn (Herrera kick)
Sea — Smith 1 run (Herrera kick)
Den — Studdard 2 pass from Morton (Turner kick)
Den — Moses 11 pass from Morton (Turner kick)
Den — Upchurch 35 pass from Morton (Turner kick)

Den — Lytle 1 run (kick failed)

FROM 24 POINTS BEHIND TO WIN:
September 23, 1979, at Cincinnati

Houston	0	10	17	0	3	— 30
Cincinnati	14	10	0	3	0	— 27

Cin — Johnson 1 run (Bahr kick)
Cin — Alexander 2 run (Bahr kick)
Cin — Johnson 1 run (Bahr kick)
Cin — FG Bahr 52
Hou — Burrough 35 pass from Pastorini (Fritsch kick)
Hou — FG Fritsch 33
Hou — Campbell 8 run (Fritsch kick)
Hou — Caster 22 pass from Pastorini (Fritsch kick)
Hou — FG Fritsch 47
Cin — FG Bahr 55
Hou — FG Fritsch 29

FROM 24 POINTS BEHIND TO WIN:
November 22, 1982, at Los Angeles

San Diego	10	14	0	0	— 24
L.A. Raiders	0	7	14	7	— 28

SD — FG Benirschke 19
SD — Scales 29 pass from Fouts (Benirschke kick)
SD — Muncie 2 run (Benirschke kick)
SD — Muncie 1 run (Benirschke kick)
Raiders — Christensen 1 pass from Plunkett (Bahr kick)
Raiders — Allen 3 run (Bahr kick)
Raiders — Allen 6 run (Bahr kick)
Raiders — Hawkins 1 run (Bahr kick)

FROM 24 POINTS BEHIND TO WIN:
September 26, 1988, at Denver

L.A. Raiders	0	0	14	13	3	— 30
Denver	7	17	0	3	0	— 27

Den — Dorsett 1 run (Karlis kick)
Den — Dorsett 1 run (Karlis kick)
Den — Sewell 7 pass from Elway (Karlis kick)
Den — FG Karlis 39
Raiders — Smith 40 pass from Schroeder (Bahr kick)
Raiders — Smith 42 pass from Schroeder (Bahr kick)
Raiders — FG Bahr 28
Raiders — Allen 4 run (Bahr kick)
Den — FG Karlis 25
Raiders — FG Bahr 44
Raiders — FG Bahr 35

FROM 24 POINTS BEHIND TO WIN:
December 6, 1992, at Tampa

L.A. Rams	0	3	21	7	— 31
Tampa Bay	6	21	0	0	— 27

TB — FG Murray 34
TB — FG Murray 47
TB — Armstrong 81 pass from Testaverde (Murray kick)
TB — Jones 26 fumble recovery (Murray kick)
Rams — FG Zendejas 18
TB — Carrier 10 pass from Testaverde (Murray kick)
Rams — Anderson 40 pass from Everett (Zendejas kick)
Rams — Chadwick 27 pass from Everett (Zendejas kick)
Rams — Lang 1 run (Zendejas kick)
Rams — Carter 8 pass from Everett (Zendejas kick)

POSTSEASON GAMES

FROM 32 POINTS BEHIND TO WIN:
AFC First-Round Playoff Game
January 3, 1993, at Buffalo

Houston	7	21	7	3	0	— 38
Buffalo	3	0	28	7	3	— 41

Hou — Jeffires 3 pass from Moon (Del Greco kick)
Buff — FG Christie 36
Hou — Slaughter 7 pass from Moon (Del Greco kick)
Hou — Duncan 26 pass from Moon (Del Greco kick)
Hou — Jeffires 27 pass from Moon (Del Greco kick)
Hou — McDowell 58 interception return (Del Greco kick)
Buff — Davis 1 run (Christie kick)
Buff — Beebe 38 pass from Reich (Christie kick)
Buff — Reed 26 pass from Reich (Christie kick)
Buff — Reed 18 pass from Reich (Christie kick)
Buff — Reed 17 pass from Reich (Christie kick)
Hou — FG Del Greco 26
Buff — FG Christie 32

FROM 24 POINTS BEHIND TO WIN:
NFC First-Round Playoff Game
January 5, 2003, at San Francisco

N.Y. Giants	7	21	10	0	— 38
San Francisco	7	7	8	17	— 39

SF — Owens 76 pass from Garcia (Chandler kick)
NYG — Toomer 12 pass from Collins (Bryant kick)
NYG — Shockey 2 pass from Collins (Bryant kick)
SF — Barlow 1 run (Chandler kick)
NYG — Toomer 8 pass from Collins (Bryant kick)
NYG — Toomer 24 pass from Collins (Bryant kick)
NYG — Barber 6 run (Bryant kick)
NYG — FG Bryant 21
SF — Owens 26 pass from Garcia (Owens from Garcia)
SF — Garcia 14 run (Owens from Garcia)
SF — Garcia 14 run (Owens from Garcia)
SF — FG Chandler 25
SF — Streets 13 pass from Garcia (2-pt attempt failed)

FROM 20 POINTS BEHIND TO WIN:
Western Conference Playoff Game
December 22, 1957, at San Francisco

Detroit	0	7	14	10	— 31
San Francisco	14	10	3	0	— 27

SF — Owens 34 pass from Tittle (Soltau kick)
SF — McElhenny 47 pass from Tittle (Soltau kick)
Det — Junker 4 pass from Rote (Martin kick)
SF — Wilson 12 pass from Tittle (Soltau kick)
SF — FG Soltau 25
SF — FG Soltau 10
Det — Tracy 2 run (Martin kick)
Det — Tracy 58 run (Martin kick)
Det — Gedman 3 run (Martin kick)
Det — FG Martin 14

FROM 18 POINTS BEHIND TO WIN:
NFC Divisional Playoff Game
December 23, 1972, at San Francisco

Dallas	3	10	0	17	— 30
San Francisco	7	14	7	0	— 28

SF — Washington 97 kickoff return (Gossett kick)
Dall — FG Fritsch 37
SF — Schreiber 1 run (Gossett kick)
SF — Schreiber 1 run (Gossett kick)
Dall — FG Fritsch 45
Dall — Alworth 28 pass from Morton (Fritsch kick)
SF — Schreiber 1 run (Gossett kick)
Dall — FG Fritsch 27
Dall — Parks 20 pass from Staubach (Fritsch kick)
Dall — Sellers 10 pass from Staubach (Fritsch kick)

FROM 18 POINTS BEHIND TO WIN:
AFC Divisional Playoff Game
January 4, 1986, at Miami

Cleveland	7	7	7	0	— 21
Miami	3	0	14	7	— 24

Mia — FG Reveiz 51
Cle — Newsome 16 pass from Kosar (Bahr kick)
Cle — Byner 21 run (Bahr kick)
Cle — Byner 66 run (Bahr kick)
Mia — Moore 6 pass from Marino (Reveiz kick)
Mia — Davenport 31 run (Reveiz kick)
Mia — Davenport 1 run (Reveiz kick)

FROM 18 POINTS BEHIND TO WIN:
AFC Divisional Playoff Game
January 21, 2007, at Indianapolis

New England	7	14	7	6	— 34
Indianapolis	3	3	15	17	— 38

NE — Mankins 0 fumble recovery (Gostkowski kick)
Ind — FG Vinatieri 42
NE — Dillon 7 run (Gostkowski kick)
NE — Samuel 39 interception return (Gostkowski kick)
Ind — FG Vinatieri 26
Ind — Manning 1 run (Vinatieri kick)
Ind — Klecko 1 pass from Manning (Harrison from Manning)
NE — Gaffney 6 pass from Brady (Gostkowski kick)
Ind — Saturday 0 fumble recovery (Vinatieri kick)
NE — FG Gostkowski 28
Ind — FG Vinatieri 36
NE — FG Gostkowski 43
Ind — Addai 3 run (Vinatieri kick)

INSIDE THE NUMBERS

RECORDS FOR NFL TEAMS FOR MOST POINTS IN A GAME (REGULAR SEASON ONLY)

Note: *When the record has been achieved more than once, only the most recent game is shown; summaries are listed in alphabetical order by conference. Bold face indicates team holding record.*

BALTIMORE RAVENS

December 19, 2005, at Baltimore

Green Bay	3	0	0	0	— 3
Baltimore	14	10	10	14	— 48

TD: Balt—Todd Heap 2, Mark Clayton, Randy Hymes, Jamal Lewis, Adalius Thomas. TD Passes: Balt—Kyle Boller 3. FG: Balt—Matt Stover 2; GB—Ryan Longwell.

BUFFALO BILLS

September 18, 1966, at Buffalo

Miami	3	7	0	14	— 24
Buffalo	21	27	3	7	— 58

TD: Buff—Bobby Burnett 2, Butch Byrd 2, Jack Spikes 2, Bobby Crockett, Jack Kemp; Mia—Dave Kocourek, Bo Roberson, John Roderick. TD Passes: Buff—Jack Kemp, Daryle Lamonica; Mia—George Wilson 3. FG: Buff—Booth Lusteg; Mia—Gene Mingo.

CINCINNATI BENGALS

December 17, 1989, at Cincinnati

Houston	0	0	0	7	— 7
Cincinnati	21	10	21	9	— 61

TD: Cin—Eddie Brown 2, Eric Ball, James Brooks, Ira Hillary, Rodney Holman, Tim McGee, Craig Taylor; Hou—Lorenzo White. TD Passes: Cin—Boomer Esiason 4, Erik Wilhelm. FG: Cin—Jim Breech 2.

CLEVELAND BROWNS

November 7, 1954, at Cleveland

Washington	0	3	0	0	— 3
Cleveland	13	14	21	14	— 62

TD: Cle—Darrell Brewster 2, Mo Bassett, Ken Gorgal, Otto Graham, Dub Jones, Dante Lavelli, Curley Morrison. TD Passes: Cle—George Ratterman 3, Otto Graham. FG: Cle—Lou Groza 2; Wash—Vic Janowicz.

DENVER BRONCOS

October 6, 1963, at Denver

San Diego	13	7	0	14	— 34
Denver	3	14	9	24	— 50

TD: Den—Lionel Taylor 2, Goose Gonsoulin, Gene Prebola, Donnie Stone; SD—Keith Lincoln 2, Lance Alworth, Paul Lowe, Jacque MacKinnon. TD Passes: Den—John McCormick 3; SD—Tobin Rote 3, John Hadl 2. FG: Den—Gene Mingo 5.

HOUSTON TEXANS

December 30, 2007 at Houston

Jacksonville	7	7	7	7	— 28
Houston	0	21	14	7	— 42

TD: Jax—Earnest Wilford 2, Matt Jones, Reggie Williams; Hou—Andre Davis 2, Ron Dayne 2, Owen Daniels, Darius Walker. TD Passes: Jax—Quinn Gray 4; Hou—Sage Rosenfels.

INDIANAPOLIS COLTS

December 12, 1976, at Baltimore

Buffalo	3	3	7	7	— 20
Baltimore Colts	7	13	28	10	— 58

TD: Balt—Roger Carr, Raymond Chester, Glenn Doughty, Roosevelt Leaks, Derrel Luce, Lydell Mitchell, Howard Stevens; Buff—Bob Chandler, O.J. Simpson. TD Passes: Balt—Bert Jones 3; Buff—Gary Marangi. FG: Balt—Toni Linhart 3; Buff—George Jakowenko 2.

JACKSONVILLE JAGUARS

December 23, 2007, at Jacksonville

Oakland	0	3	0	8	— 11
Jacksonville	14	14	7	14	— 49

TD: Oak—Zach Miller; Jac—Richard Angulo, David Garrard, Greg Jones, Matt Jones, Maurice Jones-Drew, Fred Taylor, Reggie Williams. TD Passes: Oak—JaMarcus Russell; Jac—David Garrard 2, Quinn Gray 2. FG: Oak—Sebastian Janikowski.

KANSAS CITY CHIEFS

September 7, 1963, at Denver

Kansas City	14	14	21	10	— 59
Denver	0	7	0	0	— 7

TD: KC—Chris Burford 2, Frank Jackson 2, Dave Grayson, Abner Haynes, Sherrill Headrick, Curtis McClinton; Den—Lionel Taylor. TD Passes: KC—Len Dawson 4, Curtis McClinton; Den—Mickey Slaughter. FG: KC—Tommy Brooker.

MIAMI DOLPHINS

November 24, 1977, at St. Louis

Miami	14	14	20	7	— 55
St. Louis Cardinals	7	0	0	7	— 14

TD: Mia—Nat Moore 3, Gary Davis, Duriel Harris, Leroy Harris, Benny Malone, Andre Tillman; StL—Ike Harris, Terry Metcalf. TD Passes: Mia—Bob Griese 6; StL—Jim Hart.

NEW ENGLAND PATRIOTS

November 18, 2007, at Buffalo

New England	14	21	7	14	— 56
Buffalo	7	0	3	0	— 10

TD: NE—Randy Moss 4, Kyle Eckel, Ellis Hobbs, Laurence Maroney, Benjamin Watson; Buff—Roscoe Parrish. TD Passes: NE—Tom Brady 5; Buff—J.P. Losman. FG: Buff—Rian Lindell.

NEW YORK JETS

November 17, 1985, at New York

Tampa Bay	14	7	7	0	— 28
New York Jets	17	24	14	7	— 62

TD: NYJ—Mickey Shuler 3, Johnny Hector 2, Tony Paige, Al Toon, Wesley Walker; TB—James Wilder 2, Kevin House, Calvin Magee. TD Passes: NYJ—Ken O'Brien 5; TB—Steve DeBerg 2. FG: NYJ—Pat Leahy 2.

OAKLAND RAIDERS

September 29, 2002 at Oakland

Tennessee	7	0	12	6	— 25
Oakland	21	10	7	14	— 52

TD: Oak—Tim Brown, Phillip Buchanon, Charlie Garner, Terry Kirby, Jerry Porter, Jim Rice, Rod Woodson; Tenn—Drew Bennett, Eddie George, Justin McCareins, John Simon. TD Passes: Oak—Rich Gannon 4; Tenn—Steve McNair 2. FG: Oak—Sebastian Janikowski.

PITTSBURGH STEELERS

November 30, 1952, at Pittsburgh

New York Giants	0	0	7	0	— 7
Pittsburgh	14	14	7	28	— 63

TD: Pitt—Lynn Chandnois 2, Dick Hensley 2, Jack Butler, George Hays, Ray Mathews, Ed Modzelewski, Elbie Nickel; NYG—Bill Stribling. TD Passes: Pitt—Jim Finks 4, Gary Kerkorian; NYG—Tom Landry.

SAN DIEGO CHARGERS

December 22, 1963, at San Diego

Denver	7	10	3	0	— 20
San Diego	10	16	10	22	— 58

TD: SD—Paul Lowe 2, Chuck Allen, Bobby Jackson, Dave Kocourek, Keith Lincoln, Jacque MacKinnon; Den—Billy Joe, Donnie Stone. TD Passes: SD—John Hadl, Tobin Rote; Den—Don Breaux. FG: SD—George Blair 3; Den—Gene Mingo 2.

TENNESSEE TITANS

December 9, 1990, at Houston

Cleveland	0	7	7	0	— 14
Houston Oilers	14	31	7	6	— 58

TD: Hou—Lorenzo White 4, Ernest Givins, Leonard Harris, Tony Jones, Terry Kinard; Cle—Eric Metcalf 2. TD Passes: Hou—Warren Moon 2, Cody Carlson; Cle—Bernie Kosar. FG: Hou—Teddy Garcia.

ARIZONA CARDINALS

November 13, 1949, at New York

Chicago Cardinals	7	31	14	13	— 65
New York Bulldogs	7	0	6	7	— 20

TD: Chi—Red Cochran 2, Pat Harder 2, Bill Dewell, Mel Kutner, Bob Ravensburg, Vic Schwall, Charlie Trippi; NY—Joe Golding, Frank Muehlheuser, Johnny Rauch. TD Passes: Chi—Paul Christman 3, Jim Hardy 3; NY—Bobby Layne. FG: Chi—Pat Harder.

ATLANTA FALCONS

September 16, 1973, at New Orleans

Atlanta	0	24	21	17	— 62
New Orleans	0	0	7	0	— 7

TD: Atl—Ken Burrow 2, Eddie Ray 2, Wes Chesson, Tom Hayes, Art Malone, Joe Profit; NO—Bill Butler. TD Passes: Atl—Dick Shiner 3, Bob Lee; NO—Archie Manning. FG: Atl—Nick Mike-Mayer 2.

CAROLINA PANTHERS

December 8, 2002, at Carolina

Cincinnati	7	10	14	0	— 31
Carolina	9	7	21	15	— 52

TD: Car—Steve Smith 3, Dee Brown, Muhsin Muhammad, Al Wallace, Wesley Walls; Cin—Peter Warrick 2, Jon Kitna, Takeo Spikes. TD Passes: Car—Rodney Peete 3; Cin—Jon Kitna 2. FG: Cin—Neil Rackers.

CHICAGO BEARS

December 7, 1980, at Chicago

Green Bay	0	7	0	0	— 7
Chicago	0	28	13	20	— 61

TD: Chi—Walter Payton 3, Brian Baschnagel, Robin Earl, Roland Harper, Willie McClendon, Len Walterscheid, Rickey Watts; GB—James Lofton. TD Passes: Chi—Vince Evans 3; GB—Lynn Dickey.

DALLAS COWBOYS

October 12, 1980, at Dallas

San Francisco	0	7	0	7	— 14
Dallas	14	24	14	7	— 59

TD: Dall—Drew Pearson 3, Ron Springs 2, Tony Dorsett, Billy Joe DuPree, Robert Newhouse; SF—Dwight Clark 2. TD Passes: Dall—Danny White 4; SF—Steve DeBerg 2. FG: Dall—Rafael Septien.

DETROIT LIONS

November 27, 1997, at Detroit

Chicago	14	6	0	0	— 20
Detroit	3	14	17	21	— 55

TD: Det—Herman Moore, Johnnie Morton, Ron Rivers, Barry Sanders 3, Tracy Scroggins; Chi—Raymont Harris, Ricky Proehl. TD Passes: Det—Scott Mitchell 2; Chi—Erik Kramer. FG: Det—Jason Hanson 2; Chi—Jeff Jaeger 2.

GREEN BAY PACKERS

October 7, 1945, at Milwaukee

Detroit	0	7	7	7	— 21
Green Bay	0	41	9	7	— 57

TD: GB—Don Hutson 4, Charley Brock, Irv Comp, Ted Fritsch, Clyde Goodnight; Det—Chuck Fenenbock, John Greene, Bob Westfall. TD Passes: GB—Tex McKay 4, Lou Brock, Irv Comp; Det—Dave Ryan.

MINNESOTA VIKINGS

October 18, 1970, at Minnesota

Dallas	3	3	0	7	— 13
Minnesota	14	20	17	3	— 54

TD: Minn—Clint Jones 2, Ed Sharockman 2, John Beasley, Dave Osborn; Dall—Calvin Hill. TD Pass: Minn—Gary Cuozzo. FG: Minn—Fred Cox 4; Dall—Mike Clark 2.

NEW ORLEANS SAINTS

November 24, 2008, at New Orleans

Green Bay	7	14	0	8	— 29
New Orleans	14	10	21	6	— 51

TD: NO—Lance Moore 2, Pierre Thomas 2, Billy Miller, Deuce McAllister, Marques Colston; GB—John Kuhn, Greg Jennings, Ruvell Martin, Aaron Rodgers. TD Pass: NO—Drew Brees 4; GB—Aaron Rodgers 2. FG: NO—Garrett Hartley.

NEW YORK GIANTS

November 26, 1972, at New York

Philadelphia	3	7	0	0	— 10
New York Giants	14	24	10	14	— 62

TD: NYG—Don Herrmann 2, Ron Johnson 2, Bob Tucker 2, Randy Johnson; Phil—Harold Jackson. TD Passes: NYG—Norm Snead 3, Randy Johnson 2; Phil—John Reaves. FG: NYG—Pete Gogolak 2; Phil—Tom Dempsey.

PHILADELPHIA EAGLES

November 6, 1934, at Philadelphia

Cincinnati Reds	0	0	0	0	— 0
Philadelphia	26	6	12	20	— 64

TD: Phil—Joe Carter 3, Swede Hanson 3, Marvin Ellstrom, Roger Kirkman, Ed Matesic, Ed Storm. TD Passes: Phil—Ed Matesic 2, Albert Weiner 2, Marvin Elstrom.

ST. LOUIS RAMS

October 22, 1950, at Los Angeles

Baltimore	13	0	7	7	— 27
Los Angeles Rams	21	14	14	21	— 70

TD: LA—Bob Boyd 2, Vitamin T. Smith 2, Tom Fears, Elroy (Crazylegs) Hirsch, Dick Hoerner, Ralph Pasquariello, Dan Towler, Bob Waterfield; Balt—Chet Mutryn 2, Adrian Burk, Billy Stone. TD Passes: LA—Norm Van Brocklin 2, Bob Waterfield 2, Glenn Davis; Balt—Adrian Burk 3.

SAN FRANCISCO 49ERS

October 18, 1992, at San Francisco

Atlanta	7	3	0	7	— 17
San Francisco	21	21	14	0	— 56

TD: SF—Jerry Rice 3, Ricky Watters 3, Brent Jones, Tom Rathman; Atl—Michael Haynes, Jason Phillips. TD Passes: SF—Steve Young 3; Atl—Chris Miller, Wade Wilson. FG: Atl—Norm Johnson.

SEATTLE SEAHAWKS

October 30, 1977, at Seattle

Buffalo	3	0	7	7	— 17
Seattle	14	28	7	7	— 56

TD: Sea—Steve Largent 2, Duke Fergerson, Al Hunter, David Sims, Sherman Smith, Don Testerman, Jim Zorn; Buff—Joe Ferguson, John Kimbrough. TD Passes: Sea—Jim Zorn 4; Buff—Joe Ferguson. FG: Buff—Carson Long.

TAMPA BAY BUCCANEERS

December 23, 2001, at Tampa Bay

New Orleans	0	0	7	14	— 21
Tampa Bay	17	13	3	15	— 48

TD: TB—Mike Alstott, Ronde Barber, Warrick Dunn, Dave Moore, Karl Williams; NO—Joe Horn 2, Eddie Williams. TD Passes: TB—Brad Johnson 3; NO—Aaron Brooks 3. FG: TB—Martin Gramatica 4.

WASHINGTON REDSKINS

November 27, 1966, at Washington

New York Giants	0	14	14	13	— 41
Washington	13	21	14	24	— 72

TD: Wash—A.D. Whitfield 3, Brig Owens 2, Charley Taylor 2, Rickie Harris, Joe Don Looney, Bobby Mitchell; NYG—Allen Jacobs, Homer Jones, Dan Lewis, Joe Morrison, Aaron Thomas, Gary Wood. TD Passes: Wash—Sonny Jurgensen 3; NYG—Gary Wood 2, Tom Kennedy. FG: Wash—Charlie Gogolak.

RECORDS OF NFL TEAMS SINCE 1970 AFL-NFL MERGER

AFC	W	L	T	Pct.	Division Titles	Playoff Berths	Postseason Record	Super Bowl Record
Miami	365	233	2	.610	13	22	20-20	2-3
Pittsburgh	363	235	2	.607	19	24	31-18	6-1
Denver	347	247	6	.584	10	17	17-15	2-4
Oakland	328	266	6	.552	12	18	22-15	3-1
Jacksonville**	118	106	0	.527	2	6	5-6	0-0
New England	314	286	0	.523	10	15	20-12	3-3
Baltimore***	107	100	1	.517	2	5	7-4	1-0
Kansas City	294	299	7	.496	5	11	3-11	0-0
Indianapolis	294	304	2	.492	11	17	13-15	2-0
Tennessee	293	305	2	.490	5	16	12-16	0-1
Buffalo	283	315	2	.473	7	13	12-13	0-4
San Diego	276	319	5	.464	9	11	9-11	0-1
Cleveland+	248	301	3	.452	6	11	4-11	0-0
Cincinnati	265	334	1	.443	6	8	5-8	0-2
N.Y. Jets	262	336	2	.438	2	10	6-10	0-0
Houston****	40	72	0	.357	0	0	0-0	0-0

NFC	W	L	T	Pct.	Division Titles	Playoff Berths	Postseason Record	Super Bowl Record
Dallas	356	244	0	.593	16	25	31-20	5-3
Minnesota	343	255	2	.573	15	23	16-23	0-3
San Francisco	337	260	3	.564	17	21	25-16	5-0
Washington	333	265	2	.557	6	16	20-13	3-2
St. Louis	312	284	4	.523	11	19	16-18	1-2
Philadelphia	304	288	8	.513	7	17	15-17	0-2
Green Bay	299	293	8	.505	8	13	13-12	1-1
Chicago	299	300	1	.499	9	13	9-12	1-1
N.Y. Giants	294	303	3	.493	7	14	16-11	3-1
Carolina**	109	115	0	.487	3	4	6-4	0-1
Seattle*	250	266	0	.484	6	10	7-10	0-1
Atlanta	255	340	5	.429	3	9	6-9	0-1
New Orleans	250	346	4	.420	3	6	2-6	0-0
Detroit	246	350	4	.413	3	9	1-9	0-0
Arizona	241	353	6	.406	3	5	4-5	0-1
Tampa Bay*	205	310	1	.398	6	10	6-9	1-0

**Entered NFL in 1976.*
***Entered NFL in 1995.*
****Entered NFL in 1996.*
*****Entered NFL in 2002.*
+Did not play, 1996-98.
Oakland totals include L.A. Raiders, 1982-1994.
Tennessee totals include Houston, 1970-1996.
Indianapolis totals include Baltimore, 1970-1983.
St. Louis totals include L.A. Rams, 1970-1994.
Arizona totals include St. Louis, 1970-1987, and Phoenix, 1988-1993.
Tie games before 1972 are not calculated in won-lost percentage.

HOME RECORDS OF NFL TEAMS SINCE 1970 AFL-NFL MERGER

AFC	W	L	T	Pct.
Pittsburgh	216	83	1	.722
Denver	211	86	4	.709
Miami	209	89	1	.701
Baltimore***	67	36	1	.649
Jacksonville**	69	43	0	.616
Oakland	182	116	2	.610
Kansas City	179	117	3	.604
New England	178	122	0	.593
Tennessee	167	132	1	.559
Buffalo	166	134	1	.553
Cincinnati	163	136	1	.545
San Diego	159	138	2	.535
Indianapolis	156	142	2	.523
Cleveland+	137	136	2	.502
N.Y. Jets	141	157	1	.473
Houston****	26	30	0	.464

NFC	W	L	T	Pct.
Dallas	204	96	0	.680
Minnesota	202	98	1	.673
Washington	189	108	2	.636
San Francisco	182	116	2	.610
Green Bay	179	116	5	.605
Chicago	177	122	1	.592
St. Louis	172	126	2	.577
Seattle*	149	110	0	.575
Philadelphia	170	128	3	.570
N.Y. Giants	161	139	1	.537
Detroit	160	139	1	.535
Carolina**	59	53	0	.527
Atlanta	153	147	1	.510
Tampa Bay*	128	129	1	.498
Arizona	145	151	3	.490
New Orleans	134	165	1	.448

**Entered NFL in 1976.*
***Entered NFL in 1995.*
****Entered NFL in 1996.*
*****Entered NFL in 2002.*
+Did not play, 1996-98.
Oakland totals include L.A. Raiders, 1982-1994.
Tennessee totals include Houston, 1970-1996.
Indianapolis totals include Baltimore, 1970-1983.
St. Louis totals include L.A. Rams, 1970-1994.
Arizona totals include St. Louis, 1970-1987, and Phoenix, 1988-1993.
Tie games before 1972 are not calculated in won-lost percentage.

ROAD RECORDS OF NFL TEAMS SINCE 1970 AFL-NFL MERGER

AFC	W	L	T	Pct.
Miami	156	144	1	.520
Oakland	146	150	4	.493
Pittsburgh	147	152	1	.492
Indianapolis	138	162	0	.460
Denver	136	161	2	.458
New England	136	164	0	.453
Jacksonville**	49	63	0	.438
Tennessee	126	173	1	.421
N.Y. Jets	121	179	1	.404
Cleveland+	111	165	1	.403
Buffalo	117	181	1	.393
San Diego	117	181	3	.393
Kansas City	115	182	4	.388
Baltimore***	40	64	0	.385
Cincinnati	102	198	0	.340
Houston***	14	42	0	.250

NFC	W	L	T	Pct.
San Francisco	155	144	1	.518
Dallas	152	148	0	.507
Washington	144	157	0	.478
Minnesota	141	157	1	.473
St. Louis	140	158	2	.470
Philadelphia	134	160	5	.456
N.Y. Giants	133	164	2	.448
Carolina**	50	62	0	.446
Chicago	122	178	0	.407
Green Bay	120	177	3	.405
Seattle*	101	156	0	.393
New Orleans	116	181	3	.391
Atlanta	102	193	4	.346
Arizona	96	202	3	.323
Tampa Bay**	77	181	0	.298
Detroit	86	211	3	.291

**Entered NFL in 1976.*
***Entered NFL in 1995.*
****Entered NFL in 1996.*
*****Entered NFL in 2002.*
+Did not play, 1996-98.
Oakland totals include L.A. Raiders, 1982-1994.
Tennessee totals include Houston, 1970-1996.
Indianapolis totals include Baltimore, 1970-1983.
St. Louis totals include L.A. Rams, 1970-1994.
Arizona totals include St. Louis, 1970-1987, and Phoenix, 1988-1993.
Tie games before 1972 are not calculated in won-lost percentage.

RECORDS OF TEAMS ON KICKOFF WEEKEND

AFC	W	L	T	Pct.	Longest W Strk.	Longest L Strk.	Current Streak
Denver	31	17	1	.646	4	4	W-2
Jacksonville	9	5	0	.643	6	2	L-2
San Diego	28	21	0	.571	6	6	L-1
Miami	23	19	1	.548	11	5	L-3
Pittsburgh	38	32	4	.543	6	3	W-6
Kansas City	26	23	0	.531	7	4	L-3
Tennessee	26	23	0	.531	4	3	W-2
Indianapolis	33	31	1	.516	8	8	L-1
New England	25	24	0	.510	6	3	W-5
Oakland	24	25	0	.490	5	6	L-6
Cleveland	27	29	0	.482	5	6	L-4
Cincinnati	19	22	0	.463	4	4	L-1
Houston	3	4	0	.429	2	3	L-1
N.Y. Jets	21	28	0	.429	3	5	W-1
Buffalo	20	29	0	.408	6	5	W-1
Baltimore	5	8	0	.385	2	4	W-1

NFC	W	L	T	Pct.	Longest W Strk.	Longest L Strk.	Current Streak
Dallas	33	15	1	.688	17	5	W-2
Chicago	50	34	5	.595	9	6	W-1
N.Y. Giants	47	32	5	.595	4	3	W-1
Green Bay	49	36	3	.576	5	6	W-2
Minnesota	27	20	1	.574	5	3	L-1
Detroit	42	35	2	.545	10	4	L-1
St. Louis	38	33	0	.535	5	6	L-2
Atlanta	23	20	0	.535	5	3	W-1
San Francisco	30	28	1	.517	5	3	L-1
Washington	37	36	4	.507	6	5	L-1
Carolina	6	8	0	.429	3	4	W-2
Arizona	35	51	2	.407	6	7	W-1
Philadelphia	30	44	1	.405	5	9	W-1
Tampa Bay	13	20	0	.394	3	5	L-3
New Orleans	14	28	0	.333	2	6	W-1
Seattle	11	22	0	.333	3	8	L-1

Kansas City totals include Dallas Texans, 1960-62.
Oakland totals include L.A. Raiders, 1982-1994.
San Diego totals include L.A. Chargers, 1960.
Indianapolis totals include Baltimore, 1953-1983.
Tennessee total include Houston, 1960-1996.
New England totals include Boston, 1960-1970.
St. Louis totals include Cleveland, 1937-1942 and 1944-45, and L.A. Rams, 1946-1994.
Detroit totals include Portsmouth, 1930-33.
Arizona totals include Chi. Cardinals, 1920-1959, St. Louis, 1960-1987, and Phoenix, 1988-1993.
Chicago totals include Decatur, 1920.
Washington totals include Boston Braves, 1932 and Boston Redskins, 1933-36.
NOTE: All tied games occurred prior to 1972, when calculation of ties in percentage as half-win.

INSIDE THE NUMBERS

RECORDS OF NFL TEAMS, 1999-2008

AFC	W	L	T	Pct.	Division Titles	Playoff Berths	Postseason Record	Super Bowl Record
Indianapolis	114	46	0	.713	6	9	7-8	1-0
New England	110	50	0	.688	6	6	14-3	3-1
Pittsburgh	100	59	1	.628	5	6	10-4	2-0
Tennessee	96	64	0	.600	3	6	5-6	0-1
Baltimore	91	69	0	.569	2	5	7-4	1-0
Denver	91	69	0	.569	1	4	1-4	0-0
Jacksonville	83	77	0	.519	1	3	2-3	0-0
Miami	81	79	0	.506	2	4	2-4	0-0
San Diego	80	80	0	.500	4	4	3-4	0-0
N.Y. Jets	79	81	0	.494	1	4	2-4	0-0
Kansas City	75	85	0	.469	1	2	0-2	0-0
Buffalo	71	89	0	.444	0	1	0-1	0-0
Oakland	65	95	0	.406	3	3	4-3	0-1
Cincinnati	62	97	1	.391	1	1	0-1	0-0
Houston	40	72	0	.357	0	0	0-0	0-0
Cleveland	54	106	0	.338	0	1	0-1	0-0

Houston entered NFL in 2002.

NFC	W	L	T	Pct.	Division Titles	Playoff Berths	Postseason Record	Super Bowl Record
Philadelphia	97	62	1	.609	5	7	10-7	0-1
Green Bay	92	68	0	.575	4	5	3-5	0-0
N.Y. Giants	87	73	0	.544	3	6	6-5	1-1
Tampa Bay	87	73	0	.544	4	6	4-5	1-0
Seattle	86	74	0	.538	5	6	4-6	0-1
St. Louis	83	77	0	.519	3	5	6-4	1-1
Minnesota	82	78	0	.513	2	4	3-4	0-0
Chicago	80	80	0	.500	3	3	2-3	0-1
Carolina	79	81	0	.494	2	3	5-3	0-1
Dallas	79	81	0	.494	1	4	0-4	0-0
Washington	76	84	0	.475	1	3	2-3	0-0
New Orleans	73	87	0	.456	2	2	2-2	0-0
Atlanta	71	88	1	.447	1	3	2-3	0-0
San Francisco	64	96	0	.400	1	2	1-2	0-0
Arizona	58	102	0	.363	1	1	3-1	0-1
Detroit	48	112	0	.300	0	1	0-1	0-0

Seattle was in AFC from 1999-2001.

HOME RECORDS, 1999-2008

AFC	W-L-T	Pct.
Indianapolis	60-20-0	.750
New England	58-22-0	.725
Baltimore	56-24-0	.700
Pittsburgh	53-26-1	.669
Denver	53-27-0	.663
Tennessee	52-28-0	.650
Kansas City	48-32-0	.600
San Diego	47-33-0	.588
Jacksonville	46-34-0	.575
Miami	46-34-0	.575
N.Y. Jets	43-37-0	.538
Buffalo	41-39-0	.513
Oakland	38-42-0	.475
Cincinnati	37-42-1	.469
Houston	26-30-0	.464
Cleveland	28-52-0	.350

Houston entered NFL in 2002.

NFC	W-L-T	Pct.
Minnesota	53-27-0	.663
Green Bay	52-28-0	.650
Seattle	52-28-0	.650
Tampa Bay	52-28-0	.650
Philadelphia	50-30-0	.625
Dallas	49-31-0	.613
St. Louis	48-32-0	.600
Chicago	47-33-0	.588
N.Y. Giants	43-37-0	.538
Washington	43-37-0	.538
Carolina	42-38-0	.525
Atlanta	41-39-0	.513
Arizona	40-40-0	.500
San Francisco	40-40-0	.500
New Orleans	35-45-0	.438
Detroit	33-47-0	.413

Seattle was in AFC from 1999-2001.

ROAD RECORDS, 1999-2008

AFC	W-L-T	Pct.
Indianapolis	54-26-0	.675
New England	52-28-0	.650
Pittsburgh	47-33-0	.588
Tennessee	44-36-0	.550
Denver	38-42-0	.475
Jacksonville	37-43-0	.463
N.Y. Jets	36-44-0	.450
Baltimore	35-45-0	.438
Miami	35-45-0	.438
San Diego	33-47-0	.413
Buffalo	30-50-0	.375
Kansas City	27-53-0	.338
Oakland	27-53-0	.338
Cleveland	26-54-0	.325
Cincinnati	25-55-0	.313
Houston	14-42-0	.250

Houston entered NFL in 2002.

NFC	W-L-T	Pct.
Philadelphia	47-32-1	.594
N.Y. Giants	44-36-0	.550
Green Bay	40-40-0	.500
New Orleans	38-42-0	.475
Carolina	37-43-0	.463
St. Louis	35-45-0	.438
Tampa Bay	35-45-0	.438
Seattle	34-46-0	.425
Chicago	33-47-0	.413
Washington	33-47-0	.413
Atlanta	30-49-1	.381
Dallas	30-50-0	.375
Minnesota	29-51-0	.363
San Francisco	24-56-0	.300
Arizona	18-62-0	.225
Detroit	15-65-0	.188

Seattle was in AFC from 1999-2001.

RECORDS BY MONTHS, 1999-2008

	Sept.	Oct.	Nov.	Dec.	Total	
AFC	W-L-T	W-L-T	W-L-T	W-L-T	W-L-T	Pct.
Indianapolis	25- 7-0	27-11-0	30-12-0	32-16-0	114- 46-0	.713
New England	20-12-0	29-13-0	25-15-0	36-10-0	110- 50-0	.688
Pittsburgh	17-15-0	26-12-0	24-17-1	33-15-0	100- 59-1	.628
Tennessee	17-15-0	26-15-0	22-16-0	31-18-0	96- 64-0	.600
Baltimore	18-14-0	19-21-0	26-17-0	28-17-0	91- 69-0	.569
Denver	22-13-0	22-19-0	23-14-0	24-23-0	91- 69-0	.569
Jacksonville	19-14-0	17-22-0	22-17-0	25-24-0	83- 77-0	.519
Miami	16-16-0	18-21-0	23-18-0	24-24-0	81- 79-0	.506
San Diego	15-18-0	22-19-0	16-23-0	27-20-0	80- 80-0	.500
N.Y. Jets	14-19-0	17-22-0	24-15-0	24-25-0	79- 81-0	.494
Kansas City	16-18-0	23-16-0	14-26-0	22-25-0	75- 85-0	.469
Buffalo	15-18-0	19-22-0	17-22-0	20-27-0	71- 89-0	.444
Oakland	17-16-0	16-23-0	16-24-0	16-32-0	65- 95-0	.406
Cincinnati	11-22-0	13-28-0	17-22-1	21-25-0	62- 97-1	.391
Houston	6-17-0	11-16-0	9-19-0	14-20-0	40- 72-0	.357
Cleveland	12-23-0	16-23-0	14-26-0	12-34-0	54-106-0	.338

Houston entered the NFL in 2002.
September totals include August; December totals include January.

	Sept.	Oct.	Nov.	Dec.	Total	
NFC	W-L-T	W-L-T	W-L-T	W-L-T	W-L-T	Pct.
Philadelphia	18-16-0	23-16-0	26-15-1	30-15-0	97- 62-1	.609
Green Bay	20-15-0	18-17-0	22-21-0	32-15-0	92- 68-0	.575
N.Y. Giants	20-13-0	27-13-0	17-23-0	23-24-0	87- 73-0	.544
Tampa Bay	20-13-0	18-22-0	25-14-0	24-24-0	87- 73-0	.544
Seattle	21-12-0	14-23-0	25-17-0	26-22-0	86- 74-0	.538
St. Louis	16-18-0	24-15-0	18-21-0	25-23-0	83- 77-0	.519
Minnesota	16-18-0	22-16-0	24-17-0	20-27-0	82- 78-0	.513
Chicago	12-21-0	21-18-0	23-18-0	24-23-0	80- 80-0	.500
Carolina	17-15-0	18-24-0	18-21-0	26-21-0	79- 81-0	.494
Dallas	19-13-0	21-20-0	22-19-0	17-29-0	79- 81-0	.494
Washington	17-15-0	20-21-0	15-25-0	24-23-0	76- 84-0	.475
New Orleans	15-17-0	21-21-0	17-21-0	20-28-0	73- 87-0	.456
Atlanta	16-18-0	18-21-0	18-21-1	19-28-0	71- 88-1	.447
San Francisco	13-20-0	13-27-0	16-23-0	22-26-0	64- 96-0	.400
Arizona	10-23-0	14-24-0	16-25-0	18-30-0	58-102-0	.363
Detroit	13-19-0	13-25-0	12-32-0	10-36-0	48-112-0	.300

Seattle was in the AFC from 1999-2001.
September totals include August; December totals include January.

TAKEAWAYS/GIVEAWAYS, 1999-2008

AFC	Takeaways Int.	Takeaways Fum.	Takeaways Total	Giveaways Int.	Giveaways Fum.	Giveaways Total	Net.Diff.
New England	180	121	301	139	109	248	53
Kansas City	167	134	301	154	95	249	52
Indianapolis	153	130	283	140	98	238	45
Tennessee	171	129	300	148	112	260	40
Jacksonville	160	105	265	118	109	227	38
Pittsburgh	165	132	297	158	101	259	38
N.Y. Jets	176	113	289	167	86	253	36
Baltimore	212	125	337	164	142	306	31
Denver	151	127	278	165	100	265	13
San Diego	174	106	280	167	107	274	6
Cincinnati	158	132	290	179	114	293	-3
Miami	175	123	298	175	126	301	-3
Oakland	159	101	260	149	134	283	-23
Buffalo	141	110	251	154	129	283	-32
Houston	87	71	158	114	86	200	-42
Cleveland	173	101	274	198	125	323	-49

Houston entered NFL in 2002.

NFC	Takeaways Int.	Takeaways Fum.	Takeaways Total	Giveaways Int.	Giveaways Fum.	Giveaways Total	Net.Diff.
Tampa Bay	207	117	324	144	126	270	54
Philadelphia	168	138	306	140	131	271	35
Carolina	178	141	319	171	131	302	17
Seattle	176	116	292	159	119	278	14
Green Bay	194	116	310	186	122	308	2
Atlanta	157	119	276	159	120	279	-3
N.Y. Giants	153	117	270	161	113	274	-4
Washington	162	106	268	139	133	272	-4
Chicago	172	138	310	180	136	316	-6
Detroit	148	140	288	200	104	304	-16
New Orleans	150	130	280	179	127	306	-26
San Francisco	155	98	253	160	128	288	-35
Minnesota	155	118	273	177	139	316	-43
Dallas	154	114	268	191	123	314	-46
St. Louis	171	123	294	211	145	356	-62
Arizona	151	116	267	207	137	344	-77

Seattle was in the AFC from 1999-2001.

BEST TAKEAWAY/GIVEAWAY DIFFERENTIAL, SEASON

+43 Washington, 1983
+26 Kansas City, 1990
+25 N.Y. Giants, 1997

HIGH AND LOW SINGLE-GAME YARDAGE TOTALS, 1999-2008

Most Total Yards, Game
645 Pittsburgh vs. Atlanta, Nov. 10, 2002 (OT)
614 St. Louis vs. San Diego, Oct. 1, 2000
605 Minnesota at New Orleans, Oct. 17, 2004
595 New Orleans vs. Cincinnati, Nov. 19, 2006
591 Seattle at San Diego, Dec. 29, 2002 (OT)

Fewest Total Yards, Game
26 Cleveland at Buffalo, Dec. 12, 2004
40 Cleveland vs. Pittsburgh, Sept. 12, 1999
47 Houston at Pittsburgh, Dec. 8, 2002
53 Cleveland at Jacksonville, Dec. 3, 2000
77 Oakland vs. Atlanta, Nov. 2, 2008

Most Yards Rushing, Game
407 Cincinnati vs. Denver, Oct. 22, 2000
378 Minnesota vs. San Diego, Nov. 4, 2007
375 Jacksonville vs. Indianapolis, Dec. 10, 2006
343 Baltimore vs. Cleveland, Sept. 14, 2003
337 St. Louis vs. Carolina, Nov. 11, 2001

Fewest Yards Rushing, Game
-18 Detroit at Arizona, Nov. 11, 2007
-3 Detroit vs. Minnesota, Dec. 10, 2006
1 Dallas at Washington, Dec. 30, 2007
4 Cincinnati at Baltimore, Sept. 24, 2000
5 New England at Pittsburgh, Oct. 31, 2004

Most Yards Passing, Game
504 New Orleans vs. Cincinnati, Nov. 19, 2006
499 Denver vs. Atlanta, Oct. 31, 2004
474 Kansas City at Oakland, Nov. 5, 2000
473 N.Y. Jets at Baltimore, Dec. 24, 2000
472 Indianapolis at Kansas City, Oct. 31, 2004

Fewest Yards Passing, Game
-9 Cleveland at Jacksonville, Dec. 3, 2000
-5 Houston at Oakland, Dec. 3, 2006
-3 Cleveland at Buffalo, Dec. 12, 2004
0 Oakland at San Diego, Dec. 28, 2003
6 Houston vs. Indianapolis, Oct. 23, 2005

NFL INDIVIDUAL LEADERS, 1999-2008

Points

Jason Elam	1,185
Matt Stover	1,176
Adam Vinatieri	1,130
Ryan Longwell	1,122
John Carney	1,063

Touchdowns

LaDainian Tomlinson	141
Randy Moss	119
Terrell Owens	114
Shaun Alexander	112
Marvin Harrison	107

Field Goals

Matt Stover	288
Jason Elam	267
Adam Vinatieri	248
John Carney	246
Ryan Longwell	243

Rushes

Edgerrin James	2,982
LaDainian Tomlinson	2,657
Jamal Lewis	2,399
Warrick Dunn	2,200
Curtis Martin	2,191

Rushing Yards

Edgerrin James	12,121
LaDainian Tomlinson	11,760
Jamal Lewis	10,107
Fred Taylor	10,048
Tiki Barber	9,772

Rushing TDs

LaDainian Tomlinson	126
Shaun Alexander	100
Edgerrin James	80
Priest Holmes	79
Clinton Portis	72

Pass Attempts

Brett Favre	5,524
Peyton Manning	5,385
Donovan McNabb	4,303
Kerry Collins	4,138
Jon Kitna	3,897

Completions

Peyton Manning	3,513
Brett Favre	3,402
Donovan McNabb	2,534
Kerry Collins	2,372
Drew Brees	2,334

Passing Yards

Peyton Manning	41,889
Brett Favre	38,324
Donovan McNabb	29,320
Kurt Warner	28,552
Kerry Collins	27,885

TD Passes

Peyton Manning	307
Brett Favre	251
Tom Brady	197
Donovan McNabb	194
Kurt Warner	182

Receptions

Marvin Harrison	906
Torry Holt	869
Tony Gonzalez	824
Terrell Owens	789
Hines Ward	785

Reception Yards

Torry Holt	12,660
Marvin Harrison	12,102
Randy Moss	11,888
Terrell Owens	11,569
Isaac Bruce	10,281

Receiving TDs

Randy Moss	118
Terrell Owens	113
Marvin Harrison	107
Torry Holt	74
Two tied	72

Interceptions

Darren Sharper	52
Champ Bailey	43
Ed Reed	43
Dre' Bly	40
Tory James	37

Sacks

Jason Taylor	106.5
Simeon Rice	94.5
Michael Strahan	94.5
John Abraham	84.0
Joey Porter	83.0

NFL GAMES IN WHICH A TEAM HAS SCORED 60 OR MORE POINTS

(Home team in capitals)

Regular Season

WASHINGTON 72, New York Giants 41	November 27, 1966
LOS ANGELES RAMS 70, Baltimore 27	October 22, 1950
Chicago Cardinals 65, NEW YORK BULLDOGS 20	November 13, 1949
LOS ANGELES RAMS 65, Detroit 24	October 29, 1950
PHILADELPHIA 64, Cincinnati 0	November 6, 1934
CHICAGO CARDINALS 63, New York Giants 35	October 17, 1948
AKRON 62, Oorang 0	October 29, 1922
PITTSBURGH 62, New York Giants 7	November 30, 1952
CLEVELAND 62, New York Giants 14	December 6, 1953
CLEVELAND 62, Washington 3	November 7, 1954
NEW YORK GIANTS 62, Philadelphia 10	November 26, 1972
Atlanta 62, NEW ORLEANS 7	September 16, 1973
NEW YORK JETS 62, Tampa Bay 28	November 17, 1985
CHICAGO 61, San Francisco 20	December 12, 1965
Cincinnati 61, HOUSTON 17	December 17, 1972
CHICAGO 61, Green Bay 7	December 7, 1980
CINCINNATI 61, Houston 7	December 17, 1989
ROCK ISLAND 60, Evansville 0	October 15, 1922
CHICAGO CARDINALS 60, Rochester 0	October 7, 1923

Postseason

Chicago Bears 73, WASHINGTON 0	December 8, 1940
JACKSONVILLE 62, Miami 7	January 15, 2000

YOUNGEST AND OLDEST PLAYERS IN NFL IN 2008

10 Youngest Players	Birthdate	Games	Starts	Position
Darren McFadden, Oakland	8/27/87	13	5	RB
Geno Hayes, Tampa Bay	8/10/87	9	0	LB
Letroy Guion, Minnesota	6/21/87	2	0	DT
Rashard Mendenhall, Pittsburgh	6/19/87	4	1	RB
Amobi Okoye, Houston	6/10/87	14	12	DT
Felix Jones, Dallas	5/8/87	6	0	RB
Jermichael Finley, Green Bay	3/26/87	14	1	TE
Earl Bennett, Chicago	3/23/87	10	0	WR
Jonathan Stewart, Carolina	3/21/87	16	0	RB
Martellus Bennett, Dallas	3/10/87	16	7	TE

10 Oldest Players	Birthdate	Games	Starts	Position
John Carney, N.Y. Giants	4/20/64	15	0	K
Jeff Feagles, N.Y. Giants	3/7/66	16	0	P
Matt Stover, Baltimore	1/27/68	16	0	K
Matt Turk, Houston	6/16/68	16	0	P
Brad Johnson, Dallas	9/13/68	16	3	QB
Junior Seau, New England	1/19/69	4	2	LB
Brett Favre, N.Y. Jets	10/10/69	16	16	QB
John Kasay, Carolina	10/27/69	16	0	K
Jeff Robinson, Seattle	2/20/70	16	0	LS
Jeff Garcia, Tampa Bay	2/24/70	12	11	QB

YOUNGEST AND OLDEST REGULAR STARTERS BY POSITION IN 2008

Minimum: 8 Games Started

	Youngest		Oldest	
QB	8/9/85	JaMarcus Russell, Oak.	10/10/69	Brett Favre, N.Y. Jets
RB	12/17/86	Kevin Smith, Det.	1/27/76	Fred Taylor, Jac.
WR	12/1/86	DeSean Jackson, Phi.	8/25/72	Marvin Harrison, Ind.
TE	12/11/85	Zach Miller, Oak.	2/27/76	Tony Gonzalez, K.C.
T	9/6/86	Ryan Clady, Den.	11/27/73	Jon Runyan, Phi.
G	9/21/85	Darnell Stapleton, Pit.	7/9/73	Pete Kendall, Was.
C	3/29/85	Ryan Kalil, Car.	1/23/71	Kevin Mawae, Ten.
DE	11/9/86	Derrick Harvey, Jac.	9/21/73	Kevin Carter, T.B.
DT	6/10/87	Amobi Okoye, Hou.	10/24/72	Pat Williams, Min.
LB	6/9/86	Curtis Lofton, Atl.	12/11/71	Willie McGinest, Cle.
CB	5/19/86	Brandon Carr, K.C.	8/10/74	Walt Harris, S.F.
S	11/15/85	Charles Godfrey, Car.	10/13/73	Brian Dawkins, Phi.

OLDEST INDIVIDUAL SINGLE-SEASON OR SINGLE-GAME RECORDS IN NFL RECORD & FACT BOOK

Most Points, Game—40, Ernie Nevers, Chi. Cardinals vs. Chi. Bears, Nov. 28, 1929 (6-td, 4-pat)

Most Touchdowns Rushing, Game—6, Ernie Nevers, Chi. Cardinals vs. Chi. Bears, Nov. 28, 1929

Highest Rushing Average Gain, Season (Qualifiers)—8.44, Beattie Feathers, Chi. Bears, 1934 (119-1,004)

Highest Punting Average, Season (Qualifiers)—51.40, Sammy Baugh, Washington, 1940 (35-1,799)

Highest Punting Average, Rookie, Season (Qualifiers)—45.92, Frank Sinkwich, Detroit, 1943 (12-551)

Highest Punting Average, Game (minimum: 4 punts)—61.75, Bob Cifers, Detroit vs. Chi. Bears, Nov. 24, 1946 (4-247)

Highest Average Gain, Pass Receptions, Season (minimum: 24 receptions)—32.58, Don Currivan, Boston, 1947 (24-782)

Highest Average Gain, Passing, Game (minimum: 20 passes)—18.58, Sammy Baugh, Washington vs. Boston, Oct. 31, 1948 (24-446)

Most Touchdowns, Fumble Recoveries, Game—2, Fred (Dippy) Evans, Chi. Bears vs. Washington, Nov. 28, 1948

Most Yards Gained, Intercepted Passes, Rookie, Season—301, Don Doll, Detroit, 1949

Most Passes Had Intercepted, Game—8, Jim Hardy, Chi. Cardinals vs. Philadelphia, Sept. 24, 1950

Highest Kickoff Return Average, Game (minimum: 3 returns)—73.50, Wally Triplett, Detroit vs. Los Angeles, Oct. 29, 1950 (4-294)

Highest Punt Return Average, Season (Qualifiers)—23.00, Herb Rich, Baltimore, 1950 (12-276)

Highest Punt Return Average, Rookie, Season (Qualifiers)—23.00, Herb Rich, Baltimore, 1950 (12-276)

Most Yards Passing, Game—554, Norm Van Brocklin, Los Angeles vs. N.Y. Yanks, Sept. 28, 1951

Most Touchdowns, Punt Returns, Rookie, Season—4, Jack Christiansen, Detroit, 1951

Most Interceptions By, Season—14, Dick (Night Train) Lane, Los Angeles, 1952

Most Interceptions By, Rookie, Season—14, Dick (Night Train) Lane, Los Angeles, 1952

Highest Average Gain, Passing, Season (Qualifiers)—11.17, Tommy O'Connell, Cleveland, 1957 (110-1,229)

Most Yards Gained, Pass Receptions, Rookie, Season—1,473, Bill Groman, Houston, 1960

NFL INDIVIDUAL LEADERS OVER RECENT SEASONS

Points

Last 2 Seasons		Last 3 Seasons		Last 4 Seasons	
285	Stephen Gostkowski	388	Stephen Gostkowski	493	Nate Kaeding
268	Mason Crosby	388	Robbie Gould	486	LaDainian Tomlinson
260	Rob Bironas	381	Nate Kaeding	485	Neil Rackers
252	David Akers	366	LaDainian Tomlinson	473	Jason Elam
249	Matt Bryant	358	Two tied	470	Robbie Gould

Touchdowns

Last 2 Seasons		Last 3 Seasons		Last 4 Seasons	
34	Randy Moss	61	LaDainian Tomlinson	81	LaDainian Tomlinson
30	LaDainian Tomlinson	40	Maurice Jones-Drew	49	Larry Johnson
26	Brian Westbrook	38	Terrell Owens	45	Randy Moss
25	Terrell Owens	37	Three tied	44	Terrell Owens
25	DeAngelo Williams			44	Brian Westbrook

Field Goals

Last 2 Seasons		Last 3 Seasons		Last 4 Seasons	
64	Rob Bironas	89	Robbie Gould	114	Neil Rackers
60	Matt Bryant	86	Rob Bironas	112	Matt Stover
59	Josh Brown	84	Josh Brown	110	Robbie Gould
58	Mason Crosby	83	Jason Elam	109	Rob Bironas
57	Three tied	82	Matt Stover	107	Jason Elam

Rushes

Last 2 Seasons		Last 3 Seasons		Last 4 Seasons	
667	Clinton Portis	955	LaDainian Tomlinson	1,294	LaDainian Tomlinson
607	LaDainian Tomlinson	896	Thomas Jones	1,210	Thomas Jones
601	Adrian Peterson	891	Jamal Lewis	1,160	Jamal Lewis
600	Thomas Jones	868	Willie Parker	1,154	Edgerrin James
577	Jamal Lewis	836	Steven Jackson	1,146	Clinton Portis

Rushing Yards

Last 2 Seasons		Last 3 Seasons		Last 4 Seasons	
3,101	Adrian Peterson	4,399	LaDainian Tomlinson	5,861	LaDainian Tomlinson
2,749	Clinton Portis	3,833	Frank Gore	4,976	Thomas Jones
2,584	LaDainian Tomlinson	3,641	Thomas Jones	4,972	Larry Johnson
2,431	Thomas Jones	3,601	Willie Parker	4,803	Willie Parker
2,306	Jamal Lewis	3,572	Steven Jackson	4,788	Clinton Portis

Rushing Touchdowns

Last 2 Seasons		Last 3 Seasons		Last 4 Seasons	
26	LaDainian Tomlinson	54	LaDainian Tomlinson	72	LaDainian Tomlinson
22	Adrian Peterson	34	Maurice Jones-Drew	45	Larry Johnson
22	LenDale White	31	Marion Barber	38	Shaun Alexander
22	DeAngelo Williams	28	Brandon Jacobs	38	Clinton Portis
21	Maurice Jones-Drew	27	Clinton Portis	36	Marion Barber

Passes

Last 2 Seasons		Last 3 Seasons		Last 4 Seasons	
1,287	Drew Brees	1,841	Drew Brees	2,341	Drew Brees
1,083	Jay Cutler	1,670	Brett Favre	2,277	Brett Favre
1,070	Peyton Manning	1,627	Peyton Manning	2,087	Eli Manning
1,057	Brett Favre	1,530	Eli Manning	2,080	Peyton Manning
1,049	Kurt Warner	1,406	Marc Bulger	1,733	Carson Palmer

Completions

Last 2 Seasons		Last 3 Seasons		Last 4 Seasons	
853	Drew Brees	1,209	Drew Brees	1,532	Drew Brees
708	Peyton Manning	1,070	Peyton Manning	1,414	Brett Favre
699	Brett Favre	1,042	Brett Favre	1,375	Peyton Manning
682	Kurt Warner	887	Eli Manning	1,181	Eli Manning
681	Jay Cutler	873	Philip Rivers	1,117	Carson Palmer

Passing Yards

Last 2 Seasons		Last 3 Seasons		Last 4 Seasons	
9,492	Drew Brees	13,910	Drew Brees	17,486	Drew Brees
8,042	Peyton Manning	12,439	Peyton Manning	16,186	Peyton Manning
8,023	Jay Cutler	11,512	Brett Favre	15,393	Brett Favre
8,000	Kurt Warner	10,562	Tony Romo	13,580	Eli Manning
7,659	Tony Romo	10,549	Philip Rivers	12,733	Carson Palmer

Touchdown Passes

Last 2 Seasons		Last 3 Seasons		Last 4 Seasons	
62	Drew Brees	89	Peyton Manning	117	Peyton Manning
62	Tony Romo	88	Drew Brees	112	Drew Brees
58	Peyton Manning	81	Tony Romo	100	Tom Brady
57	Kurt Warner	77	Philip Rivers	92	Eli Manning
55	Philip Rivers	74	Tom Brady	89	Carson Palmer

Receptions

Last 2 Seasons		Last 3 Seasons		Last 4 Seasons	
223	Wes Welker	294	T.J. Houshmandzadeh	372	T.J. Houshmandzadeh
206	Brandon Marshall	290	Wes Welker	368	Larry Fitzgerald
204	T.J. Houshmandzadeh	278	Andre Johnson	355	Reggie Wayne
196	Larry Fitzgerald	272	Reggie Wayne	352	Torry Holt
195	Tony Gonzalez	268	Tony Gonzalez	351	Steve Smith

Receiving Yards

Last 2 Seasons		Last 3 Seasons		Last 4 Seasons	
2,840	Larry Fitzgerald	3,965	Reggie Wayne	5,195	Larry Fitzgerald
2,655	Reggie Wayne	3,786	Larry Fitzgerald	5,152	Steve Smith
2,590	Brandon Marshall	3,589	Steve Smith	5,020	Reggie Wayne
2,584	Roddy White	3,587	Terrell Owens	4,781	Chad Ochocinco
2,501	Randy Moss	3,573	Andre Johnson	4,576	Donald Driver

Receiving Touchdowns

Last 2 Seasons		Last 3 Seasons		Last 4 Seasons	
34	Randy Moss	38	Terrell Owens	45	Randy Moss
25	Terrell Owens	37	Randy Moss	44	Terrell Owens
22	Larry Fitzgerald	28	Larry Fitzgerald	38	Larry Fitzgerald
21	Greg Jennings	26	Plaxico Burress	36	Antonio Gates
20	Anquan Boldin	26	Antonio Gates	33	Two tied

Interceptions

Last 2 Seasons		Last 3 Seasons		Last 4 Seasons	
16	Ed Reed	21	Ed Reed	23	Asante Samuel
13	Oshiomogho Atogwe	20	Asante Samuel	22	Champ Bailey
12	Antonio Cromartie	19	Charles Woodson	22	Ed Reed
11	Charles Woodson	16	Oshiomogho Atogwe	20	DeAngelo Hall
10	Three tied	15	Walt Harris	20	Charles Woodson

Sacks

Last 2 Seasons		Last 3 Seasons		Last 4 Seasons	
34.0	DeMarcus Ware	45.5	DeMarcus Ware	53.5	DeMarcus Ware
30.0	Jared Allen	37.5	Jared Allen	48.5	Jared Allen
26.5	John Abraham	37.0	Aaron Kampman	43.5	Aaron Kampman
26.0	Mario Williams	30.5	John Abraham	41.0	John Abraham
24.5	James Harrison	30.5	Mario Williams	40.5	Two tied

NFL TEAM LEADERS OVER RECENT SEASONS

Highest Won-Lost Percentage

Last 2 Seasons		Last 3 Seasons		Last 4 Seasons	
.844	New England	.813	New England	.797	Indianapolis
.781	Indianapolis	.771	Indianapolis	.766	New England
.719	Tennessee	.688	San Diego	.656	San Diego
.688	Three tied	.646	Dallas	.641	N.Y. Giants
		.646	Tennessee	.641	Pittsburgh

Most Points

Last 2 Seasons		Last 3 Seasons		Last 4 Seasons	
999	New England	1,384	New England	1,763	New England
854	Green Bay	1,343	San Diego	1,761	San Diego
851	San Diego	1,255	New Orleans	1,693	Indianapolis
842	New Orleans	1,254	Indianapolis	1,577	N.Y. Giants
831	Arizona	1,242	Dallas	1,567	Dallas

Most Total Yards

Last 2 Seasons		Last 3 Seasons		Last 4 Seasons	
12,427	New England	18,615	New Orleans	23,646	New Orleans
12,351	New Orleans	17,796	New England	23,428	New England
11,874	Denver	17,440	Philadelphia	22,976	Indianapolis
11,549	Green Bay	17,177	Indianapolis	22,591	Denver
11,450	Houston	17,135	Dallas	22,549	Philadelphia

INSIDE THE NUMBERS

Most Rushing Yards

Last 2 Seasons		Last 3 Seasons		Last 4 Seasons	
4,972	Minnesota	6,902	Atlanta	9,448	Atlanta
4,666	N.Y. Giants	6,822	N.Y. Giants	9,031	N.Y. Giants
4,308	Tennessee	6,792	Minnesota	8,665	Jacksonville
4,261	Carolina	6,706	Jacksonville	8,510	Denver
4,173	Baltimore	6,522	Tennessee	8,415	San Diego

Most Passing Yards

Last 2 Seasons		Last 3 Seasons		Last 4 Seasons	
9,291	New Orleans	13,794	New Orleans	17,137	New Orleans
8,739	Arizona	12,435	Indianapolis	16,838	Arizona
8,300	New England	12,401	Arizona	16,531	Indianapolis
8,147	Green Bay	11,942	Green Bay	15,820	New England
8,127	Indianapolis	11,785	Philadelphia	15,708	Green Bay

Fewest Turnovers

Last 2 Seasons		Last 3 Seasons		Last 4 Seasons	
36	Indianapolis	55	Indianapolis	74	Indianapolis
36	New England	59	San Diego	85	Jacksonville
42	Miami	63	New England	87	New England
44	San Diego	64	Washington	87	San Diego
45	Three tied	65	Atlanta	91	Washington

Fewest Points Allowed

Last 2 Seasons		Last 3 Seasons		Last 4 Seasons	
492	Pittsburgh	807	Pittsburgh	1,065	Pittsburgh
531	Tennessee	820	New England	1,128	Baltimore
560	Indianapolis	829	Baltimore	1,155	Chicago
583	New England	917	Philadelphia	1,158	New England
589	Philadelphia	920	Indianapolis	1,167	Indianapolis

Fewest Total Yards Allowed

Last 2 Seasons		Last 3 Seasons		Last 4 Seasons	
8,057	Pittsburgh	12,862	Pittsburgh	17,406	Pittsburgh
9,002	Baltimore	13,227	Baltimore	17,776	Baltimore
9,352	Tampa Bay	14,267	New England	19,067	Tampa Bay
9,363	Tennessee	14,620	Philadelphia	19,509	Jacksonville
9,371	Philadelphia	14,623	Tampa Bay	19,550	New England

Fewest Rushing Yards Allowed

Last 2 Seasons		Last 3 Seasons		Last 4 Seasons	
2,415	Minnesota	3,400	Minnesota	5,241	Minnesota
2,570	Baltimore	3,784	Baltimore	5,375	Baltimore
2,722	Pittsburgh	4,134	Pittsburgh	5,510	Pittsburgh
2,980	Tennessee	4,774	Jacksonville	6,315	San Diego
2,986	Washington	4,801	New England	6,381	New England

Fewest Passing Yards Allowed

Last 2 Seasons		Last 3 Seasons		Last 4 Seasons	
5,335	Pittsburgh	8,321	Indianapolis	11,472	Indianapolis
5,725	Tampa Bay	8,728	Pittsburgh	11,896	Pittsburgh
5,773	Indianapolis	8,765	Oakland	12,008	Oakland
6,263	New England	9,079	Tampa Bay	12,008	Tampa Bay
6,352	Oakland	9,429	Philadelphia	12,401	Baltimore

Most Opponents' Turnovers

Last 2 Seasons		Last 3 Seasons		Last 4 Seasons	
72	San Diego	109	Chicago	143	Chicago
65	Chicago	100	San Diego	134	Cincinnati
65	Tampa Bay	97	Baltimore	127	Minnesota
65	Tennessee	93	Tennessee	123	Baltimore
63	Indianapolis	92	Two tied	120	Two tied

RETIRED UNIFORM NUMBERS IN NFL

AFC

Team	Player	No.
Baltimore	None	
Buffalo	Jim Kelly	12
Cincinnati	Bob Johnson	54
Cleveland	Otto Graham	14
	Jim Brown	32
	Ernie Davis	45
	Don Fleming	46
	Lou Groza	76
Denver	John Elway	7
	Frank Tripucka	18
	Floyd Little	44
Houston	None	
Indianapolis	Johnny Unitas	19
	Buddy Young	22
	Lenny Moore	24
	Art Donovan	70
	Jim Parker	77
	Raymond Berry	82
	Gino Marchetti	89
Jacksonville	None	
Kansas City	Jan Stenerud	3
	Len Dawson	16
	Emmitt Thomas	18
	Abner Haynes	28
	Stone Johnson	33
	Mack Lee Hill	36
	Willie Lanier	63
	Bobby Bell	78
	Buck Buchanan	86
Miami	Bob Griese	12
	Dan Marino	13
	Larry Csonka	39
New England	Bruce Armstrong	78
	Gino Cappelletti	20
	Mike Haynes	40
	Steve Nelson	57
	John Hannah	73
	Jim Lee Hunt	79
	Bob Dee	89
New York Jets	Joe Namath	12
	Don Maynard	13
	Joe Klecko	73
Oakland	None	
Pittsburgh	Ernie Stautner	70
San Diego	Dan Fouts	14
	Lance Alworth	19
Tennessee	Warren Moon	1
	Earl Campbell	34
	Jim Norton	43
	Mike Munchak	63
	Elvin Bethea	65
	Bruce Matthews	74

NFC

Team	Player	No.
Arizona	Larry Wilson	8
	Pat Tillman	40
	Stan Mauldin	77
	J.V. Cain	88
	Marshall Goldberg	99
Atlanta	Steve Bartkowski	10
	William Andrews	31
	Jeff Van Note	57
	Tommy Nobis	60
Carolina	Sam Mills	51
Chicago	Bronko Nagurski	3
	George McAfee	5
	George Halas	7
	Willie Galimore	28
	Walter Payton	34
	Gale Sayers	40
	Brian Piccolo	41
	Sid Luckman	42
	Dick Butkus	51
	Bill Hewitt	56
	Bill George	61
	Bulldog Turner	66
	Red Grange	77
Dallas	None	
Detroit	Dutch Clark	7
	Bobby Layne	22
	Doak Walker	37
	Joe Schmidt	56
	Chuck Hughes	85
Green Bay	Tony Canadeo	3
	Don Hutson	14
	Bart Starr	15
	Ray Nitschke	66
	Reggie White	92
Minnesota	Fran Tarkenton	10
	Mick Tingelhoff	53
	Jim Marshall	70
	Korey Stringer	77
	Cris Carter	80
	Alan Page	88
New Orleans	Jim Taylor	31
	Doug Atkins	81
New York Giants	Ray Flaherty	1
	Tuffy Leemans	4
	Mel Hein	7
	Phil Simms	11
	Y.A. Tittle	14
	Frank Gifford	16
	Al Blozis	32
	Joe Morrison	40
	Charlie Conerly	42
	Ken Strong	50
	Lawrence Taylor	56
Philadelphia	Steve Van Buren	15
	Tom Brookshier	40
	Pete Retzlaff	44
	Chuck Bednarik	60
	Al Wistert	70
	Reggie White	92
	Jerome Brown	99
St. Louis	Bob Waterfield	7
	Eric Dickerson	29
	Merlin Olsen	74
	Jackie Slater	78
	Jack Youngblood	85
San Francisco	Steve Young	8
	John Brodie	12
	Joe Montana	16
	Joe Perry	34
	Jimmy Johnson	37
	Hugh McElhenny	39
	Ronnie Lott	42
	Charlie Krueger	70
	Leo Nomellini	73
	Bob St. Clair	79
	Dwight Clark	87
Seattle	"Fans/the twelfth man"	12
	Steve Largent	80
Tampa Bay	Lee Roy Selmon	63
Washington	Sammy Baugh	33

The NFL rates its passers for statistical purposes against a fixed performance standard based on statistical achievements of all qualified pro passers since 1960. The current system replaced one that rated passers in relation to their position in a total group based on various criteria. The current system, which was adopted in 1973, removes inequities that existed in the former method and, at the same time, provides a means of comparing passing performances from one season to the next.

It is important to remember that the system is used to rate passers, not quarterbacks. Statistics do not reflect leadership, play-calling, and other intangible factors that go into making a successful professional quarterback. Four categories are used as a basis for compiling a rating:

—Percentage of completions per attempt
—Average yards gained per attempt
—Percentage of touchdown passes per attempt
—Percentage of interceptions per attempt

The average standard is 1.000. The bottom is .000. To earn a 2.000 rating, a passer must perform at exceptional levels, i.e., 70 percent in completions, 10 percent in touchdowns, 1.5 percent in interceptions, and 11 yards average gain per pass attempt. The maximum a passer can receive in any category is 2.375.

For example, to gain a 2.375 in completion percentage, a passer would have to complete 77.5 percent of his passes. The NFL record is 70.55 by Ken Anderson (Cincinnati, 1982). To earn a 2.375 in percentage of touchdowns, a passer would have to achieve a percentage of 11.9. The record is 13.9 by Sid Luckman (Chicago, 1943). To gain 2.375 in percentage of interceptions, a passer would have to go the entire season without an interception. The 2.375 figure in average yards is 12.50, compared with the NFL record of 11.17 by Tommy O'Connell (Cleveland, 1957).

In order to make the rating more understandable, the point rating is then converted into a scale of 100, with 158.3 being the highest rating a passer can achieve. In cases where statistical performance has been superior, it is possible for a passer to surpass a 100 rating. For example, take Peyton Manning's record-setting season in 2004 when he completed 336 of 497 passes for 4,557 yards, 49 touchdowns, and 10 interceptions. The four calculations would be:

—Percentage of Completions—336 of 497 is 67.60 percent. Subtract 30 from the completion percentage (37.60) and multiply the result by 0.05. The result is a point rating of 1.880.
Note: If the result is less than zero (Comp. Pct. less than 30.0), award zero points. If the results are greater than 2.375 (Comp. Pct. greater than 77.5), award 2.375.

—Average Yards Gained Per Attempt—4,557 yards divided by 497 attempts is 9.17. Subtract three yards from yards-per-attempt (6.17) and multiply the result by 0.25. The result is 1.543.
Note: If the result is less than zero (yards per attempt less than 3.0), award zero points. If the result is greater than 2.375 (yards per attempt greater than 12.5), award 2.375 points.

—Percentage of Touchdown Passes—49 touchdowns in 497 attempts is 9.86 percent. Multiply the touchdown percentage by 0.2. The result is 1.972.
Note: If the result is greater than 2.375 (touchdown percentage greater than 11.875), award 2.375.

—Percentage of Interceptions—10 interceptions in 497 attempts is 2.01 percent. Multiply the interception percentage by 0.25 (0.503) and subtract the number from 2.375. The result is 1.872.
Note: If the result is less than zero (interception percentage greater than 9.5), award zero points.

The sum of the four steps is (1.880 + 1.543 + 1.972 + 1.872) 7.267. The sum is then divided by six (1.211) and multiplied by 100. In this case, the result is 121.1. This same formula can be used to determine a passer rating for any player who attempts at least one pass.

Forty-three qualifying passers have had a single-season passer rating of 100 or higher. The following is a list of the Top 25 single-season passer ratings among qualifying players:

TOP 25 NFL SINGLE-SEASON PASSER RATINGS (QUALIFYING PLAYERS)

Player, Team	Season	Rating	Att.	Comp.	Pct.	Yds.	Yds. Avg.	TD	TD Pct.	Int.	Int. Pct.
Peyton Manning, Indianapolis	2004	*121.1	497	336	67.6	4,557	9.17	49	9.9	10	2.0
Tom Brady, New England	2007	117.2	578	398	68.9	4,806	8.31	*50	8.7	8	1.4
Steve Young, San Francisco	1994	112.8	461	324	70.2	3,969	8.61	35	7.6	10	2.2
Joe Montana, San Francisco	1989	112.4	386	271	70.2	3,521	9.12	26	6.7	8	2.1
Daunte Culpepper, Minnesota	2004	110.9	548	379	69.2	4,717	8.61	39	7.1	11	2.0
Milt Plum, Cleveland	1960	110.4	250	151	60.4	2,297	9.19	21	8.4	5	2.0
Sammy Baugh, Washington	1945	109.9	182	128	70.3	1,669	9.17	11	6.0	4	2.2
Kurt Warner, St. Louis	1999	109.2	499	325	65.1	4,353	8.72	41	8.2	13	2.6
Dan Marino, Miami	1984	108.9	564	362	64.2	*5,084	9.01	48	8.5	17	3.0
Sid Luckman, Chicago Bears	1943	107.5	202	110	54.5	2,194	10.86	28	13.9	12	5.9
Steve Young, San Francisco	1992	107.0	402	268	66.7	3,465	8.62	25	6.2	7	1.7
Randall Cunningham, Minnesota	1998	106.0	425	259	60.9	3,704	8.72	34	8.0	10	2.4
Philip Rivers, San Diego	2008	105.5	478	312	65.3	4,009	8.39	34	7.1	11	2.3
Bart Starr, Green Bay	1966	105.0	251	156	62.2	2,257	8.99	14	5.6	3	1.2
Drew Brees, San Diego	2004	104.8	400	262	65.5	3,159	7.90	27	6.8	7	1.8
Roger Staubach, Dallas	1971	104.8	211	126	59.7	1,882	8.92	15	7.1	4	1.9
Y.A. Tittle, N.Y. Giants	1963	104.8	367	221	60.2	3,145	8.57	36	9.8	14	3.8
Donovan McNabb, Philadelphia	2004	104.7	469	300	64.0	3,875	8.06	31	6.6	8	1.7
Steve Young, San Francisco	1997	104.7	356	241	67.7	3,029	8.51	19	5.3	6	1.7
Bart Starr, Green Bay	1968	104.3	171	109	63.7	1,617	9.46	15	8.8	8	4.7
Chad Pennington, N.Y. Jets	2002	104.2	399	275	68.9	3,120	7.82	22	5.5	6	1.5
Ben Roethlisberger, Pittsburgh	2007	104.1	404	264	65.3	3,154	7.81	32	7.9	11	2.7
Peyton Manning, Indianapolis	2005	104.1	453	305	67.3	3,747	8.27	28	6.2	10	2.2
Ken Stabler, Oakland	1976	103.4	291	194	66.7	2,737	9.41	27	9.3	17	5.8
Brian Griese, Denver	2000	102.9	336	216	64.3	2,688	8.00	19	5.7	4	1.2

**NFL Record*

HIGHEST NFL POSTSEASON PASSER RATINGS (MINIMUM: 150 ATTEMPTS)

Player	Games	Att.	Cmp.	Pct.	Yards	Avg. Gain	TD	Int.	Rating
Bart Starr	10	213	130	61.0	1,753	8.23	15	3	104.8
Kurt Warner	11	403	261	64.8	3,368	8.36	26	13	98.9
Joe Montana	23	734	460	62.7	5,772	7.86	45	21	95.6
Ken Anderson	6	166	110	66.3	1,321	7.96	9	6	93.5
Joe Theismann	10	211	128	60.7	1,782	8.45	11	7	91.4
Troy Aikman	16	502	320	63.7	3,849	7.67	23	17	88.3
Tom Brady	17	595	372	62.5	3,954	6.65	26	12	88.0
Ben Roethlisberger	10	278	172	61.9	2,239	8.05	15	12	87.2
Steve Young	22	471	292	62.0	3,326	7.06	20	13	85.8
Brett Favre	22	721	438	60.6	5,311	7.37	39	28	85.2

HIGHEST NFL POSTSEASON PASSER RATINGS, ACTIVE PLAYERS (MINIMUM: 100 ATTEMPTS)

Player	Games	Att.	Cmp.	Pct.	Yards	Avg. Gain	TD	Int.	Rating
Kurt Warner	11	403	261	64.8	3,368	8.36	26	13	98.9
Drew Brees	3	123	78	63.4	916	7.45	5	2	92.7
Tom Brady	17	595	372	62.5	3,954	6.65	26	12	88.0
Ben Roethlisberger	10	278	172	61.9	2,239	8.05	15	12	87.2
Peyton Manning	15	564	348	61.7	4,208	7.46	22	17	85.0
Jake Delhomme	8	226	130	57.5	1,847	8.17	12	10	83.3
Daunte Culpepper	4	134	73	54.5	980	7.31	8	5	82.3
Donovan McNabb	15	540	322	59.6	3,522	6.52	23	16	80.8
Marc Bulger	3	113	68	60.2	944	8.35	4	5	80.4
Matt Hasselbeck	9	325	189	58.2	2,211	6.80	11	8	79.9

ALL-TIME RANKINGS OF PLAYERS IN FOUR CATEGORIES THAT DETERMINE NFL PASSER RATING

Minimum: 1,500 Attempts

COMPLETION PERCENTAGE	Pct.	Att.	Comp.
Chad Pennington	65.97	2,395	1,580
Kurt Warner	65.42	3,557	2,327
Peyton Manning	64.41	5,960	3,839
Steve Young	64.28	4,149	2,667
Drew Brees	63.95	3,650	2,334
Carson Palmer	63.74	2,165	1,380
Daunte Culpepper	63.35	3,042	1,927
Joe Montana	63.24	5,391	3,409
Tom Brady	62.99	3,653	2,301
Brian Griese	62.66	2,796	1,752

AVERAGE YARDS PER PASS	Avg.	Att.	Yards
Otto Graham	8.63	1,565	13,499
Sid Luckman	8.42	1,744	14,686
Norm Van Brocklin	8.16	2,895	23,611
Kurt Warner	8.04	3,557	28,591
Steve Young	7.98	4,149	33,124
Ben Roethlisberger	7.86	1,905	14,974
Ed Brown	7.85	1,987	15,600
Bart Starr	7.85	3,149	24,718
Johnny Unitas	7.76	5,186	40,239
Earl Morrall	7.74	2,689	20,809

TOUCHDOWN PERCENTAGE	Pct.	Att.	TD
Sid Luckman	7.86	1,744	137
Frank Ryan	6.99	2,133	149
Len Dawson	6.39	3,741	239
Daryle Lamonica	6.31	2,601	164
Sammy Baugh	6.24	2,995	187
Charlie Conerly	6.11	2,833	173
Bob Waterfield	6.00	1,617	97
Earl Morrall	5.99	2,689	161
Sonny Jurgensen	5.98	4,262	255
Norm Van Brocklin	5.98	2,895	173

INTERCEPTION PERCENTAGE	Pct.	Att.	Int.
Donovan McNabb	2.09	4,303	90
Neil O'Donnell	2.11	3,229	68
Jeff Garcia	2.26	3,676	83
Mark Brunell	2.31	4,594	106
Tom Brady	2.35	3,653	86
Steve Bono	2.47	1,701	42
Rich Gannon	2.47	4,206	104
Joe Montana	2.58	5,391	139
Steve Young	2.58	4,149	107
Bernie Kosar	2.59	3,365	87

INSIDE THE NUMBERS

STARTING RECORDS OF ACTIVE NFL QUARTERBACKS

Minimum: 10 starts	W-L-T	Pct.
Tom Brady	87-24-0	.784
Ben Roethlisberger	51-20-0	.718
Shaun Hill	7-3-0	.700
Tony Romo	27-12-0	.692
Joe Flacco	11-5-0	.688
Philip Rivers	33-15-0	.688
Matt Ryan	11-5-0	.688
Matt Cassel	10-5-0	.667
Peyton Manning	117-59-0	.665
Donovan McNabb	82-45-1	.645
Kyle Orton	21-12-0	.636
Vince Young	18-11-0	.621
Jake Delhomme	50-31-0	.617
Rex Grossman	19-12-0	.613
Eli Manning	42-29-0	.592
Brad Johnson	72-53-0	.576
Kurt Warner	57-44-0	.564
Matt Hasselbeck	58-45-0	.563
Chad Pennington	43-34-0	.558
Damon Huard	15-12-0	.556
Brian Griese	45-38-0	.542
Tarvaris Jackson	10-9-0	.526
Trent Edwards	12-11-0	.522
David Garrard	24-22-0	.522
Byron Leftwich	24-22-0	.522
Mark Brunell	78-72-0	.520
Drew Brees	55-51-0	.519
Todd Collins	10-10-0	.500
Jeff Garcia	58-58-0	.500
Sage Rosenfels	6-6-0	.500
Trent Green	56-57-0	.496
Carson Palmer	32-33-0	.492
Gus Frerotte	45-47-1	.489
Kerry Collins	79-85-0	.482
Derek Anderson	13-14-0	.481
Kyle Boller	20-22-0	.476
A.J. Feeley	7-8-0	.467
Chris Simms	7-8-0	.467
Marc Bulger	40-47-0	.460
Jay Cutler	17-20-0	.459
Jason Campbell	16-20-0	.444
Charlie Batch	22-28-0	.440
Matt Leinart	7-9-0	.438
Daunte Culpepper	41-54-0	.432
Anthony Wright	8-11-0	.421
Patrick Ramsey	10-14-0	.417
Matt Schaub	10-14-0	.417
Seneca Wallace	5-7-0	.417
Jon Kitna	46-69-0	.400
Chris Redman	4-6-0	.400
Josh McCown	12-19-0	.387
Aaron Rodgers	6-10-0	.375
Alex Smith	11-19-0	.367
Joey Harrington	26-50-0	.342
JaMarcus Russell	5-11-0	.313
J.P. Losman	10-23-0	.303
Ryan Fitzpatrick	4-10-1	.300
Charlie Frye	6-14-0	.300
Billy Volek	3-7-0	.300
David Carr	23-56-0	.291
Bruce Gradkowski	3-9-0	.250
Brooks Bollinger	2-8-0	.200
Ken Dorsey	2-11-0	.154
Tyler Thigpen	1-10-0	.091

TEAMS THAT FINISHED IN FIRST PLACE IN THEIR DIVISION THE SEASON AFTER FINISHING IN LAST PLACE

Season	Team	Record	Prior Season
1967	Houston	9-4-1	*3-11-0
1968	Minnesota	8-6-0	3- 8-3
1970	Cincinnati	8-6-0	4- 9-1
1970	San Francisco	10-3-1	4- 8-2
1972	Green Bay	10-4-0	4- 8-2
1975	Baltimore	10-4-0	2-12-0
1979	Tampa Bay	10-6-0	5-11-0
1981	Cincinnati	12-4-0	6-10-0
1987	Indianapolis	9-6-0	3-13-0
1988	Cincinnati	12-4-0	4-11-0
1990	Cincinnati	9-7-0	8- 8-0
1991	Denver	12-4-0	5-11-0
1992	San Diego	11-5-0	4-12-0
1993	Detroit	10-6-0	5-11-0
1997	N.Y. Giants	10-5-1	6-10-0
1999	Indianapolis	13-3-0	3-13-0
1999	St. Louis	13-3-0	4-12-0
2000	New Orleans	10-6-0	3-13-0
2001	Chicago	13-3-0	5-11-0
2001	New England	11-5-0	5-11-0
2003	Carolina	11-5-0	7- 9-0
2003	Kansas City	13-3-0	*8- 8-0
2004	Atlanta	11-5-0	5-11-0
2004	San Diego	12-4-0	*4-12-0
2005	Chicago	11-5-0	5-11-0
2005	Tampa Bay	11-5-0	5-11-0
2006	Baltimore	13-3-0	*6-10-0
2006	New Orleans	10-6-0	3-13-0
2006	Philadelphia	10-6-0	6-10-0
2007	Tampa Bay	9-7-0	4-12-0
2008	Miami	11-5-0	1-15-0

**tied for last place*

LONGEST WINNING STREAKS SINCE 1970

21	New England, 2006-08	(3 in 2006, 16 in 2007, 2 in 2008)
18	New England, 2003-04	(12 in 2003, 6 in 2004)
16	Miami, 1971-73	(1 in 1971, 14 in 1972, 1 in 1973)
16	Miami, 1983-84	(5 in 1983, 11 in 1984)
16	Pittsburgh, 2004-05	(14 in 2004, 2 in 2005)
15	San Francisco, 1989-90	(5 in 1989, 10 in 1990)
14	Oakland, 1976-77	(10 in 1976, 4 in 1977)
14	Denver, 1997-98	(1 in 1997, 13 in 1998)
13	Minnesota, 1974-75	(3 in 1974, 10 in 1975)
13	Chicago, 1984-85	(1 in 1984, 12 in 1985)
13	N.Y. Giants, 1989-90	(3 in 1989, 10 in 1990)
13	Indianapolis, 2005	
13	Tennessee, 2007-08	(3 in 2007, 10 in 2008)
12	Washington, 1990-91	(1 in 1990, 11 in 1991)
11	Pittsburgh, 1975	
11	Baltimore, 1975-76	(9 in 1975, 2 in 1976)
11	Chicago, 1986-87	(7 in 1986, 4 in 1987)
11	Houston, 1993	
11	San Francisco, 1997	
11	Jacksonville, 1999	
11	Indianapolis, 1999	
11	Seattle, 2005	
11	San Diego	(10 in 2006, 1 in 2007)
10	Miami, 1973	
10	Pittsburgh, 1976-77	(9 in 1976, 1 in 1977)
10	Denver, 1984	
10	San Francisco, 1994	
10	Minnesota, 1999-00	(3 in 1999, 7 in 2000)
10	Indianapolis, 2005-06	(1 in 2005, 9 in 2006)

NFL PLAYOFF APPEARANCES BY SEASONS

Team	Number of Seasons in Playoffs
N.Y. Giants	30
Dallas	29
St. Louis	27
Minnesota	25
Pittsburgh	25

Team	Number of Seasons in Playoffs
Chicago	24
Cleveland	24
Green Bay	24
Indianapolis	22
Miami	22
San Francisco	22
Washington	22
Oakland	21
Philadelphia	21
Tennessee	21
Buffalo	17
Denver	17
New England	16
San Diego	16
Kansas City	15
Detroit	14
N.Y. Jets	12
Seattle	10
Tampa Bay	10
Atlanta	9
Cincinnati	8
Arizona	7
Jacksonville	6
New Orleans	6
Baltimore	5
Carolina	4

TEAMS IN SUPER BOWL CONTENTION (1978-2008)

	With 3 Weeks to Play	With 2 Weeks to Play	With 1 Week to Play
2008	22	19	18
2007	23	20	15
2006	25	24	*20
2005	18	17	14
2004	*27	*26	17
2003	22	17	14
2002	21	21	19
2001	23	16	13
2000	19	17	16
1999	23	20	16
1998	22	19	14
1997	22	18	14
1996	23	21	13
1995	*27	21	18
1994	25	22	15
1993	20	18	16
1992	20	16	14
1991	20	18	13
1990	23	20	15
1989	21	18	17
1988	21	18	15
1987	19	19	15
1986	19	17	14
1985	21	18	13
1984	18	14	13
1983	24	19	15
1982	20	17	16
1981	21	20	16
1980	20	14	12
1979	19	15	13
1978	20	17	12

RECORD OF TEAMS ON THE ROAD (1970-2008)

Year	W	L	T	Pct
1970	72	101	9	.420
1971	74	100	8	.429
1972	87	90	5	.492
1973	66	109	7	.382
1974	82	99	1	.453
1975	81	101	0	.445
1976	83	112	1	.426
1977	83	113	0	.423
1978	93	130	1	.417
1979	92	132	0	.411
1980	101	122	1	.453
1981	84	139	1	.377
1982	57	68	1	.456
1983	104	119	1	.467
1984	94	129	1	.422
1985	80	144	0	.357
1986	104	118	2	.469
1987	95	114	1	.455
1988	92	131	1	.413
1989	95	128	1	.426
1990	93	131	0	.415
1991	92	132	0	.411
1992	88	136	0	.393
1993	101	123	0	.451
1994	96	128	0	.429
1995	96	144	0	.400
1996	91	149	0	.379
1997	93	145	2	.392
1998	89	151	0	.371
1999	100	148	0	.403
2000	110	138	0	.444
2001	112	136	0	.452
2002	107	148	1	.420
2003	99	157	0	.387
2004	111	145	0	.434
2005	105	151	0	.410
2006	120	136	0	.469
2007	109	147	0	.426
2008	109	146	1	.428

GAMES DECIDED BY 7 POINTS OR LESS AND 3 POINTS OR LESS (1970-2008)

	Games Decided by 7 Points or Less	Games Decided by 3 Points or Less
1970	59 of 182 (32.4%)	34 of 182 (18.7%)
1971	76 of 182 (41.8%)	35 of 182 (19.2%)
1972	71 of 182 (39.0%)	38 of 182 (20.9%)
1973	60 of 182 (32.9%)	28 of 182 (15.4%)
1974	91 of 182 (50.0%)	37 of 182 (20.3%)
1975	62 of 182 (34.1%)	35 of 182 (19.2%)
1976	73 of 196 (37.2%)	38 of 196 (19.4%)
1977	85 of 196 (43.4%)	36 of 196 (18.4%)
1978	108 of 224 (48.2%)	49 of 224 (21.9%)
1979	104 of 224 (46.4%)	51 of 224 (22.8%)
1980	108 of 224 (48.2%)	58 of 224 (25.9%)
1981	91 of 224 (40.6%)	60 of 224 (26.8%)
1982	61 of 126 (48.4%)	33 of 126 (26.2%)
1983	106 of 224 (47.3%)	54 of 224 (24.1%)
1984	95 of 224 (42.4%)	58 of 224 (25.9%)
1985	87 of 224 (38.8%)	38 of 224 (17.0%)
1986	106 of 224 (47.3%)	48 of 224 (21.4%)
1987	99 of 210 (47.1%)	40 of 210 (19.0%)
1988	113 of 224 (50.4%)	62 of 224 (27.7%)
1989	107 of 224 (47.8%)	55 of 224 (24.6%)
1990	97 of 224 (43.3%)	54 of 224 (24.1%)
1991	112 of 224 (50.0%)	57 of 224 (25.4%)
1992	88 of 224 (39.3%)	48 of 224 (21.4%)
1993	*105 of 224 (46.9%)	53 of 224 (23.7%)
1994	115 of 224 (51.3%)	60 of 224 (26.8%)
1995	115 of 240 (47.9%)	61 of 240 (25.4%)
1996	109 of 240 (45.4%)	47 of 240 (19.6%)
1997	111 of 240 (46.3%)	67 of 240 (27.9%)
1998	113 of 240 (47.1%)	50 of 240 (20.8%)
1999	115 of 248 (46.4%)	**64 of 248 (25.8%)
2000	109 of 248 (44.0%)	61 of 248 (24.6%)
2001	121 of 248 (48.8%)	62 of 248 (25.0%)
2002	126 of 256 (49.2%)	63 of 256 (24.6%)
2003	124 of 256 (48.4%)	60 of 256 (23.4%)
2004	116 of 256 (45.3%)	61 of 256 (23.8%)
2005	114 of 256 (44.5%)	60 of 256 (23.4%)
2006	117 of 256 (45.7%)	61 of 256 (23.8%)
2007	110 of 256 (43.0%)	55 of 256 (21.5%)

	Games Decided by 7 Points or Less	Games Decided by 3 Points or Less
2008	115 of 256 (44.9%)	50 of 256 (19.5%)

*Week record: Dec. 11-13, 1993 (Week 15), 12 of 14 games (86%) decided by 7 points or less.
**Week record: Oct. 10-11, 1999 (Week 5), 10 of 14 games (71%) decided by 3 points or less.

GAMES DECIDED BY 8 PTS. OR LESS (1994-2008)

1994	121 of 224 (54.0%)	2004	121 of 256 (47.3%)
1995	123 of 240 (51.3%)	2005	123 of 256 (48.0%)
1996	115 of 240 (47.9%)	2006	126 of 256 (49.2%)
1997	120 of 240 (50.0%)	2007	120 of 256 (46.9%)
1998	120 of 240 (50.0%)	2008	118 of 256 (46.1%)
1999	124 of 248 (50.0%)		
2000	119 of 248 (48.0%)		
2001	*128 of 248 (51.6%)		
2002	137 of 256 (53.5%)		
2003	132 of 256 (51.6%)		

*Week record: Oct. 14-15, 2001 (Week 5), 12 of 14 games (86%) decided by 8 points or less

TWO-POINT CONVERSION RESULTS (1994-2008)

1994	59 of 116 (50.9%)	2002	47 of 98 (48.0%)
1995	40 of 104 (38.5%)	2003	29 of 66 (43.9%)
1996	44 of 92 (47.8%)	2004	37 of 76 (48.7%)
1997	47 of 109 (43.1%)	2005	27 of 53 (50.9%)
1998	41 of 105 (39.1%)	2006	21 of 41 (51.2%)
1999	31 of 84 (36.9%)	2007	30 of 61 (49.2%)
2000	35 of 85 (41.2%)	2008	28 of 68 (41.2%)
2001	40 of 90 (44.4%)		

RECORDS AFTER BYE WEEKS (1990-2008)

AFC		NFC	
Baltimore	8-5	Arizona	9-11
Buffalo	14-6	Atlanta	10-10
Cincinnati	4-15-1	Carolina	6-8
Cleveland	6-9	Chicago	13-7
Denver	15-5	Dallas	15-5
Houston	2-5	Detroit	9-11
Indianapolis	11-9	Green Bay	11-9
Jacksonville	7-7	Minnesota	16-4
Kansas City	12-8	New Orleans	8-12
Miami	12-8	N.Y. Giants	5-15
New England	11-9	Philadelphia	16-4
N.Y. Jets	11-9	San Francisco	8-12
Oakland	9-11	Seattle	5-15
Pittsburgh	11-9	St. Louis	11-9
San Diego	10-9	Tampa Bay	8-12
Tennessee	12-8		

2008 RECORDS OF TEAMS IN CLOSE GAMES

AFC	Overall Record	Decided by 8 Pts. or Less	Decided By 3 Pts. or Less
Baltimore	11-5	1-3	0-2
Buffalo	7-9	3-3	1-1
Cincinnati	4-11-1	2-3-1	1-1-1
Cleveland	4-12	3-4	1-1
Denver	8-8	6-2	3-0
Houston	8-8	5-4	3-1
Indianapolis	12-4	8-1	3-1
Jacksonville	5-11	4-6	2-1
Kansas City	2-14	1-7	0-3
Miami	11-5	7-2	2-1
New England	11-5	3-2	1-2
N.Y. Jets	9-7	4-2	1-1
Oakland	5-11	2-3	1-2
Pittsburgh	12-4	6-2	2-0
San Diego	8-8	2-7	2-4
Tennessee	13-3	4-1	2-1

NFC	Overall Record	Decided by 8 Pts. or Less	Decided By 3 Pts. or Less
Arizona	9-7	3-3	0-0
Atlanta	11-5	6-2	3-0
Carolina	12-4	5-1	3-0
Chicago	9-7	5-5	2-3
Dallas	9-7	3-3	0-1
Detroit	0-16	0-5	0-1
Green Bay	6-10	1-7	0-5
Minnesota	10-6	6-5	4-1
New Orleans	8-8	3-6	0-5
N.Y. Giants	12-4	5-2	1-1
Philadelphia	9-6-1	1-5-1	0-0-1
San Francisco	7-9	4-2	3-0
Seattle	4-12	1-5	1-4
St. Louis	2-14	1-5	1-2
Tampa Bay	9-7	4-5	3-2
Washington	8-8	8-4	3-2

SUPER BOWL CHAMPIONS THAT DID NOT MAKE PLAYOFFS THE FOLLOWING YEAR

Pittsburgh—Super Bowl XL champions did not make playoffs in 2006 season.
Tampa Bay—Super Bowl XXXVII champions did not make playoffs in 2003 season.
New England—Super Bowl XXXVI champions did not make playoffs in the 2002 season.
Denver—Super Bowl XXXIII champions did not make playoffs in the 1999 season.
N.Y. Giants—Super Bowl XXV champions did not make playoffs in the 1991 season.
Washington—Super Bowl XXII champions did not make playoffs in the 1988 season.
N.Y. Giants—Super Bowl XXI champions did not make playoffs in the 1987 season.
San Francisco—Super Bowl XVI champions did not make playoffs in the 1982 season.
Oakland—Super Bowl XV champions did not make playoffs in the 1981 season.
Pittsburgh—Super Bowl XIV champions did not make playoffs in the 1980 season.
Kansas City—Super Bowl IV champions did not make playoffs in the 1970 season.
Green Bay—Super Bowl II champions did not make playoffs in the 1968 season.

NON-DIVISION WINNERS THAT PLAYED IN SUPER BOWL

2007 New York Giants ....Super Bowl XLII
(Defeated New England, 17-14)
2005 Pittsburgh Steelers ....Super Bowl XL
(Defeated Seattle, 21-10)
2000 Baltimore Ravens ....Super Bowl XXXV
(Defeated N.Y. Giants, 34-7)
1999 Tennessee Titans....................Super Bowl XXXIV
(Lost to St. Louis, 23-16)
1997 Denver Broncos....................Super Bowl XXXII
(Defeated Green Bay, 31-24)
1992 Buffalo Bills....................Super Bowl XXVII
(Lost to Dallas, 52-17)
1985 New England Patriots....................Super Bowl XX
(Lost to Chicago, 46-10)
1980 Oakland Raiders....................Super Bowl XV
(Defeated Philadelphia, 27-10)
1975 Dallas Cowboys ....Super Bowl X
(Lost to Pittsburgh, 21-17)
1969 Kansas City Chiefs ....Super Bowl IV
(Defeated Minnesota, 23-7)

TEAMS AT OR UNDER .500 IN POSTSEASON PLAY

2008 San Diego Chargers....................8-8
2006 New York Giants....................8-8
2004 Minnesota Vikings....................8-8
2004 St. Louis Rams....................8-8
1999 Dallas Cowboys....................8-8
1999 Detroit Lions....................8-8
1991 New York Jets....................8-8
1990 New Orleans Saints....................8-8

1985 Cleveland Browns....................8-8
1982 Cleveland Browns....................4-5
1982 Detroit Lions.......................4-5
1969 Houston Oilers......................6-6-2

COLDEST NFL GAMES ON RECORD

-13 degrees (-48 degree wind chill)—December 31, 1967, Lambeau Field, Green Bay, Wisconsin, NFL Championship (Green Bay 21, Dallas 17)

-9 degrees (-59 degree wind chill)—January 10, 1982, Riverfront Stadium, Cincinnati, Ohio, AFC Championship (Cincinnati 27, San Diego 7)

0 degrees (-32 degree wind chill)—January 15, 1994, Rich Stadium, Orchard Park, New York, AFC Divisional Playoff (Buffalo 29, Los Angeles Raiders 23)

TEAM LEADERS

Offense	**Most Scored**		**Fewest Scored**	
1st Quarter	114	Atlanta	33	Washington
2nd Quarter	154	New Orleans	54	Oakland
3rd Quarter	154	Arizona	20	Cincinnati
4th Quarter	152	San Diego	41	Cincinnati
Defense	**Most Scored**		**Fewest Scored**	
1st Quarter	130	St. Louis	39	N.Y. Giants
2nd Quarter	163	Detroit	58	Baltimore
3rd Quarter	115	Minnesota	29	Pittsburgh
4th Quarter	136	Houston	60	Baltimore

2008 NFL SCORE BY QUARTERS

AFC Offense	**1**	**2**	**3**	**4**	**OT**	**PTS**
San Diego	77	126	84	152	0	439
New England	84	123	106	97	0	410
N.Y. Jets	102	137	55	108	3	405
Baltimore	58	115	97	115	0	385
Indianapolis	98	71	81	127	0	377
Tennessee	63	119	67	123	3	375
Denver	106	86	70	108	0	370
Houston	77	109	78	102	0	366
Pittsburgh	47	106	87	104	3	347
Miami	85	113	65	82	0	345
Buffalo	46	113	73	104	0	336
Jacksonville	58	88	62	91	3	302
Kansas City	68	102	33	88	0	291
Oakland	46	54	73	87	3	263
Cleveland	45	76	29	82	0	232
Cincinnati	51	92	20	41	0	204

NFC Offense	**1**	**2**	**3**	**4**	**OT**	**PTS**
New Orleans	67	154	115	127	0	463
Arizona	64	117	154	86	6	427
N.Y. Giants	91	138	76	113	9	427
Green Bay	61	133	75	150	0	419
Philadelphia	85	150	73	108	0	416
Carolina	60	149	99	106	0	414
Atlanta	114	120	43	111	3	391
Minnesota	94	114	61	110	0	379
Chicago	109	101	88	71	6	375
Dallas	72	117	62	111	0	362
Tampa Bay	61	112	86	96	6	361
San Francisco	90	102	53	91	3	339
Seattle	74	95	38	87	0	294
Detroit	47	92	57	72	0	268
Washington	33	92	57	83	0	265
St. Louis	61	82	35	54	0	232

AFC Defense	**1**	**2**	**3**	**4**	**OT**	**PTS**
Pittsburgh	54	65	29	75	0	223
Tennessee	49	87	34	64	0	234
Baltimore	57	58	66	60	3	244
Indianapolis	45	111	67	75	0	298
New England	75	79	61	91	3	309
Miami	62	102	91	62	0	317
Buffalo	108	76	81	77	0	342
San Diego	64	141	59	83	0	347
Cleveland	51	119	74	106	0	350
N.Y. Jets	60	117	75	101	3	356
Cincinnati	54	94	82	131	3	364
Jacksonville	101	102	50	114	0	367
Oakland	81	115	58	134	0	388
Houston	84	85	86	136	3	394
Kansas City	77	141	106	113	3	440
Denver	84	145	88	131	0	448

NFC Defense	**1**	**2**	**3**	**4**	**OT**	**PTS**
Philadelphia	53	100	49	87	0	289
N.Y. Giants	39	121	38	96	0	294
Washington	89	66	66	75	0	296
Tampa Bay	77	86	51	106	3	323
Atlanta	52	87	60	126	0	325
Carolina	57	92	71	103	6	329
Minnesota	78	74	115	66	0	333
Chicago	47	128	72	100	3	350
Dallas	79	109	67	104	6	365
Green Bay	65	103	71	135	6	380
San Francisco	54	160	64	103	0	381
Seattle	78	137	105	69	3	392
New Orleans	80	141	69	100	3	393
Arizona	84	150	81	111	0	426
St. Louis	130	144	57	134	0	465
Detroit	126	163	109	119	0	517
NFL Totals	**2,294**	**3,498**	**2,252**	**3,187**	**48**	**11,279**

LARGEST TRADES IN NFL HISTORY
(Based on number of players or draft choices involved)

18—October 13, 1989—RB Herschel Walker from the Dallas Cowboys to Minnesota. Dallas also traded its third-round choice in 1990, its tenth-round choice in 1990, and its third-round choice in 1991 to Minnesota. Minnesota traded LB Jesse Solomon, LB David Howard, CB Issiac Holt, and DE Alex Stewart along with its first-round choice in 1990, its second-round choice in 1990, its sixth-round choice in 1990, its first-round choice in 1991, its second-round choice in 1991, its first-round choice in 1992, its second-round choice in 1992, and its third-round choice in 1992 to Dallas. Minnesota traded RB Darrin Nelson to Dallas, which traded Nelson to San Diego for the Chargers' fifth-round choice in 1990, which Dallas then sent to Minnesota.

15—March 26, 1953—T Mike McCormack, DT Don Colo, LB Tom Catlin, DB John Petitbon, and G Herschell Forester from Baltimore to Cleveland for DB Don Shula, DB Bert Rechichar, DB Carl Taseff, LB Ed Sharkey, E Gern Nagler, QB Harry Agganis, T Dick Batten, T Stu Sheets, G Art Spinney, and G Elmer Willhoite.

15—January 28, 1971—LB Marlin McKeever, first- and third-round choices in 1971, and third-, fourth-, fifth-, sixth-, and seventh-round choices in 1972 from Washington to the Los Angeles Rams for LB Maxie Baughan, LB Jack Pardee, LB Myron Pottios, RB Jeff Jordan, G John Wilbur, DT Diron Talbert, and a fifth-round choice in 1971.

12—June 13, 1952—Selection rights to Les Richter from the Dallas Texans to the Los Angeles Rams for RB Dick Hoerner, DB Tom Keane, DB George Sims, C Joe Reid, HB Billy Baggett, T Jack Halliday, FB Dick McKissack, LB Vic Vasicek, E Richard Wilkins, C Aubrey Phillips, and RB Dave Anderson.

10—March 23, 1959—HB Ollie Matson from the Chicago Cardinals to the Los Angeles Rams for T Frank Fuller, DE Glenn Holtzman, T Ken Panfil, DT Art Hauser, E John Tracey, FB Larry Hickman, HB Don Brown, the Rams second-round choice in 1960, and a player to be delivered during the 1959 training camp.

10—October 31, 1987—RB Eric Dickerson from the Los Angeles Rams to Indianapolis. The rights to LB Cornelius Bennett from Indianapolis to Buffalo. Indianapolis running back Owen Gill and the Colts' first- and second-round choices in 1988 and second-round choice in 1989, plus Bills running back Greg Bell and Buffalo's first-round choice in 1988 and first- and second-round choices in 1989 to the Rams.

2009 TOP 100 TELEVISION MARKETS
(NFL TEAM MARKETS IN BOLD)

RANK	MARKET	TV HOUSEHOLDS	% of U.S.
1	**New York**	**7,433,820**	**6.495**
2	Los Angeles	5,654,260	4.940
3	**Chicago**	**3,492,850**	**3.052**
4	**Philadelphia**	**2,950,220**	**2.578**
5	**Dallas-Ft. Worth**	**2,489,970**	**2.175**
6	**San Francisco-Oak-San Jose**	**2,476,450**	**2.164**
7	**Boston (Manchester)**	**2,409,080**	**2.105**
8	**Atlanta**	**2,369,780**	**2.070**
9	**Washington, DC (Hagrstwn)**	**2,321,610**	**2.028**
10	**Houston**	**2,106,210**	**1.840**
11	**Detroit**	**1,926,970**	**1.684**
12	**Phoenix (Prescott)**	**1,855,930**	**1.622**
13	**Tampa-St. Pete (Sarasota)**	**1,822,160**	**1.592**
14	**Seattle-Tacoma**	**1,819,970**	**1.590**
15	**Minneapolis-St. Paul**	**1,730,530**	**1.512**
16	**Miami-Ft. Lauderdale**	**1,546,920**	**1.352**
17	**Cleveland-Akron (Canton)**	**1,524,930**	**1.332**
18	**Denver**	**1,524,210**	**1.332**
19	Orlando-Daytona Bch-Melbrn	1,466,420	1.281
20	Sacramnto-Stkton-Modesto	1,399,520	1.223
21	**St. Louis**	**1,249,820**	**1.092**
22	Portland, OR	1,175,100	1.027
23	**Pittsburgh**	**1,156,460**	**1.010**
24	**Charlotte**	**1,122,860**	**0.981**
25	**Indianapolis**	**1,114,970**	**0.974**
26	**Baltimore**	**1,102,080**	**0.963**
27	Raleigh-Durham (Fayetvlle)	1,080,680	0.944
28	**San Diego**	**1,066,680**	**0.932**
29	**Nashville**	**1,016,290**	**0.888**
30	Hartford & New Haven	1,014,990	0.887
31	**Kansas City**	**937,970**	**0.819**
32	Columbus, OH	925,840	0.809
33	Salt Lake City	919,390	0.803
34	**Cincinnati**	**915,570**	**0.800**
35	Milwaukee	905,350	0.791
36	Greenvll-Spart-Ashevll-And	858,050	0.750
37	San Antonio	818,560	0.715
38	West Palm Beach-Ft. Pierce	779,430	0.681
39	Grand Rapids-Kalmzoo-B.Crk	741,420	0.648
40	Birmingham (Ann, Tusc)	739,750	0.646
41	Harrisburg-Lncstr-Leb-York	738,880	0.646
42	Las Vegas	728,410	0.636
43	Norfolk-Portsmth-Newpt Nws	718,020	0.627
44	Albuquerque-Santa Fe	689,120	0.602
45	Oklahoma City	687,300	0.600
46	Greensboro-H.Point-W.Salem	685,110	0.599
47	**Jacksonville**	**674,860**	**0.590**
48	Memphis	673,770	0.589
49	Austin	667,670	0.583
50	Louisville	667,230	0.583

2009 TOP 100 TELEVISION MARKETS (NFL TEAM MARKETS IN BOLD)

RANK	MARKET	TV HOUSEHOLDS	% of U.S.
51	**Buffalo**	**631,120**	**0.551**
52	Providence-New Bedford	622,580	0.544
53	**New Orleans**	**602,740**	**0.527**
54	Wilkes Barre-Scranton	594,570	0.519
55	Fresno-Visalia	574,900	0.502
56	Little Rock-Pine Bluff	567,060	0.495
57	Albany-Schenectady-Troy	556,750	0.486
58	Richmond-Petersburg	550,240	0.481
59	Knoxville	547,930	0.479
60	Mobile-Pensacola (Ft Walt)	537,810	0.470
61	Tulsa	529,540	0.463
62	Ft. Myers-Naples	509,530	0.445
63	Lexington	503,260	0.440
64	Dayton	483,790	0.423
65	Charleston-Huntington	479,750	0.419
66	Flint-Saginaw-Bay City	465,790	0.407
67	Roanoke-Lynchburg	461,420	0.403
68	Tucson (Sierra Vista)	456,030	0.398
69	Wichita-Hutchinson Plus	450,930	0.394
70	**Green Bay-Appleton**	**444,210**	**0.388**
71	Des Moines-Ames	432,410	0.378
72	Honolulu	429,940	0.376
73	Toledo	425,890	0.372
74	Springfield, MO	421,960	0.369
75	Spokane	416,630	0.364
76	Omaha	411,520	0.360
77	Portland-Auburn	410,890	0.359
78	Paducah-Cape Girard-Harsbg	393,260	0.344
79	Columbia, SC	393,170	0.343
80	Rochester, NY	390,590	0.341
81	Syracuse	388,000	0.339
82	Huntsville-Decatur (Flor)	386,520	0.338
83	Champaign&Sprngfld-Decatur	386,000	0.337
84	Shreveport	385,770	0.337
85	Madison	378,740	0.331
86	Chattanooga	366,780	0.320
87	Harlingen-Wslco-Brnsvl-McA	349,910	0.306
88	Cedar Rapids-Wtrlo-IWC&Dub	346,330	0.303
89	South Bend-Elkhart	334,720	0.292
90	Jackson, MS	334,650	0.292
91	Colorado Springs-Pueblo	334,390	0.292
92	Tri-Cities, TN-VA	332,840	0.291
93	Burlington-Plattsburgh	331,320	0.289
94	Waco-Temple-Bryan	329,690	0.288
95	Baton Rouge	326,390	0.285
96	Savannah	319,160	0.279
97	Davenport-R.Island-Moline	309,600	0.270
98	El Paso (Las Cruces)	308,080	0.269
99	Charleston, SC	307,610	0.269
100	Ft. Smith-Fay-Sprngdl-Rgrs	297,920	0.260
TOTAL NFL MARKETS		**53,837,240**	**47.037**
TOTAL TOP 100 MARKETS		**98,444,070**	**86.010**
TOTAL MARKETS		**114,456,650**	**100.000**

ALL-TIME REGULAR-SEASON RECORDS OF CURRENT NFL TEAMS

AFC

BALTIMORE RAVENS

	All Games			Home Games			Road Games		
Season	W	L	T	W	L	T	W	L	T
1996	4	12		4	4		0	8	
1997	6	9	1	3	4	1	3	5	
1998	6	10		4	4		2	6	
1999	8	8		4	4		4	4	
2000	12	4		6	2		6	2	
2001	10	6		6	2		4	4	
2002	7	9		4	4		3	5	
2003	10	6		7	1		3	5	
2004	9	7		6	2		3	5	
2005	6	10		6	2		0	8	
2006	13	3		7	1		6	2	
2007	5	11		4	4		1	7	
2008	11	5		6	2		5	3	
	107	100	1	67	36	1	40	64	

BUFFALO BILLS

	All Games			Home Games			Road Games		
Season	W	L	T	W	L	T	W	L	T
1960	5	8	1	3	4		2	4	1
1961	6	8		2	5		4	3	
1962	7	6	1	3	3	1	4	3	
1963	7	6	1	4	2	1	3	4	
1964	12	2		6	1		6	1	
1965	10	3	1	5	2		5	1	1
1966	9	4	1	4	2	1	5	2	
1967	4	10		2	5		2	5	
1968	1	12	1	1	6		0	6	1
1969	4	10		4	3		0	7	
1970	3	10	1	1	6		2	4	1
1971	1	13		1	6		0	7	
1972	4	9	1	2	4	1	2	5	
1973	9	5		5	2		4	3	
1974	9	5		5	2		4	3	
1975	8	6		3	4		5	2	
1976	2	12		1	6		1	6	
1977	3	11		1	6		2	5	
1978	5	11		4	4		1	7	
1979	7	9		3	5		4	4	
1980	11	5		6	2		5	3	
1981	10	6		7	1		3	5	
1982	4	5		4	1		0	4	
1983	8	8		3	5		5	3	
1984	2	14		2	6		0	8	
1985	2	14		2	6		0	8	
1986	4	12		3	5		1	7	
1987	7	8		4	4		3	4	
1988	12	4		8	0		4	4	
1989	9	7		6	2		3	5	
1990	13	3		8	0		5	3	
1991	13	3		7	1		6	2	
1992	11	5		6	2		5	3	
1993	12	4		6	2		6	2	
1994	7	9		4	4		3	5	
1995	10	6		6	2		4	4	
1996	10	6		7	1		3	5	
1997	6	10		4	4		2	6	
1998	10	6		6	2		4	4	
1999	11	5		6	2		5	3	
2000	8	8		5	3		3	5	
2001	3	13		1	7		2	6	
2002	8	8		5	3		3	5	
2003	6	10		4	4		2	6	
2004	9	7		5	3		4	4	
2005	5	11		4	4		1	7	
2006	7	9		4	4		3	5	
2007	7	9		4	4		3	5	
2008	7	9		3	5		4	4	
	348	384	8	200	167	4	148	217	4

CINCINNATI BENGALS

	All Games			Home Games			Road Games		
Season	W	L	T	W	L	T	W	L	T
1968	3	11		2	5		1	6	
1969	4	9	1	4	3		0	6	1
1970	8	6		5	2		3	4	
1971	4	10		3	4		1	6	
1972	8	6		4	3		4	3	
1973	10	4		7	0		3	4	
1974	7	7		4	3		3	4	
1975	11	3		6	1		5	2	
1976	10	4		6	1		4	3	
1977	8	6		5	2		3	4	
1978	4	12		3	5		1	7	
1979	4	12		4	4		0	8	
1980	6	10		3	5		3	5	
1981	12	4		6	2		6	2	
1982	7	2		4	0		3	2	
1983	7	9		4	4		3	5	
1984	8	8		5	3		3	5	
1985	7	9		5	3		2	6	
1986	10	6		6	2		4	4	
1987	4	11		1	7		3	4	
1988	12	4		8	0		4	4	
1989	8	8		5	3		3	5	
1990	9	7		5	3		4	4	
1991	3	13		3	5		0	8	
1992	5	11		3	5		2	6	
1993	3	13		3	5		0	8	
1994	3	13		2	6		1	7	
1995	7	9		3	5		4	4	
1996	8	8		6	2		2	6	
1997	7	9		6	2		1	7	
1998	3	13		1	7		2	6	
1999	4	12		2	6		2	6	
2000	4	12		3	5		1	7	
2001	6	10		4	4		2	6	
2002	2	14		1	7		1	7	
2003	8	8		5	3		3	5	
2004	8	8		5	3		3	5	
2005	11	5		5	3		6	2	
2006	8	8		4	4		4	4	
2007	7	9		5	3		2	6	
2008	4	11	1	3	4	1	1	7	
	272	354	2	169	144	1	103	210	1

CLEVELAND BROWNS*

	All Games			Home Games			Road Games		
Season	W	L	T	W	L	T	W	L	T
1950	10	2		5	1		5	1	
1951	11	1		6	0		5	1	
1952	8	4		4	2		4	2	
1953	11	1		6	0		5	1	
1954	9	3		5	1		4	2	
1955	9	2	1	5	1		4	1	1
1956	5	7		1	5		4	2	
1957	9	2	1	6	0		3	2	1
1958	9	3		4	2		5	1	
1959	7	5		3	3		4	2	
1960	8	3	1	4	2		4	1	1
1961	8	5	1	4	3		4	2	1
1962	7	6	1	4	2	1	3	4	
1963	10	4		5	2		5	2	

Season	All Games W	L	T	Home Games W	L	T	Road Games W	L	T
1964	10	3	1	5	1	1	5	2	
1965	11	3		5	2		6	1	
1966	9	5		5	2		4	3	
1967	9	5		6	1		3	4	
1968	10	4		5	2		5	2	
1969	10	3	1	5	1	1	5	2	
1970	7	7		4	3		3	4	
1971	9	5		4	3		5	2	
1972	10	4		4	3		6	1	
1973	7	5	2	5	1	1	2	4	1
1974	4	10		3	4		1	6	
1975	3	11		3	4		0	7	
1976	9	5		6	1		3	4	
1977	6	8		2	5		4	3	
1978	8	8		5	3		3	5	
1979	9	7		5	3		4	4	
1980	11	5		6	2		5	3	
1981	5	11		3	5		2	6	
1982	4	5		2	2		2	3	
1983	9	7		6	2		3	5	
1984	5	11		2	6		3	5	
1985	8	8		5	3		3	5	
1986	12	4		6	2		6	2	
1987	10	5		5	2		5	3	
1988	10	6		6	2		4	4	
1989	9	6	1	5	2	1	4	4	
1990	3	13		2	6		1	7	
1991	6	10		3	5		3	5	
1992	7	9		4	4		3	5	
1993	7	9		4	4		3	5	
1994	11	5		6	2		5	3	
1995	5	11		3	5		2	6	
1999	2	14		0	8		2	6	
2000	3	13		2	6		1	7	
2001	7	9		4	4		3	5	
2002	9	7		3	5		6	2	
2003	5	11		2	6		3	5	
2004	4	12		3	5		1	7	
2005	6	10		4	4		2	6	
2006	4	12		2	6		2	6	
2007	10	6		7	1		3	5	
2008	4	12		1	7		3	5	
	428	372	10	230	169	5	198	203	5

*Did not play from 1996-98.

DENVER BRONCOS

Season	All Games W	L	T	Home Games W	L	T	Road Games W	L	T
1960	4	9	1	2	4	1	2	5	
1961	3	11		2	5		1	6	
1962	7	7		3	4		4	3	
1963	2	11	1	2	5		0	6	1
1964	2	11	1	2	4	1	0	7	
1965	4	10		2	5		2	5	
1966	4	10		3	4		1	6	
1967	3	11		1	6		2	5	
1968	5	9		3	4		2	5	
1969	5	8	1	4	2	1	1	6	
1970	5	8	1	3	3	1	2	5	
1971	4	9	1	2	4	1	2	5	
1972	5	9		3	4		2	5	
1973	7	5	2	3	3	1	4	2	1
1974	7	6	1	3	3	1	4	3	
1975	6	8		5	2		1	6	
1976	9	5		6	1		3	4	
1977	12	2		6	1		6	1	
1978	10	6		6	2		4	4	
1979	10	6		6	2		4	4	
1980	8	8		4	4		4	4	
1981	10	6		8	0		2	6	
1982	2	7		1	4		1	3	
1983	9	7		6	2		3	5	
1984	13	3		7	1		6	2	
1985	11	5		6	2		5	3	
1986	11	5		7	1		4	4	
1987	10	4	1	7	1		3	3	1
1988	8	8		6	2		2	6	
1989	11	5		6	2		5	3	
1990	5	11		4	4		1	7	
1991	12	4		7	1		5	3	
1992	8	8		7	1		1	7	
1993	9	7		5	3		4	4	
1994	7	9		4	4		3	5	
1995	8	8		6	2		2	6	
1996	13	3		8	0		5	3	
1997	12	4		8	0		4	4	
1998	14	2		8	0		6	2	
1999	6	10		3	5		3	5	
2000	11	5		6	2		5	3	
2001	8	8		6	2		2	6	
2002	9	7		5	3		4	4	
2003	10	6		6	2		4	4	
2004	10	6		6	2		4	4	
2005	13	3		8	0		5	3	
2006	9	7		4	4		5	3	
2007	7	9		5	3		2	6	
2008	8	8		4	4		4	4	
	386	344	10	235	129	7	151	215	3

HOUSTON TEXANS

Season	All Games W	L	T	Home Games W	L	T	Road Games W	L	T
2002	4	12		2	6		2	6	
2003	5	11		3	5		2	6	
2004	7	9		3	5		4	4	
2005	2	14		2	6		0	8	
2006	6	10		4	4		2	6	
2007	8	8		6	2		2	6	
2008	8	8		6	2		2	6	
	40	72		26	30		14	42	

INDIANAPOLIS COLTS*

Season	All Games W	L	T	Home Games W	L	T	Road Games W	L	T
1953	3	9		2	4		1	5	
1954	3	9		2	4		1	5	
1955	5	6	1	4	1	1	1	5	
1956	5	7		4	2		1	5	
1957	7	5		4	2		3	3	
1958	9	3		6	0		3	3	
1959	9	3		4	2		5	1	
1960	6	6		4	2		2	4	
1961	8	6		5	2		3	4	
1962	7	7		3	4		4	3	
1963	8	6		4	3		4	3	
1964	12	2		7	1		5	1	
1965	10	3	1	5	2		5	1	1
1966	9	5		5	2		4	3	
1967	11	1	2	6	0	1	5	1	1
1968	13	1		6	1		7	0	
1969	8	5	1	4	2	1	4	3	
1970	11	2	1	5	1	1	6	1	
1971	10	4		5	2		5	2	
1972	5	9		2	5		3	4	
1973	4	10		3	4		1	6	
1974	2	12		0	7		2	5	

Season	All Games W	L	T	Home Games W	L	T	Road Games W	L	T
1975	10	4		5	2		5	2	
1976	11	3		6	1		5	2	
1977	10	4		6	1		4	3	
1978	5	11		2	6		3	5	
1979	5	11		3	5		2	6	
1980	7	9		2	6		5	3	
1981	2	14		1	7		1	7	
1982	0	8	1	0	3	1	0	5	
1983	7	9		3	5		4	4	
1984	4	12		2	6		2	6	
1985	5	11		4	4		1	7	
1986	3	13		1	7		2	6	
1987	9	6		4	4		5	2	
1988	9	7		6	2		3	5	
1989	8	8		6	2		2	6	
1990	7	9		3	5		4	4	
1991	1	15		0	8		1	7	
1992	9	7		4	4		5	3	
1993	4	12		2	6		2	6	
1994	8	8		5	3		3	5	
1995	9	7		5	3		4	4	
1996	9	7		6	2		3	5	
1997	3	13		2	6		1	7	
1998	3	13		3	5		0	8	
1999	13	3		7	1		6	2	
2000	10	6		6	2		4	4	
2001	6	10		3	5		3	5	
2002	10	6		5	3		5	3	
2003	12	4		5	3		7	1	
2004	12	4		7	1		5	3	
2005	14	2		7	1		7	1	
2006	12	4		8	0		4	4	
2007	13	3		6	2		7	1	
2008	12	4		6	2		6	2	
	427	388	7	231	176	5	196	212	2

**includes Baltimore Colts (1953-1983).*

JACKSONVILLE JAGUARS

Season	All Games W	L	T	Home Games W	L	T	Road Games W	L	T
1995	4	12		2	6		2	6	
1996	9	7		7	1		2	6	
1997	11	5		7	1		4	4	
1998	11	5		7	1		4	4	
1999	14	2		7	1		7	1	
2000	7	9		4	4		3	5	
2001	6	10		3	5		3	5	
2002	6	10		3	5		3	5	
2003	5	11		5	3		0	8	
2004	9	7		4	4		5	3	
2005	12	4		6	2		6	2	
2006	8	8		6	2		2	6	
2007	11	5		6	2		5	3	
2008	5	11		2	6		3	5	
	118	106		69	43		49	63	

KANSAS CITY CHIEFS*

Season	All Games W	L	T	Home Games W	L	T	Road Games W	L	T
1960	8	6		5	2		3	4	
1961	6	8		4	3		2	5	
1962	11	3		6	1		5	2	
1963	5	7	2	4	3		1	4	2
1964	7	7		4	3		3	4	
1965	7	5	2	5	2		2	3	2
1966	11	2	1	4	2	1	7	0	
1967	9	5		4	3		5	2	
1968	12	2		6	1		6	1	
1969	11	3		6	1		5	2	
1970	7	5	2	4	1	2	3	4	
1971	10	3	1	7	0		3	3	1
1972	8	6		3	4		5	2	
1973	7	5	2	5	1	1	2	4	1
1974	5	9		1	6		4	3	
1975	5	9		3	4		2	5	
1976	5	9		1	6		4	3	
1977	2	12		1	6		1	6	
1978	4	12		3	5		1	7	
1979	7	9		3	5		4	4	
1980	8	8		3	5		5	3	
1981	9	7		5	3		4	4	
1982	3	6		2	2		1	4	
1983	6	10		5	3		1	7	
1984	8	8		5	3		3	5	
1985	6	10		5	3		1	7	
1986	10	6		6	2		4	4	
1987	4	11		3	4		1	7	
1988	4	11	1	4	4		0	7	1
1989	8	7	1	5	3		3	4	1
1990	11	5		6	2		5	3	
1991	10	6		6	2		4	4	
1992	10	6		7	1		3	5	
1993	11	5		7	1		4	4	
1994	9	7		5	3		4	4	
1995	13	3		8	0		5	3	
1996	9	7		5	3		4	4	
1997	13	3		8	0		5	3	
1998	7	9		5	3		2	6	
1999	9	7		6	2		3	5	
2000	7	9		5	3		2	6	
2001	6	10		3	5		3	5	
2002	8	8		6	2		2	6	
2003	13	3		8	0		5	3	
2004	7	9		4	4		3	5	
2005	10	6		7	1		3	5	
2006	9	7		6	2		3	5	
2007	4	12		2	6		2	6	
2008	2	14		1	7		1	7	
	381	347	12	227	138	4	154	209	8

**includes Dallas Texans (1960-62).*

MIAMI DOLPHINS

Season	All Games W	L	T	Home Games W	L	T	Road Games W	L	T
1966	3	11		2	5		1	6	
1967	4	10		4	3		0	7	
1968	5	8	1	1	5	1	4	3	
1969	3	10	1	2	4	1	1	6	
1970	10	4		6	1		4	3	
1971	10	3	1	6	1		4	2	1
1972	14	0		7	0		7	0	
1973	12	2		7	0		5	2	
1974	11	3		7	0		4	3	
1975	10	4		5	2		5	2	
1976	6	8		3	4		3	4	
1977	10	4		6	1		4	3	
1978	11	5		7	1		4	4	
1979	10	6		6	2		4	4	
1980	8	8		5	3		3	5	
1981	11	4	1	6	1	1	5	3	
1982	7	2		4	0		3	2	
1983	12	4		7	1		5	3	
1984	14	2		7	1		7	1	
1985	12	4		8	0		4	4	
1986	8	8		4	4		4	4	
1987	8	7		4	3		4	4	

	All Games			Home Games			Road Games		
Season	W	L	T	W	L	T	W	L	T
1988	6	10		4	4		2	6	
1989	8	8		4	4		4	4	
1990	12	4		7	1		5	3	
1991	8	8		5	3		3	5	
1992	11	5		6	2		5	3	
1993	9	7		4	4		5	3	
1994	10	6		6	2		4	4	
1995	9	7		5	3		4	4	
1996	8	8		4	4		4	4	
1997	9	7		6	2		3	5	
1998	10	6		7	1		3	5	
1999	9	7		5	3		4	4	
2000	11	5		5	3		6	2	
2001	11	5		7	1		4	4	
2002	9	7		7	1		2	6	
2003	10	6		4	4		6	2	
2004	4	12		3	5		1	7	
2005	9	7		5	3		4	4	
2006	6	10		4	4		2	6	
2007	1	15		1	7		0	8	
2008	11	5		5	3		6	2	
	380	272	4	218	106	3	162	166	1

NEW ENGLAND PATRIOTS*

	All Games			Home Games			Road Games		
Season	W	L	T	W	L	T	W	L	T
1960	5	9		3	4		2	5	
1961	9	4	1	4	2	1	5	2	
1962	9	4	1	6	1		3	3	1
1963	7	6	1	5	1	1	2	5	
1964	10	3	1	4	2	1	6	1	
1965	4	8	2	1	4	2	3	4	
1966	8	4	2	4	2	1	4	2	1
1967	3	10	1	2	4		1	6	1
1968	4	10		2	5		2	5	
1969	4	10		2	5		2	5	
1970	2	12		1	6		1	6	
1971	6	8		5	2		1	6	
1972	3	11		2	5		1	6	
1973	5	9		3	4		2	5	
1974	7	7		3	4		4	3	
1975	3	11		2	5		1	6	
1976	11	3		6	1		5	2	
1977	9	5		6	1		3	4	
1978	11	5		5	3		6	2	
1979	9	7		6	2		3	5	
1980	10	6		6	2		4	4	
1981	2	14		2	6		0	8	
1982	5	4		3	1		2	3	
1983	8	8		5	3		3	5	
1984	9	7		5	3		4	4	
1985	11	5		7	1		4	4	
1986	11	5		4	4		7	1	
1987	8	7		5	3		3	4	
1988	9	7		7	1		2	6	
1989	5	11		3	5		2	6	
1990	1	15		0	8		1	7	
1991	6	10		4	4		2	6	
1992	2	14		1	7		1	7	
1993	5	11		3	5		2	6	
1994	10	6		5	3		5	3	
1995	6	10		3	5		3	5	
1996	11	5		6	2		5	3	
1997	10	6		6	2		4	4	
1998	9	7		6	2		3	5	
1999	8	8		5	3		3	5	
2000	5	11		3	5		2	6	
2001	11	5		6	2		5	3	

	All Games			Home Games			Road Games		
Season	W	L	T	W	L	T	W	L	T
2002	9	7		5	3		4	4	
2003	14	2		8	0		6	2	
2004	14	2		8	0		6	2	
2005	10	6		5	3		5	3	
2006	12	4		5	3		7	1	
2007	16	0		8	0		8	0	
2008	11	5		5	3		6	2	
	377	354	9	211	152	6	166	202	3

**includes Boston Patriots (1960-1970).*

NEW YORK JETS*

	All Games			Home Games			Road Games		
Season	W	L	T	W	L	T	W	L	T
1960	7	7		3	4		4	3	
1961	7	7		5	2		2	5	
1962	5	9		2	5		3	4	
1963	5	8	1	4	2	1	1	6	
1964	5	8	1	5	1	1	0	7	
1965	5	8	1	3	3	1	2	5	
1966	6	6	2	4	3		2	3	2
1967	8	5	1	4	2	1	4	3	
1968	11	3		6	1		5	2	
1969	10	4		5	2		5	2	
1970	4	10		2	5		2	5	
1971	6	8		4	3		2	5	
1972	7	7		4	3		3	4	
1973	4	10		2	4		2	6	
1974	7	7		3	4		4	3	
1975	3	11		1	6		2	5	
1976	3	11		2	5		1	6	
1977	3	11		1	6		2	5	
1978	8	8		4	4		4	4	
1979	8	8		6	2		2	6	
1980	4	12		2	6		2	6	
1981	10	5	1	6	2		4	3	1
1982	6	3		3	1		3	2	
1983	7	9		2	6		5	3	
1984	7	9		3	5		4	4	
1985	11	5		7	1		4	4	
1986	10	6		5	3		5	3	
1987	6	9		4	4		2	5	
1988	8	7	1	5	2	1	3	5	
1989	4	12		1	7		3	5	
1990	6	10		3	5		3	5	
1991	8	8		4	4		4	4	
1992	4	12		3	5		1	7	
1993	8	8		3	5		5	3	
1994	6	10		4	4		2	6	
1995	3	13		2	6		1	7	
1996	1	15		0	8		1	7	
1997	9	7		5	3		4	4	
1998	12	4		7	1		5	3	
1999	8	8		4	4		4	4	
2000	9	7		5	3		4	4	
2001	10	6		3	5		7	1	
2002	9	7		5	3		4	4	
2003	6	10		4	4		2	6	
2004	10	6		6	2		4	4	
2005	4	12		4	4		0	8	
2006	10	6		4	4		6	2	
2007	4	12		3	5		1	7	
2008	9	7		5	3		4	4	
	331	401	8	182	182	5	149	219	3

**includes New York Titans (1960-62).*

OAKLAND RAIDERS*

Season	All Games			Home Games			Road Games		
	W	L	T	W	L	T	W	L	T
1960	6	8		3	4		3	4	
1961	2	12		1	6		1	6	
1962	1	13		1	6		0	7	
1963	10	4		6	1		4	3	
1964	5	7	2	5	2		0	5	2
1965	8	5	1	5	2		3	3	1
1966	8	5	1	3	3	1	5	2	
1967	13	1		7	0		6	1	
1968	12	2		6	1		6	1	
1969	12	1	1	7	0		5	1	1
1970	8	4	2	6	1		2	3	2
1971	8	4	2	5	1	1	3	3	1
1972	10	3	1	5	1	1	5	2	
1973	9	4	1	5	2		4	2	1
1974	12	2		6	1		6	1	
1975	11	3		6	1		5	2	
1976	13	1		7	0		6	1	
1977	11	3		6	1		5	2	
1978	9	7		4	4		5	3	
1979	9	7		6	2		3	5	
1980	11	5		6	2		5	3	
1981	7	9		4	4		3	5	
1982	8	1		4	0		4	1	
1983	12	4		6	2		6	2	
1984	11	5		6	2		5	3	
1985	12	4		7	1		5	3	
1986	8	8		3	5		5	3	
1987	5	10		3	5		2	5	
1988	7	9		3	5		4	4	
1989	8	8		7	1		1	7	
1990	12	4		6	2		6	2	
1991	9	7		5	3		4	4	
1992	7	9		5	3		2	6	
1993	10	6		5	3		5	3	
1994	9	7		4	4		5	3	
1995	8	8		4	4		4	4	
1996	7	9		4	4		3	5	
1997	4	12		2	6		2	6	
1998	8	8		4	4		4	4	
1999	8	8		5	3		3	5	
2000	12	4		7	1		5	3	
2001	10	6		5	3		5	3	
2002	11	5		6	2		5	3	
2003	4	12		4	4		0	8	
2004	5	11		3	5		2	6	
2005	4	12		2	6		2	6	
2006	2	14		2	6		0	8	
2007	4	12		2	6		2	6	
2008	5	11		4	4		1	7	
	405	324	11	228	139	3	177	185	8

**includes Los Angeles Raiders (1982-1994).*

PITTSBURGH STEELERS*

Season	All Games			Home Games			Road Games		
	W	L	T	W	L	T	W	L	T
1933	3	6	2	2	3		1	3	2
1934	2	10		1	5		1	5	
1935	4	8		2	5		2	3	
1936	6	6		4	1		2	5	
1937	4	7		2	4		2	3	
1938	2	9		0	5		2	4	
1939	1	9	1	1	4		0	5	1
1940	2	7	2	1	2	2	1	5	
1941	1	9	1	1	4		0	5	1
1942	7	4		3	2		4	2	
1945	2	8		1	4		1	4	
1946	5	5	1	4	1		1	4	1
1947	8	4		5	1		3	3	
1948	4	8		4	2		0	6	
1949	6	5	1	3	2	1	3	3	
1950	6	6		2	4		4	2	
1951	4	7	1	1	4	1	3	3	
1952	5	7		2	4		3	3	
1953	6	6		3	3		3	3	
1954	5	7		4	2		1	5	
1955	4	8		3	2		1	6	
1956	5	7		3	3		2	4	
1957	6	6		4	2		2	4	
1958	7	4	1	5	1		2	3	1
1959	6	5	1	3	2	1	3	3	
1960	5	6	1	4	2		1	4	1
1961	6	8		4	3		2	5	
1962	9	5		4	3		5	2	
1963	7	4	3	5	0	2	2	4	1
1964	5	9		2	5		3	4	
1965	2	12		1	6		1	6	
1966	5	8	1	3	3	1	2	5	
1967	4	9	1	1	6		3	3	1
1968	2	11	1	1	6		1	5	1
1969	1	13		1	6		0	7	
1970	5	9		4	3		1	6	
1971	6	8		5	2		1	6	
1972	11	3		7	0		4	3	
1973	10	4		7	1		3	3	
1974	10	3	1	5	2		5	1	1
1975	12	2		6	1		6	1	
1976	10	4		6	1		4	3	
1977	9	5		6	1		3	4	
1978	14	2		7	1		7	1	
1979	12	4		8	0		4	4	
1980	9	7		6	2		3	5	
1981	8	8		5	3		3	5	
1982	6	3		4	0		2	3	
1983	10	6		4	4		6	2	
1984	9	7		6	2		3	5	
1985	7	9		5	3		2	6	
1986	6	10		4	4		2	6	
1987	8	7		4	3		4	4	
1988	5	11		4	4		1	7	
1989	9	7		4	4		5	3	
1990	9	7		6	2		3	5	
1991	7	9		5	3		2	6	
1992	11	5		7	1		4	4	
1993	9	7		6	2		3	5	
1994	12	4		7	1		5	3	
1995	11	5		6	2		5	3	
1996	10	6		7	1		3	5	
1997	11	5		7	1		4	4	
1998	7	9		5	3		2	6	
1999	6	10		2	6		4	4	
2000	9	7		4	4		5	3	
2001	13	3		7	1		6	2	
2002	10	5	1	5	2	1	5	3	
2003	6	10		4	4		2	6	
2004	15	1		8	0		7	1	
2005	11	5		5	3		6	2	
2006	8	8		5	3		3	5	
2007	10	6		7	1		3	5	
2008	12	4		6	2		6	2	
	520	488	20	306	195	9	214	293	11

**includes Pittsburgh Pirates (1933-1940).*

SAN DIEGO CHARGERS*

Season	All Games W	L	T	Home Games W	L	T	Road Games W	L	T
1960	10	4		5	2		5	2	
1961	12	2		6	1		6	1	
1962	4	10		3	4		1	6	
1963	11	3		6	1		5	2	
1964	8	5	1	4	3		4	2	1
1965	9	2	3	4	1	2	5	1	1
1966	7	6	1	5	2		2	4	1
1967	8	5	1	5	2	1	3	3	
1968	9	5		4	3		5	2	
1969	8	6		5	2		3	4	
1970	5	6	3	2	3	2	3	3	1
1971	6	8		6	1		0	7	
1972	4	9	1	2	5		2	4	1
1973	2	11	1	2	5		0	6	1
1974	5	9		3	4		2	5	
1975	2	12		1	6		1	6	
1976	6	8		3	4		3	4	
1977	7	7		3	4		4	3	
1978	9	7		5	3		4	4	
1979	12	4		7	1		5	3	
1980	11	5		6	2		5	3	
1981	10	6		5	3		5	3	
1982	6	3		3	1		3	2	
1983	6	10		4	4		2	6	
1984	7	9		4	4		3	5	
1985	8	8		6	2		2	6	
1986	4	12		2	6		2	6	
1987	8	7		4	3		4	4	
1988	6	10		3	5		3	5	
1989	6	10		4	4		2	6	
1990	6	10		3	5		3	5	
1991	4	12		3	5		1	7	
1992	11	5		6	2		5	3	
1993	8	8		4	4		4	4	
1994	11	5		5	3		6	2	
1995	9	7		5	3		4	4	
1996	8	8		5	3		3	5	
1997	4	12		2	6		2	6	
1998	5	11		4	4		1	7	
1999	8	8		4	4		4	4	
2000	1	15		1	7		0	8	
2001	5	11		4	4		1	7	
2002	8	8		5	3		3	5	
2003	4	12		2	6		2	6	
2004	12	4		7	1		5	3	
2005	9	7		4	4		5	3	
2006	14	2		8	0		6	2	
2007	11	5		7	1		4	4	
2008	8	8		5	3		3	5	
	362	367	11	206	159	5	156	208	6

includes Los Angeles Chargers (1960).

TENNESSEE TITANS*

Season	All Games W	L	T	Home Games W	L	T	Road Games W	L	T
1960	10	4		6	1		4	3	
1961	10	3	1	6	1		4	2	1
1962	11	3		6	1		5	2	
1963	6	8		4	3		2	5	
1964	4	10		3	4		1	6	
1965	4	10		3	4		1	6	
1966	3	11		3	4		0	7	
1967	9	4	1	5	2		4	2	1
1968	7	7		3	4		4	3	
1969	6	6	2	4	2	1	2	4	1
1970	3	10	1	1	6		2	4	1
1971	4	9	1	3	3	1	1	6	
1972	1	13		1	6		0	7	
1973	1	13		0	7		1	6	
1974	7	7		3	4		4	3	
1975	10	4		5	2		5	2	
1976	5	9		3	4		2	5	
1977	8	6		5	2		3	4	
1978	10	6		5	3		5	3	
1979	11	5		6	2		5	3	
1980	11	5		6	2		5	3	
1981	7	9		5	3		2	6	
1982	1	8		1	4		0	4	
1983	2	14		2	6		0	8	
1984	3	13		2	6		1	7	
1985	5	11		4	4		1	7	
1986	5	11		4	4		1	7	
1987	9	6		5	2		4	4	
1988	10	6		7	1		3	5	
1989	9	7		6	2		3	5	
1990	9	7		6	2		3	5	
1991	11	5		7	1		4	4	
1992	10	6		5	3		5	3	
1993	12	4		7	1		5	3	
1994	2	14		2	6		0	8	
1995	7	9		3	5		4	4	
1996	8	8		2	6		6	2	
1997	8	8		6	2		2	6	
1998	8	8		3	5		5	3	
1999	13	3		8	0		5	3	
2000	13	3		7	1		6	2	
2001	7	9		3	5		4	4	
2002	11	5		6	2		5	3	
2003	12	4		7	1		5	3	
2004	5	11		2	6		3	5	
2005	4	12		3	5		1	7	
2006	8	8		4	4		4	4	
2007	10	6		5	3		5	3	
2008	13	3		7	1		6	2	
	363	371	6	210	158	2	153	213	4

includes Houston (1960-1996) and Tennessee Oilers (1997-98).

NFC

ARIZONA CARDINALS*

Season	All Games W	L	T	Home Games W	L	T	Road Games W	L	T
1920	6	2	2	5	1	1	1	1	1
1921	3	3	2	3	3	1	0	0	1
1922	8	3		8	3		0	0	
1923	8	4		8	3		0	1	
1924	5	4	1	5	3	1	0	1	
1925	11	2	1	11	2		0	0	1
1926	5	6	1	3	3		2	3	1
1927	3	7	1	2	3	1	1	4	
1928	1	5		1	1		0	4	
1929	6	6	1	3	2		3	4	1
1930	5	6	2	3	2		2	4	2
1931	5	4		3	0		2	4	
1932	2	6	2	1	2	1	1	4	1
1933	1	9	1	0	4	1	1	5	
1934	5	6		2	2		3	4	
1935	6	4	2	2	2		4	2	2
1936	3	8	1	3	1	1	0	7	
1937	5	5	1	1	3		4	2	1
1938	2	9		1	4		1	5	
1939	1	10		0	4		1	6	
1940	2	7	2	2	1	1	0	6	1
1941	3	7	1	0	3	1	3	4	
1942	3	8		2	2		1	6	
1943	0	10		0	3		0	7	

Season	All Games W	L	T	Home Games W	L	T	Road Games W	L	T
1945	1	9		0	3		1	6	
1946	6	5		2	2		4	3	
1947	9	3		5	0		4	3	
1948	11	1		5	1		6	0	
1949	6	5	1	2	3	1	4	2	
1950	5	7		3	3		2	4	
1951	3	9		1	5		2	4	
1952	4	8		2	4		2	4	
1953	1	10	1	0	5	1	1	5	
1954	2	10		2	4		0	6	
1955	4	7	1	3	2	1	1	5	
1956	7	5		4	2		3	3	
1957	3	9		0	6		3	3	
1958	2	9	1	1	4	1	1	5	
1959	2	10		2	4		0	6	
1960	6	5	1	3	2	1	3	3	
1961	7	7		3	4		4	3	
1962	4	9	1	2	4	1	2	5	
1963	9	5		3	4		6	1	
1964	9	3	2	4	1	1	5	2	1
1965	5	9		2	5		3	4	
1966	8	5	1	5	1	1	3	4	
1967	6	7	1	3	3	1	3	4	
1968	9	4	1	4	2	1	5	2	
1969	4	9	1	3	4		1	5	1
1970	8	5	1	6	1		2	4	1
1971	4	9	1	1	5	1	3	4	
1972	4	9	1	2	5		2	4	1
1973	4	9	1	2	4	1	2	5	
1974	10	4		5	2		5	2	
1975	11	3		6	1		5	2	
1976	10	4		6	1		4	3	
1977	7	7		4	3		3	4	
1978	6	10		3	5		3	5	
1979	5	11		3	5		2	6	
1980	5	11		2	6		3	5	
1981	7	9		5	3		2	6	
1982	5	4		1	3		4	1	
1983	8	7	1	4	3	1	4	4	
1984	9	7		5	3		4	4	
1985	5	11		4	4		1	7	
1986	4	11	1	3	5		1	6	1
1987	7	8		4	3		3	5	
1988	7	9		4	4		3	5	
1989	5	11		2	6		3	5	
1990	5	11		3	5		2	6	
1991	4	12		2	6		2	6	
1992	4	12		3	5		1	7	
1993	7	9		4	4		3	5	
1994	8	8		5	3		3	5	
1995	4	12		3	5		1	7	
1996	7	9		5	3		2	6	
1997	4	12		3	5		1	7	
1998	9	7		5	3		4	4	
1999	6	10		4	4		2	6	
2000	3	13		3	5		0	8	
2001	7	9		3	5		4	4	
2002	5	11		3	5		2	6	
2003	4	12		4	4		0	8	
2004	6	10		5	3		1	7	
2005	5	11		3	5		2	6	
2006	5	11		3	5		2	6	
2007	8	8		6	2		2	6	
2008	9	7		6	2		3	5	
	473	664	39	278	286	22	195	378	17

**includes Chicago Cardinals (1920-1959), St. Louis Cardinals (1960-1987), and Phoenix Cardinals (1988-1993).*

ATLANTA FALCONS

Season	All Games W	L	T	Home Games W	L	T	Road Games W	L	T
1966	3	11		1	6		2	5	
1967	1	12	1	1	5	1	0	7	
1968	2	12		1	6		1	6	
1969	6	8		4	3		2	5	
1970	4	8	2	3	4		1	4	2
1971	7	6	1	4	3		3	3	1
1972	7	7		4	3		3	4	
1973	9	5		4	3		5	2	
1974	3	11		2	5		1	6	
1975	4	10		3	4		1	6	
1976	4	10		3	4		1	6	
1977	7	7		4	3		3	4	
1978	9	7		7	1		2	6	
1979	6	10		3	5		3	5	
1980	12	4		6	2		6	2	
1981	7	9		4	4		3	5	
1982	5	4		2	3		3	1	
1983	7	9		4	4		3	5	
1984	4	12		2	6		2	6	
1985	4	12		3	5		1	7	
1986	7	8	1	2	5	1	5	3	
1987	3	12		2	6		1	6	
1988	5	11		2	6		3	5	
1989	3	13		3	5		0	8	
1990	5	11		5	3		0	8	
1991	10	6		6	2		4	4	
1992	6	10		5	3		1	7	
1993	6	10		4	4		2	6	
1994	7	9		5	3		2	6	
1995	9	7		7	1		2	6	
1996	3	13		2	6		1	7	
1997	7	9		3	5		4	4	
1998	14	2		8	0		6	2	
1999	5	11		4	4		1	7	
2000	4	12		3	5		1	7	
2001	7	9		3	5		4	4	
2002	9	6	1	5	3		4	3	1
2003	5	11		2	6		3	5	
2004	11	5		7	1		4	4	
2005	8	8		4	4		4	4	
2006	7	9		3	5		4	4	
2007	4	12		3	5		1	7	
2008	11	5		7	1		4	4	
	267	383	6	160	167	2	107	216	4

CAROLINA PANTHERS

Season	All Games W	L	T	Home Games W	L	T	Road Games W	L	T
1995	7	9		5	3		2	6	
1996	12	4		8	0		4	4	
1997	7	9		2	6		5	3	
1998	4	12		2	6		2	6	
1999	8	8		5	3		3	5	
2000	7	9		5	3		2	6	
2001	1	15		0	8		1	7	
2002	7	9		4	4		3	5	
2003	11	5		6	2		5	3	
2004	7	9		3	5		4	4	
2005	11	5		5	3		6	2	
2006	8	8		4	4		4	4	
2007	7	9		2	6		5	3	
2008	12	4		8	0		4	4	
	109	115		59	53		50	62	

CHICAGO BEARS*

Season	All Games W	All Games L	All Games T	Home Games W	Home Games L	Home Games T	Road Games W	Road Games L	Road Games T
1920	10	1	2	6	0	1	4	1	1
1921	9	1	1	9	1	1	0	0	
1922	9	3		7	1		2	2	
1923	9	2	1	7	1	1	2	1	
1924	6	1	4	5	0	3	1	1	1
1925	9	5	3	7	1	1	2	4	2
1926	12	1	3	10	0	2	2	1	1
1927	9	3	2	7	1	1	2	2	1
1928	7	5	1	6	3		1	2	1
1929	4	9	2	1	5	2	3	4	
1930	9	4	1	5	2	1	4	2	
1931	8	5		6	3		2	2	
1932	7	1	6	6	1	1	1	0	5
1933	10	2	1	6	0		4	2	1
1934	13	0		5	0		8	0	
1935	6	4	2	1	2	2	5	2	
1936	9	3		3	1		6	2	
1937	9	1	1	4	1		5	0	1
1938	6	5		2	3		4	2	
1939	8	3		4	1		4	2	
1940	8	3		5	0		3	3	
1941	10	1		5	1		5	0	
1942	11	0		6	0		5	0	
1943	8	1	1	5	0		3	1	1
1944	6	3	1	4	0	1	2	3	
1945	3	7		2	3		1	4	
1946	8	2	1	4	1	1	4	1	
1947	8	4		4	2		4	2	
1948	10	2		5	1		5	1	
1949	9	3		5	1		4	2	
1950	9	3		6	0		3	3	
1951	7	5		3	3		4	2	
1952	5	7		3	3		2	4	
1953	3	8	1	1	4	1	2	4	
1954	8	4		4	2		4	2	
1955	8	4		5	1		3	3	
1956	9	2	1	6	0		3	2	1
1957	5	7		2	4		3	3	
1958	8	4		5	1		3	3	
1959	8	4		4	2		4	2	
1960	5	6	1	4	2		1	4	1
1961	8	6		5	2		3	4	
1962	9	5		4	3		5	2	
1963	11	1	2	6	0	1	5	1	1
1964	5	9		2	5		3	4	
1965	9	5		5	2		4	3	
1966	5	7	2	4	1	2	1	6	
1967	7	6	1	3	3	1	4	3	
1968	7	7		2	5		5	2	
1969	1	13		1	6		0	7	
1970	6	8		3	4		3	4	
1971	6	8		4	3		2	5	
1972	4	9	1	1	5	1	3	4	
1973	3	11		1	6		2	5	
1974	4	10		4	3		0	7	
1975	4	10		3	4		1	6	
1976	7	7		4	3		3	4	
1977	9	5		5	2		4	3	
1978	7	9		4	4		3	5	
1979	10	6		6	2		4	4	
1980	7	9		5	3		2	6	
1981	6	10		4	4		2	6	
1982	3	6		2	2		1	4	
1983	8	8		5	3		3	5	
1984	10	6		6	2		4	4	
1985	15	1		8	0		7	1	
1986	14	2		7	1		7	1	
1987	11	4		6	2		5	2	
1988	12	4		7	1		5	3	
1989	6	10		4	4		2	6	
1990	11	5		7	1		4	4	
1991	11	5		6	2		5	3	
1992	5	11		4	4		1	7	
1993	7	9		3	5		4	4	
1994	9	7		5	3		4	4	
1995	9	7		5	3		4	4	
1996	7	9		6	2		1	7	
1997	4	12		2	6		2	6	
1998	4	12		3	5		1	7	
1999	6	10		3	5		3	5	
2000	5	11		3	5		2	6	
2001	13	3		7	1		6	2	
2002	4	12		3	5		1	7	
2003	7	9		6	2		1	7	
2004	5	11		2	6		3	5	
2005	11	5		7	1		4	4	
2006	13	3		6	2		7	1	
2007	7	9		4	4		3	5	
2008	9	7		6	2		3	5	
	686	498	42	404	207	24	282	291	18

**includes Decatur Staleys (1920) and Chicago Staleys (1921).*

DALLAS COWBOYS

Season	All Games W	All Games L	All Games T	Home Games W	Home Games L	Home Games T	Road Games W	Road Games L	Road Games T
1960	0	11	1	0	6		0	5	1
1961	4	9	1	2	4	1	2	5	
1962	5	8	1	2	4	1	3	4	
1963	4	10		3	4		1	6	
1964	5	8	1	2	4	1	3	4	
1965	7	7		5	2		2	5	
1966	10	3	1	6	1		4	2	1
1967	9	5		5	2		4	3	
1968	12	2		5	2		7	0	
1969	11	2	1	6	0	1	5	2	
1970	10	4		6	1		4	3	
1971	11	3		6	1		5	2	
1972	10	4		5	2		5	2	
1973	10	4		6	1		4	3	
1974	8	6		5	2		3	4	
1975	10	4		5	2		5	2	
1976	11	3		6	1		5	2	
1977	12	2		6	1		6	1	
1978	12	4		7	1		5	3	
1979	11	5		6	2		5	3	
1980	12	4		8	0		4	4	
1981	12	4		8	0		4	4	
1982	6	3		3	2		3	1	
1983	12	4		6	2		6	2	
1984	9	7		5	3		4	4	
1985	10	6		7	1		3	5	
1986	7	9		3	5		4	4	
1987	7	8		3	4		4	4	
1988	3	13		1	7		2	6	
1989	1	15		0	8		1	7	
1990	7	9		5	3		2	6	
1991	11	5		6	2		5	3	
1992	13	3		7	1		6	2	
1993	12	4		6	2		6	2	
1994	12	4		6	2		6	2	
1995	12	4		6	2		6	2	
1996	10	6		6	2		4	4	
1997	6	10		5	3		1	7	
1998	10	6		6	2		4	4	
1999	8	8		7	1		1	7	

Season	All Games W	L	T	Home Games W	L	T	Road Games W	L	T
2000	5	11		3	5		2	6	
2001	5	11		4	4		1	7	
2002	5	11		4	4		1	7	
2003	10	6		6	2		4	4	
2004	6	10		4	4		2	6	
2005	9	7		5	3		4	4	
2006	9	7		4	4		5	3	
2007	13	3		6	2		7	1	
2008	9	7		6	2		3	5	
	423	309	6	240	125	4	183	184	2

DETROIT LIONS*

Season	All Games W	L	T	Home Games W	L	T	Road Games W	L	T
1930	5	6	3	5	1	2	0	5	1
1931	11	3		8	0		3	3	
1932	6	2	4	3	0	2	3	2	2
1933	6	5		4	1		2	4	
1934	10	3		6	2		4	1	
1935	7	3	2	5	0	1	2	3	1
1936	8	4		5	1		3	3	
1937	7	4		4	2		3	2	
1938	7	4		4	3		3	1	
1939	6	5		4	2		2	3	
1940	5	5	1	3	3		2	2	1
1941	4	6	1	3	2		1	4	1
1942	0	11		0	7		0	4	
1943	3	6	1	2	2	1	1	4	
1944	6	3	1	4	2		2	1	1
1945	7	3		4	1		3	2	
1946	1	10		1	5		0	5	
1947	3	9		2	4		1	5	
1948	2	10		2	4		0	6	
1949	4	8		2	4		2	4	
1950	6	6		4	2		2	4	
1951	7	4	1	3	3	1	4	1	
1952	9	3		6	1		3	2	
1953	10	2		5	1		5	1	
1954	9	2	1	5	0	1	4	2	
1955	3	9		3	4		0	5	
1956	9	3		5	1		4	2	
1957	8	4		5	1		3	3	
1958	4	7	1	2	4		2	3	1
1959	3	8	1	2	4		1	4	1
1960	7	5		5	1		2	4	
1961	8	5	1	2	5		6	0	1
1962	11	3		7	0		4	3	
1963	5	8	1	3	3	1	2	5	
1964	7	5	2	3	3	1	4	2	1
1965	6	7	1	2	4	1	4	3	
1966	4	9	1	3	4		1	5	1
1967	5	7	2	3	4		2	3	2
1968	4	8	2	1	4	2	3	4	
1969	9	4	1	5	2		4	2	1
1970	10	4		6	1		4	3	
1971	7	6	1	3	4		4	2	1
1972	8	5	1	5	2		3	3	1
1973	6	7	1	4	3		2	4	1
1974	7	7		5	2		2	5	
1975	7	7		4	3		3	4	
1976	6	8		5	2		1	6	
1977	6	8		5	2		1	6	
1978	7	9		5	3		2	6	
1979	2	14		2	6		0	8	
1980	9	7		6	2		3	5	
1981	8	8		7	1		1	7	
1982	4	5		2	3		2	2	
1983	9	7		6	2		3	5	
1984	4	11	1	2	5	1	2	6	
1985	7	9		6	2		1	7	
1986	5	11		1	7		4	4	
1987	4	11		1	6		3	5	
1988	4	12		2	6		2	6	
1989	7	9		4	4		3	5	
1990	6	10		3	5		3	5	
1991	12	4		8	0		4	4	
1992	5	11		3	5		2	6	
1993	10	6		5	3		5	3	
1994	9	7		6	2		3	5	
1995	10	6		7	1		3	5	
1996	5	11		4	4		1	7	
1997	9	7		6	2		3	5	
1998	5	11		4	4		1	7	
1999	8	8		6	2		2	6	
2000	9	7		4	4		5	3	
2001	2	14		2	6		0	8	
2002	3	13		3	5		0	8	
2003	5	11		5	3		0	8	
2004	6	10		3	5		3	5	
2005	5	11		3	5		2	6	
2006	3	13		2	6		1	7	
2007	7	9		5	3		2	6	
2008	0	16		0	8		0	8	
	488	569	32	305	236	14	183	333	18

**includes Portsmouth Spartans (1930-33).*

GREEN BAY PACKERS

Season	All Games W	L	T	Home Games W	L	T	Road Games W	L	T
1921	3	2	1	2	1		1	1	1
1922	4	3	3	4	1	1	0	2	2
1923	7	2	1	4	2	1	3	0	
1924	7	4		5	0		2	4	
1925	8	5		6	0		2	5	
1926	7	3	3	4	1	2	3	2	1
1927	7	2	1	6	1		1	1	1
1928	6	4	3	2	2	2	4	2	1
1929	12	0	1	5	0		7	0	1
1930	10	3	1	6	0		4	3	1
1931	12	2		8	0		4	2	
1932	10	3	1	5	0	1	5	3	
1933	5	7	1	3	2	1	2	5	
1934	7	6		4	2		3	4	
1935	8	4		5	2		3	2	
1936	10	1	1	5	1		5	0	1
1937	7	4		3	2		4	2	
1938	8	3		4	2		4	1	
1939	9	2		4	1		5	1	
1940	6	4	1	4	2		2	2	1
1941	10	1		4	1		6	0	
1942	8	2	1	4	1		4	1	1
1943	7	2	1	2	1	1	5	1	
1944	8	2		5	0		3	2	
1945	6	4		4	1		2	3	
1946	6	5		2	3		4	2	
1947	6	5	1	4	2		2	3	1
1948	3	9		2	4		1	5	
1949	2	10		1	5		1	5	
1950	3	9		3	3		0	6	
1951	3	9		2	4		1	5	
1952	6	6		3	3		3	3	
1953	2	9	1	1	5		1	4	1
1954	4	8		2	4		2	4	
1955	6	6		5	1		1	5	
1956	4	8		2	4		2	4	
1957	3	9		1	5		2	4	

Season	All Games W	L	T	Home Games W	L	T	Road Games W	L	T
1958	1	10	1	1	4	1	0	6	
1959	7	5		4	2		3	3	
1960	8	4		4	2		4	2	
1961	11	3		6	1		5	2	
1962	13	1		7	0		6	1	
1963	11	2	1	6	1		5	1	1
1964	8	5	1	4	3		4	2	1
1965	10	3	1	6	1		4	2	1
1966	12	2		6	1		6	1	
1967	9	4	1	4	2	1	5	2	
1968	6	7	1	2	5		4	2	1
1969	8	6		5	2		3	4	
1970	6	8		4	3		2	5	
1971	4	8	2	3	3	1	1	5	1
1972	10	4		4	3		6	1	
1973	5	7	2	3	2	2	2	5	
1974	6	8		4	3		2	5	
1975	4	10		3	4		1	6	
1976	5	9		4	3		1	6	
1977	4	10		2	5		2	5	
1978	8	7	1	5	2	1	3	5	
1979	5	11		4	4		1	7	
1980	5	10	1	4	4		1	6	1
1981	8	8		4	4		4	4	
1982	5	3	1	3	1		2	2	1
1983	8	8		5	3		3	5	
1984	8	8		5	3		3	5	
1985	8	8		5	3		3	5	
1986	4	12		1	7		3	5	
1987	5	9	1	2	5	1	3	4	
1988	4	12		2	6		2	6	
1989	10	6		6	2		4	4	
1990	6	10		3	5		3	5	
1991	4	12		2	6		2	6	
1992	9	7		6	2		3	5	
1993	9	7		6	2		3	5	
1994	9	7		7	1		2	6	
1995	11	5		7	1		4	4	
1996	13	3		8	0		5	3	
1997	13	3		8	0		5	3	
1998	11	5		7	1		4	4	
1999	8	8		5	3		3	5	
2000	9	7		6	2		3	5	
2001	12	4		7	1		5	3	
2002	12	4		8	0		4	4	
2003	10	6		5	3		5	3	
2004	10	6		4	4		6	2	
2005	4	12		3	5		1	7	
2006	8	8		3	5		5	3	
2007	13	3		7	1		6	2	
2008	6	10		4	4		2	6	
	643	513	36	370	209	16	273	304	20

MINNESOTA VIKINGS

Season	All Games W	L	T	Home Games W	L	T	Road Games W	L	T
1961	3	11		3	4		0	7	
1962	2	11	1	1	5	1	1	6	
1963	5	8	1	3	4		2	4	1
1964	8	5	1	4	3		4	2	1
1965	7	7		2	5		5	2	
1966	4	9	1	2	5		2	4	1
1967	3	8	3	1	4	2	2	4	1
1968	8	6		4	3		4	3	
1969	12	2		7	0		5	2	
1970	12	2		7	0		5	2	
1971	11	3		5	2		6	1	
1972	7	7		3	4		4	3	
1973	12	2		7	0		5	2	
1974	10	4		4	3		6	1	
1975	12	2		7	0		5	2	
1976	11	2	1	6	0	1	5	2	
1977	9	5		5	2		4	3	
1978	8	7	1	5	3		3	4	1
1979	7	9		5	3		2	6	
1980	9	7		5	3		4	4	
1981	7	9		5	3		2	6	
1982	5	4		4	1		1	3	
1983	8	8		3	5		5	3	
1984	3	13		2	6		1	7	
1985	7	9		4	4		3	5	
1986	9	7		5	3		4	4	
1987	8	7		5	3		3	4	
1988	11	5		7	1		4	4	
1989	10	6		8	0		2	6	
1990	6	10		4	4		2	6	
1991	8	8		4	4		4	4	
1992	11	5		5	3		6	2	
1993	9	7		4	4		5	3	
1994	10	6		6	2		4	4	
1995	8	8		6	2		2	6	
1996	9	7		5	3		4	4	
1997	9	7		5	3		4	4	
1998	15	1		8	0		7	1	
1999	10	6		6	2		4	4	
2000	11	5		7	1		4	4	
2001	5	11		5	3		0	8	
2002	6	10		4	4		2	6	
2003	9	7		6	2		3	5	
2004	8	8		5	3		3	5	
2005	9	7		6	2		3	5	
2006	6	10		3	5		3	5	
2007	8	8		5	3		3	5	
2008	10	6		6	2		4	4	
	395	322	9	229	131	4	166	191	5

NEW ORLEANS SAINTS

Season	All Games W	L	T	Home Games W	L	T	Road Games W	L	T
1967	3	11		2	5		1	6	
1968	4	9	1	3	4		1	5	1
1969	5	9		3	4		2	5	
1970	2	11	1	2	5		0	6	1
1971	4	8	2	2	4	1	2	4	1
1972	2	11	1	2	5		0	6	1
1973	5	9		5	2		0	7	
1974	5	9		4	3		1	6	
1975	2	12		2	5		0	7	
1976	4	10		2	5		2	5	
1977	3	11		2	5		1	6	
1978	7	9		3	5		4	4	
1979	8	8		3	5		5	3	
1980	1	15		0	8		1	7	
1981	4	12		2	6		2	6	
1982	4	5		2	3		2	2	
1983	8	8		5	3		3	5	
1984	7	9		3	5		4	4	
1985	5	11		3	5		2	6	
1986	7	9		4	4		3	5	
1987	12	3		6	1		6	2	
1988	10	6		5	3		5	3	
1989	9	7		5	3		4	4	
1990	8	8		5	3		3	5	
1991	11	5		6	2		5	3	
1992	12	4		6	2		6	2	
1993	8	8		4	4		4	4	

Season	All Games W	L	T	Home Games W	L	T	Road Games W	L	T
1994	7	9		3	5		4	4	
1995	7	9		4	4		3	5	
1996	3	13		2	6		1	7	
1997	6	10		3	5		3	5	
1998	6	10		4	4		2	6	
1999	3	13		3	5		0	8	
2000	10	6		3	5		7	1	
2001	7	9		3	5		4	4	
2002	9	7		4	4		5	3	
2003	8	8		5	3		3	5	
2004	8	8		3	5		5	3	
2005	3	13		1	7		2	6	
2006	10	6		4	4		6	2	
2007	7	9		3	5		4	4	
2008	8	8		6	2		2	6	
	262	375	5	142	178	1	120	197	4

NEW YORK GIANTS

Season	All Games W	L	T	Home Games W	L	T	Road Games W	L	T
1925	8	4		7	2		1	2	
1926	8	4	1	5	2	1	3	2	
1927	11	1	1	7	1		4	0	1
1928	4	7	2	1	2	2	3	5	
1929	13	1	1	7	1		6	0	1
1930	13	4		6	2		7	2	
1931	7	6	1	4	2	1	3	4	
1932	4	6	2	3	2	1	1	4	1
1933	11	3		7	0		4	3	
1934	8	5		5	1		3	4	
1935	9	3		4	2		5	1	
1936	5	6	1	3	3	1	2	3	
1937	6	3	2	4	2	1	2	1	1
1938	8	2	1	6	1		2	1	1
1939	9	1	1	6	0		3	1	1
1940	6	4	1	4	3		2	1	1
1941	8	3		5	2		3	1	
1942	5	5	1	3	2	1	2	3	
1943	6	3	1	4	2		2	1	1
1944	8	1	1	5	1		3	0	1
1945	3	6	1	2	4		1	2	1
1946	7	3	1	5	1	1	2	2	
1947	2	8	2	2	3	1	0	5	1
1948	4	8		2	4		2	4	
1949	6	6		2	4		4	2	
1950	10	2		5	1		5	1	
1951	9	2	1	5	1		4	1	1
1952	7	5		2	4		5	1	
1953	3	9		2	4		1	5	
1954	7	5		4	2		3	3	
1955	6	5	1	4	1	1	2	4	
1956	8	3	1	4	1	1	4	2	
1957	7	5		3	3		4	2	
1958	9	3		5	1		4	2	
1959	10	2		5	1		5	1	
1960	6	4	2	1	3	2	5	1	
1961	10	3	1	4	2	1	6	1	
1962	12	2		6	1		6	1	
1963	11	3		5	2		6	1	
1964	2	10	2	2	5		0	5	2
1965	7	7		3	4		4	3	
1966	1	12	1	1	6		0	6	1
1967	7	7		5	2		2	5	
1968	7	7		3	4		4	3	
1969	6	8		5	2		1	6	
1970	9	5		5	2		4	3	
1971	4	10		1	6		3	4	
1972	8	6		4	3		4	3	
1973	2	11	1	2	4	1	0	7	
1974	2	12		0	7		2	5	
1975	5	9		2	5		3	4	
1976	3	11		3	4		0	7	
1977	5	9		3	4		2	5	
1978	6	10		5	3		1	7	
1979	6	10		4	4		2	6	
1980	4	12		2	6		2	6	
1981	9	7		4	4		5	3	
1982	4	5		2	3		2	2	
1983	3	12	1	1	7		2	5	1
1984	9	7		6	2		3	5	
1985	10	6		6	2		4	4	
1986	14	2		8	0		6	2	
1987	6	9		5	3		1	6	
1988	10	6		5	3		5	3	
1989	12	4		7	1		5	3	
1990	13	3		7	1		6	2	
1991	8	8		5	3		3	5	
1992	6	10		4	4		2	6	
1993	11	5		6	2		5	3	
1994	9	7		4	4		5	3	
1995	5	11		3	5		2	6	
1996	6	10		3	5		3	5	
1997	10	5	1	6	2		4	3	1
1998	8	8		5	3		3	5	
1999	7	9		4	4		3	5	
2000	12	4		5	3		7	1	
2001	7	9		5	3		2	6	
2002	10	6		5	3		5	3	
2003	4	12		1	7		3	5	
2004	6	10		3	5		3	5	
2005	11	5		7	1		4	4	
2006	8	8		3	5		5	3	
2007	10	6		3	5		7	1	
2008	12	4		7	1		5	3	
	618	510	33	344	238	16	274	272	17

PHILADELPHIA EAGLES

Season	All Games W	L	T	Home Games W	L	T	Road Games W	L	T
1933	3	5	1	2	3	1	1	2	
1934	4	7		2	4		2	3	
1935	2	9		0	5		2	4	
1936	1	11		1	6		0	5	
1937	2	8	1	0	5	1	2	3	
1938	5	6		2	3		3	3	
1939	1	9	1	1	3	1	0	6	
1940	1	10		1	4		0	6	
1941	2	8	1	1	4	1	1	4	
1942	2	9		0	5		2	4	
1944	7	1	2	3	1	2	4	0	
1945	7	3		6	0		1	3	
1946	6	5		3	2		3	3	
1947	8	4		6	1		2	3	
1948	9	2	1	6	0		3	2	1
1949	11	1		6	0		5	1	
1950	6	6		2	4		4	2	
1951	4	8		1	5		3	3	
1952	7	5		4	2		3	3	
1953	7	4	1	5	0	1	2	4	
1954	7	4	1	5	1		2	3	1
1955	4	7	1	4	2		0	5	1
1956	3	8	1	2	3	1	1	5	
1957	4	8		3	3		1	5	
1958	2	9	1	2	4		0	5	1
1959	7	5		5	1		2	4	
1960	10	2		5	1		5	1	

Season	All Games W	L	T	Home Games W	L	T	Road Games W	L	T
1961	10	4		5	2		5	2	
1962	3	10	1	2	5		1	5	1
1963	2	10	2	1	5	1	1	5	1
1964	6	8		3	4		3	4	
1965	5	9		2	5		3	4	
1966	9	5		5	2		4	3	
1967	6	7	1	5	2		1	5	1
1968	2	12		1	6		1	6	
1969	4	9	1	2	5		2	4	1
1970	3	10	1	3	3	1	0	7	
1971	6	7	1	3	4		3	3	1
1972	2	11	1	0	6	1	2	5	
1973	5	8	1	4	3		1	5	1
1974	7	7		5	2		2	5	
1975	4	10		2	5		2	5	
1976	4	10		2	5		2	5	
1977	5	9		4	3		1	6	
1978	9	7		5	3		4	4	
1979	11	5		5	3		6	2	
1980	12	4		7	1		5	3	
1981	10	6		6	2		4	4	
1982	3	6		1	4		2	2	
1983	5	11		1	7		4	4	
1984	6	9	1	5	3		1	6	1
1985	7	9		4	4		3	5	
1986	5	10	1	2	5	1	3	5	
1987	7	8		4	4		3	4	
1988	10	6		5	3		5	3	
1989	11	5		6	2		5	3	
1990	10	6		6	2		4	4	
1991	10	6		4	4		6	2	
1992	11	5		8	0		3	5	
1993	8	8		3	5		5	3	
1994	7	9		5	3		2	6	
1995	10	6		6	2		4	4	
1996	10	6		5	3		5	3	
1997	6	9	1	6	2		0	7	1
1998	3	13		3	5		0	8	
1999	5	11		4	4		1	7	
2000	11	5		5	3		6	2	
2001	11	5		4	4		7	1	
2002	12	4		7	1		5	3	
2003	12	4		5	3		7	1	
2004	13	3		7	1		6	2	
2005	6	10		4	4		2	6	
2006	10	6		5	3		5	3	
2007	8	8		3	5		5	3	
2008	9	6	1	6	2		3	4	1
	483	526	25	274	236	12	209	290	13

ST. LOUIS RAMS*

Season	All Games W	L	T	Home Games W	L	T	Road Games W	L	T
1937	1	10		0	5		1	5	
1938	4	7		2	2		2	5	
1939	5	5	1	3	2	1	2	3	
1940	4	6	1	3	1	1	1	5	
1941	2	9		1	4		1	5	
1942	5	6		3	2		2	4	
1944	4	6		1	2		3	4	
1945	9	1		4	0		5	1	
1946	6	4	1	3	2		3	2	1
1947	6	6		3	3		3	3	
1948	6	5	1	3	2	1	3	3	
1949	8	2	2	5	1		3	1	2
1950	9	3		5	1		4	2	
1951	8	4		5	2		3	2	
1952	9	3		5	1		4	2	
1953	8	3	1	5	1		3	2	1
1954	6	5	1	3	2	1	3	3	
1955	8	3	1	5	1		3	2	1
1956	4	8		4	2		0	6	
1957	6	6		5	1		1	5	
1958	8	4		4	2		4	2	
1959	2	10		0	6		2	4	
1960	4	7	1	2	3	1	2	4	
1961	4	10		4	3		0	7	
1962	1	12	1	0	7		1	5	1
1963	5	9		3	4		2	5	
1964	5	7	2	3	2	2	2	5	
1965	4	10		3	4		1	6	
1966	8	6		5	2		3	4	
1967	11	1	2	5	1	1	6	0	1
1968	10	3	1	5	2		5	1	1
1969	11	3		5	2		6	1	
1970	9	4	1	3	3	1	6	1	
1971	8	5	1	4	2	1	4	3	
1972	6	7	1	4	3		2	4	1
1973	12	2		7	0		5	2	
1974	10	4		6	1		4	3	
1975	12	2		6	1		6	1	
1976	10	3	1	5	2		5	1	1
1977	10	4		7	0		3	4	
1978	12	4		6	2		6	2	
1979	9	7		4	4		5	3	
1980	11	5		6	2		5	3	
1981	6	10		4	4		2	6	
1982	2	7		1	4		1	3	
1983	9	7		5	3		4	4	
1984	10	6		5	3		5	3	
1985	11	5		6	2		5	3	
1986	10	6		6	2		4	4	
1987	6	9		3	4		3	5	
1988	10	6		4	4		6	2	
1989	11	5		6	2		5	3	
1990	5	11		2	6		3	5	
1991	3	13		2	6		1	7	
1992	6	10		4	4		2	6	
1993	5	11		3	5		2	6	
1994	4	12		3	5		1	7	
1995	7	9		4	4		3	5	
1996	6	10		4	4		2	6	
1997	5	11		2	6		3	5	
1998	4	12		2	6		2	6	
1999	13	3		8	0		5	3	
2000	10	6		5	3		5	3	
2001	14	2		6	2		8	0	
2002	7	9		6	2		1	7	
2003	12	4		8	0		4	4	
2004	8	8		6	2		2	6	
2005	6	10		3	5		3	5	
2006	8	8		4	4		4	4	
2007	3	13		1	7		2	6	
2008	2	14		1	7		1	7	
	503	468	20	279	201	10	224	267	10

**includes Cleveland Rams (1937-1942, 1944-45) and Los Angeles Rams (1946-1994).*

SAN FRANCISCO 49ERS

Season	All Games W	L	T	Home Games W	L	T	Road Games W	L	T
1950	3	9		3	3		0	6	
1951	7	4	1	5	1		2	3	1
1952	7	5		3	3		4	2	
1953	9	3		5	1		4	2	
1954	7	4	1	4	2		3	2	1

	All Games			Home Games			Road Games		
Season	W	L	T	W	L	T	W	L	T
1955	4	8		2	4		2	4	
1956	5	6	1	3	3		2	3	1
1957	8	4		5	1		3	3	
1958	6	6		4	2		2	4	
1959	7	5		4	2		3	3	
1960	7	5		3	3		4	2	
1961	7	6	1	5	1	1	2	5	
1962	6	8		1	6		5	2	
1963	2	12		2	5		0	7	
1964	4	10		3	4		1	6	
1965	7	6	1	4	2	1	3	4	
1966	6	6	2	4	2	1	2	4	1
1967	7	7		3	4		4	3	
1968	7	6	1	3	3	1	4	3	
1969	4	8	2	3	3	1	1	5	1
1970	10	3	1	5	1	1	5	2	
1971	9	5		4	3		5	2	
1972	8	5	1	4	2	1	4	3	
1973	5	9		3	4		2	5	
1974	6	8		3	4		3	4	
1975	5	9		2	5		3	4	
1976	8	6		4	3		4	3	
1977	5	9		3	4		2	5	
1978	2	14		2	6		0	8	
1979	2	14		2	6		0	8	
1980	6	10		4	4		2	6	
1981	13	3		7	1		6	2	
1982	3	6		0	5		3	1	
1983	10	6		4	4		6	2	
1984	15	1		7	1		8	0	
1985	10	6		5	3		5	3	
1986	10	5	1	6	2		4	3	1
1987	13	2		6	1		7	1	
1988	10	6		4	4		6	2	
1989	14	2		6	2		8	0	
1990	14	2		6	2		8	0	
1991	10	6		7	1		3	5	
1992	14	2		7	1		7	1	
1993	10	6		6	2		4	4	
1994	13	3		7	1		6	2	
1995	11	5		6	2		5	3	
1996	12	4		6	2		6	2	
1997	13	3		8	0		5	3	
1998	12	4		8	0		4	4	
1999	4	12		3	5		1	7	
2000	6	10		4	4		2	6	
2001	12	4		7	1		5	3	
2002	10	6		5	3		5	3	
2003	7	9		6	2		1	7	
2004	2	14		1	7		1	7	
2005	4	12		3	5		1	7	
2006	7	9		4	4		3	5	
2007	5	11		3	5		2	6	
2008	7	9		4	4		3	5	
	457	388	13	251	171	7	206	217	6

SEATTLE SEAHAWKS

	All Games			Home Games			Road Games		
Season	W	L	T	W	L	T	W	L	T
1976	2	12		1	6		1	6	
1977	5	9		3	4		2	5	
1978	9	7		5	3		4	4	
1979	9	7		5	3		4	4	
1980	4	12		0	8		4	4	
1981	6	10		5	3		1	7	
1982	4	5		3	2		1	3	
1983	9	7		5	3		4	4	
1984	12	4		7	1		5	3	
1985	8	8		5	3		3	5	
1986	10	6		7	1		3	5	
1987	9	6		6	2		3	4	
1988	9	7		5	3		4	4	
1989	7	9		3	5		4	4	
1990	9	7		5	3		4	4	
1991	7	9		5	3		2	6	
1992	2	14		1	7		1	7	
1993	6	10		4	4		2	6	
1994	6	10		3	5		3	5	
1995	8	8		5	3		3	5	
1996	7	9		4	4		3	5	
1997	8	8		4	4		4	4	
1998	8	8		6	2		2	6	
1999	9	7		5	3		4	4	
2000	6	10		3	5		3	5	
2001	9	7		6	2		3	5	
2002	7	9		3	5		4	4	
2003	10	6		8	0		2	6	
2004	9	7		5	3		4	4	
2005	13	3		8	0		5	3	
2006	9	7		5	3		4	4	
2007	10	6		7	1		3	5	
2008	4	12		2	6		2	6	
	250	266		149	110		101	156	

TAMPA BAY BUCCANEERS

	All Games			Home Games			Road Games		
Season	W	L	T	W	L	T	W	L	T
1976	0	14		0	7		0	7	
1977	2	12		1	6		1	6	
1978	5	11		3	5		2	6	
1979	10	6		5	3		5	3	
1980	5	10	1	2	5	1	3	5	
1981	9	7		6	2		3	5	
1982	5	4		4	1		1	3	
1983	2	14		1	7		1	7	
1984	6	10		6	2		0	8	
1985	2	14		2	6		0	8	
1986	2	14		1	7		1	7	
1987	4	11		2	5		2	6	
1988	5	11		3	5		2	6	
1989	5	11		2	6		3	5	
1990	6	10		4	4		2	6	
1991	3	13		3	5		0	8	
1992	5	11		3	5		2	6	
1993	5	11		3	5		2	6	
1994	6	10		4	4		2	6	
1995	7	9		5	3		2	6	
1996	6	10		5	3		1	7	
1997	10	6		5	3		5	3	
1998	8	8		6	2		2	6	
1999	11	5		7	1		4	4	
2000	10	6		6	2		4	4	
2001	9	7		5	3		4	4	
2002	12	4		6	2		6	2	
2003	7	9		3	5		4	4	
2004	5	11		4	4		1	7	
2005	11	5		6	2		5	3	
2006	4	12		3	5		1	7	
2007	9	7		6	2		3	5	
2008	9	7		6	2		3	5	
	205	310	1	128	129	1	77	181	

WASHINGTON REDSKINS*

	All Games			Home Games			Road Games		
Season	**W**	**L**	**T**	**W**	**L**	**T**	**W**	**L**	**T**
1932	4	4	2	2	3	1	2	1	1
1933	5	5	2	4	2		1	3	2
1934	6	6		4	3		2	3	
1935	2	8	1	2	5		0	3	1
1936	7	5		4	3		3	2	
1937	8	3		4	2		4	1	
1938	6	3	2	3	1	1	3	2	1
1939	8	2	1	5	0	1	3	2	
1940	9	2		6	0		3	2	
1941	6	5		4	2		2	3	
1942	10	1		5	1		5	0	
1943	6	3	1	4	2		2	1	1
1944	6	3	1	4	2		2	1	1
1945	8	2		6	0		2	2	
1946	5	5	1	3	2	1	2	3	
1947	4	8		4	2		0	6	
1948	7	5		4	2		3	3	
1949	4	7	1	3	3		1	4	1
1950	3	9		1	5		2	4	
1951	5	7		2	4		3	3	
1952	4	8		1	5		3	3	
1953	6	5	1	3	3		3	2	1
1954	3	9		3	3		0	6	
1955	8	4		3	3		5	1	
1956	6	6		4	2		2	4	
1957	5	6	1	2	3	1	3	3	
1958	4	7	1	3	2	1	1	5	
1959	3	9		2	4		1	5	
1960	1	9	2	1	4	1	0	5	1
1961	1	12	1	1	6		0	6	1
1962	5	7	2	3	4		2	3	2
1963	3	11		1	6		2	5	
1964	6	8		4	3		2	5	
1965	6	8		3	4		3	4	
1966	7	7		4	3		3	4	
1967	5	6	3	2	4	1	3	2	2
1968	5	9		3	4		2	5	
1969	7	5	2	4	2	1	3	3	1
1970	6	8		4	3		2	5	
1971	9	4	1	4	2	1	5	2	
1972	11	3		6	1		5	2	
1973	10	4		7	0		3	4	
1974	10	4		6	1		4	3	
1975	8	6		5	2		3	4	
1976	10	4		5	2		5	2	
1977	9	5		5	2		4	3	
1978	8	8		5	3		3	5	
1979	10	6		6	2		4	4	
1980	6	10		4	4		2	6	
1981	8	8		5	3		3	5	
1982	8	1		3	1		5	0	
1983	14	2		7	1		7	1	
1984	11	5		7	1		4	4	
1985	10	6		5	3		5	3	
1986	12	4		7	1		5	3	
1987	11	4		6	1		5	3	
1988	7	9		4	4		3	5	
1989	10	6		4	4		6	2	
1990	10	6		7	1		3	5	
1991	14	2		7	1		7	1	
1992	9	7		6	2		3	5	
1993	4	12		3	5		1	7	
1994	3	13		0	8		3	5	
1995	6	10		4	4		2	6	
1996	9	7		5	3		4	4	
1997	8	7	1	5	2	1	3	5	
1998	6	10		4	4		2	6	
1999	10	6		6	2		4	4	
2000	8	8		4	4		4	4	
2001	8	8		4	4		4	4	
2002	7	9		5	3		2	6	
2003	5	11		3	5		2	6	
2004	6	10		3	5		3	5	
2005	10	6		6	2		4	4	
2006	5	11		3	5		2	6	
2007	9	7		5	3		4	4	
2008	8	8		4	4		4	4	
	537	494	27	310	217	11	227	277	16

includes Boston Braves (1932) and Boston Redskins (1933-36).

ALL-TIME RECORDS OF NFL TEAMS

AFC	**W**	**L**	**T**	**Pct.**
Miami	380	272	4	.583
Oakland	405	324	11	.555
Cleveland	428	372	10	.535
Denver	386	344	10	.529
Jacksonville	118	106	0	.527
Indianapolis	427	388	7	.524
Kansas City	381	347	12	.523
Baltimore	107	100	1	.517
Pittsburgh	520	488	20	.516
New England	377	354	9	.516
San Diego	362	367	11	.497
Tennessee	363	371	6	.495
Buffalo	348	384	8	.475
N.Y. Jets	331	401	8	.452
Cincinnati	272	354	2	.435
Houston	40	72	0	.357

NFC	**W**	**L**	**T**	**Pct.**
Chicago	686	498	42	.579
Dallas	423	309	6	.578
Green Bay	643	513	36	.556
Minnesota	395	322	9	.551
N.Y. Giants	618	510	33	.548
San Francisco	457	388	13	.541
Washington	537	494	27	.521
St. Louis	503	468	20	.518
Carolina	109	115	0	.487
Seattle	250	266	0	.484
Philadelphia	483	526	25	.479
Detroit	488	569	32	.462
Arizona	473	664	39	.416
New Orleans	262	375	5	.411
Atlanta	267	383	6	.411
Tampa Bay	205	310	1	.398

From 1920-1971, tie games were not included in win percentage.

History

PRO FOOTBALL HALL OF FAME

The Professional Football Hall of Fame is located in Canton, Ohio, site of the organizational meeting on September 17, 1920, from which the National Football League evolved. The NFL recognized Canton as the Hall of Fame site on April 27, 1961. Canton area individuals, foundations, and companies donated almost $400,000 in cash and services to provide funds for the construction of the original two-building complex, which was dedicated on September 7, 1963. Since that time, the Hall added three buildings with major expansion projects in 1971, 1978, and 1995. The Hall's largest-ever expansion, a $9.2 million project, was completed in early fall 1995. With the new fifth building, the Hall's size is now 82,307 square feet, more than four times its original size.

The expanded Hall represents the sport of pro football in many ways—through (1) GameDay Stadium, a dynamic two-part turntable theater featuring NFL action in Cinemascope for the first time, (2) a standard theater showing NFL films hourly, (3) six large exhibition areas where the history of pro football is detailed in memento, picture, and story form, (4) an extensive archive and information center, and (5) a large museum store.

Throughout the years, the Pro Football Hall of Fame has become an extremely popular tourist attraction. Since its opening, the Hall has had more than eight million visitors.

New members of the Pro Football Hall of Fame are elected annually by a 44-member National Board of Selectors, made up of media representatives from every league city, eleven at-large representatives, and a representative of the Pro Football Writers of America. Between four and seven new members are elected each year. An affirmative vote of approximately 80 percent is needed for election.

Any fan may nominate any eligible player or contributor simply by writing to the Pro Football Hall of Fame. Players and coaches must have last played or coached at least five years before he is eligible. Contributors (administrators, owners, *et al.*) may be elected while they are still active.

The charter class of 17 enshrinees was elected in 1963 and the honor roll now stands at 253 (152 living as of May 1, 2009) with the election of a six-man class in 2009. That class consists of Bob Hayes, Randall McDaniel, Bruce Smith, Derrick Thomas, Ralph Wilson, Jr., and Rod Woodson.

ROSTER OF MEMBERS

HERB ADDERLEY
Cornerback. 6-0, 205. Born in Philadelphia, Pennsylvania, June 8, 1939. Michigan State. Inducted in 1980. 1961-69 Green Bay Packers, 1970-72 Dallas Cowboys. **Highlights:** 48 interceptions, 7 touchdowns. Played in four Super Bowls, five Pro Bowls.

TROY AIKMAN
Quarterback. 6-4, 219. Born in West Covina, California, November 21, 1966. Oklahoma, UCLA. Inducted in 2006. 1989-2000 Dallas Cowboys. **Highlights:** His 90 wins in 1990s make him winningest quarterback of any decade. Led Cowboys to three Super Bowl wins. Passed for 32,942 yards, 165 touchdowns. Named to six Pro Bowls.

GEORGE ALLEN
Coach. Born in Detroit, Michigan, April 29, 1918. Died December 31, 1990. Alma College, Eastern Michigan, Marquette, Michigan. Inducted in 2002. 1966-1970 Los Angeles Rams, 1971-77 Washington Redskins. **Highlights:** 118-54-5 overall record. Never suffered a losing season, and ranked tenth in coaching victories at time of retirement.

MARCUS ALLEN
Running back. 6-2, 210. Born in San Diego, California, March 26, 1960. Southern California. Inducted in 2003. 1982-1992 Los Angeles Raiders, 1993-1997 Kansas City Chiefs. **Highlights:** First player in NFL history to tally 10,000 rushing yards and 5,000 receiving yards. MVP, Super Bowl XVIII.

LANCE ALWORTH
Wide receiver. 6-0, 184. Born in Houston, Texas, August 3, 1940. Arkansas. Inducted in 1978. 1962-1970 San Diego Chargers, 1971-72 Dallas Cowboys. **Highlights:** 542 receptions for 10,266 yards, 85 touchdowns. All-AFL seven times, seven All-Star games.

DOUG ATKINS
Defensive end. 6-8, 275. Born in Humboldt, Tennessee, May 8, 1930. Tennessee. Inducted in 1982. 1953-54 Cleveland Browns, 1955-1966 Chicago Bears, 1967-69 New Orleans Saints. **Highlights:** Eight Pro Bowls, All-NFL four times. Played for 17 years, 205 games.

MORRIS (RED) BADGRO
End. 6-0, 190. Born in Orillia, Washington, December 1, 1902. Died July 13, 1998. Southern California. Inducted in 1981. 1927-28 New York Yankees, 1930-35 New York Giants, 1936 Brooklyn Dodgers. **Highlights:** First- or second-team All-NFL four times. Scored first touchdown in NFL Championship Game series.

LEM BARNEY
Cornerback. 6-0, 190. Born in Gulfport, Mississippi, September 8, 1945. Jackson State. Inducted in 1992. 1967-1977 Detroit Lions. **Highlights:** 56 interceptions for 1,077 yards, 11 touchdowns (7 defensive, 4 special teams). Seven Pro Bowls, All-NFL/NFC four times.

CLIFF BATTLES
Halfback. 6-1, 195. Born in Akron, Ohio, May 1, 1910. Died April 28, 1981. West Virginia Wesleyan. Inducted in 1968. 1932 Boston Braves, 1933-36 Boston Redskins, 1937 Washington Redskins. **Highlights:** NFL rushing champion 1932, 1937. First to gain more than 200 yards in a game, 1933.

SAMMY BAUGH
Quarterback. 6-2, 180. Born in Temple, Texas, March 17, 1914. Died December 17, 2008. Texas Christian. Inducted in 1963. 1937-1952 Washington Redskins. **Highlights:** Charter enshrinee. Six-time NFL passing leader. NFL passing, punting, interception champ, 1943.

CHUCK BEDNARIK
Center-linebacker. 6-3, 230. Born in Bethlehem, Pennsylvania, May 1, 1925. Pennsylvania. Inducted in 1967. 1949-1962 Philadelphia Eagles. **Highlights:** Eight Pro Bowls. Missed three games in 14 years. Named NFL all-time center, 1969.

BERT BELL
Team owner. Commissioner. Born in Philadelphia, Pennsylvania, February 25, 1895. Died October 11, 1959. Pennsylvania. Inducted in 1963. 1933-1940 Philadelphia Eagles, 1941-42 Pittsburgh Steelers, 1943 Phil-Pitt, 1944 Card-Pitt, 1945-46 Pittsburgh Steelers. Commissioner, 1946-1959. **Highlights:** Charter enshrinee. Built NFL image as commissioner, 1946-1959. Set up long-term television policies.

BOBBY BELL
Linebacker. 6-4, 225. Born in Shelby, North Carolina, June 17, 1940. Minnesota. Inducted in 1983. 1963-1974 Kansas City Chiefs. **Highlights:** 26 interceptions. All-AFL/AFC eight times. Nine career touchdowns, 1 on onside kick return.

RAYMOND BERRY
End. 6-2, 187. Born in Corpus Christi, Texas, February 27, 1933. Southern Methodist. Inducted in 1973. 1955-1967 Baltimore Colts. **Highlights:** 631 receptions for 9,275 yards, 68 touchdowns. Set NFL title game mark with 12 catches for 178 yards, 1958.

ELVIN BETHEA
Defensive end. 6-2, 260. Born in Trenton, New Jersey, March 1, 1946. North Carolina A&T. Inducted in 2003. 1968-1983 Houston Oilers. **Highlights:** Led team in sacks six times. Elected to eight Pro Bowls. Played for 16 years, 210 games.

CHARLES W. BIDWILL SR.
Team owner. Born in Chicago, Illinois, September 16, 1895. Died April 19, 1947. Loyola of Chicago. Inducted in 1967. 1933-1943 Chicago Cardinals, 1944 Card-Pitt, 1945-47 Chicago Cardinals. **Highlights:** Guiding light for NFL during depression years. Built famous "Dream Backfield."

FRED BILETNIKOFF
Wide receiver. 6-1, 190. Born in Erie, Pennsylvania, February 23, 1943. Florida State. Inducted in 1988. 1965-1978 Oakland Raiders. **Highlights:** 589 receptions for 8,974 yards, 76 touchdowns. 40 catches 10 straight years. MVP, Super Bowl XI.

GEORGE BLANDA
Quarterback-kicker. 6-2, 215. Born in Youngwood, Pennsylvania, September 17, 1927. Kentucky. Inducted in 1981. 1949-1958 Chicago Bears, 1950 Baltimore Colts, 1960-66 Houston Oilers, 1967-1975 Oakland Raiders. **Highlights:** 2,002 career points. 26-season, 340-game career longest in NFL history at retirement.

MEL BLOUNT
Cornerback. 6-3, 205. Born in Vidalia, Georgia, April 10, 1948. Southern University. Inducted in 1989. 1970-1983 Pittsburgh Steelers. **Highlights:** 57 interceptions for 736 yards. NFL defensive MVP, 1975. Played in five Pro Bowls.

TERRY BRADSHAW
Quarterback. 6-3, 210. Born in Shreveport, Louisiana, September 2, 1948. Louisiana Tech. Inducted in 1989. 1970-1983 Pittsburgh Steelers. **Highlights:** 27,989 yards passing, 212 touchdowns. MVP in Super Bowls XIII, XIV.

BOB (BOOMER) BROWN
Tackle. 6-4, 280. Born in Cleveland, Ohio, December 8, 1941. Nebraska. Inducted in 2004. 1964-68 Philadelphia Eagles, 1969-1970 Los Angeles Rams, 1971-73 Oakland Raiders. **Highlights:** All-NFL seven of 10 seasons, six Pro Bowls. Named to 1960s All-Decade Team.

JIM BROWN
Fullback. 6-2, 228. Born in St. Simons, Georgia, February 17, 1936. Syracuse. Inducted in 1971. 1957-1965 Cleveland Browns. **Highlights:** 12,312 yards rushing, 756 points. Led NFL rushers eight years. Nine consecutive Pro Bowls.

PAUL BROWN
Coach. Born in Norwalk, Ohio, September 7, 1908. Died August 5, 1991. Miami (Ohio). Inducted in 1967. 1946-49 Cleveland Browns (AAFC), 1950-1962 Cleveland Browns. **Highlights:** Built Cleveland dynasty with 167-53-8 record, four AAFC titles, three NFL crowns. Returned to coaching with Cincinnati Bengals after induction, 1968-1975.

ROOSEVELT BROWN
Tackle. 6-3, 255. Born in Charlottesville, Virginia, October 20, 1932. Died June 9, 2004. Morgan State. Inducted in 1975. 1953-1965 New York Giants. **Highlights:** All-NFL eight consecutive years, nine Pro Bowls. NFL's lineman of year, 1956.

WILLIE BROWN
Cornerback. 6-1, 210. Born in Yazoo City, Mississippi, December 2, 1940. Grambling. Inducted in 1984. 1963-66 Denver Broncos, 1967-1978 Oakland Raiders. **Highlights:** 54 interceptions for 472 yards. Scored on 75-yard interception in Super Bowl XI.

BUCK BUCHANAN
Defensive tackle. 6-7, 274. Born in Gainesville, Alabama, September 10, 1940. Died July 16, 1992. Grambling. Inducted in 1990. 1963-1975 Kansas City Chiefs. **Highlights:** Led Chiefs defensive efforts in Super Bowl I, IV. Did not miss a game in 13 years.

NICK BUONICONTI
Linebacker. 5-11, 220. Born in Springfield, Massachusetts, December 15, 1940. Notre Dame. Inducted in 2001. 1962-68 Boston Patriots, 1969-1974, 1976 Miami Dolphins. **Highlights:** All-AFL/AFC eight times. Named to AFL's All-Time Team.

DICK BUTKUS
Linebacker. 6-3, 245. Born in Chicago, Illinois, December 9, 1942. Illinois. Inducted in 1979. 1965-1973 Chicago Bears. **Highlights:** All-NFL six years, eight consecutive Pro Bowls. 27 fumble recoveries.

EARL CAMPBELL
Running back. 5-11, 233. Born in Tyler, Texas, March 29, 1955. Texas. Inducted in 1991. 1978-1984 Houston Oilers, 1984-85 New Orleans Saints. **Highlights:** 9,407 yards rushing, 74 touchdowns. 1,934 yards rushing in 1980, including four games with at least 200 yards.

TONY CANADEO
Halfback. 5-11, 195. Born in Chicago, Illinois, May 5, 1919. Died November 29, 2003. Gonzaga. Inducted in 1974. 1941-44, 1946-1952 Green Bay Packers. **Highlights:** Two-way player. Third player to rush for 1,000 yards in single season, 1949.

JOE CARR
NFL president. Born in Columbus, Ohio, October 23, 1879. Died May 20, 1939. Did not attend college. Inducted in 1963. President, 1921-1939 National Football League. **Highlights:** Charter enshrinee. NFL co-organizer, 1920. Introduced standard player contract.

HARRY CARSON
Linebacker. 6-2, 237. Born in Florence, South Carolina, November 26, 1953. South Carolina State. Inducted in 2006. 1976-1988 New York Giants. **Highlights:** 11 career interceptions. Named to nine Pro Bowls. Named first- or second-team All-NFL six times.

DAVE CASPER
Tight end. 6-4, 240. Born in Bemidji, Minnesota, February 2, 1952. Notre Dame. Inducted in 2002. 1974-1980 Oakland Raiders, 1980-83 Houston Oilers, 1983 Minnesota Vikings, 1984 Los Angeles Raiders. **Highlights:** 378 receptions for 5,216 yards, 52 touchdowns. Five consecutive Pro Bowls.

GUY CHAMBERLIN
End. Coach. 6-2, 196. Born in Blue Springs, Nebraska, January 16, 1894. Died April 4, 1967. Nebraska. Inducted in 1965. 1919 Canton Bulldogs, 1920-21 Decatur Staleys/ Chicago Staleys, player-coach 1922-23 Canton Bulldogs, 1924 Cleveland Bulldogs, 1925-26 Frankford Yellowjackets, 1927-28 Chicago Cardinals. **Highlights:** Player-coach of four NFL championship teams. Six-year coaching record of 58-16-7.

JACK CHRISTIANSEN
Safety. 6-1, 185. Born in Sublette, Kansas, December 20, 1928. Died June 29, 1986. Colorado State. Inducted in 1970. 1951-58 Detroit Lions. **Highlights:** 46 interceptions. NFL interception leader, 1953, 1957. Eight punt returns for touchdowns.

EARL (DUTCH) CLARK
Quarterback. 6-0, 185. Born in Fowler, Colorado, October 11, 1906. Died August 5, 1978. Colorado College. Inducted in 1963. 1931-32 Portsmouth Spartans, 1934-38 Detroit Lions. **Highlights:** Charter enshrinee. NFL scoring champion three years. Led Lions to 1935 NFL title.

GEORGE CONNOR
Tackle-linebacker. 6-3, 240. Born in Chicago, Illinois, January 21, 1925. Died March 31, 2003. Holy Cross, Notre Dame. Inducted in 1975. 1948-1955 Chicago Bears. **Highlights:** All-NFL at three positions—T, DT, LB. All-NFL five years. Played in first four Pro Bowls.

JIMMY CONZELMAN
Quarterback. Coach. Team owner. 6-0, 180. Born in St. Louis, Missouri, March 6, 1898. Died July 31, 1970. Washington of St. Louis. Inducted in 1964. 1920 Decatur Staleys, 1921-22 Rock Island Independents, 1922-24 Milwaukee Badgers; owner-coach 1925-26 Detroit Panthers; player-coach 1927-29, coach 1930 Providence Steam Roller; coach 1940-42, 1946-48 Chicago Cardinals. **Highlights:** Player-coach of four NFL teams in 1920's. Coached Cardinals to 1947 NFL crown.

LOU CREEKMUR
Tackle-guard. 6-4, 255. Born in Hopelawn, New Jersey. January 22, 1927. William & Mary. Inducted in 1996. 1950-59 Detroit Lions. **Highlights:** All-NFL six times, twice at guard and four times at tackle. Selected to eight Pro Bowls and played on three NFL championship teams.

LARRY CSONKA
Running back. 6-3, 235. Born in Stow, Ohio, December 25, 1946. Syracuse. Inducted in 1987. 1968-1974, 1979 Miami Dolphins, 1976-78 New York Giants. **Highlights:** 8,081 yards rushing, 68 touchdowns. MVP Super Bowl VIII. Only 21 fumbles in 1,891 carries and 106 receptions.

AL DAVIS
Team, League Administrator. Born in Brockton, Massachusetts, July 4, 1929. Wittenberg, Syracuse. Inducted in 1992. 1963-1981, 1995-present Oakland Raiders, 1982-1994 Los Angeles Raiders, 1966 American Football League. **Highlights:** Only person to serve in pros as personnel assistant, scout, assistant coach, head coach, general manager, commissioner, team owner/CEO.

WILLIE DAVIS
Defensive end. 6-3, 245. Born in Lisbon, Louisiana, July 24, 1934. Grambling. Inducted in 1981. 1958-59 Cleveland Browns, 1960-69 Green Bay Packers. **Highlights:** All-NFL five seasons, five Pro Bowls. Did not miss game in 12-year career.

LEN DAWSON
Quarterback. 6-0, 190. Born in Alliance, Ohio, June 20, 1935. Purdue. Inducted in 1987. 1957-59 Pittsburgh Steelers, 1960-61 Cleveland Browns, 1962 Dallas Texans, 1963-1975 Kansas City Chiefs. **Highlights:** 28,711 yards passing, 239 touchdowns. Four AFL passing crowns. MVP, Super Bowl IV.

FRED DEAN
Defensive end. 6-3, 230. Born in Arcadia, Louisiana, February 24, 1952. Louisiana Tech. Inducted in 2008. 1975-1981 San Diego Chargers, 1981-85 San Francisco 49ers. **Highlights:** Had career-high 17.5 sacks in 1983. Played on two Super Bowl championship teams with 49ers (Super Bowls XVI, XIX).

JOE DeLAMIELLEURE
Guard. 6-3, 254. Born in Detroit, Michigan, March 16, 1951. Michigan State. Inducted in 2003. 1973-1979, 1985 Buffalo Bills, 1980-1984 Cleveland Browns. **Highlights:** Selected All-Pro and All-AFC six consecutive times, 1975-1980. Named to six Pro Bowls. Played 13 years, 185 games.

ERIC DICKERSON
Running back. 6-3, 220. Born in Sealy, Texas, September 2, 1960. Southern Methodist. Inducted in 1999. 1983-87 Los Angeles Rams, 1987-1991 Indianapolis Colts, 1992 Los Angeles Raiders, 1993 Atlanta Falcons. **Highlights:** Rushed for 13,259 career yards, including an NFL record 2,105 yards in 1984. All-Pro five times, six Pro Bowls.

DAN DIERDORF
Tackle. 6-3, 290. Born in Canton, Ohio, June 29, 1949. Michigan. Inducted in 1996. 1971-1983 St. Louis Cardinals. **Highlights:** All-Pro five times, played in six Pro Bowls, named NFL's best blocker three times.

MIKE DITKA
Tight end. 6-3, 225. Born in Carnegie, Pennsylvania, October 18, 1939. Pittsburgh. Inducted in 1988. 1961-66 Chicago Bears, 1967-68 Philadelphia Eagles, 1969-1972 Dallas Cowboys. **Highlights:** 427 receptions for 5,812 yards, 43 touchdowns. First tight end selected to Hall of Fame. Five consecutive Pro Bowls.

ART DONOVAN
Defensive tackle. 6-3, 265. Born in Bronx, New York, June 5, 1925. Boston College. Inducted in 1968. 1950 Baltimore Colts, 1951 New York Yanks, 1952 Dallas Texans, 1953-1961 Baltimore Colts. **Highlights:** Five Pro Bowls. Vital part of Baltimore's climb to powerhouse status in 1950s.

TONY DORSETT
Running back. 5-11, 184. Born in Rochester, Pennsylvania, April 7, 1954. Pittsburgh. Inducted in 1994. 1977-1987 Dallas Cowboys, 1988 Denver Broncos. **Highlights:** 12,739 yards rushing, 398 receptions, 91 touchdowns. Ran record 99 yards for touchdown vs. Minnesota, January, 1983.

JOHN (PADDY) DRISCOLL
Quarterback. 5-11, 160. Born in Evanston, Illinois, January 11, 1896. Died June 29, 1968. Northwestern. Inducted in 1965. 1919 Hammond Pros, 1920 Decatur Staleys, 1920-25 Chicago Cardinals, 1926-29 Chicago Bears. **Highlights:** All-NFL seven times. Dropkicked record 4 field goals in one game, 1925.

BILL DUDLEY
Halfback. 5-10, 182. Born in Bluefield, Virginia, December 24, 1921. Virginia. Inducted in 1966. 1942, 1945-46 Pittsburgh Steelers, 1947-49 Detroit Lions, 1950-51, 1953 Washington Redskins. **Highlights:** Won NFL rushing, interception, punt return titles, 1946. All-NFL 1942, 1946, and 1947.

ALBERT GLEN (TURK) EDWARDS
Tackle. 6-2, 260. Born in Mold, Washington, September 28, 1907. Died January 12, 1973. Washington State. Inducted in 1969. 1932 Boston Braves, 1933-36 Boston Redskins, 1937-1940 Washington Redskins. **Highlights:** All-NFL 1932-34, 1936, 1937. Steamrolling blocker, smothering tackler.

CARL ELLER
Defensive end. 6-6, 247. Born in Winston-Salem, North Carolina, January 25, 1942. Minnesota. Inducted in 2004. 1964-1978 Minnesota Vikings, 1979 Seattle Seahawks. **Highlights:** Fixture on Vikings' "Purple People Eaters" defensive line, All-Pro five time, elected to six Pro Bowls.

JOHN ELWAY
Quarterback. 6-3, 215. Born in Port Angeles, Washington, June 28, 1960. Stanford. Inducted in 2004. 1983-1998 Denver Broncos. **Highlights:** Passed for 51,475 yards, 300 touchdowns. Named to nine Pro Bowls. NFL MVP, 1987; MVP, Super Bowl XXXIII.

WEEB EWBANK
Coach. Born in Richmond, Indiana, May 6, 1907. Died November 17, 1998. Miami (Ohio). Inducted in 1978. 1954-1962 Baltimore Colts, 1963-1973 New York Jets. **Highlights:** Only coach to win championships in both NFL, AFL. Led both Colts (1958 and 1959) and Jets (1968) to championships.

TOM FEARS
End. 6-2, 215. Born in Guadalajara, Mexico, December 3, 1922. Died January 4, 2000. Santa Clara, UCLA. Inducted in 1970. 1948-1956 Los Angeles Rams. **Highlights:** 400 receptions for 5,397 yards, 38 touchdowns. Led NFL receivers first three seasons. Had then-record 18 receptions in single game.

JIM FINKS
Administrator. Born in St. Louis, Missouri, August 31, 1927. Died May 8, 1994. Tulsa. Inducted 1995. 1964-1973 Minnesota Vikings, 1974-1982 Chicago Bears, 1986-1993 New Orleans Saints. **Highlights:** Developed Vikings, Bears, Saints—all teams with losing records—into winners.

RAY FLAHERTY
Coach. Born in Spokane, Washington, September 1, 1903. Died July 19, 1994. Gonzaga. Inducted in 1976. 1936-1942 Boston/Washington Redskins, 1946-48 New York Yankees (AAFC), 1949 Chicago Hornets (AAFC). **Highlights:** 82-41-5 coaching record. Introduced screen pass in 1937 title game and platoon system.

LEN FORD
Defensive end. 6-4, 260. Born in Washington, D.C., February 18, 1926. Died March 14, 1972. Morgan State, Michigan. Inducted in 1976. 1948-49 Los Angeles Dons (AAFC), 1950-57 Cleveland Browns, 1958 Green Bay Packers. **Highlights:** All-NFL five times, four Pro Bowls. Recovered 20 opponents' fumbles.

DAN FORTMANN
Guard. 6-0, 210. Born in Pearl River, New York, April 11, 1916. Died May 23, 1995. Colgate. Inducted in 1965. 1936-1943 Chicago Bears. **Highlights:** At 20, became youngest starter in NFL. First- or second-team All-NFL every season of career.

DAN FOUTS
Quarterback. 6-3, 210. Born in San Francisco, California, June 10, 1951. Oregon. Inducted in 1993. 1973-1987 San Diego Chargers. **Highlights:** 43,040 passing yards, 254 touchdowns. Six Pro Bowls, NFL MVP, 1982.

BENNY FRIEDMAN
Quarterback. 5-10, 183. Born in Cleveland, Ohio, March 18, 1905. Died November 23, 1982. Michigan. Inducted in 2005. 1927 Cleveland Bulldogs, 1928 Detroit Wolverines, 1929-1931 New York Giants, 1932-34 Brooklyn Dodgers. **Highlights:** NFL's first great passer. Set league mark for touchdowns with 20 in 1929. Led NFL in touchdown passes each of his first four seasons.

FRANK GATSKI
Center. 6-3, 240. Born in Farmington, West Virginia, March 18, 1919. Marshall, Auburn. Died November 22, 2005. Inducted in 1985. 1946-49 Cleveland Browns (AAFC), 1950-56 Cleveland Browns, 1957 Detroit Lions. **Highlights:** Never missed game in high school, college, or pro football. Played 11 championship games, winning eight.

BILL GEORGE
Linebacker. 6-2, 230. Born in Waynesburg, Pennsylvania, October 27, 1929. Died September 30, 1982. Wake Forest. Inducted in 1974. 1952-1965 Chicago Bears, 1966 Los Angeles Rams. **Highlights:** All-NFL eight years, eight consecutive Pro Bowls. 14 years of service, longest of any Bears player.

JOE GIBBS
Coach. Born in Mocksville, North Carolina, November 25, 1940. Cerritos (Calif.) J.C., San Diego State. Inducted in 1996. 1981-1992 Washington Redskins. **Highlights:** 124-60-0 record in regular season, 16-5 in postseason, including four Super Bowl appearances—winning three. Won 10 or more games eight times.

FRANK GIFFORD
Halfback. 6-1, 195. Born in Santa Monica, California, August 16, 1930. Southern California. Inducted in 1977. 1952-1960, 1962-64 New York Giants. **Highlights:** Starred on both offense and defense. Seven Pro Bowls, 1956 NFL player of the year.

SID GILLMAN
Coach. Born in Minneapolis, Minnesota, October 26, 1911. Died January 3, 2003. Ohio State. Inducted in 1983. 1955-59 Los Angeles Rams, 1960-69, 1971 Los Angeles/San Diego Chargers, 1973-74 Houston Oilers. **Highlights:** 123-104-7 coaching record. First to win division titles in both NFL, AFL.

OTTO GRAHAM
Quarterback. 6-1, 195. Born in Waukegan, Illinois, December 6, 1921. Died December 17, 2003. Northwestern. Inducted in 1965. 1946-49 Cleveland Browns (AAFC), 1950-55 Cleveland Browns. **Highlights:** 23,584 passing yards, 174 touchdowns. Guided Browns to 10 division or league crowns in 10 years.

HAROLD (RED) GRANGE
Halfback. 6-0, 185. Born in Forksville, Pennsylvania, June 13, 1903. Died January 28, 1991. Illinois. Inducted in 1963. 1925 Chicago Bears, 1926 New York Yankees (AFL), 1927 New York Yankees, 1929-1934 Chicago Bears. **Highlights:** Charter enshrinee. Nicknamed "Galloping Ghost." Name produced first huge pro football crowds.

BUD GRANT
Coach. Born in Superior, Wisconsin, May 20, 1927. Minnesota. Inducted in 1994. 1967-1983, 1985 Minnesota Vikings. **Highlights:** 168-108-5 coaching record. Led Vikings to 11 division championships, four Super Bowls.

DARRELL GREEN
Cornerback. 5-8, 176. Born in Houston, Texas, February 15, 1960. Texas A&I. Inducted in 2008. 1983-2002 Washington Redskins. **Highlights:** 54 interceptions, 621 yards, 6 TDs. Played 20 seasons. Recorded interception in NFL record 19 straight seasons. Selected to seven Pro Bowls.

JOE GREENE
Defensive tackle. 6-4, 260. Born in Temple, Texas, September 24, 1946. North Texas State. Inducted in 1987. 1969-1981 Pittsburgh Steelers. **Highlights:** NFL defensive player of the year, 1972, 1974. Four-time Super Bowl champion, 10 Pro Bowls.

FORREST GREGG
Tackle. 6-4, 250. Born in Birthright, Texas, October 18, 1933. Southern Methodist. Inducted in 1977. 1956, 1958-1970 Green Bay Packers, 1971 Dallas Cowboys. **Highlights:** Played 188 consecutive games. Nine Pro Bowls. Played on six NFL championship teams, three Super Bowl winners.

BOB GRIESE
Quarterback. 6-1, 190. Born in Evansville, Indiana, February 3, 1945. Purdue. Inducted in 1990. 1967-1980 Miami Dolphins. **Highlights:** 25,092 passing yards, 192 touchdowns. Led Miami to three AFC titles, Super Bowl VII, VIII wins.

LOU GROZA
Tackle-kicker. 6-3, 250. Born in Martins Ferry, Ohio, January 25, 1924. Died November 29, 2000. Ohio State. Inducted in 1974. 1946-49 Cleveland Browns (AAFC), 1950-59, 1961-67 Cleveland Browns. **Highlights:** 1,608 points in 21 years. Nine Pro Bowls, All-NFL six years. NFL player of the year, 1954.

JOE GUYON
Halfback. 6-1, 180. Born on White Earth Indian Reservation, Minnesota, November 26, 1892. Died November 27, 1971. Carlisle, Georgia Tech. Inducted in 1966. 1919-1920 Canton Bulldogs, 1921 Cleveland Indians, 1922-23 Oorang Indians, 1924 Rock Island Independents, 1924-25 Kansas City Cowboys, 1927 New York Giants. **Highlights:** Touchdown pass gave Giants victory over Bears to win 1927 championship.

GEORGE HALAS
End. Coach. Team owner. Born in Chicago, Illinois, February 2, 1895. Died October 31, 1983. Illinois. Inducted in 1963. Player-coach 1920 Decatur Staleys, 1921 Chicago Staleys, 1922-29 Chicago Bears; coach 1933-1942, 1946-1955, 1958-1967 Chicago Bears. **Highlights:** Charter enshrinee. 324 coaching wins. Only person associated with NFL throughout first 50 years. Coached Bears 40 seasons, won six NFL titles.

JACK HAM
Linebacker. 6-1, 225. Born in Johnstown, Pennsylvania, December 23, 1948. Penn State. Inducted in 1988. 1971-1982 Pittsburgh Steelers. **Highlights:** Won four Super Bowls, 21 opponents' fumbles recovered, 32 interceptions. Eight consecutive Pro Bowls.

DAN HAMPTON
Defensive tackle-defensive end. 6-5, 264. Born in Oklahoma City, Oklahoma, September 19, 1957. Arkansas. Inducted in 2002. 1979-1990 Chicago Bears. **Highlights:** A versatile player, he earned all-pro honors at both defensive tackle and defensive end. Named to four Pro Bowls.

JOHN HANNAH
Guard. 6-3, 265. Born in Canton, Georgia, April 4, 1951. Alabama. Inducted in 1991. 1973-1985 New England Patriots. **Highlights:** Renowned as premier guard of era. All-Pro 10 years, nine Pro Bowls.

FRANCO HARRIS
Running back. 6-2, 225. Born in Fort Dix, New Jersey, March 7, 1950. Penn State. Inducted in 1990. 1972-1983 Pittsburgh Steelers, 1984 Seattle Seahawks. **Highlights:** 12,120 rushing yards, 100 total touchdowns. 1,556 rushing yards in 19 postseason games. MVP in Super Bowl IX.

BOB HAYES
Wide receiver. 5-11, 185. Born in Jacksonville, Florida, December 20, 1942. Died September 18, 2002. Florida A&M. Inducted in 2009. 1965-1974 Dallas Cowboys, 1975 San Francisco 49ers. **Highlights:** Olympic gold medalist with world class speed led Cowboys in receiving three times. 371 receptions for 7,414 yards, 71 TDs. Three Pro Bowls.

MIKE HAYNES
Cornerback. 6-2, 195. Born in Denison, Texas, July 1, 1953. Arizona State. Inducted in 1997. 1976-1982 New England Patriots, 1983-89 Los Angeles Raiders. **Highlights:** Defensive rookie of the year. Selected to nine Pro Bowls and intercepted 46 passes, plus one pick in Super Bowl XVIII.

ED HEALEY
Tackle. 6-3, 220. Born in Indian Orchard, Massachusetts, December 28, 1894. Died December 9, 1978. Dartmouth. Inducted in 1964. 1920-22 Rock Island Independents, 1922-27 Chicago Bears. **Highlights:** Two-way star. Perennial all-pro with Bears.

MEL HEIN
Center. 6-2, 225. Born in Redding, California, August 22, 1909. Died January 31, 1992. Washington State. Inducted in 1963. 1931-1945 New York Giants. **Highlights:** Charter enshrinee. 60-minute regular for 15 years. All-NFL eight consecutive years.

TED HENDRICKS
Linebacker. 6-7, 235. Born in Guatemala City, Guatemala, November 1, 1947. Miami. Inducted in 1990. 1969-1973 Baltimore Colts, 1974 Green Bay Packers, 1975-1981 Oakland Raiders, 1982-83 Los Angeles Raiders. **Highlights:** 25 blocked field goals, extra points, and punts, 26 interceptions. Played in 215 consecutive games.

WILBUR (PETE) HENRY
Tackle. 6-0, 250. Born in Mansfield, Ohio, October 31, 1897. Died February 7, 1952. Washington & Jefferson. Inducted in 1963. 1920-23, 1925-26 Canton Bulldogs, 1927 New York Giants, 1927-28 Pottsville Maroons. **Highlights:** Charter enshrinee. Largest player of his time at 250 pounds. Bulwark of Canton's championship lines.

ARNIE HERBER
Quarterback. 6-0, 200. Born in Green Bay, Wisconsin, April 2, 1910. Died October 14, 1969. Wisconsin, Regis College. Inducted in 1966. 1930-1940 Green Bay Packers, 1944-45 New York Giants. **Highlights:** NFL passing leader 1932, 1934, 1936. Came out of retirement to lead 1944 Giants to NFL Eastern crown.

BILL HEWITT
End. 5-11, 191. Born in Bay City, Michigan, October 8, 1909. Died January 14, 1947. Michigan. Inducted in 1971. 1932-36 Chicago Bears, 1937-39 Philadelphia Eagles, 1943 Phil-Pitt. **Highlights:** First to be named all-NFL with two teams—1933, 1934, 1936 Bears; 1937 Eagles.

GENE HICKERSON
Guard. 6-3, 248. Born in Trenton, Tennessee, February 15, 1935. Died October 20, 2008. Mississippi. Inducted in 2007. 1958-1973 Cleveland Browns. **Highlights:** Blocked for three Hall of Fame running backs. Voted to six straight Pro Bowls. Named to NFL's All-Decade Team of the 1960s.

CLARKE HINKLE
Fullback. 5-11, 201. Born in Toronto, Ohio, April 10, 1909. Died November 9, 1988. Bucknell. Inducted in 1964. 1932-1941 Green Bay Packers. **Highlights:** 3,860 yards rushing, 379 points. Fullback on offense, linebacker on defense.

ELROY (CRAZYLEGS) HIRSCH
Halfback-end. 6-2, 190. Born in Wausau, Wisconsin, June 17, 1923. Died January 28, 2004. Wisconsin, Michigan. Inducted in 1968. 1946-48 Chicago Rockets (AAFC), 1949-1957 Los Angeles Rams. **Highlights:** 387 receptions for 7,029 yards, 60 touchdowns. Key part of Rams' revolutionary "three end" offense, 1949.

PAUL HORNUNG
Halfback. 6-2, 220. Born in Louisville, Kentucky, December 23, 1935. Notre Dame. Inducted in 1986. 1957-1962, 1964-66 Green Bay Packers. **Highlights:** 760 points. Led NFL scorers three years, including record 176 points, 1960. Record 19 points scored in 1961 NFL title game.

KEN HOUSTON
Safety. 6-3, 198. Born in Lufkin, Texas, November 12, 1944. Prairie View A&M. Inducted in 1986. 1967-1972 Houston Oilers, 1973-1980 Washington Redskins. **Highlights:** 49 interceptions, 898 yards, 9 touchdowns. NFL's premier strong safety of 1970s. 12 Pro Bowls.

ROBERT (CAL) HUBBARD
Tackle. 6-5, 250. Born in Keytesville, Missouri, October 31, 1900. Died October 17, 1977. Centenary, Geneva. Inducted in 1963. 1927-28, 1936 New York Giants, 1929-1933, 1935 Green Bay Packers, 1936 Pittsburgh Pirates. **Highlights:** Charter enshrinee. Most feared lineman of his time. All-NFL six years, 1927-29, 1931-33.

SAM HUFF
Linebacker. 6-1, 230. Born in Morgantown, West Virginia, October 4, 1934. West Virginia. Inducted in 1982. 1956-1963 New York Giants, 1964-67, 1969 Washington Redskins. **Highlights:** 30 interceptions. Played in six NFL title games, five Pro Bowls. Redskins player-coach, 1969.

LAMAR HUNT
Team owner. Born in El Dorado, Arkansas, August 2, 1932. Died December 13, 2006. Southern Methodist. Inducted in 1972. 1960-2006 Dallas Texans/Kansas City Chiefs. **Highlights:** Driving force behind organization of AFL. Spearheaded merger negotiations with NFL, 1966.

DON HUTSON
End. 6-1, 180. Born in Pine Bluff, Arkansas, January 31, 1913. Died June 26, 1997. Alabama. Inducted in 1963. 1935-1945 Green Bay Packers. **Highlights:** Charter enshrinee. 488 receptions for 7,991 yards, 99 touchdowns. NFL receiving champion eight years. NFL MVP, 1941, 1942.

MICHAEL IRVIN
Wide Receiver. 6-2, 207. Born in Ft. Lauderdale, Florida, March 5, 1966. Miami. Inducted in 2007. 1988-1999 Dallas Cowboys. **Highlights:** 750 career receptions for 11,904 yards, 65 touchdowns. Had NFL record eleven 100-yard receiving games, 1995.

JIMMY JOHNSON
Cornerback. 6-2, 187. Born in Dallas, Texas, March 31, 1938. UCLA. Inducted in 1994. 1961-1976 San Francisco 49ers. **Highlights:** 47 interceptions for 615 yards. Five Pro Bowls. Opposing passers avoided throwing in his area.

JOHN HENRY JOHNSON
Fullback. 6-2, 225. Born in Waterproof, Louisiana, November 24, 1929. St. Mary's, Arizona State. Inducted in 1987. 1954-56 San Francisco 49ers, 1957-59 Detroit Lions, 1960-65 Pittsburgh Steelers, 1966 Houston Oilers. **Highlights:** 6,803 yards rushing, 55 total touchdowns. Member of San Francisco's "Million-Dollar" backfield.

CHARLIE JOINER
Wide receiver. 5-11, 180. Born in Many, Louisiana, October 14, 1947. Grambling. Inducted in 1996. 1969-1972 Houston Oilers, 1972-75 Cincinnati Bengals, 1976-1986 San Diego Chargers. **Highlights:** 750 receptions for 12,146 yards and 65 touchdowns. Played 18 seasons, 239 games, most ever for wide receiver at time of retirement.

DAVID (DEACON) JONES
Defensive end. 6-5, 260. Born in Eatonville, Florida, December 9, 1938. South Carolina State, Mississippi Vocational. Inducted in 1980. 1961-1971 Los Angeles Rams, 1972-73 San Diego Chargers, 1974 Washington Redskins. **Highlights:** Specialized in quarterback "sacks," a term he invented. Unanimous all-league five consecutive years.

STAN JONES
Guard-defensive tackle. 6-1, 250. Born in Altoona, Pennsylvania, November 24, 1931. Maryland. Inducted in 1991. 1954-1965 Chicago Bears, 1966 Washington Redskins. **Highlights:** Seven consecutive Pro Bowls. First to rely on weightlifting for football preparation.

HENRY JORDAN
Defensive tackle, 6-3, 240. Born in Emporia, Virginia, January 26, 1935. Died February 21, 1977. Virginia. Inducted in 1995. 1957-58 Cleveland Browns, 1959-1969 Green Bay Packers. **Highlights:** Fixture at DT during Packers' dynasty. Played in four Pro Bowls, seven NFL title games, Super Bowls I, II.

SONNY JURGENSEN
Quarterback. 6-0, 203. Born in Wilmington, North Carolina, August 23, 1934. Duke. Inducted in 1983. 1957-1963 Philadelphia Eagles, 1964-1974 Washington Redskins. **Highlights:** 32,224 yards passing, 255 touchdowns, 82.63 passer rating. Surpassed 3,000 yards passing in five seasons.

JIM KELLY
Quarterback. 6-3, 225. Born in Pittsburgh, Pennsylvania, February 14, 1960. Miami. Inducted in 2002. 1986-1996 Buffalo Bills. **Highlights:** Passed for more than 3,000 yards eight times. Mastered the no-huddle offense that propelled Bills to four consecutive Super Bowls.

LEROY KELLY
Running back. 6-0, 205. Born in Philadelphia, Pennsylvania, May 20, 1942. Morgan State. Inducted in 1994. 1964-1973 Cleveland Browns. **Highlights:** 7,274 yards rushing, 90 total touchdowns, 1,000-yard rusher first three years as starter. Punt return champion, 1965.

WALT KIESLING
Guard. Coach. 6-2, 245. Born in St. Paul, Minnesota, March 27, 1903. Died March 2, 1962. St. Thomas (Minnesota). Inducted in 1966. 1926-27 Duluth Eskimos, 1928 Pottsville Maroons, 1929-1933 Chicago Cardinals, 1934 Chicago Bears, 1935-36 Green Bay Packers, 1937-38 Pittsburgh Pirates; coach, 1939 Pittsburgh Pirates, 1940-42 Pittsburgh Steelers; co-coach, 1943 Phil-Pitt, 1944 Card-Pitt; coach, 1954-56 Pittsburgh Steelers. **Highlights:** 34-year career as pro player, assistant coach, head coach. Led Steelers to first winning season, 1942.

FRANK (BRUISER) KINARD
Tackle. 6-1, 210. Born in Pelahatchie, Mississippi, October 23, 1914. Died September 7, 1985. Mississippi. Inducted in 1971. 1938-1943 Brooklyn Dodgers, 1944 Brooklyn Tigers, 1946-47 New York Yankees (AAFC). **Highlights:** First man to earn both All-NFL, All-AAFC honors. Out because of injury only once.

PAUL KRAUSE
Safety. 6-3, 200. Born in Flint, Michigan, February 19, 1942. Iowa. Inducted in 1998. 1964-67 Washington Redskins, 1968-1979 Minnesota Vikings. **Highlights:** NFL all-time leader with 81 interceptions. Played in eight Pro Bowls. Starting safety in four Super Bowls.

EARL (CURLY) LAMBEAU
Coach. Born in Green Bay, Wisconsin, April 9, 1898. Died June 1, 1965. Notre Dame. Inducted in 1963. 1919-1949 Green Bay Packers, 1950-51 Chicago Cardinals, 1952-53 Washington Redskins. **Highlights:** Charter enshrinee. 229-134-22 coaching record with six NFL championships. Founded pre-NFL Packers, 1919.

JACK LAMBERT
Linebacker. 6-4, 220. Born in Mantua, Ohio, July 8, 1952. Kent State. Inducted in 1990. 1974-1984 Pittsburgh Steelers. **Highlights:** Leader of 'Steel Curtain.' NFL defensive player of year in 1976, nine Pro Bowls.

TOM LANDRY
Coach. Born in Mission, Texas, September 11, 1924. Died February 12, 2000. Texas. Inducted in 1990. 1960-1988 Dallas Cowboys. **Highlights:** 270-178-6 coaching record. 20 consecutive winning seasons. Innovator on offense and defense.

DICK (NIGHT TRAIN) LANE
Cornerback. 6-2, 210. Born in Austin, Texas, April 16, 1928. Died January 29, 2002. Scottsbluff Junior College. Inducted in 1974. 1952-53 Los Angeles Rams, 1954-59 Chicago Cardinals, 1960-65 Detroit Lions. **Highlights:** 68 interceptions for 1,207 yards, 5 touchdowns. Record 14 interceptions as rookie. Seven Pro Bowls.

JIM LANGER
Center. 6-2, 255. Born in Little Falls, Minnesota, May 16, 1948. South Dakota State. Inducted in 1987. 1970-79 Miami Dolphins, 1980-81 Minnesota Vikings. **Highlights:** Played every offensive down in Dolphins' perfect 1972 season. Six Pro Bowls.

WILLIE LANIER
Linebacker. 6-1, 245. Born in Clover, Virginia, August 21, 1945. Morgan State. Inducted in 1986. 1967-1977 Kansas City Chiefs. **Highlights:** 27 interceptions. Defensive star in Super Bowl IV upset. Nicknamed 'Contact' for ferocious tackling.

STEVE LARGENT
Wide receiver. 5-11, 191. Born in Tulsa, Oklahoma, September 28, 1954, Tulsa. Inducted in 1995. 1976-1989 Seattle Seahawks. **Highlights:** 819 receptions for 13,089 yards, 100 touchdowns. Receptions in 177 consecutive games.

YALE LARY
Safety. 5-11, 189. Born in Fort Worth, Texas, November 24, 1930. Texas A&M. Inducted in 1979. 1952-53, 1956-1964 Detroit Lions. **Highlights:** 50 interceptions. Three NFL punting crowns, three touchdowns on punt returns. Nine Pro Bowls.

DANTE LAVELLI
End. 6-0, 199. Born in Hudson, Ohio, February 23, 1923. Died January 20, 2009. Ohio State. Inducted in 1975. 1946-49 Cleveland Browns (AAFC), 1950-56 Cleveland Browns. **Highlights:** 386 receptions for 6,488 yards, 62 touchdowns. 24 catches in six NFL title games.

BOBBY LAYNE
Quarterback. 6-2, 190. Born in Santa Anna, Texas, December 19, 1926. Died December 1, 1986. Texas. Inducted in 1967. 1948 Chicago Bears, 1949 New York Bulldogs, 1950-58 Detroit Lions, 1958-1962 Pittsburgh Steelers. **Highlights:** 26,768 yards passing, 196 touchdowns, 2,451 yards rushing. Late touchdown pass won 1953 NFL title game.

ALPHONSE (TUFFY) LEEMANS
Fullback. 6-0, 200. Born in Superior, Wisconsin, November 12, 1912. Died January 19, 1979. Oregon, George Washington. Inducted in 1978. 1936-1943 New York Giants. **Highlights:** 3,132 yards rushing, 2,318 yards passing, 422 yards receiving. Led NFL rushers as rookie, 1936.

MARV LEVY
Coach. Born in Chicago, Illinois, August 3, 1925. Wyoming, Coe College, Harvard. Inducted in 2001. 1978-1982 Kansas City Chiefs, 1986-1997 Buffalo Bills. **Highlights:** Led Bills to unprecedented four consecutive Super Bowls. Had 154-120 record. Coaching victories ranked 10th when retired.

BOB LILLY
Defensive tackle. 6-5, 260. Born in Olney, Texas, July 26, 1939. Texas Christian. Inducted in 1980. 1961-1974 Dallas Cowboys. **Highlights:** Eleven Pro Bowls. Played 196 consecutive games. Foundation of great Dallas defensive units.

LARRY LITTLE
Guard. 6-1, 265. Born in Groveland, Georgia, November 2, 1945. Bethune-Cookman. Inducted in 1993. 1967-68 San Diego Chargers, 1969-1980 Miami Dolphins. **Highlights:** Five Pro Bowls, started in three Super Bowls. Epitome of powerful Dolphins rushing game of 1970s.

JAMES LOFTON
Wide receiver. 6-3, 192. Born in Fort Ord, California, July 5, 1956. Stanford. Inducted in 2003. 1978-1986 Green Bay Packers, 1987-88 Los Angeles Raiders, 1989-1992 Buffalo Bills, 1993 Los Angeles Rams, 1993 Philadelphia Eagles. **Highlights:** Played 16 seasons, 233 games. Caught 764 passes for 75 touchdowns and a then-record 14,004 yards. All-Pro four times, eight Pro Bowls.

VINCE LOMBARDI
Coach. Born in Brooklyn, New York, June 11, 1913. Died September 3, 1970. Fordham. Inducted in 1971. 1959-1967 Green Bay Packers, 1969 Washington Redskins. **Highlights:** 105-35-6 coaching record in 10 years, including five NFL titles and victories in Super Bowls I and II.

HOWIE LONG
Defensive end. 6-5, 268. Born in Somerville, Massachusetts, January 6, 1960. Villanova. Inducted in 2000. 1981-1993 Oakland/Los Angeles Raiders. **Highlights:** All-Pro 1983, 1984, 1985. Named All-AFC four times, 1983-1986. Eight Pro Bowls.

RONNIE LOTT
Cornerback-safety. 6-0, 203. Born in Albuquerque, New Mexico, May 8, 1959. Southern California. Inducted in 2000. 1981-1990 San Francisco 49ers, 1991-92 Los Angeles Raiders, 1993-94 New York Jets. **Highlights:** Ten Pro Bowls, 63 career interceptions, and was named to the NFL's 75th Anniversary Team.

SID LUCKMAN
Quarterback. 6-0, 195. Born in Brooklyn, New York, November 21, 1916. Died July 5, 1998. Columbia. Inducted in 1965. 1939-1950 Chicago Bears. **Highlights:** 137 touchdown passes. All-NFL five times. League MVP in 1943.

WILLIAM ROY (LINK) LYMAN
Tackle. 6-2, 252. Born in Table Rock, Nebraska, November 30, 1898. Died December 28, 1972. Nebraska. Inducted in 1964. 1922-23, 1925 Canton Bulldogs, 1924 Cleveland Bulldogs, 1925 Frankford Yellowjackets, 1926-28, 1930-31, 1933-34 Chicago Bears. **Highlights:** Played for four NFL champions. In 16 seasons of college and pro football, played on one losing team.

TOM MACK
Guard. 6-3, 250. Born in Cleveland, Ohio, November 1, 1943. Michigan. Inducted in 1999. 1966-1978 Los Angeles Rams. **Highlights:** Never missed a game in entire 184-game career. Elected to 11 Pro Bowls.

JOHN MACKEY
Tight end. 6-2, 224. Born in New York, New York, September 24, 1941. Syracuse. Inducted in 1992. 1963-1971 Baltimore Colts, 1972 San Diego Chargers. **Highlights:** 331 receptions for 5,236 yards, 38 touchdowns. Second tight end to enter Hall of Fame.

JOHN MADDEN
Coach. Born in Austin, Minnesota, April 10, 1936. San Mateo Junior College, California Polytechnic College at San Luis Obispo. Inducted in 2006. 1969-1978 Oakland Raiders. **Highlights:** Became one of youngest coaches in history when hired at age 32. 112-39-7 overall record. Owns best regular season winning percentage among coaches with 100 wins.

TIM MARA
Team owner. Born in New York, New York, July 29, 1887. Died February 16, 1959. Did not attend college. Inducted in 1963. 1925-1959 New York Giants. **Highlights:** Charter enshrinee. Founder of New York Giants. Built team into powerhouse winning four NFL titles, 10 division titles.

WELLINGTON MARA
Team owner. Born in New York, New York, August 14, 1916. Died October 25, 2005. Fordham. Inducted in 1997. 1937-2005 New York Giants. **Highlights:** Lifetime contributor to NFL and New York Giants. Worked as Giants' ballboy, secretary, vice-president, president and co-CEO. NFC president 1984-present.

GINO MARCHETTI
Defensive end. 6-4, 245. Born in Smithers, West Virginia, January 2, 1927. San Francisco. Inducted in 1972. 1952 Dallas Texans, 1953-1964, 1966 Baltimore Colts. **Highlights:** Named top defensive end of NFL's first 50 years. 10 consecutive Pro Bowls. All-NFL seven times.

DAN MARINO
Quarterback. 6-4, 218. Born in Pittsburgh, Pennsylvania, September 15, 1961. Pittsburgh. Inducted in 2005. 1983-1999 Miami Dolphins. **Highlights:** Held NFL records for career passing yardage (61,361), completions (4,967), attempts (8,358), and touchdowns (420). Voted to nine Pro Bowls.

GEORGE PRESTON MARSHALL
Team owner. Born in Grafton, West Virginia, October 11, 1896. Died August 9, 1969. Randolph-Macon. Inducted in 1963. 1932 Boston Braves, 1933-36 Boston Redskins, 1937-1969 Washington Redskins. **Highlights:** Charter enshrinee. Sponsored progressive rules changes. Organized first team band, pioneered halftime shows.

OLLIE MATSON
Halfback. 6-2, 220. Born in Trinity, Texas, May 1, 1930. San Francisco. Inducted in 1972. 1952, 1954-58 Chicago Cardinals, 1959-1962 Los Angeles Rams, 1963 Detroit Lions, 1964-66 Philadelphia Eagles. **Highlights:** Nine touchdowns on kickoff, punt returns. Traded for nine players in 1959.

BRUCE MATTHEWS
Guard-tackle-center. 6-5, 289. Born in Raleigh, North Carolina, August 8, 1961. Southern California. Inducted in 2007. 1983-2001 Houston Oilers/Tennessee Oilers/Tennessee Titans. **Highlights:** Played in 296 games, most ever by positional player at time of his retirement. Named to a record-tying 14 straight Pro Bowls. All-Pro nine times, All-AFC 12 times.

DON MAYNARD
Wide receiver. 6-1, 185. Born in Crosbyton, Texas, January 25, 1935. Texas Western. Inducted in 1987. 1958 New York Giants, 1960-62 New York Titans, 1963-1972 New York Jets, 1973 St. Louis Cardinals. **Highlights:** 633 receptions for 11,834 yards, 88 touchdowns. At least 50 catches and 1,000 yards in five different seasons.

GEORGE McAFEE
Halfback. 6-0, 177. Born in Corbin, Kentucky, March 13, 1918. Died March 4, 2009. Duke. Inducted in 1966. 1940-41, 1945-1950 Chicago Bears. **Highlights:** Two-way star. 25 interceptions, 234 points. Career punt-return average of 12.78 yards per return.

MIKE McCORMACK
Tackle. 6-4, 250. Born in Chicago, Illinois, June 21, 1930. Kansas. Inducted in 1984. 1951 New York Yanks, 1954-1962 Cleveland Browns. **Highlights:** Excelled as offensive right tackle for eight years. Six Pro Bowls.

RANDALL McDANIEL
Guard. 6-3, 276. Born in Phoenix, Arizona, December 19, 1964. Arizona State. Inducted in 2009. 1988-1999 Minnesota Vikings, 2000-01 Tampa Bay Buccaneers. **Highlights:** 12 Pro Bowls, All-Pro nine straight times. Blocked for six different 1,000-yard rushers, five 3,000-yard passers.

TOMMY McDONALD
Wide receiver. 5-9, 175. Born in Roy, New Mexico, July 26, 1934. Oklahoma. Inducted in 1998. 1957-1963 Philadelphia Eagles, 1964 Dallas Cowboys, 1965-66 Los Angeles Rams, 1967 Atlanta Falcons, 1968 Cleveland Browns. **Highlights:** Recorded 495 receptions for 8,410 yards, 84 touchdowns.

HUGH McELHENNY
Halfback. 6-1, 198. Born in Los Angeles, California, December 31, 1928. Washington. Inducted in 1970. 1952-1960 San Francisco 49ers, 1961-62 Minnesota Vikings, 1963 New York Giants, 1964 Detroit Lions. **Highlights:** 5,281 rushing yards, 360 points. Totaled 11,369 yards rushing, receiving, and returning kicks.

JOHNNY (BLOOD) McNALLY
Halfback. 6-0, 185. Born in New Richmond, Wisconsin, November 27, 1903. Died November 28, 1985. Notre Dame, St. John's (Minnesota). Inducted in 1963. 1925-26 Milwaukee Badgers, 1926-27 Duluth Eskimos, 1928 Pottsville Maroons, 1929-1933, 1935-36 Green Bay Packers, 1934 Pittsburgh Pirates; player-coach, 1937-38 Pittsburgh Pirates. **Highlights:** Charter enshrinee. 49 touchdowns, 297 points in 14 seasons with five teams.

MIKE MICHALSKE
Guard. 6-0, 209. Born in Cleveland, Ohio, April 24, 1903. Died October 26, 1983. Penn State. Inducted in 1964. 1926 New York Yankees (AFL), 1927-28 New York Yankees, 1929-1935, 1937 Green Bay Packers. **Highlights:** Anchored Packers' championship lines, 1929-1931. First guard enshrined in Canton.

WAYNE MILLNER
End. 6-0, 191. Born in Roxbury, Massachusetts, January 31, 1913. Died November 19, 1976. Notre Dame. Inducted in 1968. 1936 Boston Redskins, 1937-1941, 1945 Washington Redskins. **Highlights:** Redskins' all-time leader with 124 catches when retired. 55- and 78-yard touchdown receptions in 1937 NFL Championship Game.

BOBBY MITCHELL
Running back-wide receiver. 6-0, 195. Born in Hot Springs, Arkansas, June 6, 1935. Illinois. Inducted in 1983. 1958-1961 Cleveland Browns, 1962-68 Washington Redskins. **Highlights:** 91 touchdowns, including 8 on kickoff and punt returns. 14,078 combined yards.

RON MIX
Tackle. 6-4, 255. Born in Los Angeles, California, March 10, 1938. Southern California. Inducted in 1979. 1960 Los Angeles Chargers, 1961-69 San Diego Chargers, 1971 Oakland Raiders. **Highlights:** All-AFL nine times. Only two holding penalties in 10 years with the Chargers.

ART MONK
Wide receiver. 6-3, 210. Born in White Plains, New York, December 5, 1957. Syracuse. Inducted in 2008. 1980-1993 Washington Redskins, 1994 New York Jets, 1995 Philadelphia Eagles. **Highlights:** 940 receptions, 12,721 yards, 68 TDs. Set then-single season record, 106 catches, 1984. Had 50 or more catches in a season nine times.

JOE MONTANA
Quarterback. 6-2, 200. Born in New Eagle, Pennsylvania, June, 11, 1956. Notre Dame. Inducted in 2000. 1979-1992 San Francisco 49ers, 1993-94 Kansas City Chiefs. **Highlights:** MVP in Super Bowl's XVI, XIX, and XXIV. Eight Pro Bowls and All-NFL three times.

WARREN MOON
Quarterback. 6-3, 212. Born in Los Angeles, California, November 18, 1956. West Los Angeles Junior College, Washington. Inducted in 2006. 1984-1993 Houston Oilers, 1994-1996 Minnesota Vikings, 1997-1998 Seattle Seahawks, 1999-2000 Kansas City Chiefs. **Highlights:** Passed for 49,325 yards and 291 touchdowns in 17 NFL seasons. Elected to nine Pro Bowls including eight straight. Threw for 3,000 yards in nine seasons.

LENNY MOORE
Flanker-running back. 6-1, 198. Born in Reading, Pennsylvania, November 25, 1933. Penn State. Inducted in 1975. 1956-1967 Baltimore Colts. **Highlights:** From 1963-65, scored touchdowns in record 18 consecutive games. 113 career touchdowns, 12,451 combined net yards.

MARION MOTLEY
Fullback. 6-1, 238. Born in Leesburg, Georgia, June 5, 1920. Died June 27, 1999. South Carolina State, Nevada. Inducted in 1968. 1946-49 Cleveland Browns (AAFC), 1950-53 Cleveland Browns, 1955 Pittsburgh Steelers. **Highlights:** AAFC's all-time rushing champion. Led league in rushing in first NFL season.

MIKE MUNCHAK
Guard. 6-3, 281. Born in Scranton, Pennsylvania, March 5, 1960. Penn State. Inducted in 2001. 1982-1993 Houston Oilers. **Highlights:** Devastating blocker, All-AFC seven times, elected to nine Pro Bowls.

ANTHONY MUÑOZ
Tackle. 6-6, 278. Born in Ontario, California, August 19, 1958. Southern California. Inducted in 1998. 1980-1992 Cincinnati Bengals. **Highlights:** All-Pro choice 11 consecutive years, 1981-1991. Selected to 11 straight Pro Bowls.

GEORGE MUSSO
Guard-tackle. 6-2, 270. Born in Collinsville, Illinois. April 8, 1910. Died September 5, 2000. Millikin. Inducted in 1982. 1933-1944 Chicago Bears. **Highlights:** First player to achieve All-NFL status at two positions—tackle in 1935 and guard in 1937.

BRONKO NAGURSKI
Fullback. 6-2, 225. Born in Rainy River, Ontario, Canada, November 3, 1908. Died January 7, 1990. Minnesota. Inducted in 1963. 1930-37, 1943 Chicago Bears. **Highlights:** Charter enshrinee. 2,778 rushing yards in nine seasons. All-NFL five times.

JOE NAMATH
Quarterback. 6-2, 200. Born in Beaver Falls, Pennsylvania, May 31, 1943. Alabama. Inducted in 1985. 1965-1976 New York Jets, 1977 Los Angeles Rams. **Highlights:** First quarterback to pass for more than 4,000 yards in season, 1967. Guaranteed, delivered victory over Colts in Super Bowl III.

EARLE (GREASY) NEALE
Coach. Born in Parkersburg, West Virginia, November 5, 1891. Died November 2, 1973. West Virginia Wesleyan. Inducted in 1969. 1941-42, 1944-1950 Philadelphia Eagles; co-coach, 1943 Phil-Pitt. **Highlights:** Turned Eagles into winners with three consecutive division crowns, NFL championships in 1948 and 1949.

ERNIE NEVERS
Fullback. 6-1, 205. Born in Willow River, Minnesota, June 11, 1903. Died May 3, 1976. Stanford. Inducted in 1963. 1926-27 Duluth Eskimos, 1929-1931 Chicago Cardinals. **Highlights:** Charter enshrinee. Holds NFL's longest-standing record, 40 points in one game in 1929.

OZZIE NEWSOME
Tight end. 6-2, 232. Born in Muscle Shoals, Alabama, March 16, 1956. Alabama. Inducted in 1999. 1978-1990 Cleveland Browns. **Highlights:** Finished career as all-time leader among tight ends with 662 receptions for 7,980 yards.

RAY NITSCHKE
Linebacker. 6-3, 235. Born in Elmwood Park, Illinois, December 29, 1936. Died March 8, 1998. Illinois. Inducted in 1978. 1958-1972 Green Bay Packers. **Highlights:** MVP of 1962 title game. Named NFL's all-time linebacker in 1969.

CHUCK NOLL
Coach. Born in Cleveland, Ohio, January 5, 1932. Dayton. Inducted in 1993. 1969-1991 Pittsburgh Steelers. **Highlights:** Coached for 23 years. Only coach to win four Super Bowl titles (IX, X, XIII, XIV).

LEO NOMELLINI
Defensive tackle. 6-3, 264. Born in Lucca, Italy, June 19, 1924. Died October 17, 2000. Minnesota. Inducted in 1969. 1950-1963 San Francisco 49ers. **Highlights:** Played every 49ers game for 14 seasons. 10 Pro Bowls.

MERLIN OLSEN
Defensive tackle. 6-5, 270. Born in Logan, Utah, September 15, 1940. Utah State. Inducted in 1982. 1962-1976 Los Angeles Rams. **Highlights:** Member of the Fearsome "Foursome. Named" to 14 consecutive Pro Bowls, Rams' all-time team.

JIM OTTO
Center. 6-2, 255. Born in Wausau, Wisconsin, January 5, 1938. Miami. Inducted in 1980. 1960-1974 Oakland Raiders. **Highlights:** Named AFL's all-time center. Played in 210 games, 12 AFL All-Star Games or Pro Bowls, six AFL/AFC title games.

STEVE OWEN
Tackle. Coach. 6-2, 235. Born in Cleo Springs, Oklahoma, April 21, 1898. Died May 17, 1964. Phillips. Inducted in 1966. 1924-25 Kansas City Cowboys, 1925 Cleveland Bulldogs, 1926-1931, 1933 New York Giants; coach, 1930-1953 New York Giants. **Highlights:** Both player and coach. Coached Giants to record of 155-108-17, eight divisional titles, two NFL championships.

ALAN PAGE
Defensive tackle. 6-4, 225. Born in Canton, Ohio, August 7, 1945. Notre Dame. Inducted in 1988. 1967-1978 Minnesota Vikings, 1978-1981 Chicago Bears. **Highlights:** Dominating defensive tackle played in 218 consecutive games, four Super Bowls. Won league MVP honors in 1971.

CLARENCE (ACE) PARKER
Quarterback. 5-11, 168. Born in Portsmouth, Virginia, May 17, 1912. Duke. Inducted in 1972. 1937-1941 Brooklyn Dodgers, 1945 Boston Yanks, 1946 New York Yankees (AAFC). **Highlights:** Two-way threat. Two-time All-NFL performer, league MVP in 1940.

JIM PARKER
Guard-tackle. 6-3, 273. Born in Macon, Georgia, April 3, 1934. Died July 18, 2005. Ohio State. Inducted in 1973. 1957-1967 Baltimore Colts. **Highlights:** First full-time offensive lineman elected to Hall of Fame. All-NFL eight consecutive years, eight Pro Bowls.

WALTER PAYTON
Running back. 5-10, 202. Born in Columbia, Mississippi, July 25, 1954. Died November 1, 1999. Jackson State. Inducted in 1993. 1975-1987 Chicago Bears. **Highlights:** NFL's all-time leading rusher with 16,726 yards and combined net yardage with 21,803 at time of retirement.

JOE PERRY
Fullback. 6-0, 200. Born in Stevens, Arkansas, January 22, 1927. Compton Junior College. Inducted in 1969. 1948-49 San Francisco 49ers (AAFC), 1950-1960, 1963 San Francisco 49ers, 1961-62 Baltimore Colts. **Highlights:** First player in NFL history to gain 1,000 yards two consecutive seasons. 12,532 combined yards.

PETE PIHOS
End. 6-1, 210. Born in Orlando, Florida, October 22, 1923. Indiana. Inducted in 1970. 1947-1955 Philadelphia Eagles. **Highlights:** Three-time NFL receiving champion. Caught winning touchdown in 1949 NFL Championship Game.

FRITZ POLLARD
Halfback-Coach. 5-9, 165. Born in Chicago, Illinois, January 27, 1894. Died May 11, 1986. Brown. Inducted in 2005. 1919-1921, 1925-26 Akron Pros/Indians, 1922 Milwaukee Badgers, 1923, 1925 Hammond Pros, 1925 Providence Steam Roller. **Highlights:** True pioneer as one of two African American players in the NFL in 1920 and helped lead Akron to league title that season. In 1921, became the league's first black head coach.

HUGH (SHORTY) RAY
Supervisor of officials 1938-1952. Born in Highland Park, Illinois, September 21, 1884. Died September 16, 1956. Illinois. Inducted in 1966. **Highlights:** Supervisor of Officials, 1938-1952. Streamlined rules to improve game tempo, player safety.

DAN REEVES
Team owner. Born in New York, New York, June 30, 1912. Died April 15, 1971. Georgetown. Inducted in 1967. 1941-45 Cleveland Rams, 1946-1971 Los Angeles Rams. **Highlights:** Moved Rams to Los Angeles in 1946 and opened up West Coast to pro football. First postwar owner to sign African-American player.

MEL RENFRO
Cornerback-safety. 6-0, 192. Born in Houston, Texas, December 30, 1941. Oregon. Inducted in 1996. 1964-1977 Dallas Cowboys. **Highlights:** 52 interceptions for 626 yards and 3 touchdowns. Also added 842 yards on punt returns, 2,246 yards on kickoff returns. Elected to Pro Bowl first 10 seasons.

JOHN RIGGINS
Running back. 6-2, 240. Born in Seneca, Kansas, August 4, 1949. Kansas. Inducted in 1992. 1971-75 New York Jets, 1976-79, 1981-85 Washington Redskins. **Highlights:** 11,352 rushing yards, 116 total touchdowns. MVP of Super Bowl XVII with 166 rushing yards including game-winning 43-yard touchdown.

JIM RINGO
Center. 6-2, 230. Born in Orange, New Jersey, November 21, 1931. Died November 19, 2007. Syracuse. Inducted in 1981. 1953-1963 Green Bay Packers, 1964-67 Philadelphia Eagles. **Highlights:** Ten-time Pro Bowl selection, seven-time All-NFL selection. Started in then-record 182 consecutive games.

ANDY ROBUSTELLI
Defensive end. 6-0, 230. Born in Stamford, Connecticut, December 6, 1925. Arnold College. Inducted in 1971. 1951-55 Los Angeles Rams, 1956-1964 New York Giants. **Highlights:** Anchored defense in eight championship games. Named NFL's top player in 1962.

ART ROONEY
Team owner. Born in Coulterville, Pennsylvania, January 27, 1901. Died August 25, 1988. Georgetown, Duquesne. Inducted in 1964. 1933-39 Pittsburgh Pirates, 1940-42, 1945-1988 Pittsburgh Steelers, 1943 Phil-Pitt, 1944 Card-Pitt. **Highlights:** Founded Pittsburgh Pirates in 1933 and renamed them Steelers in 1940. Team won four Super Bowls in 1970s.

DAN ROONEY
Team owner. Born in Pittsburgh, Pennsylvania, July, 20, 1932. Duquesne. Inducted in 2000. 1955-present Pittsburgh Steelers. **Highlights:** Has been on the board of directors for the NFL Trust Fund, NFL Films, and Scheduling Committee. Played a key role in the labor agreement reached in 1993 between the NFL owners and players.

PETE ROZELLE
Commissioner. Born in South Gate, California, March 1, 1926. Died December 6, 1996. Compton Junior College, San Francisco. Inducted in 1985. Commissioner, 1960-1989. **Highlights:** Negotiated first league-wide television contract in 1962. Generally recognized as premiere commissioner in all of sports. Credited with making NFL the nation's most popular sport.

BOB ST. CLAIR
Tackle. 6-9, 265. Born in San Francisco, California, February 18, 1931. San Francisco, Tulsa. Inducted in 1990. 1953-1963 San Francisco 49ers. **Highlights:** Exceptional offensive lineman. Also played goal-line defense and had 10 blocked field goals, 1956.

BARRY SANDERS
Running back. 5-8, 203. Born in Wichita, Kansas, July 16, 1968. Oklahoma State. Inducted in 2004. 1989-1998 Detroit Lions. **Highlights:** 15,269 rushing yards, 99 touchdowns. Rushed for 1,000 yards in each of 10 seasons. NFL co-MVP, 1997. Selected to 10 Pro Bowls.

CHARLIE SANDERS
Tight end. 6-4, 230. Born in Richlands, North Carolina, August 25, 1946. Minnesota. Inducted in 2007. 1968-1977 Detroit Lions. **Highlights:** 336 career receptions for 4,817 yards and 31 touchdowns. Selected to seven Pro Bowls. Named to the NFL's All-Decade Team of 1970s.

GALE SAYERS
Running back. 6-0, 200. Born in Wichita, Kansas, May 30, 1943. Kansas. Inducted in 1977. 1965-1971 Chicago Bears. **Highlights:** Broke into league by scoring rookie-record 22 touchdowns. Led league in rushing in 1966, 1969. MVP of three Pro Bowls.

JOE SCHMIDT
Linebacker. 6-0, 222. Born in Pittsburgh, Pennsylvania, January 18, 1932. Pittsburgh. Inducted in 1973. 1953-1965 Detroit Lions. **Highlights:** 24 interceptions. Lions' team captain for nine years. Mastered middle linebacker position that evolved in 1950s.

TEX SCHRAMM
Team president-general manager. Born in San Gabriel, California, June 2, 1920. Died July 15, 2003. Texas. Inducted in 1991. 1947-1956 Los Angeles Rams. 1960-1989 Dallas Cowboys. **Highlights:** Played prominent role in AFL-NFL merger. Chairman of Competition Committee from 1966-1988.

LEE ROY SELMON
Defensive end. 6-3, 250. Born in Eufaula, Oklahoma, October 20, 1954. Oklahoma. Inducted in 1995. 1976-1984 Tampa Bay Buccaneers. **Highlights:** 78½ sacks, 380 quarterback pressures, forced 28 fumbles. Six consecutive Pro Bowl selections.

BILLY SHAW
Guard. 6-2, 258. Born in Natchez, Mississippi, December 15, 1938. Georgia Tech. Inducted in 1999. 1961-69 Buffalo Bills. **Highlights:** First player who played entire career in AFL to be elected to Hall of Fame. Named to AFL's all-time team.

ART SHELL
Tackle. 6-5, 285. Born in Charleston, South Carolina, November 26, 1946. Maryland State-Eastern Shore. Inducted in 1989. 1968-82 Oakland/Los Angeles Raiders. **Highlights:** Cornerstone of Raiders' offensive line in 1970s. 207 regular-season games, 23 postseason games, eight Pro Bowls.

DON SHULA
Coach. Born in Grand River, Ohio, January 4, 1930. John Carroll. Inducted in 1997. 1963-69 Baltimore Colts, 1970-1995 Miami Dolphins. **Highlights:** Won more games (347) than any coach in NFL history. Won two Super Bowl titles, including Super Bowl VII when Dolphins recorded NFL's only perfect season (17-0).

O.J. SIMPSON
Running back. 6-1, 212. Born in San Francisco, California, July 9, 1947. City College (San Francisco), Southern California. Inducted in 1985. 1969-1977 Buffalo Bills, 1978-79 San Francisco 49ers. **Highlights:** In 1973, became first player to rush for 2,000 yards in season. Finished career with four rushing titles, 11,236 yards.

MIKE SINGLETARY
Linebacker. 6-0, 230. Born in Houston, Texas, October 9, 1958. Baylor. Inducted in 1998. 1981-1992 Chicago Bears. **Highlights:** All-Pro choice eight times and All-NFC nine consecutive seasons. Selected to 10 Pro Bowls.

JACKIE SLATER
Tackle. 6-4, 277. Born in Jackson, Mississippi, May 27, 1954. Jackson State. Inducted in 2001. 1976-1995 Los Angeles/St. Louis Rams. **Highlights:** Played 20 seasons, 259 games. Blocked for seven different 1,000-yard rushers. Seven Pro Bowls.

BRUCE SMITH
Defensive end. 6-4, 280. Born in Norfolk, Virginia, June 18, 1963. Virginia Tech. Inducted in 2009. 1985-1999 Buffalo Bills, 2000-03 Washington Redskins. **Highlights:** NFL's all-time leader in sacks with 200. Named All-Pro nine times, 11 Pro Bowls. Selected to NFL's All-Decade Team of 1980s and 1990s.

JACKIE SMITH
Tight end. 6-4, 232. Born in Columbia, Mississippi, February 23, 1940. Northwestern State (Louisiana). Inducted in 1994. 1963-1977 St. Louis Cardinals, 1978 Dallas Cowboys. **Highlights:** 480 receptions for 7,918 yards, 40 touchdowns. Third tight end to be elected to Hall of Fame.

JOHN STALLWORTH
Wide receiver. 6-2, 191. Born in Tuscaloosa, Alabama, July 15, 1952. Alabama A&M. Inducted in 2002. 1974-1987 Pittsburgh Steelers. **Highlights:** 537 receptions for 8,723 yards, 63 touchdowns. Scored go-ahead touchdown in Super Bowl XIV on 73-yard reception.

BART STARR
Quarterback. 6-1, 200. Born in Montgomery, Alabama, January 9, 1934. Alabama. Inducted in 1977. 1956-1971 Green Bay Packers. **Highlights:** Quarterbacked Packers to six division titles, five NFL titles, and first two Super Bowls in which he was MVP.

ROGER STAUBACH
Quarterback. 6-3, 202. Born in Cincinnati, Ohio, February 5, 1942. New Mexico Military Institute, Navy. Inducted in 1985. 1969-1979 Dallas Cowboys. **Highlights:** Led Cowboys to four NFC titles and victories in Super Bowls VI, XII. When retired, 83.4 career passer rating was best of all time.

ERNIE STAUTNER
Defensive tackle. 6-2, 235. Born in Prinzing-by-Cham, Bavaria, April 20, 1925. Died February 16, 2006. Boston College. Inducted in 1969. 1950-1963 Pittsburgh Steelers. **Highlights:** Played in nine Pro Bowls and won the best lineman award in 1957. Recorded 3 safeties.

JAN STENERUD
Kicker. 6-2, 190. Born in Fetsund, Norway, November 26, 1942. Montana State. Inducted in 1991. 1967-1979 Kansas City Chiefs, 1980-83 Green Bay Packers, 1984-85 Minnesota Vikings. **Highlights:** 1,699 points on 580 extra points, 373 field goals. First pure placekicker to enter Hall of Fame.

DWIGHT STEPHENSON
Center. 6-2, 255. Born in Murfreesboro, North Carolina, November 20, 1957. Alabama. Inducted in 1998. 1980-87 Miami Dolphins. **Highlights:** Recognized as premier center of his time. All-Pro, All-AFC five straight years. Selected to five Pro Bowls.

HANK STRAM
Coach. Born in Chicago, Illinois, January 3, 1923. Died July 4, 2005. Purdue. Inducted in 2003. 1960-1974 Dallas Texans/Kansas City Chiefs, 1976-1977 New Orleans Saints. **Highlights:** Overall record of 136-100-10. Recorded most wins in AFL history. Guided teams to titles in 1962, 1966, and 1969. Led Chiefs to AFL win in Super Bowl IV.

KEN STRONG
Halfback. 5-11, 210. Born in West Haven, Connecticut, April 21, 1906. Died October 5, 1979. New York University. Inducted in 1967. 1929-1932 Staten Island Stapletons, 1933-35, 1939, 1944-47 New York Giants, 1936-37 New York Yanks (AFL). **Highlights:** Scored 17 points to lead Giants to victory in 1934 'Sneakers' game, led NFL with 64 points, 1933.

JOE STYDAHAR
Tackle. 6-4, 230. Born in Kaylor, Pennsylvania, March 17, 1912. Died March 23, 1977. West Virginia. Inducted in 1967. 1936-1942, 1945-46 Chicago Bears. **Highlights:** One of stalwarts of Bears' 'Monsters of the Midway.' Played on five divisional, three NFL championship teams.

LYNN SWANN
Wide receiver. 5-11, 180. Born in Alcoa, Tennessee, March 7, 1952. Southern California. Inducted in 2001. 1974-1982 Pittsburgh Steelers. **Highlights:** All-AFC three times. Selected to three Pro Bowls. MVP, Super Bowl X.

FRAN TARKENTON
Quarterback. 6-0, 185. Born in Richmond, Virginia, February 3, 1940. Georgia. Inducted in 1986. 1961-66, 1972-78 Minnesota Vikings, 1967-1971 New York Giants. **Highlights:** At retirement, held NFL records for attempts (6,467), completions (3,686), yards (47,003), and touchdowns (342). Four touchdowns passes in first NFL game.

CHARLEY TAYLOR
Running back-wide receiver. 6-3, 210. Born in Grand Prairie, Texas, September 28, 1941. Arizona State. Inducted in 1984. 1964-1975, 1977 Washington Redskins. **Highlights:** Won rookie of year honors as running back. Switched to wide receiver and won receiving titles in 1966, 1967.

JIM TAYLOR
Fullback. 6-0, 216. Born in Baton Rouge, Louisiana, September 20, 1935. Louisiana State. Inducted in 1976. 1958-1966 Green Bay Packers, 1967 New Orleans Saints. **Highlights:** 8,597 rushing yards, 558 points. In 1962, led league in rushing and scoring with 19 touchdowns.

LAWRENCE TAYLOR
Linebacker. 6-3, 237. Born in Williamsburg, Virginia, February 4, 1959. North Carolina. Inducted in 1999. 1981-1993 New York Giants. **Highlights:** Redefined the position of outside linebacker. All-Pro nine times, 10 Pro Bowls. NFL MVP in 1986.

DERRICK THOMAS
Linebacker. 6-3, 243. Born in Miami, Florida, January 1, 1967. Died February 8, 2000. Alabama. Inducted in 2009. 1989-1999 Kansas City Chiefs. **Highlights:** Set NFL record with 7 sacks in one game. Recorded most sacks in NFL during 1990s. Nine Pro Bowls. Named to NFL's All-Decade Team of 1990s.

EMMITT THOMAS
Cornerback. 6-2, 192. Born in Angleton, Texas, June 3, 1943. Bishop. Inducted in 2008. 1966-1978 Kansas City Chiefs. **Highlights:** Undrafted free agent. 58 interceptions, 937 yards, 5 TDs. Ranked fifth all-time in interceptions at retirement. Interception leader – AFL, 1969 and NFL, 1974.

THURMAN THOMAS
Running back. 5-10, 198. Born in Houston, Texas, May 16, 1966. Oklahoma State. Inducted in 2007. 1988-1999 Buffalo Bills, 2000 Miami Dolphins. **Highlights:** Amassed 16,532 total yards including 12,074 yards rushing. Scored 88 touchdowns. Only player in history to lead league in yards from scrimmage four straight seasons.

JIM THORPE
Halfback. 6-1, 190. Born in Prague, Oklahoma, May 28, 1888. Died March 28, 1953. Carlisle. Inducted in 1963. 1915-17, 1919-1920, 1926 Canton Bulldogs, 1921 Cleveland Indians, 1922-23 Oorang Indians, 1924 Rock Island Independents, 1925 New York Giants, 1928 Chicago Cardinals. **Highlights:** Charter enshrinee. First president of American Professional Football Association, 1920. Played for 12 seasons.

ANDRE TIPPETT
Linebacker. 6-3, 240. Born in Birmingham, Alabama, December 27, 1959. Iowa; Ellsworth (IA) Jr. College. Inducted in 2008. 1982-1993 New England Patriots. **Highlights:** Recorded 100 career sacks including personal best 18.5 sacks, 1984. Named to five straight Pro Bowls, 1985-89.

Y.A. TITTLE
Quarterback. 6-0, 200. Born in Marshall, Texas, October 24, 1926. Louisiana State. Inducted in 1971. 1948-49 Baltimore Colts (AAFC), 1950 Baltimore Colts, 1951-1960 San Francisco 49ers, 1961-64 New York Giants. **Highlights:** 33,070 yards, 242 touchdowns. 33 touchdown passes in 1962 and 36 in 1963. Two-time league MVP.

GEORGE TRAFTON
Center. 6-2, 235. Born in Chicago, Illinois, December 6, 1896. Died September 5, 1971. Notre Dame. Inducted in 1964. 1920-1932 Decatur Staleys/Chicago Staleys/ Chicago Bears. **Highlights:** First center to snap with one hand. Named top NFL center of 1920s.

CHARLEY TRIPPI
Halfback-quarterback. 6-0, 185. Born in Pittston, Pennsylvania, December 14, 1922. Georgia. Inducted in 1968. 1947-1955 Chicago Cardinals. **Highlights:** One of football's most versatile performers. Played halfback five years, quarterback for two, defense for two.

EMLEN TUNNELL
Safety. 6-1, 200. Born in Bryn Mawr, Pennsylvania, March 29, 1925. Died July 22, 1975. Toledo, Iowa. Inducted in 1967. 1948-1958 New York Giants, 1959-1961 Green Bay Packers. **Highlights:** 79 interceptions. Gained more yards on kickoff, punt, and interception returns (924) in 1952 than that season's NFL rushing leader.

CLYDE (BULLDOG) TURNER
Center. 6-2, 235. Born in Plains, Texas, March 10, 1919. Died October 30, 1998. Hardin-Simmons. Inducted in 1966. 1940-1952 Chicago Bears. **Highlights:** Anchored defense for four NFL championship teams, including 4 interceptions in five title games.

JOHNNY UNITAS
Quarterback. 6-1, 195. Born in Pittsburgh, Pennsylvania, May 7, 1933. Died September 11, 2002. Louisville. Inducted in 1979. 1956-1972 Baltimore Colts, 1973 San Diego Chargers. **Highlights:** 40,239 passing yards, 290 touchdowns. Led Colts to two NFL championships. Passed for at least one touchdown in 47 consecutive games.

GENE UPSHAW
Guard. 6-5, 255. Born in Robstown, Texas, August 15, 1945. Died August 20, 2008. Texas A & I. Inducted in 1987. 1967-1981 Oakland Raiders. **Highlights:** Premier guard of his era played in 10 AFL/AFC Championship Games, three Super Bowls, seven Pro Bowls.

NORM VAN BROCKLIN
Quarterback. 6-1, 190. Born in Eagle Butte, South Dakota, March 15, 1926. Died May 2, 1983. Oregon. Inducted in 1971. 1949-1957 Los Angeles Rams, 1958-1960 Philadelphia Eagles. **Highlights:** NFL-record 554 yards passing in 1951 season opener. Guided Eagles to NFL crown as league MVP in two.

STEVE VAN BUREN
Halfback. 6-1, 200. Born in La Ceiba, Honduras, December 28, 1920. Louisiana State. Inducted in 1965. 1944-1951 Philadelphia Eagles. **Highlights:** Four-time rushing champion. Won 1944 punt-return title and was 1945 kick-off-return champion.

DOAK WALKER
Halfback. 5-11, 173. Born in Dallas, Texas, January 1, 1927. Died September 27, 1998. Southern Methodist. Inducted in 1986. 1950-55 Detroit Lions. **Highlights:** 534 points. Won two NFL scoring titles. Had winning 67-yard scoring run in 1952 title game.

BILL WALSH
Coach. Born in Los Angeles, California, November 30, 1931. Died July 30, 2007. San Jose State. Inducted in 1993. 1979-1988 San Francisco 49ers. **Highlights:** 102-63-1 coaching record. Guided 49ers to three Super Bowl titles (XVI, XIX, XXIII) in 10 years.

PAUL WARFIELD
Wide receiver. 6-0, 188. Born in Warren, Ohio, November 28, 1942. Ohio State. Inducted in 1983. 1964-69, 1976-77 Cleveland Browns, 1970-74 Miami Dolphins. **Highlights:** 8,565 yards receiving, 85 touchdowns. Eight-time Pro Bowl player. Key to both Cleveland and Miami offenses.

BOB WATERFIELD
Quarterback. 6-2, 200. Born in Elmira, New York, July 26, 1920. Died March 25, 1983. UCLA. Inducted in 1965. 1945 Cleveland Rams, 1946-1952 Los Angeles Rams. **Highlights:** NFL MVP as rookie in 1945 and led Rams to NFL title. Grabbed 20 interceptions in limited defensive duties.

MIKE WEBSTER
Center. 6-2, 260. Born in Tomahawk, Wisconsin, March 18, 1952. Died September 24, 2002. Wisconsin. Inducted in 1997. 1974-1988 Pittsburgh Steelers, 1989-1990 Kansas City Chiefs. **Highlights:** Played in 245 games, nine Pro Bowls, and won four Super Bowls during 17-year career.

ROGER WEHRLI
Cornerback. 6-0, 190. Born in New Point, Missouri, November 26, 1947. Missouri. Inducted in 2007. 1969-1982 St. Louis Cardinals. **Highlights:** 40 career interceptions. Named to the NFL's All-Decade Team of 1970s. All-Pro five times, selected to seven Pro Bowls.

ARNIE WEINMEISTER
Defensive tackle. 6-4, 235. Born in Rhein, Saskatchewan, Canada, March 23, 1923. Died June 29, 2000. Washington. Inducted in 1984. 1948-49 New York Yankees (AAFC), 1950-53 New York Giants. **Highlights:** Dominant defensive tackle of his time. Four-time All-NFL selection, four Pro Bowls.

RANDY WHITE
Defensive tackle. 6-4, 265. Born in Pittsburgh, Pennsylvania, January 15, 1953. Maryland. Inducted in 1994. 1975-1988 Dallas Cowboys. **Highlights:** Missed only one game in 14 seasons. Co-MVP of Super Bowl XII. Nine-time Pro Bowl selection.

REGGIE WHITE
Defensive end. 6-5, 291. Born in Chattanooga, Tennessee, December 19, 1961. Died December 26, 2004. Tennessee. Inducted in 2006. 1985-1992 Philadelphia Eagles, 1993-1998 Green Bay Packers, 2000 Carolina Panthers. **Highlights:** Retired as all-time sack leader with 198. Named All-Pro 13 of 15 seasons including 10 as first-team selection. Named to 13 straight Pro Bowls.

DAVE WILCOX
Linebacker. 6-3, 241. Born in Ontario, Oregon, September, 29, 1942. Boise State, Oregon. Inducted in 2000. 1964-1974 San Francisco 49ers. **Highlights:** Seven Pro Bowls, All-NFL five times. Missed only one game because of injury.

BILL WILLIS
Guard. 6-2, 215. Born in Columbus, Ohio, October 5, 1921. Died November 27, 2007. Ohio State. Inducted in 1977. 1946-1953 Cleveland Browns (AAFC/NFL). **Highlights:** Two-way player who excelled on defense. Four-time All-NFL player, played in three Pro Bowls.

LARRY WILSON
Safety. 6-0, 190. Born in Rigby, Idaho, March 24, 1938. Utah. Inducted in 1978. 1960-1972 St. Louis Cardinals. **Highlights:** 52 interceptions. Had interception in seven consecutive games in 1966. Made "safety blitz" famous.

RALPH WILSON, JR.
Owner-founder. Born in Columbus, Ohio, October 17, 1918. Virginia, Michigan. Inducted in 2009. 1960-present Buffalo Bills. **Highlights:** Founded team. Bills teams captured back-to-back AFL titles in mid-1960s. Unprecedented four straight Super Bowl appearances.

KELLEN WINSLOW
Tight end. 6-5, 250. Born in St. Louis, Missouri, November 5, 1957. Missouri. Inducted in 1995. 1979-1987 San Diego Chargers **Highlights:** 541 receptions for 6,741 yards, 45 touchdowns. 13 catches, blocked field goal in 1981 playoff win over Miami.

ALEX WOJCIECHOWICZ
Center. 6-0, 235. Born in South River, New Jersey, August 12, 1915. Died July 13, 1992. Fordham. Inducted in 1968. 1938-1946 Detroit Lions, 1946-1950 Philadelphia Eagles. **Highlights:** One of league's first iron men. Played both ways for eight years with Lions.

WILLIE WOOD
Safety. 5-10, 190. Born in Washington, D.C., December 23, 1936. Southern California. Inducted in 1989. 1960-1971 Green Bay Packers. **Highlights:** 48 interceptions. Competed in six NFL Championship Games and Super Bowls I and II.

ROD WOODSON
Cornerback-safety. 6-0, 200. Born in Fort Wayne, Indiana, March 10, 1965. Purdue. Inducted in 2009. 1987-1996 Pittsburgh Steelers, 1997 San Francisco 49ers, 1998-2001 Baltimore Ravens, 2002-03 Oakland Raiders. **Highlights:** 71 interceptions returned for 1,483 yards and NFL record 12 TDs. Named NFL Defensive Player of Year, 1993. Member of NFL's 75th Anniversary Team. 11 Pro Bowls.

RAYFIELD WRIGHT
Tackle. 6-6, 255. Born in Griffin, Georgia, August 23, 1945. Fort Valley State. Inducted in 2006. 1967-1979 Dallas Cowboys. **Highlights:** Named first- or second-team All-Pro and voted to Pro Bowl six straight seasons, 1971-76. Played in six NFC championship games and five Super Bowls. Named to NFL's All-Decade Team of 1970s.

RON YARY
Tackle. 6-5, 255. Born in Chicago, Illinois, July 16, 1946. Cerritos (Calif.) J.C., Southern California. Inducted in 2001. 1968-1981 Minnesota Vikings, 1982 Los Angeles Rams. **Highlights:** All-Pro six consecutive seasons, All-NFC eight consecutive years. Named to seven Pro Bowls. Started in four Super Bowls and five NFL/NFC Championship Games.

STEVE YOUNG
Quarterback. 6-2, 205. Born in Salt Lake City, Utah, October 11, 1961. Brigham Young. Inducted in 2005. 1985-86 Tampa Bay Buccaneers, 1987-1999 San Francisco 49ers. **Highlights:** Led the NFL in passing a record-tying six times. Passed for more than 33,000 yards and 232 touchdowns in career. MVP of Super Bowl XXIX. Elected to seven Pro Bowls.

JACK YOUNGBLOOD
Defensive end. 6-4, 247. Born in Jacksonville, Florida, January 26, 1950. Florida. Inducted in 2001. 1971-1984 Los Angeles Rams. **Highlights:** Played in club-record 201 consecutive games. Played in five NFC Championship Games, one Super Bowl. Named All-Pro five times, All-NFC seven times. Elected to seven consecutive Pro Bowls. Lions.

GARY ZIMMERMAN
Tackle. 6-6, 294. Born in Fullerton, California, December 13, 1961. Oregon. Inducted in 2008. 1986-1992 Minnesota Vikings, 1993-97 Denver Broncos. **Highlights:** Named to seven Pro Bowls. One of handful of players to be named to two NFL All-Decade Teams, 1980s and 1990s.

ENSHRINEES BY YEAR OF INDUCTION

**Deceased*
(Date of enshrinement in parentheses)

1963 CHARTER CLASS
(September 7, 1963)
Sammy Baugh*
Bert Bell*
Joe Carr*
Earl (Dutch) Clark*
Harold (Red) Grange*
George Halas*
Mel Hein*
Wilbur (Pete) Henry*
Robert (Cal) Hubbard*
Don Hutson*
Earl (Curly) Lambeau*
Tim Mara*
George Preston Marshall*
John (Blood) McNally*
Bronko Nagurski*
Ernie Nevers*
Jim Thorpe*

CLASS OF 1964
(September 6, 1964)
Jimmy Conzelman*
Ed Healey*
Clarke Hinkle*
William Roy (Link) Lyman*
Mike Michalske*
Art Rooney*
George Trafton*

CLASS OF 1965
(September 12, 1965)
Guy Chamberlin*
John (Paddy) Driscoll*
Dan Fortmann*
Otto Graham*
Sid Luckman*
Steve Van Buren
Bob Waterfield*

CLASS OF 1966
(September 17, 1966)
Bill Dudley
Joe Guyon*
Arnie Herber*
Walt Kiesling*
George McAfee*
Steve Owen*
Hugh (Shorty) Ray*
Clyde (Bulldog) Turner*

CLASS OF 1967
(August 5, 1967)
Chuck Bednarik
Charles W. Bidwill Sr.*
Paul Brown*
Bobby Layne*
Dan Reeves*
Ken Strong*
Joe Stydahar*
Emlen Tunnell*

CLASS OF 1968
(August 3, 1968)
Cliff Battles*
Art Donovan
Elroy (Crazylegs) Hirsch*
Wayne Millner*
Marion Motley*
Charley Trippi
Alex Wojciechowicz*

CLASS OF 1969
(September 13, 1969)
Albert Glen (Turk) Edwards*
Earle (Greasy) Neale*
Leo Nomellini*
Joe Perry
Ernie Stautner*

CLASS OF 1970
(August 8, 1970)
Jack Christiansen*
Tom Fears*
Hugh McElhenny
Pete Pihos

CLASS OF 1971
(July 31, 1971)
Jim Brown
Bill Hewitt*
Frank (Bruiser) Kinard*
Vince Lombardi*
Andy Robustelli
Y. A. Tittle
Norm Van Brocklin*

CLASS OF 1972
*(July 29, 1972)*Lamar Hunt*
Gino Marchetti
Ollie Matson
Clarence (Ace) Parker

CLASS OF 1973
(July 28, 1973)
Raymond Berry
Jim Parker*
Joe Schmidt

CLASS OF 1974
(July 27, 1974)
Tony Canadeo*
Bill George*
Lou Groza*
Dick (Night Train) Lane*

CLASS OF 1975
(August 2, 1975)
Roosevelt Brown*
George Connor*
Dante Lavelli*
Lenny Moore

CLASS OF 1976
(July 24, 1976)
Ray Flaherty*
Len Ford*
Jim Taylor

CLASS OF 1977
(July 30, 1977)
Frank Gifford
Forrest Gregg
Gale Sayers
Bart Starr
Bill Willis*

CLASS OF 1978
(July 29, 1978)
Lance Alworth
Weeb Ewbank*
Alphonse (Tuffy) Leemans*
Ray Nitschke*
Larry Wilson

CLASS OF 1979
(July 28, 1979)
Dick Butkus
Yale Lary
Ron Mix
Johnny Unitas*

CLASS OF 1980
(August 2, 1980)
Herb Adderley
David (Deacon) Jones
Bob Lilly
Jim Otto

CLASS OF 1981
(August 1, 1981)
Morris (Red) Badgro*
George Blanda
Willie Davis
Jim Ringo*

CLASS OF 1982
(August 7, 1982)
Doug Atkins
Sam Huff
George Musso*
Merlin Olsen

CLASS OF 1983
(July 30, 1983)
Bobby Bell
Sid Gillman*
Sonny Jurgensen
Bobby Mitchell
Paul Warfield

CLASS OF 1984
(July 28, 1984)
Willie Brown
Mike McCormack
Charley Taylor
Arnie Weinmeister*

CLASS OF 1985
(August 3, 1985)
Frank Gatski*
Joe Namath
Pete Rozelle*
O. J. Simpson
Roger Staubach

CLASS OF 1986
(August 2, 1986)
Paul Hornung
Ken Houston
Willie Lanier
Fran Tarkenton
Doak Walker*

CLASS OF 1987
(August 8, 1987)
Larry Csonka
Len Dawson
Joe Greene
John Henry Johnson
Jim Langer
Don Maynard
Gene Upshaw*

CLASS OF 1988
(July 30, 1988)
Fred Biletnikoff
Mike Ditka
Jack Ham
Alan Page

CLASS OF 1989
(August 5, 1989)
Mel Blount
Terry Bradshaw
Art Shell
Willie Wood

CLASS OF 1990
(August 4, 1990)
Buck Buchanan*
Bob Griese
Franco Harris
Ted Hendricks
Jack Lambert
Tom Landry*
Bob St. Clair

CLASS OF 1991
(July 27, 1991)
Earl Campbell
John Hannah
Stan Jones
Tex Schramm*
Jan Stenerud

CLASS OF 1992
(August 1, 1992)
Lem Barney
Al Davis
John Mackey
John Riggins

CLASS OF 1993
(July 31, 1993)
Dan Fouts
Larry Little
Chuck Noll
Walter Payton*
Bill Walsh*

CLASS OF 1994
(July 30, 1994)
Tony Dorsett
Bud Grant
Jimmy Johnson
Leroy Kelly
Jackie Smith
Randy White

CLASS OF 1995
(July 29, 1995)
Jim Finks*
Henry Jordan*
Steve Largent
Lee Roy Selmon
Kellen Winslow

CLASS OF 1996
(July 27, 1996)
Lou Creekmur
Dan Dierdorf
Joe Gibbs
Charlie Joiner
Mel Renfro

CLASS OF 1997
(July 26, 1997)
Mike Haynes
Wellington Mara*
Don Shula
Mike Webster*

CLASS OF 1998
(August 1, 1998)
Paul Krause
Tommy McDonald
Anthony Muñoz
Mike Singletary
Dwight Stephenson

CLASS OF 1999
(August 7, 1999)
Eric Dickerson
Tom Mack
Ozzie Newsome
Billy Shaw
Lawrence Taylor

CLASS OF 2000
(July 29, 2000)
Howie Long
Ronnie Lott
Joe Montana
Dan Rooney
Dave Wilcox

CLASS OF 2001
(August 4, 2001)
Nick Buoniconti
Marv Levy
Mike Munchak
Jackie Slater
Lynn Swann
Ron Yary
Jack Youngblood

CLASS OF 2002
(August 3, 2002)
George Allen*
Dave Casper
Dan Hampton
Jim Kelly
John Stallworth

CLASS OF 2003
(August 3, 2003)
Marcus Allen
Elvin Bethea
Joe DeLamielleure
James Lofton
Hank Stram*

CLASS OF 2004
(August 8, 2004)
Bob (Boomer) Brown
Carl Eller
John Elway
Barry Sanders

CLASS OF 2005
(August 7, 2005)
Benny Friedman*
Dan Marino
Fritz Pollard*
Steve Young

CLASS OF 2006
(*August 6, 2006*)
Troy Aikman
Harry Carson
John Madden
Warren Moon
Reggie White*
Rayfield Wright

CLASS OF 2007
(*August 4, 2007*)
Gene Hickerson*
Michael Irvin
Bruce Matthews
Charlie Sanders
Thurman Thomas
Roger Wehrli

CLASS OF 2008
(*August 2, 2008*)
Fred Dean
Darrell Green
Art Monk
Emmitt Thomas
Andre Tippett
Gary Zimmerman

CLASS OF 2009
(*August 8, 2009*)
Bob Hayes*
Randall McDaniel
Bruce Smith
Derrick Thomas*
Ralph Wilson, Jr.
Rod Woodson

PRO FOOTBALL HALL OF FAME GAME (46)

Date	Winner	Loser	Attendance
August 11, 1962	New York Giants 21 (tie)	St. Louis Cardinals 21 (tie)	14,000
September 8, 1963	Pittsburgh Steelers 16	Cleveland Browns 7	18,462
September 6, 1964	Baltimore Colts 48	Pittsburgh Steelers 17	11,479
September 12, 1965	Washington Redskins 20	Detroit Lions 3	14,416
1966	No game was played		
August 5, 1967	Philadelphia Eagles 28	Cleveland Browns 13	17,304
August 3, 1968	Chicago Bears 30	Dallas Cowboys 24	14,578
September 13, 1969	Green Bay Packers 38	Atlanta Falcons 24	17,411
August 8, 1970	New Orleans Saints 14	Minnesota Vikings 13	17,932
July 31, 1971	Los Angeles Rams (NFC) 17	Houston Oilers (AFC) 6	19,384
July 29, 1972	Kansas City Chiefs (AFC) 23	New York Giants (NFC) 17	19,304
July 28, 1973	San Francisco 49ers (NFC) 20	New England Patriots (AFC) 7	19,685
July 27, 1974	St. Louis Cardinals (NFC) 21	Buffalo Bills (AFC) 13	17,286
August 2, 1975	Washington Redskins (NFC) 17	Cincinnati Bengals (AFC) 9	19,360
July 24, 1976	Denver Broncos (AFC) 10	Detroit Lions (NFC) 7	17,639
July 30, 1977	Chicago Bears (NFC) 20	New York Jets (AFC) 6	19,057
July 29, 1978	Philadelphia Eagles (NFC) 17	Miami Dolphins (AFC) 3	19,255
July 28, 1979	Oakland Raiders (AFC) 20	Dallas Cowboys (NFC) 13	20,648
August 2, 1980*	San Diego Chargers (AFC) 0	Green Bay Packers (NFC) 0	19,972
August 1, 1981	Cleveland Browns (AFC) 24	Atlanta Falcons (NFC) 10	23,921
August 7, 1982	Minnesota Vikings (NFC) 30	Baltimore Colts (AFC) 14	23,379
July 30, 1983	Pittsburgh Steelers (AFC) 27	New Orleans Saints (NFC) 14	23,909
July 28, 1984	Seattle Seahawks (AFC) 38	Tampa Bay Buccaneers (NFC) 0	22,250
August 3, 1985	New York Giants (NFC) 21	Houston Oilers (AFC) 20	23,940
August 2, 1986	New England Patriots (AFC) 21	St. Louis Cardinals (NFC) 16	22,739
August 8, 1987	San Francisco 49ers (NFC) 20	Kansas City Chiefs (AFC) 7	23,826
July 30, 1988	Cincinnati Bengals (AFC) 14	Los Angeles Rams (NFC) 7	23,801
August 5, 1989	Washington Redskins (NFC) 31	Buffalo Bills (AFC) 6	23,948
August 4, 1990	Chicago Bears (NFC) 13	Cleveland Browns (AFC) 0	23,952
July 27, 1991	Detroit Lions (NFC) 14	Denver Broncos (AFC) 3	23,815
August 1, 1992	New York Jets (AFC) 41	Philadelphia Eagles (NFC) 14	23,853
July 31, 1993	Los Angeles Raiders (AFC) 19	Green Bay Packers (NFC) 3	23,863
July 30, 1994	Atlanta Falcons (NFC) 21	San Diego Chargers (AFC) 17	23,185
July 29, 1995	Carolina Panthers (NFC) 20	Jacksonville Jaguars (AFC) 14	24,625
July 27, 1996	Indianapolis Colts (AFC) 10	New Orleans Saints (NFC) 3	23,376
July 26, 1997	Minnesota Vikings (NFC) 28	Seattle Seahawks (AFC) 26	23,846
August 1, 1998	Tampa Bay Buccaneers (NFC) 30	Pittsburgh Steelers (AFC) 6	23,875
August 9, 1999	Cleveland Browns (AFC) 20	Dallas Cowboys (NFC) 17 (OT)	25,156
July 31, 2000	New England Patriots (AFC) 20	San Francisco 49ers (NFC) 0	22,840
August 6, 2001	St. Louis Rams (NFC) 17	Miami Dolphins (AFC) 10	22,736
August 5, 2002	New York Giants (NFC) 34	Houston Texans (AFC) 17	22,461
August 4, 2003**	Kansas City Chiefs (AFC) 9	Green Bay Packers (NFC) 0	22,385
August 9, 2004	Washington Redskins (NFC) 20	Denver Broncos (AFC) 17	22,177
August 8, 2005	Chicago Bears (NFC) 27	Miami Dolphins (AFC) 24	22,292
August 6, 2006	Oakland Raiders (AFC) 16	Philadelphia Eagles (NFC) 10	22,200
August 5, 2007	Pittsburgh Steelers (AFC) 20	New Orleans Saints (NFC) 7	22,302
August 3, 2008	Washington Redskins (NFC) 30	Indianapolis Colts (AFC) 16	22,216

**Game called with 5:29 remaining in the fourth quarter because of severe thunder and lightning.*
***Game called with 5:49 remaining in the third quarter because of lightning and torrential rain.*

1869
Rutgers and Princeton played a college soccer football game, the first ever, November 6. The game used modified London Football Association rules. During the next seven years, rugby gained favor with the major eastern schools over soccer, and modern football began to develop from rugby.

1876
At the Massasoit convention, the first rules for American football were written. Walter Camp, who would become known as the father of American football, first became involved with the game.

1892
In an era in which football was a major attraction of local athletic clubs, an intense competition between two Pittsburgh-area clubs, the Allegheny Athletic Association (AAA) and the Pittsburgh Athletic Club (PAC), led to the making of the first professional football player. Former Yale All-America guard William (Pudge) Heffelfinger was paid $500 by the AAA to play in a game against the PAC, becoming the first person to be paid to play football, November 12. The AAA won the game 4-0 when Heffelfinger picked up a PAC fumble and ran 35 yards for a touchdown.

1893
The Pittsburgh Athletic Club signed one of its players, probably halfback Grant Dibert, to the first known pro football contract, which covered all of the PAC's games for the year.

1895
John Brallier became the first football player to openly turn pro, accepting $10 and expenses to play for the Latrobe YMCA against the Jeannette Athletic Club.

1896
The Allegheny Athletic Association team fielded the first completely professional team for its abbreviated two-game season.

1897
The Latrobe Athletic Association football team went entirely professional, becoming the first team to play a full season with only professionals.

1898
A touchdown was changed from four points to five.

Chris O'Brien formed a neighborhood team, which played under the name the Morgan Athletic Club, on the south side of Chicago. The team later became known as the Normals, then the Racine (for a street in Chicago) Cardinals, the Chicago Cardinals, the St. Louis Cardinals, the Phoenix Cardinals, and, in 1994, the Arizona Cardinals. The team remains the oldest continuing operation in pro football.

1900
William C. Temple took over the team payments for the Duquesne Country and Athletic Club, becoming the first known individual club owner.

1902
Baseball's Philadelphia Athletics, managed by Connie Mack, and the Philadelphia Phillies formed professional football teams, joining the Pittsburgh Stars in the first attempt at a pro football league, named the National Football League. The Athletics won the first night football game ever played, 39-0 over Kanaweola AC at Elmira, New York, November 21.

All three teams claimed the pro championship for the year, but the league president, Dave Berry, named the Stars the champions. Pitcher Rube Waddell was with the Athletics, and pitcher Christy Mathewson a fullback for Pittsburgh.

The first World Series of pro football, actually a five-team tournament, was played among a team made up of players from both the Athletics and the Phillies, but simply named New York; the New York Knickerbockers; the Syracuse AC; the Warlow AC; and the Orange (New Jersey) AC at New York's original Madison Square Garden. New York and Syracuse played the first indoor football game before 3,000, December 28. Syracuse, with Glen (Pop) Warner at guard, won 6-0 and went on to win the tournament.

1903
The Franklin (Pa.) Athletic Club won the second and last World Series of pro football over the Oreos AC of Asbury Park, New Jersey; the Watertown Red and Blacks; and the Orange AC.

Pro football was popularized in Ohio when the Massillon Tigers, a strong amateur team, hired four Pittsburgh pros to play in the season-ending game against Akron. At the same time, pro football declined in the Pittsburgh area, and the emphasis on the pro game moved west from Pennsylvania to Ohio.

1904
A field goal was changed from five points to four.

Ohio had at least seven pro teams, with Massillon winning the Ohio Independent Championship, that is, the pro title. Talk surfaced about forming a state-wide league to end spiraling salaries brought about by constant bidding for players and to write universal rules for the game. The feeble attempt to start the league failed.

Halfback Charles Follis signed a contract with the Shelby (Ohio) AC, making him the first known black pro football player.

1905
The Canton AC, later to become known as the Bulldogs, became a professional team. Massillon again won the Ohio League championship.

1906
The forward pass was legalized. The first authenticated pass completion in a pro game came on October 27, when George (Peggy) Parratt of Massillon threw a completion to Dan (Bullet) Riley in a victory over a combined Benwood-Moundsville team.

Arch-rivals Canton and Massillon, the two best pro teams in America, played twice, with Canton winning the first game but Massillon winning the second and the Ohio League championship. A betting scandal and the financial disaster wrought upon the two clubs by paying huge salaries caused a temporary decline in interest in pro football in the two cities and, somewhat, throughout Ohio.

1909
A field goal dropped from four points to three.

1912
A touchdown was increased from five points to six.

Jack Cusack revived a strong pro team in Canton.

1913
Jim Thorpe, a former football and track star at the Carlisle Indian School (Pa.) and a double gold medal winner at the 1912 Olympics in Stockholm, played for the Pine Village Pros in Indiana.

1915
Massillon again fielded a major team, reviving the old rivalry with Canton. Cusack signed Thorpe to play for Canton for $250 a game.

1916
With Thorpe and former Carlisle teammate Pete Calac starring, Canton went 9-0-1, won the Ohio League championship, and was acclaimed the pro football champion.

1917
Despite an upset by Massillon, Canton again won the Ohio League championship.

1919
Canton again won the Ohio League championship, despite the team having been turned over from Cusack to Ralph Hay. Thorpe and Calac were joined in the backfield by Joe Guyon.

Earl (Curly) Lambeau and George Calhoun organized the Green Bay Packers. Lambeau's employer at the Indian Packing Company provided $500 for equipment and allowed the team to use the company field for practices. The Packers went 10-1.

1920
Pro football was in a state of confusion due to three major problems: dramatically rising salaries; players continually jumping from one team to another following the highest offer; and the use of college players still enrolled in school. A league in which all the members would follow the same rules seemed the answer. An

organizational meeting, at which the Akron Pros, Canton Bulldogs, Cleveland Indians, and Dayton Triangles were represented, was held at the Jordan and Hupmobile auto showroom in Canton, Ohio, August 20. This meeting resulted in the formation of the American Professional Football Conference.

A second organizational meeting was held in Canton, September 17. The teams were from four states—Akron, Canton, Cleveland, and Dayton from Ohio; the Hammond Pros and Muncie Flyers from Indiana; the Rochester Jeffersons from New York; and the Rock Island Independents, Decatur Staleys, and Racine Cardinals from Illinois. The name of the league was changed to the American Professional Football Association. Hoping to capitalize on his fame, the members elected Thorpe president; Stanley Cofall of Cleveland was elected vice president. A membership fee of $100 per team was charged to give an appearance of respectability, but no team ever paid it. Scheduling was left up to the teams, and there were wide variations, both in the overall number of games played and in the number played against APFA member teams.

Four other teams—the Buffalo All-Americans, Chicago Tigers, Columbus Panhandles, and Detroit Heralds—joined the league sometime during the year. On September 26, the first game featuring an APFA team was played at Rock Island's Douglas Park. A crowd of 800 watched the Independents defeat the St. Paul Ideals 48-0. A week later, October 3, the first game matching two APFA teams was held. At Triangle Park, Dayton defeated Columbus 14-0, with Lou Partlow of Dayton scoring the first touchdown in a game between Association teams. The same day, Rock Island defeated Muncie 45-0.

By the beginning of December, most of the teams in the APFA had abandoned their hopes for a championship, and some of them, including the Chicago Tigers and the Detroit Heralds, had finished their seasons, disbanded, and had their franchises canceled by the Association. Four teams—Akron, Buffalo, Canton, and Decatur—still had championship as-pirations, but a series of late-season games among them left Akron as the only undefeated team in the Association. At one of these games, Akron sold tackle Bob Nash to Buffalo for $300 and five percent of the gate receipts—the first APFA player deal.

1921

At the league meeting in Akron, April 30, the championship of the 1920 season was awarded to the Akron Pros. The APFA was reorganized, with Joe Carr of the Columbus Panhandles named president and Carl Storck of Dayton secretary-treasurer. Carr moved the Association's headquarters to Columbus, drafted a league constitution and by-laws, gave teams territorial rights, restricted player movements, developed membership criteria for the franchises, and issued standings for the first time, so that the APFA would have a clear champion.

The Association's membership increased to 22 teams, including the Green Bay Packers, who were awarded to John Clair of the Acme Packing Company.

Thorpe moved from Canton to the Cleveland Indians, but he was hurt early in the season and played very little.

A.E. Staley turned the Decatur Staleys over to player-coach George Halas, who moved the team to Cubs Park in Chicago. Staley paid Halas $5,000 to keep the name Staleys for one more year. Halas made halfback Ed (Dutch) Sternaman his partner.

Player-coach Fritz Pollard of the Akron Pros became the first black head coach.

The Staleys claimed the APFA championship with a 9-1-1 record, as did Buffalo at 9-1-2. Carr ruled in favor of the Staleys, giving Halas his first championship.

1922

After admitting the use of players who had college eligibility remaining during the 1921 season, Clair and the Green Bay management withdrew from the APFA, January 28. Curly Lambeau promised to obey league rules and then used $50 of his own money to buy back the franchise. Bad weather and low attendance plagued the Packers, and Lambeau went broke, but local merchants arranged a $2,500 loan for the club. A public nonprofit corporation was set up to operate the team, with Lambeau as head coach and manager.

The American Professional Football Association changed its name to the National Football League, June 24. The Chicago Staleys became the Chicago Bears.

The NFL fielded 18 teams, including the new Oorang Indians of Marion, Ohio, an all-Indian team featuring Thorpe, Joe Guyon, and Pete Calac, and sponsored by the Oorang dog kennels.

Canton, led by player-coach Guy Chamberlin and tackles Link Lyman and Wilbur (Pete) Henry, emerged as the league's first true powerhouse, going 10-0-2.

1923

For the first time, all of the franchises considered to be part of the NFL fielded teams. Thorpe played his second and final season for the Oorang Indians. Against the Bears, Thorpe fumbled, and Halas picked up the ball and returned it 98 yards for a touchdown, a record that would last until 1972.

Canton had its second consecutive undefeated season, going 11-0-1 for the NFL title.

1924

The league had 18 franchises, including new ones in Kansas City, Kenosha, and Frankford, a section of Philadelphia. League champion Canton, successful on the field but not at the box office, was purchased by the owner of the Cleveland franchise, who kept the Canton franchise inactive, while using the best players for his Cleveland team, which he renamed the Bulldogs. Cleveland won the title with a 7-1-1 record.

1925

Five new franchises were admitted to the NFL—the New York Giants, who were awarded to Tim Mara and Billy Gibson for $500; the Detroit Panthers, featuring Jimmy Conzelman as owner, coach, and tailback; the Providence Steam Roller; a new Canton Bulldogs team; and the Pottsville Maroons, who had been perhaps the most successful independent pro team. The NFL established its first player limit, at 16 players.

Late in the season, the NFL made its greatest coup in gaining national recognition. Shortly after the University of Illinois season ended in November, All-America halfback Harold (Red) Grange signed a contract to play with the Chicago Bears. On Thanksgiving Day, a crowd of 36,000—the largest in pro football history—watched Grange and the Bears play the Chicago Cardinals to a scoreless tie at Wrigley Field. At the beginning of December, the Bears left on a barnstorming tour that saw them play eight games in 12 days, in St. Louis, Philadelphia, New York City, Washington, Boston, Pittsburgh, Detroit, and Chicago. A crowd of 73,000 watched the game against the Giants at the Polo Grounds, helping assure the future of the troubled NFL franchise in New York. The Bears then played nine more games in the South and West, including a game in Los Angeles, in which 75,000 fans watched them defeat the Los Angeles Tigers in the Los Angeles Memorial Coliseum.

Pottsville and the Chicago Cardinals were the top contenders for the league title, with Pottsville winning a late-season meeting 21-7. Pottsville scheduled a game against a team of former Notre Dame players for Shibe Park in Philadelphia. Frankford lodged a protest not only because the game was in Frankford's protected territory, but because it was being played the same day as a Yellow Jackets home game. Carr gave three different notices forbidding Pottsville to play the game, but Pottsville played anyway, December 12. That day, Carr fined the club, suspended it from all rights and privileges (including the right to play for the NFL championship), and re-turned its franchise to the league. The Cardinals, who ended the season with the best record in the league, were named the 1925 champions.

1926

Grange's manager, C.C. Pyle, told the Bears that Grange wouldn't play for them unless he was paid a five-figure salary and given one-third ownership of the team. The Bears refused. Pyle leased Yankee Stadium in New York City, then petitioned for an NFL franchise. After he was refused, he started the first American Football League. It lasted one season and included Grange's New York Yankees and eight other teams. The AFL champion Philadelphia Quakers played a December game against the New York Giants, seventh in the NFL, and the Giants won 31-0. At the end of the season, the AFL folded.

Halas pushed through a rule that prohibited any team from signing a player whose college class had not graduated.

The NFL grew to 22 teams, including the Duluth Eskimos, who signed All-America fullback Ernie Nevers of Stanford, giving the league a gate attraction to rival Grange. The 15-member Eskimos, dubbed the Iron Men of the North, played 29 exhibition and league games, 28 on the road, and Nevers played in all but 29 minutes of them.

Frankford edged the Bears for the championship, despite Halas having obtained John (Paddy) Driscoll from the Cardinals. On December 4, the Yellow Jackets scored in the final two minutes to defeat the Bears 7-6 and move ahead of them in the standings.

1927

At a special meeting in Cleveland, April 23, Carr decided to secure the NFL's future by eliminating the financially weaker teams and consolidating the quality players onto a limited number of more successful teams. The new-look NFL dropped to 12 teams, and the center of gravity of the league left the Midwest, where the NFL had started, and began to emerge in the large cities of the East. One of the new teams was Grange's New York Yankees, but Grange suffered a knee injury and the Yankees finished in the middle of the pack. The NFL championship was won by the cross-town rival New York Giants, who posted 10 shutouts in 13 games.

1928

Grange and Nevers both retired from pro football, and Duluth disbanded, as the NFL was reduced to only 10 teams. The Providence Steam Roller of Jimmy Conzelman and Pearce Johnson won the championship, playing in the Cycledrome, a 10,000-seat oval that had been built for bicycle races.

1929

Chris O'Brien sold the Chicago Cardinals to David Jones, July 27.

The NFL added a fourth official, the field judge, July 28.

Grange and Nevers returned to the NFL. Nevers scored six rushing touchdowns and four extra points as the Cardinals beat Grange's Bears 40-6, November 28. The 40 points set a record that remains the NFL's oldest.

Providence became the first NFL team to host a game at night under floodlights, against the Cardinals, November 6.

The Packers added back Johnny Blood (McNally), tackle Cal Hubbard, and guard Mike Michalske, and won their first NFL championship, edging the Giants, who featured quarterback Benny Friedman.

1930

Dayton, the last of the NFL's original franchises, was purchased by William B. Dwyer and John C. Depler, moved to Brooklyn, and renamed the Dodgers. The Portsmouth, Ohio, Spartans entered the league.

The Packers edged the Giants for the title, but the most improved team was the Bears. Halas retired as a player and replaced himself as coach of the Bears with Ralph Jones, who refined the T-formation by introducing wide ends and a halfback in motion. Jones also introduced rookie All-America fullback-tackle Bronko Nagurski.

The Giants defeated a team of former Notre Dame players coached by Knute Rockne 22-0 before 55,000 at the Polo Grounds, December 14. The proceeds went to the New York Unemployment Fund to help those suffering because of the Great Depression, and the easy victory helped give the NFL credibility with the press and the public.

1931

The NFL decreased to 10 teams, and halfway through the season the Frankford franchise folded. Carr fined the Bears, Packers, and Portsmouth $1,000 each for using players whose college classes had not graduated.

The Packers won an unprecedented third consecutive title, beating out the Spartans, who were led by rookie backs Earl (Dutch) Clark and Glenn Presnell.

1932

George Preston Marshall, Vincent Bendix, Jay O'Brien, and M. Dorland Doyle were awarded a franchise for Boston, July 9. Despite the presence of two rookies—halfback Cliff Battles and tackle Glen (Turk) Edwards—the new team, named the Braves, lost money and Marshall was left as the sole owner at the end of the year.

NFL membership dropped to eight teams, the lowest in history. Official statistics were kept for the first time. The Bears and the Spartans finished the season in the first-ever tie for first place. After the season finale, the league office arranged for an additional regular-season game to determine the league champion. The game was moved indoors to Chicago Stadium because of bitter cold and heavy snow. The arena allowed only an 80-yard field that came right to the walls. The goal posts were moved from the end lines to the goal lines and, for safety, inbounds lines or hashmarks where the ball would be put in play were drawn 10 yards from the walls that butted against the sidelines. The Bears won 9-0, December 18, scoring the winning touchdown on a two-yard pass from Nagurski to Grange. The Spartans claimed Nagurski's pass was thrown from less than five yards behind the line of scrimmage, violating the existing passing rule, but the play stood.

1933

The NFL, which long had followed the rules of college football, made a number of significant changes from the college game for the first time and began to develop rules serving its needs and the style of play it preferred. The innovations from the 1932 championship game—inbounds line or hashmarks and goal posts on the goal lines—were adopted. Also the forward pass was legalized from anywhere behind the line of scrimmage, February 25.

Marshall and Halas pushed through a proposal that divided the NFL into two divisions, with the winners to meet in an annual championship game, July 8.

Three new franchises joined the league—the Pittsburgh Pirates of Art Rooney, the Philadelphia Eagles of Bert Bell and Lud Wray, and the Cincinnati Reds. The Staten Island Stapletons suspended operations for a year, but never returned to the league.

Halas bought out Sternaman, became sole owner of the Bears, and reinstated himself as head coach. Marshall changed the name of the Boston Braves to the Redskins. David Jones sold the Chicago Cardinals to Charles W. Bidwill.

In the first NFL Championship Game scheduled before the season, the Western Division champion Bears defeated the Eastern Division champion Giants 23-21 at Wrigley Field, December 17.

1934

G.A. (Dick) Richards purchased the Portsmouth Spartans, moved them to Detroit, and renamed them the Lions.

Professional football gained new prestige when the Bears were matched against the best college football players in the first Chicago College All-Star Game, August 31. The game ended in a scoreless tie before 79,432 at Soldier Field.

The Cincinnati Reds lost their first eight games, then were suspended from the league for defaulting on payments. The St. Louis Gunners, an independent team, joined the NFL by buying the Cincinnati franchise and went 1-2 the last three weeks.

Rookie Beattie Feathers of the Bears became the NFL's first 1,000-yard rusher, gaining 1,004 on 101 carries. The Thanksgiving Day game between the Bears and the Lions became the first NFL game broadcast nationally, with Graham McNamee the announcer for NBC radio.

In the championship game, on an extremely cold and icy day at the Polo Grounds, the Giants trailed the Bears 13-3 in the third quarter before changing to basketball shoes for better footing. The Giants won 30-13 in what has come to be known as the Sneakers Game, December 9.

The player waiver rule was adopted, December 10.

1935

The NFL adopted Bert Bell's proposal to hold an annual draft of college players, to begin in 1936, with teams selecting in an inverse order of finish, May 19. The inbounds line or hashmarks were moved nearer the center of the field, 15 yards from the sidelines.

All-America end Don Hutson of Alabama joined Green Bay. The Lions defeated the Giants 26-7 in the NFL Championship Game, December 15.

1936

There were no franchise transactions for the first year since the formation of the NFL. It also was the first year in which all member teams played the same number of games.

The Eagles made University of Chicago halfback and Heisman Trophy winner Jay Berwanger the first player ever selected in the NFL draft, February 8. The Eagles traded his rights to the Bears, but Berwanger never played pro football. The first player selected to actually sign was the number-two pick, Riley Smith of Alabama, who was selected by Boston.

A rival league was formed, and it became the second to call itself the American Football League. The Boston Shamrocks were its champions.

Because of poor attendance, Marshall, the owner of the host team, moved the Championship Game from Boston to the Polo Grounds in New York. Green Bay defeated the Redskins 21-6, December 13.

1937

Homer Marshman was granted a Cleveland franchise, named the Rams, February 12. Marshall moved the Redskins to Washington, D.C., February 13. The Redskins signed TCU All-America tailback Sammy Baugh, who led them to a 28-21 victory over the Bears in the NFL Championship Game, December 12.

The Los Angeles Bulldogs had an 8-0 record to win the AFL title, but then the 2-year-old league folded.

1938

At the suggestion of Halas, Hugh (Shorty) Ray became a technical advisor on rules and officiating to the NFL. A new rule called for a 15-yard penalty for roughing the passer.

Rookie Byron (Whizzer) White of the Pittsburgh Pirates led the NFL in rushing. The Giants defeated the Packers 23-17 for the NFL title, December 11.

Marshall, *Los Angeles Times* sports editor Bill Henry, and promoter Tom Gallery established the Pro Bowl game between the NFL champion and a team of pro all-stars.

1939

The New York Giants defeated the Pro All-Stars 13-10 in the first Pro Bowl, at Wrigley Field, Los Angeles, January 15.

Carr, NFL president since 1921, died in Columbus, May 20. Carl Storck was named acting president, May 25.

An NFL game was televised for the first time when NBC broadcast the Brooklyn Dodgers-Philadelphia Eagles game from Ebbets Field to the approximately 1,000 sets then in New York, October 22.

Green Bay defeated New York 27-0 in the NFL Championship Game, December 10 at Milwaukee. NFL attendance exceeded 1 million in a season for the first time, reaching 1,071,200.

1940

A six-team rival league, the third to call itself the American Football League, was formed, and the Columbus Bullies won its championship.

Halas' Bears, with additional coaching by Clark Shaughnessy of Stanford, defeated the Redskins 73-0 in the NFL Championship Game, December 8. The game, which was the most decisive victory in NFL history, popularized the Bears' T-formation with a man-in-motion. It was the first championship carried on network radio, broadcast by Red Barber to 120 stations of the Mutual Broadcasting System, which paid $2,500 for the rights.

Art Rooney sold the Pittsburgh franchise to Alexis Thompson, December 9, then bought part interest in the Philadelphia Eagles.

Bell and Rooney traded the Eagles to Thompson for the Pirates, then re-named their new team the Steelers.

1941

Elmer Layden was named the first Commissioner of the NFL, March 1; Storck, the acting president, resigned, April 5. NFL headquarters were moved to Chicago.

Homer Marshman sold the Rams to Daniel F. Reeves and Fred Levy, Jr.

The league by-laws were revised to provide for playoffs in case there were ties in division races, and sudden-death overtimes in case a playoff game was tied after four quarters. An official *NFL Record Manual* was published for the first time.

Columbus again won the championship of the AFL, but the two-year-old league then folded.

The Bears and the Packers finished in a tie for the Western Division championship, setting up the first divisional playoff game in league history. The Bears won 33-14, then defeated the Giants 37-9 for the NFL championship, December 21.

1942

Players departing for service in World War II depleted the rosters of NFL teams. Halas left the Bears in midseason to join the Navy, and Luke Johnsos and Heartley (Hunk) Anderson served as co-coaches as the Bears went 11-0 in the regular season. The Redskins defeated the Bears 14-6 in the NFL Championship Game, December 13.

1943

The Cleveland Rams, with co-owners Reeves and Levy in the service, were granted permission to suspend operations for one season, April 6. Levy transferred his stock in the team to Reeves, April 16.

The NFL adopted free substitution, April 7. The league also made the wearing of helmets mandatory and approved a 10-game schedule for all teams.

Philadelphia and Pittsburgh were granted permission to merge for one season, June 19. The team, known as Phil-Pitt (and called the Steagles by fans), divided home games between the two cities, and Earle (Greasy) Neale of Philadelphia and Walt Kiesling of Pittsburgh served as co-coaches. The merger automatically dissolved the last day of the season, December 5.

Ted Collins was granted a franchise for Boston, to become active in 1944.

Sammy Baugh led the league in passing, punting, and interceptions. He led the Redskins to a tie with the Giants for the Eastern Division title, and then to a 28-0 victory in a divisional playoff game. The Bears beat the Redskins 41-21 in the NFL Championship Game, December 26.

1944

Collins, who had wanted a franchise in Yankee Stadium in New York, named his new team in Boston the Yanks. Cleveland resumed operations. The Brooklyn Dodgers changed their name to the Tigers.

Coaching from the bench was legalized, April 20.

The Cardinals and the Steelers were granted permission to merge for one year under the name Card-Pitt, April 21. Phil Handler of the Cardinals and Walt Kiesling of the Steelers served as co-coaches. The merger automatically dissolved the last day of the season, December 3.

In the NFL Championship Game, Green Bay defeated the New York Giants 14-7, December 17.

1945
The inbounds lines or hashmarks were moved from 15 yards away from the sidelines to nearer the center of the field—20 yards from the sidelines.

Brooklyn and Boston merged into a team that played home games in both cities and was known simply as The Yanks. The team was coached by former Boston head coach Herb Kopf. In December, the Brooklyn franchise withdrew from the NFL to join the new All-America Football Conference; all the players on its active and reserve lists were assigned to The Yanks, who once again became the Boston Yanks.

Halas rejoined the Bears late in the season after service with the U.S. Navy. Although Halas took over much of the coaching duties, Anderson and Johnsos remained the coaches of record throughout the season.

Steve Van Buren of Philadelphia led the NFL in rushing, kickoff returns, and scoring.

After the Japanese surrendered ending World War II, a count showed that the NFL service roster, limited to men who had played in league games, totaled 638, 21 of whom had died in action.

Rookie quarterback Bob Waterfield led Cleveland to a 15-14 victory over Washington in the NFL Championship Game, December 16.

1946
The contract of Commissioner Layden was not renewed, and Bert Bell, the co-owner of the Steelers, replaced him, January 11. Bell moved the league headquarters from Chicago to the Philadelphia suburb of Bala-Cynwyd.

Free substitution was withdrawn and substitutions were limited to no more than three men at a time. Forward passes were made automatically incomplete upon striking the goal posts, January 11.

The NFL took on a truly national appearance for the first time when Reeves was granted permission by the league to move his NFL champion Rams to Los Angeles.

Halfback Kenny Washington (March 21) and end Woody Strode (May 7) signed with the Los Angeles Rams to become the first African-Americans to play in the NFL in the modern era. Guard Bill Willis (August 6) and running back Marion Motley (August 9) joined the AAFC with the Cleveland Browns.

The rival All-America Football Conference began play with eight teams. The Cleveland Browns, coached by Paul Brown, won the AAFC's first championship, defeating the New York Yankees 14-9.

Bill Dudley of the Steelers led the NFL in rushing, interceptions, and punt returns, and won the league's most valuable player award.

Backs Frank Filchock and Merle Hapes of the Giants were questioned about an attempt by a New York man to fix the championship game with the Bears. Bell suspended Hapes but allowed Filchock to play; he played well, but Chicago won 24-14, December 15.

1947
The NFL added a fifth official, the back judge.

A bonus choice was made for the first time in the NFL draft. One team each year would select the special choice before the first round began. The Chicago Bears won a lottery and the rights to the first choice and drafted back Bob Fenimore of Oklahoma A&M.

The Cleveland Browns again won the AAFC title, defeating the New York Yankees 14-3.

Charles Bidwill, Sr., owner of the Cardinals, died April 19, but his wife and sons retained ownership of the team. On December 28, the Cardinals won the NFL Championship Game 28-21 over the Philadelphia Eagles, who had beaten Pittsburgh 21-0 in a playoff.

1948
Plastic helmets were prohibited. A flexible artificial tee was permitted at the kickoff. Officials other than the referee were equipped with whistles, not horns, January 14.

Fred Mandel sold the Detroit Lions to a syndicate headed by D. Lyle Fife, January 15.

Halfback Fred Gehrke of the Los Angeles Rams painted horns on the Rams' helmets, the first modern helmet emblems in pro football.

The Cleveland Browns won their third straight championship in the AAFC, going 14-0 and then defeating the Buffalo Bills 49-7.

In a blizzard, the Eagles defeated the Cardinals 7-0 in the NFL Championship Game, December 19.

1949
Alexis Thompson sold the champion Eagles to a syndicate headed by James P. Clark, January 15. The Boston Yanks became the New York Bulldogs, sharing the Polo Grounds with the Giants.

Free substitution was adopted for one year, January 20.

The NFL had two 1,000-yard rushers in the same season for the first time—Steve Van Buren of Philadelphia and Tony Canadeo of Green Bay.

The AAFC played its season with a one-division, seven-team format. On December 9, Bell announced a merger agreement in which three AAFC franchises—Cleveland, San Francisco, and Baltimore—would join the NFL in 1950. The Browns won their fourth consecutive AAFC title, defeating the 49ers 21-7, December 11.

In a heavy rain, the Eagles defeated the Rams 14-0 in the NFL Championship Game, December 18.

1950
Unlimited free substitution was restored, opening the way for the era of two platoons and specialization in pro football, January 20.

Curly Lambeau, founder of the franchise and Green Bay's head coach since 1921, resigned under fire, February 1.

The name National Football League was restored after about three months as the National-American Football League. The American and National conferences were created to replace the Eastern and Western divisions, March 3.

The New York Bulldogs became the Yanks and divided the players of the former AAFC Yankees with the Giants. A special allocation draft was held in which the 13 teams drafted the remaining AAFC players, with special consideration for Baltimore, which received 15 choices compared to 10 for other teams.

The Los Angeles Rams became the first NFL team to have all of its games—both home and away—televised. The Washington Redskins followed the Rams in arranging to televise their games; other teams made deals to put selected games on television.

In the first game of the season, former AAFC champion Cleveland defeated NFL champion Philadelphia 35-10. For the first time, deadlocks occurred in both conferences and playoffs were necessary. The Browns defeated the Giants in the American and the Rams defeated the Bears in the National. Cleveland defeated Los Angeles 30-28 in the NFL Championship Game, December 24.

1951
The Pro Bowl game, dormant since 1942, was revived under a new format matching the all-stars of each conference at the Los Angeles Memorial Coliseum. The American Conference defeated the National Conference 28-27, January 14.

Abraham Watner returned the Baltimore franchise and its player contracts back to the NFL for $50,000. Baltimore's former players were made available for drafting at the same time as college players, January 18.

A rule was passed that no tackle, guard, or center would be eligible to catch a forward pass, January 18.

The Rams reversed their television policy and televised only road games.

The NFL Championship Game was televised coast-to-coast for the first time, December 23. The DuMont Network paid $75,000 for the rights to the game, in which the Rams defeated the Browns 24-17.

1952
Ted Collins sold the New York Yanks' franchise back to the NFL, January 19. A new fran-

chise was awarded to a group in Dallas after it purchased the assets of the Yanks, January 24. The new Texans went 1-11, with the owners turning the franchise back to the league in midseason. For the last five games of the season, the commissioner's office operated the Texans as a road team, using Hershey, Pennsylvania, as a home base. At the end of the season the franchise was canceled, the last time an NFL team failed.

The Pittsburgh Steelers abandoned the Single-Wing for the T-formation, the last pro team to do so.

The Detroit Lions won their first NFL championship in 17 years, defeating the Browns 17-7 in the title game, December 28.

1953

A Baltimore group headed by Carroll Rosenbloom was granted a franchise and was awarded the holdings of the defunct Dallas organization, January 23. The team, named the Colts, put together the largest trade in league history, acquiring 10 players from Cleveland in exchange for five.

The names of the American and National conferences were changed to the Eastern and Western conferences, January 24.

Jim Thorpe died, March 28.

Mickey McBride, founder of the Cleveland Browns, sold the franchise to a syndicate headed by Dave R. Jones, June 10.

The NFL policy of blacking out home games was upheld by Judge Allan K. Grim of the U.S. District Court in Philadelphia, November 12.

The Lions again defeated the Browns in the NFL Championship Game, winning 17-16, December 27.

1954

The Canadian Football League began a series of raids on NFL teams, signing quarterback Eddie LeBaron and defensive end Gene Brito of Washington and defensive tackle Arnie Weinmeister of the Giants, among others.

Fullback Joe Perry of the 49ers became the first player in league history to gain 1,000 yards rushing in consecutive seasons.

Cleveland defeated Detroit 56-10 in the NFL Championship Game, December 26.

1955

The sudden-death overtime rule was used for the first time in a preseason game between the Rams and Giants at Portland, Oregon, August 28. The Rams won 23-17 three minutes into overtime.

A rule change declared the ball dead immediately if the ball carrier touched the ground with any part of his body except his hands or feet while in the grasp of an opponent.

The Baltimore Colts made an 80-cent phone call to Johnny Unitas and signed him as a free agent. Another quarterback, Otto Graham, played his last game as the Browns defeated the Rams 38-14 in the NFL Championship Game, December 26. Graham had quarterbacked the Browns to 10 championship-game appearances in 10 years.

NBC replaced DuMont as the network for the title game, paying a rights fee of $100,000.

1956

The NFL Players Association was founded.

Grabbing an opponent's facemask (other than the ball carrier) was made illegal. Using radio receivers to communicate with players on the field was prohibited. A natural leather ball with white end stripes replaced the white ball with black stripes for night games.

The Giants moved from the Polo Grounds to Yankee Stadium.

Halas retired as coach of the Bears, and was replaced by Paddy Driscoll.

CBS became the first network to broadcast some NFL regular-season games to selected television markets across the nation.

The Giants routed the Bears 47-7 in the NFL Championship Game, December 30.

1957

Pete Rozelle was named general manager of the Rams. Anthony J. Morabito, founder and co-owner of the 49ers, died of a heart attack during a game against the Bears at Kezar Stadium, October 28. An NFL-record crowd of 102,368 saw the 49ers-Rams game at the Los Angeles Memorial Coliseum, November 10.

The Lions came from 20 points down to post a 31-27 playoff victory over the 49ers, December 22. Detroit defeated Cleveland 59-14 in the NFL Championship Game, December 29.

1958

The bonus selection in the draft was eliminated, January 29. The last selection was quarterback King Hill of Rice by the Chicago Cardinals.

Halas reinstated himself as coach of the Bears.

Jim Brown of Cleveland gained an NFL-record 1,527 yards rushing. In a divisional playoff game, the Giants held Brown to eight yards and defeated Cleveland 10-0.

Baltimore, coached by Weeb Ewbank, defeated the Giants 23-17 in the first sudden-death overtime in an NFL Championship Game, December 28. The game ended when Colts fullback Alan Ameche scored on a one-yard touchdown run after 8:15 of overtime.

1959

Vince Lombardi was named head coach of the Green Bay Packers, January 28. Tim Mara, the co-founder of the Giants, died, February 17.

Lamar Hunt of Dallas announced his intentions to form a second pro football league. The first meeting was held in Chicago, August 14, and consisted of Hunt representing Dallas; Bob Howsam, Denver; K.S. (Bud) Adams, Houston; Barron Hilton, Los Angeles; Max Winter and Bill Boyer, Minneapolis; and Harry Wismer, New York City. They made plans to begin play in 1960.

The new league was named the American Football League, August 22. Buffalo, owned by Ralph Wilson, became the seventh franchise, October 28. Boston, owned by William H. Sullivan, became the eighth team, November 22. The first AFL draft, lasting 33 rounds, was held, November 22. Joe Foss was named AFL Commissioner, November 30. An additional draft of 20 rounds was held by the AFL, December 2.

NFL Commissioner Bert Bell died of a heart attack suffered at Franklin Field, Philadelphia, during the last two minutes of a game between the Eagles and the Steelers, October 11. Treasurer Austin Gunsel was named president in the office of the commissioner, October 14.

The Colts again defeated the Giants in the NFL Championship Game, 31-16, December 27.

1960

Pete Rozelle was elected NFL Commissioner as a compromise choice on the twenty-third ballot, January 26. Rozelle moved the league offices to New York City.

Hunt was elected AFL president for 1960, January 26. Minneapolis withdrew from the AFL, January 27, and the same ownership was given an NFL franchise for Minnesota (to start in 1961), January 28. Dallas received an NFL franchise for 1960, January 28. Oakland received an AFL franchise, January 30.

The AFL adopted the two-point option on points after touchdown, January 28. A no-tampering verbal pact, relative to players' contracts, was agreed to between the NFL and AFL, February 9.

The NFL owners voted to allow the transfer of the Chicago Cardinals to St. Louis, March 13.

The AFL signed a five-year television contract with ABC, June 9.

The Boston Patriots defeated the Buffalo Bills 28-7 before 16,000 at Buffalo in the first AFL preseason game, July 30. The Denver Broncos defeated the Patriots 13-10 before 21,597 at Boston in the first AFL regular-season game, September 9.

Philadelphia defeated Green Bay 17-13 in the NFL Championship Game, December 26.

1961

The Houston Oilers defeated the Los Angeles Chargers 24-16 before 32,183 in the first AFL Championship Game, January 1.

Detroit defeated Cleveland 17-16 in the first Playoff Bowl, or Bert Bell Benefit Bowl, between second-place teams in each conference in Miami, January 7.

End Willard Dewveall of the Bears played out his option and joined the Oilers, becoming the first player to play out his contract and jump from the NFL to the AFL, January 14.

Ed McGah, Wayne Valley, and Robert Osborne bought out their partners in the ownership of the Raiders, January 17. The Chargers were transferred to San Diego, February 10. Dave R. Jones sold the Browns to a group headed by Arthur B. Modell, March 22. The Howsam brothers sold the Broncos to a group headed by Calvin Kunz and Gerry Phipps, May 26.

NBC was awarded a two-year contract for radio and television rights to the NFL Championship Game for $615,000 annually, $300,000 of which was to go directly into the NFL Player Benefit Plan, April 5.

Canton, Ohio, where the league that became the NFL was formed in 1920, was chosen as the site of the Pro Football Hall of Fame, April 27. Dick McCann, a former Redskins executive, was named executive director.

A bill legalizing single-network television contracts by professional sports leagues was introduced in Congress by Representative Emanuel Celler. It passed the House and Senate and was signed into law by President John F. Kennedy, September 30.

Houston defeated San Diego 10-3 for the AFL championship, December 24. Green Bay won its first NFL championship since 1944, defeating the New York Giants 37-0, December 31.

1962

The Western Division defeated the Eastern Division 47-27 in the first AFL All-Star Game, played before 20,973 in San Diego, January 7.

Both leagues prohibited grabbing any player's facemask. The AFL voted to make the scoreboard clock the official timer of the game.

The NFL entered into a single-network agreement with CBS for telecasting all regular-season games for $4.65 million annually, January 10.

Judge Roszel Thompson of the U.S. District Court in Baltimore ruled against the AFL in its antitrust suit against the NFL, May 21. The AFL had charged the NFL with monopoly and conspiracy in areas of expansion, television, and player signings. The case lasted two and a half years, the trial two months.

McGah and Valley acquired controlling interest in the Raiders, May 24. The AFL assumed financial responsibility for the New York Titans, November 8. With Commissioner Rozelle as referee, Daniel F. Reeves regained the ownership of the Rams, outbidding his partners in sealed-envelope bidding for the team, November 27.

The Dallas Texans defeated the Oilers 20-17 for the AFL championship at Houston after 17 minutes, 54 seconds of overtime on a 25-yard field goal by Tommy Brooker, December 23. The game lasted a record 77 minutes, 54 seconds.

Judge Edward Weinfeld of the U.S. District Court in New York City upheld the legality of the NFL's television blackout within a 75-mile radius of home games and denied an injunction that would have forced the championship game between the Giants and the Packers to be televised in the New York City area, December 28. The Packers beat the Giants 16-7 for the NFL title, December 30.

1963

The Dallas Texans transferred to Kansas City, becoming the Chiefs, February 8. The New York Titans were sold to a five-man syndicate headed by David (Sonny) Werblin, March 28. Weeb Ewbank became the Titans' new head coach and the team's name was changed to the Jets, April 15. They began play in the Polo Grounds.

NFL Properties, Inc., was founded to serve as the licensing arm of the NFL.

Rozelle indefinitely suspended Green Bay halfback Paul Hornung and Detroit defensive tackle Alex Karras for placing bets on their own teams and on other NFL games; he also fined five other Detroit players $2,000 each for betting on one game in which they did not participate, and the Detroit Lions Football Company $2,000 on each of two counts for failure to report information promptly and for lack of sideline supervision.

Paul Brown, head coach of the Browns since their inception, was fired and replaced by Blanton Collier. Don Shula replaced Weeb Ewbank as head coach of the Colts.

The AFL allowed the Jets and Raiders to select players from other franchises in hopes of giving the league more competitive balance, May 11.

NBC was awarded exclusive network broadcasting rights for the 1963 AFL Championship Game for $926,000, May 23.

The Pro Football Hall of Fame was dedicated at Canton, Ohio, September 7.

The U.S. Fourth Circuit Court of Appeals reaffirmed the lower court's finding for the NFL in the $10-million suit brought by the AFL, ending three and a half years of litigation, November 21.

Jim Brown of Cleveland rushed for an NFL single-season record 1,863 yards.

Boston defeated Buffalo 26-8 in the first divisional playoff game in AFL history, December 28.

The Bears defeated the Giants 14-10 in the NFL Championship Game, a record sixth and last title for Halas in his thirty-sixth season as the Bears' coach, December 29.

1964

The Chargers defeated the Patriots 51-10 in the AFL Championship Game, January 5.

William Clay Ford, the Lions' president since 1961, purchased the team, January 10. A group representing the late James P. Clark sold the Eagles to a group headed by Jerry Wolman, January 21. Carroll Rosenbloom, the majority owner of the Colts since 1953, acquired complete ownership of the team, January 23.

The AFL signed a five-year, $36-million television contract with NBC to begin with the 1965 season, January 29.

Hornung and Karras were reinstated by Rozelle, March 16.

CBS submitted the winning bid of $14.1 million per year for the NFL regular-season television rights for 1964 and 1965, January 24. CBS acquired the rights to the championship games for 1964 and 1965 for $1.8 million per game, April 17.

Pete Gogolak of Cornell signed a contract with Buffalo, becoming the first soccer-style kicker in pro football.

Buffalo defeated San Diego 20-7 in the AFL Championship Game, December 26. Cleveland defeated Baltimore 27-0 in the NFL Championship Game, December 27.

1965

The NFL teams pledged not to sign college seniors until completion of all their games, including bowl games, and empowered the Commissioner to discipline the clubs up to as much as the loss of an entire draft list for a violation of the pledge, February 15.

The NFL added a sixth official, the line judge, February 19. The color of the officials' penalty flags was changed from white to bright gold, April 5.

Commissioner Rozelle negotiated an agreement on behalf of the NFL clubs to purchase Ed Sabol's Blair Motion Pictures, which was renamed NFL Films, April.

Atlanta was awarded an NFL franchise for 1966, with Rankin Smith, Sr., as owner, June 30. Miami was awarded an AFL franchise for 1966, with Joe Robbie and Danny Thomas as owners, August 16.

Field Judge Burl Toler became the first black official in NFL history, September 19.

According to a Harris survey, sports fans chose professional football (41 percent) as their favorite sport, overtaking baseball (38 percent) for the first time, October.

Green Bay defeated Baltimore 13-10 in sudden-death overtime in a Western Conference playoff game. Don Chandler kicked a 25-yard field goal for the Packers after 13 minutes, 39 seconds of overtime, December 26. The Packers then defeated the Browns 23-12 in the NFL Championship Game, January 2.

In the AFL Championship Game, the Bills defeated the Chargers, 23-0, December 26.

CBS acquired the rights to

the NFL regular-season games in 1966 and 1967, with an option for 1968, for $18.8 million per year, December 29.

1966
The AFL-NFL war reached its peak, as the leagues spent a combined $7 million to sign their 1966 draft choices. The NFL signed 75 percent of its 232 draftees, the AFL 46 percent of its 181. Of the 111 common draft choices, 79 signed with the NFL, 28 with the AFL, and 4 went unsigned.

Buddy Young became the first African-American to work in the league office when Commissioner Rozelle named him director of player relations, February 1.

The rights to the 1966 and 1967 NFL Championship Games were sold to CBS for $2 million per game, February 14.

Foss resigned as AFL Commissioner, April 7. Al Davis, the head coach and general manager of the Raiders, was named to replace him, April 8.

Goal posts offset from the goal line, painted bright yellow, and with uprights 20 feet above the cross-bar were made standard in the NFL, May 16.

A series of secret meetings regarding a possible AFL-NFL merger were held in the spring between Hunt of Kansas City and Tex Schramm of Dallas. Rozelle announced the merger, June 8. Under the agreement, the two leagues would combine to form an expanded league with 24 teams, to be increased to 26 in 1968 and to 28 by 1970 or soon thereafter. All existing franchises would be retained, and no franchises would be transferred outside their metropolitan areas. While maintaining separate schedules through 1969, the leagues agreed to play an annual AFL-NFL World Championship Game beginning in January, 1967, and to hold a combined draft, also beginning in 1967. Preseason games would be held between teams of each league starting in 1967. Official regular-season play would start in 1970 when the two leagues would officially merge to form one league with two conferences. Rozelle was named Commissioner of the expanded league setup.

Davis rejoined the Raiders, and Milt Woodard was named president of the AFL, July 25.

The St. Louis Cardinals moved into newly constructed Busch Memorial Stadium.

Barron Hilton sold the Chargers to a group headed by Eugene Klein and Sam Schulman, August 25.

Congress approved the AFL-NFL merger, passing legislation exempting the agreement itself from antitrust action, October 21.

New Orleans was awarded an NFL franchise to begin play in 1967, November 1. John Mecom, Jr., of Houston was designated majority stockholder and president of the franchise, December 15.

The NFL was realigned for the 1967-69 seasons into the Capitol and Century Divisions in the Eastern Conference and the Central and Coastal Divisions in the Western Conference, December 2. New Orleans and the New York Giants agreed to switch divisions in 1968 and return to the 1967 alignment in 1969.

The rights to the Super Bowl for four years were sold to CBS and NBC for $9.5 million, December 13.

1967
Green Bay earned the right to represent the NFL in the first AFL-NFL World Championship Game by defeating Dallas 34-27, January 1. The same day, Kansas City defeated Buffalo 31-7 to represent the AFL. The Packers defeated the Chiefs 35-10 before 61,946 fans at the Los Angeles Memorial Coliseum in the first game between AFL and NFL teams, January 15. The winning players' share for the Packers was $15,000 each, and the losing players' share for the Chiefs was $7,500 each. The game was televised by both CBS and NBC.

The "sling-shot" goal post and a six-foot-wide border around the field were made standard in the NFL, February 22.

Baltimore made Bubba Smith, a Michigan State defensive lineman, the first choice in the first combined AFL-NFL draft, March 14.

The AFL awarded a franchise to begin play in 1968 to Cincinnati, May 23. A group with Paul Brown as part owner, general manager, and head coach, was awarded the Cincinnati franchise, September 27.

Arthur B. Modell, the president of the Cleveland Browns, was elected president of the NFL, May 28.

Defensive back Emlen Tunnell of the New York Giants became the first black player to enter the Pro Football Hall of Fame, August 5.

An AFL team defeated an NFL team for the first time, when Denver beat Detroit 13-7 in a preseason game, August 5.

Green Bay defeated Dallas 21-17 for the NFL championship on a last-minute 1-yard quarterback sneak by Bart Starr in 13-below-zero temperature at Green Bay, December 31. The same day, Oakland defeated Houston 40-7 for the AFL championship.

1968
Green Bay defeated Oakland 33-14 in Super Bowl II at Miami, January 14. The game had the first $3-million gate in pro football history.

Vince Lombardi resigned as head coach of the Packers, but remained as general manager, January 28.

Werblin sold his shares in the Jets to his partners Don Lillis, Leon Hess, Townsend Martin, and Phil Iselin, May 21. Lillis assumed the presidency of the club, but then died July 23. Iselin was appointed president, August 6.

Halas retired for the fourth and last time as head coach of the Bears, May 27.

The Oilers left Rice Stadium for the Astrodome and became the first NFL team to play its home games in a domed stadium.

The movie *Heidi* became a footnote in sports history when NBC didn't show the last 50 seconds of the Jets-Raiders game in order to permit the children's special to begin on time. The Raiders scored two touchdowns in the last 42 seconds to win 43-32, November 17.

Ewbank became the first coach to win titles in both the NFL and AFL when his Jets defeated the Raiders 27-23 for the AFL championship, December 29. The same day, Baltimore defeated Cleveland 34-0.

1969
The AFL established a playoff format for the 1969 season, with the winner in one division playing the runner-up in the other, January 11.

An AFL team won the Super Bowl for the first time, as the Jets defeated the Colts 16-7 at Miami, January 12 in Super Bowl III. The title Super Bowl was recognized by the NFL for the first time.

Vince Lombardi became part owner, executive vice-president, and head coach of the Washington Redskins, February 7.

Wolman sold the Eagles to Leonard Tose, May 1.

Baltimore, Cleveland, and Pittsburgh agreed to join the AFL teams to form the 13-team American Football Conference of the NFL in 1970, May 17. The NFL also agreed on a playoff format that would include one "wild-card" team per conference—the second-place team with the best record.

The NFL announced a three-year agreement with ABC to televise *Monday Night Football*. The new series makes the NFL the first league with a regular series of national telecasts in prime time, May 26.

George Preston Marshall, president emeritus of the Redskins, died at 72, August 9.

The NFL marked its fiftieth year by the wearing of a special patch by each of the 16 teams.

1970
Kansas City defeated Minnesota 23-7 in Super Bowl IV at New Orleans, January 11. The gross receipts of approximately $3.8 million were the largest ever for a one-day sports event.

Four-year television contracts, under which CBS would televise all NFC games and NBC all AFC games (except Monday night games) and the two would divide televising the Super Bowl and AFC-NFC Pro Bowl games, were announced, January 26.

Art Modell resigned as president of the NFL, March 12. Milt Woodard resigned as president of the AFL, March

13. Lamar Hunt was elected president of the AFC and George Halas was elected president of the NFC, March 19.

The merged 26-team league adopted rules changes putting names on the backs of players' jerseys, making a point after touchdown worth only one point, and making the scoreboard clock the official timing device of the game, March 18.

The Players Negotiating Committee and the NFL Players Association announced a four-year agreement guaranteeing approximately $4,535,000 annually to player pension and insurance benefits, August 3. The owners also agreed to contribute $250,000 annually to improve or implement items such as disability payments, widows' benefits, maternity benefits, and dental benefits. The agreement also provided for increased preseason game and per diem payments, averaging approximately $2.6 million annually.

The Pittsburgh Steelers moved into Three Rivers Stadium. The Cincinnati Bengals moved to Riverfront Stadium.

Vince Lombardi died of cancer at 57, September 3.

The Super Bowl trophy was renamed the Vince Lombardi trophy, September 10.

Tom Dempsey of New Orleans kicked a game-winning NFL-record 63-yard field goal against Detroit, November 8.

1971

Baltimore defeated Dallas 16-13 on Jim O'Brien's 32-yard field goal with five seconds to go in Super Bowl V at Miami, January 17.

The NFC defeated the AFC 27-6 in the first AFC-NFC Pro Bowl at Los Angeles, January 24.

The Boston Patriots changed their name to the New England Patriots, March 25. Their new stadium, Schaefer Stadium, was dedicated in a 20-14 preseason victory over the Giants.

The Philadelphia Eagles left Franklin Field and played their games at the new Veterans Stadium.

The San Francisco 49ers left Kezar Stadium and moved their games to Candlestick Park.

Daniel F. Reeves, the president and general manager of the Rams, died at 58, April 15.

The Dallas Cowboys moved from the Cotton Bowl into their new home, Texas Stadium, October 24.

Miami defeated Kansas City 27-24 in sudden-death overtime in an AFC Divisional Playoff Game, December 25. Garo Yepremian kicked a 37-yard field goal for the Dolphins after 22 minutes, 40 seconds of overtime, as the game lasted 82 minutes, 40 seconds overall, making it the longest game in history.

1972

Dallas defeated Miami 24-3 in Super Bowl VI at New Orleans, January 16.

The inbounds lines or hashmarks were moved nearer the center of the field, 23 yards, 1 foot, 9 inches from the sidelines, March 23. The method of determining won-lost percentage in standings changed. Tie games, previously not counted in the standings, were made equal to a half-game won and a half-game lost, May 24.

Robert Irsay purchased the Los Angeles Rams and transferred ownership of the club to Carroll Rosenbloom in exchange for the Baltimore Colts, July 13.

William V. Bidwill purchased the stock of his brother Charles (Stormy) Bidwill to become the sole owner of the St. Louis Cardinals, September 2.

The National District Attorneys Association endorsed the position of professional leagues in opposing proposed legalization of gambling on professional team sports, September 28.

Franco Harris' "Immaculate Reception" gave the Steelers their first postseason win ever, 13-7 over the Raiders, December 23.

1973

Rozelle announced that all Super Bowl VII tickets were sold and that the game would be telecast in Los Angeles, the site of the game, on an experimental basis, January 3.

Miami defeated Washington 14-7 in Super Bowl VII at Los Angeles, completing a 17-0 season, the first perfect-record regular-season and postseason mark in NFL history, January 14.

The AFC defeated the NFC 33-28 in the Pro Bowl in Dallas, the first time since 1942 that the game was played outside Los Angeles, January 21.

A jersey numbering system was adopted, April 5: 1-19 for quarterbacks and specialists, 20-49 for running backs and defensive backs, 50-59 for centers and linebackers, 60-79 for defensive linemen and interior offensive linemen other than centers, and 80-89 for wide receivers and tight ends. Players who had been in the NFL in 1972 could continue to use old numbers.

NFL Charities, a nonprofit organization, was created to derive an income from monies generated from NFL Properties' licensing of NFL trademarks and team names, June 26. NFL Charities was set up to support education and charitable activities and to supply economic support to persons formerly associated with professional football who were no longer able to support themselves.

Congress adopted experimental legislation (for three years) requiring any NFL game that had been declared a sellout 72 hours prior to kickoff to be made available for local televising, September 14. The legislation provided for an annual review to be made by the Federal Communications Commission.

The Buffalo Bills moved their home games from War Memorial Stadium to Rich Stadium in nearby Orchard Park. The Giants tied the Eagles 23-23 in the final game in Yankee Stadium, September 23. The Giants played the rest of their home games at the Yale Bowl in New Haven, Connecticut.

A rival league, the World Football League, was formed and was reported in operation, October 2. It had plans to start play in 1974.

O.J. Simpson of Buffalo became the first player to rush for more than 2,000 yards in a season, gaining 2,003.

1974

Miami defeated Minnesota 24-7 in Super Bowl VIII at Houston, the second consecutive Super Bowl championship for the Dolphins, January 13.

Rozelle was given a 10-year contract effective January 1, 1973, February 27.

Tampa Bay was awarded the twenty-seventh franchise to begin operation in 1976, April 24.

Sweeping rules changes were adopted to add action and tempo to games: one sudden-death overtime period was added for preseason and regular-season games; the goal posts were moved from the goal line to the end lines; kickoffs were moved from the 40- to the 35-yard line; after missed field goals from beyond the 20, the ball was to be returned to the line of scrimmage; restrictions were placed on members of the punting team to open up return possibilities; roll-blocking and cutting of wide receivers was eliminated; the extent of downfield contact a defender could have with an eligible receiver was restricted; the penalties for offensive holding, illegal use of the hands, and tripping were reduced from 15 to 10 yards; wide receivers blocking back toward the ball within three yards of the line of scrimmage were prevented from blocking below the waist, April 25.

Seattle was awarded the twenty-eighth NFL franchise to begin play in 1976, June 4. Lloyd W. Nordstrom, president of the Seattle Seahawks, and Hugh Culverhouse, president of the Tampa Bay Buccaneers, signed franchise agreements, December 5.

The Birmingham Americans defeated the Florida Blazers 22-21 in the WFL World Bowl, winning the league championship, December 5.

1975

Pittsburgh defeated Minnesota 16-6 in Super Bowl IX at New Orleans, the Steelers' first championship since entering the NFL in 1933, January 12.

The Memphis Southmen of the WFL signed Larry Csonka, Jim Kiick, and Paul Warfield of Miami, March 31.

The divisional winners with the highest won-loss percentage were made the home team for the divisional playoffs, and the surviving winners with the highest percentage made home teams for the championship games. Previously, the home sites were pre-determined by division on a rotating basis, June 26.

Referees were equipped with wireless microphones for all preseason, regular-season, and playoff games.

The Lions moved to the new Pontiac Silverdome. The Giants played their home games in Shea Stadium. The Saints moved into the Louisiana Superdome.

The World Football League folded, October 22.

1976
Pittsburgh defeated Dallas 21-17 in Super Bowl X in Miami. The Steelers joined Green Bay and Miami as the only teams to win two Super Bowls; the Cowboys became the first wild-card team to play in the Super Bowl, January 18.

Lloyd Nordstrom, the president of the Seahawks, died at 66, January 20. His brother Elmer succeeded him as majority representative of the team.

The owners adopted the use of two 30-second clocks for all games, visible to both players and fans to note the official time between the ready-for-play signal and snap of the ball, March 16.

A veteran player allocation was held to stock the Seattle and Tampa Bay franchises with 39 players each, March 30-31. In the college draft, Seattle and Tampa Bay each received eight extra choices, April 8-9.

The Giants moved into new Giants Stadium in East Rutherford, New Jersey.

The Steelers defeated the College All-Stars in a storm-shortened Chicago College All-Star Game, the last of the series, July 23. St. Louis defeated San Diego 20-10 in a preseason game before 38,000 in Korakuen Stadium, Tokyo, in the first NFL game outside of North America, August 16.

1977
Oakland defeated Minnesota 32-14 in Super Bowl XI at Pasadena, January 9. The paid attendance was a pro record 103,438.

The NFL Players Association and the NFL Management Council ratified a collective bargaining agreement extending until 1982, covering five football seasons while continuing the pension plan—including years 1974, 1975, and 1976—with contributions totaling more than $55 million. The total cost of the agreement was estimated at $107 million. The agreement called for a college draft at least through 1986; contained a no-strike, no-suit clause; established a 43-man active player limit; reduced pension vesting to four years; provided for increases in minimum salaries and preseason and postseason pay; improved insurance, medical, and dental benefits; modified previous practices in player movement and control; and reaffirmed the NFL Commissioner's disciplinary authority. Additionally, the agreement called for the NFL member clubs to make payments totaling $16 million the next 10 years to settle various legal disputes, February 25.

The San Francisco 49ers were sold to Edward J. DeBartolo, Jr., March 28.

A 16-game regular season, 4-game preseason was adopted to begin in 1978, March 29. A second wild-card team was adopted for the playoffs beginning in 1978, with the wild-card teams to play each other and the winners advancing to a round of eight postseason series.

The Seahawks were permanently aligned in the AFC Western Division and the Buccaneers in the NFC Central Division, March 31.

Rules changes were adopted to open up the passing game and to cut down on injuries. Defenders were permitted to make contact with eligible receivers only once; the head slap was outlawed; offensive linemen were prohibited from thrusting their hands to an opponent's neck, face, or head; and wide receivers were prohibited from clipping, even in the legal clipping zone.

Rozelle negotiated contracts with the three television networks to televise all NFL regular-season and postseason games, plus selected preseason games, for four years beginning with the 1978 season. ABC was awarded yearly rights to 16 Monday night games, four prime-time games, the AFC-NFC Pro Bowl, and the Hall of Fame games. CBS received the rights to all NFC regular-season and postseason games (except those in the ABC package) and to Super Bowls XIV and XVI. NBC received the rights to all AFC regular-season and postseason games (except those in the ABC package) and to Super Bowls XIII and XV. Industry sources considered it the largest single television package ever negotiated, October 12.

1978
Dallas defeated Denver 27-10 in Super Bowl XII, held indoors for the first time, at the Louisiana Superdome in New Orleans, January 15. Dallas' victory was the first for the NFC in six years.

According to a Louis Harris Sports Survey, 70 percent of the nation's sports fans said they followed football, compared to 54 percent who followed baseball. Football increased its lead as the country's favorite, 26 percent to 16 percent for baseball, January 19.

A seventh official, the side judge, was added to the officiating crew, March 14.

The NFL continued a trend toward opening up the game. Rules changes permitted a defender to maintain contact with a receiver within five yards of the line of scrimmage, but restricted contact beyond that point. The pass-blocking rule was interpreted to permit the extending of arms and open hands, March 17.

A study on the use of instant replay as an officiating aid was made during seven nationally televised preseason games.

The NFL played for the first time in Mexico City, with the Saints defeating the Eagles 14-7 in a preseason game, August 5.

Bolstered by the expansion of the regular-season schedule from 14 to 16 weeks, NFL paid attendance exceeded 12 million (12,771,800) for the first time. The per-game average of 57,017 was the third-highest in league history and the most since 1973.

1979
Pittsburgh defeated Dallas 35-31 in Super Bowl XIII at Miami to become the first team ever to win three Super Bowls, January 21.

NFL rules changes emphasized additional player safety. The changes prohibited players on the receiving team from blocking below the waist during kickoffs, punts, and field-goal attempts; prohibited the wearing of torn or altered equipment and exposed pads that could be hazardous; extended the zone in which there could be no crackback blocks; and instructed officials to quickly whistle a play dead when a quarterback was clearly in the grasp of a tackler, March 16.

Carroll Rosenbloom, the president of the Rams, drowned at 72, April 2. His widow, Georgia, assumed control of the club.

1980
Pittsburgh defeated the Los Angeles Rams 31-19 in Super Bowl XIV at Pasadena to become the first team to win four Super Bowls, January 20.

The AFC-NFC Pro Bowl, won 37-27 by the NFC, was played before 48,060 fans at Aloha Stadium in Honolulu, Hawaii. It was the first time in the 30-year history of the Pro Bowl that the game was played in a non-NFL city.

Rules changes placed greater restrictions on contact in the area of the head, neck, and face. Under the heading of "personal foul," players were prohibited from directly striking, swinging, or clubbing on the head, neck, or face. Starting in 1980, a penalty could be called for such contact whether or not the initial contact was made below the neck area.

CBS, with a record bid of $12 million, won the national radio rights to 26 NFL regular-season games, including Monday Night Football, and all 10 postseason games for the 1980-83 seasons.

The Los Angeles Rams moved their home games to Anaheim Stadium in nearby Orange County, California.

The Oakland Raiders joined

the Los Angeles Coliseum Commission's antitrust suit against the NFL. The suit contended the league violated antitrust laws in declining to approve a proposed move by the Raiders from Oakland to Los Angeles.

The NFL Draft is televised for the first time by ESPN, April 29.

Television ratings in 1980 were the second-best in NFL history, trailing only the combined ratings of the 1976 season. All three networks posted gains, and NBC's 15.0 rating was its best ever. CBS and ABC had their best ratings since 1977, with 15.3 and 20.8 ratings, respectively. CBS Radio reported a record audience of 7 million for Monday night and special games.

1981
Oakland defeated Philadelphia 27-10 in Super Bowl XV at the Louisiana Superdome in New Orleans, to become the first wild-card team to win a Super Bowl, January 25.

Edgar F. Kaiser, Jr., purchased the Denver Broncos from Gerald and Allan Phipps, February 26.

The owners adopted a disaster plan for re-stocking a team should the club be involved in a fatal accident, March 20.

A CBS-New York Times poll showed that 48 percent of sports fans preferred football to 31 percent for baseball.

The NFL teams hosted 167 representatives from 44 predominantly black colleges during training camps for a total of 289 days. The program was adopted for renewal during each training camp period.

ABC and CBS set all-time rating highs. ABC finished with a 21.7 rating and CBS with a 17.5 rating. NBC was down slightly to 13.9.

1982
San Francisco defeated Cincinnati 26-21 in Super Bowl XVI at the Pontiac Silverdome, in the first Super Bowl held in the North, January 24. The CBS telecast achieved the highest rating of any televised sports event ever, 49.1 with a 73.0 share.

The NFL signed a five-year contract with the three television networks (ABC, CBS, and NBC) to televise all NFL regular-season and postseason games starting with the 1982 season.

A jury ruled against the NFL in the antitrust trial brought by the Los Angeles Coliseum Commission and the Oakland Raiders, May 7. The verdict cleared the way for the Raiders to move to Los Angeles, where they defeated Green Bay 24-3 in their first preseason game, August 29.

The 1982 season was reduced from a 16-game schedule to nine as the result of a 57-day players' strike. The strike was called by the NFLPA at midnight on Monday, September 20, following the Green Bay at New York Giants game. Play resumed November 21-22 following ratification of the Collective Bargaining Agreement by NFL owners, November 17 in New York.

Under the Collective Bargaining Agreement, which was to run through the 1986 season, the NFL draft was extended through 1992 and the veteran free-agent system was left basically unchanged. A minimum salary schedule for years of experience was established; training camp and postseason pay were increased; players' medical, insurance, and retirement benefits were increased; and a severance-pay system was introduced to aid in career transition, a first in professional sports.

Despite the players' strike, the average paid attendance in 1982 was 58,472, the fifth-highest in league history.

1983
Because of the shortened season, the NFL adopted a format of 16 teams competing in a Super Bowl Tournament for the 1982 playoffs. The NFC's number-one seed, Washington, defeated the AFC's number-two seed, Miami, 27-17 in Super Bowl XVII at the Rose Bowl in Pasadena, January 30.

Super Bowl XVII was the second-highest rated live television program of all time, giving the NFL a sweep of the top 10 live programs in television history.

George Halas, the owner of the Bears and the last surviving member of the NFL's second organizational meeting, died at 88, October 31.

1984
The Los Angeles Raiders defeated Washington 38-9 in Super Bowl XVIII at Tampa Stadium, January 22.

An 11-man group headed by H.R. (Bum) Bright purchased the Dallas Cowboys from Clint Murchison, Jr., March 20. Club president Tex Schramm was designated as managing general partner.

Wellington Mara was named president of the NFC, March 20.

Patrick Bowlen purchased a majority interest in the Denver Broncos from Edgar Kaiser, Jr., March 21.

The Colts relocated to Indianapolis, March 28. Their new home became the Hoosier Dome.

The New York Jets moved their home games to Giants Stadium in East Rutherford, New Jersey.

Alex G. Spanos purchased a majority interest in the San Diego Chargers from Eugene V. Klein, August 28.

Houston defeated Pittsburgh 23-20 to mark the one-hundredth overtime game in regular-season play since overtime was adopted in 1974, December 2.

On the field, many all-time records were set: Dan Marino of Miami passed for 5,084 yards and 48 touchdowns; Eric Dickerson of the Los Angeles Rams rushed for 2,105 yards; Art Monk of Washington caught 106 passes; and Walter Payton of Chicago broke Jim Brown's career rushing mark, finishing the season with 13,309 yards.

According to a CBS Sports/*New York Times* survey, 53 percent of the nation's sports fans said they most enjoyed watching football, compared to 18 percent for baseball, December 2-4.

1985
San Francisco defeated Miami 38-16 in Super Bowl XIX at Stanford Stadium in Stanford, California, January 20. President Ronald Reagan, who took his second oath of office before tossing the coin for the game, was one of 115,936,000 viewers. Super Bowl XIX had a direct economic impact of $113.5 million on the San Francisco Bay area.

NBC Radio and the NFL entered into a two-year agreement granting NBC the radio rights to a 37-game package in each of the 1985-86 seasons, March 6. The package included 27 regular-season games and 10 postseason games.

Norman Braman, in partnership with Edward Leibowitz, bought the Philadelphia Eagles from Leonard Tose, April 29.

A group headed by Tom Benson, Jr., was approved to purchase the New Orleans Saints from John W. Mecom, Jr., June 3.

The NFL owners adopted a resolution calling for a series of overseas preseason games, beginning in 1986, with one game to be played in England/Europe and/or one game in Japan each year. The game would be a fifth preseason game for the clubs involved and all arrangements and selection of the clubs would be under the control of the Commissioner, May 23.

The league-wide conversion to videotape from movie film for coaching study was approved.

A Louis Harris poll in December revealed that pro football remained the sport most followed by Americans. Fifty-nine percent of those surveyed followed pro football, compared with 54 percent who followed baseball.

The Chicago-Miami Monday game had the highest rating, 29.6, and share, 46.0, of any prime-time game in NFL history, December 2. The game was viewed in more than 25 million homes.

The NFL showed a ratings increase on all three networks for the season, gaining 4 percent on NBC, 10 on CBS, and 16 on ABC.

1986
Chicago defeated New England 46-10 in Super Bowl XX at the Louisiana Superdome, January 26. The Patriots had earned the right to play the Bears by becoming the first wild-card team to win three consecutive games on the road. The NBC telecast replaced the final episode of

*M*A*S*H* as the most-viewed television program in history, with an audience of 127 million viewers, according to A.C. Nielsen figures. In addition to drawing a 48.3 rating and a 70 percent share in the United States, Super Bowl XX was televised to 59 foreign countries and beamed via satellite to the QE II.

The owners adopted limited use of instant replay as an officiating aid, prohibited players from wearing or otherwise displaying equipment, apparel, or other items that carry commercial names, names of organizations, or personal messages of any type, March 11.

After an 11-week trial, a jury in U.S. District Court in New York awarded the United States Football League one dollar in its $1.7 billion antitrust suit against the NFL. The jury rejected all of the USFL's television-related claims, which were the self-proclaimed heart of the USFL's case. The jury deliberated five days, July 29.

Chicago defeated Dallas 17-6 at Wembley Stadium in London in the first American Bowl. The game drew a sellout crowd of 82,699 and the NBC national telecast in this country produced a 12.4 rating and 36 percent share, making it the highest daytime preseason television audience ever with 10.65-million viewers, August 3.

ABC's *NFL Monday Night Football,* in its seventeenth season, became the longest-running prime-time series in the history of the network.

1987

The New York Giants defeated Denver 39-20 in Super Bowl XXI and captured their first NFL title since 1956. The game, played in Pasadena's Rose Bowl, drew a sellout crowd of 101,063, January 25.

New three-year TV contracts with ABC, CBS, and NBC were announced for 1987-89 at the NFL annual meeting in Maui, Hawaii, March 15. Commissioner Rozelle and Broadcast Committee Chairman Art Modell also announced a three-year contract with ESPN to televise 13 prime-time games each season. The ESPN contract was the first with a cable network. However, NFL games on ESPN also were scheduled for regular television in the city of the visiting team and in the home city if the game was sold out 72 hours in advance.

A special payment program was adopted to benefit nearly 1,000 former NFL players who participated in the League before the current Bert Bell NFL Pension Plan was created and made retroactive to the 1959 season. Players covered by the new program spent at least five years in the League and played all or part of their career prior to 1959. Each vested player would receive $60 per month for each year of service in the League for life.

NFL and CBS Radio jointly announced agreement granting CBS the radio rights to a 40-game package in each of the next three NFL seasons, 1987-89, April 7.

Over 400 former NFL players from the pre-1959 era received first payments from NFL owners, July 1.

The NFL's debut on ESPN produced the two highest-rated and most-watched sports programs in basic cable history. The Chicago at Miami game on August 16 drew an 8.9 rating in 3.81 million homes. Those records fell two weeks later when the Los Angeles Raiders at Dallas game achieved a 10.2 cable rating in 4.36 million homes.

The 1987 season was reduced from a 16-game season to 15 as the result of a 24-day players' strike. The strike was called by the NFLPA on Tuesday, September 22, following the New England at New York Jets game. Games scheduled for the third weekend were canceled but the games of weeks four, five, and six were played with replacement teams. Striking players returned for the seventh week of the season, October 25.

In a three-team deal involving 10 players and/or draft choices, the Los Angeles Rams traded running back Eric Dickerson to the Indianapolis Colts for six draft choices and two players. Buffalo obtained the rights to linebacker Cornelius Bennett from Indianapolis, sending Greg Bell and three draft choices to the Rams. The Colts added Owen Gill and three draft choices of their own to complete the deal with the Rams, October 31.

The Chicago at Minnesota game became the highest-rated and most-watched sports program in basic cable history when it drew a 14.4 cable rating in 6.5 million homes, December 6.

1988

Washington defeated Denver 42-10 in Super Bowl XXII to earn its second victory this decade in the NFL Championship Game. The game, played for the first time in San Diego Jack Murphy Stadium, drew a sellout crowd of 73,302. Doug Williams, the game's MVP, became the first African-American quarterback to play in a Super Bowl, January 31.

In a unanimous 3-0 decision, the 2nd Circuit Court of Appeals in New York upheld the verdict of the jury that in July, 1986, had awarded the United States Football League one dollar in its $1.7 billion antitrust suit against the NFL. In a 91-page opinion, Judge Ralph K. Winter said the USFL sought through court decree the success it failed to gain among football fans, March 10.

By a 23-5 margin, owners voted to continue the instant replay system for the third consecutive season with the Instant Replay Official to be assigned to a regular seven-man, on-the-field crew. At the NFL annual meeting in Phoenix, Arizona, a 45-second clock was also approved to replace the 30-second clock. For a normal sequence of plays, the interval between plays was changed to 45 seconds from the time the ball is signaled dead until it is snapped on the succeeding play.

NFL owners approved the transfer of the Cardinals' franchise from St. Louis to Phoenix; approved two supplemental drafts each year—one prior to training camp and one prior to the regular season; and voted to initiate an annual series of games in Japan/Asia as early as the 1989 preseason, March 14-18.

The NFL Annual Selection Meeting returned to a separate two-day format and for the first time originated on a Sunday. ESPN drew a 3.6 rating during their seven-hour coverage of the draft, which was viewed in 1.6 million homes, April 24-25.

Art Rooney, founder and owner of the Steelers, died at 87, August 25.

Johnny Grier became the first African-American referee in NFL history, September 4.

Commissioner Rozelle announced that two teams would play a preseason game as part of the American Bowl series on August 6, 1989, in the Korakuen Tokyo Dome in Japan, December 16.

1989

San Francisco defeated Cincinnati 20-16 in Super Bowl XXIII. The game, played for the first time at Joe Robbie Stadium in Miami, was attended by a sellout crowd of 75,129, January 22.

Commissioner Rozelle announced his retirement, pending the naming of a successor, March 22 at the NFL annual meeting in Palm Desert, California.

Following the announcement, AFC president Lamar Hunt and NFC president Wellington Mara announced the formation of a six-man search committee composed of Art Modell, Robert Parins, Dan Rooney, and Ralph Wilson. Hunt and Mara served as co-chairmen.

By a 24-4 margin, owners voted to continue the instant replay system for the fourth straight season. A strengthened policy regarding anabolic steroids and masking agents was announced by Commissioner Rozelle. NFL clubs called for strong disciplinary measures in cases of feigned injuries and adopted a joint proposal by the Long-Range Planning and Finance committees regarding player personnel rules, March 19-23.

Two hundred twenty-nine unconditional free agents signed with new teams under management's Plan B system, April 1.

Jerry Jones purchased a majority interest in the Dallas Cowboys from H.R. (Bum)

Bright, April 18.

Tex Schramm was named president of the new World League of American Football to work with a six-man committee of Dan Rooney, chairman; Norman Braman, Lamar Hunt, Victor Kiam, Mike Lynn, and Bill Walsh, April 18.

NFL and CBS Radio jointly announced agreement extending CBS's radio rights to an annual 40-game package through the 1994 season, April 18.

As of opening day, September 10, of the 229 Plan B free agents, 111 were active and 23 others were on teams' reserve lists. Ninety-two others were waived and three retired.

Art Shell was named head coach of the Los Angeles Raiders making him the NFL's first black head coach since Fritz Pollard coached the Akron Pros in 1921, October 3.

The site of the New England Patriots at San Francisco 49ers game scheduled for Candlestick Park on October 22 was switched to Stanford Stadium in the aftermath of the Bay Area Earthquake of October 17. The change was announced on October 19.

Paul Tagliabue became the seventh chief executive of the NFL on October 26 when he was chosen to succeed Commissioner Pete Rozelle on the sixth ballot of a three-day meeting in Cleveland, Ohio.

In all, 12 ballots were required to select Tagliabue. Two were conducted at a meeting in Chicago on July 6, and four at a meeting in Dallas on October 10-11. On the twelfth ballot, with Seattle absent, Tagliabue received more than the 19 affirmative votes required for election from among the 27 clubs present.

The transfer from Commissioner Rozelle to Commissioner Tagliabue took place at 12:01 A.M. on Sunday, November 5.

NFL Charities donated $1 million through United Way to benefit Bay Area earthquake victims, November 6.

1990

San Francisco defeated Denver 55-10 in Super Bowl XXIV at the Louisiana Superdome, January 28. San Francisco joined Pittsburgh as the NFL's only teams to win four Super Bowls.

The NFL announced revisions in its 1990 draft eligibility rules. College juniors became eligible but must renounce their collegiate football eligibility before applying for the NFL Draft, February 16.

Commissioner Tagliabue announced NFL teams will play their 16-game schedule over 17 weeks in 1990-92 and 16 games over 18 weeks in 1993, February 27.

The NFL revised its playoff format to include two additional wild-card teams (one per conference), which raised the total to six wild-card teams.

Commissioner Tagliabue and Broadcast Committee Chairman Art Modell announced a four-year contract with Turner Broadcasting to televise nine Sunday-night games.

New four-year TV agreements were ratified for 1990-93 for ABC, CBS, NBC, ESPN, and TNT at the NFL annual meeting in Orlando, Florida, March 12. The contracts totaled $3.6 billion, the largest in TV history.

The NFL announced plans to expand its American Bowl series of preseason games. In addition to games in London and Tokyo, American Bowl games were scheduled for Berlin, Germany, and Montreal, Canada, in 1990.

For the fifth straight year, NFL owners voted to continue a limited system of Instant Replay. Beginning in 1990, the replay official will have a two-minute time limit to make a decision. The vote was 21-7, March 12.

Commissioner Tagliabue announced the formation of a Committee on Expansion and Realignment, March 13. He also named a Player Advisory Council, comprised of 12 former NFL players, March 14.

One-hundred eighty-four Plan B unconditional free agents signed with new teams, April 2.

Commissioner Tagliabue appointed Dr. John Lombardo as the League's Drug Advisor for Anabolic Steroids, April 25 and named Dr. Lawrence Brown as the League's Advisor for Drugs of Abuse, May 17.

NFL International Week was celebrated with four preseason games in seven days in Tokyo, London, Berlin, and Montreal. More than 200,000 fans on three continents attended the four games, August 4-11.

Commissioner Tagliabue announced the NFL Teacher of the Month program in which the League furnishes grants and scholarships in recognition of teachers who provided a positive influence upon NFL players in elementary and secondary schools, September 20.

For the first time since 1957, every NFL club won at least one of its first four games, October 1.

The Super Bowl Most Valuable Player trophy was renamed the Pete Rozelle trophy, October 8.

1991

The New York Giants defeated Buffalo 20-19 in Super Bowl XXV to capture their second title in five years. The game was played before a sellout crowd of 73,813 at Tampa Stadium and became the first Super Bowl decided by one point, January 26.

New York businessman Robert Tisch purchased a 50 percent interest in the New York Giants from Mrs. Helen Mara Nugent and her children, Tim Mara and Maura Mara Concannon, February 2.

NFL clubs voted to continue a limited system of Instant Replay for the sixth consecutive year. The vote was 21-7, March 19.

The NFL launched the World League of American Football, the first sports league to operate on a weekly basis on two separate continents, March 23.

NFL Charities presented a $250,000 donation to the United Service Organization. The donation was the second largest single grant ever by NFL Charities, April 5.

Commissioner Tagliabue named Harold Henderson as Executive Vice President for Labor Relations and Chairman of the NFL Management Council Executive Committee, April 8.

NFL clubs approved a recommendation by the Expansion and Realignment Committee to add two teams for the 1994 season, resulting in six divisions of five teams each, May 22.

"NFL International Week" featured six 1990 playoff teams playing nationally televised games in London, Berlin, and Tokyo on July 28 and August 3-4. The games drew more than 150,000 fans.

Paul Brown, founder of the Cleveland Browns and Cincinnati Bengals, died at age 82, August 5.

NFL clubs approved a resolution establishing an international division. A three-year financial plan for the World League was approved by NFL clubs at a meeting in Dallas, October 23.

1992

The NFL agreed to provide a minimum of $2.5 million in financial support to the NFL Alumni Association and assistance to NFL Alumni-related programs. The agreement included contributions from NFL Charities to the Pre-59ers and Dire Need Programs for former players, January 25.

The Washington Redskins defeated the Buffalo Bills 37-24 in Super Bowl XXVI to capture their third world championship in 10 years, January 26. The game was played before a sellout crowd of 63,130 at the Hubert H. Humphrey Metrodome in Minneapolis.

The use in officiating of a limited system of Instant Replay was not approved. The vote was 17-11 in favor of approval (21 votes were required). Instant Replay had been used for six consecutive years (1986-1991), March 18.

St. Louis businessman James Orthwein purchased controlling interest in the New England Patriots from Victor Kiam, May 11.

In a Harris Poll taken during the NFL offseason, professional football again was declared the nation's most popular sport. Professional football finished atop similar surveys conducted by Harris in 1985 and 1989, May 23.

NFL clubs accepted the report of the Expansion Committee at a league meeting in Pasadena. The report names five cities as finalists for the two expansion teams—Baltimore, Charlotte, Jacksonville, Memphis, and St. Louis, May 19.

At a league meeting in Dallas, NFL clubs approved a proposal by the World League Board of Directors to restructure the World League and place future emphasis on its international success, September 17.

The Professional and Amateur Sports Protection Act made it unlawful for a government entity to operate a lottery or other betting scheme based on pro or collegiate games. Four states that already had such betting were grandfathered, October 6.

NFL teams played their 16-game regular-season schedule over 18 weeks for the only time in league history.

1993

The NFL and lawyers for the players announced a settlement of various lawsuits and an agreement on the terms of a seven-year deal that included a new player system to be in place through the 1999 season, January 6.

Commissioner Tagliabue announced the establishment of the "NFL World Partnership Program" to develop amateur football internationally through a series of clinics conducted by former NFL players and coaches, January 14.

As part of Super Bowl XXVII, the NFL announced the creation of the first NFL Youth Education Town, a facility located in south central Los Angeles for inner city youth. January 25.

The Dallas Cowboys defeated the Buffalo Bills 52-17 in Super Bowl XXVII to capture their first NFL title since 1978. The game was played before a crowd of 98,374 at the Rose Bowl in Pasadena, California, January 31.

The NFL and the NFL Players Association officially signed a 7-year Collective Bargaining Agreement in Washington, D.C., which guarantees more than $1 billion in pension, health, and post-career benefits for current and retired players—the most extensive benefits plan in pro sports. It was the NFL's first CBA since the 1982 agreement expired in 1987, June 29.

NFL Enterprises, a newly formed division of the NFL responsible for NFL Films, home video, and special domestic and international television programming was announced, August 19.

NFL announced plans to allow fans, for the first time ever, to join players and coaches in selecting the annual AFC and NFC Pro Bowl teams, October 12.

NFL clubs unanimously awarded the league's twenty-ninth franchise to the Carolina Panthers and owner Jerry Richardson at a meeting in Chicago, October 26.

At the same meeting in Chicago, NFL clubs approved a plan to form a European league with joint venture partners, October 27.

Don Shula became the winningest coach in NFL history when Miami beat Philadelphia to give Shula his 325th victory, one more than George Halas, November 14.

NFL clubs awarded the league's thirtieth franchise to the Jacksonville Jaguars and owner Wayne Weaver at a meeting in Chicago, November 30.

The NFL announced new 4-year television agreements with NBC, ABC, ESPN, TNT, and NFL newcomer FOX, which took over the NFC package from CBS, December 18.

The NFL completed its new TV agreements by announcing that NBC would retain the rights to the AFC package, December 20.

1994

The Dallas Cowboys defeated the Buffalo Bills 30-13 in Super Bowl XXVIII to become the fifth team to win back-to-back Super Bowl titles, January 30.

NFL clubs unanimously approved the transfer of the New England Patriots from James Orthwein to Robert Kraft at a meeting in Orlando, February 22.

In a move to increase offensive production, NFL clubs at the league's annual meeting in Orlando adopted a package of changes, including modifications in line play, chucking rules, and the roughing-the-passer rule, plus the adoption of the two-point conversion and moving the spot of the kickoff back to the 30-yard line, March 22.

NFL clubs approved the transfer of the majority interest in the Miami Dolphins from the Robbie family to H. Wayne Huizenga, March 23.

The NFL and FOX announced the formation of a joint venture to create a six-team World League to begin play in Europe in April, 1995, March 23.

The Carolina Panthers earned the right to select first in the 1995 NFL draft by winning a coin toss with the Jacksonville Jaguars. The Jaguars received the second selection in the 1995 draft, April 24.

NFL clubs approved the transfer of the Philadelphia Eagles from Norman Braman to Jeffrey Lurie, May 6.

The NFL launched "NFL Sunday Ticket," a new season subscription service for satellite television dish owners, June 1.

An all-time NFL record crowd of 112,376 attended the American Bowl game between Dallas and Houston in Mexico City. It concluded the biggest American Bowl series in NFL history with four games attracting a record 256,666 fans, August 15.

The NFL reached agreement on a new seven-year contract with its game officials, September 22.

The NFL Management Council and the NFL Players Association announced an agreement on the formulation and implementation of the most comprehensive drug and alcohol policy in sports, October 28.

At an NFL meeting in Chicago, Commissioner Tagliabue slotted the two new expansion teams into the AFC Central (Jacksonville Jaguars) and NFC West (Carolina Panthers) for the 1995 season only. He also appointed a special committee on realignment to make recommendations on the 1996 season and beyond, November 2.

1995

The San Francisco 49ers became the first team to win five Super Bowls when they defeated the San Diego Chargers 49-26 in Super Bowl XXIX at Joe Robbie Stadium in Miami, January 29.

Carolina and Jacksonville stocked their expansion rosters with a total of 66 players from other NFL teams in a veteran player allocation draft in New York, February 16.

CBS Radio and the NFL agreed to a new four-year contract for an annual 53-game package of games, continuing a relationship that spanned 15 of the past 17 years, February 22.

NFL clubs approved the transfer of the Tampa Bay Buccaneers from the estate of the late Hugh Culverhouse to South Florida businessman Malcolm Glazer, March 13.

After a two-year hiatus, the World League of American Football returned to action with six teams in Europe, April 8.

The NFL became the first major sports league to establish a site on the Internet system of on-line computer communication, April 10.

The transfer of the Rams from Los Angeles to St. Louis was approved by a vote of the NFL clubs at a meeting in Dallas, April 12.

ABC's *NFL Monday Night Football* finished the 1994-95 television season as the fifth highest-rated show out of 146 with a 17.8 average rating, the highest finish in the 25-year history of the series, April 18.

The Frankfurt Galaxy defeated the Amsterdam Admirals 26-22 to win the 1995 World Bowl before a crowd of 23,847 in Amsterdam's Olympic Stadium, June 23.

The transfer of the Raiders from Los Angeles to Oakland was approved by a vote of the NFL clubs at a meeting in Chicago, July 22.

Jacksonville Municipal Stadium opened in Jacksonville, Florida before a sold-out crowd of more than 70,000 as the St. Louis Rams defeated the Jacksonville Jaguars 27-10 in their first preseason game, August 18.

NFL Charities and 50 NFL players donated $1 million to the United Negro College Fund in honor of the fiftieth anniversary of the UNCF and the integration of the modern NFL, September 15.

The Trans World Dome opened in St. Louis with a sold-out crowd of 65,598 as the Rams defeated the Carolina Panthers 28-17, November 12.

On the field, many significant records and milestones were achieved: Miami's Dan Marino surpassed Pro Football Hall of Famer Fran Tarkenton in four major passing categories—attempts, completions, yards, and touchdowns—to become the NFL's all-time career leader. San Francisco's Jerry Rice became the all-time reception and receiving-yardage leader.

1996

The Dallas Cowboys won their third Super Bowl title in four years when they defeated the Pittsburgh Steelers 27-17 in Super Bowl XXX at Sun Devil Stadium in Tempe, Arizona, January 28.

An agreement between the NFL and the city of Cleveland regarding the Cleveland Browns' relocation was approved by a vote of the NFL clubs, February 9. According to the agreement, the city of Cleveland retained the Browns' heritage and records, including the name, logo, colors, history, playing records, trophies, and memorabilia, and committed to building a new 72,000-seat stadium for a reactivated Browns' franchise to begin play there no later than 1999. Art Modell received approval to move his franchise to Baltimore and rename it.

The transfer of the Oilers from Houston to Nashville for the 1998 season was approved by a vote of the NFL clubs at a meeting in Atlanta, April 30.

The Scottish Claymores defeated the Frankfurt Galaxy 32-27 to win the 1996 World Bowl in front of 38,982 at Murrayfield Stadium in Edinburgh, Scotland, June 23.

The NFL returned to Baltimore when the new Baltimore Ravens defeated the Philadelphia Eagles 17-9 in a preseason game before a crowd of 63,804 at Memorial Stadium, August 3.

Ericsson Stadium opened in Charlotte, North Carolina with a crowd of 65,350 as the Carolina Panthers defeated the Chicago Bears 30-12 in a preseason game, August 3.

Former NFL Commissioner Pete Rozelle died at his home in Rancho Santa Fe, California. Rozelle, regarded as the premiere commissioner in sports history, led the NFL for 29 years, from 1960-1989, December 6.

1997

Indianapolis Colts owner Robert Irsay died from complications related to a stroke he suffered in 1995. Irsay acquired the club in 1972 when he traded his Los Angeles Rams to Carrol Rosenbloom for the Colts. He later moved the Colts from Baltimore to Indianapolis in 1984, January 14.

The Green Bay Packers won their first NFL title in 29 years by defeating the New England Patriots 35-21 in Super Bowl XXXI at the Louisiana Superdome in New Orleans, January 26.

The rules governing cross-ownership were modified, permitting NFL club owners to also own teams in other sports in their home market or markets without NFL teams. The vote was 24-5 (one abstention) in favor of approval, March 11.

Washington Redskins owner Jack Kent Cooke died at his home in Washington, D.C. Cooke became majority owner in 1974 and the Redskins won three Super Bowls under his leadership, April 6.

The Barcelona Dragons defeated the Rhein Fire 38-24 to win the 1997 World Bowl in front of 31,100 fans at Estadi Olimpic de Montjuic in Barcelona, Spain, June 22.

NFL clubs approved the transfer of the Seattle Seahawks from Ken Behring to Paul Allen, August 19.

Jack Kent Cooke Stadium opened in Raljon, Maryland with a crowd of 78,270 as the Washington Redskins defeated the Arizona Cardinals 19-13 in overtime, September 14.

The 10,000th regular-season game in NFL history was played when the Seattle Seahawks defeated the Tennessee Oilers 16-13 at the Kingdome in Seattle, October 5.

Atlanta Falcons owner Rankin Smith died of heart failure three days prior to his seventy-third birthday. Smith was the founder of the Falcons and was instrumental in bringing Super Bowls XXVIII and XXXIV to Atlanta, October 26.

1998

The NFL reached agreement on record eight-year television contracts with four networks. ABC (*NFL Monday Night Football*) and FOX (NFC) retained their previous rights, CBS took over the AFC package from NBC, and ESPN won the right to broadcast the entire Sunday night cable package, January 13.

The World League was renamed the NFL Europe League, January 22.

The Denver Broncos won their first Super Bowl by defeating the defending champion Green Bay Packers 31-24 in Super Bowl XXXII at Qualcomm Stadium in San Diego, January 25.

The NFL clubs approved an extension of the Collective Bargaining Agreement through 2003. The extended CBA also created a $100 million fund for youth football, March 22.

The NFL clubs unanimously approved an expansion team for Cleveland to fulfill the commitment to return the Browns to the field in 1999, March 23.

The Rhein Fire defeated the Frankfurt Galaxy 34-10 to win the 1998 World Bowl in front of 47,846 fans in Frankfurt's Waldstadion—the biggest crowd to witness a World Bowl since 1991, June 14.

NFL clubs approved the transfer of the Minnesota Vikings from a 10-man ownership group to Red McCombs, July 28.

The NFL Stadium at Camden Yards opened in Baltimore, Maryland before a crowd of 65,938 as the Baltimore Ravens defeated the Chicago Bears 19-14 in a preseason game, August 8.

Raymond James Stadium opened in Tampa, Florida before a crowd of 62,410 as the Tampa Bay Buccaneers defeated the Chicago Bears 27-15, September 20.

Tennessee Oilers owner Bud Adams announced the team will change its name to the Tennessee Titans following the 1998 season. The NFL announced that the name Oilers will be retired—a first in league history, November 14.

1999

The Denver Broncos won their second consecutive Super Bowl title by defeating the NFC champion Atlanta Falcons 34-19 in Super Bowl XXXIII at Pro Player Stadium in Miami, January 31.

Jim Pyne, a center allocated by the Detroit Lions, was the first selection of the Cleveland Browns in the 1999 NFL Expansion Draft. The Browns eventually selected 37 players, February 9.

CBS Radio/Westwood One agreed to a 3-year extension of their exclusive national radio rights to NFL games, March 11.

By a vote of 28-3, the owners adopted an instant replay system as an officiating aid for the 1999 season, March 17.

New York Jets owner Leon Hess died from complications of a blood disease. Hess had been involved in the ownership of the Jets since 1963 and was sole owner of the club since 1984, May 9.

A group led by Washington area businessman Daniel Snyder is approved by NFL clubs as the new owner of the Washington Redskins at a league meeting in Atlanta, May 25.

The Frankfurt Galaxy became the first team in NFL Europe League history to win a second World Bowl by defeating the Barcelona Dragons 38-24 at Rheinstadion, in Düsseldorf, Germany, June 27.

The Cleveland Browns returned to the field for the first time since 1995 and defeated the Dallas Cowboys 20-17 in overtime in the annual Hall of Fame Game at Canton, Ohio, August 9.

Cleveland Browns Stadium opened in Cleveland, Ohio before a crowd of 71,398 as the Minnesota Vikings defeated the Browns in a preseason game, 24-17, August 21.

Adelphia Coliseum opened in Nashville, Tennessee before a crowd of 65,729 with the Tennessee Titans defeating the Atlanta Falcons 17-3 in a preseason game, August 26.

Houston, Texas and owner Robert McNair were awarded the NFL's thirty-second franchise in a vote of the NFL clubs at a league meeting in Atlanta. The team will begin play in 2002. The NFL clubs also voted to realign into eight divisions of four teams each for the 2002 season, October 6.

Walter Payton, the NFL's all-time leading rusher, died of liver cancer at the age of 45. Payton played for the Chicago Bears from 1975-1987 and rushed for an NFL-record 16,726 yards, November 1.

Former NFL Commissioner Pete Rozelle, who guided a still-developing league to its position today as America's most popular sport, was named by *The Sporting News* as the most powerful person in sports in the 20th Century, December 15.

2000

New York businessman Robert Wood Johnson IV was approved by NFL clubs as the new owner of the New York Jets at a league meeting, January 18.

The St. Louis Rams won their first Super Bowl by defeating the AFC champion Tennessee Titans 23-16 in Super Bowl XXXIV at the Georgia Dome in Atlanta, January 30.

For the first time in league history, paid attendance topped 16 million for the regular season and more than 65,000 per game, an increase of 1,300 per game over 1998. Paid attendance for all NFL games increased in 1999 for the third year in a row and was the highest ever in the 80-year history of the league. It marked the first time in league history that the 20-million paid attendance mark was reached for all games in a season, March 27.

The Rhein Fire won their second World Bowl in three years, defeating the Scottish Claymores 13-10 to win World Bowl 2000 in front of 35,680 at Frankfurt's Waldstadion, June 25.

More than 100 of the 136 living members of the Pro Football Hall of Fame gathered to celebrate Pro Football's Greatest Reunion in Canton, Ohio, July 28-31.

Paul Brown Stadium opened in Cincinnati, Ohio with a crowd of 56,180 as the Cincinnati Bengals defeated the Chicago Bears 24-20 in a preseason game, August 19.

Minnesota's Gary Anderson converted a 21-yard field goal against Buffalo to pass George Blanda as the NFL's all-time scoring leader with 2,004 points, October 22.

San Francisco's Terrell Owens set a single-game receiving record with 20 receptions (283 yards) against Chicago, surpassing the previous mark of 18 by Tom Fears of the Los Angeles Rams in 1950, December 17.

2001

NFL clubs approved additional league-wide revenue sharing at a special league meeting in Dallas. The teams agreed to pool the visiting team share of gate receipts for all preseason and regular-season games and divide the pool equally starting in 2002, January 17.

The Baltimore Ravens won their first Super Bowl by defeating the NFC champion New York Giants 34-7 in Super Bowl XXXV at Raymond James Stadium in Tampa Bay, January 28.

The *Sports Business Daily* named NFL Commissioner Paul Tagliabue the 2000 Sports Industrialist of the Year, February 28.

NFL owners unanimously approved a realignment plan for the league starting in 2002. With the addition of the Houston Texans, the league's 32 teams will be divided into eight four-team divisions. Seven clubs change divisions, and the Seattle Seahawks change conferences, moving from the AFC to the NFC. A new scheduling format ensures that every team meets every other team in the league at least once every four years, May 22.

The Berlin Thunder won their first World Bowl, defeating the Barcelona Dragons 24-17 to win World Bowl IX in front of 32,116 at Amsterdam ArenA, June 30.

Heinz Field opened in Pittsburgh, Pennsylvania before a crowd of 57,829 with the Pittsburgh Steelers defeating the Detroit Lions 20-7 in a preseason game; and INVESCO Field at Mile High opened in Denver, Colorado before a crowd of 74,063 with the Denver Broncos defeating the New Orleans Saints 31-24 in a preseason game, August 25.

President George W. Bush became the first United States President to be involved in an NFL regular-season pregame coin toss as he helped kick off the 2001 season from the White House. Via satellite, President Bush tossed the coin for the 10 regular-season games that started at 1:00 P.M. ET, September 9.

In the wake of the September 11 terrorist attacks, Commissioner Paul Tagliabue postponed the games scheduled for September 16-17, September 13.

The league's 16-game regular season was retained when the postponed Week 2 games were rescheduled for the weekend of January 6-7, September 18.

The NFL and its game officials agreed to a new six-year Collective Bargaining Agreement, ending a two-week lockout of the regular officials, who returned to work on September 23, September 19.

The NFL announced that the league's prohibition of anabolic steroids and related substances had been strengthened to include supplements containing ephedrine and other high-risk supplements, September 27.

The NFL announced that the Super Bowl would be rescheduled from January 27 to February 3 in order to retain the full playoff format for the 2002 season. It will be the first Super Bowl played in February, October 3.

President Bush designated Super Bowl XXXVI as a "National Special Security Event," allowing all security for the game to be coordinated by the Secret Service, November 26.

2002

The NFL and the NFL Players Association agreed to a fourth extension of the 1993 Collective Bargaining Agreement through 2007, January 7.

In an AFC Wild Card matchup, the Oakland Raiders defeated the New York Jets 38-24 in the NFL's first-ever prime-time playoff game, January 12.

In a special meeting in New Orleans, NFL owners voted unanimously to approve the purchase of the Atlanta Falcons to Home Depot co-founder Arthur Blank, February 2.

The New England Patriots won their first Super Bowl by defeating the NFC champion St. Louis Rams 20-17 in Super Bowl XXXVI at the Louisiana Superdome in New Orleans. The game marked the first time in Super Bowl history that the winning points came on the final play, a 48-yard field goal by Patriots kicker Adam Vinatieri, February 3.

Tony Boselli, a five-time Pro Bowl tackle allocated by the Jacksonville Jaguars, was the first selection of the Houston Texans in the 2002 NFL Expansion Draft. The Texans selected 19 players, February 18.

The NFL and Westwood One/CBS Radio Sports announced the renewal of a multiyear agreement for Westwood One/CBS Radio Sports to continue as the exclusive network radio home of the NFL, April 9.

NFL Europe kicked off its tenth season with a record 254 players allocated by NFL clubs, April 13-14.

The Berlin Thunder became the first team to win consecutive World Bowls, defeating the Rhein Fire 26-20 to win World Bowl X in front of 53,109 fans at Rheinstadion, June 22.

Seahawks Stadium opened in Seattle, Washington with an attendance of 52,902 fans as the Indianapolis Colts defeated the Seattle Seahawks 28-10 in a preseason game, August 10.

Gillette Stadium opened in Foxboro, Massachusetts with a crowd of 68,436 fans as the New England Patriots defeated the Philadelphia Eagles 16-15 in a preseason game, August 17.

Reliant Stadium opened in Houston, Texas with 69,432 fans in attendance, the largest non-Super Bowl crowd to ever watch an NFL game in Houston as the Miami Dolphins defeated the Houston Texans 24-3 in a preseason game, August 24.

For the first time, the NFL season kicked off on a Thursday night in prime time as the San Francisco 49ers defeated the New York Giants 16-13 at Giants Stadium. The game was preceded by "NFL Kickoff Live From Times Square," presented by New York City and the NFL, a football and music festival honoring the resilient spirit of New York and America, September 5.

Week 1 of the 2002 season produced the highest-scoring and most competitive Kickoff Weekend in NFL history. The 16 games averaged 49.3 points per game. A total of 788 points and 89 touchdowns were scored, the most in league history for an opening weekend. Eleven of the 16 games were decided by one score (eight points or less), a Kickoff Weekend record, September 5-9.

Johnny Unitas, the legendary quarterback for the Baltimore Colts and a Pro Football Hall of Fame member, died of a heart attack at the age of 69, September 11.

Oakland Raiders wide receiver Jerry Rice became the all-time leader in yards from scrimmage, surpassing Pro Football Hall of Fame running back Walter Payton (21,281 yards), September 29.

Cleveland Browns owner Al Lerner, the NFL Finance Committee Chairman and Chairman and CEO of MBNA Corporation, died at the age of 69, October 23.

Dallas Cowboys running back Emmitt Smith became the NFL's all-time rushing leader, surpassing Pro Football Hall of Fame running back Walter Payton (16,726 yards), October 27.

The NFL and NFLPA announced the creation of USA Football, the first national advocacy organization representing all levels of amateur football, December 5.

The 2002 season concluded with 25 overtime games, the most in NFL history, December 30.

2003

The Tampa Bay Buccaneers won their first Super Bowl by defeating the AFC champion Oakland Raiders 48-21 in Super Bowl XXXVII at Qualcomm Stadium in San Diego, January 26.

Chicago Bears chairman emeritus Edward W. McCaskey died at the age of 83, April 8.

The Frankfurt Galaxy became the first team to win three World Bowls, defeating the Rhein Fire 35-16 to win World Bowl XI in front of 28,138 fans at Hampden Park, June 14.

Tex Schramm, the legendary team president and general manager of the Dallas Cowboys and a member of the Pro Football Hall of Fame, died at the age of 83, July 15.

Lincoln Financial Field opened in Philadelphia, Pennsylvania with an attendance of 66,279 fans as the New England Patriots defeated the Philadelphia Eagles 24-12 in a preseason game, August 22.

A renovated Lambeau Field opened in Green Bay, Wisconsin with a crowd of 69,831 fans as the Carolina Panthers defeated the Green Bay Packers 20-7 in a preseason game, August 23.

A renovated Soldier Field opened in Chicago, Illinois with an attendance of 61,500 fans as the Green Bay Packers defeated the Chicago Bears 38-23 in a regular season game on ABC's *NFL Monday Night Football*, September 29.

NFL Network, the first 24-hour, year-round television channel dedicated to the NFL and the sport of football, launched on DirecTV, November 4.

2004

The New England Patriots won their second Super Bowl in three years by defeating the NFC champion Carolina Panthers 32-29 in Super Bowl XXXVIII at Reliant Stadium in Houston, February 1.

By a vote of 29-3, NFL owners extended the instant replay system for another five seasons through 2008, March 30.

Steve Bisciotti took over as the controlling owner of the Baltimore Ravens, succeeding Art Modell, who operated the franchise for 43 years, April 8.

Former Arizona Cardinals safety Pat Tillman was killed in a firefight while on combat patrol with the U.S. Army Rangers in Afghanistan, April 22.

A federal appeals court formally ruled in favor of the NFL's draft eligibility rule in Maurice Clarett's lawsuit, citing federal labor policy in permitting the NFL and the Players Association to set rules for when players can enter the league, May 24.

The Berlin Thunder defeated the Frankfurt Galaxy 30-24 to win World Bowl XII in front of 35,413 fans at Arena Auf-Schalke, June 12.

The New England Patriots defeated the New York Jets 13-7 for their NFL-record 18th consecutive regular-season victory, October 24.

The NFL reached an agreement on six-year contract extensions with two of its network television partners—CBS and FOX—to run through the 2011 season, November 8.

The NFL and DirecTV announced a five-year extension on the NFL Sunday Ticket subscription television package to run through the 2010 season, November 8.

NFL Europe named the Hamburg Sea Devils as the league's newest team, November 24.

2005

Indianapolis Colts quarterback Peyton Manning set the NFL single-season record with 49 touchdown passes, January 2.

The New England Patriots became the second team in NFL history to win three Super Bowls in four seasons by defeating the Philadelphia Eagles 24-21 in Super Bowl XXXIX at ALLTEL Stadium in Jacksonville, February 6.

The Pat Tillman USO Center opened in Afghanistan. The NFL donated $250,000 to the USO to honor the memory of the former Arizona Cardinals player who died in Afghanistan while serving in the U.S. Army, April 1.

The NFL reached long-term agreements for its Sunday and Monday primetime TV packages. NBC returned to the NFL by acquiring the Sunday night package for six years (2006-2011). ESPN agreed on an eight-year deal to televise *Monday Night Football* from 2006-2013, April 18.

The NFL strengthened its steroids program by adopting the Olympic testosterone testing standard, tripling the number of times a player can be randomly tested during the offseason from two to six, adding substances to the list of banned substances, and putting new language in the policy to allow for testing of designer drugs and other substances that may have evaded detection, April 27.

NFL owners voted unanimously to approve the sale of the Minnesota Vikings to real-estate developer Zygi Wilf, May 25.

The Amsterdam Admirals defeated the Berlin Thunder 27-21 to win World Bowl XIII in front of 35,134 fans at LTU Arena in Dússeldorf, Germany, June 11.

The NFL designated September 18-19 as "Hurricane Relief Weekend," which concluded with a telethon in conjunction with a Monday Night Football doubleheader on ABC and ESPN. The New York Giants-New Orleans Saints game, originally scheduled for the Louisiana Superdome, was moved to Giants Stadium following Hurricane Katrina. In total, the NFL, its owners, teams, players, and fans contributed $21 million to aid the Hurricane Katrina rebuilding effort, September 19.

An NFL record 103,467 fans attended the Arizona Cardinals' 31-14 victory over the San Francisco 49ers at Mexico City's Azteca Stadium, the first-ever regular-season NFL game played outside the United States, October 2.

Wellington Mara, the New York Giants' president and co-chief executive officer, died at the age of 89, October 25.

Preston Robert Tisch, the Giants' chairman and co-chief executive officer, died at the age of 79, November 15.

2006

The NFL announced that NFL Network would begin airing a "Road To The Playoffs" package of eight primetime regular season NFL games starting in 2006, January 28.

The Pittsburgh Steelers won their fifth Super Bowl, defeating the Seattle Seahawks 21-10 in Super Bowl XL at Ford Field in Detroit, Michigan, February 5.

The NFL clubs approved an extension of the Collective Bargaining Agreement through 2012, March 8.

Commissioner Tagliabue announced his decision to retire by the end of July. The NFL enjoyed an era of unrivaled prosperity in the Tagliabue Era, including labor peace throughout his 17-year tenure, March 20.

NFL clubs unanimously decided to return the name of the official game ball to "The Duke" in honor of the late New York Giants owner Wellington Mara, March 27.

The Amsterdam Admirals defeated the Berlin Thunder 22-7 to win World Bowl XIV in front of 36,286 fans at LTU Arena in Düsseldorf, Germany, May 27.

Roger Goodell became the eighth chief executive of the NFL on August 8 when he was chosen to succeed Paul Tagliabue as commissioner by a unanimous vote of the clubs at a three-day meeting in Chicago, Illinois. The transfer from Commissioner Tagliabue to Commissioner Goodell took place at 6:00 A.M. on Friday, September 1.

Cardinals Stadium opened in Glendale, Arizona with a crowd of 63,400 fans on August 12 as the Arizona Cardinals defeated the Pittsburgh Steelers 21-13 in a preseason game. The facility was later renamed University of Phoenix Stadium on September 26.

President George W. Bush signed into law HR 4954, which included the Internet Gambling Prohibition and Enforcement Act. The bill prohibits online gamblers from using credit cards, checks and electronic fund transfers to place and settle bets, strengthening enforcement of federal and state gambling laws that had been evaded by overseas gambling operations using the Internet, October 13.

NFL owners approved a resolution to stage a limited number of international regular-season games—up to two per season—beginning in 2007 and continuing through 2011, October 24.

The NFL Network broadcast its first-ever regular-season game as the Kansas City Chiefs defeated the Denver Broncos 19-10 at Arrowhead Stadium on Thanksgiving night, November 23.

San Diego Chargers running back LaDainian Tomlinson set the NFL single-season record for touchdowns with 29 on December 10. He finished the season with 31 touchdowns and also set a single-season record for points with 186.

Lamar Hunt, founder of the Kansas City Chiefs and the American Football League, died at the age of 74, December 13.

2007

The Indianapolis Colts won their second Super Bowl, defeating the Chicago Bears 29-17 in Super Bowl XLI at Dolphin Stadium in South Florida, February 4. Both teams were coached by African-Americans: Tony Dungy of the Colts and Lovie Smith of the Bears.

NFL clubs approved additional league-wide revenue sharing at a league meeting in Phoenix, Arizona. The teams agreed to redistribute up to $430 million over a four-year span, retroactive to 2006, March 26.

The NFL announced changes to its long-standing personal conduct policy and programs for players, coaches, and other team and league employees. The modifications focus on expanded educational and support programs in addition to increased levels of discipline for violations of the policy, April 10.

The NFL, NFL Players Association, NFL Retired Players Association, NFL Alumni Association, NFL Charities and Pro Football Hall of Fame formed the first-ever Alliance to coordinate medical support services for former players, May 22.

The Hamburg Sea Devils defeated the Frankfurt Galaxy 37-28 to win World Bowl XV in front of 48,125 fans at Commerzbank-Arena in Frankfurt, Germany, June 23.

The NFL announced it will focus its international business strategy on reaching the widest possible global audience, including the staging of international regular-season games, and discontinued NFL Europa after 15 seasons of operation, June 29.

NFL owners unanimously approved $10 million in additional Alliance funding for retired players to help pay for joint replacement surgeries and other medical assistance, supplementing the initial $7 million committed in July by Alliance members, October 24.

The New York Giants defeated the Miami Dolphins 13-10 at London's in front of 81,176 fans at Wembley Stadium in the first regular-season game played outside of North America, October 28.

On the field in the 2007 season, many significant records and milestones were achieved: Green Bay quarterback Brett Favre surpassed Pro Football Hall of Famer Dan Marino in both passing categories—touchdowns and yards—to become the NFL's all-time career leader. Patriots quarterback Tom Brady set the single-season record with 50 touchdown passes, including 23 to wide receiver Randy Moss—also a record. New England, which became the first team ever to finish 16-0 in the regular season, scored a record 589 points.

2008

The NFL, United States Olympic Committee, United States Anti-Doping Agency and MLB announced a partnership to form a clean competition anti-doping research collaborative, January 10.

Georgia Frontiere, majority owner of the St. Louis Rams, died at the age of 80, January 18.

The NFL announced it will stage a regular-season game in the United Kingdom during each of the next three seasons, beginning with the New Orleans Saints hosting the San Diego Chargers on October 26, 2008 at London's Wembley Stadium, February 1.

The New York Giants scored with 35 seconds remaining to win their third Super Bowl, defeating the New England Patriots 17-14 in Super Bowl XLII at University of Phoenix Stadium in Glendale, Arizona, February 3.

The NFL set an all-time paid attendance record in 2007 for the sixth consecutive season. Attendance for all 2007 games was 22,256,502, an increase of 56,790 over the previous mark. The Washington Redskins set an all-time NFL regular-season home paid attendance record of 711,471 for eight games, breaking their own record of 708,852 in 2006.

NFL clubs voted unanimously to exercise their option to shorten by two years the current Collective Bargaining Agreement, which now will run through the 2010 season and 2011 NFL Draft, May 20.

Lucas Oil Stadium opened in Indianapolis, Indiana with a crowd of 65,333 as the Buffalo Bills defeated the Indianapolis Colts by a score of 20-7 in a preseason game, August 24.

The NFL established a new fan code of conduct to help support a positive fan environment at all NFL stadiums, August 5.

NFLPA Executive Director and Pro Football Hall of Famer Gene Upshaw died at the age of 63, August 20.

For the first time, an NFL game was broadcast on NBC and also streamed live in its entirety to fans on the Internet via NFL.com and NBCSports.com as the Giants beat the Redskins 16-7 in the 2009 NFL Kickoff game, September 4.

Owners approved a restructured ownership plan for the Pittsburgh Steelers that will keep the team under the control of chairman Dan Rooney and team president Art Rooney II, December 17.

The NFL announced that the 2010 Pro Bowl will be played a week prior to Super Bowl XLIV on Sunday, January 31, 2010. Both games will be played in South Florida, December 30.

In the 256 regular-season games of 2008, 44.1 points per game were scored—the highest average since 1970.

2009

Stephen M. Ross purchased an additional 45 percent of the Miami Dolphins from Wayne Huizenga and became the team's managing partner. Coupled with his April 1, 2008 purchase of 50 percent of the franchise, the stadium, and the excess developable land, Ross now owns 95 percent of the Dolphins and the stadium while Huizenga retains a five percent share of both and remains a 50 percent partner in that land, January 20.

The NFL re-named its minority coaching internship program the Bill Walsh NFL Minority Coaching Fellowship, honoring the Pro Football Hall of Fame coach who conceived of the program, January 29.

The Pittsburgh Steelers

scored a touchdown with 42 seconds remaining to claim their NFL-record sixth Super Bowl title, defeating the Arizona Cardinals 27-23 in Super Bowl XLIII at Raymond James Stadium in Tampa Bay. The game was viewed by 151.6 million people, making it the most-watched program in U.S. television history, February 1.

The NFL and Westwood One announced a new two-year agreement for Westwood One to continue as the exclusive network radio partner of the NFL, March 12.

The NFLPA selected Washington-based attorney DeMaurice Smith as its new executive director, March 16.

The NFL and DIRECTV announced an agreement to extend DIRECTV's rights to carry NFL Sunday Ticket through the 2014 season. In addition, the NFL announced plans for a new "Red Zone Channel" that will offer fans crucial live action cut-ins of all Sunday afternoon games. The Red Zone Channel will launch no later than 2012, March 23.

NFL COMMISSIONERS AND PRESIDENTS*

1920 ....Jim Thorpe, President
1921-39....Joe Carr, President
1939-41 .Carl Storck, President
1941-46 ....Elmer Layden, Commissioner
1946-1959 ....Bert Bell, Commissioner
1960-1989.........Pete Rozelle, Commissioner
1989-2006 .....Paul Tagliabue, Commissioner
2006-present ..Roger Goodell, Commissioner

**NFL treasurer Austin Gunsel served as president in the office of the commissioner following the death of Bert Bell (Oct. 11, 1959) until the election of Pete Rozelle (Jan. 26, 1960).*

2008

AMERICAN CONFERENCE

East Division

	W	L	T	Pct.	Pts.	OP
Miami	11	5	0	.688	345	317
New England	11	5	0	.688	410	309
New York Jets	9	7	0	.563	405	356
Buffalo	7	9	0	.438	336	342

North Division

	W	L	T	Pct.	Pts.	OP
Pittsburgh	12	4	0	.750	347	223
Baltimore*	11	5	0	.688	385	244
Cincinnati	4	11	1	.281	204	364
Cleveland	4	12	0	.250	232	350

South Division

	W	L	T	Pct.	Pts.	OP
Tennessee#	13	3	0	.813	375	234
Indianapolis*	12	4	0	.750	377	298
Houston	8	8	0	.500	366	394
Jacksonville	5	11	0	.313	302	367

West Division

	W	L	T	Pct.	Pts.	OP
San Diego	8	8	0	.500	439	347
Denver	8	8	0	.500	370	448
Oakland	5	11	0	.313	263	388
Kansas City	2	14	0	.125	291	440

NATIONAL CONFERENCE

East Division

	W	L	T	Pct.	Pts.	OP
New York Giants#	12	4	0	.750	427	294
Philadelphia*	9	6	1	.594	416	289
Dallas	9	7	0	.563	362	365
Washington	8	8	0	.500	265	296

North Division

	W	L	T	Pct.	Pts.	OP
Minnesota	10	6	0	.625	379	333
Chicago	9	7	0	.563	375	350
Green Bay	6	10	0	.375	419	380
Detroit	0	16	0	.000	268	517

South Division

	W	L	T	Pct.	Pts.	OP
Carolina	12	4	0	.750	414	329
Atlanta*	11	5	0	.688	391	325
Tampa Bay	9	7	0	.563	361	323
New Orleans	8	8	0	.500	463	393

West Division

	W	L	T	Pct.	Pts.	OP
Arizona	9	7	0	.563	427	426
San Francisco	7	9	0	.438	339	381
Seattle	4	12	0	.250	294	392
St. Louis	2	14	0	.125	232	465

**Wild Card qualifier for playoffs; #Top playoff seed in conference*

Miami finished ahead of New England based on better conference record (8-4 to Patriots' 7-5). Baltimore was second Wild Card ahead of New England based on better conference record (8-4 to Patriots' 7-5). San Diego finished ahead of Denver based on better division record (5-1 to Broncos' 3-3). N.Y. Giants finished ahead of Carolina based on head-to-head victory.

Wild Card Playoff: SAN DIEGO 23, Indianapolis 17; Baltimore 27, MIAMI 9

Divisional Playoff: Baltimore 13, TENNESSEE 10 PITTSBURGH 35, San Diego 24

AFC Championship: PITTSBURGH 23, Baltimore 14

Wild Card Playoff: ARIZONA 30, Atlanta 24; Philadelphia 26, MINNESOTA 14

Divisional Playoff: Arizona 33, CAROLINA 13; Philadelphia 23, N.Y. GIANTS 11

NFC Championship: ARIZONA 32, Philadelphia 25

Super Bowl XLIII: Pittsburgh (AFC) 27, Arizona (NFC) 23 at Raymond James Stadium, Tampa, Florida

In Past Standings section, home teams in playoff games are indicated by capital letters.

Playoff Seeds

AFC
1. Tennessee
2. **Pittsburgh**
3. Miami
4. San Diego
5. Indianapolis
6. Baltimore

NFC
1. N.Y. Giants
2. Carolina
3. Minnesota
4. **Arizona**
5. Atlanta
6. Philadelphia

2007

AMERICAN CONFERENCE

East Division

	W	L	T	Pct.	Pts.	OP
New England#	16	0	0	1.000	589	274
Buffalo	7	9	0	.438	252	354
New York Jets	4	12	0	.250	268	355
Miami	1	15	0	.063	267	437

North Division

	W	L	T	Pct.	Pts.	OP
Pittsburgh	10	6	0	.625	393	269
Cleveland	10	6	0	.625	402	382
Cincinnati	7	9	0	.438	380	385
Baltimore	5	11	0	.313	275	384

South Division

	W	L	T	Pct.	Pts.	OP
Indianapolis	13	3	0	.813	450	262
Jacksonville*	11	5	0	.688	411	304
Tennessee*	10	6	0	.625	301	297
Houston	8	8	0	.500	379	384

West Division

	W	L	T	Pct.	Pts.	OP
San Diego	11	5	0	.688	412	284
Denver	7	9	0	.438	320	409
Kansas City	4	12	0	.250	226	335
Oakland	4	12	0	.250	283	398

NATIONAL CONFERENCE

East Division

	W	L	T	Pct.	Pts.	OP
Dallas#	13	3	0	.813	455	325
New York Giants*	10	6	0	.625	373	351
Washington*	9	7	0	.563	334	310
Philadelphia	8	8	0	.500	336	300

North Division

	W	L	T	Pct.	Pts.	OP
Green Bay	13	3	0	.813	435	291
Minnesota	8	8	0	.500	365	311
Detroit	7	9	0	.438	346	444
Chicago	7	9	0	.438	334	348

South Division

	W	L	T	Pct.	Pts.	OP
Tampa Bay	9	7	0	.563	334	270
Carolina	7	9	0	.438	267	347
New Orleans	7	9	0	.438	379	388
Atlanta	4	12	0	.250	259	414

West Division

	W	L	T	Pct.	Pts.	OP
Seattle	10	6	0	.625	393	291
Arizona	8	8	0	.500	404	399
San Francisco	5	11	0	.313	219	364
St. Louis	3	13	0	.188	263	438

**Wild Card qualifier for playoffs; #Top playoff seed in conference*

Pittsburgh finished ahead of Cleveland based on head-to-head sweep (2-0). Tennessee finished ahead of Cleveland based on better record vs. common opponents (4-1 to Browns' 3-2). Kansas City finished ahead of Oakland based on better record vs. common opponents (2-10 to Raiders' 1-11). Dallas finished ahead of Green Bay based on head-to-head victory. Detroit finished ahead of Chicago based on head-to-head sweep (2-0). Carolina finished ahead of New Orleans based on better conference record (7-5 to Saints' 6-6).

Wild Card Playoff: Jacksonville 31, PITTSBURGH 29 SAN DIEGO 17, Tennessee 6

Divisional Playoff: NEW ENGLAND 31, Jacksonville 20 San Diego 28, INDIANAPOLIS 24

AFC Championship: NEW ENGLAND 21, San Diego 12

Wild Card Playoff: SEATTLE 35, Washington 14 N.Y. Giants 24, TAMPA BAY 14

Divisional Playoff: GREEN BAY 42, Seattle 20 N.Y. Giants 21, DALLAS 17

NFC Championship: N.Y. Giants 23, GREEN BAY 20 (OT)

Super Bowl XLII: N.Y. Giants (NFC) 17, New England (AFC) 14 at University of Phoenix Stadium, Glendale, Arizona

Playoff Seeds

AFC
1. **New England**
2. Indianapolis
3. San Diego
4. Pittsburgh
5. Jacksonville
6. Tennessee

NFC
1. Dallas
2. Green Bay
3. Seattle
4. Tampa Bay
5. **N.Y. Giants**
6. Washington

PAST STANDINGS

2006

AMERICAN CONFERENCE

East Division

	W	L	T	Pct.	Pts.	OP
New England	12	4	0	.750	385	237
New York Jets*	10	6	0	.625	316	295
Buffalo	7	9	0	.438	300	311
Miami	6	10	0	.375	260	283

North Division

	W	L	T	Pct.	Pts.	OP
Baltimore	13	3	0	.813	353	201
Cincinnati	8	8	0	.500	373	331
Pittsburgh	8	8	0	.500	353	315
Cleveland	4	12	0	.250	238	356

South Division

	W	L	T	Pct.	Pts.	OP
Indianapolis	12	4	0	.750	427	360
Tennessee	8	8	0	.500	324	400
Jacksonville	8	8	0	.500	371	274
Houston	6	10	0	.375	267	366

West Division

	W	L	T	Pct.	Pts.	OP
San Diego#	14	2	0	.875	492	303
Kansas City*	9	7	0	.563	331	315
Denver	9	7	0	.563	319	305
Oakland	2	14	0	.125	168	332

NATIONAL CONFERENCE

East Division

	W	L	T	Pct.	Pts.	OP
Philadelphia	10	6	0	.625	398	328
Dallas*	9	7	0	.563	425	350
New York Giants*	8	8	0	.500	355	362
Washington	5	11	0	.313	307	376

North Division

	W	L	T	Pct.	Pts.	OP
Chicago#	13	3	0	.813	427	255
Green Bay	8	8	0	.500	301	366
Minnesota	6	10	0	.375	282	327
Detroit	3	13	0	.188	305	398

South Division

	W	L	T	Pct.	Pts.	OP
New Orleans	10	6	0	.625	413	322
Carolina	8	8	0	.500	270	305
Atlanta	7	9	0	.438	292	328
Tampa Bay	4	12	0	.250	211	353

West Division

	W	L	T	Pct.	Pts.	OP
Seattle	9	7	0	.563	335	341
St. Louis	8	8	0	.500	367	381
San Francisco	7	9	0	.438	298	412
Arizona	5	11	0	.313	314	389

**Wild Card qualifier for playoffs; #Top playoff seed in conference*

Indianapolis finished ahead of New England based on head-to-head victory. Cincinnati finished ahead of Pittsburgh based on better division record (4-2 to Steelers' 3-3). Tennessee finished ahead of Jacksonville based on better division record (4-2 to Jaguars' 2-4). Kansas City finished ahead of Denver based on better division record (4-2 to Broncos' 3-3). New Orleans finished ahead of Philadelphia based on head-to-head victory. N.Y. Giants finished ahead of Carolina and St. Louis based on better conference record (Giants' 7-5 to Panthers' 6-6 and Rams' 6-6) and ahead of Green Bay based on strength of victory (.422 to Packers' .383).

Wild Card Playoff: INDIANAPOLIS 23, Kansas City 8
NEW ENGLAND 37, N.Y. Jets 16

Divisional Playoff: Indianapolis 15, BALTIMORE 6
New England 24, SAN DIEGO 21

AFC Championship: INDIANAPOLIS 38, New England 34

Wild Card Playoff: SEATTLE 21, Dallas 20
PHILADELPHIA 23, N.Y. Giants 20

Divisional Playoff: NEW ORLEANS 27, Philadelphia 24
CHICAGO 27, Seattle 24 (OT)

NFC Championship: CHICAGO 39, New Orleans 14

Super Bowl XLI: Indianapolis (AFC) 29, Chicago (NFC) 17
at Dolphin Stadium, Miami, Florida

Playoff Seeds

AFC
1. San Diego
2. Baltimore
3. **Indianapolis**
4. New England
5. N.Y. Jets
6. Kansas City

NFC
1. **Chicago**
2. New Orleans
3. Philadelphia
4. Seattle
5. Dallas
6. N.Y. Giants

2005

AMERICAN CONFERENCE

East Division

	W	L	T	Pct.	Pts.	OP
New England	10	6	0	.625	379	338
Miami	9	7	0	.563	318	317
Buffalo	5	11	0	.313	271	367
N.Y. Jets	4	12	0	.250	240	355

North Division

	W	L	T	Pct.	Pts.	OP
Cincinnati	11	5	0	.688	421	350
Pittsburgh*	11	5	0	.688	389	258
Baltimore	6	10	0	.375	265	299
Cleveland	6	10	0	.375	232	301

South Division

	W	L	T	Pct.	Pts.	OP
Indianapolis#	14	2	0	.875	439	247
Jacksonville*	12	4	0	.750	361	269
Tennessee	4	12	0	.250	299	421
Houston	2	14	0	.125	260	431

West Division

	W	L	T	Pct.	Pts.	OP
Denver	13	3	0	.813	395	258
Kansas City	10	6	0	.625	403	325
San Diego	9	7	0	.563	418	312
Oakland	4	12	0	.250	290	383

NATIONAL CONFERENCE

East Division

	W	L	T	Pct.	Pts.	OP
N.Y. Giants	11	5	0	.688	422	314
Washington*	10	6	0	.625	359	293
Dallas	9	7	0	.563	325	308
Philadelphia	6	10	0	.375	310	388

North Division

	W	L	T	Pct.	Pts.	OP
Chicago	11	5	0	.688	260	202
Minnesota	9	7	0	.563	306	344
Detroit	5	11	0	.313	254	345
Green Bay	4	12	0	.250	298	344

South Division

	W	L	T	Pct.	Pts.	OP
Tampa Bay	11	5	0	.688	300	274
Carolina*	11	5	0	.688	391	259
Atlanta	8	8	0	.500	351	341
New Orleans	3	13	0	.188	235	398

West Division

	W	L	T	Pct.	Pts.	OP
Seattle#	13	3	0	.813	452	271
St. Louis	6	10	0	.375	363	429
Arizona	5	11	0	.313	311	387
San Francisco	4	12	0	.250	239	428

**Wild Card qualifier for playoffs; #Top playoff seed in conference*

Cincinnati finished ahead of Pittsburgh based on better division record (5-1 to Steelers' 4-2). Baltimore finished ahead of Cleveland based on better division record (2-4 to Browns' 1-5). Tampa Bay finished ahead of Carolina based on better division record (5-1 to Panthers' 4-2). Chicago finished ahead of Tampa Bay, and Tampa Bay finished ahead of the N.Y. Giants, based on better conference record (Bears' 10-2 to Buccaneers' 9-3 to Giants' 8-4).

Wild Card playoff: NEW ENGLAND 28, Jacksonville 3
Pittsburgh 31, CINCINNATI 17

Divisional playoff: DENVER 27, New England 13
Pittsburgh 21, INDIANAPOLIS 18

AFC Championship: Pittsburgh 34, DENVER 17

Wild Card playoffs: Washington 17, TAMPA BAY 10
Carolina 23, NEW YORK GIANTS 0

Divisional playoff: SEATTLE 20, Washington 10
Carolina 29, CHICAGO 21

NFC Championship: SEATTLE 34, Carolina 14

Super Bowl XL: Pittsburgh (AFC) 21, Seattle (NFC) 10
at Ford Field, Detroit, Michigan

Playoff Seeds

AFC
1. Indianapolis
2. Denver
3. Cincinnati
4. New England
5. Jacksonville
6. **Pittsburgh**

NFC
1. **Seattle**
2. Chicago
3. Tampa Bay
4. New York Giants
5. Carolina
6. Washington

2004

AMERICAN CONFERENCE

East Division

	W	L	T	Pct.	Pts.	OP
New England	14	2	0	.875	437	260
N.Y. Jets*	10	6	0	.625	333	261
Buffalo	9	7	0	.563	395	284
Miami	4	12	0	.250	275	354

North Division

	W	L	T	Pct.	Pts.	OP
Pittsburgh#	15	1	0	.938	372	251
Baltimore	9	7	0	.563	317	268
Cincinnati	8	8	0	.500	374	372
Cleveland	4	12	0	.250	276	390

South Division

	W	L	T	Pct.	Pts.	OP
Indianapolis	12	4	0	.750	522	351
Jacksonville	9	7	0	.563	261	280
Houston	7	9	0	.438	309	339
Tennessee	5	11	0	.313	344	439

West Division

	W	L	T	Pct.	Pts.	OP
San Diego	12	4	0	.750	446	313
Denver*	10	6	0	.625	381	304
Kansas City	7	9	0	.438	483	435
Oakland	5	11	0	.313	320	442

NATIONAL CONFERENCE

East Division

	W	L	T	Pct.	Pts.	OP
Philadelphia#	13	3	0	.813	386	260
N.Y. Giants	6	10	0	.375	303	347
Dallas	6	10	0	.375	293	405
Washington	6	10	0	.375	240	265

North Division

	W	L	T	Pct.	Pts.	OP
Green Bay	10	6	0	.625	424	380
Minnesota*	8	8	0	.500	405	395
Detroit	6	10	0	.375	296	350
Chicago	5	11	0	.313	231	331

South Division

	W	L	T	Pct.	Pts.	OP
Atlanta	11	5	0	.688	340	337
New Orleans	8	8	0	.500	348	405
Carolina	7	9	0	.438	355	339
Tampa Bay	5	11	0	.313	301	304

West Division

	W	L	T	Pct.	Pts.	OP
Seattle	9	7	0	.563	371	373
St. Louis*	8	8	0	.500	319	392
Arizona	6	10	0	.375	284	322
San Francisco	2	14	0	.125	259	452

**Wild Card qualifier for playoffs; #Top playoff seed in conference*

Indianapolis finished ahead of San Diego based on head-to-head victory. N.Y. Jets finished ahead of Denver based on better record vs. common opponents (5-0 to Broncos' 3-2). St. Louis finished ahead of New Orleans and Minnesota based on best conference record (7-5 to Saints' 6-6 to Vikings' 5-7), and Minnesota finished ahead of New Orleans based on head-to-head victory. N.Y. Giants finished ahead of Dallas and Washington based on better head-to-head record (3-1 to Cowboys' 2-2 to Redskins' 1-3), and Dallas finished ahead of Washington based on head-to-head sweep (2-0).

Wild Card playoffs: N.Y. Jets 20, SAN DIEGO 17 (OT)
INDIANAPOLIS 49, Denver 24

Divisional playoffs: PITTSBURGH 20, N.Y. Jets 17 (OT)
NEW ENGLAND 20, Indianapolis 3

AFC Championship: New England 41, PITTSBURGH 27

Wild Card playoffs: St. Louis 27, SEATTLE 20
Minnesota 31, GREEN BAY 17

Divisional playoffs: ATLANTA 47, St. Louis 17
PHILADELPHIA 27, Minnesota 14

NFC Championship: PHILADELPHIA 27, Atlanta 10

Super Bowl XXXIX: New England (AFC) 24, Philadelphia (NFC) 21 at Alltel Stadium, Jacksonville, Florida

Playoff Seeds

AFC	NFC
1. Pittsburgh	**1. Philadelphia**
2. New England	2. Atlanta
3. Indianapolis	3. Green Bay
4. San Diego	4. Seattle
5. N.Y. Jets	5. St. Louis
6. Denver	6. Minnesota

2003

AMERICAN CONFERENCE

East Division

	W	L	T	Pct.	Pts.	OP
New England#	14	2	0	.875	348	238
Miami	10	6	0	.625	311	261
Buffalo	6	10	0	.375	243	279
N.Y. Jets	6	10	0	.375	283	299

North Division

	W	L	T	Pct.	Pts.	OP
Baltimore	10	6	0	.625	391	281
Cincinnati	8	8	0	.500	346	384
Pittsburgh	6	10	0	.375	300	327
Cleveland	5	11	0	.313	254	322

South Division

	W	L	T	Pct.	Pts.	OP
Indianapolis	12	4	0	.750	447	336
Tennessee*	12	4	0	.750	435	324
Jacksonville	5	11	0	.313	276	331
Houston	5	11	0	.313	255	380

West Division

	W	L	T	Pct.	Pts.	OP
Kansas City	13	3	0	.813	484	332
Denver*	10	6	0	.625	381	301
Oakland	4	12	0	.250	270	379
San Diego	4	12	0	.250	313	441

NATIONAL CONFERENCE

East Division

	W	L	T	Pct.	Pts.	OP
Philadelphia#	12	4	0	.750	374	287
Dallas*	10	6	0	.625	289	260
Washington	5	11	0	.313	287	372
N.Y. Giants	4	12	0	.250	243	387

North Division

	W	L	T	Pct.	Pts.	OP
Green Bay	10	6	0	.625	442	307
Minnesota	9	7	0	.563	416	353
Chicago	7	9	0	.438	283	346
Detroit	5	11	0	.313	270	379

South Division

	W	L	T	Pct.	Pts.	OP
Carolina	11	5	0	.688	325	304
New Orleans	8	8	0	.500	340	326
Tampa Bay	7	9	0	.438	301	264
Atlanta	5	11	0	.313	299	422

West Division

	W	L	T	Pct.	Pts.	OP
St. Louis	12	4	0	.750	447	328
Seattle*	10	6	0	.625	404	327
San Francisco	7	9	0	.438	384	337
Arizona	4	12	0	.250	225	452

**Wild Card qualifier for playoffs; #Top playoff seed in conference*

Buffalo finished ahead of N.Y. Jets based on better division record (2-4 to Jets' 1-5). Indianapolis finished ahead of Tennessee based on head-to-head sweep (2-0). Jacksonville finished ahead of Houston based on better division record (2-4 to Texans' 1-5). Denver finished ahead of Miami based on better conference record (9-3 to Dolphins' 7-5). Oakland finished ahead of San Diego based on better conference record (3-9 to Chargers' 2-10). Philadelphia finished ahead of St. Louis based on better conference record (9-3 to Rams' 8-4). Seattle finished ahead of Dallas based on better strength of victory (65-95 to Cowboys' 62-98).

Wild Card playoffs: Tennessee 20, BALTIMORE 17;
INDIANAPOLIS 41, Denver 10

Divisional playoffs: NEW ENGLAND 17, Tennessee 14;
Indianapolis 38, KANSAS CITY 31

AFC Championship: NEW ENGLAND 24, Indianapolis 14

Wild Card playoffs: CAROLINA 29, Dallas 10;
GREEN BAY 33, Seattle 27 (OT)

Divisional playoffs: Carolina 29, ST. LOUIS 23 (2OT);
PHILADELPHIA 20, Green Bay 17 (OT)

NFC Championship: Carolina 14, PHILADELPHIA 3

Super Bowl XXXVIII: New England (AFC) 32, Carolina (NFC) 29 at Reliant Stadium, Houston, Texas

Playoff Seeds

AFC	NFC
1. New England	1. Philadelphia
2. Kansas City	2. St. Louis
3. Indianapolis	**3. Carolina**
4. Baltimore	4. Green Bay
5. Tennessee	5. Seattle
6. Denver	6. Dallas

2002

AMERICAN CONFERENCE

East Division

	W	L	T	Pct.	Pts.	OP
N.Y. Jets	9	7	0	.563	359	336
New England	9	7	0	.563	381	346
Miami	9	7	0	.563	378	301
Buffalo	8	8	0	.500	379	397

North Division

	W	L	T	Pct.	Pts.	OP
Pittsburgh	10	5	1	.656	390	345
Cleveland*	9	7	0	.563	344	320
Baltimore	7	9	0	.438	316	354
Cincinnati	2	14	0	.125	279	456

South Division

	W	L	T	Pct.	Pts.	OP
Tennessee	11	5	0	.688	367	324
Indianapolis*	10	6	0	.625	349	313
Jacksonville	6	10	0	.375	328	315
Houston	4	12	0	.250	213	356

West Division

	W	L	T	Pct.	Pts.	OP
Oakland#	11	5	0	.688	450	304
Denver	9	7	0	.563	392	344
San Diego	8	8	0	.500	333	367
Kansas City	8	8	0	.500	467	399

NATIONAL CONFERENCE

East Division

	W	L	T	Pct.	Pts.	OP
Philadelphia#	12	4	0	.750	415	241
N.Y. Giants*	10	6	0	.625	320	279
Washington	7	9	0	.438	307	365
Dallas	5	11	0	.313	217	329

North Division

	W	L	T	Pct.	Pts.	OP
Green Bay	12	4	0	.750	398	328
Minnesota	6	10	0	.375	390	442
Chicago	4	12	0	.250	281	379
Detroit	3	13	0	.188	306	451

South Division

	W	L	T	Pct.	Pts.	OP
Tampa Bay	12	4	0	.750	346	196
Atlanta*	9	6	1	.594	402	314
New Orleans	9	7	0	.563	432	388
Carolina	7	9	0	.438	258	302

West Division

	W	L	T	Pct.	Pts.	OP
San Francisco	10	6	0	.625	367	351
St. Louis	7	9	0	.438	316	369
Seattle	7	9	0	.438	355	369
Arizona	5	11	0	.313	262	417

**Wild Card qualifier for playoffs; #Top playoff seed in conference*

New York Jets finished ahead of New England based on better record in common games (8-4 to Patriots' 7-5) and Miami based on better division record (4-2 to Dolphins' 2-4). New England finished ahead of Miami based on better division record (4-2 to Dolphins' 2-4). Cleveland finished ahead of Denver and New England based on better conference record (7-5 to Broncos' 5-7 and Patriots' 6-6). Oakland finished ahead of Tennessee based on better head-to-head record (1-0). San Diego finished ahead of Kansas City based on better division record (3-3 to Chiefs' 2-4). Philadelphia finished ahead of Green Bay and Tampa Bay based on better conference record (11-1 to Packers' 9-3 and Buccaneers' 9-3). Tampa Bay finished ahead of Green Bay based on better head-to-head record (1-0). St. Louis finished ahead of Seattle based on better division record (4-2 to Seahawks' 2-4).

Wild Card playoffs: N.Y. JETS 41, Indianapolis 0; PITTSBURGH 36, Cleveland 33

Divisional playoffs: TENNESSEE 34, Pittsburgh 31 (OT); OAKLAND 30, N.Y. Jets 10

AFC Championship: OAKLAND 41, Tennessee 24

Wild Card playoffs: Atlanta 27, GREEN BAY 7; SAN FRANCISCO 39, N.Y. Giants 38

Divisional playoffs: PHILADELPHIA 20, Atlanta 6; TAMPA BAY 31, San Francisco 6

NFC Championship: Tampa Bay 27, PHILADELPHIA 10

Super Bowl XXXVII: Tampa Bay (NFC) 48, Oakland (AFC) 21 at Qualcomm Stadium, San Diego, California

Playoff Seeds

AFC

1. Oakland
2. Tennessee
3. Pittsburgh
4. N.Y. Jets
5. Indianapolis
6. Cleveland

NFC

1. Philadelphia
2. Tampa Bay
3. Green Bay
4. San Francisco
5. N.Y. Giants
6. Atlanta

2001

AMERICAN CONFERENCE

Eastern Division

	W	L	T	Pct.	Pts.	OP
New England	11	5	0	.688	371	272
Miami*	11	5	0	.688	344	290
N.Y. Jets*	10	6	0	.625	308	295
Indianapolis	6	10	0	.375	413	486
Buffalo	3	13	0	.188	265	420

Central Division

	W	L	T	Pct.	Pts.	OP
Pittsburgh#	13	3	0	.813	352	212
Baltimore*	10	6	0	.625	303	265
Cleveland	7	9	0	.438	285	319
Tennessee	7	9	0	.438	336	388
Jacksonville	6	10	0	.375	294	286
Cincinnati	6	10	0	.375	226	309

Western Division

	W	L	T	Pct.	Pts.	OP
Oakland	10	6	0	.625	399	327
Seattle	9	7	0	.563	301	324
Denver	8	8	0	.500	340	339
Kansas City	6	10	0	.375	320	344
San Diego	5	11	0	.313	332	321

NATIONAL CONFERENCE

Eastern Division

	W	L	T	Pct.	Pts.	OP
Philadelphia	11	5	0	.688	343	208
Washington	8	8	0	.500	256	303
N.Y. Giants	7	9	0	.438	294	321
Arizona	7	9	0	.438	295	343
Dallas	5	11	0	.313	246	338

Central Division

	W	L	T	Pct.	Pts.	OP
Chicago	13	3	0	.813	338	203
Green Bay*	12	4	0	.750	390	266
Tampa Bay*	9	7	0	.563	324	280
Minnesota	5	11	0	.313	290	390
Detroit	2	14	0	.125	270	424

Western Division

	W	L	T	Pct.	Pts.	OP
St. Louis#	14	2	0	.875	503	273
San Francisco*	12	4	0	.750	409	282
New Orleans	7	9	0	.438	333	409
Atlanta	7	9	0	.438	291	377
Carolina	1	15	0	.063	253	410

**Wild Card qualifier for playoffs; #Top playoff seed in conference*

New England finished ahead of Miami based on better division record (6-2 to Dolphins' 5-3). Baltimore was second Wild Card ahead of N.Y. Jets based on better record against common opponents (3-2 to Jets' 2-2). Cleveland finished ahead of Tennessee based on better division record (5-5 to Titans' 3-7). Jacksonville finished ahead of Cincinnati based on head-to-head record (2-0). N.Y. Giants finished ahead of Arizona based on head-to-head record (2-0). Green Bay was first Wild Card ahead of San Francisco based on better conference record (9-3 to 49ers' 8-4). New Orleans finished ahead of Atlanta based on better division record (4-4 to Falcons' 3-5).

Wild Card playoffs: OAKLAND 38, N.Y. Jets 24; Baltimore 20, MIAMI 3

Divisional playoffs: NEW ENGLAND 16, Oakland 13 (OT); PITTSBURGH 27, Baltimore 10

AFC Championship: New England 24, PITTSBURGH 17

Wild Card playoffs: PHILADELPHIA 31, Tampa Bay 9; GREEN BAY 25, San Francisco 15

Divisional playoffs: Philadelphia 33, CHICAGO 19; ST. LOUIS 45, Green Bay 17

NFC Championship: ST. LOUIS 29, Philadelphia 24

Super Bowl XXXVI: New England (AFC) 20, St. Louis (NFC) 17 at Louisiana Superdome, New Orleans, Louisiana

Playoff Seeds

AFC

1. Pittsburgh
2. New England
3. Oakland
4. Miami
5. Baltimore
6. N.Y. Jets

NFC

1. St. Louis
2. Chicago
3. Philadelphia
4. Green Bay
5. San Francisco
6. Tampa Bay

2000

AMERICAN CONFERENCE

Eastern Division

	W	L	T	Pct.	Pts.	OP
Miami	11	5	0	.688	323	226
Indianapolis*	10	6	0	.625	429	326
N.Y. Jets	9	7	0	.563	321	321
Buffalo	8	8	0	.500	315	350
New England	5	11	0	.313	276	338

Central Division

	W	L	T	Pct.	Pts.	OP
Tennessee#	13	3	0	.813	346	191
Baltimore*	12	4	0	.750	333	165
Pittsburgh	9	7	0	.563	321	255
Jacksonville	7	9	0	.438	367	327
Cincinnati	4	12	0	.250	185	359
Cleveland	3	13	0	.188	161	419

Western Division

	W	L	T	Pct.	Pts.	OP
Oakland	12	4	0	.750	479	299
Denver*	11	5	0	.688	485	369
Kansas City	7	9	0	.438	355	354
Seattle	6	10	0	.375	320	405
San Diego	1	15	0	.063	269	440

NATIONAL CONFERENCE

Eastern Division

	W	L	T	Pct.	Pts.	OP
N.Y. Giants#	12	4	0	.750	328	246
Philadelphia*	11	5	0	.688	351	245
Washington	8	8	0	.500	281	269
Dallas	5	11	0	.313	294	361
Arizona	3	13	0	.188	210	443

Central Division

	W	L	T	Pct.	Pts.	OP
Minnesota	11	5	0	.688	397	371
Tampa Bay*	10	6	0	.625	388	269
Green Bay	9	7	0	.563	353	323
Detroit	9	7	0	.563	307	307
Chicago	5	11	0	.313	216	355

Western Division

	W	L	T	Pct.	Pts.	OP
New Orleans	10	6	0	.625	354	305
St. Louis*	10	6	0	.625	540	471
Carolina	7	9	0	.438	310	310
San Francisco	6	10	0	.375	388	422
Atlanta	4	12	0	.250	252	413

**Wild Card qualifier for playoffs; #Top playoff seed in conference*

Green Bay finished ahead of Detroit based on better division record (5-3 to Lions' 3-5). New Orleans finished ahead of St. Louis based on better division record (7-1 to Rams' 5-3). Tampa Bay was second Wild Card based on head-to-head victory over St. Louis (1-0).

Wild Card playoffs: MIAMI 23, Indianapolis 17 (OT); BALTIMORE 21, Denver 3

Divisional playoffs: OAKLAND 27, Miami 0; Baltimore 24, TENNESSEE 10

AFC Championship: Baltimore 16, OAKLAND 3

Wild Card playoffs: NEW ORLEANS 31, St. Louis 28; PHILADELPHIA 21, Tampa Bay 3

Divisional playoffs: MINNESOTA 34, New Orleans 16; N.Y. GIANTS 20, Philadelphia 10

NFC Championship: N.Y. GIANTS 41, Minnesota 0

Super Bowl XXXV: Baltimore (AFC) 34, N.Y. Giants (NFC) 7 at Raymond James Stadium, Tampa, Florida

Playoff Seeds

AFC	NFC
1. Tennessee	**1. N.Y. Giants**
2. Oakland	2. Minnesota
3. Miami	3. New Orleans
4. Baltimore	4. Philadelphia
5. Denver	5. Tampa Bay
6. Indianapolis	6. St. Louis

1999

AMERICAN CONFERENCE

Eastern Division

	W	L	T	Pct.	Pts.	OP
Indianapolis	13	3	0	.813	423	333
Buffalo*	11	5	0	.688	320	229
Miami*	9	7	0	.563	326	336
N.Y. Jets	8	8	0	.500	308	309
New England	8	8	0	.500	299	284

Central Division

	W	L	T	Pct.	Pts.	OP
Jacksonville#	14	2	0	.875	396	217
Tennessee*	13	3	0	.813	392	324
Baltimore	8	8	0	.500	324	277
Pittsburgh	6	10	0	.375	317	320
Cincinnati	4	12	0	.250	283	460
Cleveland	2	14	0	.125	217	437

Western Division

	W	L	T	Pct.	Pts.	OP
Seattle	9	7	0	.563	338	298
Kansas City	9	7	0	.563	390	322
San Diego	8	8	0	.500	269	316
Oakland	8	8	0	.500	390	329
Denver	6	10	0	.375	314	318

NATIONAL CONFERENCE

Eastern Division

	W	L	T	Pct.	Pts.	OP
Washington	10	6	0	.625	443	377
Dallas*	8	8	0	.500	352	276
N.Y. Giants	7	9	0	.438	299	358
Arizona	6	10	0	.375	245	382
Philadelphia	5	11	0	.313	272	357

Central Division

	W	L	T	Pct.	Pts.	OP
Tampa Bay	11	5	0	.688	270	235
Minnesota*	10	6	0	.625	399	335
Detroit*	8	8	0	.500	322	323
Green Bay	8	8	0	.500	357	341
Chicago	6	10	0	.375	272	341

Western Division

	W	L	T	Pct.	Pts.	OP
St. Louis#	13	3	0	.813	526	242
Carolina	8	8	0	.500	421	381
Atlanta	5	11	0	.313	285	380
San Francisco	4	12	0	.250	295	453
New Orleans	3	13	0	.188	260	434

**Wild Card qualifier for playoffs; #Top playoff seed in conference*

Miami was third Wild Card ahead of Kansas City based on better record against common opponents (6-1 to Chiefs' 5-3). N.Y. Jets finished ahead of New England based on better division record (4-4 to Patriots' 2-6). Seattle finished ahead of Kansas City based on head-to-head sweep (2-0). San Diego finished ahead of Oakland based on better division record (5-3 to Raiders' 3-5). Dallas was second Wild Card based on better record against common opponents (3-2 to Lions' 3-3) and better conference record than Carolina (7-5 to Panthers' 6-6). Detroit was third Wild Card based on better conference record than Green Bay (7-5 to Packers' 6-6) and head-to-head victory over Carolina.

Wild Card playoffs: TENNESSEE 22, Buffalo 16; Miami 20, SEATTLE 17

Divisional playoffs: JACKSONVILLE 62, Miami 7; Tennessee 19, INDIANAPOLIS 16

AFC Championship: Tennessee 33, JACKSONVILLE 14

Wild Card playoffs: WASHINGTON 27, Detroit 13; MINNESOTA 27, Dallas 10

Divisional playoffs: TAMPA BAY 14, Washington 13; ST. LOUIS 49, Minnesota 37

NFC Championship: ST. LOUIS 11, Tampa Bay 6

Super Bowl XXXIV: St. Louis (NFC) 23, Tennessee (AFC) 16 at Georgia Dome, Atlanta, Georgia

Playoff Seeds

AFC	NFC
1. Jacksonville	**1. St. Louis**
2. Indianapolis	2. Tampa Bay
3. Seattle	3. Washington
4. Tennessee	4. Minnesota
5. Buffalo	5. Dallas
6. Miami	6. Detroit

1998

AMERICAN CONFERENCE

Eastern Division

	W	L	T	Pct.	Pts.	OP
N.Y. Jets	12	4	0	.750	416	266
Miami*	10	6	0	.625	321	265
Buffalo*	10	6	0	.625	400	333
New England*	9	7	0	.563	337	329
Indianapolis	3	13	0	.188	310	444

Central Division

	W	L	T	Pct.	Pts.	OP
Jacksonville	11	5	0	.688	392	338
Tennessee	8	8	0	.500	330	320
Pittsburgh	7	9	0	.438	263	303
Baltimore	6	10	0	.375	269	335
Cincinnati	3	13	0	.188	268	452

Western Division

	W	L	T	Pct.	Pts.	OP
Denver#	14	2	0	.875	501	309
Oakland	8	8	0	.500	288	356
Seattle	8	8	0	.500	372	310
Kansas City	7	9	0	.438	327	363
San Diego	5	11	0	.313	241	342

NATIONAL CONFERENCE

Eastern Division

	W	L	T	Pct.	Pts.	OP
Dallas	10	6	0	.625	381	275
Arizona*	9	7	0	.563	325	378
N.Y. Giants	8	8	0	.500	287	309
Washington	6	10	0	.375	319	421
Philadelphia	3	13	0	.188	161	344

Central Division

	W	L	T	Pct.	Pts.	OP
Minnesota#	15	1	0	.938	556	296
Green Bay*	11	5	0	.688	408	319
Tampa Bay	8	8	0	.500	314	295
Detroit	5	11	0	.313	306	378
Chicago	4	12	0	.250	276	368

Western Division

	W	L	T	Pct.	Pts.	OP
Atlanta	14	2	0	.875	442	289
San Francisco*	12	4	0	.750	479	328
New Orleans	6	10	0	.375	305	359
Carolina	4	12	0	.250	336	413
St. Louis	4	12	0	.250	285	378

**Wild Card qualifier for playoffs; #Top playoff seed in conference*

Miami finished ahead of Buffalo based on better net division points (6 to Bills' 0). Oakland finished ahead of Seattle based on head-to-head sweep (2-0). Carolina finished ahead of St. Louis based on head-to-head sweep (2-0).

Wild Card playoffs: MIAMI 24, Buffalo 17; JACKSONVILLE 25, New England 10

Divisional playoffs: DENVER 38, Miami 3; N.Y. JETS 34, Jacksonville 24

AFC Championship: DENVER 23, N.Y. Jets 10

Wild Card playoffs: Arizona 20, DALLAS 7; SAN FRANCISCO 30, Green Bay 27

Divisional playoffs: ATLANTA 20, San Francisco 18; MINNESOTA 41, Arizona 21

NFC Championship: Atlanta 30, MINNESOTA 27 (OT)

Super Bowl XXXIII: Denver (AFC) 34, Atlanta (NFC) 19, at Pro Player Stadium, Miami, Florida

Playoff Seeds

AFC	NFC
1. Denver	1. Minnesota
2. N.Y. Jets	**2. Atlanta**
3. Jacksonville	3. Dallas
4. Miami	4. San Francisco
5. Buffalo	5. Green Bay
6. New England	6. Arizona

1997

AMERICAN CONFERENCE

Eastern Division

	W	L	T	Pct.	Pts.	OP
New England	10	6	0	.625	369	289
Miami*	9	7	0	.563	339	327
N.Y. Jets	9	7	0	.563	348	287
Buffalo	6	10	0	.375	255	367
Indianapolis	3	13	0	.188	313	401

Central Division

	W	L	T	Pct.	Pts.	OP
Pittsburgh	11	5	0	.688	372	307
Jacksonville*	11	5	0	.688	394	318
Tennessee	8	8	0	.500	333	310
Cincinnati	7	9	0	.438	355	405
Baltimore	6	9	1	.406	326	345

Western Division

	W	L	T	Pct.	Pts.	OP
Kansas City#	13	3	0	.813	375	232
Denver*	12	4	0	.750	472	287
Seattle	8	8	0	.500	365	362
Oakland	4	12	0	.250	324	419
San Diego	4	12	0	.250	266	425

NATIONAL CONFERENCE

Eastern Division

	W	L	T	Pct.	Pts.	OP
N.Y. Giants	10	5	1	.656	307	265
Washington	8	7	1	.531	327	289
Philadelphia	6	9	1	.406	317	372
Dallas	6	10	0	.375	304	314
Arizona	4	12	0	.250	283	379

Central Division

	W	L	T	Pct.	Pts.	OP
Green Bay	13	3	0	.813	422	282
Tampa Bay*	10	6	0	.625	299	263
Detroit*	9	7	0	.563	379	306
Minnesota*	9	7	0	.563	354	359
Chicago	4	12	0	.250	263	421

Western Division

	W	L	T	Pct.	Pts.	OP
San Francisco#	13	3	0	.813	375	265
Carolina	7	9	0	.438	265	314
Atlanta	7	9	0	.438	320	361
New Orleans	6	10	0	.375	237	327
St. Louis	5	11	0	.313	299	359

**Wild Card qualifier for playoffs; #Top playoff seed in conference*

Miami finished ahead of N.Y. Jets based on head-to-head sweep (2-0). Pittsburgh finished ahead of Jacksonville based on better net division points (78 to Jaguars' 23). Oakland finished ahead of San Diego based on better division record (2-6 to Chargers' 1-7). San Francisco was top playoff seed based on better conference record than Green Bay (11-1 to Packers' 10-2). Detroit finished ahead of Minnesota based on head-to-head sweep (2-0). Carolina finished ahead of Atlanta based on head-to-head sweep (2-0).

Wild Card playoffs: DENVER 42, Jacksonville 17; NEW ENGLAND 17, Miami 3

Divisional playoffs: PITTSBURGH 7, New England 6; Denver 14, KANSAS CITY 10

AFC Championship: Denver 24, PITTSBURGH 21

Wild Card playoffs: Minnesota 23, N.Y. GIANTS 22; TAMPA BAY 20, Detroit 10

Divisional playoffs: SAN FRANCISCO 38, Minnesota 22; GREEN BAY 21, Tampa Bay 7

NFC Championship: Green Bay 23, SAN FRANCISCO 10

Super Bowl XXXII: Denver (AFC) 31, Green Bay (NFC) 24, at Qualcomm Stadium, San Diego, California

Playoff Seeds

AFC	NFC
1. Kansas City	1. San Francisco
2. Pittsburgh	**2. Green Bay**
3. New England	3. N.Y. Giants
4. Denver	4. Tampa Bay
5. Jacksonville	5. Detroit
6. Miami	6. Minnesota

1996

AMERICAN CONFERENCE

Eastern Division

	W	L	T	Pct.	Pts.	OP
New England	11	5	0	.688	418	313
Buffalo*	10	6	0	.625	319	266
Indianapolis*	9	7	0	.563	317	334
Miami	8	8	0	.500	339	325
N.Y. Jets	1	15	0	.063	279	454

Central Division

	W	L	T	Pct.	Pts.	OP
Pittsburgh	10	6	0	.625	344	257
Jacksonville*	9	7	0	.563	325	335
Cincinnati	8	8	0	.500	372	369
Houston	8	8	0	.500	345	319
Baltimore	4	12	0	.250	371	441

Western Division

	W	L	T	Pct.	Pts.	OP
Denver#	13	3	0	.813	391	275
Kansas City	9	7	0	.563	297	300
San Diego	8	8	0	.500	310	376
Oakland	7	9	0	.438	340	293
Seattle	7	9	0	.438	317	376

NATIONAL CONFERENCE

Eastern Division

	W	L	T	Pct.	Pts.	OP
Dallas	10	6	0	.625	286	250
Philadelphia*	10	6	0	.625	363	341
Washington	9	7	0	.563	364	312
Arizona	7	9	0	.438	300	397
N.Y. Giants	6	10	0	.375	242	297

Central Division

	W	L	T	Pct.	Pts.	OP
Green Bay#	13	3	0	.813	456	210
Minnesota*	9	7	0	.563	298	315
Chicago	7	9	0	.438	283	305
Tampa Bay	6	10	0	.375	221	293
Detroit	5	11	0	.313	302	368

Western Division

	W	L	T	Pct.	Pts.	OP
Carolina	12	4	0	.750	367	218
San Francisco*	12	4	0	.750	398	257
St. Louis	6	10	0	.375	303	409
Atlanta	3	13	0	.188	309	461
New Orleans	3	13	0	.188	229	339

**Wild Card qualifier for playoffs; #Top playoff seed in conference*

Jacksonville was second Wild Card ahead of Indianapolis and Kansas City based on better conference record (7-5 to Colts' 6-6 and Chiefs' 5-7). Indianapolis was third Wild Card based on head-to-head victory over Kansas City (1-0). Cincinnati finished ahead of Houston based on better net division points (19 to Oilers' 11). Oakland finished ahead of Seattle based on better division record (3-5 to Seahawks' 2-6). Dallas finished ahead of Philadelphia based on better record against common opponents (7-4 to Eagles' 6-5). Minnesota was third Wild Card based on better conference record than Washington (8-4 to Redskins' 6-6). Carolina finished ahead of San Francisco based on head-to-head sweep (2-0). Atlanta finished ahead of New Orleans based on head-to-head sweep (2-0).

Wild Card playoffs: Jacksonville 30, BUFFALO 27; PITTSBURGH 42, Indianapolis 14

Divisional playoffs: Jacksonville 30, DENVER 27; NEW ENGLAND 28, Pittsburgh 3

AFC Championship: NEW ENGLAND 20, Jacksonville 6

Wild Card playoffs: DALLAS 40, Minnesota 15; SAN FRANCISCO 14, Philadelphia 0

Divisional playoffs: GREEN BAY 35, San Francisco 14; CAROLINA 26, Dallas 17

NFC Championship: GREEN BAY 30, Carolina 13

Super Bowl XXXI: Green Bay (NFC) 35, New England (AFC) 21, at Louisiana Superdome, New Orleans, Louisiana

Playoff Seeds

AFC	NFC
1. Denver	**1. Green Bay**
2. New England	2. Carolina
3. Pittsburgh	3. Dallas
4. Buffalo	4. San Francisco
5. Jacksonville	5. Philadelphia
6. Indianapolis	6. Minnesota

1995

AMERICAN CONFERENCE

Eastern Division

	W	L	T	Pct.	Pts.	OP
Buffalo	10	6	0	.625	350	335
Indianapolis*	9	7	0	.563	331	316
Miami*	9	7	0	.563	398	332
New England	6	10	0	.375	294	377
N.Y. Jets	3	13	0	.188	233	384

Central Division

	W	L	T	Pct.	Pts.	OP
Pittsburgh	11	5	0	.688	407	327
Cincinnati	7	9	0	.438	349	374
Houston	7	9	0	.438	348	324
Cleveland	5	11	0	.313	289	356
Jacksonville	4	12	0	.250	275	404

Western Division

	W	L	T	Pct.	Pts.	OP
Kansas City#	13	3	0	.813	358	241
San Diego*	9	7	0	.563	321	323
Seattle	8	8	0	.500	363	366
Denver	8	8	0	.500	388	345
Oakland	8	8	0	.500	348	332

NATIONAL CONFERENCE

Eastern Division

	W	L	T	Pct.	Pts.	OP
Dallas#	12	4	0	.750	435	291
Philadelphia*	10	6	0	.625	318	338
Washington	6	10	0	.375	326	359
N.Y. Giants	5	11	0	.313	290	340
Arizona	4	12	0	.250	275	422

Central Division

	W	L	T	Pct.	Pts.	OP
Green Bay	11	5	0	.688	404	314
Detroit*	10	6	0	.625	436	336
Chicago	9	7	0	.563	392	360
Minnesota	8	8	0	.500	412	385
Tampa Bay	7	9	0	.438	238	335

Western Division

	W	L	T	Pct.	Pts.	OP
San Francisco	11	5	0	.688	457	258
Atlanta*	9	7	0	.563	362	349
St. Louis	7	9	0	.438	309	418
Carolina	7	9	0	.438	289	325
New Orleans	7	9	0	.438	319	348

**Wild Card qualifier for playoffs; #Top playoff seed in conference*

Indianapolis finished ahead of Miami based on head-to-head sweep (2-0). San Diego was first Wild Card based on head-to-head victory over Indianapolis (1-0). Cincinnati finished ahead of Houston based on better division record (4-4 to Oilers' 3-5). Seattle finished ahead of Denver and Oakland based on best head-to-head record (3-1 to Broncos' 2-2 and Raiders' 1-3). Denver finished ahead of Oakland based on head-to-head sweep (2-0). Philadelphia was first Wild Card ahead of Detroit based on better conference record (9-3 to Lions' 7-5). San Francisco was second playoff seed ahead of Green Bay based on better conference record (8-4 to Packers' 7-5). Atlanta was third Wild Card ahead of Chicago based on better record against common opponents (4-2 to Bears' 3-3). St. Louis finished ahead of Carolina and New Orleans based on best head-to-head record (3-1 to Panthers' 1-3 and Saints' 2-2). Carolina finished ahead of New Orleans based on better conference record (4-8 to 3-9).

Wild Card playoffs: BUFFALO 37, Miami 22; Indianapolis 35, SAN DIEGO 20

Divisional playoffs: PITTSBURGH 40, Buffalo 21; Indianapolis 10, KANSAS CITY 7

AFC Championship: PITTSBURGH 20, Indianapolis 16

Wild Card playoffs: PHILADELPHIA 58, Detroit 37; GREEN BAY 37, Atlanta 20

Divisional playoffs: Green Bay 27, SAN FRANCISCO 17; DALLAS 30, Philadelphia 11

NFC Championship: DALLAS 38, Green Bay 27

Super Bowl XXX: Dallas (NFC) 27, Pittsburgh (AFC) 17, at Sun Devil Stadium, Tempe, Arizona

Playoff Seeds

AFC	NFC
1. Kansas City	**1. Dallas**
2. Pittsburgh	2. San Francisco
3. Buffalo	3. Green Bay
4. San Diego	4. Philadelphia
5. Indianapolis	5. Detroit
6. Miami	6. Atlanta

1994

AMERICAN CONFERENCE

Eastern Division

	W	L	T	Pct.	Pts.	OP
Miami	10	6	0	.625	389	327
New England*	10	6	0	.625	351	312
Indianapolis	8	8	0	.500	307	320
Buffalo	7	9	0	.438	340	356
N.Y. Jets	6	10	0	.375	264	320

Central Division

	W	L	T	Pct.	Pts.	OP
Pittsburgh#	12	4	0	.750	316	234
Cleveland*	11	5	0	.688	340	204
Cincinnati	3	13	0	.188	276	406
Houston	2	14	0	.125	226	352

Western Division

	W	L	T	Pct.	Pts.	OP
San Diego	11	5	0	.688	381	306
Kansas City*	9	7	0	.563	319	298
L.A. Raiders	9	7	0	.563	303	327
Denver	7	9	0	.438	347	396
Seattle	6	10	0	.375	287	323

NATIONAL CONFERENCE

Eastern Division

	W	L	T	Pct.	Pts.	OP
Dallas	12	4	0	.750	414	248
N.Y. Giants	9	7	0	.563	279	305
Arizona	8	8	0	.500	235	267
Philadelphia	7	9	0	.438	308	308
Washington	3	13	0	.188	320	412

Central Division

	W	L	T	Pct.	Pts.	OP
Minnesota	10	6	0	.625	356	314
Green Bay*	9	7	0	.563	382	287
Detroit*	9	7	0	.563	357	342
Chicago*	9	7	0	.563	271	307
Tampa Bay	6	10	0	.375	251	351

Western Division

	W	L	T	Pct.	Pts.	OP
San Francisco#	13	3	0	.813	505	296
New Orleans	7	9	0	.438	348	407
Atlanta	7	9	0	.438	317	385
L.A. Rams	4	12	0	.250	286	365

**Wild Card qualifier for playoffs; #Top playoff seed in conference*

Miami finished ahead of New England based on head-to-head sweep (2-0). Kansas City finished ahead of L.A. Raiders based on head-to-head sweep (2-0). Green Bay was first Wild Card based on best head-to-head record (3-1) vs. Detroit (2-2) and Chicago (1-3) and better conference record (8-4) than N.Y. Giants (6-6). Detroit was second Wild Card based on better division record (4-4) than Chicago (3-5) and head-to-head victory over N.Y. Giants (1-0). Chicago was third Wild Card based on better record against common opponents (4-4) than N.Y. Giants (3-5). New Orleans finished ahead of Atlanta based on head-to-head sweep (2-0).

Wild Card playoffs: MIAMI 27, Kansas City 17; CLEVELAND 20, New England 13

Divisional playoffs: PITTSBURGH 29, Cleveland 9; SAN DIEGO 22, Miami 21

AFC Championship: San Diego 17, PITTSBURGH 13

Wild Card playoffs: GREEN BAY 16, Detroit 12; Chicago 35, MINNESOTA 18

Divisional playoffs: SAN FRANCISCO 44, Chicago 15; DALLAS 35, Green Bay 9

NFC Championship: SAN FRANCISCO 38, Dallas 28

Super Bowl XXIX: San Francisco (NFC) 49, San Diego (AFC) 26, at Joe Robbie Stadium, Miami, Florida

Playoff Seeds

AFC	NFC
1. Pittsburgh	**1. San Francisco**
2. San Diego	2. Dallas
3. Miami	3. Minnesota
4. Cleveland	4. Green Bay
5. New England	5. Detroit
6. Kansas City	6. Chicago

1993

AMERICAN CONFERENCE

Eastern Division

	W	L	T	Pct.	Pts.	OP
Buffalo#	12	4	0	.750	329	242
Miami	9	7	0	.563	349	351
N.Y. Jets	8	8	0	.500	270	247
New England	5	11	0	.313	238	286
Indianapolis	4	12	0	.250	189	378

Central Division

	W	L	T	Pct.	Pts.	OP
Houston	12	4	0	.750	368	238
Pittsburgh*	9	7	0	.563	308	281
Cleveland	7	9	0	.438	304	307
Cincinnati	3	13	0	.188	187	319

Western Division

	W	L	T	Pct.	Pts.	OP
Kansas City	11	5	0	.688	328	291
L.A. Raiders*	10	6	0	.625	306	326
Denver*	9	7	0	.563	373	284
San Diego	8	8	0	.500	322	290
Seattle	6	10	0	.375	280	314

NATIONAL CONFERENCE

Eastern Division

	W	L	T	Pct.	Pts.	OP
Dallas#	12	4	0	.750	376	229
N.Y. Giants*	11	5	0	.688	288	205
Philadelphia	8	8	0	.500	293	315
Phoenix	7	9	0	.438	326	269
Washington	4	12	0	.250	230	345

Central Division

	W	L	T	Pct.	Pts.	OP
Detroit	10	6	0	.625	298	292
Minnesota*	9	7	0	.563	277	290
Green Bay*	9	7	0	.563	340	282
Chicago	7	9	0	.438	234	230
Tampa Bay	5	11	0	.313	237	376

Western Division

	W	L	T	Pct.	Pts.	OP
San Francisco	10	6	0	.625	473	295
New Orleans	8	8	0	.500	317	343
Atlanta	6	10	0	.375	316	385
L.A. Rams	5	11	0	.313	221	367

**Wild Card qualifier for playoffs; #Top playoff seed in conference*

Buffalo was top playoff seed based on head-to-head victory over Houston (1-0). Denver was second Wild Card ahead of Pittsburgh and Miami based on better conference record (8-4 to Steelers' 7-5 to Dolphins' 6-6). Pittsburgh was third Wild Card ahead of Miami based on head-to-head victory. San Francisco was second playoff seed based on head-to-head victory over Detroit (1-0). Minnesota finished ahead of Green Bay based on head-to-head sweep (2-0).

Wild Card playoffs: KANSAS CITY 27, Pittsburgh 24 (OT); L.A. RAIDERS 42, Denver 24

Divisional playoffs: BUFFALO 29, L.A. Raiders 23; Kansas City 28, HOUSTON 20

AFC Championship: BUFFALO 30, Kansas City 13

Wild Card playoffs: Green Bay 28, DETROIT 24; N.Y. GIANTS 17, Minnesota 10

Divisional playoffs: SAN FRANCISCO 44, N.Y. Giants 3; DALLAS 27, Green Bay 17

NFC Championship: DALLAS 38, San Francisco 21

Super Bowl XXVIII: Dallas (NFC) 30, Buffalo (AFC) 13, at Georgia Dome, Atlanta, Georgia

Playoff Seeds

AFC	NFC
1. Buffalo	**1. Dallas**
2. Houston	2. San Francisco
3. Kansas City	3. Detroit
4. L.A. Raiders	4. N.Y. Giants
5. Denver	5. Minnesota
6. Pittsburgh	6. Green Bay

1992

AMERICAN CONFERENCE

Eastern Division

	W	L	T	Pct.	Pts.	OP
Miami	11	5	0	.688	340	281
Buffalo*	11	5	0	.688	381	283
Indianapolis	9	7	0	.563	216	302
N.Y. Jets	4	12	0	.250	220	315
New England	2	14	0	.125	205	363

Central Division

	W	L	T	Pct.	Pts.	OP
Pittsburgh#	11	5	0	.688	299	225
Houston*	10	6	0	.625	352	258
Cleveland	7	9	0	.438	272	275
Cincinnati	5	11	0	.313	274	364

Western Division

	W	L	T	Pct.	Pts.	OP
San Diego	11	5	0	.688	335	241
Kansas City*	10	6	0	.625	348	282
Denver	8	8	0	.500	262	329
L.A. Raiders	7	9	0	.438	249	281
Seattle	2	14	0	.125	140	312

NATIONAL CONFERENCE

Eastern Division

	W	L	T	Pct.	Pts.	OP
Dallas	13	3	0	.813	409	243
Philadelphia*	11	5	0	.688	354	245
Washington*	9	7	0	.563	300	255
N.Y. Giants	6	10	0	.375	306	367
Phoenix	4	12	0	.250	243	332

Central Division

	W	L	T	Pct.	Pts.	OP
Minnesota	11	5	0	.688	374	249
Green Bay	9	7	0	.563	276	296
Tampa Bay	5	11	0	.313	267	365
Chicago	5	11	0	.313	295	361
Detroit	5	11	0	.313	273	332

Western Division

	W	L	T	Pct.	Pts.	OP
San Francisco#	14	2	0	.875	431	236
New Orleans*	12	4	0	.750	330	202
Atlanta	6	10	0	.375	327	414
L.A. Rams	6	10	0	.375	313	383

**Wild Card qualifier for playoffs; #Top playoff seed in conference*

Pittsburgh was top playoff seed, and Miami was second playoff seed ahead of San Diego, based on conference record (10-2 to Dolphins' 9-3 to Chargers' 9-5). Miami finished ahead of Buffalo based on better conference record (9-3 to Bills' 7-5). Houston was second Wild Card based on head-to-head victory over Kansas City (1-0). Washington was third Wild Card based on better conference record than Green Bay (7-5 to Packers' 6-6). Tampa Bay finished ahead of Chicago and Chicago finished ahead of Detroit based on better conference record (5-9 to Bears' 4-8 and Lions' 3-9). Atlanta finished ahead of L.A. Rams based on better record against common opponents (5-7 to Rams' 4-8).

Wild Card playoffs: SAN DIEGO 17, Kansas City 0; BUFFALO 41, Houston 38 (OT)

Divisional playoffs: Buffalo 24, PITTSBURGH 3; MIAMI 31, San Diego 0

AFC Championship: Buffalo 29, MIAMI 10

Wild Card playoffs: Washington 24, MINNESOTA 7; Philadelphia 36, NEW ORLEANS 20

Divisional playoffs: SAN FRANCISCO 20, Washington 13; DALLAS 34, Philadelphia 10

NFC Championship: Dallas 30, SAN FRANCISCO 20

Super Bowl XXVII: Dallas (NFC) 52, Buffalo (AFC) 17, at Rose Bowl, Pasadena, California

Playoff Seeds

AFC	NFC
1. Pittsburgh	1. San Francisco
2. Miami	**2. Dallas**
3. San Diego	3. Minnesota
4. Buffalo	4. New Orleans
5. Houston	5. Philadelphia
6. Kansas City	6. Washington

1991

AMERICAN CONFERENCE

Eastern Division

	W	L	T	Pct.	Pts.	OP
Buffalo#	13	3	0	.813	458	318
N.Y. Jets*	8	8	0	.500	314	293
Miami	8	8	0	.500	343	349
New England	6	10	0	.375	211	305
Indianapolis	1	15	0	.063	143	381

Central Division

	W	L	T	Pct.	Pts.	OP
Houston	11	5	0	.688	386	251
Pittsburgh	7	9	0	.438	292	344
Cleveland	6	10	0	.375	293	298
Cincinnati	3	13	0	.188	263	435

Western Division

	W	L	T	Pct.	Pts.	OP
Denver	12	4	0	.750	304	235
Kansas City*	10	6	0	.625	322	252
L.A. Raiders*	9	7	0	.563	298	297
Seattle	7	9	0	.438	276	261
San Diego	4	12	0	.250	274	342

NATIONAL CONFERENCE

Eastern Division

	W	L	T	Pct.	Pts.	OP
Washington#	14	2	0	.875	485	224
Dallas*	11	5	0	.688	342	310
Philadelphia	10	6	0	.625	285	244
N.Y. Giants	8	8	0	.500	281	297
Phoenix	4	12	0	.250	196	344

Central Division

	W	L	T	Pct.	Pts.	OP
Detroit	12	4	0	.750	339	295
Chicago*	11	5	0	.688	299	269
Minnesota	8	8	0	.500	301	306
Green Bay	4	12	0	.250	273	313
Tampa Bay	3	13	0	.188	199	365

Western Division

	W	L	T	Pct.	Pts.	OP
New Orleans	11	5	0	.688	341	211
Atlanta*	10	6	0	.625	361	338
San Francisco	10	6	0	.625	393	239
L.A. Rams	3	13	0	.188	234	390

**Wild Card qualifier for playoffs; #Top playoff seed in conference*

N.Y. Jets finished ahead of Miami based on head-to-head sweep (2-0). Chicago was first Wild Card based on better conference record than Dallas (9-3 to Cowboys' 8-4). Atlanta finished ahead of San Francisco based on head-to-head sweep (2-0), and was third Wild Card ahead of Philadelphia based on better conference record (7-5 to Eagles' 6-6).

Wild Card playoffs: KANSAS CITY 10, L.A. Raiders 6; HOUSTON 17, N.Y. Jets 10

Divisional playoffs: DENVER 26, Houston 24; BUFFALO 37, Kansas City 14

AFC Championship: BUFFALO 10, Denver 7

Wild Card playoffs: Atlanta 27, NEW ORLEANS 20; Dallas 17, CHICAGO 13

Divisional playoffs: WASHINGTON 24, Atlanta 7; DETROIT 38, Dallas 6

NFC Championship: WASHINGTON 41, Detroit 10

Super Bowl XXVI: Washington (NFC) 37, Buffalo (AFC) 24, at Hubert H. Humphrey Metrodome, Minneapolis, Minnesota

Playoff Seeds

AFC	NFC
1. Buffalo	**1. Washington**
2. Denver	2. Detroit
3. Houston	3. New Orleans
4. Kansas City	4. Chicago
5. L.A. Raiders	5. Dallas
6. N.Y. Jets	6. Atlanta

1990

AMERICAN CONFERENCE

Eastern Division

	W	L	T	Pct.	Pts.	OP
Buffalo#	13	3	0	.813	428	263
Miami*	12	4	0	.750	336	242
Indianapolis	7	9	0	.438	281	353
N.Y. Jets	6	10	0	.375	295	345
New England	1	15	0	.063	181	446

Central Division

	W	L	T	Pct.	Pts.	OP
Cincinnati	9	7	0	.563	360	352
Houston*	9	7	0	.563	405	307
Pittsburgh	9	7	0	.563	292	240
Cleveland	3	13	0	.188	228	462

Western Division

	W	L	T	Pct.	Pts.	OP
L.A. Raiders	12	4	0	.750	337	268
Kansas City*	11	5	0	.688	369	257
Seattle	9	7	0	.563	306	286
San Diego	6	10	0	.375	315	281
Denver	5	11	0	.313	331	374

NATIONAL CONFERENCE

Eastern Division

	W	L	T	Pct.	Pts.	OP
N.Y. Giants	13	3	0	.813	335	211
Philadelphia*	10	6	0	.625	396	299
Washington*	10	6	0	.625	381	301
Dallas	7	9	0	.438	244	308
Phoenix	5	11	0	.313	268	396

Central Division

	W	L	T	Pct.	Pts.	OP
Chicago	11	5	0	.688	348	280
Tampa Bay	6	10	0	.375	264	367
Detroit	6	10	0	.375	373	413
Green Bay	6	10	0	.375	271	347
Minnesota	6	10	0	.375	351	326

Western Division

	W	L	T	Pct.	Pts.	OP
San Francisco#	14	2	0	.875	353	239
New Orleans*	8	8	0	.500	274	275
L.A. Rams	5	11	0	.313	345	412
Atlanta	5	11	0	.313	348	365

**Wild Card qualifier for playoffs; #Top playoff seed in conference*

Cincinnati finished ahead of Houston and Pittsburgh based on best head-to-head record (3-1 to Oilers' 2-2 to Steelers' 1-3). Houston was Wild Card based on better conference record (8-4) than Seattle (7-5) and Pittsburgh (6-6). Philadelphia finished ahead of Washington based on better division record (5-3 to Redskins' 4-4). Tampa Bay was second in NFC Central based on best head-to-head record (5-1) against Detroit (2-4), Green Bay (3-3), and Minnesota (2-4). Detroit finished third based on best net division points (minus 8) against Green Bay (minus 40). Green Bay finished ahead of Minnesota based on better conference record (5-7 to Vikings' 4-8). The L.A. Rams finished ahead of Atlanta based on net points in division (plus 1 to Falcons' minus 31).

Wild Card playoffs: MIAMI 17, Kansas City 16; CINCINNATI 41, Houston 14

Divisional playoffs: BUFFALO 44, Miami 34; L.A. RAIDERS 20, Cincinnati 10

AFC Championship: BUFFALO 51, L.A. Raiders 3

Wild Card playoffs: Washington 20, PHILADELPHIA 6; CHICAGO 16, New Orleans 6

Divisional playoffs: SAN FRANCISCO 28, Washington 10; N.Y. GIANTS 31, Chicago 3

NFC Championship: N.Y. Giants 15, SAN FRANCISCO 13

Super Bowl XXV: N.Y. Giants (NFC) 20, Buffalo (AFC) 19, at Tampa Stadium, Tampa, Florida

Playoff Seeds

AFC	NFC
1. Buffalo	1. San Francisco
2. L.A. Raiders	**2. N.Y. Giants**
3. Cincinnati	3. Chicago
4. Miami	4. Philadelphia
5. Kansas City	5. Washington
6. Houston	6. New Orleans

1989

AMERICAN CONFERENCE

Eastern Division

	W	L	T	Pct.	Pts.	OP
Buffalo	9	7	0	.563	409	317
Indianapolis	8	8	0	.500	298	301
Miami	8	8	0	.500	331	379
New England	5	11	0	.313	297	391
N.Y. Jets	4	12	0	.250	253	411

Central Division

	W	L	T	Pct.	Pts.	OP
Cleveland	9	6	1	.594	334	254
Houston*	9	7	0	.563	365	412
Pittsburgh*	9	7	0	.563	265	326
Cincinnati	8	8	0	.500	404	285

Western Division

	W	L	T	Pct.	Pts.	OP
Denver#	11	5	0	.688	362	226
Kansas City	8	7	1	.531	318	286
L.A. Raiders	8	8	0	.500	315	297
Seattle	7	9	0	.438	241	327
San Diego	6	10	0	.375	266	290

NATIONAL CONFERENCE

Eastern Division

	W	L	T	Pct.	Pts.	OP
N.Y. Giants	12	4	0	.750	348	252
Philadelphia*	11	5	0	.688	342	274
Washington	10	6	0	.625	386	308
Phoenix	5	11	0	.313	258	377
Dallas	1	15	0	.063	204	393

Central Division

	W	L	T	Pct.	Pts.	OP
Minnesota	10	6	0	.625	351	275
Green Bay	10	6	0	.625	362	356
Detroit	7	9	0	.438	312	364
Chicago	6	10	0	.375	358	377
Tampa Bay	5	11	0	.313	320	419

Western Division

	W	L	T	Pct.	Pts.	OP
San Francisco#	14	2	0	.875	442	253
L.A. Rams*	11	5	0	.688	426	344
New Orleans	9	7	0	.563	386	301
Atlanta	3	13	0	.188	279	437

**Wild Card qualifier for playoffs; #Top playoff seed in conference*

Indianapolis finished ahead of Miami based on better conference record (7-5 vs. Dolphins' 6-8). Houston finished ahead of Pittsburgh based on head-to-head sweep (2-0). The L.A. Rams did not play San Francisco in the divisional playoffs because, from 1970-1989, two teams from the same division could not meet prior to the conference championship game. Philadelphia was first Wild Card ahead of L.A. Rams based on better record against common opponents (7-3 to Rams' 5-4). Minnesota finished ahead of Green Bay based on better division record (6-2 vs. Packers' 5-3).

Wild Card playoff: Pittsburgh 26, HOUSTON 23 (OT)

Divisional playoffs: CLEVELAND 34, Buffalo 30; DENVER 24, Pittsburgh 23

AFC Championship: DENVER 37, Cleveland 21

Wild Card playoff: L.A. Rams 21, PHILADELPHIA 7

Divisional playoffs: L.A. Rams 19, N.Y. GIANTS 13 (OT); SAN FRANCISCO 41, Minnesota 13

NFC Championship: SAN FRANCISCO 30, L.A. Rams 3

Super Bowl XXIV: San Francisco (NFC) 55, Denver (AFC) 10, at Louisiana Superdome, New Orleans, Louisiana

1988

AMERICAN CONFERENCE

Eastern Division

	W	L	T	Pct.	Pts.	OP
Buffalo	12	4	0	.750	329	237
Indianapolis	9	7	0	.563	354	315
New England	9	7	0	.563	250	284
N.Y. Jets	8	7	1	.531	372	354
Miami	6	10	0	.375	319	380

Central Division

	W	L	T	Pct.	Pts.	OP
Cincinnati#	12	4	0	.750	448	329
Cleveland*	10	6	0	.625	304	288
Houston*	10	6	0	.625	424	365
Pittsburgh	5	11	0	.313	336	421

Western Division

	W	L	T	Pct.	Pts.	OP
Seattle	9	7	0	.563	339	329
Denver	8	8	0	.500	327	352
L.A. Raiders	7	9	0	.438	325	369
San Diego	6	10	0	.375	231	332
Kansas City	4	11	1	.281	254	320

NATIONAL CONFERENCE

Eastern Division

	W	L	T	Pct.	Pts.	OP
Philadelphia	10	6	0	.625	379	319
N.Y. Giants	10	6	0	.625	359	304
Washington	7	9	0	.438	345	387
Phoenix	7	9	0	.438	344	398
Dallas	3	13	0	.188	265	381

Central Division

	W	L	T	Pct.	Pts.	OP
Chicago#	12	4	0	.750	312	215
Minnesota*	11	5	0	.688	406	233
Tampa Bay	5	11	0	.313	261	350
Detroit	4	12	0	.250	220	313
Green Bay	4	12	0	.250	240	315

Western Division

	W	L	T	Pct.	Pts.	OP
San Francisco	10	6	0	.625	369	294
L.A. Rams*	10	6	0	.625	407	293
New Orleans	10	6	0	.625	312	283
Atlanta	5	11	0	.313	244	315

**Wild Card qualifier for playoffs; #Top playoff seed in conference*

Cincinnati was top playoff seed ahead of Buffalo based on head-to-head victory (1-0). Indianapolis finished ahead of New England based on better record against common opponents (7-5 to Patriots' 6-6). Cleveland finished ahead of Houston based on better division record (4-2 to Oilers' 3-3). Houston did not play Cincinnati, and Minnesota did not play Chicago in the divisional playoffs because, from 1970-1989, two teams from the same division could not meet prior to the conference championship game. Philadelphia finished first in NFC East based on head-to-head sweep of N.Y. Giants (2-0). Washington finished third in NFC East based on better division record (4-4) than Phoenix (3-5). Detroit finished fourth in NFC Central based on head-to-head sweep of Green Bay (2-0). San Francisco finished first in NFC West based on better head-to-head record (3-1) against L.A. Rams (2-2) and New Orleans (1-3). San Francisco finished with second playoff seed ahead of Philadelphia based on better record against common opponents (5-3 to Eagles' 5-4). L.A. Rams finished second in NFC West based on better division record (4-2) than New Orleans (3-3) and earned Wild-Card position based on better conference record (8-4) than N.Y. Giants (9-5) and New Orleans (6-6).

Wild Card playoff: Houston 24, CLEVELAND 23

Divisional playoffs: CINCINNATI 21, Seattle 13;
BUFFALO 17, Houston 10

AFC Championship: CINCINNATI 21, Buffalo 10

Wild Card playoff: MINNESOTA 28, L.A. Rams 17

Divisional playoffs: CHICAGO 20, Philadelphia 12;
SAN FRANCISCO 34, Minnesota 9

NFC Championship: San Francisco 28, CHICAGO 3

Super Bowl XXIII: San Francisco (NFC) 20, Cincinnati (AFC) 16,
at Joe Robbie Stadium, Miami, Florida

1987

AMERICAN CONFERENCE

Eastern Division

	W	L	T	Pct.	Pts.	OP
Indianapolis	9	6	0	.600	300	238
New England	8	7	0	.533	320	293
Miami	8	7	0	.533	362	335
Buffalo	7	8	0	.467	270	305
N.Y. Jets	6	9	0	.400	334	360

Central Division

	W	L	T	Pct.	Pts.	OP
Cleveland	10	5	0	.667	390	239
Houston*	9	6	0	.600	345	349
Pittsburgh	8	7	0	.533	285	299
Cincinnati	4	11	0	.267	285	370

Western Division

	W	L	T	Pct.	Pts.	OP
Denver#	10	4	1	.700	379	288
Seattle*	9	6	0	.600	371	314
San Diego	8	7	0	.533	253	317
L.A. Raiders	5	10	0	.333	301	289
Kansas City	4	11	0	.267	273	388

NATIONAL CONFERENCE

Eastern Division

	W	L	T	Pct.	Pts.	OP
Washington	11	4	0	.733	379	285
Dallas	7	8	0	.467	340	348
St. Louis	7	8	0	.467	362	368
Philadelphia	7	8	0	.467	337	380
N.Y. Giants	6	9	0	.400	280	312

Central Division

	W	L	T	Pct.	Pts.	OP
Chicago	11	4	0	.733	356	282
Minnesota*	8	7	0	.533	336	335
Green Bay	5	9	1	.367	255	300
Tampa Bay	4	11	0	.267	286	360
Detroit	4	11	0	.267	269	384

Western Division

	W	L	T	Pct.	Pts.	OP
San Francisco#	13	2	0	.867	459	253
New Orleans*	12	3	0	.800	422	283
L.A. Rams	6	9	0	.400	317	361
Atlanta	3	12	0	.200	205	436

**Wild Card qualifier for playoffs; #Top playoff seed in conference*

New England finished ahead of Miami based on head-to-head sweep (2-0). Houston was first Wild Card ahead of Seattle based on better conference record (7-4 to Seahawks' 5-6). Chicago was second playoff seed ahead of Washington based on better conference record (9-2 to Redskins' 9-3). Dallas finished ahead of St. Louis and Philadelphia based on better division record (4-4 to Cardinals' 3-5 and Eagles' 3-5). St. Louis finished ahead of Philadelphia based on better conference record (7-7 to Eagles' 4-7). Tampa Bay finished ahead of Detroit based on better division record (3-4 to Lions' 2-5).

Wild Card playoff: HOUSTON 23, Seattle 20 (OT)

Divisional playoffs: CLEVELAND 38, Indianapolis 21;
DENVER 34, Houston 10

AFC Championship: DENVER 38, Cleveland 33

Wild Card playoff: Minnesota 44, NEW ORLEANS 10

Divisional playoffs: Minnesota 36, SAN FRANCISCO 24;
Washington 21, CHICAGO 17

NFC Championship: WASHINGTON 17, Minnesota 10

Super Bowl XXII: Washington (NFC) 42, Denver (AFC) 10,
at San Diego Jack Murphy Stadium, San Diego, California

Note: 1987 regular season was reduced from 16 to 15 games for each team due to players' strike.

1986

AMERICAN CONFERENCE

Eastern Division

	W	L	T	Pct.	Pts.	OP
New England	11	5	0	.688	412	307
N.Y. Jets*	10	6	0	.625	364	386
Miami	8	8	0	.500	430	405
Buffalo	4	12	0	.250	287	348
Indianapolis	3	13	0	.188	229	400

Central Division

	W	L	T	Pct.	Pts.	OP
Cleveland#	12	4	0	.750	391	310
Cincinnati	10	6	0	.625	409	394
Pittsburgh	6	10	0	.375	307	336
Houston	5	11	0	.313	274	329

Western Division

	W	L	T	Pct.	Pts.	OP
Denver	11	5	0	.688	378	327
Kansas City*	10	6	0	.625	358	326
Seattle	10	6	0	.625	366	293
L.A. Raiders	8	8	0	.500	323	346
San Diego	4	12	0	.250	335	396

NATIONAL CONFERENCE

Eastern Division

	W	L	T	Pct.	Pts.	OP
N.Y. Giants#	14	2	0	.875	371	236
Washington*	12	4	0	.750	368	296
Dallas	7	9	0	.438	346	337
Philadelphia	5	10	1	.344	256	312
St. Louis	4	11	1	.281	218	351

Central Division

	W	L	T	Pct.	Pts.	OP
Chicago	14	2	0	.875	352	187
Minnesota	9	7	0	.563	398	273
Detroit	5	11	0	.313	277	326
Green Bay	4	12	0	.250	254	418
Tampa Bay	2	14	0	.125	239	473

Western Division

	W	L	T	Pct.	Pts.	OP
San Francisco	10	5	1	.656	374	247
L.A. Rams*	10	6	0	.625	309	267
Atlanta	7	8	1	.469	280	280
New Orleans	7	9	0	.438	288	287

**Wild Card qualifier for playoffs; #Top playoff seed in conference*

Denver was second playoff seed ahead of New England based on head-to-head victory (1-0). N.Y. Jets were first Wild Card based on better conference record (8-4) than Kansas City (9-5), Seattle (7-5), and Cincinnati (7-5). Kansas City was second Wild Card based on better conference record (9-5) than Seattle (7-5) and Cincinnati (7-5). N.Y. Giants were top playoff seed based on better conference record than Chicago (11-1 to Bears' 10-2). Washington did not play the N.Y. Giants in the divisional playoffs because, from 1970-1989, two teams from the same division could not meet prior to the conference championship game.

Wild Card playoff: N.Y. JETS 35, Kansas City 15
Divisional playoffs: CLEVELAND 23, N.Y. Jets 20 (OT); DENVER 22, New England 17
AFC Championship: Denver 23, CLEVELAND 20 (OT)
Wild Card playoff: WASHINGTON 19, L.A. Rams 7
Divisional playoffs: Washington 27, CHICAGO 13 N.Y. GIANTS 49, San Francisco 3
NFC Championship: N.Y. GIANTS 17, Washington 0
Super Bowl XXI: N.Y. Giants (NFC) 39, Denver (AFC) 20, at Rose Bowl, Pasadena, California

1985

AMERICAN CONFERENCE

Eastern Division

	W	L	T	Pct.	Pts.	OP
Miami	12	4	0	.750	428	320
N.Y. Jets*	11	5	0	.688	393	264
New England*	11	5	0	.688	362	290
Indianapolis	5	11	0	.313	320	386
Buffalo	2	14	0	.125	200	381

Central Division

	W	L	T	Pct.	Pts.	OP
Cleveland	8	8	0	.500	287	294
Cincinnati	7	9	0	.438	441	437
Pittsburgh	7	9	0	.438	379	355
Houston	5	11	0	.313	284	412

Western Division

	W	L	T	Pct.	Pts.	OP
L.A. Raiders#	12	4	0	.750	354	308
Denver	11	5	0	.688	380	329
Seattle	8	8	0	.500	349	303
San Diego	8	8	0	.500	467	435
Kansas City	6	10	0	.375	317	360

NATIONAL CONFERENCE

Eastern Division

	W	L	T	Pct.	Pts.	OP
Dallas	10	6	0	.625	357	333
N.Y. Giants*	10	6	0	.625	399	283
Washington	10	6	0	.625	297	312
Philadelphia	7	9	0	.438	286	310
St. Louis	5	11	0	.313	278	414

Central Division

	W	L	T	Pct.	Pts.	OP
Chicago#	15	1	0	.938	456	198
Green Bay	8	8	0	.500	337	355
Minnesota	7	9	0	.438	346	359
Detroit	7	9	0	.438	307	366
Tampa Bay	2	14	0	.125	294	448

Western Division

	W	L	T	Pct.	Pts.	OP
L.A. Rams	11	5	0	.688	340	277
San Francisco*	10	6	0	.625	411	263
New Orleans	5	11	0	.313	294	401
Atlanta	4	12	0	.250	282	452

**Wild Card qualifier for playoffs; #Top playoff seed in conference*

L.A. Raiders were top playoff seed ahead of Miami based on better record against common opponents (5-1 to 4-2). N.Y. Jets were first Wild Card based on better conference record (9-3) than New England (8-4) and Denver (8-4). New England was second Wild Card ahead of Denver based on better record against common opponents (4-2 to Broncos' 3-3). Cincinnati finished ahead of Pittsburgh based on head-to-head sweep (2-0). Seattle finished ahead of San Diego based on head-to-head sweep (2-0). Dallas finished ahead of N.Y. Giants and Washington based on better head-to-head record (4-0 to Giants' 1-3 and Redskins' 1-3). N.Y. Giants were first Wild Card based on better conference record (8-4) than San Francisco (7-5) and Washington (6-6). San Francisco was second Wild Card based on head-to-head victory over Washington (1-0). Minnesota finished ahead of Detroit based on better division record (3-5 to Lions' 2-6).

Wild Card playoff: New England 26, N.Y. JETS 14
Divisional playoffs: MIAMI 24, Cleveland 21; New England 27, L.A. RAIDERS 20
AFC Championship: New England 31, MIAMI 14
Wild Card playoff: N.Y. GIANTS 17, San Francisco 3
Divisional playoffs: L.A. RAMS 20, Dallas 0; CHICAGO 21, N.Y. Giants 0
NFC Championship: CHICAGO 24, L.A. Rams 0
Super Bowl XX: Chicago (NFC) 46, New England (AFC) 10, at Louisiana Superdome, New Orleans, Louisiana

1984

AMERICAN CONFERENCE

Eastern Division

	W	L	T	Pct.	Pts.	OP
Miami#	14	2	0	.875	513	298
New England	9	7	0	.563	362	352
N.Y. Jets	7	9	0	.438	332	364
Indianapolis	4	12	0	.250	239	414
Buffalo	2	14	0	.125	250	454

Central Division

	W	L	T	Pct.	Pts.	OP
Pittsburgh	9	7	0	.563	387	310
Cincinnati	8	8	0	.500	339	339
Cleveland	5	11	0	.313	250	297
Houston	3	13	0	.188	240	437

Western Division

	W	L	T	Pct.	Pts.	OP
Denver	13	3	0	.813	353	241
Seattle*	12	4	0	.750	418	282
L.A. Raiders*	11	5	0	.688	368	278
Kansas City	8	8	0	.500	314	324
San Diego	7	9	0	.438	394	413

NATIONAL CONFERENCE

Eastern Division

	W	L	T	Pct.	Pts.	OP
Washington	11	5	0	.688	426	310
N.Y. Giants*	9	7	0	.563	299	301
St. Louis	9	7	0	.563	423	345
Dallas	9	7	0	.563	308	308
Philadelphia	6	9	1	.406	278	320

Central Division

	W	L	T	Pct.	Pts.	OP
Chicago	10	6	0	.625	325	248
Green Bay	8	8	0	.500	390	309
Tampa Bay	6	10	0	.375	335	380
Detroit	4	11	1	.281	283	408
Minnesota	3	13	0	.188	276	484

Western Division

	W	L	T	Pct.	Pts.	OP
San Francisco#	15	1	0	.938	475	227
L.A. Rams*	10	6	0	.625	346	316
New Orleans	7	9	0	.438	298	361
Atlanta	4	12	0	.250	281	382

**Wild Card qualifier for playoffs; #Top playoff seed in conference*

N.Y. Giants finished ahead of St. Louis and Dallas based on best head-to-head record (3-1 to Cardinals' 2-2 and Cowboys' 1-3). St. Louis finished ahead of Dallas based on better division record (5-3 to Cowboys' 3-5).

Wild Card playoff: SEATTLE 13, L.A. Raiders 7

Divisional playoffs: MIAMI 31, Seattle 10; Pittsburgh 24, DENVER 17

AFC Championship: MIAMI 45, Pittsburgh 28

Wild Card playoff: N.Y. Giants 16, L.A. RAMS 13

Divisional playoffs: SAN FRANCISCO 21, N.Y. Giants 10; Chicago 23, WASHINGTON 19

NFC Championship: SAN FRANCISCO 23, Chicago 0

Super Bowl XIX: San Francisco (NFC) 38, Miami (AFC) 16, at Stanford Stadium, Stanford, California

1983

AMERICAN CONFERENCE

Eastern Division

	W	L	T	Pct.	Pts.	OP
Miami	12	4	0	.750	389	250
New England	8	8	0	.500	274	289
Buffalo	8	8	0	.500	283	351
Baltimore	7	9	0	.438	264	354
N.Y. Jets	7	9	0	.438	313	331

Central Division

	W	L	T	Pct.	Pts.	OP
Pittsburgh	10	6	0	.625	355	303
Cleveland	9	7	0	.563	356	342
Cincinnati	7	9	0	.438	346	302
Houston	2	14	0	.125	288	460

Western Division

	W	L	T	Pct.	Pts.	OP
L.A. Raiders#	12	4	0	.750	442	338
Seattle*	9	7	0	.563	403	397
Denver*	9	7	0	.563	302	327
San Diego	6	10	0	.375	358	462
Kansas City	6	10	0	.375	386	367

NATIONAL CONFERENCE

Eastern Division

	W	L	T	Pct.	Pts.	OP
Washington#	14	2	0	.875	541	332
Dallas*	12	4	0	.750	479	360
St. Louis	8	7	1	.531	374	428
Philadelphia	5	11	0	.313	233	322
N.Y. Giants	3	12	1	.219	267	347

Central Division

	W	L	T	Pct.	Pts.	OP
Detroit	9	7	0	.563	347	286
Green Bay	8	8	0	.500	429	439
Chicago	8	8	0	.500	311	301
Minnesota	8	8	0	.500	316	348
Tampa Bay	2	14	0	.125	241	380

Western Division

	W	L	T	Pct.	Pts.	OP
San Francisco	10	6	0	.625	432	293
L.A. Rams*	9	7	0	.563	361	344
New Orleans	8	8	0	.500	319	337
Atlanta	7	9	0	.438	370	389

**Wild Card qualifier for playoffs; #Top playoff seed in conference*

L.A. Raiders were top playoff seed ahead of Miami based on head-to-head victory (1-0). Seattle was first Wild Card ahead of Denver based on better division record (5-3 to Broncos' 3-5) after Cleveland was eliminated from three-way tie based on losing head-to-head to both Seattle and Denver. Seattle did not play the L.A. Raiders in the divisional playoffs because, from 1970-1989, two teams from the same division could not meet prior to the conference championship game. New England finished ahead of Buffalo based on head-to-head sweep (2-0). Baltimore finished ahead of N.Y. Jets based on better conference record (5-9 to Jets' 4-8). San Diego finished ahead of Kansas City based on head-to-head sweep (2-0). Green Bay finished ahead of Chicago based on better record against common opponents (4-4 to Bears' 3-5) after Minnesota was eliminated from three-way tie based on conference record (Chicago 7-7 and Green Bay 6-6 to Vikings' 4-8).

Wild Card playoff: SEATTLE 31, Denver 7

Divisional playoffs: Seattle 27, MIAMI 20; L.A. RAIDERS 38, Pittsburgh 10

AFC Championship: L.A. RAIDERS 30, Seattle 14

Wild Card playoff: L.A. Rams 24, DALLAS 17

Divisional playoffs: SAN FRANCISCO 24, Detroit 23; WASHINGTON 51, L.A. Rams 7

NFC Championship: WASHINGTON 24, San Francisco 21

Super Bowl XVIII: L.A. Raiders (AFC) 38, Washington (NFC) 9, at Tampa Stadium, Tampa, Florida

1982

AMERICAN CONFERENCE	W	L	T	Pct.	Pts.	OP	NATIONAL CONFERENCE	W	L	T	Pct.	Pts.	OP
L.A. Raiders#	8	1	0	.889	260	200	Washington#	8	1	0	.889	190	128
Miami	7	2	0	.778	198	131	Dallas	6	3	0	.667	226	145
Cincinnati	7	2	0	.778	232	177	Green Bay	5	3	1	.611	226	169
Pittsburgh	6	3	0	.667	204	146	Minnesota	5	4	0	.556	187	198
San Diego	6	3	0	.667	288	221	Atlanta	5	4	0	.556	183	199
N.Y. Jets	6	3	0	.667	245	166	St. Louis	5	4	0	.556	135	170
New England	5	4	0	.556	143	157	Tampa Bay	5	4	0	.556	158	178
Cleveland	4	5	0	.444	140	182	Detroit	4	5	0	.444	181	176
Buffalo	4	5	0	.444	150	154	New Orleans	4	5	0	.444	129	160
Seattle	4	5	0	.444	127	147	N.Y. Giants	4	5	0	.444	164	160
Kansas City	3	6	0	.333	176	184	San Francisco	3	6	0	.333	209	206
Denver	2	7	0	.222	148	226	Chicago	3	6	0	.333	141	174
Houston	1	8	0	.111	136	245	Philadelphia	3	6	0	.333	191	195
Baltimore	0	8	1	.056	113	236	L.A. Rams	2	7	0	.222	200	250

As the result of a 57-day players' strike, the 1982 NFL regular season schedule was reduced from 16 weeks to 9. At the conclusion of the regular season, the NFL conducted a 16-team postseason Super Bowl Tournament. Eight teams from each conference were seeded 1-8 based on their records during the season.

#Top playoff seed in conference

Miami finished ahead of Cincinnati based on better conference record (6-1 to Bengals' 6-2). Pittsburgh finished ahead of San Diego based on better record against common opponents (3-1 to Chargers' 2-1) after N.Y. Jets were eliminated from three-way tie based on conference record (Pittsburgh and San Diego 5-3 to Jets' 2-3). Cleveland finished ahead of Buffalo and Seattle based on better conference record (4-3 to Bills' 3-3 to Seahawks' 3-5). Buffalo finished ahead of Seattle based on better conference record (3-3 to Seahawks' 3-5). Minnesota (4-1), Atlanta (4-3), St. Louis (5-4), Tampa Bay (3-3) seeds were determined by best won-lost record in conference games. Detroit finished ahead of New Orleans and the N.Y. Giants based on best conference record (4-4 to Saints' 3-5 to Giants' 3-5). New Orleans finished ahead of N.Y. Giants based on better record against common opponents (1-3 to Giants' 0-4). San Francisco finished ahead of Chicago, and Chicago finished ahead of Philadelphia, based on conference record (49ers' 2-3 to Bears' 2-5 to Eagles' 1-5).

First round playoff: MIAMI 28, New England 13;
L.A. RAIDERS 27, Cleveland 10;
N.Y. Jets 44, CINCINNATI 17;
San Diego 31, PITTSBURGH 28

Second round playoff: N.Y. Jets 17, L.A. RAIDERS 14;
MIAMI 34, San Diego 13

AFC Championship: MIAMI 14, N.Y. Jets 0

First round playoff: WASHINGTON 31, Detroit 7;
GREEN BAY 41, St. Louis 16;
MINNESOTA 30, Atlanta 24;
DALLAS 30, Tampa Bay 17

Second round playoff: WASHINGTON 21, Minnesota 7;
DALLAS 37, Green Bay 26

NFC Championship: WASHINGTON 31, Dallas 17

Super Bowl XVII: Washington (NFC) 27, Miami (AFC) 17, at Rose Bowl, Pasadena, California

1981

AMERICAN CONFERENCE	W	L	T	Pct.	Pts.	OP	NATIONAL CONFERENCE	W	L	T	Pct.	Pts.	OP
Eastern Division							**Eastern Division**						
Miami	11	4	1	.719	345	275	Dallas	12	4	0	.750	367	277
N.Y. Jets*	10	5	1	.656	355	287	Philadelphia*	10	6	0	.625	368	221
Buffalo*	10	6	0	.625	311	276	N.Y. Giants*	9	7	0	.563	295	257
Baltimore	2	14	0	.125	259	533	Washington	8	8	0	.500	347	349
New England	2	14	0	.125	322	370	St. Louis	7	9	0	.438	315	408
Central Division	W	L	T	Pct.	Pts.	OP	**Central Division**	W	L	T	Pct.	Pts.	OP
Cincinnati#	12	4	0	.750	421	304	Tampa Bay	9	7	0	.563	315	268
Pittsburgh	8	8	0	.500	356	297	Detroit	8	8	0	.500	397	322
Houston	7	9	0	.438	281	355	Green Bay	8	8	0	.500	324	361
Cleveland	5	11	0	.313	276	375	Minnesota	7	9	0	.438	325	369
Western Division							Chicago	6	10	0	.375	253	324
	W	L	T	Pct.	Pts.	OP	**Western Division**						
San Diego	10	6	0	.625	478	390		W	L	T	Pct.	Pts.	OP
Denver	10	6	0	.625	321	289	San Francisco#	13	3	0	.813	357	250
Kansas City	9	7	0	.563	343	290	Atlanta	7	9	0	.438	426	355
Oakland	7	9	0	.438	273	343	Los Angeles	6	10	0	.375	303	351
Seattle	6	10	0	.375	322	388	New Orleans	4	12	0	.250	207	378

**Wild Card qualifier for playoffs; #Top playoff seed in conference*

Baltimore finished ahead of New England based on head-to-head sweep (2-0). San Diego finished ahead of Denver based on better division record (6-2 to Broncos' 5-3). Buffalo was second Wild Card based on head-to-head victory over Denver (1-0). Detroit finished ahead of Green Bay based on better record against common opponents (4-4 to Packers' 3-5).

Wild Card playoff: Buffalo 31, N.Y. JETS 27

Divisional playoffs: San Diego 41, MIAMI 38 (OT);
CINCINNATI 28, Buffalo 21

AFC Championship: CINCINNATI 27, San Diego 7

Wild Card playoff: N.Y. Giants 27, PHILADELPHIA 21

Divisional playoffs: DALLAS 38, Tampa Bay 0;
SAN FRANCISCO 38, N.Y. Giants 24

NFC Championship: SAN FRANCISCO 28, Dallas 27

Super Bowl XVI: San Francisco (NFC) 26, Cincinnati (AFC) 21, at Silverdome, Pontiac, Michigan

1980

AMERICAN CONFERENCE

Eastern Division

	W	L	T	Pct.	Pts.	OP
Buffalo	11	5	0	.688	320	260
New England	10	6	0	.625	441	325
Miami	8	8	0	.500	266	305
Baltimore	7	9	0	.438	355	387
N.Y. Jets	4	12	0	.250	302	395

Central Division

	W	L	T	Pct.	Pts.	OP
Cleveland	11	5	0	.688	357	310
Houston*	11	5	0	.688	295	251
Pittsburgh	9	7	0	.563	352	313
Cincinnati	6	10	0	.375	244	312

Western Division

	W	L	T	Pct.	Pts.	OP
San Diego#	11	5	0	.688	418	327
Oakland*	11	5	0	.688	364	306
Kansas City	8	8	0	.500	319	336
Denver	8	8	0	.500	310	323
Seattle	4	12	0	.250	291	408

NATIONAL CONFERENCE

Eastern Division

	W	L	T	Pct.	Pts.	OP
Philadelphia	12	4	0	.750	384	222
Dallas*	12	4	0	.750	454	311
Washington	6	10	0	.375	261	293
St. Louis	5	11	0	.313	299	350
N.Y. Giants	4	12	0	.250	249	425

Central Division

	W	L	T	Pct.	Pts.	OP
Minnesota	9	7	0	.563	317	308
Detroit	9	7	0	.563	334	272
Chicago	7	9	0	.438	304	264
Tampa Bay	5	10	1	.344	271	341
Green Bay	5	10	1	.344	231	371

Western Division

	W	L	T	Pct.	Pts.	OP
Atlanta#	12	4	0	.750	405	272
Los Angeles*	11	5	0	.688	424	289
San Francisco	6	10	0	.375	320	415
New Orleans	1	15	0	.063	291	487

**Wild Card qualifier for playoffs; #Top playoff seed in conference*

San Diego was top playoff seed based on better conference record than Cleveland and Buffalo (9-3 to Browns' 8-4 and Bills' 8-4). Cleveland was second playoff seed based on better record against common opponents (5-2 to Bills' 5-3). Cleveland finished ahead of Houston based on better conference record (8-4 to Oilers' 7-5). Oakland was first Wild Card based on better conference record than Houston (9-3 to Oilers' 7-5). San Diego finished ahead of Oakland based on better net points in division games (plus 60 net points to Raiders' plus 37). Oakland did not play San Diego in the divisional playoffs because, from 1970-1989, two teams from the same division could not meet prior to the conference championship game. Kansas City finished ahead of Denver based on head-to-head sweep (2-0). Atlanta was top playoff seed based on head-to-head victory over Philadelphia (1-0). Philadelphia finished ahead of Dallas based on better net points in division games (plus 84 net points to Cowboys' plus 50). Minnesota finished ahead of Detroit based on better conference record (8-4 to Lions' 9-5). Tampa Bay finished ahead of Green Bay based on better head-to-head record (1-0-1 to Packers' 0-1-1).

Wild Card playoff: OAKLAND 27, Houston 7
Divisional playoffs: SAN DIEGO 20, Buffalo 14; Oakland 14, CLEVELAND 12
AFC Championship: Oakland 34, SAN DIEGO 27
Wild Card playoff: DALLAS 34, Los Angeles 13
Divisional playoffs: PHILADELPHIA 31, Minnesota 16; Dallas 30, ATLANTA 27
NFC Championship: PHILADELPHIA 20, Dallas 7
Super Bowl XV: Oakland (AFC) 27, Philadelphia (NFC) 10, at Louisiana Superdome, New Orleans, Louisiana

1979

AMERICAN CONFERENCE

Eastern Division

	W	L	T	Pct.	Pts.	OP
Miami	10	6	0	.625	341	257
New England	9	7	0	.563	411	326
N.Y. Jets	8	8	0	.500	337	383
Buffalo	7	9	0	.438	268	279
Baltimore	5	11	0	.313	271	351

Central Division

	W	L	T	Pct.	Pts.	OP
Pittsburgh	12	4	0	.750	416	262
Houston*	11	5	0	.688	362	331
Cleveland	9	7	0	.563	359	352
Cincinnati	4	12	0	.250	337	421

Western Division

	W	L	T	Pct.	Pts.	OP
San Diego#	12	4	0	.750	411	246
Denver*	10	6	0	.625	289	262
Seattle	9	7	0	.563	378	372
Oakland	9	7	0	.563	365	337
Kansas City	7	9	0	.438	238	262

NATIONAL CONFERENCE

Eastern Division

	W	L	T	Pct.	Pts.	OP
Dallas#	11	5	0	.688	371	313
Philadelphia*	11	5	0	.688	339	282
Washington	10	6	0	.625	348	295
N.Y. Giants	6	10	0	.375	237	323
St. Louis	5	11	0	.313	307	358

Central Division

	W	L	T	Pct.	Pts.	OP
Tampa Bay	10	6	0	.625	273	237
Chicago*	10	6	0	.625	306	249
Minnesota	7	9	0	.438	259	337
Green Bay	5	11	0	.313	246	316
Detroit	2	14	0	.125	219	365

Western Division

	W	L	T	Pct.	Pts.	OP
Los Angeles	9	7	0	.563	323	309
New Orleans	8	8	0	.500	370	360
Atlanta	6	10	0	.375	300	388
San Francisco	2	14	0	.125	308	416

**Wild Card qualifier for playoffs; #Top playoff seed in conference*

San Diego was top playoff seed based on head-to-head victory over Pittsburgh (1-0). Seattle finished ahead of Oakland based on head-to-head sweep (2-0). Dallas finished ahead of Philadelphia based on better conference record (10-2 to Eagles' 9-3). Philadelphia did not play Dallas in the divisional playoffs because, from 1970-1989, two teams from the same division could not meet prior to the conference championship game. Tampa Bay finished ahead of Chicago based on a better division record (6-2 to Bears' 5-3). Chicago was second Wild Card ahead of Washington based on better net points in all games (57 to Redskins' 53).

Wild Card playoff: HOUSTON 13, Denver 7
Divisional playoffs: Houston 17, SAN DIEGO 14; PITTSBURGH 34, Miami 14
AFC Championship: PITTSBURGH 27, Houston 13
Wild Card playoff: PHILADELPHIA 27, Chicago 17
Divisional playoffs: TAMPA BAY 24, Philadelphia 17; Los Angeles 21, DALLAS 19
NFC Championship: Los Angeles 9, TAMPA BAY 0
Super Bowl XIV: Pittsburgh (AFC) 31, Los Angeles (NFC) 19, at Rose Bowl, Pasadena, California

PAST STANDINGS

1978

AMERICAN CONFERENCE

Eastern Division

	W	L	T	Pct.	Pts.	OP
New England	11	5	0	.688	358	286
Miami*	11	5	0	.688	372	254
N.Y. Jets	8	8	0	.500	359	364
Buffalo	5	11	0	.313	302	354
Baltimore	5	11	0	.313	239	421

Central Division

	W	L	T	Pct.	Pts.	OP
Pittsburgh#	14	2	0	.875	356	195
Houston*	10	6	0	.625	283	298
Cleveland	8	8	0	.500	334	356
Cincinnati	4	12	0	.250	252	284

Western Division

	W	L	T	Pct.	Pts.	OP
Denver	10	6	0	.625	282	198
Oakland	9	7	0	.563	311	283
Seattle	9	7	0	.563	345	358
San Diego	9	7	0	.563	355	309
Kansas City	4	12	0	.250	243	327

NATIONAL CONFERENCE

Eastern Division

	W	L	T	Pct.	Pts.	OP
Dallas	12	4	0	.750	384	208
Philadelphia*	9	7	0	.563	270	250
Washington	8	8	0	.500	273	283
St. Louis	6	10	0	.375	248	296
N.Y. Giants	6	10	0	.375	264	298

Central Division

	W	L	T	Pct.	Pts.	OP
Minnesota	8	7	1	.531	294	306
Green Bay	8	7	1	.531	249	269
Detroit	7	9	0	.438	290	300
Chicago	7	9	0	.438	253	274
Tampa Bay	5	11	0	.313	241	259

Western Division

	W	L	T	Pct.	Pts.	OP
Los Angeles#	12	4	0	.750	316	245
Atlanta*	9	7	0	.563	240	290
New Orleans	7	9	0	.438	281	298
San Francisco	2	14	0	.125	219	350

**Wild Card qualifier for playoffs; #Top playoff seed in conference*

New England finished ahead of Miami based on better division record (6-2 to Dolphins' 5-3). Buffalo finished ahead of Baltimore based on head-to-head sweep (2-0). Oakland finished ahead of Seattle and San Diego based on better record against common opponents (6-2 to Seahawks' 5-3 and Chargers' 4-4). Atlanta was first Wild Card ahead of Philadelphia based on better record against common opponents (5-2 to Eagles' 5-3). Houston did not play Pittsburgh, and Atlanta did not play Los Angeles in the divisional playoffs because, from 1970-1989, two teams from the same division could not meet prior to the conference championship game. Los Angeles was top playoff seed based on head-to-head victory over Dallas (1-0). St. Louis finished ahead of N.Y. Giants based on better division record (3-5 to Giants' 2-6). Minnesota finished ahead of Green Bay based on better head-to-head record (1-0-1). Detroit finished ahead of Chicago based on better division record (4-4 to Bears' 3-5).

Wild Card playoff: Houston 17, MIAMI 9

Divisional playoffs: Houston 31, NEW ENGLAND 14; PITTSBURGH 33, Denver 10

AFC Championship: PITTSBURGH 34, Houston 5

Wild Card playoff: ATLANTA 14, Philadelphia 13

Divisional playoffs: DALLAS 27, Atlanta 20; LOS ANGELES 34, Minnesota 10

NFC Championship: Dallas 28, LOS ANGELES 0

Super Bowl XIII: Pittsburgh (AFC) 35, Dallas (NFC) 31, at Orange Bowl, Miami, Florida

1977

AMERICAN CONFERENCE

Eastern Division

	W	L	T	Pct.	Pts.	OP
Baltimore	10	4	0	.714	295	221
Miami	10	4	0	.714	313	197
New England	9	5	0	.643	278	217
N.Y. Jets	3	11	0	.214	191	300
Buffalo	3	11	0	.214	160	313

Central Division

	W	L	T	Pct.	Pts.	OP
Pittsburgh	9	5	0	.643	283	243
Houston	8	6	0	.571	299	230
Cincinnati	8	6	0	.571	238	235
Cleveland	6	8	0	.429	269	267

Western Division

	W	L	T	Pct.	Pts.	OP
Denver#	12	2	0	.857	274	148
Oakland*	11	3	0	.786	351	230
San Diego	7	7	0	.500	222	205
Seattle	5	9	0	.357	282	373
Kansas City	2	12	0	.143	225	349

NATIONAL CONFERENCE

Eastern Division

	W	L	T	Pct.	Pts.	OP
Dallas#	12	2	0	.857	345	212
Washington	9	5	0	.643	196	189
St. Louis	7	7	0	.500	272	287
Philadelphia	5	9	0	.357	220	207
N.Y. Giants	5	9	0	.357	181	265

Central Division

	W	L	T	Pct.	Pts.	OP
Minnesota	9	5	0	.643	231	227
Chicago*	9	5	0	.643	255	253
Detroit	6	8	0	.429	183	252
Green Bay	4	10	0	.286	134	219
Tampa Bay	2	12	0	.143	103	223

Western Division

	W	L	T	Pct.	Pts.	OP
Los Angeles	10	4	0	.714	302	146
Atlanta	7	7	0	.500	179	129
San Francisco	5	9	0	.357	220	260
New Orleans	3	11	0	.214	232	336

**Wild Card qualifier for playoffs; #Top playoff seed in conference*

Baltimore finished ahead of Miami based on better conference record (9-3 to Dolphins' 8-4). N.Y. Jets finished ahead of Buffalo based on better point-differential in head-to-head competition (1 point). Houston finished ahead of Cincinnati based on better point-differential in head-to-head competition (2 points). Oakland did not play Denver in the divisional playoffs because, from 1970-1989, two teams from the same division could not meet prior to the conference championship game. Minnesota finished ahead of Chicago based on better point-differential in head-to-head competition (3 points). Chicago won Wild Card ahead of Washington based on better net points in conference games (48 to Redskins' 4). Philadelphia finished ahead of N.Y. Giants based on head-to-head sweep (2-0).

Divisional playoffs: DENVER 34, Pittsburgh 21; Oakland 37, BALTIMORE 31 (OT)

AFC Championship: DENVER 20, Oakland 17

Divisional playoffs: DALLAS 37, Chicago 7; Minnesota 14, LOS ANGELES 7

NFC Championship: DALLAS 23, Minnesota 6

Super Bowl XII: Dallas (NFC) 27, Denver (AFC) 10, at Louisiana Superdome, New Orleans, Louisiana

1976

AMERICAN CONFERENCE

Eastern Division

	W	L	T	Pct.	Pts.	OP
Baltimore	11	3	0	.786	417	246
New England*	11	3	0	.786	376	236
Miami	6	8	0	.429	263	264
N.Y. Jets	3	11	0	.214	169	383
Buffalo	2	12	0	.143	245	363

Central Division

	W	L	T	Pct.	Pts.	OP
Pittsburgh	10	4	0	.714	342	138
Cincinnati	10	4	0	.714	335	210
Cleveland	9	5	0	.643	267	287
Houston	5	9	0	.357	222	273

Western Division

	W	L	T	Pct.	Pts.	OP
Oakland#	13	1	0	.929	350	237
Denver	9	5	0	.643	315	206
San Diego	6	8	0	.429	248	285
Kansas City	5	9	0	.357	290	376
Tampa Bay	0	14	0	.000	125	412

NATIONAL CONFERENCE

Eastern Division

	W	L	T	Pct.	Pts.	OP
Dallas	11	3	0	.786	296	194
Washington*	10	4	0	.714	291	217
St. Louis	10	4	0	.714	309	267
Philadelphia	4	10	0	.286	165	286
N.Y. Giants	3	11	0	.214	170	250

Central Division

	W	L	T	Pct.	Pts.	OP
Minnesota#	11	2	1	.821	305	176
Chicago	7	7	0	.500	253	216
Detroit	6	8	0	.429	262	220
Green Bay	5	9	0	.357	218	299

Western Division

	W	L	T	Pct.	Pts.	OP
Los Angeles	10	3	1	.750	351	190
San Francisco	8	6	0	.571	270	190
New Orleans	4	10	0	.286	253	346
Atlanta	4	10	0	.286	172	312
Seattle	2	12	0	.143	229	429

**Wild Card qualifier for playoffs; #Top playoff seed in conference*

Baltimore finished ahead of New England based on better division record (7-1 to Patriots' 6-2). Pittsburgh finished ahead of Cincinnati based on head-to-head sweep (2-0). Washington finished ahead of St. Louis based on head-to-head sweep (2-0). New Orleans finished ahead of Atlanta based on better point-differential in head-to-head competition (27 points).

Divisional playoffs: OAKLAND 24, New England 21; Pittsburgh 40, BALTIMORE 14

AFC Championship: OAKLAND 24, Pittsburgh 7

Divisional playoffs: MINNESOTA 35, Washington 20; Los Angeles 14, DALLAS 12

NFC Championship: MINNESOTA 24, Los Angeles 13

Super Bowl XI: Oakland (AFC) 32, Minnesota (NFC) 14, at Rose Bowl, Pasadena, California

1975

AMERICAN CONFERENCE

Eastern Division

	W	L	T	Pct.	Pts.	OP
Baltimore	10	4	0	.714	395	269
Miami	10	4	0	.714	357	222
Buffalo	8	6	0	.571	420	355
N.Y. Jets	3	11	0	.214	258	433
New England	3	11	0	.214	258	358

Central Division

	W	L	T	Pct.	Pts.	OP
Pittsburgh#	12	2	0	.857	373	162
Cincinnati*	11	3	0	.786	340	246
Houston	10	4	0	.714	293	226
Cleveland	3	11	0	.214	218	372

Western Division

	W	L	T	Pct.	Pts.	OP
Oakland	11	3	0	.786	375	255
Denver	6	8	0	.429	254	307
Kansas City	5	9	0	.357	282	341
San Diego	2	12	0	.143	189	345

NATIONAL CONFERENCE

Eastern Division

	W	L	T	Pct.	Pts.	OP
St. Louis	11	3	0	.786	356	276
Dallas*	10	4	0	.714	350	268
Washington	8	6	0	.571	325	276
N.Y. Giants	5	9	0	.357	216	306
Philadelphia	4	10	0	.286	225	302

Central Division

	W	L	T	Pct.	Pts.	OP
Minnesota#	12	2	0	.857	377	180
Detroit	7	7	0	.500	245	262
Chicago	4	10	0	.286	191	379
Green Bay	4	10	0	.286	226	285

Western Division

	W	L	T	Pct.	Pts.	OP
Los Angeles	12	2	0	.857	312	135
San Francisco	5	9	0	.357	255	286
Atlanta	4	10	0	.286	240	289
New Orleans	2	12	0	.143	165	360

**Wild Card qualifier for playoffs; #Top playoff seed in conference*

Baltimore finished ahead of Miami based on head-to-head sweep (2-0). Cincinnati did not play Pittsburgh in the divisional playoffs because, from 1970-1989, two teams from the same division could not meet prior to the conference championship game. N.Y. Jets finished ahead of New England based on head-to-head sweep (2-0). Minnesota was top playoff seed based on better Point Rating system than Los Angeles (3 to 6). Chicago finished ahead of Green Bay based on better division record (2-4 to Bears' 1-5).

Divisional playoffs: PITTSBURGH 28, Baltimore 10; OAKLAND 31, Cincinnati 28

AFC Championship: PITTSBURGH 16, Oakland 10

Divisional playoffs: LOS ANGELES 35, St. Louis 23; Dallas 17, MINNESOTA 14

NFC Championship: Dallas 37, LOS ANGELES 7

Super Bowl X: Pittsburgh (AFC) 21, Dallas (NFC) 17, at Orange Bowl, Miami, Florida

1974

AMERICAN CONFERENCE

Eastern Division

	W	L	T	Pct.	Pts.	OP
Miami	11	3	0	.786	327	216
Buffalo*	9	5	0	.643	264	244
N.Y. Jets	7	7	0	.500	279	300
New England	7	7	0	.500	348	289
Baltimore	2	12	0	.143	190	329

Central Division

	W	L	T	Pct.	Pts.	OP
Pittsburgh	10	3	1	.750	305	189
Houston	7	7	0	.500	236	282
Cincinnati	7	7	0	.500	283	259
Cleveland	4	10	0	.286	251	344

Western Division

	W	L	T	Pct.	Pts.	OP
Oakland	12	2	0	.857	355	228
Denver	7	6	1	.536	302	294
Kansas City	5	9	0	.357	233	293
San Diego	5	9	0	.357	212	285

NATIONAL CONFERENCE

Eastern Division

	W	L	T	Pct.	Pts.	OP
St. Louis	10	4	0	.714	285	218
Washington*	10	4	0	.714	320	196
Dallas	8	6	0	.571	297	235
Philadelphia	7	7	0	.500	242	217
N.Y. Giants	2	12	0	.143	195	299

Central Division

	W	L	T	Pct.	Pts.	OP
Minnesota	10	4	0	.714	310	195
Detroit	7	7	0	.500	256	270
Green Bay	6	8	0	.429	210	206
Chicago	4	10	0	.286	152	279

Western Division

	W	L	T	Pct.	Pts.	OP
Los Angeles	10	4	0	.714	263	181
San Francisco	6	8	0	.429	226	236
New Orleans	5	9	0	.357	166	263
Atlanta	3	11	0	.214	111	271

**Wild Card qualifier for playoffs*

N.Y. Jets finished ahead of New England based on better conference record (5-6 to Patriots' 4-7). Houston finished ahead of Cincinnati based on head-to-head sweep (2-0). Kansas City finished ahead of San Diego based on better point-differential in head-to-head competition (3 points). St. Louis finished ahead of Washington based on head-to-head sweep (2-0).

Divisional playoffs: OAKLAND 28, Miami 26; PITTSBURGH 32, Buffalo 14

AFC Championship: Pittsburgh 24, OAKLAND 13

Divisional playoffs: MINNESOTA 30, St. Louis 14; LOS ANGELES 19, Washington 10

NFC Championship: MINNESOTA 14, Los Angeles 10

Super Bowl IX: Pittsburgh (AFC) 16, Minnesota (NFC) 6, at Tulane Stadium, New Orleans, Louisiana

From 1933-1974, sites for league/conference championship games alternated by division.

1973

AMERICAN CONFERENCE

Eastern Division

	W	L	T	Pct.	Pts.	OP
Miami	12	2	0	.857	343	150
Buffalo	9	5	0	.643	259	230
New England	5	9	0	.357	258	300
N.Y. Jets	4	10	0	.286	240	306
Baltimore	4	10	0	.286	226	341

Central Division

	W	L	T	Pct.	Pts.	OP
Cincinnati	10	4	0	.714	286	231
Pittsburgh*	10	4	0	.714	347	210
Cleveland	7	5	2	.571	234	255
Houston	1	13	0	.071	199	447

Western Division

	W	L	T	Pct.	Pts.	OP
Oakland	9	4	1	.679	292	175
Kansas City	7	5	2	.571	231	192
Denver	7	5	2	.571	354	296
San Diego	2	11	1	.179	188	386

NATIONAL CONFERENCE

Eastern Division

	W	L	T	Pct.	Pts.	OP
Dallas	10	4	0	.714	382	203
Washington*	10	4	0	.714	325	198
Philadelphia	5	8	1	.393	310	393
St. Louis	4	9	1	.321	286	365
N.Y. Giants	2	11	1	.179	226	362

Central Division

	W	L	T	Pct.	Pts.	OP
Minnesota	12	2	0	.857	296	168
Detroit	6	7	1	.464	271	247
Green Bay	5	7	2	.429	202	259
Chicago	3	11	0	.214	195	334

Western Division

	W	L	T	Pct.	Pts.	OP
Los Angeles	12	2	0	.857	388	178
Atlanta	9	5	0	.643	318	224
San Francisco	5	9	0	.357	262	319
New Orleans	5	9	0	.357	163	312

**Wild Card qualifier for playoffs*

Cincinnati finished ahead of Pittsburgh based on better conference record (8-3 to Steelers' 7-4). N.Y. Jets finished ahead of Baltimore based on head-to-head sweep (2-0). Kansas City finished ahead of Denver based on better division record (4-2 to Broncos' 3-2-1). Dallas finished ahead of Washington based on better point differential in head-to-head games (13 points). San Francisco finished ahead of New Orleans based on better division record (2-4 to Saints' 1-5).

Divisional playoffs: OAKLAND 33, Pittsburgh 14; MIAMI 34, Cincinnati 16

AFC Championship: MIAMI 27, Oakland 10

Divisional playoffs: MINNESOTA 27, Washington 20; DALLAS 27, Los Angeles 16

NFC Championship: Minnesota 27, DALLAS 10

Super Bowl VIII: Miami (AFC) 24, Minnesota (NFC) 7, at Rice Stadium, Houston, Texas

1972

AMERICAN CONFERENCE

Eastern Division

	W	L	T	Pct.	Pts.	OP
Miami	14	0	0	1.000	385	171
N.Y. Jets	7	7	0	.500	367	324
Baltimore	5	9	0	.357	235	252
Buffalo	4	9	1	.321	257	377
New England	3	11	0	.214	192	446

Central Division

	W	L	T	Pct.	Pts.	OP
Pittsburgh	11	3	0	.786	343	175
Cleveland*	10	4	0	.714	268	249
Cincinnati	8	6	0	.571	299	229
Houston	1	13	0	.071	164	380

Western Division

	W	L	T	Pct.	Pts.	OP
Oakland	10	3	1	.750	365	248
Kansas City	8	6	0	.571	287	254
Denver	5	9	0	.357	325	350
San Diego	4	9	1	.321	264	344

NATIONAL CONFERENCE

Eastern Division

	W	L	T	Pct.	Pts.	OP
Washington	11	3	0	.786	336	218
Dallas*	10	4	0	.714	319	240
N.Y. Giants	8	6	0	.571	331	247
St. Louis	4	9	1	.321	193	303
Philadelphia	2	11	1	.179	145	352

Central Division

	W	L	T	Pct.	Pts.	OP
Green Bay	10	4	0	.714	304	226
Detroit	8	5	1	.607	339	290
Minnesota	7	7	0	.500	301	252
Chicago	4	9	1	.321	225	275

Western Division

	W	L	T	Pct.	Pts.	OP
San Francisco	8	5	1	.607	353	249
Atlanta	7	7	0	.500	269	274
Los Angeles	6	7	1	.464	291	286
New Orleans	2	11	1	.179	215	361

**Wild Card qualifier for playoffs*

Dallas did not play Washington in the divisional playoffs because, from 1970-1989, two teams from the same division could not meet prior to the conference championship game.

Divisional playoffs: PITTSBURGH 13, Oakland 7; MIAMI 20, Cleveland 14

AFC Championship: Miami 21, PITTSBURGH 17

Divisional playoffs: Dallas 30, SAN FRANCISCO 28; WASHINGTON 16, Green Bay 3

NFC Championship: WASHINGTON 26, Dallas 3

Super Bowl VII: Miami (AFC) 14, Washington (NFC) 7, at Memorial Coliseum, Los Angeles, California

1971

AMERICAN CONFERENCE

Eastern Division

	W	L	T	Pct.	Pts.	OP
Miami	10	3	1	.769	315	174
Baltimore*	10	4	0	.714	313	140
New England	6	8	0	.429	238	325
N.Y. Jets	6	8	0	.429	212	299
Buffalo	1	13	0	.071	184	394

Central Division

	W	L	T	Pct.	Pts.	OP
Cleveland	9	5	0	.643	285	273
Pittsburgh	6	8	0	.429	246	292
Houston	4	9	1	.308	251	330
Cincinnati	4	10	0	.286	284	265

Western Division

	W	L	T	Pct.	Pts.	OP
Kansas City	10	3	1	.769	302	208
Oakland	8	4	2	.667	344	278
San Diego	6	8	0	.429	311	341
Denver	4	9	1	.308	203	275

NATIONAL CONFERENCE

Eastern Division

	W	L	T	Pct.	Pts.	OP
Dallas	11	3	0	.786	406	222
Washington*	9	4	1	.692	276	190
Philadelphia	6	7	1	.462	221	302
St. Louis	4	9	1	.308	231	279
N.Y. Giants	4	10	0	.286	228	362

Central Division

	W	L	T	Pct.	Pts.	OP
Minnesota	11	3	0	.786	245	139
Detroit	7	6	1	.538	341	286
Chicago	6	8	0	.429	185	276
Green Bay	4	8	2	.333	274	298

Western Division

	W	L	T	Pct.	Pts.	OP
San Francisco	9	5	0	.643	300	216
Los Angeles	8	5	1	.615	313	260
Atlanta	7	6	1	.538	274	277
New Orleans	4	8	2	.333	266	347

**Wild Card qualifier for playoffs*

New England finished ahead of N.Y. Jets based on better point-differential in head-to-head competition (13 points).

Divisional playoffs: Miami 27, KANSAS CITY 24 (OT); Baltimore 20, CLEVELAND 3

AFC Championship: MIAMI 21, Baltimore 0

Divisional playoffs: Dallas 20, MINNESOTA 12; SAN FRANCISCO 24, Washington 20

NFC Championship: DALLAS 14, San Francisco 3

Super Bowl VI: Dallas (NFC) 24, Miami (AFC) 3, at Tulane Stadium, New Orleans, Louisiana

From 1920-1971, tie games were not included in winning percentage.

1970

AMERICAN CONFERENCE

Eastern Division

	W	L	T	Pct.	Pts.	OP
Baltimore	11	2	1	.846	321	234
Miami*	10	4	0	.714	297	228
N.Y. Jets	4	10	0	.286	255	286
Buffalo	3	10	1	.231	204	337
Boston Patriots	2	12	0	.143	149	361

Central Division

	W	L	T	Pct.	Pts.	OP
Cincinnati	8	6	0	.571	312	255
Cleveland	7	7	0	.500	286	265
Pittsburgh	5	9	0	.357	210	272
Houston	3	10	1	.231	217	352

Western Division

	W	L	T	Pct.	Pts.	OP
Oakland	8	4	2	.667	300	293
Kansas City	7	5	2	.583	272	244
San Diego	5	6	3	.455	282	278
Denver	5	8	1	.385	253	264

NATIONAL CONFERENCE

Eastern Division

	W	L	T	Pct.	Pts.	OP
Dallas	10	4	0	.714	299	221
N.Y. Giants	9	5	0	.643	301	270
St. Louis	8	5	1	.615	325	228
Washington	6	8	0	.429	297	314
Philadelphia	3	10	1	.231	241	332

Central Division

	W	L	T	Pct.	Pts.	OP
Minnesota	12	2	0	.857	335	143
Detroit*	10	4	0	.714	347	202
Green Bay	6	8	0	.429	196	293
Chicago	6	8	0	.429	256	261

Western Division

	W	L	T	Pct.	Pts.	OP
San Francisco	10	3	1	.769	352	267
Los Angeles	9	4	1	.692	325	202
Atlanta	4	8	2	.333	206	261
New Orleans	2	11	1	.154	172	347

**Wild Card qualifier for playoffs*

Miami did not play Baltimore, and Detroit did not play Minnesota, in the divisional playoffs because, from 1970-1989, two teams from the same division could not meet prior to the conference championship game. Green Bay finished ahead of Chicago based on better division record (2-4 to Bears' 1-5).

Divisional playoffs: BALTIMORE 17, Cincinnati 0; OAKLAND 21, Miami 14

AFC Championship: BALTIMORE 27, Oakland 17

Divisional playoffs: DALLAS 5, Detroit 0; San Francisco 17, MINNESOTA 14

NFC Championship: Dallas 17, SAN FRANCISCO 10

Super Bowl V: Baltimore (AFC) 16, Dallas (NFC) 13, at Orange Bowl, Miami, Florida

1969 NFL

EASTERN CONFERENCE

Capitol Division

	W	L	T	Pct.	Pts.	OP
Dallas	11	2	1	.846	369	223
Washington	7	5	2	.583	307	319
New Orleans	5	9	0	.357	311	393
Philadelphia	4	9	1	.308	279	377

Century Division

	W	L	T	Pct.	Pts.	OP
Cleveland	10	3	1	.769	351	300
N.Y. Giants	6	8	0	.429	264	298
St. Louis	4	9	1	.308	314	389
Pittsburgh	1	13	0	.071	218	404

WESTERN CONFERENCE

Coastal Division

	W	L	T	Pct.	Pts.	OP
Los Angeles	11	3	0	.786	320	243
Baltimore	8	5	1	.615	279	268
Atlanta	6	8	0	.429	276	268
San Francisco	4	8	2	.333	277	319

Central Division

	W	L	T	Pct.	Pts.	OP
Minnesota	12	2	0	.857	379	133
Detroit	9	4	1	.692	259	188
Green Bay	8	6	0	.571	269	221
Chicago	1	13	0	.071	210	339

Conference championships: Cleveland 38, DALLAS 14; MINNESOTA 23, Los Angeles 20

NFL championship: MINNESOTA 27, Cleveland 7

Super Bowl IV: Kansas City (AFL) 23, Minnesota (NFL) 7, at Tulane Stadium, New Orleans, Louisiana

1969 AFL

EASTERN DIVISION

	W	L	T	Pct.	Pts.	OP
N.Y. Jets	10	4	0	.714	353	269
Houston	6	6	2	.500	278	279
Boston Patriots	4	10	0	.286	266	316
Buffalo	4	10	0	.286	230	359
Miami	3	10	1	.231	233	332

WESTERN DIVISION

	W	L	T	Pct.	Pts.	OP
Oakland	12	1	1	.923	377	242
Kansas City	11	3	0	.786	359	177
San Diego	8	6	0	.571	288	276
Denver	5	8	1	.385	297	344
Cincinnati	4	9	1	.308	280	367

Divisional playoffs: Kansas City 13, N.Y. JETS 6; OAKLAND 56, Houston 7

AFL championship: Kansas City 17, OAKLAND 7

1968 NFL

EASTERN CONFERENCE

Capitol Division

	W	L	T	Pct.	Pts.	OP
Dallas	12	2	0	.857	431	186
N.Y. Giants	7	7	0	.500	294	325
Washington	5	9	0	.357	249	358
Philadelphia	2	12	0	.143	202	351

Century Division

	W	L	T	Pct.	Pts.	OP
Cleveland	10	4	0	.714	394	273
St. Louis	9	4	1	.692	325	289
New Orleans	4	9	1	.308	246	327
Pittsburgh	2	11	1	.154	244	397

WESTERN CONFERENCE

Coastal Division

	W	L	T	Pct.	Pts.	OP
Baltimore	13	1	0	.929	402	144
Los Angeles	10	3	1	.769	312	200
San Francisco	7	6	1	.538	303	310
Atlanta	2	12	0	.143	170	389

Central Division

	W	L	T	Pct.	Pts.	OP
Minnesota	8	6	0	.571	282	242
Chicago	7	7	0	.500	250	333
Green Bay	6	7	1	.462	281	227
Detroit	4	8	2	.333	207	241

Conference championships: CLEVELAND 31, Dallas 20; BALTIMORE 24, Minnesota 14

NFL championship: Baltimore 34, CLEVELAND 0

Super Bowl III: N.Y. Jets (AFL) 16, Baltimore (NFL) 7, at Orange Bowl, Miami, Florida

1968 AFL

EASTERN DIVISION

	W	L	T	Pct.	Pts.	OP
N.Y. Jets	11	3	0	.786	419	280
Houston	7	7	0	.500	303	248
Miami	5	8	1	.385	276	355
Boston Patriots	4	10	0	.286	229	406
Buffalo	1	12	1	.077	199	367

WESTERN DIVISION

	W	L	T	Pct.	Pts.	OP
Oakland	12	2	0	.857	453	233
Kansas City	12	2	0	.857	371	170
San Diego	9	5	0	.643	382	310
Denver	5	9	0	.357	255	404
Cincinnati	3	11	0	.214	215	329

Western Division playoff: OAKLAND 41, Kansas City 6

AFL championship: N.Y. JETS 27, Oakland 23

1967 NFL

EASTERN CONFERENCE

Capitol Division

	W	L	T	Pct.	Pts.	OP
Dallas	9	5	0	.643	342	268
Philadelphia	6	7	1	.462	351	409
Washington	5	6	3	.455	347	353
New Orleans	3	11	0	.214	233	379

Century Division

	W	L	T	Pct.	Pts.	OP
Cleveland	9	5	0	.643	334	297
N.Y. Giants	7	7	0	.500	369	379
St. Louis	6	7	1	.462	333	356
Pittsburgh	4	9	1	.308	281	320

WESTERN CONFERENCE

Coastal Division

	W	L	T	Pct.	Pts.	OP
Los Angeles	11	1	2	.917	398	196
Baltimore	11	1	2	.917	394	198
San Francisco	7	7	0	.500	273	337
Atlanta	1	12	1	.077	175	422

Central Division

	W	L	T	Pct.	Pts.	OP
Green Bay	9	4	1	.692	332	209
Chicago	7	6	1	.538	239	218
Detroit	5	7	2	.417	260	259
Minnesota	3	8	3	.273	233	294

Los Angeles finished ahead of Baltimore based on better point differential in head-to-head games (net 24 points).

Conference championships: DALLAS 52, Cleveland 14; GREEN BAY 28, Los Angeles 7

NFL championship: GREEN BAY 21, Dallas 17

Super Bowl II: Green Bay (NFL) 33, Oakland (AFL) 14, at Orange Bowl, Miami, Florida

1967 AFL

EASTERN DIVISION	W	L	T	Pct.	Pts.	OP	WESTERN DIVISION	W	L	T	Pct.	Pts.	OP
Houston	9	4	1	.692	258	199	Oakland	13	1	0	.929	468	233
N.Y. Jets	8	5	1	.615	371	329	Kansas City	9	5	0	.643	408	254
Buffalo	4	10	0	.286	237	285	San Diego	8	5	1	.615	360	352
Miami	4	10	0	.286	219	407	Denver	3	11	0	.214	256	409
Boston Patriots	3	10	1	.231	280	389							

AFL championship: OAKLAND 40, Houston 7

1966 NFL

EASTERN CONFERENCE	W	L	T	Pct.	Pts.	OP	WESTERN CONFERENCE	W	L	T	Pct.	Pts.	OP
Dallas	10	3	1	.769	445	239	Green Bay	12	2	0	.857	335	163
Cleveland	9	5	0	.643	403	259	Baltimore	9	5	0	.643	314	226
Philadelphia	9	5	0	.643	326	340	Los Angeles	8	6	0	.571	289	212
St. Louis	8	5	1	.615	264	265	San Francisco	6	6	2	.500	320	325
Washington	7	7	0	.500	351	355	Chicago	5	7	2	.417	234	272
Pittsburgh	5	8	1	.385	316	347	Detroit	4	9	1	.308	206	317
Atlanta	3	11	0	.214	204	437	Minnesota	4	9	1	.308	292	304
N.Y. Giants	1	12	1	.077	263	501							

NFL championship: Green Bay 34, DALLAS 27
Super Bowl I: Green Bay (NFL) 35, Kansas City (AFL) 10, at Memorial Coliseum, Los Angeles, California

1966 AFL

EASTERN DIVISION	W	L	T	Pct.	Pts.	OP	WESTERN DIVISION	W	L	T	Pct.	Pts.	OP
Buffalo	9	4	1	.692	358	255	Kansas City	11	2	1	.846	448	276
Boston Patriots	8	4	2	.677	315	283	Oakland	8	5	1	.615	315	288
N.Y. Jets	6	6	2	.500	322	312	San Diego	7	6	1	.538	335	284
Houston	3	11	0	.214	335	396	Denver	4	10	0	.286	196	381
Miami	3	11	0	.214	213	362							

AFL championship: Kansas City 31, BUFFALO 7

1965 NFL

EASTERN CONFERENCE	W	L	T	Pct.	Pts.	OP	WESTERN CONFERENCE	W	L	T	Pct.	Pts.	OP
Cleveland	11	3	0	.786	363	325	Green Bay	10	3	1	.769	316	224
Dallas	7	7	0	.500	325	280	Baltimore	10	3	1	.769	389	284
N.Y. Giants	7	7	0	.500	270	338	Chicago	9	5	0	.643	409	275
Washington	6	8	0	.429	257	301	San Francisco	7	6	1	.538	421	402
Philadelphia	5	9	0	.357	363	359	Minnesota	7	7	0	.500	383	403
St. Louis	5	9	0	.357	296	309	Detroit	6	7	1	.462	257	295
Pittsburgh	2	12	0	.143	202	397	Los Angeles	4	10	0	.286	269	328

Western Conference playoff: GREEN BAY 13, Baltimore 10 (OT)
NFL championship: GREEN BAY 23, Cleveland 12

1965 AFL

EASTERN DIVISION	W	L	T	Pct.	Pts.	OP	WESTERN DIVISION	W	L	T	Pct.	Pts.	OP
Buffalo	10	3	1	.769	313	226	San Diego	9	2	3	.818	340	227
N.Y. Jets	5	8	1	.385	285	303	Oakland	8	5	1	.615	298	239
Boston Patriots	4	8	2	.333	244	302	Kansas City	7	5	2	.583	322	285
Houston	4	10	0	.286	298	429	Denver	4	10	0	.286	303	392

AFL championship: Buffalo 23, SAN DIEGO 0

1964 NFL

EASTERN CONFERENCE	W	L	T	Pct.	Pts.	OP	WESTERN CONFERENCE	W	L	T	Pct.	Pts.	OP
Cleveland	10	3	1	.769	415	293	Baltimore	12	2	0	.857	428	225
St. Louis	9	3	2	.750	357	331	Green Bay	8	5	1	.615	342	245
Philadelphia	6	8	0	.429	312	313	Minnesota	8	5	1	.615	355	296
Washington	6	8	0	.429	307	305	Detroit	7	5	2	.583	280	260
Dallas	5	8	1	.385	250	289	Los Angeles	5	7	2	.417	283	339
Pittsburgh	5	9	0	.357	253	315	Chicago	5	9	0	.357	260	379
N.Y. Giants	2	10	2	.167	241	399	San Francisco	4	10	0	.286	236	330

NFL championship: CLEVELAND 27, Baltimore 0

1964 AFL

EASTERN DIVISION	W	L	T	Pct.	Pts.	OP	WESTERN DIVISION	W	L	T	Pct.	Pts.	OP
Buffalo	12	2	0	.857	400	242	San Diego	8	5	1	.615	341	300
Boston Patriots	10	3	1	.769	365	297	Kansas City	7	7	0	.500	366	306
N.Y. Jets	5	8	1	.385	278	315	Oakland	5	7	2	.417	303	350
Houston	4	10	0	.286	310	355	Denver	2	11	1	.154	240	438

AFL championship: BUFFALO 20, San Diego 7

1963 NFL

EASTERN CONFERENCE	W	L	T	Pct.	Pts.	OP	WESTERN CONFERENCE	W	L	T	Pct.	Pts.	OP
N.Y. Giants	11	3	0	.786	448	280	Chicago	11	1	2	.917	301	144
Cleveland	10	4	0	.714	343	262	Green Bay	11	2	1	.846	369	206
St. Louis	9	5	0	.643	341	283	Baltimore	8	6	0	.571	316	285
Pittsburgh	7	4	3	.636	321	295	Detroit	5	8	1	.385	326	265
Dallas	4	10	0	.286	305	378	Minnesota	5	8	1	.385	309	390
Washington	3	11	0	.214	279	398	Los Angeles	5	9	0	.357	210	350
Philadelphia	2	10	2	.167	242	381	San Francisco	2	12	0	.143	198	391

NFL championship: CHICAGO 14, N.Y. Giants 10

1963 AFL

EASTERN DIVISION	W	L	T	Pct.	Pts.	OP	WESTERN DIVISION	W	L	T	Pct.	Pts.	OP
Boston Patriots	7	6	1	.538	327	257	San Diego	11	3	0	.786	399	255
Buffalo	7	6	1	.538	304	291	Oakland	10	4	0	.714	363	282
Houston	6	8	0	.429	302	372	Kansas City	5	7	2	.417	347	263
N.Y. Jets	5	8	1	.385	249	399	Denver	2	11	1	.154	301	473

Eastern Division playoff: Boston 26, BUFFALO 8
AFL championship: SAN DIEGO 51, Boston 10

1962 NFL

EASTERN CONFERENCE	W	L	T	Pct.	Pts.	OP	WESTERN CONFERENCE	W	L	T	Pct.	Pts.	OP
N.Y. Giants	12	2	0	.857	398	283	Green Bay	13	1	0	.929	415	148
Pittsburgh	9	5	0	.643	312	363	Detroit	11	3	0	.786	315	177
Cleveland	7	6	1	.538	291	257	Chicago	9	5	0	.643	321	287
Washington	5	7	2	.417	305	376	Baltimore	7	7	0	.500	293	288
Dallas Cowboys	5	8	1	.385	398	402	San Francisco	6	8	0	.429	282	331
St. Louis	4	9	1	.308	287	361	Minnesota	2	11	1	.154	254	410
Philadelphia	3	10	1	.231	282	356	Los Angeles	1	12	1	.077	220	334

NFL championship: Green Bay 16, N.Y. GIANTS 7

1962 AFL

EASTERN DIVISION	W	L	T	Pct.	Pts.	OP	WESTERN DIVISION	W	L	T	Pct.	Pts.	OP
Houston	11	3	0	.786	387	270	Dallas Texans	11	3	0	.786	389	233
Boston Patriots	9	4	1	.692	346	295	Denver	7	7	0	.500	353	334
Buffalo	7	6	1	.538	309	272	San Diego	4	10	0	.286	314	392
N.Y. Titans	5	9	0	.357	278	423	Oakland	1	13	0	.071	213	370

AFL championship: Dallas Texans 20, HOUSTON 17 (OT)

1961 NFL

EASTERN CONFERENCE	W	L	T	Pct.	Pts.	OP
N.Y. Giants	10	3	1	.769	368	220
Philadelphia	10	4	0	.714	361	297
Cleveland	8	5	1	.615	319	270
St. Louis	7	7	0	.500	279	267
Pittsburgh	6	8	0	.429	295	287
Dallas Cowboys	4	9	1	.308	236	380
Washington	1	12	1	.077	174	392

WESTERN CONFERENCE	W	L	T	Pct.	Pts.	OP
Green Bay	11	3	0	.786	391	223
Detroit	8	5	1	.615	270	258
Baltimore	8	6	0	.571	302	307
Chicago	8	6	0	.571	326	302
San Francisco	7	6	1	.538	346	272
Los Angeles	4	10	0	.286	263	333
Minnesota	3	11	0	.214	285	407

NFL championship: GREEN BAY 37, N.Y. Giants 0

1961 AFL

EASTERN DIVISION	W	L	T	Pct.	Pts.	OP
Houston	10	3	1	.769	513	242
Boston Patriots	9	4	1	.692	413	313
N.Y. Titans	7	7	0	.500	301	390
Buffalo	6	8	0	.429	294	342

WESTERN DIVISION	W	L	T	Pct.	Pts.	OP
San Diego	12	2	0	.857	396	219
Dallas Texans	6	8	0	.429	334	343
Denver	3	11	0	.214	251	432
Oakland	2	12	0	.143	237	458

AFL championship: Houston 10, SAN DIEGO 3

1960 NFL

EASTERN CONFERENCE	W	L	T	Pct.	Pts.	OP
Philadelphia	10	2	0	.833	321	246
Cleveland	8	3	1	.727	362	217
N.Y. Giants	6	4	2	.600	271	261
St. Louis	6	5	1	.545	288	230
Pittsburgh	5	6	1	.455	240	275
Washington	1	9	2	.100	178	309

WESTERN CONFERENCE	W	L	T	Pct.	Pts.	OP
Green Bay	8	4	0	.667	332	209
Detroit	7	5	0	.583	239	212
San Francisco	7	5	0	.583	208	205
Baltimore	6	6	0	.500	288	234
Chicago	5	6	1	.455	194	299
L.A. Rams	4	7	1	.364	265	297
Dallas Cowboys	0	11	1	.000	177	369

NFL championship: PHILADELPHIA 17, Green Bay 13

1960 AFL

EASTERN CONFERENCE	W	L	T	Pct.	Pts.	OP
Houston	10	4	0	.714	379	285
N.Y. Titans	7	7	0	.500	382	399
Buffalo	5	8	1	.385	296	303
Boston Patriots	5	9	0	.357	286	349

WESTERN CONFERENCE	W	L	T	Pct.	Pts.	OP
L.A. Chargers	10	4	0	.714	373	336
Dallas Texans	8	6	0	.571	362	253
Oakland	6	8	0	.429	319	388
Denver	4	9	1	.308	309	393

AFL championship: HOUSTON 24, L.A. Chargers 16

1959

EASTERN CONFERENCE	W	L	T	Pct.	Pts.	OP
N.Y. Giants	10	2	0	.833	284	170
Cleveland	7	5	0	.583	270	214
Philadelphia	7	5	0	.583	268	278
Pittsburgh	6	5	1	.545	257	216
Washington	3	9	0	.250	185	350
Chi. Cardinals	2	10	0	.167	234	324

WESTERN CONFERENCE	W	L	T	Pct.	Pts.	OP
Baltimore	9	3	0	.750	374	251
Chi. Bears	8	4	0	.667	252	196
Green Bay	7	5	0	.583	248	246
San Francisco	7	5	0	.583	255	237
Detroit	3	8	1	.273	203	275
Los Angeles	2	10	0	.167	242	315

NFL championship: BALTIMORE 31, N.Y. Giants 16

1958

EASTERN CONFERENCE	W	L	T	Pct.	Pts.	OP
N.Y. Giants	9	3	0	.750	246	183
Cleveland	9	3	0	.750	302	217
Pittsburgh	7	4	1	.636	261	230
Washington	4	7	1	.364	214	268
Chi. Cardinals	2	9	1	.182	261	356
Philadelphia	2	9	1	.182	235	306

WESTERN CONFERENCE	W	L	T	Pct.	Pts.	OP
Baltimore	9	3	0	.750	381	203
Chi. Bears	8	4	0	.667	298	230
Los Angeles	8	4	0	.667	344	278
San Francisco	6	6	0	.500	257	324
Detroit	4	7	1	.364	261	276
Green Bay	1	10	1	.091	193	382

Eastern Conference playoff: N.Y. GIANTS 10, Cleveland 0
NFL championship: Baltimore 23, N.Y. GIANTS 17 (OT)

1957

EASTERN CONFERENCE	W	L	T	Pct.	Pts.	OP
Cleveland	9	2	1	.818	269	172
N.Y. Giants	7	5	0	.583	254	211
Pittsburgh	6	6	0	.500	161	178
Washington	5	6	1	.455	251	230
Philadelphia	4	8	0	.333	173	230
Chi. Cardinals	3	9	0	.250	200	299

WESTERN CONFERENCE	W	L	T	Pct.	Pts.	OP
Detroit	8	4	0	.667	251	231
San Francisco	8	4	0	.667	260	264
Baltimore	7	5	0	.583	303	235
Los Angeles	6	6	0	.500	307	278
Chi. Bears	5	7	0	.417	203	211
Green Bay	3	9	0	.250	218	311

Western Conference playoff: Detroit 31, SAN FRANCISCO 27
NFL championship: DETROIT 59, Cleveland 14

1956

EASTERN CONFERENCE	W	L	T	Pct.	Pts.	OP
N.Y. Giants	8	3	1	.727	264	197
Chi. Cardinals	7	5	0	.583	240	182
Washington	6	6	0	.500	183	225
Cleveland	5	7	0	.417	167	177
Pittsburgh	5	7	0	.417	217	250
Philadelphia	3	8	1	.273	143	215

WESTERN CONFERENCE	W	L	T	Pct.	Pts.	OP
Chi. Bears	9	2	1	.818	363	246
Detroit	9	3	0	.750	300	188
San Francisco	5	6	1	.455	233	284
Baltimore	5	7	0	.417	270	322
Green Bay	4	8	0	.333	264	342
Los Angeles	4	8	0	.333	291	307

NFL championship: N.Y. GIANTS 47, Chi. Bears 7

1955

EASTERN CONFERENCE	W	L	T	Pct.	Pts.	OP
Cleveland	9	2	1	.818	349	218
Washington	8	4	0	.667	246	222
N.Y. Giants	6	5	1	.545	267	223
Chi. Cardinals	4	7	1	.364	224	252
Philadelphia	4	7	1	.364	248	231
Pittsburgh	4	8	0	.333	195	285

WESTERN CONFERENCE	W	L	T	Pct.	Pts.	OP
Los Angeles	8	3	1	.727	260	231
Chi. Bears	8	4	0	.667	294	251
Green Bay	6	6	0	.500	258	276
Baltimore	5	6	1	.455	214	239
San Francisco	4	8	0	.333	216	298
Detroit	3	9	0	.250	230	275

NFL championship: Cleveland 38, LOS ANGELES 14

1954

EASTERN CONFERENCE	W	L	T	Pct.	Pts.	OP
Cleveland	9	3	0	.750	336	162
Philadelphia	7	4	1	.636	284	230
N.Y. Giants	7	5	0	.583	293	184
Pittsburgh	5	7	0	.417	219	263
Washington	3	9	0	.250	207	432
Chi. Cardinals	2	10	0	.167	183	347

WESTERN CONFERENCE	W	L	T	Pct.	Pts.	OP
Detroit	9	2	1	.818	337	189
Chi. Bears	8	4	0	.667	301	279
San Francisco	7	4	1	.636	313	251
Los Angeles	6	5	1	.545	314	285
Green Bay	4	8	0	.333	234	251
Baltimore	3	9	0	.250	131	279

NFL championship: CLEVELAND 56, Detroit 10

1953

EASTERN CONFERENCE	W	L	T	Pct.	Pts.	OP	WESTERN CONFERENCE	W	L	T	Pct.	Pts.	OP
Cleveland	11	1	0	.917	348	162	Detroit	10	2	0	.833	271	205
Philadelphia	7	4	1	.636	352	215	San Francisco	9	3	0	.750	372	237
Washington	6	5	1	.545	208	215	Los Angeles	8	3	1	.727	366	236
Pittsburgh	6	6	0	.500	211	263	Chi. Bears	3	8	1	.273	218	262
N.Y. Giants	3	9	0	.250	179	277	Baltimore	3	9	0	.250	182	350
Chi. Cardinals	1	10	1	.091	190	337	Green Bay	2	9	1	.182	200	338

NFL championship: DETROIT 17, Cleveland 16

1952

AMERICAN CONFERENCE	W	L	T	Pct.	Pts.	OP	NATIONAL CONFERENCE	W	L	T	Pct.	Pts.	OP
Cleveland	8	4	0	.667	310	213	Detroit	9	3	0	.750	344	192
N.Y. Giants	7	5	0	.583	234	231	Los Angeles	9	3	0	.750	349	234
Philadelphia	7	5	0	.583	252	271	San Francisco	7	5	0	.583	285	221
Pittsburgh	5	7	0	.417	300	273	Green Bay	6	6	0	.500	295	312
Chi. Cardinals	4	8	0	.333	172	221	Chi. Bears	5	7	0	.417	245	326
Washington	4	8	0	.333	240	287	Dallas Texans	1	11	0	.083	182	427

National Conference playoff: DETROIT 31, Los Angeles 21
NFL championship: Detroit 17, CLEVELAND 7

1951

AMERICAN CONFERENCE	W	L	T	Pct.	Pts.	OP	NATIONAL CONFERENCE	W	L	T	Pct.	Pts.	OP
Cleveland	11	1	0	.917	331	152	Los Angeles	8	4	0	.667	392	261
N.Y. Giants	9	2	1	.818	254	161	Detroit	7	4	1	.636	336	259
Washington	5	7	0	.417	183	296	San Francisco	7	4	1	.636	255	205
Pittsburgh	4	7	1	.364	183	235	Chi. Bears	7	5	0	.583	286	282
Philadelphia	4	8	0	.333	234	264	Green Bay	3	9	0	.250	254	375
Chi. Cardinals	3	9	0	.250	210	287	N.Y. Yanks	1	9	2	.100	241	382

NFL championship: LOS ANGELES 24, Cleveland 17

1950

AMERICAN CONFERENCE	W	L	T	Pct.	Pts.	OP	NATIONAL CONFERENCE	W	L	T	Pct.	Pts.	OP
Cleveland	10	2	0	.833	310	144	Los Angeles	9	3	0	.750	466	309
N.Y. Giants	10	2	0	.833	268	150	Chi. Bears	9	3	0	.750	279	207
Philadelphia	6	6	0	.500	254	141	N.Y. Yanks	7	5	0	.583	366	367
Pittsburgh	6	6	0	.500	180	195	Detroit	6	6	0	.500	321	285
Chi. Cardinals	5	7	0	.417	233	287	Green Bay	3	9	0	.250	244	406
Washington	3	9	0	.250	232	326	San Francisco	3	9	0	.250	213	300
							Baltimore	1	11	0	.083	213	462

American Conference playoff: CLEVELAND 8, N.Y. Giants 3
National Conference playoff: LOS ANGELES 24, Chi. Bears 14
NFL championship: CLEVELAND 30, Los Angeles 28

1949

EASTERN DIVISION	W	L	T	Pct.	Pts.	OP	WESTERN DIVISION	W	L	T	Pct.	Pts.	OP
Philadelphia	11	1	0	.917	364	134	Los Angeles	8	2	2	.800	360	239
Pittsburgh	6	5	1	.545	224	214	Chi. Bears	9	3	0	.750	332	218
N.Y. Giants	6	6	0	.500	287	298	Chi. Cardinals	6	5	1	.545	360	301
Washington	4	7	1	.364	268	339	Detroit	4	8	0	.333	237	259
N.Y. Bulldogs	1	10	1	.091	153	368	Green Bay	2	10	0	.167	114	329

NFL championship: Philadelphia 14, LOS ANGELES 0

1948

EASTERN DIVISION	W	L	T	Pct.	Pts.	OP	WESTERN DIVISION	W	L	T	Pct.	Pts.	OP
Philadelphia	9	2	1	.818	376	156	Chi. Cardinals	11	1	0	.917	395	226
Washington	7	5	0	.583	291	287	Chi. Bears	10	2	0	.833	375	151
N.Y. Giants	4	8	0	.333	297	388	Los Angeles	6	5	1	.545	327	269
Pittsburgh	4	8	0	.333	200	243	Green Bay	3	9	0	.250	154	290
Boston	3	9	0	.250	174	372	Detroit	2	10	0	.167	200	407

NFL championship: PHILADELPHIA 7, Chi. Cardinals 0

1947

EASTERN DIVISION	W	L	T	Pct.	Pts.	OP	WESTERN DIVISION	W	L	T	Pct.	Pts.	OP
Philadelphia	8	4	0	.667	308	242	Chi. Cardinals	9	3	0	.750	306	231
Pittsburgh	8	4	0	.667	240	259	Chi. Bears	8	4	0	.667	363	241
Boston	4	7	1	.364	168	256	Green Bay	6	5	1	.545	274	210
Washington	4	8	0	.333	295	367	Los Angeles	6	6	0	.500	259	214
N.Y. Giants	2	8	2	.200	190	309	Detroit	3	9	0	.250	231	305

Eastern Division playoff: Philadelphia 21, PITTSBURGH 0
NFL championship: CHI. CARDINALS 28, Philadelphia 21

1946

EASTERN DIVISION	W	L	T	Pct.	Pts.	OP	WESTERN DIVISION	W	L	T	Pct.	Pts.	OP
N.Y. Giants	7	3	1	.700	236	162	Chi. Bears	8	2	1	.800	289	193
Philadelphia	6	5	0	.545	231	220	Los Angeles	6	4	1	.600	277	257
Washington	5	5	1	.500	171	191	Green Bay	6	5	0	.545	148	158
Pittsburgh	5	5	1	.500	136	117	Chi. Cardinals	6	5	0	.545	260	198
Boston	2	8	1	.200	189	273	Detroit	1	10	0	.091	142	310

NFL championship: Chi. Bears 24, N.Y. GIANTS 14

1945

EASTERN DIVISION	W	L	T	Pct.	Pts.	OP	WESTERN DIVISION	W	L	T	Pct.	Pts.	OP
Washington	8	2	0	.800	209	121	Cleveland	9	1	0	.900	244	136
Philadelphia	7	3	0	.700	272	133	Detroit	7	3	0	.700	195	194
N.Y. Giants	3	6	1	.333	179	198	Green Bay	6	4	0	.600	258	173
Boston	3	6	1	.333	123	211	Chi. Bears	3	7	0	.300	192	235
Pittsburgh	2	8	0	.200	79	220	Chi. Cardinals	1	9	0	.100	98	228

NFL championship: CLEVELAND 15, Washington 14

1944

EASTERN DIVISION	W	L	T	Pct.	Pts.	OP	WESTERN DIVISION	W	L	T	Pct.	Pts.	OP
N.Y. Giants	8	1	1	.889	206	75	Green Bay	8	2	0	.800	238	141
Philadelphia	7	1	2	.875	267	131	Chi. Bears	6	3	1	.667	258	172
Washington	6	3	1	.667	169	180	Detroit	6	3	1	.667	216	151
Boston	2	8	0	.200	82	233	Cleveland	4	6	0	.400	188	224
Brooklyn	0	10	0	.000	69	166	Card-Pitt	0	10	0	.000	108	328

NFL championship: Green Bay 14, N.Y. GIANTS 7

1943

EASTERN DIVISION	W	L	T	Pct.	Pts.	OP	WESTERN DIVISION	W	L	T	Pct.	Pts.	OP
Washington	6	3	1	.667	229	137	Chi. Bears	8	1	1	.889	303	157
N.Y. Giants	6	3	1	.667	197	170	Green Bay	7	2	1	.778	264	172
Phil-Pitt	5	4	1	.556	225	230	Detroit	3	6	1	.333	178	218
Brooklyn	2	8	0	.200	65	234	Chi. Cardinals	0	10	0	.000	95	238

Eastern Division playoff: Washington 28, N.Y. GIANTS 0
NFL championship: CHI. BEARS 41, Washington 21

1942

EASTERN DIVISION	W	L	T	Pct.	Pts.	OP
Washington	10	1	0	.909	227	102
Pittsburgh	7	4	0	.636	167	119
N.Y. Giants	5	5	1	.500	155	139
Brooklyn	3	8	0	.273	100	168
Philadelphia	2	9	0	.182	134	239

WESTERN DIVISION	W	L	T	Pct.	Pts.	OP
Chi. Bears	11	0	0	1.000	376	84
Green Bay	8	2	1	.800	300	215
Cleveland	5	6	0	.455	150	207
Chi. Cardinals	3	8	0	.273	98	209
Detroit	0	11	0	.000	38	263

NFL championship: WASHINGTON 14, Chi. Bears 6

1941

EASTERN DIVISION	W	L	T	Pct.	Pts.	OP
N.Y. Giants	8	3	0	.727	238	114
Brooklyn	7	4	0	.636	158	127
Washington	6	5	0	.545	176	174
Philadelphia	2	8	1	.200	119	218
Pittsburgh	1	9	1	.100	103	276

WESTERN DIVISION	W	L	T	Pct.	Pts.	OP
Chi. Bears	10	1	0	.909	396	147
Green Bay	10	1	0	.909	258	120
Detroit	4	6	1	.400	121	195
Chi. Cardinals	3	7	1	.300	127	197
Cleveland	2	9	0	.182	116	244

Western Division playoff: CHI. BEARS 33, Green Bay 14
NFL championship: CHI. BEARS 37, N.Y. Giants 9

1940

EASTERN DIVISION	W	L	T	Pct.	Pts.	OP
Washington	9	2	0	.818	245	142
Brooklyn	8	3	0	.727	186	120
N.Y. Giants	6	4	1	.600	131	133
Pittsburgh	2	7	2	.222	60	178
Philadelphia	1	10	0	.091	111	211

WESTERN DIVISION	W	L	T	Pct.	Pts.	OP
Chi. Bears	8	3	0	.727	238	152
Green Bay	6	4	1	.600	238	155
Detroit	5	5	1	.500	138	153
Cleveland	4	6	1	.400	171	191
Chi. Cardinals	2	7	2	.222	139	222

NFL championship: Chi. Bears 73, WASHINGTON 0

1939

EASTERN DIVISION	W	L	T	Pct.	Pts.	OP
N.Y. Giants	9	1	1	.900	168	85
Washington	8	2	1	.800	242	94
Brooklyn	4	6	1	.400	108	219
Philadelphia	1	9	1	.100	105	200
Pittsburgh	1	9	1	.100	114	216

WESTERN DIVISION	W	L	T	Pct.	Pts.	OP
Green Bay	9	2	0	.818	233	153
Chi. Bears	8	3	0	.727	298	157
Detroit	6	5	0	.545	145	150
Cleveland	5	5	1	.500	195	164
Chi. Cardinals	1	10	0	.091	84	254

NFL championship: GREEN BAY 27, N.Y. Giants 0

1938

EASTERN DIVISION	W	L	T	Pct.	Pts.	OP
N.Y. Giants	8	2	1	.800	194	79
Washington	6	3	2	.667	148	154
Brooklyn	4	4	3	.500	131	161
Philadelphia	5	6	0	.455	154	164
Pittsburgh	2	9	0	.182	79	169

WESTERN DIVISION	W	L	T	Pct.	Pts.	OP
Green Bay	8	3	0	.727	223	118
Detroit	7	4	0	.636	119	108
Chi. Bears	6	5	0	.545	194	148
Cleveland	4	7	0	.364	131	215
Chi. Cardinals	2	9	0	.182	111	168

NFL championship: N.Y. GIANTS 23, Green Bay 17

1937

EASTERN DIVISION	W	L	T	Pct.	Pts.	OP
Washington	8	3	0	.727	195	120
N.Y. Giants	6	3	2	.667	128	109
Pittsburgh	4	7	0	.364	122	145
Brooklyn	3	7	1	.300	82	174
Philadelphia	2	8	1	.200	86	177

WESTERN DIVISION	W	L	T	Pct.	Pts.	OP
Chi. Bears	9	1	1	.900	201	100
Green Bay	7	4	0	.636	220	122
Detroit	7	4	0	.636	180	105
Chi. Cardinals	5	5	1	.500	135	165
Cleveland	1	10	0	.091	75	207

NFL championship: Washington 28, CHI. BEARS 21

1936

EASTERN DIVISION	W	L	T	Pct.	Pts.	OP
Boston	7	5	0	.583	149	110
Pittsburgh	6	6	0	.500	98	187
N.Y. Giants	5	6	1	.455	115	163
Brooklyn	3	8	1	.273	92	161
Philadelphia	1	11	0	.083	51	206

WESTERN DIVISION	W	L	T	Pct.	Pts.	OP
Green Bay	10	1	1	.909	248	118
Chi. Bears	9	3	0	.750	222	94
Detroit	8	4	0	.667	235	102
Chi. Cardinals	3	8	1	.273	74	143

NFL championship: Green Bay 21, Boston 6, at Polo Grounds, N.Y.

1935

EASTERN DIVISION	W	L	T	Pct.	Pts.	OP
N.Y. Giants	9	3	0	.750	180	96
Brooklyn	5	6	1	.455	90	141
Pittsburgh	4	8	0	.333	100	209
Boston	2	8	1	.200	65	123
Philadelphia	2	9	0	.182	60	179

WESTERN DIVISION	W	L	T	Pct.	Pts.	OP
Detroit	7	3	2	.700	191	111
Green Bay	8	4	0	.667	181	96
Chi. Bears	6	4	2	.600	192	106
Chi. Cardinals	6	4	2	.600	99	97

NFL championship: DETROIT 26, N.Y. Giants 7
One game between Boston and Philadelphia was canceled.

1934

EASTERN DIVISION	W	L	T	Pct.	Pts.	OP
N.Y. Giants	8	5	0	.615	147	107
Boston	6	6	0	.500	107	94
Brooklyn	4	7	0	.364	61	153
Philadelphia	4	7	0	.364	127	85
Pittsburgh	2	10	0	.167	51	206

WESTERN DIVISION	W	L	T	Pct.	Pts.	OP
Chi. Bears	13	0	0	1.000	286	86
Detroit	10	3	0	.769	238	59
Green Bay	7	6	0	.538	156	112
Chi. Cardinals	5	6	0	.455	80	84
St. Louis	1	2	0	.333	27	61
Cincinnati	0	8	0	.000	10	243

NFL championship: N.Y. GIANTS 30, Chi. Bears 13

1933

EASTERN DIVISION	W	L	T	Pct.	Pts.	OP
N.Y. Giants	11	3	0	.786	244	101
Brooklyn	5	4	1	.556	93	54
Boston	5	5	2	.500	103	97
Philadelphia	3	5	1	.375	77	158
Pittsburgh	3	6	2	.333	67	208

WESTERN DIVISION	W	L	T	Pct.	Pts.	OP
Chi. Bears	10	2	1	.833	133	82
Portsmouth	6	5	0	.545	128	87
Green Bay	5	7	1	.417	170	107
Cincinnati	3	6	1	.333	38	110
Chi. Cardinals	1	9	1	.100	52	101

NFL championship: CHI. BEARS 23, N.Y. Giants 21

1932

	W	L	T	Pct.
Chicago Bears	7	1	6	.875
Green Bay Packers	10	3	1	.769
Portsmouth Spartans	6	2	4	.750
Boston Braves	4	4	2	.500
New York Giants	4	6	2	.400
Brooklyn Dodgers	3	9	0	.250
Chicago Cardinals	2	6	2	.250
Staten Island Stapletons	2	7	3	.222

Chicago Bears and Portsmouth finished regularly scheduled games tied for first place. Bears won playoff game, which counted in standings, 9-0.

1931

	W	L	T	Pct.
Green Bay Packers	12	2	0	.857
Portsmouth Spartans	11	3	0	.786
Chicago Bears	8	5	0	.615
Chicago Cardinals	5	4	0	.556
New York Giants	7	6	1	.538
Providence Steam Roller	4	4	3	.500
Staten Island Stapletons	4	6	1	.400
Cleveland Indians	2	8	0	.200
Brooklyn Dodgers	2	12	0	.143
Frankford Yellow Jackets	1	6	1	.143

1930

	W	L	T	Pct.
Green Bay Packers	10	3	1	.769
New York Giants	13	4	0	.765
Chicago Bears	9	4	1	.692
Brooklyn Dodgers	7	4	1	.636
Providence Steam Roller	6	4	1	.600
Staten Island Stapletons	5	5	2	.500
Chicago Cardinals	5	6	2	.455
Portsmouth Spartans	5	6	3	.455
Frankford Yellow Jackets	4	13	1	.222
Minneapolis Red Jackets	1	7	1	.125
Newark Tornadoes	1	10	1	.091

1929

	W	L	T	Pct.
Green Bay Packers	12	0	1	1.000
New York Giants	13	1	1	.929
Frankford Yellow Jackets	10	4	5	.714
Chicago Cardinals	6	6	1	.500
Boston Bulldogs	4	4	0	.500
Staten Island Stapletons	3	4	3	.429
Providence Steam Roller	4	6	2	.400
Orange Tornadoes	3	5	4	.375
Chicago Bears	4	9	2	.308
Buffalo Bisons	1	7	1	.125
Minneapolis Red Jackets	1	9	0	.100
Dayton Triangles	0	6	0	.000

1928

	W	L	T	Pct.
Providence Steam Roller	8	1	2	.889
Frankford Yellow Jackets	11	3	2	.786
Detroit Wolverines	7	2	1	.778
Green Bay Packers	6	4	3	.600
Chicago Bears	7	5	1	.583
New York Giants	4	7	2	.364
New York Yankees	4	8	1	.333
Pottsville Maroons	2	8	0	.200
Chicago Cardinals	1	5	0	.167
Dayton Triangles	0	7	0	.000

1927

	W	L	T	Pct.
New York Giants	11	1	1	.917
Green Bay Packers	7	2	1	.778
Chicago Bears	9	3	2	.750
Cleveland Bulldogs	8	4	1	.667
Providence Steam Roller	8	5	1	.615
New York Yankees	7	8	1	.467
Frankford Yellow Jackets	6	9	3	.400
Pottsville Maroons	5	8	0	.385
Chicago Cardinals	3	7	1	.300
Dayton Triangles	1	6	1	.143
Duluth Eskimos	1	8	0	.111
Buffalo Bisons	0	5	0	.000

1926

	W	L	T	Pct.
Frankford Yellow Jackets	14	1	2	.933
Chicago Bears	12	1	3	.923
Pottsville Maroons	10	2	2	.833
Kansas City Cowboys	8	3	0	.727
Green Bay Packers	7	3	3	.700
Los Angeles Buccaneers	6	3	1	.667
New York Giants	8	4	1	.667
Duluth Eskimos	6	5	3	.545
Buffalo Rangers	4	4	2	.500
Chicago Cardinals	5	6	1	.455
Providence Steam Roller	5	7	1	.417
Detroit Panthers	4	6	2	.400
Hartford Blues	3	7	0	.300
Brooklyn Lions	3	8	0	.273
Milwaukee Badgers	2	7	0	.222
Akron Indians	1	4	3	.200
Dayton Triangles	1	4	1	.200
Racine Tornadoes	1	4	0	.200
Columbus Tigers	1	6	0	.143
Canton Bulldogs	1	9	3	.100
Hammond Pros	0	4	0	.000
Louisville Colonels	0	4	0	.000

1925

	W	L	T	Pct.
Chicago Cardinals	11	2	1	.846
Pottsville Maroons	10	2	0	.833
Detroit Panthers	8	2	2	.800
New York Giants	8	4	0	.667
Akron Indians	4	2	2	.667
Frankford Yellow Jackets	13	7	0	.650
Chicago Bears	9	5	3	.643
Rock Island Independents	5	3	3	.625
Green Bay Packers	8	5	0	.615
Providence Steam Roller	6	5	1	.545
Canton Bulldogs	4	4	0	.500
Cleveland Bulldogs	5	8	1	.385
Kansas City Cowboys	2	5	1	.286
Hammond Pros	1	4	0	.200
Buffalo Bisons	1	6	2	.143
Duluth Kelleys	0	3	0	.000
Rochester Jeffersons	0	6	1	.000
Milwaukee Badgers	0	6	0	.000
Dayton Triangles	0	7	1	.000
Columbus Tigers	0	9	0	.000

1924

	W	L	T	Pct.
Cleveland Bulldogs	7	1	1	.875
Chicago Bears	6	1	4	.857
Frankford Yellow Jackets	11	2	1	.846
Duluth Kelleys	5	1	0	.833
Rock Island Independents	5	2	2	.714
Green Bay Packers	7	4	0	.636
Racine Legion	4	3	3	.571
Chicago Cardinals	5	4	1	.556
Buffalo Bisons	6	5	0	.545
Columbus Tigers	4	4	0	.500
Hammond Pros	2	2	1	.500
Milwaukee Badgers	5	8	0	.385
Akron Indians	2	6	0	.250
Dayton Triangles	2	6	0	.250
Kansas City Blues	2	7	0	.222
Kenosha Maroons	0	4	1	.000
Minneapolis Marines	0	6	0	.000
Rochester Jeffersons	0	7	0	.000

1923

	W	L	T	Pct.
Canton Bulldogs	11	0	1	1.000
Chicago Bears	9	2	1	.818
Green Bay Packers	7	2	1	.778
Milwaukee Badgers	7	2	3	.778
Cleveland Indians	3	1	3	.750
Chicago Cardinals	8	4	0	.667
Duluth Kelleys	4	3	0	.571
Buffalo All-Americans	5	4	3	.556
Columbus Tigers	5	4	1	.556
Racine Legion	4	4	2	.500
Toledo Maroons	3	3	2	.500
Rock Island Independents	2	3	3	.400
Minneapolis Marines	2	5	2	.286
St. Louis All-Stars	1	4	2	.200
Hammond Pros	1	5	1	.167
Dayton Triangles	1	6	1	.143
Akron Indians	1	6	0	.143
Oorang Indians	1	10	0	.091
Louisville Brecks	0	3	0	.000
Rochester Jeffersons	0	4	0	.000

1922

	W	L	T	Pct.
Canton Bulldogs	10	0	2	1.000
Chicago Bears	9	3	0	.750
Chicago Cardinals	8	3	0	.727
Toledo Maroons	5	2	2	.714
Rock Island Independents	4	2	1	.667
Racine Legion	6	4	1	.600
Dayton Triangles	4	3	1	.571
Green Bay Packers	4	3	3	.571
Buffalo All-Americans	5	4	1	.556
Akron Pros	3	5	2	.375
Milwaukee Badgers	2	4	3	.333
Oorang Indians	3	6	0	.333
Minneapolis Marines	1	3	0	.250
Louisville Brecks	1	3	0	.250
Evansville Crimson Giants	0	3	0	.000
Rochester Jeffersons	0	4	1	.000
Hammond Pros	0	5	1	.000
Columbus Panhandles	0	8	0	.000

1921

	W	L	T	Pct.
Chicago Staleys	9	1	1	.900
Buffalo All-Americans	9	1	2	.900
Akron Pros	8	3	1	.727
Canton Bulldogs	5	2	3	.714
Rock Island Independents	4	2	1	.667
Evansville Crimson Giants	3	2	0	.600
Green Bay Packers	3	2	1	.600
Dayton Triangles	4	4	1	.500
Chicago Cardinals	3	3	2	.500
Rochester Jeffersons	2	3	0	.400
Cleveland Indians	3	5	0	.375
Washington Senators	1	2	0	.333
Cincinnati Celts	1	3	0	.250
Hammond Pros	1	3	1	.250
Minneapolis Marines	1	3	0	.250
Detroit Tigers	1	5	1	.167
Columbus Panhandles	1	8	0	.111
Tonawanda Kardex	0	1	0	.000
Muncie Flyers	0	2	0	.000
Louisville Brecks	0	2	0	.000
New York Giants	0	2	0	.000

1920*

	W	L	T	Pct.
Akron Pros	8	0	3	1.000
Decatur Staleys	10	1	2	.909
Buffalo All-Americans	9	1	1	.900
Chicago Cardinals	6	2	2	.750
Rock Island Independents	6	2	2	.750
Dayton Triangles	5	2	2	.714
Rochester Jeffersons	6	3	2	.667
Canton Bulldogs	7	4	2	.636
Detroit Heralds	2	3	3	.400
Cleveland Tigers	2	4	2	.333
Chicago Tigers	2	5	1	.286
Hammond Pros	2	5	0	.286
Columbus Panhandles	2	6	2	.250
Muncie Flyers	0	1	0	.000

**No official standings were maintained for the 1920 season, and the championship was awarded to the Akron Pros in a League meeting on April 30, 1921. Clubs played schedules that included games against nonleague opponents.*

INTERNATIONAL GAMES

NFL INTERNATIONAL GAMES (60)

REGULAR SEASON GAMES (4)

(Home Team in capitals)

October 2, 2005	Mexico City, Mexico	ARIZONA 31, San Francisco 14
October 28, 2007	London, England	N.Y. Giants 13, MIAMI 10
October 26, 2008	London, England	NEW ORLEANS 37, San Diego 32
December 7, 2008	Toronto, Canada	Miami 16, BUFFALO 3

PRESEASON GAMES (56)

Date	Site	Teams
August 12, 1950	Ottawa, Canada	N.Y. Giants 27, Ottawa Rough Riders 6
August 11, 1951	Ottawa, Canada	N.Y. Giants 41, Ottawa Rough Riders 18
August 5, 1959	Toronto, Canada	Chi. Cardinals 55, Tor. Argonauts 26
August 3, 1960	Toronto, Canada	Pittsburgh 43, Toronto Argonauts 16
August 15, 1960	Toronto, Canada	Chicago 16, N.Y. Giants 7
August 2, 1961	Toronto, Canada	St. Louis 36, Toronto Argonauts 7
August 5, 1961	Montreal, Canada	Chicago 34, Montreal Allouettes 16
August 8, 1961	Hamilton, Canada	Hamilton Tiger-Cats 38, Buffalo 21
August 25, 1969	Montreal, Canada	Detroit 22, Boston 9
September 11, 1969	Montreal, Canada	Pittsburgh 17, N.Y. Giants 13
August 16, 1976	Tokyo, Japan	St. Louis 20, San Diego 10
August 5, 1978	Mexico City, Mexico	New Orleans 14, Philadelphia 7
August 6, 1983	London, England	Minnesota 28, St. Louis 10
* August 3, 1986	London, England	Chicago 17, Dallas 6
* August 9, 1987	London, England	L.A. Rams 28, Denver 27
* July 31, 1988	London, England	Miami 27, San Francisco 21
August 14, 1988	Goteborg, Sweden	Minnesota 28, Chicago 21
August 18, 1988	Montreal, Canada	N.Y. Jets 11, Cleveland 7
* August 5, 1989	Tokyo, Japan	L.A. Rams 16, San Francisco 13 (OT)
* August 6, 1989	London, England	Philadelphia 17, Cleveland 13
* August 4, 1990	Tokyo, Japan	Denver 10, Seattle 7
* August 5, 1990	London, England	New Orleans 17, L.A. Raiders 10
* August 9, 1990	Montreal, Canada	Pittsburgh 30, New England 14
* August 11, 1990	Berlin, Germany	L.A. Rams 19, Kansas City 3
* July 28, 1991	London, England	Buffalo 17, Philadelphia 13
* August 3, 1991	Berlin, Germany	San Francisco 21, Chicago 7
* August 3, 1991	Tokyo, Japan	Miami 19, L.A. Raiders 17
* August 1, 1992	Tokyo, Japan	Houston 34, Dallas 23
* August 15, 1992	Berlin, Germany	Miami 31, Denver 27
* August 16, 1992	London, England	San Francisco 17, Washington 15
* July 31, 1993	Tokyo, Japan	New Orleans 28, Philadelphia 16
* August 1, 1993	Barcelona, Spain	San Francisco 21, Pittsburgh 14
* August 7, 1993	Berlin, Germany	Minnesota 20, Buffalo 6
* August 8, 1993	London, England	Dallas 13, Detroit 13 (OT)
August 14, 1993	Toronto, Canada	Cleveland 12, New England 9
* July 31, 1994	Barcelona, Spain	L.A. Raiders 25, Denver 22
* August 6, 1994	Tokyo, Japan	Minnesota 17, Kansas City 9
* August 13, 1994	Berlin, Germany	N.Y. Giants 28, San Diego 20
* August 15, 1994	Mexico City, Mexico	Houston 6, Dallas 0
* August 5, 1995	Tokyo, Japan	Denver 24, San Francisco 10
* August 12, 1995	Toronto, Canada	Buffalo 9, Dallas 7
* July 27, 1996	Tokyo, Japan	San Diego 20, Pittsburgh 10
* August 5, 1996	Monterrey, Mexico	Kansas City 32, Dallas 6
* July 27, 1997	Dublin, Ireland	Pittsburgh 30, Chicago 17
* August 4, 1997	Mexico City, Mexico	Miami 38, Denver 19
* August 16, 1997	Toronto, Canada	Green Bay 35, Buffalo 3
* August 1, 1998	Tokyo, Japan	Green Bay 27, Kansas City 24 (OT)
* August 15, 1998	Vancouver, Canada	San Francisco 24, Seattle 21
* August 17, 1998	Mexico City, Mexico	New England 21, Dallas 3
* August 7, 1999	Sydney, Australia	Denver 20, San Diego 17
* August 5, 2000	Tokyo, Japan	Atlanta 20, Dallas 9
* August 19, 2000	Mexico City, Mexico	Indianapolis 24, Pittsburgh 23
* August 27, 2001	Mexico City, Mexico	Dallas 21, Oakland 6
* August 3, 2002	Osaka, Japan	Washington 38, San Francisco 7
* August 2, 2003	Tokyo, Japan	Tampa Bay 30, N.Y. Jets 14
* August 6, 2005	Tokyo, Japan	Atlanta 27, Indianapolis 21
August 14, 2008	Toronto, Canada	Buffalo 34, Pittsburgh 21

* *American Bowl Game*

RS=REGULAR SEASON
PS=POSTSEASON

***ARIZONA vs. ATLANTA**
RS: Cardinals lead series, 14-10
PS: Cardinals lead series, 1-0
1966—Falcons, 16-10 (A)
1968—Cardinals, 17-12 (StL)
1971—Cardinals, 26-9 (A)
1973—Cardinals, 32-10 (A)
1975—Cardinals, 23-20 (StL)
1978—Cardinals, 42-21 (StL)
1980—Falcons, 33-27 (StL) OT
1981—Falcons, 41-20 (A)
1982—Cardinals, 23-20 (A)
1986—Falcons, 33-13 (A)
1987—Cardinals, 34-21 (A)
1989—Cardinals, 34-20 (P)
1990—Cardinals, 24-13 (A)
1991—Cardinals, 16-10 (P)
1992—Falcons, 20-17 (A)
1993—Cardinals, 27-10 (A)
1994—Falcons, 10-6 (Atl)
1995—Cardinals, 40-37 (Ariz) OT
1997—Cardinals, 29-26 (Ariz)
1999—Falcons, 37-14 (Atl)
2001—Falcons, 34-14 (Ariz)
2004—Falcons, 6-3 (Atl)
2006—Falcons, 32-10 (Atl)
2007—Cardinals, 30-27 (Ariz) OT
2008—**Cardinals, 30-24 (Ariz)
(RS Pts.—Cardinals 531, Falcons 518)
(PS Pts.—Cardinals 30, Falcons 24)
**Franchise known as Phoenix prior to 1994 and in St. Louis prior to 1988*
***NFC First-Round Playoff*

***ARIZONA vs. BALTIMORE**
RS: Ravens lead series, 3-1
1997—Cardinals, 16-13 (B)
2000—Ravens, 13-7 (A)
2003—Ravens, 26-18 (A)
2007—Ravens, 26-23 (B)
(RS Pts.—Ravens 78, Cardinals 64)

***ARIZONA vs. BUFFALO**
RS: Bills lead series, 5-4
1971—Cardinals, 28-23 (B)
1975—Bills, 32-14 (StL)
1981—Cardinals, 24-0 (StL)
1984—Cardinals, 37-7 (StL)
1986—Bills, 17-10 (B)
1990—Bills, 45-14 (B)
1999—Bills, 31-21 (A)
2004—Bills, 38-14 (B)
2008—Cardinals, 41-17 (A)
(RS Pts.—Bills 210, Cardinals 203)
**Franchise known as Phoenix prior to 1994 and in St. Louis prior to 1988*

ARIZONA vs. CAROLINA
RS: Panthers lead series, 6-2
PS: Cardinals lead series, 1-0
1995—Panthers, 27-7 (C)
2001—Cardinals, 30-7 (C)
2002—Cardinals, 16-13 (C)
2003—Panthers, 20-17 (A)
2004—Panthers, 35-10 (C)
2005—Panthers, 24-20 (A)
2007—Panthers, 25-10 (A)
2008—Panthers, 27-23 (C)
*Cardinals, 33-13 (C)
(RS Pts.—Panthers 178, Cardinals 133)
(PS Pts.—Cardinals 33, Panthers 13)
**NFC Divisional Playoff*

***ARIZONA vs. **CHICAGO**
RS: Bears lead series, 55-26-6
(NP denotes Normal Park;
Wr denotes Wrigley Field;
Co denotes Comiskey Park;
So denotes Soldier Field;
all Chicago)
1920—Cardinals, 7-6 (NP)
Staleys, 10-0 (Wr)
1921—Tie, 0-0 (Wr)
1922—Cardinals, 6-0 (Co)
Cardinals, 9-0 (Co)
1923—Bears, 3-0 (Wr)
1924—Bears, 6-0 (Wr)
Bears, 21-0 (Co)
1925—Cardinals, 9-0 (Co)
Tie, 0-0 (Wr)
1926—Bears, 16-0 (Wr)
Bears, 10-0 (So)
Tie, 0-0 (Wr)
1927—Bears, 9-0 (NP)
Cardinals, 3-0 (Wr)
1928—Bears, 15-0 (NP)
Bears, 34-0 (Wr)
1929—Tie, 0-0 (Wr)
Cardinals, 40-6 (Co)
1930—Bears, 32-6 (Co)
Bears, 6-0 (Wr)
1931—Bears, 26-13 (Wr)
Bears, 18-7 (Wr)
1932—Tie, 0-0 (Wr)
Bears, 34-0 (Wr)
1933—Bears, 12-9 (Wr)
Bears, 22-6 (Wr)
1934—Bears, 20-0 (Wr)
Bears, 17-6 (Wr)
1935—Tie, 7-7 (Wr)
Bears, 13-0 (Wr)
1936—Bears, 7-3 (Wr)
Cardinals, 14-7 (Wr)
1937—Bears, 16-7 (Wr)
Bears, 42-28 (Wr)
1938—Bears, 16-13 (So)
Bears, 34-28 (Wr)
1939—Bears, 44-7 (Wr)
Bears, 48-7 (Co)
1940—Cardinals, 21-7 (Co)
Bears, 31-23 (Wr)
1941—Bears, 53-7 (Wr)
Bears, 34-24 (Co)
1942—Bears, 41-14 (Wr)
Bears, 21-7 (Co)
1943—Bears, 20-0 (Wr)
Bears, 35-24 (Co)
1945—Cardinals, 16-7 (Wr)
Bears, 28-20 (Co)
1946—Bears, 34-17 (Co)
Cardinals, 35-28 (Wr)
1947—Cardinals, 31-7 (Co)
Cardinals, 30-21 (Wr)
1948—Bears, 28-17 (Co)
Cardinals, 24-21 (Wr)
1949—Bears, 17-7 (Co)
Bears, 52-21 (Wr)
1950—Bears, 27-6 (Wr)
Cardinals, 20-10 (Co)
1951—Cardinals, 28-14 (Co)
Cardinals, 24-14 (Wr)
1952—Cardinals, 21-10 (Co)
Bears, 10-7 (Wr)
1953—Cardinals, 24-17 (Wr)
1954—Bears, 29-7 (Co)
1955—Cardinals, 53-14 (Co)
1956—Bears, 10-3 (Wr)
1957—Bears, 14-6 (Co)
1958—Bears, 30-14 (Wr)
1959—Bears, 31-7 (So)
1965—Bears, 34-13 (Wr)
1966—Cardinals, 24-17 (StL)
1967—Bears, 30-3 (Wr)
1969—Cardinals, 20-17 (StL)
1972—Bears, 27-10 (StL)
1975—Cardinals, 34-20 (So)
1977—Cardinals, 16-13 (StL)
1978—Bears, 17-10 (So)
1979—Bears, 42-6 (So)
1982—Cardinals, 10-7 (So)
1984—Cardinals, 38-21 (StL)
1990—Bears, 31-21 (P)
1994—Bears, 19-16 (A) OT
1998—Cardinals, 20-7 (A)
2001—Bears, 20-13 (C)
2003—Bears, 28-3 (C)
2006—Bears, 24-23 (A)
(RS Pts.—Bears 1,646, Cardinals 1,073)
**Franchise known as Phoenix prior to 1994, in St. Louis prior to 1988, and in Chicago prior to 1960*
***Franchise in Decatur prior to 1921 and known as Staleys prior to 1922*

***ARIZONA vs. CINCINNATI**
RS: Bengals lead series, 5-4
1973—Bengals, 42-24 (C)
1979—Bengals, 34-28 (C)
1985—Cardinals, 41-27 (StL)
1988—Bengals, 21-14 (C)
1994—Cardinals, 28-7 (A)
1997—Bengals, 24-21 (C)
2000—Bengals, 24-13 (C)
2003—Cardinals, 17-14 (A)
2007—Cardinals, 35-27 (C)
(RS Pts.—Cardinals 221, Bengals 220)
**Franchise known as Phoenix prior to 1994 and in St. Louis prior to 1988*

***ARIZONA vs. CLEVELAND**
RS: Browns lead series, 33-12-3
1950—Browns, 34-24 (Cle)
Browns, 10-7 (Chi)
1951—Browns, 34-17 (Chi)
Browns, 49-28 (Cle)
1952—Browns, 28-13 (Cle)
Browns, 10-0 (Chi)
1953—Browns, 27-7 (Chi)
Browns, 27-16 (Cle)
1954—Browns, 31-7 (Cle)
Browns, 35-3 (Chi)
1955—Browns, 26-20 (Chi)
Browns, 35-24 (Cle)
1956—Cardinals, 9-7 (Chi)
Cardinals, 24-7 (Cle)
1957—Browns, 17-7 (Chi)
Browns, 31-0 (Cle)
1958—Browns, 35-28 (Cle)
Browns, 38-24 (Chi)
1959—Browns, 34-7 (Chi)
Browns, 17-7 (Cle)
1960—Browns, 28-27 (Cle)
Tie, 17-17 (StL)
1961—Browns, 20-17 (Cle)

Browns, 21-10 (StL)
1962—Browns, 34-7 (StL)
Browns, 38-14 (Cle)
1963—Cardinals, 20-14 (Cle)
Browns, 24-10 (StL)
1964—Tie, 33-33 (Cle)
Cardinals, 28-19 (StL)
1965—Cardinals, 49-13 (Cle)
Browns, 27-24 (StL)
1966—Cardinals, 34-28 (Cle)
Browns, 38-10 (StL)
1967—Browns, 20-16 (Cle)
Browns, 20-16 (StL)
1968—Cardinals, 27-21 (Cle)
Cardinals, 27-16 (StL)
1969—Tie, 21-21 (Cle)
Browns, 27-21 (StL)
1974—Cardinals, 29-7 (StL)
1979—Browns, 38-20 (StL)
1985—Cardinals, 27-24 (Cle) OT
1988—Browns, 29-21 (P)
1994—Browns, 32-0 (Cle)
2000—Cardinals, 29-21 (A)
2003—Browns, 44-6 (Cle)
2007—Cardinals, 27-21 (A)
(RS Pts.—Browns 1,227, Cardinals 859)
**Franchise known as Phoenix prior to 1994, in St. Louis prior to 1988, and in Chicago prior to 1960*

***ARIZONA vs. DALLAS**
RS: Cowboys lead series, 55-28-1
PS: Cardinals lead series, 1-0
1960—Cardinals, 12-10 (StL)
1961—Cardinals, 31-17 (D)
Cardinals, 31-13 (StL)
1962—Cardinals, 28-24 (D)
Cardinals, 52-20 (StL)
1963—Cardinals, 34-7 (D)
Cowboys, 28-24 (StL)
1964—Cardinals, 16-6 (D)
Cowboys, 31-13 (StL)
1965—Cardinals, 20-13 (StL)
Cowboys, 27-13 (D)
1966—Tie, 10-10 (StL)
Cowboys, 31-17 (D)
1967—Cowboys, 46-21 (D)
1968—Cowboys, 27-10 (StL)
1969—Cowboys, 24-3 (D)
1970—Cardinals, 20-7 (StL)
Cardinals, 38-0 (D)
1971—Cowboys, 16-13 (StL)
Cowboys, 31-12 (D)
1972—Cowboys, 33-24 (D)
Cowboys, 27-6 (StL)
1973—Cowboys, 45-10 (D)
Cowboys, 30-3 (StL)
1974—Cardinals, 31-28 (StL)
Cowboys, 17-14 (D)
1975—Cowboys, 37-31 (D) OT
Cardinals, 31-17 (StL)
1976—Cardinals, 21-17 (StL)
Cowboys, 19-14 (D)
1977—Cowboys, 30-24 (StL)
Cardinals, 24-17 (D)
1978—Cowboys, 21-12 (D)
Cowboys, 24-21 (StL) OT
1979—Cowboys, 22-21 (StL)
Cowboys, 22-13 (D)
1980—Cowboys, 27-24 (StL)
Cowboys, 31-21 (D)
1981—Cowboys, 30-17 (D)
Cardinals, 20-17 (StL)
1982—Cowboys, 24-7 (StL)
1983—Cowboys, 34-17 (StL)
Cowboys, 35-17 (D)
1984—Cardinals, 31-20 (D)
Cowboys, 24-17 (StL)
1985—Cardinals, 21-10 (StL)
Cowboys, 35-17 (D)
1986—Cowboys, 31-7 (StL)
Cowboys, 37-6 (D)
1987—Cardinals, 24-13 (StL)
Cowboys, 21-16 (D)
1988—Cowboys, 17-14 (P)
Cardinals, 16-10 (D)
1989—Cardinals, 19-10 (D)
Cardinals, 24-20 (P)
1990—Cardinals, 20-3 (P)
Cowboys, 41-10 (D)
1991—Cowboys, 17-9 (P)
Cowboys, 27-7 (D)
1992—Cowboys, 31-20 (D)
Cowboys, 16-10 (P)
1993—Cowboys, 17-10 (P)
Cowboys, 20-15 (D)
1994—Cowboys, 38-3 (D)
Cowboys, 28-21 (A)
1995—Cowboys, 34-20 (D)
Cowboys, 37-13 (A)
1996—Cowboys, 17-3 (D)
Cowboys, 10-6 (A)
1997—Cardinals, 25-22 (A) OT
Cowboys, 24-6 (D)
1998—Cowboys, 38-10 (D)
Cowboys, 35-28 (A)
**Cardinals, 20-7 (D)
1999—Cowboys, 35-7 (D)
Cardinals, 13-9 (A)
2000—Cardinals, 32-31 (A)
Cowboys, 48-7 (D)
2001—Cowboys, 17-3 (D)
Cardinals, 17-10 (A)
2002—Cardinals, 9-6 (A) OT
2003—Cowboys, 24-7 (D)
2005—Cowboys, 34-13 (D)
2006—Cowboys, 27-10 (A)
2008—Cardinals, 30-24 (A) OT
(RS Pts.—Cowboys 1,960, Cardinals 1,437)
(PS Pts.—Cardinals 20, Cowboys 7)
**Franchise known as Phoenix prior to 1994 and in St. Louis prior to 1988*
***NFC First-Round Playoff*

***ARIZONA vs. DENVER**
RS: Broncos lead series, 7-0-1
1973—Tie, 17-17 (StL)
1977—Broncos, 7-0 (D)
1989—Broncos, 37-0 (P)
1991—Broncos, 24-19 (D)
1995—Broncos, 38-6 (D)
2001—Broncos, 38-17 (A)
2002—Broncos, 37-7 (D)
2006—Broncos, 37-20 (A)
(RS Pts.—Broncos 235, Cardinals 86)
**Franchise known as Phoenix prior to 1994 and in St. Louis prior to 1988*

***ARIZONA vs. **DETROIT**
RS: Lions lead series, 31-23-5
1930—Tie, 0-0 (Port)
Cardinals, 23-0 (C)
1931—Spartans, 13-3 (Port)
Cardinals, 20-19 (C)
1932—Tie, 7-7 (Port)
1933—Spartans, 7-6 (Port)
1934—Lions, 6-0 (D)
Lions, 17-13 (C)
1935—Tie, 10-10 (D)
Lions, 7-6 (C)
1936—Lions, 39-0 (D)
Lions, 14-7 (C)
1937—Lions, 16-7 (C)
Lions, 16-7 (D)
1938—Lions, 10-0 (D)
Lions, 7-3 (C)
1939—Lions, 21-3 (D)
Lions, 17-3 (C)
1940—Tie, 0-0 (Buffalo)
Lions, 43-14 (C)
1941—Tie, 14-14 (C)
Lions, 21-3 (D)
1942—Cardinals, 13-0 (C)
Cardinals, 7-0 (D)
1943—Lions, 35-17 (D)
Lions, 7-0 (Buffalo)
1945—Lions, 10-0 (Milwaukee)
Lions, 26-0 (D)
1946—Cardinals, 34-14 (C)
Cardinals, 36-14 (D)
1947—Cardinals, 45-21 (C)
Cardinals, 17-7 (D)
1948—Cardinals, 56-20 (C)
Cardinals, 28-14 (D)
1949—Lions, 24-7 (C)
Cardinals, 42-19 (D)
1959—Lions, 45-21 (D)
1961—Lions, 45-14 (StL)
1967—Cardinals, 38-28 (StL)
1969—Lions, 20-0 (D)
1970—Lions, 16-3 (D)
1973—Lions, 20-16 (StL)
1975—Cardinals, 24-13 (D)
1978—Cardinals, 21-14 (StL)
1980—Lions, 20-7 (D)
Cardinals, 24-23 (StL)
1989—Cardinals, 16-13 (D)
1993—Lions, 26-20 (D)
Lions, 21-14 (Phx)
1995—Cardinals, 20-17 (D)
1998—Cardinals, 17-15 (D)
1999—Cardinals, 23-19 (A)
2001—Cardinals, 45-38 (A)
2002—Cardinals, 23-20 (A) OT
2003—Lions, 42-24 (D)
2004—Lions, 26-12 (D)
2005—Lions, 29-21 (D)
2006—Cardinals, 17-10 (A)
2007—Cardinals, 31-21 (A)
(RS Pts.—Lions 1,069, Cardinals 912)
**Franchise known as Phoenix prior to 1994, in St. Louis prior to 1988, and in Chicago prior to 1960*
***Franchise in Portsmouth prior to 1934 and known as the Spartans*

***ARIZONA vs. GREEN BAY**
RS: Packers lead series, 42-22-4
PS: Packers lead series, 1-0
1921—Tie, 3-3 (C)
1922—Cardinals, 16-3 (C)
1924—Cardinals, 3-0 (C)
1925—Cardinals, 9-6 (C)
1926—Cardinals, 13-7 (GB)

Packers, 3-0 (C)
1927—Packers, 13-0 (GB)
Tie, 6-6 (C)
1928—Packers, 20-0 (GB)
1929—Packers, 9-2 (GB)
Packers, 7-6 (C)
Packers, 12-0 (C)
1930—Packers, 14-0 (GB)
Cardinals, 13-6 (C)
1931—Packers, 26-7 (GB)
Cardinals, 21-13 (C)
1932—Packers, 15-7 (GB)
Packers, 19-9 (C)
1933—Packers, 14-6 (C)
1934—Packers, 15-0 (GB)
Cardinals, 9-0 (Mil)
Cardinals, 6-0 (C)
1935—Cardinals, 7-6 (GB)
Cardinals, 3-0 (Mil)
Cardinals, 9-7 (C)
1936—Packers, 10-7 (GB)
Packers, 24-0 (Mil)
Tie, 0-0 (C)
1937—Cardinals, 14-7 (GB)
Packers, 34-13 (Mil)
1938—Packers, 28-7 (Mil)
Packers, 24-22 (Buffalo)
1939—Packers, 14-10 (GB)
Packers, 27-20 (Mil)
1940—Packers, 31-6 (Mil)
Packers, 28-7 (C)
1941—Packers, 14-13 (Mil)
Packers, 17-9 (GB)
1942—Packers, 17-13 (C)
Packers, 55-24 (GB)
1943—Packers, 28-7 (C)
Packers, 35-14 (Mil)
1945—Packers, 33-14 (GB)
1946—Packers, 19-7 (C)
Cardinals, 24-6 (GB)
1947—Cardinals, 14-10 (GB)
Cardinals, 21-20 (C)
1948—Cardinals, 17-7 (Mil)
Cardinals, 42-7 (C)
1949—Cardinals, 39-17 (Mil)
Cardinals, 41-21 (C)
1955—Packers, 31-14 (GB)
1956—Packers, 24-21 (C)
1962—Packers, 17-0 (Mil)
1963—Packers, 30-7 (StL)
1967—Packers, 31-23 (StL)
1969—Packers, 45-28 (GB)
1971—Tie, 16-16 (StL)
1973—Packers, 25-21 (GB)
1976—Cardinals, 29-0 (StL)
1982—**Packers, 41-16 (GB)
1984—Packers, 24-23 (GB)
1985—Cardinals, 43-28 (StL)
1988—Packers, 26-17 (P)
1990—Packers, 24-21 (P)
1999—Packers, 49-24 (GB)
2000—Packers, 29-3 (A)
2003—Cardinals, 20-13 (A)
2006—Packers, 31-14 (GB)
(RS Pts.—Packers 1,200, Cardinals 884)
(PS Pts.—Packers 41, Cardinals 16)
Franchise known as Phoenix prior to 1994, in St. Louis prior to 1988, and in Chicago prior to 1960
***NFC First-Round Playoff*

ARIZONA vs. HOUSTON
RS: Texans lead series, 1-0
2005—Texans, 30-19 (H)
(RS Pts.—Texans 30, Cardinals 19)

***ARIZONA vs. **INDIANAPOLIS**
RS: Colts lead series, 7-6
1961—Colts, 16-0 (B)
1964—Colts, 47-27 (B)
1968—Colts, 27-0 (B)
1972—Cardinals, 10-3 (B)
1976—Cardinals, 24-17 (StL)
1978—Colts, 30-17 (StL)
1980—Cardinals, 17-10 (B)
1981—Cardinals, 35-24 (B)
1984—Cardinals, 34-33 (I)
1990—Cardinals, 20-17 (P)
1992—Colts, 16-13 (I)
1996—Colts, 20-13 (I)
2005—Colts, 17-13 (I)
(RS Pts.—Colts 277, Cardinals 223)
Franchise known as Phoenix prior to 1994 and in St. Louis prior to 1988
***Franchise in Baltimore prior to 1984*

ARIZONA vs. JACKSONVILLE
RS: Jaguars lead series, 2-0
2000—Jaguars, 44-10 (J)
2005—Jaguars, 24-17 (A)
(RS Pts.—Jaguars 68, Cardinals 27)

***ARIZONA vs. KANSAS CITY**
RS: Chiefs lead series, 7-2-1
1970—Tie, 6-6 (KC)
1974—Chiefs, 17-13 (StL)
1980—Chiefs, 21-13 (StL)
1983—Chiefs, 38-14 (KC)
1986—Cardinals, 23-14 (StL)
1995—Chiefs, 24-3 (A)
1998—Chiefs, 34-24 (KC)
2001—Cardinals, 24-16 (A)
2002—Chiefs, 49-0 (KC)
2006—Chiefs, 23-20 (A)
(RS Pts.—Chiefs 242, Cardinals 140)
Franchise known as Phoenix prior to 1994 and in St. Louis prior to 1988

***ARIZONA vs. MIAMI**
RS: Dolphins lead series, 8-2
1972—Dolphins, 31-10 (M)
1977—Dolphins, 55-14 (StL)
1978—Dolphins, 24-10 (M)
1981—Dolphins, 20-7 (StL)
1984—Dolphins, 36-28 (StL)
1990—Dolphins, 23-3 (M)
1996—Dolphins, 38-10 (A)
1999—Dolphins, 19-16 (M)
2004—Cardinals, 24-23 (M)
2008—Cardinals, 31-10 (A)
(RS Pts.—Dolphins 279, Cardinals 153)
Franchise known as Phoenix prior to 1994 and in St. Louis prior to 1988

***ARIZONA vs. MINNESOTA**
RS: Vikings lead series, 10-9
PS: Vikings lead series, 2-0
1963—Cardinals, 56-14 (M)
1967—Cardinals, 34-24 (M)
1969—Vikings, 27-10 (StL)
1972—Cardinals, 19-17 (M)
1974—Vikings, 28-24 (StL)
**Vikings, 30-14 (M)
1977—Cardinals, 27-7 (M)
1979—Cardinals, 37-7 (StL)
1981—Cardinals, 30-17 (StL)
1983—Cardinals, 41-31 (StL)
1991—Vikings, 34-7 (M)
Vikings, 28-0 (P)
1994—Cardinals, 17-7 (A)
1995—Vikings, 30-24 (A) OT
1996—Vikings, 41-17 (M)
1997—Vikings, 20-19 (A)
1998—**Vikings, 41-21 (M)
2000—Vikings, 31-14 (M)
2003—Cardinals, 18-17 (A)
2006—Vikings, 31-26 (M)
2008—Vikings, 35-14 (A)
(RS Pts.—Vikings 446, Cardinals 434)
(PS Pts.—Vikings 71, Cardinals 35)
Franchise known as Phoenix prior to 1994 and in St. Louis prior to 1988
***NFC Divisional Playoff*

***ARIZONA vs. **NEW ENGLAND**
RS: Series tied, 6-6
1970—Cardinals, 31-0 (StL)
1975—Cardinals, 24-17 (StL)
1978—Patriots, 16-6 (StL)
1981—Cardinals, 27-20 (NE)
1984—Cardinals, 33-10 (NE)
1990—Cardinals, 34-14 (P)
1991—Cardinals, 24-10 (P)
1993—Patriots, 23-21 (P)
1996—Patriots, 31-0 (NE)
1999—Patriots, 27-3 (A)
2004—Patriots, 23-12 (A)
2008—Patriots, 47-7 (NE)
(RS Pts.—Patriots 238, Cardinals 222)
Franchise known as Phoenix prior to 1994 and in St. Louis prior to 1988
***Franchise in Boston prior to 1971*

***ARIZONA vs. NEW ORLEANS**
RS: Cardinals lead series, 13-12
1967—Cardinals, 31-20 (StL)
1968—Cardinals, 21-20 (NO)
Cardinals, 31-17 (StL)
1969—Saints, 51-42 (StL)
1970—Cardinals, 24-17 (StL)
1974—Saints, 14-0 (NO)
1977—Cardinals, 49-31 (StL)
1980—Cardinals, 40-7 (NO)
1981—Cardinals, 30-3 (StL)
1982—Cardinals, 21-7 (NO)
1983—Saints, 28-17 (NO)
1984—Saints, 34-24 (NO)
1985—Cardinals, 28-16 (StL)
1986—Saints, 16-7 (StL)
1987—Cardinals, 24-19 (StL)
1990—Saints, 28-7 (NO)
1991—Saints, 27-3 (P)
1992—Saints, 30-21 (P)
1993—Saints, 20-17 (P)
1996—Cardinals, 28-14 (NO)
1997—Saints, 27-10 (NO)
1998—Cardinals, 19-17 (A)
2000—Saints, 21-10 (A)
2004—Cardinals, 34-10 (A)
2007—Saints, 31-24 (NO)
(RS Pts.—Cardinals 562, Saints 525)
Franchise known as Phoenix prior to 1994 and in St. Louis prior to 1988

***ARIZONA vs. N.Y. GIANTS**
RS: Giants lead series, 79-41-2
1926—Giants, 20-0 (NY)
1927—Giants, 28-7 (NY)
1929—Giants, 24-21 (NY)

1930—Giants, 25-12 (NY)
Giants, 13-7 (C)
1935—Cardinals, 14-13 (NY)
1936—Giants, 14-6 (NY)
1938—Giants, 6-0 (NY)
1939—Giants, 17-7 (NY)
1941—Cardinals, 10-7 (NY)
1942—Giants, 21-7 (NY)
1943—Giants, 24-13 (NY)
1946—Giants, 28-24 (NY)
1947—Giants, 35-31 (NY)
1948—Cardinals, 63-35 (NY)
1949—Giants, 41-38 (C)
1950—Cardinals, 17-3 (C)
Giants, 51-21 (NY)
1951—Giants, 28-17 (NY)
Giants, 10-0 (C)
1952—Cardinals, 24-23 (NY)
Giants, 28-6 (C)
1953—Giants, 21-7 (NY)
Giants, 23-20 (C)
1954—Giants, 41-10 (C)
Giants, 31-17 (NY)
1955—Cardinals, 28-17 (C)
Giants, 10-0 (NY)
1956—Cardinals, 35-27 (C)
Giants, 23-10 (NY)
1957—Giants, 27-14 (NY)
Giants, 28-21 (C)
1958—Giants, 37-7 (Buffalo)
Cardinals, 23-6 (NY)
1959—Giants, 9-3 (NY)
Giants, 30-20 (Minn)
1960—Giants, 35-14 (StL)
Cardinals, 20-13 (NY)
1961—Cardinals, 21-10 (NY)
Giants, 24-9 (StL)
1962—Giants, 31-14 (StL)
Giants, 31-28 (NY)
1963—Giants, 38-21 (StL)
Cardinals, 24-17 (NY)
1964—Giants, 34-17 (NY)
Tie, 10-10 (StL)
1965—Giants, 14-10 (NY)
Giants, 28-15 (StL)
1966—Cardinals, 24-19 (StL)
Cardinals, 20-17 (NY)
1967—Giants, 37-20 (StL)
Giants, 37-14 (NY)
1968—Cardinals, 28-21 (NY)
1969—Cardinals, 42-17 (StL)
Giants, 49-6 (NY)
1970—Giants, 35-17 (NY)
Giants, 34-17 (StL)
1971—Giants, 21-20 (StL)
Cardinals, 24-7 (NY)
1972—Giants, 27-21 (NY)
Giants, 13-7 (StL)
1973—Cardinals, 35-27 (StL)
Giants, 24-13 (New Haven)
1974—Cardinals, 23-21 (New Haven)
Cardinals, 26-14 (StL)
1975—Cardinals, 26-14 (StL)
Cardinals, 20-13 (NY)
1976—Cardinals, 27-21 (StL)
Cardinals, 17-14 (NY)
1977—Cardinals, 28-0 (StL)
Giants, 27-7 (NY)
1978—Cardinals, 20-10 (StL)
Giants, 17-0 (NY)
1979—Cardinals, 27-14 (NY)
Cardinals, 29-20 (StL)
1980—Giants, 41-35 (StL)
Cardinals, 23-7 (NY)
1981—Giants, 34-14 (NY)
Giants, 20-10 (StL)
1982—Cardinals, 24-21 (StL)
1983—Tie, 20-20 (StL) OT
Cardinals, 10-6 (NY)
1984—Giants, 16-10 (NY)
Cardinals, 31-21 (StL)
1985—Giants, 27-17 (NY)
Giants, 34-3 (StL)
1986—Giants, 13-6 (StL)
Giants, 27-7 (NY)
1987—Giants, 30-7 (NY)
Cardinals, 27-24 (StL)
1988—Cardinals, 24-17 (P)
Giants, 44-7 (NY)
1989—Giants, 35-7 (NY)
Giants, 20-13 (P)
1990—Giants, 20-19 (NY)
Giants, 24-21 (P)
1991—Giants, 20-9 (NY)
Giants, 21-14 (P)
1992—Giants, 31-21 (NY)
Cardinals, 19-0 (P)
1993—Giants, 19-17 (NY)
Cardinals, 17-6 (P)
1994—Giants, 20-17 (A)
Cardinals, 10-9 (NY)
1995—Giants, 27-21 (NY) OT
Giants, 10-6 (A)
1996—Giants, 16-8 (NY)
Cardinals, 31-23 (A)
1997—Giants, 27-13 (A)
Giants, 19-10 (NY)
1998—Giants, 34-7 (NY)
Giants, 23-19 (A)
1999—Cardinals, 14-3 (A)
Cardinals, 34-24 (NY)
2000—Giants, 21-16 (NY)
Giants, 31-7 (A)
2001—Giants, 17-10 (A)
Giants, 17-13 (NY)
2002—Cardinals, 21-7 (A)
2004—Cardinals, 17-14 (A)
2005—Giants, 42-19 (NY)
2008—Giants, 37-29 (A)
(RS Pts.—Giants 2,698, Cardinals 2,075)
Franchise known as Phoenix prior to 1994, in St. Louis prior to 1988, and in Chicago prior to 1960

***ARIZONA vs. N.Y. JETS**
RS: Jets lead series, 5-2
1971—Cardinals, 17-10 (StL)
1975—Cardinals, 37-6 (NY)
1978—Jets, 23-10 (NY)
1996—Jets, 31-21 (A)
1999—Jets, 12-7 (NY)
2004—Jets, 13-3 (A)
2008—Jets, 56-35 (NY)
(RS Pts.—Jets 151, Cardinals 130)
**Franchise known as Phoenix prior to 1994 and in St. Louis prior to 1988*

***ARIZONA vs. **OAKLAND**
RS: Raiders lead series, 5-2
1973—Raiders, 17-10 (StL)
1983—Cardinals, 34-24 (LA)
1989—Raiders, 16-14 (LA)
1998—Raiders, 23-20 (A)
2001—Cardinals, 34-31 (O) OT
2002—Raiders, 41-20 (A)
2006—Raiders, 22-9 (O)
(RS Pts.— Raiders 174, Cardinals 141)
**Franchise known as Phoenix prior to 1994 and in St. Louis prior to 1988*
***Franchise in Los Angeles from 1982-1994*

***ARIZONA vs. PHILADELPHIA**
RS: Series tied, 53-53-5
PS: Cardinals lead series, 2-1
1935—Cardinals, 12-3 (C)
1936—Cardinals, 13-0 (C)
1937—Tie, 6-6 (P)
1938—Eagles, 7-0 (Erie, Pa.)
1941—Eagles, 21-14 (P)
1945—Eagles, 21-6 (P)
1947—Cardinals, 45-21 (P)
**Cardinals, 28-21 (C)
1948—Cardinals, 21-14 (C)
**Eagles, 7-0 (P)
1949—Eagles, 28-3 (P)
1950—Eagles, 45-7 (C)
Cardinals, 14-10 (P)
1951—Eagles, 17-14 (C)
1952—Eagles, 10-7 (P)
Cardinals, 28-22 (C)
1953—Eagles, 56-17 (C)
Eagles, 38-0 (P)
1954—Eagles, 35-16 (C)
Eagles, 30-14 (P)
1955—Tie, 24-24 (C)
Eagles, 27-3 (P)
1956—Cardinals, 20-6 (P)
Cardinals, 28-17 (C)
1957—Eagles, 38-21 (C)
Cardinals, 31-27 (P)
1958—Tie, 21-21 (C)
Eagles, 49-21 (P)
1959—Eagles, 28-24 (Minn)
Eagles, 27-17 (P)
1960—Eagles, 31-27 (P)
Eagles, 20-6 (StL)
1961—Cardinals, 30-27 (P)
Eagles, 20-7 (StL)
1962—Cardinals, 27-21 (P)
Cardinals, 45-35 (StL)
1963—Cardinals, 28-24 (P)
Cardinals, 38-14 (StL)
1964—Cardinals, 38-13 (P)
Cardinals, 36-34 (StL)
1965—Eagles, 34-27 (P)
Eagles, 28-24 (StL)
1966—Cardinals, 16-13 (StL)
Cardinals, 41-10 (P)
1967—Cardinals, 48-14 (StL)
1968—Cardinals, 45-17 (P)
1969—Eagles, 34-30 (StL)
1970—Cardinals, 35-20 (P)
Cardinals, 23-14 (StL)
1971—Eagles, 37-20 (StL)
Eagles, 19-7 (P)
1972—Tie, 6-6 (P)
Cardinals, 24-23 (StL)
1973—Cardinals, 34-23 (P)
Eagles, 27-24 (StL)
1974—Cardinals, 7-3 (StL)
Cardinals, 13-3 (P)
1975—Cardinals, 31-20 (StL)

Cardinals, 24-23 (P)
1976—Cardinals, 33-14 (StL)
Cardinals, 17-14 (P)
1977—Cardinals, 21-17 (P)
Cardinals, 21-16 (StL)
1978—Cardinals, 16-10 (P)
Eagles, 14-10 (StL)
1979—Eagles, 24-20 (StL)
Eagles, 16-13 (P)
1980—Cardinals, 24-14 (StL)
Eagles, 17-3 (P)
1981—Eagles, 52-10 (StL)
Eagles, 38-0 (P)
1982—Cardinals, 23-20 (P)
1983—Cardinals, 14-11 (P)
Cardinals, 31-7 (StL)
1984—Cardinals, 34-14 (P)
Cardinals, 17-16 (StL)
1985—Eagles, 30-7 (P)
Eagles, 24-14 (StL)
1986—Cardinals, 13-10 (StL)
Tie, 10-10 (P) OT
1987—Eagles, 28-23 (StL)
Cardinals, 31-19 (P)
1988—Eagles, 31-21 (P)
Eagles, 23-17 (Phx)
1989—Eagles, 17-5 (Phx)
Eagles, 31-14 (P)
1990—Cardinals, 23-21 (P)
Eagles, 23-21 (Phx)
1991—Cardinals, 26-10 (P)
Eagles, 34-14 (Phx)
1992—Eagles, 31-14 (Phx)
Eagles, 7-3 (P)
1993—Eagles, 23-17 (P)
Cardinals, 16-3 (Phx)
1994—Eagles, 17-7 (P)
Cardinals, 12-6 (A)
1995—Eagles, 31-19 (A)
Eagles, 21-20 (P)
1996—Cardinals, 36-30 (A)
Eagles, 29-19 (P)
1997—Eagles, 13-10 (P) OT
Cardinals, 31-21 (A)
1998—Cardinals, 17-3 (A)
Cardinals, 20-17 (P) OT
1999—Cardinals, 25-24 (P)
Cardinals, 21-17 (A)
2000—Eagles, 33-14 (A)
Eagles, 34-9 (P)
2001—Cardinals, 21-20 (P)
Eagles, 21-7 (A)
2002—Eagles, 38-14 (P)
2005—Cardinals, 27-21 (A)
2008—Eagles, 48-20 (P)
***Cardinals, 32-25 (A)
(RS Pts.—Eagles 2,388, Cardinals 2,153)
(PS Pts.—Cardinals 60, Eagles 53)
Franchise known as Phoenix prior to 1994, in St. Louis prior to 1988, and in Chicago prior to 1960
***NFL Championship*
****NFC Championship*

***ARIZONA vs. **PITTSBURGH**
RS: Steelers lead series, 31-23-3
PS: Steelers lead series, 1-0
1933—Pirates, 14-13 (C)
1935—Pirates, 17-13 (P)
1936—Cardinals, 14-6 (C)
1937—Cardinals, 13-7 (P)
1939—Cardinals, 10-0 (P)
1940—Tie, 7-7 (P)
1942—Steelers, 19-3 (P)
1945—Steelers, 23-0 (P)
1946—Steelers, 14-7 (P)
1948—Cardinals, 24-7 (P)
1950—Steelers, 28-17 (C)
Steelers, 28-7 (P)
1951—Steelers, 28-14 (C)
1952—Steelers, 34-28 (C)
Steelers, 17-14 (P)
1953—Steelers, 31-28 (P)
Steelers, 21-17 (C)
1954—Cardinals, 17-14 (C)
Steelers, 20-17 (P)
1955—Steelers, 14-7 (P)
Cardinals, 27-13 (C)
1956—Steelers, 14-7 (P)
Cardinals, 38-27 (C)
1957—Steelers, 29-20 (P)
Steelers, 27-2 (C)
1958—Steelers, 27-20 (C)
Steelers, 38-21 (P)
1959—Cardinals, 45-24 (C)
Steelers, 35-20 (P)
1960—Steelers, 27-14 (P)
Cardinals, 38-7 (StL)
1961—Steelers, 30-27 (P)
Cardinals, 20-0 (StL)
1962—Steelers, 26-17 (StL)
Steelers, 19-7 (P)
1963—Steelers, 23-10 (P)
Cardinals, 24-23 (StL)
1964—Cardinals, 34-30 (StL)
Cardinals, 21-20 (P)
1965—Cardinals, 20-7 (P)
Cardinals, 21-17 (StL)
1966—Steelers, 30-9 (P)
Cardinals, 6-3 (StL)
1967—Cardinals, 28-14 (P)
Tie, 14-14 (StL)
1968—Tie, 28-28 (StL)
Cardinals, 20-10 (P)
1969—Cardinals, 27-14 (P)
Cardinals, 47-10 (StL)
1972—Steelers, 25-19 (StL)
1979—Steelers, 24-21 (StL)
1985—Steelers, 23-10 (P)
1988—Cardinals, 31-14 (Phx)
1994—Cardinals, 20-17 (A) OT
1997—Steelers, 26-20 (A) OT
2003—Steelers, 28-15 (P)
2007—Cardinals, 21-14 (A)
2008—***Steelers, 27-23 (Tampa Bay)
(RS Pts.—Steelers 1,106, Cardinals 1,059)
(PS Pts.—Steelers 27, Cardinals 23)
Franchise known as Phoenix prior to 1994, in St. Louis prior to 1988, and in Chicago prior to 1960
***Steelers known as Pirates prior to 1940*
****Super Bowl XLIII*

***ARIZONA vs. **ST. LOUIS**
RS: Rams lead series, 30-28-2
PS: Rams lead series, 1-0
1937—Cardinals, 6-0 (Cle)
Cardinals, 13-7 (Chi)
1938—Cardinals, 7-6 (Cle)
Cardinals, 31-17 (Chi)
1939—Rams, 24-0 (Chi)
Rams, 14-0 (Cle)
1940—Rams, 26-14 (Cle)
Cardinals, 17-7 (Chi)
1941—Rams, 10-6 (Cle)
Cardinals, 7-0 (Chi)
1942—Cardinals, 7-0 (Buffalo)
Rams, 7-3 (Cle)
1945—Rams, 21-0 (Cle)
Rams, 35-21 (Chi)
1946—Cardinals, 34-10 (Chi)
Rams, 17-14 (LA)
1947—Rams, 27-7 (LA)
Cardinals, 17-10 (Chi)
1948—Cardinals, 27-22 (LA)
Cardinals, 27-24 (Chi)
1949—Tie, 28-28 (Chi)
Cardinals, 31-27 (LA)
1951—Rams, 45-21 (LA)
1953—Tie, 24-24 (Chi)
1954—Rams, 28-17 (LA)
1958—Rams, 20-14 (Chi)
1960—Cardinals, 43-21 (LA)
1965—Rams, 27-3 (StL)
1968—Rams, 24-13 (StL)
1970—Rams, 34-13 (LA)
1972—Cardinals, 24-14 (StL)
1975—***Rams, 35-23 (LA)
1976—Cardinals, 30-28 (LA)
1979—Rams, 21-0 (LA)
1980—Rams, 21-13 (StL)
1984—Rams, 16-13 (StL)
1985—Rams, 46-14 (LA)
1986—Rams, 16-10 (StL)
1987—Rams, 27-24 (StL)
1988—Cardinals, 41-27 (LA)
1989—Rams, 37-14 (LA)
1991—Cardinals, 24-14 (LA)
1992—Cardinals, 20-14 (LA)
1993—Cardinals, 38-10 (P)
1994—Rams, 14-12 (LA)
1996—Cardinals, 31-28 (A) OT
1998—Cardinals, 20-17 (StL)
2002—Rams, 27-14 (A)
Rams, 30-28 (StL)
2003—Rams, 37-13 (StL)
Rams, 30-27 (A) OT
2004—Rams, 17-10 (StL)
Cardinals, 31-7 (A)
2005—Rams, 17-12 (A)
Cardinals, 38-28 (StL)
2006—Rams, 16-14 (A)
Cardinals, 34-20 (StL)
2007—Cardinals, 34-31 (StL)
Cardinals, 48-19 (A)
2008—Cardinals, 34-13 (StL)
Cardinals, 34-10 (A)
(RS Pts.—Rams 1,214, Cardinals 1,164)
(PS Pts.—Rams 35, Cardinals 23)
Franchise known as Phoenix prior to 1994, in St. Louis prior to 1988, and in Chicago prior to 1960
***Franchise in Los Angeles prior to 1995 and in Cleveland prior to 1946*
****NFC Divisional Playoff*

***ARIZONA vs. SAN DIEGO**
RS: Chargers lead series, 8-3
1971—Chargers, 20-17 (SD)
1976—Chargers, 43-24 (SD)
1983—Cardinals, 44-14 (StL)
1987—Chargers, 28-24 (SD)
1989—Chargers, 24-13 (P)

1992—Chargers, 27-21 (P)
1995—Chargers, 28-25 (SD)
1998—Cardinals, 16-13 (A)
2001—Cardinals, 20-17 (SD)
2002—Chargers, 23-15 (A)
2006—Chargers, 27-20 (SD)
(RS Pts.—Chargers 264, Cardinals 239)
Franchise known as Phoenix prior to 1994, in St. Louis prior to 1988,

***ARIZONA vs. SAN FRANCISCO**
RS: 49ers lead series, 19-16
1951—Cardinals, 27-21 (SF)
1957—Cardinals, 20-10 (SF)
1962—49ers, 24-17 (StL)
1964—Cardinals, 23-13 (SF)
1968—49ers, 35-17 (SF)
1971—49ers, 26-14 (StL)
1974—Cardinals, 34-9 (SF)
1976—Cardinals, 23-20 (StL) OT
1978—Cardinals, 16-10 (SF)
1979—Cardinals, 13-10 (StL)
1980—49ers, 24-21 (SF) OT
1982—49ers, 31-20 (StL)
1983—49ers, 42-27 (StL)
1986—49ers, 43-17 (SF)
1987—49ers, 34-28 (SF)
1988—Cardinals, 24-23 (P)
1991—49ers, 14-10 (SF)
1992—Cardinals, 24-14 (P)
1993—49ers, 28-14 (SF)
1999—49ers, 24-10 (A)
2000—49ers, 27-20 (SF)
2002—49ers, 38-28 (SF)
49ers, 17-14 (A)
2003—Cardinals, 16-13 (A) OT
49ers, 50-14 (SF)
2004—49ers, 31-28 (SF) OT
49ers, 31-28 (A) OT
2005—Cardinals, 31-14 (Mex. City)
Cardinals, 17-10 (SF)
2006—Cardinals, 34-27 (A)
Cardinals, 26-20 (SF)
2007—49ers, 20-17 (SF)
49ers, 37-31 (A) OT
2008—Cardinals, 23-13 (SF)
Cardinals, 29-24 (A)
(RS Pts.—49ers 827, Cardinals 755)
Franchise known as Phoenix prior to 1994, in St. Louis prior to 1988, and in Chicago prior to 1960

***ARIZONA vs. SEATTLE**
RS: Cardinals lead series, 11-9
1976—Cardinals, 30-24 (S)
1983—Cardinals, 33-28 (StL)
1989—Cardinals, 34-24 (S)
1993—Cardinals, 30-27 (S) OT
1995—Cardinals, 20-14 (A) OT
1998—Seahawks, 33-14 (S)
2002—Cardinals, 24-13 (S)
Seahawks, 27-6 (A)
2003—Seahawks, 38-0 (A)
Seahawks, 28-10 (S)
2004—Cardinals, 25-17 (A)
Seahawks, 24-21 (S)
2005—Seahawks, 37-12 (S)
Seahawks, 33-19 (A)
2006—Seahawks, 21-10 (S)
Cardinals, 27-21 (A)
2007—Cardinals, 23-20 (A)
Seahawks, 42-21 (S)
2008—Cardinals, 26-20 (S)
Cardinals, 34-21 (A)
(RS Pts.—Seahawks 512, Cardinals 419)
Franchise known as Phoenix prior to 1994 and in St. Louis prior to 1988

***ARIZONA vs. TAMPA BAY**
RS: Series tied, 8-8
1977—Buccaneers, 17-7 (TB)
1981—Buccaneers, 20-10 (TB)
1983—Cardinals, 34-27 (TB)
1985—Buccaneers, 16-0 (TB)
1986—Cardinals, 30-19 (TB)
Cardinals, 21-17 (StL)
1987—Cardinals, 31-28 (StL)
Cardinals, 31-14 (TB)
1988—Cardinals, 30-24 (TB)
1989—Buccaneers, 14-13 (P)
1992—Buccaneers, 23-7 (TB)
Buccaneers, 7-3 (P)
1996—Cardinals, 13-9 (A)
1997—Buccaneers, 19-18 (TB)
2004—Cardinals, 12-7 (A)
2007—Buccaneers, 17-10 (TB)
(RS Pts.—Buccaneers 278, Cardinals 270)
Franchise known as Phoenix prior to 1994 and in St. Louis prior to 1988

***ARIZONA vs. **TENNESSEE**
RS: Cardinals lead series, 5-3
1970—Cardinals, 44-0 (StL)
1974—Cardinals, 31-27 (H)
1979—Cardinals, 24-17 (H)
1985—Oilers, 20-10 (StL)
1988—Oilers, 38-20 (H)
1994—Cardinals, 30-12 (H)
1997—Oilers, 41-14 (A)
2005—Cardinals, 20-10 (A)
(RS Pts.—Cardinals 193, Titans 165)
Franchise known as Phoenix prior to 1994 and in St. Louis prior to 1988
***Franchise in Houston prior to 1997; known as Oilers prior to 1999*

***ARIZONA vs. **WASHINGTON**
RS: Redskins lead series, 73-44-2
1932—Cardinals, 9-0 (B)
Braves, 8-6 (C)
1933—Redskins, 10-0 (C)
Tie, 0-0 (B)
1934—Redskins, 9-0 (B)
1935—Cardinals, 6-0 (B)
1936—Redskins, 13-10 (B)
1937—Cardinals, 21-14 (W)
1939—Redskins, 28-7 (W)
1940—Redskins, 28-21 (W)
1942—Redskins, 28-0 (W)
1943—Redskins, 13-7 (W)
1945—Redskins, 24-21 (W)
1947—Redskins, 45-21 (W)
1949—Cardinals, 38-7 (C)
1950—Cardinals, 38-28 (W)
1951—Redskins, 7-3 (C)
Redskins, 20-17 (W)
1952—Redskins, 23-7 (C)
Cardinals, 17-6 (W)
1953—Redskins, 24-13 (C)
Redskins, 28-17 (W)
1954—Cardinals, 38-16 (C)
Redskins, 37-20 (W)
1955—Cardinals, 24-10 (W)
Redskins, 31-0 (C)
1956—Cardinals, 31-3 (W)
Redskins, 17-14 (C)
1957—Redskins, 37-14 (C)
Cardinals, 44-14 (W)
1958—Cardinals, 37-10 (C)
Redskins, 45-31 (W)
1959—Cardinals, 49-21 (C)
Redskins, 23-14 (W)
1960—Cardinals, 44-7 (StL)
Cardinals, 26-14 (W)
1961—Cardinals, 24-0 (W)
Cardinals, 38-24 (StL)
1962—Redskins, 24-14 (W)
Tie, 17-17 (StL)
1963—Cardinals, 21-7 (W)
Cardinals, 24-20 (StL)
1964—Cardinals, 23-17 (W)
Cardinals, 38-24 (StL)
1965—Cardinals, 37-16 (W)
Redskins, 24-20 (StL)
1966—Cardinals, 23-7 (StL)
Redskins, 26-20 (W)
1967—Cardinals, 27-21 (W)
1968—Cardinals, 41-14 (StL)
1969—Redskins, 33-17 (W)
1970—Cardinals, 27-17 (StL)
Redskins, 28-27 (W)
1971—Redskins, 24-17 (StL)
Redskins, 20-0 (W)
1972—Redskins, 24-10 (W)
Redskins, 33-3 (StL)
1973—Cardinals, 34-27 (StL)
Redskins, 31-13 (W)
1974—Cardinals, 17-10 (W)
Cardinals, 23-20 (StL)
1975—Redskins, 27-17 (W)
Cardinals, 20-17 (StL) OT
1976—Redskins, 20-10 (W)
Redskins, 16-10 (StL)
1977—Redskins, 24-14 (W)
Redskins, 26-20 (StL)
1978—Redskins, 28-10 (StL)
Cardinals, 27-17 (W)
1979—Redskins, 17-7 (StL)
Redskins, 30-28 (W)
1980—Redskins, 23-0 (W)
Redskins, 31-7 (StL)
1981—Cardinals, 40-30 (StL)
Redskins, 42-21 (W)
1982—Redskins, 12-7 (StL)
Redskins, 28-0 (W)
1983—Redskins, 38-14 (StL)
Redskins, 45-7 (W)
1984—Cardinals, 26-24 (StL)
Redskins, 29-27 (W)
1985—Redskins, 27-10 (W)
Redskins, 27-16 (StL)
1986—Redskins, 28-21 (W)
Redskins, 20-17 (StL)
1987—Redskins, 28-21 (W)
Redskins, 34-17 (StL)
1988—Cardinals, 30-21 (P)
Redskins, 33-17 (W)
1989—Redskins, 30-28 (W)
Redskins, 29-10 (P)
1990—Redskins, 31-0 (W)
Redskins, 38-10 (P)
1991—Redskins, 34-0 (W)
Redskins, 20-14 (P)
1992—Cardinals, 27-24 (P)
Redskins, 41-3 (W)

1993—Cardinals, 17-10 (W)
Cardinals, 36-6 (P)
1994—Cardinals, 19-16 (W) OT
Cardinals, 17-15 (A)
1995—Redskins, 27-7 (W)
Cardinals, 24-20 (A)
1996—Cardinals, 37-34 (W) OT
Cardinals, 27-26 (A)
1997—Redskins, 19-13 (W) OT
Redskins, 38-28 (A)
1998—Cardinals, 29-27 (A)
Cardinals, 45-42 (W)
1999—Redskins, 24-10 (A)
Redskins, 28-3 (W)
2000—Cardinals, 16-15 (A)
Redskins, 20-3 (W)
2001—Redskins, 20-10 (A)
Redskins, 20-17 (W)
2002—Redskins, 31-23 (W)
2005—Redskins, 17-13 (A)
2007—Redskins, 21-19 (W)
2008—Redskins, 24-17 (W)
(RS Pts.—Redskins 2,645, Cardinals 2,203)
Franchise known as Phoenix prior to 1994, in St. Louis prior to 1988, and in Chicago prior to 1960
***Franchise in Boston prior to 1937 and known as Braves prior to 1933*

ATLANTA vs. ARIZONA
RS: Cardinals lead series, 14-10
PS: Cardinals lead series, 1-0;
See Arizona vs. Atlanta

ATLANTA vs. BALTIMORE
RS: Ravens lead series, 2-1
1999—Ravens, 19-13 (A) OT
2002—Falcons, 20-17 (A)
2006—Ravens, 24-10 (B)
(RS Pts.—Ravens 60, Falcons 43)

ATLANTA vs. BUFFALO
RS: Falcons lead series, 5-4
1973—Bills, 17-6 (A)
1977—Bills, 3-0 (B)
1980—Falcons, 30-14 (B)
1983—Falcons, 31-14 (A)
1989—Falcons, 30-28 (A)
1992—Bills, 41-14 (B)
1995—Bills, 23-17 (B)
2001—Falcons, 33-30 (A)
2005—Falcons, 24-16 (B)
(RS Pts.—Bills 186, Falcons 185)

ATLANTA vs. CAROLINA
RS: Falcons lead series, 17-11
1995—Falcons, 23-20 (A) OT
Panthers, 21-17 (C)
1996—Panthers, 29-6 (C)
Falcons, 20-17 (A)
1997—Panthers, 9-6 (A)
Panthers, 21-12 (C)
1998—Falcons, 19-14 (C)
Falcons, 51-23 (A)
1999—Falcons, 27-20 (A)
Panthers, 34-28 (C)
2000—Falcons, 15-10 (C)
Falcons, 13-12 (A)
2001—Falcons, 24-16 (A)
Falcons, 10-7 (C)
2002—Falcons, 30-0 (A)
Falcons, 41-0 (C)
2003—Panthers, 23-3 (C)
Falcons, 20-14 (A) OT
2004—Falcons, 27-10 (C)
Falcons, 34-31 (A) OT
2005—Panthers, 24-6 (C)
Panthers, 44-11 (A)
2006—Falcons, 20-6 (C)
Panthers, 10-3 (A)
2007—Panthers, 27-20 (A)
Falcons, 20-13 (C)
2008—Panthers, 24-9 (C)
Falcons, 45-28 (A)
(RS Pts.—Falcons 560, Panthers 507)

ATLANTA vs. CHICAGO
RS: Bears lead series, 12-11
1966—Bears, 23-6 (C)
1967—Bears, 23-14 (A)
1968—Falcons, 16-13 (C)
1969—Falcons, 48-31 (A)
1970—Bears, 23-14 (A)
1972—Falcons, 37-21 (C)
1973—Falcons, 46-6 (A)
1974—Falcons, 13-10 (A)
1976—Falcons, 10-0 (C)
1977—Falcons, 16-10 (C)
1978—Bears, 13-7 (C)
1980—Falcons, 28-17 (A)
1983—Falcons, 20-17 (C)
1985—Bears, 36-0 (C)
1986—Bears, 13-10 (A)
1990—Bears, 30-24 (C)
1992—Bears, 41-31 (C)
1993—Bears, 6-0 (C)
1998—Falcons, 20-13 (A)
2001—Bears, 31-3 (A)
2002—Bears, 14-13 (A)
2005—Bears, 16-3 (C)
2008—Falcons, 22-20 (A)
(RS Pts.—Bears 427, Falcons 401)

ATLANTA vs. CINCINNATI
RS: Bengals lead series, 7-4
1971—Falcons, 9-6 (C)
1975—Bengals, 21-14 (A)
1978—Bengals, 37-7 (C)
1981—Bengals, 30-28 (A)
1984—Bengals, 35-14 (C)
1987—Bengals, 16-10 (A)
1990—Falcons, 38-17 (A)
1993—Bengals, 21-17 (C)
1996—Bengals, 41-31 (C)
2002—Falcons, 30-3 (A)
2006—Falcons, 29-27 (C)
(RS Pts.—Bengals 254, Falcons 227)

ATLANTA vs. CLEVELAND
RS: Browns lead series, 10-2
1966—Browns, 49-17 (A)
1968—Browns, 30-7 (C)
1971—Falcons, 31-14 (C)
1976—Browns, 20-17 (A)
1978—Browns, 24-16 (A)
1981—Browns, 28-17 (C)
1984—Browns, 23-7 (A)
1987—Browns, 38-3 (C)
1990—Browns, 13-10 (C)
1993—Falcons, 17-14 (A)
2002—Browns, 24-16 (C)
2006—Browns, 17-13 (A)
(RS Pts.—Browns 294, Falcons 171)

ATLANTA vs. DALLAS
RS: Cowboys lead series, 13-8
PS: Cowboys lead series, 2-0
1966—Cowboys, 47-14 (A)
1967—Cowboys, 37-7 (D)
1969—Cowboys, 24-17 (A)
1970—Cowboys, 13-0 (D)
1974—Cowboys, 24-0 (A)
1976—Falcons, 17-10 (A)
1978—*Cowboys, 27-20 (D)
1980—*Cowboys, 30-27 (A)
1985—Cowboys, 24-10 (D)
1986—Falcons, 37-35 (D)
1987—Falcons, 21-10 (D)
1988—Cowboys, 26-20 (D)
1989—Falcons 27-21 (A)
1990—Falcons, 26-7 (A)
1991—Cowboys, 31-27 (D)
1992—Cowboys, 41-17 (A)
1993—Falcons, 27-14 (A)
1995—Cowboys, 28-13 (A)
1996—Cowboys, 32-28 (D)
1999—Cowboys, 24-7 (D)
2001—Falcons, 20-13 (A)
2003—Falcons, 27-13 (D)
2006—Cowboys, 38-28 (A)
(RS Pts.—Cowboys 512, Falcons 390)
(PS Pts.—Cowboys 57, Falcons 47)
**NFC Divisional Playoff*

ATLANTA vs. DENVER
RS: Broncos lead series, 8-4
PS: Broncos lead series, 1-0
1970—Broncos, 24-10 (D)
1972—Falcons, 23-20 (A)
1975—Falcons, 35-21 (A)
1979—Broncos, 20-17 (A) OT
1982—Falcons, 34-27 (D)
1985—Broncos, 44-28 (A)
1988—Broncos, 30-14 (D)
1994—Broncos, 32-28 (D)
1997—Broncos, 29-21 (A)
1998—*Broncos, 34-19 (South Florida)
2000—Broncos, 42-14 (D)
2004—Falcons, 41-28 (D)
2008—Broncos, 24-20 (A)
(RS Pts.—Broncos 341, Falcons 285)
(PS Pts.—Broncos 34, Falcons 19)
**Super Bowl XXXIII*

ATLANTA vs. DETROIT
RS: Lions lead series, 23-10
1966—Lions, 28-10 (D)
1967—Lions, 24-3 (D)
1968—Lions, 24-7 (A)
1969—Lions, 27-21 (D)
1971—Lions, 41-38 (D)
1972—Lions, 26-23 (A)
1973—Lions, 31-6 (D)
1975—Lions, 17-14 (A)
1976—Lions, 24-10 (D)
1977—Falcons, 17-6 (A)
1978—Falcons, 14-0 (A)
1979—Lions, 24-23 (D)
1980—Falcons, 43-28 (A)
1983—Falcons, 30-14 (D)
1984—Lions, 27-24 (A) OT
1985—Lions, 28-27 (A)
1986—Falcons, 20-6 (D)
1987—Lions, 30-13 (A)
1988—Lions, 31-17 (D)
1989—Lions, 31-24 (A)
1990—Lions, 21-14 (D)
1993—Lions, 30-13 (D)
1994—Lions, 31-28 (D) OT

1995—Falcons, 34-22 (A)
1996—Lions, 28-24 (D)
1997—Lions, 28-17 (D)
1998—Falcons, 24-17 (D)
2000—Lions, 13-10 (D)
2002—Falcons, 36-15 (A)
2004—Lions, 17-10 (A)
2005—Falcons, 27-7 (D)
2006—Lions, 30-14 (D)
2008—Falcons, 34-21 (A)
(RS Pts.—Lions 747, Falcons 669)

ATLANTA vs. GREEN BAY
RS: Packers lead series, 12-11
PS: Series tied, 1-1
1966—Packers, 56-3 (Mil)
1967—Packers, 23-0 (Mil)
1968—Packers, 38-7 (A)
1969—Packers, 28-10 (GB)
1970—Packers, 27-24 (GB)
1971—Falcons, 28-21 (A)
1972—Falcons, 10-9 (Mil)
1974—Falcons, 10-3 (A)
1975—Packers, 22-13 (GB)
1976—Packers, 24-20 (A)
1979—Falcons, 25-7 (A)
1981—Falcons, 31-17 (GB)
1982—Packers, 38-7 (A)
1983—Falcons, 47-41 (A) OT
1988—Falcons, 20-0 (A)
1989—Packers, 23-21 (Mil)
1991—Falcons, 35-31 (A)
1992—Falcons, 24-10 (A)
1994—Packers, 21-17 (Mil)
1995—*Packers, 37-20 (GB)
2001—Falcons, 23-20 (GB)
2002—Packers, 37-34 (GB) OT
*Falcons, 27-7 (GB)
2005—Packers, 33-25 (A)
2008—Falcons, 27-24 (GB)
(RS Pts.—Packers 553, Falcons 461)
(PS Pts.—Falcons 47, Packers 44)
NFC First-Round Playoff

ATLANTA vs. HOUSTON
RS: Series tied, 1-1
2003—Texans, 17-13 (H)
2007—Falcons, 26-16 (A)
(RS Pts.—Falcons 39, Texans 33)

ATLANTA vs. *INDIANAPOLIS
RS: Colts lead series, 13-1
1966—Colts, 19-7 (A)
1967—Colts, 38-31 (B)
Colts, 49-7 (A)
1968—Colts, 28-20 (A)
Colts, 44-0 (B)
1969—Colts, 21-14 (A)
Colts, 13-6 (B)
1974—Colts, 17-7 (A)
1986—Colts, 28-23 (A)
1989—Colts, 13-9 (I)
1998—Falcons, 28-21 (A)
2001—Colts, 41-27 (I)
2003—Colts, 38-7 (I)
2007—Colts, 31-13 (A)
(RS Pts.—Colts 401, Falcons 199)
Franchise in Baltimore prior to 1984

ATLANTA vs. JACKSONVILLE
RS: Jaguars lead series, 3-1
1996—Jaguars, 19-17 (J)
1999—Jaguars, 30-7 (A)
2003—Falcons, 21-14 (A)
2007—Jaguars, 13-7 (J)
(RS Pts.—Jaguars 76, Falcons 52)

ATLANTA vs. KANSAS CITY
RS: Chiefs lead series, 5-2
1972—Chiefs, 17-14 (A)
1985—Chiefs, 38-10 (KC)
1991—Chiefs, 14-3 (KC)
1994—Chiefs, 30-10 (A)
2000—Falcons, 29-13 (A)
2004—Chiefs, 56-10 (KC)
2008—Falcons, 38-14 (A)
(RS Pts.—Chiefs 182, Falcons 114)

ATLANTA vs. MIAMI
RS: Dolphins lead series, 7-3
1970—Dolphins, 20-7 (A)
1974—Dolphins, 42-7 (M)
1980—Dolphins, 20-17 (A)
1983—Dolphins, 31-24 (M)
1986—Falcons, 20-14 (M)
1992—Dolphins, 21-17 (M)
1995—Dolphins, 21-20 (M)
1998—Falcons, 38-16 (A)
2001—Dolphins, 21-14 (M)
2005—Falcons, 17-10 (M)
(RS Pts.—Dolphins 216, Falcons 181)

ATLANTA vs. MINNESOTA
RS: Vikings lead series, 15-9
PS: Series tied, 1-1
1966—Falcons, 20-13 (M)
1967—Falcons, 21-20 (A)
1968—Vikings, 47-7 (M)
1969—Falcons, 10-3 (A)
1970—Vikings, 37-7 (A)
1971—Vikings, 24-7 (M)
1973—Falcons, 20-14 (A)
1974—Vikings, 23-10 (M)
1975—Vikings, 38-0 (M)
1977—Vikings, 14-7 (A)
1980—Vikings, 24-23 (M)
1981—Falcons, 31-30 (A)
1982—*Vikings, 30-24 (M)
1984—Vikings, 27-20 (M)
1985—Falcons, 14-13 (A)
1987—Vikings, 24-13 (M)
1989—Vikings, 43-17 (M)
1991—Vikings, 20-19 (A)
1996—Vikings, 23-17 (A)
1998—**Falcons, 30-27 (M) OT
1999—Vikings, 17-14 (A)
2002—Falcons, 30-24 (M) OT
2003—Vikings, 39-26 (A)
2005—Falcons, 30-10 (A)
2007—Vikings, 24-3 (M)
2008—Falcons, 24-17 (M)
(RS Pts.—Vikings 568, Falcons 390)
(PS Pts.—Vikings 57, Falcons 54)
NFC First-Round Playoff
***NFC Championship*

ATLANTA vs. NEW ENGLAND
RS: Falcons lead series, 6-5
1972—Patriots, 21-20 (NE)
1977—Patriots, 16-10 (A)
1980—Falcons, 37-21 (NE)
1983—Falcons, 24-13 (A)
1986—Patriots, 25-17 (NE)
1989—Falcons, 16-15 (A)
1992—Falcons, 34-0 (A)
1995—Falcons, 30-17 (A)
1998—Falcons, 41-10 (NE)
2001—Patriots, 24-10 (A)
2005—Patriots, 31-28 (A)
(RS Pts.—Falcons 267, Patriots 193)

ATLANTA vs. NEW ORLEANS
RS: Falcons lead series, 44-35
PS: Falcons lead series, 1-0
1967—Saints, 27-24 (NO)
1969—Falcons, 45-17 (A)
1970—Falcons, 14-3 (NO)
Falcons, 32-14 (A)
1971—Falcons, 28-6 (A)
Falcons, 24-20 (NO)
1972—Falcons, 21-14 (NO)
Falcons, 36-20 (A)
1973—Falcons, 62-7 (NO)
Falcons, 14-10 (A)
1974—Saints, 14-13 (NO)
Saints, 13-3 (A)
1975—Falcons, 14-7 (A)
Saints, 23-7 (NO)
1976—Saints, 30-0 (NO)
Falcons, 23-20 (A)
1977—Saints, 21-20 (NO)
Falcons, 35-7 (A)
1978—Falcons, 20-17 (NO)
Falcons, 20-17 (A)
1979—Falcons, 40-34 (NO) OT
Saints, 37-6 (A)
1980—Falcons, 41-14 (NO)
Falcons, 31-13 (A)
1981—Falcons, 27-0 (A)
Falcons, 41-10 (NO)
1982—Falcons, 35-0 (A)
Saints, 35-6 (NO)
1983—Saints, 19-17 (A)
Saints, 27-10 (NO)
1984—Falcons, 36-28 (NO)
Saints, 17-13 (A)
1985—Falcons, 31-24 (A)
Falcons, 16-10 (NO)
1986—Falcons, 31-10 (NO)
Saints, 14-9 (A)
1987—Saints, 38-0 (A)
1988—Saints, 29-21 (A)
Saints, 10-9 (NO)
1989—Saints, 20-13 (NO)
Saints, 26-17 (A)
1990—Falcons, 28-27 (A)
Saints, 10-7 (NO)
1991—Saints, 27-6 (A)
Falcons, 23-20 (NO) OT
*Falcons, 27-20 (NO)
1992—Saints, 10-7 (A)
Saints, 22-14 (NO)
1993—Saints, 34-31 (A)
Falcons, 26-15 (NO)
1994—Saints, 33-32 (NO)
Saints, 29-20 (A)
1995—Falcons, 27-24 (NO) OT
Falcons, 19-14 (A)
1996—Falcons, 17-15 (A)
Falcons, 31-15 (NO)
1997—Falcons, 23-17 (NO)
Falcons, 20-3 (A)
1998—Falcons, 31-23 (A)
Falcons, 27-17 (NO)
1999—Falcons, 20-17 (NO)
Falcons, 35-12 (A)
2000—Saints, 21-19 (A)
Saints, 23-7 (NO)
2001—Falcons, 20-13 (NO)

Saints, 28-10 (NO)
2002—Falcons, 37-35 (NO)
Falcons, 24-17 (A)
2003—Saints, 45-17 (A)
Saints, 23-20 (NO) OT
2004—Falcons, 24-21 (A)
Saints, 26-13 (NO)
2005—Falcons, 34-31 (San Antonio)
Falcons, 36-17 (A)
2006—Saints, 23-3 (NO)
Saints, 31-13 (A)
2007—Saints, 22-16 (NO)
Saints, 34-14 (A)
2008—Falcons, 34-20 (A)
Saints, 29-25 (NO)
(RS Pts.—Falcons 1,715, Saints 1,565)
(PS Pts.—Falcons 27, Saints 20)
NFC First-Round Playoff

ATLANTA vs. N.Y. GIANTS
RS: Falcons lead series, 10-9
1966—Falcons, 27-16 (NY)
1968—Falcons, 24-21 (A)
1971—Giants, 21-17 (A)
1974—Falcons, 14-7 (New Haven)
1977—Falcons, 17-3 (A)
1978—Falcons, 23-20 (A)
1979—Giants, 24-3 (NY)
1981—Giants, 27-24 (A) OT
1982—Falcons, 16-14 (NY)
1983—Giants, 16-13 (A) OT
1984—Giants, 19-7 (A)
1988—Giants, 23-16 (A)
1998—Falcons, 34-20 (NY)
2000—Giants, 13-6 (A)
2002—Falcons, 17-10 (NY)
2003—Falcons, 27-7 (NY)
2004—Falcons, 14-10 (NY)
2006—Giants, 27-14 (A)
2007—Giants, 31-10 (A)
(RS Pts.—Giants 329, Falcons 323)

ATLANTA vs. N.Y. JETS
RS: Falcons lead series, 5-4
1973—Falcons, 28-20 (NY)
1980—Jets, 14-7 (A)
1983—Falcons, 27-21 (NY)
1986—Jets, 28-14 (A)
1989—Jets, 27-7 (NY)
1992—Falcons, 20-17 (A)
1995—Falcons, 13-3 (A)
1998—Jets, 28-3 (NY)
2005—Falcons, 27-14 (A)
(RS Pts.—Jets 172, Falcons 146)

ATLANTA vs. *OAKLAND
RS: Raiders lead series, 7-5
1971—Falcons, 24-13 (A)
1975—Raiders, 37-34 (O) OT
1979—Raiders, 50-19 (O)
1982—Raiders, 38-14 (A)
1985—Raiders, 34-24 (A)
1988—Falcons, 12-6 (LA)
1991—Falcons, 21-17 (A)
1994—Raiders, 30-17 (LA)
1997—Raiders, 36-31 (A)
2000—Raiders, 41-14 (O)
2004—Falcons, 35-10 (A)
2008—Falcons, 24-0 (O)
(RS Pts.—Raiders 312, Falcons 269)
Franchise in Los Angeles from 1982-1994

ATLANTA vs. PHILADELPHIA
RS: Eagles lead series, 13-10-1
PS: Eagles lead series, 2-1
1966—Eagles, 23-10 (P)
1967—Eagles, 38-7 (A)
1969—Falcons, 27-3 (P)
1970—Tie, 13-13 (P)
1973—Falcons, 44-27 (P)
1976—Eagles, 14-13 (A)
1978—*Falcons, 14-13 (A)
1979—Falcons, 14-10 (P)
1980—Falcons, 20-17 (P)
1981—Eagles, 16-13 (P)
1983—Eagles, 28-24 (A)
1984—Falcons, 26-10 (A)
1985—Eagles, 23-17 (P) OT
1986—Eagles, 16-0 (A)
1988—Falcons, 27-24 (P)
1990—Eagles, 24-23 (A)
1994—Falcons, 28-21 (A)
1996—Eagles, 33-18 (A)
1997—Falcons, 20-17 (A)
1998—Falcons, 17-12 (A)
2000—Eagles, 38-10 (P)
2002—**Eagles, 20-6 (P)
2003—Eagles, 23-16 (A)
2004—***Eagles, 27-10 (P)
2005—Falcons, 14-10 (A)
2006—Eagles, 24-17 (P)
2008—Eagles, 27-14 (P)
(RS Pts.—Eagles 491, Falcons 432)
(PS Pts.—Eagles 60, Falcons 30)
NFC First-Round Playoff
**NFC Divisional Playoff*
***NFC Championship*

ATLANTA vs. PITTSBURGH
RS: Steelers lead series, 11-2-1
1966—Steelers, 57-33 (A)
1968—Steelers, 41-21 (A)
1970—Falcons, 27-16 (A)
1974—Steelers, 24-17 (P)
1978—Steelers, 31-7 (P)
1981—Steelers, 34-20 (A)
1984—Steelers, 35-10 (P)
1987—Steelers, 28-12 (A)
1990—Steelers, 21-9 (P)
1993—Steelers, 45-17 (A)
1996—Steelers, 20-17 (A)
1999—Steelers, 13-9 (P)
2002—Tie, 34-34 (P) OT
2006—Falcons, 41-38 (A) OT
(RS Pts.—Steelers 437, Falcons 274)

ATLANTA vs. *ST. LOUIS
RS: Rams lead series, 47-25-2
PS: Falcons lead series, 1-0
1966—Rams, 19-14 (A)
1967—Rams, 31-3 (A)
Rams, 20-3 (LA)
1968—Rams, 27-14 (LA)
Rams, 17-10 (A)
1969—Rams, 17-7 (LA)
Rams, 38-6 (A)
1970—Tie, 10-10 (LA)
Rams, 17-7 (A)
1971—Tie, 20-20 (LA)
Rams, 24-16 (A)
1972—Falcons, 31-3 (A)
Rams, 20-7 (LA)
1973—Rams, 31-0 (LA)
Falcons, 15-13 (A)
1974—Rams, 21-0 (LA)
Rams, 30-7 (A)
1975—Rams, 22-7 (LA)
Rams, 16-7 (A)
1976—Rams, 30-14 (A)
Rams, 59-0 (LA)
1977—Falcons, 17-6 (A)
Rams, 23-7 (LA)
1978—Rams, 10-0 (LA)
Falcons, 15-7 (A)
1979—Rams, 20-14 (LA)
Rams, 34-13 (A)
1980—Falcons, 13-10 (A)
Rams, 20-17 (LA) OT
1981—Rams, 37-35 (A)
Rams, 21-16 (LA)
1982—Falcons, 34-17 (A)
1983—Rams, 27-21 (LA)
Rams, 36-13 (A)
1984—Falcons, 30-28 (LA)
Rams, 24-10 (A)
1985—Rams, 17-6 (LA)
Falcons, 30-14 (A)
1986—Falcons, 26-14 (A)
Rams, 14-7 (LA)
1987—Falcons, 24-20 (A)
Rams, 33-0 (LA)
1988—Rams, 33-0 (A)
Rams, 22-7 (LA)
1989—Rams, 31-21 (A)
Rams, 26-14 (LA)
1990—Rams, 44-24 (LA)
Falcons, 20-13 (A)
1991—Falcons, 31-14 (A)
Falcons, 31-14 (LA)
1992—Falcons, 30-28 (A)
Rams, 38-27 (LA)
1993—Falcons, 30-24 (A)
Falcons, 13-0 (LA)
1994—Falcons, 31-13 (A)
Falcons, 8-5 (LA)
1995—Rams, 21-19 (StL)
Falcons, 31-6 (A)
1996—Rams, 59-16 (StL)
Rams, 34-27 (A)
1997—Falcons, 34-31 (A)
Falcons, 27-21 (StL)
1998—Falcons, 37-15 (A)
Falcons, 21-10 (StL)
1999—Rams, 35-7 (StL)
Rams, 41-13 (A)
2000—Rams, 41-20 (A)
Rams, 45-29 (StL)
2001—Rams, 35-6 (A)
Rams, 31-13 (StL)
2003—Rams, 36-0 (StL)
2004—Falcons, 34-17 (A)
**Falcons, 47-17 (A)
2007—Rams, 28-16 (StL)
2008—Falcons, 31-27 (A)
(RS Pts.—Rams 1,755, Falcons 1,214)
(PS Pts.—Falcons 47, Rams 17)
Franchise in Los Angeles prior to 1995
**NFC Divisional Playoff*

ATLANTA vs. SAN DIEGO
RS: Falcons lead series, 7-1
1973—Falcons, 41-0 (SD)
1979—Falcons, 28-26 (SD)
1988—Chargers, 10-7 (A)
1991—Falcons, 13-10 (SD)
1994—Falcons, 10-9 (A)
1997—Falcons, 14-3 (SD)

2004—Falcons, 21-20 (A)
2008—Falcons, 22-16 (SD)
(RS Pts.—Falcons 156, Chargers 94)

ATLANTA vs. SAN FRANCISCO
RS: 49ers lead series, 44-27-1
PS: Falcons lead series, 1-0
1966—49ers, 44-7 (A)
1967—49ers, 38-7 (SF)
49ers, 34-28 (A)
1968—49ers, 28-13 (SF)
49ers, 14-12 (A)
1969—Falcons, 24-12 (A)
Falcons, 21-7 (SF)
1970—Falcons, 21-20 (A)
49ers, 24-20 (SF)
1971—Falcons, 20-17 (A)
49ers, 24-3 (SF)
1972—49ers, 49-14 (A)
49ers, 20-0 (SF)
1973—49ers, 13-9 (A)
Falcons, 17-3 (SF)
1974—49ers, 16-10 (A)
49ers, 27-0 (SF)
1975—Falcons, 17-3 (SF)
Falcons, 31-9 (A)
1976—49ers, 15-0 (SF)
Falcons, 21-16 (A)
1977—Falcons, 7-0 (SF)
49ers, 10-3 (A)
1978—Falcons, 20-17 (SF)
Falcons, 21-10 (A)
1979—49ers, 20-15 (SF)
Falcons, 31-21 (A)
1980—Falcons, 20-17 (SF)
Falcons, 35-10 (A)
1981—Falcons, 34-17 (A)
49ers, 17-14 (SF)
1982—Falcons, 17-7 (SF)
1983—49ers, 24-20 (SF)
Falcons, 28-24 (A)
1984—49ers, 14-5 (SF)
49ers, 35-17 (A)
1985—49ers, 35-16 (SF)
49ers, 38-17 (A)
1986—Tie, 10-10 (A) OT
49ers, 20-0 (SF)
1987—49ers, 25-17 (A)
49ers, 35-7 (SF)
1988—Falcons, 34-17 (SF)
49ers, 13-3 (A)
1989—49ers, 45-3 (SF)
49ers, 23-10 (A)
1990—49ers, 19-13 (SF)
49ers, 45-35 (A)
1991—Falcons, 39-34 (SF)
Falcons, 17-14 (A)
1992—49ers, 56-17 (SF)
49ers, 41-3 (A)
1993—49ers, 37-30 (SF)
Falcons, 27-24 (A)
1994—49ers, 42-3 (A)
49ers, 50-14 (SF)
1995—49ers, 41-10 (SF)
Falcons, 28-27 (A)
1996—49ers, 39-17 (SF)
49ers, 34-10 (A)
1997—49ers, 34-7 (SF)
49ers, 35-28 (A)
1998—49ers, 31-20 (SF)
Falcons, 31-19 (A)
*Falcons, 20-18 (A)
1999—49ers, 26-7 (SF)
Falcons, 34-29 (A)
2000—Falcons, 36-28 (A)
49ers, 16-6 (SF)
2001—49ers, 16-13 (SF) OT
49ers, 37-31 (A) OT
2004—Falcons, 21-19 (SF)
2007—Falcons, 20-16 (A)
(RS Pts.—49ers 1,746, Falcons 1,216)
(PS Pts.—Falcons 20, 49ers 18)
**NFC Divisional Playoff*

ATLANTA vs. SEATTLE
RS: Seahawks lead series, 8-3
1976—Seahawks, 30-13 (S)
1979—Seahawks, 31-28 (A)
1985—Seahawks, 30-26 (S)
1988—Seahawks, 31-20 (A)
1991—Falcons, 26-13 (A)
1997—Falcons, 24-17 (S)
2000—Seahawks, 30-10 (A)
2002—Seahawks, 30-24 (A) OT
2004—Seahawks, 28-26 (S)
2005—Seahawks, 21-18 (S)
2007—Falcons, 44-41 (A)
(RS Pts.—Seahawks 302, Falcons 259)

ATLANTA vs. TAMPA BAY
RS: Buccaneers lead series, 18-13
1977—Falcons, 17-0 (TB)
1978—Buccaneers, 14-9 (TB)
1979—Falcons, 17-14 (A)
1981—Buccaneers, 24-23 (TB)
1984—Buccaneers, 23-6 (TB)
1986—Falcons, 23-20 (TB) OT
1987—Buccaneers, 48-10 (TB)
1988—Falcons, 17-10 (A)
1990—Buccaneers, 23-17 (TB)
1991—Falcons, 43-7 (A)
1992—Falcons, 35-7 (TB)
1993—Buccaneers, 31-24 (A)
1994—Falcons, 34-13 (A)
1995—Falcons, 24-21 (TB)
1997—Buccaneers, 31-10 (A)
1999—Buccaneers, 19-10 (TB)
2000—Buccaneers, 27-14 (A)
2002—Buccaneers, 20-6 (A)
Buccaneers, 34-10 (TB)
2003—Buccaneers, 31-10 (A)
Falcons, 30-28 (TB)
2004—Falcons, 24-14 (A)
Buccaneers, 27-0 (TB)
2005—Buccaneers, 30-27 (A)
Buccaneers, 27-24 (TB) OT
2006—Falcons, 14-3 (A)
Falcons, 17-6 (TB)
2007—Buccaneers, 31-7 (A)
Buccaneers, 37-3 (TB)
2008—Buccaneers, 24-9 (TB)
Falcons, 13-10 (A) OT
(RS Pts.—Buccaneers 654, Falcons 527)

ATLANTA vs. *TENNESSEE
RS: Titans lead series, 7-5
1972—Falcons, 20-10 (A)
1976—Oilers, 20-14 (H)
1978—Falcons, 20-14 (A)
1981—Falcons, 31-27 (H)
1984—Falcons, 42-10 (A)
1987—Oilers, 37-33 (H)
1990—Falcons, 47-27 (A)
1993—Oilers, 33-17 (H)
1996—Oilers, 23-13 (A)
1999—Titans, 30-17 (T)
2003—Titans, 38-31 (A)
2007—Titans, 20-13 (T)
(RS Pts.—Falcons 298, Titans 289)
**Franchise in Houston prior to 1997; known as Oilers prior to 1999*

ATLANTA vs. WASHINGTON
RS: Redskins lead series, 14-5-1
PS: Redskins lead series, 1-0
1966—Redskins, 33-20 (W)
1967—Tie, 20-20 (A)
1969—Redskins, 27-20 (W)
1972—Redskins, 24-13 (W)
1975—Redskins, 30-27 (A)
1977—Redskins, 10-6 (W)
1978—Falcons, 20-17 (A)
1979—Redskins, 16-7 (A)
1980—Falcons, 10-6 (A)
1983—Redskins, 37-21 (W)
1984—Redskins, 27-14 (W)
1985—Redskins, 44-10 (A)
1987—Falcons, 21-20 (A)
1989—Redskins, 31-30 (A)
1991—Redskins, 56-17 (W)
*Redskins, 24-7 (W)
1992—Redskins, 24-17 (W)
1993—Redskins, 30-17 (W)
1994—Falcons, 27-20 (W)
2003—Redskins, 33-31 (A)
2006—Falcons, 24-14 (W)
(RS Pts.—Redskins 519, Falcons 372)
(PS Pts.—Redskins 24, Falcons 7)
**NFC Divisional Playoff*

BALTIMORE vs. ARIZONA
RS: Ravens lead series, 3-1;
See Arizona vs. Baltimore

BALTIMORE vs. ATLANTA
RS: Ravens lead series, 2-1;
See Atlanta vs. Baltimore

BALTIMORE vs. BUFFALO
RS: Series tied, 2-2
1999—Bills, 13-10 (Balt)
2004—Ravens, 20-6 (Balt)
2006—Ravens, 19-7 (Balt)
2007—Bills, 19-14 (Buf)
(RS Pts.—Ravens 63, Bills 45)

BALTIMORE vs. CAROLINA
RS: Panthers lead series, 3-0
1996—Panthers, 27-16 (C)
2002—Panthers, 10-7 (C)
2006—Panthers, 23-21 (B)
(RS Pts.—Panthers 60, Ravens 44)

BALTIMORE vs. CHICAGO
RS: Bears lead series, 2-1
1998—Bears, 24-3 (C)
2001—Ravens, 17-6 (B)
2005—Bears, 10-6 (C)
(RS Pts.—Bears 40, Ravens 26)

BALTIMORE vs. CINCINNATI
RS: Ravens lead series, 15-11
1996—Bengals, 24-21 (B)
Bengals, 21-14 (C)
1997—Ravens, 23-10 (B)
Bengals, 16-14 (C)
1998—Ravens, 31-24 (B)
Ravens, 20-13 (C)
1999—Ravens, 34-31 (C)
Ravens, 22-0 (B)

2000—Ravens, 37-0 (B)
Ravens, 27-7 (C)
2001—Bengals, 21-10 (C)
Ravens, 16-0 (B)
2002—Ravens, 38-27 (B)
Ravens, 27-23 (C)
2003—Bengals, 34-26 (C)
Ravens, 31-13 (B)
2004—Ravens, 23-9 (C)
Bengals, 27-26 (B)
2005—Bengals, 21-9 (B)
Bengals, 42-29 (C)
2006—Ravens, 26-20 (B)
Bengals, 13-7 (C)
2007—Bengals, 27-20 (C)
Bengals, 21-7 (B)
2008—Ravens, 17-10 (B)
Ravens, 34-3 (C)
(RS Pts.—Ravens 589, Bengals 457)

BALTIMORE vs. CLEVELAND
RS: Ravens lead series, 13-7
1999—Ravens, 17-10 (B)
Ravens, 41-9 (C)
2000—Ravens, 12-0 (C)
Ravens, 44-7 (B)
2001—Browns, 24-14 (C)
Browns, 27-17 (B)
2002—Ravens, 26-21 (C)
Browns, 14-13 (B)
2003—Ravens, 33-13 (B)
Ravens, 35-0 (C)
2004—Browns, 20-3 (C)
Ravens, 27-13 (B)
2005—Ravens, 16-3 (B)
Browns, 20-16 (C)
2006—Ravens, 15-14 (C)
Ravens, 27-17 (B)
2007—Browns, 27-13 (C)
Browns, 33-30 (B) OT
2008—Ravens, 28-10 (B)
Ravens, 37-27 (C)
(RS Pts.—Ravens 464, Browns 309)

BALTIMORE vs. DALLAS
RS: Ravens lead series, 3-0
2000—Ravens, 27-0 (B)
2004—Ravens, 30-10 (B)
2008—Ravens, 33-24 (D)
(RS Pts.—Ravens 90, Cowboys 34)

BALTIMORE vs. DENVER
RS: Series tied, 3-3
PS: Ravens lead series, 1-0
1996—Broncos, 45-34 (D)
2000—*Ravens, 21-3 (B)
2001—Ravens, 20-13 (D)
2002—Ravens, 34-23 (B)
2003—Ravens, 26-6 (B)
2005—Broncos, 12-10 (D)
2006—Broncos, 13-3 (D)
(RS Pts.—Ravens 127, Broncos 112)
(PS Pts.—Ravens 21, Broncos 3)
**AFC First-Round Playoff*

BALTIMORE vs. DETROIT
RS: Series tied, 1-1
1998—Ravens, 19-10 (B)
2005—Lions, 35-17 (D)
(RS Pts.—Lions 45, Ravens 36)

BALTIMORE vs. GREEN BAY
RS: Packers lead series, 2-1
1998—Packers, 28-10 (GB)
2001—Packers, 31-23 (GB)
2005—Ravens, 48-3 (B)
(RS Pts.—Ravens 81, Packers 62)

BALTIMORE vs. HOUSTON
RS: Ravens lead series, 3-0
2002—Ravens, 23-19 (H)
2005—Ravens, 16-15 (B)
2008—Ravens, 41-13 (H)
(RS Pts.—Ravens 80, Texans 47)

BALTIMORE vs. INDIANAPOLIS
RS: Colts lead series, 6-2
PS: Colts lead series, 1-0
1996—Colts, 26-21 (I)
1998—Ravens, 38-31 (B)
2001—Ravens, 39-27 (B)
2002—Colts, 22-20 (I)
2004—Colts, 20-10 (I)
2005—Colts, 24-7 (B)
2006—*Colts, 15-6 (B)
2007—Colts, 44-20 (B)
2008—Colts, 31-3 (I)
(RS Pts.—Colts 225, Ravens 158)
(PS Pts.—Colts 15, Ravens 6)
**AFC Divisional Playoff*

BALTIMORE vs. JACKSONVILLE
RS: Jaguars lead series, 9-7
1996—Jaguars, 30-27 (J)
Jaguars, 28-25 (B) OT
1997—Jaguars, 28-27 (B)
Jaguars, 29-27 (J)
1998—Jaguars, 24-10 (J)
Jaguars, 45-19 (B)
1999—Jaguars, 6-3 (J)
Jaguars, 30-23 (B)
2000—Ravens, 39-36 (B)
Ravens, 15-10 (J)
2001—Ravens, 18-17 (B)
Ravens, 24-21 (J)
2002—Ravens, 17-10 (B)
2003—Ravens, 24-17 (B)
2005—Jaguars, 30-3 (J)
2008—Ravens, 27-7 (B)
(RS Pts.—Jaguars 368, Ravens 328)

BALTIMORE vs. KANSAS CITY
RS: Chiefs lead series, 3-1
1999—Chiefs, 35-8 (B)
2003—Chiefs, 17-10 (B)
2004—Chiefs, 27-24 (B)
2006—Ravens, 20-10 (KC)
(RS Pts.—Chiefs 89, Ravens 62)

BALTIMORE vs. MIAMI
RS: Dolphins lead series, 5-2
PS: Ravens lead series, 2-0
1997—Dolphins, 24-13 (B)
2000—Dolphins, 19-6 (M)
2001—*Ravens, 20-3 (M)
2002—Dolphins, 26-7 (M)
2003—Dolphins, 9-6 (M) OT
2004—Ravens, 30-23 (B)
2007—Dolphins, 22-16 (M) OT
2008—Ravens, 27-13 (M)
*Ravens, 27-9 (M)
(RS Pts.—Dolphins 136, Ravens 105)
(PS Pts.—Ravens 47, Dolphins 12)
**AFC First-Round Playoff*

BALTIMORE vs. MINNESOTA
RS: Ravens lead series, 2-1
1998—Vikings, 38-28 (B)
2001—Ravens, 19-3 (B)
2005—Ravens, 30-23 (B)
(RS Pts.—Ravens 77, Vikings 64)

BALTIMORE vs. NEW ENGLAND
RS: Patriots lead series, 4-0
1996—Patriots, 46-38 (B)
1999—Patriots, 20-3 (NE)
2004—Patriots, 24-3 (NE)
2007—Patriots, 27-24 (B)
(RS Pts.—Patriots 117, Ravens 68)

BALTIMORE vs. NEW ORLEANS
RS: Ravens lead series, 3-1
1996—Ravens, 17-10 (B)
1999—Ravens, 31-8 (B)
2002—Saints, 37-25 (B)
2006—Ravens, 35-22 (NO)
(RS Pts.—Ravens 108, Saints 77)

BALTIMORE vs. N.Y. GIANTS
RS: Ravens lead series, 2-1
PS: Ravens lead series, 1-0
1997—Ravens, 24-23 (NY)
2000—*Ravens, 34-7 (Tampa)
2004—Ravens, 37-14 (B)
2008—Giants, 30-10 (NY)
(RS Pts.—Ravens 71, Giants 67)
(PS Pts.—Ravens 34, Giants 7)
**Super Bowl XXXV*

BALTIMORE vs. N.Y. JETS
RS: Ravens lead series, 5-1
1997—Jets, 19-16 (NY) OT
1998—Ravens, 24-10 (NY)
2000—Ravens, 34-20 (B)
2004—Ravens, 20-17 (NY) OT
2005—Ravens, 13-3 (B)
2007—Ravens, 20-13 (B)
(RS Pts.—Ravens 127, Jets 82)

BALTIMORE vs. OAKLAND
RS: Ravens lead series, 4-1
PS: Ravens lead series, 1-0
1996—Ravens, 19-14 (B)
1998—Ravens, 13-10 (B)
2000—*Ravens, 16-3 (O)
2003—Raiders, 20-12 (O)
2006—Ravens, 28-6 (B)
2008—Ravens, 29-10 (B)
(RS Pts.—Ravens 101, Raiders 60)
(PS Pts.—Ravens 16, Raiders 3)
**AFC Championship*

BALTIMORE vs. PHILADELPHIA
RS: Series tied, 1-1-1
1997—Tie, 10-10 (B) OT
2004—Eagles, 15-10 (P)
2008—Ravens, 36-7 (B)
(RS Pts.—Eagles 56, Ravens 32)

BALTIMORE vs. PITTSBURGH
RS: Steelers lead series, 16-10
PS: Steelers lead series, 2-0
1996—Steelers, 31-17 (P)
Ravens, 31-17 (B)
1997—Steelers, 42-34 (B)
Steelers, 37-0 (P)
1998—Steelers, 20-13 (B)
Steelers, 16-6 (P)
1999—Steelers, 23-20 (B)
Ravens, 31-24 (P)
2000—Ravens, 16-0 (P)
Steelers, 9-6 (B)
2001—Ravens, 13-10 (P)
Steelers, 26-21 (B)
*Steelers, 27-10 (P)
2002—Steelers, 31-18 (B)
Steelers, 34-31 (P)
2003—Steelers, 34-15 (P)

Ravens, 13-10 (B) OT
2004—Ravens, 30-13 (B)
Steelers, 20-7 (P)
2005—Steelers, 20-19 (P)
Ravens, 16-13 (B) OT
2006—Ravens, 27-0 (B)
Ravens, 31-7 (P)
2007—Steelers, 38-7 (P)
Ravens, 27-21 (B)
2008—Steelers, 23-20 (P) OT
Steelers, 13-9 (B)
**Steelers, 23-14 (P)
(RS Pts.—Steelers 532, Ravens 478)
(PS Pts.—Steelers 50, Ravens 24)
AFC Divisional Playoff
***AFC Championship*

BALTIMORE vs. ST. LOUIS
RS: Series tied, 2-2
1996—Ravens, 37-31 (B) OT
1999—Rams, 27-10 (StL)
2003—Rams, 33-22 (StL)
2007—Ravens, 22-3 (B)
(RS Pts.—Rams 94, Ravens 91)

BALTIMORE vs. SAN DIEGO
RS: Series tied, 3-3
1997—Chargers, 21-17 (SD)
1998—Chargers, 14-13 (SD)
2000—Ravens, 24-3 (B)
2003—Ravens, 24-10 (SD)
2006—Ravens, 16-13 (B)
2007—Chargers, 32-14 (SD)
(RS Pts.—Ravens 108, Chargers 93)

BALTIMORE vs. SAN FRANCISCO
RS: Ravens lead series, 2-1
1996—49ers, 38-20 (SF)
2003—Ravens, 44-6 (B)
2007—Ravens, 9-7 (SF)
(RS Pts.—Ravens 73, 49ers 51)

BALTIMORE vs. SEATTLE
RS: Ravens lead series, 2-1
1997—Ravens, 31-24 (B)
2003—Ravens, 44-41 (B) OT
2007—Seahawks, 27-6 (S)
(RS Pts.—Seahawks 92, Ravens 81)

BALTIMORE vs. TAMPA BAY
RS: Buccaneers lead series, 2-1
2001—Buccaneers, 22-10 (TB)
2002—Buccaneers, 25-0 (B)
2006—Ravens, 27-0 (B)
(RS Pts.—Buccaneers 47, Ravens 37)

BALTIMORE vs. *TENNESSEE
RS: Series tied, 8-8
PS: Ravens lead series, 2-1
1996—Oilers, 29-13 (H)
Oilers, 24-21 (B)
1997—Ravens, 36-10 (T)
Ravens, 21-19 (B)
1998—Oilers, 12-8 (B)
Oilers, 16-14 (T)
1999—Titans, 14-11 (T)
Ravens, 41-14 (B)
2000—Titans, 14-6 (B)
Ravens, 24-23 (T)
**Ravens, 24-10 (T)
2001—Ravens, 26-7 (B)
Ravens, 16-10 (T)
2002—Ravens, 13-12 (B)
2003—***Titans, 20-17 (B)
2005—Titans, 25-10 (T)
2006—Ravens, 27-26 (T)
2008—Titans, 13-10 (B)
**Ravens, 13-10 (T)
(RS Pts.—Ravens 297, Titans 268)
(PS Pts.—Ravens 54, Titans 40)
**Franchise in Houston prior to 1997; known as Oilers prior to 1999*
***AFC Divisional Playoff*
****AFC First-Round Playoff*

BALTIMORE vs. WASHINGTON
RS: Ravens lead series, 3-1
1997—Ravens, 20-17 (W)
2000—Redskins, 10-3 (W)
2004—Ravens, 17-10 (W)
2008—Ravens, 24-10 (B)
(RS Pts.—Ravens 64, Redskins 47)

BUFFALO vs. ARIZONA
RS: Bills lead series, 5-4;
See Arizona vs. Buffalo

BUFFALO vs. ATLANTA
RS: Falcons lead series, 5-4;
See Atlanta vs. Buffalo

BUFFALO vs. BALTIMORE
RS: Series tied, 2-2;
See Baltimore vs. Buffalo

BUFFALO vs. CAROLINA
RS: Bills lead series, 3-1
1995—Bills, 31-9 (B)
1998—Bills, 30-14 (C)
2001—Bills, 25-24 (B)
2005—Panthers, 13-9 (B)
(RS Pts.—Bills 95, Panthers 60)

BUFFALO vs. CHICAGO
RS: Bears lead series, 6-4
1970—Bears, 31-13 (C)
1974—Bills, 16-6 (B)
1979—Bears, 7-0 (B)
1988—Bears, 24-3 (C)
1991—Bills, 35-20 (B)
1994—Bears, 20-13 (C)
1997—Bears, 20-3 (C)
2000—Bills, 20-3 (B)
2002—Bills, 33-27 (B) OT
2006—Bears, 40-7 (C)
(RS Pts.—Bears 198, Bills 143)

BUFFALO vs. CINCINNATI
RS: Bills lead series, 14-9
PS: Bengals lead series, 2-0
1968—Bengals, 34-23 (C)
1969—Bills, 16-13 (B)
1970—Bengals, 43-14 (B)
1973—Bengals, 16-13 (B)
1975—Bengals, 33-24 (C)
1978—Bills, 5-0 (B)
1979—Bills, 51-24 (B)
1980—Bills, 14-0 (C)
1981—Bengals, 27-24 (C) OT
*Bengals, 28-21 (C)
1983—Bills, 10-6 (C)
1984—Bengals, 52-21 (C)
1985—Bengals, 23-17 (B)
1986—Bengals, 36-33 (C) OT
1988—Bengals, 35-21 (C)
**Bengals, 21-10 (C)
1989—Bills, 24-7 (B)
1991—Bills, 35-16 (B)
1996—Bills, 31-17 (B)
1998—Bills, 33-20 (C)
2002—Bills, 27-9 (B)
2003—Bills, 22-16 (B) OT
2004—Bills, 33-17 (C)
2005—Bills, 37-27 (C)
2007—Bills, 33-21 (B)
(RS Pts.—Bills 561, Bengals 492)
(PS Pts.—Bengals 49, Bills 31)
**AFC Divisional Playoff*
***AFC Championship*

BUFFALO vs. CLEVELAND
RS: Browns lead series, 9-5
PS: Browns lead series, 1-0
1972—Browns, 27-10 (C)
1974—Bills, 15-10 (C)
1977—Browns, 27-16 (B)
1978—Browns, 41-20 (C)
1981—Bills, 22-13 (B)
1984—Browns, 13-10 (B)
1985—Browns, 17-7 (C)
1986—Browns, 21-17 (B)
1987—Browns, 27-21 (C)
1989—*Browns, 34-30 (C)
1990—Bills, 42-0 (C)
1995—Bills, 22-19 (C)
2004—Bills, 37-7 (B)
2007—Browns, 8-0 (C)
2008—Browns, 29-27 (B)
(RS Pts.—Bills 266, Browns 259)
(PS Pts.—Browns 34, Bills 30)
**AFC Divisional Playoff*

BUFFALO vs. DALLAS
RS: Cowboys lead series, 5-3
PS: Cowboys lead series, 2-0
1971—Cowboys, 49-37 (B)
1976—Cowboys, 17-10 (D)
1981—Cowboys, 27-14 (D)
1984—Bills, 14-3 (B)
1992—*Cowboys, 52-17 (Pasadena)
1993—Bills, 13-10 (D)
**Cowboys, 30-13 (Atlanta)
1996—Bills, 10-7 (B)
2003—Cowboys, 10-6 (D)
2007—Cowboys, 25-24 (B)
(RS Pts.—Cowboys 148, Bills 128)
(PS Pts.—Cowboys 82, Bills 30)
**Super Bowl XXVII*
***Super Bowl XXVIII*

BUFFALO vs. DENVER
RS: Bills lead series, 18-15-1
PS: Bills lead series, 1-0
1960—Broncos, 27-21 (B)
Tie, 38-38 (D)
1961—Broncos, 22-10 (B)
Bills, 23-10 (D)
1962—Broncos, 23-20 (B)
Bills, 45-38 (D)
1963—Bills, 30-28 (D)
Bills, 27-17 (B)
1964—Bills, 30-13 (B)
Bills, 30-19 (D)
1965—Bills, 30-15 (D)
Bills, 31-13 (B)
1966—Bills, 38-21 (B)
1967—Bills, 17-16 (D)
Broncos, 21-20 (B)
1968—Broncos, 34-32 (D)
1969—Bills, 41-28 (B)
1970—Broncos, 25-10 (B)
1975—Bills, 38-14 (B)
1977—Broncos, 26-6 (D)
1979—Broncos, 19-16 (B)
1981—Bills, 9-7 (B)

1984—Broncos, 37-7 (B)
1987—Bills, 21-14 (B)
1989—Broncos, 28-14 (B)
1990—Bills, 29-28 (B)
1991—*Bills, 10-7 (B)
1992—Bills, 27-17 (B)
1994—Bills, 27-20 (B)
1995—Broncos, 22-7 (D)
1997—Broncos, 23-20 (B) OT
2002—Broncos, 28-23 (D)
2005—Broncos, 28-17 (B)
2007—Broncos, 15-14 (B)
2008—Bills, 30-23 (D)
(RS Pts.—Bills 798, Broncos 757)
(PS Pts.—Bills 10, Broncos 7)
AFC Championship

BUFFALO vs. DETROIT
RS: Lions lead series, 4-3-1
1972—Tie, 21-21 (B)
1976—Lions, 27-14 (D)
1979—Bills, 20-17 (D)
1991—Lions, 17-14 (B) OT
1994—Lions, 35-21 (D)
1997—Bills, 22-13 (B)
2002—Bills, 24-17 (B)
2006—Lions, 20-17 (D)
(RS Pts.—Lions 167, Bills 153)

BUFFALO vs. GREEN BAY
RS: Bills lead series, 7-3
1974—Bills, 27-7 (GB)
1979—Bills, 19-12 (B)
1982—Packers, 33-21 (Mil)
1988—Bills, 28-0 (B)
1991—Bills, 34-24 (Mil)
1994—Bills 29-20 (B)
1997—Packers, 31-21 (GB)
2000—Bills 27-18 (B)
2002—Packers, 10-0 (GB)
2006—Bills, 24-10 (B)
(RS Pts.—Bills 230, Packers 165)

BUFFALO vs. HOUSTON
RS: Bills lead series, 3-1
2002—Bills, 31-24 (H)
2003—Texans, 12-10 (B)
2005—Bills, 22-7 (B)
2006—Bills, 24-21 (H)
(RS Pts.—Bills 87, Texans 64)

BUFFALO vs. *INDIANAPOLIS
RS: Bills lead series, 34-30-1
1970—Tie, 17-17 (Balt)
Colts, 20-14 (Buff)
1971—Colts, 43-0 (Buff)
Colts, 24-0 (Balt)
1972—Colts, 17-0 (Buff)
Colts, 35-7 (Balt)
1973—Bills, 31-13 (Buff)
Bills, 24-17 (Balt)
1974—Bills, 27-14 (Balt)
Bills, 6-0 (Buff)
1975—Bills, 38-31 (Balt)
Colts, 42-35 (Buff)
1976—Colts, 31-13 (Buff)
Colts, 58-20 (Balt)
1977—Colts, 17-14 (Balt)
Colts, 31-13 (Buff)
1978—Bills, 24-17 (Buff)
Bills, 21-14 (Balt)
1979—Bills, 31-13 (Balt)
Colts, 14-13 (Buff)
1980—Colts, 17-12 (Buff)
Colts, 28-24 (Balt)
1981—Bills, 35-3 (Balt)
Bills, 23-17 (Buff)
1982—Bills, 20-0 (Buff)
1983—Bills, 28-23 (Buff)
Bills, 30-7 (Balt)
1984—Colts, 31-17 (I)
Bills, 21-15 (Buff)
1985—Colts, 49-17 (I)
Bills, 21-9 (Buff)
1986—Bills, 24-13 (Buff)
Colts, 24-14 (I)
1987—Colts, 47-6 (Buff)
Bills, 27-3 (I)
1988—Bills, 34-23 (Buff)
Colts, 17-14 (I)
1989—Colts, 37-14 (I)
Bills, 30-7 (Buff)
1990—Bills, 26-10 (Buff)
Bills, 31-7 (I)
1991—Bills, 42-6 (Buff)
Bills, 35-7 (I)
1992—Bills, 38-0 (Buff)
Colts, 16-13 (I) OT
1993—Bills, 23-9 (Buff)
Bills, 30-10 (I)
1994—Colts, 27-17 (Buff)
Colts, 10-9 (I)
1995—Bills, 20-14 (Buff)
Bills, 16-10 (I)
1996—Bills, 16-13 (Buff) OT
Colts, 13-10 (I) OT
1997—Bills, 37-35 (B)
Bills, 9-6 (I)
1998—Bills, 31-24 (I)
Bills, 34-11 (B)
1999—Colts, 31-14 (I)
Bills, 31-6 (B)
2000—Colts, 18-16 (B)
Colts, 44-20 (I)
2001—Colts, 42-26 (I)
Colts, 30-14 (B)
2003—Colts, 17-14 (B)
2006—Colts, 17-16 (I)
(RS Pts.—Bills 1,347, Colts 1,271)
Franchise in Baltimore prior to 1984

BUFFALO vs. JACKSONVILLE
RS: Bills lead series, 5-3
PS: Jaguars lead series, 1-0
1996—*Jaguars, 30-27 (B)
1997—Jaguars, 20-14 (B)
1998—Bills, 17-16 (B)
2001—Bills, 13-10 (J)
2003—Bills, 38-17 (J)
2004—Jaguars, 13-10 (B)
2006—Bills, 27-24 (B)
2007—Jaguars, 36-14 (J)
2008—Bills, 20-16 (J)
(RS Pts.—Bills 153, Jaguars 152)
(PS Pts.—Jaguars 30, Bills 27)
AFC First-Round Playoff

BUFFALO vs. *KANSAS CITY
RS: Bills lead series, 20-16-1
PS: Bills lead series, 2-1
1960—Texans, 45-28 (B)
Texans, 24-7 (D)
1961—Bills, 27-24 (B)
Bills, 30-20 (D)
1962—Texans, 41-21 (D)
Bills, 23-14 (B)
1963—Tie, 27-27 (B)
Bills, 35-26 (KC)
1964—Bills, 34-17 (B)
Bills, 35-22 (KC)
1965—Bills, 23-7 (KC)
Bills, 34-25 (B)
1966—Chiefs, 42-20 (B)
Bills, 29-14 (KC)
**Chiefs, 31-7 (B)
1967—Chiefs, 23-13 (KC)
1968—Chiefs, 18-7 (B)
1969—Chiefs, 29-7 (B)
Chiefs, 22-19 (KC)
1971—Chiefs, 22-9 (KC)
1973—Bills, 23-14 (B)
1976—Bills, 50-17 (B)
1978—Bills, 28-13 (B)
Chiefs, 14-10 (KC)
1982—Bills, 14-9 (B)
1983—Bills, 14-9 (KC)
1986—Chiefs, 20-17 (B)
Bills, 17-14 (KC)
1991—Chiefs, 33-6 (KC)
***Bills, 37-14 (B)
1993—Chiefs, 23-7 (KC)
****Bills, 30-13 (B)
1994—Bills, 44-10 (B)
1996—Bills, 20-9 (B)
1997—Chiefs, 22-16 (KC)
2000—Bills, 21-17 (KC)
2002—Chiefs, 17-16 (KC)
2003—Chiefs, 38-5 (KC)
2005—Bills, 14-3 (B)
2008—Bills, 54-31 (KC)
(RS Pts.—Bills 804, Chiefs 775)
(PS Pts.—Bills 74, Chiefs 58)
Franchise in Dallas prior to 1963 and known as Texans
***AFL Championship*
****AFC Divisional Playoff*
*****AFC Championship*

BUFFALO vs. MIAMI
RS: Dolphins lead series, 51-34-1
PS: Bills lead series, 3-1
1966—Bills, 58-24 (B)
Bills, 29-0 (M)
1967—Bills, 35-13 (B)
Dolphins, 17-14 (M)
1968—Tie, 14-14 (M)
Dolphins, 21-17 (B)
1969—Dolphins, 24-6 (M)
Bills, 28-3 (B)
1970—Dolphins, 33-14 (B)
Dolphins, 45-7 (M)
1971—Dolphins, 29-14 (B)
Dolphins, 34-0 (M)
1972—Dolphins, 24-23 (M)
Dolphins, 30-16 (B)
1973—Dolphins, 27-6 (M)
Dolphins, 17-0 (B)
1974—Dolphins, 24-16 (B)
Dolphins, 35-28 (M)
1975—Dolphins, 35-30 (B)
Dolphins, 31-21 (M)
1976—Dolphins, 30-21 (B)
Dolphins, 45-27 (M)
1977—Dolphins, 13-0 (B)
Dolphins, 31-14 (M)
1978—Dolphins, 31-24 (M)
Dolphins, 25-24 (B)

1979—Dolphins, 9-7 (B)
Dolphins, 17-7 (M)
1980—Bills, 17-7 (B)
Dolphins, 17-14 (M)
1981—Bills, 31-21 (B)
Dolphins, 16-6 (M)
1982—Dolphins, 9-7 (B)
Dolphins, 27-10 (M)
1983—Dolphins, 12-0 (B)
Bills, 38-35 (M) OT
1984—Dolphins, 21-17 (B)
Dolphins, 38-7 (M)
1985—Dolphins, 23-14 (B)
Dolphins, 28-0 (M)
1986—Dolphins, 27-14 (M)
Dolphins, 34-24 (B)
1987—Bills, 34-31 (M) OT
Bills, 27-0 (B)
1988—Bills, 9-6 (B)
Bills, 31-6 (M)
1989—Bills, 27-24 (M)
Bills, 31-17 (B)
1990—Dolphins, 30-7 (M)
Bills, 24-14 (B)
*Bills, 44-34 (B)
1991—Bills, 35-31 (B)
Bills, 41-27 (M)
1992—Dolphins, 37-10 (B)
Bills, 26-20 (M)
**Bills, 29-10 (M)
1993—Dolphins, 22-13 (B)
Bills, 47-34 (M)
1994—Bills, 21-11 (B)
Bills, 42-31 (M)
1995—Dolphins, 23-6 (M)
Bills, 23-20 (B)
***Bills, 37-22 (B)
1996—Dolphins, 21-7 (B)
Dolphins, 16-14 (M)
1997—Bills, 9-6 (B)
Dolphins, 30-13 (M)
1998—Dolphins, 13-7 (M)
Bills, 30-24 (B)
***Dolphins, 24-17 (M)
1999—Bills, 23-18 (M)
Bills, 23-3 (B)
2000—Dolphins, 22-13 (M)
Dolphins, 33-6 (B)
2001—Dolphins, 34-27 (B)
Dolphins, 34-7 (M)
2002—Bills, 23-10 (M)
Bills, 38-21 (B)
2003—Dolphins, 17-7 (M)
Dolphins, 20-3 (B)
2004—Bills, 20-13 (B)
Bills, 42-32 (M)
2005—Bills, 20-14 (B)
Dolphins, 24-23 (M)
2006—Bills, 16-6 (M)
Bills, 21-0 (B)
2007—Bills, 13-10 (M)
Bills, 38-17 (B)
2008—Dolphins, 25-16 (M)
Dolphins, 16-3 (Toronto)
(RS Pts.—Dolphins 1,859, Bills 1,615)
(PS Pts.—Bills 127, Dolphins 90)
AFC Divisional Playoff
**AFC Championship*
***AFC First-Round Playoff*

BUFFALO vs. MINNESOTA
RS: Vikings lead series, 7-4
1971—Vikings, 19-0 (M)
1975—Vikings, 35-13 (B)
1979—Vikings, 10-3 (M)
1982—Bills, 23-22 (B)
1985—Vikings, 27-20 (B)
1988—Bills, 13-10 (B)
1994—Vikings, 21-17 (B)
1997—Vikings, 34-13 (B)
2000—Vikings, 31-27 (M)
2002—Bills, 45-39 (M) OT
2006—Bills, 17-12 (B)
(RS Pts.—Vikings 260, Bills 191)

BUFFALO vs. *NEW ENGLAND
RS: Patriots lead series, 56-40-1
PS: Patriots lead series, 1-0
1960—Bills, 13-0 (Bos)
Bills, 38-14 (Buff)
1961—Patriots, 23-21 (Buff)
Patriots, 52-21 (Bos)
1962—Tie, 28-28 (Buff)
Patriots, 21-10 (Bos)
1963—Bills, 28-21 (Buff)
Patriots, 17-7 (Bos)
**Patriots, 26-8 (Buff)
1964—Patriots, 36-28 (Buff)
Bills, 24-14 (Bos)
1965—Bills, 24-7 (Buff)
Bills, 23-7 (Bos)
1966—Patriots, 20-10 (Buff)
Patriots, 14-3 (Bos)
1967—Patriots, 23-0 (Buff)
Bills, 44-16 (Bos)
1968—Patriots, 16-7 (Buff)
Patriots, 23-6 (Bos)
1969—Bills, 23-16 (Buff)
Patriots, 35-21 (Bos)
1970—Bills, 45-10 (Bos)
Patriots, 14-10 (Buff)
1971—Patriots, 38-33 (NE)
Bills, 27-20 (Buff)
1972—Bills, 38-14 (Buff)
Bills, 27-24 (NE)
1973—Bills, 31-13 (NE)
Bills, 37-13 (Buff)
1974—Bills, 30-28 (Buff)
Bills, 29-28 (NE)
1975—Bills, 45-31 (Buff)
Bills, 34-14 (NE)
1976—Patriots, 26-22 (Buff)
Patriots, 20-10 (NE)
1977—Bills, 24-14 (NE)
Patriots, 20-7 (Buff)
1978—Patriots, 14-10 (Buff)
Patriots, 26-24 (NE)
1979—Patriots, 26-6 (Buff)
Bills, 16-13 (NE) OT
1980—Bills, 31-13 (Buff)
Patriots, 24-2 (NE)
1981—Bills, 20-17 (Buff)
Bills, 19-10 (NE)
1982—Patriots, 30-19 (NE)
1983—Patriots, 31-0 (Buff)
Patriots, 21-7 (NE)
1984—Patriots, 21-17 (Buff)
Patriots, 38-10 (NE)
1985—Patriots, 17-14 (Buff)
Patriots, 14-3 (NE)
1986—Patriots, 23-3 (Buff)
Patriots, 22-19 (NE)
1987—Patriots, 14-7 (NE)
Patriots, 13-7 (Buff)
1988—Bills, 16-14 (NE)
Bills, 23-20 (Buff)
1989—Bills, 31-10 (Buff)
Patriots, 33-24 (NE)
1990—Bills, 27-10 (NE)
Bills, 14-0 (Buff)
1991—Bills, 22-17 (Buff)
Patriots, 16-13 (NE)
1992—Bills, 41-7 (NE)
Bills, 16-7 (Buff)
1993—Bills, 38-14 (Buff)
Bills, 13-10 (NE) OT
1994—Bills, 38-35 (NE)
Patriots, 41-17 (Buff)
1995—Patriots, 27-14 (NE)
Patriots, 35-25 (Buff)
1996—Bills, 17-10 (Buff)
Patriots, 28-25 (NE)
1997—Patriots, 33-6 (NE)
Patriots, 31-10 (Buff)
1998—Bills, 13-10 (Buff)
Patriots, 25-21 (NE)
1999—Bills, 17-7 (Buff)
Bills, 13-10 (NE) OT
2000—Bills, 16-13 (NE) OT
Patriots, 13-10 (Buff) OT
2001—Patriots, 21-11 (NE)
Patriots, 12-9 (Buff) OT
2002—Patriots, 38-7 (Buff)
Patriots, 27-17 (NE)
2003—Bills, 31-0 (Buff)
Patriots, 31-0 (NE)
2004—Patriots, 31-17 (Buff)
Patriots, 29-6 (NE)
2005—Patriots, 21-16 (NE)
Patriots, 35-7 (Buff)
2006—Patriots, 19-17 (NE)
Patriots, 28-6 (B)
2007—Patriots, 38-7 (NE)
Patriots, 56-10 (Buff)
2008—Patriots, 20-10 (NE)
Patriots, 13-0 (B)
(RS Pts.—Patriots 2,012, Bills 1,753)
(PS Pts.—Patriots 26, Bills 8)
Franchise in Boston prior to 1971
**Division Playoff*

BUFFALO vs. NEW ORLEANS
RS: Series tied, 4-4
1973—Saints, 13-0 (NO)
1980—Bills, 35-26 (NO)
1983—Bills, 27-21 (B)
1989—Saints, 22-19 (B)
1992—Bills, 20-16 (NO)
1998—Bills, 45-33 (NO)
2001—Saints, 24-6 (B)
2005—Saints, 19-7 (San Antonio)
(RS Pts.—Saints 174, Bills 159)

BUFFALO vs. N.Y. GIANTS
RS: Bills lead series, 6-4
PS: Giants lead series, 1-0
1970—Giants, 20-6 (NY)
1975—Giants, 17-14 (B)
1978—Bills, 41-17 (B)
1987—Bills, 6-3 (B) OT
1990—Bills, 17-13 (NY)
*Giants, 20-19 (Tampa)
1993—Bills, 17-14 (B)

1996—Bills, 23-20 (NY) OT
1999—Giants, 19-17 (B)
2003—Bills, 24-7 (NY)
2007—Giants, 38-21 (B)
(RS Pts.—Bills 186, Giants 168)
(PS Pts.—Giants 20, Bills 19)
Super Bowl XXV

BUFFALO vs. *N.Y. JETS
RS: Bills lead series, 52-44
PS: Bills lead series, 1-0
1960—Titans, 27-3 (NY)
Titans, 17-13 (B)
1961—Bills, 41-31 (B)
Titans, 21-14 (NY)
1962—Titans, 17-6 (B)
Bills, 20-3 (NY)
1963—Bills, 45-14 (B)
Bills, 19-10 (NY)
1964—Bills, 34-24 (B)
Bills, 20-7 (NY)
1965—Bills, 33-21 (B)
Jets, 14-12 (NY)
1966—Bills, 33-23 (NY)
Bills, 14-3 (B)
1967—Bills, 20-17 (B)
Jets, 20-10 (NY)
1968—Bills, 37-35 (B)
Jets, 25-21 (NY)
1969—Jets, 33-19 (B)
Jets, 16-6 (NY)
1970—Bills, 34-31 (B)
Bills, 10-6 (NY)
1971—Jets, 28-17 (NY)
Jets, 20-7 (B)
1972—Jets, 41-24 (B)
Jets, 41-3 (NY)
1973—Bills, 9-7 (B)
Bills, 34-14 (NY)
1974—Bills, 16-12 (B)
Jets, 20-10 (NY)
1975—Bills, 42-14 (B)
Bills, 24-23 (NY)
1976—Jets, 17-14 (NY)
Jets, 19-14 (B)
1977—Jets, 24-19 (B)
Bills, 14-10 (NY)
1978—Jets, 21-20 (B)
Jets, 45-14 (NY)
1979—Bills, 46-31 (B)
Bills, 14-12 (NY)
1980—Bills, 20-10 (B)
Bills, 31-24 (NY)
1981—Bills, 31-0 (B)
Jets, 33-14 (NY)
**Bills, 31-27 (NY)
1983—Jets, 34-10 (B)
Bills, 24-17 (NY)
1984—Jets, 28-26 (B)
Jets, 21-17 (NY)
1985—Jets, 42-3 (NY)
Jets, 27-7 (B)
1986—Jets, 28-24 (B)
Jets, 14-13 (NY)
1987—Jets, 31-28 (B)
Bills, 17-14 (NY)
1988—Bills, 37-14 (NY)
Bills, 9-6 (B) OT
1989—Bills, 34-3 (B)
Bills, 37-0 (NY)
1990—Bills, 30-7 (NY)
Bills, 30-27 (B)
1991—Bills, 23-20 (NY)
Bills, 24-13 (B)
1992—Bills, 24-20 (NY)
Jets, 24-17 (B)
1993—Bills, 19-10 (NY)
Bills, 16-14 (B)
1994—Jets, 23-3 (B)
Jets, 22-17 (NY)
1995—Bills, 29-10 (B)
Bills, 28-26 (NY)
1996—Bills, 25-22 (NY)
Bills, 35-10 (B)
1997—Bills, 28-22 (NY)
Bills, 20-10 (B)
1998—Jets, 34-12 (NY)
Jets, 17-10 (B)
1999—Bills, 17-3 (B)
Jets, 17-7 (NY)
2000—Jets, 27-14 (NY)
Bills, 23-20 (B)
2001—Jets, 42-36 (B)
Bills, 14-9 (NY)
2002—Jets, 37-31 (B) OT
Jets, 31-13 (NY)
2003—Jets, 30-3 (NY)
Bills, 17-6 (B)
2004—Jets, 16-14 (NY)
Bills, 22-17 (B)
2005—Bills, 27-17 (B)
Jets, 30-26 (NY)
2006—Jets, 28-20 (B)
Bills, 31-13 (NY)
2007—Bills, 17-14 (B)
Bills, 13-3 (NY)
2008—Jets, 26-17 (B)
Jets, 31-27 (NY)
(RS Pts.—Bills 1,966, Jets 1,908)
(PS Pts.—Bills 31, Jets 27)
**Jets known as Titans prior to 1963*
***AFC First-Round Playoff*

BUFFALO vs. *OAKLAND
RS: Raiders lead series, 19-16
PS: Bills lead series, 2-0
1960—Bills, 38-9 (B)
Raiders, 20-7 (O)
1961—Raiders, 31-22 (B)
Bills, 26-21 (O)
1962—Bills, 14-6 (B)
Bills, 10-6 (O)
1963—Raiders, 35-17 (O)
Bills, 12-0 (B)
1964—Bills, 23-20 (B)
Raiders, 16-13 (O)
1965—Bills, 17-12 (B)
Bills, 17-14 (O)
1966—Bills, 31-10 (O)
1967—Raiders, 24-20 (B)
Raiders, 28-21 (O)
1968—Raiders, 48-6 (B)
Raiders, 13-10 (O)
1969—Raiders, 50-21 (O)
1972—Raiders, 28-16 (O)
1974—Bills, 21-20 (B)
1977—Raiders, 34-13 (O)
1980—Bills, 24-7 (B)
1983—Raiders, 27-24 (B)
1987—Raiders, 34-21 (LA)
1988—Bills, 37-21 (B)
1990—Bills, 38-24 (B)
**Bills, 51-3 (B)
1991—Bills, 30-27 (LA) OT
1992—Raiders, 20-3 (LA)
1993—Raiders, 25-24 (B)
***Bills, 29-23 (B)
1998—Bills, 44-21 (B)
1999—Raiders, 20-14 (B)
2002—Raiders, 49-31 (B)
2004—Raiders, 13-10 (O)
2005—Raiders, 38-17 (O)
2008—Bills, 24-23 (B)
(RS Pts.—Raiders 794, Bills 716)
(PS Pts.—Bills 80, Raiders 26)
**Franchise in Los Angeles from 1982-1994*
***AFC Championship*
****AFC Divisional Playoff*

BUFFALO vs. PHILADELPHIA
RS: Eagles lead series, 6-5
1973—Bills, 27-26 (B)
1981—Eagles, 20-14 (B)
1984—Eagles, 27-17 (B)
1985—Eagles, 21-17 (P)
1987—Eagles, 17-7 (P)
1990—Bills, 30-23 (B)
1993—Bills, 10-7 (P)
1996—Bills, 24-17 (P)
1999—Bills, 26-0 (B)
2003—Eagles, 23-13 (B)
2007—Eagles, 17-9 (P)
(RS Pts.—Eagles 198, Bills 194)

BUFFALO vs. PITTSBURGH
RS: Steelers lead series, 11-8
PS: Steelers lead series, 2-1
1970—Steelers, 23-10 (P)
1972—Steelers, 38-21 (B)
1974—*Steelers, 32-14 (P)
1975—Bills, 30-21 (P)
1978—Steelers, 28-17 (B)
1979—Steelers, 28-0 (P)
1980—Bills, 28-13 (B)
1982—Bills, 13-0 (B)
1985—Steelers, 30-24 (P)
1986—Bills, 16-12 (B)
1988—Bills, 36-28 (B)
1991—Bills, 52-34 (B)
1992—Bills, 28-20 (B)
*Bills, 24-3 (P)
1993—Steelers, 23-0 (P)
1994—Steelers, 23-10 (P)
1995—*Steelers, 40-21 (P)
1996—Steelers, 24-6 (P)
1999—Bills, 24-21 (B)
2001—Steelers, 20-3 (B)
2004—Steelers, 29-24 (B)
2007—Steelers, 26-3 (P)
(RS Pts.—Steelers 441, Bills 345)
(PS Pts.—Steelers 75, Bills 59)
**AFC Divisional Playoff*

BUFFALO vs. *ST. LOUIS
RS: Bills lead series, 6-4
1970—Rams, 19-0 (B)
1974—Rams, 19-14 (LA)
1980—Bills, 10-7 (B) OT
1983—Rams, 41-17 (LA)
1989—Bills, 23-20 (B)
1992—Bills, 40-7 (B)
1995—Bills, 45-27 (StL)
1998—Rams, 34-33 (B)
2004—Bills, 37-17 (B)
2008—Bills, 31-14 (StL)

(RS Pts.—Bills 250, Rams 205)
Franchise in Los Angeles prior to 1995

BUFFALO vs. *SAN DIEGO
RS: Chargers lead series, 20-10-2
PS: Bills lead series, 2-1
1960—Chargers, 24-10 (B)
Bills, 32-3 (LA)
1961—Chargers, 19-11 (B)
Chargers, 28-10 (SD)
1962—Bills, 35-10 (B)
Bills, 40-20 (SD)
1963—Chargers, 14-10 (SD)
Chargers, 23-13 (B)
1964—Bills, 30-3 (B)
Bills, 27-24 (SD)
**Bills, 20-7 (B)
1965—Chargers, 34-3 (B)
Tie, 20-20 (SD)
**Bills, 23-0 (SD)
1966—Chargers, 27-7 (SD)
Tie, 17-17 (B)
1967—Chargers, 37-17 (B)
1968—Chargers, 21-6 (B)
1969—Chargers, 45-6 (SD)
1971—Chargers, 20-3 (SD)
1973—Chargers, 34-7 (SD)
1976—Chargers, 34-13 (B)
1979—Chargers, 27-19 (SD)
1980—Bills, 26-24 (SD)
***Chargers, 20-14 (SD)
1981—Bills, 28-27 (SD)
1985—Chargers, 14-9 (B)
Chargers, 40-7 (SD)
1998—Chargers, 16-14 (SD)
2000—Bills, 27-24 (B) OT
2001—Chargers, 27-24 (SD)
2002—Bills, 20-13 (B)
2005—Chargers, 48-10 (SD)
2006—Chargers, 24-21 (B)
2008—Bills, 23-14 (B)
(RS Pts.—Chargers 755, Bills 545)
(PS Pts.—Bills 57, Chargers 27)
Franchise in Los Angeles prior to 1961
***AFL Championship*
****AFC Divisional Playoff*

BUFFALO vs. SAN FRANCISCO
RS: Series tied, 5-5
1972—Bills, 27-20 (B)
1980—Bills, 18-13 (SF)
1983—49ers, 23-10 (B)
1989—49ers, 21-10 (SF)
1992—Bills, 34-31 (SF)
1995—49ers, 27-17 (SF)
1998—Bills, 26-21 (B)
2001—49ers, 35-0 (SF)
2004—Bills, 41-7 (SF)
2008—49ers, 10-3 (B)
(RS Pts.—49ers 208, Bills 186)

BUFFALO vs. SEATTLE
RS: Seahawks lead series, 6-5
1977—Seahawks, 56-17 (S)
1984—Seahawks, 31-28 (S)
1988—Bills, 13-3 (S)
1989—Seahawks, 17-16 (S)
1995—Bills, 27-21 (B)
1996—Seahawks, 26-18 (S)
1999—Seahawks, 26-16 (S)
2000—Bills, 42-23 (S)
2001—Seahawks, 23-20 (B)
2004—Bills, 38-9 (S)
2008—Bills, 34-10 (B)
(RS Pts.—Bills 269, Seahawks 245)

BUFFALO vs. TAMPA BAY
RS: Buccaneers lead series, 6-2
1976—Bills, 14-9 (TB)
1978—Buccaneers, 31-10 (TB)
1982—Buccaneers, 24-23 (TB)
1986—Buccaneers, 34-28 (TB)
1988—Buccaneers, 10-5 (TB)
1991—Bills, 17-10 (TB)
2000—Buccaneers, 31-17 (TB)
2005—Buccaneers, 19-3 (TB)
(RS Pts.—Buccaneers 168, Bills 117)

BUFFALO vs. *TENNESSEE
RS: Titans lead series, 24-14
PS: Bills lead series, 2-1
1960—Bills, 25-24 (B)
Oilers, 31-23 (H)
1961—Bills, 22-12 (H)
Oilers, 28-16 (B)
1962—Oilers, 28-23 (B)
Oilers, 17-14 (H)
1963—Oilers, 31-20 (B)
Oilers, 28-14 (H)
1964—Bills, 48-17 (H)
Bills, 24-10 (B)
1965—Oilers, 19-17 (B)
Bills, 29-18 (H)
1966—Bills, 27-20 (B)
Bills, 42-20 (H)
1967—Oilers, 20-3 (B)
Oilers, 10-3 (H)
1968—Oilers, 30-7 (B)
Oilers, 35-6 (H)
1969—Oilers, 17-3 (B)
Oilers, 28-14 (H)
1971—Oilers, 20-14 (B)
1974—Oilers, 21-9 (B)
1976—Oilers, 13-3 (B)
1978—Oilers, 17-10 (H)
1983—Bills, 30-13 (B)
1985—Bills, 20-0 (B)
1986—Oilers, 16-7 (H)
1987—Bills, 34-30 (B)
1988—**Bills, 17-10 (B)
1989—Bills, 47-41 (H) OT
1990—Oilers, 27-24 (H)
1992—Oilers, 27-3 (H)
***Bills, 41-38 (B) OT
1993—Bills, 35-7 (B)
1994—Bills, 15-7 (H)
1995—Oilers, 28-17 (B)
1997—Oilers, 31-14 (T)
1999—***Titans, 22-16 (T)
2000—Bills, 16-13 (B)
2003—Titans, 28-26 (T)
2006—Titans, 30-29 (B)
(RS Pts.—Titans 812, Bills 733)
(PS Pts.—Bills 74, Titans 70)
Franchise in Houston prior to 1997; known as Oilers prior to 1999
***AFC Divisional Playoff*
****AFC First-Round Playoff*

BUFFALO vs. WASHINGTON
RS: Bills lead series, 7-4
PS: Redskins lead series, 1-0
1972—Bills, 24-17 (W)
1977—Redskins, 10-0 (B)
1981—Bills, 21-14 (B)
1984—Redskins, 41-14 (W)
1987—Redskins, 27-7 (B)
1990—Redskins, 29-14 (W)
1991—*Redskins, 37-24 (Minneapolis)
1993—Bills, 24-10 (B)
1996—Bills, 38-13 (B)
1999—Bills, 34-17 (W)
2003—Bills, 24-7 (B)
2007—Bills, 17-16 (W)
(RS Pts.—Bills 217, Redskins 201)
(PS Pts.—Redskins 37, Bills 24)
Super Bowl XXVI

CAROLINA vs. ARIZONA
RS: Panthers lead series, 6-2
PS: Cardinals lead series, 1-0;
See Arizona vs. Carolina

CAROLINA vs. ATLANTA
RS: Falcons lead series, 17-11;
See Atlanta vs. Carolina

CAROLINA vs. BALTIMORE
RS: Panthers lead series, 3-0;
See Baltimore vs. Carolina

CAROLINA vs. BUFFALO
RS: Bills lead series, 3-1;
See Buffalo vs. Carolina

CAROLINA vs. CHICAGO
RS: Series tied, 2-2
PS: Panthers lead series, 1-0
1995—Bears, 31-27 (Chi)
2002—Panthers, 24-14 (Car)
2005—Bears, 13-3 (Chi)
*Panthers, 29-21 (Chi)
2008—Panthers, 20-17 (Car)
(RS Pts.—Bears 75, Panthers 74)
(PS Pts.—Panthers 29, Bears 21)
NFC Divisional Playoff

CAROLINA vs. CINCINNATI
RS: Panthers lead series, 2-1
1999—Panthers, 27-3 (Car)
2002—Panthers, 52-31 (Car)
2006—Bengals, 17-14 (Cin)
(RS Pts.—Panthers 93, Bengals 51)

CAROLINA vs. CLEVELAND
RS: Panthers lead series, 3-0
1999—Panthers, 31-17 (Cle)
2002—Panthers, 13-6 (Cle)
2006—Panthers, 20-12 (Car)
(RS Pts.—Panthers 64, Browns 35)

CAROLINA vs. DALLAS
RS: Cowboys lead series, 7-1
PS: Panthers lead series, 2-0
1996—*Panthers, 26-17 (C)
1997—Panthers, 23-13 (D)
1998—Cowboys, 27-20 (D)
2000—Cowboys, 16-13 (C) OT
2002—Cowboys, 14-13 (D)
2003—Cowboys, 24-20 (D)
**Panthers, 29-10 (C)
2005—Cowboys, 24-20 (C)
2006—Cowboys, 35-14 (C)
2007—Cowboys, 20-13 (C)
(RS Pts.—Cowboys 173, Panthers 136)
(PS Pts.—Panthers 55, Cowboys 27)
NFC Divisional Playoff
NFC First-Round Playoff

CAROLINA vs. DENVER
RS: Broncos lead series, 2-1
1997—Broncos, 34-0 (D)
2004—Broncos, 20-17 (D)
2008—Panthers, 30-10 (C)

(RS Pts.—Broncos 64, Panthers 47)

CAROLINA vs. DETROIT
RS: Panthers lead series, 4-1
1999—Lions, 24-9 (C)
2002—Panthers, 31-7 (C)
2003—Panthers, 20-14 (C)
2005—Panthers, 21-20 (D)
2008—Panthers, 31-22 (C)
(RS Pts.—Panthers 112, Lions 87)

CAROLINA vs. GREEN BAY
RS: Packers lead series, 6-4
PS: Packers lead series, 1-0
1996—*Packers, 30-13 (GB)
1997—Packers, 31-10 (C)
1998—Packers, 37-30 (C)
1999—Panthers, 33-31 (GB)
2000—Panthers, 31-14 (C)
2001—Packers, 28-7 (C)
2002—Packers, 17-14 (GB)
2004—Packers, 24-14 (C)
2005—Panthers, 32-29 (C)
2007—Packers, 31-17 (GB)
2008—Panthers, 35-31 (GB)
(RS Pts.—Packers 273, Panthers 223)
(PS Pts.—Packers 30, Panthers 13)
**NFC Championship*

CAROLINA vs. HOUSTON
RS: Texans lead series, 2-0
2003—Texans, 14-10 (H)
2007—Texans, 34-21 (C)
(RS Pts.—Texans 48, Panthers 31)

CAROLINA vs. INDIANAPOLIS
RS: Panthers lead series, 3-1
1995—Panthers, 13-10 (C)
1998—Panthers, 27-19 (I)
2003—Panthers, 23-20 (I) OT
2007—Colts, 31-7 (C)
(RS Pts.—Colts 80, Panthers 70)

CAROLINA vs. JACKSONVILLE
RS: Jaguars lead series, 3-1
1996—Jaguars, 24-14 (J)
1999—Jaguars, 22-20 (C)
2003—Panthers, 24-23 (C)
2007—Jaguars, 37-6 (J)
(RS Pts.—Jaguars 106, Panthers 64)

CAROLINA vs. KANSAS CITY
RS: Series tied, 2-2
1997—Chiefs, 35-14 (C)
2000—Chiefs, 15-14 (KC)
2004—Panthers, 28-17 (KC)
2008—Panthers, 34-0 (C)
(RS Pts.—Panthers 90, Chiefs 67)

CAROLINA vs. MIAMI
RS: Dolphins lead series, 3-0
1998—Dolphins, 13-9 (C)
2001—Dolphins, 23-6 (M)
2005—Dolphins, 27-24 (M)
(RS Pts.—Dolphins 63, Panthers 39)

CAROLINA vs. MINNESOTA
RS: Vikings lead series, 5-3
1996—Vikings, 14-12 (M)
1997—Vikings, 21-14 (M)
2000—Vikings, 31-17 (M)
2001—Panthers, 24-13 (M)
2002—Panthers, 21-14 (M)
2005—Panthers, 38-13 (C)
2006—Vikings, 16-13 (M) OT
2008—Vikings, 20-10 (M)
(RS Pts.—Panthers 149, Vikings 142)

CAROLINA vs. NEW ENGLAND
RS: Panthers lead series, 2-1
PS: Patriots lead series, 1-0
1995—Panthers, 20-17 (NE) OT
2001—Patriots, 38-6 (C)
2003—*Patriots, 32-29 (Houston)
2005—Panthers, 27-17 (C)
(RS Pts.—Patriots 72, Panthers 53)
(PS Pts.—Patriots 32, Panthers 29)
**Super Bowl XXXVIII*

CAROLINA vs. NEW ORLEANS
RS: Panthers lead series, 16-12
1995—Panthers, 20-3 (C)
Saints, 34-26 (NO)
1996—Panthers, 22-20 (NO)
Panthers, 19-7 (C)
1997—Panthers, 13-0 (NO)
Saints, 16-13 (C)
1998—Saints, 19-14 (NO)
Panthers, 31-17 (C)
1999—Saints, 19-10 (NO)
Panthers, 45-13 (C)
2000—Saints, 24-6 (NO)
Saints, 20-10 (C)
2001—Saints, 27-25 (C)
Saints, 27-23 (NO)
2002—Saints, 34-24 (C)
Panthers, 10-6 (NO)
2003—Panthers, 19-13 (C)
Panthers, 23-20 (NO) OT
2004—Panthers, 32-21 (NO)
Saints, 21-18 (C)
2005—Saints, 23-20 (C)
Panthers, 27-10 (Baton Rouge)
2006—Panthers, 21-18 (C)
Panthers, 31-21 (NO)
2007—Panthers, 16-13 (NO)
Saints, 31-6 (C)
2008—Panthers, 30-7 (C)
Panthers, 33-31 (NO)
(RS Pts.—Panthers 587, Saints 515)

CAROLINA vs. N.Y. GIANTS
RS: Series tied, 2-2
PS: Panthers lead series, 1-0
1996—Panthers, 27-17 (C)
2003—Panthers, 37-24 (NY)
2005—*Panthers, 23-0 (NY)
2006—Giants, 27-13 (C)
2008—Giants, 34-28 (NY) OT
(RS Pts.—Panthers 105, Giants 102)
(PS Pts.—Panthers 23, Giants 0)
**NFC First-Round Playoff*

CAROLINA vs. N.Y. JETS
RS: Series tied, 2-2
1995—Panthers, 26-15 (C)
1998—Jets, 48-21 (NY)
2001—Jets, 13-12 (C)
2005—Panthers, 30-3 (C)
(RS Pts.—Panthers 89, Jets 79)

CAROLINA vs. OAKLAND
RS: Series tied, 2-2
1997—Panthers, 38-14 (C)
2000—Raiders, 52-9 (O)
2004—Raiders, 27-24 (C)
2008—Panthers, 17-6 (O)
(RS Pts.— Raiders 99, Panthers 88)

CAROLINA vs. PHILADELPHIA
RS: Eagles lead series, 4-1
PS: Panthers lead series, 1-0
1996—Eagles, 20-9 (P)
1999—Panthers, 33-7 (C)
2003—Eagles, 25-16 (C)
*Panthers, 14-3 (P)
2004—Eagles, 30-8 (P)
2006—Eagles, 27-24 (P)
(RS Pts.—Eagles 109, Panthers 90)
(PS Pts.—Panthers 14, Eagles 3)
**NFC Championship*

CAROLINA vs. PITTSBURGH
RS: Steelers lead series, 3-1
1996—Panthers, 18-14 (C)
1999—Steelers, 30-20 (P)
2002—Steelers, 30-14 (P)
2006—Steelers, 37-3 (C)
(RS Pts.—Steelers 111, Panthers 55)

CAROLINA vs. ST. LOUIS
RS: Panthers lead series, 10-7
PS: Panthers lead series, 1-0
1995—Rams, 31-10 (C)
Rams, 28-17 (StL)
1996—Panthers, 45-13 (C)
Panthers, 20-10 (StL)
1997—Panthers, 16-10 (StL)
Rams, 30-18 (C)
1998—Panthers, 24-20 (StL)
Panthers, 20-13 (C)
1999—Rams, 35-10 (StL)
Rams, 34-21 (C)
2000—Panthers, 27-24 (StL)
Panthers, 16-3 (C)
2001—Rams, 48-14 (StL)
Rams, 38-32 (C)
2003—*Panthers, 29-23 (StL) 2OT
2004—Panthers, 20-7 (C)
2006—Panthers, 15-0 (C)
2007—Panthers, 27-13 (StL)
(RS Pts.—Rams 357, Panthers 352)
(PS Pts.—Panthers 29, Rams 23)
**NFC Divisional Playoff*

CAROLINA vs. SAN DIEGO
RS: Panthers lead series, 3-1
1997—Panthers, 26-7 (SD)
2000—Panthers, 30-22 (C)
2004—Chargers, 17-6 (C)
2008—Panthers, 26-24 (SD)
(RS Pts.—Panthers 88, Chargers 70)

CAROLINA vs. SAN FRANCISCO
RS: Panthers lead series, 9-7
1995—Panthers, 13-7 (SF)
49ers, 31-10 (C)
1996—Panthers, 23-7 (C)
Panthers, 30-24 (SF)
1997—49ers, 34-21 (C)
49ers, 27-19 (SF)
1998—49ers, 25-23 (SF)
49ers, 31-28 (C) OT
1999—Panthers, 31-29 (SF)
Panthers, 41-24 (C)
2000—Panthers, 38-22 (SF)
Panthers, 34-16 (C)
2001—49ers, 24-14 (SF)
49ers, 25-22 (C) OT
2004—Panthers, 37-27 (SF)
2007—Panthers, 31-14 (C)
(RS Pts.—Panthers 415, 49ers 367)

CAROLINA vs. SEATTLE
RS: Panthers lead series, 2-1
PS: Seahawks lead series, 1-0
2000—Panthers, 26-3 (C)
2004—Seahawks, 23-17 (S)

2005—*Seahawks, 34-14 (S)
2007—Panthers, 13-10 (C)
(RS Pts.—Panthers 56, Seahawks 36)
(PS Pts.—Seahawks 34, Panthers 14)
NFC Championship

CAROLINA vs. TAMPA BAY
RS: Panthers lead series, 10-7
1995—Buccaneers, 20-13 (C)
1996—Panthers, 24-0 (C)
1998—Buccaneers, 16-13 (TB)
2002—Buccaneers, 12-9 (C)
Buccaneers, 23-10 (TB)
2003—Panthers, 12-9 (TB) OT
Panthers, 27-24 (C)
2004—Panthers, 21-14 (C)
Panthers, 37-20 (TB)
2005—Panthers, 34-14 (TB)
Buccaneers, 20-10 (C)
2006—Panthers, 26-24 (TB)
Panthers, 24-10 (C)
2007—Buccaneers, 20-7 (C)
Panthers, 31-23 (TB)
2008—Buccaneers, 27-3 (TB)
Panthers, 38-23 (C)
(RS Pts.—Panthers 339, Buccaneers 299)

CAROLINA vs. *TENNESSEE
RS: Titans lead series, 2-1
1996—Panthers, 31-6 (H)
2003—Titans, 37-17 (C)
2006—Panthers, 26-24 (TB)
Panthers, 24-10 (C)
2007—Titans, 20-7 (T)
(RS Pts.—Titans 63, Panthers 55)
Franchise in Houston prior to 1997; known as Oilers prior to 1999

CAROLINA vs. WASHINGTON
RS: Redskins lead series, 7-1
1995—Redskins, 20-17 (W)
1997—Redskins, 24-10 (C)
1998—Redskins, 28-25 (C)
1999—Redskins, 38-36 (W)
2000—Redskins, 20-17 (W)
2001—Redskins, 17-14 (W) OT
2003—Panthers, 20-17 (C)
2006—Redskins, 17-13 (W)
(RS Pts.—Redskins 181, Panthers 152)

CHICAGO vs. ARIZONA
RS: Bears lead series, 55-26-6;
See Arizona vs. Chicago

CHICAGO vs. ATLANTA
RS: Bears lead series, 12-11;
See Atlanta vs. Chicago

CHICAGO vs. BALTIMORE
RS: Bears lead series, 2-1;
See Baltimore vs. Chicago

CHICAGO vs. BUFFALO
RS: Bears lead series, 6-4;
See Buffalo vs. Chicago

CHICAGO vs. CAROLINA
RS: Series tied, 2-2
PS: Panthers lead series, 1-0;
See Carolina vs. Chicago

CHICAGO vs. CINCINNATI
RS: Bengals lead series, 5-3
1972—Bengals, 13-3 (Chi)
1980—Bengals, 17-14 (Chi) OT
1986—Bears, 44-7 (Cin)
1989—Bears, 17-14 (Chi)
1992—Bengals, 31-28 (Chi) OT
1995—Bengals, 16-10 (Cin)
2001—Bears, 24-0 (Cin)
2005—Bengals, 24-7 (Chi)
(RS Pts.—Bears 147, Bengals 122)

CHICAGO vs. CLEVELAND
RS: Browns lead series, 9-4
1951—Browns, 42-21 (Cle)
1954—Browns, 39-10 (Chi)
1960—Browns, 42-0 (Cle)
1961—Bears, 17-14 (Chi)
1967—Browns, 24-0 (Cle)
1969—Browns, 28-24 (Chi)
1972—Bears, 17-0 (Cle)
1980—Browns, 27-21 (Cle)
1986—Bears, 41-31 (Chi)
1989—Browns, 27-7 (Cle)
1992—Browns, 27-14 (Cle)
2001—Bears, 27-21 (Chi) OT
2005—Browns, 20-10 (Cle)
(RS Pts.—Browns 342, Bears 209)

CHICAGO vs. DALLAS
RS: Cowboys lead series, 11-8
PS: Cowboys lead series, 2-0
1960—Bears, 17-7 (C)
1962—Bears, 34-33 (D)
1964—Cowboys, 24-10 (C)
1968—Cowboys, 34-3 (C)
1971—Bears, 23-19 (C)
1973—Cowboys, 20-17 (C)
1976—Cowboys, 31-21 (D)
1977—*Cowboys, 37-7 (D)
1979—Cowboys, 24-20 (D)
1981—Cowboys, 10-9 (D)
1984—Cowboys, 23-14 (C)
1985—Bears, 44-0 (D)
1986—Bears, 24-10 (D)
1988—Bears, 17-7 (C)
1991—**Cowboys, 17-13 (C)
1992—Cowboys, 27-14 (D)
1996—Bears, 22-6 (C)
1997—Cowboys, 27-3 (D)
1998—Bears, 13-12 (C)
2004—Cowboys, 21-7 (D)
2007—Cowboys, 34-10 (C)
(RS Pts.—Cowboys 369, Bears 322)
(PS Pts.—Cowboys 54, Bears 20)
NFC Divisional Playoff
***NFC First-Round Playoff*

CHICAGO vs. DENVER
RS: Bears lead series, 7-6
1971—Broncos, 6-3 (D)
1973—Bears, 33-14 (D)
1976—Broncos, 28-14 (C)
1978—Broncos, 16-7 (D)
1981—Bears, 35-24 (C)
1983—Bears, 31-14 (C)
1984—Bears, 27-0 (C)
1987—Broncos, 31-29 (D)
1990—Bears, 16-13 (D) OT
1993—Broncos, 13-3 (C)
1996—Broncos, 17-12 (D)
2003—Bears, 19-10 (D)
2007—Bears, 37-34 (C) OT
(RS Pts.—Bears 266, Broncos 220)

CHICAGO vs. *DETROIT
RS: Bears lead series, 89-64-5
1930—Spartans, 7-6 (P)
Bears, 14-6 (C)
1931—Bears, 9-6 (C)
Spartans, 3-0 (P)
1932—Tie, 13-13 (C)
Tie, 7-7 (P)
Bears, 9-0 (C)
1933—Bears, 17-14 (C)
Bears, 17-7 (P)
1934—Bears, 19-16 (D)
Bears, 10-7 (C)
1935—Tie, 20-20 (C)
Lions, 14-2 (D)
1936—Bears, 12-10 (C)
Lions, 13-7 (D)
1937—Bears, 28-20 (C)
Bears, 13-0 (D)
1938—Lions, 13-7 (C)
Lions, 14-7 (D)
1939—Lions, 10-0 (C)
Bears, 23-13 (D)
1940—Bears, 7-0 (C)
Lions, 17-14 (D)
1941—Bears, 49-0 (C)
Bears, 24-7 (D)
1942—Bears, 16-0 (C)
Bears, 42-0 (D)
1943—Bears, 27-21 (D)
Bears, 35-14 (C)
1944—Tie, 21-21 (C)
Lions, 41-21 (D)
1945—Lions, 16-10 (D)
Lions, 35-28 (C)
1946—Bears, 42-6 (C)
Bears, 45-24 (D)
1947—Bears, 33-24 (C)
Bears, 34-14 (D)
1948—Bears, 28-0 (C)
Bears, 42-14 (D)
1949—Bears, 27-24 (C)
Bears, 28-7 (D)
1950—Bears, 35-21 (D)
Bears, 6-3 (C)
1951—Bears, 28-23 (D)
Lions, 41-28 (C)
1952—Bears, 24-23 (C)
Lions, 45-21 (D)
1953—Lions, 20-16 (C)
Lions, 13-7 (D)
1954—Lions, 48-23 (D)
Bears, 28-24 (C)
1955—Bears, 24-14 (D)
Bears, 21-20 (C)
1956—Lions, 42-10 (D)
Bears, 38-21 (C)
1957—Bears, 27-7 (D)
Lions, 21-13 (C)
1958—Bears, 20-7 (D)
Bears, 21-16 (C)
1959—Bears, 24-14 (D)
Bears, 25-14 (C)
1960—Bears, 28-7 (C)
Lions, 36-0 (D)
1961—Bears, 31-17 (D)
Lions, 16-15 (C)
1962—Lions, 11-3 (D)
Bears, 3-0 (C)
1963—Bears, 37-21 (D)
Bears, 24-14 (C)
1964—Lions, 10-0 (C)
Bears, 27-24 (D)
1965—Bears, 38-10 (C)
Bears, 17-10 (D)
1966—Lions, 14-3 (D)

Tie, 10-10 (C)
1967—Bears, 14-3 (C)
Bears, 27-13 (D)
1968—Lions, 42-0 (D)
Lions, 28-10 (C)
1969—Lions, 13-7 (D)
Lions, 20-3 (C)
1970—Lions, 28-14 (D)
Lions, 16-10 (C)
1971—Bears, 28-23 (D)
Lions, 28-3 (C)
1972—Lions, 38-24 (C)
Lions, 14-0 (D)
1973—Lions, 30-7 (C)
Lions, 40-7 (D)
1974—Bears, 17-9 (C)
Lions, 34-17 (D)
1975—Lions, 27-7 (D)
Bears, 25-21 (C)
1976—Bears, 10-3 (C)
Lions, 14-10 (D)
1977—Bears, 30-20 (C)
Bears, 31-14 (D)
1978—Bears, 19-0 (D)
Lions, 21-17 (C)
1979—Bears, 35-7 (C)
Lions, 20-0 (D)
1980—Bears, 24-7 (C)
Bears, 23-17 (D) OT
1981—Lions, 48-17 (D)
Lions, 23-7 (C)
1982—Lions, 17-10 (D)
Bears, 20-17 (C)
1983—Lions, 31-17 (D)
Lions, 38-17 (C)
1984—Bears, 16-14 (C)
Bears, 30-13 (D)
1985—Bears, 24-3 (C)
Bears, 37-17 (D)
1986—Bears, 13-7 (C)
Bears, 16-13 (D)
1987—Bears, 30-10 (C)
1988—Bears, 24-7 (D)
Bears, 13-12 (C)
1989—Bears, 47-27 (D)
Lions, 27-17 (C)
1990—Bears, 23-17 (C) OT
Lions, 38-21 (D)
1991—Bears, 20-10 (C)
Lions, 16-6 (D)
1992—Bears, 27-24 (C)
Lions, 16-3 (D)
1993—Bears, 10-6 (D)
Lions, 20-14 (C)
1994—Lions, 21-16 (D)
Bears, 20-10 (C)
1995—Lions, 24-17 (C)
Lions, 27-7 (D)
1996—Lions, 35-16 (D)
Bears, 31-14 (C)
1997—Lions, 32-7 (C)
Lions, 55-20 (D)
1998—Bears, 31-27 (C)
Lions, 26-3 (D)
1999—Lions, 21-17 (D)
Bears, 28-10 (C)
2000—Lions, 21-14 (C)
Bears, 23-20 (D)
2001—Bears, 13-10 (C)
Bears, 24-0 (D)
2002—Lions, 23-20 (D) OT
Bears, 20-17 (C) OT
2003—Bears, 24-16 (C)
Lions, 12-10 (D)
2004—Lions, 20-16 (C)
Lions, 19-13 (D)
2005—Bears, 38-6 (C)
Bears, 19-13 (D) OT
2006—Bears, 34-7 (C)
Bears, 26-21 (D)
2007—Lions, 37-27 (D)
Lions, 16-7 (C)
2008—Bears, 34-7 (D)
Bears, 27-23 (C)
(RS Pts.—Bears 2,988, Lions 2,746)
**Franchise in Portsmouth prior to 1934 and known as the Spartans*

***CHICAGO vs. GREEN BAY**
RS: Bears lead series, 90-80-6
PS: Bears lead series, 1-0
1921—Staleys, 20-0 (C)
1923—Bears, 3-0 (GB)
1924—Bears, 3-0 (C)
1925—Packers, 14-10 (GB)
Bears, 21-0 (C)
1926—Tie, 6-6 (GB)
Bears, 19-13 (C)
Tie, 3-3 (C)
1927—Bears, 7-6 (GB)
Bears, 14-6 (C)
1928—Tie, 12-12 (GB)
Packers, 16-6 (C)
Packers, 6-0 (C)
1929—Packers, 23-0 (GB)
Packers, 14-0 (C)
Packers, 25-0 (C)
1930—Packers, 7-0 (GB)
Packers, 13-12 (C)
Bears, 21-0 (C)
1931—Packers, 7-0 (GB)
Packers, 6-2 (C)
Bears, 7-6 (C)
1932—Tie, 0-0 (GB)
Packers, 2-0 (C)
Bears, 9-0 (C)
1933—Bears, 14-7 (GB)
Bears, 10-7 (C)
Bears, 7-6 (C)
1934—Bears, 24-10 (GB)
Bears, 27-14 (C)
1935—Packers, 7-0 (GB)
Packers, 17-14 (C)
1936—Bears, 30-3 (GB)
Packers, 21-10 (C)
1937—Bears, 14-2 (GB)
Packers, 24-14 (C)
1938—Bears, 2-0 (GB)
Packers, 24-17 (C)
1939—Packers, 21-16 (GB)
Bears, 30-27 (C)
1940—Bears, 41-10 (GB)
Bears, 14-7 (C)
1941—Bears, 25-17 (GB)
Packers, 16-14 (C)
**Bears, 33-14 (C)
1942—Bears, 44-28 (GB)
Bears, 38-7 (C)
1943—Tie, 21-21 (GB)
Bears, 21-7 (C)
1944—Packers, 42-28 (GB)
Bears, 21-0 (C)
1945—Packers, 31-21 (GB)
Bears, 28-24 (C)
1946—Bears, 30-7 (GB)
Bears, 10-7 (C)
1947—Packers, 29-20 (GB)
Bears, 20-17 (C)
1948—Bears, 45-7 (GB)
Bears, 7-6 (C)
1949—Bears, 17-0 (GB)
Bears, 24-3 (C)
1950—Packers, 31-21 (GB)
Bears, 28-14 (C)
1951—Bears, 31-20 (GB)
Bears, 24-13 (C)
1952—Bears, 24-14 (GB)
Packers, 41-28 (C)
1953—Bears, 17-13 (GB)
Tie, 21-21 (C)
1954—Bears, 10-3 (GB)
Bears, 28-23 (C)
1955—Packers, 24-3 (GB)
Bears, 52-31 (C)
1956—Bears, 37-21 (GB)
Bears, 38-14 (C)
1957—Packers, 21-17 (GB)
Bears, 21-14 (C)
1958—Bears, 34-20 (GB)
Bears, 24-10 (C)
1959—Packers, 9-6 (GB)
Bears, 28-17 (C)
1960—Bears, 17-14 (GB)
Packers, 41-13 (C)
1961—Packers, 24-0 (GB)
Packers, 31-28 (C)
1962—Packers, 49-0 (GB)
Packers, 38-7 (C)
1963—Bears, 10-3 (GB)
Bears, 26-7 (C)
1964—Packers, 23-12 (GB)
Packers, 17-3 (C)
1965—Packers, 23-14 (GB)
Bears, 31-10 (C)
1966—Packers, 17-0 (C)
Packers, 13-6 (GB)
1967—Packers, 13-10 (GB)
Packers, 17-13 (C)
1968—Bears, 13-10 (GB)
Packers, 28-27 (C)
1969—Packers, 17-0 (GB)
Packers, 21-3 (C)
1970—Packers, 20-19 (GB)
Bears, 35-17 (C)
1971—Packers, 17-14 (C)
Packers, 31-10 (GB)
1972—Packers, 20-17 (GB)
Packers, 23-17 (C)
1973—Bears, 31-17 (GB)
Packers, 21-0 (C)
1974—Bears, 10-9 (C)
Packers, 20-3 (Mil)
1975—Bears, 27-14 (C)
Packers, 28-7 (GB)
1976—Bears, 24-13 (C)
Bears, 16-10 (GB)
1977—Bears, 26-0 (GB)
Bears, 21-10 (C)
1978—Packers, 24-14 (GB)
Bears, 14-0 (C)
1979—Bears, 6-3 (C)

Bears, 15-14 (GB)
1980—Packers, 12-6 (GB) OT
Bears, 61-7 (C)
1981—Packers, 16-9 (C)
Packers, 21-17 (GB)
1983—Packers, 31-28 (GB)
Bears, 23-21 (C)
1984—Bears, 9-7 (GB)
Packers, 20-14 (C)
1985—Bears, 23-7 (C)
Bears, 16-10 (GB)
1986—Bears, 25-12 (GB)
Bears, 12-10 (C)
1987—Bears, 26-24 (GB)
Bears, 23-10 (C)
1988—Bears, 24-6 (GB)
Bears, 16-0 (C)
1989—Packers, 14-13 (GB)
Packers, 40-28 (C)
1990—Bears, 31-13 (GB)
Bears, 27-13 (C)
1991—Bears, 10-0 (GB)
Bears, 27-13 (C)
1992—Bears, 30-10 (GB)
Packers, 17-3 (C)
1993—Packers, 17-3 (GB)
Bears, 30-17 (C)
1994—Packers, 33-6 (C)
Packers, 40-3 (GB)
1995—Packers, 27-24 (C)
Packers, 35-28 (GB)
1996—Packers, 37-6 (C)
Packers, 28-17 (GB)
1997—Packers, 38-24 (GB)
Packers, 24-23 (C)
1998—Packers, 26-20 (GB)
Packers, 16-13 (C)
1999—Bears, 14-13 (GB)
Packers, 35-19 (C)
2000—Bears, 27-24 (GB)
Packers, 28-6 (C)
2001—Packers, 20-12 (C)
Packers, 17-7 (GB)
2002—Packers, 34-21 (C)
Packers, 30-20 (GB)
2003—Packers, 38-23 (C)
Packers, 34-21 (GB)
2004—Bears, 21-10 (GB)
Packers, 31-14 (C)
2005—Bears, 19-7 (C)
Bears, 24-17 (GB)
2006—Bears, 26-0 (GB)
Packers, 26-7 (C)
2007—Bears, 27-20 (GB)
Bears, 35-7 (C)
2008—Packers, 37-3 (GB)
Bears, 20-17 (C) OT
(RS Pts.—Bears 3,008, Packers 2,879)
(PS Pts.—Bears 33, Packers 14)
Bears known as Staleys prior to 1922
***Division Playoff*

CHICAGO vs. HOUSTON
RS: Texans lead series, 2-0
2004—Texans, 24-5 (C)
2008—Texans, 31-24 (H)
(RS Pts.—Texans 55, Bears 29)

CHICAGO vs. *INDIANAPOLIS
RS: Colts lead series, 22-18
PS: Colts lead series, 1-0
1953—Colts, 13-9 (B)
Colts, 16-14 (C)
1954—Bears, 28-9 (C)
Bears, 28-13 (B)
1955—Colts, 23-17 (B)
Bears, 38-10 (C)
1956—Colts, 28-21 (B)
Bears, 58-27 (C)
1957—Colts, 21-10 (B)
Colts, 29-14 (C)
1958—Colts, 51-38 (B)
Colts, 17-0 (C)
1959—Bears, 26-21 (B)
Colts, 21-7 (C)
1960—Colts, 42-7 (B)
Colts, 24-20 (C)
1961—Bears, 24-10 (C)
Bears, 21-20 (B)
1962—Bears, 35-15 (C)
Bears, 57-0 (B)
1963—Bears, 10-3 (C)
Bears, 17-7 (B)
1964—Colts, 52-0 (B)
Colts, 40-24 (C)
1965—Colts, 26-21 (C)
Bears, 13-0 (B)
1966—Bears, 27-17 (C)
Colts, 21-16 (B)
1967—Colts, 24-3 (C)
1968—Colts, 28-7 (B)
1969—Colts, 24-21 (C)
1970—Colts, 21-20 (B)
1975—Colts, 35-7 (C)
1983—Colts, 22-19 (B) OT
1985—Bears, 17-10 (C)
1988—Bears, 17-13 (I)
1991—Bears, 31-17 (I)
2000—Bears, 27-24 (C)
2004—Colts, 41-10 (C)
2006—**Colts, 29-17 (South Florida)
2008—Bears, 29-13 (I)
(RS Pts.—Colts 848, Bears 808)
(PS: Pts.—Colts 29, Bears 17)
Franchise in Baltimore prior to 1984
***Super Bowl XLI*

CHICAGO vs. JACKSONVILLE
RS: Bears lead series, 3-2
1995—Bears, 30-27 (J)
1998—Jaguars, 24-23 (C)
2001—Bears, 33-13 (C)
2004—Jaguars, 22-3 (J)
2008—Bears, 23-10 (C)
(RS Pts.—Bears 112, Jaguars 96)

CHICAGO vs. KANSAS CITY
RS: Bears lead series, 6-4
1973—Chiefs, 19-7 (KC)
1977—Bears, 28-27 (C)
1981—Bears, 16-13 (KC) OT
1987—Bears, 31-28 (C)
1990—Chiefs, 21-10 (C)
1993—Bears, 19-17 (KC)
1996—Chiefs, 14-10 (KC)
1999—Bears, 20-17 (C)
2003—Chiefs, 31-3 (KC)
2007—Bears, 20-10 (C)
(RS Pts.—Chiefs 197, Bears 164)

CHICAGO vs. MIAMI
RS: Dolphins lead series, 7-3
1971—Dolphins, 34-3 (M)
1975—Dolphins, 46-13 (C)
1979—Dolphins, 31-16 (M)
1985—Dolphins, 38-24 (M)
1988—Bears, 34-7 (C)
1991—Dolphins, 16-13 (C) OT
1994—Bears, 17-14 (M)
1997—Bears, 36-33 (M) OT
2002—Dolphins, 27-9 (M)
2006—Dolphins, 31-13 (C)
(RS Pts.—Dolphins 277, Bears 178)

CHICAGO vs. MINNESOTA
RS: Vikings lead series, 51-42-2
PS: Bears lead series, 1-0
1961—Vikings, 37-13 (M)
Bears, 52-35 (C)
1962—Bears, 13-0 (M)
Bears, 31-30 (C)
1963—Bears, 28-7 (M)
Tie, 17-17 (C)
1964—Bears, 34-28 (M)
Vikings, 41-14 (C)
1965—Bears, 45-37 (M)
Vikings, 24-17 (C)
1966—Bears, 13-10 (M)
Bears, 41-28 (C)
1967—Bears, 17-7 (M)
Tie, 10-10 (C)
1968—Bears, 27-17 (M)
Bears, 26-24 (C)
1969—Vikings, 31-0 (C)
Vikings, 31-14 (M)
1970—Vikings, 24-0 (C)
Vikings, 16-13 (M)
1971—Bears, 20-17 (M)
Vikings, 27-10 (C)
1972—Bears, 13-10 (C)
Vikings, 23-10 (M)
1973—Vikings, 22-13 (C)
Vikings, 31-13 (M)
1974—Vikings, 11-7 (M)
Vikings, 17-0 (C)
1975—Vikings, 28-3 (M)
Vikings, 13-9 (C)
1976—Vikings, 20-19 (M)
Bears, 14-13 (C)
1977—Vikings, 22-16 (M) OT
Bears, 10-7 (C)
1978—Vikings, 24-20 (C)
Vikings, 17-14 (M)
1979—Bears, 26-7 (C)
Vikings, 30-27 (M)
1980—Vikings, 34-14 (C)
Vikings, 13-7 (M)
1981—Vikings, 24-21 (M)
Bears, 10-9 (C)
1982—Vikings, 35-7 (M)
1983—Vikings, 23-14 (C)
Bears, 19-13 (M)
1984—Bears, 16-7 (C)
Bears, 34-3 (M)
1985—Bears, 33-24 (M)
Bears, 27-9 (C)
1986—Bears, 23-0 (C)
Vikings, 23-7 (M)
1987—Bears, 27-7 (C)
Bears, 30-24 (M)
1988—Vikings, 31-7 (C)
Vikings, 28-27 (M)
1989—Bears, 38-7 (C)
Vikings, 27-16 (M)
1990—Bears, 19-16 (C)
Vikings, 41-13 (M)

1991—Bears, 10-6 (C)
Bears, 34-17 (M)
1992—Vikings, 21-20 (M)
Vikings, 38-10 (C)
1993—Vikings, 10-7 (M)
Vikings, 19-12 (C)
1994—Vikings, 42-14 (C)
Vikings, 33-27 (M) OT
*Bears, 35-18 (M)
1995—Bears, 31-14 (C)
Bears, 14-6 (M)
1996—Vikings, 20-14 (C)
Bears, 15-13 (M)
1997—Vikings, 27-24 (C)
Vikings, 29-22 (M)
1998—Vikings, 31-28 (C)
Vikings, 48-22 (M)
1999—Bears, 24-22 (M)
Vikings, 27-24 (C) OT
2000—Vikings, 30-27 (M)
Vikings, 28-16 (C)
2001—Bears, 17-10 (C)
Bears, 13-6 (M)
2002—Bears, 27-23 (C)
Vikings, 25-7 (M)
2003—Vikings, 24-13 (M)
Bears, 13-10 (C)
2004—Vikings, 27-22 (M)
Bears, 24-14 (C)
2005—Bears, 28-3 (C)
Vikings, 34-10 (M)
2006—Bears, 19-16 (M)
Bears, 23-13 (C)
2007—Vikings, 34-31 (C)
Vikings, 20-13 (M)
2008—Bears, 48-41 (C)
Vikings, 34-14 (M)
RS Pts.—Vikings 2,006, Bears 1,795)
(PS Pts.—Bears 35, Vikings 18)
NFC First-Round Playoff

CHICAGO vs. NEW ENGLAND
RS: Patriots lead series, 7-3
PS: Bears lead series, 1-0
1973—Patriots, 13-10 (C)
1979—Patriots, 27-7 (C)
1982—Bears, 26-13 (C)
1985—Bears, 20-7 (C)
*Bears, 46-10 (New Orleans)
1988—Patriots, 30-7 (NE)
1994—Patriots, 13-3 (C)
1997—Patriots, 31-3 (NE)
2000—Bears, 24-17 (C)
2002—Patriots, 33-30 (C)
2006—Patriots, 17-13 (NE)
(RS Pts.—Patriots 201, Bears 143)
(PS Pts.—Bears 46, Patriots 10)
Super Bowl XX

CHICAGO vs. NEW ORLEANS
RS: Bears lead series, 13-11
PS: Bears lead series, 2-0
1968—Bears, 23-17 (NO)
1970—Bears, 24-3 (NO)
1971—Bears, 35-14 (C)
1973—Saints, 21-16 (NO)
1974—Bears, 24-10 (C)
1975—Bears, 42-17 (NO)
1977—Saints, 42-24 (C)
1980—Bears, 22-3 (C)
1982—Saints, 10-0 (C)
1983—Saints, 34-31 (NO) OT
1984—Bears, 20-7 (C)
1987—Saints, 19-17 (C)
1990—*Bears, 16-6 (C)
1991—Bears, 20-17 (NO)
1992—Saints, 28-6 (NO)
1994—Bears, 17-7 (C)
1996—Saints, 27-24 (NO)
1997—Saints, 20-17 (C)
1999—Bears, 14-10 (C)
2000—Saints, 31-10 (C)
2002—Saints, 29-23 (C)
2003—Saints, 20-13 (NO)
2005—Bears, 20-17 (Baton Rouge)
2006—**Bears, 39-14 (C)
2007—Bears, 33-25 (C)
2008—Bears, 27-24 (C) OT
(RS Pts.—Bears 502, Saints 452)
(PS Pts.—Bears 55, Saints 20)
**NFC First-Round Playoff*
***NFC Championship*

CHICAGO vs. N.Y. GIANTS
RS: Bears lead series, 27-18-2
PS: Bears lead series, 5-3
1925—Bears, 19-7 (NY)
Giants, 9-0 (C)
1926—Bears, 7-0 (C)
1927—Giants, 13-7 (NY)
1928—Bears, 13-0 (C)
1929—Giants, 26-14 (C)
Giants, 34-0 (NY)
Giants, 14-9 (C)
1930—Giants, 12-0 (C)
Bears, 12-0 (NY)
1931—Bears, 6-0 (C)
Bears, 12-6 (NY)
Giants, 25-6 (C)
1932—Bears, 28-8 (NY)
Bears, 6-0 (C)
1933—Bears, 14-10 (C)
Giants, 3-0 (NY)
*Bears, 23-21 (C)
1934—Bears, 27-7 (C)
Bears, 10-9 (NY)
*Giants, 30-13 (NY)
1935—Bears, 20-3 (NY)
Giants, 3-0 (C)
1936—Bears, 25-7 (NY)
1937—Tie, 3-3 (NY)
1939—Giants, 16-13 (NY)
1940—Bears, 37-21 (NY)
1941—*Bears, 37-9 (C)
1942—Bears, 26-7 (NY)
1943—Bears, 56-7 (NY)
1946—Giants, 14-0 (NY)
*Bears, 24-14 (NY)
1948—Bears, 35-14 (C)
1949—Giants, 35-28 (NY)
1956—Tie, 17-17 (NY)
*Giants, 47-7 (NY)
1962—Giants, 26-24 (C)
1963—*Bears, 14-10 (C)
1965—Bears, 35-14 (NY)
1967—Bears, 34-7 (C)
1969—Giants, 28-24 (NY)
1970—Bears, 24-16 (NY)
1974—Bears, 16-13 (C)
1977—Bears, 12-9 (NY) OT
1985—**Bears, 21-0 (C)
1987—Bears, 34-19 (C)
1990—**Giants, 31-3 (NY)
1991—Bears, 20-17 (C)
1992—Giants, 27-14 (C)
1993—Giants, 26-20 (C)
1995—Bears, 27-24 (NY)
2000—Giants, 14-7 (C)
2004—Bears, 28-21 (NY)
2006—Bears, 38-20 (NY)
2007—Giants, 21-16 (C)
(RS Pts.—Bears 823, Giants 632)
(PS Pts.—Giants 162, Bears 142)
**NFL Championship*
***NFC Divisional Playoff*

CHICAGO vs. N.Y. JETS
RS: Bears lead series, 6-3
1974—Jets, 23-21 (C)
1979—Bears, 23-13 (C)
1985—Bears, 19-6 (NY)
1991—Bears, 19-13 (C) OT
1994—Bears, 19-7 (NY)
1997—Jets, 23-15 (C)
2000—Jets, 17-10 (NY)
2002—Bears, 20-13 (C)
2006—Bears, 10-0 (NY)
(RS Pts.—Bears 156, Jets 115)

CHICAGO vs. *OAKLAND
RS: Series tied, 6-6
1972—Raiders, 28-21 (O)
1976—Raiders, 28-27 (C)
1978—Raiders, 25-19 (C) OT
1981—Bears, 23-6 (O)
1984—Bears, 17-6 (C)
1987—Bears, 6-3 (LA)
1990—Raiders, 24-10 (LA)
1993—Raiders, 16-14 (C)
1996—Bears, 19-17 (C)
1999—Raiders, 24-17 (O)
2003—Bears, 24-21 (C)
2007—Bears, 17-6 (O)
(RS Pts.—Bears 214, Raiders 204)
**Franchise in Los Angeles from 1982-1994*

CHICAGO vs. PHILADELPHIA
RS: Bears lead series, 26-8-1
PS: Eagles lead series, 2-1
1933—Tie, 3-3 (P)
1935—Bears, 39-0 (P)
1936—Bears, 17-0 (P)
Bears, 28-7 (P)
1938—Bears, 28-6 (P)
1939—Bears, 27-14 (C)
1941—Bears, 49-14 (P)
1942—Bears, 45-14 (C)
1944—Bears, 28-7 (P)
1946—Bears, 21-14 (C)
1947—Bears, 40-7 (C)
1948—Eagles, 12-7 (P)
1949—Bears, 38-21 (C)
1955—Bears, 17-10 (C)
1961—Eagles, 16-14 (P)
1963—Bears, 16-7 (C)
1968—Bears, 29-16 (P)
1970—Bears, 20-16 (C)
1972—Bears, 21-12 (P)
1975—Bears, 15-13 (C)
1979—*Eagles, 27-17 (P)
1980—Eagles, 17-14 (P)
1983—Bears, 7-6 (P)
Bears, 17-14 (C)
1986—Bears, 13-10 (C) OT
1987—Bears, 35-3 (P)
1988—**Bears, 20-12 (C)

1989—Bears, 27-13 (C)
1993—Bears, 17-6 (P)
1994—Eagles, 30-22 (P)
1995—Bears, 20-14 (C)
1999—Eagles, 20-16 (C)
2000—Eagles, 13-9 (P)
2001—**Eagles, 33-19 (C)
2002—Eagles, 19-13 (C)
2004—Eagles, 19-9 (C)
2007—Bears, 19-16 (P)
2008—Bears, 24-20 (C)
(RS Pts.—Bears 764, Eagles 429)
(PS Pts.—Eagles 72, Bears 56)
NFC First-Round Playoff
***NFC Divisional Playoff*

CHICAGO vs. *PITTSBURGH
RS: Bears lead series, 16-7-1
1934—Bears, 28-0 (P)
1935—Bears, 23-7 (P)
1936—Bears, 27-9 (P)
Bears, 26-6 (C)
1937—Bears, 7-0 (P)
1939—Bears, 32-0 (P)
1941—Bears, 34-7 (C)
1945—Bears, 28-7 (C)
1947—Bears, 49-7 (C)
1949—Bears, 30-21 (C)
1958—Steelers, 24-10 (P)
1959—Bears, 27-21 (C)
1963—Tie, 17-17 (P)
1967—Steelers, 41-13 (P)
1969—Bears, 38-7 (C)
1971—Bears, 17-15 (C)
1975—Steelers, 34-3 (P)
1980—Steelers, 38-3 (P)
1986—Bears, 13-10 (C) OT
1989—Bears, 20-0 (P)
1992—Bears, 30-6 (C)
1995—Steelers, 37-34 (C) OT
1998—Steelers, 17-12 (P)
2005—Steelers, 21-9 (P)
(RS Pts.—Bears 530, Steelers 352)
**Steelers known as Pirates prior to 1940*

CHICAGO vs. *ST. LOUIS
RS: Bears lead series, 49-34-3
PS: Series tied, 1-1
1937—Bears, 20-2 (Cle)
Bears, 15-7 (C)
1938—Rams, 14-7 (C)
Rams, 23-21 (Cle)
1939—Bears, 30-21 (Cle)
Bears, 35-21 (C)
1940—Bears, 21-14 (Cle)
Bears, 47-25 (C)
1941—Bears, 48-21 (Cle)
Bears, 31-13 (C)
1942—Bears, 21-7 (Cle)
Bears, 47-0 (C)
1944—Rams, 19-7 (Cle)
Bears, 28-21 (C)
1945—Rams, 17-0 (Cle)
Rams, 41-21 (C)
1946—Tie, 28-28 (C)
Bears, 27-21 (LA)
1947—Bears, 41-21 (LA)
Rams, 17-14 (C)
1948—Bears, 42-21 (C)
Bears, 21-6 (LA)
1949—Rams, 31-16 (C)
Rams, 27-24 (LA)
1950—Bears, 24-20 (LA)
Bears, 24-14 (C)
**Rams, 24-14 (LA)
1951—Rams, 42-17 (C)
1952—Rams, 31-7 (LA)
Rams, 40-24 (C)
1953—Rams, 38-24 (LA)
Bears, 24-21 (C)
1954—Rams, 42-38 (LA)
Bears, 24-13 (C)
1955—Bears, 31-20 (LA)
Bears, 24-3 (C)
1956—Bears, 35-24 (LA)
Bears, 30-21 (C)
1957—Bears, 34-26 (C)
Bears, 16-10 (LA)
1958—Bears, 31-10 (C)
Rams, 41-35 (LA)
1959—Rams, 28-21 (C)
Bears, 26-21 (LA)
1960—Bears, 34-27 (C)
Tie, 24-24 (LA)
1961—Bears, 21-17 (LA)
Bears, 28-24 (C)
1962—Bears, 27-23 (LA)
Bears, 30-14 (C)
1963—Bears, 52-14 (LA)
Bears, 6-0 (C)
1964—Bears, 38-17 (C)
Bears, 34-24 (LA)
1965—Rams, 30-28 (LA)
Bears, 31-6 (C)
1966—Rams, 31-17 (LA)
Bears, 17-10 (C)
1967—Rams, 28-17 (C)
1968—Bears, 17-16 (LA)
1969—Rams, 9-7 (C)
1971—Rams, 17-3 (LA)
1972—Tie, 13-13 (C)
1973—Rams, 26-0 (C)
1975—Rams, 38-10 (LA)
1976—Rams, 20-12 (LA)
1977—Bears, 24-23 (C)
1979—Bears, 27-23 (C)
1981—Rams, 24-7 (C)
1982—Bears, 34-26 (LA)
1983—Rams, 21-14 (LA)
1984—Rams, 29-13 (LA)
1985—***Bears, 24-0 (C)
1986—Rams, 20-17 (C)
1988—Rams, 23-3 (LA)
1989—Bears, 20-10 (C)
1990—Bears, 38-9 (C)
1993—Rams, 20-6 (LA)
1994—Bears, 27-13 (C)
1995—Rams, 34-28 (StL)
1996—Bears, 35-9 (C)
1997—Bears, 13-10 (StL)
1998—Rams, 20-12 (C)
1999—Rams, 34-12 (StL)
2002—Rams, 21-16 (StL)
2003—Rams, 23-21 (C)
2006—Bears, 42-27 (StL)
2008—Bears, 27-3 (StL)
(RS Pts.—Bears 2,003, Rams 1,753)
(PS Pts.—Bears 38, Rams 24)
**Franchise in Los Angeles prior to 1995 and in Cleveland prior to 1946*
***Conference Playoff*
****NFC Championship*

CHICAGO vs. SAN DIEGO
RS: Series tied, 5-5
1970—Chargers, 20-7 (C)
1974—Chargers, 28-21 (SD)
1978—Chargers, 40-7 (SD)
1981—Bears, 20-17 (C) OT
1984—Chargers, 20-7 (SD)
1993—Bears, 16-13 (SD)
1996—Bears, 27-14 (C)
1999—Bears, 23-20 (SD) OT
2003—Bears, 20-7 (C)
2007—Chargers, 14-3 (SD)
(RS Pts.—Chargers 193, Bears 151)

CHICAGO vs. SAN FRANCISCO
RS: Bears lead series, 29-27-1
PS: 49ers lead series, 3-0
1950—Bears, 32-20 (SF)
Bears, 17-0 (C)
1951—Bears, 13-7 (C)
1952—49ers, 40-16 (C)
Bears, 20-17 (SF)
1953—49ers, 35-28 (C)
49ers, 24-14 (SF)
1954—49ers, 31-24 (C)
Bears, 31-27 (SF)
1955—49ers, 20-19 (C)
Bears, 34-23 (SF)
1956—Bears, 31-7 (C)
Bears, 38-21 (SF)
1957—49ers, 21-17 (C)
49ers, 21-17 (SF)
1958—Bears, 28-6 (C)
Bears, 27-14 (SF)
1959—49ers, 20-17 (SF)
Bears, 14-3 (C)
1960—Bears, 27-10 (C)
49ers, 25-7 (SF)
1961—Bears, 31-0 (C)
49ers, 41-31 (SF)
1962—Bears, 30-14 (SF)
49ers, 34-27 (C)
1963—49ers, 20-14 (SF)
Bears, 27-7 (C)
1964—49ers, 31-21 (SF)
Bears, 23-21 (C)
1965—49ers, 52-24 (SF)
Bears, 61-20 (C)
1966—Tie, 30-30 (C)
49ers, 41-14 (SF)
1967—Bears, 28-14 (SF)
1968—Bears, 27-19 (C)
1969—49ers, 42-21 (SF)
1970—49ers, 37-16 (C)
1971—49ers, 13-0 (SF)
1972—49ers, 34-21 (C)
1974—49ers, 34-0 (C)
1975—49ers, 31-3 (SF)
1976—Bears, 19-12 (SF)
1978—Bears, 16-13 (SF)
1979—Bears, 28-27 (SF)
1981—49ers, 28-17 (SF)
1983—Bears, 13-3 (C)
1984—*49ers, 23-0 (SF)
1985—Bears, 26-10 (SF)
1987—49ers, 41-0 (SF)
1988—Bears, 10-9 (C)
*49ers, 28-3 (C)
1989—49ers, 26-0 (SF)
1991—49ers, 52-14 (SF)
1994—**49ers, 44-15 (SF)

2000—49ers, 17-0 (SF)
2001—Bears, 37-31 (C) OT
2003—49ers, 49-7 (SF)
2004—Bears, 23-13 (C)
2005—Bears, 17-9 (C)
2006—Bears, 41-10 (C)
(RS Pts.—49ers 1,277, Bears 1,188)
(PS Pts.—49ers 95, Bears 18)
NFC Championship
**NFC Divisional Playoff*

CHICAGO vs. SEATTLE
RS: Seahawks lead series, 7-3
PS: Bears lead series, 1-0
1976—Bears, 34-7 (S)
1978—Seahawks, 31-29 (C)
1982—Seahawks, 20-14 (S)
1984—Seahawks, 38-9 (S)
1987—Seahawks, 34-21 (C)
1990—Bears, 17-0 (C)
1999—Seahawks, 14-13 (C)
2003—Seahawks, 24-17 (S)
2006—Bears, 37-6 (C)
*Bears, 27-24 (C) OT
2007—Seahawks, 30-23 (S)
(RS Pts.—Bears 214, Seahawks 204)
(PS Pts.—Bears 27, Seahawks 24)
NFC Divisional Playoff

CHICAGO vs. TAMPA BAY
RS: Bears lead series, 35-18
1977—Bears, 10-0 (TB)
1978—Buccaneers, 33-19 (TB)
Bears, 14-3 (C)
1979—Buccaneers, 17-13 (C)
Bears, 14-0 (TB)
1980—Bears, 23-0 (C)
Bears, 14-13 (TB)
1981—Bears, 28-17 (C)
Buccaneers, 20-10 (TB)
1982—Buccaneers, 26-23 (TB) OT
1983—Bears, 17-10 (C)
Bears, 27-0 (TB)
1984—Bears, 34-14 (C)
Bears, 44-9 (TB)
1985—Bears, 38-28 (C)
Bears, 27-19 (TB)
1986—Bears, 23-3 (TB)
Bears, 48-14 (C)
1987—Bears, 20-3 (C)
Bears, 27-26 (TB)
1988—Bears, 28-10 (C)
Bears, 27-15 (TB)
1989—Buccaneers, 42-35 (TB)
Buccaneers, 32-31 (C)
1990—Bears, 26-6 (TB)
Bears, 27-14 (C)
1991—Bears, 21-20 (TB)
Bears, 27-0 (C)
1992—Bears, 31-14 (C)
Buccaneers, 20-17 (TB)
1993—Bears, 47-17 (C)
Buccaneers, 13-10 (TB)
1994—Bears, 21-9 (C)
Bears, 20-6 (TB)
1995—Bears, 25-6 (TB)
Bears, 31-10 (C)
1996—Bears, 13-10 (C)
Buccaneers, 34-19 (TB)
1997—Bears, 13-7 (C)
Buccaneers, 31-15 (TB)
1998—Buccaneers, 27-15 (TB)
Buccaneers, 31-17 (C)
1999—Buccaneers, 6-3 (TB)
Buccaneers, 20-6 (C)
2000—Buccaneers, 41-0 (TB)
Bears, 13-10 (C)
2001—Bears, 27-24 (TB)
Bears, 27-3 (C)
2002—Buccaneers, 15-0 (C)
2004—Buccaneers, 19-7 (TB)
2005—Bears, 13-10 (TB)
2006—Bears, 34-31 (C) OT
2008—Buccaneers, 27-24 (C) OT
(RS Pts.—Bears 1,143, Buccaneers 835)

CHICAGO vs. *TENNESSEE
RS: Series tied, 5-5
1973—Bears, 35-14 (C)
1977—Oilers, 47-0 (H)
1980—Oilers, 10-6 (C)
1986—Bears, 20-7 (H)
1989—Oilers, 33-28 (C)
1992—Oilers, 24-7 (H)
1995—Bears, 35-32 (C)
1998—Bears, 23-20 (T)
2004—Bears, 19-17 (T) OT
2008—Titans, 21-14 (C)
(RS Pts.—Titans 225, Bears 187)
Franchise in Houston prior to 1997; known as Oilers prior to 1999

CHICAGO vs. *WASHINGTON
RS: Bears lead series, 20-18-1
PS: Redskins lead series, 4-3
1932—Tie, 7-7 (B)
1933—Bears, 7-0 (C)
Redskins, 10-0 (B)
1934—Bears, 21-0 (B)
1935—Bears, 30-14 (B)
1936—Bears, 26-0 (B)
1937—**Redskins, 28-21 (C)
1938—Bears, 31-7 (C)
1940—Redskins, 7-3 (W)
**Bears, 73-0 (W)
1941—Bears, 35-21 (C)
1942—**Redskins, 14-6 (W)
1943—Redskins, 21-7 (W)
**Bears, 41-21 (C)
1945—Redskins, 28-21 (W)
1946—Bears, 24-20 (C)
1947—Bears, 56-20 (W)
1948—Bears, 48-13 (C)
1949—Bears, 31-21 (W)
1951—Bears, 27-0 (W)
1953—Bears, 27-24 (W)
1957—Redskins, 14-3 (C)
1964—Redskins, 27-20 (W)
1968—Redskins, 38-28 (C)
1971—Bears, 16-15 (C)
1974—Redskins, 42-0 (W)
1976—Bears, 33-7 (C)
1978—Bears, 14-10 (W)
1980—Bears, 35-21 (C)
1981—Redskins, 24-7 (C)
1984—***Bears, 23-19 (W)
1985—Bears, 45-10 (C)
1986—***Redskins, 27-13 (C)
1987—***Redskins, 21-17 (C)
1988—Bears, 34-14 (W)
1989—Redskins, 38-14 (W)
1990—Redskins, 10-9 (W)
1991—Redskins, 20-7 (C)
1996—Redskins, 10-3 (W)
1997—Redskins, 31-8 (C)
1999—Redskins, 48-22 (W)
2001—Bears, 20-15 (W)
2003—Bears, 27-24 (C)
2004—Redskins, 13-10 (C)
2005—Redskins, 9-7 (W)
2007—Redskins, 24-16 (W)
(RS Pts.—Bears 779, Redskins 677)
(PS Pts.—Bears 194, Redskins 130)
Franchise in Boston prior to 1937 and known as Braves prior to 1933
**NFL Championship*
***NFC Divisional Playoff*

CINCINNATI vs. ARIZONA
RS: Bengals lead series, 5-4;
See Arizona vs. Cincinnati

CINCINNATI vs. ATLANTA
RS: Bengals lead series, 7-4;
See Atlanta vs. Cincinnati

CINCINNATI vs. BALTIMORE
RS: Ravens lead series, 15-11;
See Baltimore vs. Cincinnati

CINCINNATI vs. BUFFALO
RS: Bills lead series, 14-9
PS: Bengals lead series, 2-0;
See Buffalo vs. Cincinnati

CINCINNATI vs. CAROLINA
RS: Panthers lead series, 2-1;
See Carolina vs. Cincinnati

CINCINNATI vs. CHICAGO
RS: Bengals lead series, 5-3;
See Chicago vs. Cincinnati

CINCINNATI vs. CLEVELAND
RS: Bengals lead series, 36-35
1970—Browns, 30-27 (Cle)
Bengals, 14-10 (Cin)
1971—Browns, 27-24 (Cin)
Browns, 31-27 (Cle)
1972—Browns, 27-6 (Cle)
Browns, 27-24 (Cin)
1973—Browns, 17-10 (Cle)
Bengals, 34-17 (Cin)
1974—Bengals, 33-7 (Cin)
Bengals, 34-24 (Cle)
1975—Bengals, 24-17 (Cin)
Browns, 35-23 (Cle)
1976—Bengals, 45-24 (Cle)
Bengals, 21-6 (Cin)
1977—Browns, 13-3 (Cin)
Bengals, 10-7 (Cle)
1978—Browns, 13-10 (Cle) OT
Bengals, 48-16 (Cin)
1979—Browns, 28-27 (Cle)
Bengals, 16-12 (Cin)
1980—Browns, 31-7 (Cle)
Browns, 27-24 (Cin)
1981—Browns, 20-17 (Cin)
Bengals, 41-21 (Cle)
1982—Bengals, 23-10 (Cin)
1983—Browns, 17-7 (Cle)
Bengals, 28-21 (Cin)
1984—Bengals, 12-9 (Cin)
Bengals, 20-17 (Cle) OT
1985—Bengals, 27-10 (Cin)
Browns, 24-6 (Cle)
1986—Bengals, 30-13 (Cle)
Browns, 34-3 (Cin)
1987—Browns, 34-0 (Cin)
Browns, 38-24 (Cle)

1988—Bengals, 24-17 (Cin)
Browns, 23-16 (Cle)
1989—Bengals, 21-14 (Cin)
Bengals, 21-0 (Cle)
1990—Bengals, 34-13 (Cle)
Bengals, 21-14 (Cin)
1991—Browns, 14-13 (Cle)
Bengals, 23-21 (Cin)
1992—Bengals, 30-10 (Cin)
Browns, 37-21 (Cle)
1993—Browns, 27-14 (Cle)
Browns, 28-17 (Cin)
1994—Browns, 28-20 (Cin)
Browns, 37-13 (Cle)
1995—Browns, 29-26 (Cin) OT
Browns, 26-10 (Cle)
1999—Bengals, 18-17 (Cle)
Bengals, 44-28 (Cin)
2000—Browns, 24-7 (Cin)
Bengals, 12-3 (Cle)
2001—Bengals, 24-14 (Cin)
Browns, 18-0 (Cle)
2002—Browns, 20-7 (Cle)
Browns, 27-20 (Cin)
2003—Bengals, 21-14 (Cle)
Browns, 22-14 (Cin)
2004—Browns, 34-17 (Cle)
Bengals, 58-48 (Cin)
2005—Bengals, 27-13 (Cle)
Bengals, 23-20 (Cin)
2006—Bengals, 34-17 (Cin)
Bengals, 30-0 (Cle)
2007—Browns, 51-45 (Cle)
Bengals, 19-14 (Cin)
2008—Browns, 20-12 (Cin)
Bengals, 14-0 (Cle)
(RS Pts.—Bengals 1,499, Browns 1,456)

CINCINNATI vs. DALLAS
RS: Cowboys lead series, 6-4
1973—Cowboys, 38-10 (D)
1979—Cowboys, 38-13 (D)
1985—Bengals, 50-24 (C)
1988—Bengals, 38-24 (D)
1991—Cowboys, 35-23 (D)
1994—Cowboys, 23-20 (C)
1997—Bengals, 31-24 (C)
2000—Cowboys, 23-6 (D)
2004—Bengals, 26-3 (C)
2008—Cowboys, 31-22 (D)
(RS Pts.—Cowboys 263, Bengals 239)

CINCINNATI vs. DENVER
RS: Broncos lead series, 16-8
1968—Bengals, 24-10 (C)
Broncos, 10-7 (D)
1969—Broncos, 30-23 (C)
Broncos, 27-16 (D)
1971—Bengals, 24-10 (D)
1972—Bengals, 21-10 (C)
1973—Broncos, 28-10 (D)
1975—Bengals, 17-16 (D)
1976—Bengals, 17-7 (C)
1977—Broncos, 24-13 (C)
1979—Broncos, 10-0 (D)
1981—Bengals, 38-21 (C)
1983—Broncos, 24-17 (D)
1984—Broncos, 20-17 (D)
1986—Broncos, 34-28 (D)
1991—Broncos, 45-14 (D)
1994—Broncos, 15-13 (D)
1996—Broncos, 14-10 (C)
1997—Broncos, 38-20 (D)
1998—Broncos, 33-26 (C)
2000—Bengals, 31-21 (C)
2003—Broncos, 30-10 (C)
2004—Bengals, 23-10 (C)
2006—Broncos, 24-23 (D)
(RS Pts.—Broncos 511, Bengals 442)

CINCINNATI vs. DETROIT
RS: Bengals lead series, 6-3
1970—Lions, 38-3 (D)
1974—Lions, 23-19 (C)
1983—Bengals, 17-9 (C)
1986—Bengals, 24-17 (D)
1989—Bengals, 42-7 (C)
1992—Lions, 19-13 (C)
1998—Bengals, 34-28 (D) OT
2001—Bengals, 31-27 (D)
2005—Bengals, 41-17 (D)
(RS Pts.—Bengals 224, Lions 185)

CINCINNATI vs. GREEN BAY
RS: Series tied, 5-5
1971—Packers, 20-17 (GB)
1976—Bengals, 28-7 (C)
1977—Bengals, 17-7 (Mil)
1980—Packers, 14-9 (GB)
1983—Bengals, 34-14 (C)
1986—Bengals, 34-28 (Mil)
1992—Packers, 24-23 (GB)
1995—Packers, 24-10 (GB)
1998—Packers, 13-6 (C)
2005—Bengals, 21-14 (C)
(RS Pts.—Bengals 199, Packers 165)

CINCINNATI vs. HOUSTON
RS: Bengals lead series, 3-1
2002—Bengals, 38-3 (H)
2003—Bengals, 34-27 (C)
2005—Bengals, 16-10 (C)
2008—Texans, 35-6 (H)
(RS Pts.—Bengals 94, Texans 75)

CINCINNATI vs. *INDIANAPOLIS
RS: Colts lead series, 15-8
PS: Colts lead series, 1-0
1970—**Colts, 17-0 (B)
1972—Colts, 20-19 (C)
1974—Bengals, 24-14 (B)
1976—Colts, 28-27 (B)
1979—Colts, 38-28 (B)
1980—Bengals, 34-33 (C)
1981—Bengals, 41-19 (B)
1982—Bengals, 20-17 (B)
1983—Colts, 34-31 (C)
1987—Bengals, 23-21 (I)
1989—Colts, 23-12 (C)
1990—Colts, 34-20 (C)
1992—Colts, 21-17 (C)
1993—Colts, 9-6 (C)
1994—Colts, 17-13 (C)
1995—Bengals, 24-21 (I) OT
1996—Bengals, 31-24 (C)
1997—Bengals, 28-13 (I)
1998—Colts, 39-26 (I)
1999—Colts, 31-10 (I)
2002—Colts, 28-21 (I)
2005—Colts, 45-37 (C)
2006—Colts, 34-16 (I)
2008—Colts, 35-3 (I)
(RS Pts.—Colts 598, Bengals 511)
(PS Pts.—Colts 17, Bengals 0)
**Franchise in Baltimore prior to 1984*
***AFC Divisional Playoff*

CINCINNATI vs. JACKSONVILLE
RS: Jaguars lead series, 11-6
1995—Bengals, 24-17 (C)
Bengals, 17-13 (J)
1996—Bengals, 28-21 (C)
Jaguars, 30-27 (J)
1997—Jaguars, 21-13 (J)
Bengals, 31-26 (C)
1998—Jaguars, 24-11 (J)
Jaguars, 34-17 (C)
1999—Jaguars, 41-10 (C)
Jaguars, 24-7 (J)
2000—Jaguars, 13-0 (J)
Bengals, 17-14 (C)
2001—Jaguars, 30-13 (J)
Jaguars, 14-10 (C)
2002—Jaguars, 29-15 (C)
2005—Jaguars, 23-20 (J)
2008—Bengals, 21-19 (C)
(RS Pts.—Jaguars 393, Bengals 281)

CINCINNATI vs. KANSAS CITY
RS: Chiefs lead series, 13-12
1968—Chiefs, 13-3 (KC)
Chiefs, 16-9 (C)
1969—Bengals, 24-19 (C)
Chiefs, 42-22 (KC)
1970—Chiefs, 27-19 (C)
1972—Bengals, 23-16 (KC)
1973—Bengals, 14-6 (C)
1974—Bengals, 33-6 (C)
1976—Bengals, 27-24 (KC)
1977—Bengals, 27-7 (KC)
1978—Chiefs, 24-23 (C)
1979—Chiefs, 10-7 (C)
1980—Bengals, 20-6 (KC)
1983—Chiefs, 20-15 (KC)
1984—Chiefs, 27-22 (C)
1986—Chiefs, 24-14 (KC)
1987—Bengals, 30-27 (C) OT
1988—Chiefs, 31-28 (KC)
1989—Bengals, 21-17 (KC)
1993—Chiefs, 17-15 (KC)
2003—Bengals, 24-19 (C)
2005—Chiefs, 37-3 (KC)
2006—Bengals, 23-10 (KC)
2007—Chiefs, 27-20 (KC)
2008—Bengals, 16-6 (C)
(RS Pts.—Bengals 482, Chiefs 478)

CINCINNATI vs. MIAMI
RS: Dolphins lead series, 12-5
PS: Dolphins lead series, 1-0
1968—Dolphins, 24-22 (C)
Bengals, 38-21 (M)
1969—Bengals, 27-21 (C)
1971—Dolphins, 23-13 (C)
1973—*Dolphins, 34-16 (M)
1974—Dolphins, 24-3 (M)
1977—Bengals, 23-17 (C)
1978—Dolphins, 21-0 (M)
1980—Dolphins, 17-16 (M)
1983—Dolphins, 38-14 (M)
1987—Dolphins, 20-14 (C)
1989—Dolphins, 20-13 (C)
1991—Dolphins, 37-13 (M)
1994—Dolphins, 23-7 (C)
1995—Dolphins, 26-23 (C)
2000—Dolphins, 31-16 (C)
2004—Bengals, 16-13 (C)
2007—Bengals, 38-25 (M)
(RS Pts.—Dolphins 401, Bengals 296)

(PS Pts.—Dolphins 34, Bengals 16)
AFC Divisional Playoff

CINCINNATI vs. MINNESOTA
RS: Series tied, 5-5
1973—Bengals, 27-0 (C)
1977—Vikings, 42-10 (M)
1980—Bengals, 14-0 (C)
1983—Vikings, 20-14 (M)
1986—Bengals, 24-20 (C)
1989—Vikings, 29-21 (M)
1992—Vikings, 42-7 (C)
1995—Bengals, 27-24 (C)
1998—Vikings, 24-3 (M)
2005—Bengals, 37-8 (C)
(RS Pts.—Vikings 209, Bengals 184)

CINCINNATI vs. *NEW ENGLAND
RS: Patriots lead series, 13-8
1968—Patriots, 33-14 (B)
1969—Patriots, 25-14 (C)
1970—Bengals, 45-7 (C)
1972—Bengals, 31-7 (NE)
1975—Bengals, 27-10 (C)
1978—Patriots, 10-3 (C)
1979—Patriots, 20-14 (C)
1984—Patriots, 20-14 (NE)
1985—Patriots, 34-23 (NE)
1986—Bengals, 31-7 (NE)
1988—Patriots, 27-21 (NE)
1990—Bengals, 41-7 (C)
1991—Bengals, 29-7 (C)
1992—Bengals, 20-10 (C)
1993—Patriots, 7-2 (NE)
1994—Patriots, 31-28 (C)
2000—Patriots, 16-13 (NE)
2001—Bengals, 23-17 (C)
2004—Patriots, 35-28 (NE)
2006—Patriots, 38-13 (C)
2007—Patriots, 34-13 (C)
(RS Pts.—Bengals 447, Patriots 402)
Franchise in Boston prior to 1971

CINCINNATI vs. NEW ORLEANS
RS: Bengals lead series, 6-5
1970—Bengals, 26-6 (C)
1975—Bengals, 21-0 (NO)
1978—Saints, 20-18 (C)
1981—Saints, 17-7 (NO)
1984—Bengals, 24-21 (NO)
1987—Saints, 41-24 (C)
1990—Saints, 21-7 (C)
1993—Saints, 20-13 (NO)
1996—Bengals, 30-15 (C)
2002—Bengals, 20-13 (C)
2006—Bengals, 31-16 (NO)
(RS Pts.—Bengals 221, Saints 190)

CINCINNATI vs. N.Y. GIANTS
RS: Bengals lead series, 5-3
1972—Bengals, 13-10 (C)
1977—Bengals, 30-13 (C)
1985—Bengals, 35-30 (C)
1991—Bengals, 27-24 (C)
1994—Giants, 27-20 (NY)
1997—Giants, 29-27 (NY)
2004—Bengals, 23-22 (C)
2008—Giants, 26-23 (NY) OT
(RS Pts.—Bengals 198, Giants 181)

CINCINNATI vs. N.Y. JETS
RS: Jets lead series, 13-7
PS: Jets lead series, 1-0
1968—Jets, 27-14 (NY)
1969—Jets, 21-7 (C)
Jets, 40-7 (NY)
1971—Jets, 35-21 (NY)
1973—Bengals, 20-14 (C)
1976—Bengals, 42-3 (NY)
1981—Bengals, 31-30 (NY)
1982—*Jets, 44-17 (C)
1984—Jets, 43-23 (NY)
1985—Jets, 29-20 (C)
1986—Bengals, 52-21 (C)
1987—Jets, 27-20 (NY)
1988—Bengals, 36-19 (C)
1990—Bengals, 25-20 (C)
1992—Jets, 17-14 (NY)
1993—Jets, 17-12 (NY)
1997—Jets, 31-14 (C)
2001—Jets, 15-14 (NY)
2004—Jets, 31-24 (NY)
2007—Bengals, 38-31 (C)
2008—Jets, 26-14 (NY)
(RS Pts.—Jets 497, Bengals 448)
(PS Pts.—Jets 44, Bengals 17)
AFC First-Round Playoff

CINCINNATI vs. *OAKLAND
RS: Raiders lead series, 17-8
PS: Raiders lead series, 2-0
1968—Raiders, 31-10 (O)
Raiders, 34-0 (C)
1969—Bengals, 31-17 (C)
Raiders, 37-17 (O)
1970—Bengals, 31-21 (C)
1971—Raiders, 31-27 (O)
1972—Raiders, 20-14 (C)
1974—Raiders, 30-27 (O)
1975—Bengals, 14-10 (C)
**Raiders, 31-28 (O)
1976—Raiders, 35-20 (O)
1978—Raiders, 34-21 (C)
1980—Raiders, 28-17 (O)
1982—Bengals, 31-17 (C)
1983—Raiders, 20-10 (C)
1985—Raiders, 13-6 (LA)
1988—Bengals, 45-21 (LA)
1989—Raiders, 28-7 (LA)
1990—Raiders, 24-7 (LA)
**Raiders, 20-10 (LA)
1991—Raiders, 38-14 (C)
1992—Bengals, 24-21 (C) OT
1993—Bengals, 16-10 (C)
1995—Raiders, 20-17 (C)
1998—Raiders, 27-10 (O)
2003—Raiders, 23-20 (O)
2006—Bengals, 27-10 (C)
(RS Pts.—Raiders 600, Bengals 463)
(PS Pts.—Raiders 51, Bengals 38)
Franchise in Los Angeles from 1982-1994
***AFC Divisional Playoff*

CINCINNATI vs. PHILADELPHIA
RS: Bengals lead series, 7-3-1
1971—Bengals, 37-14 (C)
1975—Bengals, 31-0 (P)
1979—Bengals, 37-13 (C)
1982—Bengals, 18-14 (P)
1988—Bengals, 28-24 (P)
1991—Eagles, 17-10 (P)
1994—Bengals, 33-30 (C)
1997—Eagles, 44-42 (P)
2000—Eagles, 16-7 (P)
2004—Bengals, 38-10 (P)
2008—Tie, 13-13 OT (C)
(RS Pts.—Bengals 294, Eagles 195)

CINCINNATI vs. PITTSBURGH
RS: Steelers lead series, 47-30
PS: Steelers lead series, 1-0
1970—Steelers, 21-10 (P)
Bengals, 34-7 (C)
1971—Steelers, 21-10 (P)
Steelers, 21-13 (C)
1972—Bengals, 15-10 (C)
Steelers, 40-17 (P)
1973—Bengals, 19-7 (C)
Steelers, 20-13 (P)
1974—Bengals, 17-10 (C)
Steelers, 27-3 (P)
1975—Steelers, 30-24 (C)
Steelers, 35-14 (P)
1976—Steelers, 23-6 (P)
Steelers, 7-3 (C)
1977—Steelers, 20-14 (P)
Bengals, 17-10 (C)
1978—Steelers, 28-3 (C)
Steelers, 7-6 (P)
1979—Bengals, 34-10 (C)
Steelers, 37-17 (P)
1980—Bengals, 30-28 (C)
Bengals, 17-16 (P)
1981—Bengals, 34-7 (C)
Bengals, 17-10 (P)
1982—Steelers, 26-20 (P) OT
1983—Steelers, 24-14 (C)
Bengals, 23-10 (P)
1984—Steelers, 38-17 (P)
Bengals, 22-20 (C)
1985—Bengals, 37-24 (P)
Bengals, 26-21 (C)
1986—Bengals, 24-22 (C)
Steelers, 30-9 (P)
1987—Steelers, 23-20 (P)
Steelers, 30-16 (C)
1988—Bengals, 17-12 (P)
Bengals, 42-7 (C)
1989—Bengals, 41-10 (C)
Bengals, 26-16 (P)
1990—Bengals, 27-3 (C)
Bengals, 16-12 (P)
1991—Steelers, 33-27 (C) OT
Steelers, 17-10 (P)
1992—Steelers, 20-0 (P)
Steelers, 21-9 (C)
1993—Steelers, 34-7 (P)
Steelers, 24-16 (C)
1994—Steelers, 14-10 (P)
Steelers, 38-15 (C)
1995—Bengals, 27-9 (P)
Steelers, 49-31 (C)
1996—Steelers, 20-10 (P)
Bengals, 34-24 (C)
1997—Steelers, 26-10 (C)
Steelers, 20-3 (P)
1998—Bengals, 25-20 (C)
Bengals, 25-24 (P)
1999—Steelers, 17-3 (C)
Bengals, 27-20 (P)
2000—Steelers, 15-0 (P)
Steelers, 48-28 (C)
2001—Steelers, 16-7 (P)
Bengals, 26-23 (C) OT
2002—Steelers, 34-7 (C)
Steelers, 29-21 (P)
2003—Steelers, 17-10 (C)
Bengals, 24-20 (P)

2004—Steelers, 28-17 (P)
Steelers, 19-14 (C)
2005—Steelers, 27-13 (C)
Bengals, 38-31 (P)
*Steelers, 31-17 (C)
2006—Bengals, 28-20 (P)
Steelers, 23-17 (C) OT
2007—Steelers, 24-13 (C)
Steelers, 24-10 (P)
2008—Steelers, 38-10 (C)
Steelers, 27-10 (P)
(RS Pts.—Steelers 1,673, Bengals 1,366)
(PS Pts.—Steelers 31, Bengals 17)
AFC First-Round Playoff

CINCINNATI vs. *ST. LOUIS
RS: Bengals lead series, 6-5
1972—Rams, 15-12 (LA)
1976—Bengals, 20-12 (C)
1978—Bengals, 20-19 (LA)
1981—Bengals, 24-10 (C)
1984—Rams, 24-14 (C)
1990—Bengals, 34-31 (LA) OT
1993—Bengals, 15-3 (C)
1996—Rams, 26-16 (StL)
1999—Rams, 38-10 (C)
2003—Rams, 27-10 (StL)
2007—Bengals, 19-10 (C)
(RS Pts.—Rams 215, Bengals 194)
Franchise in Los Angeles prior to 1995

CINCINNATI vs. SAN DIEGO
RS: Chargers lead series, 18-10
PS: Bengals lead series, 1-0
1968—Chargers, 29-13 (SD)
Chargers, 31-10 (C)
1969—Bengals, 34-20 (C)
Chargers, 21-14 (SD)
1970—Bengals, 17-14 (SD)
1971—Bengals, 31-0 (C)
1973—Bengals, 20-13 (SD)
1974—Chargers, 20-17 (C)
1975—Bengals, 47-17 (C)
1977—Chargers, 24-3 (SD)
1978—Chargers, 22-13 (SD)
1979—Chargers, 26-24 (C)
1980—Chargers, 31-14 (C)
1981—Bengals, 40-17 (SD)
*Bengals, 27-7 (C)
1982—Chargers, 50-34 (SD)
1985—Chargers, 44-41 (C)
1987—Chargers, 10-9 (C)
1988—Bengals, 27-10 (C)
1990—Bengals, 21-16 (SD)
1992—Chargers, 27-10 (SD)
1994—Chargers, 27-10 (SD)
1996—Chargers, 27-14 (SD)
1997—Bengals, 38-31 (C)
1999—Chargers, 34-7 (C)
2001—Chargers, 28-14 (SD)
2002—Chargers, 34-6 (C)
2003—Bengals, 34-27 (SD)
2006—Chargers, 49-41 (C)
(RS Pts.—Chargers 699, Bengals 603)
(PS Pts.—Bengals 27, Chargers 7)
AFC Championship

CINCINNATI vs. SAN FRANCISCO
RS: 49ers lead series, 8-3
PS: 49ers lead series, 2-0
1974—Bengals, 21-3 (SF)
1978—49ers, 28-12 (SF)
1981—49ers, 21-3 (C)
*49ers, 26-21 (Detroit)
1984—49ers, 23-17 (SF)
1987—49ers, 27-26 (C)
1988—**49ers, 20-16 (South Florida)
1990—49ers, 20-17 (C) OT
1993—49ers, 21-8 (SF)
1996—49ers, 28-21 (SF)
1999—Bengals, 44-30 (C)
2003—Bengals, 41-38 (C)
2007—49ers, 20-13 (SF)
(RS Pts.—49ers 259, Bengals 223)
(PS Pts.—49ers 46, Bengals 37)
Super Bowl XVI
**Super Bowl XXIII*

CINCINNATI vs. SEATTLE
RS: Seahawks lead series, 9-8
PS: Bengals lead series, 1-0
1977—Bengals, 42-20 (C)
1981—Bengals, 27-21 (C)
1982—Bengals, 24-10 (C)
1984—Seahawks, 26-6 (C)
1985—Seahawks, 28-24 (C)
1986—Bengals, 34-7 (C)
1987—Bengals, 17-10 (S)
1988—*Bengals, 21-13 (C)
1989—Seahawks, 24-17 (C)
1990—Seahawks, 31-16 (S)
1991—Seahawks, 13-7 (C)
1992—Bengals, 21-3 (S)
1993—Seahawks, 19-10 (C)
1994—Bengals, 20-17 (S) OT
1995—Seahawks, 24-21 (S)
1999—Seahawks, 37-20 (S)
2003—Bengals, 27-24 (C)
2007—Seahawks, 24-21 (S)
(RS Pts.—Bengals 354, Seahawks 338)
(PS Pts.—Bengals 21, Seahawks 13)
AFC Divisional Playoff

CINCINNATI vs. TAMPA BAY
RS: Buccaneers lead series, 6-3
1976—Bengals, 21-0 (C)
1980—Buccaneers, 17-12 (C)
1983—Bengals, 23-17 (TB)
1989—Bengals, 56-23 (C)
1995—Buccaneers, 19-16 (TB)
1998—Buccaneers, 35-0 (C)
2001—Buccaneers, 16-13 (C) OT
2002—Buccaneers, 35-7 (C)
2006—Buccaneers, 14-13 (TB)
(RS Pts.— Buccaneers 176, Bengals 161)

CINCINNATI vs. *TENNESSEE
RS: Titans lead series, 39-31-1
PS: Bengals lead series, 1-0
1968—Oilers, 27-17 (C)
1969—Tie, 31-31 (H)
1970—Oilers, 20-13 (C)
Bengals, 30-20 (H)
1971—Oilers, 10-6 (H)
Bengals, 28-13 (C)
1972—Bengals, 30-7 (C)
Bengals, 61-17 (H)
1973—Bengals, 24-10 (C)
Bengals, 27-24 (H)
1974—Oilers, 34-21 (C)
Oilers, 20-3 (H)
1975—Bengals, 21-19 (H)
Bengals, 23-19 (C)
1976—Bengals, 27-7 (H)
Bengals, 31-27 (C)
1977—Bengals, 13-10 (C) OT
Oilers, 21-16 (H)
1978—Bengals, 28-13 (C)
Oilers, 17-10 (H)
1979—Oilers, 30-27 (C) OT
Oilers, 42-21 (H)
1980—Oilers, 13-10 (C)
Oilers, 23-3 (H)
1981—Oilers, 17-10 (H)
Bengals, 34-21 (C)
1982—Bengals, 27-6 (C)
Bengals, 35-27 (H)
1983—Bengals, 55-14 (H)
Bengals, 38-10 (C)
1984—Bengals, 13-3 (C)
Bengals, 31-13 (H)
1985—Oilers, 44-27 (H)
Bengals, 45-27 (C)
1986—Bengals, 31-28 (C)
Oilers, 32-28 (H)
1987—Oilers, 31-29 (C)
Oilers, 21-17 (H)
1988—Bengals, 44-21 (C)
Oilers, 41-6 (H)
1989—Oilers, 26-24 (H)
Bengals, 61-7 (C)
1990—Oilers, 48-17 (H)
Bengals, 40-20 (C)
**Bengals, 41-14 (C)
1991—Oilers, 30-7 (C)
Oilers, 35-3 (H)
1992—Oilers, 38-24 (C)
Oilers, 26-10 (H)
1993—Oilers, 28-12 (H)
Oilers, 38-3 (C)
1994—Oilers, 20-13 (H)
Bengals, 34-31 (C)
1995—Oilers, 38-28 (C)
Bengals, 32-25 (H)
1996—Oilers, 30-27 (C) OT
Bengals, 21-13 (H)
1997—Oilers, 30-7 (T)
Bengals, 41-14 (C)
1998—Oilers, 23-14 (C)
Oilers, 44-14 (T)
1999—Titans, 36-35 (T)
Titans, 24-14 (C)
2000—Titans, 23-14 (C)
Titans, 35-3 (T)
2001—Titans, 20-7 (C)
Bengals, 23-21 (T)
2002—Titans, 30-24 (C)
2004—Titans, 27-20 (T)
2005—Bengals, 31-23 (T)
2007—Bengals, 35-6 (C)
2008—Titans, 24-7 (C)
(RS Pts.—Titans 1,663, Bengals 1,636)
(PS Pts.—Bengals 41, Titans 14)
Franchise in Houston prior to 1997; known as Oilers prior to 1999
**AFC First-Round Playoff*

CINCINNATI vs. WASHINGTON
RS: Series tied, 4-4
1970—Redskins, 20-0 (W)
1974—Bengals, 28-17 (C)
1979—Redskins, 28-14 (W)
1985—Redskins, 27-24 (W)
1988—Bengals, 20-17 (C) OT
1991—Redskins, 34-27 (C)
2004—Bengals, 17-10 (W)
2008—Bengals, 20-13 (C)

(RS Pts.—Redskins 166, Bengals 150)

CLEVELAND vs. ARIZONA
RS: Browns lead series, 33-12-3;
See Arizona vs. Cleveland
CLEVELAND vs. ATLANTA
RS: Browns lead series, 10-2;
See Atlanta vs. Cleveland
CLEVELAND vs. BALTIMORE
RS: Ravens lead series, 13-7;
See Baltimore vs. Cleveland
CLEVELAND vs. BUFFALO
RS: Browns lead series, 9-5
PS: Browns lead series, 1-0;
See Buffalo vs. Cleveland
CLEVELAND vs. CAROLINA
RS: Panthers lead series, 3-0;
See Carolina vs. Cleveland
CLEVELAND vs. CHICAGO
RS: Browns lead series, 9-4;
See Chicago vs. Cleveland
CLEVELAND vs. CINCINNATI
RS: Bengals lead series, 36-35;
See Cincinnati vs. Cleveland
CLEVELAND vs. DALLAS
RS: Browns lead series, 15-11
PS: Browns lead series, 2-1
1960—Browns, 48-7 (D)
1961—Browns, 25-7 (C)
Browns, 38-17 (D)
1962—Browns, 19-10 (C)
Cowboys, 45-21 (D)
1963—Browns, 41-24 (D)
Browns, 27-17 (C)
1964—Browns, 27-6 (C)
Browns, 20-16 (D)
1965—Browns, 23-17 (C)
Browns, 24-17 (D)
1966—Browns, 30-21 (C)
Cowboys, 26-14 (D)
1967—Cowboys, 21-14 (C)
*Cowboys, 52-14 (D)
1968—Cowboys, 28-7 (D)
*Browns, 31-20 (C)
1969—Browns, 42-10 (C)
*Browns, 38-14 (D)
1970—Cowboys, 6-2 (C)
1974—Cowboys, 41-17 (D)
1979—Browns, 26-7 (C)
1982—Cowboys, 31-14 (D)
1985—Cowboys, 20-7 (D)
1988—Browns, 24-21 (C)
1991—Cowboys, 26-14 (C)
1994—Browns, 19-14 (D)
2004—Cowboys, 19-12 (D)
2008—Cowboys, 28-10 (C)
(RS Pts.—Browns 565, Cowboys 502)
(PS Pts.—Cowboys 86, Browns 83)
**Conference Championship*
CLEVELAND vs. DENVER
RS: Broncos lead series, 17-5
PS: Broncos lead series, 3-0
1970—Browns, 27-13 (D)
1971—Broncos, 27-0 (C)
1972—Browns, 27-20 (D)
1974—Browns, 23-21 (C)
1975—Broncos, 16-15 (D)
1976—Broncos, 44-13 (D)
1978—Broncos, 19-7 (C)
1980—Broncos, 19-16 (C)
1981—Broncos, 23-20 (D) OT
1983—Broncos, 27-6 (D)
1984—Broncos, 24-14 (C)
1986—*Broncos, 23-20 (C) OT
1987—*Broncos, 38-33 (D)
1988—Broncos, 30-7 (D)
1989—Browns, 16-13 (C)
*Broncos, 37-21 (D)
1990—Browns, 30-29 (D)
1991—Broncos, 17-7 (C)
1992—Broncos, 12-0 (C)
1993—Broncos, 29-14 (C)
1994—Broncos, 26-14 (D)
2000—Broncos, 44-10 (D)
2003—Broncos, 23-20 (D) OT
2006—Broncos, 17-7 (C)
2008—Broncos, 34-30 (C)
(RS Pts.—Broncos 527, Browns 323)
(PS Pts.—Broncos 98, Browns 74)
**AFC Championship*
CLEVELAND vs. DETROIT
RS: Lions lead series, 13-4
PS: Lions lead series, 3-1
1952—Lions, 17-6 (D)
*Lions, 17-7 (C)
1953—*Lions, 17-16 (D)
1954—Lions, 14-10 (C)
*Browns, 56-10 (C)
1957—Lions, 20-7 (D)
*Lions, 59-14 (D)
1958—Lions, 30-10 (C)
1963—Lions, 38-10 (D)
1964—Browns, 37-21 (C)
1967—Lions, 31-14 (D)
1969—Lions, 28-21 (C)
1970—Lions, 41-24 (C)
1975—Lions, 21-10 (D)
1983—Browns, 31-26 (D)
1986—Browns, 24-21 (C)
1989—Lions, 13-10 (D)
1992—Lions, 24-14 (D)
1995—Lions, 38-20 (D)
2001—Browns, 24-14 (C)
2005—Lions, 13-10 (C)
(RS Pts.—Lions 410, Browns 282)
(PS Pts.—Lions 103, Browns 93)
**NFL Championship*
CLEVELAND vs. GREEN BAY
RS: Packers lead series, 9-7
PS: Packers lead series, 1-0
1953—Browns, 27-0 (Mil)
1955—Browns, 41-10 (C)
1956—Browns, 24-7 (Mil)
1961—Packers, 49-17 (C)
1964—Packers, 28-21 (Mil)
1965—*Packers, 23-12 (GB)
1966—Packers, 21-20 (C)
1967—Packers, 55-7 (Mil)
1969—Browns, 20-7 (C)
1972—Packers, 26-10 (C)
1980—Browns, 26-21 (C)
1983—Packers, 35-21 (Mil)
1986—Packers, 17-14 (C)
1992—Browns, 17-6 (C)
1995—Packers, 31-20 (C)
2001—Packers, 30-7 (GB)
2005—Browns, 26-24 (GB)
(RS Pts.—Packers 367, Browns 318)
(PS Pts.—Packers 23, Browns 12)
**NFL Championship*
CLEVELAND vs. HOUSTON
RS: Series tied, 3-3
2002—Browns, 34-17 (C)
2004—Browns, 22-14 (H)
2005—Texans, 19-16 (H)
2006—Texans, 14-6 (H)
2007—Browns, 27-17 (C)
2008—Texans, 16-6 (C)
(RS Pts.—Browns 111, Texans 97)
CLEVELAND vs. *INDIANAPOLIS
RS: Browns lead series, 13-12
PS: Series tied, 2-2
1956—Colts, 21-7 (C)
1959—Browns, 38-31 (B)
1962—Colts, 36-14 (C)
1964—**Browns, 27-0 (C)
1968—Browns, 30-20 (B)
**Colts, 34-0 (C)
1971—Browns, 14-13 (B)
***Colts, 20-3 (C)
1973—Browns, 24-14 (C)
1975—Colts, 21-7 (B)
1978—Browns, 45-24 (B)
1979—Browns, 13-10 (C)
1980—Browns, 28-27 (B)
1981—Browns, 42-28 (C)
1983—Browns, 41-23 (C)
1986—Browns, 24-9 (I)
1987—Colts, 9-7 (C)
***Browns, 38-21 (C)
1988—Browns, 23-17 (C)
1989—Colts, 23-17 (I) OT
1991—Browns, 31-0 (I)
1992—Colts, 14-3 (I)
1993—Colts, 23-10 (I)
1994—Browns, 21-14 (I)
1999—Colts, 29-28 (C)
2002—Colts, 28-23 (C)
2003—Colts, 9-6 (C)
2005—Colts, 13-6 (I)
2008—Colts, 10-6 (C)
(RS Pts.—Browns 508, Colts 466)
(PS Pts.—Colts 75, Browns 68)
**Franchise in Baltimore prior to 1984*
***NFL Championship*
****AFC Divisional Playoff*
CLEVELAND vs. JACKSONVILLE
RS: Jaguars lead series, 8-3
1995—Jaguars, 23-15 (C)
Jaguars, 24-21 (J)
1999—Jaguars, 24-7 (J)
Jaguars, 24-14 (C)
2000—Jaguars, 27-7 (C)
Jaguars, 48-0 (J)
2001—Browns, 23-14 (J)
Jaguars, 15-10 (C)
2002—Browns, 21-20 (J)
2005—Jaguars, 20-14 (C)
2008—Browns, 23-17 (J)
(RS Pts.—Jaguars 256, Browns 155)
CLEVELAND vs. KANSAS CITY
RS: Series tied, 9-9-2
1971—Chiefs, 13-7 (KC)
1972—Chiefs, 31-7 (C)
1973—Tie, 20-20 (KC)
1975—Browns, 40-14 (C)
1976—Chiefs, 39-14 (KC)
1977—Browns, 44-7 (C)
1978—Chiefs, 17-3 (KC)
1979—Browns, 27-24 (KC)

1980—Browns, 20-13 (C)
1984—Chiefs, 10-6 (KC)
1986—Browns, 20-7 (C)
1988—Browns, 6-3 (KC)
1989—Tie, 10-10 (C) OT
1990—Chiefs, 34-0 (KC)
1991—Browns, 20-15 (C)
1994—Chiefs, 20-13 (KC)
1995—Browns, 35-17 (C)
2002—Chiefs, 40-39 (C)
2003—Chiefs, 41-20 (KC)
2006—Browns, 31-28 (C) OT
(RS Pts.—Chiefs 403, Browns 382)

CLEVELAND vs. MIAMI
RS: Dolphins lead series, 7-6
PS: Dolphins lead series, 2-0
1970—Browns, 28-0 (M)
1972—*Dolphins, 20-14 (M)
1973—Dolphins, 17-9 (C)
1976—Browns, 17-13 (C)
1979—Browns, 30-24 (C) OT
1985—*Dolphins, 24-21 (M)
1986—Browns, 26-16 (C)
1988—Dolphins, 38-31 (M)
1989—Dolphins, 13-10 (M) OT
1990—Dolphins, 30-13 (C)
1992—Dolphins, 27-23 (C)
1993—Dolphins, 24-14 (C)
2004—Dolphins, 10-7 (M)
2005—Browns, 22-0 (C)
2007—Browns, 41-31 (C)
(RS Pts.—Browns 271, Dolphins 243)
(PS Pts.—Dolphins 44, Browns 35)
**AFC Divisional Playoff*

CLEVELAND vs. MINNESOTA
RS: Vikings lead series, 9-3
PS: Vikings lead series, 1-0
1965—Vikings, 27-17 (C)
1967—Browns, 14-10 (C)
1969—Vikings, 51-3 (M)
*Vikings, 27-7 (M)
1973—Vikings, 26-3 (M)
1975—Vikings, 42-10 (C)
1980—Vikings, 28-23 (M)
1983—Vikings, 27-21 (C)
1986—Browns, 23-20 (M)
1989—Browns, 23-17 (C) OT
1992—Vikings, 17-13 (M)
1995—Vikings, 27-11 (M)
2005—Vikings, 24-12 (M)
(RS Pts.—Vikings 316, Browns 173)
(PS Pts.—Vikings 27, Browns 7)
**NFL Championship*

CLEVELAND vs. NEW ENGLAND
RS: Browns lead series, 11-9
PS: Browns lead series, 1-0
1971—Browns, 27-7 (C)
1974—Browns, 21-14 (NE)
1977—Browns, 30-27 (C) OT
1980—Patriots, 34-17 (NE)
1982—Browns, 10-7 (C)
1983—Browns, 30-0 (NE)
1984—Patriots, 17-16 (C)
1985—Browns, 24-20 (C)
1987—Browns, 20-10 (NE)
1991—Browns, 20-0 (NE)
1992—Browns, 19-17 (NE)
1993—Patriots, 20-17 (C)
1994—Browns, 13-6 (C)
*Browns, 20-13 (C)
1995—Patriots, 17-14 (NE)
1999—Patriots, 19-7 (C)
2000—Browns, 19-11 (C)
2001—Patriots, 27-16 (NE)
2003—Patriots, 9-3 (NE)
2004—Patriots, 42-15 (C)
2007—Patriots, 34-17 (NE)
(RS Pts.—Browns 355, Patriots 338)
(PS Pts.—Browns 20, Patriots 13)
**AFC First-Round Playoff*

CLEVELAND vs. NEW ORLEANS
RS: Browns lead series, 11-4
1967—Browns, 42-7 (NO)
1968—Browns, 24-10 (NO)
Browns, 35-17 (C)
1969—Browns, 27-17 (NO)
1971—Browns, 21-17 (NO)
1975—Browns, 17-16 (C)
1978—Browns, 24-16 (NO)
1981—Browns, 20-17 (C)
1984—Saints, 16-14 (C)
1987—Saints, 28-21 (NO)
1990—Saints, 25-20 (NO)
1993—Browns, 17-13 (C)
1999—Browns, 21-16 (NO)
2002—Browns, 24-15 (NO)
2006—Saints, 19-14 (C)
(RS Pts.—Browns 341, Saints 249)

CLEVELAND vs. N.Y. GIANTS
RS: Browns lead series, 26-19-2
PS: Series tied, 1-1
1950—Giants, 6-0 (C)
Giants, 17-13 (NY)
*Browns, 8-3 (C)
1951—Browns, 14-13 (C)
Browns, 10-0 (NY)
1952—Giants, 17-9 (C)
Giants, 37-34 (NY)
1953—Browns, 7-0 (NY)
Browns, 62-14 (C)
1954—Browns, 24-14 (C)
Browns, 16-7 (NY)
1955—Browns, 24-14 (C)
Tie, 35-35 (NY)
1956—Giants, 21-9 (C)
Browns, 24-7 (NY)
1957—Browns, 6-3 (C)
Browns, 34-28 (NY)
1958—Giants, 21-17 (C)
Giants, 13-10 (NY)
*Giants, 10-0 (NY)
1959—Giants, 10-6 (C)
Giants, 48-7 (NY)
1960—Giants, 17-13 (C)
Browns, 48-34 (NY)
1961—Giants, 37-21 (C)
Tie, 7-7 (NY)
1962—Browns, 17-7 (C)
Giants, 17-13 (NY)
1963—Browns, 35-24 (NY)
Giants, 33-6 (C)
1964—Browns, 42-20 (C)
Browns, 52-20 (NY)
1965—Browns, 38-14 (NY)
Browns, 34-21 (C)
1966—Browns, 28-7 (NY)
Browns, 49-40 (C)
1967—Giants, 38-34 (NY)
Browns, 24-14 (C)
1968—Browns, 45-10 (C)
1969—Browns, 28-17 (C)
Giants, 27-14 (NY)
1973—Browns, 12-10 (C)
1977—Browns, 21-7 (NY)
1985—Browns, 35-33 (NY)
1991—Giants, 13-10 (NY)
1994—Giants, 16-13 (C)
2000—Giants, 24-3 (C)
2004—Giants, 27-10 (NY)
2008—Browns, 35-14 (C)
(RS Pts.—Browns 1,048, Giants 873)
(PS Pts.—Giants 13, Browns 8)
**Conference Playoff*

CLEVELAND vs. N.Y. JETS
RS: Browns lead series, 12-7
PS: Browns lead series, 1-0
1970—Browns, 31-21 (C)
1972—Browns, 26-10 (NY)
1976—Browns, 38-17 (C)
1978—Browns, 37-34 (C) OT
1979—Browns, 25-22 (NY) OT
1980—Browns, 17-14 (C)
1981—Jets, 14-13 (C)
1983—Browns, 10-7 (C)
1984—Jets, 24-20 (C)
1985—Jets, 37-10 (NY)
1986—*Browns, 23-20 (C) OT
1988—Jets, 23-3 (C)
1989—Browns, 38-24 (C)
1990—Jets, 24-21 (NY)
1991—Jets, 17-14 (C)
1994—Browns, 27-7 (C)
2002—Browns, 24-21 (NY)
2004—Jets, 10-7 (C)
2006—Browns, 20-13 (C)
2007—Browns, 24-18 (NY)
(RS Pts.—Browns 405, Jets 357)
(PS Pts.—Browns 23, Jets 20)
**AFC Divisional Playoff*

CLEVELAND vs. *OAKLAND
RS: Raiders lead series, 10-7
PS: Raiders lead series, 2-0
1970—Raiders, 23-20 (O)
1971—Raiders, 34-20 (C)
1973—Browns, 7-3 (O)
1974—Raiders, 40-24 (C)
1975—Raiders, 38-17 (O)
1977—Raiders, 26-10 (C)
1979—Raiders, 19-14 (O)
1980—**Raiders, 14-12 (C)
1982—***Raiders, 27-10 (LA)
1985—Raiders, 21-20 (C)
1986—Raiders, 27-14 (LA)
1987—Browns, 24-17 (LA)
1992—Browns, 28-16 (LA)
1993—Browns, 19-16 (LA)
2000—Raiders, 36-10 (O)
2003—Browns, 13-7 (C)
2005—Browns, 9-7 (O)
2006—Browns, 24-21 (O)
2007—Raiders, 26-24 (O)
(RS Pts.—Raiders 377, Browns 297)
(PS Pts.—Raiders 41, Browns 22)
**Franchise in Los Angeles from 1982-1994*
***AFC Divisional Playoff*
****AFC First-Round Playoff*

CLEVELAND vs. PHILADELPHIA
RS: Browns lead series, 31-15-1
1950—Browns, 35-10 (P)
Browns, 13-7 (C)

1951—Browns, 20-17 (C)
Browns, 24-9 (P)
1952—Browns, 49-7 (P)
Eagles, 28-20 (C)
1953—Browns, 37-13 (C)
Eagles, 42-27 (P)
1954—Eagles, 28-10 (P)
Browns, 6-0 (C)
1955—Browns, 21-17 (C)
Eagles, 33-17 (P)
1956—Browns, 16-0 (P)
Browns, 17-14 (C)
1957—Browns, 24-7 (C)
Eagles, 17-7 (P)
1958—Browns, 28-14 (C)
Browns, 21-14 (P)
1959—Browns, 28-7 (C)
Browns, 28-21 (P)
1960—Browns, 41-24 (P)
Eagles, 31-29 (C)
1961—Eagles, 27-20 (P)
Browns, 45-24 (C)
1962—Eagles, 35-7 (P)
Tie, 14-14 (C)
1963—Browns, 37-7 (C)
Browns, 23-17 (P)
1964—Browns, 28-20 (P)
Browns, 38-24 (C)
1965—Browns, 35-17 (P)
Browns, 38-34 (C)
1966—Browns, 27-7 (C)
Eagles, 33-21 (P)
1967—Eagles, 28-24 (P)
1968—Browns, 47-13 (C)
1969—Browns, 27-20 (P)
1972—Browns, 27-17 (P)
1976—Browns, 24-3 (C)
1979—Browns, 24-19 (P)
1982—Eagles, 24-21 (C)
1988—Browns, 19-3 (C)
1991—Eagles, 32-30 (C)
1994—Browns, 26-7 (P)
2000—Eagles, 35-24 (C)
2004—Eagles, 34-31 (C) OT
2008—Eagles, 30-10 (P)
(RS Pts.—Browns 1,185, Eagles 884)

CLEVELAND vs. PITTSBURGH
RS: Steelers lead series, 57-55
PS: Steelers lead series, 2-0
1950—Browns, 30-17 (P)
Browns, 45-7 (C)
1951—Browns, 17-0 (C)
Browns, 28-0 (P)
1952—Browns, 21-20 (P)
Browns, 29-28 (C)
1953—Browns, 34-16 (C)
Browns, 20-16 (P)
1954—Steelers, 55-27 (P)
Browns, 42-7 (C)
1955—Browns, 41-14 (C)
Browns, 30-7 (P)
1956—Browns, 14-10 (P)
Steelers, 24-16 (C)
1957—Browns, 23-12 (P)
Browns, 24-0 (C)
1958—Browns, 45-12 (P)
Browns, 27-10 (C)
1959—Steelers, 17-7 (P)
Steelers, 21-20 (C)
1960—Browns, 28-20 (C)
Steelers, 14-10 (P)
1961—Browns, 30-28 (P)
Steelers, 17-13 (C)
1962—Browns, 41-14 (P)
Browns, 35-14 (C)
1963—Browns, 35-23 (C)
Steelers, 9-7 (P)
1964—Steelers, 23-7 (C)
Browns, 30-17 (P)
1965—Browns, 24-19 (C)
Browns, 42-21 (P)
1966—Browns, 41-10 (C)
Steelers, 16-6 (P)
1967—Browns, 21-10 (C)
Browns, 34-14 (P)
1968—Browns, 31-24 (C)
Browns, 45-24 (P)
1969—Browns, 42-31 (C)
Browns, 24-3 (P)
1970—Browns, 15-7 (C)
Steelers, 28-9 (P)
1971—Browns, 27-17 (C)
Steelers, 26-9 (P)
1972—Browns, 26-24 (C)
Steelers, 30-0 (P)
1973—Steelers, 33-6 (P)
Browns, 21-16 (C)
1974—Steelers, 20-16 (P)
Steelers, 26-16 (C)
1975—Steelers, 42-6 (C)
Steelers, 31-17 (P)
1976—Steelers, 31-14 (P)
Browns, 18-16 (C)
1977—Steelers, 28-14 (C)
Steelers, 35-31 (P)
1978—Steelers, 15-9 (P) OT
Steelers, 34-14 (C)
1979—Steelers, 51-35 (C)
Steelers, 33-30 (P) OT
1980—Browns, 27-26 (C)
Steelers, 16-13 (P)
1981—Steelers, 13-7 (P)
Steelers, 32-10 (C)
1982—Browns, 10-9 (C)
Steelers, 37-21 (P)
1983—Steelers, 44-17 (P)
Browns, 30-17 (C)
1984—Browns, 20-10 (C)
Steelers, 23-20 (P)
1985—Browns, 17-7 (C)
Steelers, 10-9 (P)
1986—Browns, 27-24 (P)
Browns, 37-31 (C) OT
1987—Browns, 34-10 (C)
Browns, 19-13 (P)
1988—Browns, 23-9 (P)
Browns, 27-7 (C)
1989—Browns, 51-0 (P)
Steelers, 17-7 (C)
1990—Browns, 13-3 (C)
Steelers, 35-0 (P)
1991—Browns, 17-14 (C)
Steelers, 17-10 (P)
1992—Browns, 17-9 (C)
Steelers, 23-13 (P)
1993—Browns, 28-23 (C)
Steelers, 16-9 (P)
1994—Steelers, 17-10 (C)
Steelers, 17-7 (P)
*Steelers, 29-9 (P)
1995—Steelers, 20-3 (P)
Steelers, 20-17 (C)
1999—Steelers, 43-0 (C)
Browns, 16-15 (P)
2000—Browns, 23-20 (C)
Steelers, 22-0 (P)
2001—Steelers, 15-12 (C) OT
Steelers, 28-7 (P)
2002—Steelers, 16-13 (P) OT
Steelers, 23-20 (C)
**Steelers, 36-33 (P)
2003—Browns, 33-13 (P)
Steelers, 13-6 (C)
2004—Steelers, 34-23 (P)
Steelers, 24-10 (C)
2005—Steelers, 34-21 (P)
Steelers, 41-0 (C)
2006—Steelers, 24-20 (C)
Steelers, 27-7 (P)
2007—Steelers, 34-7 (C)
Steelers, 31-28 (P)
2008—Steelers, 10-6 (C)
Steelers, 31-0 (P)
(RS Pts.—Browns 2,254, Steelers 2,241)
(PS Pts.—Steelers 65, Browns 42)
AFC Divisional Playoff
***AFC First-Round Playoff*

CLEVELAND vs. *ST. LOUIS
RS: Series tied, 9-9
PS: Browns lead series, 2-1
1950—**Browns, 30-28 (C)
1951—Browns, 38-23 (LA)
**Rams, 24-17 (LA)
1952—Browns, 37-7 (C)
1955—**Browns, 38-14 (LA)
1957—Browns, 45-31 (C)
1958—Browns, 30-27 (LA)
1963—Browns, 20-6 (C)
1965—Rams, 42-7 (LA)
1968—Rams, 24-6 (C)
1973—Rams, 30-17 (LA)
1977—Rams, 9-0 (C)
1978—Browns, 30-19 (C)
1981—Rams, 27-16 (LA)
1984—Rams, 20-17 (LA)
1987—Browns, 30-17 (C)
1990—Rams, 38-23 (C)
1993—Browns, 42-14 (LA)
1999—Rams, 34-3 (StL)
2003—Rams, 26-20 (C)
2007—Browns, 27-20 (StL)
(RS Pts.—Rams 414, Browns 408)
(PS Pts.—Browns 85, Rams 66)
Franchise in Los Angeles prior to 1995
***NFL Championship*

CLEVELAND vs. SAN DIEGO
RS: Chargers lead series, 13-7-1
1970—Chargers, 27-10 (C)
1972—Browns, 21-17 (SD)
1973—Tie, 16-16 (C)
1974—Chargers, 36-35 (SD)
1976—Browns, 21-17 (C)
1977—Chargers, 37-14 (SD)
1981—Chargers, 44-14 (C)
1982—Chargers, 30-13 (C)
1983—Browns, 30-24 (SD) OT
1985—Browns, 21-7 (SD)
1986—Browns, 47-17 (C)
1987—Chargers, 27-24 (SD) OT
1990—Chargers, 24-14 (C)

1991—Browns, 30-24 (SD) OT
1992—Chargers, 14-13 (C)
1995—Chargers, 31-13 (SD)
1999—Chargers, 23-10 (SD)
2001—Browns, 20-16 (C)
2003—Chargers, 26-20 (C)
2004—Chargers, 21-0 (C)
2006—Chargers, 32-25 (SD)
(RS Pts.—Chargers 510, Browns 411)

CLEVELAND vs. SAN FRANCISCO
RS: Browns lead series, 11-6
1950—Browns, 34-14 (C)
1951—49ers, 24-10 (SF)
1953—Browns, 23-21 (C)
1955—Browns, 38-3 (SF)
1959—49ers, 21-20 (C)
1962—Browns, 13-10 (SF)
1968—Browns, 33-21 (SF)
1970—49ers, 34-31 (SF)
1974—Browns, 7-0 (C)
1978—Browns, 24-7 (C)
1981—Browns, 15-12 (SF)
1984—49ers, 41-7 (C)
1987—49ers, 38-24 (SF)
1990—49ers, 20-17 (SF)
1993—Browns, 23-13 (C)
2003—Browns, 13-12 (SF)
2007—Browns, 20-7 (C)
(RS Pts.—Browns 352, 49ers 298)

CLEVELAND vs. SEATTLE
RS: Seahawks lead series, 11-5
1977—Seahawks, 20-19 (S)
1978—Seahawks, 47-24 (S)
1979—Seahawks, 29-24 (C)
1980—Browns, 27-3 (S)
1981—Seahawks, 42-21 (S)
1982—Browns, 21-7 (S)
1983—Seahawks, 24-9 (C)
1984—Seahawks, 33-0 (S)
1985—Seahawks, 31-13 (S)
1988—Seahawks, 16-10 (C)
1989—Browns, 17-7 (S)
1993—Seahawks, 22-5 (S)
1994—Browns, 35-9 (C)
2001—Seahawks, 9-6 (C)
2003—Seahawks, 34-7 (S)
2007—Browns, 33-30 (C) OT
(RS Pts.—Seahawks 363, Browns 271)

CLEVELAND vs. TAMPA BAY
RS: Browns lead series, 5-2
1976—Browns, 24-7 (TB)
1980—Browns, 34-27 (TB)
1983—Browns, 20-0 (C)
1989—Browns, 42-31 (TB)
1995—Browns, 22-6 (C)
2002—Buccaneers 17-3 (TB)
2006—Buccaneers, 22-7 (C)
(RS Pts.—Browns 152, Buccaneers 110)

CLEVELAND vs. *TENNESSEE
RS: Browns lead series, 33-27
PS: Titans lead series, 1-0
1970—Browns, 28-14 (C)
Browns, 21-10 (H)
1971—Browns, 31-0 (C)
Browns, 37-24 (H)
1972—Browns, 23-17 (H)
Browns, 20-0 (C)
1973—Browns, 42-13 (C)
Browns, 23-13 (H)
1974—Browns, 20-7 (C)
Oilers, 28-24 (H)
1975—Oilers, 40-10 (C)
Oilers, 21-10 (H)
1976—Browns, 21-7 (H)
Browns, 13-10 (C)
1977—Browns, 24-23 (H)
Oilers, 19-15 (C)
1978—Oilers, 16-13 (C)
Oilers, 14-10 (H)
1979—Oilers, 31-10 (H)
Browns, 14-7 (C)
1980—Oilers, 16-7 (C)
Browns, 17-14 (H)
1981—Oilers, 9-3 (C)
Oilers, 17-13 (H)
1982—Browns, 20-14 (H)
1983—Browns, 25-19 (C) OT
Oilers, 34-27 (H)
1984—Browns, 27-10 (C)
Browns, 27-20 (H)
1985—Browns, 21-6 (H)
Browns, 28-21 (C)
1986—Browns, 23-20 (H)
Browns, 13-10 (C) OT
1987—Oilers, 15-10 (C)
Browns, 40-7 (H)
1988—Oilers, 24-17 (H)
Browns, 28-23 (C)
**Oilers, 24-23 (C)
1989—Browns, 28-17 (C)
Browns, 24-20 (H)
1990—Oilers, 35-23 (C)
Oilers, 58-14 (H)
1991—Oilers, 28-24 (H)
Oilers, 17-14 (C)
1992—Browns, 24-14 (H)
Oilers, 17-14 (C)
1993—Oilers, 27-20 (C)
Oilers, 19-17 (H)
1994—Browns, 11-8 (H)
Browns, 34-10 (C)
1995—Browns, 14-7 (H)
Oilers, 37-10 (C)
1999—Titans, 26-9 (T)
Titans, 33-21 (C)
2000—Titans, 24-10 (T)
Titans, 24-0 (C)
2001—Titans, 31-15 (C)
Browns, 41-38 (T)
2002—Browns, 31-28 (T) OT
2005—Browns, 20-14 (C)
2008—Titans, 28-9 (T)
(RS Pts.—Browns 1,182, Titans 1,153)
(PS Pts.—Titans 24, Browns 23)
**Franchise in Houston prior to 1997; known as Oilers prior to 1999*
***AFC First-Round Playoff*

CLEVELAND vs. WASHINGTON
RS: Browns lead series, 33-10-1
1950—Browns, 20-14 (C)
Browns, 45-21 (W)
1951—Browns, 45-0 (C)
1952—Browns, 19-15 (C)
Browns, 48-24 (W)
1953—Browns, 30-14 (W)
Browns, 27-3 (C)
1954—Browns, 62-3 (C)
Browns, 34-14 (W)
1955—Redskins, 27-17 (C)
Browns, 24-14 (W)
1956—Redskins, 20-9 (W)
Redskins, 20-17 (C)
1957—Browns, 21-17 (C)
Tie, 30-30 (W)
1958—Browns, 20-10 (W)
Browns, 21-14 (C)
1959—Browns, 34-7 (C)
Browns, 31-17 (W)
1960—Browns, 31-10 (W)
Browns, 27-16 (C)
1961—Browns, 31-7 (C)
Browns, 17-6 (W)
1962—Redskins, 17-16 (C)
Redskins, 17-9 (W)
1963—Browns, 37-14 (C)
Browns, 27-20 (W)
1964—Browns, 27-13 (W)
Browns, 34-24 (C)
1965—Browns, 17-7 (W)
Browns, 24-16 (C)
1966—Browns, 38-14 (W)
Browns, 14-3 (C)
1967—Browns, 42-37 (C)
1968—Browns, 24-21 (W)
1969—Browns, 27-23 (C)
1971—Browns, 20-13 (W)
1975—Redskins, 23-7 (C)
1979—Redskins, 13-9 (C)
1985—Redskins, 14-7 (C)
1988—Browns, 17-13 (W)
1991—Redskins, 42-17 (W)
2004—Browns, 17-13 (C)
2008—Redskins, 14-11 (W)
(RS Pts.—Browns 1,101, Redskins 694)

DALLAS vs. ARIZONA
RS: Cowboys lead series, 55-28-1
PS: Cardinals lead series, 1-0;
See Arizona vs. Dallas

DALLAS vs. ATLANTA
RS: Cowboys lead series, 13-8
PS: Cowboys lead series, 2-0;
See Atlanta vs. Dallas

DALLAS vs. BALTIMORE
RS: Ravens lead series, 3-0;
See Baltimore vs. Dallas

DALLAS vs. BUFFALO
RS: Cowboys lead series, 5-3
PS: Cowboys lead series, 2-0;
See Buffalo vs. Dallas

DALLAS vs. CAROLINA
RS: Cowboys lead series, 7-1
PS: Panthers lead series, 2-0;
See Carolina vs. Dallas

DALLAS vs. CHICAGO
RS: Cowboys lead series, 11-8
PS: Cowboys lead series, 2-0;
See Chicago vs. Dallas

DALLAS vs. CINCINNATI
RS: Cowboys lead series, 6-4;
See Cincinnati vs. Dallas

DALLAS vs. CLEVELAND
RS: Browns lead series, 15-11
PS: Browns lead series, 2-1;
See Cleveland vs. Dallas

DALLAS vs. DENVER
RS: Broncos lead series, 5-4
PS: Cowboys lead series, 1-0
1973—Cowboys, 22-10 (Den)
1977—Cowboys, 14-6 (Dal)

*Cowboys, 27-10 (New Orleans)
1980—Broncos, 41-20 (Den)
1986—Broncos, 29-14 (Den)
1992—Cowboys, 31-27 (Den)
1995—Cowboys, 31-21 (Dal)
1998—Broncos, 42-23 (Den)
2001—Broncos, 26-24 (Dal)
2005—Broncos, 24-21 (Dal) OT
(RS Pts.—Broncos 226, Cowboys 200)
(PS Pts.—Cowboys 27, Broncos 10)
Super Bowl XII

DALLAS vs. DETROIT
RS: Cowboys lead series, 11-9
PS: Series tied, 1-1
1960—Lions, 23-14 (Det)
1963—Cowboys, 17-14 (Dal)
1968—Cowboys, 59-13 (Dal)
1970—*Cowboys, 5-0 (Dal)
1972—Cowboys, 28-24 (Dal)
1975—Cowboys, 36-10 (Det)
1977—Cowboys, 37-0 (Dal)
1981—Lions, 27-24 (Det)
1985—Lions, 26-21 (Det)
1986—Cowboys, 31-7 (Det)
1987—Lions, 27-17 (Det)
1991—Lions, 34-10 (Det)
*Lions, 38-6 (Det)
1992—Cowboys, 37-3 (Det)
1994—Lions, 20-17 (Dal) OT
2001—Lions, 15-10 (Det)
2002—Lions, 9-7 (Det)
2003—Cowboys, 38-7 (Det)
2004—Cowboys, 31-21 (Dal)
2005—Cowboys, 20-7 (Dal)
2006—Lions, 39-31 (Dal)
2007—Cowboys, 28-27 (Det)
(RS Pts.—Cowboys 513, Lions 353)
(PS Pts.—Lions 38, Cowboys 11)
NFC Divisional Playoff

DALLAS vs. GREEN BAY
RS: Cowboys lead series, 12-10
PS: Cowboys lead series, 4-2
1960—Packers, 41-7 (GB)
1964—Packers, 45-21 (D)
1965—Packers, 13-3 (Mil)
1966—*Packers, 34-27 (D)
1967—*Packers, 21-17 (GB)
1968—Packers, 28-17 (D)
1970—Cowboys, 16-3 (D)
1972—Packers, 16-13 (Mil)
1975—Packers, 19-17 (D)
1978—Cowboys, 42-14 (Mil)
1980—Cowboys, 28-7 (Mil)
1982—**Cowboys, 37-26 (D)
1984—Cowboys, 20-6 (D)
1989—Packers, 31-13 (GB)
Packers, 20-10 (D)
1991—Cowboys, 20-17 (Mil)
1993—Cowboys, 36-14 (D)
***Cowboys, 27-17 (D)
1994—Cowboys, 42-31 (D)
***Cowboys, 35-9 (D)
1995—Cowboys, 34-24 (D)
****Cowboys, 38-27 (D)
1996—Cowboys, 21-6 (D)
1997—Packers, 45-17 (GB)
1999—Cowboys, 27-13 (D)
2004—Packers, 41-20 (GB)
2007—Cowboys, 37-27 (D)
2008—Cowboys, 27-16 (GB)
(RS Pts.—Cowboys 488, Packers 477)
(PS Pts.—Cowboys 181, Packers 134)
NFL Championship
***NFC Second-Round Playoff*
****NFC Divisional Playoff*
*****NFC Championship*

DALLAS vs. HOUSTON
RS: Series tied, 1-1
2002—Texans, 19-10 (H)
2006—Cowboys, 34-6 (D)
(RS Pts.—Cowboys 44, Texans 25)

DALLAS vs. *INDIANAPOLIS
RS: Cowboys lead series, 8-5
PS: Colts lead series, 1-0
1960—Colts, 45-7 (D)
1967—Colts, 23-17 (B)
1969—Cowboys, 27-10 (D)
1970—**Colts, 16-13 (Miami)
1972—Cowboys, 21-0 (B)
1976—Cowboys, 30-27 (D)
1978—Cowboys, 38-0 (D)
1981—Cowboys, 37-13 (B)
1984—Cowboys, 22-3 (D)
1993—Cowboys, 27-3 (I)
1996—Colts, 25-24 (D)
1999—Colts, 34-24 (I)
2002—Colts, 20-3 (I)
2006—Cowboys, 21-14 (D)
(RS Pts.—Cowboys 298, Colts 217)
(PS Pts.—Colts 16, Cowboys 13)
Franchise in Baltimore prior to 1984
***Super Bowl V*

DALLAS vs. JACKSONVILLE
RS: Series tied, 2-2
1997—Cowboys, 26-22 (D)
2000—Jaguars, 23-17 (D) OT
2002—Cowboys, 21-19 (D)
2006—Jaguars, 24-17 (J)
(RS Pts.—Jaguars 88, Cowboys 81)

DALLAS vs. KANSAS CITY
RS: Cowboys lead series, 5-3
1970—Cowboys, 27-16 (KC)
1975—Chiefs, 34-31 (D)
1983—Cowboys, 41-21 (D)
1989—Chiefs, 36-28 (KC)
1992—Cowboys, 17-10 (D)
1995—Cowboys, 24-12 (D)
1998—Chiefs, 20-17 (KC)
2005—Cowboys, 31-28 (D)
(RS Pts.—Cowboys 216, Chiefs 177)

DALLAS vs. MIAMI
RS: Dolphins lead series, 7-4
PS: Cowboys lead series, 1-0
1971—*Cowboys, 24-3 (New Orleans)
1973—Dolphins, 14-7 (D)
1978—Dolphins, 23-16 (M)
1981—Cowboys, 28-27 (D)
1984—Dolphins, 28-21 (M)
1987—Dolphins, 20-14 (D)
1989—Dolphins, 17-14 (D)
1993—Dolphins, 16-14 (D)
1996—Cowboys, 29-10 (M)
1999—Cowboys, 20-0 (D)
2003—Dolphins, 40-21 (D)
2007—Cowboys, 37-20 (M)
(RS Pts.—Cowboys 221, Dolphins 215)
(PS Pts.—Cowboys 24, Dolphins 3)
Super Bowl VI

DALLAS vs. MINNESOTA
RS: Series tied, 10-10
PS: Cowboys lead series, 4-2
1961—Cowboys, 21-7 (D)
Cowboys, 28-0 (M)
1966—Cowboys, 28-17 (D)
1968—Cowboys, 20-7 (M)
1970—Vikings, 54-13 (M)
1971—*Cowboys, 20-12 (M)
1973—**Vikings, 27-10 (D)
1974—Vikings, 23-21 (D)
1975—*Cowboys, 17-14 (M)
1977—Cowboys, 16-10 (M) OT
**Cowboys, 23-6 (D)
1978—Vikings, 21-10 (D)
1979—Cowboys, 36-20 (M)
1982—Vikings, 31-27 (M)
1983—Cowboys, 37-24 (M)
1987—Vikings, 44-38 (D) OT
1988—Vikings, 43-3 (D)
1993—Cowboys, 37-20 (M)
1995—Cowboys, 23-17 (M) OT
1996—***Cowboys, 40-15 (D)
1998—Vikings, 46-36 (D)
1999—Vikings, 27-17 (M)
***Vikings, 27-10 (M)
2000—Vikings, 27-15 (D)
2004—Vikings, 35-17 (M)
2007—Cowboys, 24-14 (D)
(RS Pts.—Vikings 487, Cowboys 467)
(PS Pts.—Cowboys 120, Vikings 101)
NFC Divisional Playoff
***NFC Championship*
****NFC First-Round Playoff*

DALLAS vs. NEW ENGLAND
RS: Cowboys lead series, 7-3
1971—Cowboys, 44-21 (D)
1975—Cowboys, 34-31 (NE)
1978—Cowboys, 17-10 (D)
1981—Cowboys, 35-21 (NE)
1984—Cowboys, 20-17 (D)
1987—Cowboys, 23-17 (NE) OT
1996—Cowboys, 12-6 (D)
1999—Patriots, 13-6 (NE)
2003—Patriots, 12-0 (NE)
2007—Patriots, 48-27 (D)
(RS Pts.—Cowboys 218, Patriots 196)

DALLAS vs. NEW ORLEANS
RS: Cowboys lead series, 14-8
1967—Cowboys, 14-10 (D)
Cowboys, 27-10 (NO)
1968—Cowboys, 17-3 (NO)
1969—Cowboys, 21-17 (NO)
Cowboys, 33-17 (D)
1971—Saints, 24-14 (NO)
1973—Cowboys, 40-3 (D)
1976—Cowboys, 24-6 (NO)
1978—Cowboys, 27-7 (D)
1982—Cowboys, 21-7 (D)
1983—Cowboys, 21-20 (D)
1984—Cowboys, 30-27 (D) OT
1988—Saints, 20-17 (NO)
1989—Saints, 28-0 (NO)
1990—Cowboys, 17-13 (D)
1991—Cowboys, 23-14 (D)
1994—Cowboys, 24-16 (NO)
1998—Saints, 22-3 (NO)
1999—Saints, 31-24 (NO)
2003—Saints, 13-7 (NO)
2004—Saints, 27-13 (D)
2006—Saints, 42-17 (D)
(RS Pts.—Cowboys 434, Saints 377)

DALLAS vs. N.Y. GIANTS
RS: Cowboys lead series, 55-36-2
PS: Giants lead series, 1-0
1960—Tie, 31-31 (NY)
1961—Giants, 31-10 (D)
Cowboys, 17-16 (NY)
1962—Giants, 41-10 (D)
Giants, 41-31 (NY)
1963—Giants, 37-21 (NY)
Giants, 34-27 (D)
1964—Tie, 13-13 (D)
Cowboys, 31-21 (NY)
1965—Cowboys, 31-2 (D)
Cowboys, 38-20 (NY)
1966—Cowboys, 52-7 (D)
Cowboys, 17-7 (NY)
1967—Cowboys, 38-24 (D)
1968—Giants, 27-21 (D)
Cowboys, 28-10 (NY)
1969—Cowboys, 25-3 (D)
1970—Cowboys, 28-10 (D)
Giants, 23-20 (NY)
1971—Cowboys, 20-13 (D)
Cowboys, 42-14 (NY)
1972—Cowboys, 23-14 (NY)
Giants, 23-3 (D)
1973—Cowboys, 45-28 (D)
Cowboys, 23-10 (New Haven)
1974—Giants, 14-6 (D)
Cowboys, 21-7 (New Haven)
1975—Cowboys, 13-7 (NY)
Cowboys, 14-3 (D)
1976—Cowboys, 24-14 (NY)
Cowboys, 9-3 (D)
1977—Cowboys, 41-21 (D)
Cowboys, 24-10 (NY)
1978—Cowboys, 34-24 (NY)
Cowboys, 24-3 (D)
1979—Cowboys, 16-14 (NY)
Cowboys, 28-7 (D)
1980—Cowboys, 24-3 (D)
Giants, 38-35 (NY)
1981—Cowboys, 18-10 (D)
Giants, 13-10 (NY) OT
1983—Cowboys, 28-13 (D)
Cowboys, 38-20 (NY)
1984—Giants, 28-7 (NY)
Giants, 19-7 (D)
1985—Cowboys, 30-29 (NY)
Cowboys, 28-21 (D)
1986—Cowboys, 31-28 (D)
Giants, 17-14 (NY)
1987—Cowboys, 16-14 (NY)
Cowboys, 33-24 (D)
1988—Giants, 12-10 (D)
Giants, 29-21 (NY)
1989—Giants, 30-13 (D)
Giants, 15-0 (NY)
1990—Giants, 28-7 (D)
Giants, 31-17 (NY)
1991—Cowboys, 21-16 (D)
Giants, 22-9 (NY)
1992—Cowboys, 34-28 (NY)
Cowboys, 30-3 (D)
1993—Cowboys, 31-9 (D)
Cowboys, 16-13 (NY) OT
1994—Cowboys, 38-10 (D)
Giants, 15-10 (NY)
1995—Cowboys, 35-0 (NY)
Cowboys, 21-20 (D)
1996—Cowboys, 27-0 (D)
Giants, 20-6 (NY)
1997—Giants, 20-17 (NY)
Giants, 20-7 (D)
1998—Cowboys, 31-7 (NY)
Cowboys, 16-6 (D)
1999—Giants, 13-10 (NY)
Cowboys, 26-18 (D)
2000—Giants, 19-14 (NY)
Giants, 17-13 (D)
2001—Giants, 27-24 (NY) OT
Cowboys, 20-13 (D)
2002—Giants, 21-17 (D)
Giants, 37-7 (NY)
2003—Cowboys, 35-32 (NY) OT
Cowboys, 19-3 (D)
2004—Giants, 26-10 (D)
Giants, 28-24 (NY)
2005—Cowboys, 16-13 (D) OT
Giants, 17-10 (NY)
2006—Giants, 36-22 (D)
Cowboys, 23-20 (NY)
2007—Cowboys, 45-35 (D)
Cowboys, 31-20 (NY)
*Giants, 21-17 (D)
2008—Giants, 35-14 (NY)
Cowboys, 20-8 (D)
(RS Pts.—Cowboys 2,035, Giants 1,696)
(PS Pts.—Giants 21, Cowboys 17)
NFC Divisional Playoff

DALLAS vs. N.Y. JETS
RS: Cowboys lead series, 7-2
1971—Cowboys, 52-10 (D)
1975—Cowboys, 31-21 (NY)
1978—Cowboys, 30-7 (NY)
1987—Cowboys, 38-24 (NY)
1990—Jets, 24-9 (NY)
1993—Cowboys, 28-7 (NY)
1999—Jets, 22-21 (D)
2003—Cowboys, 17-6 (NY)
2007—Cowboys, 34-3 (D)
(RS Pts.—Cowboys 260, Jets 124)

DALLAS vs. *OAKLAND
RS: Raiders lead series, 6-3
1974—Raiders, 27-23 (O)
1980—Cowboys, 19-13 (O)
1983—Raiders, 40-38 (D)
1986—Raiders, 17-13 (D)
1992—Cowboys, 28-13 (LA)
1995—Cowboys, 34-21 (O)
1998—Raiders, 13-12 (D)
2001—Raiders, 28-21 (O)
2005—Raiders, 19-13 (O)
(RS Pts.—Cowboys 201, Raiders 191)
**Franchise in Los Angeles from 1982-1994*

DALLAS vs. PHILADELPHIA
RS: Cowboys lead series, 53-43
PS: Cowboys lead series, 2-1
1960—Eagles, 27-25 (D)
1961—Eagles, 43-7 (D)
Eagles, 35-13 (P)
1962—Cowboys, 41-19 (D)
Eagles, 28-14 (P)
1963—Eagles, 24-21 (P)
Cowboys, 27-20 (D)
1964—Eagles, 17-14 (D)
Eagles, 24-14 (P)
1965—Eagles, 35-24 (D)
Cowboys, 21-19 (P)
1966—Cowboys, 56-7 (D)
Eagles, 24-23 (P)
1967—Eagles, 21-14 (P)
Cowboys, 38-17 (D)
1968—Cowboys, 45-13 (P)
Cowboys, 34-14 (D)
1969—Cowboys, 38-7 (P)
Cowboys, 49-14 (D)
1970—Cowboys, 17-7 (P)
Cowboys, 21-17 (D)
1971—Cowboys, 42-7 (P)
Cowboys, 20-7 (D)
1972—Cowboys, 28-6 (D)
Cowboys, 28-7 (P)
1973—Eagles, 30-16 (P)
Cowboys, 31-10 (D)
1974—Eagles, 13-10 (P)
Cowboys, 31-24 (D)
1975—Cowboys, 20-17 (P)
Cowboys, 27-17 (D)
1976—Cowboys, 27-7 (D)
Cowboys, 26-7 (P)
1977—Cowboys, 16-10 (P)
Cowboys, 24-14 (D)
1978—Cowboys, 14-7 (D)
Cowboys, 31-13 (P)
1979—Eagles, 31-21 (D)
Cowboys, 24-17 (P)
1980—Eagles, 17-10 (P)
Cowboys, 35-27 (D)
*Eagles, 20-7 (P)
1981—Cowboys, 17-14 (P)
Cowboys, 21-10 (D)
1982—Eagles, 24-20 (D)
1983—Cowboys, 37-7 (D)
Cowboys, 27-20 (P)
1984—Cowboys, 23-17 (D)
Cowboys, 26-10 (P)
1985—Eagles, 16-14 (P)
Cowboys, 34-17 (D)
1986—Cowboys, 17-14 (P)
Eagles, 23-21 (D)
1987—Cowboys, 41-22 (D)
Eagles, 37-20 (P)
1988—Eagles, 24-23 (P)
Eagles, 23-7 (D)
1989—Eagles, 27-0 (D)
Eagles, 20-10 (P)
1990—Eagles, 21-20 (D)
Eagles, 17-3 (P)
1991—Eagles, 24-0 (D)
Cowboys, 25-13 (P)
1992—Eagles, 31-7 (P)
Cowboys, 20-10 (D)
**Cowboys, 34-10 (D)
1993—Cowboys, 23-10 (P)
Cowboys, 23-17 (D)
1994—Cowboys, 24-13 (D)
Cowboys, 31-19 (P)
1995—Cowboys, 34-12 (D)
Eagles, 20-17 (P)
**Cowboys, 30-11 (D)
1996—Cowboys, 23-19 (P)
Eagles, 31-21 (D)
1997—Cowboys, 21-20 (D)
Eagles, 13-12 (P)
1998—Cowboys, 34-0 (P)
Cowboys, 13-9 (D)
1999—Eagles, 13-10 (P)
Cowboys, 20-10 (D)
2000—Eagles, 41-14 (D)

Eagles, 16-13 (P) OT
2001—Eagles, 40-18 (P)
Eagles, 36-3 (D)
2002—Eagles, 44-13 (P)
Eagles, 27-3 (D)
2003—Cowboys, 23-21 (D)
Eagles, 36-10 (P)
2004—Eagles, 49-21 (D)
Eagles, 12-7 (P)
2005—Cowboys, 33-10 (D)
Cowboys, 21-20 (P)
2006—Eagles, 38-24 (P)
Eagles, 23-7 (D)
2007—Cowboys, 38-17 (P)
Eagles, 10-6 (D)
2008—Cowboys, 41-37 (D)
Eagles, 44-6 (P)
(RS Pts.—Cowboys 2,077, Eagles 1,888)
(PS Pts.—Cowboys 71, Eagles 41)
NFC Championship
**NFC Divisional Playoff*

DALLAS vs. PITTSBURGH
RS: Cowboys lead series, 14-13
PS: Steelers lead series, 2-1
1960—Steelers, 35-28 (D)
1961—Cowboys, 27-24 (D)
Steelers, 37-7 (P)
1962—Steelers, 30-28 (D)
Cowboys, 42-27 (P)
1963—Steelers, 27-21 (P)
Steelers, 24-19 (D)
1964—Steelers, 23-17 (P)
Cowboys, 17-14 (D)
1965—Steelers, 22-13 (P)
Cowboys, 24-17 (D)
1966—Cowboys, 52-21 (D)
Cowboys, 20-7 (P)
1967—Cowboys, 24-21 (P)
1968—Cowboys, 28-7 (D)
1969—Cowboys, 10-7 (P)
1972—Cowboys, 17-13 (D)
1975—*Steelers, 21-17 (Miami)
1977—Steelers, 28-13 (P)
1978—**Steelers, 35-31 (Miami)
1979—Steelers, 14-3 (P)
1982—Steelers, 36-28 (D)
1985—Cowboys, 27-13 (D)
1988—Steelers, 24-21 (P)
1991—Cowboys, 20-10 (D)
1994—Cowboys, 26-9 (P)
1995—***Cowboys, 27-17 (Tempe)
1997—Cowboys, 37-7 (P)
2004—Steelers, 24-20 (D)
2008—Steelers, 20-13 (P)
(RS Pts.—Cowboys 602, Steelers 541)
(PS Pts.—Cowboys 75, Steelers 73)
Super Bowl X
**Super Bowl XIII*
***Super Bowl XXX*

DALLAS vs. *ST. LOUIS
RS: Rams lead series, 11-10
PS: Series tied, 4-4
1960—Rams, 38-13 (D)
1962—Cowboys, 27-17 (LA)
1967—Rams, 35-13 (D)
1969—Rams, 24-23 (LA)
1971—Cowboys, 28-21 (D)
1973—Rams, 37-31 (LA)
**Cowboys, 27-16 (D)
1975—Cowboys, 18-7 (D)
***Cowboys, 37-7 (LA)
1976—**Rams, 14-12 (D)
1978—Rams, 27-14 (LA)
***Cowboys, 28-0 (LA)
1979—Cowboys, 30-6 (D)
**Rams, 21-19 (D)
1980—Rams, 38-14 (LA)
****Cowboys, 34-13 (D)
1981—Cowboys, 29-17 (D)
1983—****Rams, 24-17 (D)
1984—Cowboys, 20-13 (LA)
1985—**Rams, 20-0 (LA)
1986—Rams, 29-10 (LA)
1987—Cowboys, 29-21 (LA)
1989—Rams, 35-31 (D)
1990—Cowboys, 24-21 (LA)
1992—Rams, 27-23 (D)
2002—Cowboys, 13-10 (StL)
2005—Rams, 20-10 (D)
2007—Cowboys, 35-7 (D)
2008—Rams, 34-14 (StL)
(RS Pts.—Rams 484, Cowboys 449)
(PS Pts.—Cowboys 174, Rams 115)
Franchise in Los Angeles prior to 1995
**NFC Divisional Playoff*
***NFC Championship*
****NFC First-Round Playoff*

DALLAS vs. SAN DIEGO
RS: Cowboys lead series, 6-2
1972—Cowboys, 34-28 (SD)
1980—Cowboys, 42-31 (D)
1983—Chargers, 24-23 (SD)
1986—Cowboys, 24-21 (SD)
1990—Cowboys, 17-14 (D)
1995—Cowboys, 23-9 (SD)
2001—Chargers, 32-21 (D)
2005—Cowboys, 28-24 (SD)
(RS Pts.—Cowboys 212, Chargers 183)

DALLAS vs. SAN FRANCISCO
RS: 49ers lead series, 14-10-1
PS: Cowboys lead series, 5-2
1960—49ers, 26-14 (D)
1963—49ers, 31-24 (SF)
1965—Cowboys, 39-31 (D)
1967—49ers, 24-16 (SF)
1969—Tie, 24-24 (D)
1970—*Cowboys, 17-10 (SF)
1971—*Cowboys, 14-3 (D)
1972—49ers, 31-10 (D)
**Cowboys, 30-28 (SF)
1974—Cowboys, 20-14 (D)
1977—Cowboys, 42-35 (SF)
1979—Cowboys, 21-13 (SF)
1980—Cowboys, 59-14 (D)
1981—49ers, 45-14 (SF)
*49ers, 28-27 (SF)
1983—49ers, 42-17 (SF)
1985—49ers, 31-16 (SF)
1989—49ers, 31-14 (D)
1990—49ers, 24-6 (D)
1992—*Cowboys, 30-20 (SF)
1993—Cowboys, 26-17 (D)
*Cowboys, 38-21 (D)
1994—49ers, 21-14 (SF)
*49ers, 38-28 (SF)
1995—49ers, 38-20 (D)
1996—Cowboys, 20-17 (SF) OT
1997—49ers, 17-10 (SF)
2000—49ers, 41-24 (D)
2001—Cowboys, 27-21 (D)
2002—49ers, 31-27 (D)
2005—Cowboys, 34-31 (SF)
2008—Cowboys, 35-22 (D)
(RS Pts.—49ers 672, Cowboys 573)
(PS Pts.—Cowboys 184, 49ers 148)
NFC Championship
**NFC Divisional Playoff*

DALLAS vs. SEATTLE
RS: Cowboys lead series, 7-4
PS: Seahawks lead series, 1-0
1976—Cowboys, 28-13 (S)
1980—Cowboys, 51-7 (D)
1983—Cowboys, 35-10 (S)
1986—Seahawks, 31-14 (D)
1992—Cowboys, 27-0 (D)
1998—Cowboys, 30-22 (D)
2001—Seahawks, 29-3 (S)
2002—Seahawks, 17-14 (D)
2004—Cowboys, 43-39 (S)
2005—Seahawks, 13-10 (S)
2006—*Seahawks, 21-20 (S)
2008—Cowboys, 34-9 (D)
(RS Pts.—Cowboys 289, Seahawks 190)
(PS Pts.—Seahawks 21, Cowboys 20)
NFC First-Round Playoff

DALLAS vs. TAMPA BAY
RS: Cowboys lead series, 8-3
PS: Cowboys lead series, 2-0
1977—Cowboys, 23-7 (D)
1980—Cowboys, 28-17 (D)
1981—*Cowboys, 38-0 (D)
1982—Cowboys, 14-9 (D)
**Cowboys, 30-17 (D)
1983—Cowboys, 27-24 (D) OT
1990—Cowboys, 14-10 (D)
Cowboys, 17-13 (TB)
2000—Buccaneers, 27-7 (TB)
2001—Buccaneers, 10-6 (D)
2003—Buccaneers, 16-0 (TB)
2006—Cowboys, 38-10 (D)
2008—Cowboys, 13-9 (D)
(RS Pts.—Cowboys 187, Buccaneers 152)
(PS Pts.—Cowboys 68, Buccaneers 17)
NFC Divisional Playoff
**NFC First-Round Playoff*

DALLAS vs. *TENNESSEE
RS: Cowboys lead series, 7-5
1970—Cowboys, 52-10 (D)
1974—Cowboys, 10-0 (H)
1979—Oilers, 30-24 (D)
1982—Cowboys, 37-7 (H)
1985—Cowboys, 17-10 (H)
1988—Oilers, 25-17 (D)
1991—Oilers, 26-23 (H) OT
1994—Cowboys, 20-17 (D)
1997—Oilers, 27-14 (D)
2000—Titans, 31-0 (T)
2002—Cowboys, 21-13 (D)
2006—Cowboys, 45-14 (T)
(RS Pts.—Cowboys 280, Titans 210)
Franchise in Houston prior to 1997; known as Oilers prior to 1999

DALLAS vs. WASHINGTON
RS: Cowboys lead series, 57-37-2
PS: Redskins lead series, 2-0
1960—Redskins, 26-14 (W)
1961—Tie, 28-28 (D)
Redskins, 34-24 (W)
1962—Tie, 35-35 (D)
Cowboys, 38-10 (W)

1963—Redskins, 21-17 (W)
Cowboys, 35-20 (D)
1964—Cowboys, 24-18 (D)
Redskins, 28-16 (W)
1965—Cowboys, 27-7 (D)
Redskins, 34-31 (W)
1966—Cowboys, 31-30 (W)
Redskins, 34-31 (D)
1967—Cowboys, 17-14 (W)
Redskins, 27-20 (D)
1968—Cowboys, 44-24 (W)
Cowboys, 29-20 (D)
1969—Cowboys, 41-28 (W)
Cowboys, 20-10 (D)
1970—Cowboys, 45-21 (W)
Cowboys, 34-0 (D)
1971—Redskins, 20-16 (D)
Cowboys, 13-0 (W)
1972—Redskins, 24-20 (W)
Cowboys, 34-24 (D)
*Redskins, 26-3 (W)
1973—Redskins, 14-7 (W)
Cowboys, 27-7 (D)
1974—Redskins, 28-21 (W)
Cowboys, 24-23 (D)
1975—Redskins, 30-24 (W) OT
Cowboys, 31-10 (D)
1976—Cowboys, 20-7 (W)
Redskins, 27-14 (D)
1977—Cowboys, 34-16 (D)
Cowboys, 14-7 (W)
1978—Redskins, 9-5 (W)
Cowboys, 37-10 (D)
1979—Redskins, 34-20 (W)
Cowboys, 35-34 (D)
1980—Cowboys, 17-3 (W)
Cowboys, 14-10 (D)
1981—Cowboys, 26-10 (W)
Cowboys, 24-10 (D)
1982—Cowboys, 24-10 (W)
*Redskins, 31-17 (W)
1983—Cowboys, 31-30 (W)
Redskins, 31-10 (D)
1984—Redskins, 34-14 (W)
Redskins, 30-28 (D)
1985—Cowboys, 44-14 (D)
Cowboys, 13-7 (W)
1986—Cowboys, 30-6 (D)
Redskins, 41-14 (W)
1987—Redskins, 13-7 (D)
Redskins, 24-20 (W)
1988—Redskins, 35-17 (D)
Cowboys, 24-17 (W)
1989—Redskins, 30-7 (D)
Cowboys, 13-3 (W)
1990—Redskins, 19-15 (W)
Cowboys, 27-17 (D)
1991—Redskins, 33-31 (D)
Cowboys, 24-21 (W)
1992—Cowboys, 23-10 (D)
Redskins, 20-17 (W)
1993—Redskins, 35-16 (W)
Cowboys, 38-3 (D)
1994—Cowboys, 34-7 (W)
Cowboys, 31-7 (D)
1995—Redskins, 27-23 (W)
Redskins, 24-17 (D)
1996—Cowboys, 21-10 (D)
Redskins, 37-10 (W)
1997—Redskins, 21-16 (W)
Cowboys, 17-14 (D)
1998—Cowboys, 31-10 (W)
Cowboys, 23-7 (D)
1999—Cowboys, 41-35 (W) OT
Cowboys, 38-20 (D)
2000—Cowboys, 27-21 (W)
Cowboys, 32-13 (D)
2001—Cowboys, 9-7 (D)
Cowboys, 20-14 (W)
2002—Cowboys, 27-20 (D)
Redskins, 20-14 (W)
2003—Cowboys, 21-14 (D)
Cowboys, 27-0 (W)
2004—Cowboys, 21-18 (W)
Cowboys, 13-10 (D)
2005—Redskins, 14-13 (D)
Redskins, 35-7 (W)
2006—Cowboys, 27-10 (D)
Redskins, 22-19 (W)
2007—Cowboys, 28-23 (D)
Redskins, 27-6 (W)
2008—Redskins, 26-24 (D)
Cowboys, 14-10 (W)
(RS Pts.—Cowboys 2,216, Redskins 1,832)
(PS Pts.—Redskins 57, Cowboys 20)
NFC Championship

DENVER vs. ARIZONA
RS: Broncos lead series, 7-0-1;
See Arizona vs. Denver
DENVER vs. ATLANTA
RS: Broncos lead series, 8-4
PS: Broncos lead series, 1-0;
See Atlanta vs. Denver
DENVER vs. BALTIMORE
RS: Series tied, 3-3
PS: Ravens lead series, 1-0;
See Baltimore vs. Denver
DENVER vs. BUFFALO
RS: Bills lead series, 18-15-1
PS: Bills lead series, 1-0;
See Buffalo vs. Denver
DENVER vs. CAROLINA
RS: Broncos lead series, 2-1;
See Carolina vs. Denver
DENVER vs. CHICAGO
RS: Bears lead series, 7-6;
See Chicago vs. Denver
DENVER vs. CINCINNATI
RS: Broncos lead series, 16-8;
See Cincinnati vs. Denver
DENVER vs. CLEVELAND
RS: Broncos lead series, 17-5
PS: Broncos lead series, 3-0;
See Cleveland vs. Denver
DENVER vs. DALLAS
RS: Broncos lead series, 5-4
PS: Cowboys lead series, 1-0;
See Dallas vs. Denver
DENVER vs. DETROIT
RS: Broncos lead series, 6-4
1971—Lions, 24-20 (Den)
1974—Broncos, 31-27 (Det)
1978—Lions, 17-14 (Det)
1981—Broncos, 27-21 (Den)
1984—Broncos, 28-7 (Det)
1987—Broncos, 34-0 (Den)
1990—Lions, 40-27 (Det)
1999—Broncos, 17-7 (Det)
2003—Broncos, 20-16 (Den)
2007—Lions, 44-7 (Det)
(RS Pts.—Broncos 225, Lions 203)
DENVER vs. GREEN BAY
RS: Series tied, 5-5-1
PS: Broncos lead series, 1-0
1971—Packers, 34-13 (Mil)
1975—Broncos, 23-13 (D)
1978—Broncos, 16-3 (D)
1984—Broncos, 17-14 (D)
1987—Tie, 17-17 (Mil) OT
1990—Broncos, 22-13 (D)
1993—Packers, 30-27 (GB)
1996—Packers, 41-6 (GB)
1997—*Broncos, 31-24 (San Diego)
1999—Broncos, 31-10 (D)
2003—Packers, 31-3 (GB)
2007—Packers, 19-13 (D) OT
(RS Pts.—Packers 225, Broncos 188)
(PS Pts.—Broncos 31, Packers 24)
Super Bowl XXXII
DENVER vs. HOUSTON
RS: Series tied, 1-1
2004—Broncos, 31-13 (D)
2007—Texans, 31-13 (H)
(RS Pts.—Broncos 44, Texans 44)
DENVER vs. *INDIANAPOLIS
RS: Broncos lead series, 11-6
PS: Colts lead series, 2-0
1974—Broncos, 17-6 (B)
1977—Broncos, 27-13 (D)
1978—Colts, 7-6 (B)
1981—Broncos, 28-10 (D)
1983—Broncos, 17-10 (B)
Broncos, 21-19 (D)
1985—Broncos, 15-10 (I)
1988—Colts, 55-23 (I)
1989—Broncos, 14-3 (D)
1990—Broncos, 27-17 (I)
1993—Broncos, 35-13 (D)
2001—Colts, 29-10 (I)
2002—Colts, 23-20 (D) OT
2003—Broncos, 31-17 (I)
**Colts, 41-10 (I)
2004—Broncos, 33-14 (D)
**Colts, 49-24 (I)
2006—Colts, 34-31 (D)
2007—Colts, 38-20 (I)
(RS Pts.—Broncos 375, Colts 318)
(PS Pts.—Colts 90, Broncos 34)
**Franchise in Baltimore prior to 1984*
***AFC First-Round Playoff*
DENVER vs. JACKSONVILLE
RS: Jaguars lead series, 4-3
PS: Series tied, 1-1
1995—Broncos, 31-23 (D)
1996—*Jaguars, 30-27 (D)
1997—**Broncos, 42-17 (D)
1998—Broncos, 37-24 (D)
1999—Jaguars, 27-24 (J)
2004—Jaguars, 7-6 (J)
2005—Broncos, 20-7 (J)
2007—Jaguars, 23-14 (D)
2008—Jaguars, 24-17 (D)
(RS Pts.—Broncos 149, Jaguars 135)
(PS Pts.—Broncos 69, Jaguars 47)
**AFC Divisional Playoff*
***AFC First-Round Playoff*
DENVER vs. *KANSAS CITY
RS: Chiefs lead series, 53-44
PS: Broncos lead series, 1-0

1960—Texans, 17-14 (D)
Texans, 34-7 (Dal)
1961—Texans, 19-12 (D)
Texans, 49-21 (Dal)
1962—Texans, 24-3 (D)
Texans, 17-10 (Dal)
1963—Chiefs, 59-7 (D)
Chiefs, 52-21 (KC)
1964—Broncos, 33-27 (D)
Chiefs, 49-39 (KC)
1965—Chiefs, 31-23 (D)
Chiefs, 45-35 (KC)
1966—Chiefs, 37-10 (KC)
Chiefs, 56-10 (D)
1967—Chiefs, 52-9 (KC)
Chiefs, 38-24 (D)
1968—Chiefs, 34-2 (KC)
Chiefs, 30-7 (D)
1969—Chiefs, 26-13 (D)
Chiefs, 31-17 (KC)
1970—Broncos, 26-13 (D)
Chiefs, 16-0 (KC)
1971—Chiefs, 16-3 (D)
Chiefs, 28-10 (KC)
1972—Chiefs, 45-24 (D)
Chiefs, 24-21 (KC)
1973—Chiefs, 16-14 (KC)
Broncos, 14-10 (D)
1974—Broncos, 17-14 (KC)
Chiefs, 42-34 (D)
1975—Broncos, 37-33 (D)
Chiefs, 26-13 (KC)
1976—Broncos, 35-26 (KC)
Broncos, 17-16 (D)
1977—Broncos, 23-7 (D)
Broncos, 14-7 (KC)
1978—Broncos, 23-17 (KC) OT
Broncos, 24-3 (D)
1979—Broncos, 24-10 (KC)
Broncos, 20-3 (D)
1980—Chiefs, 23-17 (D)
Chiefs, 31-14 (KC)
1981—Chiefs, 28-14 (KC)
Broncos, 16-13 (D)
1982—Chiefs, 37-16 (D)
1983—Broncos, 27-24 (D)
Chiefs, 48-17 (KC)
1984—Broncos, 21-0 (D)
Chiefs, 16-13 (KC)
1985—Broncos, 30-10 (KC)
Broncos, 14-13 (D)
1986—Broncos, 38-17 (D)
Chiefs, 37-10 (KC)
1987—Broncos, 26-17 (KC)
Broncos, 20-17 (D)
1988—Chiefs, 20-13 (KC)
Broncos, 17-11 (D)
1989—Broncos, 34-20 (D)
Broncos, 16-13 (KC)
1990—Broncos, 24-23 (D)
Chiefs, 31-20 (KC)
1991—Broncos, 19-16 (D)
Broncos, 24-20 (KC)
1992—Broncos, 20-19 (D)
Chiefs, 42-20 (KC)
1993—Chiefs, 15-7 (KC)
Broncos, 27-21 (D)
1994—Chiefs, 31-28 (D)
Broncos, 20-17 (KC) OT
1995—Chiefs, 21-7 (D)
Chiefs, 20-17 (KC)
1996—Chiefs, 17-14 (KC)
Broncos, 34-7 (D)
1997—Broncos, 19-3 (D)
Chiefs, 24-22 (KC)
**Broncos, 14-10 (KC)
1998—Broncos, 30-7 (KC)
Broncos, 35-31 (D)
1999—Chiefs, 26-10 (KC)
Chiefs, 16-10 (D)
2000—Chiefs, 23-22 (D)
Chiefs, 20-7 (KC)
2001—Broncos, 20-6 (D)
Chiefs, 26-23 (KC) OT
2002—Broncos, 37-34 (KC) OT
Broncos, 31-24 (D)
2003—Chiefs, 24-23 (KC)
Broncos, 45-27 (D)
2004—Broncos, 34-24 (D)
Chiefs, 45-17 (KC)
2005—Broncos, 30-10 (D)
Chiefs, 31-27 (KC)
2006—Broncos, 9-6 (D) OT
Chiefs, 19-10 (KC)
2007—Broncos, 27-11 (KC)
Broncos, 41-7 (D)
2008—Chiefs, 33-19 (KC)
Broncos, 24-17 (D)
(RS Pts.—Chiefs 2,288, Broncos 1,936)
(PS Pts.—Broncos 14, Chiefs 10)
Franchise in Dallas prior to 1963 and known as Texans
***AFC Divisional Playoff*

DENVER vs. MIAMI
RS: Dolphins lead series, 11-3-1
PS: Broncos lead series, 1-0
1966—Dolphins, 24-7 (M)
Broncos, 17-7 (D)
1967—Dolphins, 35-21 (M)
1968—Broncos, 21-14 (D)
1969—Dolphins, 27-24 (M)
1971—Tie, 10-10 (D)
1975—Dolphins, 14-13 (M)
1985—Dolphins, 30-26 (D)
1998—Dolphins, 31-21 (M)
*Broncos, 38-3 (D)
1999—Dolphins, 38-21 (D)
2001—Dolphins, 21-10 (M)
2002—Dolphins, 24-22 (D)
2004—Broncos, 20-17 (D)
2005—Dolphins, 34-10 (M)
2008—Dolphins, 26-17 (D)
(RS Pts.—Dolphins 352, Broncos 260)
(PS Pts.—Broncos 38, Dolphins 3)
**AFC Divisional Playoff*

DENVER vs. MINNESOTA
RS: Vikings lead series, 7-5
1972—Vikings, 23-20 (D)
1978—Vikings, 12-9 (M) OT
1981—Broncos, 19-17 (D)
1984—Broncos, 42-21 (D)
1987—Vikings, 34-27 (M)
1990—Vikings, 27-22 (M)
1991—Broncos, 13-6 (M)
1993—Vikings, 26-23 (D)
1996—Broncos, 21-17 (M)
1999—Vikings, 23-20 (D)
2003—Vikings, 28-20 (M)
2007—Broncos, 22-19 (D) OT
(RS Pts.—Broncos 258, Vikings 253)

DENVER vs. *NEW ENGLAND
RS: Broncos lead series, 24-16
PS: Broncos lead series, 2-0
1960—Broncos, 13-10 (B)
Broncos, 31-24 (D)
1961—Patriots, 45-17 (B)
Patriots, 28-24 (D)
1962—Patriots, 41-16 (B)
Patriots, 33-29 (D)
1963—Broncos, 14-10 (D)
Patriots, 40-21 (B)
1964—Patriots, 39-10 (D)
Patriots, 12-7 (B)
1965—Broncos, 27-10 (B)
Patriots, 28-20 (D)
1966—Patriots, 24-10 (D)
Broncos, 17-10 (B)
1967—Broncos, 26-21 (D)
1968—Patriots, 20-17 (D)
Broncos, 35-14 (B)
1969—Broncos, 35-7 (D)
1972—Broncos, 45-21 (D)
1976—Patriots, 38-14 (NE)
1979—Broncos, 45-10 (D)
1980—Patriots, 23-14 (NE)
1984—Broncos, 26-19 (D)
1986—Broncos, 27-20 (D)
**Broncos, 22-17 (D)
1987—Broncos, 31-20 (D)
1988—Broncos, 21-10 (D)
1991—Broncos, 9-6 (NE)
Broncos, 20-3 (D)
1995—Broncos, 37-3 (NE)
1996—Broncos, 34-8 (NE)
1997—Broncos, 34-13 (D)
1998—Broncos, 27-21 (D)
1999—Patriots, 24-23 (NE)
2000—Patriots, 28-19 (D)
2001—Broncos, 31-20 (D)
2002—Broncos, 24-16 (NE)
2003—Patriots, 30-26 (D)
2005—Broncos, 28-20 (D)
**Broncos, 27-13 (D)
2006—Broncos, 17-7 (NE)
2008—Patriots, 41-7 (NE)
(RS Pts.—Broncos 928, Patriots 817)
(PS Pts.—Broncos 49, Patriots 30)
**Franchise in Boston prior to 1971*
***AFC Divisional Playoff*

DENVER vs. NEW ORLEANS
RS: Broncos lead series, 7-2
1970—Broncos, 31-6 (NO)
1974—Broncos, 33-17 (D)
1979—Broncos, 10-3 (D)
1985—Broncos, 34-23 (D)
1988—Saints, 42-0 (NO)
1994—Saints, 30-28 (D)
2000—Broncos, 38-23 (NO)
2004—Broncos, 34-13 (NO)
2008—Broncos, 34-32 (D)
(RS Pts.—Broncos 242, Saints 189)

DENVER vs. N.Y. GIANTS
RS: Giants lead series, 5-4
PS: Giants lead series, 1-0
1972—Giants, 29-17 (NY)
1976—Broncos, 14-13 (D)
1980—Broncos, 14-9 (NY)
1986—Giants, 19-16 (NY)
*Giants, 39-20 (Pasadena)
1989—Giants, 14-7 (D)

1992—Broncos, 27-13 (D)
1998—Giants, 20-16 (NY)
2001—Broncos, 31-20 (D)
2005—Giants, 24-23 (NY)
(RS Pts.—Broncos 165, Giants 161)
(PS Pts.—Giants 39, Broncos 20)
Super Bowl XXI

DENVER vs. *N.Y. JETS
RS: Broncos lead series, 16-14-1
PS: Broncos lead series, 1-0
1960—Titans, 28-24 (NY)
Titans, 30-27 (D)
1961—Titans, 35-28 (NY)
Broncos, 27-10 (D)
1962—Broncos, 32-10 (NY)
Titans, 46-45 (D)
1963—Tie, 35-35 (NY)
Jets, 14-9 (D)
1964—Jets, 30-6 (NY)
Broncos, 20-16 (D)
1965—Broncos, 16-13 (D)
Jets, 45-10 (NY)
1966—Jets, 16-7 (D)
1967—Jets, 38-24 (D)
Broncos, 33-24 (NY)
1968—Broncos, 21-13 (NY)
1969—Broncos, 21-19 (D)
1973—Broncos, 40-28 (NY)
1976—Broncos, 46-3 (D)
1978—Jets, 31-28 (D)
1980—Broncos, 31-24 (D)
1986—Jets, 22-10 (NY)
1992—Broncos, 27-16 (D)
1993—Broncos, 26-20 (NY)
1994—Jets, 25-22 (NY) OT
1996—Broncos, 31-6 (D)
1998—**Broncos, 23-10 (D)
1999—Jets, 21-13 (D)
2000—Broncos, 30-23 (NY)
2002—Jets, 19-13 (NY)
2005—Broncos, 27-0 (D)
2008—Broncos, 34-17 (NY)
(RS Pts.—Broncos 763, Jets 677)
(PS Pts.—Broncos 23, Jets 10)
**Jets known as Titans prior to 1963*
***AFC Championship*

DENVER vs. *OAKLAND
RS: Raiders lead series, 55-40-2
PS: Series tied, 1-1
1960—Broncos, 31-14 (D)
Raiders, 48-10 (O)
1961—Raiders, 33-19 (O)
Broncos, 27-24 (D)
1962—Broncos, 44-7 (D)
Broncos, 23-6 (O)
1963—Raiders, 26-10 (D)
Raiders, 35-31 (O)
1964—Raiders, 40-7 (O)
Tie, 20-20 (D)
1965—Raiders, 28-20 (D)
Raiders, 24-13 (O)
1966—Raiders, 17-3 (D)
Raiders, 28-10 (O)
1967—Raiders, 51-0 (O)
Raiders, 21-17 (D)
1968—Raiders, 43-7 (D)
Raiders, 33-27 (O)
1969—Raiders, 24-14 (D)
Raiders, 41-10 (O)
1970—Raiders, 35-23 (O)
Raiders, 24-19 (D)
1971—Raiders, 27-16 (D)
Raiders, 21-13 (O)
1972—Broncos, 30-23 (O)
Raiders, 37-20 (D)
1973—Tie, 23-23 (D)
Raiders, 21-17 (O)
1974—Raiders, 28-17 (D)
Broncos, 20-17 (O)
1975—Raiders, 42-17 (D)
Raiders, 17-10 (O)
1976—Raiders, 17-10 (D)
Raiders, 19-6 (O)
1977—Broncos, 30-7 (O)
Raiders, 24-14 (D)
**Broncos, 20-17 (D)
1978—Broncos, 14-6 (D)
Broncos, 21-6 (O)
1979—Raiders, 27-3 (O)
Raiders, 14-10 (D)
1980—Raiders, 9-3 (O)
Raiders, 24-21 (D)
1981—Broncos, 9-7 (D)
Broncos, 17-0 (O)
1982—Raiders, 27-10 (LA)
1983—Raiders, 22-7 (D)
Raiders, 22-20 (LA)
1984—Broncos, 16-13 (D)
Broncos, 22-19 (LA) OT
1985—Raiders, 31-28 (LA) OT
Raiders, 17-14 (D) OT
1986—Broncos, 38-36 (D)
Broncos, 21-10 (LA)
1987—Broncos, 30-14 (D)
Broncos, 23-17 (LA)
1988—Raiders, 30-27 (D) OT
Raiders, 21-20 (LA)
1989—Broncos, 31-21 (D)
Raiders, 16-13 (LA) OT
1990—Raiders, 14-9 (LA)
Raiders, 23-20 (D)
1991—Raiders, 16-13 (LA)
Raiders, 17-16 (D)
1992—Broncos, 17-13 (D)
Raiders, 24-0 (LA)
1993—Raiders, 23-20 (D)
Raiders, 33-30 (LA) OT
***Raiders, 42-24 (LA)
1994—Raiders, 48-16 (D)
Raiders, 23-13 (LA)
1995—Broncos, 27-0 (D)
Broncos, 31-28 (O)
1996—Broncos, 22-21 (O)
Broncos, 24-19 (D)
1997—Raiders, 28-25 (O)
Broncos, 31-3 (D)
1998—Broncos, 34-17 (O)
Broncos, 40-14 (D)
1999—Broncos, 16-13 (O)
Broncos, 27-21 (D) OT
2000—Broncos, 33-24 (O)
Broncos, 27-24 (D)
2001—Raiders, 38-28 (O)
Broncos, 23-17 (D)
2002—Raiders, 34-10 (D)
Raiders, 28-16 (O)
2003—Broncos, 31-10 (D)
Broncos, 22-8 (O)
2004—Broncos, 31-3 (O)
Raiders, 25-24 (D)
2005—Broncos, 31-17 (O)
Broncos, 22-3 (D)
2006—Broncos, 13-3 (D)
Broncos, 17-13 (O)
2007—Broncos, 23-20 (D) OT
Raiders, 34-20 (O)
2008—Broncos, 41-14 (O)
Raiders, 31-10 (D)
(RS Pts.—Raiders 2,098, Broncos 1,899)
(PS Pts.—Raiders 59, Broncos 44)
**Franchise in Los Angeles from 1982-1994*
***AFC Championship*
****AFC First-Round Playoff*

DENVER vs. PHILADELPHIA
RS: Eagles lead series, 6-4
1971—Eagles, 17-16 (P)
1975—Broncos, 25-10 (D)
1980—Eagles, 27-6 (P)
1983—Eagles, 13-10 (D)
1986—Broncos, 33-7 (P)
1989—Eagles, 28-24 (D)
1992—Eagles, 30-0 (P)
1995—Eagles, 31-13 (P)
1998—Broncos, 41-16 (D)
2005—Broncos, 49-21 (D)
(RS Pts.—Broncos 217, Eagles 200)

DENVER vs. PITTSBURGH
RS: Broncos lead series, 13-6-1
PS: Series tied, 3-3
1970—Broncos, 16-13 (D)
1971—Broncos, 22-10 (P)
1973—Broncos, 23-13 (P)
1974—Tie, 35-35 (D) OT
1975—Steelers, 20-9 (P)
1977—Broncos, 21-7 (D)
*Broncos, 34-21 (D)
1978—Steelers, 21-17 (D)
*Steelers, 33-10 (P)
1979—Steelers, 42-7 (P)
1983—Broncos, 14-10 (P)
1984—*Steelers, 24-17 (D)
1985—Broncos, 31-23 (P)
1986—Broncos, 21-10 (P)
1988—Steelers, 39-21 (P)
1989—Broncos, 34-7 (D)
*Broncos, 24-23 (D)
1990—Steelers, 34-17 (D)
1991—Broncos, 20-13 (D)
1993—Broncos, 37-13 (D)
1997—Steelers, 35-24 (P)
**Broncos, 24-21 (P)
2003—Broncos, 17-14 (D)
2005—**Steelers, 34-17 (D)
2006—Broncos, 31-20 (P)
2007—Broncos, 31-28 (D)
(RS Pts.—Broncos 448, Steelers 407)
(PS Pts.—Steelers 156, Broncos 126)
**AFC Divisional Playoff*
***AFC Championship*

DENVER vs. *ST. LOUIS
RS: Rams lead series, 6-5
1972—Broncos, 16-10 (LA)
1974—Rams, 17-10 (D)
1979—Rams, 13-9 (D)
1982—Broncos, 27-24 (LA)
1985—Rams, 20-16 (LA)
1988—Broncos, 35-24 (D)
1994—Rams, 27-21 (LA)
1997—Broncos, 35-14 (D)
2000—Rams, 41-36 (StL)

2002—Broncos, 23-16 (D)
2006—Rams, 18-10 (StL)
(RS Pts.—Broncos 238, Rams 224)
Franchise in Los Angeles prior to 1995

DENVER vs. *SAN DIEGO
RS: Broncos lead series, 53-44-1
1960—Chargers, 23-19 (D)
Chargers, 41-33 (LA)
1961—Chargers, 37-0 (SD)
Chargers, 19-16 (D)
1962—Broncos, 30-21 (D)
Broncos, 23-20 (SD)
1963—Broncos, 50-34 (D)
Chargers, 58-20 (SD)
1964—Chargers, 42-14 (SD)
Chargers, 31-20 (D)
1965—Chargers, 34-31 (SD)
Chargers, 33-21 (D)
1966—Chargers, 24-17 (SD)
Broncos, 20-17 (D)
1967—Chargers, 38-21 (D)
Chargers, 24-20 (SD)
1968—Chargers, 55-24 (SD)
Chargers, 47-23 (D)
1969—Broncos, 13-0 (D)
Chargers, 45-24 (SD)
1970—Chargers, 24-21 (SD)
Tie, 17-17 (D)
1971—Broncos, 20-16 (D)
Chargers, 45-17 (SD)
1972—Chargers, 37-14 (SD)
Broncos, 38-13 (D)
1973—Broncos, 30-19 (D)
Broncos, 42-28 (SD)
1974—Broncos, 27-7 (D)
Chargers, 17-0 (SD)
1975—Broncos, 27-17 (SD)
Broncos, 13-10 (D) OT
1976—Broncos, 26-0 (D)
Broncos, 17-0 (SD)
1977—Broncos, 17-14 (SD)
Broncos, 17-9 (D)
1978—Broncos, 27-14 (D)
Chargers, 23-0 (SD)
1979—Broncos, 7-0 (D)
Chargers, 17-7 (SD)
1980—Chargers, 30-13 (D)
Broncos, 20-13 (SD)
1981—Broncos, 42-24 (D)
Chargers, 34-17 (SD)
1982—Chargers, 23-3 (D)
Chargers, 30-20 (SD)
1983—Broncos, 14-6 (D)
Chargers, 31-7 (SD)
1984—Broncos, 16-13 (SD)
Broncos, 16-13 (D)
1985—Chargers, 30-10 (SD)
Broncos, 30-24 (D) OT
1986—Broncos, 31-14 (SD)
Chargers, 9-3 (D)
1987—Broncos, 31-17 (SD)
Broncos, 24-0 (D)
1988—Broncos, 34-3 (D)
Broncos, 12-0 (SD)
1989—Broncos, 16-10 (D)
Chargers, 19-16 (SD)
1990—Chargers, 19-7 (SD)
Broncos, 20-10 (D)
1991—Broncos, 27-19 (D)
Broncos, 17-14 (SD)
1992—Broncos, 21-13 (D)
Chargers, 24-21 (SD)
1993—Broncos, 34-17 (D)
Chargers, 13-10 (SD)
1994—Chargers, 37-34 (D)
Broncos, 20-15 (SD)
1995—Chargers, 17-6 (SD)
Broncos, 30-27 (D)
1996—Broncos, 28-17 (D)
Chargers, 16-10 (SD)
1997—Broncos, 38-28 (SD)
Broncos, 38-3 (D)
1998—Broncos, 27-10 (D)
Broncos, 31-16 (SD)
1999—Broncos, 33-17 (SD)
Chargers, 12-6 (D)
2000—Broncos, 21-7 (SD)
Broncos, 38-37 (D)
2001—Chargers, 27-10 (SD)
Broncos, 26-16 (D)
2002—Broncos, 26-9 (D)
Chargers, 30-27 (SD) OT
2003—Broncos, 37-13 (SD)
Broncos, 37-8 (D)
2004—Broncos, 23-13 (D)
Chargers, 20-17 (SD)
2005—Broncos, 20-17 (D)
Broncos, 23-7 (SD)
2006—Chargers, 35-27 (D)
Chargers, 48-20 (SD)
2007—Chargers, 41-3 (D)
Chargers, 23-3 (SD)
2008—Broncos, 39-38 (D)
Chargers, 52-21 (SD)
(RS Pts.—Chargers 2,100, Broncos 2,074)
Franchise in Los Angeles prior to 1961

DENVER vs. SAN FRANCISCO
RS: Broncos lead series, 6-5
PS: 49ers lead series, 1-0
1970—49ers, 19-14 (SF)
1973—49ers, 36-34 (D)
1979—Broncos, 38-28 (SF)
1982—Broncos, 24-21 (D)
1985—Broncos, 17-16 (D)
1988—Broncos, 16-13 (SF) OT
1989—*49ers, 55-10 (New Orleans)
1994—49ers, 42-19 (SF)
1997—49ers, 34-17 (SF)
2000—Broncos, 38-9 (D)
2002—Broncos, 24-14 (SF)
2006—49ers, 26-23 (D) OT
(RS Pts.—Broncos 264, 49ers 258)
(PS Pts.—49ers 55, Broncos 10)
Super Bowl XXIV

DENVER vs. SEATTLE
RS: Broncos lead series, 33-18
PS: Seahawks lead series, 1-0
1977—Broncos, 24-13 (S)
1978—Broncos, 28-7 (D)
Broncos, 20-17 (S) OT
1979—Broncos, 37-34 (D)
Seahawks, 28-23 (S)
1980—Broncos, 36-20 (D)
Broncos, 25-17 (S)
1981—Seahawks, 13-10 (S)
Broncos, 23-13 (D)
1982—Seahawks, 17-10 (D)
Seahawks, 13-11 (S)
1983—Seahawks, 27-19 (S)
Broncos, 38-27 (D)
*Seahawks, 31-7 (S)
1984—Seahawks, 27-24 (D)
Broncos, 31-14 (S)
1985—Broncos, 13-10 (D) OT
Broncos, 27-24 (S)
1986—Broncos, 20-13 (D)
Seahawks, 41-16 (S)
1987—Broncos, 40-17 (D)
Seahawks, 28-21 (S)
1988—Seahawks, 21-14 (D)
Seahawks, 42-14 (S)
1989—Broncos, 24-21 (S) OT
Broncos, 41-14 (D)
1990—Broncos, 34-31 (D) OT
Seahawks, 17-12 (S)
1991—Broncos, 16-10 (D)
Seahawks, 13-10 (S)
1992—Seahawks, 16-13 (S) OT
Broncos, 10-6 (D)
1993—Broncos, 28-17 (D)
Broncos, 17-9 (S)
1994—Broncos, 16-9 (S)
Broncos, 17-10 (D)
1995—Seahawks, 27-10 (S)
Seahawks, 31-27 (D)
1996—Broncos, 30-20 (S)
Broncos, 34-7 (D)
1997—Broncos, 35-14 (S)
Broncos, 30-27 (D)
1998—Broncos, 21-16 (S)
Broncos, 28-21 (D)
1999—Seahawks, 20-17 (S)
Broncos, 36-30 (D) OT
2000—Broncos, 38-31 (S)
Broncos, 31-24 (D)
2001—Seahawks, 34-21 (S)
Broncos, 20-7 (D)
2002—Broncos, 31-9 (S)
2006—Seahawks, 23-20 (D)
(RS Pts.—Broncos 1,191, Seahawks 997)
(PS Pts.—Seahawks 31, Broncos 7)
AFC First-Round Playoff

DENVER vs. TAMPA BAY
RS: Broncos lead series, 5-2
1976—Broncos, 48-13 (D)
1981—Broncos, 24-7 (TB)
1993—Buccaneers, 17-10 (D)
1996—Broncos, 27-23 (D)
1999—Buccaneers, 13-10 (TB)
2004—Broncos, 16-13 (TB)
2008—Broncos, 16-13 (D)
(RS Pts.—Broncos 151, Buccaneers 99)

DENVER vs. *TENNESSEE
RS: Titans lead series, 20-13-1
PS: Broncos lead series, 2-1
1960—Oilers, 45-25 (D)
Oilers, 20-10 (H)
1961—Oilers, 55-14 (D)
Oilers, 45-14 (H)
1962—Broncos, 20-10 (D)
Oilers, 34-17 (H)
1963—Oilers, 20-14 (H)
Oilers, 33-24 (D)
1964—Oilers, 38-17 (D)
Oilers, 34-15 (H)
1965—Broncos, 28-17 (D)
Broncos, 31-21 (H)
1966—Oilers, 45-7 (H)
Broncos, 40-38 (D)
1967—Oilers, 10-6 (H)

Oilers, 20-18 (D)
1968—Oilers, 38-17 (H)
1969—Oilers, 24-21 (H)
Tie, 20-20 (D)
1970—Oilers, 31-21 (H)
1972—Broncos, 30-17 (D)
1973—Broncos, 48-20 (H)
1974—Broncos, 37-14 (D)
1976—Oilers, 17-3 (H)
1977—Broncos, 24-14 (H)
1979—**Oilers, 13-7 (H)
1980—Oilers, 20-16 (D)
1983—Broncos, 26-14 (H)
1985—Broncos, 31-20 (D)
1987—Oilers, 40-10 (D)
***Broncos, 34-10 (D)
1991—Oilers, 42-14 (H)
***Broncos, 26-24 (D)
1992—Broncos, 27-21 (D)
1995—Oilers, 42-33 (H)
2004—Broncos, 37-16 (T)
2007—Broncos, 34-20 (D)
(RS Pts.—Titans 915, Broncos 749)
(PS Pts.—Broncos 67, Titans 47)
Franchise in Houston prior to 1997; known as the Oilers prior to 1999
***AFC First-Round Playoff*
****AFC Divisional Playoff*

DENVER vs. WASHINGTON
RS: Broncos lead series, 6-4
PS: Redskins lead series, 1-0
1970—Redskins, 19-3 (D)
1974—Redskins, 30-3 (W)
1980—Broncos, 20-17 (D)
1986—Broncos, 31-30 (D)
1987—*Redskins, 42-10 (San Diego)
1989—Broncos, 14-10 (W)
1992—Redskins, 34-3 (W)
1995—Broncos, 38-31 (D)
1998—Broncos, 38-16 (W)
2001—Redskins, 17-10 (D)
2005—Broncos, 21-19 (D)
(RS Pts.—Redskins 223, Broncos 181)
(PS Pts.—Redskins 42, Broncos 10)
**Super Bowl XXII*

DETROIT vs. ARIZONA
RS: Lions lead series, 31-23-5;
See Arizona vs. Detroit
DETROIT vs. ATLANTA
RS: Lions lead series, 23-10;
See Atlanta vs. Detroit
DETROIT vs. BALTIMORE
RS: Series tied, 1-1;
See Baltimore vs. Detroit
DETROIT vs. BUFFALO
RS: Lions lead series, 4-3-1;
See Buffalo vs. Detroit
DETROIT vs. CAROLINA
RS: Panthers lead series, 4-1;
See Carolina vs. Detroit
DETROIT vs. CHICAGO
RS: Bears lead series, 89-64-5;
See Chicago vs. Detroit
DETROIT vs. CINCINNATI
RS: Bengals lead series, 6-3;
See Cincinnati vs. Detroit
DETROIT vs. CLEVELAND
RS: Lions lead series, 13-4
PS: Lions lead series, 3-1;
See Cleveland vs. Detroit
DETROIT vs. DALLAS
RS: Cowboys lead series, 11-9
PS: Series tied, 1-1;
See Dallas vs. Detroit
DETROIT vs. DENVER
RS: Broncos lead series, 6-4;
See Denver vs. Detroit
***DETROIT vs. GREEN BAY**
RS: Packers lead series, 86-64-7
PS: Packers lead series, 2-0
1930—Packers, 47-13 (GB)
Tie, 6-6 (P)
1932—Packers, 15-10 (GB)
Spartans, 19-0 (P)
1933—Packers, 17-0 (GB)
Spartans, 7-0 (P)
1934—Lions, 3-0 (GB)
Packers, 3-0 (D)
1935—Packers, 13-9 (Mil)
Packers, 31-7 (GB)
Lions, 20-10 (D)
1936—Packers, 20-18 (GB)
Packers, 26-17 (D)
1937—Packers, 26-6 (GB)
Packers, 14-13 (D)
1938—Lions, 17-7 (GB)
Packers, 28-7 (D)
1939—Packers, 26-7 (GB)
Packers, 12-7 (D)
1940—Lions, 23-14 (GB)
Packers, 50-7 (D)
1941—Packers, 23-0 (GB)
Packers, 24-7 (D)
1942—Packers, 38-7 (Mil)
Packers, 28-7 (D)
1943—Packers, 35-14 (GB)
Packers, 27-6 (D)
1944—Packers, 27-6 (Mil)
Packers, 14-0 (D)
1945—Packers, 57-21 (Mil)
Lions, 14-3 (D)
1946—Packers, 10-7 (Mil)
Packers, 9-0 (D)
1947—Packers, 34-17 (GB)
Packers, 35-14 (D)
1948—Packers, 33-21 (GB)
Lions, 24-20 (D)
1949—Packers, 16-14 (Mil)
Lions, 21-7 (D)
1950—Lions, 45-7 (GB)
Lions, 24-21 (D)
1951—Lions, 24-17 (GB)
Lions, 52-35 (D)
1952—Lions, 52-17 (GB)
Lions, 48-24 (D)
1953—Lions, 14-7 (GB)
Lions, 34-15 (D)
1954—Lions, 21-17 (GB)
Lions, 28-24 (D)
1955—Packers, 20-17 (GB)
Lions, 24-10 (D)
1956—Lions, 20-16 (GB)
Packers, 24-20 (D)
1957—Lions, 24-14 (GB)
Lions, 18-6 (D)
1958—Tie, 13-13 (GB)
Lions, 24-14 (D)
1959—Packers, 28-10 (GB)
Packers, 24-17 (D)
1960—Packers, 28-9 (GB)
Lions, 23-10 (D)
1961—Lions, 17-13 (Mil)
Packers, 17-9 (D)
1962—Packers, 9-7 (GB)
Lions, 26-14 (D)
1963—Packers, 31-10 (Mil)
Tie, 13-13 (D)
1964—Packers, 14-10 (D)
Packers, 30-7 (GB)
1965—Packers, 31-21 (D)
Lions, 12-7 (GB)
1966—Packers, 23-14 (GB)
Packers, 31-7 (D)
1967—Tie, 17-17 (GB)
Packers, 27-17 (D)
1968—Lions, 23-17 (GB)
Tie, 14-14 (D)
1969—Packers, 28-17 (D)
Lions, 16-10 (GB)
1970—Lions, 40-0 (GB)
Lions, 20-0 (D)
1971—Lions, 31-28 (D)
Tie, 14-14 (Mil)
1972—Packers, 24-23 (D)
Packers, 33-7 (GB)
1973—Tie, 13-13 (GB)
Lions, 34-0 (D)
1974—Packers, 21-19 (Mil)
Lions, 19-17 (D)
1975—Lions, 30-16 (Mil)
Lions, 13-10 (D)
1976—Packers, 24-14 (GB)
Lions, 27-6 (D)
1977—Lions, 10-6 (D)
Packers, 10-9 (GB)
1978—Packers, 13-7 (D)
Packers, 35-14 (Mil)
1979—Packers, 24-16 (Mil)
Packers, 18-13 (D)
1980—Lions, 29-7 (Mil)
Lions, 24-3 (D)
1981—Lions, 31-27 (D)
Packers, 31-17 (GB)
1982—Lions, 30-10 (GB)
Lions, 27-24 (D)
1983—Lions, 38-14 (D)
Lions, 23-20 (Mil) OT
1984—Packers, 41-9 (GB)
Lions, 31-28 (D)
1985—Packers, 43-10 (GB)
Packers, 26-23 (D)
1986—Lions, 21-14 (GB)
Packers, 44-40 (D)
1987—Lions, 19-16 (GB) OT
Packers, 34-33 (D)
1988—Lions, 19-9 (Mil)
Lions, 30-14 (D)
1989—Packers, 23-20 (Mil) OT
Lions, 31-22 (D)
1990—Packers, 24-21 (D)
Lions, 24-17 (GB)
1991—Lions, 23-14 (D)
Lions, 21-17 (GB)
1992—Packers, 27-13 (D)
Packers, 38-10 (Mil)
1993—Packers, 26-17 (Mil)
Lions, 30-20 (D)
**Packers, 28-24 (D)
1994—Packers, 38-30 (Mil)

Lions, 34-31 (D)
**Packers, 16-12 (GB)
1995—Packers, 30-21 (GB)
Lions, 24-16 (D)
1996—Packers, 28-18 (GB)
Packers, 31-3 (D)
1997—Lions, 26-15 (D)
Packers, 20-10 (GB)
1998—Packers, 38-19 (GB)
Lions, 27-20 (D)
1999—Lions, 23-15 (D)
Packers, 26-17 (GB)
2000—Lions, 31-24 (D)
Packers, 26-13 (GB)
2001—Packers, 28-6 (GB)
Packers, 29-27 (D)
2002—Packers, 37-31 (D)
Packers, 40-14 (GB)
2003—Packers, 31-6 (GB)
Lions, 22-14 (D)
2004—Packers, 38-10 (D)
Packers, 16-13 (GB)
2005—Lions, 17-3 (D)
Packers, 16-13 (GB) OT
2006—Packers, 31-24 (D)
Packers, 17-9 (GB)
2007—Packers, 37-26 (D)
Packers, 34-13 (GB)
2008—Packers, 48-25 (D)
Packers, 31-21 (GB)
(RS Pts.—Packers 3,295, Lions 2,844)
(PS Pts.—Packers 44, Lions 36)
Franchise in Portsmouth prior to 1934 and known as the Spartans
***NFC First-Round Playoff*

DETROIT vs. HOUSTON
RS: Series tied, 1-1
2004—Lions, 28-16 (D)
2008—Texans, 28-21 (H)
(RS Pts.—Lions 49, Texans 44)

DETROIT vs. *INDIANAPOLIS
RS: Colts lead series, 20-18-2
1953—Lions, 27-17 (B)
Lions, 17-7 (D)
1954—Lions, 35-0 (D)
Lions, 27-3 (B)
1955—Colts, 28-13 (B)
Lions, 24-14 (D)
1956—Lions, 31-14 (B)
Lions, 27-3 (D)
1957—Colts, 34-14 (B)
Lions, 31-27 (D)
1958—Colts, 28-15 (B)
Colts, 40-14 (D)
1959—Colts, 21-9 (B)
Colts, 31-24 (D)
1960—Lions, 30-17 (D)
Lions, 20-15 (B)
1961—Lions, 16-15 (B)
Colts, 17-14 (D)
1962—Lions, 29-20 (B)
Lions, 21-14 (D)
1963—Colts, 25-21 (D)
Colts, 24-21 (B)
1964—Colts, 34-0 (D)
Lions, 31-14 (B)
1965—Colts, 31-7 (B)
Tie, 24-24 (D)
1966—Colts, 45-14 (B)
Lions, 20-14 (D)
1967—Colts, 41-7 (B)
1968—Colts, 27-10 (D)
1969—Tie, 17-17 (B)
1973—Colts, 29-27 (D)
1977—Lions, 13-10 (B)
1980—Colts, 10-9 (D)
1985—Colts, 14-6 (I)
1991—Lions, 33-24 (I)
1997—Lions, 32-10 (D)
2000—Colts, 30-18 (I)
2004—Colts, 41-9 (D)
2008—Colts, 31-21 (I)
(RS Pts.—Colts 860, Lions 778)
Franchise in Baltimore prior to 1984

DETROIT vs. JACKSONVILLE
RS: Jaguars lead series, 3-1
1995—Lions, 44-0 (D)
1998—Jaguars, 37-22 (J)
2004—Jaguars, 23-17 (J) OT
2008—Jaguars, 38-14 (D)
(RS Pts.—Jaguars 98, Lions 97)

DETROIT vs. KANSAS CITY
RS: Chiefs lead series, 7-4
1971—Lions, 32-21 (D)
1975—Chiefs, 24-21 (KC) OT
1980—Chiefs, 20-17 (KC)
1981—Lions, 27-10 (D)
1987—Chiefs, 27-20 (D)
1988—Lions, 7-6 (KC)
1990—Chiefs, 43-24 (KC)
1996—Chiefs, 28-24 (D)
1999—Chiefs, 31-21 (KC)
2003—Chiefs, 45-17 (KC)
2007—Lions, 25-20 (D)
(RS Pts.—Chiefs 275, Lions 235)

DETROIT vs. MIAMI
RS: Dolphins lead series, 7-2
1973—Dolphins, 34-7 (M)
1979—Dolphins, 28-10 (D)
1985—Lions, 31-21 (D)
1991—Lions, 17-13 (D)
1994—Dolphins, 27-20 (M)
1997—Dolphins, 33-30 (M)
2000—Dolphins, 23-8 (D)
2002—Dolphins, 49-21 (M)
2006—Dolphins, 27-10 (D)
(RS Pts.—Dolphins 255, Lions 154)

DETROIT vs. MINNESOTA
RS: Vikings lead series, 63-30-2
1961—Lions, 37-10 (M)
Lions, 13-7 (D)
1962—Lions, 17-6 (M)
Lions, 37-23 (D)
1963—Lions, 28-10 (D)
Vikings, 34-31 (M)
1964—Lions, 24-20 (M)
Tie, 23-23 (D)
1965—Lions, 31-29 (M)
Vikings, 29-7 (D)
1966—Lions, 32-31 (M)
Vikings, 28-16 (D)
1967—Tie, 10-10 (M)
Lions, 14-3 (D)
1968—Vikings, 24-10 (M)
Vikings, 13-6 (D)
1969—Vikings, 24-10 (M)
Vikings, 27-0 (D)
1970—Vikings, 30-17 (D)
Vikings, 24-20 (M)
1971—Vikings, 16-13 (D)
Vikings, 29-10 (M)
1972—Vikings, 34-10 (D)
Vikings, 16-14 (M)
1973—Vikings, 23-9 (D)
Vikings, 28-7 (M)
1974—Vikings, 7-6 (D)
Lions, 20-16 (M)
1975—Vikings, 25-19 (M)
Lions, 17-10 (D)
1976—Vikings, 10-9 (D)
Vikings, 31-23 (M)
1977—Vikings, 14-7 (M)
Vikings, 30-21 (D)
1978—Vikings, 17-7 (M)
Lions, 45-14 (D)
1979—Vikings, 13-10 (D)
Vikings, 14-7 (M)
1980—Lions, 27-7 (D)
Vikings, 34-0 (M)
1981—Vikings, 26-24 (M)
Lions, 45-7 (D)
1982—Vikings, 34-31 (D)
1983—Vikings, 20-17 (M)
Lions, 13-2 (D)
1984—Vikings, 29-28 (D)
Lions, 16-14 (M)
1985—Vikings, 16-13 (M)
Lions, 41-21 (D)
1986—Lions, 13-10 (M)
Vikings, 24-10 (D)
1987—Vikings, 34-19 (M)
Vikings, 17-14 (D)
1988—Vikings, 44-17 (M)
Vikings, 23-0 (D)
1989—Vikings, 24-17 (M)
Vikings, 20-7 (D)
1990—Lions, 34-27 (M)
Vikings, 17-7 (D)
1991—Lions, 24-20 (D)
Lions, 34-14 (M)
1992—Lions, 31-17 (D)
Vikings, 31-14 (M)
1993—Lions, 30-27 (M)
Vikings, 13-0 (D)
1994—Vikings, 10-3 (M)
Lions, 41-19 (D)
1995—Vikings, 20-10 (M)
Lions, 44-38 (D)
1996—Vikings, 17-13 (M)
Vikings, 24-22 (D)
1997—Lions, 38-15 (D)
Lions, 14-13 (M)
1998—Vikings, 29-6 (M)
Vikings, 34-13 (D)
1999—Lions, 25-23 (D)
Vikings, 24-17 (M)
2000—Vikings, 31-24 (D)
Vikings, 24-17 (M)
2001—Vikings, 31-26 (M)
Lions, 27-24 (D)
2002—Vikings, 31-24 (M)
Vikings, 38-36 (D)
2003—Vikings, 23-13 (D)
Vikings, 24-14 (M)
2004—Vikings, 22-19 (M)
Vikings, 28-27 (D)
2005—Vikings, 27-14 (M)
Vikings, 21-16 (D)
2006—Vikings, 26-17 (M)
Vikings, 30-20 (D)

2007—Lions, 20-17 (D) OT
Vikings, 42-10 (M)
2008—Vikings, 12-10 (M)
Vikings, 20-16 (D)
(RS Pts.—Vikings 2,061, Lions 1,759)

DETROIT vs. NEW ENGLAND
RS: Patriots lead series, 5-4
1971—Lions, 34-7 (NE)
1976—Lions, 30-10 (D)
1979—Patriots, 24-17 (NE)
1985—Patriots, 23-6 (NE)
1993—Lions, 19-16 (NE) OT
1994—Patriots, 23-17 (D)
2000—Lions, 34-9 (D)
2002—Patriots, 20-12 (D)
2006—Patriots, 28-21 (NE)
(RS Pts.—Lions 190, Patriots 160)

DETROIT vs. NEW ORLEANS
RS: Series tied, 9-9-1
1968—Tie, 20-20 (D)
1970—Saints, 19-17 (NO)
1972—Lions, 27-14 (D)
1973—Saints, 20-13 (NO)
1974—Lions, 19-14 (D)
1976—Saints, 17-16 (NO)
1977—Lions, 23-19 (D)
1979—Saints, 17-7 (NO)
1980—Lions, 24-13 (D)
1988—Saints, 22-14 (D)
1989—Lions, 21-14 (D)
1990—Lions, 27-10 (NO)
1992—Saints, 13-7 (D)
1993—Saints, 14-3 (NO)
1997—Saints, 35-17 (NO)
2000—Lions, 14-10 (NO)
2002—Lions, 26-21 (D)
2005—Lions, 13-12 (San Antonio)
2008—Saints, 42-7 (D)
(RS Pts.—Saints 346, Lions 315)

***DETROIT vs. N.Y. GIANTS**
RS: Lions lead series, 20-18-1
PS: Lions lead series, 1-0
1930—Giants, 19-6 (P)
1931—Spartans, 14-6 (P)
Giants, 14-0 (NY)
1932—Spartans, 7-0 (P)
Spartans, 6-0 (NY)
1933—Spartans, 17-7 (P)
Giants, 13-10 (NY)
1934—Lions, 9-0 (D)
1935—**Lions, 26-7 (D)
1936—Giants, 14-7 (NY)
Lions, 38-0 (D)
1937—Lions, 17-0 (NY)
1939—Lions, 18-14 (D)
1941—Giants, 20-13 (NY)
1943—Tie, 0-0 (D)
1945—Giants, 35-14 (NY)
1947—Lions, 35-7 (D)
1949—Lions, 45-21 (NY)
1953—Lions, 27-16 (NY)
1955—Giants, 24-19 (D)
1958—Giants, 19-17 (D)
1962—Giants, 17-14 (NY)
1964—Lions, 26-3 (D)
1967—Lions, 30-7 (NY)
1969—Lions, 24-0 (D)
1972—Lions, 30-16 (D)
1974—Lions, 20-19 (D)
1976—Giants, 24-10 (NY)
1982—Giants, 13-6 (D)
1983—Lions, 15-9 (D)
1988—Giants, 30-10 (NY)
Giants, 13-10 (D) OT
1989—Giants, 24-14 (NY)
1990—Giants, 20-0 (NY)
1994—Lions, 28-25 (NY) OT
1996—Giants, 35-7 (D)
1997—Giants, 26-20 (D) OT
2000—Lions, 31-21 (NY)
2004—Lions, 28-13 (NY)
2007—Giants, 16-10 (D)
(RS Pts.—Lions 652, Giants 560)
(PS Pts.—Lions 26, Giants 7)
**Franchise in Portsmouth prior to 1934 and known as the Spartans*
***NFL Championship*

DETROIT vs. N.Y. JETS
RS: Lions lead series, 6-5
1972—Lions, 37-20 (D)
1979—Jets, 31-10 (NY)
1982—Jets, 28-13 (D)
1985—Lions, 31-20 (D)
1988—Jets, 17-10 (D)
1991—Lions, 34-20 (D)
1994—Lions, 18-7 (NY)
1997—Lions, 13-10 (D)
2000—Lions, 10-7 (NY)
2002—Jets, 31-14 (D)
2006—Jets, 31-24 (NY)
(RS Pts.—Jets 222, Lions 214)

DETROIT vs. *OAKLAND
RS: Raiders lead series, 6-4
1970—Lions, 28-14 (D)
1974—Raiders, 35-13 (O)
1978—Raiders, 29-17 (O)
1981—Lions, 16-0 (D)
1984—Raiders, 24-3 (D)
1987—Raiders, 27-7 (LA)
1990—Raiders, 38-31 (D)
1996—Raiders, 37-21 (O)
2003—Lions, 23-13 (D)
2007—Lions, 36-21 (O)
(RS Pts.—Raiders 238, Lions 195)
**Franchise in Los Angeles from 1982-1994*

***DETROIT vs. PHILADELPHIA**
RS: Eagles lead series, 13-12-2
PS: Eagles lead series, 1-0
1933—Spartans, 25-0 (P)
1934—Lions, 10-0 (P)
1935—Lions, 35-0 (D)
1936—Lions, 23-0 (P)
1938—Eagles, 21-7 (D)
1940—Lions, 21-0 (P)
1941—Lions, 21-17 (D)
1945—Lions, 28-24 (D)
1948—Eagles, 45-21 (P)
1949—Eagles, 22-14 (D)
1951—Lions, 28-10 (P)
1954—Tie, 13-13 (D)
1957—Lions, 27-16 (P)
1960—Eagles, 28-10 (P)
1961—Eagles, 27-24 (D)
1965—Lions, 35-28 (P)
1968—Eagles, 12-0 (D)
1971—Eagles, 23-20 (D)
1974—Eagles, 28-17 (P)
1977—Lions, 17-13 (D)
1979—Eagles, 44-7 (P)
1984—Tie, 23-23 (D) OT
1986—Lions, 13-11 (P)
1995—**Eagles, 58-37 (P)
1996—Eagles, 24-17 (P)
1998—Eagles, 10-9 (P)
2004—Eagles, 30-13 (D)
2007—Eagles, 56-21 (P)
(RS Pts.—Eagles 525, Lions 499)
(PS Pts.—Eagles 58, Lions 37)
**Franchise in Portsmouth prior to 1934 and known as the Spartans*
***NFC First-Round Playoff*

DETROIT vs. *PITTSBURGH
RS: Series tied, 14-14-1
1934—Lions, 40-7 (D)
1936—Lions, 28-3 (D)
1937—Lions, 7-3 (D)
1938—Lions, 16-7 (D)
1940—Steelers, 10-7 (D)
1942—Steelers, 35-7 (D)
1946—Lions, 17-7 (D)
1947—Steelers, 17-10 (P)
1948—Lions, 17-14 (D)
1949—Steelers, 14-7 (P)
1950—Lions, 10-7 (D)
1952—Lions, 31-6 (P)
1953—Lions, 38-21 (D)
1955—Lions, 31-28 (P)
1956—Lions, 45-7 (D)
1959—Tie, 10-10 (P)
1962—Lions, 45-7 (D)
1966—Steelers, 17-3 (P)
1967—Steelers, 24-14 (D)
1969—Steelers, 16-13 (P)
1973—Steelers, 24-10 (P)
1983—Lions, 45-3 (D)
1986—Steelers, 27-17 (P)
1989—Steelers, 23-3 (D)
1992—Steelers, 17-14 (P)
1995—Steelers, 23-20 (P)
1998—Lions, 19-16 (D) OT
2001—Steelers, 47-14 (P)
2005—Steelers, 35-21 (P)
(RS Pts.—Lions 559, Steelers 475)
**Steelers known as Pirates prior to 1940*

DETROIT vs. *ST. LOUIS
RS: Rams lead series, 41-37-1
PS: Lions lead series, 1-0
1937—Lions, 28-0 (C)
Lions, 27-7 (D)
1938—Rams, 21-17 (C)
Lions, 6-0 (D)
1939—Lions, 15-7 (D)
Rams, 14-3 (C)
1940—Lions, 6-0 (D)
Rams, 24-0 (C)
1941—Lions, 17-7 (D)
Lions, 14-0 (C)
1942—Rams, 14-0 (D)
Rams, 27-7 (C)
1944—Rams, 20-17 (D)
Lions, 26-14 (C)
1945—Rams, 28-21 (D)
1946—Rams, 35-14 (LA)
Rams, 41-20 (D)
1947—Rams, 27-13 (D)
Rams, 28-17 (LA)
1948—Rams, 44-7 (LA)
Rams, 34-27 (D)
1949—Rams, 27-24 (LA)
Rams, 21-10 (D)

1950—Rams, 30-28 (D)
Rams, 65-24 (LA)
1951—Rams, 27-21 (D)
Lions, 24-22 (LA)
1952—Lions, 17-14 (LA)
Lions, 24-16 (D)
**Lions, 31-21 (D)
1953—Rams, 31-19 (D)
Rams, 37-24 (LA)
1954—Lions, 21-3 (D)
Lions, 27-24 (LA)
1955—Rams, 17-10 (D)
Rams, 24-13 (LA)
1956—Lions, 24-21 (D)
Lions, 16-7 (LA)
1957—Lions, 10-7 (D)
Rams, 35-17 (LA)
1958—Rams, 42-28 (D)
Lions, 41-24 (LA)
1959—Lions, 17-7 (LA)
Lions, 23-17 (D)
1960—Rams, 48-35 (LA)
Lions, 12-10 (D)
1961—Lions, 14-13 (D)
Lions, 28-10 (LA)
1962—Lions, 13-10 (D)
Lions, 12-3 (LA)
1963—Lions, 23-2 (LA)
Rams, 28-21 (D)
1964—Tie, 17-17 (LA)
Lions, 37-17 (D)
1965—Lions, 20-0 (D)
Lions, 31-7 (LA)
1966—Rams, 14-7 (D)
Rams, 23-3 (LA)
1967—Rams, 31-7 (D)
1968—Rams, 10-7 (LA)
1969—Lions, 28-0 (D)
1970—Lions, 28-23 (LA)
1971—Rams, 21-13 (D)
1972—Lions, 34-17 (LA)
1974—Rams, 16-13 (LA)
1975—Rams, 20-0 (D)
1976—Rams, 20-17 (D)
1980—Lions, 41-20 (LA)
1981—Rams, 20-13 (LA)
1982—Lions, 19-14 (LA)
1983—Rams, 21-10 (LA)
1986—Rams, 14-10 (LA)
1987—Rams, 37-16 (D)
1988—Rams, 17-10 (LA)
1991—Lions, 21-10 (D)
1993—Lions, 16-13 (LA)
1999—Lions, 31-27 (D)
2001—Rams, 35-0 (D)
2003—Lions, 30-20 (D)
2006—Rams, 41-34 (StL)
(RS Pts.—Rams 1,559, Lions 1,435)
(PS Pts.—Lions 31, Rams 21)
Franchise in Los Angeles prior to 1995 and in Cleveland prior to 1946
***Conference Playoff*

DETROIT vs. SAN DIEGO
RS: Chargers lead series, 6-3
1972—Lions, 34-20 (D)
1977—Lions, 20-0 (D)
1978—Lions, 31-14 (D)
1981—Chargers, 28-23 (SD)
1984—Chargers, 27-24 (SD)
1996—Chargers, 27-21 (SD)
1999—Chargers, 20-10 (D)
2003—Chargers, 14-7 (D)
2007—Chargers, 51-14 (SD)
(RS Pts.—Chargers 201, Lions 184)

DETROIT vs. SAN FRANCISCO
RS: 49ers lead series, 33-26-1
PS: Series tied, 1-1
1950—Lions, 24-7 (D)
49ers, 28-27 (SF)
1951—49ers, 20-10 (D)
49ers, 21-17 (SF)
1952—49ers, 17-3 (SF)
49ers, 28-0 (D)
1953—Lions, 24-21 (D)
Lions, 14-10 (SF)
1954—49ers, 37-31 (SF)
Lions, 48-7 (D)
1955—49ers, 27-24 (D)
49ers, 38-21 (SF)
1956—Lions, 20-17 (D)
Lions, 17-13 (SF)
1957—49ers, 35-31 (SF)
Lions, 31-10 (D)
*Lions, 31-27 (SF)
1958—49ers, 24-21 (SF)
Lions, 35-21 (D)
1959—49ers, 34-13 (D)
49ers, 33-7 (SF)
1960—49ers, 14-10 (D)
Lions, 24-0 (SF)
1961—49ers, 49-0 (D)
Tie, 20-20 (SF)
1962—Lions, 45-24 (D)
Lions, 38-24 (SF)
1963—Lions, 26-3 (D)
Lions, 45-7 (SF)
1964—Lions, 26-17 (SF)
Lions, 24-7 (D)
1965—49ers, 27-21 (D)
49ers, 17-14 (SF)
1966—49ers, 27-24 (SF)
49ers, 41-14 (D)
1967—Lions, 45-3 (SF)
1968—49ers, 14-7 (D)
1969—Lions, 26-14 (SF)
1970—Lions, 28-7 (D)
1971—49ers, 31-27 (SF)
1973—Lions, 30-20 (D)
1974—Lions, 17-13 (D)
1975—Lions, 28-17 (SF)
1977—49ers, 28-7 (SF)
1978—Lions, 33-14 (D)
1980—Lions, 17-13 (D)
1981—Lions, 24-17 (D)
1983—**49ers, 24-23 (SF)
1984—49ers, 30-27 (D)
1985—Lions, 23-21 (D)
1988—49ers, 20-13 (SF)
1991—49ers, 35-3 (SF)
1992—49ers, 24-6 (SF)
1993—49ers, 55-17 (D)
1994—49ers, 27-21 (D)
1995—Lions, 27-24 (D)
1996—49ers, 24-14 (SF)
1998—49ers, 35-13 (SF)
2001—49ers, 21-13 (SF)
2003—49ers, 24-17 (SF)
2006—49ers, 19-13 (D)
2008—49ers, 31-13 (SF)
(RS Pts.—49ers 1,306, Lions 1,258)
(PS Pts.—Lions 54, 49ers 51)
**Conference Playoff*
***NFC Divisional Playoff*

DETROIT vs. SEATTLE
RS: Seahawks lead series, 6-4
1976—Lions, 41-14 (S)
1978—Seahawks, 28-16 (S)
1984—Seahawks, 38-17 (S)
1987—Seahawks, 37-14 (D)
1990—Seahawks, 30-10 (S)
1993—Lions, 30-10 (D)
1996—Lions, 17-16 (D)
1999—Lions, 28-20 (S)
2003—Seahawks, 35-14 (S)
2006—Seahawks, 9-6 (D)
(RS Pts.—Seahawks 237, Lions 193)

DETROIT vs. TAMPA BAY
RS: Lions lead series, 27-25
PS: Buccaneers lead series, 1-0
1977—Lions, 16-7 (D)
1978—Lions, 15-7 (TB)
Lions, 34-23 (D)
1979—Buccaneers, 31-16 (TB)
Buccaneers, 16-14 (D)
1980—Lions, 24-10 (TB)
Lions, 27-14 (D)
1981—Buccaneers, 28-10 (TB)
Buccaneers, 20-17 (D)
1982—Buccaneers, 23-21 (TB)
1983—Lions, 11-0 (TB)
Lions, 23-20 (D)
1984—Buccaneers, 21-17 (TB)
Lions, 13-7 (D) OT
1985—Lions, 30-9 (D)
Buccaneers, 19-16 (TB) OT
1986—Buccaneers, 24-20 (D)
Lions, 38-17 (TB)
1987—Buccaneers, 31-27 (D)
Lions, 20-10 (TB)
1988—Buccaneers, 23-20 (D)
Buccaneers, 21-10 (TB)
1989—Lions, 17-16 (TB)
Lions, 33-7 (D)
1990—Buccaneers, 38-21 (D)
Buccaneers, 23-20 (TB)
1991—Lions, 31-3 (D)
Buccaneers, 30-21 (TB)
1992—Buccaneers, 27-23 (D)
Lions, 38-7 (TB)
1993—Buccaneers, 27-10 (TB)
Lions, 23-0 (D)
1994—Buccaneers, 24-14 (TB)
Lions, 14-9 (D)
1995—Lions, 27-24 (D)
Lions, 37-10 (TB)
1996—Lions, 21-6 (D)
Lions, 27-0 (TB)
1997—Buccaneers, 24-17 (D)
Lions, 27-9 (TB)
*Buccaneers, 20-10 (TB)
1998—Lions, 27-6 (D)
Lions, 28-25 (TB)
1999—Lions, 20-3 (D)
Buccaneers, 23-16 (TB)
2000—Buccaneers, 31-10 (D)
Lions, 28-14 (TB)
2001—Buccaneers, 20-17 (D)
Buccaneers, 15-12 (TB)
2002—Buccaneers, 23-20 (D)
2005—Buccaneers, 17-13 (TB)

2007—Lions, 23-16 (D)
2008—Buccaneers, 38-20 (D)
(RS Pts—Lions 1,094, Buccaneers 896)
(PS Pts.—Buccaneers 20, Lions 10)
NFC First-Round Playoff

DETROIT vs. *TENNESSEE
RS: Titans lead series, 7-3
1971—Lions, 31-7 (H)
1975—Oilers, 24-8 (H)
1983—Oilers, 27-17 (H)
1986—Lions, 24-13 (D)
1989—Oilers, 35-31 (H)
1992—Oilers, 24-21 (D)
1995—Lions, 24-17 (H)
2001—Titans, 27-24 (D)
2004—Titans, 24-19 (T)
2008—Titans, 47-10 (D)
(RS Pts.—Titans 245, Lions 209)
**Franchise in Houston prior to 1997; known as Oilers prior to 1999*

***DETROIT vs. **WASHINGTON**
RS: Redskins lead series, 27-10
PS: Redskins lead series, 3-0
1932—Spartans, 10-0 (P)
1933—Spartans, 13-0 (B)
1934—Lions, 24-0 (D)
1935—Lions, 17-7 (B)
Lions, 14-0 (D)
1938—Redskins, 7-5 (D)
1939—Redskins, 31-7 (W)
1940—Redskins, 20-14 (D)
1942—Redskins, 15-3 (D)
1943—Redskins, 42-20 (W)
1946—Redskins, 17-16 (W)
1947—Lions, 38-21 (D)
1948—Redskins, 46-21 (W)
1951—Lions, 35-17 (D)
1956—Redskins, 18-17 (W)
1965—Lions, 14-10 (D)
1968—Redskins, 14-3 (W)
1970—Redskins, 31-10 (W)
1973—Redskins, 20-0 (D)
1976—Redskins, 20-7 (W)
1978—Redskins, 21-19 (D)
1979—Redskins, 27-24 (D)
1981—Redskins, 33-31 (W)
1982—***Redskins, 31-7 (W)
1983—Redskins, 38-17 (W)
1984—Redskins, 28-14 (W)
1985—Redskins, 24-3 (W)
1987—Redskins, 20-13 (W)
1990—Redskins, 41-38 (D) OT
1991—Redskins, 45-0 (W)
****Redskins, 41-10 (W)
1992—Redskins, 13-10 (W)
1995—Redskins, 36-30 (W) OT
1997—Redskins, 30-7 (W)
1999—Lions, 33-17 (D)
***Redskins, 27-13 (W)
2000—Lions, 15-10 (D)
2004—Redskins, 17-10 (D)
2007—Redskins, 34-3 (W)
2008—Redskins, 25-17 (D)
(RS Pts.—Redskins 795, Lions 572)
(PS Pts.—Redskins 99, Lions 30)
**Franchise in Portsmouth prior to 1934 and known as the Spartans.*
***Franchise in Boston prior to 1937*
****NFC First-Round Playoff*
*****NFC Championship*

GREEN BAY vs. ARIZONA
RS: Packers lead series, 42-22-4
PS: Packers lead series, 1-0;
See Arizona vs. Green Bay

GREEN BAY vs. ATLANTA
RS: Packers lead series, 12-11
PS: Series tied, 1-1;
See Atlanta vs. Green Bay

GREEN BAY vs. BALTIMORE
RS: Packers lead series, 2-1;
See Baltimore vs. Green Bay

GREEN BAY vs. BUFFALO
RS: Bills lead series, 7-3;
See Buffalo vs. Green Bay

GREEN BAY vs. CAROLINA
RS: Packers lead series, 6-4
PS: Packers lead series, 1-0;
See Carolina vs. Green Bay

GREEN BAY vs. CHICAGO
RS: Bears lead series, 90-80-6
PS: Bears lead series, 1-0;
See Chicago vs. Green Bay

GREEN BAY vs. CINCINNATI
RS: Series tied, 5-5;
See Cincinnati vs. Green Bay

GREEN BAY vs. CLEVELAND
RS: Packers lead series, 9-7
PS: Packers lead series, 1-0;
See Cleveland vs. Green Bay

GREEN BAY vs. DALLAS
RS: Cowboys lead series, 12-10
PS: Cowboys lead series, 4-2;
See Dallas vs. Green Bay

GREEN BAY vs. DENVER
RS: Series tied, 5-5-1
PS: Broncos lead series, 1-0;
See Denver vs. Green Bay

GREEN BAY vs. DETROIT
RS: Packers lead series, 86-64-7
PS: Packers lead series, 2-0;
See Detroit vs. Green Bay

GREEN BAY vs. HOUSTON
RS: Series tied, 1-1
2004—Packers, 16-13 (H)
2008—Texans, 24-21 (GB)
(RS Pts.—Packers 37, Texans 37)

GREEN BAY vs. *INDIANAPOLIS
RS: Series tied, 20-20-1
PS: Packers lead series, 1-0
1953—Packers, 37-14 (GB)
Packers, 35-24 (B)
1954—Packers, 7-6 (B)
Packers, 24-13 (Mil)
1955—Colts, 24-20 (Mil)
Colts, 14-10 (B)
1956—Packers, 38-33 (Mil)
Colts, 28-21 (B)
1957—Colts, 45-17 (Mil)
Packers, 24-21 (B)
1958—Colts, 24-17 (Mil)
Colts, 56-0 (B)
1959—Colts, 38-21 (B)
Colts, 28-24 (Mil)
1960—Packers, 35-21 (GB)
Colts, 38-24 (B)
1961—Packers, 45-7 (GB)
Colts, 45-21 (B)
1962—Packers, 17-6 (B)
Packers, 17-13 (GB)
1963—Packers, 31-20 (GB)
Packers, 34-20 (B)
1964—Colts, 21-20 (GB)
Colts, 24-21 (B)
1965—Packers, 20-17 (Mil)
Packers, 42-27 (B)
**Packers, 13-10 (GB) OT
1966—Packers, 24-3 (Mil)
Packers, 14-10 (B)
1967—Colts, 13-10 (B)
1968—Colts, 16-3 (GB)
1969—Colts, 14-6 (B)
1970—Colts, 13-10 (Mil)
1974—Packers, 20-13 (B)
1982—Tie, 20-20 (B) OT
1985—Colts, 37-10 (I)
1988—Colts, 20-13 (GB)
1991—Packers, 14-10 (Mil)
1997—Colts, 41-38 (I)
2000—Packers, 26-24 (GB)
2004—Colts, 45-31 (I)
2008—Packers, 34-14 (GB)
(RS Pts.—Colts 920, Packers 895)
(PS Pts.—Packers 13, Colts 10)
**Franchise in Baltimore prior to 1984*
***Conference Playoff*

GREEN BAY vs. JACKSONVILLE
RS: Series tied, 2-2
1995—Packers, 24-14 (J)
2001—Packers, 28-21 (J)
2004—Jaguars, 28-25 (GB)
2008—Jaguars, 20-16 (J)
(RS Pts.—Packers 93, Jaguars 83)

GREEN BAY vs. KANSAS CITY
RS: Chiefs lead series, 6-2-1
PS: Packers lead series, 1-0
1966—*Packers, 35-10 (Los Angeles)
1973—Tie, 10-10 (Mil)
1977—Chiefs, 20-10 (KC)
1987—Packers, 23-3 (KC)
1989—Chiefs, 21-3 (GB)
1990—Chiefs, 17-3 (GB)
1993—Chiefs, 23-16 (KC)
1996—Chiefs, 27-20 (KC)
2003—Chiefs, 40-34 (GB) OT
2007—Packers, 33-22 (KC)
(RS Pts.—Chiefs 183, Packers 152)
(PS Pts.—Packers 35, Chiefs 10)
**Super Bowl I*

GREEN BAY vs. MIAMI
RS: Dolphins lead series, 9-3
1971—Dolphins, 27-6 (Mia)
1975—Dolphins, 31-7 (GB)
1979—Dolphins, 27-7 (Mia)
1985—Dolphins, 34-24 (GB)
1988—Dolphins, 24-17 (Mia)
1989—Dolphins, 23-20 (Mia)
1991—Dolphins, 16-13 (Mia)
1994—Dolphins, 24-14 (Mil)
1997—Packers, 23-18 (GB)
2000—Dolphins, 28-20 (Mia)
2002—Packers, 24-10 (GB)
2006—Packers, 34-24 (M)
(RS Pts.—Dolphins 286, Packers 209)

GREEN BAY vs. MINNESOTA
RS: Packers lead series, 49-45-1
PS: Vikings lead series, 1-0
1961—Packers, 33-7 (Minn)
Packers, 28-10 (Mil)
1962—Packers, 34-7 (GB)

Packers, 48-21 (Minn)
1963—Packers, 37-28 (Minn)
Packers, 28-7 (GB)
1964—Vikings, 24-23 (GB)
Packers, 42-13 (Minn)
1965—Packers, 38-13 (Minn)
Packers, 24-19 (GB)
1966—Vikings, 20-17 (GB)
Packers, 28-16 (Minn)
1967—Vikings, 10-7 (Mil)
Packers, 30-27 (Minn)
1968—Vikings, 26-13 (Mil)
Vikings, 14-10 (Minn)
1969—Vikings, 19-7 (Minn)
Vikings, 9-7 (Mil)
1970—Packers, 13-10 (Mil)
Vikings, 10-3 (Minn)
1971—Vikings, 24-13 (GB)
Vikings, 3-0 (Minn)
1972—Vikings, 27-13 (GB)
Packers, 23-7 (Minn)
1973—Vikings, 11-3 (Minn)
Vikings, 31-7 (GB)
1974—Vikings, 32-17 (GB)
Packers, 19-7 (Minn)
1975—Vikings, 28-17 (GB)
Vikings, 24-3 (Minn)
1976—Vikings, 17-10 (Mil)
Vikings, 20-9 (Minn)
1977—Vikings, 19-7 (Minn)
Vikings, 13-6 (GB)
1978—Vikings, 21-7 (Minn)
Tie, 10-10 (GB) OT
1979—Vikings, 27-21 (Minn) OT
Packers, 19-7 (Mil)
1980—Packers, 16-3 (GB)
Packers, 25-13 (Minn)
1981—Vikings, 30-13 (Mil)
Packers, 35-23 (Minn)
1982—Packers, 26-7 (Mil)
1983—Vikings, 20-17 (GB) OT
Packers, 29-21 (Minn)
1984—Packers, 45-17 (Mil)
Packers, 38-14 (Minn)
1985—Packers, 20-17 (Mil)
Packers, 27-17 (Minn)
1986—Vikings, 42-7 (Minn)
Vikings, 32-6 (GB)
1987—Packers, 23-16 (Minn)
Packers, 16-10 (Mil)
1988—Packers, 34-14 (Minn)
Packers, 18-6 (GB)
1989—Vikings, 26-14 (Minn)
Packers, 20-19 (Mil)
1990—Packers, 24-10 (Mil)
Vikings, 23-7 (Minn)
1991—Vikings, 35-21 (GB)
Packers, 27-7 (Minn)
1992—Vikings, 23-20 (GB) OT
Vikings, 27-7 (Minn)
1993—Vikings, 15-13 (Minn)
Vikings, 21-17 (Mil)
1994—Packers, 16-10 (GB)
Vikings, 13-10 (Minn) OT
1995—Packers, 38-21 (GB)
Vikings, 27-24 (Minn)
1996—Vikings, 30-21 (Minn)
Packers, 38-10 (GB)
1997—Packers, 38-32 (GB)
Packers, 27-11 (Minn)
1998—Vikings, 37-24 (GB)
Vikings, 28-14 (Minn)
1999—Packers, 23-20 (GB)
Vikings, 24-20 (Minn)
2000—Packers, 26-20 (GB) OT
Packers, 33-28 (Minn)
2001—Vikings, 35-13 (Minn)
Packers, 24-13 (GB)
2002—Vikings, 31-21 (Minn)
Packers, 26-22 (GB)
2003—Vikings, 30-25 (GB)
Packers, 30-27 (Minn)
2004—Packers, 34-31 (GB)
Packers, 34-31 (Minn)
*Vikings, 31-17 (GB)
2005—Vikings, 23-20 (Minn)
Vikings, 20-17 (GB)
2006—Packers, 23-17 (Minn)
Packers, 9-7 (GB)
2007—Packers, 23-16 (Minn)
Packers, 34-0 (GB)
2008—Packers, 24-19 (GB)
Packers, 28-27 (M)
(RS Pts.—Packers 1,975, Vikings 1,807)
(PS Pts.—Vikings 31, Packers 17)
NFC First-Round Playoff

GREEN BAY vs. NEW ENGLAND
RS: Series tied, 4-4
PS: Packers lead series, 1-0
1973—Patriots, 33-24 (NE)
1979—Packers, 27-14 (GB)
1985—Patriots, 26-20 (NE)
1988—Packers, 45-3 (Mil)
1994—Patriots, 17-16 (NE)
1996—*Packers, 35-21 (New Orleans)
1997—Packers, 28-10 (NE)
2002—Packers, 28-10 (NE)
2006—Patriots, 35-0 (GB)
(RS Pts.—Packers 188, Patriots 148)
(PS Pts.—Packers 35, Patriots 21)
Super Bowl XXXI

GREEN BAY vs. NEW ORLEANS
RS: Packers lead series, 14-7
1968—Packers, 29-7 (Mil)
1971—Saints, 29-21 (Mil)
1972—Packers, 30-20 (NO)
1973—Packers, 30-10 (Mil)
1975—Saints, 20-19 (NO)
1976—Packers, 32-27 (Mil)
1977—Packers, 24-20 (NO)
1978—Packers, 28-17 (Mil)
1979—Packers, 28-19 (Mil)
1981—Packers, 35-7 (NO)
1984—Packers, 23-13 (NO)
1985—Packers, 38-14 (Mil)
1986—Saints, 24-10 (NO)
1987—Saints, 33-24 (NO)
1989—Packers, 35-34 (GB)
1993—Packers, 19-17 (NO)
1995—Packers, 34-23 (NO)
2002—Saints, 35-20 (NO)
2005—Packers, 52-3 (GB)
2006—Saints, 34-27 (GB)
2008—Saints, 51-29 (NO)
(RS Pts.—Packers 587, Saints 457)

GREEN BAY vs. N.Y. GIANTS
RS: Packers lead series, 25-21-2
PS: Packers lead series, 4-2
1928—Giants, 6-0 (GB)
Packers, 7-0 (NY)
1929—Packers, 20-6 (NY)
1930—Packers, 14-7 (GB)
Giants, 13-6 (NY)
1931—Packers, 27-7 (GB)
Packers, 14-10 (NY)
1932—Packers, 13-0 (GB)
Giants, 6-0 (NY)
1933—Giants, 10-7 (Mil)
Giants, 17-6 (NY)
1934—Packers, 20-6 (Mil)
Giants, 17-3 (NY)
1935—Packers, 16-7 (GB)
1936—Packers, 26-14 (NY)
1937—Giants, 10-0 (NY)
1938—Giants, 15-3 (NY)
*Giants, 23-17 (NY)
1939—*Packers, 27-0 (Mil)
1940—Giants, 7-3 (NY)
1942—Tie, 21-21 (NY)
1943—Packers, 35-21 (NY)
1944—Giants, 24-0 (NY)
*Packers, 14-7 (NY)
1945—Packers, 23-14 (NY)
1947—Tie, 24-24 (NY)
1948—Giants, 49-3 (Mil)
1949—Giants, 30-10 (GB)
1952—Packers, 17-3 (NY)
1957—Giants, 31-17 (GB)
1959—Giants, 20-3 (NY)
1961—Packers, 20-17 (Mil)
*Packers, 37-0 (GB)
1962—*Packers, 16-7 (NY)
1967—Packers, 48-21 (NY)
1969—Packers, 20-10 (Mil)
1971—Giants, 42-40 (GB)
1973—Packers, 16-14 (New Haven)
1975—Packers, 40-14 (Mil)
1980—Giants, 27-21 (NY)
1981—Packers, 27-14 (NY)
Packers, 26-24 (Mil)
1982—Packers, 27-19 (NY)
1983—Giants, 27-3 (NY)
1985—Packers, 23-20 (GB)
1986—Giants, 55-24 (NY)
1987—Giants, 20-10 (NY)
1992—Giants, 27-7 (NY)
1995—Packers, 14-6 (GB)
1998—Packers, 37-3 (NY)
2001—Packers, 34-25 (NY)
2004—Giants, 14-7 (GB)
2007—Packers, 35-13 (NY)
**Giants, 23-20 (GB) OT
(RS Pts.—Packers 817, Giants 807)
(PS Pts.—Packers 131, Giants 60)
NFL Championship
***NFC Championship Game*

GREEN BAY vs. N.Y. JETS
RS: Jets lead series, 8-2
1973—Packers, 23-7 (Mil)
1979—Jets, 27-22 (GB)
1981—Jets, 28-3 (NY)
1982—Jets, 15-13 (NY)
1985—Jets, 24-3 (Mil)
1991—Jets, 19-16 (NY) OT
1994—Packers, 17-10 (GB)
2000—Jets, 20-16 (GB)
2002—Jets, 42-17 (NY)
2006—Jets, 38-10 (GB)
(RS Pts.—Jets 230, Packers 140)

GREEN BAY vs. *OAKLAND
RS: Series tied, 5-5
PS: Packers lead series, 1-0
1967—**Packers, 33-14 (Miami)
1972—Raiders, 20-14 (GB)
1976—Raiders, 18-14 (O)
1978—Raiders, 28-3 (GB)
1984—Raiders, 28-7 (LA)
1987—Raiders, 20-0 (GB)
1990—Packers, 29-16 (LA)
1993—Packers, 28-0 (GB)
1999—Packers, 28-24 (GB)
2003—Packers, 41-7 (O)
2007—Packers, 38-7 (GB)
(RS Pts.—Packers 202, Raiders 168)
(PS Pts.—Packers 33, Raiders 14)
Franchise in Los Angeles from 1982-1994
***Super Bowl II*

GREEN BAY vs. PHILADELPHIA
RS: Packers lead series, 23-13
PS: Eagles lead series, 2-0
1933—Packers, 35-9 (GB)
Packers, 10-0 (P)
1934—Packers, 19-6 (GB)
1935—Packers, 13-6 (P)
1937—Packers, 37-7 (Mil)
1939—Packers, 23-16 (P)
1940—Packers, 27-20 (GB)
1942—Packers, 7-0 (P)
1946—Packers, 19-7 (P)
1947—Eagles, 28-14 (P)
1951—Packers, 37-24 (GB)
1952—Packers, 12-10 (Mil)
1954—Packers, 37-14 (P)
1958—Packers, 38-35 (GB)
1960—*Eagles, 17-13 (P)
1962—Packers, 49-0 (P)
1968—Packers, 30-13 (GB)
1970—Packers, 30-17 (Mil)
1974—Eagles, 36-14 (P)
1976—Packers, 28-13 (GB)
1978—Eagles, 10-3 (P)
1979—Eagles, 21-10 (GB)
1987—Packers, 16-10 (GB) OT
1990—Eagles, 31-0 (P)
1991—Eagles, 20-3 (GB)
1992—Packers, 27-24 (Mil)
1993—Eagles, 20-17 (GB)
1994—Eagles, 13-7 (P)
1996—Packers, 39-13 (GB)
1997—Eagles, 10-9 (P)
1998—Packers, 24-16 (GB)
2000—Packers, 6-3 (GB)
2003—Eagles, 17-14 (GB)
**Eagles, 20-17 (P) OT
2004—Eagles, 47-17 (P)
2005—Eagles, 19-14 (P)
2006—Eagles, 31-9 (P)
2007—Packers, 16-13 (GB)
(RS Pts.—Packers 710, Eagles 579)
(PS Pts.—Eagles 37, Packers 30)
**NFL Championship*
***NFC Divisional Playoff*

GREEN BAY vs. *PITTSBURGH
RS: Packers lead series, 18-13
1933—Packers, 47-0 (GB)
1935—Packers, 27-0 (GB)
Packers, 34-14 (P)
1936—Packers, 42-10 (Mil)
1938—Packers, 20-0 (GB)
1940—Packers, 24-3 (Mil)
1941—Packers, 54-7 (P)
1942—Packers, 24-21 (Mil)
1946—Packers, 17-7 (GB)
1947—Steelers, 18-17 (Mil)
1948—Steelers, 38-7 (P)
1949—Steelers, 30-7 (Mil)
1951—Packers, 35-33 (Mil)
Steelers, 28-7 (P)
1953—Steelers, 31-14 (P)
1954—Steelers, 21-20 (GB)
1957—Packers, 27-10 (P)
1960—Packers, 19-13 (P)
1963—Packers, 33-14 (Mil)
1965—Packers, 41-9 (P)
1967—Steelers, 24-17 (GB)
1969—Packers, 38-34 (P)
1970—Packers, 20-12 (P)
1975—Steelers, 16-13 (Mil)
1980—Steelers, 22-20 (P)
1983—Steelers, 25-21 (GB)
1986—Steelers, 27-3 (P)
1992—Packers, 17-3 (GB)
1995—Packers, 24-19 (GB)
1998—Steelers, 27-20 (P)
2005—Steelers, 20-10 (GB)
(RS Pts.—Packers 719, Steelers 536)
**Steelers known as Pirates prior to 1940*

GREEN BAY vs. *ST. LOUIS
RS: Rams lead series, 45-41-2
PS: Series tied, 1-1
1937—Packers, 35-10 (C)
Packers, 35-7 (GB)
1938—Packers, 26-17 (GB)
Packers, 28-7 (C)
1939—Rams, 27-24 (GB)
Packers, 7-6 (C)
1940—Packers, 31-14 (GB)
Tie, 13-13 (C)
1941—Packers, 24-7 (Mil)
Packers, 17-14 (C)
1942—Packers, 45-28 (GB)
Packers, 30-12 (C)
1944—Packers, 30-21 (GB)
Packers, 42-7 (C)
1945—Rams, 27-14 (GB)
Rams, 20-7 (C)
1946—Rams, 21-17 (Mil)
Rams, 38-17 (LA)
1947—Packers, 17-14 (Mil)
Packers, 30-10 (LA)
1948—Packers, 16-0 (GB)
Rams, 24-10 (LA)
1949—Rams, 48-7 (GB)
Rams, 35-7 (LA)
1950—Rams, 45-14 (Mil)
Rams, 51-14 (LA)
1951—Rams, 28-0 (Mil)
Rams, 42-14 (LA)
1952—Rams, 30-28 (Mil)
Rams, 45-27 (LA)
1953—Rams, 38-20 (Mil)
Rams, 33-17 (LA)
1954—Packers, 35-17 (Mil)
Rams, 35-27 (LA)
1955—Packers, 30-28 (Mil)
Rams, 31-17 (LA)
1956—Packers, 42-17 (Mil)
Rams, 49-21 (LA)
1957—Rams, 31-27 (Mil)
Rams, 42-17 (LA)
1958—Rams, 20-7 (GB)
Rams, 34-20 (LA)
1959—Rams, 45-6 (Mil)
Packers, 38-20 (LA)
1960—Rams, 33-31 (Mil)
Packers, 35-21 (LA)
1961—Packers, 35-17 (GB)
Packers, 24-17 (LA)
1962—Packers, 41-10 (Mil)
Packers, 20-17 (LA)
1963—Packers, 42-10 (GB)
Packers, 31-14 (LA)
1964—Rams, 27-17 (Mil)
Tie, 24-24 (LA)
1965—Packers, 6-3 (Mil)
Rams, 21-10 (LA)
1966—Packers, 24-13 (GB)
Packers, 27-23 (LA)
1967—Rams, 27-24 (LA)
**Packers, 28-7 (Mil)
1968—Rams, 16-14 (Mil)
1969—Rams, 34-21 (LA)
1970—Rams, 31-21 (GB)
1971—Rams, 30-13 (LA)
1973—Rams, 24-7 (LA)
1974—Packers, 17-6 (Mil)
1975—Rams, 22-5 (LA)
1977—Rams, 24-6 (Mil)
1978—Rams, 31-14 (LA)
1980—Rams, 51-21 (LA)
1981—Rams, 35-23 (LA)
1982—Packers, 35-23 (Mil)
1983—Packers, 27-24 (Mil)
1984—Packers, 31-6 (Mil)
1985—Rams, 34-17 (LA)
1988—Rams, 34-7 (GB)
1989—Rams, 41-38 (LA)
1990—Packers, 36-24 (GB)
1991—Rams, 23-21 (LA)
1992—Packers, 28-13 (GB)
1993—Packers, 36-6 (Mil)
1994—Packers, 24-17 (GB)
1995—Rams, 17-14 (GB)
1996—Packers, 24-9 (StL)
1997—Packers, 17-7 (GB)
2001—***Rams, 45-17 (StL)
2003—Rams, 34-24 (StL)
2004—Packers, 45-17 (GB)
2006—Rams, 23-20 (GB)
2007—Packers, 33-14 (StL)
(RS Pts.—Rams 2,055, Packers 1,980)
(PS Pts.—Rams 52, Packers 45)
**Franchise in Los Angeles prior to 1995 and in Cleveland prior to 1946*
***Conference Championship*
****NFC Divisional Playoff*

GREEN BAY vs. SAN DIEGO
RS: Packers lead series, 8-1
1970—Packers, 22-20 (SD)
1974—Packers, 34-0 (GB)
1978—Packers, 24-3 (SD)
1984—Chargers, 34-28 (GB)
1993—Packers, 20-13 (SD)
1996—Packers, 42-10 (GB)
1999—Packers, 31-3 (SD)
2003—Packers, 38-21 (SD)
2007—Packers, 31-24 (GB)
(RS Pts.—Packers 270, Chargers 128)

GREEN BAY vs. SAN FRANCISCO
RS: Packers lead series, 28-25-1
PS: Packers lead series, 4-1
1950—Packers, 25-21 (GB)
49ers, 30-14 (SF)
1951—49ers, 31-19 (SF)
1952—49ers, 24-14 (SF)
1953—49ers, 37-7 (Mil)
49ers, 48-14 (SF)
1954—49ers, 23-17 (Mil)
49ers, 35-0 (SF)
1955—Packers, 27-21 (Mil)
Packers, 28-7 (SF)
1956—49ers, 17-16 (GB)
49ers, 38-20 (SF)
1957—49ers, 24-14 (Mil)
49ers, 27-20 (SF)
1958—49ers, 33-12 (Mil)
49ers, 48-21 (SF)
1959—Packers, 21-20 (GB)
Packers, 36-14 (SF)
1960—Packers, 41-14 (Mil)
Packers, 13-0 (SF)
1961—Packers, 30-10 (GB)
49ers, 22-21 (SF)
1962—Packers, 31-13 (Mil)
Packers, 31-21 (SF)
1963—Packers, 28-10 (Mil)
Packers, 21-17 (SF)
1964—Packers, 24-14 (Mil)
49ers, 24-14 (SF)
1965—Packers, 27-10 (GB)
Tie, 24-24 (SF)
1966—49ers, 21-20 (SF)
Packers, 20-7 (Mil)
1967—Packers, 13-0 (GB)
1968—49ers, 27-20 (SF)
1969—Packers, 14-7 (Mil)
1970—49ers, 26-10 (SF)
1972—Packers, 34-24 (Mil)
1973—49ers, 20-6 (SF)
1974—49ers, 7-6 (SF)
1976—49ers, 26-14 (GB)
1977—Packers, 16-14 (Mil)
1980—Packers, 23-16 (Mil)
1981—49ers, 13-3 (Mil)
1986—49ers, 31-17 (Mil)
1987—49ers, 23-12 (GB)
1989—Packers, 21-17 (SF)
1990—49ers, 24-20 (GB)
1995—*Packers, 27-17 (SF)
1996—Packers, 23-20 (GB) OT
*Packers, 35-14 (GB)
1997—**Packers, 23-10 (SF)
1998—Packers, 36-22 (GB)
***49ers, 30-27 (SF)
1999—Packers, 20-3 (SF)
2000—Packers, 31-28 (GB)
2001—***Packers, 25-15 (GB)
2002—Packers, 20-14 (SF)
2003—Packers, 20-10 (GB)
2006—Packers, 30-19 (SF)
(RS Pts.—49ers 1,096, Packers 1,079)
(PS Pts.—Packers 137, 49ers 86)
NFC Divisional Playoff
***NFC Championship*
****NFC First-Round Playoff*

GREEN BAY vs. SEATTLE
RS: Packers lead series, 7-5
PS: Packers lead series, 2-0
1976—Packers, 27-20 (Mil)
1978—Packers, 45-28 (Mil)
1981—Packers, 34-24 (GB)
1984—Seahawks, 30-24 (Mil)
1987—Seahawks, 24-13 (S)
1990—Seahawks, 20-14 (Mil)
1996—Packers, 31-10 (S)
1999—Seahawks, 27-7 (GB)
2003—Packers, 35-13 (GB)
*Packers, 33-27 (GB) OT
2005—Packers, 23-17 (GB)
2006—Seahawks, 34-24 (S)
2007—**Packers, 42-20 (GB)
2008—Packers, 27-17 (S)
(RS Pts.—Packers 304, Seahawks 264)
(PS Pts.—Packers 75, Seahawks 47)
NFC First-Round Playoff
***NFC Divisional Playoff*

GREEN BAY vs. TAMPA BAY
RS: Packers lead series, 29-20-1
PS: Packers lead series, 1-0
1977—Packers, 13-0 (TB)
1978—Packers, 9-7 (GB)
Packers, 17-7 (TB)
1979—Buccaneers, 21-10 (GB)
Buccaneers, 21-3 (TB)
1980—Tie, 14-14 (TB) OT
Buccaneers, 20-17 (Mil)
1981—Buccaneers, 21-10 (GB)
Buccaneers, 37-3 (TB)
1983—Packers, 55-14 (GB)
Packers, 12-9 (TB) OT
1984—Buccaneers, 30-27 (TB) OT
Packers, 27-14 (GB)
1985—Packers, 21-0 (GB)
Packers, 20-17 (TB)
1986—Packers, 31-7 (Mil)
Packers, 21-7 (TB)
1987—Buccaneers, 23-17 (Mil)
1988—Buccaneers, 13-10 (GB)
Buccaneers, 27-24 (TB)
1989—Buccaneers, 23-21 (GB)
Packers, 17-16 (TB)
1990—Buccaneers, 26-14 (TB)
Packers, 20-10 (Mil)
1991—Packers, 15-13 (GB)
Packers, 27-0 (TB)
1992—Buccaneers, 31-3 (TB)
Packers, 19-14 (Mil)
1993—Packers, 37-14 (TB)
Packers, 13-10 (GB)
1994—Packers, 30-3 (GB)
Packers, 34-19 (TB)
1995—Packers, 35-13 (GB)
Buccaneers, 13-10 (TB) OT
1996—Packers, 34-3 (TB)
Packers, 13-7 (GB)
1997—Packers, 21-16 (GB)
Packers, 17-6 (TB)
*Packers, 21-7 (GB)
1998—Packers, 23-15 (GB)
Buccaneers, 24-22 (TB)
1999—Packers, 26-23 (GB)
Buccaneers, 29-10 (TB)
2000—Buccaneers, 20-15 (TB)
Packers, 17-14 (GB) OT
2001—Buccaneers, 14-10 (TB)
Packers, 21-20 (GB)
2002—Buccaneers, 21-7 (TB)
2003—Packers, 20-13 (TB)
2005—Buccaneers, 17-16 (GB)
2008—Buccaneers, 30-21 (TB)
(RS Pts.—Packers 949, Buccaneers 786)
(PS Pts.—Packers 21, Buccaneers 7)
NFC Divisional Playoff

GREEN BAY vs. *TENNESSEE
RS: Titans lead series, 6-4
1972—Packers, 23-10 (H)
1977—Oilers, 16-10 (GB)
1980—Oilers, 22-3 (GB)
1983—Packers, 41-38 (H) OT
1986—Oilers, 31-3 (GB)
1992—Packers, 16-14 (H)
1998—Packers, 30-22 (GB)
2001—Titans, 26-20 (T)
2004—Titans, 48-27 (GB)
2008—Titans, 19-16 (T) OT
(RS Pts.—Titans 246, Packers 189)
**Franchise in Houston prior to 1997; known as Oilers prior to 1999*

GREEN BAY vs. *WASHINGTON
RS: Packers lead series, 17-12-1
PS: Series tied, 1-1
1932—Packers, 21-0 (B)
1933—Tie, 7-7 (GB)
Redskins, 20-7 (B)
1934—Packers, 10-0 (B)
1936—Packers, 31-2 (GB)
Packers, 7-3 (B)
**Packers, 21-6 (New York)
1937—Redskins, 14-6 (W)
1939—Packers, 24-14 (Mil)
1941—Packers, 22-17 (W)
1943—Redskins, 33-7 (Mil)
1946—Packers, 20-7 (W)
1947—Packers, 27-10 (Mil)
1948—Redskins, 23-7 (Mil)
1949—Redskins, 30-0 (W)
1950—Packers, 35-21 (Mil)
1952—Packers, 35-20 (Mil)
1958—Redskins, 37-21 (W)
1959—Packers, 21-0 (GB)
1968—Packers, 27-7 (W)
1972—Redskins, 21-16 (W)
***Redskins, 16-3 (W)
1974—Redskins, 17-6 (GB)
1977—Redskins, 10-9 (W)
1979—Redskins, 38-21 (W)
1983—Packers, 48-47 (GB)
1986—Redskins, 16-7 (GB)
1988—Redskins, 20-17 (Mil)
2001—Packers, 37-0 (GB)
2002—Packers, 30-9 (GB)
2004—Packers, 28-14 (W)
2007—Packers, 17-14 (GB)
(RS Pts.—Packers 571, Redskins 471)
(PS Pts.—Packers 24, Redskins 22)
**Franchise in Boston prior to 1937 and known as Braves prior to 1933*
***NFL Championship*
****NFC Divisional Playoff*

HOUSTON vs. ARIZONA
RS: Texans lead series, 1-0;
See Arizona vs. Houston

HOUSTON vs. ATLANTA
RS: Series tied, 1-1;
See Atlanta vs. Houston

HOUSTON vs. BALTIMORE
RS: Ravens lead series, 3-0;

See Baltimore vs. Houston
HOUSTON vs. BUFFALO
RS: Bills lead series, 3-1;
See Buffalo vs. Houston
HOUSTON vs. CAROLINA
RS: Texans lead series, 2-0;
See Carolina vs. Houston
HOUSTON vs. CHICAGO
RS: Texans lead series, 2-0;
See Chicago vs. Houston
HOUSTON vs. CINCINNATI
RS: Bengals lead series, 3-1;
See Cincinnati vs. Houston
HOUSTON vs. CLEVELAND
RS: Series tied, 3-3;
See Cleveland vs. Houston
HOUSTON vs. DALLAS
RS: Series tied, 1-1;
See Dallas vs. Houston
HOUSTON vs. DENVER
RS: Series tied, 1-1;
See Denver vs. Houston
HOUSTON vs. DETROIT
RS: Series tied, 1-1;
See Detroit vs. Houston
HOUSTON vs. GREEN BAY
RS: Series tied, 1-1;
See Green Bay vs. Houston
HOUSTON vs. INDIANAPOLIS
RS: Colts lead series, 13-1
2002—Colts, 23-3 (H)
Colts, 19-3 (I)
2003—Colts, 30-21 (I)
Colts, 20-17 (H)
2004—Colts, 49-14 (I)
Colts, 23-14 (H)
2005—Colts, 38-20 (H)
Colts, 31-17 (I)
2006—Colts, 43-24 (I)
Texans, 27-24 (H)
2007—Colts, 30-24 (H)
Colts, 38-15 (I)
2008—Colts, 31-27 (H)
Colts, 33-27 (I)
(RS Pts.—Colts 432, Texans 253)
HOUSTON vs. JACKSONVILLE
RS: Texans lead series, 8-6
2002—Texans, 21-19 (J)
Jaguars, 24-21 (H)
2003—Texans, 24-20 (H)
Jaguars, 27-0 (J)
2004—Texans, 20-6 (H)
Texans, 21-0 (J)
2005—Jaguars, 21-14 (J)
Jaguars, 38-20 (H)
2006—Texans, 27-7 (H)
Texans, 13-10 (J)
2007—Jaguars, 37-17 (J)
Texans, 42-28 (H)
2008—Jaguars, 30-27 (J) OT
Texans, 30-17 (H)
(RS Pts.—Texans 297, Jaguars 284)
HOUSTON vs. KANSAS CITY
RS: Series tied, 2-2
2003—Chiefs, 42-14 (H)
2004—Texans, 24-21 (KC)
2005—Chiefs, 45-17 (H)
2007—Texans, 20-3 (H)
(RS Pts.—Chiefs 111, Texans 75)
HOUSTON vs. MIAMI
RS: Texans lead series, 4-0
2003—Texans, 21-20 (M)
2006—Texans, 17-15 (H)
2007—Texans, 22-19 (H)
2008—Texans, 29-28 (M)
(RS Pts.—Texans 89, Dolphins 82)
HOUSTON vs. MINNESOTA
RS: Vikings lead series, 2-0
2004—Vikings, 34-28 (H) OT
2008—Vikings, 28-21 (M)
(RS Pts.—Vikings 62, Texans 49)
HOUSTON vs. NEW ENGLAND
RS: Patriots lead series, 2-0
2003—Patriots, 23-20 (H) OT
2006—Patriots, 40-7 (NE)
(RS Pts.—Patriots 63, Texans 27)
HOUSTON vs. NEW ORLEANS
RS: Series tied, 1-1
2003—Saints, 31-10 (NO)
2007—Texans, 23-10 (H)
(RS Pts.—Saints 41, Texans 33)
HOUSTON vs. N.Y. GIANTS
RS: Series tied, 1-1
2002—Texans, 16-14 (H)
2006—Giants, 14-10 (NY)
(RS Pts.—Giants 28, Texans 26)
HOUSTON vs. N.Y. JETS
RS: Jets lead series, 3-0
2003—Jets, 19-14 (H)
2004—Jets, 29-7 (NY)
2006—Jets, 26-11 (NY)
(RS Pts.—Jets 74, Texans 32)
HOUSTON vs. OAKLAND
RS: Texans lead series, 3-1
2004—Texans, 30-17 (H)
2006—Texans, 23-14 (O)
2007—Texans, 24-17 (O)
2008—Raiders, 27-16 (O)
(RS Pts.—Texans 93, Raiders 75)
HOUSTON vs. PHILADELPHIA
RS: Eagles lead series, 2-0
2002—Eagles, 35-17 (P)
2006—Eagles, 24-10 (H)
(RS Pts.—Eagles 59, Texans 27)
HOUSTON vs. PITTSBURGH
RS: Steelers lead series, 2-1
2002—Texans, 24-6 (P)
2005—Steelers, 27-7 (H)
2008—Steelers, 38-17 (P)
(RS Pts.—Steelers 71, Texans 48)
HOUSTON vs. ST. LOUIS
RS: Rams lead series, 1-0
2005—Rams, 33-27 (H) OT
(RS Pts.—Rams 33, Texans 27)
HOUSTON vs. SAN DIEGO
RS: Chargers lead series, 3-0
2002—Chargers, 24-3 (SD)
2004—Chargers, 27-20 (H)
2007—Chargers, 35-10 (SD)
(RS Pts.—Chargers 86, Texans 33)
HOUSTON vs. SAN FRANCISCO
RS: 49ers lead series, 1-0
2005—49ers, 20-17 (SF) OT
(RS Pts.—49ers 20, Texans 17)
HOUSTON vs. SEATTLE
RS: Seahawks lead series, 1-0
2005—Seahawks, 42-10
(RS Pts.—Seahawks 42, Texans 10)
HOUSTON vs. TAMPA BAY
RS: Series tied, 1-1
2003—Buccaneers, 16-3 (TB)
2007—Texans, 28-14 (H)
(RS Pts.—Texans 31, Buccaneers 30)
HOUSTON vs. TENNESSEE
RS: Titans lead series, 11-3
2002—Titans, 17-10 (T)
Titans, 13-3 (H)
2003—Titans, 38-17 (T)
Titans, 27-24 (H)
2004—Texans, 20-10 (T)
Texans, 31-21 (H)
2005—Titans, 34-20 (H)
Titans, 13-10 (T)
2006—Titans, 28-22 (T)
Titans, 26-20 (H) OT
2007—Titans, 38-36 (H)
Titans, 28-20 (T)
2008—Titans, 31-12 (T)
Texans, 13-12 (H)
(RS Pts.—Titans 336, Texans 258)
HOUSTON vs. WASHINGTON
RS: Redskins lead series, 2-0
2002—Redskins, 26-10 (W)
2006—Redskins, 31-15 (H)
(RS Pts.—Redskins 57, Texans 25)

INDIANAPOLIS vs. ARIZONA
RS: Colts lead series, 7-6;
See Arizona vs. Indianapolis
INDIANAPOLIS vs. ATLANTA
RS: Colts lead series, 13-1;
See Atlanta vs. Indianapolis
INDIANAPOLIS vs. BALTIMORE
RS: Colts lead series, 6-2
PS: Colts lead series, 1-0;
See Baltimore vs. Indianapolis
INDIANAPOLIS vs. BUFFALO
RS: Bills lead series, 34-30-1;
See Buffalo vs. Indianapolis
INDIANAPOLIS vs. CAROLINA
RS: Panthers lead series, 3-1;
See Carolina vs. Indianapolis
INDIANAPOLIS vs. CHICAGO
RS: Colts lead series, 22-18
PS: Colts lead series, 1-0;
See Chicago vs. Indianapolis
INDIANAPOLIS vs. CINCINNATI
RS: Colts lead series, 15-8
PS: Colts lead series, 1-0;
See Cincinnati vs. Indianapolis
INDIANAPOLIS vs. CLEVELAND
RS: Browns lead series, 13-12
PS: Series tied, 2-2;
See Cleveland vs. Indianapolis
INDIANAPOLIS vs. DALLAS
RS: Cowboys lead series, 8-5
PS: Colts lead series, 1-0;
See Dallas vs. Indianapolis
INDIANAPOLIS vs. DENVER
RS: Broncos lead series, 11-6
PS: Colts lead series, 2-0;
See Denver vs. Indianapolis
INDIANAPOLIS vs. DETROIT
RS: Colts lead series, 20-18-2;
See Detroit vs. Indianapolis
INDIANAPOLIS vs. GREEN BAY
RS: Series tied, 20-20-1
PS: Packers lead series, 1-0;

See Green Bay vs. Indianapolis

INDIANAPOLIS vs. HOUSTON

RS: Colts lead series, 13-1;
See Houston vs. Indianapolis

INDIANAPOLIS vs. JACKSONVILLE

RS: Colts lead series, 12-4
1995—Colts, 41-31 (J)
2000—Colts, 43-14 (I)
2002—Colts, 28-25 (J)
Colts, 20-13 (I)
2003—Colts, 23-13 (I)
Jaguars, 28-23 (J)
2004—Colts, 24-17 (J)
Jaguars, 27-24 (I)
2005—Colts, 10-3 (I)
Colts, 26-18 (J)
2006—Colts, 21-14 (I)
Jaguars, 44-17 (J)
2007—Colts, 29-7 (J)
Colts, 28-25 (I)
2008—Jaguars, 23-21 (I)
Colts, 31-24 (J)
(RS Pts.—Colts 409, Jaguars 326)

***INDIANAPOLIS vs. KANSAS CITY**

RS: Colts lead series, 9-7
PS: Colts lead series, 3-0
1970—Chiefs, 44-24 (B)
1972—Chiefs, 24-10 (KC)
1975—Colts, 28-14 (B)
1977—Colts, 17-6 (KC)
1979—Chiefs, 14-0 (KC)
Chiefs, 10-7 (B)
1980—Colts, 31-24 (KC)
Chiefs, 38-28 (B)
1985—Chiefs, 20-7 (KC)
1990—Colts, 23-19 (I)
1995—**Colts, 10-7 (KC)
1996—Colts, 24-19 (KC)
1999—Colts, 25-17 (I)
2000—Colts, 27-14 (KC)
2001—Colts, 35-28 (KC)
2003—**Colts, 38-31 (KC)
2004—Chiefs, 45-35 (KC)
2006—***Colts, 23-8 (I)
2007—Colts, 13-10 (I)
(RS Pts.—Chiefs 346, Colts 334)
(PS Pts.—Colts 71, Chiefs 46)
Franchise in Baltimore prior to 1984
***AFC Divisional Playoff*
****AFC First-Round Playoff*

***INDIANAPOLIS vs. MIAMI**

RS: Dolphins lead series, 44-23
PS: Dolphins lead series, 2-0
1970—Colts, 35-0 (B)
Dolphins, 34-17 (M)
1971—Dolphins, 17-14 (M)
Colts, 14-3 (B)
**Dolphins, 21-0 (M)
1972—Dolphins, 23-0 (B)
Dolphins, 16-0 (M)
1973—Dolphins, 44-0 (M)
Colts, 16-3 (B)
1974—Dolphins, 17-7 (M)
Dolphins, 17-16 (B)
1975—Colts, 33-17 (M)
Colts, 10-7 (B) OT
1976—Colts, 28-14 (B)
Colts, 17-16 (M)
1977—Colts, 45-28 (B)
Dolphins, 17-6 (M)
1978—Dolphins, 42-0 (B)
Dolphins, 26-8 (M)
1979—Dolphins, 19-0 (M)
Dolphins, 28-24 (B)
1980—Colts, 30-17 (M)
Dolphins, 24-14 (B)
1981—Dolphins, 31-28 (B)
Dolphins, 27-10 (M)
1982—Dolphins, 24-20 (M)
Dolphins, 34-7 (B)
1983—Dolphins, 21-7 (B)
Dolphins, 37-0 (M)
1984—Dolphins, 44-7 (M)
Dolphins, 35-17 (I)
1985—Dolphins, 30-13 (M)
Dolphins, 34-20 (I)
1986—Dolphins, 30-10 (M)
Dolphins, 17-13 (I)
1987—Dolphins, 23-10 (I)
Colts, 40-21 (M)
1988—Colts, 15-13 (I)
Colts, 31-28 (M)
1989—Dolphins, 19-13 (M)
Colts, 42-13 (I)
1990—Dolphins, 27-7 (I)
Dolphins, 23-17 (M)
1991—Dolphins, 17-6 (M)
Dolphins, 10-6 (I)
1992—Colts, 31-20 (M)
Dolphins, 28-0 (I)
1993—Dolphins, 24-20 (I)
Dolphins, 41-27 (M)
1994—Dolphins, 22-21 (M)
Colts, 10-6 (I)
1995—Colts, 27-24 (M) OT
Colts, 36-28 (I)
1996—Colts, 10-6 (I)
Dolphins, 37-13 (M)
1997—Dolphins, 16-10 (M)
Colts, 41-0 (I)
1998—Dolphins, 24-15 (I)
Dolphins, 27-14 (M)
1999—Dolphins, 34-31 (I)
Colts, 37-34 (M)
2000—Dolphins, 17-14 (I)
Colts, 20-13 (M)
***Dolphins 23-17 (M) OT
2001—Dolphins, 27-24 (I)
Dolphins, 41-6 (M)
2002—Dolphins, 21-13 (I)
2003—Colts, 23-17 (M)
2006—Colts, 27-22 (I)
(RS Pts.—Dolphins 1,516, Colts 1,143)
(PS Pts.—Dolphins 44, Colts 17)
Franchise in Baltimore prior to 1984
***AFC Championship*
****AFC First-Round Playoff*

***INDIANAPOLIS vs. MINNESOTA**

RS: Colts lead series, 14-7-1
PS: Colts lead series, 1-0
1961—Colts, 34-33 (B)
Vikings, 28-20 (M)
1962—Colts, 34-7 (M)
Colts, 42-17 (B)
1963—Colts, 37-34 (M)
Colts, 41-10 (B)
1964—Vikings, 34-24 (M)
Colts, 17-14 (B)
1965—Colts, 35-16 (B)
Colts, 41-21 (M)
1966—Colts, 38-23 (M)
Colts, 20-17 (B)
1967—Tie, 20-20 (M)
1968—Colts, 21-9 (B)
**Colts, 24-14 (B)
1969—Vikings, 52-14 (M)
1971—Vikings, 10-3 (M)
1982—Vikings, 13-10 (M)
1988—Vikings, 12-3 (M)
1997—Vikings, 39-28 (M)
2000—Colts, 31-10 (I)
2004—Colts, 31-28 (I)
2008—Colts, 18-15 (M)
(RS Pts.—Colts 562, Vikings 462)
(PS Pts.—Colts 24, Vikings 14)
Franchise in Baltimore prior to 1984
***Conference Championship*

***INDIANAPOLIS vs. **NEW ENGLAND**

RS: Patriots lead series, 42-27
PS: Patriots lead series, 2-1
1970—Colts, 14-6 (Bos)
Colts, 27-3 (Balt)
1971—Colts, 23-3 (NE)
Patriots, 21-17 (Balt)
1972—Colts, 24-17 (NE)
Colts, 31-0 (Balt)
1973—Patriots, 24-16 (NE)
Colts, 18-13 (Balt)
1974—Patriots, 42-3 (NE)
Patriots, 27-17 (Balt)
1975—Patriots, 21-10 (NE)
Colts, 34-21 (Balt)
1976—Colts, 27-13 (NE)
Patriots, 21-14 (Balt)
1977—Patriots, 17-3 (NE)
Colts, 30-24 (Balt)
1978—Colts, 34-27 (NE)
Patriots, 35-14 (Balt)
1979—Colts, 31-26 (Balt)
Patriots, 50-21 (NE)
1980—Patriots, 37-21 (Balt)
Patriots, 47-21 (NE)
1981—Colts, 29-28 (NE)
Colts, 23-21 (Balt)
1982—Patriots, 24-13 (Balt)
1983—Colts, 29-23 (NE) OT
Colts, 12-7 (Balt)
1984—Patriots, 50-17 (I)
Patriots, 16-10 (NE)
1985—Patriots, 34-15 (NE)
Patriots, 38-31 (I)
1986—Patriots, 33-3 (NE)
Patriots, 30-21 (I)
1987—Colts, 30-16 (I)
Patriots, 24-0 (NE)
1988—Patriots, 21-17 (NE)
Colts, 24-21 (I)
1989—Patriots, 23-20 (I) OT
Patriots, 22-16 (NE)
1990—Patriots, 16-14 (I)
Colts, 13-10 (NE)
1991—Patriots, 16-7 (I)
Patriots, 23-17 (NE) OT
1992—Patriots, 37-34 (I) OT
Colts, 6-0 (NE)
1993—Colts, 9-6 (I)
Patriots, 38-0 (NE)
1994—Patriots, 12-10 (I)
Patriots, 28-13 (NE)
1995—Colts, 24-10 (NE)

Colts, 10-7 (I)
1996—Patriots, 27-9 (I)
Patriots, 27-13 (NE)
1997—Patriots, 31-6 (I)
Patriots, 20-17 (NE)
1998—Patriots, 29-6 (NE)
Patriots, 21-16 (I)
1999—Patriots, 31-28 (NE)
Colts, 20-15 (I)
2000—Patriots, 24-16 (NE)
Colts, 30-23 (I)
2001—Patriots, 44-13 (NE)
Patriots, 38-17 (I)
2003—Patriots, 38-34 (I)
***Patriots, 24-14 (NE)
2004—Patriots, 27-24 (NE)
****Patriots, 20-3 (NE)
2005—Colts, 40-21 (NE)
2006—Colts, 27-20 (NE)
***Colts, 38-34 (I)
2007—Patriots, 24-20 (I)
2008—Colts, 18-15 (I)
(RS Pts.—Patriots 1,604, Colts 1,271)
(PS Pts.—Patriots 78, Colts 55)
Franchise in Baltimore prior to 1984
***Franchise in Boston prior to 1971*
****AFC Championship*
*****AFC Divisional Playoff*

***INDIANAPOLIS vs. NEW ORLEANS**
RS: Series tied, 5-5
1967—Colts, 30-10 (B)
1969—Colts, 30-10 (NO)
1973—Colts, 14-10 (B)
1986—Saints, 17-14 (I)
1989—Saints, 41-6 (NO)
1995—Saints, 17-14 (NO)
1998—Saints, 19-13 (I) OT
2001—Saints, 34-20 (NO)
2003—Colts, 55-21 (NO)
2007—Colts, 41-10 (I)
(RS Pts.—Colts 237, Saints 189)
Franchise in Baltimore prior to 1984

***INDIANAPOLIS vs. N.Y. GIANTS**
RS: Colts lead series, 7-6
PS: Colts lead series, 2-0
1954—Colts, 20-14 (B)
1955—Giants, 17-7 (NY)
1958—Giants, 24-21 (NY)
**Colts, 23-17 (NY) OT
1959—**Colts, 31-16 (B)
1963—Giants, 37-28 (B)
1968—Colts, 26-0 (NY)
1971—Colts, 31-7 (NY)
1975—Colts, 21-0 (NY)
1979—Colts, 31-7 (NY)
1990—Giants, 24-7 (I)
1993—Giants, 20-6 (NY)
1999—Colts, 27-19 (NY)
2002—Giants, 44-27 (I)
2006—Colts, 26-21 (NY)
(RS Pts.—Colts 278, Giants 234)
(PS Pts.—Colts 54, Giants 33)
Franchise in Baltimore prior to 1984
***NFL Championship*

***INDIANAPOLIS vs. N.Y. JETS**
RS: Colts lead series, 40-25
PS: Jets lead series, 2-0
1968—**Jets 16-7 (Miami)
1970—Colts, 29-22 (NY)
Colts, 35-20 (B)
1971—Colts, 22-0 (B)
Colts, 14-13 (NY)
1972—Jets, 44-34 (B)
Jets, 24-20 (NY)
1973—Jets, 34-10 (B)
Jets, 20-17 (NY)
1974—Colts, 35-20 (NY)
Jets, 45-38 (B)
1975—Colts, 45-28 (NY)
Colts, 52-19 (B)
1976—Colts, 20-0 (NY)
Colts, 33-16 (B)
1977—Colts, 20-12 (NY)
Colts, 33-12 (B)
1978—Jets, 33-10 (B)
Jets, 24-16 (NY)
1979—Colts, 10-8 (B)
Jets, 30-17 (NY)
1980—Colts, 17-14 (NY)
Colts, 35-21 (B)
1981—Jets, 41-14 (B)
Jets, 25-0 (NY)
1982—Jets, 37-0 (NY)
1983—Colts, 17-14 (NY)
Jets, 10-6 (B)
1984—Jets, 23-14 (I)
Colts, 9-5 (NY)
1985—Jets, 25-20 (NY)
Jets, 35-17 (I)
1986—Jets, 26-7 (I)
Jets, 31-16 (NY)
1987—Colts, 6-0 (I)
Colts, 19-14 (NY)
1988—Colts, 38-14 (I)
Jets, 34-16 (NY)
1989—Colts, 17-10 (NY)
Colts, 27-10 (I)
1990—Colts, 17-14 (I)
Colts, 29-21 (NY)
1991—Jets, 17-6 (I)
Colts, 28-27 (NY)
1992—Colts, 6-3 (I) OT
Colts, 10-6 (NY)
1993—Jets, 31-17 (I)
Colts, 9-6 (NY)
1994—Jets, 16-6 (NY)
Colts, 28-25 (I)
1995—Colts, 27-24 (NY) OT
Colts, 17-10 (I)
1996—Colts, 21-7 (NY)
Colts, 34-29 (I)
1997—Jets, 16-12 (I)
Colts, 22-14 (NY)
1998—Jets, 44-6 (NY)
Colts, 24-23 (I)
1999—Colts, 16-13 (NY)
Colts, 13-6 (I)
2000—Colts, 23-15 (I)
Jets, 27-17 (NY)
2001—Colts, 45-24 (NY)
Jets, 29-28 (I)
2002—***Jets, 41-0 (NY)
2003—Colts, 38-31 (I)
2006—Colts, 31-28 (NY)
(RS Pts.—Colts 1,335, Jets 1,319)
(PS Pts.—Jets 57, Colts 7)
Franchise in Baltimore prior to 1984
***Super Bowl III*
****AFC First-Round Playoff*

***INDIANAPOLIS vs. **OAKLAND**
RS: Raiders lead series, 7-4
PS: Series tied, 1-1
1970—***Colts, 27-17 (B)
1971—Colts, 37-14 (O)
1973—Raiders, 34-21 (B)
1975—Raiders, 31-20 (B)
1977—****Raiders, 37-31 (B) OT
1984—Raiders, 21-7 (LA)
1986—Colts, 30-24 (LA)
1991—Raiders, 16-0 (LA)
1995—Raiders, 30-17 (O)
2000—Raiders, 38-31 (I)
2001—Raiders, 23-18 (I)
2004—Colts, 35-14 (I)
2007—Colts, 21-14 (O)
(RS Pts.—Raiders 259, Colts 237)
(PS Pts.—Colts 58, Raiders 54)
Franchise in Baltimore prior to 1984
***Franchise in Los Angeles from 1982-1994*
****AFC Championship*
*****AFC Divisional Playoff*

***INDIANAPOLIS vs. PHILADELPHIA**
RS: Colts lead series, 10-6
1953—Eagles, 45-14 (P)
1965—Colts, 34-24 (B)
1967—Colts, 38-6 (P)
1969—Colts, 24-20 (B)
1970—Colts, 29-10 (B)
1974—Eagles, 30-10 (P)
1978—Eagles, 17-14 (B)
1981—Eagles, 38-13 (P)
1983—Colts, 22-21 (P)
1984—Eagles, 16-7 (P)
1990—Colts, 24-23 (P)
1993—Eagles, 20-10 (I)
1996—Colts, 37-10 (I)
1999—Colts, 44-17 (P)
2002—Colts, 35-13 (P)
2006—Colts, 45-21 (I)
(RS Pts.—Colts 400, Eagles 331)
Franchise in Baltimore prior to 1984

***INDIANAPOLIS vs. PITTSBURGH**
RS: Steelers lead series, 13-6
PS: Steelers lead series, 5-0
1957—Steelers, 19-13 (B)
1968—Colts, 41-7 (P)
1971—Colts, 34-21 (B)
1974—Steelers, 30-0 (P)
1975—**Steelers, 28-10 (P)
1976—**Steelers, 40-14 (B)
1977—Colts, 31-21 (B)
1978—Steelers, 35-13 (P)
1979—Steelers, 17-13 (P)
1980—Steelers, 20-17 (B)
1983—Steelers, 24-13 (B)
1984—Colts, 17-16 (I)
1985—Steelers, 45-3 (P)
1987—Steelers, 21-7 (P)
1991—Steelers, 21-3 (I)
1992—Steelers, 30-14 (P)
1994—Steelers, 31-21 (P)
1995—***Steelers, 20-16 (P)
1996—****Steelers, 42-14 (P)
1997—Steelers, 24-22 (P)
2002—Steelers, 28-10 (P)
2005—Colts, 26-7 (I)
**Steelers, 21-18 (I)
2008—Colts, 24-20 (P)

(RS Pts.—Steelers 437, Colts 322)
(PS Pts.—Steelers 151, Colts 72)
Franchise in Baltimore prior to 1984
***AFC Divisional Playoff*
****AFC Championship*
*****AFC First-Round Playoff*

***INDIANAPOLIS vs. **ST. LOUIS**
RS: Colts lead series, 22-17-2
1953—Rams, 21-13 (B)
Rams, 45-2 (LA)
1954—Rams, 48-0 (B)
Colts, 22-21 (LA)
1955—Tie, 17-17 (B)
Rams, 20-14 (LA)
1956—Colts, 56-21 (B)
Rams, 31-7 (LA)
1957—Colts, 31-14 (B)
Rams, 37-21 (LA)
1958—Colts, 34-7 (B)
Rams, 30-28 (LA)
1959—Colts, 35-21 (B)
Colts, 45-26 (LA)
1960—Colts, 31-17 (B)
Rams, 10-3 (LA)
1961—Colts, 27-24 (B)
Rams, 34-17 (LA)
1962—Colts, 30-27 (B)
Colts, 14-2 (LA)
1963—Rams, 17-16 (LA)
Colts, 19-16 (B)
1964—Colts, 35-20 (B)
Colts, 24-7 (LA)
1965—Colts, 35-20 (B)
Colts, 20-17 (LA)
1966—Colts, 17-3 (LA)
Rams, 23-7 (B)
1967—Tie, 24-24 (B)
Rams, 34-10 (LA)
1968—Colts, 27-10 (B)
Colts, 28-24 (LA)
1969—Rams, 27-20 (B)
Colts, 13-7 (LA)
1971—Colts, 24-17 (B)
1975—Rams, 24-13 (LA)
1986—Rams, 24-7 (I)
1989—Rams, 31-17 (LA)
1995—Colts, 21-18 (I)
2001—Rams, 42-17 (StL)
2005—Colts, 45-28 (I)
(RS Pts.—Rams 906, Colts 886)
**Franchise in Baltimore prior to 1984*
***Franchise in Los Angeles prior to 1995*

***INDIANAPOLIS vs. SAN DIEGO**
RS: Chargers lead series, 14-9
PS: Chargers lead series, 2-1
1970—Colts, 16-14 (SD)
1972—Chargers, 23-20 (B)
1976—Colts, 37-21 (SD)
1981—Chargers, 43-14 (B)
1982—Chargers, 44-26 (SD)
1984—Chargers, 38-10 (I)
1986—Chargers, 17-3 (I)
1987—Chargers, 16-13 (I)
Colts, 20-7 (SD)
1988—Colts, 16-0 (SD)
1989—Colts, 10-6 (I)
1992—Chargers, 34-14 (I)
Chargers, 26-0 (SD)
1993—Chargers, 31-0 (I)
1995—Chargers, 27-24 (I)
**Colts, 35-20 (SD)
1996—Chargers, 26-19 (I)
1997—Chargers, 35-19 (SD)
1998—Colts, 17-12 (I)
1999—Colts, 27-19 (SD)
2004—Colts, 34-31 (I) OT
2005—Chargers, 26-17 (I)
2007—Chargers, 23-21 (SD)
***Chargers, 28-24 (I)
2008—Colts, 23-20 (SD)
**Chargers, 23-17 (SD) OT
(RS Pts.—Chargers 539, Colts 400)
(PS Pts.—Colts 76, Chargers 71)
**Franchise in Baltimore prior to 1984*
***AFC First-Round Playoff*
****AFC Divisional Playoff*

***INDIANAPOLIS vs. SAN FRANCISCO**
RS: Colts lead series, 23-18
1953—49ers, 38-21 (B)
49ers, 45-14 (SF)
1954—Colts, 17-13 (B)
49ers, 10-7 (SF)
1955—Colts, 26-14 (B)
49ers, 35-24 (SF)
1956—49ers, 20-17 (B)
49ers, 30-17 (SF)
1957—Colts, 27-21 (B)
49ers, 17-13 (SF)
1958—Colts, 35-27 (B)
49ers, 21-12 (SF)
1959—Colts, 45-14 (B)
Colts, 34-14 (SF)
1960—49ers, 30-22 (B)
49ers, 34-10 (SF)
1961—Colts, 20-17 (B)
Colts, 27-24 (SF)
1962—49ers, 21-13 (B)
Colts, 22-3 (SF)
1963—Colts, 20-14 (SF)
Colts, 20-3 (B)
1964—Colts, 37-7 (B)
Colts, 14-3 (SF)
1965—Colts, 27-24 (B)
Colts, 34-28 (SF)
1966—Colts, 36-14 (B)
Colts, 30-14 (SF)
1967—Colts, 41-7 (B)
Colts, 26-9 (SF)
1968—Colts, 27-10 (B)
Colts, 42-14 (SF)
1969—49ers, 24-21 (B)
49ers, 20-17 (SF)
1972—49ers, 24-21 (SF)
1986—49ers, 35-14 (SF)
1989—49ers, 30-24 (I)
1995—Colts, 18-17 (I)
1998—49ers, 34-31 (SF)
2001—49ers, 40-21 (I)
2005—Colts, 28-3 (SF)
(RS Pts.—Colts 972, 49ers 822)
**Franchise in Baltimore prior to 1984*

***INDIANAPOLIS vs. SEATTLE**
RS: Colts lead series, 5-4
1977—Colts, 29-14 (S)
1978—Colts, 17-14 (S)
1991—Seahawks, 31-3 (S)
1994—Colts, 17-15 (I)
Colts, 31-19 (S)
1997—Seahawks, 31-3 (I)
1998—Seahawks, 27-23 (S)
2000—Colts, 37-24 (S)
2005—Seahawks, 28-13 (S)
(RS Pts.—Seahawks 203, Colts 173)
**Franchise in Baltimore prior to 1984*

***INDIANAPOLIS vs. TAMPA BAY**
RS: Colts lead series, 7-4
1976—Colts, 42-17 (B)
1979—Buccaneers, 29-26 (B) OT
1985—Colts, 31-23 (TB)
1987—Colts, 24-6 (I)
1988—Colts, 35-31 (I)
1991—Buccaneers, 17-3 (TB)
1992—Colts, 24-14 (TB)
1994—Buccaneers, 24-10 (TB)
1997—Buccaneers, 31-28 (I)
2003—Colts, 38-35 (TB) OT
2007—Colts, 33-14 (I)
(RS Pts.—Colts 294, Buccaneers 241)
**Franchise in Baltimore prior to 1984*

***INDIANAPOLIS vs. **TENNESSEE**
RS: Colts lead series, 16-12
PS: Titans lead series, 1-0
1970—Colts, 24-20 (H)
1973—Oilers, 31-27 (B)
1976—Colts, 38-14 (B)
1979—Oilers, 28-16 (B)
1980—Oilers, 21-16 (H)
1983—Colts, 20-10 (B)
1984—Colts, 35-21 (H)
1985—Colts, 34-16 (I)
1986—Oilers, 31-17 (H)
1987—Colts, 51-27 (I)
1988—Oilers, 17-14 (I) OT
1990—Oilers, 24-10 (H)
1992—Oilers, 20-10 (I)
1994—Colts, 45-21 (I)
1999—***Titans, 19-16 (I)
2002—Titans, 23-15 (I)
Titans, 27-17 (T)
2003—Colts, 33-7 (I)
Colts, 29-27 (T)
2004—Colts, 31-17 (T)
Colts, 51-24 (I)
2005—Colts, 31-10 (T)
Colts, 35-3 (I)
2006—Colts, 14-13 (I)
Titans, 20-17 (T)
2007—Colts, 22-20 (T)
Titans, 16-10 (I)
2008—Titans, 31-21 (T)
Colts, 23-0 (I)
(RS Pts.—Colts 706, Titans 539)
(PS Pts.—Titans 19, Colts 16)
**Franchise in Baltimore prior to 1984*
***Franchise in Houston prior to 1997; known as Oilers prior to 1999*
****AFC Divisional Playoff*

***INDIANAPOLIS vs. WASHINGTON**
RS: Colts lead series, 18-10
1953—Colts, 27-17 (B)
1954—Redskins, 24-21 (W)
1955—Redskins, 14-13 (B)
1956—Colts, 19-17 (B)
1957—Colts, 21-17 (W)
1958—Colts, 35-10 (B)
1959—Redskins, 27-24 (W)
1960—Colts, 20-0 (B)
1961—Colts, 27-6 (W)
1962—Colts, 34-21 (B)
1963—Colts, 36-20 (W)

1964—Colts, 45-17 (B)
1965—Colts, 38-7 (W)
1966—Colts, 37-10 (B)
1967—Colts, 17-13 (W)
1969—Colts, 41-17 (B)
1973—Redskins, 22-14 (W)
1977—Colts, 10-3 (B)
1978—Colts, 21-17 (B)
1981—Redskins, 38-14 (W)
1984—Redskins, 35-7 (I)
1990—Colts, 35-28 (I)
1993—Redskins, 30-24 (W)
1994—Redskins, 41-27 (I)
1996—Redskins, 31-16 (W)
1999—Colts, 24-21 (I)
2002—Redskins, 26-21 (W)
2006—Colts, 36-22 (I)
(RS Pts.—Colts 704, Redskins 551)
**Franchise in Baltimore prior to 1984*

JACKSONVILLE vs. ARIZONA
RS: Jaguars lead series, 2-0;
See Arizona vs. Jacksonville
JACKSONVILLE vs. ATLANTA
RS: Jaguars lead series, 3-1;
See Atlanta vs. Jacksonville
JACKSONVILLE vs. BALTIMORE
RS: Jaguars lead series, 9-7;
See Baltimore vs. Jacksonville
JACKSONVILLE vs. BUFFALO
RS: Bills lead series, 5-3
PS: Jaguars lead series, 1-0;
See Buffalo vs. Jacksonville
JACKSONVILLE vs. CAROLINA
RS: Jaguars lead series, 3-1;
See Carolina vs. Jacksonville
JACKSONVILLE vs. CHICAGO
RS: Bears lead series, 3-2;
See Chicago vs. Jacksonville
JACKSONVILLE vs. CINCINNATI
RS: Jaguars lead series, 11-6;
See Cincinnati vs. Jacksonville
JACKSONVILLE vs. CLEVELAND
RS: Jaguars lead series, 8-3;
See Cleveland vs. Jacksonville
JACKSONVILLE vs. DALLAS
RS: Series tied, 2-2;
See Dallas vs. Jacksonville
JACKSONVILLE vs. DENVER
RS: Jaguars lead series, 4-3
PS: Series tied, 1-1;
See Denver vs. Jacksonville
JACKSONVILLE vs. DETROIT
RS: Jaguars lead series, 3-1;
See Detroit vs. Jacksonville
JACKSONVILLE vs. GREEN BAY
RS: Series tied, 2-2;
See Green Bay vs. Jacksonville
JACKSONVILLE vs. HOUSTON
RS: Texans lead series, 8-6;
See Houston vs. Jacksonville
JACKSONVILLE vs. INDIANAPOLIS
RS: Colts lead series, 12-4;
See Indianapolis vs. Jacksonville
JACKSONVILLE vs. KANSAS CITY
RS: Jaguars lead series, 5-2
1997—Jaguars, 24-10 (J)
1998—Jaguars, 21-16 (J)
2001—Chiefs, 30-26 (J)
2002—Jaguars, 23-16 (KC)
2004—Jaguars, 22-16 (J)
2006—Chiefs, 35-30 (KC)
2007—Jaguars, 17-7 (KC)
(RS Pts.—Jaguars 163, Chiefs 130)
JACKSONVILLE vs. MIAMI
RS: Jaguars lead series, 2-1
PS: Jaguars lead series, 1-0
1998—Jaguars, 28-21 (J)
1999—*Jaguars, 62-7 (J)
2003—Dolphins, 24-10 (J)
2006—Jaguars, 24-10 (M)
(RS Pts.—Jaguars 62, Dolphins 55)
(PS Pts.—Jaguars 62, Dolphins 7)
**AFC Divisional Playoff*
JACKSONVILLE vs. MINNESOTA
RS: Vikings lead series, 3-1
1998—Vikings, 50-10 (M)
2001—Jaguars, 33-3 (M)
2004—Vikings, 27-16 (M)
2008—Vikings, 30-12 (J)
(RS Pts.—Vikings 110, Jaguars 71)
JACKSONVILLE vs. NEW ENGLAND
RS: Patriots lead series, 4-0
PS: Patriots lead series, 3-1
1996—Patriots, 28-25 (NE) OT
*Patriots, 20-6 (NE)
1997—Patriots, 26-20 (J)
1998—**Jaguars, 25-10 (J)
2003—Patriots, 27-13 (NE)
2005—**Patriots, 28-3 (NE)
2006—Patriots, 24-21 (J)
2007—***Patriots, 31-20 (NE)
(RS Pts.—Patriots 105, Jaguars 79)
(PS Pts.—Patriots 89, Jaguars 54)
**AFC Championship*
***AFC First-Round Playoff*
****AFC Divisional Playoff*
JACKSONVILLE vs. NEW ORLEANS
RS: Series tied, 2-2
1996—Saints, 17-13 (NO)
1999—Jaguars, 41-23 (J)
2003—Jaguars, 20-19 (J)
2007—Saints, 41-24 (NO)
(RS Pts.—Saints 100, Jaguars 98)
JACKSONVILLE vs. N.Y. GIANTS
RS: Series tied, 2-2
1997—Jaguars, 40-13 (J)
2000—Giants, 28-25 (NY)
2002—Giants, 24-17 (NY)
2006—Jaguars, 26-10 (J)
(RS Pts.—Jaguars 108, Giants 75)
JACKSONVILLE vs. N.Y. JETS
RS: Jaguars lead series, 5-2
PS: Jets lead series, 1-0
1995—Jets, 27-10 (NY)
1996—Jaguars, 21-17 (J)
1998—*Jets, 34-24 (NY)
1999—Jaguars, 16-6 (NY)
2002—Jaguars, 28-3 (J)
2003—Jets, 13-10 (NY)
2005—Jaguars, 26-20 (NY) OT
2006—Jaguars, 41-0 (J)
(RS Pts.—Jaguars 152, Jets 86)
(PS Pts.—Jets 34, Jaguars 24
**AFC Divisional Playoff*
JACKSONVILLE vs. OAKLAND
RS: Jaguars lead series, 3-1
1996—Raiders, 17-3 (O)
1997—Jaguars, 20-9 (O)
2004—Jaguars, 13-6 (O)
2007—Jaguars, 49-11 (J)
(RS Pts.—Jaguars 85, Raiders 43)
JACKSONVILLE vs. PHILADELPHIA
RS: Jaguars lead series, 3-0
1997—Jaguars, 38-21 (J)
2002—Jaguars, 28-25 (J)
2006—Jaguars, 13-6 (P)
(RS Pts.—Jaguars 79, Eagles 52)
JACKSONVILLE vs. PITTSBURGH
RS: Jaguars lead series, 11-9
PS: Jaguars lead series, 1-0
1995—Jaguars, 20-16 (J)
Steelers, 24-7 (P)
1996—Jaguars, 24-9 (J)
Steelers, 28-3 (P)
1997—Jaguars, 30-21 (J)
Steelers, 23-17 (P) OT
1998—Steelers, 30-15 (P)
Jaguars, 21-3 (J)
1999—Jaguars, 17-3 (P)
Jaguars, 20-6 (J)
2000—Steelers, 24-13 (J)
Jaguars, 34-24 (P)
2001—Jaguars, 21-3 (J)
Steelers, 20-7 (P)
2002—Steelers, 25-23 (J)
2004—Steelers, 17-16 (J)
2005—Jaguars, 23-17 (P) OT
2006—Jaguars, 9-0 (J)
2007—Jaguars, 29-22 (P)
*Jaguars, 31-29 (P)
2008—Steelers, 26-21 (J)
(RS Pts.—Jaguars 370, Steelers 341)
(PS Pts.—Jaguars 31, Steelers 29)
**AFC First-Round Playoff*
JACKSONVILLE vs. ST. LOUIS
RS: Rams lead series, 2-0
1996—Rams, 17-14 (StL)
2005—Rams, 24-21 (StL)
(RS Pts.—Rams 41, Jaguars 35)
JACKSONVILLE vs. SAN DIEGO
RS: Jaguars lead series, 2-1
2003—Jaguars, 27-21 (J)
2004—Chargers, 34-21 (SD)
2007—Jaguars, 24-17 (J)
(RS Pts.—Chargers 72, Jaguars 72)
JACKSONVILLE vs. SAN FRANCISCO
RS: Jaguars lead series, 2-0
1999—Jaguars, 41-3 (J)
2005—Jaguars, 10-9 (J)
(RS Pts.—Jaguars 51, 49ers 12)
JACKSONVILLE vs. SEATTLE
RS: Seahawks lead series, 3-2
1995—Seahawks, 47-30 (J)
1996—Jaguars, 20-13 (J)
2000—Seahawks, 28-21 (J)
2001—Seahawks, 24-15 (S)
2005—Jaguars, 26-14 (J)
(RS Pts.—Seahawks 126, Jaguars 112)
JACKSONVILLE vs. TAMPA BAY
RS: Jaguars lead series, 3-1
1995—Buccaneers, 17-16 (TB)
1998—Jaguars, 29-24 (J)
2003—Jaguars, 17-10 (J)
2007—Jaguars, 24-23 (TB)
(RS Pts.—Jaguars 86, Buccaneers 74)
JACKSONVILLE vs. *TENNESSEE
RS: Titans lead series, 16-12
PS: Titans lead, 1-0
1995—Oilers, 10-3 (J)

Jaguars, 17-16 (H)
1996—Oilers, 34-27 (J)
Jaguars, 23-17 (H)
1997—Jaguars, 30-24 (T)
Jaguars, 17-9 (J)
1998—Jaguars, 27-22 (T)
Oilers, 16-13 (J)
1999—Titans, 20-19 (J)
Titans, 41-14 (T)
**Titans, 33-14 (J)
2000—Titans, 27-13 (T)
Jaguars, 16-13 (J)
2001—Jaguars, 13-6 (J)
Titans, 28-24 (T)
2002—Titans, 23-14 (T)
Titans, 28-10 (J)
2003—Titans, 30-17 (J)
Titans, 10-3 (T)
2004—Jaguars, 15-12 (T)
Titans, 18-15 (J)
2005—Jaguars, 31-28 (T)
Jaguars, 40-13 (J)
2006—Jaguars, 37-7 (J)
Titans, 24-17 (T)
2007—Titans, 13-10 (J)
Jaguars, 28-13 (T)
2008—Titans, 17-10 (T)
Jaguars, 24-14 (J)
(RS Pts.—Titans 543, Jaguars 517)
(PS Pts.—Titans 33, Jaguars 14)
Franchise in Houston prior to 1997; known as Oilers prior to 1999
***AFC Championship*

JACKSONVILLE vs. WASHINGTON
RS: Redskins lead series, 3-1
1997—Redskins, 24-12 (W)
2000—Redskins, 35-16 (J)
2002—Jaguars, 26-7 (J)
2006—Redskins, 36-30 (W) OT
(RS Pts.—Redskins 102, Jaguars 84)

KANSAS CITY vs. ARIZONA
RS: Chiefs lead series, 7-2-1;
See Arizona vs. Kansas City

KANSAS CITY vs. ATLANTA
RS: Chiefs lead series, 5-2;
See Atlanta vs. Kansas City

KANSAS CITY vs. BALTIMORE
RS: Chiefs lead series, 3-1;
See Baltimore vs. Kansas City

KANSAS CITY vs. BUFFALO
RS: Bills lead series, 20-16-1
PS: Bills lead series, 2-1;
See Buffalo vs. Kansas City

KANSAS CITY vs. CAROLINA
RS: Series tied, 2-2;
See Carolina vs. Kansas City

KANSAS CITY vs. CHICAGO
RS: Bears lead series, 6-4;
See Chicago vs. Kansas City

KANSAS CITY vs. CINCINNATI
RS: Chiefs lead series, 13-12;
See Cincinnati vs. Kansas City

KANSAS CITY vs. CLEVELAND
RS: Series tied, 9-9-2;
See Cleveland vs. Kansas City

KANSAS CITY vs. DALLAS
RS: Cowboys lead series, 5-3;
See Dallas vs. Kansas City

KANSAS CITY vs. DENVER
RS: Chiefs lead series, 53-44
PS: Broncos lead series, 1-0;
See Denver vs. Kansas City

KANSAS CITY vs. DETROIT
RS: Chiefs lead series, 7-4;
See Detroit vs. Kansas City

KANSAS CITY vs. GREEN BAY
RS: Chiefs lead series, 6-2-1
PS: Packers lead series, 1-0;
See Green Bay vs. Kansas City

KANSAS CITY vs. HOUSTON
RS: Series tied, 2-2;
See Houston vs. Kansas City

KANSAS CITY vs. INDIANAPOLIS
RS: Colts lead series, 9-7
PS: Colts lead series, 3-0;
See Indianapolis vs. Kansas City

KANSAS CITY vs. JACKSONVILLE
RS: Jaguars lead series, 5-2;
See Jacksonville vs. Kansas City

KANSAS CITY vs. MIAMI
RS: Series tied, 12-12
PS: Dolphins lead series, 3-0
1966—Chiefs, 34-16 (KC)
Chiefs, 19-18 (M)
1967—Chiefs, 24-0 (M)
Chiefs, 41-0 (KC)
1968—Chiefs, 48-3 (M)
1969—Chiefs, 17-10 (KC)
1971—*Dolphins, 27-24 (KC) OT
1972—Dolphins, 20-10 (KC)
1974—Dolphins, 9-3 (M)
1976—Chiefs, 20-17 (M) OT
1981—Dolphins, 17-7 (KC)
1983—Dolphins, 14-6 (M)
1985—Dolphins, 31-0 (M)
1987—Dolphins, 42-0 (M)
1989—Chiefs, 26-21 (KC)
Chiefs, 27-24 (M)
1990—**Dolphins, 17-16 (M)
1991—Chiefs, 42-7 (KC)
1993—Dolphins, 30-10 (M)
1994—Dolphins, 45-28 (M)
**Dolphins, 27-17 (M)
1995—Dolphins, 13-6 (M)
1997—Dolphins, 17-14 (M)
2002—Chiefs, 48-30 (KC)
2005—Chiefs, 30-20 (M)
2006—Dolphins, 13-10 (M)
2008—Dolphins, 38-31 (KC)
(RS Pts.—Chiefs 501, Dolphins 455)
(PS Pts.—Dolphins 71, Chiefs 57)
**AFC Divisional Playoff*
***AFC First-Round Playoff*

KANSAS CITY vs. MINNESOTA
RS: Chiefs lead series, 5-4
PS: Chiefs lead series, 1-0
1969—*Chiefs, 23-7 (New Orleans)
1970—Vikings, 27-10 (M)
1974—Vikings, 35-15 (KC)
1981—Chiefs, 10-6 (M)
1990—Chiefs, 24-21 (KC)
1993—Vikings, 30-10 (M)
1996—Chiefs, 21-6 (M)
1999—Chiefs, 31-28 (KC)
2003—Vikings, 45-20 (M)
2007—Chiefs, 13-10 (KC)
(RS Pts.—Vikings 208, Chiefs 154)
(PS Pts.—Chiefs 23, Vikings 7)
**Super Bowl IV*

***KANSAS CITY vs. **NEW ENGLAND**
RS: Chiefs lead series, 16-12-3
1960—Patriots, 42-14 (B)
Texans, 34-0 (D)
1961—Patriots, 18-17 (D)
Patriots, 28-21 (B)
1962—Texans, 42-28 (D)
Texans, 27-7 (B)
1963—Tie, 24-24 (B)
Chiefs, 35-3 (KC)
1964—Patriots, 24-7 (B)
Patriots, 31-24 (KC)
1965—Chiefs, 27-17 (KC)
Tie, 10-10 (B)
1966—Chiefs, 43-24 (B)
Tie, 27-27 (KC)
1967—Chiefs, 33-10 (B)
1968—Chiefs, 31-17 (KC)
1969—Chiefs, 31-0 (B)
1970—Chiefs, 23-10 (KC)
1973—Chiefs, 10-7 (NE)
1977—Patriots, 21-17 (NE)
1981—Patriots, 33-17 (NE)
1990—Chiefs, 37-7 (NE)
1992—Chiefs, 27-20 (KC)
1995—Chiefs, 31-26 (KC)
1998—Patriots, 40-10 (NE)
1999—Chiefs, 16-14 (KC)
2000—Patriots, 30-24 (NE)
2002—Patriots, 41-38 (NE) OT
2004—Patriots, 27-19 (KC)
2005—Chiefs, 26-16 (KC)
2008—Patriots, 17-10 (NE)
(RS Pts.—Chiefs 752, Patriots 619)
**Franchise located in Dallas prior to 1963 and known as Texans*
***Franchise in Boston prior to 1971*

KANSAS CITY vs. NEW ORLEANS
RS: Saints lead series, 5-4
1972—Chiefs, 20-17 (NO)
1976—Saints, 27-17 (KC)
1982—Saints, 27-17 (NO)
1985—Chiefs, 47-27 (NO)
1991—Saints, 17-10 (KC)
1994—Chiefs, 30-17 (NO)
1997—Chiefs, 25-13 (KC)
2004—Saints, 27-20 (NO)
2008—Saints, 30-20 (KC)
(RS Pts.—Chiefs 206, Saints 202)

KANSAS CITY vs. N.Y. GIANTS
RS: Giants lead series, 9-2
1974—Giants, 33-27 (KC)
1978—Giants, 26-10 (NY)
1979—Giants, 21-17 (KC)
1983—Chiefs, 38-17 (KC)
1984—Giants, 28-27 (NY)
1988—Giants, 28-12 (NY)
1992—Giants, 35-21 (NY)
1995—Chiefs, 20-17 (KC) OT
1998—Giants, 28-7 (NY)
2001—Giants, 13-3 (KC)
2005—Giants, 27-17 (NY)
(RS Pts.—Giants 273, Chiefs 199)

***KANSAS CITY vs. **N.Y. JETS**
RS: Series tied, 16-16-1
PS: Series tied, 1-1
1960—Titans, 37-35 (D)
Titans, 41-35 (NY)
1961—Titans, 28-7 (NY)

Texans, 35-24 (D)
1962—Texans, 20-17 (D)
Texans, 52-31 (NY)
1963—Jets, 17-0 (NY)
Chiefs, 48-0 (KC)
1964—Jets, 27-14 (NY)
Chiefs, 24-7 (KC)
1965—Chiefs, 14-10 (NY)
Jets, 13-10 (KC)
1966—Chiefs, 32-24 (NY)
1967—Chiefs, 42-18 (KC)
Chiefs, 21-7 (NY)
1968—Jets, 20-19 (KC)
1969—Chiefs, 34-16 (NY)
***Chiefs, 13-6 (NY)
1971—Jets, 13-10 (NY)
1974—Chiefs, 24-16 (KC)
1975—Jets, 30-24 (KC)
1982—Chiefs, 37-13 (KC)
1984—Jets, 17-16 (KC)
Jets, 28-7 (NY)
1986—****Jets, 35-15 (NY)
1987—Jets, 16-9 (KC)
1988—Tie, 17-17 (NY)
Chiefs, 38-34 (KC)
1992—Chiefs, 23-7 (NY)
1998—Jets, 20-17 (KC)
2001—Jets, 27-7 (NY)
2002—Chiefs, 29-25 (NY)
2005—Chiefs, 27-7 (KC)
2007—Jets, 13-10 (NY) OT
2008—Jets, 28-24 (NY)
(RS Pts.—Chiefs 761, Jets 648)
(PS Pts.—Jets 41, Chiefs 28)
Franchise in Dallas prior to 1963 and known as Texans
**Jets known as Titans prior to 1963*
***Inter-Divisional Playoff*
****AFC First-Round Playoff*

***KANSAS CITY vs. **OAKLAND**
RS: Chiefs lead series, 51-44-2
PS: Chiefs lead series, 2-1
1960—Texans, 34-16 (O)
Raiders, 20-19 (D)
1961—Texans, 42-35 (O)
Texans, 43-11 (D)
1962—Texans, 26-16 (O)
Texans, 35-7 (D)
1963—Raiders, 10-7 (O)
Raiders, 22-7 (KC)
1964—Chiefs, 21-9 (O)
Chiefs, 42-7 (KC)
1965—Raiders, 37-10 (O)
Chiefs, 14-7 (KC)
1966—Chiefs, 32-10 (O)
Raiders, 34-13 (KC)
1967—Raiders, 23-21 (O)
Raiders, 44-22 (KC)
1968—Chiefs, 24-10 (KC)
Raiders, 38-21 (O)
***Raiders, 41-6 (O)
1969—Raiders, 27-24 (KC)
Raiders, 10-6 (O)
****Chiefs, 17-7 (O)
1970—Tie, 17-17 (KC)
Raiders, 20-6 (O)
1971—Tie, 20-20 (O)
Chiefs, 16-14 (KC)
1972—Chiefs, 27-14 (KC)
Raiders, 26-3 (O)
1973—Chiefs, 16-3 (KC)
Raiders, 37-7 (O)
1974—Raiders, 27-7 (O)
Raiders, 7-6 (KC)
1975—Chiefs, 42-10 (KC)
Raiders, 28-20 (O)
1976—Raiders, 24-21 (KC)
Raiders, 21-10 (O)
1977—Raiders, 37-28 (KC)
Raiders, 21-20 (O)
1978—Raiders, 28-6 (O)
Raiders, 20-10 (KC)
1979—Chiefs, 35-7 (KC)
Chiefs, 24-21 (O)
1980—Raiders, 27-14 (KC)
Chiefs, 31-17 (O)
1981—Chiefs, 27-0 (KC)
Chiefs, 28-17 (O)
1982—Raiders, 21-16 (KC)
1983—Raiders, 21-20 (LA)
Raiders, 28-20 (KC)
1984—Raiders, 22-20 (KC)
Raiders, 17-7 (LA)
1985—Chiefs, 36-20 (KC)
Raiders, 19-10 (LA)
1986—Raiders, 24-17 (KC)
Chiefs, 20-17 (LA)
1987—Raiders, 35-17 (LA)
Chiefs, 16-10 (KC)
1988—Raiders, 27-17 (KC)
Raiders, 17-10 (LA)
1989—Chiefs, 24-19 (KC)
Raiders, 20-14 (LA)
1990—Chiefs, 9-7 (KC)
Chiefs, 27-24 (LA)
1991—Chiefs, 24-21 (KC)
Chiefs, 27-21 (LA)
*****Chiefs, 10-6 (KC)
1992—Chiefs, 27-7 (KC)
Raiders, 28-7 (LA)
1993—Chiefs, 24-9 (KC)
Chiefs, 31-20 (LA)
1994—Chiefs, 13-3 (KC)
Chiefs, 19-9 (LA)
1995—Chiefs, 23-17 (KC) OT
Chiefs, 29-23 (O)
1996—Chiefs, 19-3 (KC)
Raiders, 26-7 (O)
1997—Chiefs, 28-27 (O)
Chiefs, 30-0 (KC)
1998—Chiefs, 28-8 (KC)
Chiefs, 31-24 (O)
1999—Chiefs, 37-34 (O)
Raiders, 41-38 (KC) OT
2000—Raiders, 20-17 (KC)
Raiders, 49-31 (O)
2001—Raiders, 27-24 (KC)
Raiders, 28-26 (O)
2002—Chiefs, 20-10 (KC)
Raiders, 24-0 (O)
2003—Chiefs, 17-10 (O)
Chiefs, 27-24 (KC)
2004—Chiefs, 34-27 (O)
Chiefs, 31-30 (KC)
2005—Chiefs, 23-17 (O)
Chiefs, 27-23 (KC)
2006—Chiefs, 17-13 (KC)
Chiefs, 20-9 (O)
2007—Chiefs, 12-10 (O)
Raiders, 20-17 (KC)
2008—Raiders, 23-8 (KC)
Chiefs, 20-13 (O)
(RS Pts.—Chiefs 2,017, Raiders 1,902)
(PS Pts.—Raiders 54, Chiefs 33)
Franchise in Dallas prior to 1963 and known as Texans
**Franchise in Los Angeles from 1982-1994*
***Division Playoff*
****AFL Championship*
*****AFC First-Round Playoff*

KANSAS CITY vs. PHILADELPHIA
RS: Eagles lead series, 3-2
1972—Eagles, 21-20 (KC)
1992—Chiefs, 24-17 (KC)
1998—Chiefs, 24-21 (P)
2001—Eagles, 23-10 (KC)
2005—Eagles, 37-31 (KC)
(RS Pts.—Eagles 119, Chiefs 109)

KANSAS CITY vs. PITTSBURGH
RS: Steelers lead series, 17-8
PS: Chiefs lead series, 1-0
1970—Chiefs, 31-14 (P)
1971—Chiefs, 38-16 (KC)
1972—Steelers, 16-7 (P)
1974—Steelers, 34-24 (KC)
1975—Steelers, 28-3 (P)
1976—Steelers, 45-0 (KC)
1978—Steelers, 27-24 (P)
1979—Steelers, 30-3 (KC)
1980—Steelers, 21-16 (P)
1981—Chiefs, 37-33 (P)
1982—Steelers, 35-14 (P)
1984—Chiefs, 37-27 (P)
1985—Steelers, 36-28 (KC)
1986—Chiefs, 24-19 (P)
1987—Steelers, 17-16 (KC)
1988—Steelers, 16-10 (P)
1989—Steelers, 23-17 (P)
1992—Steelers, 27-3 (KC)
1993—*Chiefs, 27-24 (KC) OT
1996—Steelers, 17-7 (KC)
1997—Chiefs, 13-10 (KC)
1998—Steelers, 20-13 (KC)
1999—Chiefs, 35-19 (KC)
2001—Steelers, 20-17 (KC)
2003—Chiefs, 41-20 (KC)
2006—Steelers, 45-7 (P)
(RS Pts.—Steelers 615, Chiefs 465)
(PS Pts.—Chiefs 27, Steelers 24)
AFC First-Round Playoff

KANSAS CITY vs. *ST. LOUIS
RS: Chiefs lead series, 5-4
1973—Rams, 23-13 (KC)
1982—Rams, 20-14 (LA)
1985—Rams, 16-0 (KC)
1991—Chiefs, 27-20 (LA)
1994—Rams, 16-0 (KC)
1997—Chiefs, 28-20 (StL)
2000—Chiefs, 54-34 (KC)
2002—Chiefs, 49-10 (KC)
2006—Chiefs, 31-17 (StL)
(RS Pts.—Chiefs 216, Rams 176)
Franchise in Los Angeles prior to 1995

***KANSAS CITY vs. **SAN DIEGO**
RS: Chiefs lead series, 50-46-1
PS: Chargers lead series, 1-0
1960—Chargers, 21-20 (LA)
Texans, 17-0 (D)
1961—Chargers, 26-10 (D)

Chargers, 24-14 (SD)
1962—Chargers, 32-28 (SD)
Texans, 26-17 (D)
1963—Chargers, 24-10 (SD)
Chargers, 38-17 (KC)
1964—Chargers, 28-14 (KC)
Chiefs, 49-6 (SD)
1965—Tie, 10-10 (SD)
Chiefs, 31-7 (KC)
1966—Chiefs, 24-14 (KC)
Chiefs, 27-17 (SD)
1967—Chargers, 45-31 (SD)
Chargers, 17-16 (KC)
1968—Chiefs, 27-20 (KC)
Chiefs, 40-3 (SD)
1969—Chiefs, 27-9 (SD)
Chiefs, 27-3 (KC)
1970—Chiefs, 26-14 (KC)
Chargers, 31-13 (SD)
1971—Chargers, 21-14 (SD)
Chiefs, 31-10 (KC)
1972—Chiefs, 26-14 (SD)
Chargers, 27-17 (KC)
1973—Chiefs, 19-0 (SD)
Chiefs, 33-6 (KC)
1974—Chiefs, 24-14 (SD)
Chargers, 14-7 (KC)
1975—Chiefs, 12-10 (SD)
Chargers, 28-20 (KC)
1976—Chargers, 30-16 (KC)
Chiefs, 23-20 (SD)
1977—Chargers, 23-7 (KC)
Chiefs, 21-16 (SD)
1978—Chargers, 29-23 (SD) OT
Chiefs, 23-0 (KC)
1979—Chargers, 20-14 (KC)
Chargers, 28-7 (SD)
1980—Chargers, 24-7 (KC)
Chargers, 20-7 (SD)
1981—Chargers, 42-31 (KC)
Chargers, 22-20 (SD)
1982—Chiefs, 19-12 (KC)
1983—Chargers, 17-14 (KC)
Chargers, 41-38 (SD)
1984—Chiefs, 31-13 (KC)
Chiefs, 42-21 (SD)
1985—Chargers, 31-20 (SD)
Chiefs, 38-34 (KC)
1986—Chiefs, 42-41 (KC)
Chiefs, 24-23 (SD)
1987—Chiefs, 20-13 (KC)
Chargers, 42-21 (SD)
1988—Chargers, 24-23 (KC)
Chargers, 24-13 (SD)
1989—Chargers, 21-6 (SD)
Chargers, 20-13 (KC)
1990—Chiefs, 27-10 (KC)
Chiefs, 24-21 (SD)
1991—Chiefs, 14-13 (SD)
Chiefs, 20-17 (KC) OT
1992—Chiefs, 24-10 (SD)
Chiefs, 16-14 (KC)
***Chargers, 17-0 (SD)
1993—Chiefs, 17-14 (SD)
Chiefs, 28-24 (KC)
1994—Chargers, 20-6 (SD)
Chargers, 14-13 (KC)
1995—Chiefs, 29-23 (KC) OT
Chiefs, 22-7 (SD)
1996—Chargers, 22-19 (SD)
Chargers, 28-14 (KC)
1997—Chiefs, 31-3 (KC)
Chiefs, 29-7 (SD)
1998—Chiefs, 23-7 (KC)
Chargers, 38-37 (SD)
1999—Chargers, 21-14 (SD)
Chiefs, 34-0 (KC)
2000—Chiefs, 42-10 (KC)
Chargers, 17-16 (SD)
2001—Chiefs, 25-20 (SD)
Chiefs, 20-17 (KC)
2002—Chargers, 35-34 (SD)
Chiefs, 24-22 (KC)
2003—Chiefs, 27-14 (KC)
Chiefs, 28-24 (SD)
2004—Chargers, 34-31 (KC)
Chargers, 24-17 (SD)
2005—Chargers, 28-20 (SD)
Chiefs, 20-7 (KC)
2006—Chiefs, 30-27 (KC)
Chargers, 20-9 (SD)
2007—Chiefs, 30-16 (SD)
Chargers, 24-10 (KC)
2008—Chargers, 20-19 (SD)
Chargers, 22-21 (KC)
(RS Pts.—Chiefs 2,134, Chargers 1,895)
(PS Pts.—Chargers 17, Chiefs 0)
Franchise in Dallas prior to 1963 and known as Texans
**Franchise in Los Angeles prior to 1961*
***AFC First-Round Playoff*

KANSAS CITY vs. SAN FRANCISCO
RS: 49ers lead series, 6-4
1971—Chiefs, 26-17 (SF)
1975—49ers, 20-3 (KC)
1982—49ers, 26-13 (KC)
1985—49ers, 31-3 (SF)
1991—49ers, 28-14 (SF)
1994—Chiefs, 24-17 (KC)
1997—Chiefs, 44-9 (KC)
2000—49ers, 21-7 (SF)
2002—49ers, 17-13 (SF)
2006—Chiefs, 41-10 (KC)
(PS Pts.—Chiefs 188, 49ers 186)

KANSAS CITY vs. SEATTLE
RS: Chiefs lead series, 31-18
1977—Seahawks, 34-31 (KC)
1978—Seahawks, 13-10 (KC)
Seahawks, 23-19 (S)
1979—Chiefs, 24-6 (S)
Chiefs, 37-21 (KC)
1980—Seahawks, 17-16 (KC)
Chiefs, 31-30 (S)
1981—Chiefs, 20-14 (S)
Chiefs, 40-13 (KC)
1983—Chiefs, 17-13 (KC)
Seahawks, 51-48 (S) OT
1984—Seahawks, 45-0 (S)
Chiefs, 34-7 (KC)
1985—Chiefs, 28-7 (KC)
Seahawks, 24-6 (S)
1986—Seahawks, 23-17 (S)
Chiefs, 27-7 (KC)
1987—Seahawks, 43-14 (S)
Chiefs, 41-20 (KC)
1988—Seahawks, 31-10 (S)
Chiefs, 27-24 (KC)
1989—Chiefs, 20-16 (S)
Chiefs, 20-10 (KC)
1990—Seahawks, 19-7 (S)
Seahawks, 17-16 (KC)
1991—Chiefs, 20-13 (KC)
Chiefs, 19-6 (S)
1992—Chiefs, 26-7 (KC)
Chiefs, 24-14 (S)
1993—Chiefs, 31-16 (S)
Chiefs, 34-24 (KC)
1994—Chiefs, 38-23 (KC)
Seahawks, 10-9 (S)
1995—Chiefs, 34-10 (S)
Chiefs, 26-3 (KC)
1996—Chiefs, 35-17 (S)
Chiefs, 34-16 (KC)
1997—Chiefs, 20-17 (KC) OT
Chiefs, 19-14 (S)
1998—Chiefs, 17-6 (KC)
Seahawks, 24-12 (S)
1999—Seahawks, 31-19 (KC)
Seahawks, 23-14 (S)
2000—Chiefs, 24-17 (KC)
Chiefs, 24-19 (S)
2001—Chiefs, 19-7 (KC)
Seahawks, 21-18 (S)
2002—Seahawks, 39-32 (S)
2006—Chiefs, 35-28 (KC)
(RS Pts.—Chiefs 1,143, Seahawks 933)

KANSAS CITY vs. TAMPA BAY
RS: Series tied, 5-5
1976—Chiefs, 28-19 (TB)
1978—Buccaneers, 30-13 (KC)
1979—Buccaneers, 3-0 (TB)
1981—Chiefs, 19-10 (KC)
1984—Chiefs, 24-20 (KC)
1986—Chiefs, 27-20 (KC)
1993—Chiefs, 27-3 (TB)
1999—Buccaneers, 17-10 (TB)
2004—Buccaneers, 34-31 (TB)
2008—Buccaneers, 30-27 (KC) OT
(RS Pts.—Chiefs 206, Buccaneers 186)

***KANSAS CITY vs. **TENNESSEE**
RS: Chiefs lead series, 25-20
PS: Chiefs lead series, 2-0
1960—Oilers, 20-10 (H)
Texans, 24-0 (D)
1961—Texans, 26-21 (D)
Oilers, 38-7 (H)
1962—Texans, 31-7 (H)
Oilers, 14-6 (D)
***Texans, 20-17 (H) OT
1963—Chiefs, 28-7 (KC)
Oilers, 28-7 (H)
1964—Chiefs, 28-7 (KC)
Chiefs, 28-19 (H)
1965—Chiefs, 52-21 (KC)
Oilers, 38-36 (H)
1966—Chiefs, 48-23 (KC)
1967—Chiefs, 25-20 (H)
Oilers, 24-19 (KC)
1968—Chiefs, 26-21 (H)
Chiefs, 24-10 (KC)
1969—Chiefs, 24-0 (KC)
1970—Chiefs, 24-9 (KC)
1971—Chiefs, 20-16 (H)
1973—Chiefs, 38-14 (KC)
1974—Chiefs, 17-7 (H)
1975—Oilers, 17-13 (KC)
1977—Oilers, 34-20 (H)
1978—Oilers, 20-17 (KC)
1979—Oilers, 20-6 (H)
1980—Chiefs, 21-20 (KC)

1981—Chiefs, 23-10 (KC)
1983—Chiefs, 13-10 (H) OT
1984—Oilers, 17-16 (KC)
1985—Oilers, 23-20 (H)
1986—Chiefs, 27-13 (KC)
1988—Oilers, 7-6 (H)
1989—Chiefs, 34-0 (KC)
1990—Oilers, 27-10 (KC)
1991—Oilers, 17-7 (H)
1992—Oilers, 23-20 (H) OT
1993—Oilers, 30-0 (H)
****Chiefs, 28-20 (H)
1994—Chiefs, 31-9 (KC)
1995—Chiefs, 20-13 (KC)
1996—Chiefs, 20-19 (H)
2000—Titans, 17-14 (T) OT
2004—Chiefs, 49-38 (T)
2007—Titans, 26-17 (KC)
2008—Titans, 34-10 (KC)
(RS Pts.—Chiefs 962, Titans 808)
(PS Pts.—Chiefs 48, Titans 37)
Franchise in Dallas prior to 1963 and known as Texans
**Franchise in Houston prior to 1997; known as Oilers prior to 1999*
***AFL Championship*
****AFC Divisional Playoff*

KANSAS CITY vs. WASHINGTON
RS: Chiefs lead series, 6-1
1971—Chiefs, 27-20 (KC)
1976—Chiefs, 33-30 (W)
1983—Redskins, 27-12 (W)
1992—Chiefs, 35-16 (KC)
1995—Chiefs, 24-3 (KC)
2001—Chiefs, 45-13 (W)
2005—Chiefs, 28-21, (KC)
(RS Pts.—Chiefs 204, Redskins 130)

MIAMI vs. ARIZONA
RS: Dolphins lead series, 8-2;
See Arizona vs. Miami

MIAMI vs. ATLANTA
RS: Dolphins lead series, 7-3;
See Atlanta vs. Miami

MIAMI vs. BALTIMORE
RS: Dolphins lead series, 5-2
PS: Ravens lead series, 2-0;
See Baltimore vs. Miami

MIAMI vs. BUFFALO
RS: Dolphins lead series, 51-34-1
PS: Bills lead series, 3-1;
See Buffalo vs. Miami

MIAMI vs. CAROLINA
RS: Dolphins lead series, 3-0;
See Carolina vs. Miami

MIAMI vs. CHICAGO
RS: Dolphins lead series, 7-3;
See Chicago vs. Miami

MIAMI vs. CINCINNATI
RS: Dolphins lead series, 12-5
PS: Dolphins lead series, 1-0;
See Cincinnati vs. Miami

MIAMI vs. CLEVELAND
RS: Dolphins lead series, 7-6
PS: Dolphins lead series, 2-0;
See Cleveland vs. Miami

MIAMI vs. DALLAS
RS: Dolphins lead series, 7-4
PS: Cowboys lead series, 1-0;
See Dallas vs. Miami

MIAMI vs. DENVER
RS: Dolphins lead series, 11-3-1
PS: Broncos lead series, 1-0;
See Denver vs. Miami

MIAMI vs. DETROIT
RS: Dolphins lead series, 7-2;
See Detroit vs. Miami

MIAMI vs. GREEN BAY
RS: Dolphins lead series, 9-3;
See Green Bay vs. Miami

MIAMI vs. HOUSTON
RS: Texans lead series, 4-0;
See Houston vs. Miami

MIAMI vs. INDIANAPOLIS
RS: Dolphins lead series, 44-23
PS: Dolphins lead series, 2-0;
See Indianapolis vs. Miami

MIAMI vs. JACKSONVILLE
RS: Jaguars lead series, 2-1
PS: Jaguars lead series, 1-0;
See Jacksonville vs. Miami

MIAMI vs. KANSAS CITY
RS: Series tied, 12-12
PS: Dolphins lead series, 3-0;
See Kansas City vs. Miami

MIAMI vs. MINNESOTA
RS: Dolphins lead series, 5-4
PS: Dolphins lead series, 1-0
1972—Dolphins, 16-14 (Minn)
1973—*Dolphins, 24-7 (Houston)
1976—Vikings, 29-7 (Mia)
1979—Dolphins, 27-12 (Minn)
1982—Dolphins, 22-14 (Mia)
1988—Dolphins, 24-7 (Mia)
1994—Vikings, 38-35 (Minn)
2000—Vikings, 13-7 (Minn)
2002—Vikings, 20-17 (Minn)
2006—Dolphins, 24-20 (Mia)
(RS Pts.—Dolphins 179, Vikings 167)
(PS Pts.—Dolphins 24, Vikings 7)
Super Bowl VIII

MIAMI vs. *NEW ENGLAND
RS: Dolphins lead series, 48-36
PS: Patriots lead series, 2-1
1966—Patriots, 20-14 (M)
1967—Patriots, 41-10 (B)
Dolphins, 41-32 (M)
1968—Dolphins, 34-10 (B)
Dolphins, 38-7 (M)
1969—Dolphins, 17-16 (B)
Patriots, 38-23 (Tampa)
1970—Patriots, 27-14 (B)
Dolphins, 37-20 (M)
1971—Dolphins, 41-3 (M)
Patriots, 34-13 (NE)
1972—Dolphins, 52-0 (M)
Dolphins, 37-21 (NE)
1973—Dolphins, 44-23 (M)
Dolphins, 30-14 (NE)
1974—Patriots, 34-24 (NE)
Dolphins, 34-27 (M)
1975—Dolphins, 22-14 (NE)
Dolphins, 20-7 (M)
1976—Patriots, 30-14 (NE)
Dolphins, 10-3 (M)
1977—Dolphins, 17-5 (M)
Patriots, 14-10 (NE)
1978—Patriots, 33-24 (NE)
Dolphins, 23-3 (M)
1979—Patriots, 28-13 (NE)
Dolphins, 39-24 (M)
1980—Patriots, 34-0 (NE)
Dolphins, 16-13 (M) OT
1981—Dolphins, 30-27 (NE) OT
Dolphins, 24-14 (M)
1982—Patriots, 3-0 (NE)
**Dolphins, 28-13 (M)
1983—Dolphins, 34-24 (M)
Patriots, 17-6 (NE)
1984—Dolphins, 28-7 (M)
Dolphins, 44-24 (NE)
1985—Patriots, 17-13 (NE)
Dolphins, 30-27 (M)
***Patriots, 31-14 (M)
1986—Patriots, 34-7 (NE)
Patriots, 34-27 (M)
1987—Patriots, 28-21 (NE)
Patriots, 24-10 (M)
1988—Patriots, 21-10 (NE)
Patriots, 6-3 (M)
1989—Dolphins, 24-10 (NE)
Dolphins, 31-10 (M)
1990—Dolphins, 27-24 (NE)
Dolphins, 17-10 (M)
1991—Dolphins, 20-10 (NE)
Dolphins, 30-20 (M)
1992—Dolphins, 38-17 (M)
Dolphins, 16-13 (NE) OT
1993—Dolphins, 17-13 (M)
Patriots, 33-27 (NE) OT
1994—Dolphins, 39-35 (M)
Dolphins, 23-3 (NE)
1995—Dolphins, 20-3 (NE)
Patriots, 34-17 (M)
1996—Dolphins, 24-10 (M)
Patriots, 42-23 (NE)
1997—Patriots, 27-24 (NE)
Patriots, 14-12 (M)
**Patriots, 17-3 (NE)
1998—Dolphins, 12-9 (M) OT
Patriots, 26-23 (NE)
1999—Dolphins, 31-30 (NE)
Dolphins, 27-17 (M)
2000—Dolphins, 10-3 (M)
Dolphins, 27-24 (NE)
2001—Dolphins, 30-10 (M)
Patriots, 20-13 (NE)
2002—Dolphins, 26-13 (M)
Patriots, 27-24 (NE) OT
2003—Patriots, 19-13 (M) OT
Patriots, 12-0 (NE)
2004—Patriots, 24-10 (NE)
Dolphins, 29-28 (M)
2005—Patriots, 23-16 (M)
Dolphins, 28-26 (NE)
2006—Patriots, 20-10 (NE)
Dolphins, 21-0 (M)
2007—Patriots, 49-28 (M)
Patriots, 28-7 (NE)
2008—Dolphins, 38-13 (NE)
Patriots, 48-28 (M)
(RS Pts.—Dolphins 1,878, Patriots 1,679)
(PS Pts.—Patriots 61, Dolphins 45)
Franchise in Boston prior to 1971
**AFC First-Round Playoff*
***AFC Championship*

MIAMI vs. NEW ORLEANS
RS: Dolphins lead series, 6-3
1970—Dolphins, 21-10 (M)
1974—Dolphins, 21-0 (NO)

1980—Dolphins, 21-16 (M)
1983—Saints, 17-7 (NO)
1986—Dolphins, 31-27 (NO)
1992—Saints, 24-13 (NO)
1995—Saints, 33-30 (NO)
1998—Dolphins, 30-10 (M)
2005—Dolphins, 21-6 (Baton Rouge)
(RS Pts.—Dolphins 195, Saints 143)

MIAMI vs. N.Y. GIANTS
RS: Giants lead series, 4-2
1972—Dolphins, 23-13 (NY)
1990—Giants, 20-3 (NY)
1993—Giants, 19-14 (M)
1996—Giants, 17-7 (M)
2003—Dolphins, 23-10 (NY)
2007—Giants, 13-10 (London)
(RS Pts.—Giants 92, Dolphins 80)

MIAMI vs. N.Y. JETS
RS: Jets lead series, 46-39-1
PS: Dolphins lead series, 1-0
1966—Jets, 19-14 (M)
Jets, 30-13 (NY)
1967—Jets, 29-7 (NY)
Jets, 33-14 (M)
1968—Jets, 35-17 (NY)
Jets, 31-7 (M)
1969—Jets, 34-31 (NY)
Jets, 27-9 (M)
1970—Dolphins, 20-6 (NY)
Dolphins, 16-10 (M)
1971—Jets, 14-10 (M)
Dolphins, 30-14 (NY)
1972—Dolphins, 27-17 (NY)
Dolphins, 28-24 (M)
1973—Dolphins, 31-3 (M)
Dolphins, 24-14 (NY)
1974—Dolphins, 21-17 (M)
Jets, 17-14 (NY)
1975—Dolphins, 43-0 (NY)
Dolphins, 27-7 (M)
1976—Dolphins, 16-0 (M)
Dolphins, 27-7 (NY)
1977—Dolphins, 21-17 (M)
Dolphins, 14-10 (NY)
1978—Jets, 33-20 (NY)
Jets, 24-13 (M)
1979—Jets, 33-27 (NY)
Jets, 27-24 (M)
1980—Jets, 17-14 (NY)
Jets, 24-17 (M)
1981—Tie, 28-28 (M) OT
Jets, 16-15 (NY)
1982—Dolphins, 45-28 (NY)
Dolphins, 20-19 (M)
*Dolphins, 14-0 (M)
1983—Dolphins, 32-14 (NY)
Dolphins, 34-14 (M)
1984—Dolphins, 31-17 (NY)
Dolphins, 28-17 (M)
1985—Jets, 23-7 (NY)
Dolphins, 21-17 (M)
1986—Jets, 51-45 (NY) OT
Dolphins, 45-3 (M)
1987—Jets, 37-31 (NY) OT
Dolphins, 37-28 (M)
1988—Jets, 44-30 (M)
Jets, 38-34 (NY)
1989—Jets, 40-33 (M)
Dolphins, 31-23 (NY)
1990—Dolphins, 20-16 (M)
Dolphins, 17-3 (NY)
1991—Jets, 41-23 (NY)
Jets, 23-20 (M) OT
1992—Jets, 26-14 (NY)
Dolphins, 19-17 (M)
1993—Jets, 24-14 (M)
Jets, 27-10 (NY)
1994—Dolphins, 28-14 (M)
Dolphins, 28-24 (NY)
1995—Dolphins, 52-14 (M)
Jets, 17-16 (NY)
1996—Dolphins, 36-27 (M)
Dolphins, 31-28 (NY)
1997—Dolphins, 31-20 (NY)
Dolphins, 24-17 (M)
1998—Jets, 20-9 (NY)
Jets, 21-16 (M)
1999—Jets, 28-20 (NY)
Jets, 38-31 (M)
2000—Jets, 40-37 (NY) OT
Jets, 20-3 (M)
2001—Jets, 21-17 (NY)
Jets, 24-0 (M)
2002—Dolphins, 30-3 (M)
Jets, 13-10 (NY)
2003—Dolphins, 21-10 (NY)
Dolphins, 23-21 (M)
2004—Jets, 17-9 (M)
Jets, 41-14 (NY)
2005—Jets, 17-7 (NY)
Dolphins, 24-20 (M)
2006—Jets, 20-17 (NY)
Jets, 13-10 (M)
2007—Jets, 31-28 (NY)
Jets, 40-13 (M)
2008—Jets, 20-14 (M)
Dolphins, 24-17 (NY)
(RS Pts.—Dolphins 1,903, Jets 1,863)
(PS Pts.—Dolphins 14, Jets 0)
AFC Championship

MIAMI vs. *OAKLAND
RS: Raiders lead series, 16-12-1
PS: Raiders lead series, 3-1
1966—Raiders, 23-14 (M)
Raiders, 21-10 (O)
1967—Raiders, 31-17 (O)
1968—Raiders, 47-21 (M)
1969—Raiders, 20-17 (O)
Tie, 20-20 (M)
1970—Dolphins, 20-13 (M)
**Raiders, 21-14 (O)
1973—Raiders, 12-7 (O)
***Dolphins, 27-10 (M)
1974—**Raiders, 28-26 (O)
1975—Raiders, 31-21 (M)
1978—Dolphins, 23-6 (M)
1979—Raiders, 13-3 (O)
1980—Raiders, 16-10 (O)
1981—Raiders, 33-17 (M)
1983—Raiders, 27-14 (LA)
1984—Raiders, 45-34 (M)
1986—Raiders, 30-28 (M)
1988—Dolphins, 24-14 (LA)
1990—Raiders, 13-10 (M)
1992—Dolphins, 20-7 (M)
1994—Dolphins, 20-17 (M) OT
1996—Raiders, 17-7 (O)
1997—Dolphins, 34-16 (O)
1998—Dolphins, 27-17 (O)
1999—Dolphins, 16-9 (O)
2000—**Raiders, 27-0 (O)
2001—Dolphins, 18-15 (M)
2002—Dolphins, 23-17 (M)
2005—Dolphins, 33-21 (O)
2007—Raiders, 35-17 (M)
2008—Dolphins, 17-15 (M)
(RS Pts.—Raiders 601, Dolphins 542)
(PS Pts.—Raiders 86, Dolphins 67)
**Franchise in Los Angeles from 1982-1994*
***AFC Divisional Playoff*
****AFC Championship*

MIAMI vs. PHILADELPHIA
RS: Dolphins lead series, 7-5
1970—Eagles, 24-17 (P)
1975—Dolphins, 24-16 (M)
1978—Eagles, 17-3 (P)
1981—Dolphins, 13-10 (M)
1984—Dolphins, 24-23 (M)
1987—Dolphins, 28-10 (P)
1990—Dolphins, 23-20 (M) OT
1993—Dolphins, 19-14 (P)
1996—Eagles, 35-28 (P)
1999—Dolphins, 16-13 (M)
2003—Eagles, 34-27 (M)
2007—Eagles, 17-7 (P)
(RS Pts.—Eagles 233, Dolphins 229)

MIAMI vs. PITTSBURGH
RS: Steelers lead series, 10-9
PS: Dolphins lead series, 2-1
1971—Dolphins, 24-21 (M)
1972—*Dolphins, 21-17 (P)
1973—Dolphins, 30-26 (M)
1976—Steelers, 14-3 (P)
1979—**Steelers, 34-14 (P)
1980—Steelers, 23-10 (P)
1981—Dolphins, 30-10 (M)
1984—Dolphins, 31-7 (P)
*Dolphins, 45-28 (M)
1985—Dolphins, 24-20 (M)
1987—Dolphins, 35-24 (M)
1988—Steelers, 40-24 (P)
1989—Steelers, 34-14 (M)
1990—Dolphins, 28-6 (P)
1993—Steelers, 21-20 (M)
1994—Steelers, 16-13 (P) OT
1995—Dolphins, 23-10 (M)
1996—Steelers, 24-17 (M)
1998—Dolphins, 21-0 (M)
2004—Steelers, 13-3 (M)
2006—Steelers, 28-17 (P)
2007—Steelers, 3-0 (P)
(RS Pts.—Dolphins 367, Steelers 340)
(PS Pts.—Dolphins 80, Steelers 79)
**AFC Championship*
***AFC Divisional Playoff*

MIAMI vs. *ST. LOUIS
RS: Dolphins lead series, 9-2
1971—Dolphins, 20-14 (LA)
1976—Rams, 31-28 (M)
1980—Dolphins, 35-14 (LA)
1983—Dolphins, 30-14 (M)
1986—Dolphins, 37-31 (LA) OT
1992—Dolphins, 26-10 (M)
1995—Dolphins, 41-22 (StL)
1998—Dolphins, 14-0 (M)
2001—Rams, 42-10 (StL)
2004—Dolphins, 31-14 (M)
2008—Dolphins, 16-12 (StL)
(RS Pts.—Dolphins 288, Rams 204)
**Franchise in Los Angeles prior to 1995*

MIAMI vs. SAN DIEGO
RS: Dolphins lead series, 12-10
PS: Series tied, 2-2
1966—Chargers, 44-10 (SD)
1967—Chargers, 24-0 (SD)
Dolphins, 41-24 (M)
1968—Chargers, 34-28 (SD)
1969—Chargers, 21-14 (M)
1972—Dolphins, 24-10 (M)
1974—Dolphins, 28-21 (SD)
1977—Chargers, 14-13 (M)
1978—Dolphins, 28-21 (SD)
1980—Chargers, 27-24 (M) OT
1981—*Chargers, 41-38 (M) OT
1982—**Dolphins, 34-13 (M)
1984—Chargers, 34-28 (SD) OT
1986—Chargers, 50-28 (SD)
1988—Dolphins, 31-28 (M)
1991—Chargers, 38-30 (SD)
1992—*Dolphins, 31-0 (M)
1993—Chargers, 45-20 (SD)
1994—*Chargers, 22-21 (SD)
1995—Dolphins, 24-14 (SD)
1999—Dolphins, 12-9 (M)
2000—Dolphins, 17-7 (SD)
2002—Dolphins, 30-3 (M)
2003—Dolphins, 26-10 (Ariz)
2005—Dolphins, 23-21 (SD)
2008—Dolphins, 17-10 (M)
(RS Pts.—Chargers 509, Dolphins 496)
(PS Pts.—Dolphins 124, Chargers 76)
AFC Divisional Playoff
***AFC Second-Round Playoff*

MIAMI vs. SAN FRANCISCO
RS: Dolphins lead series, 6-4
PS: 49ers lead series, 1-0
1973—Dolphins, 21-13 (M)
1977—Dolphins, 19-15 (SF)
1980—Dolphins, 17-13 (M)
1983—Dolphins, 20-17 (SF)
1984—*49ers, 38-16 (Stanford)
1986—49ers, 31-16 (M)
1992—49ers, 27-3 (SF)
1995—49ers, 44-20 (M)
2001—49ers, 21-0 (SF)
2004—Dolphins, 24-17 (SF)
2008—Dolphins, 14-9 (M)
(RS Pts.—49ers 207, Dolphins 154)
(PS Pts.—49ers 38, Dolphins 16)
Super Bowl XIX

MIAMI vs. SEATTLE
RS: Dolphins lead series, 7-3
PS: Dolphins lead series, 2-1
1977—Dolphins, 31-13 (M)
1979—Dolphins, 19-10 (M)
1983—*Seahawks, 27-20 (M)
1984—*Dolphins, 31-10 (M)
1987—Seahawks, 24-20 (S)
1990—Dolphins, 24-17 (M)
1992—Dolphins, 19-17 (S)
1996—Seahawks, 22-15 (M)
1999—**Dolphins, 20-17 (S)
2000—Dolphins, 23-0 (M)
2001—Dolphins, 24-20 (S)
2004—Seahawks, 24-17 (S)
2008—Dolphins, 21-19 (M)
(RS Pts.—Dolphins 213, Seahawks 166)
(PS Pts.—Dolphins 71, Seahawks 54)
AFC Divisional Playoff
***AFC First-Round Playoff*

MIAMI vs. TAMPA BAY
RS: Series tied, 4-4
1976—Dolphins, 23-20 (TB)
1982—Buccaneers, 23-17 (TB)
1985—Dolphins, 41-38 (M)
1988—Dolphins, 17-14 (TB)
1991—Dolphins, 33-14 (M)
1997—Buccaneers, 31-21 (TB)
2000—Buccaneers, 16-13 (M)
2005—Buccaneers, 27-13 (TB)
(RS Pts.—Buccaneers 183, Dolphins 178)

MIAMI vs. *TENNESSEE
RS: Dolphins lead series, 17-13
PS: Titans lead series, 1-0
1966—Dolphins, 20-13 (H)
Dolphins, 29-28 (M)
1967—Oilers, 17-14 (H)
Oilers, 41-10 (M)
1968—Oilers, 24-10 (M)
Dolphins, 24-7 (H)
1969—Oilers, 22-10 (H)
Oilers, 32-7 (M)
1970—Dolphins, 20-10 (H)
1972—Dolphins, 34-13 (M)
1975—Oilers, 20-19 (H)
1977—Dolphins, 27-7 (M)
1978—Oilers, 35-30 (H)
**Oilers, 17-9 (M)
1979—Oilers, 9-6 (M)
1981—Dolphins, 16-10 (H)
1983—Dolphins, 24-17 (H)
1984—Dolphins, 28-10 (M)
1985—Oilers, 26-23 (H)
1986—Dolphins, 28-7 (M)
1989—Oilers, 39-7 (H)
1991—Oilers, 17-13 (M)
1992—Dolphins, 19-16 (M)
1996—Dolphins, 23-20 (H)
1997—Dolphins, 16-13 (M) OT
1999—Dolphins, 17-0 (M)
2001—Dolphins, 31-23 (T)
2003—Titans, 31-7 (T)
2004—Titans, 17-7 (M)
2005—Dolphins, 24-10 (M)
2006—Dolphins, 13-10 (M)
(RS Pts.—Dolphins 556, Titans 544)
(PS Pts.—Titans 17, Dolphins 9)
Franchise in Houston prior to 1997; known as Oilers prior to 1999
***AFC First-Round Playoff*

MIAMI vs. WASHINGTON
RS: Dolphins lead series, 6-4
PS: Series tied, 1-1
1972—*Dolphins, 14-7 (Los Angeles)
1974—Redskins, 20-17 (W)
1978—Dolphins, 16-0 (W)
1981—Dolphins, 13-10 (M)
1982—**Redskins, 27-17 (Pasadena)
1984—Dolphins, 35-17 (W)
1987—Dolphins, 23-21 (M)
1990—Redskins, 42-20 (W)
1993—Dolphins, 17-10 (M)
1999—Redskins, 21-10 (W)
2003—Dolphins, 24-23 (M)
2007—Redskins, 16-13 (W) OT
(RS Pts.—Dolphins 188, Redskins 180)
(PS Pts.—Redskins 34, Dolphins 31)
Super Bowl VII
***Super Bowl XVII*

MINNESOTA vs. ARIZONA
RS: Vikings lead series, 10-9
PS: Vikings lead series, 2-0;
See Arizona vs. Minnesota

MINNESOTA vs. ATLANTA
RS: Vikings lead series, 15-9
PS: Series tied, 1-1;
See Atlanta vs. Minnesota

MINNESOTA vs. BALTIMORE
RS: Ravens lead series, 2-1;
See Baltimore vs. Minnesota

MINNESOTA vs. BUFFALO
RS: Vikings lead series, 7-4;
See Buffalo vs. Minnesota

MINNESOTA vs. CAROLINA
RS: Vikings lead series, 5-3;
See Carolina vs. Minnesota

MINNESOTA vs. CHICAGO
RS: Vikings lead series, 51-42-2
PS: Bears lead series, 1-0;
See Chicago vs. Minnesota

MINNESOTA vs. CINCINNATI
RS: Series tied, 5-5;
See Cincinnati vs. Minnesota

MINNESOTA vs. CLEVELAND
RS: Vikings lead series, 9-3
PS: Vikings lead series, 1-0;
See Cleveland vs. Minnesota

MINNESOTA vs. DALLAS
RS: Series tied, 10-10
PS: Cowboys lead series, 4-2;
See Dallas vs. Minnesota

MINNESOTA vs. DENVER
RS: Vikings lead series, 7-5;
See Denver vs. Minnesota

MINNESOTA vs. DETROIT
RS: Vikings lead series, 63-30-2;
See Detroit vs. Minnesota

MINNESOTA vs. GREEN BAY
RS: Packers lead series, 49-45-1
PS: Vikings lead series, 1-0;
See Green Bay vs. Minnesota

MINNESOTA vs. HOUSTON
RS: Vikings lead series, 2-0;
See Houston vs. Minnesota

MINNESOTA vs. INDIANAPOLIS
RS: Colts lead series, 14-7-1
PS: Colts lead series, 1-0;
See Indianapolis vs. Minnesota

MINNESOTA vs. JACKSONVILLE
RS: Vikings lead series, 3-1;
See Jacksonville vs. Minnesota

MINNESOTA vs. KANSAS CITY
RS: Chiefs lead series, 5-4
PS: Chiefs lead series, 1-0;
See Kansas City vs. Minnesota

MINNESOTA vs. MIAMI
RS: Dolphins lead series, 5-4
PS: Dolphins lead series, 1-0;
See Miami vs. Minnesota

MINNESOTA vs. *NEW ENGLAND
RS: Patriots lead series, 6-4
1970—Vikings, 35-14 (B)
1974—Patriots, 17-14 (M)
1979—Patriots, 27-23 (NE)
1988—Vikings, 36-6 (M)
1991—Patriots, 26-23 (NE) OT
1994—Patriots, 26-20 (NE) OT
1997—Vikings, 23-18 (M)
2000—Vikings, 21-13 (NE)

2002—Patriots, 24-17 (NE)
2006—Patriots, 31-7 (M)
(RS Pts.—Vikings 219, Patriots 202)
Franchise in Boston prior to 1971

MINNESOTA vs. NEW ORLEANS
RS: Vikings lead series, 18-7
PS: Vikings lead series, 2-0
1968—Saints, 20-17 (NO)
1970—Vikings, 26-0 (M)
1971—Vikings, 23-10 (NO)
1972—Vikings, 37-6 (M)
1974—Vikings, 29-9 (M)
1975—Vikings, 20-7 (NO)
1976—Vikings, 40-9 (NO)
1978—Saints, 31-24 (NO)
1980—Vikings, 23-20 (NO)
1981—Vikings, 20-10 (M)
1983—Saints, 17-16 (NO)
1985—Saints, 30-23 (M)
1986—Vikings, 33-17 (M)
1987—*Vikings, 44-10 (NO)
1988—Vikings, 45-3 (M)
1990—Vikings, 32-3 (M)
1991—Saints, 26-0 (NO)
1993—Saints, 17-14 (M)
1994—Vikings, 21-20 (M)
1995—Vikings, 43-24 (M)
1998—Vikings, 31-24 (M)
2000—**Vikings, 34-16 (M)
2001—Saints, 28-15 (NO)
2002—Vikings, 32-31 (NO)
2004—Vikings, 38-31 (NO)
2005—Vikings, 33-16 (M)
2008—Vikings, 30-27 (NO)
(RS Pts.—Vikings 665, Saints 436)
(PS Pts.—Vikings 78, Saints 26)
**NFC First-Round Playoff*
***NFC Divisional Playoff*

MINNESOTA vs. N.Y. GIANTS
RS: Vikings lead series, 12-8
PS: Giants lead series, 2-1
1964—Vikings, 30-21 (NY)
1965—Vikings, 40-14 (M)
1967—Vikings, 27-24 (M)
1969—Giants, 24-23 (NY)
1971—Vikings, 17-10 (NY)
1973—Vikings, 31-7 (New Haven)
1976—Vikings, 24-7 (M)
1986—Giants, 22-20 (M)
1989—Giants, 24-14 (NY)
1990—Giants, 23-15 (NY)
1993—*Giants, 17-10 (NY)
1994—Vikings, 27-10 (NY)
1996—Giants, 15-10 (NY)
1997—*Vikings, 23-22 (NY)
1999—Vikings, 34-17 (NY)
2000—**Giants, 41-0 (NY)
2001—Vikings, 28-16 (M)
2002—Giants, 27-20 (M)
2003—Giants, 29-17 (M)
2004—Giants, 34-13 (M)
2005—Vikings, 24-21 (NY)
2007—Vikings, 41-17 (NY)
2008—Vikings, 20-19 (M)
(RS Pts.—Vikings 475, Giants 381)
(PS Pts.—Giants 80, Vikings 33)
**NFC First-Round Playoff*
***NFC Championship*

MINNESOTA vs. N.Y. JETS
RS: Jets lead series, 7-1
1970—Jets, 20-10 (NY)
1975—Vikings, 29-21 (M)
1979—Jets, 14-7 (NY)
1982—Jets, 42-14 (M)
1994—Jets, 31-21 (M)
1997—Jets, 23-21 (NY)
2002—Jets, 20-7 (NY)
2006—Jets, 26-13 (M)
(RS Pts.—Jets 197, Vikings 122)

MINNESOTA vs. *OAKLAND
RS: Raiders lead series, 8-4
PS: Raiders lead series, 1-0
1973—Vikings, 24-16 (M)
1976—**Raiders, 32-14 (Pasadena)
1977—Raiders, 35-13 (O)
1978—Raiders, 27-20 (O)
1981—Raiders, 36-10 (M)
1984—Raiders, 23-20 (LA)
1987—Vikings, 31-20 (M)
1990—Raiders, 28-24 (M)
1993—Raiders, 24-7 (LA)
1996—Vikings, 16-13 (O) OT
1999—Raiders, 22-17 (M)
2003—Raiders, 28-18 (O)
2007—Vikings, 29-22 (M)
(RS Pts.—Raiders 294, Vikings 229)
(PS Pts.—Raiders 32, Vikings 14)
**Franchise in Los Angeles from 1982-1994*
***Super Bowl XI*

MINNESOTA vs. PHILADELPHIA
RS: Vikings lead series, 11-9
PS: Eagles lead series, 3-0
1962—Vikings, 31-21 (M)
1963—Vikings, 34-13 (P)
1968—Vikings, 24-17 (P)
1971—Vikings, 13-0 (P)
1973—Vikings, 28-21 (M)
1976—Vikings, 31-12 (P)
1978—Vikings, 28-27 (M)
1980—Eagles, 42-7 (M)
    *Eagles, 31-16 (P)
1981—Vikings, 35-23 (M)
1984—Eagles, 19-17 (P)
1985—Vikings, 28-23 (P)
    Eagles, 37-35 (M)
1988—Vikings, 23-21 (M)
1989—Eagles, 10-9 (P)
1990—Eagles, 32-24 (P)
1992—Eagles, 28-17 (P)
1997—Vikings, 28-19 (M)
2001—Eagles, 48-17 (P)
2004—Eagles, 27-16 (P)
    *Eagles, 27-14 (P)
2007—Eagles, 23-16 (M)
2008—**Eagles, 26-14 (M)
(RS Pts.—Eagles 463, Vikings 461)
(PS Pts.—Eagles 84, Vikings 44)
**NFC Divisional Playoff*
***NFC First-Round Playoff*

MINNESOTA vs. PITTSBURGH
RS: Vikings lead series, 8-6
PS: Steelers lead series, 1-0
1962—Steelers, 39-31 (P)
1964—Vikings, 30-10 (M)
1967—Vikings, 41-27 (P)
1969—Vikings, 52-14 (M)
1972—Steelers, 23-10 (P)
1974—*Steelers, 16-6 (New Orleans)
1976—Vikings, 17-6 (M)
1980—Steelers, 23-17 (M)
1983—Vikings, 17-14 (P)
1986—Vikings, 31-7 (M)
1989—Steelers, 27-14 (P)
1992—Vikings, 6-3 (P)
1995—Vikings, 44-24 (P)
2001—Steelers, 21-16 (P)
2005—Steelers, 18-3 (M)
(RS Pts.—Vikings 329, Steelers 256)
(PS Pts.—Steelers 16, Vikings 6)
**Super Bowl IX*

MINNESOTA vs. *ST. LOUIS
RS: Vikings lead series, 17-14-2
PS: Vikings lead series, 5-2
1961—Rams, 31-17 (LA)
    Vikings, 42-21 (M)
1962—Vikings, 38-14 (LA)
    Tie, 24-24 (M)
1963—Rams, 27-24 (LA)
    Vikings, 21-13 (M)
1964—Rams, 22-13 (LA)
    Vikings, 34-13 (M)
1965—Vikings, 38-35 (LA)
    Vikings, 24-13 (M)
1966—Vikings, 35-7 (M)
    Rams, 21-6 (LA)
1967—Rams, 39-3 (LA)
1968—Rams, 31-3 (M)
1969—Vikings, 20-13 (LA)
    **Vikings, 23-20 (M)
1970—Vikings, 13-3 (M)
1972—Vikings, 45-41 (LA)
1973—Vikings, 10-9 (M)
1974—Rams, 20-17 (LA)
    ***Vikings, 14-10 (M)
1976—Tie, 10-10 (M) OT
    ***Vikings, 24-13 (M)
1977—Rams, 35-3 (LA)
    ****Vikings, 14-7 (LA)
1978—Rams, 34-17 (M)
    ****Rams, 34-10 (LA)
1979—Rams, 27-21 (LA) OT
1985—Rams, 13-10 (LA)
1987—Vikings, 21-16 (LA)
1988—*****Vikings, 28-17 (M)
1989—Vikings, 23-21 (M) OT
1991—Vikings, 20-14 (M)
1992—Vikings, 31-17 (LA)
1998—Vikings, 38-31 (StL)
1999—****Rams, 49-37 (StL)
2000—Rams, 40-29 (StL)
2003—Rams, 48-17 (StL)
2005—Vikings, 27-13 (M)
2006—Rams, 41-21 (M)
(RS Pts.—Rams 757, Vikings 715)
(PS Pts.—Rams 150, Vikings 150)
**Franchise in Los Angeles prior to 1995*
***Conference Championship*
****NFC Championship*
*****NFC Divisional Playoff*
******NFC First-Round Playoff*

MINNESOTA vs. SAN DIEGO
RS: Series tied, 5-5
1971—Chargers, 30-14 (SD)
1975—Vikings, 28-13 (M)
1978—Chargers, 13-7 (M)
1981—Vikings, 33-31 (SD)
1984—Chargers, 42-13 (M)
1985—Vikings, 21-17 (M)
1993—Chargers, 30-17 (M)
1999—Vikings, 35-27 (M)

2003—Chargers, 42-28 (SD)
2007—Vikings, 35-17 (M)
(RS Pts.—Chargers 262, Vikings 231)

MINNESOTA vs. SAN FRANCISCO
RS: Vikings lead series, 19-18-1
PS: 49ers lead series, 4-1
1961—49ers, 38-24 (M)
49ers, 38-28 (SF)
1962—49ers, 21-7 (SF)
49ers, 35-12 (M)
1963—Vikings, 24-20 (SF)
Vikings, 45-14 (M)
1964—Vikings, 27-22 (SF)
Vikings, 24-7 (M)
1965—Vikings, 42-41 (SF)
49ers, 45-24 (M)
1966—Tie, 20-20 (SF)
Vikings, 28-3 (M)
1967—49ers, 27-21 (M)
1968—Vikings, 30-20 (SF)
1969—Vikings, 10-7 (M)
1970—*49ers, 17-14 (M)
1971—49ers, 13-9 (M)
1972—49ers, 20-17 (SF)
1973—Vikings, 17-13 (SF)
1975—Vikings, 27-17 (M)
1976—49ers, 20-16 (SF)
1977—Vikings, 28-27 (M)
1979—Vikings, 28-22 (M)
1983—49ers, 48-17 (M)
1984—49ers, 51-7 (SF)
1985—Vikings, 28-21 (M)
1986—Vikings, 27-24 (SF) OT
1987—*Vikings, 36-24 (SF)
1988—49ers, 24-21 (SF)
*49ers, 34-9 (SF)
1989—*49ers, 41-13 (SF)
1990—49ers, 20-17 (M)
1991—Vikings, 17-14 (M)
1992—49ers, 20-17 (M)
1993—49ers, 38-19 (SF)
1994—Vikings, 21-14 (M)
1995—49ers, 37-30 (SF)
1997—49ers, 28-17 (SF)
*49ers, 38-22 (SF)
1999—Vikings, 40-16 (M)
2003—Vikings, 35-7 (M)
2006—49ers, 9-3 (SF)
2007—Vikings, 27-7 (SF)
(RS Pts.—49ers 868, Vikings 851)
(PS Pts.—49ers 154, Vikings 94)
NFC Divisional Playoff

MINNESOTA vs. SEATTLE
RS: Seahawks lead series, 6-4
1976—Vikings, 27-21 (M)
1978—Seahawks, 29-28 (S)
1984—Seahawks, 20-12 (M)
1987—Seahawks, 28-17 (S)
1990—Vikings, 24-21 (S)
1996—Seahawks, 42-23 (S)
2002—Seahawks, 48-23 (S)
2003—Vikings, 34-7 (M)
2004—Seahawks, 27-23 (M)
2006—Vikings, 31-13 (S)
(RS Pts.—Seahawks 256, Vikings 242)

MINNESOTA vs. TAMPA BAY
RS: Vikings lead series, 31-20
1977—Vikings, 9-3 (TB)
1978—Buccaneers, 16-10 (M)
Vikings, 24-7 (TB)
1979—Buccaneers, 12-10 (M)
Vikings, 23-22 (TB)
1980—Vikings, 38-30 (M)
Vikings, 21-10 (TB)
1981—Buccaneers, 21-13 (TB)
Vikings, 25-10 (M)
1982—Vikings, 17-10 (M)
1983—Vikings, 19-16 (TB) OT
Buccaneers, 17-12 (M)
1984—Buccaneers, 35-31 (TB)
Vikings, 27-24 (M)
1985—Vikings, 31-16 (TB)
Vikings, 26-7 (M)
1986—Vikings, 23-10 (TB)
Vikings, 45-13 (M)
1987—Buccaneers, 20-10 (TB)
Vikings, 23-17 (M)
1988—Vikings, 14-13 (M)
Vikings, 49-20 (TB)
1989—Vikings, 17-3 (M)
Vikings, 24-10 (TB)
1990—Buccaneers, 23-20 (M) OT
Buccaneers, 26-13 (TB)
1991—Vikings, 28-13 (M)
Vikings, 26-24 (TB)
1992—Vikings, 26-20 (M)
Vikings, 35-7 (TB)
1993—Vikings, 15-0 (M)
Buccaneers, 23-10 (TB)
1994—Vikings, 36-13 (TB)
Buccaneers, 20-17 (M) OT
1995—Buccaneers, 20-17 (TB) OT
Vikings, 31-17 (M)
1996—Buccaneers, 24-13 (TB)
Vikings, 21-10 (M)
1997—Buccaneers, 28-14 (M)
Vikings, 10-6 (TB)
1998—Vikings, 31-7 (M)
Buccaneers, 27-24 (TB)
1999—Vikings, 21-14 (M)
Buccaneers, 24-17 (TB)
2000—Vikings, 30-23 (M)
Buccaneers, 41-13 (TB)
2001—Vikings, 20-16 (M)
Buccaneers, 41-14 (TB)
2002—Buccaneers, 38-24 (TB)
2005—Buccaneers, 24-13 (M)
2008—Buccaneers, 19-13 (TB)
(RS Pts.—Vikings 1,093, Buccaneers 910)

MINNESOTA vs. *TENNESSEE
RS: Vikings lead series, 7-4
1974—Vikings, 51-10 (M)
1980—Oilers, 20-16 (H)
1983—Vikings, 34-14 (M)
1986—Oilers, 23-10 (H)
1989—Vikings, 38-7 (M)
1992—Oilers, 17-13 (M)
1995—Vikings, 23-17 (M) OT
1998—Vikings, 26-16 (T)
2001—Vikings, 42-24 (M)
2004—Vikings, 20-3 (M)
2008—Titans, 30-17 (T)
(RS Pts.—Vikings 290, Titans 181)
**Franchise in Houston prior to 1997; known as Oilers prior to 1999*

MINNESOTA vs. WASHINGTON
RS: Redskins lead series, 8-6
PS: Redskins lead series, 3-2
1968—Vikings, 27-14 (M)
1970—Vikings, 19-10 (W)
1972—Redskins, 24-21 (M)
1973—*Vikings, 27-20 (M)
1975—Redskins, 31-30 (W)
1976—*Vikings, 35-20 (M)
1980—Vikings, 39-14 (W)
1982—**Redskins, 21-7 (W)
1984—Redskins, 31-17 (M)
1986—Redskins, 44-38 (W) OT
1987—Redskins, 27-24 (M) OT
***Redskins, 17-10 (W)
1992—Redskins, 15-13 (M)
****Redskins, 24-7 (M)
1993—Vikings, 14-9 (W)
1998—Vikings, 41-7 (M)
2004—Redskins, 21-18 (W)
2006—Vikings, 19-16 (W)
2007—Redskins, 32-21 (M)
(RS Pts.—Vikings 341, Redskins 295)
(PS Pts.—Redskins 102, Vikings 86)
**NFC Divisional Playoff*
***NFC Second-Round Playoff*
****NFC Championship*
*****NFC First-Round Playoff*

NEW ENGLAND vs. ARIZONA
RS: Series tied, 6-6;
See Arizona vs. New England

NEW ENGLAND vs. ATLANTA
RS: Falcons lead series, 6-5;
See Atlanta vs. New England

NEW ENGLAND vs. BALTIMORE
RS: Patriots lead series, 4-0;
See Baltimore vs. New England

NEW ENGLAND vs. BUFFALO
RS: Patriots lead series, 56-40-1
PS: Patriots lead series, 1-0;
See Buffalo vs. New England

NEW ENGLAND vs. CAROLINA
RS: Panthers lead series, 2-1
PS: Patriots lead series, 1-0;
See Carolina vs. New England

NEW ENGLAND vs. CHICAGO
RS: Patriots lead series, 7-3
PS: Bears lead series, 1-0;
See Chicago vs. New England

NEW ENGLAND vs. CINCINNATI
RS: Patriots lead series, 13-8;
See Cincinnati vs. New England

NEW ENGLAND vs. CLEVELAND
RS: Browns lead series, 11-9
PS: Browns lead series, 1-0;
See Cleveland vs. New England

NEW ENGLAND vs. DALLAS
RS: Cowboys lead series, 7-3;
See Dallas vs. New England

NEW ENGLAND vs. DENVER
RS: Broncos lead series, 24-16
PS: Broncos lead series, 2-0;
See Denver vs. New England

NEW ENGLAND vs. DETROIT
RS: Patriots lead series, 5-4;
See Detroit vs. New England

NEW ENGLAND vs. GREEN BAY
RS: Series tied, 4-4
PS: Packers lead series, 1-0;
See Green Bay vs. New England

NEW ENGLAND vs. HOUSTON
RS: Patriots lead series, 2-0;
See Houston vs. New England

NEW ENGLAND vs. INDIANAPOLIS
RS: Patriots lead series, 42-27
PS: Patriots lead series, 2-1;
See Indianapolis vs. New England

NEW ENGLAND vs. JACKSONVILLE
RS: Patriots lead series, 4-0
PS: Patriots lead series, 3-1;
See Jacksonville vs. New England

NEW ENGLAND vs. KANSAS CITY
RS: Chiefs lead series, 16-12-3;
See Kansas City vs. New England

NEW ENGLAND vs. MIAMI
RS: Dolphins lead series, 48-36
PS: Patriots lead series, 2-1;
See Miami vs. New England

NEW ENGLAND vs. MINNESOTA
RS: Patriots lead series, 6-4;
See Minnesota vs. New England

NEW ENGLAND vs. NEW ORLEANS
RS: Patriots lead series, 8-3
1972—Patriots, 17-10 (NO)
1976—Patriots, 27-6 (NE)
1980—Patriots, 38-27 (NO)
1983—Patriots, 7-0 (NE)
1986—Patriots, 21-20 (NO)
1989—Saints, 28-24 (NE)
1992—Saints, 31-14 (NE)
1995—Saints, 31-17 (NE)
1998—Patriots, 30-27 (NO)
2001—Patriots, 34-17 (NE)
2005—Patriots, 24-17 (NE)
(RS Pts.—Patriots 253, Saints 214)

***NEW ENGLAND vs. N.Y. GIANTS**
RS: Patriots lead series, 5-3
PS: Giants lead series, 1-0;
1970—Giants, 16-0 (B)
1974—Patriots, 28-20 (New Haven)
1987—Giants, 17-10 (NY)
1990—Giants, 13-10 (NE)
1996—Patriots, 23-22 (NY)
1999—Patriots, 16-14 (NE)
2003—Patriots, 17-6 (NE)
2007—Patriots, 38-35 (NY)
 **Giants, 17-14 (Arizona)
(RS Pts.—Giants 143, Patriots 142)
(PS Pts.—Giants 17, Patriots 14)
**Franchise in Boston prior to 1971*
***Super Bowl XLII*

***NEW ENGLAND vs. **N.Y. JETS**
RS: Jets lead series, 49-47-1
PS: Patriots lead series, 2-0
1960—Patriots, 28-24 (NY)
 Patriots, 38-21 (B)
1961—Titans, 21-20 (B)
 Titans, 37-30 (NY)
1962—Patriots, 43-14 (NY)
 Patriots, 24-17 (B)
1963—Patriots, 38-14 (B)
 Jets, 31-24 (NY)
1964—Patriots, 26-10 (B)
 Jets, 35-14 (NY)
1965—Jets, 30-20 (B)
 Patriots, 27-23 (NY)
1966—Tie, 24-24 (B)
 Jets, 38-28 (NY)
1967—Jets, 30-23 (NY)
 Jets, 29-24 (B)
1968—Jets, 47-31 (Birmingham)
 Jets, 48-14 (NY)
1969—Jets, 23-14 (B)
 Jets, 23-17 (NY)
1970—Jets, 31-21 (B)
 Jets, 17-3 (NY)
1971—Patriots, 20-0 (NE)
 Jets, 13-6 (NY)
1972—Jets, 41-13 (NE)
 Jets, 34-10 (NY)
1973—Jets, 9-7 (NE)
 Jets, 33-13 (NY)
1974—Patriots, 24-0 (NY)
 Jets, 21-16 (NE)
1975—Jets, 36-7 (NY)
 Jets, 30-28 (NE)
1976—Patriots, 41-7 (NE)
 Patriots, 38-24 (NY)
1977—Jets, 30-27 (NY)
 Patriots, 24-13 (NE)
1978—Patriots, 55-21 (NE)
 Patriots, 19-17 (NY)
1979—Patriots, 56-3 (NE)
 Jets, 27-26 (NY)
1980—Patriots, 21-11 (NY)
 Patriots, 34-21 (NE)
1981—Jets, 28-24 (NY)
 Jets, 17-6 (NE)
1982—Jets, 31-7 (NE)
1983—Patriots, 23-13 (NE)
 Jets, 26-3 (NY)
1984—Patriots, 28-21 (NY)
 Patriots, 30-20 (NE)
1985—Patriots, 20-13 (NE)
 Jets, 16-13 (NY) OT
 ***Patriots, 26-14 (NY)
1986—Patriots, 20-6 (NY)
 Jets, 31-24 (NE)
1987—Jets, 43-24 (NY)
 Patriots, 42-20 (NE)
1988—Patriots, 28-3 (NE)
 Patriots, 14-13 (NY)
1989—Patriots, 27-24 (NY)
 Jets, 27-26 (NE)
1990—Jets, 37-13 (NE)
 Jets, 42-7 (NY)
1991—Jets, 28-21 (NE)
 Patriots, 6-3 (NY)
1992—Jets, 30-21 (NY)
 Patriots, 24-3 (NE)
1993—Jets, 45-7 (NY)
 Jets, 6-0 (NE)
1994—Jets, 24-17 (NY)
 Patriots, 24-13 (NE)
1995—Patriots, 20-7 (NY)
 Patriots, 31-28 (NE)
1996—Patriots, 31-27 (NY)
 Patriots, 34-10 (NE)
1997—Patriots, 27-24 (NE) OT
 Jets, 24-19 (NY)
1998—Jets, 24-14 (NE)
 Jets, 31-10 (NY)
1999—Patriots, 30-28 (NY)
 Jets, 24-17 (NE)
2000—Jets, 20-19 (NY)
 Jets, 34-17 (NE)
2001—Jets, 10-3 (NE)
 Patriots, 17-16 (NY)
2002—Patriots, 44-7 (NY)
 Jets, 30-17 (NE)
2003—Patriots, 23-16 (NE)
 Patriots, 21-16 (NY)
2004—Patriots, 13-7 (NE)
 Patriots, 23-7 (NY)
2005—Patriots, 16-3 (NE)
 Patriots, 31-21 (NY)
2006—Patriots, 24-17 (NY)
 Jets, 17-14 (NE)
 ***Patriots, 37-16 (NE)
2007—Patriots, 38-14 (NY)
 Patriots, 20-10 (NE)
2008—Patriots, 19-10 (NY)
 Jets, 34-31 (NE) OT
(RS Pts.—Patriots 2,138, Jets 2,077)
(PS Pts.—Patriots 63, Jets 30)
**Franchise in Boston prior to 1971*
***Jets known as Titans prior to 1963*
****AFC First-Round Playoff*

***NEW ENGLAND vs. **OAKLAND**
RS: Series tied, 14-14-1
PS: Patriots lead series, 2-1
1960—Raiders, 27-14 (O)
 Patriots, 34-28 (B)
1961—Patriots, 20-17 (B)
 Patriots, 35-21 (O)
1962—Patriots, 26-16 (B)
 Raiders, 20-0 (O)
1963—Patriots, 20-14 (O)
 Patriots, 20-14 (B)
1964—Patriots, 17-14 (O)
 Tie, 43-43 (B)
1965—Raiders, 24-10 (B)
 Raiders, 30-21 (O)
1966—Patriots, 24-21 (B)
1967—Raiders, 35-7 (O)
 Raiders, 48-14 (B)
1968—Raiders, 41-10 (O)
1969—Raiders, 38-23 (B)
1971—Patriots, 20-6 (NE)
1974—Raiders, 41-26 (O)
1976—Patriots, 48-17 (NE)
 ***Raiders, 24-21 (O)
1978—Patriots, 21-14 (O)
1981—Raiders, 27-17 (O)
1985—Raiders, 35-20 (NE)
 ***Patriots, 27-20 (LA)
1987—Patriots, 26-23 (NE)
1989—Raiders, 24-21 (LA)
1994—Raiders, 21-17 (NE)
2001—***Patriots, 16-13 (NE) OT
2002—Raiders, 27-20 (O)
2005—Patriots, 30-20 (NE)
2008—Patriots, 49-26 (O)
(RS Pts.—Raiders 732, Patriots 653)
(PS Pts.—Patriots 64, Raiders 57)
**Franchise in Boston prior to 1971*
***Franchise in Los Angeles from 1982-1994*
****AFC Divisional Playoff*

NEW ENGLAND vs. PHILADELPHIA
RS: Eagles lead series, 6-4
PS: Patriots lead series, 1-0
1973—Eagles, 24-23 (P)
1977—Patriots, 14-6 (NE)
1978—Patriots, 24-14 (NE)
1981—Eagles, 13-3 (P)
1984—Eagles, 27-17 (P)
1987—Eagles, 34-31 (NE) OT
1990—Eagles, 48-20 (P)
1999—Eagles, 24-9 (P)
2003—Patriots, 31-10 (P)
2004—*Patriots, 24-21 (Jacksonville)
2007—Patriots, 31-28 (NE)

(RS Pts.—Eagles 228, Patriots 203)
(PS Pts.—Patriots 24, Eagles 21)
*Super Bowl XXXIX

NEW ENGLAND vs. PITTSBURGH
RS: Steelers lead series, 13-7
PS: Patriots lead series, 3-1
1972—Steelers, 33-3 (P)
1974—Steelers, 21-17 (NE)
1976—Patriots, 30-27 (P)
1979—Steelers, 16-13 (NE) OT
1981—Steelers, 27-21 (P) OT
1982—Steelers, 37-14 (P)
1983—Patriots, 28-23 (P)
1986—Patriots, 34-0 (P)
1989—Steelers, 28-10 (P)
1990—Steelers, 24-3 (P)
1991—Steelers, 20-6 (P)
1993—Steelers, 17-14 (P)
1995—Steelers, 41-27 (P)
1996—*Patriots, 28-3 (NE)
1997—Steelers, 24-21 (NE) OT
*Steelers, 7-6 (P)
1998—Patriots, 23-9 (P)
2001—**Patriots, 24-17 (P)
2002—Patriots, 30-14 (NE)
2004—Steelers, 34-20 (P)
**Patriots, 41-27 (P)
2005—Patriots, 23-20 (P)
2007—Patriots, 34-13 (NE)
2008—Steelers, 33-10 (NE)
(RS Pts.—Steelers 461, Patriots 381)
(PS Pts.—Patriots 99, Steelers 54)
*AFC Divisional Playoff
**AFC Championship

NEW ENGLAND vs. *ST. LOUIS
RS: Series tied, 5-5
PS: Patriots lead series, 1-0
1974—Patriots, 20-14 (NE)
1980—Rams, 17-14 (NE)
1983—Patriots, 21-7 (LA)
1986—Patriots, 30-28 (LA)
1989—Rams, 24-20 (NE)
1992—Rams, 14-0 (LA)
1998—Rams, 32-18 (StL)
2001—Rams, 24-17 (NE)
**Patriots, 20-17 (New Orleans)
2004—Patriots, 40-22 (StL)
2008—Patriots, 23-16 (NE)
(RS Pts.—Patriots 203, Rams 198)
(PS Pts.—Patriots 20, Rams 17)
*Franchise in Los Angeles prior to 1995
**Super Bowl XXXVI

***NEW ENGLAND vs. **SAN DIEGO**
RS: Patriots lead series, 18-14-2
PS: Patriots lead series, 2-1
1960—Patriots, 35-0 (LA)
Chargers, 45-16 (B)
1961—Chargers, 38-27 (B)
Patriots, 41-0 (SD)
1962—Patriots, 24-20 (B)
Patriots, 20-14 (SD)
1963—Chargers, 17-13 (SD)
Chargers, 7-6 (B)
***Chargers, 51-10 (SD)
1964—Patriots, 33-28 (SD)
Chargers, 26-17 (B)
1965—Tie, 10-10 (B)
Patriots, 22-6 (SD)
1966—Chargers, 24-0 (SD)
Patriots, 35-17 (B)
1967—Chargers, 28-14 (SD)
Tie, 31-31 (SD)
1968—Chargers, 27-17 (B)
1969—Chargers, 13-10 (B)
Chargers, 28-18 (SD)
1970—Chargers, 16-14 (B)
1973—Patriots, 30-14 (NE)
1975—Patriots, 33-19 (SD)
1977—Patriots, 24-20 (SD)
1978—Patriots, 28-23 (NE)
1979—Patriots, 27-21 (NE)
1983—Patriots, 37-21 (NE)
1994—Patriots, 23-17 (NE)
1996—Patriots, 45-7 (SD)
1997—Patriots, 41-7 (NE)
2001—Patriots, 29-26 (NE) OT
2002—Chargers, 21-14 (SD)
2005—Chargers, 41-17 (NE)
2006—****Patriots, 24-21 (SD)
2007—Patriots, 38-14 (NE)
*****Patriots, 21-12 (NE)
2008—Chargers, 30-10 (SD)
(RS Pts.—Patriots 802, Chargers 679)
(PS Pts.—Chargers 84, Patriots 55)
*Franchise in Boston prior to 1971
**Franchise in Los Angeles prior to 1961
***AFL Championship
****AFC Divisional Playoff
*****AFC Championship

NEW ENGLAND vs. SAN FRANCISCO
RS: 49ers lead series, 7-4
1971—49ers, 27-10 (SF)
1975—Patriots, 24-16 (NE)
1980—49ers, 21-17 (SF)
1983—49ers, 33-13 (NE)
1986—49ers, 29-24 (NE)
1989—49ers, 37-20 (SF)
1992—49ers, 24-12 (NE)
1995—49ers, 28-3 (SF)
1998—Patriots, 24-21 (NE)
2004—Patriots, 21-7 (NE)
2008—Patriots, 30-21 (SF)
(RS Pts.—49ers 264, Patriots 198)

NEW ENGLAND vs. SEATTLE
RS: Patriots lead series, 8-7
1977—Patriots, 31-0 (NE)
1980—Patriots, 37-31 (S)
1982—Patriots, 16-0 (S)
1983—Seahawks, 24-6 (S)
1984—Patriots, 38-23 (NE)
1985—Patriots, 20-13 (S)
1986—Seahawks, 38-31 (NE)
1988—Patriots, 13-7 (NE)
1989—Seahawks, 24-3 (NE)
1990—Seahawks, 33-20 (NE)
1992—Seahawks, 10-6 (NE)
1993—Seahawks, 17-14 (NE)
Seahawks, 10-9 (S)
2004—Patriots, 30-20 (NE)
2008—Patriots, 24-21 (S)
(RS Pts.—Patriots 298, Seahawks 271)

NEW ENGLAND vs. TAMPA BAY
RS: Patriots lead series, 4-2
1976—Patriots, 31-14 (TB)
1985—Patriots, 32-14 (TB)
1988—Patriots, 10-7 (NE) OT
1997—Buccaneers, 27-7 (TB)
2000—Buccaneers, 21-16 (NE)
2005—Patriots, 28-0 (NE)
(RS Pts.—Patriots 124, Buccaneers 83)

***NEW ENGLAND vs. **TENNESSEE**
RS: Patriots lead series, 20-15-1
PS: Series tied, 1-1
1960—Oilers, 24-10 (B)
Oilers, 37-21 (H)
1961—Tie, 31-31 (B)
Oilers, 27-15 (H)
1962—Patriots, 34-21 (B)
Oilers, 21-17 (H)
1963—Patriots, 45-3 (B)
Patriots, 46-28 (H)
1964—Patriots, 25-24 (B)
Patriots, 34-17 (H)
1965—Oilers, 31-10 (H)
Patriots, 42-14 (B)
1966—Patriots, 27-21 (B)
Patriots, 38-14 (H)
1967—Patriots, 18-7 (B)
Oilers, 27-6 (H)
1968—Oilers, 16-0 (B)
Oilers, 45-17 (H)
1969—Patriots, 24-0 (B)
Oilers, 27-23 (H)
1971—Patriots, 28-20 (NE)
1973—Patriots, 32-0 (H)
1975—Oilers, 7-0 (NE)
1978—Oilers, 26-23 (NE)
***Oilers, 31-14 (NE)
1980—Oilers, 38-34 (H)
1981—Patriots, 38-10 (NE)
1982—Patriots, 29-21 (NE)
1987—Patriots, 21-7 (H)
1988—Oilers, 31-6 (H)
1989—Patriots, 23-13 (NE)
1991—Patriots, 24-20 (NE)
1993—Oilers, 28-14 (NE)
1998—Patriots, 27-16 (NE)
2002—Titans, 24-7 (T)
2003—Patriots, 38-30 (NE)
***Patriots, 17-14 (NE)
2006—Patriots, 40-23 (T)
(RS Pts.—Patriots 867, Titans 749)
(PS Pts.—Titans 45, Patriots 31)
*Franchise in Boston prior to 1971
**Franchise in Houston prior to 1997; known as Oilers prior to 1999
***AFC Divisional Playoff

NEW ENGLAND vs. WASHINGTON
RS: Redskins lead series, 6-2
1972—Patriots, 24-23 (NE)
1978—Redskins, 16-14 (NE)
1981—Redskins, 24-22 (W)
1984—Redskins, 26-10 (NE)
1990—Redskins, 25-10 (NE)
1996—Redskins, 27-22 (NE)
2003—Redskins, 20-17 (W)
2007—Patriots, 52-7 (NE)
(RS Pts.—Patriots 171, Redskins 168)

NEW ORLEANS vs. ARIZONA
RS: Cardinals lead series, 13-12;
See Arizona vs. New Orleans

NEW ORLEANS vs. ATLANTA
RS: Falcons lead series, 44-35
PS: Falcons lead series, 1-0;
See Atlanta vs. New Orleans

NEW ORLEANS vs. BALTIMORE
RS: Ravens lead series, 3-1;
See Baltimore vs. New Orleans

NEW ORLEANS vs. BUFFALO
RS: Series tied, 4-4;
See Buffalo vs. New Orleans
NEW ORLEANS vs. CAROLINA
RS: Panthers lead series, 16-12;
See Carolina vs. New Orleans
NEW ORLEANS vs. CHICAGO
RS: Bears lead series, 13-11
PS: Bears lead series, 2-0;
See Chicago vs. New Orleans
NEW ORLEANS vs. CINCINNATI
RS: Bengals lead series, 6-5;
See Cincinnati vs. New Orleans
NEW ORLEANS vs. CLEVELAND
RS: Browns lead series, 11-4;
See Cleveland vs. New Orleans
NEW ORLEANS vs. DALLAS
RS: Cowboys lead series, 14-8;
See Dallas vs. New Orleans
NEW ORLEANS vs. DENVER
RS: Broncos lead series, 7-2;
See Denver vs. New Orleans
NEW ORLEANS vs. DETROIT
RS: Series tied, 9-9-1;
See Detroit vs. New Orleans
NEW ORLEANS vs. GREEN BAY
RS: Packers lead series, 14-7;
See Green Bay vs. New Orleans
NEW ORLEANS vs. HOUSTON
RS: Series tied, 1-1;
See Houston vs. New Orleans
NEW ORLEANS vs. INDIANAPOLIS
RS: Series tied, 5-5;
See Indianapolis vs. New Orleans
NEW ORLEANS vs. JACKSONVILLE
RS: Series tied, 2-2;
See Jacksonville vs. New Orleans
NEW ORLEANS vs. KANSAS CITY
RS: Saints lead series, 5-4;
See Kansas City vs. New Orleans
NEW ORLEANS vs. MIAMI
RS: Dolphins lead series, 6-3;
See Miami vs. New Orleans
NEW ORLEANS vs. MINNESOTA
RS: Vikings lead series, 18-7
PS: Vikings lead series, 2-0;
See Minnesota vs. New Orleans
NEW ORLEANS vs. NEW ENGLAND
RS: Patriots lead series, 8-3;
See New England vs. New Orleans
NEW ORLEANS vs. N.Y. GIANTS
RS: Giants lead series, 14-10
1967—Giants, 27-21 (NY)
1968—Giants, 38-21 (NY)
1969—Saints, 25-24 (NY)
1970—Saints, 14-10 (NO)
1972—Giants, 45-21 (NY)
1975—Giants, 28-14 (NY)
1978—Saints, 28-17 (NO)
1979—Saints, 24-14 (NO)
1981—Giants, 20-7 (NY)
1984—Saints, 10-3 (NY)
1985—Giants, 21-13 (NO)
1986—Giants, 20-17 (NY)
1987—Saints, 23-14 (NO)
1988—Giants, 13-12 (NO)
1993—Giants, 24-14 (NO)
1994—Saints, 27-22 (NO)
1995—Giants, 45-29 (NY)
1996—Saints 17-3 (NY)
1997—Giants, 14-9 (NY)
1999—Giants, 31-3 (NY)
2001—Giants, 21-13 (NY)
2003—Saints, 45-7 (NO)
2005—Giants, 27-10 (NY*)
2006—Saints, 30-7 (NY)
(RS Pts.—Giants 495, Saints 447)
**Saints home game*
NEW ORLEANS vs. N.Y. JETS
RS: Series tied, 5-5
1972—Jets, 18-17 (NY)
1977—Jets, 16-13 (NO)
1980—Saints, 21-20 (NY)
1983—Jets, 31-28 (NO)
1986—Jets, 28-23 (NY)
1989—Saints, 29-14 (NO)
1992—Saints, 20-0 (NY)
1995—Saints, 12-0 (NY)
2001—Jets, 16-9 (NO)
2005—Saints, 21-19 (NY)
(RS Pts.—Saints 193, Jets 162)
NEW ORLEANS vs. *OAKLAND
RS: Series tied, 5-5-1
1971—Tie, 21-21 (NO)
1975—Raiders, 48-10 (O)
1979—Raiders, 42-35 (NO)
1985—Raiders, 23-13 (LA)
1988—Saints, 20-6 (NO)
1991—Saints, 27-0 (NO)
1994—Raiders, 24-19 (LA)
1997—Saints, 13-10 (O)
2000—Raiders, 31-22 (NO)
2004—Saints, 31-26 (O)
2008—Saints, 34-3 (NO)
(RS Pts.—Saints 245, Raiders 234)
**Franchise in Los Angeles from 1982-1994*
NEW ORLEANS vs. PHILADELPHIA
RS: Eagles lead series, 15-9
PS: Series tied, 1-1
1967—Saints, 31-24 (NO)
Eagles, 48-21 (P)
1968—Eagles, 29-17 (P)
1969—Eagles, 13-10 (P)
Saints, 26-17 (NO)
1972—Saints, 21-3 (NO)
1974—Saints, 14-10 (NO)
1977—Eagles, 28-7 (P)
1978—Eagles, 24-17 (NO)
1979—Eagles, 26-14 (NO)
1980—Eagles, 34-21 (NO)
1981—Eagles, 31-14 (NO)
1983—Saints, 20-17 (P) OT
1985—Saints, 23-21 (NO)
1987—Eagles, 27-17 (P)
1989—Saints, 30-20 (NO)
1991—Saints, 13-6 (P)
1992—Eagles, 15-13 (P)
*Eagles, 36-20 (NO)
1993—Eagles, 37-26 (P)
1995—Eagles, 15-10 (NO)
2000—Eagles, 21-7 (NO)
2003—Eagles, 33-20 (P)
2006—Saints, 27-24 (NO)
**Saints, 27-24 (NO)
2007—Eagles, 38-23 (NO)
(RS Pts.—Eagles 561, Saints 442)
(PS Pts.—Eagles 60, Saints 47)
**NFC First-Round Playoff*
***NFC Divisional Playoff*
NEW ORLEANS vs. PITTSBURGH
RS: Steelers lead series, 7-6
1967—Steelers, 14-10 (NO)
1968—Saints, 16-12 (P)
Saints, 24-14 (NO)
1969—Saints, 27-24 (NO)
1974—Steelers, 28-7 (NO)
1978—Steelers, 20-14 (P)
1981—Steelers, 20-6 (NO)
1984—Saints, 27-24 (NO)
1987—Saints, 20-16 (P)
1990—Steelers, 9-6 (NO)
1993—Steelers, 37-14 (P)
2002—Saints, 32-29 (NO)
2006—Steelers, 38-31 (P)
(RS Pts.—Steelers 285, Saints 234)
NEW ORLEANS vs. *ST. LOUIS
RS: Rams lead series, 38-29
PS: Saints lead series, 1-0
1967—Rams, 27-13 (NO)
1969—Rams, 36-17 (LA)
1970—Rams, 30-17 (NO)
Rams, 34-16 (LA)
1971—Saints, 24-20 (NO)
Rams, 45-28 (LA)
1972—Rams, 34-14 (LA)
Saints, 19-16 (NO)
1973—Rams, 29-7 (LA)
Rams, 24-13 (NO)
1974—Rams, 24-0 (LA)
Saints, 20-7 (NO)
1975—Rams, 38-14 (LA)
Rams, 14-7 (NO)
1976—Rams, 16-10 (NO)
Rams, 33-14 (LA)
1977—Rams, 14-7 (LA)
Saints, 27-26 (NO)
1978—Rams, 26-20 (NO)
Saints, 10-3 (LA)
1979—Rams, 35-17 (NO)
Saints, 29-14 (LA)
1980—Rams, 45-31 (LA)
Rams, 27-7 (NO)
1981—Saints, 23-17 (NO)
Saints, 21-13 (LA)
1983—Rams, 30-27 (LA)
Rams, 26-24 (NO)
1984—Rams, 28-10 (NO)
Rams, 34-21 (LA)
1985—Rams, 28-10 (LA)
Saints, 29-3 (NO)
1986—Saints, 6-0 (NO)
Rams, 26-13 (LA)
1987—Saints, 37-10 (NO)
Saints, 31-14 (LA)
1988—Rams, 12-10 (NO)
Saints, 14-10 (LA)
1989—Saints, 40-21 (LA)
Rams, 20-17 (NO) OT
1990—Saints, 24-20 (LA)
Saints, 20-17 (NO)
1991—Saints, 24-7 (NO)
Saints, 24-17 (LA)
1992—Saints, 13-10 (NO)
Saints, 37-14 (LA)
1993—Saints, 37-6 (LA)
Rams, 23-20 (NO)
1994—Saints, 37-34 (NO)
Saints, 31-15 (LA)
1995—Rams, 17-13 (StL)

Saints, 19-10 (NO)
1996—Rams, 26-10 (NO)
Rams, 14-13 (StL)
1997—Rams, 38-24 (StL)
Rams, 34-27 (NO)
1998—Saints, 24-17 (StL)
Saints, 24-3 (NO)
1999—Rams, 43-12 (StL)
Rams, 30-14 (NO)
2000—Saints, 31-24 (StL)
Rams, 26-21 (NO)
**Saints, 31-28 (NO)
2001—Saints, 34-31 (StL)
Rams, 34-21 (NO)
2004—Saints, 28-25 (StL) OT
2005—Rams, 28-17 (StL)
2007—Rams, 37-29 (NO)
(RS Pts.—Rams 1,509, Saints 1,342)
(PS Pts.—Saints 31, Rams 28)
Franchise in Los Angeles prior to 1995
***NFC First-Round Playoff*

NEW ORLEANS vs. SAN DIEGO
RS: Chargers lead series, 7-3
1973—Chargers, 17-14 (SD)
1977—Chargers, 14-0 (NO)
1979—Chargers, 35-0 (NO)
1988—Saints, 23-17 (SD)
1991—Chargers, 24-21 (SD)
1994—Chargers, 36-22 (NO)
1997—Chargers, 20-6 (NO)
2000—Saints, 28-27 (SD)
2004—Chargers, 43-17 (SD)
2008—Saints, 37-32 (London)
(RS Pts.—Chargers 265, Saints 168)

NEW ORLEANS vs. SAN FRANCISCO
RS: 49ers lead series, 45-23-2
1967—49ers, 27-13 (SF)
1969—Saints, 43-38 (NO)
1970—Tie, 20-20 (SF)
49ers, 38-27 (NO)
1971—49ers, 38-20 (NO)
Saints, 26-20 (SF)
1972—49ers, 37-2 (NO)
Tie, 20-20 (SF)
1973—49ers, 40-0 (SF)
Saints, 16-10 (NO)
1974—49ers, 17-13 (NO)
49ers, 35-21 (SF)
1975—49ers, 35-21 (SF)
49ers, 16-6 (NO)
1976—49ers, 33-3 (SF)
49ers, 27-7 (NO)
1977—49ers, 10-7 (NO) OT
49ers, 20-17 (SF)
1978—Saints, 14-7 (SF)
Saints, 24-13 (NO)
1979—Saints, 30-21 (SF)
Saints, 31-20 (NO)
1980—49ers, 26-23 (NO)
49ers, 38-35 (SF) OT
1981—49ers, 21-14 (SF)
49ers, 21-17 (NO)
1982—Saints, 23-20 (SF)
1983—49ers, 32-13 (NO)
49ers, 27-0 (SF)
1984—49ers, 30-20 (SF)
49ers, 35-3 (NO)
1985—Saints, 20-17 (SF)
49ers, 31-19 (NO)
1986—49ers, 26-17 (SF)
Saints, 23-10 (NO)
1987—49ers, 24-22 (NO)
Saints, 26-24 (SF)
1988—49ers, 34-33 (NO)
49ers, 30-17 (SF)
1989—49ers, 24-20 (NO)
49ers, 31-13 (SF)
1990—49ers, 13-12 (NO)
Saints, 13-10 (SF)
1991—Saints, 10-3 (NO)
49ers, 38-24 (SF)
1992—49ers, 16-10 (NO)
49ers, 21-20 (SF)
1993—Saints, 16-13 (NO)
49ers, 42-7 (SF)
1994—49ers, 24-13 (SF)
49ers, 35-14 (NO)
1995—49ers, 24-22 (NO)
Saints, 11-7 (SF)
1996—49ers, 27-11 (SF)
49ers, 24-17 (NO)
1997—49ers, 33-7 (SF)
49ers, 23-0 (NO)
1998—49ers, 31-0 (NO)
49ers, 31-20 (SF)
1999—49ers, 28-21 (SF)
Saints, 24-6 (NO)
2000—Saints, 31-15 (NO)
Saints, 31-27 (SF)
2001—49ers, 28-27 (SF)
49ers, 38-0 (NO)
2002—Saints, 35-27 (NO)
2004—Saints, 30-27 (NO)
2006—Saints, 34-10 (NO)
2007—Saints, 31-10 (SF)
2008—Saints, 31-17 (NO)
(RS Pts.—49ers 1,691, Saints 1,261)

NEW ORLEANS vs. SEATTLE
RS: Series tied, 5-5
1976—Saints, 51-27 (S)
1979—Seahawks, 38-24 (S)
1985—Seahawks, 27-3 (NO)
1988—Saints, 20-19 (S)
1991—Saints, 27-24 (NO)
1997—Saints, 20-17 (NO) OT
2000—Seahawks, 20-10 (S)
2003—Seahawks, 27-10 (S)
2004—Seahawks, 21-7 (NO)
2007—Saints, 28-17 (S)
(RS Pts.—Seahawks 237, Saints 200)

NEW ORLEANS vs. TAMPA BAY
RS: Saints lead series, 20-14
1977—Buccaneers, 33-14 (NO)
1978—Saints, 17-10 (TB)
1979—Saints, 42-14 (TB)
1981—Buccaneers, 31-14 (NO)
1982—Buccaneers, 13-10 (NO)
1983—Saints, 24-21 (TB)
1984—Saints, 17-13 (NO)
1985—Saints, 20-13 (NO)
1986—Saints, 38-7 (NO)
1987—Saints, 44-34 (NO)
1988—Saints, 13-9 (NO)
1989—Buccaneers, 20-10 (TB)
1990—Saints, 35-7 (NO)
1991—Saints, 23-7 (NO)
1992—Saints, 23-21 (NO)
1994—Saints, 9-7 (TB)
1996—Buccaneers, 13-7 (TB)
1998—Saints, 9-3 (NO)
1999—Buccaneers, 31-16 (NO)
2001—Buccaneers, 48-21 (TB)
2002—Saints, 26-20 (TB) OT
Saints, 23-20 (NO)
2003—Saints, 17-14 (TB)
Buccaneers, 14-7 (NO)
2004—Buccaneers, 20-17 (NO)
Saints, 21-17 (TB)
2005—Buccaneers, 10-3 (Baton Rouge)
Buccaneers, 27-13 (TB)
2006—Saints, 24-21 (NO)
Saints, 31-14 (TB)
2007—Buccaneers, 31-14 (TB)
Buccaneers, 27-23 (NO)
2008—Saints, 24-20 (NO)
Buccaneers, 23-20 (TB)
(RS Pts.—Saints 669, Buccaneers 633)

NEW ORLEANS vs. *TENNESSEE
RS: Titans lead series, 7-4-1
1971—Tie, 13-13 (H)
1976—Oilers, 31-26 (NO)
1978—Oilers, 17-12 (NO)
1981—Saints, 27-24 (H)
1984—Saints, 27-10 (H)
1987—Saints, 24-10 (NO)
1990—Oilers, 23-10 (H)
1993—Saints, 33-21 (NO)
1996—Oilers, 31-14 (NO)
1999—Titans, 24-21 (NO)
2003—Titans, 27-12 (T)
2007—Titans, 31-14 (NO)
(RS Pts.—Titans 262, Saints 233)
Franchise in Houston prior to 1997; known as Oilers prior to 1999

NEW ORLEANS vs. WASHINGTON
RS: Redskins lead series, 15-7
1967—Redskins, 30-10 (NO)
Saints, 30-14 (W)
1968—Saints, 37-17 (NO)
1969—Redskins, 26-20 (NO)
Redskins, 17-14 (W)
1971—Redskins, 24-14 (W)
1973—Saints, 19-3 (NO)
1975—Redskins, 41-3 (W)
1979—Saints, 14-10 (W)
1980—Redskins, 22-14 (W)
1982—Redskins, 27-10 (NO)
1986—Redskins, 14-6 (NO)
1988—Redskins, 27-24 (W)
1989—Redskins, 16-14 (NO)
1990—Redskins, 31-17 (W)
1992—Saints, 20-3 (NO)
1994—Redskins, 38-24 (NO)
2001—Redskins, 40-10 (NO)
2002—Saints, 43-27 (W)
2003—Saints, 24-20 (W)
2006—Redskins, 16-10 (NO)
2008—Redskins, 29-24 (W)
(RS Pts.—Redskins 492, Saints 401)

N.Y. GIANTS vs. ARIZONA
RS: Giants lead series, 79-41-2;
See Arizona vs. N.Y. Giants

N.Y. GIANTS vs. ATLANTA
RS: Falcons lead series, 10-9;
See Atlanta vs. N.Y. Giants

N.Y. GIANTS vs. BALTIMORE
RS: Ravens lead series, 2-1
PS: Ravens lead series, 1-0;
See Baltimore vs. N.Y. Giants

N.Y. GIANTS vs. BUFFALO
RS: Bills lead series, 6-4
PS: Giants lead series, 1-0;
See Buffalo vs. N.Y. Giants
N.Y. GIANTS vs. CAROLINA
RS: Series tied, 2-2
PS: Panthers lead series, 1-0;
See Carolina vs. N.Y. Giants
N.Y. GIANTS vs. CHICAGO
RS: Bears lead series, 27-18-2
PS: Bears lead series, 5-3;
See Chicago vs. N.Y. Giants
N.Y. GIANTS vs. CINCINNATI
RS: Bengals lead series, 5-3;
See Cincinnati vs. N.Y. Giants
N.Y. GIANTS vs. CLEVELAND
RS: Browns lead series, 26-19-2
PS: Series tied, 1-1;
See Cleveland vs. N.Y. Giants
N.Y. GIANTS vs. DALLAS
RS: Cowboys lead series, 55-36-2
PS: Giants lead series, 1-0;
See Dallas vs. N.Y. Giants
N.Y. GIANTS vs. DENVER
RS: Giants lead series, 5-4
PS: Giants lead series, 1-0;
See Denver vs. N.Y. Giants
N.Y. GIANTS vs. DETROIT
RS: Lions lead series, 20-18-1
PS: Lions lead series, 1-0;
See Detroit vs. N.Y. Giants
N.Y. GIANTS vs. GREEN BAY
RS: Packers lead series, 25-21-2
PS: Packers lead series, 4-2;
See Green Bay vs. N.Y. Giants
N.Y. GIANTS vs. HOUSTON
RS: Series tied, 1-1;
See Houston vs. N.Y. Giants
N.Y. GIANTS vs. INDIANAPOLIS
RS: Colts lead series, 7-6
PS: Colts lead series, 2-0;
See Indianapolis vs. N.Y. Giants
N.Y. GIANTS vs. JACKSONVILLE
RS: Series tied, 2-2;
See Jacksonville vs. N.Y. Giants
N.Y. GIANTS vs. KANSAS CITY
RS: Giants lead series, 9-2;
See Kansas City vs. N.Y. Giants
N.Y. GIANTS vs. MIAMI
RS: Giants lead series, 4-2;
See Miami vs. N.Y. Giants
N.Y. GIANTS vs. MINNESOTA
RS: Vikings lead series, 12-8
PS: Giants lead series, 2-1;
See Minnesota vs. N.Y. Giants
N.Y. GIANTS vs. NEW ENGLAND
RS: Patriots lead series, 5-3
PS: Giants lead series, 1-0;
See New England vs. N.Y. Giants
N.Y. GIANTS vs. NEW ORLEANS
RS: Giants lead series, 14-10;
See New Orleans vs. N.Y. Giants
N.Y. GIANTS vs. N.Y. JETS
RS: Giants lead series, 7-4
1970—Giants, 22-10 (NYJ)
1974—Jets, 26-20 (New Haven) OT
1981—Jets, 26-7 (NYG)
1984—Giants, 20-10 (NYJ)
1987—Giants, 20-7 (NYG)
1988—Jets, 27-21 (NYJ)
1993—Jets, 10-6 (NYG)
1996—Giants, 13-6 (NYJ)
1999—Giants, 41-28 (NYG)
2003—Giants, 31-28 (NYJ) OT
2007—Giants, 35-24 (NYG)
(RS Pts.—Giants 236, Jets 202)
N.Y. GIANTS vs. *OAKLAND
RS: Raiders lead series, 7-3
1973—Raiders, 42-0 (O)
1980—Raiders, 33-17 (NY)
1983—Raiders, 27-12 (LA)
1986—Giants, 14-9 (LA)
1989—Giants, 34-17 (NY)
1992—Raiders, 13-10 (LA)
1995—Raiders, 17-13 (NY)
1998—Raiders, 20-17 (O)
2001—Raiders, 28-10 (NY)
2005—Giants, 30-21 (O)
(RS Pts.—Raiders 227, Giants 157)
**Franchise in Los Angeles from 1982-1994*
N.Y. GIANTS vs. PHILADELPHIA
RS: Giants lead series, 79-67-2
PS: Series tied, 2-2
1933—Giants, 56-0 (NY)
Giants, 20-14 (P)
1934—Giants, 17-0 (NY)
Eagles, 6-0 (P)
1935—Giants, 10-0 (NY)
Giants, 21-14 (P)
1936—Eagles, 10-7 (P)
Giants, 21-17 (NY)
1937—Giants, 16-7 (P)
Giants, 21-0 (NY)
1938—Eagles, 14-10 (P)
Giants, 17-7 (NY)
1939—Giants, 13-3 (P)
Giants, 27-10 (NY)
1940—Giants, 20-14 (P)
Giants, 17-7 (NY)
1941—Giants, 24-0 (P)
Giants, 16-0 (NY)
1942—Giants, 35-17 (NY)
Giants, 14-0 (P)
1944—Eagles, 24-17 (NY)
Tie, 21-21 (P)
1945—Eagles, 38-17 (P)
Giants, 28-21 (NY)
1946—Eagles, 24-14 (P)
Giants, 45-17 (NY)
1947—Eagles, 23-0 (P)
Eagles, 41-24 (NY)
1948—Eagles, 45-0 (P)
Eagles, 35-14 (NY)
1949—Eagles, 24-3 (NY)
Eagles, 17-3 (P)
1950—Giants, 7-3 (NY)
Giants, 9-7 (P)
1951—Giants, 26-24 (NY)
Giants, 23-7 (P)
1952—Giants, 31-7 (P)
Eagles, 14-10 (NY)
1953—Eagles, 30-7 (P)
Giants, 37-28 (NY)
1954—Giants, 27-14 (NY)
Eagles, 29-14 (P)
1955—Eagles, 27-17 (P)
Giants, 31-7 (NY)
1956—Giants, 20-3 (NY)
Giants, 21-7 (P)
1957—Giants, 24-20 (P)
Giants, 13-0 (NY)
1958—Eagles, 27-24 (P)
Giants, 24-10 (NY)
1959—Eagles, 49-21 (P)
Giants, 24-7 (NY)
1960—Eagles, 17-10 (NY)
Eagles, 31-23 (P)
1961—Giants, 38-21 (NY)
Giants, 28-24 (P)
1962—Giants, 29-13 (P)
Giants, 19-14 (NY)
1963—Giants, 37-14 (P)
Giants, 42-14 (NY)
1964—Eagles, 38-7 (P)
Eagles, 23-17 (NY)
1965—Giants, 16-14 (P)
Giants, 35-27 (NY)
1966—Eagles, 35-17 (P)
Eagles, 31-3 (NY)
1967—Giants, 44-7 (NY)
1968—Giants, 34-25 (P)
Giants, 7-6 (NY)
1969—Eagles, 23-20 (NY)
1970—Giants, 30-23 (NY)
Eagles, 23-20 (P)
1971—Eagles, 23-7 (P)
Eagles, 41-28 (NY)
1972—Giants, 27-12 (P)
Giants, 62-10 (NY)
1973—Tie, 23-23 (NY)
Eagles, 20-16 (P)
1974—Eagles, 35-7 (P)
Eagles, 20-7 (New Haven)
1975—Giants, 23-14 (P)
Eagles, 13-10 (NY)
1976—Eagles, 20-7 (P)
Eagles, 10-0 (NY)
1977—Eagles, 28-10 (NY)
Eagles, 17-14 (P)
1978—Eagles, 19-17 (NY)
Eagles, 20-3 (P)
1979—Eagles, 23-17 (P)
Eagles, 17-13 (NY)
1980—Eagles, 35-3 (P)
Eagles, 31-16 (NY)
1981—Eagles, 24-10 (NY)
Giants, 20-10 (P)
*Giants, 27-21 (P)
1982—Giants, 23-7 (NY)
Giants, 26-24 (P)
1983—Eagles, 17-13 (NY)
Giants, 23-0 (P)
1984—Giants, 28-27 (NY)
Eagles, 24-10 (P)
1985—Giants, 21-0 (NY)
Giants, 16-10 (P) OT
1986—Giants, 35-3 (NY)
Giants, 17-14 (P)
1987—Giants, 20-17 (P)
Giants, 23-20 (NY) OT
1988—Eagles, 24-13 (P)
Eagles, 23-17 (NY) OT
1989—Eagles, 21-19 (P)
Eagles, 24-17 (NY)
1990—Giants, 27-20 (NY)
Eagles, 31-13 (P)
1991—Eagles, 30-7 (P)
Eagles, 19-14 (NY)
1992—Eagles, 47-34 (NY)
Eagles, 20-10 (P)

1993—Giants, 21-10 (NY)
Giants, 7-3 (P)
1994—Giants, 28-23 (NY)
Giants, 16-13 (P)
1995—Eagles, 17-14 (NY)
Eagles, 28-19 (P)
1996—Eagles, 19-10 (NY)
Eagles, 24-0 (P)
1997—Giants, 31-17 (NY)
Giants, 31-21 (P)
1998—Giants, 20-0 (NY)
Giants, 20-10 (P)
1999—Giants, 16-15 (NY)
Giants, 23-17 (P) OT
2000—Giants, 33-18 (P)
Giants, 24-7 (NY)
**Giants, 20-10 (NY)
2001—Eagles, 10-9 (NY)
Eagles, 24-21 (P)
2002—Eagles, 17-3 (P)
Giants, 10-7 (NY) OT
2003—Eagles, 14-10 (NY)
Eagles, 28-10 (P)
2004—Eagles, 31-17 (P)
Eagles, 27-6 (NY)
2005—Giants, 27-17 (NY)
Giants, 26-23 (P) OT
2006—Giants, 30-24 (P) OT
Eagles, 36-22 (NY)
*Eagles, 23-20 (P)
2007—Giants, 16-3 (NY)
Giants, 16-13 (P)
2008—Giants, 36-31 (P)
Eagles, 20-14 (NY)
**Eagles, 23-11 (NY)
(RS Pts.—Giants 2,806, Eagles 2,667)
(PS Pts.—Giants 78, Eagles 77)
NFC First-Round Playoff
***NFC Divisional Playoff*

N.Y. GIANTS vs. *PITTSBURGH
RS: Giants lead series, 44-28-3
1933—Giants, 23-2 (P)
Giants, 27-3 (NY)
1934—Giants, 14-12 (P)
Giants, 17-7 (NY)
1935—Giants, 42-7 (P)
Giants, 13-0 (NY)
1936—Pirates, 10-7 (P)
1937—Giants, 10-7 (P)
Giants, 17-0 (NY)
1938—Giants, 27-14 (P)
Pirates, 13-10 (NY)
1939—Giants, 14-7 (P)
Giants, 23-7 (NY)
1940—Tie, 10-10 (P)
Giants, 12-0 (NY)
1941—Giants, 37-10 (P)
Giants, 28-7 (NY)
1942—Steelers, 13-10 (P)
Steelers, 17-9 (NY)
1945—Giants, 34-6 (P)
Steelers, 21-7 (NY)
1946—Giants, 17-14 (P)
Giants, 7-0 (NY)
1947—Steelers, 38-21 (NY)
Steelers, 24-7 (P)
1948—Giants, 34-27 (NY)
Steelers, 38-28 (P)
1949—Steelers, 28-7 (P)
Steelers, 21-17 (NY)
1950—Giants, 18-7 (P)
Steelers, 17-6 (NY)
1951—Tie, 13-13 (P)
Giants, 14-0 (NY)
1952—Steelers, 63-7 (P)
1953—Steelers, 24-14 (P)
Steelers, 14-10 (NY)
1954—Giants, 30-6 (P)
Giants, 24-3 (NY)
1955—Steelers, 30-23 (P)
Steelers, 19-17 (NY)
1956—Giants, 38-10 (NY)
Giants, 17-14 (P)
1957—Giants, 35-0 (NY)
Steelers, 21-10 (P)
1958—Giants, 17-6 (NY)
Steelers, 31-10 (P)
1959—Giants, 21-16 (P)
Steelers, 14-9 (NY)
1960—Giants, 19-17 (P)
Giants, 27-24 (NY)
1961—Giants, 17-14 (P)
Giants, 42-21 (NY)
1962—Giants, 31-27 (P)
Steelers, 20-17 (NY)
1963—Steelers, 31-0 (P)
Giants, 33-17 (NY)
1964—Steelers, 27-24 (P)
Steelers, 44-17 (NY)
1965—Giants, 23-13 (P)
Giants, 35-10 (NY)
1966—Tie, 34-34 (P)
Steelers, 47-28 (NY)
1967—Giants, 27-24 (P)
Giants, 28-20 (NY)
1968—Giants, 34-20 (P)
1969—Giants, 10-7 (NY)
Giants, 21-17 (P)
1971—Steelers, 17-13 (P)
1976—Steelers, 27-0 (NY)
1985—Giants, 28-10 (NY)
1991—Giants, 23-20 (P)
1994—Steelers, 10-6 (NY)
2000—Giants, 30-10 (NY)
2004—Steelers, 33-30 (NY)
2008—Giants, 21-14 (P)
(RS Pts.—Giants 1,480, Steelers 1,246)
**Steelers known as Pirates prior to 1940*

N.Y. GIANTS vs. *ST. LOUIS
RS: Rams lead series, 25-13
PS: Series tied, 1-1
1938—Giants, 28-0 (NY)
1940—Rams, 13-0 (NY)
1941—Giants, 49-14 (NY)
1945—Rams, 21-17 (NY)
1946—Rams, 31-21 (NY)
1947—Rams, 34-10 (LA)
1948—Rams, 52-37 (NY)
1953—Rams, 21-7 (LA)
1954—Rams, 17-16 (NY)
1959—Giants, 23-21 (LA)
1961—Giants, 24-14 (NY)
1966—Rams, 55-14 (LA)
1968—Rams, 24-21 (LA)
1970—Rams, 31-3 (NY)
1973—Rams, 40-6 (LA)
1976—Rams, 24-10 (LA)
1978—Rams, 20-17 (NY)
1979—Giants, 20-14 (LA)
1980—Rams, 28-7 (NY)
1981—Giants, 10-7 (NY)
1983—Rams, 16-6 (NY)
1984—Rams, 33-12 (LA)
**Giants, 16-13 (LA)
1985—Giants, 24-19 (NY)
1988—Rams, 45-31 (NY)
1989—Rams, 31-10 (LA)
***Rams, 19-13 (NY) OT
1990—Giants, 31-7 (LA)
1991—Rams, 19-13 (NY)
1992—Rams, 38-17 (LA)
1993—Giants, 20-10 (NY)
1994—Rams, 17-10 (LA)
1997—Rams, 13-3 (StL)
1999—Rams, 31-10 (StL)
2000—Rams, 38-24 (NY)
2001—Rams, 15-14 (StL)
2002—Giants, 26-21 (StL)
2003—Giants, 23-13 (NY)
2005—Giants, 44-24 (NY)
2008—Giants, 41-13 (StL)
(RS Pts.—Rams 884, Giants 699)
(PS Pts.—Rams 32, Giants 29)
**Franchise in Los Angeles prior to 1995 and in Cleveland prior to 1946*
***NFC First-Round Playoff*
****NFC Divisional Playoff*

N.Y. GIANTS vs. SAN DIEGO
RS: Giants lead series, 5-4
1971—Giants, 35-17 (NY)
1975—Giants, 35-24 (NY)
1980—Chargers, 44-7 (SD)
1983—Chargers, 41-34 (NY)
1986—Giants, 20-7 (NY)
1989—Giants, 20-13 (SD)
1995—Chargers, 27-17 (NY)
1998—Giants, 34-16 (SD)
2005—Chargers, 45-23 (SD)
(RS Pts.—Chargers 234, Giants 225)

N.Y. GIANTS vs. SAN FRANCISCO
RS: Giants lead series, 14-13
PS: 49ers lead series, 4-3
1952—Giants, 23-14 (NY)
1956—Giants, 38-21 (SF)
1957—49ers, 27-17 (NY)
1960—Giants, 21-19 (SF)
1963—Giants, 48-14 (NY)
1968—49ers, 26-10 (NY)
1972—Giants, 23-17 (SF)
1975—Giants, 26-23 (SF)
1977—Giants, 20-17 (NY)
1978—Giants, 27-10 (NY)
1979—Giants, 32-16 (NY)
1980—49ers, 12-0 (SF)
1981—49ers, 17-10 (SF)
*49ers, 38-24 (SF)
1984—49ers, 31-10 (NY)
*49ers, 21-10 (SF)
1985—**Giants, 17-3 (NY)
1986—Giants, 21-17 (SF)
*Giants, 49-3 (NY)
1987—49ers, 41-21 (NY)
1988—49ers, 20-17 (NY)
1989—49ers, 34-24 (SF)
1990—49ers, 7-3 (SF)
***Giants, 15-13 (SF)
1991—Giants, 16-14 (NY)
1992—49ers, 31-14 (NY)
1993—*49ers, 44-3 (SF)
1995—49ers, 20-6 (SF)

1998—49ers, 31-7 (SF)
2002—49ers, 16-13 (NY)
**49ers, 39-38 (SF)
2005—Giants, 24-6 (SF)
2007—Giants, 33-15 (NY)
2008—Giants, 29-17 (NY)
(RS Pts.—49ers 533, Giants 533)
(PS Pts.—49ers 161, Giants 156)
NFC Divisional Playoff
***NFC First-Round Playoff*
****NFC Championship*

N.Y. GIANTS vs. SEATTLE
RS: Giants lead series, 8-5
1976—Giants, 28-16 (NY)
1980—Giants, 27-21 (S)
1981—Giants, 32-0 (S)
1983—Seahawks, 17-12 (NY)
1986—Seahawks, 17-12 (S)
1989—Giants, 15-3 (NY)
1992—Giants, 23-10 (NY)
1995—Seahawks, 30-28 (S)
2001—Giants, 27-24 (NY)
2002—Giants, 9-6 (NY)
2005—Seahawks, 24-21 (S) OT
2006—Seahawks, 42-30 (S)
2008—Giants, 44-6 (NY)
(RS Pts.—Giants 308, Seahawks 216)

N.Y. GIANTS vs. TAMPA BAY
RS: Giants lead series, 10-6
PS: Giants lead series, 1-0
1977—Giants, 10-0 (TB)
1978—Giants, 19-13 (TB)
Giants, 17-14 (NY)
1979—Giants, 17-14 (NY)
Buccaneers, 31-3 (TB)
1980—Buccaneers, 30-13 (TB)
1984—Giants, 17-14 (NY)
Buccaneers, 20-17 (TB)
1985—Giants, 22-20 (NY)
1991—Giants, 21-14 (TB)
1993—Giants, 23-7 (NY)
1997—Buccaneers, 20-8 (NY)
1998—Buccaneers, 20-3 (TB)
1999—Giants, 17-13 (TB)
2003—Buccaneers, 19-13 (TB)
2006—Giants, 17-3 (NY)
2007—*Giants, 24-14 (TB)
(RS Pts.—Buccaneers 252, Giants 237)
(PS Pts.—Giants 24, Buccaneers 14)
**NFC First-Round Playoff*

N.Y. GIANTS vs. *TENNESSEE
RS: Giants lead series, 5-4
1973—Giants, 34-14 (NY)
1982—Giants, 17-14 (NY)
1985—Giants, 35-14 (H)
1991—Giants, 24-20 (NY)
1994—Giants, 13-10 (H)
1997—Oilers, 10-6 (T)
2000—Titans, 28-14 (T)
2002—Titans, 32-29 (NY) OT
2006—Titans, 24-21 (T)
(RS Pts.—Giants 193, Titans 166)
**Franchise in Houston prior to 1997; known as Oilers prior to 1999*

N.Y. GIANTS vs. *WASHINGTON
RS: Giants lead series, 87-61-4
PS: Series tied, 1-1
1932—Braves, 14-6 (B)
Tie, 0-0 (NY)
1933—Redskins, 21-20 (B)
Giants, 7-0 (NY)
1934—Giants, 16-13 (B)
Giants, 3-0 (NY)
1935—Giants, 20-12 (B)
Giants, 17-6 (NY)
1936—Giants, 7-0 (B)
Redskins, 14-0 (NY)
1937—Redskins, 13-3 (W)
Redskins, 49-14 (NY)
1938—Giants, 10-7 (W)
Giants, 36-0 (NY)
1939—Tie, 0-0 (W)
Giants, 9-7 (NY)
1940—Redskins, 21-7 (W)
Giants, 21-7 (NY)
1941—Giants, 17-10 (W)
Giants, 20-13 (NY)
1942—Giants, 14-7 (W)
Redskins, 14-7 (NY)
1943—Giants, 14-10 (NY)
Giants, 31-7 (W)
**Redskins, 28-0 (NY)
1944—Giants, 16-13 (NY)
Giants, 31-0 (W)
1945—Redskins, 24-14 (NY)
Redskins, 17-0 (W)
1946—Redskins, 24-14 (W)
Giants, 31-0 (NY)
1947—Redskins, 28-20 (W)
Giants, 35-10 (NY)
1948—Redskins, 41-10 (W)
Redskins, 28-21 (NY)
1949—Giants, 45-35 (W)
Giants, 23-7 (NY)
1950—Giants, 21-17 (W)
Giants, 24-21 (NY)
1951—Giants, 35-14 (W)
Giants, 28-14 (NY)
1952—Giants, 14-10 (W)
Redskins, 27-17 (NY)
1953—Redskins, 13-9 (W)
Redskins, 24-21 (NY)
1954—Giants, 51-21 (W)
Giants, 24-7 (NY)
1955—Giants, 35-7 (NY)
Giants, 27-20 (W)
1956—Redskins, 33-7 (W)
Giants, 28-14 (NY)
1957—Giants, 24-20 (W)
Redskins, 31-14 (NY)
1958—Giants, 21-14 (W)
Giants, 30-0 (NY)
1959—Giants, 45-14 (NY)
Giants, 24-10 (W)
1960—Tie, 24-24 (NY)
Giants, 17-3 (W)
1961—Giants, 24-21 (W)
Giants, 53-0 (NY)
1962—Giants, 49-34 (NY)
Giants, 42-24 (W)
1963—Giants, 24-14 (W)
Giants, 44-14 (NY)
1964—Giants, 13-10 (NY)
Redskins, 36-21 (W)
1965—Redskins, 23-7 (NY)
Giants, 27-10 (W)
1966—Giants, 13-10 (NY)
Redskins, 72-41 (W)
1967—Redskins, 38-34 (W)
1968—Giants, 48-21 (NY)
Giants, 13-10 (W)
1969—Redskins, 20-14 (W)
1970—Giants, 35-33 (NY)
Giants, 27-24 (W)
1971—Redskins, 30-3 (NY)
Redskins, 23-7 (W)
1972—Redskins, 23-16 (NY)
Redskins, 27-13 (W)
1973—Redskins, 21-3 (New Haven)
Redskins, 27-24 (W)
1974—Redskins, 13-10 (New Haven)
Redskins, 24-3 (W)
1975—Redskins, 49-13 (W)
Redskins, 21-13 (NY)
1976—Redskins, 19-17 (W)
Giants, 12-9 (NY)
1977—Giants, 20-17 (NY)
Giants, 17-6 (W)
1978—Giants, 17-6 (NY)
Redskins, 16-13 (W) OT
1979—Redskins, 27-0 (W)
Giants, 14-6 (NY)
1980—Redskins, 23-21 (NY)
Redskins, 16-13 (W)
1981—Giants, 17-7 (W)
Redskins, 30-27 (NY) OT
1982—Redskins, 27-17 (NY)
Redskins, 15-14 (W)
1983—Redskins, 33-17 (NY)
Redskins, 31-22 (W)
1984—Redskins, 30-14 (W)
Giants, 37-13 (NY)
1985—Giants, 17-3 (NY)
Redskins, 23-21 (W)
1986—Giants, 27-20 (NY)
Giants, 24-14 (W)
***Giants, 17-0 (NY)
1987—Redskins, 38-12 (NY)
Redskins, 23-19 (W)
1988—Giants, 27-20 (NY)
Giants, 24-23 (W)
1989—Giants, 27-24 (W)
Giants, 20-17 (NY)
1990—Giants, 24-20 (W)
Giants, 21-10 (NY)
1991—Redskins, 17-13 (NY)
Redskins, 34-17 (W)
1992—Giants, 24-7 (W)
Redskins, 28-10 (NY)
1993—Giants, 41-7 (W)
Giants, 20-6 (NY)
1994—Giants, 31-23 (NY)
Giants, 21-19 (W)
1995—Giants, 24-15 (W)
Giants, 20-13 (NY)
1996—Redskins, 31-10 (NY)
Redskins, 31-21 (W)
1997—Tie, 7-7 (W) OT
Giants, 30-10 (NY)
1998—Giants, 31-24 (NY)
Redskins, 21-14 (W)
1999—Redskins, 50-21 (NY)
Redskins, 23-13 (W)
2000—Redskins, 16-6 (NY)
Giants, 9-7 (W)
2001—Giants, 23-9 (NY)
Redskins, 35-21 (W)
2002—Giants, 19-17 (NY)
Giants, 27-21 (W)
2003—Giants, 24-21 (W) OT

Redskins, 20-7 (NY)
2004—Giants, 20-14 (NY)
Redskins, 31-7 (W)
2005—Giants, 36-0 (NY)
Redskins, 35-20 (W)
2006—Giants, 19-3 (NY)
Giants, 34-28 (W)
2007—Giants, 24-17 (W)
Redskins, 22-10 (NY)
2008—Giants, 16-7 (NY)
Giants, 23-7 (W)
(RS Pts.—Giants 3,018, Redskins 2,744)
(PS Pts.—Redskins 28, Giants 17)
**Franchise in Boston prior to 1937 and known as Braves prior to 1933*
***Division Playoff*
****NFC Championship*

N.Y. JETS vs. ARIZONA
RS: Jets lead series, 5-2;
See Arizona vs. N.Y. Jets
N.Y. JETS vs. ATLANTA
RS: Falcons lead series, 5-4;
See Atlanta vs. N.Y. Jets
N.Y. JETS vs. BALTIMORE
RS: Ravens lead series, 5-1;
See Baltimore vs. N.Y. Jets
N.Y. JETS vs. BUFFALO
RS: Bills lead series, 52-44
PS: Bills lead series, 1-0;
See Buffalo vs. N.Y. Jets
N.Y. JETS vs. CAROLINA
RS: Series tied, 2-2;
See Carolina vs. N.Y. Jets
N.Y. JETS vs. CHICAGO
RS: Bears lead series, 6-3;
See Chicago vs. N.Y. Jets
N.Y. JETS vs. CINCINNATI
RS: Jets lead series, 13-7
PS: Jets lead series, 1-0;
See Cincinnati vs. N.Y. Jets
N.Y. JETS vs. CLEVELAND
RS: Browns lead series, 12-7
PS: Browns lead series, 1-0;
See Cleveland vs. N.Y. Jets
N.Y. JETS vs. DALLAS
RS: Cowboys lead series, 7-2;
See Dallas vs. N.Y. Jets
N.Y. JETS vs. DENVER
RS: Broncos lead series, 16-14-1
PS: Broncos lead series, 1-0;
See Denver vs. N.Y. Jets
N.Y. JETS vs. DETROIT
RS: Lions lead series, 6-5;
See Detroit vs. N.Y. Jets
N.Y. JETS vs. GREEN BAY
RS: Jets lead series, 8-2;
See Green Bay vs. N.Y. Jets
N.Y. JETS vs. HOUSTON
RS: Jets lead series, 3-0;
See Houston vs. N.Y. Jets
N.Y. JETS vs. INDIANAPOLIS
RS: Colts lead series, 40-25
PS: Jets lead series, 2-0;
See Indianapolis vs. N.Y. Jets
N.Y. JETS vs. JACKSONVILLE
RS: Jaguars lead series, 5-2
PS: Jets lead series, 1-0;
See Jacksonville vs. N.Y. Jets

N.Y. JETS vs. KANSAS CITY
RS: Series tied, 16-16-1
PS: Series tied, 1-1;
See Kansas City vs. N.Y. Jets
N.Y. JETS vs. MIAMI
RS: Jets lead series, 46-39-1
PS: Dolphins lead series, 1-0;
See Miami vs. N.Y. Jets
N.Y. JETS vs. MINNESOTA
RS: Jets lead series, 7-1;
See Minnesota vs. N.Y. Jets
N.Y. JETS vs. NEW ENGLAND
RS: Jets lead series, 49-47-1
PS: Patriots lead series, 2-0;
See New England vs. N.Y. Jets
N.Y. JETS vs. NEW ORLEANS
RS: Series tied, 5-5;
See New Orleans vs. N.Y. Jets
N.Y. JETS vs. N.Y. GIANTS
RS: Giants lead series, 7-4;
See N.Y. Giants vs. N.Y. Jets
***N.Y. JETS vs. **OAKLAND**
RS: Raiders lead series, 20-14-2
PS: Series tied, 2-2
1960—Raiders, 28-27 (NY)
Titans, 31-28 (O)
1961—Titans, 14-6 (O)
Titans, 23-12 (NY)
1962—Titans, 28-17 (O)
Titans, 31-21 (NY)
1963—Jets, 10-7 (NY)
Raiders, 49-26 (O)
1964—Jets, 35-13 (NY)
Raiders, 35-26 (O)
1965—Tie, 24-24 (NY)
Raiders, 24-14 (O)
1966—Raiders, 24-21 (NY)
Tie, 28-28 (O)
1967—Jets, 27-14 (NY)
Raiders, 38-29 (O)
1968—Raiders, 43-32 (O)
***Jets, 27-23 (NY)
1969—Raiders, 27-14 (NY)
1970—Raiders, 14-13 (NY)
1972—Raiders, 24-16 (O)
1977—Raiders, 28-27 (NY)
1979—Jets, 28-19 (NY)
1982—****Jets, 17-14 (LA)
1985—Raiders, 31-0 (LA)
1989—Raiders, 14-7 (NY)
1993—Raiders, 24-20 (LA)
1995—Raiders, 47-10 (NY)
1996—Raiders, 34-13 (NY)
1997—Jets 23-22 (NY)
1999—Raiders, 24-23 (O)
2000—Raiders, 31-7 (O)
2001—Jets, 24-22 (O)
*****Raiders, 38-24 (O)
2002—Raiders, 26-20 (O)
****Raiders, 30-10 (O)
2003—Jets, 27-24 (O) OT
2005—Jets, 26-10 (NY)
2006—Jets, 23-3 (NY)
2008—Raiders, 16-13 (O) OT
(RS Pts.—Raiders 851, Jets 760)
(PS Pts.—Raiders 105, Jets 78)
**Jets known as Titans prior to 1963*
***Franchise in Los Angeles from 1982-1994*
****AFL Championship*
*****AFC Second-Round Playoff*
******AFC First-Round Playoff*
N.Y. JETS vs. PHILADELPHIA
RS: Eagles lead series, 8-0
1973—Eagles, 24-23 (P)
1977—Eagles, 27-0 (P)
1978—Eagles, 17-9 (P)
1987—Eagles, 38-27 (NY)
1993—Eagles, 35-30 (NY)
1996—Eagles, 21-20 (NY)
2003—Eagles, 24-17 (P)
2007—Eagles, 16-9 (NY)
(RS Pts.—Eagles 202, Jets 135)
N.Y. JETS vs. PITTSBURGH
RS: Steelers lead series, 15-3
PS: Steelers lead series, 1-0
1970—Steelers, 21-17 (P)
1973—Steelers, 26-14 (P)
1975—Steelers, 20-7 (NY)
1977—Steelers, 23-20 (NY)
1978—Steelers, 28-17 (NY)
1981—Steelers, 38-10 (P)
1983—Steelers, 34-7 (NY)
1984—Steelers, 23-17 (NY)
1986—Steelers, 45-24 (NY)
1988—Jets, 24-20 (NY)
1989—Steelers, 13-0 (NY)
1990—Steelers, 24-7 (NY)
1992—Steelers, 27-10 (P)
2000—Steelers, 20-3 (NY)
2001—Steelers, 18-7 (P)
2003—Jets, 6-0 (NY)
2004—Steelers, 17-6 (P)
*Steelers, 20-17 (P) OT
2007—Jets, 19-16 (NY) OT
(RS Pts.—Steelers 413, Jets 215)
(PS Pts.—Steelers 20, Jets 17)
**AFC Divisional Playoff*
N.Y. JETS vs. *ST. LOUIS
RS: Rams lead series, 9-3
1970—Jets, 31-20 (LA)
1974—Rams, 20-13 (NY)
1980—Rams, 38-13 (LA)
1983—Jets, 27-24 (NY) OT
1986—Rams, 17-3 (NY)
1989—Rams, 38-14 (LA)
1992—Rams, 18-10 (LA)
1995—Rams, 23-20 (NY)
1998—Rams, 30-10 (StL)
2001—Rams, 34-14 (NY)
2004—Rams, 32-29 (StL) OT
2008—Jets, 47-3 (NY)
(RS Pts.—Rams 297, Jets 231)
**Franchise in Los Angeles prior to 1995*
***N.Y. JETS vs. **SAN DIEGO**
RS: Chargers lead series, 19-11-1
PS: Jets lead series, 1-0
1960—Chargers, 21-7 (NY)
Chargers, 50-43 (LA)
1961—Chargers, 25-10 (NY)
Chargers, 48-13 (SD)
1962—Chargers, 40-14 (SD)
Titans, 23-3 (NY)
1963—Chargers, 24-20 (SD)
Chargers, 53-7 (NY)
1964—Tie, 17-17 (NY)
Chargers, 38-3 (SD)
1965—Chargers, 34-9 (NY)
Chargers, 38-7 (SD)
1966—Jets, 17-16 (NY)

Chargers, 42-27 (SD)
1967—Jets, 42-31 (SD)
1968—Jets, 23-20 (NY)
Jets, 37-15 (SD)
1969—Chargers, 34-27 (SD)
1971—Chargers, 49-21 (SD)
1974—Jets, 27-14 (NY)
1975—Chargers, 24-16 (SD)
1983—Jets, 41-29 (SD)
1989—Jets, 20-17 (SD)
1990—Chargers, 39-3 (NY)
Chargers, 38-17 (SD)
1991—Jets, 24-3 (NY)
1994—Chargers, 21-6 (NY)
2002—Jets, 44-13 (SD)
2004—Jets, 34-28 (SD)
***Jets, 20-17 (SD) OT
2005—Chargers, 31-26 (NY)
2008—Chargers, 48-29 (SD)
(RS Pts.—Chargers 903, Jets 654)
(PS Pts.—Jets 20, Chargers 17)
Jets known as Titans prior to 1963
**Franchise in Los Angeles prior to 1961*
***AFC First-Round Playoff*

N.Y. JETS vs. SAN FRANCISCO
RS: 49ers lead series, 9-2
1971—49ers, 24-21 (NY)
1976—49ers, 17-6 (SF)
1980—49ers, 37-27 (NY)
1983—Jets, 27-13 (SF)
1986—49ers, 24-10 (SF)
1989—49ers, 23-10 (NY)
1992—49ers, 31-14 (NY)
1998—49ers, 36-30 (SF) OT
2001—49ers, 19-17 (NY)
2004—Jets, 22-14 (NY)
2008—49ers, 24-14 (SF)
(RS Pts.—49ers 262, Jets 198)

N.Y. JETS vs. SEATTLE
RS: Seahawks lead series, 9-8
1977—Seahawks, 17-0 (NY)
1978—Seahawks, 24-17 (NY)
1979—Seahawks, 30-7 (S)
1980—Seahawks, 27-17 (NY)
1981—Seahawks, 19-3 (NY)
Seahawks, 27-23 (S)
1983—Seahawks, 17-10 (NY)
1985—Jets, 17-14 (NY)
1986—Jets, 38-7 (S)
1987—Jets, 30-14 (NY)
1991—Seahawks, 20-13 (S)
1995—Jets, 16-10 (S)
1997—Jets, 41-3 (S)
1998—Jets, 32-31 (NY)
1999—Jets, 19-9 (NY)
2004—Jets, 37-14 (NY)
2008—Seahawks, 13-3 (S)
(RS Pts.—Jets 323, Seahawks 296)

N.Y. JETS vs. TAMPA BAY
RS: Jets lead series, 8-1
1976—Jets, 34-0 (NY)
1982—Jets, 32-17 (NY)
1984—Buccaneers, 41-21 (TB)
1985—Jets, 62-28 (NY)
1990—Jets, 16-14 (TB)
1991—Jets, 16-13 (NY)
1997—Jets, 31-0 (NY)
2000—Jets, 21-17 (TB)
2005—Jets, 14-12 (NY)
(RS Pts.—Jets 247, Buccaneers 142)

***N.Y. JETS vs. **TENNESSEE**
RS: Titans lead series, 21-16-1
PS: Titans lead series, 1-0
1960—Oilers, 27-21 (H)
Oilers, 42-28 (NY)
1961—Oilers, 49-13 (H)
Oilers, 48-21 (NY)
1962—Oilers, 56-17 (H)
Oilers, 44-10 (NY)
1963—Jets, 24-17 (NY)
Oilers, 31-27 (H)
1964—Jets, 24-21 (NY)
Oilers, 33-17 (H)
1965—Oilers, 27-21 (H)
Jets, 41-14 (NY)
1966—Jets, 52-13 (NY)
Oilers, 24-0 (H)
1967—Tie, 28-28 (NY)
1968—Jets, 20-14 (H)
Jets, 26-7 (NY)
1969—Jets, 26-17 (NY)
Jets, 34-26 (H)
1972—Oilers, 26-20 (H)
1974—Oilers, 27-22 (NY)
1977—Oilers, 20-0 (H)
1979—Oilers, 27-24 (H) OT
1980—Jets, 31-28 (NY) OT
1981—Jets, 33-17 (NY)
1984—Oilers, 31-20 (H)
1988—Jets, 45-3 (NY)
1990—Jets, 17-12 (H)
1991—Oilers, 23-20 (NY)
***Oilers, 17-10 (H)
1993—Oilers, 24-0 (H)
1994—Oilers, 24-10 (H)
1995—Oilers, 23-6 (H)
1996—Oilers, 35-10 (NY)
1998—Jets, 24-3 (T)
2003—Jets, 24-17 (NY)
2006—Jets, 23-16 (T)
2007—Titans, 10-6 (T)
2008—Jets, 34-13 (T)
(RS Pts.—Titans 917, Jets 819)
(PS Pts.—Titans 17, Jets 10)
Jets known as Titans prior to 1963
**Franchise in Houston prior to 1997; known as Oilers prior to 1999*
***AFC First-Round Playoff*

N.Y. JETS vs. WASHINGTON
RS: Redskins lead series, 8-1
1972—Redskins, 35-17 (NY)
1976—Redskins, 37-16 (NY)
1978—Redskins, 23-3 (W)
1987—Redskins, 17-16 (W)
1993—Jets, 3-0 (W)
1996—Redskins, 31-16 (W)
1999—Redskins, 27-20 (NY)
2003—Redskins, 16-13 (W)
2007—Redskins 23-20 (NY) OT
(RS Pts.—Redskins 209, Jets 124)

OAKLAND vs. ARIZONA
RS: Raiders lead series, 5-2;
See Arizona vs. Oakland

OAKLAND vs. ATLANTA
RS: Raiders lead series, 7-5;
See Atlanta vs. Oakland

OAKLAND vs. BALTIMORE
RS: Ravens lead series, 4-1
PS: Ravens lead series, 1-0;
See Baltimore vs. Oakland

OAKLAND vs. BUFFALO
RS: Raiders lead series, 19-16
PS: Bills lead series, 2-0;
See Buffalo vs. Oakland

OAKLAND vs. CAROLINA
RS: Series tied, 2-2;
See Carolina vs. Oakland

OAKLAND vs. CHICAGO
RS: Series tied, 6-6;
See Chicago vs. Oakland

OAKLAND vs. CINCINNATI
RS: Raiders lead series, 17-8
PS: Raiders lead series, 2-0;
See Cincinnati vs. Oakland

OAKLAND vs. CLEVELAND
RS: Raiders lead series, 10-7
PS: Raiders lead series, 2-0;
See Cleveland vs. Oakland

OAKLAND vs. DALLAS
RS: Raiders lead series, 6-3;
See Dallas vs. Oakland

OAKLAND vs. DENVER
RS: Raiders lead series, 55-40-2
PS: Series tied, 1-1;
See Denver vs. Oakland

OAKLAND vs. DETROIT
RS: Raiders lead series, 6-4;
See Detroit vs. Oakland

OAKLAND vs. GREEN BAY
RS: Series tied, 5-5
PS: Packers lead series, 1-0;
See Green Bay vs. Oakland

OAKLAND vs. HOUSTON
RS: Texans lead series, 3-1;
See Houston vs. Oakland

OAKLAND vs. INDIANAPOLIS
RS: Raiders lead series, 7-4
PS: Series tied, 1-1;
See Indianapolis vs. Oakland

OAKLAND vs. JACKSONVILLE
RS: Jaguars lead series, 3-1;
See Jacksonville vs. Oakland

OAKLAND vs. KANSAS CITY
RS: Chiefs lead series, 51-44-2
PS: Chiefs lead series, 2-1;
See Kansas City vs. Oakland

OAKLAND vs. MIAMI
RS: Raiders lead series, 16-12-1
PS: Raiders lead series, 3-1;
See Miami vs. Oakland

OAKLAND vs. MINNESOTA
RS: Raiders lead series, 8-4
PS: Raiders lead series, 1-0;
See Minnesota vs. Oakland

OAKLAND vs. NEW ENGLAND
RS: Series tied, 14-14-1
PS: Patriots lead series, 2-1;
See New England vs. Oakland

OAKLAND vs. NEW ORLEANS
RS: Series tied, 5-5-1;
See New Orleans vs. Oakland

OAKLAND vs. N.Y. GIANTS
RS: Raiders lead series, 7-3;
See N.Y. Giants vs. Oakland

OAKLAND vs. N.Y. JETS
RS: Raiders lead series, 20-14-2
PS: Series tied, 2-2;
See N.Y. Jets vs. Oakland

***OAKLAND vs. PHILADELPHIA**
RS: Eagles lead series, 5-4
PS: Raiders lead series, 1-0
1971—Raiders, 34-10 (O)
1976—Raiders, 26-7 (P)
1980—Eagles, 10-7 (P)
**Raiders, 27-10 (New Orleans)
1986—Eagles, 33-27 (LA) OT
1989—Eagles, 10-7 (P)
1992—Eagles, 31-10 (P)
1995—Raiders, 48-17 (O)
2001—Raiders, 20-10 (P)
2005—Eagles, 23-20 (P)
(RS Pts.—Raiders 199, Eagles 151)
(PS Pts.—Raiders 27, Eagles 10)
**Franchise in Los Angeles from 1982-1994*
***Super Bowl XV*

***OAKLAND vs. PITTSBURGH**
RS: Raiders lead series, 9-8
PS: Series tied, 3-3
1970—Raiders, 31-14 (O)
1972—Steelers, 34-28 (P)
**Steelers, 13-7 (P)
1973—Steelers, 17-9 (O)
**Raiders, 33-14 (O)
1974—Raiders, 17-0 (P)
***Steelers, 24-13 (O)
1975—***Steelers, 16-10 (P)
1976—Raiders, 31-28 (O)
***Raiders, 24-7 (O)
1977—Raiders, 16-7 (P)
1980—Raiders, 45-34 (P)
1981—Raiders, 30-27 (O)
1983—**Raiders, 38-10 (LA)
1984—Steelers, 13-7 (LA)
1990—Raiders, 20-3 (LA)
1994—Steelers, 21-3 (LA)
1995—Steelers, 29-10 (O)
2000—Steelers, 21-20 (P)
2002—Raiders, 30-17 (P)
2003—Steelers, 27-7 (P)
2004—Steelers, 24-21 (P)
2006—Raiders, 20-13 (O)
(RS Pts.—Raiders 345, Steelers 329)
(PS Pts.—Raiders 125, Steelers 84)
**Franchise in Los Angeles from 1982-1994*
***AFC Divisional Playoff*
****AFC Championship*

***OAKLAND vs. **ST. LOUIS**
RS: Raiders lead series, 7-4
1972—Raiders, 45-17 (O)
1977—Rams, 20-14 (LA)
1979—Raiders, 24-17 (LA)
1982—Raiders, 37-31 (LA Raiders)
1985—Raiders, 16-6 (LA Rams)
1988—Rams, 22-17 (LA Raiders)
1991—Raiders, 20-17 (LA Raiders)
1994—Raiders, 20-17 (LA Rams)
1997—Raiders, 35-17 (O)
2002—Rams, 28-13 (StL)
2006—Rams, 20-0 (O)
(RS Pts.—Raiders 241, Rams 212)
**Franchise in Los Angeles from 1982-1994*
***Franchise in Los Angeles prior to 1995*

***OAKLAND vs. **SAN DIEGO**
RS: Raiders lead series, 54-42-2
PS: Raiders lead series, 1-0
1960—Chargers, 52-28 (LA)
Chargers, 41-17 (O)
1961—Chargers, 44-0 (SD)
Chargers, 41-10 (O)
1962—Chargers, 42-33 (O)
Chargers, 31-21 (SD)
1963—Raiders, 34-33 (SD)
Raiders, 41-27 (O)
1964—Chargers, 31-17 (SD)
Raiders, 21-20 (O)
1965—Chargers, 17-6 (O)
Chargers, 24-14 (SD)
1966—Chargers, 29-20 (O)
Raiders, 41-19 (SD)
1967—Raiders, 51-10 (O)
Raiders, 41-21 (SD)
1968—Chargers, 23-14 (O)
Raiders, 34-27 (SD)
1969—Raiders, 24-12 (SD)
Raiders, 21-16 (O)
1970—Tie, 27-27 (SD)
Raiders, 20-17 (O)
1971—Raiders, 34-0 (SD)
Raiders, 34-33 (O)
1972—Tie, 17-17 (O)
Raiders, 21-19 (SD)
1973—Raiders, 27-17 (SD)
Raiders, 31-3 (O)
1974—Raiders, 14-10 (SD)
Raiders, 17-10 (O)
1975—Raiders, 6-0 (SD)
Raiders, 25-0 (O)
1976—Raiders, 27-17 (SD)
Raiders, 24-0 (O)
1977—Raiders, 24-0 (O)
Chargers, 12-7 (SD)
1978—Raiders, 21-20 (SD)
Chargers, 27-23 (O)
1979—Chargers, 30-10 (SD)
Raiders, 45-22 (O)
1980—Chargers, 30-24 (SD) OT
Raiders, 38-24 (O)
***Raiders, 34-27 (SD)
1981—Chargers, 55-21 (O)
Chargers, 23-10 (SD)
1982—Raiders, 28-24 (LA)
Raiders, 41-34 (SD)
1983—Raiders, 42-10 (SD)
Raiders, 30-14 (LA)
1984—Raiders, 33-30 (LA)
Raiders, 44-37 (SD)
1985—Raiders, 34-21 (LA)
Chargers, 40-34 (SD) OT
1986—Raiders, 17-13 (LA)
Raiders, 37-31 (SD) OT
1987—Chargers, 23-17 (LA)
Chargers, 16-14 (SD)
1988—Raiders, 24-13 (LA)
Raiders, 13-3 (SD)
1989—Raiders, 40-14 (LA)
Chargers, 14-12 (SD)
1990—Raiders, 24-9 (SD)
Raiders, 17-12 (LA)
1991—Chargers, 21-13 (LA)
Raiders, 9-7 (SD)
1992—Chargers, 27-3 (SD)
Chargers, 36-14 (LA)
1993—Chargers, 30-23 (LA)
Raiders, 12-7 (SD)
1994—Chargers, 26-24 (LA)
Raiders, 24-17 (SD)
1995—Raiders, 17-7 (O)
Chargers, 12-6 (SD)
1996—Chargers, 40-34 (O)
Raiders, 23-14 (SD)
1997—Chargers, 25-10 (O)
Raiders, 38-13 (SD)
1998—Raiders, 7-6 (O)
Raiders, 17-10 (SD)
1999—Raiders, 28-9 (O)
Chargers, 23-20 (SD)
2000—Raiders, 9-6 (O)
Raiders, 15-13 (SD)
2001—Raiders, 34-24 (O)
Raiders, 13-6 (SD)
2002—Chargers, 27-21 (O) OT
Raiders, 27-7 (SD)
2003—Raiders, 34-31 (O) OT
Chargers, 21-14 (SD)
2004—Chargers, 42-14 (SD)
Chargers, 23-17 (O)
2005—Chargers, 27-14 (O)
Chargers, 34-10 (SD)
2006—Chargers, 27-0 (O)
Chargers, 21-14 (SD)
2007—Chargers, 28-14 ((SD)
Chargers, 30-17 (O)
2008—Chargers, 28-18 (O)
Chargers, 34-7 (SD)
(RS Pts.—Raiders 2,150, Chargers 2,090)
(PS Pts.—Raiders 34, Chargers 27)
**Franchise in Los Angeles from 1982-1994*
***Franchise in Los Angeles prior to 1961*
****AFC Championship*

***OAKLAND vs. SAN FRANCISCO**
RS: Raiders lead series, 6-5
1970—49ers, 38-7 (O)
1974—Raiders, 35-24 (SF)
1979—Raiders, 23-10 (O)
1982—Raiders, 23-17 (SF)
1985—49ers, 34-10 (LA)
1988—Raiders, 9-3 (SF)
1991—Raiders, 12-6 (LA)
1994—49ers, 44-14 (SF)
2000—Raiders, 34-28 (SF) OT
2002—49ers, 23-20 (O) OT
2006—49ers, 34-20 (SF)
(RS Pts.—49ers 261, Raiders 207)
**Franchise in Los Angeles from 1982-1994*

***OAKLAND vs. SEATTLE**
RS: Raiders lead series, 27-23
PS: Series tied, 1-1
1977—Raiders, 44-7 (O)
1978—Seahawks, 27-7 (S)
Seahawks, 17-16 (O)
1979—Seahawks, 27-10 (S)
Seahawks, 29-24 (O)
1980—Raiders, 33-14 (O)
Raiders, 19-17 (S)
1981—Raiders, 20-10 (O)
Raiders, 32-31 (S)
1982—Raiders, 28-23 (LA)
1983—Seahawks, 38-36 (S)
Seahawks, 34-21 (LA)
**Raiders, 30-14 (LA)
1984—Raiders, 28-14 (LA)
Seahawks, 17-14 (S)
***Seahawks, 13-7 (S)
1985—Seahawks, 33-3 (S)
Raiders, 13-3 (LA)
1986—Raiders, 14-10 (LA)
Seahawks, 37-0 (S)
1987—Seahawks, 35-13 (LA)

Raiders, 37-14 (S)
1988—Seahawks, 35-27 (S)
Seahawks, 43-37 (LA)
1989—Seahawks, 24-20 (LA)
Seahawks, 23-17 (S)
1990—Raiders, 17-13 (S)
Raiders, 24-17 (LA)
1991—Raiders, 23-20 (S) OT
Raiders, 31-7 (LA)
1992—Raiders, 19-0 (S)
Raiders, 20-3 (LA)
1993—Raiders, 17-13 (S)
Raiders, 27-23 (LA)
1994—Seahawks, 38-9 (LA)
Raiders, 17-16 (S)
1995—Raiders, 34-14 (O)
Seahawks, 44-10 (S)
1996—Raiders, 27-21 (S)
Seahawks, 28-21 (O)
1997—Seahawks, 45-34 (S)
Seahawks, 22-21 (O)
1998—Raiders, 31-18 (S)
Raiders, 20-17 (O)
1999—Seahawks, 22-21 (S)
Raiders, 30-21 (O)
2000—Raiders, 31-3 (O)
Seahawks, 27-24 (S)
2001—Raiders, 38-14 (O)
Seahawks, 34-27 (S)
2002—Raiders, 31-17 (O)
2006—Seahawks, 16-0 (S)
(RS Pts.—Raiders 1,117, Seahawks 1,075)
(PS Pts.—Raiders 37, Seahawks 27)
Franchise in Los Angeles from 1982-1994
**AFC Championship*
***AFC First-Round Playoff*

***OAKLAND vs. TAMPA BAY**
RS: Raiders lead series, 6-1
PS: Buccaneers lead series, 1-0
1976—Raiders, 49-16 (O)
1981—Raiders, 18-16 (O)
1993—Raiders, 27-20 (LA)
1996—Buccaneers, 20-17 (TB) OT
1999—Raiders, 45-0 (O)
2002—**Buccaneers, 48-21 (San Diego)
2004—Raiders, 30-20 (O)
2008—Raiders, 31-24 (TB)
(RS Pts.—Raiders 217, Buccaneers 116)
(PS Pts.—Buccaneers 48, Raiders 21)
Franchise in Los Angeles from 1982-1994
**Super Bowl XXXVII*

***OAKLAND vs. **TENNESSEE**
RS: Raiders lead series, 23-18
PS: Raiders lead series, 4-0
1960—Oilers, 37-22 (O)
Raiders, 14-13 (H)
1961—Oilers, 55-0 (H)
Oilers, 47-16 (O)
1962—Oilers, 28-20 (O)
Oilers, 32-17 (H)
1963—Raiders, 24-13 (H)
Raiders, 52-49 (O)
1964—Oilers, 42-28 (H)
Raiders, 20-10 (O)
1965—Raiders, 21-17 (O)
Raiders, 33-21 (H)
1966—Oilers, 31-0 (H)
Raiders, 38-23 (O)
1967—Raiders, 19-7 (H)
***Raiders, 40-7 (O)
1968—Raiders, 24-15 (H)
1969—Raiders, 21-17 (O)
****Raiders, 56-7 (O)
1971—Raiders, 41-21 (O)
1972—Raiders, 34-0 (H)
1973—Raiders, 17-6 (H)
1975—Oilers, 27-26 (O)
1976—Raiders, 14-13 (H)
1977—Raiders, 34-29 (O)
1978—Raiders, 21-17 (O)
1979—Oilers, 31-17 (H)
1980—*****Raiders, 27-7 (O)
1981—Oilers, 17-16 (H)
1983—Raiders, 20-6 (LA)
1984—Raiders, 24-14 (H)
1986—Raiders, 28-17 (H)
1988—Oilers, 38-35 (H)
1989—Oilers, 23-7 (H)
1991—Oilers, 47-17 (H)
1994—Raiders, 17-14 (LA)
1997—Oilers, 24-21 (T) OT
1999—Titans, 21-14 (T)
2001—Titans, 13-10 (O)
2002—Raiders, 52-25 (O)
******Raiders, 41-24 (O)
2003—Titans, 25-20 (T)
2004—Raiders, 40-35 (O)
2005—Raiders, 34-25 (T)
2007—Titans, 13-9 (T)
(RS Pts.—Titans 958, Raiders 937)
(PS Pts.—Raiders 164, Titans 45)
Franchise in Los Angeles from 1982-1994
**Franchise in Houston prior to 1997; known as Oilers prior to 1999*
***AFL Championship*
****Inter-Divisional Playoff*
*****AFC First-Round Playoff*
******AFC Championship*

***OAKLAND vs. WASHINGTON**
RS: Raiders lead series, 7-3
PS: Raiders lead series, 1-0
1970—Raiders, 34-20 (O)
1975—Raiders, 26-23 (W) OT
1980—Raiders, 24-21 (O)
1983—Redskins, 37-35 (W)
**Raiders, 38-9 (Tampa)
1986—Redskins, 10-6 (W)
1989—Raiders, 37-24 (LA)
1992—Raiders, 21-20 (W)
1995—Raiders, 20-8 (W)
1998—Redskins, 29-19 (O)
2005—Raiders, 16-13 (W)
(RS Pts.—Raiders 238, Redskins 205)
(PS Pts.—Raiders 38, Redskins 9)
Franchise in Los Angeles from 1982-1994
**Super Bowl XVIII*

PHILADELPHIA vs. ARIZONA
RS: Series tied, 53-53-5
PS: Cardinals lead series, 2-1;
See Arizona vs. Philadelphia

PHILADELPHIA vs. ATLANTA
RS: Eagles lead series, 13-10-1
PS: Eagles lead series, 2-1;
See Atlanta vs. Philadelphia

PHILADELPHIA vs. BALTIMORE
RS: Series tied, 1-1-1;
See Baltimore vs. Philadelphia

PHILADELPHIA vs. BUFFALO
RS: Eagles lead series, 6-5;
See Buffalo vs. Philadelphia

PHILADELPHIA vs. CAROLINA
RS: Eagles lead series, 4-1
PS: Panthers lead series, 1-0;
See Carolina vs. Philadelphia

PHILADELPHIA vs. CHICAGO
RS: Bears lead series, 26-8-1
PS: Eagles lead series, 2-1;
See Chicago vs. Philadelphia

PHILADELPHIA vs. CINCINNATI
RS: Bengals lead series, 7-3-1;
See Cincinnati vs. Philadelphia

PHILADELPHIA vs. CLEVELAND
RS: Browns lead series, 31-15-1;
See Cleveland vs. Philadelphia

PHILADELPHIA vs. DALLAS
RS: Cowboys lead series, 53-43
PS: Cowboys lead series, 2-1;
See Dallas vs. Philadelphia

PHILADELPHIA vs. DENVER
RS: Eagles lead series, 6-4;
See Denver vs. Philadelphia

PHILADELPHIA vs. DETROIT
RS: Eagles lead series, 13-12-2
PS: Eagles lead series, 1-0;
See Detroit vs. Philadelphia

PHILADELPHIA vs. GREEN BAY
RS: Packers lead series, 23-13
PS: Eagles lead series, 2-0;
See Green Bay vs. Philadelphia

PHILADELPHIA vs. HOUSTON
RS: Eagles lead series, 2-0;
See Houston vs. Philadelphia

PHILADELPHIA vs. INDIANAPOLIS
RS: Colts lead series, 10-6;
See Indianapolis vs. Philadelphia

PHILADELPHIA vs. JACKSONVILLE
RS: Jaguars lead series, 3-0;
See Jacksonville vs. Philadelphia

PHILADELPHIA vs. KANSAS CITY
RS: Eagles lead series, 3-2;
See Kansas City vs. Philadelphia

PHILADELPHIA vs. MIAMI
RS: Dolphins lead series, 7-5;
See Miami vs. Philadelphia

PHILADELPHIA vs. MINNESOTA
RS: Vikings lead series, 11-9
PS: Eagles lead series, 3-0;
See Minnesota vs. Philadelphia

PHILADELPHIA vs. NEW ENGLAND
RS: Eagles lead series, 6-4
PS: Patriots lead series, 1-0;
See New England vs. Philadelphia

PHILADELPHIA vs. NEW ORLEANS
RS: Eagles lead series, 15-9
PS; Series tied, 1-1;
See New Orleans vs. Philadelphia

PHILADELPHIA vs. N.Y. GIANTS
RS: Giants lead series, 79-67-2
PS: Series tied, 2-2;
See N.Y. Giants vs. Philadelphia

PHILADELPHIA vs. N.Y. JETS
RS: Eagles lead series, 8-0;
See N.Y. Jets vs. Philadelphia

PHILADELPHIA vs. OAKLAND
RS: Eagles lead series, 5-4
PS: Raiders lead series, 1-0;
See Oakland vs. Philadelphia

PHILADELPHIA vs. *PITTSBURGH
RS: Eagles lead series, 46-27-3
PS: Eagles lead series, 1-0
1933—Eagles, 25-6 (Phila)
1934—Eagles, 17-0 (Pitt)
Pirates, 9-7 (Phila)
1935—Pirates, 17-7 (Phila)
Eagles, 17-6 (Pitt)
1936—Pirates, 17-0 (Pitt)
Pirates, 6-0 (Johnstown, Pa.)
1937—Pirates, 27-14 (Pitt)
Pirates, 16-7 (Pitt)
1938—Eagles, 27-7 (Buffalo)
Eagles, 14-7 (Charleston, W. Va.)
1939—Eagles, 17-14 (Phila)
Pirates, 24-12 (Pitt)
1940—Steelers, 7-3 (Pitt)
Eagles, 7-0 (Phila)
1941—Eagles, 10-7 (Pitt)
Tie, 7-7 (Phila)
1942—Eagles, 24-14 (Pitt)
Steelers, 14-0 (Phila)
1945—Eagles, 45-3 (Pitt)
Eagles, 30-6 (Phila)
1946—Steelers, 10-7 (Pitt)
Eagles, 10-7 (Phila)
1947—Steelers, 35-24 (Pitt)
Eagles, 21-0 (Phila)
**Eagles, 21-0 (Pitt)
1948—Eagles, 34-7 (Pitt)
Eagles, 17-0 (Phila)
1949—Eagles, 38-7 (Pitt)
Eagles, 34-17 (Phila)
1950—Eagles, 17-10 (Pitt)
Steelers, 9-7 (Phila)
1951—Eagles, 34-13 (Pitt)
Steelers, 17-13 (Phila)
1952—Eagles, 31-25 (Pitt)
Eagles, 26-21 (Phila)
1953—Eagles, 23-17 (Phila)
Eagles, 35-7 (Pitt)
1954—Eagles, 24-22 (Phila)
Steelers, 17-7 (Pitt)
1955—Steelers, 13-7 (Pitt)
Eagles, 24-0 (Phila)
1956—Eagles, 35-21 (Pitt)
Eagles, 14-7 (Phila)
1957—Steelers, 6-0 (Pitt)
Eagles, 7-6 (Phila)
1958—Steelers, 24-3 (Pitt)
Steelers, 31-24 (Phila)
1959—Eagles, 28-24 (Phila)
Steelers, 31-0 (Pitt)
1960—Eagles, 34-7 (Phila)
Steelers, 27-21 (Pitt)
1961—Eagles, 21-16 (Phila)
Eagles, 35-24 (Pitt)
1962—Steelers, 13-7 (Pitt)
Steelers, 26-17 (Phila)
1963—Tie, 21-21 (Phila)
Tie, 20-20 (Pitt)
1964—Eagles, 21-7 (Phila)
Eagles, 34-10 (Pitt)
1965—Steelers, 20-14 (Phila)
Eagles, 47-13 (Pitt)
1966—Eagles, 31-14 (Pitt)
Eagles, 27-23 (Phila)
1967—Eagles, 34-24 (Phila)
1968—Steelers, 6-3 (Pitt)
1969—Eagles, 41-27 (Phila)
1970—Eagles, 30-20 (Phila)
1974—Steelers, 27-0 (Pitt)
1979—Eagles, 17-14 (Phila)
1988—Eagles, 27-26 (Pitt)
1991—Eagles, 23-14 (Phila)
1994—Steelers, 14-3 (Pitt)
1997—Eagles, 23-20 (Phila)
2000—Eagles, 26-23 (Pitt) OT
2004—Steelers, 27-3 (Pitt)
2008—Eagles, 15-6 (Phila)
(RS Pts.—Eagles 1,429, Steelers 1,097)
(PS Pts.—Eagles 21, Steelers 0)
**Steelers known as Pirates prior to 1940*
***Division Playoff*

PHILADELPHIA vs. *ST. LOUIS
RS: Series tied, 17-17-1
PS: Rams lead series, 2-1
1937—Rams, 21-3 (P)
1939—Rams, 35-13 (Colorado Springs)
1940—Rams, 21-13 (C)
1942—Rams, 24-14 (Akron)
1944—Eagles, 26-13 (P)
1945—Eagles, 28-14 (P)
1946—Eagles, 25-14 (LA)
1947—Eagles, 14-7 (P)
1948—Tie, 28-28 (LA)
1949—Eagles, 38-14 (P)
**Eagles, 14-0 (LA)
1950—Eagles, 56-20 (P)
1955—Rams, 23-21 (P)
1956—Rams, 27-7 (LA)
1957—Rams, 17-13 (LA)
1959—Eagles, 23-20 (P)
1964—Rams, 20-10 (LA)
1967—Rams, 33-17 (LA)
1969—Rams, 23-17 (P)
1972—Rams, 34-3 (P)
1975—Rams, 42-3 (P)
1977—Rams, 20-0 (LA)
1978—Rams, 16-14 (P)
1983—Eagles, 13-9 (P)
1985—Rams, 17-6 (P)
1986—Eagles, 34-20 (P)
1988—Eagles, 30-24 (P)
1989—***Rams, 21-7 (P)
1990—Eagles, 27-21 (LA)
1995—Eagles, 20-9 (P)
1998—Eagles, 17-14 (P)
1999—Eagles, 38-31 (P)
2001—Rams, 20-17 (P) OT
****Rams, 29-24 (StL)
2002—Eagles, 10-3 (P)
2004—Rams, 20-7 (StL)
2005—Eagles, 17-16 (StL)
2008—Eagles, 38-3 (P)
(RS Pts.—Rams 693, Eagles 660)
(PS Pts.—Rams 50, Eagles 45)
**Franchise in Los Angeles prior to 1995 and in Cleveland prior to 1946*
***NFL Championship*
****NFC First-Round Playoff*
*****NFC Championship*

PHILADELPHIA vs. SAN DIEGO
RS: Chargers lead series, 5-4
1974—Eagles, 13-7 (SD)
1980—Chargers, 22-21 (SD)
1985—Chargers, 20-14 (SD)
1986—Eagles, 23-7 (P)
1989—Chargers, 20-17 (SD)
1995—Chargers, 27-21 (P)
1998—Chargers, 13-10 (SD)
2001—Eagles, 24-14 (P)
2005—Eagles, 20-17 (P)
(RS Pts.—Eagles 163, Chargers 147)

PHILADELPHIA vs. SAN FRANCISCO
RS: 49ers lead series, 16-10-1
PS: 49ers lead series, 1-0
1951—Eagles, 21-14 (P)
1953—49ers, 31-21 (SF)
1956—Tie, 10-10 (P)
1958—49ers, 30-24 (P)
1959—49ers, 24-14 (SF)
1964—49ers, 28-24 (P)
1966—Eagles, 35-34 (SF)
1967—49ers, 28-27 (P)
1969—49ers, 14-13 (SF)
1971—49ers, 31-3 (P)
1973—49ers, 38-28 (SF)
1975—Eagles, 27-17 (P)
1983—Eagles, 22-17 (SF)
1984—49ers, 21-9 (P)
1985—49ers, 24-13 (SF)
1989—49ers, 38-28 (P)
1991—49ers, 23-7 (P)
1992—49ers, 20-14 (SF)
1993—Eagles, 37-34 (SF) OT
1994—Eagles, 40-8 (SF)
1996—*49ers, 14-0 (SF)
1997—49ers, 24-12 (P)
2001—49ers, 13-3 (SF)
2002—Eagles, 38-17 (SF)
2003—49ers, 31-28 (P) OT
2005—Eagles, 42-3 (P)
2006—Eagles, 38-24 (SF)
2008—Eagles, 40-26 (SF)
(RS Pts.—49ers 622, Eagles 618)
(PS Pts.—49ers 14, Eagles 0)
**NFC First-Round Playoff*

PHILADELPHIA vs. SEATTLE
RS: Eagles lead series, 7-5
1976—Eagles, 27-10 (P)
1980—Eagles, 27-20 (S)
1986—Seahawks, 24-20 (S)
1989—Eagles, 31-7 (P)
1992—Eagles, 20-17 (S) OT
1995—Seahawks, 26-14 (S)
1998—Seahawks, 38-0 (P)
2001—Eagles, 27-3 (S)
2002—Eagles, 27-20 (S)
2005—Seahawks, 42-0 (P)
2007—Seahawks, 28-24 (P)
2008—Eagles, 26-7 (S)
(RS Pts.—Eagles 243, Seahawks 242)

PHILADELPHIA vs. TAMPA BAY
RS: Series tied, 5-5
PS: Series tied, 2-2
1977—Eagles, 13-3 (P)
1979—*Buccaneers, 24-17 (TB)
1981—Eagles, 20-10 (P)
1988—Eagles, 41-14 (TB)
1991—Buccaneers, 14-13 (TB)
1995—Buccaneers, 21-6 (P)
1999—Buccaneers, 19-5 (P)
2000—**Eagles, 21-3 (P)
2001—Eagles, 17-13 (TB)
**Eagles, 31-9 (P)
2002—Eagles, 20-10 (P)
***Buccaneers, 27-10 (P)
2003—Buccaneers, 17-0 (P)
2006—Buccaneers, 23-21 (TB)

(RS Pts.—Eagles 156, Buccaneers 144)
(PS Pts.—Eagles 79, Buccaneers 63)
NFC Divisional Playoff
***NFC First-Round Playoff*
****NFC Championship*

PHILADELPHIA vs. *TENNESSEE
RS: Eagles lead series, 6-3
1972—Eagles, 18-17 (H)
1979—Eagles, 26-20 (H)
1982—Eagles, 35-14 (P)
1988—Eagles, 32-23 (P)
1991—Eagles, 13-6 (H)
1994—Eagles, 21-6 (P)
2000—Titans, 15-13 (P)
2002—Titans, 27-24 (T)
2006—Titans, 31-13 (P)
(RS Pts.—Eagles 195, Titans 159)
Franchise in Houston prior to 1997; known as Oilers prior to 1999

PHILADELPHIA vs. *WASHINGTON
RS: Redskins lead series, 77-65-5
PS: Redskins lead series, 1-0
1934—Redskins, 6-0 (B)
Redskins, 14-7 (P)
1935—Eagles, 7-6 (B)
1936—Redskins, 26-3 (P)
Redskins, 17-7 (B)
1937—Eagles, 14-0 (W)
Redskins, 10-7 (P)
1938—Redskins, 26-23 (P)
Redskins, 20-14 (W)
1939—Redskins, 7-0 (P)
Redskins, 7-6 (W)
1940—Redskins, 34-17 (P)
Redskins, 13-6 (W)
1941—Redskins, 21-17 (P)
Redskins, 20-14 (W)
1942—Redskins, 14-10 (P)
Redskins, 30-27 (W)
1944—Tie, 31-31 (P)
Eagles, 37-7 (W)
1945—Redskins, 24-14 (W)
Eagles, 16-0 (P)
1946—Eagles, 28-24 (W)
Redskins, 27-10 (P)
1947—Eagles, 45-42 (P)
Eagles, 38-14 (W)
1948—Eagles, 45-0 (W)
Eagles, 42-21 (P)
1949—Eagles, 49-14 (P)
Eagles, 44-21 (W)
1950—Eagles, 35-3 (P)
Eagles, 33-0 (W)
1951—Redskins, 27-23 (P)
Eagles, 35-21 (W)
1952—Eagles, 38-20 (P)
Redskins, 27-21 (W)
1953—Tie, 21-21 (P)
Redskins, 10-0 (W)
1954—Eagles, 49-21 (W)
Eagles, 41-33 (P)
1955—Redskins, 31-30 (P)
Redskins, 34-21 (W)
1956—Eagles, 13-9 (P)
Redskins, 19-17 (W)
1957—Eagles, 21-12 (P)
Redskins, 42-7 (W)
1958—Redskins, 24-14 (P)
Redskins, 20-0 (W)
1959—Eagles, 30-23 (P)
Eagles, 34-14 (W)
1960—Eagles, 19-13 (P)
Eagles, 38-28 (W)
1961—Eagles, 14-7 (P)
Eagles, 27-24 (W)
1962—Redskins, 27-21 (P)
Eagles, 37-14 (W)
1963—Eagles, 37-24 (W)
Redskins, 13-10 (P)
1964—Redskins, 35-20 (W)
Redskins, 21-10 (P)
1965—Redskins, 23-21 (W)
Eagles, 21-14 (P)
1966—Redskins, 27-13 (P)
Eagles, 37-28 (W)
1967—Eagles, 35-24 (P)
Tie, 35-35 (W)
1968—Redskins, 17-14 (W)
Redskins, 16-10 (P)
1969—Tie, 28-28 (W)
Redskins, 34-29 (P)
1970—Redskins, 33-21 (P)
Redskins, 24-6 (W)
1971—Tie, 7-7 (W)
Redskins, 20-13 (P)
1972—Redskins, 14-0 (W)
Redskins, 23-7 (P)
1973—Redskins, 28-7 (P)
Redskins, 38-20 (W)
1974—Redskins, 27-20 (P)
Redskins, 26-7 (W)
1975—Eagles, 26-10 (P)
Eagles, 26-3 (W)
1976—Redskins, 20-17 (P) OT
Redskins, 24-0 (W)
1977—Redskins, 23-17 (W)
Redskins, 17-14 (P)
1978—Redskins, 35-30 (W)
Eagles, 17-10 (P)
1979—Eagles, 28-17 (P)
Redskins, 17-7 (W)
1980—Eagles, 24-14 (P)
Eagles, 24-0 (W)
1981—Eagles, 36-13 (P)
Redskins, 15-13 (W)
1982—Redskins, 37-34 (P) OT
Redskins, 13-9 (W)
1983—Redskins, 23-13 (P)
Redskins, 28-24 (W)
1984—Redskins, 20-0 (W)
Eagles, 16-10 (P)
1985—Eagles, 19-6 (W)
Redskins, 17-12 (P)
1986—Redskins, 41-14 (W)
Redskins, 21-14 (P)
1987—Redskins, 34-24 (W)
Eagles, 31-27 (P)
1988—Redskins, 17-10 (W)
Redskins, 20-19 (P)
1989—Eagles, 42-37 (W)
Redskins, 10-3 (P)
1990—Redskins, 13-7 (W)
Eagles, 28-14 (P)
**Redskins, 20-6 (P)
1991—Redskins, 23-0 (W)
Eagles, 24-22 (P)
1992—Redskins, 16-12 (W)
Eagles, 17-13 (P)
1993—Eagles, 34-31 (P)
Eagles, 17-14 (W)
1994—Eagles, 21-17 (P)
Eagles, 31-29 (W)
1995—Eagles, 37-34 (P) OT
Eagles, 14-7 (W)
1996—Eagles, 17-14 (W)
Redskins, 26-21 (P)
1997—Eagles, 24-10 (P)
Redskins, 35-32 (W)
1998—Eagles, 17-12 (P)
Redskins, 28-3 (W)
1999—Eagles, 35-28 (P)
Redskins, 20-17 (W) OT
2000—Redskins, 17-14 (P)
Eagles, 23-20 (W)
2001—Redskins, 13-3 (P)
Eagles, 20-6 (W)
2002—Eagles, 37-7 (W)
Eagles, 34-21 (P)
2003—Eagles, 27-25 (P)
Eagles, 31-7 (W)
2004—Eagles, 28-6 (P)
Eagles, 17-14 (W)
2005—Redskins, 17-10 (W)
Redskins, 31-20 (P)
2006—Eagles, 27-3 (P)
Eagles, 21-19 (W)
2007—Redskins, 20-12 (P)
Eagles, 33-25 (W)
2008—Redskins, 23-17 (P)
Redskins, 10-3 (W)
(RS Pts.—Eagles 2,993, Redskins 2,868)
(PS Pts.—Redskins 20, Eagles 6)
Franchise in Boston prior to 1937
***NFC First-Round Playoff*

PITTSBURGH vs. ARIZONA
RS: Steelers lead series, 31-23-3
PS: Steelers lead series, 1-0;
See Arizona vs. Pittsburgh

PITTSBURGH vs. ATLANTA
RS: Steelers lead series, 11-2-1;
See Atlanta vs. Pittsburgh

PITTSBURGH vs. BALTIMORE
RS: Steelers lead series, 16-10
PS: Steelers lead series, 2-0;
See Baltimore vs. Pittsburgh

PITTSBURGH vs. BUFFALO
RS: Steelers lead series, 11-8
PS: Steelers lead series, 2-1;
See Buffalo vs. Pittsburgh

PITTSBURGH vs. CAROLINA
RS: Steelers lead series, 3-1;
See Carolina vs. Pittsburgh

PITTSBURGH vs. CHICAGO
RS: Bears lead series, 16-7-1;
See Chicago vs. Pittsburgh

PITTSBURGH vs. CINCINNATI
RS: Steelers lead series, 47-30
PS: Steelers lead series, 1-0;
See Cincinnati vs. Pittsburgh

PITTSBURGH vs. CLEVELAND
RS: Steelers lead series, 57-55
PS: Steelers lead series, 2-0;
See Cleveland vs. Pittsburgh

PITTSBURGH vs. DALLAS
RS: Cowboys lead series, 14-13
PS: Steelers lead series, 2-1;
See Dallas vs. Pittsburgh

PITTSBURGH vs. DENVER
RS: Broncos lead series, 13-6-1

PS: Series tied, 3-3;
See Denver vs. Pittsburgh
PITTSBURGH vs. DETROIT
RS: Series tied, 14-14-1;
See Detroit vs. Pittsburgh
PITTSBURGH vs. GREEN BAY
RS: Packers lead series, 18-13;
See Green Bay vs. Pittsburgh
PITTSBURGH vs. HOUSTON
RS: Steelers lead series 2-1;
See Houston vs. Pittsburgh
PITTSBURGH vs. INDIANAPOLIS
RS: Steelers lead series, 13-6
PS: Steelers lead series, 5-0;
See Indianapolis vs. Pittsburgh
PITTSBURGH vs. JACKSONVILLE
RS: Jaguars lead series, 11-9
PS: Jaguars lead series, 1-0;
See Jacksonville vs. Pittsburgh
PITTSBURGH vs. KANSAS CITY
RS: Steelers lead series, 17-8
PS: Chiefs lead series, 1-0;
See Kansas City vs. Pittsburgh
PITTSBURGH vs. MIAMI
RS: Steelers lead series, 10-9
PS: Dolphins lead series, 2-1;
See Miami vs. Pittsburgh
PITTSBURGH vs. MINNESOTA
RS: Vikings lead series, 8-6
PS: Steelers lead series, 1-0;
See Minnesota vs. Pittsburgh
PITTSBURGH vs. NEW ENGLAND
RS: Steelers lead series, 13-7
PS: Patriots lead series, 3-1;
See New England vs. Pittsburgh
PITTSBURGH vs. NEW ORLEANS
RS: Steelers lead series, 7-6;
See New Orleans vs. Pittsburgh
PITTSBURGH vs. N.Y. GIANTS
RS: Giants lead series, 44-28-3;
See N.Y. Giants vs. Pittsburgh
PITTSBURGH vs. N.Y. JETS
RS: Steelers lead series, 15-3
PS: Steelers lead series, 1-0;
See N.Y. Jets vs. Pittsburgh
PITTSBURGH vs. OAKLAND
RS: Raiders lead series, 9-8
PS: Series tied, 3-3;
See Oakland vs. Pittsburgh
PITTSBURGH vs. PHILADELPHIA
RS: Eagles lead series, 46-27-3
PS: Eagles lead series, 1-0;
See Philadelphia vs. Pittsburgh
***PITTSBURGH vs. **ST. LOUIS**
RS: Rams lead series, 15-6-2
PS: Steelers lead series, 1-0
1938—Rams, 13-7 (New Orleans)
1939—Tie, 14-14 (C)
1941—Rams, 17-14 (Akron)
1947—Rams, 48-7 (P)
1948—Rams, 31-14 (LA)
1949—Tie, 7-7 (P)
1952—Rams, 28-14 (LA)
1955—Rams, 27-26 (LA)
1956—Steelers, 30-13 (P)
1961—Rams, 24-14 (LA)
1964—Rams, 26-14 (P)
1968—Rams, 45-10 (LA)
1971—Rams, 23-14 (P)
1975—Rams, 10-3 (LA)
1978—Rams, 10-7 (LA)
1979—***Steelers, 31-19 (Pasadena)
1981—Steelers, 24-0 (P)
1984—Steelers, 24-14 (P)
1987—Rams, 31-21 (LA)
1990—Steelers, 41-10 (P)
1993—Rams, 27-0 (LA)
1996—Steelers, 42-6 (P)
2003—Rams, 33-21 (P)
2007—Steelers, 41-24 (StL)
(RS Pts.—Rams 481, Steelers 409)
(PS Pts.—Steelers 31, Rams 19)
**Steelers known as Pirates prior to 1940*
***Franchise in Los Angeles prior to 1995 and in Cleveland prior to 1946*
****Super Bowl XIV*
PITTSBURGH vs. SAN DIEGO
RS: Steelers lead series, 20-6
PS: Chargers lead series, 2-1
1971—Steelers, 21-17 (P)
1972—Steelers, 24-2 (SD)
1973—Steelers, 38-21 (P)
1975—Steelers, 37-0 (SD)
1976—Steelers, 23-0 (P)
1977—Steelers, 10-9 (SD)
1979—Chargers, 35-7 (SD)
1980—Chargers, 26-17 (SD)
1982—*Chargers, 31-28 (P)
1983—Steelers, 26-3 (P)
1984—Steelers, 52-24 (P)
1985—Chargers, 54-44 (SD)
1987—Steelers, 20-16 (SD)
1988—Chargers, 20-14 (SD)
1989—Steelers, 20-17 (P)
1990—Steelers, 36-14 (P)
1991—Steelers, 26-20 (P)
1992—Steelers, 23-6 (SD)
1993—Steelers,.16-3 (P)
1994—Chargers, 37-34 (SD)
**Chargers, 17-13 (P)
1995—Steelers, 31-16 (P)
1996—Steelers, 16-3 (P)
2000—Steelers, 34-21 (SD)
2003—Steelers, 40-24 (P)
2005—Steelers, 24-22 (SD)
2006—Chargers, 23-13 (SD)
2008—Steelers, 11-10 (P)
***Steelers, 35-24 (P)
(RS Pts.—Steelers 657, Chargers 443)
(PS Pts.—Steelers 76, Chargers 72)
**AFC First-Round Playoff*
***AFC Championship*
****AFC Divisional Playoff*
PITTSBURGH vs. SAN FRANCISCO
RS: 49ers lead series, 10-9
1951—49ers, 28-24 (P)
1952—Steelers, 24-7 (SF)
1954—49ers, 31-3 (SF)
1958—49ers, 23-20 (SF)
1961—Steelers, 20-10 (P)
1965—49ers, 27-17 (SF)
1968—49ers, 45-28 (P)
1973—Steelers, 37-14 (SF)
1977—Steelers, 27-0 (P)
1978—Steelers, 24-7 (SF)
1981—49ers, 17-14 (P)
1984—Steelers, 20-17 (SF)
1987—Steelers, 30-17 (P)
1990—49ers, 27-7 (SF)
1993—49ers, 24-13 (P)
1996—49ers, 25-15 (P)
1999—Steelers, 27-6 (SF)
2003—49ers, 30-14 (SF)
2007—Steelers, 37-16 (P)
(RS Pts.—Steelers 401, 49ers 371)
PITTSBURGH vs. SEATTLE
RS: Seahawks lead series, 8-7
PS: Steelers lead series, 1-0
1977—Steelers, 30-20 (P)
1978—Steelers, 21-10 (P)
1981—Seahawks, 24-21 (S)
1982—Seahawks, 16-0 (S)
1983—Steelers, 27-21 (S)
1986—Seahawks, 30-0 (S)
1987—Steelers, 13-9 (P)
1991—Seahawks, 27-7 (P)
1992—Steelers, 20-14 (P)
1993—Seahawks, 16-6 (S)
1994—Seahawks, 30-13 (S)
1998—Steelers, 13-10 (P)
1999—Seahawks, 29-10 (P)
2003—Seahawks, 23-16 (S)
2005—*Steelers, 21-10 (Detroit)
2007—Steelers, 21-0 (P)
(RS Pts.—Seahawks 279, Steelers 218)
(PS Pts.—Steelers 21, Seahawks 10)
**Super Bowl XL*
PITTSBURGH vs. TAMPA BAY
RS: Steelers lead series, 7-1
1976—Steelers, 42-0 (P)
1980—Steelers, 24-21 (TB)
1983—Steelers, 17-12 (P)
1989—Steelers, 31-22 (TB)
1998—Buccaneers, 16-3 (TB)
2001—Steelers, 17-10 (TB)
2002—Steelers, 17-7 (TB)
2006—Steelers, 20-3 (P)
(RS Pts.—Steelers 171, Buccaneers 91)
PITTSBURGH vs. *TENNESSEE
RS: Steelers lead series, 38-29
PS: Steelers lead series, 3-1
1970—Oilers, 19-7 (P)
Steelers, 7-3 (H)
1971—Steelers, 23-16 (P)
Oilers, 29-3 (H)
1972—Steelers, 24-7 (P)
Steelers, 9-3 (H)
1973—Steelers, 36-7 (H)
Steelers, 33-7 (P)
1974—Steelers, 13-7 (H)
Oilers, 13-10 (P)
1975—Steelers, 24-17 (P)
Steelers, 32-9 (H)
1976—Steelers, 32-16 (P)
Steelers, 21-0 (H)
1977—Oilers, 27-10 (H)
Steelers, 27-10 (P)
1978—Oilers, 24-17 (P)
Steelers, 13-3 (H)
**Steelers, 34-5 (P)
1979—Steelers, 38-7 (P)
Oilers, 20-17 (H)
**Steelers, 27-13 (P)
1980—Steelers, 31-17 (P)
Oilers, 6-0 (H)
1981—Steelers, 26-13 (P)
Oilers, 21-20 (H)
1982—Steelers, 24-10 (H)
1983—Steelers, 40-28 (H)
Steelers, 17-10 (P)

1984—Steelers, 35-7 (P)
Oilers, 23-20 (H) OT
1985—Steelers, 20-0 (P)
Steelers, 30-7 (H)
1986—Steelers, 22-16 (H) OT
Steelers, 21-10 (P)
1987—Oilers, 23-3 (P)
Oilers, 24-16 (H)
1988—Oilers, 34-14 (P)
Steelers, 37-34 (H)
1989—Oilers, 27-0 (H)
Oilers, 23-16 (P)
***Steelers, 26-23 (H) OT
1990—Steelers, 20-9 (P)
Oilers, 34-14 (H)
1991—Steelers, 26-14 (P)
Oilers, 31-6 (H)
1992—Steelers, 29-24 (H)
Steelers, 21-20 (P)
1993—Oilers, 23-3 (H)
Oilers, 26-17 (P)
1994—Steelers, 30-14 (P)
Steelers, 12-9 (H) OT
1995—Steelers, 34-17 (H)
Steelers, 21-7 (P)
1996—Steelers, 30-16 (P)
Oilers, 23-13 (H)
1997—Steelers, 37-24 (P)
Oilers, 16-6 (T)
1998—Oilers, 41-31 (P)
Oilers, 23-14 (T)
1999—Titans, 16-10 (T)
Titans, 47-36 (P)
2000—Titans, 23-20 (P)
Titans, 9-7 (T)
2001—Steelers, 34-7 (P)
Steelers, 34-24 (T)
2002—Titans, 31-23 (T)
****Titans, 34-31 (T) OT
2003—Titans, 30-13 (P)
2005—Steelers, 34-7 (P)
2008—Titans, 31-14 (T)
(RS Pts.—Steelers 1,377, Titans 1,173)
(PS Pts.—Steelers 118, Titans 75)
Franchise in Houston prior to 1997; known as Oilers prior to 1999
***AFC Championship*
****AFC First-Round Playoff*
*****AFC Divisional Playoff*

***PITTSBURGH vs. **WASHINGTON**
RS: Redskins lead series, 42-31-3
1933—Redskins, 21-6 (P)
Pirates, 16-14 (B)
1934—Redskins, 7-0 (P)
Redskins, 39-0 (B)
1935—Pirates, 6-0 (P)
Redskins, 13-3 (B)
1936—Pirates, 10-0 (P)
Redskins, 30-0 (B)
1937—Redskins, 34-20 (W)
Pirates, 21-13 (P)
1938—Redskins, 7-0 (P)
Redskins, 15-0 (W)
1939—Redskins, 44-14 (W)
Redskins, 21-14 (P)
1940—Redskins, 40-10 (P)
Redskins, 37-10 (W)
1941—Redskins, 24-20 (P)
Redskins, 23-3 (W)
1942—Redskins, 28-14 (W)
Redskins, 14-0 (P)
1945—Redskins, 14-0 (P)
Redskins, 24-0 (W)
1946—Tie, 14-14 (W)
Steelers, 14-7 (P)
1947—Redskins, 27-26 (W)
Steelers, 21-14 (P)
1948—Redskins, 17-14 (W)
Steelers, 10-7 (P)
1949—Redskins, 27-14 (P)
Redskins, 27-14 (W)
1950—Steelers, 26-7 (W)
Redskins, 24-7 (P)
1951—Redskins, 22-7 (P)
Steelers, 20-10 (W)
1952—Redskins, 28-24 (P)
Steelers, 24-23 (W)
1953—Redskins, 17-9 (P)
Steelers, 14-13 (W)
1954—Steelers, 37-7 (P)
Redskins, 17-14 (W)
1955—Redskins, 23-14 (P)
Redskins, 28-17 (W)
1956—Steelers, 30-13 (P)
Steelers, 23-0 (W)
1957—Steelers, 28-7 (P)
Redskins, 10-3 (W)
1958—Steelers, 24-16 (P)
Tie, 14-14 (W)
1959—Redskins, 23-17 (P)
Steelers, 27-6 (W)
1960—Tie, 27-27 (W)
Steelers, 22-10 (P)
1961—Steelers, 20-0 (P)
Steelers, 30-14 (W)
1962—Steelers, 23-21 (P)
Steelers, 27-24 (W)
1963—Steelers, 38-27 (P)
Steelers, 34-28 (W)
1964—Redskins, 30-0 (P)
Steelers, 14-7 (W)
1965—Redskins, 31-3 (P)
Redskins, 35-14 (W)
1966—Redskins, 33-27 (P)
Redskins, 24-10 (W)
1967—Redskins, 15-10 (P)
1968—Redskins, 16-13 (W)
1969—Redskins, 14-7 (P)
1973—Steelers, 21-16 (P)
1979—Steelers, 38-7 (P)
1985—Redskins, 30-23 (P)
1988—Redskins, 30-29 (W)
1991—Redskins, 41-14 (P)
1997—Steelers, 14-13 (P)
2000—Steelers, 24-3 (P)
2004—Steelers, 16-7 (P)
2008—Steelers, 23-6 (W)
(RS Pts.—Redskins 1,419, Steelers 1,194)
**Steelers known as Pirates prior to 1940*
***Franchise in Boston prior to 1937*

ST. LOUIS vs. ARIZONA
RS: Rams lead series, 30-28-2
PS: Rams lead series, 1-0;
See Arizona vs. St. Louis

ST. LOUIS vs. ATLANTA
RS: Rams lead series, 47-25-2
PS: Falcons lead series, 1-0;
See Atlanta vs. St. Louis

ST. LOUIS vs. BALTIMORE
RS: Series tied, 2-2;
See Baltimore vs. St. Louis

ST. LOUIS vs. BUFFALO
RS: Bills lead series, 6-4;
See Buffalo vs. St. Louis

ST. LOUIS vs. CAROLINA
RS: Panthers lead series, 10-7
PS: Panthers lead series, 1-0;
See Carolina vs. St. Louis

ST. LOUIS vs. CHICAGO
RS: Bears lead series, 49-34-3
PS: Series tied, 1-1;
See Chicago vs. St. Louis

ST. LOUIS vs. CINCINNATI
RS: Bengals lead series, 6-5;
See Cincinnati vs. St. Louis

ST. LOUIS vs. CLEVELAND
RS: Series tied, 9-9
PS: Browns lead series, 2-1;
See Cleveland vs. St. Louis

ST. LOUIS vs. DALLAS
RS: Rams lead series, 11-10
PS: Series tied, 4-4;
See Dallas vs. St. Louis

ST. LOUIS vs. DENVER
RS: Rams lead series, 6-5;
See Denver vs. St. Louis

ST. LOUIS vs. DETROIT
RS: Rams lead series, 41-37-1
PS: Lions lead series, 1-0;
See Detroit vs. St. Louis

ST. LOUIS vs. GREEN BAY
RS: Rams lead series, 45-41-2
PS: Series tied, 1-1;
See Green Bay vs. St. Louis

ST. LOUIS vs. HOUSTON
RS: Rams lead series, 1-0;
See Houston vs. St. Louis

ST. LOUIS vs. INDIANAPOLIS
RS: Colts lead series, 22-17-2;
See Indianapolis vs. St. Louis

ST. LOUIS vs. JACKSONVILLE
RS: Rams lead series, 2-0;
See Jacksonville vs. St. Louis

ST. LOUIS vs. KANSAS CITY
RS: Chiefs lead series; 5-4;
See Kansas City vs. St. Louis

ST. LOUIS vs. MIAMI
RS: Dolphins lead series, 9-2;
See Miami vs. St. Louis

ST. LOUIS vs. MINNESOTA
RS: Vikings lead series, 17-14-2
PS: Vikings lead series, 5-2;
See Minnesota vs. St. Louis

ST. LOUIS vs. NEW ENGLAND
RS: Series tied, 5-5
PS: Patriots lead series, 1-0;
See New England vs. St. Louis

ST. LOUIS vs. NEW ORLEANS
RS: Rams lead series, 38-29
PS: Saints lead series, 1-0;
See New Orleans vs. St. Louis

ST. LOUIS vs. N.Y. GIANTS
RS: Rams lead series, 25-13
PS: Series tied, 1-1;
See N.Y. Giants vs. St. Louis

ST. LOUIS vs. N.Y. JETS
RS: Rams lead series, 9-3;
See N.Y. Jets vs. St. Louis

ST. LOUIS vs. OAKLAND
RS: Raiders lead series, 7-4;
See Oakland vs. St. Louis
ST. LOUIS vs. PHILADELPHIA
RS: Series tied, 17-17-1
PS: Rams lead series, 2-1;
See Philadelphia vs. St. Louis
ST. LOUIS vs. PITTSBURGH
RS: Rams lead series, 15-6-2
PS: Steelers lead series, 1-0;
See Pittsburgh vs. St. Louis
***ST. LOUIS vs. SAN DIEGO**
RS: Rams lead series, 5-4
1970—Rams, 37-10 (LA)
1975—Rams, 13-10 (SD) OT
1979—Chargers, 40-16 (LA)
1988—Chargers, 38-24 (LA)
1991—Rams, 30-24 (LA)
1994—Chargers, 31-17 (SD)
2000—Rams, 57-31 (StL)
2002—Rams, 28-24 (StL)
2006—Chargers, 38-24 (SD)
(RS Pts.—Rams 246, Chargers 246)
**Franchise in Los Angeles prior to 1995*
***ST. LOUIS vs. SAN FRANCISCO**
RS: Rams lead series, 60-56-2
PS: 49ers lead series, 1-0
1950—Rams, 35-14 (SF)
Rams, 28-21 (LA)
1951—49ers, 44-17 (SF)
Rams, 23-16 (LA)
1952—Rams, 35-9 (LA)
Rams, 34-21 (SF)
1953—49ers, 31-30 (SF)
49ers, 31-27 (LA)
1954—Tie, 24-24 (LA)
Rams, 42-34 (SF)
1955—Rams, 23-14 (SF)
Rams, 27-14 (LA)
1956—49ers, 33-30 (SF)
Rams, 30-6 (LA)
1957—49ers, 23-20 (SF)
Rams, 37-24 (LA)
1958—Rams, 33-3 (SF)
Rams, 56-7 (LA)
1959—49ers, 34-0 (SF)
49ers, 24-16 (LA)
1960—49ers, 13-9 (SF)
49ers, 23-7 (LA)
1961—49ers, 35-0 (SF)
Rams, 17-7 (LA)
1962—Rams, 28-14 (SF)
49ers, 24-17 (LA)
1963—Rams, 28-21 (LA)
Rams, 21-17 (SF)
1964—Rams, 42-14 (LA)
49ers, 28-7 (SF)
1965—49ers, 45-21 (LA)
49ers, 30-27 (SF)
1966—Rams, 34-3 (LA)
49ers, 21-13 (SF)
1967—49ers, 27-24 (LA)
Rams, 17-7 (SF)
1968—Rams, 24-10 (LA)
Tie, 20-20 (SF)
1969—Rams, 27-21 (SF)
Rams, 41-30 (LA)
1970—49ers, 20-6 (LA)
Rams, 30-13 (SF)
1971—Rams, 20-13 (SF)
Rams, 17-6 (LA)
1972—Rams, 31-7 (LA)
Rams, 26-16 (SF)
1973—Rams, 40-20 (SF)
Rams, 31-13 (LA)
1974—Rams, 37-14 (LA)
Rams, 15-13 (SF)
1975—Rams, 23-14 (SF)
49ers, 24-23 (LA)
1976—49ers, 16-0 (LA)
Rams, 23-3 (SF)
1977—Rams, 34-14 (LA)
Rams, 23-10 (SF)
1978—Rams, 27-10 (LA)
Rams, 31-28 (SF)
1979—Rams, 27-24 (LA)
Rams, 26-20 (SF)
1980—Rams, 48-26 (LA)
Rams, 31-17 (SF)
1981—49ers, 20-17 (SF)
49ers, 33-31 (LA)
1982—49ers, 30-24 (LA)
Rams, 21-20 (SF)
1983—Rams, 10-7 (SF)
49ers, 45-35 (LA)
1984—49ers, 33-0 (LA)
49ers, 19-16 (SF)
1985—49ers, 28-14 (LA)
Rams, 27-20 (SF)
1986—Rams, 16-13 (LA)
49ers, 24-14 (SF)
1987—49ers, 31-10 (LA)
49ers, 48-0 (SF)
1988—49ers, 24-21 (LA)
Rams, 38-16 (SF)
1989—Rams, 13-12 (SF)
49ers, 30-27 (LA)
**49ers, 30-3 (SF)
1990—Rams, 28-17 (SF)
49ers, 26-10 (LA)
1991—49ers, 27-10 (SF)
49ers, 33-10 (LA)
1992—49ers, 27-24 (SF)
49ers, 27-10 (LA)
1993—49ers, 40-17 (SF)
49ers, 35-10 (LA)
1994—49ers, 34-19 (LA)
49ers, 31-27 (SF)
1995—49ers, 44-10 (StL)
49ers, 41-13 (SF)
1996—49ers, 34-0 (SF)
49ers, 28-11 (StL)
1997—49ers, 15-12 (StL)
49ers, 30-10 (SF)
1998—49ers, 28-10 (StL)
49ers, 38-19 (SF)
1999—Rams, 42-20 (StL)
Rams, 23-7 (SF)
2000—Rams, 41-24 (StL)
Rams, 34-24 (SF)
2001—Rams, 30-26 (SF)
Rams, 27-14 (StL)
2002—49ers, 37-13 (SF)
Rams, 31-20 (StL)
2003—Rams, 27-24 (StL) OT
49ers, 30-10 (SF)
2004—Rams, 24-14 (SF)
Rams, 16-6 (StL)
2005—49ers, 28-25 (SF)
49ers, 24-20 (StL)
2006—49ers, 20-13 (SF)
Rams, 20-17 (StL)
2007—49ers, 17-16 (StL)
Rams, 13-9 (SF)
2008—49ers, 35-16 (SF)
49ers, 17-16 (StL)
(RS Pts.—Rams 2,601, 49ers 2,599)
(PS Pts.—49ers 30, Rams 3)
**Franchise in Los Angeles prior to 1995*
***NFC Championship*
***ST. LOUIS vs. SEATTLE**
RS: Seahawks lead series, 12-9
PS: Rams lead series, 1-0
1976—Rams, 45-6 (LA)
1979—Rams, 24-0 (S)
1985—Rams, 35-24 (S)
1988—Rams, 31-10 (LA)
1991—Seahawks, 23-9 (S)
1997—Seahawks, 17-9 (StL)
2000—Rams, 37-34 (Sea)
2002—Rams, 37-20 (StL)
Seahawks, 30-10 (Sea)
2003—Seahawks, 24-23 (Sea)
Rams, 27-22 (StL)
2004—Rams, 33-27 (Sea) OT
Rams, 23-12 (StL)
**Rams, 27-20 (Sea)
2005—Seahawks, 37-31 (StL)
Seahawks, 31-16 (Sea)
2006—Seahawks, 30-28 (StL)
Seahawks, 24-22 (Sea)
2007—Seahawks, 33-6 (Sea)
Seahawks, 24-19 (StL)
2008—Seahawks, 37-13 (Sea)
Seahawks, 23-20 (StL)
(RS Pts.—Rams 498, Seahawks 488)
(PS Pts.—Rams 27, Seahawks 20)
**Franchise in Los Angeles prior to 1995*
***NFC First-Round Playoff*
***ST. LOUIS vs. TAMPA BAY**
RS: Rams lead series, 9-7
PS: Rams lead series, 2-0
1977—Rams, 31-0 (LA)
1978—Rams, 26-23 (LA)
1979—Buccaneers, 21-6 (TB)
**Rams, 9-0 (TB)
1980—Buccaneers, 10-9 (TB)
1984—Rams, 34-33 (TB)
1985—Rams, 31-27 (TB)
1986—Rams, 26-20 (LA) OT
1987—Rams, 35-3 (LA)
1990—Rams, 35-14 (TB)
1992—Rams, 31-27 (TB)
1994—Buccaneers, 24-14 (TB)
1999—**Rams, 11-6 (StL)
2000—Buccaneers, 38-35 (TB)
2001—Buccaneers, 24-17 (StL)
2002—Buccaneers, 26-14 (TB)
2004—Rams, 28-21 (StL)
2007—Buccaneers, 24-3 (TB)
(RS Pts.—Rams 375, Buccaneers 335)
(PS Pts.—Rams 20, Buccaneers 6)
**Franchise in Los Angeles prior to 1995*
***NFC Championship*
***ST. LOUIS vs. **TENNESSEE**
RS: Rams lead series, 6-3
PS: Rams lead series, 1-0
1973—Rams, 31-26 (H)
1978—Rams, 10-6 (H)
1981—Oilers, 27-20 (LA)

1984—Rams, 27-16 (LA)
1987—Oilers, 20-16 (H)
1990—Rams, 17-13 (LA)
1993—Rams, 28-13 (H)
1999—Titans, 24-21 (T)
***Rams, 23-16 (Atlanta)
2005—Rams, 31-27 (StL)
(RS Pts.—Rams 201, Titans 172)
(PS Pts.—Rams 23, Titans 16)
Franchise in Los Angeles prior to 1995
**Franchise in Houston prior to 1997; known as Oilers prior to 1999*
***Super Bowl XXXIV*

***ST. LOUIS vs. WASHINGTON**
RS: Redskins lead series, 20-8-1
PS: Series tied, 2-2
1937—Redskins, 16-7 (C)
1938—Redskins, 37-13 (W)
1941—Redskins, 17-13 (W)
1942—Redskins, 33-14 (W)
1944—Redskins, 14-10 (W)
1945—**Rams, 15-14 (C)
1948—Rams, 41-13 (W)
1949—Rams, 53-27 (LA)
1951—Redskins, 31-21 (W)
1962—Redskins, 20-14 (W)
1963—Redskins, 37-14 (LA)
1967—Tie, 28-28 (LA)
1969—Rams, 24-13 (W)
1971—Redskins, 38-24 (LA)
1974—Redskins, 23-17 (LA)
***Rams, 19-10 (LA)
1977—Redskins, 17-14 (W)
1981—Redskins, 30-7 (LA)
1983—Redskins, 42-20 (LA)
***Redskins, 51-7 (W)
1986—****Redskins, 19-7 (W)
1987—Rams, 30-26 (W)
1991—Redskins, 27-6 (LA)
1993—Rams, 10-6 (LA)
1994—Redskins, 24-21 (LA)
1995—Redskins, 35-23 (StL)
1996—Redskins, 17-10 (StL)
1997—Rams, 23-20 (W)
2000—Redskins, 33-20 (StL)
2002—Redskins, 20-17 (W)
2005—Redskins, 24-9 (StL)
2006—Rams, 37-31 (StL) OT
2008—Rams, 19-17 (W)
(RS Pts.—Redskins 716, Rams 559)
(PS Pts.—Redskins 94, Rams 48)
Franchise in Los Angeles prior to 1995 and in Cleveland prior to 1946
**NFL Championship*
***NFC Divisional Playoff*
****NFC First-Round Playoff*

SAN DIEGO vs. ARIZONA
RS: Chargers lead series, 8-3;
See Arizona vs. San Diego

SAN DIEGO vs. ATLANTA
RS: Falcons lead series, 7-1;
See Atlanta vs. San Diego

SAN DIEGO vs. BALTIMORE
RS: Series tied, 3-3;
See Baltimore vs. San Diego

SAN DIEGO vs. BUFFALO
RS: Chargers lead series, 20-10-2
PS: Bills lead series, 2-1;
See Buffalo vs. San Diego

SAN DIEGO vs. CAROLINA
RS: Panthers lead series, 3-1;
See Carolina vs. San Diego

SAN DIEGO vs. CHICAGO
RS: Series tied, 5-5;
See Chicago vs. San Diego

SAN DIEGO vs. CINCINNATI
RS: Chargers lead series, 18-10
PS: Bengals lead series, 1-0;
See Cincinnati vs. San Diego

SAN DIEGO vs. CLEVELAND
RS: Chargers lead series, 13-7-1;
See Cleveland vs. San Diego

SAN DIEGO vs. DALLAS
RS: Cowboys lead series, 6-2;
See Dallas vs. San Diego

SAN DIEGO vs. DENVER
RS: Broncos lead series, 53-44-1;
See Denver vs. San Diego

SAN DIEGO vs. DETROIT
RS: Chargers lead series, 6-3;
See Detroit vs. San Diego

SAN DIEGO vs. GREEN BAY
RS: Packers lead series, 8-1;
See Green Bay vs. San Diego

SAN DIEGO vs. HOUSTON
RS: Chargers lead series, 3-0;
See Houston vs. San Diego

SAN DIEGO vs. INDIANAPOLIS
RS: Chargers lead series, 14-9
PS: Chargers lead series, 2-1;
See Indianapolis vs. San Diego

SAN DIEGO vs. JACKSONVILLE
RS: Jaguars lead series, 2-1;
See Jacksonville vs. San Diego

SAN DIEGO vs. KANSAS CITY
RS: Chiefs lead series, 50-46-1
PS: Chargers lead series, 1-0;
See Kansas City vs. San Diego

SAN DIEGO vs. MIAMI
RS: Dolphins lead series, 12-10
PS: Series tied, 2-2;
See Miami vs. San Diego

SAN DIEGO vs. MINNESOTA
RS: Series tied, 5-5;
See Minnesota vs. San Diego

SAN DIEGO vs. NEW ENGLAND
RS: Patriots lead series, 18-14-2
PS: Patriots lead series, 2-1;
See New England vs. San Diego

SAN DIEGO vs. NEW ORLEANS
RS: Chargers lead series, 7-3;
See New Orleans vs. San Diego

SAN DIEGO vs. N.Y. GIANTS
RS: Giants lead series, 5-4;
See N.Y. Giants vs. San Diego

SAN DIEGO vs. N.Y. JETS
RS: Chargers lead series, 19-11-1
PS: Jets lead series, 1-0;
See N.Y. Jets vs. San Diego

SAN DIEGO vs. OAKLAND
RS: Raiders lead series, 54-42-2
PS: Raiders lead series, 1-0;
See Oakland vs. San Diego

SAN DIEGO vs. PHILADELPHIA
RS: Chargers lead series, 5-4;
See Philadelphia vs. San Diego

SAN DIEGO vs. PITTSBURGH
RS: Steelers lead series, 20-6
PS: Chargers lead series, 2-1;
See Pittsburgh vs. San Diego

SAN DIEGO vs. ST. LOUIS
RS: Rams lead series, 5-4;
See St. Louis vs. San Diego

SAN DIEGO vs. SAN FRANCISCO
RS: 49ers lead series, 6-5
PS: 49ers lead series, 1-0
1972—49ers, 34-3 (SF)
1976—Chargers, 13-7 (SD) OT
1979—Chargers, 31-9 (SD)
1982—Chargers, 41-37 (SF)
1988—49ers, 48-10 (SD)
1991—49ers, 34-14 (SF)
1994—49ers, 38-15 (SD)
*49ers, 49-26 (South Florida)
1997—49ers, 17-10 (SF)
2000—49ers, 45-17 (SD)
2002—Chargers, 20-17 (SD) OT
2006—Chargers, 48-19 (SF)
(RS Pts.—49ers 305, Chargers 222)
(PS Pts.—49ers 49, Chargers 26)
Super Bowl XXIX

SAN DIEGO vs. SEATTLE
RS: Seahawks lead series, 25-23
1977—Chargers, 30-28 (S)
1978—Chargers, 24-20 (S)
Chargers, 37-10 (SD)
1979—Chargers, 33-16 (S)
Chargers, 20-10 (SD)
1980—Chargers, 34-13 (S)
Chargers, 21-14 (SD)
1981—Chargers, 24-10 (SD)
Seahawks, 44-23 (S)
1983—Seahawks, 34-31 (S)
Chargers, 28-21 (SD)
1984—Seahawks, 31-17 (S)
Seahawks, 24-0 (SD)
1985—Seahawks, 49-35 (SD)
Seahawks, 26-21 (S)
1986—Seahawks, 33-7 (S)
Seahawks, 34-24 (SD)
1987—Seahawks, 34-3 (S)
1988—Chargers, 17-6 (SD)
Seahawks, 17-14 (S)
1989—Seahawks, 17-16 (SD)
Seahawks, 10-7 (S)
1990—Chargers, 31-14 (S)
Seahawks, 13-10 (SD) OT
1991—Seahawks, 20-9 (S)
Chargers, 17-14 (SD)
1992—Chargers, 17-6 (SD)
Chargers, 31-14 (S)
1993—Chargers, 18-12 (SD)
Seahawks, 31-14 (S)
1994—Chargers, 24-10 (S)
Chargers, 35-15 (SD)
1995—Chargers, 14-10 (SD)
Chargers, 35-25 (S)
1996—Chargers, 29-7 (SD)
Seahawks, 32-13 (S)
1997—Seahawks, 26-22 (S)
Seahawks, 37-31 (SD)
1998—Seahawks, 27-20 (SD)
Seahawks, 38-17 (S)
1999—Chargers, 13-10 (SD)
Chargers, 19-16 (S)
2000—Seahawks, 20-12 (SD)
Seahawks, 17-15 (S)
2001—Seahawks, 13-10 (S) OT
Seahawks, 25-22 (SD)

2002—Seahawks, 31-28 (SD) OT
2006—Chargers, 20-17 (Sea)
(RS Pts.—Seahawks 1,001, Chargers 992)
SAN DIEGO vs. TAMPA BAY
RS: Chargers lead series, 8-1
1976—Chargers, 23-0 (TB)
1981—Chargers, 24-23 (TB)
1987—Chargers, 17-13 (TB)
1990—Chargers, 41-10 (SD)
1992—Chargers, 29-14 (SD)
1993—Chargers, 32-17 (TB)
1996—Buccaneers, 25-17 (SD)
2004—Chargers, 31-24 (SD)
2008—Chargers, 41-24 (TB)
(RS Pts.—Chargers 255, Buccaneers 150)
***SAN DIEGO vs. **TENNESSEE**
RS: Chargers lead series, 22-13-1
PS: Titans lead series, 3-1
1960—Oilers, 38-28 (H)
Chargers, 24-21 (LA)
***Oilers, 24-16 (H)
1961—Chargers, 34-24 (SD)
Oilers, 33-13 (H)
***Oilers, 10-3 (SD)
1962—Oilers, 42-17 (SD)
Oilers, 33-27 (H)
1963—Chargers, 27-0 (SD)
Chargers 20-14 (H)
1964—Chargers, 27-21 (SD)
Chargers, 20-17 (H)
1965—Chargers, 31-14 (SD)
Chargers, 37-26 (H)
1966—Chargers, 28-22 (H)
1967—Chargers, 13-3 (SD)
Oilers, 24-17 (H)
1968—Chargers, 30-14 (SD)
1969—Chargers, 21-17 (H)
1970—Tie, 31-31 (SD)
1971—Oilers, 49-33 (H)
1972—Chargers, 34-20 (SD)
1974—Oilers, 21-14 (H)
1975—Oilers, 33-17 (H)
1976—Chargers, 30-27 (SD)
1978—Chargers, 45-24 (H)
1979—****Oilers, 17-14 (SD)
1984—Chargers, 31-14 (SD)
1985—Oilers, 37-35 (H)
1986—Chargers, 27-0 (SD)
1987—Oilers, 33-18 (H)
1989—Oilers, 34-27 (SD)
1990—Oilers, 17-7 (SD)
1992—Oilers, 27-0 (H)
1993—Chargers, 18-17 (SD)
1998—Chargers, 13-7 (T)
2004—Chargers, 38-17 (SD)
2006—Chargers, 40-7 (SD)
2007—Chargers, 23-17 (T) OT
*****Chargers, 17-6 (SD)
(RS Pts.—Chargers 895, Titans 795)
(PS Pts.—Titans 57, Chargers 50)
**Franchise in Los Angeles prior to 1961*
***Franchise in Houston prior to 1997; known as Oilers prior to 1999*
****AFL Championship*
*****AFC Divisional Playoff*
******AFC First-Round Playoff*
SAN DIEGO vs. WASHINGTON
RS: Redskins lead series, 6-2
1973—Redskins, 38-0 (W)
1980—Redskins, 40-17 (W)
1983—Redskins, 27-24 (SD)
1986—Redskins, 30-27 (SD)
1989—Redskins, 26-21 (W)
1998—Redskins, 24-20 (W)
2001—Chargers, 30-3 (SD)
2005—Chargers, 23-17 (W) OT
(RS Pts.—Redskins 205, Chargers 162)

SAN FRANCISCO vs. ARIZONA
RS: 49ers lead series, 19-16;
See Arizona vs. San Francisco
SAN FRANCISCO vs. ATLANTA
RS: 49ers lead series, 44-27-1
PS: Falcons lead series, 1-0;
See Atlanta vs. San Francisco
SAN FRANCISCO vs. BALTIMORE
RS: Ravens lead series, 2-1;
See Baltimore vs. San Francisco
SAN FRANCISCO vs. BUFFALO
RS: Series tied, 5-5;
See Buffalo vs. San Francisco
SAN FRANCISCO vs. CAROLINA
RS: Panthers lead series, 9-7;
See Carolina vs. San Francisco
SAN FRANCISCO vs. CHICAGO
RS: Bears lead series, 29-27-1
PS: 49ers lead series, 3-0;
See Chicago vs. San Francisco
SAN FRANCISCO vs. CINCINNATI
RS: 49ers lead series, 8-3
PS: 49ers lead series, 2-0;
See Cincinnati vs. San Francisco
SAN FRANCISCO vs. CLEVELAND
RS: Browns lead series, 11-6;
See Cleveland vs. San Francisco
SAN FRANCISCO vs. DALLAS
RS: 49ers lead series, 14-10-1
PS: Cowboys lead series, 5-2;
See Dallas vs. San Francisco
SAN FRANCISCO vs. DENVER
RS: Broncos lead series, 6-5
PS: 49ers lead series, 1-0;
See Denver vs. San Francisco
SAN FRANCISCO vs. DETROIT
RS: 49ers lead series, 33-26-1
PS: Series tied, 1-1;
See Detroit vs. San Francisco
SAN FRANCISCO vs. GREEN BAY
RS: Packers lead series, 28-25-1
PS: Packers lead series, 4-1;
See Green Bay vs. San Francisco
SAN FRANCISCO vs. HOUSTON
RS: 49ers lead series, 1-0;
See Houston vs. San Francisco
SAN FRANCISCO vs. INDIANAPOLIS
RS: Colts lead series, 23-18;
See Indianapolis vs. San Francisco
SAN FRANCISCO vs. JACKSONVILLE
RS: Jaguars lead series, 2-0;
See Jacksonville vs. San Francisco
SAN FRANCISCO vs. KANSAS CITY
RS: 49ers lead series, 6-4;
See Kansas City vs. San Francisco
SAN FRANCISCO vs. MIAMI
RS: Dolphins lead series, 6-4
PS: 49ers lead series, 1-0;
See Miami vs. San Francisco
SAN FRANCISCO vs. MINNESOTA
RS: Vikings lead series, 19-18-1
PS: 49ers lead series, 4-1;
See Minnesota vs. San Francisco
SAN FRANCISCO vs. NEW ENGLAND
RS: 49ers lead series, 7-4;
See New England vs. San Francisco
SAN FRANCISCO vs. NEW ORLEANS
RS: 49ers lead series, 45-23-2;
See New Orleans vs. San Francisco
SAN FRANCISCO vs. N.Y. GIANTS
RS: Giants lead series, 14-13
PS: 49ers lead series, 4-3;
See N.Y. Giants vs. San Francisco
SAN FRANCISCO vs. N.Y. JETS
RS: 49ers lead series, 9-2;
See N.Y. Jets vs. San Francisco
SAN FRANCISCO vs. OAKLAND
RS: Raiders lead series, 6-5;
See Oakland vs. San Francisco
SAN FRANCISCO vs. PHILADELPHIA
RS: 49ers lead series, 16-10-1
PS: 49ers lead series, 1-0;
See Philadelphia vs. San Francisco
SAN FRANCISCO vs. PITTSBURGH
RS: 49ers lead series, 10-9;
See Pittsburgh vs. San Francisco
SAN FRANCISCO vs. ST. LOUIS
RS: Rams lead series, 60-56-2
PS: 49ers lead series, 1-0;
See St. Louis vs. San Francisco
SAN FRANCISCO vs. SAN DIEGO
RS: 49ers lead series, 6-5
PS: 49ers lead series, 1-0;
See San Diego vs. San Francisco
SAN FRANCISCO vs. SEATTLE
RS: Seahawks lead series, 11-9
1976—49ers, 37-21 (Sea)
1979—Seahawks, 35-24 (SF)
1985—49ers, 19-6 (SF)
1988—49ers, 38-7 (Sea)
1991—49ers, 24-22 (Sea)
1997—Seahawks, 38-9 (Sea)
2002—49ers, 28-21 (Sea)
49ers, 31-24 (SF)
2003—Seahawks, 20-19 (Sea)
Seahawks, 24-17 (SF)
2004—Seahawks, 34-0 (Sea)
Seahawks, 42-27 (SF)
2005—Seahawks, 27-25 (SF)
Seahawks, 41-3 (Sea)
2006—49ers, 20-14 (SF)
49ers, 24-14 (Sea)
2007—Seahawks, 23-3 (SF)
Seahawks, 24-0 (Sea)
2008—49ers, 33-30 (Sea) OT
Seahawks, 34-13 (SF)
(RS Pts.—Seahawks 501, 49ers 394)
SAN FRANCISCO vs. TAMPA BAY
RS: 49ers lead series, 15-3
PS: Buccaneers lead series, 1-0
1977—49ers, 20-10 (SF)
1978—49ers, 6-3 (SF)
1979—49ers, 23-7 (SF)
1980—Buccaneers, 24-23 (SF)
1983—49ers, 35-21 (SF)
1984—49ers, 24-17 (SF)
1986—49ers, 31-7 (TB)
1987—49ers, 24-10 (TB)
1989—49ers, 20-16 (TB)
1990—49ers, 31-7 (SF)
1992—49ers, 21-14 (SF)
1993—49ers, 45-21 (TB)

1994—49ers, 41-16 (SF)
1997—Buccaneers, 13-6 (TB)
2002—*Buccaneers, 31-6 (TB)
2003—49ers, 24-7 (SF)
2004—Buccaneers, 35-3 (TB)
2005—49ers, 15-10 (SF)
2007—49ers, 21-19 (SF)
(RS Pts.—49ers 413, Buccaneers 257)
(PS Pts.—Buccaneers 31, 49ers 6)
NFC Divisional Playoff

SAN FRANCISCO vs. *TENNESSEE
RS: 49ers lead series, 7-4
1970—49ers, 30-20 (H)
1975—Oilers, 27-13 (SF)
1978—Oilers, 20-19 (H)
1981—49ers, 28-6 (SF)
1984—49ers, 34-21 (H)
1987—49ers, 27-20 (SF)
1990—49ers, 24-21 (H)
1993—Oilers, 10-7 (SF)
1996—49ers, 10-9 (H)
1999—49ers, 24-22 (SF)
2005—Titans, 33-22 (T)
(RS Pts.—49ers 238, Titans 209)
**Franchise in Houston prior to 1997; known as Oilers prior to 1999*

SAN FRANCISCO vs. WASHINGTON
RS: 49ers lead series, 14-9-1
PS: 49ers lead series, 3-1
1952—49ers, 23-17 (W)
1954—49ers, 41-7 (SF)
1955—Redskins, 7-0 (W)
1961—49ers, 35-3 (SF)
1967—Redskins, 31-28 (W)
1969—Tie, 17-17 (SF)
1970—49ers, 26-17 (SF)
1971—*49ers, 24-20 (SF)
1973—Redskins, 33-9 (W)
1976—Redskins, 24-21 (SF)
1978—Redskins, 38-20 (W)
1981—49ers, 30-17 (W)
1983—**Redskins, 24-21 (W)
1984—49ers, 37-31 (SF)
1985—49ers, 35-8 (W)
1986—Redskins, 14-6 (W)
1988—49ers, 37-21 (SF)
1990—49ers, 26-13 (SF)
*49ers, 28-10 (SF)
1992—*49ers, 20-13 (SF)
1994—49ers, 37-22 (W)
1996—49ers, 19-16 (W) OT
1998—49ers, 45-10 (W)
1999—Redskins, 26-20 (SF) OT
2002—49ers, 20-10 (SF)
2004—Redskins, 26-16 (SF)
2005—Redskins, 52-17 (W)
2008—49ers, 27-24 (SF)
(RS Pts.—49ers 592, Redskins 484)
(PS Pts.—49ers 93, Redskins 67)
**NFC Divisional Playoff*
***NFC Championship*

SEATTLE vs. ARIZONA
RS: Cardinals lead series, 11-9;
See Arizona vs. Seattle

SEATTLE vs. ATLANTA
RS: Seahawks lead series, 8-3;
See Atlanta vs. Seattle

SEATTLE vs. BALTIMORE
RS: Ravens lead series, 2-1;
See Baltimore vs. Seattle

SEATTLE vs. BUFFALO
RS: Seahawks lead series, 6-5;
See Buffalo vs. Seattle

SEATTLE vs. CAROLINA
RS: Panthers lead series, 2-1
PS: Seahawks lead series, 1-0;
See Carolina vs. Seattle

SEATTLE vs. CHICAGO
RS: Seahawks lead series, 7-3
PS: Bears lead series, 1-0;
See Chicago vs. Seattle

SEATTLE vs. CINCINNATI
RS: Seahawks lead series, 9-8
PS: Bengals lead series, 1-0;
See Cincinnati vs. Seattle

SEATTLE vs. CLEVELAND
RS: Seahawks lead series, 11-5;
See Cleveland vs. Seattle

SEATTLE vs. DALLAS
RS: Cowboys lead series, 7-4
PS: Seahawks lead series, 1-0;
See Dallas vs. Seattle

SEATTLE vs. DENVER
RS: Broncos lead series, 33-18
PS: Seahawks lead series, 1-0;
See Denver vs. Seattle

SEATTLE vs. DETROIT
RS: Seahawks lead series, 6-4;
See Detroit vs. Seattle

SEATTLE vs. GREEN BAY
RS: Packers lead series, 7-5
PS: Packers lead series, 2-0;
See Green Bay vs. Seattle

SEATTLE vs. HOUSTON
RS: Seahawks lead series, 1-0;
See Houston vs. Seattle

SEATTLE vs. INDIANAPOLIS
RS: Colts lead series, 5-4;
See Indianapolis vs. Seattle

SEATTLE vs. JACKSONVILLE
RS: Seahawks lead series, 3-2;
See Jacksonville vs. Seattle

SEATTLE vs. KANSAS CITY
RS: Chiefs lead series, 31-18;
See Kansas City vs. Seattle

SEATTLE vs. MIAMI
RS: Dolphins lead series, 7-3
PS: Dolphins lead series, 2-1;
See Miami vs. Seattle

SEATTLE vs. MINNESOTA
RS: Seahawks lead series, 6-4;
See Minnesota vs. Seattle

SEATTLE vs. NEW ENGLAND
RS: Patriots lead series, 8-7;
See New England vs. Seattle

SEATTLE vs. NEW ORLEANS
RS: Series tied, 5-5;
See New Orleans vs. Seattle

SEATTLE vs. N.Y. GIANTS
RS: Giants lead series, 8-5;
See N.Y. Giants vs. Seattle

SEATTLE vs. N.Y. JETS
RS: Seahawks lead series, 9-8;
See N.Y. Jets vs. Seattle

SEATTLE vs. OAKLAND
RS: Raiders lead series, 27-23
PS: Series tied, 1-1;
See Oakland vs. Seattle

SEATTLE vs. PHILADELPHIA
RS: Eagles lead series, 7-5;
See Philadelphia vs. Seattle

SEATTLE vs. PITTSBURGH
RS: Seahawks lead series, 8-7
PS: Steelers lead series, 1-0;
See Pittsburgh vs. Seattle

SEATTLE vs. ST. LOUIS
RS: Seahawks lead series, 12-9
PS: Rams lead series, 1-0;
See St. Louis vs. Seattle

SEATTLE vs. SAN DIEGO
RS: Seahawks lead series, 25-23;
See San Diego vs. Seattle

SEATTLE vs. SAN FRANCISCO
RS: Seahawks lead series, 11-9;
See San Francisco vs. Seattle

SEATTLE vs. TAMPA BAY
RS: Seahawks lead series, 7-2
1976—Seahawks, 13-10 (TB)
1977—Seahawks, 30-23 (S)
1994—Seahawks, 22-21 (S)
1996—Seahawks, 17-13 (TB)
1999—Buccaneers, 16-3 (S)
2004—Seahawks, 10-6 (TB)
2006—Seahawks, 23-7 (TB)
2007—Seahawks, 20-6 (S)
2008—Buccaneers, 20-10 (TB)
(RS Pts.—Seahawks 148, Buccaneers 122)

SEATTLE vs. *TENNESSEE
RS: Seahawks lead series, 9-4
PS: Titans lead series, 1-0
1977—Oilers, 22-10 (S)
1979—Seahawks, 34-14 (S)
1980—Seahawks, 26-7 (H)
1981—Oilers, 35-17 (H)
1982—Oilers, 23-21 (H)
1987—**Oilers, 23-20 (H) OT
1988—Seahawks, 27-24 (S)
1990—Seahawks, 13-10 (S) OT
1993—Oilers, 24-14 (H)
1994—Seahawks, 16-14 (H)
1996—Seahawks, 23-16 (S)
1997—Seahawks, 16-13 (S)
1998—Seahawks, 20-18 (S)
2005—Seahawks, 28-24 (T)
(RS Pts.—Seahawks 265, Titans 244)
(PS Pts.—Titans 23, Seahawks 20)
**Franchise in Houston prior to 1997; known as Oilers prior to 1999*
***AFC First-Round Playoff*

SEATTLE vs. WASHINGTON
RS: Redskins lead series, 10-4
PS: Seahawks lead series, 2-0
1976—Redskins, 31-7 (W)
1980—Seahawks, 14-0 (W)
1983—Redskins, 27-17 (S)
1986—Redskins, 19-14 (W)
1989—Redskins, 29-0 (S)
1992—Redskins, 16-3 (S)
1994—Seahawks, 28-7 (W)
1995—Seahawks, 27-20 (W)
1998—Seahawks, 24-14 (S)
2001—Redskins, 27-14 (W)
2002—Redskins, 14-3 (S)
2003—Redskins, 27-20 (W)
2005—Redskins, 20-17 (W) OT
*Seahawks, 20-10 (S)
2007—**Seahawks, 35-14 (S)
2008—Redskins, 20-17 (S)

(RS Pts.—Redskins 271, Seahawks 205)
(PS Pts.—Seahawks 55, Redskins 24)
NFC Divisional Playoff
***NFC First-Round Playoff*

TAMPA BAY vs. ARIZONA
RS: Series tied, 8-8;
See Arizona vs. Tampa Bay
TAMPA BAY vs. ATLANTA
RS: Buccaneers lead series, 18-13;
See Atlanta vs. Tampa Bay
TAMPA BAY vs. BALTIMORE
RS: Buccaneers lead series, 2-1;
See Baltimore vs. Tampa Bay
TAMPA BAY vs. BUFFALO
RS: Buccaneers lead series, 6-2;
See Buffalo vs. Tampa Bay
TAMPA BAY vs. CAROLINA
RS: Panthers lead series, 10-7;
See Carolina vs. Tampa Bay
TAMPA BAY vs. CHICAGO
RS: Bears lead series, 35-18;
See Chicago vs. Tampa Bay
TAMPA BAY vs. CINCINNATI
RS: Buccaneers lead series, 6-3;
See Cincinnati vs. Tampa Bay
TAMPA BAY vs. CLEVELAND
RS: Browns lead series, 5-2;
See Cleveland vs. Tampa Bay
TAMPA BAY vs. DALLAS
RS: Cowboys lead series, 8-3
PS: Cowboys lead series, 2-0;
See Dallas vs. Tampa Bay
TAMPA BAY vs. DENVER
RS: Broncos lead series, 5-2;
See Denver vs. Tampa Bay
TAMPA BAY vs. DETROIT
RS: Lions lead series, 27-25
PS: Buccaneers lead series, 1-0;
See Detroit vs. Tampa Bay
TAMPA BAY vs. GREEN BAY
RS: Packers lead series, 29-20-1
PS: Packers lead series, 1-0;
See Green Bay vs. Tampa Bay
TAMPA BAY vs. HOUSTON
RS: Series tied, 1-1;
See Houston vs. Tampa Bay
TAMPA BAY vs. INDIANAPOLIS
RS: Colts lead series, 7-4;
See Indianapolis vs. Tampa Bay
TAMPA BAY vs. JACKSONVILLE
RS: Jaguars lead series, 3-1;
See Jacksonville vs. Tampa Bay
TAMPA BAY vs. KANSAS CITY
RS: Series tied, 5-5;
See Kansas City vs. Tampa Bay
TAMPA BAY vs. MIAMI
RS: Series tied, 4-4;
See Miami vs. Tampa Bay
TAMPA BAY vs. MINNESOTA
RS: Vikings lead series, 31-20;
See Minnesota vs. Tampa Bay
TAMPA BAY vs. NEW ENGLAND
RS: Patriots lead series, 4-2;
See New England vs. Tampa Bay
TAMPA BAY vs. NEW ORLEANS
RS: Saints lead series, 20-14;
See New Orleans vs. Tampa Bay
TAMPA BAY vs. N.Y. GIANTS
RS: Giants lead series, 10-6
PS: Giants lead series, 1-0;
See N.Y. Giants vs. Tampa Bay
TAMPA BAY vs. N.Y. JETS
RS: Jets lead series, 8-1;
See N.Y. Jets vs. Tampa Bay
TAMPA BAY vs. OAKLAND
RS: Raiders lead series, 6-1
PS: Buccaneers lead series, 1-0;
See Oakland vs. Tampa Bay
TAMPA BAY vs. PHILADELPHIA
RS: Series tied, 5-5
PS: Series tied, 2-2;
See Philadelphia vs. Tampa Bay
TAMPA BAY vs. PITTSBURGH
RS: Steelers lead series, 7-1;
See Pittsburgh vs. Tampa Bay
TAMPA BAY vs. ST. LOUIS
RS: Rams lead series, 9-7
PS: Rams lead series, 2-0;
See St. Louis vs. Tampa Bay
TAMPA BAY vs. SAN DIEGO
RS: Chargers lead series, 8-1;
See San Diego vs. Tampa Bay
TAMPA BAY vs. SAN FRANCISCO
RS: 49ers lead series, 15-3
PS: Buccaneers lead series, 1-0;
See San Francisco vs. Tampa Bay
TAMPA BAY vs. SEATTLE
RS: Seahawks lead series, 7-2;
See Seattle vs. Tampa Bay
TAMPA BAY vs. *TENNESSEE
RS: Titans lead series, 7-2
1976—Oilers, 20-0 (H)
1980—Oilers, 20-14 (H)
1983—Buccaneers, 33-24 (TB)
1989—Oilers, 20-17 (H)
1995—Oilers, 19-7 (H)
1998—Oilers, 31-22 (TB)
2001—Titans, 31-28 (Tenn) OT
2003—Titans, 33-13 (Tenn)
2007—Buccaneers, 13-10 (TB)
(RS Pts.—Titans 208, Buccaneers 147)
**Franchise in Houston prior to 1997; known as Oilers prior to 1999*
TAMPA BAY vs. WASHINGTON
RS: Buccaneers lead series, 8-7
PS: Series tied, 1-1
1977—Redskins, 10-0 (TB)
1982—Redskins, 21-13 (TB)
1989—Redskins, 32-28 (W)
1993—Redskins, 23-17 (TB)
1994—Buccaneers, 26-21 (TB)
Buccaneers, 17-14 (W)
1995—Buccaneers, 14-6 (TB)
1996—Buccaneers, 24-10 (TB)
1998—Redskins, 20-16 (W)
1999—*Buccaneers, 14-13 (TB)
2000—Redskins, 20-17 (W) OT
2003—Buccaneers, 35-13 (W)
2004—Redskins, 16-10 (W)
2005—Buccaneers, 36-35 (TB)
**Redskins, 17-10 (TB)
2006—Buccaneers, 20-17 (TB)
2007—Buccaneers, 19-13 (TB)
(RS Pts.—Buccaneers 292, Redskins 271)
(PS Pts.—Redskins 30, Buccaneers 24)
**NFC Divisional Playoff*
***NFC First-Round Playoff*

TENNESSEE VS. ARIZONA
RS: Cardinals lead series, 5-3;
See Arizona vs. Tennessee
TENNESSEE vs. ATLANTA
RS: Titans lead series, 7-5;
See Atlanta vs. Tennessee
TENNESSEE vs. BALTIMORE
RS: Series tied, 8-8
PS: Ravens lead series, 2-1;
See Baltimore vs. Tennessee
TENNESSEE vs. BUFFALO
RS: Titans lead series, 24-14
PS: Bills lead series, 2-1;
See Buffalo vs. Tennessee
TENNESSEE vs. CAROLINA
RS: Titans lead series, 2-1;
See Carolina vs. Tennessee
TENNESSEE vs. CHICAGO
RS: Series tied, 5-5;
See Chicago vs. Tennessee
TENNESSEE vs. CINCINNATI
RS: Titans lead series, 39-31-1
PS: Bengals lead series, 1-0;
See Cincinnati vs. Tennessee
TENNESSEE vs. CLEVELAND
RS: Browns lead series, 33-27
PS: Titans lead series, 1-0;
See Cleveland vs. Tennessee
TENNESSEE vs. DALLAS
RS: Cowboys lead series, 7-5;
See Dallas vs. Tennessee
TENNESSEE vs. DENVER
RS: Titans lead series, 20-13-1
PS: Broncos lead series, 2-1;
See Denver vs. Tennessee
TENNESSEE vs. DETROIT
RS: Titans lead series, 7-3;
See Detroit vs. Tennessee
TENNESSEE vs. GREEN BAY
RS: Titans lead series, 6-4;
See Green Bay vs. Tennessee
TENNESSEE vs. HOUSTON
RS: Titans lead series, 11-3;
See Houston vs. Tennessee
TENNESSEE vs. INDIANAPOLIS
RS: Colts lead series, 16-12
PS: Titans lead series, 1-0;
See Indianapolis vs. Tennessee
TENNESSEE vs. JACKSONVILLE
RS: Titans lead series, 16-12
PS: Titans lead series, 1-0;
See Jacksonville vs. Tennessee
TENNESSEE vs. KANSAS CITY
RS: Chiefs lead series, 25-20
PS: Chiefs lead series, 2-0;
See Kansas City vs. Tennessee
TENNESSEE vs. MIAMI
RS: Dolphins lead series, 17-13
PS: Titans lead series, 1-0;
See Miami vs. Tennessee
TENNESSEE vs. MINNESOTA
RS: Vikings lead series, 7-4;
See Minnesota vs. Tennessee
TENNESSEE vs. NEW ENGLAND
RS: Patriots lead series, 20-15-1
PS: Series tied, 1-1;
See New England vs. Tennessee
TENNESSEE vs. NEW ORLEANS
RS: Titans lead series, 7-4-1;

See New Orleans vs. Tennessee
TENNESSEE vs. N.Y. GIANTS
RS: Giants lead series, 5-4;
See N.Y. Giants vs. Tennessee
TENNESSEE vs. N.Y. JETS
RS: Titans lead series, 21-16-1
PS: Titans lead series, 1-0;
See N.Y. Jets vs. Tennessee
TENNESSEE vs. OAKLAND
RS: Raiders lead series, 23-18
PS: Raiders lead series, 4-0;
See Oakland vs. Tennessee
TENNESSEE vs. PHILADELPHIA
RS: Eagles lead series, 6-3;
See Philadelphia vs. Tennessee
TENNESSEE vs. PITTSBURGH
RS: Steelers lead series, 38-29
PS: Steelers lead series, 3-1;
See Pittsburgh vs. Tennessee
TENNESSEE vs. ST. LOUIS
RS: Rams lead series, 6-3
PS: Rams lead series, 1-0;
See St. Louis vs. Tennessee
TENNESSEE vs. SAN DIEGO
RS: Chargers lead series, 22-13-1
PS: Titans lead series, 3-1;
See San Diego vs. Tennessee
TENNESSEE vs. SAN FRANCISCO
RS: 49ers lead series, 7-4;
See San Francisco vs. Tennessee
TENNESSEE vs. SEATTLE
RS: Seahawks lead series, 9-4
PS: Titans lead series, 1-0;
See Seattle vs. Tennessee
TENNESSEE vs. TAMPA BAY
RS: Titans lead series, 7-2;
See Tampa Bay vs. Tennessee
***TENNESSEE vs. WASHINGTON**
RS: Titans lead series, 6-4
1971—Redskins, 22-13 (W)
1975—Oilers, 13-10 (H)
1979—Oilers, 29-27 (W)
1985—Redskins, 16-13 (W)
1988—Oilers, 41-17 (H)
1991—Redskins, 16-13 (W) OT
1997—Oilers, 28-14 (T)
2000—Titans, 27-21 (W)
2002—Redskins, 31-14 (T)
2006—Titans, 25-22 (W)
(RS—Titans 216, Redskins 196)
**Franchise in Houston prior to 1997; known as Oilers prior to 1999*

WASHINGTON vs. ARIZONA
RS: Redskins lead series, 73-44-2;
See Arizona vs. Washington
WASHINGTON vs. ATLANTA
RS: Redskins lead series, 14-5-1
PS: Redskins lead series, 1-0;
See Atlanta vs. Washington
WASHINGTON vs. BALTIMORE
RS: Ravens lead series, 3-1;
See Baltimore vs. Washington
WASHINGTON vs. BUFFALO
RS: Bills lead series, 7-4
PS: Redskins lead series, 1-0;
See Buffalo vs. Washington
WASHINGTON vs. CAROLINA
RS: Redskins lead series, 7-1;
See Carolina vs. Washington
WASHINGTON vs. CHICAGO
RS: Bears lead series, 20-18-1
PS: Redskins lead series, 4-3;
See Chicago vs. Washington
WASHINGTON vs. CINCINNATI
RS: Series tied, 4-4;
See Cincinnati vs. Washington
WASHINGTON vs. CLEVELAND
RS: Browns lead series, 33-10-1;
See Cleveland vs. Washington
WASHINGTON vs. DALLAS
RS: Cowboys lead series, 57-37-2
PS: Redskins lead series, 2-0;
See Dallas vs. Washington
WASHINGTON vs. DENVER
RS: Broncos lead series, 6-4
PS: Redskins lead series, 1-0;
See Denver vs. Washington
WASHINGTON vs. DETROIT
RS: Redskins lead series, 27-10
PS: Redskins lead series, 3-0;
See Detroit vs. Washington
WASHINGTON vs. GREEN BAY
RS: Packers lead series, 17-12-1
PS: Series tied, 1-1;
See Green Bay vs. Washington
WASHINGTON vs. HOUSTON
RS: Redskins lead series, 2-0;
See Houston vs. Washington
WASHINGTON vs. INDIANAPOLIS
RS: Colts lead series, 18-10;
See Indianapolis vs. Washington
WASHINGTON vs. JACKSONVILLE
RS: Redskins lead series, 3-1;
See Jacksonville vs. Washington
WASHINGTON vs. KANSAS CITY
RS: Chiefs lead series, 6-1;
See Kansas City vs. Washington
WASHINGTON vs. MIAMI
RS: Dolphins lead series, 6-4
PS: Series tied, 1-1;
See Miami vs. Washington
WASHINGTON vs. MINNESOTA
RS: Redskins lead series, 8-6
PS: Redskins lead series, 3-2;
See Minnesota vs. Washington
WASHINGTON vs. NEW ENGLAND
RS: Redskins lead series, 6-2;
See New England vs. Washington
WASHINGTON vs. NEW ORLEANS
RS: Redskins lead series, 15-7;
See New Orleans vs. Washington
WASHINGTON vs. N.Y. GIANTS
RS: Giants lead series, 87-61-4
PS: Series tied, 1-1;
See N.Y. Giants vs. Washington
WASHINGTON vs. N.Y. JETS
RS: Redskins lead series, 8-1;
See N.Y. Jets vs. Washington
WASHINGTON vs. OAKLAND
RS: Raiders lead series, 7-3
PS: Raiders lead series, 1-0;
See Oakland vs. Washington
WASHINGTON vs. PHILADELPHIA
RS: Redskins lead series, 77-65-5
PS: Redskins lead series, 1-0;
See Philadelphia vs. Washington
WASHINGTON vs. PITTSBURGH
RS: Redskins lead series, 42-31-3;
See Pittsburgh vs. Washington
WASHINGTON vs. ST. LOUIS
RS: Redskins lead series, 20-8-1
PS: Series tied, 2-2;
See St. Louis vs. Washington
WASHINGTON vs. SAN DIEGO
RS: Redskins lead series, 6-2;
See San Diego vs. Washington
WASHINGTON vs. SAN FRANCISCO
RS: 49ers lead series, 14-9-1
PS: 49ers lead series, 3-1;
See San Francisco vs. Washington
WASHINGTON vs. SEATTLE
RS: Redskins lead series, 10-4
PS: Seahawks lead series, 2-0;
See Seattle vs. Washington
WASHINGTON vs. TAMPA BAY
RS: Buccaneers lead series, 8-7
PS: Series tied, 1-1;
See Tampa Bay vs. Washington
WASHINGTON vs. TENNESSEE
RS: Titans lead series, 6-4;
See Tennessee vs. Washington

NFL OPENING KICKOFF WEEKEND

NFL OPENING KICKOFF GAMES (7)
(Home Team in capitals)

Date	Sites*	Teams
Sept. 5, 2002	Giants Stadium (East Rutherford, New Jersey) Times Square (New York, New York)	San Francisco 16, N.Y. GIANTS 13
Sept. 4, 2003	FedExField (Landover, Maryland) National Mall (Washington, D.C.)	WASHINGTON 16, N.Y. Jets 13
Sept. 9, 2004	Gillette Stadium (Foxboro, Massachusetts) Metropolitan Park (Jacksonville, Florida)	NEW ENGLAND 27, Indianapolis 24
Sept. 8, 2005	Gillette Stadium (Foxboro, Massachusetts) Detroit, Michigan Los Angeles Coliseum (Los Angeles, California)	NEW ENGLAND 30, Oakland 20
Sept. 7, 2006	Heinz Field (Pittsburgh, Pennsylvania) Miami, Florida	PITTSBURGH 28, Miami 17
Sept. 6, 2007	RCA Dome (Indianapolis, Indianapolis)	INDIANAPOLIS 41, New Orleans 10
Sept. 4, 2008	Giants Stadium (East Rutherford, New Jersey) Columbus Circle (New York, New York)	N.Y. GIANTS 16, Washington 7

**The first site listed each year designates location of Thursday Night NFL Kickoff Weekend game; subsequent locations indicate site(s) of NFL Kickoff Weekend concert.*

SUPER BOWL COMPOSITE STANDINGS

	W	L	Pct.	Pts.	OP
San Francisco 49ers	5	0	1.000	188	89
Baltimore Ravens	1	0	1.000	34	7
New York Jets	1	0	1.000	16	7
Tampa Bay Buccaneers	1	0	1.000	48	21
Pittsburgh Steelers	6	1	.857	168	133
Green Bay Packers	3	1	.750	127	76
New York Giants	3	1	.750	83	87
Indianapolis/Baltimore Colts	2	1	.667	52	46
Dallas Cowboys	5	3	.625	221	132
Oakland/L.A. Raiders	3	2	.600	132	114
Washington Redskins	3	2	.600	122	103
New England Patriots	3	3	.500	121	165
Chicago Bears	1	1	.500	63	39
Kansas City Chiefs	1	1	.500	33	42
Miami Dolphins	2	3	.400	74	103
Denver Broncos	2	4	.333	115	206
St. Louis/L.A. Rams	1	2	.333	59	67
Arizona Cardinals	0	1	.000	23	27
Atlanta Falcons	0	1	.000	19	34
Carolina Panthers	0	1	.000	29	32
San Diego Chargers	0	1	.000	26	49
Seattle Seahawks	0	1	.000	10	21
Tennessee Titans	0	1	.000	16	23
Cincinnati Bengals	0	2	.000	37	46
Philadelphia Eagles	0	2	.000	31	51
Buffalo Bills	0	4	.000	73	139
Minnesota Vikings	0	4	.000	34	95

SUPER BOWL HOST CITIES

Miami/South Florida	9	
New Orleans	9	
Los Angeles	7	(LA Coliseum 2, Rose Bowl 5)
Tampa Bay	4	
San Diego	3	
Arizona	2	
Atlanta	2	
Detroit	2	
Houston	2	
Jacksonville	1	
Minneapolis	1	
Stanford	1	

FUTURE SUPER BOWL SITES

Super Bowl XLIV	Feb. 7, 2010	Dolphin Stadium, South Florida
Super Bowl XLV	Feb. 6, 2011	Cowboys Stadium, North Texas
Super Bowl XLVI	Feb. 5, 2012	Lucas Oil Stadium, Indianapolis, Indiana
Super Bowl XLVII	Feb. 3, 2013 *	Louisiana Superdome New Orleans, Louisiana

*Tentative date

PETE ROZELLE TROPHY/SUPER BOWL MVPs*

Super Bowl I	— QB Bart Starr, Green Bay
Super Bowl II	— QB Bart Starr, Green Bay
Super Bowl III	— QB Joe Namath, N.Y. Jets
Super Bowl IV	— QB Len Dawson, Kansas City
Super Bowl V	— LB Chuck Howley, Dallas
Super Bowl VI	— QB Roger Staubach, Dallas
Super Bowl VII	— S Jake Scott, Miami
Super Bowl VIII	— RB Larry Csonka, Miami
Super Bowl IX	— RB Franco Harris, Pittsburgh
Super Bowl X	— WR Lynn Swann, Pittsburgh
Super Bowl XI	— WR Fred Biletnikoff, Oakland
Super Bowl XII	— DT Randy White and DE Harvey Martin, Dallas
Super Bowl XIII	— QB Terry Bradshaw, Pittsburgh
Super Bowl XIV	— QB Terry Bradshaw, Pittsburgh
Super Bowl XV	— QB Jim Plunkett, Oakland
Super Bowl XVI	— QB Joe Montana, San Francisco
Super Bowl XVII	— RB John Riggins, Washington
Super Bowl XVIII	— RB Marcus Allen, L.A. Raiders
Super Bowl XIX	— QB Joe Montana, San Francisco
Super Bowl XX	— DE Richard Dent, Chicago
Super Bowl XXI	— QB Phil Simms, N.Y. Giants
Super Bowl XXII	— QB Doug Williams, Washington
Super Bowl XXIII	— WR Jerry Rice, San Francisco
Super Bowl XXIV	— QB Joe Montana, San Francisco
Super Bowl XXV	— RB Ottis Anderson, N.Y. Giants
Super Bowl XXVI	— QB Mark Rypien, Washington
Super Bowl XXVII	— QB Troy Aikman, Dallas
Super Bowl XXVIII	— RB Emmitt Smith, Dallas
Super Bowl XXIX	— QB Steve Young, San Francisco
Super Bowl XXX	— CB Larry Brown, Dallas
Super Bowl XXXI	— KR-PR Desmond Howard, Green Bay
Super Bowl XXXII	— RB Terrell Davis, Denver
Super Bowl XXXIII	— QB John Elway, Denver
Super Bowl XXXIV	— QB Kurt Warner, St. Louis
Super Bowl XXXV	— LB Ray Lewis, Baltimore
Super Bowl XXXVI	— QB Tom Brady, New England
Super Bowl XXXVII	— S Dexter Jackson, Tampa Bay
Super Bowl XXXVIII	— QB Tom Brady, New England
Super Bowl XXXIX	— WR Deion Branch, New England
Super Bowl XL	— WR Hines Ward, Pittsburgh
Super Bowl XLI	— QB Peyton Manning, Indianapolis
Super Bowl XLII	— QB Eli Manning, N.Y. Giants
Super Bowl XLIII	— WR Santonio Holmes, Pittsburgh

** Award named Pete Rozelle Trophy since Super Bowl XXV.*

SUPER BOWL MVP BY POSITION

Quarterback	22
Running Back	7
Wide Receiver	6
Defensive End	2
Linebacker	2
Safety	2
Cornerback	1
Defensive Tackle	1
Kick Returner-Punt Returner	1

A defensive end and defensive tackle shared the Super Bowl XII MVP award.

RESULTS

NFC leads AFC, 22-21

Super Bowl	Date	Winner (Share)	Loser (Share)	Score	Site	Attendance
XLIII	2-1-09	Pittsburgh ($78,000)	Arizona ($40,000)	27-23	Tampa Bay	70,774
XLII	2-3-08	N.Y. Giants ($78,000)	New England ($40,000)	17-14	Arizona	71,101
XLI	2-4-07	Indianapolis ($73,000)	Chicago ($38,000)	29-17	South Florida	74,512
XL	2-5-06	Pittsburgh ($73,000)	Seattle ($38,000)	21-10	Detroit	68,206
XXXIX	2-6-05	New England ($68,000)	Philadelphia ($36,500)	24-21	Jacksonville	78,125
XXXVIII	2-1-04	New England ($68,000)	Carolina ($36,500)	32-29	Houston	71,525
* XXXVII	1-26-03	Tampa Bay ($63,000)	Oakland ($35,000)	48-21	San Diego	67,603
* XXXVI	2-3-02	New England ($63,000)	St. Louis ($34,500)	20-17	New Orleans	72,922
XXXV	1-28-01	Baltimore ($58,000)	N.Y. Giants ($34,500)	34-7	Tampa Bay	71,921
* XXXIV	1-30-00	St. Louis ($58,000)	Tennessee ($33,000)	23-16	Atlanta	72,625
XXXIII	1-31-99	Denver ($53,000)	Atlanta ($32,500)	34-19	South Florida	74,803
XXXII	1-25-98	Denver ($48,000)	Green Bay ($29,000)	31-24	San Diego	68,912
XXXI	1-26-97	Green Bay ($48,000)	New England ($29,000)	35-21	New Orleans	72,301
XXX	1-28-96	Dallas ($42,000)	Pittsburgh ($27,000)	27-17	Arizona	76,347
XXIX	1-29-95	San Francisco ($42,000)	San Diego ($26,000)	49-26	South Florida	74,107
* XXVIII	1-30-94	Dallas ($38,000)	Buffalo ($23,500)	30-13	Atlanta	72,817
XXVII	1-31-93	Dallas ($36,000)	Buffalo ($18,000)	52-17	Pasadena	98,374
XXVI	1-26-92	Washington ($36,000)	Buffalo ($18,000)	37-24	Minneapolis	63,130
* XXV	1-27-91	N.Y. Giants ($36,000)	Buffalo ($18,000)	20-19	Tampa Bay	73,813
XXIV	1-28-90	San Francisco ($36,000)	Denver ($18,000)	55-10	New Orleans	72,919
XXIII	1-22-89	San Francisco ($36,000)	Cincinnati ($18,000)	20-16	South Florida	75,129
XXII	1-31-88	Washington ($36,000)	Denver ($18,000)	42-10	San Diego	73,302
XXI	1-25-87	N.Y. Giants ($36,000)	Denver ($18,000)	39-20	Pasadena	101,063
XX	1-26-86	Chicago ($36,000)	New England ($18,000)	46-10	New Orleans	73,818
XIX	1-20-85	San Francisco ($36,000)	Miami ($18,000)	38-16	Stanford	84,059
XVIII	1-22-84	L.A. Raiders ($36,000)	Washington ($18,000)	38-9	Tampa Bay	72,920
* XVII	1-30-83	Washington ($36,000)	Miami ($18,000)	27-17	Pasadena	103,667
XVI	1-24-82	San Francisco ($18,000)	Cincinnati ($9,000)	26-21	Pontiac	81,270
XV	1-25-81	Oakland ($18,000)	Philadelphia ($9,000)	27-10	New Orleans	76,135
XIV	1-20-80	Pittsburgh ($18,000)	Los Angeles ($9,000)	31-19	Pasadena	103,985
XIII	1-21-79	Pittsburgh ($18,000)	Dallas ($9,000)	35-31	Miami	79,484
XII	1-15-78	Dallas ($18,000)	Denver ($9,000)	27-10	New Orleans	75,583
XI	1-9-77	Oakland ($15,000)	Minnesota ($7,500)	32-14	Pasadena	103,438
X	1-18-76	Pittsburgh ($15,000)	Dallas ($7,500)	21-17	Miami	80,187
IX	1-12-75	Pittsburgh ($15,000)	Minnesota ($7,500)	16-6	New Orleans	80,997
VIII	1-13-74	Miami ($15,000)	Minnesota ($7,500)	24-7	Houston	71,882
VII	1-14-73	Miami ($15,000)	Washington ($7,500)	14-7	Los Angeles	90,182
VI	1-16-72	Dallas ($15,000)	Miami ($7,500)	24-3	New Orleans	81,023
V	1-17-71	Baltimore ($15,000)	Dallas ($7,500)	16-13	Miami	79,204
* IV	1-11-70	Kansas City ($15,000)	Minnesota ($7,500)	23-7	New Orleans	80,562
III	1-12-69	N.Y. Jets ($15,000)	Baltimore ($7,500)	16-7	Miami	75,389
II	1-14-68	Green Bay ($15,000)	Oakland ($7,500)	33-14	Miami	75,546
I	1-15-67	Green Bay ($15,000)	Kansas City ($7,500)	35-10	Los Angeles	61,946

** One week between conference championship games and Super Bowl; all others had two weeks between conference championship games and Super Bowl.*

For historical Super Bowl game recaps, box scores, and video highlights, please visit www.SuperBowl.com.

SUPER BOWL XLIII

Raymond James Stadium, Tampa, Florida
February 1, 2009, Attendance: 70,774

PITTSBURGH 27, ARIZONA 23—Santonio Holmes caught a 6-yard touchdown pass in the back right corner of the end zone with 35 seconds left as the Steelers rallied to win their record sixth Super Bowl title. Holmes' touchdown grab averted what would have been the largest comeback in Super Bowl history, as the Cardinals had scored 16 unanswered points in the fourth quarter. The Steelers began the game with a long drive. Ben Roethlisberger had a 1-yard touchdown run overturned by replay, and the Steelers settled for Jeff Reed's 18-yard field goal. Holmes' 25-yard catch began the next drive, and Gary Russell capped it with a 1-yard run for a 10-0 lead. Arizona responded immediately as Kurt Warner completed a 45-yard pass to Anquan Boldin to set up Ben Patrick's touchdown catch. Karlos Dansby's interception at the Steelers' 34 with 2:00 left in the half gave the Cardinals the opportunity to take the lead. On first-and-goal from the Steelers' 1 with 18 seconds left in the half, James Harrison stepped in front of Warner's quick-slant pass intended for Boldin. Harrison deftly maneuvered down the right sideline and raced 100 yards for a touchdown, barely breaking the plane as Steve Breaston and Larry Fitzgerald attempted to corral him. Harrison's return ended the half, was the longest play in Super Bowl history, and gave the Steelers a 17-7 lead. The Steelers utilized a 16-play, 79-yard drive in the third quarter that consumed 8:39 off the clock. The Steelers had six offensive snaps inside the Cardinals 10-yard line, but settled for Reed's 21-yard field goal and 20-7 lead. With 11:30 to play and on their own 13-yard line, the Cardinals went to a no-huddle offense and Warner completed all eight of his pass attempts, including four to Fitzgerald, capped by his leaping 1-yard catch on third-and-goal to pull the Cardinals within 20-14 with 7:33 to play. With 3:34 remaining, the Cardinals, faced with fourth-and-20 at the

Steelers' 36, punted. Ben Graham's punt was downed by Mike Adams at the 2-yard line. A penalty pushed the Steelers back to the 1-yard line, and on third-and-10, Justin Hartwig was penalized for holding in the end zone. The safety cut the lead to 20-16 with 2:58 to play. Two plays later, Warner hit Fitzgerald with a short pass over the middle, and Fitzgerald raced untouched for a 64-yard touchdown and 23-20 lead with 2:37 remaining. The Steelers began on their own 22-yard line, but a holding penalty pushed them back to their 12. On third-and-6 from their own 26 with 1:56 to play, Roethlisberger connected with Holmes on a 13-yard pass play. On second-and-6 from the Cardinals' 46 with 1:02 to play, Roethlisberger found Holmes with a pass on the right side. Holmes slipped past one defender before being tackled at the 6-yard line. On second-and-goal, Roethlisberger's pass to the back right corner appeared high, but Holmes stretched high, kept both toes on the ground, and held on to the ball despite Aaron Francisco's tight coverage. The touchdown capped an 8-play, 78-yard drive in 2:02, with the last eight plays covering 88 yards following the holding call. Warner completed a 20-yard pass to Fitzgerald and 13-yard pass to J.J. Arrington to reach the Steelers' 44 with 15 seconds left. On the next play, Warner was sacked by LaMarr Woodley. Brett Keisel recovered the ball at the Steelers' 43 with five seconds left to clinch the victory. Roethlisberger was 21 of 30 for 256 yards and 1 touchdown, with 1 interception. Holmes had 9 receptions for 131 yards and was the game's most valuable player. Woodley had his fourth consecutive 2-sack postseason game, extending his record. Warner was 31 of 43 for 377 yards and 3 touchdowns, with 1 interception. In three career Super Bowl games, Warner has the three highest passing-yardage totals in Super Bowl history. Fitzgerald had 7 receptions for 127 yards. Darnell Dockett tied Reggie White's Super Bowl record with 3 sacks.

Pittsburgh (27)	Offense	Arizona (23)
Hines Ward	WR	Larry Fitzgerald
Max Starks	LT	Mike Gandy
Chris Kemoeatu	LG	Reggie Wells
Justin Hartwig	C	Lyle Sendlein
Darnell Stapleton	RG	Deuce Lutui
Willie Colon	RT	Levi Brown
Heath Miller	TE	Leonard Pope
Matt Spaeth	TE/WR	Anquan Boldin
Ben Roethlisberger	QB	Kurt Warner
Sean McHugh	TE/RB	Edgerrin James
Willie Parker	RB/FB	Terrelle Smith
	Defense	
Aaron Smith	DE/LDE	Antonio Smith
Casey Hampton	NT	Bryan Robinson
Brett Keisel	DE/DT	Darnell Dockett
LaMarr Woodley	OLB/RDE	Gabe Watson
James Farrior	LILB/SLB	Chike Okeafor
Larry Foote	RILB/LB	Gerald Hayes
James Harrison	OLB/LB	Monty Beisel
Ike Taylor	LCB/LB	Karlos Dansby
Bryant McFadden	RCB	D. Rodgers-Cromartie
Troy Polamalu	SS	Adrian Wilson
Ryan Clark	FS	Antrel Rolle

SUBSTITUTIONS

PITTSBURGH—Specialists: K—Jeff Reed. P—Mitch Berger. LS—Jared Retkofsky. Offense: RB—Carey Davis, Mewelde Moore, Gary Russell. WR—Santonio Holmes, Limas Sweed, Nate Washington. Defense: DT—Chris Hoke. DE—Nick Eason, Travis Kirschke. LB—Patrick Bailey, Keyaron Fox, Andre Frazier, Lawrence Timmons. CB—Tyrone Carter, William Gay, Anthony Madison, Deshea Townsend. DNP: QB—Byron Leftwich. G—Jeremy Parquet. T—Trai Essex. Not Active: QB—Dennis Dixon. T—Jason Capizzi, Tony Hills. DL—Scott Paxson. DE—Orpheus Roye. LB—Bruce Davis. CB—Fernando Bryant. S—Anthony Smith.

ARIZONA—Specialists: K—Neil Rackers. P—Ben Graham. LS—Nathan Hodel. Offense: RB—J.J. Arrington, Tim Hightower. WR—Steve Breaston, Sean Morey, Jerheme Urban. TE—Ben Patrick. G/T—Elton Brown. Defense: DE—Bertrand Berry, Calais Campbell, Kenny Iwebema. DE/LB—Travis LaBoy. LB—Pago Togafau. CB—Mike Adams, Ralph Brown, Roderick Hood. S—Aaron Francisco, Matt Ware. DNP: QB—Matt Leinart. WR—Early Doucet. C—Pat Ross. Not Active: QB—Brian St. Pierre. FB—Tim Castille. TE—Jerame Tuman. T—Brandon Keith, Elliott Vallejo. DT—Alan Branch. LB—Victor Hobson. CB—Eric Green.

OFFICIALS

Referee—Terry McAulay. Umpire—Roy Ellison. Head Linesman—Derick Bowers. Line Judge—Mark Perlman. Side Judge—Michael Banks. Field Judge—Greg Gautreaux. Back Judge—Keith Ferguson. Replay Official—Bob McGrath.

SCORING

Pittsburgh (AFC)	3	14	3	7	—27
Arizona (NFC)	0	7	0	16	—23

Pitt — FG Reed 18 (9:45)
Pitt — Russell 1 run (Reed kick) (14:01)
Ariz — Patrick 1 pass from Warner (Rackers kick) (8:34)
Pitt — Harrison 100 interception return (Reed kick) (0:00)
Pitt — FG Reed 21 (2:11)
Ariz — Fitzgerald 1 pass from Warner (Rackers kick) (7:33)
Ariz — Safety, Hartwig penalized for holding in end zone (2:58)
Ariz — Fitzgerald 64 pass from Warner (Rackers kick) (2:37)
Pitt — Holmes 6 pass from Roethlisberger (Reed kick) (0:35)

TEAM STATISTICS	PITT	ARIZ
Total First Downs	20	23
Rushing	4	2
Passing	12	20
Penalty	4	1
Total Net Yardage	292	407
Total Offensive Plays	58	57
Avg. Gain Per Offensive Play	5.0	7.1
Rushes	25	12
Yards Gained Rushing (Net)	58	33
Avg. Yards per Rush	2.3	2.8
Passes Attempted	30	43
Passes Completed	21	31
Had Intercepted	1	1
Tackled Attempting to Pass	3	2
Yards Lost Attempting to Pass	22	3
Yards Gained Passing (Net)	234	374
Punts	3	5
Avg. Distance	46.3	36.0
Punt Returns	2	2
Punt Return Yardage	5	34
Kickoff Returns	4	5
Kickoff Return Yardage	80	91
Interception Return Yardage	100	(-1)
Total Return Yardage	105	33
Fumbles	0	2
Fumbles Lost	0	1
Own Fumbles Recovered	0	1
Opponent Fumbles Recovered	1	0
Penalties	7	11
Yards Penalized	56	106
Field Goals	2	0
Field Goals Attempted	2	0
Third-Down Efficiency	4/10	3/8
Fourth-Down Efficiency	0/0	0/0
Time of Possession	33:01	26:59

INDIVIDUAL STATISTICS

RUSHING: PITT: Parker 19-53-0, Moore 1-6-0, Roethlisberger 3-2-0, Russell 2-(-3)-1. ARIZ: James 9-33-0, Warner 1-0-0, Hightower 1-0-0, Arrington 1-0-0.

PASSING: PITT: Roethlisberger 30-21-256-1-1. ARIZ: Warner 43-31-377-3-1.

RECEIVING: PITT: Holmes 9-131-1, Miller 5-57-0, Ward 2-43-0, Washington 1-11-0, Davis 1-6-0, Spaeth 1-6-0, Moore 1-4-0, Parker 1-(-2)-0. ARIZ: Boldin 8-84-0, Fitzgerald 7-127-2, Breaston 6-71-0, James 4-28-0, Arrington 2-35-0, Hightower 2-13-0, Urban 1-18-0, Patrick 1-1-1.

KICKOFF RETURNS: PITT: Russell 2-42-0, Davis 2-38-0. ARIZ: Arrington 4-82-0, Breaston 1-9-0.

PUNT RETURNS: PITT: Holmes 2-5-0. ARIZ: Breaston 2-34-0.

PUNTING: PITT: Berger 3-139-46.3. ARIZ: Graham 5-180-36.0.

INTERCEPTIONS: PITT: Harrison 1-100-1. ARIZ: Dansby 1-(-1)-0.

SACKS: PITT: Woodley 2. ARIZ: Dockett 3.

AFC CHAMPIONSHIP GAME RESULTS

Includes AFL Championship Games (1960-69)

Season	Date	Winner (Share)	Loser (Share)	Score	Site	Attendance
2008	Jan. 18	Pittsburgh ($37,500)	Baltimore ($37,500)	23-14	Pittsburgh	65,350
2007	Jan. 20	New England ($37,500)	San Diego ($37,500)	21-12	Foxborough	68,756
2006	Jan. 21	Indianapolis ($37,000)	New England ($37,000)	38-34	Indianapolis	57,433
2005	Jan. 22	Pittsburgh ($37,000)	Denver ($37,000)	34-17	Denver	76,775
2004	Jan. 23	New England ($36,500)	Pittsburgh ($36,500)	41-27	Pittsburgh	65,242
2003	Jan. 18	New England ($36,500)	Indianapolis ($36,500)	24-14	Foxborough	68,436
2002	Jan. 19	Oakland ($35,000)	Tennessee ($35,000)	41-24	Oakland	62,544
2001	Jan. 27	New England ($34,500)	Pittsburgh ($34,500)	24-17	Pittsburgh	64,704
2000	Jan. 14	Baltimore ($34,500)	Oakland ($34,500)	16-3	Oakland	62,784
1999	Jan. 23	Tennessee ($33,000)	Jacksonville ($33,000)	33-14	Jacksonville	75,206
1998	Jan. 17	Denver ($32,500)	N.Y. Jets ($32,500)	23-10	Denver	75,482
1997	Jan. 11	Denver ($30,000)	Pittsburgh ($30,000)	24-21	Pittsburgh	61,382
1996	Jan. 12	New England ($29,000)	Jacksonville ($29,000)	20-6	Foxborough	60,190
1995	Jan. 14	Pittsburgh ($27,000)	Indianapolis ($27,000)	20-16	Pittsburgh	61,062
1994	Jan. 15	San Diego ($26,000)	Pittsburgh ($26,000)	17-13	Pittsburgh	61,545
1993	Jan. 23	Buffalo ($23,500)	Kansas City ($23,500)	30-13	Buffalo	76,642
1992	Jan. 17	Buffalo ($18,000)	Miami ($18,000)	29-10	Miami	72,703
1991	Jan. 12	Buffalo ($18,000)	Denver ($18,000)	10-7	Buffalo	80,272
1990	Jan. 20	Buffalo ($18,000)	L.A. Raiders ($18,000)	51-3	Buffalo	80,325
1989	Jan. 14	Denver ($18,000)	Cleveland ($18,000)	37-21	Denver	76,046
1988	Jan. 8	Cincinnati ($18,000)	Buffalo ($18,000)	21-10	Cincinnati	59,747
1987	Jan. 17	Denver ($18,000)	Cleveland ($18,000)	38-33	Denver	76,197
1986	Jan. 11	Denver ($18,000)	Cleveland ($18,000)	23-20*	Cleveland	79,973
1985	Jan. 12	New England ($18,000)	Miami ($18,000)	31-14	Miami	75,662
1984	Jan. 6	Miami ($18,000)	Pittsburgh ($18,000)	45-28	Miami	76,029
1983	Jan. 8	L.A. Raiders ($18,000)	Seattle ($18,000)	30-14	Los Angeles	91,445
1982	Jan. 23	Miami ($18,000)	N.Y. Jets ($18,000)	14-0	Miami	67,396
1981	Jan. 10	Cincinnati ($9,000)	San Diego ($9,000)	27-7	Cincinnati	46,302
1980	Jan. 11	Oakland ($9,000)	San Diego ($9,000)	34-27	San Diego	52,675
1979	Jan. 6	Pittsburgh ($9,000)	Houston ($9,000)	27-13	Pittsburgh	50,475
1978	Jan. 7	Pittsburgh ($9,000)	Houston ($9,000)	34-5	Pittsburgh	50,725
1977	Jan. 1	Denver ($9,000)	Oakland ($9,000)	20-17	Denver	75,044
1976	Dec. 26	Oakland ($8,500)	Pittsburgh ($5,500)	24-7	Oakland	53,821
1975	Jan. 4	Pittsburgh ($8,500)	Oakland ($5,500)	16-10	Pittsburgh	50,609
1974	Dec. 29	Pittsburgh ($8,500)	Oakland ($5,500)	24-13	Oakland	53,800
1973	Dec. 30	Miami ($8,500)	Oakland ($5,500)	27-10	Miami	79,325
1972	Dec. 31	Miami ($8,500)	Pittsburgh ($5,500)	21-17	Pittsburgh	50,845
1971	Jan. 2	Miami ($8,500)	Baltimore ($5,500)	21-0	Miami	76,622
1970	Jan. 3	Baltimore ($8,500)	Oakland ($5,500)	27-17	Baltimore	54,799
1969	Jan. 4	Kansas City ($7,755)	Oakland ($6,252)	17-7	Oakland	53,564
1968	Dec. 29	N.Y. Jets ($7,007)	Oakland ($5,349)	27-23	New York	62,627
1967	Dec. 31	Oakland ($6,321)	Houston ($4,996)	40-7	Oakland	53,330
1966	Jan. 1	Kansas City ($5,309)	Buffalo ($3,799)	31-7	Buffalo	42,080
1965	Dec. 26	Buffalo ($5,189)	San Diego ($3,447)	23-0	San Diego	30,361
1964	Dec. 26	Buffalo ($2,668)	San Diego ($1,738)	20-7	Buffalo	40,242
1963	Jan. 5	San Diego ($2,498)	Boston ($1,596)	51-10	San Diego	30,127
1962	Dec. 23	Dallas ($2,206)	Houston ($1,471)	20-17*	Houston	37,981
1961	Dec. 24	Houston ($1,792)	San Diego ($1,111)	10-3	San Diego	29,556
1960	Jan. 1	Houston ($1,025)	L.A. Chargers ($718)	24-16	Houston	32,183

**Sudden death overtime*

AFC CHAMPIONSHIP GAME COMPOSITE STANDINGS

	W	L	Pct.	Pts.	OP
Cincinnati Bengals	2	0	1.000	48	17
Buffalo Bills	6	2	.750	180	92
Denver Broncos	6	2	.750	189	166
New England Patriots**	6	2	.750	205	179
Kansas City Chiefs*	3	1	.750	81	61
Miami Dolphins	5	2	.714	152	115
Pittsburgh Steelers	7	7	.500	308	284
Baltimore Ravens	1	1	.500	30	26
Indianapolis Colts#	2	3	.400	95	116
Tennessee Titans##	3	5	.375	133	195
Oakland Raiders###	5	9	.357	272	304
New York Jets	1	2	.333	37	60
San Diego Chargers***	2	7	.222	140	182
Seattle Seahawks	0	1	.000	14	30
Jacksonville Jaguars	0	2	.000	20	53
Cleveland Browns	0	3	.000	74	98

* *One game played when franchise was in Dallas (Texans) (Won 20-17)*

** *One game played when franchise was in Boston (Lost 51-10)*

*** *One game played when franchise was in Los Angeles (Lost 24-16)*

\# *Two games played when franchise was in Baltimore (Won 27-17, lost 21-0)*

\#\# *Six games played when franchise was in Houston and known as Oilers (Won 2, lost 4)*

\#\#\# *Two games played when franchise was in Los Angeles (Won 30-14, lost 51-3)*

2008 AFC CHAMPIONSHIP GAME
Heinz Field, Pittsburgh, Pennsylvania
January 18, 2009, Attendance: 65,350

PITTSBURGH 23, BALTIMORE 14—Troy Polamalu's 40-yard interception return for a touchdown with 4:24 remaining helped propel the Steelers to their AFC-leading seventh Super Bowl. Ben Roethlisberger's 45-yard pass to Hines Ward on the game's third play set up Jeff Reed's 34-yard field goal. Later in the first quarter, Deshea Townsend intercepted Joe Flacco's short pass at the Ravens' 35. Reed's 42-yard field goal moments later stretched the lead to 6-0. Flacco was then stuffed for no gain on fourth-and-1 from the Steelers' 34 at the end of the first quarter. Three plays later, Roethlisberger connected on a 65-yard touchdown pass to Santonio Holmes for a 13-0 lead. Jim Leonhard's 45-yard punt return set up Willis McGahee's 3-yard touchdown run with 2:40 left in the half. The Steelers drove to the Ravens' 21 with 16 seconds left, but Roethlisberger completed a 9-yard pass to Mewelde Moore and the Steelers could not get another snap off before halftime. Reed kicked another field goal in the third quarter, and the Ravens drove 58 yards in the fourth quarter to cut the deficit to two points when McGahee scored on a 1-yard run with 9:29 to play. The Ravens' defense then forced a punt, but on third-and-13 from their own 29-yard-line, Polamalu intercepted a pass intended for Derrick Mason. Polamalu weaved through the Ravens' offense before bulling his way into the end zone for a 23-14 lead. Baltimore failed to cross midfield on its final two possessions, both ending in turnovers as Lawrence Timmons recovered a fumble and Tyrone Carter intercepted a pass. Roethlisberger was 16 of 33 for 255 yards and 1 touchdown. Flacco was 13 of 30 for 141 yards, with 3 interceptions.

Baltimore (14)	**Offense**	**Pittsburgh (23)**
Mark Clayton	WR	Hines Ward
Jared Gaither	LT	Max Starks
Ben Grubbs	LG	Chris Kemoeatu
Jason Brown	C	Justin Hartwig
Chris Chester	RG	Darnell Stapleton
Willie Anderson	RT	Willie Colon
Todd Heap	TE	Heath Miller
Derrick Mason	WR	Santonio Holmes
Joe Flacco	QB	Ben Roethlisberger
Le'Ron McClain	FB/TE	Matt Spaeth
Willis McGahee	RB	Willie Parker
	Defense	
Trevor Pryce	RDT/DE	Aaron Smith
Haloti Ngata	NT	Casey Hampton
Justin Bannan	LDT/DE	Brett Keisel
Jarret Johnson	LOLB/OLB	LaMarr Woodley
Ray Lewis	LILB/ILB	James Farrior
Bart Scott	RILB/ILB	Larry Foote
Terrell Suggs	LOLB/OLB	James Harrison
Fabian Washington	LCB	Ike Taylor
Frank Walker	RCB	Bryant McFadden
Jim Leonhard	SS	Troy Polamalu
Ed Reed	FS	Ryan Clark

SUBSTITUTIONS

BALTIMORE—Specialists: K—Steven Hauschka, Matt Stover. P—Sam Koch. LS—Matt Katula. Offense: RB—Ray Rice. FB—Lorenzo Neal. WR—Yamon Figurs, Marcus Smith. TE—Edgar Jones, Daniel Wilcox. T—Chad Slaughter, Adam Terry. Defense: DT—Brandon McKinney. DE—Marques Douglas. LB—Brendon Ayanbadejo, Nick Greisen, Jameel McClain. CB—Corey Ivy, Evan Oglesby. S—Haruki Nakamura, Daren Stone, Tom Zbikowski. DNP: QB—Troy Smith. Not Active: QB—Todd Bouman. RB—Jalen Parmele. WR—Terrance Copper. T—Oniel Cousins. G/T—David Hale. LB—Antwan Barnes, Robert McCune. CB—Samari Rolle.

PITTSBURGH—Specialists: K—Jeff Reed. P—Mitch Berger. LS—Jared Retkofsky. Offense: RB—Carey Davis, Mewelde Moore, Gary Russell. WR—Limas Sweed, Nate Washington. TE—Sean McHugh. Defense: DT—Chris Hoke. DE—Nick Eason, Travis Kirschke. LB—Patrick Bailey, Keyaron Fox, Andre Frazier, Lawrence Timmons. CB—William Gay, Anthony Madison, Deshea Townsend. S—Tyrone Carter. DNP: QB—Byron Leftwich. G—Jeremy Parquet. T—Trai Essex. Not Active: QB—Dennis Dixon. T—Jason Capizzi, Tony Hills. DT—Scott Paxson. DE—Orpheus Roye. LB—Bruce Davis. CB—Fernando Bryant. S—Anthony Smith.

OFFICIALS

Referee—William Carollo. Umpire—Ruben Fowler.
Line Judge—Byron Boston. Side Judge—Scott Steenson.
Head Linesman—Ed Camp. Back Judge—Tony Steratore.
Field Judge—Gary Cavaletto.

SCORING

Baltimore	0	7	0	7	—	14
Pittsburgh	6	7	3	7	—	23

Pitt — FG Reed 34
Pitt — FG Reed 42
Pitt — Holmes 65 pass from Roethlisberger (Reed kick)
Balt — McGahee 3 run (Stover kick)
Pitt — FG Reed 46
Balt — McGahee 1 run (Stover kick)
Pitt — Polamalu 40 interception return (Reed kick)

TEAM STATISTICS	**BALT**	**PITT**
Total First Downs	13	11
Rushing	5	1
Passing	6	9
Penalty	2	1
Total Net Yardage	198	275
Total Offensive Plays	58	65
Average Gain Per Offensive Play	3.4	4.2
Rushes	25	28
Yards Gained Rushing (Net)	73	52
Average Yards per Rush	2.9	1.9
Passes Attempted	30	33
Passes Completed	13	16
Had Intercepted	3	0
Tackled Attempting to Pass	3	4
Yards Lost Attempting to Pass	16	32
Yards Gained Passing (Net)	141	255
Punts	7	7
Average Distance	40.9	37.7
Punt Returns	6	5
Punt Return Yardage	65	26
Kickoff Returns	6	3
Kickoff Return Yardage	86	64
Interception Return Yardage	0	47
Total Return Yardage	65	73
Fumbles	3	2
Fumbles Lost	1	1
Own Fumbles Recovered	2	1
Opponent Fumbles Recovered	1	1
Penalties	6	6
Yards Penalized	53	67
Field Goals	0	3
Field Goals Attempted	0	3
Third-Down Efficiency	3/13	7/18
Fourth-Down Efficiency	0/1	0/0
Time of Possession	26:51	33:09

INDIVIDUAL STATISTICS

RUSHING: BALT: McGahee 20-60-2, Clayton 1-16-0, McClain 1-3-0, Rice 1-2-0, Flacco 2-(-8)-0. PITT: Parker 24-47-0, Moore 1-6-0, Washington 1-1-0, Roethlisberger 2-(-2)-0.

PASSING: BALT: Flacco 30-13-141-0-3.
PITT: Roethlisberger 33-16-255-1-0.

RECEIVING: BALT: Rice 3-43-0, Mason 3-41-0, Heap 3-26-0, Clayton 2-18-0, McGahee 2-13-0. PITT: Miller 3-62-0, Ward 3-55-0, Washington 3-21-0, Holmes 2-70-1, Sweed 2-20-0, Davis 1-20-0, Moore 1-9-0, Parker 1-(-2)-0.

KICKOFF RETURNS: BALT: Rice 2-31-0, Figurs 2-19-0, Zbikowski 1-22-0, Wilcox 1-14-0. PITT: Russell 2-45-0, Davis 1-19-0.
PUNT RETURNS: BALT: Leonhard 6-65-0. PITT: Holmes 3-25-0, Moore 2-1-0.

PUNTING: BALT: Koch 7-286-40.9. PITT: Berger 7-264-37.7.
INTERCEPTIONS: BALT: None. PITT: Polamalu 1-40-1, Carter 1-5-0, Townsend 1-2-0.
SACKS: BALT: Suggs 2, Douglas 1, Ngata 1. PITT: Woodley 2, Aa. Smith 1.

NFC CHAMPIONSHIP GAME RESULTS
Includes NFL Championship Games (1933-1969)

Season	Date	Winner (Share)	Loser (Share)	Score	Site	Attendance
2008	Jan. 18	Arizona ($37,500)	Philadelphia ($37,500)	32-25	Glendale	70,650
2007	Jan. 20	N.Y. Giants ($37,500)	Green Bay ($37,500)	23-20*	Green Bay	72,740
2006	Jan. 21	Chicago ($37,000)	New Orleans ($37,000)	39-14	Chicago	61,817
2005	Jan. 22	Seattle ($37,000)	Carolina ($37,000)	34-14	Seattle	67,837
2004	Jan. 23	Philadelphia ($36,500)	Atlanta ($36,500)	27-10	Philadelphia	67,717
2003	Jan. 18	Carolina ($36,500)	Philadelphia ($36,500)	14-3	Philadelphia	67,862
2002	Jan. 19	Tampa Bay ($35,000)	Philadelphia ($35,000)	27-10	Philadelphia	66,713
2001	Jan. 27	St. Louis ($34,500)	Philadelphia ($34,500)	29-24	St. Louis	66,502
2000	Jan. 14	N.Y. Giants ($34,500)	Minnesota ($34,500)	41-0	East Rutherford	79,310
1999	Jan. 23	St. Louis ($33,000)	Tampa Bay ($33,000)	11-6	St. Louis	66,396
1998	Jan. 17	Atlanta ($32,500)	Minnesota ($32,500)	30-27*	Minneapolis	64,060
1997	Jan. 11	Green Bay ($30,000)	San Francisco ($30,000)	23-10	San Francisco	68,987
1996	Jan. 12	Green Bay ($29,000)	Carolina ($29,000)	30-13	Green Bay	60,216
1995	Jan. 14	Dallas ($27,000)	Green Bay ($27,000)	38-27	Dallas	65,135
1994	Jan. 15	San Francisco ($26,000)	Dallas ($26,000)	38-28	San Francisco	69,125
1993	Jan. 23	Dallas ($23,500)	San Francisco ($23,500)	38-21	Dallas	64,902
1992	Jan. 17	Dallas ($18,000)	San Francisco ($18,000)	30-20	San Francisco	64,920
1991	Jan. 12	Washington ($18,000)	Detroit ($18,000)	41-10	Washington	55,585
1990	Jan. 20	N.Y. Giants ($18,000)	San Francisco ($18,000)	15-13	San Francisco	65,750
1989	Jan. 14	San Francisco ($18,000)	L.A. Rams ($18,000)	30-3	San Francisco	65,634
1988	Jan. 8	San Francisco ($18,000)	Chicago ($18,000)	28-3	Chicago	66,946
1987	Jan. 17	Washington ($18,000)	Minnesota ($18,000)	17-10	Washington	55,212
1986	Jan. 11	New York Giants ($18,000)	Washington ($18,000)	17-0	East Rutherford	76,891
1985	Jan. 12	Chicago ($18,000)	L.A. Rams ($18,000)	24-0	Chicago	66,030
1984	Jan. 6	San Francisco ($18,000)	Chicago ($18,000)	23-0	San Francisco	61,336
1983	Jan. 8	Washington ($18,000)	San Francisco ($18,000)	24-21	Washington	55,363
1982	Jan. 22	Washington ($18,000)	Dallas ($18,000)	31-17	Washington	55,045
1981	Jan. 10	San Francisco ($9,000)	Dallas ($9,000)	28-27	San Francisco	60,525
1980	Jan. 11	Philadelphia ($9,000)	Dallas ($9,000)	20-7	Philadelphia	71,522
1979	Jan. 6	Los Angeles ($9,000)	Tampa Bay ($9,000)	9-0	Tampa	72,033
1978	Jan. 7	Dallas ($9,000)	Los Angeles ($9,000)	28-0	Los Angeles	71,086
1977	Jan. 1	Dallas ($9,000)	Minnesota ($9,000)	23-6	Dallas	64,293
1976	Dec. 26	Minnesota ($8,500)	Los Angeles ($5,500)	24-13	Minneapolis	48,379
1975	Jan. 4	Dallas ($8,500)	Los Angeles ($5,500)	37-7	Los Angeles	88,919
1974	Dec. 29	Minnesota ($8,500)	Los Angeles ($5,500)	14-10	Minneapolis	48,444
1973	Dec. 30	Minnesota ($8,500)	Dallas ($5,500)	27-10	Dallas	64,422
1972	Dec. 31	Washington ($8,500)	Dallas ($5,500)	26-3	Washington	53,129
1971	Jan. 2	Dallas ($8,500)	San Francisco ($5,500)	14-3	Dallas	63,409
1970	Jan. 3	Dallas ($8,500)	San Francisco ($5,500)	17-10	San Francisco	59,364
1969	Jan. 4	Minnesota ($7,930)	Cleveland ($5,118)	27-7	Minneapolis	46,503
1968	Dec. 29	Baltimore ($9,306)	Cleveland ($5,963)	34-0	Cleveland	78,410
1967	Dec. 31	Green Bay ($7,950)	Dallas ($5,299)	21-17	Green Bay	50,861
1966	Jan. 1	Green Bay ($9,813)	Dallas ($6,527)	34-27	Dallas	74,152
1965	Jan. 2	Green Bay ($7,819)	Cleveland ($5,288)	23-12	Green Bay	50,777
1964	Dec. 27	Cleveland ($8,052)	Baltimore ($5,571)	27-0	Cleveland	79,544
1963	Dec. 29	Chicago ($5,899)	New York ($4,218)	14-10	Chicago	45,801
1962	Dec. 30	Green Bay ($5,888)	New York ($4,166)	16-7	New York	64,892
1961	Dec. 31	Green Bay ($5,195)	New York ($3,339)	37-0	Green Bay	39,029
1960	Dec. 26	Philadelphia ($5,116)	Green Bay ($3,105)	17-13	Philadelphia	67,325
1959	Dec. 27	Baltimore ($4,674)	New York ($3,083)	31-16	Baltimore	57,545
1958	Dec. 28	Baltimore ($4,718)	New York ($3,111)	23-17*	New York	64,185
1957	Dec. 29	Detroit ($4,295)	Cleveland ($2,750)	59-14	Detroit	55,263
1956	Dec. 30	New York ($3,779)	Chi. Bears ($2,485)	47-7	New York	56,836
1955	Dec. 26	Cleveland ($3,508)	Los Angeles ($2,316)	38-14	Los Angeles	85,693
1954	Dec. 26	Cleveland ($2,478)	Detroit ($1,585)	56-10	Cleveland	43,827
1953	Dec. 27	Detroit ($2,424)	Cleveland ($1,654)	17-16	Detroit	54,577
1952	Dec. 28	Detroit ($2,274)	Cleveland ($1,712)	17-7	Cleveland	50,934
1951	Dec. 23	Los Angeles ($2,108)	Cleveland ($1,483)	24-17	Los Angeles	57,522
1950	Dec. 24	Cleveland ($1,113)	Los Angeles ($686)	30-28	Cleveland	29,751
1949	Dec. 18	Philadelphia ($1,094)	Los Angeles ($739)	14-0	Los Angeles	27,980
1948	Dec. 19	Philadelphia ($1,540)	Chi. Cardinals ($874)	7-0	Philadelphia	36,309
1947	Dec. 28	Chi. Cardinals ($1,132)	Philadelphia ($754)	28-21	Chicago	30,759

Season	Date	Winner (Share)	Loser (Share)	Score	Site	Attendance
1946	Dec. 15	Chi. Bears ($1,975)	New York ($1,295)	24-14	New York	58,346
1945	Dec. 16	Cleveland ($1,469)	Washington ($902)	15-14	Cleveland	32,178
1944	Dec. 17	Green Bay ($1,449)	New York ($814)	14-7	New York	46,016
1943	Dec. 26	Chi. Bears ($1,146)	Washington ($765)	41-21	Chicago	34,320
1942	Dec. 13	Washington ($965)	Chi. Bears ($637)	14-6	Washington	36,006
1941	Dec. 21	Chi. Bears ($430)	New York ($288)	37-9	Chicago	13,341
1940	Dec. 8	Chi. Bears ($873)	Washington ($606)	73-0	Washington	36,034
1939	Dec. 10	Green Bay ($703.97)	New York ($455.57)	27-0	Milwaukee	32,279
1938	Dec. 11	New York ($504.45)	Green Bay ($368.81)	23-17	New York	48,120
1937	Dec. 12	Washington ($225.90)	Chi. Bears ($127.78)	28-21	Chicago	15,870
1936	Dec. 13	Green Bay ($250)	Boston ($180)	21-6	New York	29,545
1935	Dec. 15	Detroit ($313.35)	New York ($200.20)	26-7	Detroit	15,000
1934	Dec. 9	New York ($621)	Chi. Bears ($414.02)	30-13	New York	35,059
1933	Dec. 17	Chi. Bears ($210.34)	New York ($140.22)	23-21	Chicago	26,000

*Sudden death overtime

NFC CHAMPIONSHIP GAME COMPOSITE STANDINGS

	W	L	Pct.	Pts.	OP
Seattle Seahawks	1	0	1.000	34	14
Baltimore Colts	3	1	.750	88	60
Green Bay Packers	10	4	.714	323	200
Detroit Lions	4	2	.667	139	141
Arizona Cardinals**	2	1	.667	60	53
Washington Redskins*	7	5	.583	222	255
Chicago Bears	8	6	.571	325	259
Dallas Cowboys	8	8	.500	361	319
Philadelphia Eagles	5	5	.500	168	160
Minnesota Vikings	4	4	.500	135	151
Atlanta Falcons	1	1	.500	40	54
San Francisco 49ers	5	7	.417	245	222
New York Giants	7	11	.389	304	342
Cleveland Browns	4	7	.364	224	253
St. Louis Rams***	5	9	.357	163	300
Carolina Panthers	1	2	.333	41	67
Tampa Bay Buccaneers	1	2	.333	33	30
New Orleans Saints	0	1	.000	14	39

*One game played when franchise was in Boston (Lost 21-6)

**Both games played when franchise was in Chicago(Won 28-21, lost 7-0)

***One game played when franchise was in Cleveland (Won 15-14), and 11 games when franchise was in Los Angeles (Won 2, lost 9, scored 108 points, allowed 256 points).

2008 NFC CHAMPIONSHIP GAME

University of Phoenix Stadium, Glendale, Arizona

January 18, 2009, Attendance: 70,650

ARIZONA 32, PHILADELPHIA 25—Kurt Warner passed for four touchdowns, including an 8-yard pass to Tim Hightower with 2:53 remaining, as the Cardinals, who had allowed 19 consecutive points, rallied to defeat the Eagles. The victory propelled the Cardinals to their first-ever Super Bowl appearance. Larry Fitzgerald caught three touchdown passes for the Cardinals, the first of which capped a game-opening 9-play, 80-yard drive. Early in the second quarter, David Akers missed a 47-yard field-goal attempt wide right. On the next play, Warner pitched the ball to running back J.J. Arrington, who threw a lateral back across the field to Warner, who then launched a 62-yard touchdown pass to Fitzgerald for a 14-3 lead. Akers made his second field goal of the half, but Arizona answered with a 73-yard drive capped by Fitzgerald's third touchdown catch of the half for a 21-6 lead with 3:06 remaining in the second quarter. Neil Rackers made a 49-yard field goal as the half expired, and Donovan McNabb fumbled on the Eagles' first possession of the second half. But Philadelphia scored on its next three drives. Kevin Curtis caught a 50-yard pass on third-and-18 to set up Brent Celek's 6-yard touchdown catch with 4:08 left in the third quarter. The Eagles' defense forced a three-and-out, and after DeSean Jackson caught a 9-yard pass on third-and-6, McNabb connected with Celek on a 31-yard touchdown catch with 49 seconds left in the third quarter. However, Akers' extra-point attempt was wide right, and the scored remained 24-19. After another Cardinals' punt, McNabb needed just four plays to take the lead, finding Jackson for a 62-yard touchdown deep down the right side. It was the Eagles' third touchdown in eight minutes, 23 seconds, but McNabb's two-point conversion attempt pass for Brian Westbrook was incomplete, limiting the Eagles' lead to 25-24. The Cardinals drove to midfield, where Tim Hightower gained 6 yards on fourth-and-1 to keep the drive alive. On third-and-goal, Warner connected with Hightower on an 8-yard touchdown. Along with the subsequent two-point conversion pass to Ben Patrick, the Cardinals led 32-25 with 2:53 remaining. The Eagles drove to the Cardinals' 47, but McNabb had four consecutive passes fall incomplete. Warner was 21 of 28 for 279 yards and 4 touchdowns. Fitzgerald had 9 receptions for 152 yards. McNabb was 28 of 47 for 375 yards and 3 touchdowns, with 1 interception.

Philadelphia (25)	Offense	Arizona (32)
Kevin Curtis	WR	Larry Fitzgerald
Tra Thomas	LT	Mike Gandy
Todd Herremans	LG	Reggie Wells
Jamaal Jackson	C	Lyle Sendlein
Nick Cole	RG	Deuce Lutui
Jon Runyan	RT	Levi Brown
Brent Celek	TE	Leonard Pope
DeSean Jackson	WR	Anquan Boldin
Donovan McNabb	QB	Kurt Warner
Brian Westbrook	RB	Edgerrin James
Dan Klecko	FB	Terrelle Smith
	Defense	
Juqua Parker	LE	Antonio Smith
Mike Patterson	LT/NT	Bryan Robinson
Brodrick Bunkley	RT/DT	Darnell Dockett
Trent Cole	RE	Bertrand Berry
Chris Gocong	SLB	Chike Okeafor
Stewart Bradley	MLB	Gerald Hayes
Akeem Jordan	WLB	Karlos Dansby
Asante Samuel	LCB	Roderick Hood
Sheldon Brown	RCB	Dominique Rodgers-Cromartie
Quintin Mikell	SS	Adrian Wilson
Brian Dawkins	FS	Antrel Rolle

SUBSTITUTIONS

PHILADELPHIA—Specialists: K—David Akers. P—Sav Rocca. LS—Jon Dorenbos. Offense: RB—Correll Buckhalter. FB—Kyle Eckel. WR—Jason Avant, Hank Baskett, Greg Lewis. TE—L. J. Smith. T—Winston Justice. Defense: DT—Trevor Laws. DE—Victor Abiamiri, Chris Clemons, Darren Howard. LB—Tank Daniels, Omar Gaither, Tracy White. CB—Joselio Hanson, Lito Sheppard. S—Sean Considine, Quintin Demps. DNP: QB—Kevin Kolb. T—Chris Patrick. Not Active: QB—A.J. Feeley. RB—Lorenzo Booker.

WR—Reggie Brown. TE—Matt Schobel. G/T—Shawn Andrews. DE—Bryan Smith. LB—Joe Mays. CB—Dimitri Patterson. **GREEN BAY**—Specialists: K—Neil Rackers. P—Ben Graham. LS—Nathan Hodel. Offense: RB—J.J. Arrington, Tim Hightower. WR—Steve Breaston, Early Doucet, Sean Morey, Jerheme Urban. TE—Ben Patrick. G/T—Elton Brown. Defense: DT—Gabe Watson. DE—Calais Campbell, Kenny Iwebema. DE/LB—Travis LaBoy. LB—Monty Beisel, Pago Togafau. CB—Michael Adams, Ralph Brown. S—Aaron Francisco, Matt Ware. DNP: QB—Matt Leinart. C—Pat Ross. Not Active: QB—Brian St. Pierre. FB—Tim Castille. TE—Jerame Tuman. T—Brandon Keith, Elliott Vallejo. DT—Alan Branch. LB—Victor Hobson. CB—Eric Green.

OFFICIALS

Referee—Walt Anderson. Umpire—Undrey Wash. Line Judge—Tom Barnes. Side Judge—Greg Meyer. Head Linesman—Kent Payne. Back Judge—Scott Helverson. Field Judge—Jim Saracino.

SCORING

Philadelphia	3	3	13	6	—	25
Arizona	7	17	0	8	—	32

Ariz — Fitzgerald 9 pass from Warner (Rackers kick)
Phil — FG Akers 45
Ariz — Fitzgerald 62 pass from Warner (Rackers kick)
Phil — FG Akers 33
Ariz — Fitzgerald 1 pass from Warner (Rackers kick)
Ariz — FG Rackers 49
Phil — Celek 6 pass from McNabb (Akers kick)
Phil — Celek 31 pass from McNabb (kick failed)
Phil — Jackson 62 pass from McNabb (pass failed)
Ariz — Hightower 8 pass from Warner (Patrick pass from Warner)

TEAM STATISTICS	PHIL	ARIZ
Total First Downs	22	21
Rushing	5	6
Passing	16	13
Penalty	1	2
Total Net Yardage	454	369
Total Offensive Plays	67	59
Average Gain Per Offensive Play	6.8	6.3
Rushes	18	29
Yards Gained Rushing (Net)	97	102
Average Yards per Rush	5.4	3.5
Passes Attempted	47	28
Passes Completed	28	21
Had Intercepted	1	0
Tackled Attempting to Pass	2	2
Yards Lost Attempting to Pass	18	12
Yards Gained Passing (Net)	357	267
Punts	1	5
Average Distance	58.0	37.2
Punt Returns	1	1
Punt Return Yardage	13	10
Kickoff Returns	2	3
Kickoff Return Yardage	20	80
Interception Return Yardage	0	27
Total Return Yardage (excluding Kickoffs)	13	37
Fumbles	3	1
Fumbles Lost	2	1
Own Fumbles Recovered	1	0
Opponent Fumbles Recovered	1	2
Penalties	7	3
Yards Penalized	64	15
Field Goals	2	1
Field Goals Attempted	3	1
Third-Down Efficiency	7/14	5/12
Fourth-Down Efficiency	0/1	1/1
Time of Possession	30:04	29:56

INDIVIDUAL STATISTICS

RUSHING: PHIL: Westbrook 12-45-0, McNabb 2-31-0, Buckhalter 4-21-0. ARIZ: James 16-73-0, Hightower 11-33-0, Arrington 2-(-4)-0.

PASSING: PHIL: McNabb 47-28-375-3-1. ARIZ: Warner 28-21-279-4-0.

RECEIVING: PHIL: Celek 10-83-2, Jackson 6-92-1, Curtis 4-122-0, Westbrook 2-26-0, Avant 2-23-0, Baskett 1-14-0, Buckhalter 1-12-0, Smith 1-5-0, Lewis 1-(-2)-0. ARIZ: Fitzgerald 9-152-3, Boldin 4-34-0, Pope 2-21-0, Urban 1-18-0, Arrington 1-16-0, James 1-16-0, Breaston 1-10-0, Hightower 1-8-1, Warner 1-4-0.

KICKOFF RETURNS: PHIL: Buckhalter 1-20-0, Abiamiri 1-0-0. ARIZ: Arrington 2-51-0, Breaston 1-29-0.

PUNT RETURNS: PHIL: Jackson 1-13-0. ARIZ: Breaston 1-10-0.

PUNTING: PHIL: Rocca 1-58-58.0. ARIZ: Graham 5-186-37.2.

INTERCEPTIONS: PHIL: None. ARIZ: Francisco 1-27-0.

SACKS: PHIL: Abiamiri 1, Cole 1. ARIZ: Wilson 2.

AFC DIVISIONAL PLAYOFFS RESULTS

Includes Second-Round Playoff Games (1982), AFC Inter-Divisional Games (1969), and special playoff games to break ties for AFL Division Championships (1963, 1968)

Season	Date	Winner (Share)	Loser (Share)	Score	Site	Attendance
2008	Jan. 11	Pittsburgh ($20,000)	San Diego ($20,000)	35-24	Pittsburgh	63,899
	Jan. 10	Baltimore ($20,000)	Tennessee ($20,000)	13-10	Nashville	69,143
2007	Jan. 13	San Diego ($20,000)	Indianapolis ($20,000)	28-24	Indianapolis	56,950
	Jan. 12	New England ($20,000)	Jacksonville ($20,000)	31-20	Foxborough	68,756
2006	Jan. 14	New England ($19,000)	San Diego ($19,000)	24-21	San Diego	68,810
	Jan. 13	Indianapolis ($19,000)	Baltimore ($19,000)	15-6	Baltimore	71,162
2005	Jan. 15	Pittsburgh ($19,000)	Indianapolis ($19,000)	21-18	Indianapolis	57,449
	Jan. 14	Denver ($19,000)	New England ($19,000)	27-13	Denver	76,238
2004	Jan. 16	New England ($18,000)	Indianapolis ($18,000)	20-3	Foxborough	68,756
	Jan. 15	Pittsburgh ($18,000)	N.Y. Jets ($18,000)	20-17*	Pittsburgh	64,915
2003	Jan. 11	Indianapolis ($18,000)	Kansas City ($18,000)	38-31	Kansas City	79,159
	Jan. 10	New England ($18,000)	Tennessee ($18,000)	17-14	Foxborough	68,436
2002	Jan. 12	Oakland ($17,000)	N.Y. Jets ($17,000)	30-10	Oakland	62,207
	Jan. 11	Tennessee ($17,000)	Pittsburgh ($17,000)	34-31*	Nashville	68,809
2001	Jan. 20	Pittsburgh ($17,000)	Baltimore ($17,000)	27-10	Pittsburgh	63,976
	Jan. 19	New England ($17,000)	Oakland ($17,000)	16-13*	Foxborough	60,292
2000	Jan. 7	Baltimore ($16,000)	Tennessee ($16,000)	24-10	Nashville	68,527
	Jan. 6	Oakland ($16,000)	Miami ($16,000)	27-0	Oakland	61,998
1999	Jan. 16	Tennessee ($16,000)	Indianapolis ($16,000)	19-16	Indianapolis	57,097
	Jan. 15	Jacksonville ($16,000)	Miami ($16,000)	62-7	Jacksonville	75,173

Season	Date	Winner (Share)	Loser (Share)	Score	Site	Attendance
1998	Jan. 10	N.Y. Jets ($15,000)	Jacksonville ($15,000)	34-24	East Rutherford	78,817
	Jan. 9	Denver ($15,000)	Miami ($15,000)	38-3	Denver	75,729
1997	Jan. 4	Denver ($15,000)	Kansas City ($15,000)	14-10	Kansas City	76,965
	Jan. 3	Pittsburgh ($15,000)	New England ($15,000)	7-6	Pittsburgh	61,228
1996	Jan. 5	New England ($14,000)	Pittsburgh ($14,000)	28-3	Foxborough	60,188
	Jan. 4	Jacksonville ($14,000)	Denver ($14,000)	30-27	Denver	75,678
1995	Jan. 7	Indianapolis ($13,000)	Kansas City ($13,000)	10-7	Kansas City	77,594
	Jan. 6	Pittsburgh ($13,000)	Buffalo ($13,000)	40-21	Pittsburgh	59,072
1994	Jan. 8	San Diego ($12,000)	Miami ($12,000)	22-21	San Diego	63,381
	Jan. 7	Pittsburgh ($12,000)	Cleveland ($12,000)	29-9	Pittsburgh	58,185
1993	Jan. 16	Kansas City ($12,000)	Houston ($12,000)	28-20	Houston	64,011
	Jan. 15	Buffalo ($12,000)	L.A. Raiders ($12,000)	29-23	Buffalo	61,923
1992	Jan. 10	Miami ($10,000)	San Diego ($10,000)	31-0	Miami	71,224
	Jan. 9	Buffalo ($10,000)	Pittsburgh ($10,000)	24-3	Pittsburgh	60,407
1991	Jan. 5	Buffalo ($10,000)	Kansas City ($10,000)	37-14	Buffalo	80,182
	Jan. 4	Denver ($10,000)	Houston ($10,000)	26-24	Denver	75,301
1990	Jan. 13	L.A. Raiders ($10,000)	Cincinnati ($10,000)	20-10	Los Angeles	92,045
	Jan. 12	Buffalo ($10,000)	Miami ($10,000)	44-34	Buffalo	77,087
1989	Jan. 7	Denver ($10,000)	Pittsburgh ($10,000)	24-23	Denver	75,477
	Jan. 6	Cleveland ($10,000)	Buffalo ($10,000)	34-30	Cleveland	78,921
1988	Jan. 1	Buffalo ($10,000)	Houston ($10,000)	17-10	Buffalo	79,532
	Dec. 31	Cincinnati ($10,000)	Seattle ($10,000)	21-13	Cincinnati	58,560
1987	Jan. 10	Denver ($10,000)	Houston ($10,000)	34-10	Denver	75,440
	Jan. 9	Cleveland ($10,000)	Indianapolis ($10,000)	38-21	Cleveland	79,372
1986	Jan. 4	Denver ($10,000)	New England ($10,000)	22-17	Denver	75,262
	Jan. 3	Cleveland ($10,000)	N.Y. Jets ($10,000)	23-20*	Cleveland	79,720
1985	Jan. 5	New England ($10,000)	L.A. Raiders ($10,000)	27-20	Los Angeles	87,163
	Jan. 4	Miami ($10,000)	Cleveland ($10,000)	24-21	Miami	74,667
1984	Dec. 30	Pittsburgh ($10,000)	Denver ($10,000)	24-17	Denver	74,981
	Dec. 29	Miami ($10,000)	Seattle ($10,000)	31-10	Miami	73,469
1983	Jan. 1	L.A. Raiders ($10,000)	Pittsburgh ($10,000)	38-10	Los Angeles	90,380
	Dec. 31	Seattle ($10,000)	Miami ($10,000)	27-20	Miami	74,136
1982	Jan. 16	Miami ($10,000)	San Diego ($10,000)	34-13	Miami	71,383
	Jan. 15	N.Y. Jets ($10,000)	L.A. Raiders ($10,000)	17-14	Los Angeles	90,038
1981	Jan. 3	Cincinnati ($5,000)	Buffalo ($5,000)	28-21	Cincinnati	55,420
	Jan. 2	San Diego ($5,000)	Miami ($5,000)	41-38*	Miami	73,735
1980	Jan. 4	Oakland ($5,000)	Cleveland ($5,000)	14-12	Cleveland	78,245
	Jan. 3	San Diego ($5,000)	Buffalo ($5,000)	20-14	San Diego	52,253
1979	Dec. 30	Pittsburgh ($5,000)	Miami ($5,000)	34-14	Pittsburgh	50,214
	Dec. 29	Houston ($5,000)	San Diego ($5,000)	17-14	San Diego	51,192
1978	Dec. 31	Houston ($5,000)	New England ($5,000)	31-14	Foxborough	60,735
	Dec. 30	Pittsburgh ($5,000)	Denver ($5,000)	33-10	Pittsburgh	50,230
1977	Dec. 24	Oakland ($5,000)	Baltimore ($5,000)	37-31*	Baltimore	59,925
	Dec. 24	Denver ($5,000)	Pittsburgh ($5,000)	34-21	Denver	75,059
1976	Dec. 19	Pittsburgh [$]	Baltimore [$]	40-14	Baltimore	59,296
	Dec. 18	Oakland [$]	New England [$]	24-21	Oakland	53,050
1975	Dec. 28	Oakland [$]	Cincinnati [$]	31-28	Oakland	53,030
	Dec. 27	Pittsburgh [$]	Baltimore [$]	28-10	Pittsburgh	49,557
1974	Dec. 22	Pittsburgh [$]	Buffalo [$]	32-14	Pittsburgh	49,841
	Dec. 21	Oakland [$]	Miami [$]	28-26	Oakland	53,023
1973	Dec. 23	Miami [$]	Cincinnati [$]	34-16	Miami	78,928
	Dec. 22	Oakland [$]	Pittsburgh [$]	33-14	Oakland	52,646
1972	Dec. 24	Miami [$]	Cleveland [$]	20-14	Miami	78,916
	Dec. 23	Pittsburgh [$]	Oakland [$]	13-7	Pittsburgh	50,327
1971	Dec. 26	Baltimore [$]	Cleveland [$]	20-3	Cleveland	70,734
	Dec. 25	Miami [$]	Kansas City [$]	27-24*	Kansas City	50,374
1970	Dec. 27	Oakland [$]	Miami [$]	21-14	Oakland	52,594
	Dec. 26	Baltimore [$]	Cincinnati [$]	17-0	Baltimore	49,694
1969	Dec. 21	Oakland [$]	Houston [$]	56-7	Oakland	53,539
	Dec. 20	Kansas City [$]	N.Y. Jets [$]	13-6	New York	62,977
1968	Dec. 22	Oakland [$]	Kansas City [$]	41-6	Oakland	53,605
1963	Dec. 28	Boston [$]	Buffalo [$]	26-8	Buffalo	33,044

**Sudden death overtime*

$ Players received 1/14 of annual salary for playoff appearances.

2008 AFC DIVISIONAL PLAYOFF GAME
Heinz Field, Pittsburgh, Pennsylvania
January 11, 2009, Attendance: 63,899

PITTSBURGH 35, SAN DIEGO 24—Willie Parker rushed for 146 yards and 2 touchdowns as the Steelers won their first playoff game under second-year coach Mike Tomlin. Four plays into the game, it was the Chargers who scored first, as Philip Rivers lofted a 41-yard touchdown pass to Vincent Jackson on a post pattern for a 7-0 lead. Santonio Holmes tied the game with a 67-yard punt return, but the Chargers' special teams unit responded by stopping Ryan Clark for a 4-yard loss on a fake punt in the second quarter. Nate Kaeding made a 42-yard field goal for a 10-7 lead. A 41-yard pass from Ben Roethlisberger to Hines Ward set up Parker's 3-yard touchdown run with 40 seconds left in the half, giving Pittsburgh a 14-10 halftime lead. The Steelers dominated the third quarter, maintaining possession for all but one play and 17 seconds. First, Roethlisberger completed three key third-down passes on a 13-play, 77-yard drive that was capped by Heath Miller's 8-yard touchdown catch. On the next play, Larry Foote intercepted Rivers' pass. The Chargers forced a punt, but the ball hit blocker Eric Weddle and William Gay recovered at the Chargers' 23. The Chargers' defense held, but after another punt, and a 44-yard pass interference penalty, Gary Russell scored on a 1-yard run with 12:52 remaining for a 28-10 lead. Rivers responded with a touchdown pass to Legedu Naanee, but Pittsburgh drove 73 yards in nine plays, capped by Parker's 16-yard run with 4:11 remaining for a 35-17 lead. Roethlisberger was 17 of 26 for 181 yards and 1 touchdown. Parker carried 27 times for 146 yards. Rivers was 21 of 35 for 308 yards and 3 touchdowns, with 1 interception.

San Diego	7	3	0	14	—	24
Pittsburgh	7	7	7	14	—	35

SD — Jackson 41 pass from Rivers (Kaeding kick)
Pitt — Holmes 67 punt return (Reed kick)
SD — FG Kaeding 42
Pitt — Parker 3 run (Reed kick)
Pitt — Miller 8 pass from Roethlisberger (Reed kick)
Pitt — Russell 1 run (Reed kick)
SD — Naanee 4 pass from Rivers (Kaeding kick)
Pitt — Parker 16 run (Reed kick)
SD — Sproles 62 pass from Rivers (Kaeding kick)

LP Field, Nashville, Tennessee
January 10, 2009, Attendance: 69,143

BALTIMORE 13, TENNESSEE 10—Matt Stover's 43-yard field goal with 53 seconds remaining lifted the Ravens to victory over the top-seeded Titans. The Titans' defense limited Baltimore to just nine first downs and 211 yards, but the Ravens' defense forced three turnovers. Kerry Collins completed a 28-yard pass to Chris Johnson and 20-yard pass to Justin Gage to set up Johnson's 8-yard touchdown run in the first quarter. The Ravens responded immediately, as rookie Joe Flacco completed a 48-yard touchdown pass to Derrick Mason on third-and-13 to tie the game. The Titans drove to the Ravens' 32 with 4:07 left in the half, but Samari Rolle intercepted Collins' third-and-8 pass. Then, with 36 seconds remaining until halftime, Jarret Johnson forced LenDale White to fumble at the Ravens' 15. Jim Leonhard recovered the fumble to maintain a 7-7 halftime score. Rob Bironas missed a 51-yard field-goal attempt in the third quarter, and late in the quarter Flacco connected with Mark Clayton on a 37-yard pass to set up Stover's 21-yard field goal with 14:10 to play. The Titans drove to the Ravens' 13, but Alge Crumpler fumbled and Fabian Washington recovered at the Ravens' 1 with 8:57 to play. The Titans did force a punt and Bironas kicked a 27-yard field goal to tie the game with 4:23 remaining, but Flacco completed a 23-yard pass to Todd Heap on third-and-2, and Willis McGahee had a key 11-yard run to set up Stover's winning 43-yard kick. Flacco was 11 of 22 for 161 yards and 1 touchdown. Collins was 26 of 42 for 281 yards, with 1 interception. Gage had 10 catches for 135 yards.

Baltimore	7	0	0	6	—	13
Tennessee	7	0	0	3	—	10

Tenn — Johnson 8 run (Bironas kick)
Balt — Mason 48 pass from Flacco (Stover kick)
Balt — FG Stover 21
Tenn — FG Bironas 27
Balt — FG Stover 43

NFC DIVISIONAL PLAYOFFS RESULTS

Includes Second-Round Playoff Games (1982), NFL Conference Championship Games (1967-69), and special playoff games to break ties for NFL Division or Conference Championships (1941, 1943, 1947, 1950, 1952, 1957, 1958, 1965)

Season	Date	Winner (Share)	Loser (Share)	Score	Site	Attendance
2008	Jan. 11	Philadelphia ($20,000)	N.Y. Giants ($20,000)	23-11	East Rutherford	79,193
	Jan. 10	Arizona ($20,000)	Carolina ($20,000)	33-13	Charlotte	73,695
2007	Jan. 13	N.Y. Giants ($20,000)	Dallas ($20,000)	21-17	Dallas	63,660
	Jan. 12	Green Bay ($20,000)	Seattle ($20,000)	42-20	Green Bay	72,168
2006	Jan. 14	Chicago ($19,000)	Seattle ($19,000)	27-24*	Chicago	62,184
	Jan. 13	New Orleans ($19,000)	Philadelphia ($19,000)	27-24	New Orleans	70,001
2005	Jan. 15	Carolina ($19,000)	Chicago ($19,000)	29-21	Chicago	62,209
	Jan. 14	Seattle ($19,000)	Washington ($19,000)	20-10	Seattle	67,551
2004	Jan. 16	Philadelphia ($18,000)	Minnesota ($18,000)	27-14	Philadelphia	67,722
	Jan. 15	Atlanta ($18,000)	St. Louis ($18,000)	47-17	Atlanta	70,709
2003	Jan. 11	Philadelphia ($18,000)	Green Bay ($18,000)	20-17*	Philadelphia	67,707
	Jan. 10	Carolina ($18,000)	St. Louis ($18,000)	29-23*	St. Louis	66,165
2002	Jan. 12	Tampa Bay ($17,000)	San Francisco ($17,000)	31-6	Tampa	65,599
	Jan. 11	Philadelphia ($17,000)	Atlanta ($17,000)	20-6	Philadelphia	66,452
2001	Jan. 20	St. Louis ($17,000)	Green Bay ($17,000)	45-17	St. Louis	66,338
	Jan. 19	Philadelphia ($17,000)	Chicago ($17,000)	33-19	Chicago	66,944
2000	Jan. 7	N.Y. Giants ($16,000)	Philadelphia ($16,000)	20-10	East Rutherford	78,765
	Jan. 6	Minnesota ($16,000)	New Orleans ($16,000)	34-16	Minneapolis	63,881
1999	Jan. 16	St. Louis ($16,000)	Minnesota ($16,000)	49-37	St. Louis	66,194
	Jan. 15	Tampa Bay ($16,000)	Washington ($16,000)	14-13	Tampa	65,835
1998	Jan. 10	Minnesota ($15,000)	Arizona ($15,000)	41-21	Minneapolis	63,760
	Jan. 9	Atlanta ($15,000)	San Francisco ($15,000)	20-18	Atlanta	70,262
1997	Jan. 4	Green Bay ($15,000)	Tampa Bay ($15,000)	21-7	Green Bay	60,327
	Jan. 3	San Francisco ($15,000)	Minnesota ($15,000)	38-22	San Francisco	65,018

Season	Date	Winner (Share)	Loser (Share)	Score	Site	Attendance
1996	Jan. 5	Carolina ($14,000)	Dallas ($14,000)	26-17	Charlotte	72,808
	Jan. 4	Green Bay ($14,000)	San Francisco ($14,000)	35-14	Green Bay	60,787
1995	Jan. 7	Dallas ($13,000)	Philadelphia ($13,000)	30-11	Dallas	64,371
	Jan. 6	Green Bay ($13,000)	San Francisco ($13,000)	27-17	San Francisco	69,311
1994	Jan. 8	Dallas ($12,000)	Green Bay ($12,000)	35-9	Dallas	64,745
	Jan. 7	San Francisco ($12,000)	Chicago ($12,000)	44-15	San Francisco	64,644
1993	Jan. 16	Dallas ($12,000)	Green Bay ($12,000)	27-17	Dallas	64,790
	Jan. 15	San Francisco ($12,000)	N.Y. Giants ($12,000)	44-3	San Francisco	67,143
1992	Jan. 10	Dallas ($10,000)	Philadelphia ($10,000)	34-10	Dallas	63,721
	Jan. 9	San Francisco ($10,000)	Washington ($10,000)	20-13	San Francisco	64,991
1991	Jan. 5	Detroit ($10,000)	Dallas ($10,000)	38-6	Detroit	78,290
	Jan. 4	Washington ($10,000)	Atlanta ($10,000)	24-7	Washington	55,181
1990	Jan. 13	N.Y. Giants ($10,000)	Chicago ($10,000)	31-3	East Rutherford	77,025
	Jan. 12	San Francisco ($10,000)	Washington ($10,000)	28-10	San Francisco	65,292
1989	Jan. 7	L.A. Rams ($10,000)	N.Y. Giants ($10,000)	19-13*	East Rutherford	76,526
	Jan. 6	San Francisco ($10,000)	Minnesota ($10,000)	41-13	San Francisco	64,918
1988	Jan. 1	San Francisco ($10,000)	Minnesota ($10,000)	34-9	San Francisco	61,848
	Dec. 31	Chicago ($10,000)	Philadelphia ($10,000)	20-12	Chicago	65,534
1987	Jan. 10	Washington ($10,000)	Chicago ($10,000)	21-17	Chicago	65,268
	Jan. 9	Minnesota ($10,000)	San Francisco ($10,000)	36-24	San Francisco	63,008
1986	Jan. 4	N.Y. Giants ($10,000)	San Francisco ($10,000)	49-3	East Rutherford	75,691
	Jan. 3	Washington ($10,000)	Chicago ($10,000)	27-13	Chicago	65,524
1985	Jan. 5	Chicago ($10,000)	N.Y. Giants ($10,000)	21-0	Chicago	65,670
	Jan. 4	L.A. Rams ($10,000)	Dallas ($10,000)	20-0	Anaheim	66,581
1984	Dec. 30	Chicago ($10,000)	Washington ($10,000)	23-19	Washington	55,431
	Dec. 29	San Francisco ($10,000)	N.Y. Giants ($10,000)	21-10	San Francisco	60,303
1983	Jan. 1	Washington ($10,000)	L.A. Rams ($10,000)	51-7	Washington	54,440
	Dec. 31	San Francisco ($10,000)	Detroit ($10,000)	24-23	San Francisco	59,979
1982	Jan. 16	Dallas ($10,000)	Green Bay ($10,000)	37-26	Dallas	63,972
	Jan. 15	Washington ($10,000)	Minnesota ($10,000)	21-7	Washington	54,593
1981	Jan. 3	San Francisco ($5,000)	N.Y. Giants ($5,000)	38-24	San Francisco	58,360
	Jan. 2	Dallas ($5,000)	Tampa Bay ($5,000)	38-0	Dallas	64,848
1980	Jan. 4	Dallas ($5,000)	Atlanta ($5,000)	30-27	Atlanta	59,793
	Jan. 3	Philadelphia ($5,000)	Minnesota ($5,000)	31-16	Philadelphia	70,178
1979	Dec. 30	Los Angeles ($5,000)	Dallas ($5,000)	21-19	Dallas	64,792
	Dec. 29	Tampa Bay ($5,000)	Philadelphia ($5,000)	24-17	Tampa	71,402
1978	Dec. 31	Los Angeles ($5,000)	Minnesota ($5,000)	34-10	Los Angeles	70,436
	Dec. 30	Dallas ($5,000)	Atlanta ($5,000)	27-20	Dallas	63,406
1977	Dec. 26	Dallas ($5,000)	Chicago ($5,000)	37-7	Dallas	63,260
	Dec. 26	Minnesota ($5,000)	Los Angeles ($5,000)	14-7	Los Angeles	70,203
1976	Dec. 19	Los Angeles [$]	Dallas [$]	14-12	Dallas	63,283
	Dec. 18	Minnesota [$]	Washington [$]	35-20	Minneapolis	47,466
1975	Dec. 28	Dallas [$]	Minnesota [$]	17-14	Minneapolis	48,050
	Dec. 27	Los Angeles [$]	St. Louis [$]	35-23	Los Angeles	73,459
1974	Dec. 22	Los Angeles [$]	Washington [$]	19-10	Los Angeles	77,925
	Dec. 21	Minnesota [$]	St. Louis [$]	30-14	Minneapolis	48,150
1973	Dec. 23	Dallas [$]	Los Angeles [$]	27-16	Dallas	63,272
	Dec. 22	Minnesota [$]	Washington [$]	27-20	Minneapolis	48,040
1972	Dec. 24	Washington [$]	Green Bay [$]	16-3	Washington	52,321
	Dec. 23	Dallas [$]	San Francisco [$]	30-28	San Francisco	59,746
1971	Dec. 26	San Francisco [$]	Washington [$]	24-20	San Francisco	45,327
	Dec. 25	Dallas [$]	Minnesota [$]	20-12	Minneapolis	47,307
1970	Dec. 27	San Francisco [$]	Minnesota [$]	17-14	Minneapolis	45,103
	Dec. 26	Dallas [$]	Detroit [$]	5-0	Dallas	69,613
1969	Dec. 28	Cleveland [$]	Dallas [$]	38-14	Dallas	69,321
	Dec. 27	Minnesota [$]	Los Angeles [$]	23-20	Minneapolis	47,900
1968	Dec. 22	Baltimore [$]	Minnesota [$]	24-14	Baltimore	60,238
	Dec. 21	Cleveland [$]	Dallas [$]	31-20	Cleveland	81,497
1967	Dec. 24	Dallas [$]	Cleveland [$]	52-14	Dallas	70,786
	Dec. 23	Green Bay [$]	Los Angeles [$]	28-7	Milwaukee	49,861
1965	Dec. 26	Green Bay [$]	Baltimore [$]	13-10*	Green Bay	50,484
1958	Dec. 21	N.Y. Giants (#)	Cleveland (#)	10-0	New York	61,274
1957	Dec. 22	Detroit (#)	San Francisco (#)	31-27	San Francisco	60,118
1952	Dec. 21	Detroit (#)	Los Angeles (#)	31-21	Detroit	47,645
1950	Dec. 17	Los Angeles (#)	Chicago Bears (#)	24-14	Los Angeles	83,501
	Dec. 17	Cleveland (#)	N.Y. Giants (#)	8-3	Cleveland	33,054
1947	Dec. 21	Philadelphia (#)	Pittsburgh (#)	21-0	Pittsburgh	35,729
1943	Dec. 19	Washington (¢)	N.Y. Giants (¢)	28-0	New York	42,800
1941	Dec. 14	Chicago Bears (¢)	Green Bay (¢)	33-14	Chicago	43,425

**Sudden death overtime*

$ Players received 1/14 of annual salary for playoff appearances.

 # Players received 1/12 of annual salary for playoff appearances.

¢ Players received 1/10 of annual salary for playoff appearances.

2008 NFC DIVISIONAL PLAYOFF GAMES
Giants Stadium, East Rutherford, New Jersey
January 11, 2009, Attendance: 79,193

PHILADELPHIA 23, N.Y. GIANTS 11—Donovan McNabb rushed for a touchdown and passed for another as the Eagles' defense kept the Giants out of the end zone and defeated the NFC's top-seed and defending Super Bowl champion. John Carney kicked a 22-yard field goal on the Giants' first possession, but Asante Samuel intercepted a pass on their second drive. Samuel returned the ball 25 yards to the Giants' 2, and McNabb scored a few plays later for a 7-3 lead. An intentional grounding penalty in the end zone cut the score to 7-5, and Kevin Dockery's interception late in the half led to Carney's 34-yard field goal and 8-7 lead with 1:33 left in the half. McNabb completed five consecutive passes on the ensuing drive, and David Akers kicked a 25-yard field goal as the half expired for a 10-8 Eagles' lead. Two plays into the second half, Fred Robbins intercepted a pass to set up Carney's third field goal. The Eagles answered with a field goal, and after Carney missed a 47-yard attempt on the Giants' next possession, McNabb engineered a 10-play, 63-yard drive, capped by Brent Celek's 1-yard catch on the first play of the fourth quarter for a 20-11 lead. The Giants twice drove to near midfield, but Eli Manning was stopped for no gain on fourth-and-1 with 12:29 to play, and Brandon Jacobs was stopped a yard short on fourth-and-two with 6:28 remaining. McNabb was 22 of 40 for 217 yards and 1 touchdown, with 2 interceptions. Manning was 15 of 29 for 169 yards, with 2 interceptions.

Philadelphia	7	3	3	10	—	23
N.Y. Giants	3	5	3	0	—	11

NYG — FG Carney 22
Phil — McNabb 1 run (Akers kick)
NYG — Safety, McNabb flagged for intentional grounding in end zone
NYG — FG Carney 34
Phil — FG Akers 25
NYG — FG Carney 36
Phil — FG Akers 35
Phil — Celek 1 pass from McNabb (Akers kick)
Phil — FG Akers 20

Bank of America Stadium, Charlotte, North Carolina
January 10, 2009, Attendance: 73,695

ARIZONA 33, CAROLINA 13—The Cardinals' defense forced six turnovers that led to 20 points as Arizona scored 33 unanswered points to defeat the number-two seeded Panthers. Arizona maintained possession for 39 minutes, 49 seconds and converted 10 of 18 third-down situations to keep the Panthers at bay. The Panthers scored five plays into the game for a 7-0 lead, and then forced Arizona to punt. However, the Cardinals' defense forced a three-and-out, and Arizona scored on its next five possessions, spanning a total of just 14 minutes, 11 seconds, to take a 27-7 lead. The outburst began with Kurt Warner's 3-yard touchdown pass to Tim Hightower on third-and-goal. On the next play from scrimmage, Antonio Smith sacked Jake Delhomme and forced him to fumble. Smith recovered the ball at the Panthers' 13, and Edgerrin James scored two plays later. Dominique Rodgers-Cromartie then intercepted a pass near the goal line to thwart the Panthers. The Cardinals kicked field goals on their next two possessions, and Gerald Hayes' interception on the first play after Neil Rackers' second field goal led to Larry Fitzgerald's 29-yard touchdown catch with 3:32 left in the half for a 27-7 lead. The Panthers did not score again until there were just 50 seconds remaining. Warner was 21 of 32 for 220 yards and 2 touchdowns, with 1 interception. Fitzgerald had 8 receptions for 166 yards. Delhomme was 17 of 34 for 205 yards and 1 touchdown, with 5 interceptions.

Arizona	14	13	3	3	—	33
Carolina	7	0	0	6	—	13

Car — Stewart 9 run (Kasay kick)
Ariz — Hightower 3 pass from Warner (Rackers kick)
Ariz — James 4 run (Rackers kick)
Ariz — FG Rackers 49
Ariz — FG Rackers 30
Ariz — Fitzgerald 29 pass from Warner (Rackers kick)
Ariz — FG Rackers 33
Ariz — FG Rackers 20
Car — Smith 8 pass from Delhomme (pass failed)

AFC WILD CARD PLAYOFF GAMES RESULTS

Season	Date	Winner (Share)	Loser (Share)	Score	Site	Attendance
2008	Jan. 4	Baltimore ($18,000)	Miami ($20,000)	27-9	Miami	74,240
	Jan. 3	San Diego ($20,000)	Indianapolis ($18,000)	23-17*	San Diego	68,082
2007	Jan. 6	San Diego ($20,000)	Tennessee ($18,000)	17-6	San Diego	65,640
	Jan. 5	Jacksonville ($18,000)	Pittsburgh ($20,000)	31-29	Pittsburgh	63,629
2006	Jan. 7	New England ($19,000)	N.Y. Jets ($17,000)	37-16	Foxborough	68,756
	Jan. 6	Indianapolis ($19,000)	Kansas City ($17,000)	23-8	Indianapolis	57,215
2005	Jan. 8	Pittsburgh ($17,000)	Cincinnati ($19,000)	31-17	Cincinnati	65,870
	Jan. 7	New England ($19,000)	Jacksonville ($17,000)	28-3	Foxborough	68,756
2004	Jan. 9	Indianapolis ($18,000)	Denver ($15,000)	49-24	Indianapolis	56,609
	Jan. 8	N.Y. Jets ($15,000)	San Diego ($18,000)	20-17*	San Diego	67,536
2003	Jan. 4	Indianapolis ($18,000)	Denver ($15,000)	41-10	Indianapolis	56,586
	Jan. 3	Tennessee ($15,000)	Baltimore ($18,000)	20-17	Baltimore	69,452
2002	Jan. 5	Pittsburgh ($17,000)	Cleveland ($12,500)	36-33	Pittsburgh	62,595
	Jan. 4	N.Y. Jets ($17,000)	Indianapolis ($12,500)	41-0	East Rutherford	78,524
2001	Jan. 13	Baltimore ($12,500)	Miami ($12,500)	20-3	Miami	72,251
	Jan. 12	Oakland ($17,000)	N.Y. Jets ($12,500)	38-24	Oakland	61,503
2000	Dec. 31	Baltimore (12,500)	Denver ($12,500)	21-3	Baltimore	69,638
	Dec. 30	Miami ($16,000)	Indianapolis ($12,500)	23-17*	Miami	73,193
1999	Jan. 9	Miami ($10,000)	Seattle ($16,000)	20-17	Seattle	66,170
	Jan. 8	Tennessee ($10,000)	Buffalo ($10,000)	22-16	Nashville	66,672
1998	Jan. 3	Jacksonville ($15,000)	New England ($10,000)	25-10	Jacksonville	71,139
	Jan. 2	Miami ($10,000)	Buffalo ($10,000)	24-17	Miami	72,698
1997	Dec. 28	New England ($15,000)	Miami ($10,000)	17-3	Foxborough	60,041
	Dec. 27	Denver ($10,000)	Jacksonville ($10,000)	42-17	Denver	74,481
1996	Dec. 29	Pittsburgh ($14,000)	Indianapolis ($10,000)	42-14	Pittsburgh	58,078
	Dec. 28	Jacksonville ($10,000)	Buffalo ($10,000)	30-27	Buffalo	70,213
1995	Dec. 31	Indianapolis ($7,500)	San Diego ($7,500)	35-20	San Diego	61,182
	Dec. 30	Buffalo ($13,000)	Miami ($7,500)	37-22	Buffalo	73,103

Season	Date	Winner (Share)	Loser (Share)	Score	Site	Attendance
1994	Jan. 1	Cleveland ($7,500)	New England ($7,500)	20-13	Cleveland	77,452
	Dec. 31	Miami ($12,000)	Kansas City ($7,500)	27-17	Miami	67,487
1993	Jan. 9	L.A. Raiders ($7,500)	Denver ($7,500)	42-24	Los Angeles	65,314
	Jan. 8	Kansas City ($12,000)	Pittsburgh ($7,500)	27-24*	Kansas City	74,515
1992	Jan. 3	Buffalo ($6,000)	Houston ($6,000)	41-38*	Buffalo	75,141
	Jan. 2	San Diego ($10,000)	Kansas City ($6,000)	17-0	San Diego	58,278
1991	Dec. 29	Houston ($10,000)	N.Y. Jets ($6,000)	17-10	Houston	61,485
	Dec. 28	Kansas City ($6,000)	L.A. Raiders ($6,000)	10-6	Kansas City	75,827
1990	Jan. 6	Cincinnati ($10,000)	Houston ($6,000)	41-14	Cincinnati	60,012
	Jan. 5	Miami ($6,000)	Kansas City ($6,000)	17-16	Miami	67,276
1989	Dec. 31	Pittsburgh ($6,000)	Houston ($6,000)	26-23*	Houston	59,406
1988	Dec. 26	Houston ($6,000)	Cleveland ($6,000)	24-23	Cleveland	75,896
1987	Jan. 3	Houston ($6,000)	Seattle ($6,000)	23-20*	Houston	50,519
1986	Dec. 28	N.Y. Jets ($6,000)	Kansas City ($6,000)	35-15	East Rutherford	75,210
1985	Dec. 28	New England ($6,000)	N.Y. Jets ($6,000)	26-14	East Rutherford	75,945
1984	Dec. 22	Seattle ($6,000)	L.A. Raiders ($6,000)	13-7	Seattle	62,049
1983	Dec. 24	Seattle ($6,000)	Denver ($6,000)	31-7	Seattle	64,275
1982	Jan. 9	N.Y. Jets ($6,000)	Cincinnati ($6,000)	44-17	Cincinnati	57,560
	Jan. 9	San Diego ($6,000)	Pittsburgh ($6,000)	31-28	Pittsburgh	53,546
	Jan. 8	L.A. Raiders ($6,000)	Cleveland ($6,000)	27-10	Los Angeles	56,555
	Jan. 8	Miami ($6,000)	New England ($6,000)	28-13	Miami	68,842
1981	Dec. 27	Buffalo ($3,000)	N.Y. Jets ($3,000)	31-27	New York	57,050
1980	Dec. 28	Oakland ($3,000)	Houston ($3,000)	27-7	Oakland	53,333
1979	Dec. 23	Houston ($3,000)	Denver ($3,000)	13-7	Houston	48,776
1978	Dec. 24	Houston ($3,000)	Miami ($3,000)	17-9	Miami	72,445

**Sudden death overtime*

2008 AFC WILD CARD PLAYOFF GAMES

Dolphin Stadium, Miami, Florida
January 4, 2009, Attendance: 74,240

BALTIMORE 27, MIAMI 9—The Ravens' defense forced five turnovers, including Ed Reed's 64-yard interception return for a touchdown to guide Baltimore to a road victory. Joe Flacco became the first rookie quarterback to win a postseason game since Ben Roethlisberger four years earlier. With 2:30 left in the first half, Chad Pennington released a long pass downfield. Reed intercepted the pass over his shoulder and weaved his way through the entire Dolphins' offense for a 64-yard touchdown and 10-3 lead. The Ravens' defense forced a quick three-and-out, and Flacco completed a 31-yard pass to Derrick Mason to set up Matt Stover's 31-yard field goal with 16 seconds left in the half for a 13-3 lead. Fabian Washington intercepted Pennington three plays into the second half, and Terrell Suggs recovered Patrick Cobbs' fumble on the Dolphins' next possession. The latter turnover was followed four plays later by Le'Ron McClain's 8-yard touchdown run for a 20-3 lead. Reed's second interception, at the Ravens' 8, stopped another Dolphins' drive late in the third quarter. Miami scored its first touchdown with 13:09 to play, but Frank Walker blocked the extra point. The Dolphins then drove to the Ravens' 25 with 8:44 to play, but Ted Ginn fumbled the exchange on a reverse. Miami recovered, but lost 19 yards on the play and was forced to punt on fourth-and-26 with 7:37 remaining. Willis McGahee's 48-yard run set up Flacco's 5-yard scoring run on third-and-goal with 3:53 left to put the game out of reach. Flacco was 9 of 23 for 135 yards. Pennington was 25 of 38 for 252 yards and 1 touchdown, with 4 interceptions.

Baltimore	3	10	7	7	—	27
Miami	3	0	0	6	—	9

Mia — FG Carpenter 19
Balt — FG Stover 23
Balt — Reed 64 interception return (Stover kick)
Balt — FG Stover 31
Balt — McClain 8 run (Stover kick)
Mia — Brown 2 pass from Pennington (kick blocked)
Balt — Flacco 5 run (Stover kick)

Qualcomm Stadium, San Diego, California
January 3, 2009, Attendance: 68,082

SAN DIEGO 23, INDIANAPOLIS 17 (OT)—Darren Sproles raced 22 yards for a touchdown 6:20 into overtime as the Chargers knocked the Colts out of the playoffs for the second consecutive season. Peyton Manning was 6-for-6 on an 81-yard touchdown drive in the first quarter. Antonio Gates' 30-yard reception in the second quarter was followed on the next play by LaDainian Tomlinson's 3-yard scoring run to tie the game. Sproles' 9-yard run with just 42 seconds left in the half gave the Chargers a 14-10 lead. In the third quarter, on third-and-5, Manning and the Colts rushed to the line of scrimmage. Manning took a quick snap and fired a pass down the left sideline to Reggie Wayne, who had streaked past Antonio Cromartie, who had been looking at the sidelines for a play call. Wayne caught the pass for a 72-yard touchdown and 17-14 lead. San Diego drove to the Colts' 9, but Sproles fumbled and Raheem Brock recovered for a touchback. Antoine Bethea intercepted Philip Rivers' long pass at the goal line and returned it 36 yards with 12:17 remaining to stop another Chargers' scoring threat. Later in the quarter, Mike Scifres' 52-yard punt bounced out of bounds at the Colts' 1. Tim Dobbins sacked Manning on third down, and Sproles returned the punt 26 yards to the Colts' 38 with 1:48 to play. Nate Kaeding's 26-yard field goal tied the game with 31 seconds left. The Chargers won the overtime coin toss. The Colts committed three defensive penalties on the final drive, which ended on its tenth play when Sproles went over left tackle on second-and-12 for a 22-yard touchdown. Rivers was 20 of 36 for 217 yards, with 1 interception. Sproles rushed 22 times for 105 yards and 2 touchdowns. Manning was 25 of 42 for 310 yards and 1 touchdown. Wayne had 4 catches for 129 yards.

Indianapolis	7	3	7	0	0	—	17
San Diego	0	14	0	3	6	—	23

Ind — Addai 1 run (Vinatieri kick)
SD — Tomlinson 3 run (Kaeding kick)
Ind — FG Vinatieri 43
SD — Sproles 9 run (Kaeding kick)
Ind — Wayne 72 pass from Manning (Vinatieri kick)
SD — FG Kaeding 26
SD — Sproles 22 run

NFC WILD CARD PLAYOFF GAMES RESULTS

Season	Date	Winner (Share)	Loser (Share)	Score	Site	Attendance
2008	Jan. 4	Philadelphia ($18,000)	Minnesota ($20,000)	26-14	Minneapolis	61,746
	Jan. 3	Arizona ($20,000)	Atlanta ($18,000)	30-24	Glendale	62,848
2007	Jan. 6	N.Y. Giants ($18,000)	Tampa Bay ($20,000)	24-14	Tampa	65,621
	Jan. 5	Seattle ($20,000)	Washington ($18,000)	35-14	Seattle	68,297
2006	Jan. 7	Philadelphia ($19,000)	N.Y. Giants ($17,000)	23-20	Philadelphia	69,094
	Jan. 6	Seattle ($19,000)	Dallas ($17,000)	21-20	Seattle	68,058
2005	Jan. 8	Carolina ($17,000)	N.Y. Giants ($19,000)	23-0	East Rutherford	79,378
	Jan. 7	Washington ($17,000)	Tampa Bay ($19,000)	17-10	Tampa	65,514
2004	Jan. 9	Minnesota ($15,000)	Green Bay ($18,000)	31-17	Green Bay	71,075
	Jan. 8	St. Louis ($15,000)	Seattle ($18,000)	27-20	Seattle	65,397
2003	Jan. 4	Green Bay ($18,000)	Seattle ($15,000)	33-27*	Green Bay	71,457
	Jan. 3	Carolina ($18,000)	Dallas ($15,000)	29-10	Charlotte	73,014
2002	Jan. 5	San Francisco ($17,000)	N.Y. Giants ($12,500)	39-38	San Francisco	66,318
	Jan. 4	Atlanta ($12,500)	Green Bay ($17,000)	27-7	Green Bay	65,358
2001	Jan. 13	Green Bay ($12,500)	San Francisco ($12,500)	25-15	Green Bay	59,825
	Jan. 12	Philadelphia ($17,000)	Tampa Bay ($12,500)	31-9	Philadelphia	65,847
2000	Dec. 31	Philadelphia ($12,500)	Tampa Bay ($12,500)	21-3	Philadelphia	65,813
	Dec. 30	New Orleans ($16,000)	St. Louis ($12,500)	31-28	New Orleans	64,900
1999	Jan. 9	Minnesota ($10,000)	Dallas ($10,000)	27-10	Minneapolis	64,056
	Jan. 8	Washington ($16,000)	Detroit ($10,000)	27-13	Washington	79,411
1998	Jan. 3	San Francisco ($10,000)	Green Bay ($10,000)	30-27	San Francisco	66,506
	Jan. 2	Arizona ($10,000)	Dallas ($15,000)	20-7	Dallas	62,969
1997	Dec. 28	Tampa Bay ($10,000)	Detroit ($10,000)	20-10	Tampa	73,361
	Dec. 27	Minnesota ($10,000)	N.Y. Giants ($15,000)	23-22	East Rutherford	77,497
1996	Dec. 29	San Francisco ($10,000)	Philadelphia ($10,000)	14-0	San Francisco	56,460
	Dec. 28	Dallas ($14,000)	Minnesota ($10,000)	40-15	Dallas	64,682
1995	Dec. 31	Green Bay ($13,000)	Atlanta ($7,500)	37-20	Green Bay	60,453
	Dec. 30	Philadelphia ($7,500)	Detroit ($7,500)	58-37	Philadelphia	66,099
1994	Jan. 1	Chicago ($7,500)	Minnesota ($12,000)	35-18	Minnesota	60,347
	Dec. 31	Green Bay ($7,500)	Detroit ($7,500)	16-12	Green Bay	58,125
1993	Jan. 9	N.Y. Giants ($7,500)	Minnesota ($7,500)	17-10	East Rutherford	75,089
	Jan. 8	Green Bay ($7,500)	Detroit ($12,000)	28-24	Detroit	68,479
1992	Jan. 3	Philadelphia ($6,000)	New Orleans ($6,000)	36-20	New Orleans	68,893
	Jan. 2	Washington ($6,000)	Minnesota ($10,000)	24-7	Minnesota	57,353
1991	Dec. 29	Dallas ($6,000)	Chicago ($6,000)	17-13	Chicago	62,594
	Dec. 28	Atlanta ($6,000)	New Orleans ($10,000)	27-20	New Orleans	68,794
1990	Jan. 6	Chicago ($10,000)	New Orleans ($6,000)	16-6	Chicago	60,767
	Jan. 5	Washington ($6,000)	Philadelphia ($6,000)	20-6	Philadelphia	65,287
1989	Dec. 31	L.A. Rams ($6,000)	Philadelphia ($6,000)	21-7	Philadelphia	65,479
1988	Dec. 26	Minnesota ($6,000)	L.A. Rams ($6,000)	28-17	Minnesota	61,204
1987	Jan. 3	Minnesota ($6,000)	New Orleans ($6,000)	44-10	New Orleans	68,546
1986	Dec. 28	Washington ($6,000)	L.A. Rams ($6,000)	19-7	Washington	54,567
1985	Dec. 29	N.Y. Giants ($6,000)	San Francisco ($6,000)	17-3	East Rutherford	75,131
1984	Dec. 23	N.Y. Giants ($6,000)	L.A. Rams ($6,000)	16-13	Anaheim	67,037
1983	Dec. 26	L.A. Rams ($6,000)	Dallas ($6,000)	24-17	Dallas	62,118
1982	Jan. 9	Dallas ($6,000)	Tampa Bay ($6,000)	30-17	Dallas	65,042
	Jan. 9	Minnesota ($6,000)	Atlanta ($6,000)	30-24	Minnesota	60,560
	Jan. 8	Green Bay ($6,000)	St. Louis ($6,000)	41-16	Green Bay	54,282
	Jan. 8	Washington ($6,000)	Detroit ($6,000)	31-7	Washington	55,045
1981	Dec. 27	N.Y. Giants ($3,000)	Philadelphia ($3,000)	27-21	Philadelphia	71,611
1980	Dec. 28	Dallas ($3,000)	Los Angeles ($3,000)	34-13	Dallas	63,052
1979	Dec. 23	Philadelphia ($3,000)	Chicago ($3,000)	27-17	Philadelphia	69,397
1978	Dec. 24	Atlanta ($3,000)	Philadelphia ($3,000)	14-13	Atlanta	59,403

**Sudden death overtime*

2008 NFC WILD CARD PLAYOFF GAMES

Metrodome, Minneapolis, Minnesota

January 4, 2009, Attendance: 61,746

PHILADELPHIA 26, MINNESOTA 14—Brian Westbrook had a key 71-yard touchdown catch and David Akers kicked four field goals as the sixth-seeded Eagles defeated the Vikings. The Eagles kicked field goals on three consecutive possessions in the first half for a 9-7 lead, and three plays later Asante Samuel returned an interception 44 yards for a touchdown and 16-7 lead. The Vikings, however, answered with a 64-yard drive capped by Adrian Peterson's 3-yard run with 1:51 left in the half to cut the deficit to 16-14. The Eagles' defense forced the Vikings to punt on their first five second-half possessions. On the first play after the fourth punt, Westbrook took a swing pass from McNabb and raced 71 yards for a touchdown and 23-14 lead with 6:37 to play. The Vikings drove to midfield later in the quarter, but Tarvaris Jackson fumbled the snap and Juqua Parker recovered with 2:49 remaining to set up Akers' fourth field goal with 1:55 to play. McNabb was 23 of 34 for 300 yards and 1 touchdown, with 1 interception. Jackson was 15 of 35 for 164 yards, with 1 interception.

Philadelphia	6	10	0	10	—	26
Minnesota	0	14	0	0	—	14

Phil — FG Akers 43
Phil — FG Akers 51
Minn — Peterson 40 run (Longwell kick)

Phil — FG Akers 31
Phil — Samuel 44 interception return (Akers kick)
Minn — Peterson 3 run (Longwell kick)
Phil — Westbrook 71 pass from McNabb (Akers kick)
Phil — FG Akers 45

University of Phoenix Stadium, Glendale, Arizona
January 3, 2009, Attendance: 62,848
ARIZONA 30, ATLANTA 24—Kurt Warner passed for 271 yard and 2 touchdowns as the Cardinals rallied to win their first home playoff game in 61 years. Ralph Brown intercepted Matt Ryan's first career postseason pass attempt, and four plays later Warner took a flea-flicker toss and connected with Larry Fitzgerald on a long pass down the left side. Fitzgerald caught the ball in midair, in between two defenders and while falling backwards, for a 42-yard touchdown and 7-0 lead. Three plays after Jason Elam's second-quarter field goal, Anquan Boldin took a short pass that resulted into a 71-yard touchdown and 14-3 lead. Ryan responded with a 14-play, 77-yard drive, which consisted of three third-down conversions, and capped by Michael Turner's 7-yard touchdown with 2:55 left in the half. Three plays later, Chevis Jackson intercepted Warner and Ryan completed on a 2-yard touchdown pass to Justin Peelle with 23 seconds left in the half for a 17-14 Atlanta lead. Two plays into the second half, Ryan lost the snap. Antrel Rolle recovered and raced 27 yards for a go-ahead touchdown. The Cardinals converted four third-down situations on a 76-yard drive later in the third quarter, capped by Tim Hightower's 4-yard run for a 28-17 lead. After Ben Graham's 31-yard punt pinned the Falcons deep, Antonio Smith sacked Ryan for a safety and 30-17 lead with 12:37 to play. The Falcons' defense forced a punt, and on fourth-and-6, Ryan completed a short pass to Jerious Norwood that resulted in a 28-yard gain. Five plays later, White caught a 5-yard touchdown with 4:15 remaining to pull within 30-24. Warner's 23-yard pass to Stephen Spach with 2:00 remaining iced the victory. Warner was 19 of 32 for 271 yards and 2 touchdowns, with 1 interception. Fitzgerald had 6 receptions for 101 yards. Ryan was 26 of 40 for 199 yards and 2 touchdowns, with 2 interceptions. Roddy White had 11 catches for 84 yards.

Atlanta	0	17	0	7	—	24
Arizona	7	7	14	2	—	30

Ariz — Fitzgerald 42 pass from Warner (Rackers kick)
Atl — FG Elam 30
Ariz — Boldin 71 pass from Warner (Rackers kick)
Atl — Turner 7 run (Elam kick)
Atl — Peelle 2 pass from Ryan (Elam kick)
Ariz — Rolle 27 fumble return (Rackers kick)
Ariz — Hightower 4 run (Rackers kick)
Ariz — Safety, Ryan sacked by A. Smith in end zone
Atl — White 5 pass from Ryan (Elam kick)

AFC-NFC PRO BOWL RESULTS (1971-2009)

NFC leads series, 20-19

Year	Date	Winner (Share)	Loser (Share)	Score	Site	Attendance
2009	Feb. 8	NFC ($45,000)	AFC ($22,500)	30-21	Honolulu	49,958
2008	Feb. 10	NFC ($40,000)	AFC ($20,000)	42-30	Honolulu	50,044
2007	Feb. 10	AFC ($40,000)	NFC ($20,000)	31-28	Honolulu	50,410
2006	Feb. 12	NFC ($40,000)	AFC ($20,000)	23-17	Honolulu	50,190
2005	Feb. 13	AFC ($35,000)	NFC ($17,500)	38-27	Honolulu	50,225
2004	Feb. 8	NFC ($35,000)	AFC ($17,500)	55-52	Honolulu	50,127
2003	Feb. 2	AFC ($30,000)	NFC ($15,000)	45-20	Honolulu	50,125
2002	Feb. 9	AFC ($30,000)	NFC ($15,000)	38-30	Honolulu	50,301
2001	Feb. 4	AFC ($30,000)	NFC ($15,000)	38-17	Honolulu	50,128
2000	Feb. 6	NFC ($25,000)	AFC ($12,500)	51-31	Honolulu	50,112
1999	Feb. 7	AFC ($25,000)	NFC ($12,500)	23-10	Honolulu	50,075
1998	Feb. 1	AFC ($25,000)	NFC ($12,500)	29-24	Honolulu	49,995
1997	Feb. 2	AFC ($20,000)	NFC ($10,000)	26-23 (OT)	Honolulu	50,031
1996	Feb. 4	NFC ($20,000)	AFC ($10,000)	20-13	Honolulu	50,034
1995	Feb. 5	AFC ($20,000)	NFC ($10,000)	41-13	Honolulu	50,529
1994	Feb. 6	NFC ($20,000)	AFC ($10,000)	17-3	Honolulu	50,026
1993	Feb. 7	AFC ($10,000)	NFC ($5,000)	23-20 (OT)	Honolulu	50,007
1992	Feb. 2	NFC ($10,000)	AFC ($5,000)	21-15	Honolulu	50,209
1991	Feb. 3	AFC ($10,000)	NFC ($5,000)	23-21	Honolulu	50,345
1990	Feb. 4	NFC ($10,000)	AFC ($5,000)	27-21	Honolulu	50,445
1989	Jan. 29	NFC ($10,000)	AFC ($5,000)	34-3	Honolulu	50,113
1988	Feb. 7	AFC ($10,000)	NFC ($5,000)	15-6	Honolulu	50,113
1987	Feb. 1	AFC ($10,000)	NFC ($5,000)	10-6	Honolulu	50,101
1986	Feb. 2	NFC ($10,000)	AFC ($5,000)	28-24	Honolulu	50,101
1985	Jan. 27	AFC ($10,000)	NFC ($5,000)	22-14	Honolulu	50,385
1984	Jan. 29	NFC ($10,000)	AFC ($5,000)	45-3	Honolulu	50,445
1983	Feb. 6	NFC ($10,000)	AFC ($5,000)	20-19	Honolulu	49,883
1982	Jan. 31	AFC ($5,000)	NFC ($2,500)	16-13	Honolulu	50,402
1981	Feb. 1	NFC ($5,000)	AFC ($2,500)	21-7	Honolulu	50,360
1980	Jan. 27	NFC ($5,000)	AFC ($2,500)	37-27	Honolulu	49,800
1979	Jan. 29	NFC ($5,000)	AFC ($2,500)	13-7	Los Angeles	46,281
1978	Jan. 23	NFC ($5,000)	AFC ($2,500)	14-13	Tampa	51,337
1977	Jan. 17	AFC ($2,000)	NFC ($1,500)	24-14	Seattle	64,752
1976	Jan. 26	NFC ($2,000)	AFC ($1,500)	23-20	New Orleans	30,546
1975	Jan. 20	NFC ($2,000)	AFC ($1,500)	17-10	Miami	26,484
1974	Jan. 20	AFC ($2,000)	NFC ($1,500)	15-13	Kansas City	66,918
1973	Jan. 21	AFC ($2,000)	NFC ($1,500)	33-28	Dallas	37,091
1972	Jan. 23	AFC ($2,000)	NFC ($1,500)	26-13	Los Angeles	53,647
1971	Jan. 24	NFC ($2,000)	AFC ($1,500)	27-6	Los Angeles	48,222

2009 AFC-NFC PRO BOWL

Aloha Stadium, Honolulu, Hawaii
February 8, 2009, Attendance: 49,958

NFC 30, AFC 21—Larry Fitzgerald caught 2 touchdown passes, including the go-ahead score with 4:03 remaining, as the NFC rallied to defeat the AFC. Fitzgerald, who also caught a 46-yard touchdown as the first half expired, was the game's MVP with 5 receptions for 81 yards along with the 2 scores. The AFC marched 96 yards on its first possession, with Peyton Manning completing 6 of 8 passes, capped by his 19-yard scoring toss to Tony Gonzalez. The AFC had a 16-play drive in the second quarter, but on fourth-and-goal from the NFC's 1-yard line, Manning's pass for Brandon Marshall was incomplete. After a punt, Kerry Collins needed just 49 seconds to drive 52 yards, and his 9-yard touchdown pass to Owen Daniels gave the AFC a 14-3 lead with 28 seconds left in the half. However, Drew Brees lofted a long pass as the half expired. Fitzgerald caught the ball despite Cortland Finnegan's defense, and his touchdown trimmed the deficit to 14-10. Late in the third quarter, Jared Allen sacked Collins, forced him to fumble, and recovered the ball. On the next play, Adrian Peterson scored on a 10-yard run for a 17-14 NFC lead. Early in the fourth quarter, Jay Cutler engineered a 13-play, 89-yard drive, highlighted by a 13-yard pass to Reggie Wayne on third-and-8, and capped by Le'Ron McClain's 5-yard run with 6:59 remaining for a 21-17 AFC lead. Clifton Smith returned the ensuing kickoff 55 yards, and Eli Manning completed a 24-yard pass to Anquan Boldin. On third-and-goal from the AFC's 2, Manning found Fitzgerald for a 24-21 lead. Julius Peppers' interception set up John Carney's 48-yard field goal with 2:06 to play. After four consecutive incomplete passes by Cutler, the 44-year-old Carney, the oldest player in Pro Bowl history, tacked on a 26-yard field goal with 32 seconds left to clinch the victory. Brees was 11 of 19 for 142 yards and 1 touchdown, and Eli Manning was 8 of 14 for 111 yards and 1 touchdown, with 1 interception. Peterson led the NFC with 48 rushing yards, and Steve Smith had 6 receptions for 89 yards. Peyton Manning was 12 of 17 for 151 yards and 1 touchdown, while Collins was 10 of 15 for 108 yards and 1 touchdown, with 1 interception. Eli and Peyton Manning were the first brother quarterbacks to play against each in the Pro Bowl. Marshawn Lynch had 48 rushing yards for the AFC, while Gonzalez had 6 catches for 98 yards.

NFC (30)	Offense	AFC (21)
Anquan Boldin (Arizona)	WR	Andre Johnson (Houston)
Flozell Adams (Dallas)	LT	Joe Thomas (Cleveland)
Steve Hutchinson (Minnesota)	LG	Alan Faneca (Pittsburgh)
Andre Gurode (Dallas)	C	Nick Mangold (N.Y. Jets)
Chris Snee (N.Y. Giants)	RG	Kris Dielman (San Diego)
Jordan Gross (Carolina)	RT	Michael Roos (Tennessee)
Jason Witten (Dallas)	TE	Tony Gonzalez (Kansas City)
Larry Fitzgerald (Arizona)	WR	Brandon Marshall (Denver)
Kurt Warner (Arizona)	QB	Peyton Manning (Indianapolis)
Mike Sellers (Washington)	FB	Le'Ron McClain (Baltimore)
Adrian Peterson (Minnesota)	RB	Thomas Jones (N.Y. Jets)
	Defense	
Julius Peppers (Carolina)	DE	Mario Williams (Houston)
Kevin Williams (Minnesota)	UT	Albert Haynesworth (Tennessee)
Jay Ratliff (Dallas)	NT	Kris Jenkins (N.Y. Jets)
Justin Tuck (N.Y. Giants)	DE	Dwight Freeney (Indianapolis)
DeMarcus Ware (Dallas)	SLB	Joey Porter (Miami)
Patrick Willis (San Francisco)	MLB	Ray Lewis (Baltimore)
Lance Briggs (Chicago)	WLB	James Harrison (Pittsburgh)
Ronde Barber (Tampa Bay)	CB	Nnamdi Asomugha (Oakland)
Antoine Winfield (Minnesota)	CB	Cortland Finnegan (Tennessee)
Nick Collins (Green Bay)	FS	Chris Hope (Tennessee)
Adrian Wilson (Arizona)	SS	Troy Polamalu (Pittsburgh)

SUBSTITUTIONS

NFC—Specialists: K—John Carney (N.Y. Giants). P—Jeff Feagles (N.Y. Giants). KR—Clifton Smith (Tampa Bay). LS—Zak DeOssie (N.Y. Giants). ST—Sean Morey (Arizona). Offense: QB—Drew Brees (New Orleans), Eli Manning (N.Y. Giants). RB—Clinton Portis (Washington), Michael Turner (Atlanta). WR—Steve Smith (Carolina), Roddy White (Atlanta). TE—Chris Cooley (Washington). G—Davin Joseph (Tampa Bay). T—Jammal Brown (New Orleans). C—Shaun O'Hara (N.Y. Giants). Defense: DL—Pat Williams (Minnesota). DE—Jared Allen (Minnesota). LB—Jon Beason (Carolina), Julian Peterson (Seattle). CB—Al Harris (Green Bay). S—Brian Dawkins (Philadelphia). Not Active: G—Leonard Davis (Dallas). T—Walter Jones (Seattle), Chris Samuels (Washington). LB—Derrick Brooks (Tampa Bay). CB—Asante Samuel (Philadelphia), Charles Woodson (Green Bay).

AFC—Specialists: K—Stephen Gostkowski (New England). P—Shane Lechler (Oakland). KR—Leon Washington (N.Y. Jets). LS—Ryan Pontbriand (Cleveland). ST—Brendon Ayanbadejo (Baltimore). Offense: QB—Kerry Collins (Tennessee), Jay Cutler (Denver). RB—Ronnie Brown (Miami), Marshawn Lynch (Buffalo). WR—Reggie Wayne (Indianapolis), Wes Welker (New England). TE—Owen Daniels (Houston). G—Brian Waters (Kansas City). T—Jake Long (Miami). C—Casey Wiegmann (Denver). Defense: DL—Shaun Rogers (Cleveland). DE—Robert Mathis (Indianapolis). LB—James Farrior (Pittsburgh), Terrell Suggs (Baltimore). CB—Darrelle Revis (N.Y. Jets). S—Michael Griffin (Tennessee). Not Active: QB—Brett Favre (N.Y. Jets). RB—Chris Johnson (Tennessee). TE—Antonio Gates (San Diego). T—Jason Peters (Buffalo). C—Kevin Mawae (Tennessee). S—Ed Reed (Baltimore).

HEAD COACHES

AFC—John Harbaugh (Baltimore)
NFC—Andy Reid (Philadelphia)

OFFICIALS

Referee—Scott Green. Umpire—Jim Quick. Side Judge—Rick Patterson. Field Judge—Boris Cheek. Head Linesman—Paul Weidner. Back Judge—Bob Waggoner. Line Judge—Gary Arthur.

NFC	0	10	7	13	—	30
AFC	7	7	0	7	—	21

AFC — Gonzalez 19 pass from P. Manning (Gostkowski kick)
NFC — FG Carney 37
AFC — Daniels 9 pass from Collins (Gostkowski kick)
NFC — Fitzgerald 46 pass from Brees (Carney kick)
NFC — Peterson 10 run (Carney kick)
AFC — McClain 5 run (Gostkowski kick)
NFC — Fitzgerald 2 pass from E. Manning (Carney kick)
NFC — FG Carney 48
NFC — FG Carney 26

TEAM STATISTICS	NFC	AFC
Total First Downs	16	26
Rushing	2	8
Passing	12	18
Penalty	2	0
Total Net Yardage	309	415
Total Offensive Plays	57	77
Avg. Gain Per Offensive Play	5.4	5.4
Rushes	19	26
Yards Gained Rushing (Net)	77	136
Avg. Yards per Rush	4.1	5.2
Passes Attempted	35	47
Passes Completed	20	29
Had Intercepted	1	2
Tackled Attempting to Pass	3	4
Yards Lost Attempting to Pass	29	28
Yards Gained Passing (Net)	232	279
Punts	4	3
Avg. Distance	48.5	48.7
Punt Returns	2	2
Punt Return Yardage	28	2
Kickoff Returns	3	5
Kickoff Return Yardage	128	76
Interception Return Yardage	31	0
Total Return Yardage (KO excluded)	59	2
Fumbles	3	2
Fumbles Lost	1	1
Own Fumbles Recovered	2	1
Opponent Fumbles Recovered	1	1
Penalties	3	4
Yards Penalized	15	30
Field Goals	3	0
Field Goals Attempted	3	0
Third-Down Efficiency	6/14	6/12
Fourth-Down Efficiency	0/1	1/3
Time of Possession	23:46	36:14

INDIVIDUAL STATISTICS

RUSHING: NFC: Peterson 8-48-1, Portis 5-18-0, White 1-7-0, Turner 2-4-0, Sellers 1-1-0, E. Manning 2-(-1)-0. AFC: Lynch 6-48-0, Brown 7-41-0, Washington 2-22-0, Jones 6-21-0, McClain 3-5-1, Collins 1-0-0, Cutler 1-(-1)-0.

PASSING: NFC: Brees 19-11-142-1-0, E. Manning 14-8-111-1-1, Warner 2-1-8-0-0. AFC: P. Manning 17-12-151-1-0, Collins 15-10-108-1-1, Cutler 15-7-48-0-1, Brown 0-0-0-0-0.

RECEIVING: NFC: S. Smith 6-89-0, Fitzgerald 5-81-2, Boldin 2-27-0, Peterson 2-15-0, Portis 2-8-0, White 1-26-0, Witten 1-8-0, Sellers 1-7-0. AFC: Gonzalez 6-98-1, Marshall 5-44-0, Wayne 4-45-0, Brown 4-27-0, Welker 3-23-0, Daniels 2-30-1, Johnson 2-29-0, Washington 1-6-0, Jones 1-3-0, Lynch 1-2-0.

KICKOFF RETURNS: NFC: C. Smith 3-128-0. AFC: Washington 4-65-0, Griffin 1-11-0.

PUNT RETURNS: NFC: C. Smith 2-28-0. AFC: Washington 2-2-0.

PUNTING: NFC: Feagles 4-194-48.5. AFC: Lechler 3-146-48.7.

INTERCEPTIONS: NFC: Winfield 1-19, Peppers 1-12. AFC: Revis 1-0-0.

SACKS: NFC: Tuck 2, Allen 1, Peppers 1. AFC: Mathis 2, Freeney 1.

PRO BOWL ALL-TIME RESULTS

Includes AFL All-Star Game played after the 1961-69 seasons.

Date	Result/Honored players	Site (attendance)
Jan. 15, 1939	New York Giants 13, Pro All-Stars 10	Wrigley Field, Los Angeles (20,000)
Jan. 14, 1940	Green Bay 16, NFL All-Stars 7	Gilmore Stadium, Los Angeles (18,000)
Dec. 29, 1940	Chicago Bears 28, NFL All-Stars 14	Gilmore Stadium, Los Angeles (21,624)
Jan. 4, 1942	Chicago Bears 35, NFL All-Stars 24	Polo Grounds, New York (17,725)
Dec. 27, 1942	NFL All-Stars 17, Washington 14	Shibe Park, Philadelphia (18,671)
Jan. 14, 1951	American Conf. 28, National Conf. 27 Otto Graham, Cleveland, player of the game	Los Angeles Memorial Coliseum (53,676)
Jan. 12, 1952	National Conf. 30, American Conf. 13 Dan Towler, Los Angeles, player of the game	Los Angeles Memorial Coliseum (19,400)
Jan. 10, 1953	National Conf. 27, American Conf. 7 Don Doll, Detroit, player of the game	Los Angeles Memorial Coliseum (34,208)
Jan. 17, 1954	East 20, West 9 Chuck Bednarik, Philadelphia, player of the game	Los Angeles Memorial Coliseum (44,214)
Jan. 16, 1955	West 26, East 19 Billy Wilson, San Francisco, player of the game	Los Angeles Memorial Coliseum (43,972)
Jan. 15, 1956	East 31, West 30 Ollie Matson, Chi. Cardinals, player of the game	Los Angeles Memorial Coliseum (37,867)
Jan. 13, 1957	West 19, East 10 Bert Rechichar, Baltimore, outstanding back Ernie Stautner, Pittsburgh, outstanding lineman	Los Angeles Memorial Coliseum (44,177)
Jan. 12, 1958	West 26, East 7 Hugh McElhenny, San Francisco, outstanding back Gene Brito, Washington, outstanding lineman	Los Angeles Memorial Coliseum (66,634)
Jan. 11, 1959	East 28, West 21 Frank Gifford, N.Y. Giants, outstanding back Doug Atkins, Chi. Bears, outstanding lineman	Los Angeles Memorial Coliseum (72,250)
Jan. 17, 1960	West 38, East 21 Johnny Unitas, Baltimore, outstanding back Gene (Big Daddy) Lipscomb, Baltimore, outstanding lineman	Los Angeles Memorial Coliseum (56,876)
Jan. 15, 1961	West 35, East 31 Johnny Unitas, Baltimore, outstanding back Sam Huff, N.Y. Giants, outstanding lineman	Los Angeles Memorial Coliseum (62,971)
Jan. 7, 1962	AFL West 47, East 27 Cotton Davidson, Dallas Texans, player of the game	Balboa Stadium, San Diego (20,973)
Jan. 14, 1962	NFL West 31, East 30 Jim Brown, Cleveland, outstanding back Henry Jordan, Green Bay, outstanding lineman	Los Angeles Memorial Coliseum (57,409)
Jan. 13, 1963	AFL West 21, East 14 Curtis McClinton, Dallas Texans, outstanding offensive player Earl Faison, San Diego, outstanding defensive player	Balboa Stadium, San Diego (27,641)
Jan. 13, 1963	NFL East 30, West 20 Jim Brown, Cleveland, outstanding back Gene (Big Daddy) Lipscomb, Pittsburgh, outstanding lineman	Los Angeles Memorial Coliseum (61,374)
Jan. 12, 1964	NFL West 31, East 17 Johnny Unitas, Baltimore, player of the game Gino Marchetti, Baltimore, outstanding lineman	Los Angeles Memorial Coliseum (67,242)
Jan. 19, 1964	AFL West 27, East 24 Keith Lincoln, San Diego, outstanding offensive player Archie Matsos, Oakland, outstanding defensive player	Balboa Stadium, San Diego (20,016)
Jan. 10, 1965	NFL West 34, East 14 Fran Tarkenton, Minnesota, outstanding back Terry Barr, Detroit, outstanding lineman	Los Angeles Memorial Coliseum (60,598)
Jan. 16, 1965	AFL West 38, East 14 Keith Lincoln, San Diego, outstanding offensive player Willie Brown, Denver, outstanding defensive player	Jeppesen Stadium, Houston (15,446)
Jan. 15, 1966	AFL All-Stars 30, Buffalo 19 Joe Namath, N.Y. Jets, most valuable player, offense Frank Buncom, San Diego, most valuable player, defense	Rice Stadium, Houston (35,572)
Jan. 15, 1966	NFL East 36, West 7 Jim Brown, Cleveland, outstanding back Dale Meinert, St. Louis, outstanding lineman	Los Angeles Memorial Coliseum (60,124)
Jan. 21, 1967	AFL East 30, West 23 Babe Parilli, Boston, outstanding offensive player Verlon Biggs, N.Y. Jets, outstanding defensive player	Oakland-Alameda County Coliseum (18,876)
Jan. 22, 1967	NFL East 20, West 10 Gale Sayers, Chicago, outstanding back Floyd Peters, Philadelphia, outstanding lineman	Los Angeles Memorial Coliseum (15,062)

Jan. 21, 1968 AFL East 25, West 24 .... Gator Bowl, Jacksonville, Fla. (40,103)
Joe Namath and Don Maynard, N.Y. Jets, out. off. players
Leslie (Speedy) Duncan, San Diego, out. def. player

Jan. 21, 1968 NFL West 38, East 20 .... Los Angeles Memorial Coliseum (53,289)
Gale Sayers, Chicago, outstanding back
Dave Robinson, Green Bay, outstanding lineman

Jan. 19, 1969 AFL West 38, East 25 .... Gator Bowl, Jacksonville, Fla. (41,058)
Len Dawson, Kansas City, outstanding offensive player
George Webster, Houston, outstanding defensive player

Jan. 19, 1969 NFL West 10, East 7 .... Los Angeles Memorial Coliseum (32,050)
Roman Gabriel, Los Angeles, outstanding back
Merlin Olsen, Los Angeles, outstanding lineman

Jan. 17, 1970 AFL West 26, East 3 .... Astrodome, Houston (30,170)
John Hadl, San Diego, player of the game

Jan. 18, 1970 NFL West 16, East 13 .... Los Angeles Memorial Coliseum (57,786)
Gale Sayers, Chicago, outstanding back
George Andrie, Dallas, outstanding lineman

Jan. 24, 1971 NFC 27, AFC 6 .... Los Angeles Memorial Coliseum (48,222)
Mel Renfro, Dallas, outstanding back
Fred Carr, Green Bay, outstanding lineman

Jan. 23, 1972 AFC 26, NFC 13 .... Los Angeles Memorial Coliseum (53,647)
Jan Stenerud, Kansas City, outstanding offensive player
Willie Lanier, Kansas City, outstanding defensive player

Jan. 21, 1973 AFC 33, NFC 28 .... Texas Stadium, Irving (37,091)
O.J. Simpson, Buffalo, player of the game

Jan. 20, 1974 AFC 15, NFC 13 .... Arrowhead Stadium, Kansas City (66,918)
Garo Yepremian, Miami, player of the game

Jan. 20, 1975 NFC 17, AFC 10 .... Orange Bowl, Miami (26,484)
James Harris, Los Angeles, player of the game

Jan. 26, 1976 NFC 23, AFC 20 .... Louisiana Superdome, New Orleans (30,546)
Billy Johnson, Houston, player of the game

Jan. 17, 1977 AFC 24, NFC 14 .... Kingdome, Seattle (64,752)
Mel Blount, Pittsburgh, player of the game

Jan. 23, 1978 NFC 14, AFC 13 .... Tampa Stadium (51,337)
Walter Payton, Chicago, player of the game

Jan. 29, 1979 NFC 13, AFC 7 .... Los Angeles Memorial Coliseum (46,281)
Ahmad Rashad, Minnesota, player of the game

Jan. 27, 1980 NFC 37, AFC 27 .... Aloha Stadium, Honolulu (49,800)
Chuck Muncie, New Orleans, player of the game

Feb. 1, 1981 NFC 21, AFC 7 .... Aloha Stadium, Honolulu (50,360)
Eddie Murray, Detroit, player of the game

Jan. 31, 1982 AFC 16, NFC 13 .... Aloha Stadium, Honolulu (50,402)
Kellen Winslow, San Diego, and Lee Roy Selmon, Tampa Bay, players of the game

Feb. 6, 1983 NFC 20, AFC 19 .... Aloha Stadium, Honolulu (49,883)
Dan Fouts, San Diego, and John Jefferson, Green Bay, players of the game

Jan. 29, 1984 NFC 45, AFC 3 .... Aloha Stadium, Honolulu (50,445)
Joe Theismann, Washington, player of the game

Jan. 27, 1985 AFC 22, NFC 14 .... Aloha Stadium, Honolulu (50,385)
Mark Gastineau, N.Y. Jets, player of the game

Feb. 2, 1986 NFC 28, AFC 24 .... Aloha Stadium, Honolulu (50,101)
Phil Simms, N.Y. Giants, player of the game

Feb. 1, 1987 AFC 10, NFC 6 .... Aloha Stadium, Honolulu (50,101)
Reggie White, Philadelphia, player of the game

Feb. 7, 1988 AFC 15, NFC 6 .... Aloha Stadium, Honolulu (50,113)
Bruce Smith, Buffalo, player of the game

Jan. 29, 1989 NFC 34, AFC 3 .... Aloha Stadium, Honolulu (50,113)
Randall Cunningham, Philadelphia, player of the game

Feb. 4, 1990 NFC 27, AFC 21 .... Aloha Stadium, Honolulu (50,445)
Jerry Gray, L.A. Rams, player of the game

Feb. 3, 1991 AFC 23, NFC 21 .... Aloha Stadium, Honolulu (50,345)
Jim Kelly, Buffalo, player of the game

Feb. 2, 1992 NFC 21, AFC 15 .... Aloha Stadium, Honolulu (50,209)
Michael Irvin, Dallas, player of the game

Feb. 7, 1993 AFC 23, NFC 20 (OT) .... Aloha Stadium, Honolulu (50,007)
Steve Tasker, Buffalo, player of the game

Feb. 6, 1994 NFC 17, AFC 3 .... Aloha Stadium, Honolulu (50,026)
Andre Rison, Atlanta, player of the game

Feb. 5, 1995 AFC 41, NFC 13 .... Aloha Stadium, Honolulu (50,529)
Marshall Faulk, Indianapolis, player of the game

PRO BOWL ALL-TIME RESULTS

Feb. 4, 1996 NFC 20, AFC 13 ... Aloha Stadium, Honolulu (50,034)
Jerry Rice, San Francisco, player of the game

Feb. 2, 1997 AFC 26, NFC 23 (OT) ... Aloha Stadium, Honolulu (50,031)
Mark Brunell, Jacksonville, player of the game

Feb. 1, 1998 AFC 29, NFC 24 ... Aloha Stadium, Honolulu (49,995)
Warren Moon, Seattle, player of the game

Feb. 7, 1999 AFC 23, NFC 10 ... Aloha Stadium, Honolulu (50,075)
Keyshawn Johnson, N.Y. Jets and Ty Law, New England, co-players of the game

Feb. 6, 2000 NFC 51, AFC 31 ... Aloha Stadium, Honolulu (50,112)
Randy Moss, Minnesota, player of the game

Feb. 4, 2001 AFC 38, NFC 17 ... Aloha Stadium, Honolulu (50,128)
Rich Gannon, Oakland, player of the game

Feb. 9, 2002 AFC 38, NFC 30 ... Aloha Stadium, Honolulu (50,301)
Rich Gannon, Oakland, player of the game

Feb. 2, 2003 AFC 45, NFC 20 ... Aloha Stadium, Honolulu (50,125)
Ricky Williams, Miami, player of the game

Feb. 8, 2004 NFC 55, AFC 52 ... Aloha Stadium, Honolulu (50,127)
Marc Bulger, St. Louis, player of the game

Feb. 13, 2005 AFC 38, NFC 27 ... Aloha Stadium, Honolulu (50,225)
Peyton Manning, Indianapolis, player of the game

Feb. 12, 2006 NFC 23, AFC 17 ... Aloha Stadium, Honolulu (50,190)
Derrick Brooks, Tampa Bay, player of the game

Feb. 10, 2007 AFC 31, NFC 28 ... Aloha Stadium, Honolulu (50,410)
Carson Palmer, Cincinnati, player of the game

Feb. 10, 2008 NFC 42, AFC 30 ... Aloha Stadium, Honolulu (50,044)
Adrian Peterson, Minnesota, most valuable player

Feb. 8, 2009 NFC 30, AFC 21 ... Aloha Stadium, Honolulu (49,958)
Larry Fitzgerald, Arizona, most valuable player

SUNDAY NIGHT FOOTBALL, 1978-2008
(Home Team in capitals, games listed in chronological order.)

2008
Chicago 29, INDIANAPOLIS 13
Pittsburgh 10, CLEVELAND 6
Dallas 27, GREEN BAY 16
CHICAGO 24, Philadelphia 20
Pittsburgh 26, JACKSONVILLE 21
SAN DIEGO 30, New England 10
TAMPA BAY 20, Seattle 10
INDIANAPOLIS 18, New England 15
New York Giants 36, PHILADELPHIA 31
Dallas 14, WASHINGTON 10
Indianapolis 23, SAN DIEGO 20
MINNESOTA 34, Chicago 14
BALTIMORE 24, Washington 10
DALLAS 20, New York Giants 8
NEW YORK GIANTS 34, Carolina 28
SAN DIEGO 52, Denver 21

2007
DALLAS 45, New York Giants 35
NEW ENGLAND 38, San Diego 14
Dallas 34, CHICAGO 10
NEW YORK GIANTS 16, Philadelphia 3
Chicago 27, GREEN BAY 20
New Orleans 28, SEATTLE 17
DENVER 31, Pittsburgh 28
Dallas 38, PHILADELPHIA 17
SAN DIEGO 23, Indianapolis 21
New England 56, BUFFALO 10
NEW ENGLAND 31, Philadelphia 28
PITTSBURGH 24, Cincinnati 10
Indianapolis 44, BALTIMORE 20
Washington 22, NEW YORK GIANTS 10
Washington 32, MINNESOTA 21
Tennessee 16, INDIANAPOLIS 10

2006
Indianapolis 26, NEW YORK GIANTS 21
DALLAS 27, Washington 10
Denver 17, NEW ENGLAND 7
CHICAGO 37, Seattle 6
SAN DIEGO 23, Pittsburgh 13
DENVER 13, Oakland 3
Dallas 35, CAROLINA 14
Indianapolis 27, NEW ENGLAND 20
Chicago 38, NEW YORK GIANTS 20
San Diego 35, DENVER 27
INDIANAPOLIS 45, Philadelphia 21
Seattle 23, DENVER 20
New Orleans 42, DALLAS 17
SAN DIEGO 20, Kansas City 9
Green Bay 26, CHICAGO 7

2005
Indianapolis 24, BALTIMORE 7
Kansas City 23, OAKLAND 17
SAN DIEGO 45, New York Giants 23
ARIZONA 31, San Francisco 14
JACKSONVILLE 23, Cincinnati 20
SEATTLE 42, Houston 10
NEW ENGLAND 21, Buffalo 16
WASHINGTON 17, Philadelphia 10
PITTSBURGH 34, Cleveland 21
Kansas City 45, HOUSTON 17
New Orleans 21, NEW YORK JETS 19
SAN DIEGO 34, Oakland 10
GREEN BAY 16, Detroit 13
CHICAGO 16, Atlanta 3
BALTIMORE 30, Minnesota 23
St. Louis 20, DALLAS 10

2004
DENVER 34, Kansas City 24
CINCINNATI 16, Miami 13
OAKLAND 30, Tampa Bay 20
Pittsburgh 13, MIAMI 3
St. Louis 24, SAN FRANCISCO 14
Baltimore 17, WASHINGTON 10
Minnesota 38, NEW ORLEANS 31
CHICAGO 23, San Francisco 13
BALTIMORE 27, Cleveland 13
NEW ENGLAND 29, Buffalo 6
Green Bay 16, HOUSTON 13
Oakland 25, DENVER 24
Pittsburgh 17, JACKSONVILLE 16
Philadelphia 17, WASHINGTON 14
INDIANAPOLIS 20, Baltimore 10
MIAMI 10, Cleveland 7
NEW YORK GIANTS 28, Dallas 24

2003
TENNESSEE 25, Oakland 20
MINNESOTA 24, Chicago 13
MIAMI 17, Buffalo 7
Indianapolis 55, NEW ORLEANS 21
Cleveland 33, PITTSBURGH 13
SEATTLE 20, San Francisco 19
KANSAS CITY 38, Buffalo 5
Green Bay 30, MINNESOTA 27
ST. LOUIS 33, Baltimore 22
NEW ENGLAND 12, Dallas 0
MIAMI 24, Washington 23
JACKSONVILLE 17, Tampa Bay 10
ATLANTA 20, Carolina 14 (OT)
NEW ORLEANS 45, New York Giants 7
Denver 31, INDIANAPOLIS 17
BALTIMORE 13, Pittsburgh 10 (OT)

SUNDAY NIGHT FOOTBALL

2002
HOUSTON 19, Dallas 10
Oakland 30, PITTSBURGH 17
ATLANTA 30, Cincinnati 3
SEATTLE 48, Minnesota 23
Baltimore 26, CLEVELAND 21
Miami 24, DENVER 22
WASHINGTON 26, Indianapolis 21
NEW YORK GIANTS 24, Jacksonville 17
NEW YORK JETS 13, Miami 10
OAKLAND 27, New England 20
Indianapolis 23, DENVER 20 (OT)
NEW ORLEANS 23, Tampa Bay 20
GREEN BAY 26, Minnesota 22
ST. LOUIS 30, Arizona 28
New York Jets 30, NEW ENGLAND 17
Tampa Bay 15, CHICAGO 0

2001
Miami 31, TENNESSEE 23
Denver 38, ARIZONA 17
PHILADELPHIA 40, Dallas 18
SAN FRANCISCO 24, Carolina 14
Oakland 23, INDIANAPOLIS 18
New York Jets 16, NEW ORLEANS 9
SEATTLE 34, Oakland 27
St. Louis 24, NEW ENGLAND 17
Chicago 13, MINNESOTA 6
SAN FRANCISCO 35, Buffalo 0
DENVER 20, Seattle 7
Pittsburgh 26, BALTIMORE 21
New York Jets 29, INDIANAPOLIS 28
Washington 40, NEW ORLEANS 10
Philadelphia 17, TAMPA BAY 13

2000
BUFFALO 16, Tennessee 13
ARIZONA 32, Dallas 31
MIAMI 19, Baltimore 6
Washington 16, NEW YORK GIANTS 6
PHILADELPHIA 38, Atlanta 10
Baltimore 15, JACKSONVILLE 10
Minnesota 28, CHICAGO 16
Oakland 15, SAN DIEGO 13
Carolina 27, ST. LOUIS 24
INDIANAPOLIS 23, New York Jets 15
Jacksonville 34, PITTSBURGH 24
New York Giants 31, ARIZONA 7
Green Bay 28, CHICAGO 6
OAKLAND 31, New York Jets 7
New York Giants 17, DALLAS 13

1999
Pittsburgh 43, CLEVELAND 0
BUFFALO 17, New York Jets 3
NEW ENGLAND 16, New York Giants 14
SEATTLE 22, Oakland 21
GREEN BAY 26, Tampa Bay 23
Washington 24, ARIZONA 10
DETROIT 20, Tampa Bay 3
MIAMI 17, Tennessee 0
SEATTLE 20, Denver 17
JACKSONVILLE 41, New Orleans 23
CAROLINA 34, Atlanta 28
NEW ENGLAND 13, Dallas 6
KANSAS CITY 31, Minnesota 28
Buffalo 31, ARIZONA 21
Washington 26, SAN FRANCISCO 20 (OT)

1998
KANSAS CITY 28, Oakland 8
NEW ENGLAND 29, Indianapolis 6
ARIZONA 17, Philadelphia 3
BALTIMORE 31, Cincinnati 24
KANSAS CITY 17, Seattle 6
Atlanta 34, NEW YORK GIANTS 20
Buffalo 30, CAROLINA 14
Oakland 31, SEATTLE 18
Tennessee 31, TAMPA BAY 22
DETROIT 26, Chicago 3
SAN FRANCISCO 31, New Orleans 20
Denver 31, SAN DIEGO 16
MINNESOTA 48, Chicago 22
New York Jets 21, MIAMI 16
MINNESOTA 50, Jacksonville 10
DALLAS 23, Washington 7

1997
Washington 24, CAROLINA 10
ARIZONA 25, Dallas 22 (OT)
NEW ENGLAND 27, New York Jets 24 (OT)
TAMPA BAY 31, Miami 21
MINNESOTA 28, Philadelphia 19
New Orleans 20, CHICAGO 17
PITTSBURGH 24, Indianapolis 22
CAROLINA 21, Atlanta 12
GREEN BAY 20, Detroit 10
PITTSBURGH 37, Baltimore 0
Oakland 38, SAN DIEGO 13
WASHINGTON 7, New York Giants 7 (OT)
Denver 38, SAN DIEGO 28
MIAMI 33, Detroit 30
Chicago 13, ST. LOUIS 10
SEATTLE 38, San Francisco 9

1996
Buffalo 23, NEW YORK GIANTS 20 (OT)
Miami 38, ARIZONA 10
DENVER 27, Tampa Bay 23
Philadelphia 33, ATLANTA 18
WASHINGTON 31, New York Jets 16
Houston 30, CINCINNATI 27 (OT)
INDIANAPOLIS 26, Baltimore 21
NEW ENGLAND 28, Buffalo 25
San Francisco 24, NEW ORLEANS 17
CAROLINA 27, New York Giants 17
Minnesota 16, OAKLAND 13 (OT)
Green Bay 24, ST. LOUIS 9
New England 45, SAN DIEGO 7
Minnesota 24, DETROIT 22
JACKSONVILLE 20, Seattle 13
SAN DIEGO 16, Denver 10

1995
DENVER 22, Buffalo 7
Philadelphia 31, ARIZONA 19
Dallas 23, MINNESOTA 17 (OT)
Green Bay 24, JACKSONVILLE 14
Oakland 47, NEW YORK JETS 10
Denver 37, NEW ENGLAND 3
New York Giants 24, WASHINGTON 15
Miami 24, SAN DIEGO 14
PHILADELPHIA 31, Denver 13
KANSAS CITY 20, Houston 13
NEW ORLEANS 34, Carolina 26
SAN FRANCISCO 27, Buffalo 17
TAMPA BAY 13, Green Bay 10 (OT)
SEATTLE 44, Oakland 10

1994
San Diego 17, DENVER 34
New York Giants 20, ARIZONA 17
Kansas City 30, ATLANTA 10
Chicago 19, NEW YORK JETS 7
Miami 23, CINCINNATI 7
PHILADELPHIA 21, Washington 17
ARIZONA 20, Pittsburgh 17 (OT)
KANSAS CITY 13, Los Angeles Raiders 3
DETROIT 14, Tampa Bay 9
SAN FRANCISCO 31, Los Angeles Rams 27
New England 12, INDIANAPOLIS 10
Buffalo 42, MIAMI 31
New Orleans 29, ATLANTA 20
Los Angeles Raiders 17, SEATTLE 16
MIAMI 27, Detroit 20

1993
NEW ORLEANS 33, Houston 21
Los Angeles Raiders 17, SEATTLE 13
Dallas 17, PHOENIX 10
NEW YORK JETS 45, New England 7
BUFFALO 17, New York Giants 14
GREEN BAY 30, Denver 27
MIAMI 41, Indianapolis 27
Detroit 30, MINNESOTA 27
WASHINGTON 30, Indianapolis 24
Chicago 16, SAN DIEGO 13
TAMPA BAY 23, Minnesota 10
HOUSTON 23, Pittsburgh 3
SAN FRANCISCO 21, Cincinnati 8
Green Bay 20, SAN DIEGO 13
Philadelphia 20, INDIANAPOLIS 10
MINNESOTA 30, Kansas City 10
HOUSTON 24, New York Jets 0

1992
DENVER 17, Los Angeles Raiders 13
Philadelphia 31, PHOENIX 14
BUFFALO 38, Indianapolis 0
San Francisco 16, NEW ORLEANS 10
NEW YORK JETS 30, New England 21
NEW ORLEANS 13, Los Angeles Rams 10
Pittsburgh 27, KANSAS CITY 3
New York Giants 24, WASHINGTON 7
Cincinnati 31, CHICAGO 28 (OT)
DENVER 27, New York Giants 13
Kansas City 24, SEATTLE 14
SAN DIEGO 27, Los Angeles Raiders 3
Los Angeles Rams 31, TAMPA BAY 27
Green Bay 16, HOUSTON 14
MIAMI 19, New York Jets 17
HOUSTON 27, Buffalo 3

1991
WASHINGTON 45, Detroit 0
Houston 30, CINCINNATI 7
NEW ORLEANS 24, Los Angeles Rams 7
Dallas 17, PHOENIX 9
Denver 13, MINNESOTA 6
Pittsburgh 21, INDIANAPOLIS 3
Los Angeles Raiders 23, SEATTLE 20
Washington 17, NEW YORK GIANTS 13
DENVER 20, Pittsburgh 13
MIAMI 30, New England 20
HOUSTON 28, Cleveland 24
Atlanta 23, NEW ORLEANS 20 (OT)
Los Angeles Raiders 9, SAN DIEGO 7
Minnesota 26, TAMPA BAY 24
Buffalo 35, INDIANAPOLIS 7
SEATTLE 23, Los Angeles Rams 9

1990
NEW YORK GIANTS 27, Philadelphia 20
PITTSBURGH 20, Houston 9
TAMPA BAY 23, Detroit 20
Washington 38, PHOENIX 10
BUFFALO 38, Los Angeles Raiders 24
CHICAGO 38, Los Angeles Rams 9
ATLANTA 38, Cincinnati 17
MINNESOTA 27, Denver 22
San Francisco 24, DALLAS 6
CINCINNATI 27, Pittsburgh 3
Seattle 13, SAN DIEGO 10
MINNESOTA 23, Green Bay 7
MIAMI 23, Philadelphia 20
DETROIT 38, Chicago 21
SEATTLE 17, Denver 12
HOUSTON 34, Pittsburgh 14

1989
Dallas 13, WASHINGTON 3
SAN DIEGO 14, Los Angeles Raiders 12
INDIANAPOLIS 27, New York Jets 10
Los Angeles Rams 20, NEW ORLEANS 17
MINNESOTA 27, Chicago 16
MIAMI 31, New England 10
SEATTLE 23, Los Angeles Raiders 17

1988
HOUSTON 41, Washington 17
Los Angeles Raiders 13, SAN DIEGO 3
Minnesota 43, DALLAS 3
New England 6, MIAMI 3
New York Giants 13, NEW ORLEANS 12
Pittsburgh 37, HOUSTON 34
SEATTLE 42, Denver 14
Los Angeles Rams 38, SAN FRANCISCO 16

1987
NEW YORK GIANTS 17, New England 10
SAN DIEGO 16, Los Angeles Raiders 14
Miami 20, DALLAS 14
SAN FRANCISCO 38, Cleveland 24
Chicago 30, MINNESOTA 24
SEATTLE 28, Denver 21
MIAMI 23, Washington 21
SAN FRANCISCO 48, Los Angeles Rams 0

1986
LOS ANGELES RAMS 29, Dallas 10

SUNDAY/THURSDAY-SATURDAY NIGHT FOOTBALL

1985
Dallas 30, NEW YORK GIANTS 29
SAN DIEGO 54, Pittsburgh 44

1984
Denver 24, CLEVELAND 14
DALLAS 30, New Orleans 27

1983
Los Angeles Raiders 40, DALLAS 38

1982
ATLANTA 17, San Francisco 7

1981
DALLAS 29, Los Angeles 17

1980
DALLAS 42, San Diego 31

1979
DALLAS 30, Los Angeles 6

1978
New England 21, OAKLAND 14
LOS ANGELES 10, Pittsburgh 7
Denver 21, OAKLAND 6

THURSDAY-SATURDAY NIGHT FOOTBALL, 1974-2008

2008
NEW YORK GIANTS 16, Washington 7 (Thurs.)
Denver 34, CLEVELAND 30 (Thurs.)
New York Jets 34, NEW ENGLAND 31 (Thurs.)
PITTSBURGH 27, Cincinnati 10 (Thurs.)
PHILADELPHIA 48, Arizona 20 (Thurs.)
SAN DIEGO 34, Oakland 7 (Thurs.)
CHICAGO 27, New Orleans 24 (Thurs.)
Indianapolis 31, JACKSONVILLE 24 (Thurs.)
Baltimore 33, DALLAS 24 (Sat.)

2007
INDIANAPOLIS 41, New Orleans 10 (Thurs.)
Indianapolis 31, ATLANTA 13 (Thurs.)
DALLAS 37, Green Bay 27 (Thurs.)
WASHINGTON 24, Chicago 16 (Thurs.)
HOUSTON 31, Denver 13 (Thurs.)
SAN FRANCISCO 20, Cincinnati 13 (Sat.)
Pittsburgh 41, ST. LOUIS 24 (Thurs.)
Dallas 20, CAROLINA 13 (Sat.)
New England 38, NEW YORK GIANTS 35 (Sat.)

2006
PITTSBURGH 28, Miami 17 (Thurs.)
KANSAS CITY 19, Denver 10 (Thurs.)
CINCINNATI 13, Baltimore 7 (Thurs.)
PITTSBURGH 27, Cleveland 7 (Thurs.)
San Francisco 24, SEATTLE 14 (Thurs.)
Dallas 38, ATLANTA 28 (Sat.)
GREEN BAY 9, Minnesota 7 (Thurs.)
Kansas City 20, OAKLAND 9 (Sat.)
New York Giants 34, WASHINGTON 28 (Sat.)

2005
NEW ENGLAND 30, Oakland 20 (Thurs.)
Kansas City 30, MIAMI 20 (Fri.)
Denver 28, BUFFALO 17 (Sat.)
New York Giants 30, OAKLAND 21 (Sat.)

2004
NEW ENGLAND 27, Indianapolis 24 (Thurs.)
ATLANTA 34, Carolina 31 (OT) (Sat.)
Denver 37, TENNESSEE 16 (Sat.)

2003
WASHINGTON 16, New York Jets 13 (Thurs.)
New England 21, NEW YORK JETS 16 (Sat.)
Philadelphia 31, WASHINGTON 7 (Sat.)

2002
San Francisco 16, NEW YORK GIANTS 13 (Thurs.)
Philadelphia 27, DALLAS 3 (Sat.)

2001
Buffalo 13, JACKSONVILLE 10 (Thurs.)
Indianapolis 35, KANSAS CITY 28 (Thurs.)
Tennessee 13, OAKLAND 10 (Sat.)
TAMPA BAY 22, Baltimore 10 (Sat.)

2000
Detroit 28, TAMPA BAY 14 (Thurs.)
MINNESOTA 24, Detroit 17 (Thurs.)
Buffalo 42, SEATTLE 23 (Sat.)

1999
Kansas City 35, BALTIMORE 8 (Thurs.)
JACKSONVILLE 20, Pittsburgh 6 (Thurs.)
TENNESSEE 21, Oakland 14 (Thurs.)

1998
DETROIT 27, Green Bay 20 (Thurs.)
PHILADELPHIA 17, St. Louis 14 (Thurs.)

1997
KANSAS CITY 31, San Diego 3 (Thurs.)
CINCINNATI 41, Tennessee 14 (Thurs.)

1996
KANSAS CITY 34, Seattle 16 (Thurs.)
INDIANAPOLIS 37, Philadelphia 10 (Thurs.)

1995
ST. LOUIS 21, Atlanta 19 (Thurs.)
Cincinnati 27, PITTSBURGH 9 (Thurs.)
New York Giants 10, ARIZONA 6 (Thurs.)
Indianapolis 10, New England 7 (Sat.)

1994
Cleveland 11, HOUSTON 8 (Thurs.)
MINNESOTA 13, Green Bay 10 (OT) (Thurs.)
MINNESOTA 33, Chicago 27 (OT) (Thurs.)

1993
ATLANTA 30, Los Angeles Rams 24 (Thurs.)

1992
MINNESOTA 31, Detroit 14 (Thurs.)
NEW ORLEANS 22, Atlanta 14 (Thurs.)

1991
Chicago 10, GREEN BAY 0 (Thurs.)

1990
MIAMI 17, New England 10 (Thurs.)
INDIANAPOLIS 35, Washington 28 (Sat.)

1989
Cleveland 24, HOUSTON 20 (Sat.)

1987-88
None

1986
New England 20, NEW YORK JETS 6 (Thurs.)
Cincinnati 30, CLEVELAND 13 (Thurs.)
Los Angeles Raiders 37, SAN DIEGO 31 (OT) (Thurs.)
SAN FRANCISCO 24, Los Angeles Rams 14 (Fri.)

1985
KANSAS CITY 36, Los Angeles Raiders 20 (Thurs.)
Chicago 33, MINNESOTA 24 (Thurs.)
Denver 27, SEATTLE 24 (Fri.)

1984
Pittsburgh 23, NEW YORK JETS 17 (Thurs.)
Washington 31, MINNESOTA 17 (Thurs.)
SAN FRANCISCO 19, Los Angeles Rams 16 (Fri.)

1983
San Francisco 48, MINNESOTA 17 (Thurs.)
CLEVELAND 17, Cincinnati 7 (Thurs.)
Los Angeles Raiders 42, SAN DIEGO 10 (Thurs.)
MIAMI 34, New York Jets 14 (Fri.)

1982
BUFFALO 23, Minnesota 22 (Thurs.)
SAN FRANCISCO 30, Los Angeles Rams 24 (Thurs.)

1981
MIAMI 30, Pittsburgh 10 (Thurs.)
Philadelphia 20, BUFFALO 14 (Thurs.)
HOUSTON 17, Cleveland 13 (Thurs.

1980
TAMPA BAY 10, Los Angeles 9 (Thurs.)
San Diego 27, MIAMI 24 (OT) (Thurs.)
HOUSTON 6, Pittsburgh 0 (Thurs.)

1979
Los Angeles 13, DENVER 9 (Thurs.)
OAKLAND 45, San Diego 22 (Thurs.)
MIAMI 39, New England 24 (Thurs.)

1978
Minnesota 21, DALLAS 10 (Thurs.)

1977
Minnesota 30, DETROIT 21 (Sat.)

1976
Los Angeles 20, DETROIT 17 (Sat.)

1975
LOS ANGELES 10, Pittsburgh 3 (Sat.)

1974
OAKLAND 27, Dallas 23 (Sat.)

MONDAY NIGHT RECORDS

Compiled by Elias Sports Bureau
*NFL record.

MONDAY NIGHT RECORDS

SCORING
TOUCHDOWNS
Most Touchdowns, Career
- 36 Jerry Rice, San Francisco, 1985-2000; Oakland, 2001-04; Seattle 2004
- 24 Emmitt Smith, Dallas, 1990-2002; Arizona 2003-04
- 19 Marcus Allen, L.A. Raiders, 1982-1992; Kansas City, 1993-97

Most Touchdowns, Game
- 4 Ron Johnson, N.Y. Giants at Philadelphia, Oct. 2, 1972
  - Earl Campbell, Houston vs. Miami, Nov. 20, 1978
  - Marcus Allen, L.A. Raiders vs. San Diego, Sept. 24, 1984
  - Eric Dickerson, Indianapolis vs. Denver, Oct. 31, 1988
  - Emmitt Smith, Dallas at N.Y. Giants, Sept. 4, 1995
  - Marshall Faulk, St. Louis at Tampa Bay, Dec. 18, 2000

FIELD GOALS
Most Field Goals, Career
- 51 Gary Anderson, Pittsburgh, 1982-1994; Philadelphia, 1995-96; San Francisco, 1997; Minnesota, 1998-2002; Tennessee, 2003-04
- 48 Jason Elam, Denver, 1993-2007
- 41 Ryan Longwell, Green Bay, 1997-2005; Minnesota, 2006-08

Most Field Goals, Game
- 7 Chris Boniol, Dallas vs. Green Bay, Nov. 18, 1996*
  - Billy Cundiff, Dallas at N.Y. Giants, Sept. 15, 2003 (OT)*
- 5 Tim Mazzetti, Atlanta vs. Los Angeles, Oct. 30, 1978
  - Roger Ruzek, Dallas at L.A. Rams, Dec. 21, 1987
  - Rich Karlis, Minnesota vs. Cincinnati, Dec. 25, 1989
  - Nick Lowery, Kansas City vs. Denver, Sept. 20, 1993
  - Chris Jacke, Green Bay vs. San Francisco, Oct. 14, 1996 (OT)
  - Richie Cunningham, Dallas vs. Philadelphia, Sept. 15, 1997
  - Phil Dawson, Cleveland vs. Buffalo, Nov. 17, 2008

RUSHING
YARDS GAINED
Most Yards Gained, Career
- 2,434 Emmitt Smith, Dallas, 1990-2002; Arizona, 2003-04
- 1,897 Tony Dorsett, Dallas, 1977-1987; Denver, 1988
- 1,769 Thurman Thomas, Buffalo, 1988-1999; Miami, 2000

Most Yards Gained, Game
- 221 Bo Jackson, L.A. Raiders at Seattle, Nov. 30, 1987
- 216 Ricky Williams, Miami vs. Chicago, Dec. 9, 2002
- 214 Thurman Thomas, Buffalo at N.Y. Jets, Sept. 24, 1990

Longest Run From Scrimmage, Game
- 99 Tony Dorsett, Dallas at Minnesota, Jan. 3, 1983 (TD)*
- 91 Bo Jackson, L.A. Raiders at Seattle, Nov. 30, 1987 (TD)
- 83 James Lofton, Green Bay at N.Y. Giants, Sept. 20, 1982 (TD)

TOUCHDOWNS
Most Rushing Touchdowns, Career
- 23 Emmitt Smith, Dallas, 1990-2002; Arizona, 2003-04
- 17 Marcus Allen, L.A. Raiders, 1982-1992; Kansas City, 1993-97
- 14 Eric Dickerson, L.A. Rams, 1983-87; Indianapolis, 1987-1991; L.A. Raiders, 1992; Atlanta, 1993

Most Rushing Touchdowns, Game
- 4 Earl Campbell, Houston vs. Miami, Nov. 20, 1978
  - Eric Dickerson, Indianapolis vs. Denver, Oct. 31, 1988
  - Emmitt Smith, Dallas at N.Y. Giants, Sept. 4, 1995

PASSING
YARDS GAINED
Most Yards Gained, Career
- 9,654 Dan Marino, Miami, 1983-1999
- 8,149 Brett Favre, Atlanta, 1991; Green Bay, 1992-2007; N.Y. Jets, 2008
- 5,148 Joe Montana, San Francisco, 1979-1992; Kansas City, 1993-94

Most Yards Gained, Game
- 458 Joe Montana, San Francisco at L.A. Rams, Dec. 11, 1989
- 448 Marc Bulger, St. Louis at Green Bay, Nov. 29, 2004
- 447 Ken Anderson, Cincinnati vs. Buffalo, Nov. 17, 1975

Longest Pass Play
- 99 Brett Favre to Robert Brooks, Green Bay at Chicago, Sept. 11, 1995 (TD)*
- 97 Bernie Kosar to Webster Slaughter, Cleveland vs. Chicago, Oct. 23, 1989 (TD)
- 95 Joe Montana to John Taylor, San Francisco at L.A. Rams, Dec. 11, 1989 (TD)

TOUCHDOWNS
Most Touchdown Passes, Career
- 74 Dan Marino, Miami, 1983-1999
- 60 Brett Favre, Atlanta, 1991; Green Bay, 1992-2007; N.Y. Jets, 2008
- 42 Steve Young, Tampa Bay, 1985-86; San Francisco, 1987-1999

Most Touchdown Passes, Game
- 5 Dave Krieg, Seattle vs. L.A. Raiders, Nov. 28, 1988
  - Jim Kelly, Buffalo vs. Cincinnati, Oct. 21, 1991
  - Vinny Testaverde, N.Y. Jets vs. Miami, Oct. 23, 2000 (OT)
  - Ben Roethlisberger, Pittsburgh vs. Baltimore, Nov. 5, 2007

RECEIVING
PASS RECEPTIONS
Most Pass Receptions, Career
- 254 Jerry Rice, San Francisco, 1985-2000; Oakland, 2001-04; Seattle, 2004
- 124 Andre Reed, Buffalo, 1985-1999; Washington, 2000
- 123 Cris Carter, Philadelphia, 1987-89; Minnesota, 1990-2001; Miami, 2002

Most Pass Receptions, Game
- 14 Herman Moore, Detroit vs. Chicago, Dec. 4, 1995
  - Jerry Rice, San Francisco vs. Minnesota, Dec. 18, 1995
- 13 Andre Reed, Buffalo vs. Denver, Sept. 18, 1989
  - Terrell Owens, San Francisco vs. Philadelphia, Nov. 25, 2002

YARDS GAINED
Most Yards Gained, Career
- 4,029 Jerry Rice, San Francisco, 1985-2000; Oakland, 2001-04; Seattle, 2004
- 1,783 Andre Reed, Buffalo, 1985-1999; Washington, 2000
- 1,537 Art Monk, Washington, 1980-1993; N.Y. Jets, 1994; Philadelphia, 1995

Most Yards Gained, Game
- 289 Jerry Rice, San Francisco vs. Minnesota, Dec. 18, 1995
- 286 John Taylor, San Francisco at L.A. Rams, Dec. 11, 1989
- 260 Wes Chandler, San Diego vs. Cincinnati, Dec. 20, 1982

TOUCHDOWN

Most Receiving Touchdowns, Career

34 Jerry Rice, San Francisco, 1985-2000; Oakland, 2001-04; Seattle, 2004
18 Terrell Owens, San Francisco, 1996-2003; Philadelphia, 2004-05; Dallas, 2006-08
16 Randy Moss, Minnesota, 1998-2004; Oakland, 2005-06; New England, 2007-08

Most Receiving Touchdowns, Game

3 Ron Johnson, N.Y. Giants at Philadelphia, Oct. 2, 1972
Wesley Walker, N.Y. Jets at Detroit, Dec. 6, 1982
Steve Largent, Seattle at San Diego, Oct. 29, 1984
Mark Clayton, Miami vs. Dallas, Dec. 17, 1984
Jerry Rice, San Francisco vs. Chicago, Dec. 14, 1987
Jerry Rice, San Francisco vs. Minnesota, Dec. 18, 1995
Lamar Thomas, Miami vs. Denver, Dec. 21, 1998
Ed McCaffrey, Denver vs. Miami, Sept. 13, 1999
Randy Moss, Minnesota vs. N.Y. Giants, Nov. 19, 2001
Isaac Bruce, St. Louis at New Orleans, Dec. 17, 2001
Terrell Owens, Philadelphia at Dallas, Nov. 15, 2004
Drew Bennett, Tennessee vs. Kansas City, Dec. 13, 2004
Marvin Harrison, Indianapolis vs. Cincinnati, Dec. 18, 2006

YARDS FROM SCRIMMAGE

Most Scrimmage Yards, Career

4,116 Jerry Rice, San Francisco, 1985-2000; Oakland, 2001-04; Seattle, 2004
2,836 Emmitt Smith, Dallas, 1990-2002; Arizona, 2003-04
2,567 Tony Dorsett, Dallas, 1977-1987; Denver, 1988

INTERCEPTIONS BY

Most Interceptions, Career

11 Everson Walls, Dallas, 1981-89; N.Y. Giants, 1990-92; Cleveland, 1992-93
9 Merton Hanks, San Francisco, 1991-98; Seattle, 1999
8 Emmitt Thomas, Kansas City, 1966-1978

Most Interceptions, Game

4 Dick Anderson, Miami vs. Pittsburgh, Dec. 3, 1973*
3 Johnny Robinson, Kansas City at Baltimore, Sept. 28, 1970
Charlie Babb, Miami vs. Oakland, Sept. 22, 1975
Charles Phillips, Oakland vs. Denver, Dec. 8, 1975
Mark Murphy, Washington at San Diego, Oct. 31, 1983
Ken Easley, Seattle at San Diego, Oct. 29, 1984
Dwayne Harper, San Diego vs. Oakland, Nov. 27, 1995
Marcus Coleman, N.Y. Jets vs. Miami, Oct. 23, 2000 (OT)
Keith Bulluck, Tennessee vs. New Orleans, Sept. 24, 2007

Longest Interception Return

102 Eddie Anderson, L.A. Raiders at Miami, Dec. 14, 1992 (TD)
101 Lito Sheppard, Philadelphia at Dallas, Nov. 15, 2004 (TD)
98 Marcus Coleman, N.Y. Jets vs. Miami, Dec. 27, 1999 (TD)
Rod Woodson, Oakland at Denver, Nov. 11, 2002 (TD)
Brandon McDonald, Cleveland vs. Philadelphia, Dec. 15, 2008

SACKS

Most Sacks, Career

24.5 Bruce Smith, Buffalo, 1985-1999; Washington, 2000-03
20.0 Richard Dent, Chicago, 1983-1993, 1995; San Francisco, 1994; Indianapolis, 1996; Philadelphia, 1997
18.0 Kevin Greene, L.A. Rams, 1985-1992; Pittsburgh, 1993-95; Carolina, 1996, 1998-99; San Francisco, 1997

PUNTING

Highest Punt Average, Career (Minimum: 25 Punts)

47.1 Shane Lechler, Oakland, 2000-08
45.8 Dave Zastudil, Baltimore, 2002-05; Cleveland, 2006-08
44.5 Tom Tupa, Phoenix, 1988-1991; Indianapolis, 1992; Cleveland, 1994-95; New England, 1996-98; N.Y. Jets, 1999-2001; Tampa Bay, 2002-03; Washington, 2004

Longest Punt

90 Rodney Williams, N.Y. Giants at Denver, Sept. 10, 2001
83 Bryan Barker, Jacksonville vs. N.Y. Jets, Oct. 11, 1999
75 Craig Hentrich, Indianapolis vs. Tennessee, Oct. 27, 2008

PUNT RETURNS

Longest Punt Return

95 John Taylor, San Francisco vs. Washington, Nov. 21, 1988 (TD)
94 Dennis McKinnon, Chicago vs. N.Y. Giants, Sept. 14, 1987 (TD)
91 JoJo Townsell, N.Y. Jets vs. Seattle, Nov. 9, 1987 (TD)
Nate Burleson, Minnesota at Indianapolis, Nov. 8, 2004 (TD)

KICKOFF RETURNS

Longest Kickoff Return

105 Terry Fair, Detroit vs. Tampa Bay, Sept. 28, 1998 (TD)
104 Allen Rossum, San Francisco vs. Arizona, Nov. 10, 2008 (TD)
103 Terrence McGee, Buffalo vs. Dallas, Oct. 8, 2007 (TD)

FUMBLES

Longest Fumble Return

99 Don Griffin, San Francisco vs. Chicago, Dec. 23, 1991 (TD)
96 Joe Lavender, Philadelphia vs. Dallas, Sept. 23, 1974 (TD)
93 Adam Archuleta, St. Louis vs. Tampa Bay, Oct. 18, 2004 (TD)

MONDAY NIGHT FOOTBALL, 1970-2008

(Home Team in capitals, games listed in chronological order.)

2008
GREEN BAY 24, Minnesota 19
Denver 41, OAKLAND 14
DALLAS 41, Philadelphia 37
SAN DIEGO 48, New York Jets 29
PITTSBURGH 23, Baltimore 20
Minnesota 30, NEW ORLEANS 27
CLEVELAND 35, New York Giants 14
NEW ENGLAND 41, Denver 7
TENNESSEE 31, Indianapolis 21
Pittsburgh 23, WASHINGTON 6
ARIZONA 29, San Francisco 24
Cleveland 29, BUFFALO 27
NEW ORLEANS 51, Green Bay 29
HOUSTON 30, Jacksonville 17
CAROLINA 28, Tampa Bay 23
PHILADELPHIA 30, Cleveland 10
CHICAGO 20, Green Bay 17

2007
CINCINNATI 27, Baltimore 20
SAN FRANCISCO 20, Arizona 17
Washington 20, PHILADELPHIA 12
Tennessee 31, NEW ORLEANS 14
New England 34, CINCINNATI 13
Dallas 25, BUFFALO 24
New York Giants 31, ATLANTA 10
Indianapolis 29, JACKSONVILLE 7
Green Bay 19, DENVER 13 (OT)
PITTSBURGH 38, Baltimore 7
SEATTLE 24, San Francisco 0
DENVER 34, Tennessee 20
PITTSBURGH 3, Miami 0
New England 27, BALTIMORE 24
New Orleans 34, ATLANTA 14
MINNESOTA 13, Chicago 13
SAN DIEGO 23, Denver 3

2006
Minnesota 19, WASHINGTON 16
San Diego 27, OAKLAND 0
JACKSONVILLE 9, Pittsburgh 0
NEW ORLEANS 23, Atlanta 3
PHILADELPHIA 31, Green Bay 9
DENVER 13, Baltimore 3
Chicago 24, ARIZONA 23
New York Giants 36, DALLAS 22
New England 31, MINNESOTA 7
SEATTLE 16, Oakland 0
CAROLINA 24, Tampa Bay 10
JACKSONVILLE 26, New York Giants 10
SEATTLE 34, Green Bay 24
PHILADELPHIA 27, Carolina 24
Chicago 42, ST. LOUIS 27
INDIANAPOLIS 34, Cincinnati 16
New York Jets 13, MIAMI 10

2005
ATLANTA 14, Philadelphia 10
New York Giants 27, NEW ORLEANS 10
Washington 14, DALLAS 13
DENVER 30, Kansas City 10
CAROLINA 32, Green Bay 29
Pittsburgh 24, SAN DIEGO 22
INDIANAPOLIS 45, St. Louis 28
ATLANTA 27, New York Jets 14
PITTSBURGH 20, Baltimore 19
Indianapolis 40, NEW ENGLAND 21
Dallas 21, PHILADELPHIA 20
Minnesota 20, GREEN BAY 17
INDIANAPOLIS 26, Pittsburgh 7
Seattle 42, PHILADELPHIA 0
ATLANTA 36, New Orleans 17
BALTIMORE 48, Green Bay 3
New England 31, NEW YORK JETS 21

2004
Green Bay 24, CAROLINA 14
PHILADELPHIA 27, Minnesota 16
Dallas 21, WASHINGTON 18
Kansas City 27, BALTIMORE 24
Tennessee 48, GREEN BAY 27
ST. LOUIS 28, Tampa Bay 21
CINCINNATI 23, Denver 10
NEW YORK JETS 41, Miami 14
INDIANAPOLIS 31, Minnesota 28
Philadelphia 49, DALLAS 21
New England 27, KANSAS CITY 19
GREEN BAY 45, St. Louis 17
Dallas 43, SEATTLE 39
Kansas City 49, TENNESSEE 38
MIAMI 29, New England 28
ST. LOUIS 20, Philadelphia 7

2003
Tampa Bay 17, Philadelphia 0
Dallas 35, NEW YORK GIANTS 32 (OT)
DENVER 31, Oakland 10
Green Bay 38, CHICAGO 23
Indianapolis 38, TAMPA BAY 35 (OT)
ST. LOUIS 36, Atlanta 0
Kansas City 17, OAKLAND 10
Miami 26, SAN DIEGO 10
New England 30, DENVER 26
Philadelphia 17, GREEN BAY 14
SAN FRANCISCO 30, Pittsburgh 14
TAMPA BAY 19, New York Giants 13
NEW YORK JETS 24, Tennessee 17
St. Louis 26, CLEVELAND 20
Philadelphia 34, MIAMI 27
Green Bay 41, OAKLAND 7

2002
NEW ENGLAND 30, Pittsburgh 14
Philadelphia 37, WASHINGTON 7
TAMPA BAY 26, St. Louis 14
BALTIMORE 34, Denver 23
Green Bay 34, CHICAGO 21
San Francisco 28, SEATTLE 21
PITTSBURGH 28, Indianapolis 10
PHILADELPHIA 17, New York Giants 3
GREEN BAY 24, Miami 10
Oakland 34, DENVER 10
ST. LOUIS 21, Chicago 16
Philadelphia 38, SAN FRANCISCO 17
OAKLAND 26, New York Jets 20
MIAMI 27, Chicago 9
TENNESSEE 24, New England 7
Pittsburgh 17, TAMPA BAY 7
ST. LOUIS 31, San Francisco 20

2001
DENVER 31, New York Giants 20
GREEN BAY 37, Washington 0
San Francisco 19, NEW YORK JETS 17
St. Louis 35, DETROIT 0
DALLAS 9, Washington 7
Philadelphia 10, NEW YORK GIANTS 9
PITTSBURGH 34, Tennessee 7
OAKLAND 38, Denver 28
Baltimore 16, TENNESSEE 10
MINNESOTA 28, New York Giants 16
Tampa Bay 24, ST. LOUIS 17
Green Bay 28, JACKSONVILLE 21
MIAMI 41, Indianapolis 6
St. Louis 34, NEW ORLEANS 21
BALTIMORE 19, Minnesota 3

2000
ST. LOUIS 41, Denver 36
NEW YORK JETS 20, New England 19
Dallas 27, WASHINGTON 21
INDIANAPOLIS 43, Jacksonville 14
KANSAS CITY 24, Seattle 17
MINNESOTA 30, Tampa Bay 23
TENNESSEE 27, Jacksonville 13
NEW YORK JETS 40, Miami 37 (OT)
Tennessee 27, WASHINGTON 21
GREEN BAY 26, Minnesota 20 (OT)
DENVER 27, Oakland 24
Washington 33, ST. LOUIS 20
CAROLINA 31, Green Bay 14
NEW ENGLAND 30, Kansas City 24
INDIANAPOLIS 44, Buffalo 20
TAMPA BAY 38, St. Louis 35
TENNESSEE 31, Dallas 0

1999
Miami 38, DENVER 21
DALLAS 24, Atlanta 7
San Francisco 24, ARIZONA 10
Buffalo 23, MIAMI 18
Jacksonville 16, NEW YORK JETS 6
NEW YORK GIANTS 13, Dallas 10
PITTSBURGH 13, Atlanta 9
Seattle 27, GREEN BAY 7
MINNESOTA 27, Dallas 17
New York Jets 24, NEW ENGLAND 17
DENVER 27, Oakland 21 (OT)
Green Bay 20, SAN FRANCISCO 3
TAMPA BAY 24, Minnesota 17
JACKSONVILLE 27, Denver 24
MINNESOTA 24, Green Bay 20
New York Jets 38, MIAMI 31
ATLANTA 34, San Francisco 29

1998
DENVER 27, New England 21
San Francisco 45, WASHINGTON 10
Dallas 31, NEW YORK GIANTS 7
DETROIT 27, Tampa Bay 6
Minnesota 37, GREEN BAY 24
JACKSONVILLE 28, Miami 21
New York Jets 24, NEW ENGLAND 14
Pittsburgh 20, KANSAS CITY 13
Dallas 34, PHILADELPHIA 0
PITTSBURGH 27, Green Bay 20
Denver 30, KANSAS CITY 7
NEW ENGLAND 26, Miami 23
SAN FRANCISCO 31, New York Giants 7
TAMPA BAY 24, Green Bay 22
SAN FRANCISCO 35, Detroit 13
MIAMI 31, Denver 21
JACKSONVILLE 21, Pittsburgh 3

1997
GREEN BAY 38, Chicago 24
Kansas City 28, OAKLAND 27
DALLAS 21, Philadelphia 20
JACKSONVILLE 30, Pittsburgh 21
San Francisco 34, CAROLINA 21
DENVER 34, New England 13
WASHINGTON 21, Dallas 16
Buffalo 9, INDIANAPOLIS 6
Green Bay 28, NEW ENGLAND 10
Chicago 36, MIAMI 33 (OT)
KANSAS CITY 13, Pittsburgh 10
San Francisco 24, PHILADELPHIA 12
MIAMI 30, Buffalo 13
DENVER 31, Oakland 3
Green Bay 27, MINNESOTA 11
Carolina 23, DALLAS 13
SAN FRANCISCO 34, Denver 17
New England 14, MIAMI 12

1996
CHICAGO 22, Dallas 6
GREEN BAY 39, Philadelphia 13
PITTSBURGH 24, Buffalo 6
INDIANAPOLIS 10, Miami 6
Dallas 23, PHILADELPHIA 19
Pittsburgh 17, KANSAS CITY 7
GREEN BAY 23, San Francisco 20 (OT)
Oakland 23, SAN DIEGO 14
Chicago 15, MINNESOTA 13
Denver 22, OAKLAND 21
SAN DIEGO 27, Detroit 21
DALLAS 21, Green Bay 6
Pittsburgh 24, MIAMI 17
San Francisco 34, ATLANTA 10
OAKLAND 26, Kansas City 7
MIAMI 16, Buffalo 14
SAN FRANCISCO 24, Detroit 14

1995
Dallas 35, NEW YORK GIANTS 0
Green Bay 27, CHICAGO 24
MIAMI 23, Pittsburgh 10
DETROIT 27, San Francisco 24
Buffalo 22, CLEVELAND 19
KANSAS CITY 29, San Diego 23 (OT)
DENVER 27, Oakland 0
NEW ENGLAND 27, Buffalo 14
Chicago 14, MINNESOTA 6
DALLAS 34, Philadelphia 12
PITTSBURGH 20, Cleveland 3
San Francisco 44, MIAMI 20
SAN DIEGO 12, Oakland 6
DETROIT 27, Chicago 7
MIAMI 13, Kansas City 6
SAN FRANCISCO 37, Minnesota 30
Dallas 37, ARIZONA 13

1994
SAN FRANCISCO 44, L.A. Raiders 14
PHILADELPHIA 30, Chicago 22
Detroit 20, DALLAS 17 (OT)
BUFFALO 27, Denver 20
PITTSBURGH 30, Houston 14
Minnesota 27, NEW YORK GIANTS 10
Kansas City 31, DENVER 28
PHILADELPHIA 21, Houston 6
Green Bay 33, CHICAGO 6
DALLAS 38, New York Giants 10
PITTSBURGH 23, Buffalo 10
New York Giants 13, HOUSTON 10
San Francisco 35, NEW ORLEANS 14
L.A. Raiders 24, SAN DIEGO 17
MIAMI 45, Kansas City 28
Dallas 24, NEW ORLEANS 16
MINNESOTA 21, San Francisco 14

1993
WASHINGTON 35, Dallas 16
CLEVELAND 23, San Francisco 13
KANSAS CITY 15, Denver 7
Pittsburgh 45, ATLANTA 17
MIAMI 17, Washington 10
BUFFALO 35, Houston 7
L.A. Raiders 23, DENVER 20
Minnesota 19, CHICAGO 12
BUFFALO 24, Washington 10
KANSAS CITY 23, Green Bay 16
PITTSBURGH 23, Buffalo 0
SAN FRANCISCO 42, New Orleans 7
San Diego 31, INDIANAPOLIS 0
DALLAS 23, Philadelphia 17
Pittsburgh 21, MIAMI 20
New York Giants 24, NEW ORLEANS 14
SAN DIEGO 45, Miami 20
Philadelphia 37, SAN FRANCISCO 34 (OT)

1992
DALLAS 23, Washington 10
Miami 27, CLEVELAND 23
New York Giants 27, CHICAGO 14
KANSAS CITY 27, L.A. Raiders 7
PHILADELPHIA 31, Dallas 7
WASHINGTON 34, Denver 3
PITTSBURGH 20, Cincinnati 0
Buffalo 24, NEW YORK JETS 20
Minnesota 38, CHICAGO 10
San Francisco 41, ATLANTA 3
Buffalo 26, MIAMI 20
NEW ORLEANS 20, Washington 3
SEATTLE 16, Denver 13 (OT)
HOUSTON 24, Chicago 7
MIAMI 20, L.A. Raiders 7
Dallas 41, ATLANTA 17
SAN FRANCISCO 24, Detroit 6

1991
NEW YORK GIANTS 16, San Francisco 14
Washington 33, DALLAS 31
HOUSTON 17, Kansas City 7
CHICAGO 19, New York Jets 13 (OT)
WASHINGTON 23, Philadelphia 0
KANSAS CITY 33, Buffalo 6
New York Giants 23, PITTSBURGH 20
BUFFALO 35, Cincinnati 16
KANSAS CITY 24, L.A. Raiders 21
PHILADELPHIA 30, New York Giants 7
Chicago 34, MINNESOTA 17
Buffalo 41, MIAMI 27
San Francisco 33, L.A. RAMS 10
Philadelphia 13, HOUSTON 6
MIAMI 37, Cincinnati 13
NEW ORLEANS 27, L.A. Raiders 0
SAN FRANCISCO 52, Chicago 14

1990
San Francisco 13, NEW ORLEANS 12
DENVER 24, Kansas City 23
Buffalo 30, NEW YORK JETS 7
SEATTLE 31, Cincinnati 16
Cleveland 30, DENVER 29
PHILADELPHIA 32, Minnesota 24
Cincinnati 34, CLEVELAND 13
PITTSBURGH 41, L.A. Rams 10
New York Giants 24, INDIANAPOLIS 7
PHILADELPHIA 28, Washington 14
L.A. Raiders 13, MIAMI 10
HOUSTON 27, Buffalo 24
SAN FRANCISCO 7, New York Giants 3
L.A. Raiders 38, DETROIT 31
San Francisco 26, L.A. RAMS 10
NEW ORLEANS 20, L.A. Rams 17

1989
New York Giants 27, WASHINGTON 24
Denver 28, BUFFALO 14
CINCINNATI 21, Cleveland 14
CHICAGO 27, Philadelphia 13
L.A. Raiders 14, NEW YORK JETS 7
BUFFALO 23, L.A. Rams 20
CLEVELAND 27, Chicago 7
NEW YORK GIANTS 24, Minnesota 14
SAN FRANCISCO 31, New Orleans 13
HOUSTON 26, Cincinnati 24
Denver 14, WASHINGTON 10
SAN FRANCISCO 34, New York Giants 24
SEATTLE 17, Buffalo 16
San Francisco 30, L.A. RAMS 27
NEW ORLEANS 30, Philadelphia 20
MINNESOTA 29, Cincinnati 21

1988
NEW YORK GIANTS 27, Washington 20
Dallas 17, PHOENIX 14
CLEVELAND 23, Indianapolis 17
L.A. Raiders 30, DENVER 27 (OT)
NEW ORLEANS 20, Dallas 17
PHILADELPHIA 24, New York Giants 13
Buffalo 37, NEW YORK JETS 14
CHICAGO 10, San Francisco 9
INDIANAPOLIS 55, Denver 23
HOUSTON 24, Cleveland 17
Buffalo 31, MIAMI 6
SAN FRANCISCO 37, Washington 21
SEATTLE 35, L.A. Raiders 27
L.A. RAMS 23, Chicago 3
MIAMI 38, Cleveland 31
MINNESOTA 28, Chicago 27

1987
CHICAGO 34, New York Giants 19
NEW YORK JETS 43, New England 24
San Francisco 41, NEW YORK GIANTS 21
DENVER 30, L.A. Raiders 14
Washington 13, DALLAS 7
CLEVELAND 30, L.A. Rams 17
MINNESOTA 34, Denver 27
DALLAS 33, New York Giants 24
NEW YORK JETS 30, Seattle 14
DENVER 31, Chicago 29
L.A. Rams 30, WASHINGTON 26
L.A. Raiders 37, SEATTLE 14
MIAMI 37, New York Jets 28
SAN FRANCISCO 41, Chicago 0
Dallas 29, L.A. RAMS 21
New England 24, MIAMI 10

1986
DALLAS 31, New York Giants 28
Denver 21, PITTSBURGH 10
Chicago 25, GREEN BAY 12
Dallas 31, ST. LOUIS 7
SEATTLE 33, San Diego 7
CINCINNATI 24, Pittsburgh 22
NEW YORK JETS 22, Denver 10
NEW YORK GIANTS 27, Washington 20
L.A. Rams 20, CHICAGO 17
CLEVELAND 26, Miami 16
WASHINGTON 14, San Francisco 6
MIAMI 45, New York Jets 3
New York Giants 21, SAN FRANCISCO 17
SEATTLE 37, L.A. Raiders 0
Chicago 16, DETROIT 13
New England 34, MIAMI 27

1985
DALLAS 44, Washington 14
CLEVELAND 17, Pittsburgh 7
L.A. Rams 35, SEATTLE 24
Cincinnati 37, PITTSBURGH 24
WASHINGTON 27, St. Louis 10
NEW YORK JETS 23, Miami 7
CHICAGO 23, Green Bay 7
L.A. RAIDERS 34, San Diego 21
ST. LOUIS 21, Dallas 10
DENVER 17, San Francisco 16
WASHINGTON 23, New York Giants 21
SAN FRANCISCO 19, Seattle 6
MIAMI 38, Chicago 24
L.A. Rams 27, SAN FRANCISCO 20
MIAMI 30, New England 27
L.A. Raiders 16, L.A. RAMS 6

1984
Dallas 20, L.A. RAMS 13
SAN FRANCISCO 37, Washington 31
Miami 21, BUFFALO 17
L.A. RAIDERS 33, San Diego 30
PITTSBURGH 38, Cincinnati 17
San Francisco 31, NEW YORK GIANTS 10
DENVER 17, Green Bay 14
L.A. Rams 24, ATLANTA 10
Seattle 24, SAN DIEGO 0
WASHINGTON 27, Atlanta 14
SEATTLE 17, L.A. Raiders 14
NEW ORLEANS 27, Pittsburgh 24
MIAMI 28, New York Jets 17
SAN DIEGO 20, Chicago 7
L.A. Raiders 24, DETROIT 3
MIAMI 28, Dallas 21

1983
Dallas 31, WASHINGTON 30
San Diego 17, KANSAS CITY 14
L.A. RAIDERS 27, Miami 14
NEW YORK GIANTS 27, Green Bay 3
New York Jets 34, BUFFALO 10
Pittsburgh 24, CINCINNATI 14
GREEN BAY 48, Washington 47
ST. LOUIS 20, NEW YORK Giants 20 (OT)
Washington 27, SAN DIEGO 24
DETROIT 15, New York Giants 9
L.A. Rams 36, ATLANTA 13
New York Jets 31, NEW ORLEANS 28
MIAMI 38, Cincinnati 14
DETROIT 13, Minnesota 2
Green Bay 12, TAMPA BAY 9 (OT)
SAN FRANCISCO 42, Dallas 17

1982
Pittsburgh 36, DALLAS 28
Green Bay 27, NEW YORK GIANTS 19
L.A. RAIDERS 28, San Diego 24
TAMPA BAY 23, Miami 17
New York Jets 28, DETROIT 13
Dallas 37, HOUSTON 7
SAN DIEGO 50, Cincinnati 34
MIAMI 27, Buffalo 10
MINNESOTA 31, Dallas 27

1981
San Diego 44, CLEVELAND 14
Oakland 36, MINNESOTA 10
Dallas 35, NEW ENGLAND 21
Los Angeles 24, CHICAGO 7
PHILADELPHIA 16, Atlanta 13
BUFFALO 31, Miami 21
DETROIT 48, Chicago 17
PITTSBURGH 26, Houston 13
DENVER 19, Minnesota 17
DALLAS 27, Buffalo 14
SEATTLE 44, San Diego 23
ATLANTA 31, Minnesota 30
MIAMI 13, Philadelphia 10
OAKLAND 30, Pittsburgh 27
LOS ANGELES 21, Atlanta 16
SAN DIEGO 23, Oakland 10

1980
Dallas 17, WASHINGTON 3
Houston 16, CLEVELAND 7
PHILADELPHIA 35, New York Giants 3
NEW ENGLAND 23, Denver 14
CHICAGO 23, Tampa Bay 0
DENVER 20, Washington 17
Oakland 45, PITTSBURGH 34
NEW YORK JETS 17, Miami 14
CLEVELAND 27, Chicago 21
HOUSTON 38, New England 34
Oakland 19, SEATTLE 17
Los Angeles 27, NEW ORLEANS 7
OAKLAND 9, Denver 3
MIAMI 16, New England 13 (OT)
LOS ANGELES 38, Dallas 14
SAN DIEGO 26, Pittsburgh 17

1979
Pittsburgh 16, NEW ENGLAND 13 (OT)
Atlanta 14, PHILADELPHIA 10
WASHINGTON 27, New York Giants 0
CLEVELAND 26, Dallas 7
GREEN BAY 27, New England 14
OAKLAND 13, Miami 3
NEW YORK JETS 14, Minnesota 7
PITTSBURGH 42, Denver 7
Seattle 31, ATLANTA 28
Houston 9, MIAMI 6
Philadelphia 31, DALLAS 21
LOS ANGELES 20, Atlanta 14
SEATTLE 30, New York Jets 7
Oakland 42, NEW ORLEANS 35
HOUSTON 20, Pittsburgh 17
SAN DIEGO 17, Denver 7

1978
DALLAS 38, Baltimore 0
MINNESOTA 12, Denver 9 (OT)
Baltimore 34, NEW ENGLAND 27
Minnesota 24, CHICAGO 20
WASHINGTON 9, Dallas 5
MIAMI 21, Cincinnati 0
DENVER 16, Chicago 7
Houston 24, PITTSBURGH 17
ATLANTA 15, Los Angeles 7
BALTIMORE 21, Washington 17
Oakland 34, CINCINNATI 21
HOUSTON 35, Miami 30
Pittsburgh 24, SAN FRANCISCO 7
SAN DIEGO 40, Chicago 7
Cincinnati 20, LOS ANGELES 19
MIAMI 23, New England 3

1977
PITTSBURGH 27, San Francisco 0
CLEVELAND 30, New England 27 (OT)
Oakland 37, KANSAS CITY 28
CHICAGO 24, Los Angeles 23
PITTSBURGH 20, Cincinnati 14
LOS ANGELES 35, Minnesota 3
ST. LOUIS 28, New York Giants 0
BALTIMORE 10, Washington 3
St. Louis 24, DALLAS 17
WASHINGTON 10, Green Bay 9
OAKLAND 34, Buffalo 13
MIAMI 17, Baltimore 6
Dallas 42, SAN FRANCISCO 35

1976
Miami 30, BUFFALO 21
Oakland 24, KANSAS CITY 21
Washington 20, PHILADELPHIA 17 (OT)
MINNESOTA 17, Pittsburgh 6
San Francisco 16, LOS ANGELES 0
NEW ENGLAND 41, New York Jets 7
WASHINGTON 20, St. Louis 10
BALTIMORE 38, Houston 14
CINCINNATI 20, Los Angeles 12
DALLAS 17, Buffalo 10
Baltimore 17, MIAMI 16
SAN FRANCISCO 20, Minnesota 16
OAKLAND 35, Cincinnati 20

1975
Oakland 31, MIAMI 21
DENVER 23, Green Bay 13
Dallas 36, DETROIT 10
WASHINGTON 27, St. Louis 17
New York Giants 17, BUFFALO 14
Minnesota 13, CHICAGO 9
Los Angeles 42, PHILADELPHIA 3
Kansas City 34, DALLAS 31
CINCINNATI 33, Buffalo 24
Pittsburgh 32, HOUSTON 9
MIAMI 20, New England 7
OAKLAND 17, Denver 10
SAN DIEGO 24, New York Jets 16

1974
BUFFALO 21, Oakland 20
PHILADELPHIA 13, Dallas 10
WASHINGTON 30, Denver 3
MIAMI 21, New York Jets 17
DETROIT 17, San Francisco 13
CHICAGO 10, Green Bay 9
PITTSBURGH 24, Atlanta 17
Los Angeles 15, SAN FRANCISCO 13
Minnesota 28, ST. LOUIS 24
Kansas City 42, DENVER 34
Pittsburgh 28, NEW ORLEANS 7
MIAMI 24, Cincinnati 3
Washington 23, LOS ANGELES 17

1973
GREEN BAY 23, New York Jets 7
DALLAS 40, New Orleans 3
DETROIT 31, Atlanta 6
WASHINGTON 14, Dallas 7
Miami 17, CLEVELAND 9
DENVER 23, Oakland 23
BUFFALO 23, Kansas City 14
PITTSBURGH 21, Washington 16
KANSAS CITY 19, Chicago 7
ATLANTA 20, Minnesota 14
SAN FRANCISCO 20, Green Bay 6
MIAMI 30, Pittsburgh 26
LOS ANGELES 40, New York Giants 6

1972
Washington 24, MINNESOTA 21
Kansas City 20, NEW ORLEANS 17
New York Giants 27, PHILADELPHIA 12
Oakland 34, HOUSTON 0
Green Bay 24, DETROIT 23
CHICAGO 13, Minnesota 10
DALLAS 28, Detroit 24
Baltimore 24, NEW ENGLAND 17
Cleveland 21, SAN DIEGO 17
WASHINGTON 24, Atlanta 13
MIAMI 31, St. Louis 10
Los Angeles 26, SAN FRANCISCO 16
OAKLAND 24, New York Jets 16

1971
Minnesota 16, DETROIT 13
ST. LOUIS 17, New York Jets 10
Oakland 34, CLEVELAND 20
DALLAS 20, New York Giants 13
KANSAS CITY 38, Pittsburgh 16
MINNESOTA 10, Baltimore 3
GREEN BAY 14, Detroit 14
BALTIMORE 24, Los Angeles 17
SAN DIEGO 20, St. Louis 17
ATLANTA 28, Green Bay 21
MIAMI 34, Chicago 3
Kansas City 26, SAN FRANCISCO 17
Washington 38, LOS ANGELES 24

1970
CLEVELAND 31, New York Jets 21
Kansas City 44, BALTIMORE 24
DETROIT 28, Chicago 14
Green Bay 22, SAN DIEGO 20
OAKLAND 34, Washington 20
MINNESOTA 13, Los Angeles 3
PITTSBURGH 21, Cincinnati 10
Baltimore 13, GREEN BAY 10
St. Louis 38, DALLAS 0
PHILADELPHIA 23, New York Giants 20
Miami 20, ATLANTA 7
Cleveland 21, HOUSTON 10
Detroit 28, LOS ANGELES 23

MONDAY NIGHT FOOTBALL

MONDAY NIGHT WON-LOST RECORDS, 1970-2008

AMERICAN FOOTBALL CONFERENCE

	Balt.	Buff.	Cin.	Cle.	Den.	Hou.	Ind.	Jax.	K.C.	Mia.	N.E.	N.Y.J.	Oak.	Pitt.	S.D.	Tenn.
Total	4-7	17-22	9-18	15-13	26-32-1	1-0	19-11	7-5	20-15	39-34	16-21	17-22	36-24-1	37-22	17-14	18-16
2008	0-1	0-1		2-1	1-1	1-0	0-1	0-1			1-0	0-1	0-1	2-0	1-0	1-0
2007	0-3	0-1	1-1		1-2		1-0	0-1		0-1	2-0			2-0	1-0	1-1
2006	0-1		0-1		1-0		1-0	2-0	0-1	0-1	1-0	1-0	0-2	0-1	1-0	
2005	1-1				1-0		3-0		0-1		1-1	0-2		2-1	0-1	
2004	0-1		1-0		0-1		1-0		2-1	1-1	1-1	1-0				1-1
2003				0-1	1-1		1-0		1-0	1-1	1-0	1-0	0-3	0-1	0-1	0-1
2002	1-0				0-2		0-1			1-1	1-1	0-1	2-0	2-1		1-0
2001	2-0				1-1		0-1	0-1		1-0		0-1	1-0	1-0		0-2
2000		0-1			1-1		2-0	0-2	1-1	0-1	1-1	2-0	0-1			3-0
1999		1-0			1-2			2-0		1-2	0-1	2-1	0-1	1-0		
1998					2-1			2-0	0-2	1-2	1-2	1-0		2-1		
1997		1-1			2-1		0-1	1-0	2-0	1-2	1-2		0-2	0-2		
1996		0-2			1-0		1-0		0-2	1-2			2-1	3-0	1-1	
1995		1-1		0-2	1-0				1-1	2-1	1-0		0-2	1-1	1-1	
1994		1-1			0-2				1-1	1-0			1-1	2-0	0-1	0-3
1993		2-1		1-0	0-2		0-1		2-0	1-2			1-0	3-0	2-0	0-1
1992		2-0	0-1	0-1	0-2				1-0	2-1		0-1	0-2	1-0		1-0
1991		2-1	0-2						2-1	1-1		0-1	0-2	0-1		1-1
1990		1-1	1-1	1-1	1-1		0-1		0-1	0-1		0-1	2-0	1-0		1-0
1989		1-2	1-2	1-1	2-0							0-1	1-0			1-0
1988		2-0		1-2	0-2		1-1			1-1		0-1	1-1			1-0
1987				1-0	2-1					1-1	1-1	2-1	1-1			
1986			1-0	1-0	1-1					1-2	1-0	1-1	0-1	0-2	0-1	
1985			1-0	1-0	1-0					2-1	0-1	1-0	2-0	0-2	0-1	
1984		0-1	0-1		1-0					3-0		0-1	2-1	1-1	1-2	
1983		0-1	0-2						0-1	1-1		2-0	1-0	1-0	1-1	
1982		0-1	0-1							1-1		1-0	1-0	1-0	1-1	0-1
1981		1-1		0-1	1-0					1-1	0-1		2-1	1-1	2-1	0-1
1980				1-1	1-2					1-1	1-2	1-0	3-0	0-2	1-0	2-0
1979				1-0	0-2					0-2	0-2	1-1	2-0	2-1	1-0	2-0
1978			1-2		1-1		2-1			2-1	0-2		1-0	1-1	1-0	2-0
1977		0-1	0-1	1-0			1-1		0-1	1-0	0-1		2-0	2-0		
1976		0-2	1-1				2-0		0-1	1-1	1-0	0-1	2-0	0-1		0-1
1975		0-2	1-0		1-1				1-0	1-1	0-1	0-1	2-0	1-0	1-0	0-1
1974		1-0	0-1		0-2				1-0	2-0		0-1	0-1	2-0		
1973		1-0		0-1	0-0-1				1-1	2-0		0-1	0-0-1	1-1		
1972				1-0			1-0		1-0	1-0	0-1	0-1	2-0		0-1	0-1
1971				0-1			1-1		2-0	1-0		0-1	1-0	0-1	1-0	
1970			0-1	2-0			1-1		1-0	1-0		0-1	1-0	1-0	0-1	0-1

MONDAY NIGHT FOOTBALL ALL-TIME STANDINGS

AMERICAN FOOTBALL CONFERENCE

East	W	L	T	Pct.
Miami	39	34	0	.534
Buffalo	17	22	0	.436
New York Jets	17	22	0	.436
New England	16	21	0	.432

North	W	L	T	Pct.
Pittsburgh	37	22	0	.627
Cleveland	15	13	0	.536
Baltimore	4	7	0	.364
Cincinnati	9	18	0	.333

South	W	L	T	Pct.
Houston	1	0	0	1.000
Indianapolis	19	11	0	.633
Jacksonville	7	5	0	.583
Tennessee	18	16	0	.529

West	W	L	T	Pct.
Oakland	36	24	1	.598
Kansas City	20	15	0	.571
San Diego	17	14	0	.548
Denver	26	32	1	.449

From 1970-71, tie games were not included in winning percentage.

MONDAY NIGHT WON-LOST RECORDS, 1970-2008

NATIONAL FOOTBALL CONFERENCE

	Ariz.	Atl.	Car.	Chi.	Dall.	Det.	G.B.	Minn.	N.O.	N.Y.G.	Phil.	St.L.	S.F.	Sea.	T.B.	Wash.
Total	6-12-1	9-21	5-3	19-33	41-29	11-13-1	26-27-1	25-24	10-16	18-31-1	25-22	26-27	38-24	16-8	8-9	26-30
2008	1-0		1-0	1-0	1-0		1-2	1-1	1-1	0-1	1-1		0-1		0-1	0-1
2007	0-1	0-2		0-1	1-0		1-0	1-0	2-0	1-0	0-1		1-1	1-0		1-0
2006	0-1	0-1	1-1	2-0	0-1		0-2	1-1	1-0	1-1	2-0	0-1		2-0	0-1	0-1
2005		3-0	1-0		1-1		0-3	1-0	0-2	1-0	0-3	0-1		1-0		1-0
2004			0-1		2-1		2-1	0-2			2-1	2-1		0-1	0-1	0-1
2003		0-1		0-1	1-0		2-1			0-2	2-1	2-0	1-0		2-1	
2002				0-3			2-0			0-1	3-0	2-1	1-2	0-1	1-1	0-1
2001					1-0	0-1	2-0	1-1	0-1	0-3	1-0	2-1	1-0		1-0	0-2
2000			1-0		1-1		1-1	1-1				1-2		0-1	1-1	1-2
1999	0-1	1-2			1-2		1-2	2-1		1-0			1-2	1-0	1-0	
1998					2-0	1-1	0-3	1-0		0-2	0-1		3-0		1-1	0-1
1997			1-1	1-1	1-2		3-0	0-1			0-2		3-0			1-0
1996		0-1		2-0	2-1	0-2	2-1	0-1			0-2		2-1			
1995	0-1			1-2	3-0	2-0	1-0	0-2		0-1	0-1		2-1			
1994				0-2	2-1	1-0	1-0	2-0	0-2	1-2	2-0		2-1			
1993		0-1		0-1	1-1		0-1	1-0	0-2	1-0	1-1		1-2			1-2
1992		0-2		0-3	2-1	0-1		1-0	1-0	1-0	1-0		2-0	1-0		1-2
1991				2-1	0-1			0-1	1-0	2-1	2-1	0-1	2-1			2-0
1990						0-1		0-1	1-1	1-1	2-0	0-3	3-0	1-0		0-1
1989				1-1				1-1	1-1	2-1	0-2	0-2	3-0	1-0		0-2
1988	0-1			1-2	1-1			1-0	1-0	1-1	1-0	1-0	1-1	1-0		0-2
1987				1-2	2-1			1-0		0-3		1-2	2-0	0-2		1-1
1986	0-1			2-1	2-0	0-1	0-1			2-1		1-0	0-2	2-0		1-1
1985	1-1			1-1	1-1		0-1			0-1		2-1	1-2	0-2		2-1
1984		0-2		0-1	1-1	0-1	0-1		1-0	0-1		1-1	2-0	2-0		1-1
1983	0-0-1	0-1			1-1	2-0	2-1	0-1	0-1	1-1-1		1-0	1-0		0-1	1-2
1982					1-2	0-1	1-0	1-0		0-1					1-0	
1981		1-2		0-2	2-0	1-0		0-3			1-1	2-0		1-0		
1980				1-1	1-1				0-1	0-1	1-0	2-0		0-1	0-1	0-2
1979		1-2			0-2		1-0	0-1	0-1	0-1	1-1	1-0		2-0		1-0
1978		1-0		0-3	1-1			2-0				0-2	0-1			1-1
1977	2-0			1-0	1-1		0-1	0-1		0-1		1-1	0-2			1-1
1976	0-1				1-0			1-1			0-1	0-2	2-0			2-0
1975	0-1			0-1	1-1	0-1	0-1	1-0		1-0	0-1	1-0				1-0
1974	0-1	0-1		1-0	0-1	1-0	0-1	1-0	0-1		1-0	1-1	0-2			2-0
1973		1-1		0-1	1-1	1-0	1-1	0-1	0-1	0-1		1-0	1-0			1-1
1972	0-1	0-1		1-0	1-0	0-2	1-0	0-2	0-1	1-0	0-1	1-0	0-1			2-0
1971	1-1	1-0		0-1	1-0	0-1-1	0-1-1	2-0		0-1		0-2	0-1			1-0
1970	1-0	0-1		0-1	0-1	2-0	1-1	1-0		0-1	1-0	0-2				0-1

MONDAY NIGHT FOOTBALL ALL-TIME STANDINGS

NATIONAL FOOTBALL CONFERENCE

East	W	L	T	Pct.
Dallas	41	29	0	.586
Philadelphia	25	22	0	.532
Washington	26	30	0	.464
New York Giants	18	31	1	.370

North	W	L	T	Pct.
Minnesota	25	24	0	.510
Green Bay	26	27	1	.491
Detroit	11	13	1	.458
Chicago	19	33	0	.365

South	W	L	T	Pct.
Carolina	5	3	0	.625
Tampa Bay	8	9	0	.471
New Orleans	10	16	0	.385
Atlanta	9	21	0	.300

West	W	L	T	Pct.
Seattle	16	8	0	.667
San Francisco	38	24	0	.613
St. Louis	26	27	0	.491
Arizona	6	12	1	.342

From 1970-71, tie games were not included in winning percentage.

THANKSGIVING DAY FOOTBALL, 1920-2008

(Home Team in capitals, games listed in chronological order.)
(AFL)-American Football League, 1960-69.

Nov. 25, 1920	AKRON PROS 7, Canton Bulldogs 0 Decatur Staleys 6, CHICAGO TIGERS 0 ELYRIA (OH) ATHLETICS* 0, Columbus Panhandles 0 DAYTON TRIANGLES 28, Detroit Heralds 0 CHICAGO BOOSTERS* 27, Hammond Pros 0 All-Tonawanda (NY) 14, ROCHESTER JEFFERSONS 3 * Non league team. Games between league teams and non league teams counted in standings in 1920.
Nov. 24, 1921	Canton Bulldogs 14, AKRON PROS 0 Buffalo All-Americans 7, CHICAGO STALEYS 6
Nov. 30, 1922	Buffalo All-Americans 21, ROCHESTER JEFFERSONS 0 CHICAGO CARDINALS 6, Chicago Bears 0 RACINE LEGION 3, Milwaukee Badgers 0 Oorang Indians 18, COLUMBUS PANHANDLES 6 CANTON BULLDOGS 14, Akron Pros 0
Nov. 29, 1923	CANTON BULLDOGS 28, Toledo Maroons 0 CHICAGO BEARS 3, Chicago Cardinals 0 GREEN BAY PACKERS 19, Hammond Pros 0 Milwaukee Badgers 16, RACINE LEGION 0 AKRON PROS 2, Buffalo All-Americans 0
Nov. 27, 1924	AKRON PROS 22, Buffalo Bisons 0 Chicago Bears 21, CHICAGO CARDINALS 0 FRANKFORD YELLOWJACKETS 32, Dayton Triangles 7 CLEVELAND BULLDOGS 53, Milwaukee Badgers 10 (at Canton, Ohio) Green Bay Packers 17, KANSAS CITY BLUES 6
Nov. 26, 1925	CHICAGO BEARS 0, Chicago Cardinals 0 Kansas City Cowboys 17, CLEVELAND BULLDOGS 0 (at Hartford, Connecticut) Rock Island Independents 6, DETROIT PANTHERS 3 POTTSVILLE MAROONS 31, Green Bay Packers 0
Nov. 25, 1926	New York Giants 17, BROOKLYN LIONS 0 Los Angeles Buccaneers 9, DETROIT PANTHERS 6 CHICAGO BEARS 0, Chicago Cardinals 0 FRANKFORD YELLOWJACKETS 20, Green Bay Packers 14 POTTSVILLE MAROONS 8, Providence Steam Roller 0 CANTON BULLDOGS 0, Akron Pros 0
Nov. 24, 1927	Chicago Cardinals 3, CHICAGO BEARS 0 POTTSVILLE MAROONS 6, Providence Steam Roller 0 Green Bay Packers 17, FRANKFORD YELLOWJACKETS 9 Cleveland Bulldogs 30, NEW YORK YANKEES 19
Nov. 29, 1928	Providence Steam Roller 7, POTTSVILLE MAROONS 0 DETROIT WOLVERINES 33, Dayton Triangles 0 FRANKFORD YELLOWJACKETS 2, Green Bay Packers 0 CHICAGO BEARS 34, Chicago Cardinals 0
Nov. 28, 1929	New York Giants 21, STATEN ISLAND STAPLETONS 7 FRANKFORD YELLOWJACKETS 0, Green Bay Packers 0 Chicago Cardinals 40, CHICAGO BEARS 6
Nov. 27, 1930	STATEN ISLAND STAPLETONS 7, New York Giants 6 BROOKLYN DODGERS 33, Providence Steam Roller 12 Green Bay Packers 25, FRANKFORD YELLOWJACKETS 7 CHICAGO BEARS 6, Chicago Cardinals 0
Nov. 26, 1931	Green Bay Packers 38, PROVIDENCE STEAM ROLLER 7 STATEN ISLAND STAPLETONS 9, New York Giants 6 CHICAGO BEARS 18, Chicago Cardinals 7
Nov. 24, 1932	CHICAGO BEARS 34, Chicago Cardinals 0 Green Bay Packers 7, BROOKLYN DODGERS 0 STATEN ISLAND STAPLETONS 13, New York Giants 13
Nov. 30, 1933	Chicago Bears 22, CHICAGO CARDINALS 6 New York Giants 10, BROOKLYN DODGERS 0

Nov. 29, 1934	CHICAGO CARDINALS 6, Green Bay Packers 0 Chicago Bears 19, DETROIT LIONS 16 New York Giants 27, BROOKLYN DODGERS 0
Nov. 28, 1935	New York Giants 21, BROOKLYN DODGERS 0 CHICAGO CARDINALS 9, Green Bay Packers 7 DETROIT LIONS 14, Chicago Bears 2
Nov. 26, 1936	DETROIT LIONS 13, Chicago Bears 7 New York Giants 14, BROOKLYN DODGERS 0
Nov. 25, 1937	Chicago Bears 13, DETROIT LIONS 0 BROOKLYN DODGERS 13, New York Giants 13
Nov. 24, 1938	DETROIT LIONS 14, Chicago Bears 7 BROOKLYN DODGERS 7, New York Giants 7
Nov. 23, 1939#	PHILADELPHIA EAGLES 17, Pittsburgh Steelers 14
Nov. 28, 1940#	PHILADELPHIA EAGLES 7, Pittsburgh Steelers 0

In 1939 and 1940, President Roosevelt moved Thanksgiving one week earlier. Various states celebrated on the date declared by the President, while other states recognized the traditional fourth Thursday of the month. In 1941, Thanksgiving was sanctioned by Congress to be celebrated on the fourth Thursday of November, which it has been ever since.

Nov. 22, 1945	Cleveland Rams 28, DETROIT LIONS 21
Nov. 28, 1946	Boston Yanks 34, DETROIT LIONS 10
Nov. 27, 1947	Chicago Bears 34, DETROIT LIONS 14
Nov. 25, 1948	Chicago Cardinals 28, DETROIT LIONS 14
Nov. 24, 1949	Chicago Bears 28, DETROIT LIONS 7
Nov. 23, 1950	DETROIT LIONS 49, New York Yanks 14 Pittsburgh Steelers 28, CHICAGO CARDINALS 17
Nov. 22, 1951	DETROIT LIONS 52, Green Bay Packers 35
Nov. 27, 1952	DETROIT LIONS 48, Green Bay Packers 24 DALLAS TEXANS 27, Chicago Bears 23 (at Akron, Ohio)
Nov. 26, 1953	DETROIT LIONS 34, Green Bay Packers 15
Nov. 25, 1954	DETROIT LIONS 28, Green Bay Packers 24
Nov. 24, 1955	DETROIT LIONS 24, Green Bay Packers 10
Nov. 22, 1956	Green Bay Packers 24, DETROIT LIONS 20
Nov. 28, 1957	DETROIT LIONS 18, Green Bay Packers 6
Nov. 27, 1958	DETROIT LIONS 24, Green Bay Packers 14
Nov. 26, 1959	Green Bay Packers 24, DETROIT LIONS 17
Nov. 24, 1960	DETROIT LIONS 23, Green Bay Packers 10 (AFL) - NEW YORK TITANS 41, Dallas Texans 35
Nov. 23, 1961	Green Bay Packers 17, DETROIT LIONS 9 (AFL) - NEW YORK TITANS 21, Buffalo Bills 14
Nov. 22, 1962	DETROIT LIONS 26, Green Bay Packers 14 (AFL) - New York Titans 46, DENVER BRONCOS 45
Nov. 28, 1963	DETROIT LIONS 13, Green Bay Packers 13 (AFL) - Oakland Raiders 26, DENVER BRONCOS 10
Nov. 26, 1964	Chicago Bears 27, DETROIT LIONS 24 (AFL) - Buffalo Bills 27, SAN DIEGO CHARGERS 24
Nov. 25, 1965	DETROIT LIONS 24, Baltimore Colts 24 (AFL) - SAN DIEGO CHARGERS 20, Buffalo Bills 20
Nov. 24, 1966	San Francisco 49ers 41, DETROIT LIONS 14 DALLAS COWBOYS 26, Cleveland Browns 14 (AFL) - Buffalo Bills 31, OAKLAND RAIDERS 10

Nov. 23, 1967	Los Angeles Rams 31, DETROIT LIONS 7 DALLAS COWBOYS 46, St. Louis Cardinals 21 (AFL) - Oakland Raiders 44, KANSAS CITY CHIEFS 22 (AFL) - SAN DIEGO CHARGERS 24, Denver Broncos 20
Nov. 28, 1968	Philadelphia Eagles 12, DETROIT LIONS 0 DALLAS COWBOYS 29, Washington Redskins 20 (AFL) - OAKLAND RAIDERS 13, Buffalo Bills 10 (AFL) - KANSAS CITY CHIEFS 24, Houston Oilers 10
Nov. 27, 1969	Minnesota Vikings 27, DETROIT LIONS 0 DALLAS COWBOYS 24, San Francisco 49ers 24 (AFL) - KANSAS CITY CHIEFS 31, Denver Broncos 17 (AFL) - San Diego Chargers 21, HOUSTON OILERS 17
Nov. 26, 1970	DETROIT LIONS 28, Oakland Raiders 14 DALLAS COWBOYS 16, Green Bay Packers 3
Nov. 25, 1971	DETROIT LIONS 32, Kansas City Chiefs 21 DALLAS COWBOYS 28, Los Angeles Rams 21
Nov. 23, 1972	DETROIT LIONS 37, New York Jets 20 San Francisco 49ers 31, DALLAS COWBOYS 10
Nov. 22, 1973	Washington Redskins 20, DETROIT LIONS 0 Miami Dolphins 14, DALLAS COWBOYS 7
Nov. 28, 1974	Denver Broncos 31, DETROIT LIONS 27 DALLAS COWBOYS 24, Washington Redskins 23
Nov. 27, 1975	Los Angeles Rams 20, DETROIT LIONS 0 Buffalo Bills 32, ST. LOUIS CARDINALS 14
Nov. 25, 1976	DETROIT LIONS 27, Buffalo Bills 14 DALLAS COWBOYS 19, St. Louis Cardinals 14
Nov. 24, 1977	Chicago Bears 31, DETROIT LIONS 14 Miami Dolphins 55, ST. LOUIS CARDINALS 14
Nov. 23, 1978	DETROIT LIONS 17, Denver Broncos 14 DALLAS COWBOYS 37, Washington Redskins 10
Nov. 22, 1979	DETROIT LIONS 20, Chicago Bears 0 Houston Oilers 30, DALLAS COWBOYS 24
Nov. 27, 1980	Chicago Bears 23, DETROIT LIONS 17 (OT) DALLAS COWBOYS 51, Seattle Seahawks 7
Nov. 26, 1981	DETROIT LIONS 27, Kansas City Chiefs 10 DALLAS COWBOYS 10, Chicago Bears 9
Nov. 25, 1982	New York Giants 13, DETROIT LIONS 6 DALLAS COWBOYS 31, Cleveland Browns 14
Nov. 24, 1983	DETROIT LIONS 45, Pittsburgh Steelers 3 DALLAS COWBOYS 35, St. Louis Cardinals 17
Nov. 22, 1984	DETROIT LIONS 31, Green Bay Packers 28 DALLAS COWBOYS 20, New England Patriots 17
Nov. 28, 1985	DETROIT LIONS 31, New York Jets 20 DALLAS COWBOYS 35, St. Louis Cardinals 17
Nov. 27, 1986	Green Bay Packers 44, DETROIT LIONS 40 Seattle Seahawks 31, DALLAS COWBOYS 14
Nov. 26, 1987	Kansas City Chiefs 27, DETROIT LIONS 20 Minnesota Vikings 44, DALLAS COWBOYS 38 (OT)
Nov. 24, 1988	Minnesota Vikings 23, DETROIT LIONS 0 Houston Oilers 25, DALLAS COWBOYS 17
Nov. 23, 1989	DETROIT LIONS 13, Cleveland Browns 10 Philadelphia Eagles 27, DALLAS COWBOYS 0
Nov. 22, 1990	DETROIT LIONS 40, Denver Broncos 27 DALLAS COWBOYS 27, Washington Redskins 17

Nov. 28, 1991	DETROIT LIONS 16, Chicago Bears 6 DALLAS COWBOYS 20, Pittsburgh Steelers 10
Nov. 26, 1992	Houston Oilers 24, DETROIT LIONS 21 DALLAS COWBOYS 30, New York Giants 3
Nov. 25, 1993	Chicago Bears 10, DETROIT LIONS 6 Miami Dolphins 16, DALLAS COWBOYS 14
Nov. 24, 1994	DETROIT LIONS 35, Buffalo Bills 21 DALLAS COWBOYS 42, Green Bay Packers 31
Nov. 23, 1995	DETROIT LIONS 44, Minnesota Vikings 38 DALLAS COWBOYS 24, Kansas City Chiefs 12
Nov. 28, 1996	Kansas City Chiefs 28, DETROIT LIONS 24 DALLAS COWBOYS 21, Washington Redskins 10
Nov. 27, 1997	DETROIT LIONS 55, Chicago Bears 20 Tennessee Titans 27, DALLAS COWBOYS 14
Nov. 26, 1998	DETROIT LIONS 19, Pittsburgh Steelers 16 (OT) Minnesota Vikings 46, DALLAS COWBOYS 36
Nov. 25, 1999	DETROIT LIONS 21, Chicago Bears 17 DALLAS COWBOYS 20, Miami Dolphins 0
Nov. 23, 2000	DETROIT LIONS 34, New England Patriots 9 Minnesota Vikings 27, DALLAS COWBOYS 15
Nov. 22, 2001	Green Bay Packers 29, DETROIT LIONS 27 Denver Broncos 26, DALLAS COWBOYS 24
Nov. 28, 2002	New England Patriots 20, DETROIT LIONS 12 DALLAS COWBOYS 27, Washington Redskins 20
Nov. 27, 2003	DETROIT LIONS 22, Green Bay Packers 14 Miami Dolphins 40, DALLAS COWBOYS 21
Nov. 25, 2004	Indianapolis Colts 41, DETROIT LIONS 9 DALLAS COWBOYS 21, Chicago Bears 7
Nov. 24, 2005	Atlanta Falcons 27, DETROIT LIONS 7 Denver Broncos 24, DALLAS COWBOYS 21 (OT)
Nov. 23, 2006	Miami Dolphins 27, DETROIT LIONS 10 DALLAS COWBOYS 38, Tampa Bay Buccaneers 10 KANSAS CITY CHIEFS 19, Denver Broncos 10
Nov. 22, 2007	Green Bay Packers 37, DETROIT LIONS 26 DALLAS COWBOYS 34, New York Jets 3 Indianapolis Colts 31, ATLANTA FALCONS 13
Nov. 27, 2008	Tennessee Titans 41, DETROIT LIONS 10 DALLAS COWBOYS 34, Seattle Seahawks 9 PHILADELPHIA EAGLES 48, Arizona Cardinals 20

THANKSGIVING DAY RECORDS
*NFL record; stats compiled by Elias Sports Bureau.

SCORING / Most Touchdowns, Game
- 6 Ernie Nevers, Chi. Cardinals vs. Chi. Bears, Nov. 28, 1929*
- 4 Sterling Sharpe, Green Bay at Dallas, Nov. 24, 1994
- 3 By many players

RUSHING / Most Yards Rushing, Game
- 273 O.J. Simpson, Buffalo at Detroit, Nov. 25, 1976
- 198 Bob Hoernschemeyer, Detroit vs. N.Y. Yankees, Nov. 23, 1950
- 195 Earl Campbell, Houston at Dallas, Nov. 22, 1979

PASSING / Most Yards Passing, Game
- 455 Troy Aikman, Dallas vs. Minnesota, Nov. 26, 1998
- 410 Scott Mitchell, Detroit vs. Minnesota, Nov. 23, 1995
- 384 Warren Moon, Minnesota at Detroit, Nov. 23, 1995

PASS RECEIVING
RECEPTIONS / Most Pass Receptions, Game
- 12 Brett Perriman, Detroit vs. Minnesota, Nov. 23, 1995
  Marvin Harrison, Indianapolis at Detroit, Nov. 25, 2004
- 11 Daryl Johnston, Dallas vs. Miami, Nov. 25, 1993
  Michael Irvin, Dallas vs. Kansas City, Nov. 23, 1995

YARDS GAINED / Most Yards on Pass Receptions, Game
- 303 Jim Benton, Cleveland at Detroit, Nov. 22, 1945
- 185 Lance Alworth, San Diego vs. Buffalo, Nov. 26, 1964
- 184 Anthony Carter, Minnesota at Dallas, Nov. 26, 1987 (OT)

INTERCONFERENCE GAMES

AFC VS. NFC (REGULAR SEASON), 1970-2008

	Balt	Buff	Cin	Cle	Den	Hou	Ind	Jax	KC	Mia
1970		0-3	1-2	0-3	2-2		3-0		0-2-1	2-1
1971		0-3	1-2	2-1	1-3		2-1		2-1	3-0
1972		2-0-1	2-1	1-2	1-3		0-3		2-1	3-0
1973		2-1	2-1	1-2	0-3-1		2-1		1-1-1	3-0
1974		2-1	2-1	1-2	2-2		1-2		1-2	2-1
1975		1-2	3-0	1-3	2-1		2-1		2-1	3-0
1976		0-2	2-0	2-0	2-0		0-2		1-1	0-2
1977		1-1	2-1	1-1	1-1		1-1		1-1	2-0
1978		1-1	2-2	4-0	2-2		2-2		0-2	3-1
1979		2-2	2-2	3-1	3-1		1-1		0-2	4-0
1980		3-1	2-2	3-1	3-1		1-1		2-0	4-0
1981		1-3	2-2	3-1	3-1		0-4		2-2	3-1
1982		1-2	1-0	0-2	2-1		0-1-1		0-3	1-1
1983		1-3	3-1	2-2	0-2		2-0		2-2	3-1
1984		1-3	2-2	1-3	3-1		0-4		1-1	4-0
1985		0-2	2-2	1-3	3-1		3-1		2-2	3-1
1986		1-1	3-1	2-2	3-1		1-3		1-1	2-2
1987		1-2	1-2	2-2	2-1-1		1-0		1-2	3-0
1988		2-2	4-0	4-0	3-1		2-2		0-2	3-1
1989		1-3	2-2	3-1	2-2		1-3		2-0	2-0
1990		3-1	1-3	1-3	1-3		2-2		4-0	2-2
1991		3-1	1-3	0-4	2-0		0-4		2-2	3-1
1992		4-0	1-3	2-2	1-3		2-0		2-2	2-2
1993		4-0	2-2	3-1	1-3		0-4		2-2	3-1
1994		1-3	1-3	3-1	1-3		0-2		3-1	2-2
1995		3-1	2-2	1-3	2-2		2-2	0-4	3-1	2-2
1996	2-2	4-0	2-2		3-1		3-1	2-2	4-0	1-3
1997	2-1-1	1-3	2-2		3-1		1-3	2-2	4-0	1-3
1998	1-3	3-1	1-3		3-1		0-4	3-1	3-1	3-1
1999	2-1	3-1	1-2	1-2	2-2		4-0	4-0	2-2	2-2
2000	2-1	2-2	1-2	0-3	3-1		2-2	2-2	2-2	2-2
2001	2-2	1-3	1-2	1-2	3-1		1-3	1-2	1-3	2-2
2002	0-4	3-1	1-3	2-2	4-0	2-2	2-2	2-2	2-2	2-2
2003	3-1	2-2	2-2	2-2	1-3	2-2	3-1	2-2	3-1	3-1
2004	3-1	4-0	4-0	1-3	3-1	1-3	4-0	3-1	1-3	2-2
2005	2-2	0-4	4-0	2-2	3-1	1-3	3-1	3-1	1-3	2-2
2006	3-1	2-2	2-2	1-3	1-3	0-4	3-1	3-1	4-0	3-1
2007	3-1	1-3	1-3	3-1	1-3	3-1	4-0	3-1	1-3	0-4
2008	3-1	2-2	1-2-1	1-3	3-1	3-1	2-2	2-2	0-4	3-1
Total	**28-21-1**	**69-68-1**	**72-67-1**	**61-69**	**81-63-2**	**12-16**	**63-67-1**	**32-23**	**67-61-2**	**93-48**

	NE	NYJ	Oak	Pitt	SD	Sea	TB	Tenn	TOTALS
1970	0-3	2-1	1-2	0-3	1-2			0-3	12-27-1
1971	0-3	0-3	1-1-1	1-2	2-1			0-2-1	15-23-2
1972	3-0	1-2	3-0	2-1	0-3			0-3	20-19-1
1973	2-1	0-3	2-1	3-0	1-2			0-3	19-19-2
1974	3-0	2-1	3-0	3-0	1-2			0-3	23-17
1975	1-2	0-3	3-0	2-1	0-3			3-0	23-17
1976	1-1	0-2	3-0	1-1	2-0		0-1	2-0	16-12
1977	2-0	1-1	1-1	2-0	1-1	1-0		2-0	19-9
1978	2-2	1-3	4-0	3-1	2-2	3-1		2-2	31-21
1979	3-1	3-1	4-0	3-1	3-1	3-1		2-2	36-16
1980	1-3	1-3	2-2	4-0	2-2	1-3		4-0	33-19
1981	0-4	2-0	2-2	3-1	2-2	0-2		1-3	24-28
1982	0-1	4-0	3-0	1-0	1-0	1-0		0-3	15-14-1
1983	2-2	3-1	2-2	2-2	2-2	1-3		1-3	26-26
1984	0-4	0-2	3-1	3-1	4-0	4-0		0-4	26-26
1985	3-1	2-2	3-1	1-3	1-1	2-2		1-3	27-25
1986	3-1	2-2	1-3	2-2	0-4	3-1		2-2	26-26
1987	0-3	0-4	2-2	2-2	2-0	4-0		2-2	23-22-1
1988	2-2	2-0	1-3	1-3	2-2	1-3		3-1	30-22
1989	0-4	1-3	2-2	3-1	2-2	0-4		3-1	24-28
1990	0-4	2-0	3-1	3-1	1-1	2-2		1-3	26-26
1991	1-1	2-2	2-2	0-4	1-3	1-3		1-3	19-33
1992	0-4	0-4	2-2	1-3	2-0	0-4		3-1	22-30
1993	1-1	2-2	3-1	2-2	2-2	0-2		2-2	27-25
1994	4-0	1-3	3-1	2-2	2-2	2-0		0-4	25-27
1995	0-4	0-4	3-1	2-2	3-1	3-1		1-3	27-33
1996	2-2	1-3	1-3	2-2	1-3	2-2		2-2	32-28
1997	1-3	3-1	2-2	2-2	1-3	2-2		4-0	31-28-1
1998	2-2	2-2	3-1	2-2	1-3	3-1		1-3	31-29
1999	3-1	2-2	3-1	3-0	1-3	2-2		3-1	38-22
2000	0-4	3-1	4-0	1-2	0-4	2-2		4-0	30-30
2001	3-1	2-2	3-1	3-0	2-2	1-3		3-1	30-30
2002	3-1	3-1	2-2	2-1-1	2-2			2-2	34-29-1
2003	3-1	0-4	1-3	1-3	2-2			4-0	34-30
2004	4-0	3-1	2-2	4-0	3-1			2-2	44-20
2005	3-1	1-3	2-2	4-0	2-2			1-3	34-30
2006	4-0	3-1	1-3	3-1	4-0			3-1	40-24
2007	4-0	0-4	0-4	3-1	2-2			3-1	32-32
2008	4-0	2-2	1-3	2-2	1-3			4-0	34-29-1
Total	**70-68**	**59-79**	**87-58-1**	**84-55-1**	**64-71**	**44-44**	**0-1**	**72-72-1**	**1058-951-11**

NFC VS. AFC (REGULAR SEASON), 1970-2008

	Ariz	Atl	Car	Chi	Dall	Det	GB	Minn	NO
1970	2-0-1	1-2		1-2	3-0	3-0	2-1	2-1	0-3
1971	2-1	3-0		1-2	3-0	4-0	2-1	2-1	0-1-2
1972	1-2	2-2		1-2	3-0	2-0-1	2-1	1-2	0-3
1973	0-2-1	2-1		2-2	2-1	0-3	1-1-1	2-1	1-2
1974	2-1	0-3		0-3	2-1	1-2	2-1	2-1	0-3
1975	2-1	1-2		0-3	2-1	1-2	0-3	4-0	0-3
1976	1-1	0-2		0-2	2-0	2-0	0-2	2-0	1-2
1977	0-2	0-2		1-1	1-1	2-0	0-3	1-1	0-2
1978	0-4	1-3		0-4	3-1	2-2	2-2	1-3	1-3
1979	1-3	1-3		2-2	1-3	0-4	1-3	1-3	0-4
1980	1-1	2-2		0-4	3-1	0-2	1-3	1-3	1-3
1981	3-1	1-3		4-0	4-0	2-2	1-1	1-3	2-2
1982		1-1		1-1	2-1	0-1	1-1-1	1-3	1-0
1983	3-1	3-1		1-1	2-2	1-3	2-2	4-0	1-3
1984	3-1	1-3		2-2	2-2	0-4	0-4	0-4	3-1
1985	2-2	0-4		3-1	3-1	2-2	0-4	2-0	0-4
1986	1-1	1-3		4-0	1-3	1-3	1-3	1-3	1-3
1987	0-1	0-4		2-2	2-1	0-4	1-2-1	2-1	4-0
1988	1-3	1-3		3-1	0-4	1-1	1-3	2-2	4-0
1989	1-3	2-2		2-2	0-2	1-3	0-2	2-2	4-0
1990	2-2	2-2		2-2	1-1	1-3	1-3	2-2	2-2
1991	1-1	3-1		2-2	3-1	4-0	1-3	0-2	3-1
1992	0-2	2-2		1-3	4-0	2-2	3-1	3-1	3-1
1993	1-1	1-3		2-2	2-2	2-0	3-1	2-2	2-2
1994	3-1	1-3		3-1	3-1	2-2	1-3	2-2	1-3
1995	1-3	2-2	3-1	2-2	4-0	3-1	4-0	3-1	4-0
1996	0-4	0-4	3-1	2-2	2-2	1-3	3-1	1-3	1-3
1997	1-3	2-2	2-2	2-2	2-2	2-2	3-1	3-1	2-2
1998	1-3	3-1	1-3	2-2	1-3	1-3	3-1	4-0	1-3
1999	0-4	0-4	2-2	2-2	1-3	1-3	2-2	2-2	0-4
2000	1-3	1-3	2-2	2-2	1-3	2-2	1-3	3-1	1-3
2001	3-1	1-3	0-4	3-1	0-4	0-4	3-1	1-3	2-2
2002	0-4	2-1-1	3-1	1-3	2-2	0-4	3-1	1-3	2-2
2003	1-3	1-3	2-2	3-1	2-2	1-3	3-1	2-2	1-3
2004	1-3	3-1	1-3	1-3	1-3	1-3	1-3	3-1	2-2
2005	1-3	3-1	3-1	1-3	2-2	2-2	0-4	1-3	2-2
2006	0-4	2-2	2-2	2-2	3-1	1-3	1-3	0-4	1-3
2007	3-1	1-3	0-4	3-1	3-1	3-1	4-0	2-2	1-3
2008	2-2	3-1	4-0	2-2	2-2	0-4	1-3	2-2	3-1
Total	**48-79-2**	**56-88-1**	**28-28**	**68-75**	**80-60**	**54-83-1**	**61-78-3**	**71-71**	**58-84-2**

	NYG	Phil	StL	SF	Sea	TB	Wash	TOTALS
1970	3-0	2-1	2-1	4-0			2-1	27-12-1
1971	1-2	1-2	1-2	2-1			1-2	23-15-2
1972	1-2	2-1	1-2	2-1			1-2	19-20-1
1973	1-2	2-1	3-0	1-2			2-1	19-19-2
1974	1-2	2-1	3-1	0-3			2-1	17-23
1975	2-1	0-3	3-0	1-2			1-2	17-23
1976	0-2	0-2	1-1	1-1	1-0		1-1	12-16
1977	0-2	1-1	2-0	0-2		0-1	1-1	9-19
1978	1-1	3-1	2-2	1-3		2-0	2-2	21-31
1979	1-1	2-2	2-2	0-4		2-0	2-2	16-36
1980	1-3	3-1	2-2	2-2		1-3	1-3	19-33
1981	1-1	3-1	1-3	3-1		0-4	2-2	28-24
1982	1-0	2-1	1-2	1-3		2-1		14-15-1
1983	0-4	1-1	1-3	2-2		1-3	4-0	26-26
1984	2-0	3-1	3-1	3-1		1-1	3-1	26-26
1985	2-2	1-1	3-1	3-1		0-4	4-0	25-27
1986	3-1	2-2	2-2	4-0		1-1	3-1	26-26
1987	2-1	3-1	1-2	3-1		0-2	2-1	22-23-1
1988	1-1	2-2	2-2	2-2		1-3	1-3	22-30
1989	4-0	3-1	3-1	4-0		0-4	2-2	28-24
1990	3-1	1-3	2-2	4-0		0-2	3-1	26-26
1991	3-1	4-0	1-3	3-1		1-3	4-0	33-19
1992	2-2	3-1	2-2	3-1		0-2	2-2	30-22
1993	2-2	2-2	2-2	2-2		1-3	1-3	25-27
1994	3-1	1-3	2-2	3-1		1-1	1-1	27-25
1995	0-4	1-3	1-3	3-1		2-2	0-4	33-27
1996	2-2	2-2	2-2	4-0		2-2	3-1	28-32
1997	1-3	2-1-1	0-4	2-2		3-1	1-3	28-31-1
1998	3-1	0-4	3-1	2-2		2-2	2-2	29-31
1999	2-2	1-3	3-1	1-3		3-1	2-2	22-38
2000	3-1	3-1	3-1	2-2		3-1	2-2	30-30
2001	2-2	3-1	4-0	4-0		2-2	2-2	30-30
2002	2-2	1-3	2-2	2-2	2-2	3-1	3-1	29-34-1
2003	1-3	3-1	4-0	1-3	2-2	1-3	2-2	30-34
2004	1-3	2-2	1-3	0-4	1-3	1-3	0-4	20-44
2005	3-1	3-1	3-1	1-3	3-1	2-2	0-4	30-34
2006	1-3	1-3	2-2	2-2	2-2	2-2	2-2	24-40
2007	3-1	3-1	0-4	1-3	2-2	1-3	2-2	32-32
2008	3-1	2-1-1	0-4	2-2	1-3	1-3	1-3	29-34-1
Total	**68-64**	**76-63-2**	**76-69**	**81-66**	**14-15**	**42-66**	**70-69**	**951-1058-11**

INTERCONFERENCE GAMES

2008 INTERCONFERENCE GAMES

(Home Team in capital letters)

AFC 34, NFC 29, TIE 1

AFC Victories

BUFFALO 34, Seattle 10
Indianapolis 18, MINNESOTA 15
DENVER 34, New Orleans 32
N.Y. JETS 56, Arizona 35
TENNESSEE 30, Minnesota 17
Buffalo 31, ST. LOUIS 14
DENVER 16, Tampa Bay 13
New England 30, SAN FRANCISCO 21
CLEVELAND 35, N.Y. Giants 14
HOUSTON 28, Detroit 21
NEW ENGLAND 23, St. Louis 16
TENNESSEE 19, Green Bay 16 (OT)
Pittsburgh 23, WASHINGTON 6
Tennessee 21, CHICAGO 14
Jacksonville 38, DETROIT 14
MIAMI 21, Seattle 19
N.Y. JETS 47, St. Louis 3
Denver 24, ATLANTA 20
BALTIMORE 36, Philadelphia 7
Tennessee 47, DETROIT 10
Miami 16, ST. LOUIS 12
Houston 24, GREEN BAY 21
New England 24, SEATTLE 21
PITTSBURGH 20, Dallas 13
BALTIMORE 24, Washington 10
CINCINNATI 20, Washington 13
INDIANAPOLIS 31, Detroit 21
JACKSONVILLE 20, Green Bay 16
MIAMI 14, San Francisco 9
Baltimore 33, DALLAS 24
NEW ENGLAND 47, Arizona 7
San Diego 41, TAMPA BAY 24
HOUSTON 31, Chicago 24
Oakland 31, TAMPA BAY 24

NFC Victories

Chicago 29, INDIANAPOLIS 13
Carolina 26, SAN DIEGO 24
Dallas 28, CLEVELAND 10
ARIZONA 31, Miami 10
N.Y. GIANTS 26, Cincinnati 23 (OT)
ATLANTA 38, Kansas City 14
PHILADELPHIA 15, Pittsburgh 6
CAROLINA 34, Kansas City 0
ARIZONA 41, Buffalo 17
DALLAS 31, Cincinnati 22
NEW ORLEANS 34, Oakland 3
GREEN BAY 34, Indianapolis 14
WASHINGTON 14, Cleveland 11
NEW ORLEANS 37, San Diego 32 (London)
N.Y. Giants 21, PITTSBURGH 14
Tampa Bay 30, KANSAS CITY 27 (OT)
MINNESOTA 28, Houston 21
Atlanta 24, OAKLAND 0
Carolina 17, OAKLAND 6
New Orleans 30, KANSAS CITY 20
N.Y. GIANTS 30, Baltimore 10
Minnesota 30, JACKSONVILLE 12
San Francisco 10, BUFFALO 3
Atlanta 22, SAN DIEGO 16
CHICAGO 23, Jacksonville 10
SAN FRANCISCO 24, N.Y. Jets 14
PHILADELPHIA 30, Cleveland 10
CAROLINA 30, Denver 10
SEATTLE 13, N.Y. Jets 3

TIE

Philadelphia 13, CINCINNATI 13 (OT)

REGULAR SEASON INTERCONFERENCE RECORDS, 1970-2008

AMERICAN FOOTBALL CONFERENCE

East	W	L	T	Pct.
Miami	93	48	0	.660
New England	70	68	0	.507
Buffalo	69	68	1	.504
New York Jets	59	79	0	.428
North	**W**	**L**	**T**	**Pct.**
Pittsburgh	84	55	1	.604
Baltimore	28	21	1	.570
Cincinnati	72	67	1	.518
Cleveland	61	69	0	.469
South	**W**	**L**	**T**	**Pct.**
Jacksonville	32	23	0	.582
Tennessee	72	72	1	.500
Indianapolis	63	67	1	.485
Houston	12	16	0	.429
West	**W**	**L**	**T**	**Pct.**
Oakland	87	58	1	.600
Denver	81	63	2	.562
Kansas City	67	61	2	.523
San Diego	64	71	0	.474

NATIONAL FOOTBALL CONFERENCE

East	W	L	T	Pct.
Dallas	80	60	0	.571
Philadelphia	76	63	2	.546
New York Giants	68	64	0	.515
Washington	70	69	0	.504
North	**W**	**L**	**T**	**Pct.**
Minnesota	71	71	0	.500
Chicago	68	75	0	.476
Green Bay	61	78	3	.440
Detroit	54	83	1	.395
South	**W**	**L**	**T**	**Pct.**
Carolina	28	28	0	.500
New Orleans	58	84	2	.408
Atlanta	56	88	1	.390
Tampa Bay*	42	67	0	.385
West	**W**	**L**	**T**	**Pct.**
San Francisco	81	66	0	.551
St. Louis	76	69	0	.524
Seattle* #	58	59	0	.496
Arizona	48	79	2	.379

* Records include one game played between Seattle and Tampa Bay, won by the Seahawks 13-10, in their inaugural season (1976) when Seattle competed in the NFC and Tampa Bay in the AFC.

\# Seattle was a member of the AFC from 1977-2001.

From 1970-71, tie games were not included in winning percentage.

INTERCONFERENCE VICTORIES, 1970-2008

REGULAR SEASON

	AFC	NFC	Tie
1970	12	27	1
1971	15	23	2
1972	20	19	1
1973	19	19	2
1974	23	17	0
1975	23	17	0
1976	16	12	0
1977	19	9	0
1978	31	21	0
1979	36	16	0
1980	33	19	0
1981	24	28	0
1982	15	14	1
1983	26	26	0
1984	26	26	0
1985	27	25	0
1986	26	26	0
1987	23	22	1
1988	30	22	0
1989	24	28	0
1990	26	26	0
1991	19	33	0
1992	22	30	0
1993	27	25	0
1994	25	27	0
1995	27	33	0
1996	32	28	0
1997	31	28	1
1998	31	29	0
1999	38	22	0
2000	30	30	0
2001	30	30	0
2002	34	29	1
2003	34	30	0
2004	44	20	0
2005	34	30	0
2006	40	24	0
2007	32	32	0
2008	34	29	1
Total	1,058	951	11

PRESEASON

	AFC	NFC	Tie
1970	21	28	1
1971	28	28	3
1972	27	25	4
1973	23	35	2
1974	35	25	0
1975	30	26	1
1976	30	31	0
1977	38	25	0
1978	20	19	0
1979	25	18	0
1980	22	20	1
1981	18	19	0
1982	25	16	0
1983	15	24	0
1984	16	19	0
1985	10	22	1
1986	22	17	0
1987	22	22	0
1988	23	16	1
1989	16	27	0
1990	15	29	0
1991	19	27	0
1992	30	22	0
1993	17	22	0
1994	22	16	0
1995	19	26	0
1996	27	19	0
1997	26	17	0
1998	34	16	0
1999	22	25	0
2000	34	17	0
2001	28	23	0
2002	25	24	0
2003	25	21	0
2004	21	18	0
2005	21	29	0
2006	27	24	0
2007	27	24	0
2008	21	27	0
Total	926	888	14

WALTER PAYTON NFL MAN OF THE YEAR

The Walter Payton NFL Man of the Year Award is the only NFL award that recognizes a player for his community service activities as well as his excellence on the field. Renamed in 1999 for the legendary Chicago Bears Pro Football Hall of Fame running back, the Walter Payton NFL Man of the Year Award has been given annually since 1970.

YEAR	PLAYER	POS.	TEAM
1970	Johnny Unitas	QB	Baltimore Colts
1971	John Hadl	QB	San Diego Chargers
1972	Willie Lanier	LB	Kansas City Chiefs
1973	Len Dawson	QB	Kansas City Chiefs
1974	George Blanda	QB	Oakland Raiders
1975	Ken Anderson	QB	Cincinnati Bengals
1976	Franco Harris	RB	Pittsburgh Steelers
1977	Walter Payton	RB	Chicago Bears
1978	Roger Staubach	QB	Dallas Cowboys
1979	Joe Greene	DT	Pittsburgh Steelers
1980	Harold Carmichael	WR	Philadelphia Eagles
1981	Lynn Swann	WR	Pittsburgh Steelers
1982	Joe Theismann	QB	Washington Redskins
1983	Rolf Benirschke	K	San Diego Chargers
1984	Marty Lyons	T	New York Jets
1985	Dwight Stephenson	C	Miami Dolphins
1986	Reggie Williams	LB	Cincinnati Bengals
1987	Dave Duerson	S	Chicago Bears
1988	Steve Largent	WR	Seattle Seahawks
1989	Warren Moon	QB	Houston Oilers
1990	Mike Singletary	LB	Chicago Bears
1991	Anthony Muñoz	T	Cincinnati Bengals
1992	John Elway	QB	Denver Broncos
1993	Derrick Thomas	LB	Kansas City Chiefs
1994	Junior Seau	LB	San Diego Chargers
1995	Boomer Esiason	QB	New York Jets
1996	Darrell Green	CB	Washington Redskins
1997	Troy Aikman	QB	Dallas Cowboys
1998	Dan Marino	QB	Miami Dolphins
1999	Cris Carter	WR	Minnesota Vikings
2000*	Derrick Brooks	LB	Tampa Bay Buccaneers
	Jim Flanigan	DT	Chicago Bears
2001	Jerome Bettis	RB	Pittsburgh Steelers
2002	Troy Vincent	CB	Philadelphia Eagles
2003	Will Shields	G	Kansas City Chiefs
2004	Warrick Dunn	RB	Atlanta Falcons
2005	Peyton Manning	QB	Indianapolis Colts
2006*	Drew Brees	QB	New Orleans Saints
	LaDainian Tomlinson	RB	San Diego Chargers
2007	Jason Taylor	DE	Miami Dolphins
2008	Kurt Warner	QB	Arizona Cardinals

* The award was shared in 2000 and 2006.

NUMBER-ONE DRAFT CHOICES

NUMBER-ONE DRAFT CHOICES

Season	Date	Team	Player	Position	College
2009	April 25-26	Detroit	Matthew Stafford	QB	Georgia
2008	April 26-27	Miami	Jake Long	T	Michigan
2007	April 28-29	Oakland	JaMarcus Russell	QB	Louisiana State
2006	April 29-30	Houston	Mario Williams	DE	North Carolina State
2005	April 23-24	San Francisco	Alex Smith	QB	Utah
2004	April 24-25	San Diego	Eli Manning	QB	Mississippi
2003	April 26-27	Cincinnati	Carson Palmer	QB	Southern California
2002	April 20-21	Houston	David Carr	QB	Fresno State
2001	April 21-22	Atlanta	Michael Vick	QB	Virginia Tech
2000	April 15-16	Cleveland	Courtney Brown	DE	Penn State
1999	April 17-18	Cleveland	Tim Couch	QB	Kentucky
1998	April 18-19	Indianapolis	Peyton Manning	QB	Tennessee
1997	April 19-20	St. Louis	Orlando Pace	T	Ohio State
1996	April 20-21	New York Jets	Keyshawn Johnson	WR	Southern California
1995	April 22-23	Cincinnati	Ki-Jana Carter	RB	Penn State
1994	April 24-25	Cincinnati	Dan Wilkinson	DT	Ohio State
1993	April 25-26	New England	Drew Bledsoe	QB	Washington State
1992	April 26-27	Indianapolis	Steve Emtman	DT	Washington
1991	April 21-22	Dallas	Russell Maryland	DT	Miami
1990	April 22-23	Indianapolis	Jeff George	QB	Illinois
1989	April 23-24	Dallas	Troy Aikman	QB	UCLA
1988	April 24-25	Atlanta	Aundray Bruce	LB	Auburn
1987	April 28-29	Tampa Bay	Vinny Testaverde	QB	Miami
1986	April 29-30	Tampa Bay	Bo Jackson	RB	Auburn
1985	April 30-May 1	Buffalo	Bruce Smith	DE	Virginia Tech
1984	May 1-2	New England	Irving Fryar	WR	Nebraska
1983	April 26-27	Baltimore	John Elway	QB	Stanford
1982	April 27-28	New England	Kenneth Sims	DT	Texas
1981	April 28-29	New Orleans	George Rogers	RB	South Carolina
1980	April 29-30	Detroit	Billy Sims	RB	Oklahoma
1979	May 3-4	Buffalo	Tom Cousineau	LB	Ohio State
1978	May 2-3	Houston	Earl Campbell	RB	Texas
1977	May 3-4	Tampa Bay	Ricky Bell	RB	Southern California
1976	April 8-9	Tampa Bay	Lee Roy Selmon	DE	Oklahoma
1975	January 28-29	Atlanta	Steve Bartkowski	QB	California
1974	January 29-30	Dallas	Ed Jones	DE	Tennessee State
1973	January 30-31	Houston	John Matuszak	DE	Tampa
1972	February 1-2	Buffalo	Walt Patulski	DE	Notre Dame
1971	January 28-29	New England	Jim Plunkett	QB	Stanford
1970	January 27-28	Pittsburgh	Terry Bradshaw	QB	Louisiana Tech
1969	January 28-29	Buffalo (AFL)	O.J. Simpson	RB	Southern California
1968	January 30-31	Minnesota	Ron Yary	T	Southern California
1967	March 14	Baltimore	Bubba Smith	DT	Michigan State
1966	November 27, 1965	Atlanta	Tommy Nobis	LB	Texas
	November 28, 1965	Miami (AFL)	Jim Grabowski	RB	Illinois
1965	November 28, 1964	New York Giants	Tucker Frederickson	RB	Auburn
	November 28, 1964	Houston (AFL)	Lawrence Elkins	E	Baylor
1964	December 2, 1963	San Francisco	Dave Parks	E	Texas Tech
	November 30, 1963	Boston (AFL)	Jack Concannon	QB	Boston College
1963	December 3, 1962	Los Angeles	Terry Baker	QB	Oregon State
	December 1, 1962	Kansas City (AFL)	Buck Buchanan	DT	Grambling
1962	December 4, 1961	Washington	Ernie Davis	RB	Syracuse
	December 2, 1961	Oakland (AFL)	Roman Gabriel	QB	North Carolina State
1961	December 27-28, 1960	Minnesota	Tommy Mason	RB	Tulane
	November 23, 1960	Buffalo (AFL)	Ken Rice	G	Auburn
1960	Secret Draft	Los Angeles	Billy Cannon	RB	Louisiana State
	November 22, December 2, 1959	(AFL had no formal first pick)			
1959	December 2, 1958	Green Bay	Randy Duncan	QB	Iowa
1958	December 2, 1957	Chicago Cardinals	King Hill	QB	Rice
1957	November 27, 1956	Green Bay	Paul Hornung	HB	Notre Dame
1956	November 29, 1955	Pittsburgh	Gary Glick	DB	Colorado A&M

Season	Date	Team	Player	Position	College
1955	January 27-28	Baltimore	George Shaw	QB	Oregon
1954	January 28	Cleveland	Bobby Garrett	QB	Stanford
1953	January 22	San Francisco	Harry Babcock	E	Georgia
1952	January 17	Los Angeles	Bill Wade	QB	Vanderbilt
1951	January 18-19	New York Giants	Kyle Rote	HB	Southern Methodist
1950	January 21-22	Detroit	Leon Hart	E	Notre Dame
1949	December 21, 1948	Philadelphia	Chuck Bednarik	C	Pennsylvania
1948	December 19, 1947	Washington	Harry Gilmer	QB	Alabama
1947	December 16, 1946	Chicago Bears	Bob Fenimore	HB	Oklahoma A&M
1946	January 14	Boston	Frank Dancewicz	QB	Notre Dame
1945	April 6	Chicago Cardinals	Charley Trippi	HB	Georgia
1944	April 19	Boston	Angelo Bertelli	QB	Notre Dame
1943	April 8	Detroit	Frank Sinkwich	HB	Georgia
1942	December 22, 1941	Pittsburgh	Bill Dudley	HB	Virginia
1941	December 10, 1940	Chicago Bears	Tom Harmon	HB	Michigan
1940	December 9, 1939	Chicago Cardinals	George Cafego	HB	Tennessee
1939	December 8, 1938	Chicago Cardinals	Ki Aldrich	C	Texas Christian
1938	December 12, 1937	Cleveland	Corbett Davis	FB	Indiana
1937	December 12, 1936	Philadelphia	Sam Francis	FB	Nebraska
1936	February 8	Philadelphia	Jay Berwanger	HB	Chicago

Note: From 1947 through 1958, the first selection in the draft was a Bonus pick, awarded to the winner of a random draw. That club, in turn, forfeited its last-round draft choice. The winner of the Bonus choice was eliminated from future draws. The system was abolished after 1958, by which time all clubs had received a Bonus choice.

NUMBER-ONE DRAFT CHOICES BY POSITION

Quarterbacks:	28
Running Backs:	23
Defensive Linemen:	13
Offensive Linemen:	6
Wide Receivers:	6
Linebackers:	3
Defensive Backs:	1

FIRST-ROUND SELECTIONS

If club had no first-round selection, first player drafted is listed with round in parentheses.

ARIZONA CARDINALS

Year Player, College, Position

1936 Jim Lawrence, Texas Christian, B
1937 Ray Buivid, Marquette, B
1938 Jack Robbins, Arkansas, B
1939 Charles (Ki) Aldrich, TCU, C
1940 George Cafego, Tennessee, B
1941 John Kimbrough, Texas A&M, B
1942 Steve Lach, Duke, B
1943 Glenn Dobbs, Tulsa, B
1944 Pat Harder, Wisconsin, B
1945 Charley Trippi, Georgia, B
1946 Dub Jones, Louisiana State, B
1947 DeWitt (Tex) Coulter, Army, T
1948 Jim Spavital, Oklahoma A&M, B
1949 Bill Fischer, Notre Dame, G
1950 Jack Jennings, Ohio State, T (2)
1951 Jerry Groom, Notre Dame, C
1952 Ollie Matson, San Francisco, B
1953 Johnny Olszewski, California, B
1954 Lamar McHan, Arkansas, B
1955 Max Boydston, Oklahoma, E
1956 Joe Childress, Auburn, B
1957 Jerry Tubbs, Oklahoma, C
1958 King Hill, Rice, B
John David Crow, Texas A&M, B
1959 Bill Stacy, Mississippi State, B
1960 George Izo, Notre Dame, QB
1961 Ken Rice, Auburn, T
1962 Fate Echols, Northwestern, DT
Irv Goode, Kentucky, C
1963 Jerry Stovall, Louisiana State, S
Don Brumm, Purdue, DE
1964 Ken Kortas, Louisville, DT
1965 Joe Namath, Alabama, QB
1966 Carl McAdams, Oklahoma, LB
1967 Dave Williams, Washington, WR
1968 MacArthur Lane, Utah State, RB
1969 Roger Wehrli, Missouri, DB
1970 Larry Stegent, Texas A&M, RB
1971 Norm Thompson, Utah, CB
1972 Bobby Moore, Oregon, RB-WR
1973 Dave Butz, Purdue, DT
1974 J.V. Cain, Colorado, TE
1975 Tim Gray, Texas A&M, DB
1976 Mike Dawson, Arizona, DT
1977 Steve Pisarkiewicz, Missouri, QB
1978 Steve Little, Arkansas, K
Ken Greene, Washington State, DB
1979 Ottis Anderson, Miami, RB
1980 Curtis Greer, Michigan, DE
1981 E.J. Junior, Alabama, LB
1982 Luis Sharpe, UCLA, T
1983 Leonard Smith, McNeese St., DB
1984 Clyde Duncan, Tennessee, WR
1985 Freddie Joe Nunn, Mississippi, LB
1986 Anthony Bell, Michigan State, LB
1987 Kelly Stouffer, Colorado State, QB
1988 Ken Harvey, California, LB
1989 Eric Hill, Louisiana State, LB
Joe Wolf, Boston College, G
1990 Anthony Thompson, Indiana, RB (2)
1991 Eric Swann, No College, DE
1992 Tony Sacca, Penn State, QB (2)
1993 Garrison Hearst, Georgia, RB
Ernest Dye, South Carolina, T
1994 Jamir Miller, UCLA, LB
1995 Frank Sanders, Auburn, WR (2)
1996 Simeon Rice, Illinois, DE
1997 Tom Knight, Iowa, DB
1998 Andre Wadsworth, Florida St., DE
1999 David Boston, Ohio State, WR
L.J. Shelton, Eastern Michigan, T
2000 Thomas Jones, Virginia, RB
2001 Leonard Davis, Texas, T
2002 Wendell Bryant, Wisconsin, DT
2003 Bryant Johnson, Penn State, WR
Calvin Pace, Wake Forest, DE
2004 Larry Fitzgerald, Pittsburgh, WR
2005 Antrel Rolle, Miami, DB
2006 Matt Leinart, So. California, QB
2007 Levi Brown, Penn State, T
2008 Dominique Rodgers-Cromartie, Tenn. St., DB
2009 Beanie Wells, Ohio State, RB

ATLANTA FALCONS

Year Player, College, Position

1966 Tommy Nobis, Texas, LB
Randy Johnson, Texas A&I, QB
1967 Leo Carroll, San Diego St., DE (2)
1968 Claude Humphrey, Tennessee St., DE
1969 George Kunz, Notre Dame, T
1970 John Small, Citadel, LB
1971 Joe Profit, Northeast Louisiana, RB
1972 Clarence Ellis, Notre Dame, DB
1973 Greg Marx, Notre Dame, DT (2)
1974 Gerald Tinker, Kent State, WR (2)
1975 Steve Bartkowski, California, QB
1976 Bubba Bean, Texas A&M, RB
1977 Warren Bryant, Kentucky, T
Wilson Faumuina, San Jose St., DT
1978 Mike Kenn, Michigan, T
1979 Don Smith, Miami, DE
1980 Junior Miller, Nebraska, TE
1981 Bobby Butler, Florida State, DB
1982 Gerald Riggs, Arizona State, RB
1983 Mike Pitts, Alabama, DE
1984 Rick Bryan, Oklahoma, DT
1985 Bill Fralic, Pittsburgh, T
1986 Tony Casillas, Oklahoma, NT
Tim Green, Syracuse, LB
1987 Chris Miller, Oregon, QB
1988 Aundray Bruce, Auburn, LB
1989 Deion Sanders, Florida State, DB
Shawn Collins, No. Arizona, WR
1990 Steve Broussard, Washington St., RB
1991 Bruce Pickens, Nebraska, DB
Mike Pritchard, Colorado, WR
1992 Bob Whitfield, Stanford, T
Tony Smith, So. Mississippi, RB
1993 Lincoln Kennedy, Washington, T
1994 Bert Emanuel, Rice, WR (2)
1995 Devin Bush, Florida State, DB
1996 Shannon Brown, Alabama, DT (3)
1997 Michael Booker, Nebraska, DB
1998 Keith Brooking, Georgia Tech, LB
1999 Patrick Kerney, Virginia, DE
2000 Travis Claridge, So. California, T (2)
2001 Michael Vick, Virginia Tech, QB
2002 T.J. Duckett, Michigan State, RB
2003 Bryan Scott, Penn State, DB (2)
2004 DeAngelo Hall, Virginia Tech, DB
Michael Jenkins, Ohio State, WR
2005 Roddy White, Ala.-Birmingham, WR
2006 Jimmy Williams, Virginia Tech, DB (2)
2007 Jamaal Anderson, Arkansas, DE
2008 Matt Ryan, Boston College, QB
Sam Baker, So. California, T
2009 Peria Jerry, Mississippi, DT

BALTIMORE RAVENS

Year Player, College, Position

1996 Jonathan Ogden, UCLA, T
Ray Lewis, Miami, LB
1997 Peter Boulware, Florida State, DE
1998 Duane Starks, Miami, DB
1999 Chris McAlister, Arizona, DB
2000 Jamal Lewis, Tennessee, RB
Travis Taylor, Florida, WR
2001 Todd Heap, Arizona State, TE
2002 Ed Reed, Miami, DB
2003 Terrell Suggs, Arizona State, DE
Kyle Boller, California, QB
2004 Dwan Edwards, Oregon St., DT (2)
2005 Mark Clayton, Oklahoma, WR
2006 Haloti Ngata, Oregon, DT
2007 Ben Grubbs, Auburn, G
2008 Joe Flacco, Delaware, QB
2009 Michael Oher, Mississippi, T

BUFFALO BILLS

Year Player, College, Position

1960 Richie Lucas, Penn State, QB
1961 Ken Rice, Auburn, T
1962 Ernie Davis, Syracuse, RB
1963 Dave Behrman, Michigan State, C
1964 Carl Eller, Minnesota, DE
1965 Jim Davidson, Ohio State, T
1966 Mike Dennis, Mississippi, RB
1967 John Pitts, Arizona State, S
1968 Haven Moses, San Diego St., WR
1969 O.J. Simpson, So. California, RB
1970 Al Cowlings, So. California, DE
1971 J.D. Hill, Arizona State, WR
1972 Walt Patulski, Notre Dame, DE
1973 Paul Seymour, Michigan, TE
Joe DeLamielleure, Michigan St., G
1974 Reuben Gant, Oklahoma State, TE
1975 Tom Ruud, Nebraska, LB
1976 Mario Clark, Oregon, DB
1977 Phil Dokes, Oklahoma State, DT
1978 Terry Miller, Oklahoma State, RB
1979 Tom Cousineau, Ohio State, LB
Jerry Butler, Clemson, WR
1980 Jim Ritcher, North Carolina St., C
1981 Booker Moore, Penn State, RB
1982 Perry Tuttle, Clemson, WR
1983 Tony Hunter, Notre Dame, TE
Jim Kelly, Miami, QB
1984 Greg Bell, Notre Dame, RB
1985 Bruce Smith, Virginia Tech, DE
Derrick Burroughs, Memphis St., DB
1986 Ronnie Harmon, Iowa, RB
Will Wolford, Vanderbilt, T
1987 Shane Conlan, Penn State, LB
1988 Thurman Thomas, Oklahoma St., RB (2)
1989 Don Beebe, Chadron, Neb., WR (3)
1990 James Williams, Fresno State, DB
1991 Henry Jones, Illinois, DB
1992 John Fina, Arizona, T
1993 Thomas Smith, North Carolina, DB
1994 Jeff Burris, Notre Dame, DB
1995 Ruben Brown, Pittsburgh, G
1996 Eric Moulds, Mississippi St., WR

1997 Antowain Smith, Houston, RB
1998 Sam Cowart, Florida State, LB (2)
1999 Antoine Winfield, Ohio State, DB
2000 Erik Flowers, Arizona State, DE
2001 Nate Clements, Ohio State, DB
2002 Mike Williams, Texas, T
2003 Willis McGahee, Miami, RB
2004 Lee Evans, Wisconsin, WR
J.P. Losman, Tulane, QB
2005 Roscoe Parrish, Miami, WR (2)
2006 Donte' Whitner, Ohio State, DB
John McCargo, North Carolina St., DT
2007 Marshawn Lynch, California, RB
2008 Leodis McKelvin, Troy, DB
2009 Aaron Maybin, Penn State, DE
Eric Wood, Louisville, C

CAROLINA PANTHERS

Year Player, College, Position
1995 Kerry Collins, Penn State, QB
Tyrone Poole, Ft. Valley State, DB
Blake Brockermeyer, Texas, T
1996 Tim Biakabutuka, Michigan, RB
1997 Rae Carruth, Colorado, WR
1998 Jason Peter, Nebraska, DT
1999 Chris Terry, Georgia, T (2)
2000 Rashard Anderson, Jackson St., DB
2001 Dan Morgan, Miami, LB
2002 Julius Peppers, North Carolina, DE
2003 Jordan Gross, Utah, T
2004 Chris Gamble, Ohio State, DB
2005 Thomas Davis, Georgia, DB
2006 DeAngelo Williams, Memphis, RB
2007 Jon Beason, Miami, LB
2008 Jonathan Stewart, Oregon, RB
Jeff Otah, Pittsburgh, T
2009 Everette Brown, Florida St., DE (2)

CHICAGO BEARS

Year Player, College, Position
1936 Joe Stydahar, West Virginia, T
1937 Les McDonald, Nebraska, E
1938 Joe Gray, Oregon State, B
1939 Sid Luckman, Columbia, QB
Bill Osmanski, Holy Cross, B
1940 Clyde (Bulldog) Turner, Hardin-Simmons, C
1941 Tom Harmon, Michigan, B
Norm Standlee, Stanford, B
Don Scott, Ohio State, B
1942 Frankie Albert, Stanford, B
1943 Bob Steber, Missouri, B
1944 Ray Evans, Kansas, B
1945 Don Lund, Michigan, B
1946 Johnny Lujack, Notre Dame, QB
1947 Bob Fenimore, Oklahoma State, B
Don Kindt, Wisconsin, B
1948 Bobby Layne, Texas, QB
Max Bumgardner, Texas, E
1949 Dick Harris, Texas, C
1950 Chuck Hunsinger, Florida, B
Fred Morrison, Ohio State, B
1951 Bob Williams, Notre Dame, B
Billy Stone, Bradley, B
Gene Schroeder, Virginia, E
1952 Jim Dooley, Miami, B
1953 Billy Anderson, Compton (Calif.) J.C., B
1954 Stan Wallace, Illinois, B
1955 Ron Drzewiecki, Marquette, B
1956 Menan (Tex) Schriewer, Texas, E
1957 Earl Leggett, Louisiana State, T
1958 Chuck Howley, West Virginia, G
1959 Don Clark, Ohio State, B
1960 Roger Davis, Syracuse, G
1961 Mike Ditka, Pittsburgh, E
1962 Ronnie Bull, Baylor, RB
1963 Dave Behrman, Michigan State, C
1964 Dick Evey, Tennessee, DT
1965 Dick Butkus, Illinois, LB
Gale Sayers, Kansas, RB
Steve DeLong, Tennessee, T
1966 George Rice, Louisiana State, DT
1967 Loyd Phillips, Arkansas, DE
1968 Mike Hull, Southern California, RB
1969 Rufus Mayes, Ohio State, T
1970 George Farmer, UCLA, WR (3)
1971 Joe Moore, Missouri, RB
1972 Lionel Antoine, Southern Illinois, T
Craig Clemons, Iowa, DB
1973 Wally Chambers, Eastern Kentucky, DE
1974 Waymond Bryant, Tennessee St., LB
Dave Gallagher, Michigan, DT
1975 Walter Payton, Jackson State, RB
1976 Dennis Lick, Wisconsin, T
1977 Ted Albrecht, California, T
1978 Brad Shearer, Texas, DT (3)
1979 Dan Hampton, Arkansas, DT
Al Harris, Arizona State, DE
1980 Otis Wilson, Louisville, LB
1981 Keith Van Horne, So. California, T
1982 Jim McMahon, Brigham Young, QB
1983 Jim Covert, Pittsburgh, T
Willie Gault, Tennessee, WR
1984 Wilber Marshall, Florida, LB
1985 William Perry, Clemson, DT
1986 Neal Anderson, Florida, RB
1987 Jim Harbaugh, Michigan, QB
1988 Brad Muster, Stanford, RB
Wendell Davis, Louisiana St., WR
1989 Donnell Woolford, Clemson, DB
Trace Armstrong, Florida, DE
1990 Mark Carrier, So. California, DB
1991 Stan Thomas, Texas, T
1992 Alonzo Spellman, Ohio State, DE
1993 Curtis Conway, So. California, WR
1994 John Thierry, Alcorn State, DE
1995 Rashaan Salaam, Colorado, RB
1996 Walt Harris, Mississippi State, DB
1997 John Allred, So. California, TE (2)
1998 Curtis Enis, Penn State, RB
1999 Cade McNown, UCLA, QB
2000 Brian Urlacher, New Mexico, LB
2001 David Terrell, Michigan, WR
2002 Marc Colombo, Boston College, T
2003 Michael Haynes, Penn State, DE
Rex Grossman, Florida, QB
2004 Tommie Harris, Oklahoma, DT
2005 Cedric Benson, Texas, RB
2006 Danieal Manning, Abilene Christian, DB (2)
2007 Greg Olsen, Miami, TE
2008 Chris Williams, Vanderbilt, T
2009 Jarron Gilbert, San Jose State, DT (3)

CINCINNATI BENGALS

Year Player, College, Position
1968 Bob Johnson, Tennessee, C
1969 Greg Cook, Cincinnati, QB
1970 Mike Reid, Penn State, DT
1971 Vernon Holland, Tennessee St., T
1972 Sherman White, California, DE
1973 Isaac Curtis, San Diego State, WR
1974 Bill Kollar, Montana State, DT
1975 Glenn Cameron, Florida, LB
1976 Billy Brooks, Oklahoma, WR
Archie Griffin, Ohio State, RB
1977 Eddie Edwards, Miami, DT
Wilson Whitley, Houston, DT
Mike Cobb, Michigan State, TE
1978 Ross Browner, Notre Dame, DT
Blair Bush, Washington, C
1979 Jack Thompson, Washington St., QB
Charles Alexander, Louisiana St., RB
1980 Anthony Muñoz, So. California, T
1981 David Verser, Kansas, WR
1982 Glen Collins, Mississippi State, DE
1983 Dave Rimington, Nebraska, C
1984 Ricky Hunley, Arizona, LB
Pete Koch, Maryland, DE
Brian Blados, North Carolina, T
1985 Eddie Brown, Miami, WR
Emanuel King, Alabama, LB
1986 Joe Kelly, Washington, LB
Tim McGee, Tennessee, WR
1987 Jason Buck, Brigham Young, DE
1988 Rickey Dixon, Oklahoma, DB
1989 Eric Ball, UCLA, RB (2)
1990 James Francis, Baylor, LB
1991 Alfred Williams, Colorado, LB
1992 David Klingler, Houston, QB
Darryl Williams, Miami, DB
1993 John Copeland, Alabama, DE
1994 Dan Wilkinson, Ohio State, DT
1995 Ki-Jana Carter, Penn State, RB
1996 Willie Anderson, Auburn, T
1997 Reinard Wilson, Florida State, LB
1998 Takeo Spikes, Auburn, LB
Brian Simmons, North Carolina, LB
1999 Akili Smith, Oregon, QB
2000 Peter Warrick, Florida State, WR
2001 Justin Smith, Missouri, DE
2002 Levi Jones, Arizona State, T
2003 Carson Palmer, Southern California, QB
2004 Chris Perry, Michigan, RB
2005 David Pollack, Georgia, LB
2006 Johnathan Joseph, South Carolina, DB
2007 Leon Hall, Michigan, DB
2008 Keith Rivers, So. California, LB
2009 Andre Smith, Alabama, T

CLEVELAND BROWNS

Year Player, College, Position
1950 Ken Carpenter, Oregon State, B
1951 Ken Konz, Louisiana State, B
1952 Bert Rechichar, Tennessee, DB
Harry Agganis, Boston U., QB
1953 Doug Atkins, Tennessee, DE
1954 Bobby Garrett, Stanford, QB
John Bauer, Illinois, G
1955 Kurt Burris, Oklahoma, C
1956 Preston Carpenter, Arkansas, B
1957 Jim Brown, Syracuse, RB
1958 Jim Shofner, Texas Christian, DB
1959 Rich Kreitling, Illinois, DE
1960 Jim Houston, Ohio State, DE
1961 Bobby Crespino, Mississippi, TE
1962 Gary Collins, Maryland, WR
Leroy Jackson, Western Illinois, RB
1963 Tom Hutchinson, Kentucky, WR
1964 Paul Warfield, Ohio State, WR
1965 James Garcia, Purdue, T (2)
1966 Milt Morin, Massachusetts, TE

1967 Bob Matheson, Duke, LB
1968 Marvin Upshaw, Trinity, Tex., DT-DE
1969 Ron Johnson, Michigan, RB
1970 Mike Phipps, Purdue, QB
Bob McKay, Texas, T
1971 Clarence Scott, Kansas State, CB
1972 Thom Darden, Michigan, DB
1973 Steve Holden, Arizona State, WR
Pete Adams, Southern California, T
1974 Billy Corbett, Johnson C. Smith, T (2)
1975 Mack Mitchell, Houston, DE
1976 Mike Pruitt, Purdue, RB
1977 Robert Jackson, Texas A&M, LB
1978 Clay Matthews, So. California, LB
Ozzie Newsome, Alabama, TE
1979 Willis Adams, Houston, WR
1980 Charles White, So. California, RB
1981 Hanford Dixon, So. Mississippi, DB
1982 Chip Banks, So. California, LB
1983 Ron Brown, Arizona State, WR (2)
1984 Don Rogers, UCLA, DB
1985 Greg Allen, Florida State, RB (2)
1986 Webster Slaughter, San Diego St., WR (2)
1987 Mike Junkin, Duke, LB
1988 Clifford Charlton, Florida, LB
1989 Eric Metcalf, Texas, RB
1990 Leroy Hoard, Michigan, RB (2)
1991 Eric Turner, UCLA, DB
1992 Tommy Vardell, Stanford, RB
1993 Steve Everitt, Michigan, C
1994 Antonio Langham, Alabama, DB
Derrick Alexander, Michigan, WR
1995 Craig Powell, Ohio State, LB
1999 Tim Couch, Kentucky, QB
2000 Courtney Brown, Penn State, DE
2001 Gerard Warren, Florida, DT
2002 William Green, Boston College, RB
2003 Jeff Faine, Norte Dame, C
2004 Kellen Winslow, Miami, TE
2005 Braylon Edwards, Michigan, WR
2006 Kamerion Wimbley, Florida St., DE
2007 Joe Thomas, Wisconsin, T
Brady Quinn, Notre Dame, QB
2008 Beau Bell, Nevada-Las Vegas, LB (4)
2009 Alex Mack, California, C

DALLAS COWBOYS

Year Player, College, Position
1960 None
1961 Bob Lilly, Texas Christian, DT
1962 Sonny Gibbs, TCU, QB (2)
1963 Lee Roy Jordan, Alabama, LB
1964 Scott Appleton, Texas, DT
1965 Craig Morton, California, QB
1966 John Niland, Iowa, G
1967 Phil Clark, Northwestern, DB (3)
1968 Dennis Homan, Alabama, WR
1969 Calvin Hill, Yale, RB
1970 Duane Thomas, West Texas St., RB
1971 Tody Smith, So. California, DE
1972 Bill Thomas, Boston College, RB
1973 Billy Joe DuPree, Michigan St., TE
1974 Ed (Too Tall) Jones, Tennessee St., DE
Charley Young, North Carolina St., RB
1975 Randy White, Maryland, LB
Thomas Henderson, Langston, LB
1976 Aaron Kyle, Wyoming, DB
1977 Tony Dorsett, Pittsburgh, RB
1978 Larry Bethea, Michigan State, DE
1979 Robert Shaw, Tennessee, C
1980 Bill Roe, Colorado, LB (3)
1981 Howard Richards, Missouri, T
1982 Rod Hill, Kentucky State, DB
1983 Jim Jeffcoat, Arizona State, DE
1984 Billy Cannon, Jr., Texas A&M, LB
1985 Kevin Brooks, Michigan, DE
1986 Mike Sherrard, UCLA, WR
1987 Danny Noonan, Nebraska, DT
1988 Michael Irvin, Miami, WR
1989 Troy Aikman, UCLA, QB
1990 Emmitt Smith, Florida, RB
1991 Russell Maryland, Miami, DT
Alvin Harper, Tennessee, WR
Kelvin Pritchett, Mississippi, DT
1992 Kevin Smith, Texas A&M, DB
Robert Jones, East Carolina, LB
1993 Kevin Williams, Miami, WR (2)
1994 Shante Carver, Arizona State, DE
1995 Sherman Williams, Alabama, RB (2)
1996 Kavika Pittman, McNeese St., DE (2)
1997 David LaFleur, Louisiana State, TE
1998 Greg Ellis, North Carolina, DE
1999 Ebenezer Ekuban, North Carolina, DE
2000 Dwayne Goodrich, Tennessee, DB (2)
2001 Quincy Carter, Georgia, QB (2)
2002 Roy Williams, Oklahoma, DB
2003 Terence Newman, Kansas State, DB
2004 Julius Jones, Notre Dame, RB (2)
2005 DeMarcus Ware, Troy, DE
Marcus Spears, Louisiana St., DE
2006 Bobby Carpenter, Ohio State, LB
2007 Anthony Spencer, Purdue, LB
2008 Felix Jones, Arkansas, RB
Mike Jenkins, South Florida, DB
2009 Jason Williams, Western Illinois, LB (3)

DENVER BRONCOS

Year Player, College, Position
1960 Roger LeClerc, Trinity, Conn., C
1961 Bob Gaiters, New Mexico St., RB
1962 Merlin Olsen, Utah State, DT
1963 Kermit Alexander, UCLA, CB
1964 Bob Brown, Nebraska, T
1965 Dick Butkus, Illinois, LB (2)
1966 Jerry Shay, Purdue, DT
1967 Floyd Little, Syracuse, RB
1968 Curley Culp, Arizona State, DE (2)
1969 Grady Cavness, Texas-El Paso, DB (2)
1970 Bob Anderson, Colorado, RB
1971 Marv Montgomery, So. California, T
1972 Riley Odoms, Houston, TE
1973 Otis Armstrong, Purdue, RB
1974 Randy Gradishar, Ohio State, LB
1975 Louis Wright, San Jose State, DB
1976 Tom Glassic, Virginia, G
1977 Steve Schindler, Boston College, G
1978 Don Latimer, Miami, DT
1979 Kelvin Clark, Nebraska, T
1980 Rulon Jones, Utah State, DE (2)
1981 Dennis Smith, So. California, DB
1982 Gerald Willhite, San Jose St., RB
1983 Chris Hinton, Northwestern, G
1984 Andre Townsend, Mississippi, DE (2)
1985 Steve Sewell, Oklahoma, RB
1986 Jim Juriga, Illinois, T (4)
1987 Ricky Nattiel, Florida, WR
1988 Ted Gregory, Syracuse, NT
1989 Steve Atwater, Arkansas, DB
1990 Alton Montgomery, Houston, DB (2)
1991 Mike Croel, Nebraska, LB
1992 Tommy Maddox, UCLA, QB
1993 Dan Williams, Toledo, DE
1994 Allen Aldridge, Houston, LB (2)
1995 Jamie Brown, Florida A&M, T (4)
1996 John Mobley, Kutztown, LB
1997 Trevor Pryce, Clemson, DT
1998 Marcus Nash, Tennessee, WR
1999 Al Wilson, Tennessee, LB
2000 Deltha O'Neal, California, DB
2001 Willie Middlebrooks, Minnesota, DB
2002 Ashley Lelie, Hawaii, WR
2003 George Foster, Georgia, T
2004 D.J. Williams, Miami, LB
2005 Darrent Williams, Oklahoma St., DB (2)
2006 Jay Cutler, Vanderbilt, QB
2007 Jarvis Moss, Florida, DE
2008 Ryan Clady, Boise State, T
2009 Knowshon Moreno, Georgia, RB
Robert Ayers, Tennessee, DE

DETROIT LIONS

Year Player, College, Position
1936 Sid Wagner, Michigan State, G
1937 Lloyd Cardwell, Nebraska, B
1938 Alex Wojciechowicz, Fordham, C
1939 John Pingel, Michigan State, B
1940 Doyle Nave, Southern California, B
1941 Jim Thomason, Texas A&M, B
1942 Bob Westfall, Michigan, B
1943 Frank Sinkwich, Georgia, B
1944 Otto Graham, Northwestern, B
1945 Frank Szymanski, Notre Dame, C
1946 Bill Dellastatious, Missouri, B
1947 Glenn Davis, Army, B
1948 Y.A. Tittle, Louisiana State, B
1949 John Rauch, Georgia, B
1950 Leon Hart, Notre Dame, E
Joe Watson, Rice, C
1951 Dick Stanfel, San Francisco, G (2)
1952 Yale Lary, Texas A&M, B (3)
1953 Harley Sewell, Texas, G
1954 Dick Chapman, Rice, T
1955 Dave Middleton, Auburn, B
1956 Hopalong Cassady, Ohio State, B
1957 Bill Glass, Baylor, G
1958 Alex Karras, Iowa, T
1959 Nick Pietrosante, Notre Dame, B
1960 John Robinson, Louisiana State, S
1961 Danny LaRose, Missouri, T (2)
1962 John Hadl, Kansas, QB
1963 Daryl Sanders, Ohio State, T
1964 Pete Beathard, So. California, QB
1965 Tom Nowatzke, Indiana, RB
1966 Nick Eddy, Notre Dame, RB (2)
1967 Mel Farr, UCLA, RB
1968 Greg Landry, Massachusetts, QB
Earl McCullouch, So. California, WR
1969 Altie Taylor, Utah State, RB (2)
1970 Steve Owens, Oklahoma, RB
1971 Bob Bell, Cincinnati, DT
1972 Herb Orvis, Colorado, DE
1973 Ernie Price, Texas A&I, DE
1974 Ed O'Neil, Penn State, LB
1975 Lynn Boden, South Dakota St., G
1976 James Hunter, Grambling, DB
Lawrence Gaines, Wyoming, RB
1977 Walt Williams, New Mexico St., DB (2)
1978 Luther Bradley, Notre Dame, DB
1979 Keith Dorney, Penn State, T
1980 Billy Sims, Oklahoma, RB

1981 Mark Nichols, San Jose State, WR
1982 Jimmy Williams, Nebraska, LB
1983 James Jones, Florida, RB
1984 David Lewis, California, TE
1985 Lomas Brown, Florida, T
1986 Chuck Long, Iowa, QB
1987 Reggie Rogers, Washington, DE
1988 Bennie Blades, Miami, DB
1989 Barry Sanders, Oklahoma St., RB
1990 Andre Ware, Houston, QB
1991 Herman Moore, Virginia, WR
1992 Robert Porcher, South Carolina St., DE
1993 Ryan McNeil, Miami, DB (2)
1994 Johnnie Morton, So. California, WR
1995 Luther Elliss, Utah, DT
1996 Reggie Brown, Texas A&M, LB
Jeff Hartings, Penn State, G
1997 Bryant Westbrook, Texas, DB
1998 Terry Fair, Tennessee, DB
1999 Chris Claiborne, So. California, LB
Aaron Gibson, Wisconsin, T
2000 Stockar McDougle, Oklahoma, T
2001 Jeff Backus, Michigan, T
2002 Joey Harrington, Oregon, QB
2003 Charles Rogers, Michigan State, WR
2004 Roy Williams, Texas, WR
Kevin Jones, Virginia Tech, RB
2005 Mike Williams, So. California, WR
2006 Ernie Sims, Florida State, LB
2007 Calvin Johnson, Georgia Tech, WR
2008 Gosder Cherilus, Boson College, T
2009 Matthew Stafford, Georgia, QB
Brandon Pettigrew, Oklahoma St., TE

GREEN BAY PACKERS

Year Player, College, Position
1936 Russ Letlow, San Francisco, G
1937 Eddie Jankowski, Wisconsin, B
1938 Cecil Isbell, Purdue, B
1939 Larry Buhler, Minnesota, B
1940 Harold Van Every, Minnesota, B
1941 George Paskvan, Wisconsin, B
1942 Urban Odson, Minnesota, T
1943 Dick Wildung, Minnesota, T
1944 Merv Pregulman, Michigan, G
1945 Walt Schlinkman, Texas Tech, B
1946 Johnny Strzykalski, Marquette, B
1947 Ernie Case, UCLA, B
1948 Earl (Jug) Girard, Wisconsin, B
1949 Stan Heath, Nevada, B
1950 Clayton Tonnemaker, Minnesota, C
1951 Bob Gain, Kentucky, T
1952 Babe Parilli, Kentucky, QB
1953 Al Carmichael, So. California, B
1954 Art Hunter, Notre Dame, T
Veryl Switzer, Kansas State, B
1955 Tom Bettis, Purdue, G
1956 Jack Losch, Miami, B
1957 Paul Hornung, Notre Dame, B
Ron Kramer, Michigan, E
1958 Dan Currie, Michigan State, C
1959 Randy Duncan, Iowa, B
1960 Tom Moore, Vanderbilt, RB
1961 Herb Adderley, Michigan State, CB
1962 Earl Gros, Louisiana State, RB
1963 Dave Robinson, Penn State, LB
1964 Lloyd Voss, Nebraska, DT
1965 Donny Anderson, Texas Tech, RB
Lawrence Elkins, Baylor, E
1966 Jim Grabowski, Illinois, RB
Gale Gillingham, Minnesota, T
1967 Bob Hyland, Boston College, C
Don Horn, San Diego State, QB
1968 Fred Carr, Texas-El Paso, LB
Bill Lueck, Arizona, G
1969 Rich Moore, Villanova, DT
1970 Mike McCoy, Notre Dame, DT
Rich McGeorge, Elon, TE
1971 John Brockington, Ohio State, RB
1972 Willie Buchanon, San Diego St., DB
Jerry Tagge, Nebraska, QB
1973 Barry Smith, Florida State, WR
1974 Barty Smith, Richmond, RB
1975 Bill Bain, So. California, G (2)
1976 Mark Koncar, Colorado, T
1977 Mike Butler, Kansas, DE
Ezra Johnson, Morris Brown, DE
1978 James Lofton, Stanford, WR
John Anderson, Michigan, LB
1979 Eddie Lee Ivery, Georgia Tech, RB
1980 Bruce Clark, Penn State, DE
George Cumby, Oklahoma, LB
1981 Rich Campbell, California, QB
1982 Ron Hallstrom, Iowa, G
1983 Tim Lewis, Pittsburgh, DB
1984 Alphonso Carreker, Florida St., DE
1985 Ken Ruettgers, So. California, T
1986 Kenneth Davis, TCU, RB (2)
1987 Brent Fullwood, Auburn, RB
1988 Sterling Sharpe, South Carolina, WR
1989 Tony Mandarich, Michigan State, T
1990 Tony Bennett, Mississippi, LB
Darrell Thompson, Minnesota, RB
1991 Vinnie Clark, Ohio State, DB
1992 Terrell Buckley, Florida State, DB
1993 Wayne Simmons, Clemson, LB
George Teague, Alabama, DB
1994 Aaron Taylor, Notre Dame, T
1995 Craig Newsome, Arizona State, DB
1996 John Michels, Southern California, T
1997 Ross Verba, Iowa, T
1998 Vonnie Holliday, North Carolina, DT
1999 Antuan Edwards, Clemson, DB
2000 Bubba Franks, Miami, TE
2001 Jamal Reynolds, Florida State, DE
2002 Javon Walker, Florida State, WR
2003 Nick Barnett, Oregon State, LB
2004 Ahmad Carroll, Arkansas, DB
2005 Aaron Rodgers, California, QB
2006 A.J. Hawk, Ohio State, LB
2007 Justin Harrell, Tennessee, DT
2008 Jordy Nelson, Kansas State, WR (2)
2009 B.J. Raji, Boston College, DT
Clay Matthews, So. California, LB

HOUSTON TEXANS

Year Player, College, Position
2002 David Carr, Fresno State, QB
2003 Andre Johnson, Miami, WR
2004 Dunta Robinson, South Carolina, DB
Jason Babin, Western Michigan, LB
2005 Travis Johnson, Florida State, DE
2006 Mario Williams, North Carolina St., DE
2007 Amobi Okoye, Louisville, DT
2008 Duane Brown, Virginia Tech, T
2009 Brian Cushing, So. California, LB

INDIANAPOLIS COLTS

Year Player, College, Position
1953 Billy Vessels, Oklahoma, B
1954 Cotton Davidson, Baylor, B
1955 George Shaw, Oregon, B
Alan Ameche, Wisconsin, FB
1956 Lenny Moore, Penn State, B
1957 Jim Parker, Ohio State, G
1958 Lenny Lyles, Louisville, B
1959 Jackie Burkett, Auburn, C
1960 Ron Mix, Southern California, T
1961 Tom Matte, Ohio State, RB
1962 Wendell Harris, Louisiana State, S
1963 Bob Vogel, Ohio State, T
1964 Marv Woodson, Indiana, CB
1965 Mike Curtis, Duke, LB
1966 Sam Ball, Kentucky, T
1967 Bubba Smith, Michigan State, DT
Jim Detwiler, Michigan, RB
1968 John Williams, Minnesota, G
1969 Eddie Hinton, Oklahoma, WR
1970 Norman Bulaich, Texas Christian, RB
1971 Don McCauley, North Carolina, RB
Leonard Dunlap, North Texas St., DB
1972 Tom Drougas, Oregon, T
1973 Bert Jones, Louisiana State, QB
Joe Ehrmann, Syracuse, DT
1974 John Dutton, Nebraska, DE
Roger Carr, Louisiana Tech, WR
1975 Ken Huff, North Carolina, G
1976 Ken Novak, Purdue, DT
1977 Randy Burke, Kentucky, WR
1978 Reese McCall, Auburn, TE
1979 Barry Krauss, Alabama, LB
1980 Curtis Dickey, Texas A&M, RB
Derrick Hatchett, Texas, DB
1981 Randy McMillan, Pittsburgh, RB
Donnell Thompson, North Carolina, DT
1982 Johnie Cooks, Mississippi St., LB
Art Schlichter, Ohio State, QB
1983 John Elway, Stanford, QB
1984 Leonard Coleman, Vanderbilt, DB
Ron Solt, Maryland, G
1985 Duane Bickett, So. California, LB
1986 Jon Hand, Alabama, DE
1987 Cornelius Bennett, Alabama, LB
1988 Chris Chandler, Washington, QB (3)
1989 Andre Rison, Michigan State, WR
1990 Jeff George, Illinois, QB
1991 Shane Curry, Miami, DE (2)
1992 Steve Emtman, Washington, DT
Quentin Coryatt, Texas A&M, LB
1993 Sean Dawkins, California, WR
1994 Marshall Faulk, San Diego St., RB
Trev Alberts, Nebraska, LB
1995 Ellis Johnson, Florida, DT
1996 Marvin Harrison, Syracuse, WR
1997 Tarik Glenn, California, T
1998 Peyton Manning, Tennessee, QB
1999 Edgerrin James, Miami, RB
2000 Rob Morris, Brigham Young, LB
2001 Reggie Wayne, Miami, WR
2002 Dwight Freeney, Syracuse, DE
2003 Dallas Clark, Iowa, TE
2004 Bob Sanders, Iowa, DB (2)
2005 Marlin Jackson, Michigan, DB
2006 Joseph Addai, Louisiana State, RB
2007 Anthony Gonzalez, Ohio State, WR
2008 Mike Pollak, Arizona State, G (2)
2009 Donald Brown, Connecticut, RB

FIRST-ROUND SELECTIONS

JACKSONVILLE JAGUARS

Year Player, College, Position

1995 Tony Boselli, Southern California, T
James Stewart, Tennessee, RB
1996 Kevin Hardy, Illinois, LB
1997 Renaldo Wynn, Notre Dame, DT
1998 Fred Taylor, Florida, RB
Donovin Darius, Syracuse, DB
1999 Fernando Bryant, Alabama, DB
2000 R. Jay Soward, So. California, WR
2001 Marcus Stroud, Georgia, DT
2002 John Henderson, Tennessee, DT
2003 Byron Leftwich, Marshall, QB
2004 Reggie Williams, Washington, WR
2005 Matt Jones, Arkansas, WR
2006 Marcedes Lewis, UCLA, TE
2007 Reggie Nelson, Florida, DB
2008 Derrick Harvey, Florida, DE
2009 Eugene Monroe, Virginia, T

KANSAS CITY CHIEFS

Year Player, College, Position

1960 Don Meredith, So. Methodist, QB
1961 E.J. Holub, Texas Tech, C
1962 Ronnie Bull, Baylor, RB
1963 Buck Buchanan, Grambling, DT
Ed Budde, Michigan State, G
1964 Pete Beathard, So. California, QB
1965 Gale Sayers, Kansas, RB
1966 Aaron Brown, Minnesota, DE
1967 Gene Trosch, Miami, DE-DT
1968 Mo Moorman, Texas A&M, G
George Daney, Texas-El Paso, G
1969 Jim Marsalis, Tennessee State, CB
1970 Sid Smith, Southern California, T
1971 Elmo Wright, Houston, WR
1972 Jeff Kinney, Nebraska, RB
1973 Gary Butler, Rice, TE (2)
1974 Woody Green, Arizona State, RB
1975 Elmore Stephens, Kentucky, TE (2)
1976 Rod Walters, Iowa, G
1977 Gary Green, Baylor, DB
1978 Art Still, Kentucky, DE
1979 Mike Bell, Colorado State, DE
Steve Fuller, Clemson, QB
1980 Brad Budde, Southern California, G
1981 Willie Scott, South Carolina, TE
1982 Anthony Hancock, Tennessee, WR
1983 Todd Blackledge, Penn State, QB
1984 Bill Maas, Pittsburgh, DT
John Alt, Iowa, T
1985 Ethan Horton, North Carolina, RB
1986 Brian Jozwiak, West Virginia, T
1987 Paul Palmer, Temple, RB
1988 Neil Smith, Nebraska, DE
1989 Derrick Thomas, Alabama, LB
1990 Percy Snow, Michigan State, LB
1991 Harvey Williams, Louisiana St., RB
1992 Dale Carter, Tennessee, DB
1993 Will Shields, Nebraska, G (3)
1994 Greg Hill, Texas A&M, RB
1995 Trezelle Jenkins, Michigan, T
1996 Jerome Woods, Memphis, DB
1997 Tony Gonzalez, California, TE
1998 Victor Riley, Auburn, T
1999 John Tait, Brigham Young, T
2000 Sylvester Morris, Jackson St., WR
2001 Eric Downing, Syracuse, DT (3)
2002 Ryan Sims, North Carolina, DT
2003 Larry Johnson, Penn State, RB
2004 Junior Siavii, Oregon, DT (2)
2005 Derrick Johnson, Texas, LB
2006 Tamba Hali, Penn State, DE
2007 Dwayne Bowe, Louisiana State, WR
2008 Glenn Dorsey, Louisiana State, DT
Branden Albert, Virginia, T
2009 Tyson Jackson, Louisiana State, DE

MIAMI DOLPHINS

Year Player, College, Position

1966 Jim Grabowski, Illinois, RB
Rick Norton, Kentucky, QB
1967 Bob Griese, Purdue, QB
1968 Larry Csonka, Syracuse, RB
Doug Crusan, Indiana, T
1969 Bill Stanfill, Georgia, DE
1970 Jim Mandich, Michigan, TE (2)
1971 Otto Stowe, Iowa State, WR (2)
1972 Mike Kadish, Notre Dame, DT
1973 Chuck Bradley, Oregon, C (2)
1974 Donald Reese, Jackson State, DE
1975 Darryl Carlton, Tampa, T
1976 Larry Gordon, Arizona State, LB
Kim Bokamper, San Jose State, LB
1977 A.J. Duhe, Louisiana State, DT
1978 Guy Benjamin, Stanford, QB (2)
1979 Jon Giesler, Michigan, T
1980 Don McNeal, Alabama, DB
1981 David Overstreet, Oklahoma, RB
1982 Roy Foster, Southern California, G
1983 Dan Marino, Pittsburgh, QB
1984 Jackie Shipp, Oklahoma, LB
1985 Lorenzo Hampton, Florida, RB
1986 John Offerdahl, Western Michigan, LB (2)
1987 John Bosa, Boston College, DE
1988 Eric Kumerow, Ohio State, DE
1989 Sammie Smith, Florida State, RB
Louis Oliver, Florida, DB
1990 Richmond Webb, Texas A&M, T
1991 Randal Hill, Miami, WR
1992 Troy Vincent, Wisconsin, DB
Marco Coleman, Georgia Tech, LB
1993 O.J. McDuffie, Penn State, WR
1994 Tim Bowens, Mississippi, DT
1995 Billy Milner, Houston, T
1996 Daryl Gardener, Baylor, DT
1997 Yatil Green, Miami, WR
1998 John Avery, Mississippi, RB
1999 J.J. Johnson, Mississippi St., RB (2)
2000 Todd Wade, Mississippi, T (2)
2001 Jamar Fletcher, Wisconsin, DB
2002 Seth McKinney, Texas A&M, C (3)
2003 Eddie Moore, Tennessee, LB (2)
2004 Vernon Carey, Miami, T
2005 Ronnie Brown, Auburn, RB
2006 Jason Allen, Tennessee, DB
2007 Ted Ginn, Ohio State, WR
2008 Jake Long, Michigan, T
2009 Vontae Davis, Illinois, DB

MINNESOTA VIKINGS

Year Player, College, Position

1961 Tommy Mason, Tulane, RB
1962 Bill Miller, Miami, WR (3)
1963 Jim Dunaway, Mississippi, T
1964 Carl Eller, Minnesota, DE
1965 Jack Snow, Notre Dame, WR
1966 Jerry Shay, Purdue, DT
1967 Clint Jones, Michigan State, RB
Gene Washington, Michigan St., WR
Alan Page, Notre Dame, DT
1968 Ron Yary, Southern California, T
1969 Ed White, California, G (2)
1970 John Ward, Oklahoma State, DT
1971 Leo Hayden, Ohio State, RB
1972 Jeff Siemon, Stanford, LB
1973 Chuck Foreman, Miami, RB
1974 Fred McNeill, UCLA, LB
Steve Riley, Southern California, T
1975 Mark Mullaney, Colorado State, DE
1976 James White, Oklahoma State, DT
1977 Tommy Kramer, Rice, QB
1978 Randy Holloway, Pittsburgh, DE
1979 Ted Brown, North Carolina St., RB
1980 Doug Martin, Washington, DT
1981 Mardye McDole, Mississippi St., WR (2)
1982 Darrin Nelson, Stanford, RB
1983 Joey Browner, So. California, DB
1984 Keith Millard, Washington St., DE
1985 Chris Doleman, Pittsburgh, LB
1986 Gerald Robinson, Auburn, DE
1987 D.J. Dozier, Penn State, RB
1988 Randall McDaniel, Arizona State, G
1989 David Braxton, Wake Forest, LB (2)
1990 Mike Jones, Texas A&M, TE (3)
1991 Carlos Jenkins, Michigan St., LB (3)
1992 Robert Harris, Southern Univ., DE (2)
1993 Robert Smith, Ohio State, RB
1994 DeWayne Washington, N. Carolina St., DB
Todd Steussie, California, T
1995 Derrick Alexander, Florida St., DE
Korey Stringer, Ohio State, T
1996 Duane Clemons, California, DE
1997 Dwayne Rudd, Alabama, LB
1998 Randy Moss, Marshall, WR
1999 Daunte Culpepper, Central Florida, QB
Dimitrius Underwood, Michigan St., DE
2000 Chris Hovan, Boston College, DT
2001 Michael Bennett, Wisconsin, RB
2002 Bryant McKinnie, Miami, T
2003 Kevin Williams, Oklahoma State, DT
2004 Kenechi Udeze, Southern California, DE
2005 Troy Williamson, South Carolina, WR
Erasmus James, Wisconsin, DE
2006 Chad Greenway, Iowa, LB
2007 Adrian Peterson, Oklahoma, RB
2008 Tyrell Johnson, Arkansas State, DB (2)
2009 Percy Harvin, Florida, WR

NEW ENGLAND PATRIOTS

Year Player, College, Position

1960 Ron Burton, Northwestern, RB
1961 Tommy Mason, Tulane, RB
1962 Gary Collins, Maryland, WR
1963 Art Graham, Boston College, WR
1964 Jack Concannon, Boston College, QB
1965 Jerry Rush, Michigan State, DE
1966 Karl Singer, Purdue, T
1967 John Charles, Purdue, S
1968 Dennis Byrd, North Carolina St., DE
1969 Ron Sellers, Florida State, WR
1970 Phil Olsen, Utah State, DE
1971 Jim Plunkett, Stanford, QB
1972 Tom Reynolds, San Diego St., WR (2)
1973 John Hannah, Alabama, G
Sam Cunningham, So. California, RB
Darryl Stingley, Purdue, WR
1974 Steve Corbett, Boston College, G (2)

1975 Russ Francis, Oregon, TE
1976 Mike Haynes, Arizona State, DB
Pete Brock, Colorado, C
Tim Fox, Ohio State, DB
1977 Raymond Clayborn, Texas, DB
Stanley Morgan, Tennessee, WR
1978 Bob Cryder, Alabama, G
1979 Rick Sanford, South Carolina, DB
1980 Roland James, Tennessee, DB
Vagas Ferguson, Notre Dame, RB
1981 Brian Holloway, Stanford, T
1982 Kenneth Sims, Texas, DT
Lester Williams, Miami, DT
1983 Tony Eason, Illinois, QB
1984 Irving Fryar, Nebraska, WR
1985 Trevor Matich, Brigham Young, C
1986 Reggie Dupard, So. Methodist, RB
1987 Bruce Armstrong, Louisville, T
1988 John Stephens, Northwestern St., La., RB
1989 Hart Lee Dykes, Oklahoma St., WR
1990 Chris Singleton, Arizona, LB
Ray Agnew, North Carolina St., DE
1991 Pat Harlow, Southern California, T
Leonard Russell, Arizona St., RB
1992 Eugene Chung, Virginia Tech, T
1993 Drew Bledsoe, Washington St., QB
1994 Willie McGinest, So. California, DE
1995 Ty Law, Michigan, DB
1996 Terry Glenn, Ohio State, WR
1997 Chris Canty, Kansas State, DB
1998 Robert Edwards, Georgia, RB
Tebucky Jones, Syracuse, DB
1999 Damien Woody, Boston College, C
Andy Katzenmoyer, Ohio State, LB
2000 Adrian Klemm, Hawaii, T (2)
2001 Richard Seymour, Georgia, DT
2002 Daniel Graham, Colorado, TE
2003 Ty Warren, Texas A&M, DT
2004 Vince Wilfork, Miami, DT
Ben Watson, Georgia, TE
2005 Logan Mankins, Fresno State, G
2006 Laurence Maroney, Minnesota, RB
2007 Brandon Meriweather, Miami, DB
2008 Jerod Mayo, Tennessee, LB
2009 Patrick Chung, Oregon, DB (2)

NEW ORLEANS SAINTS

Year Player, College, Position
1967 Les Kelley, Alabama, RB
1968 Kevin Hardy, Notre Dame, DE
1969 John Shinners, Xavier, G
1970 Ken Burrough, Texas Southern, WR
1971 Archie Manning, Mississippi, QB
1972 Royce Smith, Georgia, G
1973 Derland Moore, Oklahoma, DE (2)
1974 Rick Middleton, Ohio State, LB
1975 Larry Burton, Purdue, WR
Kurt Schumacher, Ohio State, T
1976 Chuck Muncie, California, RB
1977 Joe Campbell, Maryland, DE
1978 Wes Chandler, Florida, WR
1979 Russell Erxleben, Texas, P-K
1980 Stan Brock, Colorado, T
1981 George Rogers, South Carolina, RB
1982 Lindsay Scott, Georgia, WR
1983 Steve Korte, Arkansas, G (2)
1984 James Geathers, Wichita State, DE
1985 Alvin Toles, Tennessee, LB
1986 Jim Dombrowski, Virginia, T
1987 Shawn Knight, Brigham Young, DT
1988 Craig Heyward, Pittsburgh, RB
1989 Wayne Martin, Arkansas, DE
1990 Renaldo Turnbull, West Virginia, DE
1991 Wesley Carroll, Miami, WR (2)
1992 Vaughn Dunbar, Indiana, RB
1993 Willie Roaf, Louisiana Tech, T
Irv Smith, Notre Dame, TE
1994 Joe Johnson, Louisville, DE
1995 Mark Fields, Washington State, LB
1996 Alex Molden, Oregon, DB
1997 Chris Naeole, Colorado, G
1998 Kyle Turley, San Diego State, T
1999 Ricky Williams, Texas, RB
2000 Darren Howard, Kansas St., DE (2)
2001 Deuce McAllister, Mississippi, RB
2002 Donte' Stallworth, Tennessee, WR
Charles Grant, Georgia, DE
2003 Johnathan Sullivan, Georgia, DT
2004 Will Smith, Ohio State, DE
2005 Jammal Brown, Oklahoma, T
2006 Reggie Bush, So. California, RB
2007 Robert Meachem, Tennessee, WR
2008 Sedrick Ellis, So. California, DT
2009 Malcolm Jenkins, Ohio State, DB

NEW YORK GIANTS

Year Player, College, Position
1936 Art Lewis, Ohio U., T
1937 Ed Widseth, Minnesota, T
1938 George Karamatic, Gonzaga, B
1939 Walt Neilson, Arizona, B
1940 Grenville Lansdell, So. California, B
1941 George Franck, Minnesota, B
1942 Merle Hapes, Mississippi, B
1943 Steve Filipowicz, Fordham, B
1944 Billy Hillenbrand, Indiana, B
1945 Elmer Barbour, Wake Forest, B
1946 George Connor, Notre Dame, T
1947 Vic Schwall, Northwestern, B
1948 Tony Minisi, Pennsylvania, B
1949 Paul Page, Southern Methodist, B
1950 Travis Tidwell, Auburn, B
1951 Kyle Rote, Southern Methodist, B
Jim Spavital, Oklahoma A&M, B
1952 Frank Gifford, Southern California, B
1953 Bobby Marlow, Alabama, B
1954 Ken Buck, Pacific, C (2)
1955 Joe Heap, Notre Dame, B
1956 Henry Moore, Arkansas, B (2)
1957 Sam DeLuca, South Carolina, T (2)
1958 Phil King, Vanderbilt, B
1959 Lee Grosscup, Utah, B
1960 Lou Cordileone, Clemson, G
1961 Bruce Tarbox, Syracuse, G (2)
1962 Jerry Hillebrand, Colorado, LB
1963 Frank Lasky, Florida, T (2)
1964 Joe Don Looney, Oklahoma, RB
1965 Tucker Frederickson, Auburn, RB
1966 Francis Peay, Missouri, T
1967 Louis Thompson, Alabama, DT (4)
1968 Dick Buzin, Penn State, T (2)
1969 Fred Dryer, San Diego State, DE
1970 Jim Files, Oklahoma, LB
1971 Rocky Thompson, West Texas St., WR
1972 Eldridge Small, Texas A&I, DB
Larry Jacobson, Nebraska, DE
1973 Brad Van Pelt, Michigan St., LB (2)
1974 John Hicks, Ohio State, G
1975 Al Simpson, Colorado State, T (2)
1976 Troy Archer, Colorado, DE
1977 Gary Jeter, Southern California, DT
1978 Gordon King, Stanford, T
1979 Phil Simms, Morehead State, QB
1980 Mark Haynes, Colorado, DB
1981 Lawrence Taylor, North Carolina, LB
1982 Butch Woolfolk, Michigan, RB
1983 Terry Kinard, Clemson, DB
1984 Carl Banks, Michigan State, LB
William Roberts, Ohio State, T
1985 George Adams, Kentucky, RB
1986 Eric Dorsey, Notre Dame, DE
1987 Mark Ingram, Michigan State, WR
1988 Eric Moore, Indiana, T
1989 Brian Williams, Minnesota, C-G
1990 Rodney Hampton, Georgia, RB
1991 Jarrod Bunch, Michigan, RB
1992 Derek Brown, Notre Dame, TE
1993 Michael Strahan, Texas Southern, DE (2)
1994 Thomas Lewis, Indiana, WR
1995 Tyrone Wheatley, Michigan, RB
1996 Cedric Jones, Oklahoma, DE
1997 Ike Hilliard, Florida, WR
1998 Shaun Williams, UCLA, DB
1999 Luke Petitgout, Notre Dame, T
2000 Ron Dayne, Wisconsin, RB
2001 Will Allen, Syracuse, DB
2002 Jeremy Shockey, Miami, TE
2003 William Joseph, Miami, DT
2004 Philip Rivers, North Carolina St., QB
2005 Corey Webster, Louisiana St., DB (2)
2006 Mathias Kiwanuka, Boston College, DE
2007 Aaron Ross, Texas, DB
2008 Kenny Phillips, Miami, DB
2009 Hakeem Nicks, North Carolina, WR

NEW YORK JETS

Year Player, College, Position
1960 George Izo, Notre Dame, QB
1961 Tom Brown, Minnesota, G
1962 Sandy Stephens, Minnesota, QB
1963 Jerry Stovall, Louisiana State, S
1964 Matt Snell, Ohio State, RB
1965 Joe Namath, Alabama, QB
Tom Nowatzke, Indiana, RB
1966 Bill Yearby, Michigan, DT
1967 Paul Seiler, Notre Dame, T
1968 Lee White, Weber State, RB
1969 Dave Foley, Ohio State, T
1970 Steve Tannen, Florida, CB
1971 John Riggins, Kansas, RB
1972 Jerome Barkum, Jackson St., WR
Mike Taylor, Michigan, LB
1973 Burgess Owens, Miami, DB
1974 Carl Barzilauskas, Indiana, DT
1975 Anthony Davis, So. California, RB (2)
1976 Richard Todd, Alabama, QB
1977 Marvin Powell, So. California, T
1978 Chris Ward, Ohio State, T
1979 Marty Lyons, Alabama, DE
1980 Johnny (Lam) Jones, Texas, WR
1981 Freeman McNeil, UCLA, RB
1982 Bob Crable, Notre Dame, LB
1983 Ken O'Brien, Cal-Davis, QB
1984 Russell Carter, So. Methodist, DB
Ron Faurot, Arkansas, DE
1985 Al Toon, Wisconsin, WR
1986 Mike Haight, Iowa, T
1987 Roger Vick, Texas A&M, RB
1988 Dave Cadigan, So. California, T
1989 Jeff Lageman, Virginia, LB

1990 Blair Thomas, Penn State, RB
1991 Browning Nagle, Louisville, QB (2)
1992 Johnny Mitchell, Nebraska, TE
1993 Marvin Jones, Florida State, LB
1994 Aaron Glenn, Texas A&M, DB
1995 Kyle Brady, Penn State, TE
Hugh Douglas, Central St., Ohio, DE
1996 Keyshawn Johnson, So. California, WR
1997 James Farrior, Virginia, LB
1998 Dorian Boose, Washington St., DE (2)
1999 Randy Thomas, Mississippi St., G (2)
2000 Shaun Ellis, Tennessee, DE
John Abraham, South Carolina, LB
Chad Pennington, Marshall, QB
Anthony Becht, West Virginia, TE
2001 Santana Moss, Miami, WR
2002 Bryan Thomas, Ala.-Birmingham, DE
2003 Dewayne Robertson, Kentucky, DT
2004 Jonathan Vilma, Miami, LB
2005 Mike Nugent, Ohio State, K (2)
2006 D'Brickashaw Ferguson, Virginia, T
Nick Mangold, Ohio State, C
2007 Darrelle Revis, Pittsburgh, DB
2008 Vernon Gholston, Ohio State, LB
Dustin Keller, Purdue, TE
2009 Mark Sanchez, So. California, QB

OAKLAND RAIDERS

Year Player, College, Position

1960 Dale Hackbart, Wisconsin, CB
1961 Joe Rutgens, Illinois, DT
1962 Roman Gabriel, North Carolina St., QB
1963 George Wilson, Alabama, RB (6)
1964 Tony Lorick, Arizona State, RB
1965 Harry Schuh, Memphis State, T
1966 Rodger Bird, Kentucky, S
1967 Gene Upshaw, Texas A&I, G
1968 Eldridge Dickey, Tennessee St., QB
1969 Art Thoms, Syracuse, DT
1970 Raymond Chester, Morgan St., TE
1971 Jack Tatum, Ohio State, S
1972 Mike Siani, Villanova, WR
1973 Ray Guy, Southern Mississippi, P
1974 Henry Lawrence, Florida A&M, T
1975 Neal Colzie, Ohio State, DB
1976 Charles Philyaw, Texas Southern, DT (2)
1977 Mike Davis, Colorado, DB (2)
1978 Dave Browning, Washington, DE (2)
1979 Willie Jones, Florida State, DE (2)
1980 Marc Wilson, Brigham Young, QB
1981 Ted Watts, Texas Tech, DB
Curt Marsh, Washington, T
1982 Marcus Allen, So. California, RB
1983 Don Mosebar, So. California, T
1984 Sean Jones, Northeastern, DE (2)
1985 Jessie Hester, Florida State, WR
1986 Bob Buczkowski, Pittsburgh, DE
1987 John Clay, Missouri, T
1988 Tim Brown, Notre Dame, WR
Terry McDaniel, Tennessee, DB
Scott Davis, Illinois, DE
1989 Jeff Francis, Tennessee, QB (6)
1990 Anthony Smith, Arizona, DE
1991 Todd Marinovich, So. California, QB
1992 Chester McGlockton, Clemson, DE
1993 Patrick Bates, Texas A&M, DB
1994 Rob Fredrickson, Michigan St., LB
1995 Napoleon Kaufman, Washington, RB
1996 Rickey Dudley, Ohio State, TE
1997 Darrell Russell, Southern California, DT
1998 Charles Woodson, Michigan, DB
Mo Collins, Florida, T
1999 Matt Stinchcomb, Georgia, T
2000 Sebastian Janikowski, Florida St., K
2001 Derrick Gibson, Florida State, DB
2002 Phillip Buchanon, Miami, DB
Napoleon Harris, Northwestern, LB
2003 Nnamdi Asomugha, California, DB
Tyler Brayton, Colorado, DE
2004 Robert Gallery, Iowa, T
2005 Fabian Washington, Nebraska, DB
2006 Michael Huff, Texas, DB
2007 JaMarcus Russell, Louisiana State, QB
2008 Darren McFadden, Arkansas, RB
2009 Darrius Heyward-Bey, Maryland, WR

PHILADELPHIA EAGLES

Year Player, College, Position

1936 Jay Berwanger, Chicago, B
1937 Sam Francis, Nebraska, B
1938 Jim McDonald, Ohio State, B
1939 Davey O'Brien, Texas Christian, B
1940 George McAfee, Duke, B
1941 Art Jones, Richmond, B (2)
1942 Pete Kmetovic, Stanford, B
1943 Joe Muha, Virginia Military, B
1944 Steve Van Buren, Louisiana St., B
1945 John Yonaker, Notre Dame, E
1946 Leo Riggs, Southern California, B
1947 Neill Armstrong, Oklahoma A&M, E
1948 Clyde (Smackover) Scott, Arkansas, B
1949 Chuck Bednarik, Pennsylvania, C
Frank Tripucka, Notre Dame, B
1950 Harry (Bud) Grant, Minnesota, E
1951 Ebert Van Buren, Louisiana St., B
Chet Mutryn, Xavier, B
1952 Johnny Bright, Drake, B
1953 Al Conway, Army, B (2)
1954 Neil Worden, Notre Dame, B
1955 Dick Bielski, Maryland, B
1956 Bob Pellegrini, Maryland, C
1957 Clarence Peaks, Michigan State, B
1958 Walt Kowalczyk, Michigan State, B
1959 J.D. Smith, Rice, T (2)
1960 Ron Burton, Northwestern, RB
1961 Art Baker, Syracuse, RB
1962 Pete Case, Georgia, G (2)
1963 Ed Budde, Michigan State, G
1964 Bob Brown, Nebraska, T
1965 Ray Rissmiller, Georgia, T (2)
1966 Randy Beisler, Indiana, DE
1967 Harry Jones, Arkansas, RB
1968 Tim Rossovich, So. California, DE
1969 Leroy Keyes, Purdue, RB
1970 Steve Zabel, Oklahoma, TE
1971 Richard Harris, Grambling, DE
1972 John Reaves, Florida, QB
1973 Jerry Sisemore, Texas, T
Charle Young, So. California, TE
1974 Mitch Sutton, Kansas, DT (3)
1975 Bill Capraun, Miami, T (7)
1976 Mike Smith, Florida, DE (4)
1977 Skip Sharp, Kansas, DB (5)
1978 Reggie Wilkes, Georgia Tech, LB (3)
1979 Jerry Robinson, UCLA, LB
1980 Roynell Young, Alcorn State, DB
1981 Leonard Mitchell, Houston, DE
1982 Mike Quick, North Carolina St., WR
1983 Michael Haddix, Mississippi St., RB
1984 Kenny Jackson, Penn State, WR
1985 Kevin Allen, Indiana, T
1986 Keith Byars, Ohio State, RB
1987 Jerome Brown, Miami, DT
1988 Keith Jackson, Oklahoma, TE
1989 Jessie Small, Eastern Kentucky, LB (2)
1990 Ben Smith, Georgia, DB
1991 Antone Davis, Tennessee, T
1992 Siran Stacy, Alabama, RB (2)
1993 Lester Holmes, Jackson State, T
Leonard Renfro, Colorado, DT
1994 Bernard Williams, Georgia, T
1995 Mike Mamula, Boston College, DE
1996 Jermane Mayberry, Texas A&M-Kingsville, T
1997 Jon Harris, Virginia, DE
1998 Tra Thomas, Florida State, T
1999 Donovan McNabb, Syracuse, QB
2000 Corey Simon, Florida State, DT
2001 Freddie Mitchell, UCLA, WR
2002 Lito Sheppard, Florida, DB
2003 Jerome McDougle, Miami, DE
2004 Shawn Andrews, Arkansas, T
2005 Mike Patterson, So. California, DT
2006 Brodrick Bunkley, Florida State, DT
2007 Kevin Kolb, Houston, QB (2)
2008 Trevor Laws, Notre Dame, DT (2)
2009 Jeremy Maclin, Missouri, WR

PITTSBURGH STEELERS

Year Player, College, Position

1936 Bill Shakespeare, Notre Dame, B
1937 Mike Basrak, Duquesne, C
1938 Byron (Whizzer) White, Colorado, B
1939 Bill Patterson, Baylor, B (3)
1940 Kay Eakin, Arkansas, B
1941 Chet Gladchuk, Boston College, C (2)
1942 Bill Dudley, Virginia, B
1943 Bill Daley, Minnesota, B
1944 Johnny Podesto, St. Mary's, Calif., B
1945 Paul Duhart, Florida, B
1946 Felix (Doc) Blanchard, Army, B
1947 Hub Bechtol, Texas, E
1948 Dan Edwards, Georgia, E
1949 Bobby Gage, Clemson, B
1950 Lynn Chandnois, Michigan St., B
1951 Butch Avinger, Alabama, B
1952 Ed Modzelewski, Maryland, B
1953 Ted Marchibroda, St. Bonaventure, B
1954 Johnny Lattner, Notre Dame, B
1955 Frank Varrichione, Notre Dame, T
1956 Gary Glick, Colorado A&M, B
Art Davis, Mississippi State, B
1957 Len Dawson, Purdue, B
1958 Larry Krutko, West Virginia, B (2)
1959 Tom Barnett, Purdue, B (8)
1960 Jack Spikes, Texas Christian, RB
1961 Myron Pottios, Notre Dame, LB (2)
1962 Bob Ferguson, Ohio State, RB
1963 Frank Atkinson, Stanford, T (8)
1964 Paul Martha, Pittsburgh, S
1965 Roy Jefferson, Utah, WR (2)
1966 Dick Leftridge, West Virginia, RB
1967 Don Shy, San Diego State, RB (2)
1968 Mike Taylor, Southern California, T
1969 Joe Greene, North Texas State, DT
1970 Terry Bradshaw, Louisiana Tech, QB
1971 Frank Lewis, Grambling, WR
1972 Franco Harris, Penn State, RB
1973 J.T. Thomas, Florida State, DB
1974 Lynn Swann, So. California, WR
1975 Dave Brown, Michigan, DB

1976 Bennie Cunningham, Clemson, TE
1977 Robin Cole, New Mexico, LB
1978 Ron Johnson, Eastern Michigan, DB
1979 Greg Hawthorne, Baylor, RB
1980 Mark Malone, Arizona State, QB
1981 Keith Gary, Oklahoma, DE
1982 Walter Abercrombie, Baylor, RB
1983 Gabriel Rivera, Texas Tech, DT
1984 Louis Lipps, So. Mississippi, WR
1985 Darryl Sims, Wisconsin, DE
1986 John Rienstra, Temple, G
1987 Rod Woodson, Purdue, DB
1988 Aaron Jones, Eastern Kentucky, DE
1989 Tim Worley, Georgia, RB
Tom Ricketts, Pittsburgh, T
1990 Eric Green, Liberty, TE
1991 Huey Richardson, Florida, DE
1992 Leon Searcy, Miami, T
1993 Deon Figures, Colorado, DB
1994 Charles Johnson, Colorado, WR
1995 Mark Bruener, Washington, TE
1996 Jamain Stephens, North Carolina A&T, T
1997 Chad Scott, Maryland, DB
1998 Alan Faneca, Louisiana State, G
1999 Troy Edwards, Louisiana Tech, WR
2000 Plaxico Burress, Michigan St., WR
2001 Casey Hampton, Texas, DT
2002 Kendall Simmons, Auburn, G
2003 Troy Polamalu, Southern California, DB
2004 Ben Roethlisberger, Miami (OH), QB
2005 Heath Miller, Virginia, TE
2006 Santonio Holmes, Ohio State, WR
2007 Lawrence Timmons, Florida State, LB
2008 Rashard Mendenhall, Illinois, RB
2009 Evander Hood, Missouri, DE

ST. LOUIS RAMS

Year Player, College, Position
1937 Johnny Drake, Purdue, B
1938 Corbett Davis, Indiana, B
1939 Parker Hall, Mississippi, B
1940 Ollie Cordill, Rice, B
1941 Rudy Mucha, Washington, C
1942 Jack Wilson, Baylor, B
1943 Mike Holovak, Boston College, B
1944 Tony Butkovich, Illinois, B
1945 Elroy (Crazylegs) Hirsch, Wisconsin, B
1946 Emil Sitko, Notre Dame, B
1947 Herman Wedemeyer, St. Mary's, Calif., B
1948 Tom Keane, West Virginia, B (2)
1949 Bobby Thomason, Virginia Military, B
1950 Ralph Pasquariello, Villanova, B
Stan West, Oklahoma, G
1951 Bud McFadin, Texas, G
1952 Bill Wade, Vanderbilt, QB
Bob Carey, Michigan State, E
1953 Donn Moomaw, UCLA, C
Ed Barker, Washington State, E
1954 Ed Beatty, Cincinnati, C
1955 Larry Morris, Georgia Tech, C
1956 Joe Marconi, West Virginia, B
Charles Horton, Vanderbilt, B
1957 Jon Arnett, Southern California, B
Del Shofner, Baylor, E
1958 Lou Michaels, Kentucky, T
Jim Phillips, Auburn, E
1959 Dick Bass, Pacific, B
Paul Dickson, Baylor, T
1960 Billy Cannon, Louisiana State, RB
1961 Marlin McKeever, So. California, E-LB
1962 Roman Gabriel, North Carolina St., QB
Merlin Olsen, Utah State, DT
1963 Terry Baker, Oregon State, QB
Rufus Guthrie, Georgia Tech, G
1964 Bill Munson, Utah State, QB
1965 Clancy Williams, Washington St., CB
1966 Tom Mack, Michigan, G
1967 Willie Ellison, Texas Southern, RB (2)
1968 Gary Beban, UCLA, QB (2)
1969 Larry Smith, Florida, RB
Jim Seymour, Notre Dame, WR
Bob Klein, Southern California, TE
1970 Jack Reynolds, Tennessee, LB
1971 Isiah Robertson, Southern, LB
Jack Youngblood, Florida, DE
1972 Jim Bertelsen, Texas, RB (2)
1973 Cullen Bryant, Colorado, DB (2)
1974 John Cappelletti, Penn State, RB
1975 Mike Fanning, Notre Dame, DT
Dennis Harrah, Miami, T
Doug France, Ohio State, T
1976 Kevin McLain, Colorado State, LB
1977 Bob Brudzinski, Ohio State, LB
1978 Elvis Peacock, Oklahoma, RB
1979 George Andrews, Nebraska, LB
Kent Hill, Georgia Tech, T
1980 Johnnie Johnson, Texas, DB
1981 Mel Owens, Michigan, LB
1982 Barry Redden, Richmond, RB
1983 Eric Dickerson, So. Methodist, RB
1984 Hal Stephens, East Carolina, DE (5)
1985 Jerry Gray, Texas, DB
1986 Mike Schad, Queen's Univ., Canada, T
1987 Donald Evans, Winston-Salem, DE (2)
1988 Gaston Green, UCLA, RB
Aaron Cox, Arizona State, WR
1989 Bill Hawkins, Miami, DE
Cleveland Gary, Miami, RB
1990 Bern Brostek, Washington, C
1991 Todd Lyght, Notre Dame, DB
1992 Sean Gilbert, Pittsburgh, DE
1993 Jerome Bettis, Notre Dame, RB
1994 Wayne Gandy, Auburn, T
1995 Kevin Carter, Florida, DE
1996 Lawrence Phillips, Nebraska, RB
Eddie Kennison, Louisiana St., WR
1997 Orlando Pace, Ohio State, T
1998 Grant Wistrom, Nebraska, DE
1999 Torry Holt, North Carolina St., WR
2000 Trung Canidate, Arizona, RB
2001 Damione Lewis, Miami, DT
Adam Archuleta, Arizona State, DB
Ryan Pickett, Ohio State, DT
2002 Robert Thomas, UCLA, LB
2003 Jimmy Kennedy, Penn State, DT
2004 Steven Jackson, Oregon State, RB
2005 Alex Barron, Florida State, T
2006 Tye Hill, Clemson, DB
2007 Adam Carriker, Nebraska, DE
2008 Chris Long, Virginia, DE
2009 Jason Smith, Baylor, T

SAN DIEGO CHARGERS

Year Player, College, Position
1960 Monty Stickles, Notre Dame, E
1961 Earl Faison, Indiana, DE
1962 Bob Ferguson, Ohio State, RB
1963 Walt Sweeney, Syracuse, G
1964 Ted Davis, Georgia Tech, LB
1965 Steve DeLong, Tennessee, DE
1966 Don Davis, Cal St.-Los Angeles, DT
1967 Ron Billingsley, Wyoming, DE
1968 Russ Washington, Missouri, DT
Jimmy Hill, Texas A&I, DB
1969 Marty Domres, Columbia, QB
Bob Babich, Miami, Ohio, LB
1970 Walker Gillette, Richmond, WR
1971 Leon Burns, Long Beach State, RB
1972 Pete Lazetich, Stanford, DE (2)
1973 Johnny Rodgers, Nebraska, WR
1974 Bo Matthews, Colorado, RB
Don Goode, Kansas, LB
1975 Gary Johnson, Grambling, DT
Mike Williams, Louisiana State, DB
1976 Joe Washington, Oklahoma, RB
1977 Bob Rush, Memphis State, C
1978 John Jefferson, Arizona State, WR
1979 Kellen Winslow, Missouri, TE
1980 Ed Luther, San Jose State, QB (4)
1981 James Brooks, Auburn, RB
1982 Hollis Hall, Clemson, DB (7)
1983 Billy Ray Smith, Arkansas, LB
Gary Anderson, Arkansas, WR
Gill Byrd, San Jose State, DB
1984 Mossy Cade, Texas, DB
1985 Jim Lachey, Ohio State, G
1986 Leslie O'Neal, Oklahoma State, DE
James FitzPatrick, So. California, T
1987 Rod Bernstine, Texas A&M, TE
1988 Anthony Miller, Tennessee, WR
1989 Burt Grossman, Pittsburgh, DE
1990 Junior Seau, So. California, LB
1991 Stanley Richard, Texas, DB
1992 Chris Mims, Tennessee, DE
1993 Darrien Gordon, Stanford, DB
1994 Isaac Davis, Arkansas, G (2)
1995 Terrance Shaw, Stephen F. Austin, DB (2)
1996 Bryan Still, Virginia Tech, WR (2)
1997 Freddie Jones, North Carolina, TE (2)
1998 Ryan Leaf, Washington State, QB
1999 Jermaine Fazande, Oklahoma, RB (2)
2000 Rogers Beckett, Marshall, DB (2)
2001 LaDainian Tomlinson, TCU, RB
2002 Quentin Jammer, Texas, DB
2003 Sammy Davis, Texas A&M, DB
2004 Eli Manning, Mississippi, QB
2005 Shawne Merriman, Maryland, LB
Luis Castillo, Northwestern, DT
2006 Antonio Cromartie, Florida State, DB
2007 Craig Davis, Louisiana State, WR
2008 Antoine Cason, Arizona, DB
2009 Larry English, Northern Illinois, LB

SAN FRANCISCO 49ERS

Year Player, College, Position
1950 Leo Nomellini, Minnesota, T
1951 Y.A. Tittle, Louisiana State, B
1952 Hugh McElhenny, Washington, B
1953 Harry Babcock, Georgia, E
Tom Stolhandske, Texas, E
1954 Bernie Faloney, Maryland, B
1955 Dickie Moegle, Rice, B
1956 Earl Morrall, Michigan State, B
1957 John Brodie, Stanford, B
1958 Jim Pace, Michigan, B
Charlie Krueger, Texas A&M, T
1959 Dave Baker, Oklahoma, B
Dan James, Ohio State, C
1960 Monty Stickles, Notre Dame, E

1961 Jimmy Johnson, UCLA, CB
Bernie Casey, Bowling Green, WR
Bill Kilmer, UCLA, QB
1962 Lance Alworth, Arkansas, WR
1963 Kermit Alexander, UCLA, CB
1964 Dave Parks, Texas Tech, WR
1965 Ken Willard, North Carolina, RB
George Donnelly, Illinois, DB
1966 Stan Hindman, Mississippi, DE
1967 Steve Spurrier, Florida, QB
Cas Banaszek, Northwestern, T
1968 Forrest Blue, Auburn, C
1969 Ted Kwalick, Penn State, TE
Gene Washington, Stanford, WR
1970 Cedrick Hardman, North Texas St., DE
Bruce Taylor, Boston U., DB
1971 Tim Anderson, Ohio State, DB
1972 Terry Beasley, Auburn, WR
1973 Mike Holmes, Texas Southern, DB
1974 Wilbur Jackson, Alabama, RB
Bill Sandifer, UCLA, DT
1975 Jimmy Webb, Mississippi St., DT
1976 Randy Cross, UCLA, C (2)
1977 Elmo Boyd, Eastern Kentucky, WR (3)
1978 Ken MacAfee, Notre Dame, TE
Dan Bunz, Cal St.-Long Beach, LB
1979 James Owens, UCLA, WR (2)
1980 Earl Cooper, Rice, RB
Jim Stuckey, Clemson, DT
1981 Ronnie Lott, So. California, DB
1982 Bubba Paris, Michigan, T (2)
1983 Roger Craig, Nebraska, RB (2)
1984 Todd Shell, Brigham Young, LB
1985 Jerry Rice, Mississippi Valley St., WR
1986 Larry Roberts, Alabama, DE (2)
1987 Harris Barton, North Carolina, T
Terrence Flagler, Clemson, RB
1988 Danny Stubbs, Miami, DE (2)
1989 Keith DeLong, Tennessee, LB
1990 Dexter Carter, Florida State, RB
1991 Ted Washington, Louisville, DT
1992 Dana Hall, Washington, DB
1993 Dana Stubblefield, Kansas, DT
Todd Kelly, Tennessee, DE
1994 Bryant Young, Notre Dame, DT
William Floyd, Florida State, RB
1995 J.J. Stokes, UCLA, WR
1996 Israel Ifeanyi, So.California, DE (2)
1997 Jim Druckenmiller, Virginia Tech, QB
1998 R.W. McQuarters, Oklahoma St., DB
1999 Reggie McGrew, Florida, DT
2000 Julian Peterson, Michigan St., LB
Ahmed Plummer, Ohio State, DB
2001 Andre Carter, California, DE
2002 Mike Rumph, Miami, DB
2003 Kwame Harris, Stanford, T
2004 Rashaun Woods, Oklahoma St., WR
2005 Alex Smith, Utah, QB
2006 Vernon Davis, Maryland, TE
Manny Lawson, North Carolina St., DE
2007 Patrick Willis, Mississippi, LB
Joe Staley, Central Michigan, T
2008 Kentwan Balmer, North Carolina, DT
2009 Michael Crabtree, Texas Tech, WR

SEATTLE SEAHAWKS

Year Player, College, Position
1976 Steve Niehaus, Notre Dame, DT
1977 Steve August, Tulsa, G
1978 Keith Simpson, Memphis St., DB
1979 Manu Tuiasosopo, UCLA, DT
1980 Jacob Green, Texas A&M, DE
1981 Ken Easley, UCLA, DB
1982 Jeff Bryant, Clemson, DE
1983 Curt Warner, Penn State, RB
1984 Terry Taylor, Southern Illinois, DB
1985 Owen Gill, Iowa, RB (2)
1986 John L. Williams, Florida, RB
1987 Tony Woods, Pittsburgh, LB
1988 Brian Blades, Miami, WR (2)
1989 Andy Heck, Notre Dame, T
1990 Cortez Kennedy, Miami, DT
1991 Dan McGwire, San Diego St., QB
1992 Ray Roberts, Virginia, T
1993 Rick Mirer, Notre Dame, QB
1994 Sam Adams, Texas A&M, DT
1995 Joey Galloway, Ohio State, WR
1996 Pete Kendall, Boston College, T
1997 Shawn Springs, Ohio State, DB
Walter Jones, Florida State, T
1998 Anthony Simmons, Clemson, LB
1999 Lamar King, Saginaw Valley St., DE
2000 Shaun Alexander, Alabama, RB
Chris McIntosh, Wisconsin, T
2001 Koren Robinson, North Carolina St., WR
Steve Hutchinson, Michigan, G
2002 Jerramy Stevens, Washington, TE
2003 Marcus Trufant, Washington State, DB
2004 Marcus Tubbs, Texas, DT
2005 Chris Spencer, Mississippi, C
2006 Kelly Jennings, Miami, DB
2007 Josh Wilson, Maryland, DB (2)
2008 Lawrence Jackson, So. California, DE
2009 Aaron Curry, Wake Forest, LB

TAMPA BAY BUCCANEERS

Year Player, College, Position
1976 Lee Roy Selmon, Oklahoma, DT
1977 Ricky Bell, Southern California, RB
1978 Doug Williams, Grambling, QB
1979 Greg Roberts, Oklahoma, G (2)
1980 Ray Snell, Wisconsin, G
1981 Hugh Green, Pittsburgh, LB
1982 Sean Farrell, Penn State, G
1983 Randy Grimes, Baylor, C (2)
1984 Keith Browner, So. California, LB (2)
1985 Ron Holmes, Washington, DE
1986 Bo Jackson, Auburn, RB
Roderick Jones, So. Methodist, DB
1987 Vinny Testaverde, Miami, QB
1988 Paul Gruber, Wisconsin, T
1989 Broderick Thomas, Nebraska, LB
1990 Keith McCants, Alabama, LB
1991 Charles McRae, Tennessee, T
1992 Courtney Hawkins, Michigan St., WR (2)
1993 Eric Curry, Alabama, DE
1994 Trent Dilfer, Fresno State, QB
1995 Warren Sapp, Miami, DT
Derrick Brooks, Florida State, LB
1996 Regan Upshaw, California, DE
Marcus Jones, North Carolina, DT
1997 Warrick Dunn, Florida State, RB
Reidel Anthony, Florida, WR
1998 Jacquez Green, Florida, WR (2)
1999 Anthony McFarland, Louisiana St., DT
2000 Cosey Coleman, Tennessee, G (2)
2001 Kenyatta Walker, Florida, T
2002 Marquise Walker, Michigan, WR (3)
2003 Dewayne White, Louisville, DE (2)
2004 Michael Clayton, Louisiana St., WR
2005 Carnell Williams, Auburn, RB
2006 Davin Joseph, Oklahoma, G
2007 Gaines Adams, Clemson, DE
2008 Aqib Talib, Kansas, DB
2009 Josh Freeman, Kansas State, QB

TENNESSEE TITANS

Year Player, College, Position
1960 Billy Cannon, Louisiana State, RB
1961 Mike Ditka, Pittsburgh, E
1962 Ray Jacobs, Howard Payne, DT
1963 Danny Brabham, Arkansas, LB
1964 Scott Appleton, Texas, DT
1965 Lawrence Elkins, Baylor, WR
1966 Tommy Nobis, Texas, LB
1967 George Webster, Michigan St., LB
Tom Regner, Notre Dame, G
1968 Mac Haik, Mississippi, WR (2)
1969 Ron Pritchard, Arizona State, LB
1970 Doug Wilkerson, N. Carolina Central, G
1971 Dan Pastorini, Santa Clara, QB
1972 Greg Sampson, Stanford, DE
1973 John Matuszak, Tampa, DE
George Amundson, Iowa State, RB
1974 Steve Manstedt, Nebraska, LB (4)
1975 Robert Brazile, Jackson State, LB
Don Hardeman, Texas A&I, RB
1976 Mike Barber, Louisiana Tech, TE (2)
1977 Morris Towns, Missouri, T
1978 Earl Campbell, Texas, RB
1979 Mike Stensrud, Iowa State, DE (2)
1980 Angelo Fields, Michigan St., T (2)
1981 Michael Holston, Morgan St., WR (3)
1982 Mike Munchak, Penn State, G
1983 Bruce Matthews, So. California, T
1984 Dean Steinkuhler, Nebraska, T
1985 Ray Childress, Texas A&M, DE
Richard Johnson, Wisconsin, DB
1986 Jim Everett, Purdue, QB
1987 Alonzo Highsmith, Miami, RB
Haywood Jeffires, North Carolina St., WR
1988 Lorenzo White, Michigan State, RB
1989 David Williams, Florida, T
1990 Lamar Lathon, Houston, LB
1991 Mike Dumas, Indiana, DB (2)
1992 Eddie Robinson, Alabama St., LB (2)
1993 Brad Hopkins, Illinois, T
1994 Henry Ford, Arkansas, DE
1995 Steve McNair, Alcorn State, QB
1996 Eddie George, Ohio State, RB
1997 Kenny Holmes, Miami, DE
1998 Kevin Dyson, Utah, WR
1999 Jevon Kearse, Florida, DE
2000 Keith Bulluck, Syracuse, LB
2001 Andre Dyson, Utah, DB (2)
2002 Albert Haynesworth, Tennessee, DT
2003 Andre Woolfolk, Oklahoma, DB
2004 Ben Troupe, Florida, TE (2)
2005 Adam Jones, West Virginia, DB
2006 Vince Young, Texas, QB
2007 Michael Griffin, Texas, DB
2008 Chris Johnson, East Carolina, RB
2009 Kenny Britt, Rutgers, WR

WASHINGTON REDSKINS

Year Player, College, Position
1936 Riley Smith, Alabama, B
1937 Sammy Baugh, Texas Christian, B
1938 Andy Farkas, Detroit, B
1939 I.B. Hale, Texas Christian, T

1940 Ed Boell, New York U., B
1941 Forest Evashevski, Michigan, B
1942 Orban (Spec) Sanders, Texas, B
1943 Jack Jenkins, Missouri, B
1944 Mike Micka, Colgate, B
1945 Jim Hardy, Southern California, B
1946 Cal Rossi, UCLA, B*
1947 Cal Rossi, UCLA, B
1948 Harry Gilmer, Alabama, B
Lowell Tew, Alabama, B
1949 Rob Goode, Texas A&M, B
1950 George Thomas, Oklahoma, B
1951 Leon Heath, Oklahoma, B
1952 Larry Isbell, Baylor, B
1953 Jack Scarbath, Maryland, B
1954 Steve Meilinger, Kentucky, E
1955 Ralph Guglielmi, Notre Dame, B
1956 Ed Vereb, Maryland, B
1957 Don Bosseler, Miami, B
1958 Mike Sommer, George Washington, B (2)
1959 Don Allard, Boston College, B
1960 Richie Lucas, Penn State, QB
1961 Norman Snead, Wake Forest, QB
Joe Rutgens, Illinois, DT
1962 Ernie Davis, Syracuse, RB
1963 Pat Richter, Wisconsin, TE
1964 Charley Taylor, Arizona St., RB-WR
1965 Bob Breitenstein, Tulsa, T (2)
1966 Charlie Gogolak, Princeton, K
1967 Ray McDonald, Idaho, RB
1968 Jim Smith, Oregon, DB
1969 Eugene Epps, Texas-El Paso, DB (2)
1970 Bill Bundige, Colorado, DT (2)
1971 Cotton Speyrer, Texas, WR (2)
1972 Moses Denson, Maryland St., RB (8)
1973 Charles Cantrell, Lamar, G (5)
1974 Jon Keyworth, Colorado, TE (6)
1975 Mike Thomas, Nevada-Las Vegas, RB (6)
1976 Mike Hughes, Baylor, G (5)
1977 Duncan McColl, Stanford, DE (4)
1978 Tony Green, Florida, RB (6)
1979 Don Warren, San Diego St., TE (4)
1980 Art Monk, Syracuse, WR
1981 Mark May, Pittsburgh, T
1982 Vernon Dean, San Diego St., DB (2)
1983 Darrell Green, Texas A&I, DB
1984 Bob Slater, Oklahoma, DT (2)
1985 Tory Nixon, San Diego St., DB (2)
1986 Markus Koch, Boise State, DE (2)
1987 Brian Davis, Nebraska, DB (2)
1988 Chip Lohmiller, Minnesota, K (2)
1989 Tracy Rocker, Auburn, DT (3)
1990 Andre Collins, Penn State, LB (2)
1991 Bobby Wilson, Michigan State, DT
1992 Desmond Howard, Michigan, WR
1993 Tom Carter, Notre Dame, DB
1994 Heath Shuler, Tennessee, QB
1995 Michael Westbrook, Colorado, WR
1996 Andre Johnson, Penn State, T
1997 Kenard Lang, Miami, DE
1998 Stephen Alexander, Oklahoma, TE (2)
1999 Champ Bailey, Georgia, DB
2000 LaVar Arrington, Penn State, LB
Chris Samuels, Alabama, T
2001 Rod Gardner, Clemson, WR
2002 Patrick Ramsey, Tulane, QB
2003 Taylor Jacobs, Florida, WR (2)
2004 Sean Taylor, Miami, DB
2005 Carlos Rogers, Auburn, DB
Jason Campbell, Auburn, QB
2006 Rocky McIntosh, Miami, LB (2)
2007 LaRon Landry, Louisiana State, DB
2008 Devin Thomas, Michigan State, WR (2)
2009 Brian Orakpo, Texas, DE

Choice lost because of ineligibility

2008/POSTSEASON OVERTIME GAMES

PRESEASON
Aug. 9, 2008 Carolina 23, Indianapolis 20, at Carolina
Aug. 16, 2008 Seattle 29, Chicago 26, at Seattle

** indicates Monday-night game*
 # indicates Thursday/Saturday/Sunday-night game
+ indicates Thanksgiving Day game

REGULAR SEASON

Sept. 14, 2008—San Francisco 33, Seattle 30, at Seattle; 49ers win toss. Touchback. Drive begins at 49ers 20. Nedney kicks 40-yard field goal at 5:40.

Sept. 21, 2008—New York Giants 26, Cincinnati 23, at New York; Giants win toss. Touchback. Drive begins on Giants 20. Drive ends on Giants 44. Feagles punts 41 yards. Chatman returns punt 10 yards. Drive begins on Bengals 25. Drive ends on Bengals 27. Larson punts 46 yards. Hixon returns punt 7 yards. Drive begins at Giants 34. Carney kicks 22-yard field goal at 7:21.

Sept. 21, 2008—Tampa Bay 27, Chicago 24, at Chicago; Buccaneers win toss. Clayton returns kickoff 23 yards. Drive begins on Buccaneers 23. Drive ends on Bears 49. Bidwell punts 35 yards. Fair catch. Drive begins on Bears 14. Drive ends on Bears 47. Maynard punts 46 yards out of bounds. Drive begins on Buccaneers 7. Bryant kicks 21-yard field goal at 11:39.

Sept. 28, 2008—Jacksonville 30, Houston 27, at Jacksonville; Jaguars win toss. Witherspoon returns kickoff 29 yards. Drive begins on Jaguars 30. Scobee kicks 37-yard field goal at 4:35.

* **Sept. 29, 2008—Pittsburgh 23, Baltimore 20,** at Pittsburgh; Ravens win the toss. Figurs returns kickoff 51 yards. Penalty (offensive holding) on play. Drive begins on Ravens 15. Drive ends on Ravens 12. Koch punts 49 yards. Holmes returns punt 4 yards. Drive begins on Steelers 43. Reed kicks 46-yard field goal 7:05.

Oct. 12, 2008—Arizona 30, Dallas 24, at Arizona; Cowboys win toss. Austin returns kickoff 25 yards. Drive begins on Cowboys 22. Drive ends on Cowboys 15. McBriar has punt blocked by Morey. Recovered at Cowboys 3 and returned for touchdown by Beisel at 1:00. Penalty on Carpenter for ineligible man downfield is declined.

Oct. 19, 2008—Oakland 16, New York Jets 13, at Oakland; Jets win toss. L. Washington returns kickoff 23 yards. Drive begins on Jets 22. Drive ends on Jets 41. Hodges punts 39 yards. Higgins returns punt 0 yards. Drive begins on Raiders 20. Drive ends on Raiders 24. Lechler punts 55 yards. L. Washington returns punt -1 yard. Penalty on Carroll for illegal block above the waist. Penalty accepted. Drive begins on Jets 10. Drive ends on Jets 16. Hodges punts 50 yards. Higgins returns punt 11 yards. Drive begins on Raiders 45. Drive ends on Raiders 46. Lechler punts 36 yards. Downed. Drive begins on Jets 18. Drive ends on Jets 38. Hodges punts 43 yards. Fair catch. Drive begins on Raiders 19. Janikowski kicks 57-yard field goal at 13:30.

Nov. 2, 2008—Tampa Bay 30, Kansas City 27, at Kansas City; Buccaneers win toss. C. Smith returns kickoff 22 yards. Drive begins on Buccaneers 26. Bryant kicks 34-yard field goal at 5:36.

Nov. 2, 2008—Tennessee 19, Green Bay 16, at Tennessee; Titans win toss. Carr returns kickoff 23 yards. Drive begins on Titans 22. Bironas kicks 41-yard field goal at 6:24.

Nov. 13, 2008—New York Jets 34, New England 31, at New England. Jets win toss. Touchback. Drive begins on Jets 20. Feely kicks 34-yard field goal at 8:50.

Nov. 16, 2008—Cincinnati 13, Philadelphia 13, at Cincinnati; Eagles win toss. Demps returns kickoff 20 yards. Drive begins on Eagles 23. Drive ends on Eagles 42. Rocca punts 37 yards. Houshmandzadeh returns punt 22 yards. Drive begins on Bengals 43. Drive ends on Eagles 47. Larson punts 38 yards. D. Jackson returns punt 3 yards. Drive begins on Eagles 12. Drive ends on Eagles 21. Rocca punts 34 yards out of bounds. Drive begins on Bengals 45. Drive ends on Eagles 47. Larson punts 35 yards. D. Jackson returns punt 1 yard. Drive begins on Eagles 13. Drive ends on Eagles 22. Rocca punts 37 yards. Downed. Drive begins on Bengals 41. Graham misses 47-yard field goal. Drive begins on Eagles 37, and on the next play McNabb's long pass falls incomplete shy of the end zone as time expires.

Dec. 11, 2008—Chicago 27, New Orleans 24, at Chicago; Bears win toss. Manning returns kickoff 20 yards. Drive begins on Bears 30. Gould kicks 35-yard field goal at 3:46.

Dec. 14, 2008—Atlanta 13, Tampa Bay 10, at Atlanta; Buccaneers win toss. C. Smith returns kickoff 21 yards. Drive begins on Buccaneers 21. Drive ends on Buccaneers 24. Bidwell punts 47 yards. Fair catch. Drive begins on Falcons 29. Elam kicks 34-yard field goal at 11:56.

Dec. 21, 2008—New York Giants 34, Carolina 28, at New York; Giants win toss. Touchback. Drive begins on Giants 20. Drive ends on Giants 26. Feagles punts 48 yards. M. Jones returns punt 13 yards. Drive begins on Panthers 39. Drive ends on Panthers 46. Baker punts 35 yards. McQuarters muffs punt and recovers at Giants 13. Drive begins on Giants 13. Jacobs runs for 2-yard touchdown at 6:03.

* **Dec. 22, 2008—Chicago 20, Green Bay 17,** at Chicago; Bears win toss. Manning returns kickoff 24 yards. Drive begins on Bears 33. Gould kicks 38-yard field goal at 4:42.

POSTSEASON

Dec. 28, 1958—Baltimore 23, New York Giants 17, at New York in NFL Championship Game; Giants win toss. Maynard returns kickoff to Giants' 20. Chandler punts and Taseff returns one yard to Colts' 20. Ameche scores on 1-yard run at 8:15.

Dec. 23, 1962—Dallas Texans 20, Houston Oilers 17, at Houston in AFL Championship Game; Texans win toss and kick off. Jancik returns kickoff to Oilers' 33. Norton punts and Jackson makes fair catch on Texans' 22. Wilson punts and Jancik makes fair catch on Oilers' 45. Robinson intercepts Blanda's pass and returns 13 yards to Oilers' 47. Wilson's punt rolls dead at Oilers' 12. Hull intercepts Blanda's pass and returns 23 yards to midfield. Brooker kicks 25-yard field goal at 17:54.

Dec. 26, 1965—Green Bay 13, Baltimore 10, at Green Bay in NFL Divisional Playoff Game; Packers win toss. Moore returns kickoff to Packers' 22. Chandler punts and Haymond returns nine yards to Colts' 41. Gilburg punts and Wood makes fair catch at Packers' 21. Chandler punts and Haymond returns one yard to Colts' 41. Michaels misses 47-yard field goal. Chandler kicks 25-yard field goal at 13:39.

Dec. 25, 1971—Miami 27, Kansas City 24, at Kansas City in AFC Divisional Playoff Game; Chiefs win toss. Podolak, after a lateral from Buchanan, returns kickoff to Chiefs' 46. Stenerud's 42-yard field goal is blocked. Seiple punts and Podolak makes fair catch at Chiefs' 17. Wilson punts and Scott returns 18 yards to Dolphins' 39. Yepremian misses 62-yard field goal. Scott intercepts Dawson's pass and returns 13 yards to Dolphins' 46. Seiple punts and Podolak loses one yard to Chiefs' 15. Wilson punts and Scott makes fair catch on Dolphins' 30. Yepremian kicks 37-yard field goal at 22:40.

Dec. 24, 1977—Oakland 37, Baltimore 31, at Baltimore in AFC Divisional Playoff Game; Colts win toss. Raiders start on own 42 following a punt late in the first overtime. Oakland works way into field-goal range on Stabler's 19-yard pass to Branch at Colts' 26. Four plays later, on the second play of the second overtime, Stabler hits Casper with a 10-yard touchdown pass at 15:43.

Jan. 2, 1982—San Diego 41, Miami 38, at Miami in AFC Divisional Playoff Game; Chargers win toss. San Diego drives from its 13 to Miami 8. On second-and-goal, Benirschke misses 27-yard field goal attempt wide left at 9:15. Miami has the ball twice and San Diego twice more before the Dolphins get their third possession. Miami drives from the San Diego 46 to Chargers' 17 and on fourth-and-two, von Schamann's 34-yard field goal attempt is blocked by San Diego's Winslow after 11:27. Fouts then completes four of five passes, including a 39-yarder to Joiner that puts the ball on Dolphins' 10. On first down, Benirschke kicks a 29-yard field goal at 13:52.

Jan. 3, 1987—Cleveland 23, New York Jets 20, at Cleveland in AFC Divisional Playoff Game; Jets win toss. Jets' punt downed at Browns' 26. Moseley's 23-yard field goal attempt is wide right. Teams trade punts. Jets' second punt downed at Browns' 31. First overtime period expires eight plays later with Browns in possession at Jets' 42. Moseley kicks 27-yard field goal four plays into second overtime at 17:02.

Jan. 11, 1987—Denver 23, Cleveland 20, at Cleveland in AFC Championship Game; Browns win toss. Broncos hold Browns on four downs. Browns' punt returned four yards to Denver's 25. Elway completes 22- and 28-yard passes to set up Karlis's 33-yard field goal nine plays into drive at 5:38.

Jan. 3, 1988—Houston 23, Seattle 20, at Houston in AFC Wild Card Game; Seahawks win toss. Rodriguez punts to K.

Johnson who returns one yard to Houston 15. Zendejas kicks 32-yard field goal 12 plays later at 8:05.

Dec. 31, 1989—Pittsburgh 26, Houston 23, at Houston in AFC Wild Card Playoff Game; Steelers win toss. Steelers punt to Oilers. Oilers' fumble recovered by Woodson and returned three yards. Four plays and 13 yards later, Anderson kicks a 50-yard field goal at 3:26.

Jan. 7, 1990—Los Angeles Rams 19, New York Giants 13, at New York in NFC Divisional Game; Rams win toss. Everett completes two passes to move ball to Giants' 48. White called for pass interference; ball spotted on Giants' 25. Everett hits Anderson with a 30-yard touchdown pass at 1:06.

Jan. 3, 1993—Buffalo 41, Houston 38, at Buffalo in AFC Wild Card Game; Oilers win toss. Oilers begin at 20. After 2 plays, Moon's pass is intercepted by Odomes who returns ball 2 yards to Houston 35. After 2 plays, Christie kicks 32-yard field goal at 3:06.

Jan. 8, 1994—Kansas City 27, Pittsburgh 24, at Kansas City in AFC Wild Card Game; Chiefs win toss. Hughes returns kickoff 20 yards to Kansas City 25. After 3 plays, Barker punts 48 yards to Pittsburgh 18 where Woodson returns 8 yards to the 26. After 6 plays, Royals punts 30 yards to Kansas City 20. Kansas City drives to Pittsburgh 14 where Lowery kicks 32-yard field goal at 11:03.

Jan. 17, 1999—Atlanta 30, Minnesota 27, at Minnesota in NFC Championship Game; Vikings win toss. Palmer returns kickoff 30 yards to Minnesota 29. After four plays, Berger punts 51 yards to Atlanta 7 where Dwight returns 8 yards to Atlanta 15. Falcons drive to Atlanta 36. Stryzinski punts 37 yards to Vikings' 27. Palmer calls fair catch. Vikings drive to Minnesota 39. Berger punts 52 yards to Atlanta 9. Downed by Vikings. Atlanta drives to Minnesota 21 where Andersen kicks 38-yard field goal at 11:52.

Dec. 30, 2000—Miami 23, Indianapolis 17, at Miami in AFC Wild Card Game; Dolphins win toss. Williams returns kickoff 18 yards to Miami 20. Offensive holding penalty on Freeman, 10 yards, ball spotted on Miami 10. Dolphins drive to Miami 29 where Turk punts 53 yards to Indianapolis 18. Colts drive to Miami 31 where Vanderjagt misses 49-yard field-goal attempt wide right. Dolphins drive to Indianapolis 17 where Smith rushes for a 17-yard touchdown at 11:16.

Jan. 19, 2002—New England 16, Oakland 13, at New England in AFC Divisional Playoff Game; Patriots win toss. Pass returns kickoff 24 yards to New England 34. Patriots drive to Oakland 5. Vinatieri kicks 23-yard field goal at 8:29.

Jan. 11, 2003—Tennessee 34, Pittsburgh 31, at Tennessee in AFC Divisional Playoff Game; Tennessee wins toss. Reed kicks 60 yards. Returned by Simon 21 yards to Tennessee 31. Titans drive to Pittsburgh 8. Nedney's 26-yard field goal is good at 2:15.

Jan. 4, 2004—Green Bay 33, Seattle 27, at Green Bay in NFC Wild Card Game; Seahawks win toss. Morris returns kick to Seattle 33. Seahawks drive to Seattle 42. Rouen's 44-yard punt returned by Chatman to Green Bay 26. Packers drive to Green Bay 31. Bidwell punts 35 yards to Seattle 34. Seahawks drive to Seattle 45. Hasselbeck's pass to Bannister intercepted by Packers' Harris and returned 52 yards for touchdown at 4:25.

Jan. 10, 2004—Carolina 29, St. Louis 23, at St. Louis in NFC Divisional Game; Panthers win toss. Smart returns kick to Carolina 32. Panthers drive to St. Louis 27. Kasay's 45-yard field-goal attempt no good. Rams take over at own 35 and drive to Carolina 35. Wilkins' 53-yard field-goal attempt no good. Panthers take over at Carolina 43, drive to Carolina 47. Sauerbrun punts 40 yards to St. Louis 13. Rams drive to Carolina 38. Bulger's pass intercepted by Manning at Carolina 35. Panthers drive to Carolina 31. First overtime ends. On first play of second overtime, Delhomme passes to Smith for 69-yard touchdown at 15:10.

Jan. 11, 2004—Philadelphia 20, Green Bay 17, at Philadelphia in NFC Divisional Game; Eagles win toss. Thrash returns kick to Philadelphia 28. Eagles drive to Philadelphia 24. Johnson punts 49 yards and Packers start at own 32 after holding penalty. Favre's pass intercepted by Dawkins at Philadelphia 31 and returned to Green Bay 34. Eagles drive to Green Bay 13. Akers kicks 31-yard field goal at 4:48.

Jan. 8, 2005—New York Jets 20, San Diego 17, at San Diego in AFC Wild Card Game; Chargers win toss. Dwight returns kick to San Diego 26. Chargers drive to San Diego 35. Scifres punts 39 yards and ball is downed at the New York 26. Jets gain no yards. Gowin punts 41 yards. Parker loses 3 yards on return. San Diego starts on own 30. Chargers drive to New York 22. Kaeding's 40-yard field-goal attempt no good. Jets drive to San Diego 10. Brien kicks 28-yard field goal at 14:55.

Jan. 15, 2005—Pittsburgh 20, New York Jets 17, at Pittsburgh in AFC Divisional Game; Jets win toss. Cotchery returns kick to New York 31. Jets drive to New York 41. Gowin punts 54 yards. Randle El returns 8 yards to Pittsburgh 13. Steelers drive to New York 15. Reed kicks 33-yard field goal at 11:04.

Jan. 14, 2007—Chicago 27, Seattle 24, at Chicago in NFC Divisional Playoff Game; Seahawks win the toss. Burleson returns kickoff 25 yards to Seahawks 30. Plackemeier punts 18 yards. Drive begins at Bears 34. Gould kicks 49-yard field goal at 4:53.

Jan. 20, 2008—New York Giants 23, Green Bay 20, at Green Bay in NFC Championship Game; Packers win toss. K. Robinson returns kick 19 yards to Green Bay 26. Favre pass intercepted by Webster and returned 9 yards to Green Bay 34. Tynes kicks 47-yard field goal at 12:34.

Jan. 3, 2009—San Diego Chargers 23, Indianapolis 17, at San Diego in AFC Wild Card Playoffs; Chargers win toss. Sproles returns kick 31 yards to San Diego 25. Sproles scores on 22-yard touchdown run at 6:12.

NFL POSTSEASON OVERTIME GAMES (BY LENGTH OF GAME)

Dec. 25, 1971	Miami 27, KANSAS CITY 24	82:40
Dec. 23, 1962	Dallas Texans 20, HOUSTON 17	77:54
Jan. 3 1987	CLEVELAND 23, N.Y. Jets 20	77:02
Dec. 24, 1977	Oakland 37, BALTIMORE 31	75:43
Jan. 10, 2004	Carolina 29, ST. LOUIS 23	75:10
Jan. 8, 2005	N.Y. Jets 20, SAN DIEGO 17	74:55
Jan 2, 1982	San Diego 41, MIAMI 38	73:52
Dec. 26, 1965	GREEN BAY 13, Baltimore 10	73:39
Jan 17, 1999	Atlanta 30, MINNESOTA 27	71:52
Dec. 30, 2000	MIAMI 23, Indianapolis 17	71:16
Jan. 15, 2005	PITTSBURGH 20, N.Y. Jets 17	71:04
Jan 8, 1994	KANSAS CITY 27, Pittsburgh 24	71:03
Jan. 19, 2002	NEW ENGLAND 16, Oakland 13	68:29
Dec. 28, 1958	Baltimore 23, N.Y. GIANTS 17	68:15
Jan. 3, 1988	HOUSTON 23, Seattle 20	68:05
Jan. 3, 2009	SAN DIEGO 23, Indianapolis 17	66:12
Jan. 11, 1987	Denver 23, CLEVELAND 20	65:38
Jan. 14, 2007	CHICAGO 27, Seattle 24	64:53
Jan. 11, 2004	PHILADELPHIA 20, Green Bay 17	64:48
Jan. 4, 2004	GREEN BAY 33, Seattle 27	64:25
Dec. 31, 1989	Pittsburgh 26, HOUSTON 23	63:26
Jan. 3, 1993	BUFFALO 41, Houston 38	63:06
Jan. 20, 2008	N.Y. Giants 23, GREEN BAY 20	62:26
Jan. 11, 2003	TENNESSEE 34, Pittsburgh 31	62:15
Jan. 7, 1990	L.A. Rams 19, N.Y. GIANTS 13	61:06

Home team in CAPS

There have been 25 overtime postseason games dating back to 1958. In 21 cases, both teams have had at least one possession. Last time: 1/23/09, SAN DIEGO 23, Indianapolis 17.

OVERTIME GAMES

OVERTIME WON-LOST RECORDS, 1974-2008 (REGULAR SEASON)

Team	Win	Loss	Tie	Pct.
AFC				
Baltimore	6	6	1	.500
Buffalo	17	9	0	.654
Cincinnati	14	11	1	.558
Cleveland	16	13	1	.550
Denver	21	15	2	.579
Houston	0	6	0	.000
Indianapolis	12	9	1	.568
Jacksonville	6	3	0	.667
Kansas City	10	15	2	.407
Miami	12	18	1	.403
New England	16	19	0	.457
N.Y. Jets	16	15	2	.515
Oakland	14	17	0	.452
Pittsburgh	17	12	2	.581
San Diego	12	17	0	.414
Tennessee	13	16	0	.448
NFC				
Arizona	18	14	2	.559
Atlanta	12	17	2	.419
Carolina	4	9	0	.308
Chicago	21	15	0	.583
Dallas	13	12	0	.520
Detroit	12	15	1	.446
Green Bay	11	13	4	.464
Minnesota	17	16	2	.514
New Orleans	7	9	0	.438
N.Y. Giants	17	14	2	.545
Philadelphia	11	16	4	.419
St. Louis	12	8	1	.595
San Francisco	18	13	1	.578
Seattle	8	17	0	.320
Tampa Bay	13	15	1	.466
Washington	19	11	1	.629

OVERTIME GAMES BY YEAR (REGULAR SEASON)

2008-15	1999-11	1990-10	1981-10
2007-15	1998-7	1989-11	1980-13
2006-11	1997-17	1988- 9	1979-12
2005-14	1996-14	1987-13	1978-11
2004-12	1995-21	1986-16	1977-6
2003-23	1994-16	1985-10	1976-5
2002-25*	1993-7	1984- 9	1975-9
2001-17	1992-10	1983-19	1974-2
2000-13	1991-15	1982- 4	

**Record*

OVERTIME GAME SUMMARY—1974-2008

There have been 432 overtime games in regular season play since the rule was adopted in 1974 (15 in 2008 season). Breakdown follows:

RESULTS

232(10) times the team which won the toss won the game (53.7%)

183 (4) times the team which lost the toss won the game (42.4%)

17 (1) games ended tied (3.9%). Last time: Nov. 16, 2008, Philadelphia 13 at Cincinnati 13.

POSSESSIONS

302 (8) times both teams had at least one possession (69.9%)

130 (7) times the team which won the toss drove for winning score (95 FG, 35 TD) (30.1%)

Of the 432 overtime games, there were 13 miscellaneous situations in which non-standard possessions took place:

9 (1) times the defense or special teams won without registering an official possession (5 interceptions, 2 blocked punts, 1 fumble recovery, 1 blocked field goal) (2.1%)

1 (0) times the special teams forced a fumble on the opening kickoff and drove for the winning score (0.23%)

1 (0) times the punting team recovered a muffed punt and drove for winning score with team muffing punt having no official possessions (0.23%)

2 (0) times the team that won the toss elected to kick and the team receiving the ball drove for winning score (0.46%)

SCORING

301(12) games were decided by a field goal (69.7%)

112 (2) games were decided by a touchdown (25.9%)

2 (0) games were decided by a safety (0.46%)

17 (1) games ended tied (3.9%). Last time: Nov. 16, 2008, Philadelphia 13 at Cincinnati 13.

COIN TOSS

423(15) times the team which won the toss elected to receive (97.9%)

9 (0) times the team which won the toss elected to kick off (4 wins) (2.1%)

Note: The number in parentheses is the 2008 Season Total.

MOST OVERTIME GAMES, SEASON

5	Green Bay Packers, 1983
4	Denver Broncos, 1985, 2007
	Cleveland Browns, 1989
	Minnesota Vikings, 1994
	Arizona Cardinals, 1995
	Minnesota Vikings, 1995
	Arizona Cardinals, 1997
	San Francisco 49ers, 2001
	Atlanta Falcons, 2002
	San Diego Chargers, 2002
	Carolina Panthers, 2003

LONGEST CONSECUTIVE GAME STREAKS WITHOUT OVERTIME (Current)

91 Buffalo Bills (Last OT Game, 10/5/03 vs. Cincinnati Bengals)

(Record: 110, St. Louis/Phoenix Cardinals, 12/7/86-12/19/93)

SHORTEST OVERTIME GAMES

0:14	New York Jets 37, BUFFALO 31; 9/8/02
0:16	CHICAGO 37, San Francisco 31; 10/28/01
0:16	Green Bay 19, DENVER 13; 10/29/07
0:17	NEW ORLEANS 20, Seattle 17; 11/16/97
0:21	Chicago 23, DETROIT 17; 11/27/80
0:30	Baltimore 29, NEW ENGLAND 23; 9/4/83
0:34	San Diego 23, WASHINGTON 17; 11/27/05
0:55	New York Giants 16, PHILADELPHIA 10; 9/29/85

LONGEST OVERTIME GAMES (ALL POSTSEASON GAMES)

22:40	Miami 27, KANSAS CITY 24; 12/25/71
17:54	Dallas Texans 20, HOUSTON 17; 12/23/62
17:02	CLEVELAND 23, New York Jets 20; 1/3/87
15:43	Oakland 37, BALTIMORE 31; 12/24/77
15:10	Carolina 29, ST. LOUIS 23; 1/10/04

OVERTIME SCORING SUMMARY

301 were decided by a field goal
51 were decided by a touchdown pass
31 were decided by a touchdown run
17 were decided by an interception (Atlanta 40, New Orleans 34, 9/2/79; Atlanta 47, Green Bay 41, 11/27/83; New York Giants 16, Philadelphia 10, 9/29/85; Indianapolis 23, Cleveland 17, 12/10/89; Cleveland 30, San Diego 24, 10/20/91; Kansas City 23, Oakland 17, 9/17/95; New York Giants 27, Arizona 21, 10/8/95; Washington 36, Detroit 30, 10/22/95; Arizona 20, Seattle 14, 10/29/95; Cincinnati 34, Detroit 28, 9/13/98; New York Giants 23, Philadelphia 17, 10/31/99; Chicago 37, San Francisco 31, 10/28/01; Chicago 27, Cleveland 21, 11/4/01; New Orleans 26, Tampa Bay 20, 9/8/02; Atlanta 20, Carolina 14, 12/7/03; Jacksonville 23, Pittsburgh 17, 10/16/05; Chicago 19, Detroit 13, 10/30/05)
3 were decided by a fumble recovery (Baltimore 29, New England 23, 9/4/83; Denver 36, Seattle 30, 12/19/99; San Francisco 37, Arizona 31, 11/24/07)
2 were decided on a fake field goal/touchdown pass (Minnesota 22, Chicago 16, 10/16/77; Cleveland 23, Minnesota 17, 12/17/89)
2 were decided by a kickoff return (Chicago 23, Detroit 17, 11/27/80; New York Jets 37, Buffalo 31, 9/8/02)
2 were decided by a safety (Minnesota 23, Los Angeles Rams 21, 11/5/89; Chicago 19, Tennessee 17, 11/14/04)
1 was decided by a punt return (Kansas City 29, San Diego 23, 10/9/95)
1 was decided on a fake field goal/touchdown run (Los Angeles Rams 27, Minnesota 21, 12/2/79)
1 was decided on a blocked field goal (Denver 30, San Diego 24, 11/17/85)
1 was decided on a blocked field goal/recovery by kicker (Green Bay 12, Chicago 6, 9/7/80)
1 was decided on a blocked field goal/recovery by kicking team (Philadelphia 23, New York Giants 17, 11/20/88)
1 was decided by a blocked punt (Arizona 30, Dallas 24, 10/12/08)
16 ended tied

OVERTIME RECORDS

Longest Touchdown Pass

99 Yards — Ron Jaworski to Mike Quick, Philadelphia 23, Atlanta 17 (11/10/85)
82 Yards — Tom Brady to Troy Brown, New England 19, Miami 13 (10/19/03); Brett Favre to Greg Jennings, Green Bay 19, Denver 13 (10/29/07)
76 Yards — Troy Aikman to Raghib Ismail, Dallas 41, Washington 35 (9/12/99)

Longest Touchdown Run

96 Yards — Garrison Hearst, San Francisco 36, New York Jets 30 (9/6/98)
60 Yards — Herschel Walker, Dallas 23, New England 17 (11/15/87)
46 Yards — Michael Vick, Atlanta 30, Minnesota 24 (12/1/02)

Longest Field Goal

57 Yards — Sebastian Janikowski, Oakland 16, New York Jets 13 (10/19/08)
53 Yards — Chris Jacke, Green Bay 23, San Francisco 20 (10/4/96)
52 Yards — Mike Cofer, Indianapolis 27, New York Jets 24 (9/10/95)

Longest Touchdown Plays

99 Yards — (Pass) Ron Jaworski to Mike Quick, Philadelphia 23, Atlanta 17 (11/10/85)
96 Yards — (Run) Garrison Hearst, San Francisco 36, New York Jets 30 (9/6/98)
96 Yards — (Kickoff return) Chad Morton, New York Jets 37, Buffalo 31 (9/8/02)
95 Yards — (Kickoff return) Dave Williams, Chicago 23, Detroit 17 (11/27/80)
86 Yards — (Punt return) Tamarick Vanover, Kansas City 29, San Diego 23 (10/9/95)

ASSOCIATED PRESS NFL MOST OUTSTANDING/VALUABLE PLAYERS

THE FOLLOWING AWARDS WERE NAMED BY ASSOCIATED PRESS IN BALLOTING BY A NATIONWIDE PANEL OF MEDIA.

NFL MOST OUTSTANDING PLAYER AWARD

YEAR	PLAYER	POS.	TEAM	ACCOMPLISHMENTS
1957	Jim Brown	RB	Cleveland Browns	Rushed for league-leading 942 yards and added 9 touchdowns as a rookie.
1958	Jim Brown	RB	Cleveland Browns	Rushed for NFL-record 1,527 yards and added 17 touchdowns. Led Browns to 9-3 record.
1959	Charley Conerly	QB	New York Giants	Passed for 14 touchdowns and only 4 interceptions. Led offense to division-leading 284 points.
1960	Norm Van Brocklin	QB	Philadelphia Eagles	Guided Eagles to first division title since 1949. Passed for 2,471 yards and 24 touchdowns.

NFL MOST VALUABLE PLAYER AWARD

YEAR	PLAYER	POS.	TEAM	ACCOMPLISHMENTS
1961	Paul Hornung	RB	Green Bay Packers	Led league in scoring for second straight season with 146 points (10 TD, 15 FG, 41 PAT).
1962	Jim Taylor	RB	Green Bay Packers	League rushing champion with 1,474 yards. Scored all-time record 19 touchdowns.
1963	Y.A. Tittle	QB	New York Giants	Set all-time season record with 36 touchdown passes. Guided league's top offense (5,024 yards).
1964	Johnny Unitas	QB	Baltimore Colts	Guided Colts to NFL's best record (12-2) and league's top offensive attack (4,779 yards).
1965	Jim Brown	RB	Cleveland Browns	Leader of NFL's top rushing attack. Led league with 1,544 yards, added 21 total touchdowns.
1966	Bart Starr	QB	Green Bay Packers	Passed for 14 touchdowns and only 3 interceptions. Led Packers to league-best 12-2 record.
1967	Johnny Unitas	QB	Baltimore Colts	Passed for 3,428 yards and 20 touchdowns. Led Colts to 11-1-2 record.
1968	Earl Morrall	QB	Baltimore Colts	Guided Colts to NFL-best 13-1 record. Led league with 26 touchdown passes.
1969	Roman Gabriel	QB	Los Angeles Rams	Led NFL with 24 touchdown passes. Guided Rams to 11-3 record.
1970	John Brodie	QB	San Francisco 49ers	Took 49ers to first division title. Threw NFL-best 24 touchdown passes.
1971	Alan Page	DT	Minnesota Vikings	Led defense that allowed NFL-low 139 points. Vikings won fourth straight NFC Central title.
1972	Larry Brown	RB	Washington Redskins	Led conference with 1,216 rushing yards. Redskins had NFC-best 11-3 record.
1973	O.J. Simpson	RB	Buffalo Bills	Rushed for all-time record 2,003 yards, including three 200-yard performances.
1974	Ken Stabler	QB	Oakland Raiders	Led league with 26 touchdown passes and only 12 interceptions. Raiders had NFL-best 12-2 record.
1975	Fran Tarkenton	QB	Minnesota Vikings	Tied for league-best 12-2 record. Led NFC with 91.7 passer rating.
1976	Bert Jones	QB	Baltimore Colts	Threw 24 touchdowns and only 9 interceptions for 102.5 passer rating.
1977	Walter Payton	RB	Chicago Bears	Rushed for league-leading 1,852 yards and 16 total touchdowns.
1978	Terry Bradshaw	QB	Pittsburgh Steelers	Led Steelers to league-leading 14-2 mark. Set club record with 28 touchdown passes.
1979	Earl Campbell	RB	Houston Oilers	Led league with 1,697 rushing yards and 19 touchdowns.
1980	Brian Sipe	QB	Cleveland Browns	NFL-best 91.4 passer rating. Set Browns' records with 30 touchdown passes and 4,132 yards.
1981	Ken Anderson	QB	Cincinnati Bengals	Led Bengals to first division title since 1973. NFL-high 98.5 passer rating.
1982	Mark Moseley	K	Washington Redskins	Converted 20 of 21 FGs. Set consecutive field-goal record at 23 (including last three in '81).
1983	Joe Theismann	QB	Washington Redskins	Leader of offense that scored NFL record 541 points. Redskins had NFL-best 14-2 record.
1984	Dan Marino	QB	Miami Dolphins	Set NFL records with 5,084 yards and 48 touchdown passes. Led Dolphins to AFC-best 14-2 mark.
1985	Marcus Allen	RB	Los Angeles Raiders	Rushed for league-leading 1,759 yards. Tied for AFC lead with 11 rushing touchdowns.
1986	Lawrence Taylor	LB	New York Giants	Recorded league-high 20.5 sacks, and led Giants' second-ranked defense (297.3).
1987	John Elway	QB	Denver Broncos	In 12 games, passed for 19 touchdowns and 3,198 yards, including four 300-yard games.
1988	Boomer Esiason	QB	Cincinnati Bengals	Led NFL with 97.4 passer rating. Tied for AFC lead with 28 TD passes.
1989	Joe Montana	QB	San Francisco 49ers	Set NFL record with 112.4 passer rating, including 70.2 completion percentage.
1990	Joe Montana	QB	San Francisco 49ers	Led 49ers to league-best 14-2 record. Completed NFC-high 61.7 percent of passes.
1991	Thurman Thomas	RB	Buffalo Bills	Recorded league-high 2,038 yards from scrimmage (1,407 rushing, 631 receiving).
1992	Steve Young	QB	San Francisco 49ers	NFL's top passer with 107.0 rating. Led 49ers to NFL-best 14-2 record.

ASSOCIATED PRESS NFL MOST OUTSTANDING/VALUABLE PLAYERS

Year	Player	Pos.	Team	Achievement
1993	Emmitt Smith	RB	Dallas Cowboys	Led league in rushing (1,486 yards) for third straight year despite missing first two games.
1994	Steve Young	QB	San Francisco 49ers	Compiled NFL all-time best 112.8 passer rating. Completed more than 70 percent of his passes.
1995	Brett Favre	QB	Green Bay Packers	Led league with 38 touchdown passes and NFC with 99.5 passer rating.
1996	Brett Favre	QB	Green Bay Packers	Led Packers to top conference record (13-3). Threw NFL-best 39 touchdown passes.
1997*	Brett Favre	QB	Green Bay Packers	Led league with 35 touchdown passes. Led NFC with 3,867 passing yards.
	Barry Sanders	RB	Detroit Lions	Rushed for all-time second-best 2,053 yards, including record 14 straight 100-yard games.
1998	Terrell Davis	RB	Denver Broncos	Rushed for 2,008 yards and scored league-best 23 total touchdowns.
1999	Kurt Warner	QB	St. Louis Rams	Became the second QB in history to have 40 touchdown passes in a season (41).
2000	Marshall Faulk	RB	St. Louis Rams	Set NFL record with 26 touchdowns and led NFC with 2,189 yards from scrimmage.
2001	Kurt Warner	QB	St. Louis Rams	Led NFL with 4,830 passing yards, 36 touchdowns, 68.7 completion percentage, and 101.4 passer rating.
2002	Rich Gannon	QB	Oakland Raiders	Set single-season records with 10 300-yard passing games and 418 completions, and led NFL with 4,689 passing yards.
2003*	Peyton Manning	QB	Indianapolis Colts	Led NFL with 4,267 passing yards, had AFC-best 29 touchdown passes, and posted 99.0 passer rating.
	Steve McNair	QB	Tennessee Titans	Posted NFL-best 100.4 passer rating, passing for 3,215 yards with 24 touchdowns against 7 interceptions.
2004	Peyton Manning	QB	Indianapolis Colts	Set NFL records with 49 touchdown passes and 121.1 passer rating while passing for 4,557 yards.
2005	Shaun Alexander	RB	Seattle Seahawks	Set NFL record with 28 touchdowns and led league with 1,880 rushing yards.
2006	LaDainian Tomlinson	RB	San Diego Chargers	Set NFL record for touchdowns (31) and points scored (186). Rushed for team-record 1,815 yards.
2007	Tom Brady	QB	New England Patriots	Set NFL record with 50 passing touchdowns. Led New England to first 16-0 regular-season record in league history. interceptions.
2008	Peyton Manning	QB	Indianapolis Colts	Threw for 4,002 yards and 27 touchdowns and 95.0 passer rating. Led Indianapolis to 12-4 record.

Total Associated Press NFL MVPs: 50
Three-time Winner: Brett Favre, Peyton Manning
Two-time Winners: Joe Montana, Johnny Unitas, Kurt Warner, Steve Young
* The award was shared in 1997 and 2003.

ASSOCIATED PRESS MVPs WHO WON SUPER BOWL/ NFL CHAMPIONSHIP IN SAME SEASON: 14

1960	Norm Van Brocklin	Philadelphia Eagles
1961	Paul Hornung	Green Bay Packers
1962	Jim Taylor	Green Bay Packers
1966	Bart Starr	Green Bay Packers
1968	Earl Morrall	Baltimore Colts
1978	Terry Bradshaw	Pittsburgh Steelers
1982	Mark Moseley	Washington Redskins
1986	Lawrence Taylor	New York Giants
1989	Joe Montana	San Francisco 49ers
1993	Emmitt Smith	Dallas Cowboys
1994	Steve Young	San Francisco 49ers
1996	Brett Favre	Green Bay Packers
1998	Terrell Davis	Denver Broncos
1999	Kurt Warner	St. Louis Rams

ASSOCIATED PRESS NFL MVP BY POSITION

Position		Position	
Quarterback:	32	**Kicker:**	1
Running Back:	15	**Linebacker:**	1
Defensive Tackle:	1		

ASSOCIATED PRESS MVPs BY TEAM

7 Indianapolis/Baltimore Colts

6 Green Bay Packers

5 San Francisco 49ers

4 St. Louis/Los Angeles Rams

3 Oakland/Los Angeles Raiders
Washington Redskins

2 Buffalo Bills
Cincinnati Bengals
Cleveland Browns
Denver Broncos
Houston Oilers/Tennessee Titans
Minnesota Vikings
New York Giants

1 Chicago Bears
Dallas Cowboys
Detroit Lions
Miami Dolphins
New England Patriots
Pittsburgh Steelers
San Diego Chargers
Seattle Seahawks

ASSOCIATED PRESS NFL AWARDS

AP OFFENSIVE PLAYER OF THE YEAR

1973	O.J. Simpson	RB	Buffalo Bills
1974	Ken Stabler	QB	Oakland Raiders
1975	Fran Tarkenton	QB	Minnesota Vikings
1976	Bert Jones	QB	Baltimore Colts
1977	Walter Payton	RB	Chicago Bears
1978	Earl Campbell	RB	Houston Oilers
1979	Earl Campbell	RB	Houston Oilers
1980	Earl Campbell	RB	Houston Oilers
1981	Ken Anderson	QB	Cincinnati Bengals
1982	Dan Fouts	QB	San Diego Chargers
1983	Joe Theismann	QB	Washington Redskins
1984	Dan Marino	QB	Miami Dolphins
1985	Marcus Allen	RB	Los Angeles Raiders
1986	Eric Dickerson	RB	Los Angeles Rams
1987	Jerry Rice	WR	San Francisco 49ers
1988	Roger Craig	RB	San Francisco 49ers
1989	Joe Montana	QB	San Francisco 49ers
1990	Warren Moon	QB	Houston Oilers
1991	Thurman Thomas	RB	Buffalo Bills
1992	Steve Young	QB	San Francisco 49ers
1993	Jerry Rice	WR	San Francisco 49ers
1994	Barry Sanders	RB	Detroit Lions
1995	Brett Favre	QB	Green Bay Packers
1996	Terrell Davis	RB	Denver Broncos
1997	Barry Sanders	RB	Detroit Lions
1998	Terrell Davis	RB	Denver Broncos
1999	Marshall Faulk	RB	St. Louis Rams
2000	Marshall Faulk	RB	St. Louis Rams
2001	Marshall Faulk	RB	St. Louis Rams
2002	Priest Holmes	RB	Kansas City Chiefs
2003	Jamal Lewis	RB	Baltimore Ravens
2004	Peyton Manning	QB	Indianapolis Colts
2005	Shaun Alexander	RB	Seattle Seahawks
2006	LaDainian Tomlinson	RB	San Diego Chargers
2007	Tom Brady	QB	New England Patriots
2008	Drew Brees	QB	New Orleans Saints

AP OFFENSIVE ROOKIE OF THE YEAR

1957	Jim Brown	RB	Cleveland Browns
1958	Jimmy Orr	WR	Pittsburgh Steelers
1959	Nick Pietrosante	RB	Detroit Lions
1960	Gail Cogdill	WR	Detroit Lions
1961	Mike Ditka	TE	Chicago Bears
1962	Ron Bull	RB	Chicago Bears
1963	Paul Flatley	WR	Minnesota Vikings
1964	Charley Taylor	WR	Washington Redskins
1965	Gale Sayers	RB	Chicago Bears
1966	Johnny Roland	RB	St. Louis Cardinals
1967	Mel Farr	RB	Detroit Lions
1968	Earl McCullouch	WR	Detroit Lions
1969	Calvin Hill	RB	Dallas Cowboys
1970	Duane Thomas	RB	Dallas Cowboys
1971	John Brockington	RB	Green Bay Packers
1972	Franco Harris	RB	Pittsburgh Steelers
1973	Chuck Foreman	RB	Minnesota Vikings
1974	Don Woods	RB	San Diego Chargers
1975	Mike Thomas	RB	Washington Redskins
1976	Sammy White	WR	Minnesota Vikings
1977	Tony Dorsett	RB	Dallas Cowboys
1978	Earl Campbell	RB	Houston Oilers
1979	Ottis Anderson	RB	St. Louis Cardinals
1980	Billy Sims	RB	Detroit Lions
1981	George Rogers	RB	New Orleans Saints
1982	Marcus Allen	RB	Los Angeles Raiders
1983	Eric Dickerson	RB	Los Angeles Rams
1984	Louis Lipps	WR	Pittsburgh Steelers
1985	Eddie Brown	WR	Cincinnati Bengals
1986	Rueben Mayes	RB	New Orleans Saints
1987	Troy Stradford	RB	Miami Dolphins
1988	John Stephens	RB	New England Patriots
1989	Barry Sanders	RB	Detroit Lions
1990	Emmitt Smith	RB	Dallas Cowboys
1991	Leonard Russell	RB	New England Patriots
1992	Carl Pickens	WR	Cincinnati Bengals
1993	Jerome Bettis	RB	Los Angeles Rams
1994	Marshall Faulk	RB	Indianapolis Colts
1995	Curtis Martin	RB	New England Patriots
1996	Eddie George	RB	Houston Oilers
1997	Warrick Dunn	RB	Tampa Bay Buccaneers
1998	Randy Moss	WR	Minnesota Vikings
1999	Edgerrin James	RB	Indianapolis Colts
2000	Mike Anderson	RB	Denver Broncos
2001	Anthony Thomas	RB	Chicago Bears
2002	Clinton Portis	RB	Denver Broncos
2003	Anquan Boldin	WR	Arizona Cardinals
2004	Ben Roethlisberger	QB	Pittsburgh Steelers
2005	Carnell Williams	RB	Tampa Bay Buccaneers
2006	Vince Young	QB	Tennessee Titans
2007	Adrian Peterson	RB	Minnesota Vikings
2008	Matt Ryan	QB	Atlanta Falcons

AP DEFENSIVE PLAYER OF THE YEAR

1971	Alan Page	DT	Minnesota Vikings
1972	Joe Greene	DT	Pittsburgh Steelers
1973	Dick Anderson	S	Miami Dolphins
1974	Joe Greene	DT	Pittsburgh Steelers
1975	Mel Blount	CB	Pittsburgh Steelers
1976	Jack Lambert	LB	Pittsburgh Steelers
1977	Harvey Martin	DE	Dallas Cowboys
1978	Randy Gradishar	LB	Denver Broncos
1979	Lee Roy Selmon	DE	Tampa Bay Buccaneers
1980	Lester Hayes	CB	Oakland Raiders
1981	Lawrence Taylor	LB	New York Giants
1982	Lawrence Taylor	LB	New York Giants
1983	Doug Betters	DE	Miami Dolphins
1984	Kenny Easley	S	Seattle Seahawks
1985	Mike Singletary	LB	Chicago Bears
1986	Lawrence Taylor	LB	New York Giants
1987	Reggie White	DT	Philadelphia Eagles
1988	Mike Singletary	LB	Chicago Bears
1989	Keith Millard	DT	Minnesota Vikings
1990	Bruce Smith	DE	Buffalo Bills
1991	Pat Swilling	LB	New Orleans Saints
1992	Cortez Kennedy	DT	Seattle Seahawks
1993	Rod Woodson	CB	Pittsburgh Steelers
1994	Deion Sanders	CB	San Francisco 49ers
1995	Bryce Paup	LB	Buffalo Bills
1996	Bruce Smith	DE	Buffalo Bills
1997	Dana Stubblefield	DT	San Francisco 49ers
1998	Reggie White	DE	Green Bay Packers
1999	Warren Sapp	DT	Tampa Bay Buccaneers
2000	Ray Lewis	LB	Baltimore Ravens
2001	Michael Strahan	DE	New York Giants
2002	Derrick Brooks	LB	Tampa Bay Buccaneers
2003	Ray Lewis	LB	Baltimore Ravens
2004	Ed Reed	S	Baltimore Ravens
2005	Brian Urlacher	LB	Chicago Bears
2006	Jason Taylor	DE	Miami Dolphins
2007	Bob Sanders	S	Indianapolis Colts
2008	James Harrison	LB	Pittsburgh Steelers

AP DEFENSIVE ROOKIE OF THE YEAR

1967	Lem Barney	CB	Detroit Lions
1968	Claude Humphrey	DE	Atlanta Falcons
1969	Joe Greene	DT	Pittsburgh Steelers

1970	Bruce Taylor	CB	San Francisco 49ers
1971	Isiah Robertson	LB	Los Angeles Rams
1972	Willie Buchanon	CB	Green Bay Packers
1973	Wally Chambers	DT	Chicago Bears
1974	Jack Lambert	LB	Pittsburgh Steelers
1975	Robert Brazile	LB	Houston Oilers
1976	Mike Haynes	S	New England Patriots
1977	A.J. Duhe	DT	Miami Dolphins
1978	Al Baker	DE	Detroit Lions
1979	Jim Haslett	LB	Buffalo Bills
1980*	Buddy Curry	LB	Atlanta Falcons
	Al Richardson	LB	Atlanta Falcons
1981	Lawrence Taylor	LB	New York Giants
1982	Chip Banks	LB	Cleveland Browns
1983	Vernon Maxwell	LB	Baltimore Colts
1984	Bill Maas	NT	Kansas City Chiefs
1985	Duane Bickett	LB	Indianapolis Colts
1986	John Offerdahl	LB	Miami Dolphins
1987	Shane Conlan	LB	Buffalo Bills
1988	Erik McMillan	S	New York Jets
1989	Derrick Thomas	LB	Kansas City Chiefs
1990	Mark Carrier	S	Chicago Bears
1991	Mike Croel	LB	Denver Broncos
1992	Dale Carter	CB	Kansas City Chiefs
1993	Dana Stubblefield	DT	San Francisco 49ers
1994	Tim Bowens	DT	Miami Dolphins
1995	Hugh Douglas	DE	New York Jets
1996	Simeon Rice	DE	Arizona Cardinals
1997	Peter Boulware	LB	Baltimore Ravens
1998	Charles Woodson	CB	Oakland Raiders
1999	Jevon Kearse	DE	Tennessee Titans
2000	Brian Urlacher	LB	Chicago Bears
2001	Kendrell Bell	LB	Pittsburgh Steelers
2002	Julius Peppers	DE	Carolina Panthers
2003	Terrell Suggs	LB	Baltimore Ravens
2004	Jonathan Vilma	LB	New York Jets
2005	Shawne Merriman	LB	San Diego Chargers
2006	DeMeco Ryans	LB	Houston Texans
2007	Patrick Willis	LB	San Francisco 49ers
2008	Jerod Mayo	LB	New England Patriots

*The award was shared in 1980.

AP COMEBACK PLAYER OF THE YEAR

1998	Doug Flutie	QB	Buffalo Bills
1999	Bryant Young	DT	San Francisco 49ers
2000	Joe Johnson	DE	New Orleans Saints
2001	Garrison Hearst	RB	San Francisco 49ers
2002	Tommy Maddox	QB	Pittsburgh Steelers
2003	Jon Kitna	QB	Cincinnati Bengals
2004	Drew Brees	QB	San Diego Chargers
2005*	Steve Smith	WR	Carolina Panthers
	Tedy Bruschi	LB	New England Patriots
2006	Chad Pennington	QB	New York Jets
2007	Greg Ellis	DE	Dallas Cowboys
2008	Chad Pennington	QB	Miami Dolphins

*The award was shared in 2005.

AP COACH OF THE YEAR

1957	George Wilson	Detroit Lions
1958	Weeb Ewbank	Baltimore Colts
1959	Vince Lombardi	Green Bay Packers
1960	Buck Shaw	Philadelphia Eagles
1961	Allie Sherman	New York Giants
1962	Allie Sherman	New York Giants
1963	George Halas	Chicago Bears
1964	Don Shula	Baltimore Colts
1965	George Halas	Chicago Bears
1966	Tom Landry	Dallas Cowboys
1967*	George Allen	Los Angeles Rams
	Don Shula	Baltimore Colts
1968	Don Shula	Baltimore Colts
1969	Bud Grant	Minnesota Vikings
1970	Paul Brown	Cincinnati Bengals
1971	George Allen	Washington Redskins
1972	Don Shula	Miami Dolphins
1973	Chuck Knox	Los Angeles Rams
1974	Don Coryell	St. Louis Cardinals
1975	Ted Marchibroda	Baltimore Colts
1976	Forrest Gregg	Cleveland Browns
1977	Red Miller	Denver Broncos
1978	Jack Patera	Seattle Seahawks
1979	Jack Pardee	Washington Redskins
1980	Chuck Knox	Buffalo Bills
1981	Bill Walsh	San Francisco 49ers
1982	Joe Gibbs	Washington Redskins
1983	Joe Gibbs	Washington Redskins
1984	Chuck Knox	Seattle Seahawks
1985	Mike Ditka	Chicago Bears
1986	Bill Parcells	New York Giants
1987	Jim Mora	New Orleans Saints
1988	Mike Ditka	Chicago Bears
1989	Lindy Infante	Green Bay Packers
1990	Jimmy Johnson	Dallas Cowboys
1991	Wayne Fontes	Detroit Lions
1992	Bill Cowher	Pittsburgh Steelers
1993	Dan Reeves	New York Giants
1994	Bill Parcells	New England Patriots
1995	Ray Rhodes	Philadelphia Eagles
1996	Dom Capers	Carolina Panthers
1997	Jim Fassel	New York Giants
1998	Dan Reeves	Atlanta Falcons
1999	Dick Vermeil	St. Louis Rams
2000	Jim Haslett	New Orleans Saints
2001	Dick Jauron	Chicago Bears
2002	Andy Reid	Philadelphia Eagles
2003	Bill Belichick	New England Patriots
2004	Marty Schottenheimer	San Diego Chargers
2005	Lovie Smith	Chicago Bears
2006	Sean Payton	New Orleans Saints
2007	Bill Belichick	New England Patriots
2008	Mike Smith	Atlanta Falcons

*The award was shared in 1967.

ATTENDANCE/TV RATINGS

NFL'S 10 HIGHEST SCORING WEEKENDS

Point Total	Date	Weekend
837	November 20-24, 2008	12th
788	December 29-30, 2007	17th
788	December 5-6, 2004	13th
788	September 5, 8-9, 2002	1st
762	November 10-11, 1996	11th
761	October 16-17, 1983	7th
753	December 8-9, 2002	14th
752	November 29, December 2-3, 2007	13th
751	September 23-24, 2007	3rd
748	December 18-20, 2004	15th

TOP 10 TELEVISED SPORTS EVENTS OF ALL-TIME

(Based on A.C. Nielsen Figures)

Program	Date	Network	Share	Rating
Super Bowl XVI	1/24/82	CBS	73%	49.1
Super Bowl XVII	1/30/83	NBC	69%	48.6
Winter Olympics	2/23/94	CBS	64%	48.5
Super Bowl XX	1/26/86	NBC	70%	48.3
Super Bowl XII	1/15/78	CBS	67%	47.2
Super Bowl XIII	1/21/79	NBC	74%	47.1
Super Bowl XVIII	1/22/84	CBS	71%	46.4
Super Bowl XIX	1/20/85	ABC	63%	46.4
Super Bowl XIV	1/20/80	CBS	67%	46.3
Super Bowl XXX	1/28/96	NBC	68%	46.0

TEN MOST WATCHED TV PROGRAMS & ESTIMATED TOTAL NUMBER OF VIEWERS

(Based on A.C. Nielsen Figures)

Program	Date	Network	*Total Viewers
Super Bowl XLIII	Feb. 1, 2009	NBC	151,600,000
Super Bowl XLII	Feb. 3, 2008	FOX	148,300,000
Super Bowl XXXVIII	Feb. 1, 2004	CBS	144,400,000
Super Bowl XL	Feb. 5, 2006	ABC	141,400,000
Super Bowl XLI	Feb. 4, 2007	CBS	139,800,000
Super Bowl XXXVII	Jan. 26, 2003	ABC	138,900,000
Super Bowl XXX	Jan. 28, 1996	NBC	138,488,000
Super Bowl XXVIII	Jan. 30, 1994	NBC	134,800,000
Super Bowl XXXIX	Feb. 6, 2005	FOX	133,700,000
Super Bowl XXXII	Jan. 25, 1998	NBC	133,400,000

**Watched some portion of the broadcast*

NFL'S TOP FIVE PAID ATTENDANCE TOTALS FOR ALL GAMES

Year	Preseason	Regular Season	Postseason	All Games
2007	4,119,278	17,345,205	792,019	22,256,502
2006	4,083,282	17,340,879	775,551	22,199,712
2008	3,995,942	17,055,982	806,840	21,858,764
2005	3,977,388	17,012,453	802,255	21,792,096
2004	3,918,848	17,000,811	788,965	21,708,624

TEN HIGHEST-RATED *NFL MONDAY NIGHT FOOTBALL* GAMES OF ALL-TIME

(Based on A.C. Nielsen Figures)

Game	Date	Share	Rating
Chicago at Miami	12/2/85	46%	29.6
N.Y. Giants at San Francisco	12/3/90	42%	26.9
Dallas at Washington	10/2/78	43%	26.8
Pittsburgh at San Diego	12/22/80	40%	25.3
Philadelphia at Miami	11/30/81	40%	25.3
Pittsburgh at Houston	12/10/79	40%	25.1
Dallas at Miami	12/17/84	40%	25.1
Pittsburgh at Dallas	9/13/82	42%	24.9
Cincinnati at Oakland	12/6/76	40%	24.7
Dallas at Washington	10/8/73	40%	24.6
Minnesota at Atlanta	11/19/73	40%	24.6

NFL'S 10 BIGGEST SINGLE-GAME ATTENDANCE TOTALS

Date	Site	Game	Teams	Attendance
August 15, 1994	Azteca Stadium	American Bowl (Mexico City)	Cowboys vs. Oilers	112,376
August 17, 1998	Azteca Stadium	American Bowl (Mexico City)	Cowboys vs. Patriots	106,424
August 22, 1947	Soldier Field	College All-Star	Bears vs. All-Stars	105,840
August 4, 1997	Estadio Guillermo Canedo	American Bowl (Mexico City)	Broncos vs. Dolphins	104,629
January 20, 1980	Rose Bowl	Super Bowl XIV	Steelers vs. Rams	103,985
January 30, 1983	Rose Bowl	Super Bowl XVII	Redskins vs. Dolphins	103,667
October 2, 2005	Azteca Stadium	Regular Season	49ers at Cardinals	103,467
January 9, 1977	Rose Bowl	Super Bowl XI	Raiders vs. Vikings	103,438
November 10, 1957	L.A. Coliseum	Regular Season	49ers at Rams	102,368
January 25, 1987	Rose Bowl	Super Bowl XXI	Giants vs. Broncos	101,643

NFL'S TOP 10 PAID ATTENDANCE WEEKENDS

Weekend	Games	Attendance
September 8, 11-12, 2005	16	1,115,018
December 6, 9-10, 2007	16	1,113,376
November 20-21, 2005	16	1,112,555
December 27-28, 2003	16	1,106,818
November 19-20, 2006	16	1,106,739
September 23-24, 2007	16	1,103,570
December 24-26, 2005	16	1,102,701
September 7, 10-11, 2006	16	1,102,102
September 9, 12-13, 2004	16	1,101,332
December 7, 10-11, 2006	16	1,099,794

NFL'S TOP 10 TEAM SINGLE-SEASON HOME PAID ATTENDANCE TOTALS

Year	Club	Games	Attendance
2007	Washington Redskins	8	711,471
2008	Washington Redskins	8	710,049
2006	Washington Redskins	8	708,952
2004	Washington Redskins	8	707,920
2005	Washington Redskins	8	707,614
2003	Washington Redskins	8	667,033
2002	Washington Redskins	8	663,536
2001	Washington Redskins	8	661,970
2000	Washington Redskins	8	656,599
1980	Detroit Lions	8	634,204

NFL PAID ATTENDANCE

For detailed 2008 attendance, see page 244.

Year	Regular Season			Average	Postseason	Total
2008	17,055,982	(256 games)		66,625	806,840 (12)	17,862,822
2007	17,345,205	(256 games)		#67,755	792,019 (12)	#18,137,224
2006	17,340,879	(256 games)		67,738	775,551 (12)	18,116,430
2005	17,012,453	(256 games)		66,455	802,255 (12)	17,814,708
2004	17,000,811	(256 games)		66,409	788,965 (12)	17,789,776
2003	16,913,584	(255 games***)		66,328	805,546 (12)	17,719,130
2002	16,833,310	(256 games)		65,755	781,944 (12)	17,615,254
2001	16,166,258	(248 games)		65,187	766,905 (12)	16,933,163
2000	16,387,289	(248 games)		66,078	809,132 (12)	17,196,421
1999	16,206,640	(248 games)		65,349	793,759 (12)	17,000,399
1998	15,364,873	(240 games)		64,020	822,885 (12)	16,187,758
1997	14,967,314	(240 games)		62,364	801,879 (12)	15,769,193
1996	14,612,417	(240 games)		60,885	769,310 (12)	15,381,727
1995	15,043,562	(240 games)		62,682	790,906 (12)	15,834,468
1994	14,030,435	(224 games)		62,636	779,738 (12)	14,810,173
1993	13,966,843	(224 games)		62,352	814,607 (12)	14,781,450
1992	13,828,887	(224 games)		61,736	815,910 (12)	14,644,797
1991	13,841,459	(224 games)		61,792	813,247 (12)	14,654,706
1990	13,959,896	(224 games)		62,321	847,543 (12)	14,807,439
1989	13,625,662	(224 games)		60,829	685,771 (10)	14,311,433
1988	13,539,848	(224 games)		60,446	658,317 (10)	14,198,165
1987	11,406,166	(210 games**)		54,315	656,977 (10)	12,063,143
1986	13,588,551	(224 games)		60,663	734,002 (10)	14,322,553
1985	13,345,047	(224 games)		59,567	710,768 (10)	14,055,815
1984	13,398,112	(224 games)		59,813	665,194 (10)	14,063,306
1983	13,277,222	(224 games)		59,273	675,513 (10)	13,952,735
1982	7,367,438	(126 games*)		58,472	#1,033,153 (16)	8,400,591
1981	13,606,990	(224 games)		60,745	637,763 (10)	14,244,753
1980	13,392,230	(224 games)		59,787	624,430 (10)	14,016,660
1979	13,182,039	(224 games)		58,848	630,326 (10)	13,812,365
1978	12,771,800	(224 games)		57,017	624,388 (10)	13,396,188
1977	11,018,632	(196 games)		56,218	534,925 (8)	11,553,557
1976	11,070,543	(196 games)		56,482	492,884 (8)	11,563,427
1975	10,213,193	(182 games)		56,116	475,919 (8)	10,689,112
1974	10,236,322	(182 games)		56,244	438,664 (8)	10,674,986
1973	10,730,933	(182 games)		58,961	525,433 (8)	11,256,366
1972	10,445,827	(182 games)		57,395	483,345 (8)	10,929,172
1971	10,076,035	(182 games)		55,363	483,891 (8)	10,559,926
1970	9,533,333	(182 games)		52,381	458,493 (8)	9,991,826
1969	6,096,127	(112 games)	NFL	54,430	162,279 (3)	6,258,406
	2,843,373	(70 games)	AFL	40,620	167,088 (3)	3,010,461
1968	5,882,313	(112 games)	NFL	52,521	215,902 (3)	6,098,215
	2,635,004	(70 games)	AFL	37,643	114,438 (2)	2,749,442
1967	5,938,924	(112 games)	NFL	53,026	166,208 (3)	6,105,132
	2,295,697	(63 games)	AFL	36,439	53,330 (1)	2,349,027
1966	5,337,044	(105 games)	NFL	50,829	74,152 (1)	5,411,196
	2,160,369	(63 games)	AFL	34,291	42,080 (1)	2,202,449
1965	4,634,021	(98 games)	NFL	47,286	100,304 (2)	4,734,325
	1,782,384	(56 games)	AFL	31,828	30,361 (1)	1,812,745
1964	4,563,049	(98 games)	NFL	46,562	79,544 (1)	4,642,593
	1,447,875	(56 games)	AFL	25,855	40,242 (1)	1,488,117
1963	4,163,643	(98 games)	NFL	42,486	45,801 (1)	4,209,444
	1,208,697	(56 games)	AFL	21,584	63,171 (2)	1,271,868

PAID ATTENDANCE

Year	Regular Season			Average	Postseason	Total
1962	4,003,421	(98 games)	NFL	40,851	64,892 (1)	4,068,313
	1,147,302	(56 games)	AFL	20,487	37,981 (1)	1,185,283
1961	3,986,159	(98 games)	NFL	40,675	39,029 (1)	4,025,188
	1,002,657	(56 games)	AFL	17,904	29,556 (1)	1,032,213
1960	3,128,296	(78 games)	NFL	40,106	67,325 (1)	3,195,621
	926,156	(56 games)	AFL	16,538	32,183 (1)	958,339
1959	3,140,000	(72 games)		43,617	57,545 (1)	3,197,545
1958	3,006,124	(72 games)		41,752	123,659 (2)	3,129,783
1957	2,836,318	(72 games)		39,393	119,579 (2)	2,955,897
1956	2,551,263	(72 games)		35,434	56,836 (1)	2,608,099
1955	2,521,836	(72 games)		35,026	85,693 (1)	2,607,529
1954	2,190,571	(72 games)		30,425	43,827 (1)	2,234,398
1953	2,164,585	(72 games)		30,064	54,577 (1)	2,219,162
1952	2,052,126	(72 games)		28,502	97,507 (2)	2,149,633
1951	1,913,019	(72 games)		26,570	57,522 (1)	1,970,541
1950	1,977,753	(78 games)		25,356	136,647 (3)	2,114,400
1949	1,391,735	(60 games)		23,196	27,980 (1)	1,419,715
1948	1,525,243	(60 games)		25,421	36,309 (1)	1,561,552
1947	1,837,437	(60 games)		30,624	66,268 (2)	1,903,705
1946	1,732,135	(55 games)		31,493	58,346 (1)	1,790,481
1945	1,270,401	(50 games)		25,408	32,178 (1)	1,302,579
1944	1,019,649	(50 games)		20,393	46,016 (1)	1,065,665
1943	969,128	(40 games)		24,228	71,315 (2)	1,040,443
1942	887,920	(55 games)		16,144	36,006 (1)	923,926
1941	1,108,615	(55 games)		20,157	55,870 (2)	1,164,485
1940	1,063,025	(55 games)		19,328	36,034 (1)	1,099,059
1939	1,071,200	(55 games)		19,476	32,279 (1)	1,103,479
1938	937,197	(55 games)		17,040	48,120 (1)	985,317
1937	963,039	(55 games)		17,510	15,878 (1)	978,917
1936	816,007	(54 games)		15,111	29,545 (1)	845,552
1935	638,178	(53 games)		12,041	15,000 (1)	653,178
1934	492,684	(60 games)		8,211	35,059 (1)	527,743

 # Record

**Players' 57-day strike reduced 224-game schedule to 126 games.*

***Players' 24-day strike reduced 224-game schedule to 210 games.*

****The Week 8 Miami at San Diego game is not included. The game was moved to Arizona due to the San Diego wildfires and tickets were distributed at no charge.*

Records

Compiled by Elias Sports Bureau.

The following records reflect all available official information on the National Football League from its formation in 1920 to date. Also included are all applicable records from the American Football League, 1960-69.

Individuals eligible for Rookie records are players who were in their first season of professional football and had not been on the roster of another professional football team, including teams in other leagues, for any regular-season or postseason games in a previous season. Eligible players, therefore, include those who were under contract to a National Football League club for a previous season but were terminated prior to their club's first regular-season game and not re-signed, or who were placed on Reserve/Injured (or another category of the Reserve List) prior to their club's first regular-season game and were not activated during the rest of the regular season or postseason.

INDIVIDUAL RECORDS

SERVICE

Most Seasons

26 George Blanda, Chi. Bears, 1949, 1950-58; Baltimore, 1950; Houston, 1960-66; Oakland, 1967-1975
25 Morten Andersen, New Orleans, 1982-1994; Atlanta, 1995-2000; N.Y. Giants, 2001; Kansas City, 2002-03; Minnesota, 2004; Atlanta, 2006-07
23 Gary Anderson, Pittsburgh, 1982-1994; Philadelphia, 1995-96; San Francisco, 1997; Minnesota, 1998-2002; Tennessee, 2003-04

Most Seasons, One Club

20 Jackie Slater, L.A. Rams, 1976-1994; St. Louis, 1995
Darrell Green, Washington, 1983-2002
19 Jim Marshall, Minnesota, 1961-1979
Bruce Matthews, Houston, 1983-1996; Tennessee, 1997-2001
18 Jim Hart, St. Louis, 1966-1983
Jeff Van Note, Atlanta, 1969-1986
Pat Leahy, N.Y. Jets, 1974-1991

Most Games Played, Career

382 Morten Andersen, New Orleans, 1982-1994; Atlanta, 1995-2000; N.Y. Giants, 2001; Kansas City, 2002-03; Minnesota, 2004; Atlanta, 2006-07
353 Gary Anderson, Pittsburgh, 1982-1994; Philadelphia, 1995-96; San Francisco, 1997; Minnesota, 1998-2002; Tennessee, 2003-04
340 George Blanda, Chi. Bears, 1949, 1950-58; Baltimore, 1950; Houston, 1960-66; Oakland, 1967-1975

Most Consecutive Games Played, Career

336 Jeff Feagles, New England, 1988-89; Philadelphia, 1990-93; Arizona, 1994-97; Seattle, 1998-2002; N.Y. Giants, 2003-08 (current)
282 Jim Marshall, Cleveland, 1960; Minnesota, 1961-1979
271 Brett Favre, Green Bay, 1992-2007; N.Y. Jets, 2008 (current)

SCORING

Most Seasons Leading League

5 Don Hutson, Green Bay, 1940-44
Gino Cappelletti, Boston, 1961, 1963-66
3 Earl (Dutch) Clark, Portsmouth, 1932; Detroit, 1935-36
Pat Harder, Chi. Cardinals, 1947-49
Paul Hornung, Green Bay, 1959-1961
2 Jack Manders, Chi. Bears, 1934, 1937
Gordy Soltau, San Francisco, 1952-53
Doak Walker, Detroit, 1950, 1955
Gene Mingo, Denver, 1960, 1962
Jim Turner, N.Y. Jets, 1968-69
Fred Cox, Minnesota, 1969-1970
Chester Marcol, Green Bay, 1972, 1974
John Smith, New England, 1979-1980
Marshall Faulk, St. Louis, 2000-01

Most Consecutive Seasons Leading League

5 Don Hutson, Green Bay, 1940-44
4 Gino Cappelletti, Boston, 1963-66
3 Pat Harder, Chi. Cardinals, 1947-49
Paul Hornung, Green Bay, 1959-1961

POINTS

Most Points, Career

2,544 Morten Andersen, New Orleans, 1982-1994; Atlanta, 1995-2000; N.Y. Giants, 2001; Kansas City, 2002-03; Minnesota, 2004; Atlanta, 2006-07 (849-pat, 565-fg)
2,434 Gary Anderson, Pittsburgh, 1982-1994; Philadelphia 1995-96; San Francisco, 1997; Minnesota, 1998-2002; Tennessee, 2003-04 (820-pat, 538-fg)
2,002 George Blanda, Chi. Bears, 1949, 1950-58; Baltimore, 1950; Houston, 1960-66; Oakland, 1967-1975 (9-td, 943-pat, 335-fg)

Most Points, Season

186 LaDainian Tomlinson, San Diego, 2006 (31-td)
176 Paul Hornung, Green Bay, 1960 (15-td, 41-pat, 15-fg)
168 Shaun Alexander, Seattle, 2005 (28-td)

Most Points, No Touchdowns, Season

164 Gary Anderson, Minnesota, 1998 (59-pat, 35-fg)
163 Jeff Wilkins, St. Louis, 2003 (46-pat, 39-fg)
161 Mark Moseley, Washington, 1983 (62-pat, 33-fg)

Most Seasons, 100 or More Points

16 Jason Elam, Denver, 1993-2007; Atlanta, 2008
14 Gary Anderson, Pittsburgh, 1983-85, 1988, 1991-94; Philadelphia 1996; San Francisco, 1997; Minnesota, 1998-2000; Tennessee, 2003
Morten Andersen, New Orleans, 1985-89, 1991-94; Atlanta, 1995, 1997-98; Kansas City, 2002-03
13 Adam Vinatieri, New England, 1996-2005; Indianapolis, 2006-08

Most Points, Rookie, Season

144 Kevin Butler, Chicago, 1985 (51-pat, 31-fg)
141 Mason Crosby, Green Bay, 2007, (48-pat, 31-fg)
132 Gale Sayers, Chicago, 1965 (22-td)

Most Points, Game

40 Ernie Nevers, Chi. Cardinals vs. Chi. Bears, Nov. 28, 1929 (6-td, 4-pat)
36 Dub Jones, Cleveland vs. Chi. Bears, Nov. 25, 1951 (6-td)
Gale Sayers, Chicago vs. San Francisco, Dec. 12, 1965 (6-td)
33 Paul Hornung, Green Bay vs. Baltimore, Oct. 8, 1961 (4-td, 6-pat, 1-fg)

Most Consecutive Games Scoring

360 Morten Andersen, New Orleans, 1983-1994; Atlanta, 1995-2000; N.Y. Giants, 2001; Kansas City, 2002-03; Minnesota, 2004; Atlanta, 2006-07
252 Jason Elam, Denver, 1993-2007; Atlanta, 2008 (current)
186 Jim Breech, Oakland, 1979; Cincinnati, 1980-1992

TOUCHDOWNS

Most Seasons Leading League

8 Don Hutson, Green Bay, 1935-38, 1941-44
3 Jim Brown, Cleveland, 1958-59, 1963
Lance Alworth, San Diego, 1964-66
Emmitt Smith, Dallas, 1992, 1994-95
2 By many players

Most Consecutive Seasons Leading League

4 Don Hutson, Green Bay, 1935-38, 1941-44

3 Lance Alworth, San Diego, 1964-66
2 By many players

Most Touchdowns, Career
208 Jerry Rice, San Francisco, 1985-2000; Oakland, 2001-04; Seattle, 2004 (10-r, 197-p, 1-ret)
175 Emmitt Smith, Dallas, 1990-2002; Arizona, 2003-04 (164-r, 11-p)
145 Marcus Allen, L.A. Raiders, 1982-1992; Kansas City, 1993-97 (123-r, 21-p, 1-ret)

Most Touchdowns, Season
31 LaDainian Tomlinson, San Diego, 2006 (28-r, 3-p)
28 Shaun Alexander, Seattle, 2005 (27-r, 1-p)
27 Priest Holmes, Kansas City, 2003 (27-r)

Most Touchdowns, Rookie, Season
22 Gale Sayers, Chicago, 1965 (14-r, 6-p, 2-ret)
20 Eric Dickerson, L.A. Rams, 1983 (18-r, 2-p)
17 Randy Moss, Minnesota, 1998 (17-p)
Fred Taylor, Jacksonville, 1998 (14-r, 3-p)
Edgerrin James, Indianapolis, 1999 (13-r, 4-p)
Clinton Portis, Denver, 2002 (15-r, 2-p)

Most Touchdowns, Game
6 Ernie Nevers, Chi. Cardinals vs. Chi. Bears, Nov. 28, 1929 (6-r)
Dub Jones, Cleveland vs. Chi. Bears, Nov. 25, 1951 (4-r, 2-p)
Gale Sayers, Chicago vs. San Francisco, Dec. 12, 1965 (4-r, 1-p, 1-ret)
5 Jimmy Conzelman, Rhode Island vs. Evansville, Oct. 15, 1922 (5-r)
Bob Shaw, Chi. Cardinals vs. Baltimore, Oct. 2, 1950 (5-p)
Jim Brown, Cleveland vs. Baltimore, Nov. 1, 1959 (5-r)
Abner Haynes, Dall. Texans vs. Oakland, Nov. 26, 1961 (4-r, 1-p)
Billy Cannon, Houston vs. N.Y. Titans, Dec. 10, 1961 (3-r, 2-p)
Cookie Gilchrist, Buffalo vs. N.Y. Jets, Dec. 8, 1963 (5-r)
Paul Hornung, Green Bay vs. Baltimore, Dec. 12, 1965 (3-r, 2-p)
Kellen Winslow, San Diego vs. Oakland, Nov. 22, 1981 (5-p)
Jerry Rice, San Francisco vs. Atlanta, Oct. 14, 1990 (5-p)
James Stewart, Jacksonville vs. Philadelphia, Oct. 12, 1997 (5-r)
Shaun Alexander, Seattle vs. Minnesota, Sept. 29, 2002 (4-r, 1-p)
Clinton Portis, Denver vs. Kansas City, Dec. 7, 2003 (5-r)
4 By many players. Last time:
DeAngelo Williams, Carolina vs. N.Y. Giants, Dec. 21, 2008 (OT) (4-r)

Most Consecutive Games Scoring Touchdowns
18 Lenny Moore, Baltimore, 1963-65
LaDainian Tomlinson, San Diego, 2004-05
14 O.J. Simpson, Buffalo, 1975
13 John Riggins, Washington, 1982-83
George Rogers, Washington, 1985-86
Jerry Rice, San Francisco, 1986-87

POINTS AFTER TOUCHDOWN

Most Seasons Leading League
8 George Blanda, Chi. Bears, 1956; Houston, 1961-62; Oakland, 1967-69, 1972, 1974
4 Bob Waterfield, Cleveland, 1945; Los Angeles, 1946, 1950, 1952
3 Earl (Dutch) Clark, Portsmouth, 1932; Detroit, 1935-36 Jack Manders, Chi. Bears, 1933-35
Don Hutson, Green Bay, 1941-42, 1945

Most (Kicking) Points After Touchdown Attempted, Career
959 George Blanda, Chi. Bears, 1949, 1950-58; Baltimore, 1950; Houston, 1960-66; Oakland, 1967-1975
859 Morten Andersen, New Orleans, 1982-1994; Atlanta, 1995-2000; N.Y. Giants, 2001; Kansas City, 2002-03; Minnesota, 2004; Atlanta, 2006-07
827 Gary Anderson, Pittsburgh, 1982-1994; Philadelphia 1995-96; San Francisco, 1997; Minnesota, 1998-2002; Tennessee, 2003-04

Most (Kicking) Points After Touchdown Attempted, Season
74 Stephen Gostkowski, New England, 2007
70 Uwe von Schamann, Miami, 1984
65 George Blanda, Houston, 1961

Most (Kicking) Points After Touchdown Attempted, Game
10 Charlie Gogolak, Washington vs. N.Y. Giants, Nov. 27, 1966
9 Pat Harder, Chi. Cardinals vs. N.Y. Giants, Oct. 17, 1948; vs. N.Y. Bulldogs, Nov. 13, 1949
Bob Waterfield, Los Angeles vs. Baltimore, Oct. 22, 1950
Bob Thomas, Chicago vs. Green Bay, Dec. 7, 1980
8 By many players

Most (One-Point) Points After Touchdown, Career
943 George Blanda, Chi. Bears, 1949, 1950-58; Baltimore, 1950; Houston, 1960-66; Oakland, 1967-1975
849 Morten Andersen, New Orleans, 1982-1994; Atlanta, 1995-2000; N.Y. Giants, 2001; Kansas City, 2002-03; Minnesota, 2004, Atlanta, 2006-07
820 Gary Anderson, Pittsburgh, 1982-1994; Philadelphia 1995-96; San Francisco, 1997; Minnesota, 1998-2002; Tennessee, 2003-04

Most (One-Point) Points After Touchdown, Season
74 Stephen Gostkowski, New England, 2007
66 Uwe von Schamann, Miami, 1984
64 George Blanda, Houston, 1961
Jeff Wilkins, St. Louis, 1999

Most (One-Point) Points After Touchdown, Game
9 Pat Harder, Chi. Cardinals vs. N.Y. Giants, Oct. 17, 1948
Bob Waterfield, Los Angeles vs. Baltimore, Oct. 22, 1950
Charlie Gogolak, Washington vs. N.Y. Giants, Nov. 27, 1966
8 By many players

Most Consecutive (Kicking) Points After Touchdown
389 Matt Stover, Baltimore, 1996-2008 (current)
371 Jason Elam, Denver, 1993-2002
Jeff Wilkins, St. Louis, 1999-2007
301 Norm Johnson, Atlanta, 1991-94; Pittsburgh, 1995-98; Philadelphia, 1999

Highest (Kicking) Points After Touchdown Percentage, Career (200 points after touchdown)
100.000 Rian Lindell, Seattle, 2000-02; Buffalo, 2003-08 (282-282)
99.61 Nate Kaeding, San Diego, 2004-08 (253-254)
99.59 Josh Brown, Seattle, 2003-07; St. Louis, 2008 (242-243)

Most (Kicking) Points After Touchdown, No Misses, Season
74 Stephen Gostkowski, New England, 2007
64 Jeff Wilkins, St. Louis, 1999
59 Gary Anderson, Minnesota, 1998

Most (Kicking) Points After Touchdown, No Misses, Game
9 Pat Harder, Chi. Cardinals vs. N.Y. Giants, Oct. 17, 1948
Bob Waterfield, Los Angeles vs. Baltimore, Oct. 22, 1950
8 By many players

Most Two-Point Conversions, Career
Two-point conversions include AFL (1960-69) and NFL (since 1994).
7 Marshall Faulk, Indianapolis, 1994-98; St. Louis, 1999-2005
6 Terance Mathis, Atlanta, 1994-2001; Pittsburgh, 2002
5 Cris Carter, Minnesota, 1994-2001; Miami, 2002
Rob Moore, N.Y. Jets, 1994; Arizona, 1995-99
Willie Jackson, Jacksonville, 1995-97; Cincinnati, 1998-99; New Orleans, 2000-01; Washington, 2002
Keenan McCardell, Cleveland, 1994-95; Jacksonville, 1996-2001; Tampa Bay, 2002-03; San Diego, 2004-06, Washington, 2007
Marvin Harrison, Indianapolis, 1996-2008
Marcus Pollard, Indianapolis, 1995-2004; Detroit, 2005-06; Seattle, 2007; Atlanta, 2008
Todd Heap, Baltimore, 2001-08
Hines Ward, Pittsburgh, 1998-2008
Edgerrin James, Indianapolis, 1999-2005; Arizona, 2006-08

Most Two-Point Conversions, Season
4 Todd Heap, Baltimore, 2003
3 Gino Cappelletti, Boston, 1960
Richie Lucas, Buffalo, 1961
Ronnie Harmon, San Diego, 1994
Haywood Jeffires, Houston, 1994
Tom Tupa, Cleveland, 1994
Terance Mathis, Atlanta, 1995
Lamar Smith, Seattle, 1996
Cris Carter, Minnesota, 1997
Terrell Davis, Denver, 1997
James Stewart, Detroit, 2000
Hines Ward, Pittsburgh, 2002
Brian Finneran, Atlanta, 2005
Reggie Bush, New Orleans, 2007
2 By many players

Most Two-Point Conversions, Game
2 Brett Perriman, Detroit vs. Green Bay, Nov. 6, 1994
Michael Jackson, Baltimore vs. New England, Oct. 6, 1996
Terrell Davis, Denver vs. Atlanta, Sept. 28, 1997
Charles Johnson, Pittsburgh vs. Tennessee, Nov. 1, 1998
Marshall Faulk, St. Louis vs. Atlanta, Oct. 15, 2000
Todd Heap, Baltimore vs. Cincinnati, Oct. 19, 2003
Reggie Bush, New Orleans vs. St. Louis, Nov. 11, 2007
Tarvaris Jackson, Minnesota vs. Denver, Dec. 30, 2007 (OT)

FIELD GOALS

Most Seasons Leading League
5 Lou Groza, Cleveland, 1950, 1952-54, 1957
4 Jack Manders, Chi. Bears, 1933-34, 1936-37
Ward Cuff, N.Y. Giants, 1938-39, 1943; Green Bay, 1947
Mark Moseley, Washington, 1976-77, 1979, 1982
3 Bob Waterfield, Los Angeles, 1947, 1949, 1951
Gino Cappelletti, Boston, 1961, 1963-64
Fred Cox, Minnesota, 1965, 1969-1970
Jan Stenerud, Kansas City, 1967, 1970, 1975

Most Consecutive Seasons Leading League
3 Lou Groza, Cleveland, 1952-54
2 Jack Manders, Chi. Bears, 1933-34
Armand Niccolai, Pittsburgh, 1935-36
Jack Manders, Chi. Bears, 1936-37
Ward Cuff, N.Y. Giants, 1938-39
Clark Hinkle, Green Bay, 1940-41
Cliff Patton, Philadelphia, 1948-49
Gino Cappelletti, Boston, 1963-64
Jim Turner, N.Y. Jets, 1968-69
Fred Cox, Minnesota, 1969-1970
Mark Moseley, Washington, 1976-77
Chip Lohmiller, Washington, 1991-92
Pete Stoyanovich, Miami, 1991-92

Most Field Goals Attempted, Career
709 Morten Andersen, New Orleans, 1982-1994; Atlanta, 1995-2000; N.Y. Giants, 2001; Kansas City, 2002-03; Minnesota, 2004; Atlanta, 2006-07
672 Gary Anderson, Pittsburgh, 1982-1994; Philadelphia 1995-96; San Francisco, 1997; Minnesota, 1998-2002; Tennessee, 2003-04
641 George Blanda, Chi. Bears, 1949, 1950-58; Baltimore, 1950; Houston, 1960-66; Oakland, 1967-1975

Most Field Goals Attempted, Season
49 Bruce Gossett, Los Angeles, 1966
Curt Knight, Washington, 1971
48 Chester Marcol, Green Bay, 1972
47 Jim Turner, N.Y. Jets, 1969
David Ray, Los Angeles, 1973
Mark Moseley, Washington, 1983

Most Field Goals Attempted, Game
9 Jim Bakken, St. Louis vs. Pittsburgh, Sept. 24, 1967
8 Lou Michaels, Pittsburgh vs. St. Louis, Dec. 2, 1962
Garo Yepremian, Detroit vs. Minnesota, Nov. 13, 1966
Jim Turner, N.Y. Jets vs. Buffalo, Nov. 3, 1968
Billy Cundiff, Dallas vs. N.Y. Giants, Sept. 15, 2003 (OT)
Rob Bironas, Tennessee vs. Houston, Oct. 21, 2007
7 By many players

Most Field Goals, Career
565 Morten Andersen, New Orleans, 1982-1994; Atlanta, 1995-2000; N.Y. Giants, 2001; Kansas City, 2002-03; Minnesota, 2004; Atlanta, 2006-07
538 Gary Anderson, Pittsburgh, 1982-1994; Philadelphia, 1995-96; San Francisco, 1997; Minnesota, 1998-2002; Tennessee, 2003-04
462 Matt Stover, Cleveland, 1991-95; Baltimore, 1996-2008

Most Field Goals, Season
40 Neil Rackers, Arizona, 2005
39 Olindo Mare, Miami, 1999
Jeff Wilkins, St. Louis, 2003
37 John Kasay, Carolina, 1996
Mike Vanderjagt, Indianapolis, 2003

Most Field Goals, Rookie, Season
35 Ali Haji-Sheikh, N.Y. Giants, 1983
34 Richie Cunningham, Dallas, 1997
33 Chester Marcol, Green Bay, 1972

Most Field Goals, Game
8 Rob Bironas, Tennessee vs. Houston, Oct. 21, 2007
7 Jim Bakken, St. Louis vs. Pittsburgh, Sept. 24, 1967
Rich Karlis, Minnesota vs. L.A. Rams, Nov. 5, 1989 (OT)
Chris Boniol, Dallas vs. Green Bay, Nov. 18, 1996
Billy Cundiff, Dallas vs. N.Y. Giants, Sept. 15, 2003 (OT)
Shayne Graham, Cincinnati vs. Baltimore, Nov. 11, 2007
6 By many players

Most Field Goals, One Quarter
4 Garo Yepremian, Detroit vs. Minnesota, Nov. 13, 1966 (second quarter)
Curt Knight, Washington vs. N.Y. Giants, Nov. 15, 1970 (second quarter)
Roger Ruzek, Dallas vs. N.Y. Giants, Nov. 2, 1987 (fourth quarter)
Cary Blanchard, Indianapolis vs. Buffalo, Sept. 21 1997 (second quarter)
Sebastian Janikowski, Oakland vs. Chicago, Oct. 5, 2003 (second quarter)

Jeff Wilkins, St. Louis vs. Baltimore, Nov. 9, 2003 (fourth quarter)
Lawrence Tynes, Kansas City vs. New England, Nov. 27, 2005 (second quarter)
Shayne Graham, Cincinnati vs. Baltimore, Nov. 11, 2007 (fourth quarter)
3 By many players

Most Consecutive Games Scoring Field Goals
38 Matt Stover, Baltimore, 1999-2001
31 Fred Cox, Minnesota, 1968-1970
28 Jim Turner, N.Y. Jets, 1970; Denver, 1971-72
Chip Lohmiller, Washington, 1988-1990

Most Consecutive Field Goals
42 Mike Vanderjagt, Indianapolis, 2002-04
40 Gary Anderson, San Francisco, 1997; Minnesota, 1998
36 Matt Stover, Baltimore, 2005-06

Longest Field Goal
63 Tom Dempsey, New Orleans vs. Detroit, Nov. 8, 1970
Jason Elam, Denver vs. Jacksonville, Oct. 25, 1998
62 Matt Bryant, Tampa Bay vs. Philadelphia, Oct. 22, 2006
60 Steve Cox, Cleveland vs. Cincinnati, Oct. 21, 1984
Morten Andersen, New Orleans vs. Chicago, Oct. 27, 1991
Rob Bironas, Tennessee vs. Indianapolis, Dec. 3, 2006

Highest Field Goal Percentage, Career (100 field goals)
86.47 Mike Vanderjagt, Indianapolis, 1998-2005; Dallas, 2006 (230-266)
86.13 Nate Kaeding, San Diego, 2004-08 (118-137)
85.94 Robbie Gould, Chicago, 2005-08 (110-128)

Highest Field Goal Percentage, Season (Qualifiers)
100.00 Tony Zendejas, L.A. Rams, 1991 (17-17)
Gary Anderson, Minnesota, 1998 (35-35)
Jeff Wilkins, St. Louis, 2000 (17-17)
Mike Vanderjagt, Indianapolis, 2003 (37-37)
96.43 Chris Boniol, Dallas, 1995 (28-27)
96.30 Norm Johnson, Atlanta, 1993 (27-26)
Pete Stoyanovich, Kansas City, 1997 (27-26)

Most Field Goals, No Misses, Game
8 Rob Bironas, Tennessee vs. Houston, Oct. 21, 2007
7 Rich Karlis, Minnesota vs. L.A. Rams, Nov. 5, 1989 (OT)
Chris Boniol, Dallas vs. Green Bay, Nov. 18, 1996
Shayne Graham, Cincinnati vs. Baltimore, Nov. 11, 2007
6 By many players

Most Field Goals, 50 or More Yards, Career
41 Jason Hanson, Detroit, 1992-2008
40 Morten Andersen, New Orleans, 1982-1994; Atlanta, 1995-2000; N.Y. Giants, 2001; Kansas City, 2002-03; Minnesota, 2004; Atlanta, 2006-07
38 Jason Elam, Denver, 1993-2007; Atlanta, 2008

Most Field Goals, 50 or More Yards, Season
8 Morten Andersen, Atlanta, 1995
Jason Hanson, Detroit, 2008
6 Dean Biasucci, Indianapolis, 1988
Chris Jacke, Green Bay, 1993
Tony Zendejas, L.A. Rams, 1993
Mike Vanderjagt, Indianapolis, 1998
Neil Rackers, Arizona, 2005
Sebastian Janikowski, Oakland, 2007
Josh Brown, St. Louis, 2008
Ryan Longwell, Minnesota, 2008
5 Fred Steinfort, Denver, 1980
Norm Johnson, Seattle, 1986
Kevin Butler, Chicago, 1993
Jason Elam, Denver, 1995
Cary Blanchard, Indianapolis, 1996
Jason Elam, Denver, 1999
Martín Gramatica, Tampa Bay, 2000, 2002
Paul Edinger, Chicago, 2002
Neil Rackers, Arizona, 2004
Josh Brown, Seattle, 2005
Kris Brown, Houston, 2007
Matt Prater, Denver, 2008

Most Field Goals, 50 or More Yards, Game
3 Morten Andersen, Atlanta vs. New Orleans, Dec. 10, 1995
Neil Rackers, Arizona vs. Seattle, Oct. 24, 2004
Kris Brown, Houston vs. Miami, Oct. 7, 2007
2 By many players. Last time: Jason Hanson, Detroit vs. Houston, Oct. 19, 2008

SAFETIES

Most Safeties, Career
4 Ted Hendricks, Baltimore, 1969-1973; Green Bay, 1974; Oakland, 1975-1981; L.A. Raiders, 1982-83
Doug English, Detroit, 1975-79, 1981-85
3 Bill McPeak, Pittsburgh, 1949-1957
Charlie Krueger, San Francisco, 1959-1973
Ernie Stautner, Pittsburgh, 1950-1963
Jim Katcavage, N.Y. Giants, 1956-1968
Roger Brown, Detroit, 1960-66; Los Angeles, 1967-69
Bruce Maher, Detroit, 1960-67; N.Y. Giants, 1968-69
Ron McDole, St. Louis, 1961; Houston, 1962; Buffalo, 1963-1970; Washington, 1971-78
Alan Page, Minnesota, 1967-1978; Chicago, 1979-1981
Lyle Alzado, Denver, 1971-78; Cleveland, 1979-1981; L.A. Raiders, 1982-85
Rulon Jones, Denver, 1980-88
Steve McMichael, New England, 1980; Chicago, 1981-1993; Green Bay, 1994
Kevin Greene, L.A. Rams, 1985-1992; Pittsburgh, 1993-95; Carolina, 1996, 1998-99; San Francisco, 1997
Burt Grossman, San Diego, 1989-1993; Philadelphia, 1994
Eric Swann, Phoenix, 1991-93; Arizona, 1994-99; Carolina, 2000
Dan Saleaumua, Detroit, 1987-88; Kansas City, 1989-1996; Seattle, 1997-98
Derrick Thomas, Kansas City, 1989-1999
Bryant Young, San Francisco, 1994-2007
2 By many players

Most Safeties, Season
2 Tom Nash, Green Bay, 1932
Roger Brown, Detroit, 1962
Ron McDole, Buffalo, 1964
Alan Page, Minnesota, 1971
Fred Dryer, Los Angeles, 1973
Benny Barnes, Dallas, 1973
James Young, Houston, 1977
Doug English, Detroit, 1983
Don Blackmon, New England, 1985
Tim Harris, Green Bay, 1988
Brian Jordan, Atlanta, 1991
Burt Grossman, San Diego, 1992
Rod Stephens, Seattle, 1993
Bryant Young, San Francisco, 1996
Jared Allen, Minnesota, 2008
Jameel McClain, Baltimore, 2008

Most Safeties, Game
2 Fred Dryer, Los Angeles vs. Green Bay, Oct. 21, 1973

RUSHING

Most Seasons Leading League

8 Jim Brown, Cleveland, 1957-1961, 1963-65
4 Steve Van Buren, Philadelphia, 1945, 1947-49
O.J. Simpson, Buffalo, 1972-73, 1975-76
Eric Dickerson, L.A. Rams, 1983-84, 1986; Indianapolis, 1988
Emmitt Smith, Dallas, 1991-93, 1995
Barry Sanders, Detroit, 1990, 1994, 1996-97
3 Earl Campbell, Houston, 1978-1980

Most Consecutive Seasons Leading League

5 Jim Brown, Cleveland, 1957-1961
3 Steve Van Buren, Philadelphia, 1947-49
Jim Brown, Cleveland, 1963-65
Earl Campbell, Houston, 1978-1980
Emmitt Smith, Dallas, 1991-93
2 Bill Paschal, N.Y. Giants, 1943-44
Joe Perry, San Francisco, 1953-54
Jim Nance, Boston, 1966-67
Leroy Kelly, Cleveland, 1967-68
O.J. Simpson, Buffalo, 1972-73; 1975-76
Eric Dickerson, L.A. Rams, 1983-84
Barry Sanders, Detroit, 1996-97
Edgerrin James, Indianapolis, 1999-2000
LaDainian Tomlinson, San Diego, 2006-07

ATTEMPTS

Most Seasons Leading League

6 Jim Brown, Cleveland, 1958-59, 1961, 1963-65
4 Steve Van Buren, Philadelphia, 1947-1950
Walter Payton, Chicago, 1976-79
3 Cookie Gilchrist, Buffalo, 1963-64; Denver, 1965
Jim Nance, Boston, 1966-67, 1969
O.J. Simpson, Buffalo, 1973-75
Eric Dickerson, L.A. Rams, 1983, 1986; Indianapolis, 1988
Emmitt Smith, Dallas, 1991, 1994-95

Most Consecutive Seasons Leading League

4 Steve Van Buren, Philadelphia, 1947-1950
Walter Payton, Chicago, 1976-79
3 Jim Brown, Cleveland, 1963-65
Cookie Gilchrist, Buffalo, 1963-64; Denver, 1965
O.J. Simpson, Buffalo, 1973-75
2 By many players

Most Attempts, Career

4,409 Emmitt Smith, Dallas, 1990-2002; Arizona, 2003-04
3,838 Walter Payton, Chicago, 1975-1987
3,518 Curtis Martin, New England, 1995-97; N.Y. Jets, 1998-2005

Most Attempts, Season

416 Larry Johnson, Kansas City, 2006
410 Jamal Anderson, Atlanta, 1998
407 James Wilder, Tampa Bay, 1984

Most Attempts, Rookie, Season

390 Eric Dickerson, L.A. Rams, 1983
378 George Rogers, New Orleans, 1981
369 Edgerrin James, Indianapolis, 1999

Most Attempts, Game

45 Jamie Morris, Washington vs. Cincinnati, Dec. 17, 1988 (OT)
43 Butch Woolfolk, N.Y. Giants vs. Philadelphia, Nov. 20, 1983
James Wilder, Tampa Bay vs. Green Bay, Sept. 30, 1984 (OT)
Rudi Johnson, Cincinnati vs. Houston, Nov. 9, 2003
42 James Wilder, Tampa Bay vs. Pittsburgh, Oct. 30, 1983
Terrell Davis, Denver vs. Buffalo, Oct. 26, 1997 (OT)
Ricky Williams, Miami vs. Buffalo, Sept. 21, 2003

YARDS GAINED

Most Yards Gained, Career

18,355 Emmitt Smith, Dallas, 1990-2002; Arizona, 2003-04
16,726 Walter Payton, Chicago, 1975-1987
15,269 Barry Sanders, Detroit, 1989-1998

Most Seasons, 1,000 or More Yards Rushing

11 Emmitt Smith, Dallas, 1991-2001
10 Walter Payton, Chicago, 1976-1981, 1983-86
Barry Sanders, Detroit, 1989-1998
Curtis Martin, New England, 1995-97; N.Y. Jets, 1998-2004
8 Franco Harris, Pittsburgh, 1972, 1974-79, 1983
Tony Dorsett, Dallas, 1977-1981, 1983-85
Thurman Thomas, Buffalo, 1989-1996
Jerome Bettis, L.A. Rams, 1993-94; Pittsburgh, 1996-2001
LaDainian Tomlinson, San Diego, 2001-08

Most Consecutive Seasons, 1,000 or More Yards Rushing

11 Emmitt Smith, Dallas, 1991-2001
10 Barry Sanders, Detroit, 1989-1998
Curtis Martin, New England, 1995-97; N.Y. Jets, 1998-2004
8 Thurman Thomas, Buffalo, 1989-1996
LaDainian Tomlinson, San Diego, 2001-08

Most Yards Gained, Season

2,105 Eric Dickerson, L.A. Rams, 1984
2,066 Jamal Lewis, Baltimore, 2003
2,053 Barry Sanders, Detroit, 1997

Most Yards Gained, Rookie, Season

1,808 Eric Dickerson, L.A. Rams, 1983
1,674 George Rogers, New Orleans, 1981
1,605 Ottis Anderson, St. Louis, 1979

Most Yards Gained, Game

296 Adrian Peterson, Minnesota vs. San Diego, Nov. 4, 2007
295 Jamal Lewis, Baltimore vs. Cleveland, Sept. 14, 2003
278 Corey Dillon, Cincinnati vs. Denver, Oct. 22, 2000

Most Games, 200 or More Yards Rushing, Career

6 O.J. Simpson, Buffalo, 1969-1977; San Francisco, 1978-79
5 Tiki Barber, N.Y. Giants, 1997-2006
4 Jim Brown, Cleveland, 1957-1965
Earl Campbell, Houston, 1978-1984; New Orleans, 1984-85
Barry Sanders, Detroit, 1989-1998
LaDainian Tomlinson, San Diego, 2001-08

Most Games, 200 or More Yards Rushing, Season

4 Earl Campbell, Houston, 1980
3 O.J. Simpson, Buffalo, 1973
Tiki Barber, N.Y. Giants, 2005
2 Jim Brown, Cleveland, 1963
O.J. Simpson, Buffalo, 1976
Walter Payton, Chicago, 1977
Eric Dickerson, L.A. Rams, 1984
Greg Bell, L.A. Rams, 1989
Terrell Davis, Denver, 1997
Barry Sanders, Detroit, 1997
Corey Dillon, Cincinnati, 2000
Marshall Faulk, St. Louis, 2000
LaDainian Tomlinson, San Diego, 2002
Ricky Williams, Miami, 2002
Jamal Lewis, Baltimore, 2003
LaDainian Tomlinson, San Diego, 2003
Larry Johnson, Kansas City, 2005
Willie Parker, Pittsburgh, 2006
Adrian Peterson, Minnesota, 2007
Michael Turner, Atlanta, 2008

Most Consecutive Games, 200 or More Yards Rushing
2 O.J. Simpson, Buffalo, 1973, 1976
Earl Campbell, Houston, 1980
Ricky Williams, Miami, 2002

Most Games, 100 or More Yards Rushing, Career
78 Emmitt Smith, Dallas, 1990-2002; Arizona, 2003-04
77 Walter Payton, Chicago, 1975-1987
76 Barry Sanders, Detroit, 1989-1998

Most Games, 100 or More Yards Rushing, Season
14 Barry Sanders, Detroit, 1997
12 Eric Dickerson, L.A. Rams, 1984
Barry Foster, Pittsburgh, 1992
Jamal Anderson, Atlanta, 1998
Jamal Lewis, Baltimore, 2003
11 O.J. Simpson, Buffalo, 1973
Earl Campbell, Houston, 1979
Marcus Allen, L.A. Raiders, 1985
Eric Dickerson, L.A. Rams, 1986
Emmitt Smith, Dallas, 1995
Terrell Davis, Denver, 1998
Shaun Alexander, Seattle, 2005
Larry Johnson, Kansas City, 2006

Most Consecutive Games, 100 or More Yards Rushing
14 Barry Sanders, Detroit, 1997
11 Marcus Allen, L.A. Raiders, 1985-86
9 Walter Payton, Chicago, 1985
Fred Taylor, Jacksonville, 2000
Deuce McAllister, New Orleans, 2003
Larry Johnson, Kansas City, 2005
LaDainian Tomlinson, San Diego, 2006

Longest Run From Scrimmage
99 Tony Dorsett, Dallas vs. Minnesota, Jan. 3, 1983 (TD)
98 Ahman Green, Green Bay vs. Denver, Dec. 28, 2003 (TD)
97 Andy Uram, Green Bay vs. Chi. Cardinals, Oct. 8, 1939 (TD)
Bob Gage, Pittsburgh vs. Chi. Bears, Dec. 4, 1949 (TD)

AVERAGE GAIN

Highest Average Gain, Career (750 attempts)
6.36 Randall Cunningham, Philadelphia, 1985-1995; Minnesota, 1997-99; Dallas, 2000; Baltimore, 2001 (775-4,928)
5.22 Jim Brown, Cleveland, 1957-1965 (2,359-12,312)
5.14 Eugene (Mercury) Morris, Miami, 1969-1975; San Diego, 1976 (804-4,133)

Highest Average Gain, Season (Qualifiers)
8.45 Michael Vick, Atlanta, 2006 (123-1,039)
8.44 Beattie Feathers, Chi. Bears, 1934 (119-1,004)
7.98 Randall Cunningham, Philadelphia, 1990 (118-942)

Highest Average Gain, Game (10 attempts)
17.30 Michael Vick, Atlanta vs. Minnesota, Dec. 1, 2002 (OT) (10-173)
17.09 Marion Motley, Cleveland vs. Pittsburgh, Oct. 29, 1950 (11-188)
16.70 Bill Grimes, Green Bay vs. N.Y. Yanks, Oct. 8, 1950 (10-167)

TOUCHDOWNS

Most Seasons Leading League
5 Jim Brown, Cleveland, 1957-59, 1963, 1965
4 Steve Van Buren, Philadelphia, 1945, 1947-49
3 Abner Haynes, Dall. Texans, 1960-62
Cookie Gilchrist, Buffalo, 1962-64
Paul Lowe, L.A. Chargers, 1960; San Diego, 1961, 1965
Leroy Kelly, Cleveland, 1966-68
Emmitt Smith, Dallas, 1992, 1994-95
LaDainian Tomlinson, San Diego, 2004, 2006-07

Most Consecutive Seasons Leading League
3 Steve Van Buren, Philadelphia, 1947-49
Jim Brown, Cleveland, 1957-59
Abner Haynes, Dall. Texans, 1960-62
Cookie Gilchrist, Buffalo, 1962-64
Leroy Kelly, Cleveland, 1966-68

Most Touchdowns, Career
164 Emmitt Smith, Dallas, 1990-2002; Arizona, 2003-04
126 LaDainian Tomlinson, San Diego, 2001-08
123 Marcus Allen, L.A. Raiders, 1982-1992; Kansas City, 1993-97

Most Touchdowns, Season
28 LaDainian Tomlinson, San Diego, 2006
27 Priest Holmes, Kansas City, 2003
Shaun Alexander, Seattle, 2005
25 Emmitt Smith, Dallas, 1995

Most Touchdowns, Rookie, Season
18 Eric Dickerson, L.A. Rams, 1983
15 Ickey Woods, Cincinnati, 1988
Mike Anderson, Denver, 2000
Clinton Portis, Denver, 2002
14 Gale Sayers, Chicago, 1965
Barry Sanders, Detroit, 1989
Curtis Martin, New England, 1995
Fred Taylor, Jacksonville, 1998

Most Touchdowns, Game
6 Ernie Nevers, Chi. Cardinals vs. Chi. Bears, Nov. 28, 1929
5 Jimmy Conzelman, Rhode Island vs. Evansville, Oct. 15, 1922
Jim Brown, Cleveland vs. Baltimore, Nov. 1, 1959
Cookie Gilchrist, Buffalo vs. N.Y. Jets, Dec. 8, 1963
James Stewart, Jacksonville vs. Philadelphia, Oct. 12, 1997
Clinton Portis, Denver vs. Kansas City, Dec. 7, 2003
4 By many players

Most Consecutive Games Rushing for Touchdowns
18 LaDainian Tomlinson, San Diego, 2004-05
13 John Riggins, Washington, 1982-83
George Rogers, Washington, 1985-86
11 Lenny Moore, Baltimore, 1963-64
Emmitt Smith, Dallas, 1994-95
Emmitt Smith, Dallas, 1995
Priest Holmes, Kansas City, 2002

PASSING

Most Seasons Leading League
6 Sammy Baugh, Washington, 1937, 1940, 1943, 1945, 1947, 1949
Steve Young San Francisco, 1991-94, 1996-97
4 Len Dawson, Dall. Texans; 1962; Kansas City, 1964, 1966, 1968
Roger Staubach, Dallas, 1971, 1973, 1978-79
Ken Anderson, Cincinnati, 1974-75, 1981-82
3 Arnie Herber, Green Bay, 1932, 1934, 1936
Norm Van Brocklin, Los Angeles, 1950, 1952, 1954
Bart Starr, Green Bay, 1962, 1964, 1966
Peyton Manning, Indianapolis, 2004-06

Most Consecutive Seasons Leading League
4 Steve Young, San Francisco, 1991-94
3 Peyton Manning, Indianapolis, 2004-06
2 Cecil Isbell, Green Bay, 1941-42
Milt Plum, Cleveland, 1960-61
Ken Anderson, Cincinnati, 1974-75, 1981-82
Roger Staubach, Dallas, 1978-79
Steve Young, San Francisco, 1996-97

PASSER RATING

Highest Passer Rating, Career (1,500 attempts)

96.8 Steve Young, Tampa Bay, 1985-86; San Francisco, 1987-1999
94.7 Peyton Manning, Indianapolis, 1998-2008
93.8 Kurt Warner, St. Louis, 1998-2003; N.Y. Giants, 2004; Arizona, 2005-08

Highest Passer Rating, Season (Qualifiers)

121.1 Peyton Manning, Indianapolis, 2004
117.2 Tom Brady, New England, 2007
112.8 Steve Young, San Francisco, 1994

Highest Passer Rating, Rookie, Season (Qualifiers)

98.1 Ben Roethlisberger, Pittsburgh, 2004
96.0 Dan Marino, Miami, 1983
88.2 Greg Cook, Cincinnati, 1969

ATTEMPTS

Most Seasons Leading League

5 Dan Marino, Miami, 1984, 1986, 1988, 1992, 1997
4 Sammy Baugh, Washington, 1937, 1943, 1947-48
Johnny Unitas, Baltimore, 1957, 1959-1961
George Blanda, Chi. Bears, 1953; Houston, 1963-65
3 Arnie Herber, Green Bay, 1932, 1934, 1936
Sonny Jurgensen, Washington, 1966-67, 1969
Drew Bledsoe, New England, 1994-96
Brett Favre, Green Bay, 1999, 2005-06

Most Consecutive Seasons Leading League

3 Johnny Unitas, Baltimore, 1959-1961
George Blanda, Houston, 1963-65
Drew Bledsoe, New England, 1994-96
2 By many players

Most Passes Attempted, Career

9,280 Brett Favre, Atlanta, 1991; Green Bay, 1992-2007; N.Y. Jets, 2008
8,358 Dan Marino, Miami, 1983-1999
7,250 John Elway, Denver, 1983-1998

Most Passes Attempted, Season

691 Drew Bledsoe, New England, 1994
655 Warren Moon, Houston, 1991
652 Drew Brees, New Orleans, 2007

Most Passes Attempted, Rookie, Season

575 Peyton Manning, Indianapolis, 1998
540 Chris Weinke, Carolina, 2001
486 Rick Mirer, Seattle, 1993

Most Passes Attempted, Game

70 Drew Bledsoe, New England vs. Minnesota, Nov. 13, 1994 (OT)
69 Vinny Testaverde, N.Y. Jets vs. Baltimore, Dec. 24, 2000
68 George Blanda, Houston vs. Buffalo, Nov. 1, 1964
Jon Kitna, Cincinnati vs. Pittsburgh, Dec. 30, 2001 (OT)

COMPLETIONS

Most Seasons Leading League

6 Dan Marino, Miami, 1984-86, 1988, 1992, 1997
5 Sammy Baugh, Washington, 1937, 1943, 1945, 1947-48
4 George Blanda, Chi. Bears, 1953; Houston, 1963-65
Sonny Jurgensen, Philadelphia, 1961; Washington, 1966-67, 1969

Most Consecutive Seasons Leading League

3 George Blanda, Houston, 1963-65
Dan Marino, Miami, 1984-86
2 By many players

Most Passes Completed, Career

5,720 Brett Favre, Atlanta, 1991; Green Bay, 1992-2007; N.Y. Jets, 2008
4,967 Dan Marino, Miami, 1983-1999
4,123 John Elway, Denver, 1983-1998

Most Passes Completed, Season

440 Drew Brees, New Orleans, 2007
418 Rich Gannon, Oakland, 2002
413 Drew Brees, New Orleans, 2008

Most Passes Completed, Rookie, Season

326 Peyton Manning, Indianapolis, 1998
293 Chris Weinke, Carolina, 2001
274 Rick Mirer, Seattle, 1993

Most Passes Completed, Game

45 Drew Bledsoe, New England vs. Minnesota, Nov. 13, 1994 (OT)
43 Rich Gannon, Oakland vs. Pittsburgh, Sept. 15, 2002
42 Richard Todd, N.Y. Jets vs. San Francisco, Sept. 21, 1980
Vinny Testaverde, N.Y. Jets vs. Seattle, Dec. 6, 1998

Most Consecutive Passes Completed

24 Donovan McNabb, Philadelphia vs. N.Y. Giants (10), Nov. 28, 2004; vs. Green Bay (14), Dec. 5, 2004
23 Peyton Manning, Indianapolis vs. Detroit (6), Dec. 14, 2008; vs. Jacksonville (17), Dec. 18, 2008
22 Joe Montana, San Francisco vs. Cleveland (5), Nov. 29, 1987; vs. Green Bay (17), Dec. 6, 1987
Mark Brunell, Washington vs. Houston, Sept. 24, 2006
David Carr, Houston vs. Buffalo, Nov. 19, 2006

COMPLETION PERCENTAGE

Most Seasons Leading League

8 Len Dawson, Dall. Texans, 1962; Kansas City, 1964-69, 1975
7 Sammy Baugh, Washington, 1940, 1942-43, 1945, 1947-49
5 Joe Montana, San Francisco, 1980-81, 1985, 1987, 1989
Steve Young, San Francisco, 1992, 1994-97

Most Consecutive Seasons Leading League

6 Len Dawson, Kansas City, 1964-69
4 Steve Young, San Francisco, 1994-97
3 Sammy Baugh, Washington, 1947-49
Otto Graham, Cleveland, 1953-55
Milt Plum, Cleveland, 1959-1961
Kurt Warner, St. Louis, 1999-2001

Highest Completion Percentage, Career (1,500 attempts)

65.97 Chad Pennington, N.Y. Jets, 2000-07; Miami, 2008 (2,395-1,580)
65.42 Kurt Warner, St. Louis, 1998-2003; N.Y. Giants, 2004; Arizona, 2005-08 (3,557-2,327)
64.41 Peyton Manning, Indianapolis, 1998-2008 (5,960-3,839)

Highest Completion Percentage, Season (Qualifiers)

70.55 Ken Anderson, Cincinnati, 1982 (309-218)
70.33 Sammy Baugh, Washington, 1945 (182-128)
70.28 Steve Young, San Francisco, 1994 (461-324)

Highest Completion Percentage, Rookie, Season (Qualifiers)

66.44 Ben Roethlisberger, Pittsburgh, 2004 (295-196)
61.06 Matt Ryan, Atlanta, 2008 (434-265)
60.05 Joe Flacco, Baltimore, 2008 (428-257)

Highest Completion Percentage, Game (20 attempts)

91.30 Vinny Testaverde, Cleveland vs. L.A. Rams, Dec. 26, 1993 (23-21)
90.91 Ken Anderson, Cincinnati vs. Pittsburgh, Nov. 10, 1974 (22-20)
90.48 Lynn Dickey, Green Bay vs. New Orleans, Dec. 13, 1981 (21-19)

YARDS GAINED

Most Seasons Leading League

5 Sonny Jurgensen, Philadelphia, 1961-62; Washington, 1966-67, 1969
Dan Marino, Miami, 1984-86, 1988, 1992
4 Sammy Baugh, Washington, 1937, 1940, 1947-48
Johnny Unitas, Baltimore, 1957, 1959-1960, 1963
Dan Fouts, San Diego, 1979-1982
3 Arnie Herber, Green Bay, 1932, 1934, 1936
Sid Luckman, Chi. Bears, 1943, 1945-46
John Brodie, San Francisco, 1965, 1968, 1970
John Hadl, San Diego, 1965, 1968, 1971
Joe Namath, N.Y. Jets, 1966-67, 1972

Most Consecutive Seasons Leading League

4 Dan Fouts, San Diego, 1979-1982
3 Dan Marino, Miami, 1984-86
2 By many players

Most Yards Gained, Career

65,127 Brett Favre, Atlanta, 1991; Green Bay, 1992-2007; N.Y. Jets, 2008
61,361 Dan Marino, Miami, 1983-1999
51,475 John Elway, Denver, 1983-1998

Most Seasons, 3,000 or More Yards Passing

17 Brett Favre, Green Bay, 1992-2007; N.Y. Jets, 2008
13 Dan Marino, Miami, 1984-1992, 1994-95, 1997-98
12 John Elway, Denver, 1985-1991, 1993-97

Most Yards Gained, Season

5,084 Dan Marino, Miami, 1984
5,069 Drew Brees, New Orleans, 2008
4,830 Kurt Warner, St. Louis, 2001

Most Yards Gained, Rookie, Season

3,739 Peyton Manning, Indianapolis, 1998
3,440 Matt Ryan, Atlanta, 2008
2,971 Joe Flacco, Baltimore, 2008

Most Yards Gained, Game

554 Norm Van Brocklin, Los Angeles vs. N.Y. Yanks, Sept. 28, 1951
527 Warren Moon, Houston vs. Kansas City, Dec. 16, 1990
522 Boomer Esiason, Arizona vs. Washington, Nov. 10, 1996

Most Games, 400 or More Yards Passing, Career

13 Dan Marino, Miami, 1983-1999
7 Joe Montana, San Francisco, 1979-1990, 1992; Kansas City, 1993-94
Warren Moon, Houston, 1984-1993; Minnesota, 1994-96; Seattle, 1997-98; Kansas City, 1999-2000
Peyton Manning, Indianapolis, 1998-2008
6 Dan Fouts, San Diego, 1973-1987
Drew Bledsoe, New England, 1993-2001; Buffalo, 2002-04; Dallas, 2005-06

Most Games, 400 or More Yards Passing, Season

4 Dan Marino, Miami, 1984
3 Dan Marino, Miami, 1986
2 By many players

Most Consecutive Games, 400 or More Yards Passing

2 Dan Fouts, San Diego, 1982
Dan Marino, Miami, 1984
Phil Simms, N.Y. Giants, 1985
Billy Volek, Tennessee, 2004
Matt Cassel, New England, 2008

Most Games, 300 or More Yards Passing, Career

63 Dan Marino, Miami, 1983-1999
55 Brett Favre, Atlanta, 1991; Green Bay, 1992-2007; N.Y. Jets, 2008
51 Dan Fouts, San Diego, 1973-1987

Most Games, 300 or More Yards Passing, Season

10 Rich Gannon, Oakland, 2002
Drew Brees, New Orleans, 2008
9 Dan Marino, Miami, 1984
Warren Moon, Houston, 1990
Kurt Warner, St. Louis, 1999
Kurt Warner, St. Louis, 2001
8 Dan Fouts, San Diego, 1980
Kurt Warner, St. Louis, 2000
Trent Green, Kansas City, 2004
Marc Bulger, St. Louis, 2006
Drew Brees, New Orleans, 2006
Tom Brady, New England, 2007
Jay Cutler, Denver, 2008

Most Consecutive Games, 300 or More Yards Passing

6 Steve Young, San Francisco, 1998
Kurt Warner, St. Louis, 2000
Rich Gannon, Oakland, 2002
5 Joe Montana, San Francisco, 1982
Kerry Collins, N.Y. Giants, 2001-02
Drew Brees, New Orleans, 2006
Kurt Warner, Arizona, 2008
4 Dan Fouts, San Diego, 1979
Dan Fouts, San Diego, 1980-81
Bill Kenney, Kansas City, 1983
Joe Montana, San Francisco, 1985-86
Joe Montana, San Francisco, 1990
Warren Moon, Houston, 1990
Drew Bledsoe, New England, 1993-94
Kurt Warner, St. Louis, 1999
Brian Griese, Denver, 2002
Daunte Culpepper, Minnesota, 2004
Trent Green, Kansas City, 2004
Drew Brees, New Orleans, 2008

Longest Pass Completion (All TDs except as noted)

99 Frank Filchock (to Farkas), Washington vs. Pittsburgh, Oct. 15, 1939
George Izo (to Mitchell), Washington vs. Cleveland, Sept. 15, 1963
Karl Sweetan (to Studstill), Detroit vs. Baltimore, Oct. 16, 1966
Sonny Jurgensen (to Allen), Washington vs. Chicago, Sept. 15, 1968
Jim Plunkett (to Branch), L.A. Raiders vs. Washington, Oct. 2, 1983
Ron Jaworski (to Quick), Philadelphia vs. Atlanta, Nov. 10, 1985
Stan Humphries (to Martin), San Diego vs. Seattle, Sept. 18, 1994
Brett Favre (to Brooks), Green Bay vs. Chicago, Sept. 11, 1995
Trent Green (to Boerigter), Kansas City vs. San Diego, Dec. 22, 2002
Jeff Garcia (to Davis), Cleveland vs. Cincinnati, Oct. 17, 2004
Gus Frerotte (to Berrian), Minnesota vs. Chicago, Nov. 30, 2008
98 Doug Russell (to Tinsley), Chi. Cardinals vs. Cleveland, Nov. 27, 1938
Ogden Compton (to Lane), Chi. Cardinals vs. Green Bay, Nov. 13, 1955
Bill Wade (to Farrington), Chicago Bears vs. Detroit, Oct. 8, 1961
Jacky Lee (to Dewveall), Houston vs. San Diego, Nov. 25, 1962
Earl Morrall (to Jones), N.Y. Giants vs. Pittsburgh, Sept. 11, 1966
Jim Hart (to Moore), St. Louis vs. Los Angeles, Dec. 10, 1972 (no TD)
Bobby Hebert (to Haynes), Atlanta vs. New Orleans, Sept. 12, 1993
Charlie Batch (to Morton), Detroit vs. Chicago, Oct. 4, 1998

97 Pat Coffee (to Tinsley), Chi. Cardinals vs. Chi. Bears, Dec. 5, 1937
Bobby Layne (to Box), Detroit vs. Green Bay, Nov. 26, 1953
George Shaw (to Tarr), Denver vs. Boston, Sept. 21, 1962
Bernie Kosar (to Slaughter), Cleveland vs. Chicago, Oct. 23, 1989
Steve Young (to Taylor), San Francisco vs. Atlanta, Nov. 3, 1991

AVERAGE GAIN

Most Seasons Leading League
7 Sid Luckman, Chi. Bears, 1939-1943, 1946-47
5 Steve Young, San Francisco, 1991-94, 1997
3 Arnie Herber, Green Bay, 1932, 1934, 1936
Norm Van Brocklin, Los Angeles, 1950, 1952, 1954
Len Dawson, Dall. Texans, 1962; Kansas City, 1966, 1968
Bart Starr, Green Bay, 1966-68
Kurt Warner, St. Louis, 1999-2001

Most Consecutive Seasons Leading League
5 Sid Luckman, Chi. Bears, 1939-1943
4 Steve Young, San Francisco, 1991-94
3 Bart Starr, Green Bay, 1966-68
Kurt Warner, St. Louis, 1999-2001

Highest Average Gain, Career (1,500 attempts)
8.63 Otto Graham, Cleveland, 1950-55 (1,565-13,499)
8.42 Sid Luckman, Chi. Bears, 1939-1950 (1,744-14,686)
8.16 Norm Van Brocklin, Los Angeles, 1949-1957; Philadelphia, 1958-1960

Highest Average Gain, Season (Qualifiers)
11.17 Tommy O'Connell, Cleveland, 1957 (110-1,229)
10.86 Sid Luckman, Chi. Bears, 1943 (202-2,194)
10.55 Otto Graham, Cleveland, 1953 (258-2,722)

Highest Average Gain, Rookie, Season (Qualifiers)
9.411 Greg Cook, Cincinnati, 1969 (197-1,854)
9.409 Bob Waterfield, Cleveland, 1945 (171-1,609)
8.88 Ben Roethlisberger, Pittsburgh, 2004 (295-2,621)

Highest Average Gain, Game (20 attempts)
18.58 Sammy Baugh, Washington vs. Boston, Oct. 31, 1948 (24-446)
18.50 Johnny Unitas, Baltimore vs. Atlanta, Nov. 12, 1967 (20-370)
17.71 Joe Namath, N.Y. Jets vs. Baltimore, Sept. 24, 1972 (28-496)

TOUCHDOWNS

Most Seasons Leading League
4 Johnny Unitas, Baltimore, 1957-1960
Len Dawson, Dall. Texans, 1962; Kansas City, 1963, 1965-66
Steve Young, San Francisco, 1992-94, 1998
Brett Favre, Green Bay, 1995-97, 2003
3 Arnie Herber, Green Bay, 1932, 1934, 1936
Sid Luckman, Chi. Bears, 1943, 1945-46
Y.A. Tittle, San Francisco, 1955; N.Y. Giants, 1962-63
Dan Marino, Miami, 1984-86
Peyton Manning, Indianapolis, 2000, 2004, 2006
2 By many players

Most Consecutive Seasons Leading League
4 Johnny Unitas, Baltimore, 1957-1960
3 Dan Marino, Miami, 1984-86
Steve Young, San Francisco, 1992-94
Brett Favre, Green Bay, 1995-97
2 By many players

Most Touchdown Passes, Career
464 Brett Favre, Atlanta, 1991; Green Bay, 1992-2007; N.Y. Jets, 2008
420 Dan Marino, Miami, 1983-1999
342 Fran Tarkenton, Minnesota, 1961-66, 1972-78; N.Y. Giants, 1967-1971

Most Touchdown Passes, Season
50 Tom Brady, New England, 2007
49 Peyton Manning, Indianapolis, 2004
48 Dan Marino, Miami, 1984

Most Touchdown Passes, Rookie, Season
26 Peyton Manning, Indianapolis, 1998
22 Charlie Conerly, N.Y. Giants, 1948
20 Dan Marino, Miami, 1983

Most Touchdown Passes, Game
7 Sid Luckman, Chi. Bears vs. N.Y. Giants, Nov. 14, 1943
Adrian Burk, Philadelphia vs. Washington, Oct. 17, 1954
George Blanda, Houston vs. N.Y. Titans, Nov. 19, 1961
Y.A. Tittle, N.Y. Giants vs. Washington, Oct. 28, 1962
Joe Kapp, Minnesota vs. Baltimore, Sept. 28, 1969
6 By many players. Last time:
Brett Favre, N.Y. Jets vs. Arizona, Sept. 28, 2008

Most Games, Four or More Touchdown Passes, Career
21 Dan Marino, Miami, 1983-1999
20 Brett Favre, Atlanta, 1991; Green Bay, 1992-2007; N.Y. Jets, 2008
17 Johnny Unitas, Baltimore, 1956-1972; San Diego, 1973
Peyton Manning, Indianapolis, 1998-2008

Most Games, Four or More Touchdown Passes, Season
6 Dan Marino, Miami, 1984
Peyton Manning, Indianapolis, 2004
5 Dan Marino, Miami, 1986
Brett Favre, Green Bay, 1996
Donovan McNabb, Philadelphia, 2004
Tom Brady, New England, 2007
4 George Blanda, Houston, 1961
Vince Ferragamo, Los Angeles, 1980
Steve Young, San Francisco, 1994
Randall Cunningham, Minnesota, 1998
Daunte Culpepper, Minnesota, 2004
Tony Romo, Dallas, 2007

Most Consecutive Games, Four or More Touchdown Passes
5 Peyton Manning, Indianapolis, 2004
4 Dan Marino, Miami, 1984
2 By many players

Most Consecutive Games, Touchdown Passes
47 Johnny Unitas, Baltimore, 1956-1960
36 Brett Favre, Green Bay, 2002-2004
30 Dan Marino, Miami, 1985-87

HAD INTERCEPTED

Most Consecutive Passes Attempted, None Intercepted
308 Bernie Kosar, Cleveland, 1990-91
294 Bart Starr, Green Bay, 1964-65
279 Jeff George, Indianapolis, 1993; Atlanta, 1994

Most Passes Had Intercepted, Career
310 Brett Favre, Atlanta, 1991; Green Bay, 1992-2007; N.Y. Jets, 2008
277 George Blanda, Chi. Bears, 1949, 1950-58; Baltimore, 1950; Houston, 1960-66; Oakland, 1967-1975
268 John Hadl, San Diego, 1962-1972; Los Angeles, 1973-74; Green Bay, 1974-75; Houston, 1976-77

Most Passes Had Intercepted, Season
42 George Blanda, Houston, 1962
35 Vinny Testaverde, Tampa Bay, 1988
34 Frank Tripucka, Denver, 1960

Most Passes Had Intercepted, Game
8 Jim Hardy, Chi. Cardinals vs. Philadelphia, Sept. 24, 1950

7 Parker Hall, Cleveland vs. Green Bay, Nov. 8, 1942
Frank Sinkwich, Detroit vs. Green Bay, Oct. 24, 1943
Bob Waterfield, Los Angeles vs. Green Bay, Oct. 17, 1948
Zeke Bratkowski, Chicago vs. Baltimore, Oct. 2, 1960
Tommy Wade, Pittsburgh vs. Philadelphia, Dec. 12, 1965
Ken Stabler, Oakland vs. Denver, Oct. 16, 1977
Steve DeBerg, Tampa Bay vs. San Francisco, Sept. 7, 1986
Ty Detmer, Detroit vs. Cleveland, Sept. 23, 2001
6 By many players

Most Attempts, No Interceptions, Game
70 Drew Bledsoe, New England vs. Minnesota, Nov. 13, 1994 (OT)
63 Rich Gannon, Minnesota vs. New England, Oct. 20, 1991 (OT)
60 Davey O'Brien, Philadelphia vs. Washington, Dec. 1, 1940

LOWEST PERCENTAGE, PASSES HAD INTERCEPTED

Most Seasons Leading League, Lowest Percentage, Passes Had Intercepted
5 Sammy Baugh, Washington, 1940, 1942, 1944-45, 1947
3 Charlie Conerly, N.Y. Giants, 1950, 1956, 1959
Bart Starr, Green Bay, 1962, 1964, 1966
Roger Staubach, Dallas, 1971, 1977, 1979
Ken Anderson, Cincinnati, 1972, 1981-82
Ken O'Brien, N.Y. Jets, 1985, 1987-88
2 By many players

Lowest Percentage, Passes Had Intercepted, Career (1,500 attempts)
2.09 Donovan McNabb, Philadelphia, 1999-2008 (4,303-90)
2.11 Neil O'Donnell, Pittsburgh, 1991-95; N.Y. Jets, 1996-97; Cincinnati, 1998; Tennessee, 1999-2003 (3,229-68)
2.26 Jeff Garcia, San Francisco 1999-2003; Cleveland, 2004; Detroit, 2005; Philadelphia, 2006; Tampa Bay, 2007-08 (3,676-83)

Lowest Percentage, Passes Had Intercepted, Season (Qualifiers)
0.41 Damon Huard, Kansas City, 2006 (244-1)
0.66 Joe Ferguson, Buffalo, 1976 (151-1)
0.90 Steve DeBerg, Kansas City, 1990 (444-4)

Lowest Percentage, Passes Had Intercepted, Rookie, Season (Qualifiers)
1.98 Charlie Batch, Detroit, 1998 (303-6)
2.03 Dan Marino, Miami, 1983 (296-6)
2.10 Gary Wood, N.Y. Giants, 1964 (143-3)

TIMES SACKED

Times Sacked has been compiled since 1963.

Most Times Sacked, Career
516 John Elway, Denver, 1983-1998
494 Dave Krieg, Seattle, 1980-1991; Kansas City, 1992-93; Detroit, 1994; Arizona, 1995; Chicago, 1996; Tennessee, 1997-98
484 Randall Cunningham, Philadelphia, 1985-1995; Minnesota, 1997-99; Dallas, 2000; Baltimore, 2001

Most Times Sacked, Season
76 David Carr, Houston, 2002
72 Randall Cunningham, Philadelphia, 1986
68 David Carr, Houston, 2005

Most Times Sacked, Game
12 Bert Jones, Baltimore vs. St. Louis, Oct. 26, 1980
Warren Moon, Houston vs. Dallas, Sept. 29, 1985
Donovan McNabb, Philadelphia vs. N.Y. Giants, Sept. 30, 2007
11 Charley Johnson, St. Louis vs. N.Y. Giants, Nov. 1, 1964
Bart Starr, Green Bay vs. Detroit, Nov. 7, 1965
Jack Kemp, Buffalo vs. Oakland, Oct. 15, 1967
Bob Berry, Atlanta vs. St. Louis, Nov. 24, 1968
Greg Landry, Detroit vs. Dallas, Oct. 6, 1975
Ron Jaworski, Philadelphia vs. St. Louis, Dec. 18, 1983
Paul McDonald, Cleveland vs. Kansas City, Sept. 30, 1984
Archie Manning, Minnesota vs. Chicago, Oct. 28, 1984
Steve Pelluer, Dallas vs. San Diego, Nov. 16, 1986
Randall Cunningham, Philadelphia vs. L.A. Raiders, Nov. 30, 1986 (OT)
David Norrie, N.Y. Jets vs. Dallas, Oct. 4, 1987
Troy Aikman, Dallas vs. Philadelphia, Sept. 15, 1991
Bernie Kosar, Cleveland vs. Indianapolis, Sept. 6, 1992
10 By many players

RECEIVING

Most Seasons Leading League
8 Don Hutson, Green Bay, 1936-37, 1939, 1941-45
5 Lionel Taylor, Denver, 1960-63, 1965
3 Tom Fears, Los Angeles, 1948-1950
Pete Pihos, Philadelphia, 1953-55
Billy Wilson, San Francisco, 1954, 1956-57
Raymond Berry, Baltimore, 1958-1960
Lance Alworth, San Diego, 1966, 1968-69
Sterling Sharpe, Green Bay, 1989, 1992-93

Most Consecutive Seasons Leading League
5 Don Hutson, Green Bay, 1941-45
4 Lionel Taylor, Denver, 1960-63
3 Tom Fears, Los Angeles, 1948-1950
Pete Pihos, Philadelphia, 1953-55
Raymond Berry, Baltimore, 1958-1960

Most Pass Receptions, Career
1,549 Jerry Rice, San Francisco, 1985-2000; Oakland, 2001-04; Seattle, 2004
1,102 Marvin Harrison, Indianapolis, 1996-2008
1,101 Cris Carter, Philadelphia, 1987-89; Minnesota, 1990-2001; Miami, 2002

Most Seasons, 50 or More Pass Receptions
17 Jerry Rice, San Francisco, 1986-1996, 1998-2000; Oakland, 2001-03
13 Andre Reed, Buffalo, 1986-1994, 1996-99
12 Isaac Bruce, St. Louis, 1995-97, 1999-2004, 2006-07; San Francisco, 2008
Marvin Harrison, Indianapolis, 1996-2006, 2008

Most Pass Receptions, Season
143 Marvin Harrison, Indianapolis, 2002
123 Herman Moore, Detroit, 1995
122 Cris Carter, Minnesota, 1994
Cris Carter, Minnesota, 1995
Jerry Rice, San Francisco, 1995

Most Pass Receptions, Rookie, Season
101 Anquan Boldin, Arizona, 2003
91 Eddie Royal, Denver, 2008
90 Terry Glenn, New England, 1996

Most Pass Receptions, Game
20 Terrell Owens, San Francisco vs. Chicago, Dec. 17, 2000
18 Tom Fears, Los Angeles vs. Green Bay, Dec. 3, 1950
Brandon Marshall, Denver vs. San Diego, Sept. 14, 2008
17 Clark Gaines, N.Y. Jets vs. San Francisco, Sept. 21, 1980

Most Consecutive Games, Pass Receptions

274 Jerry Rice, San Francisco, 1985-2000; Oakland, 2001-04
190 Marvin Harrison, Indianapolis, 1996-2008 (current)
183 Art Monk, Washington, 1983-1993; N.Y. Jets, 1994; Philadelphia, 1995
Terrell Owens, San Francisco, 1996-2003; Philadelphia, 2004-05; Dallas, 2006-08 (current)

YARDS GAINED

Most Seasons Leading League

7 Don Hutson, Green Bay, 1936, 1938-39, 1941-44
6 Jerry Rice, San Francisco, 1986, 1989-1990, 1993-95
3 Raymond Berry, Baltimore, 1957, 1959-1960
Lance Alworth, San Diego, 1965-66, 1968

Most Consecutive Seasons Leading League

4 Don Hutson, Green Bay, 1941-44
3 Jerry Rice, San Francisco, 1993-95
2 By many players

Most Yards Gained, Career

22,895 Jerry Rice, San Francisco, 1985-2000; Oakland, 2001-04; Seattle, 2004
14,944 Isaac Bruce, L.A. Rams, 1994; St. Louis, 1995-2007; San Francisco, 2008
14,934 Tim Brown, L.A. Raiders, 1988-1994; Oakland, 1995-2003; Tampa Bay, 2004

Most Seasons, 1,000 or More Yards, Pass Receiving

14 Jerry Rice, San Francisco, 1986-1996, 1998; Oakland, 2001-02
9 Tim Brown, L.A. Raiders, 1993-94; Oakland, 1995-2001
Jimmy Smith, Jacksonville, 1996-2002, 2004-05
Randy Moss, Minnesota, 1998-2003; Oakland, 2005; New England, 2007-08
Terrell Owens, San Francisco, 1998, 2000-03; Philadelphia, 2004; Dallas, 2006-08
8 Steve Largent, Seattle, 1978-1981, 1983-86
Cris Carter, Minnesota, 1993-2000
Rod Smith, Denver, 1997-2002, 2004-05
Isaac Bruce, St. Louis, 1995-96, 1999-2002, 2004, 2006
Marvin Harrison, Indianapolis, 1999-2006
Torry Holt, St. Louis, 2000-07

Most Yards Gained, Season

1,848 Jerry Rice, San Francisco, 1995
1,781 Isaac Bruce, St. Louis, 1995
1,746 Charley Hennigan, Houston, 1961

Most Yards Gained, Rookie, Season

1,473 Bill Groman, Houston, 1960
1,377 Anquan Boldin, Arizona, 2003
1,313 Randy Moss, Minnesota, 1998

Most Yards Gained, Game

336 Willie Anderson, L.A. Rams vs. New Orleans, Nov. 26, 1989 (OT)
309 Stephone Paige, Kansas City vs. San Diego, Dec. 22, 1985
303 Jim Benton, Cleveland vs. Detroit, Nov. 22, 1945

Most Games, 200 or More Yards Pass Receiving, Career

5 Lance Alworth, San Diego, 1962-1970; Dallas, 1971-72
4 Don Hutson, Green Bay, 1935-45
Charley Hennigan, Houston, 1960-66
Jerry Rice, San Francisco, 1985-2000; Oakland, 2001-04; Seattle, 2004
3 Don Maynard, N.Y. Giants, 1958; N.Y. Jets, 1960-1972; St. Louis, 1973
Wes Chandler, New Orleans, 1978-1981; San Diego, 1981-87; San Francisco, 1988
Isaac Bruce, L.A. Rams, 1994; St. Louis, 1995-2007; San Francisco, 2008

Most Games, 200 or More Yards Pass Receiving, Season

3 Charley Hennigan, Houston, 1961
2 Don Hutson, Green Bay, 1942
Gene Roberts, N.Y. Giants, 1949
Lance Alworth, San Diego, 1963
Don Maynard, N.Y. Jets, 1968

Most Games, 100 or More Yards Pass Receiving, Career

76 Jerry Rice, San Francisco, 1985-2000; Oakland, 2001-04; Seattle, 2004
59 Marvin Harrison, Indianapolis, 1996-2008
Randy Moss, Minnesota, 1998-2004; Oakland, 2005-06; New England, 2007-08
50 Don Maynard, N.Y. Giants, 1958; N.Y. Titans, 1960-62; N.Y. Jets, 1963-1972; St. Louis, 1973

Most Games, 100 or More Yards Pass Receiving, Season

11 Michael Irvin, Dallas, 1995
10 Charley Hennigan, Houston, 1961
Herman Moore, Detroit, 1995
Marvin Harrison, Indianapolis, 2002
Torry Holt, St. Louis, 2003
9 Elroy (Crazylegs) Hirsch, Los Angeles, 1951
Bill Groman, Houston, 1960
Lance Alworth, San Diego, 1965
Don Maynard, N.Y. Jets, 1967
Stanley Morgan, New England, 1986
Mark Carrier, Tampa Bay, 1989
Robert Brooks, Green Bay, 1995
Isaac Bruce, St. Louis, 1995
Jerry Rice, San Francisco, 1995
Marvin Harrison, Indianapolis, 1999
Jimmy Smith, Jacksonville, 1999
David Boston, Arizona, 2001
Steve Smith, Carolina, 2005
Randy Moss, New England, 2007

Most Consecutive Games, 100 or More Yards Pass Receiving

7 Charley Hennigan, Houston, 1961
Michael Irvin, Dallas, 1995
6 Raymond Berry, Baltimore, 1960
Bill Groman, Houston, 1961
Pat Studstill, Detroit, 1966
Isaac Bruce, St. Louis, 1995
5 Elroy (Crazylegs) Hirsch, Los Angeles, 1951
Bob Boyd, Los Angeles, 1954
Terry Barr, Detroit, 1963
Lance Alworth, San Diego, 1966
Don Maynard, N.Y. Jets, 1968-69
Harold Jackson, Philadelphia, 1971-72
Patrick Jeffers, Carolina, 1999
Terrell Owens, Philadelphia, 2004
Anquan Boldin, Arizona, 2005

Longest Pass Reception (All TDs except as noted)

99 Andy Farkas (from Filchock), Washington vs. Pittsburgh, Oct. 15, 1939
Bobby Mitchell (from Izo), Washington vs. Cleveland, Sept. 15, 1963
Pat Studstill (from Sweetan), Detroit vs. Baltimore, Oct. 16, 1966
Gerry Allen (from Jurgensen), Washington vs. Chicago, Sept. 15, 1968
Cliff Branch (from Plunkett), L.A. Raiders vs. Washington, Oct. 2, 1983
Mike Quick (from Jaworski), Philadelphia vs. Atlanta, Nov. 10, 1985
Tony Martin (from Humphries), San Diego vs. Seattle, Sept. 18, 1994
Robert Brooks (from Favre), Green Bay vs. Chicago, Sept. 11, 1995

Marc Boerigter (from Green), Kansas City vs. San Diego, Dec. 22, 2002
Andre Davis (from Garcia), Cleveland vs. Cincinnati, Oct. 17, 2004
Bernard Berrian (from Frerotte), Minnesota vs. Chicago, Nov. 30, 2008
98 Gaynell Tinsley (from Russell), Chi. Cardinals vs. Cleveland, Nov. 17, 1938
Dick (Night Train) Lane (from Compton), Chi. Cardinals vs. Green Bay, Nov. 13, 1955
John Farrington (from Wade), Chicago vs. Detroit, Oct. 8, 1961
Willard Dewveall (from Lee), Houston vs. San Diego, Nov. 25, 1962
Homer Jones (from Morrall), N.Y. Giants vs. Pittsburgh, Sept. 11, 1966
Bobby Moore (from Hart), St. Louis vs. Los Angeles, Dec. 10, 1972 (no TD)
Michael Haynes (from Hebert), Atlanta vs. New Orleans, Sept. 12, 1993
Johnnie Morton (from Batch), Detroit vs. Chicago, Oct. 4, 1998
97 Gaynell Tinsley (from Coffee), Chi. Cardinals vs. Chi. Bears, Dec. 5, 1937
Cloyce Box (from Layne), Detroit vs. Green Bay, Nov. 26, 1953
Jerry Tarr (from Shaw), Denver vs. Boston, Sept. 21, 1962
Webster Slaughter (from Kosar), Cleveland vs. Chicago, Oct. 23, 1989
John Taylor (from Young), San Francisco vs. Atlanta, Nov. 3, 1991

AVERAGE GAIN

Highest Average Gain, Career (200 receptions)
22.26 Homer Jones, N.Y. Giants, 1964-69; Cleveland, 1970 (224-4,986)
20.83 Buddy Dial, Pittsburgh, 1959-1963; Dallas, 1964-66 (261-5,436)
20.24 Harlon Hill, Chi. Bears, 1954-1961; Pittsburgh, 1962; Detroit, 1962 (233-4,717)

Highest Average Gain, Season (24 receptions)
32.58 Don Currivan, Boston, 1947 (24-782)
31.44 Bucky Pope, Los Angeles, 1964 (25-786)
28.60 Bobby Duckworth, San Diego, 1984 (25-715)

Highest Average Gain, Game (3 receptions)
63.00 Torry Holt, St. Louis vs. Atlanta, Sept. 24, 2000 (3-189)
60.67 Bill Groman, Houston vs. Denver, Nov. 20, 1960 (3-182)
Homer Jones, N.Y. Giants vs. Washington, Dec. 12, 1965 (3-182)
60.33 Don Currivan, Boston vs. Washington, Nov. 30, 1947 (3-181)

TOUCHDOWNS

Most Seasons Leading League
9 Don Hutson, Green Bay, 1935-38, 1940-44
6 Jerry Rice, San Francisco, 1986-87, 1989-1991, 1993
4 Randy Moss, Minnesota, 1998, 2000, 2003; New England, 2007

Most Consecutive Seasons Leading League
5 Don Hutson, Green Bay, 1940-44
4 Don Hutson, Green Bay, 1935-38
3 Lance Alworth, San Diego, 1964-66
Jerry Rice, San Francisco, 1989-1991

Most Touchdowns, Career
197 Jerry Rice, San Francisco, 1985-2000; Oakland, 2001-04; Seattle, 2004
139 Terrell Owens, San Francisco, 1996-2003; Philadelphia, 2004-05; Dallas, 2006-08
135 Randy Moss, Minnesota, 1998-2004; Oakland, 2005-06; New England, 2007-08

Most Touchdowns, Season
23 Randy Moss, New England, 2007
22 Jerry Rice, San Francisco, 1987
18 Mark Clayton, Miami, 1984
Sterling Sharpe, Green Bay, 1994

Most Touchdowns, Rookie, Season
17 Randy Moss, Minnesota, 1998
13 Bill Howton, Green Bay, 1952
John Jefferson, San Diego, 1978
12 Harlon Hill, Chi. Bears, 1954
Bill Groman, Houston, 1960
Mike Ditka, Chicago, 1961
Bob Hayes, Dallas, 1965

Most Touchdowns, Game
5 Bob Shaw, Chi. Cardinals vs. Baltimore, Oct. 2, 1950
Kellen Winslow, San Diego vs. Oakland, Nov. 22, 1981
Jerry Rice, San Francisco vs. Atlanta, Oct. 14, 1990
4 By many players. Last time:
Randy Moss, New England vs. Buffalo, Nov. 18, 2007
Terrell Owens, Dallas vs. Washington, Nov. 18, 2007

Most Consecutive Games, Touchdowns
13 Jerry Rice, San Francisco, 1986-87
11 Elroy (Crazylegs) Hirsch, Los Angeles, 1950-51
Buddy Dial, Pittsburgh, 1959-1960
10 Carl Pickens, Cincinnati, 1994-95
Randy Moss, Minnesota, 2003-04

YARDS FROM SCRIMMAGE

Most Scrimmage Yards, Career
23,540 Jerry Rice, San Francisco 1985-2000; Oakland, 2001-04; Seattle, 2004
21,579 Emmitt Smith, Dallas, 1990-2002; Arizona, 2003-04
21,264 Walter Payton, Chicago, 1975-1987

Most Scrimmage Yards, Season
2,429 Marshall Faulk, St. Louis, 1999 (1,381 rush., 1,048 rec.)
2,390 Tiki Barber, N.Y. Giants, 2005 (1,860 rush., 530 rec.)
2,370 LaDainian Tomlinson, San Diego, 2003 (1,645 rush., 725 rec.)

Most Scrimmage Yards, Rookie, Season
2,212 Eric Dickerson, L.A. Rams, 1983 (1,808 rush., 404 rec.)
2,139 Edgerrin James, Indianapolis, 1999 (1,553 rush., 586 rec.)
1,924 Billy Sims, Detroit, 1980 (1,303 rush., 621 rec.)

Most Scrimmage Yards, Game
336 Flipper Anderson, L.A. Rams vs. New Orleans, Nov. 26, 1989 (OT) (336 rec.)
330 Billy Cannon, Houston vs. N.Y. Titans, Dec. 10, 1961 (216 rush., 114 rec.)
315 Adrian Peterson, Minnesota vs. San Diego, Nov. 4, 2007 (296 rush, 19 pass)

INTERCEPTIONS BY

Most Seasons Leading League
3 Everson Walls, Dallas, 1981-82, 1985
2 Dick (Night Train) Lane, Los Angeles, 1952; Chi. Cardinals, 1954
Jack Christiansen, Detroit, 1953, 1957
Milt Davis, Baltimore, 1957, 1959
Dick Lynch, N.Y. Giants, 1961, 1963
Johnny Robinson, Kansas City, 1966, 1970
Bill Bradley, Philadelphia, 1971-72
Emmitt Thomas, Kansas City, 1969, 1974
Ronnie Lott, San Francisco, 1986; L.A. Raiders, 1991

Rod Woodson, Baltimore, 1999; Oakland, 2002
Ty Law, New England, 1998; N.Y. Jets, 2005
Ed Reed, Baltimore, 2004, 2008

Most Interceptions By, Career
81 Paul Krause, Washington, 1964-67; Minnesota, 1968-1979
79 Emlen Tunnell, N.Y. Giants, 1948-1958; Green Bay, 1959-1961
71 Rod Woodson, Pittsburgh, 1987-1996; San Francisco, 1997; Baltimore, 1998-2001; Oakland, 2002-03

Most Interceptions By, Season
14 Dick (Night Train) Lane, Los Angeles, 1952
13 Dan Sandifer, Washington, 1948
Orban (Spec) Sanders, N.Y. Yanks, 1950
Lester Hayes, Oakland, 1980
12 By nine players

Most Interceptions By, Rookie, Season
14 Dick (Night Train) Lane, Los Angeles, 1952
13 Dan Sandifer, Washington, 1948
12 Woodley Lewis, Los Angeles, 1950
Paul Krause, Washington, 1964

Most Interceptions By, Game
4 Sammy Baugh, Washington vs. Detroit, Nov. 14, 1943
Dan Sandifer, Washington vs. Boston, Oct. 31, 1948
Don Doll, Detroit vs. Chi. Cardinals, Oct. 23, 1949
Bob Nussbaumer, Chi. Cardinals vs. N.Y. Bulldogs, Nov. 13, 1949
Russ Craft, Philadelphia vs. Chi. Cardinals, Sept. 24, 1950
Bobby Dillon, Green Bay vs. Detroit, Nov. 26, 1953
Jack Butler, Pittsburgh vs. Washington, Dec. 13, 1953
Austin (Goose) Gonsoulin, Denver vs. Buffalo, Sept. 18, 1960
Jerry Norton, St. Louis vs. Washington, Nov. 20, 1960; vs. Pittsburgh, Nov. 26, 1961
Dave Baker, San Francisco vs. L.A. Rams, Dec. 4, 1960
Bobby Ply, Dall. Texans vs. San Diego, Dec. 16, 1962
Bobby Hunt, Kansas City vs. Houston, Oct. 4, 1964
Willie Brown, Denver vs. N.Y. Jets, Nov. 15, 1964
Dick Anderson, Miami vs. Pittsburgh, Dec. 3, 1973
Willie Buchanon, Green Bay vs. San Diego, Sept. 24, 1978
Deron Cherry, Kansas City vs. Seattle, Sept. 29, 1985
Kwamie Lassiter, Arizona vs. San Diego, Dec. 27, 1998
Deltha O'Neal, Denver vs. Kansas City, Oct. 7, 2001

Most Consecutive Games, Passes Intercepted By
8 Tom Morrow, Oakland, 1962-63
7 Tom Landry, N.Y. Giants, 1950-51
Paul Krause, Washington, 1964
Larry Wilson, St. Louis, 1966
Ben Davis, Cleveland, 1968
6 By many players.
Last time: Brian Russell, Minnesota, 2003

YARDS GAINED

Most Seasons Leading League
2 Dick (Night Train) Lane, Los Angeles, 1952; Chi. Cardinals, 1954
Herb Adderley, Green Bay, 1965, 1969
Dick Anderson, Miami, 1968, 1970
Darren Sharper, Green Bay, 2002; Minnesota, 2005

Most Yards Gained, Career
1,483 Rod Woodson, Pittsburgh, 1987-1996; San Francisco, 1997; Baltimore, 1998-2001; Oakland, 2002-03
1,331 Deion Sanders, Atlanta, 1989-1993; San Francisco, 1994; Dallas, 1995-99; Washington, 2000; Baltimore, 2004-05
1,282 Emlen Tunnell, N.Y. Giants, 1948-1958; Green Bay, 1959-1961

Most Yards Gained, Season
358 Ed Reed, Baltimore, 2004
349 Charlie McNeil, San Diego, 1961
303 Deion Sanders, San Francisco, 1994

Most Yards Gained, Rookie, Season
301 Don Doll, Detroit, 1949
298 Dick (Night Train) Lane, Los Angeles, 1952
275 Woodley Lewis, Los Angeles, 1950

Most Yards Gained, Game
177 Charlie McNeil, San Diego vs. Houston, Sept. 24, 1961
170 Louis Oliver, Miami vs. Buffalo, Oct. 4, 1992
167 Dick Jauron, Detroit vs. Chicago, Nov. 18, 1973

Longest Return (All TDs)
107 Ed Reed, Baltimore vs. Philadelphia, Nov. 23, 2008
106 Ed Reed, Baltimore vs. Cleveland, Nov. 7, 2004
103 Vencie Glenn, San Diego vs. Denver, Nov. 29, 1987
Louis Oliver, Miami vs. Buffalo, Oct. 4, 1992

TOUCHDOWNS

Most Touchdowns, Career
12 Rod Woodson, Pittsburgh, 1987-1996; San Francisco, 1997; Baltimore, 1998-2001; Oakland, 2002-03
9 Ken Houston, Houston, 1967-1972; Washington, 1973-1980
Aeneas Williams, Phoenix, 1991-93; Arizona, 1994-2000; St. Louis, 2001-04
Deion Sanders, Atlanta, 1989-1993; San Francisco, 1994; Dallas, 1995-99; Washington, 2000; Baltimore, 2004-05
8 Eric Allen, Philadelphia, 1988-1994; New Orleans, 1995-97; Oakland, 1998-2001
Darren Sharper, Green Bay, 1997-2004; Minnesota, 2005-08

Most Touchdowns, Season
4 Ken Houston, Houston, 1971
Jim Kearney, Kansas City, 1972
Eric Allen, Philadelphia, 1993
3 Dick Harris, San Diego, 1961
Dick Lynch, N.Y. Giants, 1963
Herb Adderley, Green Bay, 1965
Lem Barney, Detroit, 1967
Miller Farr, Houston, 1967
Monte Jackson, Los Angeles, 1976
Rod Perry, Los Angeles, 1978
Ronnie Lott, San Francisco, 1981
Lloyd Burruss, Kansas City, 1986
Wayne Haddix, Tampa Bay, 1990
Robert Massey, Phoenix, 1992
Ray Buchanan, Indianapolis, 1994
Deion Sanders, San Francisco, 1994
Mark McMillian, Kansas City, 1997
Otis Smith, N.Y. Jets, 1997
Jimmy Hitchcock, Minnesota, 1998
Eric Allen, Oakland, 2000
Derrick Brooks, Tampa Bay, 2002
Antrel Rolle, Arizona, 2007
Nick Collins, Green Bay, 2008
2 By many players

Most Touchdowns, Rookie, Season
3 Lem Barney, Detroit, 1967
Ronnie Lott, San Francisco, 1981
2 By many players

Most Touchdowns, Game
2 Bill Blackburn, Chi. Cardinals vs. Boston, Oct. 24, 1948
Dan Sandifer, Washington vs. Boston, Oct. 31, 1948
Bob Franklin, Cleveland vs. Chicago, Dec. 11, 1960

Bill Stacy, St. Louis vs. Dall. Cowboys, Nov. 5, 1961
Jerry Norton, St. Louis vs. Pittsburgh, Nov. 26, 1961
Miller Farr, Houston vs. Buffalo, Dec. 7, 1968
Ken Houston, Houston vs. San Diego, Dec. 19, 1971
Jim Kearney, Kansas City vs. Denver, Oct. 1, 1972
Lemar Parrish, Cincinnati vs. Houston, Dec. 17, 1972
Dick Anderson, Miami vs. Pittsburgh, Dec. 3, 1973
Prentice McCray, New England vs. N.Y. Jets, Nov. 21, 1976
Kenny Johnson, Atlanta vs. Green Bay, Nov. 27, 1983 (OT)
Mike Kozlowski, Miami vs. N.Y. Jets, Dec. 16, 1983
Dave Brown, Seattle vs. Kansas City, Nov. 4, 1984
Lloyd Burruss, Kansas City vs. San Diego, Oct. 19, 1986
Henry Jones, Buffalo vs. Indianapolis, Sept. 20, 1992
Robert Massey, Phoenix vs. Washington, Oct. 4, 1992
Eric Allen, Philadelphia vs. New Orleans, Dec. 26, 1993
Ken Norton, San Francisco vs. St. Louis, Oct. 22, 1995
Otis Smith, N.Y. Jets vs. Tampa Bay, Dec. 14, 1997
Dewayne Washington, Pittsburgh vs. Jacksonville, Nov. 22, 1998
Aaron Glenn, Houston vs. Pittsburgh, Dec. 8, 2002
Ronde Barber, Tampa Bay vs. Philadelphia, Oct. 22, 2006
Antrel Rolle, Arizona vs. Cincinnati, Nov. 18, 2007

PUNTING

Most Seasons Leading League
4 Sammy Baugh, Washington, 1940-43
Jerrel Wilson, Kansas City, 1965, 1968, 1972-73
3 Yale Lary, Detroit, 1959, 1961, 1963
Jim Fraser, Denver, 1962-64
Ray Guy, Oakland, 1974-75, 1977
Rohn Stark, Baltimore, 1983; Indianapolis, 1985-86
Shane Lechler, Oakland, 2003-04, 2007
2 By many players

Most Consecutive Seasons Leading League
4 Sammy Baugh, Washington, 1940-43
3 Jim Fraser, Denver, 1962-64
2 By many players

PUNTS

Most Punts, Career
1,649 Jeff Feagles, New England, 1988-89; Philadelphia, 1990-93; Arizona, 1994-97; Seattle, 1998-2002; N.Y. Giants, 2003-08
1,401 Sean Landeta, N.Y. Giants, 1985-1993; L.A. Rams, 1993-94; St. Louis, 1995-96; Tampa Bay, 1997; Green Bay, 1998; Philadelphia, 1999-2002; St. Louis, 2003-04; Philadelphia, 2005
1,226 Lee Johnson, Houston, 1985-87; Cleveland, 1987-88; Cincinnati, 1988-1998; New England, 1999-2001; Minnesota, 2001; Philadelphia, 2002

Most Punts, Season
114 Bob Parsons, Chicago, 1981
Chad Stanley, Houston, 2002
111 Brad Maynard, N.Y. Giants, 1997
109 John James, Atlanta, 1978

Most Punts, Rookie, Season
111 Brad Maynard, N.Y. Giants, 1997
108 John Teltschik, Philadelphia, 1986
101 Daniel Pope, Kansas City, 1999

Most Punts, Game
16 Leo Araguz, Oakland vs. San Diego, Oct. 11, 1998
15 John Teltschik, Philadelphia vs. N.Y. Giants, Dec. 6, 1987 (OT)
14 Dick Nesbitt, Chi. Cardinals vs. Chi. Bears, Nov. 30, 1933
Keith Molesworth, Chi. Bears vs. Green Bay, Dec. 10, 1933
Sammy Baugh, Washington vs. Philadelphia, Nov. 5, 1939
Carl Kinscherf, N.Y. Giants vs. Detroit, Nov. 7, 1943
George Taliaferro, N.Y. Yanks vs. Los Angeles, Sept. 28, 1951

Longest Punt
98 Steve O'Neal, N.Y. Jets vs. Denver, Sept. 21, 1969
94 Joe Lintzenich, Chi. Bears vs. N.Y. Giants, Nov. 16, 1931
93 Shawn McCarthy, New England vs. Buffalo, Nov. 3, 1991

AVERAGE YARDAGE

Highest Average, Punting, Career (250 punts)
46.78 Shane Lechler, Oakland, 2000-08 (682-31,902)
45.23 Donnie Jones, Seattle, 2004; Miami, 2005-06; St. Louis, 2007-08 (359-16,239)
45.10 Sammy Baugh, Washington, 1937-1952 (338-15,245)

Highest Average, Punting, Season (Qualifiers)
51.40 Sammy Baugh, Washington, 1940 (35-1,799)
50.00 Donnie Jones, St. Louis, 2008 (82-4,100)
49.11 Shane Lechler, Oakland, 2007 (73-3,585)

Highest Average, Punting, Rookie, Season (Qualifiers)
46.74 Brett Kern, Denver, 2008 (46-2,150)
45.92 Frank Sinkwich, Detroit, 1943 (12-551)
45.91 Shane Lechler, Oakland, 2000 (65-2,984)

Highest Average, Punting, Game (4 punts)
61.75 Bob Cifers, Detroit vs. Chi. Bears, Nov. 24, 1946 (4-247)
61.60 Roy McKay, Green Bay vs. Chi. Cardinals, Oct. 28, 1945 (5-308)
59.50 Darren Bennett, San Diego vs. Pittsburgh, Oct. 1, 1995 (4-238)

NET AVERAGE

Net average has been compiled since 1976.

Highest Net Average, Punting, Career (250 punts)
38.94 Mike Scifres, San Diego, 2003-08 (342-13,317)
38.34 Donnie Jones, Seattle, 2004; Miami, 2005-06; St. Louis, 2007-08 (361-13,839)
38.32 Dustin Colquitt, Kansas City, 2005-08 (302-11,572)

Highest Net Average, Punting, Season (Qualifiers)
41.18 Shane Lechler, Oakland, 2008 (90-3,706)
41.097 Donnie Jones, St. Louis, 2008 (82-3,370)
41.096 Shane Lechler, Oakland, 2007 (73-3,000)

Highest Net Average, Punting, Rookie, Season (Qualifiers)
38.00 Dale Hatcher, L.A. Rams, 1985 (88-3,344)
37.955 Shane Lechler, Oakland, 2000 (66-2,505)
37.946 Ben Graham, N.Y. Jets, 2005 (74-2,808)

Highest Net Average, Punting, Game (4 punts)
59.50 Rohn Stark, Indianapolis vs. Houston, Sept. 13, 1992 (4-238)
52.80 Mike Horan, Denver vs. L.A. Raiders, Sept. 26, 1988 (OT) (5-264)
52.33 Tom Rouen, Denver vs. San Diego, Nov. 11, 2001 (6-314)

PUNTS HAD BLOCKED

Most Consecutive Punts, None Blocked
1,177 Chris Gardocki, Chicago, 1992-94; Indianapolis, 1995-98; Cleveland, 1999-2003; Pittsburgh, 2004-06 (current)
878 Bryan Barker, Kansas City, 1993; Philadelphia, 1994; Jacksonville, 1995-2000; Washington, 2001-03 Green Bay, 2004; St. Louis, 2005

638 Tom Tupa, New England, 1997-98; N.Y. Jets, 1999-2001; Tampa Bay, 2002-03; Washington, 2004

Most Punts Had Blocked, Career

14 Herman Weaver, Detroit, 1970-76; Seattle, 1977-1980
Harry Newsome, Pittsburgh, 1985-89; Minnesota, 1990-93
12 Jerrel Wilson, Kansas City, 1963-1977; New England, 1978
Tom Blanchard, N.Y. Giants, 1971-73; New Orleans, 1974-78; Tampa Bay, 1979-1981
Jeff Feagles, New England, 1988-89; Philadelphia, 1990-93; Arizona, 1994-97; Seattle, 1998-2002; N.Y. Giants, 2003-08
11 David Lee, Baltimore, 1966-1978

Most Punts Had Blocked, Season

6 Harry Newsome, Pittsburgh, 1988
4 Bryan Wagner, Cleveland, 1990
3 By many players

PUNTS INSIDE THE 20

Punts Inside the 20 have been compiled since 1976.

Most Punts Inside the 20, Career

531 Jeff Feagles, New England, 1988-89; Philadelphia, 1990-93; Arizona, 1994-97; Seattle, 1998-2002; N.Y. Giants, 2003-08
396 Craig Hentrich, Green Bay, 1994-97; Tennessee, 1998-2008
381 Sean Landeta, N.Y. Giants, 1985-1993; L.A. Rams, 1993-94; St. Louis, 1995-96; Tampa Bay, 1997; Green Bay, 1998; Philadelphia, 1999-2002; St. Louis, 2003-04; Philadelphia, 2005

Most Punts Inside the 20, Season

42 Andy Lee, San Francisco, 2007
40 Brad Maynard, Chicago, 2008
39 Kyle Richardson, Baltimore, 1999

Most Punts Inside the 20, Game

8 Mark Royals, Pittsburgh vs. Houston, Nov. 6, 1994 (OT)
Bryan Barker, Jacksonville vs. Baltimore, Nov. 14, 1999
7 Josh Miller, Pittsburgh vs. Cincinnati, Dec. 20, 1998
6 By many players

PUNT RETURNS

Most Seasons Leading League

3 Les (Speedy) Duncan, San Diego, 1965-66; Washington, 1971
Rick Upchurch, Denver, 1976, 1978, 1982
2 Dick Christy, N.Y. Titans, 1961-62
Claude Gibson, Oakland, 1963-64
Billy (White Shoes) Johnson, Houston, 1975, 1977
Mel Gray, New Orleans, 1987; Detroit, 1991
Jermaine Lewis, Baltimore, 1997, 2000
Roscoe Parrish, Buffalo, 2007-08

PUNT RETURNS

Most Punt Returns, Career

463 Brian Mitchell, Washington, 1990-99; Philadelphia, 2000-02; N.Y. Giants, 2003
351 Eric Metcalf, Cleveland, 1989-1994; Atlanta, 1995-96; San Diego, 1997; Arizona, 1998; Carolina, 1999; Washington, 2001; Green Bay, 2002
349 David Meggett, N.Y. Giants, 1989-1994; New England, 1995-97; N.Y. Jets, 1998

Most Punt Returns, Season

70 Danny Reece, Tampa Bay, 1979
62 Fulton Walker, Miami-L.A. Raiders, 1985
58 J.T. Smith, Kansas City, 1979
Greg Pruitt, L.A. Raiders, 1983
Leo Lewis, Minnesota, 1988
Desmond Howard, Green Bay, 1996
Nate Burleson, Seattle, 2007

Most Punt Returns, Rookie, Season

57 Lew Barnes, Chicago, 1986
55 B.J. Sams, Baltimore, 2004
54 James Jones, Dallas, 1980

Most Punt Returns, Game

11 Eddie Brown, Washington vs. Tampa Bay, Oct. 9, 1977
10 Theo Bell, Pittsburgh vs. Buffalo, Dec. 16, 1979
Mike Nelms, Washington vs. New Orleans, Dec. 26, 1982
Ronnie Harris, New England vs. Pittsburgh, Dec. 5, 1993
9 Rodger Bird, Oakland vs. Denver, Sept. 10, 1967
Ralph McGill, San Francisco vs. Atlanta, Oct. 29, 1972
Ed Podolak, Kansas City vs. San Diego, Nov. 10, 1974
Anthony Leonard, San Francisco vs. New Orleans, Oct. 17, 1976
Butch Johnson, Dallas vs. Buffalo, Nov. 15, 1976
Larry Marshall, Philadelphia vs. Tampa Bay, Sept. 18, 1977
Nesby Glasgow, Baltimore vs. Kansas City, Sept. 2, 1979
Mike Nelms, Washington vs. St. Louis, Dec. 21, 1980
Leon Bright, N.Y. Giants vs. Philadelphia, Dec. 11, 1982
Pete Shaw, N.Y. Giants vs. Philadelphia, Nov. 20, 1983
Cleotha Montgomery, L.A. Raiders vs. Detroit, Dec. 10, 1984
Phil McConkey, N.Y. Giants vs. Philadelphia, Dec. 6, 1987 (OT)
Andre Hastings, Pittsburgh vs. Cleveland, Nov. 13, 1995
Steve Smith, Carolina vs. Detroit, Sept. 15, 2002
Reggie Swinton, Arizona vs. Philadelphia, Dec. 24, 2005

FAIR CATCHES

Most Fair Catches, Career

231 Brian Mitchell, Washington, 1990-99; Philadelphia, 2000-02; N.Y. Giants, 2003
162 Tim Brown, L.A. Raiders, 1988-1994; Oakland, 1995-2003; Tampa Bay, 2004
144 Glyn Milburn, Denver, 1993-95; Detroit, 1996-97; Chicago, 1998-2001; San Diego, 2001

Most Fair Catches, Season

33 Brian Mitchell, Philadelphia, 2000
29 Wes Welker, Miami, 2006
27 Leo Lewis, Minnesota, 1989
Antonio Chatman, Green Bay, 2004

Most Fair Catches, Game

7 Bake Turner, N.Y. Jets vs. Miami, Nov. 20, 1966
Lem Barney, Detroit vs. Chicago, Nov. 21, 1976
Bobby Morse, Philadelphia vs. Buffalo, Dec. 27, 1987
Chris Carr, Tennessee vs. Jacksonville, Nov. 16, 2008
6 Jake Scott, Miami vs. Buffalo, Dec. 20, 1970
Greg Pruitt, L.A. Raiders vs. Seattle, Oct. 7, 1984
Phil McConkey, San Diego vs. Kansas City, Dec. 17, 1989
Gerald McNeil, Houston vs. Pittsburgh, Sept. 16, 1990
Bobby Engram, Chicago vs. Minnesota, Sept. 15, 1996
Eddie Kennison, New Orleans vs. Baltimore, Dec. 19, 1999

R.W. McQuarters, N.Y. Giants vs. Atlanta, Oct. 15, 2007
5 By many players

YARDS GAINED

Most Seasons Leading League

3 Alvin Haymond, Baltimore, 1965-66; Los Angeles, 1969
2 Bill Dudley, Pittsburgh, 1942, 1946
Emlen Tunnell, N.Y. Giants, 1951-52
Dick Christy, N.Y. Titans, 1961-62
Claude Gibson, Oakland, 1963-64
Rodger Bird, Oakland, 1966-67
J.T. Smith, Kansas City, 1979-1980
Vai Sikahema, St. Louis, 1986-87
David Meggett, N.Y. Giants, 1989-1990
Tamarick Vanover, Kansas City, 1995, 1999

Most Yards Gained, Career

4,999 Brian Mitchell, Washington, 1990-99; Philadelphia, 2000-02; N.Y. Giants, 2003
3,708 David Meggett, N.Y. Giants, 1989-1994; New England, 1995-97; N.Y. Jets, 1998
3,601 Darrien Gordon, San Diego, 1993-94, 1996; Denver, 1997-98; Oakland, 1999-2000; Atlanta, 2001; Green Bay, 2002

Most Yards Gained, Season

875 Desmond Howard, Green Bay, 1996
692 Fulton Walker, Miami-L.A. Raiders, 1985
666 Greg Pruitt, L.A. Raiders, 1983

Most Yards Gained, Rookie, Season

656 Louis Lipps, Pittsburgh, 1984
655 Neal Colzie, Oakland, 1975
619 Leon Johnson, N.Y. Jets, 1997

Most Yards Gained, Game

207 LeRoy Irvin, Los Angeles vs. Atlanta, Oct. 11, 1981
205 George Atkinson, Oakland vs. Buffalo, Sept. 15, 1968
199 Eddie Drummond, Detroit vs. Jacksonville, Nov. 14, 2004 (OT)

Longest Punt Return (All TDs)

103 Robert Bailey, L.A. Rams vs. New Orleans, Oct. 23, 1994
98 Gil LeFebvre, Cincinnati vs. Brooklyn, Dec. 3, 1933
Charlie West, Minnesota vs. Washington, Nov. 3, 1968
Dennis Morgan, Dallas vs. St. Louis, Oct. 13, 1974
Terance Mathis, N.Y. Jets vs. Dallas, Nov. 4, 1990
97 Greg Pruitt, L.A. Raiders vs. Washington, Oct. 2, 1983

AVERAGE YARDAGE

Highest Average, Career (75 returns)

13.96 Roscoe Parrish, Buffalo, 2005-08 (94-1,312)
12.78 George McAfee, Chi. Bears, 1940-41, 1945-1950 (112-1,431)
12.75 Jack Christiansen, Detroit, 1951-58 (85-1,084)

Highest Average, Season (Qualifiers)

23.00 Herb Rich, Baltimore, 1950 (12-276)
21.47 Jack Christiansen, Detroit, 1952 (15-322)
21.28 Dick Christy, N.Y. Titans, 1961 (18-383)

Highest Average, Rookie, Season (Qualifiers)

23.00 Herb Rich, Baltimore, 1950 (12-276)
20.88 Jerry Davis, Chi. Cardinals, 1948 (16-334)
20.73 Frank Sinkwich, Detroit, 1943 (11-228)

Highest Average, Game (3 returns)

51.00 Steve Smith, Carolina vs. Cincinnati, Dec. 8, 2002 (3-153)
47.67 Chuck Latourette, St. Louis vs. New Orleans, Sept. 29, 1968 (3-143)
47.33 Johnny Roland, St. Louis vs. Philadelphia, Oct. 2, 1966 (3-142)

TOUCHDOWNS

Most Touchdowns, Career

10 Eric Metcalf, Cleveland, 1989-1994; Atlanta, 1995-96; San Diego, 1997; Arizona, 1998; Carolina, 1999; Washington, 2001; Green Bay, 2002
9 Brian Mitchell, Washington, 1990-99; Philadelphia 2000-02; N.Y. Giants, 2003
8 Jack Christiansen, Detroit, 1951-58
Rick Upchurch, Denver, 1975-1983
Desmond Howard, Washington, 1992-94; Jacksonville, 1995; Green Bay, 1996, 1999; Oakland, 1997-98; Detroit, 1999-2002

Most Touchdowns, Season

4 Jack Christiansen, Detroit, 1951
Rick Upchurch, Denver, 1976
Devin Hester, Chicago, 2007
3 Emlen Tunnell, N.Y. Giants, 1951
Billy (White Shoes) Johnson, Houston, 1975
LeRoy Irvin, Los Angeles, 1981
Desmond Howard, Green Bay, 1996
Darrien Gordon, Denver, 1997
Eric Metcalf, San Diego, 1997
Devin Hester, Chicago, 2006
Adam Jones, Tennessee, 2006
Reggie Bush, New Orleans, 2008
Johnnie Lee Higgins, Oakland, 2008
2 By many players

Most Touchdowns, Rookie, Season

4 Jack Christiansen, Detroit, 1951
3 Devin Hester, Chicago, 2006
2 By many players

Most Touchdowns, Game

2 Jack Christiansen, Detroit vs. Los Angeles, Oct. 14, 1951; vs. Green Bay, Nov. 22, 1951
Dick Christy, N.Y. Titans vs. Denver, Sept. 24, 1961
Rick Upchurch, Denver vs. Cleveland, Sept. 26, 1976
LeRoy Irvin, Los Angeles vs. Atlanta, Oct. 11, 1981
Vai Sikahema, St. Louis vs. Tampa Bay, Dec. 21, 1986
Todd Kinchen, L.A. Rams vs. Atlanta, Dec. 27, 1992
Eric Metcalf, Cleveland vs. Pittsburgh, Oct. 24, 1993; San Diego vs. Cincinnati, Nov. 2, 1997
Darrien Gordon, Denver vs. Carolina, Nov. 9, 1997
Jermaine Lewis, Baltimore vs. Seattle, Dec. 7, 1997; Baltimore vs. N.Y. Jets, Dec. 24, 2000
Steve Smith, Carolina vs. Cincinnati, Dec. 8, 2002
Eddie Drummond, Detroit vs. Jacksonville, Nov. 14, 2004 (OT)
Reggie Bush, New Orleans vs. Minnesota, Oct. 6, 2008

KICKOFF RETURNS

Most Seasons Leading League

3 Abe Woodson, San Francisco, 1959, 1962-63
2 Lynn Chandnois, Pittsburgh, 1951-52
Bobby Jancik, Houston, 1962-63
Travis Williams, Green Bay, 1967; Los Angeles, 1971
Mel Gray, Detroit, 1991, 1994
Michael Bates, Carolina, 1996-97

KICKOFF RETURNS

Most Kickoff Returns, Career

607 Brian Mitchell, Washington, 1990-99; Philadelphia 2000-02; N.Y. Giants, 2003
506 Allen Rossum, Philadelphia, 1998-99; Green Bay, 2000-01; Atlanta, 2002-06; Pittsburgh, 2007; San Francisco, 2008
426 Dante Hall, Kansas City, 2000-06; St. Louis, 2007-08

Most Kickoff Returns, Season
82 MarTay Jenkins, Arizona, 2000
73 Josh Scobey, Arizona, 2003
Chris Carr, Oakland, 2005
70 Tyrone Hughes, New Orleans, 1996
Michael Lewis, New Orleans, 2002

Most Kickoff Returns, Rookie, Season
73 Josh Scobey, Arizona, 2003
Chris Carr, Oakland, 2005
67 Ronney Jenkins, San Diego, 2000
64 Tab Perry, Cincinnati, 2005

Most Kickoff Returns, Game
10 Desmond Howard, Oakland vs. Seattle, Oct. 26, 1997
Richard Alston, Cleveland vs. Cincinnati, Nov. 28, 2004
9 Noland Smith, Kansas City vs. Oakland, Nov. 23, 1967
Dino Hall, Cleveland vs. Pittsburgh, Oct. 7, 1979
Paul Palmer, Kansas City vs. Seattle, Sept. 20, 1987
Eric Metcalf, Atlanta vs. San Francisco, Sept. 29, 1996; vs. St. Louis, Nov. 10, 1996
Michael Bates, Carolina vs. Atlanta, Oct. 4, 1998
Nate Jacquet, Minnesota vs. Philadelphia, Nov. 11, 2001
Ahmad Merritt, Chicago vs. San Francisco, Sept. 7, 2003
Josh Scobey, Arizona vs. Cleveland, Nov. 16, 2003
Maurice Hicks, San Francisco vs. San Diego, Oct. 15, 2006
Aveion Cason, Detroit vs. San Diego, Dec. 16, 2007
Allen Rossum, San Francisco vs. Philadelphia, Oct. 12, 2008
Steve Breaston, Arizona vs. New England, Dec. 21, 2008
8 By many players

YARDS GAINED

Most Seasons Leading League
3 Bruce Harper, N.Y. Jets, 1977-79
Tyrone Hughes, New Orleans, 1994-96
2 Marshall Goldberg, Chi. Cardinals, 1941-42
Woodley Lewis, Los Angeles, 1953-54
Al Carmichael, Green Bay, 1956-57
Timmy Brown, Philadelphia, 1961, 1963
Bobby Jancik, Houston, 1963, 1966
Ron Smith, Atlanta, 1966-67
Chris Carr, Oakland, 2005-06

Most Yards Gained, Career
14,014 Brian Mitchell, Washington, 1990-99; Philadelphia, 2000-02; N.Y. Giants, 2003
11,779 Allen Rossum, Philadelphia, 1998-99; Green Bay, 2000-01; Atlanta, 2002-06; Pittsburgh, 2007; San Francisco, 2008
10,250 Mel Gray, New Orleans, 1986-88; Detroit, 1989-1994; Houston, 1995-96; Tennessee, 1997; Philadelphia, 1997

Most Yards Gained, Season
2,186 MarTay Jenkins, Arizona, 2000
1,809 Josh Cribbs, Cleveland, 2007
1,807 Michael Lewis, New Orleans, 2002

Most Yards Gained, Rookie, Season
1,752 Chris Carr, Oakland, 2005
1,684 Josh Scobey, Arizona, 2003
1,577 Justin Miller, N.Y. Jets, 2005

Most Yards Gained, Game
304 Tyrone Hughes, New Orleans vs. L.A. Rams, Oct. 23, 1994
294 Wally Triplett, Detroit vs. Los Angeles, Oct. 29, 1950
278 Chad Morton, N.Y. Jets vs. Buffalo, Sept. 8, 2002 (OT)

Longest Kickoff Return (All TDs)
108 Ellis Hobbs, New England, vs. N.Y. Jets, Sept. 9, 2007
106 Al Carmichael, Green Bay vs. Chi. Bears, Oct. 7, 1956
Noland Smith, Kansas City vs. Denver, Dec. 17, 1967
Roy Green, St. Louis vs. Dallas, Oct. 21, 1979
105 Frank Seno, Chi. Cardinals vs. N.Y. Giants, Oct. 20, 1946
Ollie Matson, Chi. Cardinals vs. Washington, Oct. 14, 1956
Abe Woodson, San Francisco vs. Los Angeles, Nov. 8, 1959
Timmy Brown, Philadelphia vs. Cleveland, Sept. 17, 1961
Jon Arnett, Los Angeles vs. Detroit, Oct. 29, 1961
Eugene (Mercury) Morris, Miami vs. Cincinnati, Sept. 14, 1969
Travis Williams, Los Angeles vs. New Orleans, Dec. 5, 1971
Terry Fair, Detroit vs. Tampa Bay, Sept. 28, 1998

AVERAGE YARDAGE

Highest Average, Career (75 returns)
30.56 Gale Sayers, Chicago, 1965-1971 (91-2,781)
29.57 Lynn Chandnois, Pittsburgh, 1950-56 (92-2,720)
28.69 Abe Woodson, San Francisco, 1958-1964; St. Louis, 1965-66 (193-5,538)

Highest Average, Season (Qualifiers)
41.06 Travis Williams, Green Bay, 1967 (18-739)
37.69 Gale Sayers, Chicago, 1967 (16-603)
35.50 Ollie Matson, Chi. Cardinals, 1958 (14-497)

Highest Average, Rookie, Season (Qualifiers)
41.06 Travis Williams, Green Bay, 1967 (18-739)
33.08 Tom Moore, Green Bay, 1960 (12-397)
32.88 Duriel Harris, Miami, 1976 (17-559)

Highest Average, Game (3 returns)
73.50 Wally Triplett, Detroit vs. Los Angeles, Oct. 29, 1950 (4-294)
67.33 Lenny Lyles, San Francisco vs. Baltimore, Dec. 18, 1960 (3-202)
65.33 Ken Hall, Houston vs. N.Y. Titans, Oct. 23, 1960 (3-196)

TOUCHDOWNS

Most Touchdowns, Career
6 Ollie Matson, Chi. Cardinals, 1952, 1954-58; L.A. Rams, 1959-1962; Detroit, 1963; Philadelphia, 1964
Gale Sayers, Chicago, 1965-1971
Travis Williams, Green Bay, 1967-1970; Los Angeles, 1971
Mel Gray, New Orleans, 1986-88; Detroit, 1989-1994; Houston, 1995-96; Tennessee, 1997; Philadelphia, 1997
Dante Hall, Kansas City, 2000-06; St. Louis, 2007-08
5 Bobby Mitchell, Cleveland, 1958-1961; Washington, 1962-68
Abe Woodson, San Francisco, 1958-1964; St. Louis, 1965-66
Timmy Brown, Green Bay, 1959; Philadelphia, 1960-67; Baltimore, 1968
Michael Bates, Seattle, 1993-94; Cleveland, 1995; Carolina, 1996-2000, 2002; Washington, 2001; N.Y. Jets, 2003; Dallas, 2003
Terrence McGee, Buffalo, 2003-08
Josh Cribbs, Cleveland, 2005-08
Justin Miller, N.Y. Jets, 2005-08; Oakland, 2008
Allen Rossum, Philadelphia, 1998-99; Green Bay, 2000-01; Atlanta, 2002-06; Pittsburgh, 2007; San Francisco, 2008

4 Cecil Turner, Chicago, 1968-1973
Ron Brown, L.A. Rams, 1984-89, 1991; L.A. Raiders, 1990
Jon Vaughn, New England, 1991-92; Seattle, 1993-94; Kansas City, 1994
Andre Coleman, San Diego, 1994-96; Seattle, 1997; Pittsburgh, 1997-98
Tamarick Vanover, Kansas City, 1995-99, San Diego, 2002
Tony Horne, St. Louis, 1998-2000
Brian Mitchell, Washington, 1990-99; Philadelphia, 2000-02; N.Y. Giants, 2003
Darrick Vaughn, Atlanta, 2000-01; Houston, 2003
André Davis, Cleveland, 2002-04; New England, 2005; Buffalo, 2006; Houston, 2007-08
Devin Hester, Chicago, 2006-08
Leon Washington, N.Y. Jets, 2006-08

Most Touchdowns, Season

4 Travis Williams, Green Bay, 1967
Cecil Turner, Chicago, 1970
3 Verda (Vitamin T) Smith, Los Angeles, 1950
Abe Woodson, San Francisco, 1963
Gale Sayers, Chicago, 1967
Raymond Clayborn, New England, 1977
Ron Brown, L.A. Rams, 1985
Mel Gray, Detroit, 1994
Darrick Vaughn, Atlanta, 2000
Terrence McGee, Buffalo, 2004
André Davis, Houston, 2007
Leon Washington, N.Y. Jets, 2007
2 By many players

Most Touchdowns, Rookie, Season

4 Travis Williams, Green Bay, 1967
3 Raymond Clayborn, New England, 1977
Darrick Vaughn, Atlanta, 2000
2 By many players

Most Touchdowns, Game

2 Timmy Brown, Philadelphia vs. Dallas, Nov. 6, 1966
Travis Williams, Green Bay vs. Cleveland, Nov. 12, 1967
Ron Brown, L.A. Rams vs. Green Bay, Nov. 24, 1985
Tyrone Hughes, New Orleans vs. L.A. Rams, Oct. 23, 1994
Chad Morton, N.Y. Jets vs. Buffalo, Sept. 8, 2002 (OT)
Devin Hester, Chicago vs. St. Louis, Dec. 11, 2006
André Davis, Houston vs. Jacksonville, Dec. 30, 2007

COMBINED KICK RETURNS

Most Combined Kick Returns, Career

1,070 Brian Mitchell, Washington, 1990-99; Philadelphia, 2000-02; N.Y. Giants, 2003 (p-463, k-607)
801 Allen Rossum, Philadelphia, 1998-99; Green Bay, 2000-01; Atlanta, 2002-06; Pittsburgh, 2007; San Francisco, 2008 (p-295, k-506)
711 Glyn Milburn, Denver, 1993-95; Detroit, 1996-97; Chicago, 1998-2001; San Diego, 2001 (p-304, k-407)

Most Combined Kick Returns, Season

114 Michael Lewis, New Orleans, 2002 (p-44, k-70)
B.J. Sams, Baltimore, 2004 (p-55, k-59)
107 Chris Carr, Oakland, 2005 (p-34, k-73)
Dante Hall, Kansas City, 2005 (p-42, k-65)
105 Reggie Swinton, Arizona, 2005 (p-42, k-63)

Most Combined Kick Returns, Game

13 Stump Mitchell, St. Louis vs. Atlanta, Oct. 18, 1981 (p-6, k-7)
Ronnie Harris, New England vs. Pittsburgh, Dec. 5, 1993 (p-10, k-3)
12 Mel Renfro, Dallas vs. Green Bay, Nov. 29, 1964 (p-4, k-8)
Larry Jones, Washington vs. Dallas, Dec. 13, 1975 (p-6, k-6)
Eddie Brown, Washington vs. Tampa Bay, Oct. 9, 1977 (p-11, k-1)
Nesby Glasgow, Baltimore vs. Denver, Sept. 2, 1979 (p-9, k-3)
Tim Dwight, Atlanta vs. Detroit, Nov. 12, 2000 (p-8, k-4)
Wes Welker, Miami vs. Buffalo, Dec. 5, 2004 (p-6, k-6)
Reggie Swinton, Arizona vs. Philadelphia, Dec. 24, 2005 (p-9, k-3)
Devin Hester, Chicago vs. Detroit, Sept. 30, 2007 (p-5, k-7)
11 By many players

YARDS GAINED

Most Yards Returned, Career

19,013 Brian Mitchell, Washington, 1990-99; Philadelphia, 2000-02; N.Y. Giants, 2003 (p-4,999; k-14,014)
14,751 Allen Rossum, Philadelphia, 1998-99; Green Bay, 2000-01; Atlanta, 2002-06; Pittsburgh, 2007; San Francisco, 2008 (p-2,972, k-11,779)
13,003 Mel Gray, New Orleans, 1986-88; Detroit, 1989-1994; Houston, 1995-96; Tennessee, 1997; Philadelphia, 1997 (p-2,753; k-10,250)

Most Yards Returned, Season

2,432 Michael Lewis, New Orleans, 2002 (p-625, k-1,807)
2,214 Josh Cribbs, Cleveland, 2007 (p-405, k-1,809)
2,187 MarTay Jenkins, Arizona, 2000 (p-1, k-2,186)

Most Yards Returned, Game

347 Tyrone Hughes, New Orleans vs. L.A. Rams, Oct. 23, 1994 (p-43, k-304)
314 Devin Hester, Chicago vs. Detroit, Sept. 30, 2007 (p-95, k-219)
306 Josh Cribbs, Cleveland vs. Baltimore, Nov. 18, 2007 (OT) (p-61, k-245)

TOUCHDOWNS

Most Touchdowns, Career

13 Brian Mitchell, Washington, 1990-99; Philadelphia, 2000-02; N.Y. Giants, 2003 (p-9, k-4)
12 Eric Metcalf, Cleveland, 1989-1994; Atlanta, 1995-96; San Diego, 1997; Arizona, 1998; Carolina, 1999; Washington, 2001; Green Bay, 2002 (p-10, k-2)
Dante Hall, Kansas City, 2000-06; St. Louis, 2007-08 (p-6, k-6)
11 Devin Hester, Chicago, 2006-08 (p-7, k-4)

Most Touchdowns, Season

6 Devin Hester, Chicago, 2007 (p-4, k-2)
5 Devin Hester, Chicago, 2006 (p-3, k-2)
4 Jack Christiansen, Detroit, 1951 (p-4)
Emlen Tunnell, N.Y. Giants, 1951 (p-3, k-1)
Gale Sayers, Chicago, 1967 (p-1, k-3)
Travis Williams, Green Bay, 1967 (k-4)
Cecil Turner, Chicago, 1970 (k-4)
Billy Johnson, Houston, 1975 (p-3, k-1)
Rick Upchurch, Denver, 1976 (p-4)
Dante Hall, Kansas City, 2003 (p-2, r-2)
Eddie Drummond, Detroit, 2004 (p-2, k-2)

Most Touchdowns, Game

2 Jack Christiansen, Detroit vs. Los Angeles, Oct. 14, 1951 (p-2); vs. Green Bay, Nov. 22, 1951 (p-2)
Jim Patton, N.Y. Giants vs. Washington, Oct. 30, 1955 (p-1, k-1)
Bobby Mitchell, Cleveland vs. Philadelphia, Nov. 23, 1958 (p-1, k-1)

Dick Christy, N.Y. Titans vs. Denver, Sept. 24, 1961 (p-2)
Al Frazier, Denver vs. Boston, Dec. 3, 1961 (p-1, k-1)
Timmy Brown, Philadelphia vs. Dallas, Nov. 6, 1966 (k-2)
Travis Williams, Green Bay vs. Cleveland, Nov. 12, 1967 (k-2); vs. Pittsburgh, Nov. 2, 1969 (p-1, k-1)
Gale Sayers, Chicago vs. San Francisco, Dec. 3, 1967 (p-1, k-1)
Rick Upchurch, Denver vs. Cleveland, Sept. 26, 1976 (p-2)
Eddie Payton, Detroit vs. Minnesota, Dec. 17, 1977 (p-1, k-1)
LeRoy Irvin, Los Angeles vs. Atlanta, Oct. 11, 1981 (p-2)
Ron Brown, L.A. Rams vs. Green Bay, Nov. 24, 1985 (k-2)
Vai Sikahema, St. Louis vs. Tampa Bay, Dec. 21, 1986 (p-2)
Todd Kinchen, L.A. Rams vs. Atlanta, Dec. 27, 1992 (p-2)
Eric Metcalf, Cleveland vs. Pittsburgh, Oct. 24, 1993 (p-2); San Diego vs. Cincinnati, Nov. 2, 1997 (p-2)
Tyrone Hughes, New Orleans vs. L.A. Rams, Oct. 23, 1994 (k-2)
Darrien Gordon, Denver vs. Carolina, Nov. 9, 1997 (p-2)
Jermaine Lewis, Baltimore vs. Seattle, Dec. 7, 1997 (p-2); Baltimore vs. N.Y. Jets, Dec. 24, 2000 (p-2)
Chad Morton, N.Y. Jets vs. Buffalo, Sept. 8, 2002 (OT) (k-2)
Michael Lewis, New Orleans vs. Washington, Oct. 13, 2002 (p-1, k-1)
Dante Hall, Kansas City vs. St. Louis, Dec. 8, 2002 (p-1, k-1)
Steve Smith, Carolina vs. Cincinnati, Dec. 8, 2002 (p-2)
Eddie Drummond, Detroit vs. Jacksonville, Nov. 14, 2004 (OT) (p-2)
Devin Hester, Chicago vs. St. Louis, Dec. 11, 2006 (k-2)
Darren Sproles, San Diego vs. Indianapolis, Nov. 11, 2007 (p-1, k-1)
Devin Hester, Chicago vs. Denver, Nov. 25, 2007 (p-1, k-1)
André Davis, Houston vs. Jacksonville, Dec. 30, 2007 (k-2)
Reggie Bush, New Orleans vs. Minnesota, Oct. 6, 2008

FUMBLES

Most Fumbles, Career

161 Warren Moon, Houston, 1984-1993; Minnesota, 1994-96; Seattle, 1997-98; Kansas City, 1999-2000
157 Brett Favre, Atlanta, 1991; Green Bay, 1992-2007; N.Y. Jets, 2008
153 Dave Krieg, Seattle, 1980-1991; Kansas City, 1992-93; Detroit, 1994; Arizona, 1995; Chicago, 1996; Tennessee, 1997-98

Most Fumbles, Season

23 Kerry Collins, N.Y. Giants, 2001
Daunte Culpepper, Minnesota, 2002
21 Tony Banks, St. Louis, 1996
David Carr, Houston, 2002
18 Dave Krieg, Seattle, 1989
Warren Moon, Houston, 1990

Most Fumbles, Game

7 Len Dawson, Kansas City vs. San Diego, Nov. 15, 1964
6 Sam Etcheverry, St. Louis vs. N.Y. Giants, Sept, 17, 1961
Dave Krieg, Seattle vs. Kansas City, Nov. 5, 1989
Brett Favre, Green Bay vs. Tampa Bay, Dec. 7, 1998
Kurt Warner, St. Louis vs. N.Y. Giants, Sept. 7, 2003
Chad Pennington, N.Y. Jets vs. Kansas City, Sept. 11, 2005
5 Paul Christman, Chi. Cardinals vs. Green Bay, Nov. 10, 1946
Joe Perry, San Francisco vs. Cleveland, Nov. 12, 1950
Charlie Conerly, N.Y. Giants vs. San Francisco, Dec. 1, 1957
Tom Yewcic, Boston vs. Oakland, Dec. 16, 1962
Jack Kemp, Buffalo vs. Houston, Oct. 29, 1967
Roman Gabriel, Philadelphia vs. Oakland, Nov. 21, 1976
Randall Cunningham, Philadelphia vs. L.A. Raiders, Nov. 30, 1986 (OT)
Willie Totten, Buffalo vs. Indianapolis, Oct. 4, 1987
Dave Walter, Cincinnati vs. Seattle, Oct. 11, 1987
Dave Krieg, Seattle vs. San Diego, Nov. 25, 1990 (OT)
Andre Ware, Detroit vs. Green Bay, Dec. 6, 1992
Steve Beuerlein, Carolina vs. San Francisco, Nov. 8, 1998
Patrick Ramsey, Washington vs. Green Bay, Oct. 20, 2002
Eli Manning, N.Y. Giants vs. Buffalo, Dec. 23, 2007

FUMBLES RECOVERED

Most Fumbles Recovered, Career, Own and Opponents'

56 Warren Moon, Houston, 1984-1993; Minnesota, 1994-96; Seattle, 1997-98; Kansas City, 1999-2000 (56 own)
47 Dave Krieg, Seattle, 1980-1991; Kansas City, 1992-93; Detroit, 1994; Arizona, 1995; Chicago, 1996; Tennessee, 1997-98 (47 own)
45 Boomer Esiason, Cincinnati, 1984-1992, 1997; N.Y. Jets, 1993-95; Arizona, 1996 (45 own)

Most Fumbles Recovered, Season, Own and Opponents'

12 David Carr, Houston, 2002 (12 own)
9 Don Hultz, Minnesota, 1963 (9 opp)
Dave Krieg, Seattle, 1989 (9 own)
Brian Griese, Denver, 1999 (9 own)
Jon Kitna, Seattle, 2000 (9 own)
8 Paul Christman, Chi. Cardinals, 1945 (8 own)
Joe Schmidt, Detroit, 1955 (8 opp)
Bill Butler, Minnesota, 1963 (8 own)
Kermit Alexander, San Francisco, 1965 (4 own, 4 opp)
Jack Lambert, Pittsburgh, 1976 (1 own, 7 opp)
Danny White, Dallas, 1981 (8 own)
Dan Marino, Miami, 1988 (7 own, 1 opp)
Tony Banks, St. Louis, 1998 (8 own)
Ryan Fitzpatrick, Cincinnati, 2008 (8 own)

Most Fumbles Recovered, Game, Own and Opponents'

4 Otto Graham, Cleveland vs. N.Y. Giants, Oct. 25, 1953 (4 own)
Sam Etcheverry, St. Louis vs. N.Y. Giants, Sept. 17, 1961 (4 own)
Roman Gabriel, Los Angeles vs. San Francisco, Oct. 12, 1969 (4 own)
Joe Ferguson, Buffalo vs. Miami, Sept. 18, 1977 (4 own)
Randall Cunningham, Philadelphia vs. L.A. Raiders, Nov. 30, 1986 (OT) (4 own)

3 By many players

OWN FUMBLES RECOVERED

Most Own Fumbles Recovered, Career

56 Warren Moon, Houston, 1984-1993; Minnesota, 1994-96; Seattle, 1997-98; Kansas City, 1999-2000
47 Dave Krieg, Seattle, 1980-1991; Kansas City, 1992-93; Detroit, 1994; Arizona, 1995; Chicago, 1996; Tennessee, 1997-98
45 Boomer Esiason, Cincinnati, 1984-1992, 1997; N.Y. Jets, 1993-95; Arizona, 1996

Most Own Fumbles Recovered, Season

12 David Carr, Houston, 2002
9 Dave Krieg, Seattle, 1989
Brian Griese, Denver, 1999
Jon Kitna, Seattle, 2000
8 Paul Christman, Chi. Cardinals, 1945
Bill Butler, Minnesota, 1963
Danny White, Dallas, 1981
Tony Banks, St. Louis, 1998
Ryan Fitzpatrick, Cincinnati, 2008

Most Own Fumbles Recovered, Game

4 Otto Graham, Cleveland vs. N.Y. Giants, Oct. 25, 1953
Sam Etcheverry, St. Louis vs. N.Y. Giants, Sept. 17, 1961
Roman Gabriel, Los Angeles vs. San Francisco, Oct. 12, 1969
Joe Ferguson, Buffalo vs. Miami, Sept. 18, 1977
Randall Cunningham, Philadelphia vs. L.A. Raiders, Nov. 30, 1986 (OT)
3 By many players

OPPONENTS' FUMBLES RECOVERED

Most Opponents' Fumbles Recovered, Career

29 Jim Marshall, Cleveland, 1960; Minnesota, 1961-1979
28 Rickey Jackson, New Orleans, 1981-1993; San Francisco, 1994-95
26 Kevin Greene, L.A. Rams, 1985-1992; Pittsburgh, 1993-95; Carolina, 1996, 1998-99; San Francisco, 1997
Cornelius Bennett, Buffalo, 1987-1995; Atlanta, 1996-98; Indianapolis, 1999-2000
Jason Taylor, Miami, 1997-2007; Washington, 2008

Most Opponents' Fumbles Recovered, Season

9 Don Hultz, Minnesota, 1963
8 Joe Schmidt, Detroit, 1955
7 Alan Page, Minnesota, 1970
Jack Lambert, Pittsburgh, 1976
Ray Childress, Houston, 1988
Rickey Jackson, New Orleans, 1990

Most Opponents' Fumbles Recovered, Game

3 Corwin Clatt, Chi. Cardinals vs. Detroit, Nov. 6, 1949
Vic Sears, Philadelphia vs. Green Bay, Nov. 2, 1952
Ed Beatty, San Francisco vs. Los Angeles, Oct. 7, 1956
Ron Carroll, Houston vs. Cincinnati, Oct. 27, 1974
Maurice Spencer, New Orleans vs. Atlanta, Oct. 10, 1976
Steve Nelson, New England vs. Philadelphia, Oct. 8, 1978
Charles Jackson, Kansas City vs. Pittsburgh, Sept. 6, 1981
Willie Buchanon, San Diego vs. Denver, Sept. 27, 1981
Joey Browner, Minnesota vs. San Francisco, Sept. 8, 1985
Ray Childress, Houston vs. Washington, Oct. 30, 1988
John Thierry, Chicago vs. Houston, Oct. 22, 1995
Stephen Boyd, Detroit vs. Chicago, Oct. 4, 1998
Darryl Williams, Seattle vs. Kansas City, Oct. 4, 1998
Rod Woodson, Oakland vs. Pittsburgh, Sept. 15, 2002
Brian Young, St. Louis vs. Baltimore, Nov. 9, 2003
2 By many players

YARDS RETURNING FUMBLES

Longest Fumble Run (All TDs)

104 Jack Tatum, Oakland vs. Green Bay, Sept. 24, 1972
Aeneas Williams, Arizona vs. Washington, Nov. 5, 2000
102 Travis Davis, Pittsburgh vs. Carolina, Dec. 26, 1999
100 Chris Martin, Kansas City vs. Miami, Oct. 13, 1991

TOUCHDOWNS

Most Touchdowns, Career (Total)

5 Jessie Tuggle, Atlanta, 1987-2000
Jason Taylor, Miami, 1997-2007; Washington, 2008
4 Bill Thompson, Denver, 1969-1981
Derrick Thomas, Kansas City, 1989-1999
Keith Bulluck, Tennessee, 2000-08
Ronde Barber, Tampa Bay, 1997-2008
3 By many players

Most Touchdowns, Season (Total)

2 Harold McPhail, Boston, 1934
Harry Ebding, Detroit, 1937
John Morelli, Boston, 1944
Frank Maznicki, Boston, 1947
Fred (Dippy) Evans, Chi. Bears, 1948
Ralph Heywood, Boston, 1948
Art Tait, N.Y. Yanks, 1951
John Dwyer, Los Angeles, 1952
Leo Sugar, Chi. Cardinals, 1957
Doug Cline, Houston, 1961
Jim Bradshaw, Pittsburgh, 1964
Royce Berry, Cincinnati, 1970
Ahmad Rashad, Buffalo, 1974
Tim Gray, Kansas City, 1977
Charles Phillips, Oakland, 1978
Kenny Johnson, Atlanta, 1981
George Martin, N.Y. Giants, 1981
Del Rodgers, Green Bay, 1982
Mike Douglass, Green Bay, 1983
Shelton Robinson, Seattle, 1983
Erik McMillan, N.Y. Jets, 1989
Les Miller, San Diego, 1990
Seth Joyner, Philadelphia, 1991
Robert Goff, New Orleans, 1992
Willie Clay, Detroit, 1993
Tyrone Hughes, New Orleans, 1994
Chad Brown, Seattle, 1997
Marcus Robertson, Tennessee, 1997
Dwayne Rudd, Minnesota, 1998
Keith McKenzie, Green Bay, 1999
Ronde Barber, Tampa Bay, 2004
Leonard Little, St. Louis, 2004
Antwan Odom, Tennessee, 2005
Adalius Thomas, Baltimore, 2005
Kevin Curtis, Philadelphia, 2007

Most Touchdowns, Career (Own recovered)

2 Ken Kavanaugh, Chi. Bears, 1940-41, 1945-1950
Mike Ditka, Chicago, 1961-66; Philadelphia, 1967-68; Dallas, 1969-1972
Gail Cogdill, Detroit, 1960-68; Baltimore, 1968; Atlanta, 1969-1970
Ahmad Rashad, St. Louis, 1972-73; Buffalo, 1974; Minnesota, 1976-1982
Jim Mitchell, Atlanta, 1969-1979
Drew Pearson, Dallas, 1973-1983
Del Rodgers, Green Bay, 1982, 1984; San Francisco, 1987-88

Alan Ricard, Baltimore, 2001-05
Kevin Curtis, St. Louis, 2003-06; Philadelphia, 2007-08

Most Touchdowns, Season (Own recovered)
2 Ahmad Rashad, Buffalo, 1974
Del Rodgers, Green Bay, 1982
Kevin Curtis, Philadelphia, 2007
1 By many players

Most Touchdowns, Career (Opponents' recovered)
5 Jessie Tuggle, Atlanta, 1987-2000
Jason Taylor, Miami, 1997-2007; Washington, 2008
4 Derrick Thomas, Kansas City, 1989-1999
Keith Bulluck, Tennessee, 2000-08
Ronde Barber, Tampa Bay, 1997-2008
3 By many players

Most Touchdowns, Season (Opponents' recovered)
2 Harold McPhail, Boston, 1934
Harry Ebding, Detroit, 1937
John Morelli, Boston, 1944
Frank Maznicki, Boston, 1947
Fred (Dippy) Evans, Chi. Bears, 1948
Ralph Heywood, Boston, 1948
Art Tait, N.Y. Yanks, 1951
John Dwyer, Los Angeles, 1952
Leo Sugar, Chi. Cardinals, 1957
Doug Cline, Houston, 1961
Jim Bradshaw, Pittsburgh, 1964
Royce Berry, Cincinnati, 1970
Tim Gray, Kansas City, 1977
Charles Phillips, Oakland, 1978
Kenny Johnson, Atlanta, 1981
George Martin, N.Y. Giants, 1981
Mike Douglass, Green Bay, 1983
Shelton Robinson, Seattle, 1983
Erik McMillan, N.Y. Jets, 1989
Les Miller, San Diego, 1990
Seth Joyner, Philadelphia, 1991
Robert Goff, New Orleans, 1992
Willie Clay, Detroit, 1993
Tyrone Hughes, New Orleans, 1994
Chad Brown, Seattle, 1997
Marcus Robertson, Tennessee, 1997
Dwayne Rudd, Minnesota, 1998
Keith McKenzie, Green Bay, 1999
Ronde Barber, Tampa Bay, 2004
Leonard Little, St. Louis, 2004
Antwan Odom, Tennessee, 2005
Adalius Thomas, Baltimore, 2005

Most Touchdowns, Game (Opponents' recovered)
2 Fred (Dippy) Evans, Chi. Bears vs. Washington, Nov. 28, 1948

COMBINED NET YARDS GAINED

Rushing, receiving, interception returns, punt returns, kickoff returns, and fumble returns

Most Seasons Leading League
5 Jim Brown, Cleveland, 1958-1961, 1964
4 Brian Mitchell, Washington, 1994-96, 1998
3 Cliff Battles, Boston, 1932-33; Washington, 1937
Gale Sayers, Chicago, 1965-67
Eric Dickerson, L.A. Rams, 1983-84, 1986
Thurman Thomas, Buffalo, 1989, 1991-92

Most Consecutive Seasons Leading League
4 Jim Brown, Cleveland, 1958-1961
3 Gale Sayers, Chicago, 1965-67
Brian Mitchell, Washington, 1994-96
2 Cliff Battles, Boston, 1932-33
Charley Trippi, Chi. Cardinals, 1948-49
Timmy Brown, Philadelphia, 1962-63
Floyd Little, Denver, 1967-68
James Brooks, San Diego, 1981-82
Eric Dickerson, L.A. Rams, 1983-84
Thurman Thomas, Buffalo, 1991-92
Dante Hall, Kansas City, 2003-04

ATTEMPTS

Most Attempts, Career
4,939 Emmitt Smith, Dallas, 1990-2002; Arizona, 2003-04
4,368 Walter Payton, Chicago, 1975-1987
4,016 Curtis Martin, New England, 1995-97; N.Y. Jets, 1998-2005

Most Attempts, Season
496 James Wilder, Tampa Bay, 1984
458 Larry Johnson, Kansas City, 2006
455 Eddie George, Tennessee, 2000

Most Attempts, Rookie, Season
442 Eric Dickerson, L.A. Rams, 1983
433 Edgerrin James, Indianapolis, 1999
401 Curtis Martin, New England, 1995

Most Attempts, Game
48 James Wilder, Tampa Bay vs. Pittsburgh, Oct. 30, 1983
LaDainian Tomlinson, San Diego vs. Denver, Dec. 1, 2002 (OT)
47 James Wilder, Tampa Bay vs. Green Bay, Sept. 30, 1984 (OT)
Terrell Davis, Denver vs. Buffalo, Oct. 26, 1997 (OT)
46 Gerald Riggs, Atlanta vs. L.A. Rams, Nov. 17, 1985

YARDS GAINED

Most Yards Gained, Career
23,546 Jerry Rice, San Francisco, 1985-2000; Oakland, 2001-04; Seattle, 2004
23,330 Brian Mitchell, Washington, 1990-99; Philadelphia, 2000-02; N.Y. Giants, 2003
21,803 Walter Payton, Chicago, 1975-1987

Most Yards Gained, Season
2,690 Derrick Mason, Tennessee, 2000
2,647 Michael Lewis, New Orleans, 2002
2,535 Lionel James, San Diego, 1985

Most Yards Gained, Rookie, Season
2,317 Tim Brown, L.A. Raiders, 1988
2,272 Gale Sayers, Chicago, 1965
2,250 Maurice Jones-Drew, Jacksonville, 2006

Most Yards Gained, Game
404 Glyn Milburn, Denver vs. Seattle, Dec. 10, 1995
373 Billy Cannon, Houston vs. N.Y. Titans, Dec. 10, 1961
361 Adrian Peterson, Minnesota vs. Chicago, Oct. 4, 2007

SACKS

Sacks have been compiled since 1982.

Most Seasons Leading League
2 Mark Gastineau, N.Y. Jets, 1983-84
Reggie White, Philadelphia, 1987-88
Kevin Greene, Pittsburgh, 1994; Carolina, 1996
Michael Strahan, N.Y. Giants, 2001, 2003

Most Sacks, Career
200.0 Bruce Smith, Buffalo, 1985-1999; Washington, 2000-03
198.0 Reggie White, Philadelphia, 1985-1992; Green Bay, 1993-98; Carolina, 2000
160.0 Kevin Greene, L.A. Rams, 1985-1992; Pittsburgh, 1993-95; Carolina, 1996, 1998-99; San Francisco, 1997

Most Sacks, Season
22.5 Michael Strahan, N.Y. Giants, 2001
22.0 Mark Gastineau, N.Y. Jets, 1984
21.0 Reggie White, Philadelphia, 1987
Chris Doleman, Minnesota, 1989

Most Sacks, Rookie, Season
14.5 Jevon Kearse, Tennessee, 1999
13.0 Dwight Freeney, Indianapolis, 2002
12.5 Leslie O'Neal, San Diego, 1986
Simeon Rice, Arizona, 1996

Most Sacks, Game
7.0 Derrick Thomas, Kansas City vs. Seattle, Nov. 11, 1990
6.0 Fred Dean, San Francisco vs. New Orleans, Nov. 13, 1983
Derrick Thomas, Kansas City vs. Oakland, Sept. 6, 1998
Osi Umenyiora, N.Y. Giants vs. Philadelphia, Sept. 30, 2007
5.5 William Gay, Detroit vs. Tampa Bay, Sept. 4, 1983

Most Seasons, 10 or More Sacks
13 Bruce Smith, Buffalo, 1986-1990, 1992-98; Washington, 2000
12 Reggie White, Philadelphia, 1985-1992; Green Bay, 1993, 1995, 1997-98
10 Kevin Greene, L.A. Rams, 1988-1990, 1992; Pittsburgh, 1993-94; Carolina, 1996, 1998-99; San Francisco, 1997

Most Consecutive Seasons, 10 or More Sacks
9 Reggie White, Philadelphia, 1985-1992; Green Bay, 1993
8 John Randle, Minnesota, 1992-99
7 Lawrence Taylor, N.Y. Giants, 1984-1990
Bruce Smith, Buffalo, 1992-98

Most Consecutive Games, Sack
10 Simon Fletcher, Denver, Nov. 15, 1992-Sept. 20, 1993
DeMarcus Ware, Dallas, Dec. 16, 2007-Oct. 19, 2008
9 Bruce Smith, Buffalo, Nov. 16, 1986-Oct. 25, 1987
Kevin Greene, San Francisco-Carolina, Dec. 7, 1997-Oct. 18, 1998
8 By many players

MISCELLANEOUS

Longest Return of Missed Field Goal (All TDs)
109 Antonio Cromartie, San Diego vs. Minnesota, Nov. 4, 2007
108 Nathan Vasher, Chicago vs. San Francisco, Nov. 13, 2005
Devin Hester, Chicago vs. N.Y. Giants, Nov. 12, 2006
107 Chris McAlister, Baltimore vs. Denver, Sept. 30, 2002

TEAM RECORDS

CHAMPIONSHIPS

Most Seasons League Champion
12 Green Bay, 1929-1931, 1936, 1939, 1944, 1961-62, 1965-67, 1996
9 Chi. Bears, 1921, 1932-33, 1940-41, 1943, 1946, 1963, 1985
7 N.Y. Giants, 1927, 1934, 1938, 1956, 1986, 1990, 2007

Most Consecutive Seasons League Champion
3 Green Bay, 1929-1931
Green Bay, 1965-67
2 Canton, 1922-23
Chi. Bears, 1932-33
Chi. Bears, 1940-41
Philadelphia, 1948-49
Detroit, 1952-53
Cleveland, 1954-55
Baltimore, 1958-59
Houston, 1960-61
Green Bay, 1961-62
Buffalo, 1964-65
Miami, 1972-73
Pittsburgh, 1974-75
Pittsburgh, 1978-79
San Francisco, 1988-89
Dallas, 1992-93
Denver, 1997-98
New England, 2003-04

Most Times Finishing First, Regular Season
22 N.Y. Giants, 1927, 1933-35, 1938-39, 1941, 1944, 1946, 1956, 1958-59, 1961-63, 1986, 1989-1990, 1997, 2000, 2005, 2008
21 Chi. Bears, 1921, 1932-34, 1937, 1940-43, 1946, 1956, 1963, 1984-88, 1990, 2001, 2005-06
Green Bay, 1929-1931, 1936, 1938-39, 1944, 1960-62, 1965-67, 1972, 1995-97, 2002-04, 2007
20 Dallas, 1966-1971, 1973, 1976-79, 1981, 1985, 1992-96, 1998, 2007

Most Consecutive Times Finishing First, Regular Season
7 Los Angeles, 1973-79
6 Cleveland, 1950-55
Dallas, 1966-1971
Minnesota, 1973-78
Pittsburgh, 1974-79
5 Oakland, 1972-76
Chicago, 1984-88
San Francisco, 1986-1990
Dallas, 1992-96
Indianapolis, 2003-07
New England, 2003-07

GAMES WON

Most Consecutive Games Won
21 New England, 2006-08
18 New England, 2003-04
17 Chi. Bears, 1933-34

Most Consecutive Games Without Defeat
25 Canton, 1921-23 (won 22, tied 3)
24 Chi. Bears, 1941-43 (won 23, tied 1)
23 Green Bay, 1928-1930 (won 21, tied 2)

Most Games Won, Season
16 New England, 2007
15 San Francisco, 1984
Chicago, 1985
Minnesota, 1998
Pittsburgh, 2004
14 By many teams

Most Consecutive Games Won, Season
16 New England, 2007, entire season
14 Miami, 1972, entire season
Pittsburgh, 2004
13 Chi. Bears, 1934, entire season
Denver, 1998
Indianapolis, 2005

Most Consecutive Games Won, Start of Season
16 New England, 2007, entire season
14 Miami, 1972, entire season
13 Chi. Bears, 1934, entire season
Denver, 1998
Indianapolis, 2005

Most Consecutive Games Won, End of Season
16 New England, 2007, entire season
14 Miami, 1972, entire season
Pittsburgh, 2004
13 Chi. Bears, 1934, entire season

Most Consecutive Games Without Defeat, Season
16 New England, 2007 (won 16), entire season
14 Miami, 1972 (won 14), entire season
Pittsburgh, 2004 (won 14)
13 Chi. Bears, 1926 (won 11, tied 2)
Green Bay, 1929 (won 12, tied 1)

Chi. Bears, 1934 (won 13), entire season
Baltimore, 1967 (won 11, tied 2)
Denver, 1998 (won 13)
Indianapolis, 2005 (won 13)

Most Consecutive Games Without Defeat, Start of Season
16 New England, 2007 (won 16), entire season
14 Miami, 1972 (won 14), entire season
13 Chi. Bears, 1926 (won 11, tied 2)
Green Bay, 1929 (won 12, tied 1), entire season
Chi. Bears, 1934 (won 13), entire season
Baltimore, 1967 (won 11, tied 2)
Denver, 1998 (won 13)
Indianapolis, 2005 (won 13)

Most Consecutive Games Without Defeat, End of Season
16 New England, 2007 (won 16), entire season
14 Miami, 1972 (won 14), entire season
Pittsburgh, 2004 (won 14)
13 Green Bay, 1929 (won 12, tied 1), entire season
Chi. Bears, 1934 (won 13), entire season

Most Consecutive Home Games Won
27 Miami, 1971-74
25 Green Bay, 1995-98
24 Denver, 1996-98

Most Consecutive Home Games Without Defeat
30 Green Bay, 1928-1933 (won 27, tied 3)
27 Miami, 1971-74 (won 27)
25 Chi. Bears, 1923-25 (won 19, tied 6)
Green Bay, 1995-98 (won 25)

Most Consecutive Road Games Won
18 San Francisco, 1988-1990
12 New England, 2006-08
11 L.A. Chargers/San Diego, 1960-61
San Francisco, 1987-88
Pittsburgh, 2004-05

Most Consecutive Road Games Without Defeat
18 San Francisco, 1988-1990 (won 18)
13 Chi. Bears, 1941-43 (won 12, tied 1)
12 Green Bay, 1928-1930 (won 10, tied 2)
New England, 2006-08 (won 12)

Most Shutout Games Won or Tied, Season
10 Pottsville, 1926 (won 9, tied 1)
N.Y. Giants, 1927 (won 9, tied 1)
9 Akron, 1921 (won 8, tied 1)
Canton, 1922 (won 7, tied 2)
Frankford, 1926 (won 9)
Frankford, 1929 (won 6, tied 3)
8 By many teams

Most Consecutive Shutout Games Won or Tied
13 Akron, 1920-21 (won 10, tied 3)
7 Pottsville, 1926 (won 6, tied 1)
Detroit, 1934 (won 7)
6 Buffalo, 1920-21 (won 5, tied 1)
Frankford, 1926 (won 6)
Detroit, 1926 (won 4, tied 2)
N.Y. Giants, 1926-27 (won 5, tied 1)

GAMES LOST

Most Consecutive Games Lost
26 Tampa Bay, 1976-1977
19 Chi. Cardinals, 1942-43, 1945
Oakland, 1961-62
18 Houston, 1972-73

Most Consecutive Games Without Victory
26 Tampa Bay, 1976-77 (lost 26)
23 Rochester, 1922-25 (lost 21, tied 2)
Washington, 1960-61 (lost 20, tied 3)
19 Dayton, 1927-29 (lost 18, tied 1)
Chi. Cardinals, 1942-43, 1945 (lost 19)
Oakland, 1961-62 (lost 19)

Most Games Lost, Season
16 Detroit, 2008
15 New Orleans, 1980
Dallas, 1989
New England, 1990
Indianapolis, 1991
N.Y. Jets, 1996
San Diego, 2000
Carolina, 2001
Miami, 2007
14 By many teams

Most Consecutive Games Lost, Season
16 Detroit, 2008, entire season
15 Carolina, 2001
14 Tampa Bay, 1976
New Orleans, 1980
Baltimore, 1981
New England, 1990

Most Consecutive Games Lost, Start of Season
16 Detroit, 2008, entire season
14 Tampa Bay, 1976, entire season
New Orleans, 1980
13 Oakland, 1962
Indianapolis, 1986
Miami, 2007

Most Consecutive Games Lost, End of Season
16 Detroit, 2008, entire season
15 Carolina, 2001
14 Tampa Bay, 1976, entire season
New England, 1990

Most Consecutive Games Without Victory, Season
16 Detroit, 2008 (lost 16), entire season
15 Carolina, 2001 (lost 15)
14 Tampa Bay, 1976 (lost 14), entire season
New Orleans, 1980 (lost 14)
Baltimore, 1981 (lost 14)
New England, 1990 (lost 14)

Most Consecutive Games Without Victory, Start of Season
16 Detroit, 2008 (lost 16), entire season
14 Tampa Bay, 1976 (lost 14), entire season
New Orleans, 1980 (lost 14)
13 Washington, 1961 (lost 12, tied 1)
Oakland, 1962 (lost 13)
Indianapolis, 1986 (lost 13)
Miami, 2007 (lost 13)

Most Consecutive Games Without Victory, End of Season
16 Detroit, 2008 (lost 16), entire season
15 Carolina, 2001
14 Tampa Bay, 1976, (lost 14), entire season
New England, 1990 (lost 14)

Most Consecutive Home Games Lost
14 Dallas, 1988-89
13 Houston, 1972-73
Tampa Bay, 1976-77
N.Y. Jets, 1995-97
11 Oakland, 1961-62
Los Angeles, 1961-63
Cincinnati, 1998-99

Most Consecutive Home Games Without Victory
14 Dallas, 1988-89 (lost 14)
13 Houston, 1972-73 (lost 13)
Tampa Bay, 1976-77 (lost 13)
N.Y. Jets, 1995-97 (lost 13)
Philadelphia, 1936-38 (lost 12, tied 1)

Most Consecutive Road Games Lost
24 Detroit, 2001-03
23 Houston, 1981-84
22 Buffalo, 1983-86

Most Consecutive Road Games Without Victory
24 Detroit, 2001-03 (lost 24)

23 Houston, 1981-84 (lost 23)
22 Buffalo, 1983-86 (lost 22)

Most Shutout Games Lost or Tied, Season
8 Frankford, 1927 (lost 6, tied 2)
Brooklyn, 1931 (lost 8)
7 Dayton, 1925 (lost 6, tied 1)
Orange, 1929 (lost 4, tied 3)
Frankford, 1931 (lost 6, tied 1)
6 By many teams

Most Consecutive Shutout Games Lost or Tied
8 Rochester, 1922-24 (lost 8)
7 Hammond, 1922-23 (lost 6, tied 1)
6 Providence, 1926-27 (lost 5, tied 1)
Brooklyn, 1942-43 (lost 6)

TIE GAMES

Most Tie Games, Season
6 Chi. Bears, 1932
5 Frankford, 1929
4 Chi. Bears, 1924
Orange, 1929
Portsmouth, 1932

Most Consecutive Tie Games
3 Chi. Bears, 1932
2 By many teams

SCORING

Most Seasons Leading League
10 Chi. Bears, 1932, 1934-35, 1939, 1941-43, 1946-47, 1956
9 San Francisco, 1953, 1965, 1970, 1987, 1989, 1992-95
L.A./St. Louis Rams, 1950-52, 1957, 1967, 1973, 1999-2001
7 Green Bay, 1931, 1936-38, 1961-62, 1996

Most Consecutive Seasons Leading League
4 San Francisco, 1992-1995
3 Green Bay, 1936-38
Chi. Bears, 1941-43
Los Angeles, 1950-52
Oakland, 1967-69
St. Louis, 1999-2001
2 By many teams

POINTS

Most Points, Season
589 New England, 2007
556 Minnesota, 1998
541 Washington, 1983

Fewest Points, Season (Since 1932)
37 Cincinnati/St. Louis, 1934
38 Cincinnati, 1933
Detroit, 1942
51 Pittsburgh, 1934
Philadelphia, 1936

Most Points, Game
72 Washington vs. N.Y. Giants, Nov. 27, 1966
70 Los Angeles vs. Baltimore, Oct. 22, 1950
66 Rochester vs. *Fort Porter, Oct. 10, 1920
**Not a member of the American Professional Football Association*

Most Points, Both Teams, Game
113 Washington (72) vs. N.Y. Giants (41), Nov. 27, 1966
106 Cincinnati (58) vs. Cleveland (48), Nov. 28, 2004
101 Oakland (52) vs. Houston (49), Dec. 22, 1963

Fewest Points, Both Teams, Game
0 In many games. Last time: N.Y. Giants vs. Detroit, Nov. 7, 1943

Most Points, Shutout Victory, Game
66 Rochester vs. *Fort Porter, Oct. 10, 1920
**Not a member of the American Professional Football Association*
64 Philadelphia vs. Cincinnati, Nov. 6, 1934
62 Akron vs. Oorang, Oct. 29, 1922

Fewest Points, Shutout Victory, Game
2 Akron vs. Buffalo, Nov. 29, 1923
Kansas City vs. Buffalo, Nov. 21, 1926
Frankford vs. Green Bay, Nov. 29, 1928
Green Bay vs. Chi. Bears, Oct. 16, 1932
Chi. Bears vs. Green Bay, Sept. 18, 1938

Most Points Overcome to Win Game
28 San Francisco vs. New Orleans, Dec. 7, 1980 (OT) (trailed 7-35, won 38-35)
26 Buffalo vs. Indianapolis, Sept., 21, 1997 (trailed 0-26, won 37-35)
25 St. Louis vs. Tampa Bay, Nov. 8, 1987 (trailed 3-28, won 31-28)

Most Points Overcome to Tie Game
31 Denver vs. Buffalo, Nov. 27, 1960 (trailed 7-38, tied 38-38)
28 Los Angeles vs. Philadelphia, Oct. 3, 1948 (trailed 0-28, tied 28-28)

Most Points, Each Half
1st: 49 Green Bay vs. Tampa Bay, Oct. 2, 1983
48 Buffalo vs. Miami, Sept. 18, 1966
45 Green Bay vs. Cleveland, Nov. 12, 1967
Indianapolis vs. Denver, Oct. 31, 1988
Houston vs. Cleveland, Dec. 9, 1990
Seattle vs. Minnesota, Sept. 29, 2002
2nd: 49 Chi. Bears vs. Philadelphia, Nov. 30, 1941
48 Chi. Cardinals vs. Baltimore, Oct. 2, 1950
N.Y. Giants vs. Baltimore, Nov. 19, 1950
45 Cincinnati vs. Houston, Dec. 17, 1972

Most Points, Both Teams, Each Half
1st: 70 Houston (35) vs. Oakland (35), Dec. 22, 1963
63 Philadelphia (42) vs. Detroit (21), Sept. 23, 2007
62 N.Y. Jets (41) vs. Tampa Bay (21), Nov. 17, 1985
Indianapolis (35) vs. Cincinnati (27), Nov. 20, 2005
2nd: 66 Cleveland (35) vs. Cincinnati (31), Nov. 28, 2004
65 Washington (38) vs. N.Y. Giants (27), Nov. 27, 1966
62 L.A. Raiders (31) vs. San Diego (31), Jan. 2, 1983
Baltimore (38) vs. Seattle (24), Nov. 23, 2003

Most Points, One Quarter
41 Green Bay vs. Detroit, Oct. 7, 1945 (second quarter)
Los Angeles vs. Detroit, Oct. 29, 1950 (third quarter)
37 Los Angeles vs. Green Bay, Sept. 21, 1980 (second quarter)
35 Chi. Cardinals vs. Boston, Oct. 24, 1948 (third quarter)
Green Bay vs. Cleveland, Nov. 12, 1967 (first quarter)
Green Bay vs. Tampa Bay, Oct. 2, 1983 (second quarter)

Most Points, Both Teams, One Quarter
49 Oakland (28) vs. Houston (21), Dec. 22, 1963 (second quarter)
48 Green Bay (41) vs. Detroit (7), Oct. 7, 1945 (second quarter)
Los Angeles (41) vs. Detroit (7), Oct. 29, 1950 (third quarter)
Detroit (34) vs. Chicago (14), Sept. 30, 2007 (fourth quarter)
47 St. Louis (27) vs. Philadelphia (20), Dec. 13, 1964 (second quarter)

Most Points, Each Quarter
1st: 35 Green Bay vs. Cleveland, Nov. 12, 1967
31 Buffalo vs. Kansas City, Sept. 13, 1964

28 By eight teams
2nd: 41 Green Bay vs. Detroit, Oct. 7, 1945
37 Los Angeles vs. Green Bay, Sept. 21, 1980
35 Green Bay vs. Tampa Bay, Oct. 2, 1983
3rd: 41 Los Angeles vs. Detroit, Oct. 29, 1950
35 Chi. Cardinals vs. Boston, Oct. 24, 1948
28 By 10 teams
4th: 34 Detroit vs. Chicago, Sept. 30, 2007
31 Oakland vs. Denver, Dec. 17, 1960
Oakland vs. San Diego, Dec. 8, 1963
Atlanta vs. Green Bay, Sept. 13, 1981
30 N.Y. Jets vs. Miami, Oct. 23, 2000

Most Points, Both Teams, Each Quarter
1st: 42 Green Bay (35) vs. Cleveland (7), Nov. 12, 1967
41 Tennessee (24) vs. Indianapolis (17), Dec. 5, 2004
35 Dall. Texans (21) vs. N.Y. Titans (14), Nov. 11, 1962
Dallas (28) vs. Philadelphia (7), Oct. 19, 1969
Kansas City (21) vs. Seattle (14), Dec. 11, 1977
Detroit (21) vs. L.A. Raiders (14), Dec. 10, 1990
Dallas (21) vs. Atlanta (14), Dec. 22, 1991
Indianapolis (21) vs. Green Bay (14), Sept 26, 2004
Miami (21) vs. Buffalo (14), Dec. 5, 2004
Philadelphia (21) vs. New Orleans (14), Dec. 23, 2007
2nd: 49 Oakland (28) vs. Houston (21), Dec. 22, 1963
48 Green Bay (41) vs. Detroit (7), Oct. 7, 1945
47 St. Louis (27) vs. Philadelphia (20), Dec. 13, 1964
3rd: 48 Los Angeles (41) vs. Detroit (7), Oct. 29, 1950
42 Washington (28) vs. Philadelphia (14), Oct. 1, 1955
41 Green Bay (21) vs. N.Y. Yanks (20), Oct. 8, 1950
4th: 48 Detroit (34) vs. Chicago (14), Sept. 30, 2007
43 Atlanta (28) vs. Carolina (15), Nov. 23, 2008
42 Chi. Cardinals (28) vs. Philadelphia (14), Dec. 7, 1947
Green Bay (28) vs. Chi. Bears (14), Nov. 6, 1955
N.Y. Jets (28) vs. Boston (14), Oct. 27, 1968
Pittsburgh (21) vs. Cleveland (21), Oct. 18, 1969
New England (21) vs. Kansas City (21), Sept. 22, 2002

Most Consecutive Games Scoring
420 San Francisco, 1977-2004
274 Cleveland, 1950-1971
261 Denver, 1992-2008 (current)

TOUCHDOWNS

Most Seasons Leading League, Touchdowns
13 Chi. Bears, 1932, 1934-35, 1939, 1941-44, 1946-48, 1956, 1965
7 Dallas, 1966, 1968, 1971, 1973, 1977-78, 1980
San Francisco, 1953, 1970, 1987, 1992-95
L.A./St. Louis Rams, 1949-1952, 1999-2001
San Diego, 1963, 1965, 1979, 1981-82, 1985, 2006
6 Oakland, 1967-69, 1972, 1974, 1977
Green Bay, 1932, 1937-38, 1961-62, 1996
Baltimore/Indianapolis Colts, 1957-59, 1964, 1976, 2004

Most Consecutive Seasons Leading League, Touchdowns
4 Chi. Bears, 1941-44
Los Angeles, 1949-1952
San Francisco, 1992-95
3 Chi. Bears, 1946-48
Baltimore, 1957-59
Oakland, 1967-69
St. Louis, 1999-2001
2 By many teams

Most Touchdowns, Season
75 New England, 2007
70 Miami, 1984
67 St. Louis, 2000

Fewest Touchdowns, Season (Since 1932)
3 Cincinnati, 1933
4 Cincinnati/St. Louis, 1934
5 Detroit, 1942

Most Touchdowns, Game
10 Rochester vs. *Fort Porter, Oct. 10, 1920
**Not a member of the American Professional Football Association*
Philadelphia vs. Cincinnati, Nov. 6, 1934
Los Angeles vs. Baltimore, Oct. 22, 1950
Washington vs. N.Y. Giants, Nov. 27, 1966
9 Rock Island vs. Evansville, Oct. 15, 1922
Akron vs. Oorang, Oct. 29, 1922
Racine vs. Louisville, Nov. 5, 1922
Chi. Cardinals vs. Rochester, Oct. 7, 1923
Chi. Cardinals vs. Milwaukee, Dec. 10, 1925
Chi. Cardinals vs. N.Y. Giants, Oct. 17, 1948
Chi. Cardinals vs. N.Y. Bulldogs, Nov. 13, 1949
Los Angeles vs. Detroit, Oct. 29, 1950
Pittsburgh vs. N.Y. Giants, Nov. 30, 1952
Chicago vs. San Francisco, Dec. 12, 1965
Chicago vs. Green Bay, Dec. 7, 1980
8 By many teams

Most Touchdowns, Both Teams, Game
16 Washington (10) vs. N.Y. Giants (6), Nov. 27, 1966
14 Chi. Cardinals (9) vs. N.Y. Giants (5), Oct. 17, 1948
Los Angeles (10) vs. Baltimore (4), Oct. 22, 1950
Houston (7) vs. Oakland (7), Dec. 22, 1963
13 New Orleans (7) vs. St. Louis (6), Nov. 2, 1969
Kansas City (7) vs. Seattle (6), Nov. 27, 1983 (OT)
San Diego (8) vs. Pittsburgh (5), Dec. 8, 1985
N.Y. Jets (7) vs. Miami (6), Sept. 21, 1986 (OT)
Cincinnati (7) vs. Cleveland (6), Nov. 28, 2004

Most Consecutive Games Scoring Touchdowns
166 Cleveland, 1957-1969
101 San Diego, 2002-08 (current)
97 Oakland, 1966-1973
Minnesota, 1995-2001

POINTS AFTER TOUCHDOWN

Most (One-Point) Points After Touchdown, Season
74 New England, 2007
66 Miami, 1984
65 Houston, 1961

Fewest (One-Point) Points After Touchdown, Season
2 Chi. Cardinals, 1933
3 Cincinnati, 1933
Pittsburgh, 1934
4 Cincinnati/St. Louis, 1934

Most (One-Point) Points After Touchdown, Game
10 Los Angeles vs. Baltimore, Oct. 22, 1950
9 Chi. Cardinals vs. N.Y. Giants, Oct. 17, 1948
Pittsburgh vs. N.Y. Giants, Nov. 30, 1952
Washington vs. N.Y. Giants, Nov. 27, 1966
8 By many teams

Most (One-Point) Points After Touchdown, Both Teams, Game
14 Chi. Cardinals (9) vs. N.Y. Giants (5), Oct. 17, 1948
Houston (7) vs. Oakland (7), Dec. 22, 1963
Washington (9) vs. N.Y. Giants (5), Nov. 27, 1966
13 Los Angeles (10) vs. Baltimore (3), Oct. 22, 1950
Cincinnati (7) vs. Cleveland (6), Nov. 28, 2004
12 In many games

Most Two-Point Conversions, Season
6 Miami, 1994
Minnesota, 1997
5 Arizona, 1995
Baltimore, 1996
Jacksonville, 1996
Chicago, 1997
San Francisco, 1998
Pittsburgh, 2002
4 By many teams

Most Two-Point Conversions, Game
4 St. Louis vs. Atlanta, Oct. 15, 2000
3 Baltimore vs. New England, Oct. 6, 1996
Pittsburgh vs. Tennessee, Nov. 1, 1998
2 By many teams

Most Two-Point Conversions, Both Teams, Game
5 Baltimore (3) vs. New England (2), Oct. 6, 1996
St. Louis (4) vs. Atlanta (1), Oct. 15, 2000
3 Seattle (2) vs. Kansas City (1), Oct. 23, 1994
Minnesota (2) vs. Seattle (1), Nov. 10, 1996
Pittsburgh (3) vs. Tennessee (0), Nov. 1, 1998
2 In many games

FIELD GOALS

Most Seasons Leading League, Field Goals
11 Green Bay, 1935-36, 1940-43, 1946-47, 1955, 1972, 1974
8 Washington, 1945, 1956, 1971, 1976-77, 1979, 1982, 1992
L.A./St. Louis Rams, 1949, 1951, 1958, 1966, 1973, 1978, 2003, 2006
N.Y. Giants, 1933, 1937, 1939, 1941, 1944, 1959, 1983, 2008
6 Boston/New England Patriots, 1961, 1963, 1964, 1986, 2004, 2008

Most Consecutive Seasons Leading League, Field Goals
4 Green Bay, 1940-43
3 Cleveland, 1952-54
2 By many teams

Most Field Goals Attempted, Season
49 Los Angeles, 1966
Washington, 1971
48 Green Bay, 1972
47 N.Y. Jets, 1969
Los Angeles, 1973
Washington, 1983

Fewest Field Goals Attempted, Season (Since 1938)
0 Chi. Bears, 1944
2 Cleveland, 1939
Card-Pitt, 1944
Boston, 1946
Chi. Bears, 1947
3 Chi. Bears, 1945
Cleveland, 1945

Most Field Goals Attempted, Game
9 St. Louis vs. Pittsburgh, Sept. 24, 1967
8 Pittsburgh vs. St. Louis, Dec. 2, 1962
Detroit vs. Minnesota, Nov. 13, 1966
N.Y. Jets vs. Buffalo, Nov. 3, 1968
Dallas vs. N.Y. Giants, Sept. 15, 2003 (OT)
Tennessee vs. Houston, Oct. 21, 2007
7 By many teams

Most Field Goals Attempted, Both Teams, Game
11 St. Louis (6) vs. Pittsburgh (5), Nov. 13, 1966
Washington (6) vs. Chicago (5), Nov. 14, 1971
Green Bay (6) vs. Detroit (5), Sept. 29, 1974
Washington (6) vs. N.Y. Giants (5), Nov. 14, 1976
10 In many games

Most Field Goals, Season
43 Arizona, 2005
39 Miami, 1999
St. Louis, 2003
37 Carolina, 1996
Indianapolis, 2003

Fewest Field Goals, Season (Since 1932)
0 Boston, 1932, 1935
Chi. Cardinals, 1932, 1945
Green Bay, 1932, 1944
N.Y. Giants, 1932
Brooklyn, 1944
Card-Pitt, 1944
Chi. Bears, 1944, 1947
Boston, 1946
Baltimore, 1950
Dallas, 1952

Most Field Goals, Game
8 Tennessee vs. Houston, Oct. 21, 2007
7 St. Louis vs. Pittsburgh, Sept. 24, 1967
Minnesota vs. L.A. Rams, Nov. 5, 1989 (OT)
Dallas vs. Green Bay, Nov. 18, 1996
Dallas vs. N.Y. Giants, Sept. 15, 2003 (OT)
Cincinnati vs. Baltimore, Nov. 11, 2007
6 By many teams

Most Field Goals, Both Teams, Game
9 San Diego (5) vs. Kansas City (4), Sept. 29, 1996
Miami (6) vs. New England (3), Oct. 17, 1999
Houston (5) vs. Miami (4), Oct. 7, 2007
8 Cleveland (4) vs. St. Louis (4), Sept. 20, 1964
Chicago (5) vs. Philadelphia (3), Oct. 20, 1968
Washington (5) vs. Chicago (3), Nov. 14, 1971
Kansas City (5) vs. Buffalo (3), Dec. 19, 1971
Detroit (4) vs. Green Bay (4), Sept. 29, 1974
Cleveland (5) vs. Denver (3), Oct. 19, 1975
New England (4) vs. San Diego (4), Nov. 9, 1975
San Francisco (6) vs. New Orleans (2), Oct. 16, 1983
Seattle (5) vs. L.A. Raiders (3), Dec. 18, 1988
Atlanta (6) vs. New Orleans (2), Nov. 13, 1994
Indianapolis (4) vs. San Diego (4), Nov. 3, 1996
Dallas (7) vs. N.Y. Giants (1), Sept. 15, 2003 (OT)
Oakland (5) vs. Chicago (3), Oct. 5, 2003
Buffalo (5) vs. Tennessee (3), Dec. 24, 2006
Tennessee (8) vs. Houston (0), Oct. 21, 2007
Buffalo (5) vs. Washington (3), Dec. 2, 2007
Kansas City (4) vs. Denver (4), Sept. 28, 2008
San Francisco (4) vs. Philadelphia (4), Oct. 12, 2008
7 In many games

Most Consecutive Games Scoring Field Goals
38 Baltimore, 1999-2001
31 Minnesota, 1968-1970
28 Washington, 1988-1990

SAFETIES

Most Safeties, Season
4 Cleveland, 1927
Detroit, 1962
Seattle, 1993
San Francisco, 1996
Tennessee, 1999
3 By many teams

Most Safeties, Game
3 L.A. Rams vs. N.Y. Giants, Sept. 30, 1984
2 N.Y. Giants vs. Pottsville, Oct. 30, 1927
Chi. Bears vs. Pottsville, Nov. 13, 1927
Detroit vs. Brooklyn, Dec. 1, 1935
N.Y. Giants vs. Pittsburgh, Sept. 17, 1950
N.Y. Giants vs. Washington, Nov. 5, 1961
Chicago vs. Pittsburgh, Nov. 9, 1969
Dallas vs. Philadelphia, Nov. 19, 1972
Los Angeles vs. Green Bay, Oct. 21, 1973
Oakland vs. San Diego, Oct. 26, 1975
Denver vs. Seattle, Jan. 2, 1983
New Orleans vs. Cleveland, Sept. 13, 1987
Buffalo vs. Denver, Nov. 8, 1987
San Francisco vs. St. Louis, Sept. 8, 1996
Jacksonville vs. Pittsburgh, Oct. 3, 1999
Minnesota vs. Atlanta, Oct. 5, 2003
Dallas vs. Arizona, Oct. 5, 2003
Buffalo vs. Houston, Nov. 16, 2003
Minnesota vs. Green Bay, Nov. 9, 2008

Most Safeties, Both Teams, Game

3 L.A. Rams (3) vs. N.Y. Giants (0), Sept. 30, 1984
2 Chi. Cardinals (1) vs. Frankford (1), Nov. 19, 1927
Chi. Cardinals (1) vs. Cincinnati (1), Nov. 12, 1933
Chi. Bears (1) vs. San Francisco (1), Oct. 19, 1952
Cincinnati (1) vs. Los Angeles (1), Oct. 22, 1972
Chi. Bears (1) vs. San Francisco (1), Sept. 19, 1976
Baltimore (1) vs. Miami (1), Oct. 29, 1978
Atlanta (1) vs. Detroit (1), Oct. 5, 1980
Houston (1) vs. Philadelphia (1), Oct. 2, 1988
Cleveland (1) vs. Seattle (1), Nov. 14, 1993
Arizona (1) vs. Houston (1), Dec. 4, 1994
(Also see previous record)

FIRST DOWNS

Most Seasons Leading League

9 Chi. Bears, 1935, 1939, 1941, 1943, 1945, 1947-49, 1955
7 San Diego, 1965, 1969, 1980-83, 1985
L.A./St. Louis Rams, 1946, 1950-51, 1954, 1957, 1973, 2001
6 San Francisco, 1965, 1987, 1989, 1993-94, 1998
Baltimore/Indianapolis Colts, 1958-59, 1967, 2003, 2005-06

Most Consecutive Seasons Leading League

4 San Diego, 1980-83
3 Chi. Bears, 1947-49
2 By many teams

Most First Downs, Season

398 Kansas City, 2004
393 New England, 2007
387 Miami, 1984

Fewest First Downs, Season

51 Cincinnati, 1933
64 Pittsburgh, 1935
67 Philadelphia, 1937

Most First Downs, Game

39 N.Y. Jets vs. Miami, Nov. 27, 1988
Washington vs. Detroit, Nov. 4, 1990 (OT)
38 Los Angeles vs. N.Y. Giants, Nov. 13, 1966
37 Green Bay vs. Philadelphia, Nov. 11, 1962

Fewest First Downs, Game

0 N.Y. Giants vs. Green Bay, Oct. 1, 1933
Pittsburgh vs. Boston, Oct. 29, 1933
Philadelphia vs. Detroit, Sept. 20, 1935
N.Y. Giants vs. Washington, Sept. 27, 1942
Denver vs. Houston, Sept. 3, 1966

Most First Downs, Both Teams, Game

64 Seattle (32) vs. Kansas City (32), Nov. 24, 2002
62 San Diego (32) vs. Seattle (30), Sept. 15, 1985
Oakland (31) vs. Kansas City (31), Nov. 5, 2000
59 Miami (31) vs. Buffalo (28), Oct. 9, 1983 (OT)
Seattle (33) vs. Kansas City (26), Nov. 27, 1983 (OT)
N.Y. Jets (32) vs. Miami (27), Sept. 21, 1986 (OT)
N.Y. Jets (39) vs. Miami (20), Nov. 27, 1988
Oakland (31) vs. San Francisco (28), Oct. 8, 2000 (OT)

Fewest First Downs, Both Teams, Game

7 Chi. Cardinals (2) vs. Detroit (5), Sept. 15, 1940
9 Pittsburgh (1) vs. Boston (8), Oct. 27, 1935
Boston (4) vs. Brooklyn (5), Nov. 24, 1935
N.Y. Giants (3) vs. Detroit (6), Nov. 7, 1943
Pittsburgh (4) vs. Chi. Cardinals (5), Nov. 11, 1945
N.Y. Bulldogs (1) vs. Philadelphia (8), Sept. 22, 1949
10 Philadelphia (4) vs. Brooklyn (6), Nov. 5, 1944
N.Y. Giants (4) vs. Washington (6), Dec. 11, 1960

Most First Downs, Rushing, Season

181 New England, 1978
177 Los Angeles, 1973
176 Chicago, 1985

Fewest First Downs, Rushing, Season

36 Cleveland, 1942
Boston, 1944
39 Brooklyn, 1943
40 Philadelphia, 1940
Detroit, 1945

Most First Downs, Rushing, Game

25 Philadelphia vs. Washington, Dec. 2, 1951
23 St. Louis vs. New Orleans, Oct. 5, 1980
21 Cleveland vs. Philadelphia, Dec. 13, 1959
Green Bay vs. Philadelphia, Nov. 11, 1962
Los Angeles vs. New Orleans, Nov. 25, 1973
Pittsburgh vs. Kansas City, Nov. 7, 1976
New England vs. Denver, Nov. 28, 1976
Oakland vs. Green Bay, Sept. 17, 1978
Buffalo vs. Washington, Nov. 3, 1996
San Francisco vs. Detroit, Dec. 14, 1998
Kansas City vs. Atlanta, Oct. 24, 2004

Fewest First Downs, Rushing, Game

0 By many teams. Last time:
Arizona vs. Philadelphia, Nov. 27, 2008

Most First Downs, Rushing, Both Teams, Game

36 Philadelphia (25) vs. Washington (11), Dec. 2, 1951
31 Detroit (18) vs. Washington (13), Sept. 30, 1951
30 Los Angeles (17) vs. Minnesota (13), Nov. 5, 1961
New Orleans (17) vs. Green Bay (13), Sept. 9, 1979
New Orleans (16) vs. San Francisco (14), Nov. 11, 1979
New England (16) vs. Kansas City (14), Oct. 4, 1981
Indianapolis (18) vs. Denver (12), Sept. 30, 2007

Fewest First Downs, Rushing, Both Teams, Game

1 Oakland (0) vs. Tennessee (1), Sept. 7, 2003
Carolina (0) vs. Detroit (1), Oct. 16, 2005
2 Houston (0) vs. Denver (2), Dec. 2, 1962
N.Y. Jets, (1) vs. St. Louis (1), Dec. 3, 1995
Miami (1) vs. San Diego (1), Dec. 19, 1999
New Orleans (0) vs. Baltimore (2), Dec. 19, 1999
Baltimore (0) vs. Tennessee (2), Sept. 18, 2005
Pittsburgh (1) vs. Baltimore (1), Nov. 5, 2007
3 In many games

Most First Downs, Passing, Season

259 San Diego, 1985
251 Houston, 1990
250 Miami, 1986

Fewest First Downs, Passing, Season

18 Pittsburgh, 1941
23 Brooklyn, 1942
N.Y. Giants, 1944
24 N.Y. Giants, 1943

Most First Downs, Passing, Game

29 N.Y. Giants vs. Cincinnati, Oct. 13, 1985
28 Tennessee vs. Oakland, Dec. 19, 2004
27 San Diego vs. Seattle, Sept. 15, 1985

Fewest First Downs, Passing, Game

0 By many teams. Last time:
Oakland vs. Atlanta, Nov. 2, 2008

Most First Downs, Passing, Both Teams, Game

43 San Diego (23) vs. Cincinnati (20), Dec. 20, 1982
Miami (24) vs. N.Y. Jets (19), Sept. 21, 1986 (OT)
Tennessee (28) vs. Oakland (15), Dec. 19, 2004
42 San Francisco (22) vs. San Diego (20), Dec. 11, 1982
Seattle (22) vs. Cleveland (20), Nov. 4, 2007 (OT)
41 San Diego (27) vs. Seattle (14), Sept. 15, 1985
Miami (26) vs. Cleveland (15), Dec. 12, 1988
Kansas City (23) vs. Oakland (18), Nov. 5, 2000

Fewest First Downs, Passing, Both Teams, Game

0 Brooklyn vs. Pittsburgh, Nov. 29, 1942
1 Green Bay (0) vs. Cleveland (1), Sept. 21, 1941
Pittsburgh (0) vs. Brooklyn (1), Oct. 11, 1942
N.Y. Giants (0) vs. Detroit (1), Nov. 7, 1943
Pittsburgh (0) vs. Chi. Cardinals (1), Nov. 11, 1945

N.Y. Bulldogs (0) vs. Philadelphia (1), Sept. 22, 1949
Chicago (0) vs. Buffalo (1), Oct. 7, 1979
2 In many games

Most First Downs, Penalty, Season
47 Buffalo, 2002
Indianapolis, 2004
44 Dallas, 2005
43 Denver, 1994

Fewest First Downs, Penalty, Season
2 Brooklyn, 1940
4 Chi. Cardinals, 1940
N.Y. Giants, 1942, 1944
Washington, 1944
Cleveland, 1952
Kansas City, 1969
5 Brooklyn, 1939
Chi. Bears, 1939
Detroit, 1953
Los Angeles, 1953
Houston, 1982

Most First Downs, Penalty, Game
11 Denver vs. Houston, Oct. 6, 1985
9 Chi. Bears vs. Cleveland, Nov. 25, 1951
Baltimore vs. Pittsburgh, Oct. 30, 1977
N.Y. Jets vs. Houston, Sept. 18, 1988
Dallas vs. Detroit, Nov. 20, 2005
8 Philadelphia vs. Detroit, Dec. 2, 1979
Cincinnati vs. N.Y. Jets, Oct. 6, 1985
Buffalo vs. Houston, Sept. 20, 1987
Houston vs. Atlanta, Sept. 9, 1990
Kansas City vs. L.A. Raiders, Oct. 3, 1993
San Francisco vs. New Orleans, Oct. 11, 1998
Oakland vs. San Francisco, Oct. 8, 2000 (OT)
Philadelphia vs. Chicago, Nov. 3, 2002
Detroit vs. Baltimore, Oct. 9, 2005

Most First Downs, Penalty, Both Teams, Game
12 Buffalo (7) vs. San Francisco (5), Oct. 4, 1998
Detroit (8) vs. Baltimore (4), Oct. 9, 2005
11 Chi. Bears (9) vs. Cleveland (2), Nov. 25, 1951
Cincinnati (8) vs. N.Y. Jets (3), Oct. 6, 1985
Denver (11) vs. Houston (0), Oct. 6, 1985
Detroit (6) vs. Dallas (5), Nov. 8, 1987
N.Y. Jets (9) vs. Houston (2), Sept. 18, 1988
Kansas City (8) vs. L.A. Raiders (3), Oct. 3, 1993
Detroit (6) vs. San Diego (5), Nov. 11, 1996
Philadelphia (8) vs. Chicago (3), Nov. 3, 2002
Arizona (6) vs. St. Louis (5), Dec. 3, 2006
Indianapolis (6) vs. Green Bay (5), Oct. 19, 2008
10 In many games

NET YARDS GAINED RUSHING AND PASSING

Most Seasons Leading League
12 Chi. Bears, 1932, 1934-35, 1939, 1941-44, 1947, 1949, 1955-56
9 L.A./St. Louis Rams, 1946, 1950-51, 1954, 1957, 1973, 1999-2001
7 San Diego, 1963, 1965, 1980-83, 1985

Most Consecutive Seasons Leading League
4 Chi. Bears, 1941-44
San Diego, 1980-83
3 Baltimore, 1958-1960
Houston, 1960-62
Oakland, 1968-1970
St. Louis, 1999-2001
2 By many teams

Most Yards Gained, Season
7,075 St. Louis, 2000
6,936 Miami, 1984
6,800 San Francisco, 1998

Fewest Yards Gained, Season
1,150 Cincinnati, 1933
1,443 Chi. Cardinals, 1934
1,486 Chi. Cardinals, 1933

Most Yards Gained, Game
735 Los Angeles vs. N.Y. Yanks, Sept. 28, 1951
683 Pittsburgh vs. Chi. Cardinals, Dec. 13, 1958
682 Chi. Bears vs. N.Y. Giants, Nov. 14, 1943

Fewest Yards Gained, Game
–7 Seattle vs. Los Angeles, Nov. 4, 1979
–5 Denver vs. Oakland, Sept. 10, 1967
14 Chi. Cardinals vs. Detroit, Sept. 15, 1940

Most Yards Gained, Both Teams, Game
1,133 Los Angeles (636) vs. N.Y. Yanks (497), Nov. 19, 1950
1,102 San Diego (661) vs. Cincinnati (441), Dec. 20, 1982
1,095 Kansas City (590) vs. Indianapolis (505), Oct. 31, 2004

Fewest Yards Gained, Both Teams, Game
30 Chi. Cardinals (14) vs. Detroit (16), Sept. 15, 1940
136 Chi. Cardinals (50) vs. Green Bay (86), Nov. 18, 1934
154 N.Y. Giants (51) vs. Washington (103), Dec. 11, 1960

Most Consecutive Games, 400 or More Yards Gained
11 San Diego, 1982-83
9 New England, 2006-07
8 St. Louis, 1999-2000

Most Consecutive Games, 300 or More Yards Gained
36 Minnesota, 2002-04
30 Minnesota, 1999-2000
St. Louis, 2000-02
29 Los Angeles, 1949-1951

RUSHING

Most Seasons Leading League
16 Chi. Bears, 1932, 1934-35, 1939-1942, 1951, 1955-56, 1968, 1977, 1983-86
7 Buffalo, 1962, 1964, 1973, 1975, 1982, 1991-92
6 Cleveland, 1958-59, 1963, 1965-67
San Francisco, 1952-54, 1987, 1998-99

Most Consecutive Seasons Leading League
4 Chi. Bears, 1939-1942
Chi. Bears, 1983-86
3 Detroit, 1936-38
San Francisco, 1952-54
Cleveland, 1965-67
Atlanta, 2004-06
2 By many teams

ATTEMPTS

Most Rushing Attempts, Season
681 Oakland, 1977
674 Chicago, 1984
671 New England, 1978

Fewest Rushing Attempts, Season
211 Philadelphia, 1982
219 San Francisco, 1982
225 Houston, 1982

Most Rushing Attempts, Game
72 Chi. Bears vs. Brooklyn, Oct. 20, 1935
70 Chi. Cardinals vs. Green Bay, Dec. 5, 1948
69 Chi. Cardinals vs. Green Bay, Dec. 6, 1936
Kansas City vs. Cincinnati, Sept. 3, 1978

Fewest Rushing Attempts, Game
6 Chi. Cardinals vs. Boston, Oct. 29, 1933
New England vs. Pittsburgh, Oct. 31, 2004
Arizona vs. Minnesota, Nov. 26, 2006
7 Oakland vs. Buffalo, Oct. 5, 1963
Houston vs. N.Y. Giants, Dec. 8, 1985
Seattle vs. L.A. Raiders, Nov. 17, 1991
Green Bay vs. Miami, Sept. 11, 1994
Detroit vs. Minnesota, Dec. 2, 2007

Arizona vs. Minnesota, Dec. 14, 2008
8 Denver vs. Oakland, Dec. 17, 1960
Buffalo vs. St. Louis, Sept. 9, 1984
Detroit vs. San Francisco, Oct. 20, 1991
Atlanta vs. Detroit, Sept. 5, 1993
St. Louis vs. San Francisco, Nov. 2, 2003
N.Y. Jets vs. Denver, Nov. 20, 2005
St. Louis vs. Carolina, Nov. 19, 2006
Detroit vs. Arizona, Nov. 11, 2007

Most Rushing Attempts, Both Teams, Game
108 Chi. Cardinals (70) vs. Green Bay (38), Dec. 5, 1948
105 Oakland (62) vs. Atlanta (43), Nov. 30, 1975 (OT)
104 Chi. Bears (64) vs. Pittsburgh (40), Oct. 18, 1936

Fewest Rushing Attempts, Both Teams, Game
16 Chi. Cardinals (6) vs. Boston (10), Oct. 22, 1933
30 Minnesota (15) vs. New England (15), Oct. 30, 2006
34 Atlanta (12) vs. Houston (22), Dec. 5, 1993
Atlanta (15) vs. San Francisco (19), Dec. 24, 1995
Philadelphia (14) vs. San Diego (20), Oct. 23, 2005

YARDS GAINED

Most Yards Gained Rushing, Season
3,165 New England, 1978
3,088 Buffalo, 1973
2,986 Kansas City, 1978

Fewest Yards Gained Rushing, Season
298 Philadelphia, 1940
467 Detroit, 1946
471 Boston, 1944

Most Yards Gained Rushing, Game
426 Detroit vs. Pittsburgh, Nov. 4, 1934
423 N.Y. Giants vs. Baltimore, Nov. 19, 1950
420 Boston vs. N.Y. Giants, Oct. 8, 1933

Fewest Yards Gained Rushing, Game
–53 Detroit vs. Chi. Cardinals, Oct. 17, 1943
–36 Philadelphia vs. Chi. Bears, Nov. 19, 1939
–33 Brooklyn vs. Phil-Pitt, Oct. 2, 1943

Most Yards Gained Rushing, Both Teams, Game
595 Los Angeles (371) vs. N.Y. Yanks (224), Nov. 18, 1951
574 Chi. Bears (396) vs. Pittsburgh (178), Oct. 10, 1934
558 Boston (420) vs. N.Y. Giants (138), Oct. 8, 1933

Fewest Yards Gained Rushing, Both Teams, Game
–15 Detroit (–53) vs. Chi. Cardinals (38), Oct. 17, 1943
4 Detroit (–10) vs. Chi. Cardinals (14), Sept. 15, 1940
45 San Diego (21) vs. Philadelphia (24), Oct. 23, 2005

AVERAGE GAIN

Highest Average Gain, Rushing, Season
5.74 Cleveland, 1963
5.65 San Francisco, 1954
5.56 San Diego, 1963

Lowest Average Gain, Rushing, Season
0.94 Philadelphia, 1940
1.45 Boston, 1944
1.55 Pittsburgh, 1935

TOUCHDOWNS

Most Touchdowns, Rushing, Season
36 Green Bay, 1962
33 Pittsburgh, 1976
32 Kansas City, 2003
San Diego, 2006

Fewest Touchdowns, Rushing, Season
1 Brooklyn, 1934
2 Chi. Cardinals, 1933
Cincinnati, 1933
Pittsburgh, 1934
Philadelphia, 1935
Philadelphia, 1936
Philadelphia, 1937
Philadelphia, 1938
Pittsburgh, 1940
Philadelphia, 1972
N.Y. Jets, 1995
Arizona, 2005
3 By many teams

Most Touchdowns, Rushing, Game
9 Rock Island vs. Evansville, Oct. 15, 1922
Racine vs. Louisville, Nov. 5, 1922
8 Chi. Cardinals vs. Rochester, Oct. 7, 1923
Kansas City vs. Atlanta, Oct. 24, 2004
7 By many teams

Most Touchdowns, Rushing, Both Teams, Game
9 Rock Island (9) vs. Evansville (0), Oct. 15, 1922
Racine (9) vs. Louisville (0), Nov. 5, 1922
8 Chi. Cardinals (8) vs. Rochester (0), Oct. 7, 1923
Canton (7) vs. Cleveland (1), Nov. 25, 1923
Los Angeles (6) vs. N.Y. Yanks (2), Nov. 18, 1951
Chi. Bears (5) vs. Green Bay (3), Nov. 6, 1955
Denver (5) vs. Kansas City (3), Dec. 7, 2003
Kansas City (8) vs. Atlanta (0), Oct. 24, 2004
7 In many games

PASSING

ATTEMPTS

Most Passes Attempted, Season
709 Minnesota, 1981
699 New England, 1994
686 New England, 1995

Fewest Passes Attempted, Season
102 Cincinnati, 1933
106 Boston, 1933
120 Detroit, 1937

Most Passes Attempted, Game
70 New England vs. Minnesota, Nov. 13, 1994 (OT)
69 N.Y. Jets vs. Baltimore, Dec. 24, 2000
68 Houston vs. Buffalo, Nov 1, 1964
Cincinnati vs. Pittsburgh, Dec. 30, 2001 (OT)

Fewest Passes Attempted, Game
0 Green Bay vs. Portsmouth, Oct. 8, 1933
Detroit vs. Cleveland, Sept. 10, 1937
Pittsburgh vs. Brooklyn, Nov. 16, 1941
Pittsburgh vs. Los Angeles, Nov. 13, 1949
Cleveland vs. Philadelphia, Dec. 3, 1950

Most Passes Attempted, Both Teams, Game
112 New England (70) vs. Minnesota (42), Nov. 13, 1994
104 Miami (55) vs. N.Y. Jets (49), Oct. 18, 1987 (OT)
N.Y. Jets (58) vs. San Francisco (46), Sept. 6, 1998 (OT)
103 Cincinnati (68) vs. Pittsburgh (35), Dec. 30, 2001 (OT)
Seattle (53) vs. San Diego (50), Dec. 29, 2002 (OT)

Fewest Passes Attempted, Both Teams, Game
4 Chi. Cardinals (1) vs. Detroit (3), Nov. 3, 1935
Detroit (0) vs. Cleveland (4), Sept. 10, 1937
6 Chi. Cardinals (2) vs. Detroit (4), Sept. 15, 1940
8 Brooklyn (2) vs. Philadelphia (6), Oct. 1, 1939

COMPLETIONS

Most Passes Completed, Season
440 New Orleans, 2007
432 San Francisco, 1995
419 Arizona, 2005

Fewest Passes Completed, Season
25 Cincinnati, 1933
33 Boston, 1933
34 Chi. Cardinals, 1934

Most Passes Completed, Game
45 New England vs. Minnesota, Nov. 13, 1994 (OT)
43 Washington vs. Detroit, Nov. 4, 1990 (OT)
Oakland vs. Pittsburgh, Sept. 15, 2002

42 N.Y. Jets vs. San Francisco, Sept. 21, 1980
N.Y. Jets vs. Seattle, Dec. 6, 1998

Fewest Passes Completed, Game
0 By many teams. Last time: Buffalo vs. N.Y. Jets, Sept. 29, 1974

Most Passes Completed, Both Teams, Game
71 New England (45) vs. Minnesota (26), Nov. 13, 1994
68 San Francisco (37) vs. Atlanta (31), Oct. 6, 1985
Denver (34) vs. Oakland (34), Nov. 11, 2002
66 Cincinnati (40) vs. San Diego (26), Dec. 20, 1982

Fewest Passes Completed, Both Teams, Game
1 Chi. Cardinals (0) vs. Philadelphia (1), Nov. 8, 1936
Detroit (0) vs. Cleveland (1), Sept. 10, 1937
Chi. Cardinals (0) vs. Detroit (1), Sept. 15, 1940
Brooklyn (0) vs. Pittsburgh (1), Nov. 29, 1942
2 Chi. Cardinals (0) vs. Detroit (2), Nov. 3, 1935
Buffalo (0) vs. N.Y. Jets (2), Sept. 29, 1974
Chi. Cardinals (0) vs. Green Bay (2), Nov. 18, 1934
3 In seven games

YARDS GAINED

Most Seasons Leading League, Passing Yardage
10 San Diego, 1965, 1968, 1971, 1978-1983, 1985
8 Chi. Bears, 1932, 1939, 1941, 1943, 1945, 1949, 1954, 1964
Washington, 1938, 1940, 1944, 1947-48, 1967, 1974, 1989
7 Houston, 1960-61, 1963-64, 1990-92
L.A./St. Louis Rams, 1946, 1950-51, 1956, 1999-2001
Balt./Indianapolis, 1957, 1959, 1960, 1963, 1976, 2003-04

Most Consecutive Seasons Leading League, Passing Yardage
6 San Diego, 1978-1983
4 Green Bay, 1934-37
3 Miami, 1986-88
Houston, 1990-92
St. Louis, 1999-2001

Most Yards Gained, Passing, Season
5,232 St. Louis, 2000
5,018 Miami, 1984
4,977 New Orleans, 2008

Fewest Yards Gained, Passing, Season
302 Chi. Cardinals, 1934
357 Cincinnati, 1933
459 Boston, 1934

Most Yards Gained, Passing, Game
554 Los Angeles vs. N.Y. Yanks, Sept. 28, 1951
530 Minnesota vs. Baltimore, Sept. 28, 1969
521 Miami vs. N.Y. Jets, Oct. 23, 1988

Fewest Yards Gained, Passing, Game
–53 Denver vs. Oakland, Sept. 10, 1967
–52 Cincinnati vs. Houston, Oct. 31, 1971
–39 Atlanta vs. San Francisco, Oct. 23, 1976

Most Yards Gained, Passing, Both Teams, Game
884 N.Y. Jets (449) vs. Miami (435), Sept. 21, 1986 (OT)
883 San Diego (486) vs. Cincinnati (397), Dec. 20, 1982
874 Miami (456) vs. New England (418), Sept. 4, 1994

Fewest Yards Gained, Passing, Both Teams, Game
–11 Green Bay (–10) vs. Dallas (–1), Oct. 24, 1965
1 Chi. Cardinals (0) vs. Philadelphia (1), Nov. 8, 1936
7 Brooklyn (0) vs. Pittsburgh (7), Nov. 29, 1942

TIMES SACKED

Most Seasons Leading League, Fewest Times Sacked
10 Miami, 1973, 1982-1990
5 N.Y. Jets, 1965-66, 1968, 1993, 2000
Indianapolis, 1999-2000, 2004-06
4 San Diego, 1963-64, 1967-68
San Francisco, 1964-65, 1970-71
Hou. Oilers/Tenn. Titans, 1961-62, 1978, 2008

Most Consecutive Seasons Leading League, Fewest Times Sacked
9 Miami, 1982-1990
3 St. Louis, 1974-76
Indianapolis, 2004-06
2 By many teams

Most Times Sacked, Season
104 Philadelphia, 1986
78 Arizona, 1997
76 Houston, 2002

Fewest Times Sacked, Season
7 Miami, 1988
8 San Francisco, 1970
St. Louis, 1975
9 N.Y. Jets, 1966
Washington, 1991

Most Times Sacked, Game
12 Pittsburgh vs. Dallas, Nov. 20, 1966
Baltimore vs. St. Louis, Oct. 26, 1980
Detroit vs. Chicago, Dec. 16, 1984
Houston vs. Dallas, Sept. 29, 1985
Philadelphia vs. N.Y. Giants, Sept. 30, 2007
11 St. Louis vs. N.Y. Giants, Nov. 1, 1964
Los Angeles vs. Baltimore, Nov. 22, 1964
Denver vs. Buffalo, Dec. 13, 1964
Green Bay vs. Detroit, Nov. 7, 1965
Buffalo vs. Oakland, Oct. 15, 1967
Denver vs. Oakland, Nov. 5, 1967
Atlanta vs. St. Louis, Nov. 24, 1968
Detroit vs. Dallas, Oct. 6, 1975
Philadelphia vs. St. Louis, Dec. 18, 1983
Cleveland vs. Kansas City, Sept. 30, 1984
Minnesota vs. Chicago, Oct. 28, 1984
Atlanta vs. Cleveland, Nov. 18, 1984
Dallas vs. San Diego, Nov. 16, 1986
Philadelphia vs. Detroit, Nov. 16, 1986
Philadelphia vs. L.A. Raiders, Nov. 30, 1986 (OT)
L.A. Raiders vs. Seattle, Dec. 8, 1986
N.Y. Jets vs. Dallas, Oct. 4, 1987
Philadelphia vs. Chicago, Oct. 4, 1987
Dallas vs. Philadelphia, Sept. 15, 1991
Cleveland vs. Indianapolis, Sept. 6, 1992
10 By many teams

Most Times Sacked, Both Teams, Game
18 Green Bay (10) vs. San Diego (8), Sept. 24, 1978
17 Buffalo (10) vs. N.Y. Titans (7), Nov. 23, 1961
Pittsburgh (12) vs. Dallas (5), Nov. 20, 1966
Atlanta (9) vs. Philadelphia (8), Dec. 16, 1984
Philadelphia (11) vs. L.A. Raiders (6), Nov. 30, 1986 (OT)
16 Los Angeles (11) vs. Baltimore (5), Nov. 22, 1964
Buffalo (11) vs. Oakland (5), Oct. 15, 1967

COMPLETION PERCENTAGE

Most Seasons Leading League, Completion Percentage
14 San Francisco, 1952, 1957-58, 1965, 1981, 1983, 1987, 1989, 1992-97
11 Washington, 1937, 1939-1940, 1942-45, 1947-48, 1969-1970
8 Green Bay, 1936, 1941, 1961-62, 1964, 1966, 1968, 1998

Most Consecutive Seasons Leading League, Completion Percentage
6 San Francisco, 1992-97
4 Washington, 1942-45
Kansas City, 1966-69
3 Cleveland, 1953-55
St. Louis, 1999-2001

Highest Completion Percentage, Season
70.65 Cincinnati, 1982 (310-219)
70.25 San Francisco, 1994 (511-359)

70.19 San Francisco, 1989 (483-339)

Lowest Completion Percentage, Season

22.9 Philadelphia, 1936 (170-39)
24.5 Cincinnati, 1933 (102-25)
25.0 Pittsburgh, 1941 (168-42)

TOUCHDOWNS

Most Touchdowns, Passing, Season

51 Indianapolis, 2004
50 New England, 2007
49 Miami, 1984

Fewest Touchdowns, Passing, Season

0 Cincinnati, 1933
Pittsburgh, 1945
1 Boston, 1932
Boston, 1933
Chi. Cardinals, 1934
Cincinnati/St. Louis, 1934
Detroit, 1942
2 Chi. Cardinals, 1932
Stapleton, 1932
Chi. Cardinals, 1935
Brooklyn, 1936
Pittsburgh, 1942

Most Touchdowns, Passing, Game

7 Chi. Bears vs. N.Y. Giants, Nov. 14, 1943
Philadelphia vs. Washington, Oct. 17, 1954
Houston vs. N.Y. Titans, Nov. 19, 1961
Houston vs. N.Y. Titans, Oct. 14, 1962
N.Y. Giants vs. Washington, Oct. 28, 1962
Minnesota vs. Baltimore, Sept. 28, 1969
San Diego vs. Oakland, Nov. 22, 1981
6 By many teams

Most Touchdowns, Passing, Both Teams, Game

12 New Orleans (6) vs. St. Louis (6), Nov. 2, 1969
11 N.Y. Giants (7) vs. Washington (4), Oct. 28, 1962
Oakland (6) vs. Houston (5), Dec. 22, 1963
Cincinnati (6) vs. Cleveland, (5), Sept. 16, 2007
10 San Diego (5) vs. Seattle (5), Sept. 15, 1985
Miami (6) vs. N.Y. Jets (4), Sept. 21, 1986 (OT)
San Francisco (6) vs. Atlanta (4), Oct. 14, 1990

PASSES HAD INTERCEPTED

Most Passes Had Intercepted, Season

48 Houston, 1962
45 Denver, 1961
41 Card-Pitt, 1944

Fewest Passes Had Intercepted, Season

5 Cleveland, 1960
Green Bay, 1966
Kansas City, 1990
N.Y. Giants, 1990
6 Green Bay, 1964
St. Louis, 1982
Dallas, 1993
Jacksonville, 2005
Washington, 2008
7 Los Angeles, 1969
Denver, 2005
Miami, 2008

Most Passes Had Intercepted, Game

9 Detroit vs. Green Bay, Oct. 24, 1943
Pittsburgh vs. Philadelphia, Dec. 12, 1965
8 Green Bay vs. N.Y. Giants, Nov. 21, 1948
Chi. Cardinals vs. Philadelphia, Sept. 24, 1950
N.Y. Yanks vs. N.Y. Giants, Dec. 16, 1951
Denver vs. Houston, Dec. 2, 1962
Chi. Bears vs. Detroit, Sept. 22, 1968
Baltimore vs. N.Y. Jets, Sept. 23, 1973
7 By many teams. Last time: Detroit vs. Cleveland, Sept. 23, 2001

Most Passes Had Intercepted, Both Teams, Game

13 Denver (8) vs. Houston (5), Dec. 2, 1962
11 Philadelphia (7) vs. Boston (4), Nov. 3, 1935
Boston (6) vs. Pittsburgh (5), Dec. 1, 1935
Cleveland (7) vs. Green Bay (4), Oct. 30, 1938
Green Bay (7) vs. Detroit (4), Oct. 20, 1940
Detroit (7) vs. Chi. Bears (4), Nov. 22, 1942
Detroit (7) vs. Cleveland (4), Nov. 26, 1944
Chi. Cardinals (8) vs. Philadelphia (3), Sept. 24, 1950
Washington (7) vs. N.Y. Giants (4), Dec. 8, 1963
Pittsburgh (9) vs. Philadelphia (2), Dec 12, 1965
10 In many games

PUNTING

Most Seasons Leading League (Average Distance)

7 Denver 1962-64, 1966-67, 1982, 1999
Oakland, 1974-75, 1977-78, 2003-04, 2007
6 Washington, 1940-43, 1945, 1958
Kansas City, 1968, 1971-73, 1979, 1984
L.A. Rams, 1946, 1949, 1955-56, 1994, 2008
4 By many teams

Most Consecutive Seasons Leading League (Average Distance)

4 Washington, 1940-43
3 Cleveland, 1950-52
Denver, 1962-64
Kansas City, 1971-73

Most Punts, Season

116 Houston, 2002
114 Chicago, 1981
113 Boston, 1934
Brooklyn, 1934
Dallas, 2002

Fewest Punts, Season

23 San Diego, 1982
31 Cincinnati, 1982
32 Chi. Bears, 1941

Most Punts, Game

17 Chi. Bears vs. Green Bay, Oct. 22, 1933
Cincinnati vs. Pittsburgh, Oct. 22, 1933
16 Cincinnati vs. Portsmouth, Sept. 17, 1933
Chi. Cardinals vs. Chi. Bears, Nov. 30, 1933
Chi. Cardinals vs. Detroit, Sept. 15, 1940
Oakland vs. San Diego, Oct. 11, 1998
15 Chi. Cardinals vs. Cincinnati, Nov. 12, 1933
N.Y. Giants vs. Chi. Bears, Nov. 17, 1935
Philadelphia vs. N.Y. Giants, Dec. 6, 1987 (OT)

Fewest Punts, Game

0 By many teams. Last time:
Denver vs. Buffalo, Dec. 21, 2008
New Orleans vs. Detroit, Dec. 21, 2008

Most Punts, Both Teams, Game

31 Chi. Bears (17) vs. Green Bay (14), Oct. 22, 1933
Cincinnati (17), vs. Pittsburgh (14), Oct. 22, 1933
29 Chi. Cardinals (15) vs. Cincinnati (14), Nov. 12, 1933
Chi. Cardinals (16) vs. Chi. Bears (13), Nov. 30, 1933
Chi. Cardinals (16) vs. Detroit (13), Sept. 15, 1940
28 Philadelphia (14) vs. Washington (14), Nov. 5, 1939

Fewest Punts, Both Teams, Game

0 Buffalo vs. San Francisco, Sept. 13, 1992
1 Baltimore (0) vs. Cleveland (1), Nov. 1, 1959
Dall. Cowboys (0) vs. Cleveland (1), Dec. 3, 1961
Chicago (0) vs. Detroit (1), Oct. 1, 1972
San Francisco (0) vs. N.Y. Giants (1), Oct. 15, 1972
Green Bay (0) vs. Buffalo (1), Dec. 5, 1982
Miami (0) vs. Buffalo (1), Oct. 12, 1986
Green Bay (0) vs. Chicago (1), Dec. 17, 1989
Oakland (0) vs. Seattle (1), Dec. 5, 1999

Tampa Bay (0) vs. Minnesota (1), Oct. 29, 2000
New Orleans (0) vs. San Francisco (1), Oct. 20, 2002
2 In many games

AVERAGE YARDAGE

Highest Average Distance, Punting, Season
49.6 St. Louis, 2008 (83-4,120)
49.1 Oakland, 2007 (73-3,585)
48.8 Oakland, 2008 (90-4,391)

Lowest Average Distance, Punting, Season
32.7 Card-Pitt, 1944 (60-1,964)
33.8 Cincinnati, 1986 (59-1,996)
33.9 Detroit, 1969 (74-2,510)

PUNT RETURNS

Most Seasons Leading League (Average Return)
9 Detroit, 1943-45, 1951-52, 1962, 1966, 1969, 1991
7 Chi. Cardinals/St. Louis, 1948-49, 1955-56, 1959, 1986-87
6 Green Bay, 1950, 1953-54, 1961, 1972, 1996
Dallas/Kansas City, 1960, 1968, 1970, 1979-1980, 2003

Most Consecutive Seasons Leading League (Average Return)
3 Detroit, 1943-45
2 By many teams

Most Punt Returns, Season
71 Pittsburgh, 1976
Tampa Bay, 1979
L.A. Raiders, 1985
67 Pittsburgh, 1974
Los Angeles, 1978
L.A. Raiders, 1984
65 San Francisco, 1976

Fewest Punt Returns, Season
12 Baltimore, 1981
San Diego, 1982
14 Los Angeles, 1961
Philadelphia, 1962
Baltimore, 1982
15 Houston, 1960
Washington, 1960
Oakland, 1961
N.Y. Giants, 1969
Philadelphia, 1973
Kansas City, 1982

Most Punt Returns, Game
12 Philadelphia vs. Cleveland, Dec. 3, 1950
11 Chi. Bears vs. Chi. Cardinals, Oct. 8, 1950
Washington vs. Tampa Bay, Oct. 9, 1977
10 Philadelphia vs. N.Y. Giants, Nov. 26, 1950
Philadelphia vs. Tampa Bay, Sept. 18, 1977
Pittsburgh vs. Buffalo, Dec. 16, 1979
Washington vs. New Orleans, Dec. 26, 1982
Philadelphia vs. Seattle, Dec. 13, 1992 (OT)
New England vs. Pittsburgh, Dec. 5, 1993

Most Punt Returns, Both Teams, Game
17 Philadelphia (12) vs. Cleveland (5), Dec. 3, 1950
16 N.Y. Giants (9) vs. Philadelphia (7), Dec. 12, 1954
Washington (11) vs. Tampa Bay (5), Oct. 9, 1977
Oakland (8) vs. San Diego (8), Oct. 11, 1998
15 Detroit (8) vs. Cleveland (7), Sept. 27, 1942
Los Angeles (8) vs. Baltimore (7), Nov. 27, 1966
Pittsburgh (8) vs. Houston (7), Dec. 1, 1974
Philadelphia (10) vs. Tampa Bay (5), Sept. 18, 1977
Baltimore (9) vs. Kansas City (6), Sept. 2, 1979
Washington (10) vs. New Orleans (5), Dec. 26, 1982
L.A. Raiders (8) vs. Cleveland (7), Nov. 16, 1986

FAIR CATCHES

Most Fair Catches, Season
34 Baltimore, 1971
33 Philadelphia, 2000
32 San Diego, 1969
Oakland, 2001

Fewest Fair Catches, Season
0 San Diego, 1975
New England, 1976
Tampa Bay, 1976
Pittsburgh, 1977
Dallas, 1982
1 Cleveland, 1974
San Francisco, 1975
Kansas City, 1976
St. Louis, 1976
San Diego, 1976
L.A. Rams, 1982
St. Louis, 1982
Tampa Bay, 1982
Arizona, 2001
2 By many teams

Most Fair Catches, Game
7 Minnesota vs. Dallas, Sept. 25, 1966
N.Y. Jets vs. Miami, Nov. 20, 1966
Detroit vs. Chicago, Nov. 21, 1976
Philadelphia vs. Buffalo, Dec. 27, 1987
Tennessee vs. Jacksonville, Nov. 16, 2008
6 By many teams

YARDS GAINED

Most Yards, Punt Returns, Season
875 Green Bay, 1996
785 L.A. Raiders, 1985
781 Chi. Bears, 1948

Fewest Yards, Punt Returns, Season
27 St. Louis, 1965
35 N.Y. Giants, 1965
37 New England, 1972

Most Yards, Punt Returns, Game
231 Detroit vs. San Francisco, Oct. 6, 1963
225 Oakland vs. Buffalo, Sept. 15, 1968
219 Los Angeles vs. Atlanta, Oct. 11, 1981

Fewest Yards, Punt Returns, Game
-28 Washington vs. Dallas, Dec. 11, 1966
-23 N.Y. Giants vs. Buffalo, Oct. 20, 1975
Pittsburgh vs. Houston, Sept. 20, 1970
-20 New Orleans vs. Pittsburgh, Oct. 20, 1968

Most Yards, Punt Returns, Both Teams, Game
282 Los Angeles (219) vs. Atlanta (63), Oct. 11, 1981
245 Detroit (231) vs. San Francisco (14), Oct. 6, 1963
244 Oakland (225) vs. Buffalo (19), Sept. 15, 1968

Fewest Yards, Punt Returns, Both Teams, Game
-18 Buffalo (-18) vs. Pittsburgh (0), Oct. 29, 1972
-14 Miami (-14) vs. Boston (0), Nov. 30, 1969
Tennessee (-14) vs. New Orleans (0), Sept. 21, 2003
-13 N.Y. Giants (-13) vs. Cleveland (0), Nov. 14, 1965

AVERAGE YARDS RETURNING PUNTS

Highest Average, Punt Returns, Season
20.2 Chi. Bears, 1941 (27-546)
19.1 Chi. Cardinals, 1948 (35-669)
18.2 Chi. Cardinals, 1949 (30-546)

Lowest Average, Punt Returns, Season
1.2 St. Louis, 1965 (23-27)
1.5 N.Y. Giants, 1965 (24-35)
1.7 Washington, 1970 (27-45)

TOUCHDOWNS RETURNING PUNTS

Most Touchdowns, Punt Returns, Season

5 Chi. Cardinals, 1959
4 Chi. Cardinals, 1948
Detroit, 1951
N.Y. Giants, 1951
Denver, 1976
Chicago, 2007
3 Washington, 1941
Detroit, 1952
Pittsburgh, 1952
Houston, 1975
Los Angeles, 1981
Cleveland, 1993
Green Bay, 1996
Denver, 1997
San Diego, 1997
Chicago, 2006
Tennessee, 2006
New Orleans, 2008
Oakland, 2008

Most Touchdowns, Punt Returns, Game

2 Detroit vs. Los Angeles, Oct. 14, 1951
Detroit vs. Green Bay, Nov. 22, 1951
Chi. Cardinals vs. Pittsburgh, Nov. 1, 1959
Chi. Cardinals vs. N.Y. Giants, Nov. 22, 1959
N.Y. Titans vs. Denver, Sept. 24, 1961
Denver vs. Cleveland, Sept. 26, 1976
Los Angeles vs. Atlanta, Oct. 11, 1981
St. Louis vs. Tampa Bay, Dec. 21, 1986
L.A. Rams vs. Atlanta, Dec. 27, 1992
Cleveland vs. Pittsburgh, Oct. 24, 1993
San Diego vs. Cincinnati, Nov. 2, 1997
Denver vs. Carolina, Nov. 9, 1997
Baltimore vs. Seattle, Dec. 7, 1997
Baltimore vs. N.Y. Jets, Dec. 24, 2000
Oakland vs. Tennessee, Sept. 29, 2002
Carolina vs. Cincinnati, Dec. 8, 2002
Detroit at Jacksonville, Nov. 14, 2004 (OT)
New Orleans vs. Minnesota, Oct. 6, 2008

Most Touchdowns, Punt Returns, Both Teams, Game

2 Philadelphia (1) vs. Washington (1), Nov. 9, 1952
Kansas City (1) vs. Buffalo (1), Sept. 11, 1966
Baltimore (1) vs. New England (1), Nov. 18, 1979
L.A. Raiders (1) vs. Philadelphia (1), Nov. 30, 1986 (OT)
Cincinnati (1) vs. Green Bay (1), Sept. 20, 1992
Oakland (1) vs. Seattle (1), Nov. 15, 1998
Atlanta (1) vs. Tennessee (1), Nov. 23, 2003

(Also see previous record)

KICKOFF RETURNS

Most Seasons Leading League (Average Return)

8 Washington, 1942, 1947, 1962-63, 1973-74, 1981, 1995
6 Chicago Bears, 1943, 1948, 1958, 1966, 1972, 1985
N.Y. Giants, 1944, 1946, 1949, 1951, 1953, 2004
5 Green Bay, 1954, 1964, 1967, 1993, 1998
New England, 1977, 1980, 1982, 1997, 2006
Hou. Oilers/ Tenn. Titans, 1960, 1962-63, 1968, 2008

Most Consecutive Seasons Leading League (Average Return)

3 Denver, 1965-67
2 By many teams

Most Kickoff Returns, Season

89 Cleveland, 1999
88 New Orleans, 1980
87 Atlanta, 1996
New Orleans, 2001

Fewest Kickoff Returns, Season

17 N.Y. Giants, 1944
20 N.Y. Giants, 1941, 1943
Chi. Bears, 1942
23 Washington, 1942

Most Kickoff Returns, Game

12 N.Y. Giants vs. Washington, Nov. 27, 1966
11 Kansas City vs. Buffalo, Nov. 23, 2008
10 By many teams

Most Kickoff Returns, Both Teams, Game

19 N.Y. Giants (12) vs. Washington (7), Nov. 27, 1966
Cleveland (10) vs. Cincinnati (9), Nov. 28, 2004
18 Houston (10) vs. Oakland (8), Dec. 22, 1963
17 Washington (9) vs. Green Bay (8), Oct. 17, 1983
San Diego (9) vs. Pittsburgh (8), Dec. 8, 1985
Detroit (9) vs. Green Bay (8), Nov. 27, 1986
L.A. Raiders (9) vs. Seattle (8), Dec. 18, 1988
Oakland (10) vs. Seattle (7), Oct. 26, 1997
Buffalo (9) vs. Minnesota (8), Sept. 15, 2002 (OT)
Cincinnati (10) vs. Cleveland (7), Sept. 16, 2007
Kansas City (11) vs. Buffalo (6), Nov. 23, 2008

YARDS GAINED

Most Yards, Kickoff Returns, Season

2,296 Arizona, 2000
2,173 Houston, 2005
2,039 Detroit, 2002

Fewest Yards, Kickoff Returns, Season

282 N.Y. Giants, 1940
381 Green Bay, 1940
424 Chicago, 1963

Most Yards, Kickoff Returns, Game

367 Baltimore vs. Minnesota, Dec. 13, 1998
362 Detroit vs. Los Angeles, Oct. 29, 1950
304 Chi. Bears vs. Green Bay, Nov. 9, 1952
New Orleans vs. L.A. Rams, Oct. 23, 1994

Most Yards, Kickoff Returns, Both Teams, Game

560 Detroit (362) vs. Los Angeles (198), Oct. 29, 1950
511 Baltimore (367) vs. Minnesota (144), Dec. 13, 1998
501 New Orleans (304) vs. L.A. Rams (197), Oct. 23, 1994

AVERAGE YARDAGE

Highest Average, Kickoff Returns, Season

29.4 Chicago, 1972 (52-1,528)
28.9 Pittsburgh, 1952 (39-1,128)
28.2 Washington, 1962 (61-1,720)

Lowest Average, Kickoff Returns, Season

14.7 N.Y. Jets, 1993 (46-675)
15.8 N.Y. Giants, 1993 (32-507)
15.9 Tampa Bay, 1993 (58-922)

TOUCHDOWNS

Most Touchdowns, Kickoff Returns, Season

4 Green Bay, 1967
Chicago, 1970
Detroit, 1994
Houston, 2007
3 Los Angeles, 1950
Chi. Cardinals, 1954
San Francisco, 1963
Denver, 1966
Chicago, 1967
New England, 1977
L.A. Rams, 1985
Atlanta, 2000
Buffalo, 2004
N.Y. Jets, 2007
2 By many teams

Most Touchdowns, Kickoff Returns, Game

2 Chi. Bears vs. Green Bay, Sept. 22, 1940
Chi. Bears vs. Green Bay, Nov. 9, 1952
Philadelphia vs. Dallas, Nov. 6, 1966

Green Bay vs. Cleveland, Nov. 12, 1967
L.A. Rams vs. Green Bay, Nov. 24, 1985
New Orleans vs. L.A. Rams, Oct. 23, 1994
Baltimore vs. Minnesota, Dec. 13, 1998
N.Y. Jets vs. Buffalo, Sept. 8, 2002 (OT)
Chicago vs. St. Louis, Dec. 11, 2006
Houston vs. Jacksonville, Dec. 30, 2007

Most Touchdowns, Kickoff Returns, Both Teams, Game
3 Baltimore (2) vs. Minnesota (1), Dec. 13, 1998
2 In many games

FUMBLES

Most Fumbles, Season
56 Chi. Bears, 1938
San Francisco, 1978
54 Philadelphia, 1946
51 New England, 1973

Fewest Fumbles, Season
7 Kansas City, 2002
8 Cleveland, 1959
10 Indianapolis, 1998
Minnesota, 1998

Most Fumbles, Game
10 Phil-Pitt vs. N.Y. Giants, Oct. 9, 1943
Detroit vs. Minnesota, Nov. 12, 1967
Kansas City vs. Houston, Oct. 12, 1969
San Francisco vs. Detroit, Dec. 17, 1978
9 Philadelphia vs. Green Bay, Oct. 13, 1946
Boston at Oakland, Dec. 16, 1962
Kansas City vs. San Diego, Nov. 15, 1964
N.Y. Giants vs. Buffalo, Oct. 20, 1975
St. Louis vs. Washington, Oct. 25, 1976
San Diego vs. Green Bay, Sept. 24, 1978
Pittsburgh vs. Cincinnati, Oct. 14, 1979
Cleveland vs. Seattle, Dec. 20, 1981
Cleveland vs. Pittsburgh, Dec. 23, 1990
Oakland vs. Seattle, Dec. 22, 1996
8 By many teams

Most Fumbles, Both Teams, Game
14 Chi. Bears (7) vs. Cleveland (7), Nov. 24, 1940
St. Louis (8) vs. N.Y. Giants (6), Sept. 17, 1961
Kansas City (10) vs. Houston (4), Oct. 12, 1969
13 Washington (8) vs. Pittsburgh (5), Nov. 14, 1937
Philadelphia (7) vs. Boston (6), Dec. 8, 1946
N.Y. Giants (7) vs. Washington (6), Nov. 5, 1950
Kansas City (9) vs. San Diego (4), Nov. 15, 1964
Buffalo (7) vs. Denver (6), Dec. 13, 1964
N.Y. Jets (7) vs. Houston (6), Sept. 12, 1965
Cleveland (7) vs. New Orleans (6), Dec. 12, 1971
Houston (8) vs. Pittsburgh (5), Dec. 9, 1973
St. Louis (9) vs. Washington (4), Oct. 25, 1976
Cleveland (9) vs. Seattle (4), Dec. 20, 1981
Green Bay (7) vs. Detroit (6), Oct. 6, 1985
12 In many games

FUMBLES LOST

Most Fumbles Lost, Season
36 Chi. Cardinals, 1959
31 Green Bay, 1952
29 Chi. Cardinals, 1946
Pittsburgh, 1950
Cleveland, 1978

Fewest Fumbles Lost, Season
2 Kansas City, 2002
3 Philadelphia, 1938
Minnesota, 1980
N.Y. Giants, 2008
4 San Francisco, 1960
Kansas City, 1982
Minnesota, 1998
Detroit, 2003

Most Fumbles Lost, Game
8 St. Louis vs. Washington, Oct. 25, 1976
Cleveland vs. Pittsburgh, Dec. 23, 1990
7 Cincinnati vs. Buffalo, Nov. 30, 1969
Pittsburgh vs. Cincinnati, Oct. 14, 1979
Cleveland vs. Seattle, Dec. 20, 1981
6 By many teams

FUMBLES RECOVERED

Most Fumbles Recovered, Season, Own and Opponents'
58 Minnesota, 1963 (27 own, 31 opp)
51 Chi. Bears, 1938 (37 own, 14 opp)
San Francisco, 1978 (24 own, 27 opp)
50 Philadelphia, 1987 (23 own, 27 opp)

Fewest Fumbles Recovered, Season, Own and Opponents'
9 San Francisco, 1982 (5 own, 4 opp)
10 Jacksonville, 2006 (6 own, 4 opp)
11 Cincinnati, 1982 (5 own, 6 opp)
Denver, 2008 (4 own, 7 opp)
Washington, 2008 (6 own, 5 opp)

Most Fumbles Recovered, Game, Own and Opponents'
10 Denver vs. Buffalo, Dec. 13, 1964 (5 own, 5 opp)
Pittsburgh vs. Houston, Dec. 9, 1973 (5 own, 5 opp)
Washington vs. St. Louis, Oct. 25, 1976 (2 own, 8 opp)
9 St. Louis vs. N.Y. Giants, Sept. 17, 1961 (6 own, 3 opp)
Houston vs. Cincinnati, Oct. 27, 1974 (4 own, 5 opp)
Kansas City vs. Dallas, Nov. 10, 1975 (4 own, 5 opp)
Green Bay vs. Detroit, Oct. 6, 1985 (5 own, 4 opp)
Pittsburgh vs. Cleveland, Dec. 23, 1990 (1 own, 8 opp)
8 By many teams

Most Own Fumbles Recovered, Season
37 Chi. Bears, 1938
28 Pittsburgh, 1987
27 Philadelphia, 1946
Minnesota, 1963

Fewest Own Fumbles Recovered, Season
1 Indianapolis, 2006
Philadelphia, 2008
2 Washington, 1958
Miami, 2000
3 Detroit, 1956
Cleveland, 1959
Houston, 1982
New Orleans, 2005

Most Opponents' Fumbles Recovered, Season
31 Minnesota, 1963
29 Cleveland, 1951
28 Green Bay, 1946
Houston, 1977
Seattle, 1983

Fewest Opponents' Fumbles Recovered, Season
3 Los Angeles, 1974
Green Bay, 1995
4 Philadelphia, 1944
San Francisco, 1982
Jacksonville, 2006
Jacksonville, 2008
5 Baltimore, 1982
Arizona, 1997
Baltimore, 1998
Chicago, 2003
Oakland, 2006
N.Y. Giants, 2008
Washington, 2008

Most Opponents' Fumbles Recovered, Game
8 Washington vs. St. Louis, Oct. 25, 1976

Pittsburgh vs. Cleveland, Dec. 23, 1990
7 Buffalo vs. Cincinnati, Nov. 30, 1969
Cincinnati vs. Pittsburgh, Oct. 14, 1979
Seattle vs. Cleveland, Dec. 20, 1981
6 By many teams

TOUCHDOWNS

Most Touchdowns, Fumbles Recovered, Season, Own and Opponents'
5 Chi. Bears, 1942 (1 own, 4 opp)
Los Angeles, 1952 (1 own, 4 opp)
San Francisco, 1965 (1 own, 4 opp)
Oakland, 1978 (2 own, 3 opp)
4 Chi. Bears, 1948 (1 own, 3 opp)
Boston, 1948 (4 opp)
Denver, 1979 (1 own, 3 opp)
Atlanta, 1981 (1 own, 3 opp)
Denver, 1984 (4 opp)
St. Louis, 1987 (4 opp)
Minnesota, 1989 (4 opp)
Atlanta, 1991 (4 opp)
Philadelphia, 1995 (4 opp)
Atlanta, 1998 (4 opp)
New Orleans, 1998 (4 opp)
Kansas City, 1999 (4 opp)
3 By many teams

Most Touchdowns, Own Fumbles Recovered, Season
2 Chi. Bears, 1953
New England, 1973
Buffalo, 1974
Denver, 1975
Oakland, 1978
Green Bay, 1982
New Orleans, 1983
Cleveland, 1986
Green Bay, 1989
Miami, 1996
Buffalo, 2000
Philadelphia, 2007

Most Touchdowns, Opponents' Fumbles Recovered, Season
4 Detroit, 1937
Chi. Bears, 1942
Boston, 1948
Los Angeles, 1952
San Francisco, 1965
Denver, 1984
St. Louis, 1987
Minnesota, 1989
Atlanta, 1991
Philadelphia, 1995
Atlanta, 1998
New Orleans, 1998
Kansas City, 1999
3 By many teams

Most Touchdowns, Fumbles Recovered, Game, Own and Opponents'
2 By many teams

Most Touchdowns, Fumbles Recovered, Game, Both Teams, Own and Opponents'
3 Detroit (2) vs. Minnesota (1), Dec. 9, 1962 (2 own, 1 opp)
Green Bay (2) vs. Dallas (1), Nov. 29, 1964 (3 opp)
Oakland (2) vs. Buffalo (1), Dec. 24, 1967 (3 opp)
Oakland (2) vs. Philadelphia (1), Sept. 24, 1995 (3 opp)
Tennessee (2) vs. Pittsburgh (1), Jan. 2, 2000 (3 opp)

Most Touchdowns, Own Fumbles Recovered, Game
2 Miami vs. New England, Sept.1, 1996

Most Touchdowns, Opponents' Fumbles Recovered, Game
2 Many times. Last time:
Philadelphia vs. Dallas, Dec. 28, 2008

Most Touchdowns, Opponents' Fumbles Recovered, Game, Both Teams
3 Green Bay (2) vs. Dallas (1), Nov. 29, 1964
Oakland (2) vs. Buffalo (1), Dec. 24, 1967
Oakland (2) vs. Philadelphia (1), Sept. 24, 1995
Tennessee (2) vs. Pittsburgh (1), Jan. 2, 2000

TURNOVERS

(Number of times losing the ball on interceptions and fumbles.)

Most Turnovers, Season
65 Denver, 1961
63 San Francisco, 1978
58 Chi. Bears, 1947
Pittsburgh, 1950
N.Y. Giants, 1983

Fewest Turnovers, Season
12 Kansas City, 1982
13 Miami, 2008
N.Y. Giants, 2008
14 N.Y. Giants, 1943
Cleveland, 1959
N.Y. Giants, 1990

Most Turnovers, Game
12 Detroit vs. Chi. Bears, Nov. 22, 1942
Chi. Cardinals vs. Philadelphia, Sept. 24, 1950
Pittsburgh vs. Philadelphia, Dec. 12, 1965
11 San Diego vs. Green Bay, Sept. 24, 1978
10 Washington vs. N.Y. Giants, Dec. 4, 1938
Pittsburgh vs. Green Bay, Nov. 23, 1941
Detroit vs. Green Bay, Oct. 24, 1943
Chi. Cardinals vs. Green Bay, Nov. 10, 1946
Chi. Cardinals vs. N.Y. Giants, Nov. 2, 1952
Minnesota vs. Detroit, Dec. 9, 1962
Houston vs. Oakland, Sept. 7, 1963
Washington vs. N.Y. Giants, Dec. 8, 1963
Chicago vs. Detroit, Sept. 22, 1968
St. Louis vs. Washington, Oct. 25, 1976
N.Y. Jets vs. New England, Nov. 21, 1976
San Francisco vs. Dallas, Oct. 12, 1980
Cleveland vs. Seattle, Dec. 20, 1981
Detroit vs. Denver, Oct. 7, 1984

Most Turnovers, Both Teams, Game
17 Detroit (12) vs. Chi. Bears (5), Nov. 22, 1942
Boston (9) vs. Philadelphia (8), Dec. 8, 1946
16 Chi. Cardinals (12) vs. Philadelphia (4), Sept. 24, 1950
Chi. Cardinals (8) vs. Chi. Bears (8), Dec. 7, 1958
Minnesota (10) vs. Detroit (6), Dec. 9, 1962
Houston (9) vs. Kansas City (7), Oct. 12, 1969
15 Philadelphia (8) vs. Chi. Cardinals (7), Oct. 3, 1954
Denver (9) vs. Houston (6), Dec. 2, 1962
Washington (10) vs. N.Y. Giants (5), Dec. 8, 1963
St. Louis (9) vs. Kansas City (6), Oct. 2, 1983

PENALTIES

Most Seasons Leading League, Fewest Penalties
13 Miami, 1968, 1976-1984, 1986, 1990-91
9 Pittsburgh, 1946-47, 1950-52, 1954, 1963, 1965, 1968
8 Boston/New England, 1962, 1964-65, 1973, 1987, 1989, 1993, 2008

Most Consecutive Seasons Leading League, Fewest Penalties
9 Miami, 1976-1984
3 Pittsburgh, 1950-52
2 By many teams

Most Seasons Leading League, Most Penalties
16 Chi. Bears, 1941-44, 1946-49, 1951, 1959-1961, 1963, 1965, 1968, 1976
15 Oakland/L.A. Raiders, 1963, 1966, 1968-69, 1975, 1982, 1984, 1991, 1993-96, 2003-05
7 L.A./St. Louis Rams, 1950, 1952, 1962, 1969, 1978, 1980, 1997

Most Consecutive Seasons Leading League, Most Penalties
4 Chi. Bears, 1941-44, 1946-49
Oakland/L.A. Raiders, 1993-96
3 Chi. Cardinals, 1954-56
Chi. Bears, 1959-1961
Oakland, 2003-05

Fewest Penalties, Season
19 Detroit, 1937
21 Boston, 1935
24 Philadelphia, 1936

Most Penalties, Season
158 Kansas City, 1998
156 L.A. Raiders, 1994
Oakland, 1996
149 Houston, 1989

Fewest Penalties, Game
0 By many teams. Last time:
Philadelphia vs. Dallas, Dec. 28, 2008

Most Penalties, Game
22 Brooklyn vs. Green Bay, Sept. 17, 1944
Chi. Bears vs. Philadelphia, Nov. 26, 1944
San Francisco vs. Buffalo, Oct. 4, 1998
21 Cleveland vs. Chi. Bears, Nov. 25, 1951
Baltimore vs. Detroit, Oct. 9, 2005
20 Tampa Bay vs. Seattle, Oct. 17, 1976
Oakland vs. Denver, Dec. 15, 1996

Fewest Penalties, Both Teams, Game
0 Brooklyn vs. Pittsburgh, Oct. 28, 1934
Brooklyn vs. Boston, Sept. 28, 1936
Cleveland vs. Chi. Bears, Oct. 9, 1938
Pittsburgh vs. Philadelphia, Nov. 10, 1940

Most Penalties, Both Teams, Game
37 Cleveland (21) vs. Chi. Bears (16), Nov. 25, 1951
35 Tampa Bay (20) vs. Seattle (15), Oct. 17, 1976
34 San Francisco (22) vs. Buffalo (12), Oct. 4, 1998

YARDS PENALIZED

Most Seasons Leading League, Fewest Yards Penalized
13 Miami, 1967-68, 1973, 1977-1984, 1990-91
10 Boston/Washington, 1935, 1953-54, 1956-58, 1970, 1985, 1995, 1997
8 Boston/New England, 1962, 1964-66, 1987, 1989, 1993, 2008

Most Consecutive Seasons Leading League, Fewest Yards Penalized
8 Miami, 1977-1984
3 Washington, 1956-58
Boston, 1964-66
2 By many teams

Most Seasons Leading League, Most Yards Penalized
15 Chi. Bears, 1935, 1937, 1939-1944, 1946-47, 1949, 1951, 1961-62, 1968
12 Oakland/L.A. Raiders, 1963-64, 1968-69, 1975, 1982, 1984, 1991, 1993-94, 1996, 2003
6 Buffalo, 1962, 1967, 1970, 1972, 1981, 1983
Houston, 1961, 1985-86, 1988-1990

Most Consecutive Seasons Leading League, Most Yards Penalized
6 Chi. Bears, 1939-1944
3 Houston, 1988-1990
2 By many teams

Fewest Yards Penalized, Season
139 Detroit, 1937
146 Philadelphia, 1937
159 Philadelphia, 1936

Most Yards Penalized, Season
1,304 Kansas City, 1998
1,274 Oakland, 1969
1,266 Oakland, 1996

Fewest Yards Penalized, Game
0 By many teams. Last time:
Philadelphia vs. Dallas, Dec. 28, 2008

Most Yards Penalized, Game
212 Tennessee vs. Baltimore, Oct. 10, 1999
209 Cleveland vs. Chi. Bears, Nov. 25, 1951
191 Philadelphia vs. Seattle, Dec. 13, 1992 (OT)

Fewest Yards Penalized, Both Teams, Game
0 Brooklyn vs. Pittsburgh, Oct. 28, 1934
Brooklyn vs. Boston, Sept. 28, 1936
Cleveland vs. Chi. Bears, Oct. 9, 1938
Pittsburgh vs. Philadelphia, Nov. 10, 1940

Most Yards Penalized, Both Teams, Game
374 Cleveland (209) vs. Chi. Bears (165), Nov. 25, 1951
310 Tampa Bay (190) vs. Seattle (120), Oct. 17, 1976
309 Green Bay (184) vs. Boston (125), Oct. 21, 1945

DEFENSE

SCORING

Most Seasons Leading League, Fewest Points Allowed
11 N.Y. Giants, 1927, 1935, 1938-39, 1941, 1944, 1958-59, 1961, 1990, 1993
Chi. Bears, 1932, 1936-37, 1942, 1948, 1963, 1985-86, 1988, 2001, 2005
7 Cleveland, 1951, 1953-57, 1994
Green Bay, 1929, 1935, 1947, 1962, 1965-66, 1996
6 Dallas/Kansas City, 1960, 1962, 1968-69, 1995, 1997

Most Consecutive Seasons Leading League, Fewest Points Allowed
5 Cleveland, 1953-57
3 Buffalo, 1964-66
Minnesota, 1969-1971
2 By many teams

Fewest Points Allowed, Season (Since 1932)
44 Chi. Bears, 1932
54 Brooklyn, 1933
59 Detroit, 1934

Most Points Allowed, Season
533 Baltimore, 1981
517 Detroit, 2008
501 N.Y. Giants, 1966

Fewest Touchdowns Allowed, Season (Since 1932)
6 Chi. Bears, 1932
Brooklyn, 1933
7 Detroit, 1934
8 Green Bay, 1932

Most Touchdowns Allowed, Season
68 Baltimore, 1981
66 N.Y. Giants, 1966
63 Baltimore, 1950
Detroit, 2008

FIRST DOWNS

Fewest First Downs Allowed, Season
77 Detroit, 1935
79 Boston, 1935
82 Washington, 1937

Most First Downs Allowed, Season
406 Baltimore, 1981
371 Seattle, 1981
368 Cleveland, 1999

Fewest First Downs Allowed, Rushing, Season
35 Chi. Bears, 1942
40 Green Bay, 1939
41 Brooklyn, 1944

Most First Downs Allowed, Rushing, Season
179 Detroit, 1985
178 New Orleans, 1980
175 Seattle, 1981

Fewest First Downs Allowed, Passing, Season
33 Chi. Bears, 1943
34 Pittsburgh, 1941
Washington, 1943
35 Detroit, 1940
Philadelphia, 1940, 1944

Most First Downs Allowed, Passing, Season
230 Atlanta, 1995
227 Kansas City, 2002
222 Minnesota, 2007

Fewest First Downs Allowed, Penalty, Season
1 Boston, 1944
3 Philadelphia, 1940
Pittsburgh, 1945
Washington, 1957
4 Cleveland, 1940
Green Bay, 1943
N.Y. Giants, 1943

Most First Downs Allowed, Penalty, Season
56 Kansas City, 1998
48 Houston, 1985
46 Houston, 1986

NET YARDS ALLOWED RUSHING AND PASSING

Most Seasons Leading League, Fewest Yards Allowed
8 Chi. Bears, 1942-43, 1948, 1958, 1963, 1984-86
Pittsburgh, 1957, 1974, 1976, 1990, 2001, 2004, 2007-08
6 N.Y. Giants, 1938, 1940-41, 1951, 1956, 1959
Philadelphia, 1944-45, 1949, 1953, 1981, 1991
Minnesota, 1969-1970, 1975, 1988-89, 1993

Most Consecutive Seasons Leading League, Fewest Yards Allowed
3 Boston/Washington, 1935-37
Chicago, 1984-86
2 By many teams

Fewest Yards Allowed, Season
1,539 Chi. Cardinals, 1934
1,703 Chi. Bears, 1942
1,789 Brooklyn, 1933

Most Yards Allowed, Season
6,793 Baltimore, 1981
6,470 Detroit, 2008
6,403 Green Bay, 1983

RUSHING

Most Seasons Leading League, Fewest Yards Allowed
10 Chi. Bears, 1937, 1939, 1942, 1946, 1949, 1963, 1984-85, 1987-88
7 Detroit, 1938, 1950, 1952, 1962, 1970, 1980-81
Philadelphia, 1944-45, 1947-48, 1953, 1990-91
Dallas, 1966-69, 1972, 1978, 1992
Pittsburgh, 1961, 1976, 1982, 1997, 2001-02, 2004
5 N.Y. Giants, 1940, 1951, 1956, 1959, 1986
L.A./St. Louis Rams, 1964-65, 1973-74, 1999
Minnesota, 1975, 1994, 2006-08

Most Consecutive Seasons Leading League, Fewest Yards Allowed
4 Dallas, 1966-69
3 Minnesota, 2006-08
2 By many teams

Fewest Yards Allowed, Rushing, Season
519 Chi. Bears, 1942
558 Philadelphia, 1944
762 Pittsburgh, 1982

Most Yards Allowed, Rushing, Season
3,228 Buffalo, 1978
3,106 New Orleans, 1980
3,010 Baltimore, 1978

Fewest Touchdowns Allowed, Rushing, Season
2 Detroit, 1934
N.Y. Giants, 1944
Dallas, 1968
Minnesota, 1971
3 By many teams

Most Touchdowns Allowed, Rushing, Season
36 Oakland, 1961
31 N.Y. Giants, 1980
Tampa Bay, 1986
Detroit, 2008
30 Baltimore, 1981

PASSING

Most Seasons Leading League, Fewest Yards Allowed
10 Green Bay, 1947-48, 1962, 1964-68, 1996, 2005
7 Washington, 1939, 1942, 1945, 1952-53, 1980, 1985
Philadelphia 1934, 1936, 1940, 1949, 1981, 1991, 1998
Pittsburgh, 1941, 1946, 1951, 1955, 1974, 1990, 2008
6 Chi. Bears, 1938, 1943-44, 1958, 1960, 1963
Minnesota, 1969-1970, 1972, 1975-76, 1989

Most Consecutive Seasons Leading League, Fewest Yards Allowed
5 Green Bay, 1964-68
2 By many teams

Fewest Yards Allowed, Passing, Season
545 Philadelphia, 1934
558 Portsmouth, 1933
585 Chi. Cardinals, 1934

Most Yards Allowed, Passing, Season
4,541 Atlanta, 1995
4.427 San Francisco, 2005
4,389 N.Y. Jets, 1986

Fewest Touchdowns Allowed, Passing, Season
1 Portsmouth, 1932
Philadelphia, 1934
2 Brooklyn, 1933
Chi. Bears, 1934
3 Chi. Bears, 1932
Green Bay, 1932
Green Bay, 1934
Chi. Bears, 1936
New York, 1939
New York, 1944

Most Touchdowns Allowed, Passing, Season
40 Denver, 1963
38 St. Louis, 1969
37 Washington, 1961
Baltimore, 1981

SACKS

Most Seasons Leading League
5 Oakland/L.A. Raiders, 1966-68, 1982, 1986
Dallas, 1966, 1968-69, 1978, 2008
4 New England/Boston, 1961, 1963, 1977, 1979
Dallas/Kansas City, 1960, 1965, 1969, 1990
L.A./St. Louis Rams, 1968, 1970, 1988, 1999
N.Y. Giants, 1963, 1985, 1998, 2007
3 San Francisco, 1967, 1972, 1976
N.Y. Giants, 1963, 1985, 1998
New Orleans, 1992, 1997, 2000

Pittsburgh, 1974, 1994, 2001
San Diego, 1962, 1980, 2006

Most Consecutive Seasons Leading League
3 Oakland, 1966-68
2 Dallas, 1968-69

Most Sacks, Season
72 Chicago, 1984
71 Minnesota, 1989
70 Chicago, 1987

Fewest Sacks, Season
10 Kansas City, 2008
11 Baltimore, 1982
12 Buffalo, 1982
13 Baltimore, 1981

Most Sacks, Game
12 Dallas vs. Pittsburgh, Nov. 20, 1966
St. Louis vs. Baltimore, Oct. 26, 1980
Chicago vs. Detroit, Dec. 16, 1984
Dallas vs. Houston, Sept. 29, 1985
N.Y. Giants vs. Philadelphia, Sept. 30, 2007
11 N.Y. Giants vs. St. Louis, Nov. 1, 1964
Baltimore vs. Los Angeles, Nov. 22, 1964
Buffalo vs. Denver, Dec. 13, 1964
Detroit vs. Green Bay, Nov. 7, 1965
Oakland vs. Buffalo, Oct. 15, 1967
Oakland vs. Denver, Nov. 5, 1967
St. Louis vs. Atlanta, Nov. 24, 1968
Dallas vs. Detroit, Oct. 6, 1975
St. Louis vs. Philadelphia, Dec. 18, 1983
Kansas City vs. Cleveland, Sept. 30, 1984
Chicago vs. Minnesota, Oct. 28, 1984
Cleveland vs. Atlanta, Nov. 18, 1984
Detroit vs. Philadelphia, Nov. 16, 1986
San Diego vs. Dallas, Nov. 16, 1986
L.A. Raiders vs. Philadelphia, Nov. 30, 1986 (OT)
Seattle vs. L.A. Raiders, Dec. 8, 1986
Chicago vs. Philadelphia, Oct. 4, 1987
Dallas vs. N.Y. Jets, Oct. 4, 1987
Philadelphia vs. Dallas, Sept. 15, 1991
Indianapolis vs. Cleveland, Sept. 6, 1992
10 By many teams

Most Opponents Yards Lost Attempting to Pass, Season
666 Oakland, 1967
583 Chicago, 1984
573 San Francisco, 1976

Fewest Opponents Yards Lost Attempting to Pass, Season
62 Kansas City, 2008
72 Jacksonville, 1995
75 Green Bay, 1956

INTERCEPTIONS BY

Most Seasons Leading League
10 N.Y. Giants, 1933, 1937-39, 1944, 1948, 1951, 1954, 1961, 1997
8 Green Bay, 1940, 1942-43, 1947, 1955, 1957, 1962, 1965
Chi. Bears, 1935-36, 1941-42, 1946, 1963, 1985, 1990
6 Kansas City, 1966-1970, 1974

Most Consecutive Seasons Leading League
5 Kansas City, 1966-1970
3 N.Y. Giants, 1937-39
2 By many teams

Most Passes Intercepted By, Season
49 San Diego, 1961
42 Green Bay, 1943
41 N.Y. Giants, 1951

Fewest Passes Intercepted By, Season
3 Houston, 1982
4 Detroit, 2008
5 Baltimore, 1982
Oakland, 2005

Most Passes Intercepted By, Game
9 Green Bay vs. Detroit, Oct. 24, 1943
Philadelphia vs. Pittsburgh, Dec. 12, 1965
8 N.Y. Giants vs. Green Bay, Nov. 21, 1948
Philadelphia vs. Chi. Cardinals, Sept. 24, 1950
N.Y. Giants vs. N.Y. Yanks, Dec. 16, 1951
Houston vs. Denver, Dec. 2, 1962
Detroit vs. Chicago, Sept. 22, 1968
N.Y. Jets vs. Baltimore, Sept. 23, 1973
7 By many teams. Last time:
Cleveland vs. Detroit, Sept. 23, 2001

Most Consecutive Games, One or More Interceptions By
46 L.A. Chargers/San Diego, 1960-63
37 Detroit, 1960-63
36 Boston, 1944-47

Most Yards Returning Interceptions, Season
929 San Diego, 1961
712 Los Angeles, 1952
700 Baltimore, 2004

Fewest Yards Returning Interceptions, Season
5 Los Angeles, 1959
16 Detroit, 2008
25 Washington, 2006

Most Yards Returning Interceptions, Game
325 Seattle vs. Kansas City, Nov. 4, 1984
314 Los Angeles vs. San Francisco, Oct. 18, 1964
245 Houston vs. N.Y. Jets, Oct. 15, 1967

Most Yards Returning Interceptions, Both Teams, Game
356 Seattle (325) vs. Kansas City (31), Nov. 4, 1984
338 Los Angeles (314) vs. San Francisco (24), Oct. 18, 1964
308 Dallas (182) vs. Los Angeles (126), Nov. 2, 1952

Most Touchdowns, Returning Interceptions, Season
9 San Diego, 1961
8 Seattle, 1998
7 Seattle, 1984
St. Louis, 1999

Most Touchdowns Returning Interceptions, Game
4 Seattle vs. Kansas City, Nov. 4, 1984
3 Baltimore vs. Green Bay, Nov. 5, 1950
Cleveland vs. Chicago, Dec. 11, 1960
Philadelphia vs. Pittsburgh, Dec. 12, 1965
Baltimore vs. Pittsburgh, Sept. 29, 1968
Buffalo vs. N.Y. Jets, Sept. 29, 1968
Houston vs. San Diego, Dec. 19, 1971
Cincinnati vs. Houston, Dec. 17, 1972
Tampa Bay vs. New Orleans, Dec. 11, 1977
Minnesota vs. N.Y. Giants, Nov. 25, 2007
2 By many teams

Most Touchdown Returning Interceptions, Both Teams, Game
4 Philadelphia (3) vs. Pittsburgh (1), Dec. 12, 1965
Seattle (4) vs. Kansas City (0), Nov. 4, 1984
3 Los Angeles (2) vs. Detroit (1), Nov. 1, 1953
Cleveland (2) vs. N.Y. Giants (1), Dec. 18, 1960
Pittsburgh (2) vs. Cincinnati (1), Oct. 10, 1983
Kansas City (2) vs. San Diego (1), Oct. 19, 1986
Arizona (2) vs. St. Louis (1), Dec. 30, 2007
(Also see previous record)

PUNT RETURNS

Fewest Opponents Punt Returns, Season
7 Washington, 1962
San Diego, 1982
10 Buffalo, 1982
11 Boston, 1962
New England, 2008

Most Opponents Punt Returns, Season
71 Tampa Bay, 1976, 1977

69 N.Y. Giants, 1953
Cleveland, 2000
68 Cleveland, 1974
Cleveland, 1999

Fewest Yards Allowed, Punt Returns, Season
22 Green Bay, 1967
30 Buffalo, 1982
34 Washington, 1962

Most Yards Allowed, Punt Returns, Season
932 Green Bay, 1949
913 Boston, 1947
906 New Orleans, 1974

Lowest Average Allowed, Punt Returns, Season
1.20 Chi. Cardinals, 1954 (46-55)
1.22 Cleveland, 1959 (32-39)
1.55 Chi. Cardinals, 1953 (44-68)

Highest Average Allowed, Punt Returns, Season
18.6 Green Bay, 1949 (50-932)
18.0 Cleveland, 1977 (31-558)
17.9 Boston, 1960 (20-357)

Most Touchdowns Allowed, Punt Returns, Season
4 New York, 1959
Atlanta, 1992
Minnesota, 2008
3 Green Bay, 1949
Chi. Cardinals, 1951
L.A. Rams, 1951, 1994
Washington, 1952
Dallas, 1952
Pittsburgh, 1959, 1993
N.Y. Jets, 1968
Cleveland, 1977
Atlanta, 1986
Tampa Bay, 1986
Arizona, 2002
Cincinnati, 2002
Tennessee, 2002
2 By many teams

KICKOFF RETURNS

Fewest Opponents Kickoff Returns, Season
10 Brooklyn, 1943
13 Denver, 1992
15 Detroit, 1942
Brooklyn, 1944

Most Opponents Kickoff Returns, Season
93 Indianapolis, 2003
92 Indianapolis, 2004
New England, 2007
91 Washington, 1983

Fewest Yards Allowed, Kickoff Returns, Season
225 Brooklyn, 1943
254 Denver, 1992
293 Brooklyn, 1944

Most Yards Allowed, Kickoff Returns, Season
2,194 St. Louis, 2001
2,115 St. Louis, 1999
2,053 Kansas City, 2005

Lowest Average Allowed, Kickoff Returns, Season
14.3 Cleveland, 1980 (71-1,018)
14.9 Indianapolis, 1993 (37-551)
15.0 Seattle, 1982 (24-361)

Highest Average Allowed, Kickoff Returns, Season
29.5 N.Y. Jets, 1972 (47-1,386)
29.4 Los Angeles, 1950 (48-1,411)
29.1 New England, 1971 (49-1,427)

Most Touchdowns Allowed, Kickoff Returns, Season
4 Minnesota, 1998
3 Minnesota, 1963, 1970
Dallas, 1966
Detroit, 1980
Pittsburgh, 1986
Buffalo, 1997
Atlanta, 2000
Arizona, 2005
Indianapolis, 2007
2 By many teams

FUMBLES

Fewest Opponents Fumbles, Season
11 Cleveland, 1956
Baltimore, 1982
Tennessee, 1998
12 Green Bay, 1995
Cincinnati, 1998
Jacksonville, 2006
Baltimore, 2007
13 Los Angeles, 1956
Chicago, 1960
Cleveland, 1963
Cleveland, 1965
Detroit, 1967
San Diego, 1969
New England, 2005
Cleveland, 2006

Most Opponents Fumbles, Season
50 Minnesota, 1963
San Francisco, 1978
48 N.Y. Giants, 1980
N.Y. Jets, 1986
47 N.Y. Giants, 1977
Seattle, 1984

TURNOVERS

(Number of times losing the ball on interceptions and fumbles.)

Fewest Opponents Turnovers, Season
11 Baltimore, 1982
12 Washington, 2006
13 San Francisco, 1982
Denver, 2008

Most Opponents Turnovers, Season
66 San Diego, 1961
63 Seattle, 1984
61 Washington, 1983

Most Opponents Turnovers, Game
12 Chi. Bears vs. Detroit, Nov. 22, 1942
Philadelphia vs. Chi. Cardinals, Sept. 24, 1950
Philadelphia vs. Pittsburgh, Dec. 12, 1965
11 Green Bay vs. San Diego, Sept. 24, 1978
10 By 14 teams

ANNUAL SCORING LEADERS

Year	Player, Team	TD	FG	PAT	TP
2008	Stephen Gostkowski, New England, AFC	0	36	40	148
	David Akers, Philadelphia, NFC	0	33	45	144
2007	*Mason Crosby, Green Bay, NFC	0	31	48	141
	Randy Moss, New England, AFC	23	0	0	138
2006	LaDainian Tomlinson, AFC	31	0	0	186
	Robbie Gould, Chicago, NFC	0	32	47	143
2005	Shaun Alexander, Seattle, NFC	28	0	0	168
	Shayne Graham, Cincinnati, AFC	0	28	47	131
2004	Adam Vinatieri, New England, AFC	0	31	48	141
	David Akers, Philadelphia, NFC	0	27	41	122
2003	Jeff Wilkins, St. Louis, NFC	0	39	46	163
	Priest Holmes, Kansas City, AFC	27	0	0	162
2002	Priest Holmes, Kansas City, AFC	24	0	0	144
	Jay Feely, Atlanta, NFC	0	32	42	138
2001	Marshall Faulk, St. Louis, NFC	21	0	0	#128
	Mike Vanderjagt, Indianapolis, AFC	0	28	41	125
2000	Marshall Faulk, St. Louis, NFC	26	0	0	##160
	Matt Stover, Baltimore, AFC	0	35	30	135
1999	Mike Vanderjagt, Indianapolis, AFC	0	34	43	145
	Jeff Wilkins, St. Louis, NFC	0	20	64	124
1998	Gary Anderson, Minnesota, NFC	0	35	59	164
	Steve Christie, Buffalo, AFC	0	33	41	140
1997	Mike Hollis, Jacksonville, AFC	0	31	41	134
	Richie Cunningham, Dallas, NFC	0	34	24	126
1996	John Kasay, Carolina, NFC	0	37	34	145
	Cary Blanchard, Indianapolis, AFC	0	36	27	135
1995	Emmitt Smith, Dallas, NFC	25	0	0	150
	Norm Johnson, Pittsburgh, AFC	0	34	39	141
1994	John Carney, San Diego, AFC	0	34	33	135
	Fuad Reveiz, Minnesota, NFC	0	34	30	132
1993	Jeff Jaeger, L.A. Raiders, AFC	0	35	27	132
	Jason Hanson, Detroit, NFC	0	34	28	130
1992	Pete Stoyanovich, Miami, AFC	0	30	34	124
	Morten Andersen, New Orleans, NFC	0	29	33	120
	Chip Lohmiller, Washington, NFC	0	30	30	120
1991	Chip Lohmiller, Washington, NFC	0	31	56	149
	Pete Stoyanovich, Miami, AFC	0	31	28	121
1990	Nick Lowery, Kansas City, AFC	0	34	37	139
	Chip Lohmiller, Washington, NFC	0	30	41	131
1989	Mike Cofer, San Francisco, NFC	0	29	49	136
	*David Treadwell, Denver, AFC	0	27	39	120
1988	Scott Norwood, Buffalo, AFC	0	32	33	129
	Mike Cofer, San Francisco, NFC	0	27	40	121
1987	Jerry Rice, San Francisco, NFC	23	0	0	138
	Jim Breech, Cincinnati, AFC	0	24	25	97
1986	Tony Franklin, New England, AFC	0	32	44	140
	Kevin Butler, Chicago, NFC	0	28	36	120
1985	*Kevin Butler, Chicago, NFC	0	31	51	144
	Gary Anderson, Pittsburgh, AFC	0	33	40	139
1984	Ray Wersching, San Francisco, NFC	0	25	56	131
	Gary Anderson, Pittsburgh, AFC	0	24	45	117
1983	Mark Moseley, Washington, NFC	0	33	62	161
	Gary Anderson, Pittsburgh, AFC	0	27	38	119
1982	*Marcus Allen, L.A. Raiders, AFC	14	0	0	84
	Wendell Tyler, L.A. Rams, NFC	13	0	0	78
1981	Ed Murray, Detroit, NFC	0	25	46	121
	Rafael Septien, Dallas, NFC	0	27	40	121
	Jim Breech, Cincinnati, AFC	0	22	49	115
	Nick Lowery, Kansas City, AFC	0	26	37	115
1980	John Smith, New England, AFC	0	26	51	129
	*Ed Murray, Detroit, NFC	0	27	35	116
1979	John Smith, New England, AFC	0	23	46	115
	Mark Moseley, Washington, NFC	0	25	39	114
1978	*Frank Corral, Los Angeles, NFC	0	29	31	118
	Pat Leahy, N.Y. Jets, AFC	0	22	41	107
1977	Errol Mann, Oakland, AFC	0	20	39	99
	Walter Payton, Chicago, NFC	16	0	0	96

YEARLY STATISTICAL LEADERS

Year	Player, Team	TD	FG	PAT	TP
1976	Toni Linhart, Baltimore, AFC	0	20	49	109
	Mark Moseley, Washington, NFC	0	22	31	97
1975	O.J. Simpson, Buffalo, AFC	23	0	0	138
	Chuck Foreman, Minnesota, NFC	22	0	0	132
1974	Chester Marcol, Green Bay, NFC	0	25	19	94
	Roy Gerela, Pittsburgh, AFC	0	20	33	93
1973	David Ray, Los Angeles, NFC	0	30	40	130
	Roy Gerela, Pittsburgh, AFC	0	29	36	123
1972	*Chester Marcol, Green Bay, NFC	0	33	29	128
	Bobby Howfield, N.Y. Jets, AFC	0	27	40	121
1971	Garo Yepremian, Miami, AFC	0	28	33	117
	Curt Knight, Washington, NFC	0	29	27	114
1970	Fred Cox, Minnesota, NFC	0	30	35	125
	Jan Stenerud, Kansas City, AFC	0	30	26	116
1969	Jim Turner, N.Y. Jets, AFL	0	32	33	129
	Fred Cox, Minnesota, NFL	0	26	43	121
1968	Jim Turner, N.Y. Jets, AFL	0	34	43	145
	Leroy Kelly, Cleveland, NFL	20	0	0	120
1967	Jim Bakken, St. Louis, NFL	0	27	36	117
	George Blanda, Oakland, AFL	0	20	56	116
1966	Gino Cappelletti, Boston, AFL	6	16	35	119
	Bruce Gossett, Los Angeles, NFL	0	28	29	113
1965	*Gale Sayers, Chicago, NFL	22	0	0	132
	Gino Cappelletti, Boston, AFL	9	17	27	132
1964	Gino Cappelletti, Boston, AFL	7	25	36	#155
	Lenny Moore, Baltimore, NFL	20	0	0	120
1963	Gino Cappelletti, Boston, AFL	2	22	35	113
	Don Chandler, N.Y. Giants, NFL	0	18	52	106
1962	Gene Mingo, Denver, AFL	4	27	32	137
	Jim Taylor, Green Bay, NFL	19	0	0	114
1961	Gino Cappelletti, Boston, AFL	8	17	48	147
	Paul Hornung, Green Bay, NFL	10	15	41	146
1960	Paul Hornung, Green Bay, NFL	15	15	41	176
	*Gene Mingo, Denver, AFL	6	18	33	123
1959	Paul Hornung, Green Bay	7	7	31	94
1958	Jim Brown, Cleveland	18	0	0	108
1957	Sam Baker, Washington	1	14	29	77
	Lou Groza, Cleveland	0	15	32	77
1956	Bobby Layne, Detroit	5	12	33	99
1955	Doak Walker, Detroit	7	9	27	96
1954	Bobby Walston, Philadelphia	11	4	36	114
1953	Gordy Soltau, San Francisco	6	10	48	114
1952	Gordy Soltau, San Francisco	7	6	34	94
1951	Elroy (Crazylegs) Hirsch, Los Angeles	17	0	0	102
1950	*Doak Walker, Detroit	11	8	38	128
1949	Pat Harder, Chi. Cardinals	8	3	45	102
	Gene Roberts, N.Y. Giants	17	0	0	102
1948	Pat Harder, Chi. Cardinals	6	7	53	110
1947	Pat Harder, Chi. Cardinals	7	7	39	102
1946	Ted Fritsch, Green Bay	10	9	13	100
1945	Steve Van Buren, Philadelphia	18	0	2	110
1944	Don Hutson, Green Bay	9	0	31	85
1943	Don Hutson, Green Bay	12	3	36	117
1942	Don Hutson, Green Bay	17	1	33	138
1941	Don Hutson, Green Bay	12	1	20	95
1940	Don Hutson, Green Bay	7	0	15	57
1939	Andy Farkas, Washington	11	0	2	68
1938	Clarke Hinkle, Green Bay	7	3	7	58
1937	Jack Manders, Chi. Bears	5	8	15	69
1936	Earl (Dutch) Clark, Detroit	7	4	19	73
1935	Earl (Dutch) Clark, Detroit	6	1	16	55
1934	Jack Manders, Chi. Bears	3	10	31	79
1933	Ken Strong, N.Y. Giants	6	5	13	64
	Glenn Presnell, Portsmouth	6	6	10	64
1932	Earl (Dutch) Clark, Portsmouth	6	3	10	55

**First season of professional football.*
#Cappelletti's total and Faulk's total in 2001 include a two-point conversion.
##Faulk's total in 2000 includes 2 two-point conversions.

ANNUAL TOUCHDOWN LEADERS

Year	Player, Team	TD	Rush	Pass	Ret.
2008	DeAngelo Williams, Carolina, NFC	20	18	2	0
	Thomas Jones, N.Y. Jets, AFC	15	13	2	0
	LenDale White, Tennessee, AFC	15	15	0	0
2007	Randy Moss, New England, AFC	23	0	23	0
	Terrell Owens, Dallas, NFC	15	0	15	0
2006	LaDainian Tomlinson, San Diego, AFC	31	28	3	0
	Marion Barber, Dallas, NFC	16	14	2	0
	Steven Jackson, St. Louis, NFC	16	13	3	0
2005	Shaun Alexander, Seattle, NFC	28	27	1	0
	Larry Johnson, Kansas City, AFC	21	20	1	0
2004	Shaun Alexander, Seattle, NFC	20	16	4	0
	LaDainian Tomlinson, San Diego, AFC	18	17	1	0
2003	Priest Holmes, Kansas City, AFC	27	27	0	0
	Ahman Green, Green Bay, NFC	20	15	5	0
2002	Priest Holmes, Kansas City, AFC	24	21	3	0
	Shaun Alexander, Seattle, NFC	18	16	2	0
2001	Marshall Faulk, St. Louis, NFC	21	12	9	0
	Shaun Alexander, Seattle, AFC	16	14	2	0
2000	Marshall Faulk, St. Louis, NFC	26	18	8	0
	Edgerrin James, Indianapolis, AFC	18	13	5	0
1999	Stephen Davis, Washington, NFC	17	17	0	0
	*Edgerrin James, Indianapolis, AFC	17	13	4	0
1998	Terrell Davis, Denver, AFC	23	21	2	0
	*Randy Moss, Minnesota, NFC	17	0	17	0
1997	Karim Abdul-Jabbar, Miami, AFC	16	15	1	0
	Barry Sanders, Detroit, NFC	14	11	3	0
1996	Terry Allen, Washington, NFC	21	21	0	0
	Curtis Martin, New England, AFC	17	14	3	0
1995	Emmitt Smith, Dallas, NFC	25	25	0	0
	Carl Pickens, Cincinnati, AFC	17	0	17	0
1994	Emmitt Smith, Dallas, NFC	22	21	1	0
	*Marshall Faulk, Indianapolis, AFC	12	11	1	0
	Natrone Means, San Diego, AFC	12	12	0	0
1993	Jerry Rice, San Francisco, NFC	16	1	15	0
	Marcus Allen, Kansas City, AFC	15	12	3	0
1992	Emmitt Smith, Dallas, NFC	19	18	1	0
	Thurman Thomas, Buffalo, AFC	12	9	3	0
1991	Barry Sanders, Detroit, NFC	17	16	1	0
	Mark Clayton, Miami, AFC	12	0	12	0
	Thurman Thomas, Buffalo, AFC	12	7	5	0
1990	Barry Sanders, Detroit, NFC	16	13	3	0
	Derrick Fenner, Seattle, AFC	15	14	1	0
1989	Dalton Hilliard, New Orleans, NFC	18	13	5	0
	Christian Okoye, Kansas City, AFC	12	12	0	0
	Thurman Thomas, Buffalo, AFC	12	6	6	0
1988	Greg Bell, L.A. Rams, NFC	18	16	2	0
	Eric Dickerson, Indianapolis, AFC	15	14	1	0
	*Ickey Woods, Cincinnati, AFC	15	15	0	0
1987	Jerry Rice, San Francisco, NFC	23	1	22	0
	Johnny Hector, N.Y. Jets, AFC	11	11	0	0
1986	George Rogers, Washington, NFC	18	18	0	0
	Sammy Winder, Denver, AFC	14	9	5	0
1985	Joe Morris, N.Y. Giants, NFC	21	21	0	0
	Louis Lipps, Pittsburgh, AFC	15	1	12	2
1984	Marcus Allen, L.A. Raiders, AFC	18	13	5	0
	Mark Clayton, Miami, AFC	18	0	18	0
	Eric Dickerson, L.A. Rams, NFC	14	14	0	0
	John Riggins, Washington, NFC	14	14	0	0
1983	John Riggins, Washington, NFC	24	24	0	0
	Pete Johnson, Cincinnati, AFC	14	14	0	0
	*Curt Warner, Seattle, AFC	14	13	1	0
1982	*Marcus Allen, L.A. Raiders, AFC	14	11	3	0
	Wendell Tyler, L.A. Rams, NFC	13	9	4	0
1981	Chuck Muncie, San Diego, AFC	19	19	0	0
	Wendell Tyler, Los Angeles, NFC	17	12	5	0

Year	Player, Team	TD	Rush	Pass	Ret.
1980	*Billy Sims, Detroit, NFC	16	13	3	0
	Earl Campbell, Houston, AFC	13	13	0	0
	*Curtis Dickey, Baltimore, AFC	13	11	2	0
	John Jefferson, San Diego, AFC	13	0	13	0
1979	Earl Campbell, Houston, AFC	19	19	0	0
	Walter Payton, Chicago, NFC	16	14	2	0
1978	David Sims, Seattle, AFC	15	14	1	0
	Terdell Middleton, Green Bay, NFC	12	11	1	0
1977	Walter Payton, Chicago, NFC	16	14	2	0
	Nat Moore, Miami, AFC	13	1	12	0
1976	Chuck Foreman, Minnesota, NFC	14	13	1	0
	Franco Harris, Pittsburgh, AFC	14	14	0	0
1975	O.J. Simpson, Buffalo, AFC	23	16	7	0
	Chuck Foreman, Minnesota, NFC	22	13	9	0
1974	Chuck Foreman, Minnesota, NFC	15	9	6	0
	Cliff Branch, Oakland, AFC	13	0	13	0
1973	Larry Brown, Washington, NFC	14	8	6	0
	Floyd Little, Denver, AFC	13	12	1	0
1972	Emerson Boozer, N.Y. Jets, AFC	14	11	3	0
	Ron Johnson, N.Y. Giants, NFC	14	9	5	0
1971	Duane Thomas, Dallas, NFC	13	11	2	0
	Leroy Kelly, Cleveland, AFC	12	10	2	0
1970	Dick Gordon, Chicago, NFC	13	0	13	0
	MacArthur Lane, St. Louis, NFC	13	11	2	0
	Gary Garrison, San Diego, AFC	12	0	12	0
1969	Warren Wells, Oakland, AFL	14	0	14	0
	Tom Matte, Baltimore, NFL	13	11	2	0
	Lance Rentzel, Dallas, NFL	13	0	12	1
1968	Leroy Kelly, Cleveland, NFL	20	16	4	0
	Warren Wells, Oakland, AFL	12	1	11	0
1967	Homer Jones, N.Y. Giants, NFL	14	1	13	0
	Emerson Boozer, N.Y. Jets, AFL	13	10	3	0
1966	Leroy Kelly, Cleveland, NFL	16	15	1	0
	Dan Reeves, Dallas, NFL	16	8	8	0
	Lance Alworth, San Diego, AFL	13	0	13	0
1965	*Gale Sayers, Chicago, NFL	22	14	6	2
	Lance Alworth, San Diego, AFL	14	0	14	0
	Don Maynard, N.Y. Jets, AFL	14	0	14	0
1964	Lenny Moore, Baltimore, NFL	20	16	3	1
	Lance Alworth, San Diego, AFL	15	2	13	0
1963	Art Powell, Oakland, AFL	16	0	16	0
	Jim Brown, Cleveland, NFL	15	12	3	0
1962	Abner Haynes, Dallas, AFL	19	13	6	0
	Jim Taylor, Green Bay, NFL	19	19	0	0
1961	Bill Groman, Houston, AFL	18	1	17	0
	Jim Taylor, Green Bay, NFL	16	15	1	0
1960	Paul Hornung, Green Bay, NFL	15	13	2	0
	Sonny Randle, St. Louis, NFL	15	0	15	0
	Art Powell, N.Y. Titans, AFL	14	0	14	0
1959	Raymond Berry, Baltimore	14	0	14	0
	Jim Brown, Cleveland	14	14	0	0
1958	Jim Brown, Cleveland	18	17	1	0
1957	Lenny Moore, Baltimore	11	3	7	1
1956	Rick Casares, Chi. Bears	14	12	2	0
1955	*Alan Ameche, Baltimore	9	9	0	0
	Harlon Hill, Chi. Bears	9	0	9	0
1954	*Harlon Hill, Chi. Bears	12	0	12	0
1953	Joseph Perry, San Francisco	13	10	3	0
1952	Cloyce Box, Detroit	15	0	15	0
1951	Elroy (Crazylegs) Hirsch, Los Angeles	17	0	17	0
1950	Bob Shaw, Chi. Cardinals	12	0	12	0
1949	Gene Roberts, N.Y. Giants	17	9	8	0
1948	Mal Kutner, Chi. Cardinals	15	1	14	0
1947	Steve Van Buren, Philadelphia	14	13	0	1
1946	Ted Fritsch, Green Bay	10	9	1	0
1945	Steve Van Buren, Philadelphia	18	15	2	1
1944	Don Hutson, Green Bay	9	0	9	0
	Bill Paschal, N.Y. Giants	9	9	0	0

Year	Player, Team	TD	Rush	Pass	Ret.
1943	Don Hutson, Green Bay	12	0	11	1
	*Bill Paschal, N.Y. Giants	12	10	2	0
1942	Don Hutson, Green Bay	17	0	17	0
1941	Don Hutson, Green Bay	12	2	10	0
	George McAfee, Chi. Bears	12	6	3	3
1940	John Drake, Cleveland	9	9	0	0
	Richard Todd, Washington	9	4	4	1
1939	Andrew Farkas, Washington	11	5	5	1
1938	Don Hutson, Green Bay	9	0	9	0
1937	Cliff Battles, Washington	7	5	1	1
	Clarke Hinkle, Green Bay	7	5	2	0
	Don Hutson, Green Bay	7	0	7	0
1936	Don Hutson, Green Bay	9	0	8	1
1935	*Don Hutson, Green Bay	7	0	6	1
1934	*Beattie Feathers, Chi. Bears	9	8	1	0
1933	*Charlie (Buckets) Goldenberg, Green Bay	7	4	1	2
	John (Shipwreck) Kelly, Brooklyn	7	2	3	2
	*Elvin (Kink) Richards, N.Y. Giants	7	4	3	0
1932	Earl (Dutch) Clark, Portsmouth	6	3	3	0
	Red Grange, Chi. Bears	6	3	3	0

**First season of professional football.*

ANNUAL LEADERS—MOST FIELD GOALS MADE

Year	Player, Team	Att.	Made	Pct.
2008	Stephen Gostkowski, New England, AFC	40	36	90.0
	John Carney, N.Y. Giants, NFC	38	35	92.1
2007	Rob Bironas, Tennessee, AFC	39	35	89.7
	*Mason Crosby, Green Bay, NFC	39	31	79.5
	Robbie Gould, Chicago, NFC	36	31	86.1
2006	Robbie Gould, Chicago, NFC	36	32	88.9
	Jeff Wilkins, St. Louis, NFC	37	32	86.5
	Matt Stover, Baltimore, AFC	30	28	93.3
2005	Neil Rackers, Arizona, NFC	42	40	95.2
	Matt Stover, Baltimore, AFC	34	30	88.2
2004	Adam Vinatieri, New England, AFC	33	31	93.9
	David Akers, Philadelphia, NFC	32	27	84.4
2003	Jeff Wilkins, St. Louis, NFC	42	39	92.9
	Mike Vanderjagt, Indianapolis, AFC	37	37	100.0
2002	Jay Feely, Atlanta, NFC	40	32	80.0
	Martín Gramatica, Tampa Bay, NFC	39	32	82.1
	Adam Vinatieri, New England, AFC	30	27	90.0
2001	Jason Elam, Denver, AFC	36	31	86.1
	*Jay Feely, Atlanta, NFC	37	29	78.4
2000	Matt Stover, Baltimore, AFC	39	35	89.7
	Ryan Longwell, Green Bay, NFC	38	33	86.8
1999	Olindo Mare, Miami, AFC	46	39	84.8
	*Martin Gramatica, Tampa Bay, NFC	32	27	84.4
1998	Al Del Greco, Tennessee, AFC	39	36	92.3
	Gary Anderson, Minnesota, NFC	35	35	100.0
1997	Richie Cunningham, Dallas, NFC	37	34	91.9
	Cary Blanchard, Indianapolis, AFC	41	32	78.1
1996	John Kasay, Carolina, NFC	45	37	82.2
	Cary Blanchard, Indianapolis, AFC	40	36	90.0
1995	Norm Johnson, Pittsburgh, AFC	41	34	82.9
	Morten Andersen, Atlanta, NFC	37	31	83.8
1994	John Carney, San Diego, AFC	38	34	89.5
	Fuad Reveiz, Minnesota, NFC	39	34	87.2
1993	Jeff Jaeger, L.A. Raiders, AFC	44	35	79.5
	Jason Hanson, Detroit, NFC	43	34	79.1
1992	Pete Stoyanovich, Miami, AFC	37	30	81.1
	Chip Lohmiller, Washington, NFC	40	30	75.0
1991	Pete Stoyanovich, Miami, AFC	37	31	83.8
	Chip Lohmiller, Washington, NFC	43	31	72.1
1990	Nick Lowery, Kansas City, AFC	37	34	91.9
	Chip Lohmiller, Washington, NFC	40	30	75.0
1989	Rich Karlis, Minnesota, NFC	39	31	79.5
	*David Treadwell, Denver, AFC	33	27	81.8

YEARLY STATISTICAL LEADERS

Year	Player, Team	Att.	Made	Pct.
1988	Scott Norwood, Buffalo, AFC	37	32	86.5
	Mike Cofer, San Francisco, NFC	38	27	71.1
1987	Morten Andersen, New Orleans, NFC	36	28	77.8
	Dean Biasucci, Indianapolis, AFC	27	24	88.9
	Jim Breech, Cincinnati, AFC	30	24	80.0
1986	Tony Franklin, New England, AFC	41	32	78.0
	Kevin Butler, Chicago, NFC	41	28	68.3
1985	Gary Anderson, Pittsburgh, AFC	42	33	78.6
	Morten Andersen, New Orleans, NFC	35	31	88.6
	*Kevin Butler, Chicago, NFC	37	31	83.8
1984	*Paul McFadden, Philadelphia, NFC	37	30	81.1
	Gary Anderson, Pittsburgh, AFC	32	24	75.0
	Matt Bahr, Cleveland, AFC	32	24	75.0
1983	*Ali-Haji-Sheikh, N.Y. Giants, NFC	42	35	83.3
	*Raul Allegre, Baltimore, AFC	35	30	85.7
1982	Mark Moseley, Washington, NFC	21	20	95.2
	Nick Lowery, Kansas City, AFC	24	19	79.2
1981	Rafael Septien, Dallas, NFC	35	27	77.1
	Nick Lowery, Kansas City, AFC	36	26	72.2
1980	*Ed Murray, Detroit, NFC	42	27	64.3
	John Smith, New England, AFC	34	26	76.5
	Fred Steinfort, Denver, AFC	34	26	76.5
1979	Mark Moseley, Washington, NFC	33	25	75.8
	John Smith, New England, AFC	33	23	69.7
1978	*Frank Corral, Los Angeles, NFC	43	29	67.4
	Pat Leahy, N.Y. Jets, AFC	30	22	73.3
1977	Mark Moseley, Washington, NFC	37	21	56.8
	Errol Mann, Oakland, AFC	28	20	71.4
1976	Mark Moseley, Washington, NFC	34	22	64.7
	Jan Stenerud, Kansas City, AFC	38	21	55.3
1975	Jan Stenerud, Kansas City, AFC	32	22	68.8
	Toni Fritsch, Dallas, NFC	35	22	62.9
1974	Chester Marcol, Green Bay, NFC	39	25	64.1
	Roy Gerela, Pittsburgh, AFC	29	20	69.0
1973	David Ray, Los Angeles, NFC	47	30	63.8
	Roy Gerela, Pittsburgh, AFC	43	29	67.4
1972	*Chester Marcol, Green Bay, NFC	48	33	68.8
	Roy Gerela, Pittsburgh, AFC	41	28	68.3
1971	Curt Knight, Washington, NFC	49	29	59.2
	Garo Yepremian, Miami, AFC	40	28	70.0
1970	Jan Stenerud, Kansas City, AFC	42	30	71.4
	Fred Cox, Minnesota, NFC	46	30	65.2
1969	Jim Turner, N.Y. Jets, AFL	47	32	68.1
	Fred Cox, Minnesota, NFL	37	26	70.3
1968	Jim Turner, N.Y. Jets, AFL	46	34	73.9
	Mac Percival, Chicago, NFL	36	25	69.4
1967	Jim Bakken, St. Louis, NFL	39	27	69.2
	Jan Stenerud, Kansas City, AFL	36	21	58.3
1966	Bruce Gossett, Los Angeles, NFL	49	28	57.1
	Mike Mercer, Oakland-Kansas City, AFL	30	21	70.0
1965	Pete Gogolak, Buffalo, AFL	46	28	60.9
	Fred Cox, Minnesota, NFL	35	23	65.7
1964	Jim Bakken, St. Louis, NFL	38	25	65.8
	Gino Cappelletti, Boston, AFL	39	25	64.1
1963	Jim Martin, Baltimore, NFL	39	24	61.5
	Gino Cappelletti, Boston, AFL	38	22	57.9
1962	Gene Mingo, Denver, AFL	39	27	69.2
	Lou Michaels, Pittsburgh, NFL	42	26	61.9
1961	Steve Myhra, Baltimore, NFL	39	21	53.8
	Gino Cappelletti, Boston, AFL	32	17	53.1
1960	Tommy Davis, San Francisco, NFL	32	19	59.4
	*Gene Mingo, Denver, AFL	28	18	64.3
1959	Pat Summerall, N.Y. Giants	29	20	69.0
1958	Paige Cothren, Los Angeles	25	14	56.0
	*Tom Miner, Pittsburgh	28	14	50.0
1957	Lou Groza, Cleveland	22	15	68.2
1956	Sam Baker, Washington	25	17	68.0
1955	Fred Cone, Green Bay	24	16	66.7
1954	Lou Groza, Cleveland	24	16	66.7

Year	Player, Team	Att.	Made	Pct.
1953	Lou Groza, Cleveland	26	23	88.5
1952	Lou Groza, Cleveland	33	19	57.6
1951	Bob Waterfield, Los Angeles	23	13	56.5
1950	Lou Groza, Cleveland	19	13	68.4
1949	Cliff Patton, Philadelphia	18	9	50.0
	Bob Waterfield, Los Angeles	16	9	56.3
1948	Cliff Patton, Philadelphia	12	8	66.7
1947	Ward Cuff, Green Bay	16	7	43.8
	Pat Harder, Chi. Cardinals	10	7	70.0
	Bob Waterfield, Los Angeles	16	7	43.8
1946	Ted Fritsch, Green Bay	17	9	52.9
1945	Joe Aguirre, Washington	13	7	53.8
1944	Ken Strong, N.Y. Giants	12	6	50.0
1943	Ward Cuff, N.Y. Giants	9	3	33.3
	Don Hutson, Green Bay	5	3	60.0
1942	Bill Daddio, Chi. Cardinals	10	5	50.0
1941	Clarke Hinkle, Green Bay	14	6	42.9
1940	Clarke Hinkle, Green Bay	14	9	64.3
1939	Ward Cuff, N.Y. Giants	16	7	43.8
1938	Ward Cuff, N.Y. Giants	9	5	55.6
	Ralph Kercheval, Brooklyn	13	5	38.5
1937	Jack Manders, Chi. Bears		8	
1936	Jack Manders, Chi. Bears		7	
	Armand Niccolai, Pittsburgh		7	
1935	Armand Niccolai, Pittsburgh		6	
	Bill Smith, Chi. Cardinals		6	
1934	Jack Manders, Chi. Bears		10	
1933	*Jack Manders, Chi. Bears		6	
	Glenn Presnell, Portsmouth		6	
1932	Earl (Dutch) Clark, Portsmouth		3	

**First season of professional football.*

ANNUAL RUSHING LEADERS

Year	Player, Team	Att.	Yards	Avg.	TD
2008	Adrian Peterson, Minnesota, NFC	363	1,760	4.9	10
	Thomas Jones, N.Y. Jets, AFC	290	1,312	4.5	13
2007	LaDainian Tomlinson, San Diego, AFC	315	1,474	4.7	15
	*Adrian Peterson, Minnesota, NFC	238	1,341	5.6	12
2006	LaDainian Tomlinson, San Diego, AFC	348	1,815	5.2	28
	Frank Gore, San Francisco, NFC	312	1,695	5.4	8
2005	Shaun Alexander, Seattle, NFC	370	1,880	5.1	27
	Larry Johnson, Kansas City, AFC	336	1,750	5.2	20
2004	Curtis Martin, N.Y. Jets, AFC	371	1,697	4.6	12
	Shaun Alexander, Seattle, NFC	353	1,696	4.8	16
2003	Jamal Lewis, Baltimore, AFC	387	2,066	5.3	14
	Ahman Green, Green Bay, NFC	355	1,883	5.3	15
2002	Ricky Williams, Miami, AFC	383	1,853	4.8	16
	Deuce McAllister, New Orleans, NFC	325	1,388	4.3	13
2001	Priest Holmes, Kansas City, AFC	327	1,555	4.8	8
	Stephen Davis, Washington, NFC	356	1,432	4.0	5
2000	Edgerrin James, Indianapolis, AFC	387	1,709	4.4	13
	Robert Smith, Minnesota, NFC	295	1,521	5.2	7
1999	*Edgerrin James, Indianapolis, AFC	369	1,553	4.2	13
	Stephen Davis, Washington, NFC	290	1,405	4.8	17
1998	Terrell Davis, Denver, AFC	392	2,008	5.1	21
	Jamal Anderson, Atlanta, NFC	410	1,846	4.5	14
1997	Barry Sanders, Detroit, NFC	335	2,053	6.1	11
	Terrell Davis, Denver, AFC	369	1,750	4.7	15
1996	Barry Sanders, Detroit, NFC	307	1,553	5.1	11
	Terrell Davis, Denver, AFC	345	1,538	4.5	13
1995	Emmitt Smith, Dallas, NFC	377	1,773	4.7	25
	*Curtis Martin, New England, AFC	368	1,487	4.0	14
1994	Barry Sanders, Detroit, NFC	331	1,883	5.7	7
	Chris Warren, Seattle, AFC	333	1,545	4.6	9
1993	Emmitt Smith, Dallas, NFC	283	1,486	5.3	9
	Thurman Thomas, Buffalo, AFC	355	1,315	3.7	6
1992	Emmitt Smith, Dallas, NFC	373	1,713	4.6	18
	Barry Foster, Pittsburgh, AFC	390	1,690	4.3	11

YEARLY STATISTICAL LEADERS

Year	Player, Team	Att.	Yards	Avg.	TD
1991	Emmitt Smith, Dallas, NFC	365	1,563	4.3	12
	Thurman Thomas, Buffalo, AFC	288	1,407	4.9	7
1990	Barry Sanders, Detroit, NFC	255	1,304	5.1	13
	Thurman Thomas, Buffalo, AFC	271	1,297	4.8	11
1989	Christian Okoye, Kansas City, AFC	370	1,480	4.0	12
	*Barry Sanders, Detroit, NFC	280	1,470	5.3	14
1988	Eric Dickerson, Indianapolis, AFC	388	1,659	4.3	14
	Herschel Walker, Dallas, NFC	361	1,514	4.2	5
1987	Charles White, L.A. Rams, NFC	324	1,374	4.2	11
	Eric Dickerson, Indianapolis, AFC	223	1,011	4.5	5
1986	Eric Dickerson, L.A. Rams, NFC	404	1,821	4.5	11
	Curt Warner, Seattle, AFC	319	1,481	4.6	13
1985	Marcus Allen, L.A. Raiders, AFC	380	1,759	4.6	11
	Gerald Riggs, Atlanta, NFC	397	1,719	4.3	10
1984	Eric Dickerson, L.A. Rams, NFC	379	2,105	5.6	14
	Earnest Jackson, San Diego, AFC	296	1,179	4.0	8
1983	*Eric Dickerson, L.A. Rams, NFC	390	1,808	4.6	18
	*Curt Warner, Seattle, AFC	335	1,449	4.3	13
1982	Freeman McNeil, N.Y. Jets, AFC	151	786	5.2	6
	Tony Dorsett, Dallas, NFC	177	745	4.2	5
1981	*George Rogers, New Orleans, NFC	378	1,674	4.4	13
	Earl Campbell, Houston, AFC	361	1,376	3.8	10
1980	Earl Campbell, Houston, AFC	373	1,934	5.2	13
	Walter Payton, Chicago, NFC	317	1,460	4.6	6
1979	Earl Campbell, Houston, AFC	368	1,697	4.6	19
	Walter Payton, Chicago, NFC	369	1,610	4.4	14
1978	*Earl Campbell, Houston, AFC	302	1,450	4.8	13
	Walter Payton, Chicago, NFC	333	1,395	4.2	11
1977	Walter Payton, Chicago, NFC	339	1,852	5.5	14
	Mark van Eeghen, Oakland, AFC	324	1,273	3.9	7
1976	O.J. Simpson, Buffalo, AFC	290	1,503	5.2	8
	Walter Payton, Chicago, NFC	311	1,390	4.5	13
1975	O.J. Simpson, Buffalo, AFC	329	1,817	5.5	16
	Jim Otis, St. Louis, NFC	269	1,076	4.0	5
1974	Otis Armstrong, Denver, AFC	263	1,407	5.3	9
	Lawrence McCutcheon, Los Angeles, NFC	236	1,109	4.7	3
1973	O.J. Simpson, Buffalo, AFC	332	2,003	6.0	12
	John Brockington, Green Bay, NFC	265	1,144	4.3	3
1972	O.J. Simpson, Buffalo, AFC	292	1,251	4.3	6
	Larry Brown, Washington, NFC	285	1,216	4.3	8
1971	Floyd Little, Denver, AFC	284	1,133	4.0	6
	*John Brockington, Green Bay, NFC	216	1,105	5.1	4
1970	Larry Brown, Washington, NFC	237	1,125	4.7	5
	Floyd Little, Denver, AFC	209	901	4.3	3
1969	Gale Sayers, Chicago, NFL	236	1,032	4.4	8
	Dickie Post, San Diego, AFL	182	873	4.8	6
1968	Leroy Kelly, Cleveland, NFL	248	1,239	5.0	16
	*Paul Robinson, Cincinnati, AFL	238	1,023	4.3	8
1967	Jim Nance, Boston, AFL	269	1,216	4.5	7
	Leroy Kelly, Cleveland, NFL	235	1,205	5.1	11
1966	Jim Nance, Boston, AFL	299	1,458	4.9	11
	Gale Sayers, Chicago, NFL	229	1,231	5.4	8
1965	Jim Brown, Cleveland, NFL	289	1,544	5.3	17
	Paul Lowe, San Diego, AFL	222	1,121	5.0	7
1964	Jim Brown, Cleveland, NFL	280	1,446	5.2	7
	Cookie Gilchrist, Buffalo, AFL	230	981	4.3	6
1963	Jim Brown, Cleveland, NFL	291	1,863	6.4	12
	Clem Daniels, Oakland, AFL	215	1,099	5.1	3
1962	Jim Taylor, Green Bay, NFL	272	1,474	5.4	19
	Cookie Gilchrist, Buffalo, AFL	214	1,096	5.1	13
1961	Jim Brown, Cleveland, NFL	305	1,408	4.6	8
	Billy Cannon, Houston, AFL	200	948	4.7	6
1960	Jim Brown, Cleveland, NFL	215	1,257	5.8	9
	*Abner Haynes, Dall. Texans, AFL	156	875	5.6	9
1959	Jim Brown, Cleveland	290	1,329	4.6	14
1958	Jim Brown, Cleveland	257	1,527	5.9	17
1957	*Jim Brown, Cleveland	202	942	4.7	9
1956	Rick Casares, Chi. Bears	234	1,126	4.8	12
1955	*Alan Ameche, Baltimore	213	961	4.5	9

Year	Player, Team	Att.	Yards	Avg.	TD
1954	Joe Perry, San Francisco	173	1,049	6.1	8
1953	Joe Perry, San Francisco	192	1,018	5.3	10
1952	Dan Towler, Los Angeles	156	894	5.7	10
1951	Eddie Price, N.Y. Giants	271	971	3.6	7
1950	Marion Motley, Cleveland	140	810	5.8	3
1949	Steve Van Buren, Philadelphia	263	1,146	4.4	11
1948	Steve Van Buren, Philadelphia	201	945	4.7	10
1947	Steve Van Buren, Philadelphia	217	1,008	4.6	13
1946	Bill Dudley, Pittsburgh	146	604	4.1	3
1945	Steve Van Buren, Philadelphia	143	832	5.8	15
1944	Bill Paschal, N.Y. Giants	196	737	3.8	9
1943	*Bill Paschal, N.Y. Giants	147	572	3.9	10
1942	*Bill Dudley, Pittsburgh	162	696	4.3	5
1941	Clarence (Pug) Manders, Brooklyn	111	486	4.4	5
1940	Byron (Whizzer) White, Detroit	146	514	3.5	5
1939	*Bill Osmanski, Chicago	121	699	5.8	7
1938	*Byron (Whizzer) White, Pittsburgh	152	567	3.7	4
1937	Cliff Battles, Washington	216	874	4.0	5
1936	*Alphonse (Tuffy) Leemans, N.Y. Giants	206	830	4.0	2
1935	Doug Russell, Chi. Cardinals	140	499	3.6	0
1934	*Beattie Feathers, Chi. Bears	119	1,004	8.4	8
1933	Jim Musick, Boston	173	809	4.7	5
1932	*Cliff Battles, Boston	148	576	3.9	3

**First season of professional football.*

ANNUAL PASSING LEADERS

(Current rating system implemented in 1973)

Year	Player, Team	Att.	Comp.	Yards	TD	Int.	Rating
2008	Philip Rivers, San Diego, AFC	478	312	4,009	34	11	105.5
	Kurt Warner, Arizona, NFC	598	401	4,583	30	14	96.9
2007	Tom Brady, New England, AFC	578	398	4,806	50	8	117.2
	Tony Romo, Dallas, NFC	520	335	4,211	36	19	97.4
2006	Peyton Manning, Indianapolis, AFC	557	362	4,397	31	9	101.0
	Drew Brees, New Orleans, NFC	554	356	4,418	26	11	96.2
2005	Peyton Manning, Indianapolis, AFC	453	305	3,747	28	10	104.1
	Matt Hasselbeck, Seattle, NFC	449	294	3,459	24	9	98.2
2004	Peyton Manning, Indianapolis, AFC	497	336	4,557	49	10	121.1
	Daunte Culpepper, Minnesota, NFC	548	379	4,717	39	11	110.9
2003	Steve McNair, Tennessee, AFC	400	250	3,215	24	7	100.4
	Daunte Culpepper, Minnesota, NFC	454	295	3,479	25	11	96.4
2002	Chad Pennington, N.Y. Jets, AFC	399	275	3,120	22	6	104.2
	Brad Johnson, Tampa Bay, NFC	451	281	3,049	22	6	92.9
2001	Kurt Warner, St. Louis, NFC	546	375	4,830	36	22	101.4
	Rich Gannon, Oakland, AFC	549	361	3,828	27	9	95.5
2000	Brian Griese, Denver, AFC	336	216	2,688	19	4	102.9
	Trent Green, St. Louis, NFC	240	145	2,063	16	5	101.8
1999	Kurt Warner, St. Louis, NFC	499	325	4,353	41	13	109.2
	Peyton Manning, Indianapolis, AFC	533	331	4,135	26	15	90.7
1998	Randall Cunningham, Minnesota, NFC	425	259	3,704	34	10	106.0
	Vinny Testaverde, N.Y. Jets, AFC	421	259	3,256	29	7	101.6
1997	Steve Young, San Francisco, NFC	356	241	3,029	19	6	104.7
	Mark Brunell, Jacksonville, AFC	435	264	3,281	18	7	91.2
1996	Steve Young, San Francisco NFC	316	214	2,410	14	6	97.2
	John Elway, Denver, AFC	466	287	3,328	26	14	89.2
1995	Jim Harbaugh, Indianapolis, AFC	314	200	2,575	17	5	100.7
	Brett Favre, Green Bay, NFC	570	359	4,413	38	13	99.5
1994	Steve Young, San Francisco, NFC	461	324	3,969	35	10	112.8
	Dan Marino, Miami, AFC	615	385	4,453	30	17	89.2
1993	Steve Young, San Francisco, NFC	462	314	4,023	29	16	101.5
	John Elway, Denver, AFC	551	348	4,030	25	10	92.8
1992	Steve Young, San Francisco, NFC	402	268	3,465	25	7	107.0
	Warren Moon, Houston, AFC	346	224	2,521	18	12	89.3
1991	Steve Young, San Francisco, NFC	279	180	2,517	17	8	101.8
	Jim Kelly, Buffalo, AFC	474	304	3,844	33	17	97.6
1990	Jim Kelly, Buffalo, AFC	346	219	2,829	24	9	101.2
	Phil Simms, N.Y. Giants, NFC	311	184	2,284	15	4	92.7
1989	Joe Montana, San Francisco, NFC	386	271	3,521	26	8	112.4
	Boomer Esiason, Cincinnati, AFC	455	258	3,525	28	11	92.1

YEARLY STATISTICAL LEADERS

Year	Player, Team	Att.	Comp.	Yards	TD	Int.	Rating
1988	Boomer Esiason, Cincinnati, AFC	388	223	3,572	28	14	97.4
	Wade Wilson, Minnesota, NFC	332	204	2,746	15	9	91.5
1987	Joe Montana, San Francisco, NFC	398	266	3,054	31	13	102.1
	Bernie Kosar, Cleveland, AFC	389	241	3,033	22	9	95.4
1986	Tommy Kramer, Minnesota, NFC	372	208	3,000	24	10	92.6
	Dan Marino, Miami, AFC	623	378	4,746	44	23	92.5
1985	Ken O'Brien, N.Y. Jets, AFC	488	297	3,888	25	8	96.2
	Joe Montana, San Francisco, NFC	494	303	3,653	27	13	91.3
1984	Dan Marino, Miami, AFC	564	362	5,084	48	17	108.9
	Joe Montana, San Francisco, NFC	432	279	3,630	28	10	102.9
1983	Steve Bartkowski, Atlanta, NFC	432	274	3,167	22	5	97.6
	*Dan Marino, Miami, AFC	296	173	2,210	20	6	96.0
1982	Ken Anderson, Cincinnati, AFC	309	218	2,495	12	9	95.3
	Joe Theismann, Washington, NFC	252	161	2,033	13	9	91.3
1981	Ken Anderson, Cincinnati, AFC	479	300	3,754	29	10	98.4
	Joe Montana, San Francisco, NFC	488	311	3,565	19	12	88.4
1980	Brian Sipe, Cleveland, AFC	554	337	4,132	30	14	91.4
	Ron Jaworski, Philadelphia, NFC	451	257	3,529	27	12	91.0
1979	Roger Staubach, Dallas, NFC	461	267	3,586	27	11	92.3
	Dan Fouts, San Diego, AFC	530	332	4,082	24	24	82.6
1978	Roger Staubach, Dallas, NFC	413	231	3,190	25	16	84.9
	Terry Bradshaw, Pittsburgh, AFC	368	207	2,915	28	20	84.7
1977	Bob Griese, Miami, AFC	307	180	2,252	22	13	87.8
	Roger Staubach, Dallas, NFC	361	210	2,620	18	9	87.0
1976	Ken Stabler, Oakland, AFC	291	194	2,737	27	17	103.4
	James Harris, Los Angeles, NFC	158	91	1,460	8	6	89.6
1975	Ken Anderson, Cincinnati, AFC	377	228	3,169	21	11	93.9
	Fran Tarkenton, Minnesota, NFC	425	273	2,994	25	13	91.8
1974	Ken Anderson, Cincinnati, AFC	328	213	2,667	18	10	95.7
	Sonny Jurgensen, Washington, NFC	167	107	1,185	11	5	94.5
1973	Roger Staubach, Dallas, NFC	286	179	2,428	23	15	94.6
	Ken Stabler, Oakland, AFC	260	163	1,997	14	10	88.3
1972	Norm Snead, N.Y. Giants, NFC	325	196	2,307	17	12	
	Earl Morrall, Miami, AFC	150	83	1,360	11	7	
1971	Roger Staubach, Dallas, NFC	211	126	1,882	15	4	
	Bob Griese, Miami, AFC	263	145	2,089	19	9	
1970	John Brodie, San Francisco, NFC	378	223	2,941	24	10	
	Daryle Lamonica, Oakland, AFC	356	179	2,516	22	15	
1969	Sonny Jurgensen, Washington, NFL	442	274	3,102	22	15	
	*Greg Cook, Cincinnati, AFL	197	106	1,854	15	11	
1968	Len Dawson, Kansas City, AFL	224	131	2,109	17	9	
	Earl Morrall, Baltimore, NFL	317	182	2,909	26	17	
1967	Sonny Jurgensen, Washington, NFL	508	288	3,747	31	16	
	Daryle Lamonica, Oakland, AFL	425	220	3,228	30	20	
1966	Bart Starr, Green Bay, NFL	251	156	2,257	14	3	
	Len Dawson, Kansas City, AFL	284	159	2,527	26	10	
1965	Rudy Bukich, Chicago, NFL	312	176	2,641	20	9	
	John Hadl, San Diego, AFL	348	174	2,798	20	21	
1964	Len Dawson, Kansas City, AFL	354	199	2,879	30	18	
	Bart Starr, Green Bay, NFL	272	163	2,144	15	4	
1963	Y.A. Tittle, N.Y. Giants, NFL	367	221	3,145	36	14	
	Tobin Rote, San Diego, AFL	286	170	2,510	20	17	
1962	Len Dawson, Dallas Texans, AFL	310	189	2,759	29	17	
	Bart Starr, Green Bay, NFL	285	178	2,438	12	9	
1961	George Blanda, Houston, AFL	362	187	3,330	36	22	
	Milt Plum, Cleveland, NFL	302	177	2,416	18	10	
1960	Milt Plum, Cleveland, NFL	250	151	2,297	21	5	
	Jack Kemp, L.A. Chargers, AFL	406	211	3,018	20	25	
1959	Charlie Conerly, N.Y. Giants	194	113	1,706	14	4	
1958	Eddie LeBaron, Washington	145	79	1,365	11	10	
1957	Tommy O'Connell, Cleveland	110	63	1,229	9	8	
1956	Ed Brown, Chicago Bears	168	96	1,667	11	12	
1955	Otto Graham, Cleveland	185	98	1,721	15	8	
1954	Norm Van Brocklin, Los Angeles	260	139	2,637	13	21	
1953	Otto Graham, Cleveland	258	167	2,722	11	9	
1952	Norm Van Brocklin, Los Angeles	205	113	1,736	14	17	
1951	Bob Waterfield, Los Angeles	176	88	1,566	13	10	
1950	Norm Van Brocklin, Los Angeles	233	127	2,061	18	14	

Year	Player, Team	Att.	Comp.	Yards	TD	Int.	Rating
1949	Sammy Baugh, Washington	255	145	1,903	18	14	
1948	Tommy Thompson, Philadelphia	246	141	1,965	25	11	
1947	Sammy Baugh, Washington	354	210	2,938	25	15	
1946	Bob Waterfield, Los Angeles	251	127	1,747	18	17	
1945	Sammy Baugh, Washington	182	128	1,669	11	4	
	Sid Luckman, Chicago Bears	217	117	1,725	14	10	
1944	Frank Filchock, Washington	147	84	1,139	13	9	
1943	Sammy Baugh, Washington	239	133	1,754	23	19	
1942	Cecil Isbell, Green Bay	268	146	2,021	24	14	
1941	Cecil Isbell, Green Bay	206	117	1,479	15	11	
1940	Sammy Baugh, Washington	177	111	1,367	12	10	
1939	*Parker Hall, Cleveland	208	106	1,227	9	13	
1938	Ed Danowski, N.Y. Giants	129	70	848	7	8	
1937	*Sammy Baugh, Washington	171	81	1,127	8	14	
1936	Arnie Herber, Green Bay	173	77	1,239	11	13	
1935	Ed Danowski, N.Y. Giants	113	57	794	10	9	
1934	Arnie Herber, Green Bay	115	42	799	8	12	
1933	*Harry Newman, N.Y. Giants	136	53	973	11	17	
1932	Arnie Herber, Green Bay	101	37	639	9	9	

**First season of professional football.*

ANNUAL PASSING TOUCHDOWN LEADERS

Year	Player, Team	TD
2008	Drew Brees, New Orleans, NFC	34
	Philip Rivers, San Diego, AFC	34
2007	Tom Brady, New England, AFC	50
	Tony Romo, Dallas, NFC	36
2006	Peyton Manning, Indianapolis, AFC	31
	Drew Brees, New Orleans, NFC	26
2005	Carson Palmer, Cincinnati, AFC	32
	Jake Delhomme, Carolina, NFC	24
	Matt Hasselbeck, Seattle, NFC	24
	Eli Manning, N.Y. Giants, NFC	24
2004	Peyton Manning, Indianapolis, AFC	49
	Daunte Culpepper, Minnesota, NFC	39
2003	Brett Favre, Green Bay, NFC	32
	Peyton Manning, Indianapolis, AFC	29
2002	Tom Brady, New England, AFC	28
	Aaron Brooks, New Orleans, NFC	27
	Brett Favre, Green Bay, NFC	27
2001	Kurt Warner, St. Louis, NFC	36
	Rich Gannon, Oakland, AFC	27
2000	Daunte Culpepper, Minnesota, NFC	33
	Peyton Manning, Indianapolis, AFC	33
1999	Kurt Warner, St. Louis, NFC	41
	Peyton Manning, Indianapolis, AFC	26
1998	Steve Young, San Francisco, NFC	36
	Vinny Testaverde, N.Y. Jets, AFC	29
1997	Brett Favre, Green Bay, NFC	35
	Jeff George, Oakland, AFC	29
1996	Brett Favre, Green Bay, NFC	39
	Vinny Testaverde, Baltimore, AFC	33
1995	Brett Favre, Green Bay, NFC	38
	Jeff Blake, Cincinnati, AFC	28
1994	Steve Young, San Francisco, NFC	35
	Dan Marino, Miami, AFC	30
1993	Steve Young, San Francisco, NFC	29
	John Elway, Denver, AFC	25
1992	Steve Young, San Francisco, NFC	25
	Dan Marino, Miami, AFC	24
1991	Jim Kelly, Buffalo, AFC	33
	Mark Rypien, Washington, NFC	28
1990	Warren Moon, Houston, AFC	33
	Randall Cunningham, Philadelphia, NFC	30
1989	Jim Everett, L.A. Rams, NFC	29
	Boomer Esiason, Cincinnati, AFC	28
1988	Jim Everett, L.A. Rams, NFC	31
	Boomer Esiason, Cincinnati, AFC	28
	Dan Marino, Miami, AFC	28
1987	Joe Montana, San Francisco, NFC	31
	Dan Marino, Miami, AFC	26
1986	Dan Marino, Miami, AFC	44
	Tommy Kramer, Minnesota, NFC	24
1985	Dan Marino, Miami, AFC	30
	Joe Montana, San Francisco, NFC	27
1984	Dan Marino, Miami, AFC	48
	Neil Lomax, St. Louis, NFC	28
	Joe Montana, San Francisco, NFC	28
1983	Lynn Dickey, Green Bay, NFC	32
	Joe Ferguson, Buffalo, AFC	26
	Brian Sipe, Cleveland, AFC	26
1982	Terry Bradshaw, Pittsburgh, AFC	17
	Dan Fouts, San Diego, AFC	17
	Joe Montana, San Francisco, NFC	17
1981	Dan Fouts, San Diego, AFC	33
	Steve Bartkowski, Atlanta, NFC	30
1980	Steve Bartkowski, Atlanta, NFC	31
	Dan Fouts, San Diego, AFC	30
	Brian Sipe, Cleveland, AFC	30
1979	Steve Grogan, New England, AFC	28
	Brian Sipe, Cleveland, AFC	28
	Roger Staubach, Dallas, NFC	27
1978	Terry Bradshaw, Pittsburgh, AFC	28
	Roger Staubach, Dallas, NFC	25
	Fran Tarkenton, Minnesota, NFC	25
1977	Bob Griese, Miami, AFC	22
	Ron Jaworski, Philadelphia, NFC	18
	Roger Staubach, Dallas, NFC	18
1976	Ken Stabler, Oakland, AFC	27
	Jim Hart, St. Louis, NFC	18
1975	Joe Ferguson, Buffalo, AFC	25
	Fran Tarkenton, Minnesota, NFC	25
1974	Ken Stabler, Oakland, AFC	26
	Jim Hart, St. Louis, NFC	20
1973	Roman Gabriel, Philadelphia, NFC	23
	Roger Staubach, Dallas, NFC	23
	Charley Johnson, Denver, AFC	20
1972	Billy Kilmer, Washington, NFC	19
	Joe Namath, N.Y. Jets, AFC	19
1971	John Hadl, San Diego, AFC	21
	John Brodie, San Francisco, NFC	18
1970	John Brodie, San Francisco, NFC	24
	John Hadl, San Diego, AFC	22
	Daryle Lamonica, Oakland, AFC	22
1969	Daryle Lamonica, Oakland, AFL	34
	Roman Gabriel, Los Angeles, NFL	24
1968	John Hadl, San Diego, AFL	27
	Earl Morrall, Baltimore, NFL	26
1967	Sonny Jurgensen, Washington, NFL	31
	Daryle Lamonica, Oakland, AFL	30

YEARLY STATISTICAL LEADERS

Year	Player, Team	TD
1966	Frank Ryan, Cleveland, NFL	29
	Len Dawson, Kansas City, AFL	26
1965	John Brodie, San Francisco, NFL	30
	Len Dawson, Kansas City, AFL	21
1964	Babe Parilli, Boston, AFL	31
	Frank Ryan, Cleveland, NFL	25
1963	Y.A. Tittle, N.Y. Giants, NFL	36
	Len Dawson, Kansas City, AFL	26
1962	Y.A. Tittle, N.Y. Giants, NFL	33
	Len Dawson, Dallas, AFL	29
1961	George Blanda, Houston, AFL	36
	Sonny Jurgensen, Philadelphia, NFL	32
1960	Al Dorow, N.Y. Titans, AFL	26
	Johnny Unitas, Baltimore, NFL	25
1959	Johnny Unitas, Baltimore	32
1958	Johnny Unitas, Baltimore	19
1957	Johnny Unitas, Baltimore	24
1956	Tobin Rote, Green Bay	18
1955	Tobin Rote, Green Bay	17
	Y.A. Tittle, San Francisco	17
1954	Adrian Burk, Philadelphia	23
1953	Robert Thomason, Philadelphia	21
1952	Jim Finks, Pittsburgh	20
	Otto Graham, Cleveland	20
1951	Bobby Layne, Detroit	26
1950	George Ratterman, N.Y. Yanks	22
1949	Johnny Lujack, Chi. Bears	23
1948	Tommy Thompson, Philadelphia	25
1947	Sammy Baugh, Washington	25
1946	Sid Luckman, Chi. Bears	17
	Bob Waterfield, Los Angeles	17
1945	Sid Luckman, Chi. Bears	14
	*Bob Waterfield, Cleveland	14
1944	Frank Filchock, Washington	13
1943	Sid Luckman, Chi. Bears	28
1942	Cecil Isbell, Green Bay	24
1941	Cecil Isbell, Green Bay	15
1940	Sammy Baugh, Washington	12
1939	Frank Filchock, Washington	11
1938	Bob Monnett, Green Bay	9
1937	Bernie Masterson, Chi. Bears	9
1936	Arnie Herber, Green Bay	11
1935	Ed Danowski, N.Y. Giants	10
1934	Arnie Herber, Green Bay	8
1933	*Harry Newman, N.Y. Giants	11
1932	Arnie Herber, Green Bay	9

**First season of professional football.*

ANNUAL PASS RECEIVING LEADERS

Year	Player, Team	No.	Yards	Avg.	TD
2008	Andre Johnson, Houston, AFC	115	1,575	13.7	8
	Larry Fitzgerald, Arizona, NFC	96	1,431	14.9	12
2007	T.J. Houshmandzadeh, Cincinnati, AFC	112	1,143	10.2	12
	Wes Welker, New England, AFC	112	1,175	10.5	8
	Larry Fitzgerald, Arizona, NFC	100	1,409	14.1	10
2006	Andre Johnson, Houston, AFC	103	1,147	11.1	5
	Mike Furrey, Detroit, NFC	98	1,086	11.1	6
2005	Steve Smith, Carolina, NFC	103	1,563	15.2	12
	Larry Fitzgerald, Arizona, NFC	103	1,409	13.7	10
	Chad Ochocinco, Cincinnati, AFC	97	1,432	14.8	9
2004	Tony Gonzalez, Kansas City, AFC	102	1,258	12.3	7
	Joe Horn, New Orleans, NFC	94	1,399	14.9	11
	Torry Holt, St. Louis, NFC	94	1,372	14.6	10
2003	Torry Holt, St. Louis, NFC	117	1,696	14.5	12
	LaDainian Tomlinson, San Diego, AFC	100	725	7.3	4
2002	Marvin Harrison, Indianapolis, AFC	143	1,722	12.0	11
	Randy Moss, Minnesota, NFC	106	1,347	12.7	7
2001	Rod Smith, Denver, AFC	113	1,343	11.9	11
	Keyshawn Johnson, Tampa Bay, NFC	106	1,266	11.9	1
2000	Marvin Harrison, Indianapolis, AFC	102	1,413	13.9	14
	Muhsin Muhammad, Carolina, NFC	102	1,183	11.6	6
1999	Jimmy Smith, Jacksonville, AFC	116	1,636	14.1	6
	Muhsin Muhammad, Carolina, NFC	96	1,253	13.1	8
1998	O.J. McDuffie, Miami, AFC	90	1,050	11.7	7
	Frank Sanders, Arizona, NFC	89	1,145	12.9	3
1997	Tim Brown, Oakland, AFC	104	1,408	13.5	5
	Herman Moore, Detroit, NFC	104	1,293	12.4	8
1996	Jerry Rice, San Francisco, NFC	108	1,254	11.6	8
	Carl Pickens, Cincinnati, AFC	100	1,180	11.8	12
1995	Herman Moore, Detroit, NFC	123	1,686	13.7	14
	Carl Pickens, Cincinnati, AFC	99	1,234	12.5	17
1994	Cris Carter, Minnesota, NFC	122	1,256	10.3	7
	Ben Coates, New England, AFC	96	1,174	12.2	7
1993	Sterling Sharpe, Green Bay, NFC	112	1,274	11.4	11
	Reggie Langhorne, Indianapolis, AFC	85	1,038	12.2	3
1992	Sterling Sharpe, Green Bay, NFC	108	1,461	13.5	13
	Haywood Jeffires, Houston, AFC	90	913	10.1	9
1991	Haywood Jeffires, Houston, AFC	100	1,181	11.8	7
	Michael Irvin, Dallas, NFC	93	1,523	16.4	8
1990	Jerry Rice, San Francisco, NFC	100	1,502	15.0	13
	Haywood Jeffires, Houston, AFC	74	1,048	14.2	8
	Drew Hill, Houston, AFC	74	1,019	13.8	5

Year	Player, Team	No.	Yards	Avg.	TD
1989	Sterling Sharpe, Green Bay, NFC	90	1,423	15.8	12
	Andre Reed, Buffalo, AFC	88	1,312	14.9	9
1988	Al Toon, N.Y. Jets, AFC	93	1,067	11.5	5
	Henry Ellard, L.A. Rams, NFC	86	1,414	16.4	10
1987	J.T. Smith, St. Louis, NFC	91	1,117	12.3	8
	Al Toon, N.Y. Jets, AFC	68	976	14.4	5
1986	Todd Christensen, L.A. Raiders, AFC	95	1,153	12.1	8
	Jerry Rice, San Francisco, NFC	86	1,570	18.3	15
1985	Roger Craig, San Francisco, NFC	92	1,016	11.0	6
	Lionel James, San Diego, AFC	86	1,027	11.9	6
1984	Art Monk, Washington, NFC	106	1,372	12.9	7
	Ozzie Newsome, Cleveland, AFC	89	1,001	11.2	5
1983	Todd Christensen, L.A. Raiders, AFC	92	1,247	13.6	12
	Roy Green, St. Louis, NFC	78	1,227	15.7	14
	Charlie Brown, Washington, NFC	78	1,225	15.7	8
	Earnest Gray, N.Y. Giants, NFC	78	1,139	14.6	5
1982	Dwight Clark, San Francisco, NFC	60	913	15.2	5
	Kellen Winslow, San Diego, AFC	54	721	13.4	6
1981	Kellen Winslow, San Diego, AFC	88	1,075	12.2	10
	Dwight Clark, San Francisco, NFC	85	1,105	13.0	4
1980	Kellen Winslow, San Diego, AFC	89	1,290	14.5	9
	*Earl Cooper, San Francisco, NFC	83	567	6.8	4
1979	Joe Washington, Baltimore, AFC	82	750	9.1	3
	Ahmad Rashad, Minnesota, NFC	80	1,156	14.5	9
1978	Rickey Young, Minnesota, NFC	88	704	8.0	5
	Steve Largent, Seattle, AFC	71	1,168	16.5	8
1977	Lydell Mitchell, Baltimore, AFC	71	620	8.7	4
	Ahmad Rashad, Minnesota, NFC	51	681	13.4	2
1976	MacArthur Lane, Kansas City, AFC	66	686	10.4	1
	Drew Pearson, Dallas, NFC	58	806	13.9	6
1975	Chuck Foreman, Minnesota, NFC	73	691	9.5	9
	Reggie Rucker, Cleveland, AFC	60	770	12.8	3
	Lydell Mitchell, Baltimore, AFC	60	544	9.1	4
1974	Lydell Mitchell, Baltimore, AFC	72	544	7.6	2
	Charles Young, Philadelphia, NFC	63	696	11.0	3
1973	Harold Carmichael, Philadelphia, NFC	67	1,116	16.7	9
	Fred Willis, Houston, AFC	57	371	6.5	1
1972	Harold Jackson, Philadelphia, NFC	62	1,048	16.9	4
	Fred Biletnikoff, Oakland, AFC	58	802	13.8	7
1971	Fred Biletnikoff, Oakland, AFC	61	929	15.2	9
	Bob Tucker, N.Y. Giants, NFC	59	791	13.4	4
1970	Dick Gordon, Chicago, NFC	71	1,026	14.5	13
	Marlin Briscoe, Buffalo, AFC	57	1,036	18.2	8
1969	Dan Abramowicz, New Orleans, NFL	73	1,015	13.9	7
	Lance Alworth, San Diego, AFL	64	1,003	15.7	4
1968	Clifton McNeil, San Francisco, NFL	71	994	14.0	7
	Lance Alworth, San Diego, AFL	68	1,312	19.3	10
1967	George Sauer, N.Y. Jets, AFL	75	1,189	15.9	6
	Charley Taylor, Washington, NFL	70	990	14.1	9
1966	Lance Alworth, San Diego, AFL	73	1,383	18.9	13
	Charley Taylor, Washington, NFL	72	1,119	15.5	12
1965	Lionel Taylor, Denver, AFL	85	1,131	13.3	6
	Dave Parks, San Francisco, NFL	80	1,344	16.8	12
1964	Charley Hennigan, Houston, AFL	101	1,546	15.3	8
	Johnny Morris, Chicago, NFL	93	1,200	12.9	10
1963	Lionel Taylor, Denver, AFL	78	1,101	14.1	10
	Bobby Joe Conrad, St. Louis, NFL	73	967	13.2	10
1962	Lionel Taylor, Denver, AFL	77	908	11.8	4
	Bobby Mitchell, Washington, NFL	72	1,384	19.2	11
1961	Lionel Taylor, Denver, AFL	100	1,176	11.8	4
	Jim (Red) Phillips, Los Angeles, NFL	78	1,092	14.0	5
1960	Lionel Taylor, Denver, AFL	92	1,235	13.4	12
	Raymond Berry, Baltimore, NFL	74	1,298	17.5	10
1959	Raymond Berry, Baltimore	66	959	14.5	14
1958	Raymond Berry, Baltimore	56	794	14.2	9
	Pete Retzlaff, Philadelphia	56	766	13.7	2
1957	Billy Wilson, San Francisco	52	757	14.6	6
1956	Billy Wilson, San Francisco	60	889	14.8	5
1955	Pete Pihos, Philadelphia	62	864	13.9	7

Year	Player, Team	No.	Yards	Avg.	TD
1954	Pete Pihos, Philadelphia	60	872	14.5	10
	Billy Wilson, San Francisco	60	830	13.8	5
1953	Pete Pihos, Philadelphia	63	1,049	16.7	10
1952	Mac Speedie, Cleveland	62	911	14.7	5
1951	Elroy (Crazylegs) Hirsch, Los Angeles	66	1,495	22.7	17
1950	Tom Fears, Los Angeles	84	1,116	13.3	7
1949	Tom Fears, Los Angeles	77	1,013	13.2	9
1948	*Tom Fears, Los Angeles	51	698	13.7	4
1947	Jim Keane, Chi. Bears	64	910	14.2	10
1946	Jim Benton, Los Angeles	63	981	15.6	6
1945	Don Hutson, Green Bay	47	834	17.7	9
1944	Don Hutson, Green Bay	58	866	14.9	9
1943	Don Hutson, Green Bay	47	776	16.5	11
1942	Don Hutson, Green Bay	74	1,211	16.4	17
1941	Don Hutson, Green Bay	58	738	12.7	10
1940	*Don Looney, Philadelphia	58	707	12.2	4
1939	Don Hutson, Green Bay	34	846	24.9	6
1938	Gaynell Tinsley, Chi. Cardinals	41	516	12.6	1
1937	Don Hutson, Green Bay	41	552	13.5	7
1936	Don Hutson, Green Bay	34	536	15.8	8
1935	*Tod Goodwin, N.Y. Giants	26	432	16.6	4
1934	Joe Carter, Philadelphia	16	238	14.9	4
	Morris (Red) Badgro, N.Y. Giants	16	206	12.9	1
1933	John (Shipwreck) Kelly, Brooklyn	22	246	11.2	3
1932	Ray Flaherty, N.Y. Giants	21	350	16.7	3

**First season of professional football.*

ANNUAL PASS RECEIVING LEADERS (YARDS)

Year	Player, Team	No.	Yards	Avg.	TD
2008	Andre Johnson, Houston, AFC	115	1,575	13.7	8
	Larry Fitzgerald, Arizona, NFC	96	1,431	14.9	12
2007	Reggie Wayne, Indianapolis, AFC	104	1,510	14.5	10
	Larry Fitzgerald, Arizona, NFC	100	1,409	14.1	10
2006	Chad Ochocinco, Cincinnati, AFC	87	1,369	15.7	7
	Roy Williams, Detroit, NFC	82	1,310	16.0	7
2005	Steve Smith, Carolina, NFC	103	1,563	15.2	12
	Chad Ochocinco, Cincinnati, AFC	97	1,432	14.8	9
2004	Muhsin Muhammad, Carolina, NFC	93	1,405	15.1	16
	Chad Ochocinco, Cincinnati, AFC	95	1,274	13.4	9
2003	Torry Holt, St. Louis, NFC	117	1,696	14.5	12
	Chad Ochocinco, Cincinnati, AFC	90	1,355	15.1	10
2002	Marvin Harrison, Indianapolis, AFC	143	1,722	12.0	11
	Randy Moss, Minnesota, NFC	106	1,347	12.7	7
2001	David Boston, Arizona, NFC	98	1,598	16.3	8
	Marvin Harrison, Indianapolis, AFC	109	1,524	14.0	15
2000	Torry Holt, St. Louis, NFC	82	1,635	19.9	6
	Rod Smith, Denver, AFC	100	1,602	16.0	8
1999	Marvin Harrison, Indianapolis, AFC	115	1,663	14.5	12
	Randy Moss, Minnesota, NFC	80	1,413	17.7	11
1998	Antonio Freeman, Green Bay, NFC	84	1,424	17.0	14
	Eric Moulds, Buffalo, AFC	67	1,368	20.4	9
1997	Rob Moore, Arizona, NFC	97	1,584	16.3	8
	Tim Brown, Oakland, AFC	104	1,408	13.5	5
1996	Isaac Bruce, St. Louis, NFC	84	1,338	15.9	7
	Jimmy Smith, Jacksonville, AFC	83	1,244	15.0	7
1995	Jerry Rice, San Francisco, NFC	122	1,848	15.1	15
	Tim Brown, Oakland, AFC	89	1,342	15.1	10
1994	Jerry Rice, San Francisco, NFC	112	1,499	13.4	13
	Tim Brown, L.A. Raiders, AFC	89	1,309	14.7	9
1993	Jerry Rice, San Francisco, NFC	98	1,503	15.3	15
	Tim Brown, L.A. Raiders, AFC	80	1,180	14.8	7
1992	Sterling Sharpe, Green Bay, NFC	108	1,461	13.5	13
	Anthony Miller, San Diego, AFC	72	1,060	14.7	7
1991	Michael Irvin, Dallas, NFC	93	1,523	16.4	8
	Haywood Jeffires, Houston, AFC	100	1,181	11.8	7
1990	Jerry Rice, San Francisco, NFC	100	1,502	15.0	13
	Haywood Jeffires, Houston, AFC	74	1,048	14.2	8
1989	Jerry Rice, San Francisco, NFC	82	1,483	18.1	17
	Andre Reed, Buffalo, AFC	88	1,312	14.9	9

Year	Player, Team	No.	Yards	Avg.	TD
1988	Henry Ellard, L.A. Rams, NFC	86	1,414	16.4	10
	Eddie Brown, Cincinnati, AFC	53	1,273	24.0	9
1987	J.T. Smith, St. Louis, NFC	91	1,117	12.3	8
	Carlos Carson, Kansas City, AFC	55	1,044	19.0	7
1986	Jerry Rice, San Francisco, NFC	86	1,570	18.3	15
	Stanley Morgan, New England, AFC	84	1,491	17.8	10
1985	Steve Largent, Seattle, AFC	79	1,287	16.3	6
	Mike Quick, Philadelphia, NFC	73	1,247	17.1	11
1984	Roy Green, St. Louis, NFC	78	1,555	19.9	12
	John Stallworth, Pittsburgh, AFC	80	1,395	17.4	11
1983	Mike Quick, Philadelphia, NFC	69	1,409	20.4	13
	Carlos Carson, Kansas City, AFC	80	1,351	16.9	7
1982	Wes Chandler, San Diego, AFC	49	1,032	21.1	9
	Dwight Clark, San Francisco, NFC	60	913	15.2	5
1981	Alfred Jenkins, Atlanta, NFC	70	1,358	19.4	13
	Frank Lewis, Buffalo, AFC	70	1,244	17.8	4
	Steve Watson, Denver, AFC	60	1,244	20.7	13
1980	John Jefferson, San Diego, AFC	82	1,340	16.3	13
	James Lofton, Green Bay, NFC	71	1,226	17.3	4
1979	Steve Largent, Seattle, AFC	66	1,237	18.7	9
	Ahmad Rashad, Minnesota, NFC	80	1,156	14.5	9
1978	Wesley Walker, N.Y. Jets, AFC	48	1,169	24.4	8
	Harold Carmichael, Philadelphia, NFC	55	1,072	19.5	8
1977	Drew Pearson, Dallas, NFC	48	870	18.1	2
	Ken Burrough, Houston, AFC	43	816	19.0	8
1976	Roger Carr, Baltimore, AFC	43	1,112	25.9	11
	*Sammy White, Minnesota, NFC	51	906	17.8	10
1975	Ken Burrough, Houston, AFC	53	1,063	20.1	8
	Mel Gray, St. Louis, NFC	48	926	19.3	11
1974	Cliff Branch, Oakland, AFC	60	1,092	18.2	13
	Drew Pearson, Dallas, NFC	62	1,087	17.5	2
1973	Harold Carmichael, Philadelphia, NFC	67	1,116	16.7	9
	*Isaac Curtis, Cincinnati, AFC	45	843	18.7	9
1972	Harold Jackson, Philadelphia, NFC	62	1,048	16.9	4
	Rich Caster, N.Y. Jets, AFC	39	833	21.4	10
1971	Otis Taylor, Kansas City, AFC	57	1,110	19.5	7
	Gene Washington, San Francisco, NFC	46	884	19.2	4
1970	Gene Washington, San Francisco, NFC	53	1,100	20.8	12
	Marlin Briscoe, Buffalo, AFC	57	1,036	18.2	8
1969	Warren Wells, Oakland, AFL	47	1,260	26.8	14
	Harold Jackson, Philadelphia, NFL	65	1,116	17.2	9
1968	Lance Alworth, San Diego, AFL	68	1,312	19.3	10
	Roy Jefferson, Pittsburgh, NFL	58	1,074	18.5	11
1967	Don Maynard, N.Y. Jets, AFL	71	1,434	20.3	10
	Ben Hawkins, Philadelphia, NFL	59	1,265	21.4	10
1966	Lance Alworth, San Diego, AFL	73	1,383	18.9	13
	Pat Studstill, Detroit, NFL	67	1,266	18.9	5
1965	Lance Alworth, San Diego, AFL	69	1,602	23.2	14
	Dave Parks, San Francisco, NFL	80	1,344	16.8	12
1964	Charley Hennigan, Houston, AFL	101	1,546	15.3	8
	Johnny Morris, Chicago, NFL	93	1,200	12.9	10
1963	Bobby Mitchell, Washington, NFL	69	1,436	20.8	7
	Art Powell, Oakland, AFL	73	1,304	17.8	16
1962	Bobby Mitchell, Washington, NFL	72	1,384	19.2	11
	Art Powell, N.Y. Titans, AFL	64	1,130	17.6	8
1961	Charley Hennigan, Houston, AFL	82	1,746	21.3	12
	Tommy McDonald, Philadelphia, NFL	64	1,144	17.9	13
1960	*Bill Groman, Houston, AFL	72	1,473	20.5	12
	Raymond Berry, Baltimore, NFL	74	1,298	17.5	10
1959	Raymond Berry, Baltimore	66	959	14.5	14
1958	Del Shofner, Los Angeles	51	1,097	21.5	8
1957	Raymond Berry, Baltimore	47	800	17.0	6
1956	Billy Howton, Green Bay	55	1,188	21.6	12
1955	Pete Pihos, Philadelphia	62	864	13.9	7
1954	Bob Boyd, Los Angeles	53	1,212	22.9	6
1953	Pete Pihos, Philadelphia	63	1,049	16.7	10
1952	*Billy Howton, Green Bay	53	1,231	23.2	13
1951	Elroy (Crazylegs) Hirsch, Los Angeles	66	1,495	22.7	17
1950	Tom Fears, Los Angeles	84	1,116	13.3	7

Year	Player, Team	No.	Yards	Avg.	TD
1949	Bob Mann, Detroit	66	1,014	15.4	4
1948	Mal Kutner, Chi. Cardinals	41	943	23.0	14
1947	Mal Kutner, Chi. Cardinals	43	944	21.9	7
1946	Jim Benton, Los Angeles	63	981	15.5	6
1945	Jim Benton, Cleveland	45	1,067	23.7	8
1944	Don Hutson, Green Bay	58	866	14.6	9
1943	Don Hutson, Green Bay	47	776	16.5	11
1942	Don Hutson, Green Bay	74	1,211	16.4	17
1941	Don Hutson, Green Bay	58	738	12.7	10
1940	*Don Looney, Philadelphia	58	707	12.2	4
1939	Don Hutson, Green Bay	34	846	24.9	6
1938	Don Hutson, Green Bay	32	548	17.1	9
1937	*Gaynell Tinsley, Chi. Cardinals	36	675	18.8	5
1936	Don Hutson, Green Bay	34	526	15.5	8
1935	Charley Malone, Boston	22	433	19.7	2
1934	Harry Ebding, Detroit	9	257	28.6	2
1933	*Paul Moss, Pittsburgh	18	383	21.3	2
1932	Johnny (Blood) McNally, Green Bay	19	326	17.2	3

**First season of professional football.*

ANNUAL PUNT RETURN LEADERS

Year	Player, Team	No.	Yards	Avg.	Long	TD
2008	Roscoe Parrish, Buffalo, AFC	21	322	15.3	63	1
	*Clifton Smith, Tampa Bay, NFC	23	324	14.1	70	1
2007	Roscoe Parrish, Buffalo, AFC	27	440	16.3	74	1
	Devin Hester, Chicago, NFC	42	651	15.5	89	4
2006	Pacman Jones, Tennessee, AFC	34	440	12.9	90	3
	*Devin Hester, Chicago, NFC	47	600	12.8	84	3
2005	Reno Mahe, Philadelphia, NFC	21	269	12.8	44	0
	B.J. Sams, Baltimore, AFC	33	401	12.2	51	0
2004	Eddie Drummond, Detroit, NFC	24	316	13.2	83	2
	Dennis Northcutt, Cleveland, AFC	36	432	12.0	44	0
2003	Dante Hall, Kansas City, AFC	29	472	16.3	93	2
	Brian Westbrook, Philadelphia, NFC	20	306	15.3	84	2
2002	Jimmy Williams, San Francisco, NFC	20	336	16.8	89	1
	Santana Moss, N.Y. Jets, AFC	25	413	16.5	63	2
2001	Troy Brown, New England, AFC	29	413	14.2	85	2
	Darrien Gordon, Atlanta, NFC	31	437	14.1	74	0
2000	Jermaine Lewis, Baltimore, AFC	36	578	16.1	89	2
	Az-Zahir Hakim, St. Louis, NFC	32	489	15.3	86	1
1999	*Charlie Rogers, Seattle, AFC	22	318	14.5	94	1
	*Mac Cody, Arizona, NFC	32	373	11.7	31	0
1998	Deion Sanders, Dallas, NFC	24	375	15.6	69	2
	Reggie Barlow, Jacksonville, AFC	43	555	12.9	85	1
1997	Jermaine Lewis, Baltimore, AFC	28	437	15.6	89	2
	David Palmer, Minnesota, NFC	34	444	13.1	57	0
1996	Desmond Howard, Green Bay, NFC	58	875	15.1	92	3
	Darrien Gordon, San Diego, AFC	36	537	14.9	81	1
1995	David Palmer, Minnesota, NFC	26	342	13.2	74	1
	Andre Coleman, San Diego, AFC	28	326	11.6	88	1
1994	Brian Mitchell, Washington, NFC	32	452	14.1	78	2
	Darrien Gordon, San Diego, AFC	36	475	13.2	90	2
1993	*Tyrone Hughes, New Orleans, NFC	37	503	13.6	83	2
	Eric Metcalf, Cleveland, AFC	36	464	12.9	91	2
1992	Johnny Bailey, Phoenix, NFC	20	263	13.2	65	0
	Rod Woodson, Pittsburgh, AFC	32	364	11.4	80	1
1991	Mel Gray, Detroit, NFC	25	385	15.4	78	1
	Rod Woodson, Pittsburgh, AFC	28	320	11.4	40	0
1990	Clarence Verdin, Indianapolis, AFC	31	396	12.8	36	0
	*Johnny Bailey, Chicago, NFC	36	399	11.1	95	1
1989	Walter Stanley, Detroit, NFC	36	496	13.8	74	0
	Clarence Verdin, Indianapolis, AFC	23	296	12.9	49	1
1988	John Taylor, San Francisco, NFC	44	556	12.6	95	2
	JoJo Townsell, N.Y. Jets, AFC	35	409	11.7	59	1
1987	Mel Gray, New Orleans, NFC	24	352	14.7	80	0
	Bobby Joe Edmonds, Seattle, AFC	20	251	12.6	40	0
1986	*Bobby Joe Edmonds, Seattle, AFC	34	419	12.3	75	1
	*Vai Sikahema, St. Louis, NFC	43	522	12.1	71	2

Year	Player, Team	No.	Yards	Avg.	Long	TD
1985	Irving Fryar, New England, AFC	37	520	14.1	85	2
	Henry Ellard, L.A. Rams, NFC	37	501	13.5	80	1
1984	Mike Martin, Cincinnati, AFC	24	376	15.7	55	0
	Henry Ellard, L.A. Rams, NFC	30	403	13.4	83	2
1983	*Henry Ellard, L.A. Rams, NFC	16	217	13.6	72	1
	Kirk Springs, N.Y. Jets, AFC	23	287	12.5	76	1
1982	Rick Upchurch, Denver, AFC	15	242	16.1	78	2
	Billy Johnson, Atlanta, NFC	24	273	11.4	71	0
1981	LeRoy Irvin, Los Angeles, NFC	46	615	13.4	84	3
	*James Brooks, San Diego, AFC	22	290	13.2	42	0
1980	J.T. Smith, Kansas City, AFC	40	581	14.5	75	2
	*Kenny Johnson, Atlanta, NFC	23	281	12.2	56	0
1979	John Sciarra, Philadelphia, NFC	16	182	11.4	38	0
	*Tony Nathan, Miami, AFC	28	306	10.9	86	1
1978	Rick Upchurch, Denver, AFC	36	493	13.7	75	1
	Jackie Wallace, Los Angeles, NFC	52	618	11.9	58	0
1977	Billy Johnson, Houston, AFC	35	539	15.4	87	2
	Larry Marshall, Philadelphia, NFC	46	489	10.6	48	0
1976	Rick Upchurch, Denver, AFC	39	536	13.7	92	4
	Eddie Brown, Washington, NFC	48	646	13.5	71	1
1975	Billy Johnson, Houston, AFC	40	612	15.3	83	3
	Terry Metcalf, St. Louis, NFC	23	285	12.4	69	1
1974	Lemar Parrish, Cincinnati, AFC	18	338	18.8	90	2
	Dick Jauron, Detroit, NFC	17	286	16.8	58	0
1973	Bruce Taylor, San Francisco, NFC	15	207	13.8	61	0
	Ron Smith, San Diego, AFC	27	352	13.0	84	2
1972	Ken Ellis, Green Bay, NFC	14	215	15.4	80	1
	Chris Farasopoulos, N.Y. Jets, AFC	17	179	10.5	65	1
1971	Les (Speedy) Duncan, Washington, NFC	22	233	10.6	33	0
	Leroy Kelly, Cleveland, AFC	30	292	9.7	74	0
1970	Ed Podolak, Kansas City, AFC	23	311	13.5	60	0
	*Bruce Taylor, San Francisco, NFC	43	516	12.0	76	0
1969	Alvin Haymond, Los Angeles, NFL	33	435	13.2	52	0
	*Bill Thompson, Denver, AFL	25	288	11.5	40	0
1968	Bob Hayes, Dallas, NFL	15	312	20.8	90	2
	Noland Smith, Kansas City, AFL	18	270	15.0	80	1
1967	Floyd Little, Denver, AFL	16	270	16.9	72	1
	Ben Davis, Cleveland, NFL	18	229	12.7	52	1
1966	Les (Speedy) Duncan, San Diego, AFL	18	238	13.2	81	1
	Johnny Roland, St. Louis, NFL	20	221	11.1	86	1
1965	Leroy Kelly, Cleveland, NFL	17	265	15.6	67	2
	Les (Speedy) Duncan, San Diego, AFL	30	464	15.5	66	2
1964	Bobby Jancik, Houston, AFL	12	220	18.3	82	1
	Tommy Watkins, Detroit, NFL	16	238	14.9	68	2
1963	Dick James, Washington, NFL	16	214	13.4	39	0
	Claude (Hoot) Gibson, Oakland, AFL	26	307	11.8	85	2
1962	Dick Christy, N.Y. Titans, AFL	15	250	16.7	73	2
	Pat Studstill, Detroit, NFL	29	457	15.8	44	0
1961	Dick Christy, N.Y. Titans, AFL	18	383	21.3	70	2
	Willie Wood, Green Bay, NFL	14	225	16.1	72	2
1960	*Abner Haynes, Dall. Texans, AFL	14	215	15.4	46	0
	Abe Woodson, San Francisco, NFL	13	174	13.4	48	0
1959	Johnny Morris, Chi. Bears	14	171	12.2	78	1
1958	Jon Arnett, Los Angeles	18	223	12.4	58	0
1957	Bert Zagers, Washington	14	217	15.5	76	2
1956	Ken Konz, Cleveland	13	187	14.4	65	1
1955	Ollie Matson, Chi. Cardinals	13	245	18.8	78	2
1954	*Veryl Switzer, Green Bay	24	306	12.8	93	1
1953	Charley Trippi, Chi. Cardinals	21	239	11.4	38	0
1952	Jack Christiansen, Detroit	15	322	21.5	79	2
1951	Claude (Buddy) Young, N.Y. Yanks	12	231	19.3	79	1
1950	*Herb Rich, Baltimore	12	276	23.0	86	1
1949	Verda (Vitamin T) Smith, Los Angeles	27	427	15.8	85	1
1948	George McAfee, Chi. Bears	30	417	13.9	60	1
1947	*Walt Slater, Pittsburgh	28	435	15.5	33	0
1946	Bill Dudley, Pittsburgh	27	385	14.3	52	0
1945	*Dave Ryan, Detroit	15	220	14.7	56	0
1944	*Steve Van Buren, Philadelphia	15	230	15.3	55	1
1943	Andy Farkas, Washington	15	168	11.2	33	0

Year	Player, Team	No.	Yards	Avg.	Long	TD
1942	Merlyn Condit, Brooklyn	21	210	10.0	23	0
1941	Byron (Whizzer) White, Detroit	19	262	13.8	64	0

First season of professional football.

ANNUAL KICKOFF RETURN LEADERS

Year	Player, Team	No.	Yards	Avg.	Long	TD
2008	Danieal Manning, Chicago, NFC	36	1,070	29.7	83	1
	Ellis Hobbs, New England, AFC	45	1,281	28.5	95	1
2007	Josh Cribbs, Cleveland, AFC	59	1,809	30.7	100	2
	*Aundrae Allison, Minnesota, NFC	20	574	28.7	104	1
2006	Justin Miller, N.Y. Jets, AFC	46	1,304	28.3	103	2
	*Devin Hester, Chicago, NFC	20	528	26.4	96	2
2005	Terrence McGee, Buffalo, AFC	46	1,391	30.2	99	1
	Koren Robinson, Minnesota, NFC	47	1,221	26.0	86	1
2004	Willie Ponder, N.Y. Giants, NFC	36	967	26.9	91	1
	Terrence McGee, Buffalo, AFC	52	1,370	26.3	104	3
2003	Jerry Azumah, Chicago, NFC	41	1,191	29.0	89	2
	*Bethel Johnson, New England, AFC	30	847	28.2	92	1
2002	MarTay Jenkins, Arizona, NFC	20	559	28.0	95	1
	Kevin Faulk, New England, AFC	26	725	27.9	87	2
2001	Ronney Jenkins, San Diego, AFC	58	1,541	26.6	93	2
	*Steve Smith, Carolina, NFC	56	1,431	25.6	99	2
2000	*Darrick Vaughn, Atlanta, NFC	39	1,082	27.7	100	3
	Derrick Mason, Tennessee, AFC	42	1,132	27.0	66	0
1999	Tony Horne, St. Louis, NFC	30	892	29.7	101	2
	Tremain Mack, Cincinnati, AFC	51	1,382	27.1	99	1
1998	*Terry Fair, Detroit, NFC	51	1,428	28.0	105	2
	Corey Harris, Baltimore, AFC	35	965	27.6	95	1
1997	Michael Bates, Carolina, NFC	47	1,281	27.3	56	0
	Aaron Glenn, N.Y. Jets, AFC	28	741	26.5	96	1
1996	Michael Bates, Carolina, NFC	33	998	30.2	93	1
	Tamarick Vanover, Kansas City, AFC	33	854	25.9	97	1
1995	Ron Carpenter, N.Y. Jets, AFC	20	553	27.7	58	0
	Brian Mitchell, Washington, NFC	55	1,408	25.6	59	0
1994	Mel Gray, Detroit, NFC	45	1,276	28.4	102	3
	Randy Baldwin, Cleveland, AFC	28	753	26.9	85	1
1993	Robert Brooks, Green Bay, NFC	23	611	26.6	95	1
	*Raghib Ismail, L.A. Raiders, AFC	25	605	24.2	66	0
1992	Jon Vaughn, New England, AFC	20	564	28.2	100	1
	Deion Sanders, Atlanta, NFC	40	1,067	26.7	99	2
1991	Mel Gray, Detroit, NFC	36	929	25.8	71	0
	Nate Lewis, San Diego, AFC	23	578	25.1	95	1
1990	Kevin Clark, Denver, AFC	20	505	25.3	75	0
	David Meggett, N.Y. Giants, NFC	21	492	23.4	58	0
1989	Rod Woodson, Pittsburgh, AFC	36	982	27.3	84	1
	Mel Gray, Detroit, NFC	24	640	26.7	57	0
1988	*Tim Brown, L.A. Raiders, AFC	41	1,098	26.8	97	1
	Donnie Elder, Tampa Bay, NFC	34	772	22.7	51	0
1987	Sylvester Stamps, Atlanta, NFC	24	660	27.5	97	1
	Paul Palmer, Kansas City, AFC	38	923	24.3	95	2
1986	Dennis Gentry, Chicago, NFC	20	576	28.8	91	1
	Lupe Sanchez, Pittsburgh, AFC	25	591	23.6	64	0
1985	Ron Brown, L.A. Rams, NFC	28	918	32.8	98	3
	Glen Young, Cleveland, AFC	35	898	25.7	63	0
1984	*Bobby Humphery, N.Y. Jets, AFC	22	675	30.7	97	1
	Barry Redden, L.A. Rams, NFC	23	530	23.0	40	0
1983	Fulton Walker, Miami, AFC	36	962	26.7	78	0
	Darrin Nelson, Minnesota, NFC	18	445	24.7	50	0
1982	*Mike Mosley, Buffalo, AFC	18	487	27.1	66	0
	Alvin Hall, Detroit, NFC	16	426	26.6	96	1
1981	Mike Nelms, Washington, NFC	37	1,099	29.7	84	0
	Carl Roaches, Houston, AFC	28	769	27.5	96	1
1980	Horace Ivory, New England, AFC	36	992	27.6	98	1
	Rich Mauti, New Orleans, NFC	31	798	25.7	52	0
1979	Larry Brunson, Oakland, AFC	17	441	25.9	89	0
	Jimmy Edwards, Minnesota, NFC	44	1,103	25.1	83	0
1978	Steve Odom, Green Bay, NFC	25	677	27.1	95	1
	*Keith Wright, Cleveland, AFC	30	789	26.3	86	0

Year	Player, Team	No.	Yards	Avg.	Long	TD
1977	*Raymond Clayborn, New England, AFC	28	869	31.0	101	3
	*Wilbert Montgomery, Philadelphia, NFC	23	619	26.9	99	1
1976	*Duriel Harris, Miami, AFC	17	559	32.9	69	0
	Cullen Bryant, Los Angeles, NFC	16	459	28.7	90	1
1975	*Walter Payton, Chicago, NFC	14	444	31.7	70	0
	Harold Hart, Oakland, AFC	17	518	30.5	102	1
1974	Terry Metcalf, St. Louis, NFC	20	623	31.2	94	1
	Greg Pruitt, Cleveland, AFC	22	606	27.5	88	1
1973	Carl Garrett, Chicago, NFC	16	486	30.4	67	0
	*Wallace Francis, Buffalo, AFC	23	687	29.9	101	2
1972	Ron Smith, Chicago, NFC	30	924	30.8	94	1
	*Bruce Laird, Baltimore, AFC	29	843	29.1	73	0
1971	Travis Williams, Los Angeles, NFC	25	743	29.7	105	1
	Eugene (Mercury) Morris, Miami, AFC	15	423	28.2	94	1
1970	Jim Duncan, Baltimore, AFC	20	707	35.4	99	1
	Cecil Turner, Chicago, NFC	23	752	32.7	96	4
1969	Bobby Williams, Detroit, NFL	17	563	33.1	96	1
	*Bill Thompson, Denver, AFL	18	513	28.5	63	0
1968	Preston Pearson, Baltimore, NFL	15	527	35.1	102	2
	*George Atkinson, Oakland, AFL	32	802	25.1	60	0
1967	*Travis Williams, Green Bay, NFL	18	739	41.1	104	4
	*Zeke Moore, Houston, AFL	14	405	28.9	92	1
1966	Gale Sayers, Chicago, NFL	23	718	31.2	93	2
	*Goldie Sellers, Denver, AFL	19	541	28.5	100	2
1965	Tommy Watkins, Detroit, NFL	17	584	34.4	94	0
	Abner Haynes, Denver, AFL	34	901	26.5	60	0
1964	*Clarence Childs, N.Y. Giants, NFL	34	987	29.0	100	1
	Bo Roberson, Oakland, AFL	36	975	27.1	59	0
1963	Abe Woodson, San Francisco, NFL	29	935	32.2	103	3
	Bobby Jancik, Houston, AFL	45	1,317	29.3	53	0
1962	Abe Woodson, San Francisco, NFL	37	1,157	31.3	79	0
	*Bobby Jancik, Houston, AFL	24	826	30.3	61	0
1961	Dick Bass, Los Angeles, NFL	23	698	30.3	64	0
	*Dave Grayson, Dall. Texans, AFL	16	453	28.3	73	0
1960	*Tom Moore, Green Bay, NFL	12	397	33.1	84	0
	Ken Hall, Houston, AFL	19	594	31.3	104	1
1959	Abe Woodson, San Francisco	13	382	29.4	105	1
1958	Ollie Matson, Chi. Cardinals	14	497	35.5	101	2
1957	*Jon Arnett, Los Angeles	18	504	28.0	98	1
1956	*Tom Wilson, Los Angeles	15	477	31.8	103	1
1955	Al Carmichael, Green Bay	14	418	29.9	100	1
1954	Billy Reynolds, Cleveland	14	413	29.5	51	0
1953	Joe Arenas, San Francisco	16	551	34.4	82	0
1952	Lynn Chandnois, Pittsburgh	17	599	35.2	93	2
1951	Lynn Chandnois, Pittsburgh	12	390	32.5	55	0
1950	Verda (Vitamin T) Smith, Los Angeles	22	742	33.7	97	3
1949	*Don Doll, Detroit	21	536	25.5	56	0
1948	*Joe Scott, N.Y. Giants	20	569	28.5	99	1
1947	Eddie Saenz, Washington	29	797	27.5	94	2
1946	Abe Karnofsky, Boston	21	599	28.5	97	1
1945	Steve Van Buren, Philadelphia	13	373	28.7	98	1
1944	Bob Thurbon, Card.-Pitt.	12	291	24.3	55	0
1943	Ken Heineman, Brooklyn	16	444	27.8	69	0
1942	Marshall Goldberg, Chi. Cardinals	15	393	26.2	95	1
1941	Marshall Goldberg, Chi. Cardinals	12	290	24.2	41	0

**First season of professional football.*

ANNUAL INTERCEPTION LEADERS

Year	Player, Team	No.	Yards	TD
2008	Ed Reed, Baltimore, AFC	9	264	2
	Nick Collins, Green Bay, NFC	7	295	3
	Charles Woodson, Green Bay, NFC	7	169	2
2007	Antonio Cromartie, San Diego, AFC	10	144	1
	O.J. Atogwe, St. Louis, NFC	8	125	1
2006	Champ Bailey, Denver, AFC	10	162	1
	Asante Samuel, New England, AFC	10	120	0
	Walt Harris, San Francisco, NFC	8	84	1
	Charles Woodson, Green Bay, NFC	8	61	1
2005	Ty Law, N.Y. Jets, AFC	10	195	1
	Deltha O'Neal, Cincinnati, AFC	10	103	0
	Darren Sharper, Minnesota, NFC	9	276	2
2004	Ed Reed, Baltimore, AFC	9	358	1
	Ken Lucas, Seattle, NFC	6	46	1
	*Chris Gamble, Carolina, NFC	6	15	0
2003	Tony Parrish, San Francisco, NFC	9	202	0
	Brian Russell, Minnesota, NFC	9	185	0
	Ed Reed, Baltimore, AFC	7	132	1
	Marcus Coleman, Houston, AFC	7	95	0
	Patrick Surtain, Miami, AFC	7	59	0

YEARLY STATISTICAL LEADERS

Year	Player, Team	No.	Yards	TD
2002	Rod Woodson, Oakland, AFC	8	225	2
	Brian Kelly, Tampa Bay, NFC	8	68	0
2001	*Anthony Henry, Cleveland, AFC	10	177	1
	Ronde Barber, Tampa Bay, NFC	10	86	1
2000	Darren Sharper, Green Bay, NFC	9	109	0
	Samari Rolle, Tennessee, AFC	7	140	1
	Brian Walker, Miami, AFC	7	80	0
1999	Rod Woodson, Baltimore, AFC	7	195	2
	Sam Madison, Miami, AFC	7	164	1
	James Hasty, Kansas City, AFC	7	98	2
	Donnie Abraham, Tampa Bay, NFC	7	115	2
	Troy Vincent, Philadelphia, NFC	7	91	0
1998	Ty Law, New England, AFC	9	133	1
	Kwamie Lassiter, Arizona, NFC	8	80	0
1997	Ryan McNeil, St. Louis, NFC	9	127	1
	Mark McMillian, Kansas City, AFC	8	274	3
	Darryl Williams, Seattle, AFC	8	172	1
1996	Tyrone Braxton, Denver, AFC	9	128	1
	Keith Lyle, St. Louis, NFC	9	152	0
1995	*Orlando Thomas, Minnesota, NFC	9	108	1
	Willie Williams, Pittsburgh, AFC	7	122	1
1994	Eric Turner, Cleveland, AFC	9	199	1
	Aeneas Williams, Arizona, NFC	9	89	0
1993	Eugene Robinson, Seattle, AFC	9	80	0
	Nate Odomes, Buffalo, AFC	9	65	0
	Deion Sanders, Atlanta, NFC	7	91	0
1992	Henry Jones, Buffalo, AFC	8	263	2
	Audray McMillian, Minnesota, NFC	8	157	2
1991	Ronnie Lott, L.A. Raiders, AFC	8	52	0
	Ray Crockett, Detroit, NFC	6	141	1
	Deion Sanders, Atlanta, NFC	6	119	1
	*Aeneas Williams, Phoenix, NFC	6	60	0
	Tim McKyer, Atlanta, NFC	6	24	0
1990	*Mark Carrier, Chicago, NFC	10	39	0
	Richard Johnson, Houston, AFC	8	100	1
1989	Felix Wright, Cleveland, AFC	9	91	1
	Eric Allen, Philadelphia, NFC	8	38	0
1988	Scott Case, Atlanta, NFC	10	47	0
	Erik McMillan, N.Y. Jets, AFC	8	168	2
1987	Barry Wilburn, Washington, NFC	9	135	1
	Mike Prior, Indianapolis, AFC	6	57	0
	Mark Kelso, Buffalo, AFC	6	25	0
	Keith Bostic, Houston, AFC	6	-14	0
1986	Ronnie Lott, San Francisco, NFC	10	134	1
	Deron Cherry, Kansas City, AFC	9	150	0
1985	Everson Walls, Dallas, NFC	9	31	0
	Albert Lewis, Kansas City, AFC	8	59	0
	Eugene Daniel, Indianapolis, AFC	8	53	0
1984	Ken Easley, Seattle, AFC	10	126	2
	*Tom Flynn, Green Bay, NFC	9	106	0
1983	Mark Murphy, Washington, NFC	9	127	0
	Ken Riley, Cincinnati, AFC	8	89	2
	Vann McElroy, L.A. Raiders, AFC	8	68	0
1982	Everson Walls, Dallas, NFC	7	61	0
	Ken Riley, Cincinnati, AFC	5	88	1
	Bobby Jackson, N.Y Jets, AFC	5	84	1
	Dwayne Woodruff, Pittsburgh, AFC	5	53	0
	Donnie Shell, Pittsburgh, AFC	5	27	0
1981	*Everson Walls, Dallas, NFC	11	133	0
	John Harris, Seattle, AFC	10	155	2
1980	Lester Hayes, Oakland, AFC	13	273	1
	Nolan Cromwell, Los Angeles, NFC	8	140	1
1979	Mike Reinfeldt, Houston, AFC	12	205	0
	Lemar Parrish, Washington, NFC	9	65	0
1978	Thom Darden, Cleveland, AFC	10	200	0
	Ken Stone, St. Louis, NFC	9	139	0
	Willie Buchanon, Green Bay, NFC	9	93	1

Year	Player, Team	No.	Avg.	Long
1977	Lyle Blackwood, Baltimore, AFC	10	163	0
	Rolland Lawrence, Atlanta, NFC	7	138	0
1976	Monte Jackson, Los Angeles, NFC	10	173	3
	Ken Riley, Cincinnati, AFC	9	141	1
1975	Mel Blount, Pittsburgh, AFC	11	121	0
	Paul Krause, Minnesota, NFC	10	201	0
1974	Emmitt Thomas, Kansas City, AFC	12	214	2
	Ray Brown, Atlanta, NFC	8	164	1
1973	Dick Anderson, Miami, AFC	8	163	2
	Mike Wagner, Pittsburgh, AFC	8	134	0
	Bobby Bryant, Minnesota, NFC	7	105	1
1972	Bill Bradley, Philadelphia, NFC	9	73	0
	Mike Sensibaugh, Kansas City, AFC	8	65	0
1971	Bill Bradley, Philadelphia, NFC	11	248	0
	Ken Houston, Houston, AFC	9	220	4
1970	Johnny Robinson, Kansas City, AFC	10	155	0
	Dick LeBeau, Detroit, NFC	9	96	0
1969	Mel Renfro, Dallas, NFL	10	118	0
	Emmitt Thomas, Kansas City, AFL	9	146	1
1968	Dave Grayson, Oakland, AFL	10	195	1
	Willie Williams, N.Y. Giants, NFL	10	103	0
1967	Miller Farr, Houston, AFL	10	264	3
	*Lem Barney, Detroit, NFL	10	232	3
	Tom Janik, Buffalo, AFL	10	222	2
	Dave Whitsell, New Orleans, NFL	10	178	2
	Dick Westmoreland, Miami, AFL	10	127	1
1966	Larry Wilson, St. Louis, NFL	10	180	2
	Johnny Robinson, Kansas City, AFL	10	136	1
	Bobby Hunt, Kansas City, AFL	10	113	0
1965	W.K. Hicks, Houston, AFL	9	156	0
	Bobby Boyd, Baltimore, NFL	9	78	1
1964	Dainard Paulson, N.Y. Jets, AFL	12	157	1
	*Paul Krause, Washington, NFL	12	140	1
1963	Fred Glick, Houston, AFL	12	180	1
	Dick Lynch, N.Y. Giants, NFL	9	251	3
	Roosevelt Taylor, Chicago, NFL	9	172	1
1962	Lee Riley, N.Y. Titans, AFL	11	122	0
	Willie Wood, Green Bay, NFL	9	132	0
1961	Billy Atkins, Buffalo, AFL	10	158	0
	Dick Lynch, N.Y. Giants, NFL	9	60	0
1960	*Austin (Goose) Gonsoulin, Denver, AFL	11	98	0
	Dave Baker, San Francisco, NFL	10	96	0
	Jerry Norton, St. Louis, NFL	10	96	0
1959	Dean Derby, Pittsburgh	7	127	0
	Milt Davis, Baltimore	7	119	1
	Don Shinnick, Baltimore	7	70	0
1958	Jim Patton, N.Y. Giants	11	183	0
1957	Milt Davis, Baltimore	10	219	2
	Jack Christiansen, Detroit	10	137	1
	Jack Butler, Pittsburgh	10	85	0
1956	Linden Crow, Chi. Cardinals	11	170	0
1955	Will Sherman, Los Angeles	11	101	0
1954	Dick (Night Train) Lane, Chi. Cardinals	10	181	0
1953	Jack Christiansen, Detroit	12	238	1
1952	*Dick (Night Train) Lane, Los Angeles	14	298	2
1951	Otto Schnellbacher, N.Y. Giants	11	194	2
1950	Orban (Spec) Sanders, N.Y. Yanks	13	199	0
1949	Bob Nussbaumer, Chi. Cardinals	12	157	0
1948	*Dan Sandifer, Washington	13	258	2
1947	Frank Reagan, N.Y. Giants	10	203	0
	Frank Seno, Boston	10	100	0
1946	Bill Dudley, Pittsburgh	10	242	1
1945	Roy Zimmerman, Philadelphia	7	90	0
1944	*Howard Livingston, N.Y. Giants	9	172	1
1943	Sammy Baugh, Washington	11	112	0
1942	Clyde (Bulldog) Turner, Chi. Bears	8	96	1
1941	Marshall Goldberg, Chi. Cardinals	7	54	0
	*Art Jones, Pittsburgh	7	35	0

Year	Player, Team	No.	Avg.	Long
1940	Clarence (Ace) Parker, Brooklyn	6	146	1
	Kent Ryan, Detroit	6	65	0
	Don Hutson, Green Bay	6	24	0

*First season of professional football.

ANNUAL PUNTING LEADERS

Year	Player, Team	No.	Avg.	Long
2008	Donnie Jones, St. Louis, NFC	82	50.0	68
	Shane Lechler, Oakland, AFC	90	48.8	70
2007	Shane Lechler, Oakland, AFC	73	49.1	70
	Andy Lee, San Francisco, NFC	105	47.3	74
2006	Mat McBriar, Dallas, NFC	56	48.2	75
	Shane Lechler, Oakland, AFC	77	47.5	67
2005	Brian Moorman, Buffalo, AFC	71	45.7	68
	Josh Bidwell, Tampa Bay, NFC	90	45.6	61
2004	Shane Lechler, Oakland, AFC	73	46.7	67
	Tom Tupa, Washington, NFC	103	44.1	61
2003	Shane Lechler, Oakland, AFC	96	46.9	73
	Todd Sauerbrun, Carolina, NFC	77	44.6	64
2002	Todd Sauerbrun, Carolina, NFC	104	45.5	67
	Chris Hanson, Jacksonville, AFC	81	44.2	64
2001	Todd Sauerbrun, Carolina, NFC	93	47.5	73
	Shane Lechler, Oakland, AFC	73	46.2	65
2000	Darren Bennett, San Diego, AFC	92	46.2	66
	Mitch Berger, Minnesota, NFC	62	44.7	60
1999	Tom Rouen, Denver, AFC	84	46.5	65
	Mitch Berger, Minnesota, NFC	61	45.4	75
1998	Craig Hentrich, Tennessee, AFC	69	47.2	71
	Mark Royals, New Orleans, NFC	88	45.6	64
1997	Mark Royals, New Orleans, NFC	88	45.9	66
	Tom Tupa, New England, AFC	78	45.8	73
1996	John Kidd, Miami, AFC	78	46.3	63
	Matt Turk, Washington, NFC	75	45.1	63
1995	Rick Tuten, Seattle, AFC	83	45.0	73
	Sean Landeta, St. Louis, NFC	83	44.3	63
1994	Sean Landeta, L.A. Rams, NFC	78	44.8	62
	Jeff Gossett, L.A. Raiders, AFC	77	43.9	65
1993	Greg Montgomery, Houston, AFC	54	45.6	77
	Jim Arnold, Detroit, NFC	72	44.5	68
1992	Greg Montgomery, Houston, AFC	53	46.9	66
	Harry Newsome, Minnesota, NFC	72	45.0	84
1991	Reggie Roby, Miami, AFC	54	45.7	64
	Harry Newsome, Minnesota, AFC	68	45.5	65
1990	Mike Horan, Denver, AFC	58	44.4	67
	Sean Landeta, N.Y. Giants, NFC	75	44.1	67
1989	Rich Camarillo, Phoenix, NFC	76	43.4	58
	Greg Montgomery, Houston, AFC	56	43.3	63
1988	Harry Newsome, Pittsburgh, AFC	65	45.4	62
	Jim Arnold, Detroit, NFC	97	42.4	69
1987	Rick Donnelly, Atlanta, NFC	61	44.0	62
	Ralf Mojsiejenko, San Diego, AFC	67	42.9	57
1986	Rohn Stark, Indianapolis, AFC	76	45.2	63
	Sean Landeta, N.Y. Giants, NFC	79	44.8	61
1985	Rohn Stark, Indianapolis, AFC	78	45.9	68
	*Rick Donnelly, Atlanta, NFC	59	43.6	68
1984	Jim Arnold, Kansas City, AFC	98	44.9	63
	*Brian Hansen, New Orleans, NFC	69	43.8	66
1983	Rohn Stark, Baltimore, AFC	91	45.3	68
	Frank Garcia, Tampa Bay, NFC	95	42.2	64
1982	Luke Prestridge, Denver, AFC	45	45.0	65
	Carl Birdsong, St. Louis, NFC	54	43.8	65
1981	Pat McInally, Cincinnati, AFC	72	45.4	62
	Tom Skladany, Detroit, NFC	64	43.5	74
1980	Dave Jennings, N.Y. Giants, NFC	94	44.8	63
	Luke Prestridge, Denver, AFC	70	43.9	57
1979	*Bob Grupp, Kansas City, AFC	89	43.6	74
	Dave Jennings, N.Y. Giants, NFC	104	42.7	72
1978	Pat McInally, Cincinnati, AFC	91	43.1	65
	*Tom Skladany, Detroit, NFC	86	42.5	63
1977	Ray Guy, Oakland, AFC	59	43.3	74
	Tom Blanchard, New Orleans, NFC	82	42.4	66
1976	Marv Bateman, Buffalo, AFC	86	42.8	78
	John James, Atlanta, NFC	101	42.1	67
1975	Ray Guy, Oakland, AFC	68	43.8	64
	Herman Weaver, Detroit, NFC	80	42.0	61
1974	Ray Guy, Oakland, AFC	74	42.2	66
	Tom Blanchard, New Orleans, NFC	88	42.1	71
1973	Jerrel Wilson, Kansas City, AFC	80	45.5	68
	*Tom Wittum, San Francisco, NFC	79	43.7	62
1972	Jerrel Wilson, Kansas City, AFC	66	44.8	69
	Dave Chapple, Los Angeles, NFC	53	44.2	70
1971	Dave Lewis, Cincinnati, AFC	72	44.8	56
	Tom McNeill, Philadelphia, NFC	73	42.0	64
1970	Dave Lewis, Cincinnati, AFC	79	46.2	63
	*Julian Fagan, New Orleans, NFC	77	42.5	64
1969	David Lee, Baltimore, NFL	57	45.3	66
	Dennis Partee, San Diego, AFL	71	44.6	62
1968	Jerrel Wilson, Kansas City, AFL	63	45.1	70
	Billy Lothridge, Atlanta, NFL	75	44.3	70
1967	Bob Scarpitto, Denver, AFL	105	44.9	73
	Billy Lothridge, Atlanta, NFL	87	43.7	62
1966	Bob Scarpitto, Denver, AFL	76	45.8	70
	*David Lee, Baltimore, NFL	49	45.6	64
1965	Gary Collins, Cleveland, NFL	65	46.7	71
	Jerrel Wilson, Kansas City, AFL	69	45.4	64
1964	Bobby Walden, Minnesota, NFL	72	46.4	73
	Jim Fraser, Denver, AFL	73	44.2	67
1963	Yale Lary, Detroit, NFL	35	48.9	73
	Jim Fraser, Denver, AFL	81	44.4	66
1962	Tommy Davis, San Francisco, NFL	48	45.6	82
	Jim Fraser, Denver, AFL	55	43.6	75
1961	Yale Lary, Detroit, NFL	52	48.4	71
	Billy Atkins, Buffalo, AFL	85	44.5	70
1960	Jerry Norton, St. Louis, NFL	39	45.6	62
	*Paul Maguire, L.A. Chargers, AFL	43	40.5	61
1959	Yale Lary, Detroit	45	47.1	67
1958	Sam Baker, Washington	48	45.4	64
1957	Don Chandler, N.Y. Giants	60	44.6	61
1956	Norm Van Brocklin, Los Angeles	48	43.1	72
1955	Norm Van Brocklin, Los Angeles	60	44.6	61
1954	Pat Brady, Pittsburgh	66	43.2	72
1953	Pat Brady, Pittsburgh	80	46.9	64
1952	Horace Gillom, Cleveland	61	45.7	73
1951	Horace Gillom, Cleveland	73	45.5	66
1950	*Fred (Curly) Morrison, Chi. Bears	57	43.3	65
1949	*Mike Boyda, N.Y. Bulldogs	56	44.2	61
1948	Joe Muha, Philadelphia	57	47.3	82
1947	Jack Jacobs, Green Bay	57	43.5	74
1946	Roy McKay, Green Bay	64	42.7	64
1945	Roy McKay, Green Bay	44	41.2	73
1944	Frank Sinkwich, Detroit	45	41.0	73
1943	Sammy Baugh, Washington	50	45.9	81
1942	Sammy Baugh, Washington	37	48.2	74
1941	Sammy Baugh, Washington	30	48.7	75
1940	Sammy Baugh, Washington	35	51.4	85
1939	*Parker Hall, Cleveland	58	40.8	80

*First season of professional football.

ANNUAL LEADERS IN SACKS (SINCE 1982)

Year	Player, Team	Sacks
2008	DeMarcus Ware, Dallas, NFC	20.0
	Joey Porter, Miami, AFC	17.5
2007	Jared Allen, Kansas City, AFC	15.5
	Patrick Kerney, Seattle, NFC	14.5

Year	Player, Team	Sacks
2006	Shawne Merriman, San Diego, AFC	17.0
	Aaron Kampman, Green Bay, NFC	15.5
2005	Derrick Burgess, Oakland, AFC	16.0
	Osi Umenyiora, N.Y. Giants, NFC	14.5
2004	Dwight Freeney, Indianapolis, AFC	16.0
	Bertrand Berry, Arizona, NFC	14.5
2003	Michael Strahan, N.Y. Giants, NFC	18.5
	Adewale Ogunleye, Miami, AFC	15.0
2002	Jason Taylor, Miami, AFC	18.5
	Simeon Rice, Tampa Bay, NFC	15.5
2001	Michael Strahan, N.Y. Giants, NFC	22.5
	Peter Boulware, Baltimore, AFC	15.0
2000	La'Roi Glover, New Orleans, NFC	17.0
	Trace Armstrong, Miami, AFC	16.5
1999	Kevin Carter, St. Louis, NFC	17.0
	*Jevon Kearse, Tennessee, AFC	14.5
1998	Michael Sinclair, Seattle, AFC	16.5
	Reggie White, Green Bay, NFC	16.0
1997	John Randle, Minnesota, NFC	15.5
	Bruce Smith, Buffalo, AFC	14.0
1996	Kevin Greene, Carolina, NFC	14.5
	Michael McCrary, Seattle, AFC	13.5
	Bruce Smith, Buffalo, AFC	13.5
1995	Bryce Paup, Buffalo, AFC	17.5
	William Fuller, Philadelphia, NFC	13.0
	Wayne Martin, New Orleans, NFC	13.0
1994	Kevin Greene, Pittsburgh, AFC	14.0
	Ken Harvey, Washington, NFC	13.5
	John Randle, Minnesota, NFC	13.5
1993	Neil Smith, Kansas City, AFC	15.0
	Renaldo Turnbull, New Orleans, NFC	13.0
	Reggie White, Green Bay, NFC	13.0
1992	Clyde Simmons, Philadelphia, NFC	19.0
	Leslie O'Neal, San Diego, AFC	17.0
1991	Pat Swilling, New Orleans, NFC	17.0
	William Fuller, Houston, AFC	15.0
1990	Derrick Thomas, Kansas City, AFC	20.0
	Charles Haley, San Francisco, NFC	16.0
1989	Chris Doleman, Minnesota, NFC	21.0
	Lee Williams, San Diego, AFC	14.0
1988	Reggie White, Philadelphia, NFC	18.0
	Greg Townsend, L.A. Raiders, AFC	11.5
1987	Reggie White, Philadelphia, NFC	21.0
	Andre Tippett, New England, AFC	12.5
1986	Lawrence Taylor, N.Y. Giants, NFC	20.5
	Sean Jones, L.A. Raiders, AFC	15.5
1985	Richard Dent, Chicago, NFC	17.0
	Andre Tippett, New England, AFC	16.5
1984	Mark Gastineau, N.Y. Jets, AFC	22.0
	Richard Dent, Chicago, NFC	17.5
1983	Mark Gastineau, N.Y. Jets, AFC	19.0
	Fred Dean, San Francisco, NFC	17.5
1982	Doug Martin, Minnesota, NFC	11.5
	Jesse Baker, Houston, AFC	7.5

First season of professional football.

POINTS SCORED

Year	Team	Points
2008	New Orleans, NFC	463
	San Diego, AFC	439
2007	New England, AFC	589
	Dallas, NFC	455
2006	San Diego, AFC	492
	Chicago, NFC	427
2005	Seattle, NFC	452
	Indianapolis, AFC	439
2004	Indianapolis, AFC	522
	Green Bay, NFC	424
2003	Kansas City, AFC	484
	St. Louis, NFC	447
2002	Kansas City, AFC	467
	New Orleans, NFC	432
2001	St. Louis, NFC	503
	Indianapolis, AFC	413
2000	St. Louis, NFC	540
	Denver, AFC	485
1999	St. Louis, NFC	526
	Indianapolis, AFC	423
1998	Minnesota, NFC	556
	Denver, AFC	501
1997	Denver, AFC	472
	Green Bay, NFC	422
1996	Green Bay, NFC	456
	New England, AFC	418
1995	San Francisco, NFC	457
	Pittsburgh, AFC	407
1994	San Francisco, NFC	505
	Miami, AFC	389
1993	San Francisco, NFC	473
	Denver, AFC	373
1992	San Francisco, NFC	431
	Buffalo, AFC	381
1991	Washington, NFC	485
	Buffalo, AFC	458
1990	Buffalo, AFC	428
	Philadelphia, NFC	396
1989	San Francisco, NFC	442
	Buffalo, AFC	409
1988	Cincinnati, AFC	448
	L.A. Rams, NFC	407
1987	San Francisco, NFC	459
	Cleveland, AFC	390
1986	Miami, AFC	430
	Minnesota, NFC	398
1985	San Diego, AFC	467
	Chicago, NFC	456
1984	Miami, AFC	513
	San Francisco, NFC	475
1983	Washington, NFC	541
	L.A. Raiders, AFC	442
1982	San Diego, AFC	288
	Dallas, NFC	226
	Green Bay, NFC	226
1981	San Diego, AFC	478
	Atlanta, NFC	426
1980	Dallas, NFC	454
	New England, AFC	441
1979	Pittsburgh, AFC	416
	Dallas, NFC	371
1978	Dallas, NFC	384
	Miami, AFC	372
1977	Oakland, AFC	351
	Dallas, NFC	345
1976	Baltimore, AFC	417
	Los Angeles, NFC	351
1975	Buffalo, AFC	420
	Minnesota, NFC	377
1974	Oakland, AFC	355
	Washington, NFC	320
1973	Los Angeles, NFC	388
	Denver, AFC	354
1972	Miami, AFC	385
	San Francisco, NFC	353
1971	Dallas, NFC	406
	Oakland, AFC	344
1970	San Francisco, NFC	352
	Baltimore, AFC	321

Year	Team	Points
1969	Minnesota, NFL	379
	Oakland, AFL	377
1968	Oakland, AFL	453
	Dallas, NFL	431
1967	Oakland, AFL	468
	Los Angeles, NFL	398
1966	Kansas City, AFL	448
	Dallas, NFL	445
1965	San Francisco, NFL	421
	San Diego, AFL	340
1964	Baltimore, NFL	428
	Buffalo, AFL	400
1963	N.Y. Giants, NFL	448
	San Diego, AFL	399
1962	Green Bay, NFL	415
	Dall. Texans, AFL	389
1961	Houston, AFL	513
	Green Bay, NFL	391
1960	N.Y. Titans, AFL	382
	Cleveland, NFL	362
1959	Baltimore	374
1958	Baltimore	381
1957	Los Angeles	307
1956	Chi. Bears	363
1955	Cleveland	349
1954	Detroit	337
1953	San Francisco	372
1952	Los Angeles	349
1951	Los Angeles	392
1950	Los Angeles	466
1949	Philadelphia	364
1948	Chi. Cardinals	395
1947	Chi. Bears	363
1946	Chi. Bears	289
1945	Philadelphia	272
1944	Philadelphia	267
1943	Chi. Bears	303
1942	Chi. Bears	376
1941	Chi. Bears	396
1940	Washington	245
1939	Chi. Bears	298
1938	Green Bay	223
1937	Green Bay	220
1936	Green Bay	248
1935	Chi. Bears	192
1934	Chi. Bears	286
1933	N.Y. Giants	244
1932	Chi. Bears	160

TOTAL YARDS GAINED

Year	Team	Yards
2008	New Orleans, NFC	6,571
	Denver, AFC	6,333
2007	New England, AFC	6,580
	Green Bay, NFC	5,931
2006	New Orleans, NFC	6,264
	Indianapolis, AFC	6,070
2005	Kansas City, AFC	6,192
	Seattle, NFC	5,915
2004	Kansas City, AFC	6,695
	Green Bay, NFC	6,357
2003	Minnesota, NFC	6,294
	Kansas City, AFC	5,910
2002	Oakland, AFC	6,237
	Minnesota, NFC	6,192
2001	St. Louis, NFC	6,690
	Indianapolis, AFC	5,955
2000	St. Louis, NFC	7,075
	Denver, AFC	6,554
1999	St. Louis, NFC	6,412
	Indianapolis, AFC	5,726
1998	San Francisco, NFC	6,800
	Denver, AFC	6,092
1997	Denver, AFC	5,872
	Detroit, NFC	5,798
1996	Denver, AFC	5,791
	Philadelphia, NFC	5,627
1995	Detroit, NFC	6,113
	Denver, AFC	6,040
1994	Miami, AFC	6,078
	San Francisco, NFC	6,060
1993	San Francisco, NFC	6,435
	Miami, AFC	5,812
1992	San Francisco, NFC	6,195
	Buffalo, AFC	5,893
1991	Buffalo, AFC	6,252
	San Francisco, NFC	5,858
1990	Houston, AFC	6,222
	San Francisco, NFC	5,895
1989	San Francisco, NFC	6,268
	Cincinnati, AFC	6,101
1988	Cincinnati, AFC	6,057
	San Francisco, NFC	5,900
1987	San Francisco, NFC	5,987
	Denver, AFC	5,624
1986	Cincinnati, AFC	6,490
	San Francisco, NFC	6,082
1985	San Diego, AFC	6,535
	San Francisco, NFC	5,920
1984	Miami, AFC	6,936
	San Francisco, NFC	6,366
1983	San Diego, AFC	6,197
	Green Bay, NFC	6,172
1982	San Diego, AFC	4,048
	San Francisco, NFC	3,242
1981	San Diego, AFC	6,744
	Detroit, NFC	5,933
1980	San Diego, AFC	6,410
	Los Angeles, NFC	6,006
1979	Pittsburgh, AFC	6,258
	Dallas, NFC	5,968
1978	New England, AFC	5,965
	Dallas, NFC	5,959
1977	Dallas, NFC	4,812
	Oakland, AFC	4,736
1976	Baltimore, AFC	5,236
	St. Louis, NFC	5,136
1975	Buffalo, AFC	5,467
	Dallas, NFC	5,025
1974	Dallas, NFC	4,983
	Oakland, AFC	4,718
1973	Los Angeles, NFC	4,906
	Oakland, AFC	4,773
1972	Miami, AFC	5,036
	N.Y. Giants, NFC	4,483
1971	Dallas, NFC	5,035
	San Diego, AFC	4,738
1970	Oakland, AFC	4,829
	San Francisco, NFC	4,503
1969	Dallas, NFL	5,122
	Oakland, AFL	5,036
1968	Oakland, AFL	5,696
	Dallas, NFL	5,117
1967	N.Y. Jets, AFL	5,152
	Baltimore, NFL	5,008
1966	Dallas, NFL	5,145
	Kansas City, AFL	5,114

YEARLY STATISTICAL LEADERS

Year	Team	Yards
1965	San Francisco, NFL	5,270
	San Diego, AFL	5,188
1964	Buffalo, AFL	5,206
	Baltimore, NFL	4,779
1963	San Diego, AFL	5,153
	N.Y. Giants, NFL	5,024
1962	N.Y. Giants, NFL	5,005
	Houston, AFL	4,971
1961	Houston, AFL	6,288
	Philadelphia, NFL	5,112
1960	Houston, AFL	4,936
	Baltimore, NFL	4,245
1959	Baltimore	4,458
1958	Baltimore	4,539
1957	Los Angeles	4,143
1956	Chi. Bears	4,537
1955	Chi. Bears	4,316
1954	Los Angeles	5,187
1953	Philadelphia	4,811
1952	Cleveland	4,352
1951	Los Angeles	5,506
1950	Los Angeles	5,420
1949	Chi. Bears	4,873
1948	Chi. Cardinals	4,705
1947	Chi. Bears	5,053
1946	Los Angeles	3,793
1945	Washington	3,549
1944	Chi. Bears	3,239
1943	Chi. Bears	4,045
1942	Chi. Bears	3,900
1941	Chi. Bears	4,265
1940	Green Bay	3,400
1939	Chi. Bears	3,988
1938	Green Bay	3,037
1937	Green Bay	3,201
1936	Detroit	3,703
1935	Chi. Bears	3,454
1934	Chi. Bears	3,900
1933	N.Y. Giants	2,973
1932	Chi. Bears	2,755

YARDS RUSHING

Year	Team	Yards
2008	N.Y. Giants, NFC	2,518
	Baltimore, AFC	2,376
2007	Minnesota, NFC	2,634
	Jacksonville, AFC	2,391
2006	Atlanta, NFC	2,939
	San Diego, AFC	2,578
2005	Atlanta, NFC	2,546
	Denver, AFC	2,539
2004	Atlanta, NFC	2,672
	Pittsburgh, AFC	2,464
2003	Baltimore, AFC	2,674
	Green Bay, NFC	2,558
2002	Minnesota, NFC	2,507
	Miami, AFC	2,502
2001	Pittsburgh, AFC	2,774
	San Francisco, NFC	2,244
2000	Oakland, AFC	2,470
	Minnesota, NFC	2,129
1999	San Francisco, NFC	2,095
	Jacksonville, AFC	2,091
1998	San Francisco, NFC	2,544
	Denver, AFC	2,468
1997	Pittsburgh, AFC	2,479
	Detroit, NFC	2,464
1996	Denver, AFC	2,362
	Washington, NFC	1,910
1995	Kansas City, AFC	2,222
	Dallas, NFC	2,201
1994	Pittsburgh, AFC	2,180
	Detroit, NFC	2,080
1993	N.Y. Giants, NFC	2,210
	Seattle, AFC	2,015
1992	Buffalo, AFC	2,436
	Philadelphia, NFC	2,388
1991	Buffalo, AFC	2,381
	Minnesota, NFC	2,201
1990	Philadelphia, NFC	2,556
	San Diego, AFC	2,257
1989	Cincinnati, AFC	2,483
	Chicago, NFC	2,287
1988	Cincinnati, AFC	2,710
	San Francisco, NFC	2,523
1987	San Francisco, NFC	2,237
	L.A. Raiders, AFC	2,197
1986	Chicago, NFC	2,700
	Cincinnati, AFC	2,533
1985	Chicago, NFC	2,761
	Indianapolis, AFC	2,439
1984	Chicago, NFC	2,974
	N.Y. Jets, AFC	2,189
1983	Chicago, NFC	2,727
	Baltimore, AFC	2,695
1982	Buffalo, AFC	1,371
	Dallas, NFC	1,313
1981	Detroit, NFC	2,795
	Kansas City, AFC	2,633
1980	Los Angeles, NFC	2,799
	Houston, AFC	2,635
1979	N.Y. Jets, AFC	2,646
	St. Louis, NFC	2,582
1978	New England, AFC	3,165
	Dallas, NFC	2,783
1977	Chicago, NFC	2,811
	Oakland, AFC	2,627
1976	Pittsburgh, AFC	2,971
	Los Angeles, NFC	2,528
1975	Buffalo, AFC	2,974
	Dallas, NFC	2,432
1974	Dallas, NFC	2,454
	Pittsburgh, AFC	2,417
1973	Buffalo, AFC	3,088
	Los Angeles, NFC	2,925
1972	Miami, AFC	2,960
	Chicago, NFC	2,360
1971	Miami, AFC	2,429
	Detroit, NFC	2,376
1970	Dallas, NFC	2,300
	Miami, AFC	2,082
1969	Dallas, NFL	2,276
	Kansas City, AFL	2,220
1968	Chicago, NFL	2,377
	Kansas City, AFL	2,227
1967	Cleveland, NFL	2,139
	Houston, AFL	2,122
1966	Kansas City, AFL	2,274
	Cleveland, NFL	2,166
1965	Cleveland, NFL	2,331
	San Diego, AFL	2,085
1964	Green Bay, NFL	2,276
	Buffalo, AFL	2,040
1963	Cleveland, NFL	2,639
	San Diego, AFL	2,203
1962	Buffalo, AFL	2,480
	Green Bay, NFL	2,460

Year	Team	Yards
1961	Green Bay, NFL	2,350
	Dall. Texans, AFL	2,189
1960	St. Louis, NFL	2,356
	Oakland, AFL	2,056
1959	Cleveland	2,149
1958	Cleveland	2,526
1957	Los Angeles	2,142
1956	Chi. Bears	2,468
1955	Chi. Bears	2,388
1954	San Francisco	2,498
1953	San Francisco	2,230
1952	San Francisco	1,905
1951	Chi. Bears	2,408
1950	N.Y. Giants	2,336
1949	Philadelphia	2,607
1948	Chi. Cardinals	2,560
1947	Los Angeles	2,171
1946	Green Bay	1,765
1945	Cleveland	1,714
1944	Philadelphia	1,661
1943	Phil-Pitt	1,730
1942	Chi. Bears	1,881
1941	Chi. Bears	2,263
1940	Chi. Bears	1,818
1939	Chi. Bears	2,043
1938	Detroit	1,893
1937	Detroit	2,074
1936	Detroit	2,885
1935	Chi. Bears	2,096
1934	Chi. Bears	2,847
1933	Boston	2,260
1932	Chi. Bears	1,770

YARDS PASSING

Leadership in this category has been based on net yards since 1952.

Year	Team	Yards
2008	New Orleans, NFC	4,977
	Denver, AFC	4,471
2007	New England, AFC	4,731
	Green Bay, NFC	4,334
2006	New Orleans, NFC	4,503
	Indianapolis, AFC	4,308
2005	Arizona, NFC	4,437
	New England, AFC	4,120
2004	Indianapolis, AFC	4,623
	Minnesota, NFC	4,516
2003	Indianapolis, AFC	4,179
	St. Louis, NFC	3,961
2002	Oakland, AFC	4,475
	St. Louis, NFC	4,154
2001	St. Louis, NFC	4,663
	Indianapolis, AFC	3,989
2000	St. Louis, NFC	5,232
	Indianapolis, AFC	4,282
1999	St. Louis, NFC	4,353
	Indianapolis, AFC	4,066
1998	Minnesota, NFC	4,328
	N.Y. Jets, AFC	3,836
1997	Seattle, AFC	3,959
	Green Bay, NFC	3,705
1996	Jacksonville, AFC	4,110
	Philadelphia, NFC	3,745
1995	San Francisco, NFC	4,608
	Miami, AFC	4,210
1994	New England, AFC	4,444
	Minnesota, NFC	4,324
1993	Miami, AFC	4,353
	San Francisco, NFC	4,302
1992	Houston, AFC	4,029
	San Francisco, NFC	3,880
1991	Houston, AFC	4,621
	San Francisco, NFC	3,997
1990	Houston, AFC	4,805
	San Francisco, NFC	4,177
1989	Washington, NFC	4,349
	Miami, AFC	4,216
1988	Miami, AFC	4,516
	Washington, NFC	4,136
1987	Miami, AFC	3,876
	San Francisco, NFC	3,750
1986	Miami, AFC	4,779
	San Francisco, NFC	4,096
1985	San Diego, AFC	4,870
	Dallas, NFC	3,861
1984	Miami, AFC	5,018
	St. Louis, NFC	4,257
1983	San Diego, AFC	4,661
	Green Bay, NFC	4,365
1982	San Diego, AFC	2,927
	San Francisco, NFC	2,502
1981	San Diego, AFC	4,739
	Minnesota, NFC	4,333
1980	San Diego, AFC	4,531
	Minnesota, NFC	3,688
1979	San Diego, AFC	3,915
	San Francisco, NFC	3,641
1978	San Diego, AFC	3,375
	Minnesota, NFC	3,243
1977	Buffalo, AFC	2,530
	St. Louis, NFC	2,499
1976	Baltimore, AFC	2,933
	Minnesota, NFC	2,855
1975	Cincinnati, AFC	3,241
	Washington, NFC	2,917
1974	Washington, NFC	2,978
	Cincinnati, AFC	2,804
1973	Philadelphia, NFC	2,998
	Denver, AFC	2,519
1972	N.Y. Jets, AFC	2,777
	San Francisco, NFC	2,735
1971	San Diego, AFC	3,134
	Dallas, NFC	2,786
1970	San Francisco, NFC	2,923
	Oakland, AFC	2,865
1969	Oakland, AFL	3,271
	San Francisco, NFL	3,158
1968	San Diego, AFL	3,623
	Dallas, NFL	3,026
1967	N.Y. Jets, AFL	3,845
	Washington, NFL	3,730
1966	N.Y. Jets, AFL	3,464
	Dallas, NFL	3,023
1965	San Francisco, NFL	3,487
	San Diego, AFL	3,103
1964	Houston, AFL	3,527
	Chicago, NFL	2,841
1963	Baltimore, NFL	3,296
	Houston, AFL	3,222
1962	Denver, AFL	3,404
	Philadelphia, NFL	3,385
1961	Houston, AFL	4,392
	Philadelphia, NFL	3,605
1960	Houston, AFL	3,203
	Baltimore, NFL	2,956
1959	Baltimore	2,753
1958	Pittsburgh	2,752
1957	Baltimore	2,388

Year	Team	Yards
1956	Los Angeles	2,419
1955	Philadelphia	2,472
1954	Chi. Bears	3,104
1953	Philadelphia	3,089
1952	Cleveland	2,566
1951	Los Angeles	3,296
1950	Los Angeles	3,709
1949	Chi. Bears	3,055
1948	Washington	2,861
1947	Washington	3,336
1946	Los Angeles	2,080
1945	Chi. Bears	1,857
1944	Washington	2,021
1943	Chi. Bears	2,310
1942	Green Bay	2,407
1941	Chi. Bears	2,002
1940	Washington	1,887
1939	Chi. Bears	1,965
1938	Washington	1,536
1937	Green Bay	1,398
1936	Green Bay	1,629
1935	Green Bay	1,449
1934	Green Bay	1,165
1933	N.Y. Giants	1,348
1932	Chi. Bears	1,013

FEWEST POINTS ALLOWED

Year	Team	Points
2008	Pittsburgh, AFC	223
	Philadelphia, NFC	289
2007	Indianapolis, AFC	262
	Tampa Bay, NFC	270
2006	Baltimore, AFC	201
	Chicago, NFC	255
2005	Chicago, NFC	202
	Indianapolis, AFC	247
2004	Pittsburgh, AFC	251
	Philadelphia, NFC	260
2003	New England, AFC	238
	Dallas, NFC	260
2002	Tampa Bay, NFC	196
	Miami, AFC	301
2001	Chicago, NFC	203
	Pittsburgh, AFC	212
2000	Baltimore, AFC	165
	Philadelphia, NFC	245
1999	Jacksonville, AFC	217
	Tampa Bay, NFC	235
1998	Miami, AFC	265
	Dallas, NFC	275
1997	Kansas City, AFC	232
	Tampa Bay, NFC	263
1996	Green Bay, NFC	210
	Pittsburgh, AFC	257
1995	Kansas City, AFC	241
	San Francisco, NFC	258
1994	Cleveland, AFC	204
	Dallas, NFC	248
1993	N.Y. Giants, NFC	205
	Houston, AFC	238
1992	New Orleans, NFC	202
	Pittsburgh, AFC	225
1991	New Orleans, NFC	211
	Denver, AFC	235
1990	N.Y. Giants, NFC	211
	Pittsburgh, AFC	240
1989	Denver, AFC	226
	N.Y. Giants, NFC	252
1988	Chicago, NFC	215
	Buffalo, AFC	237
1987	Indianapolis, AFC	238
	San Francisco, NFC	253
1986	Chicago, NFC	187
	Seattle, AFC	293
1985	Chicago, NFC	198
	N.Y. Jets, AFC	264
1984	San Francisco, NFC	227
	Denver, AFC	241
1983	Miami, AFC	250
	Detroit, NFC	286
1982	Washington, NFC	128
	Miami, AFC	131
1981	Philadelphia, NFC	221
	Miami, AFC	275
1980	Philadelphia, NFC	222
	Houston, AFC	251
1979	Tampa Bay, NFC	237
	San Diego, AFC	246
1978	Pittsburgh, AFC	195
	Dallas, NFC	208
1977	Atlanta, NFC	129
	Denver, AFC	148
1976	Pittsburgh, AFC	138
	Minnesota, NFC	176
1975	Los Angeles, NFC	135
	Pittsburgh, AFC	162
1974	Los Angeles, NFC	181
	Pittsburgh, AFC	189
1973	Miami, AFC	150
	Minnesota, NFC	168
1972	Miami, AFC	171
	Washington, NFC	218
1971	Minnesota, NFC	139
	Baltimore, AFC	140
1970	Minnesota, NFC	143
	Miami, AFC	228
1969	Minnesota, NFL	133
	Kansas City, AFL	177
1968	Baltimore, NFL	144
	Kansas City, AFL	170
1967	Los Angeles, NFL	196
	Houston, AFL	199
1966	Green Bay, NFL	163
	Buffalo, AFL	255
1965	Green Bay, NFL	224
	Buffalo, AFL	226
1964	Baltimore, NFL	225
	Buffalo, AFL	242
1963	Chicago, NFL	144
	San Diego, AFL	255
1962	Green Bay, NFL	148
	Dall. Texans, AFL	233
1961	San Diego, AFL	219
	N.Y. Giants, NFL	220
1960	San Francisco, NFL	205
	Dall. Texans, AFL	253
1959	N.Y. Giants	170
1958	N.Y. Giants	183
1957	Cleveland	172
1956	Cleveland	177
1955	Cleveland	218
1954	Cleveland	162
1953	Cleveland	162
1952	Detroit	192
1951	Cleveland	152
1950	Philadelphia	141
1949	Philadelphia	134

Year	Team	Yards
1948	Chi. Bears	151
1947	Green Bay	210
1946	Pittsburgh	117
1945	Washington	121
1944	N.Y. Giants	75
1943	Washington	137
1942	Chi. Bears	84
1941	N.Y. Giants	114
1940	Brooklyn	120
1939	N.Y. Giants	85
1938	N.Y. Giants	79
1937	Chi. Bears	100
1936	Chi. Bears	94
1935	Green Bay	96
	N.Y. Giants	96
1934	Detroit	59
1933	Brooklyn	54
1932	Chi. Bears	44

FEWEST TOTAL YARDS ALLOWED

Year	Team	Yards
2008	Pittsburgh, AFC	3,795
	Philadelphia, NFC	4,389
2007	Pittsburgh, AFC	4,262
	Tampa Bay, NFC	4,454
2006	Baltimore, AFC	4,225
	Chicago, NFC	4,706
2005	Tampa Bay, NFC	4,444
	Pittsburgh, AFC	4,544
2004	Pittsburgh, AFC	4,134
	Washington, NFC	4,281
2003	Dallas, NFC	4,056
	Buffalo, AFC	4,313
2002	Tampa Bay, NFC	4,044
	Miami, AFC	4,656
2001	Pittsburgh, AFC	4,137
	St. Louis, NFC	4,471
2000	Tennessee, AFC	3,813
	Washington, NFC	4,474
1999	Buffalo, AFC	4,045
	Tampa Bay, NFC	4,280
1998	San Diego, AFC	4,208
	Tampa Bay, NFC	4,345
1997	San Francisco, NFC	4,013
	Denver, AFC	4,671
1996	Green Bay, NFC	4,156
	Pittsburgh, AFC	4,362
1995	San Francisco, NFC	4,398
	Kansas City, AFC	4,549
1994	Dallas, NFC	4,313
	Pittsburgh, AFC	4,326
1993	Minnesota, NFC	4,406
	Pittsburgh, AFC	4,531
1992	Dallas, NFC	3,931
	Houston, AFC	4,211
1991	Philadelphia, NFC	3,549
	Denver, AFC	4,549
1990	Pittsburgh, AFC	4,115
	N.Y. Giants, NFC	4,206
1989	Minnesota, NFC	4,184
	Kansas City, AFC	4,293
1988	Minnesota, NFC	4,091
	Buffalo, AFC	4,578
1987	San Francisco, NFC	4,095
	Cleveland, AFC	4,264
1986	Chicago, NFC	4,130
	L.A. Raiders, AFC	4,804
1985	Chicago, NFC	4,135
	L.A. Raiders, AFC	4,603
1984	Chicago, NFC	3,863
	Cleveland, AFC	4,641
1983	Cincinnati, AFC	4,327
	New Orleans, NFC	4,691
1982	Miami, AFC	2,312
	Tampa Bay, NFC	2,442
1981	Philadelphia, NFC	4,447
	N.Y. Jets, AFC	4,871
1980	Buffalo, AFC	4,101
	Philadelphia, NFC	4,443
1979	Tampa Bay, NFC	3,949
	Pittsburgh, AFC	4,270
1978	Los Angeles, NFC	3,893
	Pittsburgh, AFC	4,168
1977	Dallas, NFC	3,213
	New England, AFC	3,638
1976	Pittsburgh, AFC	3,323
	San Francisco, NFC	3,562
1975	Minnesota, NFC	3,153
	Oakland, AFC	3,629
1974	Pittsburgh, AFC	3,074
	Washington, NFC	3,285
1973	Los Angeles, NFC	2,951
	Oakland, AFC	3,160
1972	Miami, AFC	3,297
	Green Bay, NFC	3,474
1971	Baltimore, AFC	2,852
	Minnesota, NFC	3,406
1970	Minnesota, NFC	2,803
	N.Y. Jets, AFC	3,655
1969	Minnesota, NFL	2,720
	Kansas City, AFL	3,163
1968	Los Angeles, NFL	3,118
	N.Y. Jets, AFL	3,363
1967	Oakland, AFL	3,294
	Green Bay, NFL	3,300
1966	St. Louis, NFL	3,492
	Oakland, AFL	3,910
1965	San Diego, AFL	3,262
	Detroit, NFL	3,557
1964	Green Bay, NFL	3,179
	Buffalo, AFL	3,878
1963	Chicago, NFL	3,176
	Boston, AFL	3,834
1962	Detroit, NFL	3,217
	Dall. Texans, AFL	3,951
1961	San Diego, AFL	3,726
	Baltimore, NFL	3,782
1960	St. Louis, NFL	3,029
	Buffalo, AFL	3,866
1959	N.Y. Giants	2,843
1958	Chi. Bears	3,066
1957	Pittsburgh	2,791
1956	N.Y. Giants	3,081
1955	Cleveland	2,841
1954	Cleveland	2,658
1953	Philadelphia	2,998
1952	Cleveland	3,075
1951	N.Y. Giants	3,250
1950	Cleveland	3,154
1949	Philadelphia	2,831
1948	Chi. Bears	2,931
1947	Green Bay	3,396
1946	Washington	2,451
1945	Philadelphia	2,073
1944	Philadelphia	1,943
1943	Chi. Bears	2,262
1942	Chi. Bears	1,703
1941	N.Y. Giants	2,368

Year	Team	Yards
1940	N.Y. Giants	2,219
1939	Washington	2,116
1938	N.Y. Giants	2,029
1937	Washington	2,123
1936	Boston	2,181
1935	Boston	1,996
1934	Chi. Cardinals	1,539
1933	Brooklyn	1,789

FEWEST RUSHING YARDS ALLOWED

Year	Team	Yards
2008	Minnesota, NFC	1,230
	Pittsburgh, AFC	1,284
2007	Minnesota, NFC	1,185
	Baltimore, AFC	1,268
2006	Minnesota, NFC	985
	Baltimore, AFC	1,214
2005	San Diego, AFC	1,349
	Carolina, NFC	1,465
2004	Pittsburgh, AFC	1,299
	Washington, NFC	1,304
2003	Tennessee, AFC	1,295
	Dallas, NFC	1,425
2002	Pittsburgh, AFC	1,375
	Tampa Bay, NFC	1,554
2001	Pittsburgh, AFC	1,195
	Chicago, NFC	1,313
2000	Baltimore, AFC	970
	N.Y. Giants, NFC	1,156
1999	St. Louis, NFC	1,189
	Baltimore, AFC	1,231
1998	San Diego, AFC	1,140
	Atlanta, NFC	1,203
1997	Pittsburgh, AFC	1,318
	San Francisco, NFC	1,366
1996	Denver, AFC	1,331
	Green Bay, NFC	1,416
1995	San Francisco, NFC	1,061
	Pittsburgh, AFC	1,321
1994	Minnesota, NFC	1,090
	San Diego, AFC	1,404
1993	Houston, AFC	1,273
	Minnesota, NFC	1,536
1992	Dallas, NFC	1,244
	Buffalo, AFC	1,395
	San Diego, AFC	1,395
1991	Philadelphia, NFC	1,136
	N.Y. Jets, AFC	1,442
1990	Philadelphia, NFC	1,169
	San Diego, AFC	1,515
1989	New Orleans, NFC	1,326
	Denver, AFC	1,580
1988	Chicago, NFC	1,326
	Houston, AFC	1,592
1987	Chicago, NFC	1,413
	Cleveland, AFC	1,433
1986	N.Y. Giants, NFC	1,284
	Denver, AFC	1,651
1985	Chicago, NFC	1,319
	N.Y. Jets, AFC	1,516
1984	Chicago, NFC	1,377
	Pittsburgh, AFC	1,617
1983	Washington, NFC	1,289
	Cincinnati, AFC	1,499
1982	Pittsburgh, AFC	762
	Detroit, NFC	854
1981	Detroit, NFC	1,623
	Kansas City, AFC	1,747

Year	Team	Yards
1980	Detroit, NFC	1,599
	Cincinnati, AFC	1,680
1979	Denver, AFC	1,693
	Tampa Bay, NFC	1,873
1978	Dallas, NFC	1,721
	Pittsburgh, AFC	1,774
1977	Denver, AFC	1,531
	Dallas, NFC	1,651
1976	Pittsburgh, AFC	1,457
	Los Angeles, NFC	1,564
1975	Minnesota, NFC	1,532
	Houston, AFC	1,680
1974	Los Angeles, NFC	1,302
	New England, AFC	1,587
1973	Los Angeles, NFC	1,270
	Oakland, AFC	1,470
1972	Dallas, NFC	1,515
	Miami, AFC	1,548
1971	Baltimore, AFC	1,113
	Dallas, NFC	1,144
1970	Detroit, NFC	1,152
	N.Y. Jets, AFC	1,283
1969	Dallas, NFL	1,050
	Kansas City, AFL	1,091
1968	Dallas, NFL	1,195
	N.Y. Jets, AFL	1,195
1967	Dallas, NFL	1,081
	Oakland, AFL	1,129
1966	Buffalo, AFL	1,051
	Dallas, NFL	1,176
1965	San Diego, AFL	1,094
	Los Angeles, NFL	1,409
1964	Buffalo, AFL	913
	Los Angeles, NFL	1,501
1963	Boston, AFL	1,107
	Chicago, NFL	1,442
1962	Detroit, NFL	1,231
	Dall. Texans, AFL	1,250
1961	Boston, AFL	1,041
	Pittsburgh, NFL	1,463
1960	St. Louis, NFL	1,212
	Dall. Texans, AFL	1,338
1959	N.Y. Giants	1,261
1958	Baltimore	1,291
1957	Baltimore	1,174
1956	N.Y. Giants	1,443
1955	Cleveland	1,189
1954	Cleveland	1,050
1953	Philadelphia	1,117
1952	Detroit	1,145
1951	N.Y. Giants	913
1950	Detroit	1,367
1949	Chi. Bears	1,196
1948	Philadelphia	1,209
1947	Philadelphia	1,329
1946	Chi. Bears	1,060
1945	Philadelphia	817
1944	Philadelphia	558
1943	Phil-Pitt	793
1942	Chi. Bears	519
1941	Washington	1,042
1940	N.Y. Giants	977
1939	Chi. Bears	812
1938	Detroit	1,081
1937	Chi. Bears	933
1936	Boston	1,148
1935	Boston	998
1934	Chi. Cardinals	954
1933	Brooklyn	964

FEWEST PASSING YARDS ALLOWED

Leadership in this category has been based on net yards since 1952.

Year	Team	Yards
2008	Pittsburgh, AFC	2,511
	Philadelphia, NFC	2,913
2007	Tampa Bay, NFC	2,728
	Indianapolis, AFC	2,764
2006	Oakland, AFC	2,413
	New Orleans, NFC	2,854
2005	Green Bay, NFC	2,680
	N.Y. Jets, AFC	2,755
2004	Tampa Bay, NFC	2,579
	Miami, AFC	2,592
2003	Dallas, NFC	2,631
	Buffalo, AFC	2,707
2002	Tampa Bay, NFC	2,490
	Indianapolis, AFC	2,917
2001	Miami, AFC	2,829
	Philadelphia, NFC	2,864
2000	Tennessee, AFC	2,423
	Washington, NFC	2,621
1999	Buffalo, AFC	2,675
	Tampa Bay, NFC	2,873
1998	Philadelphia, NFC	2,720
	Oakland, AFC	2,876
1997	Dallas, NFC	2,522
	Indianapolis, AFC	2,820
1996	Green Bay, NFC	2,740
	Pittsburgh, AFC	2,947
1995	N.Y. Jets, AFC	2,740
	Philadelphia, NFC	2,816
1994	Dallas, NFC	2,752
	Houston, AFC	2,795
1993	New Orleans, NFC	2,606
	Cincinnati, AFC	2,798
1992	New Orleans, NFC	2,470
	Kansas City, AFC	2,537
1991	Philadelphia, NFC	2,413
	Denver, AFC	2,755
1990	Pittsburgh, AFC	2,500
	Dallas, NFC	2,639
1989	Minnesota, NFC	2,501
	Kansas City, AFC	2,527
1988	Kansas City, AFC	2,434
	Minnesota, NFC	2,489
1987	San Francisco, NFC	2,484
	L.A. Raiders, AFC	2,727
1986	St. Louis, NFC	2,637
	New England, AFC	2,978
1985	Washington, NFC	2,746
	Pittsburgh, AFC	2,783
1984	New Orleans, NFC	2,453
	Cleveland, AFC	2,696
1983	New Orleans, NFC	2,691
	Cincinnati, AFC	2,828
1982	Miami, AFC	1,027
	Tampa Bay, NFC	1,384
1981	Philadelphia, NFC	2,696
	Buffalo, AFC	2,870
1980	Washington, NFC	2,171
	Buffalo, AFC	2,282
1979	Tampa Bay, NFC	2,076
	Buffalo, AFC	2,530
1978	Buffalo, AFC	1,960
	Los Angeles, NFC	2,048
1977	Atlanta, NFC	1,384
	San Diego, AFC	1,725
1976	Minnesota, NFC	1,575
	Cincinnati, AFC	1,758
1975	Minnesota, NFC	1,621
	Cincinnati, AFC	1,729
1974	Pittsburgh, AFC	1,466
	Atlanta, NFC	1,572
1973	Miami, AFC	1,290
	Atlanta, NFC	1,430
1972	Minnesota, NFC	1,699
	Cleveland, AFC	1,736
1971	Atlanta, NFC	1,638
	Baltimore, AFC	1,739
1970	Minnesota, NFC	1,438
	Kansas City, AFC	2,010
1969	Minnesota, NFL	1,631
	Kansas City, AFL	2,072
1968	Houston, AFL	1,671
	Green Bay, NFL	1,796
1967	Green Bay, NFL	1,377
	Buffalo, AFL	1,825
1966	Green Bay, NFL	1,959
	Oakland, AFL	2,118
1965	Green Bay, NFL	1,981
	San Diego, AFL	2,168
1964	Green Bay, NFL	1,647
	San Diego, AFL	2,518
1963	Chicago, NFL	1,734
	Oakland, AFL	2,589
1962	Green Bay, NFL	1,746
	Oakland, AFL	2,306
1961	Baltimore, NFL	1,913
	San Diego, AFL	2,363
1960	Chicago, NFL	1,388
	Buffalo, AFL	2,124
1959	N.Y. Giants	1,582
1958	Chi. Bears	1,769
1957	Cleveland	1,300
1956	Cleveland	1,103
1955	Pittsburgh	1,295
1954	Cleveland	1,608
1953	Washington	1,751
1952	Washington	1,580
1951	Pittsburgh	1,687
1950	Cleveland	1,581
1949	Philadelphia	1,607
1948	Green Bay	1,626
1947	Green Bay	1,790
1946	Pittsburgh	939
1945	Washington	1,121
1944	Chi. Bears	1,052
1943	Chi. Bears	980
1942	Washington	1,093
1941	Pittsburgh	1,168
1940	Philadelphia	1,012
1939	Washington	1,116
1938	Chi. Bears	897
1937	Detroit	804
1936	Philadelphia	853
1935	Chi. Cardinals	793
1934	Philadelphia	545
1933	Portsmouth	558

OUTSTANDING PERFORMERS

1,000 YARDS RUSHING IN A SEASON

Year	Player, Team	Att.	Yards	Avg.	Long	TD
2008	Adrian Peterson, Minnesota[2]	363	1,760	4.9	67	10
	Michael Turner, Atlanta	376	1,699	4.5	70	17
	DeAngelo Williams, Carolina	273	1,515	5.6	69	18
	Clinton Portis, Washington[6]	342	1,487	4.4	31	9
	Thomas Jones, N.Y. Jets[4]	290	1,312	4.5	59	13
	*Steve Slaton, Houston	268	1,282	4.8	71	9
	*Matt Forté, Chicago	316	1,238	3.9	50	8
	*Chris Johnson, Tennessee	251	1,228	4.9	66	9
	Ryan Grant, Green Bay	312	1,203	3.9	57	4
	LaDainian Tomlinson, San Diego[8]	292	1,110	3.8	45	11
	Brandon Jacobs, N.Y. Giants[2]	219	1,089	5.0	44	15
	Steven Jackson, St. Louis[4]	253	1,042	4.1	56	7
	Frank Gore, San Francisco[3]	240	1,036	4.3	41	6
	Marshawn Lynch, Buffalo[2]	250	1,036	4.1	50	8
	Derrick Ward, N.Y. Giants	182	1,025	5.6	51	2
	Jamal Lewis, Cleveland[7]	279	1,002	3.6	29	4
2007	LaDainian Tomlinson, San Diego[7]	315	1,474	4.7	49	15
	*Adrian Peterson, Minnesota	238	1,341	5.6	73	12
	Brian Westbrook, Philadelphia[2]	278	1,333	4.8	36	7
	Willie Parker, Pittsburgh[3]	321	1,316	4.1	32	2
	Jamal Lewis, Cleveland[6]	298	1,304	4.4	66	9
	Clinton Portis, Washington[5]	325	1,262	3.9	32	11
	Edgerrin James, Arizona[7]	324	1,222	3.8	27	7
	Willis McGahee, Baltimore[3]	294	1,207	4.1	46	7
	Fred Taylor, Jacksonville[7]	223	1,202	5.4	80	5
	Thomas Jones, N.Y. Jets[3]	310	1,119	3.6	36	1
	*Marshawn Lynch, Buffalo	280	1,115	4.0	56	7
	LenDale White, Tennessee	303	1,110	3.7	28	7
	Frank Gore, San Francisco[2]	260	1,102	4.2	43	5
	Joseph Addai, Indianapolis[2]	261	1,072	4.1	23	12
	Justin Fargas, Oakland	222	1,009	4.6	48	4
	Brandon Jacobs, N.Y. Giants	202	1,009	5.0	43	4
	Steven Jackson, St. Louis[3]	237	1,002	4.2	54	5
2006	LaDainian Tomlinson, San Diego[6]	348	1,815	5.2	85	28
	Larry Johnson, Kansas City[2]	416	1,789	4.3	47	17
	Frank Gore, San Francisco	312	1,695	5.4	72	8
	Tiki Barber, N.Y. Giants[6]	327	1,662	5.1	55	5
	Steven Jackson, St. Louis[2]	346	1,528	4.4	59	13
	Willie Parker, Pittsburgh[2]	337	1,494	4.4	76	13
	Rudi Johnson, Cincinnati[3]	341	1,309	3.8	22	12
	Brian Westbrook, Philadelphia	240	1,217	5.1	71	7
	Chester Taylor, Minnesota	303	1,216	4.0	95	6
	Travis Henry, Tennessee[3]	270	1,211	4.5	70	7
	Thomas Jones, Chicago[2]	296	1,210	4.1	30	6
	Edgerrin James, Arizona[6]	337	1,159	3.4	18	6
	Ladell Betts, Washington	245	1,154	4.7	26	4
	Fred Taylor, Jacksonville[6]	231	1,146	5.0	76	5
	Warrick Dunn, Atlanta[5]	286	1,140	4.0	90	4
	Jamal Lewis, Baltimore[5]	314	1,132	3.6	52	9
	Julius Jones, Dallas	267	1,084	4.1	77	4
	*Joseph Addai, Indianapolis	226	1,081	4.8	41	7
	Ahman Green, Green Bay[6]	266	1,059	4.0	70	5
	Deuce McAllister, New Orleans[4]	244	1,057	4.3	57	10
	Michael Vick, Atlanta	123	1,039	8.5	51	2
	Tatum Bell, Denver	233	1,025	4.4	51	2
	Ronnie Brown, Miami	241	1,008	4.2	47	5
2005	Shaun Alexander, Seattle[5]	370	1,880	5.1	88	27
	Tiki Barber, N.Y. Giants[5]	357	1,860	5.2	95	9
	Larry Johnson, Kansas City	336	1,750	5.2	49	20
	Clinton Portis, Washington[4]	352	1,516	4.3	47	11
	Edgerrin James, Indianapolis[5]	360	1,506	4.2	33	13
	LaDainian Tomlinson, San Diego[5]	339	1,462	4.3	62	18
	Rudi Johnson, Cincinnati[2]	337	1,458	4.3	33	12
	Warrick Dunn, Atlanta[4]	280	1,416	5.1	65	3
	Thomas Jones, Chicago	314	1,335	4.3	42	9
	Willis McGahee, Buffalo[2]	325	1,247	3.8	27	5
	Reuben Droughns, Cleveland[2]	309	1,232	4.0	75	2
	Willie Parker, Pittsburgh	255	1,202	4.7	80	4

Year	Player, Team	Att.	Yards	Avg.	Long	TD
	*Carnell Williams, Tampa Bay	290	1,178	4.1	71	6
	Steven Jackson, St. Louis	254	1,046	4.1	51	8
	LaMont Jordan, Oakland	272	1,025	3.8	26	9
	Mike Anderson, Denver[2]	239	1,014	4.2	44	12
2004	Curtis Martin, N.Y. Jets[10]	371	1,697	4.6	25	12
	Shaun Alexander, Seattle[4]	353	1,696	4.8	44	16
	Corey Dillon, New England[7]	345	1,635	4.7	44	12
	Edgerrin James, Indianapolis[4]	334	1,548	4.6	40	9
	Tiki Barber, N.Y. Giants[4]	322	1,518	4.7	72	13
	Rudi Johnson, Cincinnati	361	1,454	4.0	52	12
	LaDainian Tomlinson, San Diego[4]	339	1,335	3.9	42	17
	Clinton Portis, Washington[3]	343	1,315	3.8	64	5
	Reuben Droughns, Denver	275	1,240	4.5	51	6
	Fred Taylor, Jacksonville[5]	260	1,224	4.7	46	2
	Domanick Davis, Houston[2]	302	1,188	3.9	44	13
	Ahman Green, Green Bay[5]	259	1,163	4.5	90	7
	*Kevin Jones, Detroit	241	1,133	4.7	74	5
	Willis McGahee, Buffalo	284	1,128	4.0	41	13
	Warrick Dunn, Atlanta[3]	265	1,106	4.2	60	9
	Deuce McAllister, New Orleans[3]	269	1,074	4.0	71	9
	Chris Brown, Tennessee	220	1,067	4.9	52	6
	Jamal Lewis, Baltimore[4]	235	1,006	4.3	75	7
2003	Jamal Lewis, Baltimore[3]	387	2,066	5.3	82	14
	Ahman Green, Green Bay[4]	355	1,883	5.3	98	15
	LaDainian Tomlinson, San Diego[3]	313	1,645	5.3	73	13
	Deuce McAllister, New Orleans[2]	351	1,641	4.7	76	8
	Clinton Portis, Denver[2]	290	1,591	5.5	65	14
	Fred Taylor, Jacksonville[4]	345	1,572	4.6	62	6
	Stephen Davis, Carolina[4]	318	1,444	4.5	40	8
	Shaun Alexander, Seattle[3]	326	1,435	4.4	55	14
	Priest Holmes, Kansas City[4]	320	1,420	4.4	31	27
	Ricky Williams, Miami[4]	392	1,372	3.5	45	9
	Travis Henry, Buffalo[2]	331	1,356	4.1	64	10
	Curtis Martin, N.Y. Jets[9]	323	1,308	4.1	56	2
	Edgerrin James, Indianapolis[3]	310	1,259	4.1	43	11
	Tiki Barber, N.Y. Giants[3]	278	1,216	4.4	27	2
	*Domanick Davis, Houston	238	1,031	4.3	51	8
	Eddie George, Tennessee[7]	312	1,031	3.3	27	5
	Kevan Barlow, San Francisco	201	1,024	5.1	78	6
	Anthony Thomas, Chicago[2]	244	1,024	4.2	67	6
2002	Ricky Williams, Miami[3]	383	1,853	4.8	63	16
	LaDainian Tomlinson, San Diego[2]	372	1,683	4.5	76	14
	Priest Holmes, Kansas City[3]	313	1,615	5.2	56	21
	*Clinton Portis, Denver	273	1,508	5.5	59	15
	Travis Henry, Buffalo	325	1,438	4.4	34	13
	Deuce McAllister, New Orleans	325	1,388	4.3	62	13
	Tiki Barber, N.Y. Giants[2]	304	1,387	4.6	70	11
	Jamal Lewis, Baltimore[2]	308	1,327	4.3	75	6
	Fred Taylor, Jacksonville[3]	287	1,314	4.6	63	8
	Corey Dillon, Cincinnati[6]	314	1,311	4.2	67	7
	Michael Bennett, Minnesota	255	1,296	5.1	85	5
	Ahman Green, Green Bay[3]	286	1,240	4.3	43	7
	Shaun Alexander, Seattle[2]	295	1,175	4.0	58	16
	Eddie George, Tennessee[6]	343	1,165	3.4	35	12
	Curtis Martin, N.Y. Jets[8]	261	1,094	4.2	35	7
	Duce Staley, Philadelphia[3]	269	1,029	3.8	57	5
	James Stewart, Detroit[2]	231	1,021	4.4	56	4
2001	Priest Holmes, Kansas City[2]	327	1,555	4.8	41	8
	Curtis Martin, N.Y. Jets[7]	333	1,513	4.5	47	10
	Stephen Davis, Washington[3]	356	1,432	4.0	32	5
	Ahman Green, Green Bay[2]	304	1,387	4.6	83	9
	Marshall Faulk, St. Louis[7]	260	1,382	5.3	71	12
	Shaun Alexander, Seattle	309	1,318	4.3	88	14
	Corey Dillon, Cincinnati[5]	340	1,315	3.9	96	10
	Ricky Williams, New Orleans[2]	313	1,245	4.0	46	6
	*LaDainian Tomlinson, San Diego	339	1,236	3.6	54	10
	Garrison Hearst, San Francisco[4]	252	1,206	4.8	43	4
	*Anthony Thomas, Chicago	278	1,183	4.3	46	7
	Antowain Smith, New England[2]	287	1,157	4.0	44	12

Year	Player, Team	Att.	Yards	Avg.	Long	TD
	*Dominic Rhodes, Indianapolis	233	1,104	4.7	77	9
	Jerome Bettis, Pittsburgh[8]	225	1,072	4.8	48	4
	Emmitt Smith, Dallas[11]	261	1,021	3.9	44	3
2000	Edgerrin James, Indianapolis[2]	387	1,709	4.4	30	13
	Robert Smith, Minnesota[4]	295	1,521	5.2	72	7
	Eddie George, Tennessee[5]	403	1,509	3.7	35	14
	*Mike Anderson, Denver	297	1,487	5.0	80	15
	Corey Dillon, Cincinnati[4]	315	1,435	4.6	80	7
	Fred Taylor, Jacksonville[2]	292	1,399	4.8	71	12
	*Jamal Lewis, Baltimore	309	1,364	4.4	45	6
	Marshall Faulk, St. Louis[6]	253	1,359	5.4	36	18
	Jerome Bettis, Pittsburgh[7]	355	1,341	3.8	30	8
	Stephen Davis, Washington[2]	332	1,318	4.0	50	11
	Ricky Watters, Seattle[7]	278	1,242	4.5	55	7
	Curtis Martin, N.Y. Jets[6]	316	1,204	3.8	55	9
	Emmitt Smith, Dallas[10]	294	1,203	4.1	52	9
	James Stewart, Detroit	339	1,184	3.5	34	10
	Ahman Green, Green Bay	263	1,175	4.5	39	10
	Charlie Garner, San Francisco[2]	258	1,142	4.4	42	7
	Lamar Smith, Miami	309	1,139	3.7	68	14
	Warrick Dunn, Tampa Bay[2]	248	1,133	4.6	70	8
	James Allen, Chicago	290	1,120	3.9	29	2
	Tyrone Wheatley, Oakland	232	1,046	4.5	80	9
	Jamal Anderson, Atlanta[4]	282	1,024	3.6	42	6
	Tiki Barber, N.Y. Giants	213	1,006	4.7	78	8
	Ricky Williams, New Orleans	248	1,000	4.0	26	8
1999	*Edgerrin James, Indianapolis	369	1,553	4.2	72	13
	Curtis Martin, N.Y. Jets[5]	367	1,464	4.0	50	5
	Stephen Davis, Washington	290	1,405	4.8	76	17
	Emmitt Smith, Dallas[9]	329	1,397	4.3	63	11
	Marshall Faulk, St. Louis[5]	253	1,381	5.5	58	7
	Eddie George, Tennessee[4]	320	1,304	4.1	40	9
	Duce Staley, Philadelphia[2]	325	1,273	3.9	29	4
	Charlie Garner, San Francisco	241	1,229	5.1	53	4
	Ricky Watters, Seattle[6]	325	1,210	3.7	45	5
	Corey Dillon, Cincinnati[3]	263	1,200	4.6	50	5
	*Olandis Gary, Denver	276	1,159	4.2	71	7
	Jerome Bettis, Pittsburgh[6]	299	1,091	3.7	35	7
	Dorsey Levens, Green Bay[2]	279	1,034	3.7	36	9
	Robert Smith, Minnesota[3]	221	1,015	4.6	70	2
1998	Terrell Davis, Denver[4]	392	2,008	5.1	70	21
	Jamal Anderson, Atlanta[3]	410	1,846	4.5	48	14
	Garrison Hearst, San Francisco[3]	310	1,570	5.1	96	7
	Barry Sanders, Detroit[10]	343	1,491	4.3	73	4
	Emmitt Smith, Dallas[8]	319	1,332	4.2	32	13
	Marshall Faulk, Indianapolis[4]	324	1,319	4.1	68	6
	Eddie George, Tennessee[3]	348	1,294	3.7	37	5
	Curtis Martin, N.Y. Jets[4]	369	1,287	3.5	60	8
	Ricky Watters, Seattle[5]	319	1,239	3.9	39	9
	*Fred Taylor, Jacksonville	264	1,223	4.6	77	14
	Robert Smith, Minnesota[2]	249	1,187	4.8	74	6
	Jerome Bettis, Pittsburgh[5]	316	1,185	3.8	42	3
	Corey Dillon, Cincinnati[2]	262	1,130	4.3	66	4
	Antowain Smith, Buffalo	300	1,124	3.7	30	8
	*Robert Edwards, New England	291	1,115	3.8	53	9
	Duce Staley, Philadelphia	258	1,065	4.1	64	5
	Gary Brown, N.Y. Giants[2]	247	1,063	4.3	45	5
	Adrian Murrell, Arizona[3]	274	1,042	3.8	32	8
	Warrick Dunn, Tampa Bay	245	1,026	4.2	50	2
	Priest Holmes, Baltimore	233	1,008	4.3	56	7
1997	Barry Sanders, Detroit[9]	335	2,053	6.1	82	11
	Terrell Davis, Denver[3]	369	1,750	4.7	50	15
	Jerome Bettis, Pittsburgh[4]	375	1,665	4.4	34	7
	Dorsey Levens, Green Bay	329	1,435	4.4	52	7
	Eddie George, Tennessee[2]	357	1,399	3.9	30	6
	Napoleon Kaufman, Oakland	272	1,294	4.8	83	6
	Robert Smith, Minnesota	232	1,266	5.5	78	6
	Curtis Martin, New England[3]	274	1,160	4.2	70	4
	*Corey Dillon, Cincinnati	233	1,129	4.8	71	10

Year	Player, Team	Att.	Yards	Avg.	Long	TD
	Ricky Watters, Philadelphia[4]	285	1,110	3.9	28	7
	Adrian Murrell, N.Y. Jets[2]	300	1,086	3.6	43	7
	Emmitt Smith, Dallas[7]	261	1,074	4.1	44	4
	Marshall Faulk, Indianapolis[3]	264	1,054	4.0	45	7
	Raymont Harris, Chicago	275	1,033	3.8	68	10
	Garrison Hearst, San Francisco[2]	234	1,019	4.4	51	4
	Jamal Anderson, Atlanta[2]	290	1,002	3.5	39	7
1996	Barry Sanders, Detroit[8]	307	1,553	5.1	54	11
	Terrell Davis, Denver[2]	345	1,538	4.5	71	13
	Jerome Bettis, Pittsburgh[3]	320	1,431	4.5	50	11
	Ricky Watters, Philadelphia[3]	353	1,411	4.0	56	13
	*Eddie George, Houston	335	1,368	4.1	76	8
	Terry Allen, Washington[4]	347	1,353	3.9	49	21
	Adrian Murrell, N.Y. Jets	301	1,249	4.1	78	6
	Emmitt Smith, Dallas[6]	327	1,204	3.7	42	12
	Curtis Martin, New England[2]	316	1,152	3.6	57	14
	Anthony Johnson, Carolina	300	1,120	3.7	29	6
	*Karim Abdul-Jabbar, Miami	307	1,116	3.6	29	11
	Jamal Anderson, Atlanta	232	1,055	4.5	32	5
	Thurman Thomas, Buffalo[8]	281	1,033	3.7	36	8
1995	Emmitt Smith, Dallas[5]	377	1,773	4.7	60	25
	Barry Sanders, Detroit[7]	314	1,500	4.8	75	11
	*Curtis Martin, New England	368	1,487	4.0	49	14
	Chris Warren, Seattle[4]	310	1,346	4.3	52	15
	Terry Allen, Washington[3]	338	1,309	3.9	28	10
	Ricky Watters, Philadelphia[2]	337	1,273	3.8	57	11
	Errict Rhett, Tampa Bay[2]	332	1,207	3.6	21	11
	Rodney Hampton, N.Y. Giants[5]	306	1,182	3.9	32	10
	*Terrell Davis, Denver	237	1,117	4.7	60	7
	Harvey Williams, Oakland	255	1,114	4.4	60	9
	Craig Heyward, Atlanta	236	1,083	4.6	31	6
	Marshall Faulk, Indianapolis[2]	289	1,078	3.7	40	11
	*Rashaan Salaam, Chicago	296	1,074	3.6	42	10
	Garrison Hearst, Arizona	284	1,070	3.8	38	1
	Edgar Bennett, Green Bay	316	1,067	3.4	23	3
	Thurman Thomas, Buffalo[7]	267	1,005	3.8	49	6
1994	Barry Sanders, Detroit[6]	331	1,883	5.7	85	7
	Chris Warren, Seattle[3]	333	1,545	4.6	41	9
	Emmitt Smith, Dallas[4]	368	1,484	4.0	46	21
	Natrone Means, San Diego	343	1,350	3.9	25	12
	*Marshall Faulk, Indianapolis	314	1,282	4.1	52	11
	Thurman Thomas, Buffalo[6]	287	1,093	3.8	29	7
	Rodney Hampton, N.Y. Giants[4]	327	1,075	3.3	27	6
	Terry Allen, Minnesota[2]	255	1,031	4.0	45	8
	Jerome Bettis, L.A. Rams[2]	319	1,025	3.2	19	3
	*Errict Rhett, Tampa Bay	284	1,011	3.6	27	7
1993	Emmitt Smith, Dallas[3]	283	1,486	5.3	62	9
	*Jerome Bettis, L.A. Rams	294	1,429	4.9	71	7
	Thurman Thomas, Buffalo[5]	355	1,315	3.7	27	6
	Erric Pegram, Atlanta	292	1,185	4.1	29	3
	Barry Sanders, Detroit[5]	243	1,115	4.6	42	3
	Leonard Russell, New England	300	1,088	3.6	21	7
	Rodney Hampton, N.Y. Giants[3]	292	1,077	3.7	20	5
	Chris Warren, Seattle[2]	273	1,072	3.9	45	7
	*Reggie Brooks, Washington	223	1,063	4.8	85	3
	*Ron Moore, Phoenix	263	1,018	3.9	20	9
	Gary Brown, Houston	195	1,002	5.1	26	6
1992	Emmitt Smith, Dallas[2]	373	1,713	4.6	68	18
	Barry Foster, Pittsburgh	390	1,690	4.3	69	11
	Thurman Thomas, Buffalo[4]	312	1,487	4.8	44	9
	Barry Sanders, Detroit[4]	312	1,352	4.3	55	9
	Lorenzo White, Houston	265	1,226	4.6	44	7
	Terry Allen, Minnesota	266	1,201	4.5	51	13
	Reggie Cobb, Tampa Bay	310	1,171	3.8	25	9
	Harold Green, Cincinnati	265	1,170	4.4	53	2
	Rodney Hampton, N.Y. Giants[2]	257	1,141	4.4	63	14
	Cleveland Gary, L.A. Rams	279	1,125	4.0	63	7
	Herschel Walker, Philadelphia[2]	267	1,070	4.0	38	8
	Chris Warren, Seattle	223	1,017	4.6	52	3

OUTSTANDING PERFORMERS

Year	Player, Team	Att.	Yards	Avg.	Long	TD
	Ricky Watters, San Francisco	206	1,013	4.9	43	9
1991	Emmitt Smith, Dallas	365	1,563	4.3	75	12
	Barry Sanders, Detroit[3]	342	1,548	4.5	69	16
	Thurman Thomas, Buffalo[3]	288	1,407	4.9	33	7
	Rodney Hampton, N.Y. Giants	256	1,059	4.1	44	10
	Earnest Byner, Washington[3]	274	1,048	3.8	32	5
	Gaston Green, Denver	261	1,037	4.0	63	4
	Christian Okoye, Kansas City[2]	225	1,031	4.6	48	9
1990	Barry Sanders, Detroit[2]	255	1,304	5.1	45	13
	Thurman Thomas, Buffalo[2]	271	1,297	4.8	80	11
	Marion Butts, San Diego	265	1,225	4.6	52	8
	Earnest Byner, Washington[2]	297	1,219	4.1	22	6
	Bobby Humphrey, Denver[2]	288	1,202	4.2	37	7
	Neal Anderson, Chicago[3]	260	1,078	4.1	52	10
	Barry Word, Kansas City	204	1,015	5.0	53	4
	James Brooks, Cincinnati[3]	195	1,004	5.1	56	5
1989	Christian Okoye, Kansas City	370	1,480	4.0	59	12
	*Barry Sanders, Detroit	280	1,470	5.3	34	14
	Eric Dickerson, Indianapolis[7]	314	1,311	4.2	21	7
	Neal Anderson, Chicago[2]	274	1,275	4.7	73	11
	Dalton Hilliard, New Orleans	344	1,262	3.7	40	13
	Thurman Thomas, Buffalo	298	1,244	4.2	38	6
	James Brooks, Cincinnati[2]	221	1,239	5.6	65	7
	*Bobby Humphrey, Denver	294	1,151	3.9	40	7
	Greg Bell, L.A. Rams[3]	272	1,137	4.2	47	15
	Roger Craig, San Francisco[3]	271	1,054	3.9	27	6
	Ottis Anderson, N.Y. Giants[6]	325	1,023	3.1	36	14
1988	Eric Dickerson, Indianapolis[6]	388	1,659	4.3	41	14
	Herschel Walker, Dallas	361	1,514	4.2	38	5
	Roger Craig, San Francisco[2]	310	1,502	4.8	46	9
	Greg Bell, L.A. Rams[2]	288	1,212	4.2	44	16
	*John Stephens, New England	297	1,168	3.9	52	4
	Gary Anderson, San Diego	225	1,119	5.0	36	3
	Neal Anderson, Chicago	249	1,106	4.4	80	12
	Joe Morris, N.Y. Giants[3]	307	1,083	3.5	27	5
	*Ickey Woods, Cincinnati	203	1,066	5.3	56	15
	Curt Warner, Seattle[4]	266	1,025	3.9	29	10
	John Settle, Atlanta	232	1,024	4.4	62	7
	Mike Rozier, Houston	251	1,002	4.0	28	10
1987	Charles White, L.A. Rams	324	1,374	4.2	58	11
	Eric Dickerson, L.A. Rams-Indianapolis[5]	283	1,288	4.6	57	6
1986	Eric Dickerson, L.A. Rams[4]	404	1,821	4.5	42	11
	Joe Morris, N.Y. Giants[2]	341	1,516	4.4	54	14
	Curt Warner, Seattle[3]	319	1,481	4.6	60	13
	*Rueben Mayes, New Orleans	286	1,353	4.7	50	8
	Walter Payton, Chicago[10]	321	1,333	4.2	41	8
	Gerald Riggs, Atlanta[3]	343	1,327	3.9	31	9
	George Rogers, Washington[4]	303	1,203	4.0	42	18
	James Brooks, Cincinnati	205	1,087	5.3	56	5
1985	Marcus Allen, L.A. Raiders[3]	390	1,759	4.6	61	11
	Gerald Riggs, Atlanta[2]	397	1,719	4.3	50	10
	Walter Payton, Chicago[9]	324	1,551	4.8	40	9
	Joe Morris, N.Y. Giants	294	1,336	4.5	65	21
	Freeman McNeil, N.Y. Jets[2]	294	1,331	4.5	69	3
	Tony Dorsett, Dallas[8]	305	1,307	4.3	60	7
	James Wilder, Tampa Bay[2]	365	1,300	3.6	28	10
	Eric Dickerson, L.A. Rams[3]	292	1,234	4.2	43	12
	Craig James, New England	263	1,227	4.7	65	5
	Kevin Mack, Cleveland	222	1,104	5.0	61	7
	Curt Warner, Seattle[2]	291	1,094	3.8	38	8
	George Rogers, Washington[3]	231	1,093	4.7	35	7
	Roger Craig, San Francisco	214	1,050	4.9	62	9
	Earnest Jackson, Philadelphia[2]	282	1,028	3.6	59	5
	Stump Mitchell, St. Louis	183	1,006	5.5	64	7
	Earnest Byner, Cleveland	244	1,002	4.1	36	8
1984	Eric Dickerson, L.A. Rams[2]	379	2,105	5.6	66	14
	Walter Payton, Chicago[8]	381	1,684	4.4	72	11
	James Wilder, Tampa Bay	407	1,544	3.8	37	13
	Gerald Riggs, Atlanta	353	1,486	4.2	57	13

Year	Player, Team	Att.	Yards	Avg.	Long	TD
	Wendell Tyler, San Francisco[3]	246	1,262	5.1	40	7
	John Riggins, Washington[5]	327	1,239	3.8	24	14
	Tony Dorsett, Dallas[7]	302	1,189	3.9	31	6
	Earnest Jackson, San Diego	296	1,179	4.0	32	8
	Ottis Anderson, St. Louis[5]	289	1,174	4.1	24	6
	Marcus Allen, L.A. Raiders[2]	275	1,168	4.2	52	13
	Sammy Winder, Denver	296	1,153	3.9	24	4
	*Greg Bell, Buffalo	262	1,100	4.2	85	7
	Freeman McNeil, N.Y. Jets	229	1,070	4.7	53	5
1983	*Eric Dickerson, L.A. Rams	390	1,808	4.6	85	18
	William Andrews, Atlanta[4]	331	1,567	4.7	27	7
	*Curt Warner, Seattle	335	1,449	4.3	60	13
	Walter Payton, Chicago[7]	314	1,421	4.5	49	6
	John Riggins, Washington[4]	375	1,347	3.6	44	24
	Tony Dorsett, Dallas[6]	289	1,321	4.6	77	8
	Earl Campbell, Houston[5]	322	1,301	4.0	42	12
	Ottis Anderson, St. Louis[4]	296	1,270	4.3	43	5
	Mike Pruitt, Cleveland[4]	293	1,184	4.0	27	10
	George Rogers, New Orleans[2]	256	1,144	4.5	76	5
	Joe Cribbs, Buffalo[3]	263	1,131	4.3	45	3
	Curtis Dickey, Baltimore	254	1,122	4.4	56	4
	Tony Collins, New England	219	1,049	4.8	50	10
	Billy Sims, Detroit[3]	220	1,040	4.7	41	7
	Marcus Allen, L.A. Raiders	266	1,014	3.8	19	9
	Franco Harris, Pittsburgh[8]	279	1,007	3.6	19	5
1981	*George Rogers, New Orleans	378	1,674	4.4	79	13
	Tony Dorsett, Dallas[5]	342	1,646	4.8	75	4
	Billy Sims, Detroit[2]	296	1,437	4.9	51	13
	Wilbert Montgomery, Philadelphia[3]	286	1,402	4.9	41	8
	Ottis Anderson, St. Louis[3]	328	1,376	4.2	28	9
	Earl Campbell, Houston[4]	361	1,376	3.8	43	10
	William Andrews, Atlanta[3]	289	1,301	4.5	29	10
	Walter Payton, Chicago[6]	339	1,222	3.6	39	6
	Chuck Muncie, San Diego[2]	251	1,144	4.6	73	19
	*Joe Delaney, Kansas City	234	1,121	4.8	82	3
	Mike Pruitt, Cleveland[3]	247	1,103	4.5	21	7
	Joe Cribbs, Buffalo[2]	257	1,097	4.3	35	3
	Pete Johnson, Cincinnati	274	1,077	3.9	39	12
	Wendell Tyler, Los Angeles[2]	260	1,074	4.1	69	12
	Ted Brown, Minnesota	274	1,063	3.9	34	6
1980	Earl Campbell, Houston[3]	373	1,934	5.2	55	13
	Walter Payton, Chicago[5]	317	1,460	4.6	69	6
	Ottis Anderson, St. Louis[2]	301	1,352	4.5	52	9
	William Andrews, Atlanta[2]	265	1,308	4.9	33	4
	*Billy Sims, Detroit	313	1,303	4.2	52	13
	Tony Dorsett, Dallas[4]	278	1,185	4.3	56	11
	*Joe Cribbs, Buffalo	306	1,185	3.9	48	11
	Mike Pruitt, Cleveland[2]	249	1,034	4.2	56	6
1979	Earl Campbell, Houston[2]	368	1,697	4.6	61	19
	Walter Payton, Chicago[4]	369	1,610	4.4	43	14
	*Ottis Anderson, St. Louis	331	1,605	4.8	76	8
	Wilbert Montgomery, Philadelphia[2]	338	1,512	4.5	62	9
	Mike Pruitt, Cleveland	264	1,294	4.9	77	9
	Ricky Bell, Tampa Bay	283	1,263	4.5	49	7
	Chuck Muncie, New Orleans	238	1,198	5.0	69	11
	Franco Harris, Pittsburgh[7]	267	1,186	4.4	71	11
	John Riggins, Washington[3]	260	1,153	4.4	66	9
	Wendell Tyler, Los Angeles	218	1,109	5.1	63	9
	Tony Dorsett, Dallas[3]	250	1,107	4.4	41	6
	*William Andrews, Atlanta	239	1,023	4.3	23	3
1978	*Earl Campbell, Houston	302	1,450	4.8	81	13
	Walter Payton, Chicago[3]	333	1,395	4.2	76	11
	Tony Dorsett, Dallas[2]	290	1,325	4.6	63	7
	Delvin Williams, Miami[2]	272	1,258	4.6	58	8
	Wilbert Montgomery, Philadelphia	259	1,220	4.7	47	9
	Terdell Middleton, Green Bay	284	1,116	3.9	76	11
	Franco Harris, Pittsburgh[6]	310	1,082	3.5	37	8
	Mark van Eeghen, Oakland[3]	270	1,080	4.0	34	9
	*Terry Miller, Buffalo	238	1,060	4.5	60	7

Year	Player, Team	Att.	Yards	Avg.	Long	TD
	Tony Reed, Kansas City	206	1,053	5.1	62	5
	John Riggins, Washington[2]	248	1,014	4.1	31	5
1977	Walter Payton, Chicago[2]	339	1,852	5.5	73	14
	Mark van Eeghen, Oakland[2]	324	1,273	3.9	27	7
	Lawrence McCutcheon, Los Angeles[4]	294	1,238	4.2	48	7
	Franco Harris, Pittsburgh[5]	300	1,162	3.9	61	11
	Lydell Mitchell, Baltimore[3]	301	1,159	3.9	64	3
	Chuck Foreman, Minnesota[3]	270	1,112	4.1	51	6
	Greg Pruitt, Cleveland[3]	236	1,086	4.6	78	3
	Sam Cunningham, New England	270	1,015	3.8	31	4
	*Tony Dorsett, Dallas	208	1,007	4.8	84	12
1976	O.J. Simpson, Buffalo[5]	290	1,503	5.2	75	8
	Walter Payton, Chicago	311	1,390	4.5	60	13
	Delvin Williams, San Francisco	248	1,203	4.9	80	7
	Lydell Mitchell, Baltimore[2]	289	1,200	4.2	43	5
	Lawrence McCutcheon, Los Angeles[3]	291	1,168	4.0	40	9
	Chuck Foreman, Minnesota[2]	278	1,155	4.2	46	13
	Franco Harris, Pittsburgh[4]	289	1,128	3.9	30	14
	Mike Thomas, Washington	254	1,101	4.3	28	5
	Rocky Bleier, Pittsburgh	220	1,036	4.7	28	5
	Mark van Eeghen, Oakland	233	1,012	4.3	21	3
	Otis Armstrong, Denver[2]	247	1,008	4.1	31	5
	Greg Pruitt, Cleveland[2]	209	1,000	4.8	64	4
1975	O.J. Simpson, Buffalo[4]	329	1,817	5.5	88	16
	Franco Harris, Pittsburgh[3]	262	1,246	4.8	36	10
	Lydell Mitchell, Baltimore	289	1,193	4.1	70	11
	Jim Otis, St. Louis	269	1,076	4.0	30	5
	Chuck Foreman, Minnesota	280	1,070	3.8	31	13
	Greg Pruitt, Cleveland	217	1,067	4.9	50	8
	John Riggins, N.Y. Jets	238	1,005	4.2	42	8
	Dave Hampton, Atlanta	250	1,002	4.0	22	5
1974	Otis Armstrong, Denver	263	1,407	5.3	43	9
	*Don Woods, San Diego	227	1,162	5.1	56	7
	O.J. Simpson, Buffalo[3]	270	1,125	4.2	41	3
	Lawrence McCutcheon, Los Angeles[2]	236	1,109	4.7	23	3
	Franco Harris, Pittsburgh[2]	208	1,006	4.8	54	5
1973	O.J. Simpson, Buffalo[2]	332	2,003	6.0	80	12
	John Brockington, Green Bay[3]	265	1,144	4.3	53	3
	Calvin Hill, Dallas[2]	273	1,142	4.2	21	6
	Lawrence McCutcheon, Los Angeles	210	1,097	5.2	37	2
	Larry Csonka, Miami[3]	219	1,003	4.6	25	5
1972	O.J. Simpson, Buffalo	292	1,251	4.3	94	6
	Larry Brown, Washington[2]	285	1,216	4.3	38	8
	Ron Johnson, N.Y. Giants[2]	298	1,182	4.0	35	9
	Larry Csonka, Miami[2]	213	1,117	5.2	45	6
	Marv Hubbard, Oakland	219	1,100	5.0	39	4
	*Franco Harris, Pittsburgh	188	1,055	5.6	75	10
	Calvin Hill, Dallas	245	1,036	4.2	26	6
	Mike Garrett, San Diego[2]	272	1,031	3.8	41	6
	John Brockington, Green Bay[2]	274	1,027	3.7	30	8
	Eugene (Mercury) Morris, Miami	190	1,000	5.3	33	12
1971	Floyd Little, Denver	284	1,133	4.0	40	6
	*John Brockington, Green Bay	216	1,105	5.1	52	4
	Larry Csonka, Miami	195	1,051	5.4	28	7
	Steve Owens, Detroit	246	1,035	4.2	23	8
	Willie Ellison, Los Angeles	211	1,000	4.7	80	4
1970	Larry Brown, Washington	237	1,125	4.7	75	5
	Ron Johnson, N.Y. Giants	263	1,027	3.9	68	8
1969	Gale Sayers, Chicago[2]	236	1,032	4.4	28	8
1968	Leroy Kelly, Cleveland[3]	248	1,239	5.0	65	16
	*Paul Robinson, Cincinnati	238	1,023	4.3	87	8
1967	Jim Nance, Boston[2]	269	1,216	4.5	53	7
	Leroy Kelly, Cleveland[2]	235	1,205	5.1	42	11
	Hoyle Granger, Houston	236	1,194	5.1	67	6
	Mike Garrett, Kansas City	236	1,087	4.6	58	9
1966	Jim Nance, Boston	299	1,458	4.9	65	11
	Gale Sayers, Chicago	229	1,231	5.4	58	8
	Leroy Kelly, Cleveland	209	1,141	5.5	70	15
	Dick Bass, Los Angeles[2]	248	1,090	4.4	50	8

Year	Player, Team	Att.	Yards	Avg.	Long	TD
1965	Jim Brown, Cleveland[7]	289	1,544	5.3	67	17
	Paul Lowe, San Diego[2]	222	1,121	5.0	59	7
1964	Jim Brown, Cleveland[6]	280	1,446	5.2	71	7
	Jim Taylor, Green Bay[5]	235	1,169	5.0	84	12
	John Henry Johnson, Pittsburgh[2]	235	1,048	4.5	45	7
1963	Jim Brown, Cleveland[5]	291	1,863	6.4	80	12
	Clem Daniels, Oakland	215	1,099	5.1	74	3
	Jim Taylor, Green Bay[4]	248	1,018	4.1	40	9
	Paul Lowe, San Diego	177	1,010	5.7	66	8
1962	Jim Taylor, Green Bay[3]	272	1,474	5.4	51	19
	John Henry Johnson, Pittsburgh	251	1,141	4.5	40	7
	Cookie Gilchrist, Buffalo	214	1,096	5.1	44	13
	Abner Haynes, Dall. Texans	221	1,049	4.7	71	13
	Dick Bass, Los Angeles	196	1,033	5.3	57	6
	Charlie Tolar, Houston	244	1,012	4.1	25	7
1961	Jim Brown, Cleveland[4]	305	1,408	4.6	38	8
	Jim Taylor, Green Bay[2]	243	1,307	5.4	53	15
1960	Jim Brown, Cleveland[3]	215	1,257	5.8	71	9
	Jim Taylor, Green Bay	230	1,101	4.8	32	11
	John David Crow, St. Louis	183	1,071	5.9	57	6
1959	Jim Brown, Cleveland[2]	290	1,329	4.6	70	14
	J.D. Smith, San Francisco	207	1,036	5.0	73	10
1958	Jim Brown, Cleveland	257	1,527	5.9	65	17
1956	Rick Casares, Chi. Bears	234	1,126	4.8	68	12
1954	Joe Perry, San Francisco[2]	173	1,049	6.1	58	8
1953	Joe Perry, San Francisco	192	1,018	5.3	51	10
1949	Steve Van Buren, Philadelphia[2]	263	1,146	4.4	41	11
	Tony Canadeo, Green Bay	208	1,052	5.1	54	4
1947	Steve Van Buren, Philadelphia	217	1,008	4.6	45	13
1934	*Beattie Feathers, Chi. Bears	119	1,004	8.4	82	8

**First season of professional football.*

200 YARDS RUSHING IN A GAME

Date	Player, Team, Opponent	Att.	Yards	TD
Dec. 28, 2008	Michael Turner, Atlanta vs. St. Louis	25	208	1
Dec. 21, 2008	Derrick Ward, N.Y. Giants vs. Carolina (OT)	15	215	0
Sept. 7, 2008	Michael Turner, Atlanta vs. Detroit	22	220	2
Nov. 4, 2007	*Adrian Peterson, Minnesota vs. San Diego	30	296	3
Oct. 14, 2007	*Adrian Peterson, Minnesota vs. Chicago	20	224	3
Sept. 16, 2007	Jamal Lewis, Cleveland vs. Cincinnati	27	216	1
Dec. 30, 2006	Tiki Barber, N.Y. Giants vs. Washington	23	234	3
Dec. 7, 2006	Willie Parker, Pittsburgh vs. Cleveland	32	223	1
Nov. 27, 2006	Shaun Alexander, Seattle vs. Green Bay	40	201	0
Nov. 19, 2006	Frank Gore, San Francisco vs. Seattle	24	212	0
Nov. 12, 2006	Willie Parker, Pittsburgh vs. New Orleans	22	213	2
Jan. 1, 2006	Larry Johnson, Kansas City vs. Cincinnati	26	201	3
Dec. 31, 2005	Tiki Barber, N.Y. Giants vs. Oakland	28	203	1
Dec. 17, 2005	Tiki Barber, N.Y. Giants vs. Kansas City	29	220	2
Nov. 20, 2005	Larry Johnson, Kansas City vs. Houston	36	211	2
Oct. 30, 2005	Tiki Barber, N.Y. Giants vs. Washington	24	206	1
Nov. 28, 2004	Rudi Johnson, Cincinnati vs. Cleveland	26	202	2
Nov. 21, 2004	Edgerrin James, Indianapolis vs. Chicago	23	204	1
Dec. 28, 2003	Ahman Green, Green Bay vs. Denver	20	218	2
Dec. 28, 2003	LaDainian Tomlinson, San Diego vs. Oakland	31	243	2
Dec. 21, 2003	Jamal Lewis, Baltimore vs. Cleveland	22	205	2
Dec. 7, 2003	Clinton Portis, Denver vs. Kansas City	22	218	5
Oct. 19, 2003	LaDainian Tomlinson, San Diego vs. Cleveland	26	200	1
Sept. 14, 2003	Jamal Lewis, Baltimore vs. Cleveland	30	295	2
Dec. 29, 2002	*Clinton Portis, Denver vs. Arizona	24	228	2
Dec. 28, 2002	Tiki Barber, N.Y. Giants vs. Philadelphia	32	203	0
Dec. 9, 2002	Ricky Williams, Miami vs. Chicago	31	216	2
Dec. 1, 2002	LaDainian Tomlinson, San Diego vs. Denver	37	220	3
Dec. 1, 2002	Ricky Williams, Miami vs. Buffalo	27	228	2
Sept. 29, 2002	LaDainian Tomlinson, San Diego vs. New England	27	217	2
Dec. 23, 2001	Marshall Faulk, St. Louis vs. Carolina	30	202	2
Nov. 11, 2001	Shaun Alexander, Seattle vs. Oakland	35	266	3
Dec. 24, 2000	Marshall Faulk, St. Louis vs. New Orleans	32	220	2
Dec. 3, 2000	Corey Dillon, Cincinnati vs. Arizona	35	216	1
Dec. 3, 2000	Warrick Dunn, Tampa Bay vs. Dallas	22	210	2
Dec. 3, 2000	*Mike Anderson, Denver vs. New Orleans	37	251	4

OUTSTANDING PERFORMERS

Date	Player, Team, Opponent	Att.	Yards	TD
Dec. 3, 2000	Curtis Martin, N.Y. Jets vs. Indianapolis	30	203	1
Nov. 19, 2000	Fred Taylor, Jacksonville vs. Pittsburgh	30	234	3
Oct. 22, 2000	Corey Dillon, Cincinnati vs. Denver	22	278	2
Oct. 15, 2000	Marshall Faulk, St. Louis vs. Atlanta	25	208	1
Oct. 15, 2000	Edgerrin James, Indianapolis vs. Seattle	38	219	3
Sept. 24, 2000	Charlie Garner, San Francisco vs. Dallas	36	201	1
Sept. 3, 2000	Duce Staley, Philadelphia vs. Dallas	26	201	1
Nov. 22, 1998	Priest Holmes, Baltimore vs. Cincinnati	36	227	1
Oct. 11, 1998	Terrell Davis, Denver vs. Seattle	30	208	1
Dec. 4, 1997	*Corey Dillon, Cincinnati vs. Tennessee	39	246	4
Nov. 23, 1997	Barry Sanders, Detroit vs. Indianapolis	24	216	2
Oct. 26, 1997	Terrell Davis, Denver vs. Buffalo (OT)	42	207	1
Oct. 19, 1997	Napoleon Kaufman, Oakland vs. Denver	28	227	1
Oct. 12, 1997	Barry Sanders, Detroit vs. Tampa Bay	24	215	2
Sept. 21, 1997	Terrell Davis, Denver vs. Cincinnati	27	215	1
Aug. 31, 1997	Eddie George, Tennessee vs. Oakland (OT)	35	216	1
Sept. 22, 1996	LeShon Johnson, Arizona vs. New Orleans	21	214	2
Nov. 13, 1994	Barry Sanders, Detroit vs. Tampa Bay	26	237	0
Dec. 12, 1993	*Jerome Bettis, L.A. Rams vs. New Orleans	28	212	1
Oct. 31, 1993	Emmitt Smith, Dallas vs. Philadelphia	30	237	1
Nov. 24, 1991	Barry Sanders, Detroit vs. Minnesota	23	220	4
Dec. 23, 1990	James Brooks, Cincinnati vs. Houston	20	201	1
Oct. 14, 1990	Barry Word, Kansas City vs. Detroit	18	200	2
Sept. 24, 1990	Thurman Thomas, Buffalo vs. N.Y. Jets	18	214	0
Dec. 24, 1989	Greg Bell, L.A. Rams vs. New England	26	210	1
Sept. 24, 1989	Greg Bell, L.A. Rams vs. Green Bay	28	221	2
Sept. 17, 1989	Gerald Riggs, Washington vs. Philadelphia	29	221	1
Dec. 18, 1988	Gary Anderson, San Diego vs. Kansas City	34	217	1
Nov. 30, 1987	*Bo Jackson, L.A. Raiders vs. Seattle	18	221	2
Nov. 15, 1987	Charles White, L.A. Rams vs. St. Louis	34	213	1
Dec. 7, 1986	Rueben Mayes, New Orleans vs. Miami	28	203	2
Oct. 5, 1986	Eric Dickerson, L.A. Rams vs. Tampa Bay (OT)	30	207	2
Dec. 21, 1985	George Rogers, Washington vs. St. Louis	34	206	1
Dec. 21, 1985	Joe Morris, N.Y. Giants vs. Pittsburgh	36	202	3
Dec. 9, 1984	Eric Dickerson, L.A. Rams vs. Houston	27	215	2
Nov. 18, 1984	*Greg Bell, Buffalo vs. Dallas	27	206	1
Nov. 4, 1984	Eric Dickerson, L.A. Rams vs. St. Louis	21	208	0
Sept. 2, 1984	Gerald Riggs, Atlanta vs. New Orleans	35	202	2
Nov. 27, 1983	*Curt Warner, Seattle vs. Kansas City (OT)	32	207	3
Nov. 6, 1983	James Wilder, Tampa Bay vs. Minnesota	31	219	1
Sept. 18, 1983	Tony Collins, New England vs. N.Y. Jets	23	212	3
Sept. 4, 1983	George Rogers, New Orleans vs. St. Louis	24	206	2
Dec. 21, 1980	Earl Campbell, Houston vs. Minnesota	29	203	1
Nov. 16, 1980	Earl Campbell, Houston vs. Chicago	31	206	0
Oct. 26, 1980	Earl Campbell, Houston vs. Cincinnati	27	202	2
Oct. 19, 1980	Earl Campbell, Houston vs. Tampa Bay	33	203	0
Nov. 26, 1978	*Terry Miller, Buffalo vs. N.Y. Giants	21	208	2
Dec. 4, 1977	*Tony Dorsett, Dallas vs. Philadelphia	23	206	2
Nov. 20, 1977	Walter Payton, Chicago vs. Minnesota	40	275	1
Oct. 30, 1977	Walter Payton, Chicago vs. Green Bay	23	205	2
Dec. 5, 1976	O.J. Simpson, Buffalo vs. Miami	24	203	1
Nov. 25, 1976	O.J. Simpson, Buffalo vs. Detroit	29	273	2
Oct. 24, 1976	Chuck Foreman, Minnesota vs. Philadelphia	28	200	2
Dec. 14, 1975	Greg Pruitt, Cleveland vs. Kansas City	26	214	3
Sept. 28, 1975	O.J. Simpson, Buffalo vs. Pittsburgh	28	227	1
Dec. 16, 1973	O.J. Simpson, Buffalo vs. N.Y. Jets	34	200	1
Dec. 9, 1973	O.J. Simpson, Buffalo vs. New England	22	219	1
Sept. 16, 1973	O.J. Simpson, Buffalo vs. New England	29	250	2
Dec. 5, 1971	Willie Ellison, Los Angeles vs. New Orleans	26	247	1
Dec. 20, 1970	John (Frenchy) Fuqua, Pittsburgh vs. Philadelphia	20	218	2
Nov. 3, 1968	Gale Sayers, Chicago vs. Green Bay	24	205	0
Oct. 30, 1966	Jim Nance, Boston vs. Oakland	38	208	2
Oct. 10, 1964	John Henry Johnson, Pittsburgh vs. Cleveland	30	200	3
Dec. 8, 1963	Cookie Gilchrist, Buffalo vs. N.Y. Jets	36	243	5
Nov. 3, 1963	Jim Brown, Cleveland vs. Philadelphia	28	223	1
Oct. 20, 1963	Clem Daniels, Oakland vs. N.Y. Jets	27	200	2
Sept. 22, 1963	Jim Brown, Cleveland vs. Dallas	20	232	2
Dec. 10, 1961	Billy Cannon, Houston vs. N.Y. Titans	25	216	3
Nov. 19, 1961	Jim Brown, Cleveland vs. Philadelphia	34	237	4
Dec. 18, 1960	John David Crow, St. Louis vs. Pittsburgh	24	203	0
Nov. 15, 1959	Bobby Mitchell, Cleveland vs. Washington	14	232	3

Date	Player, Team, Opponent	Att.	Yards	TD
Nov. 24, 1957	*Jim Brown, Cleveland vs. Los Angeles	31	237	4
Dec. 16, 1956	*Tom Wilson, Los Angeles vs. Green Bay	23	223	0
Nov. 22, 1953	Dan Towler, Los Angeles vs. Baltimore	14	205	1
Nov. 12, 1950	Gene Roberts, N.Y. Giants vs. Chi. Cardinals	26	218	2
Nov. 27, 1949	Steve Van Buren, Philadelphia vs. Pittsburgh	27	205	0
Oct. 8, 1933	Cliff Battles, Boston vs. N.Y. Giants	16	215	1

**First season of professional football.*

TIMES 200 OR MORE

113 times by 69 players…Simpson 6; Barber 5; Brown, Campbell, Sanders, Tomlinson 4; Bell, Davis, Dickerson, Dillon, Faulk, Lewis 3; Alexander, James, Johnson, Parker, Payton, Peterson, Portis, Riggs, Rogers, Turner, Williams 2.

4,000 YARDS PASSING IN A SEASON

Year	Player, Team	Att.	Comp.	Pct.	Yards	TD	Int.
2008	Drew Brees, New Orleans[3]	635	413	65.0	5,069	34	17
	Kurt Warner, Arizona[3]	598	401	67.1	4,583	30	14
	Jay Cutler, Denver	616	384	62.3	4,526	25	18
	Aaron Rodgers, Green Bay	536	341	63.6	4,038	28	13
	Philip Rivers, San Diego	478	312	65.3	4,009	34	11
	Peyton Manning, Indianapolis[9]	555	371	66.8	4,002	27	12
2007	Tom Brady, New England[2]	578	398	68.9	4,806	50	8
	Drew Brees, New Orleans[2]	652	440	67.5	4,423	28	18
	Tony Romo, Dallas	520	335	64.4	4,211	36	19
	Brett Favre, Green Bay[5]	535	356	66.5	4,155	28	15
	Carson Palmer, Cincinnati[2]	575	373	64.9	4,131	26	20
	Jon Kitna, Detroit[2]	561	355	63.3	4,068	18	20
	Peyton Manning, Indianapolis[8]	515	337	65.4	4,040	31	14
2006	Drew Brees, New Orleans	554	356	64.3	4,418	26	11
	Peyton Manning, Indianapolis[7]	557	362	65.0	4,397	31	9
	Marc Bulger, St. Louis	588	370	62.9	4,301	24	8
	Jon Kitna, Detroit	596	372	62.4	4,208	21	22
	Carson Palmer, Cincinnati	520	324	62.3	4,035	28	13
2005	Tom Brady, New England	530	334	63.0	4,110	26	14
	Trent Green, Kansas City[3]	507	317	62.5	4,014	17	10
2004	Daunte Culpepper, Minnesota	548	379	69.2	4,717	39	11
	Trent Green, Kansas City[2]	556	369	66.4	4,591	27	17
	Peyton Manning, Indianapolis[6]	497	336	67.6	4,557	49	10
	Jake Plummer, Denver	521	303	58.2	4,089	27	20
	Brett Favre, Green Bay[4]	540	346	64.1	4,088	30	17
2003	Peyton Manning, Indianapolis[5]	566	379	67.0	4,267	29	10
	Trent Green, Kansas City	523	330	63.1	4,039	24	12
2002	Rich Gannon, Oakland	618	418	67.6	4,689	26	10
	Drew Bledsoe, Buffalo[3]	610	375	61.5	4,359	24	15
	Peyton Manning, Indianapolis[4]	591	392	66.3	4,200	27	19
	Kerry Collins, N.Y. Giants	545	335	61.5	4,073	19	14
2001	Kurt Warner, St. Louis[2]	546	375	68.7	4,830	36	22
	Peyton Manning, Indianapolis[3]	547	343	62.7	4,131	26	23
2000	Peyton Manning, Indianapolis[2]	571	357	62.5	4,413	33	15
	Jeff Garcia, San Francisco	561	355	63.3	4,278	31	10
	Elvis Grbac, Kansas City	547	326	59.6	4,169	28	14
1999	Steve Beuerlein, Carolina	571	343	60.1	4,436	36	15
	Kurt Warner, St. Louis	499	325	65.1	4,353	41	13
	Peyton Manning, Indianapolis	533	331	62.1	4,135	26	15
	Brett Favre, Green Bay[3]	595	341	57.3	4,091	22	23
	Brad Johnson, Washington	519	316	60.9	4,005	24	13
1998	Brett Favre, Green Bay[2]	551	347	63.0	4,212	31	23
	Steve Young, San Francisco[2]	517	322	62.3	4,170	36	12
1996	Mark Brunell, Jacksonville	557	353	63.4	4,367	19	20
	Vinny Testaverde, Baltimore	549	325	59.2	4,177	33	19
	Drew Bledsoe, New England[2]	623	373	59.9	4,086	27	15
1995	Brett Favre, Green Bay	570	359	63.0	4,413	38	13
	Scott Mitchell, Detroit	583	346	59.3	4,338	32	12
	Warren Moon, Minnesota[4]	606	377	62.2	4,228	33	14
	Jeff George, Atlanta	557	336	60.3	4,143	24	11
1994	Drew Bledsoe, New England	691	400	57.9	4,555	25	27
	Dan Marino, Miami[6]	615	385	62.6	4,453	30	17
	Warren Moon, Minnesota[3]	601	371	61.7	4,264	18	19

OUTSTANDING PERFORMERS

Year	Player, Team	Att.	Comp.	Pct.	Yards	TD	Int.
1993	John Elway, Denver	551	348	63.2	4,030	25	10
	Steve Young, San Francisco	462	314	68.0	4,023	29	16
1992	Dan Marino, Miami[5]	554	330	59.6	4,116	24	16
1991	Warren Moon, Houston[2]	655	404	61.7	4,690	23	21
1990	Warren Moon, Houston	584	362	62.0	4,689	33	13
1989	Don Majkowski, Green Bay	599	353	58.9	4,318	27	20
	Jim Everett, L.A. Rams	518	304	58.7	4,310	29	17
1988	Dan Marino, Miami[4]	606	354	58.4	4,434	28	23
1986	Dan Marino, Miami[3]	623	378	60.7	4,746	44	23
	Jay Schroeder, Washington	541	276	51.0	4,109	22	22
1985	Dan Marino, Miami[2]	567	336	59.3	4,137	30	21
1984	Dan Marino, Miami	564	362	64.2	5,084	48	17
	Neil Lomax, St. Louis	560	345	61.6	4,614	28	16
	Phil Simms, N.Y. Giants	533	286	53.7	4,044	22	18
1983	Lynn Dickey, Green Bay	484	289	59.7	4,458	32	29
	Bill Kenney, Kansas City	603	346	57.4	4,348	24	18
1981	Dan Fouts, San Diego[3]	609	360	59.1	4,802	33	17
1980	Dan Fouts, San Diego[2]	589	348	59.1	4,715	30	24
	Brian Sipe, Cleveland	554	337	60.8	4,132	30	14
1979	Dan Fouts, San Diego	530	332	62.6	4,082	24	24
1967	Joe Namath, N.Y. Jets	491	258	52.5	4,007	26	28

400 YARDS PASSING IN A GAME

Date	Player, Team, Opponent	Att.	Comp.	Yards	TD
Dec. 7, 2008	Matt Schaub, Houston vs. Green Bay	42	28	414	2
Nov. 23, 2008	Matt Cassel, New England vs. Miami	43	30	415	3
Nov. 13, 2008	Matt Cassel, New England vs. N.Y. Jets (OT)	51	30	400	3
Nov. 9, 2008	Drew Brees, New Orleans vs. Atlanta	58	31	422	2
Nov. 6, 2008	Jay Cutler, Denver vs. Cleveland	42	24	447	3
Sept. 28, 2008	Kurt Warner, Arizona vs. N.Y. Jets	57	40	472	2
Sept. 21, 2008	Drew Brees, New Orleans vs. Denver	48	39	421	1
Sept. 21, 2008	Brian Griese, Tampa Bay vs. Chicago (OT)	67	38	407	2
Nov. 25, 2007	Kurt Warner, Arizona vs. San Francisco (OT)	48	34	484	2
Nov. 4, 2007	Drew Brees, New Orleans vs. Jacksonville	49	35	445	3
Sept. 23, 2007	Jon Kitna, Detroit vs. Philadelphia	46	29	446	2
Sept. 16, 2007	Carson Palmer, Cincinnati vs. Cleveland	50	33	401	6
Dec. 10, 2006	Chris Weinke, Carolina vs. N.Y. Giants	61	34	423	1
Nov. 26, 2006	Matt Leinart, Arizona vs. Minnesota	51	31	405	1
Nov. 19, 2006	Drew Brees, New Orleans vs. Cincinnati	52	37	510	2
Nov. 12, 2006	Carson Palmer, Cincinnati vs. San Diego	42	31	440	3
Nov. 5, 2006	Ben Roethlisberger, Pittsburgh vs. Denver	54	38	433	1
Oct. 22, 2006	Joey Harrington, Miami vs. Green Bay	62	33	414	2
Sept. 17, 2006	Peyton Manning, Indianapolis vs. Houston	38	26	400	3
Oct. 2, 2005	Marc Bulger, St. Louis vs. N.Y. Giants	62	40	442	2
Jan. 2, 2005	Marc Bulger, St. Louis vs. N.Y. Jets (OT)	39	29	450	3
Dec. 19, 2004	Daunte Culpepper, Minnesota vs. Detroit	35	25	404	3
Dec. 19, 2004	Billy Volek, Tennessee vs. Oakland	60	40	492	4
Dec. 13, 2004	Billy Volek, Tennessee vs. Kansas City	43	29	426	4
Dec. 6, 2004	Matt Hasselbeck, Seattle vs. Dallas	40	28	414	3
Dec. 5, 2004	Peyton Manning, Indianapolis vs. Tennessee	33	25	425	3
Dec. 5, 2004	Donovan McNabb, Philadelphia vs. Green Bay	43	32	464	5
Nov. 29, 2004	Marc Bulger, St. Louis vs. Green Bay	53	35	448	2
Nov. 28, 2004	Kelly Holcomb, Cleveland vs. Cincinnati	39	30	413	5
Oct. 31, 2004	Peyton Manning, Indianapolis vs. Kansas City	44	25	472	5
Oct. 31, 2004	Jake Plummer, Denver vs. Atlanta	55	31	499	4
Oct. 17, 2004	Daunte Culpepper, Minnesota vs. New Orleans	37	26	425	5
Oct. 10. 2004	Tim Rattay, San Francisco vs. Arizona (OT)	57	38	417	2
Nov. 16, 2003	Peyton Manning, Indianapolis vs. N.Y. Jets	36	27	401	1
Oct. 12, 2003	Trent Green, Kansas City vs. Green Bay (OT)	45	27	400	3
Oct. 12, 2003	Steve McNair, Tennessee vs. Houston	27	18	421	3
Dec. 29, 2002	Matt Hasselbeck, Seattle vs. San Diego (OT)	53	36	449	2
Dec. 1, 2002	Matt Hasselbeck, Seattle vs. San Francisco	55	30	427	3
Nov. 10, 2002	Marc Bulger, St. Louis vs. San Diego	48	36	453	4
Nov. 10, 2002	Tommy Maddox, Pittsburgh vs. Atlanta (OT)	41	28	473	4
Oct. 6, 2002	Drew Bledsoe, Buffalo vs. Oakland	53	32	417	2
Sept. 22, 2002	Tom Brady, New England vs. Kansas City (OT)	54	39	410	4
Sept. 15, 2002	Drew Bledsoe, Buffalo vs. Minnesota (OT)	49	35	463	3
Sept. 15, 2002	Rich Gannon, Oakland vs. Pittsburgh	64	43	403	1
Dec. 30, 2001	Jon Kitna, Cincinnati vs. Pittsburgh	68	35	411	2

Date	Player, Team, Opponent	Att.	Comp.	Yards	TD
Dec. 23, 2001	Chris Chandler, Atlanta vs. Buffalo	40	28	431	2
Nov. 18, 2001	Charlie Batch, Detroit vs. Arizona	62	36	436	3
Nov. 18, 2001	Kurt Warner, St. Louis vs. New England	42	30	401	3
Sept. 23, 2001	Peyton Manning, Indianapolis vs. Buffalo	29	23	421	4
Dec. 24, 2000	Vinny Testaverde, N.Y. Jets vs. Baltimore	69	36	481	2
Dec. 17, 2000	Jeff Garcia, San Francisco vs. Chicago	44	36	402	2
Dec. 3, 2000	Aaron Brooks, New Orleans vs. Denver	48	30	441	2
Nov. 19, 2000	Gus Frerotte, Denver vs. San Diego	58	36	462	5
Nov. 5, 2000	Elvis Grbac, Kansas City vs. Oakland	53	39	504	2
Nov. 5, 2000	Trent Green, St. Louis vs. Carolina	42	29	431	2
Sept. 25, 2000	Peyton Manning, Indianapolis vs. Jacksonville	36	23	440	4
Sept. 4, 2000	Kurt Warner, St. Louis vs. Denver	35	25	441	3
Dec. 26, 1999	Brad Johnson, Washington vs. San Francisco (OT)	47	32	471	2
Dec. 5, 1999	Jeff Garcia, San Francisco vs. Cincinnati	49	33	437	3
Nov. 28, 1999	Jim Harbaugh, San Diego vs. Minnesota	39	25	404	1
Nov. 14, 1999	Jim Miller, Chicago vs. Minnesota (OT)	48	34	422	3
Sept. 26, 1999	Peyton Manning, Indianapolis vs. San Diego	54	29	404	2
Dec. 6, 1998	Vinny Testaverde, N.Y. Jets vs. Seattle	63	42	418	2
Dec. 6, 1998	John Elway, Denver vs. Kansas City	32	22	400	2
Nov. 26, 1998	Troy Aikman, Dallas vs. Minnesota	57	34	455	1
Nov. 23, 1998	Drew Bledsoe, New England vs. Miami	54	28	423	2
Nov. 15, 1998	Jake Plummer, Arizona vs. Dallas	56	31	465	3
Oct. 5, 1998	Randall Cunningham, Minnesota vs. Green Bay	32	20	442	4
Sept. 6, 1998	Glenn Foley, N.Y. Jets vs. San Francisco (OT)	58	30	415	3
Nov. 2, 1997	Tony Banks, St. Louis vs. Atlanta	34	23	401	2
Oct. 26, 1997	Warren Moon, Seattle vs. Oakland	44	28	409	5
Nov. 10, 1996	Boomer Esiason, Arizona vs. Washington (OT)	59	35	522	3
Nov. 3, 1996	Drew Bledsoe, New England vs. Miami	41	30	419	3
Oct. 27, 1996	Vinny Testaverde, Baltimore vs. St. Louis (OT)	51	31	429	3
Oct. 20, 1996	Mark Brunell, Jacksonville vs. St. Louis	52	37	421	0
Sept. 22, 1996	Mark Brunell, Jacksonville vs. New England (OT)	39	23	432	3
Dec. 18, 1995	Steve Young, San Francisco vs. Minnesota	49	30	425	3
Nov. 26, 1995	Dave Krieg, Arizona vs. Atlanta (OT)	43	27	413	4
Nov. 23, 1995	Scott Mitchell, Detroit vs. Minnesota	45	30	410	4
Oct. 1, 1995	Dan Marino, Miami vs. Cincinnati	48	33	450	2
Nov. 20, 1994	Warren Moon, Minnesota vs. N.Y. Jets	50	33	400	2
Nov. 13, 1994	Drew Bledsoe, New England vs. Minnesota (OT)	70	45	426	3
Nov. 6, 1994	Warren Moon, Minnesota vs. New Orleans	57	33	420	3
Sept. 25, 1994	Dan Marino, Miami vs. Minnesota	54	29	431	3
Sept. 4, 1994	Dan Marino, Miami vs. New England (OT)	42	23	473	5
Sept. 4, 1994	Drew Bledsoe, New England vs. Miami (OT)	51	32	421	4
Dec. 19, 1993	Steve Beuerlein, Phoenix vs. Seattle	53	34	431	3
Dec. 5, 1993	Brett Favre, Green Bay vs. Chicago	54	36	402	2
Nov. 28, 1993	Steve Young, San Francisco vs. L.A. Rams	32	26	462	4
Oct. 31, 1993	Jeff Hostetler, L.A. Raiders vs. San Diego	32	20	424	2
Sept. 13, 1992	Steve Young, San Francisco vs. Buffalo	37	26	449	3
Sept. 13, 1992	Jim Kelly, Buffalo vs. San Francisco	33	22	403	3
Nov. 10, 1991	Warren Moon, Houston vs. Dallas (OT)	56	41	432	0
Nov. 10, 1991	Mark Rypien, Washington vs. Atlanta	31	16	442	6
Oct. 13, 1991	Warren Moon, Houston vs. N.Y. Jets	50	35	423	2
Dec. 16, 1990	Warren Moon, Houston vs. Kansas City	45	27	527	3
Nov. 4, 1990	Joe Montana, San Francisco vs. Green Bay	40	25	411	3
Oct. 14, 1990	Joe Montana, San Francisco vs. Atlanta	49	32	476	6
Oct. 7, 1990	Boomer Esiason, Cincinnati vs. L.A. Rams (OT)	45	31	490	3
Dec. 23, 1989	Warren Moon, Houston vs. Cleveland	51	32	414	2
Dec. 11, 1989	Joe Montana, San Francisco vs. L.A. Rams	42	30	458	3
Nov. 26, 1989	Jim Everett, L.A. Rams vs. New Orleans (OT)	51	29	454	1
Nov. 26, 1989	Mark Rypien, Washington vs. Chicago	47	30	401	4
Oct. 2, 1989	Randall Cunningham, Philadelphia vs. Chicago	62	32	401	1
Sept. 24, 1989	Joe Montana, San Francisco vs. Philadelphia	34	25	428	5
Sept. 24, 1989	Dan Marino, Miami vs. N.Y. Jets	55	33	427	3
Sept. 17, 1989	Randall Cunningham, Philadelphia vs. Washington	46	34	447	5
Dec. 18, 1988	Dave Krieg, Seattle vs. L.A. Raiders	32	19	410	4
Dec. 12, 1988	Dan Marino, Miami vs. Cleveland	50	30	404	4
Oct. 23, 1988	Dan Marino, Miami vs. N.Y. Jets	60	35	521	3
Oct. 16, 1988	Vinny Testaverde, Tampa Bay vs. Indianapolis	42	25	469	2
Sept. 11, 1988	Doug Williams, Washington vs. Pittsburgh	52	30	430	2
Nov. 29, 1987	Tom Ramsey, New England vs. Philadelphia	53	34	402	3

Date	Player, Team, Opponent	Att.	Comp.	Yards	TD
Nov. 22, 1987	Boomer Esiason, Cincinnati vs. Pittsburgh	53	30	409	0
Sept. 20, 1987	Neil Lomax, St. Louis vs. San Diego	61	32	457	3
Dec. 21, 1986	Boomer Esiason, Cincinnati vs. N.Y. Jets	30	23	425	5
Dec. 14, 1986	Dan Marino, Miami vs. L.A. Rams (OT)	46	29	403	5
Nov. 23, 1986	Bernie Kosar, Cleveland vs. Pittsburgh (OT)	46	28	414	2
Nov. 17, 1986	Joe Montana, San Francisco vs. Washington	60	33	441	0
Nov. 16, 1986	Dan Marino, Miami vs. Buffalo	54	39	404	4
Nov. 10, 1986	Bernie Kosar, Cleveland vs. Miami	50	32	401	0
Nov. 2, 1986	Tommy Kramer, Minnesota vs. Washington (OT)	35	20	490	4
Nov. 2, 1986	Ken O'Brien, N.Y. Jets vs. Seattle	32	26	431	4
Oct. 27, 1986	Jay Schroeder, Washington vs. N.Y. Giants	40	22	420	1
Oct. 12, 1986	Steve Grogan, New England vs. N.Y. Jets	42	23	401	3
Sept. 21, 1986	Ken O'Brien, N.Y. Jets vs. Miami (OT)	43	29	479	4
Sept. 21, 1986	Dan Marino, Miami vs. N.Y. Jets (OT)	50	30	448	6
Sept. 21, 1986	Tony Eason, New England vs. Seattle	45	26	414	3
Dec. 20, 1985	John Elway, Denver vs. Seattle	42	24	432	1
Nov. 10, 1985	Dan Fouts, San Diego vs. L.A. Raiders (OT)	41	26	436	4
Oct. 13, 1985	Phil Simms, N.Y. Giants vs. Cincinnati	62	40	513	1
Oct. 13, 1985	Dave Krieg, Seattle vs. Atlanta	51	33	405	4
Oct. 6, 1985	Phil Simms, N.Y. Giants vs. Dallas	36	18	432	3
Oct. 6, 1985	Joe Montana, San Francisco vs. Atlanta	57	37	429	5
Sept. 19, 1985	Tommy Kramer, Minnesota vs. Chicago	55	28	436	3
Sept. 15, 1985	Dan Fouts, San Diego vs. Seattle	43	29	440	4
Dec. 16, 1984	Neil Lomax, St. Louis vs. Washington	46	37	468	2
Dec. 9, 1984	Dan Marino, Miami vs. Indianapolis	41	29	404	4
Dec. 2, 1984	Dan Marino, Miami vs. L.A. Raiders	57	35	470	4
Nov. 25, 1984	Dave Krieg, Seattle vs. Denver	44	30	406	3
Nov. 4, 1984	Dan Marino, Miami vs. N.Y. Jets	42	23	422	2
Oct. 21, 1984	Dan Fouts, San Diego vs. L.A. Raiders	45	24	410	3
Sept. 30, 1984	Dan Marino, Miami vs. St. Louis	36	24	429	3
Sept. 2, 1984	Phil Simms, N.Y. Giants vs. Philadelphia	30	23	409	4
Dec. 11, 1983	Bill Kenney, Kansas City vs. San Diego	41	31	411	4
Nov. 20, 1983	Dave Krieg, Seattle vs. Denver	42	31	418	3
Oct. 9, 1983	Joe Ferguson, Buffalo vs. Miami (OT)	55	38	419	5
Oct. 2, 1983	Joe Theismann, Washington vs. L.A. Raiders	39	23	417	3
Sept. 25, 1983	Richard Todd, N.Y. Jets vs. L.A. Rams (OT)	50	37	446	2
Dec. 26, 1982	Vince Ferragamo, L.A. Rams vs. Chicago	46	30	509	3
Dec. 20, 1982	Dan Fouts, San Diego vs. Cincinnati	40	25	435	1
Dec. 20, 1982	Ken Anderson, Cincinnati vs. San Diego	56	40	416	2
Dec. 11, 1982	Dan Fouts, San Diego vs. San Francisco	48	33	444	5
Nov. 21, 1982	Joe Montana, San Francisco vs. St. Louis	39	26	408	3
Nov. 15, 1981	Steve Bartkowski, Atlanta vs. Pittsburgh	50	33	416	2
Oct. 25, 1981	Brian Sipe, Cleveland vs. Baltimore	41	30	444	4
Oct. 25, 1981	David Woodley, Miami vs. Dallas	37	21	408	3
Oct. 11, 1981	Tommy Kramer, Minnesota vs. San Diego	43	27	444	4
Dec. 14, 1980	Tommy Kramer, Minnesota vs. Cleveland	49	38	456	4
Nov. 16, 1980	Doug Williams, Tampa Bay vs. Minnesota	55	30	486	4
Oct. 19, 1980	Dan Fouts, San Diego vs. N.Y. Giants	41	26	444	3
Oct. 12, 1980	Lynn Dickey, Green Bay vs. Tampa Bay (OT)	51	35	418	1
Sept. 21, 1980	Richard Todd, N.Y. Jets vs. San Francisco	60	42	447	3
Oct. 3, 1976	James Harris, Los Angeles vs. Miami	29	17	436	2
Nov. 17, 1975	Ken Anderson, Cincinnati vs. Buffalo	46	30	447	2
Nov. 18, 1974	Charley Johnson, Denver vs. Kansas City	42	28	445	2
Dec. 11, 1972	Joe Namath, N.Y. Jets vs. Oakland	46	25	403	1
Sept. 24, 1972	Joe Namath, N.Y. Jets vs. Baltimore	28	15	496	6
Dec. 21, 1969	Don Horn, Green Bay vs. St. Louis	31	22	410	5
Sept. 28, 1969	Joe Kapp, Minnesota vs. Baltimore	43	28	449	7
Sept. 9, 1968	Pete Beathard, Houston vs. Kansas City	48	23	413	2
Nov. 26, 1967	Sonny Jurgensen, Washington vs. Cleveland	50	32	418	3
Oct. 1, 1967	Joe Namath, N.Y. Jets vs. Miami	39	23	415	3
Sept. 17, 1967	Johnny Unitas, Baltimore vs. Atlanta	32	22	401	2
Nov. 13, 1966	Don Meredith, Dallas vs. Washington	29	21	406	2
Nov. 28, 1965	Sonny Jurgensen, Washington vs. Dallas	43	26	411	3
Oct. 24, 1965	Fran Tarkenton, Minnesota vs. San Francisco	35	21	407	3
Nov. 1, 1964	Len Dawson, Kansas City vs. Denver	38	23	435	6
Oct. 25, 1964	Cotton Davidson, Oakland vs. Denver	36	23	427	5
Oct. 16, 1964	Babe Parilli, Boston vs. Oakland	47	25	422	4
Dec. 22, 1963	Tom Flores, Oakland vs. Houston	29	17	407	6

Date	Player, Team, Opponent	Att.	Comp.	Yards	TD
Nov. 17, 1963	Norm Snead, Washington vs. Pittsburgh	40	23	424	2
Nov. 10, 1963	Don Meredith, Dallas vs. San Francisco	48	30	460	3
Oct. 13, 1963	Charley Johnson, St. Louis vs. Pittsburgh	41	20	428	2
Dec. 16, 1962	Sonny Jurgensen, Philadelphia vs. St. Louis	34	15	419	5
Nov. 18, 1962	Bill Wade, Chicago vs. Dall. Cowboys	46	28	466	2
Oct. 28, 1962	Y.A. Tittle, N.Y. Giants vs. Washington	39	27	505	7
Sept. 15, 1962	Frank Tripucka, Denver vs. Buffalo	56	29	447	2
Dec. 17, 1961	Sonny Jurgensen, Philadelphia vs. Detroit	42	27	403	3
Nov. 19, 1961	George Blanda, Houston vs. N.Y. Titans	32	20	418	7
Oct. 29, 1961	George Blanda, Houston vs. Buffalo	32	18	464	4
Oct. 29, 1961	Sonny Jurgensen, Philadelphia vs. Washington	41	27	436	3
Oct. 13, 1961	Jacky Lee, Houston vs. Boston	41	27	457	2
Dec. 13, 1958	Bobby Layne, Pittsburgh vs. Chi. Cardinals	49	23	409	2
Nov. 8, 1953	Bobby Thomason, Philadelphia vs. N.Y. Giants	44	22	437	4
Oct. 4, 1952	Otto Graham, Cleveland vs. Pittsburgh	49	21	401	3
Sept. 28, 1951	Norm Van Brocklin, Los Angeles vs. N.Y. Yanks	41	27	554	5
Dec. 11, 1949	Johnny Lujack, Chi. Bears vs. Chi. Cardinals	39	24	468	6
Oct. 31, 1948	Sammy Baugh, Washington vs. Boston	24	17	446	4
Oct. 31, 1948	Jim Hardy, Los Angeles vs. Chi. Cardinals	53	28	406	3
Nov. 14, 1943	Sid Luckman, Chi. Bears vs. N.Y. Giants	32	21	433	7

TIMES 400 OR MORE

201 times by 105 players...Marino 13; Manning, Montana, Moon 7; Bledsoe, Fouts 6; Jurgensen, Krieg 5; Brees, Bulger, Esiason, Kramer, Testaverde, Warner 4; Cunningham, Hasselbeck, Namath, Simms, Young 3; Anderson, Blanda, Brunell, Cassel, Culpepper, Elway, Garcia, Green, Johnson, Kitna, Kosar, Lomax, Meredith, O'Brien, Palmer, Plummer, Rypien, Todd, Volek, Williams 2.

100 PASS RECEPTIONS IN A SEASON

Year	Player, Team	No.	Yards	Avg.	Long	TD
2008	Andre Johnson, Houston[2]	115	1,575	13.7	65	8
	Wes Welker, New England[2]	111	1,165	10.5	64	3
	Brandon Marshall, Denver[2]	104	1,265	12.2	47	6
2007	T.J. Houshmandzadeh, Cincinnati	112	1,143	10.2	42	12
	Wes Welker, New England	112	1,175	10.5	42	8
	Reggie Wayne, Indianapolis	104	1,510	14.5	64	10
	Derrick Mason, Baltimore	103	1,087	10.6	79	5
	Brandon Marshall, Denver	102	1,325	13.0	68	7
	Larry Fitzgerald, Arizona[2]	100	1,409	14.1	48	10
2006	Andre Johnson, Houston	103	1,147	11.1	53	5
2005	Larry Fitzgerald, Arizona	103	1,409	13.7	47	10
	Steve Smith, Carolina	103	1,563	15.2	80	12
	Anquan Boldin, Arizona[2]	102	1,402	13.7	54	7
	Torry Holt, St. Louis[2]	102	1,331	13.0	44	9
2004	Tony Gonzalez, Kansas City	102	1,258	12.3	32	7
2003	Torry Holt, St. Louis	117	1,696	14.5	48	12
	Randy Moss, Minnesota[2]	111	1,632	14.7	72	17
	*Anquan Boldin, Arizona	101	1,377	13.6	71	8
	LaDainian Tomlinson, San Diego	100	725	7.3	73	4
2002	Marvin Harrison, Indianapolis[4]	143	1,722	12.0	69	11
	Hines Ward, Pittsburgh	112	1,329	11.9	72	12
	Randy Moss, Minnesota	106	1,347	12.7	60	7
	Eric Moulds, Buffalo	100	1,292	12.9	70	10
	Terrell Owens, San Francisco	100	1,300	13.0	76	13
2001	Rod Smith, Denver[2]	113	1,343	11.9	65	11
	Jimmy Smith, Jacksonville[2]	112	1,373	12.3	35	8
	Marvin Harrison, Indianapolis[3]	109	1,524	14.0	68	15
	Keyshawn Johnson, Tampa Bay	106	1,266	11.9	47	1
	Troy Brown, New England	101	1,199	11.9	60	5
	Marty Booker, Chicago	100	1,071	10.7	66	8
2000	Marvin Harrison, Indianapolis[2]	102	1,413	13.9	78	14
	Muhsin Muhammad, Carolina	102	1,183	11.6	36	6
	Ed McCaffrey, Denver	101	1,317	13.0	61	9
	Rod Smith, Denver	100	1,602	16.0	49	8
1999	Jimmy Smith, Jacksonville	116	1,636	14.1	62	6
	Marvin Harrison, Indianapolis	115	1,663	14.5	57	12
1997	Tim Brown, Oakland	104	1,408	13.5	59	5
	Herman Moore, Detroit[3]	104	1,293	12.4	79	8
1996	Jerry Rice, San Francisco[4]	108	1,254	11.6	39	8

Year	Player, Team	No.	Yards	Avg.	Long	TD
	Herman Moore, Detroit[2]	106	1,296	12.2	50	9
	Carl Pickens, Cincinnati	100	1,180	11.8	61	12
1995	Herman Moore, Detroit	123	1,686	13.7	69	14
	Jerry Rice, San Francisco[3]	122	1,848	15.1	81	15
	Cris Carter, Minnesota[2]	122	1,371	11.2	60	17
	Isaac Bruce, St. Louis	119	1,781	15.0	72	13
	Michael Irvin, Dallas	111	1,603	14.4	50	10
	Brett Perriman, Detroit	108	1,488	13.8	91	9
	Eric Metcalf, Atlanta	104	1,189	11.4	62	8
	Robert Brooks, Green Bay	102	1,497	14.7	99	13
	Larry Centers, Arizona	101	962	9.5	32	2
1994	Cris Carter, Minnesota	122	1,256	10.3	65	7
	Jerry Rice, San Francisco[2]	112	1,499	13.4	69	13
	Terance Mathis, Atlanta	111	1,342	12.1	81	11
1993	Sterling Sharpe, Green Bay[2]	112	1,274	11.4	54	11
1992	Sterling Sharpe, Green Bay	108	1,461	13.5	76	13
1991	Haywood Jeffires, Houston	100	1,181	11.8	44	7
1990	Jerry Rice, San Francisco	100	1,502	15.0	64	13
1984	Art Monk, Washington	106	1,372	12.9	72	7
1964	Charley Hennigan, Houston	101	1,546	15.3	53	8
1961	Lionel Taylor, Denver	100	1,176	11.8	52	4

**First season of professional football.*

1,000 YARDS PASS RECEIVING IN A SEASON

Year	Player, Team	No.	Yards	Avg.	Long	TD
2008	Andre Johnson, Houston[3]	115	1,575	13.7	65	8
	Larry Fitzgerald, Arizona[3]	96	1,431	14.9	78	12
	Steve Smith, Carolina[5]	78	1,421	18.2	65	6
	Roddy White, Atlanta[2]	88	1,382	15.7	70	7
	Calvin Johnson, Detroit	78	1,331	17.1	96	12
	Greg Jennings, Green Bay	80	1,292	16.1	63	9
	Brandon Marshall, Denver[2]	104	1,265	12.2	47	6
	Antonio Bryant, Tampa Bay[2]	83	1,248	15.0	71	7
	Wes Welker, New England[2]	111	1,165	10.5	64	3
	Reggie Wayne, Indianapolis[5]	82	1,145	14.0	65	6
	Vincent Jackson, San Diego	59	1,098	18.6	60	7
	Tony Gonzalez, Kansas City[4]	96	1,058	11.0	35	10
	Terrell Owens, Dallas[9]	69	1,052	15.2	75	10
	Santana Moss, Washington[3]	79	1,044	13.2	67	6
	Hines Ward, Pittsburgh[5]	81	1,043	12.9	49	7
	Anquan Boldin, Arizona[4]	89	1,038	11.7	79	11
	Derrick Mason, Baltimore[7]	80	1,037	13.0	54	5
	Dwayne Bowe, Kansas City	86	1,022	11.9	36	7
	Lee Evans, Buffalo[2]	63	1,017	16.1	87	3
	Donald Driver, Green Bay[6]	74	1,012	13.7	71	5
	Randy Moss, New England[9]	69	1,008	14.6	76	11
	Steve Breaston, Arizona	77	1,006	13.1	58	3
2007	Reggie Wayne, Indianapolis[4]	104	1,510	14.5	64	10
	Randy Moss, New England[8]	98	1,493	15.2	65	23
	Chad Ochocinco, Cincinnati[6]	93	1,440	15.5	70	8
	Larry Fitzgerald, Arizona[2]	100	1,409	14.1	48	10
	Terrell Owens, Dallas[8]	81	1,355	16.7	52	15
	Brandon Marshall, Denver	102	1,325	13.0	68	7
	Braylon Edwards, Cleveland	80	1,289	16.1	78	16
	Marques Colston, New Orleans[2]	98	1,202	12.3	45	11
	Roddy White, Atlanta	83	1,202	14.5	69	6
	Torry Holt, St. Louis[8]	93	1,189	12.8	40	7
	Wes Welker, New England	112	1,175	10.5	42	8
	Tony Gonzalez, Kansas City[3]	99	1,172	11.8	31	5
	Bobby Engram, Seattle	94	1,147	12.2	49	6
	Jason Witten, Dallas	96	1,145	11.9	53	7
	T.J. Houshmandzadeh, Cincinnati[2]	112	1,143	10.2	42	12
	Jerricho Cotchery, N.Y. Jets	82	1,130	13.8	50	2
	Kevin Curtis, Philadelphia	77	1,110	14.4	75	6
	Kellen Winslow, Cleveland	82	1,106	13.5	49	5
	Derrick Mason, Baltimore[6]	103	1,087	10.6	79	5
	Donald Driver, Green Bay[5]	82	1,048	12.8	47	2
	Plaxico Burress, N.Y. Giants[4]	70	1,025	14.6	60	12
	Joey Galloway, Tampa Bay[6]	57	1,014	17.8	69	6

Year	Player, Team	No.	Yards	Avg.	Long	TD
	Steve Smith, Carolina[4]	87	1,002	11.5	74	7
2006	Chad Ochocinco, Cincinnati[5]	87	1,369	15.7	74	7
	Marvin Harrison, Indianapolis[8]	95	1,366	14.4	68	12
	Reggie Wayne, Indianapolis[3]	86	1,310	15.2	51	9
	Roy Williams, Detroit	82	1,310	16.0	60	7
	Donald Driver, Green Bay[4]	92	1,295	14.1	82	8
	Lee Evans, Buffalo	82	1,292	15.8	83	8
	Anquan Boldin, Arizona[3]	83	1,203	14.5	64	4
	Torry Holt, St. Louis[7]	93	1,188	12.8	67	10
	Terrell Owens, Dallas[7]	85	1,180	13.9	56	13
	Steve Smith, Carolina[3]	83	1,166	14.1	72	8
	Andre Johnson, Houston[2]	103	1,147	11.1	53	5
	Isaac Bruce, St. Louis[8]	74	1,098	14.8	45	3
	Laveranues Coles, N.Y. Jets[2]	91	1,098	12.1	58	6
	Mike Furrey, Detroit	98	1,086	11.1	31	6
	Javon Walker, Denver[2]	69	1,084	15.7	83	8
	T.J. Houshmandzadeh, Cincinnati	90	1,081	12.0	40	9
	Joey Galloway, Tampa Bay[5]	62	1,057	17.1	64	7
	Terry Glenn, Dallas[4]	70	1,047	15.0	54	6
	*Marques Colston, New Orleans	70	1,038	14.8	86	8
2005	Steve Smith, Carolina[2]	103	1,563	15.2	80	12
	Santana Moss, Washington[2]	84	1,483	17.7	78	9
	Chad Ochocinco, Cincinnati[4]	97	1,432	14.8	70	9
	Larry Fitzgerald, Arizona	103	1,409	13.7	47	10
	Anquan Boldin, Arizona[2]	102	1,402	13.7	54	7
	Torry Holt, St. Louis[6]	102	1,331	13.0	44	9
	Joey Galloway, Tampa Bay[4]	83	1,287	15.5	80	10
	Donald Driver, Green Bay[3]	86	1,221	14.2	59	5
	Plaxico Burress, N.Y. Giants[3]	76	1,214	16.0	78	7
	Marvin Harrison, Indianapolis[7]	82	1,146	14.0	80	12
	Terry Glenn, Dallas[3]	62	1,136	18.3	71	7
	Chris Chambers, Miami	82	1,118	13.6	77	11
	Rod Smith, Denver[8]	85	1,105	13.0	72	6
	Eddie Kennison, Kansas City[2]	68	1,102	16.2	55	5
	Antonio Gates, San Diego	89	1,101	12.4	38	10
	Derrick Mason, Baltimore[5]	86	1,073	12.5	39	3
	Reggie Wayne, Indianapolis[2]	83	1,055	12.7	66	5
	Jimmy Smith, Jacksonville[9]	70	1,023	14.6	45	6
	Antonio Bryant, Cleveland	69	1,009	14.6	54	4
	Randy Moss, Oakland[7]	60	1,005	16.8	79	8
2004	Muhsin Muhammad, Carolina[3]	93	1,405	15.1	51	16
	Joe Horn, New Orleans[4]	94	1,399	14.9	57	11
	Javon Walker, Green Bay	89	1,382	15.5	79	12
	Torry Holt, St. Louis[5]	94	1,372	14.6	75	10
	Isaac Bruce, St. Louis[7]	89	1,292	14.5	56	6
	Chad Ochocinco, Cincinnati[3]	95	1,274	13.4	53	9
	Tony Gonzalez, Kansas City[2]	102	1,258	12.3	32	7
	Drew Bennett, Tennessee	80	1,247	15.6	48	11
	Reggie Wayne, Indianapolis	77	1,210	15.7	71	12
	Donald Driver, Green Bay[2]	84	1,208	14.4	50	9
	Terrell Owens, Philadelphia[6]	77	1,200	15.6	59	14
	Darrell Jackson, Seattle[3]	87	1,199	13.8	56	7
	*Michael Clayton, Tampa Bay	80	1,193	14.9	75	7
	Jimmy Smith, Jacksonville[8]	74	1,172	15.8	65	6
	Derrick Mason, Tennessee[4]	96	1,168	12.2	37	7
	Rod Smith, Denver[7]	79	1,144	14.5	85	7
	Andre Johnson, Houston	79	1,142	14.5	54	6
	Marvin Harrison, Indianapolis[6]	86	1,113	12.9	59	15
	Eddie Kennison, Kansas City	62	1,086	17.5	70	8
	Ashley Lelie, Denver	54	1,084	20.1	58	7
	Brandon Stokley, Indianapolis	68	1,077	15.8	69	10
	Eric Moulds, Buffalo[4]	88	1,043	11.9	49	5
	Nate Burleson, Minnesota	68	1,006	14.8	68	9
	Hines Ward, Pittsburgh[4]	80	1,004	12.6	58	4
2003	Torry Holt, St. Louis[4]	117	1,696	14.5	48	12
	Randy Moss, Minnesota[6]	111	1,632	14.7	72	17
	*Anquan Boldin, Arizona	101	1,377	13.6	71	8
	Chad Ochocinco, Cincinnati[2]	90	1,355	15.1	82	10
	Derrick Mason, Tennessee[3]	95	1,303	13.7	50	8

Year	Player, Team	No.	Yards	Avg.	Long	TD
	Marvin Harrison, Indianapolis[5]	94	1,272	13.5	79	10
	Laveranues Coles, Washington[2]	82	1,204	14.7	64	6
	Keenan McCardell, Tampa Bay[5]	84	1,174	14.0	76	8
	Hines Ward, Pittsburgh[3]	95	1,163	12.2	50	10
	Darrell Jackson, Seattle[2]	68	1,137	16.7	80	9
	Steve Smith, Carolina	88	1,110	12.6	67	7
	Santana Moss, N.Y. Jets	74	1,105	14.9	65	10
	Terrell Owens, San Francisco[5]	80	1,102	13.8	75	9
	Amani Toomer, N.Y. Giants[5]	63	1,057	16.8	77	5
2002	Marvin Harrison, Indianapolis[4]	143	1,722	12.0	69	11
	Randy Moss, Minnesota[5]	106	1,347	12.7	60	7
	Amani Toomer, N.Y. Giants[4]	82	1,343	16.4	82	8
	Hines Ward, Pittsburgh[2]	112	1,329	11.9	72	12
	Plaxico Burress, Pittsburgh[2]	78	1,325	17.0	62	7
	Joe Horn, New Orleans[3]	88	1,312	14.9	63	7
	Torry Holt, St. Louis[3]	91	1,302	14.3	58	4
	Terrell Owens, San Francisco[4]	100	1,300	13.0	76	13
	Eric Moulds, Buffalo[3]	100	1,292	12.9	70	10
	Laveranues Coles, N.Y. Jets	89	1,264	14.2	43	5
	Peerless Price, Buffalo	94	1,252	13.3	73	9
	Koren Robinson, Seattle	78	1,240	15.9	83	5
	Jerry Rice, Oakland[14]	92	1,211	13.2	75	7
	Marty Booker, Chicago[2]	97	1,189	12.3	54	6
	Chad Ochocinco, Cincinnati	69	1,166	16.9	72	5
	Keyshawn Johnson, Tampa Bay[4]	76	1,088	14.3	76	5
	Isaac Bruce, St. Louis[6]	79	1,075	13.6	34	7
	Donald Driver, Green Bay	70	1,064	15.2	85	9
	Jimmy Smith, Jacksonville[7]	80	1,027	12.8	47	7
	Rod Smith, Denver[6]	89	1,027	11.5	46	5
	Derrick Mason, Tennessee[2]	79	1,012	12.8	40	5
	Rod Gardner, Washington	71	1,006	14.2	43	8
2001	David Boston, Arizona[2]	98	1,598	16.3	61	8
	Marvin Harrison, Indianapolis[3]	109	1,524	14.0	68	15
	Terrell Owens, San Francisco[3]	93	1,412	15.2	60	16
	Jimmy Smith, Jacksonville[6]	112	1,373	12.3	35	8
	Torry Holt, St. Louis[2]	81	1,363	16.8	51	7
	Rod Smith, Denver[5]	113	1,343	11.9	65	11
	Keyshawn Johnson, Tampa Bay[3]	106	1,266	11.9	47	1
	Joe Horn, New Orleans[2]	83	1,265	15.2	56	9
	Randy Moss, Minnesota[4]	82	1,233	15.0	73	10
	Troy Brown, New England	101	1,199	11.9	60	5
	Tim Brown, Oakland[9]	91	1,165	12.8	46	9
	Johnnie Morton, Detroit[4]	77	1,154	15.0	76	4
	Jerry Rice, Oakland[13]	83	1,139	13.7	40	9
	Derrick Mason, Tennessee	73	1,128	15.5	71	9
	Curtis Conway, San Diego[3]	71	1,125	15.8	72	6
	Keenan McCardell, Jacksonville[4]	93	1,110	11.9	45	6
	Isaac Bruce, St. Louis[5]	64	1,106	17.3	51	6
	Kevin Johnson, Cleveland	84	1,097	13.1	55	9
	Darrell Jackson, Seattle	70	1,081	15.4	64	8
	Marty Booker, Chicago	100	1,071	10.7	66	8
	Qadry Ismail, Baltimore[2]	74	1,059	14.3	77	7
	Amani Toomer, N.Y. Giants[3]	72	1,054	14.6	60	5
	Willie Jackson, New Orleans	81	1,046	12.9	63	5
	Plaxico Burress, Pittsburgh	66	1,008	15.3	43	6
	Hines Ward, Pittsburgh	94	1,003	10.7	34	4
2000	Torry Holt, St. Louis	82	1,635	19.9	85	6
	Rod Smith, Denver[4]	100	1,602	16.0	49	8
	Isaac Bruce, St. Louis[4]	87	1,471	16.9	78	9
	Terrell Owens, San Francisco[2]	97	1,451	15.0	69	13
	Randy Moss, Minnesota[3]	77	1,437	18.7	78	15
	Marvin Harrison, Indianapolis[2]	102	1,413	13.9	78	14
	Derrick Alexander, Kansas City[3]	78	1,391	17.8	81	10
	Joe Horn, New Orleans	94	1,340	14.3	52	8
	Eric Moulds, Buffalo[2]	94	1,326	14.1	52	5
	Ed McCaffrey, Denver[3]	101	1,317	13.0	61	9
	Cris Carter, Minnesota[8]	96	1,274	13.3	53	9
	Jimmy Smith, Jacksonville[5]	91	1,213	13.3	65	8
	Keenan McCardell, Jacksonville[3]	94	1,207	12.8	67	5

Year	Player, Team	No.	Yards	Avg.	Long	TD
	Tony Gonzalez, Kansas City	93	1,203	12.9	39	9
	Muhsin Muhammad, Carolina[2]	102	1,183	11.6	36	6
	David Boston, Arizona	71	1,156	16.3	70	7
	Tim Brown, Oakland[8]	76	1,128	14.8	45	11
	Amani Toomer, N.Y. Giants[2]	78	1,094	14.0	54	7
1999	Marvin Harrison, Indianapolis	115	1,663	14.5	57	12
	Jimmy Smith, Jacksonville[4]	116	1,636	14.1	62	6
	Randy Moss, Minnesota[2]	80	1,413	17.7	67	11
	Marcus Robinson, Chicago	84	1,400	16.7	80	9
	Tim Brown, Oakland[7]	90	1,344	14.9	47	6
	Germane Crowell, Detroit	81	1,338	16.5	77	7
	Muhsin Muhammad, Carolina	96	1,253	13.1	60	8
	Cris Carter, Minnesota[7]	90	1,241	13.8	68	13
	Michael Westbrook, Washington	65	1,191	18.3	65	9
	Amani Toomer, N.Y. Giants	79	1,183	15.0	80	6
	Keyshawn Johnson, N.Y. Jets[2]	89	1,170	13.2	65	8
	Isaac Bruce, St. Louis[3]	77	1,165	15.1	60	12
	Terry Glenn, New England[2]	69	1,147	16.6	67	4
	Albert Connell, Washington	62	1,132	18.3	62	7
	Johnnie Morton, Detroit[3]	80	1,129	14.1	48	5
	Qadry Ismail, Baltimore	68	1,105	16.3	76	6
	Raghib Ismail, Dallas[2]	80	1,097	13.7	76	6
	Patrick Jeffers, Carolina	63	1,082	17.2	88	12
	Antonio Freeman, Green Bay[3]	74	1,074	14.5	51	6
	Bill Schroeder, Green Bay	74	1,051	14.2	51	5
	Marshall Faulk, St. Louis	87	1,048	12.1	57	5
	Tony Martin, Miami[4]	67	1,037	15.5	69	5
	Darnay Scott, Cincinnati	68	1,022	15.0	76	7
	Rod Smith, Denver[3]	79	1,020	12.9	71	4
	Ed McCaffrey, Denver[2]	71	1,018	14.3	78	7
	Terance Mathis, Atlanta[4]	81	1,016	12.5	52	6
1998	Antonio Freeman, Green Bay[2]	84	1,424	17.0	84	14
	Eric Moulds, Buffalo	67	1,368	20.4	84	9
	*Randy Moss, Minnesota	69	1,313	19.0	61	17
	Rod Smith, Denver[2]	86	1,222	14.2	58	6
	Jimmy Smith, Jacksonville[3]	78	1,182	15.2	72	8
	Tony Martin, Atlanta[3]	66	1,181	17.9	62	6
	Jerry Rice, San Francisco[12]	82	1,157	14.1	75	9
	Frank Sanders, Arizona[2]	89	1,145	12.9	42	3
	Terance Mathis, Atlanta[3]	64	1,136	17.8	78	11
	Keyshawn Johnson, N.Y. Jets	83	1,131	13.6	41	10
	Terrell Owens, San Francisco	67	1,097	16.4	79	14
	Wayne Chrebet, N.Y. Jets	75	1,083	14.4	63	8
	Michael Irvin, Dallas[7]	74	1,057	14.3	51	1
	Ed McCaffrey, Denver	64	1,053	16.5	48	10
	O.J. McDuffie, Miami	90	1,050	11.7	61	7
	Joey Galloway, Seattle[3]	65	1,047	16.1	81	10
	Johnnie Morton, Detroit[2]	69	1,028	14.9	98	2
	Raghib Ismail, Carolina	69	1,024	14.8	62	8
	Carl Pickens, Cincinnati[4]	82	1,023	12.5	67	5
	Tim Brown, Oakland[6]	81	1,012	12.5	49	9
	Cris Carter, Minnesota[6]	78	1,011	13.0	54	12
1997	Rob Moore, Arizona[3]	97	1,584	16.3	47	8
	Tim Brown, Oakland[5]	104	1,408	13.5	59	5
	Yancey Thigpen, Pittsburgh[2]	79	1,398	17.7	69	7
	Jimmy Smith, Jacksonville[2]	82	1,324	16.1	75	4
	Irving Fryar, Philadelphia[5]	86	1,316	15.3	72	6
	Herman Moore, Detroit[4]	104	1,293	12.4	79	8
	Antonio Freeman, Green Bay	81	1,243	15.3	58	12
	Michael Irvin, Dallas[6]	75	1,180	15.7	55	9
	Rod Smith, Denver	70	1,180	16.9	78	12
	Keenan McCardell, Jacksonville[2]	85	1,164	13.7	60	5
	Jake Reed, Minnesota[4]	68	1,138	16.7	56	6
	Shannon Sharpe, Denver[3]	72	1,107	15.4	68	3
	Andre Rison, Kansas City[5]	72	1,092	15.2	45	7
	Cris Carter, Minnesota[5]	89	1,069	12.0	43	13
	Johnnie Morton, Detroit	80	1,057	13.2	73	6
	Joey Galloway, Seattle[2]	72	1,049	14.6	53	12
	Frank Sanders, Arizona	75	1,017	13.6	70	4

OUTSTANDING PERFORMERS

Year	Player, Team	No.	Yards	Avg.	Long	TD
	Robert Brooks, Green Bay[2]	60	1,010	16.8	48	7
	Derrick Alexander, Baltimore[2]	65	1,009	15.5	92	9
1996	Isaac Bruce, St. Louis[2]	84	1,338	15.9	70	7
	Jake Reed, Minnesota[3]	72	1,320	18.3	82	7
	Herman Moore, Detroit[3]	106	1,296	12.2	50	9
	Jerry Rice, San Francisco[11]	108	1,254	11.6	39	8
	Jimmy Smith, Jacksonville	83	1,244	15.0	62	7
	Michael Jackson, Baltimore	76	1,201	15.8	86	14
	Irving Fryar, Philadelphia[4]	88	1,195	13.6	42	11
	Carl Pickens, Cincinnati[3]	100	1,180	11.8	61	12
	Tony Martin, San Diego[2]	85	1,171	13.8	55	14
	Cris Carter, Minnesota[4]	96	1,163	12.1	43	10
	*Terry Glenn, New England	90	1,132	12.6	37	6
	Keenan McCardell, Jacksonville	85	1,129	13.3	52	3
	Tim Brown, Oakland[4]	90	1,104	12.3	42	9
	Derrick Alexander, Baltimore	62	1,099	17.7	64	9
	Shannon Sharpe, Denver[2]	80	1,062	13.3	51	10
	Curtis Conway, Chicago[2]	81	1,049	13.0	58	7
	Andre Reed, Buffalo[4]	66	1,036	15.7	67	6
	Brett Perriman, Detroit[2]	94	1,021	10.9	44	5
	Rob Moore, Arizona[2]	58	1,016	17.5	69	4
	Henry Ellard, Washington[7]	52	1,014	19.5	51	2
	Charles Johnson, Pittsburgh	60	1,008	16.8	70	3
1995	Jerry Rice, San Francisco[10]	122	1,848	15.1	81	15
	Isaac Bruce, St. Louis	119	1,781	15.0	72	13
	Herman Moore, Detroit[2]	123	1,686	13.7	69	14
	Michael Irvin, Dallas[5]	111	1,603	14.4	50	10
	Robert Brooks, Green Bay	102	1,497	14.7	99	13
	Brett Perriman, Detroit	108	1,488	13.8	91	9
	Cris Carter, Minnesota[3]	122	1,371	11.2	60	17
	Tim Brown, Oakland[3]	89	1,342	15.1	80	10
	Yancey Thigpen, Pittsburgh	85	1,307	15.4	43	5
	Jeff Graham, Chicago	82	1,301	15.9	51	4
	Carl Pickens, Cincinnati[2]	99	1,234	12.5	68	17
	Tony Martin, San Diego	90	1,224	13.6	51	6
	Eric Metcalf, Atlanta	104	1,189	11.4	62	8
	Jake Reed, Minnesota[2]	72	1,167	16.2	55	9
	Quinn Early, New Orleans	81	1,087	13.4	70	8
	Anthony Miller, Denver[5]	59	1,079	18.3	62	14
	Bert Emanuel, Atlanta	74	1,039	14.0	52	5
	*Joey Galloway, Seattle	67	1,039	15.5	59	7
	Terance Mathis, Atlanta[2]	78	1,039	13.3	54	9
	Curtis Conway, Chicago	62	1,037	16.7	76	12
	Henry Ellard, Washington[6]	56	1,005	17.9	59	5
	Mark Carrier, Carolina[2]	66	1,002	15.2	66	3
	Brian Blades, Seattle[4]	77	1,001	13.0	49	4
1994	Jerry Rice, San Francisco[9]	112	1,499	13.4	69	13
	Henry Ellard, Washington[5]	74	1,397	18.9	73	6
	Terance Mathis, Atlanta	111	1,342	12.1	81	11
	Tim Brown, L.A. Raiders[2]	89	1,309	14.7	77	9
	Andre Reed, Buffalo[2]	90	1,303	14.5	83	8
	Irving Fryar, Miami[3]	73	1,270	17.4	54	7
	Cris Carter, Minnesota[2]	122	1,256	10.3	65	7
	Michael Irvin, Dallas[4]	79	1,241	15.7	65	6
	Jake Reed, Minnesota	85	1,175	13.8	59	4
	Ben Coates, New England	96	1,174	12.2	62	7
	Herman Moore, Detroit	72	1,173	16.3	51	11
	Fred Barnett, Philadelphia[2]	78	1,127	14.4	54	5
	Carl Pickens, Cincinnati	71	1,127	15.9	70	11
	Sterling Sharpe, Green Bay[4]	94	1,119	11.9	49	18
	Anthony Miller, Denver[4]	60	1,107	18.5	76	5
	Andre Rison, Atlanta[3]	81	1,088	13.4	69	8
	Brian Blades, Seattle[3]	81	1,088	13.4	45	4
	Rob Moore, N.Y. Jets	78	1,010	12.9	41	6
	Shannon Sharpe, Denver	87	1,010	11.6	44	4
1993	Jerry Rice, San Francisco[8]	98	1,503	15.3	80	15
	Michael Irvin, Dallas[3]	88	1,330	15.1	61	7
	Sterling Sharpe, Green Bay[4]	112	1,274	11.4	54	11
	Andre Rison, Atlanta[3]	86	1,242	14.4	53	15

Year	Player, Team	No.	Yards	Avg.	Long	TD
	Tim Brown, L.A. Raiders	80	1,180	14.8	71	7
	Anthony Miller, San Diego[3]	84	1,162	13.8	66	7
	Cris Carter, Minnesota	86	1,071	12.5	58	9
	Reggie Langhorne, Indianapolis	85	1,038	12.2	72	3
	Irving Fryar, Miami[2]	64	1,010	15.8	65	5
1992	Sterling Sharpe, Green Bay[3]	108	1,461	13.5	76	13
	Michael Irvin, Dallas[2]	78	1,396	17.9	87	7
	Jerry Rice, San Francisco[7]	84	1,201	14.3	80	10
	Andre Rison, Atlanta[2]	93	1,119	12.0	71	11
	Fred Barnett, Philadelphia	67	1,083	16.2	71	6
	Anthony Miller, San Diego[2]	72	1,060	14.7	67	7
	Eric Martin, New Orleans[3]	68	1,041	15.3	52	5
1991	Michael Irvin, Dallas	93	1,523	16.4	66	8
	Gary Clark, Washington[5]	70	1,340	19.1	82	10
	Jerry Rice, San Francisco[6]	80	1,206	15.1	73	14
	Haywood Jeffires, Houston[2]	100	1,181	11.8	44	7
	Michael Haynes, Atlanta	50	1,122	22.4	80	11
	Andre Reed, Buffalo[2]	81	1,113	13.7	55	10
	Drew Hill, Houston[5]	90	1,109	12.3	61	4
	Mark Duper, Miami[4]	70	1,085	15.5	43	5
	James Lofton, Buffalo[6]	57	1,072	18.8	77	8
	Mark Clayton, Miami[5]	70	1,053	15.0	43	12
	Henry Ellard, L.A. Rams[4]	64	1,052	16.4	38	3
	Art Monk, Washington[5]	71	1,049	14.8	64	8
	Irving Fryar, New England	68	1,014	14.9	56	3
	John Taylor, San Francisco[2]	64	1,011	15.8	97	9
	Brian Blades, Seattle[2]	70	1,003	14.3	52	2
1990	Jerry Rice, San Francisco[5]	100	1,502	15.0	64	13
	Henry Ellard, L.A. Rams[3]	76	1,294	17.0	50	4
	Andre Rison, Atlanta	82	1,208	14.7	75	10
	Gary Clark, Washington[4]	75	1,112	14.8	53	8
	Sterling Sharpe, Green Bay[2]	67	1,105	16.5	76	6
	Willie Anderson, L.A. Rams[2]	51	1,097	21.5	55	4
	Haywood Jeffires, Houston	74	1,048	14.2	87	8
	Stephone Paige, Kansas City	65	1,021	15.7	86	5
	Drew Hill, Houston[4]	74	1,019	13.8	57	5
	Anthony Carter, Minnesota[3]	70	1,008	14.4	56	8
1989	Jerry Rice, San Francisco[4]	82	1,483	18.1	68	17
	Sterling Sharpe, Green Bay	90	1,423	15.8	79	12
	Mark Carrier, Tampa Bay	86	1,422	16.5	78	9
	Henry Ellard, L.A. Rams[2]	70	1,382	19.7	53	8
	Andre Reed, Buffalo	88	1,312	14.9	78	9
	Anthony Miller, San Diego	75	1,252	16.7	69	10
	Webster Slaughter, Cleveland	65	1,236	19.0	97	6
	Gary Clark, Washington[3]	79	1,229	15.6	80	9
	Tim McGee, Cincinnati	65	1,211	18.6	74	8
	Art Monk, Washington[4]	86	1,186	13.8	60	8
	Willie Anderson, L.A. Rams	44	1,146	26.0	78	5
	Ricky Sanders, Washington[2]	80	1,138	14.2	68	4
	Vance Johnson, Denver	76	1,095	14.4	69	7
	Richard Johnson, Detroit	70	1,091	15.6	75	8
	Eric Martin, New Orleans[2]	68	1,090	16.0	53	8
	John Taylor, San Francisco	60	1,077	18.0	95	10
	Mervyn Fernandez, L.A. Raiders	57	1,069	18.8	75	9
	Anthony Carter, Minnesota[2]	65	1,066	16.4	50	4
	Brian Blades, Seattle	77	1,063	13.8	60	5
	Mark Clayton, Miami[4]	64	1,011	15.8	78	9
1988	Henry Ellard, L.A. Rams	86	1,414	16.4	68	10
	Jerry Rice, San Francisco[3]	64	1,306	20.4	96	9
	Eddie Brown, Cincinnati	53	1,273	24.0	86	9
	Anthony Carter, Minnesota	72	1,225	17.0	67	6
	Ricky Sanders, Washington	73	1,148	15.7	55	12
	Drew Hill, Houston[3]	72	1,141	15.8	57	10
	Mark Clayton, Miami[3]	86	1,129	13.1	45	14
	Roy Green, Phoenix[3]	68	1,097	16.1	52	7
	Eric Martin, New Orleans	85	1,083	12.7	40	7
	Al Toon, N.Y. Jets[2]	93	1,067	11.5	42	5
	Bruce Hill, Tampa Bay	58	1,040	17.9	42	9
	Lionel Manuel, N.Y. Giants	65	1,029	15.8	46	4

OUTSTANDING PERFORMERS

Year	Player, Team	No.	Yards	Avg.	Long	TD
1987	J.T. Smith, St. Louis[2]	91	1,117	12.3	38	8
	Jerry Rice, San Francisco[2]	65	1,078	16.6	57	22
	Gary Clark, Washington[2]	56	1,066	19.0	84	7
	Carlos Carson, Kansas City[3]	55	1,044	19.0	81	7
1986	Jerry Rice, San Francisco	86	1,570	18.3	66	15
	Stanley Morgan, New England[3]	84	1,491	17.8	44	10
	Mark Duper, Miami[3]	67	1,313	19.6	85	11
	Gary Clark, Washington	74	1,265	17.1	55	7
	Al Toon, N.Y. Jets	85	1,176	13.8	62	8
	Todd Christensen, L.A. Raiders[3]	95	1,153	12.1	35	8
	Mark Clayton, Miami[2]	60	1,150	19.2	68	10
	*Bill Brooks, Indianapolis	65	1,131	17.4	84	8
	Drew Hill, Houston[2]	65	1,112	17.1	81	5
	Steve Largent, Seattle[8]	70	1,070	15.3	38	9
	Art Monk, Washington[3]	73	1,068	14.6	69	4
	*Ernest Givins, Houston	61	1,062	17.4	60	3
	Cris Collinsworth, Cincinnati[4]	62	1,024	16.5	46	10
	Wesley Walker, N.Y. Jets[2]	49	1,016	20.7	83	12
	J.T. Smith, St. Louis	80	1,014	12.7	45	6
	Mark Bavaro, N.Y. Giants	66	1,001	15.2	41	4
1985	Steve Largent, Seattle[7]	79	1,287	16.3	43	6
	Mike Quick, Philadelphia[3]	73	1,247	17.1	99	11
	Art Monk, Washington[2]	91	1,226	13.5	53	2
	Wes Chandler, San Diego[4]	67	1,199	17.9	75	10
	Drew Hill, Houston	64	1,169	18.3	57	9
	James Lofton, Green Bay[5]	69	1,153	16.7	56	4
	Louis Lipps, Pittsburgh	59	1,134	19.2	51	12
	Cris Collinsworth, Cincinnati[3]	65	1,125	17.3	71	5
	Tony Hill, Dallas[3]	74	1,113	15.0	53	7
	Lionel James, San Diego	86	1,027	11.9	67	6
	Roger Craig, San Francisco	92	1,016	11.0	73	6
1984	Roy Green, St. Louis[2]	78	1,555	19.9	83	12
	John Stallworth, Pittsburgh[3]	80	1,395	17.4	51	11
	Mark Clayton, Miami	73	1,389	19.0	65	18
	Art Monk, Washington	106	1,372	12.9	72	7
	James Lofton, Green Bay[4]	62	1,361	22.0	79	7
	Mark Duper, Miami[2]	71	1,306	18.4	80	8
	Steve Watson, Denver[3]	69	1,170	17.0	73	7
	Steve Largent, Seattle[6]	74	1,164	15.7	65	12
	Tim Smith, Houston[2]	69	1,141	16.5	75	4
	Stacey Bailey, Atlanta	67	1,138	17.0	61	6
	Carlos Carson, Kansas City[2]	57	1,078	18.9	57	4
	Mike Quick, Philadelphia[2]	61	1,052	17.2	90	9
	Todd Christensen, L.A. Raiders[2]	80	1,007	12.6	38	7
	Kevin House, Tampa Bay[2]	76	1,005	13.2	55	5
	Ozzie Newsome, Cleveland[2]	89	1,001	11.2	52	5
1983	Mike Quick, Philadelphia	69	1,409	20.4	83	13
	Carlos Carson, Kansas City	80	1,351	16.9	50	7
	James Lofton, Green Bay[3]	58	1,300	22.4	74	8
	Todd Christensen, L.A. Raiders	92	1,247	13.6	45	12
	Roy Green, St. Louis	78	1,227	15.7	71	14
	Charlie Brown, Washington	78	1,225	15.7	75	8
	Tim Smith, Houston	83	1,176	14.2	47	6
	Kellen Winslow, San Diego[3]	88	1,172	13.3	46	8
	Earnest Gray, N.Y. Giants	78	1,139	14.6	62	5
	Steve Watson, Denver[2]	59	1,133	19.2	78	5
	Cris Collinsworth, Cincinnati[2]	66	1,130	17.1	63	5
	Steve Largent, Seattle[5]	72	1,074	14.9	46	11
	Mark Duper, Miami	51	1,003	19.7	85	10
1982	Wes Chandler, San Diego[3]	49	1,032	21.1	66	9
1981	Alfred Jenkins, Atlanta[2]	70	1,358	19.4	67	13
	James Lofton, Green Bay[2]	71	1,294	18.2	75	8
	Steve Watson, Denver	60	1,244	20.7	95	13
	Frank Lewis, Buffalo[2]	70	1,244	17.8	33	4
	Steve Largent, Seattle[4]	75	1,224	16.3	57	9
	Charlie Joiner, San Diego[4]	70	1,188	17.0	57	7
	Kevin House, Tampa Bay	56	1,176	21.0	84	9
	Wes Chandler, N.O.-San Diego[2]	69	1,142	16.6	51	6
	Dwight Clark, San Francisco	85	1,105	13.0	78	4

Year	Player, Team	No.	Yards	Avg.	Long	TD
	John Stallworth, Pittsburgh[2]	63	1,098	17.4	55	5
	Kellen Winslow, San Diego[2]	88	1,075	12.2	67	10
	Pat Tilley, St. Louis	66	1,040	15.8	75	3
	Stanley Morgan, New England[2]	44	1,029	23.4	76	6
	Harold Carmichael, Philadelphia[3]	61	1,028	16.9	85	6
	Freddie Scott, Detroit	53	1,022	19.3	48	5
	*Cris Collinsworth, Cincinnati	67	1,009	15.1	74	8
	Joe Senser, Minnesota	79	1,004	12.7	53	8
	Ozzie Newsome, Cleveland	69	1,002	14.5	62	6
	Sammy White, Minnesota	66	1,001	15.2	53	3
1980	John Jefferson, San Diego[3]	82	1,340	16.3	58	13
	Kellen Winslow, San Diego	89	1,290	14.5	65	9
	James Lofton, Green Bay	71	1,226	17.3	47	4
	Charlie Joiner, San Diego[3]	71	1,132	15.9	51	4
	Ahmad Rashad, Minnesota[2]	69	1,095	15.9	76	5
	Steve Largent, Seattle[3]	66	1,064	16.1	67	6
	Tony Hill, Dallas[2]	60	1,055	17.6	58	8
	Alfred Jenkins, Atlanta	57	1,026	18.0	57	6
1979	Steve Largent, Seattle[2]	66	1,237	18.7	55	9
	John Stallworth, Pittsburgh	70	1,183	16.9	65	8
	Ahmad Rashad, Minnesota	80	1,156	14.5	52	9
	John Jefferson, San Diego[2]	61	1,090	17.9	65	10
	Frank Lewis, Buffalo	54	1,082	20.0	55	2
	Wes Chandler, New Orleans	65	1,069	16.4	85	6
	Tony Hill, Dallas	60	1,062	17.7	75	10
	Drew Pearson, Dallas[2]	55	1,026	18.7	56	8
	Wallace Francis, Atlanta	74	1,013	13.7	42	8
	Harold Jackson, New England[3]	45	1,013	22.5	59	7
	Charlie Joiner, San Diego[2]	72	1,008	14.0	39	4
	Stanley Morgan, New England	44	1,002	22.8	63	12
1978	Wesley Walker, N.Y. Jets	48	1,169	24.4	77	8
	Steve Largent, Seattle	71	1,168	16.5	57	8
	Harold Carmichael, Philadelphia[2]	55	1,072	19.5	56	8
	*John Jefferson, San Diego	56	1,001	17.9	46	13
1976	Roger Carr, Baltimore	43	1,112	25.9	79	11
	Cliff Branch, Oakland[2]	46	1,111	24.2	88	12
	Charlie Joiner, San Diego	50	1,056	21.1	81	7
1975	Ken Burrough, Houston	53	1,063	20.1	77	8
1974	Cliff Branch, Oakland	60	1,092	18.2	67	13
	Drew Pearson, Dallas	62	1,087	17.5	50	2
1973	Harold Carmichael, Philadelphia	67	1,116	16.7	73	9
1972	Harold Jackson, Philadelphia[2]	62	1,048	16.9	77	4
	John Gilliam, Minnesota	47	1,035	22.0	66	7
1971	Otis Taylor, Kansas City[2]	57	1,110	19.5	82	7
1970	Gene Washington, San Francisco	53	1,100	20.8	79	12
	Marlin Briscoe, Buffalo	57	1,036	18.2	48	8
	Dick Gordon, Chicago	71	1,026	14.5	69	13
	Gary Garrison, San Diego[2]	44	1,006	22.9	67	12
1969	Warren Wells, Oakland[2]	47	1,260	26.8	80	14
	Harold Jackson, Philadelphia	65	1,116	17.2	65	9
	Roy Jefferson, Pittsburgh[2]	67	1,079	16.1	63	9
	Dan Abramowicz, New Orleans	73	1,015	13.9	49	7
	Lance Alworth, San Diego[7]	64	1,003	15.7	76	4
1968	Lance Alworth, San Diego[6]	68	1,312	19.3	80	10
	Don Maynard, N.Y. Jets[5]	57	1,297	22.8	87	10
	George Sauer, N.Y. Jets[3]	66	1,141	17.3	43	3
	Warren Wells, Oakland	53	1,137	21.5	94	11
	Gary Garrison, San Diego	52	1,103	21.2	84	10
	Roy Jefferson, Pittsburgh	58	1,074	18.5	62	11
	Paul Warfield, Cleveland	50	1,067	21.3	65	12
	Homer Jones, N.Y. Giants[3]	45	1,057	23.5	84	7
	Fred Biletnikoff, Oakland	61	1,037	17.0	82	6
	Lance Rentzel, Dallas	54	1,009	18.7	65	6
1967	Don Maynard, N.Y. Jets[4]	71	1,434	20.2	75	10
	Ben Hawkins, Philadelphia	59	1,265	21.4	87	10
	Homer Jones, N.Y. Giants[2]	49	1,209	24.7	70	13
	Jackie Smith, St. Louis	56	1,205	21.5	76	9
	George Sauer, N.Y. Jets[2]	75	1,189	15.9	61	6
	Lance Alworth, San Diego[5]	52	1,010	19.4	71	9

OUTSTANDING PERFORMERS

Year	Player, Team	No.	Yards	Avg.	Long	TD
1966	Lance Alworth, San Diego[4]	73	1,383	18.9	78	13
	Otis Taylor, Kansas City	58	1,297	22.4	89	8
	Pat Studstill, Detroit	67	1,266	18.9	99	5
	Bob Hayes, Dallas[2]	64	1,232	19.3	95	13
	Charlie Frazier, Houston	57	1,129	19.8	79	12
	Charley Taylor, Washington	72	1,119	15.5	86	12
	George Sauer, N.Y. Jets	63	1,081	17.2	77	5
	Homer Jones, N.Y. Giants	48	1,044	21.8	98	8
	Art Powell, Oakland[5]	53	1,026	19.4	46	11
1965	Lance Alworth, San Diego[3]	69	1,602	23.2	85	14
	Dave Parks, San Francisco	80	1,344	16.8	53	12
	Don Maynard, N.Y. Jets[3]	68	1,218	17.9	56	14
	Pete Retzlaff, Philadelphia	66	1,190	18.0	78	10
	Lionel Taylor, Denver[4]	85	1,131	13.3	63	6
	Tommy McDonald, Los Angeles[3]	67	1,036	15.5	51	9
	*Bob Hayes, Dallas	46	1,003	21.8	82	12
1964	Charley Hennigan, Houston[3]	101	1,546	15.3	53	8
	Art Powell, Oakland[4]	76	1,361	17.9	77	11
	Lance Alworth, San Diego[2]	61	1,235	20.2	82	13
	Johnny Morris, Chicago	93	1,200	12.9	63	10
	Elbert Dubenion, Buffalo	42	1,139	27.1	72	10
	Terry Barr, Detroit[2]	57	1,030	18.1	58	9
1963	Bobby Mitchell, Washington[2]	69	1,436	20.8	99	7
	Art Powell, Oakland[3]	73	1,304	17.9	85	16
	Buddy Dial, Pittsburgh[2]	60	1,295	21.6	83	9
	Lance Alworth, San Diego	61	1,205	19.8	85	11
	Del Shofner, N.Y. Giants[4]	64	1,181	18.5	70	9
	Lionel Taylor, Denver[3]	78	1,101	14.1	72	10
	Terry Barr, Detroit	66	1,086	16.5	75	13
	Charley Hennigan, Houston[2]	61	1,051	17.2	83	10
	Sonny Randle, St. Louis[2]	51	1,014	19.9	68	12
	Bake Turner, N.Y. Jets	71	1,009	14.2	53	6
1962	Bobby Mitchell, Washington	72	1,384	19.2	81	11
	Sonny Randle, St. Louis	63	1,158	18.4	86	7
	Tommy McDonald, Philadelphia[2]	58	1,146	19.8	60	10
	Del Shofner, N.Y. Giants[3]	53	1,133	21.4	69	12
	Art Powell, N.Y. Titans[2]	64	1,130	17.7	80	8
	Frank Clarke, Dall. Cowboys	47	1,043	22.2	66	14
	Don Maynard, N.Y. Titans[2]	56	1,041	18.6	86	8
1961	Charley Hennigan, Houston	82	1,746	21.3	80	12
	Lionel Taylor, Denver[2]	100	1,176	11.8	52	4
	Bill Groman, Houston[2]	50	1,175	23.5	80	17
	Tommy McDonald, Philadelphia	64	1,144	17.9	66	13
	Del Shofner, N.Y. Giants[2]	68	1,125	16.5	46	11
	Jim Phillips, Los Angeles	78	1,092	14.0	69	5
	*Mike Ditka, Chicago	56	1,076	19.2	76	12
	Dave Kocourek, San Diego	55	1,055	19.2	76	4
	Buddy Dial, Pittsburgh	53	1,047	19.8	88	12
	R.C. Owens, San Francisco	55	1,032	18.8	54	5
1960	*Bill Groman, Houston	72	1,473	20.5	92	12
	Raymond Berry, Baltimore	74	1,298	17.5	70	10
	Don Maynard, N.Y. Titans	72	1,265	17.6	65	6
	Lionel Taylor, Denver	92	1,235	13.4	80	12
	Art Powell, N.Y. Titans	69	1,167	16.9	76	14
1958	Del Shofner, Los Angeles	51	1,097	21.5	92	8
1956	Bill Howton, Green Bay[2]	55	1,188	21.6	66	12
	Harlon Hill, Chi. Bears[2]	47	1,128	24.0	79	11
1954	Bob Boyd, Los Angeles	53	1,212	22.9	80	6
	*Harlon Hill, Chi. Bears	45	1,124	25.0	76	12
1953	Pete Pihos, Philadelphia	63	1,049	16.7	59	10
1952	*Bill Howton, Green Bay	53	1,231	23.2	90	13
1951	Elroy (Crazylegs) Hirsch, Los Angeles	66	1,495	22.7	91	17
1950	Tom Fears, Los Angeles[2]	84	1,116	13.3	53	7
	Cloyce Box, Detroit	50	1,009	20.2	82	11
1949	Bob Mann, Detroit	66	1,014	15.4	64	4
	Tom Fears, Los Angeles	77	1,013	13.2	51	9
1945	Jim Benton, Cleveland	45	1,067	23.7	84	8
1942	Don Hutson, Green Bay	74	1,211	16.4	73	17

**First season of professional football.*

250 YARDS PASS RECEIVING IN A GAME

Date	Player, Team, Opponent	No.	Yards	TD
Nov. 19, 2006	Lee Evans, Buffalo vs. Houston	11	265	2
Nov. 12, 2006	Chad Ochocinco, Cincinnati vs. San Diego	11	260	2
Nov. 10, 2002	Plaxico Burress, Pittsburgh vs. Atlanta (OT)	9	253	2
Dec. 17, 2000	Terrell Owens, San Francisco vs. Chicago	20	283	1
Sept. 10, 2000	Jimmy Smith, Jacksonville vs. Baltimore	15	291	3
Dec. 12, 1999	Qadry Ismail, Baltimore vs. Pittsburgh	6	258	3
Dec. 18, 1995	Jerry Rice, San Francisco vs. Minnesota	14	289	3
Dec. 11, 1989	John Taylor, San Francisco vs. L.A. Rams	11	286	2
Nov. 26, 1989	Willie Anderson, L.A. Rams vs. New Orleans (OT)	15	336	1
Oct. 18, 1987	Steve Largent, Seattle vs. Detroit	15	261	3
Oct. 4, 1987	Anthony Allen, Washington vs. St. Louis	7	255	3
Dec. 22, 1985	Stephone Paige, Kansas City vs. San Diego	8	309	2
Dec. 20, 1982	Wes Chandler, San Diego vs. Cincinnati	10	260	2
Sept. 23, 1979	*Jerry Butler, Buffalo vs. N.Y. Jets	10	255	4
Nov. 4, 1962	Sonny Randle, St. Louis vs. N.Y. Giants	16	256	1
Oct. 28, 1962	Del Shofner, N.Y. Giants vs. Washington	11	269	1
Oct. 13, 1961	Charley Hennigan, Houston vs. Boston	13	272	1
Oct. 21, 1956	Billy Howton, Green Bay vs. Los Angeles	7	257	2
Dec. 3, 1950	Cloyce Box, Detroit vs. Baltimore	12	302	4
Nov. 22, 1945	Jim Benton, Cleveland vs. Detroit	10	303	1

**First season of professional football.*

2,000 COMBINED NET YARDS GAINED IN A SEASON

Year	Player, Team	Rushing Att.-Yds.	Pass Rec.	Punt Ret.	Kickoff Ret.	Fum. Ret.	Total Yds.
2008	Leon Washington, N.Y. Jets[2]	76-448	47-355	29-303	48-1,231	4-(-5)	204-2,332
	Darren Sproles, San Diego	61-330	29-342	22-249	53-1,376	1-(-2)	166-2,295
	Jerious Norwood, Atlanta[2]	95-489	36-338	0-0	51-1,311	0-0	182-2,138
2007	Josh Cribbs, Cleveland	9-61	3-37	30-405	59-1,809	2-0	103-2,312
	Jerious Norwood, Atlanta	103-613	28-277	0-0	52-1,317	0-0	183-2,207
	Brian Westbrook, Philadelphia	278-1,333	90-771	4-79	0-0	0-0	372-2,183
	*Ted Ginn Jr., Miami	4-3	34-420	24-230	63-1,433	2-(-9)	127-2,077
	Leon Washington, N.Y. Jets	71-353	36-213	20-183	47-1,291	1-0	175-2,040
	*Adrian Peterson, Minnesota	238-1,341	19-268	0-0	16-412	3-0	276-2,014
	Maurice Jones-Drew, Jacksonville[2]	167-768	40-407	3-28	31-811	0-0	241-2,014
2006	Steven Jackson, St. Louis	346-1,528	90,806	0-0	0-0	2-0	438-2,334
	LaDainian Tomlinson, San Diego[3]	348-1,815	56-508	0-0	0-0	1-0	405-2,323
	*Maurice Jones-Drew, Jacksonville	166-941	46-436	1-13	31-860	0-0	244-2,250
	Larry Johnson, Kansas City[2]	416-1,789	41-410	0-0	0-0	1-0	458-2,199
	Frank Gore, San Francisco	312-1,695	61-485	0-0	0-0	0-0	373-2,180
	Wes Welker, Miami[2]	0-0	67-687	41-378	48-1,064	1-0	157-2,129
	Tiki Barber, N.Y. Giants[4]	327-1,662	58-465	0-0	0-0	1-0	386-2,127
	Chris Carr, Oakland	0-0	0-0	35-216	69-1,762	1-0	106-2,078
2005	Tiki Barber, N.Y. Giants[3]	357-1,860	54-530	0-0	0-0	1-0	412-2,390
	Dante Hall, Kansas City[4]	7-11	34-436	42-276	65-1,560	2-0	150-2,283
	Wes Welker, Miami	1-5	29-434	43-390	61-1,379	4-0	138-2,208
	Larry Johnson, Kansas City	336-1,750	33-343	0-0	0-0	3-0	372-2,093
2004	Dante Hall, Kansas City[3]	8-56	25-230	23-232	68-1,718	0-0	124-2,236
	Tiki Barber, N.Y. Giants[2]	322-1,518	52-578	0-0	0-0	2-0	376-2,096
	Edgerrin James, Indianapolis[3]	334-1,548	51-483	0-0	0-0	1-0	386-2,031
2003	Dante Hall, Kansas City[2]	16-73	40-423	29-472	57-1,478	0-0	142-2,446
	LaDainian Tomlinson, San Diego[2]	313-1,645	100-725	0-0	0-0	2-0	415-2,370
	Jamal Lewis, Baltimore	387-2,066	26-205	0-0	0-0	1-0	414-2,271
	Ahman Green, Green Bay	355-1,883	50-367	0-0	0-0	2-0	407-2,250
	Deuce McAllister, New Orleans	351-1,641	69-516	0-0	0-0	3-(-3)	423-2,154
	Priest Holmes, Kansas City[3]	320-1,420	74-690	0-0	0-0	0-0	394-2,110
2002	Michael Lewis, New Orleans	1-15	8-200	44-625	70-1,807	2-0	125-2,647
	Priest Holmes, Kansas City[2]	313-1,615	70-672	0-0	0-0	0-0	383-2,287
	Ricky Williams, Miami	383-1,853	47-363	0-0	0-0	1-0	431-2,216
	LaDainian Tomlinson, San Diego	372-1,683	79-489	0-0	0-0	0-0	451-2,172
	Dante Hall, Kansas City	11-54	20-322	29-390	57-1,354	1-0	118-2,120
2001	Priest Holmes, Kansas City	327-1,555	62-614	0-0	0-0	0-0	389-2,169
	Marshall Faulk, St. Louis[4]	260-1,382	83-765	0-0	0-0	2-0	345-2,147
	Derrick Mason, Tennessee[2]	0-0	73-1,128	20-128	34-748	1-0	128-2,004
2000	Derrick Mason, Tennessee	1-1	63-895	51-662	42-1,132	1-0	158-2,690
	MarTay Jenkins, Arizona	1-(-4)	17-219	1-1	82-2,186	0-0	101-2,402
	Edgerrin James, Indianapolis[2]	387-1,709	63-594	0-0	0-0	0-0	450-2,303

OUTSTANDING PERFORMERS

Year	Player, Team	Rushing Att.-Yds.	Pass Rec.	Punt Ret.	Kickoff Ret.	Fum. Ret.	Total Yds.
	Marshall Faulk, St. Louis[3]	253-1,359	81-830	0-0	1-18	2-0	337-2,207
	Tiki Barber, N.Y. Giants	213-1,006	70-719	39-332	1-28	5-0	328-2,085
1999	Marshall Faulk, St. Louis[2]	253-1,381	87-1,048	0-0	0-0	0-0	340-2,429
	*Edgerrin James, Indianapolis	369-1,553	62-586	0-0	0-0	2-0	433-2,139
	*Terrence Wilkins, Indianapolis	1-2	42-565	41-388	51-1,134	1-0	136-2,089
	Glyn Milburn, Chicago[2]	16-102	20-151	30-346	61-1,426	2-0	129-2,025
1998	Brian Mitchell, Washington[4]	39-208	44-306	44-506	59-1,337	0-0	186-2,357
	Marshall Faulk, Indianapolis	324-1,319	86-908	0-0	0-0	2-13	412-2,240
	Terrell Davis, Denver[2]	392-2,008	25-217	0-0	0-0	1-0	418-2,225
	Jamal Anderson, Atlanta	410-1,846	27-319	0-0	0-0	1-0	438-2,165
	Garrison Hearst, San Francisco	310-1,570	39-535	0-0	0-0	1-0	350-2,105
1997	Barry Sanders, Detroit[2]	335-2,053	33-305	0-0	0-0	1-0	369-2,358
	Kevin Williams, Arizona	1-(-2)	20-273	40-462	59-1,458	1-0	121-2,191
	Brian Mitchell, Washington[3]	23-107	36-438	38-442	47-1,094	0-0	144-2,081
	Terrell Davis, Denver	369-1,750	42-287	0-0	0-0	2-(-7)	413-2,030
	Jermaine Lewis, Baltimore	3-35	42-648	28-437	41-905	2-0	116-2,025
1995	Brian Mitchell, Washington[2]	46-301	38-324	25-315	55-1,408	0-0	164-2,348
	Emmitt Smith, Dallas[2]	377-1,773	62-375	0-0	0-0	0-0	439-2,148
	Glyn Milburn, Denver	49-266	22-191	31-354	47-1,269	0-0	149-2,080
	Ernie Mills, Pittsburgh	5-39	39-679	0-0	54-1,306	0-0	98-2,024
1994	Brian Mitchell, Washington	78-311	26-236	32-452	58-1,478	0-0	194-2,477
	Barry Sanders, Detroit	331-1,883	44-283	0-0	0-0	0-0	375-2,166
1992	Thurman Thomas, Buffalo[2]	312-1,487	58-626	0-0	0-0	1-0	371-2,113
	Emmitt Smith, Dallas	373-1,713	59-335	0-0	0-0	1-0	433-2,048
	Barry Foster, Pittsburgh	390-1,690	36-344	0-0	0-0	2-(–20)	428-2,014
1991	Thurman Thomas, Buffalo	288-1,407	62-631	0-0	0-0	0-0	350-2,038
1990	Herschel Walker, Minnesota[2]	184-770	35-315	0-0	44-966	4-0	267-2,051
1988	*Tim Brown, L.A. Raiders	14-50	43-725	49-444	41-1,098	7-0	154-2,317
	Roger Craig, San Francisco[2]	310-1,502	76-534	0-0	2-32	2-0	390-2,068
	Eric Dickerson, Indianapolis[4]	388-1,659	36-377	0-0	0-0	1-0	425-2,036
	Herschel Walker, Dallas	361-1,514	53-505	0-0	0-0	3-0	417-2,019
1986	Eric Dickerson, L.A. Rams[3]	404-1,821	26-205	0-0	0-0	2-0	432-2,026
	Gary Anderson, San Diego	127-442	80-871	25-227	24-482	2-0	258-2,022
1985	Lionel James, San Diego	105-516	86-1,027	25-213	36-779	1-0	253-2,535
	Marcus Allen, L.A. Raiders	380-1,759	67-555	0-0	0-0	2-(–6)	449-2,308
	Roger Craig, San Francisco	214-1,050	92-1,016	0-0	0-0	0-0	306-2,066
	Walter Payton, Chicago[4]	324-1,551	49-483	0-0	0-0	1-0	374-2,034
1984	Eric Dickerson, L.A. Rams[2]	379-2,105	21-139	0-0	0-0	4-15	404-2,259
	James Wilder, Tampa Bay	407-1,544	85-685	0-0	0-0	4-0	496-2,229
	Walter Payton, Chicago[3]	381-1,684	45-368	0-0	0-0	1-0	427-2,052
1983	*Eric Dickerson, L.A. Rams	390-1,808	51-404	0-0	0-0	1-0	442-2,212
	William Andrews, Atlanta[2]	331-1,567	59-609	0-0	0-0	2-0	392-2,176
	Walter Payton, Chicago[2]	314-1,421	53-607	0-0	0-0	2-0	369-2,028
1981	*James Brooks, San Diego	109-525	46-329	22-290	40-949	2-0	219-2,093
	William Andrews, Atlanta	289-1,301	81-735	0-0	0-0	0-0	370-2,036
1980	Bruce Harper, N.Y. Jets[2]	45-126	50-634	28-242	49-1,070	3-0	175-2,072
1979	Wilbert Montgomery, Philadelphia	338-1,512	41-494	0-0	1-6	2-0	382-2,012
1978	Bruce Harper, N.Y. Jets	58-303	13-196	30-378	55-1,280	1-0	157-2,157
1977	Walter Payton, Chicago	339-1,852	27-269	0-0	2-95	5-0	373-2,216
	Terry Metcalf, St. Louis[3]	149-739	34-403	14-108	32-772	1-0	230-2,022
1975	Terry Metcalf, St. Louis[2]	165-816	43-378	23-285	35-960	2-23	268-2,462
	O.J. Simpson, Buffalo[2]	329-1,817	28-426	0-0	0-0	1-0	358-2,243
1974	Mack Herron, New England	231-824	38-474	35-517	28-629	3-0	335-2,444
	Otis Armstrong, Denver	263-1,407	38-405	0-0	16-386	1-0	318-2,198
	Terry Metcalf, St. Louis	152-718	50-377	26-340	20-623	7-0	255-2,058
1973	O.J. Simpson, Buffalo	332-2,003	6-70	0-0	0-0	0-0	338-2,073
1966	Gale Sayers, Chicago[2]	229-1,231	34-447	6-44	23-718	3-0	295-2,440
	Leroy Kelly, Cleveland	209-1,141	32-366	13-104	19-403	0-0	273-2,014
1965	*Gale Sayers, Chicago	166-867	29-507	16-238	21-660	4-0	236-2,272
1963	Timmy Brown, Philadelphia[2]	192-841	36-487	16-152	33-945	2-3	279-2,428
	Jim Brown, Cleveland	291-1,863	24-268	0-0	0-0	0-0	315-2,131
1962	Timmy Brown, Philadelphia	137-545	52-849	6-81	30-831	4-0	229-2,306
	Dick Christy, N.Y. Titans	114-535	62-538	15-250	38-824	2-0	231-2,147
1961	Billy Cannon, Houston	200-948	43-586	9-70	18-439	2-0	272-2,043
1960	*Abner Haynes, Dallas Texans	156-875	55-576	14-215	19-434	4-0	248-2,100

**First season of professional football.*

300 COMBINED NET YARDS GAINED IN A GAME

Date	Player, Team, Opponent	No.	Yards	TD
Sept. 28, 2008	Steve Breaston, Arizona vs. N.Y. Jets	19	324	0
Sept. 14, 2008	Darren Sproles, San Diego vs. Denver	14	317	2
Nov. 18, 2007	Josh Cribbs, Cleveland vs. Baltimore (OT)	12	309	0
Nov. 4, 2007	*Adrian Peterson, Minnesota vs. San Diego	31	315	3
Oct. 14, 2007	*Adrian Peterson, Minnesota vs. Chicago	25	361	3
Sept. 30, 2007	Devin Hester, Chicago vs. Detroit	13	317	1
Dec. 10, 2006	*Maurice Jones-Drew, Jacksonville vs. Indianapolis	19	303	3
Dec. 14, 2003	Derrick Mason, Tennessee vs. Buffalo	21	302	0
Nov. 16, 2003	Jonathan Carter, N.Y. Jets vs. Indianapolis	7	304	2
Dec. 8, 2002	Steve Smith, Carolina vs. Cincinnati	9	313	3
Nov. 24, 2002	Priest Holmes, Kansas City vs. Seattle	30	307	3
Oct. 13, 2002	Michael Lewis, New Orleans vs. Washington	8	356	2
Dec. 24, 1999	Jason Tucker, Dallas vs. New Orleans	13	331	1
Dec. 7, 1997	Jermaine Lewis, Baltimore vs. Seattle	10	308	3
Dec. 25, 1995	Kevin Williams, Dallas vs. Arizona	16	307	2
Dec. 10, 1995	Glyn Milburn, Denver vs. Seattle	33	404	0
Oct. 23, 1994	Tyrone Hughes, New Orleans vs. L.A. Rams	11	347	2
Dec. 11, 1989	John Taylor, San Francisco vs. L.A. Rams	14	321	2
Nov. 26, 1989	Willie Anderson, L.A. Rams vs. New Orleans (OT)	15	336	1
Nov. 28, 1988	*Tim Brown, L.A. Raiders vs. Seattle	12	308	1
Dec. 22, 1985	Stephone Paige, Kansas City vs. San Diego	8	309	2
Nov. 10, 1985	Lionel James, San Diego vs. L.A. Raiders (OT)	23	345	0
Sept. 22, 1985	Lionel James, San Diego vs. Cincinnati	20	316	2
Dec. 21, 1975	*Walter Payton, Chicago vs. New Orleans	32	300	1
Nov. 23, 1975	Greg Pruitt, Cleveland vs. Cincinnati	28	304	2
Nov. 1, 1970	Eugene (Mercury) Morris, Miami vs. Baltimore	17	302	0
Oct. 4, 1970	O.J. Simpson, Buffalo vs. N.Y. Jets	26	303	2
Dec. 6, 1969	Jerry LeVias, Houston vs. N.Y. Jets	18	329	1
Nov. 2, 1969	Travis Williams, Green Bay vs. Pittsburgh	11	314	3
Dec. 18, 1966	Gale Sayers, Chicago vs. Minnesota	20	339	2
Dec. 12, 1965	*Gale Sayers, Chicago vs. San Francisco	17	336	6
Nov. 17, 1963	Gary Ballman, Pittsburgh vs. Washington	12	320	2
Dec. 16, 1962	Timmy Brown, Philadelphia vs. St. Louis	19	341	2
Dec. 10, 1961	Billy Cannon, Houston vs. N.Y. Titans	32	373	5
Nov. 19, 1961	Jim Brown, Cleveland vs. Philadelphia	38	313	4
Dec. 3, 1950	Cloyce Box, Detroit vs. Baltimore	13	302	4
Oct. 29, 1950	Wally Triplett, Detroit vs. Los Angeles	11	331	1
Nov. 22, 1945	Jim Benton, Cleveland vs. Detroit	10	303	1

**First season of professional football.*

2,000 SCRIMMAGE YARDS GAINED IN A SEASON

Year	Player, Team	Att.	Rushing Yards	Receptions	Receiving Yards	Scrimm. Yards
2007	Brian Westbrook, Philadelphia	278	1,333	90	771	2,104
2006	Steven Jackson, St. Louis	346	1,528	90	806	2,334
	LaDainian Tomlinson, San Diego[3]	348	1,815	56	508	2,323
	Larry Johnson, Kansas City[2]	416	1,789	41	410	2,199
	Frank Gore, San Francisco	312	1,695	61	485	2,180
	Tiki Barber, N.Y. Giants[3]	327	1,662	58	465	2,127
2005	Tiki Barber, N.Y. Giants[2]	357	1,860	54	530	2,390
	Larry Johnson, Kansas City	336	1,750	33	343	2,093
2004	Tiki Barber, N.Y. Giants	322	1.518	52	578	2,096
	Edgerrin James, Indianapolis[3]	334	1,548	51	483	2,031
2003	LaDainian Tomlinson, San Diego[2]	313	1,645	100	725	2,370
	Jamal Lewis, Baltimore	387	2,066	26	205	2,271
	Ahman Green, Green Bay	355	1,883	50	367	2,250
	Deuce McAllister, New Orleans	351	1,641	69	516	2,157
	Priest Holmes, Kansas City[3]	320	1,420	74	690	2,110
2002	Priest Holmes, Kansas City[2]	313	1,615	70	672	2,287
	Ricky Williams, Miami	383	1,853	47	363	2,216
	LaDainian Tomlinson, San Diego	372	1,683	79	489	2,172
2001	Priest Holmes, Kansas City	327	1,555	62	614	2,169
	Marshall Faulk, St. Louis[4]	260	1,382	83	765	2,147
2000	Edgerrin James, Indianapolis[2]	387	1,709	63	594	2,303
	Marshall Faulk, St. Louis[3]	253	1,359	81	830	2,189
1999	Marshall Faulk, St. Louis[2]	253	1,381	87	1,048	2,429
	*Edgerrin James, Indianapolis	369	1,553	62	586	2,139
1998	Marshall Faulk, Indianapolis	324	1,319	86	908	2,227
	Terrell Davis, Denver[2]	392	2,008	25	217	2,225

Year	Player, Team	Att.	Yards	Receptions	Yards	Yards
	Jamal Anderson, Atlanta	410	1,846	27	319	2,165
	Garrison Hearst, San Francisco	310	1,570	39	535	2,105
1997	Barry Sanders, Detroit[2]	335	2,053	33	305	2,358
	Terrell Davis, Denver	369	1,750	42	287	2,037
1995	Emmitt Smith, Dallas[2]	377	1,773	62	375	2,148
1994	Barry Sanders, Detroit	331	1,883	44	283	2,166
1992	Thurman Thomas, Buffalo[2]	312	1,487	58	626	2,113
	Emmitt Smith, Dallas	373	1,713	59	335	2,048
	Barry Foster, Pittsburgh	390	1,690	36	344	2,034
1991	Thurman Thomas, Buffalo	288	1,407	62	631	2,038
1988	Roger Craig, San Francisco[2]	310	1,502	76	534	2,036
	Eric Dickerson, Indianapolis[4]	388	1,659	36	377	2,036
	Herschel Walker, Dallas	361	1,514	53	505	2,019
1986	Eric Dickerson, L.A. Rams[3]	404	1,821	26	205	2,026
1985	Marcus Allen, L.A. Raiders	380	1,759	67	555	2,314
	Roger Craig, San Francisco	214	1,050	92	1,016	2,066
	Walter Payton, Chicago[4]	324	1,551	49	483	2,034
1984	Eric Dickerson, L. A. Rams[2]	379	2,105	21	139	2,244
	James Wilder, Tampa Bay	407	1,544	85	685	2,229
	Walter Payton, Chicago[3]	381	1,684	45	368	2,052
1983	*Eric Dickerson, L.A. Rams	390	1,808	51	404	2,212
	William Andrews, Atlanta[2]	331	1,567	59	609	2,176
	Walter Payton, Chicago[2]	314	1,421	53	607	2,028
1981	William Andrews, Atlanta	289	1,301	81	735	2,036
1979	Wilbert Montgomery, Philadelphia	338	1,512	41	494	2,006
1977	Walter Payton, Chicago	339	1,852	27	269	2,121
1975	O.J. Simpson, Buffalo[2]	329	1,817	28	426	2,243
1973	O.J. Simpson, Buffalo	332	2,003	6	70	2,073
1963	Jim Brown, Cleveland	91	1,863	24	268	2,131

First season of professional football.

300 SCRIMMAGE YARDS GAINED IN A GAME

Date	Player, Team, Opponent	Att.	Yards	TD
Nov. 4, 2007	*Adrian Peterson, Minnesota vs. San Diego	31	315	3
Nov. 24, 2002	Priest Holmes, Kansas City vs. Seattle	30	307	3
Nov. 26, 1989	Flipper Anderson, L.A. Rams vs. New Orleans (OT)	15	336	1
Dec. 22, 1985	Stephone Paige, Kansas City vs. San Diego	8	309	2
Dec. 10, 1961	Billy Cannon, Houston vs. N.Y. Titans	30	330	5
Dec. 3, 1950	Cloyce Box, Detroit vs. Baltimore	12	302	4
Nov. 22, 1945	Jim Benton, Cleveland vs. Detroit	10	303	1

First season of professional football.

TOP 20 SCORERS

	Player	Years	TD	FG	PAT	TP
1.	Morten Andersen	25	0	565	849	2,544
2.	Gary Anderson	23	0	538	820	2,434
3.	George Blanda	26	9	335	942	2,002
4.	John Carney	21	0	460	575	1,955
5.	Matt Stover	18	0	462	558	1,944
6.	Jason Elam	16	0	424	643	1,915
7.	Jason Hanson	17	0	406	529	1,747
8.	Norm Johnson	18	0	366	638	1,736
9.	Nick Lowery	18	0	383	562	1,711
10.	Jan Stenerud	19	0	373	580	1,699
11.	John Kasay	17	0	386	476	1,634
12.	Eddie Murray	19	0	352	538	1,594
13.	Al Del Greco	17	0	347	543	1,584
14.	Adam Vinatieri	13	0	331	497	1,492
15.	Steve Christie	15	0	336	468	1,476
16.	Pat Leahy	18	0	304	558	1,470
17.	Jim Turner	16	1	304	521	1,439
18.	Matt Bahr	17	0	300	522	1,422
19.	Jeff Wilkins	14	0	307	495	1,416
20.	Mark Moseley	16	0	300	482	1,382

TOP 20 TOUCHDOWN SCORERS

	Player	Years	Rush	Rec.	Total Returns	TD
1.	Jerry Rice	20	10	197	1	208
2.	Emmitt Smith	15	164	11	0	175
3.	Marcus Allen	16	123	21	1	145
4.	Terrell Owens	13	2	139	0	141
	LaDainian Tomlinson	8	126	15	0	141
6.	Marshall Faulk	12	100	36	0	136
	Randy Moss	11	0	135	1	136
8.	Cris Carter	16	0	130	1	131
9.	Marvin Harrison	13	0	128	0	128
10.	Jim Brown	9	106	20	0	126
11.	Walter Payton	13	110	15	0	125
12.	John Riggins	14	104	12	0	116
13.	Lenny Moore	12	63	48	2	113
14.	Shaun Alexander	9	100	12	0	112
15.	Barry Sanders	10	99	10	0	109
16.	Tim Brown	17	1	100	4	105
	Don Hutson	11	3	99	3	105
18.	Steve Largent	14	1	100	0	101
19.	Franco Harris	13	91	9	0	100
	Curtis Martin	11	90	10	0	100

TOP 20 RUSHERS

	Player	Years	Att.	Yards	Avg.	Long	TD
1.	Emmitt Smith	15	4,409	18,355	4.2	75	164
2.	Walter Payton	13	3,838	16,726	4.4	76	110
3.	Barry Sanders	10	3,062	15,269	5.0	85	99
4.	Curtis Martin	11	3,518	14,101	4.0	70	90
5.	Jerome Bettis	13	3,479	13,662	3.9	71	91
6.	Eric Dickerson	11	2,996	13,259	4.4	85	90
7.	Tony Dorsett	12	2,936	12,739	4.3	99	77
8.	Jim Brown	9	2,359	12,312	5.2	80	106
9.	Marshall Faulk	12	2,836	12,279	4.3	71	100
10.	Marcus Allen	16	3,022	12,243	4.1	61	123
11.	Edgerrin James	10	2,982	12,121	4.1	72	80
12.	Franco Harris	13	2,949	12,120	4.1	75	91
13.	Thurman Thomas	13	2,877	12,074	4.2	80	65
14.	LaDainian Tomlinson	8	2,657	11,760	4.4	85	126
15.	John Riggins	14	2,916	11,352	3.9	66	104
16.	Fred Taylor	11	2,428	11,271	4.6	80	62
17.	Corey Dillon	10	2,618	11,241	4.3	96	82
18.	O.J. Simpson	11	2,404	11,236	4.7	94	61
19.	Warrick Dunn	12	2,669	10,967	4.1	90	49
20.	Ricky Watters	10	2,622	10,643	4.1	57	78

OUTSTANDING PERFORMERS

TOP 20 LEADERS IN PASSES COMPLETED

1.	Brett Favre	5,720
2.	Dan Marino	4,967
3.	John Elway	4,123
4.	Warren Moon	3,988
5.	Drew Bledsoe	3,839
	Peyton Manning	3,839
7.	Vinny Testaverde	3,787
8.	Fran Tarkenton	3,686
9.	Joe Montana	3,409
10.	Dan Fouts	3,297
11.	Kerry Collins	3,160
12.	Dave Krieg	3,105
13.	Boomer Esiason	2,969
14.	Troy Aikman	2,898
15.	Steve DeBerg	2,874
	Jim Kelly	2,874
17.	Jim Everett	2,841
18.	Johnny Unitas	2,830
19.	Mark Brunell	2,738
20.	Steve McNair	2,733

TOP 20 LEADERS IN PASSING YARDS

1.	Brett Favre	65,127
2.	Dan Marino	61,361
3.	John Elway	51,475
4.	Warren Moon	49,325
5.	Fran Tarkenton	47,003
6.	Vinny Testaverde	46,233
7.	Peyton Manning	45,628
8.	Drew Bledsoe	44,611
9.	Dan Fouts	43,040
10.	Joe Montana	40,551
11.	Johnny Unitas	40,239
12.	Dave Krieg	38,147
13.	Boomer Esiason	37,920
14.	Kerry Collins	37,393
15.	Jim Kelly	35,467
16.	Jim Everett	34,837
17.	Jim Hart	34,665
18.	Steve DeBerg	34,241
19.	John Hadl	33,503
20.	Phil Simms	33,462

TOP 20 LEADERS IN TOUCHDOWN PASSES

1.	Brett Favre	464
2.	Dan Marino	420
3.	Fran Tarkenton	342
4.	Peyton Manning	333
5.	John Elway	300
6.	Warren Moon	291
7.	Johnny Unitas	290
8.	Vinny Testaverde	275
9.	Joe Montana	273
10.	Dave Krieg	261
11.	Sonny Jurgensen	255
12.	Dan Fouts	254
13.	Drew Bledsoe	251
14.	Boomer Esiason	247
15.	John Hadl	244
16.	Len Dawson	239
17.	Jim Kelly	237
18.	George Blanda	236
19.	Steve Young	232
20.	John Brodie	214

TOP 20 LEADERS IN RECEPTION YARDS

1.	Jerry Rice	22,895
2.	Isaac Bruce	14,944
3.	Tim Brown	14,934
4.	Marvin Harrison	14,580
5.	Terrell Owens	14,122
6.	James Lofton	14,004
7.	Cris Carter	13,899
8.	Henry Ellard	13,777
9.	Randy Moss	13,201
10.	Andre Reed	13,198
11.	Steve Largent	13,089
12.	Irving Fryar	12,785
13.	Art Monk	12,721
14.	Torry Holt	12,660
15.	Jimmy Smith	12,287
16.	Charlie Joiner	12,146
17.	Michael Irvin	11,904
18.	Don Maynard	11,834
19.	Rod Smith	11,389
20.	Keenan McCardell	11,373

TOP 20 COMBINED YARDS GAINED

Player	Years	Tot.	Rush.	Rec.	Int. Ret.	Punt Ret.	Kickoff Ret.	Fumble Ret.
1. Jerry Rice	20	23,546	645	22,895	0	0	6	0
2. Brian Mitchell	14	23,330	1,967	2,336	0	4,999	14,014	14
3. Walter Payton	13	21,803	16,726	4,538	0	0	539	0
4. Emmitt Smith	15	21,564	18,355	3,224	0	0	0	-15
5. Tim Brown	17	19,682	190	14,934	0	3,320	1,235	3
6. Marshall Faulk	12	19,190	12,279	6,875	0	0	18	18
7. Barry Sanders	10	18,308	15,269	2,921	0	0	118	0
8. Herschel Walker	12	18,168	8,225	4,859	0	0	5,084	0
9. Marcus Allen	16	17,648	12,243	5,411	0	0	0	-6
10. Curtis Martin	11	17,421	14,101	3,329	0	0	0	-9
11. Tiki Barber	10	17,359	10,449	5,183	0	1,181	544	2
12. Eric Metcalf	13	17,230	2,392	5,572	0	3,453	5,813	0
13. Thurman Thomas	13	16,532	12,074	4,458	0	0	0	0
14. Tony Dorsett	12	16,326	12,739	3,554	0	0	0	54
15. Henry Ellard	16	15,718	50	13,777	0	1,527	364	0
16. Warrick Dunn	12	15,665	10,967	4,339	0	48	310	1
17. Irving Fryar	17	15,594	242	12,785	0	2,055	505	7
18. LaDainian Tomlinson	8	15,561	11,760	3,801	0	0	0	0
19. Edgerrin James	10	15,466	12,121	3,345	0	0	0	0
20. Jim Brown	9	15,459	12,312	2,499	0	0	648	0

TOP 20 YARDS FROM SCRIMMAGE

Player	Years	Scrimmage Yards	Rushing Yards	Receiving Yards
1. Jerry Rice	20	23,540	645	22,895
2. Emmitt Smith	15	21,579	18,355	3,224
3. Walter Payton	13	21,264	16,726	4,538
4. Marshall Faulk	12	19,154	12,279	6,875
5. Barry Sanders	10	18,190	15,269	2,921
6. Marcus Allen	16	17,654	12,243	5,411
7. Curtis Martin	11	17,430	14,101	3,329
8. Thurman Thomas	13	16,532	12,074	4,458
9. Tony Dorsett	12	16,293	12,739	3,554
10. Tiki Barber	10	15,632	10,449	5,183
11. LaDainian Tomlinson	8	15,561	11,760	3,801
12. Edgerrin James	10	15,446	12,121	3,345
13. Eric Dickerson	11	15,396	13,259	2,137
14. Warrick Dunn	12	15,306	10,967	4,339
15. Tim Brown	17	15,124	190	14,934
16. Jerome Bettis	13	15,111	13,662	1,449
17. Isaac Bruce	15	15,091	147	14,944
18. Ricky Watters	10	14,891	10,643	4,248
19. Jim Brown	9	14,811	12,312	2,499
20. Marvin Harrison	13	14,608	28	14,580

TOP 20 PASSERS

Player	Years	Att.	Comp.	Pct. Comp.	Yards	Avg. Gain	TD	Pct. TD	Int.	Pct. Int.	Rating
1. Steve Young	15	4,149	2,667	64.3	33,124	7.98	232	5.6	107	2.6	96.8
2. Peyton Manning	11	5,960	3,839	64.4	45,628	7.66	333	5.6	165	2.8	94.7
3. Kurt Warner	11	3,557	2,327	65.4	28,591	8.04	182	5.1	114	3.2	93.8
4. Tom Brady	9	3,653	2,301	63.0	26,446	7.24	197	5.4	86	2.4	92.9
5. Joe Montana	15	5,391	3,409	63.2	40,551	7.52	273	5.1	139	2.6	92.3
6. Chad Pennington	9	2,395	1,580	66.0	17,391	7.26	101	4.2	62	2.6	90.6
7. Ben Roethlisberger	5	1,905	1,189	62.4	14,974	7.86	101	5.3	69	3.6	89.4
8. Drew Brees	8	3,650	2,334	63.9	26,258	7.19	168	4.6	99	2.7	89.4
9. Daunte Culpepper	10	3,042	1,927	63.3	23,208	7.63	146	4.8	100	3.3	89.0
10. Carson Palmer	5	2,165	1,380	63.7	15,630	7.22	107	4.9	67	3.1	88.9
11. Jeff Garcia	10	3,676	2,264	61.6	25,537	6.95	161	4.4	83	2.3	87.5
12. Dan Marino	17	8,358	4,967	59.4	61,361	7.34	420	5.0	252	3.0	86.4
13. Trent Green	11	3,740	2,266	60.6	28,475	7.61	162	4.3	114	3.0	86.0
14. Donovan McNabb	10	4,303	2,534	58.9	29,320	6.81	194	4.5	90	2.1	85.9
15. Marc Bulger	7	2,924	1,829	62.6	21,345	7.30	117	4.0	87	3.0	85.6
16. Brett Favre	18	9,280	5,720	61.6	65,127	7.02	464	5.0	310	3.3	85.4
17. Jake Delhomme	8	2,434	1,452	59.7	17,877	7.34	115	4.7	76	3.1	85.1
18. Rich Gannon	16	4,206	2,533	60.2	28,743	6.83	180	4.3	104	2.5	84.7
19. Matt Hasselbeck	10	3,347	2,013	60.1	23,549	7.04	147	4.4	94	2.8	84.5
20. Jim Kelly	11	4,779	2,874	60.1	35,467	7.42	237	5.0	175	3.7	84.4

1,500 or more attempts. The passing ratings are based on performance standards established for completion percentage, interception percentage, touchdown percentage, and average gain. Please consult page 364 for more information.

OUTSTANDING PERFORMERS

TOP 20 PASS RECEIVERS

Player	Years	No.	Yards	Avg.	Long	TD
1. Jerry Rice	20	1,549	22,895	14.8	96	197
2. Marvin Harrison	13	1,102	14,580	13.2	80	128
3. Cris Carter	16	1,101	13,899	12.6	80	130
4. Tim Brown	17	1,094	14,934	13.7	80	100
5. Isaac Bruce	15	1,003	14,944	14.9	80	91
6. Terrell Owens	13	951	14,122	14.8	91	139
Andre Reed	16	951	13,198	13.9	83	87
8. Art Monk	16	940	12,721	13.5	79	68
9. Tony Gonzalez	12	916	10,940	11.9	73	76
10. Keenan McCardell	16	883	11,373	12.9	76	63
11. Torry Holt	10	869	12,660	14.6	85	74
12. Jimmy Smith	12	862	12,287	14.3	75	67
13. Irving Fryar	17	851	12,785	15.0	80	84
14. Rod Smith	12	849	11,389	13.4	85	68
15. Randy Moss	11	843	13,201	15.7	82	135
16. Larry Centers	14	827	6,797	8.2	54	28
17. Steve Largent	14	819	13,089	16.0	74	100
18. Shannon Sharpe	14	815	10,060	12.3	82	62
19. Henry Ellard	16	814	13,777	16.9	81	65
Keyshawn Johnson	11	814	10,571	13.0	76	64

TOP 20 INTERCEPTORS

Player	Years	No.	Yards	Avg.	Long	TD
1. Paul Krause	16	81	1,185	14.6	81	3
2. Emlen Tunnell	14	79	1,282	16.2	55	4
3. Rod Woodson	17	71	1,483	20.9	98	12
4. Dick (Night Train) Lane	14	68	1,207	17.8	80	5
5. Ken Riley	15	65	596	9.2	66	5
6. Ronnie Lott	14	63	730	11.6	83	5
7. Dave Brown	15	62	698	11.3	90	5
Dick LeBeau	14	62	762	12.3	70	3
9. Emmitt Thomas	13	58	937	16.2	73	5
10. Mel Blount	14	57	736	12.9	52	2
Bobby Boyd	9	57	994	17.4	74	4
Eugene Robinson	16	57	762	13.4	49	1
Johnny Robinson	12	57	741	13.0	57	1
Everson Walls	13	57	504	8.8	40	1
15. Lem Barney	11	56	1,077	19.2	71	7
Pat Fischer	17	56	941	16.8	69	4
17. Aeneas Williams	14	55	807	14.7	65	9
18. Eric Allen	14	54	826	15.3	94	8
Willie Brown	16	54	472	8.7	45	2
Darrell Green	20	54	621	11.5	83	6
Darren Sharper	12	54	1,036	19.2	92	8

TOP 20 PUNTERS (MINIMUM 250 PUNTS)

Player	Years	No.	Yards	Avg.	Long	Blk.
1. Shane Lechler	9	682	31,902	46.8	73	3
2. Donnie Jones	5	359	16,239	45.2	80	2
3. Sammy Baugh	16	338	15,245	45.1	85	9
4. Mat McBriar	5	299	13,463	45.0	75	1
5. Tommy Davis	11	511	22,833	44.7	82	2
6. Chris Kluwe	4	318	14,158	44.5	70	1
7. Andy Lee	5	455	20,185	44.4	82	2
8. Yale Lary	11	503	22,279	44.3	74	4
9. Todd Sauerbrun	13	889	39,208	44.1	73	9
10. Mike Scifres	6	341	15,038	44.1	71	1
11. Bob Scarpitto	8	283	12,408	43.8	87	4
12. Horace Gillom	7	385	16,872	43.8	80	5
13. Jerry Norton	11	358	15,671	43.8	78	2
14. Dave Lewis	4	285	12,447	43.7	63	0
15. Dustin Colquitt	4	301	13,141	43.7	81	1
16. Greg Montgomery	9	524	22,831	43.6	77	8
17. Don Chandler	12	660	28,678	43.5	90	4
18. Tom Rouen	12	810	35,189	43.4	76	9
19. Rick Tuten	11	741	32,190	43.4	73	2
20. Darren Bennett	11	836	36,316	43.4	66	3

TOP 20 KICKOFF RETURNERS (MINIMUM 75 RETURNS)

Player	Years	No.	Yards	Avg.	Long	TD
1. Gale Sayers	7	91	2,781	30.6	103	6
2. Lynn Chandnois	7	92	2,720	29.6	93	3
3. Abe Woodson	9	193	5,538	28.7	105	5
4. Buddy Young	6	90	2,514	27.9	104	2
5. Ellis Hobbs	4	105	2,913	27.7	108	3
6. Travis Williams	5	102	2,801	27.5	105	6
7. Joe Arenas	7	139	3,798	27.3	96	1
8. Clarence Davis	8	79	2,140	27.1	76	0
9. Steve Van Buren	8	76	2,030	26.7	98	3
10. Lenny Lyles	12	81	2,161	26.7	103	3
11. Justin Miller	4	141	3,745	26.6	103	5
12. Mercury Morris	8	111	2,947	26.5	105	3
13. Bobby Jancik	6	158	4,185	26.5	61	0
14. Mel Renfro	14	85	2,246	26.4	100	2
15. Bobby Mitchell	14	102	2,690	26.4	98	5
16. Josh Cribbs	4	209	5,507	26.3	100	5
17. Terrence McGee	6	206	5,420	26.3	104	5
18. Ollie Matson	14	143	3,746	26.2	105	6
19. Alvin Haymond	10	170	4,438	26.1	98	2
20. Noland Smith	3	82	2,137	26.1	106	1

TOP 20 PUNT RETURNERS (MINIMUM 75 RETURNS)

Player	Years	No.	Yards	Avg.	Long	TD
1. Roscoe Parrish	4	94	1,312	14.0	82	3
2. George McAfee	8	112	1,431	12.8	74	2
3. Jack Christiansen	8	85	1,084	12.8	89	8
4. Claude Gibson	5	110	1,381	12.6	85	3
5. Bill Dudley	9	124	1,515	12.2	96	3
6. Rick Upchurch	9	248	3,008	12.1	92	8
7. Santana Moss	8	101	1,216	12.0	80	3
8. Devin Hester	3	121	1,449	12.0	89	7
9. Desmond Howard	11	244	2,895	11.9	95	8
10. Billy Johnson	14	282	3,317	11.8	87	6
11. Mack Herron	3	84	982	11.7	66	0
12. Billy Thompson	13	157	1,814	11.6	60	0
13. Darrien Gordon	9	314	3,601	11.5	94	6
14. Henry Ellard	16	135	1,527	11.3	83	4
15. Rodger Bird	3	94	1,063	11.3	78	0
16. Bosh Pritchard	6	95	1,072	11.3	81	2
17. Terry Metcalf	6	84	936	11.1	69	1
18. Bob Hayes	11	104	1,158	11.1	90	3
19. Jermaine Lewis	9	295	3,282	11.1	89	6
20. Floyd Little	9	81	893	11.0	72	2

TOP 20 LEADERS IN SACKS

Player	*Years	No.
1. Bruce Smith	19	200.0
2. Reggie White	15	198.0
3. Kevin Greene	15	160.0
4. Chris Doleman	15	150.5
5. Michael Strahan	15	141.5
6. Richard Dent	15	137.5
John Randle	14	137.5
8. Leslie O'Neal	13	132.5
Lawrence Taylor	12	132.5
10. Rickey Jackson	14	128.0
11. Derrick Thomas	11	126.5
12. Simeon Rice	12	122.0
13. Clyde Simmons	15	121.5
14. Jason Taylor	12	120.5
15. Sean Jones	13	113.0
16. Greg Townsend	13	109.5
17. Pat Swilling	12	107.5
18. Trace Armstrong	15	106.0
19. Kevin Carter	14	104.5
Neil Smith	13	104.5

**Years played since 1982 when sacks became an official statistic.*

OUTSTANDING PERFORMERS

POSTSEASON LEADERS

TOP 10 POSTSEASON RUSHERS

Player	Att.	Yards	Avg.	Long	TD
1. Emmitt Smith	349	1,586	4.5	65	19
2. Franco Harris	400	1,556	3.9	50	16
3. Thurman Thomas	339	1,442	4.3	40	16
4. Tony Dorsett	302	1,383	4.6	53	9
5. Marcus Allen	267	1,347	5.0	74	11
6. Terrell Davis	204	1,140	5.6	62	12
7. John Riggins	251	996	4.0	43	12
8. Larry Csonka	225	891	4.0	49	9
9. Chuck Foreman	229	860	3.8	62	7
10. Edgerrin James	218	852	3.9	34	6

TOP 10 POSTSEASON PASSERS

Player	Att.	Comp.	Pct. Comp.	Yards	Avg. Gain	TD	Pct. TD	Int.	Pct. Int.	Rating
1. Bart Starr	213	130	61.0	1,753	8.23	15	7.0	3	1.4	104.8
2. Kurt Warner	403	261	64.8	3,368	8.36	26	6.5	13	3.2	98.9
3. Joe Montana	734	460	62.7	5,772	7.86	45	6.1	21	2.9	95.6
4. Ken Anderson	166	110	66.3	1,321	7.96	9	5.4	6	3.6	93.5
5. Joe Theismann	211	128	60.7	1,782	8.45	11	5.2	7	3.3	91.4
6. Troy Aikman	502	320	63.7	3,849	7.67	23	4.6	17	3.4	88.3
7. Tom Brady	595	372	62.5	3,954	6.7	26	4.4	12	2.0	88.0
8. Ben Roethlisberger	278	172	61.9	2,239	8.05	15	5.4	12	4.3	87.2
9. Steve Young	471	292	62.0	3,326	7.06	20	4.2	13	2.8	85.8
10. Brett Favre	721	438	60.7	5,311	7.4	39	5.4	28	3.9	85.2

TOP 10 POSTSEASON PASS RECEIVERS

Player	No.	Yards	Avg.	Long	TD
1. Jerry Rice	151	2,245	14.9	72	22
2. Michael Irvin	87	1,315	15.1	53	8
3. Andre Reed	85	1,229	14.5	72	9
4. Thurman Thomas	76	672	8.8	27	5
Hines Ward	76	1,064	14.0	45	8
6. Cliff Branch	73	1,289	17.7	72	5
7. Fred Biletnikoff	70	1,167	16.7	57	10
8. Art Monk	69	1,062	15.4	48	7
9. Drew Pearson	67	1,105	16.5	83	8
10. Reggie Wayne	66	963	14.6	72	8

TOP 10 POSTSEASON INTERCEPTION LEADERS

Player	Interceptions
1. Ronnie Lott	9
Bill Simpson	9
Charlie Waters	9
4. Lester Hayes	8
5. Willie Brown	7
Rodney Harrison	7
Asante Samuel	7
Dennis Thurman	7
9. Bobby Bryant	6
Eric Davis	6
Glen Edwards	6
Darrell Green	6
Cliff Harris	6
Ty Law	6
Vernon Perry	6
Aeneas Williams	6

TOP 10 POSTSEASON SACK LEADERS

Player	Sacks
1. Willie McGinest	16.0
2. Bruce Smith	14.5
3. Reggie White	12.0
4. Charles Haley	11.0
5. Richard Dent	10.5
6. Trace Armstrong	10.0
Charles Mann	10.0
Tony Tolbert	10.0
9. Neil Smith	9.5
Michael Strahan	9.5

**Sacks became an official statistic in 1982.*

Compiled by Elias Sports Bureau

Super Bowl I, 1/15/67
Super Bowl II, 1/14/68
Super Bowl III, 1/12/69
Super Bowl IV, 1/11/70
Super Bowl V, 1/17/71
Super Bowl VI, 1/16/72
Super Bowl VII, 1/14/73
Super Bowl VIII, 1/13/74
Super Bowl IX, 1/12/75
Super Bowl X, 1/18/76
Super Bowl XI, 1/9/77
Super Bowl XII, 1/15/78
Super Bowl XIII, 1/21/79
Super Bowl XIV, 1/20/80
Super Bowl XV, 1/25/81
Super Bowl XVI, 1/24/82
Super Bowl XVII, 1/30/83
Super Bowl XVIII, 1/22/84
Super Bowl XIX, 1/20/85
Super Bowl XX, 1/26/86
Super Bowl XXI, 1/25/87
Super Bowl XXII, 1/31/88
Super Bowl XXIII, 1/22/89
Super Bowl XXIV, 1/28/90
Super Bowl XXV, 1/27/91
Super Bowl XXVI, 1/26/92
Super Bowl XXVII, 1/31/93
Super Bowl XXVIII, 1/30/94
Super Bowl XXIX, 1/29/95
Super Bowl XXX, 1/28/96
Super Bowl XXXI, 1/26/97
Super Bowl XXXII, 1/25/98
Super Bowl XXXIII, 1/31/99
Super Bowl XXXIV, 1/30/00
Super Bowl XXXV, 1/28/01
Super Bowl XXXVI, 2/3/02
Super Bowl XXXVII, 1/26/03
Super Bowl XXXVIII, 2/1/04
Super Bowl XXXIX, 2/6/05
Super Bowl XL, 2/5/06
Super Bowl XLI, 2/4/07
Super Bowl XLII, 2/3/08
Super Bowl XLIII, 2/1/09

INDIVIDUAL RECORDS

SERVICE

Most Games

6 Mike Lodish, Buffalo, XXV-XXVIII; Denver, XXXII-XXXIII
5 Marv Fleming, Green Bay, I-II; Miami, VI-VIII
Larry Cole, Dallas, V-VI, X, XII-XIII
Cliff Harris, Dallas, V-VI, X, XII-XIII
Charles Haley, San Francisco, XXIII-XXIV; Dallas, XXVII-XXVIII, XXX
D.D. Lewis, Dallas, V-VI, X, XII-XIII
Preston Pearson, Baltimore, III; Pittsburgh, IX; Dallas, X, XII-XIII
Charlie Waters, Dallas, V-VI, X, XII-XIII
Rayfield Wright, Dallas, V-VI, X, XII-XIII
Cornelius Bennett, Buffalo, XXV-XXVIII; Atlanta, XXXIII
John Elway, Denver, XXI-XXII, XXIV, XXXII-XXXIII
Glenn Parker, Buffalo, XXV-XXVIII; N.Y. Giants, XXXV
Bill Romanowski, San Francisco, XXIII-XXIV; Denver, XXXII-XXXIII; Oakland, XXXVII
Adam Vinatieri, New England, XXXI, XXXVI, XXXVIII, XXXIX; Indianapolis, XLI
Tedy Bruschi, New England, XXXI, XXXVI, XXXVIII-XXXIX, XLII
4 By many players

Most Games, Winning Team

5 Charles Haley, San Francisco, XXIII-XXIV; Dallas, XXVII-XXVIII, XXX
4 By many players

Most Games, Coach

6 Don Shula, Baltimore, III; Miami, VI-VIII, XVII, XIX
5 Tom Landry, Dallas, V-VI, X, XII-XIII
4 Bud Grant, Minnesota, IV, VIII-IX, XI
Chuck Noll, Pittsburgh, IX-X, XIII-XIV
Joe Gibbs, Washington, XVII-XVIII, XXII, XXVI
Marv Levy, Buffalo, XXV-XXVIII
Dan Reeves, Denver, XXI-XXII, XXIV; Atlanta, XXXIII
Bill Belichick, New England, XXXVI, XXXVIII-XXXIX, XLII

Most Games, Winning Team, Coach

4 Chuck Noll, Pittsburgh, IX-X, XIII-XIV
3 Bill Walsh, San Francisco, XVI, XIX, XXIII
Joe Gibbs, Washington, XVII, XXII, XXVI
Bill Belichick, New England, XXXVI, XXXVIII-XXXIX
2 Vince Lombardi, Green Bay, I-II
Tom Landry, Dallas, VI, XII
Don Shula, Miami, VII-VIII
Tom Flores, Oakland, XV; L.A. Raiders, XVIII
Bill Parcells, N.Y. Giants, XXI, XXV
Jimmy Johnson, Dallas, XXVII-XXVIII
George Seifert, San Francisco, XXIV, XXIX
Mike Shanahan, Denver, XXXII-XXXIII

Most Games, Losing Team, Coach

4 Bud Grant, Minnesota, IV, VIII-IX, XI
Don Shula, Baltimore, III; Miami, VI, XVII, XIX
Marv Levy, Buffalo, XXV-XXVIII
Dan Reeves, Denver, XXI-XXII, XXIV; Atlanta, XXXIII
3 Tom Landry, Dallas, V, X, XIII

SCORING

POINTS

Most Points, Career

48 Jerry Rice, San Francisco-Oakland, 4 games (8-td)
34 Adam Vinatieri, New England-Indianapolis, 5 games (7-fg, 13-xp)
30 Emmitt Smith, Dallas, 3 games (5-td)

Most Points, Game

18 Roger Craig, San Francisco vs. Miami, XIX (3-td)
Jerry Rice, San Francisco vs. Denver, XXIV (3-td); vs. San Diego, XXIX (3-td)
Ricky Watters, San Francisco vs. San Diego, XXIX (3-td)
Terrell Davis, Denver vs. Green Bay, XXXII (3-td)
15 Don Chandler, Green Bay vs. Oakland, II (3-pat, 4-fg)
14 Ray Wersching, San Francisco vs. Cincinnati, XVI (2-pat, 4-fg)
Kevin Butler, Chicago vs. New England, XX (5-pat, 3-fg)

TOUCHDOWNS

Most Touchdowns, Career

8 Jerry Rice, San Francisco-Oakland, 4 games (8-p)
5 Emmitt Smith, Dallas, 3 games (5-r)
4 Franco Harris, Pittsburgh, 4 games (4-r)
Roger Craig, San Francisco, 3 games (2-r, 2-p)
Thurman Thomas, Buffalo, 4 games (4-r)
John Elway, Denver, 5 games (4-r)

Most Touchdowns, Game

3 Roger Craig, San Francisco vs. Miami, XIX (1-r, 2-p)
Jerry Rice, San Francisco. vs. Denver, XXIV (3-p); vs. San Diego, XXIX (3-p)
Ricky Watters, San Francisco vs. San Diego, XXIX (1-r, 2-p)
Terrell Davis, Denver vs. Green Bay, XXXII (3-r)
2 Max McGee, Green Bay vs. Kansas City, I (2-p)
Elijah Pitts, Green Bay vs. Kansas City, I (2-r)
Bill Miller, Oakland vs. Green Bay, II (2-p)
Larry Csonka, Miami vs. Minnesota, VIII (2-r)
Pete Banaszak, Oakland vs. Minnesota, XI (2-r)
John Stallworth, Pittsburgh vs. Dallas, XIII (2-p)
Franco Harris, Pittsburgh vs. Los Angeles, XIV (2-r)
Cliff Branch, Oakland vs. Philadelphia, XV (2-p)
Dan Ross, Cincinnati vs. San Francisco, XVI (2-p)
Marcus Allen, L.A. Raiders vs. Washington, XVIII (2-r)
Jim McMahon, Chicago vs. New England, XX (2-r)
Ricky Sanders, Washington vs. Denver, XXII (2-p)
Timmy Smith, Washington vs. Denver, XXII (2-r)
Tom Rathman, San Francisco vs. Denver, XXIV (2-r)
Gerald Riggs, Washington vs. Buffalo, XXVI (2-r)
Michael Irvin, Dallas vs. Buffalo, XXVII (2-p)
Emmitt Smith, Dallas vs. Buffalo, XXVIII (2-r)
Emmitt Smith, Dallas vs. Pittsburgh, XXX (2-r)
Antonio Freeman, Green Bay vs. Denver, XXXII (2-p)
Howard Griffith, Denver vs. Atlanta, XXXIII (2-r)
Eddie George, Tennessee vs. St. Louis, XXXIV (2-r)

Keenan McCardell, Tampa Bay vs. Oakland, XXXVII (2-r)
Dwight Smith, Tampa Bay vs. Oakland, XXXVII (2-ret)
Larry Fitzgerald, Arizona vs. Pittsburgh, XLIII (2-p)

POINTS AFTER TOUCHDOWN

Most (One-Point) Points After Touchdown, Career

13 Adam Vinatieri, New England-Indianapolis, 5 games (13 att)
9 Mike Cofer, San Francisco, 2 games (10 att)
8 Don Chandler, Green Bay, 2 games (8 att)
Roy Gerela, Pittsburgh, 3 games (9 att)
Chris Bahr, Oakland-L.A. Raiders, 2 games (8 att)
Jason Elam, Denver, 2 games (8 att)

Most (One-Point) Points After Touchdown, Game

7 Mike Cofer, San Francisco vs. Denver, XXIV (8 att)
Lin Elliott, Dallas vs. Buffalo, XXVII (7 att)
Doug Brien, San Francisco vs. San Diego, XXIX (7 att)
6 Ali Hají-Sheikh, Washington vs. Denver, XXII (6 att)
Martín Gramatica, Tampa Bay vs. Oakland, XXXVII (6 att)
5 Don Chandler, Green Bay vs. Kansas City, I (5 att)
Roy Gerela, Pittsburgh vs. Dallas, XIII (5 att)
Chris Bahr, L.A. Raiders vs. Washington, XVIII (5 att)
Ray Wersching, San Francisco vs. Miami, XIX (5 att)
Kevin Butler, Chicago vs. New England, XX (5 att)

Most Two-Point Conversions, Game

1 Mark Seay, San Diego vs. San Francisco, XXIX
Alfred Pupunu, San Diego vs. San Francisco, XXIX
Mark Chmura, Green Bay vs. New England, XXXI
Kevin Faulk, New England vs. Carolina, XXXVIII

FIELD GOALS

Field Goals Attempted, Career

10 Adam Vinatieri, New England-Indianapolis, 5 games
6 Jim Turner, N.Y. Jets-Denver, 2 games
Roy Gerela, Pittsburgh, 3 games
Rich Karlis, Denver, 2 games
Jeff Wilkins, St. Louis, 2 games
5 Efren Herrera, Dallas, 1 game
Ray Wersching, San Francisco, 2 games
Jason Elam, Denver, 2 games

Most Field Goals Attempted, Game

5 Jim Turner, N.Y. Jets vs. Baltimore, III
Efren Herrera, Dallas vs. Denver, XII
4 Don Chandler, Green Bay vs. Oakland, II
Roy Gerela, Pittsburgh vs. Dallas, X
Ray Wersching, San Francisco vs. Cincinnati, XVI
Rich Karlis, Denver vs. N.Y. Giants, XXI
Mike Cofer, San Francisco vs. Cincinnati, XXIII
Jason Elam, Denver vs. Atlanta, XXXIII
Jeff Wilkins, St. Louis vs. Tennessee, XXXIV
Adam Vinatieri, Indianapolis vs. Chicago, XLI

Most Field Goals, Career

7 Adam Vinatieri, New England-Indianapolis, 5 games (10 att)
5 Ray Wersching, San Francisco, 2 games (5 att)
4 Don Chandler, Green Bay, 2 games (4 att)
Jim Turner, N.Y. Jets-Denver, 2 games (6 att)
Uwe von Schamann, Miami, 2 games (4 att)
Jeff Wilkins, St. Louis, 2 games (6 att)

Most Field Goals, Game

4 Don Chandler, Green Bay vs. Oakland, II
Ray Wersching, San Francisco vs. Cincinnati, XVI
3 Jim Turner, N.Y. Jets vs. Baltimore, III
Jan Stenerud, Kansas City vs. Minnesota, IV
Uwe von Schamann, Miami vs. San Francisco, XIX
Kevin Butler, Chicago vs. New England, XX
Jim Breech, Cincinnati vs. San Francisco, XXIII
Chip Lohmiller, Washington vs. Buffalo, XXVI
Eddie Murray, Dallas vs. Buffalo, XXVIII
Jeff Wilkins, St. Louis vs. Tennessee, XXXIV
Adam Vinatieri, Indianapolis vs. Chicago, XLI

Longest Field Goal

54 Steve Christie, Buffalo vs. Dallas, XXVIII
51 Jason Elam, Denver vs. Green Bay, XXXII
50 Jeff Wilkins, St. Louis vs. New England, XXXVI
John Kasay, Carolina vs. New England, XXXVIII

SAFETIES

Most Safeties, Game

1 Dwight White, Pittsburgh vs. Minnesota, IX
Reggie Harrison, Pittsburgh vs. Dallas, X
Henry Waechter, Chicago vs. New England, XX
George Martin, N.Y. Giants vs. Denver, XXI
Bruce Smith, Buffalo vs. N.Y. Giants, XXV

RUSHING

ATTEMPTS

Most Attempts, Career

101 Franco Harris, Pittsburgh, 4 games
70 Emmitt Smith, Dallas, 3 games
64 John Riggins, Washington, 2 games

Most Attempts, Game

38 John Riggins, Washington vs. Miami, XVII
34 Franco Harris, Pittsburgh vs. Minnesota, IX
33 Larry Csonka, Miami vs. Minnesota, VIII

YARDS GAINED

Most Yards Gained, Career

354 Franco Harris, Pittsburgh, 4 games
297 Larry Csonka, Miami, 3 games
289 Emmitt Smith, Dallas, 3 games

Most Yards Gained, Game

204 Timmy Smith, Washington vs. Denver, XXII
191 Marcus Allen, L.A. Raiders vs. Washington, XVIII
166 John Riggins, Washington vs. Miami, XVII

Longest Run From Scrimmage

75 Willie Parker, Pittsburgh vs. Seattle, XL (TD)
74 Marcus Allen, L.A. Raiders vs. Washington, XVIII (TD)
58 Tom Matte, Baltimore vs. N.Y. Jets, III
Timmy Smith, Washington vs. Denver, XXII (TD)

AVERAGE GAIN

Highest Average Gain, Career (20 attempts)

9.6 Marcus Allen, L.A. Raiders, 1 game (20-191)
9.3 Timmy Smith, Washington, 1 game (22-204)
5.4 Dominic Rhodes, Indianapolis, 1 game (21-113)

Highest Average Gain, Game (10 attempts)

10.5 Tom Matte, Baltimore vs. N.Y. Jets, III (11-116)
9.6 Marcus Allen, L.A. Raiders vs. Washington, XVIII (20-191)
9.3 Willie Parker, Pittsburgh vs. Seattle, XL (10-93)

TOUCHDOWNS

Most Touchdowns, Career

5 Emmitt Smith, Dallas, 3 games
4 Franco Harris, Pittsburgh, 4 games
Thurman Thomas, Buffalo, 4 games
John Elway, Denver, 5 games
3 Terrell Davis, Denver, 2 games

Most Touchdowns, Game

3 Terrell Davis, Denver vs. Green Bay, XXXII
2 Elijah Pitts, Green Bay vs. Kansas City, I
Larry Csonka, Miami vs. Minnesota, VIII
Pete Banaszak, Oakland vs. Minnesota, XI
Franco Harris, Pittsburgh vs. Los Angeles, XIV
Marcus Allen, L.A. Raiders vs. Washington, XVIII
Jim McMahon, Chicago vs. New England, XX
Timmy Smith, Washington vs. Denver, XXII

Tom Rathman, San Francisco vs. Denver, XXIV
Gerald Riggs, Washington vs. Buffalo, XXVI
Emmitt Smith, Dallas vs. Buffalo, XXVIII
Emmitt Smith, Dallas vs. Pittsburgh, XXX
Howard Griffith, Denver vs. Atlanta, XXXIII
Eddie George, Tennessee vs. St. Louis, XXXIV

PASSING

PASSER RATING

Highest Passer Rating, Career (40 attempts)
127.8 Joe Montana, San Francisco, 4 games
122.8 Jim Plunkett, Oakland-L.A. Raiders, 2 games
112.8 Terry Bradshaw, Pittsburgh, 4 games

ATTEMPTS

Most Passes Attempted, Career
156 Tom Brady, New England, 4 games
152 John Elway, Denver, 5 games
145 Jim Kelly, Buffalo, 4 games

Most Passes Attempted, Game
58 Jim Kelly, Buffalo vs. Washington, XXVI
51 Donovan McNabb, Philadelphia vs. New England, XXXIX
50 Dan Marino, Miami vs. San Francisco, XIX
Jim Kelly, Buffalo vs. Dallas, XXVIII

COMPLETIONS

Most Passes Completed, Career
100 Tom Brady, New England, 4 games
83 Joe Montana, San Francisco, 4 games
Kurt Warner, St. Louis-Arizona, 3 games
81 Jim Kelly, Buffalo, 4 games

Most Passes Completed, Game
32 Tom Brady, New England vs. Carolina, XXXVIII
31 Jim Kelly, Buffalo vs. Dallas, XXVIII
Kurt Warner, Arizona vs. Pittsburgh, XLIII
30 Donovan McNabb, Philadelphia vs. New England, XXXIX

Most Consecutive Completions, Game
13 Joe Montana, San Francisco vs. Denver, XXIV
10 Phil Simms, N.Y. Giants vs. Denver, XXI
Troy Aikman, Dallas vs. Pittsburgh, XXX
Kurt Warner, Arizona vs. Pittsburgh, XLIII
9 Jim Kelly, Buffalo vs. Dallas, XXVIII
Neil O'Donnell, Pittsburgh vs. Dallas, XXX
Steve McNair, Tennessee vs. St. Louis, XXXIV
Peyton Manning, Indianapolis vs. Chicago, XLI

COMPLETION PERCENTAGE

Highest Completion Percentage, Career (40 attempts)
70.0 Troy Aikman, Dallas, 3 games, (80-56)
68.0 Joe Montana, San Francisco, 4 games (122-83)
64.1 Tom Brady, New England, 4 games (156-100)

Highest Completion Percentage, Game (20 attempts)
88.0 Phil Simms, N.Y. Giants vs. Denver, XXI (25-22)
75.9 Joe Montana, San Francisco vs. Denver, XXIV (29-22)
73.5 Ken Anderson, Cincinnati vs. San Francisco, XVI (34-25)

YARDS GAINED

Most Yards Gained, Career
1,156 Kurt Warner, St. Louis-Arizona, 3 games
1,142 Joe Montana, San Francisco, 4 games
1,128 John Elway, Denver, 5 games

Most Yards Gained, Game
414 Kurt Warner, St. Louis vs. Tennessee, XXXIV
377 Kurt Warner, Arizona vs. Pittsburgh, XLIII
365 Kurt Warner, St. Louis vs. New England, XXXVI

Longest Pass Completion
85 Jake Delhomme (to Muhammad), Carolina vs. New England, XXXVIII (TD)
81 Brett Favre (to Freeman), Green Bay vs. New England, XXXI (TD)
80 Jim Plunkett (to King), Oakland vs. Philadelphia, XV (TD)
Doug Williams (to Sanders), Washington vs. Denver, XXII (TD)
John Elway (to R. Smith), Denver vs. Atlanta, XXXIII (TD)

AVERAGE GAIN

Highest Average Gain, Career (40 attempts)
11.10 Terry Bradshaw, Pittsburgh, 4 games (84-932)
9.62 Bart Starr, Green Bay, 2 games (47-452)
9.41 Jim Plunkett, Oakland-L.A. Raiders, 2 games (46-433)

Highest Average Gain, Game (20 attempts)
14.71 Terry Bradshaw, Pittsburgh vs. Los Angeles, XIV (21-309)
12.80 Jim McMahon, Chicago vs. New England, XX (20-256)
12.43 Jim Plunkett, Oakland vs. Philadelphia, XV (21-261)

TOUCHDOWNS

Most Touchdown Passes, Career
11 Joe Montana, San Francisco, 4 games
9 Terry Bradshaw, Pittsburgh, 4 games
8 Roger Staubach, Dallas, 4 games

Most Touchdown Passes, Game
6 Steve Young, San Francisco vs. San Diego, XXIX
5 Joe Montana, San Francisco vs. Denver, XXIV
4 Terry Bradshaw, Pittsburgh vs. Dallas, XIII
Doug Williams, Washington vs. Denver, XXII
Troy Aikman, Dallas vs. Buffalo, XXVII

HAD INTERCEPTED

Lowest Percentage, Passes Had Intercepted, Career (40 attempts)
0.00 Jim Plunkett, Oakland-L.A. Raiders, 2 games (46-0)
Joe Montana, San Francisco, 4 games (122-0)
0.64 Tom Brady, New England, 4 games (156-1)
1.25 Troy Aikman, Dallas, 3 games (80-1)

Most Attempts, Without Interception, Game
48 Tom Brady, New England vs. N.Y. Giants, XLII
45 Kurt Warner, St. Louis vs. Tennessee, XXXIV
36 Joe Montana, San Francisco vs. Cincinnati, XXIII
Steve Young, San Francisco vs. San Diego, XXIX
Steve McNair, Tennessee vs. St. Louis, XXXIV

Most Passes Had Intercepted, Career
8 John Elway, Denver, 5 games
7 Craig Morton, Dallas-Denver, 2 games
Jim Kelly, Buffalo, 4 games
6 Fran Tarkenton, Minnesota, 3 games

Most Passes Had Intercepted, Game
5 Rich Gannon, Oakland vs. Tampa Bay, XXXVII
4 Craig Morton, Denver vs. Dallas, XII
Jim Kelly, Buffalo vs. Washington, XXVI
Drew Bledsoe, New England vs. Green Bay, XXXI
Kerry Collins, N.Y. Giants vs. Baltimore, XXXV
3 By 11 players

PASS RECEIVING

RECEPTIONS

Most Receptions, Career
33 Jerry Rice, San Francisco-Oakland, 4 games
27 Andre Reed, Buffalo, 4 games
21 Deion Branch, New England, 2 games

Most Receptions, Game
11 Dan Ross, Cincinnati vs. San Francisco, XVI
Jerry Rice, San Francisco vs. Cincinnati, XXIII
Deion Branch, New England vs. Philadelphia, XXXIX

Wes Welker, New England vs. N.Y. Giants, XLII
10 Tony Nathan, Miami vs. San Francisco, XIX
Jerry Rice, San Francisco vs. San Diego, XXIX
Andre Hastings, Pittsburgh vs. Dallas, XXX
Deion Branch, New England vs. Carolina, XXXVIII
Joseph Addai, Indianapolis vs. Chicago, XLI
9 Ricky Sanders, Washington vs. Denver, XXII
Antonio Freeman, Green Bay vs. Denver, XXXII
Terrell Owens, Philadelphia vs. New England, XXXIX
Santonio Holmes, Pittsburgh vs. Arizona, XLIII

YARDS GAINED

Most Yards Gained, Career

589 Jerry Rice, San Francisco-Oakland, 4 games
364 Lynn Swann, Pittsburgh, 4 games
323 Andre Reed, Buffalo, 4 games

Most Yards Gained, Game

215 Jerry Rice, San Francisco vs. Cincinnati, XXIII
193 Ricky Sanders, Washington vs. Denver, XXII
162 Isaac Bruce, St. Louis vs. Tennessee, XXXIV

Longest Reception

85 Muhsin Muhammad (from Delhomme), Carolina vs. New England, XXXVIII
81 Antonio Freeman (from Favre), Green Bay vs. New England, XXXI (TD)
80 Kenny King (from Plunkett), Oakland vs. Philadelphia, XV (TD)
Ricky Sanders (from Williams), Washington vs. Denver, XXII (TD)
Rod Smith (from Elway), Denver vs. Atlanta, XXXIII

AVERAGE GAIN

Highest Average Gain, Career (8 receptions)

24.4 John Stallworth, Pittsburgh, 4 games (11-268)
23.4 Ricky Sanders, Washington, 2 games (10-234)
22.8 Lynn Swann, Pittsburgh, 4 games (16-364)

Highest Average Gain, Game (3 receptions)

40.33 John Stallworth, Pittsburgh vs. Los Angeles, XIV (3-121)
40.25 Lynn Swann, Pittsburgh vs. Dallas, X (4-161)
38.33 John Stallworth, Pittsburgh vs. Dallas, XIII (3-115)

TOUCHDOWNS

Most Touchdowns, Career

8 Jerry Rice, San Francisco-Oakland, 4 games
3 John Stallworth, Pittsburgh, 4 games
Lynn Swann, Pittsburgh, 4 games
Cliff Branch, Oakland-L.A. Raiders, 3 games
Antonio Freeman, Green Bay, 2 games
2 Max McGee, Green Bay, 2 games
Bill Miller, Oakland, 1 game
Butch Johnson, Dallas, 2 games
Dan Ross, Cincinnati, 1 game
Roger Craig, San Francisco, 3 games
Ricky Sanders, Washington, 2 games
John Taylor, San Francisco, 3 games
Gary Clark, Washington, 2 games
Don Beebe, Buffalo-Green Bay, 4 games
Michael Irvin, Dallas, 3 games
Ricky Watters, San Francisco, 1 game
Jay Novacek, Dallas, 3 games
Keenan McCardell, Tampa Bay, 1 game
Ricky Proehl, St. Louis-Carolina, 3 games
David Givens, New England, 2 games
Mike Vrabel, New England, 4 games
Muhsin Muhammad, Carolina-Chicago, 2 games
Larry Fitzgerald, Arizona, 1 game

Most Touchdowns, Game

3 Jerry Rice, San Francisco vs. Denver, XXIV; vs. San Diego, XXIX
2 Max McGee, Green Bay vs. Kansas City, I
Bill Miller, Oakland vs. Green Bay, II
John Stallworth, Pittsburgh vs. Dallas, XIII
Cliff Branch, Oakland vs. Philadelphia, XV
Dan Ross, Cincinnati vs. San Francisco, XVI
Roger Craig, San Francisco vs. Miami, XIX
Ricky Sanders, Washington vs. Denver, XXII
Michael Irvin, Dallas vs. Buffalo, XXVII
Ricky Watters, San Francisco vs. San Diego, XXIX
Antonio Freeman, Green Bay vs. Denver, XXXII
Keenan McCardell, Tampa Bay vs. Oakland, XXXVII
Larry Fitzgerald, Arizona vs. Pittsburgh, XLIII

INTERCEPTIONS BY

Most Interceptions By, Career

3 Chuck Howley, Dallas, 2 games
Rod Martin, Oakland-L.A. Raiders, 2 games
Larry Brown, Dallas, 3 games
2 Randy Beverly, N.Y. Jets, 1 game
Jake Scott, Miami, 3 games
Mike Wagner, Pittsburgh, 3 games
Mel Blount, Pittsburgh, 4 games
Eric Wright, San Francisco, 4 games
Barry Wilburn, Washington, 1 game
Brad Edwards, Washington, 1 game
Thomas Everett, Dallas, 2 games
James Washington, Dallas, 2 games
Darrien Gordon, San Diego-Denver-Oakland, 4 games
Dexter Jackson, Tampa Bay, 1 game
Dwight Smith, Tampa Bay, 1 game
Rodney Harrison, San Diego-New England, 4 games

Most Interceptions By, Game

3 Rod Martin, Oakland vs. Philadelphia, XV
2 Randy Beverly, N.Y. Jets vs. Baltimore, III
Chuck Howley, Dallas vs. Baltimore, V
Jake Scott, Miami vs. Washington, VII
Barry Wilburn, Washington vs. Denver, XXII
Brad Edwards, Washington vs. Buffalo, XXVI
Thomas Everett, Dallas vs. Buffalo, XXVII
Larry Brown, Dallas vs. Pittsburgh, XXX
Darrien Gordon, Denver vs. Atlanta, XXXIII
Dexter Jackson, Tampa Bay vs. Oakland, XXXVII
Dwight Smith, Tampa Bay vs. Oakland, XXXVII
Rodney Harrison, New England vs. Philadelphia, XXXIX

YARDS GAINED

Most Yards Gained, Career

108 Darrien Gordon, San Diego-Denver-Oakland, 4 games
100 James Harrison, Pittsburgh, 2 games
94 Dwight Smith, Tampa Bay, 1 game

Most Yards Gained, Game

108 Darrien Gordon, Denver vs. Atlanta, XXXIII
100 James Harrison, Pittsburgh vs. Arizona, XLIII
94 Dwight Smith, Tampa Bay vs. Oakland, XXXVII

Longest Return

100 James Harrison, Pittsburgh vs. Arizona, XLIII
76 Kelly Herndon, Seattle vs. Pittsburgh, XL
75 Willie Brown, Oakland vs. Minnesota, XI (TD)

TOUCHDOWNS

Most Touchdowns, Game

2 Dwight Smith, Tampa Bay vs. Oakland, XXXVII
1 Herb Adderley, Green Bay vs. Oakland, II
Willie Brown, Oakland vs. Minnesota, XI
Jack Squirek, L.A. Raiders vs. Washington, XVIII
Reggie Phillips, Chicago vs. New England, XX
Duane Starks, Baltimore vs. N.Y. Giants, XXXV

Ty Law, New England vs. St. Louis, XXXVI
Derrick Brooks, Tampa Bay vs. Oakland, XXXVII
Kelvin Hayden, Indianapolis vs. Chicago, XLI
James Harrison, Pittsburgh vs. Arizona, XLIII

PUNTING

Most Punts, Career

17 Mike Eischeid, Oakland-Minnesota, 3 games
Mike Horan, Denver-St. Louis, 4 games
16 Brad Maynard, N.Y. Giants-Chicago, 2 games
15 Larry Seiple, Miami, 3 games

Most Punts, Game

11 Brad Maynard, N.Y. Giants vs. Baltimore, XXXV
10 Kyle Richardson, Baltimore vs. N.Y. Giants, XXXV
9 Ron Widby, Dallas vs. Baltimore, V

Longest Punt

63 Lee Johnson, Cincinnati vs. San Francisco, XXIII
62 Rich Camarillo, New England vs. Chicago, XX
61 Jerrel Wilson, Kansas City vs. Green Bay, I

AVERAGE YARDAGE

Highest Average, Punting, Career (10 punts)

46.5 Jerrel Wilson, Kansas City, 2 games (11-511)
43.8 Tom Rouen, Denver-Seattle, 3 games (11-482)
43.0 Kyle Richardson, Baltimore, 1 game (10-430)
Tom Tupa, New England-Tampa Bay, 2 games (12-516)

Highest Average, Punting, Game (4 punts)

50.2 Tom Rouen, Seattle vs. Pittsburgh, XL (6-301)
48.8 Bryan Wagner, San Diego vs. San Francisco, XXIX (4-195)
48.7 Chris Gardocki, Pittsburgh vs. Seattle, XL (6-292)

PUNT RETURNS

Most Punt Returns, Career

8 Troy Brown, New England, 3 games
6 Willie Wood, Green Bay, 2 games
Jake Scott, Miami, 3 games
Theo Bell, Pittsburgh, 2 games
Mike Nelms, Washington, 1 game
John Taylor, San Francisco, 3 games
Desmond Howard, Green Bay, 1 game
David Meggett, N.Y. Giants-New England, 2 games
Darrien Gordon, San Diego-Denver-Oakland, 4 games
5 Dana McLemore, San Francisco, 1 game

Most Punt Returns, Game

6 Mike Nelms, Washington vs. Miami, XVII
Desmond Howard, Green Bay vs. New England, XXXI
5 Willie Wood, Green Bay vs. Oakland, II
Dana McLemore, San Francisco vs. Miami, XIX
4 By nine players

Most Fair Catches, Game

4 Jermaine Lewis, Baltimore vs. N.Y. Giants, XXXV
Karl Williams, Tampa Bay vs. Oakland, XXXVII
3 Ron Gardin, Baltimore vs. Dallas, V
Golden Richards, Dallas vs. Pittsburgh, X
Greg Pruitt, L.A. Raiders vs. Washington, XVIII
Al Edwards, Buffalo vs. N.Y. Giants, XXV
David Meggett, N.Y. Giants vs. Buffalo, XXV

YARDS GAINED

Most Yards Gained, Career

94 John Taylor, San Francisco, 3 games
90 Desmond Howard, Green Bay, 1 game
67 David Meggett, N.Y. Giants-New England, 2 games

Most Yards Gained, Game

90 Desmond Howard, Green Bay vs. New England, XXXI
56 John Taylor, San Francisco vs. Cincinnati, XXIII
52 Mike Nelms, Washington vs. Miami, XXII

Longest Return

45 John Taylor, San Francisco vs. Cincinnati, XXIII
34 Darrell Green, Washington vs. L.A. Raiders, XVIII
Desmond Howard, Green Bay vs. New England, XXXI
Jermaine Lewis, Baltimore vs. N.Y. Giants, XXXV
Steve Breaston, Arizona vs. Pittsburgh, XLIII
32 Desmond Howard, Green Bay vs. New England, XXXI

AVERAGE YARDAGE

Highest Average, Career (4 returns)

15.7 John Taylor, San Francisco, 3 games (6-94)
15.0 Desmond Howard, Green Bay, 1 game (6-90)
11.2 David Meggett, N.Y. Giants-New England, 2 games (6-67)

Highest Average, Game (3 returns)

18.7 John Taylor, San Francisco vs. Cincinnati, XXIII (3-56)
15.0 Desmond Howard, Green Bay vs. New England, XXXI (6-90)
14.0 Terrence Wilkins, Indianapolis vs. Chicago, XLI (3-42)

TOUCHDOWNS

Most Touchdowns, Game

None

KICKOFF RETURNS

Most Kickoff Returns, Career

10 Ken Bell, Denver, 3 games
8 Larry Anderson, Pittsburgh, 2 games
Fulton Walker, Miami, 2 games
Andre Coleman, San Diego, 1 game
Marcus Knight, Oakland, 1 game
7 Preston Pearson, Baltimore-Pittsburgh-Dallas, 5 games
Stephen Starring, New England, 1 game
David Meggett, N.Y. Giants-New England, 2 games

Most Kickoff Returns, Game

8 Andre Coleman, San Diego vs. San Francisco, XXIX
Marcus Knight, Oakland vs. Tampa Bay, XXXVII
7 Stephen Starring, New England vs. Chicago, XX
6 Darren Carrington, Denver vs. San Francisco, XXIV
Antonio Freeman, Green Bay vs. Denver, XXXII
Ron Dixon, N.Y. Giants vs. Baltimore, XXXV

YARDS GAINED

Most Yards Gained, Career

283 Fulton Walker, Miami, 2 games
244 Andre Coleman, San Diego, 1 game
210 Tim Dwight, Atlanta, 1 game

Most Yards Gained, Game

244 Andre Coleman, San Diego vs. San Francisco, XXIX
210 Tim Dwight, Atlanta vs. Denver, XXXIII
190 Fulton Walker, Miami vs. Washington, XVII

Longest Return

99 Desmond Howard, Green Bay vs. New England, XXXI (TD)
98 Fulton Walker, Miami vs. Washington, XVII (TD)
Andre Coleman, San Diego vs. San Francisco, XXIX (TD)
97 Ron Dixon, N.Y. Giants vs. Baltimore, XXXV (TD)

AVERAGE YARDAGE

Highest Average, Career (4 returns)

42.0 Tim Dwight, Atlanta, 1 game (5-210)
38.5 Desmond Howard, Green Bay, 1 game (4-154)
35.4 Fulton Walker, Miami, 2 games (8-283)

Highest Average, Game (3 returns)

47.5 Fulton Walker, Miami vs. Washington, XVII (4-190)
42.0 Tim Dwight, Atlanta vs. Denver, XXXIII (5-210)
38.5 Desmond Howard, Green Bay vs. New England, XXXI (4-154)

TOUCHDOWNS

Most Touchdowns, Game

1 Fulton Walker, Miami vs. Washington, XVII
Stanford Jennings, Cincinnati vs. San Francisco, XXIII
Andre Coleman, San Diego vs. San Francisco, XXIX
Desmond Howard, Green Bay vs. New England, XXXI
Tim Dwight, Atlanta vs. Denver, XXXIII
Ron Dixon, N.Y. Giants vs. Baltimore, XXXV
Jermaine Lewis, Baltimore vs. N.Y. Giants, XXXV
Devin Hester, Chicago vs. Indianapolis, XLI

FUMBLES

Most Fumbles, Career

5 Roger Staubach, Dallas, 4 games
4 Jim Kelly, Buffalo, 4 games
Kurt Warner, St. Louis-Arizona, 3 games
3 Franco Harris, Pittsburgh, 4 games
Terry Bradshaw, Pittsburgh, 4 games
John Elway, Denver, 5 games
Frank Reich, Buffalo, 4 games
Thurman Thomas, Buffalo, 4 games

Most Fumbles, Game

3 Roger Staubach, Dallas vs. Pittsburgh, X
Jim Kelly, Buffalo vs. Washington, XXVI
Frank Reich, Buffalo vs. Dallas, XXVII
2 Franco Harris, Pittsburgh vs. Minnesota, IX
Butch Johnson, Dallas vs. Denver, XII
Terry Bradshaw, Pittsburgh vs. Dallas, XIII
Joe Montana, San Francisco vs. Cincinnati, XXIII
John Elway, Denver vs. San Francisco, XXIV
Thurman Thomas, Buffalo vs. Dallas, XXVIII
Rex Grossman, Chicago vs. Indianapolis, XLI
Eli Manning, N.Y. Giants vs. New England, XLII
Kurt Warner, Arizona vs. Pittsburgh, XLIII

RECOVERIES

Most Fumbles Recovered, Career

2 Jake Scott, Miami, 3 games (1 own, 1 opp)
Fran Tarkenton, Minnesota, 3 games (2 own)
Franco Harris, Pittsburgh, 4 games (2 own)
Roger Staubach, Dallas, 4 games (2 own)
Bobby Walden, Pittsburgh, 2 games (2 own)
John Fitzgerald, Dallas, 4 games (2 own)
Randy Hughes, Dallas, 3 games (2 opp)
Butch Johnson, Dallas, 2 games (2 own)
Mike Singletary, Chicago, 1 game (2 opp)
John Elway, Denver, 5 games (2 own)
Jimmie Jones, Dallas, 2 games (2 opp)
Kenneth Davis, Buffalo, 4 games (2 own)
Kurt Warner, St. Louis-Arizona, 3 games (2 own)

Most Fumbles Recovered, Game

2 Jake Scott, Miami vs. Minnesota, VIII (1 own, 1 opp)
Roger Staubach, Dallas vs. Pittsburgh, X (2 own)
Randy Hughes, Dallas vs. Denver, XII (2 opp)
Butch Johnson, Dallas vs. Denver, XII (2 own)
Mike Singletary, Chicago vs. New England, XX (2 opp)
Jimmie Jones, Dallas vs. Buffalo, XXVII (2 opp)

YARDS GAINED

Most Yards Gained, Game

64 Leon Lett, Dallas vs. Buffalo, XXVII (opp)
49 Mike Bass, Washington vs. Miami, VII (opp)
46 James Washington, Dallas vs. Buffalo, XXVIII (opp)

Longest Return

64 Leon Lett, Dallas vs. Buffalo, XXVII
49 Mike Bass, Washington vs. Miami, VII (TD)
46 James Washington, Dallas vs. Buffalo, XXVIII (TD)

TOUCHDOWNS

Most Touchdowns, Game

1 Mike Bass, Washington vs. Miami, VII (opp 49 yds)
Mike Hegman, Dallas vs. Pittsburgh, XIII (opp 37 yds)
Jimmie Jones, Dallas vs. Buffalo, XXVII (opp 2 yds)
Ken Norton, Dallas vs. Buffalo, XXVII (opp 9 yds)
James Washington, Dallas vs. Buffalo, XXVIII (opp 46 yds)

COMBINED NET YARDS GAINED

(Rushing, receiving, interception returns, punt returns, kickoff returns, and fumble returns)

ATTEMPTS

Most Attempts, Career

108 Franco Harris, Pittsburgh, 4 games
81 Emmitt Smith, Dallas, 3 games
72 Roger Craig, San Francisco, 3 games
Thurman Thomas, Buffalo, 4 games

Most Attempts, Game

39 John Riggins, Washington vs. Miami, XVII
35 Franco Harris, Pittsburgh vs. Minnesota, IX
34 Matt Snell, N.Y. Jets vs. Baltimore, III
Emmitt Smith, Dallas vs. Buffalo, XXVIII

YARDS GAINED

Most Yards Gained, Career

604 Jerry Rice, San Francisco-Oakland, 4 games
468 Franco Harris, Pittsburgh, 4 games
410 Roger Craig, San Francisco, 3 games

Most Yards Gained, Game

244 Andre Coleman, San Diego vs. San Francisco, XXIX
Desmond Howard, Green Bay vs. New England, XXXI
235 Ricky Sanders, Washington vs. Denver, XXII
230 Antonio Freeman, Green Bay vs. Denver, XXXII

SACKS

Sacks have been compiled since XVII.

Most Sacks, Career

4.5 Charles Haley, San Francisco-Dallas, 5 games
3.0 Danny Stubbs, San Francisco, 2 games
Leonard Marshall, N.Y. Giants, 2 games
Jeff Wright, Buffalo, 4 games
Reggie White, Green Bay, 2 games
Willie McGinest, New England, 4 games
Tedy Bruschi, New England, 5 games
Mike Vrabel, New England, 4 games
Darnell Dockett, Arizona, 1 game
2.5 Dexter Manley, Washington, 3 games
Michael Strahan, N.Y. Giants, 2 games

Most Sacks, Game

3.0 Reggie White, Green Bay vs. New England, XXXI
Darnell Dockett, Arizona vs. Pittsburgh, XLIII
2.0 Dwaine Board, San Francisco vs. Miami, XIX
Dennis Owens, New England vs. Chicago, XX
Otis Wilson, Chicago vs. New England, XX
Leonard Marshall, N.Y. Giants vs. Denver, XXI
Alvin Walton, Washington vs. Denver, XXII
Charles Haley, San Francisco vs. Cincinnati, XXIII
Danny Stubbs, San Francisco vs. Denver, XXIV
Jeff Wright, Buffalo vs. Dallas, XXVIII
Raylee Johnson, San Diego vs. San Francisco, XXIX
Chad Hennings, Dallas vs. Pittsburgh, XXX
Tedy Bruschi, New England vs. Green Bay, XXXI
Michael McCrary, Baltimore vs. N.Y. Giants, XXXV
Simeon Rice, Tampa Bay vs. Oakland, XXXVII
Mike Vrabel, New England vs. Carolina, XXXVIII
Adalius Thomas, New England vs. N.Y. Giants, XLII
Justin Tuck, N.Y. Giants vs. New England, XLII
LaMarr Woodley, Pittsburgh vs. Arizona, XLIII

TEAM RECORDS

GAMES, VICTORIES, DEFEATS

Most Games

8 Dallas, V-VI, X, XII-XIII, XXVII-XXVIII, XXX
7 Pittsburgh, IX-X, XIII-XIV, XXX, XL, XLIII
6 Denver, XII, XXI-XXII, XXIV, XXXII-XXXIII
New England, XX, XXXI, XXXVI, XXXVIII-XXXIX, XLII

Most Consecutive Games

4 Buffalo, XXV-XXVIII
3 Miami, VI-VIII
2 Green Bay, I-II; XXXI-XXXII
Dallas, V-VI; XII-XIII; XXVII-XXVIII
Minnesota, VIII-IX
Pittsburgh, IX-X; XIII-XIV
Washington, XVII-XVIII
Denver, XXI-XXII; XXXII-XXXIII
San Francisco, XXIII-XXIV
New England, XXXVIII-XXXIX

Most Games Won

6 Pittsburgh, IX-X, XIII-XIV, XL, XLIII
5 San Francisco, XVI, XIX, XXIII-XXIV, XXIX
Dallas, VI, XII, XXVII-XXVIII, XXX
3 Oakland/L.A. Raiders, XI, XV, XVIII
Washington, XVII, XXII, XXVI
Green Bay, I-II, XXXI
New England, XXXVI, XXXVIII-XXXIX
N.Y. Giants, XXI, XXV, XLII

Most Consecutive Games Won

2 Green Bay, I-II
Miami, VII-VIII
Pittsburgh, IX-X, XIII-XIV
San Francisco, XXIII-XXIV
Dallas, XXVII-XXVIII
Denver, XXXII-XXXIII
New England, XXXVIII-XXXIX

Most Games Lost

4 Minnesota, IV, VIII-IX, XI
Denver, XII, XXI-XXII, XXIV
Buffalo, XXV-XXVIII
3 Dallas, V, X, XIII
Miami, VI, XVII, XIX
New England, XX, XXXI, XLII
2 Washington, VII, XVIII
Cincinnati, XVI, XXII
L.A./St. Louis Rams, XIV, XXXVI
Oakland/L.A. Raiders, II, XXXVII
Philadelphia, XV, XXXIX

Most Consecutive Games Lost

4 Buffalo, XXV-XXVIII
2 Minnesota, VIII-IX
Denver, XXI-XXII

SCORING

Most Points, Game

55 San Francisco vs. Denver, XXIV
52 Dallas vs. Buffalo, XXVII
49 San Francisco vs. San Diego, XXIX

Fewest Points, Game

3 Miami vs. Dallas, VI
6 Minnesota vs. Pittsburgh, IX
7 By five teams

Most Points, Both Teams, Game

75 San Francisco (49) vs. San Diego (26), XXIX
69 Dallas (52) vs. Buffalo (17), XXVII
Tampa Bay (48) vs. Oakland (21), XXXVII
66 Pittsburgh (35) vs. Dallas (31), XIII

Fewest Points, Both Teams, Game

21 Washington (7) vs. Miami (14), VII
22 Minnesota (6) vs. Pittsburgh (16), IX
23 Baltimore (7) vs. N.Y. Jets (16), III

Largest Margin of Victory, Game

45 San Francisco vs. Denver, XXIV (55-10)
36 Chicago vs. New England, XX (46-10)
35 Dallas vs. Buffalo, XXVII (52-17)

Most Points, Each Half

1st: 35 Washington vs. Denver, XXII
2nd: 30 N.Y. Giants vs. Denver, XXI

Most Points, Each Quarter

1st: 14 Miami vs. Minnesota, VIII
Oakland vs. Philadelphia, XV
Dallas vs. Buffalo, XXVII
San Francisco vs. San Diego, XXIX
New England vs. Green Bay, XXXI
Chicago vs. Indianapolis, XLI
2nd: 35 Washington vs. Denver, XXII
3rd: 21 Chicago vs. New England, XX
4th: 21 Dallas vs. Buffalo, XXVII

Most Points, Both Teams, Each Half

1st: 45 Washington (35) vs. Denver (10), XXII
2nd: 46 Tampa Bay (28) vs. Oakland (18), XXXVII

Fewest Points, Both Teams, Each Half

1st: 2 Minnesota (0) vs. Pittsburgh (2), IX
2nd: 7 Miami (0) vs. Washington (7), VII
Denver (0) vs. Washington (7), XXII

Most Points, Both Teams, Each Quarter

1st: 24 New England (14) vs. Green Bay (10), XXXI
2nd: 35 Washington (35) vs. Denver (0), XXII
3rd: 24 Washington (14) vs. Buffalo (10), XXVI
4th: 37 Carolina (19) vs. New England (18), XXXVIII

TOUCHDOWNS

Most Touchdowns, Game

8 San Francisco vs. Denver, XXIV
7 Dallas vs. Buffalo, XXVII
San Francisco vs. San Diego, XXIX
6 Washington vs. Denver, XXII
Tampa Bay vs. Oakland, XXXVII

Fewest Touchdowns, Game

0 Miami vs. Dallas, VI
1 By 19 teams

Most Touchdowns, Both Teams, Game

10 San Francisco (7) vs. San Diego (3), XXIX
9 Pittsburgh (5) vs. Dallas (4), XIII
San Francisco (8) vs. Denver (1), XXIV
Dallas (7) vs. Buffalo (2), XXVII
Tampa Bay (6) vs. Oakland (3), XXXVII
8 Carolina (4) vs. New England (4), XXXVIII

Fewest Touchdowns, Both Teams, Game

2 Baltimore (1) vs. N.Y. Jets (1), III
3 In six games

POINTS AFTER TOUCHDOWN

Most (One-Point) Points After Touchdown, Game

7 San Francisco vs. Denver, XXIV
Dallas vs. Buffalo, XXVII
San Francisco vs. San Diego, XXIX
6 Washington vs. Denver, XXII
Tampa Bay vs. Oakland, XXXVII
5 Green Bay vs. Kansas City, I
Pittsburgh vs. Dallas, XIII
L.A. Raiders vs. Washington, XVIII
San Francisco vs. Miami, XIX
Chicago vs. New England, XX

Most (One-Point) Points After Touchdown, Both Teams, Game

9 Pittsburgh (5) vs. Dallas (4), XIII
Dallas (7) vs. Buffalo (2), XXVII
8 San Francisco (7) vs. Denver (1), XXIV
San Francisco (7) vs. San Diego (1), XXIX

7 Washington (6) vs. Denver (1), XXII
Washington (4) vs. Buffalo (3), XXVI
Denver (4) vs. Green Bay (3), XXXII

Fewest (One-Point) Points After Touchdown, Both Teams, Game
2 Baltimore (1) vs. N.Y. Jets (1), III
Baltimore (1) vs. Dallas (1), V
Minnesota (0) vs. Pittsburgh (2), IX

Most Two-Point Conversions, Game
2 San Diego vs. San Francisco, XXIX

Most Two-Point Conversions, Both Teams, Game
2 San Diego (2) vs. San Francisco (0), XXIX

FIELD GOALS

Most Field Goals Attempted, Game
5 N.Y. Jets vs. Baltimore, III
Dallas vs. Denver, XII
4 Green Bay vs. Oakland, II
Pittsburgh vs. Dallas, XX
San Francisco vs. Cincinnati, XVI; XXIII
Denver vs. N.Y. Giants, XXI
Denver vs. Atlanta, XXXIII
St. Louis vs. Tennessee, XXXIV
Indianapolis vs. Chicago, XLI

Most Field Goals Attempted, Both Teams, Game
7 N.Y. Jets (5) vs. Baltimore (2), III
San Francisco (4) vs. Cincinnati (3), XXIII
St. Louis (4) vs. Tennessee (3), XXXIV
Denver (4) vs. Atlanta (3), XXXIII
6 Dallas (5) vs. Denver (1), XII
5 Green Bay (4) vs. Oakland (1), II
Pittsburgh (4) vs. Dallas (1), X
Oakland (3) vs. Philadelphia (2), XV
Denver (4) vs. N.Y. Giants (1), XXI
Dallas (3) vs. Buffalo (2), XXVIII
Indianapolis (4) vs. Chicago (1), XLI

Fewest Field Goals Attempted, Both Teams, Game
1 Minnesota (0) vs. Miami (1), VIII
San Francisco (0) vs. Denver (1), XXIV
Philadelphia (0) vs. New England (1), XXXIX
New England (0) vs. N.Y. Giants (1), XLII
2 Green Bay (0) vs. Kansas City (2), I
Miami (1) vs. Washington (1), VII
Minnesota (1) vs. Pittsburgh (1), IX
Dallas (1) vs. Pittsburgh (1), XIII
Dallas (1) vs. Buffalo (1), XXVII
San Diego (1) vs. San Francisco (1), XXIX
Denver (1) vs. Green Bay (1), XXXII
Arizona (0) vs. Pittsburgh (2), XLIII

Most Field Goals, Game
4 Green Bay vs. Oakland, II
San Francisco vs. Cincinnati, XVI
3 N.Y. Jets vs. Baltimore, III
Kansas City vs. Minnesota, IV
Miami vs. San Francisco, XIX
Chicago vs. New England, XX
Cincinnati vs. San Francisco, XXIII
Washington vs. Buffalo, XXVI
Dallas vs. Buffalo, XXVIII
St. Louis vs. Tennessee, XXXIV
Indianapolis vs. Chicago, XLI

Most Field Goals, Both Teams, Game
5 Cincinnati (3) vs. San Francisco (2), XXIII
Dallas (3) vs. Buffalo (2), XXVIII
4 Green Bay (4) vs. Oakland (0), II
San Francisco (4) vs. Cincinnati (0), XVI
Miami (3) vs. San Francisco (1), XIX
Chicago (3) vs. New England (1), XX
Washington (3) vs. Buffalo (1), XXVI
Atlanta (2) vs. Denver (2), XXXIII
St. Louis (3) vs. Tennessee (1), XXXIV
Indianapolis (3) vs. Chicago (1), XLI
3 In 13 games

Fewest Field Goals, Both Teams, Game
0 Miami vs. Washington, VII
Pittsburgh vs. Minnesota, IX
1 Green Bay (0) vs. Kansas City (1), I
Minnesota (0) vs. Miami (1), VIII
Pittsburgh (0) vs. Dallas (1), XIII
Washington (0) vs. Denver (1), XXII
San Francisco (0) vs. Denver (1), XXIV
San Francisco (0) vs. San Diego (1), XXIX
Philadelphia (0) vs. New England (1), XXXIX
Pittsburgh (0) vs. Seattle (1), XLI
New England (0) vs. N.Y. Giants (1), XLII

SAFETIES

Most Safeties, Game
1 Pittsburgh vs. Minnesota, IX; vs. Dallas, X
Chicago vs. New England, XX
N.Y. Giants vs. Denver, XXI
Buffalo vs. N.Y. Giants, XXV
Arizona vs. Pittsburgh, XLIII

FIRST DOWNS

Most First Downs, Game
31 San Francisco vs. Miami, XIX
29 New England vs. Carolina, XXXVIII
28 San Francisco vs. Denver, XXIV
San Francisco vs. San Diego, XXIX

Fewest First Downs, Game
9 Minnesota vs. Pittsburgh, IX
Miami vs. Washington, XVII
10 Dallas vs. Baltimore, V
Miami vs. Dallas, VI
11 Denver vs. Dallas, XII
N.Y. Giants vs. Baltimore, XXXV
Oakland vs. Tampa Bay, XXXVII
Chicago vs. Indianapolis, XLI

Most First Downs, Both Teams, Game
50 San Francisco (31) vs. Miami (19), XIX
Tennessee (27) vs. St. Louis (23), XXXIV
49 Buffalo (25) vs. Washington (24), XXVI
48 San Francisco (28) vs. San Diego (20), XXIX

Fewest First Downs, Both Teams, Game
24 Dallas (10) vs. Baltimore (14), V
N.Y. Giants (11) vs. Baltimore (13), XXXV
26 Minnesota (9) vs. Pittsburgh (17), IX
27 Pittsburgh (13) vs. Dallas (14), X

RUSHING

Most First Downs, Rushing, Game
16 San Francisco vs. Miami, XIX
15 Dallas vs. Miami, VI
14 Washington vs. Miami, XVII
San Francisco vs. Denver, XXIV
Denver vs. Green Bay, XXXII

Fewest First Downs, Rushing, Game
1 New England vs. Chicago, XX
St. Louis vs. Tennessee, XXXIV
Oakland vs. Tampa Bay, XXXVII
2 Minnesota vs. Kansas City, IV; vs. Pittsburgh, IX; vs. Oakland, XI
Pittsburgh vs. Dallas, XIII
Miami vs. San Francisco, XIX
N.Y. Giants vs. Baltimore, XXXV
Arizona vs. Pittsburgh, XLIII
3 Miami vs. Dallas, VI
Philadelphia vs. Oakland, XV
New England vs. Green Bay, XXXI
Carolina vs. New England, XXXVIII

Chicago vs. Indianapolis, XLII
New England vs. N.Y. Giants, XLII

Most First Downs, Rushing, Both Teams, Game
21 Washington (14) vs. Miami (7), XVII
19 Washington (13) vs. Denver (6), XXII
San Francisco (14) vs. Denver (5), XXIV
18 Dallas (15) vs. Miami (3), VI
Miami (13) vs. Minnesota (5), VIII
San Francisco (16) vs. Miami (2), XIX
N.Y. Giants (10) vs. Buffalo (8), XXV
Denver (14) vs. Green Bay (4), XXXII

Fewest First Downs, Rushing, Both Teams, Game
6 Arizona (2) vs. Pittsburgh (4), XLIII
7 Oakland (1) vs. Tampa Bay (6), XXXVIII
New England (3) vs. N.Y. Giants (4), XLII
8 Baltimore (4) vs. Dallas (4), V
Pittsburgh (2) vs. Dallas (6), XIII
N.Y. Giants (2) vs. Baltimore (6), XXXV

PASSING

Most First Downs, Passing, Game
20 Arizona vs. Pittsburgh, XLIII
19 New England vs. Carolina, XXXVIII
18 Buffalo vs. Washington, XXVI
St. Louis vs. Tennessee, XXXIV
Philadelphia vs. New England, XXXIX

Fewest First Downs, Passing, Game
1 Denver vs. Dallas, XII
2 Miami vs. Washington, XVII
4 Miami vs. Minnesota, VIII

Most First Downs, Passing, Both Teams, Game
32 Miami (17) vs. San Francisco (15), XIX
Philadelphia (18) vs. New England (14), XXXIX
Arizona (20) vs. Pittsburgh (12), XLIII
31 San Francisco (17) vs. San Diego (14), XXIX
St. Louis (18) vs. Tennessee (13), XXXIV
New England (19) vs. Carolina (12), XXXVIII
30 Buffalo (18) vs. Washington (12), XXVII
New England (17) vs. N.Y. Giants (13), XLII

Fewest First Downs, Passing, Both Teams, Game
9 Denver (1) vs. Dallas (8), XII
10 Minnesota (5) vs. Pittsburgh (5), IX
11 Dallas (5) vs. Baltimore (6), V
Miami (2) vs. Washington (9), XVII

PENALTY

Most First Downs, Penalty, Game
4 Baltimore vs. Dallas, V
Miami vs. Minnesota, VIII
Cincinnati vs. San Francisco, XVI
Buffalo vs. Dallas, XXVII
St. Louis vs. Tennessee, XXXIV
Pittsburgh vs. Arizona, XLIII
3 Kansas City vs. Minnesota, IV
Minnesota vs. Oakland, XI
Buffalo vs. Washington, XXVI
Green Bay vs. Denver, XXXII
N.Y. Giants vs. Baltimore, XXXV
St. Louis vs. New England, XXXVI
Tampa Bay vs. Oakland, XXXVII
New England vs. Carolina, XXXVIII

Most First Downs, Penalty, Both Teams, Game
6 Cincinnati (4) vs. San Francisco (2), XVI
St. Louis (4) vs. Tennessee (2), XXXIV
5 Baltimore (4) vs. Dallas (1), V
Miami (4) vs. Minnesota (1), VIII
Buffalo (3) vs. Washington (2), XXVI
Green Bay (3) vs. Denver (2), XXXII
New England (3) vs. Carolina (2), XXXVIII
Pittsburgh (4) vs. Arizona (1), XLIII
4 Kansas City (3) vs. Minnesota (1), IV
Buffalo (4) vs. Dallas (0), XXVII
N.Y. Giants (3) vs. Baltimore (1), XXXV
St. Louis (3) vs. New England (1), XXXVI
Tampa Bay (3) vs. Oakland (1), XXXVII

Fewest First Downs, Penalty, Both Teams, Game
0 Dallas vs. Miami, VI
Miami vs. Washington, VII
Dallas vs. Pittsburgh, X
Miami vs. San Francisco, XIX
Pittsburgh vs. Seattle, XL
1 Green Bay (0) vs. Kansas City (1), I
Miami (0) vs. Washington (1), XVII
Cincinnati (0) vs. San Francisco (1), XXIII
San Francisco (0) vs. Denver (1), XXIV
Dallas (0) vs. Buffalo (1), XXVIII
Dallas (0) vs. Pittsburgh (1), XXX
Denver (0) vs. Atlanta (1), XXXIII
Chicago (0) vs. Indianapolis (1), XLI

NET YARDS GAINED RUSHING AND PASSING

Most Yards Gained, Game
602 Washington vs. Denver, XXII
537 San Francisco vs. Miami, XIX
481 New England vs. Carolina, XXXVIII

Fewest Yards Gained, Game
119 Minnesota vs. Pittsburgh, IX
123 New England vs. Chicago, XX
152 N.Y. Giants vs. Baltimore, XXXV

Most Yards Gained, Both Teams, Game
929 Washington (602) vs. Denver (327), XXII
868 New England (481) vs. Carolina (387), XXXVIII
851 San Francisco (537) vs. Miami (314), XIX

Fewest Yards Gained, Both Teams, Game
396 N.Y. Giants (152) vs. Baltimore (244), XXXV
452 Minnesota (119) vs. Pittsburgh (333), IX
481 Washington (228) vs. Miami (253), VII
Denver (156) vs. Dallas (325), XII

RUSHING

ATTEMPTS

Most Attempts, Game
57 Pittsburgh vs. Minnesota, IX
53 Miami vs. Minnesota, VIII
52 Oakland vs. Minnesota, XI
Washington vs. Miami, XVII

Fewest Attempts, Game
9 Miami vs. San Francisco, XIX
11 New England vs. Chicago, XX
Oakland vs. Tampa Bay, XXXVII
12 Arizona vs. Pittsburgh, XLIII

Most Attempts, Both Teams, Game
81 Washington (52) vs. Miami (29), XVII
78 Pittsburgh (57) vs. Minnesota (21), IX
Oakland (52) vs. Minnesota (26), XI
77 Miami (53) vs. Minnesota (24), VIII
Pittsburgh (46) vs. Dallas (31), X

Fewest Attempts, Both Teams, Game
37 Arizona (12) vs. Pittsburgh (25), XLIII
42 New England (16) vs. N.Y. Giants (26), XLII
45 Philadelphia (17) vs. New England (28), XXXIX

YARDS GAINED

Most Yards Gained, Game
280 Washington vs. Denver, XXII
276 Washington vs. Miami, XVII
266 Oakland vs. Minnesota, XI

Fewest Yards Gained, Game
7 New England vs. Chicago, XX
17 Minnesota vs. Pittsburgh, IX

19 Oakland vs. Tampa Bay, XXXVII

Most Yards Gained, Both Teams, Game
377 Washington (280) vs. Denver (97), XXII
372 Washington (276) vs. Miami (96), XVII
338 N.Y. Giants (172) vs. Buffalo (166), XXV

Fewest Yards Gained, Both Teams, Game
91 Arizona (33) vs. Pittsburgh (58), XLIII
136 New England (45) vs. N.Y. Giants (91), XLII
157 Philadelphia (45) vs. New England (112), XXXIX

AVERAGE GAIN

Highest Average Gain, Game
7.00 L.A. Raiders vs. Washington, XVIII (33-231)
Washington vs. Denver, XXII (40-280)
6.64 Buffalo vs. N.Y. Giants, XXV (25-166)
6.22 Baltimore vs. N.Y. Jets, III (23-143)

Lowest Average Gain, Game
0.64 New England vs. Chicago, XX (11-7)
0.81 Minnesota vs. Pittsburgh, IX (21-17)
1.73 Oakland vs. Tampa Bay, XXXVII (11-19)

TOUCHDOWNS

Most Touchdowns, Game
4 Chicago vs. New England, XX
Denver vs. Green Bay, XXXII
3 Green Bay vs. Kansas City, I
Miami vs. Minnesota, VIII
San Francisco vs. Denver, XXIV
Denver vs. Atlanta, XXXIII
2 Oakland vs. Minnesota, XI
Pittsburgh vs. Los Angeles, XIV
L.A. Raiders vs. Washington, XVIII
San Francisco vs. Miami, XIX
N.Y. Giants vs. Denver, XXI
Washington vs. Denver, XXII; vs. Buffalo, XXVI
Buffalo vs. N.Y. Giants, XXV
Dallas vs. Buffalo, XXVIII; vs. Pittsburgh, XXX
Tennessee vs. St. Louis, XXXIV
Pittsburgh vs. Seattle, XL

Fewest Touchdowns, Game
0 By 29 teams

Most Touchdowns, Both Teams, Game
4 Miami (3) vs. Minnesota (1), VIII
Chicago (4) vs. New England (0), XX
San Francisco (3) vs. Denver (1), XXIV
Denver (4) vs. Green Bay (0), XXXII
3 In nine games

Fewest Touchdowns, Both Teams, Game
0 Pittsburgh vs. Dallas, X
Oakland vs. Philadelphia, XV
Cincinnati vs. San Francisco, XXIII
1 In 14 games

PASSING

ATTEMPTS

Most Passes Attempted, Game
59 Buffalo vs. Washington, XXVI
55 San Diego vs. San Francisco, XXIX
51 Philadelphia vs. New England, XXXIX

Fewest Passes Attempted, Game
7 Miami vs. Minnesota, VIII
11 Miami vs. Washington, VII
14 Pittsburgh vs. Minnesota, IX

Most Passes Attempted, Both Teams, Game
93 San Diego (55) vs. San Francisco (38), XXIX
92 Buffalo (59) vs. Washington (33), XXVI
85 Miami (50) vs. San Francisco (35), XIX

Fewest Passes Attempted, Both Teams, Game
35 Miami (7) vs. Minnesota (28), VIII
39 Miami (11) vs. Washington (28), VII
40 Pittsburgh (14) vs. Minnesota (26), IX
Miami (17) vs. Washington (23), XVII

COMPLETIONS

Most Passes Completed, Game
32 New England vs. Carolina, XXXVIII
31 Buffalo vs. Dallas, XXVIII
Arizona vs. Pittsburgh, XLIII
30 Philadelphia vs. New England, XXXIX

Fewest Passes Completed, Game
4 Miami vs. Washington, XVII
6 Miami vs. Minnesota, VIII
8 Miami vs. Washington, VII
Denver vs. Dallas, XII

Most Passes Completed, Both Teams, Game
53 Miami (29) vs. San Francisco (24), XIX
Philadelphia (30) vs. New England (23), XXXIX
52 San Diego (27) vs. San Francisco (25), XXIX
Arizona (31) vs. Pittsburgh (21), XLIII
50 Buffalo (31) vs. Dallas (19), XXVIII

Fewest Passes Completed, Both Teams, Game
19 Miami (4) vs. Washington (15), XVII
20 Pittsburgh (9) vs. Minnesota (11), IX
22 Miami (8) vs. Washington (14), VII

COMPLETION PERCENTAGE

Highest Completion Percentage, Game (20 attempts)
88.0 N.Y. Giants vs. Denver, XXI (25-22)
75.0 San Francisco vs. Denver, XXIV (32-24)
73.5 Cincinnati vs. San Francisco, XVI (34-25)

Lowest Completion Percentage, Game (20 attempts)
32.0 Denver vs. Dallas, XII (25-8)
37.9 Denver vs. San Francisco, XXIV (29-11)
38.5 Denver vs. Washington, XXII (39-15)
N.Y. Giants vs. Baltimore, XXXV (39-15)

YARDS GAINED

Most Yards Gained, Game
407 St. Louis vs. Tennessee, XXXIV
374 Arizona vs. Pittsburgh, XLIII
354 New England vs. Carolina, XXXVIII

Fewest Yards Gained, Game
35 Denver vs. Dallas, XII
63 Miami vs. Minnesota, VIII
69 Miami vs. Washington, VII

Most Yards Gained, Both Teams, Game
649 New England (354) vs. Carolina (295), XXXVIII
615 San Francisco (326) vs. Miami (289), XIX
St. Louis (407) vs. Tennessee (208), XXXIV
608 Arizona (374) vs. Pittsburgh (234), XLIII

Fewest Yards Gained, Both Teams, Game
156 Miami (69) vs. Washington (87), VII
186 Pittsburgh (84) vs. Minnesota (102), IX
204 Miami (80) vs. Washington (124), XVII

TIMES SACKED

Most Times Sacked, Game
7 Dallas vs. Pittsburgh, X
New England vs. Chicago, XX
6 Kansas City vs. Green Bay, I
Washington vs. L.A. Raiders, XVIII
Denver vs. San Francisco, XXIV
5 Dallas vs. Denver, XII; vs. Pittsburgh, XIII
Cincinnati vs. San Francisco, XVI; XXIII
Denver vs. Washington, XXII
Buffalo vs. Washington, XXVI
Green Bay vs. New England, XXXI
New England vs. Green Bay, XXXI
Oakland vs. Tampa Bay, XXXVIII
New England vs. N.Y. Giants, XLII

Fewest Times Sacked, Game
0 Baltimore vs. N.Y. Jets, III; vs. Dallas, V
Minnesota vs. Pittsburgh, IX
Pittsburgh vs. Los Angeles, XIV
Philadelphia vs. Oakland, XV
Washington vs. Buffalo, XXVI
Denver vs. Green Bay, XXXII; vs. Atlanta, XXXIII
Tampa Bay vs. Oakland, XXXVII
New England vs. Carolina, XXXVIII
1 By 16 teams

Most Times Sacked, Both Teams, Game
10 New England (7) vs. Chicago (3), XX
Green Bay (5) vs. New England (5), XXXI
9 Kansas City (6) vs. Green Bay (3), I
Dallas (7) vs. Pittsburgh (2), X
Dallas (5) vs. Denver (4), XII
Dallas (5) vs. Pittsburgh (4), XIII
Cincinnati (5) vs. San Francisco (4), XXIII
8 Washington (6) vs. L.A. Raiders (2), XVIII
New England (5) vs. N.Y. Giants (3), XLII

Fewest Times Sacked, Both Teams, Game
1 Philadelphia (0) vs. Oakland (1), XV
Denver (0) vs. Green Bay (1), XXXII
2 Baltimore (0) vs. N.Y. Jets (2), III
Baltimore (0) vs. Dallas (2), V
Minnesota (0) vs. Pittsburgh (2), IX
Denver (0) vs. Atlanta (2), XXXIII
Chicago (1) vs. Indianapolis (1), XLI
3 In five games

TOUCHDOWNS

Most Touchdowns, Game
6 San Francisco vs. San Diego, XXIX
5 San Francisco vs. Denver, XXIV
4 Pittsburgh vs. Dallas, XIII
Washington vs. Denver, XXII
Dallas vs. Buffalo, XXVII

Fewest Touchdowns, Game
0 By 19 teams

Most Touchdowns, Both Teams, Game
7 Pittsburgh (4) vs. Dallas (3), XIII
San Francisco (6) vs. San Diego (1), XXIX
6 Carolina (3) vs. New England (3), XXXVIII
5 Washington (4) vs. Denver (1), XXII
San Francisco (5) vs. Denver (0), XXIV
Dallas (4) vs. Buffalo (1), XXVII
Philadelphia (3) vs. New England (2), XXXIX

Fewest Touchdowns, Both Teams, Game
0 N.Y. Jets vs. Baltimore, III
Miami vs. Minnesota, VIII
Buffalo vs. Dallas, XXVIII
1 In seven games

INTERCEPTIONS BY

Most Interceptions By, Game
5 Tampa Bay vs. Oakland, XXXVII
4 N.Y. Jets vs. Baltimore, III
Dallas vs. Denver, XII
Washington vs. Buffalo, XXVI
Dallas vs. Buffalo, XXVII
Green Bay vs. New England, XXXI
Baltimore vs. N.Y. Giants, XXXV
3 By 13 teams

Most Interceptions By, Both Teams, Game
6 Baltimore (3) vs. Dallas (3), V
Tampa Bay (5) vs. Oakland (1), XXXVII
5 Washington (4) vs. Buffalo (1), XXVI
4 In 10 games

Fewest Interceptions By, Both Teams, Game
0 Buffalo vs. N.Y. Giants, XXV
St. Louis vs. Tennessee, XXXIV
1 Oakland (0) vs. Green Bay (1), II
Miami (0) vs. Dallas (1), VI
Minnesota (0) vs. Miami (1), VIII
N.Y. Giants (0) vs. Denver (1), XXI
Cincinnati (0) vs. San Francisco (1), XXIII
New England (0) vs. Carolina (1), XXXVIII
N.Y. Giants (0) vs. New England (1), XLII

YARDS GAINED

Most Yards Gained, Game
172 Tampa Bay vs. Oakland, XXXVII
136 Denver vs. Atlanta, XXXIII
100 Pittsburgh vs. Arizona, XLIII

Most Yards Gained, Both Teams, Game
184 Tampa Bay (172) vs. Oakland (12), XXXVII
137 Denver (136) vs. Atlanta (1), XXXIII
100 Seattle (76) vs. Pittsburgh (24), XL
Indianapolis (94) vs. Chicago (6), XLI

TOUCHDOWNS

Most Touchdowns, Game
3 Tampa Bay vs. Oakland, XXXVII
1 Green Bay vs. Oakland, II
Oakland vs. Minnesota, XI
L.A. Raiders vs. Washington, XVIII
Chicago vs. New England, XX
Baltimore vs. N.Y. Giants, XXXV
New England vs. St. Louis, XXXVI
Indianapolis vs. Chicago, XLI
Pittsburgh vs. Arizona, XLIII

PUNTING

Most Punts, Game
11 N.Y. Giants vs. Baltimore, XXXV
10 Baltimore vs. N.Y. Giants, XXXV
9 Dallas vs. Baltimore, V

Fewest Punts, Game
1 Atlanta vs. Denver, XXXIII
Denver vs. Atlanta, XXXIII
2 Pittsburgh vs. Los Angeles, XIV
Denver vs. N.Y. Giants, XXI
St. Louis vs. Tennessee, XXXIV
3 By 12 teams

Most Punts, Both Teams, Game
21 N.Y. Giants (11) vs. Baltimore (10), XXXV
15 Washington (8) vs. L.A. Raiders (7), XVIII
New England (8) vs. Green Bay (7), XXXI
13 Dallas (9) vs. Baltimore (4), V
Pittsburgh (7) vs. Minnesota (6), IX

Fewest Punts, Both Teams, Game
2 Atlanta (1) vs. Denver (1), XXXIII
5 Denver (2) vs. N.Y. Giants (3), XXI
St. Louis (2) vs. Tennessee (3), XXXIV
6 Oakland (3) vs. Philadelphia (3), XV

AVERAGE YARDAGE

Highest Average, Game (4 punts)
50.17 Seattle vs. Pittsburgh, XL (6-301)
48.75 San Diego vs. San Francisco, XXIX (4-195)
48.67 Pittsburgh vs. Seattle, XL (6-292)

Lowest Average, Game (4 punts)
31.00 Tampa Bay vs. Oakland, XXXVII (5-155)
31.20 Washington vs. Miami, VII (5-156)
32.38 Washington vs. L.A. Raiders, XVIII (8-259)

PUNT RETURNS

Most Punt Returns, Game
6 Washington vs. Miami, XVII
Green Bay vs. New England, XXXI

5 By seven teams

Fewest Punt Returns, Game

0 Minnesota vs. Miami, VIII
Buffalo vs. N.Y. Giants, XXV
Washington vs. Buffalo, XXVI
Denver vs. Green Bay, XXXII
Green Bay vs. Denver, XXXII
Atlanta vs. Denver, XXXIII
Denver vs. Atlanta, XXXIII
1 By 21 teams

Most Punt Returns, Both Teams, Game

10 Green Bay (6) vs. New England (4), XXXI
9 Pittsburgh (5) vs. Minnesota (4), IX
8 Green Bay (5) vs. Oakland (3), II
Baltimore (5) vs. Dallas (3), V
Washington (6) vs. Miami (2), XVII
N.Y. Giants (5) vs. Baltimore (3), XXXV

Fewest Punt Returns, Both Teams, Game

0 Denver vs. Green Bay, XXXII
Atlanta vs. Denver, XXXIII
2 Dallas (1) vs. Miami (1), VI
Denver (1) vs. N.Y. Giants (1), XXI
Buffalo (0) vs. N.Y. Giants (2), XXV
Buffalo (1) vs. Dallas (1), XXVIII
3 Kansas City (1) vs. Minnesota (2), IV
Minnesota (0) vs. Miami (3), VIII
Washington (1) vs. Denver (2), XXII
Washington (0) vs. Buffalo (3), XXVI
Dallas (1) vs. Pittsburgh (2), XXX
Tennessee (1) vs. St. Louis (2), XXXIV

YARDS GAINED

Most Yards Gained, Game

90 Green Bay vs. New England, XXXI
56 San Francisco vs. Cincinnati, XXIII
52 Washington vs. Miami, XVII

Fewest Yards Gained, Game

–1 Dallas vs. Miami, VI
Tennessee vs. St. Louis, XXXIV
0 By 12 teams

Most Yards Gained, Both Teams, Game

120 Green Bay (90) vs. New England (30), XXXI
80 N.Y. Giants (46) vs. Baltimore (34), XXXV
74 Washington (52) vs. Miami (22), XVII

Fewest Yards Gained, Both Teams, Game

0 Denver vs. Green Bay, XXXII
Atlanta vs. Denver, XXXIII
7 Tennessee (-1) vs. St. Louis (8), XXXIV
9 Washington (0) vs. Buffalo (9), XXVI

AVERAGE RETURN

Highest Average, Game (3 returns)

18.7 San Francisco vs. Cincinnati, XXIII (3-56)
15.0 Green Bay vs. New England, XXXI (6-90)
14.0 Indianapolis vs. Chicago, XLI (3-42)

TOUCHDOWNS

Most Touchdowns, Game

None

KICKOFF RETURNS

Most Kickoff Returns, Game

9 Denver vs. San Francisco, XXIV
Oakland vs. Tampa Bay, XXXVII
8 San Diego vs. San Francisco, XXIX
7 By eight teams

Fewest Kickoff Returns, Game

1 N.Y. Jets vs. Baltimore, III
L.A. Raiders vs. Washington, XVIII
Washington vs. Buffalo, XXVI
2 By 10 teams

Most Kickoff Returns, Both Teams, Game

13 Oakland (9) vs. Tampa Bay (4), XXXVII
12 Denver (9) vs. San Francisco (3), XXIV
San Diego (8) vs. San Francisco (4), XXIX
11 Los Angeles (6) vs. Pittsburgh (5), XIV
Miami (7) vs. San Francisco (4), XIX
New England (7) vs. Chicago (4), XX
Green Bay (6) vs. Denver (5), XXXII

Fewest Kickoff Returns, Both Teams, Game

5 N.Y. Jets (1) vs. Baltimore (4), III
Miami (2) vs. Washington (3), VII
Washington (1) vs. Buffalo (4), XXVI
6 In five games

YARDS GAINED

Most Yards Gained, Game

244 San Diego vs. San Francisco, XXIX
227 Atlanta vs. Denver, XXXIII
222 Miami vs. Washington, XVII

Fewest Yards Gained, Game

16 Washington vs. Buffalo, XXVI
17 L.A. Raiders vs. Washington, XVIII
25 N.Y. Jets vs. Baltimore, III

Most Yards Gained, Both Teams, Game

292 San Diego (244) vs. San Francisco (48), XXIX
289 Green Bay (154) vs. New England (135), XXXI
281 N.Y. Giants (170) vs. Baltimore (111), XXXV

Fewest Yards Gained, Both Teams, Game

78 Miami (33) vs. Washington (45), VII
82 Pittsburgh (32) vs. Minnesota (50), IX
92 San Francisco (40) vs. Cincinnati (52), XVI

AVERAGE GAIN

Highest Average, Game (3 returns)

44.0 Cincinnati vs. San Francisco, XXIII (3-132)
38.5 Green Bay vs. New England, XXXI (4-154)
37.0 Miami vs. Washington, XVII (6-222)

TOUCHDOWNS

Most Touchdowns, Game

1 Miami vs. Washington, XVII
Cincinnati vs. San Francisco, XXIII
San Diego vs. San Francisco, XXIX
Green Bay vs. New England, XXXI
Atlanta vs. Denver, XXXIII
Baltimore vs. N.Y. Giants, XXXV
N.Y. Giants vs. Baltimore, XXXV
Chicago vs. Indianapolis, XLI

Most Touchdowns, Both Teams, Game

2 Baltimore (1) vs. N.Y. Giants (1), XXXV

PENALTIES

Most Penalties, Game

12 Dallas vs. Denver, XII
Carolina vs. New England, XXXVIII
11 Arizona vs. Pittsburgh, XLIII
10 Dallas vs. Baltimore, V

Fewest Penalties, Game

0 Miami vs. Dallas, VI
Pittsburgh vs. Dallas, X
Denver vs. San Francisco, XXIV
Atlanta vs. Denver, XXXIII
1 Green Bay vs. Oakland, II
Miami vs. Minnesota, VIII; vs. San Francisco, XIX
Buffalo vs. Dallas, XXVIII
2 By six teams

Most Penalties, Both Teams, Game

20 Dallas (12) vs. Denver (8), XII
Carolina (12) vs. New England (8), XXXVIII

18 Arizona (11) vs. Pittsburgh (7), XLIII
16 Cincinnati (8) vs. San Francisco (8), XVI
Green Bay (9) vs. Denver (7), XXXII

Fewest Penalties, Both Teams, Game
2 Pittsburgh (0) vs. Dallas (2), X
3 Miami (0) vs. Dallas (3), VI
Miami (1) vs. San Francisco (2), XIX
4 Denver (0) vs. San Francisco (4), XXIV
Atlanta (0) vs. Denver (4), XXXIII

YARDS PENALIZED

Most Yards Penalized, Game
133 Dallas vs. Baltimore, X
122 Pittsburgh vs. Minnesota, IX
106 Arizona vs. Pittsburgh, XLIII

Fewest Yards Penalized, Game
0 Miami vs. Dallas, VI
Pittsburgh vs. Dallas, X
Denver vs. San Francisco, XXIV
Atlanta vs. Denver, XXXIII
4 Miami vs. Minnesota, VIII
10 Miami vs. San Francisco, XIX
San Francisco vs. Miami, XIX
Buffalo vs. Dallas, XXVIII

Most Yards Penalized, Both Teams, Game
164 Dallas (133) vs. Baltimore (31), V
162 Arizona (106) vs. Pittsburgh (56), XLIII
154 Dallas (94) vs. Denver (60), XII

Fewest Yards Penalized, Both Teams, Game
15 Miami (0) vs. Dallas (15), VI
20 Pittsburgh (0) vs. Dallas (20), X
Miami (10) vs. San Francisco (10), XIX
38 Denver (0) vs. San Francisco (38), XXIV

FUMBLES

Most Fumbles, Game
8 Buffalo vs. Dallas, XXVII
6 Dallas vs. Denver, XII
Buffalo vs. Washington, XXVI
5 Baltimore vs. Dallas, V

Fewest Fumbles, Game
0 By 20 teams

Most Fumbles, Both Teams, Game
12 Buffalo (8) vs. Dallas (4), XXVII
10 Dallas (6) vs. Denver (4), XII
8 Dallas (4) vs. Pittsburgh (4), X

Fewest Fumbles, Both Teams, Game
0 Los Angeles vs. Pittsburgh, XIV
Green Bay vs. New England, XXXI
Pittsburgh vs. Seattle, XL
1 Oakland (0) vs. Minnesota (1), XI
Oakland (0) vs. Philadelphia (1), XV
Denver (0) vs. Washington (1), XXII
N.Y. Giants (0) vs. Buffalo (1), XXV
Denver (0) vs. Atlanta (1), XXXIII
2 In nine games

Most Fumbles Lost, Game
5 Buffalo vs. Dallas, XXVII
4 Baltimore vs. Dallas, V
Denver vs. Dallas, XII
New England vs. Chicago, XX
3 Chicago vs. Indianapolis, XLI

Most Fumbles Lost, Both Teams, Game
7 Buffalo (5) vs. Dallas (2), XXVII
6 Denver (4) vs. Dallas (2), XII
New England (4) vs. Chicago (2), XX
5 Baltimore (4) vs. Dallas (1), V
Chicago (3) vs. Indianapolis (2), XLI

Fewest Fumbles Lost, Both Teams, Game
0 Green Bay vs. Kansas City, I
Dallas vs. Pittsburgh, X
Los Angeles vs. Pittsburgh, XIV
Denver vs. N.Y. Giants, XXI; vs. Washington, XXII
Buffalo vs. N.Y. Giants, XXV
San Diego vs. San Francisco, XXIX
Dallas vs. Pittsburgh, XXX
Green Bay vs. New England, XXXI
St. Louis vs. Tennessee, XXXIV
Oakland vs. Tampa Bay, XXXVII
Pittsburgh vs. Seattle, XL

Most Fumbles Recovered, Game
8 Dallas vs. Denver, XII (4 own, 4 opp.)
6 Dallas vs. Buffalo, XXVII (1 own, 5 opp.)
5 Chicago vs. New England, XX (1 own, 4 opp.)

TURNOVERS

(Number of times losing the ball on interceptions and fumbles.)

Most Turnovers, Game
9 Buffalo vs. Dallas, XXVII
8 Denver vs. Dallas, XII
7 Baltimore vs. Dallas, V

Fewest Turnovers, Game
0 Green Bay vs. Oakland, II
Miami vs. Minnesota, VIII
Pittsburgh vs. Dallas, X
Oakland vs. Minnesota, XI; vs. Philadelphia, XV
N.Y. Giants vs. Denver, XXI; vs. Buffalo, XXV
San Francisco vs. Denver, XXIV; vs. San Diego, XXIX
Buffalo vs. N.Y. Giants, XXV
Dallas vs. Pittsburgh, XXX
Green Bay vs. New England, XXXI
St. Louis vs. Tennessee, XXXIV
Tennessee vs. St. Louis, XXXIV
Baltimore vs. N.Y. Giants, XXXV
New England vs. St. Louis, XXXVI
1 By many teams

Most Turnovers, Both Teams, Game
11 Baltimore (7) vs. Dallas (4), V
Buffalo (9) vs. Dallas (2), XXVII
10 Denver (8) vs. Dallas (2), XII
8 New England (6) vs. Chicago (2), XX
Chicago (5) vs. Indianapolis (3), XLI

Fewest Turnovers, Both Teams, Game
0 Buffalo vs. N.Y. Giants, XXV
St. Louis vs. Tennessee, XXXIV
1 N.Y. Giants (0) vs. Denver (1), XXI
2 Green Bay (1) vs. Kansas City (1), I
Miami (0) vs. Minnesota (2), VIII
Cincinnati (1) vs. San Francisco (1), XXIII
Carolina (1) vs. New England (1), XXXVIII
New England (1) vs. N.Y. Giants (1), XLII

POSTSEASON RECORDS

Compiled by Elias Sports Bureau

Throughout this all-time postseason record section, the following abbreviations are used to indicate various levels of postseason games:

SB — Super Bowl (1966 to date)
AFC — AFC Championship Game (1970 to date) or AFL Championship Game (1960-69)
NFC — NFC Championship Game (1970 to date) or NFL Championship Game (1933-69)
AFC-D — AFC Divisional Playoff Game (1970 to date), AFC Second-Round Playoff Game (1982), AFL Inter-Divisional Playoff Game (1969), or special playoff game to break tie for AFL Division Championship (1963, 1968)
NFC-D — NFC Divisional Playoff Game (1970 to date), NFC Second-Round Playoff Game (1982), NFL Conference Championship Game (1967-69), or special playoff game to break tie for NFL Division or Conference Championship (1941, 1943, 1947, 1950, 1952, 1957, 1958, 1965)
AFC-FR — AFC First-Round Playoff Game (1978 to date)
NFC-FR — NFC First-Round Playoff Game (1978 to date)

Year indicates season in which game took place and does not necessarily reflect calendar year.

POSTSEASON GAME COMPOSITE STANDINGS

	W	L	PCT.	PTS.	OP
Baltimore Ravens	7	4	.636	202	130
Green Bay Packers	25	15	.625	950	766
Pittsburgh Steelers	31	19	.620	1,180	1,020
New England Patriots#	21	13	.618	730	666
Carolina Panthers	6	4	.600	219	203
San Francisco 49ers	25	17	.595	1,044	853
Oakland Raiders**	25	18	.581	1,028	797
Washington Redskins*	23	17	.575	819	707
Dallas Cowboys	32	24	.571	1,318	1,050
Denver Broncos	17	15	.531	694	794
Philadelphia Eagles	19	18	.514	727	665
Miami Dolphins	20	20	.500	789	875
Indianapolis Colts***	17	18	.486	702	718
Chicago Bears	16	17	.485	702	681
Buffalo Bills	14	15	.483	681	658
Arizona Cardinals††††	5	6	.455	240	271
Jacksonville Jaguars	5	6	.455	262	288
New York Giants	20	24	.455	763	833
St. Louis Rams††	19	24	.442	770	944
Tennessee Titans†	14	19	.424	579	762
New York Jets	8	11	.421	388	389
Minnesota Vikings	18	25	.419	838	983
Detroit Lions	7	10	.412	365	404
Seattle Seahawks	7	10	.412	356	367
Atlanta Falcons	6	9	.400	322	361
San Diego Chargers†††	10	15	.400	474	575
Tampa Bay Buccaneers	6	9	.400	230	279
Cincinnati Bengals	5	8	.385	263	288
Kansas City Chiefs****	8	13	.381	340	445
Cleveland Browns	11	20	.355	629	728
New Orleans Saints	2	6	.250	144	248

* *One game played when franchise was in Boston (lost 21-6).*
** *12 games played when franchise was in Los Angeles (won 6, lost 6, 268 points scored, 224 points allowed).*
*** *15 games played when franchise was in Baltimore (won 8, lost 7, 264 points scored, 262 points allowed).*
**** *One game played when franchise was Dallas Texans (won 20-17).*
\# *Two games played when franchise was in Boston (won 26-8, lost 51-10).*
† *22 games played when franchise was in Houston and known as the Oilers (won 9, lost 13, 371 points scored, 533 points allowed).*
†† *One game played when franchise was in Cleveland (won 15-14), 32 games played when franchise was in Los Angeles (won 12, lost 20, 486 points scored, 683 points allowed).*
††† *One game played when franchise was in Los Angeles (lost 24-16).*
†††† *Two games played when franchise was in Chicago (won 28-21, lost 7-0), three games played when franchise was in St. Louis (lost 30-14, lost 35-23, lost 41-16).*

INDIVIDUAL RECORDS

SERVICE

Most Games, Career
29 Jerry Rice, San Francisco-Oakland-Seattle (SB 4, NFC 6, AFC 1, NFC-D 11, AFC-D 2, NFC-FR 4, AFC-FR 1)
27 D.D. Lewis, Dallas (SB 5, NFC 9, NFC-D 12, NFC-FR 1)
26 Larry Cole, Dallas (SB 5, NFC 8, NFC-D 12, NFC-FR 1)
Bill Romanowski, San Francisco-Philadelphia-Denver-Oakland (SB 5, NFC 5, AFC 3, NFC-D 6, AFC-D 4, NFC-FR 1, AFC-FR 2)

Most Games, Head Coach
36 Tom Landry, Dallas
Don Shula, Baltimore-Miami
24 Chuck Noll, Pittsburgh
Mike Holmgren, Green Bay-Seattle
Joe Gibbs, Washington
22 Bud Grant, Minnesota

Most Championships Won, Head Coach
6 George Halas, Chicago
Curly Lambeau, Green Bay
5 Vince Lombardi, Green Bay
4 Guy Chamberlin, Canton Bulldogs-Cleveland Bulldogs-Frankford Yellow Jackets
Chuck Noll, Pittsburgh

Most Games Won, Head Coach
20 Tom Landry, Dallas
19 Don Shula, Baltimore-Miami
17 Joe Gibbs, Washington

Most Games Lost, Head Coach
17 Don Shula, Baltimore-Miami
16 Tom Landry, Dallas
13 Marty Schottenheimer, Cleveland-Kansas City-San Diego

SCORING

POINTS

Most Points, Career
177 Adam Vinatieri, New England-Indianapolis, 23 games (51-pat, 42-fg)
153 Gary Anderson, Pittsburgh-Philadelphia-San Francisco-Minnesota-Tennessee, 22 games (57-pat, 32-fg)
132 Jerry Rice, San Francisco-Oakland-Seattle, 29 games (22-td)

Most Points, Game
30 Ricky Watters, NFC-D: San Francisco vs. N.Y. Giants, 1993 (5-td)
19 Pat Harder, NFC-D: Detroit vs. Los Angeles, 1952 (2-td, 4-pat, 1-fg)
Paul Hornung, NFC: Green Bay vs. N.Y. Giants, 1961 (1-td, 4-pat, 3-fg)
18 By many players

Most Consecutive Games Scoring
23 Adam Vinatieri, New England-Indianapolis, 1996-2008 (current)
19 George Blanda, Chi. Bears-Houston-Oakland, 1956-1975
17 David Akers, Philadelphia, 2000-08 (current)

TOUCHDOWNS

Most Touchdowns, Career
22 Jerry Rice, San Francisco-Oakland-Seattle, 29 games (22-p)
21 Thurman Thomas, Buffalo, 21 games (16-r, 5-p)
Emmitt Smith, Dallas, 17 games (19-r, 2-p)

17 Franco Harris, Pittsburgh, 19 games (16-r, 1-p)

Most Touchdowns, Game

5 Ricky Watters, NFC-D: San Francisco vs. N.Y. Giants, 1993 (5-r)

3 Andy Farkas, NFC-D: Washington vs. N.Y. Giants, 1943 (3-r)
Tom Fears, NFC-D: Los Angeles vs. Chi. Bears, 1950 (3-p)
Otto Graham, NFC: Cleveland vs. Detroit, 1954 (3-r)
Gary Collins, NFC: Cleveland vs. Baltimore, 1964 (3-p)
Craig Baynham, NFC-D: Dallas vs. Cleveland, 1967 (2-r, 1-p)
Fred Biletnikoff, AFC-D: Oakland vs. Kansas City, 1968 (3-p)
Tom Matte, NFC: Baltimore vs. Cleveland, 1968 (3-r)
Larry Schreiber, NFC-D: San Francisco vs. Dallas, 1972 (3-r)
Larry Csonka, AFC: Miami vs. Oakland, 1973 (3-r)
Franco Harris, AFC-D: Pittsburgh vs. Buffalo, 1974 (3-r)
Preston Pearson, NFC: Dallas vs. Los Angeles, 1975 (3-p)
Dave Casper, AFC-D: Oakland vs. Baltimore, 1977 (OT) (3-p)
Alvin Garrett, NFC-FR: Washington vs. Detroit, 1982 (3-p)
John Riggins, NFC-D: Washington vs. L.A. Rams, 1983 (3-r)
Roger Craig, SB: San Francisco vs. Miami, 1984 (1-r, 2-p)
Jerry Rice, NFC-D: San Francisco vs. Minnesota, 1988 (3-p)
Jerry Rice, SB: San Francisco vs. Denver, 1989 (3-p)
Kenneth Davis, AFC: Buffalo vs. L.A. Raiders, 1990 (3-r)
Andre Reed, AFC-FR: Buffalo vs. Houston, 1992 (OT) (3-p)
Sterling Sharpe, NFC-FR: Green Bay vs. Detroit, 1993 (3-p)
Napoleon McCallum, AFC-FR: L.A. Raiders vs. Denver, 1993 (3-r)
Thurman Thomas, AFC: Buffalo vs. Kansas City, 1993 (3-r)
William Floyd, NFC-D: San Francisco vs. Chicago, 1994 (3-r)
Ricky Watters, SB: San Francisco vs. San Diego, 1994 (1-r, 2-p)
Jerry Rice, SB: San Francisco vs. San Diego, 1994 (3-p)
Emmitt Smith, NFC: Dallas vs. Green Bay, 1995 (3-r)
Curtis Martin, AFC-D: New England vs. Pittsburgh, 1996 (3-r)
Terrell Davis, SB: Denver vs. Green Bay, 1997 (3-r)
Mario Bates, NFC-D: Arizona vs. Minnesota, 1998 (3-r)
Leroy Hoard, NFC-D: Minnesota vs. Arizona, 1998 (2-r, 1-p)
Willie Jackson, NFC-FR: New Orleans vs. St. Louis, 2000 (3-p)
Amani Toomer, NFC-FR: N.Y. Giants vs. San Francisco, 2002 (3-p)
Shaun Alexander, NFC-FR: Seattle vs. Green Bay, 2003 (OT) (3-r)
Ryan Grant, NFC-D: Green Bay vs. Seattle, 2007 (3-r)
Larry Fitzgerald, NFC: Arizona vs. Philadelphia, 2008 (3-p)

Most Consecutive Games Scoring Touchdowns

9 Thurman Thomas, Buffalo, 1992-98

8 John Stallworth, Pittsburgh, 1978-1983
Emmitt Smith, Dallas, 1993-96

7 John Riggins, Washington, 1982-84
Marcus Allen, L.A. Raiders, 1982-85
Terrell Davis, Denver, 1996-98
David Givens, New England, 2003-05

POINTS AFTER TOUCHDOWN

Most (One-Point) Points After Touchdown, Career

57 Gary Anderson, Pittsburgh-Philadelphia-San Francisco-Minnesota-Tennessee, 22 games (57 att)

51 Adam Vinatieri, New England-Indianapolis, 23 games (51 att)

49 George Blanda, Chi. Bears-Houston-Oakland, 19 games (49 att)

Most (One-Point) Points After Touchdown, Game

8 Lou Groza, NFC: Cleveland vs. Detroit, 1954 (8 att)
Jim Martin, NFC: Detroit vs. Cleveland, 1957 (8 att)
George Blanda, AFC-D: Oakland vs. Houston, 1969 (8 att)
Mike Hollis, AFC-D: Jacksonville vs. Miami, 1999 (8 att)

7 Danny Villanueva, NFC-D: Dallas vs. Cleveland, 1967 (7 att)
Raul Allegre, NFC-D: N.Y. Giants vs. San Francisco, 1986 (7 att)
Mike Cofer, SB: San Francisco vs. Denver, 1989 (8 att)
Lin Elliott, SB: Dallas vs. Buffalo, 1992 (7 att)
Doug Brien, SB: San Francisco vs. San Diego, 1994 (7 att)
Gary Anderson, NFC-FR: Philadelphia vs. Detroit, 1995 (7 att)
Jeff Wilkins, NFC-D: St. Louis vs. Minnesota, 1999 (7 att)
Mike Vanderjagt, AFC-FR: Indianapolis vs. Denver, 2004 (7 att)

6 George Blair, AFC: San Diego vs. Boston, 1963 (6 att)
Mark Moseley, NFC-D: Washington vs. L.A. Rams, 1983 (6 att)
Uwe von Schamann, AFC: Miami vs. Pittsburgh, 1984 (6 att)
Ali Haji-Sheikh, SB: Washington vs. Denver, 1987 (6 att)
Scott Norwood, AFC: Buffalo vs. L.A. Raiders, 1990 (7 att)
Jeff Jaeger, AFC-FR: L.A. Raiders vs. Denver, 1993 (6 att)
Jason Elam, AFC-FR: Denver vs. Jacksonville, 1997 (6 att)
Jeff Wilkins, NFC-D: St. Louis vs. Green Bay, 2001 (6 att)
Martín Gramatica, SB: Tampa Bay vs. Oakland, 2002 (6 att)
Jay Feely, NFC-D: Atlanta vs. St. Louis, 2004 (6 att)
Mason Crosby, NFC-D: Green Bay vs. Seattle, 2007 (6 att)

Most (Kicking) Points After Touchdown, No Misses, Career

57 Gary Anderson, Pittsburgh-Philadelphia-San Francisco-Minnesota-Tennessee, 22 games

51 Adam Vinatieri, New England-Indianapolis, 23 games

49 George Blanda, Chi. Bears-Houston-Oakland, 19 games

Most Two-Point Conversions, Career

2 Terrell Owens, San Francisco-Philadelphia-Dallas, 12 games
Kevin Faulk, New England, 17 games

Most Two-Point Conversions, Game

2 Terrell Owens, NFC-FR: San Francisco vs. N.Y. Giants, 2002

FIELD GOALS

Most Field Goals Attempted, Career

51 Adam Vinatieri, New England-Indianapolis, 23 games

40 Gary Anderson, Pittsburgh-Philadelphia-San Francisco-Minnesota-Tennessee, 22 games

39 George Blanda, Chi. Bears-Houston-Oakland, 19 games

Most Field Goals Attempted, Game

6 George Blanda, AFC: Oakland vs. Houston, 1967
David Ray, NFC-D: Los Angeles vs. Dallas, 1973
Mark Moseley, AFC-D: Cleveland vs. N.Y. Jets, 1986 (OT)
Matt Bahr, NFC: N.Y. Giants vs. San Francisco, 1990
Steve Christie, AFC: Buffalo vs. Miami, 1992
Jeff Wilkins, NFC-D: St. Louis vs. Carolina, 2003 (2 OT)

5 By many players

Most Field Goals, Career

42 Adam Vinatieri, New England-Indianapolis, 23 games

32 Gary Anderson, Pittsburgh-Philadelphia-San Francisco-Minnesota-Tennessee, 22 games

30 David Akers, Philadelphia, 17 games

Most Field Goals, Game

5 Chuck Nelson, NFC-D: Minnesota vs. San Francisco, 1987
Matt Bahr, NFC: N.Y. Giants vs. San Francisco, 1990
Steve Christie, AFC: Buffalo vs. Miami, 1992
Brad Daluiso, NFC-FR: N.Y. Giants vs. Minnesota, 1997
John Kasay, NFC-FR: Carolina vs. Dallas, 2003
Jeff Wilkins, NFC-D: St. Louis vs. Carolina, 2003 (2 OT)
Adam Vinatieri, AFC: New England vs. Indianapolis, 2003
Adam Vinatieri, AFC-D: Indianapolis vs. Baltimore, 2006

4 Gino Cappelletti, AFC-D: Boston vs. Buffalo, 1963
George Blanda, AFC: Oakland vs. Houston, 1967
Don Chandler, SB: Green Bay vs. Oakland, 1967
Curt Knight, NFC: Washington vs. Dallas, 1972
George Blanda, AFC-D: Oakland vs. Pittsburgh, 1973
Ray Wersching, SB: San Francisco vs. Cincinnati, 1981
Tony Franklin, AFC-FR: New England vs. N.Y. Jets, 1985
Jess Atkinson, NFC-FR: Washington vs. L.A. Rams, 1986
Luis Zendejas, NFC-D: Philadelphia vs. Chicago, 1988
Gary Anderson, AFC-FR: Pittsburgh vs. Houston, 1989 (OT)
Norm Johnson, AFC-D: Pittsburgh vs. Buffalo, 1995
Chris Boniol, NFC-FR: Dallas vs. Minnesota, 1996
John Kasay, NFC-D: Carolina vs. Dallas, 1996

Mike Hollis, AFC-D: Jacksonville vs. New England, 1998
Al Del Greco, AFC-D: Tennessee vs. Indianapolis, 1999
David Akers, NFC-D: Philadelphia vs. Chicago, 2001
Nate Kaeding, AFC-D: San Diego vs. New England, 2007
David Akers, NFC-FR: Philadelphia vs. Minnesota, 2008
Neil Rackers, NFC-D: Arizona vs. Carolina, 2008
3 By many players

Most Consecutive Games Scoring Field Goals
13 Toni Fritsch, Dallas-Houston, 1972-79
12 Adam Vinatieri, New England, 1997-2004
11 Jason Elam, Denver-Atlanta, 1997-2000, 2003-05, 2008 (current)

Most Consecutive Field Goals
19 David Akers, Philadelphia, 2000-04, 2006, 2008
16 Gary Anderson, Pittsburgh-Philadelphia, 1989-1995
15 Rafael Septien, Dallas, 1978-1982

Longest Field Goal
58 Pete Stoyanovich, AFC-FR: Miami vs. Kansas City, 1990
55 Jeff Wilkins, NFC-D: St. Louis vs. Atlanta, 2004
54 Ed Murray, NFC-D: Detroit vs. San Francisco, 1983
Steve Christie, SB: Buffalo vs. Dallas, 1993
John Carney, AFC-FR: San Diego vs. Indianapolis, 1995

Highest Field Goal Percentage, Career (10 field goals)
92.9 Martín Gramatica, Tampa Bay-Indianapolis-Dallas, 9 games (14-13)
91.3 John Kasay, Carolina, 10 games (23-21)
90.9 Chuck Nelson, L.A. Rams-Minnesota, 6 games (11-10)

SAFETIES

Most Safeties, Game
1 Bill Willis, NFC-D: Cleveland vs. N.Y. Giants, 1950
Carl Eller, NFC-D: Minnesota vs. Los Angeles, 1969
George Andrie, NFC-D: Dallas vs. Detroit, 1970
Alan Page, NFC-D: Minnesota vs. Dallas, 1971
Dwight White, SB: Pittsburgh vs. Minnesota, 1974
Reggie Harrison, SB: Pittsburgh vs. Dallas, 1975
Jim Jensen, NFC-D: Dallas vs. Los Angeles, 1976
Ted Washington, AFC: Houston vs. Pittsburgh, 1978
Randy White, NFC-D: Dallas vs. Los Angeles, 1979
Henry Waechter, SB: Chicago vs. New England, 1985
Rulon Jones, AFC-FR: Denver vs. New England, 1986
George Martin, SB: N.Y. Giants vs. Denver, 1986
D.D. Hoggard, AFC: Cleveland vs. Denver, 1987
Bruce Smith, SB: Buffalo vs. N.Y. Giants, 1990
Reggie White, NFC-FR: Philadelphia vs. New Orleans, 1992
Willie Clay, NFC-FR: Detroit vs. Green Bay, 1994
Carnell Lake, AFC-D: Pittsburgh vs. Cleveland, 1994
Reuben Davis, AFC-D: San Diego vs. Miami, 1994
Jevon Kearse, AFC-FR: Tennessee vs. Buffalo, 1999
Brady Smith, NFC-D: Atlanta vs. St. Louis, 2004
Antonio Smith, NFC-FR: Arizona vs. Atlanta, 2008

RUSHING

ATTEMPTS

Most Attempts, Career
400 Franco Harris, Pittsburgh, 19 games
349 Emmitt Smith, Dallas, 17 games
339 Thurman Thomas, Buffalo, 21 games

Most Attempts, Game
40 Lamar Smith, AFC-FR: Miami vs. Indianapolis, 2000 (OT)
38 Ricky Bell, NFC-D: Tampa Bay vs. Philadelphia, 1979
John Riggins, SB: Washington vs. Miami, 1982
37 Lawrence McCutcheon, NFC-D: Los Angeles vs. St. Louis, 1975
John Riggins, NFC-D: Washington vs. Minnesota, 1982

YARDS GAINED

Most Yards Gained, Career
1,586 Emmitt Smith, Dallas, 17 games
1,556 Franco Harris, Pittsburgh, 19 games
1,442 Thurman Thomas, Buffalo, 21 games

Most Yards Gained, Game
248 Eric Dickerson, NFC-D: L.A. Rams vs. Dallas, 1985
209 Lamar Smith, AFC-FR: Miami vs. Indianapolis, 2000 (OT)
206 Keith Lincoln, AFC: San Diego vs. Boston, 1963

Most Games, 100 or More Yards Rushing, Career
7 Emmitt Smith, Dallas, 17 games
Terrell Davis, Denver, 8 games
6 John Riggins, Washington, 9 games
Thurman Thomas, Buffalo, 21 games
5 Franco Harris, Pittsburgh, 19 games
Marcus Allen, L.A. Raiders-Kansas City, 16 games

Most Consecutive Games, 100 or More Yards Rushing
7 Terrell Davis, Denver, 1997-98
6 John Riggins, Washington, 1982-83
4 Thurman Thomas, Buffalo, 1990-91

Longest Run From Scrimmage
90 Fred Taylor, AFC-D: Jacksonville vs. Miami, 1999 (TD)
80 Roger Craig, NFC-D: San Francisco vs. Minnesota, 1988 (TD)
Charlie Garner, AFC-FR: Oakland vs. N.Y. Jets, 2001 (TD)
78 Curtis Martin, AFC-D: New England vs. Pittsburgh, 1996 (TD)

AVERAGE GAIN

Highest Average Gain, Career (100 attempts)
5.59 Terrell Davis, Denver, 8 games (204-1,140)
5.04 Marcus Allen, L.A. Raiders-Kansas City, 16 games (267-1,347)
4.89 Eric Dickerson, L.A. Rams-Indianapolis, 7 games (148-724)

Highest Average Gain, Game (10 attempts)
15.90 Elmer Angsman, NFC: Chi. Cardinals vs. Philadelphia, 1947 (10-159)
15.85 Keith Lincoln, AFC: San Diego vs. Boston, 1963 (13-206)
11.31 Zack Crockett, AFC-FR: Indianapolis vs. San Diego, 1995 (13-147)

TOUCHDOWNS

Most Touchdowns, Career
19 Emmitt Smith, Dallas, 17 games
16 Franco Harris, Pittsburgh, 19 games
Thurman Thomas, Buffalo, 21 games
12 John Riggins, Washington, 9 games
Terrell Davis, Denver, 8 games

Most Touchdowns, Game
5 Ricky Watters, NFC-D: San Francisco vs. N.Y. Giants, 1993
3 Andy Farkas, NFC-D: Washington vs. N.Y. Giants, 1943
Otto Graham, NFC: Cleveland vs. Detroit, 1954
Tom Matte, NFC: Baltimore vs. Cleveland, 1968
Larry Schreiber, NFC-D: San Francisco vs. Dallas, 1972
Larry Csonka, AFC: Miami vs. Oakland, 1973
Franco Harris, AFC-D: Pittsburgh vs. Buffalo, 1974
John Riggins, NFC-D: Washington vs. L.A. Rams, 1983
Kenneth Davis, AFC: Buffalo vs. L.A. Raiders, 1990
Napoleon McCallum, AFC-FR: L.A. Raiders vs. Denver, 1993
Thurman Thomas, AFC: Buffalo vs. Kansas City, 1993
William Floyd, NFC-D: San Francisco vs. Chicago, 1994
Emmitt Smith, NFC: Dallas vs. Green Bay, 1995
Curtis Martin, AFC-D: New England vs. Pittsburgh, 1996
Terrell Davis, SB: Denver vs. Green Bay, 1997
Mario Bates, NFC-D: Arizona vs. Minnesota, 1998
Shaun Alexander, NFC-FR: Seattle vs. Green Bay, 2003 (OT)
Ryan Grant, NFC-D: Green Bay vs. Seattle, 2007

Most Consecutive Games Rushing for Touchdowns
8 Emmitt Smith, Dallas, 1993-96
Thurman Thomas, Buffalo, 1992-98
7 John Riggins, Washington, 1982-84
Terrell Davis, Denver, 1996-98
5 Franco Harris, Pittsburgh, 1974-75
Franco Harris, Pittsburgh, 1977-79
Curtis Martin, New England-N.Y. Jets, 1996-98
Jerome Bettis, Pittsburgh, 2004-05

PASSING

PASSER RATING

Highest Passer Rating, Career (150 attempts)

104.8 Bart Starr, Green Bay, 10 games
98.9 Kurt Warner, St. Louis-Arizona, 11 games
95.6 Joe Montana, San Francisco-Kansas City, 23 games

ATTEMPTS

Most Passes Attempted, Career

734 Joe Montana, San Francisco-Kansas City, 23 games
721 Brett Favre, Green Bay, 22 games
687 Dan Marino, Miami, 18 games

Most Passes Attempted, Game

65 Steve Young, NFC-D: San Francisco vs. Green Bay, 1995
64 Bernie Kosar, AFC-D: Cleveland vs. N.Y. Jets, 1986 (OT)
Dan Marino, AFC-FR: Miami vs. Buffalo, 1995
58 Jim Kelly, SB: Buffalo vs. Washington, 1991

COMPLETIONS

Most Passes Completed, Career

460 Joe Montana, San Francisco-Kansas City, 23 games
438 Brett Favre, Green Bay, 22 games
385 Dan Marino, Miami, 18 games

Most Passes Completed, Game

36 Warren Moon, AFC-FR: Houston vs. Buffalo, 1992 (OT)
33 Dan Fouts, AFC-D: San Diego vs. Miami, 1981 (OT)
Bernie Kosar, AFC-D: Cleveland vs. N.Y. Jets, 1986 (OT)
Dan Marino, AFC-FR: Miami vs. Buffalo, 1995
Peyton Manning, AFC-D: Indianapolis vs. San Diego, 2007
32 Neil Lomax, NFC-FR: St. Louis vs. Green Bay, 1982
Danny White, NFC-FR: Dallas vs. L.A. Rams, 1983
Warren Moon, AFC-D: Houston vs. Kansas City, 1993
Neil O'Donnell, AFC: Pittsburgh vs. San Diego, 1994
Steve Young, NFC-D: San Francisco vs. Green Bay, 1995
Tom Brady, AFC-D: New England vs. Oakland, 2001 (OT)
Tom Brady, SB: New England vs. Carolina, 2003

COMPLETION PERCENTAGE

Highest Completion Percentage, Career (150 attempts)

66.3 Ken Anderson, Cincinnati, 6 games (166-110)
64.8 Kurt Warner, St. Louis-Arizona, 11 games (403-261)
64.3 Warren Moon, Houston-Minnesota, 10 games (403-259))

Highest Completion Percentage, Game (15 completions)

92.9 Tom Brady, AFC-D: New England vs. Jacksonville, 2007 (28-26)
88.0 Phil Simms, SB: N.Y. Giants vs. Denver, 1986 (25-22)
86.7 Joe Montana, NFC: San Francisco vs. L.A. Rams, 1989 (30-26)

YARDS GAINED

Most Yards Gained, Career

5,772 Joe Montana, San Francisco-Kansas City, 23 games
5,311 Brett Favre, Green Bay, 22 games
4,964 John Elway, Denver, 22 games

Most Yards Gained, Game

489 Bernie Kosar, AFC-D: Cleveland vs. N.Y. Jets, 1986 (OT)
458 Peyton Manning, AFC-FR: Indianapolis vs. Denver, 2004
433 Dan Fouts, AFC-D: San Diego vs. Miami, 1981 (OT)

Most Games, 300 or More Yards Passing, Career

6 Joe Montana, San Francisco-Kansas City, 23 games
Peyton Manning, Indianapolis, 15 games
5 Dan Fouts, San Diego, 7 games
Kurt Warner, St. Louis-Arizona, 11 games
4 Warren Moon, Houston-Minnesota, 10 games
Troy Aikman, Dallas, 16 games
Dan Marino, Miami, 18 games
John Elway, Denver, 22 games

Most Consecutive Games, 300 or More Yards Passing

4 Dan Fouts, San Diego, 1979-1981
3 Jim Kelly, Buffalo, 1989-1990
Warren Moon, Houston, 1991-93
2 Daryle Lamonica, Oakland, 1968
Ken Anderson, Cincinnati, 1981-82
Terry Bradshaw, Pittsburgh, 1979-1982
Joe Montana, San Francisco, 1983-84
Dan Marino, Miami, 1984
Troy Aikman, Dallas, 1994
Steve Young, San Francisco, 1994-95
Kurt Warner, St. Louis, 1999-2000
Peyton Manning, Indianapolis, 2003
Marc Bulger, St. Louis, 2003-04
Matt Hasselbeck, Seattle, 2003-04
Peyton Manning, Indianapolis, 2007-08
Donovan McNabb, Philadelphia, 2004, 2008

Longest Pass Completion

96 Trent Dilfer (to Sharpe), AFC: Baltimore vs. Oakland, 2000 (TD)
94 Troy Aikman (to Harper), NFC-D: Dallas vs. Green Bay, 1994 (TD)
93 Daryle Lamonica (to Dubenion), AFC-D: Buffalo vs. Boston, 1963 (TD)

AVERAGE GAIN

Highest Average Gain, Career (150 attempts)

8.45 Joe Theismann, Washington, 10 games (211-1,782)
8.43 Jim Plunkett, Oakland/L.A. Raiders, 10 games (272-2,293)
8.41 Terry Bradshaw, Pittsburgh, 19 games (456-3,833)

Highest Average Gain, Game (20 attempts)

14.71 Terry Bradshaw, SB: Pittsburgh vs. Los Angeles, 1979 (21-309)
14.50 Peyton Manning, AFC-FR: Indianapolis vs. Denver, 2003 (26-377)
13.88 Peyton Manning, AFC-FR: Indianapolis vs. Denver, 2004 (33-458)

TOUCHDOWNS

Most Touchdown Passes, Career

45 Joe Montana, San Francisco-Kansas City, 23 games
39 Brett Favre, Green Bay, 22 games
32 Dan Marino, Miami, 18 games

Most Touchdown Passes, Game

6 Daryle Lamonica, AFC-D: Oakland vs. Houston, 1969
Steve Young, SB: San Francisco vs. San Diego, 1994
5 Sid Luckman, NFC: Chi. Bears vs. Washington, 1943
Daryle Lamonica, AFC-D: Oakland vs. Kansas City, 1968
Joe Montana, SB: San Francisco vs. Denver, 1989
Kurt Warner, NFC-D: St. Louis vs. Minnesota, 1999
Kerry Collins, NFC: N.Y. Giants vs. Minnesota, 2000
Peyton Manning, AFC-FR: Indianapolis vs. Denver, 2003
4 Otto Graham, NFC: Cleveland vs. Los Angeles, 1950
Tobin Rote, NFC: Detroit vs. Cleveland, 1957
Bart Starr, NFC: Green Bay vs. Dallas, 1966
Ken Stabler, AFC-D: Oakland vs. Miami, 1974
Roger Staubach, NFC: Dallas vs. Los Angeles, 1975
Terry Bradshaw, SB: Pittsburgh vs. Dallas, 1978
Don Strock, AFC-D: Miami vs. San Diego, 1981 (OT)
Lynn Dickey, NFC-FR: Green Bay vs. St. Louis, 1982
Dan Marino, AFC: Miami vs. Pittsburgh, 1984
Phil Simms, NFC-D: N.Y. Giants vs. San Francisco, 1986
Doug Williams, SB: Washington vs. Denver, 1987
Jim Kelly, AFC-D: Buffalo vs. Cleveland, 1989
Joe Montana, NFC-D: San Francisco vs. Minnesota, 1989
Warren Moon, AFC-FR: Houston vs. Buffalo, 1992 (OT)
Frank Reich, AFC-FR: Buffalo vs. Houston, 1992 (OT)
Troy Aikman, SB: Dallas vs. Buffalo, 1992
Jeff George, NFC-D: Minnesota vs. St. Louis, 1999
Aaron Brooks, NFC-FR: New Orleans vs. St. Louis, 2000
Kerry Collins, NFC-FR: N.Y. Giants vs. San Francisco, 2002
Peyton Manning, AFC-FR: Indianapolis vs. Denver, 2004
Daunte Culpepper, NFC-FR: Minnesota vs. Green Bay, 2004
Kurt Warner, NFC: Arizona vs. Philadelphia, 2008

Most Consecutive Games, Touchdown Passes

18 Brett Favre, Green Bay, 1995-2007 (current)
15 Tom Brady, New England, 2001-07 (current)
13 Dan Marino, Miami, 1983-1995

HAD INTERCEPTED

Lowest Percentage, Passes Had Intercepted, Career (150 attempts)

1.41 Bart Starr, Green Bay, 10 games (213-3)
2.02 Tom Brady, New England, 17 games (595-12)
2.15 Phil Simms, N.Y. Giants, 10 games (279-6)

Most Attempts Without Interception, Game

54 Neil O'Donnell, AFC: Pittsburgh vs. San Diego, 1994
48 Warren Moon, AFC-FR: Houston vs. Pittsburgh, 1989 (OT)
Randall Cunningham, NFC: Minnesota vs. Atlanta, 1998 (OT)
Tom Brady, SB: New England vs. N.Y. Giants, 2007
47 Daryle Lamonica, AFC: Oakland vs. N.Y. Jets, 1968

Most Passes Had Intercepted, Career

28 Jim Kelly, Buffalo, 17 games
Brett Favre, Green Bay, 22 games
26 Terry Bradshaw, Pittsburgh, 19 games
24 Dan Marino, Miami, 18 games

Most Passes Had Intercepted, Game

6 Frank Filchock, NFC: N.Y. Giants vs. Chi. Bears, 1946
Bobby Layne, NFC: Detroit vs. Cleveland, 1954
Norm Van Brocklin, NFC: Los Angeles vs. Cleveland, 1955
Brett Favre, NFC-D: Green Bay vs. St. Louis, 2001
5 Frank Filchock, NFC: Washington vs. Chi. Bears, 1940
George Blanda, AFC: Houston vs. San Diego, 1961
George Blanda, AFC: Houston vs. Dall. Texans, 1962 (OT)
Y.A. Tittle, NFC: N.Y. Giants vs. Chicago, 1963
Mike Phipps, AFC-D: Cleveland vs. Miami, 1972
Dan Pastorini, AFC: Houston vs. Pittsburgh, 1978
Dan Fouts, AFC-D: San Diego vs. Houston, 1979
Tommy Kramer, NFC-D: Minnesota vs. Philadelphia, 1980
Dan Fouts, AFC-D: San Diego vs. Miami, 1982
Richard Todd, AFC: N.Y. Jets vs. Miami, 1982
Gary Danielson, NFC-D: Detroit vs. San Francisco, 1983
Jay Schroeder, AFC: L.A. Raiders vs. Buffalo, 1990
Rich Gannon, SB: Oakland vs. Tampa Bay, 2002
Jake Delhomme, NFC-D: Carolina vs. Arizona, 2008
4 By many players

PASS RECEIVING

RECEPTIONS

Most Receptions, Career

151 Jerry Rice, San Francisco-Oakland-Seattle, 29 games
87 Michael Irvin, Dallas, 16 games
85 Andre Reed, Buffalo, 21 games

Most Receptions, Game

13 Kellen Winslow, AFC-D: San Diego vs. Miami, 1981 (OT)
Thurman Thomas, AFC-D: Buffalo vs. Cleveland, 1989
Shannon Sharpe, AFC-FR: Denver vs. L.A. Raiders, 1993
Chad Morton, NFC-D: New Orleans vs. Minnesota, 2000
12 Raymond Berry, NFC: Baltimore vs. N.Y. Giants, 1958
Michael Irvin, NFC: Dallas vs. San Francisco, 1994
Darrell Jackson, NFC-FR: Seattle vs. St. Louis, 2004
Steve Smith, NFC-D: Carolina vs. Chicago, 2005
11 Dante Lavelli, NFC: Cleveland vs. Los Angeles, 1950
Dan Ross, SB: Cincinnati vs. San Francisco, 1981
Franco Harris, AFC-FR: Pittsburgh vs. San Diego, 1982
Steve Watson, AFC-D: Denver vs. Pittsburgh, 1984
John L. Williams, AFC-D: Seattle vs. Cincinnati, 1988
Jerry Rice, SB: San Francisco vs. Cincinnati, 1988
Ernest Givins, AFC-FR: Houston vs. Pittsburgh, 1989 (OT)
Amp Lee, NFC-D: Minnesota vs. Chicago, 1994
Jay Novacek, NFC-D: Dallas vs. Green Bay, 1994
O.J. McDuffie, AFC-FR: Miami vs. Buffalo, 1995
Jerry Rice, NFC-D: San Francisco vs. Green Bay, 1995
Hines Ward, AFC-FR: Pittsburgh vs. Cleveland, 2002
Deion Branch, SB: New England vs. Philadelphia, 2004
Plaxico Burress, NFC: N.Y. Giants vs. Green Bay, 2007 (OT)
Wes Welker, SB: New England vs. N.Y. Giants, 2007
Roddy White, NFC-FR: Atlanta vs. Arizona, 2008

Most Consecutive Games, Pass Receptions

28 Jerry Rice, San Francisco-Oakland, 1985-2002
22 Drew Pearson, Dallas, 1973-1983
18 Paul Warfield, Cleveland-Miami, 1964-1974
Cliff Branch, Oakland/L.A. Raiders, 1974-1983
Thurman Thomas, Buffalo, 1989-1998
Shannon Sharpe, Denver-Baltimore-Denver, 1991-2003

YARDS GAINED

Most Yards Gained, Career

2,245 Jerry Rice, San Francisco-Oakland-Seattle, 29 games
1,315 Michael Irvin, Dallas, 16 games
1,289 Cliff Branch, Oakland/L.A. Raiders, 22 games

Most Yards Gained, Game

240 Eric Moulds, AFC-FR: Buffalo vs. Miami, 1998
227 Anthony Carter, NFC-D: Minnesota vs. San Francisco, 1987
221 Reggie Wayne, AFC-FR: Indianapolis vs. Denver, 2004

Most Games, 100 or More Yards Receiving, Career

8 Jerry Rice, San Francisco-Oakland-Seattle, 29 games
6 Michael Irvin, Dallas, 16 games
5 John Stallworth, Pittsburgh, 18 games
Andre Reed, Buffalo, 21 games
Hines Ward, Pittsburgh, 14 games

Most Consecutive Games, 100 or More Yards Receiving, Career

4 Larry Fitzgerald, Arizona, 2008 (current)
3 Tom Fears, Los Angeles, 1950-51
Jerry Rice, San Francisco, 1988-89
Randy Moss, Minnesota, 1999-2000
2 By many players

Longest Reception

96 Shannon Sharpe (from Dilfer), AFC: Baltimore vs. Oakland, 2000 (TD)
94 Alvin Harper (from Aikman), NFC-D: Dallas vs. Green Bay, 1994 (TD)
93 Elbert Dubenion (from Lamonica), AFC-D: Buffalo vs. Boston, 1963 (TD)

AVERAGE GAIN

Highest Average Gain, Career (20 receptions)

27.3 Alvin Harper, Dallas, 10 games (24-655)
23.7 Willie Gault, Chicago-L.A. Raiders, 12 games (21-497)
22.8 Harold Jackson, L.A. Rams-New England-Minnesota-Seattle, 14 games (24-548)

Highest Average Gain, Game (3 receptions)

46.3 Harold Jackson, NFC: Los Angeles vs. Minnesota, 1974 (3-139)
42.7 Billy Cannon, AFC: Houston vs. L.A. Chargers, 1960 (3-128)
42.0 Lenny Moore, NFC: Baltimore vs. N.Y. Giants, 1959 (3-126)

TOUCHDOWNS

Most Touchdowns, Career

22 Jerry Rice, San Francisco-Oakland-Seattle, 29 games
12 John Stallworth, Pittsburgh, 18 games
10 Fred Biletnikoff, Oakland, 19 games
Antonio Freeman, Green Bay-Philadelphia-Green Bay, 16 games
Randy Moss, Minnesota-New England, 11 games

Most Touchdowns, Game

3 Tom Fears, NFC-D: Los Angeles vs. Chi. Bears, 1950
Gary Collins, NFC: Cleveland vs. Baltimore, 1964
Fred Biletnikoff, AFC-D: Oakland vs. Kansas City, 1968
Preston Pearson, NFC: Dallas vs. Los Angeles, 1975
Dave Casper, AFC-D: Oakland vs. Baltimore, 1977 (OT)
Alvin Garrett, NFC-FR: Washington vs. Detroit, 1982
Jerry Rice, NFC-D: San Francisco vs. Minnesota, 1988
Jerry Rice, SB: San Francisco vs. Denver, 1989
Andre Reed, AFC-FR: Buffalo vs. Houston, 1992 (OT)
Sterling Sharpe, NFC-FR: Green Bay vs. Detroit, 1993
Jerry Rice, SB: San Francisco vs. San Diego, 1994
Willie Jackson, NFC-FR: New Orleans vs. St. Louis, 2000
Amani Toomer, NFC-FR: N.Y. Giants vs. San Francisco, 2002
Larry Fitzgerald, NFC: Arizona vs. Philadelphia, 2008

Most Consecutive Games, Touchdown Passes Caught

8 John Stallworth, Pittsburgh, 1978-1983
7 David Givens, New England, 2003-05

5 James Lofton, Green Bay-Buffalo, 1982-1990
Randy Moss, Minnesota, 1998-2000
Antonio Freeman, Green Bay, 1997-2001
Hines Ward, Pittsburgh, 2002-05

INTERCEPTIONS BY

Most Interceptions, Career

9 Charlie Waters, Dallas, 25 games
Bill Simpson, Los Angeles-Buffalo, 11 games
Ronnie Lott, San Francisco-L.A. Raiders, 20 games
8 Lester Hayes, Oakland/L.A. Raiders, 13 games
7 Willie Brown, Oakland, 17 games
Dennis Thurman, Dallas, 14 games
Rodney Harrison, San Diego-New England, 13 games
Asante Samuel, New England-Philadelphia, 17 games

Most Interceptions, Game

4 Vernon Perry, AFC-D: Houston vs. San Diego, 1979
3 Joe Laws, NFC: Green Bay vs. N.Y. Giants, 1944
Charlie Waters, NFC-D: Dallas vs. Chicago, 1977
Rod Martin, SB: Oakland vs. Philadelphia, 1980
Dennis Thurman, NFC-D: Dallas vs. Green Bay, 1982
A.J. Duhe, AFC: Miami vs. N.Y. Jets, 1982
Ty Law, AFC: New England vs. Indianapolis, 2003
Ricky Manning Jr., NFC: Carolina vs. Philadelphia, 2003
2 By many players

Most Consecutive Games, Interceptions

4 Aeneas Williams, Arizona-St. Louis, 1998-2001
Rodney Harrison, New England, 2004, 2007
3 By many players. Last time:
Ed Reed, Baltimore, 2006, 2008

YARDS GAINED

Most Yards Gained, Career

227 Asante Samuel, New England-Philadelphia, 17 games
196 Willie Brown, Oakland, 17 games
187 Ronnie Lott, San Francisco-L.A.-Raiders, 20 games

Most Yards Gained, Game

108 Darrien Gordon, SB: Denver vs. Atlanta, 1998
101 George Teague, NFC-FR: Green Bay vs. Detroit, 1993
100 Champ Bailey, AFC-D: Denver vs. New England, 2005
James Harrison, SB: Pittsburgh vs. Arizona, 2008

Longest Return

101 George Teague, NFC-FR: Green Bay vs. Detroit, 1993 (TD)
100 Champ Bailey, AFC-D: Denver vs. New England, 2005
James Harrison, SB: Pittsburgh vs. Arizona, 2008 (TD)
98 Darrol Ray, AFC-FR: N.Y. Jets vs. Cincinnati, 1982 (TD)

TOUCHDOWNS

Most Touchdowns, Career

4 Asante Samuel, New England-Philadelphia, 17 games
3 Willie Brown, Oakland, 17 games
2 Lester Hayes, Oakland/L.A. Raiders, 13 games
Ronnie Lott, San Francisco-L.A. Raiders, 20 games
Darrell Green, Washington, 18 games
Melvin Jenkins, Seattle-Detroit, 5 games
George Teague, Green Bay-Dallas-Miami-Dallas, 12 games
Aeneas Williams, Arizona-St. Louis, 6 games
Dwight Smith, Tampa Bay, 4 games

Most Touchdowns, Game

2 Aeneas Williams, NFC-D: St. Louis vs. Green Bay, 2001
Dwight Smith, SB: Tampa Bay vs. Oakland, 2002
1 By many players

PUNTING

Most Punts, Career

111 Ray Guy, Oakland/L.A. Raiders, 22 games
101 Craig Hentrich, Green Bay-Tennessee, 22 games
84 Danny White, Dallas, 18 games
Sean Landeta, N.Y. Giants-Tampa Bay-Green Bay-Philadelphia-St. Louis, 18 games

Most Punts, Game

14 Dave Jennings, AFC-D: N.Y. Jets vs. Cleveland, 1986 (OT)
12 David Lee, AFC-D: Baltimore vs. Oakland, 1977 (OT)
11 Ken Strong, NFC: N.Y. Giants vs. Chi. Bears, 1933
Jim Norton, AFC: Houston vs. Oakland, 1967
Ode Burrell, AFC-D: Houston vs. Oakland, 1969
Dale Hatcher, NFC: L.A. Rams vs. Chicago, 1985
Brad Maynard, SB: N.Y. Giants vs. Baltimore, 2000

Longest Punt

76 Ed Danowski, NFC: N.Y. Giants vs. Detroit, 1935
Mike Horan, AFC: Denver vs. Buffalo, 1991
72 Charlie Conerly, NFC-D: N.Y. Giants vs. Cleveland, 1950
Yale Lary, NFC: Detroit vs. Cleveland, 1953
71 Ray Guy, AFC: Oakland vs. San Diego, 1980

AVERAGE YARDAGE

Highest Average, Career (25 punts)

44.5 Rich Camarillo, New England, 6 games (35-1,559)
44.4 Todd Sauerbrun, Carolina-Denver-New England, 9 games (43-1,911)
44.0 Hunter Smith, Indianapolis, 15 games (52-2,288)

Highest Average, Game (4 punts)

56.0 Ray Guy, AFC: Oakland vs. San Diego, 1980 (4-224)
53.3 Craig Hentrich, AFC-D: Tennessee vs. Baltimore, 2008 (4-213)
52.8 Hunter Smith, AFC: Indianapolis vs. New England, 2006 (4-211)

PUNT RETURNS

Most Punt Returns, Career

34 David Meggett, N.Y. Giants-New England-N.Y. Jets, 13 games
Brian Mitchell, Washington-Philadelphia, 16 games
33 Troy Brown, New England, 20 games
25 Theo Bell, Pittsburgh-Tampa Bay, 10 games

Most Punt Returns, Game

7 Ron Gardin, AFC-D: Baltimore vs. Cincinnati, 1970
Carl Roaches, AFC-FR: Houston vs. Oakland, 1980
Gerald McNeil, AFC-D: Cleveland vs. N.Y. Jets, 1986 (OT)
Phil McConkey, NFC-D: N.Y. Giants vs. San Francisco, 1986
David Meggett, AFC-D: New England vs. Pittsburgh, 1996
Reggie Barlow, AFC-FR: Jacksonville vs. New England, 1998
6 George McAfee, NFC-D: Chi. Bears vs. Los Angeles, 1950
Eddie Brown, NFC-D: Washington vs. Minnesota, 1976
Theo Bell, AFC: Pittsburgh vs. Houston, 1978
Eddie Brown, NFC: Los Angeles vs. Tampa Bay, 1979
John Sciarra, NFC: Philadelphia vs. Dallas, 1980
Kurt Sohn, AFC: N.Y. Jets vs. Miami, 1982
Mike Nelms, SB: Washington vs. Miami, 1982
Anthony Carter, NFC-FR: Minnesota vs. New Orleans, 1987
Desmond Howard, SB: Green Bay vs. New England, 1996
Nate Jacquet, AFC-FR: Miami vs. Seattle, 1999
Derrick Mason, AFC-FR: Tennessee vs. Baltimore, 2003
Antonio Chatman, AFC-D: Green Bay vs. Philadelphia, 2003
Nate Burleson, NFC-FR: Seattle vs. Washington, 2007
Jim Leonhard, AFC: Baltimore vs. Pittsburgh, 2008
5 By many players

YARDS GAINED

Most Yards Gained, Career

339 Brian Mitchell, Washington-Philadelphia, 16 games
315 Troy Brown, New England, 20 games
312 David Meggett, N.Y. Giants-New England-N.Y. Jets, 13 games

Most Yards Gained, Game

152 Allen Rossum, NFC-D: Atlanta vs. St. Louis, 2004
143 Anthony Carter, NFC-FR: Minnesota vs. New Orleans, 1987
141 Bob Hayes, NFC-D: Dallas vs. Cleveland, 1967

Longest Return

88 Jermaine Lewis, AFC-D: Baltimore vs. Pittsburgh, 2001 (TD)
84 Anthony Carter, NFC-FR: Minnesota vs. New Orleans, 1987 (TD)
81 Hugh Gallarneau, NFC-D: Chi. Bears vs. Green Bay, 1941 (TD)

AVERAGE YARDAGE

Highest Average, Career (10 returns)

23.9 Allen Rossum, Green Bay-Atlanta, 6 games (10-239)
15.3 Robert Brooks, Green Bay, 11 games (14-214)
15.2 Anthony Carter, Minnesota-Detroit, 9 games (17-259)

Highest Average Gain, Game (3 returns)

50.7 Allen Rossum, NFC-D: Atlanta vs. St. Louis, 2004 (3-152)
47.0 Bob Hayes, NFC-D: Dallas vs. Cleveland, 1967 (3-141)
33.0 Jermaine Lewis, AFC-D: Baltimore vs. Pittsburgh, 2001 (3-99)

TOUCHDOWNS

Most Touchdowns

1 Hugh Gallarneau, NFC-D: Chicago Bears vs. Green Bay, 1941
Bosh Pritchard, NFC-D: Philadelphia vs. Pittsburgh, 1947
Charley Trippi, NFC: Chicago Cardinals vs. Philadelphia, 1947
Verda (Vitamin T) Smith, NFC-D: Los Angeles vs. Detroit, 1952
George (Butch) Byrd, AFC: Buffalo vs. San Diego, 1965
Golden Richards, NFC: Dallas vs. Minnesota, 1973
Wes Chandler, AFC-D: San Diego vs. Miami, 1981 (OT)
Shaun Gayle, NFC-D: Chicago vs. N.Y. Giants, 1985
Anthony Carter, NFC-FR: Minnesota vs. New Orleans, 1987
Darrell Green, NFC-D: Washington vs. Chicago, 1987
Antonio Freeman, NFC-FR: Green Bay vs. Atlanta, 1995
Desmond Howard, NFC-D: Green Bay vs. San Francisco, 1996
Jermaine Lewis, AFC-D: Baltimore vs. Pittsburgh, 2001
Troy Brown, AFC: New England vs. Pittsburgh, 2001
Antwaan Randle El, AFC-FR: Pittsburgh vs. Cleveland, 2002
Santana Moss, AFC-D: N.Y. Jets vs. Pittsburgh, 2004 (OT)
Allen Rossum, NFC-D: Atlanta vs. St. Louis, 2004
Steve Smith, NFC: Carolina vs. Seattle, 2005
Santonio Holmes, AFC: Pittsburgh vs. San Diego, 2008

KICKOFF RETURNS

Most Kickoff Returns, Career

36 Brian Mitchell, Washington-Philadelphia, 16 games
31 Kevin Williams, Dallas-Buffalo, 12 games
29 Fulton Walker, Miami-L.A. Raiders, 10 games

Most Kickoff Returns, Game

8 Marc Logan, AFC-D: Miami vs. Buffalo, 1990
Andre Coleman, SB: San Diego vs. San Francisco, 1994
Marcus Knight, SB: Oakland vs. Tampa Bay, 2002
7 Don Bingham, NFC: Chi. Bears vs. N.Y. Giants, 1956
Reggie Brown, NFC-FR: Atlanta vs. Minnesota, 1982
David Verser, AFC-FR: Cincinnati vs. N.Y. Jets, 1982
Del Rodgers, NFC-D: Green Bay vs. Dallas, 1982
Henry Ellard, NFC-D: L.A. Rams vs. Washington, 1983
Stephen Starring, SB: New England vs. Chicago, 1985
Darick Holmes, AFC-D: Buffalo vs. Pittsburgh, 1995
Antonio Freeman, NFC: Green Bay vs. Dallas, 1995
Roell Preston, NFC-FR: Green Bay vs. San Francisco, 1998
Robert Tate, NFC-D: Minnesota vs. St. Louis, 1999
Fred McAfee, NFC-D: New Orleans vs. Minnesota, 2000
Michael Bates, NFC-FR: Dallas vs. Carolina, 2003
Dante Hall, AFC-D: Kansas City vs. Indianapolis, 2003
Michael Lewis, NFC: New Orleans vs. Chicago, 2006
6 By many players

YARDS GAINED

Most Yards Gained, Career

875 Brian Mitchell, Washington-Philadelphia, 16 games
677 Fulton Walker, Miami-L.A. Raiders, 10 games
632 Kevin Williams, Dallas-Buffalo, 12 games

Most Yards Gained, Game

244 Andre Coleman, SB: San Diego vs. San Francisco, 1994
220 Ellis Hobbs, AFC: New England vs. Indianapolis, 2006
210 Tim Dwight, SB: Atlanta vs. Denver, 1998

Longest Return

100 Brian Mitchell, NFC-D: Washington vs. Tampa Bay, 1999 (TD)
99 Desmond Howard, SB: Green Bay vs. New England, 1996 (TD)
98 Fulton Walker, SB: Miami vs. Washington, 1982 (TD)
Andre Coleman, SB: San Diego vs. San Francisco, 1994 (TD)

AVERAGE YARDAGE

Highest Average, Career (10 returns)

30.1 Carl Garrett, Oakland, 5 games (16-481)
30.0 Reggie Barlow, Jacksonville, 8 games (12-360)
29.2 Chad Morton, New Orleans-N.Y. Jets-N.Y. Giants, 6 games (14-409)

Highest Average, Game (3 returns)

56.7 Les (Speedy) Duncan, NFC-D: Washington vs. San Francisco, 1971 (3-170)
51.3 Ed Podolak, AFC-D: Kansas City vs. Miami, 1971 (OT) (3-154)
49.0 Les (Speedy) Duncan, AFC: San Diego vs. Buffalo, 1964 (3-147)

TOUCHDOWNS

Most Touchdowns, Career

2 Ron Dixon, N.Y. Giants, 4 games
1 By many players

Most Touchdowns, Game

1 Vic Washington, NFC-D: San Francisco vs. Dallas, 1972
Nat Moore, AFC-D: Miami vs. Oakland, 1974
Marshall Johnson, AFC-D: Baltimore vs. Oakland, 1977 (OT)
Fulton Walker, SB: Miami vs. Washington, 1982
Stanford Jennings, SB: Cincinnati vs. San Francisco, 1988
Eric Metcalf, AFC-D: Cleveland vs. Buffalo, 1989
Andre Coleman, SB: San Diego vs. San Francisco, 1994
Desmond Howard, SB: Green Bay vs. New England, 1996
Chuck Levy, NFC: San Francisco vs. Green Bay, 1997
Tim Dwight, SB: Atlanta vs. Denver, 1998
Kevin Dyson, AFC-FR: Tennessee vs. Buffalo, 1999
Charlie Rogers, AFC-FR: Seattle vs. Miami, 1999
Brian Mitchell, NFC-D: Washington vs. Tampa Bay, 1999
Tony Horne, NFC-D: St. Louis vs. Minnesota, 1999
Derrick Mason, AFC: Tennessee vs. Jacksonville, 1999
Ron Dixon, NFC-D: N.Y. Giants vs. Philadelphia, 2000; SB: N.Y. Giants vs. Baltimore, 2000
Jermaine Lewis, SB: Baltimore vs. N.Y. Giants, 2000
Dante Hall, AFC-D: Kansas City vs. Indianapolis, 2003
Miles Austin, NFC-FR: Dallas vs. Seattle, 2006
Devin Hester, SB: Chicago vs. Indianapolis, 2006

FUMBLES

Most Fumbles, Career

16 Warren Moon, Houston-Minnesota, 10 games
14 John Elway, Denver, 22 games
13 Tony Dorsett, Dallas, 17 games
Donovan McNabb, Philadelphia, 15 games

Most Fumbles, Game

5 Warren Moon, AFC-D: Houston vs. Kansas City, 1993
4 Brian Sipe, AFC-D: Cleveland vs. Oakland, 1980
Randall Cunningham, NFC-FR: Minnesota vs. N.Y. Giants, 1997
3 By many players

RECOVERIES

Most Own Fumbles Recovered, Career

8 Warren Moon, Houston-Minnesota, 10 games
7 John Elway, Denver, 22 games
6 Jim Kelly, Buffalo, 17 games

Most Opponents' Fumbles Recovered, Career

4 Cliff Harris, Dallas, 21 games
Harvey Martin, Dallas, 22 games
Ted Hendricks, Baltimore-Oakland/L.A. Raiders, 21 games
Alvin Walton, Washington, 9 games
Monte Coleman, Washington, 21 games
Dave Thomas, Dallas-Jacksonville-N.Y. Giants, 13 games
3 Paul Krause, Minnesota, 19 games
Jack Lambert, Pittsburgh, 18 games
Fred Dryer, Los Angeles, 14 games
Charlie Waters, Dallas, 25 games
Jack Ham, Pittsburgh, 16 games
Mike Hegman, Dallas, 16 games
Tom Jackson, Denver, 10 games
Rich Milot, Washington, 13 games
Mike Singletary, Chicago, 12 games
Darryl Grant, Washington, 16 games
Wes Hopkins, Philadelphia, 3 games
Wilber Marshall, Chicago-Washington, 15 games
Tyrone Braxton, Denver-Miami-Denver, 19 games
Neil Smith, Kansas City-Denver, 16 games
Tony Brackens, Jacksonville, 7 games
Phil Hansen, Buffalo, 14 games
Carnell Lake, Pittsburgh-Jacksonville-Baltimore, 17 games
Jason Gildon, Pittsburgh, 13 games
Tedy Bruschi, New England, 22 games
2 By many players

Most Fumbles Recovered, Game, Own and Opponents'

3 Jack Lambert, AFC: Pittsburgh vs. Oakland, 1975 (3 opp)
Ron Jaworski, NFC-FR: Philadelphia vs. N.Y. Giants, 1981 (3 own)
Devin Hester, NFC-D: Chicago vs. Seattle, 2006 (3-own)
2 By many players

YARDS GAINED

Longest Return

93 Andy Russell, AFC-D: Pittsburgh vs. Baltimore, 1975 (opp, TD)
79 Neil Smith, AFC-D: Denver vs. Miami, 1998 (opp, TD)
64 Leon Lett, SB: Dallas vs. Buffalo, 1992 (opp)

TOUCHDOWNS

Most Touchdowns

1 By many players

COMBINED NET YARDS GAINED

Rushing, receiving, interception returns, punt returns, kickoff returns, and fumble returns.

ATTEMPTS

Most Attempts, Career

454 Franco Harris, Pittsburgh, 19 games
417 Thurman Thomas, Buffalo, 21 games
397 Emmitt Smith, Dallas, 17 games

Most Attempts, Game

43 Lamar Smith, AFC-FR: Miami vs. Indianapolis, 2000 (OT)
42 Curtis Martin, AFC-D: N.Y. Jets vs. Jacksonville, 1998
40 Lawrence McCutcheon, NFC-D: Los Angeles vs. St. Louis, 1975

YARDS GAINED

Most Yards Gained, Career

2,289 Jerry Rice, San Francisco-Oakland-Seattle, 29 games
2,124 Thurman Thomas, Buffalo, 21 games
2,060 Franco Harris, Pittsburgh, 19 games

Most Yards Gained, Game

350 Ed Podolak, AFC-D: Kansas City vs. Miami, 1971 (OT)
329 Keith Lincoln, AFC: San Diego vs. Boston, 1963
328 Darren Sproles, AFC-FR: San Diego vs. Indianapolis, 2008 (OT)

SACKS

Sacks have been compiled since 1982.

Most Sacks, Career

16.0 Willie McGinest, New England, 18 games
14.5 Bruce Smith, Buffalo, 20 games
12.0 Reggie White, Philadelphia-Green Bay, 19 games

Most Sacks, Game

4.5 Willie McGinest, AFC-FR: New England vs. Jacksonville, 2005
3.5 Rich Milot, NFC-D: Washington vs. Chicago, 1984
Richard Dent, NFC-D: Chicago vs. N.Y. Giants, 1985
3.0 Richard Dent, NFC-D: Chicago vs. Washington, 1984
Garin Veris, AFC-FR: New England vs. N.Y. Jets, 1985
Gary Jeter, NFC-D: L.A. Rams vs. Dallas, 1985
Carl Hairston, AFC-D: Cleveland vs. N.Y. Jets, 1986 (OT)
Charles Mann, NFC-D: Washington vs. Chicago, 1987
Kevin Greene, NFC-FR: L.A. Rams vs. Minnesota, 1988
Greg Townsend, AFC-D: L.A. Raiders vs. Cincinnati, 1990
Wilber Marshall, NFC: Washington vs. Detroit, 1991
Fred Stokes, NFC-FR: Washington vs. Minnesota, 1992
Pierce Holt, NFC-D: San Francisco vs. Washington, 1992
Tony Casillas, NFC: Dallas vs. San Francisco, 1992
Gerald Williams, AFC-FR: Pittsburgh vs. Kansas City, 1993
Chad Brown, AFC-FR: Pittsburgh vs. Indianapolis, 1996
Reggie White, SB: Green Bay vs. New England, 1996
Warren Sapp, NFC-D: Tampa Bay vs. Green Bay, 1997
Trace Armstrong, AFC-FR: Miami vs. Seattle, 1999
Michael McCrary, AFC-FR: Baltimore vs. Denver, 2000
Willie McGinest, AFC-D: New England vs. Tennessee, 2003
Darnell Dockett, SB: Arizona vs. Pittsburgh, 2008

TEAM RECORDS

CHAMPIONSHIPS

Most Seasons League Champion

12 Green Bay, 1929-1931, 1936, 1939, 1944, 1961-62, 1965-67, 1996
9 Chi. Bears, 1921, 1932-33, 1940-41, 1943, 1946, 1963, 1985
7 N.Y. Giants, 1927, 1934, 1938, 1956, 1986, 1990, 2007

Most Consecutive Seasons League Champion

3 Green Bay, 1929-1931
Green Bay, 1965-67
2 Canton, 1922-23
Chi. Bears, 1932-33
Chi. Bears, 1940-41
Philadelphia, 1948-49
Detroit, 1952-53
Cleveland, 1954-55
Baltimore, 1958-59
Houston, 1960-61
Green Bay, 1961-62
Buffalo, 1964-65
Miami, 1972-73
Pittsburgh, 1974-75
Pittsburgh, 1978-79
San Francisco, 1988-89
Dallas, 1992-93
Denver, 1997-98
New England, 2003-04

GAMES, VICTORIES, DEFEATS

Most Seasons Participating in Postseason Games

30 N.Y. Giants, 1933-35, 1938-39, 1941, 1943-44, 1946, 1950, 1956, 1958-59, 1961-63, 1981, 1984-86, 1989-1990, 1993, 1997, 2000, 2002, 2005-08

29 Dallas, 1966-1973, 1975-1983, 1985, 1991-96, 1998-99, 2003, 2006-07
27 Cleveland/L.A./St. Louis Rams, 1945, 1949-1952, 1955, 1967, 1969, 1973-1980, 1983-86, 1988-89, 1999-2001, 2003-04

Most Consecutive Seasons Participating in Postseason Games
9 Dallas, 1975-1983
8 Dallas, 1966-1973
Pittsburgh, 1972-79
Los Angeles, 1973-1980
San Francisco, 1983-1990
7 Houston, 1987-1993
San Francisco, 1992-98
Indianapolis, 2002-08

Most Games
56 Dallas, 1966-1973, 1975-1983, 1985, 1991-96, 1998-99, 2003, 2006-07
50 Pittsburgh, 1947, 1972-79, 1982-84, 1989, 1992-97, 2001-02, 2004-05, 2007-08
44 N.Y. Giants, 1933-35, 1938-39, 1941, 1943-44, 1946, 1950, 1956, 1958-59, 1961-63, 1981, 1984-86, 1989-1990, 1993, 1997, 2000, 2002, 2005-08

Most Games Won
32 Dallas, 1967, 1970-73, 1975, 1977-78, 1980-82, 1991-96
31 Pittsburgh, 1972, 1974-76, 1978-79, 1984, 1989, 1994-97, 2001-02, 2004-05, 2008
25 Oakland/L.A. Raiders, 1967-1970, 1973-77, 1980, 1982-83, 1990, 1993, 2000-02
San Francisco, 1970-71, 1981, 1983-84, 1988-1990, 1992-94, 1996-98, 2002
Green Bay, 1936, 1939, 1944, 1961-62, 1965-67, 1982, 1993-97, 2001, 2003, 2007

Most Consecutive Games Won
10 New England, 2001, 2003-05
9 Green Bay, 1961-62, 1965-67
7 Pittsburgh, 1974-76
San Francisco, 1988-1990
Dallas, 1992-94
Denver, 1997-98

Most Games Lost
25 Minnesota, 1968-1971, 1973-78, 1980, 1982, 1987-89, 1992-94, 1996-2000, 2004, 2008
24 L.A./St. Louis Rams, 1949-1950, 1952, 1955, 1967, 1969, 1973-1980, 1983-86, 1988-89, 2000-01, 2003-04
Dallas, 1966-1970, 1972-73, 1975-76, 1978-1983, 1985, 1991, 1994, 1996, 1998-99, 2003, 2006-07
N.Y. Giants, 1933, 1935, 1939, 1941, 1943-44, 1946, 1950, 1958-59, 1961-63, 1981, 1984-85, 1989, 1993, 1997, 2000, 2002, 2005-06, 2008
20 Cleveland, 1951-53, 1957-58, 1965, 1967-69, 1971-72, 1980, 1982, 1985-89, 1994, 2002
Miami, 1970-71, 1974, 1978-79, 1981-85, 1990, 1992, 1994-95, 1997-2001, 2008

Most Consecutive Games Lost
6 N.Y. Giants, 1939, 1941, 1943-44, 1946, 1950
Cleveland, 1969, 1971-72, 1980, 1982, 1985
Minnesota, 1988-89, 1992-94, 1996
Detroit, 1991, 1993-95, 1997, 1999 (current)
Seattle, 1984, 1987-88, 1999, 2003-04
Kansas City, 1993-95, 1997, 2003, 2006 (current))
Dallas, 1996, 1998-99, 2003, 2006-07 (current)
5 N.Y. Giants, 1958-59, 1961-63
Los Angeles, 1952, 1955, 1967, 1969, 1973
Denver, 1977-79, 1983-84
Baltimore/Indianapolis, 1971, 1975-77, 1987
Philadelphia, 1980-81, 1988-1990
Indianapolis, 1995-96, 1999-2000, 2002
4 Washington, 1972-74, 1976
Miami, 1974, 1978-79, 1981
Chi. Cardinals/St. Louis, 1948, 1974-75, 1982
Boston/New England, 1963, 1976, 1978, 1982
New Orleans, 1987, 1990-92
Buffalo, 1995-96, 1998-99 (current)
N.Y. Giants, 2000, 2002, 2005-06
San Diego, 1994-95, 2004, 2006

SCORING

Most Points, Game
73 NFC: Chi. Bears vs. Washington, 1940
62 AFC-D: Jacksonville vs. Miami, 1999
59 NFC: Detroit vs. Cleveland, 1957

Most Points, Both Teams, Game
95 NFC-FR: Philadelphia (58) vs. Detroit (37), 1995
86 NFC-D: St. Louis (49) vs. Minnesota (37), 1999
79 AFC-D: San Diego (41) vs. Miami (38), 1981 (OT)
AFC-FR: Buffalo (41) vs. Houston (38), 1992 (OT)

Fewest Points, Both Teams, Game
5 NFC-D: Detroit (0) vs. Dallas (5), 1970
7 NFC: Chi. Cardinals (0) vs. Philadelphia (7), 1948
9 NFC: Tampa Bay (0) vs. Los Angeles (9), 1979

Largest Margin of Victory, Game
73 NFC: Chi. Bears vs. Washington, 1940 (73-0)
55 AFC-D: Jacksonville vs. Miami, 1999 (62-7)
49 AFC-D: Oakland vs. Houston, 1969 (56-7)

Most Points, Shutout Victory, Game
73 NFC: Chi. Bears vs. Washington, 1940
41 NFC: N.Y. Giants vs. Minnesota, 2000
AFC-FR: N.Y. Jets vs. Indianapolis, 2002
38 NFC-D: Dallas vs. Tampa Bay, 1981

Most Points Overcome to Win Game
32 AFC-FR: Buffalo vs. Houston, 1992 (trailed 3-35, won 41-38) (OT)
24 NFC-FR: San Francisco vs. N.Y. Giants, 2002 (trailed 14-38, won 39-38)
20 NFC-D: Detroit vs. San Francisco, 1957 (trailed 7-27, won 31-27)

Most Points, Each Half
1st: 41 AFC: Buffalo vs. L.A. Raiders, 1990
AFC-D: Jacksonville vs. Miami, 1999
38 NFC-D: Washington vs. L.A. Rams, 1983
NFC-FR: Philadelphia vs. Detroit, 1995
35 NFC: Cleveland vs. Detroit, 1954
AFC-D: Oakland vs. Houston, 1969
SB: Washington vs. Denver, 1987
AFC-FR: Indianapolis vs. Denver, 2004
2nd: 45 NFC: Chi. Bears vs. Washington, 1940
35 AFC-FR: Buffalo vs. Houston, 1992
NFC-D: St. Louis vs. Minnesota, 1999
32 AFC: Indianapolis vs. New England, 2006

Most Points, Each Quarter
1st: 28 AFC-D: Oakland vs. Houston, 1969
24 AFC-D: San Diego vs. Miami, 1981
AFC-D: Jacksonville vs. Miami, 1999
21 NFC: Chi. Bears vs. Washington, 1940
AFC: San Diego vs. Boston, 1963
AFC-D: Oakland vs. Kansas City, 1968
AFC: Oakland vs. San Diego, 1980
AFC: Buffalo vs. L.A. Raiders, 1990
NFC: San Francisco vs. Dallas, 1994
2nd: 35 SB: Washington vs. Denver, 1987
31 NFC-FR: Philadelphia vs. Detroit, 1995
26 AFC-D: Pittsburgh vs. Buffalo, 1974
3rd: 28 AFC-FR: Buffalo vs. Houston, 1992
26 NFC: Chi. Bears vs. Washington, 1940
21 NFC-D: Dallas vs. Cleveland, 1967
NFC-D: Dallas vs. Tampa Bay, 1981
AFC-D: L.A. Raiders vs. Pittsburgh, 1983
SB: Chicago vs. New England, 1985
NFC-D: N.Y. Giants vs. San Francisco, 1986
AFC: Cleveland vs. Denver, 1987
AFC: Cleveland vs. Denver, 1989
NFC-D: St. Louis vs. Minnesota, 1999

4th: 27 NFC: N.Y. Giants vs. Chi. Bears, 1934
26 NFC-FR: Philadelphia vs. New Orleans, 1992
24 NFC: Baltimore vs. N.Y. Giants, 1959
OT: 6 NFC: Baltimore vs. N.Y. Giants, 1958
AFC-D: Oakland vs. Baltimore, 1977
NFC-D: L.A. Rams vs. N.Y. Giants, 1989
AFC-FR: Miami vs. Indianapolis, 2000
NFC-FR: Green Bay vs. Seattle, 2003
NFC-D: Carolina vs. St. Louis, 2003
AFC-FR: San Diego vs. Indianapolis, 2008

TOUCHDOWNS

Most Touchdowns, Game

11 NFC: Chi. Bears vs. Washington, 1940
8 NFC: Cleveland vs. Detroit, 1954
NFC: Detroit vs. Cleveland, 1957
AFC-D: Oakland vs. Houston, 1969
SB: San Francisco vs. Denver, 1989
AFC-D: Jacksonville vs. Miami, 1999
7 AFC: San Diego vs. Boston, 1963
NFC-D: Dallas vs. Cleveland, 1967
NFC-D: N.Y. Giants vs. San Francisco, 1986
AFC: Buffalo vs. L.A. Raiders, 1990
SB: Dallas vs. Buffalo, 1992
SB: San Francisco vs. San Diego, 1994
NFC-FR: Philadelphia vs. Detroit, 1995
NFC-D: St. Louis vs. Minnesota, 1999
AFC-FR: Indianapolis vs. Denver, 2004

Most Touchdowns, Both Teams, Game

12 NFC-FR: Philadelphia (7) vs. Detroit (5), 1995
NFC-D: St. Louis (7) vs. Minnesota (5), 1999
11 NFC: Chi. Bears (11) vs. Washington (0), 1940
10 NFC: Detroit (8) vs. Cleveland (2), 1957
AFC-D: Miami (5) vs. San Diego (5), 1981 (OT)
AFC: Miami (6) vs. Pittsburgh (4), 1984
AFC-FR: Buffalo (5) vs. Houston (5), 1992 (OT)
SB: San Francisco (7) vs. San Diego (3), 1994
NFC-FR: San Francisco (5) vs. N.Y. Giants (5), 2002
AFC-FR: Indianapolis (7) vs. Denver (3), 2004

Fewest Touchdowns, Both Teams, Game

0 NFC-D: N.Y. Giants vs. Cleveland, 1950
NFC-D: Dallas vs. Detroit, 1970
NFC: Los Angeles vs. Tampa Bay, 1979
AFC-D: Baltimore vs. Indianapolis, 2006
1 NFC: Chi. Cardinals (0) vs. Philadelphia (1), 1948
NFC-D: Cleveland (0) vs. N.Y. Giants (1), 1958
AFC: San Diego (0) vs. Houston (1), 1961
AFC-D: N.Y. Jets (0) vs. Kansas City (1), 1969
NFC-D: Green Bay (0) vs. Washington (1), 1972
NFC-FR: New Orleans (0) vs. Chicago (1), 1990
NFC: N.Y. Giants (0) vs. San Francisco (1), 1990
AFC-FR: L.A. Raiders (0) vs. Kansas City (1), 1991
AFC-D: New England (0) vs. Pittsburgh (1), 1997
NFC: Tampa Bay (0) vs. St. Louis (1), 1999
AFC: Oakland (0) vs. Baltimore (1), 2000
2 In many games

POINTS AFTER TOUCHDOWN

Most (One-Point) Points After Touchdown, Game

8 NFC: Cleveland vs. Detroit, 1954
NFC: Detroit vs. Cleveland, 1957
AFC-D: Oakland vs. Houston, 1969
AFC-D: Jacksonville vs. Miami, 1999
7 NFC: Chi. Bears vs. Washington, 1940
NFC-D: Dallas vs. Cleveland, 1967
NFC-D: N.Y. Giants vs. San Francisco, 1986
SB: San Francisco vs. Denver, 1989
SB: Dallas vs. Buffalo, 1992
SB: San Francisco vs. San Diego, 1994
NFC-FR: Philadelphia vs. Detroit, 1995
NFC-D: St. Louis vs. Minnesota, 1999
AFC-FR: Indianapolis vs. Denver, 2004
6 AFC: San Diego vs. Boston, 1963
NFC-D: Washington vs. L.A. Rams, 1983
AFC: Miami vs. Pittsburgh, 1984
SB: Washington vs. Denver, 1987
AFC: Buffalo vs. L.A. Raiders, 1990
AFC-FR: L.A. Raiders vs. Denver, 1993
AFC-FR: Denver vs. Jacksonville, 1997
NFC-D: St. Louis vs. Green Bay, 2001
SB: Tampa Bay vs. Oakland, 2002
NFC-D: Atlanta vs. St. Louis, 2004)
NFC-FR: Green Bay vs. Seattle, 2007

Most (One-Point) Points After Touchdown, Both Teams, Game

10 NFC: Detroit (8) vs. Cleveland (2), 1957
AFC-D: Miami (5) vs. San Diego (5), 1981 (OT)
AFC: Miami (6) vs. Pittsburgh (4), 1984
AFC-FR: Buffalo (5) vs. Houston (5), 1992 (OT)
NFC-FR: Philadelphia (7) vs. Detroit (3), 1995
AFC-FR: Indianapolis (7) vs. Denver (3), 2004
9 In many games

Fewest (One-Point) Points After Touchdown, Both Teams, Game

0 NFC-D: N.Y. Giants vs. Cleveland, 1950
NFC-D: Dallas vs. Detroit, 1970
NFC: Los Angeles vs. Tampa Bay, 1979
NFC: St. Louis vs. Tampa Bay, 1999
AFC-D: Baltimore vs. Indianapolis, 2006

Most Two-Point Conversions, Game

2 SB: San Diego vs. San Francisco, 1994
NFC-FR: Detroit vs. Philadelphia, 1995
NFC-FR: San Francisco vs.. N.Y. Giants, 2002
1 By many teams

FIELD GOALS

Most Field Goals, Game

5 NFC-D: Minnesota vs. San Francisco, 1987
NFC: N.Y. Giants vs. San Francisco, 1990
AFC: Buffalo vs. Miami, 1992
NFC-FR: N.Y. Giants vs. Minnesota, 1997
NFC-FR: Carolina vs. Dallas, 2003
NFC-D: St. Louis vs. Carolina, 2003 (2 OT)
AFC: New England vs. Indianapolis, 2003
AFC-D: Indianapolis vs. Baltimore, 2006
4 AFC-D: Boston vs. Buffalo, 1963
AFC: Oakland vs. Houston, 1967
SB: Green Bay vs. Oakland, 1967
NFC: Washington vs. Dallas, 1972
AFC-D: Oakland vs. Pittsburgh, 1973
SB: San Francisco vs. Cincinnati, 1981
AFC-FR: New England vs. N.Y. Jets, 1985
NFC-FR: Washington vs. L.A. Rams, 1986
NFC-D: Philadelphia vs. Chicago, 1988
AFC-FR: Pittsburgh vs. Houston, 1989 (OT)
AFC-D: Pittsburgh vs. Buffalo, 1995
NFC-FR: Dallas vs. Minnesota, 1996
NFC-D: Carolina vs. Dallas, 1996
AFC-FR: Jacksonville vs. New England, 1998
AFC-D: Tennessee vs. Indianapolis, 1999
NFC-D: Philadelphia vs. Chicago, 2001
AFC: San Diego vs. New England, 2007
NFC-FR: Philadelphia vs. Minnesota, 2008
NFC-D: Arizona vs. Carolina, 2008
3 By many teams

Most Field Goals, Both Teams, Game

8 NFC-FR: N.Y. Giants (5) vs. Minnesota (3), 1997
NFC-D: St. Louis (5) vs. Carolina (3), 2003 (2 OT)
7 AFC-FR: Pittsburgh (4) vs. Houston (3), 1989 (OT)
NFC: N.Y. Giants (5) vs. San Francisco (2), 1990
NFC-D: Carolina (4) vs. Dallas (3), 1996
AFC-D: Tennessee (4) vs. Indianapolis (3), 1999
AFC-D: Indianapolis (5) vs. Baltimore (2), 2006
6 NFC-D: Minnesota (5) vs. San Francisco (1), 1987
NFC-D: Philadelphia (4) vs. Chicago (2), 1988
AFC: Buffalo (5) vs. Miami (1), 1992

NFC-FR: Carolina (5) vs. Dallas (1), 2003
AFC-FR: New England (3) vs. N.Y. Jets (3), 2006
NFC-D: N.Y. Giants (3) vs. Philadelphia (3), 2008

Most Field Goals Attempted, Game

6 AFC: Oakland vs. Houston, 1967
NFC-D: Los Angeles vs. Dallas, 1973
AFC-D: Cleveland vs. N.Y. Jets, 1986 (OT)
NFC: N.Y. Giants vs. San Francisco, 1990
AFC: Buffalo vs. Miami, 1992
NFC-D: St. Louis vs. Carolina, 2003 (2 OT)
5 By many teams

Most Field Goals Attempted, Both Teams, Game

11 NFC-D: St. Louis (6) vs. Carolina (5), 2003 (2 OT)
9 NFC-D: Philadelphia (5) vs. Chicago (4), 1988
NFC-FR: N.Y. Giants (5) vs. Minnesota (4), 1997
8 NFC-D: Los Angeles (6) vs. Dallas (2), 1973
NFC-D: Detroit (5) vs. San Francisco (3), 1983
AFC-D: Cleveland (6) vs. N.Y. Jets (2), 1986 (OT)
NFC-D: Minnesota (5) vs. San Francisco (3), 1987
AFC-FR: Houston (4) vs. Pittsburgh (4), 1989 (OT)
NFC-FR: Chicago (4) vs. New Orleans (4), 1990
NFC: N.Y. Giants (6) vs. San Francisco (2), 1990
NFC-D: N.Y. Giants (5) vs. Philadelphia (3), 2008

SAFETIES

Most Safeties, Game

1 By many teams

Most Safeties, Both Teams, Game

1 In many games

FIRST DOWNS

Most First Downs, Game

34 AFC-D: San Diego vs. Miami, 1981 (OT)
33 AFC-D: Cleveland vs. N.Y. Jets, 1986 (OT)
32 AFC: Indianapolis vs. New England, 2006

Fewest First Downs, Game

6 NFC: N.Y. Giants vs. Green Bay, 1961
AFC-D: Baltimore vs. Tennessee, 2000
7 NFC: Green Bay vs. Boston, 1936
NFC-D: Pittsburgh vs. Philadelphia, 1947
NFC: Chi. Cardinals vs. Philadelphia, 1948
NFC: Los Angeles vs. Philadelphia, 1949
NFC-D: Cleveland vs. N.Y. Giants, 1958
AFC-D: Cincinnati vs. Baltimore, 1970
NFC-D: Detroit vs. Dallas, 1970
NFC: Tampa Bay vs. Los Angeles, 1979
AFC-D: Baltimore vs. Pittsburgh, 2001
AFC-FR: Kansas City vs. Indianapolis, 2006
8 By many teams

Most First Downs, Both Teams, Game

59 AFC-D: San Diego (34) vs. Miami (25), 1981 (OT)
55 AFC-FR: San Diego (29) vs. Pittsburgh (26), 1982
54 AFC-FR: Buffalo (28) vs. Miami (26), 1995

Fewest First Downs, Both Teams, Game

15 NFC: Green Bay (7) vs. Boston (8), 1936
19 NFC: N.Y. Giants (9) vs. Green Bay (10), 1939
NFC: Washington (9) vs. Chi. Bears (10), 1942
20 NFC-D: Cleveland (9) vs. N.Y. Giants (11), 1950

RUSHING

Most First Downs, Rushing, Game

19 NFC-FR: Dallas vs. Los Angeles, 1980
18 AFC-D: Miami vs. Cincinnati, 1973
AFC: Miami vs. Oakland, 1973
AFC-D: Pittsburgh vs. Buffalo, 1974
AFC-FR: Buffalo vs. Miami, 1995
AFC-FR: Denver vs. Jacksonville, 1997
17 AFC-D: Cincinnati vs. Seattle, 1988
AFC: Buffalo vs. Kansas City, 1993

Fewest First Downs, Rushing, Game

0 NFC: Los Angeles vs. Philadelphia, 1949
AFC-D: Buffalo vs. Boston, 1963
AFC: Oakland vs. Pittsburgh, 1974
NFC-FR: New Orleans vs. Minnesota, 1987
NFC: L.A. Rams vs. San Francisco, 1989
NFC-D: Chicago vs. N.Y. Giants, 1990
AFC-FR: Indianapolis vs. Pittsburgh, 1996
AFC-FR: Seattle vs. Miami, 1999
AFC-D: Miami vs. Jacksonville, 1999
AFC-D: Miami vs. Oakland, 2000
AFC-D: Baltimore vs. Pittsburgh, 2001
AFC-D: Indianapolis vs. New England, 2004
1 By many teams

Most First Downs, Rushing, Both Teams, Game

26 AFC: Buffalo (14) vs. L.A. Raiders (12), 1990
25 NFC-FR: Dallas (19) vs. Los Angeles (6), 1980
23 NFC: Cleveland (15) vs. Detroit (8), 1952
AFC-D: Miami (18) vs. Cincinnati (5), 1973
AFC-D: Pittsburgh (18) vs. Buffalo (5), 1974
AFC-FR: Buffalo (18) vs. Miami (5), 1995

Fewest First Downs, Rushing, Both Teams, Game

2 NFC-FR: New Orleans (1) vs. St. Louis (1), 2000
5 AFC-D: Buffalo (0) vs. Boston (5), 1963
NFC-D: Washington (1) vs. Tampa Bay (4), 1999
AFC-FR: Cleveland (2) vs. Pittsburgh (3), 2002
6 NFC: Green Bay (2) vs. Boston (4), 1936
NFC-D: Baltimore (2) vs. Minnesota (4), 1968
AFC-D: Houston (1) vs. Oakland (5), 1969
AFC-FR: N.Y. Jets (1) vs. Houston (5), 1991
AFC-FR: Denver (1) vs. Baltimore (5), 2000
AFC: Pittsburgh (1) vs. Baltimore (5), 2008
SB: Arizona (2) vs. Pittsburgh (4), 2008

PASSING

Most First Downs, Passing, Game

24 AFC-FR: Pittsburgh vs. Cleveland, 2002
21 AFC-D: Miami vs. San Diego, 1981 (OT)
AFC-D: San Diego vs. Miami, 1981 (OT)
AFC-D: Cleveland vs. N.Y. Jets, 1986 (OT)
NFC-D: Philadelphia vs. Chicago, 1988)
AFC-D; Indianapolis vs. San Diego, 2007
20 NFC-FR: Dallas vs. L.A. Rams, 1983
AFC-D: Buffalo vs. Cleveland, 1989
AFC-FR: Miami vs. Buffalo, 1995
NFC-FR: Detroit vs. Philadelphia, 1995
AFC-FR: San Diego vs. Indianapolis, 1995
NFC-D: Minnesota vs. St. Louis, 1999
AFC: Indianapolis vs. New England, 2006
SB: Arizona vs. Pittsburgh, 2008

Fewest First Downs, Passing, Game

0 NFC: Philadelphia vs. Chi. Cardinals, 1948
1 NFC-D: N.Y. Giants vs. Washington, 1943
NFC: Cleveland vs. Detroit, 1953
SB: Denver vs. Dallas, 1977
2 By many teams

Most First Downs, Passing, Both Teams, Game

42 AFC-D: Miami (21) vs. San Diego (21), 1981 (OT)
AFC-FR: Pittsburgh (24) vs. Cleveland (18), 2002
38 AFC-FR: Pittsburgh (19) vs. San Diego (19), 1982
NFC-D: Minnesota (20) vs. St. Louis (18), 1999
36 NFC: Minnesota (19) vs. Atlanta (17), 1998 (OT)

Fewest First Downs, Passing, Both Teams, Game

2 NFC: Philadelphia (0) vs. Chi. Cardinals (2), 1948
4 NFC-D: Cleveland (2) vs. N.Y. Giants (2), 1950
5 NFC: Detroit (2) vs. N.Y. Giants (3), 1935
NFC: Green Bay (2) vs. N.Y. Giants (3), 1939

PENALTY

Most First Downs, Penalty, Game

7 AFC-D: New England vs. Oakland, 1976
AFC: Tennessee vs. Oakland, 2002
6 AFC-D: Cleveland vs. N.Y. Jets, 1986 (OT)
NFC-D: Chicago vs. Carolina, 2005
5 AFC-FR: Cleveland vs. L. A. Raiders, 1982

NFC-D: San Francisco vs. Minnesota, 1997
AFC-FR: Miami vs. Buffalo, 1998
NFC-D: Arizona vs. Minnesota, 1998
AFC: Pittsburgh vs. New England, 2001
AFC-D: Pittsburgh vs. Tennessee, 2002 (OT)

Most First Downs, Penalty, Both Teams, Game
10 AFC: Tennessee (7) vs. Oakland (3), 2002
9 AFC-D: New England (7) vs. Oakland (2), 1976
8 NFC-FR: Atlanta (4) vs. Minnesota (4), 1982
AFC-FR: Miami (5) vs. Buffalo (3), 1998

NET YARDS GAINED RUSHING AND PASSING

Most Yards Gained, Game
610 AFC: San Diego vs. Boston, 1963
602 SB: Washington vs. Denver, 1987
569 AFC: Miami vs. Pittsburgh, 1984

Fewest Yards Gained, Game
86 NFC-D: Cleveland vs. N.Y. Giants, 1958
99 NFC: Chi. Cardinals vs. Philadelphia, 1948
114 NFC-D: N.Y. Giants vs. Washington, 1943
NFC: Minnesota vs. N.Y. Giants, 2000

Most Yards Gained, Both Teams, Game
1,038 AFC-FR: Buffalo (536) vs. Miami (502), 1995
1,036 AFC-D: San Diego (564) vs. Miami (472), 1981 (OT)
1,024 AFC: Miami (569) vs. Pittsburgh (455), 1984

Fewest Yards Gained, Both Teams, Game
331 NFC: Chi. Cardinals (99) vs. Philadelphia (232), 1948
332 NFC-D: N.Y. Giants (150) vs. Cleveland (182), 1950
336 NFC: Boston (116) vs. Green Bay (220), 1936

RUSHING

ATTEMPTS

Most Attempts, Game
65 NFC: Detroit vs. N.Y. Giants, 1935
61 NFC: Philadelphia vs. Los Angeles, 1949
59 AFC: New England vs. Miami, 1985

Fewest Attempts, Game
8 AFC-D: Miami vs. San Diego, 1994
9 SB: Miami vs. San Francisco, 1984
NFC: Minnesota vs. N.Y. Giants, 2000
10 NFC: L.A. Rams vs. San Francisco, 1989
NFC-FR: Atlanta vs. Green Bay, 1995
NFC-FR: Detroit vs. Washington, 1999

Most Attempts, Both Teams, Game
109 NFC: Detroit (65) vs. N.Y. Giants (44), 1935
97 AFC-D: Baltimore (50) vs. Oakland (47), 1977 (OT)
91 NFC: Philadelphia (57) vs. Chi. Cardinals (34), 1948

Fewest Attempts, Both Teams, Game
32 AFC-D: Houston (14) vs. Kansas City (18), 1993
37 SB: Arizona (12) vs. Pittsburgh (25), 2008
38 NFC-D: Detroit (16) vs. Dallas (22), 1991

YARDS GAINED

Most Yards Gained, Game
382 NFC: Chi. Bears vs. Washington, 1940
341 AFC-FR: Buffalo vs. Miami, 1995
338 NFC-FR: Dallas vs. Los Angeles, 1980

Fewest Yards Gained, Game
– 4 NFC-FR: Detroit vs. Green Bay, 1994
7 AFC-D: Buffalo vs. Boston, 1963
SB: New England vs. Chicago, 1985
14 AFC-D: Miami vs. Denver, 1998
AFC: N.Y. Jets vs. Denver, 1998

Most Yards Gained, Both Teams, Game
430 NFC-FR: Dallas (338) vs. Los Angeles (92), 1980
426 NFC: Cleveland (227) vs. Detroit (199), 1952
411 AFC-FR: Buffalo (341) vs. Miami (70), 1995

Fewest Yards Gained, Both Teams, Game
77 NFC-FR: Detroit (–4) vs. Green Bay (81), 1994
84 NFC-FR: St. Louis (34) vs. New Orleans (50), 2000
90 AFC-D: Buffalo (7) vs. Boston (83), 1963
NFC-D: Tampa Bay (44) vs. Washington (46), 1999

AVERAGE GAIN

Highest Average Gain, Game
9.94 AFC: San Diego vs. Boston, 1963 (32-318)
9.29 NFC-D: Green Bay vs. Dallas, 1982 (17-158)
8.18 NFC-D: Atlanta vs. St. Louis, 2004 (40-327)

Lowest Average Gain, Game
– 0.27 NFC-FR: Detroit vs. Green Bay, 1994 (15-(– 4))
0.58 AFC-D: Buffalo vs. Boston, 1963 (12-7)
0.64 SB: New England vs. Chicago, 1985 (11-7)

TOUCHDOWNS

Most Touchdowns, Game
7 NFC: Chi. Bears vs. Washington, 1940
6 NFC-D: San Francisco vs. N.Y. Giants, 1993
5 NFC: Cleveland vs. Detroit, 1954
NFC-D: San Francisco vs. Chicago, 1994
AFC-FR: Pittsburgh vs. Indianapolis, 1996
AFC-FR: Denver vs. Jacksonville, 1997

Most Touchdowns, Both Teams, Game
7 NFC: Chi. Bears (7) vs. Washington (0), 1940
6 NFC: Cleveland (5) vs. Detroit (1), 1954
NFC-D: San Francisco (6) vs. N.Y. Giants (0), 1993
NFC-D: San Francisco (5) vs. Chicago (1), 1994
AFC-FR: Denver (5) vs. Jacksonville (1), 1997
5 NFC: Chi. Cardinals (3) vs. Philadelphia (2), 1947
AFC: San Diego (4) vs. Boston (1), 1963
AFC-D: Cincinnati (3) vs. Buffalo (2), 1981
AFC-FR: Pittsburgh (5) vs. Indianapolis (0), 1996
NFC-D: Arizona (3) vs. Minnesota (2), 1998
NFC-FR: Seattle (3) vs. Green Bay (2), 2003 (OT)

PASSING

ATTEMPTS

Most Attempts, Game
66 AFC-FR: Miami vs. Buffalo, 1995
65 AFC-D: Cleveland vs. N.Y. Jets, 1986 (OT)
NFC-D: San Francisco vs. Green Bay, 1995
61 NFC-FR: Minnesota vs. Chicago, 1994

Fewest Attempts, Game
5 NFC: Detroit vs. N.Y. Giants, 1935
6 AFC: Miami vs. Oakland, 1973
7 SB: Miami vs. Minnesota, 1973

Most Attempts, Both Teams, Game
102 AFC-D: San Diego (54) vs. Miami (48), 1981 (OT)
96 AFC: N.Y. Jets (49) vs. Oakland (47), 1968
95 AFC-D: Cleveland (65) vs. N.Y. Jets (30), 1986 (OT)

Fewest Attempts, Both Teams, Game
18 NFC: Detroit (5) vs. N.Y. Giants (13), 1935
23 NFC: Chi. Cardinals (11) vs. Philadelphia (12), 1948
24 NFC-D: Cleveland (9) vs. N.Y. Giants (15), 1950

COMPLETIONS

Most Completions, Game
36 AFC-FR: Houston vs. Buffalo, 1992 (OT)
34 AFC-D: Cleveland vs. N.Y. Jets, 1986 (OT)
AFC-FR: Miami vs. Buffalo, 1995
33 AFC-D: San Diego vs. Miami, 1981 (OT)
NFC-FR: Minnesota vs. Chicago, 1994)
AFC-D: Indianapolis vs. San Diego, 2007

Fewest Completions, Game
2 NFC: Detroit vs. N.Y. Giants, 1935
NFC: Philadelphia vs. Chi. Cardinals, 1948
3 NFC: N.Y. Giants vs. Chi. Bears, 1941
NFC: Green Bay vs. N.Y. Giants, 1944
NFC: Chi. Cardinals vs. Philadelphia, 1947
NFC: Chi. Cardinals vs. Philadelphia, 1948
NFC-D: Cleveland vs. N.Y. Giants, 1950
NFC-D: N.Y. Giants vs. Cleveland, 1950
NFC: Cleveland vs. Detroit, 1953
AFC: Miami vs. Oakland, 1973
4 NFC: N.Y. Giants vs. Detroit, 1935
NFC-D: N.Y. Giants vs. Washington, 1943

NFC-D: Pittsburgh vs. Philadelphia, 1947
NFC-D: Dallas vs. Detroit, 1970
AFC: Miami vs. Baltimore, 1971
SB: Miami vs. Washington, 1982
AFC-FR: Seattle vs. L.A. Raiders, 1984

Most Completions, Both Teams, Game
64 AFC-D: San Diego (33) vs. Miami (31), 1981 (OT)
57 AFC-FR: Houston (36) vs. Buffalo (21), 1992 (OT)
NFC-FR: N.Y. Giants (29) vs. San Francisco (28), 2002
56 NFC-D: Dallas (28) vs. Green Bay (28), 1993
NFC: Minnesota (29) vs. Atlanta (27), 1998 (OT)
NFC-D: Minnesota (29) vs. St. Louis (27), 1999
AFC-FR: Pittsburgh (30) vs. Cleveland (26), 2002

Fewest Completions, Both Teams, Game
5 NFC: Philadelphia (2) vs. Chi. Cardinals (3), 1948
6 NFC: Detroit (2) vs. N.Y. Giants (4), 1935
NFC-D: Cleveland (3) vs. N.Y. Giants (3), 1950
11 NFC: Green Bay (3) vs. N.Y. Giants (8), 1944
NFC-D: Dallas (4) vs. Detroit (7), 1970

COMPLETION PERCENTAGE

Highest Completion Percentage, Game (20 attempts)
92.9 AFC-D: New England vs. Jacksonville, 2007 (28-26)
88.0 SB: N.Y. Giants vs. Denver, 1986 (25-22)
87.1 NFC: San Francisco vs. L.A. Rams, 1989 (31-27)

Lowest Completion Percentage, Game (20 attempts)
18.5 NFC: Tampa Bay vs. Los Angeles, 1979 (27-5)
20.0 NFC-D: N.Y. Giants vs. Washington, 1943 (20-4)
25.8 NFC: Chi. Bears vs. Washington, 1937 (31-8)

YARDS GAINED

Most Yards Gained, Game
483 AFC-D: Cleveland vs. N.Y. Jets, 1986 (OT)
454 AFC-FR: Indianapolis vs. Denver, 2004
435 AFC: Miami vs. Pittsburgh, 1984

Fewest Yards Gained, Game
3 NFC: Chi. Cardinals vs. Philadelphia, 1948
7 NFC: Philadelphia vs. Chi. Cardinals, 1948
9 NFC-D: N.Y. Giants vs. Cleveland, 1950
NFC: Cleveland vs. Detroit, 1953

Most Yards Gained, Both Teams, Game
809 AFC-D: San Diego (415) vs. Miami (394), 1981 (OT)
762 NFC-D: Minnesota (388) vs. St. Louis (374), 1999
752 AFC-FR: Cleveland (409) vs. Pittsburgh (343), 2002

Fewest Yards Gained, Both Teams, Game
10 NFC: Chi. Cardinals (3) vs. Philadelphia (7), 1948
38 NFC-D: N.Y. Giants (9) vs. Cleveland (29), 1950
102 NFC-D: Dallas (22) vs. Detroit (80), 1970

TIMES SACKED

Most Times Sacked, Game
9 AFC: Kansas City vs. Buffalo, 1966
NFC: Chicago vs. San Francisco, 1984
AFC-D: N.Y. Jets vs. Cleveland, 1986 (OT)
AFC-D: Houston vs. Kansas City, 1993
8 NFC: Green Bay vs. Dallas, 1967
NFC: Minnesota vs. Washington, 1987
NFC-D: Philadelphia vs. Green Bay, 2003 (OT)
7 NFC-D: Dallas vs. Los Angeles, 1973
SB: Dallas vs. Pittsburgh, 1975
AFC-FR: Houston vs. Oakland, 1980
NFC-D: Washington vs. Chicago, 1984
SB: New England vs. Chicago, 1985
AFC-FR: Kansas City vs. San Diego, 1992
AFC-D: Pittsburgh vs. Buffalo, 1992

Most Times Sacked, Both Teams, Game
13 AFC: Kansas City (9) vs. Buffalo (4), 1966
AFC-D: N.Y. Jets (9) vs. Cleveland (4), 1986 (OT)
12 NFC-D: Dallas (7) vs. Los Angeles (5), 1973
NFC-D: Washington (7) vs. Chicago (5), 1984
NFC: Chicago (9) vs. San Francisco (3), 1984
AFC-FR: Kansas City (7) vs. San Diego (5), 1992
11 AFC-D: Houston (9) vs. Kansas City (2), 1993

Fewest Times Sacked, Both Teams, Game
0 AFC-D: Buffalo vs. Pittsburgh, 1974
AFC-FR: Pittsburgh vs. San Diego, 1982
AFC: Miami vs. Pittsburgh, 1984
AFC-D: Buffalo vs. Miami, 1990
AFC-D: Denver vs. Houston, 1991
AFC-FR: Buffalo vs. Miami, 1995
AFC-D: Indianapolis vs. Tennessee, 1999)
AFC-D: Indianapolis vs. San Diego, 2007
NFC-D: N.Y. Giants vs. Philadelphia, 2008
1 In many games

TOUCHDOWNS

Most Touchdowns, Game
6 AFC-D: Oakland vs. Houston, 1969
SB: San Francisco vs. San Diego, 1994
5 NFC: Chi. Bears vs. Washington, 1943
NFC: Detroit vs. Cleveland, 1957
AFC-D: Oakland vs. Kansas City, 1968
SB: San Francisco vs. Denver, 1989
NFC-D: St. Louis vs. Minnesota, 1999
NFC: N.Y. Giants vs. Minnesota, 2000
AFC-FR: Indianapolis vs. Denver, 2003
4 By many teams

Most Touchdowns, Both Teams, Game
9 NFC-D: St. Louis (5) vs. Minnesota (4), 1999
8 AFC-FR: Buffalo (4) vs. Houston (4), 1992 (OT)
7 NFC: Chi. Bears (5) vs. Washington (2), 1943
AFC-D: Oakland (6) vs. Houston (1), 1969
SB: Pittsburgh (4) vs. Dallas (3), 1978
AFC-D: Miami (4) vs. San Diego (3), 1981 (OT)
AFC: Miami (4) vs. Pittsburgh (3), 1984
AFC-D: Buffalo (4) vs. Cleveland (3), 1989
SB: San Francisco (6) vs. San Diego (1), 1994
NFC-FR: Detroit (4) vs. Philadelphia (3), 1995
NFC-FR: New Orleans (4) vs. St. Louis (3), 2000
NFC-FR: N.Y. Giants (4) vs. San Francisco (3), 2002
NFC: Arizona (4) vs. Philadelphia (3), 2008

INTERCEPTIONS BY

Most Interceptions By, Game
8 NFC: Chi. Bears vs. Washington, 1940
7 NFC: Cleveland vs. Los Angeles, 1955
6 NFC: Green Bay vs. N.Y. Giants, 1939
NFC: Chi. Bears vs. N.Y. Giants, 1946
NFC: Cleveland vs. Detroit, 1954
AFC: San Diego vs. Houston, 1961
AFC: Buffalo vs. L.A. Raiders, 1990
NFC-FR: Philadelphia vs. Detroit, 1995
NFC-D: St. Louis vs. Green Bay, 2001

Most Interceptions By, Both Teams, Game
10 NFC: Cleveland (7) vs. Los Angeles (3), 1955
AFC: San Diego (6) vs. Houston (4), 1961
9 NFC: Green Bay (6) vs. N.Y. Giants (3), 1939
8 NFC: Chi. Bears (8) vs. Washington (0), 1940
NFC: Chi. Bears (6) vs. N.Y. Giants (2), 1946
NFC: Cleveland (6) vs. Detroit (2), 1954
AFC-FR: Buffalo (4) vs. N.Y. Jets (4), 1981
AFC: Miami (5) vs. N.Y. Jets (3), 1982

YARDS GAINED

Most Yards Gained, Game
172 SB: Tampa Bay vs. Oakland, 2002
161 NFC-D: St. Louis vs. Green Bay, 2001
138 AFC-FR: N.Y. Jets vs. Cincinnati, 1982

Most Yards Gained, Both Teams, Game
184 SB: Tampa Bay (172) vs. Oakland (12), 2002
161 NFC-D: St. Louis (161) vs. Green Bay (0), 2001
156 NFC: Green Bay (123) vs. N.Y. Giants (33), 1939

TOUCHDOWNS

Most Touchdowns, Game

3 NFC: Chi. Bears vs. Washington, 1940
NFC-D: St. Louis vs. Green Bay, 2001
SB: Tampa Bay vs. Oakland, 2002
2 NFC-D: Los Angeles vs. St. Louis, 1975
NFC-FR: Philadelphia vs. Detroit, 1995)
NFC-FR: Seattle vs. Washington, 2007
1 In many games

Most Touchdowns, Both Teams, Game

3 NFC: Chi. Bears (3) vs. Washington (0), 1940
NFC-D: St. Louis (3) vs. Green Bay (0), 2001
SB: Tampa Bay (3) vs. Oakland (0), 2002
2 NFC-D: Los Angeles (2) vs. St. Louis (0), 1975
NFC-D: Dallas (1) vs. Green Bay (1), 1982
NFC-D: Minnesota (1) vs. San Francisco (1), 1987
NFC-FR: Detroit (1) vs. Green Bay (1), 1993
NFC-FR: Philadelphia (2) vs. Detroit (0), 1995
AFC-FR: Buffalo (1) vs. Jacksonville (1), 1996)
NFC-FR: Seattle (2) vs. Washington (0), 2007
1 In many games

PUNTING

Most Punts, Game

14 AFC-D: N.Y. Jets vs. Cleveland, 1986 (OT)
13 NFC: N.Y. Giants vs. Chi. Bears, 1933
AFC-D: Baltimore vs. Oakland, 1977 (OT)
11 AFC: Houston vs. Oakland, 1967
AFC-D: Houston vs. Oakland, 1969
NFC: L.A. Rams vs. Chicago, 1985
SB: N.Y. Giants vs. Baltimore, 2000

Fewest Punts, Game

0 NFC-FR: St. Louis vs. Green Bay, 1982
AFC-FR: N.Y. Jets vs. Cincinnati, 1982
AFC-FR: Indianapolis vs. Denver, 2003
AFC-D: Kansas City vs. Indianapolis, 2003
AFC-D: Indianapolis vs. Kansas City, 2003
1 By many teams

Most Punts, Both Teams, Game

23 NFC: N.Y. Giants (13) vs. Chi. Bears (10), 1933
22 AFC-D: N.Y. Jets (14) vs. Cleveland (8), 1986 (OT)
21 AFC-D: Baltimore (13) vs. Oakland (8), 1977 (OT)
NFC: L.A. Rams (11) vs. Chicago (10), 1985
SB: N.Y. Giants (11) vs. Baltimore (10), 2000

Fewest Punts, Both Teams, Game

0 AFC-D: Kansas City vs. Indianapolis, 2003
1 NFC-FR: St. Louis (0) vs. Green Bay (1), 1982
2 AFC-FR: N.Y. Jets (0) vs. Cincinnati (2), 1982
SB: Atlanta (1) vs. Denver (1), 1998
AFC-FR: Indianapolis (0) vs. Denver (2), 2003)
AFC-D: New England (1) vs. Jacksonville (1), 2007

AVERAGE YARDAGE

Highest Average, Punting, Game (4 punts)

56.0 AFC: Oakland vs. San Diego, 1980
53.3 AFC-D: Tennessee vs. Baltimore, 2008
52.8 AFC: Indianapolis vs. New England, 2006

Lowest Average, Punting, Game (4 punts)

24.9 NFC: Washington vs. Chi. Bears, 1937
25.3 AFC-FR: Pittsburgh vs. Houston, 1989
25.5 NFC: Green Bay vs. N.Y. Giants, 1962

PUNT RETURNS

Most Punt Returns, Game

8 NFC: Green Bay vs. N.Y. Giants, 1944
7 By many teams

Most Punt Returns, Both Teams, Game

13 AFC-FR: Houston (7) vs. Oakland (6), 1980
12 AFC-D: New England (7) vs. Pittsburgh (5), 1996
11 NFC: Green Bay (8) vs. N.Y. Giants (3), 1944
NFC-D: Green Bay (6) vs. Baltimore (5), 1965
AFC-FR: Jacksonville (7) vs. New England (4), 1998
AFC: Baltimore (6) vs. Pittsburgh (5), 2008

Fewest Punt Returns, Both Teams, Game

0 NFC: Chi. Bears vs. N.Y. Giants, 1941
AFC: Boston vs. San Diego, 1963
NFC-FR: Green Bay vs. St. Louis, 1982
AFC-FR: Houston vs. N.Y. Jets, 1991
AFC-D: Denver vs. Houston, 1991
NFC-D: San Francisco vs. Washington, 1992
SB: Denver vs. Green Bay, 1997
SB: Atlanta vs. Denver, 1998
AFC-FR: Oakland vs. N.Y. Jets, 2001
AFC-D: N.Y. Jets vs. Oakland, 2002
AFC-FR: Denver vs. Indianapolis, 2003
NFC-D: Carolina vs. St. Louis, 2003
AFC-D: Indianapolis vs. Kansas City, 2003
1 In many games

YARDS GAINED

Most Yards Gained, Game

155 NFC-D: Dallas vs. Cleveland, 1967
152 NFC-D: Atlanta vs. St. Louis, 2004
150 NFC: Chi. Cardinals vs. Philadelphia, 1947

Fewest Yards Gained, Game

–10 NFC: Green Bay vs. Cleveland, 1965
–9 NFC: Dallas vs. Green Bay, 1966
AFC-D: Kansas City vs. Oakland, 1968
–7 NFC-D: San Francisco vs. Atlanta, 1998

Most Yards Gained, Both Teams, Game

166 NFC-D: Dallas (155) vs. Cleveland (11), 1967
AFC-D: Baltimore (99) vs. Pittsburgh (67), 2001
160 NFC: Chi. Cardinals (150) vs. Philadelphia (10), 1947
152 NFC-D: Atlanta (152) vs. St. Louis (0), 2004

Fewest Yards Gained, Both Teams, Game

–9 NFC: Dallas (–9) vs. Green Bay (0), 1966
–6 AFC-D: Miami (–5) vs. Oakland (–1), 1970
–3 NFC-D: San Francisco (–5) vs. Dallas (2), 1972

TOUCHDOWNS

Most Touchdowns, Game

1 By 19 teams

KICKOFF RETURNS

Most Kickoff Returns, Game

10 NFC-D: L.A. Rams vs. Washington, 1983
NFC-FR: Detroit vs. Philadelphia, 1995
9 NFC: Chi. Bears vs. N.Y. Giants, 1956
AFC: Boston vs. San Diego, 1963
AFC: Houston vs. Oakland, 1967
SB: Denver vs. San Francisco, 1989
AFC-D: Miami vs. Buffalo, 1990
AFC: L.A. Raiders vs. Buffalo, 1990
AFC-D: Miami vs. Jacksonville, 1999
SB: Oakland vs. Tampa Bay, 2002
8 By many teams

Most Kickoff Returns, Both Teams, Game

15 AFC-D: Miami (9) vs. Buffalo (6), 1990
14 NFC-FR: Detroit (10) vs. Philadelphia (4), 1995
13 NFC-D: Green Bay (7) vs. Dallas (6), 1982
NFC-FR: Green Bay (7) vs. San Francisco (6), 1998
AFC-FR: N.Y. Jets (8) vs. Oakland (5), 2001
NFC-FR: San Francisco (7) vs. N.Y. Giants (6), 2002
AFC-D: Tennessee (7) vs. Pittsburgh (6), 2002
SB: Oakland (9) vs. Tampa Bay (4), 2002
NFC-FR: Seattle (7) vs. Green Bay (6), 2003 (OT)
AFC-D: Kansas City (7) vs. Indianapolis (6), 2003
AFC: Pittsburgh (8) vs. New England (5), 2004
AFC: New England (8) vs. Indianapolis (5), 2006

Fewest Kickoff Returns, Both Teams, Game

1 NFC: Green Bay (0) vs. Boston (1), 1936
AFC-FR: San Diego (0) vs. Kansas City (1), 1992
2 NFC-D: Los Angeles (0) vs. Chi. Bears (2), 1950
AFC: Houston (0) vs. San Diego (2), 1961

AFC-D: Oakland (1) vs. Pittsburgh (1), 1972
AFC-D: N.Y. Jets (0) vs. L.A. Raiders (2), 1982
AFC: Miami (1) vs. N.Y. Jets (1), 1982
NFC: N.Y. Giants (0) vs. Washington (2), 1986
3 In many games

YARDS GAINED

Most Yards Gained, Game
244 SB: San Diego vs. San Francisco, 1994
231 AFC: New England vs. Indianapolis, 2006
227 SB: Atlanta vs. Denver, 1998

Most Yards Gained, Both Teams, Game
379 AFC-D: Baltimore (193) vs. Oakland (186), 1977 (OT)
348 NFC-D: Minnesota (174) vs. St. Louis (174), 1999
323 AFC-D: New England (231) vs. Indianapolis (92), 2006

Fewest Yards Gained, Both Teams, Game
5 AFC-FR: San Diego (0) vs. Kansas City (5), 1992
15 NFC: N.Y. Giants (0) vs. Washington (15), 1986
31 NFC-D: Los Angeles (0) vs. Chi. Bears (31), 1950

TOUCHDOWNS

Most Touchdowns, Game
1 NFC-D: San Francisco vs. Dallas, 1972
AFC-D: Miami vs. Oakland, 1974
AFC-D: Baltimore vs. Oakland, 1977 (OT)
SB: Miami vs. Washington, 1982
SB: Cincinnati vs. San Francisco, 1988
AFC-D: Cleveland vs. Buffalo, 1989
SB: San Diego vs. San Francisco, 1994
SB: Green Bay vs. New England, 1996
NFC: San Francisco vs. Green Bay, 1997
SB: Atlanta vs. Denver, 1998
AFC-FR: Tennessee vs. Buffalo, 1999
AFC-FR: Seattle vs. Miami, 1999
NFC-D: Washington vs. Tampa Bay, 1999
NFC-D: St. Louis vs. Minnesota, 1999
AFC: Tennessee vs. Jacksonville, 1999
NFC-D: N.Y. Giants vs. Philadelphia, 2000
SB: Baltimore vs. N.Y. Giants, 2000
SB: N.Y. Giants vs. Baltimore, 2000
AFC-D: Kansas City vs. Indianapolis, 2003
NFC-FR: Dallas vs. Seattle, 2006
SB: Chicago vs. Indianapolis, 2006

Most Touchdowns, Both Teams, Game
2 SB: Baltimore (1) vs. N.Y. Giants (1), 2000

PENALTIES

Most Penalties, Game
17 AFC-FR: L.A. Raiders vs. Denver, 1993
14 AFC-FR: Oakland vs. Houston, 1980
NFC-D: San Francisco vs. N.Y. Giants, 1981
AFC: Oakland vs. Tennessee, 2002
13 AFC-FR: Houston vs. Cleveland, 1988
AFC-D: Houston vs. Denver, 1991
NFC-D: Arizona vs. Minnesota, 1998
NFC-D: Carolina vs. St. Louis, 2003 (2 OT)

Fewest Penalties, Game
0 NFC: Philadelphia vs. Green Bay, 1960
NFC-D: Detroit vs. Dallas, 1970
AFC-D: Miami vs. Oakland, 1970
SB: Miami vs. Dallas, 1971
NFC-D: Washington vs. Minnesota, 1973
SB: Pittsburgh vs. Dallas, 1975
NFC: San Francisco vs. Chicago, 1988
SB: Denver vs. San Francisco, 1989
AFC-D: L.A. Raiders vs. Cincinnati, 1990
AFC-D: Miami vs. San Diego, 1992
SB: Atlanta vs. Denver, 1998
AFC-FR: N.Y. Jets vs. Oakland, 2001
NFC-FR: Carolina vs. Dallas, 2003
1 By many teams

Most Penalties, Both Teams, Game
27 AFC-FR: L.A. Raiders (17) vs. Denver (10), 1993
22 AFC-FR: Oakland (14) vs. Houston (8), 1980
NFC-D: San Francisco (14) vs. N.Y. Giants (8), 1981
AFC-FR: Houston (13) vs. Cleveland (9), 1988
NFC-D: Arizona (13) vs. Minnesota (9), 1998
21 AFC-D: Oakland (11) vs. New England (10), 1976
AFC: Oakland (14) vs. Tennessee (7), 2002

Fewest Penalties, Both Teams, Game
1 AFC-D: L.A. Raiders (0) vs. Cincinnati (1), 1990
2 NFC: Washington (1) vs. Chi. Bears (1), 1937
NFC-D: Washington (0) vs. Minnesota (2), 1973
SB: Pittsburgh (0) vs. Dallas (2), 1975
NFC-FR: Carolina (0) vs. Dallas (2), 2003
3 AFC: Miami (1) vs. Baltimore (2), 1971
NFC: San Francisco (1) vs. Dallas (2), 1971
SB: Miami (0) vs. Dallas (3), 1971
AFC-D: Pittsburgh (1) vs. Oakland (2), 1972
AFC-D: Miami (1) vs. Cincinnati (2), 1973
SB: Miami (1) vs. San Francisco (2), 1984
NFC: San Francisco (0) vs. Chicago (3), 1988
AFC: New England (1) vs. Pittsburgh (2), 2004
AFC: San Diego (1) vs. New England (2), 2007

YARDS PENALIZED

Most Yards Penalized, Game
145 NFC-D: San Francisco vs. N.Y. Giants, 1981
133 SB: Dallas vs. Baltimore, 1970
130 AFC-FR: L.A. Raiders vs. Denver, 1993

Fewest Yards Penalized, Game
0 By many teams

Most Yards Penalized, Both Teams, Game
227 AFC-FR: L.A. Raiders (130) vs. Denver (97), 1993
206 NFC-D: San Francisco (145) vs. N.Y. Giants (61), 1981
201 NFC-FR: Detroit (126) vs. Washington (75), 1999

Fewest Yards Penalized, Both Teams, Game
5 AFC-D: L.A. Raiders (0) vs. Cincinnati (5), 1990
9 NFC-D: Washington (0) vs. Minnesota (9), 1973
11 NFC-FR: Carolina (0) vs. Dallas (11), 2003

FUMBLES

Most Fumbles, Game
8 SB: Buffalo vs. Dallas, 1992
7 AFC-D: Houston vs. Kansas City, 1993
6 By 12 teams

Most Fumbles, Both Teams, Game
12 AFC: Houston (6) vs. Pittsburgh (6), 1978
SB: Buffalo (8) vs. Dallas (4), 1992
10 NFC: Chi. Bears (5) vs. N.Y. Giants (5), 1934
SB: Dallas (6) vs. Denver (4), 1977
AFC: Jacksonville (5) vs. Tennessee (5), 1999
9 NFC-D: San Francisco (6) vs. Detroit (3), 1957
NFC-D: San Francisco (5) vs. Dallas (4), 1972
NFC: Dallas (5) vs. Philadelphia (4), 1980

Most Fumbles Lost, Game
5 SB: Buffalo vs. Dallas, 1992
AFC-D: Miami vs. Jacksonville, 1999
4 NFC: N.Y. Giants vs. Baltimore, 1958 (OT)
AFC: Kansas City vs. Oakland, 1969
SB: Baltimore vs. Dallas, 1970
AFC: Pittsburgh vs. Oakland, 1975
SB: Denver vs. Dallas, 1977
AFC: Houston vs. Pittsburgh, 1978
AFC: Miami vs. New England, 1985
SB: New England vs. Chicago, 1985
NFC-FR: L.A. Rams vs. Washington, 1986
NFC-FR: Minnesota vs. Dallas, 1996
AFC-FR: Buffalo vs. Miami, 1998
AFC: N.Y. Jets vs. Denver, 1998
AFC: Jacksonville vs. Tennessee, 1999
3 By many teams

Fewest Fumbles, Both Teams, Game

0 NFC: Green Bay vs. Cleveland, 1965
AFC-D: Houston vs. San Diego, 1979
NFC-D: Dallas vs. Los Angeles, 1979
SB: Los Angeles vs. Pittsburgh, 1979
AFC-D: Buffalo vs. Cincinnati, 1981
NFC: Minnesota vs. Washington, 1987
NFC-D: San Francisco vs. Washington, 1990
NFC: Dallas vs. Green Bay, 1995
AFC-D: New England vs. Pittsburgh, 1996
SB: Green Bay vs. New England, 1996
AFC-FR: Miami vs. Seattle, 1999
AFC-FR: Miami vs. Indianapolis, 2000 (OT)
AFC-D: Baltimore vs. Tennessee, 2000
SB: Pittsburgh vs. Seattle, 2005

1 In many games

RECOVERIES

Most Total Fumbles Recovered, Game

8 SB: Dallas vs. Denver, 1977 (4 own, 4 opp)

7 NFC: Chi. Bears vs. N.Y. Giants, 1934 (5 own, 2 opp)
NFC-D: San Francisco vs. Detroit, 1957 (4 own, 3 opp)
NFC-D: San Francisco vs. Dallas, 1972 (4 own, 3 opp)
AFC: Pittsburgh vs. Houston, 1978 (3 own, 4 opp)

6 AFC: Houston vs. San Diego, 1961 (4 own, 2 opp)
AFC-D: Cleveland vs. Baltimore, 1971 (4 own, 2 opp)
AFC-D: Cleveland vs. Oakland, 1980 (5 own, 1 opp)
NFC: Philadelphia vs. Dallas, 1980 (3 own, 3 opp)
SB: Dallas vs. Buffalo, 1992 (1 own, 5 opp)
NFC-D: Green Bay vs. San Francisco, 1996 (4 own, 2 opp)
AFC: Denver vs. N.Y. Jets, 1998 (2 own, 4 opp)
AFC: Tennessee vs. Jacksonville, 1999 (2 own, 4 opp)

Most Own Fumbles Recovered, Game

5 NFC: Chi. Bears vs. N.Y. Giants, 1934
AFC-D: Cleveland vs. Oakland, 1980

4 By many teams

TOUCHDOWNS

Most Touchdowns, Game

2 SB: Dallas vs. Buffalo, 1992

TURNOVERS

Numbers of times losing the ball on interceptions and fumbles.

Most Turnovers, Game

9 NFC: Washington vs. Chi. Bears, 1940
NFC: Detroit vs. Cleveland, 1954
AFC: Houston vs. Pittsburgh, 1978
SB: Buffalo vs. Dallas, 1992

8 NFC: N.Y. Giants vs. Chi. Bears, 1946
NFC: Los Angeles vs. Cleveland, 1955
NFC: Cleveland vs. Detroit, 1957
SB: Denver vs. Dallas, 1977
NFC-D: Minnesota vs. Philadelphia, 1980
NFC-D: Green Bay vs. St. Louis, 2001

7 In many games

Fewest Turnovers, Game

0 By many teams

Most Turnovers, Both Teams, Game

14 AFC: Houston (9) vs. Pittsburgh (5), 1978

13 NFC: Detroit (9) vs. Cleveland (4), 1954
AFC: Houston (7) vs. San Diego (6), 1961

12 AFC: Pittsburgh (7) vs. Oakland (5), 1975

Fewest Turnovers, Both Teams, Game

0 SB: Buffalo vs. N.Y. Giants, 1990
AFC-FR: Kansas City vs. Pittsburgh, 1993 (OT)
NFC-FR: Detroit vs. Green Bay, 1994
AFC-FR: Denver vs. Jacksonville, 1996
SB: St. Louis vs. Tennessee, 1999

1 AFC-D: Baltimore (0) vs. Cincinnati (1), 1970
AFC-D: Pittsburgh (0) vs. Buffalo (1), 1974
AFC: Oakland (0) vs. Pittsburgh (1), 1976
NFC-D: Minnesota (0) vs. Washington (1), 1982
NFC-D: Chicago (0) vs. N.Y. Giants (1), 1985
SB: N.Y. Giants (0) vs. Denver (1), 1986
NFC: Washington (0) vs. Minnesota (1), 1987
AFC-D: Cincinnati (0) vs. L.A. Raiders (1), 1990
NFC: N.Y. Giants (0) vs. San Francisco (1), 1990
NFC-FR: N.Y. Giants (0) vs. Minnesota (1), 1993
AFC-FR: L.A. Raiders (0) vs. Denver (1), 1993
NFC: Dallas (0) vs. San Francisco (1), 1993
AFC: Indianapolis (0) vs. Pittsburgh (1), 1995
NFC-D: San Francisco (0) vs. Minnesota (1), 1997
AFC-D: Indianapolis (0) vs. Tennessee (1), 1999
AFC-FR: Baltimore (0) vs. Denver (1), 2000
AFC-D: Baltimore (0) vs. Tennessee (1), 2000
AFC-D: Oakland (0) vs. New England (1), 2001
NFC-FR: Green Bay (0) vs. Seattle (1), 2003 (OT)
AFC-D: Indianapolis (0) vs. Kansas City (1), 2003
AFC-FR: N.Y. Jets (0) vs. San Diego (1), 2004 (OT)
NFC: Philadelphia (0) vs. Atlanta (1), 2003
NFC-FR: Philadelphia (0) vs. N.Y. Giants (1), 2006
NFC-D: Philadelphia (0) vs. New Orleans (1), 2006
NFC-D: N.Y. Giants (0) vs. Dallas (1), 2007

2 In many games

AFC-NFC PRO BOWL RECORDS

Includes records of AFC-NFC Pro Bowls, 1971-2009
Compiled by Elias Sports Bureau

INDIVIDUAL RECORDS

SERVICE

Most Games

12 Randall McDaniel, Minnesota 1990-2000; Tampa Bay 2001
Will Shields, Kansas City, 1996-2007
11 *Reggie White, Philadelphia, 1987-1993; Green Bay, 1994, 1996-97, 1999
Junior Seau, San Diego, 1992-2002
Rod Woodson, Pittsburgh, 1990-95, 1997; Baltimore, 2000-02; Oakland, 2003
10 Lawrence Taylor, N.Y. Giants, 1982-1991
Ronnie Lott, San Francisco, 1982-85, 1987-1991; L.A. Raiders 1992
Mike Singletary, Chicago, 1984-1993
**Bruce Matthews, Houston, 1989-1995, 1997; Tennessee, 2000, 2002
***Jerry Rice, San Francisco, 1987-88, 1990-94, 1996, 1999; Oakland, 2003

**Also selected, but did not play, in two additional games*
***Also selected, but did not play, in four additional games*
****Also selected but did not play, in three additional games*

SCORING

POINTS

Most Points, Career

45 Morten Andersen, New Orleans, 1986-89, 1991, 1993; Atlanta, 1996 (15-pat, 10-fg)
30 Jan Stenerud, Kansas City, 1971-72, 1976; Minnesota, 1985 (6-pat, 8-fg)
Jimmy Smith, Jacksonville, 1998-2001 (5-td)
Marvin Harrison, Indianapolis, 2000-06 (5-td)
Tony Gonzalez, Kansas City, 2000-01, 2003-09 (5-td)
29 David Akers, Philadelphia, 2002-03, 2005 (8-pat, 7-fg)

Most Points, Game

18 John Brockington, Green Bay, 1973 (3-td)
Mike Alstott, Tampa Bay, 2000 (3-td)
Jimmy Smith, Jacksonville, 2000 (3-td)
Shaun Alexander, Seattle, 2004 (3-td)
15 Garo Yepremian, Miami, 1974 (5-fg)
Jason Hanson, Detroit, 2000 (6-pat, 3-fg)
14 Jan Stenerud, Kansas City, 1972 (2-pat, 4-fg)

TOUCHDOWNS

Most Touchdowns, Career

5 Jimmy Smith, Jacksonville, 1998-2001 (5-p)
Marvin Harrison, Indianapolis, 2000-06 (5-p)
Tony Gonzalez, Kansas City, 2000-01, 2003-09 (5-p)
4 Mike Alstott, Tampa Bay, 1998-2003 (3-r, 1-p)
Hines Ward, Pittsburgh, 2002-05 (3-p, 1-ret)
Terrell Owens, San Francisco, 2001-04; Dallas, 2008 (4-p)
3 John Brockington, Green Bay, 1972-74 (2-r, 1-p)
Earl Campbell, Houston, 1979-1982, 1984 (3-r)
Chuck Muncie, New Orleans, 1980; San Diego, 1982-83 (3-r)
William Andrews, Atlanta, 1981-84 (1-r, 2-p)
Marcus Allen, L.A. Raiders, 1983, 1985-86, 1988; Kansas City, 1994 (2-r, 1-p)
Cris Carter, Minnesota, 1994-2001 (3-p)
Curtis Martin, New England, 1996-97; N.Y. Jets, 1999, 2002 (2-r, 1-p)
Shaun Alexander, Seattle, 2004 (2-r, 1-p)
Torry Holt, St. Louis, 2001-02, 2004-06, 2008 (3-p)
Larry Fitzgerald, Arizona, 2006, 2008-09 (3-p)
Adrian Peterson, Minnesota, 2008-09 (3-r)

Most Touchdowns, Game

3 John Brockington, Green Bay, 1973 (2-r, 1-p)
Mike Alstott, Tampa Bay, 2000 (3-r)
Jimmy Smith, Jacksonville, 2000 (3-p)
Shaun Alexander, Seattle, 2004 (2-r, 1-p)
2 Mel Renfro, Dallas, 1971 (2-ret)
Earl Campbell, Houston, 1980 (2-r)
Chuck Muncie, New Orleans, 1980 (2-r)
William Andrews, Atlanta, 1984 (2-p)
Herschel Walker, Dallas, 1989 (2-r)
Johnny Johnson, Phoenix, 1991 (2-r)
Eric Green, Pittsburgh, 1995 (2-p)
Marvin Harrison, Indianapolis, 2001 (2-p)
Ricky Williams, Miami, 2003 (2-r)
Hines Ward, Pittsburgh, 2005 (1-p, 1-ret)
T.J. Houshmandzadeh, Cincinnati, 2008 (2-p)
Terrell Owens, Dallas, 2008 (2-p)
Adrian Peterson, Minnesota, 2008 (2-r)
Larry Fitzgerald, Arizona, 2009 (2-p)

POINTS AFTER TOUCHDOWN

Most Points After Touchdown, Career

15 Morten Andersen, New Orleans, 1986-89, 1991, 1993; Atlanta, 1996 (15 att)
11 Adam Vinatieri, New England, 2003, 2005 (11 att)
9 Jason Hanson, Detroit, 1998, 2000 (9 att)

Most Points After Touchdown, Game

7 Mike Vanderjagt, Indianapolis, 2004 (7 att)
6 Ali Haji-Sheikh, N.Y. Giants, 1984 (6 att)
Jason Hanson, Detroit, 2000 (6 att)
Adam Vinatieri, New England, 2003 (6 att)
Nick Folk, Dallas, 2008 (6 att)
5 John Carney, San Diego, 1995 (5 att)
Matt Stover, Baltimore, 2001 (5 att)
Jason Elam, Denver, 2002 (5 att)
Jeff Wilkins, St. Louis, 2004 (5 att)
Adam Vinatieri, New England, 2005 (5 att)

FIELD GOALS

Most Field Goals Attempted, Career

18 Morten Andersen, New Orleans, 1986-89, 1991, 1993; Atlanta, 1996
15 Jan Stenerud, Kansas City, 1971-72, 1976; Minnesota, 1985
10 Nick Lowery, Kansas City, 1982, 1991, 1993

Most Field Goals Attempted, Game

6 Jan Stenerud, Kansas City, 1972
Eddie Murray, Detroit, 1981
Mark Moseley, Washington, 1983
5 Garo Yepremian, Miami, 1974
4 Jan Stenerud, Kansas City, 1976
Nick Lowery, Kansas City, 1991, 1993
Morten Andersen, New Orleans, 1993
Cary Blanchard, Indianapolis, 1997
John Kasay, Carolina, 1997
David Akers, Philadelphia, 2002
Jeff Wilkins, St. Louis, 2004

Most Field Goals, Career

10 Morten Andersen, New Orleans, 1986-89, 1991, 1993; Atlanta, 1996
8 Jan Stenerud, Kansas City, 1971-72, 1976; Minnesota, 1985
7 Nick Lowery, Kansas City, 1982, 1991, 1993
David Akers, Philadelphia, 2002-03, 2005

Most Field Goals, Game

5 Garo Yepremian, Miami, 1974 (5 att)
4 Jan Stenerud, Kansas City, 1972 (6 att)

Eddie Murray, Detroit, 1981 (6 att)
3 Nick Lowery, Kansas City, 1991 (4 att)
Nick Lowery, Kansas City, 1993 (4 att)
Jason Elam, Denver, 1999 (3 att)
Jason Hanson, Detroit, 2000 (3 att)
David Akers, Philadelphia, 2002 (4 att)
Neil Rackers, Arizona, 2006 (3 att)
Rob Bironas, Tennessee, 2008 (3 att)
John Carney, N.Y. Giants, 2009 (3 att)

Longest Field Goal
53 David Akers, Philadelphia, 2003
51 Morten Andersen, New Orleans, 1989
Jason Hanson, Detroit, 2000
49 Fuad Reveiz, Minnesota, 1995
David Akers, Philadelphia, 2002

SAFETIES
Most Safeties, Game
1 Art Still, Kansas City, 1983
Mark Gastineau, N.Y. Jets, 1985
Greg Townsend, L.A. Raiders, 1992

RUSHING
ATTEMPTS
Most Attempts, Career
81 Walter Payton, Chicago, 1977-1981, 1984-87
68 O.J. Simpson, Buffalo, 1973-77
66 Barry Sanders, Detroit, 1990-93, 1995-98

Most Attempts, Game
19 O.J. Simpson, Buffalo, 1974
17 Marv Hubbard, Oakland, 1974
16 O.J. Simpson, Buffalo, 1973
Marcus Allen, L.A. Raiders, 1986
Adrian Peterson, Minnesota, 2008

YARDS GAINED
Most Yards Gained, Career
368 Walter Payton, Chicago, 1977-1981, 1984-87
356 O.J. Simpson, Buffalo, 1973-77
271 Marshall Faulk, Indianapolis, 1995-96, 1999; St. Louis, 2000, 2002-03

Most Yards Gained, Game
180 Marshall Faulk, Indianapolis, 1995
129 Adrian Peterson, Minnesota, 2008
127 Chris Warren, Seattle, 1995

Longest Run From Scrimmage
49 Marshall Faulk, Indianapolis, 1995 (TD)
41 Lawrence McCutcheon, Los Angeles, 1976
Natrone Means, San Diego, 1995
Marshall Faulk, Indianapolis, 1995
39 Chris Warren, Seattle, 1994
Priest Holmes, Kansas City, 2002
Adrian Peterson, Minnesota, 2008

AVERAGE GAIN
Highest Average Gain, Career (20 attempts)
9.36 Chris Warren, Seattle, 1994-96, (25-234)
7.38 Adrian Peterson, Minnesota, 2008-09 (24-177)
6.45 Marshall Faulk, Indianapolis, 1995-96, 1999; St. Louis, 2000, 2002-03 (42-271)

Highest Average Gain, Game (10 attempts)
13.85 Marshall Faulk, Indianapolis, 1995 (13-180)
9.07 Chris Warren, Seattle, 1995 (14-127)
8.06 Adrian Peterson, Minnesota 2008 (16-129)

TOUCHDOWNS
Most Touchdowns, Career
3 Earl Campbell, Houston, 1979-1982, 1984
Chuck Muncie, New Orleans, 1980; San Diego, 1982-83
Mike Alstott, Tampa Bay, 1998-2003
Adrian Peterson, Minnesota, 2008-09
2 John Brockington, Green Bay, 1972-74
O.J. Simpson, Buffalo, 1973-77
Walter Payton, Chicago, 1977-1981, 1984-87
Marcus Allen, L.A. Raiders, 1983, 1985-86, 1988; Kansas City, 1994
Herschel Walker, Dallas, 1988-89
Johnny Johnson, Phoenix, 1991
Barry Sanders, Detroit, 1990-93, 1995-98
Curtis Martin, New England, 1996-97; N.Y. Jets, 1999, 2002
Ricky Williams, Miami, 2003
Shaun Alexander, Seattle, 2004-06
LaDainian Tomlinson, San Diego, 2003, 2005-07

Most Touchdowns, Game
3 Mike Alstott, Tampa Bay, 2000
2 John Brockington, Green Bay, 1973
Earl Campbell, Houston, 1980
Chuck Muncie, New Orleans, 1980
Herschel Walker, Dallas, 1989
Johnny Johnson, Phoenix, 1991
Ricky Williams, Miami, 2003
Shaun Alexander, Seattle, 2004
Adrian Peterson, Minnesota, 2008

PASSING
ATTEMPTS
Most Attempts, Career
179 Peyton Manning, Indianapolis, 2000-01, 2003-09
120 Dan Fouts, San Diego, 1980-84, 1986
101 Steve Young, San Francisco, 1993-96, 1998-99

Most Attempts, Game
41 Peyton Manning, Indianapolis, 2004
32 Bill Kenney, Kansas City, 1984
Steve Young, San Francisco, 1993
30 Dan Fouts, San Diego, 1983

COMPLETIONS
Most Completions, Career
107 Peyton Manning, Indianapolis, 2000-01, 2003-09
63 Dan Fouts, San Diego, 1980-84, 1986
48 Steve Young, San Francisco, 1993-96, 1998-99

Most Completions, Game
22 Peyton Manning, Indianapolis, 2004
21 Joe Theismann, Washington, 1984
18 Steve Young, San Francisco, 1993

COMPLETION PERCENTAGE
Highest Completion Percentage, Career (40 attempts)
68.9 Joe Theismann, Washington, 1983-84 (45-31)
67.9 Rich Gannon, Oakland, 2000-03 (53-36)
64.4 Jim Kelly, Buffalo, 1988, 1991-92 (45-29)

Highest Completion Percentage, Game (10 attempts)
90.0 Archie Manning, New Orleans, 1980 (10-9)
85.7 Rich Gannon, Oakland, 2001 (14-12)
80.0 Rich Gannon, Oakland, 2002 (10-8)
Jeff Garcia, Tampa Bay, 2008 (10-8)

YARDS GAINED
Most Yards Gained, Career
1,496 Peyton Manning, Indianapolis, 2000-01, 2003-09
890 Dan Fouts, San Diego, 1980-84, 1986
614 Steve Young, San Francisco, 1993-96, 1998-99

Most Yards Gained, Game
342 Peyton Manning, Indianapolis, 2004
274 Dan Fouts, San Diego, 1983
270 Peyton Manning, Indianapolis, 2000

Longest Completion

93 Jeff Blake, Cincinnati (to Thigpen, Pittsburgh), 1996 (TD)
90 Steve McNair, Tennessee (to Johnson, Cincinnati), 2004 (TD)
80 Mark Brunell, Jacksonville (to Brown, Oakland), 1997 (TD)

AVERAGE GAIN

Highest Average Gain, Career (40 attempts)

8.36 Peyton Manning, Indianapolis, 2000-01, 2003-09 (179-1,496)
8.19 Rich Gannon, Oakland, 2000-03 (53-434)
8.12 Brett Favre, Green Bay, 1993-94, 1996-97 (57-463)

Highest Average Gain, Game (10 attempts)

15.27 Randall Cunningham, Philadelphia, 1991 (11-168)
13.70 Rich Gannon, Oakland, 2002 (10-137)
13.00 Brett Favre, Green Bay, 1997 (11-143)
Peyton Manning, Indianapolis, 2005 (10-130)

TOUCHDOWNS

Most Touchdowns, Career

14 Peyton Manning, Indianapolis, 2000-01, 2003-09
7 Rich Gannon, Oakland, 2000-03
4 Steve Young, San Francisco, 1993-96, 1998-99
Marc Bulger, St. Louis, 2004, 2007

Most Touchdowns, Game

4 Marc Bulger, St. Louis, 2004
3 Joe Theismann, Washington, 1984
Phil Simms, N.Y. Giants, 1986
Peyton Manning, Indianapolis, 2004
Peyton Manning, Indianapolis, 2005
2 James Harris, Los Angeles, 1975
Mike Boryla, Philadelphia, 1976
Ken Anderson, Cincinnati, 1977
Jim Kelly, Buffalo, 1991
Mark Rypien, Washington, 1992
Steve Young, San Francisco, 1998
Peyton Manning, Indianapolis, 2000
Rich Gannon, Oakland, 2001
Peyton Manning, Indianapolis, 2001
Rich Gannon, Oakland, 2002
Donovan McNabb, Philadelphia, 2002
Rich Gannon, Oakland, 2003
Brad Johnson, Tampa Bay, 2003
Carson Palmer, Cincinnati, 2007
Tony Romo, Dallas, 2008

HAD INTERCEPTED

Most Passes Had Intercepted, Career

8 Dan Fouts, San Diego, 1980-84, 1986
Peyton Manning, Indianapolis, 2000-01, 2003-09
6 Jim Hart, St. Louis, 1975-78
5 Ken Stabler, Oakland, 1974-75, 1978
Donovan McNabb, Philadelphia, 2001-03, 2005
Jeff Garcia, San Francisco, 2001-03; Tampa Bay, 2008

Most Passes Had Intercepted, Game

5 Jim Hart, St. Louis, 1977
4 Ken Stabler, Oakland, 1974
3 Dan Fouts, San Diego, 1986
Mark Rypien, Washington, 1990
Steve Young, San Francisco, 1993
Jim Harbaugh, Indianapolis, 1996
Vinny Testaverde, N.Y. Jets, 1999
Jeff Garcia, San Francisco, 2003
Peyton Manning, Indianapolis, 2006

Most Attempts, Without Interception, Game

27 Joe Theismann, Washington, 1984
Phil Simms, N.Y. Giants, 1986
26 John Brodie, San Francisco, 1971
Danny White, Dallas, 1983
23 Dave Krieg, Seattle, 1990

PERCENTAGE, PASSES HAD INTERCEPTED

Lowest Percentage, Passes Had Intercepted, Career (40 attempts)

0.00 Joe Theismann, Washington, 1983-84 (45-0)
1.89 Rich Gannon, Oakland, 2000-03 (53-1)
2.13 Dave Krieg, Seattle, 1985, 1989-1990 (47-1)

PASS RECEIVING

RECEPTIONS

Most Receptions, Career

39 Tony Gonzalez, Kansas City, 2000-01, 2003-09
37 Jerry Rice, San Francisco, 1987-88, 1990-94, 1996, 1999; Oakland, 2003
30 Marvin Harrison, Indianapolis, 2000-06

Most Receptions, Game

9 Randy Moss, Minnesota, 2000
8 Steve Largent, Seattle, 1986
Michael Irvin, Dallas, 1992
Andre Rison, Atlanta, 1993
Jimmy Smith, Jacksonville, 2000
Marvin Harrison, Indianapolis, 2001
Terrell Owens, San Francisco, 2002
Steve Smith, Carolina, 2006
Terrell Owens, Dallas, 2008
7 John Stallworth, Pittsburgh, 1983
Jerry Rice, San Francisco, 1992
Isaac Bruce, St. Louis, 1997
Keyshawn Johnson, N.Y. Jets, 1999
Randy Moss, Minnesota, 1999
Warrick Dunn, Tampa Bay, 2001
Torry Holt, St. Louis, 2001
Torry Holt, St. Louis, 2004

YARDS GAINED

Most Yards Gained, Career

590 Tony Gonzalez, Kansas City, 2000-01, 2003-09
495 Jerry Rice, San Francisco, 1987-88, 1990-94, 1996, 1999; Oakland, 2003
462 Marvin Harrison, Indianapolis, 2000-06

Most Yards Gained, Game

212 Randy Moss, Minnesota, 2000
156 Chad Johnson, Cincinnati, 2004
137 Tim Brown, Oakland, 1997
Reggie Wayne, Indianapolis, 2007

Longest Reception

93 Yancey Thigpen, Pittsburgh (from Blake, Cincinnati), 1996 (TD)
90 Chad Johnson, Cincinnati (from McNair, Tennessee), 2004 (TD)
80 Tim Brown, Oakland (from Brunell, Jacksonville), 1997 (TD)

TOUCHDOWNS

Most Touchdowns, Career

5 Jimmy Smith, Jacksonville, 1998-2001
Marvin Harrison, Indianapolis, 2000-06
Tony Gonzalez, Kansas City, 2000-01, 2003-09
4 Terrell Owens, San Francisco, 2001-04; Dallas, 2008
3 Cris Carter, Minnesota, 1994-2001
Torry Holt, St. Louis, 2001-02, 2004-06, 2008
Hines Ward, Pittsburgh, 2002-05
Larry Fitzgerald, Arizona, 2006, 2008-09

Most Touchdowns, Game

3 Jimmy Smith, Jacksonville, 2000
2 William Andrews, Atlanta, 1984
Eric Green, Pittsburgh, 1995

Marvin Harrison, Indianapolis, 2001
T.J. Houshmandzadeh, Cincinnati, 2008
Terrell Owens, Dallas, 2008
Larry Fitzgerald, Arizona, 2009

INTERCEPTIONS BY

Most Interceptions By, Career

4 Everson Walls, Dallas, 1982-84, 1986
Deion Sanders, Atlanta, 1992-94; San Francisco, 1995; Dallas, 1999
Champ Bailey, Washington, 2001-04; Denver, 2005-08
3 Ken Houston, Houston, 1971-73; Washington, 1974-79
Jack Lambert, Pittsburgh, 1976-1984
Ted Hendricks, Baltimore, 1972-74; Green Bay, 1975; Oakland, 1981-82; L.A. Raiders, 1983-84
Mike Haynes, New England, 1978-1981, 1983; L.A. Raiders, 1985-87
Ty Law, New England, 1999, 2002-04; N.Y. Jets, 2006
2 By 21 players

Most Interceptions By, Game

2 Mel Blount, Pittsburgh, 1977
Everson Walls, Dallas, 1982, 1983
LeRoy Irvin, L.A. Rams, 1986
David Fulcher, Cincinnati, 1990
Brian Dawkins, Philadelphia, 2000
Rod Woodson, Oakland, 2003
Ed Reed, Baltimore, 2007
Antonio Cromartie, San Diego, 2008

YARDS GAINED

Most Yards Gained, Career

147 Ty Law, New England, 1999, 2002-04; N.Y. Jets, 2006
103 Deion Sanders, Atlanta, 1992-94; San Francisco, 1995; Dallas, 1999
88 Rod Woodson, Pittsburgh, 1990-95, 1997; Baltimore, 2000-02; Oakland, 2003

Most Yards Gained, Game

87 Deion Sanders, Dallas, 1999
77 Antonio Cromartie, San Diego, 2008
73 Rod Woodson, Pittsburgh, 1994

Longest Gain

87 Deion Sanders, Dallas, 1999
73 Rod Woodson, Pittsburgh, 1994 (lateral)
67 Ty Law, New England, 1999 (TD)

TOUCHDOWNS

Most Touchdowns, Career

2 Ty Law, New England, 1999, 2002-04; N.Y. Jets, 2006
Derrick Brooks, Tampa Bay, 1998-2001, 2003, 2006-07
1 By many

Most Touchdowns, Game

1 Bobby Bell, Kansas City, 1973
Nolan Cromwell, L.A. Rams, 1984
Joey Browner, Minnesota, 1986
Jerry Gray, L.A. Rams, 1990
Mike Johnson, Cleveland, 1990
Junior Seau, San Diego, 1993
Ken Harvey, Washington, 1996
Ashley Ambrose, Cincinnati, 1997
Ty Law, New England, 1999
Derrick Brooks, Tampa Bay, 2000
Aeneas Williams, Arizona, 2000
Ray Lewis, Baltimore, 2002
Ty Law, New England, 2003
Dre' Bly, Detroit, 2004
Derrick Brooks, Tampa Bay, 2006

PUNTING

Most Punts, Career

33 Ray Guy, Oakland, 1974-79, 1981
23 Rohn Stark, Indianapolis, 1986-87, 1991, 1993
22 Reggie Roby, Miami, 1985, 1990; Washington, 1995

Most Punts, Game

10 Reggie Roby, Miami, 1985
9 Tom Wittum, San Francisco, 1974
Rohn Stark, Indianapolis, 1987
8 Jerrel Wilson, Kansas City, 1971
Tom Skladany, Detroit, 1982
Reggie Roby, Washington, 1995

Longest Punt

73 Shane Lechler, Oakland, 2002
70 Shane Lechler, Oakland, 2002
65 Shane Lechler, Oakland, 2009

AVERAGE YARDAGE

Highest Average, Career (10 punts)

52.90 Shane Lechler, Oakland, 2002, 2005, 2008-09 (10-529)
47.30 Jeff Feagles, Arizona, 1996; N.Y. Giants, 2009 (10-473)
46.73 Reggie Roby, Miami, 1985, 1990; Washington, 1995 (22-1,028)

Highest Average, Game (4 punts)

60.75 Shane Lechler, Oakland, 2002 (4-243)
55.50 Darren Bennett, San Diego, 1996 (4-222)
52.00 Matt Turk, Washington, 1999 (4-208)

PUNT RETURNS

Most Punt Returns, Career

13 Rick Upchurch, Denver, 1977, 1979-1980, 1983
11 Vai Sikahema, St. Louis, 1987-88
Eric Metcalf, Cleveland 1994-95; San Diego 1998
10 Mike Nelms, Washington, 1981-83

Most Punt Returns, Game

7 Vai Sikahema, St. Louis, 1987
6 Henry Ellard, L.A. Rams, 1985
Gerald McNeil, Cleveland, 1988
Eric Metcalf, Cleveland, 1995
5 Rick Upchurch, Denver, 1980
Mike Nelms, Washington, 1981
Carl Roaches, Houston, 1982
Johnny Bailey, Phoenix, 1993

Most Fair Catches, Game

2 Jerry Logan, Baltimore, 1971
Dick Anderson, Miami, 1974
Henry Ellard, L.A. Rams, 1985
Isaac Bruce, St. Louis, 1997
Desmond Howard, Detroit, 2001

YARDS GAINED

Most Yards Gained, Career

183 Billy Johnson, Houston, 1976, 1978; Atlanta, 1984
138 Mel Renfro, Dallas, 1971-72, 1974
Rick Upchurch, Denver, 1977, 1979-1980, 1983
135 Eric Metcalf, Cleveland, 1994-95; San Diego 1998

Most Yards Gained, Game

159 Billy Johnson, Houston, 1976
138 Mel Renfro, Dallas, 1971
117 Wally Henry, Philadelphia, 1980

Longest Punt Return

90 Billy Johnson, Houston, 1976 (TD)
86 Wally Henry, Philadelphia, 1980 (TD)
82 Mel Renfro, Dallas, 1971 (TD)

AFC-NFC PRO BOWL RECORDS

AVERAGE YARDAGE

Highest Average, Career (4 returns)

22.88 Billy Johnson, Houston, 1976, 1978; Atlanta, 1984 (8-183)
21.50 Tony Green, Washington, 1979 (4-86)
15.67 David Meggett, N.Y. Giants, 1990; New England, 1997

Highest Average, Game (3 returns)

39.75 Billy Johnson, Houston, 1976 (4-159)
39.00 Wally Henry, Philadelphia, 1980 (3-117)
21.50 Tony Green, Washington, 1979 (4-86)

TOUCHDOWNS

Most Touchdowns, Game

2 Mel Renfro, Dallas, 1971
1 Billy Johnson, Houston, 1976
Wally Henry, Philadelphia, 1980

KICKOFF RETURNS

Most Kickoff Returns, Career

17 Michael Bates, Carolina, 1997-2001
14 Mel Gray, Detroit, 1991-92, 1995
11 Eric Metcalf, Cleveland, 1994-95; San Diego, 1998
Derrick Mason, Tennessee, 2001, 2004

Most Kickoff Returns, Game

8 Derrick Mason, Tennessee, 2004
7 Mel Gray, Detroit, 1995
Jerry Azumah, Chicago, 2004
6 Greg Pruitt, L.A. Raiders, 1984
David Meggett, New England, 1997
Michael Bates, Carolina, 1998
Steve Smith, Carolina, 2002
Josh Cribbs, Cleveland, 2008

YARDS GAINED

Most Yards Gained, Career

488 Michael Bates, Carolina, 1997-2001
309 Greg Pruitt, Cleveland, 1974-75, 1977-78; L.A. Raiders, 1984
294 Mel Gray, Detroit, 1991-92, 1995

Most Yards Gained, Game

228 Jerry Azumah, Chicago, 2004
217 Michael Lewis, New Orleans, 2003
192 Greg Pruitt, L.A. Raiders, 1984

Longest Kickoff Return

66 Michael Bates, Carolina, 2000
62 Greg Pruitt, L.A. Raiders, 1984
61 Eugene (Mercury) Morris, Miami, 1972

AVERAGE YARDAGE

Highest Average, Career (4 returns)

43.40 Michael Lewis, New Orleans, 2003 (5-217)
35.00 Les (Speedy) Duncan, Washington, 1972 (5-175)
32.57 Jerry Azumah, Chicago, 2004 (7-228)

Highest Average, Game (3 returns)

43.40 Michael Lewis, New Orleans, 2003 (5-217)
42.67 Clifton Smith, Tampa Bay, 2009 (3-128)
42.00 Michael Bates, Carolina, 2000 (4-168)

TOUCHDOWNS

Most Touchdowns, Game

1 Hines Ward, Pittsburgh, 2005

FUMBLES

Most Fumbles, Career

6 Dan Fouts, San Diego, 1980-84, 1986
4 Lawrence McCutcheon, Los Angeles, 1974-78
Franco Harris, Pittsburgh, 1973-76, 1978-1981
Jay Schroeder, Washington, 1987
Vai Sikahema, St. Louis, 1987-88
Trent Green, Kansas City, 2004, 2006
3 O.J. Simpson, Buffalo, 1973-77
William Andrews, Atlanta, 1981-84
Joe Montana, San Francisco, 1982, 1984-85, 1988
Walter Payton, Chicago, 1977-1981, 1984-87
Neil Lomax, St. Louis, 1985, 1988
Jim Kelly, Buffalo, 1988, 1991-92
Chris Chandler, Atlanta, 1998-99
Peyton Manning, Indianapolis, 2000-01, 2003-09
Marc Bulger, St. Louis, 2004, 2007

Most Fumbles, Game

4 Jay Schroeder, Washington, 1987
Trent Green, Kansas City, 2004
3 Dan Fouts, San Diego, 1982
Vai Sikahema, St. Louis, 1987
2 By 19 players

RECOVERIES

Most Fumbles Recovered, Career

3 Harold Jackson, Philadelphia, 1973; Los Angeles, 1974, 1976, 1978 (3-own)
Dan Fouts, San Diego, 1980-84, 1986 (3-own)
Randy White, Dallas, 1978, 1980-86 (3-opp)
Trent Green, Kansas City, 2004, 2006 (3-own)
Peyton Manning, Indianapolis, 2000-01, 2003-09 (3-own)
2 By many players

Most Fumbles Recovered, Game

3 Trent Green, Kansas City, 2004 (3-own)
2 Dick Anderson, Miami, 1974 (1-own, 1-opp)
Harold Jackson, Los Angeles, 1974 (2-own)
Dan Fouts, San Diego, 1982 (2-own)
Joey Browner, Minnesota, 1990 (2-opp)
Jessie Armstead, N.Y. Giants, 1999 (1-own, 1-opp)
Steve Beuerlein, Carolina, 2000 (2-own)

YARDAGE

Longest Fumble Return

83 Art Still, Kansas City, 1985 (TD, opp)
70 Adalius Thomas, Baltimore, 2007 (TD, opp)
51 Phil Villapiano, Oakland, 1974 (opp)

TOUCHDOWNS

Most Touchdowns, Game

1 Art Still, Kansas City, 1985
Keith Millard, Minnesota, 1990
Adalius Thomas, Baltimore, 2007

SACKS

Sacks have been compiled since 1983.

Most Sacks, Career

9.5 Reggie White, Philadelphia, 1987-1993; Green Bay, 1994, 1996-97, 1999
9.0 Howie Long, L.A. Raiders, 1984-88, 1990, 1993-1994
7.5 Bruce Smith, Buffalo, 1988-1991, 1995-96, 1998-99

Most Sacks, Game

4 Mark Gastineau, N.Y. Jets, 1985
Reggie White, Philadelphia, 1987
3 Richard Dent, Chicago, 1985
Bruce Smith, Buffalo, 1991
2.5 Bruce Smith, Buffalo, 1998

Rules

2009 NFL ROSTER OF OFFICIALS

Mike Pereira, Vice President of Officiating
Ed Coukart, Supervisor of Officials
Neely Dunn, Supervisor of Officials
Johnny Grier, Supervisor of Officials
Gary Slaughter, Supervisor of Officials
Bill Vinovich, Supervisor of Officials

No.	Name	Position	College
20	Anderson, Barry	Side Judge	North Carolina State
66	Anderson, Walt	Referee	Texas
108	Arthur, Gary	Line Judge	Wright State
26	Baltz, Mark	Head Linesman	Ohio
72	Banks, Michael	Side Judge	Illinois State
55	Barnes, Tom	Line Judge	Minnesota
56	Baynes, Allen	Side Judge	Auburn
32	Bergman, Jeff	Line Judge	Robert Morris
91	Bergman, Jerry	Head Linesman	Robert Morris
34	Blakeman, Clete	Field Judge	Nebraska
23	Boger, Jerome	Referee	Morehouse College
18	Boston, Byron	Line Judge	Austin
74	Bowers, Derick	Head Linesman	East Central
98	Bradley, Greg	Side Judge	Tennessee
31	Brown, Chad	Umpire	East Texas State
43	Brown, Terry	Field Judge	Tennessee-Knoxville
11	Bryan, Fred	Umpire	Northern Iowa
86	Buchanan, Jimmy	Field Judge	South Carolina State
134	Camp, Ed	Head Linesman	William Paterson
126	Carey, Don	Referee	California-Riverside
94	Carey, Mike	Referee	Santa Clara
39	Carlsen, Don	Side Judge	Cal State-Chico
60	Cavaletto, Gary	Field Judge	Hancock
41	Cheek, Boris	Field Judge	Morgan State
51	Cheffers, Carl	Referee	California-Irvine
95	Coleman, James	Side Judge	Arkansas
65	Coleman, Walt	Referee	Arkansas
99	Corrente, Tony	Referee	Cal State-Fullerton
70	Dawson, Scott	Umpire	Virginia Tech
58	DeBell, Jimmy	Side Judge	SUNY-Brockport
53	DeFelice, Garth	Umpire	San Diego State
6	Dornan, Kirk	Back Judge	Central Washington
27	Dyer, Lee	Back Judge	Tennessee-Chattanooga
3	Edwards, Scott	Field Judge	Alabama
81	Ellison, Roy	Umpire	Savannah State
61	Ferguson, Keith	Back Judge	San Jose State
64	Ferrell, Dan	Umpire	Cal State-Fullerton
71	Fowler, Ruben	Umpire	Huston-Tillotson
133	Freeman, Steve	Back Judge	Mississippi State
80	Gautreaux, Greg	Field Judge	S.W. Louisiana
19	Green, Scott	Referee	Delaware
49	Hall, Rich	Umpire	Arizona
40	Hannah, Butch	Umpire	Middle Tennessee State
125	Hayes, Laird	Side Judge	Princeton
54	Hayward, George	Head Linesman	Missouri Western
93	Helverson, Scott	Back Judge	Iowa
97	Hill, Tom	Side Judge	Carson Newman
28	Hittner, Mark	Head Linesman	Pittsburg State
85	Hochuli, Ed	Referee	Texas-El Paso
82	Horton, Buddy	Field Judge	Oregon State
37	Howey, Jim	Field Judge	Erskine College
35	Hussey, John	Line Judge	Idaho State
76	Jenkins, Darrell	Umpire	San Jose State
101	Johnson, Carl	Line Judge	Nicholls State
121	King, Paul	Umpire	Nicholls State
103	Lamberth, Jeff	Side Judge	Texas A&M
73	Larrew, Joe	Side Judge	St. Louis
17	Lawing, Bob	Back Judge	North Carolina State
127	Leavy, Bill	Referee	San Jose State
130	Lewis, Darryll	Line Judge	Dartmouth
89	Lucivansky, Jon	Field Judge	Minnesota
106	Mackie, Wayne	Head Linesman	Colgate
52	Mapp, Julian	Head Linesman	Grambling State
107	Marinucci, Ron	Line Judge	Glassboro State
77	McAulay, Terry	Referee	Louisiana State

No.	Name	Position	College
5	McGrath, John	Head Linesman	Kentucky
8	McKenzie, Dana	Head Linesman	Toledo
110	McKinnely, Phil	Head Linesman	UCLA
48	Mello, Jim	Head Linesman	Northeastern
78	Meyer, Greg	Side Judge	Texas Christian
115	Michalek, Tony	Umpire	Indiana
111	Miles, Terrence	Back Judge	Arizona State
135	Morelli, Pete	Referee	St. Mary's
124	Paganelli, Carl	Umpire	Michigan State
105	Paganelli, Dino	Back Judge	Aquinas College
46	Paganelli, Perry	Back Judge	Hope College
132	Parry, John	Referee	Purdue
15	Patterson, Rick	Side Judge	Wofford
79	Payne, Kent	Head Linesman	Nebraska Wesleyan
9	Perlman, Mark	Line Judge	Salem
10	Phares, Ron	Line Judge	Virginia Tech
47	Podraza, Tim	Line Judge	Nebraska
109	Prioleau, Dyrol	Field Judge	Johnson C. Smith
30	Prukop, Todd	Back Judge	Cal State-Fullerton
83	Reels, Richard	Back Judge	Chicago State
44	Rice, Jeff	Umpire	Northwestern
57	Riveron, Alberto	Referee	Miami
128	Rose, Larry	Side Judge	Florida
67	Rosenbaum, Doug	Field Judge	Illinois Wesleyan
21	Schleyer, John	Head Linesman	Millersville
122	Schmitz, Bill	Back Judge	Colorado State
129	Schuster, Bill	Umpire	Alfred
45	Seeman, Jeff	Line Judge	Minnesota
2	Smith, Billy	Back Judge	East Carolina
90	Spanier, Mike	Line Judge	St. Cloud State
24	Stabile, Tom	Head Linesman	Slippery Rock
12	Steed, Greg	Back Judge	Howard
88	Steenson, Scott	Field Judge	North Texas
84	Steinkerchner, Mark	Line Judge	Akron
22	Stelljes, Steve	Head Linesman	Friends
68	Stephan, Tom	Line Judge	Pittsburg State
114	Steratore, Gene	Referee	Kent State
112	Steratore, Tony	Back Judge	California
62	Stewart, Charles	Line Judge	Long Beach State
102	Stritesky, Bruce	Umpire	Embry Riddle
100	Symonette, Tom	Line Judge	Florida
42	Triplette, Jeff	Referee	Wake Forest
75	Vernatchi, Rob	Field Judge	California-Riverside
36	Veteri, Tony	Head Linesman	Manhattan College
25	Waggoner, Bob	Back Judge	Juniata College
96	Wash, Undrey	Umpire	Texas-Arlington
7	Washington, Keith	Side Judge	Virginia Military Institute
116	Weatherford, Mike	Side Judge	Oklahoma State
50	Weir, Mike	Field Judge	Missouri
119	Wilson, Greg	Back Judge	USC
29	Wilson, Steve	Umpire	Whitworth College
14	Winter, Ron	Referee	Michigan State
4	Wrolstad, Craig	Field Judge	Washington
16	Wyant, David	Side Judge	Virginia
33	Zimmer, Steve	Field Judge	Hofstra

Roster as of May 2009

NUMERICAL ROSTER

No.	Name	Position
2	Billy Smith	BJ
3	Scott Edwards	FJ
4	Craig Wrolstad	FJ
5	John McGrath	HL
6	Kirk Dornan	BJ
7	Keith Washington	SJ
8	Dana McKenzie	HL
9	Mark Perlman	LJ
10	Ron Phares	LJ
11	Fred Bryan	U
12	Greg Steed	BJ
14	Ron Winter	R
15	Rick Patterson	SJ
16	David Wyant	SJ
17	Bob Lawing	BJ
18	Byron Boston	LJ
19	Scott Green	R
20	Barry Anderson	SJ
21	John Schleyer	HL
22	Steve Stelljes	HL
23	Jerome Boger	R
24	Tom Stabile	HL
25	Bob Waggoner	BJ
26	Mark Baltz	HL
27	Lee Dyer	BJ
28	Mark Hittner	HL
29	Steve Wilson	U
30	Todd Prukop	BJ
31	Chad Brown	U
32	Jeff Bergman	LJ
33	Steve Zimmer	FJ
34	Clete Blakeman	FJ
35	John Hussey	LJ
36	Tony Veteri	HL
37	Jim Howey	FJ
39	Don Carlsen	SJ
40	Butch Hannah	U
41	Boris Cheek	FJ
42	Jeff Triplette	R
43	Terry Brown	FJ
44	Jeff Rice	U
45	Jeff Seeman	LJ
46	Perry Paganelli	BJ
47	Tim Podraza	LJ
48	Jim Mello	HL
49	Rich Hall	U
50	Mike Weir	FJ
51	Carl Cheffers	R
52	Julian Mapp	HL
53	Garth DeFelice	U
54	George Hayward	HL
55	Tom Barnes	LJ
56	Allen Baynes	SJ
57	Alberto Riveron	R
58	Jimmy DeBell	SJ
60	Gary Cavaletto	FJ
61	Keith Ferguson	BJ
62	Charles Stewart	LJ
64	Dan Ferrell	U
65	Walt Coleman	R
66	Walt Anderson	R
67	Doug Rosenbaum	FJ
68	Tom Stephan	LJ
70	Scott Dawson	U
71	Ruben Fowler	U
72	Michael Banks	SJ
73	Joe Larrew	SJ
74	Derick Bowers	HL
75	Rob Vernatchi	FJ
76	Darrell Jenkins	U
77	Terry McAulay	R
78	Greg Meyer	SJ
79	Kent Payne	HL
80	Greg Gautreaux	FJ
81	Roy Ellison	U
82	Buddy Horton	FJ
83	Richard Reels	BJ
84	Mark Steinkerchner	LJ
85	Ed Hochuli	R
86	Jimmy Buchanan	FJ
88	Scott Steenson	FJ
89	Jon Lucivanksy	FJ
90	Mike Spanier	LJ
91	Jerry Bergman	HL
93	Scott Helverson	BJ
94	Mike Carey	R
95	James Coleman	SJ
96	Undrey Wash	U
97	Tom Hill	SJ
98	Greg Bradley	SJ
99	Tony Corrente	R
100	Tom Symonette	LJ
101	Carl Johnson	LJ
102	Bruce Stritesky	U
103	Jeff Lamberth	SJ
105	Dino Paganelli	BJ
106	Wayne Mackie	HL
107	Ron Marinucci	LJ
108	Gary Arthur	LJ
109	Dyrol Prioleau	FJ
110	Phil McKinnely	HL
111	Terrence Miles	BJ
112	Tony Steratore	BJ
114	Gene Steratore	R
115	Tony Michalek	U
116	Mike Weatherford	SJ
119	Greg Wilson	BJ
121	Paul King	U
122	Bill Schmitz	BJ
124	Carl Paganelli	U
125	Laird Hayes	SJ
126	Don Carey	R
127	Bill Leavy	R
128	Larry Rose	SJ
129	Bill Schuster	U
130	Darryll Lewis	LJ
132	John Parry	R
133	Steve Freeman	BJ
134	Ed Camp	HL
135	Pete Morelli	R

Roster as of May 2009

OFFICIALS

2009 OFFICIALS AT A GLANCE

REFEREES

Walt Anderson, No. **66,** Texas, college officiating coordinator, retired dentist, 14th year.
Jerome Boger, No. **23,** Morehouse College, commercial insurance underwriter, 6th year.
Don Carey, No. **126,** California-Riverside, contract manager, 15th year.
Mike Carey, No. **94,** Santa Clara, owner, skiing accessories, 20th year.
Carl Cheffers, No. **51,** California-Irvine, sales manager, 10th year.
Walt Coleman, No. **65,** Arkansas, manager dairy processor, 21st year.
Tony Corrente, No. **99,** Cal State-Fullerton, educator, 15th year.
Scott Green, No. **19,** Delaware, president, government support services, 19th year.
Ed Hochuli, No. **85,** Texas-El Paso, attorney, 20th year.
Bill Leavy, No. **127,** San Jose State, retired firefighter, 15th year.
Terry McAulay, No. **77,** Louisiana State, senior computer scientist, 12th year.
Pete Morelli, No. **135,** St. Mary's, high school principal, 13th year.
John Parry, No. **132,** Purdue, financial advisor, 10th year.
Alberto Riveron, No. **57,** Miami, sales, commercial restaurant equipment, 6th year.
Gene Steratore, No. **114,** Kent State, co-owner, supply company, 7th year.
Jeff Triplette, No. **42,** Wake Forest, vice president, world-wide energy company, 14th year.
Ron Winter, No. **14,** Michigan State, university professor, 15th year.

UMPIRES

Chad Brown, No. **31,** East Texas State, executive manager of facilities/student affairs administration, 18th year.
Fred Bryan, No. **11,** Northern Iowa, superintendent, juvenile correctional facility, 1st year.
Scott Dawson, No. **70,** Virginia Tech, president/owner, commercial construction company, 15th year.
Garth DeFelice, No. **53,** San Diego State, distribution center manager, beverage company, 12th year.
Roy Ellison, No. **81,** Savannah State, technical staff member, 7th year.
Dan Ferrell, No. **64,** Cal State-Fullerton, director, parts logistics, 7th year.
Ruben Fowler, No. **71,** Huston-Tillotson, retired firefighter, 4th year.
Rich Hall, No. **49,** Arizona, custom cabinetry, 6th year.
Butch Hannah, No. **40,** Middle Tennessee State, federal probation officer, 11th year.
Darrell Jenkins, No. **76,** San Jose State, retired, 8th year.
Paul King, No. **121,** Nicholls State, teacher, 1st year.
Tony Michalek, No. **115,** Indiana, eurodollar futures trader, 8th year.
Carl Paganelli, No. **124,** Michigan State, federal probation officer, 11th year.
Jeff Rice, No. **44,** Northwestern, attorney, 15th year.
Bill Schuster, No. **129,** Alfred, insurance broker, 10th year.
Bruce Stritesky, No. **102,** Embry Riddle, airline pilot, 4th year.
Undrey Wash, No. **96,** Texas-Arlington, claims manager, 10th year.
Steve Wilson, No. **29,** Whitworth College, pastor, 11th year.

HEAD LINESMEN

Mark Baltz, No. **26,** Ohio, sales consultant, 21st year.
Jerry Bergman, No. **91,** Robert Morris, sales executive, 8th year.
Derick Bowers, No. **74,** East Central, purchasing supervisor, 7th year.
Ed Camp, No. **134,** William Paterson, physical education teacher, 10th year.
George Hayward, No. **54,** Missouri Western, vice-president and manager, warehouse company, 19th year.
Mark Hittner, No. **28,** Pittsburg State, investment broker, 13th year.
Wayne Mackie, No. **106,** Colgate, director of housing, 3rd year.
Julian Mapp, No. **52,** Grambling State, project leader, 1st year.
John McGrath, No. **5,** Kentucky, senior account executive, 8th year.
Dana McKenzie, No. **8,** Toledo, claims adjuster, 2nd year.
Phil McKinnely, No. **110,** UCLA, inventory control, 7th year.
Jim Mello, No. **48,** Northeastern, facilities manager, 6th year.
Kent Payne, No. **79,** Nebraska Wesleyan, teacher, 6th year.
John Schleyer, No. **21,** Millersville, medical sales, 20th year.
Tom Stabile, No. **24,** Slippery Rock, secondary educational administrator, 15th year.
Steve Stelljes, No. **22,** Friends, business planning manager, 8th year.
Tony Veteri, No. **36,** Manhattan College, physical education teacher, 18th year.

LINE JUDGES

Gary Arthur, No. **108,** Wright State, president, commercial printing company, 13th year.
Tom Barnes, No. **55,** Minnesota, manufacturing representative, 24th year.
Jeff Bergman, No. **32,** Robert Morris, president and chief executive officer, medical services, 18th year.
Byron Boston, No. **18,** Austin, tax consultant, 15th year.
John Hussey, No. **35,** Idaho State, sales representative, retail logistics group, 8th year.
Carl Johnson, No. **101,** Nicholls State, district sales manager, 9th year.
Darryll Lewis, No. **130,** Dartmouth, associate professor, 11th year.
Ron Marinucci, No. **107,** Glassboro State, vice president, novelty cone company, 13th year.
Mark Perlman, No. **9,** Salem, teacher, 9th year.
Ron Phares, No. **10,** Virginia Tech, president, construction company, 25th year.
Tim Podraza, No. **47,** Nebraska, banker, 2nd year.
Jeff Seeman, No. **45,** Minnesota, brokerage sales, 8th year.
Mike Spanier, No. **90,** St. Cloud State, middle school principal, 11th year.
Mark Steinkerchner, No. **84,** Akron, vice-president, 16th year.
Tom Stephan, No. **68,** Pittsburg State, business broker, 11th year.
Charles Stewart, No. **62,** Long Beach State, retired human services administrator, 18th year.
Tom Symonette, No. **100,** Florida, certified public accountant, 6th year.

Roster as of May 2009

FIELD JUDGES

Clete Blakeman, No. **34,** Nebraska, attorney, 2nd year.
Terry Brown, No. **43,** Tennessee-Knoxville, probation supervisor, 4th year.
Jimmy Buchanan, No. **86**, South Carolina State, insurance agent, 1st year.
Gary Cavaletto, No. **60,** Hancock, general manager, agricultural operations, 7th year.
Boris Cheek, No. **41,** Morgan State, director of operations and management, 14th year.
Scott Edwards, No. **3,** Alabama, environmental engineer, 11th year.
Greg Gautreaux, No. **80,** S.W. Louisiana, athletic programs manager, 8th year.
Buddy Horton, No. **82,** Oregon State, water service worker, 11th year.
Jim Howey, No. **37,** Erskine College, director of adult education, 11th year.
Jon Lucivansky, No. **89,** Minnesota, high school associate principal, 1st year.
Dyrol Prioleau, No. **109,** Johnson C. Smith, manager, law firm, 3rd year.
Doug Rosenbaum, No. **67,** Illinois Wesleyan, financial consultant, 9th year.
Scott Steenson, No. **88,** North Texas, commercial real estate broker, 19th year.
Rob Vernatchi, No. **75,** California-Riverside, enforcement investigator, 6th year.
Mike Weir, No. **50,** Missouri, owner, sporting goods store, 8th year.
Craig Wrolstad, No. **4,** Washington, athletic director, 7th year.
Steve Zimmer, No. **33,** Hofstra, attorney, 13th year.

SIDE JUDGES

Barry Anderson, No. **20,** North Carolina State, builder/developer, 3rd year.
Michael Banks, No. **72,** Illinois State, carpenter foreman, 8th year.
Allen Baynes, No. **56,** Auburn, realtor, 2nd year.
Greg Bradley, No. **98,** Tennessee, chemical engineer, 1st year.
Don Carlsen, No. **39,** Cal State-Chico, retired county school superintendent, 21st year.
James Coleman, No. **95,** Arkansas, electrical engineer, 5th year.
Jimmy DeBell, No. **58,** SUNY-Brockport, high school teacher, 1st year.
Laird Hayes, No. **125,** Princeton, professor, physical education & athletics, 15th year.
Tom Hill, No. **97,** Carson Newman, teacher, 11th year.
Jeff Lamberth, No. **103,** Texas A&M, attorney, 8th year.
Joe Larrew, No. **73,** St. Louis, attorney, 8th year.
Greg Meyer, No. **78,** Texas Christian, banker, 8th year.
Rick Patterson, No. **15,** Wofford, banker, 14th year.
Larry Rose, No. **128,** Florida, financial planner, 13th year.
Keith Washington, No. **7,** Virginia Military Institute, program financial analyst, 2nd year.
Mike Weatherford, No. **116,** Oklahoma State, energy trader, 8th year.
David Wyant, No. **16,** Virginia, consulting engineer, 19th year.

BACK JUDGES

Kirk Dornan, No. **6,** Central Washington, purchasing manager, 16th year.
Lee Dyer, No. **27,** Tennessee-Chattanooga, sales manager, 7th year.
Keith Ferguson, No. **61,** San Jose State, sales, 10th year.
Steve Freeman, No. **133,** Mississippi State, custom home builder, 9th year.
Scott Helverson, No. **93,** Iowa, sales, printing and promotions, 7th year.
Bob Lawing, No. **17,** North Carolina State, certified property management, 13th year.
Terrence Miles, No. **111,** Arizona State, quality control manager, 2nd year.
Dino Paganelli, No. **105,** Aquinas College, educator, 4th year.
Perry Paganelli, No. **46,** Hope College, retired high school administrator, 12th year.
Todd Prukop, No. **30,** Cal State-Fullerton, medical sales representative, 1st year.
Richard Reels, No. **83,** Chicago State, director of security, court services, 17th year.
Bill Schmitz, No. **122,** Colorado State, general sales manager, 21st year.
Billy Smith, No. **2,** East Carolina, retired federal government, 16th year.
Greg Steed, No. **12,** Howard, computer systems analyst, 7th year.
Tony Steratore, No. **112,** California, PA., co-owner, supply company, 10th year.
Bob Waggoner, No. **25,** Juniata College, probation officer, 13th year.
Greg Wilson, No. **119,** USC, law enforcement, 2nd year.

Roster as of May 2009

OFFICIAL SIGNALS

1

TOUCHDOWN, FIELD GOAL, or SUCCESSFUL TRY
Both arms extended above head.

2

SAFETY
Palms together above head.

3

FIRST DOWN
Arm pointed toward defensive team's goal.

4

DEAD BALL or NEUTRAL ZONE ESTABLISHED
One arm above head with an open hand.
With fist closed: **Fourth Down.**

5

BALL ILLEGALLY TOUCHED, KICKED, or BATTED
Fingertips tap both shoulders.

6

TIME OUT
Hands crisscrossed above head.
Same signal followed by placing one hand on top of cap: **Referee's Time Out.**
Same signal followed by arm swung at side: **Touchback.**

7

NO TIME OUT or TIME IN WITH WHISTLE
Full arm circled to simulate moving clock.

8

DELAY OF GAME or EXCESS TIME OUT
Folded arms.

9

FALSE START, ILLEGAL FORMATION, or KICKOFF or SAFETY KICK OUT OF BOUNDS or KICKING TEAM PLAYER VOLUNTARILY OUT OF BOUNDS DURING A PUNT
Forearms rotated over and over in front of body.

10

PERSONAL FOUL
One wrist striking the other above head.
Same signal followed by swinging leg: **Roughing the Kicker.**
Same signal followed by raised arm swinging forward: **Roughing the Passer.**
Same signal followed by grasping facemask: **Major Facemask.**

11

HOLDING
Grasping one wrist, the fist clenched, in front of chest.

12

ILLEGAL USE OF HANDS, ARMS, or BODY
Grasping one wrist, the hand open and facing forward, in front of chest.

13

PENALTY REFUSED, INCOMPLETE PASS, PLAY OVER, or MISSED FIELD GOAL or EXTRA POINT
Hands shifted in horizontal plane.

14

PASS JUGGLED INBOUNDS AND CAUGHT OUT OF BOUNDS
Hands up and down in front of chest (following incomplete pass signal).

15

ILLEGAL FORWARD PASS
One hand waved behind back followed by loss of down signal (23), when appropriate.

16

INTENTIONAL GROUNDING OF PASS
Parallel arms waved in a diagonal plane across body. Followed by loss of down signal (23).

17

INTERFERENCE WITH FORWARD PASS or FAIR CATCH
Hands open and extended forward from shoulders with hands vertical.

18

INVALID FAIR-CATCH SIGNAL
One hand waved above head.

19

INELIGIBLE RECEIVER or INELIGIBLE MEMBER OF KICKING TEAM DOWNFIELD
Right hand touching top of cap.

20

ILLEGAL CONTACT
One open hand extended forward.

21

OFFSIDE, ENCROACHMENT, or NEUTRAL ZONE INFRACTION
Hands on hips.

22

ILLEGAL MOTION AT SNAP
Horizontal arc with one hand.

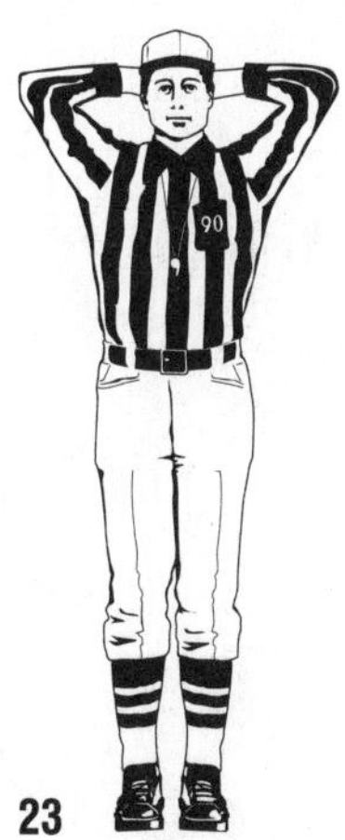

23

LOSS OF DOWN
Both hands held behind head.

24

INTERLOCKING INTERFERENCE, PUSHING, or HELPING RUNNER
Pushing movement of hands to front with arms downward.

25

TOUCHING A FORWARD PASS or SCRIMMAGE KICK
Diagonal motion of one hand across another.

26

UNSPORTSMANLIKE CONDUCT
Arms outstretched, palms down.

27

ILLEGAL CUT
Hand striking front of thigh.
ILLEGAL BLOCK BELOW THE WAIST
One hand striking front of thigh preceded by personal-foul signal (10).
CHOP BLOCK
Both hands striking side of thighs preceded by personal-foul signal (10).
CLIPPING
One hand striking back of calf preceded by personal-foul signal (10).

28

ILLEGAL CRACKBACK
Strike of an open right hand against the right mid-thigh preceded by personal foul signal (10).

29

PLAYER DISQUALIFIED
Ejection signal.

30

TRIPPING
Repeated action of right foot in back of left heel.

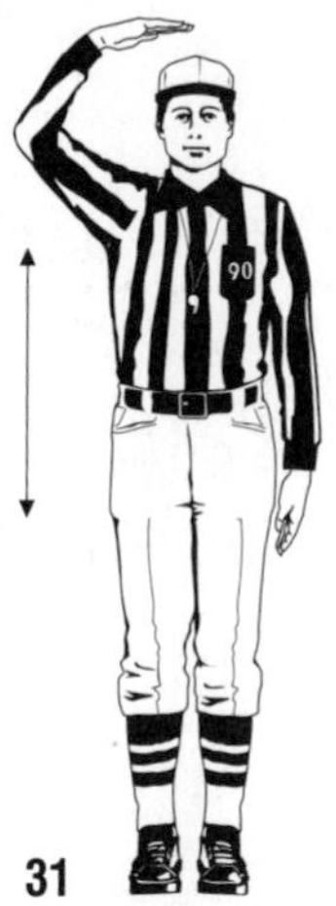

31

UNCATCHABLE FORWARD PASS
Palm of right hand held parallel to ground above head and moved back and forth.

32

TWELVE MEN IN OFFENSIVE HUDDLE or TOO MANY MEN ON THE FIELD
Both hands on top of head.

33

FACEMASK
Grasping facemask with one hand.

34

ILLEGAL SHIFT
Horizontal arcs with two hands.

35

RESET PLAY CLOCK– 25 SECONDS
Pump one arm vertically.

36

RESET PLAY CLOCK– 40 SECONDS
Pump two arms vertically.

NATIONAL FOOTBALL LEAGUE, 2009

280 Park Avenue, New York, New York 10017 (212) 450-2000

NFL Internet Network: www.NFL.com

Commissioner: Roger Goodell

Executive Vice President/Football Operations: Ray Anderson

Executive Vice President of Media/President and Chief Executive Officer of NFL Network: Steve Bornstein

Executive Vice President of Communications and Public Affairs: Joe Browne

Executive Vice President of NFL Ventures and Business Operations: Eric Grubman

Executive Vice President of Finance/Chief Financial Officer: Anthony Noto

Executive Vice President of Labor/League Counsel: Jeff Pash